HOLINSHED'S

CHRONICLES

OF

ENGLAND, SCOTLAND,

AND

IRELAND.

IN SIX VOLUMES.

VOL. III.

ENGLAND.

LONDON:

PRINTED FOR J. JOHNSON; F. C. AND J. RIVINGTON; T. PAYNE; WILKIE
AND ROBINSON; LONGMAN, HURST, REES, AND ORME;
CADELL AND DAVIES; AND J. MAWMAN.

1808.

AMS PRESS INC.

NEW YORK

1965

AMS   PRESS   INC.

NEW YORK, N.Y. 10003

1965

MANUFACTURED in the U.S.A.

THE

THIRD VOLUME

OF

CHRONICLES,

BEGINNING AT

DUKE WILLIAM THE NORMAN, COMMONLIE CALLED THE CONQUEROR;

AND

DESCENDING BY DEGREES OF YEERES

TO ALL THE

KINGS AND QUEENES OF ENGLAND

IN THEIR

ORDERLIE SUCCESSIONS:

FIRST COMPILED BY

RAPHAELL HOLINSHED,

AND BY HIM EXTENDED TO THE

YEARE 1577.

NOW NEWLIE RECOGNISED, AUGMENTED, AND CONTINUED

(WITH OCCURRENCES AND ACCIDENTS OF FRESH MEMORIE)

TO THE YEARE 1586.

WHEREIN ALSO ARE CONTEINED MANIE MATTERS OF SINGULAR DISCOURSE AND RARE OBSERUATION,

FRUITFULL TO SUCH AS BE STUDIOUS IN ANTIQUITIES,

OR

TAKE PLEASURE IN THE GROUNDS OF ANCIENT HISTORIES.

With a third table (peculiarlie seruing this third volume) both of names and matters memorable.

◆

HISTORIÆ PLACEANT NOSTRATES AC PEREGRNÆ.

HENRIE THE FOURTH,

Cousine Germane to Richard the Second, latelie depriued.

―――――――――

WHEN king Richard had resigned (as before is specified) the scepter and crowne; Henrie Plantagenet borne at Bullingbroke in the countie of Lincolne, duke of Lancaster and Hereford, earle of Derbie, Leicester, and Lincolne, sonne to Iohn of Gant duke of Lancaster, with generall consent both of the lords & commons, was published, proclamed, and declared king of England and of France, and lord of Ireland, the last daie of September, in the yeare of the world 5366, of our Lord 1399, of the reigne of the emperour Wenceslaus the two and twentith, of Charles the first king of France the twentith, and the tenth of Robert the third king of Scots. After that king Richard had surrendered his title, and dispossessed himselfe (which Chr. Okl. noteth in few words, saieing;

In Angl. præliis.

―――――――post breue tempus
Exüit insigni sese diademate, sceptrum
Henrico Lancastrensi regale relinquens)

king Henrie made certeine new officers. And first in right of his earledome of Leicester he gaue the office of high steward of England (belonging to the same earledome) vnto his second sonne the lord Thomas, who by his fathers commandement exercised that office, being assisted (by reason of his tender age) by Thomas Persie earle of Worcester. The earle of Northumberland was made constable of England: sir Iohn Scirlie lord chancellor, Iohn Norburie esquier lord treasuror, sir Richard Clifford lord priuie seale. Forsomuch as by king Richards resignation and the admitting of a new king, all plées in euerie court and place were ceased, and without daie discontinued, new writs were made for summoning of the parlement vnder the name of king Henrie the fourth, the same to be holden, as before was appointed, on mondaie next insuing. Vpon the fourth day of October, the lord Thomas second sonne to the king sat as lord high steward of England by the kings commandement in the White-hall of the kings palace at Westminster, and as belonged to his office, he caused inquirie to be made what offices were to be exercised by anie maner of persons the daie of the kings coronation, and what fées were belonging to the same, causing proclamation to be made, that what noble man or other that could claime anie office that daie of the solemnizing the kings coronation, they should come and put in their bils cōprehending their demands. Wheruppon diuers offices & fees were claimed, as well by bils as otherwise by spéech of mouth, in forme as here insueth.

First, the lord Henrie, the kings eldest sonne, to whome he as in right of his duchie of Lancaster had appointed that office, claimed to beare before the king the principall sword called Curtana, and had his sute granted. Iohn erle of Summerset, to whom the king as in right of his earledome of Lincolne, had granted to be caruer the daie of his coronation, and had it confirmed. Henrie Persie earle of Northumberland, and high constable of England, by the kings grant claimed that office, and obteined it to inioy at pleasure. The same earle in right of the Ile of Man, which at that present was granted to him, and to his heires by the king, claimed to beare on the

Side notes:
New officers made.
The parlemēt new sūmoned.
Record Turris.
Claiming of offices at the coronation.
Curtana.
The earle of Summer-et.
The earle of Northumberland.
The Ile of Man.

kings left side a naked sword, with which the king was girded, when before his coronation he entered as duke of Lancaster into the parts of Holdernesse, which sword
was called Lancasters sword. Rafe erle of Westmerland, and earle marshall of England, by the kings grant claimed the same office, and obteined it, notwithstanding
that the attornies of the duke of Norfolke, presented to the lord steward their petition on the dukes behalfe, as earle marshall, to exercise the same. Sir Thomas Erpingham knight exercised the office of lord great Chamberleine, and gaue water to
the king when he washed, both before and after dinner, hauing for his fées, the bason,
ewer, and towels, with other things whatsoeuer belonging to his office: notwithstanding Auberie de Veer earle of Orenford put in his petitions to haue that office as due
vnto him from his ancestors. Thomas Beauchampe earle of Warwike by right of inheritance, bare the third sword before the king, and by like right was pantler at the
coronation. Sir William Argentine knight, by reason of the tenure of his manour of
Wilmundale in the countie of Hertford, serued the king of the first cup of drinke
which he tasted of at his dinner the daie of his coronation: the cup was of siluer vngilt,
which the same knight had for his fées: notwithstanding the petition which Iuon Fitzwarren presented to the lord steward, requiring that office in right of his wife the
ladie Maud, daughter and heire to sir Iohn Argentine knight. Sir Thomas Neuill lord
Furniuall, by reason of his manour of Ferneham, with the hamlet of Cere, which he
held by the courtesie of England after the decesse of his wife, the ladie Ione decessed,
gaue to the king a gloue for his right hand, and susteined the kings right arme so long
as he bare the scepter.

The lord Reginald Graie of Ruthen, by reason of his manour of Ashleie in Norfolke
couered the tables, and had for his fees all the tableclothes, as well those in the hall,
as else-where, when they were taken vp; notwithstanding a petition exhibited by sir
Iohn Draiton to haue had that office. The same lord Graie of Ruthen, bare the kings
great spurs before him in the time of his coronation by right of inheritance, as heire to
Iohn Hastings earle of Penbroke. Iohn erle of Summerset, by the kings assignement
bare the second sword before him at his coronation, albeit that the said lord Graie of
Ruthen by petition exhibited before the lord steward demanded the same office, by
reason of his castell & tower of Penbroke, and of his towne of Denbigh. Thomas earle
of Arundell cheefe butler of England, obteined to exercise that office the daie of the
coronation, and had the fées thereto belonging granted to him, to wit, the goblet with
which the king was serued, and other things to that his office apperteining (the vessels of wine excepted) that laie vnder the bar, which were adiudged vnto the said lord
steward, the said earle of Arundels claime notwithstanding.

The citizens of London chosen foorth by the citie, serued in the hall, as assistants
to the lord cheefe butler, whilest the king sate at dinner, the daie of his coronation:
and when the king entered into his chamber after dinner, and called for wine, the lord
maior of London brought to him a cup of gold with wine, and had the same cup
given to him, togither with the cup that conteined water to allay the wine. After the
king had drunke, the said lord maior and the aldermen of London had their table to
dine at, on the left hand of the king in the hall. Thomas Dimocke, in right of his
moother Margaret Dimocke, by reason of the tenure of his manor of Scriuelbie,
claimed to be the kings champion at his coronation, and had his sute granted; notwithstanding a claime exhibited by Baldwin Freuill, demanding that office by reason of
of his castell of Tamworth in Warwikeshire. The said Dimocke had for his fees one
of the best coursers in the kings stable, with the kings saddle and all the trappers &
harnesse apperteining to the same horsse or courser: he had likewise one of the best armors that was in the kings armorie for his owne bodie, with all that belonged wholie
therevnto.

Iohn lord Latimer, although he was vnder age, for himselfe and the duke of Norfolke,

Lancaster
sword.

The earl of
Westmerland.

The duke of
Norffolke.

Sir Thomas Er-
pingham.

The earle of
Warwike.

Sir William Ar-
gentine.

Iuon Fitzwar-
ren.

The lord Fur-
niuall.

The lord
Graie.

Great spurs.

The second
sword.

The earle of
Arundell.

The citizens of
London.

Thomas Di-
mocke.

Baldwin Freuill.

The lord La-
timer.

folke, notwithstanding that his possessions were in the kings hands, by his atturnie sir Thomas Graie knight, claimed and had the office of almoner for that daie, by reason of certeine lands which sometime belonged to the lord William Beuchampe of Bedford.　They had a towell of fine linnen cloth prepared, to put in the siluer that was appointed to be giuen in almes; and likewise they had the distribution of the cloth that couered the pauement and floors from the kings chamber doore, vnto the place in the church of Westminster where the pulpit stood.　The residue that was spread in the church, the sexten had.　William le Venour, by reason he was tenant of the manor of Liston, claimed and obteined to exercise the office of making wafers for the king the daie of his coronation.　The barons of the fiue ports claimed, and it was granted them, to beare a canopie of cloth of gold ouer the K. with foure staues, & foure bels at the foure corners, euerie staffe hauing foure of those barons to beare it: also to dine and sit at the table next to the king on his right hand in the hall the daie of his coronation, and for their fees to haue the forsaid canopie of gold, with the bels and staues, notwithstanding the abbat of Westminster claimed the same.　Edmund Chambers claimed and obteined the office of principall larderer for him and his deputies, by reason of his manour of Skulton, otherwise called Burdellebin Skulton, in the countie of Norfolke.　Thus was euerie man appointed to exercise such office as to him of right apperteined, or at the least was thought requisit for the time present.　On mondaie then next insuing, when the states were assembled in parlement, order was taken, that by reason of such preparation as was to be made for the coronation, they should sit no more till the morow after saint Edwards daie.　On the sundaie following, being the euen of saint Edward, the new king lodged in the Tower, and there made fortie & six knights of the Bath, to wit: thrée of his sonnes, the earle of Arundell, the earle of Warwike his sonne, the earle of Stafford, two of the earle of Deuonshires sonnes, the lord Beaumont, the lord Willoughbies brother, the earle of Staffords brother, the lord Camois his sonne, the lord of Maule, Thomas Beauchampe, Thomas Pelham, Iohn Luttrell, Iohn Lisleie, William Haukeford iustice, William Brinchleie iustice, Bartholomew Rathford, Giles Daubenie, William Butler, Iohn Ashton, Richard Sanape, Iohn Tiptost, Richard Francis, Henrie Persie, Iohn Arundell, William Strall, Iohn Turpington, Ailmer Saint, Edward Hastings, Iohn Greisleie, Gerald Satill, Iohn Arden, Robert Chalons, Thomas Dimocke, Hungerford, Gibethorpe, Newport, and diuerse other, to the number of fortie and six.

On the morow being saint Edwards daie, and the thirteenth of October, the lord maior of London road towards the Tower to attend the king, with diuerse worshipfull citizens clothed all in red, and from the Tower the king rode through the citie to Westminster, where he was consecrated, anointed, and crowned king by the archbishop of Canturburie with all ceremonies and roiall solemnitie as was due and requisit.　Though all other reioised at his aduancement, yet suerlie Edmund Mortimer earle of March, which was coosine and heire to Lionell duke of Clarence, the third begotten sonne of king Edward the third, & Richard earle of Cambridge, sonne to Edmund duke of Yorke, which had married Anne sister to the same Edmund, were with these dooings neither pleased nor contented: insomuch that now the diuision once begun, the one linage ceassed not to persecute the other, till the heires males of both the lines were cléerlie destroied and extinguished.

At the daie of the coronation, to the end he should not séeme to take vpon him the crowne and scepter roiall by plaine extorted power, and iniurious intrusion: he was aduised to make his title as heire to Edmund (surnamed or vntrulie feined) Crookebacke, sonne to king Henrie the third, and to saie that the said Edmund was elder brother to king Edward the first, and for his deformitie put by from the crowne, to whom by his mother Blanch, daughter and sole heire to Henrie duke of Lancaster, he was next of blood, and undoubted heire.　But because not onelie his

Marginal notes:

William le Venour.

The barons of the cinque ports.

Knights of the Bath.

The lord maior of London.

The earle of March enuied the K. preferment.

Edmund erle of Lancaster vntrulie feined to be surnamed Crookebacke.

fréends, but also his priuie enimies, knew that this was but a forged title, considering they were suerlie informed, not onelie that the said Edmund was yoonger sonne to king Henrie the third, but also had true knowledge, that Edmund was neither crooke backed, nor a deformed person, but a goodlie gentleman, and a valiant capteine, and so much fauored of his louing father, that he to preferre him in marriage to the queene Dowager of Nauarre, hauing a great liuelihood, gaue to him the countie palantine of Lancaster, with manie notable honours, high segniories, and large priuileges. Therefore they aduised him to publish it, that he challenged the realme not onelie by conquest, but also because he by king Richard was adopted as heire, and declared by resignation as his lawfull successor, being next heire male to him of the blood roiall.

But to procéed to other dooings. The solemnitie of the coronation being ended, the morow after being tuesdaie, the parlement began againe, and the next daie sir Iohn

Sir Iohn Chenie speaker of the parlement dismissed, and William Durward admitted.
Acts repealed.
Acts confirmed.

Cheinie that was speaker, excusing himselfe, by reason of his infirmitie and sicknesse, not to be able to exercise that roome, was dismissed, and one William Durward esquier was admitted. Herewith were the acts established in the parlement of the one & twentith yeare of king Richards reigne repealed and made void, and the ordinances deuised in the parlement holden the eleuenth yeare of the same king, confirmed, and againe established for good and profitable. ¶ On the same daie, the kings eldest sonne lord Henrie, by assent of all the states in the parlement, was created prince of Wales, duke of Cornwall, and earle of Chester, then being of the age of twelue yeares.

Upon the thursdaie, the commons came and rehearsed all the errors of the last parlement holden in the one and twentith yeare of king Richard, & namelie in certeine fiue of them.

1 First, that where the king that now is, was readie to arraigne an appeale against the duke of Norfolke, he dooing what perteined to his dutie in that behalfe, was yet banished afterwards without anie reasonable cause.

2 Secondlie, the archbishop of Canturburie, metropolitan of the realme, was foreiudged without answer.

3 Thirdlie, the duke of Glocester was murthered, and after foreiudged.

4. Fourthlie, where the earle of Arundell alledged his charters of pardon, the same might not be allowed.

5 Fiftlie, that all the power of that euill parlement was granted and assigned ouer to certeine persons, and sith that such heinous errors could not be committed (as was thought) without the assent and aduise of them that were of the late kings councell, they made sute that they might be put vnder arrest, and committed to safe kéeping, till order might be further taken for them.

Thus much adoo there was in this parlement, speciallie about them that were thought to be guiltie of the duke of Glocesters death, and of the condemning of the other lords that were adiudged traitors in the forsaid late parlement holden in the said one and

Fabian.
Sir Iohn Bagot discloseth secrets.

twentith yeare of king Richards reigne. Sir Iohn Bagot knight then prisoner in the Tower, disclosed manie secrets, vnto the which he was priuie; and being brought on a daie to the barre, a bill was read in English which he had made, conteining certeine euill practises of king Richard; and further what great affection the same king bare to the duke of Aumarle, insomuch that he heard him say, that if he should renounce the gouernement of the kingdome, he wished to leaue it to the said duke, as to the most able man (for wisdome and manhood) of all other: for though he could like bet-

Henrie the fourth suspected not to be well affected towards the church before his comming to the crowne.

ter of the duke of Hereford, yet he said that he knew if he were once king, he would proue an extreame enimie and cruell tyrant to the church.

It was further conteined in that bill, that as the same Bagot rode on a daie behind the duke of Norfolke in the Sauoy stréet toward Westminster, the duke asked him what he knew of the manner of the duke of Glocester his death, and he answered that he knew nothing at all: but the people (quoth he) do say that you have murthered

thered him. Wherevnto the duke sware great othes that it was vntrue, and that he had saued his life contrarie to the will of the king, and certeine other lords, by the space of thrée wéeks, and more; affirming withall, that he was neuer in all his life-time more affraid of death, than he was at his comming home againe from Calis at that time, to the kings presence, by reason he had not put the duke to death. And then (said he) the king appointed one of his owne seruants, and certeine other that were seruants to other lords to go with him to see the said duke of Glocester put to death, swearing that as he should answer afore God, it was neuer his mind that he should haue died in the fort, but onelie for feare of the king, and sauing of his owne life. Neuerthelesse, there was no man in the realme to whom king Richard was so much be- The duke of holden, as to the duke of Aumarle: for he was the man that to fulfill his mind, had Aumarle ac-
cused. set him in hand with all that was doone against the said duke, and the other lords. There was also conteined in that bill, what secret malice king Richard had conceiued against the duke of Hereford being in exile, whereof the same Bagot had sent intel-ligence vnto the duke into France, by one Rogert Smart, who certified it to him by Piers Buckton, and others, to the intent he should the better haue regard to himselfe. There was also conteined in the said bill, that Bagot had heard the duke of Aumarle say, that he had rather than twentie thousand pounds that the duke of Hereford were dead, not for anie feare he had of him, but for the trouble and mischéefe that he was like to procure within the realme.

After that the bill had béene read and heard, the duke of Aumarle rose vp and said, The duke of Au-
marle his answer
vnto Bagots bill. that as touching the points conteined in the bill concerning him, they were vtterlie false and vntrue, which he would proue with his bodie, in what manner soeuer it should be thought requisit. Therewith also the duke of Excester rose vp, and willed Bagot that if he could say anie thing against him to speak it openlie. Bagot answered, that for his part he could say nothing against him: But there is (said he) a yeoman in Newgat one Iohn hall that can say somewhat. "Well then (said the duke of Ex- Iohn Hall a
yeoman. cester) this that I doo and shall say is true, that the late king, the duke of Nor-folke, and thou being at Woodstoke, made me to go with you into the chappell, and there the doore being shut, ye made me to sweare vpon the altar, to kéepe counsell in that ye had to say to me, and then ye rehearsed that we should neuer haue our purpose, so long as the duke of Lancaster liued, & therefore ye purposed to haue councell at Lichfield, & there you would arrest the duke of Lancaster, in such sort as by colour of his disobeieng the arrest, he should be dispatched out of life. And in this manner ye imagined his death. To the which I answered, that it were conuenient the king should send for his councell, and if they agréed herevnto, I would not be against it, and so I departed." To this Bagot made no answer.

After this, the king commanded that the lords, Berklei, and Louell, and six knights of the lower house, should go after dinner to examine the said Hall. This was on a thursdaie being the fiftéenth of October. On the saturdaie next insuing, sir William Bagot and the said Iohn Hall were brought both to the barre, and Bagot was examined Bagott and Hall
brought to the
barre. of certeine points, and sent againe to prison. The lord Fitzwater herewith rose vp, and said to the king, that where the duke of Aumarle excuseth himselfe of the duke of Glocesters death, I say (quoth he) that he was the verie cause of his death, and The lord Fitz-
water appealeth
the duke of Au-
marle of treason. so he appealed him of treason, offering by throwing downe his hood as a gage to proue it with his bodie. There were twentie other lords also that threw downe their hoods, as pledges to proue the like matter against the duke of Aumarle. The duke of Aumarle threw downe his hood to trie it against the lord Fitzwater, as against him that lied falselie, in that he had charged him with, by that his appeale. These gages were deliuered to the constable and marshall of England, and the parties put vnder arrest.

The duke of Surrie stood vp also against the lord Fitzwater, auouching that where
he

he had said that the appellants were causers of the duke of Glocesters death, it was false, for they were constrained to sue the same appeale, in like manner as the said lord Fitzwater was compelled to giue iudgement against the duke of Glocester, and the earle of Arundell; so that the suing of the appeale was doone by constraint, and if he said contrarie he lied: and therewith he threw downe his hood. The lord Fitzwater answered herevnto, that he was not present in the parlement house, when iudgement was giuen against them, and all the lords bare witnesse thereof. Moreouer, where it was alledged that the duke of Aumarle should send two of his seruants to Calis, to murther the duke of Glocester, the said duke of Aumarle said, that if the duke of Norfolke affirme it, he lied falselie, and that he would proue with his bodie, throwing downe an other hood which he had borowed. The same was likewise deliuered to the constable and marshall of England, and the king licenced the duke of Norfolke to returne, that he might arraigne his appeale. After this was Iohn Hall condemned of treason by authoritie of the parlement, for that he had confessed himself to be one of them that put the duke of Glocester to death at Calis, and so on the mondaie following, he was drawne from the Tower to Tiburne, and there hanged, bowelled, headed, and quartered: his head being sent to Calis there to be set vp, where the duke was murthered.

On Wednesdaie following, request was made by the commons, that sith king Richard had resigned, and was lawfullie deposed from his roiall dignitie, he might haue iudgement decréed against him, so as the realme were not troubled by him, and that the causes of his deposing might be published through the realme for satisfieng of the people: which demand was granted. Wherevpon the bishop of Carleill, a man both learned, wise, and stout of stomach, boldlie shewed foorth his opinion concerning that demand; affirming that there was none amongst them woorthie or meet to giue iudgement vpon so noble a prince as king Richard was, whom they had taken for their souereigne and liege lord, by the space of two & twentie yeares and more; "And I assure you (said he) there is not so ranke a traitor, nor so errant a théef, nor yet so cruell a murtherer apprehended or deteined in prison for his offense, but he shall be brought before the iustice to heare his iudgement; and will ye procéed to the iudgement of an anointed king, hearing neither his answer nor excuse? I say, that the duke of Lancaster whom ye call king, hath more trespassed to K. Richard & his realme, than king Richard hath doone either to him, or vs: for it is manifest & well knowne, that the duke was banished the realme by K. Richard and his councell, and by the iudgement of his owne father, for the space of ten yeares, for what cause ye know, and yet without licence of king Richard, he is returned againe into the realme, and (that is woorse) hath taken vpon him the name, title, & preheminence of king, And therfore I say, that you haue doone manifest wrong, to procéed in anie thing against king Richard, without calling him openlie to his answer and defense." ¶ As soone as the bishop had ended this tale, he was attached by the earle marshall, and committed to ward in the abbei of saint Albons.

Moreouer, where the king had granted to the earle of Westmerland the countie of Richmond, the duke of Britaine pretending a right thereto by an old title, had sent his letters ouer vnto the estates assembled in this parlement, offering to abide such order as the law would appoint in the like case to anie of the kings subiects. Wherevpon the commons for the more suertie of the intercourse of merchants, besought the king that the matter might be committed to the ordering of the councell of either of the parties, and of his counsell, so as an end might be had therein, which request was likewise granted. After this, the records of the last parlement were shewed, with the appeales, & the commission made to twelue persons, to determine things that were motioned in the same last parlement. Héerevpon the commons praied that they might haue iustice Markham, and maister Gascoigne a sergeant at the law ioined with them for counsell, touching the perusing of the records, which was granted them, and day giuen ouer
till

Fabian.

Iohn Hall executed.

Iohn Stow.
The request of the commons.

Hall.
A bold bishop and a faithfull.

The duke of Britaine.

till the next morrow in the White-hall, where they sat about these matters thrée daies togither.

On the morrow following, being the éeuen of Simon and Iude the apostles, the commons required to heare the iudgément of king Richard. Wherevpon the arch- K. Richard appointed to be kept in perpetuall prison. *Hall.* bishop of Canturburie appointed to speake, declared how that the king that now is, had granted king Richard his life; but in such wise as he should remaine in perpetuall prison, so safelie kept, that neither the king nor realme should be troubled with him. It was also concluded, that if anie man went about to deliuer him, that then he should be the first that should die for it. After this, the commons praied that the lords and other that were of king Richards counsell, might be put to their answers for their sundrie misdemeanors, which was granted. On Wednesday following, being the morrow after the feast of Simon and Iude, all the processe of the parlement holden the 21 yéere of king Richards reigne was read openlie, in which it was found, how the The earle of Warwike. earle of Warwike had confessed himselfe guiltie of treason, and asked pardon and mercie for his offense: but the earle denied that euer he acknowledged anie such thing by woord of mouth, and that he would prooue in what manner soeuer should be to him appointed. Therein was also the appeale found of the dukes of Aumarle, Surrie, and Excester, the marquesse Dorset, the earles of Salisburie and Glocester; vnto the which ech of them answered by himselfe, that they neuer assented to that appeale of their owne frée wils, but were compelled thereto by the king: and this they affirmed by their othes, and offered to prooue it by what manner they should be appointed.

Sir Walter Clopton said then to the commons; If ye will take aduantage of the Sir Water Clopton. processe of the last parlement, take it, and ye shall be receiued therevnto. Then rose vp the lord Morlie, and said to the earle of Salisburie, that he was chiefe of counsell with the duke of Glocester, and likewise with king Richard, & so discouered the dukes counsell to the king, as a traitor to his maister, and that he said he would with his bodie prooue against him, throwing downe his hood as a pledge. The earle of Salisburie sore mooued héerewith, told the lord Morlie, that he falslie béelied him, for he The lord Morlie appeleth the earle of Salisburie. was neuer traitor, nor false to his maister all his life time, and therewith threw downe his gloue to wage battell against the lord Morlie. Their gages were taken vp, and deliuered to the constable and marshall of England, and the parties were arrested, and day to them giuen till another time.

On Mondaie following, being the morrow after All soules day, the commons made request, that they might not be entred in the parlement rols, as parties to the iudgement giuen in this parlement, but there as in verie truth they were priuie to the same: for the iudgement otherwise belonged to the king, except where anie iudgment is giuen by statute enacted for the profit of the common-wealth, which request was granted. Diuers other petitions were presented on the behalfe of the commons, part whereof were granted, and to some there was none answere made at that time. Finallie, to auoid further inconuenience, and to qualifie the minds of the enuious, it was finallie enacted, that such as were appellants in the last parlement against the duke of Glocester and other, should in this wise following be ordred. The dukes of Aumarle, Dukes and others depriued of their titles. Surrie, and Excester there present, were iudged to loose their names of dukes, togither with the honors, titles and dignities therevnto belonging. The marquesse Dorset being likewise there present, was adiudged to lose his title and dignitie of marquesse; and the earle of Glocester being also present, was in semblable maner iudged to lose his name, title and dignitie of earle.

Moreouer, it was further decréed against them, that they and euerie of them should *Tho. Walsi.* lose and forfeit all those castels, lordships, manors, lands, possessions, rents, seruices, liberties and reuenues, whatsoeuer had beene giuen to them, at or since the last parlement, belonging aforetime to any of those persons whom they had appealed, and all other their castels, manors, lordships, lands, possessions, rents, seruices, liberties,

and

and reuenues whatsoeuer, which they held of the late kings gift, the daie of the arrest of the said duke of Glocester, or at any time after, should also remaine in the kings disposition from thencefoorth, and all letters patents and charters, which they or any of them had of the same names, castels, manors, lordships, lands, possessions, and liberties, should be surrendered vp into the chancerie, there to be cancelled. Diuerse other things were enacted in this parlement, to the preiudice of those high estates, to satisfie mens minds that were sore displeased with their dooings in the late kings daies, as now it manifestlie appéered. For after it was vnderstood that they should be no further

The hatred which the cõmons had cõmitted against the appellãts.

punished than as before is mentioned, great murmuring rose among the people against the king, the archbishop of Canturburie, the earle of Northumberland, and other of the councell, for sauing the liues of men whom the commons reputed most wicked, and not worthie in anie wise to liue. But the king thought it best, rather with courtesie to reconcile them, than by cutting them off by death to procure the hatred of their freends and alies, which were manie, and of no small power.

The earle of Salisburie his request.

After that the foresaid iudgement was declared with protestation by sir William Thirning iustice, the earle of Salisburie came and made request, that he might haue his protestation entered against the lord Morlie, which lord Morlie rising vp from his seat, said, that so he might not haue; bicause in his first answer he made no protestation, and therefore he was past it now. The earle praied day of aduisement, but the lord Morlie praied that he might lose his aduantage, sith he had not entered sufficient

Sir Mathew Gournie.

plee against him. Then sir Matthew Gournie sitting vnderneath the king said to the earle of Salisburie, that forsomuch as at the first day in your answers, ye made no protestation at all, none is entered of record, and so you are past that aduantage: and therefore asked him if he would saie any other thing. Then the earle desired that he might

The earle of Salisburie mainprised.

put in mainprise, which was granted: and so the earle of Kent, sir Rafe Ferrers, sir Iohn Roch, & sir Iohn Draiton knights, mainprised the said earle bodie for bodie. For the lord Morlie all the lords and barons offred to vndertake, and to be suerties for him; but yet foure of them had their names entered, that is to saie, the lords Wil-

The lord Morlie mainprised.

loughbie, Beauchampe, Scales, and Berkelie: they had day till the fridaie after to make their libell.

The lord Fitz-walter.

After this came the lord Fitzwater, and praied to haue day and place to arreigne his appeale against the earle of Rutland. The king said he would send for the duke of Norffolke to returne home, and then vpon his returne he said he would proceed in that matter. Manie statutes were established in this parlement, as well concerning the whole bodie of the common-wealth (as by the booke thereof imprinted may appeare) as also concerning diuerse priuate persons then presentlie liuing, which partlie we haue touched, and partlie for doubt to be ouer-tedious, we doo omit. But this among

The archb. of Canturburie restored to his sée.

other is not to be forgotten that the archbishop of Canturburie was not onelie restored to his former dignitie, being remooued from it by king Richard, who had procured one Roger Walden to be placed therein (as before ye haue heard) but also the said Walden was established Bishop of London, wherewith he séemed well content.

Thom. Wals. Hall.

The crowne intailed.

Moreouer, the kings eldest sonne Henrie alreadie created (as heire to his father, and to the crowne) prince of Wales, duke of Cornewall, and earle of Chester, was also intituled duke of Aquitaine: and to auoid all titles, claimes, and ambiguities, there was an act made for the vniting of the crowne vnto king Henrie the fourth, and to the heires of his bodie lawfullie begotten, his foure sonnes, Henrie, Thomas, Iohn, and Humfrie, being named, as to whom the right should descend successiuelie by waie of intaile, in case where heires failed to any of them. By force of this act king Henrie thought himselfe firmelie set on a sure foundation, not néeding to feare any storme of aduerse fortune. But yet shortlie after he was put in danger to haue béene set besides the seat, by a conspiracie begun in the abbat of Westminsters house, which, had it

not

not béene hindred, it is doubtfull whether the new king should haue inioied his roialtie, or the old king (now a prisoner) restored to his principalitie. But God (of whome the poet saith,

——————humana rotat
Instar volucris pulueris acti
Turbine celeri mobilis auræ)

had purposed a disappointment of their coniuration, and therefore no maruell though the issue of their labours were infortunat by their flattering hope.

But now to make an end with this parlement. After that things were concluded and granted, so as was thought to stand with the suertie of the king, and good quiet of the realme, the king granted a free pardon to all his subiects, those excepted that were at the murther of the duke of Glocester, and such as had committed wilfull murther, or rape, or were knowne to be notorious théeues. And those that were to take benefit by this pardon, were appointed to sue foorth the charters therof, betwixt that present and the feast of All saints next insuing, and so was this parlement dissolued. Immediatlie after, the king (according to an order taken in the same parlement, to giue to vnderstand vnto all princes and countries about him, by what title and occasion he had taken to him the kingdome) sent ambassadors vnto them to signifie the same. Into Rome were sent, Iohn Treneuant bishop of Hereford, sir Iohn Cheinie knight, & Iohn Cheinie esquier. Into France, master Walter Skirlow bishop of Durham, and Thomas Persie earle of Worcester. Into Spaine, Iohn Trenour bishop of saint Asaph, and sir William Parre knight. Into Almanie the bishop of Bangor, and two others. *Tho. Walsi.* *Ambassadors sent to forren princes.*

The Scots in time of the late parlement, taking occasion of the absence of the northerne lords, and also by reason of great mortalitie that afflicted the northerne people that yeare, inuaded the borders, tooke the castell of Warke, that was assigned to the safe kéeping of sir Thomas Greie knight, who then was at the parlement, as one of the knights of the shire, by meanes of whose absence, the enimies the sooner (as is to be thought) obteined their desire, and so kept that castell a certeine time, and finallie spoiled it, and ouerthrew it to the ground. Besides all this they did manie other mischéefes in the countrie, to the vndooing of manie of the kings subiects. *The castell of Warke taken by the Scots. Sir Thom. Greie.* This yeare Thomas Mowbraie duke of Norffolke died in exile at Venice, whose death might haue béene worthilie bewailed of all the realme, if he had not béene consenting to the death of the duke of Glocester. The same yeare deceassed the duchesse of Glocester, thorough sorrow (as was thought) which she conceiued for the losse of hir sonne and heire the lord Humfrie, who being sent for foorth of Ireland (as before ye haue heard) was taken with the pestilence, and died by the waie. *The death of the duke of Norffolke.* *The duchesse of Glocester deceasseth.*

But now to speake of the conspiracie, which was contriued by the abbat of Westminster as chéefe instrument thereof. Ye shall vnderstand, that this abbat (as it is reported) vpon a time heard king Henrie saie, when he was but earle of Derbie, and yoonge of yeares, that princes had too little, and religious men too much. He therefore doubting now, least if the king continued long in the estate, he would remooue the great beame that then gréeued his eies, and pricked his conscience, became an instrument to search out the minds of the nobilitie, and to bring them to an assemblie and councell, where they might consult and commen togither, how to bring that to effect, which they earnestlie wished and desired; that was, the destruction of king Henrie, and the restoring of king Richard. For there were diuerse lords that shewed themselues outwardlie to fauor king Henrie, where they secretlie wished & sought his confusion. The abbat after he had felt the minds of sundrie of them, called to his house on a day in the terme time, all such lords & other persons which he either knew or thought to be as affectioned to king Richard, so enuious to the prosperitie of king Henrie, whose names were, Iohn Holland earle of Huntington late duke of Excester, *Hall.* *What mooued the abbat of Westminster to conspire against the king.*

The lords that
conspiredagainst
the duke.
Thomas Holland earle of Kent late duke of Surrie, Edward earle of Rutland late duke
of Aumarle sonne to the duke of Yorke, Iohn Montacute earle of Salisburie, Hugh
lord Spenser late earle of Glocester, Iohn the bishop of Carleill, sir Thomas Blunt,
and Maudelen a priest one of king Richards chappell, a man as like him in stature
and proportion in all lineaments of bodie, as vnlike in birth, dignitie, and conditions.

The abbat highlie feasted these lords, his speciall freends, and when they had well
dined, they withdrew into a secret chamber, where they sat downe in councell, and
after much talke & conference had about the bringing of their purpose to passe concerning the destruction of king Henrie, at length by the aduise of the earle of Huntington it was deuised, that they should take vpon them a solemne iusts to be enter-
A iusts deuised
to be holden at
Oxford.
prised betweene him and 20 on his part, & the earle of Salisburie and 20 with him at
Oxford, to the which triumph k. Henrie should be desired, & when he should be most
busilie marking the martiall pastime, he suddenlie should be slaine and destroied, and
so by that means king Richard, who as yet liued, might be restored to libertie, and
haue his former estate & dignitie. It was further appointed, who should assemble
the people, the number and persons which should accomplish and put in execution
An indenture
sextipartite.
their deuised enterprise. Hervpon was an indenture sextipartite made, sealed with
their seales, and signed with their hands, in the which each stood bound to other, to
do their whole indeuour for the accomplishing of their purposed exploit. Moreouer,
they sware on the holie euangelists to be true and secret each to other, euen to the
houre and point of death.
He is desired to
come and see
the iusts.
When all things were thus appointed, the earle of Huntington came to the king
vnto Windsore, earnestlie requiring him, that he would vouchsafe to be at Brentford
on the daie appointed of their iustes, both to behold the same, and to be the discouerer
and indifferent iudge (if anie ambiguitie should rise) of their couragious acts and
dooings. The king being thus instantlie required of his brother in law, and nothing
lesse imagining than that which was pretended, gentlie granted to fulfill his request.
Which thing obteined, all the lords of the conspiracie departed home to their houses,
as they noised it, to set armorers on worke about the trimming of their armour against
the iusts, and to prepare all other furniture and things readie, as to such a high &
solemne triumph apperteined. The earle of Huntington came to his house and raised
men on euerie side, and prepared horsse and harness for his compassed purpose, and
when he had all things readie, he departed towards Brenford, and at his comming
thither, he found all his mates and confederates there, well appointed for their purpose, except the earle of Rutland, by whose follie their practised conspiracie was
brought to light and disclosed to king Henrie. For this earle of Rutland departing
before from Westminster to sée his father the duke of Yorke, as he sat at dinner,
had his counterpane of the indenture of the confederacie in his bosome.
The duke of
Yorke taketh
the indenture
from his son.
The father espieing it, would néeds sée what it was: and though the sonne humblie
denied to shew it, the father being more earnest to sée it, by force tooke it out of his
bosome ; and perceiuing the contents thereof, in a great rage caused his horsses to be
sadled out of hand, and spitefullie reproouing his sonne of treason, for whome he was
become suertie and mainpernour for his good abearing in open parlement, he incontinentlie mounted on horssebacke to ride towards Windsore to the king, to declare vnto
him the malicious intent of his complices. The earle of Rutland séeing in what danger
he stood, tooke his horsse and rode another waie to Windsore in post, so that he got
thither before his father, and when he was alighted at the castell gate, he caused the
The earle ofRut-
land vttereth the
whole conspira-
cie to the king.
gates to be shut, saieing that he must néeds deliuer the keies to the king. When he
came before the kings presence, he kneeled downe on his knées, beséeching him of
mercie and forgiuenesse, and declaring the whole matter vnto him in order as euerie
thing had passed, obteined pardon. Therewith came his father, and being let in,
deliuered

deliuered the indenture which he had taken from his sonne, vnto the king, who thereby perceiuing his sonnes words to be true, changed his purpose for his going to Brenford, and dispatched messengers foorth to signifie vnto the earle of Northumberland his high constable, and to the earle of Westmerland his high marshall, and to other his assured freends, of all the doubtfull danger and perillous ieopardie.

The conspirators being at Brenford, at length perceiued by the lacke of the earle of Rutland, that their enterprise was reuealed to the king, and thereupon determined now openlie with speare and shield to bring that to passe which before they couertlie attempted, and so they adorned Maudelen, a man most resembling king Richard, in roiall and princelie vesture, and named him to be king Richard, affirming that by fauour of his kéepers he was escaped out of prison, and so they came forwards in order of warre, to the intent to destroie king Henrie. Whilest the confederators with their new published idoll, accompanied with a strong armie of men, tooke the direct waie towards Windsore, king Henrie admonished thereof, with a few horssemen in the night came to the Tower of London about twelue of the clocke, where in the morning he caused the maior of the citie to apparell in armour the best and most couragious persons of the citie, which brought to him thrée thousand archers, and three thousand bill-men, besides them that were appointed to kéepe and defend the citie. *Magdalen counterfeited to be king Richard.* *The K. cometh to the tower of London.*

The conspirators comming to Windsore, entered the castell, and vnderstanding that the king was gon from thence to London, determined with all spéed to make towards the citie: but changing that determination as they were on their waie, they turned to Colbroke, and there staied. King Henrie issuing out of London with twentie thousand men, came streight to Hunslo heath, and there pitched his campe to abide the comming of his enimies: but when they were aduertised of the kings puissance, amazed with feare, and forthinking their begun enterprise, as men mistrusting their owne companie, departed from thence to Berkhamstéed, and so to Circester, & there the lords tooke their lodging. The earle of Kent, and the earle of Salisburie in one Inne, and the earle of Huntington and lord Spenser in an other, and all the host laie in the fields, wherevpon in the night season, the bailiffe of the towne with fourescore archers set on the house, where the erle of Kent and the other laie, which house was manfullie assaulted and stronglie defended a great space. The earle of Huntington being in an other Inne with the lord Spenser, set fire on diuerse houses in the towne, thinking that the assailants would leaue the assault and rescue their goods, which thing they nothing regarded. The host lieng without, hearing noise, and seeing this fire in the towne, thought verelie that king Henrie had béene come thither with his puissance, and therevpon fled without measure, euerie man making shift to saue himselfe, and so that which the lords deuised fo. their helpe, wrought their destruction; for if the armie that laie without the towne had not mistaken the matter, when they saw the houses on fire, they might easilie haue succoured their chéefeteins in the towne, that were assailed but with a few of the townesmen, in comparison of the great multitude that laie abroad in the fields. But such was the ordinance of the mightie Lord of hostes, who disposeth althings at his pleasure. *The lords come to Windesore.* *The king goeth foorth against them.* *They retire.* *They come to Circester.* *The bailiffe of Circester setteth vpon them on their lodgings.* *The lords set fire on their lodgings.* *Hall. Froissard.*

The earle of Huntington and his companie seeing the force of the townesmen to increase, fled out on the backside, intending to repaire to the armie which they found dispersed and gone. Then the earle seeing no hope of comfort, fled into Essex. The other lords which were left fighting in the towne of Circester, were wounded to death and taken, and their heads stricken off and sent to London. Thus writeth Hall of this conspiracie, in following what author I know not. But Thomas Walsingham and diuerse other séeme somewhat to dissent from him in relation of this matter; for they write that the conspiratours ment vpon the sudden to haue set vpon the king in the castell of Windsore, vnder colour of a maske or mummerie, and so to haue *Thom. Wals.* *A maske.*

dispatched

dispatched him; and restoring king Richard vnto the kingdome, to haue recouered their former titles of honour, with the possessions which they had lost by iudgement of the last parlement. But the king getting knowledge of their pretensed treasons, got him with all spéed vnto London.

The conspirators, to wit, the earles of Kent and Salisburie, sir Rafe Lumlie, and others, supposing that the king had not vnderstood their malicious purpose, the first sundaie of the new yeare, which fell in the octaues of the Innocents, came in the twilight of the euening into Windsore with foure hundred armed men, where vnderstanding that the king was withdrawne vpon warning had of their purposed intention, they forthwith returned backe, and came first vnto Sunnings, a manor place not farre from Reading, where the quéene wife to king Richard then laie. Here setting a good countenance of the matter, the earle of Kent declared in presence of the queenes servants that the lord Henrie of Lancaster was fled from his presence with his children and fréends, and had shut up himselfe & them in the Tower of London, as one afraid to come abroad, for all the brags made heretofore of his manhood: and therefore (saith he) my intention is (my lords) to go to Richard that was, is, and shall be our king, who being alreadie escaped foorth of prison, lieth now at Pomfret, with an hundred thousand men. And to cause his spéech the better to be be beléeued, he tooke awaie the kings cognisances from them that ware the same, as the collars from their necks, and the badges of cressants from the sleeues of the seruants of houshold, and throwing them awaie, said that such cognisances were no longer to be borne.

Thus hauing put the quéene in a vaine hope of that which was nothing so, they departed from thence vnto Wallingford, and after to Abington, intising the people by all meanes possible vnto rebellion, all the waie as they went, and sending their agents abroad for the same purpose: at length they came to Circester in the darke of the night, and tooke vp their lodgings. The inhabitants of that towne suspecting the matter, and iudging (as the truth was) these rumors which the lords spred abroad to be but dreams, they tooke thereupon counsell togither, got them to armor, and stopped all the entries and outgates of the Innes where these new ghestes were lodged, insomuch that when they about midnight secretlie attempted to haue come foorth, and gone their waies, the townesmen with bow and arrowes were readie to slaie them, and keepe them in. The lords perceiuing the danger, got them to their armor and weapons, and did their best by force to breake through and repell the townesmen. But after they had fought from midnight till three of the clocke in the afternoone of the next daie, and perceiued they could not preuaile, they yeelded themselues to the townesmen, beseeching them to haue their liues saued, till they might come to the kings presence.

This request they had obteined, if a préest that was chapleine to one of them, had not in the meane time set fire vpon certeine houses in the towne, to the end that whiles the townesmen should busie themselues to quench the fire, the lords might find meanes to escape. But it came nothing to passe as he imagined, for the townesmen leauing all care to saue their houses from the rage of the fire, were kindled more in furie towards the lords, and so to reuenge themselues of them, they brought them foorth of the abbei where they had them in their hands, and in the twilight of the euening, stroke of their heads. ¶ The earle of Salisburie (saith Thomas Walsingham) who in all his life time had béene a fauourer of the Lollards or Wickleuists, a despiser of images, a contemner of canons, and a scorner of the sacraments, ended his daies (as it was reported) without the * sacrament of confession. These be the words of Thom. Wals. which are set downe, to signifie that the earle of Salisburie was a bidden ghest to blockham feast with the rest: and (as it should séeme by his relation) the more maligned, bicause he was somwhat estranged fro the corruption of the religion then receiued, and leaned to a sect pursued with spitefulnesse and reuenge.

Iohn

1400.

Harding.

The words of the earle of Kent.

The lords yéeld themselues.

A priest set fire on the houses of Circester.

Abr. Fl. out of *Tho. Walsin.* pag. 404.

* He died vnconfessed.

Iohn Holland earle of Huntington (as Thomas Walsingham writeth) was not with the lords at the castell of Windsore, but staied about London to behold the end of his businesse: and hearing how the matter went, farre contrarie to that he wished, he sought to flie by sea; but not able to get awaie, by reason the wind being contrarie would not permit him, he tooke his horsse, and hauing a knight with him called sir Iohn Shellie, he road into Essex, attempting to haue fled from thence by sea: but still the wind was so against him, that he was continuallie driuen backe when he was about to make saile, and so comming againe to land, he was taken one euening at Pitwell in Essex, in a mill (that belonged to one of his trustie freends) as he sat there at supper, togither with the said sir Iohn Shellie. The commons of the countrie that tooke him, brought him first to Chelmesford, and after to Plashie, where on the daie of S. Maurie, that is the fiftéenth of Ianuarie, about sun setting he was beheaded, in the verie place in which the duke of Glocester was arrested by king Richard. He confessed with lamentable repentance (as writers doo record) that diuers & manie waies he had offended God and his prince, because that vnderstanding the purpose of the other lords, he had not reuealed the same.

The lord *Hugh Spenser, otherwise called earle of Glocester, as he would haue fled into Wales, was taken and carried to Bristow, where (according to the earnest desires of the commons) he was beheaded. Maudelen fléeing into Scotland, was taken by the waie, and brought to the Tower. Manie other that were priuie to this conspiracie, were taken, and put to death, some at Oxford, as sir Thomas Blunt, sir Benet Cilie knight, and Thomas Wintercell esquier; but sir Leonard Brokas, and sir Iohn Shellie knights, Iohn Maudelen, and William Ferbie chapleins, were drawne, hanged, and beheaded at London. There were ninetéene in all executed in one place and other, and the heads of the cheefe conspirators were set on polles ouer London bridge, to the terror of others. Shortlie after, the abbat of Westminster, in whose house the conspiracie was begun (as is said) gooing betweene his monasterie & mansion, for thought fell into a sudden palsie, and shortlie after, without speech, ended his life. The bishop of Carleill was impeached, and condemned of the same conspiracie; but the king of his mercifull clemencie, pardoned him of that offense, although he died shortly after, more through feare than force of sicknesse, as some haue written. Thus all the associats of this vnhappie conspiracie tasted the painefull penance of their plesant pastime.

Thus haue yee heard what writers haue recorded of this matter, with some difference betwixt them that write, how the king should haue béene made awaie at a iusts; and other that testifie, how it should haue béene at a maske or mummerie: but whether they meant to haue dispatched him at a mumming, or at a iusts, their purpose being reuealed by the earle of Rutland, they were brought to confusion (as before yée haue heard.) And immediatlie after, king Henrie, to rid himselfe of anie such like danger to be attempted against him thereafter, caused king Richard to die of a violent death, that no man should afterward faine himselfe to represent his person, though some haue said, he was not priuie to that wicked offense. The common fame is, that he was euerie daie serued at the table with costlie meat, like a king, to the intent that no creature should suspect anie thing done contrarie to the order taken in the parlement; and when the meat was set before him, he was forbidden once to touch it; yea, he was not permitted so much as to smell to it, and so he died of forced famine.

¶ But Thomas Walsingham is so farre from imputing his death to compulsorie famine, that he referreth it altogither to voluntarie pining of himselfe. For when he heard that the complots and attempts of such his fauourers, as sought his restitution, and their owne aduancement, annihilated; and the chéefe agents shamefullie executed; he tooke such a conceit at these misfortunes (for so Thomas Walsingham termed them) and was so beaten out of hart, that wilfullie he starued himselfe, and so died in Pomfret

Marginal notes:
The lords beheaded.
Chr. S. Alb.
The earle of Huntington taken.
He is beheaded
* Thomas Spenser, saith *Wal.* & others.
Hall.
Execution.
Tho. Walsing. Hall.
The abbat of Westminster dieth suddenlie. *Thom. Wals.*
The bishop of Carleill dieth through feare, or rather thorough gréefe of mind, to sée the wicked prosper as he tooke it. *Hall.*
The sundrie reports of K. Richar. death.
Abr. Fl. out of Thom. Walsi. pag. 404, 405.

fret castell on S. Valentines daie : a happie daie to him, for it was the beginning of his ease, and the ending of his paine : so that death was to him daintie and swéet, as the poet saith, and that verie well in bréefe,

> Dulce mori miseris,
> Neque est melius morte in malis rebus.

Corn. Gall.

Thom. Walsin. Sir Piers de Exton a murtherer of king Richard.

One writer, which séemeth to haue great knowledge of king Richards dooings, saith, that king Henrie, sitting on a daie at his table, sore sighing, said, " Have I no faithfull fréend which will deliuer me of him, whose life will be my death, and whose death will be the preseruation of my life ;" This saieng was much noted of them which were present, and especiallie of one called sir Piers of Exton. This knight incontinentlie departed from the court, with eight strong persons in his companie, and came to Pomfret, commanding the esquier that was accustomed to sew and take the assaie before king Richard, to doo so no more, saieng ; " Let him eat now, for he shall not long eat." King Richard sat downe to dinner, and was serued without courtesie or assaie, whereupon much maruelling at the sudden change, he demanded of the esquier whie he did not his dutie ; " Sir (said he) I am otherwise commanded by sir Piers of Exton, which is newlie come from K. Henrie." When king Richard heard that word, he tooke the keruing knife in his hand, and strake the esquier on the head, saieng The diuell take Henrie of Lancaster and thée togither. And with that word, sir Piers entred the chamber, well armed, with eight tall men likewise armed, euerie of them hauing a bill in his hand.

The desperat manhood of king Richard.

K. Richard murthered.

King Richard perceiuing this, put the table from him, & steping to the formost man, wrung the bill out of his hands, & so valiantlie defended himselfe, that he slue foure of those that thus came to assaile him. Sir Piers being halfe dismaied herewith, lept into the chaire where king Richard was wont to sit, while the other foure persons fought with him, and chased him about the chamber. And in conclusion, as king Richard trauersed his ground, from one side of the chamber to an other, & comming by the chaire, where sir Piers stood, he was felled with a stroke of a pollax which sir Piers gaue him upon the head, and therewith rid him out of life, without giuing him respit once to call to God for mercie of his passed offenses. It is said, that sir Piers of Exton, after he had thus slaine him, wept right bitterlie, as one striken with the pricke of a giltie conscience, for murthering him, whome he had so long time obeied as king. After he was thus dead, his bodie was imbalmed, and séered, and couered with lead, all saue the face, to the intent that all men might sée him, and perceiue that he was departed this life : for as the corps was conueied from Pomfret to Lon don, in all the townes and places where those that had the conueiance of it did staie with it all night, they caused dirige to be soong in the euening, and masse of requiem in the morning ; and as well after the one seruice as the other, his face discouered, was shewed to all that courted to behold it.

The dead bodie of K. Richard brought to the Tower.

Thus was the corps first brought to the Tower, and after through the citie, to the cathedrall church of saint Paule bare faced, where it laie thrée daies togither, that all men might behold it. There was a solemne obsequie doone for him, both at Paules, and after at Wesminster, at which time, both at dirige ouernight, and in the morning at the masse of requiem, the king and the citizens of London were present. When

He is buried at Langlie.

the same was ended, the corps was commanded to be had vnto Langlie, there to be buried in the church of the friers preachers. The bishop of Chester, the abbats of saint Albons and Waltham, celebrated the exequies for the buriall, none of the nobles nor anie of the commons (to accompt of) being present : neithei was there anie to bid them to dinner after they had laid him in the ground, and finished the funerall seruice. He was after by king Henrie the fift remooued to Westminster, and there honorablie intoomed with quéene Anne his wife, although the Scots vntrulie write, that he escaped out of prison, and led a vertuous and a solitarie life in Scotland, and there died,

                                                      & is

& is buried (as they hold) in the blacke friers at Sterling. ¶ But Fabian and others doo *Abr. Fl. out of Fabian pag. 378.*
as it were point out the place of his interrement, saieng that he lieth intoomed on the
south side of saint Edwards shrine, with an epitaph expressing partlie his proportion
of bodie and partlie his properties of mind, as after followeth in a rimed hexas-
tichon:

> Prudens & mundus, Richardus iure secundus,
> Perfatum victus, iacet hic sub marmore pictus,
> Verax sermone, fuit & plenus ratione,
> Corpore procerus, animo prudens vt Homerus,
> Ecclesiæ fauit, elatus suppeditauit,
> Quemuis prostrauit, regalia qui violauit.

When the newes of king Richards deposing was reported in France, king Charles *Forren princes not without cause abhorre to heare of the shamefull murther of king Richard.*
and all his court woondering, detested and abhorred such an iniurie doone to an an-
nointed king, to a crowned prince, and to the head of a realme: but in especiall,
Walerane earle of saint Paule, which had married king Richards halfe sister, mooued
with great disdaine towards king Henrie, ceassed not to stirre king Charles & his
councell to make warres against the Englishmen, and he himselfe sent letters of defiance into England. The earles sute was easilie agréed vnto, and an armie roiall appointed with all speed, to inuade England. The armie was come downe into Picardie,
redie to be transported into England: but when it was certeinelie knowen, that king
Richard was dead, and that the enterprise of his deliuerance (which was chéeflie meant)
was frustrate and void, the armie was dissolued. But when the certeintie of K. Richards death was intimate to the Gascoignes, the most part of the wisest men of the
countrie were right pensiue: for they iudged verelie, that hereby the English nation *How the Gascoignes tooke the death of K. Richard*
should be brought to dishonour, and losse of their ancient fame and glorie, for com-
mitting so heinous an offense against their king and souereigne lord, the memorie
whereof (as they thought) would neuer die: and chéeflie, the citizens of Burdeaux
tooke the matter verie sore at the stomach: for they bare excéeding fauour to king
Richard, because he was borne and brought vp in their citie, and therefore more than
all the residue they shewed themselves to abhorre so heinous a déed.

The Frenchmen hauing understanding hereof, thought with themselues that now
was the time for them to practise with the Gascoignes to reduce them from the
English obeisance, vnder their subiection. Herevpon came Lewes duke of Burbon *The duke of Burbon.*
vnto Agen, and wrote to diuerse cities and townes, on the confines of Guien, exhorting them with large promises, and faire sugred words, to reuolt from the Englishmen,
and to become subiects to the crowne of France; but his trauell preuailed not: for the
people vnderstanding that the English yoke was but easie in comparison to the French
bondage, determined to abide rather in their old subiection, than for a displeasure irrecouerable to aduenture themselues on a new doubtfull perill; yet it was doubted, least *Froissard.*
the cities of Burdeaux, Dar, and Baion, would haue reuolted, if the lords of the
marches about those places had leaned to them in that purpose, for they sent their
commissioners to Agen, to treate with the duke of Burbon. But forsomuch as the
lords, Pomiers, Mucident, Duras, Landuras, Copane, Rosem, & Langurant, were
minded to continue still English, those cities durst not without them turne to the
French obeisance, for they could not haue stirred out of their gates, but those lords
would haue béene readie at their elbowes, to haue caught them by the sléeues.

King Henrie being aduertised of the Frenchmens couert meanings, and also of the
wauering minds of the Gascoignes, sent Thomas Persie earle of Worcester with two
hundred men of armes, and four hundred archers into Guien, to aid and assist sir
Robert Knols, his lieutenant there. The chiefest capteines that accompanied the
earle in this iournie were these: first, his nephew sir Hugh Hastings, sir Thomas *Polydor.*
Colleuill, sir William Lisle, Iohn de Graillie base sonne to the capitall de Boeuf, sir *Froissard.*
                                                        William

William Draiton, sir Iohn Daubreticourt: also there went with him the bishop of London, and master Richard Doall or Dolleie. The earle at his arriual so wiselie intreated the noble men, so grauelie persuaded the magistrats of the cities and townes, and so gentlie and familiarlie vsed and treated the commons, that he not onelie appeased their furie and malice, but brought them to louing and vniforme obeisance, receiuing of them othes of obedience, & loiall fealtie, which doone, he returned againe into England with great thanks.

The French king perceiuing he could not bring his purpose about, neither by inuading England, nor by practising with the Gascoignes, sent a solemne ambassage into England, requiring to haue his daughter the ladie Isabell, sometime espoused to king Richard, restored to him againe. King Henrie gentlie receiued those that were sent to him about this message, and for answer, promised to send his commissioners vnto Calis, which should further commune and conclude with them. ¶ This seemeth

dissonant from the report of Fabian deriued out of Gagwine. For he saith that Charles hearing of the suppression of K. Richard, sent 2 of his houshold knights into England, requiring king Henrie the fourth, then newlie made king, to send home his daughter Isabell, latelie married vnto king Richard, with such dowrie as with hir was promised. In dooing of which message king Henrie took such displeasure, that he threw the said two knights in prison; where through one of them (named Blanchet) died in England, and the other called Henrie, after great sicknesse returned into France: wherefore if Fabian plaie not the fabler, those that were sent on the said message were not gentlie receiued of king Henrie; vnlesse to be cast in prison and discourteouslie dealt withall stand countable for beneuolence & gentle interteinment. But to remit this and the like variances among writers to such as can reconcile them, let vs returne to the storie.

It was not inough that K. Henrie was thus troubled now in the first yere of his reigne, with ciuill sedition, and the couert practises of Frenchmen; but that the Scots also tooke vpon them to make open warre against him: it chanced (as in the Scotish chronicles more at large appeareth) that George of Dunbar, earle of the

marches of Scotland, being in displeasure with Robert king of Scots, fled into England, to Henrie earle of Northumberland, wherevpon the Scotish king depriued him of all his dignities and possessions, and caused his goods to be confiscate, and after wrote to the king of England, requiring him if he would haue the truce anie longer to continue, either to deliuer into his possession the earle of March and other traitors to his person, or else to banish them out of his realmes and dominions. King Henrie dis-

créetly answerd the herald of Scotland, that the words of a prince ought to be kept: and his writings and seale to be inuiolate: and considering that he had granted a safe conduct to the earle and his companie, he should neither without cause reasonable breake his promise, nor yet deface his honor. Which answer declared to the king of

Scots, he incontinentlie proclaimed open warre against the king of England, with fire and sword. Herevpon, one sir Robert Logon, a Scotish knight, with certeine ships well appointed for the warre, meant to haue destroied the English fléet that was come on the coasts of Scotland, about Aberden, to fish there: but (as it chanced) he met

with certeine ships of Lin, that fought with him, and tooke him prisoner, with the residue of his companie, so that he quite failed of his purpose, and came to the losse himselfe.

At the same time, the Englishmen spoiled also certeine of the Iles of Orkenie. This summer, great death chanced in this land, manie dieing of the pestilence, wherewith sundrie places were infected. King Henrie perceiuing that policie often-

times preuenteth perill, and vnderstanding the naughtie purposes of the Scots, gathered a great armie, and entred into Scotland, burning townes, villages, and castels, with a great part of the townes of Edenburgh and Léeth, and besieged the castell

of

of Edenburgh in the end of September, whereof was capteine Dauid duke of Roth- The duke of Rothsaie.
saie, and a prince of the realme, with Archembald earle of Dowglas, hauing with
them manie hardie men of warre. Robert duke of Albanie, that was appointed The duke of Albanie.
gouernour of the realme, because the king was sicke and not méet to rule, sent an
herald vnto king Henrie, promising him battell within six daies at the furthest,
if he would so long tarrie, which king Henrie promised to doo right gladlie, and *Anno Reg. 2.*
gaue to the herald for bringing him so acceptable newes, a gowne of silke, and a
chéine of gold. But king Henrie staied six daies, and sixtéene too, without hearing
any word of the gouernors comming. Then the winter beginning to wax cold,
and foule weather still increasing, caused the king to breake vp his siege, and so returned without battell or skirmish offered.

In the meane time that the king was thus in Scotland, the Scots made a rode into King Henrie returneth home.
Northumberland, and burned diuerse townes in Bamburroughshire. At the kings The Scots burne in Northumberland.
comming backe to Yorke, there were two strangers, the one a Frenchman, and the
other an Italian, requiring to accomplish certeine feats of armes, against sir Iohn Iusts at Yorke.
Cornewall, and Ianico de Artois. Their request was granted, and the strangers were
put to the worst, whereby sir Iohn Cornewall obteined the kings fauour so farre Sir Iohn Cornewall marrieth the kings sister.
foorth, that he married the kings sister, the widow of Iohn Holland, earle of Hun-
tington. Yet some said, that the knight and the countesse were agréed aforehand,
without the kings consent. In the kings absence, whilest he was foorth of the realme
in Scotland against his enimies, the Welshmen tooke occasion to rebell vnder the The welshmen rebell by the setting on of Owen Glendouer.
conduct of their capteine Owen Glendouer, dooing what mischéefe they could deuise, *Iohn Stow.*
vnto their English neighbours. This Owen Glendouer was sonne to an esquier of Owen Glendouer what he was.
Wales, named Griffith Vichan: he dwelled in the parish of Conwaie, within the countie of Merioneth in North Wales, in a place called Glindourwie, which is as much
to saie in English, as The vallie by the side of the water of Dée, by occasion whereof
he was surnamed Glindour Dew.

He was first set to studie the lawes of the realme, and became an vtter barrester,
or an apprentise of the law (as they terme him) and serued king Richard at Flint
castell, when he was taken by Henrie duke of Lancaster, though other haue written
that he serued this king Henrie the fourth, before he came to atteine the crowne, *Tho. Walsi.*
in roome of an esquier, and after, by reason of variance that rose betwixt him and
the lord Reginald Gréie of Ruthin, about the lands which he claimed to be his by
right of inheritance: when he saw that he might not preuaile, finding no such fauor
in his sute as he looked for, he first made warre against the said lord Greie, wasting The occasion that mooued him to rebell.
his lands and possessions with fire and sword, cruellie killing his seruants and tenants.
The king aduertised of such rebellious exploits, enterprised by the said Owen, and The king entreth into wales, meaning to chastise the rebels.
his vnrulie complices, determined to chastise them, as disturbers of his peace, and
so with an armie entered into Wales; but the Welshmen with their capteine withdrew into the mounteines of Snowdon, so to escape the reuenge, which the king
meant towards them. The king therefore did much hurt in the countries with fire
and sword, sleing diuerse that with weapon in hand came foorth to resist him, and
so with a great bootie of beasts and cattell he returned.

The emperour of Constantinople comming into England to sue for aid against the The emperor of Constantinople cometh into Englād.
Turkes, was met by the king on Blackeheath, vpon the feast day of saint Thomas the
apostle, and brought vnto London with great honor. The king bare all his charges,
presenting him with gifts at his departure, meet for such an estate. After the feast 1401
of the Epiphanie, a parlement was holden, in which an act was made, against those
that held opinions in religion, contrarie to the receiued doctrine of the church of A parlement.
Rome; ordeining, that wheresoeuer any of them were found and prooued to set
foorth such doctrine, they should be apprehended, and deliuered to the bishop their
diocesane; and if they stood stiffelie in their opinions, and would not be reformed,

they should be deliuered to the secular power, to be burnt to ashes. The first that tasted the smart of this statute, was one William Hawtrée or Sawtrée a priest, that being apprehended was burnt in Smithfield, in time of this parlement.

One burnt in Smithfield.

Additions of the chronicles of Flanders.

There was also the erle of Deuonshire, as Froissard saith.

The hath Froissard. Commissioners met to treat of peace.

About the same time, king Henrie (according to promise made (as ye haue heard) vnto the French ambassadors, sent ouer into the countrie of Guisnes, Edward earle of Rutland, otherwise in king Richards daies intitled duke of Aumarle, son to Edmund duke of Yorke, Henrie earle of Northumberland, and his sonne the lord Henrie Persie, the lord Yuan Fitzwarren, the bishops of Winchester and Lincolne: where the duke of Burbon, the lords Charles d'Albert, Charles de Hangest, Iohn de Chastelmorant, the Patriarche of Ierusalem, and the bishops of Paris and Beauuois, were readie there to commune with them, and so they assembling togither at sundrie times and places, the Frenchmen required to haue queene Isabell to them restored, but the Englishmen séemed loth to depart with hir, requiring to haue hir married to Henrie Prince of Wales, one in bloud and age in all things to hir equall;

The French king troubled with a frensie,

but the Frenchmen would in no wise condescend thereto, without their kings consent, who at that present was not in case to vtter his mind, being troubled with his woonted disease. The commissioners then began treat of peace, and at length renewed the truce to endure for six and twentie yeares yet to come; wherevnto the foure yeares passed being added, made vp the number of thirtie yeares, according to the conclusion agreed vpon, in the life time of king Richard.

Truce for 26 yeares.

Hall.

The Frenchmen demand a dower for quéene Isabell.

Some authors affirme, that there was a new league concluded, to continue, during the liues of both the princes. The Frenchmen diuerse times required to haue some dower assigned foorth for queene Isabell, but that was at all times vtterlie denied, for that the marriage betwixt hir and king Richard was neuer consummate, by reason whereof she was not dowable. Neuerthelesse, she was shortlie after sent home, vnder the conduct of the earle of Worcester, associat with diuerse other noble and honorable personages, both men and women, hauing with hir all the iewels, ornaments, and plate which she brought into England, with a great surplusage besides

Additions of the chron. of Flanders.

She is deliuered home.

giuen to hir by the king. She was deliuered betwixt Bullongne and Calis, to Valeran earle of saint Paule, the French kings lieutenant in Picardie, who being accompanied with the bishop of Chartres, the lord de Hugueuile, the ladie of Monpensier sister to the erle of March, the ladie of Lucenburgh sister to the said earle of saint Paule, & diuerse other ladies and gentlewomen, which receiued hir with great ioy and gladnesse, and taking leaue of the English lords and ladies, they conueied hir to the dukes of Burgognie and Burbon, that attended for hir, not far off, upon a hill,

She is conueied to Paris,

with a great number of people. They first conueied hir to Bullogne, & after to Abuile, from whence the duke of Orleance conueied hir to Paris, vnto the presence of the king hir father, and the queene hir mother: she was after giuen in marriage vnto Charles, sonne to Lewes duke of Orleance.

Hir second marriage.

Anno Reg. 3. Owen Glendouer.

The danger of the king to haue béene destroied.

About the same time, Owen Glendouer and his Welshmen did much hurt to the the kings subiects. One night as the king was going to bed, he was in danger to haue beene destroied; for some naughtie traitorous persons had conueied into his bed a certeine iron made with smiths craft, like a caltrop, with three long prickes, sharp and small, standing vpright, it such sort, that when he had laid him downe, & that the weight of his bodie should come vpon the bed, he should have beene thrust in with those pricks, and peraduenture slaine: but as God would, the king not thinking of any such thing, chanced yet to féele and perceiue the instrument before he laid him downe, and so escaped the danger. ¶Howbeit he was not so soone deliuered from feare; for he might well haue his life in suspicion, & prouide for the preseruation of the same; sith perils of death crept into his secret chamber, and laie lurking in the bed of downe where his bodie was to be reposed and to take rest. Oh what a suspected state therefore is that of a king holding his regiment with the hatred of

his

his people, the hart grudgings of his courtiers, and the peremtorie practises of both togither? Could he confidentlie compose or setle himselfe to sleepe for feare of strangling? Durst he boldly eat and drinke without dread of poisoning? Might he aduenture to shew himselfe in great méetings or solemne assemblies without mistrust of mischeefe against his person intended? What pleasure or what felicitie could he take in his princelie pompe, which he knew by manifest and fearfull experience, to be enuied and maligned to the verie death? The state of such a king is noted by the poet in Dionysius, as in a mirror, concerning whom it is said,

Districtus ensis cui super impia
Ceruice pendet, non Siculæ dapes
Dulcem elaborabunt saporem,
Non auium cytharæq. cantus.

Hor. lib. ca. 3.
Ode. 1.

This yeare, the eight day of April deceassed the lord Thomas Beauchampe earle of Warwike. In the moneth of March appeared a blasing starre, first betwéene the east part of the firmament and the North, flashing foorth fire and flames round about it, and lastlie shooting foorth fierie beams towards the north, foreshewing (as was thought) the great effusion of bloud that followed, about the parts of Wales and Northumberland. For much about the same time, Owen Glendouer (with his Welshmen) fought with the lord Greie of Ruthen, comming foorth to defend his possessions, which the same Owen wasted and destroied: and as the fortune of that daies worke fell out, the lord Greie was taken prisoner, and manie of his men were slaine. This hap lifted the Welshmen into high pride, and increased meruelouslie their wicked and presumptuous attempts,

1402
The earle of Warwike departeth this life.
A blasing starre.

The lord Greie of Ruthen taken in fight by Owē Glendouer.

About Whitsuntide a conspiracie was deuised by certeine persons, that wished the kings death, mainteining and bruting abroad, that king Richard was aliue, and therefore exhorted men to stand with him, for shortlie he would come to light, and reward such as tooke his part with iust recompense. Herewith, there was a priest taken at Ware, or (as some books haue) at Warwike, who had a kalendar or roll, in which a great number of Names were written, more than were in any wise guiltie of the fact, as afterwards appeared by the same priests confession. For being examined, whether he knew such persons as he had so inrolled, & were there present before him, he said he neuer knew them at all; and being demanded wherefore he had then so recorded their names, he answered, because he thought they would gladlie doo what mischief they could against king Henrie, vpon any occasion offered in reuenge of the iniuries doone to king Richard, by whom they had beene aduanced, and princelie preferred. When therefore there appeared no more credit in the man, he was condemned, drawen, hanged, and quartered, and diuerse that had beene apprehended about that matter, were released, and set at libertie. Shortlie after, the prior of Laund (who for his euil gouernment had béene depriued of his state and dignitie) was likewise executed, not for attempting any thing of himselfe, but onlie for that he confessed, that he knew euil counsell and concealed it. His name was Walter Baldocke, a canon sometime in Dunstable, and by king Richard promoted to the priorship of Laund.

A brute was spred abroad that king Richard was liuing.
A priest takē.

He is executed.

The prior of Laund apprehended.

Also the same time, certeine greie friers were apprehended for treason which they had deuised to bring to passe, and one of them, whose name was Richard Frisebie, being asked what he would doo if king Richard had béene aliue, and present with them, answered stoutlie, that he would fight against any man in his quarrell, euen to death. Herevpon, he was condemned, drawen, and hanged in his friers wéed, to the great confusion of his brethren; but they made earnest instance to haue his bodie taken downe, and buried with diriges and exequies, and had their sute granted. Sir Roger of Claringdon knight was also put to death about this conspiracie, with two of his seruants, the one an esquier, the other a yeoman. He was base sonne (as

Greie friers apprehended.

A greie frier hanged in his habit.

Sir Roger Claringdon.

D 2

was

The diuell appeareth in likenesse of a greie frier.

was reported) vnto Edward, eldest sonne to king Edward the third, surnamed the blacke prince. On Corpus Christi daie at euensong time, the diuell (as was thought) appeared in a towne of Essex called Danburie, entring into the church in likenesse of a greie frier, behauing himselfe verie outragiouslie, plaieng his parts like a diuell indéed, so that the parishioners were put in a maruellous great fright.

At the same instant, there chanced such a tempest of wind, thunder, and lightning, that the highest part of the roofe of that church was blowen downe, and the chancell was all to shaken, rent, and torne in péeces. Within a small while after,

Eight friers executed.

eight of those greie friers that had practised treason against the king were brought to open iudgement, and conuicted were drawen and headed at London; and two other suffered at Leicester, all which persons had published king Richard to be aliue. Owen Glendouer, according to his accustomed manner, robbing and spoiling within the English borders, caused all the forces of the shire of Hereford to assemble togither against them, vnder the conduct of Edmund Mortimer earle of March. But cōming to trie the matter by battell, whether by treason or otherwise, so it

The earle of March taken prisoner in batell by Owen Glendouer.

fortuned, that the English power was discomfited, the earle taken prisoner, and aboue a thousand of his people slaine in the place. The shamefull villanie vsed by the Welshwomen towards the dead carcasses, was such, as honest eares would be ashamed to heare, and continent toongs to speake thereof. The dead bodies might not be buried, without great summes of monie giuen for libertie to conueie them awaie.

The suspicion of K. Henrie grounded vpō a guiltie conscience.

The king was not hastie to purchase the deliuerance of the earle March, bicause his title to the crowne was well inough knowen, and therefore suffered him to remaine in miserable prison, wishing both the said earle, and all other of his linage out of this life, with God and his saincts in heauen, so they had béene out of the waie, for then all had béene well inough as he thought. But to let these things

The kings daughter maried into Germanie.

passe, the king this yeare sent his eldest daughter Blanch, accōpanied with the earle of Summerset, the bishop of Worcester, the lord Clifford, and others, into Almanie, which brought hir to Colin, and there with great triumph she was married to William duke of Bauier, sonne and heire to Lewes the emperour. About mid of August, the king to chastise the presumptuous attempts of the Welshmen, went with a great power of men into Wales, to pursue the capteine of the Welsh rebell Owen Glendouer, but in effect he lost his labor; for Owen conueied himselfe out of the waie, into his knowen lurking places, and (as was thought) through art ma-

Intemperat weather.

gike, he caused such foule weather of winds, tempest, raine, snow, and haile to be raised, for the annoiance of the kings armie, that the like had not béene heard of; in such sort, that the king was constreined to returne home, hauing caused his people yet to spoile and burne first a great part of the countrie. The same time,

The deceasse of the duke of Yorke.

Scots ouerthrowen.

the lord Edmund of Langlie duke of Yorke departed this life, and was buried at Langlie with his brethren. The Scots vnder the leding of Patrike Hepborne, of the Hales the yoonger, entring into England, were ouerthrowen at Nesbit, in the marches, as in the Scotish chronicle ye may find more at large. This battell was fought the two and twentith of Iune, in this yeare of our Lord 1402.

Archembald earle Dowglas sore displeased in his mind for this ouerthrow, procured a commission to inuade England, and that to his cost, as ye may likewise read in

Scots vanquished at Homildon.

the Scotish histories. For at a place called Homildon, they were so fiercelie assailed by the Englishmen, vnder the leding of the lord Persie, surnamed Henrie Hotspur, and George earle of March, that with violence of the English shot they were quite vanquished and put to flight, on the Rood daie in haruest, with a great slaughter made by the Englishmen. We know that the Scotish writers note this battell to haue chanced in the yeare 1403. But we following Tho. Walsingham in this place, and other English writers, for the accompt of times, haue thought good to place

it

it in this yeare 1402, as in the same writers we find it.　There were slaine of men The number slaine. of estimation, sir Iohn Swinton, sir Adam Gordon, sir Iohn Leuiston, sir Alexander Ramsie of Dalehousie, and three and twentie knights, besides ten thousand of the commons: and of prisoners among other were these, Mordacke earle of Fife, son Prisoners taken. to the gouernour Archembald earle Dowglas, which in the fight lost one of his eies, Thomas erle of Murrey, Robert earle of Angus, and (as some writers haue) the earles of Atholl & Menteith, with fiue hundred other of meaner degrées.　After this, the lord Persie, hauing bestowed the prisoners in suer kéeping, entered Tiuidale, wasting and destroieng the whole countrie, and then besieged the castell of Cocklawes, The castell of Cocklawes besieged by the lord Persie. whereof was capteine one sir Iohn Grenlow, who compounded with the Englishmen, that if the castell were not succoured within three moneths, then he would deliuer it into their hands.

The first two moneths passed, and no likelihood of rescue appeared; but yer the third moneth was expired, the Englishmen being sent for to go with the king into Wales, raised their siege and departed, leauing the noble men prisoners with the earle of Northumberland, and with his sonne the lord Persie, to kéepe them to the kings vse.　In this meane while, such as misliked with the doctrine and ceremonies The professors of wicklifs doctrine. then vsed in the church, ceassed not to vtter their consciences, though in secret, to those in whome they had affiance.　But as in the like cases it commonlie hapneth, they were bewraied by some that were thought chieflie to fauour their cause, as by sir Lewes Clifford knight, who hauing leaned to the doctrine a long time, did now (as Thomas Walsingham writeth) disclose all that he knew vnto the archbishop of Canturburie, to shew himselfe as it were to haue erred rather of simplenesse and ignorance, than of frowardnesse or stubborn malice.　The names of such as taught the articles and conclusions mainteined by those which then they called Lollards or heretikes, the said sir Lewes Clifford gaue in writing to the said archbishop. Sir Lewes Clifford bewraieth his fellowes. Edmund Mortimer earle of March, prisoner with Owen Glendouer, whether for The earle of March marieth the daughter of Owen Glendouer. irksomnesse of cruell captiuitie, or feare of death, or for what other cause, it is vncerteine, agréed to take part with Owen, against the king of England, and tooke to wife the daughter of the said Owen.

Strange wonders happened (as men reported) at the natiuitie of this man, for the same night he was borne, all his fathers horsses in the stable were found to stand in bloud vp to the bellies.　The morow after the feast of saint Michaell, a parlement began at Westminster, which continued the space of seauen weekes, in the *Anno Reg.* 4. A parlement. same was a tenth and a halfe granted by the cleargie, and a fiftéenth by the communaltie.　Moreouer, the commons in this parlement besought the king to haue the person of George earle of March a Scotishman, recommended to his maiestie, for George earle of March recommended to the king by parlement. that the same earle shewed himselfe faithfull to the king & his realme.　¶ There was also a statute made, that the friers beggers should not receiue any into their order, vnder the age of fourteene yeares.　In this fourth yeare of king Henries reigne, 1403. ambassadors were sent ouer into Britaine, to bring from thence the duches of Bri- Ambassadors. taine, the ladie Iane de Nauarre, the widow of Iohn de Montford, late duke of Britaine, surnamed the conqueror, with whom by procurators the king had contracted matrimonie.　In the beginning of Februarie, those that were sent returned with hir in safetie, but not without tasting the bitter stormes of the wind and weather, that tossed them sore to and fro, before they could get to land.　The king met hir at Winchester, where the seuenth of Februarie, the marriage was solemnized betwixt them.

Whilest these things were thus in dooing in England, Waleran earl of saint Paule, bearing still a deadlie and malicious hatred toward king Henrie, hauing assembled sixtéene or seuentéene hundred men of warre, imbarked them at Har- The earle of saint Paule in the Ile of Wight. flew, and taking the sea, landed in the Ile of Wight, in the which he burned two villages,

villages, and foure simple cotages, and for a triumph of so noble an act, made foure knights. But when he heard that the people of the Ile were assembled and approched to fight with him, he hasted to his ships and returned home : wherewith the noble men of his companie were displeased, considering his prouision to be great and his gaine small. In the same verie season, Iohn earle of Cleremont sonne to the duke of Bourbon, wan in Gascoigne out of the Englishmens possession, the castels of saint Peter, saint Marie, and the New castell ; and the lord de la Bret wan the castell of Carlassin, which was no small losse to the English nation.

The earle of
Cleremont in
Gascoigne.

Henrie earle of Northumberland, with his brother Thomas earle of Worcester, and his sonne the lord Henrie Persie, surnamed Hotspur, which were to king Henrie in the beginning of his reigne, both faithfull freends, and earnest aiders, began now to enuie his wealth and felicitie ; and especiallie they were gréeued, bicause the king demanded of the earle and his sonne such Scotish prisoners as were taken at Homeldon and Nesbit : for of all the captiues which were taken in the conflicts foughten in those two places, there was deliuered to the kings possession onlie Mordake earle of Fife, the duke of Albanies sonne, though the king did diuers and sundrie times require deliuerance of the residue, and that with great threatnings : wherewith the Persies being sore offended, for that they claimed them as their owne proper prisoners, and their peculiar preies, by the counsell of the lord Thomas Persie earle of Worcester, whose studie was euer (as some write) to procure malice, and set things in a broile, came to the king vnto Windsore (vpon a purpose to prooue him) and there required of him, that either by ransome or otherwise, he would cause to be deliuered out of prison Edmund Mortimer earle of March, their cousine germane, whome (as they reported) Owen Glendouer kept in filthie prison, shakled with irons, onelie for that he tooke his part, and was to him faithfull and true.

The request of
the Persies.

The king began not a little to muse at this request, and not without cause : for in déed it touched him somewhat neere, sith this Edmund was sonne to Roger earle of March, sonne to the ladie Philip, daughter of Lionell duke of Clarence, the third sonne of king Edward the third ; which Edmund at king Richards going into Ireland, was proclamed heire apparant to the crowne and realme, whose aunt called Elianor, the lord Henrie Persie had married ; and therefore king Henrie could not well heare, that anie man should be in earnest about the aduancement of that linage. The king when he had studied on the matter made answer that the earle of March was not taken prisoner for his cause, nor in his seruice, but willinglie suffered himselfe to be taken, bicause he would not withstand the attempts of Owen Glendouer and his complices, and therefore he would neither ransome him, nor reléeue him.

The Persies with this answer and fraudulent excuse were not a little fumed, insomuch that Henrie Hotspur said openlie : Behold, the heire of the relme is robbed of his right, and yet the robber with his owne will not redeeme him. So in this furie the Persies departed, minding nothing more than to depose king Henrie from the high type of his roialtie, and to place in his seat their cousine Edmund earle of March, whom they did not onlie deliuer out of captiuitie, but also (to the high displeasure of king Henrie) entered in league with the foresaid Owen Glendouer. Héerewith, they by their deputies in the house of the archdeacon of Bangor, diuided the realme amongst them, causing a tripartite indenture to be made and sealed with their seales, by the couenants whereof, all England from Seuerne and Trent, south and eastward, was assigned to the earle of March : all Wales, & the lands beyond Seuerne westward, were appointed to Owen Glendouer : and all the remnant from Trent northward, to the lord Persie.

The saieng of
the L. Persie.

The conspiracies
of the Persies
with Owen
Glendouer.
An indenture
tripartite.

A diuision of
that which they
had not.

A vaine prophe-
sie.

This was doone (as some haue said) through a foolish credit giuen to a vaine
prophesie,

prophesie, as though king Henrie was the moldwarpe, cursed of Gods owne mouth, and they three were the dragon, the lion, and the woolfe, which should diuide this realme betwéene them.   Such is the deuiation (saith Hall) and not diuination of those blind and fantasticall dreames of the Welsh prophesiers.   King Henrie not knowing of this new confederacie, and nothing lesse minding than that which after happened, gathered a great armie to go againe into Wales, whereof the earle of Northumberland and his sonne were aduertised by the earle of Worcester, and with all diligence raised all the power they could make, and sent to the Scots which before were taken prisoners at Homeldon, for aid of men, promising to the earle of Dowglas the towne of Berwike, and a part of Northumberland, and to other Scotish lords great lordships and seigniories, if they obteined the upper hand.   The Scots in hope of gaine, and desirous to be reuenged of their old greefes, came to the earle with a great companie well appointed.

The Persies raise their powers.

They craue aid of Scots.

The Persies to make their part séeme good, deuised certeine articles, by the aduise of Richard Scroope, archbishop of Yorke, brother to the lord Scroope, whome king Henrie had caused to be beheaded at Bristow.   These articles being shewed to diuerse noblemen, and other states of the realme, mooued them to fauour their purpose, in so much that manie of them did not onelie promise to the Persies aid and succour by words, but also by their writings and seales confirmed the same.   Howbeit when the matter came to triall, the most part of the confederates abandoned them, and at the daie of the conflict left them alone.   Thus after that the conspirators had discouered themselues, the lord Henrie Persie desirous to procéed in the enterprise, vpon trust to be assisted by Owen Glendouer, the earle of March, & other, assembled an armie of men of armes and archers foorth of Cheshire and Wales.   Incontinentlie his vncle Thomas Persie earle of Worcester, that had the gouernement of the prince of Wales, who as then laie at London in secret manner, conueied himselfe out of the princes house, and comming to Stafford (where he met his nephue) they increased their power by all waies and meanes they could deuise.   The earle of Northumberland himselfe was not with them, but being sicke, had promised vpon his amendement to repaire vnto them (as some write) with all conuenient spéed.

The archbish. of Yorke of counsell with the Persies in conspiracie.
Thom. Wals.

The earle of Worcester gouernour to the prince slippeth from him.
Hall.

These noble men, to make their conspiracie to séem excusable, besides the articles aboue mentioned, sent letters abroad, wherein was conteined, that their gathering of an armie tended to none other end, but onlie for the safegard of their owne persons, and to put some better gouernment in the commonwealth.   For whereas taxes and tallages were dailie leuied, vnder pretense to be imploied in defence of the realme, the same were vainlie wasted, and vnprofitablie consumed: and where through the slanderous reports of their enimies, the king had taken a greeuous displeasure with them, they durst not appeare personallie in the kings presence, vntill the prelats and barons of the realme had obteined of the king licence for them to come and purge themselues before him, by lawfull triall of their péeres, whose iudgement (as they pretended) they would in no wise refuse.   Manie that saw and heard these letters, did commend their diligence, and highlie praised their assured fidelitie and trustinesse towards the commonwealth.

The pretense of the Persies, as they published it abroad.

But the king vnderstanding their cloaked drift, deuised (by what meanes he might) to quiet and appease the commons, and deface their contriued forgeries; and therefore he wrote an answer to their libels, that he maruelled much, sith the earle of Northumberland, and the lord Henrie Persie his sonne, had receiued the most part of the summes of monie granted to him by the cleargie and communaltie, for defence of the marches, as he could euidentlie prooue what should mooue them to complaine and raise such manifest slanders.   And whereas he vnderstood, that the earles of Northumberland and Worcester, and the lord Persie had by their letters signified to their freends abroad, that by reason of the slanderous reports of their enimies,

The kings answer to the Persies libell.

enimies, they durst not appeare in his presence, without the mediation of the prelats and nobles of the realme, so as they required pledges, whereby they might safelie come afore him, to declare and alledge what they had to saie in proofe of their innocencie, he protested by letters sent foorth vnder his seale, that they might safelie come and go, without all danger, or anie manner of indamagement to be offered to their persons.

But this could not satisfie those men, but that resolued to go forwards with their enterprise, they marched towards Shrewsburie, vpon hope to be aided (as men thought) by Owen Glendouer, and his Welshmen, publishing abroad throughout the countries on each side, that king Richard was aliue, whome if they wished to sée, they willed them to repaire in armour vnto the castell of Chester, where (without all doubt) he was at that present, and redie to come forward. This tale being raised, though it were most vntrue, yet it bred variable motions in mens minds, causing them to wauer, so as they knew not to which part they should sticke; and verelie, diuers were well affected towards king Richard, speciallie such as had tasted of his princelie bountifulnes, of which there was no small number. And to speake a truth, no maruell it was, if manie enuied the prosperous state of king Henrie, sith it was euident inough to the world, that he had with wrong vsurped the crowne, and not onelie violentlie deposed king Richard, but also cruellie procured his death; for the which vndoubtedlie, both he and his posteritie tasted such troubles, as put them still in danger of their states, till their direct suceeeding line was quite rooted out by the contrarie faction, as in Henrie the sixt and Edward the fourth it may appeare.

But now to returne where we left. King Henrie aduertised of the proceedings of the Persies, foorthwith gathered about him such power as he might make, and being earnestlie called vpon by the Scot, the earle of March, to make hast and giue battell to his enimies, before their power by delaieng of time should still too much increase, he passed forward with such spéed, that he was in sight of his

enimies, lieng in campe néere to Shrewesburie, before they were in doubt of anie such thing, for the Persies thought that he would have staid at Burton vpon Trent, till his councell had come thither to him to giue their aduise what he were best to doo. But herein the enimie was deceiued of his expectation, sith the king had great regard of expedition and making speed for the safetie of his own person, whereunto the earle of March incited him, considering that in delaie is danger, & losse in lingering, as the poet in the like case saith:

Tolle moras, nocuit semper differre paratis,
Dum trepidant nullo firmatæ robore partes.

By reason of the kings sudden cōming in this sort, they staied from assaulting the towne of Shrewesburie, which enterprise they were readie at that instant to haue taken in hand, and foorth with the lord Persie (as a capteine of high courage) began to exhort the capteines and souldiers to prepare themselues to battell, sith the matter was growen to that point, that by no meanes it could be auoided, so that (said he) this daie shall either bring vs all to aduancement & honor, or else if it shall chance vs to be ouercome, shall deliuer vs from the kings spitefull malice and cruell disdaine: for plaieng the men (as we ought to doo) better it is to die in battell for the commonwealths cause, than through cowardlike feare to prolong life, which after shall be taken from vs, by sentence of the enimie.

Hereupon, the whole armie being in number about fourtéene thousand chosen men, promised to stand with him so long as life lasted. There were with the Persies as chiefteines of this armie, the earle of Dowglas a Scotish man, the baron of Kinderton, sir Hugh Browne, and sir Richard Vernon knights, with diuerse other stout and right valiant capteins. Now when the two armies were incamped, the
one

one against the other, the earle of Worcester and the lord Persie with their complices The Persies sent their articles to the king.
sent the articles (whereof I spake before) by Thomas Caiton, and Thomas Saluain
esquiers to king Henrie, vnder their hands and seales, which articles in effect charged King Henrie charged with periurie.
him with manifest periurie, in that (contrarie to his oth receiued vpon the euangelists
at Doncaster, when he first entred the realme after his exile) he had taken vpon
him the crowne and roiall dignitie, imprisoned king Richard, caused him to resigne
his title, and finallie to be murthered. Diuerse other matters they laid to his charge,
as leuieng of taxes and tallages, contrarie to his promise, infringing of lawes & customes of the realme, and suffering the earle of March to remaine in prison, without
trauelling to haue him deliuered. All which things they as procurors & protectors Procurors & protectors of the commonwealth,
of the common-wealth, tooke vpon them to prooue against him, as they protested
vnto the whole world.

King Henrie after he had read their articles, with the defiance which they
annexed to the same, answered the esquiers, that he was readie with dint of sword The kings answer to the messengers that brought the articles.
and fierce battell to prooue their quarrell false, and nothing else than a forged
matter, not doubting, but that God would aid and assist him in his righteous
cause, against the disloiall and false forsworne traitors. The next daie in the morning
earlie, being the euen of Marie Magdalene, they set their battels in order on both
sides, and now whilest the warriors looked when the token of battell should be
giuen, the abbat of Shrewesburie, and one of the clearks of the priuie seale, were
sent from the king vnto the Persies, to offer them pardon, if they would come to any The king offereth to pardon his aduersaries,
reasonable agréement. By their persuasions, the lord Henrie Persie began to giue
eare vnto the kings offers, & so sent with them his vncle the earle of Worcester,
to declare vnto the king the causes of those troubles, and to require some effectuall
reformation in the same.

It was reported for a truth, that now when the king had condescended vnto
all that was resonable at his hands to be required, and seemed to humble himselfe
more than was meet for his estate, the earle of Worcester (vpon his returne to his The earle of worcesters double dealing in wrong reporting the kings words.
nephue) made relation cleane contrarie to that the king had said, in such sort that
he set his nephues hart more in displeasure towards the king, than euer it was
before, driuing him by that meanes to fight whether he would or not: then suddenlie
blew the trumpets, the kings part crieng S. George vpon them, the aduersaries cried
Esperance Persie, and so the two armies furiouslie ioined. The archers on both
sides shot for the best game, laieng on such load with arrowes, that manie died, and
were driuen downe that neuer rose againe.

The Scots (as some write) which had the fore ward on the Persies side, intend- *Hall.* The Scots.
ing to be reuenged of their old displeasures doone to them by the English nation, set
so fiercelie on the kings fore ward, led by the earle of Stafford, that they made the
same draw backe, and had almost broken their aduersaries arraie. The Welshmen
also which before had laine lurking in the woods, mounteines, and marishes, hearing
of this battell toward, came to the aid of the Persies, and refreshed the wearied people The welshmen come to aid the Persies.
with new succours. The king perceiuing that his men were thus put to distresse,
what with the violent impression of the Scots, and the tempestuous stormes of arrowes, that his aduersaries discharged fréely against him and his people, it was no
need to will him to stirre: for suddenlie with his fresh battell, he approached and relieued his men; so that the battell began more fierce than before. Here the lord
Henrie Persie, and the earle Dowglas, a right stout and hardie capteine, not regarding the shot of the kings battell, nor the close order of the ranks, pressing forward
togither bent their whole forces towards the kings person, comming vpon him with
speares and swords so fiercelie, that the earle of March the Scot, perceiuing their The earle or March. *Tho. Walsi*
purpose, withdrew the king from that side of the field (as some write) for his great
benefit and safegard (as it appeared) for they gaue such a violent onset vpon them

that stood about the kings standard, that slaieing his standard-bearer sir Walter Blunt, and ouerthrowing the standard, they made slaughter of all those that stood about it, as the earle of Stafford, that daie made by the king constable of the realme, and diuerse other.

Hall.
The valiance of the yoong prince.

The prince that daie holpe his father like a lustie yoong gentleman: for although he was hurt in the face with an arrow, so that diuerse noble men that were about him, would haue conueied him foorth of the field, yet he would not suffer them so to doo, least his departure from amongst his men might happilie haue striken some feare into their harts: and so without regard of his hurt, he continued with his men, & neuer ceassed, either to fight where the battell was most hot, or to

A sore battell & well mainteined.

incourage his men where it séemed most néed. This battell lasted thrée long houres, with indifferent fortune on both parts, till at length, the king crieng saint George victorie, brake the arraie of his enimies, and aduentured so farre, that (as some write)

The valiant dooings of the earle Dowglas.

the earle Dowglas strake him downe, & at that instant slue sir Walter Blunt, and thrée other, apparelled in the kings sute and clothing, saieng: I maruell to sée so many kings thus suddenlie arise one in the necke of an other. The king in deed

The high manhood of the king.

was raised, & did that daie manie a noble feat of armes, for as it is written, he slue that daie with his owne hands six and thirtie persons of his enimies. The other on his part incouraged by his doings, fought valiantlie, and slue the lord Persie,

The lord Persie slaine.

called sir Henrie Hotspurre. To conclude, the kings enimies were vanquished, and put to flight, in which flight, the earle of Dowglas, for hast, falling from the crag

The earle Dowglas taken prisoner.

of an hie mounteine, brake one of his cullions, and was taken, and for his valiantnesse, of the king frankelie and freelie deliuered.

The earle of Worcester taken.

There was also taken the earle of Worcester, the procuror and setter foorth of all this mischéefe, sir Richard Vernon, and the baron of Kinderton, with diuerse other.

Knights slaine on the kings part.

There were slaine vpon the kings part, beside the earle of Stafford, to the number of ten knights, sir Hugh Shorlie, sir Iohn Clifton, sir Iohn Cokaine, sir Nicholas Gausell, sir Walter Blunt, sir Iohn Caluerleie, sir Iohn Massie of Podington, sir Hugh Mortimer, and sir Robert Gausell, all the which receiued the same morning the order of knighthood: sir Thomas Wendesleie was wounded to death, and so passed out of this life shortlie after. There died in all vpon the kings side sixteene hundred, and foure thousand were gréeuouslie wounded. On the contrarie side were slaine, besides the lord Persie, the most part of the knights and esquiers of the countie

The slaughter of Cheshire men at this battell.

of Chester, to the number of two hundred, besides yeomen and footmen, in all there died of those that fought on the Persies side, about fiue thousand. This battell was fought on Marie Magdalene euen, being saturdaie. Vpon the mondaie folowing,

The earle of Worcester and others beheaded.

the earle of Worcester, the baron of Kinderton, and sir Richard Vernon knights, were condemned and beheaded. The earles head was sent to London, there to be set on the bridge.

The earle of Northumberland was now marching forward with great power, which he had got thither, either to aid his sonne and brother (as was thought) or at least

The earle of westmerland raiseth a power against the earle of Northumberland.

towards the king, to procure a peace: but the earle of Westmerland, and sir Robert Waterton knight, had got an armie on foot, and meant to meet him. The earle of Northumberland, taking neither of them to be his freend, turned suddenlie back, and withdrew himselfe into Warkewoorth castell. The king hauing set a staie in

The king goeth to Yorke.

things about Shrewesburie, went straight to Yorke, from whence he wrote to the earle of Northumberland, willing him to dismisse his companies that he had with him,

The earle of Northumberland commeth to the king.

and to come vnto him in peaceable wise. The earle vpon receipt of the kings letters came vnto him the morow after saint Laurence daie, hauing but a few of his seruants to attend him, and so excused himselfe, that the king (bicause the earle had Berwike in his possession, and further, had his castels of Alnewike, Warkewoorth, and other, fortified with Scots) dissembled the matter, gaue him faire words, and

suffered

suffered him (as saith Hall) to depart home, although by other it should séeme, that he was committed for a time to safe custodie.

The king returning foorth of Yorkeshire, determined to go into Northwales, to chastise the presumptuous dooings of the vnrulie Welshmen, who (after his comming from Shrewesburie, and the marches there) had doone much harme to the English subiects. But now where the king wanted monie to furnish that enterprise, and to wage his souldiers, there were some that counselled him to be bold with the bishops, and supplie his want with their surplusage. But as it fortuned, the archbishop of Canturburie was there present, who in the name of all the rest boldlie made answer, that none of his prouince should be spoiled by anie of those naughtie disposed persons; but that first with hard stripes they should vnderstand the price of their rash enterprise. But the king neuerthelesse so vsed the matter with the bishops for their good wils, that the archbishop at length to pleasure him, calling the cleargie togither, got a grant of a tenth, towards the kings necessarie charges.

The welshmen molest the English subiects.

It was spoken like a prelat.

A tenth leuied of the cleargie.

The Britaines vnder the conduct of the lord of Cassils, spoiled and burnt the towne of Plimmouth, and returned without receiuing anie damage, but immediatlie there-vpon, the westerne men manning foorth a fléet, vnder the gouernement of one William Wilford esquier, made saile ouer to the coasts of Britaine, where they tooke aboue fortie ships laden with oile, sope, and Rochell wine, to the quantitie of a thousand tunne, or much thereabouts. In returning homewards, they burnt fortie other vessels, and landing at Pennarch, they burnt townes and villages six leagues within the countrie, togither with the towne of saint Matthew, and all the buildings there, thrée leagues round about the same towns. About the feast of All saints, a parlement began at Couentrie, and continued there till saint Andrewes tide: but at length, bicause vittels waxed déere, and lodging was streict, it was adiorned from thence vnto London, there to begin againe in the octaues of the Epiphanie. The same time, a pardon was granted and proclamed, for all such as had taken part with the Persies against the king, and likewise for other offendors, those excepted that had consented to betraie Calis, whom the king sent thither to suffer for their offences. A little before Christmas the Frenchmen meant to haue robbed and spoiled the Ile of Wight, but when a thousand of them were set on land, and had got togither a great bootie of cattell, suddenlie there came vpon them such number of people that they were constreined to withdraw to their ships, leauing their preie behind them, and no small number of their men to paie for their shot, so that they wan little by that iournie, returning home with shame and dishonor.

William Wilford.

Ships taken.

Anno Reg. 5.

A parlement at Couentrie.

Adiorned to London.

A pardon.

Frenchmen inuade the Ile of Wight.

They are repelled.

This yeare in the parlement holden at London (beginning the morow after the feast of saint Hilarie, and continuing twelue wéeks) the earle of Northumberland was restored vnto his former dignities, lands and goods, the Ile of Man onlie excepted, which by reason of the forfeiture made by the earle of Salisburie, the king had first giuen vnto him, and now depriued him thereof, where all his other lands, possessions, and liuings were wholie to him and his heires restored. By authoritie of the same parlement a subsidie was also granted to the king, of euerie knights fée twentie shillings, whether the same were holden of him by menaltie, or otherwise. Moreouer, euerie man and woman that might dispend in lands the value of twentie shillings & so vpward, aboue the reprises, whether the same lands belonged to the laie fee, or to the church, paied for euerie pound twelue pence: and those that were valued to be woorth in goods twentie pounds and vpwards, paid also after the rate of lands, that is, twelue pence for euerie pound. ¶ This séemeth to be that subsidie which Thomas Walsingham calleth a sore surcharging subsidie, or an vnaccustomed tax: the forme and maner wherof (saith he) I had here interlaced, but that the verie granters and authors thereof had rather that the posteritie should

1404.

The parlement beginneth againe.

The earle of Northumberland restored.

The Ile of Man.

A subsidie

Abr. Fl. out of Tho. Walsin. Hypod. pag. 164.

be vtterlie ignorant thereof, and neuer heare of it; sithens it was granted vpon this condition, that hereafter it should not be drawne into example; neither might the euidences thereof be kept in the kings treasurie, nor in the excheker; but the records thereof presentlie (after the iust accounts giuen vp) burned; neither should writs or commissions be sent abroad against the collectors or inquirers hereof for their better inquest.

The Frenchmens demand of the Ile of Wight.

The Frenchmen about the same time came before the Ile of Wight with a great nauie, and sent certeine of their men to the shore, to demand in name of king Richard, and of his wife quéene Isabell, a tribute or speciall subsidie in monie,

The answer of the Ilandmen.

of the inhabitants of that Ile; who answered, that king Richard was dead, and quéene Isabell sometime his wife had béene sent home to hir parents and countrie, without condition of anie dowrie or tribute : wherefore, they answered reasonablie, that none they would giue: but if the Frenchmen had desire to fight, they willed them to come on land, and there should be none to resist them; and after they were on land, they promised to giue them respit for six houres space to refresh themselues, and that time being once expired, they should not faile to haue battell. When the Frenchmen heard of this stout answer made by the Ilandmen, they had no lust to approch néere to the land, but returned without further attempt.

The duke of Orleance his challenge.

About this season, the duke of Orleance, brother to the French king, a man of no lesse pride than hautinesse of courage, wrote letters to king Henrie, aduertising him, that for the loue he bare to the noble feats of chiualrie, he could imagine nothing either more honorable or cōmendable to them both, than to meet in the field each part with an hundred knights and esquiers, all being gentlemen, both of name and armes, armed at all points, and furnished with speares, axes, swords, and daggers, and there to fight and combat to the yéelding; and euerie person, to whome God should send victorie, to haue his prisoner, & him to ransome at his pleasure, offering himselfe with his companie to come to his citie of Angulesme, so that the king would come to the lands of Burdeaux, and there defend this challenge.

The answer of king Henrie.

The king of England grauelie answered herevnto, that he maruelled why the duke vnder colour of dooing déeds of armes for a vaine-glorie, would now séeke to breake the peace betwixt the realmes of England and France, he being sworne to mainteine same peace sith he might further vnderstand, that no king annointed, of verie dutie, was bound to answer anie challenge, but to his péere of equall state and dignitie : and further declared, that when opportunitie serued, he would passe the sea, and come into his countrie of Gascoigne, with such companie as he thought conuenient, and then might the duke set forward with his band, for the accomplishment of his couragious desire, promising him in the word of a prince, not thence to depart, till the duke either by fulfilling his owne desire in manner aforesaid, or by singular combat betwéene them two onelie, for auoiding of more effusion of Christian bloud, should thinke himselfe fullie satisfied. To this and much more conteined in the kings answer, the duke replied, and the king againe reioined, not without tawnts and checks vnfitting for their estates. The duke of Orleance offended highlie (as he might séeme) furnished against the king of England with an armie of six thousand men, entered into Guien, and besieged the towne of

The duke of Orleance besiegeth Vergi in Guien.

Vergi, whereof was capteine sir Robert Antlfield, a right hardie and valiant knight, hauing with him onelie thrée hundred Englishmen, which defended the fortresse so manfullie, that the duke (after he had laine three moneths) and lost manie of his men, without honour or spoile returned into France.

After this, the admerall of Britaine highlie incouraged, for that the last yeere he had taken certeine English ships laden with wines, accompanied with the lord du Chastell, a valiant baron of Britaine, and twelue hundred men of armes, sailed

foorth

foorth with thirtie ships from S. Malos, and came before the towne of Dartmouth, and would haue landed; but by the puissance of the townesmen and aid of the countrie, they were repelled, in the which conflict, the lord du Chastell, and two *The lord du Chastell slaine.* of his brethren, with foure hundred other were slaine, and aboue two hundred taken prisoners and put to their ransoms, amongst whom the lord of Baqueuille the marshall of Britaine was one. All this summer, Owen Glendouer and his *Owen Glendouer wasted the English marches.* adherents, robbed, burned, and destroied the countries adioining néere to the places where he hanted, and one while by sleight & guileful policie, an other while by open force, he tooke and slue manie Englishmen, brake downe certeine castels which he wan, and some he fortified and kept for his owne defense. Iohn Trenor bishop of Assaph, considering with himselfe how things prospered vnder the hands of this Owen, fled to him, and tooke his part against the king. About the same time, the Britaines and the Flemings tooke certeine ships of ours laden with mer- *Crueltie of the Britains & Flemings.* chandize, and slue all the mariners, or else hanged them.

Also, the old countesse of Oxford, mother to Robert Veere late duke of Ireland, *The countes of Oxford.* that died at Louaine, caused certeine of hir seruants, and other such as she durst trust, to publish and brute abroad, thorough all the parts of Essex, that king Richard was aliue, and that he would shortlie come to light, and claime his former *K. Richard once againe aliue.* estate, honor, and dignitie. She procured a great number of harts to be made of siluer and gold, such as king Richard was woont to giue vnto his knights, esquiers, & fréends, to weare as cognizances, to the end that in bestowing them in king Richards name, she might the sooner allure men to further hir lewd practises: and where the fame went abroad, that king Richard was in Scotland with a great power of Frenchmen and Scots, readie to come to recouer his realme, manie gaue the more light credit vnto this brute thus set foorth by the said countesse.

The persuasions also of one Serlo, that in times past was one of king Richards *Serlo one of K. Richards chamber.* chamber, greatlie increased this errour, for the same Serlo, hearing in France (whither he was fled) that his maister king Richard was in Scotland aliue, conueied himselfe thither, to vnderstand the truth of that matter, and finding there one indeed that greatlie resembled him in all lineaments of bodie, but yet was not the man himselfe (as he well perceiued) vpon malice that he bare to king Henrie, aduertised by letters sent vnto diuerse of king Richards freends, that he was aliue indéed, and shortlie would come to shew himselfe openlie to the world, when he had once made his waie readie to recouer his kingdome, to the confusion of his enimies, and comfort of his fréends. These forged inuentions caused manie to beléeue the brute raised by the countesse of Oxford, for the which they came in trouble, were apprehended and committed to prison. The countesse hir selfe was shut vp in close prison, and all hir goods were *The countesse of Oxford committed to prison.* confiscat, and hir secretarie drawen and hanged, that had spred abroad this fained report, in going vp and downe the countrie, blowing into mens eares that king Richard *Hir secretarie executed.* was aliue, & affirming that he had spoken with him in such a place and in such a place, apparelled in this raiment and that raiment, with such like circumstances.

About the feast of saint Iohn Baptist, at the kings commandement, the earle of *The earle of Northumberland cometh to the king.* Northumberland came to Pomfret, and brought with him his nephues, and his nephues sonnes, whereby he cleared himselfe of a great deale of suspicion, manie doubting before his comming that he had giuen euill counsell to the yoong men, whereby to mooue them to rebellion, and to withstand the king. Sir William Clifford also came *Sir William Clifford bringeth Serlo to the king.* with the earle, and brought the foresaid Serlo with him, whom he had apprehended vpon his comming to him at Berwike, in hope to haue found succour at his hands; in consideration whereof the king pardoned the said sir William Clifford of his disobedience shewed, in keeping the castell of Berwike against him, in which dooing he had committed manifest treason.

This Serlo being knowen to be the man that had béene the chiefe murtherer of the *Serlo examined for the duke of Glocesters death.*

the duke of Glocester, when he was made awaie at Calis, was diligentlie examined who were helpers with him in the execution thereof, and after what sort they made him awaie: Serlo knowing there was no waie with him but death, would not vtter any other, but confessed for his owne part, he was worthie for that wicked deed to die ten thousand deaths, and shewed such outward appearance of repentance, that manie sore lamented his case, and promised to hire priests to sing masses, (as the manner was) for his soule, of their owne costs and charges. He was con-

demned to die at Pomfret, and was drawen from thence through euerie good towne, through which those that had the conueiance of him passed with him till they came to London, where he was executed, confessing euerie thing to be true concerning his wicked pretense, as before is recited: and further, that when he perceiued how their counterfeit practise would come to light and be openlie reuealed, he meant to haue returned into France, but wanting monie, he thought to haue béene relieued with some portion at the hand of the said sir William Clifford, and this caused him to come vnto Berwike, to shew him his necessitie, who to make his owne peace, did apprehend him, and present him to the king, as before ye haue heard.

King Henrie wanting monie in the feast of saint Faith the virgine, assembled at Couentrie his high court of parlement, in the which, the lord Stephan Scroope of Masham, and the lord Henrie Fitz Hugh obteined first to haue places of barons.

Moreouer, it is to be noted, that this was called The laie mans parlement, bicause the shiriffes were appointed to haue a speciall regard, that none should be chosen knights for the counties, nor burgesses for the cities and townes, that had any skill in the lawes of the land. This was doone, and when they came togither to talke of the weightie affaires of the realme, speciallie how the king might be relieued with monie, to beare such charges as he was knowen to be at, as well in defending the realme from the Scots and Welshmen at home, as from the Britains, Flemings, and

Frenchmen abroad, it was thought most expedient, that the spiritualtie should be depriued of their temporall possessions, to the reliefe of the kings necessitie. Herevpon rose great altercation betwixt the cleargie and the laitie; the knights affirming, that they had oftentimes serued the king, not onelie with their goods, but also with their persons in great dangers and ieopardies, whilest the spiritualtie sat at home,

and holp the king nothing at all. Thomas Arundell, archbishop of Canturburie stoutlie answered herevnto, that the cleargie had alwaie giuen to the king as much as the laitie had doone, considering they had oftener giuen their tenths to him than the laitie their fiftéens: also, that more of their tenants went foorth into the kings warres, than the tenants of them of the laie fée: beside this, they praied day and night for the kings good successe against his enimies.

When the speaker named sir Iohn Cheinie, in replieng by plaine speach, séemed little to esteeme such praiers of the church, the archbishop was set in a great chafe, and with sharpe words declaring what he thought must needs follow, both of the king and kingdome, when praiers and suffrages of churchmen came to be so little set by, he grew to such impatiencie, that he flatlie told the speaker, that although

he séemed little to estéeme of the religion of the cleargie, he would not haue him to thinke, that he should take awaie the possessions of the church, without finding such as would seeke to withstand him, for if (said he) the archbishop of Canturburie maie liue, thou shalt haue hot taking awaie any manner of thing that is his. After this, when the archbishop perceiued that the king winked at these matters, he rose from his place and comming before the king, knéeled downe, and besought him to consider, how through the fauour and grace of the almightie God, he had atteined to the kingdome, and therefore he ought to remember his first purpose and intent, which was, to saue vnto euerie man his right, so far as in him laie.

He

He willed him likewise to haue in consideration the oth which he willinglie had receiued, that is, that he should aduance the honor of the church, and the ministers thereof cherish and mainteine. Also, to haue in mind the danger and dishonour that redounded to such as brake their othes: so that he besought him to permit and suffer the church to inioy the priuileges and liberties, which in time of his predecessors it had inioied, requesting him to stand in awe of that king, by whom all kings did reigne; and to feare the censures and condemnation that those incurred, which tooke and bereft from the church any good or right belonging to it, who most certeinelie (said he) are accursed. When the archbishop had vsed this, or the like speach, the king commanded him to go to his seat againe, assuring him, that his intent and purpose was to leaue the church in as good state, or better, than he found it. The kings answer to the archbishop.

The archbishop herewith turning to the knights and burgesses of the parlement, said vnto them; " You, and such other as you be, haue giuen counsell vnto the king and his predecessors, to confiscate and take into their hands the goods and possessions of the celles, which the Frenchmen and Normans possessed here in England, and affirmed that by the same he and they should heape vp great riches, and indéed those goods and possessions (as is to be prooued) were worth manie thousands of gold: and yet it is most true, that the king at this day is not halfe one marke of siluer the richer thereby, for you haue begged and gotten them out of his hands, and haue appropriated the same vnto your selues, so that we may coniecture verie well, that you request to haue our temporalties, not to aduance the kings profit, but to satisfie your owne greedie covetousnesse, for vndoubtedlie if the king (as God forbid he should) did accomplish your wicked purposes and minds, he should not be one farthing the richer the yeare next after: and trulie, sooner will I suffer this head of mine to be cut off from my shoulders, than that the church should lose the least right that apperteineth to it."

The knights said little, but yet they procéeded in their sute to haue their purpose forward, which the archbishop perceiuing (as an other Argus, hauing his eie on each side, to marke what was doone) laboured so to disappoint their dooings, that he wan the favour of certeine of the temporall lords to assist him, who constantlie auouched by their consents, that the church should neuer be spoiled of the temporalties, and herein they acquited the archbishop and prelats, one pleasure for an other, which they had doone for them before, when the commons in this parlement required, that all such lands and reuenues as sometime belonged to the crowne, and had béene giuen awaie, either by the king, or by his predecessors king Edward, and king Richard, should be againe restored to the kings vse; vnto which request, the archbishop and other the prelats would in no wise consent: thus by the stout diligence of the archbishop Arundell that petition of the commons, touching the spiritual temporalties, came to none effect. [Yea the knights themselues, who verie instantlie had stood in this error, acknowledging their maliciousnesse & guiltinesse herein, besought the archbishop of Canturburie to pardon them; and gaue thanks that by his couragiousnesse the church in this so troublesome a time reuiued, calling to mind the saieing of an ethnike, by way of application, to the said archbishops hie praise: *Abr. Fl. out of Thom. Walsi. Hypod.* pag. 167.

—————sub principe duro
    Temporibúsq; malis ausus es esse bonus.]

Two fiftéens were granted by the commons, with condition, that the same should be paid vnto the hands of the lord Furniuall, who should sée that monie imploied for maintenance of the kings warres. Moreouer, at the importunate sute of the commons, the letters patents that had béene made to diuerse persons of annuities to them granted by king Edward and king Richard, were called in, and made void, Two fiftéens granted. Letters patents reuoked.

not

A tenth and a halfe granted by the cleargie.

not without some note of dishonor to the king. The cleargie granted to the king a tenth and a halfe, notwithstanding that the halfe of one tenth latelie granted was yet behind, and appointed to be paid vpon saint Martins daie now next comming. About this season, great losse happened in Kent, by breaking in of waters, that ouerflowed

Ouerflowing of the sea.

the sea banks, as well in the archbishop of Canturburies grounds, as other mens, whereby much cattell was drowned. Neither did England alone bewaile her losses by such breakings in of the sea, but also Zealand, Flanders, & Holland tasted of the like damage.

The death of Williā Wickhaɱ.

William Wickham bishop of Winchester, being a man of great age, deceassed this yeare, leauing behind him a perpetuall memorie of his name, for the notable monuments which he erected, in building two colleges, one at Winchester for grammarians, and the other at Oxenford called the new college, purchasing lands and reuenues for the maintenance of students there, to the great commoditie of the commonwealth: for from thence, as out of a good nursserie, haue come foorth diuerse men in all ages excellentlie learned in all sciences. ¶ And héere I haue not thought it impertinent to speake somewhat of this worthie prelat (considering that by him so great a benefit hath returned to the commonwealth) according to such notes as I haue séene collected by that painfull traueller in search of antiquities Iohn Leland, who saith, that as some haue supposed, the said Wickham, otherwise called Perot, was base sonne to one Perot, the towne-clerke of Wickham in Hampshire, of which place he tooke his surname, and that one maister Wodall a gentleman, dwelling in the said towne, brought him vp at schoole, where he learned his grammar, and to write verie faire, in so much that the constable of Winchester castell, a great ruler in those daies in Hampshire, got him of maister Wodall, and reteined him to be his secretarie, with whome he continued, till king Edward the third, comming to Winchester, conceiued some good liking of the yoong man, and tooke him to his seruice, and withall vnderstanding that he was minded to be a churchman, he first made him parson and deane of saint Martins in London, then archdeacon of Buckingham.

But for so much as his seruice was right acceptable to the king, as he that with great dexteritie could handle such affaires of the state, or other matters of charge as were committed to his hands, the king still kept him about his person, as one of his chéefe chapleins of houshold, and imploied him in sundrie offices, as occasions serued: and first he made him surueior of his works and buildings, namelie at Windsore, in reparing of that castell, and also at Quinburrough, where, by the kings appointment, a strong fortresse was raised, for defence of the realme

He was also at one time treasuror of England (as *Leland* gathereth.)

on that side. After this, he was aduanced to the kéeping of the priuie seale, made ouerséer of the wards and forrests, also treasuror of the kings reuenues in France, and at length was made bishop of Winchester. Yet the Blacke prince did not greatlie fauour him, wherevpon Wickham procured to kéepe him occupied in warres beyond the seas. But at length Iohn duke of Lancaster, and Alice Perers king Edwards concubine, conceiuing some great displeasure against him, found meane to procure the king to banish him the realme, and then he remained in Normandie and Picardie for the space of seauen yeares, or thereabout, and might not be restored so long as king Edward liued. But after his deceasse, about the second yeare of king Richard the seconds reigne, he was restored home, and purchased a general pardon for all matters past that might be surmized against him, or laid to his charge.

Afterwards he bare himselfe so uprightlie in that dangerous time, when such misliking and priuie enuie reigned betwixt the king and his nobles, that both parts séemed to like of him, insomuch that when the king made him lord chancellor, there was not anie that greatlie repined thereat; and verelie in that the king made

choise

choise of him before others to occupie that place, it argueth there was not so euill a disposition in the king, nor lacke of discretion in order of gouernment, as writers seeme to charge him with. But where other could not so well beare iniuries at others hands as happilie Wickham could, the fire of dissention cheeflie kindled thereof. For if the duke of Ireland, and the earle of Suffolke, with those of that faction could haue refrained to shew their displeasures, when the duke of Glocester and other his complices pinched at them (for that they saw the king haue them in more estimation than they wished) matters might haue béene qualified peraduenture with lesse adoo, and without danger to haue insued to either part. But howsoeuer it went with them, it may doubtlesse be easilie coniectured, that Wickham was a man of singular wisedome, and politike forecast, that could from meane degrée in such wise clime aloft, and afterwards passe through the chances and changes of variable fortune, kéeping himselfe euer so in state, that he grew at length to be able to furnish the chargeable expenses of two such notable foundations which he left behind him, to make his name immortall. But leauing the consideration hereof to others, I will returne to the purpose from whence I haue thus far stepped.

In this sixt yeare, the fridaie after saint Valentines daie, the earle of March *1405.* his sonnes earlie in the morning were taken foorth of Windsore castell, and conueied awaie, it was not knowne whither at the first, but such search and inquirie was made for them that shortlie after they were heard of, and brought backe againe. The smith that counterfeited the keies, by the which they that conueied them thence got into the chamber where they were lodged, had first his hands cut off, and after his head striken from his shoulders. The ladie Spenser, sister to the duke of Yorke and widow of the lord Thomas Spenser, executed at Bristow (as before yée haue heard) being apprehended and committed to close prison, accused hir brother the duke of Yorke, as chéefe authour in stealing awaie the said earle of March his sonnes. And further, that the said duke ment to haue broken into the manor of Eltham the last Christmasse, by scaling the wals in the night season, the king being there the same time, to the intent to haue murthered him. For to prooue hir accusation true she offered that if there were anie knight, or esquier, that would take vpon him to fight in hir quarrell, if he were ouercome, she would be content to be burnt for it.

One of hir esquiers named William Maidstone, hearing what answer his ladie and mistresse propounded, cast downe his hood, and proffered in hir cause the combat. The duke likewise cast downe his hood, readie by battell to cleare his innocencie. But yet the kings sonne lord Thomas of Lancaster arrested him, and put him vnder safe kéeping in the Tower, till it were further knowne what order should be taken with him, and in the meane time were all his goods confiscate. The same time was Thomas Mowbraie earle marshall accused, as priuie to the purpose of the duke of Yorke, touching the withdrawing of the earle of March his children, who confessed indéed that he knew of the dukes purpose: but yet in no wise gaue his consent therevnto, and therefore besought the king to be good and gratious lord vnto him for concealing the matter, and so he obteined pardon of that offense.

The king had assembled at the same time the most part of the nobilitie at London, to consult with them for diuerse weightie matters, concerning the state of the common-wealth, and about some aid of monie which he required: but the lords shewed themselues not willing to satisfie his request. He therefore caused the spirituall lords as well as the temporall, to méet at S. Albons in the Lent season, about the same matter; but yet obteined not his purpose, by reason the barons were sore against him, and so at length on Palme sundaie they went their waie, each man to his home, hauing gratified the king in nothing concerning his demand. In the meane time, to wit the fiftéenth of March at a place in Wales called Huske, in a

The earle of Marches sonnes Thom. Walsin.

The ladie Spenser cōmitted to ward.

She accuseth hir brother the duke of Yorke.

Williā Maidstone esquier offred to fight in his ladies quarrell.

The earle marshall accused.

The k. wanteth monie & can get none of the lords.

conflict fought betwixt the Welshmen and certeine of the princes companie, the sonne of Owen Glendouer was taken, and fiftéene hundred Welshmen taken and slaine. Also' in Maie about the feast daie of S. Dunstane, was the chancellor of the said Owen taken prisoner, and a great number of other taken and slaine. The prisoners were brought vp to London, where the chancellor was commited to safe keeping in the Tower.

Abr. Fl. out of Thom. Wals. Hypod. pag. 159.

¶ This was a shrewd discomfiture to the Welsh by the English, on whome sinister lot lowred, at such time as more than a thousand of them were slaine in a hot skirmish; and such shamefull villanie executed vpon the carcasses of the dead men by the Welshwomen; as the like (I doo belieue) hath neuer or sildome beene practised. For though it was a cruell déed of Tomyris quéene of the Massagets in Scythia, against whome when Cyrus the great king of Persia came, and had slaine hir sonne, she by hir policie trained him into such streicts, that she slue him and all his host; and causing a great vessel to be filled with the bloud of Cyrus and other Persians, did cast his head thereinto, saieng; Bloud thou hast thirsted and now drinke théreof thy fill: againe, though it was a cruell déed of Fuluia the wife of Marcus Antonius (at whose commandement Popilius cut off the head and hands of that golden mouthed orator Tullie, which afterwards were nailed vp ouer the place of common plées at Rome) to hold in her hands the toong of that father of eloquence cut out of his head after the same was parted from his shoulders, and to pricke it all ouer with pins and néedels: yet neither the cru-eltie of Tomyris nor yet of Fuluia is comparable to this of the Welshwomen; which is worthie to be recorded to the shame of a sex pretending the title of weake vessels, and yet raging with such force of fiercenesse and barbarisme. For the dead bodies of the Englishmen, being aboue a thousand lieng vpon the ground imbrued in their owne bloud, was a sight (a man would thinke) gréeuous to looke vpon, and so farre from exciting and stirring vp affections of crueltie; that it should rather haue mooued the beholders to commiseration and mercie: yet did the women of Wales cut off their priuities, and put one part thereof into the mouthes of euerie dead man, in such sort that the cullions hoong downe to their chins; and not so contented, they did cut off their noses and thrust them into their tailes as they laie on the ground mangled and defaced. This was a verie ignominious déed, and a woorsse not committed among the barbarous: which though it make the reader to read it, and the hearer to heare it, ashamed: yet bicause it was a thing doone in open sight, and left testified in historie; I see little reason whie it should not be imparted in our mother toong to the knowledge of our owne countrimen, as well as vnto strangers in a language vnknowne. And thus much by waie of notifieng the inhumanitie and detestable demeanour of those Welshwomen, after the conflict betwéene the English and the Welsh, whereof desultorie mention is made before pag. 520, where Edmund Mortimer earle of March was taken prisoner.

Iust. lib. 1. *He-rod. lib.* 1 *Val. Max. lib.* 8. *cap.* 7.

The castell of Marke besieged about the mid-dest of Maie as Iac. Meir. saith. Sir Philip Hall.

Valeran earle of S. Paule, by the assent of the French king, assembled fiue hun-dred men of armes, fiue hundred Genowaies with crossebowes, and a thousand Flem-ings on foot, with the which he laid siege to the castell of Marke, thrée leagues from Calis, vpon the fiftéenth daie of Iulie. Capteine of the castell as then for the king of England was one sir Philip Hall, hauing with him foure score archers, and four and twentie other soldiers, which defended the place so manfullie, that the earle retired into the towne, and there lodged, fortifieng it for feare of rescue that might come from Calis. The next daie he gaue an other assault to the castell, and tooke the vtter court, wherin was found a great number of horsses, kine, and other cattell. The next daie there issued foorth of Calis two hundred men of armes, two hundred archers, and three hundred footmen, with ten or twelue wagons laden with

with vittels and artillerie, conducted by sir Richard Aston knight, lieutenant of the English pale for the earle of Summerset, capteine generall of those marches.

The Frenchmen aduertised that the Englishmen were comming to remooue the siege, issued not foorth of their lodgings, but kept them within their closure. Neuerthelesse, the Englishmen shot so sharpelie and closelie togither, that the Flemings and footmen began to flie : the men of armes fearing the slaughter of their horsses, ran awaie with a light gallop. The Genowaies which had spent the most part of their shot at the assaults made to the castell, shewed small resistance, and so all the number of the French part were slaine and put to flight. The earle of S. Paule and diuerse other escaped awaie, and by S. Omers got to Therouenne, or (as others saie) to saint Omers. But there were taken to the number of thrée or foure score, and amongst other the lord de Dampier seneshall of Ponthien, monsieur de Weriners, monsieur de Vineles, monsieur de Noielles, monsieur Iohn de Hangests capteine of Bullongne, the lord de Rambures, monsieur Lionell Darreis capteine of Graueling, monsieur Peter Rasser capteine of Arde, also Combernard capteine of Tirouan, Boid Chanon capteine of Montoire, Iohn Chanon capteine of Lisle, Stenebecke capteine of Ralingham, the bastard of Burneuill capteine of Burburgh. There were slaine about 60, and among them as cheefe sir Robert Berengueuill, the lord of Quercus, Morell de Saucuses, the lord Courbet de Rempeupret, and others. *The earle of S. Paule put to flight.* *Ia. Meir.*

The Englishmen had the spoile of the earls campe, and being returned to Calis, within fiue daies after there issued foorth about fiue hundred men meaning to haue woone the towne of Arde with a sudden assault, which they gaue to it in the night time. But sir Manfrid de Bois, and the lord Rigine, did so valiantlie defend it, that the Englishmen with losse of fortie of their men were constreined, to returne vnto Calis, after they had burnt the dead bodies in an old house, for that the enimies should not perceiue what losse the Englishmen had susteined. After this, the French king, to auoid perils, laid in garison at Bullongne, and in other places, the marques of Pount, sonne to the duke of Bar, the earle of Dampnie, and sir Iohn Harpadan a knight of great renowne and estimation. The duke of Burgognie likewise sent a number of soldiers vnto Graueling, vnder the leading of one Iohn Vandenwall, and to other fortresses alongst the coast he sent new supplies, for doubt of the Englishmens inuasions. *Arde assaulted by Englishmen.* *The marques du Pount.*

The king of England in deed hearing of the preparation made for warre by the Frenchmen, leuied fore thousand men which he sent vnto Calis, and to the sea, of the which 3000 were vnder the conduct of the kings sonne. The lord Thomas of Lancaster, and the earle of Kent, the two and twentith daie of Maie (as some write) came vpon the coast of Flanders, and entring the hauen of Sluis, burnt foure great ships which they found there lieng at anchor. On the fift daie after their comming into that hauen they went on land, thinking to haue fought with the duke of Burgognie. But as other write, after they had besieged the castell that stood in the mouth of the hauen, and loosing thrée score of their men, amongst which they name one to beare the title of earle of Penbroke (whom they buried for the time in the church of Mude) fiue daies after their comming thither they determined to depart from thence, perceiuing the castell would not easilie be woone, but first they spoiled the countrie about them, and burnt Heis fléet, otherwise called Condekirke, and diuerse other places thereabout. *An armie sent to Calis and to the sea.* *Chr. Fland. Ia. Meir. The English men besieged the castell of Sluis.*

This doone, they tooke vp the bodie of him whom the Flemish writers call the earle of Penbroke, and got them againe to the sea, for that they were aduertised how the duke of Burgognie meant to besiege Calis. Wherevpon raising their siege thus from Sluis castell, they returned vnto the defense of the towne of Calis, so much desired of the French nation. As they returned homewards, they met with three caricks of Genoa, of the which one hauing the wind with hir, meant to haue ouerthrowne

throwne the ship wherein the lord Thomas of Lancaster was aboord : but by the good foresight of the master of the ship that ruled the sterne, suddenlie turning the same, the violent swaie of that huge vessell comming so vpon them, was auoided ; but yet the caricke stroke off the nose of the English ship, and brused hir on the side. Then began the fight verie cruell, till the earle of Kent came to the rescue : and so finallie after a great conflict and bloudie battell betwixt the caricks and English ships, the victorie remained with the Englishmen, who taking the caricks, turned their sailes towards Normandie, where they arriued and burnt the townes of Hoggue, Mountburge, Berflie, saint Petronils and other, to the number of thirtie six, passing foorth into the countrie without resistance, the space of thirtie miles, spoiling all that came in their waie. This doone, they returned, and brought the caricks into the chamber at Rie, where one of them by misfortune of fire perished, to the losse & no gaine of either of the parties.

A great fight by sea.
Three caricks are taken.
Townes in Normandie burnt.

Iohn duke of Burgognie hauing obtained licence to besiege Calis, prepared an armie of six thousand men of armes, fiftéene hundred crosbowes, & twelue thousand footmen, the which being assembled, and all necessarie prouision readie at saint Omers, he was by the French king countermanded, and not suffered to proceed anie further in that weightie enterprise. And this was thought to be partlie the cause of the malice that he conceiued against the duke of Orleance, supposing that through him (enuieng his glorie) he was thus disappointed of his purpose. Whilest such dooings were in hand betwixt the English and French, as the besieging of Marke castell by the earle of saint Paule, and the sending foorth of the English fléet, vnder the gouernance of the lord Thomas of Lancaster, and the earle of Kent, the king was minded to haue gone into Wales against the Welsh rebels, that vnder their chéefteine Owen Glendouer, ceassed not to doo much mischéefe still against the English subiects.

The duke of Burgognie prepareth to besiege Calis.

The chéefe root of the malice betwixt the dukes of Burgognie & Orleance.

But at the same time, to his further disquieting, there was a conspiracie put in practise against him at home by the earle of Northumberland, who had conspired with Richard Scroope archbishop of Yorke Thomas Mowbraie earle marshall sonne to Thomas duke of Norfolke, who for the quarrell betwixt him and king Henrie had béene banished (as ye haue heard) the lords Hastings, Fauconbridge, Berdolfe, and diuerse others. It was appointed that they should meet altogither with their whole power, vpon Yorkeswold, at a daie assigned, and tha the earle of Northumberland should be cheefteine, promising to bring with him a great number of Scots. The archbishop accompanied with the earle marshall, deuised certeine articles of such matters, as it was supposed that not onelie the commonaltie of the Realme, but also the nobilitie found themselues gréeued with : which articles they shewed first vnto such of their adherents as were néere about them, & after sent them abroad to their fréends further off, assuring them that for redresse of such oppressions, they would shed the last drop of blood in their bodies, if néed were.

A new cōspiracie against king Henrie by the earle of Northumberland & others.

The archbishop not meaning to staie after he saw himselfe accompanied with a a great number of men, that came flocking to Yorke to take his part in this quarrell, foorthwith discouered his enterprise, causing the articles aforesaid to be set vp in the publike stréets of the citie of Yorke, and vpon the gates of the monasteries, that ech man might vnderstand the cause that mooued him to rise in armes against the king, the reforming whereof did not yet apperteine vnto him. Herevpon knights, esquiers, gentlemen, yeomen, and other of the commons, as well of the citie, townes and countries about, being allured either for desire of change, or else for desire to see a reformation in such things as were mentioned in the articles, assembled togither in great numbers; and the archbishop comming foorth amongst them clad in armor, incouraged, exhorted, and (by all meanes he could) pricked them foorth to take the enterprise in hand, and manfullie to continue in their begun purpose, promising forgiuenesse of sinnes to all them, whose hap it was to die in the quarrell : and thus not
onelie

The archbishop of yorke one of the chéefe conspirators.

The archbishop in armor.

onelie all the citizens of Yorke, but all other in the countries about, that were able to beare weapon, came to the archbishop, and the earle marshall. In déed the respect that men had to the archbishop, caused them to like the better of the cause, since the grauitie of his age, his integritie of life, and incomparable learning, with the reuerend aspect of his amiable personage, mooued all men to haue him in no small estimation.

The estimation which men had of the archbishop of Yorke.

The king aduertised of these matters, meaning to preuent them, left his iournie into Wales, and marched with all spéed towards the north parts. Also Rafe Neuill earle of Westmerland, that was not farre off, togither with the lord Iohn of Lancaster the kings sonne, being informed of this rebellious attempt, assembled togither such power as they might make, and together with those which were appointed to attend on the said lord Iohn to defend the borders against the Scots, as the lord Henrie Fitzhugh, the lord Rafe Eeuers, the lord Robert Umfreuill, & others, made forward against the rebels, and comming into a plaine within the forrest of Galtree, caused their standards to be pitched downe in like sort as the archbishop had pitched his, ouer against them, being farre stronger in number of people than the other, for (as some write) there were of the rebels at the least twentie thousand men.

The earle of westmerland and the lord Iohn of Lancaster the kings sonne prepare themselues to resist the kings enimies.

The forest of Galtree.

When the earle of Westmerland perceiued the force of the aduersaries, and that they laie still and attempted not to come forward vpon him, he subtillie deuised how to quaile their purpose, and foorthwith dispatched messengers vnto the archbishop to vnderstand the cause as it were of that great assemblie, and for what cause (contrarie to the kings peace) they came so in amour. The archbishop answered, that he tooke nothing in hand against the kings peace, but that whatsoeuer he did, tended rather to aduance the peace and quiet of the common-wealth, than otherwise; and where he and his companie were in armes, it was for feare of the king, to whom he could haue no free accesse, by reason of such a multitude of flatterers as were about him; and therefore he mainteined that his purpose to be good & profitable, as well for the king himselfe, as for the realme, if men were willing to vnderstand a truth: & herewith he shewed foorth a scroll, in which the articles were written wherof before ye haue heard.

The subtill policie of the earle of westmerland.

The archbishops protestation why he had on him armes.

The messengers returning to the earle of Westmerland, shewed him what they had heard & brought from the archbishop. When he had read the articles, he shewed in word and countenance outwardly that he liked of the archbishops holie and vertuous intent and purpose, promising that he and his would prosecute the same in assisting the archbishop, who reioising hereat, gaue credit to the earle, and persuaded the earle marshall (against his will as it were) to go with him to a place appointed for them to commune togither. Here when they were met with like number on either part, the articles were read ouer, and without anie more adoo, the earle of Westmerland and those that were with him agréed to doo their best, to see that a reformation might be had, according to the same.

The earle of Westmerland vsing more policie then the rest: "Well (said he) then our trauell is come to the wished end: and where our people haue beene long in armour, let them depart home to their woonted trades and occupations: in the meane time let vs drinke togither in signe of agreement, that the people on both sides maie sée it, and know that it is true, that we be light at a point." They had no sooner shaken hands togither, but that a knight was sent streight waies from the archbishop, to bring word to the people that there was peace concluded, commanding ech man to laie aside his armes, and to resort home to their houses. The people beholding such tokens of peace, as shaking of hands, and drinking togither of the lords in louing manner, they being alreadie wearied with the vnaccustomed trauell of warre, brake vp their field and returned homewards: but in the meane time, whilest the people of the archbishops side withdrew awaie, the number of the contrarie part increased, according to order giuen by the earle of Westmerland; and yet the archbishop perceiued not

The earle of westmerlāds politike dealing.

not

The archbishop of Yorke and the earle marshall arrested.
Eiton.
not that he was deceiued, vntill the earle of Westmerland arrested both him and the earle marshall with diuerse other. Thus saith Walsingham.

But others write somwhat otherwise of this matter, affirming that the earle of Westmerland in deed, and the lord Rafe Eeuers, procured the archbishop & the earle marshall, to come to a communication with them, vpon a ground iust in the midwaie betwixt both the armies, where the earle of Westmerland in talke declared to them how perilous ans enterprise they had taken in hand, so to raise the people, and to mooue warre again t the king, aduising them therefore to submit themselues without further delaie vnto the kings mercie, and his sonne the lord Iohn, who was present there in the field with banners spred, redie to trie the matter by dint of sword if they refused this counsell : and therefore he willed them to remember themselues well : & if they would not yeeld and craue the kings pardon, he bad them doo their best to defend themselues.

Herevpon as well the archbishop as the earle marshall submitted themselues vnto the king, and to his sonne the lord Iohn that was there present, and returned not to their armie. Wherevpon their troops scaled and fled their waies : but being pursued, manie were taken, manie slaine, and manie spoiled of that that they had about them, & so permitted to go their waies. Howsoeuer the matter was handled, true it is that the archbishop, and the earle marshall were brought to Pomfret to the king, who in this meane while was aduanced thither with his power, and from thence he went to Yorke,

The archbishop of Yorke, the earle marshall, & others put to death.
Abr. Fl. out of *Thom. Walsin. Hypod.* pag. 168.
whither the prisoners were also brought, and there beheaded the morrow after Whitsundaie in a place without the citie, that is to vnderstand, the archbishop himselfe, the earle marshall, sir Iohn Lampleie, and sir Robert Plumpton. ¶ Vnto all which persons though indemnitie were promised, yet was the same to none of them at anie hand performed. By the issue hereof, I meane the death of the foresaid, but speciallie of the archbishop, the prophesie of a sickelie canon of Bridlington in Yorkshire fell out to be true, who darklie inough foretold this matter, & the infortunate euent thereof in these words hereafter following, saieng :

Pacem tractabunt, sed fraudem subter arabunt,

Pro nulla marca, saluabitur ille* hierarcha.

* *Archiepiscopus.*

The archbishop reputed a martyr.
The archbishop suffered death verie constantlie, insomuch as the common people tooke it he died a martyr, affirming that certeine miracles were wrought as well in the field where he was executed, as also in the place where he was buried : and immediatlie vpon such bruits, both men and women began to worship his dead carcasse, whom they loued so much, when he was aliue, till they were forbidden by the kings freends, and for feare gaue ouer to visit the place of his sepulture. The earle marshalls bodie by the kings leaue was buried in the cathedrall church, manie lamenting his destinie ; but his head was set on a pole aloft on the wals for a certeine space, till by the kings permission [after the same had suffered manie a hot sunnie daie, and manie a wet shower of raine] it was taken downe and buried togither with the bodie.

After the king, accordinglie as seemed to him good, had ransomed and punished by greeuous fines the citizens of Yorke (which had borne armour on their archbishops side against him) he departed frō Yorke with an armie of thirtie and seuen thousand fighting men, furnished with all prouision necessarie, marching northwards against
The lords executed.
the earle of Northumberland. At his cōming to Durham, the lord Hastings, the lord Fauconbridge, sir Iohn Colleuill of the Dale, and sir Iohn Griffith, being conuicted of the conspiracie, were there beheaded. The earle of Northumberland, hearing that his counsell was bewraied, and his confederats brought to confusion, through too much hast of the archbishop of Yorke, with thrée hundred horsse got him to Berwike. The king comming forward quickelie, wan the castell of Warkewoorth. Wherevpon
The earle of Northumberland.
the earle of Northumberland, not thinking himselfe in suertie at Berwike, fled with the lord Berdolfe into Scotland, where they were receiued of Dauid lord Fleming.

The

The king comming to Berwike, commanded them that kept the castell against him to render it into his hands, and when they flatlie denied so to doo, he caused a péece of artillerie to be planted against one of the towers, and at the first shot ouerthrowing *Berwike castell* part thereof, they within were put in such feare, that they simplie yéelded themselues *yéelded to the* without any maner of condition, wholie to remaine at the kings pleasure. Herevpon *king.* the chiefest of them, to wit, sir Willian Greistoke, sonne to Rafe baron of Greistoke, *The sonne of the* sir Henrie Beinton, and Iohn Blenkinsop, with foure or fiue other were put to death, *lord Greistoke* and diuerse other were kept in prison. Some write that the earle of Northumberland *death.* at his entring into Scotland, deliuered the towne of Berwike vnto the Scots, who *Exton.* hearing of king Henries approch, and despairing to defend the towne against him, set fire on it and departed. There was not one house that was left vnburnt, except the friers and the church.

After that the king had disposed things in such conuenient order as stood with his pleasure at Berwike, he came backe, and had the castell of Alnewike deliuered vnto *The castell of* him, with all other the castels that belonged to the erle of Northumberland in the *Alnewike yéeld-* north parts, as Prodhow, Langlie, Cockermouth, Aluham, and Newstéed. Thus *ed to the king.* hauing quieted the north parts, he tooke his iournie directlie into Wales, where he *The K. passeth* found fortune nothing fauourable vnto him, for all his attempts had euill successe, *into wales.* in somuch that losing fiftie of his cariages through abundance of raine and waters, he *He looseth his* returned; and comming to Worcester, he sent for the archbishop of Canturburie, *He returneth.* and other bishops, declaring to them the misfortune that had chanced to him, in consideration whereof he requested them to helpe him with some portion of monie, towards the maintenance of his warres, for the taming of the presumptuous and vnquiet Welshmen.

In the meane time, the French king had appointed one of the marshals of France *Hall.* called Montmerancie, and the master of his crosbowes, with twelue thousand men to *The marshall* saile into Wales to aid Owen Glendouer. They tooke shipping at Brest, and hauing *Mõtmerãcie sent* the wind prosperous, landed at Milford hauen, with an hundred and fourtie ships, as *to aid Owen* Thomas Walsingham saith; though Enguerant de Monstrellet maketh mention but *Glendouer.* of an hundred and twentie. The most part of their horsses were lost by the waie for lacke of fresh water. The lord Berkleie, and Henrie Paie, espieng their aduantage, burnt fiftéene of those French ships, as they laie at road there in the hauen of Milford: and shortlie after the same lord Berkleie, and sir Thomas Swinborne, with the said Henrie Paie, tooke other fourtéene ships, as they came that waie with prouision of vittels and munition foorth of France to the aid of the other.

In the meane while the marshall Montmerancie, with his armie, besieged the towne of Carmarden, and wan it by composition, granting to the men of warre that kept *Carmarden* it against him, licence to depart whither they would, & to take with them all their *woone by the* mooueable goods: the castell of Penbroke they assaulted not, estéeming it to be so *French.* well manned, that they shuld but lose their labour in attempting it. Notwithstanding they besieged the towne of Hereford west, which neuerthelesse was so well defended *Hereford west* by the earle of Arundell and his power, that they lost more than they wan, and so *manfullie de-* they departed towards the towne of Denbigh, where they found Owen Glendouer *fended.* abiding for their comming, with ten thousand of his Welshmen. Here were the French-*Enguerant de* men ioifullie receiued of the Welsh rebels, and so when all things were prepared, they *Monstrellet* passed by Glamorganshire towards Worcester, and there burnt the suburbes: but *saith they burnt* hearing of the kings approch, they suddenlie returned towards Wales. *the townes but could not win the castell.*

The suburbs of worcester burnt.

The king with a great puissance followed, and found them imbattelled on a high mounteine, where there was a great vallie betwixt both the armies, so that either armie might plainelie perceiue the other, and either host looked to be assailed of his aduersarie, & therefore sought to take the aduantage of ground. Thus they continued for the space of eight daies from morning till night, readie to abide, but not to giue battell.

             There

French lords slaine.
There were manie skirmishes, and diuerse proper feats of armes wrought in that meane while, in the which the French lost manie of their nobles and gentlemen, as the lord Patroullars de Tries, brother to the marshall of France, the lord Matelonne or Martelonne, the lord de la Valle, and the bastard of Bourbon, with other, to the number (as some haue written) of fiue hundred. But Enguerant de Monstrellet affirmeth, that vpon their returne into France, there wanted not aboue thréescore persons of all their companies.

After they had laine thus one against another the space of eight daies (as before is said) vittels began to faile, so that they were inforced to dislodge. The French and Welshmen withdrew into Wales, and though the Englishmen followed, yet impeached with the desart grounds and barren countrie, thorough which they must passe, as our felles and craggie mounteins, from hill to dale, from marish to wood, from naught to woorsse (as Hall saith) without vittels or succour, the king was of force constrained to retire with his armie, and returne againe to Worcester, in which returne the enimies tooke certeine cariages of his laden with vittels. The Frenchmen after the armies

The Frenchmen returne home. *Anno Reg.* 7.
were thus withdrawne, returned into Britaine, making small brags of their painefull iournie.

This yeare at London, the earle of Arundell maried the bastard daughter of the king of Portingale, the king of England and the quéene with their presence honoring the solemnitie of that feast, which was kept with all sumptuous roialtie, the morrow after saint Katharins daie. ¶ And on the daie of the Conception of our ladie, the ladie Philip king Henries daughter was proclamed quéene of Denmarke, Norwaie, and Sweden, in presence of such ambassadors, as the last summer came hither from the king of those countries, to demand hir in marriage for him, and had so trauelled in

Abr. Fl. out of *Thom. Walsin.* Roiston burned.
the matter, that finallie they obteined it. ¶ On the daie of the translation of saint Martine, the towne of Roiston was on fire. This yeare the first of March a parlement

1406

A parlement.
began, which continued almost all this yeare: for after that in the lower house they had denied a long time to grant to any subsidie: yet at length, a little before Christ-

A fiftéenth grã-ted by the tem-poraltie.
masse, in the eight yeare of his reigne they granted a fifteenth to the losse and great damage of the communaltie, for through lingering of time, the expenses of knights and burgesses grew almost in value to the summe that was demanded.

A new kind of subsidie granted by the cleargie.
Moreouer, by the clergie a new kind of subsidie was granted, to the king, to be leuied of stipendarie priests and friers mendicants, and other such religious men as soong for the dead, celebrating (as they termed it) anniuersaries: euerie of them gaue halfe a marke, in reliefe of other of the cleargie that had still borne the burthen for them before. Whervpon now they murmured and grudged sore, for that they were thus charged at that present. The same time the earle of Northumberland, and the lord Bardolfe, warned by the lord Dauid Fleming, that there was a conspiracie practised to deliuer them into the king of Englands hands, fled into Wales to Owen

The lord Flem-ing lost his life for giuing know-ledge to the earle of Northumber-land of that which was meant against him.
Glendouer. This cost the lord Fleming his life: for after it was knowne that he had disclosed to the earle of Northumberland what was meant against him, and that the earle therevpon was shifted awaie, certeine of the Scots slue the said lord Fleming.

Wherevpon no small grudge rose betwixt those that so slue him, and the said lord

Dissention amõg the Scotish nobi-litie.
Flemings friends. For this and other matters, such dissention sproong vp amongst the Scotish nobilitie, that one durst not trust another, so that they were glad to sue for a truce betwixt England and them, which was granted to indure for one yeare, as in some books we find recorded. This truce being obteined, Robert king of Scot-land (vpon considerations, as in the Scotish historie ye may read more at large) sent

Eleuen years saith *Harding.* The prince of Scotland staid here in England.
his eldest son Iames intituled prince of Scotland (a child not past nine yeares of age) to be conueied into France, vnder the conduct of the earle of Orkenie, and a bishop, in hope that he might there both remaine in safetie, and also learne the French toong.

                                                      But

But it fortuned, that as they sailed neare to the English coast about Flambrough head in Holdernesse, their ship was taken and staied by certeine mariners of Claie (a towne in Norffolke) that were abroad the same time; and so he and all his companie being apprehended the thirtith of March, was conueied to Windsore, where though he had letters from his father, which he presented to the king, conteining a request in his sonnes behalfe for fauour to be shewed towards him, if by chance he landed within any of his dominions: yet was he deteined, and as well he himselfe as the earle of Orkenie was committed to safe keeping in the Tower of London, but the bishop got away and escaped (as some write) by what means I know not. By the Scotish writers we find that this chanced in the yeare 1404, that is two yeares before the time noted in diuerse English writers, as Thomas Walsingham and other. But Harding saith it was in the ninth yeare of king Henries reigne, to wit, in the yeare 1408.

But whensoeuer it chanced, it is to be thought, that there was no truce at that present betweene the two realmes, but that the warre was rather open, sith diuerse English rebels still remained in Scotland, and were there succored to the high *Hall.* displeasure of king Henrie. ¶ By authoritie of the parlement that all this time continued, the Britons that serued the quéene, with two of hir daughters were banished the realme. Robert Halome chancellor of Oxford, as then being in the *Robert Halome archb. of Yorke.* popes court at Rome, was created archbishop of Yorke. ¶ Moreouer the same time, the pope gaue vnto Thomas Langlie the bishoprike of Durham, which by the death of Walter Skirlow was then void. In the summer of this yeare, the ladie Philip the kings yoonger daughter was sent ouer to hir affianced husband, Erike king of Denmarke, Norwaie, and Sweden, being conueied thither with great pompe, and *The king and the* there married to the said king, where she tasted (according to the common spéech *quéene brought* vsed in praieng for the successe of such as match togither in mariage) both ioy and *she tooke ship-* some sorrow among. There attended hir thither Henrie Bowet bishop of Bath, and *Tho. Walsi.* the lord Richard brother to the duke of Yorke.

There was a iusts held at London, betwixt the earle of Kent and the erle of Marre a Scotishman; also sir Iohn Cornewall, and the lord Beaumont, against other two Scotish knights, whereof the honor remained with the Englishmen. In the parle-*An. Reg.* 8. ment which yet continued, the duke of Yorke was restored to his former libertie, *The duke of* estate and dignitie, where manie supposed that he had beene dead long before that *to libertie.* time in prison. Edmund Holland earle of Kent was in such fauour with king Henrie, *The earle of* that he not onelie aduanced him to high offices and great honors, but also to his great *Kent in fauor* costs and charges obteined for him the ladie Lucie, eldest daughter, and one of the *He marrieth a* heirs of the lord Barnabo of Millane, which Barnabo paied to him 100000 ducates, *daughter of* in the church of S. Marie Oueries in Southwarke, by the hands of Don Alfonso de *Millane.* Cainuola, vpon the day of the solemnization of the marriage, which was the foure and twentith of Ianuarie.

¶ In this yeare Roger of Walden departed this life; who hauing béene tossed vp and *Abr. Fl. out of* downe with sundrie changes of fortune, tried in a short time how inconstant, vncerteine, *Thom. Walsi.* variable, wandering, vnstable, and flitting she is; which when she is thought firmelie *Hypod.* pag. 161. to stand, she slipperinglie falleth; and with a dissembling looke counterfaiteth false ioies. For by the meanes of hir changeablenesse, the said Roger of a poore fellow, *Roger of waldens* grew vp to be high lord treasuror of the realme, and shortlie after archbishop of Can-*variable fortune.* turburie; but by what right, the world knoweth; considering that the lord Thomas Arundell was then liuing. Anon after he was deposed from his dignitie, and lead the life of an ordinarie priuat man a long time; within a while after againe he was pro-moted and made bishop of London, which sée he had not possessed a full yeare, but was depriued, and Nicholas Hobwith succeeded in his roome. So that hereby men are taught not to be proud of their preferment, nor to reckon of them as of perpetuities, sithens they may be as soone dispossessed as possessed of them; and for that all estates & degrées depend vpon Gods power and prouidence, whereof the poet diuinelie saieth,

Ouid. lib. de
Pont. 4.

Ludit in humanis diuina potentia rebus,
Et certam præsens vix habet hora fidem.

An addition of Francis Thin.

In this yeare the seuenth of Maie was Thomas Langlie consecrated bishop of Durham after the decease of Walter Skirlow. In which place he continued one and thirtie yeares. He among other his beneficiall déeds beautified the church of Durham for euer with a chanterie of two chapleines. Besides which for the increase of learning (wherwith himselfe was greatlie furnished) he built two schooles, the one for grammar to instruct youth, whereby in following time they might be made more able to benefit themselues and serue their countrie: and the other of musicke, wherein children might be made apt to serue God and the church, both which schooles he erected in a parcell of ground cōmonlie called The plaie gréene. To which buildings (for he was one that delighted much therein, and like vnto the philosopher Anaxagoras supposed that there was not any more earthlie felicitie, than to erect sumptuous palaces, wherby after their death the memorie of the founders might haue continuance) he added manie sumptuous parts of the palace of Durham. In the towne whereof he did also from the ground (of most statelie stone) erect a new gaole with the gatehouse to the same, in that place where of old it remained, and then by iniurie of time fallen downe and consumed. This man inioied the sée of Durham almost the whole time of thrée kings, that is; about six yeares and six moneths in the time of Henrie the fourth, nine yeares and fiue moneths in the time of Henrie the fift, and fifteene yeares in the time of Henrie the sixt; during the gouernment of all which princes, he was all his life time highlie estéemed and reuerenced for his singular wisedome, and for the great authoritie he bare in publike, betwéene whome and the maior of Newcastell arose great contention, about a bridge called Tinebridge in the towne of Gateshed or Goteshed, in Latine called Caput capræ. But in the yeare of our redemption 1416, and of Henrie the fift, the fourth, and of his bishoprike the eleuenth, this bishop had the recouerie thereof, as appeareth by the letter of atturnie of the said bishop, made to diuerse to take possession of the same.

The letter of atturnie wherby the bishop authorised diuerse to take possession of Tinebridge.

THOMAS Dei gratiâ episcopus Dunelmensis omnibus ad quos præsentes litteræ peruenerint salutem. Sciatis quòd assignauimus & deputauimus dilectos & fideles nostros Radulphum de Ewrie cheualier senescallum nostrū Dunelmiæ, Williamum Chanceler cancellarium, infra comitatum & libertatem Dunelmiæ, ac Williamum Claxton vicecomitem nostrum Dunelmiæ coniunctim & diuisim, ad plenam & pacificam seisinam, de duabus partibus medietatis cuiusdam pontis vocati Tinebridge, in villa nostra de Gatesheued, infra comitatum & libertatem Dunelmiæ existentis. Quæ quidem duæ partes medietatis prædictæ, continent & faciuut tertiam partem eiusdem pontis vsque austrum, in prædicta villa de Gatesheued. Super quas duas partes nuper maior & communitas villæ Noui castri super Tinam, quandam turrim de nouo ædificare cæperūt, & quas quidem duas partes cum franchesiis, iurisdictionibus, & iuribus regalibus super easdem duas partes medietatis prædictæ, nuper in curia domini regis versus maiorem & communitatem dictæ villæ Noui castri recuperauimus nobis & successoribus nostris episcopis Dunelmiæ, & in iure ecclesiæ nostræ sancti Cuthberti Dunelmiæ possidendas de vicecomite Westmerlandiæ, prætextu eiusdē breuis dicti domini regis sibi directi nomine nostro recipiendas; & turrim prædictā ad opus nostrum saluò & securè custodiēdam. Ratum & gratum habiturus quicquid
idē

idē Radulphus, Williamus & Willielmus nomine nostro fecerint in præmissis. In cuius rei testimonium has litteras nostras fierifecimus patentes. Datum Dunelmiæ per manus Williami Cancellarii nostri 26 Octobris, anno pontificatus nostri vndecimo.

According wherevnto in the said yeare, possession was deliuered in the presence of these persons, whose names I thinke not vnmeet for their posterities cause to be remembred, being persons of good credit and of antiquitie, that is to saie, Iohn Lomelie, Rafe Ewraie, Robert Hilton, William Fulthrop, William Tempest, Thomas Suerties, Robert *Cogniers, William Claxton shiriffe of Durham, Robert de *Egle, Iohn Bertram, Iohn Widerington, and Iohn Middleton knights of Northumberland, Christopher Morslie, Will. Osmunderlaw knights of Westmerland; and also in the presence of these esquiers, Robert Hilton, Robert Ewrie, William Bowes, Iohn Coniers, William Lampton the elder, Iohn de Morden, William Lampton the yoonger, Hugh Burunghell, Iohn Britlie, William Bellingham, Robert Belthis, Henrie Talboies; Thomas Garbois, Iohn de Hutton, William Hutton, Thomas Cooke of Fisburn, and fiue others. This bishop also procured certeine liberties from the pope in the church of Durham, by vertue of which grant they which were excommunicate (and might not inioy the priuilege of any sacraments, in other places throughout the bishoprike) should yet baptise their children in a font of that church, in an especiall place appointed therefore, and also receiue the other sacraments there to be administred vnto them. He died the eight and twentith of Nouember in the yeare of our redemption 1437, and was buried in the church of Durham in the chanterie which he had before erected. Before whose death at his manour of Holdon he builded all the west gates there of goodlie stone and lime, with the chambers thereto belonging on which he placed his armes.]

The duke of Orleance hauing leuied a mightie armie, had besieged the townes of Burge and Blaie in Gascoigne, meaning with force to win the same; but so it fortuned, that for the space of eight wéekes togither, there passed not one daie without tempest of raine, snow, and haile, mixed with winds and lightnings, which killed as well men as cattell, by reason whereof he lost (as was reported) six thousand men, so that he was constreined to breake vp his camps from before both those townes, and to get him awaie with dishonor, for all his brags and boasts made at his first comming thither. The same time, Henrie Paie and certeine other persons of the fiue ports, with fiftéene ships, tooke an hundred and twentie prises, which laie at anchor in and about the coast of Britaine, laden with iron, salt, oile, & Rochell wines.

In this season also billes were set vp in diuerse places of London, and on the doore of Paules church, in which was conteined that king Richard being aliue and in health, would come shortlie with great magnificence & power to recouer againe his kingdome: but the contriuer of this deuise was quicklie found out, apprehended, and punished according to his demerits. ¶ The citie of London this yeare in the summer was so infected with pestilent mortalitie, that the king durst not repaire thither, nor come neere to it. Whervpon he being at the castell of Leeds in Kent, and departing from thence, tooke ship at Quinburgh in the Ile of Shepie, to saile ouer vnto Lée in Essex, and so to go to Plaschie, there to passe the time till the mortalitie was ceassed.

As he was vpon the sea, certeine French pirats which laie lurking at the Thames mouth to watch for some preie, got knowledge by some meanes (as was supposed) of the kings passage, and therevpon as he was in the middest of his course, they entred among his fléet, and tooke foure vessels next to the kings ship, and in one of the same vessels sir Thomas Rampston the kings vicechamberlaine, with all his chamber stuffe and apparell. They followed the king so néere, that if his ship had not béene swift, he had landed sooner in France than in Essex: but such was his good hap, that he escaped and arriued at his appointed port. The lord Camois, that was commanded

*Coniers.
*Ogle.

1407
The duke of Orleance besiegeth townes in Gascoigne.

Henrie Paie a valiant seaman.

K. Richard still aliue as was feigned.

The king in danger to be taken by French pirats.

Sir Thomas Rampston taken.
The king escaped through swiftnesse of his ship.

G 2   with

The lord Camois put in blame. with certeine ships of warre to waft the king ouer (whether the wind turned so that he could not kéepe his direct course, or that his ship was but a slug) ran so far in the kings displeasure, that he was attached & indited, for that (as was surmized against him) he had practised with the Frenchmen, that the king might by them haue béene taken in his passage.

Yée haue heard that the pope by vertue of his prouision had giuen the arch-bishoprike of Yorke vnto maister Robert Halom; but the king was so offended there-with, that the said Robert might in no wise inioy that benefice, and so at length, to Henrie Bowet archbishop of Yorke. satisfie the kings pleasure, maister Henrie Bowet was translated from Bath vnto Yorke, and maister Robert Halom was made bishop of Salisburie then void by remoouing of Henrie Chichellie to S. Dauids. The lord Henrie prince of Wales this yeare in the Abiruscwith. summer season besieged the castell of Abiruscwith, and constreined them within to compound with him vnder certeine conditions for truce; but the prince was no sooner, Owen Glen-douer. from thence departed, but that Owen Glendouer by subtill craft entered the castell, put out the kéepers, and charging them with treason for concluding an agréement without his consent, placed other in that fortresse to defend it to his vse.

About the feast of the Assumption of our ladie, that ancient warriour and worthie Sir Robert Knols departeth this life. knight sir Robert Knols departed this life: he was (as before yée haue heard) borne of Bermondsey. meane parentage, but growen into such estimation for his valiant prowesse, as he was thought méet to haue the leading of whole armies, and the rule and gouernment of large prouinces. For not long before his deceasse, he being gouernour of Aquitaine, S. Albons. incumbred with age, resigned his office vnto sir Thomas Belfort, a right valiant capteine, and therewith returned into England, where he died at a manour place of his in Norffolke, & from thence brought to London in a litter, with great pompe and much He was buried in the white fri-ers. torch light, was buried in the church of White friers in Fleetstreet by the ladie Constance his wife, where was doone for him a solemne obsequie, with a great feast, and liberall dole to the poore.

Besides the diuerse noble exploits, and famous warlike enterprises atchiued by this valiant sonne of Mars, he (to continue the perpetuall memorie of his name) builded He built Ro-chester bridge commonlie called Knols bridge. the bridge of Rochester, ouer the riuer of Medwaie with a chappell at the end thereof; he repared also the bodie of the church of the White friers where he was buried, which church was first founded by the ancestour of the lord Greie of Codner. He also *Thom. Wals.* founded a college of secular priests at Pomfret, and did manie other things in his life right commendable. Sir Thomas Rampston constable of the tower was drowned, in comming from the court as he would haue shut the bridge, the streame being so big, An. Reg. 9. that it ouerturned his barge. This yeare the twentith of October began a parlement holden at Glocester, but remooued to London as should appeare in Nouember; for *Thom Wals.* A subsidie. (as we find) in that moneth this yéere 1407, and ninth of this kings reign, a subsidie was granted by authoritie of a parlement then assembled at London, to be leuied through the whole realme.

The lord Camois arreigned & ac-quited. The lord Camois was arreigned the last of October, before Edmund earle of Kent that daie high steward of England, and by his péeres acquit of the offense, whereof he had béene indicted (as before yee haue heard) and so dismissed at the barre, was restored againe both to his goods, lands, and offices. ¶ This yeare the winter was excéeding sharpe through frost and snow that continued & couered the ground by all the moneths of December, Ianuarie, Februarie, and March, insomuch that thrushes, blackbirds, and manie thousand birds of the like smaller size, perished with verie cold and hunger.

1408 The earle of Northumberland, and the lord Bardolfe, after they had béene in Wales in France and Flanders, to purchase aid against king Henrie, were returned backe into Scotland, and had remained there now for the space of a whole yeare: and as their euill fortune would, whilest the king held a councell of the nobilitie at London, the said earle of of Northumberland and lord Bardolfe, in a dismall houre, with a great power of Scots The earle of Northumb. & the lord Bardolfe returne into Englãd. returned into England, recouering diuerse of the earls castels and seigniories, for the people in great numbers resorted vnto them. Héerevpon incouraged with hope of good successe, they entred into Yorkeshire, & there began to destroie the countrie. At their cōming to Threske, they published a proclamation, signifieng that they were come in comfort of the English nation, as to reléeue the common-wealth, willing all such as loued the libertie of their countrie, to repaire vnto them, with their armor on their backes, and in defensible wise to assist them.

The king aduertised hereof, caused a great armie to be assembled, and came forward with the same towards his enimies: but yer the king came to Notingham, sir Thomas, or (as other copies haue) Rafe Rokesbie shiriffe of Yorkeshire, assembled The shiriffe of Yorkeshire. the forces of the countrie to resist the earle and his power, comming to Grimbaut brigs, beside Knaresborough, there to stop them the passage; but they returning aside, got to Weatherbie, and so to Tadcaster, and finallie came forward vnto Bramham more, neere to Haizelwood, where they chose their ground méet to fight vpon. The shiriffe was as readie to giue battell as the earle to receiue it, and His hardie corage to fight. so with a standard of S. George spred, set fiercelie vpon the earle, who vnder a standard of his owne armes incountered his aduersaries with great manhood. There was a sore incounter and cruell conflict betwixt the parties but in the end the victorie fell to the shiriffe. The lord Bardolfe was taken, but sore wounded, so that he shortlie after died of the hurts. ¶ As for the earle of Northumberland, he The earle of Northumberland slaine. was slaine outright: so that now the prophesie was fulfilled, which gaue an inkling of this his heauie hap long before; namelie, *Abr. Fl.* out of *Tho. Walsin. Hypod*, pag. 172

Stirps Persitina periet confusa ruina.

For this earle was the stocke and maine root of all that were left aliue called by the name of Persie; and of manie more by diuerse slaughters dispatched. For whose misfortune the people were not a little sorrie, making report of the gentlemans valiantnesse, renowne, and honour, and applieng vnto him certeine lamentable verses out of Lucane, saieng;

> Sed nos nec sanguis, nec tantùm vulnera nostri
> Affecere senis; quantum gestata per vrbem
> Ora ducis, quæ transfixo deformia pilo
> Vidimus.

For his head, full of siluer horie heares, being put vpon a stake, was openlie carried through London and set vpon the bridge of the same citie: in like maner was the lord Bardolfes. The bishop of Bangor was taken and pardoned by the king, for that when he was apprehended, he had no armor on his backe. This battell was fought the ninteenth day of Februarie. ¶ The king to purge the North parts of all rebellion, and to take order for the punishment of those that were accused to haue succoured and assisted the earle of Northumberland, went to Yorke, where when manie were condemned, and diuerse put to great fines, and the countrie brought to quietnesse, he caused the abbat of Hailes to be hanged, who had béene in armour The abbat of Hails hanged. against him with the foresaid earle.

In the beginning of March, the king sent Edmund Holland earle of Kent with The earle of Kent sent to the sea. an armie of men imbarked in certeine ships of warre vnto the sea, bicause he had knowledge that diuerse rouers were wafting about the coasts of this land, and did much hurt. When the earle had serched the coasts, and could meet with no enimie abrode, he was aduertised by espials, that the pirats hearing of his comming to sea were withdrawne into Britaine: wherefore the said earle intending to be reuenged on them, whome he sought, directed his course thither, and finding that they had laid vp their ships in the hauens, so as he could not fight with them by sea, he lanched out his boates, and with his fierce souldiers tooke land, and manfullie

assaulted

assaulted the towne of Briake standing by the sea side. They within stoutlie defended themselues, dooing their best to repell the Englishmen, with throwing darts,
casting stones, and shooting quarels; in which conflict the earle receiued a wound in
his head, so that he died thereof within fiue daies after.

The Englishmen not dismaied with his death, but the more desirous to obteine
their purpose, continued their assaults, till by fine force they entered the towne,
set it on fire, and slue all that made resistance; and after for want of a generall
to command what should be doone, they being pestered with preies and prisoners,
returned into England. ¶ The countesse of Kent that was daughter (as yée haue
heard) to Bernabo viscont lord of Millaine, hauing no issue by hir husband, was
now mooued by the king after hir husbands death, to marrie with his bastard
brother the earle of Dorset, a man verie aged and euill visaged; wherevpon she
misliking him, meant rather to satisfie hir owne fancie, and therefore chose for hir
husband Henrie Mortimer, a goodlie yoong bacheller, by whome she had issue a
daughter named Anne, married to sir Iohn Awbemond.

This yeare, the next daie after the feast daie of Marie Magdalen, in a councell
holden at London by the cleargie, the doctors of the vniuersities of Cambridge
and Oxenford being there, with the rest assembled, debated the matter, whether
they ought to withdraw from the pope, paiments of monie, and their accustomed
obedience, considering that contrarie to his word and promise so solemnlie made,
and with an oth confirmed, he withdrewe himselfe from the place where he (according
to couenants) should haue béene present, to aduance an agréement and concord in
the church. ¶ Vpon the euen of the Natiuitie of our ladie, there chanced such
flouds through abundance of raine, as the like had not béene séene afore by anie
man then liuing. Also about the feast of All saints, the cardinal of Burges came
into England, to informe the king and the cleargie of the inconstant dealing of
pope Gregorie, in like maner as he had informed the French king and the Frenchmen,
to the end that he might persuade both these kings which were accounted the
chéefe in christendome, to put vnto their helping hands, that the same pope Gregorie
might be induced to obserue and performe that oth, which he had receiued, so as
by the roiall authoritie of those two kings, concord might be had in the church.
The French king (as this cardinall alleged) following the aduise of the learned men
of the vniuersities of Paris, Bologna, Orleans, Tholouse, and Montpellier, to auoid
the danger of fauouring schisme, determined to obeie neither the one nor the other
that contended for the papasie, vntill peace and concord might be restored in Christes
church. The king vnderstanding the purpose of the cardinall, shewed him what
courtesie might be deuised, offering to beare his charges, so long as it pleased him to
remaine in England, and promising him to consider aduisedlie of the matter.

This yeare after the Epiphanie the archbishop of Canturburie called the cleargie of
the prouince of Canturburie to a conuocation in Paules church at London, to choose sufficient persons that might go vnto the generall councell, appointed to be kept at Pisa:
herevpon were chosen Robert Halom bishop of Salisburie, Henrie Chichleie bishop of
saint Dauid, & Thomas Chillingden prior of Christes church in Canturburie. The
king before this had sent ambassadors vnto pope Gregorie, and also to the cardinals; to
wit, sir Iohn Coluill knight, and maister Nicholas Rixton clearke, with letters, signifieng the gréefe he had conceiued for the inconuenience that fell in the christian
common-wealth thorough the schisme; and withall putting the pope in remembrance
what mischéefe and destruction of people had chanced by the same schisme. These
and the like matters, to vtter what desire he had to haue a vnitie in the church, he
declared frankelie in his letters directed to the pope, so as it might appear to the
world, how soberlie and modestlie he sought to induce the pope to procure peace &
concord in the church. ¶ Certeine collections of which letters (as I find them in
                                                                         Thomas

Thomas Walsingham) I haue here set downe in commendation of this king so excel- *Abr. Fl. out of Thom. Wals. Hypod. pag. 159.*
lentlie minded.

An extract of the kings letter to pope Gregorie.

MOST holie father, if the seat apostolicall would vouchsafe by prouidence to consider, how great dangers haue inuaded the whole world vnder the- pretext of
schisme, and speciallie the slaughter of christian people, which is of aboue two
hundred thousand (as it is auouched) by the outrage of warres and battell sproong
vp in sundrie parts of the world; & now latelie to the number of thirtie thousand
(by meanes of the dissention about the bishoprike of Leods betweene two, one contending vnder the authoritie of true pope, and the other vnder the title of antipape)
slaine in a foughten field, whereof we make report with greefe; trulie the said seat
would be pensiue in spirit, and with due sorow troubled in mind; yea at the motion
of a good conscience, it would rather giue ouer the honour of that apostolicall
seat, than suffer such detestable deeds further to be committed, vnder the cloke of
dissimulation, taking example of the true and naturall mother, which pleading before king Salomon, chose rather to part with hir owne child, than to see him cut
in sunder. And although by that new creation of nine cardinals, against your oth
(that we maie vse the words of others) made by you, wherof a vehement cause of
woondering is risen, it maie in some sort be supposed (as it is likelie) that your intent respecteth not anie end of schisme; yet farre be it alwaies from the world, that
your circumspect seat should be charged by anie person with so great inconstancie of
mind, whereby the last errour might be counted woorsse than the first, &c.

An extract of the said kings letter to the cardinals.

WE being desirous to shew how great zeale we had, & haue, that peace might
be granted & given to the church by the consent of the states of our realme, haue
sent ouer our letters to our lord the pope, according to the tenure of a copie inclosed within these presents effectuallie to be executed. Wherefore we doo earnestlie
beseech the reuerend college of you; that if happilie the said Gregorie be present
at the generall councell holden at Pisa, about the yeelding vp of the papasie, according
to the promise and oth by him manie a time made, to fulfill your and our desires, as
we wish and beare our selues in hand he will doo; that you will so order things
concerning his estate, that thereby God maie cheeflie be pleased, and as well Gregorie
himselfe, as we, who deseruedlie doo tender his honour and commoditie with all our
harts, maie be beholden to giue you and euerie of you manifold thanks.

This yeare certeine learned men in Oxford and other places, publikelie in their ser- *Wicklifs doctrine mainteined by the learned.*
mons mainteined and set foorth the opinions and conclusions of Wickliffe. This
troubled the bishops and other of the clergie sore, insomuch that in their conuocation house, the six and twentith of Iune, by a speciall mandat of the lord chancellor
in presence of the procurators, regents, and others, as Richard Courtneie, Richard
Talbot, Nicholas Zouch, Walter Midford, & such like in great multitude: sentence *Sentēce pro-nounced against Wicklifs books.*
was pronounced by Iohn Wels, doctor of the canon law against the books of Iohn
Wickliffe doctor of diuinitie, intituled De sermone in monte, Triologorum de simonia,
De perfectione statuum, De ordine Christiano, De gradibus cleri ecclesiæ: and to
these was added the third treatise, which he compiled of logike or sophistrie. These
books and the conclusions in the same conteined, the chancellor of the vniuersitie
of Oxford by common consent and assent of the regents and non regents of the
same

same vniuersitie, reproued, disanulled and condemned, inhibiting on paine of the great cursse and depriuation of all degrées scholasticall, that none from thencefoorth should affirme, teach, or preach by anie manner of meanes or waies, the same hereticall books (as they tearmed them) conteining anie the like opinions as he taught and set foorth in the same books.

Fabian.
Iusts in Smithfield.
Owen Glendouer endeth his life in great miserie.

This yeare about Midsummer, were roiall iusts holden at London in Smithfield betwixt the seneschall of Heinault, and certeine Henewers challengers, and the earle of Summerset, and certeine Englishmen defendants. The Welsh rebell Owen Glendouer made an end of his wretched life in this tenth yeare of king Henrie his reigne, being driuen now in his latter time (as we find recorded) to such miserie, that in manner despairing of all comfort, he fled into desert places and solitarie caues, where being destitute of all releefe and succour, dreading to shew his face to anie creature, and finallie lacking meat to ·susteine nature, for méere hunger and lacke of

An. Reg. 11.
Officers made.
__1410__
A parlement.

food, miserablie pined awaie and died. This yeare Thomas Beaufort earle of Surrie was made chancellor, and Henrie Scroope lord treasuror. A parlement began this yeare in the quindene of saint Hilarie, in which the commons of the lower house exhibited a bill to the king and lords of the vpper house, conteining effect as followeth.

A supplication to the king.

Tho. Walsi.
Fabian.

TO the most excellent lord our k. and to all the nobles in this present parlement assembled, your faithfull commons doo humblie signifie, that our souereigne lord the king might haue of the temporall possessions, lands & reuenues which are lewdlie spent, consumed and wasted by the bishops, abbats, and priors, within this realme, so much in value as would suffice to find and susteine one hundred and fiftie earles, one thousand & fiue hundred knights, six thousand and two hundred esquiers, and one hundred hospitals more than now be.

Thom. Wals.

The king (as some write) vpon aduised consideration hereof had, misliked of the motion, & therevpon commanded that from thenceefoorth they should not presume to studie about anie such matters. An other thing the commons sued to haue granted vnto them, but could not obteine: which was, that clearks conuicted should not from thence foorth be deliuered to the bishops prison. Moreouer they demanded to haue the statute either reuoked or qualified, which had béene established by authoritie of parlement, in the second yeare of this kings reigne, against such as were reputed to be heretiks, or Lollards. By force whereof it was prouided, that wheresoeuer such manner of persons should be found and knowne to preach or teach their erronious doctrine, they should be attached with the kings writ, and brought

King Henrie a fauorer of the clergie.

to the next goale : but the king séemed so highlie to fauour the cleargie, that the commons were answered plainelie, they should not come by their purpose, but rather that the said statute should be made more rigorous and sharpe for the punishment of such persons.

Iohn Badbie burnt.
Tho Walsi.
The prince being present at the execution offereth him pardon.

During this parlement one Iohn Badbie a tailor, or (as some write) a smith, being conuict of heresie, was brought into Smithfield, and there in a tun or pipe burnt to death, in pitifull manner. The kings eldest sonne the lord Henrie prince of Wales being present, offered him his pardon, first before the fire was kindled, if he would haue recanted his opinions; and after when the fire was kindled, hearing him make a roring noise verie pitifullie, the prince caused the fire to be plucked backe, and exhorting him being with pitifull paine almost dead, to remember himselfe, and renounce his opinions, promising him not onelie life, but also thrée pence a daie so long as he liued to be paid out of the kings coffers : but he hauing recouered his

his spirits againe, refused the princes offer, choosing eftsoones to tast the fire, and Notable constancie of Badbie. so to die, than to forsake his opinions. Wherevpon the prince commanded, that he should be put into the tun againe, from thencefoorth not to haue anie fauour or pardon at all, and so it was doone, and the fire put to him againe, and he consumed to ashes.

The king demanded in this parlement, that it might be granted to him, to haue The kings demand in parlement. euerie yeare in which he held no parlement a tenth of the cleargie, and a fifteenth of the laitie; but the estates would not agrée therevnto, by reason whereof, the par- A long parlement. A fiftéenth granted. lement continued till almost the middle of Maie. At length they granted to giue him a fiftéenth, not without murmuring and grudging of the commonaltie. About Earle of Surrie deceasseth. this season died the lord Thomas Beauford earle of Surrie. The eleuenth of April or therabouts, the towne of saint Omers was burnt by casuall fire togither with the abbeie, in which towne was such strange and maruellous prouision of engines, and all manner of furniture and preparation for the winning of Calis, as the like had Preparation made to win Calis. *Thom. Walsi.* neuer béene séene nor heard of. Some write, that they of Calis standing in doubt of such purueiance, & great preparation deuised to annoie them, procured a yoong man to kindle a fire, whereby all that dreadfull prouision was consumed to ashes, and so they within Calis deliuered of a great great deale of care and feare which they had thereof.

¶ But Tho. Walsingham maketh a full & complet declaration, both concerning the dukes deuise, & also of the Calesians deliuerance from the danger of the same; which because it perfecteth the report of this present matter, I haue thought good to set downe word for word as I find it in his Hypodigme. About the ninth of April *Abr. Fl.* out of *Thom. Wals. Hypod.* pag. 175. (saith he) the towne of saint Andomaire was burned with the abbeie, wherein was hidden and laid vp the execrable prouision of the duke of Burgognie, who had vowed either to destroie the towne of Calis, or else to subdue it to the will and pleasure of the French. There a great manie engines to this daie no where séene, The engines of the duke of Burgognie against Calis that shot out barrels of poison. there an excéeding sort of vessels cónteining poison in them were kept in store, which he had aforehand prouided to cast out to the destruction of the said towne. For he had gathered togither serpents, scorpions, todes, and other kinds of venemous things, which he had closed and shut vp in little barrels, that when the flesh or substance of those noisome creatures was rotten, and dissolued into filthie matter, he might laie siege to Calis, and cast the said barrels let out of engines into the towne; which with the violence of the throw being dasht in péeces, might choke them that were within, poison the harnessed men touched therewith, & with their scattered venem infect all the stréets, lanes, & passages of the towne. In the meane time, a certeine yoong man allured with couetousnesse of gold, or lead with affec- tion and loue towards the kings towne, asked of the gouernours what reward he should deserue, that would discharge and set frée the towne from so great a feare, and would burne all the prouision which they suspected. Herevpon they leuied a summe of that yellow metall (namelie gold) wherewith the yoong man contented, went his waie, and with fire readie made for the purpose, did not onelie burne the said venemous matter and infected stuffe, but also togither with the monasterie almost the whole towne.]

Moreouer this yeare sir Robert Umfreuill vice-admeral of England, annoied the Sir Robert Umfreuill viceadmerall. *Harding.* His exploit in Scotland. countries on the sea coasts of Scotland: for comming into the Forth with ten ships of warre, and lieng there fourtéene daies togither, he landed euerie daie on the one side of the riuer or the other, taking preies, spoiles & prisoners; notwithstanding the duke of Albanie, and the earle Dowglas were readie there, with a great power to resist him: he burnt the galliot of Scotland (being a ship of great account) with manie other vessels lieng the same time at the Blackenesh ouer against Lieth. At his returne from thence, he brought with him fourtéene good ships, and manie other great prises of cloathes, both woollen, and linnen, pitch, tarre, woad, flower, meale, wheat and rie, which being sold abroad, the markets were well holpen thereby, so that his surname of Robert Mendmarket séemed verie well to agrée with his qualities, which name he got by this occasion.

About foure years before this, he burnt the towne of Peples on the market daie, causing his men to meat the cloathes which they got there with their bowes, & so to sell them awaie, wherevpon the Scots named him Robert Mendmarket. Shortlie after his returne from the sea now in this eleuenth yeare of king Henries reigne, he made a road into Scotland by land, hauing with him his nephue yoong Gilbert Umfreuill earle of Angus (commonlie called earle of Kime) being then but fourtéene yeares of age, and this was the first time that the said earle spread his banner. They burnt at that time Iedwoorth, and the most part of Tiuidale. This yeare there died of the bloudie flix in the citie of Burdeaux fourtéene thousand persons, and so sore raged that disease in Gascoigne and Guien, that there wanted people to dresse their vines, and presse their grapes.

Iohn Prendergest knight, & William Long scowred the seas, as no pirat durst appeare, but that merchants & passengers might passe to & fro in safetie. But yet through disdaine of some that enuied their good successe, the same Prendergest and Long were accused of robberies which they should practise, in spoling such ships as they met with, of diuerse things against the owners wils. Prendergest was driuen to take sanctuarie at Westminster, and could not be suffered to lodge in anie mans house for feare of the kings displeasure, commanding, that none should receiue him, and so was constreined to set vp a tent within the porch of saint Peters church there, and to haue his seruants to watch nightlie about him for doubt to be murthered of his aduersaries: but his associat William Long laie still at the sea, till the lord admerall hauing prepared certeine vessels went to the sea himselfe in person to fetch him: but yet he could not catch him vntill he had promised him pardon, and vndertaken vpon his fidelitie that he should haue no harme: but notwithstanding all promises, vpon his comming in he was shut vp fast in the Tower, and so for a time remained in durance. The archbishop of Canturburie minding in this season to visit the vniuersitie of Oxenford, could not be suffered, in consideration of priuileges which they pretended to haue.

The realme of France in this meane while was disquieted, with the two factions of Burgognie and Orleance, in most miserable wise, as in the French histories it maie further appeare. Neither could the king, being a lunatike person, and féeble of braine, take any full order for reforming of such mischéefs, so that the whole state of the kingdome was maruellouslie brought in decaie: neither tooke those troubles end by the death of the duke of Orleance (murthered at length through the practise of the duke of Burgognie) but rather more perilouslie increased. For the yoong duke of Orleance Charles, sonne to duke Lewes thus murthered, alied himselfe with the dukes of Berrie and Burbon, and with the earles of Alanson & Arminacke, whereby he was so stronglie banded against the duke of Burgognie, whome he defied as his mortall fo and enimie, that the duke of Burgognie fearing the sequele of the matter, thought good (because there was a motion of mariage betwixt the prince of Wales & his daughter) to require aid of king Henrie, who foreséeing that this ciuill discord in France (as it after hapned) might turne his realme to honor and profit, sent to the duke of Burgognie, Thomas earle of Arundell, Gilbert Umfreuill earle of Angus (commonlie called the earle of Kime) sir Robert Umfreuill, vncle to the same Gilbert, sir Iohn Oldcastell lord Cobham, sir Iohn Greie, and William Porter, with twelue hundred archers.

They tooke shipping at Douer, & landed at Sluis, from whence with speedie iournies in the latter end of this twelfth yeare of king Henries reigne they came to Arras, where they found the duke of Burgognie, of whom they were ioifullie receiued, &

& from thence he appointed them to go vnto Peron, where he assembled a power also of his owne subiects, and remoouing from thence, he marched through the countrie, by Roie, Bretueill, Beauois, and Gisors, till he came with his armie vnto Pontois, where he remained about the space of thrée wéeks. From Pontois the two and twentith of October, the duke of Burgognie marched towards Paris, and passing the An.Reg.13. riuer of Saine at Pont Meulene, he staid not till he came to Paris, into the which he entred the 23 of October, late in the euening. The duke of Orleance laie at the same time at saint Denis, with the more part of his armie, & the residue kept the towne of S. Clou, where a bridge laie ouer the riuer of Saine. On the 9 of Nouember, with hard & sharpe fight the Englishmen gat the towne of saint Clou, with the bridge, slue *Saint Clou taken* & drowned nine hundred souldiors that were set there to defend that passage, besides *by the helpe of* *the Englishmen.* 400 that were taken prisoners. They tooke also aboue 12 hundred horsses, which they found in the towne, with great riches, whereof the men of warre made their profit.

Among other prisoners, sir Manserd de Bos a valiant capteine was taken, and *Sir Manserd de* shortlie after put to death, as diuerse other were which the Burgognians bought of *Bos put to death.* the Englishmen that had taken them prisoners. The tower that stood at the end of the bridge could not be woon. At an other bickering also, it chanced that the Englishmen, vnder the leading of the earle of Angus or Kime, had the vpper hand, *Harding.* and tooke manie prisoners, whom the duke of Burgognie would that they should haue béene likewise put to death as traitors to their countrie, but the said earle of Angus answered for himselfe, and the residue of the Englishmen, that they would rather die all in the place, than suffer their prisoners to be vsed otherwise than as men of war ought to be, that is, to haue their liues saued, and to be ransomed according as the law of armes required, and by that meanes they were preserued. The duke of Burgognie hauing the world at will (for the duke of Orleance immediatlie after the losse of saint Clou, departing from saint Denis, got him into the high countries) sent home the Englishmen with hartie thanks, and great rewards.

This yeare, the king created his brother Thomas Beauford earle of Dorset; and *Recor. Turris.* his sonne the lord Thomas of Lancaster, that was lord steward of England, and earle *Creations of* *noblemen.* of Aubemarle, he created duke of Clarence. Iohn duke of Burgognie, hauing now *Hall.* the gouernance both of the French king and his relme, so persecuted the duke of Or- *The Orleantiall* leance and his complices, that finallie they for their last refuge required aid of king *factiō sueth to* *the K. of Eng-* Henrie, sending ouer vnto him certeine persons as their lawfull procurators (of the *land for aid.* which one was called Albert Aubemont, a man of great wit, learning, & audacitie) to offer in name of the confederates vnto the said king Henrie and to his sonnes, certeine conditions, which were made and concluded the yeare of our lord 1412, the eight of Maie. The names of the chiefe confederats were these, Iohn duke of Berrie *The confederates* and earle of Poictou, Charles duke of Orleance, and Valois erle of Blois, and Beaumont *of the Orleantiall* *faction.* lord of Coucie and Ach, Iohn duke of Bourbon, and Auuergne earle of Clearmont forest, and Lisle lord of Beauieu, and Casteau Chinon, Iohn duke of Alanson, Barnard earle of Arminacke, and others. The effect of the articles which these confederats were agréed vpon touching their offer to the king of England, were as followeth.

The articles of couenants which they offered to the king of England.

1 FIRST, they offered their bodies, finances, and lands, to serue the king of England, his heires, and successors, in all iust causes and actions, sauing alwaies their allegiance, knowing that he would not further inquire of them.

2 Secondlie, they offered their sonnes and daughters, néeces and nephues, and all other their kinsfolks to be bestowed in marriages accordingly to the pleasure of the king of England.

H 2   3 Thirdlie,

3 Thirdlie, they offered their castels, townes, treasures, & all their other goods, to serue the forsaid king.

4 Fourthlie, they offered their fréends, alies, and well-willers to serue him, being the most part of all the nobles of France, churchmen, clearkes, and honest citizens, as it should well appeare.

5 Fiftlie, they offered to put him in possession of the duchie of Guien, which they were readie to protest to belong vnto the king of England, in like and semblable wise, in libertie and franchises, as any other king of England his predecessor had held and inioied the same.

6 Sixtlie, that they would be readie to recognise the lands which they possessed within that duchie, to hold the same of the king of England, as of the verie true duke of Guien, promising all seruices and homages after the best maner that might be.

7 Seuenthlie, they promised to deliuer vnto the king, as much as laie in them, all townes and castels apperteining to the roialtie and seigniorie of the king of England, which are in number twentie townes and castels: and as to the regard of other townes & fortresses which were not in their hands, they would to the vttermost of their powers, helpe the king of England and his heires to win them out of his aduersaries hands.

8 Eightlie, that the duke of Berrie, as vassall to the king of England, and likewise the duke of Orleance his subiect and vassall, should hold of him by homage and fealtie, the lands and seigniories hereafter following, that is to saie; the duke of Berrie to hold onelie the countie of Ponthieu during his life, and the duke of Orleance to hold the countie of Angulesme during his life, and the countie of Perigourt for euer, and the earle of Arminacke to hold foure castels vpon certeine suerties and conditions, as by indenture should be appointed. For the which offers, couenants and agreements, they requested of the king of England to condescend vnto these conditions insuing.

The conditions which they requested of the king of England.

1 FIRST, that the king of England, as duke of Guien should defend and succor them as he ought to doo, against all men, as their verie lord and souereigne, and speciallie vntill they had executed iustice fullie vpon the duke of Burgognie, for the crime which he committed vpon the person of the duke of Orleance.

2 Secondlie, that he should assist them against the said duke of Burgognie and his fautors, to recouer againe their goods, which by occasion of the said duke and his fréends they had lost and béene depriued of.

3 Thirdlie, that he should likewise aid them in all iust quarels, for recouering of damages doone to their fréends, vassals and subiects.

4 Fourthlie, to helpe and assist them for the concluding and establishing of a firme peace betwixt both the realmes, so far as was possible. ¶ And further they besought the king of England to send vnto them eight thousand men, to aid them against the duke of Burgognie and his complices, which dailie procured the French king to make war vpon them séeking by all waies & meanes how to destroie them.

The king of England louinglie interteined the messengers, and vpon consideration had of their offers, as well for that he detested the shamefull murther of the duke of Orleance (which remained vnpunished by support of such as mainteined the duke of Burgognie, who (as it appeared) would keepe promise no longer than serued his owne turne) as also for that the same offers seemed to make greatlie both for his honor and profit, thought that by the office of a king he was bound in dutie to succour them that cried for iustice, and could not haue it; and namelie sith in right they were his subiects

iects and vassals, he ought to defend them in maintenance of his superioritie and seigniorie. Herevpon as duke of Guien, he tooke vpon him to succor and defend them against all men, as their verie lord and souereigne, and so sending awaie the messengers, promised to send them aid verie shortlie.

The king of England taketh vpō him to defend the Orleantiall faction.

This feat was not so secretlie wrought, but that it was knowne streightwaies in France. Wherefore the French kings councell sent the earle of saint Paule downe into Picardie, with fifteéne hundred horssemen, and a great number of footmen, who approching to Guisnes, attempted to assault the castell, but was repelled and beaten backe, so that he retired to the towne of saint Quintines, as one that neuer wan gaine at the Engiishmens hands, but euer departed from them with losse and dishonor. In this meane season the French king being led by the duke of Burgognie, pursued them that tooke part with the duke of Orleance, commonlie called Arminacks, and after the winning of diuerse townes he besieged the citie of Burges in Berrie, comming before it vpon saturdaie the eleuenth of Iune, with a right huge armie. Within this citie were the dukes of Berrie and Burbon, the earle of Auxerre, the lord Dalbret, the archbishops of Sens and Burges, the bishops of Paris and Chartres, hauing with them fifteene hundred armed men, and foure hundred archers and arcubalisters.

The earle of saint Paule assaulteth the castell of Guisnes.

His fortune against Englishmen.

There were with the king at this siege, his sonne the duke of Aquitane, otherwise called the Dolphin, the dukes of Burgognie and Bar, and a great number of other earles, lords, knights, and gentlemen; so that the citie was besieged euen till within the Faux burges of that side towards Dun le Roie. The siege continued, till at length through mediation of Philibert de Lignac, lord great maister of the Rhodes, and the marshall of Sauoie, that were both in the kings campe, trauelling betwixt the parties, there were appointed commissioners on both sides to treat for peace, to wit the master of the crosbowes, and the seneshall of Heinalt, and certeine other for the king; and the archbishop of Burges, with the lord of Gaucourt & others for the Orlientiall side. These cōming togither on a fridaie, the fifteenth of Iulie in the Dolphins tent, vsed the matter with such discretion, that they concluded a peace, & so on the wednesdaie next following, the campe brake vp, & the king returned.

A peace concluded betwixt the two factions of Burgognie & Orleance.

Whilest these things were a dooing in France, the lord Henrie prince of Wales, eldest sonne to king Henrie, got knowledge that certeine of his fathers seruants were busie to giue informations against him whereby discord might arise betwixt him and his father: for they put into the kings head, not onelie what euill rule (according to the course of youth) the prince kept to the offense of manie: but also what great resort of people came to his house, so that the court was nothing furnished with such a traine as dailie followed the prince. These tales brought no small suspicion into the kings head, least his sonne would presume to vsurpe the crowne, he being yet aliue, through which suspicious gelousie, it was perceiued that he fauoured not his sonne, as in times past he had doone.

The prince of Wales accused to his father. *Iohn Stow.*

The suspicious gelousie of the king toward his son.

The Prince sore offended with such persons, as by slanderous reports, sought not onelie to spot his good name abrode in the realme, but to sowe discord also betwixt him and his father, wrote his letters into euerie part of the realme, to reproue all such slanderous deuises of those that sought his discredit. And to cleare himselfe the better, that the world might vnderstand what wrong he had to be slandered in such wise: about the feast of Peter and Paule, to wit, the nine and twentith daie of Iune, he came to the court with such a number of noble men and other his freends that wished him well, as the like traine had béene sildome seene repairing to the court at any one time in those daies. He was apparelled in a gowne of blew satten, full of small oilet holes, at euerie hole the néedle hanging by a silke thred with which it was sewed. About his arme he ware an hounds collar set full of S S of gold, and the tirets likewise being of the same metall.

The prince goeth to the court with a great traine.

His strange apparell.

The court was then at Westminster, where he being entred into the hall, not one of

his

his companie durst once aduance himselfe further than the fire in the same hall, notwithstanding they were earnestlie requested by the lords to come higher : but they regarding what they had in commandement of the prince, would not presume to doo in any thing contrarie there vnto. He himself onelie accompanied with those of the kings house, was streight admitted to the presence of tbe king his father, who being at that time gréeuouslie diseased, yet caused himselfe in his chaire to be borne into his priuie chamber, where in the presence of thrée or foure persons, in whome he had most *The prince cō-* confidence, he commanded the prince to shew what he had to saie concerning the *meth to the kings* cause of his comming.
preséce.

His words to his   The prince knéeling downe before his father said: " Most redoubted and souereigne
father. lord and father, I am at this time come to your presence as your liege man, and as your naturall sonne, in all things to be at your commandement. And where I vnder-stand you haue in suspicion my demeanour against your grace, you know verie well, that if I knew any man within this realme, of whome you should stand in feare, my duetie were to punish that person, thereby to remooue that greefe from your heart. Then how much more ought I to suffer death, to ease your grace of that gréefe which you haue of me, being your naturall sonne and liege man : and to that end I haue this daie made my selfe readie by confession and receiuing of the sacrament. And there-fore I beseech you most redoubted lord and deare father, for the honour of God, to ease your heart of all such suspicion as you haue of me, and to dispatch me héere be-fore your knees, with this same dagger" [and withall he deliuered vnto the king his dagger, in all humble reuerence ; adding further, that his life was not so deare to him, that he wished to liue one daie with his displeasure] " and therefore in thus ridding me out of life, and your selfe from all suspicion, here in presence of these lords, and before God at the daie of the generall iudgement, I faithfullie protest clearlie to forgiue you."

The kings wordes   The king mooued herewith, cast from him the dagger, and imbracing the prince
to the prince his kissed him, and with shedding teares confessed, that in déed he had him partlie in
son. suspicion, though now (as he perceiued) not with iust cause, and therefore from thencefoorth no misreport should cause him to haue him in mistrust, and this he promised of his honour. So by his great wisedome was the wrongfull suspicion which his father had conceiued against him remooued, and he restored to his fauour. And *Eiton.* further, where he could not but gréeuouslie complaine of them that had slandered him so greatlie, to the defacing not onelie of his honor, but also putting him in danger of *The princes re-* his life, he humblie besought the king that they might answer their vniust accusation;
quest to haue his and in case they were found to haue forged such matters vpon a malicious purpose,
accusors to an- that then they might suffer some punishment for their faults, though not to the full of
swer their wrōg- that they had deserued. The king séeming to grant his resonable desire, yet told him
ful slanders. that he must tarrie a parlement, that such offendors might be punished by iudgement of their péeres : and so for that time he was dismissed, with great loue and signes of fatherlie affection.

Abr. Fl. out of ¶ Thus were the father and the sonne reconciled, betwixt whom the said pick-
Angl. præliis. thanks had sowne diuision, insomuch that the sonne vpon a vehement conceit of vnkindnesse sproong in the father, was in the waie to be worne out of fauour. Which was the more likelie to come to passe, by their informations that priuilie charged him with riot and other vnciuill demeanor vnséemelie for a prince. Indeed he was youth-fullie giuen, growne to audacitie, and had chosen him companions agréeable to his age; with whome he spent the time in such recreations, exercises, and delights as he fansied. But yet (it should séeme by the report of some writers) that his behauiour was not offensiue or at least tending to the damage of anie bodie ; sith he had a care to auoid dooing of wrong, and to tender his affections within the tract of vertue, whereby he opened vnto himselfe a redie passage of good liking among the prudent sort, and
                                                                      was

was beloued of such as could discerne his disposition, which was in no degree so excessiue, as that he deserued in such vehement maner to be suspected. In whose dispraise I find little, but to his praise verie much, parcell whereof I will deliuer by the waie as a metyard whereby the residue may be measured. The late poet that versified the warres of the valorous Englishmen, speaking of the issue of Henrie the fourth saith of this prince (among other things) as followeth :

> ————procero qui natu maximus hæres
> Corpore, progressus cùm pubertatis ad annos
> Esset, res gessit multas iuueniliter audax,
> Asciscens comites quo spar sibi iunxerat ætas,
> Nil tamen iniustè commisit, nil tamen vnquam
> Extra virtutis normam, sapientibus æquè
> Ac aliis charus.

In Angl. prœliis, sub. Hen. 4.

About the same time, Iohn Prendergest knight, being restored to the kings fauour, with thirtie ships scowred the seas, tooke good prises of wine and vitels, which reléeued the commons greatlie. Amongst other enterprises, he landed vpon the sudden at Craal on the faire day, tooke the towne, and robbed the faire, so as they that were come thither to sell their wares, had quicke vtterance and slow paiment. King Henrie vnderstanding that the French king by setting on of the duke of Burgognie in pursuing the contrarie faction, had besieged the citie of Burges (as before yée haue heard) determined with all spéed to aid the duke of Orleance, & so about the feast of the Assumption of our ladie, he sent ouer an armie of eight hundred men of armes, and nine thousand archers, vnder the leading of his second sonne the duke of Clarence accompanied with Edward duke of Yorke, Thomas earle of Dorset and diuerse other noble men and worthie capteins. They landed in the Baie de la Hogue saint Wast, in the countrie of Constantine. The Englishmen swarmed like bées round about the countrie, robbing and spoiling the same.

Sir Iohn Prendergest restored to the kings fauour is sent to sea.

The duke of Clarence sent to aid the duke of Orleance.

Shortlie after their departure from the place where they landed, there came to them six hundred armed men of Gascoignes that were inrolled at Burdeaux. When newes thereof came to the French court, being then at Auxerre, incontinentlie the earles of Alanson and Richmond were dispatched to go vnto the English campe, bicause they had euer béene partakers with the duke of Orleance, to giue them thanks for their paines, and to aduertise them of the peace that had beene latelie concluded betwixt the parties, and therefore to take order with them, that they might be satisfied, so as they should not spoile & waste the countrie, as they had begun. But whereas the Englishmen were gréedie to haue, and the duke of Orleance was not rich to paie, they marched on towards Guien in good order, and what by sacking of townes, and ransoming of rich prisoners, they got great treasure, and manie good preies and booties.

Enguerant.

The earle of Alanson and Richmond sent to the duke of Clarence.

The duke of Clarence marcheth toward Guien.

Being passed the riuer of Loire they spoiled the towne of Beaulieu, and with fire and sword wasted the countries of Touraine and Maine. The lord de Rambures appointed to resist such violence, was easilie vanquished. Moreouer, to the aid of the duke of Orleance, the king of England sent ouer to Calis the earls of Kent and Warwike, with two thousand fighting men, which spoiled and wasted the countrie of Bullennois, burnt the towne of Samer de Bois, and tooke with assault the fortresse of Russalt, and diuerse other. This yeare, the king abased the coines of his gold and siluer, causing the same to be currant in this realme, at such value as the other was valued before, where indéed the noble was woorsse by foure pence than the former, and so likewise of the siluer, the coines whereof he appointed to be currant after the same rate. ¶ In this yeare, and vpon the twelfth day of October, were thrée flouds in the Thames, the one following vpon the other, & no ebbing betweene: which thing no man then liuing could remember the like to be seene.

Enguerant.

The lord of Rambures.

The earles of Kent & Warwike sent ouer to Calis.

Fabian.

Coine changed.

Abr. Fl. out of Fabian, pag. 388.

Thrée floods without ebbing betwéen.

¶ In

Abrf Fl. out of *R. Grafton,* pag. 433, 434, in folio.

¶ In this kings time, and in the eighth yeare of his reigne (as Richard Grafton hath recorded) a worthie citizen of London named Richard Whitington, mercer and alderman, was elected maior of the said citie, and bare that office three times. This man so bestowed his goods and substance, that he hath well deserued to be registred in chronicles. First he erected one house or church in London to be a house of praier,

Whitington college erected.

and named the same after his owne name, Whitington college, remaining at this daie. In the said church, besides certeine preests and clearks, he placed a number of poore aged men and women, builded for them houses and lodgings, and allowed them wood

Charitie.

Newgate builded.

coles, cloth, and wéekelie monie to their great reléefe and comfort. This man also at his owne cost builded the gate of London called Newgate in the yéere of our Lord 1422, which before was a most ouglie and lothsome prison. He also builded more

S. Bartholomews hospital.

than the halfe of S. Bartholomews hospitall in west Smithfield. He builded likewise the beautifull librarie in the graie friers in London now called Christs hospitall, standing in the north part of the cloister thereof, where in the wall his armes be grauen in stone. He also builded for the ease of the maior of London, his brethren, and the worshipfull citizens, on the solemne daies of their assemblie, a chapell adioining to the

Guildhall chapell.

Guildhall; to the intent that before they entered into anie of their worldlie affaires, they should begin with praier and inuocation to God for his assistance: at the end ioining to the south part of the said chapell, he builded for the citie a librarie of stone, for the custodie of their records and other bookes. He also builded a great part of

Guildhall inlarged.

the east end of Guildhall; and did manie other good déeds worthie of imitation. By a writing of this mans owne hand, which he willed to be fixed as a schedule to his last will and testament, it appeareth what a pitifull and relenting heart he had at other mens miseries, and did not onelie wish but also did what he could procure for their releefe. In so much that he charged and commanded his executors, as they would answer before God at the daie of the resurrection of all flesh, that if they found anie debtor of his, whome if in conscience they thought not to be well worth three times as much as they owght him, and also out of other mens debt, and well able to paie, that then they should neuer demand it; for he clearelie forgaue it: and that they should put no man in sute for anie debt due to him: A worthie memoriall of a notable minded gentleman.

An. Reg. 14.

The duke of Orleance cōmeth to the English armie.

Yée haue heard how the duke of Clarence and his armie did much hurt in the realme of France, in places as he passed: wherevpon at length, the duke of Orleance being earnestlie called vpon to dispatch the Englishmen out of France, according to an article comprised in the conclusion of the peace, he came to the duke of Clarence, rendering to him and his armie a thousand gramersies, and disbursed to them as much monie as he or his fréends might éasilie spare; and for the rest being two hundred and nine thousand frankes remaining vnpaid, he deliuered in gage his second brother, Iohn duke of Angolesme, which was grandfather to king Francis the first, that reigned in our daies, sir Marcell de Burges, and sir Iohn de Samoures, sir Archembald Viliers, and diuerse other, which earle continued long in England, as after shall appeare. When this agreement was thus made betwixt the dukes of Orleance and Clarence, the English armie with rich preies, booties and prisoners came to Burdéaux, making warre on

The lord of Helie marshall of France.

the frontiers of France, to their great gaine. In this meane while, the lord of Helie, one of the marshals of France, with an armie of foure thousand men, besieged a certeine fortresse in Guien, which an English knight, one sir Iohn Blunt kept, who

Sir Iohn Blunt.

with thrée hundred men that came to his aid, discomfited, chased, and ouerthrew the French power, tooke prisoners twelue men of name, and other gentlemen to the number of six score, and amongst other, the said marshall, who was sent ouer into England, and put in the castell of Wissebet, from whence he escaped, and got ouer into France, where seruing the duke of Orleance at the battell of Agincort he was slaine among other.

In

In this fourtéenth and last yeare of king Henries reigne, a councell was holden in *Fabian.* the white friers in London, at the which, among other things, order was taken for ships The K. meant to haue made a iournie against the Infidels. and gallies to be builded and made readie, and all other things necessarie to be pro- uided for a voiage which he meant to make into the holie land, there to recouer the citie of Ierusalem from the Infidels. For it gréeued him to consider the great malice of christian princes, that were bent vpon a mischéefous purpose to destroie one another, to the perill of their owne soules, rather than to make war against the enimies of the christian faith, as in conscience (it séemed to him) they were bound. He held his Christmas this yeare at Eltham, being sore vexed with sicknesse, so that it was The king is vexed with sick- nesse. thought sometime, that he had beene dead; notwithstanding it pleased God that he somwhat recouered his strength againe, and so passed that Christmasse with as much ioy as he might.

The morrow after Candlemas daie began a parlement, which he had called at 1413. London, but he departed this life before the same parlement was ended: for now that A parlement. his prouisions were readie, and that he was furnished with sufficient treasure, soldiers, capteins, vittels, munitions, tall ships, strong gallies, and all things necessarie for such a roiall iournie as he pretended to take into the holie land, he was eftsoons taken with a sore sicknesse, which was not a leprosie, striken by the hand of God (saith The k. sick of an apoplexie. maister Hall) as foolish friers imagined; but a verie apoplexie, of the which he lan- *Hall.* guished till his appointed houre, and had none other gréefe nor maladie; so that what man ordeineth, God altereth at his good will and pleasure, not giuing place more to the prince, than to the poorest creature liuing, when he séeth his time to dispose of him this waie or that, as to his omnipotent power and diuine prouidence seemeth expedient. During this his last sicknesse, he caused his crowne (as some write) to *Hall.* be set on a pillow at his beds head, and suddenlie his pangs so sore troubled him, that he laie as though all his vitall spirits had beene from him departed. Such as were about him, thinking verelie that he had béene departed, couered his face with a linnen cloth.

The prince his sonne being hereof aduertised, entered into the chamber, tooke The prince taketh awaie the crowne before his father was dead. awaie the crowne, and departed. The father being suddenlie reuiued out of that trance, quicklie perceiued the lacke of his crowne; and hauing knowledge that the prince his sonne had taken it awaie, caused him to come before his presence, requiring of him what he meant so to misuse himselfe. The prince with a good audacitie He is blamed of the king. His answer. answered; "Sir, to mine and all mens iudgements you seemed dead in this world, wherefore I as your next heire apparant tooke that as mine owne, and not as yours." Well faire sonne (said the king with a great sigh) what right I had to it, A guiltie con- science in extre- mitie of sicknesse pincheth sore. God knoweth. Well (said the prince) if you die king, I will haue the garland, and trust to kéepe it with the sword against all mine enimies as you haue doone. Then said the king, "I commit all to God, and remember you to doo well." With that he The death of Henrie the fourth. turned himselfe in his bed, and shortlie after departed to God in a chamber of the abbats of Westminster called Ierusalem, the twentith daie of March, in the yeare 1413, and in the yeare of his age 46, when he had reigned thirteene yeares, fiue moneths and od daies, in great perplexitie and little pleasure [or fourtéene yeares, as some haue noted, who name not the disease whereof he died, but refer it to sicknesse absolutelie, whereby his time of departure did approach and fetch him out of the world: as Ch. Okl. saith, whose words may serue as a funerall epigramme in me- moriall of the said king Henrie:

> Henricus quartus bis septem rexerat annos
> Anglorum gentem summa cum laude & amore,
> Iàmq; senescenti fatalis terminus æui
> Ingruerat, morbus fatalem accerserat horam.]

Ab, Fl. out of *Angl. præl. sub. Len.* 4

Fabian.

We find, that he was taken with his last sickenesse, while he was making his praiers at saint Edwards shrine, there as it were to take his leaue, and so to proceed foorth on his iournie: he was so suddenlie and greeuouslie taken, that such as were about him, feared least he would haue died presentlie, wherfore to reléeue him (if it were possible) they baré him into a chamber that was next at hand, belonging to the abbat of Westminster, where they laid him on a pallet before the fire, and vsed all remedies to reuiue him. At length, he recouered his spéech, and vnderstanding and perceiuing himselfe in a strange place which he knew not, he willed to know if the chamber had anie particular name, wherevnto answer was made, that it was called Ierusalem. Then said the king; " Lauds be giuen to the father of heauen, for now I know that I shall die heere in this chamber, according to the prophesie of me declared, that I should depart this life in Ierusalem."

Whether this was true that so he spake, as one that gaue too much credit to foolish prophesies & vaine tales, or whether it was fained, as in such cases it commonlie happeneth, we leaue it to the aduised reader to iudge. His bodie with all *He is buried at* funerall pompe was conueied vnto Canturburie, and there solemnlie buried, leauing *Canturburie.* behind him by the ladie Marie daughter to the lord Humfrie Bohun earle of Hereford *His issue.* and Northampton, Henrie prince of Wales, Thomas duke of Clarence, Iohn duke of Bedford, Humfrie duke of Glocester, Blanch duchesse of Bauier, and Philip quéene of Denmarke: by his last wife Iane, he had no children. This king was of a meane *His stature.* stature, well proportioned, and formallie compact, quicke and liuelie, and of a stout courage. In his latter daies he shewed himselfe so gentle, that he gat more loue amongst the nobles and people of this realme, than he had purchased malice and euill will in the beginning.

But yet to speake a truth, by his proceedings, after he had atteined to the crowne, what with such taxes, tallages, subsidies, and exactions as he was constreined to charge the people with; and what by punishing such as mooued with disdeine to see him vsurpe the crowne (contrarie to the oth taken at his entring into this land, vpon his returne from exile) did at sundrie times rebell against him, he wan himselfe more hatred, than in all his life time (if it had beene longer by manie yeares than it was) had beene possible for him to haue weeded out & remooued. And yet doubtlesse, woorthie were his subiects to tast of that bitter cup, sithens they were so readie to ioine and clappe hands with him, for the deposing of their rightfull and naturall prince king Richard, whose chéefe fault rested onlie in that, that he was too bountifull to his fréends, and too mercifull to his foes; speciallie if he had not béene drawne by others, to séeke reuenge of those that abused his good and courteous nature. ¶ But now to returne to the matter present. The duke of Clarence immediatlie vpon knowlege had of his father king Henrie the fourth his death, returned out of Guien into England, with the earle of Angolesme, and other prisoners.

Now will we rehearse what writers of our English nation liued in the daies of this king. That renowmed poet Geffrie Chaucer is woorthilie named as principall, a man so exquisitlie learned in all sciences, that his match was not lightlie found any where in those daies; and for reducing our English toong to a perfect conformitie, he hath excelled therein all other; he departed this life about the *John Stow.* yeare of our Lord 1402, as Bale gathereth: but by other it appeareth, that he deceassed the fiue and twentith of October in the yeare 1400, and lieth buried at Westminster, in the south part of the great church there, as by a monument erected by Nicholas Brigham it doth appeare. Iohn Gower descended of that worthie familie of the Gowers of Stitenham in Yorkeshire (as Leland noteth) studied not onelie the common lawes of this realme, but also other kinds of literature, and great knowledge in the same, namelie in poeticall inuentions, applieng his indeuor

with

with Chaucer, to garnish the English toong, in bringing it from a rude vnper-
fectnesse, vnto a more apt elegancie: for whereas before those daies, the learned
vsed to write onelie in Latine or French, and not in English, our toong remained
verie barren, rude, and vnperfect; but now by the diligent industrie of Chaucer
and Gower, it was within a while greatlie amended, so as it grew not onelie verie
rich and plentifull in words, but also so proper and apt to expresse that which
the mind conceiued, as anie other vsuall language. Gower departed this life shortlie
after the deceasse of his déere and louing freend Chaucer; to wit, in the yeare
1402, being then come to great age, and blind for a certeine time before his death.
He was buried in the church of saint Marie Oueries in Southwarke.

Moreouer, Hugh Legat borne in Hertfordshire, and a monke of saint Albons,
wrote scholies vpon Architrenius of Iohn Hanuill, and also vpon Boetius De conso-
latione; Roger Alington, chancellor of the vniuersitie of Oxford, a great sophister,
& an enimie to the doctrine of Wickliffe; Iohn Botrell, a logician; Nicholas Gorham,
borne in a village of the same name in Hertfordshire, a Dominike frier, first proceeded
master of art in Oxenford, and after going to Paris, became the French kings confessor, and therefore hath béene of some taken to be a Frenchman; Iohn Lilleshull,
so called of a monasterie in the west parties of this realme whereof he was gouernour;
Walter Disse, so called of a towne in Norfolke where he was borne, first a Carmelite
frier professed in Norwich, and after going to Cambridge, he there procéeded doctor,
he was also confessor to the duke of Lancaster, and to his wife the duchesse Constance,
& a great setter foorth of pope Urbans cause against the other popes that were by
him and those of his faction named the antipapes; Thomas Maldon, so called of
the towne of that name in Essex where he was borne: Iohn Edo, descended out of
Wales by linage, and borne in Herefordshire, a Franciscane frier.

Adde to the forenamed, Nicholas Fakingham, borne in Norfolke, a greie frier,
procéeded doctor in Oxenford, a great diuine, and an excellent philosopher, prouinciall
of his order here in England; Laurence Holbecke, a monke of Ramsie, well séene
in the Hebrue toong, and wrote thereof a dictionarie; Iohn Colton, archbishop of
Ardmach; Iohn Marrie, so called of a village in Yorkeshire where he was borne,
a Carmelite of Doncaster; Richard Chefer borne in Norfolke, a diuine, and an Augustine frier in Norwich; Iohn Lathburie, a Franciscane frier of Reading; Nicholas
Poutz; Richard Scroope brother to William Scroope, lord treasuror of England,
studied in Cambridge, and proceeded there doctor of both the lawes, became an
aduocat in the court of Rome, and afterwards was aduanced to the gouernement
of the see of Couentrie and Lichfield, and at length was remooued from thence,
and made archbishop of Yorke, he wrote an inuectiue against king Henrie, and
at length lost his head, as before ye haue heard; Iohn Wrotham, a Carmelite frier
of London, and after made warden of an house of his order in Calis.

Furthermore, Iohn Colbie, a Carmelite frier of Norwich; William Thorpe a northerne man borne, and student in Oxenford, an excellent diuine, and an earnest
follower of that famous clearke Iohn Wickliffe, a notable preacher of the word, ^{Acts and mo-}
and expressing his doctrine no lesse in trade of life, than in speech, he was at ^{ments of *Iohn*}
length apprehended by commandement of the archbishop of Canturburie Thomas ^{*Fox.*}
Arundell, and committed to prison in Saltwood castell, where at length he died;
Stephen Patrington, borne in Yorkeshire, a frier Carmelite, prouinciall of his order
through England, of which brood there were at that season 1500 within this land,
he was bishop of saint Dauids, and confessor to king Henrie the fift, about the
fift yeare of whose reigne he deceassed; Robert Mascall, a Carmelite frier of Ludlow,
confessor also to the said K. who made him bishop of Hereford; Reginald Langham,
a frier minor of Norwich: Actonus Dommicanus; Thomas Palmer, warden of the
Blacke friers within the citie of London; Boston of Burie, a monke of the abbeie

of Burie in Suffolke, wrote a catalog of all the writers of the church, and other treatises.

Moreouer, Thomas Peuerell, a frier Carmelite, borne in Suffolke, he was aduanced to the sée of Ossorie in Ireland by Richard the second, and after by pope Boniface the ninth remooued to Landaffe in Wales, and from thence called by Henrie the fourth, with consent of pope Gregorie the twelfe, to gouerne the sée of Worcester, and so continued bishop of that citie, vntill he ended his life in the yeare of our Lord 1418, which was about the sixt yeare of the reigne of king Henrie the fift; Iohn Purueie, an excellent diuine, procéeded master of art in Oxenford, he was apprehended for such doctrine as he taught, contrarie to the ordinances of the church of Rome, and was at length compelled by Thomas Arundell, archbishop of Canturburie, to recant at Paules crosse seuen speciall articles, he wrote diuerse treatises, & was the second time committed to prison in king Henrie the fift his daies, by Henrie Chichleie, that succeeded Arundell in gouernement of the church of Canturburie; William Holme, a greie frier (and a good physician for curing diseases of the bodie, whatsoeuer his physicke was for the soule) he liued vntill Henrie the fift his daies, and deceassed about the fourth yeare of his reigne; Nicholas Baiard, a blacke frier, a doctor of diuinitie professed at Oxenford; Thomas Rudburne, archdeacon of Sudburie, and bishop of saint Dauids in Wales, succéeding after Stephan Patrington, he wrote a chronicle, and certeine epistles (as Iohn Bale noteth.)

Sée maister *Fox*, in his booke of Acts and monuments.

Finallie and to conclude, Nicholas Riston, who being sore greeued in mind, as diuerse other in those daies, to consider what inconuenience redounded to the church, by reason of the strife and bralling among the prelats for the acknowleging of a lawfull pope, two or thrée still contending for that dignitie, wrote a booke, intituled De tollendo schismate; Iohn Walter, an excellent mathematician, being first brought vp of a scholer in the college of Winchester, and after studied at Oxenford; Thomas of Newmarket, taking that surname of the towne in Cambridgeshire where he was borne, he for his worthinesse (as was thought) was made bishop of Careleill, well séene both in other sciences, and also in diuinitie; William Auger a Franciscane frier, of an house of that order in Bridgewater; Peter Russell a graie frier, and of his order the prouinciall héere in England; Iohn Langton, a Carmelite; Robert Wantham a moonke of Cernelie in Dorsetshire, wrote a booke in verse, of the originall and signification of words; William Norton, a Franciscane frier of Couentrie; Hugh Sueth, a blacke frier, and a great preacher; Richard Folsham a moonke of Norwich; Robert Wimbeldon, a singular diuine, and an excellent preacher, as appeareth by the sermon which he made vpon this text, Redde rationem villicationis tuæ.

Acts and monuments.

Thus farre Henrie Plantagenet sonne to Iohn of Gaunt duke of Lancaster.

<hr>

HENRIE THE FIFT, PRINCE OF WALES,

sonne and heire to Henrie the fourth.

An. Reg. 1.   HENRIE prince of Wales, son and heire to K. Henrie the fourth, borne in Wales at Monmouth on the riuer of Wie, after his father was departed, tooke vpon him the regiment of this realme of England, the twentith of March, the morrow after proclamed

proclamed king, by the name of Henrie the fift, in the yeare of the world 5375, after the birth of our sauior, by our account 1413, the third of the emperor Sigismund: the thrée and thirtith of Charles the sixt French king, and in the seuenth yeare of gouernance in Scotland vnder Robert brother to him that (before entrance into his kingdome 1390) had Iohn to name, which by deuise and order of the states was changed into Robert the third, who at Rotsaie (a towne in the Iland of Got, 1406) deceassed by occasion thus. As vpon hope in this gouernor to himselfe conceiued how to come to the crowne, he at the castell of Faikland, latelie had famisht his coosine Dauid the kings elder sonne and heire (a dissolute yoong prince) yet to his fathers excéeding sorrow, at whose deceasse the father verie carefull, and casting for the safegard of Iames his yoonger son and heire, from Basse the rocke in a well appointed ship, vnder charge of Henrie Saintcleere earle of Orkeneie, into France to his old fréend king Charles for good education and safetie this yoong prince he sent: who in the course, whether for tempest or tendernes of stomach, tooke land in Yorkeshire at Flamborrow, that after by wisedome and good consideration of the king and his councell was thought verie necessarie here to be reteined. But by the sudden newes of this staie, the father (at supper as he sat) so stroken at hart that well nie streight had he fallen downe dead, yet borne into his chamber, where for greefe and pine within thrée daies next he deceassed. The yoong king Iames his sonne after an eightéene yeares staie, in which time he had béene well trained in princehood, at last with right honorable marriage at saint Marie Oueries vnto Ione daughter to the earle of Summerset, coosine vnto Henrie the sixt then king, and with manie other high gratuities here beside was sent and set in his rule and kingdome at home.

Wil. Patten.
Buchanan
rer. Scoticar.
lib. 10.

Such great hope, and good expectation was had of this mans fortunate successe to follow, that within thrée daies after his fathers deceasse, diuerse noble men and honorable personages did to him homage, and sware to him due obedience, which had not béene seene doone to any of his predecessors kings of this realme, till they had béene possessed of the crowne. He was crowned the ninth of Aprill being Passion sundaie, which was a sore, ruggie, and tempestuous day, with wind, snow and sléet, that men greatlie maruelled thereat, making diuerse interpretations what the same might signifie. But this king euen at first appointing with himselfe, to shew that in his person princelie honors should change publike manners, he determined to put on him the shape of a new man. For whereas aforetime he had made himselfe a companion vnto misrulie mates of dissolute order and life, he now banished them all from his presence (but not vnrewarded, or else vnpreferred) inhibiting them vpon a great paine, not once to approch, lodge, or soiourne within ten miles of his court or presence: and in their places he chose men of grauitie, wit, and high policie, by whose wise councell he might at all times rule to his honour and dignitie; calling to mind how once to hie offence of the king his father, he had with his fist striken the chéefe iustice for sending one of his minions (vpon desert) to prison, when the iustice stoutlie commanded himselfe also streict to ward, & he (then prince) obeied. The king after expelled him out of his priuie councell, banisht him the court, and made the duke of Clarence (his yoonger brother) president of councell in his steed. This reformation in the new king Christ. Okl. hath reported, fullie consenting with this. For saith he,

Homage doone to K. Henrie before his coronation.
The day of king Henries coronation a verie tempestuous day.
A notable example of a woorthie prince.

> Ille inter iuuenes paulo lasciuior antè,
> Defuncto genitore grauis constànsq; repentè,
> Moribus ablegat corruptis regis ab aula
> Assuetos socios, & nugatoribus acrem
> Pœnam (si quisquam sua tecta reuiserit) addit,
> Atq; ita mutatus facit omnia principe digna,
> Ingenio magno post consultoribus vsus, &c.

In Angl. præl.
sub. Hen. 5.

But

But now that the king was once placed in the roiall seat of the realme, he vertuouslie considering in his mind, that all goodnesse commeth of God, determined
to begin with some thing acceptable to his diuine maiestie, and therefore commanded
the cleargie sincerelie and trulie to preach the word of God, and to liue accordinglie,
that they might be the lanternes of light to the temporaltie, as their profession
required. The laie men he willed to serue God, and obeie their prince, prohibiting
them aboue all things breach of matrimonie, custome in swearing; and namelie,
willfull periurie. Beside this, he elected the best learned men in the lawes of the
realme, to the offices of iustice; and men of good liuing, he preferred to high degrées

A parlement. and authoritie. Immediatlie after Easter he called a parlement, in which diuerse
good statutes, and wholesome ordinances, for the preseruation and aduancement of
Thom. Walsin.
The funerals of
king Henrie the
fourth kept at
Canturburie. the common-wealth were deuised and established. On Trinitie sundaie were the
solemne exequies doone at Canturburie for his father, the king himselfe being
present thereat.

S. Georges day
made a double
feast. About the same time, at the speciall instance of the king, in a conuocation of
the cleargie holden at Paules in London, it was ordeined, that saint George his
daie should be celebrate and kept as a double feast. The archbishop of Canturburie
meant to haue honored saint Dunstaines daie with like reuerence, but it tooke not
effect. When the king had setled things much to his purpose, he caused the bodie
of king Richard to be remooued with all funerall dignitie conuenient for his estate,
from Langlie to Westminster, where he was honorablie interred with quéene Anne
his first wife, in a solemne toome erected and set vp at the charges of this king.

Abr. Fl. out of
Polychron. ¶ Polychronicon saith, that after the bodie of the dead king was taken vp out of
the earth, this new king (happilie tendering the magnifice of a prince, and abhorring
obscure buriall) caused the same to be conueied to Westminster in a roiall seat
(or chaire of estate) couered all ouer with blacke veluet, & adorned with banners
of diuers armes round about. All the horsses likewise (said this author) were apparelled
with blacke, and bare sundrie sutes of armes. Manie other solemnities were had
at his interrement, according to the qualitie of the age wherein he liued and died.

Also in this first yéere of this kings reigne, sir Iohn Oldcastell, which by his
wife was called lord Cobham, a valiant capteine and a hardie gentleman, was accused
to the archbishop of Canturburie of certeine points of heresie, who knowing him
to be highlie in the kings fauour, declared to his highnesse the whole accusation.
The king first hauing compassion of the noble man, required the prelats, that if
he were a straied shéepe, rather by gentlenes than by rigor to reduce him to the
fold. And after this, he himselfe sent for him, and right earnestlie exhorted him,
and louinglie admonished him to reconcile himselfe to God and to his lawes. The
lord Cobham not onelie thanked him for his most fauorable clemencie, but also
declared first to him by mouth, and afterwards by writing, the foundation of his
ith, and the ground of his beliefe, affirming his grace to be his supreme head and
competent iudge, and none other person, offering an hundred knights and esquiers
to come to his purgation, or else to fight in open lists in defence of his iust cause.

The king vnderstanding and persuaded by his councell, that by order of the lawes
of his realme, such accusations touching matters of faith ought to be tried by his
spirituall prelats, sent him to the Tower of London, there to abide the determination
of the clergie, according to the statutes in that case prouided, after which time a
solemne session was appointed in the cathedrall church of saint Paule, vpon the thrée
and twentith day of September, and an other the fiue and twentith daie of the same
moneth, in the hall of the Blacke friers at London, in which places the said lord was
examined, apposed, and fullie heard, and in conclusion by the archbishop of Canturburie denounced an heretike, & remitted againe to the Tower of London, from which
                                                                              place

place, either by helpe of fréends, or fauour of kéepers, he priuilie escaped and came into Sir Iohn Oldcastell escaped out of the Tower. Wales, where he remained for a season.

After this, the king kéeping his Christmasse at his manor of Eltham, was aduertised, *Titus Liuius.* that sir Roger Acton knight a man of great wit and possessions, Iohn Browne esquier, 1414 Iohn Beuerlie priest, and a great number of other were assembled in armour against *Hall.* the king, his brethren, the clergie and realme. These newes came to the king, on the A commotion raised by sir Roger Acton and others. *Titus Liuius.* twelfth daie in Christmasse, wherevpon vnderstanding that they were in a place called Ficket field beside London, on the backe side of saint Giles, he streight got him to his palace at Westminster, in as secret wise as he might, and there calling to him certeine bands of armed men, he repaired into saint Giles fields, néere to the said place (where The rebels surprised. he vnderstood they should fullie méet about midnight) and so handled the matter, that he tooke some, and slue some, euen as stood with his pleasure. The capteins of them afore mentioned, being apprehended, were brought to the kings presence, and to him declared the causes of their commotion & rising, accusing a great number of their *Thom. Walsin.* complices.

The king vsed one policie, which much serued to the discomfiting of the aduersaries (as Thom. Walsingham saith) which was this: he gaue order, that all the gates of London should be streictlie kept and garded, so as none should come in or out, but such as were knowen to go to the king. Hereby came it to passe, that the chiefest succour appointed to come to the capteins of the rebels, was by that meanes cut off, where otherwise suerlie (had it not beene thus preuented and staied) there had issued foorth of London to haue ioined with them, to the number (as it was thought) of fiftie By this excessiue number it may appeare, that *Walsingham* reporteth this matter according to the cõmon fame, and not as one that searched out an exquisite truth. thousand persons, one and other, seruants, prentises, and citizens, confederate with them that were thus assembled in Ficket field. Diuerse also that came from sundrie parts of the realme, hasting towards the place, to be there at their appointed time, chanced to light among the kings men, who being taken and demanded whither they went with such spéed, answered, they came to meet with their capteine the lord Cobham.

But whether he came thither at all, or made shift for himselfe to get awaie, it dooth not appeare; for he could not be heard of that time (as Thomas Walsingham confesseth) although the king by proclamation promised a thousand marks to him that could bring him foorth, with great liberties to the cities or townes that would discouer where he was. By this it maie appeare, how greatlie he was beloued, that there could not one be found, that for so great a reward would bring him to light. Among other that were taken was one William Murlie, who dwelt in Dunstable, a man of great wealth, William Murlie. and by his occupation a brewer, an earnest mainteiner of the lord Cobhams opinions, and (as the brute ran) in hope to be highlie aduanced by him if their purposed deuise had taken place, apparant by this; that he had two horsses trapped with guilt harnesse led after him, and in his bosome a paire of gilt spurs (as it was déemed) prepared for himselfe to weare, looking to be made knight by the lord Cobhams hands at that present time. But when he saw how their purpose quailed, he withdrew into the citie with great feare to hide himselfe; howbeit he was perceiued, taken, and finallie executed among others.

To conclude, so manie persons herevpon were apprehended, that all the prisons in and about London were full, the chiefe of them were condemned by the cleargie of Sir Roger Acton & his complices condemned of treason and heresie. heresie, and atteinted of high treason in the Guildhall of London, and adiudged for that offense to be drawen and hanged, and for herésie to be consumed with fire, gallowes and all, which iudgement was executed the same moneth, on the said sir Roger Acton, and eight and twentie others. ¶ Some saie, that the occasion of their death was onelie for the conueieng of the lord Cobham out of prison. Others write, that it was both for treason and heresie, and so it appeareth by the record. Certeine affirme, that it was for feined causes surmized by the spiritualtie, more vpon displeasure than

truth,

truth, and that they were assembled to heare their preacher (the foresaid Beuerlie) in that place there, out of the waie from resort of people, sith they might not come togither openlie about any such matter, without danger to be apprehended; as the manner is, and hath beene euer of the persecuted flocke, when they are prohibited publikelie the exercise of their religion. But howsoeuer the matter went with these men, apprehended they were, and diuerse of them executed (as before ye haue heard) whether for rebellion or heresie, or for both (as the forme of the indictment importeth) I néed not to spend manie words, sith others haue so largelie treated thereof; and therefore I refer those that wish to be more fullie satisfied herein vnto their reports.

Whilest in the Lent season the king laie at Killingworth, there came to him from Charles Dolphin of France certeine ambassadors, that brought with them a barrell of Paris balles, which from their maister they presented to him for a token that was taken in verie ill part, as sent in scorne, to signifie, that it was more méet for the king to passe the time with such childish exercise, than to attempt any worthie exploit. Wherefore the K. wrote to him, that yer ought long, he would tosse him some London balles that perchance should shake the walles of the best court in France. ¶ This

yeare, Thom. Arundell archbishop of Canturburie departed this life, a stout prelat, and an earnest mainteiner of the Romish religion: Henrie Chichelie bishop of saint Dauid succeeded the same Arundell in the sée of Canturburie, and the kings confessor Stephan Patrington a Carmelite frier was made bishop of S. Dauid. Henrie Persie then but a child, sonne to the lord Henrie Persie surnamed Hotspur, after his fathers deceasse, that was slaine at Shrewesburie field, was conueied into Scotland, and there left by his grandfather, where euer since he had remained: the king therefore pitied

his case, and so procured for him, that he came home, and was restored to all his lands and earledome of Northumberland, which lands before had béene giuen to the lord Iohn, the kings brother.

A case verie strange, and for manie causes alwaies right worthie of remembrance, in this yeare 1414, the second of this kings reigne did befall, which conteining in it so manie matters for knowledge of Gods great power and iustice of wilfull breaking his diuine lawes, of the easie slip into ruine where his mercie dooth not staie vs, the busie bogging of the diuell alwaies, our weakenesse in combat with him, into what outrage and confusion he haleth where he is not withstood, with what tyrannie he tormenteth where he vanquisheth, what the will and power of a souereigne ouer a subiect may force in cases of iniquitie, where by vertue and grace he be not restrained: the zeale of a parent, the pangs of a child, but chéeflie the verie plague of Gods wrath and indignation vpon wilfull and obstinate offendors, all which at those daies though touched in Naples, yet at all times and euerie where so well seruing for example and warning, it hath beene thought verie conuenient the same in our stories also héere to be noted, which was thus. At this time newes were brought into France, how king Lancelot (the aduersarie to Lewes king of Sicill) was departed, and in manner thus. It hapned that he fell in loue with a yoong damosell his owne physicians daughter (a puzell verie beautifull) and he in hope to inioy hir the easilier, caused hir father for his consent to be talked withall in the matter, which he vtterlie refused to grant, and shewed foorth manie reasons for him; but at last all causes & excuses reiected, sith (though constreined) he must néeds assent, feined himselfe willing and content. And forceing talke with his daughter vpon his mind in the matter, chéeflie how méet it were she vsed his counsell how best with the king to keepe hir still in grace, he gaue hir a little box of ointment, and instruction withall, that when the king should come to haue his will, she should afore with that balme annoint all hir wombe; the damosell ōn good obseruation did after (at oportunitie) as hir father taught hir. Héerevpon so pittifullie came it to passe that the verie same night the king laie with hir, his bellie and hirs were by and by set as it were all on a sindging fier, with

torments

torments of such vnquenchable scorching and burning euen into the verie entrailes, that he of his kingdome, his life, his loue; and she of hir princelie promotion, thus soone both togither made a sorrowfull end. After the plaie of this lamentable tragedie, the physician fled for his safetie, and straight vpon the newes king Lewes gathered a great assemblie, wherewith to passe towards Naples, and sent before a good companie vnder the lord Longnie marshall of France.

In the second yeare of his reigne, king Henrie called his high court of parlement, the last daie of Aprill in the towne of Leicester, in which parlement manie profitable lawes were concluded, atd manie petitions mooued, were for that time deferred. Amongst which, one was, that a bill exhibited in the parlement holden at Westminster in the eleuenth yeare of king Henrie the fourth (which by reason the king was then troubled with ciuill discord, came to none effect) might now with good deliberation be pondered, and brought to some good conclusion. The effect of which supplication was, that the temporall lands deuoutlie giuen, and disordinatlie spent by religious, and other spirituall persons, should be seized into the kings hands, sith the same might suffice to mainteine, to the honor of the king, and defense of the realme, fiftéene earles, fiftéene hundred knights, six thousand and two hundred esquiers, and a hundred almesse-houses, for reliefe onelie of the poore, impotent, and needie persons, and the king to haue cleerelie to his coffers twentie thousand pounds, with manie other prouisions and values of religious houses, which I passe ouer.

An. Reg. 2. 1414

A bill exhibited to the parlemēt against the clergie.

This bill was much noted, and more feared among the religious sort, whom suerlie it touched verie neere, and therefore to find remedie against it, they determined to assaie all waies to put by and ouerthrow this bill: wherein they thought best to trie if they might mooue the kings mood with some sharpe inuention, that he should not regard the importunate petitions of the commons. Wherevpon, on a daie in the parlement, Henrie Chichelie archbishop of Canturburie made a pithie oration, wherein he declared, how not onelie the duchies of Normandie and Aquitaine, with the counties of Aniou and Maine, and the countrie of Gascoigne, were by vndoubted title apperteining to the king, as to the lawfull and onelie heire of the same; but also the whole realme of France, as heire to his great grandfather king Edward the third.

The archbishop of Canturburies oration in the parlement house.

Herein did he much inueie against the surmised and false fained law Salike, which the Frenchmen alledge euer against the kings of England in barre of their iust title to the crowne of France. The verie words of that supposed law are these, In terram Salicam mulieres ne succedant, that is to saie, Into the Salike land let not women succeed. Which the French glossers expound to be the realme of France, and that this law was made by king Pharamond; whereas yet their owne authors affirme, that the land Salike is in Germanie, betwéene the riuers of Elbe and Sala; and that when Charles the great had ouercome the Saxons, he placed there certeine Frenchmen, which hauing in disdeine the dishonest maners of the Germane women, made a law, that the females should not succéed to any inheritanee within that land, which at this daie is called Meisen, so that if this be true, this law was not made for the realme of France, nor the Frenchmen possessed the land Salike, till foure hundred and one and twentie yeares after the death of Pharamond, the supposed maker of this Salike law, for this Pharamond deceassed in the yeare 426, and Charles the great subdued the Saxons, and placed the Frenchmen in those parts beyond the riuer of Sala in the yeare 805.

The Salike law.

Mesina.

Moreouer, it appeareth by their owne writers, that king Pepine, which deposed Childerike, claimed the crowne of France, as heire generall, for that he was descended of Blithild daughter to king Clothair the first: Hugh Capet also, who vsurped the crowne vpon Charles duke of Loraine, the sole heire male of the line and stocke of Charles the great, to make his title seeme true, and appeare good, though in déed it was starke naught, conueied himselfe as heire to the ladie Lingard, daughter to king

Charlemaine, sonne to Lewes the emperour, that was son to Charles the great. King Lewes also the tenth otherwise called saint Lewes, being verie heire to the said vsurper Hugh Capet, could neuer be satisfied in his conscience how he might iustlie keepe and possesse the crowne of France, till he was persuaded and fullie instructed, that quéene Isabell his grandmother was lineallie descended of the ladie Ermengard daughter and heire to the aboue named Charles duke of Loraine, by the which marriage, the bloud and line of Charles the great was againe vnited and restored to the crowne & scepter of France, so that more cléere than the sunne it openlie appeareth, that the title of king Pepin, the claime of Hugh Capet, the possession of Lewes, yea and the French kings to this daie, are deriued aud conueied from the heire female, though they would vnder the colour of such a fained law, barre the kings and princes of this realme of England of their right and lawfull inheritance.

The archbishop further alledged out of the booke of Numbers this saieng: " When a man dieth without a sonne, let the inheritance descend to his daughter." At length, hauing said sufficientlie for the proofe of the kings iust and lawfull title to the crowne of France, he exhorted him to aduance foorth his banner to fight for his right, to conquer his inheritance, to spare neither bloud, sword, nor fire, sith his warre was iust, his cause good, and his claime true. And to the intent his louing chapleins and obedient subiects of the spiritualtie might shew themselues willing and desirous to aid his maiestie, for the recouerie of his ancient right and true inheritance, the archbishop declared that in their spirituall conuocation, they had granted to his highnesse such a summe of monie, as neuer by no spirituall persons was to any prince before those daies giuen or aduanced.

The earle of Westmerland persuadeth the king to the conquest of Scotland.

When the archbishop had ended his prepared tale, Rafe Neuill earle of Westmerland, and as then lord Warden of the marches against Scotland, vnderstanding that the king vpon a couragious desire to recouer his right in France, would suerlie take the wars in hand, thought good to mooue the king to begin first with Scotland, and therevpon declared how easie a matter it should be to make a conquest there, and how greatlie the same should further his wished purpose for the subduing of the Frenchmen, concluding the summe of his tale with this old saieng: that Who so will France win, must with Scotland first begin. Manie matters he touched, as well to shew how necessarie the conquest of Scotland should be, as also to prooue how iust a cause the king had to attempt it, trusting to persuade the king and all other to be of his opinion.

The duke of Excester his wise and pithie answer to the earle of Westmerlãds saieng.

A true saieng.

But after he had made an end, the duke of Excester, vncle to the king, a man well learned and wise, (who had béene sent into Italie by his father intending that he should haue béen a preest) replied against the erle of Westmerlands oration, affirming rather that he which would Scotland win, he with France must first begin. For if the king might once compasse the conquest of France, Scotland could not long resist; so that conquere France, and Scotland would soone obeie. For where should the Scots lerne policie and skill to defend themselues, if they had not their bringing vp and training in France? If the French pensions mainteined not the Scotish nobilitie, in what case should they be? Then take awaie France, and the Scots will soone be tamed; France being to Scotland the same that the sap is to the trée, which being taken awaie, the trée must néeds die and wither.

To be briefe, the duke of Excester vsed such earnest and pithie persuasions, to induce the king and the whole assemblie of the parlement to credit his words, that immediatlie after he had made an end, all the companie began to crie; Warre, warre; France, France. Hereby the bill for dissoluing of religious houses was cléerelie set aside, and nothing thought on but onelie the recouering of France, according as the archbishop had mooued. And vpon this point, after a few acts besides for the wealth of the realme established, the parlement was proroged vnto Westminster. ¶ Some write, that in this

this parlement it was enacted, that Lollards and heretikes with their mainteiners and fauourers should be Ipso facto adiudged guiltie of high treason: but in the statute made in the same parlement against Lollards, we find no such words: albeit by force of that statute it was ordeined, that persons so conuicted & executed, should lose their lands holden in fée simple, and all other their goods and cattels, as in cases of felonie.

During this parlement, there came to the king ambassadors, as well from the French king that was then in the hands of the Orlientiall faction, as also from the duke of Burgognie, for aid against that faction; promising more (as was said) than laie well in his power to performe. The king shortlie after sent ambassadors to them both, as the bishop of Durham, and Norwich, with others. Moreouer at this parlement, Iohn the kings brother was created duke of Bedford, and his brother Humfrie duke of Glocester. Also, Thomas Beaufort, marquesse Dorset, was created duke of Excester. Immediatlie after, the king sent ouer into France his vncle the duke of Excester, the lord Greie admerall of England, the archbishop of Dubline, and the bishop of Norwich, ambassadors vnto the French king, with fiue hundred horsse, which were lodged in the temple house in Paris, keeping such triumphant cheere in their lodging, and such a solemne estate in their riding through the citie, that the Parisiens and all the Frenchmen had no small meruell at their honorable port.

Ambassadors from the Frēch king and from the duke of Burgognie.

Creation of dukes.

Harding.

Ambassadors sent to Frāce.

The French king receiued them verie honorablie, and banketted them right sumptuouslie, shewing to them iusts and Martiall pastimes, by the space of thrée daies togither, in the which iusts the king himselfe, to shew his courage and actiuitie to the Englishmen, manfullie brake speares and lustilie tournied. When the triumph was ended, the English ambassadors, hauing a time appointed them to declare their message, admitted to the French kings presence, required of him to deliuer vnto the king of England the realme and crowne of France, with the entier duchies of Aquiteine, Normandie and Aniou, with the countries of Poictiou and Maine. Manie other requests they made: and this offered withall, that if the French king would without warre and effusion of christian bloud, render to the king their maister his verie right & lawfull inheritance, that he would be content to take in mariage the ladie Katharine, daughter to the French king, and to indow hir with all the duchies and countries before rehearsed; and if he would not so doo, then the king of England did expresse and signifie to him, that with the aid of God, and helpe of his people, he would recouer his right and inheritance wrongfullie withholden from him, with mortall warre, and dint of sword. ¶ This in effect dooth our English poet comprise in his report of the occasion, which Henrie the fift tooke to arrere battell against the French king: putting into the mouthes of the said king of Englands ambassadors an imagined speech, the conclusion whereof he maketh to be either restitution of that which the French had taken and deteined from the English, or else fire and sword. His words are these,

Abr. Fl. out of In Angl. præl. sub Hen. 5.

———raptum nobis aut redde Britannis,
Aut ferrum expectes, vltrices insuper ignes.

The Frenchmen being not a little abashed at these demands, thought not to make anie absolute answer in so weightie a cause, till they had further breathed; and therefore praied the English ambassadors to saie to the king their maister, that they now hauing no opportunitie to conclude in so high a matter, would shortlie send ambassadors into England, which should certifie & declare to the king their whole mind, purpose, and intent. The English ambassadors returned with this answer, making relation of euerie thing that was said or doone. King Henrie after the returne of his ambassadors, determined fullie to make warre in France, conceiuing a good and perfect hope to haue fortunate successe, sith victorie for the most part followeth where right leadeth, being aduanced forward by iustice, and set foorth by equitie.

And bicause manie Frenchmen were promoted to ecclesiasticall dignities, as some to benefices, and some to abbeies and priories within the realme, and sent dailie innumerable summes of monie into France for the reléefe of their naturall countrimen and kinsfolke, he therefore in fauour of the publike wealth of his realme and subiects, in a councell called at London, about Michaelmas, caused to be ordeined, that no stranger hereafter should be promoted to anie spirituall dignitie or degree within this realme, without his especiall licence, and roiall consent; and all they that should be admitted, should find sufficient suerties, not to disclose the secrets of this realme to anie forren person, nor to minister aid or succour to anie of them with monie, or by anie other meanes. This was confirmed in a conuocation called at the same time by the new archbishop of Canturburie.

Thom. Wals.
It is not like that in this councell writers meane the parlement that was adiorned from Leicester to Westminster, where it began in the octaues of saint Martin, in *th*is second yeare *1415.*

The councell of Constance.

Moreouer, such as were to go vnto the generall councell holden at Constance, were named and appointed to make them readie: for the king hauing knowledge from the emperor Sigismund, of the assembling of that councell, thought it not conuenient to sit still as an hearer, and no partaker in so high a cause, which touched the whole state of the christian common-wealth, as then troubled by reason of the schisme that yet continued. Wherefore he sent thither Richard earle of Warwike, the bishops of Salisburie, Bath, and Hereford, the abbat of Westminster, and the prior of Worcester, with diuerse other doctors and learned men of the spiritualtie; besides knights and esquiers. They were in number eight hundred horsses, so well appointed and furnished, as well the men as horsses, that all nations maruelled to see such an honorable companie come from a countrie so far distant.

The earle of Warwike and others sent to the generall councell.

Diuerse other things were concluded at that present: for the king had caused not onelie the lords of the spiritualtie, but also of the temporaltie to assemble here at London the same time, to treat speciallie of his iournie that he purposed to make shortlie into France: and herevpon meanes was made for the gathering of monie; which was granted with so good a will both of the spiritualtie and temporaltie, that there was leuied the summe of thrée hundred thousand markes English: and herewith order was giuen to gather a great hoast of men, thorough all his dominions. And for the more increasing of his nauie, he sent into Holland, Zeland, and Frizeland, to conduct and hire ships for the transporting and conueieng ouer of his men and munitions of war, and finallie prouided for armour, victuals, monie, artillerie, cariage, boates to passe ouer riuers couered with leather, tents, and all other things requisite for so high an enterprise.

Enguerant.

Great preparation for the French wars.

The Frenchmen hauing knowledge hereof, the Dolphin, who had the gouernance of the realme, bicause his father was fallen into his old disease of frensie, sent for the dukes of Berrie and Alanson, and all the other lords of the councell of France: by whose aduise it was determined, that they should not onelie prepare a sufficient armie to resist the king of England, when so euer he arriued to inuade France, but also to stuffe and furnish the townes on the frontiers and sea coasts with conuenient garrisons of men: and further to send to the king of England a solemne ambassage, to make to him some offers according to the demands before rehearsed. The charge of this ambassage was committed to the earle of Vandosme, to maister William Bouratier archbishop of Burges, and to maister Peter Fremell bishop of Liseur, to the lords of Yvry and Braquemont, and to maister Gaultier Cole the kings secretarie, and diuerse others.

An. Reg. 3.
Ambassadors out of France.

These ambassadors accompanied with 350 horsses, passed the sea at Calis, and landed at Douer, before whose arriuall the king was departed from Windsore to Winchester, intending to haue gone to Hampton, there to haue surueied his nauie; but hearing of the ambassadors approching, he tarried still at Winchester, where the said French lords shewed themselues verie honorablie before the king and his nobilitie. At time prefixed, before the kings presence, sitting in his throne imperiall, the archbishop of Burges made an eloquent and a long oration, dissuading warre, and praising peace;

peace; offering to the king of England a great summe of monie, with diuerse countries, being in verie déed but base and poore, as a dowrie with the ladie Catharine in
mariage, so that he would dissolue his armie, and dismisse his soldiers, which he had
gathered and put in a readinesse.

When his oration was ended, the king caused the ambassadors to be highlie feasted,
and set them at his owne table. And after a daie assigned in the foresaid hall, the archbishop of Canturburie to their oration made a notable answer, the effect whereof was,
that if the French king would not giue with his daughter in mariage the duches of
Aquiteine, Aniou, and all other seigniories and dominions sometimes apperteining to
the noble progenitors of the king of England, he would in no wise retire his armie,
nor breake his iournie; but would with all diligence enter into France, and destroie
the people, waste the countrie, and subuert the townes with blood, sword, and fire, and
neuer ceasse till he had recouered his ancient right and lawfull patrimonie. The king
auowed the archbishops saieng, and in the word of a prince promised to performe it
to the vttermost.

The archbishop of Burges much gréeued, that his ambassage was no more regarded, A proud pre-
sumptuous pre-
lat.
after certeine brags blustered out with impatience, as more presuming vpon his pre-
lasie, than respecting his dutie of considerance to whom he spake and what became
him to saie, he praied safe conduct to depart. Which the king gentlie granted, and
added withall to this effect: " I little estéeme your French brags, & lesse set by your The wise answer
of the k. to the
bishop.
power and strength; I know perfectlie my right to my region, which you vsurpe; &
except you denie the apparant truth, so doo your selues also; if you neither doo nor
will know it, yet God and the world knoweth it. The power of your master you sée,
but my puissance ye haue not yet tasted. If he haue louing subiects, I am (I thanke
God) not vnstored of the same: and I saie this vnto you, that before one yeare passe,
I trust to make the highest crowne of your countrie to stoope, and the proudest miter
to learne his humiliatedo. In the meane time tell this to the vsurper your master,
that within thrée moneths, I will enter into France, as into mine owne true and lawfull
patrimonie, appointing to acquire the same, not with brag of words, but with déeds of men,
and dint of sword, by the aid of God, in whome is my whole trust and confidence.
Further matter at this present I impart not vnto you, sauing that with warrant you
maie depart suerlie and safelie into your countrie, where I trust sooner to visit you,
than you shall haue cause to bid me welcome." With this answer the ambassadors
sore displeased in their minds (although they were highlie interteined and liberallie
rewarded) departed into their countrie, reporting to the Dolphin how they had
sped.

After the French ambassadors were departed, the king like a prouident prince,
thought good to take order for the resisting of the Scots, if (according to their maner)
they should attempt anie thing against his subiects in his absence. For that point appointed he the earle of Westmerland, the lord Scroope, the baron of Greistocke, sir
Robert Umfreuill, & diuerse other valiant capteins to kéepe the frontiers & marches of
Scotland, which sir Robert Umfreuill on the daie of Marie Madgdalen fought with the
Scots at the towne of Gedering, hauing in his companie onelie thrée hundred archers,
and seuen score spears, where he (after long conflict) slue of his enimies sixtie and odde, Harding.
tooke thrée hundred and sixtie prisoners, discomfited and put to flight one thousand and An ouerthrow
to the Scots by
sir Robert Um-
freuill.
more, whome he followed in chace aboue twelue miles, but their hands full of preies
and prisoners, retired homeward (not vnhurt) to the castell of Rockesborough, of the
which he was capteine.

When the king had all prouisions readie, and ordered all things for the defense of his
realme, he leauing behind him for gouernour of the realme, the quéene his moother in The quéene
mother gouer-
nour of the
realme.
law, departed to Southampton, to take ship into France. And first princelie appointing
to aduertise the French king of his comming, therefore dispatched Antelope his purseu-

ant

ant at armes with letters to him for restitution of that which he wrongfully withheld, contrarie to the lawes of God and man : the king further declaring how sorie he was that he should be thus compelled for repeting of his right and iust title of inheritance, to make warre to the distruction of christian people, but sithens he had offered peace which could not be receiued, now for fault of iustice, he was forced to take armes. Neuerthelesse exhorted the French king in the bowels of Iesu Christ, to render him that which was his owne, whereby effusion of Christian bloud might be auoided. These letters chéeflie to this effect and purpose, were written and dated from Hampton the fift of August. When the same were presented to the French King, and by his councell well perused, answer was made, that he would take aduise, and prouide therein as time and place should be conuenient, so the messenger licenced to depart at his pleasure.

When king Henrie had fullie furnished his nauie with men, munition, & other prouisions, perceiuing that his capteines misliked nothing so much as delaie, determined his souldiors to go a ship-boord and awaie. But see the hap, the night before the daie appointed for their departure, he was crediblie informed, that Richard earle of Cambridge brother to Edward duke of Yorke, and Henrie lord Scroope of Masham lord treasuror, with Thomas Graie a knight of Northumberland, being confederat togither, had conspired his death : wherefore he caused them to be apprehended. The said lord Scroope was in such fauour with the king, that he admitted him sometime to be his bedfellow, in whose fidelitie the king reposed such trust, that when anie priuat or publike councell was in hand, this lord had much in the determination of it. For he represented so great grauitie in his countenance, such modestie in behauiour, and so vertuous zeale to all godlinesse in his talke, that whatsoeuer he said was thought for the most part necessarie to be doone and followed. Also the said sir Thomas Graie (as some write) was of the kings priuie councell.

The earle of Cambridge & other lords apprehended for treason.
Thom. Wals.

These prisoners vpon their examination, confessed, that for a great summe of monie which they had receiued of the French king, they intended verelie either to haue deliuered the king aliue into the hands of his enimies, or else to haue murthered him before he should arriue in the duchie of Normandie. When king Henrie had heard all things opened, which he desired to know, he caused all his nobilitie to come before his presence, before whome he caused to be brought the offendors also, and to them said. " Hauing thus conspired the death and destruction of me, which am the head of the realme and gouernour of the people, it maie be (no doubt) but that you likewise haue sworne the confusion of all that are here with me, and also the desolation of your owne countrie. To what horror (O lord) for any true English hart to consider, that such an execrable iniquitie should euer so bewray you, as for pleasing of a forren enimie to imbrue your hands in your bloud, and to ruine your owne natiue soile. Reuenge herein touching my person, though I séeke not ; yet for the safegard of you, my déere fréends, & for due perseruation of all sorts, I am by office to cause example to be shewed. Get ye hence therefore ye poore miserable wretches to the receiuing of your iust reward, wherein Gods maiestie giue you grace of his mercie and repentance of your heinous offenses." And so immediatlie they were had to execution.

Hall.

King Henries words to the traitours.

The earle of Cambridge and the other traitors executed.

This doone, the king calling his lords againe afore him, said in words few and with good grace. Of his enterprises he recounted the honor and glorie, whereof they with him were to be partakers, the great confidence he had in their noble minds, which could not but remember them of the famous feats that their ancestors aforetime in France had atchiued, whereof the due report for euer recorded remained yet in register. The great mercie of God that had so gratiouslie reuealed vnto him the treason at hand, whereby the true harts of those afore him made so eminent & apparant in his eie, as they might be right sure he would neuer forget it. The doubt of

danger

danger to be nothing in respect of the certeintie of honor that they should acquire, wherein himselfe (as they saw) in person would be lord and leader through Gods grace. To whose maiestie as chéeflie was knowne the equitie of his demand: euen so to his mercie did he onelie recommend the successe of his trauels. When the king had said, all the noble men knéeled downe, & promised faithfullie to serue him, dulie to obeie him, and rather to die than to suffer him to fall into the hands of his enimies.

This doone, the king thought that suerlie all treason and conspiracie had beene vtterlie extinct: not suspecting the fire which was newlie kindled, and ceassed not to increase, till at length it burst out into such a flame, that catching the beames of his house and familie, his line and stocke was cleane consumed to ashes. ¶ Diuerse write that Richard earle of Cambridge did not conspire with the lord Scroope & Thomas Graie for the murthering of king Henrie to please the French king withall, but onelie to the intent to exalt to the crowne his brother in law Edmund earle of March as heire to Lionell duke of Clarence: after the death of which earle of March, for diuerse secret impediments, not able to haue issue, the earle of Cambridge was sure that the crowne should come to him by his wife, and to his children, of hir begotten. And therefore (as was thought) he rather confessed himselfe for need of monie to be corrupted by the French king, than he would declare his inward mind, and open his verie intent and secret purpose, which if it were espied, he saw plainlie that the earle of March should haue tasted of the same cuppe that he had drunken, and what should haue come to his owne children he much doubted. Therefore destitute of comfort & in despaire of life to saue his children, he feined that tale, desiring rather to saue his succession than himselfe, which he did in déed: for his sonne Richard duke of Yorke not priuilie but openlie claimed the crowne, and Edward his sonne both claimed it, & gained it, as after it shall appeare. Which thing if king Henrie had at this time either doubted, or foreséene, had neuer béene like to haue come to passe, as Hall saith.

But whatsoeuer hath beene reported of the confession of the earle of Cambridge, certeine it is that indicted he was by the name of Richard earle of Cambridge of Conesburgh in the countie of Yorke knight, and with him Thomas Graie of Heton in the countie of Northumberland knight; for that they the twentith daie of Iulie, in the third yeare of king Henrie the fifts reigne, at Southampton, and in diuerse other places within this realme, had conspired togither with a power of men to them associat, without the kings licence, to haue led awaie the lord Edmund earle of March into Wales, and then to haue procured him to take vpon him the supreme gouernment of the realme, in case that king Richard the second were dead: and herwith had purposed to set foorth a proclamation there in Wales, in name of the said earle of March, as heire of the crowne against king Henrie, by the name of Henrie of Lancaster the vsurper, to the end that by such meanes they might draw the more number of the kings liege people vnto the said earle; and further to haue conueied a banner of the armes of England, and a certeine crowne of Spaine set vpon a pallet, and laid in gage to the said earle of Cambridge, by the king, togither with the said earle of March into the parties of Wales aforesaid.

Further, that the said earle of Cambridge, and sir Thomas Graie had appointed certeine of the kings liege people to repaire into Scotland, and to bring from thence one Thomas Trumpington; also an other resembling in shape, fauour, and countenance king Richard, and Henrie Persie, togither with a great multitude of people to fight with the king, and him to destroie in open field. Beside this, that they had meant to win certeine castels in Wales, and to kéepe them against the king: and manie other treasons they had contriued, as by the indictement was specified, to the intent they might destroie the king and his brethren, the dukes of Bedford and Glocester, and other the great lords & peers of the realme. And Henrie Scroope of

                                                        Masham,

The effect of the earle of Cambridges indictement.

A iewell

Masham, of Flarflet, in the countie of Yorke was likewise indicted, as consenting to the premisses. So that it appeareth their purpose was well inough then perceiued, although happilie not much bruted abroad, for considerations thought necessarie to haue it rather husht and kept secret.

About the selfe same time the lord Cobham with his freends, whether as one of counsell in the conspiracie with the earle of Cambridge or not, was determined to haue made some attempt against the lord of Aburgauennie, who being aduertised thereof, got for his defense from Worcester, Persore, Teukesburie, and other places thereabout, to the number of fiue thousand archers, and other armed men, which came to him vnto his castell of Haneleie: whereof when the lord Cobham was ad-uertised, he withdrew againe to such secret places about Maluerne, as he had pro-uided for his suertie, to resort vnto: but a priest that belonged vnto him, was taken, and diuerse other, who disclosed to the lord Aburgauennie, one of the places where the said lord Cobham with his men vsed to kéepe themselues close. Vnto that place the lord Aburgauennie went, where he found indéed monie and armor piled vp be-twixt two wals, handsomelie conueied and framed for the purpose; but the lord Cobham with his folkes were withdrawne into some other place, after they once heard, that the earle of Cambridge and the lord Scroope were executed.

But now to proceed with king Henries dooings. After this, when the wind came about prosperous to his purpose, he caused the mariners to weie vp anchors, and

hoise vp sailes, and to set forward with a thousand ships, on the vigill of our ladie daie the Assumption, and tooke land at Caur, commonlie called Kidcaur, where the riuer of Saine runneth into the sea, without resistance. At his first comming on land, he caused proclamation to be made, that no person should be so hardie on paine of death, either to take anie thing out of anie church that belonged to the same, or to hurt or doo anie violence either to priests, women, or anie such as should be found with-out weapon or armor, and not readie to make resistance: also that no man should

renew anie quarell or strife, whereby anie fraie might arise to the disquieting of the armie.

The next daie after his landing, he marched toward the towne of Harflue, standing on the riuer of Saine betwéene two hils; he besieged it on euerie side, raising bul-warks and a bastell, in which the two earles of Kent & Huntington were placed, with Cornwall, Graie, Steward, and Porter. On that side towards the sea, the king lodged with his field, and the duke of Clarence on the further side towards Rone. There were within the towne the lords de Touteuill and Gaucourt, with diuerse other that valiantlie defended the siege, dooing what damage they could to their aduer-saries; and damming vp the riuer that hath his course through the towne, the water rose so high betwixt the kings campe, and the duke of Clarence campe (diuided by the same riuer) that the Englishmen were constreined to withdraw their artillerie from one side, where they had planted the same.

The French king being aduertised, that king Henrie was arriued on that coast, sent in all hast the lord de la Breth constable of France, the seneshall of France, the lord Bouciqualt marshall of France, the seneshall of Henault, the lord Lignie with other, which fortified townes with men, victuals, and artillerie on all those

frontiers towards the sea. And hearing that Harflue was besieged, they came to the castell of Caudebecke, being not farre from Harflue, to the intent they might succor their freends which were besieged, by some policie or meanes: but the Englishmen, notwithstanding all the damage that the Frenchmen could worke against them, for-raied the countrie, spoiled the villages, bringing manie a rich preie to the campe be-fore Harflue. And dailie was the towne assaulted: for the duke of Glocester, to whome the order of the siege was committed, made thrée mines vnder the ground,

and

and approching to the wals with his engins and ordinance, would not suffer them within to take anie rest.

For although they with their countermining somwhat disappointed the Englishmen, & came to fight with them hand to hand within the mines, so that they went no further forward with that worke; yet they were so inclosed on ech side, as well by water as land, that succour they saw could none come to them: for the king lieng with his battell on the hill side on the one partie, and the duke of Clarence beyond the riuer that passeth by the towne, and runneth into Saine on the other partie, beside other lords and capteins that were lodged with their retinues for their most aduantage: none could be suffered to go in, or come foorth, without their licence; insomuch that such pouder as was sent to haue béene conueied into the towne by water, was taken by the English ships that watched the riuer.

The capteins within the towne, perceiuing that they were not able long to resist the continuall assaults of the Englishmen, knowing that their wals were vndermined, and like to be ouerthrowne (as one of their bulwarks was alredie, where the earles of Huntington and Kent had set vp their banners) sent an officer at armes foorth about midnight after the feast daie of saint Lambert, which fell that yeare vpon the tuesdaie, to beseech the king of England to appoint some certeine persons as commissioners from him, with whome they within might treat about some agréement. The duke of Clarence, to whome this messenger first declared his errand, aduertised the king of their request, who granting thereto, appointed the duke of Excester, with the lord Fitz Hugh, and sir Thomas Erpingham, to vnderstand their minds, who at the first requested a truce vntill sundaie next following the feast of saint Michaell, in which meane time if no succour came to remooue the siege, they would vndertake to deliuer the towne into the kings hands, their liues and goods saued.

The king aduertised hereof, sent them word, that except they would surrender the towne to him the morow next insuing, without anie condition, they should spend no more time in talke about the matter. But yet at length through the earnest sute of the French lords, the king was contented to grant them truce vntill nine of the clocke the next sundaie, being the two and twentith of September; with condition, that if in the meane time no rescue came, they should yéeld the towne at that houre, with their bodies and goods to stand at the kings pleasure. And for assurance thereof, they deliuered into the kings hands thirtie of their best capteins and merchants within that towne as pledges. But other write, that it was couenanted, that they should deliuer onelie twelue pledges, and that if the siege were not raised by the French kings power within six daies next following, then should they deliuer the towne into the king of England hands, and thirtie of the chéefest personages within the same, to stand for life or death at his will and pleasure: and as for the residue of the men of warre and townesmen, they should depart whether they would, without carieng foorth either armour, weapon, or goods.

The king neuerthelesse was after content to grant a respit vpon certeine conditions, that the capteins within might haue time to send to the French king for succour (as before ye haue heard) least he intending greater exploits, might lose time in such small matters. When this composition was agreed vpon, the lord Bacqueuill was sent vnto the French king, to declare in what point the towne stood. To whome the Dolphin answered, that the kings power was not yet assembled, in such number as was conuenient to raise so great a siege. This answer being brought vnto the capteins within the towne, they rendered it vp to the king of England, after that the third daie was expired, which was on the daie of saint Maurice being the seuen and thirtith daie after the siege was first laid. The souldiors were ransomed, and the towne sacked, to the great gaine of the Englishmen. ¶Some writing of this yeelding vp of Harflue, doo in like sort make mention of the distresse whereto the people

Titus Liuius.

Harding.
Thom. Walsi.

The seuentéenth
of September
they within Harflue praie parlée.

A fiue daies
respit.

Harflue yéelded
and sacked.

Abr. Fl. out of
Angl. prœl.
sub. Hen. 5. and
Polychron.

people, then expelled out of their habitations, were driuen : insomuch as parents with their children, yoong maids and old folke went out of the towne gates with heauie harts (God wot) as put to their present shifts to séeke them a new abode. Besides that, king Henrie caused proclamation to be made within his owne dominions of England, that whosoeuer (either handicraftesman, merchantman, gentleman, or plowman) would inhabit in Harflue, should haue his dwelling giuen him gratis, and his heire after him also inioy the like grace and fauour : insomuch that great multitudes flocked to the sea coasts, waiting wind and wether for their transportage into Harflue, where being arriued woonderfull it is to tell, within how short a time the towne was peopled. This doth Anglorum prælia report, saieng (not without good ground, I beléeue) as followeth :

> ———tum flentes tenera cum prole parentes
> Virgineúsque chorus veteres liquêre penates :
> Tum populus cunctus de portis Gallicus exit
> Mœstus, inarmatus, vacuus, miser, æger, inópsq;
> Vtque nouas sedes quærat migrare coactus :
> Oppidulo belli potiuntur iure Britanni, &c.

All this doone, the king ordeined capteine to the towne his vncle the duke of Excester, who established his lieutenant there, one sir Iohn Fastolfe, with fifteene hundred men, or (as some haue) two thousand and thirtie six knights, whereof the baron of Carew, and sir Hugh Lutterell, were two councellors. And bicause manie of his nobles whilest this siege laie before Harflue, fell sicke of the flix and other diseases, diuerse also dead, amongst whom the earle of Stafford, the bishop of Norwich, the lords Molins and Burnell were foure (beside others) the king licenced his brother the duke of Clarence, Iohn earle marshall, and Iohn earle of Arundell, being infected with that disease, to returne into England.

King Henrie, after the winning of Harflue, determined to haue procéeded further in the winning of other townes and fortresses : but bicause the dead time of the winter approched, it was determined by aduise of his councell, that he should in all conuenient spéed set forward, and march through the countrie towards Calis by land, least his returne as then homewards should of slanderous toongs be named a running

awaie : and yet that iournie was adiudged perillous, by reason that the number of his people was much minished by the flix and other feuers, which sore vexed and brought to death aboue fifteene hundred persons of the armie : and this was the cause that his returne was the sooner appointed and concluded.

But before his departing thence, he entered into the towne of Harflue, & went to the church of saint Martines, and there offered. All the men of warre which had

not paid their ransoms, he sware them on the holie euangelists, to yeeld themselues prisoners at Calis by the feast of saint Martine in Nouember next. There were two strong towers standing on the hauen side at Harflue, which looking for aid, did not yéeld, till ten daies after the towne was rendered. When the king had repaired the walles, bulwarks and rampiers about the towne, and furnished it with vittels and artillerie, he remooued from Harflue toward Ponthoise, intending to passe the riuer of Some with his armie, before the bridges were either withdrawen or broken. Such vittels and other necessaries as were to be caried with the armie, he appointed to be laid on horsses, leauing the carts and wagons behind for lesse incombre.

The French king hearing that the towne of Harflue was gotten, and that the king of England was marching forward into the bowels of the realme of France, sent out proclamations, and assembled people on euerie side, committing the whole charge of

his armie to his sonne the Dolphine and duke of Aquitaine, who incontinentlie caused the bridges to be broken, and the passages to be kept. Also they caused all the corne and vittels to be conueied awaie, or destroied in all places, where it was coniectured

that

that the Englishmen would passe. The king of England nothing dismaied herewith, kept his iournie in spite of his enimies, constreining them within diuerse townes and holds to furnish him with vittels: but yet as he passed by the towne of Ew, the garrison of the towne issued foorth, and gaue the Englishmen a skirmish, who beat them into the towne with losse, namelie of a right valiant man of armes, named Lancelot Piers. There were manie Englishmen hurt with quarels shot off from the loops and wals, as they pursued the enimies vnto the gates. *A skirmish with the garrison of Ew.*
Enguerant.

At length the king approched the riuer of Some, & finding all the bridges broken, he came to the passage of Blanchetake, where his great grandfather king Edward the third a little before had striken the battell of Cressie: but the passage was now so impeached with stakes in the botome of the foord, that he could not passe, his enimies besides there awaie so swarming on all sides. He therefore marched forwards to Arames, marching with his armie, and passing with his carriage in so martiall a maner, that he appeared so terrible to his enimies, as they durst not offer him battell. And yet the lord Dalbreth constable of France, the marshall Boncequault, the earle of Vendosme great master of France, the duke of Alanson, and the earle of Richmont, with all the puissance of the Dolphin laie at Abuile, but euer kept the passages, and coasted aloofe, like a hauke though eager yet not hardie on hir preie. The king of England kept on his iournie till he came to the bridge of saint Marence, where he found aboue thirtie thousand Frenchmen, and there pitched his field, looking suerlie to be fought withall. *Blanchetake.*

Wherefore to incourage his capteins the more, he dubbed certeine of his hardie and valiant gentlemen knights, as Iohn lord Ferrers of Grobie, Reginald of Greistocke, Piers Tempest, Christopher Morisbie, Thomas Pikering, William Huddleston, Iohn Hosbalton, Henrie Mortimer, Philip Hall, and William his brother, Iaques de Ormond, and diuerse other: but the French making no semblance to fight, he departed in good order of battell by the towne of Amiens, to another towne néere to a castell called Bowes, and there laie two daies looking for their bidding of battell euerie houre. From thence he came néere to Corbie, where he was staied that night, for that the common people and pezants mightilie there assembled, hauing gotten them some head and hartening by meanes of their number that was great, and by trust of a strength (then ioined vnto them) made of men at armes (manie too tall and well appointed for fight) all of the garrison of Corbie: a strong towne well walled and warded. Herevpon at a streict (which they had preoccupied) they stoutlie from our armie not onelie kept the passage, but also vpon vs gaue a proud onset: wherein sir Hugh Stafford knight lord Bourghchier, cheéfteine of a wing to the king vnder his standard of Guien, and as then neerest to the enimie, though far inferior in number, yet with readie and valiant incounter receiued them. The force and slaughter grew great both on the one side and the other, by the French in especiall, at first right fiercelie pursued, in so much as with an hardie charge vpon our men, they had both beat downe the standard, and also from vs quite woone it awaie, to their hie incouragement, and our incredible despite and dismaie. Whereat one Iohn Bromley of Bromley in Staffordshire esquier, a neere kinsman vnto the lord Bourghchier, was euen streight so pearsed at hart, as he could not conteine him, but by and by ran eagerlie vpon the French; and with his souldiers (in whom wrath and teéne had alreadie inflamed furie and desire of reuenge) did so fiercelie set vpon them, that they were not onlie beaten backe, but also forced to abandon the place. At this push the capteine cutting through the thickest, strake downe the champion that bare the standard, and so glóriouslie recouered it againe, and after during the fight (where as manie of the French lost their liues) couragiouslie ouer his souldiers aduanced it himselfe. The rest that fled awaie our people pursued in chasing & slaughter vnto Corbie verie gates. So in victorie, honor, and great ioy, with our small losse (in comparison) *Diuerse capteins knights.*

W. P.

Standing in Picardie betwéene Amiens & Peron all vp̄ the riuer of Some.
Sir Hugh Stafford lord Bourghchier.

Iohn Bromley. He came of a yoonger brother in the linage of the right honorable the lord chancelor that now is 1585.

The kings standard recouered.

thanks

thanks vnto Gods maiestie, the cheefteine brought his host into his campe and order againe. The singular prowes of this worthie capteine the noble man highlie regarding, in an ample testimonie thereof and vpon his owne honorable consideration, by a faire ancient déed yet extant at these daies did giue him reward of fortie pounds annuitie for his life. The monument so plainelie declaring the truth of the matter, with the maner and dignitie of the feat, as it was doone, hath béene thought verie meet for the storie in hand here now to place it as followeth.

1585.

A copie of the said deed.

HOC præsens scriptum testatur, quòd nos Hugo de Stafford dominus le Bourgh-chier concessimus & per præsentes confirmauimus prædilecto consanguineo nostro Iohanni Bromley de Bromley armigero, pro suo magno auxilio nobis impenso in op-pugnatione contra Françcos prope le Corbie; & præcipuè pro suo laudabili seruitio in recuperatione & supportatione vexilli domini regis de Guien sub nostra conductione, vnam annuitatem siue annualem redditum quadraginta librarum legalis monetæ annuatim percipiendum, durante tota vita naturali prædicti Iohannis de Bromley, de & in omnibus manerijs, terris, & tenementis nostris cum pertinentibus in comitatu Stafford & Warwik, ad festa Penthecostes & sancti Martini in hyeme æquis portionibus. Et si contingat prædictam annuitatem siue annualem redditum quadraginta li-brarum, à retro fore in parte vel in toto, ad aliquod festum quo solui debeat, tunc bene licebit prædicto Iohāni & assignatis suis in prædictis manerijs, ac in omnibus alijs terris & tenimentis cum suis pertinentibus præscriptis, distringere & districtiones effugare & retinere, quousque de prædicta annuitate simul cum arreragijs, si quæ fuerint, plenariè sibi fuerit satisfactum & persolutum. Et vt hæc nostra concessio, & scripti huius confirmatio (durante tota vita prædicti Iohannis de Bromley vt præfertur) rata & stabilis permaneat, hoc scriptum impressione sigilli armorum meorum roboraui. Hijs testibus, Iohanne de Holland, Richardo le Greuyll, Richardo de Hor-wood, Thoma le Forestar, & alijs. Datum apud Madeley decimo die mensis Martij, anno regni regis Henrici quinti post conquestum quarto.

w. P.

For that by the armes in the seale it may the better be knowne of what stem this noble man sproong (a matter which this storie seemes iùstlie to require) vnder-stand yée thus were the same. In his shield, a cheuorne charged with a mullet; his crest, a swans head couped betweene two wings displaied all out of a crowne supported by two greihounds; about the shéeld ingrauen, Signa Hugonis de Stafford militis. Héereby is gathered that he was a third brother of the duke of Bucking-

King Henrie passeth the riuer of Some with his host.

hams house.] This feat thus well doone, the king the same daie found a shallow, betwéene Corbie and Peron, which neuer was espied before, at which he with his armie and carriages the night insuing, passed the water of Some without let or danger, and therewith determined to make haste towards Calis, and not to seeke for battell, except he were thereto constreined, bicause that his armie by sicknesse

The kings armie but of 15000.

was sore diminished, in so much that he had but onelie two thoussand horssemen and thirteene thousand archers, bilmen, and of all sorts of other footmen.

The English armie sore afflict-ed.

The Englishmen were brought into some distresse in this iornie, by reason of their vittels in maner spent, and no hope to get more: for the enimies had de-stroied all the corne before they came. Rest could they none take, for their enimies with alarmes did euer so infest them: dailie it rained, and nightlie it fréesed: of fuell there was great scarsitie, of fluxes plentie: monie inough, but wares for their reléefe to bestow it on, had they none. Yet in this great necessitie, the poore people of the countrie were not spoiled, nor anie thing taken of them without paiment, nor

anie

anie outrage or offense doone by the Englishmen, except one, which was, that a Iustice in warre.
souldier tooke a pix out of a church, for which he was apprehended, and the king
not once remooued till the box was restored, and the offendor strangled. The peo- Note the force of
ple of the countries thereabout, hearing of such zeale in him, to the maintenance of iustice.
iustice, ministred to his armie victuals, and other necessaries, although by open *Hall.*
proclamation so to doo they were prohibited.

The French king being at Rone, and hearing that king Henrie was passed the The French
riuer of Some, was much displeased therewith, and assembling his councell to the king cōsulteth
how to deale
number of fiue and thirtie, asked their aduise what was to be doone. There was with the English-
men.
amongst these fiue and thirtie, his sonne the Dolphin, calling himselfe king of Dolphin king
Sicill; the dukes of Berrie and Britaine, the earle of Pontieu the kings yoongest of Sicill.
sonne, and other high estates. At length thirtie of them agréed, that the Englishmen should not depart vnfought withall, and fiue were of a contrarie opinion, but
the greater number ruled the matter: and so Montioy king at armes was sent to the The French k.
king of England to defie him as the enimie of France, and to tell him that he should sendeth defiance
to king Henrie.
shortlie haue battell. King Henrie aduisedlie answered: " Mine intent is to doo as K. Henries an-
it pleaseth God, I will not séeke your maister at this time; but if he or his séeke swer to the de-
fiance.
me, I will meet with them God willing. If anie of your nation attempt once to stop me
in my iournie now towards Calis, at their ieopardie be it; and yet I wish not anie of
you so vnaduised, as to be the occasion that I die your tawnie ground with your red
bloud."

When he had thus answered the herald, he gaue him a princelie reward, and
licence to depart. Vpon whose returne, with this answer, it was incontinentlie on
the French side proclamed, that all men of warre should resort to the constable to
fight with the king of England. Wherevpon, all men apt for armor and desirous of
honour, drew them toward the field. The Dolphin sore desired to haue béene at the
battell, but he was prohibited by his father: likewise Philip earle of Charolois would
gladlie haue béene there, if his father the duke of Burgognie would haue suffered
him: manie of his men stale awaie, and went to the Frenchmen. The king of England hearing that the Frenchmen approched, and that there was an other riuer for
him to passe with his armie by a bridge, and doubting least if the same bridge
should be broken, it would be greatlie to his hinderance, appointed certeine capteins
with their bands, to go thither with all speed before him, and to take possession
thereof, and so to keepe it, till his comming thither.

Those that were sent, finding the Frenchmen busie to breake downe their bridge,
assailed them so vigorouslie, that they discomfited them, and tooke and slue them;
and so the bridge was preserued till the king came, and passed the riuer by the
same with his whole armie. This was on the two and twentith day of October.
The duke of Yorke that led the vauntgard (after the armie was passed the riuer)
mounted vp to the heigth of an hill with his people, and sent out scowts to discouer
the countrie, the which vpon their returne aduertised him, that a great armie of
Frenchmen was at hand, approching towards them. The duke declared to the
king what he had heard, and the king therevpon, without all feare or trouble of
mind, caused the battell which he led himselfe to staie, and incontinentlie rode King Henrie
foorth to view his aduersaries, and that doone, returned to his people, and with rideth foorth to
take view of the
chéerefull countenance caused them to be put in order of battell, assigning to euerie French armie.
capteine such roome and place, as he thought conuenient, and so kept them still
in that order till night was come, and then determined to seeke a place to incampe &
lodge his armie in for that night.

There was not one amongst them that knew any certeine place whither to go, in
that vnknowne countrie: but by chance they happened vpon a beaten waie, white
in sight; by the which they were brought vnto a little village, where they were
refreshed

refreshed with meat and drinke somewhat more plenteouslie than they had béene diuerse daies before. Order was taken by commandement from the king after the armie was first set in battell arraie, that no noise or clamor should be made in the host; so that in marching foorth to this village, euerie man kept himselfe quiet: but at their comming into the village, fiers were made to giue light on euerie side, as there likewise were in the French host, which was incamped not past two hundred and fiftie pases distant from the English. The cheefe leaders of the French host were these: the constable of France, the marshall, the admerall, the lord Rambures maister of the crosbowes, and other of the French nobilitie, which came and pitched downe their standards and banners in the countie of saint Paule, within the territorie of Agincourt, hauing in their armie (as some write) to the number of thréescore thousand horssemen, besides footmen, wagoners and other.

They were lodged euen in the waie by the which the Englishmen must needs passe towards Calis, and all that night after their comming thither, made great cheare, and were verie merie, pleasant, and full of game. The Englishmen also for their parts were of good comfort, and nothing abashed of the matter, and yet they were both hungrie, wearie, sore trauelled, and vexed with manie cold diseases. Howbeit reconciling themselues with God by hoossell and shrift, requiring assistance at his hands that is the onelie giuer of victorie, they determined rather to die, than to yéeld, or flée. The daie following was the fiue and twentith of October in the yeare 1415, being then fridaie, and the feast of Crispine and Crispinian, a daie faire and fortunate to the English, but most sorrowfull and vnluckie to the French.

In the morning, the French capteins made thrée battels, in the vaward were eight thousand healmes of knights and esquiers, foure thousand archers, and fifteene hundred crosbowes which were guided by the lord de la Breth, constable of France, hauing with him the dukes of Orleance and Burbon, the earles of Ewe and Richmond, the marshall Bouciquault, and the maister of the crosbowes, the lord Dampier admerall of France, and other capteins. The earle of Vandosme with sixtéene hundred men of armes were ordered for a wing to that battell. And the other wing was guided by sir Guichard Dolphine, sir Clugnet of Brabant, and sir Lewes Bourdon, with eight hundred men of armes, of elect chosen persons. And to breake the shot of the Englishmen, were appointed sir Guilliam de Saueuses, with Hector and Philip his brethren, Ferrie de Maillie, and Allen de Gaspanes, with other eight hundred of armes.

In the middle ward, were assigned as manie persons, or more, as were in the formost battell, and the charge thereof was committed to the dukes of Bar and Alanson, the earles of Neuers, Vaudemont, Blamont, Salinges, Grant Prée, & of Russie. And in the rereward were all the other men of armes guided by the earles of Marle, Dampmartine, Fauconberg, and the lord of Lourreie capteine of Arde, who had with him the men of the frontiers of Bolonois. Thus the Frenchmen being ordered vnder their standards and banners, made a great shew: for suerlie they were estéemed in number six times as manie or more, than was the whole companie of the Englishmen, with wagoners, pages and all. They rested themselues, waiting for the bloudie blast of the terrible trumpet, till the houre betwéene nine and ten of the clocke of the same daie, during which season, the constable made vnto the capteins and other men of warre a pithie oration, exhorting and incouraging them to doo valiantlie, with manie comfortable words and sensible reasons. King Henrie also like a leader, and not as one led; like a souereigne, and not an inferior, perceiuing a plot of ground verie strong & méet for his purpose, which on the backe halfe was fensed with the village, wherein he had lodged the night before, and on both sides defended with hedges and bushes, thought good there to imbattell his host, and so ordered his men in the same place, as he saw occasion, and as stood for his most aduantage.

First

First he sent priuilie two hundred archers into a lowe medow, which was néere to the vauntgard of his enimies; but separated with a great ditch, commanding them there to kéepe themselues close till they had a token to them giuen, to let driue at their aduersaries: beside this, he appointed a vaward, of the which he made capteine Edward duke of Yorke, who of an haultie courage had desired that office, and with him were the lords Beaumont, Willoughbie, and Fanhope, and this battell was all of archers. The middle ward was gouerned by the king himselfe, with his brother the duke of Glocester, and the earles of Marshall, Oxenford, and Suffolke, in the which were all the strong bilmen. The duke of Excester vncle to the king led the rereward, which was mixed both with bilmen and archers. The horssemen like wings went on euerie side of the battell. The order of the English armie and archers. The vaward all of archers.

Thus the king hauing ordered his battels, feared not the puissance of his enimies, but yet to prouide that they should not with the multitude of horssemen breake the order of his archers, in whome the force of his armie consisted [¶ For in those daies the yeomen had their lims at libertie, sith their hosen were then fastened with one point, and their iackes long and easie to shoot in; so that they might draw bowes of great strength, and shoot arrowes of a yard long; beside the head] he caused stakes bound with iron sharpe at both ends, of the length of fiue or six foot to be pitched before the archers, and of ech side the footmen like an hedge, to the intent that if the barded horsses ran rashlie vpon them, they might shortlie be gored and destroied. Certeine persons also were appointed to remooue the stakes, as by the mooueing of the archers occasion and time should require, so that the footmen were hedged about with stakes, and the horssemen stood like a bulwarke betwéene them and their enimies, without the stakes. This deuise of fortifieng an armie, was at this time first inuented: but since that time they haue deuised caltraps, harrowes, and other new engins against the force of horssemen; so that if the enimies run hastilie vpon the same, either are their horsses wounded with the stakes, or their féet hurt with the other engins, so as thereby the beasts are gored, or else made vnable to mainteine their course. Archers the greatest force of the English armie. *Abr. F.* out of *Fabian* pag. 392. and *Polychron.* A politike inuention. *Hall.*

King Henrie, by reason of his small number of people to fill vp his battels, placed his vauntgard so on the right hand of the maine battell, which himselfe led, that the distance betwixt them might scarse be perceiued, and so in like case was the rereward ioined on the left hand, that the one might the more readilie succour an other in time of néed. When he had thus ordered his battels, he left a small companie to kéepe his campe and cariage, which remained still in the village, and then calling his capteins and soldiers about him, he made to them a right graue oration, moouing them to plaie the men, whereby to obteine a glorious victorie, as there was hope certeine they should, the rather if they would but remember the iust cause for which they fought, and whome they should incounter, such faint-harted people as their ancestors had so often ouercome. To conclude, manie words of courage he vttered, to stirre them to doo manfullie, assuring them that England should neuer be charged with his ransome, nor anie Frenchman triumph ouer him as a captiue; for either by famous death or glorious victorie would he (by Gods grace) win honour and fame. K. Henries oration to his men.

It is said that as he heard one of host vtter his wish to another thus: " I would to God there were with vs now so manie good soldiers as are at this houre within England! the king answered: I would not wish a man more here than I haue, we are indeed in comparison to the enimies but a few, but, if God of his clemencie doo fauour vs, and our iust cause (as I trust he will) we shall spéed well inough. But let no man ascribe victorie to our owne strength and might, but onelie to Gods assistance, to whome I haue no doubt we shall worthilie haue cause to giue thanks therefore. And if so be that for our offenses sakes we shall be deliuered into the hands of our enimies, A wish. A noble courage of a valiant prince.

enimies, the lesse number we be, the lesse damage shall the realme of England susteine: but if we should fight in trust of multitude of men, and so get the victorie (our minds being prone to pride) we should thervpon peraduenture ascribe the victorie not so much to the gift of God, as to our owne puissance, and thereby prouoke his high indignation and displeasure against vs: and if the enimie get the vpper hand, then should our realme and countrie suffer more damage and stand in further danger. But be you of good comfort, and shew your selues valiant, God and our iust quarrell shall defend vs, and deliuer these our proud aduersaries with all the multitude of them which you sée (or at the least the most of them) into our hands." Whilest the king was yet thus in spéech, either armie so maligned the other, being as then in open sight, that euerie man cried; Forward, forward. The dukes of Clarence, Glocester, and Yorke, were of the same opinion, yet the king staied a while, least anie ieopardie were not foreséene, or anie hazard not preuented. The Frenchmen in the meane while, as though they had béene sure of victorie, made great triumph, for the capteins had determined before, how to diuide the spoile, and the soldiers the night before had plaid the Englishmen at dice. The noble men had deuised a chariot, wherein they might triumphantlie conueie the king captiue to the citie of Paris, crieng to their soldiers; Haste you to the spoile, glorie and honor; little weening (God wot) how soone their brags should be blowne awaie.

Hall.
Here we may not forget how the French thus in their iolitie, sent an herald to king Henrie, to inquire what ransome he would offer. Wherevnto he answered, that within two or thrée houres he hoped it would so happen, that the Frenchmen should be glad to common rather with the Englishmen for their ransoms, than the English to take thought for their deliuerance, promising for his owne part, that his dead carcasse should rather be a prize to the Frenchmen, than that his liuing bodie should paie anie ransome. When the messenger was come backe to the French host, the men of warre put on their helmets, and caused their trumpets to blow to the battell. They thought themselues so sure of victorie, that diuerse of the noble men made such hast towards the battell, that they left manie of their seruants and men of warre behind them, and some of them would not once staie for their standards: as amongst other the duke of Brabant, when his standard was not come, caused a baner to be taken from a trumpet and fastened to a speare, the which he commanded to be borne before him in stéed of his standard.

But when both these armies comming within danger either of other, set in full order of battell on both sides, they stood still at the first, beholding either others demeanor, being not distant in sunder past thrée bow shoots. And when they had on both parts thus staied a good while without dooing anie thing, (except that certeine of the French horsemen aduancing forwards, betwixt both the hosts, were by the English archers constreined to returne backe) aduise was taken amongst the Englishmen, what was best for them to doo. Therevpon all things considered, it was determined, that sith the Frenchmen would not come forward, the king with his armie imbattelled (as yee haue hard) should march towards them, and so leauing their trusse and baggage in the village where they lodged the night before, onelie with their weapons, armour, and stakes prepared for the purpose, as yee haue heard.

The English gaue the onset.
These made somewhat forward, before whome there went an old knight sir Thomas Erpingham (a man of great experience in the warre) with a warder in his hand; and when he cast vp his warder, all the armie shouted, but that was a signe to the archers in the medow, which therwith shot wholie altogither at the vauward of the Frenchmen, who when they perceiued the archers in the medow, and saw they
The two armies ioine battell.
could not come at them for a ditch that was betwixt them, with all hast set vpon the fore ward of king Henrie, but yer they could ioine, the archers in the forefront, and

and the archers on that side which stood in the medow, so wounded the footmen, galled the horsses, and combred the men of armes, that the footmen durst not go forward, the horssemen ran togither vpō plumps without order, some ouerthrew such as were next them, and the horsses ouerthrew their masters, and so at the first ioining, the Frenchmen were foulie discomforted, and the Englishmen highlie incouraged.

When the French vauward was thus brought to confusion, the English archers cast awaie their bowes, & tooke into their hands, axes, malls, swords, bils, and other hand-weapons, and with the same slue the Frenchmen, vntil they came to the middle ward. Then approched the king, and so incouraged his people, that shortlie the second battell of the Frenchmen was ouerthrowne, and dispersed, not without great slaughter of men: howbeit, diuerse were releeued by their varlets, and conueied out of the field. The Englishmen were so busied in fighting, and taking of the prisoners at hand, that they followed not in chase of their enimies, nor would once breake out of their arraie of battell. Yet sundrie of the Frenchmen stronglie withstood the fiercenesse of the English, when they came to handie strokes, so that the fight sometime was doubtfull and perillous. Yet as part of the French horssemen set their course to haue entered vpon the kings battell, with the stakes ouerthrowne, they were either taken or slaine. Thus this battell continued thrée long houres. *The vauward of the French discomfited.* *Their battell beaten.*

The king that daie shewed himselfe a valiant knight, albeit almost felled by the duke of Alanson; yet with plaine strength he slew two of the dukes companie, and felled the duke himselfe; whome when he would haue yelded, the kings gard (contrarie to his mind) slue out of hand. In conclusion, the king minding to make an end of that daies iornie, caused his horssemen to fetch a compasse about, and to ioine with him against the rerereward of the Frenchmen, in the which was the greatest number of people. When the Frenchmen perceiued his intent, they were suddenlie amazed and ran awaie like sheepe, without order or arraie. Which when the king perceiued, he incouraged his men, and followed so quickelie vpon the enimies, that they ran hither and thither, casting awaie their armour: manie on their knees desired to haue their liues saued. *A valiant king.* *The French rerereward discomfited.*

In the meane season, while the battell thus continued, and that the Englishmen had taken a great number of prisoners, certeine Frenchmen on horssebacke, whereof were capteins Robinet of Borneuille, Rifflart of Clamas, Isambert of Agincourt, and other men of armes, to the number of six hundred horssemen, which were the first that fled, hearing that the English tents & pauillions were a good waie distant from the armie, without anie sufficient gard to defend the same, either vpon a couetous meaning to gaine by the spoile, or vpon a desire to be reuenged, entred vpon the kings campe, and there spoiled the hails, robbed the tents, brake vp chests, and carried awaie caskets, and slue such seruants as they found to make anie resistance. For which treason and haskardie in thus leauing their camp at the very point of fight, for winning of spoile where none to defend it, verie manie were after committed to prison, and had lost their liues, if the Dolphin had longer liued. *The kings campe robbed.*

But when the outcrie of the lackies and boies, which ran awaie for feare of the Frenchmen thus spoiling the campe, came to the kings eares, he doubting least his enimies should gather togither againe, and begin a new field; and mistrusting further that the prisoners would be an aid to his enimies, or the verie enimies to their takers in déed if they were suffered to liue, contrarie to his accustomed gentleness, commanded by sound of trumpet, that euerie man (vpon paine of death) should incontinentlie slaie his prisoner. When this dolorous decree, and pitifull proclamation was pronounced, pitie it was to sée how some Frenchmen were suddenlie sticked with daggers, some were brained with pollaxes, some slaine with malls, other *All the prisoners slaine.*

had their throats cut, and some their bellies panched, so that in effect, hauing respect to the great number, few prisoners were saued.

When this lamentable slaughter was ended, the Englishmen disposed themselues in order of battell, readie to abide a new field, and also to inuade, and newlie set on their enemies, with great force they assailed the earles of Marle and Faucon-bridge, and the lords of Louraie, and of Thine, with six hundred men of armes, who had all that daie kept togither, but now slaine and beaten downe out of hand.

A fresh onset.

¶ Some write, that the king perceiuing his enimies in one part to assemble togither, as though they meant to giue a new battell for preseruation of the prisoners, sent to them an herald, commanding them either to depart out of his sight, or else to come forward at once, and giue battel: promising herewith, that if they did offer to fight againe, not onelie those prisoners which his people alreadie had taken; but also so manie of them as in this new conflict, which they thus attempted should fall into his hands, should die the death without redemption.

A right wise and valiant challenge of the king.

The Frenchmen fearing the sentence of so terrible a decrée, without further delaie parted out of the field. And so about foure of the clocke in the after noone, the king when he saw no appearance of enimies, caused the retreit to be blowen; and gather-ing his armie togither, gaue thanks to almightie God for so happie a victorie, causing his prelats and chapleins to sing this psalme : In exitu Israel de Aegypto, and com-manded euerie man to knéele downe on the ground at this verse : Non nobis Domine, non nobis, sed nomini tuo da gloriam. Which doone, he caused Te Deum, with cer-teine anthems to be soong, giuing laud and praise to God, without boasting of his owne force or anie humane power. That night he and his people tooke rest, and re-freshed themselues with such victuals as they found in the French campe, but lodged in the same village where he laie the night before.

Thanks giuen to God for the vic-torie.

A woorthie ex-ample of a godlie prince.

Titus Liuius.

In the morning, Montioie king at armes and foure other French heralds came to' the K. to know the number of prisoners, and to desire buriall for the dead. Before he made them answer (to vnderstand what they would saie) he demanded of them whie they made to him that request, considering that he knew not whether the vic-torie was his or theirs? When Montioie by true and iust confession had cléered that doubt to the high praise of the king, he desired of Montioie to vnderstand the name of the castell néere adioining: when they had told him that it was called Agincourt, he said, Then shall this conflict be called the battell of Agincourt. He feasted the French officers of armes that daie, and granted them their request, which busilie sought through the field for such as were slaine. But the Englishmen suffered them not to go alone, for they searched with them, & found manie hurt, but not in ieopardie of their liues, whom they tooke prisoners, and brought them to their tents. When the king of England had well refreshed himselfe, and his souldiers, that had taken the spoile of such as were slaine, he with his prisoners in good order returned to his towne of Calis.

The battell of Agincourt.

When tidings of this great victorie was blowne into England, solemne processions and other praisings to almightie God with boune-fires and ioifull triumphes, were ordeined in euerie towne, citie, and burrow, and the maior & citizens of London went the morow after the daie of saint Simon and Iude from the church of saint Paule to the church of saint Peter at Westminster in deuout maner, rendring to God hartie thanks for such fortunate lucke sent to the king and his armie. The same sundaie that the king remooued from the campe at Agincourt towards Calis, diuerse French-men came to the field to view againe the dead bodies; and the pezants of the coun-trie spoiled the carcasses of all such apparell and other things as the Englishmen had left : who tooke nothing but gold and siluer, iewels, rich apparell and costlie armour. But the plowmen and pezants left nothing behind, neither shirt nor clout: so that the bodies laie starke naked vntill wednesdaie. On the which daie diuerse of the

The same day that the new maior went to Westminster to receiue his oth, the aduertise-ment of this no-ble victorie came to the citie in the morning betimes yer men were vp from their beds.
Register of maiors.

noble

noble men were conueied into their countries, and the remnant were by Philip earle Charolois (sore lamenting the chance, and mooued with pitie) at his costs & charges buried in a square plot of ground of fifteene hundred yards; in the which he caused to be made thrée pits, wherein were buried by account fiue thousand and eight hundred persons, beside them that were caried awaie by their fréends and seruants, and others, which being wounded died in hospitals and other places.

Thrée graues that held fiue thousand and eight hundred corpses.

After this their dolorous iournie & pitifull slaughter, diuerse clearks of Paris made manie a lamentable verse, complaining that the king reigned by will, and that councellors were parciall, affirming that the noble men fled against nature, and that the commons were destroied by their prodigalitie, declaring also that the cleargie were dumbe, and durst not saie the truth, and that the humble commons dulie obeied, & yet euer suffered punishment, for which cause by diuine persecution the lesse number vanquished the greater: wherefore they concluded, that all things went out of order, and yet was there no man that studied to bring the vnrulie to frame. It was no maruell though this battell was lamentable to the French nation, for in it were taken and slaine the flower of all the nobilitie of France.

There were taken prisoners, Charles duke of Orleance nephue to the French king, Iohn duke of Burbon, the lord Bouciqualt one of the marshals of France (he after died in England) with a number of other lords, knights, and esquiers, at the least fiftéene hundred, besides the common people. There were slaine in all of the French part to the number of ten thousand men, whereof were princes and noble men bearing baners one hundred twentie and six; to these of knights, esquiers, and gentlemen, so manie as made vp the number of eight thousand and foure hundred (of the which fiue hundred were dubbed knights the night before the battell) so as of the meaner sort, not past sixtéene hundred. Amongst those of the nobilitie that were slaine, these were the chéefest, Charles lord de la Breth high constable of France, Iaques of Chatilon lord of Dampier admerall of France, the lord Rambures master of the crossebowes, sir Guischard Dolphin great master of France, Iohn duke of Alanson, Anthonie duke of Brabant brother to the duke of Burgognie, Edward duke of Bar, the earle of Neuers an other brother to the duke of Burgognie, with the erles of Marle, Vaudemont, Beaumont, Grandprée, Roussie, Fauconberge, Fois and Lestrake, beside a great number of lords and barons of name.

Noble men prisoners.

The number slaine on the French part.

Of Englishmen, there died at this battell, Edward duke Yorke, the earle of Suffolke, sir Richard Kikelie, and Dauie Gamme esquier, and of all other not aboue fiue and twentie persons, as some doo report; but other writers of greater credit affirme, that there were slaine aboue fiue or six hundred persons. Titus Liuius saith, that there were slaine of Englishmen, beside the duke of Yorke, and the earle of Suffolke, an hundred persons at the first incounter. The duke of Glocester the kings brother was sore wounded about the hips, and borne downe to the grouud, so that he fell backwards, with his féet towards his enimies, whom the king bestrid, and like a brother valiantlie rescued from his enimies, & so sauing his life, caused him to be conueied out of the fight, into a place of more safetie. ¶ The whole order of this conflict which cost manie a mans life, and procured great bloudshed before it was ended, is liuelie described in Anglorum prælijs; where also, besides the manner of disposing the armies, with the exploits on both sides, the number also of the slaine, not much differing (though somewhat) from the account here named, is there touched, which remembrance verie fit for this place, it were an errour (I thinke) to omit; and therefore here inserted (with the shortest) as followeth.

Englishmen slaine.

Rich. Grafton.
Titus Liuius.

Ab{1} Fl. out of Anglorum prælijs sub Henr. 5.

     ——equitatus ordine primo,
Magnanimi satrapæ, post hos cecidere secundo
Nauarræ comes, & tuus archiepiscopus (ô Sans)
Præterea comites octo periere cruentis
         M 2   Vulneribus

Vulneribus, trita appellant quos voce barones
Plus centum, clari generis plus mille cadebant
Sexcenti, notiq; decem plus millia vulgi
Ex Francorum, ter centum perdidit Anglus:
Et penes Henricum belli victoria mansit.

Hall.   After that the king of England had refreshed himselfe, and his people at Calis, and that such prisoners as he had left at Harflue (as ye haue heard) were come to Calis vnto him, the sixt daie of Nouember, he with all his prisoners tooke shipping, and the same daie landed at Douer, hauing with him the dead bodies of the duke of Yorke, and the earle of Suffolke, and caused the duke to be buried at his colledge of Fodringhey, and the earle at new Elme. In this passage, the seas were so rough and troublous that two ships belonging to sir Iohn Cornewall, lord Fanhope, were driuen into Zeland; howbeit, nothing was lost, nor any person perisht. ¶ The maior of London, and the aldermen, apparelled in orient grained scarlet, and foure hundred commoners clad in beautifull murrie, well mounted, and trimlie horssed, with rich collars, & great chaines, met the king on Blackheath, reioising at his returne: and the clergie of London, with rich crosses, sumptuous copes, and massie censers, receiued him at saint Thomas of Waterings with solemne procession.

Titus Liuius.   The king like a graue and sober personage, and as one remembring from whome all victories are sent, séemed little to regard such vaine pompe and shewes as were in triumphant sort deuised for his welcomming home from so prosperous a iournie, in so *The great mo-* much that he would not suffer his helmet to be caried with him, whereby might haue *destie of the* appeared to the people the blowes and dints that were to be seene in the same; neither *king.* would he suffer any ditties to be made and soong by minstrels of his glorious victorie, for that he would wholie haue the praise and thanks altogither giuen to God. The news of this bloudie battell being reported to the French king as then soiourning at Rone, filled the court full of sorrow. But to remedie such danger as was like to insue, it was decreed by councell, to ordeine new officers in places of them that were slaine: and first he elected his chiefe officer for the wars, called the constable, the earle of Arminacke, a wise and politike capteine, and an ancient enimie to the Englishmen. Sir Iohn de Corsie was made maister of the crossebowes. Shortlie after, either for melancholie that he had for the losse at Agincourt, or by some sudden *The death of the* disease Lewes Dolphin of Viennois, heire apparant to the French king, departed this *Dolphin of* life without issue, which happened well for Robinet of Bourneuill, and his fellowes, *France.* *Part of those* as ye haue heard before, for his death was their life, & his life would haue béene *that spoiled the* *English campe.* their death.

1416.   After the French king had created new officers, in hope to relieue the state of his ———————— realme and countrie, sore shaken by the late great ouerthrow, it chanced, that Thomas duke of Excester capteine of Harflue, accompanied with thrée thousand Englishmen, made a great rode into Normandie, almost to the citie of Rone, in which iournie he got great abundance both of riches and prisoners: but in his returne, the earle of Arminacke newlie made constable of France, intending in his first enterprise to win the spurs, hauing with him aboue fiue thousand horssemen, incountred with the duke. *A sore conflict.*   The fight was handled on both parts verie hotlie, but bicause the Englishmen were not able to resist the force of the Frenchmen, the duke was constreined to retire with losse at the least of thrée hundred of his footmen.

Howbeit being withdrawen into an orchard, which was stronglie fensed and hedged about with thornes, the Frenchmen were not able to enter vpon the Englishmen; but yet they tooke from them all their horsses and spoile, & assaulted them till it was night, and then retired backe to the towne, not far distant from the place where they fought, called Vallemont: this was vpon the 14 day of March. In the morning vpon the breake of the daie, the Englishmen issued foorth of the orchard,

orchard, where they had kept themselues all the night, & drew towards Harflue, wherof the Frenchmen being aduertised, followed them, & ouertooke them vpon the sands néere to Chiefe de Caux, and there set on them: but in the end, the Frenchmen were discomfited, and a great number of them slaine by the Englishmen, which afterwards returned without more adoo, vnto Harflue. The French writers blame the constable for this losse, bicause he kept on the high ground with a number of men of war, and would not come downe to aid his fellowes.

In this fourth yeare of king Henries reigne, the emperour Sigismund, coosine germane to king Henrie, came into England, to the intent that he might make an attonement betwéene king Henrie and the French king: with whom he had beene before, bringing with him the archbishop of Remes, as ambassadour for the French king. At Calis he was honorablie recciued by the earle of Warwike lord deputie there, and diuerse other lords sent thither of purpose to attend him. More-ouer, the king sent thither thirtie great ships to bring him and his traine ouer. At Douer the duke of Glocester, and diuerse other lords were readie to receiue him, who at his approching to land, entered the water with their swords in their hands drawen; and by the mouth of the said duke declared to him, that if he intended to enter the land as the kings fréend, and as a mediator to intreat for peace, he should be suffered to arriue: but if he would enter as an emperour into a land claimed to be vnder his empire, then were they readie to resist him. This was thought necessarie to be doone for sauing of the kings prerogatiue, who hath full preheminence within his owne realme, as an absolute emperour.

When the emperour herevpon answered that he was come as the kings fréend, and as a mediator for peace, and not with any imperiall authoritie, he was of the duke and other his associats receiued with all such honor as might be deuised. The king with all his nobilitie receiued him on Blackheath the seuenth day of Maie, and brought him through London to Westminster with great triumph. Shortlie after there came also into England Albert duke of Holland, who was likewise fréend-lie interteined. Both these princes, the emperour and the duke of Holland were conueied to Windsore to saint Georges feast, and elected companions of the noble order of the garter, and had the collar and habit of the same to them deliuered, and sat in their stals all the solemnitie of the feast. Shortlie after that the feast was finished, the duke of Holland returned into his countrie; but the emperour tarried still, and assaied all maner of meanes to persuade the king to a peace with the Frenchmen.

But their euill hap, as they that were appointed by Gods prouidence to suffer more damage at the Englishmens hands, would not permit his persuasions to take place: for whereas peace was euen almost entring in at the gates, the king was sud-denlie stirred to displeasure vpon a new occasion, for he being aduertised of the losse of his men at the late conflict in the territorie of Rone (as ye haue heard) refused to heare this word peace once named. The emperour like a wise prince passed ouer that time till another season, that some fauourable aspect of the planets should séeme to further his purpose. And when he thought the same was come, he broched againe the vessell of concord and amitie, which he put in so faire a cup, and pre-sented it with such effectuous words, that suerlie the king had tasted it, if word had not béen brought about the same time that Harflue was besieged of the French both by water and land, as it was in déed: for the constable of France incouraged by his last conflict (though the same was not much to his praise) assembled an armie, and vpon a sudden laid siege to the towne. At the same instant Iohn vicount of Narbon the vice-admerall of France, brought the whole nauie to the riuage and shore adioining to the towne, in purpose to haue entered by the waterside; but the duke of Excester defeated his intent, and defended the towne verie manfullie.

King

An. Reg. 4.

The emperor Sigismund commeth into England.

Titus Liuius.

The strange manner of re-ceiuing the em-perour at Douer.

Albert duke of Holland cometh into England.

The emperor an earnest mediator for peace.

Harflue besieged by the French.

King Henrie aduertised hereof, meant at the first to haue gone with his nauie in person to the succors of his men; but the emperor dissuaded him from that purpose, aduising him rather to send some one of his capteins. The king following his louing and reasonable aduertisement, appointed his brother the duke of Bedford accompani-ed with the earles of March, Marshall, Oxford, Huntington, Warwike, Arundell, *Titus Liuius.* Salisburie, Deuonshire, and diuerse barons, with two hundred saile, to passe into Nor-mandie, for rescue of the towne of Harflue; which vsing great diligence shipped at Rie, and after some hinderance by contrarie winds, at length came to the mouth of the riuer of Seine on the daie of the Assumption of our ladie. When the vicount of Narbon perceiued the English nauie to approch, he couragiouslie set forward, and gat the possession of the mouth of the hauen. The duke of Bedford séeing his enimies

A great ouer-throw by sea giuen to the French by the duke of Bedford. thus fiercelie to come forward, set before certeine strong ships which at the first incoun-ter vanquished and tooke two French ships, the capteins whereof were too rash and forward.

The duke followed with all his puissance, and set on his enimies. The fight was long, but not so long as perillous, nor so perillous as terrible (for battels on the sea are desperate) till at length the victorie fell to the Englishmen, so that almost all the whole nauie of France, in the which were manie ships, hulkes, carikes, and other small *The French nauie of fiue hundred vessels vanquished. Titus Liuius.* vessels, to the number of fiue was sunke & taken. Amongst other vessels that were taken, thrée great carikes of Genoa, a citie in Italie, were sent into England. In the same conflict were slaine of the Frenchmen no small number, as appeared by the dead bodies, which were séene euerie daie swimming about the English ships. After this, *Titus Liuius. Harflue rescued by the English-men.* the duke of Bedford sailed vp to Harflue, & refreshed the towne both with vittels and monie; notwitstanding certeine other French gallies did what they could to haue letted that enterprise. When the earle of Arminacke heard that the puissant name of France was vanquished, he raised his siege & returned to Paris.

After this discomfiture and losse, the puissance of the Frenchmen began to decaie, for now the princes and nobles of the realme fell into diuision and discord among themselues, studieng how to reuenge their old priuat iniuries, & refused to take paine *Ciuill discord amongst the no-bles of France.* for succour of the publike weale and safegard of their countrie: wherevpon their power began to wax slender, their state brought into imminent danger of perpetuall bondage; which thing no doubt had fallen vpon them if king Henrie had longer liued. For as vpon once inconuenience suffered, manie doo follow, so was it in France at *Charles the French king not of souud memo-rie.* that time: for the king was not of sound memorie, the warre that was toward both doubtfull and perillous: the princes vntrustie and at discord: with a hundred things more (which might bring a realme to ruine) out of frame and order in France in those daies. After that the duke of Bedford was returned backe againe into Eng-land with great triumph and glorie, he was not so much thanked of the king his brother, as praised of the emperour Sigismund, being to him a stranger, which said openlie, that happie are those subiects which haue such a king, but more happie is the king that hath such subiects.

When the emperor perceiued that it was in vaine to mooue further for peace, he left off that treatie, and entered himselfe into a league with king Henrie, the con-*Titus Liuius. The emperor en-tereth into league with king Henrie.* tents of which league consisted cheeflie in these articles, that both the said emperour and king, their heires, and successors, should be freends ech to other, as alies and confederats against all manner of persons, of what estate or dégree so euer they *The côtents of the league.* were (the church of Rome, and the pope for that time being onlie excepted) and that neither they, nor their heires, nor successors should be present in councell or other place, where either of them, or his heires or successors might susteine damage, in lands, goods, honors, states, or persons: and that if anie of them should vnder-stand of losse or hinderance to be like to fall or happen to the others, they should impeach the same, or if that laie not in their powers, they should aduertise the others
thereof

thereof with all conuenient spéed: and that either of them, and their heires and successors should aduance the others honor and commoditie without fraud or deceipt. Moreouer, that neither of them, nor their heires and successors should permit their subiects to leauie warres against the others, and that it should be lawfull and frée for ech of their subiects, to passe into the others countrie, and there to remaine and make merchandize, either by sea or land, paieng the customes, gabels, and duties due and accustomed, according to the lawes and ordinances of the places and countries where they chanced to traffike.

Furthermore, that neither of the said princes, nor their heires nor successors should receiue any rebell, banished man, or traitor of the others wittinglie; but should cause euerie such person to auoid out of their countries, realmes, dominions, and iurisdictions. Againe, that neither of the said princes, their heires, nor successors should begin any wars against any other person, other than such as they had warres with at that present, without consent of the other his confederate, except in defence of themselues, their countries and subiects, in case of inuasion made vpon them. Also, that it should be lawful for the king of England, to prosecute his warres against the Frenchmen for recouerie of his right, as should séeme to him expedient; and likewise to the emperor, for recouerie of any part of his right in France, so that neither of them did preiudice the others right in that behalfe. Lastlie, that either of them should assist other, in recouerie & conquest of their rights, lands, and dominions, occupied, with-holden, and kept from them, by him that called himselfe king of France, and other the princes and barons of France. This aliance, with other conditions, agréements, and articles, was concluded & established on the nineteenth daie of October, in the yeare of our Lord 2416. This *Titus Liuius.* doone, the emperor returned homewards, to passe into Germanie; and the king partlie to shew him honor, and partlie bicause of his owne affaires, associated him to his towne of Calis.

During the time of their abode there, the duke of Burgognie offered to come to Calis, to speake with the emperor and the king, bicause he had knowledge of the league that was concluded betwixt them: the king sent his brother the duke of Glocester, and the earle of March to the water of Graueling, to be hostages for the duke of Burgognie: and also the earle of Warwike, with a noble companie to conduct him to his presence. At Graueling foord the dukes met, and after salutations doone, the duke of Burgognie was conueied to Calis, where of the emperor and the king he was highly welcomed and feasted. Here is to be noted, that in Iune last, *Continuation de la chronicles de Flanders.* the king of England had sent the earle of Warwike, and other, vnto the duke of Burgognie, as then remaining at Lisle, where by the diligent trauell of those English ambassadors, a truce was concluded betwixt the king of England and the duke *A truce betwéene the k. and the duke of Burgognie.* of Burgognie, touching onelie the counties of Flanders and Arthois, to indure from the feast of saint Iohn Baptist in that present yeare 1416, vnto the feast of saint Michaell, in the yeare next insuing. Which truce at the dukes being now at Calis (when no further agreement could be concluded) was prolonged vnto the feast of saint Michaell, that should be in the yeare 1419. The duke of Glocester was receiued at Graueling, by the earle Charolois, and by him honorablie conueied to saint Omers, and there lodged that night.

The next day, the earle Charolois came with diuerse noble men, to visit the duke of Glocester in his lodging, and when he entered into the chamber, the dukes backe was towards him, talking with some one of his seruants, and did not sée nor welcome the earle at his first entrie; but after he said to him shortlie without any great reuerence, or comming towards him; You be welcome faire cousine, and so passed foorth his tale with his seruants. The earle Charolois for all his youth, was not well content therewith, but yet suffered for that time. When the duke of Burgognie

gognie had doone all his businesse at Calis, after the ninth daie he returned to Graueling, where the duke of Glocester and he met againe, and louinglie departed, the one to Calis, and the other to saint Omers; for the which voiage the duke of Burgognie was suspected to be enemie to the crowne of France. After the dukes departing from Calis, the emperor was highlie feasted and rewarded, and at his pleasure sailed into Holland, & so rode towards Beame. The king likewise tooke ship, and returned into England on saint Lukes euen.

Titus Linius.
W. P.
About the same time, the king sent new ambassadors vnto the generall councell, which still continued at Constance, whither the emperour Sigismund also returned, chéefelie for chasing awaie of that pestilent smoke of schisme then blasted vp betwéene Iohn the thrée and twentith, Gregorie the twelfth, and Benet the thirteenth (as they intituled themselues) the thrée peruerse prelats, that all at once with such eager malice stroue togither for the sacred see of papasie Gods vicarage (that was) who to be highest here in earth. The infectious smother of this venemous vapor by the spirit of these holie men thus raised vp thorough faction and parts taking, had béene readie to choke all christendome, had not by the wisedome and autho-
The prerogatiue of the English nation in the generall councell.
ritie of the princes there, the same the sooner béene vented away. Here by the consent also of all nations it was ordeined in this councell, that this realme should haue the name of the English nation, and be called and reputed for one of the fiue principall nations of the councell, which to grant before that time, through enuie, other nations had vtterlie refused.

Thom. Walsi.

The kings oration.
The nineteenth of October, the parlement that had béene broken vp, by reason of the emperours comming, began againe at Westminster, and there the king made to them a short and pithie oration, declaring the iniuries latelie doone and committed by the French nation, shewing also the iust and lawful occasion of his warres: signifieng furthermore the great discord and ciuill dissention which reigned amongst the nobilitie of France, rehearsing manie things, for the which it were necessarie to follow the warres now in hand against them, and that without delaie. He therefore desired them to prouide for monie and treasure, that nothing should be wanting when nced required: his request heerein was granted, for euerie man was willing and glad to further that voiage, so that the cleargie granted two dismes, and the laitie a whole fiftéenth. In this parlement also Iohn Duke of Bedford was made gouernour
The duke of Bedford regent of England.

Tho. Walsi.
or regent of the realme, to hold and enioie the office so long as the king was occupied in the French wars. Moreouer, in this parlement, the king gaue to the duke of Excester a thousand pounds by yeare, to be paid out of his owne cofers; besides fortie pounds yearelie, which he was to receiue of the towne of Excester, of the kings reuenues there, and had the same grant confirmed by authoritie of the parlement, insomuch that some write, that in this parlement he was made duke of Excester, and not before.

Libels against the cleargie.
The king kept his Christmasse at Killingworth, and the morrow after Christmasse daie were certeine writings cast abroad, in great mens houses, and almost in euerie inne within the townes of S. Albons, Northampton, and Reading, conteining sharpe reproofes against all estates of the church, and it could not be knowne from whence those writings came, nor who was the author of them. The king verie earnestlie
1417
procured all things to be made readie for the warre, meaning to passe the next summer ouer into France. to recouer his right by force, which by no other meane he saw how to obteine. ¶ In this meane while had the Frenchmen hired a great num-
An. Reg. 5.
Tit. Liuius.
ber of Genowaies and Italians, with certeine carickes and gallies well appointed, the which being ioined with the French fléet, laie at the mouth of the riuer of Seine, and vp within the same riuer, both to stop all succour by sea that should come to them within Harflue, and also to waft abroad, and doo what damage they could vnto the English, as occasion serued.

The

The king therefore yer he passed ouer himselfe, sent the erle of Huntington to search and scowre the seas. This lustie earle, called Iohn Holland (sonne to the earle of Huntington, otherwise called duke of Excester, beheaded at Circester, in the time of king Henrie the fourth, and cousine to the king) with a great nauie of ships searched the sea, from the one coast to the other, and in conclusion incountred with nine of those great carickes of Genes (the which the lord Iaques the bastard of Burbon had reteined to serue the French king) and set on them sharplie. The conflict was great, and the fight long (continuing the more part of a summers daie) but in conclusion, the Frenchmen and Italians were ouercome and fled. Thrée of the greatest caricks with their patrons, and monsieur Iaques de Burbon their admerall were taken, with as much monie as should haue paid the soldiers of the whole fléet for halfe a yeare, and three other caricks were bowged. *A great exploit by sea doone by the earle of Huntington.* *Tit. Liuius.*

The earle returning backe with this good lucke, found the king at Hampton, who receiued him with thankes, as he had well deserued. Shortlie after, vpon the thrée and twentith of Iulie, the king tooke his ship at Portesmouth, accompanied with the dukes of Clarence and Glocester; the earls of Huntington, Marshall, War- wike, Deuonshire, Salisburie, Suffolke, and Summerset; the lords Rosse, Willoughbie, Fitz Hugh, Clinton, Scroope, Matreuers, Burchier, Ferreis of Grobie, and Ferreis of Chartleie, Fanhope, Graie of Codnore, sir Gilbert Umfreuile, sir Gilbert Talbot, and diuerse other; and so hauing wind and weather to his desire, the first daie of August he landed in Normandie, néere to a castell called Touque, where he consulted with his capteins, what waie was best for him to take concerning his high enterprise. *Tit. Liuius.*

His armie conteined the number of sixtéene thousand and foure hundred soldiers and men of warre of his owne purueiance, beside others. The duke of Clarence had in his retinue a hundred lances, and thrée hundred archers: and beside him, there were thrée earles, which had two hundred and fortie lances, and seauenteene hun- dred and twentie archers. The duke of Glocester foure hundred and seauentie lances, and fourteene hundred and ten archers. The earles of March, Marshall, Warwike, and Salisburie, each of them one hundred lances, and thrée hundred archers a peece. The earle of Huntington fortie lances, and six score archers. The earle of Suffolke thirtie lances, and fourescore and ten archers. Beside these, there were thirtéene lords, as Aburgauennie, Matreuers, Fitz Hugh, Clifford, Graie, Willoughbie, Talbot, Courtnie, Burchier, Roos, Louell, Ferrers of Chartlie, and Harington, the which had in their retinue the number of fiue hundred and six lances, and fiftéene hundred and fourescore archers. Also, there were in this armie thréescore and seauentéene knights, which had vnder them nine hundred and fortie fiue lances, and two thousand eight hundred and fiftie two archers; so that in all, there were fiue and twentie thousand, fiue hundred, and eight and twentie fighting men: of which number euerie fourth man was a lance. Beside the soldiers and men of warre, there were a thousand masons, carpenters, and other labourers. *The number of the armie 16400. of his owne pur- ueiance.* *Tit. Liuius.*

The Normans hearing of the kings arriuall, were suddenlie striken with such feare, that they fled out of their houses, leauing the townes and villages, and with their wiues and children, bag and baggage, got them into the walled townes, pre- paring there to defend themselues, & with all speed sent to the French king, requiring him to prouide for the defense and preseruation of his louing subiects. Héereupon, the men of war were appointed to resort into the strong townes, to lie within the same in garrisons, to resist the power of the Englishmen, so that all the walled townes and castels in Normandie were furnished with men, munition, and vittels. The king of England, when he had resolued with his councell for his proceeding in his enterprises, laid siege vnto the castell of Touque. The duke of Glocester that led the fore ward, had the charge of that siege, the which by force of assaults, and other warlike meanes, brought to that point, that they within yeelded the place *The Norm̃as flée to the walled townes.* *Touque castell besieged by the Englishmen & taken.*

into his hands, the ninth daie of August. The earle of Salisburie, who led the

Amberuilliers
castell taken.

battell, tooke the castell of Amberuilliers, the which was giuen to him by the king, and so this earle was the first that had anie territorie giuen him of the king in this new conquest. The king made at the winning of Touque eight and twentie knights, and left sir Robert Kirkelie capteine there.

After this, on deliberate aduise taken how to proceed, the k. set forward toward the towne of Caen in most warlike order, wasting the countrie on euerie side as he passed. Which towne standeth in a plaine fertile countrie, no stronger walled, than deepe ditched, and as then well vittelled and replenished with people : for the citizens fearing the kings comming, had there prouided all things necessarie and defensible. But his maiestie doubting least the Frenchmen, vpon their vnderstanding of his approch to the towne, would haue burned the suburbs and buildings without the walles, sent the duke of Clarence with a thousand men before him, to preuent that mischéefe. The duke comming thither, found the suburbs alreadie set on fire, but vsed such diligence to quench the same, that the most part was saued. He also wan the abbeie church of saint Stephan, which the Frenchmen were in hand to haue ouerthrowne, by vndermining the pillers ; but the duke obteining the place, filled vp the mines, and so preserued the church. He also wan a cell of nunnes, verie stronglie fensed, after the manner of warre.

Caen besieged.

Then came the king before the towne, who caused foorthwith to be cast a deepe trench, with an high mount, to kéepe them within from issuing foorth, and that doone, began fiercelie to assault the towne : but they within stood manfullie to their defense, so that there was sore and cruell fight betwixt them, and their enimies. But when king Henrie perceiued that he lost more than he wan by his dailie assaults, he left off anie more to assault it, and determined to ouerthrow the wals, with vndermining. Wherefore with all diligence, the pioners cast trenches, made mines, and brought timber : so that within a few daies, the wals stood onelie vpon posts,

Tit. Liuius.

readie to fall, when fire should be put to them. The king meaning now to giue a generall assault, caused all the capteins to assemble before him in councell, vnto whome he declared his purpose, commanding them not before the next daie to vtter it ; till by sound of trumpet they should haue warning to set forward towards the wals, least his determination being disclosed to the enimies, might cause them to

The order of the assault.

prouide the better for their owne defense. He also prescribed vnto them, what order he would haue them to keepe, in giuing the assault, and that was this ; that euerie capteine deuiding his band into three seuerall portions, they might be readie one to succéed in an others place, as those which fought should happilie be driuen backe and repelled.

In the morning next following, being the fourth of September, somewhat before the breake of the daie, he caused his people to approch the wals, and to shew countenance, as though they would giue a generall assault ; and whilest they were busied in assailing and defending on both sides, the Englishmen pearsed and brake thorough the wals by diuerse holes and ouertures made by the pioners, vnder the foundation : yet the king vpon diuerse respects, offered them within pardon of life if they would yeeld themselues and the towne to his mercie ; but they refusing that to doo, the assault was newlie begun, and after sore fight continued for the space of an houre, the Englishmen preuailed, and slew so manie as they found with weapon in hand, readie to resist them.

Titus Liuius.

The duke of Clarence was the first that entred with his people, and hauing got the one part of the towne, assailed them that kept the bridge, & by force beating them backe, passed the same, and so came to the wals on the other side of the towne, where the fight was sharpe and fierce betwixt the assailants and defendants ; but the duke with his people setting on the Frenchmen behind, as they stood at defense on

the

the wals, easilie vanquished them, so that the Englishmen entred at their pleasure. Caen taken by
the Englishmen. Thus when the king was possessed of the towne, he incontinentlie commanded all armours & weapons of the vanquished, to be brought into one place, which was immediatlie doone.

Then the miserable people came before the kings presence, and kneeling on their knées, held vp their hands, and cried; Mercie, mercie: to whome the king gaue certeine comfortable words, & bad them stand vp. All the night following, he caused his armie to kéepe themselues in order of battell within the towne, and on the next morning called all the magistrats & gouernors of the towne to the senat house, where some for their wilfull stubbornesse were adiudged to die, other were sore fined and ransomed. Then he calling togither his souldiers and men of warre, not onelie Diuision of
spoile. gaue them great praises and high commendations for their manlie dooings, but also distributed to euerie man, according to his desert, the spoile and gaine gotten in the towne, chéeflie bicause at the assault they had shewed good proofe of their man-hood and valiant courages.

After that the towne was thus woone, the lord Montainie, capteine of the castell, The capteine of
the castell held
out. would not yéeld, but made semblance, as though he meant to defend the place, to the vtterance: but after that he was sharplie called vpon by king Henrie, either to yéeld it, or else that he should be assured to haue all mercie and fauour se-questred from him, he tooke better aduise, and therevpon being in despaire of reléefe, made this composition, that if he were not rescued of the French power by a certeine daie, he should render the fortresse into the kings hands, with condition, that he and his souldiers should be suffered to depart with all their goods, the habiliments of warre onelie excepted. Herevpon twelue hostages were deliuered to the king, and when the daie came, being the twentith of September, they within *Titus Liuius.* rendred the castell into the kings hands; and thus, both the towne and castell Caen castell
yéelded. of Caen became English.

Whilest the king was thus occupied about his warres in Normandie, the Scots in *Titus Liuius.*
The Scots inuade
the English bor-
ders. great number, entring England, wasted the countrie with fire and sword whersoeuer they came. The English lords that were left in trust with the keeping of those parties of the realme, raised the whole power of the countries, so that there came togither the number of an hundred thousand men vpon Baw moore, where the generall *Titus Liuius.*
A great armie to
resist the Scots. assemblie was made, and as it chanced, the duke of Excester, vncle to the king, who had latelie before mustered a certeine number of men to conueie them ouer to the king as a new supplie to his armie there, was the same time in the north parts on pilgrimage at Bridlington; and hearing of this inuasion made by the Scots, tooke vpon him to be *Thom. Walsin.* generall of the armie prepared against them, and to giue them battell. Also, the archbishop of Yorke, although he was not able to sit on horssebacke by reason of his great age, caused himselfe to be caried foorth in a charet in that iournie, the better to incourage other. But the Scots hearing that the Englishmen approched toward them with such puissance, withdrew backe into their countrie, and durst not abide the The Scots recoile
home. bickering; either because they mistrusted an infortunat euent on their side, by reason of the English prowesse; or else for that they had learned by others ouerthrowes to auoid the like, wherein standeth a profitable point of wisedome, as the poet verie sententiouslie saith,

Feliciter sapit qui in alieno periculo sapit. *Plautus.*

The same time, the lord Cobham, sir Iohn Oldcastell, whilest he shifted from place Sir Iohn Oldcas-
tell. to place to escape the hands of them, who he knew would be glad to laie hold on The seruants of
the abbat of S. him, had conueied himselfe in secret wise into an husbandmans house, not farre from Albons go about S. Albons, within the precinct of a lordship belonging to the abbat of that towne. to catch the lord The abbats seruants getting knowledge hereof, came thither by night, but they missed Cobham. their purpose, for he was gone; but they caught diuerse of his men, whome they

N 2   caried

caried streict to prison. The lord Cobham herewith was sore dismaied, for that some of them that were taken were such as he trusted most, being of counsell in all his deuises. In the same place, were found books written in English, and some of those books in times past had beene trimlie gilt, limned, and beautified with images, the heads whereof had béene scraped off, and in the Letanie they had boltted foorth the name of our ladie, and of other saints, till they came to the verse Parce nobis Domine. Diuerse writings were found there also, in derogation of such honor as then was thought due our ladie. The abbat of saint Albons sent the booke so difigured with scrapings & blottings out, with other such writings as there were found, vnto the king; who sent the booke againe to the archbishop, to shew the same in his sermons at Paules crosse in London, to the end that the citizens and other people of the realme might vnderstand the purposes of those that then were called Lollards, to bring them further in discredit with the people.

In this meane time that the king of England was occupied about Caen, the French-men had neither anie sufficient power to resist him, nor were able to assemble an host togither in their necessitie, by reason of the dissention among themselues: for their king was so simple, that he was spoiled both of treasure and kingdome, so that euerie

Commendation of the Dolphin of France.

man spent and wasted he cared not what. Charles the Dolphin being of the age of sixtéene or seauentéene yeares, bewailed the ruine and decaie of his countrie, he onelie studied the reléefe of the common-wealth, and deuised how to resist his enimies; but hauing neither men nor monie, was greatlie troubled and disquieted in mind. In conclusion, by the aduise and counsell of the earle of Arminacke the constable of France, he found a meane to get all the treasure & riches which his moother queene Isabell had gotten and hoorded in diuerse secret places: and for the common defense and profit of his countrie he wiselie bestowed it in waging souldiers, and preparing of things necessarie for the warre.

The yoong Dolphin fléeced his old moother of hir treasure, what mischéefe rose vpon it.

The duke of Burgognie chéefe dooer in France.

The quéene forgetting the great perill that the realme then stood in, remembring onelie the displeasure to hir by this act doone, vpon a womanish malice, set hir husband Iohn duke of Burgognie in the highest authoritie about the king, giuing him the regiment and direction of the king and his realme, with all preheminence & souereigntie. The duke of Burgognie hauing the sword in his hand, in reuenge of old iniuries, began to make warre on the Dolphin, determining, that when he had tamed this yoong vnbrideled gentleman, then would he go about to withstand, and beat backe the common enimies of the realme. The like reason mooued the Dolphin, for he minded first to represse the authours of ciuill discord, before he would set vpon forreine enimies, and therefore prepared to subdue and destroie the duke of Burgognie, as the cheefe head of that mischeefe, whereby the realme was vnquieted, decaied, and in manner brought to vtter ruine. Thus was France afflicted, and in euerie part troubled with warre and diuision, and no man to prouide remedie, nor once put foorth his finger for helpe or succour.

King Henrie in the meane time following victorie and his good successe, sent the duke of Clarence to the sea coast, where (with great difficultie) he got the

Baieux také.

Liseaux taken.

towne of Baieux, whereof the lord Matreuers was appointed capteine. The duke of Glocester also finding small resistance, tooke the citie of Liseaux, of which citie sir Iohn Kirkleie was ordeined capteine. King Henrie himselfe taried still at Caen, fortifieng the towne and castell, and put out fiftéene hundred women and impotent

Caen peopled with English inhabitants.

A worthie & rare example of equitie in king Henrie.

persons, replenishing the towne with English people. Where while the king soiourned, he kept a solemne feast, and made manie knights; beside that, he shewed there an example of great pitie and clemencie: for in searching the castell, he found innumerable substance of plate and monie belonging to the citizens, whereof he would not suffer one penie to be touched, but restored the same to the owners, deliuering to euerie man that which was his owne.

When

When the fame of his mercifull dealing herein, of his bountie to captiues, and of his fauourable vsing of those that submitted themselues to his grace, was spred abroad, all the capteins of the townes adioining, came willinglie to his presence, offering to him themselues, their townes, and their goods, whervpon he made proclamation, that all men, which had, or would become his subiects, and sweare to him allegiance, should inioy their goods, and liberties, in as large or more ample maner, than they did be-fore: which gentle interteining of the stubborne Normans, was the verie cause, why they were not onlie content, but also glad to remooue and turne from the French part, and become subiects to the crowne of England. The Normans willinglie sworne English.

When the king had set Caen in good order, he left there for capteins, the one of the towne, the other of the castell, sir Gilbert-Umfreuill earle of Kime or Angus, & sir Gilbert Talbot, and made bailiffe there sir Iohn Popham, and so departed from Caen the first of October, and comming to the castell of Courfie, within three daies had it rendred to him. From whence, the fourth of October, he came vnto Argenton; they within that towne and castell offered, that if no rescue came by a daie limited, they would deliuer both the towne and castell into the kings hands, so that such as would abide and become the kings faithfull subiects should be receiued, the other to depart with their goods and liues saued whither they would: the king accepted their offer. When the daie limited came, and no succours appeared, they yéelded according to the couenants, and the king performed all that on his behalfe was promised. The lord Graie of Codnor was appointed capteine there. After this, resorted dailie to the king, of the Normans, people of all sorts aud degrées, to sweare to him fealtie and homage. The citie of Sées which was well inhabited, and wherein were two abbeies of great strength, one of them yéelded to the king, and so likewise did diuerse other townes in those parties, without stroke striken. The castell of Courfie render-ed. Argenton build-ed. The voluntarie subiection of the French. Sées yéelded.

The towne of Alanson abode a siege for the space of eight daies, they within defend-ing it right valiantlie at the first; but in the end, considering with themselues, what small hope there was for anie succours to come to remooue the siege, they grew to a compo-sition, that if within a certeine daie they were not reléeued, they should yéeld both the towne and castell into the kings hands, which was doone: for no succours could be heard of. The king appointed capteine of this towne, the duke of Glocester, and his lieutenant sir Ralfe Lentall. The duke of Britaine vnder safe conduct came to the king, as he was thus busie in the conquest of Normandie, and after sundrie points treated of betwixt them, a truce was taken, to indure from the seuenth daie of Nouem-ber, vnto the last of September, in the yeare next following, betwixt them, their soul-diers, men of warre, and subiects. The like truce was granted vnto the quéene of Ierusalem and Sicill, & to hir sonne Lewes, for the duchie of Aniou, and the countie of Maine, the duke of Britaine being their deputie for concluding of the same truce. Alanson besieged and yéelded vp. *Titus Liuius.* A truce taken be-twéene king Henrie and the duke of Britaine.

About the same time also, at the sute of Charles the Dolphin, a treatie was in hand at Tonque, for a finall peace, but it came to none effect. From Alanson the king set forward towards the towne and castell of Faleis, meaning to besiege the same, where the Frenchmen appointed to the kéeping of it, had fortified the towne by all meanes possible, and prepared themselues to defend it to the vttermost. The earle of Salisburie was first sent thither before with certeine bands of souldiers to inclose the enimies within the towne, & to view the strength thereof. After him came the king with his whole armie, about the first of December, and then was the towne besieged on ech side. The king lodged before the gate that leadeth to Caen, the duke of Clarence before the castell that standeth on a rocke and the duke of Glocester laie on the kings right hand, and other lords & noble men were assigned to their places as was thought expedient. And to be sure from taking damage by anie sudden inuasion of the eni-mies, Faleis besieged.

mies,

mies, there were great trenches and rampiers cast and made about their seuerall campes, for defense of the same.

The Frenchmen notwithstanding this siege, valiantlie defended their wals, and sometimes made issues foorth, but small to their gaine: and still the Englishmen with their guns and great ordinance made batterie to the wals and bulworks. The winter season was verie cold, with sharpe frost, & hard weather; but the Englishmen made such shift for prouision of all things necessarie to serue their turns, that they were sufficientlie prouided, both against hunger and cold: so that in the end, the Frenchmen perceiuing they could not long indure against them, offered to talke, and agréed to giue ouer the towne, if no rescue came by a certeine daie appointed. About the same season was sir Iohn Oldcastell, lord Cobham taken, in the countrie of Powes land, in the borders of Wales, within a lordship belonging to the lord Powes, not without danger and hurts of some that were at the taking of him: for they could not take him, till he was wounded himselfe.

Thom. Wals.

Sir Iohn Old-castell taken.

At the same time, the states of the realme were assembled at London, for the leuieng of monie, to furnish the kings great charges, which he was at about the maintenance of his wars in France: it was therefore determined, that the said sir Iohn Oldcastell should be brought, and put to his triall, yer the assemblie brake vp. The lord Powes therefore was sent to fetch him, who brought him to London in a litter, wounded as he was: herewith, being first laid fast in the Tower, shortlie after he was brought before the duke of Bedford, regent of the realme, and the other estates, where in the end he was condemned; and finallie was drawen from the Tower vnto saint Giles field, and there hanged in a chaine by the middle, and after consumed with fire, the gallowes and all.

Sir Iohn Old-castell executed.

When the daie was come, on the which it was couenanted that the towne of Faleis should deliuered, to wit, the second of Ianuarie, because no succours appeared, the towne was yéelded to the king: but the castell held out still, into the which the capteine and gouernour both of the towne and castell had withdrawne themselues, with all the souldiers; and being streictlie besieged, the capteine defended himselfe and the place right stoutlie, although he was sore laid to, vntill at length, perceiuing his people wearied with continuall assaults, and such approches as were made to and within the verie wals, he was driuen to compound with the king, that if he were not succoured by the sixt of Februarie, then should he yeeld himselfe prisoner, and deliuer the castell; so that the souldiers should haue licence to depart, with their liues onelie saued. When the daie came, the couenants were performed, and the castell rendered to the kings hands, for no aid came to the rescue of them within. The capteine named Oliuer de Mannie was kept as prisoner, till the castell was repared at his costs and charges, because the same, through his obstinat wilfulnesse, was sore beaten and defaced, with vnd'erminings and batterie. Capteine there, by the king, was appointed sir Henrie Fitz Hugh.

1418

Faleis rendered vp to king Henrie.

After this, king Henrie returned to Caen, and by reason of a proclamation which he had caused to be made for the people of Normandie, that had withdrawne themselues foorth of the baliwicks of Caen and Faleis, he granted awaie to his owne people the lands of those that came not in vpon that proclamation, and in speciall, he gaue to the duke of Clarence, during his life, the vicounties of Auge, Orbec, and Ponteau de Mer, with all the lands of those that were withdrawne foorth of the same vicounties. This gift was made the sixteenth of Februarie, in this fift yeare of this kings reigne. All the Lent season, the king laie at Baieux with part of his armie, but the residue were sent abroad, for the atchiuing of certeine enterprises, because they should not lie idle.

Histoir des ducs de Normandie.

Tho. Walsin.
Titus Liuius.

¶ In this yeare 1418, and in the first yeare of the reigne of this victorious king, Henrie the fift, on Easter daie in the after noone (a time which required deuotion) at

Abr. Fl. out of *Fabian* pag. 397. and *Iohn Stow.* pag. 598.

a sermon

a sermon in saint Dunstans in the east of London, a great fraie happened in the said church, where through manie people were sore wounded, and one Thomas Petwarden Slaughter and bloudshed in S. fishmonger that dwelt at Sprots keie was slaine outright; as they (vpon a good intent) Dunstans church did what they could (to their owne perill as vnfortunatlie it befell) to appease the on Easter day. turmoile, and to procure the kéeping of the kings peace. Herevpon the church was suspended, and the beginners of the broile, namelie the lord Strange and sir Iohn Trussell knight (betwéene whome such coles of vnkindnesse were kindled (at the instigation of their wiues, gentlewomen of euill disposition and at curssed hatred Women full of one with another) that their husbands ment at their méeting in the said church to haue mischéefe. slaine one another) were committed to the counter in the Pultrie. Two wise gentle-men (I wisse) and well aduised (no doubt) who without regard of day, place, people, preacher, or perill that might insue; were so forward to become the instrument of their mischieuous wiues malice; the fulfilling wherof they would haue forborne, if with discretion they had pondered the verdict of the poet concerning the said sex:

Fœmina lætalis, fœmina plena malis.

The archbishop of Canturburie, when he had intelligence giuen of this outragious *Record. Cant.* prophanation of the church, caused the offendors to be excommunicat, as well at Paules, as in all other parish churches of London. Shortlie after, to wit on the one and twentith of Aprill, the said archbishop sat at saint Magnus, vpon inquisition for the authors of the said disorder, and found the fault to consist speciallie in the lord Strange and his wife. So that vpon the first daie of Maie next following in Paules The principall church, before the said archbishop, the maior of London, and others, the said offen-offendors pu-dors submitted themselues to doo penance, and sware to doo it in such sort as to them nishment. it was inioined; namelie, as followeth. That immediatlie all their seruants should (in their shirts) go before the parson of saint Dunstans, from Paules to the said saint Dunstans church; and the lord Strange bare headed, with his ladie barefooted; Reignold Kenwood archdeacon of London following them. Also it was appointed them, that at the consecrating or hallowing of the said church (which they had prophaned) the ladie should fill all the vessels with * water, and offer likewise to the * Not teares of altar an ornament of ten pounds; and the lord hir husband a pix of siluer of fiue hir cōplaint (I trust) for sorrow pounds. Which doone by waie of a satisfactorie expiation, it is likelie they were of hir sinne. absolued: but the lord Strange had first made the wife of the said Petwarden slaine in the fraie, large amends: as Fabian saith, though in what sort he maketh no mention.]

Whilest the king of England wan thus in Normandie, his nauie lost nothing on the sea, but so scowred the streames, that neither Frenchmen nor Britons durst once appeare; howbeit, on a daie there arose such a storme and hideous tempest, that if the earles of March and Huntington had not taken the hauen of Southhampton, the whole nauie had perished; & yet the safegard was strange, for in the same hauen, two A sore tēpest. balingers, and two great carickes, laden with merchandize were drowned, and the broken mast of another caricke was blowen ouer the wall of the towne. When the A violent tem-furie of this outragious wind and weather was asswaged, and the sea waxed calme, pest of wind the earles of March and Huntington passed ouer with all their companie, and landing in Normandie, they marched through the countrie, destroieng the French villages, and taking preies on each hand, till they came to the king where he then was.

In the sixt yeare of king Henries reigne, he sent the earle of Warwike, and the An. Reg. 6. lord Talbot, to besiege the strong castell of Dampfront. The duke of Clarence was also sent to besiege and subdue other townes, vnto whome, at one time and other, we find, that these townes vnderwritten were yéelded, wherein he put capteins as Townes in Nor-followeth. In Courton Iohn Aubin, in Barney William Houghton, in Chambis Iames mandie yéelded Neuill, in Bechelouin the earle Marshall, in Harecourt Richard Wooduill esquier, in to K. Henrie. Fangernon Iohn S. Albon, in Creueper sir Iohn Kirbie to whom it was giuen, in

Anuilliers,

Anuilliers Robert Hornebie, in Bagles sir Iohn Arthur, in Fresnie le vicont sir Robert Brent.

The duke of Glocester the same time, accompanied with the earle of March, the lord Greie of Codner, and other was sent to subdue the townes in the Ile of Constantine, vnto whome these townes hereafter mentioned were yéelded, where he appointed capteins as followeth. At Carentine the lord Botreux, at Saint Lo Reginald West, at Valoignes Thomas Burgh, at Pont Done Dauie Howell, at the Haie de Pais sir Iohn Aston, at saint Sauieur le vicont sir Iohn Robsert, at Pontorson sir Robert Gargraue, at Hamberie the earle of Suffolke lord of that place by gift, at Briqueuill the said earle also by gift, at Auranches sir Philip Hall bailiffe of Alanson, at Vire the lord Matreuers, at S. Iames de Beumeron the same lord.

Chierburgh be-
sieged by the
English.

After that the duke had subdued to the kings dominion, the most part of all the townes in that Ile of Constantine, Chierburgh excepted, he returned to the king, and forthwith was sent thither againe to besiege that strong fortresse, which was fenced with men, munition, vittels, and strong walles, towers, and turrets, in most defensible wise, by reason whereof it was holden against him the space of fiue moneths, although he vsed all waies and meanes possible to annoie them within, so that manie fierce assaults, skirmishes, issues, and other exploits of warre were atchieued, betwixt the Frenchmen within, and the Englishmen without: yet at length, the Frenchmen were so constreined by power of baterie, mines, and other forceable waies of approchings, that they were glad to compound to deliuer the place, if no rescue came to raise the siege, either from the Dolphin, that then was retired into Aquitane, or from the duke of Burgognie that then laie at Paris, within the terme of thrée score and two daies (for so long respit the duke granted) but they trusting further vpon his lenitie and gentlenesse hoped to get a far longer terme.

Now were the Dolphin and the duke of Burgognie growen to a certeine agréement, by mediation of cardinals sent from the pope, so that the Englishmen suerlie thought that they would leauie a power, and come downe to rescue Chierburg. The duke of Glocester therefore caused his camps to be stronglie intrenched, and manie defensible blockehouses of timber to be raised, like to small turrets, that the same might be a safegard to his people, and to conclude, left nothing vnforeséene nor vndoone, that was auailable for the defense of his armie. The king doubting least some power should be sent downe, to the danger of his brother, and those that were with him at this siege, caused two thousand men to be imbarked in thirtie ships of the west countrie, by order sent vnto certeine lords there.

Chierburgh
yéelded to the
Englishmen.

The Frenchmen within the towne, perceiuing those succors to approch neere to the towne, thought verelie that there had béene a power of Frenchmen comming to their aid: but when they saw them receiued as fréends into the English campe, their comfort was soone quailed; and so when the daie appointed came, being the nineteenth of October, or rather about the later end of Nouember (as the historie of the dukes of Normandie hath) they rendred vp both the towne and castell, according to the couenants. The lord Greie of Codnore was made the kings lieutenant there, and after his deceasse, sir Water Hungerford. About the same time, or rather before, as Titus Liuius

The castell of
Dampfront
yéelded.

W. P.

writeth, to wit, the two and twentith of Iune, the strong castell of Dampfront was yéelded into the hands of the earle of Warwike, to the kings vse. But the historie writen of the dukes of Normandie affirmeth, that it was surrendred the two and twentith of September, after the siege had cōtinued about it from Aprill last. The king by honorable report of other, and of his owne speciall knowledge, so rightlie asserteined of the great valure that (for feats at armes and policie in warre) was alwaies found in the person of that Iohn Bromley esquier (spoken of a little here before) for which his maiestie so sundrie waies roiallie rewarded him againe; some specialtie yet of the gentlemans merits togither with the souereignes bountie to him among other, séemes here (at mention of this Dampfront, whereof shortlie after he was capteine) verie

verie well to deserue a place: and to that purpose as the king in Iulie went ouer againe, and this Iohn Bromley in Iune the same yeare, with conduct of charge was sent afore, imploieng himselfe still in venturous actiuitie with great annoie to the enimie: his highnesse for good liking of the same, and for hartening and example to other (in Aprill next following) gaue fourtie pounds land to him and his heires males by letters patents in words as followeth, and remaining yet of record in the Tower of London.

A copie of the said letters patents.

HENRICUS Dei gratiâ rex Angliæ & Franciæ & dominus Hiberniæ, omnibus ad quos præsentes litteræ peruenerint salutem. Sciatis quòd de gratia nostra speciali & pro bono seruitio quod dilectus seruiens noster Iohannes Bromley nobis impendit & impendet in futurum: dedimus & concessimus ei hospitium de Molay Bacon, infra comitatum nostrum de Baieux, ac omnes terras, tenementa, redditus, hæreditates, & possessiones infra ducatum nostrum Normandiæ, quæ fuerunt Alani de Beaumont nobis rebellis, vt dicitur. Habendum & tenendum præfato Iohanni & hæredibus suis masculis de corpore suo procreatis, hospitium, terras, & tenementa, redditus, hæreditates, & possessiones supradictas, vna cum omnimodis franchesijs, priulegijs, iurisdictionibus, wardis, maritagijs, releuijs, eschetis, forisfacturis, feodis militum, aduocationibus ecclesiarum, & aliorum beneficiorum ecclesiasticorū quorumcúnq; terris, pratis, pasturis, boscis, warēnis, chaseis, aquis, vijs, stagnis, molēdinis, viuarijs, moris, mariscis, ac alijs cōmoditatibus quibuscúnq; dictis hospitio, terris, tenementis, redditibus, hæreditatibus, & possessionibus pertinentibus siue spectantibus, ad valorem quadraginta librarum sterlingorum per annum, tenendis de nobis & hæredibus nostris per homagium, &c.: ac reddendo nobis, & eisdem hæredibus nostris apud castrum nostrum de Baieux vnam zonam pro lorica, ad festum Natuitatis sancti Iohannis Baptistæ singulis annis: nec non faciendo alia seruitia, &c. Reseruato, &c. Prouiso semper, &c. Castro seu ciuitati nostro de Baieux, &c. Quódq; prædictum hospitium, &c. In cuius rei, &c. Teste me ipso apud dictam ciuitatem nostram de Baieux, 18 die Aprilis, anno regni nostri sexto, per ipsum regem.

Yet heereat the noble prince not staieng his bountie, but rather regarding euer how iustlie new merits doo deserue new dignities, and peraduenture the more mooued somewhat to reare vp the degrée of this esquire, toward the state of his stocke, who a long time before had béene indued with knighthood, and also bicause that vnto the duke of Buckingham he was of bloud, which his behauiour alwaies had from staine so farre preserued, as rather brought to it some increase of glorie, did (in the most worthie wise which to that order belongeth) dub him knight of warfare in field, made him also capteine generall of this strong castell of Dampfront, seneshall and great constable of Bosseuile le Rosse, with other offices and titles of worship, as partlie may appeare by a déed, in which this knight taking patterne at his princes benignitie had giuen an annuitie of twentie pounds to his kinsman Walter Audeley.

Sir Iohn Bromley made capteine of Dampfrōt.

A copie of that writing sundrie waies so well seruing to the truth of the storie was thought right necessarie heere to be added, thus.

OMNIBUS ad quos hoc præsens scriptum peruenerit, Iohānes de Bromley miles, capitaneus generalis de Dampfront, senescallus & magnus constabularius de Bosseuile le Rosse & March ibidem, salutem. Sciatis quòd pro bono & fideli seruitio quod dilectus consanguineus meus Gualterus de Audeley mihi fecerit, tam infra regnum

Angliæ quàm extra, & præcipuè contra Francos : dedisse & concessisse, & hac præsenti charta mea confirmasse eidem Gualtero vnum annualem redditum viginti librarum, exeuntem de manerio meo de Bromley, & omnibus alijs terris & tenementis meis infra regnum Angliæ, vna cum herbagio pro quatuor equis habendo infra boscos meos de Bromley & Willoughbridge, & octo carucatis fœni capiendis infra prata mea de Shurlebrooke & Foordsmedo annuatim, durante tota vita prædicti Gualteri, in festo sancti Iacobi apostoli.   Et si contingat prædictum annualem redditum, a retrò fore in aliquo festo, durante termino prædicto ; tunc bene licebit eidem Gualtero, in manerio meo, & omnibus alijs terris meis prædictis distringere, & districtiones inde captas penes se retinere, quousq; de redditu prædicto, vna cum arreragijs (si quæ fuerint) plenariè fuerit persolutum & satisfactum.   Et vlteriùs volo, quòd prædictus Gualterus habebit liberum egressum & regressum cum equis suis prædictis, & ad asportandum fœnum predictū, quandocunq; voluerit, per omnes semitas & vias, sine aliqua contradictione mei prædicti Iohannis, aut hæredum meorum aliquali.   Reddendo inde mihi ipsi Gualtero annuatim in festo sancti Georgij martyris, si tunc fuerim infra regnum Angliæ, vnum par calcarium deauratorum, pro omnibus.   Et etiam volo & concedo quòd prædictus Gualterus liber sit, durante tota vita sua, ad volandum, venandum, piscandum, & alias commoditates percipiendum, tam infra manerium meum de Bromley quàm in omnibus alijs manerijs, terris, & tenementis meis infra regnum Angliæ, sine aliqua contradictione vel impedimento mei præfati Iohannis de Bromley militis, hæredum, aut assignatorum meorum aliquali.   Et vt fidele testimonium præsentibus habeatur, sigillum meum apposui : hijs testibus Roberto de Bruyn milite, Iohanne de Holland, Gulihelmo de Brereton, Richardo le Greuill, Iohanne de Egerton, Richardo le Beston, Thoma le Creu, & alijs.   Datum apud Dampfront prædicto, 12 die mensis Augusti, anno regni regis Henrici quinti post conquestum sexto.

The old armes of the house of Bromley being quarterlie gules and ore per fesse indented, had in the seale to this déed, an inscutchen charged with a griffin surgiant ; his creast, out of a crowne, a demilion supporting a standard charged with a lion passant gardant ; about the shield was ingrauen, Sigillum Iohannis de Bromley militis. That inscutchen and creast (as like is) giuen him in laudable remembrance for his valiant recouerie of the standard at the sharpe and bloodie skirmish by Corbie.]   The earle of Warwike, and the lord Talbot, after the winning of this fortresse, made speed to come vnto the siege of Rone, where they were imploied, as after shall appeare. And in like manner, the duke of Glocester, hauing once got the possession of Chierburgh, hasted towards the same siege : for the better furnishing of which enterprise, he had first caused an armie of fiftéene thousand men to be brought ouer to him vnder the leading of his vncle the duke of Excester, who imbarking with the same, about the feast of the holie Trinitie, was appointed by the king to besiege the citie of Eureux, as the earle of Augus, otherwise called earle of Kime, was sent to win the castell of Millie Leuesche.   These townes being deliuered to the kings vse, the duke ordeined capteine of Eureux sir Gilbert Halsall knight.

The king now determining with all spéed to besiege Rone, prepared all things necessarie for his purpose.   Into this citie the Normans had conueied out of euerie part their monie, iewels, and houshold stuffe, as into the most sure and strongest place of the whole duchie.   For since his arriuall, they had not onlie walled that citie, and fortified it with rampiers and strong bulworks, but also furnished it with valiant capteins, and hardie soldiers, to the number of foure thousand, beside such of the citizens as were appointed for the warre, according to their estates, of the which there were at the least fiftéene thousand readie to serue in defense of the citie, as soldiers, and men of warre in all places where they should be assigned.   King Henrie

to

to haue the countrie free, before he would besiege this citie, thought good first to win such townes as laie in his waie, and therefore departing from Caen (where he had kept the feast of saint George) the ninth daie of Iune, he marched streight vnto the towne *Titus Liuius.* of Louiers, and laid his siege about the same.

> *Louiers besieged.*

They within the towne, being well furnished of all things necessarie for the defending of a siege, manfullie resisted the Englishmens inforcements, which spared not to deuise all waies and means how to approch the walles, and to batter the same with their great artillerie, till at length they brought the Frenchmen to that extremitie, that they were contented to yéeld the towne on these conditions; that if by the thrée and twentith of Iune there came no succour from the French king to raise the siege, the towne should be deliuered into the kings hands, the soldiers of the garrison should serue vnder the king for a time, and the townesmen should remaine in their dwellings as they did before, as subiects to the king: but the gunners that had discharged *Louiers yéelded* anie péece against the Englishmen should suffer death. When the daie came, and no *vp.* aid appeared, the couenants were performed accordinglie. From thence went the king with all spéed vnto Point de Larch, standing vpon the riuer of Seine, eight miles aboue Rone towards Paris: he came thither about the seauen and twentith of Iune.

When the Frenchmen which kept the passage there heard of the kings approach, they gathered togither a great number of men of warre, minding to defend the passage against him, appointing an other band of men (if they failed) to kéepe the further side of the bridge; and to watch, that neither by boate nor vessell he should come ouer the riuer by anie maner of meanes. At his comming néere to the towne, he perceiued that it was not possible to passe by the bridge without great losse of his people, and therfore he retired almost a mile backeward, where, in a pleasant and commodious place by the riuer side he pitched his campe, and in the night season, what with boates and barges, and what with hogsheads and pipes, he conueied ouer the broad *The English armie passeth the* riuer of Seine a great companie of his soldiers, without anie resistance made by his *riuer of Seine.* enimies. For they which were on the hither side of Seine, thinking that the Englishmen had gone to winne some other place, followed them not, but studied how to defend their towne, which was inough for them to doo.

And to put the French men in doubt, least the Englishmen should séeke passage somewhere else, the king appointed certeine of the soldiers which had skill in swimming, to go to a place thrée miles from the siege by the riuer side, and there to enter *A good policie.* into the water, making great clamor and noise, as though they had meant to haue passed; but they had in commandement not to trauerse past halfe the riuer, so to procure the Frenchmen to make thitherwards, whilest the king in one place, and his brother the duke of Clarence in another, got ouer their men, and that in such number, before the Frenchmen had anie vnderstanding thereof, that when they made towards them, and perceiued that they were not able to incounter them, they fled backe, and durst not abide the English footmen, which would faine haue beene dooing with them.

When the king saw that his men were on the other side of the water, he (the next daie earlie) returned to the towne, & assaulted it on both sides. When the inhabitants therefore saw themselues compassed on both sides, contrarie to their expectation, with humble heart and small ioy they rendered vp the towne vnto the kings hands. After *Pont de larch* this, the king hauing no let nor impediment, determined foorthwith to besiege the *rendred vp to* citie of Rone, and first sent before him his vncle the duke of Excester, with a great *the Englishmē.* companie of horssemen & archers to view the place, & thervpon with banner displaied came before the citie, and sent Windsore an herauld at armes to the capteins within, willing them to deliuer the citie vnto the king his maister, or else he would pursue them with fire and sword. To whome they proudlie answered, that none

they

they receiued of him, nor anie they would deliuer him, except by fine force they were therevnto compelled : and herewith there issued out of the towne a great band of men of armes, and incountered fiercelie with the Englishmen, the which receiuing them with like manhood, and great force, draue the Frenchmen into the towne againe to their losse, for they left thirtie of their fellowes behind prisoners and dead in the field.

The duke returned with this good speed and proud answer of the Frenchmen vnto the king, who remained yet at Pont de Larch, and had giuen the towne of Louiers to his brother the duke of Clarence, which made there his deputie sir Iohn Godard knight. After that the duke of Excester was returned to Pont Larch, the French capteins within Rone set fire on the suburbs, beat downe churches, cut downe trées, shred the bushes, destroied the vines round about the citie, to the intent that the Englishmen should haue no reléefe nor comfort either of lodging or fewell. When the king heard of these despitefull dooings, he with his whole armie remooued from Pont Larch, and the last daie of Iulie came before the citie of Rone, and compassed it round about with a strong siege. This citie was verie rich in gold, siluer, and other pretious things, in so much that when the same was taken and seized vpon by the English, the spoile was verie great and excéeding aduantagable : which the compiler of Anglorum prælia hath verie well noted, in a few lines, but pithie; saieng

Vltima Rothomagus restat, quæ mercibus, auro,

Argento, vasis pretiosis diues abundat :

Rothomagus capitur, iámq; Anglus adeptus opimas

Prædas, in patriam perpulchra trophæa remittit.

The king laie with a great puissance at the Chartreux house, on the east side of the citie, and the duke of Clarence lodged at S. Geruais before the port of Caux on the west part. The duke of Excester tooke his place on the north side : at port S. Denis, betweene the dukes of Excester and Clarence, was appointed the earle marshall, euen before the gate of the castell; to whome were ioined the earle of Ormond, and the lords Harington and Talbot, vpon his comming from Dampfront : and from the duke of Excester toward the king were incamped the lords Ros, Willoughbie, Fits Hugh, and sir William Porter, with a great band of northerne men, euen before the port of saint Hilarie. The earles of Mortaigne and Salisburie were assigned to lodge about the abbie of saint Katharine. Sir Iohn Greie was lodged directlie against the chappell called mount S. Michaell : sir Philip Léech treasuror of the warres kept the hill next the abbeie, and the baron of Carew kept the passage on the riuer of Seine, and to him was ioined that valiant esquier Ienico Dartois.

On the further side of the riuer were lodged the earles of Warren and Huntington, the lords Neuill and Ferrers, sir *Gilbert Umfreuile with a well furnished companie of warlike soldiers directlie before the gate called Port de Pont. And to the intent that no aid should passe by the riuer toward the citie, there was a great chaine of iron deuised at Pont Larch, set on piles from the one side of the water to the other : and beside that chaine, there was set vp a new forced bridge, sufficient both for cariage and passage, to passe the riuer from one campe to another. The erle of Warwike that had latelie woone Dampfront, was sent to besiege Cawdebecke, a towne stand-ing on the riuer side, betweene the sea and the citie of Rone. [A memorable feat in seruice néere to that place was doone at that time by a well minded man then noted soone after in writing : which matter vnable to be better reported than by him that had so well marked it, nor like to be more trulie expressed than by the ancient simplicitie (and yet effectuall) of the selfe same words wherein they were written, therefore thought méetest to haue them rehearsed as they were in order, thus.

The

Rone besieged by K. Henrie.

Angl. præl. sub. Hen. 5.

Before Pont S. Hiliarie.

Titus Liuius.

The order of the siege.

Before the gate called Marke-uile.

Titus Liuius.

Salisburie & Huntington on the other side of the riuer of Seine.

*Umfreuile.

The lord Talbot.

W. P.

The truth of the said memorable feat as it was reported in writing.

MEMORANDUM, that my lord the earle of Warwike did send out my cosin sir Iohn Bromley and my cosin George Umfreuile with an hundred archers, and about two hundred soldiers a strett, to keepe at a little castell called the Stroo neere to Cawdebeke, where they wearen met with aboue eight hundred Frenchmen A conflict neere to Cawdebeke. & the fraie betweene them long yfought, and the Englishmen in great dread and perill: till at length by the might of God and saint George, the feeld did fall to our Englishmen, and the Frenchmen wearen put to flizt, and thear wearen yslaine aboue two hundred Frenchmen, and as manie ytaken prisoners, and their capteine who was ycalled the lord of Estrisles was thear also yslaine, and thear wearen The L. of Estrisles slaine. yslaine of our Englishmen my said cosin George Umfreuile and about twentie mo: George Umfreuile slaine. on whose solles Iesus haue mercie, and thear wearen hurt in the face my said cosin sir Iohn Bromley & my cosin Walter Audeley sore wounded and maimed in the right Walter Audeley sore wouded. arme of his bodie, he then being but of the age of eighteene yeares. But thankes be giuen to the blessed Trinitee, thear wearen manie noble victories ywoon by the said noble erle of Warwike and his folke, as in his officiall booke (written by maister Iohn le Tucke then present with the said noble earle) is amply recorded. My said cosin Walter Audeley died at Warwike the seauenteenth daie of Iulie* anno Domini * And this sir Iohn Bromley departed from this life the one thousand foure hundred and twentie, and was buried at Acton in Cheshire, neere fourth day of the bodie of my said cosin sir Iohn Bromley: on whose solles Iesus haue mercie. Sept. 1419. By me sir Richard Braie, chapleine to my ladie the old countesse of Warwike; which was in Iesus Maria, Amen, Pater noster, Aue Maria. anno reg. 7. as
by the office take
after his death

After this conflict, this towne was so hardlie handled with fierce and continuall remaining of
record in the assaults, that the capteins within offered to suffer the English nauie to passe by castell of Chester dooth manifestlie appeare. their towne without impeachment, vp to the citie of Rone. And also if Rone yeelded, they promised to render the towne without delaie. Héerevpon the English nauie, to the number of an hundred sailes, passed by Cawdebecke, and came to Rone, and so besieged it on the water side. There came also to this siege the duke of Glocester, with the earle of Suffolke, and the lord Aburgauennie, which had taken (as before yee haue heard) the towne of Chierburgh, & lodged before the port of S. Hilarie, néerer to their enimies by fortie rodes than any other person of the armie.

During this siege also, there arriued at Harflue the lord of Kilmaine in Ireland, The lord of Kilmaine capteine of the Irishmen. with a band of sixteene hundred Irishmen, in maile, with darts and skains after the maner of their countrie, all of them being tall, quicke and nimble persons, which came and presented themselues before the king lieng still at the siege, of whom they were not onelie gentlie receiued & welcomed; but also because it was thought that the French king and the duke of Burgognie would shortlie come, and either attempt to raise the siege, or vittell and man the towne by the north gate, they were appointed to kéepe the north side of the armie, and speciallie the waie that commeth from the forest of Lions. Which charge the lord of Kilmaine and his companie ioifullie accepted, and did so their deuoir therein, that no men The good seruice of the Irishmen at this siege. were more praised, nor did more damage to their enimies than they did: for suerlie their quicknesse & swiftnesse of foot did more preiudice to their enimies, than their barded horsses did hurt or damage to the nimble Irishmen. Also the kings *Titus Liuius.* coosine germane and alie (the king of Portingale) sent a great nauie of well appointed The king of Portingale sendeth aid to king Henrie. ships vnto the mouth of the riuer of Seine, to stop that no French vessels should enter the riuer, and passe vp the same, to the aid of them within Rone.

Thus was the faire citie of Rone compassed about with enimies, both by water
and

and land, hauing neither comfort nor aid of King, Dolphin, or Duke. And yet although the armie was strong without, there lacked not within both hardie capteins and manfull souldiers. And as for people, they had more than inough: for as it is written by some that had good cause to know the truth, and no occasion to erre from the same, there were in the citie at the time of the siege, two hundred and ten thousand persons. Dailie were issues made out of the citie at diuerse gates, sometime to the losse of the one partie, and sometime of the other, as chances of warre in such aduentures happen. The Frenchmen in déed preferring fame before worldlie riches, and despising pleasure (the enimie to warlike prowesse) sware ech to other neuer to render or deliuer the citie, while they might either hold sword in hand or speare in rest.

The king of England aduertised of their haultie courages, determined to conquer them by famine, which would not be tamed with weapon. Wherefore he stopped all the passages, both by water and land, that no vittels could be conueied to the citie: he cast trenches round about the wals, and set them full of stakes, and defended with archers, so that there was left neither waie for them within to issue out, nor for anie that were abroad to enter in without his licence. To rehearse the great paines, trauell and diligence, which the king tooke vpon him in his owne person at this siege, a man might woonder. And because diuerse of the souldiers had lodged themselues for their more ease, in places so farre distant one from an other, that they might easilie haue béene surprised by their enimies, yer anie of their fellowes could haue come to their succors; he caused proclamation to be made, that no man vpon paine of death should lodge without the precinct appointed them, nor go further abroad from the campe than such bounds as were assigned.

Now as it chanced, the king in going about the campe, to surueie and view the warders, he espied two souldiers that were walking abroad without the limits assigned, whom he caused straightwaies to be apprehended and hanged vpon a tree of great height, for a terrour to others, that none should be so hardie to breake such orders as he commanded them to obserue. Whilest the king laie thus with his power about the mightie citie of Rone, the Frenchmen sought to indamage as well those that were at that siege, as other of the Englishmen that laie in garrisons within the townes that were alreadie in the king of Englands possession, insomuch that (as some haue written) within the octaues of the Assumption, three notable victories chanced to the Englishmen in thrée seuerall places. First an hundred Englishmen at Kilbeuf tooke three great lords of the Frenchmen, besides fourescore other persons, and put thrée hundred to flight.

Also vpon the thursdaie within the same octaues, foure hundred Frenchmen that were entered within the suburbes of Eureux were repelled by eleuen Englishmen, that tooke foure of those Frenchmen prisoners, slue twelue of them, and tooke fortie horsses. On the saturdaie following, the Frenchmen tooke in hand to steale vpon them that laie in garrison within Louiers, in hope to surprise the towne earlie in the morning: but the capteine perceiuing their purpose, sallied foorth with a hundred of his men, and putting the Frenchmen to flight, being a thousand, tooke an hundred and fourescore of them being all gentlemen. But to returne to them before Rone. The siege thus continuing from Lammas, almost to Christmas, diuerse enterprises were attempted, and diuerse policies practised, how euerie part might indamage his aduersaries: no parte greatlie reioised of their gaine. But in the meane time vittels began sore to faile them within, that onelie vinegar and water serued for drinke.

If I should rehearse (according to the report of diuerse writers) how déerelie dogs, rats, mise, and cats were sold within the towne, and how greedilie they were by the poore

The number within Rone.

Titus Liuius.

King Henrie his iustice.

Thom. Wals.

Thrée great victories on the English side within a short time togither.

Extreame famine within Rone.

poore people eaten and deuoured, and how the people dailie died for fault of food, and yoong infants laie sucking in the stréets on their moothers breasts lieng dead, starued for hunger; the reader might lament their extreme miseries. A great number of poore sillie creaturs were put out at the gates, which were by the Englishmen that kept the trenches beaten and driuen backe againe to the same gates, which they found closed and shut against them. And so they laie betweene the wals of the citie and the trenches of the enimies, still crieng for helpe and reléefe, for lacke whereof great numbers of them dailie died.

Howbeit, king Henrie mooued with pitie, vpon Christmasse daie, in the honor of Christes Natiuitie, refreshed all the poore people with vittels, to their great comfort and his high praise: yet if the duke of Burgognies letters had not béene conueied into the citie, it was thought they within would neuer haue made resistance so long time as they did; for by those letters they were assured of rescue to come. Diuerse lords of France hauing written to them to the like effect, they were put in such comfort herewith, that immediatlie, to expresse their great reioising, all the bels in the citie were roong foorth chéerefullie, which during all the time of the siege till that present had kept silence. In déed by reason of a faint kind of agréement procured betwixt the Dolphin and the duke of Burgognie, it was thought verelie that a power should haue béene raised for preseruation of that noble citie, the loosing or sauing thereof being a matter of such importance. *A vertuous and charitable prince.*

The king of England, to preuent the enimies purpose, caused a large trench to be cast without his campe, which was pight full of sharpe stakes, with a great rampire fensed with bulworks, and turnepikes, in as defensible wise as might be deuised. Sir Robert Bapthorpe, knight, was appointed comptroller, to see this worke performed, which he did with all diligence accomplish; in like case as he had doone, when the other trench and rampire stronglie staked and hedged was made at the first betwixt the campe and the citie, to restreine such as in the begining of the siege rested not to pricke foorth of the gates on horsse backe. And so by this meanes was the armie defended both behind and before. *Chron. S. Alb.* A large trech without the campe.

Finallie, the whole number of the Frenchmen within the citie were brought to such an extremitie for want of vittels, that they were in danger all to haue starued. Whereupon being now past hope of reléefe, they determined to treat with the king of England, and so vpon Newyeares euen there came to the wals such as they had chosen amongst them for commissioners, which made a signe to the Englishmen lieng without the gate of the bridge, to speake with some gentleman, or other person of authoritie. The earle of Huntington, which kept that part, sent to them sir Gilbert Umfreuile; vnto whom they declared, that if they might haue a safe conduct, they would gladlie come foorth to speake with the king. Sir Gilbert reparing to the duke of Clarence, and other of the kings councell, aduertised them of this request. 1419

Herevpon the duke of Clarence with the other councellors resorted to the kings lodging, to informe him of the matter, and to know his pleasure therein; who after good aduisement and deliberation taken, willed sir Gilbert to aduertise them, that he was content to heare twelue of them, which should be safelie conueied into his presence. This answer being brought to the Frenchmen by the said sir Gilbert, on the next daie in the morning, foure knights, foure learned men, and foure sage burgesses, all clothed in blacke, came foorth of the citie, and were receiued at the port saint Hilarie by sir Gilbert Umfreuile, accompanied with diuerse gentlemen and yeomen of the kings houshold, commonlie called yeomen of the crowne, by whome they were conueied to the kings lodging, whome they found at masse, which being ended, the king came out of his trauerse, sternelie, and princelie beholding the French messengers, and passed by them into his chamber. And incontinentlie after he commanded that they should be brought in before his presence, to heare what they had to say. *They within Rone demand parlée.*

One

One of them séene in the ciuill lawes, was appointed to declare the message in all
A presumptuous
orator.
their names, who shewing himselfe more rash than wise, more arrogant than learned,
first tooke vpon him to shew wherin the glorie of victorie consisted, aduising the
king not to shew his manhood in famishing a multitude of poore, simple, and innocent people, but rather suffer such miserable wretches as laie betwixt the wals of the
citie, and the trenches of his siege, to passe through the campe, that they might get
their liuing in other places, and then if he durst manfullie assault the citie, and by
force subdue it, he should win both worldlie fame and merit great méed at the hands
of almightie God, for hauing compassion of the poore, needie, and indigent people.

When this orator had said, the king who no request lesse suspected, than that
which was thus desired, began a while to muse; and after he had well considered the
craftie cautell of his enimies, with a fierce countenance, and bold spirit he reprooued
The kings an-
swer to this proud
message.
them, both for their subtill dealing with him, and their malapert presumption, in that
they should seeme to go about to teach him what belonged to the dutie of a conquerour. "And therefore since it appeared that the same was vnknowne vnto them, he
declared that the goddesse of battell called Bellona, had thrée handmaidens, euer of
necessitie attending vpon hir, as blood, fire, and famine. And whereas it laie in his
choise to vse them all thrée; yea, two, or one of them at his pleasure, he had appointed onelie the méekest maid of those thrée damsels to punish them of that citie,
till they were brought to reason.

And whereas the gaine of a capteine atteined by anie of the said thrée handmaidens,
was both glorious, honourable, and woorthie of triumph : yet of all the thrée, the
yoongest maid, which he meant to vse at that time was most profitable and commodious. And as for the poore people lieng in the ditches, if they died through famine, the fault was theirs, that like cruell tyrants had put them out of the towne,
to the intent he should slaie them; and yet had he saued their liues, so that if anie
lacke of charitie was, it rested in them, and not in him. But to their cloked request,
he meant not to gratifie them within so much, but they should kéepe them still to
helpe to spend their vittels. And as to assault the towne, he told them that he
would they should know, he was both able and willing thereto, as he should sée occasion : but the choise was in his hand, to tame them either with blood, fire, or
famine, or with them all, whereof he would take the choice at his pleasure, and not
at theirs."

This answer put the French ambassadors in a great studie, musing much at his
excellent wit and hawtinesse of courage. Now after they had dined (as his commandement was they should) with his officers, they vpon consultation had togither,
required once againe to haue accesse to his roiall presence, which being granted, they
A truce for eight
daies.
humbling themselues on their knees, besought him to take a truce for eight daies,
during the which they might by their commissioners take some end and good conclusion with him and his councell. The king like a mercifull prince granted to them
their asking, with which answer they ioifullie returned. After their departure were
appointed and set vp three tents, the one for the lords of England, the second for
the commissioners of the citie, and the third for both parties to assemble in, and to
treat of the matter.

The commissioners for the English part were the earles of Warwike and Salisburie,
the lord Fitz Hugh, sir Walter Hungerford, sir Gilbert Umfreuile, sir Iohn Robsert,
and Iohn de Vasques de Almada. And for the French part were appointed, sir
Cõmissioners
appointed.
Guie de Butteler, and six others. These commissioners met euery daie, arguing and
reasoning about a conclusion, but nothing was doone the space of eight daies nor
so much as one article concluded : wherfore the Englishmen tooke downe the tents,
& the Frenchmen tooke their leaue : but at their departing they remembering themselues

selues, required the English lords (for the loue of God) that the truce might indure till the sunne rising the next daie, to the which the lords assented.

When the French commissioners were returned into the citie without any con-clusion of agréement, the poore people ran about the streets, crieng, and calling the capteins and gouernors murtherers and manquellers, saieng that for their pride and stiffe stomachs all this miserie was happened, threatning to flea them if they would not agrée vnto the king of Englands demand. The magistrats herewith amazed, called all the townesmen togither to know their minds and opinions. The whole voice of the commons was, to yeeld rather than to sterue. Then the Frenchmen in the euening came to the tent of sir Iohn Robsert, requiring him of gentlenes to mooue the king, that the truce might be prolonged for foure daies. The king therevnto agréed, and appointed the archbishop of Canturburie, and the other seuen before named for his part, and the citizens appointed a like number for them.

The tents were againe set vp, and dailie they met togither, and on the fourth daie *The articles cōcerning the yeélding vp of Rone.* they accorded on this wise, that the citie and castell of Rone should be deliuered vnto the king of England, at what time after the middest of the ninetéenth daie of that present moneth of Ianuarie, the said king willed the same; and that all the capteins and other men whatsoeuer, dwelling or being within the said citie and castell, should submit them in all things to the grace of the said king: and further, that they should paie to the said king thrée hundred thousand scutes of gold, whereof alwaies two should be woorth an English noble, or in stead of euerie scute thirtie great blankes white, or fiftéene grotes.

Moreouer it was accorded, that euerie soldier and stranger, being in the said citie and castell, should sweare on the euangelists before their departure, not to beare armour against the king of England, before the first daie of Ianuarie next to come. Also they within the towne should suffer all the poore people lieng in ditches, or about the ditches of the citie, which for penurie were chased out, to enter the citie againe, and to find them sufficient food till the said ninetéenth daie of Ianuarie. There were diuerse other articles, in all to the number of two and twentie agréed as well on the behalfe of the citizens, as of king Henrie, who granted, that all the soul-diers, strangers, and other within the said citie and castell at that time, being not willing to become his lieges, should depart, after that the citie and castell was once yéelded, fréelie without let, leauing to the said king all their armors, horsses, har-nesse, and goods, except the Normans, which if they should refuse to become lieges to him, were appointed to remaine as his prisoners, togither with one Luca Italico, and *Luca Italico.* certeine others.

When the daie of appointment came, which was the daie of saint Wolstane, sir *The vicar gene-rall of the archbi-shoprike of Rone for denouncing the king accursed was deliuered to him and deteined in prison till he died.* Guie de Buttler, and the burgesses, deliuered the keies of the citie and castell vnto the king of England, beséeching him of fauour and compassion. The king inconti-nentlie appointed the duke of Excester, with a great companie to take possession of the citie, who like a valiant capteine mounted on a goodlie courser first entered into the citie, and after into the castell. The next daie being fridaie, the king in *Titus Liuius.* great triumph, like a conquerour, accompanied with foure dukes, ten earles, eight *One Alane Blan-chart was like-wise deliuered to him, & by his cōmandement put to death. Trãslator of Titus Liuius.* bishops, sixtéene barons, and a great multitude of knights, esquiers, and men of war e entered into Rone, where he was receiued by the cleargie, with two and fourtie crosses; and then met him the senat, and the burgesses of the towne, offering to him diuerse faire and costlie presents.

In this manner he passed through the citie to our ladie church, and there hauing *King Hēries en-trie into Rone.* said his orisons, he caused his chapleins to sing this antheme: Quis est tam mag-nus dominus: Who is so great a lord as our God. This doone, he came to the castell, where he continued a good space after, receiuing homages and fealties of the burgesses and townesmen, and setting orders amongst them. He also reedified diuerse fortresses, and townes, during which time he made proclamation, that all men which would become his subiects, should enioy their goods, lands & offices, which proclamation made manie townes to yéeld, and manie men to become English the same season.

Titus Liuius.

The duke of Britaine, vnderstanding that if the king of England should continue in possession of Normandie, his countrie could not but be in great danger, if he prouided not to haue him his freend, vpon safe conduct obteined for him & his retinue, came to Rone with fiue hundred horsses, and being honorablie receiued of the king, after conference had betwixt them of diuerse things, at length they agréed vpon a league on this wise, that neither of them should make warre vnto the other, nor to any of the others people or subiects, except he that meant to make war denounced the same six moneths before. Thus this league being concluded, the duke tooke leaue of the king and so returned into Britaine.

A league concluded betwéene king Henrie and the duke of Britaine.

About the same time, at the sute of certeine bishops and abbats of Nomandie, the king confirmed vnto them their ancient priuileges, granted by the former dukes of Normandie and kings of France, except such as were granted by those whome he reputed for vsurpers, and no lawfull kings or dukes. He also established at Caen the chamber of accounts of the reuenues of his dukedome of Normandie. In Rone he began the foundation of a strong tower behind the castell, that from the castell to the tower, and from the tower to his palace, the men of warre appointed there in garrison, might passe in suertie without danger of the citie, if perhaps the citizens should attempt any rebellion.

She was comitted to the safe kéeping of Pelham, who appointed hir nine seruants to attend hir & conueied hir to the castell of Pompsey.
Tho. Walsin.
Frier Rãdoll.

In this sixt yeare, whilest these things were adooing in Normandie, quéene Ione late wife of king Henrie the fourth, and mother in law to this king, was arrested by the duke of Bedford the kings lieutenant in his absence, and by him committed to safe kéeping in the castell of Leeds in Kent, there to abide the kings pleasure. About the same time, one frier Randoll of the order of Franciscanes that professed diuinitie, and had beene confessor to the same queene, was taken in the Ile of Gernesey; and being first brought ouer into Normandie, was by the kings commandement sent hither into England, and committed to the Tower, where he remained till the parson of the Tower quarelling with him, by chance slue him there within the Tower ward. It was reported that he had conspired with the quéene by sorcerie and necromancie to destroie the king.

Whilest the king remained in Rone, to set things in order for the establishment of good policie in that citie, he sent abroad diuerse of his capteins, with conuenient forces to subdue certeine townes & castels in those parties, as his brother the duke of Clarence, who wan the strong towne of Vernon and Mante. In Vernon was sir William Porter made capteine, and in Mant the earle of March. The earle of Salisburie wan Hunflue, after he had besieged it from the fourth of Februarie vntill the twelfth of March. This towne was giuen afterwards vnto the duke of Clarence. Also the said earle of Salisburie wan the townes of Monster de Villiers, Ew, Newcastell, and finallie all the places in that quarter, which till that present were not vnder the English obeisance. At Newcastell sir Philip Léech was made capteine.

Vernon and Mante taken by the English.
Titus Liuius.
Hunflue takē.

After Candlemasse, the king departed from Rone to go to Eureux, whither he promised to come in like case, as the Dolphin promised to be at Dreux, to the end that they might aduise vpon a conuenient place where to méet, to intreat of peace to be concluded betwixt the two realms. But the Dolphin by sinister persuasion of some enimies to concord, brake promise, and came not. When the king saw that thorough default of his aduersarie, no treatie would be had, he remooued to Vernon, and there a while remained. Now from Eureux the king had dispatched the earle of Warwike vnto the siege of la Roch Guion, which fortresse he so constreined, that it

An. Reg. 7.
Roch Guion rendered vp.

                                                                                                   was

was yeelded into his hands, the sixt of Aprill, in the beginning of this seuenth yeare of king Henries reigne, and giuen to sir Guie Buttler late capteine of Rone, of the kings frée and liberall grant.

About the same time, the duke of Excester laid siege vnto Chateau Galiard, Chateau Galiard besieged. which siege continued from the last of March, vnto the latter end of September, or (as some write) vnto the twentith of December, as after shall appeare. The duke of Glocester being sent to win the towne and castell of Yuri, tooke the Yuri taken by assault. towne by assault, and the castell was deliuered by composition after fortie daies siege. After this the Englishmen ouerran the countrie about Chartres, and did much hurt to their enimies in all places where they came. The hearts of the Frenchmen were sore discouraged with the losse of Rone, and the other townes which yeelded one after another thus to the Englishmen, so that such as loued the wealth of their countrie sore lamented the imminent mischéefes, which they saw by the diuision of the nobilitie, like shortlie to fall on their heads, namelie bicause they saw no remidie prepared.

But who euer else was disquieted with this matter, Iohn duke of Burgognie raged and swelled, yea and so much freated therewith, that he wist not what to saie, and lesse to doo: for he knew well that he was neither free from disdaine, nor yet deliuered from the scope of malice, bicause that he onelie ruled the king, and had the whole dooings in all matters about him. And therefore he considered, that all such mishaps as chanced to the state of the common-wealth would be imputed to his negligence and disordred gouernement. To find some remedie against such dangers at hand, he thought first to assaie, if he might by any reasonable means conclude a peace betwixt the two mightie kings of England and France, which if he might bring to passe, he doubted not to reuenge his quarell easilie inough against the Dolphin Charles, and to represse all causes of grudge and disdaine.

Herewith intending to build vpon this fraile foundation, he sent letters and ambas- Ambassadors sent on either side. sadors to the king of England, aduertising him, that if he would personallie come to a communication to be had betweene him and Charles the French king, he doubted not but by his onelie meanes, peace should be brought in place, and bloudie battell cléerelie exiled. King Henrie giuing courteous eare to these ambassadors, sent with *Titus Liuius.* them the earle of Warwike as his ambassador, accompanied with two hundred gentlemen to talke wirh the duke, as then remaining in the French court at the towne of Prouince. The earle was assailed by the waie as he iournied, by a great number of rebellious persons, gotten into armour of purpose to haue spoiled him of such monie and things as he and his companie had about them. But by the high valiancie of the English people, with the aid of their bowes, the Frenchmeˆ were discomfited and chased.

The earle at his comming to Prouince was honorablie receiued, and hauing doone the effect of his message, returned; and with him the earle of saint Paule, and the sonne and heire of the duke of Burbon were also sent as ambassadors from the French king, to conclude vpon the time and place of the méeting, with all the circumstances. Wherevpon the king of England agréed to come to the towne of Mante, with condition that the duke of Burgognie, and other for the French king should come to Pontoise, that either part might méet other in a conuenient place betwixt those two townes néere to Meulan. According to this appointment, K. Henrie came to Mante, where in the feast of Pentecost he kept a liberall house to all commers, and sate himselfe in great estate. Vpon the which daie, either for good seruice alreadie by them doone, or for the good expectation of things to come, he created Gascoigne de Fois, Creation of earles. otherwise called the captau or captall de Buef a valiant Gascoigne, earle of Longueuile; and sir Iohn Greie earle of Tankeruile, and the lord Bourchier, earle of Ew.

After this solemne feast ended, the place of enteruiew and méeting was appointed

to

to be beside Meulan on the riuer of Seine, where in a faire place euerie part was by
commissioners appointed to their ground. When the daie of appointment approched,
which was the last daie of Maie, the king of England accompanied with the dukes
of Clarence, and Glocester, his brethren, the duke of Excester his vncle, and Henrie
Beauford clerke his other vncle, which after was bishop of Winchester and cardinall,
with the earles of March, Salisburie, and others, to the number of a thousand men of
warre, entered into his ground, which was barred about and ported, wherin his tents
were pight in a princelie maner.

Likewise for the French part came Isabell the French quéene, bicause hir husband
was fallen into his old frantike disease, hauing in hir companie the duke of Burgognie,
and the earle of saint Paule, and she had attending vpon hir the faire ladie Katharine
hir daughter, with six and twentie ladies and damosels; and had also for hir furniture a thousand men of warre. The said ladie Katharine was brought by hir mother
onelie to the intent that the king of England beholding hir excellent beautie, should
be so inflamed and rapt in hir loue, that he to obteine hir to his wife, should the sooner
agrée to a gentle peace and louing concord. But though manie words were spent in
this treatie, and that they met at eight seuerall times, yet no effeet insued, nor any
conclusion was taken by this freendlie consultation, so that both parties after a princelie fashion tooke leaue ech of other, and departed; the Englishmen to Mante, and
the Frenchmen to Pontoise.

Some authors write that the Dolphin to staie that no agréement should passe, sent
sir Taneguie de Chastell to the duke of Burgognie, declaring that if he would breake
off the treatie with the Englishmen, he would then common with him; and take
such order, that not onelie they but the whole realme of France should thereof be
glad and reioise. Howsoeuer it came to passe, truth it is that where it was agréed,
that they should eftsooues haue met in the same place on the third of Iulie; the king
according to that appointment came: but there was none for the French part, neither quéene nor duke that once appeared; so that it was manifest inough how the
fault rested not in the Englishmen, but in the Frenchmen. By reason wherof no
conclusion sorted to effect of all this communication, saue onlie that a certeine
sparke of burning loue was kindled in the kings heart by the sight of the ladie
Katharine.

The king without doubt was highlie displeased in his mind, that this communication
came to no better passe. Wherefore he mistrusting that the duke of Burgognie was
the verie let and stop of his desires, said vnto him before his departure: " Coosine, we
will haue your kings daughter, and all things that we demand with hir, or we will
driue your king and you out of his realme. Well (said the duke of Burgognie) before
you driue the king and me out of his realme, you shall be well wearied, and thereof
we doubt little." Shortlie after, the duke of Burgognie and the Dolphin met in the
plaine fields besides Melun, and there comming togither, concluded apparantlie an
open peace and amitie, which was proclamed in Paris, Amiens, and Pontoise.

This agréement was made the sixt of Iulie in the yeare 1419. It was ingrossed by
notaries, signed with their hands, and sealed with their great seales of armes: but
as the sequele shewed, hart thought not what toong spake, nor mind meant not that
hand wrote. Whiles these things were a dooing, diuerse of the Frenchmen in Rone
went about a conspiracie against the Englishmen, whereof the king being well aduertised, sent thither certeine of his nobles, which tried out these conspirators, caused
them to be apprehended, had them in examination, and such as they found guiltie
were put to death; and so setting the citie in quietnes, returned to the king, who counted it great honor to kéepe the countries which he woone by conquest in obedience and
aw; sith such victories are not obteined without sore labour and toile, both of prince
and people, as the poet rightlie saith:

Quærere

Quærere regna, labor; virtus est parta tueri
  Maxima.

In Angl. prœl. sub Hen. 5.

The king of England, perceiuing, by this new aliance, that nothing was lesse to be looked for, than peace at the hands of the Frenchmen, deuised still how to win townes and fortresses, which were kept against him: and now that the truce was expired, on the thirtith daie of Iulie, he being as then within the towne of Mante, appointed certeine bands of souldiers in the after noone to passe out of the gates, giuing onelie knowledge to the capteins what he would haue them to doo. And to the intent that no inkling of the enterprise should come to the enimies eare, he kept the gates himselfe as porter. These that were thus sent foorth being guided by the earle of Longueuile, otherwise called the captau de Buef, were commanded in secret maner as they could to draw toward the towne of Pontoise, and to keepe themselues in couert till the darke of the night, and then approch the walles of that towne, and vpon espieng their aduantage to enter it by scaling, hauing ladders and all things necessarie with them for the purpose.

Hall. These bands belonged to the earle of Longueuile & to the lord de Lespar Gascoignes. *Hist. des ducz de Normand* The king plaieth the porters part.

Moreouer, about the closing of the daie and night in the euening, he sent foorth the erle of Huntington with other bands of soldiers, to succor and assist the other, if they chanced to enter the towne according to the order taken. Those that were first sent foorth (according to their instructions) conueid themselues so closelie to their appointed places, that the enimies heard nothing of their dooings. Wherevpon when the night was come, they came in secret wise vnder the walles, and there watched their time till the morning began to draw on. In the meane time, whilest the watch was departed, and before other were come into their places to relieue it, the English-men setting vp their ladders, entered and brake open one of the gates to receiue the other that followed.

This captau was brother to the earle of Fois.

Hall.

Pontoise surprised by the Englishmen.

The Frenchmen perceiuing that the walles were taken, and their enimies entered into the towne, at the first were sore amazed: but after perceiuing the small number of the Englishmen, they assembled togither and fiercelie assailed them, so that they were constreined to retire to the walles and turrets which they had taken, and with much adoo defended the same; some leaping downe into the diches, and hiding them in the vines, till at length the earle of Huntington, with his companies came to their succors, and entring by the gate which was open, easilie did beat backe the enimies, & got the market place. Which when the lord Lisle Adam capteine of the towne perceiued, he opened the gate towards Paris, by the which he with all his retinue, and diuerse of the townesmen to the nsmber of ten thousand in all, (as Enguerant de Monstr. recounteth) fled towards Paris, taking awaie with them their coine, iewels, and plate. Some of them fleeing towards Beauuois were met with, and stripped of that they had, by Iehan de Guigni, and Iehan de Claw, two capteins that serued the Orlientiall faction.

Hall.

Hall.

There were within the towne of Pontoise at that time when it was thus taken by the Englishmen, a thousand lances, and two thousand arcubalisters, as Thomas Wil-singham affirmeth, and of Englishmen and Gascoignes that went first foorth of Mante with the captau de Buef, not past fiftéene hundred, as Hall reporteth: although Enguerant de Monstrellet saith, they were about thrée thousand. But how manie soeuer they were, they durst not at the first, by reason of their small number (as may be thought) once diuide themselues, or deale with booties, till about the houre of prime, that the duke of Clarence came to their aid with fiue thousand men, who much praising the valiantnesse of the earle and his retinue that had thus woone the towne, gaue to them the chéefe spoile of the which there was great plentie.

Then went the duke foorth towards Paris, and comming thither, lodged before it two daies and two nights, without perceiuing anie proffer of issue to be made foorth against him by his enimies, and therefore seeing they durst not once looke vpon him,

The duke of Clarence cōmeth before Paris with his armie.

he

he returned to Pontoise, for the taking of which towne the whole countrie of France, and speciallie the Parisians were sore dismaied: sith now there was no fortresse able to withstand the English puissance; for that the Irishmen ouerran all the Isle of France, did to the Frenchmen damages innumerable, (as their writers affirme) brought dailie preies to the English armie, burst vp houses, laid beds on the backes of the kine, rid vpon them, carried yoong children before them, and sold them to the Englishmen for slaues. These strange dooings so feared the Frenchmen within the territorie of Paris, and the countrie about, that the sorie people fled ont of the villages with all their stuffe into the citie.

The Irishmē spoile the Ile of France.

The French king, and the duke of Burgognie lieng at saint Denis, in this season, departed from thence with the quéene and hir daughter, and went to Trois in Champaigne, there to consult of their businesse, hauing left at Paris the earle of S. Paule, and the lord Lisle Adam, with a great puissance to defend the citie. The king of England immediatlie after that Pontoise was woone (as before yee haue heard) came thither in person, as well to giue order for the placing of a sufficient garrison there for defense thereof; as to proceed further into the countrie for the getting of other townes and places: and so after he had well prouided for the good gouernment, & safe kéeping thereof, the eighteenth daie of August he departed out of the same with his maine armie.

Titus Liuius.

And bicause they of the garrison that laie in the castell of Vancon Villers had doone, and dailie did diuerse and sundrie displeasures to the Englishmen, he pight downe his field néere to the same, the better to restraine them from their hostile attempts, and withall sent part of his armie to besiege the castell, which put them in such feare, that they despairing of all reléefe or succour, and perceiuing they should not be able long to defend the place against the kings puissance, yéelded the place, with all their coine and other goods into the kings hands. The soldiers of that garrison, and the inhabitants, at the contemplation of a certeine ladie there amongst them, were licenced by the king to depart without armor or weapon, onelie with their liues saued. Iohn of Burgh that was after bailiffe of Gisours, was appointed capteine of this castell.

The castell of Vancon Villers besieged and taken.

Titus Liuius.

After this, all the townes and castels within a great circuit offered to yéeld themselues vnto the English obeisance; the strong towne and castell of Gisours onelie excepted, which still held out, & would shew no token of will to yeeld. Héerevpon the king the last of August began to approch the same, but at the first he could not come néere, by reason of the marishes and fennes: but yet such was the diligence of the Englishmen, aduanced by the presence of the king, readie in all places to commend them that were forward in their businesse, and to chastise such as slacked their duetie, that dailie they came neerer and néerer, although the Frenchmen issued foorth dailie to encounter them, giuing them manie sharpe skirmishes. For the towne being double walled and fensed with those broad marishes, so incouraged them within, that they thought no force had béene able to haue subdued them.

Gisours besieged & yéelded to the Englishmen.

But at length calling to remembrance, that the king of England came before no towne nor fortresse, from which he would depart before he had brought it vnder his subiection, they offered to come to a parlée, and in the end compounded to render the towne into the kings hands the eight daie of September next insuing, and the castell (bicause it was the stronger péece) they couenanted to deliuer the foure and twentith of the same, if in the meane time no rescue came to raise the siege. Herevpon when no such releefe could be heard of, at the daies limited, the soldiers of the garrison, and the more part of the townsmen also submitted themselues, and receiued an oth to be true subiects to the king, and so remained still in their roomes. The earle of Worcester was made capteine there.

Thom. Wals.

Duke of Clarence saith Rich. Grafton.

About the same time, to wit, the thrée and twentith of September (as some write)

Titus Liuius.

was

was castell Galiard surrendred to the hands of the duke of Excester, which had beene besieged euer since the last daie of March (as before yée haue heard.) But others write that it held out seauen moneths, and was not deliuered vp till the twentith of December. This castell was not onelie strong by situàtion, standing vpon the top of a stéepe hill, but also closed with mightie thicke walles, and furnished with men and all maner of munition and things necessarie. The king appointed the lord Ros capteine of it. After that Gisours and castell Galeard were thus yéelded to the English obeisance, all the other townes and castels thereabout, and in the countrie of Veulquessin, shortlie after yéelded to the king, as Gourneie, Chauniount, Neaufle, Dangu, and other small fortresses. Of Gourneie, was sir Gilbert Umfreuile made capteine; at Neaufle, the earle of Worcester; and at Dangu, Richard Wooduile. Shortlie after was the castell Daumall yéelded to the earle of Warwike, to whome it was giuen. And thus was the whole duchie of Normandie (Mont saint Michael onelie excepted) reduced to the possession of the right heire, which had béene wrongfullie deteined from the kings of England euer since the daies of king Iohn, who lost it about the yeare one thousand two hundred and seauen. *Normandie brought into the kings subiection, that had béene lost & deteined a long time frō the English.*

To satisfie those that be desirous to know what capteins were appointed by the king in diuerse townes that were yéelded to him (of which we haue made no mention heretofore but in generall) here their names doo follow, and of the townes, as we find them in the chronicles of maister Hall. At Crewleie sir Henrie Tanclux an Almaine; at Torignie, sir Iohn Popham, to whome it was giuen; at Chamboie, the lord Fitz Hugh; at Vernueil in Perch, sir Iohn Neuill; at Essaie, sir William Huddleston bailiffe of Alanson; at Crulie sir Lois Robsert; at Conde Norean sir Iohn Fastolfe; at Cawdebecke, sir Lois Robsert; at Deepe, William lord Bourchier earle of Eu; at Aubemarle, the earle of Warwike, and his deputie thereof William Montfort; at Bellincombre, sir Thomas Ramston lord thereof by gift; at Longueuille, the capitall de Beuf or Buz, earle thereof by gift; at Danuille, sir Christopher Burden; at Couches, sir Robert Marburie; at Chierburg, sir Iohn Gedding; at Bacqueuille, the lord Ros; at Arques sir Iames Fines, bailiffe of Caux; at Monceaux, sir Philip Leech; at Estrie Pagnie, Richard Abraham; at Sentler Surget, William Basset; at Bretueill, sir Henrie Mortimer bailiffe of Hunflew.

But now to returne where we left. The wise and graue personages of the realme of France, sore lamenting & bewailing the miserie of their countrie, saw they had puissance inough to defend their enimies, if they were of perfect concord amongst themselues. And therefore to remooue all rancor and displeasure betwixt the Dolphin, and the duke of Burgognie, they procured a new méeting, which was appointed to be at Monstreau ou fault Yonne, where the two princes at the daie assigned met. But such was the fortune of France, that the duke of Burgognie was there murthered, as he knéeled before the Dolphin: wherevpon insued greater debate than before. For Philip earle of Charolois, the sonne and heire of the said duke, tooke the matter verie gréeuouslie, as he had no lesse cause, and determined to be reuenged on the Dolphin, and other that were guiltie of the murther: so that now there was great expectation of slaughter and bloudshed, but no hope for the most part of tranquillitie & peace. France therefore, what with ouerthrowes giuen by the English, & diuision among themselues, was verie sore afflicted; insomuch that one miserie riding on anothers necke, the whole land was in danger of desolation by ciuill dissention & mutuall mutinies; as the poet noteth: *The duke of Burgognie murthered.*

————accessit ad ista

Tunc mala Celtarum Burgundio fraude peremptus

Sparsaq; ciuilis tota dissensio terra. *Anglorum prælia sub Henr.* 5.

When he had well considered of the matter, and taken aduise with his councell, he first sent ambassadours to the king of England, then lieng at Gisours to treat and con-clude *Ambassadors sent to king Henrie. Titus Liuius.*

clude a truce betwéene them both for a certeine space, that they might talke of some conclusion of agréement. King Henrie receiued the ambassadors verie courteouslie, and granted that communication might be had of peace, but vtterlie denied anie abstinence from warre, bicause he would not lose time, if the treatie sorted not to good effect. Herevpon hauing his armie assembled at Maunt, he diuided the same into thrée parts, appointing the duke of Glocester with one part to go vnto the castell of S. Germane in Laie, and to laie siege therevnto. The duke according to his commission, comming before that castell, within a while constreined them within by continuall skirmishes and assaults to diliuer vp the place into his hands. An other part of the armie was sent vnto the castell of Montioie, which likewise by such fierce assaults and manfull approchcs, as the Englishmen made thereto, was shortlie giuen ouer and yéelded. The third part of the hoast went to Meulanc, a verie strong towne compassed about with the riuer of Seine.

A wise and princelie caution.

The castell of S. Germane in Laie and Montioie yéelded to the Englishmen.

A policie for redie bridges.

But the king deuised to fasten botes and barges togither, and to rere vp certeine frames of timber aloft on the same for defense of his soldiers, that should by that meanes approch the walles, wherewith those that had the towne in kéeping were so put in feare, that their capteine was glad to come to a communication, & agréed to deliuer the towne into the kings hands, if no rescue came before the thirtith daie of October next insuing. On which daie, for that no succours appeared, the towne (according to the couenants) was giuen vp into the kings hands. Sir Thomas Ramston was made capteine there, and after him sir Iohn Fastolfe. The king, whilest these places were besieged, and thus brought vnder his subiection, continued for the most part at Maunt; but yet oftentimes he went foorth to visit his campes, and to sée that nothing should be wanting, that might further the spéedie dispatch of his enterprises.

The strong town of Meulanc yéelded to the English.

About the same time, there came againe ambassadours to him from Charles the French king, & from the yoong duke of Burgognie to treat with him of some good conclusion of peace to be had; who had no such trust in their sute, but that he doubted their meaning, and therefore ceassed not to procéed in the winning of townes and castels, as he was in hand. Now when Christmasse approched, the king withdrew to Rone, and there kept the solemnization of that feast, appointing in the meane time his men of warre to be occupied as occasion serued. The earle of Salisburie was sent to besiege the towne of Fresneie, the which after stout resistance madé at the first, shortlie after was deliuered to him to the kings vse. The earles Marshall and Huntington, sir Iohn Gréene Cornewall, sir Philip Léech, and diuerse other, were sent into the countrie of Maine, where, not farre from the citie of Mens they were incountered by a power of Frenchmen, which the Dolphin had sent against them. There was at the first a sharpe bickering betwixt them, but in the end the victorie remained with the Englishmen; so that manie of the Frenchmen were slaine, and taken, and the residue chased out of the field. There were slaine (as Thomas Walsingham saith) at the point of fiue thousand, and two hundred taken prisoners, among whome was the marshall de Rous, and diuerse other of good account. The two English earles remained there as victors, in the countrie which was by the king to them assigned.

1420

An. Reg. 8.

A great victorie on the English side.

Whilest these victorious exploits were thus happilie atchiued by the Englishmen, and that the king laie still at Rone, in giuing thanks to almightie God for the same, there came to him eftsoones ambassadours from the French king and the duke of Burgognie to mooue him to peace. The king minding not to be reputed for a destroier of the countrie, which he coueted to preserue, or for a causer of christian bloud still to be spilt in his quarell, began so to incline and giue eare vnto their sute and humble request, that at length (after often sending to and fro) and that the bishop of Arras, and other men of honor had béene with him, and likewise the

King Henrie condescendeth to a treatie of peace.

the earle of Warwike, and the bishop of Rochester had béene with the duke of Burgognie, they both finallie agreed vpon certeine articles, so that the French king and his commons would thereto assent.

Now was the French king and the quéene with their daughter Katharine at Trois in Champaigne gouerned and ordered by them, which so much fauoured the duke of Burgognie, that they would not for anie earthlie good, once hinder or pull backe one iot of such articles as the same duke should séeke to preferre. And therefore what néedeth manie words, a truce tripartite was accorded betwéene the two kings and the duke, and their countries, and order taken that the king of England should send in the companie of the duke of Burgognie his ambassadours vnto Trois in Champaigne sufficientlie authorised to treat and conclude of so great matter. The king of England, being in good hope that all his affaires should take good successe as he could wish or desire, sent to the duke of Burgognie his vncle, the duke of Excester, the earle of Salisburie, the bishop of Elie, the lord Fanhope, the lord Fitz Hugh, sir Iohn Robsert, and sir Philip Hall, with diuerse doctors, to the number of fiue hundred horsse, which in the companie of the duke of Burgognie came to the citie of Trois the eleuenth of March. The king, the quéene, and the ladie Katharine them receiued, and hartilie welcomed, shewing great signes and tokens of loue and amitie.

A truce tripartite.

Ambassadors from K. Henrie to the French king.

After a few daies they fell to councell, in which at length it was concluded, that king Henrie of England should come to Trois, and marie the ladie Katherine; and the king hir father after his death should make him heire of his realme, crowne and dignitie. It was also agréed, that king Henrie, during his father in lawes life, should in his stéed haue the whole gouernment of the realme of France, as regent thereof, with manie other couenants and articles, as after shall appeere. To the performance whereof, it was accorded, that all the nobles and estates of the realme of France, as well spirituall as temporall, and also the cities and commonalties, citizens and burgesses of townes, that were obeisant at that time to the French king, should take a corporall oth. These articles were not at the first in all points brought to a perfect conclusion. But after the effect and meaning of them was agréed vpon by the commissioners, the Englishmen departed towards the king their maister, and left sir Iohn Robsert behind, to giue his attendance on the ladie Katharine.

The articles of the peace concluded betwéene king Henrie and the French king.

King Henrie being informed by them of that which they had doone, was well content with the agréement and with all diligence prepared to go vnto Trois, and therevpon hauing all things in readinesse, he being accompanied with his brethren the dukes of Clarence and Glocester, the earles of Warwike, Salisburie, Huntington, Eu, Tankeruile, and Longuile, and fiftéene thousand men of warre, went from Rone to Pontoise; & departing from thence the eight daie of Maie, came to saint Denis two leagues from Paris, and after to Pontcharenton, where he left a strong garison of men, with sir William Gascoigne, to keepe the passage; and so then entering into Brie, he tooke by the waie a castell which was kept against him, causing them that so kept it, some to be hanged, and the residue to be led foorth with him as prisoners. And after this keeping on his iournie by Prouins, and Nogent, at length he came to Trois.

Thom. Wals.

Titus Liuius.

The duke of Burgognie accompanied with manie noble men, receiued him two leagues without the towne, and conueied him to his lodging. All his armie was lodged in small villages thereabout. And after that he had reposed himselfe a little, he went to visit the French king, the quéene, and the ladie Katharine, whome he found in saint Peters church, where was a verie ioious méeting betwixt them (and this was on the twentith daie of Maie) and there the king of England, and the ladie Katharine were affianced. After this, the two kings and their councell assembled togither diuerse daies, wherein the first concluded agreement was in diuerse

King Henrie commeth to Trois to the French king.

King Henrie affieth the French kings daughter.

points altered and brought to a certeinetie, according to the effect aboue mentioned. When this great matter was finished, the kings sware for their parts to obserue all the couenants of this league and agreement. Likewise the duke of Burgognie and a great number of other princes and nobles which were present, receiued an *Titus Liuius.* oth, the tenor whereof (as the duke of Burgognie vttered it in solemne words) thus insueth, accordinglie as the same is exemplified by Titus Liuius De Foro Liuisiis in Latine.

The oth of the duke of Burgognie.

EGO Philippus Burgundiæ dux, per me meósque hæredes, ad sacra Dei euangelia domino regi Henrico Angliæ, Franciæque, pro Carolo rege regenti iuro, quòd humiliter ipsi Henrico fidelitérq; cunctis in rebus, quæ rempublicam spectant & Franciæ coronam, obediemus, & statim post mortem Caroli domini nostri, domino Henrico regi suisque successoribus in perpetuum ligei fideles erimus; nec alium quempiam pro domino nostro supremo Franciæ rege, quàm Henricum & suos hæredes habebimus, néque patiemur. Non erimus præterea in consilio vel consensu cuiusquam damni regis Henrici, suorúmue successorum, vbi quicquam detrimenti patiantur capitis siue membri, vel vitam perdant; sed prædicta (quantum in nobis fuerit) quàm citissimis literis vel nuntijs, vt sibi meliùs prouidere valeant, eis significabimus.

The same in English.

I PHILIP duke of Burgognie, for my selfe, and for mine heires, doo here sweare vpon the holie euangelists of God, to Henrie king of England, and regent of France for king Charles, that we shall humblie and faithfullie obeie the said Henrie in all things which concerne the common-wealth and crowne of France. And immediatlie after the deceasse of our souereigne lord king Charles, we shall be faithfull liegemen vnto the said king Henrie, and to his successors for euer. Neither shall we take or suffer anie other souereigne lord and supreme king of France, but the same Henrie and his heires: neither shall we be of councell or consent of anie hurt towards the said king Henrie or his successors, wherby they may suffer losse & detriment of life or lim, but that the same so farre as in vs may lie, we shall signifie to them with all speed, by letters or messengers, that they may the better prouide for themselues in such cases.

The like oth a great number of the princes and nobles both spirituall and temporall which were present, receiued at the same time. This doone, the morow after Trinitie sundaie, being the third of Iune, the mariage was solemnized and fullie consummate betwixt the king of England, and the said ladie Katharine. Herewith was the king of England named and proclamed heire and regent of France. And as the French king sent the copie of this treatie to euerie towne in France: so the king of England sent the same in English vnto euerie citie and market towne within his realme, to be proclamed and published. The true copie whereof, as we find it in the chronicles of maister Hall, we haue thought good here to set downe, for the more full satisfieng of those that shall desire to peruse euerie clause and article thereof as followeth.

The articles & appointments of peace betweene the realmes of England and France.

HENRIE by the grace of God king of England, heire and regent of France, lord of Ireland, to perpetuall mind of christian people, and all those that be vnder our obeisance,

sance, we notifie and declare, that though there hath béene here before diuerse treaties betwéene the most excellent prince Charles our father of France and his progenitors, for the peace to be had betwéene the two realmes of France and England, the which heretofore haue borne no fruit: we considering the great harmes, the which haue not onelie fallen betwéene those two realmes, for the great diuision of that hath béene betwéene them, but to all holy church; we haue taken a treatie with our said father, in which treatie betwixt our said father and vs, it is concluded & accorded in the forme after the manner that followeth.

1 First, it is accorded betwéene our father and vs, that forsomuch as by the bond of matrimonie made for the good of the peace betweene vs and our most deere beloued Katharine, daughter of our said father, & of our most déere moother Isabell his wife; the same Charles and Isabell beene made our father and moother: therefore them as our father and moother we shall haue and worship, as it fitteth and séemeth so worthie a prince and princesse to be worshipped, principallie before all other temporall persons of the world.

2 Also we shall not distrouble, diseason or let our father aforesaid, but that he hold and possede as long as he liueth, as he holdeth and possedeth at this time, the crowne and dignitie roiall of France, with rents and profits for the same, of the sustenance of his estate and charges of the realme. And our foresaid moother also hold as long as she liueth, the state and dignitie of quéene, after the manner of the same realme, with conuenable conuenient part of the said rents and profits.

3 Also that the foresaid ladie Katharine shall take and haue dower in our realme of England as queenes of England here tofore were woont for to take and haue, that is to saie, to the summe of fortie thousand scutes, of the which two algate shall be a noble English.

4 And that by the waies, manners, and meanes that we without transgression or offense of other made by vs, for to speake the lawes, customes, vsages and rights of our said realme of England, shall done our labour and pursuit, that the said Katharine, all so soone as it maie be doone, be made sure to take, and for to haue in our said realme of England, from the time of our death, the said dower of fortie thousand scutes yearelie, of the which twaine algate be worth a noble English.

5 Also if it happe the said Katharine to ouerliue vs, we shall take and haue the realme of France immediatlie, from the time of our death, dower to the summe of twentie thousand franks yearelie, of and vpon the lands, places and lordships that held and had Blanch sometime wife of Philip Beasaill to our said father.

6 Also that after the death of our said father aforesaid, and from thence forward, the crowne and the realme of France, with all the rights and appurtenances, shall remaine and abide to vs, and béene of vs and of our heires for euermore.

7 And forsomuch as our said father is withholden with diuerse sickenesse, in such manner as he maie not intend in his owne person for to dispose for the néeds of the foresaid realme of France: therefore during the life of our foresaid father, the faculties and exercise of the gouernance and disposition of the publick & common profit of the said realme of France, with councell, and nobles, and wisemen of the same realme of France, shall be and abide to vs; so that from thencefoorth we maie gouerne the same realme by vs. And also to admit to our counsell and assistance of the said nobles, such as we shall thinke méet. The which faculties and exercise of gouernance thus being toward vs, we shall labour and purpose vs spéedfullie, diligentlie, and trulie, to that that maie be and ought for to be vnto the worship of God, and our said father and moother, and also to the common good of the said realme, and that realme with the councell & helpe of the worthie and great nobles of the same realme for to be defended, peased and gouerned after right and equitie.

8 Also that we of our owne power shall doo the court of parlement in France to

be

be kept and obserued in his authoritie and souereignetie, and in all that is doone to it in all manner of places that now or in time comming is or shall be subiect to our said father.

9 Also we to our power shall defend and helpe all and euerie of the péeres, nobles, cities, townes, communalties, and singular persons, now or in time comming, subiects to our father in their rights, customes, priuileges, freedomes, and franchises, longing or due to them in all manner of places now or in time comming subiect to our father

10 Also we diligentlie and truelie shall trauell to our power, and doo that iustice be administred and doone in the same realme of France after the lawes, customes, and rights of the same realme, without personall exception. And that we shall kéepe and hold the subiects of the same realme in tranquillitie, and peace, and to our power we shall defend them against all manner of violence and oppression.

11 Also we to our power shall prouide, and doo to our power, that able persons and profitable béene taken to the offices as well of iustices and other offices belonging to the gouernance of the demaines, and of other offices of the said realme of France, for the good right and peaceable iustice of the same, and for the administration that shall be committed vnto them; and that they be such persons, that after the lawes and rights of the same realme, and for the vtilitie and profit of our said father, shall minister, and that the foresaid realme shall be taken and departed to the same offices.

12 Also that we of our power, so soone as it may commodiouslie be doone, shall trauell to put into the obedience of our said father, all manner of cities, townes, and castels, places, countries, and persons within the realme of France, disobedient, and rebels to our said father, holding with them which beene called the Dolphin or Arminacke.

13 Also that we might the more commodiouslie, suerlie and fréelie doone, exercise, & fulfill these things aforesaid, it is accorded that all worthie nobles and estates of the same realme of France, as well spirituals as temporals, and also cities notable and communalties, and citizens, burgesses of townes of the realme of France, that béene obeisant at this time to our said father, shall make these othes that followen.

14 First to vs hauing the facultie, exercise, disposition, and gouernance of the foresaid common profit to our hests and commandements, these shall meekelie & obedientlie obeie and intend in all manner of things concerning the exercise of gouernance of the same realme.

15 Also that the worthie, great, and noble estates of the said realme as well spirituals as temporals, and also cities and notable communalties, and citizens and burgesses of the same realme, in all manner of things well and trulie shall kéepe and to their power shall doo to be kept of so much as to them belongeth, or to anie of them, all those things that béene appointed and accorded betwéene our foresaid father and moother and vs, with the counsell of them whome vs list to call to vs.

16 And that continuallie from the death, and after the death of our said father Charles, they shall be our true liegemen, and our heires; and they shall receiue and admit vs for their liege and souereigne and verie king of France, and for such to obeie vs without opposition, contradiction, or difficultie, as they béene to our foresaid father during his life, neuer after this realme of France shall obey to man as king or regent of France, but to vs and our heires. Also they shall not be in counsell, helpe, or assent that we léese life or limme, or be take with euill taking, or that we suffer harme, or diminution in person, estate worship, or goods; but if they know anie such thing for to be cast or imagined against vs, they shall let it to their power, & they shall doone vs to weeten thereof, as hastilie as they maie by themselfe, by message, or by letters.

17 Also that all maner of conquests that should be made by vs in France vpon the
said.

said inobedients, out of the duchie of Normandie, shall be doone to the profit of our said father; and that to our power we shall doo, that all maner of lands and lordships that béene in the places so for to be conquered, longing to persons obeieng to our fore-said father, which shall sweare for to kéepe this present accord, shall be restored to the same persons to whom they long to.

18 Also that all manner of persons of the holie church, beneficed in the duchie of Normandie, or any other places in the realme of France, subiect to our father, and fauouring the partie of the dukes of Burgognie, which shall sweare to kéepe this present accord, shall inioy peaceablie their benefices of holie church in the duchie of Normandie, or in other places next aforesaid.

19 Also likewise, all maner of persons of holie church, obedient to vs and beneficed in the realme of France, and places subiect to our father, that shall sweare to keepe this present accord, shall inioy peaceablie their benefices of holie church in places next abouesaid.

20 Also that all maner of churches, vniuersities, and studies generall, and all colleges of studies, and other colleges of holie church, being in places now or in time comming subiect to our father, or in the duchie of Normandie, or other places in the realme of France subiect to vs, shall inioy their rights and possessions, rents, prerogatiues, liberties, & franchises, longing or due to them in any maner of wise in the said relme of France, sauing the right of the crowne of France, and euerie other person.

21 Also by Gods helpe, when it happeneth vs to come to the crowne of France, the duchie of Normandie, and all other places conquered by vs in the realme of France, shall bow vnder the commandement, obeisance, and monarchie of the crowne of France.

22 Also that we shall force vs, & doo to our power, that recompense be made by our said father without diminution of the crowne of France to persons obeieng to him, and fauoring to that partie that is said Burgognie, to whom longeth lands, lordships, rents, or possessions in the said duchie of Normandie, or other places in the realme of France, conquered by vs hithertoward giuen by vs in places and lands gotten, or to be gotten, and ouercome, in the name of our said father vpon rebels and inobedients to him. And if so be that such maner of recompense be not made to the said persons, by the life of our said father, we shall make that recompense in such maner and places, of goods, when it happeneth by Gods grace to the crowne of France. And if so be that the lands, lordships, rents, or possessions, the which longeth to such maner of persons in the said duchie and places be not giuen by vs, the same persons shall be restored to them without any delaie.

23 And during the life of our father, in all places now or in time comming subiect to him, letters of common iustice, and also grants of offices and gifts, pardons or remissions, and priuileges shall be written and proceed vnder the name and seale of our said father. And for somuch as some singular case maie fall, that maie not be foreséene by mans wit, in the which it might be necessarie and behoouefull, that we doo write our letters; in such maner case, if any hap for the good and suertie of our father, and for the gouernance that longeth to vs, as is beforesaid; and for to eschewen perils that otherwise might fall, to the preiudice of our said father, to write our letters, by the which we shall command, charge, and defend after the nature and qualitie of the néed, in our fathers behalfe and ours as regent of France.

24 Also, that during our fathers life, we shall not call nor write vs king of France; but verelie we shall absteine vs from that name, as long as our father liueth.

25 Also that our said father, during his life shall name, call, and write vs in French in this maner: Nostre treschier filz Henry roy d'Engleterre heretere de France. And in Latine in this maner: Præclarissimus filius noster Henricus rex Angliæ & hæres Franciæ.

26 Also that we shall put none impositions or exactions, or doo charge the subiects of our said father without cause reasonable and necessarie, ne otherwise than for common good of the realme of France, and after the saieng and asking of the lawes and customes reasonable approoued of the same realme.

27 Also that we shall trauell to our power to the effect and intent, that by the assent of the thrée estates of either of the realmes of France and England, that all maner of obstacles maie be doone awaie, and in this partie, that it be ordeined and prouided; that from the time that we or any of our heires come to the crowne of France, both the crownes, that is to saie, of France and England perpetuallie be togither in one & in the same person, that is to saie, from our fathers life to vs, and from the tearme of our life thenceforward in the persons of our heires, that shall be one after an other, and that both realmes shall be gouerned from that we or any of our heires come to the same, not seuerallie vnder diuerse kiugs in one time, but vnder the same person which for the time shall be king of both realmes, and our souereigne lord (as it is before said) kéeping neuerthelesse in all maner of other things to either of the same realmes, their rights, liberties, customes, vsages, and lawes, not making subiect in any maner of wise one of the same realmes, to the rights, lawes, or vsages of that other.

28 Also that thenceforward, perpetuallie, shall be still rest, and that in all maner of wise, dissentions, hates, rancors, enuies and wars, betweene the same realmes of France and England, and the people, of the same realmes, drawing to accord of the same peace, may ceasse and be broken.

29 Also that there shall be from henceforward for euermore, peace, and tranquillitie, & good accord and common affection, and stable friendship betwéene the said realmes, and their subiects before said. The same realmes shall kéepe themselues with their councell, helps, and common assistance against all maner of men that inforce them for to dooen or to imagine wrongs, harmes, displeasures, or grieuances to them or either of them. And they shall be conuersant and merchandizen fréelie and suerlie togither, paieng the custome due and accustomed. And they shall be conuersant also, that all the confederats and alies of our said father and the realme of France aforesaid, and also our confederats of the realme of England aforesaid, shall in eight moneths from the time of this accord of peace, as it is notified to them, declare by their letters, that they will draw to this accord, and will be comprehended vnder the treaties and accord of this peace, sauing neuerthelesse either of the same crownes, and also all maner actions, rights and reuenues, that longen to our said father and his subiects, and to vs and our subiects, against all maner of such alies and confederats.

30 Also neither our father, neither our brother the duke of Burgognie shall begin, ne make with Charles, cleping himselfe the Dolphin of Viennes, any treatie, or peace, or accord, but by councell and assent of all and ech of vs thrée, or of other the thrée estates of either of the said realmes aboue named.

31 Also that we with assent of our said brother of Burgognie, and other of the nobles of the realme of France, the which thereto owen to be called, shall ordeine for the gouernance of our said father sckerlie, louinglie, & honestlie, after the asking of his roiall estate and dignitie, by the maner that shall be to the worship of God, and of our father, and of the realme of France.

32 Also all maner of persons, that shall be about our father to doo him personall seruice, not onelie in office, but in all other seruices, aswell the nobles and gentlenes as other, shall be such as hath beene borne in the realme of France, or in places longing to France, good, wise, true, and able to that foresaid seruice. And our said father shall dwell in places notable of his obedience, and no where else. Wherefore we charge and command our said liege subiects, and other being vnder our obedience,

dience, that they keepe and doo to be kept in all that longeth to them, this accord and peace, after the forme and maner as it is accorded; and that they attempt in no maner wise, any thing that may be preiudiciall or contrarie to the same accord and peace, vpon paine of life and lim, and all that they may forfeit against vs. Yeuen at Troes, the thirtith day of Maie, 1420, & proclamed in London the twentith day of Iune.

33 Also that we for the things aforesaid, and euerie one of them, shall giue our assent by our letters patents, sealed with our seale vnto our said father, with all approbation and confirmation of vs, and all other of our bloud roiall, and all other of the cities and townes to vs obedient. Sealed with our seales accustomed. And further, our said father, besides his letters patents sealed with our great seale, shall make or cause to be made letters approbatorie, and confirmations of the peeres of his realme, and of the lords, citizens, and burgesses of the same, vnder his obedience. All which articles we haue sworne to keepe vpon the holie euangelists.

On the fourteenth of Iune being fridaie, there was a solemn procession at London, *Tho. Walsi.* and a sermon at Paules crosse, in which the preacher openlie declared the effect of the kings mariage, and the articles concluded vpon the same, by reason whereof (he said) there must be a new great seale deuised, and the old broken, and in the new the kings name with a new addition of his title as regent of France, and heire apparant of that kingdome was to be ingrauen. Beside the league thus concluded by king Henrie *A league be-* with the French king, and the whole bodie of the realme of France, there was a *tweene king* priuat league accorded betwixt him and the duke of Burgognie, the effect wherof *duke of Bur-* was comprehended in articles as followeth. *gognie.*

1 First, that the duke of Burgognie should procure this peace latelie before concluded, to be obserued firme and stable in all couenants and points therof, so far as he by any meanes might further the same: in consideration whereof, one of the brethren of king Henrie should take to wife one of the said duke of Burgognies sisters. 2 That king Henrie should euer haue in singular fauour the said duke of Burgognie, as his most deere brother, and support him in all his rights. 3 That the said duke, after the deceasse of king Charles, should take an oth of fealtie to be true to K. Henrie & his heires, according to the forme & tenor thereof before expressed, & should in all things be friend to king Henrie and his heires for euer. 4 That king Henrie should doo his vttermost indeuour, that due punishment might be had for the murther of duke Iohn, father to the said duke of Burgognie, aswell vpon Charles that named himselfe Dolphin, as vpon others that were guiltie and priuie to that murther.

5 If the said Dolphin chanced to be taken, in battell or towne besieged, or if anie other chanced so to be taken, that should be prooued guiltie or priuie to the murther of the said duke Iohn, he should not be deliuered without iust punishment for his deeds, nor without the consent of the two kings Charles and Henrie, & of the three estates of both the realmes. 6 In consideration of the great diligence, and painfull trauell susteined by the duke of Burgognie, it was also agreed, that he should haue by patent granted of king Charles and queene Isabell a fee of twentie thousand pounds Parisien, of yeerelie reuenues, assigned foorth neere to the confines of his countrie, to inioy the same to him and to his wife the duches Michaell, and to the heires males betwixt them two, lawfullie begotten, to the obteining whereof, king Henrie should shew all his furtherance; & if it might not be brought to passe till king Henrie had obteined the crowne of France, then should he see the same performed, vpon the receiuing of his homage.

The king of England, after all the articles of the said treaties and agreements were *The effect of* concluded, passed and sworne vnto, made to the French king, the duke of Burgognie, *king Henries* and other the French lords, a sumptuous banket; and before they departed from the *French king.* same, he sadlie and with great grauitie made to them a right pithie and sententious oration, declaring to them both how profitable the ioining of the two kingdomes should

should be to the subiects of the same, and also the right that he had thereto, being by lineall descent of the womans side (which is the surest) rather a Frenchman than an Englishman. And though he was an Englishman borne, yet he assured them to tender the wealth of the realme of France, as much as he would the aduancement of his owne natiue countrie of England.

Herewith, he inueied against Charles the Dolphin, being the head and onelie mainteiner of all the ciuill discord, whose wicked nature, and cruell disposition, did well appeare in the murther of the late duke of Burgognie. He therefore willed them, according to their dutie, oth, and agréement, to stand with him, and helpe to reduce such a stubborne and disloiall sonne vnto the obeisance of his father king Charles, that he might shew himselfe conformable vnto such orders and decrées, as they had taken, appointed, and agréed vpon: and for his part, he promised to worship, loue, and honor his father in law the said K. Charles, in place of his owne father, according to the true mening of this concord and agréement, trusting the same to be a peace finall.

And to conclude, he promised, that if they shewed themselues true and loiall to him, according to the same agréement; the Ocean sea should sooner ceasse to flow, and the bright sunne lose his light, than he would desist from dooing that which became a prince to doo to his subiect, or a father to his naturall child. When he had thus persuaded the nobilitie, and dispatched his businesse at Troies, he with all his armie, hauing with him the French king, and the duke of Burgognie, departed from thence the fourth of Iune; and vpon the seauenth daie of the same moneth, came before the towne of Sens in Burgognie, which held on the Dolphins part: but after foure daies siege, it was yéelded vnto the king, and there he made capteine, the lord Genuille. From thence, he remooued to Monstreau ou fault Yonne, which towne was taken on the three and twentith daie of Iune, by assault, so that manie of the Dolphins part were apprehended, before they could get to the castell.

It was rendered vp the tenth of Iune
Titus Liuius
Sens & Mostreau besieged and taken.
The siege was laid the 16 of Iune.

Whilest the siege laie there, and before the towne was entred, the duke of Bedford came thither vnto the king, bringing with him a faire retinue of soldiers out of England. After the getting of the towne, the castell being well vittelled and manned, denied to render, and therefore was it enuironed with a strong siege. During the which, the duke of Burgognie was informed, in what place of the towne the duke his father was buried, who was slaine there (as before you haue heard) and now his corps was taken vp againe by his sonnes appointment, and seared, and so conueied vnto Digeon in high Burgognie, and there buried by his father Philip: to the end that the remembrance of him should remaine to posterities, by the reseruation of some monument abiding in the place of his interment, after that his bodie was consumed, and his naturall countenance forgotten. Which is the last point of reuerend dutie (as we may well thinke) which pietie of children towards their parents dooth require; namelie, that they be decentlie buried when they be departed; and that their graues or toome stones may put vs that are aliue in mind of going the same waie, and to set no more by this flitting life, than standeth with the vncerteintie and shortnesse of the same; as one right well saith:

Cùm tumulum cernis, cur non mortalia spernis?
Esto memor mortis, quo viuis tempore fortis.

Bicause they within the castell of Monstreau, gaue opprobrious words vnto the kings herald that was sent to them, the king caused a gibet to be set vp before the castle, on the which were hanged twelue of those spitefull offendors, all gentlemen & freends to the capteine named monsieur de Guitrie, who at length, perceiuing that by no means he could be succoured; and fearing to be taken by force, began to treat with the king of England, who for the space of eight daies would hearken to none of his offers; but in conclusion, he and his rendred themselues simplie, their liues onelie saued, six wéekes after they had béene besieged. The earle of Warwike was made capteine, both of the towne and castell, who fortified it with men, munition, and vittels.

It held not out so long as should appeare by *Tit. Liuius*, who saith, that it was rendred the fourth of Iulie.

[About

[About this time Robert the gouernour of Scotland, the fifteenth yéere after his *W. P.* brothers reigne, and in the thirtith yeare of his owne regiment deceassed, in whose *Buchan. lib.* 10. steed and office his sonne Mordac duke of Albanie was by and by chosen, who had sonnes three, Walter, Alexander, and Iames, whereof the two eldest beginning betimes to be obstinate, grew soone after verie graceles and wicked: that in one flagitious feat among the rest by this Walter verie impiouslie against his parents was vttered. The gouernour had a faire, a gentle, and well flieng falcon, whereby he set great store. The sonne verie desirous of the same, made manie meanes and mótions to haue hir, not without note of malapert importunitie and lacke of reuerence toward his parents pleasure, which the father dissembling to sée, would not yet in anie wise forgo his hawke. Whereat this child reiecting regard of dutie, and receiuing an vnnaturall hate and heat by broth of iniquitie set a boiling in his brest, came in on a time, where standing a while at a sudden braid, pluckt awaie the bird from his fathers fist, and straight before his face wrang of hir necke. The gouernour heereat sore astonied, for verie greefe gaue a great grone; "Well sonne (quod he) since yée cannot bridle your brunts for dutie and reuerence toward me your parent and souereigne, I will bring in one that shall bridle vs both." Heerevpon soone after, he with one Calen Campbell, a noble man & of much authoritie (vnto whome this Walter had doone a great despight) and with other of the nobilitie fell straight in consultation about the calling home of their king. Which all with one assent they did right well allow, whereby soone after (as is touched afore, and followeth more at large) he was by them in his kingdome right roiallie placed. But this came of it. These mischéefous children Walter and Alexander, the verie cause of their fathers confusion and their owne, within few yeares after condemned by law, vpon a hill by Sterling castell, had their heads chopt off at once. Walters wife with hir two sonnes, Andrew and Alexander, ran for refuge awaie into Ireland; thus for their long iniquities their hires iustlie paid all in a daie.]

Now to procéed in our processe of France. After the thus winning of the towne *Melun besieged* and castell of Monstreau; the king departing from thence, came to Melun vpon Seine, *by king Henrie.* the thirteenth daie of Iulie, and besieged it round about, hauing then in companie with him the French king, and the yoong king of Scots, the dukes of Burgognie, *The king of* Clarence, Bedford, Glocester, and Bar, the prince of Orainge, and one and twentie *Scots in K.* earles, besides lords, barons, & knights, equall to lords in degree, to the number of *Héries armie.* seauen and fiftie, what of England and France; and beside also fiftéene maister soldiers. This siege continued the space almost of seuen moneths, or (as Thomas *Eightéene* Walsingham saith) fouretéene wéekes, and foure daies, with skirmishing, scaling *wéekes haue the* assaulting, and defending, to the losse (no doubt) of both parts. Capteine of this *Flanders.* towne was one monsieur de Barbason, a Gascoine of such experience and approoued *Monsieur de* valiancie in wars, that his renowme and fame was spred through the world. *valiãt captein.*

At the first laieng of the siege, he called all the soldiers there in garrison, and likewise the townesmen afore him, and warned them all on paine of death, that none of them should be so hardie, as to treat, or once to motion anie word of surrendring the towne, or of comming to anie composition or agréement with the two kings; except they made him being their capteine priuie thereto, before they attempted anie such thing. ¶ In the meane season, the French queene, the queene of England, and the duches of Burgognie, lieng at Corbeill, came diuers times to visit their husbands, and to sée their fréends; whome the king of England highlie feasted and louinglie interteined, that euerie creature reported great honour of him. This *Titus Liuius.* towne of Melun séemed verie strong, both by reason of the riuer of Seine, which compassed part thereof, and also by strong walles, turrets, ditches, and bulworks made about it.

The king therefore, to take awaie all the issues and entries from them within, made a bridge ouer the riuer, able to beare horsses and carriage: and againe, appointed diuerse botes furnished with men of warre, to kéepe the streame; so that they within should haue no waie to come abroad, either by water or land; yet on a daie, the Frenchmen sailed foorth, and assailed the English lodgings, where the earle of Warwike was incamped on the east side of the towne, not farre from the duke of Burgognie; but by the valiant prowesse and manlie courage of the Englishmen, the enimies were easilie beaten backe and constreined to retire into the towne againe with their losse. Héere is to be remembred, that during this siege before Melun, there came to the king the duke of Bauiere, the kings brother in law (but the kings sister that had béene married to him, was not then liuing) and brought with him seauen hundred well appointed horssemen, which were reteined to serue the king, and right worthilie they bare themselues, and therefore most liberallie recompensed at the kings hand, for the time they continued in his seruice.

The duke of Bauiere commeth to king Henrie with a number of horssemen.

The king inforced this siege by all waies and meanes possible, to bring the towne into subiection, as well by mines as otherwise, but they within the towne so valiantlie behaued themselues, as well by countermines (whereby at length they entered into the kings mines) as by other waies of resistance, that by force of assaults it was not thought anie easie matter to win the same. It fortuned on a daie, that whilest there rose a contention betwixt two lords of the kings host, who should haue the honor to go first into the mine, to incounter with the Frenchmen, that now had brought their mine through into the English mines, and made barriers betwixt, that they might safelie come and fight with the Englishmen: the king (to auoid the strife) entered the mine himselfe first of all other, and by chance came to fight hand to hand with the lord Barbason, who was likewise entered the mine before all other of them within the towne.

The trãslator of Tit. Liuius.

K. Henrie and mõsieur Barbason fight hand to hand.

After they had fought a good season togither, at length they agreed to discouer either to other their names; so as the lord Barbason, first declaring what he was; the king likewise told him, that he was the king of England. Wherevpon, Barbason perceiuing with whome he had fought, caused the barriers foorthwith to be closed, and withdrew into the citie, and the king returned backe to his campe. At length, vittels within the towne began to faile, and the pestilence began to wax hot, so that the lord Barbason began to treat; and in conclusion, about the middest of Nouember (as Fabian saith) the towne was yéelded vpon certeine conditions, whereof one was, that all that were consenting to the death of the duke of Burgognie, should be deliuered to the king of England, of whome the lord Barbason was suspected to be one. The king sent them vnder the conduct of his brother the duke of Clarence, to the citie of Paris, whereof the French king made him capteine, and so at his comming thither, he tooke possession of the Bastill of S. Anthonie, the Loure, the house of Néelle, and the place of Bois de Vincennes.

It was surrendred about Alhalontide, as Thom. Wal. noteth.

Melun yéelded vp to king Henrie.

Monsieur de Barbason was accused by the duke of Burgognie, and his sisters as guiltie to their fathers death; but he in open court defended himselfe as not guiltie of that crime, granting indeed and confessing, that he was one of the familiar seruants to the Dolphin, but that he was priuie or consenting to the death of the duke of Burgognie, he vtterlie denied. Wherevpon he was not condemned, neither yet acquited, by reason of such presumptions and coniectures as were alledged and brought against him, so that he remained in prison at Paris and else-where, the space of nine yeares, till at length, being brought vnto castell Galliard, it chanced that the same castell was woone by those of the Dolphins part, and he being as then prisoner there, escaped out of danger, and so by that means was set at libertie, as after shall appeare.

Titus Liuius.

Some write, that he had béene put to death, if he had not appealed from king Henries sentence, vnto the iudgement of the officers at armes; alledging, that by the lawe of armes,

Note this appeale.

armes, no man hauing his brother in armes within his danger, afterwards ought to put him to death for any cause or quarell. And that he was the kings brother in armes he prooued it, for that he had fought with him hand to hand within the mines (as before yee haue heard) which combat was thought of equall force by the heralds, as if he had fought with the king bodie to bodie, within solemne lists. The credit of this matter we leaue to the consideration of the readers. The earle of Huntington was made capteine of Melum. In defense of this towne and castell, the French had gotten vnto them manie Scots. At the siege héere the king kept with him yoong Iames of Scotland, who sent to those Scots, that they should come out and yeeld them vnto him, and not to stand in armes against their liege lord and king; but they gaue word backe againe, they could not take him for king, that was in the power of another, and so kept them in hold and in their armor still. King Henrie vpon winning of these forts, for their rebellion against their prince, which they would haue to be counted constancie, and for their contemptuous answer vnto him, twentie of the proudest, in example of the rest, caused he there to be hanged at once.

From thence the king departed with his armie vnto Corbeill, where the French king and the two queenes then soiourned; and after, both the kings, accompanied with the dukes of Bedford, Burgognie, Glocester, and Excester, and the earls of Warwike and Salisburie, with a great number of noble men and knights, set foorth towards Paris, whome the citizens in good order met without the gates, and the cleargie also with solemne procession. All the streets were hanged with rich clothes, the two kings rode togither (the king of England giuing the vpper hand to his father in lawe) though the great citie of Paris, to our ladie church, where after they had said their deuotions, they departed vnto their lodgings; the French king to the house of S. Paule, and the king of England to the castell of Louer.

The next daie, the two queenes made their entrie and were receiued with like solemnities, as their husbands were the day before. During all the season that these two kings laie in Paris, there was a great assemblie called, as well of the spiritualtie, as of the nobles of the temporaltie, in the which, the kings set as iudges, before whom the duches of Burgognie by hir proctor, appealed the Dolphin, and seauen other, for the murther of duke Iohn hir husband. To the which appeale, the counsell of the other part made diuerse offers of amends, as well of foundations of chantries for préests, to praie for the soule, as recompense of monie to the widow and children; for the finall determination whereof, the kings, to take further aduise and counsell therein, appointed another daie.

At this same time, the thrée estates of the realme of France assembled at Paris, and there euerie person seuerallie sware vpon the holie euangelists, to keepe, support, mainteine and defend the treatie and finall accord, which was concluded betwéene the two kings and thereto euerie noble man, spirituall gouernour and temporall ruler, set to their seales, which instruments were sent to the kings treasurie of his eschecker at Westminster safelie to be kept, where they yet remaine. The French king at the same time being in good and perfect state of health, openlie there in parlement declared, that peace was concluded, accorded, and made by his frée assent, and with the aduise of all the councell of France, and that he would for his owne part and that his successors ought for their parts, obserue and kéepe the same, with all the articles therein conteined. And likewise, that all his subiects were bound for euer, to obserue and kéepe the same, without breaking or dooing anie thing preiudiciall therevnto.

During the time that the two kings thus soiourned in Paris, the French king kept a small port, verie few, and those of the meaner sort resorting vnto his court: but the king of England kept such a solemne state, with so plentifull an house, and shewed himselfe so bountifull in gifts, and setting foorth of warlike shewes and

R 2　　　　　　　　　　　　　　　　　　　　　princelie

A note in law of armes.

w. p.

King Henrie is receiued in at Paris.

The duches of Burgognie hir appeale.

The oth of the thrée estates of Frāce.

princelie pastimes, that all the noble men and other resorted to his palace to see his

King Henrie taketh vpon him the office of regent of France. The coine salute,
estate, and to doo him honor.   He tooke vpon him as regent of France, to redresse causes, remooue officers, reforme things that were amisse, and caused a new coine to be made, called a salute, wherein were the armes of France, and the armes of England and France quarterlie stamped.   Also, to set all things in quiet, he constituted sir Gilbter Umfreuile capteine of Melun, with a good number of valiant soldiers, to remaine there in garrison, and the earle of Huntington (coosine germane to the king) was deputed capteine at Blois de Vincenes; and the duke of Excester, with fiue hundred men of warre, was assigned to keepe Paris.   Thus had king Henrie (when he was constituted gouernour of the land) the disposing of prouinces, townes, and castels at his pleasure; and the making of lawes and ordinances, standing with the drift of his policie to kéepe both people in due obedience; as Anglorum prælia bréefelie noteth; saieng :

> Rectorem patriæ postquam rex Gallus & omnes
> Vnanimes proceres Henricum constituerunt;
> Plantageneta dabat princeps iam iura duabus
> Gentibus, effrænes ductis cohibebat habenis.

The duke of Bauier & his troope with the kings fauor departeth.
The duke of Bauier about the same time, with the kings licence, departed into his countrie, both he and his retinue, receiuing large gifts of the kings great liberalitie, and amongst other things, the king gaue him a cup of gold, garnished and set with pretious stones of great price and value.   Moreouer, he had a pension giuen him of a thousand markes by yeare, vnder the kings letters patents, to be had and receiued of the kings frée and liberall grant, during the life of the said duke.   A right roiall reward & worthie the maiestie of a king, bestowed vpon the said duke, and his retinue, partlie in respect of the aliance betwixt the king and him (for he had maried the kings sister) but speciallie for the notable seruice which they did him at the siege before Melun.   So that hereby is commended vnto vs an example of gratitude and beneficence; teaching vs, that to such as haue béene good and gratious vnto vs, we should be alwaies forward with a right hand and readie mind to make amends in some proportion and measure.

1421
When the king had thus ordered his businesse, he with the quéene his wife, the princes, & nobles of the realme departed from Paris, the sixt of Ianuarie, and came to Rone, but first before his departing, he caused processe to be made and awarded foorth against Charles the Dolphin, commanding him to appéere at the marble table at Paris; where for lacke of appearance, he was with all solemnitie in such case
Sentence against the Dolphin.
requisite, denounced guiltie of the murther and homicide of Iohn duke of Burgognie, and by the sentence of parlement banished the realme; but the Dolphin withdrew into Languedoc, and after to Poictiers, getting to him such fréends as he could; and namelie, he found the earle of Arminacke verie faithfull to him, not onelie aiding him with men, but also with his owne person he continuallie serued him against all his aduersaries.

These counties they inioied of the kings gift.
The king of England comming to Rone, soiourned there a certeine time, and receiued the homage of all the nobles of Normandie, amongst whome, the earle of Stafford did homage for the countie of Perch, and Arthur of Britaine likewise for the countie of Yurie.   He also ordeined his lieutenant generall, both of France and Normandie, his brother Thomas duke of Clarence; and his deputie in Normandie was the earle of Salisburie.   When the feast of Christmasse was passed, he departed from Rone, with the quéene his wife, and by Amiens came to Calis, where he tooke
He landed at Douer vpon Candlemasse éeue saith *Tho. Walsingham.*
ship the morow after Candlemasse daie, and landed at Douer, and came to Canturburie and from thence to Eltham, and so through London to Westminster.   I passe ouer to write what ioy and triumph was shewed by the citizens of London, and of all other his subiects in euerie place where he came.

The

The king himselfe, to render vnto God his most humble & hartie thanks, caused King Henrie solemne processions to be obserued and kept fiue daies togither in euerie citie and returneth into England with his towne. After that doone, he made great purueiance for the coronation of his quéene new wife. & spouse, the faire ladie Katharine: which was doone the daie of S. Matthew, *Thomas Wal-singham* saith, being the twentie fourth of Februarie, with all such ceremonies and princelie solemni- she was crowned the first in Lent tie as apperteined. Which because it was full of roialtie and honour (the qualitie of which that yere, fell vpon the of the principall personages requiring no lesse) and recorded by writers of former ninth of Febru- ages, it séemeth necessarie and conuenient in this place to report it, in such sort as arie. The coronation it is found at large in some, though others glansinglie passe by it, as a matter of no of quéene great obseruation. But it is worth the noting, to consider and take a view of the Katharine. goodlie order and reuerend dutifulnesse exhibited on all sides to the new quéene; of whome Anglorum prælia saith,

More coronatur maiorum regia coniux,
Ingeminans rex ô viuat, regináque vulgus,
Altisonis suprema ferit clamoribus astra.

¶ After the great solemnization at the foresaid coronation in the church of saint *Abr. Fl.* out of Peters at Westminster was ended, the queene was conueied into the great hall of *Fabian* pag. 402, 403. Westminster, and there set to dinner. Vpon whose right hand sat at the end of A roiall banket. the table the archbishop of Canturburie, & Henrie surnamed the Rich cardinall of Winchester. Vpon the left hand of the quéene sat the king of Scots in his estate, who was serued with couered messe, as were the forenamed bishops; but yet after them. Vpon the same hand and side, néere the boords end, sat the duchesse of Yorke and the countesse of Huntington. The earle of March, holding a scepter in his hand, knéeled vpon the right side: the earle marshall in like manner on the left of the quéene. The countesse of Kent sat vnder the table at the right foot, and the countesse marshall at the left. The duke of Glocester sir Humfrie was that daie ouerseer, and stood before the queene bareheaded. Sir Richard Neuill was that daie caruer to the quéene, the earles brother of Suffolke cupbearer, sir Iohn Steward sewar, the lord Clifford pantler in the earle of Warwikes stéed, the lord Willoughbie buttler in steed of the erle of Arundell, the lord Graie Ruthin or Riffin naperer, the lord Audleie almoner in stéed of the earle of Cambridge, the earle of Worcester was that daie earle marshall in the earle marshals absence; who rode about the hall vpon a great courser with a multitude of tipped staues about him, to make and kéepe roome in the said hall. Of the which hall the barons of the cinque ports began the table vpon the right hand, toward saint Stephans chappell; and beneath them at the table sat the vowchers of the chancerie. Vpon the left hand next to the cupboord sat the maior and his brethren the aldermen of London. The bishops began the table against the barons of the cinque ports; and the ladies against the maior. Of which two tables, for the bishops, began the bishop of London and the bishop of Durham; and for the ladies, the countesse of Stafford, and the countesse of March.

The feast was all of fish, for the ordering of the seruice whereof were diuerse lords appointed head officers, as steward, controller, surueior, and other honourable officers. For the which were appointed the earles of Northumberland and Westmer-land, the lord Fitz Hugh, the lord Furneuall, the lord Graie of Wilton, the lord Ferres of Grobie, the lord Poinings, the lord Harrington, the lord Darcie, the lord Dacres, and the lord de la Ware. These with others ordered the seruice of the feast as followeth; and thus for the first course. Brawne and mustard, eeles in The first course. burneur, frument with balten, pike in herbarge, lamprie powdered, trowt, codling, plaice fried, martine fried, crabs, leech lumbard flourished, tartes; and a deuise called a pellican, sitting on hir nest with hir birds, and an image of saint Katharine holding

holding a booke, and disputing with doctors, holding this poesie in hir right hand, written in faire and legible letters, Madame le Royne; and the pellican answering.

C'e est la signe & du roy, pour tenir ioy,
Et a tout sa gent, elle mette sa entent.

The second course was: gellie coloured with columbine flowers, white potage or creame of almonds, breame of the sea, coonger, soles, cheuen, barbill and roch, fresh salmon, halibut, gurnard, rochet broiled, smelts fried, creuis or lobster; léech damaske, with the kings poesie flourished therevpon, vne sans plus; lamprie fresh baked, flampeine flourished with a scutchion roiall, and therein thrée crownes of gold planted with flourdeluces and floure of camomill wrought of confection: with a deuise of a panther, and an image of saint Katharine with a whéele in one hand, & a scroll with a poesie in the other, to wit,

La royne ma file, in cesta ile,
Per bon resoun, aues renoun.

The third course was, dates in compost, creame motle, carpe deore, turbut, tench, pearch with goion, fresh sturgion with welks, porperous rosted, mennes fried, creuisse de eau doure, pranis, éeles rosted with lamprie, a léech called the white leech flourished with hawthorne leaues & red hawes; a marchpane garnished with diuerse figures of angels, among which was set an image of S. Katharine, holding this posie,

Il est escript, pur voir & eit,
Per marriage pure, cest guerre ne dure.

And lastlie a deuise of a tiger looking in a mirror, and a man sitting on horssebacke all armed, holding in his armes a tigers whelpe with this poesie; Per force sans resounie ay prise ceste best: and with his owne hand making a countenance of throwing of mirrors at the great tiger, which held this poesie; Gile che mirrour ma feste distour. Thus with all honour was finished the solemne coronation, after which the quéene soiourned in the palace of Westminster till Palmesundaie following; and on the morow she tooke hir iournie towards Windsor; where the king and she held their Easter.]

After the solemne feast of the coronation was ended, the king as well to visit certeine places for deuotion by waie of pilgrimage, as also to see in what state and order diuerse parts of his realme stood, departed from the queene, appointing daie and place where she should méet him, and so iournied foorth from place to place, thorough sundrie countries, as well of Wales as England, and in euerie quarter where he came, he heard with diligent eare the complaints of sutors, and tooke order for the administration of iustice both to high and low, causing manie misdemeanours to be reformed. At length he came to the towne of Leicester, where he found the quéene according to the appointment before taken. Here at Leicester, he held the feast of Easter. ¶ How then standeth this with the report of Fabian, who saith, that the king and quéene kept their Easter at Windsor; and that when the said festiuall time was expired, the king made prouision for his warres in France, during the tearme of Richard Whitinghams meraltie of London, which was in the eight yeare of this king Henries reigne: Suerlie there must needs be an errour, either in mistaking the yeare or the place: vnlesse we will grant the king and queene (with their court of attendants) to haue béene Híc ibi simul, which priuilege is granted to none but Ubiquitaries.

But while these things were thus adooing in England, the duke of Clarence, the kings lieutenant in France and Normandie, assembled togither all the garrisons of Normandie, at the towne of Bernaie, and from thence departed to the countrie of Maine, and at Pont le Gene he passed the riuer of Yonne, and rode through all the countrie to Lucie, where he passed the riuer of Loire, and entered into Aniou, and came before the citie of Angiers, where he made manie knights, that

is

The second course.

The third course.

Iustice ministred by king Henrie in progresse.

Abr. Fl.

An. Reg. 9.

The duke of Clarēce made a rode into Aniou.

to saie, sir William Ros, sir Henrie Goddard, sir Rowland Rider, sir Thomas Beaufort, called the bastard of Clarence, and diuerse other; and after that he had forraied, burnt, and spoiled the countrie, he returned with preie and pillage to the towne of Beaufort in the vallie, where he was aduertised, that a great number of his enimies, Frenchmen, Scots, Spaniards, and other were assembled togither, at a place called Viell Bauge, that is Old Baugie, with the duke of Alanson, calling himselfe lieutenant generall for the Dolphin. Viell Baugē or Baugie.

The duke of Clarence had a Lombard resorting vnto him, reteined with the part aduerse (his name was Andrew Forgusa) of whom the duke inquired the number of his enimies, to whome he reported, that their number was but small, & not of puissance to match with halfe the power of his strong armie, intising him with assurance of victorie, to set on the Frenchmen. The duke like a couragious prince, assembled togither all the horssemen of the armie, and left the archers vnder the guiding of the bastard of Clarence, and two Portingales, capteins of Fresnie le vicount, saieng, that he onelie and the nobles would haue the honor of that iournie. When the duke was passed a certeine streict and narrow passage, he espied his enimies ranged in good order of battell, by the monition of the Lombard, which had sold him to his enimies, & his aduersaries had laid such ambushments at the streicts, that the duke by no waie without battell could either retire or flée. Forgusa, a Lumbard betraieth the duke of Clarence.

The Englishmen séeing this, valiantlie set on their enimies, who were foure to one, by reason whereof at length the Englishmen were oppressed with multitude, and brought to confusion. There were slaine, the duke of Clarencé, the earle of Tankeruile, the lord Ros, sir Gilbert Umfreuile earle of Angus, and sir Iohn Lomlie, sir Robert Verend, and almost two thousand Englishmen: & the earles of Summerset, Suffolke, and Perch, the lord Fitz Water, sir Iohn Berkelie, sir Rafe Neuile, sir Henrie Inglis, sir Wiliam Bowes, sir Wiliam Longton, sir Thomas Borough, and diuerse other taken prisoners. And of the Frenchmen were slaine aboue twelue hundred of the best men of warre they had, so that they gained not much. The Englishmen discomfited. The duke of Clarence and diuerse nobles of England slaine.

The bastard of Clarence which tarried at Beaufort, being informed of the great number of the Frenchmen, made forward with all the archers, to come to the succor of the duke, but they came too late. For the Frenchmen, hearing of the approching of the archers, fled with their prisoners, and left the bodie of the duke, and other the dead carcases behind them. The archers buried them all sauing the dukes corpse, which with great solemnitie was sent to England, and buried at Canturburie beside his father. After this the Englishmen burnt and spoiled the countrie of Maine, and so returned to Alanson, and after departed euerie man to his garrison. This battell was fought on Easter euen, in the yeare 1421. But now to returne to the king.

After he had kept his Easter at Leicester, he with the quéene remooued and went northward, till they came to Yorke, where they were receiued with great ioy of the citizens, and other the nobles and gentlemen of the countrie. The king went vnto Beuerlie, to visit the shrine of saint Iohn, and immediatlie vpon his departure from thence, the sorowfull newes of his brother the duke of Clarences death, came to him, for which he was right pensife. But sith mourning would not auaile, he called to remembrance what he had to doo, and therevpon without delaie, sent Edmund earle of Mortaigne, brother to the earle of Summerset into Normandie, giuing to him like authoritie and preheminence, as his brother the late deceassed duke of Clarence had before enioied. The earle of Mortaigne made lieutenant of Normandie.

After this, he called his high court of parlement, in the which he declared with such great wisedome & grauitie, the acts which had béene doone in France, the state of the time present, and what was necessarie to be prouided for the time to come (if they would looke to haue that iewell and high kingdome, for the which they A parlement.

had so long laboured and sought) that the communaltie gladlie granted a fiftéenth, & the clergie beneuolentlie offred a double disme. And bicause no delaie should be in the kings affaires for lacke of paiment, the bishop of Winchester the kings vncle lent vnto him twentie thousand pounds, to be paid him againe of the same dismes. When all things necessarie for this iournie were readie and prepared, he sent his brother the duke of Bedford before him to Calis with all his armie, being (as some write) foure thousand men of armes, and twentie thousand archers and others; though some haue written, that the whole armie passed not twelue thousand of one and other.

The bishop of Winchester lent the king 20000.

King Henrie saileth into France againe.

The king himselfe shortlie after, about the middle of Maie, passed the seas to Calis, and so from thence he marched through the countrie vnto Boies de Vincennes, where the French king and the queene as then soiourned. The duke of Burgognie also that had receiued him at Monstruell, attended him to Dowast in Ponthieu, and there hauing taking leaue of him for six daies, returned now againe to him, according to his promise. Then did they consult togither about their affaires, and appointed in all hast to fight with the Dolphin, and to raise the siege of Chartres which he had there planted. Herevpon, the king of England with all his puissance, came to the towne of Mante, and thither repaired the duke of Burgognie; but yer they departed from thence, they had knowledge, that the Dolphin hearing of the puissant armie of the king of England approching towards him, was recoiled with his people towards Towers in Touraine.

He tooke sea at Douer the fourth of Iune, as Titus Liuius saith, and so saie the chronicles of Flanders.

Herevpon the king of England incontinentlie, did not onelie send backe the duke of Burgognie into Picardie, to resist the attempts of sir Iaques de Harecourt, which made war in that countrie for the Dolphin; but also appointed the king of Scots, with the duke of Glocester, to besiege the towne of Dreux. They comming thither about the eighteenth of Iulie, planted siege on euerie side, both of the towne and castell; and what with power of batrie, and other forcible meanes, so constreined them within, that on the eight daie of August they compounded, that if no sufficient rescue came to raise the siege, before the end of twelue daies next insuing, both the towne and castell should be deliuered to the king of Englands vse, so as the soldiers might depart with their goods whither they would, except one Englishman, which was knowen to be amongst them, being fled for treason out of the kings dominions.

The king of Scots serueth king Henrie. Dreux besieged & rendred to the Englishmen.

On the twentith daie of August, which was the day of the appointment, the king of Scots receiued the towne and castell to the behoofe of his souereigne lord the king of England, who (during all the time of the siege) laie at Moraumall. The townesmen that would remaine still in their houses, were sworne to be true subiects to the king; and the other which refused, departed with the souldiers. The Englishman that was excepted, was deliuered according to the couenants; and after executed, as he had deserued. The earle of Worcester was made capteine of Dreux, and sir Henrie Mortimer bailiffe there. This doone, the king hearing that the Dolphin should be at Baugencie, assembling his power, hasted thitherwards: but at his comming into those parties, he found no appearance of enimies in the field, and so he remained there fiftéene daies.

In which meane while, the earle of Suffolke was sent foorth to discouer the countrie, and the king wan by assault the towne of Baugencie, and after when vittels began to faile, he marched forward, meaning to pursue the Dolphin. But the Dolphin douting the English puissance, conueied all the vittels foorth of those quarters, and retired himselfe to Burges in Berrie, choosing that place as his first refuge, & therefore determined there to remaine, till fortune turning hir whéele shuld looke on them with a more fauorable countenance, hereof in scorne was he commonlie called king of Berrie. The king of England followed, till vittels and forrage began

King Henrie pursueth the Dolphin.

The Dolphin, why called king of Berrie.

sore

sore to faile on all sides, and then returning, passed towards Orleance, taking the castell of Rouge Mont by assault.

He staied thrée daies before Orleance, and from thence, for want of vittels, marched through Gastinois, till he came to Vignie sur Yonne, where he remained for a season, to refresh his people that were sore trauelled, in that painefull passed iournie: *Titus Liuius.* in which the king lost not onelie manie of his men for lacke of vittels, but also a great number of horsses and carriages. Some haue written, that about the same time, he should win the citie of Sens, otherwise called the kings new towne by sur- *Les histories des* render; but after he had remained for a time at Vignie, we find that he remoued to *ducz de Norman-* Paris, where he was honorablie receiued. ¶ For he came among them as one hauing *die.* empire and dominion in his hand, so that to him they were no lesse forward in submission for feare of his indignation, than readie to giue him all the interteinement that they could deuise for the keeping of his fauour: the lacke whereof they knew stood with the hazard of their safetie, as the contrarie tended to their welfare.

Shortlie after, considering with himselfe that the towne of Meaux in Brie, being replenished with enimies, was not to be suffered to remaine in that state, in the middes of his new gotten subiects; he determined to take awaie the open scruple that might poison and infect the members, dwelling hard by: wherefore with a great number of earles and barons in his companie, he came to besiege it. This towne was no lesse well vittelled than manned, and no better manned than fortified; so that the king could neither haue it to him deliuered at his pleasure, nor gaine it by assault, without the great losse of his people: yet neuerthelesse, he determined not to depart till he had got it by one meane or other. The riuer of Marne diuided this towne into two parts, so that there was no enterie from the one into the other, but by a bridge, raised vp, and made ouer the riuer, susteined with manie arches. The one part is called the citie, and the other la March being the strongest and best fortified. The *The strong towne of Meaux* king first lodged a mile off in a castell, and sent the duke of Excester to begin the *besieged by the* siege, which he did according to his instructions, vpon the sixt of October. *Englishmen.*

Shortlie after, the king himselfe came, and lodged in the abbeie of Pharon, the duke of Excester in the abbeie de Chage, the earle of March at the greie friers, and the earle of Warwike directlie against that part that is called la March. They within defended themselues right valiantlie, so that the Englishmen were not all at their ease, but specialie through lacke of vittels manie died, and manie fell sicke, by reason whereof, no small number returned home into England; where in the meane time, on the first of December, a parlement was called and holden at Westminster, by the *A parlement* duke of Bedford, gouernour of the realme in the kings absence. ¶ In this parlement, *called by the duke of Bedford,* a fifteenth was granted to the king towards the the maintenance of the warres, the *the king being in* one moitie to be paid at Candlemasse, and the other at Martinmasse, of such monie as *France.* at the time of the grant was currant.

This yeare at Windsore on the daie of saint Nicholas in December, the quéene was *Windsore.* deliuered of a sonne named Henrie, whose godfathers were Iohn duke of Bedford, *The birth of* and Henrie bishop of Winchester, and Iaquet, or (as the Frenchmen called hir) Iaque- *king Henrie the* line of Bauier, countesse of Holland was his godmother. The king being certified *sixt.* hereof, as he laie at siege before Meaux, gaue God thanks, in that it had pleased his diuine prouidence to send him a sonne, which might succeed in his crowne and scepter. But when he heard reported the place of his natiuitie; were it that he warned by some prophesie, or had some foreknowledge, or else iudged himselfe of his sonnes fortune, *King Henrie* he said vnto the lord Fitz Hugh his trustie chamberleine these words; "My lord, I *prophesieth of* Henrie borne at Monmouth, shall small time reigne, & much get; and Henrie borne at *his sonne.* Windsore, shall long reigne, and all loose: but as God will, so be it."

The king held his Christmasse at the siege before Meaux, for he would not giue ouer that siege, although his armie was greatlie diminished, by reason of lacke of vittels,

Titus Liuius.

1422

extreame cold, foule weather, and other discommodities that bred great store of diseases and sickenesse among his people; notwithstanding, all the helps and means that might be, he deuised to remedie the same: so that beside such as died, as well of sickenesse as by the enimies hand, manie returned home into their countries. But yet he ceassed not to continue the siege, beating the walles with his ordinance, and casting downe bulworkes and rampiers on ech side the towne, made approches as well by water as land, with mightie engines deuised of boords to defend the Englishmen, as they approched the walles, and gaue assaults. The walles also were in diuerse places vndermined.

After this, the Englishmen found meanes, by bridges made of boats, to passe the riuer; but yet the souldiers and other within defended their rampiers and breaches most stoutlie, and with guns and quarrels still shot at the Englishmen, of whome they slue manie; and among other the earle of Worcester was slaine, with a bullet of the great artillerie, & the lord Clifford with a quarrell of a crossebow; yet the Englishmen still wan ground, and got neerer and neerer to the walles. They also woone the chiefest part of a bridge from the enimies, and kept watch and ward vpon and about the same. The earle of Warwike had also taken a Vaumure from them of the market place, built on the southside thereof, able to receiue and lodge a good number of men, which seruing to good purpose, for the better brideling of them within, he caused to be kept, and thus were they within Meaux sore oppressed on euerie side.

Herevpon in Februarie, the capteins doubting least the citie could not be defended long, caused all the vittels and goods to be conueied into the market place, and retired all the men of warre into the same, leauing none in the other part of the citie, but the commons, and such as were not able to doo any auaileable seruice in the warre. The king aduertised hereof commanded in all hast to assault the citie, which was quicklie

Meaux taken by assault. doone; so that the citie by fine force was within thrée houres taken and spoiled; and the same daie the market place besieged round about, and a mill woone adioining vnto

An. Reg. 10. the same. In Aprill, the quéene passed ouer into France, with a faire retinue of men,

Quéene Katharine saileth into France. vnder the conduct of the duke of Bedford, the duke of Glocester remaining lord gouernour of the realme in his place. At hir comming thither, she was so welcommed and honorablie receiued, first of hir husband, and after of hir father and mother, that she appeared to be no lesse loued of hir noble husband, than of hir déere and naturall parents.

Oliuer Mannie. Whilest the siege still continued before Meaux, Oliuer Mannie a valiant man of warre of the Dolphins part (which before was capteine of Faleis, and yéelding it, sware neuer to beare armour against the king of England) assembled a great number of men of warre, as well Britaines as Frenchmen, that is to saie, the lord Monthorchier, the lord of Coinon, the lord of Chatelgiron, the lord Tintignace, the lord de la Howssaie, and diuerse other, which entered into the countrie of Constantine in Normandie, and robbed and killed the Englishmen, where they might either espie or take them at their due aduantage. But the earle of Suffolke kéeper of the marches, hearing of their dooings, sent for the lord Scales, sir Iohn Aston bailiffe of Constantine, sir William Hall, sir Iohn Banaster, and many other, out of the garrisons within that territorie, the which incountred with their enimies at a place called Le parke leues que, in English, The bishops parke.

A sore cõflict. There was a sore fight and a long betwixt them, but finallie the Frenchmen were put to flight, so that in the conflict and chace were slaine, the lord of Coinon, the lord of Chatellgiron, and thrée hundred other: and there were taken prisoners, the lord de la Howssaie, and sir Oliuer Mannie, with threescore others. The king pardoned sir Oliuer Mannie his life, though he ill deserued so great a benefit, for that he had broken his oth and promise, but he was sent into England, there to learne to speake English, and so being brought to London, shortlie after died, being as then a

verie

verie aged man, & was buried in the white friers.   ¶ But here note (by the waie) the *Ab. Fl.*
roiall hart of this king, who as he tempered all his actions with singular circumspection; so with a pitifull mind he pondered the miserie of his enimies; so that when he
might (Iure belli, by the law of armes) haue spoiled them of goods and life, he diuerse
times spared both; with clemencie cōmonlie making conquest of them, who séemed
by open hostilitie scarse conquerable.

The king lieng still before the market place at Meaux in Brie (as ye haue heard)
sore beat the wals with his ordinance, and cast downe bulworkes and rampiers on euerie
side the towne, so that he had made an open breach for his people to enter.   Wherof
the lord of Offemont being aduertised, with a companie of chosen persons sent by
the Dolphin, assaied in the night season to enter the towne, to the succours of them
within.   But though diuerse of his people got ouer the walles, by helpe of ladders
which they had set vp; yet such was his chance, that as he passed a planke, to haue
come to the walles, he fell into a déepe ditch; and in the meane time, the Englishmen
perceiuing by the noise what the matter meant, came running to the ditch, tooke the
lord of Offemont, and slue diuerse of his companie that stood in defense.

The capteins within, perceiuing in what case they stood, by reason their succours *Continuation de la chronicles de Flanders.*
were thus intercepted, and doubting to be taken by assault, for that they wanted
munition and weapon, began to treat with the king of England, who appointed the
earle of Warwike, and the lord Hungerford, to commune with them; and in conclusion an accord was taken, and so the towne and market place with all the goods
were deliuered into the king of Englands hands, the tenth daie of Maie, in the yeare
1422.   The appointment taken with them of this towne was this, that they should *Titus Liuius.* The conditions
yéeld themselues simplie vnto the kings pleasure, their liues onlie saued: and herevpon of the surrender
manie of them were sent ouer into England, amongst whome was the bishop of that of Meaux into the kings hands.
towne, which shortlie after his arriuall here fell sicke and died.

There were also foure persons excepted, against whome the king might by order of
law and iustice procéed as he saw cause, for their faults and trespasses committed.
As first, the capteine of the towne, named the bastard of Vaureu, the which had
doone manie gréeuous oppressions to the people of the countrie thereabouts, in spoiling them of their goods and ransoming them at his pleasure.   He had also put diuerse
to death most cruellie, when they were not able to paie such finance and ransomes as
he demanded.   Wherevpon, being now put to death himselfe, his bodie was hanged
vpon a trée that stood on an hill without the towne, on the which he had caused both
husbandmen and townesmen, with other prisoners, to be hanged before time.   His
standard also, which was woont to be borne before him in battell, was set vp in the
same trée.   The bailiffe also of the towne, and two of the chéefest burgesses that had
béene of counsell with him in his vnlawfull dooings, were likewise executed.   Also
beside these, there were found in this towne diuerse that were accused to be guiltie of
the duke of Burgognies death, wherefore they were put to their triall, in the parlement
at Paris, and some of them being found guiltie, were executed.

When the deliuerie of the strong towne of Meaux was published thorough out the
countrie, all the townes and fortresses in the Ile of France, in Lannois, in Brie, & in
Champaigne, yéelded themselues to the king of England, which appointed in the
same valiant capteins, and hardie soldiers.   After that he had thus got possession of
Meaux, and the other fortresses, he returned againe to Bois de Vincennes, and being
there receiued of the king and quéene of France, and of the queene his wife the
thirtith daie of Maie, being Whitsun éeuen, they remooued all togither vnto Paris,
where the king of England lodged in the castell of Loure, and the French king in the
house of saint Paule.   These two kings kept great estate with their quéenes, at this The roiall port
high feast of Pentecost, but the king of Englands court greatlie excéeded, so that all of the K. of England.
the resort was thither.   The Parisiens that beheld his princélie port & high magnificence,

ficence, iudged him rather an emperour then a king, and their owne king to be in respect of him like a duke or marquesse.

The Dolphin hauing knowledge by espials where the king of England and his power laie, came with all his puissance ouer the riuer of Loire, and besieged Cosneie, a towne situate vpon that riuer, a six score miles distant from Paris, and appointed part of his armie to waste and destroie the confines of the duchie of Burgognie, to the intent to diuide the power of the king of England, from the strength of the duke of Burgognie, supposing (as it came to passe indéed) that the duke would make hast towards Burgognie, to defend his owne lands. In the meane time they within Cosneie were so hard handled, that they promised to render their towne to the Dolphin, if they were not rescued by the king of England within ten daies. King Henrie hearing these newes would not send anie one creature, but determined to go himselfe to the raising of that siege, and so with all diligence came to the towne of Corbeill, and so to Senlis, where (whether it were with heat of the aire, or that he with his dailie labour were féebled or weakened) he began to wax sicke, yea and so sicke, that he was constreined to tarrie, and send his brother the duke of Bedford to rescue them of Cosneie, which he did to his nigh honor. For the Dolphin hearing that the duke of Bedford was comming to raise his siege departed thence into Berrie, to his great dishonor, and lesse gaine

About the same time, the duke of Britaine sent his chancellor the bishop of Maunts, with the bishop of Vannes, and others of his councell, as ambassadors from him vnto king Henrie, with full commission, to ratifie and allow for him and his people the peace concluded at Troies: but by reason of the kings gréeuous sicknesse, nothing was then doone in that matter. Neuerthelesse, the duke himselfe in person came afterwards to Amiens, and there performed that which he had appointed his ambassadors at this time, in his name, to haue doone and accomplished. In the meane season, king Henrie waxed sicker and sicker, and so in an horsselitter was conueied to Bois de Vincennes, to whome shortlie after repaired the dukes of Bedford and Glocester, & the earles of Salisburie and Warwike, whome the king louinglie welcomed, and séemed glad of their presence.

Now, when he saw them pensife for his sicknesse, and great danger of life wherein he presentlie laie, he with manie graue, courteous, and pithie words, recomforted them the best he could, and therewith exhorted them to be trustie and faithfull vnto his sonne, and to sée that he might be well and vertuouslie brought vp. And as concerning the rule and gouernance of his realms, during the minoritie and yoong yeares of his said sonne, he willed them to ioine togither in fréendlie loue and concord, keeping continuall peace and amitie with the duke of Burgognie, and neuer to make treatie with Charles that called himselfe Dolphin of Vienne, by the which anie part either of the crowne of France, or of the duches of Normandie and Guien may be lessened or diminished; and further, that the duke of Orleance, and the other princes should still remaine prisoners, till his sonne came to lawfull age, least returning home againe, they might kindle more fire in one daie than might be quenched in thrée.

He further aduised them, that if they thought it necessarie, that it should be good to haue his brother Humfreie duke of Glocester to be protector of England, during the nonage of his sonne, and his brother the duke of Bedford, with the helpe of the duke of Burgognie to rule and to be regent of France, commanding him with fire and sword to persecute the Dolphin, till he had either brought him to reason and obeisance, or else to driue and expell him out of the realme of France. And herewith he protested vnto them, that neither the ambitious desire to inlarge his dominions, neither to purchase vaine renowme and worldlie fame, nor anie other consideration had mooued him to take the warres in hand; but onelie that in prosecuting his iust

title,

Marginal notes:

Cosneie besieged by the Dolphin.

The king falleth sicke.

Cosneie rescued by the duke of Bedford.

Titus Liuius. The duke of Britaine sendeth ambassadors to the K. of England.

The king of England is brought sicke to Bois de Vincennes.

His aduise vpon his death bed.

Titus Liuius

title, he might in the end atteine to a perfect peace, and come to enioie those péeces of his inheritance, which to him of right belonged: and that before the beginning of the same warres, he was fullie persuaded by men both wise and of great holinesse of life, that vpon such intent he might and ought both begin the same warres, and follow them, till he had brought them to an end iustlie and rightlie, and that without all danger of Gods displeasure or perill of soule. Chéeftie Chichelie archb. of Cantur. for dashing the bill against the clergie, as appeares before, pag. 65.

The noble men present, promised to obserue his precepts, and to performe his desires; but their hearts were so pensife, and replenished with sorrow, that one could not for weeping behold an other. Then he said the seauen psalmes, and receiued the sacrament, and in saieng the psalmes of the passion ended his daies héere in this world, at Bois saint Vincent, the last of August, in the yeare a thousand foure hundred twentie and two. This Henrie was a king, of life without spot, a prince whome all men loued, and of none disdained, a capteine against whome fortune neuer frowned, nor mischance once spurned, whose people him so seuere a iusticer both loued and obeied (and so humane withall) that he left no offense vnpunished, nor fréendship vnrewarded; a terrour to rebels, and suppressour of sedition, his vertues notable, his qualities most praise-worthie. He departed this life the last of August 1422. The commédation of king Henrie the fift as is expressed by maist. *Hall.*

In strength and nimblenesse of bodie from his youth few to him comparable, for in wrestling, leaping, and running, no man well able to compare. In casting of great iron barres and heauie stones he excelled commonlie all men, neuer shrinking at cold, nor slothfull for heat; and when he most laboured, his head commonlie vncouered; no more wearie of harnesse than a light cloake, verie valiantlie abiding at needs both hunger and thirst; so manfull of mind as neuer seene to quinch at a wound, or to smart at the paine; nor to turne his nose from euill sauour, nor close his eies from smoke or dust; no man more moderate in eating and drinking, with diet not delicate, but rather more meet for men of warre, than for princes, or tender stomachs. Euerie honest person was permitted to come to him, sitting at meale, where either secretlie or openlie to declare his mind. High and weightie causes as well betweene men of warre and other he would gladlie heare, and either determined them himselfe, or else for end committed them to others. He slept verie little, but that verie soundlie, in so much that when his soldiers soong at nights, or minstrels plaied, he then slept fastest; of courage inuincible, of purpose vnmutable, so wisehardie alwaies, as feare was banisht from him; at euerie alarum he first in armor and formost in ordering. In time of warre such was his prouidence, bountie and hap, as he had true intelligence not onelie what his enimies did, but what they said and intended; of his deuises and purposes few, before the thing was at the point to be done, should be made priuie.

He had such knowledge in ordering and guiding an armie, with such a gift to incourage his people, that the Frenchmen had constant opinion he could neuer be vanquished in battell. Such wit, such prudence, and such policie withall, that he neuer enterprised any thing, before he had fullie debated and forecast all the maine chances that might happen, which doone with all diligence and courage he set his purpose forward. What policie he had in finding present remedies for sudden mischeeues, and what engines in sauing himselfe and his people in sharpe distresses: were it not that by his acts they did plainlie appeare, hard were it by words to make them credible. Wantonnesse of life and thirst in auarice had he quite quenched in him; vertues in deed in such an estate of souereigntie, youth, and power, as verie rare, so right commendable in the highest degrée. So staied of mind and countenance beside, that neuer iolie or triumphant for victorie, nor sad or damped for losse or misfortune. For bountifulnesse and liberalitie, no man more frée, gentle, and franke, in bestowing rewards to all persons, according to their deserts: for his saieng was, that he neuer desired monie to kéepe but to giue and spend.

Although

Although that storie properlie serues not for theme of praise or dispraise, yet what in breuitie may well be remembred, in truth would not be forgotten by sloth, were it but onlie to remaine as a spectacle for magnanimitie to haue alwaies in eie, and for incouragement to nobles in honourable enterprises. Knowen be it therefore, of person and forme was this prince rightlie representing his heroicall affects, of stature and proportion tall and manlie, rather leane than grose, somewhat long necked and blacke haired, of countenance amiable, eloquent and graue was his spéech, and of great grace and power to persuade: for conclusion, a maiestie was he that both liued & died a paterne in princehood, a lode-starre in honour, and mirrour of magnificence: the more highlie exalted in his life, the more déepelie lamented at his death, and famous to the world alwaie. Peter Basset (a chéefe man in his chamber) affirmed that he deceassed of a pleurisie, though the Scots and French set it downe to be of saint Feacres disease, that they saie was a palsie with a crampe, which Enguerant reports to be saint Anthonies fire, but neither of them trulie. ¶ Anglorum prælia saith, that it was a sharpe feuer, which happening vnto him (wearied with the broiles of warre) in a verie vnseasonable time of the yeare, namelie the dogdaies, tormented him the sorer, and grew to be not onelie dangerous, but also desperat; for it left him not till life was extinguished: the poets report is, as followeth:

Abr. Fl. out of
Angl. præl.
sub. Hen. 5.

> Interea fractúmq; æstu nimióq; labore
> Corripit Henricum languentem febris acuta,
> Cœli intemperies, sextili Sirius ardens
> Virus * pestiferi fecit ingrandescere * morbi

* A pestilent
feuer.

His bodie imbalmed and closed in lead, was laid in a chariot roiall, richlie apparelled with cloth of gold. Vpon his coffin was laid a representation of his person, adorned with robes, diadem, scepter, & ball, like a king; the which chariot, six horsses drew richlie trapped, with seuerall appointments; the first with the armes of S. George, the second with the armes of Normandie, the third of king Arthur, the fourth of saint Edward, the fift of France, and the sixt with the armes of England and France. On this same chariot gaue attendance Iames K. of Scots, the principall mourner, king Henries vncle Thomas duke of Excester, Richard earle of Warwike, the earle of March Edmund, the earle of Stafford Humfrie, the earle of Mortaigne Edmund Beaufort, the lord Fitz Hugh Henrie, the lord Hungerford Walter, sir Robert Robsert lord Bourchier, sir Iohn Cornwall lord Fanhope, and the lord Crumwell were the other mourners. The lord Louell, the lord Audeleie, the lord Morleie, the lord Sowch bare the baners of saints and auoouries, as then they were called; the baron of Dudleie bare the standard, and the earle of Longuile the baner. The hachments were caried onelie by capteins to the number of twelue; and round about the chariot rode fiue hundred men of armes all in blacke armour, their horsses barbed blacke, and theywith the but ends of their speares vpwards.

Lord Crumwell.

The conduct of this dolorous funerall was committed to sir William Philip, treasuror of the kings houshold, and to sir William Porter, his cheefe caruer, and others. Beside this, on euerie side of the chariot went thrée hundred persons, holding long torches, & lords bearing baners, banerols, and penons. With this funerall appointment was he conueied from Bois de Vincennes, to Paris, and so to Rone, to Abuile, to Calis, to Douer, from thence thorough London to Westminster, where he was interred with such solemne ceremonies, mourning of lords, praier of priests and such lamenting of commons, as neuer before then the like was seene in England. Shortlie after this solemne buriall, his sorowfull quéene returned into England, and kept hir estate with the yoong king hir sonne.

Thus ended this puissant prince his most noble and fortunate reigne, whose life (saith Hall) though cruell Atropos abbreuiated; yet neither fire, malice nor fretting time shall appall his honour, or blot out the glorie of him that in so small time had
doone

doone so manie and roiall acts. [In this yeare, the one and twentith of October *W. P.* d ceassed the gentle and welbeloued Charles French king the sixt of that name, who was buried at S. Denis.] ¶ So that betwéene the death of these two kings, namelie *Abr. Fl.* out of the one of England, the other of France, there was no great space of time; sith *Angl. præl.* Charles departed in October, and Henrie in August: by the priuation of whose liues, which of the two realmes susteined the greater losse, it is a question not to be discussed. Certeine it is that they were both souereigns tenderlie loued of their subiects, as they were princes greatlie fauouring their people. Finallie, in memorie of this Henrie the fift, a king of a roiall hart, and euerie waie indued with imperiall vertues, I find so fit a report conspiring in truth with his properties and disposition, that I thinke it verie conuenient here to be inserted in place of an epitaph:

> Henrici illustris properans mors occupat artus,
> Ille suæ patriæ decus immortale per æuum
> Venturum, virtutis & indelebile lumen,
> Celso animo prorsus, leni quoque pectore ciues
> Non solùm, at iustos hostes fidéíque probatæ
> Dilexit, niueo raró iracundior ore.

Of learned men and writers, these I find remembred by Bale and others, to haue liued in the daies of this noble and valiant king Henrie the fift. First. Alaine de Lin, borne in Lin, and professed a Carmelite frier in that towne, he at length became prior of that conuent, procéeded doctor of diuinitie in Cambridge, and wrote manie treatises; Thomas Otterborne that wrote an historie of England, is thought to liue about this season, he was a Franciscan or graie frier, as they called them, a great student both in diuinitie and philosophie: Iohn Seguard an excellent poet, and a rhetorician, kept a schoole, and read to his scholers in Norwich, as is supposed, writing sundrie treatises, reprouuing as well the profaning of the christian religion in monks and priests, as the abuse of poetrie in those that tooke vpon them to write filthie verses and rimes; Robert Rose a frier of the Carmelites order in Norwich commonlie called the white friers, both an excellent philosopher, and diuine, procéeded doctor at Oxenford, promoted to be prior of his house, and writing diuerse treatises: amongst all the sophists of his time (as saith Bale) he offended none of the Wickleuists, who in that season set foorth purelie the word of God, as maie appeare by his workes.

Moreouer, Iohn Lucke, a doctor of diuinitie in Oxenford, a sore enimie to the Wickleuists; Richard Caister borne in Norfolke, vicar of saint Stephans in Norwich, a man of great holinesse and puritie in life, fauouring (though secretlie) the doctrine of the Wickleuists, and reprouuing in his sermons, the vnchast manners and filthie example that appeared in the cleargie. Of sir Iohn Oldcastell lord Cobham ye haue heard before; William Walleis a blacke frier in Lin, and prouinciall of his order here in England, made a booke of moralizations vpon Ouids Metamorphóseis, *W. P.* comparable to postils vpon Aesops Fables; Richard Snetisham, a student in Oxenford, where he profited so greatlie in learning and wisedome, that he was accounted the chéefest in all that vniuersitie, in respect whereof he was made chancellor of the same, chosen also to be one of the twelue to examine and iudge vpon Wickliffes doctrine by the archbishop of Canturburie; Iohn Langdene a monke of Christes church in Canturburie, an other of those twelue; William Tailor a priest, and a master of art in Oxenford, a stedfast follower of Wickliffes doctrine, & burnt for the same in Smithfield at London, the second day of March, in the yeare of our Lord 1422, & last of king Henrie the fift his reigne.

Furthermore, Richard Grasdale student in Oxenford, one of those twelue also; William Lindwood a lawier excellentlie learned, as well in the ciuill as canon lawes, aduanced to the seruice of this king, and made by him kéeper of the priuie seale, sent

in

in ambassage both to the kings of Spaine and Portingale, about businesse of most weightie importance. It is said that he was promoted to the bishoprike of saint Dauid; Bartholomew Florarius, supposed (as Bale saith) by Nicholas Brigham, to be an Englishman, wrote a treatise called Florarium, whereof he tooke his surname; and also an other treatise of abstinence, in which he reprooueth certeine corrupt manners in the cleargie, and the profession of friers mendicants; Adam Hemmelington, a Carmelite frier, studied both in Oxenford and Paris; William Batecombe is placed by Bale about the time of other learned men that liued in this kings time, he was an excellent mathematician, as by the title of his works which he wrote it should appeare.

Titus Liuius de Foro Luuisiis liued also in these daies, an Italian borne: but sith he was both resiant here, and wrote the life of this king, I haue thought good to place him among other of our English writers. One there was that translated the said historie into English, adding (as it were by waie of notes in manie places of that booke) sundrie things for the more large vnderstanding of the historie; a copie whereof I haue séene belonging to Iohn Stow citizen of London. There was also about the same time an other writer, who (as I remember) hath followed the said Liuius in the order of his booke, as it were chapter for chapter, onelie changing a good, familiar and easie stile, which the said Liuius vsed, into a certeine poeticall kind of writing: a copie whereof I haue séene (& in the life of this king partlie followed) belonging to master Iohn Twine of Kent, who (as I was informed) meant to leaue to posteritie some fruits of his labours for the due vnderstanding thereof.

Thus farre Henrie the fift sonne and successor to Henrie the fourth.

HENRIE THE SIXT,

sonne and heire to Henrie the fift.

AFTER that death had bereft the world of that noble prince king Henrie the fift, his onelie sonne prince Henrie, being of the age of nine moneths, or thereabouts, with the sound of trumpets was openlie proclamed king of England and France the thirtith daie of August, by the name of Henrie the sixt; in the yeare of the world fiue thousand, three hundred, eightie and nine, after the birth of our Sauiour 1422, about the twelfe yeare of the emperour Frederike the third, the fortith and two and

last of Charles the sixt, and the third yeare of Mordaks regiment (after his father Robert) gouernour of Scotland. The custodie of this yoong prince was appointed to Thomas duke of Excester, & to Henrie Beauford bishop of Winchester. The duke of Bedford was deputed regent of France, and the duke of Glocester was ordeined protectour of England; who taking vpon him that office, called to him wise and graue councellors, by whose aduise he prouided and tooke order as well for the good gouernment of the realme & subiects of the same at home, as also for the maintenance of the warres abroad, and further conquest to be made in France, appointing valiant and expert capteins, which should be readie, when need required. Besides this, he gathered great summes of monie to mainteine men of warre, and left nothing forgotten that might aduance the good estate of the realme.

While

While these things were a dooing in England, the duke of Bedford regent of France studied most earnestlie, not onelie to keepe and well order the countries by king Henrie late conquered; but also determined not to leaue off warre & trauell, till Charles the Dolphin (which was now aflote, because king Charles his father in the moneth of October in this present yeare was departed to God) should either be subdued, or brought to obeisance. And suerlie the death of this king Charles caused alterations in France. For a great manie of the nobilitie, which before, either for feare of the English puissance, or for the loue of this king Charles (whose authoritie they followed) held on the English part, did now reuolt to the Dolphin, with all indeuour to driue the English nation out of the French territories. Whereto they were the more earnestlie bent, and thought it a thing of greater facilitie, because of king Henries yoong yeares; whome (because he was a child) they estéemed not, but with one consent reuolted from their sworne fealtie: as the recorder of the Englishmens battels with forren nations, verie aptlie doth note, saieng:

> Hîc Franci puerum regem neglectui habentes
> Desciscunt, violátque fidem gens perfida sacro
> Consilio ante datam.

The duke of Bedford being greatlie mooued with these sudden changes, fortified his townes both with garrisons of men, munition, and vittels, assembled also a great armie of Englishmen and Normans, and so effectuouslie exhorted them to continue faithfull to their liege and lawfull lord yoong king Henrie, that manie of the French capteins willinglie sware to king Henrie fealtie and obedience, by whose example the communaltie did the same. Thus the people quieted, and the countrie established in order, nothing was minded but warre, and nothing spoken of but conquest.

The Dolphin which lay the same time in the citie of Poitiers, after his fathers deceasse, caused himselfe to be proclamed king of France, by the name of Charles the seuenth: and in good hope to recouer his patrimonie, with an haultie courage preparing war, assembled a great armie: and first the warre began by light skirmishes, but after it grew into maine battels. The Dolphin thinking not to lose anie occasions   *Pont Meulan* of well dooing, sent the lord Grauile to the towne of Pont Meulan, standing on the   *surprised by the* *Frech.* riuer of Seine, who comming to the same vpon the sudden, the fourtéenth of Ianuarie,   1423. tooke it and slue a great number of English souldiors, which he found within it.   *Enguerant.*

When the duke of Bedford the regent, aduertised of this sudden surprise, appointed the lord Thomas Montacute earle of Salisburie (a man both for policie and courage, liker to the old Romans than to men of his daies) accompanied with the earle of Suffolke, the lord Scales, the yoong lord Poinings, sir Iohn Fastolfe maister of the houshold, with himselfe and diuerse others, to besiege the said towne of Pont Meulan, which after two moneths siege was rendred to the said earle, and the lord Grauile sware to be true to the king of England euer after that day: but short-   *Lord Grauile* lie after, forgetting his oth, he turned French againe.   *falsified his oth.*

The earle of Salisburie appointed sir Henrie Mortimer, and sir Richard Vernon, capteins of the towne, and from thence went into Champaigne, and there besieged the towne of Sens, tooke it, and sir William Marin the capteine within it, and slue all the souldiors that kept it, made capteins there sir Hugh Godding, and sir Richard Aubemond. ¶ In this season, Humfrie duke of Glocester, either striken in loue, or vpon some other occasion, maried the ladie Iaquet or Iaquelin, daughter and sole heire to William of Bauier duke of Holland, which was lawfull wife to Iohn duke of Brabant then liuing, who afterwards (as after ye shall heare) recouered hir out of the dukes hands.

The chances thus happening (as you before haue heard) Iohn duke of Bedford, Philip duke of Burgognie, and Iohn duke of Britaine made a fréendlie méeting in the citie of Amiens, where they renewed the old league and ancient amitie made betwéene the noble prince king Henrie the fift and them, adding thereto these conditions and agréements, ech of them to be to the other fréend and aider; and the enimie of the one to be enimie to the other; and all they to be fréends and aiders to the king of England, welwiller to his welwillers, and aduersarie to his aduersa-

ries. And (bicause that affinitie is commonlie the bond of amitie) there was concluded a mariage betwéene the duke of Bedford, and the ladie Anne sister to the duke of Burgognie, which was after solemnized at Trois in Champaigne, in the presence of the duke of Burgognie brother to the bride, and of hir vncle the duke of Brabant, the earles of Salisburie and Suffolke, and of nine hundred lords, knights, and esquiers, with such feast and triumph, as before that time had not béene séene of the Burgognions.

Whilest these matters were in hand, the Parisiens, thinking to blind the eies of the duke of Bedford, wrote to him how diuerse castels and fortresses lieng about their territories, were replenished with their enimies, dailie stopping their passages, and robbing their merchants, to their vtter vndooing, if they by his helpe were not relieued. But this was but a glose of the Parisiens, meaning to cause him to go about the winning of some strong hold, whilest they in his absence might bring

into the citie Charles the Dolphin, that then called himselfe French king; for so had they appointed, assigning to him the daie of his comming, and the post of his entrie. But their practise being discouered to the duke of Bedford, he with a great power entered into Paris, one daie before the faire was appointed, & two nights before he was looked for of his enimies being vnprouided, and suddenlie caused the conspirators within the citie to be apprehended, and openlie to be put to execution.

This doone, putting a mistrust in the Parisiens, he caused the castels and fortresses néere and adioining to the citie, to be furnished with Englishmen. And to auoid all night-watchers about Paris, and the confines thereof, he first tooke into his possession either by assault or composition, the towne of Trainelle and Braie vpon Seine. And bicause two castels, the one called Pacie, and the other Coursaie were also euil neighbours to the Parisiens, he sent sir Iohn Fastolfe great maister of his houshold with a notable armie to win the same castels; which he did, and with preie and prisoners returned backe againe to his maister the regent.

In this verie season, the Dolphin sent the lord William Steward earle of Buchquhane that was constable of France, and the earle of Ventadour in Auuergne, and manie other noble men of his part, to laie siege to the towne of Crauant in the countie of Auxerre, within the parts of Burgognie. Wherof hearing the lord regent, and the duke of Burgognie they assembled a great armie, and appointed the earle of Salisburie to haue the guiding thereof; who with his capteins and men of warre, English and Burgognions, came in good arraie to giue battell to the besiegers. And bicause the riuer of Yonne, which runneth by the said towne, was betwéene the English armie, and their aduersaries, they could not well assaile their enimies, which defended the bankes and passages verie stronglie : yet notwithstanding, both

both horssemen and footmen of the English part couragiouslie put themselues into the riuer, and with fine force recouered the banke, whome the Burgognions incontinentlie followed.

When they were all gotten into the plaine, the archers shot, the bill men strake, and long was the fight in doubtfull balance. But in conclusion the Frenchmen not able to resist the force of the English nation, were discomfited, slaine, and chased, leauing a glorious victorie to the Englishmen and Burgognions. There were slaine of the Frenchmen an eightéene hundred knights and esquiers, beside commons : of Scots néere hand thrée thousand. Amongest the Frenchmen these were chiefest that were slaine : the earle of Lestrake, the earl of Comigens, the earle of Tonnoire, the lord
Coquart

Coquart de Comeron, the bastard of Arminake, the viscount of Touraine, the bastard of Forrestes, the lord de Port, and the lord Memorancie.

Of Scots the lord of saint Iohns towne, sir Iohn of Balgarie, sir Iohn Turnbull, sir Iohn Holiburton, sir Robert Lislie, sir William Coningham, sir William Dowglas, sir Alexander Hume, sir William Lislie, sir Iohn Rotherford, sir William Craiford, sir Thomas Seton, sir William Hamilton, and his sonne, Iohn Pillot. There were taken the earle of Buchquhane constable of France, which lost his eie, the earle of Venta-dour, sir Alexander Meldrine, sir Lewes Ferignie, and two and twentie hundred gentlemen of the French part. Of Englishmen there were slaine sir Iohn Greie, sir William Hall, sir Gilbert Halsall one of the marshals of the field, Richard ap Madocke, and one and twentie hundred souldiers and men of warre.

After this fortunate victorie was the earle of Salisburie made (by the lord regent) *An. Reg. 3* lieutenant and vicegerent for the king and the said lord regent in the countries of France, Brie, and Champaigne; and sir Iohn Fastolf was substituted deputie vnder the lord regent within the duchie of Normandie on this side the riuer of Seine; and withall he was also made gouernour of the countries of Aniou and Maine. The earle of Salisburie after fiue moneths siege, wan by surrender the towne and castell of Montaguillon in Brie; the capteins whereof, the one named Pregent of Cotinie, and Guille Bourgois Britons, sware neuer to beare armour against the Englishmen on this side the riuer of Loire. In the mean time of that siege, the earle of Suf-folke tooke by force the castell of Coucie, and the strong castell of la Roch in Mas-connois he got by appointment.

In this second yeare of king Henrie the sixt, Iames (the first of that name & the *1424* hundred & second K. of Scotland, tooke to wife the ladie Iane, daughter to Iohn *Ann. 1423, per* earle of Summerset deceassed, and sister to Iohn then duke of Summerset, and also *Buchanan.* coosine germane remoued to king Henrie, and neece to the duke of Winchester, and to the duke of Excester) was set at libertie, couenanting to paie a small portion of monie more than was allowed to him for his wiues marriage monie, and left hostages for the same. But before his departure out of the realme, he did his homage vnto the *Homage doone* the yoong king of England Henrie the sixt at the castell of Windsor, before three *by the king of* dukes, two archbishops, twelue earles, ten bishops, twentie barons, and two hun- *Henrie the sixt.* dred knights and esquiers, beside others, in order of words according to the tenour hereafter following.

The formall recognisance or acknowledgement of the said homage.

I, IAMES STEWARD, K. of Scots, shall be true and faithfull vnto you lord Henrie by the grace of God king of England & France, the noble and superiour lord of the kingdome of Scotland; and to you I make my fidelitie for the same kingdome of Scotland, which I hold and claime of you; and I shall beare you my faith and fide-litie of life and lim, and worldlie honour against all men; and faithfullie I shall knowledge and shall doo you seruice due for the kingdome of Scotland aforesaid. So God helpe me, and these holie euangelists.

But notwithstanding this his oth, and the great bounteous liberalitie of the mother & vncles of his wife, in bestowing on him abundance of plate & treasure, with rich clothes of arras; he had not béene long at home, but that soone out of France into *Buchan. lib. 10.* Scotland ouer came there Iames Steward, who (after manie of the Scotish nobilitie *An. 1425.* *W. P.* by diuerse occasions in France consumed) grew to be capteine of the horssemen there. With him came the archbishop of Remes with power and commission for concluding a league betweene France and Scotland, and also of a mariage betwéene Lewes the Dol-

phins

phins sonne and Margaret Iameses daughter, though both verie yoong. Which matters acordinglie accomplished, to France againe they got them. So Iames became as firm French as any of his predecessours.]

But now to leaue the Scotish king amongst his countriemen in Scotland, and returne to the dooings of England. I find that the duke of Glocester, being protector and gouernour of the realme, prepared an armie of ten thousand men, and sent them ouer to his brother the regent into France; who comming into the territorie of Paris, were ioifullie of him receiued. About the same time the Frenchmen got by stealth diuerse townes out of the Englishmens hands, and amongst other the faire towne of Compiegne was one, and the pretie towne of Crotoie an other. When the duke of Bedford was aduertised hereof, he determined not to let the matter passe in such sort, but with all conuenient spéed sent foorth a force to recouer these townes againe. And first the earle of Suffolke with the earle of Lignie, and diuerse other capteins of the Englishmen went to besiege Compiegne, and lodged on the one side of the riuer of Sohame, as the lord Lisle Adham, sir Thomas Ramston, and the prouost of Paris laie on the other side. The Frenchmen within the towne well furnished with good souldiers, munition, and vittels, couragiouslie defended themselues.

Compiegne surrendred to the English by a policie.

The Englishmen remembring that Guilliam Remond, other wise called Mariolaine had béen the leader of the souldiers within the towne (which Mariolaine before at Pacie was taken prisoner by sir Iohn Fastolfe) caused him to be brought from Paris vnto the campe, and set him in a chariot with an halter about his necke, and conueied him to the gibet without the towne, sending word to them within, that if they would not without delaie render the towne, their capteine should incontinentlie be strangled afore their faces. Which moued the souldiers so much, by reason of the loue they bare to their old capteine and gouernour, that for the deliuerance of him and partlie of themselues they yeelded the towne, so that both he and they might depart with horsse and harnesse onelie in sure conduct and safetie. Yet yer this towne of Compiegne was deliuered, sir Philip Hall, which was sent to Crotoie by the lord regent with eight hundred men to besiege it, got it suddenlie by assault yer the Frenchmen had either disposed their garrison, or appointed their lodgings.

Compeigne & Crotoie recouered from the French.

About the same time sir Iohn de la Poole brother to the duke of Suffolke, being capteine of Auranches in Normandie, assembled all the garrisons of the base marches of the countrie of Aniou, and came before the citie of Angiers, burnt the suburbes, spoiled and destroied the whole countrie; and hauing as manie prisoners as his men might go awaie with, he was incountered by the earle of Aumarle, the vicount of Narbonne, and six thousand Frenchmen; which finding the Englishmen out of araie, incumbred with carriage of their great spoile, suddenlie set on them, gaue them the ouerthrow, slue thrée hundred and tooke manie prisoners; as the said sir Iohn de la Poole, sir Iohn Basset, Iohn Aufort lieutenant of Faleise, Iohn Clifton, Henrie Mortimer, and other to the number of six hundred.

But though the Frenchmen got here in this place, they went not awaie with like gaine in an other: for the bastard de la Baulme, and the lord Craignar capteins of Courallon, with a great band made rode into Masconnois, whom by chance Matthew *Gough and other Englishmen, which were also abroad in the countrie, met and incountred. There was a sore fight betwéene the parties, being of Courage and number in maner equall. But after long conflict, the Frenchmen almost all were slaine and taken, and the bastard being well horssed, fled; after whome followed vpon the spurres, Matthew *Gough chasing him euen to his castell gate, and there tooke him: for the which act he was much praised of the erle of Salisburie (to whom he presented the said bastard) and had not onelie the rights giuen him that belonged to the prisoner but also was rewarded with a goodlie courser at the earles hands.

* Or rather Goche.

* Goche.

About

About this season, Arthur brother to Iohn duke of Britaine, commonlie called the earle of Richmond, hauing neither profit of the name, nor of the countrie, notwithstanding that king Henrie the fift had created him earle of Yurie in Normandie, and gaue him not onelie a great pension, but also the whole profits of the same towne of Yurie; yet now, bicause that the duke his brother was returned to the part of the Dolphin, he likewise reuolting from the English obeisance, came to the Dolphin to Poictiers, and there offered himselfe to serue him, whom the Dolphin gladlie accepted, reioising more thereof, than if he had gained an hundred thousand crownes: for the Britons within the towne of Yurie, hearing that their maister was ioined with the Dolphin, kept both the towne and castell against the duke of Bedford, furnishing it dailie with new men and munition.

The lord regent aduertised hereof, raised an armie of Englishmen and Normans, to the number of eighteene hundred men of armes, and eight thousand archers and other. He had in his companie the earles of Salisburie and Suffolke, the lords Scales, Willoughbie, and Poinings, sir Reginald Graie, sir Iohn Fastolfe, sir Iohn Saluaine, sir Lancelot Lisle, sir Philip Hall, sir Iohn Pashleie, sir Iohn Greie, sir Thomas Blunt, sir Robert Harling, sir William Oldhall, and manie other, both knights and esquiers, with whom he came before the towne of Yurie, which was well defended, till they within perceiued themselues in danger, by reason of a mine which the Englishmen made, wherevpon they yeelded the towne. But the capteins of the castell would not presentlie render the place, howbeit they promised to deliuer it, if the same were not rescued at a day assigned by the Dolphin or his power.

Vpon this promise, hostages were deliuered into the possession of the lord regent, by whose licence an herald was sent to the Dolphin, to aduertise him of the time determined; who vnderstanding the distresse of his freends, incontinentlie sent Iohn duke of Alanson, as his lieutenant generall, the erle Douglas, whome at their setting foorth he made duke of Touraine, and the earle Buchquhane as then constable of France, the erls of Aumarle, Ventadoure, Tonnere, Maulieurier, and Forests, the vicounts of Narbonne, and Touars, the lords of Grauile, Gaules, Malicorne, Mannie, Ballaie, Fountains, Montfort, and manie other noble knights and esquiers, to the number of fifteene thousand Frenchmen and Britons, besides fiue thousand Scots, whome the earle Dowglas had but latelie transported out of Scotland.

This roiall armie approched within two miles of Yurie. But when the duke of Alanson understood by such as he had sent to view the conduct of the Englishmen, that he could not get anie aduantage by assailing them (although the Dolphin had giuen him strict commandement to fight with the regent) he retired backe with his whole armie to the towne of Vernueill in Perch, that belonged to the king of England; sending word to the garrison, that he had discomfited the English armie, and that the regent with a small number with him by swiftnesse of horsse had saued himselfe. The inhabitants of Vernueill, giuing too light credit herevnto receiued the duke of Alanson with all his armie into the towne.

Verneuil gotten from the English-men by crediting a lie.

In the meane time came the daie of the rescues of Yurie, which for want thereof was deliuered to the duke of Bedford by the capteine called Gerard de la Pallier, who presenting vnto the duke of Bedford the keies of the castell, shewed him a letter also signed and sealed with the hands and seales of eighteene great lords, who the daie before promised by the tenour of the same letter to giue the duke battell, and to raise the siege. "Well (said the duke) if their hearts would haue serued, their puissance was sufficient once to haue proffered, or to haue performed this faithfull promise: but sith they disdaine to seeke me, God and saint George willing, I shall not desist to follow the tract of their horsses till one part of us be by battell ouerthrowne." And herewith he sent foorth the earle of Suffolke with six hundred horssemen, to espie the dooings of the Frenchmen, and where they were lodged. The earle

earle riding foorth, passed by Dampuile, and came to Bretueill, where he heard certeine newes where the Frenchman had gotten Verneueill, and remained there still.

These newes he sent by post vnto the duke of Bedford, the which incontinentlie vpon that aduertisement set forward in great hast towards his enimies. The French-men hearing of his comming, set their people in arraie, and made all one maine battell without fore ward or rere ward; and appointed foure hundred horssemen,

The ordering of their battels. Lombards and others to breake the arraie of the Englishmen, either behind, or at the sides, of the which was capteine sir Stephan de Vinoiles, called the Hire. The duke of Bedford likewise made one entier battell, and suffered no man to be on horssebacke, and set the archers (euerie one hauing a sharpe stake) both on the front of the battell, and also on the sides, like wings. And behind were all their horsses tied togither, either by the reins or by the tailes, with the carts and cariages, to the defense whereof were two thousand archers appointed.

Héerewith either part being come almost to the ioining, the duke of Alanson, on the one side, exhorted his people to plaie the men, declaring vnto them, that the conclusion of this battell should either deliuer them out of vile seruitude, or place them in the vale of bondage. On the other side, the duke of Bedford, to incourage his men, willed them to remember how oft they had subdued those their aduersa-ries in battell (with whome they should now cope) for the most part, euer being the lesse number against the greater. Againe, he declared how necessarie it was to tame the bold attempts of the presumptuous Dolphin now in the beginning, least if the fire were suffered further to burne, it must haue néed of the more water to quench it.

Manie words he vttered, to put them in hope of good successe and victorie. But scarse had he ended his exhortation, when the Englishmen rushed foorth, and boldlie set on their enimies, crieng, Saint George, a Bedford, a Bedford: and the Frenchmen

The battell of Vernoile the 28 of August, 1424. likewise cried Montioy saint Denis. Then began the battell right fierce on both sides, continuing for the space of three houres in doubtfull balance, fortune shewing hir selfe so equall, that no eie could iudge to whether part she was more fauourable. But at length, after that those foure hundred horssemen, which were appointed, as yée haue hard, to brake the arraie of the Englishmen, had passed thorough on the one side vnto the place where the cariages and horsses stood, and could not passe further, by reason of the fierce shot of the English bowes, they falling to the spoile made a hand, and therewith departed. Those archers then that were appointed to kéepe the cariages, being now at libertie, came forward, and so fiercelie shot at the thickest prease of their enimies fighting on foot, that in the end they were not able longer to indure, but were borne downe by fine force, and so vanquished.

This battell was fought the eight and twentith of August, in the yeare of our Lord a thousand foure hundred twentie and foure, in the which battell were slaine of the Frenchmen the earles of Aumarle, Ventadour, Forest, Marie, the lords Gra-uile, Gaules, Fountaines, Ambois, Touars, Montenie, Combreste, Brunell, Tumble, and Poisie, beside thrée hundred knights. The vicount Narbonne was hanged on a gibbet, bicause he was one of the murtherers of the duke of Burgognie. Of Scots also were slaine, Archembald earle Dowglas, that was made (as before is mentioned) duke of Touraine, Iames Dowglas sonne to the said Archembald earle of Wicton, Iohn earle of Bouqhen newlie made constable of France, sir Alexander Meldrin, sir Henrie Balglauie, sir Iohn Sterling, William of Homelsdon, sir Iames Graie, sir Robert Randen, sir Alexander Linsaie, sir Robert Steward, sir Robert Swinton, and seauen and twentie hundred Scots of name and armes, beside others.

Fiue thousād saith *Aemilius*, but *Nicholas Giles* saith there died but foure thousād on both parts. So that in this battell were slaine by report of Montioy king at armes in France, and the English haralds there present, of Frenchmen & Scots nine thousand and seauen hundred: and of Englishmen one and twentie hundred, but no man of name, sau-ing fiue yoong esquiers. And there were taken prisoners, Iohn duke of Alanson, the

bastard

bastard of Alanson, the lord of Faiect, the lord of Hormit, sir Piers Harison, sir Dudley and Charleton, two of the English nobilitie, were slaine at this battell, as *Ia. Meir* saith. Lois de Gaucourt, sir Robert Brusset, sir Iohn Turnebull a Scot, and two hundred gentlemen, beside common soldiers. The Frenchmen within Vernoill, séeing the Dolphins armie thus ouerthrowne, deliuered the towne to the regent, their liues saued. Then was sir Philip Hall appointed capteine there, and the lord regent returned, and came to Rone, and after to Paris.

The Dolphin that called himselfe king of France, was sore appalled with the ouerthrow of his armie: for he was driuen out of all the countries in maner, that apperteined to the crowne of France, & might resort to none except to Bourbonois, Aluergne, Berrie, Poictow, Touraine, a part of Aniow, and Languedoc: yet to shew himselfe as king, he erected his court of parlement, his chancerie, & all other courts in the citie of Poictiers, and there established his great seale, with all due circumstances thereto apperteining: where he continued fouretéene yeares togither, and then was remooued to Paris, after he had got that citie, and expelled the Englishmen, as after shall appeare.

The duke of Bedford lieng at Paris, sent the lord Scales, sir Iohn Montgomerie, sir Iohn Fastolfe, with two thousand men to winne the countries of Aniow, and The lord Scales sent to conquer Aniow and Maine. Maine, vnto whom were rendred without assault, the strong castels of Beaumont le Vicount, Teune, Sillie, Osce, Courceriers, Roussie, Vasse, Couetemenant, and twentie other, which I doo heere passe ouer. Such was then the opinion conceiued of the English puissance, so oft tried, prooued, and preuailing, that the Frenchmen thought the Englishmen would haue all which they wished for or wrought for.

The earle of Salisburie, with the said lord Scales, and the other capteins before named, were appointed with an armie of ten thousand men, to besiege the rich and strong citie of Mans, the chéefe citie of all the countrie of Maine; whither when they came, they made their approches, and planted their batterie to the wals, so that with the shot of their great péeces (which kind of engins before that time had not béene much séene nor heard of in France) the citie was within a few daies despoiled of all hir towers and outward defenses. The citizens and soldiers, perceiuing in what Mans deliuered to the Englishmen. danger they stood, & knowing not how to remedie the matter, offered the towne vpon this condition, that all persons which would tarrie within the towne, might abide; and all that would depart with horsse and harnesse onelie, should be permitted: which offers were accepted, and the towne rendered, whereof the earle made capteine the earle of Suffolke, and his lieutenant sir Iohn Fastolfe.

After this, the earle of Salisburie besieged the faire towne of saint Susan, whereof was capteine one Ambrose de Lore, a right valiant chéefteine. The earle caused the towne to be assaulted at his first comming to it; but he lost more than he gained, and therefore left off his assaults, and caused a trench to be cast about the towne, and so planted his batterie, by force whereof he ouerthrew the walles, in such sort that the capteine offered for himselfe and his soldiers 200000 crownes, so that they might depart in their doublets onelie, which summe (bicause winter approched) was accepted, and the towne yéelded. Of this towne sir Iohn Popham was made capteine. Then the erle went to Maine la Iuhez, which towne after fiue wéekes siege was yéelded, and appointed to the kéeping of sir Iohn Montgomerie, knight.

After the feast of the Purification of our ladie, the earle of Salisburie besieged the castell de la Fert Barnard; during which siege a sale was made of the towne of Alanson being in the Englishmens possession, by a Gascoigne that was one of the garrison there. But this sale being opened to the erle of Salisburie by the same Gascoigne at the daie appointed, the lord Willoughbie and sir Iohn Fastolfe, with two thousand men were sent to incounter with the buiers of that towne; so that when Charles de Villiers chéefe merchant of this ware, came earlie in a morning with two hundred horsemen, and three hundred footmen, and approached the towne, abiding for the
Gascoigne,

Gascoigne, yer he was aware, the Englishmen had compassed him and his companie round about, and setting vpon the Frenchmen, slue and tooke all the whole number of them, saue Peter Danthenazie and fiue and twentie other, which by the swiftnesse of their horsses saued themselues.

After this conflict, the lord Willoughbie returned to the earle of Salisburie, lieng still at siege before the towne de la Fert Barnard, which shortlie after was rendered vp into the erle of Salisburies hands, to whome the lord regent gaue it, to inioie to him and his heires for euer. Beside this, the said earle partlie by assalt, & partlie by composition tooke diuers other, as saint Kales; where he made capteine Richard Gethin

* Or rather
Goche.

esquier; Thanceaux Lermitage, where he made gouernour Matthew * Gough; Guerland, of the which he assigned ruler Iohn Banaster; Malicorne, whereof he made capteine William Glasdale esquier; Lisle Soubz Boulton, whereof was made capteine sir Lancelot Lisle knight; Loupelland, whereof was made capteine Henrie Branch; Montseur, of the which was made capteine sir William Oldhall knight: la Suze was assigned to the kéeping of Iohn Suffolke, esquier. And besides this, aboue fortie castels and piles were ouerthrowne and destroied. The newes hereof reported in England, caused great reioising among the people, not onelie for the conquest of so manie townes & fortresses, but also for that it had pleased God to giue them victorie in a

Generall proces-
sions after vic-
torie.

pitched field: whereof generall processions were appointed, to render vnto God humble thanks for his fauour so bestowed vpon them.

An. Reg. 3.

This yeare after Easter, the king called a parlement at Westminster, by aduise of the péeres; and comming to the parlement house himselfe, he was conueied through the citie vpon a great courser, with great triumph, the people flocking into the stréets to behold the child, whome they iudged to haue the liuelie image and countenance of his father, and like to succeed him, and be his heire in all princelie qualities, martiall policies, and morall vertues, aswell as in his realmes, seigniories and

A subsidie of
tunnage and
poundage.

dominions. In this parlement was granted to the king a subsidie of twelue pence the pound, towards the maintenance of his warres, of all merchandize, comming in or going out of the realme, as well of Englishmen as strangers.

The prince of
Portingale com-
meth to London.

During which parlement, came to London Peter duke of Quimbre, sonne to the king of Portingale, cousine germane remooued to the king; which of the duke of Excester and the bishop of Winchester his vncles was highlie feasted, he was also elected into the order of the garter. During the same season, Edmund Mortimer, the last earle of March, of that name (which long time had beene restreined from his libertie, and finallie waxed lame) deceassed without issue, whose inheritance descended to the lord Richard Plantagenet, sonne and heire to Richard earle of Cambridge, beheaded (as before yée haue heard) at the towne of Southampton. ¶ In the time of this parlement also was sir Iohn Mortimer cousine to the same earle, either for desert or malice, atteinted of treason, and put to execution, of whose death no small slander arose amongst the common people.

After all these things doone in England and in France, Humfreie duke of Glocester, who had married the ladie Iaquet, or Iaqueline of Bauier, countesse of Heinault, Holland, and Zeland (notwithstanding she was coupled in marriage afore to Iohn duke of Brabant, as yet liuing, and had continued with him a long space) passed now the sea with the said ladie, and went to Mons or Bergen in Heinault, where the more part of the people of that countrie came and submitted themselues vnto him, as to their souereigne lord, in right of his said wife, the ladie Iaquet or Iaqueline: with which dooing hir former husband was greatlie mooued. And likewise the duke of Burgognie, being great friend to the same duke of Brabant, was much offended: who of old familiaritie wrote louinglie to the duke of Glocester, requiring him to reforme himselfe according to reason, and to forsake his vngodlie life, both in

kéeping

kéeping of an other mans wife, and also in séeking to vsurpe other mens rights and titles.

Herevpon went letters betwixt them for a time, but at length when the duke of Burgognie perceiued that the duke of Glocester meant to mainteine his interest, & to make warre against the duke of Brabant; he tooke part with the duke of Brabant so earnestlie, that he consented to fight with the duke of Glocester bodie to bodie within lists in defence of the duke of Brabants quarell, and further aided the duke of Brabant in his warres against the duke of Glocester, with all his puissance, insomuch that in the end (after the duke of Glocesters returne into England) the duke of Brabant recouered all the towns in Heinault, which the ladie Iaquet or Iaqueline held against him. And further the same ladie was by composition deliuered by them of the towne of Mons vnto the duke of Burgognie; who caused hir to be conueied vnto Gant, from whence she made shift to escape into Holland, where she was obeied as countesse of the countrie.

Then made she warre in hir owne defense against the dukes of Burgognie and Brabant, who sought to spoile hir of all hir towns and lands: but they procured pope Martin the fift (before whome the matter was) to giue sentence that the first matrimonie with the duke of Brabant was good, and the second with the duke of Glocester to be vnlawfull. But in the meane time, the lord Fitz Walter was sent ouer to the aid of the ladie Iaquet or Iaquelin, with a power of Englishmen, landed in Zeland, neere vnto the towne of Zerixe, aginst whome came the duke of Burgognie, and incountering with them and other such Hollanders and Zelanders, as were ioined with them, néere to a place called Brewers hauen, there discomfited them; so that of English, Hollanders, and Zelanders, with the said lord Fitz Walter, were slaine seauen or eight hundred, and the residue chased to the water. At length, when the duke of Glocester vnderstood the sentence pronounced against him by the pope, he began to wax wearie of his wife the said ladie Iaquet, by whome he neuer had profit, but losse, and tooke in a second marriage Eleanor Cobham, daughter to the lord Cobham of Sterberow, which before (as the fame went) was his souereigne paramour, to his slander and dishonour.

A little before this time, sir Thomas Rampston, sir Philip Branch, sir Nicholas Burdet, and other Englishmen, to the number of fiue hundred men of warre, repared and fortified the towne of S. Iames de Beuuron, situate on the frontiers of Norman- Alias Bowron. die towards Britaine, within halfe a league of the duke of Britains ground, with whome as then they had open warre; and so began to doo manie displeasures to his people. Wherevpon Arthur earle of Richmont and Yurie, brother to the said duke, and latelie before created constable of France, assembled an huge power of men to the number of fortie thousand (as some haue written) and with the same came before Twentie thou- the said towne of S. Iames de Beuuron, and planted his siege verie stronglie about it, sand hath inforcing with his great ordinance to ouerthrow the wals. And one day amongst *Nicholas Giles.* S. Iames de other, he determined to giue the assault, and so did, the which continued a long Beuuron besieg- space verie hot and earnest. ed.

The Britons Britonants were come downe into a low bottome, where there was a little pond or fish poole, and they must néeds passe by a streict waie to come to the walles in great danger. On that side of the towne was a little bulworke, which sir Nicholas Burdet kept, hauing with him a fortie or eightie fighting men: and ouer Sir Nicholas against the same bulworke there was a gate well furnished also with English souldiers; Burdet. so that the Britons which came downe into the ditches in great number to giue the assault, heard on either side them the Englishmen (within the said bulworke and gate) make a great noise, in crieng Salisburie and Suffolke; with the which crie the Britons being maruelouslie astonied, began to recoile in great disorder. And therewith the said sir Nicholas Burdet issued foorth vpon them, and pursuing them right

Enguerant de Monstreller.
valiantlie, slue them downe, so that there died of them what by the sword, and what by drowning in the said poole, about seauen thousand or eight hundred, and to the number of fiftie were taken prisoners. And beside this, those Englishmen gained eightéene standards and one baner.

Incontinentlie the newes hereof were reported to the constable of France, who was busie at the assault on the other side of the towne, whereof he was sore displeased, and no lesse amazed; so that he caused the retreit to be sounded, for all the siege on that side toward the poole was alreadie raised. After this, vpon counsell taken amongst the Frenchmen, it was determined that they should dislodge: and so about the middest of the next night, the constable and all the residue of his people departed toward Fougiers, leauing behind them great plentie of artillerie both great and small, with victuals, and all their other prouisions: as fourteene great guns and fortie barrels of powder, thrée hundred pipes of wine, two hundred pipes of bisket and flower, two hundred frailes of figs and reisins, and fiue hundred barrels of herrings.

Somewhat before this season fell a great diuision in the realme of England, which of a sparkle was like to haue grown to a great flame. For whether the bishop of *Dissention be-twixt the duke of Glocester and the bishop of Winchester.* Winchester called Henrie Beaufort, sonne to Iohn duke of Lancaster by his third wife, enuied the authoritie of Humfrie duke of Glocester, protectour of the realme; or whether the duke disdained at the riches and pompous estate of the bishop: sure it is that the whole realme was troubled with them and their partakers: so that the citizens of London were faine to kéepe dailie and nightlie watches, and to shut vp their shops for feare of that which was doubted to haue insued of their assembling of people about them. The archbishop of Canturburie and the duke of Quimbre, called the prince of Portingale, rode eight times in one daie betwéene the two parties, and so the matter was staied for a time. But the bishop of Winchester, to cléere himselfe of blame so farre as he might, and to charge his nephue the lord protectour with all the fault, wrote a letter to the regent of France, the tenor whereof insueth.

The bishop of Winchesters letter excusatorie.

RIGHT high and mightie prince, and my right noble, and after one, lieuest lord, I recommend me vnto you with all my hart. And as you desire the welfare of the king our souereigne lord, and of his realmes of England and France, your owne health, and ours also: so hast you hither. For by my truth, if you tarie, we shall put this land in aduenture with a field; such a brother you haue here, God make him a good man. For your wisedome knoweth, that the profit of France standeth in the welfare of England, &c. Written in great hast on All hallowen euen. By your true seruant to my liues end, Henrie Winchester.

The duke of Bedford being sore gréeued and disquieted with these newes, constituted the earle of Warwike, which was latelie come into France with six thousand men, his lieutenant in the French dominions, and in the duchie of Normandie; and so with a small companie, he with the duchesse his wife returned againe ouer the seas into England, and the tenth daie of Ianuarie he was with all solemnitie receiued into London, to whome the citizens gaue a paire of basins of siluer and gilt, and a thousand markes in monie. Then from London he rode to Westminster, and was lodged *A parlement holden at Lei-cester.* in the kings palace. The fiue and twentith daie of March after his comming to London, a parlement began at the towne of Leicester; where the duke of Bedford openlie rebuked the lords in generall, bicause that they in the time of warre, thorough their priuie malice and inward grudge, had almost mooued the people to warre and commotion, in which time all men ought or should be of one mind, hart, and consent:

sent: requiring them to defend, serue, & dread their souereigne lord king Henrie, in performing his conquest in France, which was in manner brought to conclusion. In this parlement the duke of Glocester laid certeine articles to the bishop of Winchester his charge, the which with the answers hereafter doo insue; as followeth.

The articles of accusation and accord betweene the lord of Glocester, and the lord of Winchester.

HERE insueth the articles, as the kings councell hath conceiued, the which the high and mightie prince my lord of Glocester hath surmised vpon my lord of Winchester chancellor of England, with the answer to the same.

Articles set foorth by the duke of Glocester, against Henrie bishop of Winchester.

1 First, whereas he being protectour, and defendour of this land, desired the Tower to be opened to him, and to lodge him therein; Richard Wooduile esquier (hauing at that time the charge of the keeping of the Tower) refused his desire and kept the same Tower against him vndulie and against reason, by the commandement of my said lord of Winchester; and afterward in approouing of the said refusall, he receiued the said Wooduile, and cherished him against the state and worship of the king, and of my said lord of Glocester.

2 Item, my said lord of Winchester, without the aduise and assent of my said lord of Glocester, or of the kings councell, purposed and disposed him to set hand on the kings person, and to haue remooued him from Eltham, the place that he was in, to Windsor, to the intent to put him in gouernance as him list.

3 Item, that were my said lord of Glocester (to whome of all persons that should be in the land, by the waie of nature and birth, it belongeth to see the gouernance of the kings person) informed of the said vndue purpose of my said lord of Winchester declared in the article next abouesaid, and in letting thereof, determining to haue gone to Eltham vnto the king to haue prouided as the cause required; my said lord of Winchester vntrulie, and against the kings peace, to the intent to trouble my said lord of Glocester going to the king, purposing his death, in case that he had gone that waie, set men of armes and archers at the end of London bridge next Suthworke: and in forebarring of the kings high waie, let draw the chaine of the stoupes there, and set vp pipes and hurdles in manner and forme of bulworks: and set men in chambers, cellars & windowes, with bowes and arrowes and other weapons, to the intent to bring finall destruction to my said lord of Glocesters person, as well as of those that then should come with him.

4 Item, my said lord of Glocester saith and affirmeth, that our souereigne lord his brother that was king Henrie the fift, told him on a time, when our souereigne lord being prince was lodged in the palace of Westminster in the great chamber, by the noise of a spaniell, there was on a night a man spied and taken behind a * tapet of the said chamber, the which man was deliuered to the earle of Arundell to be examined vpon the cause of his being there at that time; the which so examined, at that time confessed that he was there by the stirring and procuring of my said lord of Winchester, ordeined to haue slaine the said prince there in his bed: wherefore the said earle of Arundell let sacke him foorthwith, and drowned him in the Thames.

* Or hanging.

5 Item, our souereigne lord that was, king Henrie the fift, said vnto my said lord of Glocester, that his father king Henrie the fourth liuing, and visited then greatlie with sickenesse by the hand of God, my said lord of Winchester said vnto the king (Henrie the fift then being prince) that the king his father so visited with sicknesse was not personable, & therfore not disposed to come in conuersation and gouernance of the people; and for so much, counselled him to take the gouernance and crowne of this land vpon him.

The

The answer of the bishop.

HERE insue the answers to the accusations made by my lord of Winchester chancellour of England, vnto the causes and matters of heauinesse, declared in the articles
against him by my lord of Glocester.

1 First, as of the refusall made vnto my lord of Glocester, of opening the Tower
to him, of his lodging therein, by the commandement of my said lord of Winchester;
he answereth, that in the presence of my said lord of Glocester before his comming out
of his countrie of Heinault, for causes such as were thought resonable, it séemeth
lawfull that the Tower should haue béene notablie stored and kept with vittels: howbeit it was not foorthwith executed, and that in likewise after that my said lord of
Glocester, was gone into his said countrie of Heinault, for seditious and odious billes
and languages, cast and vsed in the citie of London, sounding of insurrection and rebellion against the kings peace, and destruction aswell of diuerse estates of this land,
as strangers being vnder the defense, in so much that in doubt thereof, strangers in
great number fled the land. And for the more sure kéeping of the said Tower, Richard
Wooduile esquier so trusted with our souereigne lord the king that dead is (as well ye
know) & also chamberlaine and councellor vnto my lord of Bedford, with a certeine
number of defensible persons assigned vnto him, was made deputie there by the assent
of the kings councell, being that time at London, for to abide therein, for the safegard thereof; and streictlie charged by the said councell, that during that time of his
said charge, he should not suffer any man to be in the Tower stronger than himselfe,
without speciall charge or commandement of the king by the aduise of his councell.

2 Item, that soone after (vpon the comming of my said lord of Glocester into this
land from his countrie of Heinault) the said lords of the kings councell were informed,
that my said lord of Glocester grudged with the said maner of inforcing the Tower,
and let saie to them of London, that he had well vnderstand that they had béene
heauilie threatened for the time of his absence, and other wise than they should haue
beene, if he had bécne in this land. Wherefore he was right euill contented, and
especiallie of the said forcing of the Tower, set vpon them in manner of a chased
villain, considering the good equitie and truth that they had alwaies kept vnto the
king, offering them there vpon remedie if they would.

3 Item, that after this, Richard Scot lieutenant of the Tower, by the commandement of my said lord of Glocester, brought vnto him frier Randolph, the which had
long before confessed treason doone by him against the kings person that dead is, for
the which knowlege he was put to be kept in the said Tower, & streictlie commanded
vnder great paine giuen vnto the said Scot, to kéepe him streictlie & suerlie, & not to
let him out of the said Tower without cõmandment of the king by aduise of his councell. The which frier Randolph, my said lord of Glocester kept then with himselfe
(not witting to the said Scot) as he declared to my said lord of Winchester, soone after
that he had brought the said frier Randolph to my lord of Glocester; saieng to my lord
of Winchester, that he was vndoone but he helped him, & expressed, as for cause of
the withholding of frier Randolph: and saieng moreouer, that when he desired of my
Frier Randolph. said lord of Glocester, the deliuerance of the said frier Randolph, to lead him againe
vnto the Tower, or sufficient warrant for his discharge: my said lord of Glocester
answered him, that his commandement was sufficient warrant and discharge for him.
In the which thing abouesaid, it was thought to my lord of Winchester, that my
said lord of Glocester tooke vpon him further than his authoritie stretched vnto, and
caused him to doubt and dread, least that he would haue procéeded further. And at
such time as the said Wooduile came vnto him, to aske his aduice and counsell, of
lodging my said lord of Glocester in the Tower; he aduised and charged him, that
before

before he suffered my said lord of Glocester, or any person to lodge therein stronger than himselfe, he should purueie him a sufficient warrant therof, of the king, by the aduise of his councell.

4 Item, as to the said article of the foresaid causes of heauinesse, my said lord chancellor answereth, that he neuer purposed to set hand on the kings person, nor to remoue him, or that he should be remoued, or put in any manner of gouernance, but by the aduice of the kings councell, For he could not perceiue any manner of goodnesse or of aduantage that might haue growne to him thereof, but rather great perill and charge; and hereof my said lord of Winchester is readie to make proofe, in time and place conuenient.

5 Item, as to the third article of the foresaid causes and heauines, my lord chancellor answereth, that he was oft and diuerse times warned, by diuerse credible persons, aswell at the time of the kings last parlement, holden at Westminster, as before and since, that my said lord of Glocester purposed him bodilie harme, & was warned therof and counselled by the said persons, and that diuerse times, to absteine him from comming to Westminster as my said lord of Winchester declared vnto my said lord of Glocester.

6 Item, that in the time of the said parlement, diuerse persons of low estate of the citie of London, in great number assembled on a day vpon the wharfe, at the crane of the vinetrée, and wished and desired that they had there the person of my lord of Winchester, saieng that they would haue throwen him into the Thames, to haue taught him to swim with wings. Whereof billes and language of slander and threatnings were cast and spoken in the said citie by my said lord the chancellor, which caused him to suppose that they that so said and did, willed and desired his destruction, although they had no cause.

7 Item, that after the comming to London of sir Rafe Botiller, and maister Lewes, sent from my lord of Bedford, to the rest of the lords of the councell, they being informed, that my said lord of Glocester did beare displeasure to my said lord of Winchester, they came to the said lord of Glocester to his In, the second sundaie next before All hallondaie, and there opened vnto him, that they had knowledge and vnderstanding of the said displeasure, praieng him to let them know if he bare such displeasure against my said lord of Winchester, and also the causes thereof. At the which time (as my said lord of Winchester was afterwards informed) my said lord of Glocester affirmed that he was heauie toward him, and not without causes that peraduenture he would put in writing.

8 Item, that after the mondaie next before Allhallondaie last past in the night, the people of the said citie of London, by the commandement of my said lord of Glocester, as it was said (for what cause my lord the chancellor wist not) assembled in the citie, armed and arraied, and so continued all the night. Amongst diuerse of the which (the same night by what excitation, my said lord the chancellor wist not) seditious and heauie language was vsed, and in especiall against the person of my lord the chancellor. And so the same mondaie at night, my said lord of Glocester sent vnto the Ins of court at London, charging them of the court dwelling in the same, to be with him vpon the morrow at eight of the clocke in their best arraie.

9 Item, that on the morrow being tuesdaie next following, my said lord of Glocester sent earlie vnto the maior and aldermen of the said citie of London, to ordeine him to the number of three hundred persons on horsse backe, to accompanie him vnto such a place as he disposed him to ride, which (as it was said) was vnto the king, to the intent to haue his person, and to remoue him from the place that he was in, without assent or aduise of the kings councell. The which thing was thought vnto my said lord the chancellor, that he ought in no wise to haue doone, nor had not béene seene sobefore.

10 Item, that my said lord the chancellor, considering the things aboue said, and
doubting

doubting therefore of perils that might haue insued thereof, intending to purueie there against, and namelie for his owne suertie and defense, according to the law of nature, ordeined to let, that no force of people should come on the bridge of London towards him, by the which he or his might haue béene indangered or noied, not intending in any wise bodilie harme vnto my said lord of Glocester, nor to any other person, but onelie his owne defense, in eschewing the perill abouesaid.

11 Item, as toward the fourth and fift of the said articles, my lord the chancellor answereth, that he was euer true to all those that were his souereigne lords and reigned vpon him, and that he neuer purposed treason or vntruth against any of their persons, and in especiall against the person of our said souereigne lord Henrie the fift. The which considering the great wisdome, truth, and manhood that all men knew in him, he would not for the time that he was king, haue set on my said lord the chancellor so great trust as he did, if he had found or thought in him such vntruth. The which thing my said lord the chancellor offered to declare and shew, as it belongeth to a man of his estate to doo, requiring thérvpon my lord of Bedford and all the lords spirituall and temporall in this parlement, that it might be seene that there were iudges conuenient in this case, that they would doo him right, or else that he might haue leaue of the king by their aduise to go sue his right, before him that ought to be his iudge.

12 And as toward the letter sent by my lord of Winchester vnto my lord of Bedford, of the which the tenor is before rehearsed, of the which my lord of Glocester complained him of the malicious and vntrue purpose of my said lord of Winchester, as toward the assembling of the people, and gathering of a field in the kings land, in troubling thereof, and against the kings peace: my said lord of Winchester answereth, that if his said letters duelie vnderstand, and in such wise as he vnderstood and meant in the writing of them, it maie not reasonablie be gathered and taken, that my said lord of Winchester intended to gather any field, or assemble people in troubling of the kings land, and against the kings peace, but rather purposed to acquite him to the king in his truth, and to kéepe the rest and peace in the kings land, and to eschew rebellion, disobedience and all trouble. For by that that in the beginning of the said letter, he calleth my said lord of Bedford his lieuest lord after one, that is the king, whome he ought to accept of dutie of his truth, the which he hath euer kept, and will kéepe.

13 Moreouer, in the said letter he desireth the comming home of my lord of Bedford, for the welfare of the king and of his realmes of England and of France, which stand principallie in kéeping of his rest and peace, and praieth my said lord of Bedford to spéed his cōming into England, in eschewing of ieopardie of the land, and of a field, which he dread him might haue followed if he had long taried. As toward those words; "If ye tarie, we shall put this land in aduenture with a field, such a brother ye haue here, &c." My said lord of Winchester saith, the sooth is: before or he wrote the said letter, by the occasion of certeine ordinances made by the maior and aldermen of London against the excessiue taking of masons, carpentars, tilers, plasterers, and other labourers for their dailie iournies, and approued by the kings deuise and councell, there were cast manie heauinesses and seditious billes vnder the names of such labourers, threatning rising with manie thousands, and menacing of estates of the land, and likewise seditious and euill language sowen and so continued and likelie to haue insued, of purpose and intent of disobedience and rebellion. To the redressing of which, it seemed to my lord the chancellor, that my said lord of Glocester did not his indeuour nor diligence that he might haue shewed. For lacke of which diligence, they that were disposed to doo disobeisance were incouraged & imboldned, so that it was like, that they should haue made a gathering, and that the king and his true subiects should haue béene compelled to haue made a field to

haue

haue withstand them; the which field making, had béene aduenturing of this land, and in tokening that it was neuer my said lord chancellors intent, to gather no field, but as truth most stirred him against such as riotouslie would make such assemblie against our souereigne lord, and the weale of this land, he desired so hastilie the comming of my said lord of Bedford: the which he would in no wise haue so greatlie desired, if he would haue purposed him vnto any vnlawful making of a field; for he wist well, that my said lord of Bedford would most sharplie haue chastised and punished all those, that so would make any riotous assemblie.

When this answer was made, the duke caused this writing following openlie to be proclamed.

BE it knowne to all folkes, that it is the intent of my lord of Bedford, and all the lords spirituall & temporall, assembled in this present parlement, to acquite him and them, and to proceed truelie, iustlie, and indifferentlie, without any parcialitie in any maner or matter or quarels, moued or to be moued betweene my lord of Glocester on that one partie, & my lord of Winchester chancellor of England on that other partie. And for suer keeping of the kings peace it is accorded by my said lord of Bedford, & by my said lords spirituall and temporall, an oth to be made in forme as followeth, that is to saie.

The oth of the lords.

THAT my said lord of Bedford, and my said lords, spirituall and temporall, and ech of them shall (as far forth as their cunnings and discretions suffice) trulie, iustlie, and indifferentlie counsell and aduise the king, and also procéed and acquit themselues in all the said matters, and quarels, without that they or any of them shall priuilie and apertlie make or shew himselfe to be partie or parciall therein, not leauing or eschewing so to doo for affection, loue, meed, doubt, or dread of any person or persons. And that they shall in all wise keepe secret all that shall be commoned by waie of councell, in the matters and quarrels abouesaid, in the said parlement, without that they or any of them shall by word, writing of the king, or in any wise open or discouer it to any of the said parties, or to any other person that is not of the said councell: but if he haue a speciall commandement or leaue therevnto of the king or my said lord of Bedford. And that ech of them shall with all his might and power, assist by waie of counsell, or else shew it vnto the king, my lord of Beford, and to the rest of my said lords to put the said parties to reason; and not to suffer that any of the said parties by them, or by their assistance, proceed or attempt by way of fight against the kings peace; nor helpe, assist, or comfort any of them thereto: but let them with all their might and power withstand them, and assist vnto the king, and my said lord of Bedford, in keeping of the kings peace, and redressing all such manner of procéeding by waie of fight or force.

Dukes: the duke of Bedford, the duke of Norffolke, the duke of Excester. Bishops: the archbishop of Canturburie, the bishop of Carleill, the bishop of Bath, the bishop of Landaffe, the bishop of Rochester, the bishop of Chichester, the bishop of Worcester, the bishop of saint Dauids, the bishop of London, the bishop of Duresme. Earles: the earle of Northumberland, the earle of Stafford, the earle of Oxford. Lords: the lord Hungerford, the lord Tiptost, the lord Poinings, the lord Cromwell, the lord Borough, the lord Louell, the lord Botreux, the lord Clinton, the lord Zouch, the lord Audeleie, the lord Ferreis of Groubie, the lord Talbot, the
lord

lord Roos, the lord Greie, the lord Greie of Ruthen, the lord Fitz Walter, the lord Barkeleie. Abbats: the abbat of Waltham, the abbat of Glastenburie, the abbat of S. Augustines in Canturburie, the abbat of Westminster, the abbat of S. Maries in Yorke, the abbat of S. Albons not sworne bicause he was not present. ¶ Which oth in manner and forme aboue rehearsed, all the lords aswell spirituall as temporall, being in this parlement at Leicester assembled, the fourth day of March, promised vpon their faith, dutie, and allegiance, which they owe to the king their souereigne lord, truelie to obserue and kéepe, according to the true meaning and purport of the same.

The Arbitrement.

IN the name of God Amen. We Henrie archbishop of Canturburie, Thomas duke of Excester, Iohn duke of Norffolke, Thomas bishop of Duresme, Philip bishop of Worcester, Iohn bishop of Bath, Humfrie earle of Stafford, William Alnwicke kéeper of the kings priuie seale, Rafe lord Cromwell, arbitrators in all maner of causes, matters and quarels of heauinesses & greeuances, with all incidents, circumstances, dependents, or connexes being and hanging betweene the high & worthie prince Humfrie duke of Glocester on the one partie, and the worshipful father in God Henrie bishop of Winchester and chancellor of England on the other partie, by either of them, for the pleasing of the said quarrels and debates taken and chosen in maner and forme as it is conteined more plainelie in a compromise made therevpon, of the which the tenor insueth in this forme.

1424
———
An. Reg. 4. Memorandum, the seauenth daie of March in the fourth yeare of our souereigne lord the king, Henrie the sixt, the high and mightie prince Humfrie duke of Glocester at the reuerence of God, and for the good of the king our souereigne lord in this land, & namelie at the reuerence, and especiallie at the request and praier of the mightie and high prince my lord of Bedford his brother, agréed him to put, and putteth all maner matters and quarels indéed, with all their incidents, circumstances, dependents and connexes that touchen him and his person, that he hath in anie wise doo, or féeleth himselfe gréeued or heauie against my lord his vncle, my lord of Winchester: or else that my lord of Winchester findeth him agréeued against him, in as much as they touch him or his person from the beginning of the world vnto this daie, in the aduise, ordinance and arbitrement of the worthie father in God, Henrie archbishop of Canturburie, the high and noble prince Thomas duke of Excester, and Iohn duke of Norffolke, the worshipful father in God Thomas bishop of Duresme, Philip bishop of Worcester, Iohn bishop of Bath, the noble lord Humfrie earle of Stafford, the worshipfull persons maister William Alnewicke kéeper of the kings priuie seale, and Rafe lord Cromwell, promising and behighting by the faith of his bodie, & word of his princehood and kings sonne, to doo, kéepe, obserue, and fulfill for him and his behalfe, all that shall be declared, ordeined, and arbitrated, by the foresaid archbishop, dukes, bishops, earle, keeper of the priuie seale, and lord Cromwell in all matters and quarels abouesaid.

Granting also and promising ouer that, to be comprehended in the foresaid arbitrement, as toward putting awaie all heauinesses and displeasures, in anie wise conteined, by my lord of Glocester against all those that haue in anie wise assisted, counselled, or fauoured vnto his said vncle of Winchester, and as toward anie matters that be touching my lord of Glocester, remitteth it, and the gouernance thereof vnto the king & his councell, they to déeme it by the aduise of his councell, as him thinketh it to be doone. In witnesse of the which thing to this present compromise my said lord of Glocester hath subscribed his name with his owne hand: Humfreie Glocester. And in like forme my lord of Winchester in another compromise hath subscribed

scribed with his owne hand vnder the word of his priesthood, to stand at the aduise,
ordinance, & arbitrement of the persons abouesaid, Mutatis mutandis.

A decree or order taken by the kings councell for the pacifieng of the quarels and
　variances that were betweene the duke of Glocester, and the bishop of Win-
　chester.

THE causes aforesaid and quarels by vs séene, heard, and diligentlie examined
and decréed, by the assent of the said parties, ordeine and award, that my lords of
Glocester and of Winchester, for any thing doone or spoken, by that one partie
against that other, or by anie of theirs, or anie other person or persons, afore the
seuenth daie of this present moneth of March, neuer hereafter take causes, quarels,
displeasures, or heauinesses, that one against the other, ne neither against the counsellers, adherents, or fauourers of that other for anie thing or things that are past.
And that my said lord of Glocester be good lord to my said lord of Winchester, &
haue him in loue and affection as his kinsman & vncle. And that my said lord of
Winchester haue to my said lord of Glocester true and sad loue and affection, doo
and be readie to doo him such seruice as apperteineth of honestie to my said lord
of Winchester and his estate to doo. And that each of them be good lord vnto
all those adherents, counsellers, and fauourers of that other, and shew them at all
times fauourable loue and affection, as for anie thing by them doone or said, before
the seauenth daie of March.
　And we decrée, ordeine, and award, that my said lord of Winchester, in the presence of the king our souereigne lord, my lord of Bedford, and my lord of Glocester, and the residue of the lords spirituall and temporall, and commons being in this
this present parlement, saie and declare in maner and forme that followeth: My
souereigne lord, I haue well vnderstand, that I am noised among the states of your
land, how that the king our souereigne lord that was, at that time being prince,
and lodged in the great chamber at Westminster, by the baieng of a spaniell, there
was on a night taken behind a * tapet in the same chamber, a man, that should haue　*Or hanging.
confessed, that he was there by mine excitation and procuring, to haue slaine the
foresaid prince there in his bed; wherevpon he was sacked, and foorthwith also
drowned in the Thames.
　Furthermore, I am accused, how that I should haue stirred the king that last died,
the time also that he was prince, to haue taken the gouernance of this realme, and
the crowne vpon him, his father liuing the same time, being king. Through which
language and noising, I féele my name and fame greatlie enblemished in diuerse mens
opinions. Wherevpon, I take first God to my witnes, and after all the world, that I
haue béene at all times, and am true louer, and true man, to you my souereigne lord,
and shall be all my life. And also, I haue béene to my souereigne lord that was your
father, all the time of his reigne, true man, and for such he tooke me, trusted me
and cherished me to his liues end; and as I trust, no man will affirme the contrarie,
nor neuer in my life procuring nor imagining death nor destruction of his person, ne
assenting to any such thing, or like thereto, the time that he was king or prince, or
else in other state.
　I was likewise true man to king Henrie the fourth, all the time that he was my
souereigne lord, and reigned vpon me. In which matters, in all maner of wise that
it liketh to you my souereigne lord for to command me, I am readie for to declare me:
and furthermore, where, how, and when it shall like you, by the aduise of your
councell, to assigne me. Wherefore I beséech you my souereigne lord, as humblie
as I can, considering that there is no grounded processe, by the which I might law-

fullie in these matters abouesaid, be conuict (blessed be God) to hold me, and declare me, by the aduise of all the lords, spirituall and temporall, being in this preseut parlement, true man to you my souereigne lord, and so to haue beene vnto my souereigne lords that were your father and grandfather, and true man also to haue béene at all times to your said father whilest he was prince, or else in anie other estate, the said slander and noise notwithstanding, and this same declaration to be inacted in this your said present parlement.

The which words declared in maner as it is abouesaid, it seemeth to my said lords the arbitrators, that it is méet, that my said lord of Winchester draw him apart, and in the meane time, the lords being present, be singularlie examined therevpon, and saie their aduise. And if it be assented by them, in maner as my said lord of Winchester desireth, let him be called againe, and that then my lord of Bedford haue these words in effect that follow: Faire vncle, the king my lord by the aduise of his councell, hath commanded me to saie to you, that he hath well vnderstand and considered all the matters which yée haue heere openlie declared in his presence, and therevpon yée desire a petition, that he will declare you, and by the aduise and assent of the lords spirituall and temporall, being in this present parlement, he declareth you a true man to him, and that yée haue so béene to my lord his father, and grandfather, also true man to my lord his father while he was prince, or else in anie other estate, the said dislander and noising notwithstanding, and will that the said declaration be so inacted in this present perlement.

After the which words thus said (as before is declared) it was decréed also by the said lords arbitrators, that the said lord of Winchester should haue these words that follow vnto my said lord of Glocester: My lord of Glocester, I haue conceiued to my great heauinesse, that yée should haue receiued by diuerse reports, that I should haue purposed and imagined against your person, honor, and estate, in diuerse maners, for the which, yée haue taken against me great displeasure: Sir, I take God to my witnesse, that what reports so euer haue béene to you of me, peraduenture of such as haue had no great affection to me, God forgiue it them, I neuer imagined, ne purposed anie thing that might be hindering or preiudice to your person, honor, or estate: and therefore I praie you, that yee be vnto me good lord from this time foorth; for by my will, I gaue neuer other occasion, nor purpose not to doo hereafter by the grace of God. The which words so by him said, it was decréed by the same arbitrators, that my lord of Glocester, should answer and saie: Faire vncle, sith yée declare you such a man, as yée saie, I am right glad that it is so, and for such a man I take you. And when this was doone, it was decréed by the same arbitrators, that euerie each of my lord of Glocester, and Winchester, should take either other by the hand, in the presence of the king and all the parlement, in signe and token of good loue & accord, the which was doone, and the parlement adiorned till after Easter.

At this reconciliation, such as loued peace reioised (sith it it is a fowle & pernicious thing for priuat men, much more for noblemen to be at variance, sith vpon them depend manie in affections diuerse, whereby factions might grow to the shedding of bloud) though others, to whom contention & hartgrudge is delight, wished to see the vttermost mischéefe that might therof insue, which is the vtter ouerthrow and desolation of populous tribes, euen as with a litle sparkle whole houses are manie times consumed to ashes; as the old prouerbe saith, and that verie well and aptlie;

Sola scintilla perit hæc domus aut domus illa

But when the great fier of this dissention, betwéene these two noble personages, was thus by the arbitrators (to their knowledge and iudgement) vtterlie quenched out, and laid vnder boord; all other controuersies betwéene other lords, taking part with the one partie or the other, were appeased, and brought to concord, so that for

ioy

ioy the king caused a solemne fest to be kept on Whitsundaie; on which daie he created Richard Plantagenet, sonne and heire to the erle of Cambridge, (whome his father at Southampton had put to death, as before yee haue heard) duke of Yorke, not foreseeing that this preferment should be his destruction, nor that his séed should of his generation be the extreame end and finall conclusion. He the same daie also promoted Iohn lord Mowbraie, and earle marshall, sonne and heire to Thomas duke of Norffolke (by king Richard the second exiled this realme) to the title, name, and stile of duke of Norffolke.

During this feast, the duke of Bedford adorned the king with the high order of knighthood, who on the same daie dubbed with the sword these knights, whose names insue: Richard duke of Yorke, Iohn duke of Norffolke; the earle of West-merland, Henrie lord Persie, Iohn lord Butler, sonne to the earle of Ormond, the lord Rosse, the lord Matrauers, the lord Welles, the lord Barkelie; sir Iames Butler, sir Henrie Greie of Tankaruile, sir Iohn Talbot, sir Rafe Greie of Warke, sir Robert Véere, sir Richard Greie, sir Edmund Hungerford, sir Water Wingfield, sir Iohn Butler, sir Reginald Cobham, sir Iohn Passheleu, sir Thomas Tunstall, sir Iohn Chedocke, sir Rafe Langstre, sir William Drurie, sir William ap Thomas, sir Richard Carnonell, sir Richard Wooduile, sir Iohn Shirdlow, sir Nicholas Blunket, sir William Cheinie iustice, sir William Babington, sir Rafe Butler, sir Robert Beauchampe, sir Edmund Trafford, sir Iohn Iune cheefe baron, and diuerse others.

After this solemne feast ended, a great aid and subsidie was granted for the con-tinuance of the conquest in France, and so therevpon monie was gathered, and men were prepared in euerie citie, towne, and countrie. During which businesse, Thomas duke of Excester, great vncle to the king, a right sage and discréet councellor, de-parted out of this mortall life, at his manor of Gréenewich, and with all funerall pómpe was conueied through London to Berrie, and there buried. ¶ In the same yeare also died the ladie Elizabeth, halfe sister to the same duke, and of the whole bloud with king Henrie the fourth, maried first to the lord Iohn Holland, duke of Excester, and after to the lord Fanhope, buried at the blacke friers of London. The duke of Excester dieth.

[Philip Morgan after the death of Iohn Fortham (sometime treasuror of England, bishop of Elie and Durham, both which bishopriks, for anie thing that I can yet sée, he inioied both at one time) was made bishop of Elie in the yeare of our redemption 1425, in this sort. Henrie the sixt and manie of the nobilitie had written to the conuent of the church of Elie, to choose William Alnewicke (doctor of both lawes confessor to the king and kéeper of the priuie seale) to be their bishop. Notwithstanding which (they hauing more regard to their owne priuileges and benefit) chose Peter the prior of Elie to succéed in the place of Iohn Fortham. But none of both these inioied that roome; for Martin bishop of Rome (stepping into the matter to make the third part, neither fauouring the kings motion nor approouing the monks elec-tion) remooued this William Morgan from the see of Worcester vnto Elie, sometime called Helix: as I haue séene it set downe in Saxon characters in an ancient booke of the liues of saints written in the Saxon toong, about the yeare of Christ 1010, be-fore the time of Edward the confessor, and much about the time of Albo Floria-censis. This Morgan sat at Elie nine yeares, twentie and six wéeks, and foure daies, departing this life in his manour of Hatfield, in the yeare 1434, and was buried at the Charterhouse of London; being the twentie and fourth bishop that was installed in that place.] *Fr. Thin.*
1425

While these things were thus a dooing in England, the earle of Warwike, lieu-tenant for the regent in France, entered into the countrie of Maine, & besieged the towne of Chateau de loire, the which shortlie to him was rendered, whereof he made capteine Matthew* Gough, esquier. After this, he tooke by assault the castell of Maiet, and gaue it for his valiantnesse to Iohn Winter esquier, and after that he con- 1426
* Or rather Goche.
Iohn Winter.

X 2   quered

quered the castell of Lude, and made there capteine William Gladesdale gentleman. Here he was informed, that the Frenchmen were assembled in the countrie of Beausse, wherevpon he hasted thitherwards to haue giuen them battell, but they hauing knowledge of his approch, durst not abide to trie the matter with him by a pight field, but fled before he came néere them.

The earle of Warwike made gouernour of the yoong king.

The earle in his returne wan the castell of Montdublean by surrender; where he left the valiant lord Willoughbie, and then returned to Paris. During which season, he was ordeined by the thrée estates of the realme of England, to be gouernour of the yoong king in the place of the duke of Excester deceassed; howbeit, he did not as yet returne into England, but remained in France for a season, and atchiued manie worthie enterprises. Whilest the lord regent of France was thus in England, meanes was made by the duke of Burgognie, for the deliuerie of the duke of Alanson, taken at the battell of Vernoile, and now for the summe of two hundred thousand crownes he was set at libertie; but he would not by anie meanes acknowlege the king of England to be his liege and souereigne lord.

An. Reg. 5.

1427.

After that the duke of Bedford had set all things in good order in England, he tooke leaue of the king, and togither with his wife returned into France, first landing at Calis, where the bishop of Winchester (that also passed the seas with him) receiued the habit, hat, and dignitie of a cardinall, with all ceremonies to it apperteining: which promotion, the late K. right deeplie persing into the vnrestrainable ambitious mind of the man, that euen from his youth was euer to checke at the highest; and also right well ascerteined with what intollerable pride his head should soone be swollen vnder such a hat: did therefore all his life long kéepe this prelat backe from that presumptuous estate. But now the king being yoong and the regent his fréend, he obteined his purpose, to his great profit, and the impouerishing of the spiritualtie of this realme. For by a bull legantin, which he purchased from Rome, he gathered so much treasure, that no man in maner had monie but he: so that he was called the rich cardinall of Winchester.

The bishop of Winchester made a cardinall.
W. P.

After that the lord regent was arriued in France, the lord of Rustinian, marshall of Britaine, assembled a great companie of the British nation, which fortified and repared the towne of Pontorson: and after the said marshall, with a thousand men, entered into the countrie of Constantine, and comming before the towne of Auranches, was incountered by the Englishmen of that garrison; & after long fight, his people were put to the worse, chased, and discomfited, and he himselfe taken prisoner in the field. The duke of Bedford, hearing that the towne of Pontorson, situate within leagues of Mont Saint Michaell, was newlie fortified, and stronglie defended, sent thither the earle of Warwike, accompanied with the lord Scales, and other valiant capteins and souldiers, to the number of seauen thousand men, to besiege the towne; who so inuironed it on euerie side, that no man could steale neither in nor out.

The lord of Rustinian taken and his people slaine and discomfited.

The siege thus long continuing, vittels began to wax scant in the English armie: wherefore the lord Scales, hauing in his companie sir Iohn Harpeleie bailiffe of Constantine, sir William Brearton bailiffe of Caen, sir Rafe Tesson, sir Iohn Carbonell, and three thousand good men of warre, departed from the siege to get vittels, powder, and other things necessarie for their purpose. And as they were returning with their cariages by the sea coast, néere to Saint Michaels Mount, they suddenlie were incountered by their enimies, whereof were chéefe, the baron of Coloses, the lord Dausebost, capteine of the said Mount, the lord Mountabon, the lord Montburchier, the lord of Chateaugiron, the lord of Tintignat, the lord of Chateaubrian, with six thousand men of warre.

The lord Scales and his companie, perceiuing themselues beset on the one side with the sea, & on the other with their enimies, alighted from their horsses, and like couragious persons, there in an vnspeakeable furie, set on their enimies. The fight was fierce

A hot skirmish.

fierce & cruell. The Englishmen kept themselues close togither; so that their enimies could get no aduantage of them. At the last, the lord Scales cried S. George they flée. Wherevpon, the Englishmen tooke such courage, and the Frenchmen that fought before, were so dismaied, that they began to flee in deed. The Englishmen _{placeholder} leaped on horsse-backe, and followed them so, that they slue and tooke aboue eleuen hundred persons, among the which were taken the baron of Coloses, the vicount of Rone, and others. The lord of Chateaugiron, with a Scotish capteine, & diuerse other men of name were slaine. After this victorie, the lord Scales with his vittels, prouision, and prisoners, returned to the siege, where he was of the earle and other noble men ioiouslie receiued.

On the cene thursdaie.

Enguerant.

Whilest the siege continued thus before Pontorson, Christopher Hanson, and other souldiers of the garrison of Saint Susan, made a rode into the countrie of Aniou, and came to a castell called Ramfort, which castell was so priuilie scaled, that the capteine within, and his companie, were taken or slaine, before they knew of their enimies approching. When knowledge hereof was giuen vnto the Frenchmen which were assembled, to the number of twentie thousand, to raise the siege that laie before Pontorson, they left that enterprise, and went to recouer the said castell of Ramfort, and so comming before it, planted their siege so on ech side of it, that at length by composition the Englishmen within, doubting to be taken by force, rendered vp the castell, hauing libertie to depart with bag and baggage.

Shortlie after, the lord of Raix, calling himselfe lieutenant generall for the Dolphin, entred into Maine with an armie of three thousand men, and by force tooke the castell of Malicorne, wherof was capteine an Englishman, one Oliuer Osbatersbie. In like maner, they tooke the little castell of Lude, and therein William Blackborne, lieutenant for William Glasdale esquier. After this, the Frenchmen returned backe to the Dolphin, and kept not on their iourneie to Pontorson, for that they vnderstood by espials, that the earle of Warwike, and the Englishmen there, determined to giue them battell, if they once attempted to raise the siege. They within the towne, being streictlie besieged, perceiuing no likelihood of succours, and seeing the English armie dailie increase, fell to treatie for doubt to be taken by force, and so rendered the towne vpon condition, that they might depart with horsse and harnesse onelie. Which being granted to them, the erle like a valiant capteine entred into the towne, and there appointed for gouernors, the lord Ros, and the lord Talbot, and leauing there a conuenient garrison, returned to the lord regent.

Pontorson rendered to the Englishmen.

After the taking of this towne of Pontorson, there was a league and treatie concluded betweene the regent and the duke of Britaine; by the articles of which agréement, the townes of Pontorson and saint Iames de Beuuron were beaten downe to the ground and raced. When the lord of Raix was departed out of Maine (as ye haue heard) Christopher Hanson, Philip * Gough, Martin Godfrie, called the Scaler, tooke by stealth the castell of saint Laurence de Mortiers. At the same time, when the capteine and the most part of his companie were gone foorth to heare masse, in a church ouer against the same castell, and kéeping themselues close, till the capteine returned, they tooke him as he was entered within the first gate, & so was this castell stuffed with Englishmen, and capteine thereof was appointed sir William Oldhall.

* Or rather Goche.

The same season, sir Iohn Fastolfe, gouernour of the countries of Aniou and Maine, assembled a great puissance of men warre, and laid siege before the castell of saint Owen Distais, beside the towne of Lauall; and after he had laine there ten daies, the castell was deliuered, they within departing with their liues and armour onelie to them granted, by the tenor of the composition, which they tooke with the same sir Iohn Fastolfe. After the winning of this castell, the Englishmen remooued to the strong castell of Grauile, and after twelue daies, they within offered to yeeld the castell by a daie, if they were not succoured by the Dolphin or his power: the offer was taken and pledges deliuered.

Then

Then sir Iohn Fastolfe returned in post to the regent, aduertising him of this composition and agreement; wherefore, the said regent raised a great power to fight with the Frenchmen at the daie appointed, and in his companie were the earles of Mortaigne and Warwike, the lord Ros and Talbot, sir Iohn Fastolfe, sir Iohn Aubemond, sir Iohn Ratcliffe, and diuerse other, to the number of twentie thousand men; and so marched forwards, in hope to meet and ioine battell with their aduersaries. But the French power, being not far off from the place, durst not approch. Wherefore, the regent sent to sir Iohn Fastolfe incontinentlie, to receiue the castell; but they within (contrarie to promise and appointment) had newlie vitteled & manned the place, and

Hostages execut-
ed for promise
broken. so forsaking the pledges, and their fellowes in armes, refused to render the fortresse; wherefore, the pledges were brought before their sight, and there before the castell openlie put to death.

The lord Talbot,
a valiant cap-
teine. After this the lord Talbot was made gouernour of Aniou and Maine, and sir Iohn Fastolfe was assigned to an other place, which lord Talbot, being both of noble birth, and of haultie courage, after his comming into France, obteined so manie glorious victories of his enimies, that his onelie name was & yet is dreadfull to the French nation, and much renowmed amongst all other people. This lustie and most valiant capteine entered into Maine, where he slue men, destroied castels, burnt townes, and in conclusion suddenlie tooke the towne of Lauall. The lord Loehac, and diuerse other, withdrew into the castell, in the which they were so streictlie besieged, that in the end they agréed to paie the lord Talbot an hundred thousand crownes, for licence to depart, with all their bag and baggage.

* Or rather
Goche. Then was this castell deliuered to the keeping of Gilbert Halsall, which after was slaine at the siege of Orleance, in whose place Matthew * Gough was made capteine there: who being at the iournie of Senlis, by treason of a miller that kept a mill adioining to the wall, the Frenchmen entered into the towne, and brought it againe into their subiection. Now the duke of Bedford hearing that the towne of Montargis, in the territorie of Orleance, was but slenderlie kept, and not thoroughlie furnished, sent the erle of Suffolke, with his brother sir Iohn Poole, and sir Henrie Bisset, hauing in their companie a six thousand men, to assalt that towne; but when they came thither and found the towne both well manned and stronglie fortified, contrarie to their expectation, they surceassed from giuing the assault, and onelie laid their siege round about it.

The earle of Warwike was appointed to lie with a great number of men of warre, at S. Mathelines de Archempe, to incounter the Frenchmen, if they would attempt to aid or vittell those within the towne. The situation of this towne was such, that by reason of waters and marishes, the English armie must néeds seuer it selfe into thrée parts, so that the one could not easilie helpe the other, but either by boats or bridges. This siege continued aboue two moneths, so that in the meane time the Frenchmen had leasure to prouide for the succour thereof; and so it came to passe, that the constable of France Arthur of Britaine, the lord Boisac one of the marshals, Stephan la Hire, Pothon de Saintreiles, the lord Grauile, and diuerse others, to the number of three thousand horssemen, were sent foorth by the Dolphin.

A great slaughter
by negligence of
the watch at
Montargis. These priuilie in the night season came on that side, where sir Iohn de la Poole and sir Henrie Bisset laie, whome they found so out of order, and without good watch, that the Frenchmen entered into their lodgings, slue manie in their beds, and spared none, for their resistance was but small. Sir Iohn de la Poole with his horsse saued himselfe, and sir Henrie Bisset escaped by a boat, and eight other with him. The residue fléeing in plumpes, and striuing to passe by a bridge of timber, the which was pestered with preasse of the multitude, brake, and so there were a great number drowned: insomuch that there were slaine by the enimies swoord, and drowned in the water, fiftéene hundred men.

The

The earle of Warwike hearing of this misfortune, departed from saint Mathelines with all spéed, and comming before Montargis, offered battell to the French capteins, which answered, that they had manned and vittelled the towne, and intended to doo no more at that time. The Englishmen héerevpon came softlie backe againe with all their ordinance to the duke of Bedford. Yet had not the French so great cause to vaunt of their successe: for at this verie time, sir Nicholas Burdet, appointed by the duke of Summerset to indamage his enimies in the coasts of Britaine, sent horssemen into euerie part, woorking all the displeasure to the people that might be deuised. The countrie, through which he passed, was wasted, the townes were burnt, the houses spoiled, and great number of prisoners taken, the small villages were destroied, and the walled townes ransomed, and so without hurt or damage the said sir Nicholas Burdet returned into Normandie. *Sir Nicholas Burdet. Polydor.*

These newes being signified to the constable, and other the French capteins, asswaged their great mirth and triumphant ioy, conceiued for the victorie of Montargis, that loth they were to attempt anie further enterprises against the English nation. But the duke of Alanson, who (as ye haue heard) was latelie deliuered out of captiuitie, reuiued againe the dulled spirits of the Dolphin, and somewhat aduanced, in hope of good spéed, the fainting harts of his capteins; so that (some occasion offered) they determined to atchiue a notable feat (as they tooke it) against the Englishmen, which was the recouerie of the city of Mans out of their hands: for so it happened, that diuers of the chéefe rulers in that citie, and namelie diuerse spirituall persons, meaning to reuolt to the Dolphins side, aduertised him by letters of their whole minds, which letters were conueied vnto him by certeine friers.

The Dolphin glad of those newes, appointed the lords de la Breth and Faiet, marshals of France, accompanied with the lords of Mount Iehan, of Buell, Doruall, Torsie, Beaumanor, the Hire, and his brother Guilliam, with fiue hundred other valiant capteins and souldiers, to the accomplishing of this enterprise; who comming thither at the daie assigned, in the night season approched towards the walles, making a little fire on an hill, in sight of the towne, to signifie their comming, which perceiued by the citizens that néere to the great church were watching for the same, a burning cresset was shewed out of the steeple, which suddenlie was put out and quenched. What néedeth manie words?

The capteins on horsseback came to the gate, the traitors within slue the porters and watchmen, and let in their fréends, whereby the footmen entered first, and the men of armes waited at the barriers, to the intent that if néed required, they might fight it out in open field. Hereby manie Englishmen were slaine, and a great crie and garboile raised through the towne, as in such surprises is woont. The cause of this mischéefe was not knowen to any, but onelie to the conspirators; for the remnant of the citizens being no partakers, imagined, that the Englishmen had made hauocke in the towne, and put all to the sword. The Englishmen on the other side iudged, that the citizens had begun some new rebellion against them, or else had striuen amongst themselues. *Mans lost by treason of the citizens.*

The earle of Suffolke, which was gouernour of the towne, hauing perfect knowledge by such as scaped from the wals, how the matter went, withdrew without any tarriance into the castell, which standeth at the gate of saint Vincent, whereof was constable Thomas Gower esquier, whither also fled manie Englishmen; so as for vrging the enimie, prease of the number, and lacke of vittels, they could not haue indured long; wherefore they priuilie sent a messenger to the lord Talbot, which then laie at Alanson, certifieng him in how hard a case they were. The lord Talbot hearing these newes, like a carefull capteine in all hast assembled togither about seuen hundred men, & in the euening departed from Alanson, so as in the morning he came to a castell called Guierch, two miles from Mans, and there staied a while, till he had

sent

* Or rather Coche.

sent out Matthew **Gough, as an espiall, to vnderstand how the Frenchmen demeaned themselues.

* Goche.

Mathew ** Gough so well sped his businesse, that priuilie in the night he came into the castell, where he learned that the Frenchmen verie negligentlie vsed themselues, without taking heed to their watch, as though they had béene out of all danger: which well vnderstood, he returned againe, and within a mile of the citie met the lord Talbot, and the lord Scales, and opened vnto them all things, according to his credence. The lords then, to make hast in the matter, bicause the daie approched, with all spéed possible came to the posterne gate, and alighting from their horsses, about six of the clocke in the morning, they issued out of the castell, crieng, saint George, Talbot.

Mans recouered.

The Frenchmen being thus suddenlie taken, were sore amazed, in so much that some of them, being not out of their beds, got vp in their shirts, and lept ouer the walles. Other ran naked out of the gates to saue their liues, leauing all their apparell, horsses, armour, and riches behind them, none was hurt but such as resisted.

Abr. Fl.

¶ Hard shift was made on all hands for safetie of life, and happie was he that could find a place of refuge where to lurke vnspide and vnhurt of the enimie; who in the execution of their vengeance were so peremptorie, that it was a matter of great difficultie or rather impossibilitie to escape their force. To be short, there were slaine and taken, to the number of foure hundred gentlemen, the priuat souldiers were

Traitors executed.

frankelie let go. After this, inquisition was made of the authors of the treason, and there were found & condemned thirtie citizens, twentie priests, and fifteene friers, who according to their demerits were all hanged.

An. Reg. 6.

The citie of Mans being thus recouered, the lord Talbot returned to Alanson, and shortlie after the earle of Warwike departed into England, to be gouernour of the yoong

Duke of Excester deceassed.

king, in steed of Thomas duke of Excester, latelie departed to God, and then was the lord Thomas Montacute earle of Salisburie sent into France, to supplie the roome

1428.

of the said earle of Warwike, who landed at Calis with fiue thousand men, and so came to the duke of Bedford as then lieng in Paris, where they fell in councell togither concerning the affaires of France, and namelie the earle of Salisburie began maruellouslie to phantasie the gaining of the citie & countrie of Orleance.

This earle was the man at that time, by whose wit, strength, and policie, the English name was much fearefull and terrible to the French nation, which of himselfe might both appoint, command, and doo all things in manner at his pleasure, in

Montacute earle of Salisburie a politike and valiant man.

whose power (as it appeared after his death) a great part of the conquest consisted: for suerlie, he was a man both painefull, diligent, and readie to withstand all dangerous chances that were at hand, prompt in counsell, and of courage inuincible, so that in no one man, men put more trust; nor any singular person wan the harts so much of all men.

Herevpon, after this great enterprise had long béene debated in the priuie councell, the earle of Salisburies deuise therein was of them all granted and allowed, so that he being replenished with good hope of victorie, and furnished with artillerie & munition apperteining to so great an enterprise, accompanied with the earle of Suffolke, and the lord Talbot, and with a valiant armie, to the number of ten thousand men, departed from Paris, and passed through the countrie of Beausse. There he tooke by assault the towne of Genuille, and within fiue daies after had the castell deliuered vnto him, by them that were fled into it for their safegard. He also tooke the towne of Baugencie, suffering euerie man which would become subiect to the king of England, to inioie their lands and goods. The townes of Meun vpon Loire, and Iargeaulx, hearing of these dooings, presented to them the keies of their townes vpon like agréement.

W. P.
Les grandes chroniques de Britaigne.

[About Maie in this 1428, the towne of Naunts and territories there with a fearefull earthquake were shaken, houses castels and strong buildings in such terrour, as it was thought the end of the world had béene come.]

After

After this, in the moneth of September the earle came before the citie of Orleance, and planted his siege on the one side of the riuer of Loire; but before his comming, the bastard of Orleance, the bishop of the citie, and a great number of Scots, hearing of the earles intent, made diuerse fortifications about the towne, and destroied the suburbes, in which were twelue parish churches, and foure orders of friers. They cut also downe all the vines, trees, and bushes, within fiue leagues of the citie, so that the Englishmen should haue neither refuge nor succour.

An. Reg. 7. Orleance besieged. Bastard of Orleance.

After the siege had continued full thrée weekes, the bastard of Orleance issued out of the gate of the bridge, and fought with the Englishmen; but they receiued him with so fierce and terrible strokes, that he was with all his companie compelled to retire and flee backe into the citie. But the Englishmen followed so fast, in killing and taking of their enimies, that they entered with them. ¶ The bulworke of the bridge, with a great tower standing at the end of the same, was taken incontinentlie by the Englishmen, who behaued themselues right valiantlie vnder the conduct of their couragious capteine, as at this assault, so in diuerse skirmishes against the French; partlie to kéepe possession of that which Henrie the fift had by his magnanimitie & puissance atchiued, as also to inlarge the same. But all helped not. For who can hold that which will awaie: In so much that some cities by fraudulent practises, othersome by martiall prowesse were recouered by the French, to the great discouragement of the English and the appalling of their spirits; whose hope was now dashed partlie by their great losses and discomfitures (as after you shall heare) but chéeflie by the death of the late deceassed Henrie their victorious king; as Chr. Okland verie trulie and agréeablie to the storie noteth:

A bulworke at Orleance taken. *Abr. Fl.*

> Delphinus comitésque eius fera prælia tentant,
> Fraude domi capiunt alias, virtute receptæ
> Sunt vrbes aliæ quædam sublapsa refertur
> Anglûm spes retrò languescere pectora dicas,
> Quippe erat Henricus quintus, dux strenuus olim,
> Mortuus: hinc damni grauior causa atque doloris.

In this conflict, manie Frenchmen were taken, but more were slaine, and the kéeping of the tower and bulworke was committed to William Glasdale esquier. By the taking of this bridge the passage was stopped, that neither men nor vittels could go or come by that waie. After this, the earle caused certeine bulworkes to be made round about the towne, casting trenches betwéene the one and the other, laieng ordinance in euerie place where he saw that any batterie might be deuised. When they within saw that they were enuironed with fortresses and ordinance, they laid gun against gun, and fortified towers against bulworkes, and within cast new rampiers, and fortified themselues as stronglie as might be deuised.

The bastard of Orleance and the Hire were appointed to see the walles and watches kept, and the bishop saw that the inhabitants within the citie were put in good order, and that vittels were not vainelie spent. In the tower that was taken at the bridge end (as before you haue heard) there was an high chamber, hauing a grate full of barres of iron, by the which a man might looke all the length of the bridge into the citie; at which grate manie of the chéefe capteins stood manie times, viewing the citie, and deuising in what place it was best to giue the assault. They within the citie well perceiued this tooting hole, and laid a péece of ordinance directlie against the window.

It so chanced, that the nine and fiftith daie after the siege was laid, the earle of Salisburie, sir Thomas Gargraue, and William Glasdale, with diuerse other went into the said tower, and so into the high chamber, and looked out at the grate, and within a short space, the sonne of the maister-gunner, perceiuing men looking out at the window, tooke his match (as his father had taught him) who was gone downe to din-

ner, and fired the gun; the shot whereof brake, and shiuered the iron barres of the
grate, so that one of the same bars strake the earle so violentlie on the head, that it
stroke awaie one of his eies, and the side of his chéeke. Sir Thomas Gargraue was
likewise striken, and died within two daies.

The earle was conueied to Meun on Loire, where after eight daies he likewise departed this world, whose bodie was conueied into England with all funerall appointment, and buried at Bissam by his progenitors, leauing behind him an onelie daughter
named Alice, married to Richard Neuill, sonne to Rafe earle of Westmerland, of
whome more shall be said héereafter. The damage that the realme of England receiued by the losse of this noble man, manifestlie appeared; in that immediatlie after
his death, the prosperous good lucke, which had followed the English nation, began
to decline, and the glorie of their victories gotten in the parties beyond the sea fell in
decaie.

Though all men were sorowfull for his death, yet the duke of Bedford was most
striken with heauinesse, as he that had lost his onelie right hand, and chéefe aid in time
of necessitie. But sith that dead men cannot helpe the chances of men that be liuing,
he like a prudent gouernour appointed the earle of Suffolke to be his lieutenant and
capteine of the siege, and ioined with him the lord Scales, the lord Talbot, sir Iohn
Fastolfe, and diuerse other right valiant capteins. These persons caused bastilles to
be made round about the citie, and left nothing vnattempted, that might aduance
their purpose, which to bring to wished effect there was not anie want, as of no cautelous policie, so of no valiant enterprise, tending to the enimies ouerthrow.

In the Lent season, vittels and artillerie began to waxe scant in the English campe,
wherefore the earle of Suffolke appointed sir Iohn Fastolfe, sir Thomas Rampston,
and sir Philip Hall, with their retinues, to ride to Paris, to the lord regent, to informe
him of their lacke, who incontinentlie vpon that information prouided vittels, artillerie,
and munitions necessarie, and loded therewith manie chariots, carts, and horsses:
and for the sure conueieng of the same, he appointed sir Simon Morhier, prouost
of Paris, with the gard of the citie, and diuerse of his owne houshold-seruants
to accompanie sir Iohn Fastolfe and his complices, to the armie lieng at the siege
of Orleance. They were in all to the number of fifteene hundred men, of the which
there were not past fiue or six hundred Englishmen.

These departing in good order of battell out of Paris, came to Genuille in Beausse,
and in a morning earlie, in a great frost, they departed from thence toward the siege;
and when they came to a towne called Rowraie, in the lands of Beausse, they perceiued their enimies comming towards them, being to the number of nine or ten thousand of Frenchmen and Scots, of whome were capteins Charles of Cleremont, sonne
to the duke of Bourbon then being prisoner in England; sir William Steward constable of Scotland, a little before deliuered out of captiuitie, the earle of Perdriake,
the lord Iohn Vandosme, the Vidame of Chartres, the lord of Toures, the lord of
Lohar, the lord of Eglere, the lord of Beauiew, the bastard Tremoile, and manie
other valiant capteins.

Wherefore sir Iohn Fastolfe set all his companie in good order of battell, and
pitched stakes before euerie archer, to breake the force of the horssemen. At their
backes they set all the wagons and carriages, and within them they tied all their horsses.
In this maner stood they still, abiding the assault of their enimies. The Frenchmen
by reason of their great number, thinking themselues sure of the victorie, egerlie set
on the Englishmen, which with great force them receiued, and themselues manfullie

defended. At length, after long and cruell fight, the Englishmen droue backe and
vanquished the proud Frenchmen, & compelled them to flée. In this conflict were
slaine the lord William Steward constable of Scotland, and his brother the lord Dor-
ualle, the lord Chateaubriam, sir Iohn Basgot, and other Frenchmen and Scots, to
                                                                                      the

the number of fiue and twentie hundred, and aboue eleuen hundred taken prisoners, although the French writers affirme the number lesse.

After this fortunate victorie, sir Iohn Fastolfe and his companie (hauing lost no one man of anie reputation) with all their cariages, vittels, and prisoners, marched foorth and came to the English campe before Orleance, where they were ioifullie receiued, and highlie commended for their valiancie and worthie prowesse shewed in the battell; the which bicause most part of the cariage was herring and lenton stuffe, the Frenchmen called it the battell of herrings. The earle of Suffolke being thus vittelled, continued the siege, and euerie daie almost skirmished with the Frenchmen within, who (at length being in despaire of all succours) offered to treat, and in conclusion, to saue themselues and the citie from captiuitie of their enimies, they deuised to submit the citie, themselues, and all theirs vnder the obeisance of Philip duke of Burgognie, bicause he was extract out of the stocke and bloud roiall of the ancient kings of France, thinking by this means (as they did in deed) to breake or diminish the great amitie betwéene the Englishmen and him.

The battell of herrings.

This offer was signified by them vnto the duke of Burgognie, who with thanks certified them againe, that he would gladlie receiue them, if the lord regent would therewith be contented. Herevpon he dispatched messengers to the duke of Bedford, who though some counselled that it should be verie good and necessarie for him to agrée to that maner of yéelding; yet he and other thought it neither conuenient nor honourable, that a citie so long besieged by the king of England, should be deliuered vnto anie other prince, than to him, or to his regent, for that might be a verie bad president to other townes in anie like case. Herevpon the regent answered the Burgognian ambassadors: that after so long a siege on his part, and obstinat a resistance of theirs, he might not receiue rendring and conditions at their appointment. At this answer the duke hoong the groine, as conceiuing that our side should enuie his glorie, or not to be so forward in aduancing his honour as he would haue it.

W. P.

In time of this siege at Orleance (French stories saie) the first wéeke of March 1428, vnto Charles the Dolphin, at Chinon as he was in verie great care and studie how to wrestle against the English nation, by one Peter Badricourt capteine of Vacouleur, (made after marshall of France by the Dolphins creation) was caried a yoong wench of an eightéene yeeres old, called Ione Are, by name of hir father (a sorie sheepheard) Iames of Are, and Isabell hir mother, brought vp poorelie in their trade of kéeping cattell, borne at Domprin (therefore reported by Bale, Ione Domprin) vpon Meuse in Loraine within the diocesse of Thoule. Of fauour was she counted likesome, of person stronglie made and manlie, of courage great, hardie, and stout withall, an vnderstander of counsels though she were not at them, great semblance of chastitie both of bodie and behauiour, the name of Iesus in hir mouth about all hir businesses, humble, obedient, and fasting diuerse daies in the weeke. A person (as their bookes make hir) raised vp by power diuine, onelie for succour to the French estate then déepelie in distresse, in whome, for planting a credit the rather, first the companie that toward the Dolphin did conduct hir, through places all dangerous, as holden by the English, where she neuer was afore, all the waie and by nightertale safelie did she lead; then at the Dolphins sending by hir assignement, from saint Katharins church of Fierbois in Touraine (where she neuer had béene and knew not) in a secret place there among old iron, appointed she hir sword to be sought out and brought hir, that with fiue floure delices was grauen on both sides, wherewith she fought & did manie slaughters by hir owne hands. On warfar rode she in armour * cap a pie & mustered as a man, before hir an ensigne all white, wherin was Iesus Christ painted with a floure delice in his hand.

W. P.
Ieha de Tillet.
Les chronic.
de Bretaigne:
Le Rosier calleth him Robert.
Ione de Are
Puseli de dieu.
In vita Bund-vicæ.

Grand chro. 4.

* From head to foot.

Vnto the Dolphin into his gallerie when first she was brought, and he shadowing himselfe behind, setting other gaie lords before him to trie hir cunning from all the

companie,

This salutation appeareth after héere.

companie, with a salutation (that indeed marz all the matter) she pickt him out alone, who therevpon had hir to the end of the gallerie, where she held him an houre in secret and priuate talke, that of his priuie chamber was thought verie long, and therefore would haue broken it off; but he made them a sign to let hir saie on.   In which (among other) as likelie it was, she set out vnto him the singular feats (forsooth)

Les grand chronic.

giuen her to vnderstand by reuelation diuine, that in vertue of that sword shée should atchiue, which were, how with honor and victorie shee would raise the siege at Orleance, set him in state of the crowne of France, and driue the English out of the countrie, thereby he to inioie the kingdome alone.   Héerevpon he hartened at full, appointed hir a sufficient armie with absolute power to lead them, and they obedientlie to doo as she bad them.   Then fell she to worke, and first defeated indéed the siege at Orleance, by and by incouraged him to crowne himselfe king of France at Reims, that a little before from the English she had woone.   Thus after pursued she manie bold enterprises to our great displeasure a two yeare togither, for the time she kept in state vntill she were taken and for heresie and witcherie burned : as in particularities hereafter followeth.   But in hir prime time she armed at all points (like a iolie capteine) roade from Poictiers to Blois, and there found men of warre, vittels, and munition, ready to be conueied to Orleance.

Héere was it knowne that the Englishmen kept not so diligent watch as they had béene accustomed to doo, and therefore this maid (with other French capteins) comming forward in the dead time of the night, and in a great raine and thunder entred into the citie with all their vittels, artillerie, and other necessarie prouisions. The next daie the Englishmen boldlie assaulted the towne, but the Frenchmen defended the walles so, as no great feat worthie of memorie chanced that daie betwixt them, though the Frenchmen were amazed at the valiant attempt of the Englishmen, whervpon the bastard of Orleance gaue knowledge to the duke of Alanson, in what danger the towne stood without his present helpe, who comming within two leagues of the citie, gaue knowledge to them within, that they should be readie the next daie to receiue him.

This accordinglie was accomplished: for the Englishmen willinglie suffered him and his armie also to enter, supposing that it should be for their aduantage to haue so great a multitude to enter the citie, whereby their vittels (whereof they within had great scarsitie) might the sooner be consumed.   On the next daie in the morning, the Frenchmen altogither issued out of the towne, woone by assault the bastile of saint Lou, and set it on fire.   And after they likewise assaulted the tower at the bridge foot, which was manfullie defended.   But the Frenchmen (more in number) at length tooke it, yer the lord Talbot could come to the succours, in the which William Gladesdale the capteine was slaine, with the lord Moolins, and lord Poinings also.

The Frenchmen puffed vp with this good lucke, fetched a compasse about, and in good order of battell marched toward the bastile, which was in the kéeping of the lord Talbot: the which vpon the enimies approch, like a capteine without all feare or dread of that great multitude, issued foorth againt them, and gaue them so sharpe an incounter, that they not able to withstand his puissance, fled (like shéepe before the woolfe) againe into the citie, with great losse of men and small artillerie.   Of Englishmen were lost in the two Bastiles, to the number of six hundred persons, or thereabout, though the French writers multiplie this number of hundreds to thousands, as their maner is.

The earle of Suffolke, the lord Talbot, the lord Scales, and other capteins assembled togither in councell, and after causes shewed to and fro, it was amongst them determined to leaue their fortresses and bastiles, and to asssmble in the plaine field, and there to abide all the daie, to sée if the Frenchmen would issue foorth to fight with them.   This conclusion taken was accordinglie executed: but when the Frenchmen

durst

durst not once come foorth to shew their heads, the Englishmen set fire of their lodgings, and departed in good order of Battell from Orleance. The next daie, which was the eight daie of Maie, the earle of Suffolke rode to Iargeaux with foure hundred Englishmen, and the lord Talbot with an other companie returned to Mehun. And after he had fortified that towne, he went to the towne of Lauall, and woone it, togither with the castell, sore punishing the townsmen for their cankered obstinacie against them. The siege of Orleance broken vp.

Thus when the Englishmen had seuered themselues into garrisons, the duke of Alanson, the bastard of Orleance, Ione le Pusell, the lord Gawcourt, and diuerse other capteins of the Frenchmen, came the twelfe daie of Iune, before the towne of Iargeaux, where the earle of Suffolke and his two brethren soiourned, & gaue to the towne so fierce an assault on thrée parts, that Poiton de Sentrailes, perceiuing an other part void of defendants, scaled the wals on that side, and without difficultie tooke the towne, and slue sir Alexander Poole, brother to the erle, and manie other, to the number of two hundred. But the Frenchmen gained not much thereby, for they lost thrée hundred good men and more. Of the Englishmen fortie were taken, with the earle and his other brother named Iohn.

The Frenchmen, as they returned to Orleance, fell at variance for their prisoners, and slue them all, sauing the earle and his brother. Shortlie after, the same French armie came to Mehun, where they tooke the tower at the bridge foot, and put therein a garrison. From thence they remooued to Baugencie, and constreined them that were within the towne to yéeld, vpon condition they might depart with bag and baggage. At the same place there came to the duke of Alanson, the new constable Arthur of Britaine, and with him the lord Dalbret, and other. Also after this the earle of Vandosme came to them, so that by the dailie repaire of such as assembled togither to strengthen the French part, they were in all to the number betweene twentie and thrée and twentie thousand men. Prisoners slaine by the French as they were taken.

All which being once ioined in one armie, shortlie after fought with the lord Talbot (who had with him not past six thousand men) néere vnto a village in Beausse called Pataie: at which battell the charge was giuen by the French so vpon a sudden, that the Englishmen had not leisure to put themselues in arraie, after they had put vp their stakes before their archers, so that there was no remedie but to fight at aduenture. This battell continued by the space of three long houres; for the Englishmen, though they were ouerpressed with multitude of their enimies, yet they neuer fled backe one foot, till their capteine the lord Talbot was sore wounded at the backe, and so taken. Nichol. Giles.
Fiue thousãd saith Hall.

Then their hearts began to faint, and they fled, in which flight were slaine aboue twelue hundred, and fortie taken, of whome the lord Talbot, the lord Scales, the lord Hungerford, & sir Thomas Rampston were chéefe. Diuerse archers, after they had shot all their arrowes, hauing onelie their swords, defended themselues, and with helpe of some of thei horsemen came safe to Mehun. This ouerthrow, and speciallie the taking of the lord Talbot, did not so much reioise the Frenchmen; but it did as much abash the Englishmen: so that immediatlie therevpon, the townes of Ienuile, Mehun, Fort, and diuerse other, returned from the English part, and became French. From this battell departed without anie stroke striken sir Iohn Fastolfe, the same yeare for his valiantnesse elected into the order of the garter. But for doubt of misdealing at this brunt, the duke of Bedford tooke from him the image of saint George, and his garter; though afterward by meanes of freends, and apparant causes of good excuse, the same were to him againe deliuered against the mind of the lord Talbot. Great losse on the English side. The lords Talbot, Scales, and Hungerford taken.

Charles the Dolphin that called himselfe French K. perceiuing fortune to smile thus vpon him, assembled a great power, and determined to conquer the citie of Reimes, that he might be there sacred, crowned, and annointed, according to the custome of

his

his progenitours, that all men might iudge that he was by all lawes and decrees a iust and lawfull king. In his waie thitherwards he besieged the citie of Auxerre, the citizens whereof compounded with him to yéeld, if they were not rescued within certeine daies. From thence he came before Trois, and after twelue daies siege had that citie deliuered vnto him, by composition, that the capteine sir Philip Hall (with his people and mooueables) might depart in safetie. After that Trois was yéelded, the communaltie of Chaalons rebelled against sir Iohn Aubemond their capteine, and constreined him to deliuer the towne vpon like composition. In semblable manner did they of Reimes, desiring him to giue safe conduct to all the Englishmen safelie to depart. When Reimes was thus become French, the foresaid Charles the Dolphin in the presence of the dukes of Lorraine and Barré, and of all the noble men of his fac-

The French king crowned.

tion, was sacred there king of France by the name of Charles the seauenth, with all rites and ceremonies thereto belonging. They of Auxerre, when the terme of their appointment was expired, submitted themselues to him; and so likewise did all the cities and townes adioining.

The duke of Bedford aduertised of all these dooings, assembled his power about him, and hauing togither ten thousand good Englishmen (beside Normans) departed out of Paris in warlike fashion, and passing thorough Brie to Monstreau fault Yonne, sent by his herald Bedford, letters to the French king, signifieng to him; that where he had (contrarie to the finall conclusion accorded betwéene his noble brother K. Henrie

Ione taken to be a witch.

the fift, & king Charles the sixt, father to him that was the vsurper) by allurement of a deuelish witch, taken vpon him the name, title, & dignitie of the king of France; and further had by murther, stealing, craft, and deceitfull meanes, violentlie gotten, and wrongfullie kept diuerse cities and townes belonging to the king of England his nephue; for proofe thereof he was come downe from Paris with his armie, into the countrie of Brie, by dint of sword and stroke of battell to prooue his writing and cause true, willing his enimie to choose the place, and in the same he would giue him battell.

The new French king being come from Reimes to Dampmartine, studieng how to compasse them of Paris, was halfe abashed at this message. But yet to set a good countenance on the matter, he answered the herald, that he would sooner séeke his maister, than his maister should néed to pursue him. The duke of Bedford hearing this answer, marched toward the king, and pitched his field in a strong place. The French king, though at the first he meant to haue abidden battell; yet when he vnderstood that the duke was equall to him in number of people, he changed his purpose, and turned with his armie a little out of the waie. The duke of Bedford, perceiuing his faint courage, followed him by the hils and dales, till he came to a town not far from Senlis, where he found the French king and his armie lodged; wherefore he ordered his battels like an expert cheefteine in martiall science, setting the archers before, and himselfe with the noblemen in the maine battell, and put the Normans on both sides for wings. The French king also ordered his battels with the aduise of his capteins.

Thus these two armies laie two daies and two nights either in sight of other, with-out anie great dooing, except a few skirmishes, wherein the dukes light horssemen did

The French ar-mie fled in the night.
Boheme.

verie valiantlie. At length in the dead of the night (as priuilie as might be) the French king brake vp his campe, and fled to Braie. The duke of Bedford had much adoo to staie his people in the morning from pursuit of the French armie: but for that he mistrusted the Parisiens, he would not depart farre from that citie, and so re-turned thither againe. ¶ In this season pope Martin the fift of that name, meaning to subdue the Bohemers that dissented from the church of Rome in matters of religion, appointed Henrie Beaufort Bishop of Winchester & cardinall of saint Eusebie, to be his legat in an armie that should inuade the kingdome of Boheme, and to bring a

power

power of men with him out of England.   And because the warre touched religion, he
licenced the cardinall to take the tenth part of euerie spirituall dignitie, benefice, and
promotion.

This matter was opened in the parlement house, and assented to: wherevpon the
bishop gathered the monie, and assembled foure thousand men & aboue, not without
great grudge of the people, which dailie were with tallages and aids wearied and sore
burdened.   As this bishop was come to Douer readie to passe the seas ouer into Flanders, the duke of Glocester hauing receiued letters from the duke of Bedford, conteining an earnest request to reléeue him with some spéedie aid of men of warre, was
constreined to write vnto the bishop of Winchester, willing him in time of such néed,
when all stood vpon losse or gaine, to passe with all his armie toward the duke of
Bedford, to assist him against his aduersaries; which thing doone, and to his honour
atchiued, he might performe his iournie against the vngratious Bohemers.   The cardinall (though not well contented with this countermand) yet least he should run into
the note of infamie, if he refused to aid the regent of France in so great a cause, passed
ouer with his power, and brought the same vnto his coosine to the citie of Paris.

About the same season, the French king, in hope to be receiued into the townes
of Campaigne and Beauuois (by reason of the fauour and good will which the inhabitants bare towards him) was come with an armie towards Campaigne.   Whereof
the duke of Bedford being aduertised, and hauing now his host augmented with the
new supplie, which the cardinall had of late brought vnto him, marched forward
with great speed toward the place where he vnderstood the French king was lodged:
and comming to Senlis, he perceiued how his enimies were incamped vpon the mount
Pilioll, betweene Senlis and Campaigne.

Here might either armie behold the other: wherevpon for the auoiding of dangers that might insue, the campes were trenched, and the battels pitched, and the
fields ordered as though they should haue tried the matter by battell: but nothing
was doone except with skirmishes, in the which the Normans sore vexed the Frenchmen; and therefore receiued great commendations and praises of the lord regent:
who vndoubtedlie determined to haue giuen battell to his enimies if they would haue
abidden it.   But after the armies had thus lien ether in sight of other, for the space
of two daies together, the French king not determining to aduenture in an open
battell the whole chance of the game, least he might thereby receiue a perpetuall
checkemate, in the night season remooued his campe, and fled to Crespie, though
his number was double to the English armie.   The duke of Bedford, seeing that *An. Reg.* 8.
the French king was thus cowardlie recoiled with all his power and armie, returned
againe to Paris, euer suspecting the deceitfull faith of the Parisiens.

The bishop of Winchester, after that the French king was retreated backe, went
into Boheme, and there did somewhat, though shortlie after without anie great _{Boheme.}
praise or gaine he returned into England, more glad of his comming backe than of
his aduancing forward.   Anon after the pope vnlegated him, and set an other in his <sub>The pope did
vnlegat the car-</sub>
place, wherewith he was nothing contented.   On the sixt daie of Nouember, be- _{dinall of Win-}
ing the daie of saint Leonard, king Henrie in the eight yeare of his reigne was at <sub>chester.
K. Henries coro-</sub>
Westminster with all pompe and honour crowned king of this realme of England. _{nation at Westminster.}
In the same yere the French king was receiued into the towne of Campaigne, and
shortlie after were the townes of Senlis and Beauuois rendered to him.   And the
lord Longueall tooke by stelth the castell of Aumarle, and slue all the Englishmen
within it.

Also about the same time, the Frenchmen recouered castell Gaillard foorth of the _{Thom. Wals.}
Englishmens hands, where the lord Barbason was found in a dungeon, inclosed
within a great grate of iron like to a little chamber, and foorthwith they brake open the
grate: but Barbason would not come foorth; because he had giuen his faith and
                                                                              promise

promise to one Kingston that was capteine of that fortresse for the king of England, to be true prisoner, vntill the Frenchmen had sent to the same Kingston (that was departed vpon such couenants as they were agréed vpon at the deliuerie of that fortresse) willing him to come backe againe vpon safe conduct. Which at their earnest request he did, and withall discharged the lord Barbason of his oth; and so then he came foorth, and remained at his libertie, to the great reioising of the Frenchmen, which iudged that he had béene rather dead than aliue all that time of his imprisonment.

About the same time also the French king sought by all meanes possible to breake the amitie betwixt the realme of England, and the house of Burgognie. Whereof the duke of Bedford hauing intelligence, thought it stood him vpon the more earnestlie to looke to his charge; and namelie as it were an anchorhold, he determined to prouide that he might defend and safelie kéepe the duchie of Normandie, and therefore appointing the bishop of Terrowen and Elie, named Lewes of Lutzenburgh, chancellor for king Henrie of the realme of France, to remaine at Paris vpon the defense of that citie, with a conuenient number of Englishmen, he departed into A parlement at Rone called by the duke of Bedford. Normandie, and comming to Rone, called a parlement there of the thrée estates of the duchie, in the which he declared manie things vnto them, touching the happie life, and great freedome which they might be assured to inioy, so long as they continued vnder the English obeisance: and therefore he exhorted them to abide constant in their allegiance, faith, and promise made and sworne to his noble brother king Henrie the fift.

The French got saint Denis. Whilest the duke of Bedford was busie to reteine the Normans in their due obedience, the French king departed from Senlis; and comming to the towne of saint Denis, found it in maner desolate, so that he entered there without resistance, and lodged his armie at Mount Martyr and Amberuilliers, néere vnto the citie of Paris; and from thence sent Iohn duke of Alanson, and his sorceresse Ione la Pusell, with thrée thousand light horssemen to asssault the citie, and followed himselfe, in hope to get it, either by force or treatie. But the English capteins euerie one kéeping his ward and place assigned, so manfullie defended themselues, their walles and towers with the assistance of the Parisiens, that they repelled the Frenchmen, and threw Ione had a hurt in the leg and a fall, drawen all durtie out of the mire. downe Ione their great goddesse into the bottome of the towne ditch, where she lay behind the backe of an asse sore hurt in the leg, till the time that she (all filthie with mire and durt) was drawne out by Guischard of Thienbrone, seruant to the duke of Alanson.

The French king, perceiuing that he could not preuaile in this enterprise, left the dead bodies behind him, and taking with him the wounded capteins, returned into Berrie. But in the meane waie, the inhabitants of Laignie submitted themselues vnto him. The duke of Bedford being in Normandie, hearing of this sudden attempt, with all hast possible came to Paris, where he gaue manie great thanks, with high commendations vnto the capteins, souldiers and citizens for their assured fidelitie, great hardinesse & manlie dooing. Which his gentle words so incouraged the harts of the Parisiens, that they sware, promised and concluded, to be fréends for euer to the king of England, and his fréends, and enimies alwaies to his foes and aduersaries, making proclamation by this stile: " Fréends to K. Henrie, freends to the Parisiens; Enimies to England, enimies to Paris." Marie whether this was vttered from their harts, it is hard so to saie, for the sequeale of their acts seemed to proue the contrarie.

Soone after these dooings, came to Paris with a great companie Philip duke of Burgognie, and then vpon long consultation had for the recouerie of their losses, it was agreed that the duke of Bedford should raise an armie, & that the duke of Burgognie should be his deputie, and tarie at Paris for the defense of the citie. The duke of
Bedford,

Bedford then without any great resistance recouered againe the towne of saint Denis, Saint Denis by vs recouered againe. with diuerse other fortresses. And after this he sent the bastard of Clarence to laie siege to the castell of Torsie, the which (notwithstanding the great strength therof) after six moneths siege, was rendred vp into his hands. During the siege of this castell, sir Thomas Kiriell knight, with foure hundred Englishmen departed from Gourneie in Normandie, and rode by Beauuois, spoiling and wasting the countrie to the suburbes of Cleremont. Whereof the earle of that towne hauing aduertisement, assembled all the men of warre of the garrisons adioining, and with the same set forward to fight with the Englishmen, whom he found in a streict place néere to Beauuois.

The earle of Cleremont, perceiuing that he could not hurt them with his men of armes, by reason of the strength, came downe on foot with all his companie, and fiercelie set on the Englishmen: but by the terrible shot of the English archers, the Frenchmen in the end were constreined to flée; and the Englishmen perceiuing the matter, streight leapt on horssebacke and followed the chase. In the which were taken two hundred prisoners, and thrise as manie slaine. The earle escaped by the swiftnesse of his horsse. At the same season the earle of Suffolke besieging the towne of Aumarle (whereof was capteine the lord of Rambures) after foure and twentie great assaults, had the towne and castell simplie to him rendred. Thus by little and little the Englishmen recouered manie townes which before they had lost. Howbeit about the verie same time, the Frenchmen stale the towne of Lauall, by treason wrought by a miller, which kéeping a mill that ioined to the wall, suffered the French to passe through his mill into the towne. Shortlie after also sir Steuen de Vignoilles, surnamed la Hire, tooke by scaling the towne of Louiers in Normandie. La Hire. The Englishmen in the cold moneth of December besieged the towne of Laignie in Laignie besieged by the Englishmen. the which was the Pusell, and diuerse other good capteins.

[In the moneth of Maie 1430, with a valiant man in feats of armes on the duke *W. P.* of Burgognions side, one Franquet and his band of three hundred souldiers, making 1430 all towards the maintenance of the siege, the Pusell Ione and a foure hundred with *Le Rosier.* hir did méet. In great courage and force did she and hir people sundrie times assaile him, but he with his (though much vnder in number) by meanes of his archers in good order set, did so hardilie withstand them, that for the first and second push she rather lost than wan? Wherat this captinesse striken into a fretting chafe, called out in all hast the garrison of Laignie, and from other the forts thereabout, who thicke and threefold came downe with might and maine, in armour and number so far excéeding Franquets, that though they had doone hir much hurt in hir horsemen; yet by the verie multitude were they oppressed, most in hir ??rie put to the sword; & as for to Franquet that worthie capteine himselfe, hir rage not appeased, till out of hand she had his head stroken off: contrarie to all manhood (but she was a woman, if she were that) & contrarie to common right & law of armes. The man for his merits was verie much lamented, and she by hir malice then found of what spirit she was.]

After this the duke of Bourgognie accompanied with the earles of Arundell, and Suffolke, and the lord Iohn of Lutzenburgh besieged the towne of Campiegne with Campiegne besieged. a great puissance. This towne was well walled, manned and vittelled, so that the besiegers were constreined to cast trenches, and make mines, for otherwise they saw not how to compasse their purpose. In the meane time it happened in the night of the Ascension of our lord, that Poiton de Saintreiles, Ione la Pusell, and fiue or six hundred men of armes issued out by the bridge toward Mondedier, intending to set fire in the tents and lodgings of the lord Bawdo de Noielle.

¶ In this yeare of our Lord, among diuerse notable men of learning and knowledge, *Abr. Fl. ex Gesnero.* one Richard Fleming, English borne, a doctor of diuinitie professed in Oxford, did flourish:

flourish: who by the prouidence of God grew in such fauour with this king Henrie the sixt, & the nobles néere & about him, that he was preferred to the bishops see of Lincolne. This man founded Lincolne college in Oxford, in which vniuersitie he had beene a profitable student. Diuerse bookes he wrote (as the vniuersitie librarie dooth beare witnesse) whereof these following haue béene séene vnder their names and titles ; to wit: A protestation against the Spaniards, the Frenchmen, and the Scots, made in th egenerall councell holden at Sens: one booke of the Etymologie of England; besides diuerse other treatises, as Gesner reporteth Ex bibliotheca Oxonii, aforesaid.]

Richard Fle-ming bishop of Lincolne.
The books that he wrote.

At the verie same time that Campeigne was besieged (as before is said) sir Iohn of Lutzenburgh, with eight other gentlemen, chanced to be néere vnto the lodging of the said lord Bawdo, where they espied the Frenchmen, which began to cut downe tents, ouerthrow pauilions, & kill men in their beds: wherevpon they with all speed assembled a great number of men, as well English as Burgognions, and couragiouslie set on the Frenchmen, and in the end beat them backe into the towne, so that they fled so fast that one letted another, as they would haue entered. In the chase and pursute was the Pusell taken, with diuerse other, besides those that were slaine, which were no small number. Diuerse were hurt also on both parts. Among the Englishmen, sir Iohn Montgomerie had his arme broken, and sir Iohn Steward was shot into the thigh with a quarell.

Ione the Pusell taken.

[As before ye haue heard somewhat of this damsels strange beginning and proceedings, so sith the ending of all such miraclemongers dooth (for the most part) plainelie decipher the vertue and power that they worke, by hir shall ye be aduertised what at last became of hir; cast your opinions as ye haue cause. Of hir louers (the Frenchmen) reporteth one, how in Campeigne thus besieged, Guillamne de Flauie the capteine hauing sold hir aforehand to the lord of Lutzenburgh, vnder colour of hasting hir with a band out of the towne towards their king, for him with spéed to come and leauie the siege there, so gotten hir foorth he shut the gates after hir, when anon by the Burgognians set vpon and ouermatcht in the conflict she was taken : marie yet (all things accounted) to no small maruell how it could come so to passe, had she béene of any deuotion or of true beléefe, and no false miscreant, but all holie as she made it. For earlie that morning she gat hir to saint Iameses church ,confessed hir, and receiued hir maker (as the booke termes it) and after setting hir selfe to a piller, manie of the townesmen that with a fiue or six score of their children stood about there to see hir, vnto them " (quod she) Good children and my déere freends, I tell you plaine one hath sold me. I am betraied and shortlie shall be deliuered to death; I beséech you praie to God for me, for I shall neuer haue more power to doo seruice either to the king or to the realme of France againe."

W. P.

Chroniques de Britaigne.

Saith another booke, she was intrapt by a Picard capteine of Soissons, who sold that citie to the duke of Burgognie, and he then put it ouer into the hands of the lord of Lutzenburgh, so by that meanes the Burgognians approched and besieged Campeigne, for succour whereof as damsell Ione with hir capteins from Laignie was thither come, and dailie to the English gaue manie a hot skirmish, so happened it one a daie in an outsallie that she made by a Picard of the lord of Lutzenburghs band, in the fiercest of hir fight she was taken, and by him by and by to his lord persented, who sold hir ouer againe to the English, who for witchcraft and sorcerie burnt hir at Rone. Tillet telleth it thus, that she was caught at Campeigne by one of the earle of Ligneis soldiers, from him had to Beaureuoir castell, where kept a thrée months, she was after for ten thousand pounds in monie and thrée hundred pounds rent (all Turnois) sold into the English hands.

Le Rosier.

In la vie du Charles sep-tiesme.
Fiue thousand pounds frech crowns in monie.
An hundred and fiftie crownes rent.

In which for hir pranks so vncouth and suspicious, the lord regent by Peter Chauchon bishop of Beauuois (in whose diocesse she was taken) caused hir life and beléefe, after order of law to be inquired vpon and examined. Wherein found though a

virgin,

virgin, yet first shamefullie reiecting hir sex abominablie in acts and apparell to haue counterfeit mankind, and then all damnablie faithlesse, to be a pernicious instrument to hostilitie and bloudshed in diuelish witchcraft and sorcerie, sentence accordinglie was pronounced against hir. Howbeit vpon humble confession of hir iniquities with a counterfeit contrition pretending a carefull sorow for the same, execution spared and all mollified into this, that from thencefoorth she should cast off hir vnnaturall wearing of mans abilliments, and kéepe hir to garments of hir owne kind, abiure hir pernicious practises of sorcerie and witcherie, and haue life and leasure in perpetuall prison to bewaile hir misdeeds. Which to performe (according to the maner of abiuration) a solemne oth verie gladlie she tooke.

But herein (God helpe vs) she fullie afore possest of the feend, not able to hold hir in anie towardnesse of grace, falling streight waie into hir former abominations (and yet séeking to eetch out life as long as she might) stake not (though the shift were shamefull) to confesse hir selfe a strumpet, and (vnmaried as she was) to be with child. For triall, the lord regents lenitie gaue hir nine moneths staie, at the end wherof she found herein as false as wicked in the rest, an eight daies after, vpon a further definitiue sentence declared against hir to be relapse and a renouncer of hir oth and repentance, was she therevpon deliuered ouer to secular power, and so executed by consumption of fire in the old market place at Rone, in the selfe same stéed where now saint Michaels church stands, hir ashes afterward without the towne wals shaken into the wind. Now recounting altogither, hir pastorall bringing vp, rude without any vertuous instruction, hir campestrall conuersation with wicked spirits, whome in hir first salutation to Charles the Dolphin, she vttered to be our Ladie, saint Katharine, and saint Annes, that in this behalfe came and gaue hir commandements from God hir maker, as she kept hir fathers lambs in the fields (where saints in warres among christen men were (be we sure) neuer so parciall patrons or partners to maintenance of horrible slaughters, rapines, and bloudshed) hereto hir murtherous mind in killing of Franquet hir owne prisoner, hir two yeares continùance in hir abominations and deadlie mischiefe without anie hir trauell or motion betwéene the princes for peace, hir relapse at last & falling againe into hir abiured iniquities, by hir virginitie (if it were anie) by hir holie words, hir fasting and praiers what they might be, sith satan (after S. Paule) can change himselfe into an angell of light, the déeplier to deceiue.

Polydo. 2°. *in H.* 6.

Les grand chron.

Les grandes chronic. le 4 *liure.*

These matters may verie rightfullie denounce vnto all the world hir execrable abhominations, and well iustifie the iudgement she had, and the execution she was put to for the same. A thing yet (God wot) verie smallie shadowed, and lesse holpen by the verie trauell of the Dolphin, whose dignitie abroad foul'e spotted in this point, that contrarie to the holie degrée of a right christen prince (as he called himselfe) for maintenance of his quarels in warre would not reuerence to prophane his sacred estate, as dealing in diuelish practises with misbeléeuers and witches. Which maladie he full sorilie salued (like one that to kill the strong sent of onions would cheaw a cloue of garlike) so a six and twentie yeares after, he pact with pope Calixt the third, by whose mandat directed to his thrée delegats, the bishops of Paris, Reimes, and Constance, at the cathedrall church of Paris, in presence of Ione (the pusels mother) Iohn and Peter hir brethren, the seuen and twentith daie of Nouember 1455, the validitie and goodnesse of the processe and sentence vpon hir was called in question, and in great solemnitie sit vpon,

Christianissimus rex.

Tillet. This prelate at his death left a hundred and fiftéene crownes in gold, that vnder colour of warres with the infidels he had fléesed from christen princes. *Platina.*

Wherein the cause was so sincerelie canuassed among them, that afterward, on the eight of Iulie 1456, a quite contrarie sentence was there declared; of effect, that this Ione (forsooth) was a damsell diuine, no fault in the Dolphin for his counsell and witcherie practises with hir; the processe, iudgement, and condemnation against hir all wrong and iniurious. And for iustification and remembrance aswell of hir innocencie

in

Li. 23. in vita.
H. 6.

in life and death, as also of the sinceritie of their later sentence, a new crosse in that old market to be reared. In this tale of Tillets is she further likened to Debora, Iahell, and Iudith, and vnto Romane Clelia compared by Polydor, that shames not somewhat also to carpe at hir iudgment, and much pitieth hir paine. But what puritie or regard of deuotion or conscience is in these writers trow yée, who make no consideration of hir heinous enormities, or else any difference betwéene one stirred vp by mercie diuine, or naturall loue, and a damnable sorcerer suborned by satan? And thus much of this gentle Ione, and of hir good oratours that haue said so well for hir: now iudge as ye list.]

After the bestowing of this Pusell in sort as yée haue heard, the siege still continued before Campiegne, and the duke of Bedford sent to the duke of Burgognie lieng at the siege, the earle of Huntington, and sir Iohn Robsert (two iollie gentlemen, of no lesse prudence to parle with the enimie, than puissance to incounter them) with a thousand archers (whose actiuitie, I warrant you, stood not then vpon the first triall) which dailie skirmished with them within, and made such bastiles & fortresses, that the towne had béene rendred into their hands, but that the duke of Burgognie departed from the siege to go into Brabant, to receiue the possession of that duchie, by the death of his cousin Philip the duke of that countrie, as then departed this world.

An. Reg. 9.

Sir Iohn de Lutzenburgh was left by the duke of Burgognie as generall of the siege before Campiegne, the which he raised within a short space after, contrarie to the minds of the Englishmen, which were verie desirous to haue lien there till the towne had béene rendered, which if the siege had béene continued but eight daies longer, must needs haue come to passe; by reason that pestilence and famine had almost consumed all the souldiers within the towne, so that it remained in maner without defense. After the breaking vp of this siege, Iohn duke of Norffolke tooke againe the townes of Dampmartine, and the Chasse Mongaie, with diuerse other townes. Also the earle of Stafford tooke the towne of Brin countie Robert, and from thence forraged all the countrie to Sens, and after tooke Quesnoie in Brie, Grand Puis, and Rampellon.

1431.

During this time, the Frenchmen on the otherside tooke Louiers and Villeneuf. Then also did the towne of Melun rebell, and had such aid of other townes adioining, that the English souldiers were faine to leaue Melun, Morret, and Corbell. Thus did things wauer in doubtfull balance betwixt the two nations English and French. But bicause the English sore mistrusted further danger, it was concluded, that king Henrie in his roiall person with a new armie should come into France, partlie to visit and comfort his owne subiects there, and partlie either by feare or fauour (bicause a child of his age and beautie dooth commonlie procure them loue of elder persons) to moue the Frenchmen to continue their due obeisance towards him.

Wherefore after a great host conuenient for that purpose assembled, and monie for maintenance of the warre readie gathered, and the realme set in an order vnder the go-uernement of the duke of Glocester protector (which during the kings absence appeased diuerse riots, and punished the offendors) the king with a great power tooke shipping at Douer on saint Georges euen within night, and landed at Calis on the morrow being saint Georges daie, and sundaie, by seuen of the clocke in the morning. He remained in Calis a good space, and from thence he remoued to Rone, being there receiued with all triumph. He taried in that citie a long time, his nobles dailie consulting on their great businesse & weightie affaires.

King Henrie the
sixt in person
goeth with an ar-
mie into France.
S. Albons.
Ed. Hall.

Abr. Fl. ex Poly-
chron.
A widow with-
out Algate mur-
thered in hir bed
by a Breton
whome she cha-
ritablie reléeued.

* O fowle ingra-
titude.

¶ In this kings time, & somewhat about this yeare, a certeine Breton, whom a good honest widow had receiued into hir house, and conceiued well of him in opinion, was by hir mainteined of hir owne pursse, & (as Polychronicon saith) she found him of almes and for Gods sake. This charitable deed of hirs deserued a deuout mind to God ward, and a thankfull hart to hir. But (good soule) how was she recompensed? *Euen murthered in hir bed by the hands of that villaine whome so
bountifullie

bountifullie she succored, and motherlike tendered. Vnto which bloudie fact (which was a preparatiue to a further mischeefe bred in his vnnaturall hart) he added another offense : for when he had dispatched the woman, vsing the riddance of hir to his aduantage, and as he had obteined oportunitie (to his thinking) he conueied all that she had awaie with him for his owne releefe. Then being persecuted with guiltinesse of conscience, which troubleth offendors with ceaselesse vexations, and forceth them from place to place to séeke corners of euasion and shift, he tooke priuilege of holie church at saint Georges in Southwarke, where laieng hands on the crosse, as a shield of sufficient safegard, he abiured this land, and by that meanes thought himselfe frée from afterclaps.

Neuerthelesse, God (whose mercifull nature abhorreth the effusion of mans bloud) prepared a punishment for the malefactor, who passing through the suburbs of London, without Algate (the place where he had commited the murther) the women of the same parish and stréet (as it were inraged) came out with stones, staues, kenell doong, and other things, wherewith they so bethwackt him on all parts of his bodie, that they laid him a stretching, and rid him quite of life. In the wreking of this their teene they were so fell and fierce, that the constables with their assistants (which were no small number) dooing what they could by their authoritie and maine strength, were not able to rescue him out of the womens hands; who had sworne in their hearts (as it séemed by the maner of their reuenge which was void of all mercie) to sée the end of such a villaine as most vnnaturallie had slaine a woman, a neighbour, a widow, a pitifull woman, a good neighbour, an honest widow; the wretch himselfe being a fugitiue, a stranger borne, a begger, and he to whome she shewed hir selfe the staffe of his support. O singular ingratitude which nature abhorreth, law dissalloweth, heauen disclaimeth, God detesteth, humanitie condemneth, and euerie good bodie to the verie death defieth; as the old distichon excellentlie and with good sense noteth;

Lex & natura, cœlum, Deus, omnia iura
Damnant ingratum, mœrent illum quoq; natum.

(margin: The murther reuenged by women at the appointment of Gods iustice.)

But to returne to the affaires of king Henrie, who in the moneth of Nouember remooued from Rone to Pontoise, and so to saint Denis, to the intent to make his entrie into Paris, and there to be sacred king of France. There were in his companie of his owne nation, his vncle the cardinall of Winchester, the cardinall and archbishop of Yorke, the dukes of Bedford, Yorke, and Norffolke, the earles of Warwike, Salisburie, Oxenford, Huntington, Ormond, Mortaigne, and Suffolke. Of Gascoigns, there were the earles of Longuille and Marche, besides manie other noble men of England, Guien, and Normandie. And the chéefe of the French nation were the dukes of Burgognie, and Lewes of Lutzenburgh, cardinall and chancellor of France for king Henrie: the bishops of Beauuois and Noion, both péeres of France, beside the bishop of Paris, and diuerse other bishops; the earle of Vaudemount, and other noble men, whose names were superfluous to rehearse. And he had in a gard about his person three thousand price archers, some on horssebacke, and part on foot.

To speake with what honour he was receiued into the citie of Paris, what pageants were prepared, and how richlie the gates, streets, and bridges on euerie side were hanged with costlie clothes of arras & tapestrie, it would be too long a processe, and therefore I doo héere passe it ouer with silence. On the seauentéenth daie of December, he was crowned king of France, in our ladie church of Paris, by the cardinall of Winchester, the bishop of Paris not being contented that the cardinall should doo such an high ceremonie in his church and iurisdiction. After all the ceremonies were finished, the king returned toward the palace, hauing one crowne on his head, and another borne before him; and one scepter in his hand, and the second borne before him. As touching other the roiall seruices and princelie appointments, they are verie diligentlie & at large set out in the French chronicle of that time. This coronation

(margin: King Henrie the sixt crowned in Paris.)

(margin: Le Rofier historial.)

of

of the king, Anglorum prælia as manie other good and memorable matters, so this also he hath noted, saieng thereof in comelie breuitie and truth, as after followeth:

Aeternæ famæ paulo post rege sepulto,
Parisijs, diadema vias & compita circum
Iunior Henricus portat lepidissimus infans.

This high and ioious feast passed not without some spot of displeasure among the English nobilitie: for the cardinall of Winchester, which at this time would haue no man be equall with him, commanded the duke of Bedford to leaue off the name of regent, during the time that the king was in France, affirming the cheefe ruler being in presence, the authoritie of the substitute to be cleerlie derogate, according to the common saieng; In the presence of the higher power, the smaller giueth place. The duke of Bedford tooke such a secret displeasure with this dooing, that he neuer after fauoured the cardinall, but stood against him in all things that he would haue forward. This was the root (as some haue thought) of that diuision amongst the English nobilitie, where through their glorie within the realme of France began first to decline.

The next daie after the solemne feast of the kings coronation, were kept triumphant iusts and torneis, in the which the earle of Arundell, and the bastard of S. Paule, by the iudgement of the ladies woone the price. The king kept open hall the space of fiue daies to all commers, and after (bicause the aire of Paris séemed contrarie to his pure complexion) by the aduise of his councell, he remooued to Rone, where he kept his Christmasse. But before his departure from Paris, the noble men as well of France and Normandie did to him homage, and the common people sware to him fealtie. In this meane time, sir Francis called the Aragoignois, a noble capteine of the English part in Normandie, tooke by force and policie the towne of

Montargis, with a great preie of treasure and prisoners, and put therein a garrison, leauing it well furnished with vittels and munition.

About the same time, the earle of Arundell, being truelie informed that the lord Bousac, marshall of France, was come to Beauuois, intending to doo some feat in Normandie, assembled the number of thrée and twentie hundred men, and comming néere to the said towne of Beauuois, sent a great number of light horssemen to run before the towne, to traine out the Frenchmen within; the which issuing out and following the English horssemen vnto their stale, were so inclosed and fought with, that in maner all the number of them, saue a few which fled backe into the towne with the marshall, were slaine or taken. Amongst other of the cheefest prisoners,

that valiant capteine Pouton de Santrails was one, who without delaie was exchanged for the lord Talbot, before taken prisoner at the battell of Pataie. There was also

taken one called the sheepheard, a simple man, and a sillie soule; but yet of such reputation for his supposed holinesse amongst the Frenchmen, that if he touched the wall of any of their aduersaries townes, they beléeued verelie it would incontinentlie fall downe.

This chance succéeded not fortunatlie alone vnto the English nation, for Richard Beauchampe earle of Warwike had a great skirmish before the towne of Gournie, where he discomfited and repelled his enimies: and beside those that were slaine, he tooke fortie horssemen, all being gentlemen of name and armes. Like chance happened to the fréends of king Charles, towards the marches of Loraine, where Reigner

duke of Bar besieged the towne of Vaudemont perteining to the earle thereof named Anthonie, coosine to the same duke Reigner. This earle, before the dukes approching, left a conuenient crue within the towne to defend it, and with all spéed rode to the dukes of Bedford and Burgognie, being then at the foresaid great triumph at Paris, where he purchased such fauour at their hands, bicause he had euer taken their parts, that not onelie sir Iohn Fastolfe was appointed to go with him, hauing

iij

in his companie six hundred archers, but also the duke of Burgognies marshall named sir Anthonie Toulongon, accompanied with fiftéene hundred other men of warre.

When the duke of Bar heard that his enimies were thus comming towards him, like a hardie capteine he raised his siege, and met face to face with the earle and his companie, betwéene whome was a cruell and mortall battell. The horssemen of the French side endured long, but in conclusion the English archers so galled their horsses, and so wounded the men, that the Barrois, Almains, and other of duke Reigners side were compelled to flee. In the chase was taken the duke of Bar, the bishop of Metz, the lord of Roquedemaque, sir Euerard of Salseburgh, the vicont Darcie, and two hundred other, beside three thousand which were slaine.

In this luckie time also, no lesse occasion of victorie was offered to the Englishmen in an other part, if they could haue vsed it with such circumspect warinesse as had beene expedient. For Robert lord Willoughbie, and Matthew * Gough, a valiant Welshman, with fifteene hundred Englishmen, laid siege to a towne in Aniou called saint Seuerine. Whereof Charles the French king being aduertised, sent with all speed the lord Ambrose de Lore, with manie noble men to the succours of them within the towne, wherof the same lord Ambrose was capteine: and therefore made the more hast to releeue his deputie, and the other being streictlie besieged, but yet staied at the towne of Beaumont, till his whole power might come to him.

* Or rather Goche. Saint Seuerine besieged.

The Englishmen aduertised of this intent of the capteine, came vpon him in the night, and found the Frenchmens watch so out of order, that a thousand men were entered into the campe before they were espied; by reason whereof the Englishmen found small resistance. But when the daie began to appeare, and that the sunne had set foorth his bright beames abroad, that all things might be seene, the Englishmen giuen wholie to spoile, followed not their enimies in chase, but being contented with their preie and gaine, began to retreit toward the siege againe, which the lord Willoughbie still mainteined with a part of the armie.

But sée the chance. The Frenchmen which were cōming after, hearing by the noise of the people that some fraie was at hand, put spurres to their horsses, and set on the Englishmen pestered with bag and baggage of the spoile and preie which they had gotten in the French campe. The other of the Frenchmen which before had fled, returned againe, and aided their fellowes; so that the Englishmen being taken out of order, were compelled to flée, of whome Matthew * Gough and diuerse other were taken prisoners. And yet of the other part manie were slaine, and a great number taken: amongst whom was the lord de Lore, who (for all that the Frenchmen could doo) was kept, and not deliuered. The lord Willoughbie hearing of this mishap, raised his siege, and departed verie sore displeased in his mind, but could not remedie it.

* Goche.

About this season, Nicholas the cardinall of the holie crosse was sent into France, as a legat from Eugenie the fourth as then bishop of Rome, to treat a peace betwéene the Englishmen and Frenchmen. But when after great instance and labour made betweene the parties, he saw their obstinate and froward minds, nothing inclined to anie agréement, he wan so much at their hands by earnest sute, that a truce was granted to indure for six yeares to come: but as the same was hardlie granted, so was it of the Frenchmen soone and lightlie broken. For the bastard of Orleance newlie made earle of Dunois, tooke by treson the towne of Chartres from the Englishmen, affirming by the law of armes, that stealing or buieng a towne, without inuasion or assault, was no breach of league, amitie, or truce. In which towne he slue the bishop, bicause he was a Burgognian. Hereby did new malice increase, and mortall warre began eftsoones to be put in vre.

A legat from Rome sent to treat a peace betwixt the English and French.

A truce for six yeares.

Chartres taken by treason notwithstanding the truce.

Whilest these things were dooing in France, the cardinall of Winchester was come
backe

backe againe into England, to appease certeine commotions and sturres attempted by sundrie persons vnder colour of religion: but after that William Mandeuile, and Iohn Sharpe the chéefe authors thereof were apprehended and executed by the

The two errours.

gouernour and the kings iustices, the residue yeelded and confessed their offenses, whereof two articles were these (as some write) that priests should haue no possessions, and that all things by the order of charitie among christian people should be in common. Other thought their opinions were not such errours, but that their enimies spread abroad such rumors of them, to make them more odious to the people.

A parlement called by the duke of Glocester the king be-1:·g in France. A peace con-cluded with the Scots.

After that, a parlement was called by the duke of Glocester, in the which monie was assigned to be leuied, and men appointed, which should passe ouer into France to the aid of the duke of Bedford, for the maintenance of the warres: bicause it was sus-pected the truce would not long continue. During this parlement, Iames the king of Scots sent ambassadors to conclude a peace with the duke of Glocester, who (bicause the king was absent) referred the matter to the thrée estates. After long consultation, not without great arguments, a peace was concluded. When the parlement was ended, the cardinall well furnished with men & monie, departed out of England, and came to Rone to the king, to whome also resorted the duke of Bedford from Paris, to consult of things not vnlikelie to follow.

Herevpon a great councell was kept in the castell of Rone, and manie doubts mooued, and few weightie things out of hand concluded. At length, after great disputation, with manie arguments ended, the dukes of Bedford and Yorke, and Edmund late earle of Mortaigne, and now (by the death of Iohn duke of Summerset, leauing behind him a sole daughter and heire, maried to the earle, and called Margaret after the countesse of Richmond) atteined to the name and title of duke of Summerset, approoued the reason of those, that held it expedient to haue an armie in a redinesse for defense, least the Frenchmen suddenlie should attempt anie enterprise to the danger of the Englishmen, and losse of those townes and countries that were vnder them.

1432

King Henrie re-turneth out of France into En-gland.

When all things were agréed, king Henrie came to Calis, from thence to Douer; and so by easie iournies the one and twentith daie of Februarie to London, where he was triumphantlie receiued, and richlie presented, as in the chronicles of Robert Fabian it maie at large appeare. After that the king was departed into England, the duke of Bedford regent of France, and capteine of Calis, taried behind in the marches of Picardie, where he was informed certeine souldiers of Calis grudging at the restraint of woolles, began to murmur against the king and his councell, to some danger of the towne. The duke vpon due examination had, caused diuerse to be put to death, and manie banished that towne and marches for euer.

The duchesse of Bedford sister to the duke of Bur-gognie deceass-ed.

In the meane time, the ladie Anne duchesse of Bedford departed this life at Paris, by whose death the fast knot of faithful friendship betwixt the duke of Bedford and his brother in law the duke of Burgognie began somewhat to slacken. Shortlie after, to wit, about the beginning of the next yeare 1433, the said duke of Bedford being thus a widower, through the persuasion of the lord Lewes of Lutzenburgh bishop of Terwine and Elie, and chancellor of France for king Henrie, agréed to

The duke of Bed-ford marieth with the earle of saint Paules daughter.

marie the ladie Iaquet, daughter to Peter earle of saint Paule, and néece to the said bishop, and to the lord Iohn of Lutzenburgh.

The mariage was solemnized at Terwine with great triumph. Which ended, the duke with his new spouse (being about the age of seauenteene yeares) came vnto Calis, and so into England, from whence in the moneth of August next he returned to Paris. The duke of Burgognie, though nothing pleased with this new aliance contracted by the duke of Bedford, with the house of Lutzenburgh, but yer not able to doo anie thing to let it; bicause of the mariage consummate yer he could find any power or knowledge to hinder it. Whilest these things were a dooing, in some

places

places the French souldiers of the Dolphins, lacking wages (as the time serued) tooke both Englishmen and Burgognians, ransoming. and spoiling them at their pleasure. Herewith the regent much mooued, prepared for warre after six moneths the truce had béene taken: and so the warre againe was renewed.

The Frenchmen anon as open truce-breakers, raised a crue, and suddenlie tooke the towne of saint Valerie in Normandie, néere to the mouth of the riuer of Some. An other armie, vnder the leading of sir Ambrose de Lore, wasted and destroied all the countrie about Caen. The duke of Bedford on his part sent the earle of Arun-dell, the earle of Warwikes sonne, the lord Lisle Adam marshall of France for king Henrie, and twelue hundred men of warre with ordinance and munition to be-siege the town of Laignie vpon the riuer of Marne. The earle with shot of canon brake the arch of the bridge, and got from the Frenchmen their bulworke, and set it on fire. Diuerse assaults were attempted, but the towne was well defended: for there were within it an eight hundred men of armes, besides other meane souldiers. The Frenchmen breake the peace and take the town of Saint Valerie. Laignie be-sieged.

The duke of Bedford herewith gathered an armie of six thousand men, whereof were capteins; Robert lord Willoughbie, sir Andrew Ogard chamberlaine to the duke, sir Iohn Saluaine bailiffe of Rone, sir Iohn Montgomerie bailiffe of Caux, sir Philip Hall bailiffe of Vernoill, sir Richard Ratcliffe deputie of Calis, sir Rafe Neuill, sir Rafe Standish, sir Iohn Hanford, sir Richard Euthin, sir Richard Harington bailiffe of Eureux, sir William Fulthorpe, sir Thomas Griffin of Ireland, Dauid Hall, Thomas Stranguish, Leonard Ormstone esquiers, and Thomas Gerard. All gentle-men of courage, and as forward to giue the French the foile, as the French for their liues to giue them the discomfiture. But vnto which side the victorie should befall, vncerteine it was before the triall of both their chances had determined the doubt by the euent of the conflict.

The duke of Bedford furnished with this armie and companie of worthie capteins came to the siege before Laignie, where he made a bridge of boats, and brought his ordinance so néere the towne, that to all people it séemed not long able to resist. But the earle of Dunois, otherwise called the bastard of Orleance, with diuerse hardie capteins, as valiantlie defended as the Englishmen assaulted. At length the French king, perceiuing this towne to be the thrée cornerd keie betwéene the territories Bur-gognion, English, and French, and the losse thereof should turne him to irreuocable damage, sent the lord of Rieux, Poiton, the Hire, the lord Gawcourt, and six thou-sand men, with great plentie of vittels, to the intent either to raise the siege, or else to vittell the towne.

The Frenchmen made a brag, as though they would haue assailed the Englishmen in their campe, but when they perceiued the courage of the lord regent, and the desire he had to fight, they framed themselues so in order of battell, as though they could doo all things, and yet in effect did nothing: but that whilest part of them mainteined a skirmish, a sort of rude & rusticall persons were appointed to conueie into the towne thirtie oxen, and other small vittels. But this swéet gaine was déerelie paied for, if the losse with the gaine be pondered in equall balance: for hauing regard to their 30 leane oxen, in the skirmish were slaine the lord Saintreiles brother to that valiant capteine Poiton de Saintreiles, also capteine Iohn brother to the lord Gawcourt, and fiftie other noble and valiant personages.

The Frenchmen thus politiklie hauing doone their feat, in the beginning of August, remooued their armie vnto Fort vnder Yer, where, by a bridge of tuns they passed into the Ile of France. The duke of Bedford (like a wise prince) not minding to leaue the more in ieopardie for hope of the lesse, nor the accident for the substance, raised his siege, and returned to Paris, nothing more minding than to trie his quarrell with dint of sword against the enimies, if they would thereto agrée. And herevpon sent Bedford his herald to the lord Gawcourt and other capteins of the *An.* Reg. 11

French armie, offering them battell and a pitched field within a conuenient time, and where they would appoint. The French capteins answered the English herald, that there was time to gaine, and time to lose: and for choise of times they would vse their owne discretions.

1433
The castell of
Rone like to be
taken by treason
of the capteine.

Shortlie after, Piers Audebeufe constable of the castell of Rone, corrupted with monie, suffered the marshall of France, with two hundred other, as persons disguised to enter the place by stealth: but they were soone espied, and driuen to the dungeon, where they were constrained to yéeld themselues prisoners: of the which some were hanged, some headed, and some ransomed, at the pleasure of the regent. This pageant thus plaied, the lord regent sent the earle of sainte Paule, and Robert lord Willoughbie, with a competent number of men to besiege the town of S. Valerie, which the Frenchmen a little before had taken. This siege continued the space of thrée wéeks; at the end whereof the Frenchmen within yéelded the towne, and departed with their horsse and harnesse onelie to them saued.

The earle put there in garrison fresh and valiant souldiers, and appointed capteine there, sir Iohn Aubemond. ¶In the same towne (whether by infection of aire, or by corrupt vittels, which the townesmen did eat) a great pestilence shortlie after happened, which consumed within a small time two parts of the people. The earle of saint Paule, and the lord Willoughbie returning backe to the regent, were ioifullie receiued, and within a while after, the earle departed from Paris to laie siege to the

castell of Mouchas. But being incamped néere the towne of Blangie, he by a sunden maladie departed this life, the last of August, leauing his seigniories to Lewes de Lutzenburg his sonne and heire. Bicause this dead earle was father in law to the regent, solemne obsequies were kept for him both in Paris and in London.

In the meane season, the Frenchmen entering into high Burgognie, burnt, tooke, and destroied diuerse townes; wherevpon the Burgognians assembled a great armie, both to reuenge their quarrels, and to recouer their townes taken from them. To whome as to his freends the duke of Bedford sent the lord Willoughbie, and sir Thomas Kiriell, with a conuenient number of souldiers, which entering into the lands of Laonnois, were incountered with a great power of their enimies. But after long fight, the Frenchmen were ouerthrowne, and of them left dead in the field an hundred and sixtie horssemen, beside prisoners, which after vpon vrgent cause were

all killed.

Whilest these things happened thus in France, Iohn lord Talbot gathered togither a crue of chosen men of warre in England, to the number of eight hundred, and sailed into Normandie, and passed by Rone to Paris. In his waie he tooke the strong castell of Ioing betwéene Beauuois and Gisours, and caused all the Frenchmen within to be taken and hanged, and after raced and defaced the castell. After he had rested himselfe a while at Paris, and taken aduise with the councell there, what waie it should be best for him to take, without prolonging time; he with the lord de Lisle Adam and others, departed from thence, hauing in their retinues sixtéene hundred men of warre. And comming to the castell of Beaumont vpon Oise, whereof was capteine sir Amadour de Vignoils brother to the Hire, they found it abandoned by them that had it in kéeping, who were withdrawne to the towne of Creill.

Thither therefore the lord Talbot followed, who slaieng in a skirmish the said Amadour, he wan at length the said towne of Creill, and after the townes of Pont S. Marence, Neufuile in Esmoie, la Rouge maison, Crespie in Valois, & Cleremont in Beauuois, and after with great riches and good prisoners returned to Paris. Neither

had the lord Talbot such good and prosperous successe alone, but the earle of Arundell also at the verie same season tooke the castell of Bomeline. & raced it to the ground, after he got by force the castell of Dorle, & from thence came to S. Selerine, where
the

the lord Ambrose de Lore, being capteine, issued out and fought with the Englishmen so egerlie, that he droue them backe an arrow shoot by fine force: but the earle so incouraged his men, that they gaue a fresh onset vpon the Frenchmen, and followed it so fiercelie, that they slue a great number of them, and droue the residue into the towne.

After this victorie, he besieged Louiers, whereof was capteine the Hire, and his Louiers besieged brother, who rendered the towne without assault. Then the earle assembling togither a great armie, returned againe to S. Selerine, & inuironed the towne with a strong siege. When he had lien there almost thrée moneths, euerie daie attempting or dooing somewhat, he finallie gaue so fierce an assault, that by force he entered the towne, Saint Selerine and slue Iohn Almaigne, and Guilliam saint Albine, the chéefe capteins, and eight won by assault. hundred other men of warre. The children of le seigneur de Lore were taken prisoners. The earle put new men of warre into the towne, and made capteine there sir Iohn Cornewall. After this, he before the strong towne of Sillie pitched his campe. The inhabitants terrified at the losse of saint Selerine, deliuered him pledges, vpon condition, that if they were not rescued within thirtie daies next, then they (their liues saued) should render the towne into his possession: which offer was receiued.

The French king, being aduertised hereof by a post, appointed (as some saie) Arthur earle of Richmont (or as other write, Iohn duke of Alanson) with a great companie of men of warre to go to the rescue of this towne. But whether it was the earle or duke, certeine it is at his approching to the siege, he incamped himselfe by a brooke side, ouer the which a man might haue striden, & perceiuing how stronglie the English were incamped against him, he thought it not for his profit to giue battell; & so in the night season raised & went his waie without further attempt. When they within the towne knew that their succours failed, they rendered themselues to the mercie of the earle of Arundell, who gentlie receiued them, and leauing a garrison in the towne, departed to Mans, and in his waie tooke the castels of Mellaie and saint Laurence. About this time the lord Willoughbie & sir Thomas Kiriell, returning with great victorie out of Burgognie, passing by the towne of Louiers, latelie reduced to the English obeisance, furnished it both with men and munition.

Among so manie good chances, some euill are accustomed to happen, or else the An insurrection gainers would not know themselues. And so at this time it happened, that a great in Normandie. number of the common and rusticall people in Normandie dwelling by the sea coast, either prouoked by the French king, or desirous of alteration and change (which thing the commons much couet and desire) made an insurrection, put on harnesse, and by force expelled certeine English garrisons out of their holds, publishing and proclaming openlie, that their onelie purpose and intent was to expell and banish the whole English nation out of their countries and coasts. Wherefore it maie be likelie, that the blacke Morian will sooner become white, than the people bred in France will heartilie loue an English borne. For it standeth not with their enuious nature to alter their malicious maners; as the old prouerbe saith truelie of them:

Celtica natura semper sequitur sua iura.

These rebels thus frantikelie assembled, with all spéed marched toward Caen, to the intent there both to increase their number, and also to consult what waie they should follow in their new begun enterprise. But the dukes of Yorke and Summerset, then lieng in Normandie, hauing perfect knowledge hereof, immediatlie sent foorth the earle of Arundell, and the lord Willoughbie with six thousand archers, and thirtéene hundred light horssemen, to staie and kéepe them from making anie further progresse. The earle of Arundell appointed the lord Willoughbie, with two thousand archers, and certeine horssemen to go afore him, and lie in a stale within

A a 2

some

some couert place. Which doone, the earle followed ; & so keeping in the multitude at the backe, droue them before him as deare into a buckestale : and when the
miserable wretches came néere to the stale, the earle made a token, whereat a gun
shot off for a signe. Therewith the lord Willoughbie set on them before, and the
earle behind, shooting so fiercelie, that the poore caitiues, wounded and galled with
the shot of arrowes, threw awaie their harnesse, and cried out instantlie for mercie.

The earle of Arundell mooued with compassion, caused his souldiers to staie from
further slaughter, and apprehending those that were knowen to be stirrers and leaders
of the rest, let the other returne home without further damage : but yet, yer the
souldiers could be brought backe vnder their standards, there were aboue a thousand
of the rebels slaine. And this commotion thus appeased, vpon inquirie of the principall offendors, such as were found guiltie were put to terrible executions ; as they
had well deserued. During which rebellion, Peter Rokeford and his companie gat by
treason the towne of Diepe and diuerse other holds thereto adioining. After the earle
of Arundell had obteined so good successe in his enterprises (as partlie ye haue heard)
he attempted another, which was the last worke and finall labour of his liuing daies.
For the duke of Bedford, being informed that his aduersaries had gotten the towne of
Rue, and therein put a garrison, which sore vexed the countries of Ponthieu, Arthois,
and Bolennois, sent word to the earle that he without delaie should besiege the said
towne.

The earle obeieng his commandement assembled his people, and came to Gourneie, where he heard tell how there was a castell néere to Beauuois called Gerberoie,
the which being fallen in decaie, Charles the French king had appointed sir Stephan
de Vignoils, commonlie called the Hire, to repare and newlie to fortifie, bicause it
stood commodiouslie to serue as a countergarrison against the English townes and
fortresses on those frontiers. The earle aduertised hereof, and perceiuing that this
new building would be greatlie preiudicial to the Englishmen, determined first to
dispossesse his enimies of that place, supposing to find small resistance : but he was
deceiued. For there was the said Hire, and three thousand men of warre with him.
The erle comming thither, incamped himselfe with fiue hundred horssemen in a little
close not farre from the castell.

The Frenchmen, perceiuing that the earle and his horsses were wearie, and that his
archers were not yet come, determined to set vpon him before the comming of his
footmen, the which they knew to be little more than a mile behind. Wherfore for
a policie, they set foorth fiftie horssemen, as though there had beene no mo within the
castell. The earle perceiuing this, sent foorth sir Randolfe Standish to incounter
them, hauing with him an hundred horsses. The Frenchmen fought couragiouslie
awhile, and suddenlie came out all the remnant, and slue sir Randolfe Standish and all
his companie, and boldlie set on the earle and his band, which manfullie resisted the
Frenchmen, till at length the Hire caused thrée culuerings to be shot off amongst the
Englishmen, wherof one strake the earle on the ancle, and so brake his leg, that for
paine he fell from his horsse.

Then the Frenchmen entered amongst the Englishmen, tooke the earle lieng on the
ground, with sir Richard Wooduile, and six score more, and there were slaine almost
two hundred. The residue saued themselues as well as they might. The earle was
caried to Beauuois, where of his hurt he shortlie died, & was buried in the frier
Minors. He was a man of singular vertue, constancie, and grauitie, whose death in
so troublous a season did sore appall the harts of the English people. Thus oftentimes
varied the chance of doubtfull warre, so that one time the Englishmen got by assault,
and yeelded diuerse strong townes, castels, and piles : and at another season the French
people, sometime by bargaine, sometime by assault, obteined the same againe, or other
in their stéed.

The earle of
Arundell de-
ceassed.

About

About the moneth of Iune in this twelfth yeare, Iohn duke of Bourbon and Auuergne, taken prisoner at the battell of Agincourt eighteene yéeres past (as before ye
haue heard) now paieng his ransome, which was eightéene thousand pounds sterling,
was taken with a most sore and grieuous feuer, the which made an end of his life in *The duke of*
the citie of London, on the same daie that was appointed for his departure towards *Bourbon dieth*
France, whose corpse was interred in the graie friers of the same citie. ¶ This yeare *at London.*
also about the latter end of Maie, was a méeting appointed to be had at saint Omers
betwixt the dukes of Bedford and Burgognie, for the qualifieng of certeine displeasures
and grudges betwixt them kindled and mainteined by some flattering taletellers, who
raising matters of reproch touching their honors, bred such grudges, that all loue *w. p.*
betwixt them ceassed, all affinitie reiected, and all old fréendship forgotten; such
enuie insueth where enimitie once hath princes harts possessed.

These two dukes come into the towne of saint Omers, the duke of Bedford being
then regent of France, sonne, brother, and vncle to kings, thought that the duke of
Burgognie should haue come and visited him in his lodging. The duke of Burgognie
on the other part, being lord and souereigne of the towne, iudged it as much vnméet
for him to go to the regent where he was lodged. Howbeit by intreatie of fréends,
to meet in a place indifferent betweene both their lodgings was appointed; which
offer not accepted, both parties departed discontent, and neuer after saw nor communed togither. Thus by the proud disdaine and enuious discord of these two high
stomached princes, Bedford not minding to haue anie péere, and Burgognie not
willing to abide anie superior, shortlie after England much lost, and Burgognie
greatlie gained not, as by the sequeale may appeare.

The bastard of Orleance, called the earle of Dunois, the lord Rochford marshall *An. Reg.* 13.
of France, with other, in the beginning of this thirtéenth yeare, tooke the towne of
S. Denis by treason, skirmished with them of Paris, and leauing behind them a
great garrison, tooke the towne of Howdone, and Pont saint Marence by composition. And at the same time was the towne of Pont Meulan taken by the sudden
scaling of two fishermen, who entered vp at a common priuie standing in the wall. *A towne sur-*
Thus warre continuallie lasted betwixt these two mightie nations, English and *prised by en-*
French, within the realme of France (than which therefore no countrie thought more *trance of a*
miserable.) And though the poore people and inhabitants of the good townes and *common priuie.*
villages, susteined most losse in their substance, yet the men of warre oftentimes *The fruits of*
paied déerest for the bargaine, being daily slaine, wounded, and taken prisoners; for *warre.*
warre seldome beareth anie other fruit.

[It may serue verie well here to recount, how somewhat before these daies, Martin *w. p.*
the fift, in the fifteenth yeare of his popedome, An. 1431, agreeing vpon a generall
councell to be holden at Basill the same yeare, did anon after deceasse: whom Eu- *1434.*
genie the fourth succeeding, and liking right well of the time and place, by his au- *Onuphrius*
thoritie signified and sent with Iulian Cesarine his legat, did confirme the choise. *Panuinius.*
Wherevpon as the councell the ninetéenth of Iulie the same 1431 was there begun,
and his holinesse soone after aduertised how malapertlie his ghostlie children had im-
busied themselues in checking at their holie fathers faults, and about reformation of
his church at Rome; his sublimitie therat highlie offended (for great cause it had)·
commanded his legat by and by to dissolue that synod, and in his name to appoint
a new at Ferrar, and so come his waie: vnder colour forsooth how that place was·
méetest for the prelats of the Greeke church, who had to confer with the Latine·
councell about points of religion, wherein they long had remained at square.

But these Basilien clerks, there still fastlie conteining themselues, so smallie regarded this summons of Eugenie (who then with his prelats, as the time was run on,
vpon prorogation from Ferrar kept an other councell at Florence 1439) as by a con-
fident countermand cited Eugenie and all his cardinals to come to them at their
　　　　　　　　　　　　　　　　　　　　　　　　　　　　　　　　　　solemne

solemne set councell at Basill.   Which his supremassie (for so best became it; not-withstanding sundrie citations) vtterlie contemning to doo, they soone after like verie impious imps, first for contumacie accurssed his holie fatherhood, then depriued him of his papasie, and out of hand chose another in his office, one Amedius late duke of Sauoie, who afore that time hauing giuen vp his possessions & dignitie vnto his children, became an heremite in a monasterie of his own building by mount Ge-uenna in Sauoie nigh the lake Leman, where he by title of Decanus militum Iesu Christi, and ten more of nobilitie with him, had setled themselues to liue.

The vertuous minded man thus chosen pope by spirituall counsell inueigled, left the holie life (such as it was) that he had profest, tooke the papasie vpon him the same 1439, and called Felix the fift, which promotion yet he not long inioied.   For after, by his successour Nicholas the fifts ambition, that had suborned emperour Frederike to be a worker in the matter, this sillie Amedius was coosined of his popes golden crowne for a cardinalls felt hat.   Then (good man) at last could he find, whether were néerer to christen profession, the life of a vertuous prince ruling in iustice, of a solitarie heremite vertuouslie occupied, of an imperious pope that may know no péere, or of a licentious cardinall to liue as he list.   This poore prince had experience of all, and then knew the best : when well might he lament him, but too late repent him.

And in the fift yeare of this Basilien councell that had a continuance of eleuen yeare (whereof an eight were run yer Felix was chosen, in which Eugenie remaining remaining pope still, though of curst hart he neuer came at them) motion was made among Sigismund the emperour and other christen kings (who for appeasing this schisme betwéene the pope and his prelats, were all present by person or proxie) that sith such horror of bloudshed betwéene the two nations continuallie so lamentablie raged in France, some mediation might be made for accord : whereof one thing seemed to minister occasion of the more hope, bicause the duke of Burgognie was willing (so that it were not of his owne sute) to returne and reconcile himselfe with the French king his mortall enimie and ancient aduersarie.]

Héerevpon by authoritie of this generall councell, two graue prelats, the one Nicholas Albergat a Carthusian frier, intituled a préest cardinall of the holie crosse; the other Hugh Lusignan a Cyprian, Gréeke, bishop cardinall of Prenest in Italie, came to the towne of Arras in Arthois, whither were sent from the king of England, Henrie Beauford cardinall of Winchester, Henrie archbishop of Yorke, William de la Poole earle of Suffolke, and Iohn Holland earle of Huntington, with diuerse other knights and esquiers.   And for the French king were there present Charles duke of Bourbon, Lewes erle of Vandosme, Arthur of Britaine constable of France, the arch-bishop of Reimes, and sir Philip Harecourt.   The duke of Burgognie was there in proper person, accompanied with the duke of Guelders, and the earles of Estampes, Lignie, S. Paule, Vaudemont, Neures, and Daniell sonne to the prince of Orange, with a great gard and a gallant companie.

Vpon the daie of the first session, the cardinall of S. Crosse declared to the thrée parties the innumerable mischeefes, that had followed to the whole state of the chris-tian common-wealth by their continual dissention and dailie discord, exhorting them for the honour of God, & for the loue which they ought to beare towards the ad-uancement of his faith and true religion, to conforme themselues to reason, and to laie aside all rancor, malice and displeasure ; so that in concluding a godlie peace, they might receiue profit and quietnesse heere in this world, and of God an euer-lasting reward in heauen.   After this admonition, and diuerse daies of communica-tion, euerie partie brought in their demands, which were most contrarie, and farre from anie likelihood of comming to a good conclusion.

The Englishmen would that king Charles should haue nothing but what it pleased
the

the king of England, and that not as dutie, but as a benefit by him of his méere liberalitie giuen and distributed. The Frenchmen on the other part would that K. Charles should haue the kingdome franklie and fréelie, and that the king of England should leaue the name, armes, and title of the king of France, and to be content with the dukedomes of Aquitaine and Normandie, and to forsake Paris, and all the townes which they possessed in France, betwéene the riuers of Some and Loire, being no parcell of the duchie of Normandie. To be bréefe, the demands of all parts were betwéene them so farre out of square, as hope of concord there was none at all.

The cardinals séeing them so farre in sunder, minded not to dispute their titles, but offered them reasonable conditions of truce and peace for a season, which notwithstanding, either of frowardnesse, or of disdaine on both parts, were openlie refused. Insomuch that the Englishmen in great displeasure, departed to Calis, and so into England. ¶ One writer affirmeth, that they being warned of a secret conspiracie mooued against them, suddenlie departed from Arras, and so returned into their countrie. But what cause soeuer hindered their accord and vnitie (sith this and that *Abr. Fl.* may be surmized,) certeine it is, that the onelie and principal cause was, for that the God of peace and loue was not among them, without whom no discord is quenched, no knot of concord fastened, no bond of peace confirmed, no distracted minds reconciled, no true fréendship mainteined : for had he beene among them, their dissenting and waiward willes had sounded the swéet harmonie of amiable peace, which of all things that God hath bestowed vpon man is the verie best, and more to be set by than manie triumphs, as the poet excellentlie well saith :

Sil. Ital. lib. 11.

　　　　　　———pax optima rerum
　　　　Quas homini nouisse datum : pax vna triumphis
　　　　Innumeris potior, pax custodire salutem
　　　　Et ciues æquare potens.

Now whiles this treatie of peace was in hand, the lord Talbot, the lord Willoughbie, the lord Scales, with the lord Lisle Adam, and fiue thousand men of warre, besieged the towne of saint Denis with a strong band. The earle of Dunois hearing hereof, accompanied with the lord Lohac, and the lord Bueill, with a great companie of horssemen hasted thitherwards to raise the siege, and by the waie incountred with sir Thomas Kiriell, and Matthew * Gough, riding also toward saint Denis, be- *Or rather Goche.* twéene whom was a great conflict. But suddenlie came to the aid of the Frenchmen the garrison of Pont Meulan, which caused the Englishmen to returne without anie great harme or damage : sauing that Matthew * Gough by foundering of his *Or Goche.* horsse was taken, and carried to Pont Meulan.

In the meane time was the towne of saint Denis rendered to the Englishmen, the *S. Denis taken* which raced the walles and fortifications, sauing the walles of the abbeie, and of the *by the English-* tower called Venin. Shortlie after the towne of Pontois, where sir Iohn Ruppelleie *men.* was capteine, rebelled ; and by force the Englishmen were expelled, the inhabitants yeelding themselues to the French king. This towne was small, but the losse was great, bicause it was the keie that opened the passage betwixt the cities of Paris and Rone. But now to returne to the communication at Arras, which after the departure of the English commissioners held betwixt the Frenchmen and Burgognians, till at *A peace betwéen* length a peace was concluded, accorded, and sworne betwixt king Charles and duke *Charles of France* Philip of Burgognie, vpon certeine conditions, as in the French histories more plainlie *Burgognie.* appeareth.

And after, the duke of Burgognie, to set a veile before the king of Englands eies, sent Thoison Dore his chéefe herald to king Henrie with letters, excusing the matter by way of information, that he was constreined to enter in this league with K. Charles, by the dailie outcries, complaints, and lamentations of his people ; alledging against
　　　　　　　　　　　　　　　　　　　　　　　　　him

him, that he was the onlie cause of the long continuance of the wars, to the vtter impouerishing of his owne people, and the whole nation of France. Therefore sith he could not otherwise doo, but partlie to content his owne people, and chéefelie to satisfie the request of the whole generall councell, was in manner compelled for his part to growe vnto a peace and amitie with king Charles.

He likewise wished that king Henrie, vpon reasonable and honorable conditions of agréement offered, should in no wise refuse the same : whereby the long conti-nued warre at length might ceasse and take end, to the pleasure of almightie God, which is the author of peace and vnitie : & hereto he promised him his aid and fur-therance, with manie gaie words, which I passe ouer. The superscription of this letter was thus [To the high and mightie prince, Henrie by the grace of God king of England, his welbeloued cousine.] Neither náming him king of France, nor his souereigne lord, according as (euer before that time) he was accustomed to doo. This letter was much maruelled at of the councell, after they had throughlie considered all the contents thereof, & they could not but be much disquieted, so far foorth that diuerse of them offended so much with the vntruth of the duke, that they could not temper their passions, but openlie called him traitor.

But when the rumor of the dukes reuolting was published amongst the people, they left words, and fell to bestowing of stripes : for being pricked with these euill tidings, they ran in great outrage vpon all the Flemings, Hollanders, and Burgog-nions, which then inhabited within the citie of London, and the suburbes of the same, and slue and hurt a great number of them before they, by the kings proclamation, could be staied from such iniurious dooing : for the king nothing more minded than to saue innocent bloud, and to defend them that had not offended. The officer at armes was willed to tell his maister, that it stood not with his honor to be enimie to the English nation ; and that his dutie had béene to kéepe his ancient truth and al-legiance, rather than to be occasion of new warre. And what a new reconciled eni-mie was in respect of an old tried fréend, he might shortlie find. [When the messenger with this answer was dispatched, and vpon consultation found, a matter standing both with good policie in forceing the proud subiect to know his obedi-ence, and also with great equitie to twitch a quareller with such pinsars as wherewith afore he had nipt an other, so was it anon brought about, that sundrie of his good townes and cities rebelled against him, whereby (lesse to his liking than to his deseruing) he was verie well made to bite of a chokepeare of his own grafting.]

Spoile vpon the
Burgognian peo-
ple in London.

An. Reg. 14.
The death of the
duke of Bedford
regent of Fráce.

This yeare the fourtéeth daie of September died Iohn duke of Bedford, regent of France, a man both politike in peace, and hardie in warre, and yet no more hardie than mercifull when he had the victorie, whose bodie was with all funerall solem-nitie buried in the cathedrall church of our ladie in Rone, on the north side of the high altar, vnder a sumptuous and costlie monument. Which toome when king Lewes the eleauenth, by certeine vndiscreet persons was counselled to deface, af-firming that it was a great dishonour both to the king and to the realme, to see the enimie of his father and theirs to haue so solemne and rich a memorial : he answered saieng, " What honour shall it be to vs, or to you, to breake this monument, and to pull out of the ground the dead bones of him, whome in his life neither my father nor your progenitors, with all their power, puissance, and fréends were once able to to make flée one foot backward ; but by his strengh, wit, and policie, kept them all out of the principall dominions of the realme of France, and out of this noble and fa-mous duchie of Normandie? Wherefore I saie, first, God haue his soule, and let his bodie now lie in rest, which when he was aliue, would haue disquieted the proudest of vs all. And as for the toome, I assure you, it is not so decent nor conuenient, as his honour and acts deserued, although it were much richer, and more beautifull."

The frost was so extreame this yeare, beginning about the fiue and twentith daie

of

of Nouember, and continuing till the tenth of Februarie, that the ships with merchandize arriuing at the Thames mouth, could not come vp the riuer : so their lading
there faine to be discharged, was brought to the citie by land.   After the death of
that noble prince the duke of Bedford, the bright sunne in France toward Englishmen, began to be cloudie, and dailie to darken, the Frenchmen began not onelie to
withdrawe their obedience by oth to the king of England, but also tooke sword in
hand & openlie rebelled.   Howbeit all these mishaps could not anie thing abash the
valiant courages of the English people : for they hauing no mistrust in God and good
fortune, set vp a new saile, began the warre afresh, and appointed for regent in
France, Richard duke of Yorke, sonne to Richard earle of Cambridge.

The duke of Yorke made regent of France.

Although the duke of Yorke was worthie (both for birth and courage) of this honor
and preferment, yet so disdeined of Edmund duke of Summerset being cousine to
the king, that by all means possible he sought his hindrance, as one glad of his
losse, and sorie of his well dooing : by reason whereof, yer the duke of Yorke could
get his dispatch, Paris and diuerse other of the cheefest places in France were gotten
by the French king. The duke of Yorke perceiuing his euill will, openlie dissembled
that which he inwardlie minded, either of them working things to the others displeasure, till through malice & diuision betwéene them, at length by mortall warre
they were both consumed, with almost all their whole liues and ofspring.

The Normans of the countrie of Caux, being heartened by the death of the
duke of Bedford, began a new rebellion, slue diuerse Englishmen, robbed manie
townes that were vnder the English obeisance, and tooke the towne of Harflue by
assault, and diuerse other townes.   But the lord regent being aduertised, sent foorth
the lord Scales, sir Thomas Kiriell, and the lord Hoo, which so afflicted those rebels
of Caux, that they slue aboue fiue thousand persons, and burnt all the townes and
villages in the countrie, not being walled : so that in that part was neither habitation nor tillage, for all the people fled into Britaine, and all the beasts of the
countrie were brought to Caudebecke, where a good sheepe was sold for an English
penie, and a cow for twelue pence.   Dailie was skirmishing and fighting in euerie
part, in so much that the lord Scales at the Rie beside Rone, discomfited the Hirc,
and fiftéene hundred valiant Frenchmen ; of the which, aboue thrée hundred were
taken prisoners, beside the gaine of seauen faire coursers.

Amongst other of the prisoners, were sir Richard Reginald de Fountaines, sir Alain
Gerond, Alain Monsaie, and Geffrie Grame, capteine of the Scots.   But yet this
victorie and others the like, staied not the Frenchmen from working treason dailie,
insomuch that diuers townes turned to the part of K. Charles, and some were taken
by practise, as Diepe, Bois, Vincennes, and others. ¶ So that here partlie was accomplished the prophesie of Henrie the fift, giuen out in the ninth yeare of his
reigne when he laie at siege before Meaux, that Henrie of Windsore should loose all
that Henrie of Monmouth had gotten (for so they are named according to the place
of their natiuitie) and this prediction was complet and full by that time the yeares of
his regiment were expired.

Abr. Fl. See before pag. 129.

But heere is one cheefe point to be noted, that either the disdeine amongest the
cheef péeres of the realme of England (as yée haue heard) or the negligence of
the kings councell (which did not foresée dangers to come) was the losse of the
whole dominion of France, betwéene the riuers of Sone and Marne, and in especiall,
of the noble citie of Paris.   For where before, there were sent ouer thousands for
defense of the holds and fortresses, now were sent hundreds, yea and scores, some
rascals, and some not able to draw a bowe, or carrie a bill : for the lord Willoughbie,
and the bishop of Terwine, which had the gouernance of the great citie of Paris,
had in their companie not two thousand Englishmen.

1436

Which weakenesse king Charles well perceiued, and therefore by authoritie appointed the constable, Arthur of Britaine, the earle of Dunois, the lords de la Roch, and Lisle Adam, with other valiant capteins and men of warre, as well Burgognions as French, to go before Paris, trusting by fauour of certeine citizens, with whome he had intelligence, shortlie to be lord of the citie, without great losse or battell. So these capteins came before the citie of Paris. But perceiuing that all things succeeded not according to their expectation, they returned to Mont Martyr, and the next daie suddenlie set on the towne of saint Denis, and constreined the Englishmen that kept it, to flée into the abbeie, and into the tower Venin. In this conflict two hundred Englishmen were slaine, the residue vpon reasonable composition rendered vp the place, and departed to Paris.

Thomas lord Beaumont, who of late was come to Paris with eight hundred men, issued foorth with six hundred souldiers, intending to view the dooings and number of the French armie; but suddenlie compassed about, within a small space was discomfited and taken, with him fourescore prisoners, beside two hundred slaine in the field, the remnant chased to the verie gates of the citie. The Parisiens, and especiallie the maister of the halles, and some of the vniuersitie, and Michaell Lallier, and manie notable burgesses of the citie (who euer with an English countenance couered a French hart) perceiuing the weaknesse of the Englishmen, and force of the French; signified to the French capteins their toward minds willing them with all diligence to come & receiue so rich a preie without anie difficultie, readie to be giuen and deliuered into their hands.

The constable delaieng no time, came with his power, lodged by the charter house: and the lord Lisle Adam, approching to the walles, shewed to the citizens a charter, The treson of the Parisiens. sealed with the great seale of king Charles, by the which he had pardoned them their offenses, and granted to them all their old liberties, and ancient priuileges, so that they would hereafter be to him true and obedient: which thing to them declared, they ran about the towne, crieng; S. Denis, liue king Charles. The Englishmen perceiuing this, determined to kéepe the gate S. Denis, but they were deceiued: for the cheines were drawne in euerie stréet, and women and children cast downe stones and scalding water on the Englishmens heads, and the citizens in armour fought with them and chased them from stréet to stréet, and from lane to lane, and slue and hurt diuerse and manie of them.

The bishop of Terwine, chancellor there for king Henrie, the lord Willoughbie, and sir Simon Moruiher, tooke great paine to appease the people: but when they saw that all auailed not, they withdrew into the bastile of saint Anthonie, which fortresse they had well vittelled, and furnished with men and munitions. Whilest this rumor was in the towne, the earle of Dunois and others scaled the walles, and some passed the Paris yéelded to the French king. riuer by botes, and opened gate of saint Iames, by the which the constable with his banner displaied, entered, at whose entrie the Parisiens made great ioy. The bishop and the lord Willoughbie, with their small companie, defended their fortresse ten daies, looking for aid: but when they saw that no comfort appeared, they yéelded their fortresse, so that they and theirs, with certeine baggage, might peaceablie returne to Rone. Thus was the citie of Paris brought into the possession of Charles the French king, through the vntrue demeanour of the citizens, who contrarie to their oths, and promised allegiance, like false and inconstant people, so reuolted from the English.

After this glorious gaine, the Frenchmen besieged the towne of Craill vpon Oise, wherof sir William Chamberlaine was capteine, the which with fiue hundred Englishmen issued out of the towne, and after long fight, discomfited his enimies, & slue two hundred, and tooke a great number prisoners: the remnant not liking the market departed to Campaigne, and other townes adioining. During which season, twelue burgesses of the towne of Gisours sold it for monie vnto Poiton de Xantrailes. But

he

he had not the castell deliuered, & therefore with all his power he besieged the same; whereof the lord Talbot being aduertised, sent for the lord Scales, and they both with eightéene hundred men rescued the castell, tooke the towne, and discomfited their enimies, and slue of them foure hundred persons.

Now according to the old saieng (when the steed is stolen shut the stable doore) the duke of Yorke appointed at the last parlement to be regent of France (after that Paris, Saint Denis, Saint Germans in Laie, and diuerse other townes iu France were taken and betraied for lacke of conuenient succours) was sent ouer into Normandie with eight thousand men, and in his companie, the earles of Salisburie, and Suffolke, and the lord Fawconbridge, and diuerse other valiant capteins. When he was landed, the earle of Salisburie besieged the castell of Chambois which shortlie was to him rendered. Then the duke remooued to Rone, where he set good orders, and did great iustice to the countrie; wherefore the Normans in their chronicles highlie extoll him for that point. Howbeit they saie, that he gat by long siege the towne and abbeie of Fecampe, and did none other notable act, during the time of his rule and gouernment. *The duke set into France too late.*

In this fourtéenth yeare, the duke of Burgognie determined by the aduise of his councell, to attempt the winning of Calis. The prouision was woonderous great which was made for the atchiuing of this enterprise: whereof sir Iohn Ratcliffe, deputie of the towne of Calis, hauing perfect intelligence, aduertised king Henrie, and his councell, who incontinentlie sent thither the earle of Mortaigne, sonne to the duke of Summerset, and the lord Camois, with fifteene hundred men, and great foison of vittels, that issued out of Calis, and came before Grauelin, where they were incountered with a great number of Flemings, who were shortlie discomfited, foure hundred of them slaine, and six score taken prisoners. Within two daies after, the Englishmen draue by fine force the lords of Warren and Bado to the barriers of Ard, and discomfited their whole companie, to the number of fifteene hundred, slue seauen valiant capteins, and tooke manie gentlemen prisoners. *The duke of Burgonie prepareth an armie against Calis.*

The duke of Burgognie, remaining still in his former purpose, assembled togither, of Flemings, Picards, Hollanders, and Heneweirs, a great armie, to the number of fortie thousand, so well armed, so well vitteled, so well furnished with ordinance, and garnished in all things, that they thought and blazed amongst themselues, that the Calisians would leaue their towne desolate, and flee for their safegard, hearing onelie of the dukes approch: but they reckoned without their host; and so paid a déerer shot than they looked for. Now when this mightie armie was past the water of Grauelin, the duke intending to begin his feats, assaulted the little poore castell of Oie, which hauing in it but fiftie souldiers, whereof twelue sold their liues deerelie; the remnant (compelled by necessitie) yéelded themselues to the dukes mercie. Which to please the Gantois (being of number most puissant in all the armie) liberallie gaue to them, both the castell and prisoners, who (rude and cruell people) not onelie raced the castell, but also hanged nine and twentie of the captiues, and had so doone with the residue, if the duke, offended at their crueltie, had not willed a staie. *The duke of Burgognie with fortie thousand mē.*

After this feat doone, the Picards besieged the castell of Marke, and gaue thrée assaults to it. The Englishmen within, being in number two hundred and six, vnder the gouernement of their capteine sir Iohn Gedding, valiantlie defended the place; vntill at length, despairing of succours, they yéelded themselues (their liues and lims saued.) The castell of Marke being thus deliuered, was raced to the ground. Then the duke, accompanied with the duke of Cleues, the earle of Estampes, the lords of Dantoing, Croie, Crisquie, Humiers, and manie other barons and knights, with his great armie, came before Calis, & placed his siege about the same most to his aduantage: he gaue thrée assaults, and gained nothing by them, but *Calis besieged by the duke of Burgognie.*

           constreined

constreined to kéepe them further off.   At the first assault, the Hire which was come to sée the duke of Burgognie, was sore wounded and hurt.   A cooling card it was also vnto them, still to sée ships arriued in the hauen out of England, openlie before their faces, laden with vittels, munition and men

The duke ón a daie riding about to view the situation of the towne, to the intent to take his most aduantage (either by assault or otherwise) was quickelie espied, and with the shot of a canon, a trumpetter, which rode next before him, and thrée horsses in his companie were slaine out of hand.   The lord of Croie, and a conuenient number with him, was appointed to besiege the castell of Guisnes, where he got little profit, and did lesse harme.   Moreouer, for the better aduancing of his enterprise, the duke minded to stop vp the hauen; so that no succours should enter there.

The dukes enterprise to bar the hauen.

Herevpon, he caused foure great hulkes to be fraught with great square stones, cemented and ioined togither with lead, to the intent they should lie still like a mount, and not seuer in sunder.

These ships, with the residue of the dukes nauie, were conueied into the mouth of Calis hauen, and at a full sea, by craft and policie, were soonke downe to the ground. But whether God would not that the hauen should be destroied, either the conueiers of the hulkes knew not the verie chanell; these foure great ships, at the low water, laie openlie vpon the sands, without hurting the rode or chanell.   Which when the souldiers perceiued, they issued out of the towne, brake the ships, and caried both the stones and timber into the towne.   An other deuise the duke had, which was the building of a strong bastile vpon a little mountaine, which he furnished with foure hundred men, and much artillerie, that did impeach the Englishmen from issuing foorth of the towne, to their great displeasure.

Whilest these things were adooing, there came to the duke an herald called Penbroke, belonging to duke of Glocester, who declared to the duke of Burgognie, that the protector of England his maister (if God would send him wind & weather) would giue him battell, either there, or in anie other place within his owne countrie, where he would appoint, and that with spéed, if God vouchsafed him wind and weather. The duke answered the herald; "Sir, saie to your maister, that his chalenge is both honorable and reasonable: howbeit, he shall not néed to take the paines to séeke me in mine owne countrie, for (God willing) he shall find me héere, till I haue my will of the towne, readie to abide him and all the power he can bring."   After the herald had receiued this answer, he was highlie chéered, and had a cup and an hundred guildens to him giuen in reward, and so he returned to Calis.

After whose departure, the duke called a councell in the chéefe pauilion of the Gantois, about this message of the English herald, where it was determined with great courage, that they would abide the battell, if the duke of Glocester came to offer it.   Whilest this great matter was in consultation, the Calisians, not well content with the bastile which the duke had newlie builded, issued out of the towne in great number, part on horssebacke and part on foot.   The footmen ran to assault the bastile, and the horssemen went betwéene the armie & the assailants, to stop the aid and succours that might come.   Vpon the sounding of the alarme, the duke himselfe in person was comming on foot, to reléeue his men: but being kept backe a space by the Eng

The dukes bastile woone.

lish horssemen, in that delaie of time, the bastile was woone by fine force, and eight score persons of those that kept it slaine, beside the residue which were taken prisoners. and led to Calis with all the ordinance and artillerie, to the high displeasure of the duke and his prudent councell.   The next daie after, there sprang a rumor in the armie (no man could tell how) that the duke of Glocester with a great puissance was alreadie

The duke of Burgognie breaketh vp the siege before Calis, and fléeth, the 26 of Iulie.

imbarked, and would arriue at the next tide.   The same night the duke fled awaie, and sent in all hast to the lord of Croie, to raise his siege before Guisnes, which tidings were to him verie ioious, for he neither got nor saued.   So these two capteins de

parted,

parted, leauing behind them, both ordinance, vittels, & great riches. ¶ The French writers (to saue the honor of the duke of Burgognie) saie, that there was a certeine discord and commotion amongst the Flemings and Duch nation, affirming, that the great lords and the Picards (whome the Frenchmen greatlie extoll) would betraie and sell the Flemings and their freends, and that for the same cause in a great furie they cried; Home, home: and would not tarrie for anie request that the duke could make, and so by their misgouernance, the duke was inforced to raise his siege, and to depart. The Flemish authors affirme the contrarie, saieng, that they were readie to abide the comming of the duke of Glocester: but the duke of Burgognie fearing to be intrapped betwéene the English armie without, and the garrison within the towne of Calis, fled awaie in the night, giuing to them no warning thereof before, so that for lacke of time, and conuenient space to lade and carrie their stuffe, and being commanded vpon the sudden to dislodge with all spéed, they left behind them their vittels, tents, and other things, to their great losse and detriment.

Howsoeuer the matter was, the truth is, that he fled the six and twentith daie of Iulie, in the night. And the next daie in the morning, the duke of Glocester landed in Calis hauen, & streight went into the campe, where his enimies the night before were lodged, and there he found manie faire peeces of ordinance, and speciallie one called Digeon: so named, after the cheefe towne of Burgognie; beside pauilions, wine, beere, meale, and innumerable vittels. The duke of Glocester, seeing his enimies reculed, hauing in his companie fiue and twentie thousand men, entered into Flanders, burning houses, killing such as made resistance, destroieng the countrie on euerie part, setting fire in the townes of Poperinch, Bailleul, and others. Also, they wasted the suburbes of diuerse closed townes, and after passed by Newcastell, Rimesture, and Valon chapell: and then entering into Artois, they came to Arques and Blandesques, setting fire in euerie part where they came. Thus they passed by saint Omers, and finallie by Arde returned to Guisnes: and so to Calis at the six wéeks end, with great booties of cattell and riches. *A gun called Digeon. The duke of Glocester spoileth Flanders.*

In all this their iournie, they had but small store of bread, which caused much faintnesse and diuerse diseases in the armie, whereof a greater number died than did of the enimies sword: and yet the Flemings write, that they of Bruges distressed to the number of two thousand Englishmen in this iournie. Howbeit, the French writers affirme, that the Englishmen lost more of their companie in the marches about Ard, than they did in all other places where they had béene before, hauing passed through the parties of Flanders, without incounter, or any damage doone to them by the enimies. After that, the duke of Glocester returned into England, where he was aduertised, that Iames king of Scots had besieged the castell of Rockesburgh with thirtie thousand men: but the capteine thereof, sir Rafe Greie defended it so manfullie, for the space of twentie daies, that king Iames being then aduertised, that the earle of Northumberland was comming to fight with him, fled with no lesse losse than dishonor, and inough of both. *Barland. Enguerant. The king of Scots fled from his siege at Rockesburgh.*

Shortlie after that the duke of Burgognie had béene before Calis, at the desire of princes, a truce for a time was moued to be had betwéene the king of England & the said duke. For which cause were sent to Grauelin for the king of England, Henrie Beauford cardinall of Winchester, Iohn lord Mowbraie duke of Northfolke, Humfrie earle of Stafford, and diuerse other well learned & honorable personages. And for the duke of Burgognie, there appeared the duchesse his wife, the bishop of Arras, the lord of Croie, and diuerse other. At this treatie, a truce was taken for a small time, and for a lesse obserued, which was concluded betwéene the king of England, and the duchesse of Burgognie (interlacing the duke and his name.) *An. Reg. 15. A truce taken betwéene the king of England and the duchesse of Burgognie.*

Some thinke, that the king of England would neuer enter in league with him, bicause he had broken his promise, oth, and writing sealed to him, and to his father. *Hall.*

Other

Other imagined this to be doone of a cautell, to cast a mist before the French kings eies, to the intent he should beléeue that this feat was wrought by the duchesse, without assent or knowledge of the duke or his councell; and so he was not bound to accomplish anie act or thing doone in his wiues treatie. Thus may you sée, that princes sometime with such vaine glosses and scornefull expositions will hide their dooings, and cloke their purposes; to the intent they would not either be espied, or else that they may plucke their heads out of the collar at their pleasure. But (as the common opinion goeth) he which is a promise-breaker escapeth not alwaies with impunitie. For it is well seene by dailie and vsuall euents both in princes and priuat persons, that for violating their faith, and breaking of promise, manie discommodities arise, and inconueniences not a few doo follow. To the due keeping whereof the heathen bare such a religious conscience, that a prophane man in respect of others, preferreth it before sacrifice, the sentence is of great excellencie out of a pagans mouth:

Non boue mactato cœlestia numina gaudent,
Sed quæ præstanda est & sine teste fide.

1437.

Katharine mother to king Henrie maried Owen Teuther.

About this season, queene Katharine mother to the king of England departed out of this life, and was buried by hir husband in the abbeie of Westminster. This woman, after the death of king Henrie the fift hir husband, being yoong and lustie, following more hir owne wanton appetite than fréendlie counsell, and regarding more priuate affection than princelike honour, tooke to husband priuilie a galant gentleman and a right beautifull person, indued with manie goodlie gifts both of bodie & mind, called Owen Teuther, a man descended of the noble linage and ancient line of Cadwallader last king of the Britains. By this Owen she brought foorth thrée goodlie sonnes, Edmund, Iasper, and another that was a monke in Westminster and liued a small time: also a daughter which in hir youth departed out of this transitorie life.

King Henrie, after the death of his mother, bicause, they were his brethren of one wombe, créated Edmund earle of Richmund, and Iasper earle of Penbroke: which Edmund of Margaret daughter and sole heire to Iohn duke of Summerset begat Henrie, who after was king of this realme, called Henrie the seuenth, of whome ye shall heare more in place conuenient. This Owen, after the death of the quéene his wife, was apprehended and committed to ward, bicause that (contrarie to the statute made in the sixt yeare of this king) he presumptuouslie had maried the quéene, without the kings especiall assent, out of which prison he escaped, and let out other with him, but was

Abr Fl.

againe apprehended, and after escaped againe. ¶ Polychronicon saith that he was a squier of low birth and like degrée, the same author also reporteth that he was commanded to Newgate by the duke of Glocester then lord protector of the realme: out of which prison he brake by the helpe of a preest that was his chapline. Neuerthelesse he was apprehended afterwards by the lord Beaumont, & brought againe to Newgate, whence (when he had remained there a while) he was deliuered and set at libertie.]

The duchesse of Bedford also, sister to Lewes erle of S. Paule, more for affection than increase of honour, without councell of hir freends, maried a lustie yoong knight, called sir Richard Wooduile, to the great displeasure of hir vncle the bishop of Terwine, and the earle hir brother. This sir Richard was made baron of Riuers, and after earle, and had by this ladie manie noble sonnes, and faire daughters, of the which one

Quéene Elizabeth.

was the ladie Elizabeth, after queene of England, by reason she was married vnto Edward the fourth. ¶ Whilest this marriage was a celebrating, Iane late quéene of England, and before duchesse of Britaine, daughter to the king of Nauarre, and wife to king Henrie the fourth, died at the manor of Hauering, and was buried by hir husband at Canturburie. ¶ About the same time, deceassed also the countesse of Warwike, and Henrie archbishop of Yorke.

In this yeare also, the duke of Summerset, accompanied with the lords of Fauconbridge,

bridge, Talbot, sir Francis Surien, the Arrogonnois, Matthew * Gough, Thomas Paulet, * Or rather
Goche.
Thomas Harington, Walter Limbrike, Iohn Gedding, William Watton, esquiers, and
Thomas Hilton bailiffe of Rone, with a great companie of the English partie, besieged
the towne of Harflue (latelie before gotten by the Frenchmen) both by water and Harflue besieged
land : the capteine within the towne was one sir Iohn d' Estouteuille, hauing his brother and woon by the
Englishmen.
Robert with him, and a six hundred good fighting men. The assailants cast trenches
and so fortified themselues in their campe and lodgings, that when the earles of Ew
and Dunois, the valiant bastard of Bourbon, the lord Gawcourt, and other famous
capteins, with a foure thousand men, sent to the rescue of them within, came before
the towne, they could not succour their freends, nor annoie their enimies by any
meanes they could deuise ; & so for feare to lose honour, they returned backe againe,
with much trauell and little profit.

The capteins within the towne perceiuing they could not be aided, did shortlie
after render the towne to the duke of Summerset ; who after committed it to the
kéeping of Thomas Paulet, William Limbrike, Christopher Barber, and George saint
George, which manie yeares (till the diuision began in England) manfullie and valiantlie defended both the towne and the hauen. But afterward, when this duke of The duke of
Summerset was regent and gouernour of Normandie, he not onlie lost this towne of Summersets in-
fortunatnes.
Harflue, but also the citie of Rone, and the whole duchie of Normandie, whereas
now (being but a deputie) he got it to his high praise and glorie. In this yeare was Iames king of
Iames king of Scots murthered by certeine traitors of his own subiects [euen in his Scots murthered.
Abr. Fl. ex
Polychr.
bedchamber by night, which king (saith Polychr.) had beene prisoner in England
fiftéene yeares, the murtherers of whom being afterwards taken, were terriblie executed.]

The lord Talbot besieged Tankeruile, and after foure moneths had it simplie to
him rendered. This towne was no great gaine to the Englishmen, for in the meane
season, the French king in his owne person besieged the strong towne of Monstreau
fault Yonne ; whereof Thomas Gerard being capteine, more for desire of reward,
than for feare of enimies, sold the towne to the French king, and had of him great
gifts and interteinement, as afterwards was openlie knowen. This towne had béene
rescued of the French king fought withall, if one chance had not happened. For the
duke of Yorke about that time was discharged of his office, and the earle of Warwike The earle of
preferred to the same, so that the duke of Yorke, lieng as then at Rone, would haue Warwike made
regent of France.
gladlie rescued the towne, if his authoritie had not surceassed ; and the earle of War-
wike could not come in time, for the wind was contrarie to him.

This present yeare was a parlement holden at Westminster, in the which manie good
and profitable acts for the preseruation of concord at home, and defense against the
enimies abroad, were ordeined and deuised. ¶ Arthur of Britaine constable of France,
and Iohn duke of Alanson, were sent by the French king into Normandie, with a
great armie, to besiege the towne of Auranches, standing vpon the knop of an hill :
where after they had laien a certeine space without gaine, the lord Talbot with a valiant companie of men came thither, and offered the enimies battell. Which when
they at all hands refused, the lord Talbot perceiuing their faint harts, raised his field,
and in the open sight of them all, entered into the towne, and the next daie issued out ;
and finding the Frenchmen riding abroad to destroie the plaine countrie, he compassed
them about, and slue manie of them, and tooke diuerse prisoners. Although the
Frenchmen got neither honor nor profit by this iournie, yet they enterprised a greater
matter, as the winning of Rone ; in so much that Pouton de Santreils, and the Hire,
with manie other notable capteins, hauing promise of certeine burgesses of that citie
to haue entrie made them, secretlie in the night came forward to a towne called Rise
or Riz, not past foure leagues from Rone, and there lodged.

The lord Talbot, the lord Scales, and sir Thomas Kiriell hearing of their approch,
set

set out of Rone at midnight, & with great paine came to Rise so couertlie in the morning, that the French suddenlie surprised and set vpon, like men all amazed ran awaie and fled. In the chase were taken the lord of Fontains, sir Aleine Geron, sir Lewes de Balle, and thréescore knights, and esquiers, beside others; and there were slaine two hundred and more. The Hire escaped verie narrowlie, by swiftnesse of his horsse, though not vnwounded. The Englishmen returned to the towne of Rise, and found there great number of horsses & other baggages, which they ioiouslie brought with them to Rone.

An. Reg. 16.

The earle of Warwike regent came into France.

On the sixt daie of Nouember this present yeare, the earle of Warwike, as regent of France, passed the sea, after he had beene seuen times shipped and vnshipped, and landed at Homflue with a thousand fresh souldiers, and came to Rone, and then the duke of Yorke returned into England. Betwéene the change of these two capteins, the duke of Burgognie (which sore enuied the glorie of the Englishmen) besieged the

Croitoy besieged by the duke of Burgognie.

towne of Crotoy, with ten thousand men and more, hauing with him great plentie of guns and goodlie ordinance. The earle of Warwike aduertised hereof, sent the lord Fauconbridge, sir Thomas Kiriell, sir Iohn Montgomerie, Thomas Limbrike, Thomas Chandois, Dauid Hall, and diuerse other knights and esquiers, and an host of fiue thousand men, which passed the riuer of Some, beside the towne of saint Valerie, wading in the water vp to the chin, so glad were they to rescue their felowes.

Croitoy rescued.

When the duke of Burgognie was informed of the approching of the lord Talbot, he with all his power (sauing foure hundred, which were left in a bastile by him there newlie builded) fled to Abuile, the bastile was soone gained by the Englishmen, and those within either slaine or taken. After this, the lord Talbot sent to the duke of Burgognie, signifieng that except he would come foorth, and bide by a battell, he would vtterlie wast his countrie of Picardie. According whereunto (the duke of Burgognie shrinking) he burnt townes, spoiled and slue manie people in Picardie. But for all those his doings, the duke of Burgognie appeared not, but got him from Abuile to Amiens, so that the lord Talbot abode twentie daies full in Picardie and Arthois, destroieng all afore him, and after returned vntouched. In the meane season, sir Thomas Kiriell had gotten all the dukes cariages and ordinance, and left as much vittell in the towne of Croitoy, as would serue six hundred men a whole yeare, and conueied the residue to the earle of Warwike, who highlie praised them for their hardie dooings.

1438

After this, Henrie earle of Mortaigne, sonne to Edmund duke of Summerset, ariued at Chierburgh with foure hundred archers, & thrée hundred speares, and passed through Normandie, till he came into the countie of Maine, where he besieged a castell called saint Anian, in the which were thrée hundred Scots, besides Frenchmen. This castell he tooke by assault, slue the Scots, and hanged the Frenchmen, bicause they were once sworne English. After this he got also another castell, two miles from saint Iulians, called Alegerche, which was shortlie after recouered; and the lord of Camewis, which came to the rescue of the same, in the meane waie was intrapped and taken. Thus flowed the victorie, sometime on the one partie, and sometime on the other. For about the same time the townes of Meaux in Brie, and saint Susan were sold and deliuered to the French part, by the vntruth of the burgesses and inhabitants of the same towns, about the latter end of this sixteenth yeare.

An. Reg. 17.

Dearth of vittels.

1439

Abr. Fl. ex Polychr.

This yeare (by reason of great tempests) raging winds, and raine, there rose such scarsitie, that wheat was sold at three shillings foure pense the bushell, wine at twelue pense the gallon, baisalt at fourtéene pense the bushell, and malt at thirtéene shillings foure pense the quarter, and all other graines at excessiue prices aboue the old rate. ¶ Wherevpon Steuen Browne (saith Polychronicon) at the same season maior of London, tendering the state of the citie in this want of breadcorne, sent into Pruse certeine ships, which returned loden with plentie of rie: wherwith he did much good to the

the people in that hard time speciallie to them of the citie, where the want of corne was not so extreame as in some other places of the land, where the poore distressed people that were hungerbitten, made them bred of ferne roots, and vsed other hard shifts, till God prouided remedie for their penurie by good successe of husbandrie.] —Bread made of ferne roots.

In the moneth of Iune, the earle of Huntington (as Steward of Guien) with two thousand archers, and foure hundred speares was sent into Gascoigne, as a supplie to the countrie and cōmons of the same: for the king of England and his councell were informed, that the earle of Dunois laie in the frontiers of Tholouse secretlie, by rewards and faire promises practising to procure diuerse townes in Guien to become French. Wherefore this earle (like a politike warrior) altered not onelie the capteins in euerie A feat of a politike capteine & wise councellor. towne and citie, but also remoued the magistrates, and changed the officers from towne to towne, and roome to roome; so that by this meanes, the earle of Dunois at that time lost both trauell and cost.

In the same moneth also, sir Richard Wooduile, sir William Chamberleine, sir William Peito, and sir William Storie, with a thousand men, were sent to stuffe the townes in Normandie, which at that time had therof great néed: for the English capteins had small confidence in the Normans, and not too much in some of their own nation. For that harlot briberie, with hir fellow couetousnesse, ran so fast abroad Two shrewd persuaders. with French crownes, that hard was it to remaine vncorrupted. In this yeare, the Dolphin of France alied with Iohn duke of Alanson and Iohn duke of Burgognie, rebelled against his father king Charles: but in the end, by wise persuasions, and wittie handling of the matter, the knot of that seditious faction was dissolued, and the king with his sonne, and the other confederates openlie and apparantlie pacified. The Englishmen taking aduantage of this domesticall diuision in France, raised an armie, and recouered againe diuerse townes, which had béene surprised from them before, and prepared also to haue recouered the citie of Paris, till they hard of the agréement betwixt the father and the sonne, and then they left off that enterprise.

In Nouember of this yeare, there was such a great frost, and after that so déepe a An. Reg. 18. snow, that all the ground was couered therwith, and all the diches frosen. Which wether put the Englishmen in hope to recouer againe the towne of Ponthoise, by Ponthoise recouered by the English. the French king gotten before, by corrupting with monie diuerse burgesses of the towne. Hervpon the Englishmen clothed all in white, with Iohn lord Clifford their capteine, came in the night to the diches, passed them without danger by reason of the frost, scaled the walles, slue the watch, and tooke the towne, with manie profitable prisoners. ¶ After the regaining of this towne, the lord Richard Beauchampe earle of Warwike died in the castell of Rone, from whence conueied into England, he was with solemne ceremonies buried at his college of Warwike, in a verie faire and sumptuous sepulchre.

About the beginning of Lent, the duke of Summerset, and the lord Talbot, with An. Reg. 19. other capteins and men of warre to the number of two thousand, which they had assembled in the marches of Normandie towards Rone, marching forward towards Picardie, passed ouer the riuer of Sone; and through the towne of Monteruell, came before the fortresse of Folleuile, which the duke besieged, whilest the lord Talbot entered further into the countrie. After that the duke had mounted his great artil- *Enguerant.* lerie, and began to batter the hold, the capteine within chanced to be slaine with a shot of the same artillerie, & shortlie after, the batterie being still continued, the rest of the men of warre that serued vnder him yéelded the place, in which the duke left a competent garrison of souldiers, which afterwards sore indamaged the countrie.

This doone, the duke followed the lord Talbot, who was alreadie entered a good waie within the countrie of Santhois, and now ioining their powers togither, they came to a fortresse called Lihons in Santhois, which was also rendered vnto them, after they had burnt the church; which the countrie people kept against them, and would not yeeld it, till they were fired out, burnt, and slaine; to the number of thrée hundred. After the fortresse was deliuered into their hands by composition, the duke with his power laie there about ten daies, sending diuerse troops of his men of warre abroad into the countrie, which spoiled the same, tooke the fortresse of Herbonneres, and the lord thereof within it, who for his ransome, and to haue his subiects and house saued from spoile and fire, compounded with his takers for a thousand saluz of gold, which he paid to them. Finallie, after the duke of Summerset, and the lord Talbot with their power, had laine in Lihons about ten daies, they departed from thence, and returned into Normandie, without anie impeachment.

After the death of the earle of Warwike, the duke of Yorke was againe made regent of France, which accompanied with the earle of Oxenford, the lord Bourchier called earle of Ewe, sir Iames of Ormond, the lord Clinton, sir Richard Wooduile, & diuerse other noble men, sailed into Normandie. Before whose ariuall, the French king sore gréeued with the taking of the towne of Ponthoise, assembled a great armie, and besieged the said towne himselfe in person, inuironing it with bastiles, trenches, and ditches, beating the walles and bulworks with shot of great ordinance, and giuing therevnto diuerse great and fierce assaults. But Iohn lord Clifford, like a valiant capteine, defended the towne so manfullie, that the Frenchmen rather lost than woone.

The duke of Yorke at his landing receiued true aduertisement of this siege, wherevpon he sent for the lord Talbot, and a great number of soldiers, and so came neere to the towne of Ponthoise, and there incamped himselfe; who therewith sent word to the French king, that thither he was come to giue him battell, if he would come out of his strength and bastiles. But the French king by aduise of his councell, determined not to venture his person with men of so base degrée, but meant to kéepe his ground, bidding the lord regent to enter at his perill, and in the meane season did what he could to stop the passage of the riuer of Oise, so that no vittels should be brought to the English armie by that waie, in hope so to cause them to recule backe.

The duke of Yorke, perceiuing that the French king minded not to fight, purposed to passe ouer the riuer of Oise, and so to fight with him in his lodging. Whervpon he remooued his campe, and appointed the lord Talbot and other, to make a countenance, as they would passe the riuer by force at the port of Beaumont: and appointed an other companie in boates of timber and leather, and bridges made of cords and ropes (whereof he had great plentie caried with him in chariots) to passe ouer beneath the abbie. Whilest the lord Talbot made a crie, as though he would assault the gate, certeine Englishmen passed the water in botes, and drew a bridge of cords

ouer, so that a great number of them were got to the other side, yer the Frenchmen were aduised what had happened. When they saw the chance, they ran like mad men, to haue stopped the passage, but it was too late: for the most part of the Englishmen were got ouer, in so much that they chased their enimies backe, and slue sir Guilliam de Chastell, nephue to the lord Taneguie du Chastell, and diuerse others.

The Frenchmen séeing their euill hap irrecouerable, returned to the French king, and told him what had chanced: wherevpon he doubting to be assailed to his disaduantage, thought not good longer to tarrie, but with all spéed remoouing his ordinance into the bastile of saint Martin, which he had newlie made, dislodged in the night from Maubuisson, and went to Poissie, leauing the lord de Cotignie admerall of France, with thrée thousand men to kéepe the bastile. If he had taried still at Maubuisson, the lord Talbot which had passed the riuer of Oise in two small leather

botes, had either taken or slaine him the same night. The Englishmen the next daie in good order of battell came before the towne of Ponthoise, thinking there to haue found the French king, but he was gone: and in his lodging they found great riches,

                                                                                                    and

and much stuffe which he could not haue space for to carrie awaie for feare of the sudden inuasion.

Then the duke with his power entred into the towne, and sent for new vittels, and repaired the towers and bulworks about the towne, & diuerse times assaulted the bastile of the Frenchmen, of the which he made no great accompt, bicause they were not of power either to assault or stop the vittels or succors from the towne. After this, the duke intending once againe to offer the French king battell, left behind him at Ponthoise for capteine there, sir Geruais Clifton, sir Nicholas Burdet, Henrie Chandos, and a thousand soldiers, and therewith remoouing with his whole armie, came before Poissie, where he set himselfe and his men in good order of battell readie to fight. There issued out some of the French gentlemen to skirmish with the Englishmen, but to their losse: for diuerse of them were slaine, and foure valiant horssemen taken prisoners. The duke perceiuing the faint hearts of the Frenchmen, and that they durst not incounter in field with the English power, dislodged from Poissie, and came to Maunt, and soone after to Rone.

When the regent and the lord Talbot were returned againe into Normandie, the French king considering how much it should redound to his dishonour to let rest the towne of Ponthoise in his enimies hands, sith he had beene at such charges and trauell about the winning thereof, he eftsoones assembled all his puissance. And returning suddenlie vnto Ponthoise, he first by assault got the church, and after the whole towne, tooke the capteine, and diuerse other Englishmen, and slue to the number of foure hundred, which sold their liues dearelie: for one French writer affirmeth, that the French king lost there thrée thousand men; and the whole garrison of the Englishmen was but onelie a thousand. Among other that were slaine here of the defendants, was sir Nicholas Burdet knight, cheefe butler of Normandie. After this hot tempest, the weather began somewhat to wax more calme: for king Henrie and king Charles agréed to send ambassadors to commen of some good conclusion of peace: so that king Henrie sent the cardinall of Winchester, with diuerse other noble personages of his councell to Calis, with whome was also sent Charles duke of Orleance yet prisoner in England, to the intent that he might be both author of the peace, and also procurer of his owne deliuerance.

The French king sent the archbishop of Reimes, and the earle of Dunois: and the duke of Burgognie sent the lord de Creuecueur, and diuerse other. All these met at Calis, where the duke of Orleance courteouslie receiued the earle of Dunois (his bastard brother) thanking him greatlie for his paines taken in gouerning his lands & countrie, during the time of his captiuitie and absence. Diuerse communications were had, as well for the deliuerance of the duke as for a finall peace; but nothing was concluded, sauing that an other méeting was appointed, so that in the meane season the demands of either partie might be declared to their souereigne lords and maisters: and herevpon the commissioners brake vp their assemblie, and returned into their countries. The Englishmen (as the French writers record) required not onelie to possesse peaceablie the two duches of Aquitane and Normandie, discharged of all resort, superioritie, and souereigntie against the realme of France, the kings and gouernours of the same; but also to be restored to all the townes, cities, and places, which they within thirtie yéeres next before gone and past, had conquered in the realme of France. Which request the Frenchmen thought verie vnreasonable, and so both parties, minding rather to gaine or saue than to loose, departed for that time, as yée haue heard.

After this méeting thus proroged, Philip duke of Burgognie, partlie mooued in conscience to make amends to Charles duke of Orleance (as yet prisoner in England for the death of duke Lewes his father, whome duke Iohn, father to this duke Philip cruellie murthered in the citie of Paris; and partlie intending the aduancement of hi

C c 2

neece, the ladie Marie, daughter to Adolfe duke of Cleue (by the which aliance, he trusted, that all old rancor should ceasse, contriued waies to haue the said duke of Orleance set at libertie, vpon promise by him made to take the said ladie Marie vnto wife. This duke had beene prisoner in England euer since the battell was fought at Agincourt, vpon the daie of Crispine and Crispinian, in the yeare 1415, and was set now at libertie in the moneth of Nouember, in the yeare 1440, paieng for his ransome foure hundred thousand crownes, though other saie but thrée hundred thousand.

The cause whie he was deteined so long in captiuitie, was to pleasure thereby the duke of Burgognie: for so long as the duke of Burgognie continued faithfull to the king of England, it was not thought necessarie to suffer the duke of Orleance to be ransomed, least vpon his deliuerance he would not ceasse to séeke meanes to be reuenged vpon the duke of Burgognie. for the old grudge and displeasure betwixt their two families, and therefore such ransome was demanded for him as he was neuer able to pay. But after the duke of Burgognie had broken his promise, and was turned to the French part, the councell of the king of England deuised how to deliuer the duke of Orleance, that thereby they might displeasure the duke of Burgognie. Which thing the duke of Burgognie perceiuing, doubted what might follow if he were deliuered without his knowledge, and therefore to his great cost practised his deliuerance, paid his ransome, and ioined with him amitie and aliance by mariage of his néece.

'1 he duke of Orleance de-liuered.

This duke being now deliuered, and speaking better English than French, after his arriuall in France, repaired to the duke of Burgognie, and according to his promise and conuention, maried the ladie Marie of Cleue, in the towne of saint Omers, on

Lewes the twelfe.
W P.

whome he begat a sonne, which after was French king, and called Lewes the twelfe. [Festered sores that rankle inward, as they may perchance be palliat by sleight of surgerie; so sildome come they to sound cure, but often doo burst out againe to greater paine and perill of patient than euer afore: and so befell it betwéene these two noble houses of Orleance and Burgognie, who for all this mariage and plausible peace (that continued a twentie yeares) fell out yet after at square vnattonablie :] their children and cousins, to the great vnquietting of much part of christendome, speci-allie in the times of king Francis the first, and his sonne Henrie the second, heires of the house of Orleance. For Iohn earle of Angolesme, vncle to this duke Charles, begat Charles, father to the said king Francis : which earle Iohn had beene as pledge in England for the debt of Lewes duke of Orleance, from the last yeare of king Henrie the fourth; till that now his nephue being deliuered, made shift for monie, and ransomed him also, and at length restored him to his countrie.

In the beginning of this twentith yeare, Richard duke of Yorke, regent of France, and gouernour of Normandie, determined to inuade the territories of his enimies both by sundrie armies, and in seuerall places, and thereupon without delaie of time he sent the lord of Willoughbie with a great crue of soldiers to destroie the countrie of Amiens, and Iohn lord Talbot was appointed to besiege the towne of Diepe; and the regent himselfe accompanied with Edmund duke of Summerset, set forward into the duchie of Aniou. The lord Willoughbie, according to his commission, entred into the countrie of his enimies in such wise vpon the sudden, that a great number of people were taken yer they could withdraw into anie place of safegard.

The Frenchmen in the garrisons adioining, astonied with the clamour and crie of the poore people, issued out in good order, and manfullie fought with the English-men. But in the end, the Frenchmen séeing their fellowes in the forefront slaine downe, and kild without mercie, turned their backes, and fled: the Englishmen followed, and slue manie in the chase; and such as escaped the sword, were robbed

Earle of saint Paule fréend to the English.

by the earle of saint Paule, who was comming to aid the Englishmen. In this conflict were slaine aboue six hundred men of armes, and a great number taken. The dukes

　　　　　　　　　　　　　　　　　　　　　　　　　　　　　　　　　　of

of Yorke and Summerset likewise entered into Aniou and Maine, and there destroied townes, and spoiled the people, and with great preies and prisoners repaired againe into Normandie, whither also the lord Willoughbie withdrew, after his valiant enterprise atchiued (as before yée haue heard) with rich spoiles and good prisoners.

The duke of Summerset vpon further valiance, entered into the marches of Britaine, and tooke by fierce assault a towne named la Gerche, apperteining to the duke of Alanson, spoiling and burning the same. This doone, he went to Ponzaie, where he soiorned two moneths, sending foorth dailie his men of war to destroie the countries of Aniou, Traonnois, and Chatragonnois. The French king sent the marshall Loiach with foure thousand men to resist the inuasions of the duke of Summerset, which marshall intended to haue set on the duke in his lodgings in the dead time of the night: but that (as by a wise and hardie capteine) well foreséene, he marched forward, and met the Frenchmen halfe the waie, and after long fight, discomfited them, slue an hundred of the marshals men, and tooke thrée score and two prisoners, wherof the chéefe were the lord Dausignie, sir Lewes de Buell, all the other (almost) were knights and esquiers. This should be as *Enguerant* noteth two yeares after this present yere 19, to wit, *An.* 1440.

After this incounter, the duke tooke the towne of Beaumont le vicount, and manned all the fortresses on the frontiers of his enimies, and with rich booties and prisoners returned againe to the duke of Yorke. In this meane time the lord Talbot, besieging the towne of Diepe, inuironed it with déepe trenches; building also vpon the mount Paulet a strong and noisome bastile. But at length perceiuing the towne to be stronglie defended, and that he lacked such furniture of men, vittels and ordinance as was necessarie for the winning of it, he deliuered the custodie of the bastile, with the gouernance of the siege to his bastard sonne, a valiant yoong gentleman, and departed to Rone for aid, monie, and munition. The French king aduertised hereof, sent his sonne the Dolphin of Vienne with the earle of Dunois, and fiftéene thousand men to raise the siege from Diepe. Thrée thousand hath *Nicholas Giles*.

Thrée daies they assailed the bastile, in the which six hundred Englishmen were inclosed, and at length bicause powder and weapon failed them within, the Frenchmen wan it, and tooke the bastard Talbot prisoner, with sir William Peitow, and sir Iohn Repleie, which shortlie after were redéemed. the other English souldiers séeing the bastile woone by the Frenchmen, stood all a daie in good order of battell, and in the night following, politikelie saued themselues and returned to Rone, without losse or damage. In the assaulting of the bastile, the Frenchmen saie, they slue two hundred Englishmen; and denie not but that they lost fiue hundred of their owne men, beside those that were hurt. Whilest these things were a dooing, Philip duke of Burgognie made sharpe warre against the earle of saint Paule, in taking from him his townes and castels, that made him to renounce his allegiance swoorne and promised to the king of England, and returned to the French part. The earle of saint Paule reuolteth to the French.

The English capteins in Guien besieged the strong towne of Tartas, belonging to the lord Dalbreth their old and ancient enimie. The towne perceiuing that it was not able to resist the force of the Englishmen anie long time, tooke appointment, that the towne should remaine neuter. For assurance therof, they deliuered Cadet the sonne of the lord de la Breth in pledge, vpon this condition; that if the said lord de la Breth would not assent to the agreement, then he should signifie his refusall to the English capteins within thrée moneths next insuing, and he to haue his pledge, and they to doo their best. The French king, at the request of the lords of Guien, caused the lord de la Breth to signifie his disagréement vnto the earle of Huntington, as then lieutenant to the king of England in the duchie of Aquitaine. And therewith to gratifie the lords of Guien, he assembled an armie of thréescore thousand men, & came to Tholouse, and so to Tartas, to whome the chéeftcins of the towne, séeing no succours 1441. Tartas besieged.

cours

cours comming from the king of England, rendred the towne: and Cadet de la Breth, which was left there as a pledge, was also deliuered.

The French king, after the yeelding of Tartas, remoued to saint Seuerine, which towne he tooke by force, slue thrée hundred persons, and tooke sir Thomas Rampston prisoner. After this, he came to the citie of Arques, tooke a bulworke by force, and had the towne yéelded to him by composition. The capteine, which was the lord of Montferrant, departed with all the English crue to Burdeaux, where he found the earle of Longuile, the Capdau de Beufe, and sir Thomas Rampston, which was a little before deliuered. After this, the fortresses of the Rioll and Mermandie were also yéelded to the French king: who notwithstanding at length was constreined for lacke of vittels (which were cut off by the Englishmen that laie abroad in diuerse fortresses for the purpose) to breake vp his armie, & to retire into France. And then after his departure, the Englishmen recouered againe the citie of Arques, & the other townes by the French king gained, and tooke prisoner his lieutenant called Reginald Guilliam the Burgognion, and manie other gentlemen, and all the meane souldiers were either slaine or hanged.

While the French king was in Guien, the lord Talbot tooke the towne of Couchet, and after marched toward Galliardon, which was besieged by the bastard of Orleance, otherwise called the earle of Dunois: which earle hearing of the lord Talbots approch, raised his siege, and saued himselfe. The Frenchmen a little before this season, had taken the towne of Eureux by treason of a fisher. Sir Francis the Arragonois hearing of that chance, apparelled six strong fellowes, like men of the countrie, with sacks and baskets, as cariers of corne and vittels, and sent them to the castell of Cornill, in the which diuerse Englishmen were kept as prisoners, and he with an ambush of Englishmen laie in a vallie nigh to the fortresse.

The six counterfet husbandmen entered the castell vnsuspected, and streight came to the chamber of the capteine, & laieng hauds on him, gaue knowledge to them that laie in ambush to come to their aid. The which suddenlie made foorth, and entered the castell, slue and tooke all the Frenchmen, and set the Englishmen at libertie: which thing doone, they set fire in the castell, and departed to Rone with their bootie and prisoners. This exploit they had not atchiued peraduenture by force (as happilie they mistrusted) and therefore by subtiltie and deceit sought to accomplish it, which meanes to vse in warre is tollerable, so the same warre be lawfull; though both fraud & bloudshed otherwise be forbidden euen by the instinct of nature to be put in practise and vse; and that dooth the poet insinuat in a proper sententious verse, saieng:

Fraus absit, vacuas cædis habete manus.

But now to speake somewhat of the dooings in England in the meane time. Whilest the men of war were thus occupied in martiall feates, and dailie skirmishes, within the realme of France: ye shall vnderstand, that after the cardinall of Winchester. and the duke of Glocester, were (as it séemed) reconciled either to other, yet the cardinall, and the archbishop of Yorke ceassed not to doo manie things without the consent of the king or of the duke, being (during the minoritie of the king) gouernor and protector of the realme, whereas the duke (as good cause he had) greatlie offended, therevpon in writing declared to the king, wherein the cardinall and the archbishop had offended both his maiestie, and the lawes of the realme. This complaint of the duke of Glocester was conteined in foure and twentie articles, which chieflie rested, in that the cardinall had from time to time, through his ambitious desire to surmount all others in high degrées of honor and dignitie, sought to inrich himselfe, to the great and notorious hinderance of the king, as in defrauding him not onelie of his treasure, but also in dooing and practising things greatlie preiudiciall to his affaires in France, and

namelie

Margin notes:

The change in warre.

The lord Talbot.

The earle of Dunois. An excellent finesse in warre.

A new breach betwéene the duke of Glocester, and the bishop of Winchester.

namelie by setting at libertie the king of Scots, vpon so easie conditions, as the kings maiestie greatlie lost thereby as in particularities thus followeth.

A complaint made to king Henrie the sixt, by the duke of Glocester, vpon the cardinall of Winchester.

1 THESE be in part, the points and articles, which I Humfrie duke of Glocester, for *Ex Ed. Hall.* my truth & acquitall, said late, I would giue in writing (my right redoubted lord) vnto 143, 144, 145, your highnesse, aduertising your excellencie, of such things in part, as haue béene 146. doone in your tender age, in derogation of your noble estate, and hurt of both your realmes, and yet be doone and vsed dailie.

2 First, the cardinall then being bishop of Winchester, tooke vpon him the state of cardinall, which was naied and denaied him, by the king of most noble memorie, my lord your father (whome God assoile) saieng that he had as leefe set his crowne beside him, as sée him weare a cardinals hat, he being a cardinall. For he knew full well, the pride and ambition that was in his person, then being but a bishop, should haue so greatlie extolled him into more intollerable pride, when that he were a cardinall: and also he thought it against his fréedome, of the chéefe church of this realme, which, that he worshipped, as dulie as euer did prince, that blessed be his soule. And howbeit, that my said lord your father (whome God assoile) would haue agreed him to haue had certeine clearks of this land cardinals, and to haue no bishoprikes in England; yet his intent was neuer to doo so great derogation to the church of Canturburie, to make them that were his suffragans, to sit aboue their ordinarie and metropolitan. But the cause was that in generall, and in all matters which might concerne the weale of him, and of his realme, he should haue proctors of his nation, as other kings Christen had, in the court of Rome, and not to abide in this land, nor to be in anie part of his councels, as béene all the spirituall and temporall, at parlements and other great councels, when you list to call them. And therefore, though it please you to doo him that worshop, to set him in your priuie councell after your pleasure:, yet in your parlement, where euerie lord both spirituall and temporall, hath his place, he ought to occupie but his place as a bishop.

3 Item, the said bishop, now being cardinall, was assoiled of his bishoprike of Winchester, wherevpon he sued vnto our holie father, to haue a bull declaratorie, notwithstanding he was assumpt to the state of cardinall, that the sée was not void, where in déed it stood void by a certeine time, yer the said bull were granted; and so he was exempt from his ordinarie, by the taking on him the state of Cardinall, and the church bishoprike of Winchester, so standing void, he tooke againe of the pope (you not learned thereof ne knowing whereby he was fallen into the case of prouision) so that all his good was lawfullie & cléerlie forfeited to you my right doubted lord, with more; as the statute declareth plainelie for your aduantage.

4 Item, it is not vnknowen to you (doubted lord) how thorough your lands it is noised, that the said cardinall and the archbishop of Yorke had and haue the gouernance of you, and all your land, the which none of your true liege men ought to vsurpe nor take vpon them. And haue also estranged me your sole vncle, my coosine of Yorke, my coosine of Huntington, and manie other lords of your kin, to haue anie knowledge of anie great matter, that might touch your high estate, or either of your realmes. And of lords spirituall, of right, the archbishop of Canturburie should be your chéefe councellor, the which is also estranged and set aside. And so be manie other right sad lords, and well aduised, as well spirituall as temporall, to the great hurt of you my right doubted lord, and of your realmes, like as the experience and workes shewen cléerelie and euidentlie, more harme it is.

5 Item,

5 Item, in the tender age of you, my right doubted lord, for the necessitie of an armie, the said cardinall lent you foure thousand pounds vpon certeine iewels, prised at two and twentie thousand markes, with a letter of sale, that and they were not quited at a certeine daie, you should léese them. The said cardinall séeing your monie readie to haue quited your iewels, caused your treasuror of England, at that daie being, to paie the same monie, in part of an other armie, in defrauding you my right doubted lord of your said iewels, kéeping them yet all awaie to his owne vse, to your right great losse, and his singular profit and auaile.

6 Item, the said cardinall, then being bishop of Winchester, and chancellour of England, deliuered the king of Scots, vpon certeine appointments (as maie be shewed) presumptuouslie, and of his owne authoritie, contrarie to the act of parlement. I haue heard notable men of law say, that they neuer heard the like thing doone among them: which was too great a defamation to your highnesse, and also to wed his neece to the said king, whom that my lord of notable memorie, your father, whome God assoile, would neuer haue so deliuered. And there as he should haue paid for his costs fortie thousand pounds, the said cardinall, chancellour of England, caused you to pardon him thereof ten thousand marks, whereof the greater summe he paied you, right a little, what, I report me to your highnesse.

7 Item, where the said cardinall lent you, my redoubted lord, great and notable summes, he hath had and his assignes, the rule and profit of the port of Hampton, where the customers béene his seruants, where (by likelihood and as it is to be suppos-ed) standing the chéefe merchant of the wools of your land, that you be greatlie defrauded, and vnder that rule, what wools and other merchandizes haue béene ship-ped, and maie be from time to time, hard is to estéeme, to the great hurt and pre-iudice of you my right doubted lord, and of all your people.

8 Item, howbeit that the said cardinall hath diuerse times lent you great summes of monie, since the time of your reigne, yet his loane hath béene so deferred and delaied, that for the most part, the conuenable season of the imploieng of the good lent was passed. So that litle fruit or none came thereof, as by experience both your realmes haue sufficientlie in knowledge.

9 Item, where there was iewels and plate prised at eleuen thousand pounds in weight, of the said cardinall, forfeited to you my right redoubted lord, he gat him a restorement thereof for a loane of a little parcell of the same: and so defrauded you wholie of them, to your great hurt, and his auaile, the which good might greatlie haue eased your highnesse, in sparing as much of the poore commons..

10 Item, the cardinall being feoft of my said lord your father (whome God assoile) against his intent, gaue Elizabeth Beauchampe, three hundred markes liuelihood, where that his will was, that and she were wedded within a yeare, then to haue it, or else not, where in déed it was two or thrée years after, to your great hurt, and diminishing of your inheritance.

11 Item, notwithstanding that the said cardinall hath no maner of authoritie nor interest in the crowne, nor none maie haue by anie possibilitie; yet he presumeth and taketh vpon him in partie, your estate roiall, in calling before him, into great abusion of all your land, and derogation of your highnesse, which hath not béene séene nor vsed in no daies heretofore, in greater estate than he is, without your expresse ordi-nance and commandement.

12 Item, the said cardinall, nothing considering the necessitie of you my right doubted lord, hath sued a pardon of dismes, that he should paie for the church of Winchester, for terme of his life, giuing thereby occasion to all other lords spiri-tuall, to draw their good will for anie necessitie, to grant anie disme: and so to laie all the charge vpon the temporaltie, and the poore people.

13 Item, by the gouernance and labour of the said cardinall, and archbishop of
Yorke,

Yorke, there hath béene lost and dispended much notable and great good, by diuerse ambassadors sent out of this realme. First to Arras, for a feigned colourable peace, whereas by likelinesse it was thought and supposed, that it should neuer turne to the effectuall auaile of you my right doubted lord, nor to your said realmes: but vnder colour thereof, was made the peace of your aduersarie, and the duke of Burgognie. For else your partie aduerse, & the said duke, might not well haue found meanes nor waies to haue communed togither, nor to haue concluded with other their confederations and conspirations made and wrought there, then, at that time, against your highnesse, whereby you might haue (right doubted lord) the greater partie of your obeisance, as well in your realme of France, as in your duchie of Normandie, and much other thing gone greatlie, as through the said colourable treatie, & otherwise, since the death of my brother of Bedford (whome God assoile.)

14 Item, now of late was sent an other ambassador to Calis, by the labour and counsell of the said cardinall, and archbishop of Yorke, the cause why of the beginning, is to me your sole vncle, and other lords of your kin and councell vnknowen, to your great charge, and against the publike good of your realme; as it openlie appeareth. The which good if it be imploied for the defense of your lands, the merchandizes of the same might haue had other course, and your said lands not to haue stand in so great mischéefe as they doo.

15 Item, after that, to your great charge, and hurt of both your realmes, the said cardinall & archbishop of Yorke went to your said towne of Calis, and diuerse lords of your kin, and of your councell in their fellowship, and there, as there was naturall warre betwéene the duke of Orleance, and the duke of Burgognie, for murther of their fathers, a capitall enimitie like to haue indured for euer: the said cardinall and archbishop of Yorke licenced and suffered the said duke of Orleance, to intreat and common apart with the councell of your said aduersaries, as well as with the duchies of Burgognie: by which meane the peace and aliance was made betwéene the two dukes, to the greatest fortifieng of your said capitall aduersaries that could be thought, and consequentlie (my deere redoubted lord) to your greatest charge, and hurt to both your realmes. Vnder colour of which treatie, your said aduersaries in meane time wan your citie of Meaux, and the countrie thereabout, and manie diuerse roades made into your duchie of Normandie, to the great noisance and destruction of your people, as it sheweth openlie.

16 Item, the said archbishop of Yorke, sent with other into this your realme from the said cardinall, after communication had with your aduerse partie, at your said towne of Calis, made at his comming into your notable presence at Windesor, all the suasions and colour, all motions in the most apparant wi.. that he could, to induce your highnesse to your agréement, to the desires of your capitall aduersaries, as I saw there in your noble presence of his writing, at which time (as I vnderstood) it was his singular opinion, that is to saie: that you should leaue your right, your title, and your honour of your crowne, and nomination of you king of France, during certeine yeares, & that you should vtterlie absteine you and be content onelie in writing, with Rex Angliæ, &c: to the great note of infamie that euer fell to you or anie of your noble progenitours, since the taking of them first, the said title and right of your realme and crowne of France. To which matter in your presence there, after that it had liked your said highnesse, to aske mine aduise therevpon, with other of your blood and councell; I answerd and said, that I would neuer agrée me thereto to die therfore, and of the same disposition I am yet, and will be while I liue in conseruation of your honour, and of your oth made vnto your said crowne, in time of your coronation there.

17 Item, the said cardinall and archbishop of Yorke, haue so laboured vnto your highnesse, that you should intend to a new daie of conuention, in March or Aprill

next comming, where it is noised to be more against your worship than with it. And where it was euident to all the world, that the rupture and breaking of the said peace, should haue fallen heretofore, of your aduerse partie; because of the great vntruths. Now by that meanes it is like peraduenture to be laid vnto the verie great slander of you my doubted lord, like to come to none other purpose nor effect, than other conuentions haue doone afore time: and so by subtilties and counsell of your said enimies, your land (they in hope and trust of the said treatie, not mightilie nor puissantlie purueied for) shall be like vnder the colour of the same treatie to be burnt vp and destroied, lost, and vtterlie turned from your obeisance.

18 Item it is said, that the deliuerance of the said duke of Orleance, is vtterlie appointed by the mediation, counsell, and stirring of the said cardinall and archbishop of Yorke; and for that cause diuerse persons béene come from your aduersaries, into this your realme, and the said duke also brought to your citie of London, where as my lord your father (whom God assoile) peising so greatlie the inconueniences; and harme that might fall, onlie by his deliuerance, concluded, ordeined, and determined in his last will, vtterlie in his wisedome, his conquest in his realme of France. And yet then it is to be doone, by as great deliberation, solemnitie and suertie, as may be deuised or thought. And séeing now the disposition of your realme of France, the puissance and might of your enimies, and what aid they haue gotten against you there, aswell vnder the colour of the said treatie, as otherwise; what may or ought to be thought or said, for that laboring the said duke (all things considered) by such particular persons, the lords of your bloud not called therevnto, I report me vnto your noble grace and excellencie, and vnto the said wise true men of this your realme.

19 Item, where that euerie true councellor, speciallie vnto anie king or prince, ought of truth and of dutie, to counsell, promote, increase, prefer, and aduance the weale and prosperitie of his lord: the said cardinall, being of your councell (my right doubted lord) hath late purchased of your highnesse, certeine great lands and liuelode: as the castell and lordship of Chirke in Wales, and other lands in this your realme; vnto which I was called suddenlie, and so in eschewing the breaking and losse of your armies then againe, séeing none other remedie, gaue therevnto mine assent, thinking that who that euer laboured, moued or stirred the matter first vnto your lordship, counselled you neither for your worship nor profit.

20 More, the said cardinall hath you bound apart, to make him a sure estate of all the said lands, by Easter next comming, as could be deuised by anie learned counsell; or else that suertie not made, the said cardinall to haue and reioy to him, and his heirs for euermore, the lands of the duchie of Lancaster, in Norffolke, to the value of seuen or eight hundred marks by yeare. Which thing séemeth right strange and vnseene, and vnhard waies of anie liege man, to séeke vpon his souereigne lord, both in his inheritance and in his iewels and goods. For it is thought, but if right and extreame necessitie caused it, there should, nor ought no such things to be doone: from which necessitie God (for his mercie) euer preserue your noble person. Wherfore my redoubted lord, seeing that ye should be so counselled, or stirred to leaue your crowne and inheritance in England; and also by fraud and subtill meanes, as is afore rehearsed, so to lose your iewels: in my truth and in mine acquitall (as me séemeth) I may not nor ought not counsell so great an hurt to you and to all your land.

21 Item, it is not vnknowen to you my right doubted lord, how oftentimes I haue offered my seruice, to and for the defense of your realme of France, and duchie of Normandie, where I haue béene put therefro by the labour of the said cardinall, in preferring other after his singular affection. Which hath caused a great part of the said duchie of Normandie, aswell as of your realme of France to be lost, as it is well knowen. And what good (my right doubted lord) was lost on that armie that

was

last sent thither, which the earle of Mortaigne, your councell of France, hath well & cleerelie declared to your highnesse here before?

22 Item, my right doubted lord, it is not vnknowen, that it had not beene possible to the said cardinall, to haue come to his great riches, but by such meanes, for of his church it might not rise, and inheritance he had none. Wherfore my right doubted lord, sith there is great good behouefull at this time, for the weale and safegard of your realmes, the pouertie, necessitie, & indigence of your liege people; in highnesse vnderstand, like it vnto your noble grace, to consider the said lucre of the said cardinall, and the great deceipts that you be receiued in by the labour of him & of the archbishop, aswell in this your realme as in your realme of France and duchie of Normandie, where neither office, liuelode, nor capteine may be had, without too great good giuen vnto him, wherby a great part of all the losse that is lost, they haue béene the causers of; for who that would giue most, his was the price, not considering the merits, seruice, nor sufficiance of persons. Furthermore, it is greatlie to be considered, how, when the said cardinall had forfeited all his goods, bicause of prouision, as the statute therevpon more plainelie declareth; by hauing the rule of you my right doubted lord, purchased himselfe in great defraudation of your highnesse, a charter of pardon, the which good and it had be well gouerned, might manie yeares haue susteined your warres, without anie tallage of your poore people.

23 Item, my redoubted lord, whereas I write much thing for the weale of you and of your realms, peraduenture some will saie and vnderstand, that I would or haue written by waie of accusement of all your councell, which God knoweth, I doo not: for your highnesse may well sée, that I name them that be causers of the said inordinate rule. Wherfore, considering that the said cardinall and archbishop of Yorke beene they, that pretend the gouernance of you, and of your realmes and lordships: please it vnto your highnesse, of your right wisenesse to estrange them of your councell, to that intent, that men may be at their freedome, to say what they thinke of truth.

24 For truth, I dare speake of my truth, the poore dare not doo so. And if the cardinall and the archbishop of Yorke, may afterward declare themselues, of that is, and shalbe said of them; you my right doubted lord may then restore them againe to your councell, at your noble pleasure.

When the king had heard the accusations thus laid by the duke of Glocester against the cardinall, he committed the examination thereof to his councell, whereof the more part were spirituall persons; so that what for feare, and what for fauor, the matter was winked at, and nothing said to it : onelie faire countenance was made to the duke, as though no malice had béene conceiued against him. But venem will breake out, & inward grudge will soone appeare, which was this yeare to all men apparant: for diuers secret attempts were aduanced forward this season against this noble man Humfreie duke of Glocester a far off, which in conclusion came so néere, that they beereft him both of life and land; as shall hereafter more plainelie appéere.

For first this yeare, dame Eleanor Cobham, wife to the said duke, was accused of treason; for that she by sorcerie and inchantment intended to destroie the king, to the intent to aduance hir husband vnto the crowne. Vpon this, she was examined in saint Stephans chappell before the bishop of Canturburie, and there by examination conuict, and iudged to doo open penance in thrée open places within the citie of London. [Polychronicon saith she was inioined to go through Cheapside with a *Abr. Fl. ex* taper in hir hand] and after that adiudged to perpetuall imprisonment in the Ile of *Polychron.* Man, vnder the kéeping of sir Iohn Stanlie knight. At the same season were arrested, arreigned, and adiudged giltie, as aiders to the duchesse, Thomas Southwell priest, and canon of S. Stephans at Westminster, Iohn Hun priest, Roger Bolingbrooke *Alias* Iohn Hum.

a cunning

a cunning necromancer (as it was said) and Margerie Iordeine, surnamed the witch of Eie.

The matter laid against them, was, for that they (at the request of the said duchesse) had deuised an image of wax representing the king, which by their sorcerie by little and little consumed, intending thereby in conclusion to waste and destroie the kings person. Margerie Iordeine was burnt in Smithfield, and Roger Bolingbrooke was drawne to Tiborne, and hanged and quartered; taking vpon his death that there was neuer anie such thing by them imagined. Iohn Hun had his pardon, and Southwell died in the Tower the night before his execution: [for (saith Polychr.) he did prophesie of himselfe, that he should die in his bed, and not by iustice.] The duke of Glocester bare all these things patientlie, and said little. Edward sonne to the duke of Yorke was borne this yeare the nine and twentith of Aprill at Rone, his father being the kings lieutenant in Normandie. ¶ In this yeare was a great fraie in Fléetstréet in the night time, betwéene gentlemen of courts and inhabitants of London; insomuch that much bloud was spilt, diuerse slaine outright, and some mortallie wounded; besides great harme otherwise doone and suffered.]

¶ Vpon the daie of the translation of saint Edward, or the twelfth of October, vpon which daie the maior and his brethren for the yeare following, and daie when the commoners of the citie, after their ancient custome had chosen two aldermen, such as before had béene shiriffes of London and of Middlesex, namelie Robert Clopton draper, and Rafe Holland tailor, and them presented by name vnto the maior and his brethren, then sitting in the vtter chamber where the maiors courts be kept, to the intent that the said maior and his brethren might choose one of the said two, such as they thought most necessarie and worshipfull for the roome; the said maior and his brethren choosing Robert Clopton, brought him after downe vpon his right hand towards the hall. Whereof when certeine tailors there present were aware, and saw that Rafe Holland was not chosen, anon they cried; Nay, nay: not this, but Rafe Holland. Wherewith the old maior being astonished, stood still vpon the staire, and commanded them to keepe silence, and so held on his waie to the east end of the hall, where he sat him downe, and his brethren about him. In the meane time, the said tailors continued their crie, and incensed others of base trades of the citie (as simple persons) to take their part, and to crie as fast as they, not proffering to cease their misrule for all that the maior could saie, no nor yet when the maiors sergeant at armes had cried O-yes. Herevpon the maior, to appease the rumor, sent downe the shiriffes, and commanded them to take the offendors, and send them to the goale; which precept was fulfilled, & about twelue or sixtéene of the principall committed to Newgate, where some of them abode a long time imprisoned; and others that were fined set at libertie. This is reported by Polychronicon, but in somewhat a differing maner.]

The councell of England forgat not the late enterprise of the French king, atchiued in the duchie of Guien, and therefore doubting some other the like attempt, they sent thither sir William Wooduile with eight hundred men, to strengthen the frontiers, and further, set foorth a proclamation, that all men which would transport anie corne, chéese, or other vittels thither, should paie no maner of custome or tallage: which licence caused the countrie of Aquitaine to be well furnished of all things necessarie. About this season Iohn the valiant lord Talbot for his approued prowesse and wisdome, aswell in England as in France, both in peace & warre so well tried, was created earle of Shrewesburie, and with a companie of three thousand men sent againe into Normandie, for the better defense of the same.

* This yéere died Lodowike or Lewes Lischburne, bishop of Elie, being the fiue and twentith that inioied that place, who came to the same after this maner. After the death of Philip Morgan bishop of that sée, the moonks of Elie chose for their pastor Robert fitz Hugh bishop of London; but he dieng at saint Osees before his confirmation,

Abr. Fl.

King Edward the fourth borne.

Abr. Fl. A great fraie by night.

Abr. Fl. ex Fabian. 438.

Tailors maleportnesse at the election of an alderman.

1442 ——— *An.* Reg. 21.

Iohn lord Talbot created earle of Shrewesburie.

Fr. Thin. ——— 1443

confirmation, neuer possessed the honour thereof. Wherevpon the king directed his letters to the couent of Elie, to make election of Thomas Rudburne (bishop of S. Dauids in Wales) for their bishop. But they contrarie therevnto (taking it now for a custome, hauing so often vsed it before, as did well appeare) made choise of Thomas Bourchier (borne of a noble house, sonne to the countesse of Stafford, chancellor of Oxenford, and bishop of Worcester) to succéed Philip Morgan. Which Bourchier, the king (offended with the moonkes for the little regard had to his request) vtterlie refused, and would not admit him vnto that place. Wherevpon there were buls procured from Eugenius the fourth (then bishop of Rome) which were sent into England to confirme the Election of the said Bourchier.

But he wiselie fearing to fall into the dangerous statute of Premunire, durst not receiue or execute the tenor of the popes commandement. By reason whereof least the see might otherwise remaine void, (if speedie remedie were not prouided) the king did in commendam bestow the bishoprike of Elie vpon this Lodowike Lischburne archbishop of Rone, by office, Card. 4. Coronat. Cancellar. Franciæ & Normanniæ, and kinsman to the said king. Which doone, Eugenius (when he saw no other remedie) did reuoke his buls made before to Thomas Bourchier, in the yeare of Christ 1437. This Lodowike remaining bishop six yeares and so manie moneths, died in the yeare as before, the eighteenth of September, at his manor of Hatfield, whose bowels were buried in the said church: his hart was caried to Rone, and there honourablie intoomed, and his bodie was committed to the earth, in the church of Elie, betweene two marble pillors next to the altar of the relikes.]

In this yeare died in Guien the countesse of Comings, to whome the French king and also the earle of Arminacke pretended to be heire, in so much that the earle entred into all the lands of the said ladie. And bicause he knew the French king would not take the matter well, to haue a Rouland for an Oliuer; he sent solemne ambassadours to the king of England, offering him his daughter in mariage, with promise to be bound (beside great summes of monie, which he would giue with hir) to deliuer into the king of Englands hands, all such castels and townes, as he or his ancestors deteined from him within anie part of the duchie of Aquitaine, either by conquest of his progenitors, or by gift and deliuerie of anie French king: and further to aid the same king with monie for the recouerie of other cities within the same duchie, from the French king; or from anie other person that against king Henrie vniustlie kept, and wrongfullie withholden them.

This offer séemed so profitable and also honorable to king Henrie and the realme, that the ambassadours were well heard, honorablie receiued, and with rewards sent home into their countrie. After whome were sent for the conclusion of the marriage into Guien, sir Edward Hull, sir Robert Ros, and Iohn Gralton deane of S. Seuerines, the which (as all the chronographers agrée) both concluded the mariage, and by proxie affied the yoong ladie. The French king not a little offended herewith, sent his eldest sonne Lewes the Dolphin of Vienne into Rouergue with a puissant armie, which tooke the earle and his yoongest sonne, with both his daughters, and by force obteined the countries of Arminacke, Louuergne, Rouergue, and Moulessonois, beside the cities Seuerac & Cadeac, chasing the bastard of Arminacke out of his countries, and so by reason hereof, the concluded mariage was deferred, and that so long that it neuer tooke effect; as hereafter it may appeare.

The earle of Arminacks daughter affied vnto king Henrie.

The erle with his ladie, his sonne and two daughters taken.

¶ In this yeare was an act made by authoritie of the common councell of London, that vpon the sundaie no maner of thing within the franchises and liberties of the said citie should be bought or sold; neither vittels nor other thing. It was also enacted by the same common councell with full consent, and ratified by the authoritie of the law-makers, that no artificer or handicrafts man should bring his wares, commodities, or worke, vnto anie person or persons to be worne or occupied on that daie: bicause

Abr. Fl. ex Fabian 441.

A law against buieng and selling on the sundaie.

it

it was iudged a foule prophanation thereof. And peoples minds giuen to couetousnesse, make no exception of times or places in a case of aduantage and gaine. In consideration whereof, and for the suppressing of this abuse, this law was ordeined and made:
the force whereof did principallie extend to tailors and shoomakers (who as on that daie
bring home their garments and shoos to the parties for whome they are made) and
likewise to all other occupations and trades. But this ordinance (saith mine author)
was too good for so bad an age, and therefore died within a short time after the
magistrate had giuen it life.

Abr. Fl. er
Fabian. 441.
& Polychr.
Paules stéeple
burnt.

¶ On Candlemasse éeue this yeere by lightning in a tempest that fell with claps of
thunder at afternoone, Paules steeple was set on fier in the middest of the speare or
shaft in the verie timber worke; which was quenched by the painfulnesse of diuerse
persons, and specialie by the diligent labour of a préest of Bow in Cheape. Howbeit
the same was thought vnpossible to be quenched, but that the grace of God was chéefe
worker in the same. This stéeple hath diuerse times beene ouerthrowne and defaced,
partlie by winds, and partlie by lightning, as may be obserued in the reading of this
volume: yea when the same hath béene repared by the choisest workemen, and of
the substantiallest stuffe, aud all meanes (that stood with the déepe deuise of man)
vsed to make it so sure that it might continue, as a monument of perpetuitie for
posteritie to woonder at and admire. But to returne to the historie

An. Reg. 22.

The diet at
Tours for a
peace to be had
betwéene Eng-
land and France.

Whilest England was vnquieted (as you haue heard) and France by spoile, slaughter,
and burning sore defaced (a mischéefe in all places much lamented) therefore to a grée
the two puissant kings, all the princes of christendome trauelled so effectuouslie by
their oratours and ambassadours, that a diet was appointed to be kept at the citie of
Tours in Touraine; where for the king of England appeared William de la Poole earle
of Suffolke, doctor Adam Molins kéeper of the kings priuie seale, also sir Robert Ros,
and diuers other. And for the French king were appointed Charles duke of Orleance,
Lewes de Bourbon earle of Vandosme, great maister of the French kings houshold,
Piers de Bresse steward of Poictou, and Bertram Beauuan lord of Presignie.

There were also sent thither ambassadours from the empire, from Spaine, from Denmarke, & from Hungarie; to be mediatours betwixt the two princes. The assemblie
was great, but the cost was much greater, insomuch that euerie part for the honour of
their prince and praise of their countrie, set foorth themselues, as well in fare as apparell, to the vttermost. Manie meetings were had, and manie things mooued for a
finall peace: but in conclusion, by reason of manie doubts which rose on both parties,
no full concord could be agreed vpon; but in hope to come to a peace, a certeine truce,
A truce for 18
moneths.
as well by sea as by land, was concluded by the commissioners for eighteene moneths,
which afterward againe was prolonged to the yeare of our Lord 1449.

1444

In treating of this truce, the earle of Suffolke aduenturing somewhat vpon his commission, without the assent of his associats, imagined, that the next waie to come to
a perfect peace, was to contriue a mariage betwéene the French kings kinsewoman,
the ladie Margaret daughter to Reiner duke of Aniou, and his souereigne lord king
Henrie. This Reiner duke of Aniou named himselfe king of Sicill, Naples, and Ierusalem, hauing onlie the name and stile of those realmes; without anie penie, profit,
or foot of possession. This mariage was made strange to the earle at the first, and
one thing seemed to be a great hinderance to it; which was, bicause the king of England occupied a great part of the duchie of Aniou, and the whole countie of Maine,
apperteining (as was alledged) to king Reiner.

The earle of Suffolke (I cannot saie either corrupted with bribes, or too much affectioned to this vnprofitable mariage, condescended, that the duchie of Aniou and the
countie of Maine should be deliuered to the king, the brides father demanding for hir mariage neither penie nor farthing: as who would saie, that this new affinitie passed all
riches, and excelled both gold and pretious stones. And to the intent that of this truce
might

might insue a finall concord, a daie of enteruiew was appointed betwéene the two kings in a place conuenient betwéene Chartres and Rone. When these things were concluded, the earle of Suffolke with his companie returned into England, where he forgat not to declare what an honourable truce he had taken, out of the which there was a great hope that a finall peace might grow the sooner for that honorable mariage, which he had concluded, omitting nóthing that might extoll and set foorth the personage of the ladie, or the nobilitie of hir kinred.

But although this mariage pleased the king and diuerse of his councell, yet Humfrie duke of Glocester protector of the realme was much ágainst it, alledging that it should be both contrarie to the lawes of God, and dishonorable to the prince, if he should breake that promise and contract of mariage, made by ambassadours sufficientlie thereto instructed, with the daughter of the earle of Arminacke, vpon conditions both to him and his realme, as much profitable as honorable. But the dukes words could not be heard, for the earles dooings were onelie liked and allowed. So that for performance of the conclusions, the French king sent the earle of Vandosme, great maister of his house, and the archbishop of Reimes first peere of France, and diuerse other into England, where they were honorablie receiued; and after that the instruments were once sealed and deliuered on both parts, the said ambassadours returned againe into their countries with great gifts and rewards. *The protector misliked this second motion of the kings mariage.*

When these things were doone, the king both for honour of his realme, and to assure to himselfe mo fréends, created Iohn Holland earle of Huntington duke of Excester as his father was: Humfrie earle of Stafford was made duke of Buckingham: and Henrie earle of Warwike was elected to the title of duke of Warwike, to whome the king also gaue the castell of Bristowe, with the Ile of Iernesenie, and Garnescie. Also the earle of Suffolke was made marquesse of Suffolke, which marquesse with his wife and manie honorable personages of men and women richlie adorned both with apparell & iewels, hauing with them manie costlie chariots and gorgeous horslitters, sailed into France for the conueiance of the nominated queene into the realme of England. For king Reiner hir father, for all his long stile had too short a pursse to send his daughter honorablie to the king hir spouse. *Creations of estates.*

This noble companie came to the citie of Tours in Touraine, where they were honorablie receiued both of the French king and of the king of Sicill. The marquesse of Suffolke as procurator to king Henrie, espoused the said ladie in the church of saint Martins. At the which mariage were present the father and mother of the bride; the French king himselfe, which was vncle to the husband; and the French quéene also, which was aunt to the wife. There were also the dukes of Orleance, of Calabre, of Alanson, and of Britaine, seauen earls, twelue barons, twentie bishops, beside knights and gentlemen. When the feast, triumph, bankets and iusts were ended, the ladie was deliuered to the marquesse, who in great estate conueied hir through Normandie vnto Diepe, and so transported hir into England, where she landed at Portesmouth in the moneth of Aprill. This ladie excelled all other, aa well in beautie and fauour, as in wit and policie, and was of stomach and courage more like to a man than a woman.

Shortlie after hir arriuall, she was conueied to the towne of Southwike in Hamshire, where she with all nuptiall ceremonies was coupled in matrimonie to king Henrie the sixt of that name. ¶ On the eightéenth of Maie she came to London, all the lords of England in most sumptuous sort méeting and receiuing hir vpon the waie, and speciallie the duke of Glocester with such honour as stood with the dignitie of his person. Now when she came to Blackheath, the maior, aldermen, and men of occupations, in blew gownes imbrodered with some deuise, expressing their art and trades whereby to be knowne, did all shew themselues, with congratulation of hir comming; from whence they attended hir to London, where with goodlie pageants and sundrie gallant *Margaret daughter to Reiner K. of Sicill & Ierusalem maried to Henrie the sixt.*
Abr. Fl. ex Polychron.

historicall

historicall shewes in diuerse places erected, she was verie magnificallie welcomed. The maner and order of which pompe in sundrie places exhibited to the high honour of the king, queene, & states, is verie amplie set foorth by Fabian, pag. 423, 424, 425, 426, 427. Vpon the thirtith of Maie next following, she was crowned queene of this realme of England at Westminster, with all the solemnitie thereto apperteining.]

This mariage séemed to manie both infortunate and vnprofitable to the realme of England, and that for manie causes. First, the king had not one penie with hir; and for the fetching of hir, the marquesse of Suffolke demanded a whole fifteenth in open parlement. And also there was deliuered for hir the duchie of Aniou, the citie of Mans, and the whole countie of Maine, which countries were the verie staies and backestands to the duchie of Normandie. And furthermore, the earle of Arminacke tooke such displeasure with the king of England for this mariage, that he became vtter enimie to the crowne of England, and was the cheefe cause that the Englishmen were expelled out of the whole duchie of Aquitaine.

But most of all it should séeme, that God was displeased with this mariage: for after the confirmation thereof, the kings freends fell from him, both in England and in France, the lords of his realme fell at diuision, and the commons rebelled in such sort, that finallie after manie fields foughten, and manie thousands of men slaine, the king at length was deposed, and his sonne killed, and this quéene sent home againe, with as much miserie and sorrow as she was receiued with pompe and triumph: such is the instabilitie of worldlie felicitie, and so waucring is false flattering fortune. Which mutation and change of the better for the worse could not but nettle and sting hir with pensiuenesse, yea and anie other person whatsoeuer, that hauing béene in good estate, falleth into the contrarie: whereto the saieng of the poet giueth credit, in these few words following;

Ouid. 2. de art.

Quem res plus nimio delectauere secundæ,
Mutatæ quatiunt.

This yeare, after the deceasse of Henrie Chicheleie archbishop of Canturburie, succeeded Iohn Stafford in that sée, being translated from Bath and Wels. He was the thréescore and one archbishop, as Polydor noteth. During the time of the truce, Richard duke of Yorke and diuerse other capteins repaired into England, both to visit their wiues, children, and fréends, and also to consult what should be doone, if the truce ended. For the which cause a parlement was called, in the which it was especiallie concluded, that by good foresight Normandie might be so furnished for defense before the end of the truce, that the French king should take no aduantage through want of timelie prouision: for it was knowne, that if a peace were not concluded, the French king did prepare to imploie his whole puissance to make open warre. Héerevpon monie was granted, an armie leuied, and the duke of Summerset appointed to be regent of Normandie, and the duke of Yorke thereof discharged.

I haue séene in a register booke belonging sometime to the abbeie of saint Albons that the duke of Yorke was established regent of France, after the deceasse of the duke of Bedford, to continue in that office for the tearme of fiue yeares; which being expired, he returned home, and was ioifullie receiued of the king with thanks for his good seruice, as he had full well deserued in time of that his gouernement: and further, that now when a new regent was to be chosen and sent ouer, to abide vpon safegard of the countries beyond the seas as yet subiect to the English dominion, the said duke of Yorke was eftsoones (as a man most méet to supplie that roome) appointed to go ouer againe, as regent of France with all his former allowances.

But the duke of Summerset still maligning the duke of Yorkes aduancement, as he had sought to hinder his dispatch at the first when he was sent ouer to be regent, as before yée haue heard: he likewise now wrought so, that the king reuoked his grant made

An ominous mariage.

An. Reg. 24.

1446

The duke of Summerset made regent of Normãdie, and the duke of Yorke discharged.

The duke of Yorke appointed to the charge againe.

made to the duke of Yorke for enioieng of that office the terme of other fiue yéeres, and with helpe of William marquesse of Suffolke obteined that grant for himselfe. The appointmēt disappointed, and pointed to the marquesse of Suffolke. Which malicious deling the duke of Yorke might so euill beare, that in the end the heate of displeasure burst out into such a flame, as consumed at length not onelie both those two noble personages, but also manie thousands of others, though in diuers times and seasons, as in places hereafter (as occasion serueth) it shall more euidentlie appeare. But now to returne to the parlement.

The marques of Suffolke, supposing all men had as well liked his dooings (during The marques of Suffolks request. the time of his legation in France) as himselfe, the second daie of Iune in the first session of this parlement in the higher house openlie, eloquentlie, and boldlie declared his paine, trauell, and diligence susteined in his said legation, as well for the taking and concluding an abstinence of warre, as in the making of the mariage ; remembring them also that the said truce expired the first of Aprill next, except a finall peace, or a further truce were concluded in the meane season : and therefore he aduised them to prouide and foresée things necessarie for the warre (as though no concord should succeed) least happilie the Frenchmen perceiuing them vnprouided, would take their aduantage, and agrée neither to peace nor amitie; saieng vnto them further, that sith he had admonished the king and them according to his dutie, if anie thing happened otherwise than well, he was thereof innocent and guiltlesse and had acquited himselfe like a true and louing subiect, and a faithfull councellour, práieng the lords to haue it in remembrance.

Likewise on the morow after, he descended into the common house, accompanied with certeine lords, and there declared the same matter to the knights, citizens, and burgesses, praieng the commons for his discharge, that as well all his dooings and procéedings in the kings affaires beyond the sea, as also his aduertisement and counsell opened to the lords and commons now togither assembled, might be by the king and them inacted and inrolled in the records of the parlement. Wherevpon the next daie after, the speaker William Burghleie, and the companie of the lower house, repaired vnto the kings presence, sitting amongst the lords of the vpper house, & there humblie required that the request of the marquesse might be granted. And so likewise the lords made the like petition kneeling on their knées, insomuch that the king condescended to their desires : and so the labours, demeanours, diligences, and declarations of the said marquesse, togither with the desires not onelie of the lords, but also of the commons, as well for the honour of him and his posteritie, as for his acquitall and discharge, were inacted and inrolled in the records of the parlement.

By the quéenes meanes shortlie after also was the said marquesse aduanced so in The marques of Suffolke, chéefest in fauour and authoritie with the king and quéene. authoritie, that he ruled the king at his pleasure, and to his high preferment obteined the wardships both of the bodie and lands of the countesse of Warwike, and of the ladie Margaret sole heire to Iohn duke of Summerset, which ladie was afterward moother to king Henrie the seauenth : and besides that, caused the king to create Iohn de Fois, sonne vnto Gaston de Fois, earle of Longuile, and the Capdau de Beufe earle of Kendall, which Iohn had married his néece, and by his procurement the king elected to the order of the garter the said Gaston, and Iohn his sonne, giuing to the sonne towards the maintenance of his degrée, lands and castels, amounting to the summe of one thousand pounds, which lands, name, and stile the issue and line of the said earle of Kendall at this daie haue and inioy.

These things being thus in dooing, the French king, seeing that the towne of Mans was not deliuered according to the appointment taken by force of the marriage, raised an armie for to recouer the same. Whereof the king of England being aduertised (least the breach of the truce should come by him) caused the towne to be deliuered without anie force. This yeare was a great commotion in Norwich against A commotion in Norwich. the prior of the place. At length the citizens opened the gates to the duke of of Norffolke, whō came thither to appease the matter, though at the first they would not suffer him to enter. The chéefe offendors were (according to their demerits) gréeuouslie punished and executed, and the maior was discharged of his office, and sir Iohn Clifton was made gouernour there, vntil the king had restored the citizens to their ancient liberties. This commotion was begun for certeine new exactions which the prior claimed and tooke of the citizens, contrarie to their ancient fréedome. But herein a wrong taken for getting of right was worthilie corrected.

¶ In the foure and twentith yeare of this kings reigne, the prior of Kilmaine appeached the earle of Ormond of treason. For triall whereof the place of combat was assigned in Smithfield, & the barriers for the same there readie pitcht. Howbeit, in the meane time a doctor of diuinitie, named maister Gilbert Worthington, parson of saint Andrews in Holborne, and other honest men, made such sute with diligent labour and paines-taking to the kings councell, that when the daie of combat approched, the quarell was taken into the kings hands, and there ended. ¶ In the same yeare also, a certeine armourer was appeached of treason by a seruant of his owne. For proofe whereof a daie was giuen them to fight in Smithfield, insomuch that in conflict the said armourer was ouercome and slaine; but yet by misgouerning of himselfe. For on the morow, when he should come to the field fresh and fasting, his neighbours came to him, and gaue him wine and strong drinke in such excessiue sort, that he was therewith distempered, and réeled as he went, and so was slaine without guilt. As for the false seruant, he liued not long vnpunished; for being conuict of felonie in court of assise, he was iudged to be hanged, and so was, at Tiburne.

Whilest the warres betwéene the two nations of England & France ceassed (by occasion of the truce) the minds of men were not so quiet, but that such as were bent to malicious reuenge, sought to compasse their prepensed purpose, not against forren foes and enimies of their countrie, but against their owne countriemen, and those that had deserued verie well of the common-wealth: and this speciallie for ouermuch mildnesse in the king, who by his authoritie might haue ruled both parts, and ordered all differences betwixt them, but that in déed he was thought too soft for gouernor of a kingdome. The quéene contrariwise, a ladie of great wit, and no lesse courage, desirous of honour, and furnished with the gifts of reason, policie, and wisdome; but yet sometime (according to hir kind) when she had béene fullie bent on a matter, suddenlie like a weather cocke, mutable and turning.

This ladie disdaining that hir husband should be ruled rather than rule, could not abide that the duke of Gloucester should doo all things concerning the order of weightie affaires, least it might be said, that she had neither wit nor stomach, which would permit and suffer hir husband, being of most perfect age, like a yoong pupill to be gouerned by the direction of an other man. Although this toy entered first into hir braine thorough hir owne imagination, yet was she pricked forward to the matter both by such of hir husbands counsell, as of long time had borne malice to the duke for his plainesse vsed in declaring their vntruth (as partlie ye haue heard) and also by counsell from king Reiner hir father, aduising that she and the king should take vpon them the rule of the realme, and not to be kept vnder, as wards and mastered orphanes.

What néedeth manie words? The quéene persuaded by these meanes, first of all excluded the duke of Glocester from all rule and gouernance, not prohibiting such as she knew to be his mortall foes to inuent and imagine causes and gréefs against him and his, insomuch that by hir procurement, diuerse noblemen conspired against him. Of the which diuerse writers affirme the marquesse of Suffolke, and the duke of Buckingham to be the chéefe, not vnprocured by the cardinall of Winchester, and the archbishop of Yorke. Diuerse articles were laid against him in open councell, and

The liberties of Norwich seized into the kings hands.
Indirect meanes to reforme wrongs.

Abr. Fl. ex Fabian. 343.
Polychron.
Combats in cases of appeales touching treason.

Drunkennese the ouerthrow of right and manhood.

An. Reg. 25.

The description of the quéene.

The quéene taketh vpon hir the gouernement, and dischargeth the duke of Glocester.

and in especiallie one; That he had caused men adiudged to die, to be put to other The faint quarell piked to the duke of Glocester.
execution, than the law of the land assigned. Suerlie the duke verie well learned in
the law ciuill, detesting malefactors, and punishing offenses in seueritie of iustice,
gat him hatred of such as feared condigne reward for their wicked dooings. And
although the duke sufficientlie answered to all things against him obiected : yet because his death was determined, his wisedome and innocencie nothing auailed.

But to auoid danger of tumult that might be raised, if a prince so well beloued of
the people should be openlie executed; his enimies determined to worke their feats in
his destruction, yer he should haue anie warning. For effecting whereof, a parlement 1447.
was summoned to be kept at Berrie, whither resorted all the péeres of the realme, and A parlement at saint Edmundes-burie.
amongst them the duke of Glocester; which on the second daie of the session was
by the lord Beaumont, then high constable of England, accompanied with the duke
of Buckingham, and others arrested, apprehended, and put in ward, and all his
seruants sequestred from him, and thirtie two of the chéefe of his retinue were sent to
diuerse prisons, to the great admiration of the people. The duke the night after he The duke of Glocester suddenlie murthered.
was thus committed to prison, being the foure and twentith of Februarie, was found
dead in his bed, and his bodie shewed to the lords and commons, as though he had died
of a palsie, or of an imposteme.

But all indifferent persons (as saith Hall) might well vnderstand that he died of some *Edw. Hall.*
violent death. Some iudged him to be strangled, some affirme that an hot spit was
put in at his fundament, other write that he was smouldered betweene two featherbeds,
and some haue affirmed that he died of verie gréefe, for that he might not come openlie
to his answer. His dead corpse was conueied to saint Albons, and there buried. After
his death, none of his seruants suffered: although fiue of them, to wit, sir Roger
Chamberline knight, Middleton, Herbert, Arteise esquiers, and Richard Nedham
gentleman, were arreigned, condemned, and drawen to Tiborne, where they were
hanged, let downe quicke, and stripped to haue béene bowelled and quartered: but
the marques of Suffolke comming at that instant brought their pardons, shewed the A pardon at a pinch.
the same openlie, and so their liues were saued.

Some thinke that the name and title of Glocester hath béene vnluckie to diuerse, Dukes of Glocester vnfortunate.
which for their honours haue béene erected by creation of princes to that stile and
dignitie, as Hugh Spenser, Thomas of Woodstoke, sonne to king Edward the third,
and this duke Humfreie: which three persons by miserable death finished their daies;
and after them king Richard the third also, duke of Glocester in ciuill warre slaine.
So that this name duke of Glocester is taken for an vnhappie stile, as the prouerbe
speaketh of Seians horsse, whose rider was euer vnhorssed, & whose possessor was
euer brought to miserie. But suerlie, by the pitifull death of this noble duke and
politike gouernour, the publike wealth of the realme came to great decaie, as by
sequele here may more at large appeare.

[Oft times it hapneth that a man in quenching of smoke, burneth his fingers in the *W. P.*
fire:] so the quéene in casting how to kéepe hir husband in honor, and hir selfe in
authoritie, in making awaie of this noble man, brought that to passe, which she had
most cause to haue feared, which was the deposing of hir husband, & the decaie of
the house of Lancaster, which of likelihood had not chanced if this duke had liued:
for then durst not the duke of Yorke haue attempted to set foorth his title to the
crowne, as he afterwards did, to the great trouble of the realme, and destruction of
king Henrie, and of manie other noble men beside. This is the opinion of men, but
Gods iudgements are vnsearchable, against whose decrée and ordinance preuaileth no
humane counsell.

But to conclude of this noble duke: he was an vpright and politike gouernour,
bending all his indeuours to the aduancement of the common-wealth, verie louing to
the poore commons, and so beloued of them againe; learned, wise, full of courtesie,

void

void of pride and ambition (a vertue rare in personages of such high estate) but where it is most commendable. But sith the praise of this noble man deserueth a large discourse, and meet for such as haue cunning how to handle the same (sith the ornaments of his mind were both rare & admirable, the feats of chiualrie by him commensed and atchiued valiant and fortunate, his grauitie in counsell, and soundnesse of policie profound and singular, all which with a traine of other excellent properties linked togither, require a man of manifold gifts to aduance them according to their dignitie) I refer the readers vnto maister Foxes booke of Acts and Monuments. Onelie this I ad, that in respect of his noble indowments, and his demeanor full of decencie, which he daily vsed, it séemeth he might well haue giuen this pretty poesie,

Virtute duce non sanguine nitor.

An. Reg. 26.   In this six and twentith yeare of the reigne of this king, but in the first of the rule of the quéene, I find nothing doone worthie of rehersall within the realme of England; but that the marquesse of Suffolke, by great fauour of the king, & more

Marquesse of Suffolke made duke.   desire of the quéene, was erected to the title and dignitie of duke of Suffolke, which he a short time inioied. For Richard duke of Yorke being greatlie alied by his wife to the chiefe peeres and potentates of the realme, beside his own progenie, perceiuing the king to be no ruler, but the whole burthen of the realme to rest in direction of the quéene, & the duke of Suffolke, began secretlie to allure his friends of the nobilitie;

The duke of Yorke tempering about his title to the crowne.   and priuilie declared vnto them his title and right to the crowne, and likewise did he to certeine wise gouernours of diuerse cities and townes. Which attempt was so politikelie handled, and so secretlie kept, that prouision to his purpose was readie, before his purpose was openlie published; and his friends opened themselues, yer the contrarie part could them espie: for in conclusion all shortlie in mischiefe burst out, as ye may hereafter heare.

1448   During these dooings, Henrie Beauford bishop of Winchester, and called the rich cardinall, departed out of this world, & buried at Westminster. He was son to

The death of the bishop of Winchester & his discriptiō.   Iohn Duke of Lancaster, descended of an honorable linage, but borne in hast, more noble in blood than notable in learning, hautie in stomach, and high of countenance, rich aboue measure, but not verie liberall, disdainefull to his kin, and dreadfull to his louers, preferring monie before friendship, manie things beginning and few performing, sauing in malice and mischiefe; his insatiable couetousnesse and hope of long life made him both to forget God, his prince, and himselfe, Of the getting of his goods both by power legantine, and spirituall briberie, I will not speake; but the keeping of them, which he chiefelie gathered for ambitious purpose, was both great losse to his naturall prince and natiue countrie: for his hidden riches might haue well holpen the king, and his secret treasure might haue relieued the communaltie, when monie was scant and charges great.

W. P. Lib. 23.   [Of this catholike clerke such were the déeds, that with king and ech estate else (saith Polydor) the lighter was the losse, bicause as for his hat he was a prelate proud inough, so for a bishop was there a better soone set in his roome. One William Patin, son and heire to Richard his father, and eldest brother to Iohn that deceassed deane of Chichester, and to Richard that liued and died at Baslo in Derbishire. This William was a person by parentage borne a gentleman, for vertue and learning first consecrate bishop of Winchester, then anon after for wisedome and integritie chosen lord chancellor of England: wherein his prudence made eminent, in warilie wielding the weight of that office at those daies, which were so dangerous for all estates to liue in.

His vertuous disposition was right apparent, and it were but by this the godlie erection of that worthie worke, Magdalene colledge in Oxford, a plot right aptlie chosen out for studie at first, with strength and workemanship soone after builded
according

according, in proportion beautifull outward, and for vse verie commodious within, sorted into a faire mansion for the president, seuerall and méet for a man to that office of worship and grauitie, and also into other roomes for the fellowes, officers, and yoonger students. Not without a vertuous remembrance of the verie tenderlings, who might appeare to be toward and teachable; whereof part to be trained vp in the diuine science of musike iustlie reported in a distichon, that

Gaudiasi superûm res sit mortalibus vlla,
Integra quæ referat; musica sola refert:

the vse of it commendablie serving by sweet harmonie to praise God in church, and for delectable recreation to a gentlemanlie mind any where else: and part of these yoong ones to be taught the grammar in a faire schoole well appointed therefore, out of which as out of a nursserie of it owne, for supplement certeine to keepe full the number, these budlings at néed from time to time to be dulie deriued and drawen.

Now somewhat in casting vpon this deuout mans deuise and compasse; to consider the companie of students there, that in seuerall sciences and sundrie professions are not a few; then their assigned studies and exercises in them, their steps in rising & reward for diligence, from the lowest logician to the highest degrées of doctrine in schooles, their officers in house, their orders for gouernance in maners, in safegard of health and helpe in sicknesse: and that chiefest is, the reuenues certeine for prouision and maintenance of all, it may be a question not easie to answer: whether at first in this founders meditation vpon such a worke were a mind more magnifike, or a more amplitude of abilitie after in so absolute a forme to performe it, or else a profounder wisedome for perpetuitie into so perfect an order in all points to haue fixt it.

It was a fashion at those daies, long also afore, & since, from a learned spirituall man to take awaie the fathers surname (were it neuer so worshipfull or ancient) and giue him for it the name of the towne he was borne in: and so was Richard Notingham *Bale.* a learned frier minorite in king Edward the seconds daies called of Notingham where he was borne; Iohn Olneie a learned monke in those daies also, named of an Iland wherein he was borne nie Glocester; of Barton in Lincolnshire one William Barton in Richard the seconds reigne, for that time a famous doctor and chancellor of Oxford; Water Disse, of Disse in Suffolke a learned Carmelite frier, confessour to the duke and duchesse of Lancaster in king Henrie the fourths reigne; Richard Hampoole of a towne in Yorkshire, a zelous doctor, and after a vertuous heremit in king Henrie the sixts daies.

And after this sort manie hundreds more that had their names so altered; as euen in like maner vnto this reuerend prelat in the prime of his towardnesse was changed his fathers surname Paten to Wainfleet of the towne where he was borne in Lincolnshire: *Willā Wain-* a matter right proueable aswell by the records of the house there extant, as by a *fléet bishop of* faire deed remaining among other his proper euidences, in the hands of the worshipful *lord chancellor* maister Thomas Fanshaw esquier, the quéenes maiesties remembrancer in the escheker *of England,* at Westminster. And as the names of Germin, German, Germi, are but for one name *deline college in* though diuerslie wrested, and all to remember Germanie, the countrie their ancestors *Oxford.* came from; and also as Iute, Iud, and Chute, are all but for the race of Iudes, one of the three first Germane nations that came in with Horsus and Hengist; and Caltrap, *An. Dom.* 448. Caltrop and Calthorp was all but for Caldthorp (that signifieth a cold towne) howeuer *Malmesburie.* it be otherwise wried: euen so Paten, Patin, Patten, or Patent, is but a mention of the old Saxon name, that trulie at first was Patan; of Pate, the sole of the foot, and thereof Patan to signifie flat footed, as among the Latines they were called Plautus or Plancus: so Cicero of a chiche or tare; Nasones, Labiones and

                                          Labieni,

Labieni, well nosed and lipt; & manie more after that sort in manie toongs else so deriued.

That right manie students skilful in the profoundest sciences and learned toongs, manie venerable clerks, who in most weightie causes with singular wisedome, successe and faith, haue serued their prince and countrie this college hath brought foorth : hereto that manie toward wits it still to haue, hath had the good hap (which happilie yet to it dooth reteine) may here with modestie a litle be touched, neither to comparison that were contentious folie, nor yet to seeke glorie that cannot be but vaine, but onlie in storie to mind, how vnto purposes vértuouslie deuised and wiselie pursued, Gods goodnesse alwaies giveth chéeuing and thrift according.]

Abr. Fl. ex F.bian. 447.

¶ In this seuen and twentith yeare of king Henries reigne, as witnesse the English chronicles, a knight of France called sir Lewes de Bueill challenged an esquier of England, named Rafe Chalons, to triall of certeine feats of warre. Herevpon (as was thought conuenient) a day was appointed them to make proofe thereof; the place also was assigned of their meeting, to wit, at a towne in France called Maunt or Maunce, where the French king at the same time was personallie present. But fortune (saith mine auther) was to Chalons so fauourable, and leaned so much to his side, that he ran the French knight through with the point of his fatall speare.

A combat vpon triall of manhood betwéene a French and an Englishman.

Hunc illi finem lingua superba dedit.

The English esquier seeing the infortunate euent of this triall to fall to the shame of the challenger, was so far from reioising at his ouerthrow, that he was touched with christian compassion, and moorned for his enimie, for whome also he kept an obsequie as if he had béene his own naturall brother, and descended of the same parents. For which merciful motions of mind inwardlie working, and outwardlie appearing, he was of the king greatlie commended, But doubtfull it is, whether the other, if he had suruiued, and got the vpper hand, would haue had the like reuerend care of the Englishmans dead bodie, as to haue vouchsafed it a solemne interrement.]

The compassion of the Englishman to his enimie.

An. Reg. 27.

Sir Francis Suriennes.

As the affaires in France now were neither well looked to, nor the gouernours there well aduised, an English capteine called sir Francis Suriennes, surnamed the Aragonois, of the countrie where he was borne, a man for his wit and actiuitie admitted into the order of the garter, tooke by scaling suddenlie in the night of the euen of our ladie day in Lent, a towne on the frontiers of Normandie, belonging to the duke of Britaine called Fougiers, spoiling the same, and killing the inhabitants. The duke of Britaine, being hereof aduertised, sent word by the bishop of Reimes to the French king, beseeching him of his aid and counsell in the matter.

Fougiers.

The French king foorthwith sent his caruer Iohn Hauart, and Iohn Cosinet one of the maisters of his requests to the king of England: and to the duke of Summerset he dispatched Peter de Fonteins the maister of his horsse. To which messengers answer was made aswell by the king as the duke, that the fact was doone without their knowledge. And for the truce to be kept, and not onelie restitution, but also amends to be made to the duke of Britaine, a daie of diet was appointed to be kept at Louuiers, where the commissioners on both parts being assembled, the Frenchmen demanded amends, with no small recompense. The Englishmen answered, that without offense, nothing by iustice ought to be satisfied; affirming the dooing of sir Francis Sureinnes to be onelie his act, without consent eithcr of the king of England, or of the duke of Summerset his lieutenant and regent.

Pŏt de Larch taken by the Frēchmen by a subtill sleight.

But whiles with long delaie they talked of this matter at Louuiers, certeine French men by aduertisement of a wagoner of Louuiers, vnderstanding that the towne of Pont de Larch was but slenderlie manned; the wagoner laded his wagon and passed forward, hauing in his companie two strong varlets clad like carpentars, with great axes on their shoulders. And hereto le seineur de Bresse with a chosen companie of men of armes, lodged himselfe in ambushment neere to the gate of S. Andrew, and

Capteine

capteine Floquet, accompanied with sir Iames de Cleremont, and another great companie priuilie lurked vnder a wood toward Louuiers. When all things were appointed for the purpose, earlie in a morning about the beginning of October, the wagoner came to the gate, and called the porter by name, praieng him to open the gate, that he might passe to Rone, and returne againe the same night.

The porter (which well knew the voice of his customer) tooke little heed to the other two companions, and so opened the one gate, and sent another fellow of his to open the formost gate. When the chariot was on the draw-bridge betweene both the gates, the chariot-maister gaue the porter monie, and for the nonce let one peece fall on the ground: and while the porter stooped to take it vp, the wagoner with his dagger stroke him in at his throat, so that he cried for no helpe, and the two great lubbers slue the other porters, and with their axes cut the axeltrée of the wagon, so that the draw-bridge could not be shortlie drawen vp. This doone they made a signe to capteine Floquet, which with all spéed entered the towne, slue and tooke all the Englishmen: and amongst other, the lord Fauconbridge capteine of the said towne was taken prisoner. The losse of this place was of no small importance, being the verie keie and passage ouer the riuer of Seine, from France into Normandie, being distant from Rone onelie foure leagues.

When request was made to haue it restored againe to the Englishmen, answer was made, that if they restored vnto the duke of Britaine, the towne of Fougiers, with condigne amends for the damages doone there, the towne of Pont Larch should then be againe deliuered, or else not. And shortlie after, in hope of like successe the French king assembled an armie, and diuiding the same in three parts, got by surrender (after sundrie assaults, and losse of diuerse of his men) the townes of Louuiers, & Gerborie, whereof William Harper was capteine. Also the towne, castell, and great tower of Verneueill in Perch were rendered into the French kings hands, after twentie daies of respit granted, to sée if rescues would haue come. The French writers affirme the towne to be taken by assault.

Thus was the warre renewed before the terme of truce fullie expired, & the English capteins brought to their wits end, what with appeasing dailie rumors within the townes; and what with studie how to recouer castels lost and taken: for while they studied how to kéepe and defend one place, foure or fiue other turned to the French part. The chiefe cause of which reuolting was, for that it was blowen abroad thorough France, how the realme of England, after the death of the duke of Glocester by the seuerall factions of princes was diuided in two parts; and that William de la Poole latelie created duke of Suffolke, and diuerse other, which were the occasion of the said duke of Glocesters death, vexed and oppressed the poore people, so that mens minds were not intentiue to outward affaires: but all their studie giuen to keepe off wrongs offered at home. The warres renewed befor the end of the truce.

The king little regarding the matter, & the queene led by euill counsell, rather furthered such mischiefes as dailie began to grow by ciuil discord, than sought to reforme them: so that the Normans and Gascoignes vnderstanding in what state things stood here, turned to the French part, as hereafter it may appeare. About the same time also, began a new rebellion in Ireland; but Richard duke of Yorke being sent thither to appease the same, so asswaged the furie of the wild and sauage people there, that he wan him such fauour amongst them, as could neuer be separated from him and his linage, which in the sequele of this historie may more plainelie appeare. A rebellion in Ireland.

The Frenchmen, hauing perfect vnderstanding of the vnreadinesse of the realme of England, diplaied their banners, and set foorth their armies, and in short space got (by yeelding) Constance, Gisors, castell Galliard, Ponteau de Mere, saint Lo, Festampe, Newcastell, Tonque, Mauleon, Argenton, Lisieux, and diuerse other townes The English loose all in France.

and

and places within the countrie of Normandie. Likewise in Guien was the towne of Maulisson rendered to the earle of Fois. These townes were not yeelded voluntarilie by the English souldiers: but they were compelled thereto by the inhabitants of the townes, which hauing intelligence of the féeble estate of the realme of England, rose against the capteins, opened the gates to the enimies, or constreined them to render

Rone yéelded to the Frenchmen. vpon composition. By which inforcement was the rich citie of Rone deliuered: for suerlie the duke of Summerset and the earle of Shrewesburie had well kept that citie, if they had béene no more vexed with the citizens, than they were with their enimies.

For after that the French king had giuen summons to the citie, the inhabitants streightwaies did not onelie deuise which waie they might betraie the citie, but also put on armor, and rebelled openlie against their capteins: who perceiuing the vntruth of them, and their owne danger, retired into the castell or palace, where (for a certeine

Harflue besieged. Sir Thomas Curson. space) with arrowes & handguns they sore molested the vntrue citizens. But at length, vnderstanding the great puissance of the French king at hand, and despairing of all aid and succour, they yeelded vpon condition; that with all their goods and armour they should safelie depart to Caen, and that certeine townes should be deliuered by a day. And till the same townes were rendred, the earle of Shrewsburie and the lord Butler, sonne to the earle of Ormond, were left behind as pledges, which were sent to the castell of Eureux, bicause they sore feared the malice of the citizens of Rone.

The Frenchmen, following the successe in hand, came to Harflue, and fiercelie assaulted the walles: but by the high prowesse and vndanted valiancie of the capteine, sir Thomas Curson, they were to their great losse manfullie by him repelled, and beaten. The Frenchmen learning wit by this great perill, left their scaling, and deuised dailie how to batter the walles, & make the breaches reasonable for them to

Harflue yéelded to the French. enter. This siege long continued to the great losse of both parties. When sir Thomas Curson saw no likelihood of gaine, but great appéerance of present losse, he fell at

An. Reg. 28. composition with the enimies, and so departed with all his goods. After which towne rendered, the fortresse of Hunflue was vpon like composition yeelded. And beside these townes surrendred in Normandie, the duke of Britaine recouered againe Fougiers, saint Iames de Beuuron, and diuerse other.

1450

Sir Thomas Kiriell with a new band into France. In the meane season the king of England sent into Normandie (with a new supplie of a thousand fiue hundred men) a right valiant capteine called sir Thomas Kiriell, who ioining himselfe with other English capteins recouered the townes of Lisieux and Valongnes, and hauing with him power sufficient (as he tooke it) to kéepe the fields, he departed the twelfe of Aprill from Valongnes, meaning to passe towards Baieux, and after to Caen. But the eighteenth daie of the same moneth, he was incountred at a place called Formignie betwixt Carenten and Baieux, by the earle of Cleremont, & other Frenchmen with Scots. At the first onset, the Englishmen receiued their enimies with such manhood, that the Frenchmen were driuen backe, and the Englishmen tooke from them two culuerings.

But yet in the end, by the comming of the constable of France, Arthur de Britaine earle of Richmond, who brought two hundred or twelue score men of armes, and an

The Englishmen ouerthrowne at Formigne. eight hundred archers or demilances, the Englishmen were discomfited, put to flight, and slaine to the number of three thousand, seauen hundred, three score and thirtéene as Enguerant noteth, beside prisoners, of whome there were diuerse personages of accompt, as the said sir Thomas Kiriell himselfe, sir Henrie Norberie, sir Thomas Drew, sir Thomas Kirklie, Christopher Auberton, Arpell, Helice, Alengour, Iennequin, Vacquier, Gobart, Caleuille, and sundrie other. Sir Robert Veer, and sir

* Or rather Goche. Matthew * Gough that valiant Welshman, and manie other escaped so well as they might, some to Baieux, some to Caen, and other to other places as best they could.

Caen besieged and yéelded to the French. After this ouerthrow obteined, the French king assembled an armie roiall, and comming before Caen, besieged it on all sides: and after making his approches, fierce-

lie

lie assaulted the walles. But the duke of Summerset, and the other capteins within the towne, manfullie withstood their enimies, shewing both force and great policie in defending and beating backe the assailants. The French king, perceiuing he could not preuaile that waie, sent for all his great ordinance to Paris, which being brought, he dailie shot at the wals, and did some hurt: but to the castell which stood on a rocke, and in it a dungeon vnable to be beaten downe, he did no harme at all.

Though the duke of Summerset was the kings lieutenant, yet sir Dauid Hall, as capteine of this towne for his maister the duke of Yorke owner therof, tooke vpon him the chéefe charge. Sir Robert Véer was capteine of the castell, and sir Henrie Radford capteine of the dungeon. Dailie the shot was great, but more terrible than hurtfull: sauing on a daie a stone shot into the towne, fell betweene the duchesse of Summerset, and hir children, which being amazed with this chance, besought hir husband kneeling on hir knées, to haue mercie and compassion of his small infants, and that they might be deliuered out of the towne in safegard. Which intretie made with teares and submission, what eare could but listen to, what heart but yerne at; vnlessse both eare and heart were made of flint or marble, or hewen out of a hard rocke, and so void of all passions, of all remorse, of all affections belonging to humanitie?

The duke pitifull, mooued with the sorrow of his wife, and loue of his children, rendered the towne against the mind of sir Dauid Hall, whose counsell and faithfull diligence (in acquiting himselfe to answer the trust committed to him by his maister) if others had followed; the French had susteined more trauell and losse, yer they should haue so easilie atteined their purpose. The conditions of the surrender were, that the duke of Summerset and his might depart in safegard with all their goods and substance. Sir Dauid Hall with diuerse of his trustie freends departed to Chierburgh, and from thence sailed into Ireland to the duke of Yorke, making relation to him of all these dooings, which thing kindled so great a rancor in the dukes heart and stomach, that he neuer left persecuting the duke of Summerset, vntill he had brought him to his fatall end & confusion. Such is the nature of rancor and malice, of wrath and anger, which furthereth the hands euen of weaklings, on them to wreake their teene, with whome they are offended and pricked to reuengment, as the poet saith: The irreconciliable hate betwéene the two dukes.

> Quaslibet infirmas adiuuat ira manus.

After the obteining of Caen, the earle of Cleremont besieged the citie of Lisieux, whereof was capteine Matthew * Gough with thrée hundred Englishmen, who in the end deliuered that towne, vpon condition, that he and his people might depart to Chierburgh. Then was Falais besieged, whereof were capteins for the earle of Shrewsburie (that was the owner) Andrew Trollop, and Thomas Cotton esquiers, who being in despaire of all succors, agreed to deliuer it vpon two conditions. The one was, that the earle their maister, which remained in pledge for the performance of certeine appointments, concluded at the deliuerie of Rone (as ye haue hard) should be set at libertie. The other, that if they were not rescued within twelue daies, that then they and theirs should depart with armor, and all their goods mooueable, whither it pleased them. * Goche.

At the daie appointed, the towne was rendered, and so likewise was the towne of Dampfront vpon the semblable agréement. Now rested onelie English the towne of Chierburgh, whereof was capteine one Thomas Conuille, which suerlie as long as vittels and munition serued, defended the towne right manfullie: but without hope of repaire, consumed, and he els destitute of all comfort and aid, vpon a reasonable composition, yéelded the towne, and went to Calis, where the duke of Summerset and manie other Englishmen then soiorned. Thus was Normandie lost cleerelie out of the Englishmens hands, after it had continued in their possession the space of thirtie yeares by the conquest of Henrie the fift. All Normandie lost.

The state of it.
In this duchie were an hundred strong townes and fortresses, able to be kept and holden, beside them which were destroied by the warres; and in the same is one arch-
The causes of the losse.
bishoprike, and six bishopriks. Some saie that the Englishmen were not of puissance either to man the townes, as they should haue béene; or to inhabit the countrie, which was the cause they could not keepe it. Other saie, that the duke of Summerset for his owne peculiar lucre, kept not halfe the number of souldiours for which he was appointed and allowed, but put the wages in his purse. But the cheefe and onelie cause
The mortall mischéefe of malice and diuision in a realme.
vndoubtedlie, was the diuision within the realme, euerie great man desiring rather to be reuenged on his foe at home, than on the common enimie abroad, as by that which followeth you may plainelie perceiue.

An. Reg. 29.
W. P.
[For whilest the French thus triumphed in Normandie, thrée cruell enimies among manie (as by ciuill warre and sedition insuing appeared) sore vrged the vtter ruine of this realme at home. One was presumption in gouernance, by some that were most vnméet to rule, as the queene with hir priuie counsellors and minions; then the deadlie malice and pride, with insatiable couetise in the states both spirituall and temporall: and lastlie the generall grudge of the people, for the vniuersall smart that through misgouernment euerie where they suffered; who thus forweried with the peise of bur thens too heauie for them anie longer to beare.

Heerewith perceiuing how (through want of prouident wisedome in the gouernour) all things went to wracke, as well within the realme as without; they began to make
The commōs exclame against the duke of Suffolke.
exclamation against the duke of Suffolke, charging him to be the onelie cause of the deliuerie of Aniou, and Maine, the chéefe procuror of the duke of Glocesters death, the verie occasion of losse of Normandie, the swallower vp of the kings treasure, the remoouer of good and vertuous councellours from about the prince, and the aduancer of vicious persons, and of such as by their dooings shewed themselues apparant aduersaries to the common-wealth.

The parlemēt adiourned frō London to Leicester, and from thence to Westminster.
The quéene hereat doubting not onelie the dukes destruction, but also hir owne confusion, caused the parlement before begun at the Blackfriers, to be adiourned to Leicester, thinking there, by force and rigor of law, to suppresse and subdue all the malice and euill will conceiued against the duke & hir. At which place few of the nobilitie would appeare: wherefore it was againe adiourned to Westminster, where was a full appearance. In the which session the commons of the nether house put vp to
Edw. Hall.
the king and the lords manie articles of treason, misprision, and euill demeanor, against the duke of Suffolke: the effect whereof with his answers héere insueth.

Articles proponed by the commons against the duke of Suffolke.

1 FIRST they alleged that he had traitorouslie excited, prouoked, and councelled Iohn earle of Dunois bastard of Orleance, Bertram lord Presignie, William Cosinet, enimies to the king, and fréends and ambassadours to Charles, calling himselfe French king, to enter into this realme; and to leauie warre against the king and his people, to the intent to destroie the king and his fréends, and to make Iohn his sonne king of this realme, marieng him to Margaret, sole heire to Iohn duke of Summerset, pretending and declaring hir to be next heire inheritable to the crowne, for lacke of issue, of the kings bodie lawfullie begotten.

2 Item, the said duke, being of the kings priuie and néere councell, allured by great rewards and faire promises, made by the said earle of Dunois, caused the king to deliuer and set at libertie, Charles duke of Orleance, enimie to the king, and the kings noble father: which deliuerance was prohibited by expresse words, in the last will of the kings most victorious father.

3 Item, that before the departing of the said duke of Orleance, the aforenamed
duke

duke of Suffolke traitorouslie fast cleauing to Charles called the French king, counselled, prouoked, and intised the said duke of Orleance, to mooue the same king to make warre against England, both in France and Normandie. According to which procurement & counsell, the said French king hath recouered the whole realme of France, and all the duchie of Normandie, and taken prisoners the earle of Shrewesburie, the lord Fauconbridge, and manie other valiant capteins. ¶ These thrée articles afornamed he denied, either for fact or thought.]

4 Further it was alleged, that he being ambassadour to the king of England, to Charles calling himselfe the French king, promised to Reiner king of Sicill, and to Charles d'Angiers his brother, enimies to the king, the release of Aniou, with the deliuerance of the countie of Maine, and the city of Maunt or Mans, without the knowledge of the other ambassadours with him accompanied. Which promise, after his returne, he caused to be performed, to the kings disinheritance and loss irrecouerable, and to the strength of his enimies, and feeblishment of the duchie of Normandie. ¶ To this article he answered, that his commission was to conclude, and doo all things according to his discretion, for the obteining of a peace : & bicause without deliuerie of those countries, he perceiued that the truce could not be obteined, he agreed to the release and deliuerance of them.]

5 Also they had great cause to iudge by the sequele, that the said duke being in France in the kings seruice, and one of the priuiest of his councell there, traitorouslie declared and opened to the capteins and conductors of warre, apperteining to the kings enimies, the kings counsell, purueiance of his armies, furniture of his townes, & all other ordinances, whereby the kings enimies (instructed aforehand by his traitorous information) haue gotten townes and fortresses, and the king by that meanes depriued of his inheritance.

6 Item, the said duke declared to the earle of Dunois, to the lord Presignie, and William Cosinet ambassadours for the French king lieng in London, the priuities of the kings councell, both for the prouision of further warre, and also for the defense of the duchie of Normandie : by the disclosing whereof, the Frenchmen knowing the king secrets, defeated the kings appointments, and they obteined their purpose.

7 Item, that the said duke, at such time as the king sent ambassadours to the French king, for the intreating of peace, traitorouslie before their comming to the French court, certified king Charles of their commission, authoritie, and instructions : by reason whereof, ncither peace nor amitie succéeded, and the kings inheritance lost, and by his enimies possessed.

8 Item, the said duke said openlie in the Star-chamber before the lords of the councell, that he had as high a place in the councell-house of the French king, as he had there : and was as well trusted there as here, and could remooue from the French king the priuiest man of his councell, if he would.

9 Item, when armies haue béene prepared, and souldiers readie waged to passe ouer the sea, to deale with the kings enimies : the said duke, corrupted by rewards of the French king, hath restreined & staid the said armies to passe any further.

10 Item, the said duke being ambassadour for the king, comprised not in the league (as the kings alies) neither the king of Aragon, neither the duke of Britaine : but suffered them to be comprised on the contrarie part. By reason whereof, the old amitie of the k. of Aragon is estranged from this realme, and the duke of Britaine became enimie to the same : Giles his brother, the kings sure freend, cast in strong prison, and there lie to end his daies.]

All these obiections he vtterlie denied, or faintlie auoided : but none fullie excused. Diuerse other crimes were laid to his charge, as inriching himselfe with the kings
                                                                            goods

goods and lands, gathering togither and making a monopolie of offices, fées, wards, and farmes, by reason whereof, the kings estate was greatlie diminished and decaied, and he and his kin highlie exalted & inriched : with manie other points, which bicause they be not notable nor of great force or strength, I omit and ouer-passe.

The duke of Suffolke cō-mitted to the Tower.

The quéene, which intierlie loued the duke, doubting some commotion and trouble to arise, if he were let go vnpuished, caused him for a colour to be committed to the Tower : where he remained not past a moneth, but was againe deliuered and re-stored to the kings fauour, as much as euer he was before. This dooing so much dis-pleased the people, that if politike prouision had not béene, great mischeefe had im-mediatlie insued. For the commons in sundrie places of the realme assembled togither in great companies, and chose to them a capteine, whom they called Blew-beard : but yer they had attempted anie enterprise, their leaders were apprehended ; & so the matter pacified without anie hurt committed.

Blewbeard cap-teine of the re-bels.

After this outrage thus asswaged, the parlement was adiourned to Leicester, whither came the king and quéene in great estate, and with them the duke of Suf-folke as chéefe councellour. The commons of the lower house, not forgetting their old grudge, besought the king, that such persons as assented to the release of Aniou, and deliuerance of Maine, might be dulie punished. And to be priuie to that fact, they accused as principall, the duke of Suffolke, with Iohn bishop of Salisburie, and sir Iames Fines, lord Saie, and diuerse others. When the king per-ceiued that there was no remedie to appease the peoples furie by anie colourable waies, shortlie to pacifie so long an hatred, he first sequestred the lord Saie being treasuror of England, and other the dukes adherents from their offices and roomes, and after banished the duke of Suffolke, as the abhorred tode and common noiance of the whole realme, for tearme of fiue yeares, meaning by this exile to appease the malice of the people for the time, and after (when the matter should be forgotten) to reuoke him home againe.

But Gods iustice would not that so vngratious a person should so escape : for when he shipped in Suffolke, intending to transport himselfe ouer into France, he was incountered with a ship of warre, apperteining to the duke of Excester, con-stable of the Tower of London, called the Nicholas of the Tower. The capteine of that barke with small fight entered into the dukes ship, and perceiuing his person present, brought him to Douer road, and there on the one side of a cocke bote caused his head to be striken off, and left his bodie with the head lieng there on the sands. Which corps being there found by a chapleine of his, was conueied to Wingfield col-lege in Suffolke, and there buried. This end had William de la Poole duke of Suf-folke, as men iudge by Gods prouidence ; for that he had procured the death of that good duke of Glocester, as before is partlie touched.

The wretched death of the duke of Suf-folke.

Soone after an other disquiet befell here. Those that fauoured the duke of Yorke, and wished the crowne vpon his head, for that (as they iudged) he had more right thereto than he that ware it, procured a commotion in Kent on this manner. A cer-teine yoong man of a goodlie stature and right pregnant of wit, was intised to take vpon him the name of Iohn Mortimer coosine to the duke of Yorke (although his name was Iohn Cade, or (of some) Iohn Mend-all) [an Irishman as Polychronicon saith] and not for a small policie, thinking by that surname, that those which fauoured the house of the earle of March would be assistant to him. And so in déed it came to passe (as in such cases there is no bréeder of a broile but he shall find adherents enow, no lesse forward to further his pernicious enterprise by their foolehardines, than him-selfe was in the plot of his deuise) though in fine (as it is the vnluckie lot of such tumults) their attempts were withstood, and their offense dulie rewarded, as in pro-cesse of the storie shall more at large appeare ; according to the wisemans sentence :

Iacke Cades re-bellion in Kent.

Sæpe in magistrum scelera redeunt sua.

                                                   This

This capteine assembling a great companie of tall personages, assured them, that the enterprise which he tooke in hand, was both honourable to God and the king, and profitable to the whole realme. For if either by force or policie they might get the king and quéene into their hands, he would cause them to be honourablie vsed, and take such order for the punishing and reforming of the misdemeanours of their bad councellours, that neither fiftéens should hereafter be demanded, nor once anie impositions or taxes be spoken of. The Kentish people mooued at these persuasions & other faire promises of reformation, in good order of battell (though not in great number) came with their capteine vnto the plaine of Blackeheath, betwéene Eltham and Gréenewich, and there kept the field more than a month, pilling the countrie about; to whome the citie of London at that time was verie fauourable. ¶ And the said capteine (as I find recorded saith Iohn Stow) sent for such citizens of London as it pleased him to command to repaire vnto him, vnder letters of safe conduct, as *Abr. Fl. ex I. S.* followeth. *653.*

The safegard and signe manuell of the capteine of Kent, sent to Thomas Cocke draper of London, by the capteine of the great assemblie in Kent.

BY this our writing insealed, we grant & will permit trulie, that Thomas Cocke of London draper, shall come in good suertie and in safegard to our presence, without anie hurt of his person, and so auoid from vs againe at his pleasure, with all other persons assigned at his denomination with him comming in likewise.

The commandement by the capteine of Kent, sent vnto Thomas Cocke aboue said.

FOR your instruction, first ye shall charge all Lumbards and strangers, being merchants, Genowais, Venetians, Florentines, and others, this daie to draw them togither, and to ordeine for vs the capteine, twelue harnesses complet of the best fashion, foure & twentie brigandins, twelue battel axes, twelue glaues, six horsses with sadle and bridle completlie harnessed, and a thousand markes of readie monie. And if this our demand be not obserued & doone, we shall haue the heads of as manie as we can get of them.

And to the intent the cause of this glorious capteins comming thither, might be shadowed vnder a cloke of good meaning (though his intent nothing so) he sent vnto the king an humble supplication, affirming that his comming was not against his grace, but against such of his councellours, as were louers of themselues, and oppressors of the poore commonaltie; flatterers of the king, and enimies to his honor; suckers of his purse, and robbers of his subiects; parciall to their fréends, and extreame to their enimies: thorough bribes corrupted, and for indifferencie dooing nothing. ¶ Here, bicause a full report of this insurrection maie passe to the knowledge *Abr. Fl. ex I. S.* of the readers; it is necessarie to set downe the articles of the commons complaints *654, 655, 656,* touching the premisses, whereof a copie was sent to the parlement then holden at *657, &c.* Westminster, with their bill of requests concerning abuses to be reformed.

The

The complaint of the commons of Kent, and causes of their assemblie on the Blackheath

1 INPRIMIS, it is openlie noised that Kent should be destroied with a roiall power,
& made a wild forrest, for the death of the duke of Suffolke, of which the commons
of Kent thereof were neuer giltie.

2 Item, the king is stirred to liue onelie on his commons, and other men to haue
the reuenues of the crowne, the which hath caused pouertie in his excellencie, and
great paiments of the people, now late to the king granted in his parlement.

3 Item, that the lords of his roiall bloud beene put from his dailie presence, and
other meane persons of lower nature exalted and made chéefe of his priuie councell,
the which stoppeth matters of wrongs done in the realme from his excellent audience,
and maie not be redressed as law will; but if bribes and gifts be messengers to the
hands of the said councell.

4 Item, the people of this realme be not paid of debts owing for stuffe and purueiance taken to the vse of the kings houshold, in vndooing of the said people, and the
poore commons of the realme.

5 Item, the kings meniall seruants of houshold, and other persons, asken dailie
goods and lands, of impeached or indicted of treason, the which the king granteth
anon, yer they so indangered be conuicted. The which causeth the receiuers thereof
to inforge labours and meanes applied to the death of such people, so appeached or
indicted, by subtill meanes, for couetise of the said grants: and the people so impeached or indicted, though it be vntrue, maie not e committed to the law for their
deliuerance, but held still in prison, to their vttermost vndooing & destruction, for
couetise of goods.

6 Item, though diuerse of the poore people and commons of the realme, haue
neuer so great right, truth, and perfect title to their land: yet by vntrue claime of
infeoffement made vnto duierse states, gentles, and the kings meniall seruants in
maintenances against the right, the true owners dare not hold, claime, nor pursue
their right.

7 Item, it is noised by common voices, that the kings lands in France béene
aliened and put awaie from the crowne, and his lords and people there destroied with
vntrue meanes of treason; of which it is desired, inquiries thorough all the realme to
be made how and by whome; & if such traitors maie be found giltie, them to haue
execution of law without anie pardon, in example of others.

8 Item, collectors of the fiftéenth penie in Kent be greatlie vexed and hurt, in
paieng great summes of monie in the excheker, to sue out a writ called Quorum nomina,
for the alowance of the barons of the ports, which now is desired, that hereafter
in the lieu of thé collectors, the barons aforesaid maie sue it out for their ease at their
owne costs.

9 Item, the shiriffes and vndershiriffes let to farme their offices and bailiwickes,
taking great suertie therefore, the which causeth extortions doone by them and by
their bailiffes to the people.

10 Item, simple and poore people that vse not hunting, be greatlie oppressed by
indictements feined & doone by the said shiriffes, vndershiriffes, bailiffes, and other of
their assent, to cause their increase for paieng of their said farme.

11 Item, they returne in names of inquests in writing into diuerse courts of the
king not summoned nor warned, where through the people dailie léese great summes
of monie, well nigh to the vttermost of their vndooing : and make leuie of amercements
called the gréene wax, more in summes of monie than can be found due of record in
the kings books.

12 Item,

12 Item, the ministers of the court of Douer in Kent vex and arrest diuerse people thorough all the shire out of Castle ward, passing their bounds and libertie vsed of old time, by diuerse subtill and vntrue meanes and actions falselie feined, taking great fées at their lust in great hurt of the people on all the shire of Kent.

13 Item, the people of the said shire of Kent, maie not haue their frée election in the choosing of knights of the shire: but letters béene sent from diuerse estates to the great rulers of all the countrie, the which imbraceth their tenants and other people by force to choose other persons than the cōmons will is.

14 Item. whereas knights of the shire should choose the king collectors indifferentlie without any bride taking, they haue sent now late to diuerse persons, notifieng them to be collectors: wherevpon gifts and bribes be taken, & so the collectors office is bought and sold extortionouslie at the knights lust.

15 Item, the people be sore vexed in costs and labour, called to the sessions of peace in the said shire, appearing from the furthest and vttermost part of the west vnto the east; the which causeth to some men fiue daies iournie: wherevpon they desire the said appearance to be diuided into two parts; the which one part, to appeare in one place; an other part, in an other place; in reléeuing of the gréeuances and intollerable labours & vexatiōns of the said people

The requests by the capteine of the great assemblie in Kent.

INPRIMIS, desireth thecap teine of the commons, the welfare of our souereigne lord the king, and all his true lords spirituall and temporall, desiring of our said souereigne lord, and of all the true lords of his councell, he to take in all his demaines, that he maie reigne like a king roiall, according as he is borne our true and christian king annointed: and who so will saie the contrarie, we all will liue and die in the quarell as his true liege men.

Item, desireth the said capteine, that he will auoid all the false progenie and affinitie of the duke of Suffolke, the which beene openlie knowne, and they to be punished after the custome and law of this land, and to take about his noble person the true lords of his roiall bloud of this his realme, that is to saie, the high and mightie prince the duke of Yorke, late exiled from our said souereigne lords presence (by the motion and stirring of the traitorous and false disposed the duke of Suffolke and his affinitie) and the mightie princes & dukes of Excester, Buckingham, and Norffolke, and all the earles and barons of this land: and then shall he be the richest king christian.

Item, desireth the said capteine and commons punishment vnto the false traitors, the which contriued and imagined the death of the high, mightfull and excellent prince the duke of Glocester, the which is too much to rehearse; the which duke was proclamed as traitor. Vpon the which quarell, we purpose all to liue and die vpon that that it is false.

Item, the duke of Excester, our holie father the cardinall, the noble prince the duke of Warwike, and also the realme of France, the duchie of Normandie, Gascoigne, and Guion, Aniou, and Maine, were deliuered and lost by the meanes of the said traitors: and our true lords, knights, and esquiers, and manie a good yeoman lost and sold yer they went, the which is great pitie to heare, of the great and gréeuous losse to our souereigne lord and his realme.

Item, desireth the said capteine and commons, that all extortions vsed dailie among the common people, might be laid downe, that is to saie, the gréene wax; the which is falselie vsed, to the perpetuall destruction of the kings true commons of Kent. Also the kings Bench, the which is too gréefefull to the shire of Kent, without prouision

sion of our souereigne lord and his true councell.   And also in taking of wheat and
other graines, béefe, mutton, & all other vittels, the which is importable to the said
commons, without the bréefe prouision of our said souereigne lord and his true
councell, they maie no longer beare it.   And also vnto the statute of labourers, and
the great extortioners, the which is to saie the false traitors, Sleg. Cromer, Isle, and
Robert Est.

These billes when the councell had well perused, they did not onelie disalow and
condemne them and the authors, as proud and presumptuous; but also persuaded
the king rather to suppresse those rebels by force, than by faire promises.   Wherevpon
the king remoued from Westminster vnto Greenewich, from whence he would haue
sent certeine lords with a power to haue distressed the Kentishmen, but the men said
to their lords they would not fight against them that laboured to amend the common-
weale: wherefore the lords were driuen to leaue their purpose.   And bicause the
Kentishmen cried out against the lord Saie the kings chamberline, he was by the

King Henrie
went against the
Kentishmen
with a great
power.

king committed to the Tower of London.   Then went the king againe to London,
& within two dais after went against the Kentishmen with fiftéene thousand men well
prepared for the war: but the said Kentishmen fled the night before his comming into
the wood countrie neere vnto Senocke.   Wherevpon the king returned againe to London.

The quéene (that bare rule) being of his retrait aduertised, sent sir Humfreie Stafford knight, and William his brother, with manie other gentlemen, to follow the
Kentishmen, thinking that they had fled: but they were deceiued, for at the first

The Staffords
slaine at Senocke
by Iacke Cade.

skirmish both the Staffords were slaine, & all their companie discomfited.   The kings
armie by this time comen to Blackheath, hearing of this discomfiture, began to
murmur amongst themselues: some wishing the duke of Yorke at home to aid the
capteine his cousine: some vndutifullie coueting the ouerthrow of the king and his
councell: other openlie crieng out on the quéene and hir complices.

This rumor published abroad, caused the king and certeine of his councell (for the
appeasing thereof) to commit the lord Saie treasuror of England to the Tower of London;
and if other (against whome like displeasure was borne) had béene present, they had
béene likewise committed.   Iacke Cade vpon victorie against the Staffords apparelled
himselfe in sir Humfries brigandine set full of guilt nailes, and so in some glorie
returned againe toward London; diuerse idle and vagarant persons out of Sussex,
Surreie and other places, still increasing his number.   Thus this glorious capteine,
garded with a multitude of rusticall people, came againe to the plaine of Blackheath,
& there stronglie incamped himselfe: to whome were sent from the king, the archbishop
of Canturburie, and Humfrie duke of Buckingham, to common with him of his gréefes
and requests.

These lords found him sober in talke, wise in reasoning, arrogant in hart, and
stiffe in opinion; as who that by no means would grant to dissolue his armie, except
the king in person would come to him, and assent to the things he would require.
The K. vpon the presumptuous answers & requests of this villanous rebell, begining
asmuch to doubt his owne meniall seruants, as his vnknowen subiects (which spared
not to speake, that the capteins cause was profitable for the common-wealth) departed
in all hast to the castell of Killingworth in Warwikeshire. leauing onlie behind him
the lord Scales to kéepe the Tower of London.   The Kentish capteine being aduertised
of the kings absence, came first into Southwarke, and there lodged at the white hart,
prohibiting to all his retinue, murder, rape, and robberie; by which colour of well
meaning, he the more allured to him the harts of the common people.

After that, he entered into London, cut the ropes of the draw bridge, & strooke
his sword on London stone; saieng, Now is Mortimer lord of this citie.   And after
                                                              a glosing

a glosing declaration made to the maior touching the cause of his thither comming he departed againe into Southwarke, and vpon the third daie of Iulie he caused sir Iames Fines, lord Saie, and treasuror of England, to be brought to the Guildhall, and there to be arreigned: who being before the kings iustices put to answer, desired to be tried by his péeres, for the longer delaie of his life. The capteine perceiuing his dilatorie plee, by force tooke him from the officers, and brought him to the standard in Cheape, and there (before his confession ended) caused his head to be striken off, and pitched it vpon an high pole, which was openlie borne before him thorough the stréets. _{The lord Saie beheaded at the stãdard in Cheap.}

And not content herewith, he went to Mile end, and there apprehended sir Iames Cromer then shiriffe of Kent, and sonne in law to the said lord Saie, causing him likewise (without confession or excuse heard) to be beheaded, and his head to be fixed on a pole: and with these two heads this bloudie wretch entred into the citie againe, and as it were in a spite caused them in euerie stréet to kisse togither, to the great detestation of all the beholders. After this succéeded open rapine, and manifest robberie in diuerse houses within the citie, and speciallie in the house of Philip Malpas alderman of London, and diuerse other; ouer and beside ransoming and fining of diuers notable merchants, for the suertie of their liues and goods; as Robert Horne alderman, which paid fiue hundred marks. He also put to execution in Southwarke diuerse persons, some for breaking his ordinance, and other being of his old acquaintance, lest they should bewraie his base linage, disparaging him for his vsurped surname of Mortimer.

The maior and other the magistrates of London, perceiuing themselues neither to be sure of goods, nor of life well warranted, determined to repell and keepe out of their citie such a mischieuous caitife and his wicked companie. And to be the better able so to doo, they made the lord Scales, and that renowmed capteine Matthew * Gough priuie both of their intent and enterprise, beséeching them of their helpe and furtherance therein. The lord Scales promised them his aid, with shooting off the artillerie in the Tower; and Matthew Gough was by him appointed to assist the maior and Londoners in all that he might, and so he and other capteins, appointed for defense of the citie, tooke vpon them in the night to keepe the bridge, and would not suffer the Kentishmen once to approch. The rebels, who neuer soundlie slept for feare of sudden assaults, hearing that the bridge was thus kept, ran with great hast to open that passage, where betwéene both parties was a fierce and cruell fight. _{* Or rather Goche.}

Matthew * Gough, perceiuing the rebels to stand to their tackling more manfullie than he thought they would haue doone, aduised his companie not to aduance anie further toward Southwarke, till the daie appeared; that they might sée where the place of ieopardie rested, and so to prouide for the same: but this little auailed. For the rebels with their multitude draue backe the citizens from the stoops at the bridge foot to the draw bridge, & began to set fire in diuerse houses. Great ruth it was to behold the miserable state, wherein some desiring to eschew the fire died vpon their enimies weapon; women with children in their armes lept for feare into the riuer, other in a deadlie care how to saue themselues, betwéene fire water, and sword, were in their houses choked and smothered. Yet the capteins not sparing, fought on the bridge all the night valiantlie: but in conclusion, the rebels gat the draw bridge, and drowned manie, and slue Iohn Sutton alderman, and Robert Heisand, a hardie citizen, with manie other, beside Matthew * Gough, a man of great wit and much experience in feats of chiualrie, the which in continuall warres had spent his time in seruice of the king and his father. _{* Or rather Goche. The skirmish betwéene the citizens and the rebels vpon London bridge.} _{Matthew Goche famous for his acts abroad now slaine on Lõdõ bridge.}

This sore conflict indured in doubtfull wise on the bridge, till nine of the clocke in the morning: for somtime, the Londoners were beaten backe to saint Magnus corner: and suddenlie againe, the rebels were repelled to the stoops in Southwarke, so that both parts being faint and wearie, agréed to leaue off from fighting till the next daie;

A staie by assent. vpon condition, that neither Londoners should passe into Southwarke, nor Kentishmen into London.   Vpon this abstinence, this rakehell capteine for making him more friends, brake vp the gailes of the kings Bench and Marshalsie, and so were manie mates set at libertie verie méet for his matters in hand.

The archbishop of Canturburie being chancellor of England, and as then for his suertie lieng within the Tower, called to him the bishop of Winchester, who for some safegard laie then at Haliwell.   These two prelats, séeing the furie of the Kentish people, by their late repulse, to be somewhat asswaged, passed by the riuer of Thames from the Tower into Southwarke, bringing with them vnder the kings great seale, a generall pardon vnto all the offendors, and caused the same to be openlie published. Proclamatiō of pardon dispersed the rebels. The poore people were so glad of this pardon, and so readie to receiue it, that without bidding farewell to their capteine, they withdrew themselues the same night euerie man towards his home.

Abr. Fl. ex I. S. pag. 661, 662. *in Quart.* ¶ But Iacke Cade despairing of succours, and fearing the reward of his lewd dealings, put all his pillage and goods that he had robbed, into a barge, and sent it to Rochester by water, and himselfe went by land, and would haue entred into the castle of Quinborow with a few men that were left about him; but he was there let of his purpose: wherefore he disguised in strange attire, priuilie fled into the wood countrie beside Lewes in Sussex, hoping so to scape.   The capteine & his people being thus departed, not long after proclamations were made in diuerse places of Kent, Sussex, and Southerie, that whosoeuer could take the foresaid capteine aliue or dead, should haue a thousand markes for his trauell.   A copie of which proclamation, touching the apprehension of the said Cade and his complices, hereafter followeth.

A copie of the said writ and proclamation by the king, for the taking of the said Cade and his felowship.

HENRICUS Dei gratia rex Angliæ & Franciæ, & dominus Hiberniæ, vniuersis & singulis custodibus, &c.   For so much as one Iohn Cade borne in Ireland, which calleth himselfe Iohn Mortimer & in some writing calleth himselfe capteine of Kent, the which Iohn Cade the last yeare tofore his dwelling in Sussex with a knight, called sir Thomas Dagre, slue there a woman with child, and for that cause tooke the gréeth of the church, and after for that cause forsware the kings land: the which Iohn Cade also after this, was sworne to the French part, and dwelled with them; which hath now of late time (to the intent to inrich himselfe by robbing and despoiling of the kings liegemen, as it is now openlie knowne, to bring himselfe to great and high estate) falslie and vntruelie deceiued manie of the kings people, and vnder colour of holie and good intents made them to assemble with him against the kings regalitie & his lawes, & nought setting by the kings grace and pardons, granted not onelie to him but to all the kings subiects, the which by his deceit haue assembled with him, the which he with great reuerence receiued on mondaie last passed, and so did all that were assembled with him.   Notwithstanding all this, he laboureth now of new to assemble the kings people againe, and to that intent beareth them on hand, that the kings letters of pardon granted to him and them, be not auaileable, nor of none effect, without authoritie of parlement: whereas the contrarie is true, as it is openlie knowne by that, that the king granteth from time to time his charters of pardon to such as him list, of all manner of crimes and offenses both generall and speciall.

The king therefore willeth and commandeth, that none of his subiects giue faith nor credence to the said false informations of the said false traitor nor accompanie with him in anie wise, nor comfort nor susteine him nor his with vittels, nor with anie
                                                                                                    other

other things: but will, whosoeuer of the kings subiects may take him, shall take him; and that who so euer taketh him, and bringeth him quicke or dead to the king or to his councell, shall haue a thousand markes for his labour trulie paid him, without faile or delaie by the prouision of the kings councell. And who so euer taketh anie of those that from this daie foorth accompanie with him, shall haue fiue marks for his reward, trulie to be paid in maner and forme aboue said. And ouer this commanding all constables, ministers, and officers of the said shire, that none of them (on paine of death) take vpon them to execute anie commandement by word or writing sent or made vnto them by the said Cade, calling himselfe Mortimer and capteine, be it to reare any people, or to any other intent: but to arest and make so be arested such, as take vpon them to bring anie such commandement by writing or by word. Et hoc nullatenus omittatis. Teste me ipso apud Westm. 10 die Iulij, anno regni 28.]

After which proclamation thus published, a gentleman of Kent named Alexander Eden awaited so his time, that he tooke the said Cade in a garden in Sussex: so that there he was slaine at Hothfield, and brought to London in a cart, where he was quartered; his head set on London bridge, and his quarters sent to diuerse places to be set vp in the shire of Kent. After this, the king himselfe came into Kent, and there set in iudgment vpon the offendors: and if he had not mingled his iustice with mercie; more than fiue hundred by rigor of law had beene iustlie put to execution. Yet he punishing onelie the stubborne heads, & disordered ringleaders, pardoned the ignorant and simple persons, to the great reioising of all his subiects. ¶ But saith another, the king sent his commissioners into Kent, and caused inquirie to be made of this riot in Canturburie, where for the same eight men were iudged and executed, and in other townes of Kent and Sussex was doone the like execution. *Capteine of Kent taken & beheaded.* *Abr. Fl. ex I. St. 663, 664.*

This yeare the commons also in diuerse parts of England, as in Sussex, Salisburie, Wiltshire, and other places, did much harme to manie persons, among the which, on the nine and twentith of Iune, William Ascoth bishop of Salisburie (after he had said masse at Edington) was by his owne tenants drawne from the altar, in his albe with his stole about his necke to the top of an hill, and there by them shamefullie murthered, and after spoiled to the naked skin: they renting his bloudie shirt, tooke euerie man a péece, and made boast of their wickednesse. The daie before, his chariot was robbed, to the value of ten thousand markes. Soldiours made a fraie against the maior of London the same daie he tooke his charge at Westminster, at night comming from saint Thomas of Acres, after he had béene at Paules.] *The bishop of Salisburie murthered.* *A fray in Lōdon against the maior.*

The French king vnderstanding all the ciuill discord and rebellious sturs in England, made therof his foundation, hoping to get into his hands and possession the duchie of Aquitaine: and thereupon sent the earles of Pontheieuure and Perigort to laie siege to the towne of Bergerat, situate vpon the riuer of Dourdon, of which towne was capteine Iohn Gedding, who vpon reasonable conditions rendred the towne. But yet the lord Camois, sir George Seimor, and sir Iohn Arundell, with diuers other valiant capteins hauing gouernance of the countrie, manned townes, gathered people, and recomforted the fainting harts of the Gascoignes in all that they could, and withall sent letters ouer into England, certifieng to the kings maiestie, that without spéedie aid and readie succours, the whole countrie was like to be conquered and woone out of the Englishmens possession.

Manie letters were sent, and manie faire answers were brought; but reléefe neither appeared, nor one man of warre was thither shipped: by reason whereof the Frenchmen pursuing the victorie, got the fortresses of Iansacke, and S. Foie, with diuerse other péeces of importance thereabouts. Also, about the same time, the lord Doruall, third sonne to the lord de la Breth, with a great number of men, as well on horssebacke as on foot, departed from Basas, to conquer and destroie the Ile of Medoc. Wherevpon

the

the maior of Burdeaux issuing out, and incountring with his enimies, was vanquished, losing six hundred Englishmen and Gascoignes: albeit the Frenchmen gained not this victorie with cléere hands, for there were slaine of them to the number of eight hundred persons.

1451

After this, the bastard of Orleance, with his brother Iohn earle of Angolesme, which had béene long prisoner in England, and manie other valiant capteins, besieged the castell of Montguion, which to them was rendered. Afterwards, they besieged the towne of Blaie, standing on the riuer of Garonne, the which in conclusion by verie force was conquered and woone. The bastard of Kendall, capteine of the castell, séeing the towne lost, vpon certeine reasonable conditions deliuered his fortresse to the bastard of Orleance, the French kings lieutenant. After this, the townes of Burgh and Liborne, after fiue wéekes siege, were likewise yéelded to the Frenchmen. Then was the citie of Acques besieged by the erle of Fois, and the vicount de Law-trec his brother, and other noble men. So likewise was the strong towne of Rion by the earle of Arminacke, extreame enimie to the realme of England, for breach of the mariage concluded betwéene k ng Henrie and his daughter. The earle of Ponthieuure laid siege to Chatillon in Perigort, and the earle of Dunois inuironned with great puissance the towne of Fronsacke.

The earle of Arminack an open enimie.

The Englishmen perceiuing in what state they stood within the towne, couenanted with the said earle, that if the towne were not succoured, and the Frenchmen fought with before the feast of the natiuitie of saint Iohn Baptist next insuing; that then the towne of Fronsacke should be yéelded to them, which was the strongest fortresse in all that countrie, and the verie keie of Guien. Héereof were pledges deliuered, and writings made & sealed. Which agreement once blowne through the countrie, the citie of Burdeaux, and all other townes (except Baion) made the like agréement. So did all the noble men and gentlemen which were subiects and vassels to the crowne of England. Euerie daie was looking for aid, but none came.

Through dissention at home, all lost abroad.

And whie? Euen bicause the diuelish diuision that reigned in England, so incombred the heads of the noble men there, that the honor of the realme was cléerelie forgotten, so that (to conclude) the daie appointed came, but succour looked for came not. By reason whereof, all the townes of Aquitaine (except Baion) deliuered their keies, and became vassals to the French nation; yet the citizens of Burdeaux, in hope of rescue, required a longer daie of battell, which was granted. But at the daie appointed, when no reléefe came, they rendred themselues and the citie to their aduersaries, their liues and goods saued, with licence and safe conduct to all persons which would depart and saile into England. Then finallie was the citie of Baion besieged, and with mines and batterie constreined to yéeld it selfe into the Frenchmens hands.

Beside the agreements taken and made with the townes, diuerse noble men made seuerall compositions, as Gaston de Fois, & Capdaw de Buef, whome king Henrie the fift made earle of Longeuile, and knight of the garter; whose ancestors were euer true to England. Which agréed, that he and his sonne Iohn de Fois, whome king Henrie the sixt made earle of Kendale, and also knight of the garter, should enioy all their lands in Aquitaine, giuen to them by the kings of England, or by the dukes of Aquitaine. And sith their intent was still to serue the king of England, they agréed to deliuer into the custodie of the earle of Fois, the sonne and heire of the said earle of Kendale, being of the age of thrée yeares; to the intent that if he at his full age denied to become subiect to the French king, or before that time deceassed; that then (after the death of his father and grandfather) all the said lands should wholie remaine to the next heire of their bloud, either male or female, being vnder the obeisance of the French king or his heires.

Manie other noble men, whose hearts were good English, made like compositions, and some came into England, and others went to Calis, and bare great offices there:

as

as the lord Duras, which was marshall of that towne; and monsieur Vauclere, which was deputie there vnder the earle of Warwike.   Thus were the Englishmen cléerelie displaced and lost the possession of all the countries, townes, castels, and places *All lost in* within the realme of France; so that onelie Calis, Hammes and Guines, with the *France.* marches thereof remained in their hands, of all those their dominions and seigniories which they sometime held in the parties beyond the seas.   Whereby England suffered a partile but not a totall eclipse of hir glorie, in continuall loosing & nothing gaining of the enimie.   ¶Which recouerie was of great facilitie to the French, for that where *Abr. Fl. ex* they came, they found litle or no resistance, but rather a voluntarie submission & *Anglorum præ-* yéelding as it were with holding vp of hands, yer they came to handstroks.   So that *lijs sub Henr. 6.* in such victories and conquests consisted small renowme, sith without slaughter & bloudshed hardie enterprises are not atchiued.   Notablie therefore speaketh Anglorum prælia of these bloudlesse and sweatlesse victories, saieng:

> Delphinus totos (nullo prohibente) per agros
> Francorum transit, priùs expugnata receptans
> Oppida: perfacile est populum domüisse volentem,
> Tendentemq; manus vltrò; nec clarior ornat
> Gloria vincentem fuso sine sanguine regna.

[This yeare the king made a generall progresse and came to the citie of Excester, *An. Reg. 30.* on mondaie the sixteenth of Iulie at after noone, being the feast daie of saint *Iohn Hooker,* Kenelme; and was receiued from place to place verie honorablie through the *alias Voxcell.* whole countrie.   Before he came to this citie, he was met by all the cleargie in their *The king re-* degrées, some thrée miles, some two miles, and some at the citie, all in their copes, *cester.* censing all the waies as they went.   As soone as he came to this citie, he was first conducted to the cathedrall church in all most honourable order.   When he had doone his oblations, he was conueied and lodged in the bishops house.   During his abode here, there was a sessions kept before the duke of Summerset, and certeine men condemned to die for treason, and had iudgement to be executed to death. The bishop and his clergie vnderstanding hereof, with open mouth complained vnto the king, that he caused a sessions to be kept within his sanctuarie, contrarie to the priuilege of his church: and that all their dooings (being doone against law) were of no effect.   And notwithstanding the king and his councell had discoursed *The bishop &* vnto them the iust and orderlie procéeding, the heinousnesse of the offendors, and *his cleargie* the necessitie of their punishment: yet all could not auaile, for holie church nor the *and the duke of* sanctuarie might be prophaned (as they said) with the deciding of temporall matters. *in defense of* Wherevpon the king in the end yéelding to their exclaimes, released a couple of *their ecclesiasti-* arrant traitors, and reuersed all his former lawfull procéedings, and so vpon the wednes-*call priuilege.* daie he departed and returned towards London.]

The duke of Yorke pretending (as yée haue heard) a right to the crowne, as heire *The duke of* to Lionell duke of Clarence, came this yeare out of Ireland vnto London, in the par-*Yorke maketh* lement time, there to consult with his speciall fréends: as Iohn duke of Northfolke, *crowne.* Richard earle of Salisburie, and the lord Richard his sonne, which after was earle of Warwike; Thomas Courtneie earle of Deuonshire, and Edward Brooke lord Cobham. After long deliberation and aduise taken, it was thought expedient, to kéepe their chéefe purpose secret; and that the duke should raise an armie of men, vnder a pre-text to remooue diuerse councellors about the king, and to reuenge the manifest in-iuries doone to the common-wealth by the same rulers.   Of the which as principall, the duke of Summerset was namelie accused, both for that he was greatlie hated of the commons for the losse of Normandie: and for that it was well knowne, that he would be altogither against the duke of Yorke in his chalenge to be made (when time serued) to the crowne; insomuch that his goods by the commons were foulie despoiled *Iohn Stow.* and borne awaie from the Blacke friers.   After which riot, on the next morrow pro-
                                                               clamation

clamation was made through the citie, that no man should spoile or rob, on paine of death. But on the same daie at the standard in Cheape was a man beheaded for dooing contrarie to the proclamation.

Whethasted.
The duke of Yorke raiseth a power, for recouerie of his right to the crowne.

Therefore when the duke of Yorke had thus, by aduise of his speciall fréends, framed the foundation of his long intended enterprise, he assembled a great hoast, to the number of ten thousand able men, in the marches of Wales; publishing openlie, that the cause of this his gathering of people, was for the publike wealth of the realme. The king much astonied at the matter, by aduise of his councell raised a great power, and marched forward toward the duke. But he being thereof aduertised, turned out of that way, which by espials he vnderstood that the king held, and made streight toward London: and hauing knowledge that he might not be suffered to passe through the citie, he crossed ouer the Thames at Kingston bridge, and so kept on towards Kent, where he knew that he had both fréends & well-willers, and there on Burnt heath, a mile from Dertford, and twelue miles from London, he imbatelled, and incamped himselfe verie stronglie, inuironing his field with artillerie and trenches. The king hereof aduertised, brought his armie with all diligence vnto Blackeheath, and there pight his tents.

Whethamsted

Whilest both these armies laie thus imbattelled, the king sent the bishop of Winchester, and Thomas Bourchier, bishop of Elie, Richard Wooduile, lord Riuers, & Richard Andrew, the kéeper of his priuie seale, to the duke: both to know the cause of so great a commotion, and also to make a concord; if the requests of the duke and his companie séemed consonant to reason. The duke hearing the message of the bishops, answered; that his comming was neither to damnifie the king in honour, nor in person, neither yet anie good man: but his intent was, to remooue from him certeine euill disposed persons of his councell, bloud-succours of the nobilitie, pollers of the cleargie, and oppressours of the poore people.

The dukes answer to the kings mesage.

Amongst these, he chéeflie named Edmund duke of Summerset, whome if the king would commit to ward, to answer such articles as against him in open parlement should be both proponed and proued, he promised not onelie to dissolue his armie; but also offered himselfe (like an obedient subiect) to come to the kings presence, and to doo him true and faithfull seruice, according to his loiall and bounden dutie. ¶ But a further vnderstanding of the dukes meaning by this his forceable entering of the realme (as himselfe pretended) maie appeare by certeine letters by him written to the king, and also the kings answers vnto the same: both which I thinke good here to set downe, as I find them recorded.

Abr. Fl. ex I. S.
pag. 666. 667.
in Quart.

Richard duke of Yorke his letter to king Henrie.

PLEASE it your highnesse to conceiue, that since my departing out of this your realme, by your commandement, and being in your seruice in your land of Ireland, I haue beene informed, that diuerse language hath beene said of me to your most excellent estate, which should sound to my dishonour and reproch, and charge of my person: howbeit, that I haue béene, and euer will be, your true liegeman and seruant. And if there be anie man that will or dare saie the contrarie, or charge me otherwise; I beséech your rightwisenesse to call him before your high presence, and I will declare me for my discharge as a true knight ought to doo. And if I doo not, as I doubt not but I shall, I beseech you to punish me as the poorest man of your land. And if he be found vntrue in his suggestion and information, I beséech you of your highnesse that he be punished after his desert, in example of all other.

Please it your excellencie to know, that as well before my departing out of this
your

your realme, for to go into your land of Ireland, in your full noble seruice, as since, certeine persons haue lien in wait for to hearken vpon me, as sir Iohn Talbot knight at the castell of Holt; sir Thomas Standleie knight in Cheshire; Pulford at Chester; Elton at Worcester; Brooke at Glocester; and Richard, groome of your chamber at Beaumaris: which had in charge (as I am informed) to take me and put me into your castell of Conwaie, and to strike off the head of sir William Oldhall knight, and to haue put in prison sir William Deuereux knight, & sir Edmund Malso knight, withouten inlarging, vntill the time that your highnesse had appointed their deliuerance.

Item, at such time as I was purposed for to haue arriued at your hauen of Beaumaris, for to haue come to your noble presence to declare me your true man and subiect, as my dutie is, my landing was stopped and forebarred by Henrie Norice, Thomas Norice, William Buckleie, William Grust, and Bartholomew Bould, your officers in Northwales, that I should not land there, nor haue vittels nor refreshing for me and my fellowship, as I haue written to your excellencie here before. So farre foorth that Henrie Norice, deputie to the chamberlaine of Northwales, said vnto me, that he had in commandement that I should in no wise haue landing, refreshing, nor lodging, for men nor horsse, nor other thing that might turne to my worship or ease: putting the blame vpon William Saie vsher of your chamber, saieng and affirming that I am against your intent, and as a traitor, as I am informed. And moreouer, certeine letters were made and deliuered vnto Chester, Shrewesburie, and to other places for to let mine entrie into the same.

Item, aboue all wrongs and iniuries aboue said doone vnto me of malice, without anie cause, I being in your land of Ireland, in your honourable seruice, certeine commissions were made and directed vnto diuerse persons; which for the execution of the same, sat in certeine places, and the iuries impanelled and charged. Vnto the which iuries certeine persons laboured instantlie to haue me indicted of treason, to the intent for to haue vndoone me and mine issue, and corrupted my bloud, as it is openlie published. Beséeching your maiestie roiall, of your righteousnesse, to doo examine these matters, and therevpon to doo such iustice in his behalfe as the cause requireth: for mine intent is fullie to pursue to your highnesse for the conclusion these matters.

The ansvver of king Henrie to the duke of Yorke.

COOSINE, we haue séene the bill that ye tooke vs late, and also vnderstand the good humble obedience that ye in your selfe shew vnto us, as well in word as in deed: wherefore our intent is, the more hastilie to ease you of such things as were in your said bill. Howbeit, that at our more leasure we might answer you to your said bill, yet we let you wit, that for the causes aforesaid, we will declare you now our intent in these matters: sith it is that a long time among the people hath béene vpon you many strange language, and in especiall anon after your disordinate and vnlawful slaieng of the bishop of Chester, diuerse and manie of the vntrue shipmen and other said (in their maner) words against our estate, making manace to our owne person by your saiengs, that ye should be fetched with manie thousands, and ye should take vpon you that, which ye neither ought, nor as we doubt not, ye will not attempt: so farre foorth that it was said to our person by diuerse, & especiallie we remember of one Wasnes, which had like words to vs.

And also there were diuerse of such false people, that went on and had like language in diuerse of out townes of our land, which by our subiects were taken and dulie executed. Wherefore we sent to diuerse of our courts and places, to hearken and to take héed if anie such maner comming were; and if there had béene, for to

resist

resist it: but comming into our land our true subiect as ye did, our intent was not that ye, nor lesse of estate of our subiects, nor none of your seruants, should not haue beene letted nor warned, but in goodlie wise receiued; howbeit that peraduenture your sudden comming, without certeine warning, caused our seruants to doo as they did, considering the causes aboue said. And as to the indictement that ye spoke of, we thinke verilie, and hold for certeine, that there was none such. And if ye may trulie prooue that anie person was thereabouts, the matter shall be demeaned as the case shall require: so that he shall know it is to our great displeasure. Vpon this, for the easing of your heart in all such matters, we declare, repute, and admit you as our true and faithful subiect, and as our faithfull coosine.

Richard duke of Yorke to king Henrie againe.

PLEASE it your highnesse tenderlie to consider, that great murmur and grudging is vniuersallie in this your realme, in that iustice is not dulie ministred to such as trespasse and offend against you lawes, and in especiall of them that be indicted of treason, and other being openlie noised of the same; whereby great incoueniencies haue fallen, and great is like to fall hereafter in your said realme, which God defend: but if by your highnesse prouision conuenable be made for due reformation and punishment in this behalfe. Wherefore I your humble subiect and true liegeman, Richard duke of Yorke, willing as effectuallie as I can, and desiring the suertie and prosperitie of your most roiall person, and the welfare of this your noble realme, counsell and aduertise your excellencie, for the conseruation of good tranquillitie and peaceable rule among all other subiects, for to ordeine and prouide, that true iustice be had, against all such that so be indicted, or openlie named: wherein I offer my selfe, and will put my indeuour for to execute your commandement in the premises, for the punishing of such offendors, and redresse of the said misrules, to my might and power. And for the hastie execution hereof, like it your highnesse, to addresse these letters of priuie seale and writs to your officers and ministers, to doo, take, and arrest, all such persons so noised and indicted, of what estate, degree, or condition soeuer they be, and them to commit to the Tower of London, and to other of your prisons, there to abide without baile or maineprise, vntill the time they be vtterlie tried, and determined after the course of your lawes.

The ansvver of king Henrie to the duke of Yorke.

COOSINE, as touching your bill last put vp to vs, we vnderstand well that ye (of good heart) counsell and aduertise vs to the setting vp of iustice, and to the spéedie punishing of some persons indicted or noised, offering your seruice to be readie at commandement in the same, sith it is that for manie causes moouing vs to haue determined in our soule, to stablish a sad, and a substantiall councell, giuing them more ample authoritie and power than euer we did before this, in the which we haue appointed you to be one. But sith it is not accustomed, sure, nor expedient, to take a conclusion & conduct by aduise or counsell of one person by himselfe for the conseruation, it is obserued that the greatest and the best, the rich and the poore, in libertie, vertue, and effect of your voices be equall. We haue therfore determined within our selfe to send for our chancellour of England, and for other lords of our councell, yea and all other, togither within short time ripelie to common of these and other our great matters. In which communication, such conclusion (by the grace of God) shall
be

be taken, as shall sound to his pleasure, the weale of vs and our land, as well in these matters as in anie other.

After all this adoo, it was so agreed vpon by aduise, for the auoiding of bloudshed, and pacifieng of the duke and his people, that the duke of Summerset was committed to ward, as some say; or else commanded to kéepe himselfe priuie in his owne house for a time. But it should seeme by that which some haue written, that the duke of Yorke was deceiued of the hope which he had, to be aided of the Kentishmen; insomuch that when he saw himselfe ouermatched by the king in number of people, who had got togither thrice as manie men as the duke had there with him, the duke was the more easie to be dealt with. And so comming to the king, and submitting himselfe by mediation of certeine of the nobilitie, he obteined pardon of that his former presumptuous enterprise. And within a few daies after his comming to London with the king, he openlie in the church of S. Paule (the king being present) receiued a solemne oth, that from thenceforth, he should no more commit any such offence, nor attempt anie thing, either against the king, or any other of his liege people, contrarie to the order of law and iustice.

Whethamsted.

The duke of Yorks reconciliation to the king.

Howsoeuer the matter went, truth it is, that the duke of Yorke, the first of March, dissolued his armie, brake vp his campe, & came to the king's tent, where contrarie to his expectation, & against promise made by the king (as other write) he found the duke of Summerset going at large and set at libertie, whome the duke of Yorke boldlie accused of treason, briberie, oppression, and manie other crimes. The duke of Summersett not onelie made answer to the dukes obiections, but also accused him of high treason, affirming, that he with his fautors and complices had consulted togither, how to come by the scepter and regall crowne of this realme. By meanes of which words the king remooued streight to London, and the duke of Yorke (as prisoner) rode before him, and so was kept a while.

The duke of Yorke accuseth the duke ef Sumerset.

A mutuall charge betwéene the two dukes, Yorke and Summerset of hie treason.

The king assembled togither a great councell at Westminster to heare the accusations of the two dukes, the one obiecting to the other manie heinous and greeuous crimes. But the duke of Summerset, which now conceiued in his mind the thing that shortlie followed, incessantlie exhorted the councell, that the duke of Yorke, by compulsion or otherwise, might be driuen to confesse his offence, that so being attainted of treason, he might suffer execution, and his children to be taken as aduersaries to their natiue countrie; to the intent that by the extinction of him and his sequeale, all ciuill warre and inward diuision might ceasse and be repressed: beseeching almightie God, that so great an enimie to the king and his bloud, might neuer escape punishment, nor continue long in life.

The duke of Summerset set foorth this matter the more vehementlie, bicause he knew perfectlie, that the duke of Yorke dailie imagined with himselfe, how to get the crowne, and to depose and destroie both the king and him. But destinie cannot by anie mans deuise be letted, and manie things (to appearance) declared the duke of Yorkes innocencie in this case. First, his free and voluntarie comming to the king, without constreint, when he was partlie of puissance able to haue incountred with the kings whole power. Secondlie, his humble submission, and reasonable requests, as well on his owne behalfe, as for the poore commons: which might argue that he sought for no souereigntie.

Destinie cannot be auoided.

Whilest the councell treated of sauing or dispatching of this duke of Yorke, a rumor sprang through London, that Edward earle of March, sonne and heire apparent to the saide duke, with a great armie of Marchmen, was comming toward London: which tidings sore appalled the quéene and the whole councell. Beside this, the verie same daie came ambassadours from the cheefe citizens and magistrats of the citie of Burdeaux: whereof the chéefe were, the earle of Kendalc, and the

1452

lord de Lesparre; which signified to the councell, that if they would send an armie
into Gascoigne, the people of the countrie would reuolt from the French part, and
eftsoones become English.   These two things sore troubled the heads of the councell,
which, least inward sedition might hinder outward conquests, set the duke of Yorke

*Occasion that
set the duke of
Yorke frée.* at libertie, and permitted him to go to his castell of Wigmore, in the marches of
Wales, by whose absence the duke of Summerset rose in such high fauour, both with
the king and quéene, that his word onelie ruled, and his voice alone was heard.

*Abr. rt. ex I. S.
pag 671, 672,
in Quart.* ¶ Neuerthelesse the said duke of Yorke had first made his submission, and tooke
his oth to be true, faithfull, and obedient subiect to king Henrie the sixt king of
England, in saint Pauls church at London, there being present the king, and most
of his nobilitie, that is to saie, the dukes of Buckingham, Northampton, and Summerset: the earls of Warwike, Arundell, Salisburie, Shropshire, Deuonshire, Wiltshire, Northumberland, Stafford and Dorset, vicounts of Beaumont and Welles:
barons, Fitz Warren, Sainmound, Cobham, Dowglas, and others: bishops, the
cardinall, archbishop of Yorke and Canturburie, Winchester, Elie, and London, in
these words following.

The tenor of the duke of Yorks submission to king Henrie, vnder his oth.

I RICHARD duke of Yorke confesse and beknow, that I am & ought to be
humble subiect and liegeman to you my souereigne lord king Henrie the sixt, and
owe therefore to beare you faith and truth, as to my souereigne liege lord, and shall
doo all daies vnto my liues end; and shall not at anie time will or assent, that any
thing attempted or doone against your most noble person: but where so euer I shall
haue knowledge of anie such thing imagined or purposed, I shall with all speed and
diligence possible to me, make that your highnesse shall haue knowledge thereof:
and ouer that, doo all that shall be possible to me, to the withstanding and let
thereof, to the vttermost of my life.   I shall not anie thing take vpon against your
roiall estate or obeisance that is due thereto, nor suffer anie other man to doo, as
farre foorth as it shall be in my power to let it: and also shall come at your commandement when so euer I shall be called by the same, in humble and obeisant wise:
but if I be letted by anie sickenesse or impotence of my person, or by such other
cause as shall be thought by you my souereigne lord reasonable.   I shall neuer hereafter take vpon me to gather anie rout, nor to make anie assemblie of your people,
without your commandement or licence, or in my lawfull defense.   In interpretation
or declaration of the which my lawful defence, I shall report me at all times to your
highnesse, and if the case require, to my peeres; nor any thing attempt against anie
of your subiects, of what estate, degree, or condition that they be.   But when
so euer I find my selfe wronged and agreeued, I shall sue humblie for remedie to
your highnesse: and proceed after the course of your lawes, and in none otherwise:
sauing in mine owne lawfull defense in maner aboue said, and otherwise haue to
your highnesse as an humble and true subiect ought to haue him to his souereigne
lord.
     All these things aboue said I promise you trulie to obserue and keepe, by the holie
euangelists conteined in the booke that I laie my hand herevpon, and by the holie
crosse I here touch, and by the blessed sacrament of our Lords bodie, that I shall
now with his mercie receiue.   And ouer I agree me and will, that if I anie time
hereafter, as by the grace of our Lord God I neuer shall, anie thing attempt by waie
of feat or otherwise against your roiall maiestie, and obeisance that I owe therto, or
anie thing take vpon me otherwise than is aboue expressed, I from that time foorth be
vnabled, held, and taken as an vntrue and openlie forsworne man, and vnable to all
                                                                                                    maner

maner of worship, estate, and degree, be it such as I now occupie, or anie other that might in anie wise grow vnto me hereafter. And this I haue here promised and sworne, proceedeth of mine owne desire and free voluntee, and by no constraining or coaction. In witnesse of all the which things aboue written, I Richard duke of Yorke (aboue named) subscribe with mine owne hand and seale.

The councell not forgetting the offer of the Gascoignes, and that they might now haue the citie of Burdeaux, with the countrie round about, by request of the inhabitants, appointed the valiant capteine Iohn lord Talbot earle of Shrewesburie, to go thither with an armie: who arriuing in the Isle of Madre, passed foorth with his power, being scant thrée thousand men, and tooke the strong towne of Fronsacke, and diuerse other townes & fortresses. The inhabitants of Burdeaux, hearing of the earles arriual, sent to him messengers in the darke night, requiring him with all spéed to come and receiue the citie. The earle lost not one houre, but hasted foorth, & came before that citie, yer the Frenchmen within vnderstood anie thing of the citizens purpose. When they were aduertised that there was a gate set open for the Englishmen to enter, they thought to haue escaped secretlie by a posterne: but they were pursued, slaine, and taken by the lord de Lespar, and other of the English armie.

After the regaining of Burdeaux, there arriued at Blaie the bastard of Summerset, sir Iohn Talbot, lord Lisle by his wife, sonne to the said erle of Shrewesburie, the lord Molins, the lord Harington, the lord Camois, sir Iohn Howard, sir Iohn Montgomerie, sir Iohn Vernon, with two and twentie hundred men, with vittels and munitions. When the earle was thus (according to his intent) of all things furnished, first he fortified Burdeaux with Englishmen, and store of vittels; and after that he rode into the countrie abroad, where he obteined cities, and got townes without stroke or dint of sword, for the people alreadie wearied of the French seruitude, and longing sore to return to the English libertie, seemed to desire nothing more than to haue the earle to receiue them into the English obeisance, Amongst other townes, the towne and castell of Chastillon in Perigort was to him deliuered, the which he fortified with men and ordinance verie stronglie.

The French people soone wearie of the French gouernment.

In the meane time, the French king, being aduertised of all these dooings, raised an armie to resist this inuasion made by the erle of Shrewesburie. And first he appointed his capteins to besiege the towne of Chastillon, to the rescue whereof the earle hasted forward, hauing in his companie eight hundred horssemen, vnder the leading of his sonne the lord Lisle, the lord Molins, the lord Camois, sir Edward Hull, sir Iohn Howard, and sir Iohn Vernon. He appointed also fiue thousand footmen, vnder the conduct of the earle of Kendall, and the lord de Lespar, to follow him with all spéed. In his waie, he tooke by fine force a tower which the Frenchmen had taken, and slue all that he found within it. And after by the waie, he met fiue hundred Frenchmen going a foraging, of whome he slue the more part, and chased the other to the campe.

The Frenchmen that laie at the siege, perceiuing by those good runners away that the earle approched, left the siege, and retired in good order into the place which they had trenched, diched, and fortified with ordinance. The earle aduertised how the siege was remoued, hasted forward towards his enimies, doubting most, least they would haue béene quite fled and gone before his comming. But they fearing the displeasure of the French king (who was not far off) if they should haue fled, abode the earles comming, and so receiued him: who though he first with manfull courage, and sore fighting wan the entrie of their campe; yet at length they compassed him about, and shooting him through the thigh with an handgun, slue his horsse, and finally killed him lieng on the ground, whome they durst neuer looke in the face, while he stood on his feet.

The valiant earle of Shrewesburie and his son manfullie slaine.

It

It was said, that after he perceiued there was no remedie, but present losse of the battell, he counselled his sonne the lord Lisle, to saue himselfe by flight, sith the same could not redound to anie great reproch in him, this being the first iournie in which he had béene present. Manie words he vsed to persuade him to haue saued his life: but nature so wrought in the son, that neither desire of life, nor feare of death, could either cause him to shrinke, or conueie himselfe out of the danger, and so there manfullie ended his life with his said father. There died also the earles bastard sonne Henrie Talbot, and sir Edward Hull elect to the order of the garter, and thirtie other men of name and right valiant personages of the English nation. The lord Molins was taken prisoner with thréescore others. The residue of the English people fled to Burdeaux and other places, of whome in the flight were slaine aboue a thousand persons.

Thus at this battell of Chatillon, fought the thirteenth daie of Iulie in this yeare, ended his life Iohn lord Talbot, and of his progenie the first earle of Shrewesburie: after that he with much fame and most victorie, had valiantlie made warre, and serued his prince and countrie by the space of foure and twentie yeares, in the parties beyond the seas, whose corps was left on ground, and after was found by his fréends, and conueied to Whitchurch in Shropshire where it was interred. After this discomfiture diuerse lords fled to Burdeaux, but the earle of Candall, the lords of Montferrant, of Rosaine, & of Dangladas entered into the castell of Chatillon, which by the space of ten daies they defended: but in the end despairing of all succours, they rendred the fortresse, and came safe to Burdeaux.

After this, the townes of saint Million, Liborne, and all other, which the erle of Shrewesburie had conquered, rendred themselues to the Frenchmen, Burdeaux onelie excepted. Which citie, being the last refuge of the English people, the French king in person besieged with all his puissance; and in conclusion constreined both the garrisons and inhabitants to yéeld, so that the Englishmen & Gascoignes might safelie

depart into England or into Calis, with all their substance; and that the lords de Lesparre, Duras, and thirtie others, should neuer (vpon paine of death) be found within anie of the French kings dominions, which lord de Lesparre being after taken in Gascoigne disguised, was made shorter by the head. When this composition was agréed and sealed, the Englishmen were shortlie transported ouer into England, in the moneth of October this present yeare.

Thus was the duchie of Aquitaine, which had continued in the English possession, from the yeare of our Lord 1155, vnto this present yeare, which is neere hand thrée hundred yeares, by the mariage of Elenor daughter and heire to William duke of Aquitaine, wife to king Henrie the second, finallie reduced and brought againe to the

French obedience and seruitude. Within that onlie duchie be foure archbishops, foure and twentie bishops, fifteene earledomes, two hundred and two baronies, and aboue a thousand capteinships and baliffewikes: whereby ye may consider, what a losse this was to the realme of England. On the thirteenth daie of October this yeare, was

the quéene deliuered at Westminster of a faire sonne, who was christened, and named Edward.

His mother susteined not a little slander and obloquie of the common people, who had an opinion that the king was not able to get a child; and therefore sticked not to saie, that this was not his sonne, with manie slanderous words, greatlie sounding to the quéenes dishonour; much part perchance vntrulie. After the birth of this child, he highlie aduanced his brethren on his mothers side; for Edmund he made earle of Richmond, which was father to king Henrie the seuenth, and Iasper he created erle of Penbroke, which died without issue. ¶This yeare, Iohn Stafford archbishop of Canturburie departed this life, and Iohn Kempe archbishop of Yorke was remoued from that see, to succeed in place of the said Stafford, being the thrée score and second

cond archbishop there, & Iohn Booth bishop of Couentrie and Lichfield was translated to Yorke, being the one and fiftith archbishop of that church.

¶ On Bartholomew daie at the wrestling neere vnto Clerkenwell, a gentleman belonging to the prior of saint Iohns, made a rumor or tumult, for the which (by the commandement of the maior) he was arested by Richard Allie one of the shiriffes, and deliuered to Paris a sergeant.   But such resistance was made by parts taking, that the shiriffe was faine to craue helpe of the maior, who with his brethren the aldermen arose from the game, and strengthened the shiriffes.   And for the rescue of the said gentleman, one named Calis, came out of saint Iohns with a great strength of archers, to resist the maior, in the which fraie a yeoman of saint Iohns was slaine, and manie other sore hurt.   The maior himselfe escaped hardlie, for his cap was smitten from his head with an arrow: but the maior with his citizens put the other to flight, sent the principall of them to Newgate, and then tooke his place againe till the games were ended: by which time the citizens had gathered themselues in great number, and fetched him home, neuer maior so stronglie nor so honorablie.]

Abr. Fl. et I. St. pag. 673.

The maior, shiriffes and aldermen, resisted and abused in a fraie neere Clerkenwell.

* This yeare was Thomas Bourchier bishop of Elie (sonne to the countesse of Stafford, and brother to Henrie Bourchier earle of Essex) remooued to the see of Canturburie; who in the yeare after the word became flesh and appeared in humane shape 1443, first obtained the see of Elie (although once before he was by the king put backe from thence after his election of the couent thereunto, and confirmation of the pope) being translated from Worcester to the said sée of Elie, the twelfth daie of March in the said yeare 1443.   This man (after that he had remained at Elie ten yeares, thrée and twentie wéekes, and fiue daies) was (as is before said) in this yeare 1454 remooued to Canturburie by Nicholas the fift then bishop of Rome.   After this he was made chancellor, which office he obteined the seauenth of March, in the yeare 1455, being the thrée and thirtith yeare of king Henrie the sixts reigne.   Lastlie he was aduanced to the dignitie of cardinall by pope Paule the second, in the yeare of our Lord 1465, of whome is made a more liberall discourse in a * tretise of the liues of the chancellors of England: a place of no small authoritie and reputation.]

Fr. Thin. An. Reg. 32. 1454

* In a tretise hereafter following.

After the warres foulie ended in forren parties, ciuill dissention began againe at home, diuided speciallie into two factions.   As K. Henrie descended of the house of Lancaster possessed the crowne from his grandfather king Henrie the fourth (first author of that title) so Richard duke of Yorke, as heire to Lionell duke of Clarence, third sonne to king Edward the third, inforced.   By reason whereof, the nobles as well as the common people were into parts diuided, to the vtter destruction of manie a man, and to the great ruine and decaie of this region: for while the one partie sought to destroie the other, all care of the common-wealth was set aside, and iustice and equitie clearelie exiled.

The duke of Yorke (aboue all things) first sought means how to stir vp the malice of the people against the duke of Summerset, imagining that he being made awaie, his purpose should the sooner take effect.   He also practised to bring the king into the hatred of the people, as that he should not be a man apt to the gouernment of a realme, wanting both wit and stomach sufficient to supplie such a roome.   Manie of the high estates, not liking the world, and disalowing the dooings both of the king and his councell, were faine inough of some alteration.   Which thing the duke well vnderstanding, chiefelie sought the fauour of the two Neuils, both named Richard, one earle of Salisburie, the other earle of Warwike, the first being the father, and the second the sonne.

The duke of Yorke séeks the destructiō of the duke of Summerset.

He banded himselfe with the Neuils.

This earle of Salisburie was second son to Rafe Neuill earle of Westmerland, whose daughter the duke of Yorke had maried, and the said Richard was espoused to ladie Alice, the onelie child and sole heire of Thomas Montacute earle of Salisburie, slaine at the siege of Orleance (as before is declared) of which woman he begat Richard,

The issue of Richard earle Salisburie.

Iohn

Iohn, and George: Richard the eldest sonne espoused Anne, the sister and heire of the entire bloud of lord Henrie Beauchamp earle and after duke of Warwike, in whose right and title he was created and named earle of Warwike. [Full fraught was this nobleman with good qualities right excellent and manie, all which a certeine naturall grace did vnto all estates so farfoorth recommend, that with high and low he was in singular fauour and good liking so as (vnsought for) it séemed, in authoritie among them, he grew able to command all alone.

W. P.

An. Reg. 33.

When the duke of Yorke had fastened his chaine betwéene these two strong pillers, he with his frends wrought so effectuouslie, and handled his businesse so politikelie, that the duke of Summerset was arested in the quéenes great chamber, and sent to the Tower of London, where he kept his Christmasse without great solemnitie. Against whom, soone after in open parlement were laid diuerse and heinous articles of high treason, as well for the losse of Normandie, as for the late mischance which happened in Guien. The king at that time was sicke at Clarendon, and conueied to London, by reason whereof no finall determination procéeded in this weightie cause; but all was put in suspense, till the next assemblie of the high court of parlement. Some doo write, that whilest the king was sicke, the duke of Yorke bare all the rule, and gouerned as regent or viceroie, by authoritie committed to him by the lords of the realme, then assembled in councell; he to sée to the preseruation and good gouernement of the common-wealth, during the kings sicknesse, which was so gréeuous (as it was said) that he laie senselesse, and was not able for a time either to go or stand.

The duke of Summerset arrested.

1455

The king sicke.

Whethamsted.

The duke of Yorke hauing aforehand obteined an absolution of the pope, in discharge of his oth before taken, did now discouer his stomach against the duke of Summerset. But when the king was amended againe, and resumed to him his former gouernement, either of his owne mind, or by the quéenes procurement, the duke of Summerset was set at libertie; by which doing, great enuie and displeasure grew. That notwithstanding, the quéene (which then bare the chiefe rule) caused the duke of Summerset to be preferred to the capteineship of Calis, wherwith not onlie the commons, but also manie of the nobilitie were greatlie gréeued and offended, saieng, that he had lost Normandie, and so would he doo Calis.

The duke of Summerset set at libertie.

Made deputie of Calis.

The duke of Yorke and his adherents, perceiuing that neither exhortation nor charging him with his crimes preuailed against the duke of Summerset, they meant to mend the matter by open war: & soone after he being in the marches of Wales, accompanied with his speciall friends, the earles of Salisburie, and Warwike, the lord Cobham, and others, assembled a power, and in warlike maner marched toward London. The king informed hereof, assembled likewise a great host, and meaning to méet with the duke, rather in the north parts than about London, where it was thought he had too manie friends, he accompanied with the dukes of Summerset and Buckingham, the earles of Penbroke, Stafford, Northumberland, Deuonshire, Dorset, and Wilshire, the lords Clifford, Sudlie, Berneis, Roos, and others, being in all aboue two thousand men of warre, departed from Westminster the twentith, or (as some haue) the one and twentith of Maie, and laie the first night at Wadford.

The duke of Yorke assembled an armie.

Whethamsted.

The king with two thousand.

Of whose dooings the duke of Yorke by espials hauing still aduertisement, with all his power, being not past thrée thousand men (as some write) coasted the countrie, and came to saint Albons the third daie next insuing. The king there had pight his standard in a place called Goselow, otherwise Sandiford, in saint Peters street: the lord Clifford kept the barriers of the towne, to stop, that the duke being assembled in Keie field, should not enter the towne. ¶ The duke of Yorke (saith one moderne chronographer) knowing the strength made against him, abiding in the field aforesaid, from seuen of the clocke in the morning vntill it was almost ten of the clocke without anie stroke smitten on either part, by the aduise of his councell sent vnto the king vnder these words following.

The duke with thrée thousand.

Abr. Fl. ex I. S. pag. 675, 676, 677, in Quart.

Words

Words in writing by the duke of Yorke to the king.

PLEASE it vnto your excellent grace, Richard duke of Yorke, to take him as your true liege man and humble subiect; and to consider and tender at the reuerence of God, and in the waie of charitie, the true intent of my comming, and to be good and gratious souereigne vnto me, & all other your true liege men, which, that with all their power and might will be readie to liue and die with you in your right, and to doo all things as shall like your maiestie roiall to command vs, if it be to the worship of the crowne of England, and the welfare of this your noble realme. Moreouer, gratious lord, please it vnto your maiestie roiall, of your great goodnesse and rightwisenesse, to incline your will to heare & féele the rightwise part of vs your true subiects and liege men. First, praieng and beséeching to your souereigne, Christ Iesus, of his high and mightie power, to giue you vertue of prudence, and that through the praier of the glorious martyr S. Albon giue you verie knowledge of our truths, and to know the intent of our assembling at this time: for God that is in heauen knoweth, our intent is rightfull and true. And therefore we praie vnto that mightie Lord in these words: Domine sis clypeus defensionis nostræ. Wherfore gratious lord, please it your maiestie roiall, to deliuer such as we will accuse, and they to haue like as they haue deserued: and this doone, you to be honorablie worshipped as most rightfull king and our true gouernour. And if we should now at this time be promised, as afore this time (is not vnknowen) haue béene promises broken which haue béene full faithfullie promised, and therevpon great othes sworne, we will not now cease for no such promises, nor oth, till we haue them which haue deserued death, or else we to die therefore.

The answer by the king to the duke of Yorke.

I KING Henrie charge and command, that no manner of person, of what degrée, estate or what condition soeuer he be, abide not; but that they auoid the field, and not be so hardie to make resistance against me in my owne realme. For I shall know what traitour dare be so bold to raise anie people in mine owne land, wherethrough I am in great disease and heauines. By the faith I owe vnto S. Edward, and vnto the crowne of England, I shall destroie them euerie mothers sonne, and eke they to be hanged, drawne, and quartered, that may be taken afterward of them, in example to make all such traitors to beware for to make anie rising of people within mine owne land, and so traitorouslie to abide their king and gouernour. And for a conclusion, rather than they shall haue anie lord, that here is with me at this time, I shall this day for their sake in this quarell my selfe liue and die.

The words of the duke of Yorke to all gentlemen and other assembled with him.

SIRS, the king our souereigne lord will not be reformed at our beséeching ne praier, nor will not in no wise vnderstand the intent wherfore we be here assembled and gathered at this time, but onelie is in full purpose to destroie vs all. And thervpon a great oth hath made, that is none other waie, but that he with all his power will pursue vs; and if we be taken, to giue vs a shamefull death, léesing our liuelod and goods, and also our heires shamed for euer. Therefore sirs, now sith it will none otherwise be, but that we shall vtterlie die; better it is for vs to die in the field, than
cowardlie

cowardlie to be put to an vtter rebuke and shamefull death, for the right of England standeth in vs. Considering also in what perill it standeth at this time, and for to redresse the mischéefe thereof, let euerie man helpe to his power this daie, and in that quarell to quite vs like men, to the crowne of England; praieng and beséeching vnto that Lord, the which is eternall, that reigneth in the glorious kingdome celestiall, to kéepe and saue vs this daie in our right, and through the gifts of his holie grace we may be made strong to withstand the great, abhominable, and horrible malice of them that purpose to destroie vs and the realme of England, and put vs to a shamefull death. Praie we therefore to the Lord to be our comfort and our defendour, saieng these words, Domine sis clypeus defensionis nostræ.]

Whethamsted.
The duke of Buckingham sent to the duke of Yorke.

But another historie-writer saith, that the king, when first he heard of the duke of Yorks approch, sent to him messengers, the duke of Buckingham, and others to vnderstand what he meant by his comming thus in maner of warre. The duke of Buckingham to his message was answered by the duke of Yorke and his complices, that they were all of them the kings faithfull liege subiects, and intended no harme to him at all: but the cause of our comming (saie they) is not in meaning anie hurt to his person. But let that wicked and naughtie man the duke of Summerset be

The duke of Summerset burded with all things that had happened amisse.
W. P.

deliuered vnto vs, who hath lost Normandie, and taken no regard to the preseruation of Gascoigne; and furthermore, hath brought the realme vnto this miserable estate; that where it was the floure of nations, and the princesse of prouinces [now is it haled into desolation & spoile, not so dreadfull by malice of forren enimie, that indéed vtterlie (as yée know) seeketh our ruine, as by the intollerable outrages of him that so long ago & euen still appeares to haue sworne the confusion of our king and realme.] If it therefore please the king to deliuer that bad man into our hands, we are readie without trouble or breach of peace, to returne into our countrie. But if the king be not minded so to do, bicause he cannot misse him; let him vnderstand, that we will rather die in the field, than suffer such a mischéefe vnredressed.

The king aduertised of this answer, more wilfull than tollerable, appointed him rather to trie battell, than deliuer the duke of Summerset to his enimies. Whereof they ascerteined made no longer staie, but streightwaie sounded the trumpet to battell: or rather (as Hall saith) while king Henrie sent foorth his ambassadours to treat of

The first battell of saint Albons.
Whethamsted.

peace at the one end of the towne, the earle of Warwike with his Marchmen entred at the other end, and fiercelie setting on the kings fore-ward, within a small time discomfited the same. The place where they first brake into the towne, was about the middle of saint Peters stréet. The fight for a time was right sharpe and cruell, for the duke of Summerset, with the other lords, comming to the succours of their companions that were put to the woorse, did what they could to beat backe the enimies: but the duke of Yorke sent euer fresh men to succour the wearie, and to supplie the

Edw. Hall.

places of them that were hurt, whereby the kings armie was finallie brought low, and all the cheefteins of the field slaine and beaten downe.

The duke of Summerset slaine.

For there died vnder the signe of the castell, Edmund duke of Summerset, who (as hath béene reported) was warned long before to auoid all castels: and beside him laie Henrie the second of that name earle of Northumberland, Humfrie earle of Stafford

Thomas lord Clifford, saith Whethamsted.

sonne to the duke of Buckingham, Iohn lord Clifford, sir Barthram Antwisell knight, a Norman borne (who forsaking his natiue countrie to continue in his loiall obedience to king Henrie, came ouer to dwell here in England when Normandie was lost) William Zouch, Iohn Boutreux, Rafe Bapthorp, with his sonne William Corwin, William Cotton, Gilbert Faldinger, Reginald Griffon, Iohn Dawes, Elice Wood, Iohn Eith, Rafe Woodward, Gilbert Sharlock, and Rafe Willoughbie esquiers, with manie other, in all to the number of eight thousand, as Edward Hall saith in his chronicle: if there escaped not a fault in the impression, as 8000 for 800, sith hundreds in verie déed would better agree
with

with the number of the kings whole power, which he brought with him to that battell, being not manie aboue two thousand, as by writers appeareth.

Humfrie duke of Buckingham, being wounded, and Iames Butler earle of Ormond and Wilshire, and Thomas Thorp lord chéefe baron of the escheker, séeing fortune thus against them, left the king alone, and with a number fled awaie. Those that thus fled, made the best shift they could to get awaie through gardens and backesides, through shrubs, hedges and woods, séeking places where to hide themselues, vntill that dangerous tempest of the battell were ouerblowne. Diuerse of the kings house The kings part also that could better skill to plaie the courtiers than warriors, fled with the first; and vanquished. those of the east parts of the realme were likewise noted of too much lacke of courage, for their spéedie withdrawing themselues, and leauing the king in danger of his aduersaries: who perceiuing his men thus fled from him, withdrew into a poore mans house to saue himselfe from the shot of arrowes, that flue about him as thicke as snow.

¶ This doone, saith one historien, the duke of Yorke, the earles of Warwike, and *Abr. Fl. ex I. S.* Salisburie, came vnto the king where he was, and besought him on their knées of grace *pag.* 678, 679.
in Quart. and forgiuenesse for that they had doone in his presence, and besought him of his highnesse to take them to grace, and as his true liege men. The king desiring them to cease their people, that there should be no more hurt doone, and to obeie his commandement, did cause to be proclamed in the kings name, that all manner of people should cease off their malice, and not to smite one stroke more, and so ceassed the battell. And vpon the day next after, the king and the duke of Yorke, the earles of Warwike & Salisburie, came all to London; and were lodged in the bishops palace of London, where they kept their Whitsuntide with great ioy and solemnitie, concluding there to hold a parlement, the same to begin on the ninth daie of Iulie next following.]

Another historien saith, that the duke of Yorke, aduertised of the place into the which the king was withdrawne for the safetie of himselfe, and taking him into his power, comforted him in the best wise he could; assuring him, that now that the common enimie of the realme was dispatched, to wit, the duke of Summerset, he had cause rather to reioise, than to be sorie, sith his destruction was the kings preseruation. And for himselfe and all his adherents he vndertooke, that they were and would remaine, during life, his most faithfull liege people, readie in all points to serue him, as his trustie and obedient subiects. After he had vsed such words, as wherewith best to comfort him, he brought the king foorth of that simple house with all due reuerence shewed toward him first to the shrine, and after to his chamber.

Whilest the duke of Yorke was about thus to comfort the king, the soldiers that had the victorie now in their hands, applied the spoile, namelie, the Northerne men, stripping not onelie those that had borne armor against them, but also the townsmen and other, with whom they might méet. So that it was thought, if the king had taken vp his lodging at his first comming thither, within the abbeie, as he did not (but in the middest of the towne, to prouide the better to resist his enimies) the abbeie had béene spoiled also. This was the end of the first battell at saint Albons, Battell of S. Albons on thursday which was fought vpon the thursdaie next before the feast of Penthecost, being the the 23 of Maie. thrée and twentith day of Maie, in this three and thirtith yeare of the kings reigne. An. Reg. 33. The bodies of the noble men were buried in the monasterie in our ladies chappell, and Foure of the to the meane people in other places. This Edmund duke of Summerser left behind him wit, the duke of Sumerset, the thrée sonnes, Henrie, Edmund and Iohn, which to the extremitie of death tooke part earle of Northumberland, and with the line of king Henrie. the lord Clifford,
were buried in
our ladie chapell.
Whethamsted.

[There was this yeare a great fight & fraie vpon Clift heath, distant about two miles from Excester, betwéene Thomas Courtneie earle of Deuonshire, against William lord Bonuile of Shut, and sundrie men of both parts were slaine. But yet the lord Bon- *Iohn Hooker aliàs Vowell.* uile

uile preuailed & had the victorie, who foorthwith came to this citie, and the gates before being shut, were opened and he receiued; which thing so greeued the earle, that he continuallie sought thencefoorth to be reuenged. But not long after in the quarell betwéen king Henrie the sixt, and king Edward the fourth, he ended his daies, and was beheaded at Yorke, and was the last of that line.]

The duke of Yorke, hauing gotten the victorie, remembred well, that he had published abroad how the onelie cause of this warre was, for the aduancement of the common-wealth, and therefore vsing all courtesie, would not touch the kings person after anie violent sort; but with all honour and due reuerence conueied him to London **A parlement.** and so to Westminster. To which place was summoned a parlement, which began the ninth daie of Iulie, in the which session, the late duke of Glocester was openlie declared a true subiect, both to the king and to the realme. Beside this, it was enacted, that no person should either iudge or report anie point of vntruth of the duke of Yorke, the earles of Salisburie and Warwike, or of anie knight, esquier, archer, or other, for comming in warlike araie against the king, at saint Albons; considering their enterprise was onelie to sée the kings person in safegard.

Whethamsted. **Collaterall.** But all the blame was put vpon the duke of Summerset, Thomas Thorp, baron of **A letter kept** the escheker, and William Iosep esquier, the kings collaterall companion; bicause that **from the king of** they, vpon malicious purpose, kept a certeine letter from the kings knowledge, and **purpose.** would in no wise suffer it to be deliuered vnto him, notwithstanding the same made to the aduancement of some good peace, had it béene throughlie and aduisedlie read, weied & considered. In which letter they declared, that as faithfull and humble subiects, they required onelie, that it would please the king (whose honor, health, suertie, and preseruation, they chéefelie wished) not to giue credence to their ad-uersaries malicious suggestions, till their comming to his presence, vnto the which they humblie besought him that they might be admitted as his faithfull liege people, to shew the intent and purpose of their commings; which was to none other end, than to declare their fidelitie and allegiance towards his most roiall person, intending to put themselues with as much diligence and trauell in all things that might aduance his honour, health, and safegard, as any subiect he had liuing.

The kéeping backe of this letter from the kings sight and knowledge, did minister matter sufficient vnto the parlement, to colour and iustifie for well doone all transgres-**The duke of** sions committed in the late battell and chase at saint Albons. In this parlement also, **Yorkes comming** the duke of Yorke was made protector of the realme, and the earle of Salisburie was **against the king** appointed to be lord chancellour, and had the great seale to him deliuered, and the **iustified** **The duke of** earle of Warwike wss elected to the office of the capteineship of Calis, and the **Yorke made pro-** **tector of the** territories of the same; and thus the rule of the realme rested in the orders of the **realme.** duke and chancellour, and all warlike affaires remained, principallie in the earle of **The king to** Warwike.   And so amongest them it was agréed, that king Henrie should reigne still **reigne in name** in name and dignitie, but neither in déed nor in authoritie; not minding to destroie **but not in au-** **thoritie.** him, least they might suddenlie prouoke the furie of the common people against them, bicause that of the simple sort of people he was for his holinesse of life, and abundant clemencie, much fauoured and highlie estéemed.

Whethamsted. In this parlement also it was enacted, that the king should resume, take into his **An act for the K.** hands againe, haue and reteine into his possession, all honours, castels, lordships, **to reuoke cer-** **teine grants.** townes, villages, manours, lands, tenements, wasts, forests, chases, rents, reuersions, fées, farmes, seruices, issues, profits, counties, aduousons of priories, churches, hos-pitals, and free chapels, and all other reuenues with their appurtenances, the which had passed from him since the first daie of his reigne vnto that present; either by his letters patents, or authoritie of parlement, and manie other meanes, whether by grant, confirmation, or release from him made 'in fée simple, or fée taile, for tearme of life or yeares, to anie maner of person and persons in England, Wales, Scotland, or the marches;

marches; in Ireland, or in the townes of Calis, & Guisnes, & the marches there. And likewise all grants made of such things as are aboue mentioned, being parcell of the duchie of Lancaster; and further all grants of offices, roomes, fées, wages, or commodities, not accustomed to belong to anie office or charge before the said first daie of the kings reigne, were likewise reuoked.

Diuerse other things were also conteined within this reuocation and generall resumption; with certeine exceptions yet and prouisoes had, as were thought conuenient, and as by the same act it dooth appeare. Moreouer, now that the duke of Yorke and his adherents had wrested the whole rule & gouernement into their hands; all such persons as the king either loued, or the quéene fauoured, were put beside the priuie councell; and such put in their places, as were knowne to fauour the house of Yorke. Also the officers were changed thoroughout the realme, at the will and disposition of the protector, chancellour, and capteine of Calis; so that they constituted as it were a triumuirat, ruling all things at discretion of these thrée. And yet in all their rule I find not that anie mention is made of their deferring of iustice, or of anie polling or briberie: as was openlie prooued by such as gouerned before their time. Onelie they were noted of diuerse spirituall persons, and namelie of the abbat of Westminster and his moonks, for a great offense: bicause they tooke out of the sanctuarie at Westminster, Iohn Holland duke of Excester, all against the order taken in the last parlement, and sent him to the castell of Pomfret. *Shifting of officers.*

But now the lord Henrie Beauford, newlie duke of Summerset by the death of duke Edmund his father, slaine at the battell of saint Albons (as aboue is rehearsed) and Humfrie duke of Buckingham (who then & there lost his sonne and heire) and other of estate taking the part of king Henrie, whose case they did much bewaile & doubt, as perceiuing whereto the courtesie of the duke of Yorke did draw: they therefore thinking it necessarie to purueie for a remedie yer the mischeefe happened, consulted with the quéene. By whose aduise was a great councell called at Gréenewich, where the duke of Yorke was discharged of his protectorship, & the earle of Salisburie depriued also of his office. ¶ This sudden change amongst the nobilitie caused alterations, and seditious attempts in the commonaltie, and in especiall within London: whereof this was one. A yoong merchant, which before time had béene in diuerse cities of Italie, and there forbidden by the magistrats (as the law and maner is) to weare anie weapon, now challenged an Italian in Cheapside for wearing a dagger, telling him it was against his owne countrie lawes: wherto bicauae the Italian answered somewhat disdainefullie, the merchant not onelie tooke by force from him his dagger, but also with the same brake his pate. *Henrie duke of Summerset.* *The duke of Yorke discharged of his office.* 1456

This Italian in great hast complained to the maior, so that at the next court holden at the Guildhall, the merchant was sent for, and vpon charge of his offense, he was commanded to ward. Wherevpon diuerse other light persons within the citie, assembled togither in great plumps, by force constreined the maior to deliuer the prisoner out of Newgate: and not so satisfied, like mad men ran to the seuerall houses of diuerse Venetians, Lucases, and Florentins, and them spoiled, robbed, and rifled without reason or measure. The maior, perceiuing this enormious dooing, assembled a number of substantiall and graue citizens; who (not without bloudshed and maiming of sundrie) appeased the rage, and caused the misruled people to depart to their houses. The beginner of this vprore got him to Westminster, and there registred himselfe for a sanctuarie man. *An vprore in the citie of London.* *A foule disorder.*

The quéene, which now againe ruled all, being aduertised of this vnlawfull misdemeanour, sent the dukes of Excester and Buckingham, with other noble men to London, with a commission oier and terminer, for the inquirie and punishment of so seditious an offense. But when the maior, the two dukes, and the two cheefe iustices were set in the Guildhall vpon their commission, intelligence was giuen, that a

number

number of light persons were approching in armor to rescue the prisoners apprehended for the late robberie and riot, as they were caried to their arraignment. The two dukes and the other commissioners quickelie thense departed, and left their inquirie for that daie, though in déed in no such danger as they doubted: for certeine discréet and sage citizens so handled the matter, that no misorder followed of that furie.

A common councell called. The maior on the next daie called a common councell, whereof the number was an hundred fourescore and od, who ordeined that all wardens of mysteries shuld assemble their companies in their halles, where exhortation should be to the obseruation of peace; and if they spied any man either readie to stirre a rumor, or make to the deliuerance of such as were in prison, their names should be secretlie written, and so deliuered to the maior: which policie well appeased this outrage. Wherevpon after the commissioners sat in Guildhall, where manie of the robbers were attainted & put to execution, beside diuerse great fines set on the heads of diuerse merchants, & paid, for winking at the matter. ¶ This yeare Iohn Kempe archbishop of Canturburie departed this life, & Thomas Burstlier bishop of Elie remooued to his place, being the threescore and third archbishop of that see.

Abr. Fl. ex I. S. 681. 1457. Fabian. ¶ In the moneth of Nouember, in the Ile of Portland not farre from the towne of Weimouth, was seene a cocke comming out of the sea, hauing a great crest vpon his head, and a great red beard, and legs of halfe a yard long: he stood on the water & crowed foure times, and euerie time turned him about, and beckened with his head, toward the north, the south, and the west, and was of colour like a fesant, & when he had crowed thrée times, he vanished awaie. And shortlie after were taken at Erith within twelue miles of London, foure great and woonderfull fishes whereof one was called Mors marina, the second a sword fish, the other two were whales.]

An. Reg. 35. The French nation, hearing of the ciuall dissention within the realme here, and for an old grudge séeking our annoie, two nauies appointed they to inuade the townes standing vpon the riuage of the sea. The capteins of the one fléet was William lord Pomiers, and of the other sir Peter Bressie, a great ruler in Normandie. These two capteins, taking their course out of the mouth of Saine, seuered themselues the one westward; and the other eastward, which was sir Peter Bressie, who sailing alongst the coasts of Sussex and Kent, durst not yet take land, but staid in the Downes: and there hauing Sandwich spoiled by the French. by espiall perfect notice that Sandwich was neither peopled nor fortified (because that a little before, the rulers of the towne were from thense departed, for to auoid the plague, which sore there afflicted and slue the people) he entered the hauen, spoiled the towne, and after such poore stuffe as he there found rifled and taken, he fearing an assemblie of the countrie, shortlie gat him awaie.

Fulnaie. The Scots inuade England. The lord Pomiers likewise tooke his course westward, & by night burning certeine houses in Fulnaie with a little pillage retired into Britaine. The Scots also (busie like flies where no flap to fraie them) entered into Northumberland (king Iames the second being there in person) & burned certeine poore houses, and little cottages: but in the verie middest of their great enterprise, they hearing of the duke of Yorkes marching toward them with a great host, with much paine and no gaine in all hast returned to their countrie. But now to passe ouer outward inuasions, & to intreat of the dailie disorder amongest the nobles at home. So was it, that a great conflict fell betwéene the lord Egremond, & the sonnes of the erle of Salisburie; in which manie persons were slaine, & a great number hurt. The lord Egremond, séeking to get awaie but The lord Egremond committed to Newgate. could not, by force was taken & brought before the councell: where the king and the queene, to shew themselues indifferent, adiudged him to paie to the earle of Salisburie a great summe of monie; and for his heinous offense against the lawes, was committed He made an escape. to Newgate in London, out of which he escaped, to the great trouble of the shiriffes. The queene nothing more séeking than the ouerthrow of the duke of Yorke and his

his friends, and preceiuing she could attempt nothing against nim neere to London, because the duke was in more estimation there, than either the king hir husband, or hir selfe; therefore she caused the king to make a progresse into Warwikeshire for his health and recreation. And so in semblance of hawking and hunting came to Couentree, where diuerse waies were studied to fulfill the queenes desire: for the accomplishing whereof, the duke of Yorke, the earles of Salisburie, and Warwike (whose destructions was chieflie sought) were sent for to Couentrée by the kings letters, vnder his priuie seale, to which place the said lords without suspicion of danger obedientlie resorted.

A practise to haue intrapped the duke of Yorke.

But being admonished by secret friends, what was intended against them, they by flight auoided that danger, where otherwise their liues had béene lost without all remedie. And so without bidding anie farewell, they departed from the court; the duke vnto Wigmoore in the marches of Wales, the earle of Salisburie to his castell of Middleham in the north, and the earle of Warwike sailed to Calis. The bodies of which thrée noble personages though thus separated, yet their hearts knit in one, and still went messengers & letters betwixt them, to communicat their deuises, and giue signification of their minds and purposes.

In this yéere Reginald Peacocke bishop of Chichester, abiured at Paules crosse, all his bookes burnt, and he himselfe commanded to keepe his owne house during his naturall life: because that he (verie well learned, and better stomached) began to mooue questions, not priuilie but openlie, in the vniuersities, concerning the annates, Peter pence, and other iurisdictions & authorities, which the pope vsurped; and not onelie put foorth such questions, but declared his mind and opinion in the same. Some saie he held that spirituall persons by Gods law ought to haue no temporall possessions, nor that personall tithes by Gods law were due [nor that christian men were to beléeue in the catholike church, nor in the communion of saints, but to beléeue that a catholike church and a communion of saints there is] and that he held how the vniuersall church might erre in matters of faith; and that it is not of necessitie to beléeue all that which is ordeined by generall councels, nor all that which they call the vniuersall church ought to be allowed and holden of all christian people.

An. Reg. 36.

1458

The bishop abiured for moouing against the popes extortion.

W. P.

Moreouer, that it was méet to euerie man to vnderstand the scriptures in the true and plaine sense, & none bound to glosses of anie other sense, vpon anie necessitie of saluation. ¶ But because I find a larger report héereof elsewhere, and as more methodicall, so also (as it seemeth) in such forme as it was Res gesta, a déed doone, it shall not be amisse to insert the same. This bishop was a secular doctor of diuinitie, that had labored manie yéeres to translate the holie scripture into English, & was accused to haue passed the bounds of diuinitie and christian beléefe in certeine articles, of the which he was conuict before the archbishop of Canturburie, and other bishops and clearks, and after vtterlie abiured, reuoked, and renounced those articles openlie at Paules crosse in his mother toong on the fourth day of December, as followeth.

Abr. Fl. ex I. S. pag. 682, 683, 684, 685, 686, *in Quart.*

The forme of his abiuration.

IN the name of the trinitie, father, sonne, and holie-ghost, I Reinold Peacocke bishop of Chichester vnworthie, of mine owne power and will without anie maner coaction or dread, confesse and knowledge that I here, before this time, presuming of my naturall wit, and preferring my iudgement and naturall reason before the new and the old testament, and the authoritie & determination of our mother holie church, haue held, written and taught otherwise than the holie Romane and vniuersall church teacheth, preacheth, or obserueth. And one is against the true catholike and apostles faith, I haue written, taught, and published manie & diuerse perilous doctrines, books, works,

works, and writings, conteining heresies and errors, contrarie to the faith catholike, and determination of holie church: and speciallie these heresies and errours following, that is to saie in particular.

In primis, quòd non est de necessitate fidei credere, quòd dominus noster Iesus Christus post mortem descendit ad inferos.

Item, quòd non est de necessitate salutis credere in sanctorum communionem.

Item, quòd ecclesia vniuersalis potest errare in hijs quæ sunt fidei.

Item, quòd non est de necessitate salutis credere & tenere illud, quod consilium generale & vniuersalis ecclesia statuit, approbat, seu determinat, in fauorem fidei, & ad salutem animarum, est ab vniuersis Christi fidelibus approbandum & tenendum.

Wherefore I miserable sinner, which here before long time haue walked in darkenesse, and now by the mercie and infinit goodnesse of God reduced into the right waie, and light of truth, and considering my selfe gréeuouslie haue sinned and wickedlie haue informed and infected the people of God, returne and come againe to the vnitie of our mother holie church, and all heresies and errors written and conteined in my said books, works and writings, here solemnelie and openlie reuoke & renounce. Which heresies and errors, and all other spices of heresies I haue before this time before the most reuerend father in God, and my good lord of Canturburie, in diuerse and lawfull forme iudiciallie abiured, submitting my selfe, being then and also now at this time verie contrite and penitent sinner, to the correction of the church and of my said lord of Canturburie.

And ouer this, exhorting & requiring in the name & vertue of almightie God, in the saluation of your soules and mind, that no man hereafter giue faith and credence to my said pernicious doctrines, heresies and errors; neither my said books kéepe, hold, or read in anie wise; but that they all such books, works and writings suspect of heresies, deliuer in all goodlie hast vnto my said lord of Canturburie, or to his commissioners and deputies, in eschewing of manie inconueniences and great perils of soules, the which else might be cause of the contrarie. And ouer this declaration of my conuersion and repentance, I here openlie assent, that my said books, works, and writings, for declaration and cause aboue rehearsed, be deputed vnto the fire, and openlie burnt in example and terror of all other, &c.

After this, he was depriued of his bishoprike, hauing a certeine pension assigned vnto him for to liue on in an abbeie, and soone after died. His books were intituled: 1 Of christian religion, and a booke perteining therevnto. 2 Of matrimonie. 3 Iust expressing of holie scripture, diuided into three parts. 4 The donet of christian religion. 5 The follower of the donet. 6 The booke of faith. 7 The booke filling the foure tables. 8 The booke of worshipping. 9 The prouoker of christian men. 10 The booke of councell.

In the moneth of Ianuarie died the earle of Deuonshire in the abbeie of Abindon, poisoned (as men said) being there at that time with quéene Margaret, to appeasé the malice betweene the yoong lords, whose fathers wee slaine at saint Albons, and they that held with the duke of Yorke. The thirtéenth of Aprill there was a great fraie in Fléetstreet, betweene men of court and the inhabitants of the same stréet, in which fraie the quéenes atturnie was slaine. For this fact the king committed the principall gouernours of Furniuals, Cliffords, and Barnards In to prison in the castell of Hertford; and William Tailor alderman of that ward, with manie other were sent to Windsor castell the seuenth of Maie. On thursdaie in Whitsunweeke, the duke of Summerset with Anthonie Riuers and other foure kept iustes before the quéene in the Tower of London against three esquiers of the queenes. And in like maner at Gréenewich the sundaie following.]

The quéenes atturnie slain.

Iusting in the Tower of London.

King Henrie and his councell, perceiuing the duke of Yorke laie still and stirred not

not, returned to London, and there called a great councell, openlie declaring how the French and Scots (imboldened by the ciuill discord within this realme) attempted to annoie the same, as of late they had shewed apparant tokens, and likelie not ceasse vpon occasions to doo further displeasures, till a perfect concord were concluded betwéene him and his fréends, and those of the contrarie part and confederacie. And to the intent that he would be the cheefe author of peace, he promised of his dignitie so to interteine the duke of Yorke and his fréends, that all old grudges should be not onelie inwardlie forgotten, but also outwardlie forgiuen, which should be cause of perpetuall loue and assured amitie,

This deuise was of all men iudged for the best. Wherevpon diuerse graue persons were sent to the duke of Yorke, and all other the great estates of the realme, who since the battell of saint Albons neuer met nor communed togither, commanding them for great causes to repaire to the kings court without delaie. At his com- ^{The peeres of the realme called to a treatie.} mandement came to London Richard duke of Yorke, with foure hundred men, and was lodged at Bainards castell being his owne house; and after him came the earle of Salisburie with fiue hundred men, and was likewise lodged at his owne house called the Herbour. Then came the dukes of Excester and Summerset with eight hundred men, and were lodged without Temple barre; and the earle of Northumberland, the lord Egremond, and the lord Clifford came with fiftéene hundred men, and lodged without the citie. The earle of Warwike also came from Calis with six hundred men in red iackets, imbrodered with white ragged staues behind and before, and was lodged at the graie friers.

Thus were all those of the one part lodged within the citie, and those of the other without, in Holborne towards Westminster, and in other places of the suburbs, all vpon wise consideration: for that the Yorke faction and the Lancastrians could not well haue béene mingled without danger of discord. After that these lords were thus come vnto London, the king and the quéene shortlie followed, comming thither the seuentéenth daie of March, and lodged in the bishops palace. Bicause no riotous attempt or bickering should be begun betwéene anie of the parties or their retinues, ^{The prouidence of the citie for safegard of peace.} the maior and aldermen of the citie kept great watch, as well by daie as by night, riding about the citie by Holborne, and Fléetstréet, with fiue thousand men well armed and arraied, to sée good order and peace on all sides kept.

The lords which lodged within the citie held a dailie councell at blacke friers; the other part soiourning without the walles, assembled likewise in the chapiter house at Westminster. At length by the diligent trauell and good exhortation of the archbishop of Canturburie, and other prelats; both parties were persuaded to come to communication, and so did. Where, after long debating of grieuances on both sides, they ^{The lords are brought to agrée.} promising to forget all old rancors, and to be freends each to other, & both obedient to the king, were accorded by award, wherof writings were sealed, signed, and deliuered to effect as followeth.

The award made at Westminster on the three and twentith of March, Anno regni regis 36.

FIRST, that at the costs, charges, and expenses of the duke of Yorke, the earles ^{The clergie were sure in those daies to loose nothing by these contentions howsoeuer the world went.} of Warwike, and Salisburie, fourtie & fiue pounds of yearelie rent should be assured by waie of a mortisement for euer, vnto the monasterie of S. Albons, for suffrages and obits to be kept, and almes to be imploied for the soules of Edmund late duke of Summerset, Henrie late erle of Northumberland, and Thomas late lord Clifford late slaine in the battell of saint Albons, and buried in the abbeie church, and also for the soules of all other slaine in the same battell. The said duke of Summerset, the earle of of Northumberland, and lord Clifford, by vertue of the same award, were declared for true and faithfull liegemen to the king, and so to be holden and reputed in the daie of their deaths, aswell as the said duke of Yorke, the earles of Warwike and Salisburie.

Moreouer it was decreed, that the duke of Yorke should giue to Elenor duchesse of Summerset, and to Henrie duke of Summerset hir sonne, the summe of fiue thousand markes of good assignements of debts, which the king owght him for his wages, due during the time of his seruice in Ireland, to be diuided as the king should thinke conuenient, betwixt the brethren & sisters of the said duke of Summerset. Also that the earle of Warwike should giue vnto the lord Clifford, the summe of a thousand markes, in good and sufficient assignements of debts, which the king owght him, to be distributed betwixt the said lord Clifford his brethren and sisters.

The lord Egremond.

Also where Thomas Persie knight, lord Egremond, and Richard Persie his brother, sonnes of the ladie Elenor countesse of Northumberland, had béen in a sessions holden within the countie of Yorke before Richard Bingham, and Rafe Pole the kings iustices and other commissioners, condemned vnto the earle of Salisburie in the summe of eight thousand markes; and to the same earle, and to his wife Alice in the summe of fiue thousand marks; and to Thomas Neuill knight, son to the said earle of Salisburie, in the summe of a thousand marks; and to the said Thomas and Mawd his wife, in the summe of two thousand marks; and to Iohn Neuill knight, sonne to the said earle of Salisburie, in the summe of eight hundred marks: for transgressions and trespasses there found to be doone by the said lord Egremond, and Richard his brother, vnto the said earle of Salisburie, Alice, Thomas Neuill, Mawd and Iohn Neuill, as by the record appéered.

They were shiriffes, an. 1456.

It was ordeined, that the said earle and his sonnes should release all the said summes of monie, and the executions thereof, and likewise release vnto Rafe Verneie, and Iohn Steward late shiriffes of London, vnto whose custodie the said lord Egremond had beene for the same condemnations committed and from them escaped, all actions which they or anie of them might haue against the said Verneie and Steward for the same escape. Yet it was decreed by this award, that the said lord Egremond should be bound by recognisance in the chancerie, to kéepe the peace toward the said erle and his wife, children, seruants, and tenants.

Also were diuerse knights, esquiers, and other seruants and tenants to the said earle of Northumberland, and to the said lord Egremond, were by their seuerall obligations bound, by occasion of the said debates, vnto the said duke of Yorke, earle of Salisburie, or anie of their children, to stand to their order and gouernement; it was ordeined that the same obligations should be deliuered to them that so stood bound, before the feast of saint Peter ad vincula next insuing at the citie of Yorke; or else that the parties so bound, should haue sufficient acquitances in discharge of the same obligations.

It was further awarded, that all variances, discords, debates, controuersies, appeales, and actions personals, that were or had béene betwixt any of the said persons, or any of their seruants, or tenants, should be for euer determined & ended, sauing to euerie one his title, action and right, which he had by any euidence of arrerages of rents or seruices, accounts, detinues, or debts due by reason of anie lawfull contract or deed, had and made for anie reasonable considerations, other than the variance before said.

And for the more assurance of both parties, it was ordeined that either should release to other all maner of actions, that were méere personals and appeales, which anie of them might haue against the other, by reason of the variances and discords before mentioned.

Also it was decreed, that if anie action, sute or quarell chanced betwixt anie of the seruants or tenants of anie of the parties, for matter or title supposed to be had,

occasioned

occasioned or mooued before this time; that from thenceforth, none of the said parties should mainteine, support, or aid any of them that will so sue and mooue strife
and debate: but should rather so deale, as the matter may be brought to peace and
quietnesse.

It was further awarded, that if anie man complained, pretended, or surmised, that
this award was not kept, but in some point broken by anie of the parties, for the which
breach he would haue a Scire facias, or some other action prosecuted in the kings name
vpon anie recognisance made to the king for the performance of this award: yet should
not the same Scire facias or action be prosecuted, till the kings councell might be
throughlie certified of the matter by the complainant, and vpon consideration sée
iust cause whie the same Scire facias, or action ought to be had and prosecuted in the
kings name.

And if anie variance rose betwixt the councell of both the parties in making of the
recognisances, releases, acquittances, or other writings; the same variance should be
determined by the two lords cheefe iustices, that should be fullie instructed of the
kings intention in this behalfe.

And besides this, it was notified and declared by the same award, that the parties
being seuerallie bound in the Chancerie in great sums to obeie and performe this
award, ordinance & iudgement made by the king; it was the kings will and pleasure,
that the same recognisances should stand in force, and no parcels of the summes
therein conteined to be pardoned in anie wise, without the agréement and consent of
the partie, for whose assurance the same recognisance was taken.

And if anie of the said summes, or anie parcell thereof should be recouered by
action or execution taken and prosecuted in the kings name, vpon anie of the said
recognisances; the partie to whose hinderance the award was broken, should haue the
one halfe of the monie so recouered; and the other moitie should be assigned to the
treasuror of the kings house. ¶ This ordinance, award and agréement, was giuen
vp vnder the kings great seale, at the kings palace of Westminster, the foure and
twentith daie of March in the six and thirtith yeare of his reigne.

For the open publishing of this ioifull agréement, there was (vpon our ladie daie A solemne pro-
in March) a solemne procession celebrated within the cathedrall church of saint cession at Paules.
Paule in London, at the which the king was present in habit roiall, with his crowne 1459
on his head. Before him went hand in hand the duke of Summerset, the earle of
Salisburie, the duke of Excester, and the earle of Warwike; and so one of the one
faction, and another of the other: and behind the king the duke of Yorke, and the An. Reg. 37.
quéene with great familiaritie in appeerence leading hand in hand. [But what shall be *W. P.*
said? As goodlie apples corrupted at core, (how faire coated so euer they seeme) can
neuer be made to become sound againe: nor rotten walles new plastered without, can
euer the more staie their mooldering inward, till the putrified matter fret through the
crust laie all in the mire: so fared it on all parts in this dissembled and counterfet
concord.] For after this apparant peace (but inward discord) diuerse of the nobles
smallie regarding their honors, forgot their oth, and brake their promise boldlie.

Not long after this, of pretensed purpose (as it was thought) a fraie was made
vpon a yeoman of the earle of Warwiks, by one of the kings seruants, in the which
the assailant was sore hurt, but the earles man fled. Héerevpon the kings meniall seruants, séeing their fellow hurt, and the offendor escaped, assembled togither and
watched the earle, when he returned from the councell chamber toward his barge, The earle of Warwike as-
and suddenlie set on him, the yeomen with swords, the blacke gard with spits and fier- saulted.
forks. After long fight, and manie of the earls men maimed and hurt, by helpe of
his fréends he gat a wherrie, and so escaped to London. The quéene aduertised héerof, The quéenes
-purpose.

incontinentlie commanded that he should be apprehended and committed to the tower, where (if he had béene taken) he had shortlie ended his daies.

By this vnhappie fraie, there arose anon after such trouble and terrible warre, that the whole realme was thereby disquieted. For after this displeasure doone to the earle, and the quéenes good mind towards him by his secret fréends reuealed; he with all diligence tooke his iournie to Warwike, and after into Yorkeshire, where he found the duke of Yorke, and the earle of Salisburie, declaring vnto them the assault made vpon him by the kings seruants, and the pretensed euill purpose of the quéene. After which complaint made, he fearing to be dispossessed of his roome at Calis, with great spéed imbarked himselfe and sailed thither. He was not onelie deputie or lieutenant of Calis, but also high admerall of the seas, which office was to him confirmed for the space of fiue yeares. Wherevpon, whether before his arriuall now at Calis, or shortlie after, I cannot say; but this yeare about the middest of summer, the said earle, hauing with him a fouretéene well appointed ships, sailed abroad to scowre the seas, and by chance met with fiue great ships, whereof thrée were caraks of Genoa, and the other two were of Spaine, bigger in heigth and length than the caraks.

Whethamsted
*The earle of
Warwike lord
admerall.*

The earle, though he was scarse able to deale against them, yet he valiantlie incountred them. There was a verie sore and long continued battell fought betwixt them, for it lasted almost the space of two daies. Yet in the end the victorie fell to the English, so that two of those ships being forced to saue themselues by flight, the other thrée were taken, which the earle brought vnto Calis, with all the merchandize aboord the same; the value whereof in wine, oile, wax, iron, cloth of gold, and other riches, was estéemed to the summe of ten thousand pounds & aboue. By reason whereof, that was sold now for twelue pense, which would not haue béene bought before for two shillings. There were taken a great number of prisoners, beside a thousand of the enimies slaine in fight. Of the earles part there were fiftie slaine. The earles fame héereby increased not a little, and manie a blessing he had for this peece of seruice.

A rich prise.

*Abr. Fl. ex
I. S. pag.* 686,
687.
*Printing first
inuented.*

¶ The noble science of Printing was about this time found in Germanie at Magunce by one Iohn Cuthembergus a knight: one Conradus an Almaine brought it into Rome: William Caxton of London mercer brought it into England about the yeare 1471: and first practised the same in the abbie of saint Peter at Westminster; after which time it was likewise practised in the abbies of S. Augustine at Canturburie, saint Albons, and other monasteries of England. In a little towne in Bedfordshire there fell a bloudie raine, whereof the red drops appéered in shéets, the which a woman had hanged out for to drie.]

It rained bloud.

An. Reg. 38

But now to the former purpose. After that the earle was gone ouer to Calis, the duke of Yorke and the earle of Salisburie, falling in consultation togither, it was at length agréed betwixt them, with aduise of their fréends, that the said earle of Salisburie with a warlike companie should march toward the king; and signifie to him by waie of complaint, both the manifest iniurie doone to his sonne, and also the vncourteous breach of the sworne amitie and late agréement. In which sute if he preuailed, he should not then let passe the occasion giuen for reuenge of displeasures to him doone, both by the quéene and hir sinister councellors. After conclusion of this deuise, the earle of Salisburie remooued from Middleham castell, accompanied with foure or fiue thousand men, and tooke his waie through Lancashire, to passe that waie towards London.

The earle of
Salisburie gath-
ereth a power.

Thrée thou-
sand sa th
Whetharnsted.

In the meane season, the quéene, assisted and ruled by the dukes of Summerset and Buckingham, hauing a vigilant eie to all hir businesse, imagined that the earle of Warwike had kindled this fier, to the intent to set the crowne on the duke of Yorks head. Wherefore she appointed Iames Twichet lord Audelie (bicause his power laie in those parties by the which the earle of Salisburie must passe) to raise an hoast of men with all speed, and to giue battell to the same earle, if he saw cause and place conuenient.

The lord
Audelie.

She

She had deuised a cognisance of the white swan, which she willed all such (as she *Ex vetusto codice.* knew to beare fauor vnto hir sonne) to weare, for a signification of their good minds and hartie loue towards him: which cognisance she had giuen to manie gentlemen of Chesshire, and other countries thereabout.

The quéene hir selfe laie the same time at Ecclesale in Staffordshire, but the K. remained at Colleshill in Warwikeshire, whither the earle of Salisburie meant to come, in pretense to haue communed with him for a reformation of matters depending in controuersie betwixt himselfe, the duke of Yorke, and others. But the queene construing that they ment no good, neither to hir nor hir husband, requested the lord Audelie to apprehend him, if by anie means he might. The lord Audelie (according *Whethamsted.* to his commission) assembled aboue ten thousand men of Chesshire and Salopshire, and knowing by his espials which waie the earle kept, approached néere to him vpon a faire plaine called Bloreheath, within a mile of a towne called Draiton in Shropshire. Bloreheath. The earle, perceiuing in what ieopardie he stood, determined to abide the aduenture with fame and honour, rather than to flie with shame and reproach; and so incamped himselfe all the night on the side of a little brooke, not verie brode, but somewhat deepe.

In the morning earlie, being the daie of saint Tecle, he caused his souldiers to shoot The 23 of September. their flights towards the lord Audelies companie, which laie on the other side of the said water, and then he and all his people made a signe of retreit. The lord Audelie, supposing his aduersaries had fled in déed, caused his trumpets quicklie to blow vp, and setting foorth his voward, speedilie passed the water. The earle of Salisburie, Policie oft times passeth force. which knew the sleights of warlike policie, suddenlie returned, and set vpon the lord Audelie and his cheefe capteins, yer the residue of his armie could passe the water. The fight was sore and dreadfull. The earle desiring the sauing of his life, and his aduersaries coueting his destruction, fought sore for the obteining of their purpose: but in conclusion, the earles armie, as men not looking for other succours nor meane to escape, but by their owne manhood, so egerlie assaulted their foes, that they slue The lord Audelie slaine. the lord Audelie and all his capteins, and discomfited all the remnant of his people.

In this battell were slaine foure and twentie hundred persons, but the greatest losse fell The number slaine in the battell of Bloreheath. vpon the Chesshire men, bicause one halfe of the shire was on the one part, and the other halfe on the other: of which number were sir Thomas Dutton, sir Iohn Doune and sir Hugh Venables, sir Richard Molineux, sir William Trowtbecke, sir Iohn Legh of the Both, and sir Iohn Egerton, knights; Iohn Done, and Iohn Dutton esquiers. But the earles two sonnes, the one called sir Iohn Neuill, and the other sir Thomas Neuill, were sore wounded, the which soberlie iornieng into the north countrie, were apprehended by the quéenes fréends, and togither with sir Thomas Harington that was The earle of Salisburies sonne apprehended. likewise taken, were conueied to Chester; but their kéepers deliuered them shortlie after, or else had the Marchmen destroied the goales. Such fauour bare the commons of Wales to the duke of Yorks band, that they could not suffer anie wrong to be offered, or euill word to be spoken against him or his freends.

After this battell at Bloreheath, the said duke of Yorke, perceiuing the destruction of him and his fréends was intended, and that his deuises were alreadie disclosed to the king and the queene, he thought now no longer to linger his businesse, but with all diligence to set forward the same. And therfore sending for his cheefe freend the earle of Salisburie, after long conference of their weightie affaires, they determined The duke of Yorke assembleth an armie. to raise an armie, and by fine force either to win their purpose, or end their liues in the same. Héerevpon were men foorthwith assembled, freends sent for, and a puissant armie gathered, both of Northerne and Welshmen, who in good order came into the marches of Wales adioining to Shropshire, determining there to abide their enimies, or to méet them; if occasion serued.

There came to him from Calis the earle of Warwike bringing with him from that

towne

towne a great number of expert men in martiall feates, whereof two were capteins knowne for men of great experience and approoued policie, as they had well declared

Andrew Trollop. the same in the warres of Normandie and Guien, the one called Andrew Trollop,
Iohn Blunt. and the other Iohn Blunt. The king, hauing aduertisement of the dukes dooings, sent foorth commissioners to leuie a power in all parts of the realme, where he
The king raiseth an armie. thought to haue any faithfull fréends or fauourers: by reason whereof a great number of men of warre was assembled. Manie for the loue they bare to the king resorted to his side, but more for feare of the quéenes displesure, whose frowning countenance was their vndooing, and hir indignation their death.

To be bréefe, the king accompanied with the dukes of Summerset and Excester, and other of the line of Lancaster, determined either by force or by policie to bring the duke of Yorke to confusion; and therevpon marching forward they came vnto Worcester, where as well to refresh his people, as to take further aduise what was best to be doone, he staied for a time. And at length it was determined, that the K. should first send vnto the aduersaries, a messenger of good account, as the bishop of Salis-

Whethamsted.
The bishop of Salisburie sent to the duke of Yorke and others. burie Richard Beauchampe, to offer vnto them a cleere and free generall pardon of all trespasses, offenses, and transgressions whatsoeuer; if they would giue ouer their enter-prise, and become true and obedient subiects.

When the bishop was come vnto them, and had declared his message, they first withdrew themselues apart, and fell togither in councell: and after they gaue answer
Their answer touching the par-don offred. by the mouth of the erle of Warwike, which consisted in thrée points. First, that as concerning the pardon, they durst not trust vnto it, considering they had diuerse pardons before, and the same confirmed by parlement, and yet nothing auaileable to their assurance. Secondlie, that notwithstanding such pardons, those that were about the king, were persumptuous and vnrulie, that they cared not at all to breake the kings commandements, nor were any thing abashed to be noted for the breach thereof.

Thirdlie, although by law of the land, and right of the statute, euerie lord by ver-tue of the kings writ, being called to the parlement, ought safelie to come, safelie there to remaine, and safelie to depart and returne home: this notwithstanding, the said earle of Warwike himselfe, at a certeine councell holden at Westminster, by vertue of the kings writ of priuie seale, being there in person, & labouring to his knowledge to giue good aduise and councell for the profit of the common-wealth, was yet in danger of death, if the Lord aboue had not the better prouided for his escape, more than anie humane power or force of the kings pardon. "For the which cause (quoth he) sith the kings pardon maie be likened in these daies to a buckler of glasse, or to a staffe of réed, in which is no trust, we dare not commit our selues vnto the de-fense of anie such pardons." But if anie other waie might be deuised for their suerties, wherevnto they might safelie trust (he said) they were readie to come to his grace, and to sue for his fauour.

The king receiuing such answer in these words, or other to the like effect, was nothing contented therewith, and so commanded his standards eftsoones to aduance.
A letter from the lords to the king. But yet before he came neere to the place where they were incamped, the said lords wrote to him a letter in their owne excuse, protesting they meant no harme in the world against his person, as by their demeanors and proceedings it might well appeare, who had euer fled & withdrawne themselues from place to place, from towne to towne, from village to village, and from countie to countie. Which might serue for an euident token, that they sought for nothing but onelie their owne safegards & quiet-nesse of the realme, with so much fauour, as in good and safe suertie they might come to his presence, to declare certeine things which in their opinions might turne to the wealth of the realme: and further to make answer to all things that had béene obiected against them. And now (said they) we are here remaining in the vttermost parts of the land (that is) in the marches towards Wales, not farre from Ludlow, not

vpon

vpon anie presumptuous meaning, but rather in all humble lowlinesse of mind and bodie to abide his graces comming: which they besought of God might be in some peaceable maner and fauourable in their behalfes.

The king hauing receiued this letter, and coniecturing that some bitter meaning laie vnder so swéet a spéech, cōmanded his armie againe to march foorth; and comming within halfe a mile of the aduersaries campe, pitched downe his field, and foorthwith caused proclamation to be made, that who so euer of his aduersaries would giue ouer *A proclamation.* his lewd begun enterprise, and repaire to his presence to sue for mercie, he would pardon him of all offenses. This proclamation, comming to the vnderstanding of them in the duke of Yorks hoast, caused a great number that were there with him against the king, to get awaie & come to the kings side. Moreouer, there rose among the residue great murmuring: so as they seemed verie like to grow to a greeuous mutinie.

Amongst other of those that came to the kings campe, Andrew Trollop was chéefe, *Andrew Trollop forsaketh the* who with the other Calisians, which had long serued the king, and liued a long time *lords.* by his wages, perceiuing now that they should fight against their souereigne lord himselfe (whose true subiect they estéemed before that time the earle of Warwike euer to haue beene, and in no wise his enimie) in the dead of the night before the daie of the battell secretlie departed from the dukes campe, and submitted themselues to the king, admonishing him of all things deuised against him. Wherof part was, that the duke of Yorke by his expert capteins appointed vpon a waie how to set vpon his *Whethamsted.* enimies, & easilie to discomfitt hem; so as on the next morning he meant to haue assailed the king and his people, yer they could haue béene readie or warie of his comming

But now by the going awaie thus of his capteins and people, that purpose was disappointed. And Andrew Trollop thus departed, he was now as much discomforted, as before by trust in him he was incouraged: for all his councell and purpose by Andrew disclosed, he thought it better for him & his to depart in suertie, than to abide *The estimation* the imminent danger. Whervpon he with his yoonger sonne Edmund earle of Rutland, *of Andrew Trollop.* secretlie fled into Wales, and so passed into Ireland, where he was with all ioy and *The duke of* honour gladlie receiued, all the Irish offering to liue and die with him; as if they had *Yorke and his complices flée.* béene his liege subiects, and he their lord and prince naturallie borne.

The earle of March sonne and heire apparant to the said duke, accompanied with the earles of Salisburie and Warwike, and sir Iohn Wenlocke, got awaie the same night, and came into Deuonshire: where, by the meanes of Iohn Dinham esquier (which after was high treasuror of England, in the daies of king Henrie the seauenth) they bought a ship which cost a hundred and ten marks at Exmouth, and sailed into Gerneseie, after came to Calis, where being let in at the posterne, they were ioifullie welcomed of their fréends, namelie of sir William Neuill lord Fauconbridge, that was the earle of Warwikes vncle, and brother to the earle of Salisburie, who had the towne and castell in kéeping. All these being assembled cast their heads togither, and euerie one seuerallie had his deuise for the perfecting of their purpose, whereto there wanted in them neither will nor hardinesse.

But now to returne to the king. When in the morning he was aduertised that the duke of Yorke and his partakers were fled and gone, he caused all his horssemen to follow them; although in vaine: for they were got farre enough out of danger (as before ye haue heard.) The king pardoned all the poore souldiers, sauing certeine ringleaders; of the which some he punished and fined, and some he hanged and quartered. After this he remooued to Ludlow, and there brake vp his host, and spoiling the towne and castell, he sent the duchesse of Yorke with hir two yoong sonnes to be kept in ward with the duchesse of Buckingham hir sister. This doone, he proclamed *The lords pro-* these lords, traitors to him, enimies to their countrie, and rebels to the crowne, con- *clamed traitors.*

fiscating

fiscating their lands, goods, and offices : and committed the gouernance of the north parts to the earle of Northumberland, and to the lord Clifford, as to his trustie and most faithfull fréends, & of his towne of Calis he made capteine Henrie the new duke of Summerset.

This duke reioising much in his new office, chose foorth diuerse valiant and hardie souldiers, and with great pompe shortlie after tooke the seas, and sailed towards Calis. But when he thought to haue entred the hauen, the artillerie shot so hotlie, both out of the towne, and from Risebanke, that he suffering there a sore repulse, was faine to land at Whitsandbaie; and sent word to the capteines of the towne to receiue him as the kings lieutenant, shewing to them his letters patents. But neither he nor his writing was once regarded : and so of necessitie he resorted to the castell of Guisnes, dailie skirmishing with the garrison of Calis, more to his losse than gaine. Diuerse of the mariners of those ships that went ouer with him, after his arriuall, owing more good will to the earle of Warwike than to this yoong duke, conueied their ships into the hauen of Calis, and in them diuerse of the earle of Warwikes enimies, as Iamin Findill, Iohn Felow, and diuerse others, the which being presented vnto the earle of

Hastie heading

Warwike, he caused their heads foorthwith to be striken off.

Shortlie after, Richard lord Riuers, and sir Anthonie Wooduile his valiant sonne that was after lord Scales, accompanied with foure hundred warlike persons, were appointed to passe ouer to Guisnes, to aid the duke of Summerset against his aduersaries, which laie in Calis. But as they soiourned at Sandwich abiding for wind and weather to transport them ouer, the earles of March and Warwike had knowledge

Iohn Dinham.

thereof, and sent Iohn Dinham with a small number of men (but a multitude of valiant hearts) vnto the towne of Sandwich, which suddenlie entered the same, and

The lord Riuers taken.

tooke the lord Riuers and his sonne also in their beds, robbing houses, and spoiling ships. And beside this, they tooke the principall ships of the kings nauie, and had

Iohn Stow.

them awaie with them to Calis [one excepted called Grace de Dieu which might not be had awaie bicause she was broken in the bottome] and there presented them to the earle of March, of whome he was ioifullie receiued. For though in the fight he was sore hurt & maimed in the leg, so as he halted euer after, yet he bare himselfe so worthilie in that enterprise, that his praise was great amongst all men.

Abr. Fl. ex I. S. pag. 692.
1460
Sir Baldwine Fulford his enterprise.

¶ Sir Baldwine Fulford vndertooke on paine of loosing his head, that he would destroie the earle of Warwike : but when he had spent the king a thousand marks in monie, he returned againe.] After this good fortune thus chanced to the lords, diuerse of the best ships taken in the hauen of Sandwich, were well vittelled and manned, and with them the earle of Warwike sailed into Ireland, to common with the duke of Yorke of their great affaires and businesse. The weather and wind were so fauourable to the earles purpose, that within lesse than thirtie 'daies he passed and repassed from Calis to Dublin, and backe againe.

The duke of Excester, being chéefe admerall of the sea, laie in the west countrie, and durst not once meddle with the earle of Warwikes nauie, as he came by ; by reason of the mistrust which he had in the capteins and mariners of his owne nauie : who by their murmuring well shewed that they wished the earle of Warwikes good

Abr. Fl. ex I. S. pag. 688, 689, 690, 691.

successe. ¶ But here is to be remembred, that after the great discomfiture of the lords (as before you haue heard) and proclamation made against them as traitors, the duke of Yorke and the earles of Salisburie and Warwike had conference; and thervpon concluded with one assent, to write a letter excusatorie (supposing thereby to salue vp the sore) in all their names to the king : and so did, as followeth :

A copie of the said letter excusatorie written by the said duke and earles.

MOST christian king, right high and mightie prince, and our most dread souereigne lord, after as humble recommendations to your high excellencie as will suffice. Our

Our true intent to the prosperitie and augmentation of your high estate, and to the common-weale of this realme, hath beene shewed vnto your highnesse in such writing as we make thereof. And ouer that, an indenture signed by our hands in the church cathedrall of Worcester, comprehending the proofe of the truth and dutie that (God knoweth) we beare to your said estate, and to the preheminence and prerogatiue thereof, we sent vnto your good grace by the prior of the said church, and diuerse other doctors, and among other, by maister William Linwood doctor of diuinitie, which ministred vnto vs seuerallie the blessed sacrament of the bodie of Iesus, where-vpon we and euerie of vs deposed for our said truth and dutie, according to the tenor of the said indenture.

And since that time we haue certified at large in writing and by mouth, by Garter king of armes, not onelie to your said highnesse, but also to the good and worthie lords being about your most noble presence, the largenesse of our said truth and dutie, and our intent and disposition, to search all the motions that might serue conuenientlie to the affirmation thereof, and to our perfect suerties from such in-conuenient and vnreuerent ieopardies as we haue beene put in diuerse times here be-fore. Whereof we haue cause to make, and ought to make such exclamation and complaint, not without reason, as is not vnknowen to all the said worthie lords, and to all this land; and will offer vs to your high presence, to the same intent, if we might so doo, with our said suertie, which onelie causeth vs to keepe such fellowship as we doo in our leeful manner.

And hereto we haue forborne, and auoided all things that might serue to the effu-sion of christian bloud, of the dread that we haue of God, and of your roiall ma-iestie: and haue also eschued to approch your said most noble presence, for the hum-ble obeisance and reuerence wherein we haue, and (during our life) will haue the same. And yet neuerthelesse we heare, that we be proclamed and defamed in our name vn-rightlie, vnlawfullie, and (sauing your high reuerence) vntrulie, and otherwise (as God knoweth) than we haue giuen cause; knowing certeinelie, that the blessed and noble intent of your said good grace, and righteousnesse thereof is, to take, repute; and accept your true and lawfull subiects; and that it accordeth neither with your said intent, nor with your will or pleasure, that we should be otherwise taken or reputed. And ouer that, our lordships and tenants beene of high violence robbed and spoiled, against your peace and lawes, and all righteousnesse.

We therfore, as we suffice, beseech your said good grace, to take, repute, and receiue therevnto our said truth and intent, which to God is knowne, as we shew it by the said tenor of the same indenture. And not applie your said blessednesse, ne the great righteousnesse and equitie wherewith God hath euer indued your high nobilitie, to the importune impatience and violence of such persons, as intend of extreame malice to proceed (vnder the shadow of your high might and presence) to our destruction, for such inordinate couetise (whereof God is not pleased) as they haue to our lands, offices, and goods, not letting or sparing therefore, to put such things in all lamentable and too sorowfull ieopardie, as might in all wise take effect, by the mysterie of Gods will and power.

Not hauing regard to the effusion of christian bloud, ne anie tendernesse to the noble bloud of this land, such as serue to the tuition and defence thereof, ne not waieng the losse of your true liege men of your said realme, that God defend, which knoweth our intent, and that we haue auoided there-from as farre as we may with our suerties; not of anie dread that we haue of the said persons, but onelie of the dread of God and of your said highnesse, and will not vse our said defense vntill the time that we be prouoked of necessitie, whereof we call heauen and earth vnto witnesse and record, and therein beseech God to be our iudge, and to deliuer vs according to our

said

said intent, and our said truth & dutie to your said highnesse, and to the said common-weale.

Most christian king, right high and mightie prince, and most dread souereigne lord we beseech our blessed Lord to preserue your honour and estate in ioy and felicitie. Written at Ludlow the tenth daie of October: R. Yorke, R. Warwike, R. Salisburie.

A parlement at
Couentrie.

Duke of Yorke
and others
attainted.

During this time the king called a parlement in the citie of Couentrie, which began the twentith of September, in the which were attainted of high treason, Richard duke of Yorke, Edward erle of March his sonne and heire, Richard earle of Warwike Edmund earle of Rutland, Richard earle of Salisburie, Iohn lord Clifford, lord Clinton, sir Thomas Harington, sir Iohn Wenlock, Thomas Neuill & Iohn Neuill sons of the earle of Salisburie, Iames Pickering, Iohn Coniers, Thomas Par, William Oldhall, and Henrie Ratford knights; Iohn Bowser, Thomas Cooke, Iohn Claie, Richard Giton, Robert Browne, Edward Bowser, Thomas Vaughan, Iohn Roger, Richard Greie, Walter Deuoreux, Walter Hopton, Roger Kinderton, Will. Bowes, Foulke Stafford, the lord Powis, and Alice countesse of Salisburie, their goods and possessions escheted, and their heires disherited vnto the ninth degrée, their tenants spoiled of

Ludlow spoiled.

their goods, maimed and slaine; the towne of Ludlow, belonging to the duke of Yorke, was robbed to the bare wals, & the dutches of Yorke spoiled of hir goods.]

Whethamsted.

But (saith another) when the king should come to giue his consent vnto the acts passed in the same parlement, and that the clerke of the parlement had read that statute of the attaindor of those lords; such was the kings modestie and great zeale

The kings in-
clination to
mercie.

vnto mercie, that he caused a prouiso to be put in, and added vnto the same statute, that it might be lawfull vnto him at all times fullie without authoritie of anie other parlement, to pardon the same noble men, and restore them againe to their former estats, degrees, and dignities in all things, so they would come in vnto him, and in the spirit of humblenesse beseech him of grace and fauour. ¶ Wherin the king gaue

Abr. Fl.

euident testimonie, that he was indued with those qualities of mind which the poet ascribed vnto Cesar (namelie slow to punish, & sad when he was constreined to be seuere: sith the one commended his lenitie, the other sauoured of tyrannie) in this distichon of like termination:

*Ouid. de Ponto.
lib.* 1.

Est piger ad pœnas princeps, ad præmia velox,
Cuíq; dolet quoties cogitur esse ferox.]

Herewith also order was taken for the defense of the hauens & landing places

Osbert Mōtford
esquier saith
Whethamsted,
who should also
haue gone ouer
to Guines with
fiue hundred
souldiers to the
aid of the duke
of Summerset
The lord Faucō-
bridge was chiefe
of this enterprise
saith *Whetham-
sted.*
Thirtéene be-
headed at once.
Abr. Fl. ex I. S.
pag. 695, 693,
694, 695, 696,
697, *in Quart.*

alongst the sea coasts. Sir Simon Montford, with a great crew of men, was appointed to keepe the downes, and the fiue ports; and all men passing into Flanders were vpon paine of death prohibited to passe by Calis, least the lords there should borrow of them anie prest monie, as they did latelie before of the merchants of the staple the summe of eighteene thousand pounds. The lords were not ignorant of all the kings prouisions made against them, but were ascerteined dailie what was doone euen in the kings priuie chamber: wherefore first they sent a companie to Sandwich vnder the gouernance of the lord Fauconbridge, who tooke the towne, & sir Simon or Osbert Montford within it, and sent him with all his mates to Calis, where incontinentlie he with twelue of his chiefe fellowes lost their heads on the sand before Risebanke

¶ The earles at Calis sent to the archbishop of Canturburie, and to the commons of England at large certeine articles in writing, beginning thus: Worshipfull sirs, we the duke of Yorke, the earles of March, Warwike, and Salisburie, sued and offered to haue come to the king our souereigne lords most noble presence, to haue declared there afore him for our dutie to God and to his highnesse, and to the prosperitie and welfare of his noble estate, and to the common-weale of all his land as true liege men, the matters following.

Articles

Articles sent from the duke of Yorke, and the earles, to the archbishop of Canturburie
and the commons.

IN primis, the great oppression, extortion, robberie, murther, and other violences
doone to Gods church, and to his ministers thereof, against Gods and mans law.

2 Item, the pouertie and miserie that to our great heauinesse our souereigne lord
standeth in, not hauing anie liuelod of the crowne of England whereof he may keepe
his honorable houshold, which causeth the spoiling of his said liege men by the takers
of his said houshold, which liuelod is in their hands that haue beene destroiers of his
said estate, and of the said common-weale.

3 Item, how his lawes be parciallie and vnrightfullie guided, and that by them that
should most loue and tender his said lawes, the said oppression and extortion is most
fauoured and supported; and generallie, that all righteousnesse and iustice is exiled
out of the said land, and that no man dreadeth to offend against the said lawes.

4 Item, that it will please his said good grace to liue vpon his owne liuelod, wherevpon his noble progenitors haue in daies heretofore liued as honorablie and as worthilie
as anie christian princes, and not to suffer the destroiers of the said land, and of his true
subiects, to liue therevpon, and therefore to lacke the sustenances that should be belonging to his said estate, and find his said houshold vpon his poore commons, without
paiement, which neither accordeth with Gods nor mans law.

5 Item, how oft the said commons haue beene greatlie and maruellouslie charged
with taxes and tallages to their great impouerishing, whereof little good hath either
growne to the king or to the said land, and of the most substance thereof the king
hath left to his part not halfe so much; and other lords and persons, enimies to the
said common-weale, haue to their owne vse, suffering all the old possessions that the
king had in France and Normandie, Aniou and Maine, Gascoine, and Guien, woone
and gotten by his father of most noble memorie, and other his noble progenitors, to
be shamefullie lost or sold.

6 Item, how they can not ceasse therewith, but now begin a new charge of imposition and tallages vpon the said people, which neuer afore was seene; that is to saie,
euerie towneship to find men for the kings gard, taking example therein of our enimies
and aduersaries of France. Which imposition & tallage, if it be continued to heire,
heires, and successors, will be the heauiest charge and worst example that euer grew in
England; and the foresaid subiects, and the said heires and successors in such bondage,
as their ancestors were neuer charged with.

7 Item, where the king hath now no more liuelod out of his realme of England, but
onelie the land of Ireland, and the towne of Calis, and that no king christened hath
such a land and a towne without his realme; diuerse lords haue caused his highnesse to
write letters vnder his priuie seale, vnto his Irish enimies, which neuer king of England did heretofore, wherby they may haue comfort to enter into the conquest of the
said land, which letters the same Irish enimies sent vnto me the said duke of Yorke,
and maruelled greatlie that anie such letters should be to them sent, speaking therin
great shame and villanie of the said realme.

8 Item, in like wise the king by excitation and labour of the same lords, wrote
other letters to his enimies and aduersaries in other lands, that in no wise they should
shew anie fauour or good will to the towne of Calis, whereby they had comfort inough
to procéed to the winning thereof. Considered also, that it is ordeined by the labour
of the said lords, that no where vittels nor other thing of refreshing or defense should
come out of England, to the succour or reliefe of the said towne, to the intent that
they would haue it lost, as it may openlie appeare.

9 Item, it is déemed and ought greatlie to be déemed, that after the same lords would put the same rule of England, if they might haue their purpose and intent, into the hands and gouernance of the said enimies.

10 Item, how continuallie since the pitious, shamefull, and sorrowfull murther to all England, of that noble, worthie, and christian prince Humfreie duke of Glocester the kings true vncle, at Burie, it hath beene laboured, studied and conspired, to haue destroied and murthered the said duke of Yorke, and the issue that it pleased God to send me of the roiall bloud, and also of vs the said earles of Warwike and Salisburie, for none other cause but for the true hart that (God knoweth) we euer haue borne, and beare to the profit of the kings estate, to the common-weale of the same realme, and defense thereof.

11 Item, how the earles of Shrewesburie and Wilshire, and the lord Beaumont, our mortall and extreme enimies now, and of long time past, hauing the guiding about the most noble person of our said souereigne lord, whose highnesse they haue restreined & kept from the libertie & freedome that belongeth to his said estate, & the supporters & fauourers of all the premisses, would not suffer the kings said good grace to receiue and accept vs, as he would haue doone, if he might haue had his owne will, into his said presence, dreading the charge that would haue beene laid vpon them, of the miserie, destruction, and wretchednesse of the said realme, whereof they be causes, and not the king, which is himselfe as noble, as vertuous, as righteous and blessed of disposition, as anie prince earthlie.

12 Item, the earles of Wilshire and Shrewesburie, and the lord Beaumont, not satisfied nor content with the kings possessions and his goods, stirred and excited his said highnesse to hold his parlement at Couentrie, where an act is made by their prouocation and labour, against vs the said duke of Yorke, my sonnes March and Rutland, and the earles of Warwike and Salisburie, and the sonnes of the said earle of Salisburie, and manie other knights and esquiers of diuerse matters falselie and vntrulie imagined, as they will answer afore almightie God in the daie of doome; the which the said earles of Shrewesburie & Wilshire, and the lord Beaumont prouoked to be made, to the intent of our destruction and of our issue; and that they might haue our liuelod and goods, as they haue openlie robbed and despoiled all our places and our tenements, and manie other true men, and now procéed to hanging and drawing of men by tyrannie, and will therin shew the largenesse of their violence and malice as vengeablie as they can, if no remedie be prouided at the kings highnes, whose blessednes is neither assenting nor knowing thereof.

We therefore, seeing all the said michiefes, hearing also that the French king maketh in his land great assemblie of his people, which is greatlie to be dread for manie causes, purpose yet againe with Gods grace to offer vs to come againe to the said presence of our said souereigne lord to open and declare vnto him there, the mischiefes aboue declared; and in the name of the land to sue, in as reuerent and lowlie wise as we can, to his said good grace, to haue pittie and compassion vpon his said true subiects, and not to suffer the same mischiefs to reigne vpon them. Requiring you in Gods behalfe, and praieng you in our owne, therein to assist vs, dooing alwaie the dutie of liege men in our persons to our souereigne lord, to his estate, perogatiue, and preheminence, and to the suertie of his most noble person, wherevnto we haue euer béene and will be as true as anie of his subiects aliue, whereof we call God, our ladie saint Marie, and all the saints in heauen to witnesse.

The earle of Wilshire and other spoiled Newberie.

In the meane time, the earle of Wilshire treasuror of England, the lord Scales & the lord Hungerford went to Newberie, which belonged to the duke of Yorke, and there made inquisition of all them that in anie wise had fauoured the said duke; whereof some were found guiltie, and were drawen, hanged, and quartered, and all the inhabitants

of

of the towne were spoiled of their goods.　From thence the earle of Wilshire went to *The earle of*
Southampton; where, vnder colour to take the earle of Warwike, he armed fiue great *Wilshire stale*
caracks of Iene with souldiers, taking vittels of the kings price without paiment, and *ouer the seas.*
put a great part of his treasure into the said caracks, and after sailed about in the sea,
and at last stale into Dutchland, sending backe againe his souldiers into England.
Then were the kings priuie seales directed to all bishops, abbats, priors, and other *Priuie seales for*
states, to lend the king monie, therewith to wage souldiers to kéepe the sea coasts.] *monie.*

　　After the kings nauie was gained, and his capteins (as before yee haue heard) on the
sea taken; the lords lieng at Calis, being aduertised from the lord Fauconbridge (who
after the taking of Montford laie still in Kent) that the people of that countrie and
other parts were altogither bent in their fauour [and no lesse addicted to doo them ser- *Abr. Flem.*
uice both with bodie and goods, than the Irishmen séemed to be at their receiuing of
the said duke of Yorke, and his yoonger sonne Edmund earle of Rutland, whom they
so highlie honoured, that they offered to liue and die in their quarell] they conceiued
therevpon so great hope in their fréends within the realme, that they determined to
passe the sea, and therewith entring their ships with fiftéene hundred men landed all
at Sandwich.

　　[But it is to be read in a late writer, that the commons of Kent dreading the like *Abr. Fl. ex I. S.*
vengeance towards them, as fell vpon them of Newburie, sent priuilie messengers to *pag. 697.*
Calis to the foresaid erles, beséeching them in all hast possible to come to their suc- *The men of Kent*
cour.　Wherevpon the said earles sent ouer into Kent the lord Fauconbridge, to know *sent to Calis for*
if their déeds would accord with their words: so that anon the people of Kent and the *the earles.*
other shires adioining, resorted to the said lord Fauconbridge in great number.
Wherefore when the earles knew the willing harts of those people, they prepared to
come into this land.　Against whose comming, a long ballet was fixed vpon the gates
of Canturburie, made in fauour of the duke of Yorke and the said earles, beginning
thus: In the daie of fast and spirituall affliction, the celestiall influence of bodies
transitorie, &c.

　　Now as they passed through Kent, there came to them the lord Cobham, Iohn Gil- *Whethamsted.*
ford, William Pech, Robert Horne, and manie other gentlemen; so that before they 　　1460
approched to London, their number was esteemed aboue fourtie thousand fighting men
for the fame of their landing being once knowen, gentlemen and yeomen resorted to
them out of all the south parts of the relme.　Vpon which rumor, Thomas lord Scales,
a man in great fauour with the king & quéene, accompanied with the earle of Kendall
a Gascoigne, and the lord Louell, resorted to London with a great companie of armed
men, declaring to the maior, that their repaire onelie was to defend and kéepe the
citie from spoile of such traitors as the king was credible informed were thither comming.　To whom the maior answered, that he needed no fellow helper, either to defend or gouerne the citie to him committed in charge.　With which answer the lord
Scales and his associats nothing contented, entred into the Tower, dailie deuising waies
how to grieue the citizens, whom he perceiued to fauour rather the duke of Yorks part
than the kings.

　　But shortlie after the earles of March and Warwike, and other of their affinitie,
came to London, and were of the maior and citizens ioiouslie receiued, to whome
resorted Thomas archbishop of Canturburie, the bishops of London, Lincolne, Salisburie, Elie, and Excester, with manie other prelats and religious persons: amongst
whome also was the popes legat to treat of peace, if need so required.　Vpon good
deliberation and aduise had and taken amongst these lords how to go forward with
their weightie enterprise, the earles of March and Warwike, William lord Fauconbridge, Henrie lord Bourchier, called earle of Eu, with a great number of men which
came out of Kent, Essex, Surrie, and Sussex, to the number (as some writers affirme)
of fiue and twentie thousand persons, departed from London toward the king lieng at

Couentrie the quéenes secret harbour.

Couentrie, then called the quéenes secret harbour, leauing behind them to kéepe the Londoners in their promised fréendship, the earle of Salisburie, the lord Cobham, and sir Iohn Wenlocke, which tooke such order, and watched the gates and entries on ech side so diligentlie, that no succours might come to the lord Scales lodging in the tower; who tooke therewith such displeasure, that he shot out his great ordinance against them within the citie, and they likewise shot at him againe, to the hurt and no pleasure of both parts.

The king hauing knowledge of all these dooings, assembled a great armie, and accompanied with the duke of Summerset (latelie come from Guisnes) and the duke of Buckingham, and diuerse other great lords that tooke his part, came to Northamp-

The quéene the better capteine.

ton; where the quéene perceiuing hir puissance to be able to match in fight with the aduersaries, tooke vpon hir to incourage hir fréends and well-willers: for the king studied of nothing but of peace, quietnesse, and solitarie life. When the whole hoast of the kings part was assembled, the same issued foorth of the towne, and passing ouer the riuer of Tine, lodged in the new field betweene Harsington and Sandifford,

Whethamsted.

stronglie fensing themselues about with high banks, and déepe trenches. On the other part, the lords being herewith aduanced verie neere the place where the kings people laie without Northampton; the bishops that were there with them, by the aduise and consent of the said lords, sent vnto the king the bishop of Salisburie, to vnderstand his mind, and to mooue him vnto some treatie of peace, and to admit the archbishop of Canturburie, and the other bishops there present, to be mediatours in the matter, that some good accord might be concluded betwixt the parties, so as an vniuersall peace might be restored in all parts through the whole realme.

The bishop of Salisburie dooing this message not so circumspectlie as had béene conuenient, returned without bringing anie towardlie answer; but rather words of high despite and vtter defiance. For the lords that were about the king, trusting in their warlike engines and strength of place, in which they were incamped, though otherwise inferior in number of men, purposed to abide the brunt of battell; and so led with the spirit of rashnesse, sent none other answer backe againe by the bishop, but contumelious words sounding greatlie to the reproch of their aduersaries; who being sore offended therewith determined to seeke reuenge with dint of sword. The earle of March as then being in the floure of his lustie and most couragious youth, lieng betweene Toucetor and Northampton, determined to set on the kings armie without longer delaie: and thereupon in the night season remooued his campe toward Northampton, and in marching forward set his men in order of battell: whereof the vant-ward was led by the earle of Warwike, which either by strength or stealth wan a streict which the lord Beaumont kept, going toward the kings campe; and herewith

The battell of Northamptō.

entring freshlie with his people, began the battell about seauen of the clocke the ninth daie of Iulie. After him followed the earle of March with the banner of his

Whethamsted.

father. ¶ Others write, that the earle of March led the fore-ward, the erle of Warwike the middleward, and the lord Fauconbridge the rere-ward.

The L. Graie of Ruthen.

Moreouer, that Edmund lord Greie of Ruthen who was on the kings side, failed in the trust committed to him: for where the enimies could not (without great danger) enter vpon the kings campe, by reason of a mightie trench and rampire pight full of piles and sharpe stakes, wherewith the campe was compassed about: the said lord Graie came with his men, and with helping hands pulled the enimies vp, and receiued them into the field where the battell was begun with great force & violence. For being now entred the field, they set vpon the kings people so fiercelie, that it séemed they ment either to obteine the victorie, or to die for it, euen all the whole number of

Edw. Hall.
The kings part discomfited.

them. The fight continued right fierse and cruell, with vncerteine victorie, till the houre of nine: at which time the kings armie was discomfited, and of the same slaine

and.

and drowned in the riuer, few lesse than ten thousand; and the king himselfe left *The K. taken.* comfortlesse alone was taken by the aduersaries, as a man in great miserie.

At this battell fought at Northampton, were slaine Humfreie duke of Buckingham, Iohn Talbot earle of Shrewburie, a valiant person, and not degenerating from his noble parents, Thomas lord Egremond, Iohn viscont Beaumont, and sir William Lucie, which made great hast to come to part of the fight, and at his first approch was striken in the head with an ax. Besides these that were slaine, manie were taken prisoners, bicause they left their horsses, alighting to fight on foot. The duke of Summerset, and other, which narrowlie escaped, fled with the quéene and prince into the bishoprike of Durham. The earles, hauing got the victorie in this bloudie battell, conueied the king to London, and lodged him in the bishops palace. After whose comming to the *The Tower deliuered to the earle of March.* citie, the Tower was deliuered to the erle of March, vpon a certeine composition; but the lord Scales suspecting the sequele of the deliuerie thereof, tooke a wherrie priuilie, intending to haue fled to the quéene; but he was espied by diuerse watermen belonging to the earle of Warwike (which waited for his foorth comming on the Thames) and suddenlie taken, was shortlie slaine with manie darts & daggers, and his bodie left *The lord Scales slaine.* naked and all bloudie at the gate of the clinke, and after was buried in the church adioining.

Then were diuerse persons apprehended, and indited of treason, wherof some were pardoned, and some executed. Thomas Thorpe second baron of the escheker, was *Thomas Thorpe.* committed to the Tower, where he remained long after, for that he was knowne to be great fréend to the house of Lancaster. ¶ When queene Margaret heard that the K. *Abr. Fl. ex I. S. pag. 700.* was taken, she with hir sonne, and eight persons fled to the castell of Hardlagh in Wales, and was robbed by the waie in Lancashire of all hir goods, to the value of ten thousand markes: from thence she went into Scotland. Thus you sée what fruits the trée of ciuill discord dooth bring foorth; that euill tree, which whilest some haue taken paine to plant, and some to proine and nourish, for others confusion (to whome they haue giuen a taste of those apples which it bare, far more bitter than coloquintida) themselues haue béene forced to take such share as befell them by lot. For as it is not possible that a cōmon fier, whose heat & flame is vniuersallie spred, should spare any particular place (for so should it not be generall) no more is it likelie that in ciuill commotions, rebellions, insurrections, and partakings in conflicts and pitched feelds (speciallie vnder ringleaders of great countenance and personage, such as be the péeres and states of kingdoms) anie one should, though perhaps his life, yet (a thousand to one) not saue his bloud vnspilt, nor his goods vnspoiled.] During this trouble, a *An. Reg. 39.* parlement was summoned to begin at Westminster, in the moneth of October next following.

In the meane time the duke of Yorke, aduertised of all these things, sailed from *Whethamsted* Dubline towards England, and landed at the red bank néere to the citie of Chester, *The duke of Yorke commeth foorth of Ireland.* with no small companie: and frõm Chester by long iournies he came to the citie of London, which he entred the fridaie before the feast of S. Edward, the Confessor, with a sword borne naked before him, with trumpets also sounding, and accompanied with a great traine of men of armes, and other of his fréends and seruants. At his *Whethamsted* comming to Westminster he entred the palace, and passing foorth directlie through the great hall, staied not till he came to the chamber, where the king and lords vsed to sit in the parlement time, cōmonlie called the vpper house, or chamber of the *A strange demeanor of the duke of Yorke.* péeres, and being there entred, stept vp vnto the throne roiall, and there laieng his hand vpon the cloth of estate, seemed as if he meant to take possession of that which was his right (for he held his hand so vpon that cloth a good pretie while) and after withdrawing his hand, turned his face towards the people, beholding their preassing togither, and marking what countenance they made.

Whilest he thus stood and beheld the people, supposing they reioiced to see his presence,

sence, the archbishop of Canturburie (Thomas Bourcher) came to him, & after due salutations, asked him if he would come and see the king.   With which demand he seeming to take disdaine, answered breefelie, and in few words thus: I remember not that I know anie within this realme, but that it beseemeth him rather to come and see my person, than I to go and see his.   The archbishop hearing his answer, went backe to the king, and declared what answer he had receiued of the dukes owne mouth.   After the archbishop was departed to the king that laie in the queenes lodging, the duke also departed, and went to the most principall lodging that the king had within all his palace, breaking vp the loekes and doores, and so lodged himselfe therein, more like to a king than a duke, continuing in the same lodging for a time to the great indignation of manie, that could not in aniewise like of such presumptuous attempts made by the duke, to thrust himselfe in possession of the crowne, and to depose king Henrie, who had reigned ouer them so long a time.

Maister Edward Hall in his chronicle maketh mention of an oration, which the duke of Yorke vttered, sitting in the regall seat there in the chamber of the peeres, either at this his first comming in amongst them, or else at some one time after, the which we haue thought good also to set downe: though Iohn Whethamsted the abbat of saint Albons, who liued in those daies, and by all likelihood was there present at the parlement, maketh no further recitall of anie words, which the duke should vtter at that time in that his booke of records, where he intreateth of this matter.   But for the oration (as maister Hall hath written thereof) we find as followeth.   ¶ During the time (saith he) of this parlement, the duke of Yorke with a bold countenance entered into the chamber of the peeres, and sat downe in the throne roiall, vnder the cloth of estate (which is the kings peculiar seat) and in the presence of the nobilitie, as well spirituall as temporall (after a pause made) he began to declare his title to the crowne, in this forme and order as insueth.

The duke of Yorks oration made to the lords of the parlement.

MY singular good lords, maruell not that I approch vnto this throne: for I sit here as in the place to me by verie iustice lawfullie belonging; & here I rest, as to whom this chaire of right apperteineth, not as he which requireth of you fauour, parcialitie, or bearing, but equall right, friendlie indifferencie, and true administration of iustice.   For I beeing the partie greeued, and complainant, can not minister to my selfe the medicine that should helpe me (as expert leeches & cunning surgians maie) except you be to me both faithfull aiders & also true councellors.   Nor yet this noble realme and our naturall countrie shall neuer be vnbuckled from hir dailie feuer, except I (as the principall physician, and you as the true and trustie apothecaries) consult togither in making of the potion, and trie out the cleane and pure stuffe from the corrupt and putrified drugs.

For vndoubtedlie, the root and bottome of this long festured canker is not yet extirpate, nor the feeble foundation of this fallible building is not yet espied, which hath beene and is the dailie destruction of the nobilitie, and the continuall confusion of the poore communaltie of this realme and kingdome.   For all you know (or should know) that the high and mightie prince king Richard the second, was the true and vndoubted heire to the valiant conqueror and renowmed prince king Edward the third, as sonne & heire to the hardie knight and couragious capteine Edward prince of Wales, duke of Aquitaine and Cornewall, eldest sonne to the said king Edward the third: which king was not onelie in deed, but also of all men reputed and taken for the true and infallible heire to the wise and politike prince king Henrie the third, as sonne and heire to king Edward the second, sonne and heire to king Edward the first, the very
                                                                                            heire

heire and first begotten sonne of the said noble and vertuous prince king Henrie the third.

Which king Richard of that name the second, was lawfullie & iustlie possessed of the crowne and diadem of this realme and region, till Henrie of Derbie duke of Lancaster and Hereford, sonne to Iohn of Gant duke of Lancaster, the fourth begotten sonne to the said king Edward the third, and yoonger brother to my noble ancestor Lionell duke of Clarence, the third begotten sonne of the said king Edward, by force and violence, contrarie both to the dutie of his allegiance, and also to his homage to him both doone and sworne, raised warre and battell at the castle of Flint in North-wales, against the said king Richard, and him apprehended, and imprisoned within the Tower of London : during whose life and captiuitie, he wrongfullie vsurped and intruded vpon the roiall power, and high estate of this realme and region, taking vpon him the name, stile, and authoritie of king and gouernour of the same.

And not therewith satisfied, and contented, compassed and accomplished the death and destruction of his naturall prince, and most worthie souereigne lord, not as a common homicide and butcherlie murtherer, but as a regicide, and destroier of his king. After whose pitious death, and execrable murther, the right and title of the crowne, and superioritie of this realme was lawfullie reuerted & returned to Roger Mortimer earle of March, sonne and heire to ladie Philip the onelie child of the aboue rehearsed Lionell duke of Clarence, vnto which Rogers daughter called Anne, my most deerest and welbeloued moother, I am the verie true and lineall heire, which descent all you can not iustlie gainesay, nor yet trulie denie. Then remember this, if the title be mine, why am I put from it? If I be true heire to the crowne (as I am in deed) why is my right withholden? If my claime be good, why haue I not iustice? For suerlie, learned men of great science and knowledge say and affirme, that lineall descent, nor vsurped possession can nothing preuaile, if continuall claime be lawfullie made, or openlie published.

For the auoiding of which scruple and ambiguitie : Edmund earle of March my most welbeloued vncle, in the time of the first vsurper, in deed but not by right called king Henrie the fourth, by his coosines the earle of Northumberland, & the lord Persie, he being then in captiuitie with Owen Glendouer the rebell in Wales, made his title & righteous claime to the destruction of both the noble persons. Likewise my most deerest lord and father, so farre set foorth that right and title, that he lost his life & worldlie ioy at the towne of Southampton, more by power than indifferent iustice. Since whose death, I comming to my full age, haue neuer desisted to pursue my title, and require my right, which by meanes of sinister counsell and vniust detention, I can neither obteine nor recouer. So that of fine force I am compelled to vse power in steed of praier, and force in steed of request; not (as I said before) for my priuat emolument and peculiar profit : but to restore peace, loue, and quietnesse to this our naturall region, which euer since the first vngodlie vsurpation of the aforenamed Henrie, vntrulie called king Henrie the fourth, hath beene cleerelie banished, and out of the same vniustlie exiled.

What murthers and manslaughters haue beene perpetrated and committed within this countrie, since the beginning of that vngratious vsurpation? What number of noble men haue beene slaine, destroied, & executed since that unfortunate daie? It is too lamentable and manifest. For although Henrie of Lancaster earle of Derbie tooke vpon him the scepter and the crowne, and wrongfullie bare the name and stile of a king; and was not much tickled with mine vncle the earle of March, at that time being within age : yet was he neuer in suertie of himselfe, nor had or inioied any profit & quietnesse either in mind or in bodie. " For suerlie, a corrupt conscience neuer feeleth rest, but looketh when the sword of vengeage will descend and strike." His sonne also called king Henrie the fift, obteined notable victories, and immortal praises

for

for his noble acts doone in the realme of France: yet God (for the offense of his vn-true parent) suddenlie touched him, vnbodieng his soule in the flower of his youth, and in the glorie of his conquest.

And although he had a faire sonne and a yoong heire apparant: yet was this orphan such a one (as preachers say) that God threatned to send for a punishment to his vn-rulie and vngratious people, saieng by his prophet Esaie; " I shall giue you children to be your princes, and infants without wisedome shall haue the gouernance of you." The prophet lied not, if you note all things in an order: for after this Henrie the fift (whose fame no man can iustlie reprooue or deface) succeeded his sonne, whom all we haue called our naturall prince, and obeied as his heire. In whose time and wrong-full reigne, I require you diligentlie to consider, with what great torments and af-flictions God hath whipped & scourged this miserable Ile: yea with such and so manie scourges and plagues, as no nation (the Ægyptians onelie excepted) were euer tormented or afflicted withall. I will not speake of rebellious murthers and oppres-sions, which of late haue beene doone and exercised heere among vs. But I will declare & manifest to you, how the crowne and glorie of this realme is by the negli-gence of this sillie man, and his vnwise councell minished, defaced, and also dis-honoured.

Is not Normandie, which his father gat, regained & conquered againe, by the in-solencie of him & his couetous councell? Is not the whole duchie of Aquitaine, by two hundred and od yeares peaceablie possessed by the kings of this realme, in one yeare and a little more, gotten out of our hands & seigniorie? What should I speak of Aniou & Maine, or the losse of the Ile of France, with the rich citie of Paris. Alas it is too apparant. Neither will I molest you with the recitall of all the parti-culars thereof. But now in the middest of this affliction, and to make an end of the same: God of his ineffable goodnesse, looking on this countrie with his eies of pitie & mercie, hath sent me in the truth, to restore againe this decaid kingdome to his ancient fame and old renowme whereof heere in open parlement, according to my iust & true title, I haue and doo take possession of this roiall throne: not putting dif-fidence, but firme hope in Gods grace, that by his diuine aid, and assistance of you the peeres of this realme, I shall beautifie & mainteine the same to the glorie of him, honour of my bloud, and to the publike wealth as well of you all heere present, as of all the poore commons and subiects of this kingdome and regiment.

When the duke had made an end of his oration, the lords sat still as men striken into a certeine amazednesse, neither whispering nor speaking foorth a word, as though their mouthes had beene sowed vp. The duke not verie well content with their si-lence, aduised them to consider throughlie, and ponder the whole effect of his words and saiengs: and so neither fullie displeased, nor yet altogither content, departed to his lodging in the kings palace. While he was declaring thus his title in the higher house among the peeres, there happened a strange chance in the verie same instant amongest the commons in the nether house. A crowne which did hang in the middle

Prodigious tokens.

of the same, to garnish a branch to set lights vpon, without touch of man, or blast of wind, suddenlie fell downe. About the same time also fell downe the crowne which stood on the top of Douer castell. Which chances where construed to be signes, that the crowne of the realme should some waie haue a fall.

The lords forgot not the dukes demand, and to take some direction therein, diuerse of them as spirituall and temporall, with manie graue and sage persons of the com-monaltie dailie assembled at the Blackefriers, and other places, to treat of this matter, being of so great importance. During which time the duke of Yorke, although he and the king were both lodged in the palace of Westminster; yet would he not for anie praiers or requests once visit the king, till some conclusion were taken in this

                                                          matter:

matter: saieng, that he was subiect to no man, but only to God, vnder whose mercie none here superiour but he. ¶ The king of Scots, partlie incouraged thorough the ciuill discord here in England, and partlie for the displeasure which he had conceiued for the death of Edmund duke of Summerset his moothers brother, this yeare be- The castell of Roxburgh be-sieged. sieged the castell of Roxburgh: and by the breaking of a bombard, as the same was shot off against the castell, he chanced to be slaine. Yet the Scots left not off their The king of Scots thorough misfortune slaine. enterprise, assaulting the castell till they gat it, and then defended it a long time after, till Richard duke of Glocester wan it againe, and raced it.

After long debating of the matter and deliberate consultation amongest the peeres, The determina-tion of the parle-ment cōcerning the intailing of crowne. prelats, and commons, vpon the vigill of all saints, it was condescended: for so much as king Henrie had béene taken as king by the space of thirtie and eight yeares and more, that he should inioy the name and title of king, and haue possession of the realme during his naturall life. And if he either died, or resigned, or forfeited the same, by breaking or going against anie point of this concord, then the said crowne & autho-ritie roiall should immediatlie be deuoluted and come to the duke of Yorke, if he then liued; or else to the next heire of his linage. And that the duke of Yorke from thense foorth should be protector and regent of the land. ¶ This was the determina- *Abr. Fl. ex J. S. pag.* 700, 701, *&c. in Quart.* tion of the parlement to & fro, tending to peace betwéene the king & the duke (which was ratified accordinglie) as by the articles insuing dooth appeare.

The articles betvvixt king Henrie and the duke of Yorke.

BLESSED be Iesu, in whose hands and bountie resteth and is the peace and vnitie betwixt princes, and the weale of euerie relme: by whose direction (I know) agreed it is, appointed, and accorded as followeth, betwixt the most high and most mightie prince king Henrie the sixt, king of England and of France, and lord of Ireland, on the one partie, and the right high & mightie prince Richard Plantagenet duke of Yorke on the other partie: vpon certeine matters of variance mooued betwixt them, and especiallie vpon the claime and title vnto the crownes of England and of France, and roiall power, estate and dignitie apperteining to the same, and lordship of Ireland, opened, shewed, and declared by the said duke, before all the lords spirituall and tem-porall, being in this present parlement.

First, where the said Richard duke of Yorke hath declared and opened (as his aboue said) title & claime in maner as followeth.

That the right noble and woorthie prince, Henrie king of England the third had issue, and lawfullie got Edward the first begotten sonne, borne at Westminster, the fiftéenth kalends of Iulie, in the yeare of our Lord 1239, & Edmund his second sonne which was borne on S. Marcels daie, the yere 1200, the which Edward, after the death of king Henrie his father, intituled & called king Edward the first, had issue, Edward his first begotten sonne, called (after the deceasse of his father) king Edward the second, the which had issue, Edward the third; which Edward the third had issue, Edward prince of Wales; William of Hatfield his second sonne; Lionell the third, duke of Clarence; Iohn of Gant fourth duke of Lancaster; Edmund of Langlie fift, duke of Yorke; Thomas of Woodstoke sixt, duke of Glocester; and William of Windsor seauenth.

The said Edward prince of Wales, which died in the life time of his father, had issue Richard, which succéeded Edward the third his grandsire; Richard died without issue; William of Hatfield the second sonne of Edward the third, died without issue; Lionell the third sonne of Edward the third, duke of Clarence, had issue Philip his daughter and heire, which was coupled in matrimonie vnto Edmund Mortimer earle of March, and had issue Roger Mortimer earle of March hir sonne and heire; which

Roger had issue of Edmund erle of March, Roger Mortimer, Anne, Elianor; which Edmund, Roger, and Elianor died without issue.

And the said Anne coupled in matrimonie to Richard earle of Cambridge, the sonne of Edmund of Langleie, the fift sonne of Henrie the third, and had issue Richard Plantagenet, commonlie called duke of Yorke; Iohn of Gant, the fourth sonne of Edward and the yoonger brother of the said Lionell, had issue Henrie earle of Derbie, who incontinentlie after that king Richard resigned the crownes of the realmes and lordship of Ireland, vnrighteouslie entered vpon the same, then being aliue Edmund Mortimer earle of March, sonne to Roger Mortimer earle of March, sonne and heire of the said Philip, daughter and heire of the said Lionell, the third sonne of the said king Edward the third, to the which Edmund the right and title of the said crownes and lordship by law and custome belonged. To the which Richard duke of Yorke, as sonne to Anne daughter to Roger Mortimer earle of March, sonne and heire of the said Philip, daughter and heire of the said Lionell, the third sonne of king Edward the third, the right, title, dignitie roiall, and estate of the crownes of the realmes of England and France, and the lordship of Ireland perteineth and belongeth afore anie issue of the said Iohn of Gant, the fourth sonne of the same king Edward.

The said title notwithstanding, and without preiudice of the said Richard duke of Yorke, tenderlie desiring the wealth, rest, and prosperitie of this land, and to set apart all that might be trouble to the same, and considering the possession of the said king Henrie the sixt, and that he hath for his time béene named, taken, and reputed for king of England and of France, and lord of Ireland, is contented, agréed, and consenteth, that he be had, reputed, and taken for king of England and France, with the roiall estate, dignitie, and preheminence belonging therevnto, and lord of Ireland during his naturall life. And for that time, the said duke, without hurt or preiudice of his said right, and title, shall take, worship, and honour him for his souereigne lord.

Item, the said Richard duke of Yorke, shall promit and bind him by his solemne oth, in maner and forme as followeth.

The oth of Richard duke of Yorke. In the name of God Amen: I Richard duke of Yorke, promise and sweare by the faith and truth that I owe to almightie God, that I shall neuer consent, procure, or stirre, directlie or indirectlie, in priuie or apert, neither (as much as in me is) shall suffer to be doone, consented, procured, or stirred, anie thing that may sound to the abridgement of the naturall life of king Henrie the sixt, or to the hurt or diminishing of his reigne or dignitie roiall, by violence, or anie other waie, against his freedome or libertie: but if any person or persons would doo or presume anie thing to the contrarie, I shall with all my might and power withstand it, and make it to be withstood, as far as my power will stretch therevnto, so helpe me God and his holie euangelists.

Item, Edward earle of March, and Edmund earle of Rutland, sonnes of the said duke of Yorke, shall make like oth.

Item, it is accorded, appointed, and agréed that the said Richard duke of Yorke, shall be called and reputed from hencefoorth, verie and rightfull heire to the crownes, roiall estate, dignitie and lordship aboue said; and after the deceasse of the said king Henrie, or when he will laie from him the said crownes, estate, dignitie, and lordship, the said duke and his heires shall immediatlie succéed to the said crownes, roiall estate, dignitie and lordship.

Item, the said Richard du e of Yorke, shall haue by authoritie of this present parlement, castels, manors, lands, and tenements, with the wards, marriages, reliefes, seruices, fines, amercements, offices, aduousons, fées, and other appurtenances to them belonging, what soeuer they be, to the yearelie value of ten thousand marks, ouer all charges and reprises; whereof fiue thousand marks shall be to his owne state, thrée thousand fiue hundred marks to Edward his first begotten sonne earle of March for

his

his estate, and one thousand pounds to Edmund earle of Rutland his second sonne for his yearlie sustentation, in such consideration and such intent as shall be declared by the lords of the kings councell.

Item, if anie person or persons imagine or compasse the death of the said duke, and thereof probablie be attainted of open déed doone by folkes of other condition, that it be déemed & adiuged high treason.

Item, for the more establishing of the said accord, it is appointed and consented, that the lords spirituall and temporall, being in this present parlement, shall make oths, to accept, take, worship, and repute the said Richard duke of Yorke and his heires, as aboue is rehearsed, and kéepe, obserue, and strengthen (in as much as apperteineth vnto them) all the things abouesaid, and resist to their power, all them that would presume the contrarie, according to their estates and degrées.

Item, the said Richard duke of Yorke, earles of Mareh, and Rutland, shall permit and make other to helpe, aid, and defend the said lords, and euerie of them against all those that will quarell, or anie thing attempt against the said lords, or anie of them, by occasion of agréement or consenting to the said accord, or assistance giuing to the duke and earles, or anie of them.

Item, it is agréed and appointed, that this accord, and euerie article thereof, be opened and notified by the kings letters patents, or otherwise, at such times and places, and in maner as it shall be thought expedient to the said Richard duke of Yorke, with the aduise of the lords of the kings councell. The king vnderstandeth certeinelie the said title of the said Richard duke of Yorke, iust, lawfull, and sufficient, by the aduise and assent of the lords spirituall and temporall, and the commons in this parlement assembled; and by authoritie of the same parlement declareth, approoueth, ratifieth, confirmeth, and accepteth the said title, iust, good, lawfull, and true, and therevnto giueth his assent and agréement of his frée will and libertie.

And ouer that, by the said aduise and authoritie declareth, intituleth, calleth, cstablisheth, affirmeth, & reputeth the said Richard duke of Yorke, verie true and rightfull heire to the crownes, roiall estate, and dignitie of the realmes of England and of France, and of the lordship of Ireland aforesaid; and that according to the worship and reuerence that thereto belongeth, he be taken, accepted and reputed, in worship & reuerence, by all the states of the said realme of England, and of all his subiects thereof; sauing and ordeining by the same authoritie, the king to haue the said crownes, realme, roiall estate, dignitie, and preheminence of the same, and the said lordship of Ireland during his life naturall.

And furthermore, by the same aduise and authoritie willeth, consenteth and agréeth, that after his deceasse, or when it shall please his highnesse to laie from him the said crownes, estate, dignitie, and lordship, the said Richard duke of Yorke and his heires shall immediatlie succéed him in the said crownes, roiall estate, dignitie, and worship, and them then haue and inioie: anie act of parlement, statute, or ordinance, or other thing to the contrarie made, or interruption, or discontinuance of possession notwithstanding.

And moreouer, by the said aduise and authoritie, establisheth, granteth, confirmeth, approueth, ratifieth, and accepteth the said accord, and all things therein conteined, and therevnto fréelie and absolutelie assenteth, agréeth; and by the same aduise and authoritie ordeineth and establisheth, that if anie person or persons imagine or compasse the death of the said duke, & probablie be attainted of open déed doone by folks of that condition, that it be déemed and adiudged high treason.

And furthermore ordeineth and establisheth by the said aduise and authoritie, that all statutes, ordinances, and acts of parlement, made in the time of the said king Henrie the fourth, by the which he and the heires of his bodie, comming of Henrie late king of England the fift, the sonne and heire of the said king Henrie the fourth, and the heires of king Henrie the fift, were or be inheritable to the said crownes and realmes, or to the heritage of the same, be annulled, repealed, damned, cancelled, void, and of none effect.

And ouer this, the king by the said aduise, assent and authoritie, órdeineth and establisheth, that all other acts and statutes made afore this time by act of parlement, not repealed or annulled by like authoritie, or otherwise void, be in such force, effect, and vertue, as they were afore the making of these ordinances; and that no letters patents, roialx of record, nor acts iudiciall, made or doone afore this time not repealed, reuersed, ne otherwise void by law, be preiudiced or hurt by this present act.]

This agreement put in articles, was ingrossed, sealed, and sworne vnto by the two parties, and also enacted in the parlement. For ioy whereof the king, hauing in his companie the duke of Yorke, road to the cathedrall church of saint Paule in London, and there on the day of all saints with the crowne on his head went solemnelie in procession, and was lodged a good space after in the bishops palace, néer to the said church. And vpon the saturdaie next insuing, Richard duke of Yorke was by sound of trumpet solemnelie proclamed heire apparant to the crowne of England, and protectour of the realme. After this, the parlement kept at Couentrie the last yeare, was declared to be a diuelish councell, and onelie had for destruction of the nobilitie, and was indéed no lawfull parlement: bicause they which were returned, were neuer elected according to the due order of the law, but secretlie named by them which desired rather the destruction than the aduancement of the common-wealth. When these agréements were enacted, the king dissolued his parlement, which was the last parlement that euer he ended.

The duke of Yorke proclamed heire apparant & protectour of the realme.
The parlemēt at Couentrie made frustrat.

The duke of Yorke, well knowing that the quéene would spurne against all this, caused both hir and hir sonne to be sent for by the king. But she as woont rather to rule, than to be ruled, and thereto counselled by the dukes of Excester and Summerset not onelie denied to come, but also assembled a great armie, intending to take the king by fine force out of the lords hands. The protector in London hauing knowledge of all these dooings, assigned the duke of Norffolke, and erle of Warwike his trustie fréends to be about the king, while he with the earles of Salisburie and Rutland and a conuenient number departed out of London the second daie of December northward, and appointed the earle of March his eldest sonne to follow him with all his power. The duke came to his castell of Sandall beside Wakefield on Christmasse éeuen, & there began to make muster of his tenants and fréends. The quéene thereof ascerteined, determined to cope with him yer his succour were come.

Now she, hauing in hir companie the prince hir sonne, the dukes of Excester and Summerset, the earle of Deuonshire, the lord Clifford, the lord Ros, and in effect all the lords of the north parts, with eightéene thousand men, or (as some write) two and twentie thousand, marched from Yorke to Wakefield, and bad base to the duke, euen before his castell gates. He hauing with him not fullie fiue thousand persons, contrarie to the minds of his faithfull councellors, would needs issue foorth to fight with his enimies. The duke of Summerset and the quéenes part, casting vpon their most aduantage, appointed the lord Clifford to lie in one stale, and the earle of Wilshire in another, and the duke with other to kéepe the manie battell. The duke of Yorke with his people descended downe the hill in good order and arraie, aud was suffered to passe on towards the maine battell.

The battell Wakefield.

The duke of Yorke slaine.

But when he was in the plaine field betweene his castell and the towne of Wakefield, he was inuironed on euerie side, like fish in a net, so that though he fought manfullie, yet was he within halfe an houre slaine and dead, and his whole armie discomfited: with him died of his trustie fréends, his two bastard vncles, sir Iohn and sir Hugh Mortimers, sir Dauie Hall, sir Hugh Hastings, sir Thomas Neuill,
William

William and Thomas Aparre, both brethren; and two thousand and eight hundred Onelie seauen hundred southerne men saith *Wheth**msted.* others, whereof manie were yoong gentlemen, and heires of great parentage in the south parts, whose kin reuenged their deaths within foure moneths next, as after shall appeare.

In this conflict was wounded and taken prisoner, Richard earle of Salisburie, sir Richard Limbricke, Rafe Stanleie, Iohn Harow, capteine Hanson, and diuerse others. The lord Clifford, perceiuing where the earle of Rutland was conueied out of the field (by one of his fathers chapleins, and scholemaister to the same earle) and ouertaking The cruell murther of the yoong earle of Rutland. him, stabbed him to the heart with a dagger as he kneeled afore him. This earle was but a child at that time of twelue yeares of age, whome neither his tender yeares, nor dolorous countenance, with holding vp both his hands for mercie (for his speach was gone for feare) could mooue the cruell heart of the lord Clifford to take pitie vpon him, so that he was noted of great infamie for that his vnmercifull murther vpon that yoong gentleman.

But the same lord Clifford not satisfied herewith, came to the place where the dead corpse of the duke of Yorke laie, caused his head to be striken off, and set on it a crowne of paper, fixed it to a pole and presented it on the quéene, not lieng farre from the field, in great despite, at which great reioising was shewed: but they laughed then that shortlie after lamented, and were glad then of other mens deaths that knew not their owne to be so néere at hand. ¶ Some write that the duke was taken *WhethamsteL* aliue, and in derision caused to stand vpon a molehill, on whose head they put a garland in steed of a crowne, which they had fashioned and made of sedges or bulrushes; and hauing so crowned him with that garland, they knéeled downe afore him (as the Iewes did vnto Christ) in scorne, saieng to him; "Haile king without rule, haile king without heritage, haileduke and prince without people or possessions." And at length hauing thus scorned him with these and diuerse other the like despitefull words, they stroke off his head, which (as yee haue heard) they presented to the quéene.

Manie déemed that this miserable end chanced to the duke of Yorke, as a due punishment for breaking his oth of allegiance vnto his souereigne lord king Henrie: A purchase of Gods cursse with the popes blessing. but others held him discharged thereof, bicause he obteined a dispensation from the pope, by such suggestion as his procurators made vnto him, whereby the same oth was adiudged void, as that which was receiued vnaduisedlie, to the preiudice of himselfe, and disheriting of all his posteritie. After this victorie by the quéene, the earle The prisoners beheaded. of Salisburie and all the prisoners were sent to Pomfret, and there beheaded, whose heads (togither with the duke of Yorkes head) were conueied to Yorke, and there set 1461. on poles ouer the gate of the citie, in despite of them and their linage. The earle of March, now after the death of his father, verie duke of Yorke, lieng at Glocester, The earle of March now duke of Yorke. was woonderfullie amazed, when the sorrowfull newes of these mishaps came vnto him: but after comfort giuen to him by his faithfull louers and assured alies, he remooued to Shrewesburie, declaring to the inhabitants of that towne, and to them of the other townes in those parties the murther of his father, the ieopardie of himselfe, and the present ruine of the common-wealth.

The people on the marches of Wales, for the fauour which they bare to the Mortimers linage, more gladlie offered him their aid and assistance than he could desire the same; so that he had incontinentlie a puissant armie, to the number of thrée and twentie thousand, readie to go against the quéene, and the murtherers of his father. But when he was setting forward, newes was brought to him, that Iasper The earle of Penbroke. earle of Penbroke halfe brother to king Henrie, and Iames Butler earle of Ormund and Wilshire, had assembled a great number of Welsh and Irish people to take him: he herewith quickned, retired backe and met with his enimies in a faire plaine, néere to The battell of Mortimers crosse. Mortimers crosse, not far from Hereford east, on Candlemasse daie in the morning.

At

At which time the sunne (as some write) appeared to the earle of March like thrée sunnes, and suddenlie ioined altogither in one. Vpon which sight he tooke such courage, that he fiercelie setting on his enimies, put them to flight: and for this cause men imagined, that he gaue the sunne in his full brightnesse for his badge or

cognisance. Of his enimies were left dead on the ground thrée thousand and eight hundred.

The earles of Penbroke and Wilshire fled, but sir Owen Teuther father to the said

earle of Penbroke (which Owen had married king Henries mother, as yee haue heard before) with Dauid Floid, Morgan ap Reuther, and diuerse other were taken, and beheaded at Hereford. The quéene neuer the lesse incouraged by hir late victorie, with a multitude of northerne people, marched toward London, intending to vndoo all that

had beene ordeined in the last parlement. These northerne people, after they were once passed ouer the riuer of Trent, spoiled and wasted the countrie afore them, in maner as if they had béene in the land of forren enimies. At length, they approched to saint Albons, hearing that the duke of Northfolke, and the earle of Warwike, with other whome the duke of Yorke had left to gouerne the king in his absence, had (by the kings assent) assembled a great hoast, and were incamped neere to that towne.

Those northerne lords and other that were with the queene, made forward, and entring into S. Albons, meant to passe through the towne, and so to coape with their enimies; but finding a sort of archers ranged néere to the great crosse in the market place, to defend their passage, they were receiued with such a storme of arrowes, which came flieng about their eares as thicke as haile, that they were quicklie repelled backe, and with losse driuen to retire in hast vnto the west end of the towne; where by a lane that leadeth northwards vp to saint Peters stréet, they made their entrie, and had there also a sharpe incounter against certeine bands of the kings people. But

after great slaughter on both parts, they got through, and vpon the heath that lieth at the north end of the towne, called Barnard heath, they had a farre greater conflict with foure or fiue thousand of the kings armie, that séemed as they had beene auant courrers.

These gaue the onset so fiercelie at the beginning, that the victorie rested doubtfull a certeine time, so that if the easterne and southerne men had continued as they began, the field had beene theirs; but after they had stood to it a pretie while, and perceiued none of their fellowes from the great armie to come and assist them, they began to

faint, and turning their backes, fled amaine ouer hedge and ditch, through thicke and thin, woods and bushes, séeking so to escape the hands of their cruell enimies that followed them with eger minds, to make slaughter vpon them, namelie, the northern prickers, now in the chase pursued most hotlie, and bare downe manie, and more had doone, if the night comming vpon, had not staied them.

When the daie was closed, those that were about the king (in number a twentie thousand) hearing how euill their fellowes had sped, began vtterlie to despair of the victorie, and so fell without anie long tarriance to running awaie. By reason whereof, the nobles that were about the king, perceiuing how the game went, and withall saw no comfort in the king, but rather a good will and affection towards the contrarie part, they withdrew also, leauing the king accompanied with the lord Bonneuille, & sir Thomas Kiriell of Kent; which vpon assurance of the kings promise, tarried still with him, and fled not. But their trust deceiued them, for at the queenes departing from saint Albons, they were both beheaded; though contrarie to the mind and promise of hir husband. Sir Thomas Thorp, baron of the escheker, was also beheaded the same daie, at Highgate, by the commons of Kent.

Such was the successe of this second battell fought at S. Albons, vpon Shrouetues-

daie, the seuentéenth of Februarie, in which were slaine thrée and twentie hundred men,

men, of whom no noble man is remembred, saue sir Iohn Graie, which the same Sir Iohn Graie laine.
daie was made knight, with twelue other, at the village of Colneie. Now after
that the noble men and other were fled, and the king left in maner alone without anie
power of men to gard his person, he was counselled by an esquier called Thomas
Hoo, a man well languaged, and well seene in the lawes, to send some conuenient
messenger to the northerne lords, aduertising them, that he would now gladlie come
vnto them (whome he knew to be his verie fréends, and had assembled themselues
togither for his seruice) to the end he might remaine with them, as before he had
remained vnder the gouernement of the southerne lords.

According to the aduise and counsell of this esquier, the king thought it good to
send vnto them, and withall appointed the same esquier to beare the message, who Thomas Hoo esquier sent to the northerne lords.
first went and declared the same vnto the earle of Northumberland, and returning
backe to the king, brought certeine lords with him, who conueied the king first vnto
the lord Cliffords tent, that stood next to the place where the kings people had incamped.
This done, they went and brought the quéene and hir sonne prince Edward vnto his
presence, whome he ioifullie receiued, imbracing and kissing them in most louing wise,
and yeelding hartie thanks to almightie God, whome it had pleased thus to strengthen
the forces of the northerne men, to restore his déerlie belooued and onelie sonne againe
into his possession. Thus was the quéene fortunate in hir two battels, but vnfortunate *Edw. Hall.*
was the king in all his enterprises: for where his person was present, the victorie still
fled from him to the contrarie part. The quéene caused the king to dub hir sonne Prince Edward made knight.
prince Edward knight, with thirtie other persons, which the day before fought on hir
side against his part.

This doone, they went to abbeie, where, of the abbat and moonks they were
receiued with hymnes and songs, and so brought to the high altar, and after to the
shrine, and so to the chamber in which the king was woont to lodge. The abbat
made sute that order might be taken to restreine the northerne men from spoiling the
towne: and proclamation indéed was made to that effect, but it auailed not: for they
mainteined, that the spoile of things was granted them by couenant, after they were
once passed ouer the riuer of Trent: and so not regarding anie proclamation or other
commandement, they spared nothing that they could laie hands vpon, if the same The northern men spoile the towne of saint Albons.
were meet for them to carie awaie. The queene, hauing thus got the victorie, sent
to the maior of London, commanding him without delaie to send certeine carts, laden
with Lenton vittels, for the refreshing of hir and hir armie. The maior incontinentlie The quéene sendeth to the maior of London for vittels
caused carts to be laden, and would haue sent them forward; but the commons of the
citie would not suffer them to passe, but staied them at Criplegate, notwithstanding Vittels sent by the maior and staid by the commons.
the maior did what he could by gentle persuasions to quiet them.

During which controuersie, diuerse of the northerne horssemen, came and robbed
in the suburbs of the citie, and would haue entred at Criplegate; but they were repelled by the commoners, and three of them slaine. Wherevpon, the maior sent
the recorder to Barnet to the kings counsell there, to excuse the matter; and the
duches of Bedford, the ladie Scales, with diuerse fathers of the spiritualtie, went to
the quéene, to asswage hir displeasure conceiued against the citie. The queene at
this humble request, by aduise of hir councell, appointed certeine lords and knights,
with foure hundred tall persons, to ride to the citie, and there to view and sée the
demeanor and disposition of the people: and diuerse aldermen were appointed to
méet them at Barnet, and to conueie them to London. But what man purposeth,
God disposeth. All these deuises were shortlie altered to another forme, bicause true
report came not onelie to the queene, but also to the citie; that the earle of March,
hauing vanquished the earles of Penbroke and Wilshire, had met with the earle
of Warwike (after this last battell at saint Albons) at Chipping Norton by Cotsold;
and that they with both their powers were coming toward London. The queene The quéene returneth northward.
hauing

hauing little trust in Essex, and lesse in Kent, but least of all in London, with hir husband and sonne, departed from saint Albons, into the north countrie, where the foundation of hir aid and refuge onelie rested.

The duches of Yorke, séeing hir husband and sonne slaine, and not knowing what should succéed of hir eldest sonnes chance, sent hir two yonger sonnes, George and Richard, ouer the sea, to the citie of Utrecht in Almaine, where they were of Philip duke of Burgognie well receiued; and so remained there, till their brother Edward had got the crowne and gouernement of the realme. The earles of March and Warwike, hauing perfect knowlege that the king & queene, with their adherents, were departed from S. Albons, rode straight to London, entring there with a great number of men of warre, the first weeke of Lent. Whose cōming thither was no sooner knowne, but that the people resorted out of Kent, Essex, and other the counties adioining, in great numbers, to sée, aid, and comfort this lustie prince and flower of chiualrie, in whome the hope of their ioy and trust of their quietnesse onelie consisted.

The great hope of the people conceiued of the erle of March.

This prudent yoong prince, minding to take time when time serued, called a great councell, both of the lords spirituall and temporall, and to them repeated the title and right that he had to the crowne, rehearsing also the articles concluded betwéene king Henrie and his father, by their writings signed and sealed, and also confirmed by act of parlement; the breaches whereof he neither forgat, nor left vndeclared. After the lords had considered of this matter, they determined by authoritie of the said councell, that because king Henrie had doone contrarie to the ordinances in the last parlement concluded, and was insufficient of himselfe to rule the realme, he was therfore to be depriued of all kinglie estate: and incontinentlie was Edward earle of March, sonne and heire to Richard duke of Yorke, by the lords in the said councell assembled, named, elected, and admitted for king and gouernour of the realme.

The earle of March elected king.

On which daie, the people of the earles part, being in their muster in S. Iohns field, and a great number of the substantiall citizens there assembled, to behold their order; the lord Fauconbridge, who tooke the musters, wiselie anon declared to the people the offenses and breaches of the late agréement, committed by king Henrie the sixt; and demanded of the people, whether they would haue him to rule and reigne anie longer ouer them? To whome they with whole voice answered; Naie, naie. Then he asked them, if they would serue, loue, honour, and obeie the erle of March, as their onlie king and souereigne lord: To which question they answered; Yea, yea: crieng (king Edward) with manie great shouts & clapping of hands in assent and gladnesse of the same.

The lord Fauconbridge.

The lords were shortlie aduertised of the louing consent which the commons frankelie and fréelie had giuen. Wherupon incontinentlie, they all with a conuenient number of the most substantiall commons repaired to the erle at Bainards castell, making iust and true report of their election and admission, and the louing assent of the commons. The earle, after long pausing, first thanked God of his great grace and benefit towards him shewed; then the lords and commons for their fauour and fidelitie: notwithstanding, like a wise prince, he alleged his insufficiencie for so great a roome and weightie burthen, as lacke of knowledge, want of experience, and diuerse other qualities to a gouernour apperteining. But yet in conclusion, being persuaded by the archbishop of Canturburie, the bishop of Excester, and other lords then present, he agréed to their petition, and tooke vpon him the charge of the kingdome, as forfeited to him by breach of the couenants established in parlement:

The earle of March taketh vpon him as king.

Abr. Flem.

¶ Thus farre touching the tragicall state of this land vnder the rent regiment of king Henrie, who (besides the bare title of roialtie and naked name of king) had little apperteining to the port of a prince. For whereas the dignitie of princedome standeth in souereigntie; there were of his nobles that imbecilled his prerogatiue by sundrie

practises,

practises, speciallie by maine force; as seeking either to suppresse, or to exile, or to obscure, or to make him awaie: otherwise what should be the meaning of all those foughten fields from time to time, most miserablie falling out both to prince, peere, and people? As at saint Albons, at Bloreheath, at Northampton, at Banberie, at Barnet, & at Wakefield; to the effusion of much bloud, and pulling on of manie a plage, which otherwise might haue béene auoided. All which battels, togither with those that were tried betweene Edward the fourth, after his inthronization; and Henrie the sixt after his extermination (as at Exham, Doncaster, and Teukesburie) are remembred by Anglorum prælia in good order of pithie poetrie, as followeth:

> Nobilitata inter plures hæc sunt loca cæde,
> Albani fanum, Blorum, borealis & Ampton,
> Banbrecum campis, Barnettum collibus hærens,
> *Experrectorum pagus, fanúmq; secundò
> Albani, propior Scoticis confinibus Exam,
> Contiguóq; istis habitantes rure coloni,
> Mœrentes hodie, quoties proscindit arator
> Arua propinqua locis dentale reuellere terra
> Semisepulta virûm sulcis Cerealibus ossa:
> Mœsta execrantur planctu ciuile duellum,
> Quo periere hominum plus centum millia cæsa,
> Nobile Todcastrum clades accepta coegit
> Millibus enectis ter denis nomen habere.
> Vltima postremæ locus est Teuxburia pugnæ,
> Oppidulis his accedens certissima testis,
> Bello intestino fluuios fluxisse cruoris]

* Wakefield.

But now before we procéed anie further, sith the reigne of king Henrie maie séeme here to take end, we will specifie some such learned men as liued in his time. Iohn Leland, surnamed the elder (in respect of the other Iohn Leland, that painefull antiquarie of our time) wrote diuerse treatises, for the instruction of grammarians; Iohn Hainton, a Carmelit or white frier (as they called them) of Lincolne; Robert Colman, a Franciscane frier of Norwich, and chancellor of the vniuersitie of Oxenford; William White a priest of Kent, professing the doctrine of Wickliffe, and forsaking the order of the Romane church, married a wife, but continued his office of preaching, till at length, in the yeare 1428, he was apprehended, and by William bishop of Norwich, and the doctors of the friers mendicants, charged with thirtie articles which he mainteined, contrarie to the doctrine of the Romane church, and in September the same yeare suffered death by fire.

Alexander Carpentar, a learned man, set foorth a booke called Destructorium vitiorum, wherein he inueieth against the prelats of the church of that time, for their crueltie vsed, in persecuting the poore and godlie christians; Richard Kendall, an excellent grammarian; Iohn Bate, warden of the white friers in Yorke, but borne in the borders of Wales, an excellent philosopher, and a diuine, he was also séene in the Gréeke toong, a thing rare in those daies; Peter Basset, esquier of the priuie chamber to king Henrie the fift, whose life he wrote; Iohn Pole a priest, that wrote the life of saint Walburgh, daughter to one Richard, a noble man of this realme of England, which Walburgh (as he affirmeth) builded our ladie church in Antwerpe; Thomas Ismaelit, a monke of Sion; Walter Hilton, a Chartreaux monke also of Shiene, either of those wrote certeine treatises full of superstition, as Iohn Bale noteth.

Peter Basset wrote king Henrie the fift his life.

Thomas Walden so called of the towne where he was borne, but his fathers surname was Netter, a white frier of London, and the thrée and twentith prouinciall gouernour of his order, a man vndoubtedlie learned, and thoroughlie furnished with cunning of the schooles, but a sore enimie to them that professed the doctrine of

Wickliffe, writing sundrie great volumes and treatises against them, he died at Rone
in Normandie, the second of Nouember, in the yeare one thousand foure hundred and
thirtie; Richard Ullerston, borne in Lancashire, wrote diuerse treatises of diuinitie;
Peter Clearke, a student in Oxenford, and a defendor of Wickliffes doctrine, wherevpon when he feared persecution here in England, he fled into Boheme, but yet at length

Fabian and *Cax-ton.* he was apprehended by the imperialists, and died for it, as some write, but in what
order, is not expressed.

Robert Hounslow, a religious man of an house in Hounslow beside London, whereof
he tooke his surname; Thomas Walsingham, borne in Norffolke, in a towne there of
the same name, but professed a monke in the abbeie of saint Albons, a diligent historiographer; Iohn Tilneie, a white frier of Yermouth, but a student in Cambridge, and
prooued an excellent diuine; Richard Fleming, a doctor of diuinitie in Oxenford, of
whome more at large before, pag. 169. Iohn Low borne in Worcestershire, an Augustine frier, a doctor of diuinitie, and prouinciall in England of his order, and by king
Henrie the sixt, made first bishop of saint Asaph, and after remooued from thense to
Rochester; Thomas Ringsted the yoonger, not the same that was bishop, but a doctor
of the law, and vicar of Mildenhall in Suffolke, a notable preacher, and wrote diuerse
treatises.

Iohn Felton, a doctor of diuinitie of Magdalen college in Oxenford; Nicholas
Botlesham, a Carmelit frier borne in Cambridgeshire, and student first in the vniuersitie
of Cambridge, and after in Paris, where he proceeded doctor of diuinitie; Thomas Rudburne, a monke of Winchester, and an historiographer; Iohn Holbrooke, borne in
Surrie, a great philosopher, and well séene in the mathematiks; Peter Paine, an earnest
professor of Wickliffes doctrine, and fearing persecution here in England, fled into
Boheme, where he remained in great estimation for his great learning & no lesse wisedome; Nicholas Upton, a ciuilian, wrote of heraldrie, of colours in armorie, and of
the dutie of chiualrie; William Beckeleie, a Carmelit frier of Sandwich, & warden of
the house there, a diuine, and professed degree of schoole in Cambridge; Iohn Torpe,
a Carmelit frier of Norwich.

Iohn Capgraue borne in Kent, an Augustine frier, procéeded doctor of diuinitie in
Oxenford, was admitted prouinciall of his order, and prooued (without controuersie)
the best learned of anie of that order of friers here in England, as Iohn Bale affirmeth,
he wrote manie notable volumes, and finallie departed this life at Lin in Norffolke, the
twelfth of August, in the yere 1464, which was in the fourth yeare of king Edward
the fourth; Humfrie duke of Glocester, earle of Penbroke, and lord chamberlaine of
England, also protector of the realme, during the minoritie of his nephue king
Henrie the sixt, was both a great fauourer of learned men, and also verie well learned
himselfe, namelie in astrologie, whereof (beside other things) he wrote a speciall
treatise intituled, Tabula directionum.

Iohn Wethamsted, otherwise called Frumentarius, was abbat of saint Albons, and
highlie in fauor with the good duke of Glocester last remembred, he wrote diuerse
treatises, and among others, a booke as it were of the records of things, chancing
whilest he was abbat, which booke I haue séene, and partlie in some parcell of this
kings time haue also followed; Roger Onleie, borne in the west countrie (as Bale
thinketh) was accused of treason, for practising with the ladie Eleanor Cobham, by
sorcerie to make the king awaie, and was thereof condemned, and died for it, though
he were innocent thereof, as some haue thought, he wrote a treatise intituled, Contra
vulgi superstitiones, also another De sua innocentia; Nicholas Cantlow, a Welshman
borne, descended of an ancient familie in Southwales, as by Bale it should appeare, he
became a frier Carmelit in Bristow; Henrie Wichingham, a Carmelit frier of Norwich,
a notable diuine, a great preacher, and wrote also sundrie treatises of diuinitie.

Iohn Lidgate, a monke of Burie, an excellent poet, and chiefe in his time in that
                                                                              facultie,

facultie, of all other that practised the same within this land, he trauelled thorough France and Italie to learne the languages and sciences, how greatlie he profited in atteining to knowlege, the workes which he wrote doo sufficientlie testifie; Nicholas Hostresham, an excellent physician; Iohn Blackeneie, a religious man, of the order of the Trinitie intituled, De redemptione captiuorum, and prior of an house of the same order, at Ingham in Norffolke, he was surnamed Blackeneie, of the towne where he was borne; Thomas Beckington, bishop of Bath, wrote against the law Salique, by which law the Frenchmen would seclude the princes of this realme from their title vnto the crowne of France; Iohn Baringham, a Carmelite frier of Gippeswich in Suffolke; Dauid Bois, borne in Wales, and a frier Carmelit, professed in Glocester, a doctor of diuinitie.

Iohn Brome, an Augustine frier; Michaell Trigurie, a Cornishman borne, whome for his excellencie and learning, king Henrie the fift appointed to be gouernour of that schoole or vniuersitie, which he instituted in the citie of Caen in Normandie, after he had brought it vnder his subiection; Iohn Amundisham, a moonke of saint Albons; Oswald Anglicus, a moonke of the Chartreux order; Iohn Keningale, a Carmelit frier of Norwich; Peter De sancta fide, a Carmelit also of Norwich; Reginald Pecocke, bishop of Chichester, of whome ye haue heard before, he was borne in Wales, and student in Oriall college in Oxenford, where he procéeded doctor of diuinitie, he wrote manie treatises touching the christian religion; Iohn surnamed Burie of the towne where he was borne, an Augustine frier in the towne of Clare in Suffolke.

Robert Fleming, a man perfect in the Gréeke and Latine toong [among whose works some haue béene séene vnder these titles: namelie, Lucubrationum Tiburtinarm lib. 1. a dictionarie in Gréeke and Latine, and a worke in verse of sundrie kinds, this man was of most fame in the yeare of our Lord 1470, which was in the tenth yeare of Edward the fourth, though he were not obscure also in the daies of this Henrie the sixt;] Thomas Gascoigne, borne at Hunfléete in Yorkeshire, of that worshipfull familie of the Gascoignes there, a doctor of diuinitie, and chancellor of the vniuersitie of Oxenford; William Stapilhart, borne in Kent, but by profession a white frier in London; Robert Fimingham borne in Norffolke a Franciscan frier in Norwich; Nicholas Montacute, an historiographer; Iohn Chandler, chancellor of Welles; William Botoner, descended of a good house, a knight by degrée, and borne in Bristow, verie studious in antiquities, and other sciences.

Iohn Stow, a monke of Norwich, but student in Oxenford, where he procéeded doctor of diuinitie; Thomas Langleie, a monke of Hulme; Nicholas Bungeie, borne in a towne of Norffolke of that name, wrote an historie, called Adunationes chronicorum; Henrie Beauford bishop of Winchester, base sonne to Iohn duke of Lancaster, of whome before we haue made sufficient mention, made cardinall by pope Martine the fourth, in the yeare 1426; Adam Homlington, a Carmelit frier; William Coppinger, maister of the vniuersitie of Oxenford; Thomas Stacie, an expert mathematician, and no lesse skilfull in astronomie; Iohn Talaugerne, a moonke of Worcester; William Sutton, an astrologian; Robert Balsacke, wrote a booke intituled De re militari, that is to saie, of warre or chiualrie, so that (as is thought) he was both a good souldier, and a painefull student of good letters.

Thomas Dando, a Carmelit frier of Marleburgh, he wrote the life of Alphred king of west Saxons; William Graie, borne of the noble house of the Graies of Codnor, he went to atteine to some excellencie of learning in Italie, where he heard that noble clearke Guarinus Veronensis read in Ferrara, he was preferred to the bishoprike of Elie, in the yéere 1454, by pope Nicholas the fift, when Thomas Bourchier was translated from thense to Canturburie; Iohn Kempe, archbishop of Yorke, and after remooued from thense to Canturburie (as before ye haue heard) he was made cardinall

                                       of

of S. Albin, by pope Eugenie the fourth; Adam Molins (as Bale calleth him) kéeper of the kings priuie seale, excellentlie learned, in time of the ciuill warre betwixt king Henrie, and the duke of Yorke, in which he lost his head.

Thomas Chillenden, a doctor both of the law ciuill and canon, became at length a moonke in Canturburie; Robert Bale, surnamed the elder, excellentlie learned in the lawes of the realme, recorder of London, gathered as it were a chronicle of the customes, lawes, foundations, changes, restoring magistrats, offices, orders, and publike assemblies of the citie of London, with other matters, touching the perfect description of the same citie; he wrote other works also touching the state of the same citie, and the acts of king Edward the third; he departed this life in the yeare of our Lord 1461, euen about the beginning of the reigne of king Edward the fourth, vnto whome we will now againe returne.

Thus farre the tragicall historie of Henrie the sixt
depriued of his roialtie.

EDWARD THE FOURTH, EARLE OF MARCH,

sonne and heire to Richard duke of Yorke.

An. Reg. I.
The earle of March taketh vpon him as king.

His title declared.

AFTER that this prince Edward earle of March had taken vpon him the gouernement of this realme of England (as before ye haue heard) the morow next insuing, being the fourth of March, he rode to the church of saint Paule, and there offered: and after Te Deum soong, with great solemnitie he was conueied to Westminster, and there set in the hall with the scepter roiall in his hand, whereto people in great numbers assembled. His claime to the crowne was declared to be by two maner of waies, the first, as sonne and heire to duke Richard his father, right inheritor to the same; the second, by authoritie of parlement, and forfeiture committed by king Henrie. Wherevpon it was againe demanded of the commons, if they would admit and take the said erle as their prince and souereigne lord, which all with one voice cried; yea, yea.

This part thus plaied, he entered into Westminster church vnder a canopie with solemne procession, and there as king offered; and herewith taking the homages of all the nobles there present, he returned by water to London, and was lodged in the

He is proclamed king. bishops palace; and on the morrow after, he was proclamed king by the name of Edward the fourth, throughout the citie. This was in the yeare of the world 5427, and after the birth of our Saviour 1461 after our accompt, beginning the yeare at Christmasse; but after the vsuall accompt of the church of England 1460, the twentith of emperour Frederike the third; the nine and thirtith and last of Charles the seuenth French king; and first yeare of the reigne of Iames the third king of Scots.

Whilest these things were adooing in the southparts, king Henrie being in the north countrie, assembled a great armie, trusting (for all this) to subdue his enimies; namelie, sith their chiefe ringleader the duke of Yorke was dispatched out of the waie. But he was deceiued: for out of the ded stocke sprang a branch more mightie than the stem; this Edward the fourth, a prince so highlie fauoured of the people, for his great liberalitie, clemencie, vpright dealing, and courage, that aboue all other, he with them stood in grace alone: by reason whereof, men of all ages and degrees to him dailie repaired, some offering themselues and their men to ieopard their liues with

him,

him, and other plentiouslie gaue monie to support his charges, and to mainteine his right.

By which meanes, he gathered togither a puissant armie, to the intent by battell (sithens none other waies would serue) at once to make an end of all. So, his armie and all things prepared, he departed out of London the twelfe daie of March, and by easie iournies came to the castell of Pomfret, where he rested, appointing the lord Fitz Walter to kéepe the passage at Ferribridge with a good number of tall men. King Henrie on the other part, hauing his armie in readinesse, committed the gouernance thereof to the duke of Summerset, the earle of Northumberland, and the lord Clifford, as men desiring to reuenge the death of their parents, slaine at the first battell at saint Albons. These capteins leauing king Henrie, his wife, and sonne, for the most safegard within the citie of Yorke, passed the riuer of Wharfe with all their power, intending to stop king Edward of his passage ouer the riuer of Aire.

And the better to bring that to passe, the lord Clifford determined to make a charge vpon them that kept the passage of Ferribridge; and so he departed with his light horssemen from the great armie on the saturdaie before Plamesundaie; and earelie yer his enimies were aware, slue the kéepers and wan the bridge. The lord Fitz Walter hearing the noise, suddenlie rose out of his bed, and vnarmed with a pollax in his hand, thinking that it had béene but a fraie amongst his men, came downe to appease the same; but yer he knew what the matter meant was slaine, and with him the bastard of Salisburie brother to the earle of Warwike, a valiant yoong gentleman, and of great audacitie. _The lord Fitzwater slaine._

When the earle of Warwike was informed hereof, like a man desperat, he mounted on his hacknie, and hasted puffing and blowing to king Edward, saieng; "Sir, I praie God haue mercie of their soules, which in the beginning of your enterprise haue lost their liues. And bicause I sée no succors of the world but in God, I remit the vengeance to him our creator and redéemer." With that he alighted downe, and slue his horse with his sword, saieng; Let him flée that will, for suerlie I will tarrie with him that will tarrie with me: and kissed the crosse of his sword as it were for a vow to the promise. King Edward, perceiuing the courage of his trustie friend the earle of Warwike, made proclamation, that all men which were afraid to fight, should depart: and to all those that tarried the battell, he promised great rewards, with addition, that anie souldier which voluntarilie would abide, and afterwards either in or before the fight should séeme to flée or turne his backe, then he that could kill him, should haue a great reward and double wages. _The earle of Warwike._ _A proclamation._

After this proclamation ended, the lord Fauconbridge, sir Walter Blunt, Robert Horne with the fore-ward passed the riuer at Castelford, three miles from Ferribridge, intending to haue inuironed the lord Clifford and his companie, but they being therof aduertised, departed in great hast toward king Henries armie; yet they met with some that they looked not for, & were so trapt yer they were aware. For the lord Clifford, either for heat or paine, putting off his gorget, suddenlie with an arrow (as some saie) without an head, was striken into the throte, and immediatlie rendred his spirit; and the earle of Westmerlands brother and all his companie almost were there slaine, at a place called Dintingdale, not far from Towton. This end had the lord Clifford, which slue the earle of Rutland kneeling on his knees, whose yoong sonne Thomas Clifford was brought vp with a shéepheard in poore habit, euer in feare to be knowne, till king Henrie the seuenth obteined the crowne, by whom he was restored to his name and possessions. _The lord Clifford slain._ _Dintingdale._ _Crueltie paid with sudden mischiefe._

When this conflict was ended at Ferribridge, the lord Fauconbridge, hauing the fore-ward, bicause the duke of Norffolke was fallen sicke, valiantlie vpon Palmesundaie in the twilight set foorth his armie and came to Saxton, where he might apparantlie behold the host of his aduersaries, which were accompted thréescore thousand men, _The lord Fauconbridge._ _Saxton._

and

Whethamsted saith, that K. Heries power exceeded in number king Edwards by twentie thousand men.
An heauie proclamatiõ.
Palmesundaie field.
and thereof aduertised king Edward, whose whole armie amounted to eight and fortie thousand six hundred and thréescore persons: which incontinentlie with the earle of Warwike set forward, leauing the rere-ward vnder the gouernance of sir Iohn Wenlocke, sir Iohn Dinham, and other. And first of all, he made proclamation, that no prisoner should be taken. So the same daie about nine of the clocke, which was the nine and twentith daie of March, being Palmesundaie, both the hostes approched in a faire plaine field, betwéene Towton and Saxton.

When ech part perceiued other, they made a great shout; and at the same instant there fell a small sléete or snow, which by violence of the wind that blew against them, was driuen into the faces of king Henries armies, so that their sight was somewhat dimmed. The lord Fauconbridge, leading K. Edwards fore-ward, caused euerie archer vnder his standard to shoot one flight (which before he caused them to prouide) and then made them to stand still. The northerne men feeling the shot, but by reason of the sléet, not well viewing the distance betwéene them and their enimies, like forward men shot their sheafe arrowes as fast as they might: but all to losse, for they came short of the southerne men by thréescore yards.

So their shot almost spent, the lord Fauconbridge marched forward with his archers, which not onelie shot their whole sheafes, but also gathered the arrowes of their enimies, and let a great part flie against their first owners, and suffered a great sort of them to stand, which sore troubled the legs of the northerne men, when the battell

The earle of Northumberland.
ioined. The earle of Northumberland and Andrew Trollop, chiefe capteins of king Henries vawward, séeing their shot not to preuaile, hasted to ioine with their enimies, and the other part slacked not their pase. This battell was sore foughten, for hope of life

The obstinate minds of both parts.
was set aside on either part, & taking of prisoners proclamed a great offense, so euerie man determined to vanquish or die in the field.

This deadlie conflict continued ten houres in doubtfull state of victorie, vncerteinlie heauing and setting on both sides; but in the end, king Edward so couragiouslie com-

King Henries part discomfited.
forted his men, that the other part was discomfited and ouercome, who like men amazed, fled toward Tadcaster bridge to saue themselues, where in the mid waie is a little

Cocke or riuer.
brooke called Cocke, not verie broad, but of a great déepenesse, in which, what for hast to escape, and what for feare of their followers, a great number was drowned there. It was reported, that men aliue passed the riuer vpon dead carcasses, and that the great riuer of Wharfe whereinto that brooke dooth run, and of all the water comming from Towton, was coloured with bloud.

The chase continued all night, and the most part of the next daie, and euer the northerne men (as they saw anie aduantage) returned againe, and fought with their enimies, to the great losse of both parts. For in these two daies were slaine (as they

The number slaine in battell of Saxtõ, otherwise called Palmesundaie field.
that knew it wrote) on both parts six and thirtie thousand seuen hundred thréescore & sixteene persons, all Englishmen and of one nation, whereof the chiefe were the earles of Northumberland and Westmerland, the lord Dacres, and the lord Welles, sir Iohn Neuill, Andrew Trollop, Robert Horne, and manie other knights and esquiers, and the earle of Deuonshire was taken prisoner, but the dukes of Summerset and Excester fled from the field and saued themselues.

After this great victorie, king Edward rode to Yorke, where he was with all solemnitie receiued; and first he caused the heads of his father, the earle of Salisburie, and other his freends, to be taken from the gates, and to be buried with their bodies: and there he caused the earle of Deuonshire, and thrée other to be beheaded, and set

King Henrie withdraweth to Berwike, & from thence into Scotland.
their heads in the same place. King Henrie, after he heard of the irrecouerable losse of his armie, departed incontinentlie with his wife and sonne to the towne of Berwike, and leauing the duke of Summerset there, went into Scotland, and comming to the king of Scots, required of him and his councell, aid, and comfort.

The yoong king of Scots, lamenting the miserable state of king Henrie, comforted
him

him with faire words and friendlie promises, and assigned to him a competent pension to liue on, during his abode in Scotland. King Henrie, in recompense of this courtesie and friendship, deliuered to the king of Scots the towne of Berwike, whereof he had got possession. He faithfullie supported the part of king Henrie, and concluded a mariage betwixt his sister, and the yoong prince of Wales, but the same was neuer consummate, as after ye shall heare. When king Henrie was somwhat setled in the relme of Scotland, he sent his wife and sonne into France to king Reiner hir father, trusting by his aid and succour to assemble an armie, and once againe to recouer his right and dignitie: but he in the meane time made his aboad in Scotland, to see what waie his friends in England would studie for his restitution.

Quéene Margaret with hir sonne goeth into France.

The quéene being in France, did obteine of the yoong French king then Lewes the eleuenth, that all hir husbands friends, and those of the Lancastriall band, might safelie and suerlie haue resort into anie part of the realme of France, prohibiting all other of the contrarie faction anie accesse, or repair into that countrie. ¶ Thus ye haue heard, how king Henrie the sixt, after he had reigned eight and thirtie yeares & od moneths, was driuen out of this realme. But now leauing him with the princes of his part, consulting togither in Scotland, and queene Margaret his wife gathering of men in France, I will returne where I left, to proceed with the dooings of king Edward.

This yoong prince, hauing with prosperous success obteined so glorious a victorie in the mortall battell at Towton, and chased all his aduersaries out of the realme, or at the least waies put them to silence, returned after the maner and fashion of a triumphant conquerour, with great pompe vnto London; where according to the old custome of the realme, he called a great assemblie of persons of all degrees, and the nine & twentith daie of Iune was at Westminster with solemnitie crowned and annointed king. ¶ In which yeare, this king Edward called his high court of parlement at Westminster, in the which, the state of the realme was greatlie reformed, and all the statutes made in Henrie the sixt his time (which touched either his title or profit) were reuoked.

In the same parlement, the earle of Oxford far striken in age, and his sonne and heire the lord Awbreie Véer, either through malice of their enimies, or for that they had offended the king, were both, with diuerse of their councellors, attainted, and put to execution; which caused Iohn earle of Oxford euer after to rebell. There were also beheaded the same time, sir Thomas Tudenham knight, William Tirell, and Iohn Montgomerie esquiers, and after them diuerse others. Also after this, he created his two yoonger brethren dukes, that is to saie, lord George duke of Clarence, lord Richard duke of Glocester; and the lord Iohn Neuill, brother to Richard earle of Warwike, he first made lord Montacute, and afterwards created him marques Montacute.

Beside this, Henrie Bourchier brother to Thomas archbishop of Canturburie, was created earle of Essex; and William lord Fauconbridge was made earle of Kent. To this Henrie lord Bourchier, a man highlie renowmed in martiall feats, Richard duke of Yorke long before this time, had giuen his sister Elizabeth in mariage, of whome he begat foure sonnes, William, Thomas, Iohn and Henrie: the which William being a man of great industrie, wit, and prouidence in graue and weightie matters, maried the ladie Anne Wooduile, decended of high parentage, whose mother Iaquet was daughter to Peter of Lutzenburgh earle of saint Paule, by the which Anne he had lord Henrie earle of Essex, one daughter named Cicile, maried to Water lord Ferrers of Chartleie and an other called Isabell, which died vnmaried.

The earle of Kent was appointed about this time to kéepe the seas, being accompanied with the lord Audelie, the lord Clinton, sir Iohn Howard, sir Richard Walgraue, and others, to the number of ten thousand, who landing in Britaine, wan the towne of Conquet, and the Isle of Reth, and after returned. When all things were brought

1462
Iohn Stow.

in

An. Reg. 2.

The duke of
Summerset &
other, submit
them to king
Edward.

in order, and framed as king Edward in maner could wish, Henrie duke of Summerset, sir Rafe Persie, and diuerse other, being in despaire of all good chance to happen vnto king Henrie, came humblie, & submitted themselues vnto king Edward, whome he gentlie receiued. Which clemencie notwithstanding, both the one and the other (when time serued) reuolted from king Edward, and betooke themselues to take part with Henrie, vnto whom they had béene adherents before: bicause they grew in hope that in the end the confederats, to whom they so closelie did cleaue both in effection and seriousnesse of labour (though they pretended a temporall renunciation of all dutie and seruice for their securitie sake) should haue the honor of victorie against their gainstanders. But as commonlie the euents of enterprises fall out flat contrarie to mens expectation and hope; so came it to passe with these, whose hope though it were gréene aad flourie in the prosecuting of their affaires, yet in the knitting vp of the matter and vnluckie successe thereof, it fell out in triall to be a flattering, a false, and a fruitlesse hope: and therefore that is a true and a wise sentence of the comicall poet & well seruing the purpose:

Plaut. in Mostel.

        Insperata accidunt magis sæpè qnàm quæ speres.

1463
———
An. Reg. 3.

The Quéene
returneth foorth
of France.

All this season was king Henrie in Scotland, and quéene Margaret (being in France) found such friendship at the French kings hands, that she obteined a crue of fiue hundred Frenchmen, with the which she arriued in Scotland. And after that she had reposed hir selfe a time, she sailed with hir gallant band of those ruffling Frenchmen toward Newcastell, and landed at Tinmouth. But whether she were afraid of hir owne shadow, or that the Frenchmen cast too manie doubts; the truth is, that the whole armie returned to their ships, and a tempest rose so suddenlie, that if she had not taken a small carauell, and that with good spéed arriued at Berwike, she had béene taken at that present time by hir aduersaries.

And although fortune was so fauourable to hir, yet hir companie with stormie blasts was driuen on the shore before Banburgh castell, where they set their ships on fire, and fled to an Iland called holie Iland, where they were so assailed by the bastard Ogle, and an esquier called Iohn Manners, with other of king Edwards freends, that manie of them were slaine, and almost foure hundred taken prisoners: but their coronell Peter Bressie, otherwise called monsieur de Varenne, happened vpon a fisherman, and so came to Berwike vnto queene Margaret, who made him capteine of the castell of Alnewike, which he with his Frenchmen kept, till they were rescued.

Shortlie after quéene Margaret obteined a great companie of Scots, and other of hir friends, and so bringing hir husband with hir, and leauing hir sonne called prince Edward in the towne of Berwike, entered Northumberland, tooke the castell of Banburgh, and stuffed it with Scotishmen, and made thereof capteine sir Rafe Greie, and came

Banburgh
castell.

The duke of
Summerset
reuolteth.

forward toward the bishoprike of Durham. When the duke of Summerset heard these newes, he without delaie reuolted from king Edward, and fled to king Henrie. So likewise did sir Rafe Persie, and manie other of the kings friends. But manie mo followed king Henrie, in hope to get by the spoile: for his armie spoiled and burned townes, and destroied fields whersoeuer he came. King Edward aduertised of all these things, prepared an armie both by sea and land.

Some of his ships were rigged and vittelled at Lin, and some at Hull, and well furnished with souldiers were herewith set foorth to the sea. Also the lord Montacute was sent into Northumberland, there to raise the people to withstand his enimies. And after this, the king in his proper person, accompanied with his brethren, and a great part of the nobilitie of his realme, came to the citie of Yorke, furnished with a mightie armie, sending a great part thereof to the aid of the lord Montacute, least peraduenture he giuing too much confidence to the men of the bishoprike and Northumberland, might through them be deceiued.

The lord Monta-
cute.

The lord Montacute then hauing such with him as he might trust, marched foorth
towards

towards his enimies, and by the waie was incountered with the lord Hungerford, the lord Roos, sir Rafe Persie, and diuerse other, at a place called Hegelie moore, where Hegelie moore. suddenlie the said lords, in maner without stroke strikeng, fled; and onelie sir Rafe Percie abode, and was there manfullie slaine, with diuerse other, saieng when he was Sir Rafe Persie. dieng; I haue saued the bird in my bosome: meaning that he had kept his promise and oth made to king Henrie: forgetting (belike) that he in king Henries most necessitie abandoned him, and submitted him to king Edward, as before you haue heard.

The lord Montacute séeing fortune thus prosperouslie leading his saile, aduanced forward; & learning by espials, that king Henrie with his host was incamped in a faire plaine called Liuels, on the water of Dowill in Examshire, hasted thither, and manfullie set on his enimies in their owne campe, which like desperate persons with no small courage receiued him. There was a sore foughten field, and long yer either Exham field. part could haue anie aduantage of the other: but at length the victorie fell to the lord Móntacute, who by fine force entered the battell of his enimies, and constreined them to flie, as despairing of all succours. In which flight, and chase were taken Henrie duke of Summerset, which before was reconciled to king Edward, the lord Roos, the The duke of Summerset taken. lord Molins, the lord Hungerford, sir Thomas Wentworth, sir Thomas Husseie, sir Iohn Finderne, and manie other.

King Henrie was a good horsseman that day, for he rode so fast awaie that no man King Henrie fled. might ouertake him; and yet he was so neere pursued, that certeine of his henchmen were taken, their horsses trapped in blue veluet, and one of them had on his head the said king Henries helmet, or rather (as may be thought, & as some say) his high cap of estate, called Abacot, garnished with two rich crownes, which was presented to king Edward at Yorke the fourth day of Maie. The duke of Summerset was incontinentlie The duke of Summerset beheaded. beheaded at Exham; the other lords and knights were had to Newcastell, and there (after a little respit) were likewise put to death. Beside these, diuerse other, to the number of fiue and twentie, were executed at Yorke, and in other places.

Sir Humfrie Neuill, and William Tailbois, calling himselfe earle of Kime, sir Rafe Greie, and Richard Tunstall, with diuerse other, which escaped from this battell, hid themselues in secret places: but yet they kept not themselues so close, but that they were espied and taken. The earle of Kime was apprehended in Riddesdale, and The earle of Kime, otherwise Angus, beheaded. brought to Newcastell, and there beheaded. Sir Humfrie Neuill was taken in Holdernesse, and at Yorke lost his head. After this battell called Exham field, king Edward came to the citie of Durham, and sent from thence into Northumberland the earle of Warwike, the lord Montacute, the lords Fauconbridge & Scroope, to recouer such castels as his enimies there held, and with force defended.

They first besieged the castell of Alnewike, which sir Peter Bressie and the French-Alnewike castell besieged. men kept, and in no wise would yéeld, sending for aid to the Scots. Whervpon sir George Dowglas erle of Angus, with thirteene thousand chosen men, in the day time came and rescued the Frenchmen out of the castell; the Englishmen looking on, which thought it much better to haue the castell without losse of their men, than to leese both the castell and their men, considering the great power of the Scots, & their owne small number; and so they entered the castell and manned it. After this, they woone the castell of Dunstanburgh by force, and likewise the castell of Banburgh. Iohn Gois, seruant to the duke of Summerset, being taken within Dunstanburgh, was brought to Yorke, and there beheaded.

Sir Rafe Greie being taken in Banburgh, for that he had sworne to be true to king Edward, was disgraded of the high order of knighthood at Dóncaster, by cutting off his gilt spurs, renting his cote of armes, and breaking his sword ouer his head: and finallie, he was there beheaded for his manifest periurie. After this, king Edward returned to Yorke, where (in despite of the earle of Northumberland, who then kept himselfe in the realme of Scotland) he created sir Iohn Neuill, lord Montacute earle of Northumberland; and in reproofe of Iasper earle of Penbrooke he created William lord Herbert earle of the same place. But after, when by mediation of friends, the earle of Northumberland was reconciled to his fauour, he restored him to his possessions, name, and dignitie; and preferred the lord Montacute to the title of marques Montacute: so that in degree, he was aboue his elder brother the earle of Warwike; but in power, policie, & possessions, far mener.

1464.

An. Reg. 4.

King Edward, though all things might séeme now to rest in good case, yet he was not negligent in making necessarie prouision against all attempts of his aduersarie king Henrie, and his partakers; and therefore raised bulworks, and builded fortresses on ech side of his realme, where anie danger was suspected for the landing of anie armie. He caused also espials to be laid vpon the marches, fore against Scotland, that no person should go out of the realme to king Henrie and his companie, which then soiourned in Scotland. But all the doubts of trouble that might insue by the means of king Henries being at libertie, were shortlie taken away and ended: for he himselfe, whether he was past all fear; or that hée was not well established in his wits and perfect mind; or for that he could not long kéepe himselfe secret, in disguised atire boldlie entred into England.

King Henrie
taken.

He was no sooner entred, but he was knowne and taken of one Cantlow, and brought toward the king, whom the earle of Warwike met on the way by the kings commandement, and brought him through London to the Tower, & there he was

Abr. Fl. ex I.S.
pag. 717.

laid in sure hold. ¶ But it is woorthie the noting, which I haue obserued in a late chronographers report touching this matter; namelie, that king Henrie was taken in Cletherwood, beside Bungerleie Hippingstons in Lancashire, by Thomas Talbot sonne and heire to sir Edward Talbot of Basshall, and Iohn Talbot his cosin of Colebrie, which deceiued him being at his dinner at Wadington Hall, and brought him toward London, with his legs bound to the stirrups, where he was met by the earle of Warwike, and arested at Esildon; doctor Manning deane of Windsor, doctor Bedle, and yoong Ellerton being in his companie, with their feet bound vnder the horse bellies were brought also to the Tower of London.]

Quéene Margaret hearing of the captiuitie of hir husband, mistrusting the chance of hir sonne, all desolate and comfortlesse departed out of Scotland, and passed into France, where she remained with hir father duke Reiner, till she returned into England to hir harme, as after ye shall heare. The new duke of Summerset, and his brother Iohn, sailed into France, where they also liued in great miserie; till duke Charles, bicause he was of their kin, as descended of the house of Lancaster by his mother, succoured them with a small pension, which was to them a great comfort.

The earle of
Penbroke.

Ab. Flem.

The earle of Penbroke went from countrie to countrie, not alwaies at his hearts ease, nor in safetie of life. [As for his dignitie and reputation, it was the more obscured, for that he had lost the title of his honor, and left at his wits end, doubtfull and vncerteine in contrarie factions (as manie more) what to say or doo for his best securitie. Neuerthelesse he concealed his inward discontentment, and as oportunitie of time ministred matter, so he grew in courage, and fell to practises of force (with other complices) therby to accomplish the cloudie conceits of his troubled mind, being persuaded, that temporall misfortunes are, if not vtterlie auoidable, yet manfullie to be withstood, or at least with audacitie & courage to be suffered, as the poet properlie saith:

Vir. Aen. 6.

Tu ne cede malis, sed contra audentior ito.]

King Edward being thus in more suertie of his life than before, distributed the possessions of such as tooke part with king Henrie the sixt, to his souldiers and capteins, which he thought had well deserued: and besides this, he left no other point of liberalitie vnshewed, whereby he might allure to him the beneuolent minds and louing hearts of his people. And moreouer to haue the loue of all men, he

shewed

shewed himselfe more familiar both with the nobilitie and commonaltie, than (as some men thought) was conuenient, either for his estate, or for his honor: notwithstanding the same liberalitie be euer after vsed. The lawes of the realme, in part he reformed, and in part he newlie augmented. The coine both gold and siluer (which yet at this day is) he newlie deuised, and diuided; for the gold he named roials and nobles, and the siluer he called grotes and halfe grotes. New coine stamped.

¶ In Michaelmasse terme were made sergeants at law, Thomas Yoong, Nicholas Geneie, Richard Neale, Thomas Brian, Richard Pigot, Iohn Greenfield, Iohn Catesbie, and Gwie Fairfax, which held their feast in the bishop of Elies place in Holborne. To the which feast the maior of London, with the aldermen, shiriffes, and commons of diuerse crafts being bidden, repaired. But when the maior looked to be set to keepe the state in the hall, as it beene vsed in all places of the citie and liberties, out of the kings presence (vnknowne to the sergeants and against their wils, as they said) the lord Graie of Ruthen then treasuror of England was there placed. Wherevpon the maior, aldermen, and commons departed home, and the maior made all the aldermen to dine with him. Howbeit he and all the citizens were greatlie displeased that he was so dealt with, and the new sergeants and others were right sorie therefore, and had rather than much good it had not so happened. This was then (as my record reporteth more at large) registred to be a president in time to come.] *Abr. Fl. ex I. S. pag. 716.* Sergeants feast. *Register of maiors.* The maior of London departeth from the sergeants feast.

After that king Edward had reduced the state of the publike affaires vnto his liking; to purchase himselfe a good opinion, and fauourable iudgement among the commons, he made proclamations, that all persons, which were adherents to his aduersaries part, & would leaue their armour, and submit themselues wholie to his grace and mercie, should be cléerelie pardoned and forgiuen. By this kind of courteous dealing he wan him such fauour of the people, that euer after, in all his warres, he was (thorough their aid and support) a victor and conquerour. When his realme was thus brought into a good and quiet estate, it was thought méet by him and those of his councell, that a marriage were prouided for him in some conuenient place; and therefore was the earle of Warwike sent ouer into France, to demand the ladie Bona, daughter to Lewes duke of Sauoie, and sister to the ladie Carlot, then quéene of France; which Bona was at that time in the French court.

The earle of Warwike, comming to the French king, then lieng at Tours, was of him honourablie receiued, and right courteouslie interteined. His message was so well liked, and his request thought so honourable for the aduancement of the ladie Bona, that hir sister quéene Carlot obteined both the good will of the king hir husband, and also of hir sister the foresaid ladie: so that the matrimonie on that side was cléerelie assented to, and the erle of Dampmartine appointed (with others) to saile into England, for the full finishing of the same. But here consider the old prouerbe to be true, which saith, that mariage goeth by destinie. For, during the time that the earle of Warwike was thus in France, and (according to his instructions) brought the effect of his commission to passe, the king being on hunting in the forest of Wichwood besides Stonistratford, came for his recreation to the manor of Grafton, where the duchesse of Bedford then soiourned, wife to sir Richard Wooduile lord Riuers, on whome was then attendant a daughter of hirs, called the ladie Elizabeth Graie, widow of sir Iohn Graie knight, slaine at the last battell of saint Albons, as before ye haue heard. The earle of Warwike sent into France about a marriage. The ladie Elizabeth Graie.

This widow, hauing a sute to the king for such lands as hir husband had giuen hir in iointure, so kindled the kings affection towards hir, that he not onelie fauoured hir sute, but more hir person; for she was a woman of a more formall countenance than of excellent beautie; and yet both of such beautie and fauour, that with hir sober demeanour, sweete looks, and comelie smiling (neither too wanton, nor too bashfull) besides hir pleasant toong and trim wit, she so alured and made subiect vnto hir the heart of that great prince, that after she had denied him to be his paramour, with so good maner, and words so well set as better could not be deuised; he finallie resolued with himselfe to marrie hir, not asking counsell of anie man, till they might perceiue it was no bootie to aduise him to the contrarie of that his concluded purpose; sith he was so farre gone that he was not reuocable, and therefore had fixed his heart vpon the last resolution: namelie, to applie an holesome, honest, and honourable remedie to his affections fiered with the flames of loue, and not to permit his heart to the thraldome of vnlawful lust; which purpose was both princelie and profitable; as the poet saith:

Ou:d. de rem.
am. lib. 1.

$$\text{Vtile propositum est sæuas extinguere flammas,}$$
$$\text{Nec seruum vitijs pectus habere suum.}$$

But yet the duchesse of Yorke his moother letted this match as much as in hir laie: & when all would not serue, she caused a precontract to be alleged, made by him with ladie Elizabeth Lucie. But all doubts resolued, all things made cléere, and all cauillations auoided, priuilie in a morning he married the said ladie Elizabeth Graie at Grafton beforesaid, where he first began to fansie hir. And in the next yere after

1465
———
An. Reg. 5.

she was with great solemnitie crowned quéene at Westminster. Hir father also was created earle Riuers, and made high constable of England: hir brother lord Anthonie was married to the sole heire of Thomas lord Scales: sir Thomas Graie sonne to sir Iohn Graie the quéenes first husband, was created marques Dorset, and married to Cicelie heire to the lord Bonuille. The French king was not well pleased to be thus dallied with; but he shortlie (to appease the gréefe of his wife and hir sister the ladie Bona) married the said ladie Bona to the duke of Millan.

Now when the earle of Warwike had knowledge by letters sent to him out of England from his trustie friends, that king Edward had gotten him a new wife, he was not a little troubled in his mind, for that he tooke it his credence thereby was

The earle of Warwike offended with the kings mariage.

greatlie minished, and his honour much stained, namelie in the court of France: for that it might be iudged he came rather like an espiall, to mooue a thing neuer minded, and to treat a marriage determined before not to take effect. Suerlie he thought himselfe euill vsed, that when he had brought the matter to his purposed intent and wished conclusion, then to haue it quaile on his part; so as all men might thinke at the least wise, that his prince made small account of him, to send him on such a sléuelesse errand.

All men for the most part agrée, that this marriage was the onlie cause, why the earle of Warwike conceiued an hatred against king Edward, whome he so much before fauoured. Other affirme other causes; and one speciallie, for that king Edward did attempt a thing once in the earles house, which was much against the earles honestie (whether he would haue defloured his daughter or his néece, the certeintie was not for both their honours openlie reuealed) for suerlie, such a thing was attempted by king Edward; which loued well both to behold and also to féele faire damsels. But whether the iniurie that the earle thought he receiued at the kings hands, or the disdaine of authoritie that the earle had vnder the king, was the cause of the breach of amitie betwixt them: truth it is, that the priuie intentions of their harts brake into so many small pieces, that England, France, and Flanders, could neuer ioine them againe, during their naturall liues.

But though the earle of Warwike was earnestlie inflamed against the king, for that he had thus married himselfe without his knowledge, hauing regard onelie to the

The earle of Warwike keepeth his gréefe secret.

satisfieng of his wanton appetite, more than to his honour or suertie of his estate; yet did he so much dissemble the matter at his returne into England, as though he had not vnderstood anie thing thereof: but onelie declared what he had doone, with such reuerence, and shew of fréendlie countenance, as he had béene accustomed. And
when

when he had taried in the court a certeine space, he obteined licence of the king to depart to his castell of Warwike, meaning (when time serued) to vtter to the world, that which he then kept secret, that is to saie, his inward grudge, which he bare towards the king, with desire of reuenge, to the vttermost of his power. Neuerthelesse, at that time he departed (to the outward shew) so farre in the kings fauour, that manie gentlemen of the court for honours sake gladlie accompanied him into his countrie.

¶ This yéere it was proclamed in England, that the beakes or pikes of shooes and boots should not passe two inches, vpon paine of cursing by the cleargie, and forfeiting twentie shillings, to be paid one noble to the king, and other to the cordwainers of London, and the third to the chamber of London; and for other cities and townes the like order was taken. Before this time, and since the yeare of our Lord 1382, the pikes of shooes and boots were of such length, that they were faine to be tied vp vnto the knees with chaines of siluer and gilt, or at the least with silken laces.] *Abr. Fl. ex I. S. pag.* 717. Long piked shooes forbidden.

In this yeare also, the kings daughter, the ladie Elizabeth, after wife to king Henrie the seauenth, was borne; king Edward concluded an amitie and league with Henrie king of Castile, and Iohn king of Aragon; at the concluding whereof, he granted licence for certeine Cotteshold sheepe, to be transported into the countrie of Spaine (as people report) which haue there so multiplied and increased, that it hath turned the commoditie of England much to the Spanish profit. Beside this, to haue an amitie with his next neighbour the king of Scots, he winked at the losse of Berwike, and was contented to take a truce for fiftéene yeares. Thus king Edward, though for refusall of the French kings sister in law he wan him enimies in France; yet in other places he procured him fréends: but those fréends had stood him in small stéed, if fortune had not holpe him to an other, euen at his elbow. 1466. An. Reg. 6. Cotteshold shéepe transported into Spaine. Truce with Scots.

This was Charles earle of Charolois, the sonne and heire apparant vnto Philip duke of Burgognie, which Charles being then a widower, was councelled to be suter vnto king Edward, for to haue in mariage the ladie Margaret, sister to the said king, a ladie of excellent beautie, and indued with so manie worthie gifts of nature, grace, and fortune, that she was thought not vnworthie to match with the greatest prince of the world. The lord Anthonie bastard brother to the said earle Charolois, commonlie called the bastard of Burgognie, a man of great wit, courage, and valiantnesse, was appointed by his father duke Philip, to go into England in ambassage, about this sute; who being furnished of plate and apparell, necessarie for his estate, hauing in his companie gentlemen, and other expert in all feats of chiualrie and martiall prowesse, to the number of foure hundred horsses, tooke his ship, and arriued in England, where he was of the king & nobles honourablie receiued. 1467 An. Reg. 7. The bastard of Burgognie ambassadour into England.

This message being declared, ye may be sure the same was ioifullie heard of the king and his councell; the which by that affinitie, saw how they might be assured of a buckler against France. But yet the earle of Warwike, bearing his heartie fauour vnto the French king, did as much as in him laie by euill reports to hinder this mariage: but this notwithstanding, at length, the king granted to the bastards request; and the the said bastard openlie in the kings great chamber contracted the said ladie Margaret, for, and in the name of his brother the said earle of Charolois. After this mariage thus concluded, the bastard challenged the lord Scales, brother to the queene, a man both equall in hart and valiantnesse with the bastard, to fight with him both on horssebacke, and on foot: which demand the lord Scales gladlie accepted. Iusts betwixt the bastard of Burgognie & the lord Scales.

The king causing lists to be prepared in West-smithfield for these champions, and verie faire and costlie galleries for the ladies, was present at this martiall enterprise himselfe. The first daie they ran togither diuerse courses with sharpe speares, and departed with equall honor. The next day they turneied on horssebacke. The lord Scales horsse had on his chafron a long sharpe pike of steele, and as the two champions

pions

pions coped togither, the same horsse (whether thorough custome or by chance) thrust his pike into the nosethrils of the bastards horsse; so that for verie paine he mounted so high, that he fell on the one side with his maister, and the lord Scales rode round about him with his sword in his hand, vntill the king commanded the marshall to helpe vp the bastard, which openlie said; " I can not hold me by the clouds, for though my horsse faileth me, surelie I will not faile my contercompanion." The king would not suffer them to doo anie more that daie.

The morow after, the two noblemen came into the field on foot, with two polaxes, and fought valiantlie: but at the last, the point of the polax of the lord Scales happened to enter into the sight of the bastards helme, and by fine force might haue plucked him on his knees: the king suddenlie cast downe his warder, and then the marshals them seuered. The bastard not content with this chance, and trusting on the cunning which he had at the polax, required the king of iustice, that he might performe his enterprise. The lord Scales refused it not, but the king said, he would aske councell: and so calling to him the constable, and the marshall, with the officers of armes, after consultation had, and the lawes of armes rehearsed, it was declared
The law of armes. for a sentence definitiue, by the duke of Clarence, then constable of England, and the duke of Norffolke, then marshall; that if he would go forward with his attempted challenge, he must by the law of armes be deliuered to his aduersarie, in the same state and like condition as he stood when he was taken from him.

The bastard hearing this iudgement, doubted the sequele of the matter; and so relinquished his challenge. Other challenges were doone, and valiantlie atchiued by
The death of the duke of Burgognie. the Englishmen, which I passe ouer. Shortlie after came sorowfull tidings to the bastard, that his father duke Philip was dead, who therevpon taking his leaue of king Edward, and of his sister the new duchesse of Burgognie, liberallie rewarded with plate and iewels, with all spéed returned to his brother the new duke, who was not a little glad of the contract made for him with the said ladie, as after well appeared.
George Neuill archbishop of Yorke. In this same yeare, king Edward, more for the loue of the marques Montacute, than for anie fauour he bare to the earle of Warwike, promoted George Neuill their brother to the archbishoprike of Yorke.

1468
———
An. Reg. 8. Charles duke of Burgognie reioising that he had so well sped, for conclusion of marriage with king Edwards sister, was verie desirous to sée hir, of whome he had heard so great praise, & wrote to king Edward, requiring him to send his sister ouer vnto him, according to the couenants passed betwixt them. King Edward being not slacke in this matter, appointed the dukes of Excester and Suffolke, with their wiues, being both sisters to the ladie Margaret, to attend hir, till she came to hir husband. And so after that ships, and all other necessarie prouisions were readie, they being accompanied with a great sort of lords and ladies, and others, to the number of fiue
The ladie Margaret sister to king Edward, sent ouer to the duke of Burgognie. hundred horsse, in the beginning of Iune departed out of London to Douer, and so sailed to Sluis, and from thense was conueied to Bruges, where the marriage was solemnized betwixt the duke and hir, with great triumphs, and princelie feastings. Touching the pompe had and vsed at the setting forward of this ladie on hir voiage it is a note worth the reading; and therefore necessarilie here interlaced for honours sake.

On the eightéenth of Iune, Margaret sister to K. Edward the fourth began hir ior-
Abr. Fl. ex. I. S. pag. 719, 720. in Quart. nie from the Wardrobe in London, toward hir marriage with Charles duke of Burgognie: first she offered in the church of saint Paule, and then rode thorough the citie, the earle of Warwike riding before hir, with earles and barons a great number; the duchesse of Norffolke, with other ladies and gentlewomen in great number. And at hir entrie into Cheape, the maior of London and his brethren the aldermen presented hir with a paire of rich basons, & in them an hundred pounds of gold and that night she
lodged

lodged at the abbeie of Stratford, where the king then laie: from thense she tooke hir iournie to Canturburie.

The king riding after to sée hir shipping, on the first of Iulie, she tooke the sea at Margate, and there tooke leaue of the king hir brother, and departed. There returned backe againe with the king, the duke of Clarence, the duke of Glocester, the earles of Warwike, Shrewesburie, and Northumberland. And there abode with hir in the ship, the lord Scales, the lord Dacres, hir chamberlaine, sir Iohn Wooduile, sir Iohn Howard, and manie other famous knights and esquiers. She was shipped in the new Ellen of London, and in hir nauie the Iohn of Newcastell, the Marie of Salisburie, and manie other roiall ships, and on the morrow landed at Sluis in Flanders. Now as soone as hir ship & companie of ships were entered into the hauen, there receiued hir sir Simon de Lelein and the water bailiffe, in diuerse boats and barks apparelled readie for hir landing.

The first estate that receiued hir was the bishop of Utright well accompanied, and the countesse of Shorne bastard daughter to duke Philip of Burgognie, and with hir manie ladies and gentlewomen; and so procéeding in at the gate of the towne, the same towne was presented to hir, she to be souereigne ladie thereof: also they gaue to hir twelue marks of gold Troie weight, the which was two hundred pounds of English monie: and so procéeded thorough the towne to hir lodging, euerie housholder standing in the street with a torch in his hand burning. On the morow the old duchesse of Burgognie came to hir, accompanied with manie great estates. On the third of Iulie came the duke of Burgognie to Sluis, with twentie persons secretlie, and was there openlie affianced to the ladie Margaret, by the bishop of Salisburie and the lord Scales, in presence of the lord Dacres, the duchesse of Norffolke, the ladie Scales, and all the knights & esquiers, gentlewomen inuironing the chamber.

On the 8 of Iulie (being saturdaie) by the duke of Burgognies appointment, the lady Margaret remoued by water to the Dame. And on the sunday in the morning betwixt fiue and six of the clocke, the mariage was solemnized betwixt them, by the bishops of Salisburie and of Turneie; there being present the old duches of Burgognie, the lord Scales, the lord Dacres, with the knights, esquiers, ladies and gentlewomen that came out of England. The great triumphs, feastings, shewes of pageants, with other strange deuises, and iustings, were such as I haue not read the like, and would be ouer long in this place to set downe.

¶ Of this aliance with other more mention is honorablie made in the * declaration of the causes that moued the Quéene of England to giue aid to the defense of the people afflicted & oppressed in the low countries by the Spaniards, namelie for the maintenance of perpetuall amitie. Which declaration is so set foorth in this booke, as the same in the seuen and twentith yeare of hir maiesties reigne was published: vnto which yeare I remit the reader (for the further search thereof) for that it conteineth much memorable matter, touching the manifest causes of concord to be continued betwéene them of the low countries and vs English.] *Abr. Fl.* * Giuen at Richmont on the first of Octoer. *An. Dom.* 1585. *& An. Reg.* 27.

Sir Thomas Cooke late maior of London, was by one named Hawkins appeached of treason, for the which he was sent to the Tower, and his place within London seized by the lord Riuers, and his wife and seruants cleerelie put out therof. The cause was this. The forenamed Hawkins came vpon a season vnto the said sir Thomas, requesting him to lend a thousand markes vpon good suertie, wherevnto he answered, that first he would know for whome it should be and for what intent. *Fabian.* 497. Sir Thomas Cooke.

At length, vnderstanding it should be for the vse of queene Margaret, he answered he had no currant wares whereof anie shifts might be made without too much losse: and therefore required Hawkins to mooue him no further in that matter, for he intended not to deale withall: yet the said Hawkins exhorted him to remember, what bene-

fits

fits he had receiued by hir when she was in prosperitie, as by making him hir ward-rober, and customer of Hampton, &c.

But by no meanes the said Cooke would grant goods nor monie, although at last the said Hawkins required but an hundred pounds, he was faine to depart without the value of a penie, and neuer came againe to mooue him, which so rested two or three years after, till the said Hawkins was cast in the Tower, and at length brought to the brake, called the duke of Excesters daughter, by meanes of which paine he shewed manie things, amongst the which the motion was one that he had made to sir Thomas Cooke, and accused himselfe so farre, that he was put to death.

By meane of which confession, the said sir Thomas was troubled (as before is shewed) when the said sir Thomas had laine in the Tower from Whitsuntide till about Michaelmas, in the which season manie inquiries were made to find him guiltie, and euer quit, till one iurie (by meanes of sir Iohn Fog) indicted him of treason, after which an oier and terminer was kept at the Guildhall, in which sat with the maior the duke of Clarence, the earle of Warwike, the lord Riuers, sir Iohn Fog, with other of the kings councell.

To the which place the said Thomas was brought, and there arreigned vpon life and death, where he was acquited of the said indictement, and had to the counter in Bread street, and from thence to the kings bench. After a certeine time that he was thus acquited, his wife got againe the possession of hir house, the which she found in an euill plight; for such seruants of the lord Riuers and sir Iohn Fog, as were assigned to kéepe it, made hauocke of what they listed.

Also at his place in Essex named Giddihall, were set an other sort to kéepe that place, the which destroied his déere in his parke, his conies, and his fish without reason, and spared not brasse, pewter, bedding, & all that they might carie, for the which might neuer one penie be gotten in recompense, yet could not sir Thomas Cooke be deliuered, till he had paied eight thousand pounds to the king, and eight hundred pounds to the quéene.]

In this meane time, the earle of Warwike bearing a continuall grudge in his hart toward king Edward, since his last returne out of France, persuaded so with his two brethren, the archbishop, and the marques, that they agreed to ioine with him in anie attempt which he should take in hand against the said king. The archbishop was easilie allured to the earles purpose, but the marques could by no meanes be reduced to take anie part against king Edward of a long time, till the earle had both promised him great rewards and promotions, and also assured him of the aid and power of the greatest princes of the realme. And euen as the marques was loth to consent to his vnhappie conspiracie, so with a faint hart he shewed himselfe an enimie vnto king Ed-

Abr. Fl. ex Edw. Hall. in Edw. 4. fol. cxcviij, &c.

ward, which double dissimulation was both the destruction of him and his brethren. ¶ And that they were persuasions of no small force, which the earle of Warwike vsed to the archbishop and marques, I haue thought good here to interlace, as I find remembred by Edward Hall in forme following.

The persuasions of the earle of Warwike vnto his two brethren against king Edward the fourth

MY deere and welbeloued brethren, the incredible faithfulnesse, the secret sobernesse, and the politike prudence that I haue euer by long continuance of time experimented in you both, dooth not onelie incourage my heart, yea and setteth me in great hope of obteining my purpose, but also putteth me out of all dread and mistrust, firmelie beleeuing, and suerlie iudging, that you both will with tooth and naile endeuour your selues, to the vttermost of your power, to bring to effect and pur-

pose

pose the thing that I now shall declare vnto you. Suerlie, I would in no wise that you should thinke, that that which I shall speake to you of king Edward and king Henrie, should rise of any lightnesse or phantasie of my mind, or anie trifeling toie latelie fallen into my imagination; but the true experience and iust iudgement that I haue of them both, their qualities and conditions, in manner compell and constraine me to saie as I say and to doo as I doo.

For suerlie, king Henrie is a godlie, good, and a vertuous person, neither forgetting his freends, nor putting in obliuion anie benefit by him of a meane person receiued, nor yet anie paine for his causes susteined hath he left vnrewarded: to whome God hath sent a sonne, called prince Edward, borne to be of great worthinesse and praise, of much bountifulnesse and liberalitie, of whome men may manie laudable things coniecture, considering the paine, labour, and trauell, that he taketh to helpe his father out of captiuitie and thraldome. King Edward on the contrarie side, is a man contumelious, opprobrious, and an iniurious person; to them that deserue kindnesse he sheweth vnkindnesse, and them that loue him he deadlie hateth, now detesting to take anie paine for the preferment or maintenance of the publike wealth of this realme, but all giuen to pastime, pleasure, and daliance; sooner preferring to high estate men descended of low bloud and base degree, than men of old and vndefiled houses, which haue both supported him and the commonwealth of his realme.

So that I now perceiue, that it is euen come to this point, that he will destroie all the nobilitie; or else the nobilitie must shortlie of verie necessitie destroie and confound him. But reason would, that we that were first hurt, should first reuenge our cause: for it is not vnknowen to you both, how that he, immediatlie after he had obteined the crowne, began first secretlie, and then openlie to enuie, disdaine, and impugne the fame, glorie, and renowme of our house and familie; as who said, that all the honor, preferment, and authoritie that we haue, we had onelie receiued at his hands, and that we had neither obteined dignitie nor rule by our great labour, aid and trauell. Which to all men may seeme vntrue, that consider that our name, chiefe title, and principall authoritie, was to vs giuen by king Henrie the sixt, and not by him. But if euery man will remember, who first toke part with his father, when hee claimed the crowne (who at that time, for that cause was in great ieopardie, and almost slaine by the kings meniall seruants, and who neuer left this man in prosperitie nor aduersitie, till he had the garland, and the realme in quietnesse) shall manifestlie perceiue, that we and our bloud haue shewed our selues more like fathers to him, than he like a freend to vs.

If we haue receiued any benefits of him, suerlie they be not so much as we haue deserued, nor so much as we looked for; and yet they be much more than he would we shuld inioy, as ye both well perceiue and know. Let these things ouerpasse, and speake of the vngentle, vntrue, and vnprincelie handling of me in the last ambassage, being sent to the French king for to treat a mariage for him, hauing full authoritie to bind and to lose, to contract and conclude. Which thing when I had finished & accomplished: how lightlie his mind changed, how priuilie he vowed, and how secretlie he maried, both you know better than I. So that by this meanes, I was almost out of all credence in the court of France, both with the king and queene, as though I had come thither like an espiall, to moue a thing neuer minded; or to treat of a mariage determined before neuer to take effect. Whereby the fame of all our estimation, which all kings and princes haue conceiued in vs (partlie obteined by the vertue & prowesse of our noble ancestors, and partlie atchiued by our owne paines & forward acts) shall now be obfuscate, vtterlie extinguished, and nothing set by.

What worme is touched, and will not once turne againe? What beast is striken, that will not rore or sound? What innocent child is hurt that will not crie? If the poore and vnreasonable beasts, if the selie babes that doo lacke discretion, grone against harmé to them proffered; how ought an honest man to be angrie, when things that touch his honestie be dailie against him attempted? But if a meane person in that case be angrie: how much more ought a noble man to fume & stirre coales, when the high type of his honour is touched, his fame in maner brought to infamie, and his honour almost blemished & appalled, without his offense or desert? All this brethren you know to be true, the dishonor of one is the dishonor of vs all, and the hurt of one is the hurt of all: wherefore, rather than I will liue vnreuenged, or suffer him to reigne, which hath sought my decaie and dishonor, I will suerlie spend my life, lands, and goods, in setting vp that iust and good man king Henrie the sixt: and in deposing this vntrue, vnfaithful, and vnkind prince (by our onelie means) called king Edward the fourth.

Beside all this, the earle of Warwike, being a far casting prince, perceiued somewhat in the duke of Clarence, whereby he iudged that he bare no great good will towards the king his brother; and therevpon, feeling his mind by such talke as he of purpose ministred, vnderstood how he was bent, and so wan him to his purpose: and for better assurance of his faithful friendship, he offered him his eldest daughter in mariage, with the whole halfe deale of his wiues inheritance. And herevpon, after consultation had of their weightie businesse and dangerous affaires, they sailed ouer to Calis, of the which towne the earle was capteine, where his wife & two daughters then soiourned, whome the duke (being in loue with hir person) had great desire to visit.

But the earle, hauing in continuall remembrance his purposed enterprise, appointed his brethren, the archbishop and the marquesse, that they should by some meanes in his absence stir vp some new rebellion in the countie of Yorke, and other places adioining, so that this ciuill warre should séeme to all men to haue béene begun without

<table>
<tr><td>1469
An. Reg. 9.</td></tr>
</table>

his assent or knowlege, being on the further side of the seas. The duke of Clarence being come to Calis with the earle of Warwike, after he had sworne on the sacrament

A commotion in Yorkeshire.

to kéepe his promise and pact made with the said earle whole and inuiolate, he married the ladie Isabell, eldest daughter to the earle, in our ladies church there. Shortlie after, according as he had béene aforehand deuised, a commotion was begun in Yorkshire, to the great disquieting of that countrie. The same chanced by this means.

Saint Leonards hospital in Yorke.

There was in the citie of Yorke an old and rich hospitall, dedicated to saint Leonard, for the harbourough and reléeuing of poore people. Certeine euill disposed persons of the earle of Warwikes faction, intending to set a broile in the countrie, persuaded the husbandmen to refuse to giue anie thing to the said hospitall, affirming that the corne giuen to that good intent, came not to the vse of the poore; but was conuerted to the behoofe of the maister of the hospitall, and the preests, whereby they grew to be rich, and the poore people wanted their due succour and reléefe. And not content with these saiengs, they fell to dooings: for when the proctors of the hospitall, according to their vsage, went about the countrie to gather the accustomed corne, they were sore beaten, wounded, and euill intreated.

A rebellion.

Shortlie after, the conspiracie of the euill disposed people grew to an open rebellion, so that there assembled to the number of fifteene thousand men, euen readie bent to set on the citie of Yorke. But the lord marquesse Montacute, gouernour and president of that countrie for the king, taking speedie counsell in the matter, with a small number of men, but well chosen, incountered the rebels before the gates of Yorke:

Robert Huldorne capteine of the rebels taken and beheaded.

where (after a long conflict) he tooke Robert Huldorne their capteine, and before them commanded his head to be striken off, and then (bicause it was a darke euening) he caused his souldiers to enter into Yorke, and there to refresh them. Héere manie men haue maruelled, whie the marquesse thus put to death the capteine of those people, which had procured this their rebellious enterprise.

Some

Some saie he did it, to the intent to séeme innocent and faultlesse of his brothers dooings. But other iudge, that he did it, for that contrarie to his promise made to his brother, he was determined to take part with king Edward, with whome (as it shall after appéare) he in small space entered into grace and fauour. The rebels being nothing dismaied with the death of their capteine, but rather the more bent on mischéefe, by faire meanes and craftie persuasions got to them Henrie, sonne to the lord Fitz Hugh, and sir Henrie Neuill sonne and heire to the lord Latimer, the one being nephue and the other cousine germane to the erle of Warwike. Although these yoong gentlemen bare the names of capteins, yet they had a gouernour that was sir Iohn Coniers, a man of such courage & valiantnesse, as few are to be found in his daies within the north parts. Sir Iohn Coniers.

After they saw that they could not get Yorke, bicause they wanted ordinance, they determined with all speed to march toward London, intending to raise such a toie in the peoples minds, that they should thinke king Edward neither to be a lawfull prince, nor yet profitable to the common-wealth. King Edward hauing perfect knowledge of all the dooings of the earle of Warwike, and of his brother the duke of Clarence, was by diuerse letters certified of the great armie of the northerne men, with all spéed comming toward London; and therefore in great hast he sent to William lord Herbert, whom (as yée haue heard) he had created earle of Penbroke; requiring him without delaie to raise his power, and incounter with the northerne men. The earle of Penbroke.

The earle of Penbroke, commonlie called the lord Herbert, both readie to obeie the kings commandement, according to his dutie, and also desirous to reuenge the malice which he bare to the earle of Warwike, for that he knew how he had béene the onelie let whie he obteined not the wardship of the lord Bonneuilles daughter and heire for his eldest sonne, accompanied with his brother sir Richard Herbert, a valiant knight, and aboue six or seauen thousand Welshmen, well furnished, marched forward to incounter with the northerne men. And to assist him with archers, was appointed Humfrie lord Stafford of Southwike, named but not created earle of De-uonshire by the king, in hope that he would serue valiantlie in that iournie: he had with him eight hundred archers. The lord Staf-
ford.

When these two lords were met at Cotteshold, they heard how the northerne men were going toward Northampton: wherevpon the lord Stafford, and sir Richard Herbert, with two thousand well horsed Welshmen, rode foorth afore the maine armie, to sée the demeanour of the northerne men: and at length, vnder a woods side, they couertlie espied them passing forward, and suddenlie set on the rere-ward: but the northerne men with such nimblenesse turned about, that in a moment the Welsh-men were discomfited, and manie taken, the remnant returned to the armie with small gaine. The northerne men well cooled with this small victorie, went no further southwards, but tooke their waie toward Warwike, looking for aid of the earle, which was latelie come from Calis, with his sonne in law the duke of Clarence, and was raising men to aid his freends and kinsfolke. The Welshmen
discomfited.

The king likewise assembled people to aid the erle of Penbroke, but before either part receiued succour from his fréend or partaker, both the armies met by chance in a faire plaine, néere to a towne called Hedgecote, foure miles distant from Banberie, where there are thrée hilles, not in equall quantitie, but lieng in maner (although not fullie) triangle. The Welshmen got first the west hill, hoping to haue recouered the east hill also, which if they might haue obteined, the victorie had beene theirs, as their foolish prophesiers told them before. These northerne men incamped on the south hill; the earle of Penbroke and the lord Stafford of Southwike were lodged in Banberie, the daie before the field, which was saint Iames daie, and there the earle of Penbroke put the lord Stafford out of an Inne, wherein he delighted much to be, Hedgecote.
Baberie field.Discord what
it breedeth.

                          for

for the loue of a damosell that dwelled in the house: and yet it was agréed betwixt them, that which of them soeuer obteined first a lodging, should not be displaced.

The lord Stafford in great despite departed with his whole band of archers, leauing the earle of Penbroke almost desolate in the towne, who with all diligence returned to his host, lieng in the field vnpurueied of archers. Sir Henrie Neuill, sonne to the lord Latimer, tooke with him certeine light horssemen, and skirmished with the Welshmen in the euening, iust before their campe, where dooing right valiantlie, but a little too hardilie aduenturing himselfe, was taken and yeelded, and yet cruellie slaine. Which vnmercifull act the Welshmen sore rued the next day yer night: for the northerne men sore displeased for the death of this nobleman, in the next morning valiantlie set on the Welshmen, and by force of archers caused them quicklie to descend the hill, into the vallie, where both the hoasts fought.

The valiant manhood of sir Richard Herbert.
The earle of Penbroke did right valiantlie, and so likewise did his brother sir Richard Herbert, in so much that with his polax in his hand, he twise by fine force passed thorough the battell of his aduersaries, and without anie hurt or mortall wound returned. But sée the hap, euen as the Welshmen were at point to haue obteined the victorie, Iohn Clappam esquier, seruant to the earle of Warwike, mounted vp the side of the east hill, accompanied onelie with fiue hundred men, gathered of the rascals of the towne of Northampton, and other villages about, hauing borne before them the standard of the earle of Warwike, with the white beare, crieng; A Warwike, a Warwike.

Iohn Clappam.

The Welshmen, thinking that the earle of Warwike had come on them with all his puissance, suddenlie as men amazed, fled: the northerne men them pursued, and slue

The Welshmen slaine.
without mercie, so that there died of the Welshmen that daie, aboue fiue thousand, besides them that fled and were taken. The earle of Penbroke, and his brother sir Richard Herbert, with diuerse gentlemen, were taken and brought to Banberie, where the earle with his brother, and other gentlemen, to the number of ten, that were likewise taken, lost their heads. But great mone was made for that noble and hardie gentleman, sir Richard Herbert, being able for his goodlie personage and high valiancie to haue serued the greatest prince in christendome. [But what policie or puissance can either preuent or impugne the force of fate, whose law as it standeth vpon an ineuitable necessitie; so was it not to be dispensed withall; and therfore destinie hauing preordeined the maner of his deth, it was patientlie to be suffered, sith puissantlie it could not be auoided, nor politikelie preuented, nor violentlie resisted: for

Abr. Fiem.

——— sua quenq; dies ad funera raptat.]

The Northamptonshire men, with diuerse of the northerne men by them procured, in this furie made them a capteine, called Robert Hilliard, but they named him Robin of Reddesdale, and suddenlie came to Grafton, where they tooke the earle Riuers, father to the quéene, and his son sir Iohn Wooduile, whome they brought to Northampton, and there beheaded them both without iudgement. The king aduertised of these mischances, wrote to the shiriffes of Summersetshire, aud Deuonshire, that if they might by anie meanes take the lord Stafford of Southwike, they should without delaie put him to death. Herevpon search was made for him, till at length he was found in a village within Brentmarch, and after brought to Bridgewater where he was beheaded.

Robin of Reddesdale.
The erle Riuers and his sonne beheaded.

The lord Stafford of Southwike beheaded.

After the battell was thus fought at Hedgecote commonlie called Banberie field, the northerne men resorted toward Warwike, where the earle had gathered a great multitude of people, which earle receiued the northerne men with great gladnes, thanking sir Iohn Coniers, and other their capteins for their paines taken in his cause. The king in this meane time had assembled his power, and was comming toward the earle, who being aduertised thereof, sent to the duke of Clarence, requiring him to come and ioine with him. The duke being not farre off, with all speed repaired to the earle,

earle, and so they ioined their powers togither, and vpon secret knowledge had, that the king (bicause they were entered into termes by waie of communication to haue a peace) tooke small héed to himselfe, nothing doubting anie outward attempt of his enimies.

The earle of Warwike, intending not to léese such opportunitie of aduantage, in the dead of the night, with an elect companie of men of warre (as secretlie as was possible) set on the kings field, killing them that kept the watch, and yer the king was ware (for he thought of nothing lesse than of that which then hapned) at a place called Wolnie, foure miles from Warwike, he was taken prisoner and brought to the castell of Warwike. And to the intent his friends should not know what was become of him, the earle caused him by secret iournies in the night to be conueied to Middleham castell in Yorkeshire, and there to be kept vnder the custodie of the archbishop of Yorke, and other his freends in those parties. King Edward being thus in captiuitie, spake euer faire to the archbishop, and to his other kéepers, so that he had leaue diuerse daies to go hunt. [Which exercise he vsed, as it should séeme not so much for regard of his recreation, as for the recouerie of his libertie: which men esteeme better than gold, and being counted a diuine thing, dooth passe all the wealth, pleasure, and treasure of the world; according to the old saieng:

Non bene profuluo libertas venditur auro,

Hoc cœleste bonum præterit orbis opes.]

Now on a daie vpon a plaine when he was thus abrode, there met with him sir William Stnaleie, sir Thomas a Borough, and diuerse other of his friends, with such a great band of men, that neither his keepers would, nor once durst moue him to returne vnto prison againe. Some haue thought that his kéepers were corrupted with monie, or faire promises, and therefore suffred him thus to scape out of danger, After that he was once at libertie, he came to Yorke, where he was ioifullie receiued, and taried there two daies: but when he perceiued he could get no armie togither in that countrie to attend him to London, he turned from Yorke to Lancaster, where he found his chamberleine the lord Hastings well accompanied, by whose aid and such others as drew to him, being well furnished, he came safelie to the citie of London.

When the earle of Warwike, and the duke of Clarence had knowledge how king Edward by the treason or negligence of them (whome they had put in trust) was escaped their hands, they were in a wonderfull chafe: but sith the chance was past, they began eftsoones to prouide for the warre, which they saw was like to insue; and found much comfort, in that a great number of men, deliting more in discord than in concord, offered themselues to aid their side. But other good men desirous of common quiet, and lamenting the miserable state of the realme, to redresse such mischiefe as appeared to be at hand by these tumults, tooke paine, and road betweene the king, the earle, and the duke, to reconcile them ech to other.

Their charitable motion and causes alledged, bicause they were of the chiefest of the nobilitie, and therfore caried both credit and authoritie with them, so asswaged the moods both of the king, the duke, and the earle, that ech gaue faith to other to came and go safelie without ieopardie. In which promise both the duke and earle putting perfect confidence, came both to London. At Westminster, the king, the duke, and the earle, had long communication togither for to haue come to an agreement: but they fell at such great words vpon rehersall of old matters, that in great furie without any conclusion they departed, the king to Canturburie, and the duke and the earle to Warwike, where the earle procured a new armie to be raised in Lincolneshire, and made capteine thereof sir Robert Welles, sonne to Richard lord Welles, a man of great experience in warre.

The king aduertised hereof without delaie prepared an armie, and out of hand he sent to Richard lord Welles, willing him vpon the sight of his letters, to repaire vnto him:

Marginal notes:
King Edward taken prisoner.
Middleham castell.
Abr. Flem.
Sir William Stanleie.
K. Edward is deliuered out of captiuitie.
He commeth to London.
1470

him: which to doo he had oftentimes refused, excusing himselfe by sickenesse and feeblenesse of bodie. But when that excuse serued not, he thinking to purge himselfe sufficientlie of all offense and blame before the kings presence, tooke with him sir

Sir Thomas Dimmocke. Thomas Dimmocke, who had maried his sister, and so came to London. And when he was come vp, being admonished by his fréends that the king was greatlie with him displeased, he with his brother in law tooke the sanctuarie at Westminster.

But king Edward, trusting to pacifie all this busie tumult without anie further bloudshed, promised both those persons their pardons, causing them vpon his promise to come out of sanctuarie to his presence, and calling to him the lord Welles, willed him to write to his sonne to leaue off the warre, and in the meane season he with his **An. Reg. 10.** armie went forward, hauing with him the lord Welles, and sir Thomas Dimmocke. And being not past two daies iournie from Stamford, where his enimies had pitched their field, and hearing that sir Robert Welles, not regarding his fathers letters, kept

The lord Welles and Thomas Dimmocke beheaded. his campe still, he caused the lord Welles, father to the said sir Robert, and sir Thomas Dimmocke to be beheaded, contrarie to his promise.

Sir Robert Welles, hearing that the king approched, and that his father and sir Thomas Dimmocke were beheaded, though he was somewhat doubtfull to fight, before the earle of Warwike were with his power assembled, yet hauing a yoong and lustie courage, manfullie set on his enimies. The battell was sore fought on both sides, and manie a man slaine; till sir Robert, perceiuing his people at point to flie, was busilie in hand to exhort them to tarie, and in the meane time compassed about with enimies was there taken, & with him sir Thomas de Land knight, and manie more. After the taking of their capteine, the Lincolneshire men amazed, threw awaie their coats the lighter to run awaie, and fled amaine, and therefore this battell is called there

Losecote field yet vnto this daie, Losecote field.

The king reioising at this victorie, caused sir Robert Welles, and diuerse other to be put to execution in the same place. The fame went at this battell were slaine ten thousand men at the least. The earle of Warwike laie at the same time at his castell of Warwike, and meant to haue set forward the next daie toward his armie in Lincolneshire. But when he heard that the same was ouerthrowne, he tooke new counsell, and with all diligence imagined how to compassé Thomas lord Stanleie, which had maried his sister, that he might be one of the conspiracie. Which thing when he

The faithfulnesse of the lord Stanleie. could not bring to passe (for the lord Stanleie had answered him, that he would neuer make warre against king Edward) he thought no longer to spend time in wast; and mistrusting he was not able to méet with his enimies, he with his sonne in law the

The duke of Clarence and the earle of Warwike take the sea. duke of Clarence departed to Excester, and there tarieng a few daies, determined to saile into France, to purchase aid of king Lewes.

Now resting vpon this point, he hired ships at Dartmouth: and when the same were readie trimmed and decked, the duke and the earle with their wiues, and a great number of seruants imbarked themselues, and first tooke their course towards Calis, whereof the earle was capteine, thinking there to haue left his wife and daughters, till he had returned out of France. But when they were come before the towne of

The earle of Warwike kept out of Calis. Calis, they could not be suffered to enter: for the lord Vauclere a Gascoigne, being the earles deputie in that towne, whether he did it by dissimulation, or bearing good will to king Edward (as by the sequele it may be doubted whether he did or no) in steed of receiuing his master with triumph, he bent and discharged against him diuerse peeces of ordinance, sending him word he should not there take land.

This nauie lieng thus before Calis at anchor, the duchesse of Clarence was there deliuered of a faire sonne, which child the earles deputie would scarse suffer to be christened within the towne; nor without great intreatie would permit two flagons of wine to be conueied aboord to the ladies lieng in the hauen. The king of England aduertised

aduertised of the refusall made by monsieur de Vauclere to the earle of Warwike, Monsieur de Vauclere made deputie of Calis. was so much pleased therewith, that incontinentlie he made him chiefe capteine of the towne of Calis by his letters patents, which he sent to him out of hand, and thereof discharged the earle as a traitor and rebell. Thus was the one in respect of his accepted seruice honorablie aduanced; and the other, in regard of his disloialtie shamefullie disgraced: whereof as the one tooke occasion of inward delight; so the othe could not be void of grudging conceipts,

The duke of Burgognie (vnto whome king Edward had written, that in no wise he should receiue the earle of Warwike, nor anie of his friends within his countries) was so well pleased with the dooings of monsieur de Vauclere, that he sent to him his seruant Philip de Cumins, and gaue him yéerelie a thousand crownes in pension, praieng and requiring him to continue in truth and fidelitie toward king Edward, as he had shewed and begun. But although monsieur de Vauclere sware in the said Philips presence, trulie to take king Edwards part; yet he sent priuilie to the earle of Warwike lieng at Whitsanbaie, that if he landed, hee should be taken and lost: for all The double dealing of monsieur de Vauclere. England (as he said) tooke part against him; the duke of Burgognie, and all the inhabitants of the towne, with the lord Duras the kings marshall, and all the retinue The lord Duras was a Gascoigne also. of the garrison were his enimies.

The earle, hauing this aduertisement from his feigned enimie, with his nauie sailed toward Normandie, and by the waie spoiled and tooke manie ships of the duke of Burgognies subiects, and at the last (with all his nauie and spoiles) he tooke land at Diepe in Normandie, where the gouernor of the countrie friendlie welcomed him, and The earle of Warwike landed at Diepe. aduertised king Lewes of his arriuall. The French king, desirous of nothing more than to haue occasion to pleasure the erle of Warwike, of whom the hie renowme caused all men to haue him in admiration, sent vnto him, requiring both him and his sonne in law the duke of Clarence, to come vnto his castell of Ambois, where he Ambois. then soiourned. The duke of Burgognie, hearing that the duke and earle were thus receiued in France, sent a post with letters vnto king Lewes, partlie by waie of request, and partlie by way of menacing, to dissuade him from aiding of his aduersaries, the said duke and earle.

But the French king little regarded this sute of the duke of Burgognie, and therefore answered, that he might and would succour his friends, and yet breake no leage with him at all. In the meane time, K. Edward made inquirie for such as were knowne to be aiders of the earle of Warwike within his realme, of whom some he apprehended as guiltie, and some (doubting themselues) fled to sanctuarie, and other trusting to the kings pardon, submitted themselues, as Iohn marques Montacute, Iohn marques Montacute. whom he courteouslie receiued. When quéene Margaret that soiourned with duke Reiner hir father, heard tell that the earle of Warwike was come to the French court, with all diligence shée came to Ambois to sée him, with hir onelie sonne prince Edward.

With hir also came Iasper earle of Penbroke, and Iohn earle of Oxford, which The earles of Penbroke & Oxford. after diuerse imprisonments latelie escaped, fled out of England into France, and came by fortune to this assemblie. These persons, after intreatie had of their affaires, determined by meanes of the French king to conclude a league and amitie betweene them. And first to begin withall, for the sure foundation of their new intreatie, A league. Edward prince of Wales wedded Anne second daughter to the earle of Warwike, Edward prince of Wales maried. which ladie came with hir mother into France. After which mariage, the duke and the earles tooke a solemne oth, that they should neuer leaue the warre, till either king Henrie the sixt, or his sonne prince Edward, were restored to the crowne: and that the quéene and the prince should depute and appoint the duke and the earle to be gouernors & conseruators of the common wealth, till time the prince were come to estate.

Manie

Manie other conditions were agréed, as both reason & the weightinesse of so great businesse required.

Whilest these things were thus in dooing in the French court, there landed a damsell, belonging to the duchesse of Clarence; as she said: which made monsieur de Vaucléere beleeue, that she was sent from king Edward to the duke of Clarence and the earle of Warwike with a plaine ouerture and declaration of peace. Of the which tidings Vaucléere was verie glad for the earles sake. But this damsell comming to the duke, persuaded him so much to leaue off the pursute of his conceiued displeasure towards his brother king Edward, that he promised at his returne into England, not to be so extreme enimie against his brother as he was taken to be: and this promise afterward he did kéepe. With this answer the damsell returned into England, the earle of Warwike being thereof clearelie ignorant.

The French king lent both ships, men, and monie vnto quéene Margaret, and to hir partakers, and appointed the bastard of Burbon, admerall of France, with a great nauie to defend them against the nauie of the duke of Burgognie, which he laid at the mouth of the riuer Saine, readie to incounter them, being of greater force than both the French nauie and the English fléet. And yet king Reiner did also helpe his daughter with men and munition of warre. When their ships and men were come togither to Harflue, the erle of Warwike thought not to linger time: bicause he was certified by letters from his friends out of England, that assoone as he had taken land, there would be readie manie thousands to doo him what seruice and pleasure they could or might. And beside this, diuerse noble men wrote that they would helpe him with men, armor, monie, and all things necessarie for the warre, and further to aduenture their owne bodies in his quarell.

Suerlie his presence was so much desired of all the people, that almost all men were readie in armour, looking for his arriuall: for they iudged that the verie sunne was taken from the world when hée was absent. When he had receiued such letters of comfort, he determined with the duke, and the earles of Oxford and Pembroke (bicause quéene Margaret and hir sonne were not yet fullie furnished for the iournie) to go before with part of the nauie, and part of the armie. And euen as fortune would, the nauie of the duke of Burgognie at the same time by a tempest was scattered, & driuen beside the coast of Normandie: so that the earle of Warwike in hope of a bonne voiage, caused sailes to be halsed vp, and with good spéed landed at Darmouth in Deuonshire, from whence almost six moneths passed hé tooke his iournie toward France (as before ye haue heard.) When the earle had taken land, he made proclamation in the name of king Henrie the sixt, vpon high paines commanding and charging all men able to beare armor, to prepare themselues to fight against Edward duke of Yorke, which contrarie to right had vsurped the crowne. It is almost not to be beléeued, how manie thousands men of warre at the first tidings of the earles landing resorted vnto him.

King Edward wakened with the newes of the earles landing, and the great repaire of people that came flocking in vnto him, sent foorth letters into all parts of his realme to raise an armie: but of them that were sent for, few came, and yet of those few the more part came with no great good willes. Which when he perceiued, he began to doubt the matter, and therefore being accompanied with the duke of Glocester his brother, the lord Hastings his chamberlaine, which had maried the earles sister, and yet was euer true to the king his maister, and the lord Scales brother to the quéene, he departed into Lincolneshire. And bicause he vnderstood that all the realme was vp against him, and some part of the earle of Warwiks power was within halfe a daies iournie of him, following the aduise of his counsell, with all hast possible he passed the Washes in great ieopardie, & comming to Lin found there an English ship, and two hulkes of Holland readie (as fortune would) to make saile.

Where-

Wherevpon he with his brother the duke of Glocester, the lord Scales, and diuerse other his trustie friends, entered into the ship. The lord Hastings taried a while after, *The lord Hastings.* exhorting all his acquaintance, that of necessitie should tarie behind, to shew them selues openlie as friends to king Henrie for their owne safegard, but hartilie required them in secret to continue faithfull to king Edward. This persuasion declared, he entered the ship with the other, and so they departed, being in number in that one ship *The number that passed ouer with king Edward.* and two hulkes, about seuen or eight hundred persons, hauing no furniture of apparell, or other necessarie things with them, sauing apparell for warre. [For it was *Abr. Fl.* no taking of leasure to prouide their corporall necessaries (though the want of them could hardlie be borne) in a case of present danger; considering that they were made against by the contrarie faction with such swift pursute. And it had bene a point of extreme follie, to be carefull for the accidents, permitting in the meane time the substance vnto the spoile.]

As king Edward with saile and ore was thus making course towards the duke of Burgognies countrie (whither he determined at the first to go) it chanced that seuen or eight gallant ships of Easterlings, open enimies both to England and France, were abrode on those seas, and espieng the kings vessels, began to chase him. The kings *King Edward arriued at Alquemare.* ship was good of saile, and so much gat of the Easterlings, that he came on the coast of Holland, and so descended lower before a towne in the countrie called Alquemare, and there cast anchor as néere the towne as was possible, bicause they could not enter the hauen at an ebbing water. The Easterlings also approched the English ship, as néere as their great ships should come at the law water, intending at the floud to haue their preie: as they were verie like to haue atteined it in déed, if the lord Gronture, gouernor of that countrie for the duke of Burgognie, had not by chance béene *The lord Gronture.* at the same time in that towne.

This lord (vpon knowledge had of king Edwards arriuall there in the hauen, and in what danger he stood by reason of the Easterlings) commanded them not to be so hardie as once to meddle with anie Englishmen, being both the dukes fréends and alies. Then did king Edward & all his companie come on land. Who after they had beene well refreshed & gentlie comforted by the lord Gronture, they were by him brought to the Hagh, a rich towne in Holland, where they remained a while, hauing all things necessarie ministred to them by order of the duke of Burgognie, sent vnto the lord Gronture, immediatlie vpon certificat from the said lord Gronture of king Edwards arriuall. [Héere we sée in what perplexities king Edward and his retinue were, partlie by enimies at home in his owne countrie, whose hands he was constreined to flée from by the helpe of the sea; partlie also by aduersaries abroad, seeking opportunitie to offer him not the incounter onelie, but the ouerthrow. And suerly, had not good fortune fauoured him, in preparing readie meanes for him to auoid those imminent dangers; he had doubtlesse fallen among the weapons of his owne countrimen, and so neuer haue feared forren force: but in escaping both the one and the other, euen with shift of so spéedie expedition, it is a note (if it be well looked into) of happinesse, if anie happinesse may be in preseruation from ruine and reproch.]

Now let all Englishmen (saith Edward Hall) consider (as before is rehearsed) what *Edw. Hall. fol. ccix.* profit, what commoditie, and what helpe in distresse, the mariage of the ladie Margaret, king Edwards sister to the duke Charles, did to him in his extreame necessitie; and but by that meane vncurable extremitie: for his alies and confederats in Castile and Arragon were too far from him, either speedilie to flie to, or shortlie to come fro with anie aid or armie. The French king was his extreme enimie, and freend to king Henrie, for whose cause in the king of Scots (for all the leage betwéene them) he did put little confidence and lesse trust. The states and all Eastland were with him at open war, and yet by this marriage, God prouided him a place to flie to, both for refuge and reléefe.

Abr. Flem.

[But for the further and cleerer explanation of these stratagems, or rather ciuill tu-mults, it shall not be amisse to insert in this place (sith I cannot hit vpon one more conuenient) a verie good note or addition receiued from the hands of maister Iohn Hooker chamberlaine of Excester; the contents whereof are of such qualitie, that they cannot stand in concurrence with anie matter introduced within the compasse of the ninth yeare of this kings reigne (as he had quoted it) and therfore I thought it méet to transfer the same to this tenth yeare; considering that some part of the matter by him largelie touched, is briefelie in the premisses alreadie remembred.]

¶ This yeare (saith he) was verie troublesome, and full of ciuill wars and great

Iohn Hooker, alias Vowell.

discords. For after that king Edward the fourth was escaped out of prison, at Wol-neie besides Warwike, he mustered and prepared a new armie. Wherevpon the earle of Warwike and the duke of Clarence, mistrusting themselues, prepared to passe the seas ouer to Calis, and first of all sent awaie the duches of Clarence daughter to the said earle, who was then great with child, and she being accompanied with the lord

Lord Dinhā, and baron Ca-rew, with their power come to Excester.

Fitz Warren, the lord Dinham, and the baron of Carew, and a thousand fighting men came to this citie of Excester the eightéenth daie of March, and was lodged in the bishops palace. Sir Hugh, or (as some saie) sir William Courtneie, who then fa-uoured the partie of king Edward the fourth, assembled a great troope and armie of all the fréends he could make, and inuironing the citie, besieged the same; he pulled downe all the bridges, rampered vp all the waies, and stopped all the passages, so that no vittels at all could be brought to this citie for twelue daies togither, which being doone vpon a sudden and vnlooked for, vittels waxed short and scant within the citie, and by reason of so great a multitude within the same, the people for want of food began to murmur and mutter.

The duches and the lords of hir companie, mistrusting what might and would be the sequele hereof, began to deale with the maior, and required to haue the keies of the gates to be deliuered into their hands and that they would vndertake the safe custodie of the citie. Likewise sir William Courtneie did send his messenger to the maior, and required the gates to be opened and to giue him entrance: or els he would with sword and fier destroie the same. The maior and his brethren being in great perplexities, and hauing to answer not onelie the lords within and the knight without, but most of all doubting the common people within, who being impatient of penurie, were deafe to all persuasions and listen to any counsels: did so order and handle the matter, as that by good spéeches and courteous vsages, euerie partie was stopped and staied, vntill by means and mediations of certeine good and godlie men, an intreatie was made, the matter was compounded and the siege raised, and euerie man set at libertie.

The duke of Clarence and the earle of Warwike soiorne at Excester, and are pursued of the king.

The next daie after which conclusion, the gates being opened, to wit, the third of Aprill 1470, the earle of Warwike and the duke of Clarence came to this citie, and here rested, and soiorned themselues vntill sufficient shipping was prouided for their passage ouer the seas, and then they all imbarked themselues, and passed ouer to Calis. The king in this meane time mustered his armie, and prepared with all spéed all things necessarie to follow and pursue his said aduersaries, and came to this citie, thinking to find them here the fourtéenth of Aprill being saturdaie 1470, with fortie thousand fighting men: but the birds were fled awaie before his comming. Neuer-thelesse the king came and entred into the citie, being accompanied with sundrie no-ble men; namelie, the bishop of Elie then lord treasuror, the duke of Norffolke earle marshall, the duke of Suffolke, the earle of Arundell, the earle of Wilshire sonne to the duke of Buckingham, the earle of Worcester constable of England, the earle of Shrewesburie, the earle Riuers, the lord Hastings, the lord Graie of Codnor, the lord Audelie, the lord Saie, the lord Sturton, the lord Dacres, the lord Montioie, the lord Stanlei, the lord Ferris, and the baron of Dudlei.

Before

Before whose comming, the maior being aduertised thereof, tooke order, and gaue The king is receiued verie honorablie into the citie of Excester. commandement to euerie citizen and inhabitant, being of abilitie, to prouide and prepare for himselfe a gowne of the cities liuerie, which was then red colour, and to be in a readinesse for receiuing of the king, which was accordinglie doone. And when the king was come neere to the citie, the maior being verie well attended with foure hundred persons well and séemelie apparelled in the cities liuerie, went to the south gate, and without the same attended the kings comming. Who when he was come, the maior did his most humble obeisance, and therewith Thomas Dowrish then recorder of the citie made vnto his grace an humble oration, congratulating his comming to the citie: which ended, the maior deliuered vnto the king the keies of the gates and the maces of his office, and therewith a pursse of one hundred nobles in The citizens beneuolence to the king. gold, which his grace tooke verie thankfullie. The monie he kept, but the keies and the maces he deliuered backe to the maior; and then the maior tooke the mace and did beare it through the citie bare-headed before the king, vntill he came to his lodging.

The next daie following, being Palmesundaie, the king in most princelie and roiall maner came to the cathedrall church of saint Peters, to heare the diuine seruice, where he followed and went in procession after the maner as was then vsed, round about the churchyard, to the great ioy and comfort of all the people: he continued in the citie thrée daies vntill the tuesdaie then following; who when he had dined tooke his horsse How long the king continued in the citie. and departed backe towards London, and gaue to the maior great good thanks for his interteinement. About foure moneths after this, in August, the duke of Clarence and the erle of Warwike returned againe from Calis, with all their retinue, & landed The duke of Clarence and the earle of Warwike arriue on the English coasts. some at Plimmouth, some at Dartmouth, and some at Exmouth: but all met in this citie, and from hence they all passed towards London, and at euerie place they proclamed king Henrie the sixt, which when king Edward heard, he was very much troubled therewith: and not able then to withstand their force, he passed the seas to his brother in law the duke of Burgognie.

This yeare also, being verie troublesome, and the gouernement vncerteine, men were in great perplexities, & wist not what to doo. And among manie there was one spe- The practise of a knight being chiefe iustice at the law to rid himselfe of life. ciallie to be remembred, who to rid himselfe out of these troubles, did deuise this practise: his name was sir William Haukesford knight, a man verie well learned in the lawes of the realme, and one of the chiefe iustices at the law: he dwelled at Annorie in Deuonshire, a gentleman of great possessions, and hauing neuer a sonne, the lord Fitz Warren, sir Iohn Sentleger, & sir William Bulleine, who maried his daughters, were his heires. This man being one of the chiefest lawiers in the land, was dailie sought to and his councell asked: and he considering that when the sword ruled, law had a small course, and finding by experience what fruits insue such counsell as dooth not best like the parties, was verie heauie, sorrowfull, and in great agonies.

Herevpon suddenlie he called vnto him the keeper of his parke, with whom he fell An vniust or surmised charge of the knight against the kéeper of his parke. out and quareled, bicause (as he said) he was slothfull and careles, and did not walke in the nights about the parke, but suffered his game to be spoiled and his deere to be stolen, wherefore he willed him to be more vigilant and carefull of his charge, and also commanded him that if he met anie man in his circuit and walke in the night time, and would not stand nor speake vnto him, he should not spare to kill him what so euer he were. This knight, hauing laid this foundation, and minding to performe what he had purposed for the ending of his dolefull daies, did in a certeine darke night secretlie conueie himselfe out of his house, and walked alone in his parke. Then the kéeper in his night walke hearing one stirring and comming towards him, asked who was there? but no answer was made at all.

Then the keeper willed him to stand, which when he would not doo, the kéeper The kéeper killeth his maister the knight with an arrow. nocked his arrow and shot vnto him, and killed him; who when he perceiued that it

was

was his maister, then he called to remembrance his maisters former commandement. And so this knight, otherwise learned and wise, being affraid to displease man, did displease God, and verie disorderlie ended his life. It is inrolled amongst the records of this citie, of a commission directed to Iohn earle of Deuonshire, & from him sent to the maior of the citie of Excester to be proclamed. The words be these: Decimoquarto die Aprilis, vz. in vigilia Paschæ, An. 49. Hen. 6. commissio domini regis directa Iohanni comiti Deuon. missa est maiori vt proclamaretur. And likewise in an other place: Quatuor marcæ sunt solutæ Iohanni comiti Deuon. ex assensu maioris.

Howbeit, certeine it is there was no such earle of that name, onelie there was Iohn Holland then liuing duke of Excester, wherefore something is mistaken herein.

Abr. Flem

But was this a practise (thinke you) beséeming a man of worship, learning, and iudgement, to make awaie himselfe, bicause he saw a temporall interruption of his prosperitie? Suerlie how much learning so euer he had in the lawes of the land, litle at all or none (as appeareth) had he in suffering the forces of aduersitie, whom the feare of it did so terrifie, that it droue him to his end. Wise therefore is the counsel of the comedie-writer, and worthie of imitation, that a man, when he is in best case and highest degrée of welfare, should euen then meditate with himselfe how to awaie with hardnesse, with penurie, perils, losse, banishment, and other afflictions: for so shall he prepare himselfe to beare them with patience when they happen: as souldiers trained vp in militarie exercises at home, are so much the forwarder for the field, & fitter to incounter their foes (with lesse dread of danger) when they come abroad to be tried: and therefore it is wiselie (& to the purpose) said of Virgil:

Aeneid. 5.

————superando omnis fortuna ferendo est.]

K. Edwards fréends take sanctuarie.

Quéene Elizabeth deliuered of a prince.

Ab. Flem.

But to returne to the princes affaires. When the fame was once spred abroad that K. Edward was fled the relme, an innumerable number of people resorted to the earle of Warwike to take his part, but all K. Edwards trustie fréends went to diuerse sanctuaries, and amongst other his wife quéene Elizabeth tooke sanctuarie at Westminster, and there in great penurie forsaken of all hir friends, was deliuered of a faire son called Edward, which was with small pompe like a poore mans child christened, the godfathers being the abbat and prior of Westminster, and the godmother the ladie Scroope. [But what might be the heauinesse of this ladies hart (thinke we) vpon consideration of so manie counterblasts of vnhappinesse inwardlie conceiued? Hir husband had taken flight, his adherents and hir fréends sought to shroud themselues vnder the couert of a new protector, she driuen in distresse forsooke not that simple refuge which hir hard hap forced vpon hir; and (a kings wife) wanted in hir necessitie such things as meane mens wiues had in superfluitie, & (a corosiue to a noble mind) a prince of renowmed parentage was (by constreint of vnkind fortune) not vouchsafed the solemnitie of christendome due and decent for so honorable a personage.]

The Kentishmen make an hurlie burlie.

The Kentishmen in this seson (whose minds be euer moueable at the change of princes) came to the subvrbs of London, spoiled mansions, robbed béerehouses, and by the counsell of sir Geffrie Gates and other sanctuarie men, they brake vp the kings Bench and deliuered prisoners, and fell at Ratcliffe, Limehouse, & S. Katharins, to burning of houses, slaughter of people, and rauishing of women. Which small sparkle had growne to a greater flame, if the earle of Warwike with a great power had not suddenlie quenched it, and punished the offendors: which benefit by him doone, caused him much more to be estéemed and liked amongst the commons than

King Henrie fetched out of the Tower & restored to his kinglie gouernement.

he was before. When he had settled all things at his pleasure, vpon the twelfe daie of October he rode to the Tower of London, and there deliuered king Henrie out of the ward, where he before was kept, and brought him to the kings lodging, where he was serued according to his degrée.

On the fiue and twentith day of the said moneth, the duke of Clarence accompanied with the earles of Warwike and Shrewesburie, the lord Strange, and other lords and gentlemen,

men, some for feare, and some for loue, and some onelie to gaze at the wauering world, went to the Tower, and from tnense brought king Henrie apparelled in a long gowne of blew veluet, through London to the church of saint Paule, the people on euerie side the streets reioising and crieng; God saue the king: as though ech thing had succéeded as they would haue had it: and when he had offered (as kings vse to doo) he was conueied to the bishops palace, where he kept his houshold like a king. [Thus was the principalitie posted ouer somtimes to Henrie, sometimes to Edward; according to the swaie of the partie preuailing: ambition and disdaine still casting fagots on the fire, whereby the heat of hatred gathered the greater force to the consumption of the péeres and the destruction of the people. In the meane time, neither part could securelie possesse the regalitie, when they obteined it; which highmindednesse was in the end the ouerthrow of both principals and accessaries, according to the nature thereof noted in this distichon by the poet:

Fastus habet lites, offensis fastus abundat,

Fastus ad interitum præcipitare solet.]

When king Henrie had thus readepted and eftsoons gotten his regall power and authoritie, he called his high court of parlement to begin the six and twentith day of Nouember at Westminster; in the which king Edward was adiudged a traitor to the countrie, and an vsurper of the realme. His goods were confiscat and forfeited. The like sentence was giuen against all his partakers and freends. And besides this it was inacted, that such as for his sake were apprehended, and were either in captiuitie or at large vpon suerties, should be extremelie punished according to their demerits, amongst whome was the lord Tiptoft earle of Worcester lieutenant for king Edward in Ireland, exercising there more extreme crueltie than princelie pietie, and namelie on two infants being sonnes to the earle of Desmond. *[A parlement. K. Edward adiudged an vsurper.]*

[This earle of Worcester, being found in the top of an high trée, in the forest of Waibridge, in the countie of Huntington, was brought to London, and either for treason to him laid, or malice against him conceiued, was atteinted, and beheaded at the Tower hill, and after buried at the Blacke friers.] Moreouer, all statutes made by king Edward were clearlie reuoked, and the crownes of the realmes of England and France were by authoritie of the same parlement intailed to king Henrie the sixt, and to his heires male; and for default of such heires, to remaine to George duke of Clarence, & to his heires male: and further, the said duke was inabled to be next heire to his father Richard duke of Yorke, and to take from him all his landes and dignities, as though he had béene his eldest sonne at the time of his death. Iasper earle of Penbroke, and Iohn earle of Oxford, with diuerse other by king Edward atteinted, were restored to their old names, possessions, and ancient dignities. *[Abr. Fl, ex I. S. pag. 725. The earle Tiptoft beheaded. The crowne intailed.]*

Beside this, the earle of Warwike, as one to whom the common-wealth was much bounden [and euer had in great fauour of the commons of this land, by reason of the exceeding houshold which he dailie kept in all countries where euer he soiourned or laie: and when he came to London, he held such an house, that six oxen were eaten at a breakefast, and euerie tauerne was full of his meat, for who that had anie acquaintance in that house, he should haue had as much sod and rost as he might carrie vpon a long dagger] he (I saie) was made gouernour of the realme, with whom as fellow was associat George duke of Clarence. And thus was the state of the realme quite altered. *[Abr. Fl. ex I. S. pag. 722, 723. The earle of Warwike his housekéeping. Fabian. The earle of Warwike instituted gouernour of the realme.]*

To this parlement came the marquesse Montacute, excusing himselfe, that for feare of death he declined to take king Edwards part, which excuse was accepted. When quéene Margaret vnderstood by hir husbands letters, that the victorie was gotten by their fréends, she with hir sonne prince Edward and hir traine entered their ships, to take their voiage into England: but the winter was so sharpe, the weather so stormie, and the wind so contrarie, that she was faine to take land againe, and to deferre hir iournie till another season.

About

Iasper earle of
Penbroke.

About the same season, Iasper earle of Penbroke went into Wales, to visit his lands in Penbrokeshire, where he found lord Henrie sonne to his brother Edmund earle of Richmond, hauing not full ten yeares of age; he being kept in maner like a captiue, but honorablie brought vp by the ladie Herbert, late wife to William earle of Penbroke, beheaded

Margaret coun-
tesse of Rich-
m nd and Der-
bie.

at Banburie (as ye before haue heard.) This Henrie was borne of Margaret the onelie daughter and heire of Iohn the first duke of Summerset, then not being full ten yeares of age, the which ladie though she were after ioined in mariage with lord Henrie sonne to Humfreie duke of Buckingham, and after to Thomas Stanleie earle of Derbie, both being yoong and apt for generation, yet she had neuer anie more children, as though she had doone hir part to bring foorth a man child, and the same to be a king (as he after was indéed) intituled by the name of Henrie the seuenth (as after ye shall heare.

The earle of Penbroke tooke this child, being his nephue, out of the custodie of

The saieng of
king Henrie the
sixt, of Henrie
of Richmond
after king Hen-
rie the seuenth.

the ladie Herbert, and at his returne brought the child with him to London to king Henrie the sixt, whome when the king had a good while beheld, he said to such princes as were with him: Lo, suerlie this is he, to whom both we and our aduersaries leauing the possession of all things shall hereafter giue roome and place. So this holie man shewed before the chance that should happen, that this earle Henrie so ordeined

Ab. Flem.

by God, should in time to come (as he did indéed) haue and inioy the kingdome and whole rule of this realme of England. ¶ So that it might seeme probable by the coherence of holie Henries predictions with the issue falling out in truth with the same; that for the time he was indued with a propheticall spirit. And suerlie the epithet or title of holie is not for naught attributed vnto him, for it is to be read in writers, that he was by nature giuen to peaceablenesse, abhorring bloud and slaughter, detesting ciuill tumults, addicted to deuotion, verie frequent in praier, and not esteeming so highlie of courtlie gallantnesse as stood with the dignitie of a prince. In consideration wherof, he procured against himselfe an apostasie of his people both natiue and forren; who reuolted and fell from fealtie. And whie? The reason is rendred by the same writer, namelie:

Quòd tales homines populus sceleratior odit,
Fastidit, detestatur: non conuenit inter
Virtutem & vitium, lucem fugère tenebræ.]

The earle of Warwike, vnderstanding that his enimie the duke of Burgognie had receiued king Edward, and meant to aid him for recouerie of the kingdome, he first sent ouer to Calis foure hundred archers on horssebacke to make warre on the dukes countries; and further, prepared foure thousand valiant men to go ouer shortlie, that the duke might haue his hands euen full of trouble at home. And where ye haue heard that the erle of Warwike was kept out of Calis at his fléeing out of England into France, ye shall note that within a quarter of an houre after it was knowne that he was returned into England; and had chased king Edward out of the realme; not onelie monsieur de Vaucléere, but also all other of the garrison & towne shewed themselues to be his fréends; so that the ragged staffe was taken vp and worne in euerie

The ragged
staffe.

mans cap, some ware it of gold enameled, some of siluer; and he that could haue it neither of gold nor siluer, had it of whitish silke or cloth: such wauering minds haue the common people, bending like a reed with euerie wind that bloweth.

The duke of Burgognie, hauing an armie readie at the same time to inuade the frontiers of France, to recouer the townes of saint Quintines and Amiens, latelie by the French king taken from him, doubted to be hindered greatlie by the Englishmen, if he should be constreined to haue warre with them: for the duke of Burgognie held not onlie at that season Flanders, but also Bulleine, and Bullennois, and all Artois, so

The duke of
Burgognie
sendeth ambassa-
dors to Calis.

that he was thereby in danger to receiue harme out of Calis on ech side. Therefore he sent ambassadors thither, which did so much with the councell there, that the
league

league was newlie confirmed betwixt the realme of England and the dukes countries; onelie the name of Henrie put in the writing in stéed of Edward. This matter hindered sore the sute of king Edward, dailie suing to the duke for aid at his hands, the more earnestlie indéed, bicause of such promises as by letters were made vnto him out of England, from his assured fréends there.

But duke Charles would not consent openlie to aid king Edward; but yet secretlie vnder hand by others he lent vnto him fiftie thousand florens of the crosse of S. Andrew, and further caused foure great ships to be appointed for him in the hauen of de Véere, otherwise called Camphire in Zeland, which in those daies was free for all men to come vnto, and the duke hired for him fouretéene ships of the Easterlings well appointed, & for the more suertie tooke a bond of them to serue him trulie, till he were landed in England, and fifteene daies after. The Easterlings were glad of this iournie, trusting if he got againe the possession of England, they should the sooner come to a peace, and obteine restitution of their liberties and franchises, which they claimed of former time to haue within this realme. The duke of Burgognie cared not much on whose side the victorie fell, sauing for paiment of his monie: for he would oft saie, that he was fréend to both parties, and either part was fréendlie to him.

In déed, as he was brother in law to the one, so was he of kin to the other, as by his grandmother being daughter to Iohn of Gant duke of Lancaster. When therefore all king Edwards furniture and prouision for his iournie were once readie, hauing now with him about two thousand able men of warre, beside mariners, he entered into the ships with them, in the hauen before Flishing in Zeland, vpon the second day of March: and bicause the wind fell not good for his purpose, he taried still aboord for the space of nine daies, before it turned méet for his iournie. But after that the wind once came about (as he wisht) the sails were hoissed vp on the 11 of March being monday, & forward they sailed, directing their course streight ouer towards the coast of Norffolke. On the next day being tuesday, & the twelfe of March, toward the euening, they road before Cromer, where the king sent to land sir Robert Chamberleine, with sir Gilbert Debenham knights, and diuerse other, to the end they might discouer the countrie, and vnderstand how the people within the land were bent towards him, especiallie those countries there next adioining.

Vpon their returne, he vnderstood that there was no suertie for him to land in those parties, by reason of the good order which the earle of Warwike, and the earle of Oxford especiallie had taken in that countrie to resist him: for not onelie the duke of Norffolke, but all other the gentlemen (whome the earle of Warwike had in anie suspicion) were by letters of priuie seale sent for, and either committed to safe kéeping about London, or else inforced to find suertie for their loiall demeanor towards king Henrie: yet those knights and other that were thus sent foorth to make inquirie, were well receiued of their frends, and had good cheare. But after the king perceiued by their report, how things stood thereabouts, he caused his ships to make course towards the north parts.

The same night folowing, a great storme of winds and weather rose, sore troubling the seas, and continued till the fourtéenth day of that moneth being thursday, on the which day with greater danger, by reason of the tempestuous rage and torment of the troubled seas, he arriued at the head of Humber, where the other ships were scattered from him, each one seuered from other; so that of necessitie they were driuen to land in sunder where they best might, for doubt to be cast awaie in that perillous tempest. The king with the lord Hastings his chamberleine, and other to the number of fiue hundred men being in one ship, landed within Humber on Holdernesse side, at a place called Rauenspurgh, euen in the same place where Henrie erle of Derbie, after called king Henrie the fourth landed, when he came to depriue king Richard the second of the crowne, and to vsurpe it to himselfe.

Richard

Margin notes:

1471.

He aideth K. Edward vnder hand.

W. Fleetwood.

He arriueth on the coast of Norffolke.

An. Reg. 11.

The earle of Oxford.

He arriueth at the head of Humber.

He landeth at Rauenspurgh.

Richard duke of Glocester, and three hundred men in his companie, tooke land in another place foure miles distant from thence, where his brother king Edward did land. The earle Riuers, and with him two hundred men, landed at a place called Pole, fourtéene miles from the hauen where the king came on land. The residue of his people landed some here some there, in place where for their suerties they thought best. On the morrow, being the fifteenth of March, now that the tempest ceased, and euerie man being got to land, they drew from euerie of their landing places towards the king, who for the first night was lodged in a poore village, two miles from the place where he first set foot on land. [As for his traine, though the season of the yeere was naturallie cold, & therfore required competent refection by warmth, it is to be supposed, that all their lodgings were hard inough, sith the principals prouision was sorie inough. But what of that? Better (in cases of extremitie) an hard shift than none at all.]

Touching the folks of the countrie, there came few or none to him. For by the incensing of such as had bin sent into those parts from the erle of Warwike, and other his aduersaries, the people were shrewdlie induced to stand against him. But yet, in respect of the good will that manie of them had borne to his father, they could haue béene content, that he should haue inioied his right to his due inheritance of the duchie of Yorke, but in no wise to the title of the crowne. And herevpon they suffered him to passe, not séeking to annoie him, till they might vnderstand more of his purposed meaning. The king, perceiuing how the people were bent, noised abroad that hée came to make none other chalenge but to his inheritance of the duchie of Yorke: and withall ment to passe first into the citie of Yorke, and so forward towards London, to incounter with his aduersaries that were in the south parts.

For although his néerest waie had béene through Lincolneshire: yet bicause in taking that waie hée must haue gone againe to the water, in passing ouer Humber; he doubted least it would haue bin thought that he had withdrawne himselfe to the sea for feare. And to auoid the rumors that might haue beene spred thereof, to the hinderance of his whole cause, he refused that waie, and tooke this other, still bruting it (as before we said) that his comming was not to chalenge the crowne, but onelie to be restored vnto his fathers right and inheritance of the duchie of Yorke, which was descended to him from his father. And here it séemed that the colour of iustice hath euer such a force in it selfe amongst all men, that where before few or none of the commons could be found that would offer themselues to take his part: yet now that he did (as they thought) claime nothing but that which was his right, they began streight to haue a liking of his cause.

Martine de la Mare or Martine of the sea. He passeth toward Yorke.

And where there were gathered to the number of six or seuen thousand men in diuerse places, vnder the leading chieflie of a priest and of a gentleman called Martine de la Mare, in purpose to haue stopped his passage: now the same persons tooke occasion to assist him. And when he perceiued mens minds to bée well qualified with this feined deuise, he marched foorth till he came to Beuerleie, which stood in his direct waie as he passed toward Yorke. He sent also to Kingston vpon Hull, distant from thence six miles, willing that he might be there receiued: but the inhabitants, who had bene laboured by his aduersaries, refused in anie wise to grant therevnto.

The earle of Warwike aduertised by messengers of king Edwards arriuall, and of his turning toward Yorke, with all hast wrote to his brother the marquesse Montacute, who had laine at the castell of Pomfret all the last winter with a great number of souldiers, willing him to consider in what case their affaires stood, and therevpon with all spéed to set vpon king Edward, or else to keepe the passages, and to staie him from comming anie further forward, till he himselfe as then being in Warwikeshire busie to assemble an armie, might come to his aid with the same. [Thus laboured the earle of Warwike by policie and puissance, as well of his owne as others power, to further his

owne

owne purpose, hauing sworne in heart a due performance of that, which he had Sée before page 277. solemnlie vowed and promised before.]

But this notwithstanding, although there were great companies of people of the countries there abouts assembled, yet they came not in sight of the king, but suffered him quietlie to passe; either bicause they were persuaded that he ment (as he in outward words pretended) not to claime anie title to the crowne, but onelie his right to the duchie of Yorke; or else for that they doubted to set vpon him, although his number were farre vnequall to theirs; knowing that not onelie he himselfe, but also his companie were minded to sell their liues dearlie, before they would shrinke an inch from anie that was to incounter them. It maie be that diuerse of the capteins also were corrupted: and although outwardlie they shewed to be against him, yet in heart they bare him right good will, and in no wise minded to hinder him. So forward he marched, till he came to Yorke, on a monday being the eighteenth day of March. K. Edward without interruption passeth forward to Yorke.

Before he came to the citie by the space of thrée miles, the recorder of Yorke, whose name was Thomas Coniers (one knowne in déed not to beare him anie faithfull good will) came vnto him; & gaue him to vnderstand, that it stood in no wise with his suertie, to presume to approch the citie: for either hée should be kept out by force, or if he did enter, he shuld be in danger to be cast away by his aduersaries that were within. King Edward neuerthelesse, sith he was come thus farre forward, knew well inough there was no going backe for him, but manfullie to procéed forward with his begun iournie, and therefore kept on his way. And shortlie after there came to him out of the citie, Robert Clifford, and Richard Burgh, who assured him that in the quarell which he pretended to pursue, to wit, for the obteining of his right to the duchie of Yorke, he should not faile but be receiued into the citie. Thomas Coniers recorder of Yorke.

But immediatlie after came the said Coniers againe, with the like tale and information as he had brought before. And thus king Edward one while put in comfort, and another while discouraged, marched foorth till he came to the gates of the citie, where his people staied; whilest he and about sixtéene or seuentéene other such as he thought méetest, went forth and entred the citie with the said Clifford & Burgh. And (as some write) there was a priest readie to saie masse, in which masse time the king receiued the sacrament of the communion, & there solemnlie sware to kéepe and obserue two speciall articles: although it was farre vnlike that he minded to obserue either of them: the one was that he should vse the citizens after a gentle and courteous maner: and the other, that he should be faithfull and obedient vnto king Henries commandements. K. Edward commeth to Yorke. He receiueth an oth.

For this wilfull periurie (as hath béene thought) the issue of this king suffered (for the fathers offense the depriuation not onelie of lands and worldlie possessions, but also of their naturall liues, by their cruell vncle K. Richard the third. [And it may well be. For it is not likelie that God, in whose hands is the bestowing of all souereigntie, will suffer such an indignatie to be doone to his sacred maiestie, and will suffer the same to passe with impunitie, And suerlie, if an oth among priuate men is religiouslie to be kept, sith in the same is an exact triall of faith and honestie; doubtlesse of princes it is verie nicelie and preciselie to be obserued: yea they should rather susteine a blemish and disgrace in their roialtie, than presume to go against their oth and promise, speciallie if the same stand vpon conditions of equitie: otherwise they prooue themselues to be impugners of fidelitie, which is a iewell surpassing gold in price and estimation, as the poet prudentlie saith:

Charior est auro non simulata fides.

When king Edward had thus gotten into the citie of Yorke, he made such meanes among the citizens, that he got of them a certeine summe of monie; and leauing a garison within the citie contrarie to his oth, for fear least the citizens after his departure, might happilie mooue some rebellion against him, he set forward the next day toward

Todcaster, a towne ten miles from thence, belonging to the earle of Northumberland. The next day he tooke his waie toward Wakefield and Sendall, a castell and lordship belonging to the inheritance of the dukes of Yorke, leauing the castell of Pomfret vpon his left hand, where the marques Montacute with his armie laie, and did not once offer to stop him.

The marques Montacute suffereth king Edward to passe by him.

Whether the marques suffered him to passe by so, with his good will or no, diuerse haue diuerslie coniectured. Some thinke that it lay not in the power of the marques greatlie to annoie him, both for that the king was well beloued in those parties; & againe, all the lords & commons there for the most part were towards the earle of Northumberland, and without him or his commandement they were not willing to stirre. And therefore the earle in sitting still and not moouing to and fro, was thought to doo king Edward as good seruice as if he had come to him, and raised people to assist him; for diuerse happilie that should haue come with him, remembring displeasures past, would not haue béene so faithfull as the earle himselfe, if it had come to the iumpe of anie hazard of battell.

About Wakefield and the parts there adioining, some companie of his freends came to him, whereby his power was increased; but nothing in such numbers as he looked for. From Wakefield he crossed on the left hand, so to come againe into the high waie, and came to Doncaster, and from thence vnto Notingham. Here came to him sir William Parre, and sir Iames Harrington, with six hundred men well armed and appointed also there came to him sir Thomas Burgh, & sir Thomas Montgomerie with their aids, which caused him at their first comming to make proclamation in his owne name, to wit, of K. Edward the fourth, boldlie affirming to him, that they would serue no man but a king.

K. Edward commeth to Northamptō.

Edw. Hall.

Whilest he remained at Notingham, and also before he came there, he sent abroad diuerse of his auaunt courrers to discouer the countrie, and to vnderstand if there were anie power gathered against him. Some of them that were thus sent, approached to Newarke, and vnderstood that within the towne there, the duke of Excester, the earle of Oxenford, the lord Bardolfe, and other were lodged with a great power to the number of foure thousand men, which they had assembled in Essex, Norffolke, Suffolke, and in the shires of Cambridge, Huntington, and Lincolne. The duke of Excester, and the earle of Oxenford, with other the chéefe capteins, aduertised that king Edwards foreriders had béene afore the towne in the euening, supposed verelie that he and his whole armie were comming towards them.

The duke of Excester with a power at Newarke.

Héerevpon, they not thinking it good to abide longer there, determined with all spéed to dislodge, and so about two of the clocke after midnight they departed from Newarke, leauing some of their people behind, which either stale awaie from them, and taried of purpose, or could not get awaie so soone as their fellowes. In déed the foreriders that so discouered them within the towne of Newarke, aduertised the king thereof in all post hast, who incontinentlie assembled his people, and foorthwith marched towards them: but before he came within thrée miles of the towne, he had knowledge that they were fled and gone from Newarke. Whervpon he returned againe to Notingham, intending to keépe on his neerest waie towards the earle of Warwike, whome he vnderstood to be departed from London, and to be come into Warwikeshire, where & in the countries adioining he was busied in leuieng an armie, with the which he purposed to distresse him.

The king then from Notingham came to Leicester, where three thousand able men, and well furnished for the warre came vnto him. These were such as he knew would liue and die in his quarrell, the most part of them belonging vnto the lord Hastings, the kings chamberlaine. And thus he, being more stronglie accompanied than before, departed from Leicester, and came before the wals of the citie of Couentrie, the nine and twentith daie of March. The earle of Warwike was withdrawne into this citie,

K. Edward commeth to Leicester.

The earle of Warwike in Couentrie.

kéeping

kéeping himselfe inclosed therein with his people, being in number six or seauen thousand men. The king sent to him, and willed him to come foorth into the field, and there to make an end of the quarell in plaine battell: but the earle at that present refused so to doo,

For although, vnder pretense of king Henries authoritie, he was reputed the kings generall lieutenant of the whole realme, whereby he had got such power togither, as was thought able inough to match with the king for number; yet bicause he doubted how they were bent in his fauour, he durst not commit the matter vnto the doubtfull chance of battell, till he had more of his trustie fréends about him. The king therefore thrée daies togither prouoked him to come foorth, but when he saw it would not be, he remooued to Warwike an eight miles from Couentrie, where he was receiued as king, and so made his proclamations from that time foorth in all places where he came vnder his accustomed name snd title of king. K. Edward prouoketh the earle of Warwike to fight He cōmeth to Warwike.

He lodged héere at Warwike, the rather (as was thought) to prouoke the earle to issue foorth of Couentrie to giue him battell, howbeit that deuise nothing auailed. But yet there came dailie diuerse persons on the earls behalfe to treat with the king about a peace, that some good composition might haue béene concluded; & the king for the aduancement of peace and tranquillitie within the realme, offered large conditions; as a frée pardon of life to the earle, and all his people, with manie other beneficiall articles on their behalfes, which to manie seemed verie reasonable, considering their heinous offenses. But the earle would not accept anie offers, except he might haue compounded so as it pleased himselfe, & as was thought in no wise to stand with the king honour, and suertie of his estate. A treatie for peace.

In this meane while, the earle of Warwike still looked for the duke of Clarence, who by the said earls appointment had assembled a power of men of war about London: but when the earle perceiued that the duke lingered foorth the time, and did not vse such diligence as was requisit, as one that had béene in doubt of warre or peace, he began to suspect that the duke was of his brother corrupted, and therein he was nothing deceiued. For true it is, that whilest the king was as yet beyond the seas, in the dominion of the duke of Burgognie, the duke of Clarence began to weie with himselfe the great inconuenience into the which as well his brother king Edward as himselfe and his yoonger brother the duke of Glocester were fallen, through the dissention betwixt them: (which had béene compassed and brought to passe by the politike working of the earle of Warwike and his complices.) The duke of Clarence.

As first the disheriting of them all from their rightfull title to the crowne; secondlie the mortall and detestable war that could not but insue betwixt them, to such mischéefe, that to whether part the victorie inclined, the victor should remaine in no more suertie of his owne person or estate after the vpper hand got, than before; and thirdlie he well perceiued alreadie, that he was had in great suspicion, and not heartilie belooued of anie the lords and rulers that were assured partakers with king Henrie and the Lancastrian faction: insomuch they sticked not dailie to go about to breake and make void the appointments, articles, and couenants, made and promised to him, and of likelihood would dailie more and more intend thereto: for in truth he saw, that they purposed nothing so much as the destruction both of him and all his bloud.

All which things throughlie considered, with manie other as they were laid afore him by right wise and circumspect persons, which in this behalfe had conference with him, he consented that by some secret waies and meanes a reconciliation might be had betwixt him and his brethren, the king and the duke of Glocester. The which to bring to some good and full effect, these honorable personages following became dealers therein. First of all the duches of Yorke their mother, the duches of Excester and the duches of Suffolke their sisters; the lord cardinall of Canturburie, the bishop of Bath, the earle of Essex; but most speciallie the duches of Burgognie their sister also, and diuerse other right wise and prudent personages, who wrought by mediation of certeine preests, and others, such as they vsed for messengers betwixt them.

Preests vsed for priuie messengers.

Finallie, by the earnest trauell and diligence shewed by the said duches of Burgognie (who incessantlie sent to and fro such hir trustie messengers now to the king being on that side the seas, and then to the duke remaining heere in England) at length they were made freends, and a perfect agreement concluded and ratified, with assurance betwixt them so stronglie as might be. To the furthering whereof the kings chamberlaine the lord Hastings failed not to doo his best, so as by his good diligence, it was thought the king was the sooner induced to with to ioine eftsoones in true freendship with his said brother of Clarence. And as it well appeared, the duke of Clarence acquitted himselfe faithfullie therein.

K. Edward and his brother of Clarence reconciled vnwitting to the earle of Warwike.

For hearing now that his brother king Edward was landed and comming forward towards London, he gathered his people, outwardlie pretending to passe with them to the aid of the earle of Warwike against his brother: although inwardlie he meant the contrarie, and so accompanied with aboue foure thousand men, he marched foorth towards the place where he thought to find his brother. King Edward being then at Warwike, and vnderstanding that his brother of Clarence approched, in an afternoone issued foorth of that towne with all his forces, and passed on till he came into a faire large field three miles distant from Warwike towards Banburie, where he might behold his brother of Clarence in good arraie of battell, comming towards him.

The dissimulation of the duke of Clarence.

When they were now within halfe a mile approched togither, the king placed his people in order of battell vnder their baners, and so left them standing still, and appointed them to keepe their ground, whilest he taking with him his brother of Glocester, the lord Riuers, the lord Hastings, & a few other, went foorth to meet his brother of Clarence: and in like sort the duke of Clarence tooke with him a few of the nobilitie that were about him, and leauing his armie in good order, departed from them to meet the king, and so they met betwixt both the hosts, with so sweet salutations, louing demeanor, and good countenances, as better might not be deuised betwixt brethren of so high and noble estate. O what a hearts ioy was this to the people, to see such an accord and mutuall attonement betweene these peeres! It was the onelie pleasure in the world, to the which all other compared are but counterfet, and that dooth the psalmist testifie,

The brethren meet louinglie togither.

Nil charitate mutua fratrum, nihil
Iucundius concordia,

Buchan. in psal. 133.

Besides this the like freendlie intertainment, and courteous demeanour appeared in the salutings of other noble men that were on them attendant; wherof all such as saw it, and loued them, greatlie reioised; giuing God thankes for that ioifull meeting, vnitie, and concord, appearing thus manifestlie betwixt them: and herewith the trumpets and other instruments sounded, & the king withall brought the duke vnto his armie, whome he saluting in most courteous wise, welcomed them into the land; and they humblie thanking him, did to him such reuerence as apperteined to the honour of such a worthie personage. This was a goodlie and a gratious reconcilement, beneficiall to the princes, profitable to the peeres, and pleasurable to the people, whose part had beene deepest in dangers and losse, if discord had not beene discontinued.

This doone, the king leauing his hoast againe, keeping their ground with the same few persons which he tooke with him before, went with his brother of Clarence vnto his armie, and saluting them with sweete and courteous words, was ioifullie of them welcomed: and so after this, they all came togither ioining in one. And either part shewing themselues glad thus to meet as freends with the other, they went louinglie togither vnto Warwike with the king, where and in the countrie thereabouts they lodged, as they thought stood most with their ease and safeties. Herewith the duke of

Clarence

Clarence desired aboue all things to procure some good and perfect accord betwixt his brother the king, and the earle of Warwike.

In this was he the more studious, bicause he saw that such an accord should bring great quietnesse to the land, and deliuer the common-wealth of manie dangers that might insue by reason of such numbers of partakers, as well lords as other that were confederat with the earle. The said duke treated with the king present, and sent messengers vnto Couentrie to the earle, moouing as well the one as the other most instantlie to frame their minds vnto a pacification. The king at the instance of his brother was contented to offer large conditions, and verie beneficiall for the earle and his partakers, if they would haue accepted them.

The duke of Clarence seeketh to make peace betwixt the king and the earle of Warwike.

But the earle, whether vtterlie despairing of his owne safetie, if he should agrée to anie peace; or else happilie for that he thought it stood with his honour to stand vnto such promises and couenants as he had made with the French king, and with the quéene Margaret, and hir sonne prince Edward (to whome he was bound by oth not to shrinke or swarue from the same) he refused all maner of such conditions as were offered. Insomuch that when the duke had sent to him, both to excuse himselfe of the act which he had doone, and also to require him to take some good waie with king Edward, now while he might, the earle (after he had patientlie heard the dukes message) he séemed greatlie to abhorre his vnfaithfull dealing, in turning thus from his confederats and alies contrarie to his oth and fidelitie.

To the messengers (as some write) he gaue none other answer but this, that he had rather be like himselfe, than like a false and periured duke; and that he was fullie determined neuer to leaue warre, till he had either lost his owne life, or vtterlie subdued his enimies. At it was thought, the earle of Oxenfords persuasion wanted not, to make him the more stiffe to hold out; and rather to trie the vttermost hazard of warre, than to agrée to acknowledge king Edward for his lawfull souereigne lord and king. Whervpon no appointment nor anie agréement at all could be brought to passe; and so all that treatie, which the duke of Clarence had procured, brake off & tooke none effect. There came to the earle of Warwike, whilest he laie thus at Couentrie (besides the earle of Oxenford) the duke of Excester, and the lord marquesse Montacute, by whose comming that side was greatlie strengthened, and the number much increased.

The earle of Warwiks answer to the duke of Clarence message.

The king, vpon consideration hereof and perceiuing he could not get the earle to come foorth of Couentrie, departed from Warwike, and eftsoones shewing himselfe with his people before the citie of Couentrie, desired the earle and his power to come foorth into the fields, that they might end their quarrell by battell: which the earle and the other lords with him vtterlie refused as then to doo. This was the fift of Aprill being fridaie. The king herevpon was resolued to march towards London, where his principall aduersarie king Henrie remained, vsing his kinglie authoritie by diuerse such of the nobilitie as were about him, whereby king Edward was barred and disappointed of manie aids and assistants, which he was sure to haue, if he could once breake that force of the roiall authoritie, that was still thus exercised against him in king Henries name.

K. Edward passeth London.

Wherefore (by the aduise of his brethren and others of his councell) accordinglie as it had beene ordeined before this his last setting foorth from Warwike, he kept on his waie towards London, comming to Dantrie on the saturdaie at night: & on the morow being Palmesundaie, he heard seruice in the church there, & after rode to Northhampton, where he was ioifullie receiued. From thense he tooke the next way towards London, leauing continuallie behind him (as he passed foorth) a competent band of speares and archers, to beat backe such of the earle of Warwiks people, as peraduenture he might send abroad to trouble him and his armie by the waie. Which prouidence and foresight it not vnnecessarie to vse; for that he knew well enough, that the

heart

heart of an enimie, frieng in the fire of hatefull hostilitie, will pretermit no opportunitie either of time or place to laie in wait for his destruction, against whom he beareth an inward grudge, with a desire of vengeance to the death.

In this meane while, that things passed in maner (as before ye haue hard) Edmund duke of Summerset, & his brother Iohn marquesse Dorset, Thomas Courtneie earle of Deuonshire, and others being at London, had knowledge by aduertisements out of France, that quéene Margaret with hir sonne prince Edward, the countesse of Warwike, the prior of S. Iohns, the lord Wenlocke, and diuerse others their adherents and partakers, with all that they might make, were readie at the sea side, purposing with all spéed to saile ouer into England, and to arriue in the west countrie. Wherevpon they departed foorth of London, and with all hast possible drew westward, there to raise what forces they could, to ioine with those their fréends, immediatlie after they should once come on land, and so to assist them against king Edward and his partakers.

True it is, that the quéene with hir sonne, and the other persons before mentioned, tooke their ships, the foure and twentith daie of March, continuing on the seas before they could land (thorough tempests and contrarie winds) by the space of twentie daies, that is, till the thirtéenth of Aprill: on which daie, or rather on the fourteenth, they landed at Weimouth, as after shall appeare. But now touching king Edwards procéeding forward on his iournie toward London, ye haue to vnderstand, that vpon the tuesdaie the ninth of Aprill he came to saint Albons, from whense he sent comfortable aduertisements to the queene his wife remaining within the sanctuarie at Westminster, and to others his faithfull fréends in and about London, to vnderstand by couert meanes how to deale to obteine the fauour of the citizens, so as he might be of them receiued.

The earle of Warwike, vnderstanding all his dooings and purposes, wrote to the Londoners, willing & charging them in anie wise to keepe king Edward out of their citie, and in no condition to permit him to enter: and withall he sent to his brother the archbishop of Yorke, willing him by all meanes possible to persuade the Londoners not to receiue him; but to defend the citie against him for the space of two or thrée daies at the least: promising not to faile but to come after him, and to be readie to assaile him on the backe, not doubting but wholie to distresse his power and to bring him to vtter confusion. The archbishop herevpon, on the ninth of Aprill, called vnto him at Paules, all such lords, knights, and gentlemen, with others that were partakers on that side, to the number in all of six or seauen thousand men in armour.

Herewith also he caused king Henrie to mount on horssebacke, and to ride from Paules thorough Cheape downe to Walbroke, & so to fetch a compasse (as the custome was when they made their generall processions) returning backe againe to Paules vnto the bishops palace, where at that time he was lodged. The archbishop supposed, that shewing the king thus riding thorough the stréets, he should haue allured the citizens to assist his part. True it is, the maior & aldermen had caused the gates to be kept with watch and ward: but now they well perceiued that king Henries power was too weake, as by that shew it had well appeared, to make full resistance against king Edward, and so not for them to trust vnto, if king Edward came forward, and should attempt to enter the citie by force: for it was not vnknowne vnto them, that manie of the worshipfull citizens, and others of the commons in great numbers, were fullie bent to aid king Edward, in all that they might, as occasion serued.

Thus, what thorough loue that manie bare to king Edward, and what thorough feare that diuerse stood in, least the citie being taken by force might happilie haue beene put to the sacke, with the losse of manie an innocent mans life; the maior, aldermen, and others the worshipfull of the citie fell at a point among themselues, to

kéepe

kéepe the citie to K. Edwards vse, so as he might haue free passage and entrie into the same at his pleasure. The archbishop of Yorke, perceiuing the affections of the people, and how the most part of them were now bent in fauour of king Edward vpon the said kings approch towards the citie, he sent foorth secretlie a messenger to him, beséeching him to receiue him againe into his fauour, promising to be faithfull to him in time to come, and to acquit this good turne hereafter with some singular benefit and pleasure. The archbishop of Yorke.

The king, vpon good causes and considerations therevnto him moouing, was contented to receiue him againe into his fauour. The archbishop hereof assured, reioised greatlie, well & truelie acquiting him concerning his promise made to the king in that behalfe. The same night following was the Tower of London recouered to king Edwards vse. And on the morow being thursdaie, and the eleuenth of Aprill, king Edward quietlie made his entrie into the citie with his power, hauing fiue hundred smokie gunners marching foremost, being strangers, of such as he had brought ouer with him. He first rode vnto Paules church, & from thense he went to the bishops palace, where the archbishop of Yorke presented himselfe vnto him, and hauing king Henrie by the hand, deliuered him vnto king Edward, who being seized of his person, and diuerse other his aduersaries, he went from Paules to Westminster, where he made his deuout praiers, giuing God most heartie thanks for his safe returne thither againe. The Tower recouered to king Edwards vse.
K. Edward entereth into London.
King Henrie is deliuered to him.

This doone, he went to the quéene to comfort hir, who with great patience had abidden there a long time, as a sanctuarie woman, for doubt of hir enimies; and in the meane season was deliuered of a yoong prince, whom she now presented vnto him, to his great hearts reioising & comfort. From Westminster the king returned that night vnto London againe, hauing the quéene with him, and lodged in the house of the duchesse his moother. On the morow being good fridaie, he tooke aduise with the lords of his bloud, and other of his councell, for such businesse as he had in hand; namelie, how to subdue his enimies as sought his destruction. Thus with consultation preuenting his actions, he obteined fortunate successe, wherwith his hart was the more aduanced to ioine issue with his aduersaries, whome (rather than they should triumph ouer him) he was resolutelie minded to vanquish, if his procéedings might proue prosperous as his present good lucke.

The earle of Warwike, calling himselfe lieutenant of England, vnder the pretensed authoritie of King Henrie, hoping that king Edward should haue much a doo to enter into London, marched foorth from Couentrie with all his puissance, following the king by Northhampton, in hope to haue some great aduantage to assaile him, speciallie if the Londoners kept him out of their citie, as he trusted they would; for then he accounted himselfe sure of the vpper hand: or if he were of them receiued, yet he hoped to find him vnprouided in celebrating the feast of Easter; and so by setting vpon him on the sudden, he doubted not by that meanes to distresse him. But king Edward, hauing intelligence of the earles intention, prouided all things necessarie for battell; & hearing that the earle of Warwike was now come vnto S. Albons with his armie, he determined to march foorth to incounter him before he should approch neere the citie. The earle of Warwike foloweth the king.

The earle of Warwike accompanied with Iohn duke of Excester, Edmund duke of Summerset, Iohn earle of Oxford, and Iohn Neuill marquesse Montacute his brother, vnderstanding that king Edward was not onelie receiued into London, but also had got king Henrie into his hands, perceiued that the triall of the matter must néeds be committed to the hazard of battell; and therefore being come to the towne of saint Albons, he rested there a while, partlie to refresh his souldiers, and partlie to take counsell how to procéed in his enterprise. At length, although he knew that his brother the marquesse Montacute was not fullie well persuaded with himselfe, to like of this quarell which they had in hand; yet the brotherlie affection betwixt them *Edw. Hall.*

tooke

tooke awaie all suspicion from the earle, and so he vtterlie resolued to giue battell, meaning to trie whereto all this tumult would grow; and counting it a blemish to his honor, not to prosequute that with the sword, which he had solemnelie vowed to doo on his word.]

Hervpon remoued they towards Barnet, a towne standing in the midwaie betwixt London and saint Albons aloft on a hill; at the end whereof towards saint Albons there is a faire plaine for two armies to meet vpon, named Gladmore heath. On the further side of which plaine towards saint Albons the earle pight his campe. king Edward on the other part, being furnished with a mightie armie (hauing ioined to that power which he brought with him certeine new supplies) upon Easter euen the thirteenth of Aprill in the after noone marched foorth, hauing his said armie diuided into foure battels. He tooke with him king Henrie, and came that euening vnto Barnet, ten small miles distant from London; in which towne his foreriders finding certeine of the earle of Warwikes foreriders, beat them out, & chased them somewhat further than halfe a mile from the towne, where, by an hedge side they found readie assembled a great number of the earle of Warwiks people.

Gladmore heath.

The ordering of the kings armie.

The king after this comming to Barnet, would not suffer a man to remaine in the towne (that were of his host) but commanded them all to the field, and with them drew toward his enimies, and lodged with his armie more neere to them than he was aware of, by reason it was darke, so as he could not well discerne where they were incamped, fortifieng the field the best he could for feare of some sudden inuasion. He tooke his ground not so euen afore them as he would haue doone, if he might haue discouered the place where they had lien; and by reason thereof he incamped somewhat aside slips of them, causing his people to kéepe as much silence as was possible, [least making anie noise with the busseling of their armour and weapons or otherwise with their toongs, the enimie might haue come to some knowledge of the kings priuie purpose, and so by preuention haue disappointed his policie by some prouident deuise; which bicause they wanted for the present time, it turned to their disaduantage; after the old prouerbe:

K. Edward lodged before his enimies.

Nescit prodesse qui nescit prouidus esse.]

They had great artillerie on both parts, but the earle was better furnished therewith than the king, and therefore in the night time they shot off from his campe in maner continuallie; but dooing little hurt to the kings people, still ouershooting them, by reason they laie much néerer than the earle or anie of his men did estéeme. And such silence was kept in the kings campe, that no noise bewraied them where they laie. For to the end it should not be knowne to the enimies, how neere the king with his armie was lodged vnto them, the king would not suffer anie of his gunnes in all that night to be shot off, least thereby they might haue gessed the ground, and so leuelled their artillerie to his annoiance.

Artillerie.

A good policie.

Earelie on the next morning betwixt foure and fiue of the clocke, notwithstanding there was a great mist that letted the sight of both parts to discouer the fields, the king aduanced his banners, and caused his trumpets to sound to the battell. On the other part, the earle of Warwike, at the verie breake of the daie, had likewise set his men in order of battell in this maner. In the right wing he placed the marquesse Montacute, and the earle of Oxford with certeine horssemen, and he with the duke of Excester tooke the left wing. And in the middest betweene both, he set archers, appointing the duke of Summerset to guide them as their chiefteine. King Edward had set the duke of Glocester in the fore-ward. The middle-ward he himselfe with the duke of Clarence, hauing with them king Henrie, did rule & gouerne. The lord Hastings led the rere-ward, and beside these thrée battels, he kept a companie of fresh men in store, which did him great pleasure before the end of the battell.

Edw. Hall.

The order of battell of both sides.

Here is to be remembered, that aswell the king on his part, as the earle of Warwike

on

on his, vsed manie comfortable words to incourage their people, not forgetting to set
foorth their quarels as iust and lawfull; the king naming his aduersaries traitors and
rebels, & the earle accounting him a tyrant, & an iniurious vsurper. But when the
time came that they once got sight either of other, the battell began verie sharpe and
cruell, first with shot, and after by ioining at hand blowes. Yet at the first they
ioined not front to front, as they should haue doone, by reason of the mist that tooke
awaie the sight of either armie, and suffered the one not to discerne perfectlie the
order of the other; insomuch that the one end of the earle of Warwikes armie ouer-
raught the contrarie end of the kings battell which stood westward, and by reason
thereof (through the valiancie of the earle of Oxford that led the earles voward) the **The valiancie**
kings people on that part were ouermatched, so that manie of them fled towards **of the earle of**
Barnet, and so to London, bringing newes that the erle of Warwike had woone the **Oxford.**
field.

[Which report happilie might haue béene iustified and fallen out to be true, had not *Abr. Fl. ex I. S.*
preposterous fortune happened to the earle of Oxford and his men, who had a starre *pag. 727.*
with streames on their liueries; as king Edwards men had the sunne with streames on
their liueries: wherevpon the earle of Warwiks men, by reason of the mist not well
discerning the badges so like, shot at the earle of Oxfords men that were on their
owne part, and then the earle of Oxford and his men cried treason, and fled with
eight hundred men.]

But touching the kings people which were pursued in the chase as they fled, and
were put to the worst, manie were wounded, and manie slaine outright. But the residue of those that fought in other parts could not perceiue this distresse of the kings
people, bicause the thicke mist would not suffer them to sée anie space farre off, but
onelie at hand: and so the kings battell that saw not anie thing what was doone beside
them, was nothing discouraged. For (a few excepted that stood next to that part)
there was not anie one that wist of that discomfiture; and the other of the earle of
Warwikes men, that fought in other places somewhat distant from them, were no- **The manfull**
thing the more incouraged by this prosperous successe of their fellowes, for they per- **courage of the**
ceiued it not. And in like case as at the west end the earles battell ouer-reached the **wike.**
kings, so at the east end the kings ouer-reached the earls, and with like successe put
the earls people in that place to the worse.

At length after sore fight, and greater slaughter made on both sides, king Edward
hauing the greater number of men (as some write, though other affirme the contrarie)
began somewhat to preuaile: but the earle on the other side remembring his ancient
fame and renowme, manfullie stucke to it, and incouraged his people, still supplieng
with new succors in places where he saw expedient, and so the fight renewed more
cruell, fierce, & bloudie than before, insomuch that the victorie remained still doubtfull, though they had fought from morning till it was now far in the daie. K. Edward therefore willing to make an end of so long a conflict, caused new power of fresh
men (which he had for this purpose kept in store) to set on his enimies.

The earle of Warwike was nothing abashed herewith, but vnderstanding that this
was all the residue of king Edwards power, comforted his men to beare out this last
brunt, and in so dooing the victorie was sure on their side, and the battell at an end:
but king Edward so manfullie and valiantlie assailed his aduersaries, in the middle and
strongest part of their battell, that with great violence he bare downe all that stood
in his waie; for he was followed and assisted by a number of most hardie and faithfull men of warre, that shewed notable proofe of tried manhood in that instant necessitie. The earle of Warwike (when his souldiers all wearied with long fight, and
sore weakened with woundes and hurts receiued in the battell) gaue little heed to his
words (being a man of an inuincible stomach) rushed into the middest of his enimies, whereas he (aduenturing so farre from his companie, to kill and slea his aduer-

The earle of Warwike slaine. saries, that he could not be rescued) was amongst the preasse of his enimies striken downe and slaine.

The marquesse Montacute slaine. Abr. Flem. The marquesse Montacute, thinking to succour his brother, was likewise ouerthrowne and slaine, with manie other of good calling, as knights and esquiers, beside other gentlemen. [But some saie that the said marquesse, hauing agreed priuilie with king Edward, did weare his liuerie, whome one of his brother the earle of Warwiks men espieng, fell vpon him and killed him outright.] Some write that this battell was so driuen to the vttermost point, that king Edward was constreined to fight in his owne person, and that the earle of Warwike, which was wont euer to ride on horsebacke from place to place, and from ranke to ranke, comforting, his men, was now aduised by the marquesse his brother, to leaue his horsse, and to trie the extremitie by *Abr. Fl. ex I. S. pag. 727.* hand strokes, [which may be probable & likelie. But by the report of some it séemeth that he was not slaine in the heat of the conflict, among the rout of the fighting men, but afterwards in this sort. For when he saw the kings power preuaile and his owne sore impaired and past hope of good speed, with the slaughter of his adherents (gentlemen of name) and himselfe in the verie mouth of the enimie in possibilitie to be deuoured, he lept vpon a horsse to flie, and comming into a wood where was no passage, one of king Edwards men came to him, killed him, and spoiled him to the naked skin. Sir William Tirrell knight was killed on the earle of Warwikes part.]

The number slaine at Barnet field. On both parties were slaine (as Ed. Hall saith) ten thousand at the least, where Fabian saith but fifteene hundred and somewhat aboue. Other write that there died in all about three thousand. Vpon the kings part were slaine, the lord Crumwell, the lord Saie, the lord Montiois sonne and heire, sir Humfrie Bourchier sonne to the lord Berners, and diuerse other knights, esquiers, and gentlemen. The battell indured the space of thrée hours verie doubtfull by reason of the mist, and in skirmishing and fighting, now in this place, now in that, but finallie the victorie fell on the kings side; and yet it could not be estéemed that his whole armie passed nine thousand fighting men (as some write) where his aduersaries (as by the same writers appeareth) were farre aboue that number. But bicause those that so write, séeme altogither to fauor king Edward, we maie beléeue as we list.

The duke of Summerset and the earle of Oxford. Hall. The duke of Summerset, and the earle of Oxford fled in companie of certeine northerne men, which had béene at the battell; and (as some write) the earle of Oxford kept foorth with them, and retired after into Scotland. But yet as well the duke of Summerset, as the said earle of Oxford, in fléeing toward Scotland, changed their purpose vpon the waie, and turned into Wales to Iasper earle of Penbroke. The duke of *The duke of Excester.* Excester being striken downe and sore wounded, was left for dead in the field, amongst other the dead bodies, bicause he was not knowne, and by reason thereof comming to himselfe, got vp, and in great danger escaped vnto Westminster, and there tooke sanctuarie. [But some say, that after hée had lien in the field, spoiled, wounded, and *Abr. Flem.* (to sée to) void of life, from seuen of the clocke in the morning, till foure at after noone, he was caried to a seruants house of his there by (named Ruthland) where (after his wounds were searched and dressed by a surgian) he was conueied into Westminster sanctuarie.]

Edw. Hall. King Edward hauing got this victorie, refreshing himselfe and his people a while at Barnet, returned the same daie vnto London, like a triumphant conqueror, leading with him king Henrie as a captiue prisoner: & so making a solemne entrie at the church of saint Paule, offred his standard. The dead bodies of the earle and marques were brought to London in a coffin, & before they were buried, by the space of thrée daies laie open visaged in the cathedrall church of S. Paule, to the intent that all men might easilie perceiue, that they vnfeinedlie were dead. The common brute ran, that the king was not so ioious of the erles death, as sorowfull for the losse of the marques, whom he full well knew (and no lesse was euident to other) to be his faith

full

full friend and well-willer; for whose onelie sake, he caused both their bodies to be buried with their ancestors in the priorie of Bissam.

On the tuesdaie in Easter wéeke came knowledge to king Edward, that quéene Margaret the wife of king Henrie, with hir sonne prince Edward was landed vpon Easter day at Weimouth in Dorsetshire, accompanied with Iohn Longstrother prior of saint Iohns, commonlie called lord treasuror of England, who went ouer into France to fetch them; also the lord Wenlocke, a man made onelie by king Edward, beside diuerse other knights and esquiers, of whome part had béene long foorth of the realme, and part newlie gone ouer thither to them, in companie of the lord treasuror. They tooke their ships at Hunflue, the foure and twentith of March (as before you haue heard) but through contrarie winds and tempests, they were driuen backe, and constreined to abide for conuenient wind. *Quéene Margaret landeth with a power out of France.*

Now, although it came sometimes about fit for their purpose, yet it continued not long in that end; so as if therevpon they tooke the sea at anie time, they were forced to returne backe againe to land yer they could passe halfe the way ouer. And thus being diuerse times vnder saile, in hope to passe the seas hither into England, they were still driuen backe againe, till the thirtéenth of Aprill being Easter éeuen; on which day the wind comming fauorablie about, they tooke the seas, and sailed forward towards this land. The countesse of Warwike, hauing a ship of aduantage, arriued before the other at Portesmouth, and from thence she went to Southampton, meaning to haue gone to Weimouth, where she vnderstood that the quéene was landed: but here had shee knowledge of the losse of Barnet field, and that hir husband was there slaine. Wherevpon she went no further towards the quéene, but secretlie got hir ouer the water into the new forest, and tooke sanctuarie within the abbeie of Beaulieu. *The countesse of Warwike taketh sanctuarie.*

Quéene Margaret, and hir sonne prince Edward, with the other that landed at Weimouth, went from thence to an abbeie néere by called Ceerne. Thither came vnto them Edmund duke of Summerset, and Thomas Courtneie earle of Deuonshire, with others, and welcommed them into England, comforting the quéene in the best maner they could, and willed hir not to despaire of good successe; for albeit they had lost one field (whereof the queene had knowledge the same day being mondaie in easter wéeke, the fiftéenth of Aprill, and was therefore right sorrowfull) yet they doubted not but to assemble such a puissance (and that verie shortlie) foorth of diuerse parts of the realme, as being faithfull, and wholie bent to spend their liues, and shed the best bloud in their bodies for hir sake, & hir sonnes, it should be hard for king Edward to resist them with all the power he had or could make. *The duke of Summerset, and the earle of Deuonshire cöfort quéene Margaret.*

The presence of these noble men greatlie comforted hir, and relieued hir of the sorrowes that in maner ouerwhelmed hir pensiue heart: for she doubted sore the end of all these procéedings, the which they concluded to follow vpon the aduancement of hir and hirs. Speciallie it misgaue hir, that some euill should chance to hir sonne prince Edward for shee greatlie weied not of hir owne perill (as she hir selfe confessed) and therefore she would gladlie haue had them either to haue deferred the battell till a more conuenient time: or else that hir sonne might haue béene conueied ouer into France againe, there to haue remained in safetie, till the chance of the next battell were tried: but they being of a contrarie mind, and namelie the duke of Summerset, she at length consented vnto that which they were resolued vpon. *Edw. Hall.*

The feare which quéene Margaret had for hir sonne.

Thus euerie man being bent to battell, gathered his power by himselfe, first in Summersetshire, Dorsetshire, and part of Wiltshire, and after in Deuonshire and Cornewall. For the better incouraging of which countries to ioine with them in their quarrell, they repaired to Excester. Here they sent for sir Iohn Arundell, and sir Hugh Courtenie, and manie other in whom they had anie confidence. To be short, they wrought so, that they raised the whole powers of Cornewall and Deuon-

shire.

shire, and with a great armie departing foorth of Excester, they tooke the right waie to Glastenburie, and from thence to Bath, raising the people in all parts where they came: for those countries had bene so laboured, first by the earle of Warwike, and after by the duke of Summerset, and the earle of Deuonshire (which two noble men were reckoned as old inheritors of the same countries) that the people séemed there greatlie inclined to the fauor of king Henrie.

King Edward, being at London, was dailie aduertised by faithfull espials of all the dooings of his aduersaries, and was in no small agonie, bicause he could not learne what waie his enimies ment to take; for he purposed to incounter them in one place or other before they should approch neere to London. And vpon such resolution, with such an armie as he had got about London, furnished with all artillerie and other prouisions necessarie, he set forward the nintéenth of Aprill, and came to Windsor, where he staied a season, as well to celebrate the feast of saint George, as to abide the comming of such bands as he had appointed to repaire thither vnto him, making there his generall assemblie.

K. Edward
setteth forward
against his
enimies.

The enimies to masker him the more, sent foorth their foreriders vnto sundrie townes, both aswell to raise people in the countries about, as to make the king beléeue that their purpose was to passe those waies, where they ment not once to come. And herevpon when they departed from Excester, they sent first their foreriders streight to Shaftesburie, and after to Salisburie, and then they tooke the streight waie to Taunton, Glastenburie, and after to Wels, where houering about in the countrie, they sent another time their foreriders to a towne called Yuell, and to Bruton, as if their meaning had béene to draw towards Reading, and so through Barkeshire, and Oxford-shire to haue marched streight to London, or else to haue set vpon the king at some aduantage, if it were offered.

But king Edward, considering aduisedlie of the matter, perceiued well that they being in an angle of the realme, if they ment to go to London, they must either hold the streight waie foorth by Salisburie, or else drawing vp to the sea side, passe alongst through Hampshire, Sussex and Kent; or happilie if they mistrusted their owne strengths, as not able to match with his puissance, they would then slip on the left hand, and draw towards Chesshire, and Lancashire, there to increase their forces, and peraduenture by the waie to ioine with a power of Welshmen, vnder the leading of Iasper earle of Penbroke, who had béene sent into Wales long afore, to frame and put in a readines the people there to asist king Henries friends at their comming thitherwards. And such was their purpose in deed, for they had great confidence in such aid, as they trusted to haue of the Chesshire and Lancashire men.

King Edward, meaning to approch néerer vnto them, that he might the sooner make waie to stop them of their passage, on which hand soéuer they drew, departed from Windesore the morrow after saint Georges day, being the foure and twentith day of Aprill, kéeping foorth his iournie, till on saturdaie the twentie and seuenth of Aprill he came to Abington, where he laie sundaie all daie. On mondaie he marched forward to Chichester, where he had sure aduertisement, that they intended to be at Bath the next daie being tuesdaie, and on wednesdaie to come forward to giue him battell. Wherevpon king Edward, desirous to sée his people in order of battell, drew them foorth of the towne, and incamped in the field thrée miles distant from thence, still busieng himselfe about his necessarie affaires affoording no time to idlenesse or loiter-ing: for he knew that there was no waie more expedite and readie to tire him in trauell, than to be giuen to negligence and slouth, the two weáriers of well dooing, as the old saieng is:

Desidia pressus erit in studio citó fessus.

On the morrow, hearing no certeintie of their comming forward, he marched to Malmesburie, still seeking to incounter them: but heere he had knowledge, that they
hauing

hauing changed their purpose, meant not to giue him battell; and therefore were turned aside, and gone to Bristow, where they were receiued, reléeued and well refreshed by such as fauoured their cause, as well with vittels, men, and monie, as good store of artillerie. Wherevpon they were so incouraged, that the thursdaie after they tooke the field againe, purposing to giue king Edward battell indéed; and for the same intent had sent their foreriders to a towne, distant from Bristow nine miles, called Sudburie, appointing a ground for their field, a mile from the same towne, toward the kings campe, called Sudburie hill. Sudburie. hill.

The king heereof aduertised, the same thursdaie, being the first of Maie, with his armie faire ranged in order of battell, came towards the place by them appointed for their field: but they came not there. For hearing that king Edward did thus approach vpon a new change of resolution, they left that waie: albeit some of their herbingers were come as farre as Sudburie towne, and there surprised fiue or six of the kings partie, which were rashlie entred that towne, attending onelie to prouide lodgings for their maisters. The lords thus hauing eftsoones changed their purpose, not meaning as yet to fight with the king, directed their waie streight towards Berkelie, trauelling all that night. From Berkelie they marched forward towards Glocester.

The king in the meane time, on the thursdaie in the afternoone, came to the same ground called Sudburie hill, and there staied a certeine space, sending foorth scowriers, to hearken what they might vnderstand of the enimies, whome he tooke to be somewhere at hand. But when he could not heare anie certeintie of them, he aduanced forward, lodging his vant-gard in a vallie beyond the hill, towards the towne of Sudburie, and laie himselfe (with the residue of his people) at the same place, called Sudburie hill. About thrée of the clocke after midnight, he was aduertised, that his enimies had taken their waie by Berkeleie, towards Glocester. Héerevpon, taking aduise of his councell what was best to doo, he was counselled to send some of his seruants with all spéed vnto Glocester, to Richard Beauchampe, sonne and heire to the lord Beauchampe of Powike, to whome he had (before this present) committed the rule and custodie of the towne and castell of Glocester.

The king sent therefore with all spéed vnto him, commanding him to doo his best to defend the towne and castell against his enimies, if they came to assaile the same, as it was supposed they intended: and if they so did, he promised to come with his whole armie presentlie to the rescue. The messengers did their diligence, and so being ioifullie receiued into Glocester, the towne and castell, by the vigilant regard of the said Richard Beauchampe, was put in safe keeping. And this message was doone in good time, for true it is, there were diuerse in the towne, that could haue béene well contented that the quéene, and the lords with hir, should haue béene receiued there, and would haue aduentured to haue brought it to passe, if they had not béene thus preuented.

Againe, the quéene and the lords with hir had good intelligence, with diuerse in the towne, so as they were put in great hope to haue entred the same: wherevpon they trauelled their people right sore all that night and morning, comming before the towne of Glocester vpon the fridaie about tén of the clocke. And when they perceiued that they were disappointed of their purpose, and their entrie flatlie denied, they were highlie therewith displeased; for they knew verie well, that diuerse within the towne bare their good willes towards them: but after they had vsed certeine menacing braueries, and made a shew as if they had meant to assalt the gates and walles, & so to haue entred by force, they departed their waies, marching with all speed possible towards Teukesburie.

It might be maruelled at, whie they attempted not the winning of Glocester indéed, considering the freends which they knew they had within it. But the cause which mooued them cheeflie to forbeare, was, for that as well they without, as the other Glocester whie it was not assaulted.
within

within the towne, knew that king Edward approached at hand, and was readie to set vpon them on the backes, if they had once begun to haue assaulted the towne; and so, neither they within the towne that were the kings freends doubted the enimies forces, nor the enimie indeed durst attempt anie such enterprise against them. About foure of the clocke in the afternoone, they came to Teukesburie, hauing trauelled

A long march. that night last past, and that daie, six and thirtie long miles, in a foule countrie, all in lanes and stonie waies, betwixt woods, without anie good refreshing, so that as well the men as the horsses were right wearie.

And where the more part of their armie consisted of footmen, the capteins could not haue gone anie further, except they would haue left their footmen behind them, and so of necessitie they were driuen to staie there, determining to abide the aduenture that God would send them. For well they knew that the king followed them verie néere at hand, so as if they should haue gone further, and left the most part of their companie behind, as it could not otherwise haue chanced, he would haue béene

The place where the lords in-camped. readie to haue taken the aduantage wholie, so to distresse them. Héerevpon they pight their field in a close, euen hard at the townes end, hauing the towne and the abbeie at their backes; and directlie before them, and vpon each side of them, they were defended with cumbersome lanes, déepe ditches, and manie hedges. beside hils and dales, so as the place séemed as noisome as might be to approach vnto.

The king on this fridaie, verie erlie in the morning, aduanced his standards and in good order of battell hauing diuided his armie into thrée wards, marched through the the plaines of Cotteswold. The daie was verie hot, and hauing in his armie aboue thrée thousand footmen, he trauelled with them and the residue thirtie miles and

The painfull march of king Edward with his armie. more. By all which waie, they could find neither horssemeat, nor mans meat, no not so much as water for their horsses, except one little brooke, of the which they receiued no great reléefe; for what with the horsses and carriages that passed thorough it, the water became so troubled, that it serued them to no vse: and still all that daie king Edward with his armie was within fiue or six miles of his enimies, he in the plaine countrie, and they among the woods.

King Edward had euer good espials, to aduertise him still what his enimies did, and which waie they tooke. At length he came with all his armie vnto a village called

Chiltenham. Chiltenhám, like a fiue miles distant from Teukesburie, where he had certeine knowledge that his enimies were alreadie come to Teukesburie, and were incamped there, purposing to abide him in that place, and to deliuer him battell. King Edward therevpon made no long delaie, but tooke a little refection himselfe, and caused his people to doo the like, with such prouision of vittels as he had appointed to be conueied foorth with him for the releefe of himselfe and his armie. This doone, he set forward towards his enimies, and lodged that night in a field not past thrée miles distant from them.

On the morrow being saturdaie, and fourth of Maie, he drew towards his enimies,

The ordering of king Edwards battell. and marshalled his armie, diuided into thrée battels in this sort. He put his brother the duke of Glocester in the foreward, and himselfe in the midle-ward. The lord Marques, and the lord Hastings led the rere-ward. Heerwith he approached the enimies campe, which was right hard to be assailed, by reason of the deepe ditches, hedges, trées, bushes, and cumbersome lanes, wherewith the same was fensed, both a front, and on the sides, so as the king could not well approach them to anie aduantage: and to be the better in a readinesse to beat backe the kings power, when he should come to assault them, they were imbattelled in this order.

The ordering of the lords hoast. The duke of Summerset, and his brother the lord Iohn of Summerset led the foreward. The middle-ward was gouerned by the prince, vnder the conduct of the lord of saint Iohn, and the lord Wenlocke (whome king Edward had aduanced to the degrée of a baron.) The rere-ward was appointed to the rule of the earle of Deuonshire.

shire. Thus may yée perceiue, that king Edward was put to his shifts, how (to anie aduantage) to assault his enimies. Neuerthelesse, he being well furnished with great artillerie, the same was aptlie lodged to annoie the enimies, that they receiued great da- *The duke of Glocester.* mage thereby; and the duke of Glocester, who lacked no policie, galled them greeuouslie with the shot of arrowes: and they rewarded their aduersaries home againe with like paiment, both with shot of arrowes, and great artillerie, although they had not the like *Teukesburie field.* plentie of guns as the king had. The passages were so cumbersome, that it was not possible to come vpon anie euen hand, to ioine at handblowes.

The duke of Glocester, vpon a politike purpose (as some haue written) reculed backe with all his companie, which when the duke of Summerset perceiued, either mooued therewith, or else bicause he was too sore annoied with the shot in that place *The duke of Summerset.* where he and his fore-ward stood, like a knight more couragious than circumspect, came out of his strength with his whole battell, and aduanced himselfe somewhat aside slips the kings voward, and by certeine passages aforehand, and for that purpose prouided (to the kings part, although vnknowne) he passed a lane, and came into a faire open close right before the king, where he was imbattelled, not doubting but the prince and the lord Wenlocke, with the midle-ward, had followed iust at his backe. But whether the lord Wenlocke dissembled the matter for king Edwards sake, or whether his hart serued him not, still he stood, and gaue the looking on.

The king, or (as other haue) the duke of Glocester, taking the aduantage that he *Edw. Hall.* aduentured for, turned againe face to face vnto the duke of Summerset his battell, and winning the hedge and ditch of him, entred the close, and with great violence put him and his people vp towards the hill from whence they were decended. Héere is to be noted, that when the king was come before his enimies, yer he gaue the onset, he per- ceiued that vpon the right hand of their campe there was a parke, and much store of wood growing therein; and doubting least his aduersaries had laid an ambush within that wood, he chose foorth of his companies two hundred speares, commanding them *The politike foresight of the king.* to kéepe a stale, like a quarter of a mile from the field, to attend vpon that corner of the wood out of the which the ambush, if anie were, was to issue, and to incounter with them, as occasion serued: but if they perceiued that there was no ambush at all, then to imploie their seruice as they should see it expedient and behouefull for the time.

This politike prouision for danger that might haue insued (although there was none that waie foorth) serued yet before the end of the battell, to great good purpose. For when those speares perfectlie vnderstood that there was no ambush within the wood, and withall saw conuenient time to imploie themselues, they came and brake with full randon vpon the duke of Summerset and his voward a flanke, in so violent wise vpon the sudden, that where they had before inough to doo with those with whom *The vatgard of the lords distres- sed.* they were first matched, now with this new charge giuen on them by those two hundred speares, they were not a little dismaied; and to conclude, so discouraged, that streightwaie they tooke them to flight. Some fled into the parke, other into the meadow there at hand, some into the lanes, & some hid them in ditches, each one making what shift he could, by the which he hoped best to escape: but manie neuer- thelesse were beaten downe, slaine, and taken prisoners.

The duke of Summerset séeing this vnfortunate chance, as some write, turned to the midle-ward, and there finding the lord Wenlocke standing still, after he had re- *A terrible stroke.* uiled him, and called him traitor, with his ax he stroke the braines out of his head. The duke of Glocester pursuing after them that fled with the duke of Summerset to their campe, where the rest of their armie stood, entred the trench, and after him the king, where he bare himselfe so knightlie, that therevpon the queenes part went to wracke, and was put to flight; the king and other falling in chase after them, so that manie were slaine, but especiallie at a mill in the meadow fast by the towne a great

sort

scrt were drowned. Manie ran towards the towne, some to the church, and diuerse to the abbeie, and other to other places, where they thought best to saue themselues. [This was the last fought field or pight battell tried betwéene the potentats of this land in king Edward the fourths daies (which chanced on the fourth of Maie, being saturdaie, in the eleauenth yeare of his reigne, and in the year of Lord, 1471) as Anglorum prælia affirmeth, saieng:

Vltima postremæ locus est Teuxburia pugnæ.]

In the winning of the campe, such as stood to it were slaine out of hand. Prince Edward was taken as he fled towards the towne, by sir Richard Crofts, and kept close. In the field and chase were slaine, the lord Iohn of Summerset, called marquesse Dorset, Thomas Courtenie earle of Deuonshire, sir Iohn Delues, sir Edward Hampden, sir Robert Whitingham, and sir Iohn Leukener, with thrée thousand others. After the field was ended, proclamation was made, that whosoeuer could bring foorth prince Edward aliue or dead, should haue an annuitie of a hundred pounds during his life, and the princes life to be saued, if he were brought foorth aliue. Sir Richard Crofts, nothing mistrusting the kings promise, brought foorth his prisoner prince Edward, being a faire and well proportioned yoong gentleman; whom when king Edward had well aduised, he demanded of him, how he durst so presumptuouslie enter into his realme with banner displaied.

Wherevnto the prince boldlie answered, saieng; "To recouer my fathers kingdome & heritage, from his father and grandfather to him and from him after him to me lineallie desended." At which words king Edward said nothing, but with his hand thrust him from him, or (as some saie) stroke him with his gantlet; whome incontinentlie, George duke of Clarence, Richard duke of Glocester, Thomas Greie marquesse Dorcet, and William lord Hastings that stood by, suddenlie murthered: for the which cruell act, the more part of the dooers in their latter daies dranke of the like cup, by the righteous iustice and due punishment of God. His bodie was homelie interred with the other simple corpses, in the church of the monasterie of blacke monks in Teukesburie.

After the victorie was thus atchiued, the king repaired to the abbeie church there, to giue God thanks for that good successe, which it had pleased him to blesse him with: and there finding a great number of his enimies, that were fled thither to saue themselues, he gaue them all his free pardon; albeit there was no franchise there for rebels, but that he might haue commanded them to haue béene drawen foorth without breach of anie liberties of that church. He granted also that the dead bodies, as well of the lords as other, slaine in that battell, might be buried in the same church, or else where it pleased their friends or seruants, without anie quartering & heading, or setting vp heads or quarters in any publike places. O the patience and clemencie of this good king, who (besides the putting vp of wrongs doone to him by violence of foes without vengeance) fréelie forgaue the offendors, and did so honorablie temper his affections!]

There were found in the abbeie and other places of the towne, Edmund duke of Summerset, Iohn Lonstrother lord prior of S. Iohn, sir Thomas Tressham, sir Gerueis Clifton, and diuerse other knights and esquiers, which were apprehended, and all of them being brought before the duke of Glocester, sitting as constable of England, and the duke of Norffolke, as marshall in the middest of the towne, they were arreigned, condemned, and iudged to die; and so vpon the tuesdaie, being the seuenth of Maie, the said duke and the lord prior, with the two forenamed knights, and twelue other knights, were on a scaffold, set vp in the middle of the towne for that purpose, beheaded, and permitted to be buried, without anie other dismembring, or setting vp of their heads in anie one place or other.

The same tuesdaie, the king departed from Teukesburie towards Worcester, and by the waie had knowledge that quéene Margaret was found in a poore house of religion,

not

Marginal notes:

Abr. Flem.

Edw. Hall. Prince Edward taken. Nobles slaine.

Sir Richard Crofts deliuereth the prince in hope that his life should haue béene saued.

Prince Edward murthered.

The duke of Summerset & others beheaded.

not far from thence, into the which she was withdrawen for safegard of hir selfe, on Quéene Margaret taken.
saturdaie in the morning, being the daie of the battell. She was after brought to
London as prisoner, and so kept, till hir father ransomed hir with great summes of
monie, which he borowed of Lewes the eleuenth king of France. And bicause he
was not able to make repaiment thereof, he sold vnto the said Lewes (as the French
writers affirme) the kingdomes of Naples, and both the Sicils, with the countie of
Prouance. King Edward being at Worcester, had aduertisements brought foorth of
the north parts, that the people there were about to assemble in armour against him,
in fauour of king Henrie: wherevpon he left the right way to London, and rode to
Couentrie, meaning to increase the number of his people, and so with a puissant
armie to go northwards.

Herevpon, comming to Couentrie the eleuenth of Maie, and remaining there thrée
daies, he well refreshed such as had béene with him at Teukesburie field. Hither was
brought to him queene Margaret, from whence she was conueied to London, there to
remaine in safe keeping (as before you haue hard.) Whilest he was busie in sending
abroad vnto his friends to leauie an armie, he was aduertised that the commotion in
the north was pacified. For after it was knowen abroad, how he obteined the victorie,
as well at Teukesburie, as at Barnet, and in manner subdued all his enimies, the capteins that had stirred the people to that rebellion, began to quaile, and forsooke their
companies.

Diuerse of them made sute to the earle of Northumberland, that it might please
him to be a mediator to the king for their pardon; so that now, there was no rebel-
lion in all the north parts, but that as well the citie of Yorke, as all other places, were Rebellion in the north pacified.
at the kings commandement, readie in all things to obei him as true and loiall subiects.
And this was confirmed by the earle of Northumberlands owne mouth, who on the The earle of Northumberland.
fouretéenth of Maie came to the king, as yet remaining at Couentrie: by reason
whereof it was not thought néedfull, that the king should trauell anie further northward at that time, either about the pacifieng of the people, or to see execution doone
vpon the offendors, sith all was there in good tranquillitie and quiet.

But now when all things séemed to be at rest, and no rebellion after so happie vic
tories doubted, newes came to him before his cōming to Couentrie, from the lords of
his bloud, abiding at London, that one Thomas Neuill, bastard sonne to that valiant
capteine the lord Thomas Fauconbridge (who had latelie before beene sent to the sea Thomas Neuill bastard Faucon-bridge
by the earle of Warwike, and after fallen to practise pirasie) had spoiled diuerse mer-
chants ships, Portingals and others, in breach of the ancient amitie that long had continued betwixt the realms of England and Portingale; and furthermore, had now got
to him a great number of mariners, out of all parts of the land, and manie traitors
and misgouerned people from each quarter of the realme, beside diuerse also foorth
of other countries that delighted in theft and robberies, meaning to worke some exploit against the king.

And verelie, his puissance increased dailie, for hauing béene at Calis, and brought
from thence into Kent manie euill disposed persons, he began to gather his power in
that countrie, meaning (as was thought) to attempt some great and wicked enter-
prise. After the kings comming to Couentrie, he receiued aduertisements, that this The bastard Fauconbridge before London with an armie.
bastard was come before London, with manie thousands of men by land, and also in
ships by water, purposing to rob and spoile the citie. Manie Kentishmen were willing to assist him in this mischieuous enterprise, and other were forced against their
wils to go with him, or else to aid him with their substance and monie, insomuch that
within a short time, he had got togither sixtéene or seuentene thousand men, as they
accomted themselues.

With these he came before the citie of London the twelfe of Maie, in the quarrell (as
he pretended) of king Henrie, whom he also meant to haue out of the Tower, & to restore him againe vnto his crowne & roiall dignitie. And for that intent, he required

to enter the citie with his people, that receiuing king Henrie foorth of the Tower, they might passe with him through the citie, and so to march streight towards king Edward, whose destruction they vowed to pursue, with all their vttermost indeuors. But the maior and aldermen of the citie would not in anie wise agree to satisfie their request herein, vtterlie refusing to receiue him or anie of his companie into the citie.

King Edward from time to time by posts was informed of all these dooings, & by aduise of his councell, the foureteenth of Maie, sent to the succors of the maior and aldermen fiftéene hundred of the choisest souldiers he had about him, that they might helpe to resist the enimies, till he had got such an armie togither as was thought necessarie, meaning with all conuenient spéed to come therewith to the rescue of the citie, and preseruation of the quéene, prince, and his daughters, that were within the Tower, not in verie good safegard, considering the euill dispositions of manie within the citie of London, that for the fauour they had borne to the earle of Warwike, and desire to be partakers of the spoile, cared not if the bastard might haue atteined to his full purpose and wished intent.

On the sixtenth of Maie, king Edward set foorth of Couentrie towards London. But here ye haue to vnderstand, that when the bastard could not be receiued into the citie, neither by gentle persuasions, nor gréeuous threatnings, he made semblance to passe ouer the Thames at Kingston bridge, ten miles from London, and thitherwards

he drew with his whole power by land, leauing his ships afore saint Katharines and thereabouts. His pretense was, to spoile and destroie Westminster, and the suburbs of the citie on that side, and after to assault the citie it selfe, to trie if he might enter by force, and so be reuenged of the citizens that had refused to receiue him. [Notwithstanding all which stirring of coles & proud port, with haughtinesse of hart & violence of hand thinking to beare downe the people, as an inundation or flowing of water streams dooth all before it: yet he came short of his purpose, and pulled vpon his owne pate finall destruction: though he thought himselfe a man ordeined to glorie, & was tickled with the like flatring persuasion that one had in his hart, who said:

Magnum iter ascendo, sed dat mihi gloria vires.]

Now as he was onwards vpon his iornie, he was aduertised, that king Edward was preparing to come forwards against him, assisted in manner with all the great lords of the realme, and others in great number, more than he had béene at anie time before. By reason whereof, doubting what might follow, if passing the riuer he should fortune so to be inclosed, that he should be driuen thereby to incounter with the kings power at such ods, he thought it best to alter his purpose; and so returning, came backe againe before London, & mustered his people in S. Georges field, ranged and placed in one entier battell.

And to the intent they might worke their purposed feat, before the kings comming to the rescue, they resolued with all their forces to assault the citie, and to enter it if they could by plaine strength, that putting it to the sacke, they might conueie the riches to their ships, which laie in the riuer betwixt saint Katharins and Blackewall, neere to Ratcliffe. Herevpon hauing brought certeine peeces of artillerie foorth of their ships, they planted the same alongst the water side, right ouer against the citie, and shot off lustilie, to annoie them within so much as was possible.

But the citizens on the other side lodged their great artillerie against their aduersaries, and with violent shot therof so galled them, that they durst not abide in anie place alongst the water side, but were driuen euen from their owne ordinance. Yet the bastard not meaning to leaue anie waie vnassaied that might aduance his purpose, appointed a great number of his retinue to set fire on the bridge, so to open the passage, and to enter into the citie that way forth; and withall, he caused aboue thrée thousand other to passe by ships ouer the Thames; giuing order, that when they were got ouer, they should diuide themselues into two battels, the one to assault Algate, and the other Bishops gate, which order accordinglie was executed.

For

For they did their best at both places to force the gates, not sparing to bend and Algate and Bishops gate assaulted. discharge such guns as they had brought with them against the same, nor ceassing with arrowes to annoie those that there stood at defense: whereby much hurt was doone, as well at the one place as the other, fire being set on both the gates, in purpose to haue burnt them vp, and so to haue entered. The fire which they had kindled Houses burnt on the bridge. on the bridge little auailed them, although they burnt there to the number of a thréescore houses. For the citizens had laid such péeces of ordinance directlie in their waie, that although the passage had béene wholie open, they should haue had hard entering that waie foorth. The maior, aldermen, and other worshipfull citizens were in good arraie, and each man appointed and bestowed where was thought néedfull.

The earle of Essex, and manie knights, esquiers, and gentlemen, with their fréends and seruants, came to aid the citizens, taking great paine to place them in order, for defense of the gates and walles: and furthermore, deuised how and in what sort they might make a sallie foorth vpon the enimies to distresse them: and suerlie, by the intermingling of such gentlemen and lords seruants in euerie part with the citizens, they were greatlie incouraged to withstand their enimies. Yet the rebels, vnder the leading of one Spising, bare themselues so stoutlie at Algate, that they wan the bulworks there, and droue the citizens backe within the portculice, & entered with them, to the number of six or eight: but some of them were slaine with the fall of the portculice that was let downe vpon them, to kéepe the residue out, and those that were entered within the gate were suddenlie dispatched.

Héerewith they lashed fréelie the one part at the other with guns and bowes, although no great hurt was doone with shot; till at length Robert Basset alderman The valiancie of Robert Basset alderman. (that was appointed to the kéeping of this gate, with the most part of the citizens, and the recorder, named Ursewike, either of them being well armed in strong iackes, commanded the portculice to be drawen vp, and maintenantlie rushed foorth vpon their enimies, putting them backe vnto saint Bothulpes church. At the same instant, the earle Riuers, hauing got togither a foure or fiue hundred men, well chosen and apparelled for the warre, issued foorth at the posterne by the Tower, and assailing the Kentishmen, euen vpon the point as they were thus put backe, mightilie laid vpon them.

And first he plaged them with the swift and thicke flight of his arrowes, and after ioining with them at handstrokes, slue and tooke manie of them prisoners; so that the rebels were fullie put to flight, and followed first to Mile-end, and from thense some vnto Poplar, some to Stratford, and Stepnith, and in maner each waie foorth about that part of the citie, the chase being followed for the space of two miles in length. Manie of them were of Essex, and so made their course homewards; but the more part of them fled to the water side, and getting to their ships, passed ouer the Thames to the rest of their companie. The other likewise that were busie to assault Bishops gate, when they vnderstood that their fellowes were discomfited and fled from Algate, they likewise slipped awaie, and made the best shift they could to saue themselues.

There were a seauen hundred of them that fled from Algate, and other places, slaine outright, beside the prisoners. And yet there were fiers burning all at once at Algate, Bishops gate, & on the bridge, and manie houses consumed with the same fiers. But now the bastard, vnder whome that companie was directed that had set fire on the bridge, when he saw that he might not preuaile, and vnderstood the euill succes of those which he had set ouer the Thames, he withdrew also, and left the bridge. Here the hardie manhood of Rafe Iosselin alderman Rafe Iosselin, is not to be passed with silence; who (after he had valiantlie resisted the bastard & his band that assaulted the bridge) vpon their retire sallied foorth vpon them, and following

T t 2

lowing

lowing them in chase alongst the water side, till they came beyond Ratcliffe, slue and tooke verie manie of them.

The bastard incampeth on Blackeheath.

The bastard notwithstanding gathered his companies togither, and with such as were willing to remaine with him incamped on Blackeheath, by the space of thrée daies next insuing, to wit, the sixteenth, seauentéenth, and eightéenth of Maie, vtterlie despairing of his wished preie, sith he had béene repelled from London, to his vtter confusion. And now to conclude, hearing that king Edward was comming with a right puissant armie, the said bastard and his people durst no longer abide; but brake vp and dispersed themselues, some one waie, and some an other. They of Calis got them thither againe with all spéed, and such as were of other countries repaired likewise to their homes, and manie of the Kentishmen went also to their houses. The bastard with his mariners, and such riotous rebels, robbers, and wicked persons, as sought nothing but spoile, got them to shipboord, and with all their vessels drew downe to the coast.

King Edward, hauing assembled an armie of thirtie thousand men (as some write) and accompanied in maner with all the great lords of England, came to London the one and twentith of Maie, being tuesdaie, where he was honourablie receiued by the maior, aldermen, and other worshipfull citizens: where euen vpon their first meeting with him he dubbed diuerse of them knights; as the maior, the recorder, & other aldermen, and worshipfull commoners of the citie, which had manfullie and valiantlie acquit themselues against the bastard Fauconbridge & his wicked companie of rebels. Moreouer, here is to be remembred, that poore king Henrie the sixt, a little before depriued (as ye haue heard) of his realme and imperiall crowne, was now in the Tower

Edw. Hall. King Henrie the sixt murthered in the Tower.

spoiled of his life, by Richard duke of Glocester (as the constant fame ran) who (to the intent that his brother king Edward might reigne in more suertie) murthered the said king Henrie with a dagger.

Howbeit, some writers of that time, fauoring altogither the house of Yorke, haue recorded, that after he vnderstood what losses had chanced vnto his fréends, and how not onelie his sonne, but also all other his chéefe partakers were dead and dispatched, he tooke it so to hart, that of pure displeasure, indignation, and melancholie, he died the three and twentith of Maie. The dead corps on the Ascension euen was conueied

The nine and twentith of Maie.

with billes and glaues pompouslie (if you will call that a funerall pompe) from the Tower to the church of saint Paule, and there laid on a beire or coffen bare faced, the same in presence of the beholders did bléed; where it rested the space of one whole daie. From thense he was caried to the Blackfriers, and bled there likewise: and on the next daie after, it was conueied in a boat, without priest or clerke, torch or taper, singing or saieng, vnto the monasterie of Chertseie, distant from London fiftéene miles, and there was it first buried: but after, it was remooued to Windesor, and there in a new vawt, newlie intoomed. He reigned eight and thirtie yeares, six moneths and od daies, and after his readeption of the crowne six moneths. He liued two and fiftie yeares, hauing by wife one onelie sonne, called Edward, prince of Wales.

He was of a séemelie stature, of bodie slender, to which proportion all other members were answerable; his face beautifull, wherein continuallie was resident the bountie of mind with the which he was inwardlie indued. Of his owne naturall inclination he abhorred all the vices as well of the bodie as of the soule. His patience was such that of all the iniuries to him doone (which were innumerable) he neuer asked vengeance, thinking that for such aduersitie as chanced to him, his sinnes should be forgotten and forgiuen. What losses soeuer happened vnto him, he neuer esteemed, nor made anie account therof; but if anie thing were doone, that might sound as an offense towards God, he sore lamented, and with great repentance sorowed for it.

So then verie vnlike it is, that he died of anie wrath, indignation, and displeasure bicause

bicause his businesse about the kéeping of the crowne on his head tooke no better successe: except peraduenture ye will saie, that it gréeued him, for that such slaughters and mischéeues as had chanced within this land, came to passe onelie through his follie and default in gouernment: or (that more is) for his fathers, his grandfathers, and his owne vniust vsurping and deteining of the crowne. But howsoeuer it was, for these before remembred, and other the like properties of reputed holinesse, which was said to rest in him, it pleased God to worke miracles for him in his life time as men haue listed to report.

By reason whereof, king Henrie the seauenth sued to Pope Iulio the second, to haue Canonizing of kings, déere. him canonized a saint. But for that the canonizing of a king séemed to be more costlie than for a bishop, the said king left off his sute in that behalfe; thinking better to saue his monie, than to purchase a new holie daie of saint Henrie with so *Abr. Fl. ex I. S. pag.* 730, 731, &c. great a price, remitting to God the iudgement of his will and intent. ¶ But bicause princes princelie qualified, can not be too highlie praised, I will here record a collection of his commendable conditions, dooings, and saiengs, as I find them set downe to my hand, to his perpetuall renowme; and right worthie of imitation. not onelie of such as are singled out from among infinite thousands, to be magnified with roialtie; but also of priuat and meane men that conuerse and liue one with an other in the world.

This king hauing inioied as great prosperitie as fauourable fortune could afoord, & as great troubles on the other side as she frowning could powre out; yet in both the states he was patient and vertuous, that he maie be a patterne of most perfect vertue, as he was a worthie example of fortunes inconstancie. He was plaine, vpright, farre from fraud, wholie giuen to praier, reading of scriptures, and almesdeeds; of such integritie of life, that the bishop which had béene his confessour ten yeares, auouched that he had not all that time committed anie mortall crime: so continent, as suspicion of vnchast life neuer touched him: and hauing in Christmasse a shew of yoong women with their bare breasts laid out presented before him, he immediatlie departed with these words: "Fie, fie, for shame; forsooth you be too blame."

Before his marriage, he liked not that women should enter his chamber, and for this respect he committed his two brethren by the moothers side, Iasper and Edmund to most honest & vertuous prelats to be brought vp. So farre he was from couetousnesse, that when the executors of his vncle the bishop of Winchester, surnamed the rich cardinall, would haue giuen him two thousand pounds, he plainelie refused it, willing them to discharge the will of the departed, and would scarselie condescend at length to accept the same summe of monie toward the indowing of his colleges in Cambridge & Eaton. He was religiouslie affected (as the time then was) that at principall holidaies, he would weare sackecloth next his skin. Oth he vsed none, but in most earnest matters these words: Forsooth and forsooth.

He was so pitifull, that when he saw the quarter of a traitor against his crowne ouer Criplegate, he willed it to be taken awaie, with these words: "I will not haue anie christian so cruellie handled for my sake." Manie great offenses he willinglie pardoned and receiuing at a time a great blow by a wicked man which compassed his death, he onelie said; "Forsooth forsooth, yée doo fowlie to smite a king annointed so." An other also which thrust him into the side with a sword when he was prisoner in the Tower, was by him pardoned when he was restored to his state and kingdome. Not long before his death, being demanded whie he had so long held the crowne of England vniustlie; he replied: "My father was king of England, quietlie inioieng the crowne all his reigne: and his father my grandsire was also king of England, and I euen a child in my cradell was proclamed and crowned king without anie interruption; and so held it fortie yeares well-neere, all the states dooing homage vnto me, as to my antecessors: wherefore I maie saie with king Dauid; The lot is fallen vnto me in a
faire

faire ground; yea, I haue a goodlie heritage, my helpe is from the Lord which saueth the vpright in heart."

The kings colledge in Cambridge.

This good king being of himselfe alwaies naturallie inclined to doo good, and fearing least he might séeme vnthankefull to almightie God for his great benefits bestowed vpon him, since the time he first tooke vpon him the regiment of his realme, determined about the six and twentith yeare of his reigne, for his primer notable worke (as by the words of his will I find expressed) to erect and found two famous colledges in the honor and worship of his holy name, and for the increase of vertue, the dilatation of cunning, and establishment of christian faith, whereof the one in Cambridge to be called his colledge roiall of our ladie and saint Nicholas: and the other at Eaton beside Windsore, to be called his colledge of our blessed ladie.

And for the performance of this his deuout purpose, he infeoffed certeine bishops, with other noble and worshipfull personages, by his letters patents, with lands and possessions, parcell of his inheritance of the duchie of Lancaster, to the cleare value of well néere foure & thirtie hundred pounds by yéere. Which letters patents he after confirmed by his act of parlement, declaring also by his will vnto his said feoffées, his intent and meaning, how the same shuld be imploied vpon the edifications of his said two colledges. Whereof (in my iudgement) the deuise is so excellent, and the buildings so princelie and apt for that purpose, as I cannot omit to set foorth vnto you the verie plot of the whole colledge in Cambridge, euen as I find mentioned almost verbatim in his will, supposing that if the rest of the house had procéeded according to the chappell alreadie finished (as his full intent and meaning was) the like colledge could scant haue béene found againe in anie christian land. The words of the will are thus.

The chappell.

As touching the dimensions of the church of my said colledge of our ladie and S. Nicholas of Cambridge, I haue deuised and appointed, that the same church shall conteine in length 288 foot of assise, without anie Iles, and all of the widenesse of

The bodie of the church.
The quiere.

fortie foot. And the length of the same church from the west end vnto the altars at the quiere doore, shall conteine an hundred and twentie foot. And from the prouosts stall, vnto the gréece called Gradus chori ninetie foot; for thirtie six stalles on either side of the same quiere, answering to threescore and ten fellowes, and ten priests conducts, which must be De prima forma. And from the said stalles vnto the east end of the said church, threescore & two foot of assise. Also a reredosse bearing the

The roodloft.

roodloft, departing the quiere and the bodie of the church conteining in length fortie foot, and in breadth fourtéene foot. The walles of the same church to be in

The height of the chappell.
The east window.

height ninetie foot imbattelled, vawted and charerooffed, sufficientlie butteraced, and euerie butterace fined with finials. And in the east end of the same church, shall be a window of nine daies, and betwixt euerie butterace a window of fiue daies.

The side chappels.

And betwixt euerie of the same butteraces in the bodie of the church, on both sides of the same church, a closet with an altar therein, conteining in length twentie foot, and in breadth ten foot, vawted and finished vnder the soile of the Ile windowes. And the pauement of the church to be inhanced foure foot and aboue the ground without. And the height of the pauement of the quiere one foot and an halfe aboue the pauement of the church. And the pauement of the altar thrée foot aboue that. And on the

The vestrie.

north side of the quiere a vestrie conteining in length fiftie foot, and in breadth twentie and two foot, departed into two houses beneath, & two houses aboue, which shall conteine in height twentie two foot in all, with an entrie from the quiere vawted.

The cloister.

And at the west end of the church a cloister square, the east pane conteining in length an hundred seuentie and fiue foot, and the west pane as much. The north pane two hundred foot, and the south pane as much, of the which the deambulatorie thirtéene foot wide, and in height twentie foot to the corbill table, with cleare stories

and

and butteraces with finials, vawted & imbattelled. And the ground thereof foure foot lower than the church ground.

And in the middle of the west pane of the cloister a strong tower square, contein- The steeple. ing foure and twentie foot within the walles. And in the height one hundred and twentie foot to the corbill table. And foure small turrets ouer that fined with pinacles. And a doore into the said cloister inward, but outward none. And as touching the dimensions of the housing of the said colledge, I haue deuised and The base court. appointed in the southside of the said church a quadrant, closing to both ends of the same church; the east pane whereof shall conteine two hundred and thirtie foot in length, and in breadth within the walles two and twentie foot. In the same panes The east pane. middle, a tower for a gatehouse, conteining in length thirtie foot, and in breadth two and twentie, and in height thréescore foot, with thrée chambers ouer the gate, euerie one ouer the other. And on either side of the same gate foure chambers, euerie one The great gate. conteining in length fiue & twentie foot, and in bredth two and twentie foot. And ouer euerie of these chambers, two chambers aboue of the same measure or more, with two towers outward, and two towers inward.

The south pane shall conteine in length two hundred thirtie and eight foot, and The south pane. in breadth two and twentie foot within, in which shalbe seuen chambers, euerie one conteining in length nine and twentie foot, and in breadth twentie and two, with a chamber parcell of the prouosts lodging, conteining in length thirtie and fiue foot, and with a chamber in the east corner of the same pane, conteining in length twentie and fiue foot, and in breadth thirtie and two foot. And ouer euerie of all these chambers, two chambers, and with fiue towers outward, and thrée towers inward. The west pane The west pane. shall conteine in length two hundred and thirtie foot, and in breadth within twentie & foure foot, in which at the end toward the church shall be a librarie, conteining in The librarie. length an hundred and ten foot, and in breadth twentie and foure foot. And vnder it a large house for reading and disputations, conteining in length eleuen foot. And The disputation two chambers vnder the same librarie, each conteining twentie and nine foot in house. length, and in breadth foure and twentie foot.

And ouer the said librarie a house of the same largenesse, for diuerse stuffe of the The wardrobe. said colledge. In the other end of the same pane a hall, conteining in length an hun- The hall. dred foot, vpon a vawt of twelue foot high, ordeined for the cellar and butterie: and the breadth of the hall six and thirtie foot. On euerie side thereof a baie window. And in the nether end of the same hall toward the middle of the same pane, a pan- The pantrie and trie & butterie, euerie of them in length twentie foot, and in breadth seuentéene foot. butterie. And ouer that two chambers for officers. And at the nether end of the hall toward The colledge the west, a goodlie kitchin. And the same pane shall haue inward two towers, ordei- kitchin. ned for the waies into the hall and librarie. And in euerie corner of the said quadrant, shall be two corner towers, one inward, and one outward, more than the towers aboue rehearsed.

And at the vpper end of the hall, the prouosts lodging, that is to wit, more than The prouosts the chambers for him aboue specified, a parlour on the ground, conteining six and lodging. thirtie foot in length, and two and twentie foot in breadth, & two chambers aboue of the same quantitie. And westward closing thereto a kitchin for him, a larderhouse, stables, and other necessarie housings and ground. And westward beyond these houses, and the said kitchin ordeined for the hall, a bakehouse, brewhouse, and other houses of office: betwixt which there is left a ground square of fourscore foot in euerie pane The bakhouse for wood and such stuffe. And in the middle of the said large quadrant, shall be a conduit, and brewhouse. goodlie deuised for the ease of the same colledge. And I will, that the edification The woodyard. proceed in large forme of my said colledge cleane and substantiall, setting apart conduit. The water superfluitie of so great curious workes of intaile and busie moulding.

And I haue deuised and appointed that the precinct of my said colledge, as well on

both

The precinct of the colledge. both sides of the garden from the colledge to the water, as in all other places of the same precinct, be inclosed with s substantiall wall, of the height of fourtéene foot, with a large tower at the principall entrie against the middle of the east pane, out of the *The water gate.* high stréet. And in the same tower a large gate, and another tower in the middle of the west end at the new bridge. And the same wall to be creasted, imbattelled, and fortified with towers, as manie as shall be thought conuenient therevnto. And I will that my said colledge be edified of most substantiall & best abiding stuffe, of stone, lead, glasse, and iron, that maie best be had and prouided thereto. ¶ Thus much I haue inlarged by occasion of reading this good kings will: the cunning deuise where-of I leaue to the considerate iudgement of such as be expert in architecture, heartilie desiring almightie God to put into the heart of some noble prince of this land, one day to make perfect this roiall worke so charitablie begun.]

But now to returne to king Edward. Ye shall vnderstand, that after his comming to London, hée rested there but one daie, or two at the most, taking his iournie foorth-right into Kent with all his armie, folowing the bastard, and other his complices, to supppresse them, if they were in anie place assembled againe to resist him. But after they were once dispersed, they durst not shew themselues againe in armor, those onlie *Sandwich kept by the rebels.* excepted that were withdrawne vnto Sandwich with the bastard; which for the more part were mariners, about eight or nine hundred, beside certeine other euill disposed persons, that accompanied him as his souldiers, and men of warre, with whose as-sistance the bastard kept that towne by strength, hauing in the hauen seuen and fortie ships great and small, vnder his gouernance.

The rebels sue to r pardon. But vpon the kings approching néere vnto those parties, they sent to him for pardon, promising that vpon a reasonable appointment, for the safegard of their liues, and other indemnities to be had for their benefit, they would become his faithfull subiects, and deliuer into his hands all the ships. Their offer the king vpon great considera-tions, and by good deliberate aduise of counsell, thought best to accept: and therevpon (being at that time in Canturburie) hée granted to their petitions, and sent immediat-lie vnto Sandwich his brother Richard duke of Glocester, to receiue them to mercie, togither with all the ships, which according to their promise they deliuered into his hands.

But notwithstanding that (as some write) the bastard Fauconbridge, and other of his companie that were got to Sandwich, had thus their pardons by composition at the kings hand; we find neuerthelesse, that the said bastard Fauconbridge, being afterwards *The bastard of Fauconbridge beheaded.* at sea (a rouing belike, as he had vsed before) came at length into the open hauen at Southhampton, and there taking land, was apprehended, and shortlie after beheaded. This chanced (as should appeare by Fabian) about the latter end of October. More-*Roger Vaughan taken and be-headed.* ouer, Roger Vaughan that had béene sent by king Edward into Wales, anon after Teukesburie field (being a man of great power in that countrie) to intrap and surprise by some secret sleight the earle of Penbroke, the said earle being thereof aduertised, tooke the same Roger, and without delay stroke off his head.

After this, was the earle besieged in the towne of Penbroke by Morgan Thomas; *Dauid Thomas.* but the siege was raised by Dauid Thomas, brother to the said Morgan, a faithfull friend to the earle; and then the earle by his helpe was conueied to Tinbie, where hé *The earle of Penbroke with his nephue the earle of Rich-mond passe ouer into Britaine.* got ships, and with his nephue the lord Henrie earle of Richmond sailed into Britaine. where, of the duke they were courteouslie interteined; with assurance made, that no creature should doo them anie wrong or iniurie within his dominions. King Edward visiting diuerse places in Kent, sate in iudgement on such as had aided the bastard in the last commotion, of whome diuerse were condemned and executed, as Spising one of the capteins that assaulted Algate, whose head was set vp ouer the same gate: and *Execution.* so likewise was the head of one Quintine, a butcher, that was an other capteine amongest them, and chiefe of those that assaulted Bishops gate, as some write.

Moreouer

Moreouer, at Canturburie the maior of that citie was executed, and diuerse other at Rochester, Maidston and Blackeheath : for the lord marshall and other iudges, being appointed to hold their oier and determiner in that countrie of Kent, there were aboue an hundred indicted and condemned.   Diuerse also of Essex men that had béene partakers in this rebellion with the bastard, & holpe to set fire on Bishops gate and Algate, were hanged betwixt Stratford and London.   Manie also of the wealthie commons in Kent were put to grieuous fines.

Now when the king had made an end of his businesse in that countrie, he returned to London, comming thither againe vpon Whitsun éeuen, being the first of Iune. *Fabian.* And hauing thus within the space of eleuen wéekes recouered in maner the whole possession of his realme, being relieued of the most part of all his doubtfull feare, he ment to remooue all stops out of the waie.   Wherefore he sent the archbishop of The archbishop of Yorke. Yorke, brother to the earle of Warwike, and to the marques Montacute ouer to Guisnes, there to be kept in safe custodie within the castell, where he continued a long season, till at length he was by friendship deliuered, and shortlie after (through verie anguish of mind) departed this life; whome Laurence Bath, and after him Thomas Rotheram in the sée of Yorke, did ordinarilie succeed.   Beside this, Iohn earle of The earle of Oxford, which after Barnet field both manfullie and valiantlie kept saint Michaels Oxford. mount in Cornewall, either for lacke of aid, or persuaded by his friends, gaue vp the mount, and yeelded himselfe to king Edward (his life onelie saued) which to him was granted.   But to be out of all doutfull imaginations, king Edward also sent him ouer the sea to the castell of Hammes, where, by the space of twelue yeeres hée was in   1472 strong prison shut vp and warilie looked to.

King Edward was not a litle disquieted in mind, for that the earls of Penbroke & An. Reg. 12. Richmond were not onlie escaped out of the realme, but also well receiued and no woorsse interteined of the duke of Britaine : he sent therefore in secret wise graue & Messengers sent close messengers to the said duke, the which should not sticke to promise the duke great to the duke of Britaine. and rich rewards, so that he would deliuer both the earles into their hands and possession. The duke, after he had heard them that were sent, made this answer, that he could not with his honor deliuer them, to whome he had giuen his faith to sée them preserued from all iniurie : but this (he said) he would doo for the king of England, that they should be so looked vnto, as he néeded not to doubt of any attempt to be made against him by them, or by their meanes.

The king receiuing this answer, wrote louinglie to the duke of Britaine that he would consider his fréendship with conuenient rewards, if it should please him to be as good as his promise.   The duke, perceiuing gaine comming by the abode of the two English earles in his countrie, caused them to be separated in sunder, and all their seruants being Englishmen to be sequestred from them, and in their places appointed Britains to attend them.   In the thirtéenth yeare of his reigne, king Edward called   1473 his high court of parlement at his palace of Westminster, in the which all lawes and An. Reg. 13. ordinances made by him before that daie were confirmed, and those that king Henrie A parlement. had abrogated, after his readeption of the crowne, were againe reuiued.   Also lawes were made for the confiscation of traitors goods, and for the restoring of them that were for his sake fled the realme, which of his aduersaries had béene atteinted of high treason, and condemned to die.

Moreouer, towards his charges of late susteined, a competent summe of monie was A subsidie. demanded, and fréelie granted.   There was also a pardon granted almost for all A pardon. offenses ; and all men then being within the realme, were released and discharged of all high treasons and crimes, although they had taken part with his aduersaries against him.   In this season the duke of Burgognie had sore wars with the French king; and Ambassadors to be the more spéedelie reuenged on his aduersarie, he sent ambassadors into England, to from the duke of persuade king Edward to make warre also on the French king, for the recouerie of his B..rgognie.

ancient

ancient right to the realme of France, by the same French king against all equitie withholden and deteined. In which atttempt of his, there was some fauour of discréet policie, and a prouident forecast for his greater safetie, besides the likelie possibilitie to obteine that whereto he made chalenge: sith the huger hosts (if the hardier hearts) are of most force, according to that saieng:

Virtus vnita fortior.

And therefore, by procuring the king of Englands power to ioine with his, he supposed his purpose atchiueable with the more facilitie. King Edward not so much for the loue he bare to the duke of Burgognie, as for desire to be reuenged on the French king, whome he tooke to be his enimie for aiding the earle of Warwike, quéene Margaret, and hir sonne prince Edward, with their complices, gaue good eare to the duke of Burgognie his messengers, and finallie (after he had taken aduise of his councell) the said messengers were answered, that king Edward in the beginning of the next yeare would land at Calis with a puissant armie, both to reuenge such iniuries as he had receiued at the French kings hands, and also to recouer his right, which he wrongfullie deteined from him.

Opportunitie not to be neglected. In déed the time serued verie well for the Englishmen to atchiue some high enterprise in France at that present. For not onelie the duke of Burgognie as then made warre against the French king, but also manie great men within the realme of France, misliking the manners of their king, began to haue secret intelligence with the said The earle of S. Paule. duke; and namelie Lewes of Lutzenburgh earle of saint Paule constable of France was secretlie confederate with the duke of Burgognie, intending verelie to bring the French king to some great hinderance, the better to haue his purpose accomplished in certeine weightie matters. King Edward vnderstanding all these things, was greatlie incouraged to make a iournie into France, and therevpon with all diligence prepared all things readie for the same.

But bicause he wanted monie, and could not well charge his commons with a new subsidie, for that he had receiued the last yeare great summes of monie granted to him A shift to recouer monie. by parlement, he deuised this shift, to call afore him a great number of the wealthiest sort of people in his realme; and to them declaring his néed, and the requisite causes thereof, he demanded of euerie of them some portion of monie, which they sticked not to giue. And therefore the king willing to shew that this their liberalitie was verie acceptable to him, he called this grant of monie, A beneuolence: notwithstanding that manie with grudge gaue great sums toward that new found aid which of them might be called, A meleuolence. But the king vsed such gentle fashions toward them, with freendlie praier of their assistance in his necessitie, that they could not otherwise doo, but franklie and fréelie yeeld and giue him a reasonable and competent summe.

Abr. Flem. ex Edw. Hall. fol. Ccxxvj. ¶ But here I will not let passe a pretie conceipt that happened in this gathering, in the which you shall not onelie note the humilitie of a king, but more the fantasie of a woman. King Edward had called before him a widow, much abounding in substance, and no lesse growne in yeares, of whome he merilie demanded what she gladlie would giue him toward his great charges? By my trueth quoth she, for thy louelie countenance thou shalt haue euen twentie pounds. The king looking scarse for the halfe of that summe, thanked hir, and louinglie kist hir. Whether the flauor of his breath did so comfort hir stomach, or she esteemed the kisse of a king so pretious a iewell, she swore incontinentlie, that he should haue twentie pounds more, which she *Iohn Stow.* with the same will paied that she offered it. ¶ This yeare the duke of Excester was found dead in the sea betwéene Douer and Calis, but how he came there the certeintie could not be knowne.]

1474
An. Reg. 14. When all things conuenient for such an enterprise were in a readinesse, the king came to Douer, where he found fiue hundred ships and hoies readie to transport him

and

and his armie. And so the fourth daie of Iulie he passed ouer, and landed at Calis with *The K. with an armie passeth ouer into France.* great triumph; but his armie, horsses, and munitions of war scarse passed ouer in twentie daies. In this armie (being one of the best appointed that had passed out of England into France in manie yeares before) were fifteene hundred men of armes well horssed, of the which the most part were barded and richlie trapped, and manie of them trimmed in one sute. There were also fiftéene thousand archers with bowes and arrowes, of the which a great number were on horsbacke. There were also a great companie of other fighting men, and of such as serued to set vp tents and pauilions, to attend the artillerie and to inclose their campe, and otherwise to labour and be imploied in seruice.

In all this armie was there not one page. The king of England was at his ariuall highlie displeased with the duke of Burgognie, who in the word of a prince had promised to meet him at his landing, with two thousand men of armes and light horssemen, besides a great number of lanceknights and halberdiers, and that he would haue begun the war three moneths before the kings transporting; whereas contrarilie the duke laie lingering at the siege of Nusse, and let passe the occasion of atchiuing *The siege of Nusse.* a more profitable enterprise. King Edward incontinentlie dispatched the lord Scales *The lord Scales.* in post vnto the duke, to put him in remembrance of his promise, and to aduise him to come and ioine with him before the summer were spent.

Before king Edward departed from Douer, he sent an officer of armes vnto the French king with a defiance. The French king, receiuing the king of Englands letters *A defiance sent to the French king.* at the messengers hand, read the same; and after he had considered thereof at leasure, he called the English herald aside, and to him declared the little trust that was to be put in the duke of Burgognie and the constable, by whose procurement he knew that king Edward was procured to come at that season into France; and therefore it should be better for him to haue peace with an old enimie, than to staie vpon the promises and familiaritie of a new dissembling freend, which peace did highlie please God, & was the thing that he most desired. ¶ But to giue the greater grace to the matter in *Abr. Fl. ex Edw. Hall. fol. Ccxxvij.* hand, it is good to laie downe the forme of the French kings spéech to the said herald, to whome he vttered these words in his wardrobe, as Edward Hall reporteth.

" Sir I know and well wot, that the king of England your maister, is neither decended in these parts of his owne frée motion, nor yet of vs required; but onelie entised and prouoked by the duke of Burgognie, and somewhat inforced by the commons of his realme. But now you may sée that the season of the yeare passeth, and the duke of Burgognie is in poore estate, returning from Nusse almost discomforted. The constable also, with whome the king your souereigne lord (I am sure) hath some intelligence, for fauour that your maister hath maried his néece, is not so sure a freend as he is taken for. And if all the world knew how I haue promoted him, and what I haue doone for him, they would little thinke, that he would so vntrulie handle me as he dooth. For I assure you, he is a déepe dissembler, & in continuall dissimulation intendeth to lead his life, interteining all men for his owne profit. And although the king your maister be vnsure of all his other promises, yet of one thing he shall be sure, that is, he shall be euer dissembled withall. And therefore I saie to you, and not to your maister, that he were better haue a peace with an old enimie, than the promises and familiaritie of a new dissembling fréend, which peace most pleaseth God, and is the thing that I most doo desire."]

When he had thus said, he gaue the herald thrée hundred crownes, promising him a thousand crownes if anie good appointment came to passe. This herald was borne *The office of an herald.* in Normandie, who being more couetous of the crownes than secret (according as of dutie by his office he ought to haue beene) promised to doo all things that in him laie, and further shewed waies by the which the French king might enter into the port of treatie for peace, the which he doubted not would sort to a good conclusion. The

U u 2
French

French king glad to heare these things, gaue to the herald when he should depart, beside the other reward, a péece of Crimson veluet of thirtie yards long. The lord Scales, comming to the duke of Burgognie before Nusse, could not persuade him to raise his field, and (as it stood him vpon) to come and ioine with king Edward, till

The duke of Burgognie commeth to king Edward.

at length constreined thereto by other means, he left Nusse vnconquered and sending the most part of his armie into Lorraine, came with a small companie to king Edward lieng before Calis.

King Edward at the first comming of the duke vnto him, séemed much to reprooue his vnwise dealing, in making so slow hast to ioine with him at this time, sith for his sake, and at his sute, he had passed the seas with his armie, to the intent to make wars in France in reuenge of both their iniuries; the time seruing their turnes so well as they could wish or desire, the opportunitie whereof could neuer happilie be recouered againe. The duke after he had excused himselfe, with alledging the dishonour that should haue redounded to him, if he had left the siege of Nusse without meane of some shew of composition, incouraged king Edward to aduance forward with manie golden promises, aswell of his owne part, as of the constable. The king agréed to the dukes persuasion, and so set forward.

But yet when he was entred into the dukes countries, the Englishmen were not so freendlie interteined as they looked to haue béene: for at their comming to Peronne, there were but a few suffered to enter the gates, the remnant were driuen to lodge in the fields, better purueied of their owne, than of the dukes prouision. And at their

The constable of France a déepe dissembler.

comming before saint Quintines (which towne the constable had promised to deliuer into the hands of the duke of Burgognie) the artillerie shot off, and they of the towne came foorth both on horssebacke and foot to skirmish with them that approached, of the which two or three were slaine. This interteinment seemed strange to king Edward, pondering the last daies promise with this daies dooing. But the duke excused the matter, and would haue persuaded him to make countenance to besiege the towne, that the constable might haue a colour to render it into his hands, as though he did it by constraint.

But the king, remembring what had béene told to his herald by the French K. how he should be dissembled with, perceiued the French kings words to be too true, and therefore thought it more sure to heare the faire words of the constable and the duke, than to giue credit to their vntrue and deceitfull dooings. The Englishmen re-

The duke of Burgoguie departeth.

turned vnto their campe in a great chafe towards the constable; and the next daie to increase their displeasure, an other corosiue was ministred, that smarted sorer. For duke Charles of Burgognie tooke his leaue suddenlie of king Edward, alledging that he must néeds see his armie in Artois, promising shortlie with all his puissance to returne againe to the great commoditie of them both. This departing much troubled the king of England, bicause he looked for no such thing; but thought rather that he should haue had the duke his continuall fellow in armes: and therefore this dissembling and vnstedfast working caused the king to thinke that he neuer thought, and to doo tha the neuer intended.

The French king in this meane while had assembled a mightie power; ouer the which he had made monsieur Robert de Estoutuile capteine, whome he sent to Artois, to defend the frontiers there against the king of Englands entrie, and he himselfe tarried still at Senlis: but though he shewed countenance thus of warre, yet inwardlie desirous of peace, according to the aduise giuen him by the English herald, he caused a varlet or yeoman (as I may call him) to be put in a coat of armour of France, which for hast was made of a trumpet baner. For king Lewes was a man nothing precise in outward shewes of honor, oftentimes hauing neither officer of armes, trumpet in his court, nor other roiall appurtenances belonging to the port of a prince, which should be glorious and replenished with pompe, as the poet saith:

Regia mirifici fulgent insignia regis.

This

This counterfeit herald, being throughlie instructed in his charge, was sent to the A messenger sent to the king of England. king of England, and so passing foorth: when he approched the English campe, he put on his coat of armes, & being espied of the outriders, was brought to a tent, where the lord Howard and the lord Stanleie were at dinner, of whome he was courteouslie receiued, and by them conueied to the kings presence, vnto whom he declared his message so wittilie, that in the end he obteined a safe conduct for one hundred horsses, for such persons as his maister should appoint to meet, as manie to be assigned by king Edward in some indifferent place betwéene both armies, to haue a like safe conduct from his said maister, as he receiued from him. ¶ The words of which herald are *Abr. Fl. ex Edw. Hall. fol.* Ccxxix, ccxxx. woorth the noting, reported in writers as followeth.

The heralds oration to the king vttered with boldnesse of face and libertie of toong.

RIGHT high and mightie prince, right puissant and noble king, if your excellent wisedome did perfectlie know, or your high knowledge did apparantlie perceiue, what inward affection and feruent desire the king my maister hath alwaies had, to haue a perfect peace, a sure vnitie, & a brotherlie concord betweene your noble person and your realme, and his honorable personage and his dominions, you would & (for truths sake) should confesse and saie, that neuer christian prince more thirsted for an amitie, nor yet no louer hath more sought to atteine to the fauour of his para mor, than he hath sought to haue with you a perpetuall freendship, amitie, and aliance: to the intent that the subiects of both the relms, quietlie liuing vnder two princes, confederate and combined togither in an indissoluble confederacie and league, may mutuallie imbrace ech other in their harts, may personallie haue resort and frequent each others princes territories and dominions, with their merchandizes and wares: and finallie, the one to liue with the other, as freend with freend, brother with brother, companion with companion, in continuall loue, rest, and tranquilitie. And for his part he dooth affirme & saie, that since he receiued first the crowne of his kingdome, and was annointed with the holie ampull, he neuer attempted, nor yet once imagined anie war, or thing preiudiciall toward yout roiall person, your realme, or your people.

If you peraduenture will saie, that he supported & mainteined the earle of Warwike against your maiestie, he suerlie that dooth & will denie: for he aided him against the duke of Burgognié, whome he knew not onelie to be his extreame enimie, but also to laie in wait (both by sea and land) either to take him, or vtterlie to destroie him. Which duke of Burgognie, onelie for his owne cause, hath excited and solicited your highnesse to come ouer the troublous and tempestuous seas, to the intent to cause (yea in maner to compell) the king my master, to condescend to such treatie and appointment, as should be to his onlie profit, and neither to your honour, nor yet to your gaine. For if he & such other as dailie flattered him for their peculiar profits (as he had manie in deed that dailie sucked at his elbow) had once obteined the thing that they breathed for, all your affaires were put in obliuion, and left at large for them, or their assistants, euen as they be at this daie. Hath not the duke of Burgognie caused you first to come into France; after to set forward your armie; and in conclusion, for lacke of his promise, to loose the faire season of the yeare, and to lie in the fields in winter. Which warre (if it continue) shall neither be profitable to you, nor to your nobilitie, nor yet pleasant but painefull to your communaltie: and finallie to both the realmes, and especiallie to merchant men shall bring both miserie, pouertie, and calamitie.

Came the duke of Burgognie from Nusse to Calis, onlie to visit you? Rode he all that post hast onelie to blind you? Returned he backe into Loraine againe for anie cause but

but onelie to leaue you desolate, & to abandon you? Did he or the constable keepe anie one promise with you? Why doo you then beleeue, and yet still trust them, in whome you neuer found faith nor fidelitie? Bnt if God will it so ordeine, that you and my master may ioine in league and amitie, I dare both saie and sweare, that the fine steele neuer cleaued faster to the adamant stone than he will sticke & claspe with you, both in wealth and wo, in prosperitie and aduersitie. And if it shall please you, to harken to anie reasonable treatie, I being a poore man, shall (on ieopardie of my life which is my chiefe treasure) vndertake, that this communication shall sort and come to such an effect, that both you & your nobilitie shall be glad and reioise, and your commons shall be contented and pleased; and they that haue deceiued you, shall be both abashed and ashamed. Most humblie beseeching your highnesse, if your pleasure shall incline this waie, that I may haue a sure safe conduct for one hundred horsses, for such personages as the king my master shall send vnto you with further intimation of his mind and purpose. And if your pleasure shall be to haue the communication in anie place indifferent betweene both the armies, then shall I warrant you the like safe conduct for your men, as you doo send for ours.

When he had accomplished his message and instructions, the king of England and his councell highlie commended his audacitie, his toong, and his sobernesse, giuing to him in reward a faire gilt cup, with a hundred angels: deliuering him a safe conduct according to his request and demand, with the which he with speed departed, hauing with him an English herald to bring a like safe conduct from the French king.]

After that the safe conducts were deliuered on both parts, the ambassadours met at a village beside Amiens. On the king of Englands side, the lord Howard; sir Thomas Saintleger; doctor Morton after bishop of Elie, & chancellor of England, were cheefe. For the French king, the bastard of Burbon admerall of France; the lord Saint Pierre; & the bishop of Eureux called Heberge, were appointed as principall. The Englishmen demanded the whole realme of France, or at the least Normandie and whole Aquitaine. The allegations were proued by the Englishmen, and politikelie defended by the Frenchmen, so that with arguments, without conclusion, the day passed, and the commissioners departed, and made relation to their maisters. The French king and his councell would not consent, that the Englishmen should haue one foot of land within France; but rather determined to put him selfe & the whole realme in hazard and aduenture.

At the next meeting the commissioners agreed vpon certeine articles, which were of both the princes accepted and allowed. It was first accorded, that the French king should paie to the king of England without delaie seauentie & fiue thousand crownes of the sunne; and yearelie fiftie thousand crownes to be paid at London during king Edwards life. And further it was agreed, that Charles the Dolphin should marrie the ladie Elizabeth, eldest daughter to king Edward, and they two to haue for the maintenance of their estates the whole duchie of Guien, or else fiftie thousand crownes yearelie to be paid within the Tower of London by the space of nine yeares; and at the end of that terme, the Dolphin and his wife to haue the whole duchie of Guien, and of the charge the French king to be cleerelie acquit. And it was also concluded, that the two princes should come to an interview, and there take a corporall oth for the performance of this peace, either in sight of other.

On the king of Englands part were comprised as alies (if they would thereto assent) the dukes of Burgognie and Britaine. It was also couenanted, that after the whole summe aforesaid of seuentie and fiue thousand crownes were paid to king Edward, he should leaue in hostage the lord Howard, and sir Iohn Cheinie maister of his horsse, vntill he with all his armie was passed the seas. This agreement was verie acceptable to the French king; for he saw himselfe and his realme thereby deliuered of great

　　　　　　　　　　　　　　　　　　　　　　　　　　　　　　　　　　　perill

perill that was at hand: for not onelie he should haue béene assailed (if this peace had not taken place) both by the power of England and Burgognie, but also by the duke of Britaine, and diuerse of his owne people, as the constable and others. The king of England also vnderstanding his owne state, for want of monie, to mainteine the warres, if they should long continue (though otherwise he desired to haue attempted some high enterprise against the Frenchmen) was the more easilie induced to agrée by those of his councell, that loued peace better than warre, and their wiues soft beds better than hard armor and a stonie lodging.

But the duke of Glocester & others, whose swords thirsted for French bloud, cried out on this peace; saieng that all their trauell, paines, & expenses were to their shame lost and cast awaie, and nothing gained but a continuall mocke [and dailie derision of the French king and all his minions. This imagination tooke effect without delaie. For a gentleman of the French kings chamber, after the peace was concluded, did demand of an Englishman, how manie battels king Edward had vanquisht? He answered, nine: wherein he himselfe personallie had béene. "A great honoure" said the Frenchman. "But I praie you (quoth he smiling) how manie hath he lost?" The Englishman perceiuing what he meant, said: "one, which you by policie, and by no strength, haue caused him to loose."

The duke of Glocester an enimie to peace. *Abr. Fl. ex Edw. Hall. fol.* Ccxxxj.

"Well" said the Frenchman, "you maie ponder in a paire of balance, the gaine of nine gotten battels, and the rebuke of this one in this maner lost: for I tell you, that we haue this saieng; the force of England hath and dooth surmount the force of France: but the ingenious wits of the Frenchmen excell the dull braines of Englishmen. For in all battels you haue béene the gainers, but in leagues and treaties our wits haue made you loosers: so that you maie content your selues with the losse in treaties, for the spoile that you gat in warres and battels." This communication was reported to the French king, who priuilie sent for the Englishman to supper, and not onlie made him good cheere, but also gaue him a thousand crownes, to praise the peace and to helpe to mainteine the same. Yet neuerthelesse, he being not a little mooued with these brags, declared all the communication to the duke of Glocester; who sware, that he would neuer haue set foot out of England, if he had not thought to haue made the Frenchmen once to assaie the strength & puissance of the Englishmen: but what so euer he thought, all things were transferred vnto an other end than he could imagine.]

When the duke of Burgognie heard that there was a peace in hand betwixt king Edward and the French king, he came in no small hast from Lutzenburg, onelie accompanied with sixteene horsses into the king of Englands lodging, and began as one in a great chafe sore to blame his dooings, declaring in plaine termes how dishonorable this peace should be vnto him, hauing atchiued nothing of that about the which he came. The king of England, after he had giuen him leaue to speake his fansie, answered him somewhat roundlie againe, openlie reproouing him for his promise-breaking and vncourteous dealing with him: where for his cause cheeflie he had passed the seas, and now found him not to keepe touch in anie one point which he had couenanted. ¶ But to adde more weight to the matter in hand, sith it was so seriouslie debated betwéene the two potentats, let vs heare what talke historiens report to haue béene interchanged betwéene them. The king of England (saith mine author) not a little abashed both at the dukes sudden comming, and his fierce countenance, like one that would rather bite than whine, demanded of him the cause of his sudden comming. The duke sharpelie answered, to know whether he had either entered into anie communication, or onelie had absolutelie concluded a peace betwéene the French king and him. King Edward declared how that for sundrie and diuerse great and yrgent causes, touching as well the vniuersall publike wealth of the whole christianitie, as their

The duke of Burgognie commeth in hast to the king of England.

Abr. Fl. ex Edw. Hall. fol. Ccxxxj.

their owne priuate commoditie and the quietnesse of their realmes, he and the French king had concluded a peace and amitie for terme of nine years, in the which were comprised, as fellowes and fréends, both he and the duke of Britaine, requiring him to condescend and agrée to the same.

" Oh Lord, oh saint George (quoth the duke of Burgognie) haue you thus doone in deed? Haue you passed the seas, entered into France, and without killing of a poore flie, or burning of a séelie shéepecote, and haue taken a shamefull truce? Did your noble ancestor, K. Edward the third, euer make armie into France (as he made manie) in the which he did not either gaine victorie in battell, or profit in conquering cities, townes, and countries? That victorious prince, as neere kin to me, as you to king Henrie the fift, I meane whose bloud you haue either rightfullie or wrongfullie (God knoweth) extinguished & destroied, with a small puissance entered into France, conquered whole Normandie, and not alonelie conquered it, but peaceablie kept it, and neuer would either commen or agrée to anie league, vntill he had the whole realme of France offered him; & was thereof made regent and heire apparant. And you without anie thing dooing, or anie honour or profit gaining, haue condescended to a peace, both as honourable and as profitable to you as a peasecod, and not so wholesome as a pomegranat. Think you that I either mooued you, or once intised you to take this iournie for my peculiar aduantage or commoditie (which of my power am able to reuenge mine owne causes, without helpe of others) but onelie to haue you recouer your old rights and possessions, which were from you both tortiouslie and wrongfullie withholden? And to the intent that you shall know that I haue no néed of your aid, I will neither enter into your league, nor take truce with the French king, till you be passed the sea, and haue béene there thrée moneths.

When duke Charles had thus said, he furiouslie threw downe his chaire, and would haue departed. But the king him staid and said: " Brother Charles, sith you haue spoken at leasure what you would, you must and shall heare again what you would not. And first, as concerning our entrie into France, no man liuing knoweth that occasion, neither so well, nor hath cause halfe so well to remember it as you: for if you haue not fullie put your greatest things (to be had in memorie) in your box of obliuion, you be not yet out of mind how the French king, for all your power, tooke from you the faire towne of Amiens, and the strong pile of saint Quintins, with diuerse other townes, which you neither durst nor yet were able either to rescue or defend. Since which time, how he hath plagued you, how he hath taken from you your fréends; yea, of your priuie chamber and secret councell (by whome all your secrets be to him reuealed and made open) yon know or haue better cause to remember, and not to forget them. And when you determined to besiege the towne of Nusse, you thought your selfe in a great doubt, whether you should loose more at home by your absence (the French king dreaming and waiting like a fox for his preie) or gaine more in Germanie by your power and presence. And to kéepe the woolfe from the fold, that is, the French king from your castels and dominions, was the chéefe and principall cause whie you so faire praid me, so sore laboured and intised me to passe ouer the sea, promising mounteins of gold, which turned into snow and wasted into water, boasting and craking to send horssemen and footmen; and yet shewing neither lackie nor page. If we had made our enterprise for our selfe solie and in our owne quarell, thinke you that we would haue expected your comming? If the aduenture had béene for to haue recouered our right, imagine you that we would haue passed the sea so slenderlie as we did, looking for your aid? Nay, nay, you should haue well knowen, if we had intended a conquest, that we would haue so stronglie inuaded & set on the realme of France, that what with sauour of burning of townes, and infection of the aier, corrupted by the multitude of dead carcases of our slaine enimies, your countries of Flanders & Brabant should haue had causes enow to wonder at: trusting that that
which

which we had gotten, we would haue kept as well as anie of our ancestors haue doone.

" But bicause the verie occasion of the warre was yours, and that you wilfullie (I will not saie cowardlie) did not prosecute the same, the French king, who neuer offended me nor my subiects (except in mainteining the earle of Warwike, for the displeasure that you bare him against me) offered me, being destitute of all your succour and aid, both honourable and honest ouertures of peace, which offers I was in maner inforced (by verie reason) to incline to and accept, and so haue concluded a truce, which (God willing) I will both keepe and obserue." " God send you ioy" (quoth the duke) and so abruptlie ended his talke for that time.]

Heerwith (being in a great rage) he bad the king of England farewell, and suddenlie tooke his horsse, and rode againe to Lutzenburgh, promising not to enter into anie league with the French king, till king Edward was passed the seas againe into England, and had béene there thrée moneths: but this promise was not performed, for of necessitie he tooke a wiser waie, and agréed with the French king vpon a truce immediatly after the departure of the English armie out of his countrie. The constable of France also, doubting that his vntruth would be disclosed to his destruction, by means of this agréement betwéene the kings of England and France, as soone as he heard they were entred into communication thereof, sent to king Edward, requiring him not to credit the French kings promises, which he would no longer obserue, than vntill he should once vnderstand, that he was on the other side of the sea: and rather than he should agrée for want of monie, he offered to lend him fiftie thousand crownes. But the king of England, sith the accord was passed and agréed, would not change anie thing for the promises of so slipper a merchant as he knew the constable to be.

¶ Then was the constable in maner on all sides in despaire, but yet he wrote to the French king by his messengers, beséeching him to giue no credit or beléefe to anie tale told or fained against him, without hearing his answer, affirming that the king had alwaies knowen his truth and fidelitie toward the crowne of France, and so should he still find him till his dieng daie; promising and warranting him, if that it should stand with his pleasure, that he would so compasse the duke of Burgognie, that they two should vtterlie destroie the king of England and his armie yer they returned. The councellors of the French king made answer, that their master and the king of England were ioined and confedered in a sure amitie. Wherfore they would in no wise know nor condescend to anie thing that might be either preiudiciall, or once sound to the detriment of the Englishmen: but they said, that the king their master much trusted the constable, and that for his sake he would talke with them in his priuie chamber. The French king, before their entrie into his chamber, caused the lord of Contaie, seruant vnto the duke of Burgognie, accompanied with the lord of Argenton, one of his priuie councell, to stand secretlie behind a séeling or hanging in his chamber, & he himselfe sat in a chaire directlie before that place, so that what soeuer were purposed to him, they standing behind the cloth, might plainlie sée and easilie heare the same.

Lewes de Creuell and his fellow entered into the kings chamber, of nothing thinking lesse than of the spirits inclosed. They declared what paine their master had taken for the French kings sake, to send, mooue and entise the duke of Burgognie to leaue, and cléerelie to forsake the king of England, which duke they found in such a rage and furie against the Englishmen, that at their request he was not onelie vtterlie determined to forsake and refuse their amitie, but also would send out aduenturers and lanceknights, to rob and spoile them in their returning. And in speaking these words (thinking suerlie much to please the king) the said Lewes counterfeited the fashion and gesture of the duke of Burgognie, and began to stampe with his foot on the ground, and beat with his fist on the table, swearing by saint George that

He departeth from the king in a rage.

The constable of France his offer to K. Edward.

Abr. Fl. ex Edw. Hall. fol. Ccxxxij, Ccxxxiij.

Shamefull &
slanderous words
against the K.
of England.
the king of England was not extracted of anie noble house, but was a yeomans sonne; and that when he was not woorth one halfepenie, he was restored to his kingdome, and made king onelie by his aid, reprouing and reuiling him with such ill words, and so shamefull termes, that all the hearers abhorred it.

The French king, faining that he was thicke of hearing, caused him to reiterate his saieng againe, who so counterfeited the verie gesture of the dukes angrie countenance and roring voice, that no man hath séene a better counterfeitor or actor in anie comedie or tragedie. The lord of Contaie was sore displeased to sée his master made a iesting stocke; but he kept all these things secret, till his returne to his master. When the pageant was plaied, the king bad the messengers of the constable to haue him commended to his brother their master; and to declare to him that as newes rose & grew, he would therof aduertise him, & so gaue them licence to depart to their master, who thought himselfe now to be in great suertie of his estate, when in déed he was neuer so neere his fall and perdition: estéeming the duke of Burgognie to be his assured fréend, who hated him more than a Painime or Turke, accompting also the French king to haue no ill suspicion in him, who neither trusted nor yet beléeued anie word, writing or message that was either written or sent from him. Such end hath dissimulation, such fruit springeth of double dealing and craftie conueieng. For if either the constable had béene faithfull to the king his master, as of bounden dutie and allegiance he ought to be, or else had kept his promise made to the king of England and duke of Burgognie, and not dallied and dissembled with them, he had suerlie in his extremitie béene aided, succoured and comforted of one of these three at the least; where now he was of all three forsaken, and yet not forsaken, but sought for, looked for, and watched for; not for his profit or promotion, but for his vndooing and destruction: whereof he was the principall procurer, as manie a one besides; wherto tbe poet had an eie, when he made this outcrie of inward gréefe seasoned with sorrow and repentance:

Heu patior telis vulnera facta meis.]

After the peace was concluded, the Englishmen were permitted to enter into the towne of Amiens, and there to buie all such necessarie things as they wanted, and had plentie of wine (for the French king had sent into their armie a hundred carts of the best wine that could be gotten) and good cheere made them of his owne costs. For at the enterie of euerie gate, there were two long tables set on euerie side of the street where they should passe; and at euerie table fiue or six gentlemen of the best companions of all the countrie were appointed to interteine the Englishmen as they
*Abr. Flem. ex
Edw. Hall.
fol.* Ccxxxiij.
entered, not onelie to sée them serued without lacking [but also to drinke and make good cheere, and kéepe companie with them. And euer as they entered into the towne, they were taken by the bridels and in maner inforced to drinke, wheresoeuer they came they paied no monie, but were sent scot free.] This chéere lasted thrée or foure daies not onelie to the French kings cost, but also to his vnquietnesse at length, doubting to haue béene dispossessed of his towne.

For on a daie there entered the number of nine thousand Englishmen well armed in sundrie companies, so that no Frenchman durst once forbid them to enter. But finallie, order was taken by the king of England, who meant no deceit, that no greater number should enter than was conuenient, and the other were called backe; so that the French king and his councell were well quieted, and rid of casting further perils than néed required. After this, both the kings enteruiewed togither at Picquenie on the water of Some thrée leagues aboue Amiens, shewing great courtesie either to
The enterview
betwixt king
Edward the
fourth, & the
French king.
other. The letters of both their agréements were opened and red, & then either prince laid his right hand on the missall, and his left hand on the holie crosse (as it was termed) and tooke there a solemne oth to obserue and kéepe the treatie for nine yeares concluded betwéene them, with all their confederates and alies, comprised,

men-

mentioned and specified in the same, and further to accomplish the marriage or their children.

There was with either prince twelue noble men at this méeting, which was vpon a bridge cast ouer the water of Some, a grate being set ouerthwart the same in the midst, so from side to side, that the one prince could not come vnto the other; but onelie to imbrace ech other, in putting their armes through the holes of the * grate. There were foure Englishmen appointed to stand with the Frenchmen on the bridge to sée their demeanour; and likewise foure Frenchmen were appointed to the Englishmen for the same purpose. There were with the king of England his brother the duke of Clarence, the earle of Northumberland, the bishop of Elie his chancellor, the lord Hastings his chamberleine, and eight others. They had louing and verie familiar talke togither a good space, both afore their companie, and secretlie alone, whilest their companie (of courtesie) withdrew somewhat backe.

   ¶ But it is noteworthie which I read touching both the kings méeting, the manner of their attire, and demeanour; namelie that when the token of méeting by the shot of the artillerie was knowne, the French king with twelue noble men entered the bridge, and came to the closure, with whome was Iohn duke of Burbon, and the cardinal his brother, a prelat more méet for a ladies carpet, than for an ecclesiasticall pulpit, and ten other, amongst whome the lord of Argenton was in like disguised attire as the French king ware, for so was his pleasure that daie to haue him adorned. The king of England and foure other with him were apparelled in cloth of gold frised, hauing on his bonet of blacke veluet a flower delice of gold, set with verie rich and orient stones; he was a goodlie faire and beautifull prince, beginning a litle to grow in flesh. Now when he approched néere the grate, hée tooke off his cap, and made a low and solemne obeisance: the French king made to him an humble reuerence; but after his fashion somewhat homelie. King Lewes imbraced king Edward through the barriers, saieng: "Coosine you be right heartilie welcome into these parties, assuring you that there is no man in the world that I haue more desired to sée and speake with, than with you: and now lauded be almightie God, we be here met togither for a good and godlie purpose, whereof I doubt not but that we shall haue cause to reioise." The king of England thanked him, and answered to his words so soberlie, so grauelie, and so princelie, that the Frenchmen thereat not a litle mused. The chancellor of England made there a solemne oration in laud and praise of peace, concluding on a prophesie, which said that at Picquenie should be concluded a peace both honorable and profitable to the realmes of England and France.

When the oth was taken and sworne (as before you haue heard) the French king said merilie to king Edward; "Brother, if you will take pains to come to Paris, you shall be feasted and interteined with ladies; and I shall appoint you the cardinall of Burbon for your confessor, which shall gladlie absolue you of such sinnes, if anie be commited." The king of England tooke these words pleasantlie and thankfullie, for he was informed that the cardinall was a good companion, and a chapleine méet for such a dalieng pastime. When this communication was merilie ended, the French king, intending to shewe himselfe like a maister amongst his seruants, made all his companie to draw backe from him, meaning to commune with the king of England secretlie. The Englishmen withdrew them without any commandement. Then the two kings communed alone secretlie, I thinke not to the profit of the constable of France. The French king demanded of king Edward, whether the duke of Burgognie would accept the truce? King Edward answered that he would once againe make an offer; and then vpon the refusall, he would referre and report the truth to them both. Then king Lewes began to speake of the duke of Britaine, whome he would faine haue excepted out of the league. To whome the king of England answered: Brother, I require you to mooue no warre to the duke of Britaine;

Marginal notes:

* Of timber like to the grate where the lions be kept in the Tower.

Abr. Fl. ex Edw. Hall. fol. Ccxxxiiij.

The manerlie English and vamanerlie French.

taine; for on my fidelitie, in the time of my néed and aduersitie, I neuer found a more friendlie, sure and stedfast louer than he.

Then king Lewes called his companie againe, and with most lowlie and amiable commendations tooke his leaue of the king of England, speaking certeine friendlie words to euerie Englishman: king Edward dooing likewise to the Frenchmen. Then both at one time departed from the barriers, & mounted on horssebacke, and departed; the French king to Amiens, and king Edward to his armie. To whom was sent out of the French kings house, all things necessarie for a prince, insomuch that neither torches nor torchets lacked vnsent. When the French king was departed from Picquenie, he called to him the lord Argenton, saieng: " By the peace of God, the king of England is an amorous and a faire prince, he at the first becke would gladlie see Paris, where he might fortune to find such pleasant and talkatiue dames, which with faire words & pleasant pastimes might so allure him to their fantasies, that it might breed occasion in him to come ouer the sea againe, which I would not gladlie see. For his progenitors haue beene too long and too often both in Paris and Nor-

French loue. mandie. On this side the sea I loue neither his sight nor his companie; but when he is at home I loue him as my brother, and take him as my friend."

The French king, after this departing, sore desired to make warre on the duke of Britaine: which he could not doo, except he were left out of the treatie. Wherefore he sent the lord of Bouchage, and the lord of saint Pierre, to the king of England, intreating him by all waies and motions possible, to leaue the duke of Britaine for his alie, and not to haue him comprehended in the league. The king of England hearing them so seriouslie and so feruentlie speake against the duke of Britaine; with an earnest countenance answered, saieng: " My lords, I assure you, if I were peaceablie at home in my realme, yet for the defense of the duke of Britaine and his countrie, I would passe the seas againe, against all them that either would doo him iniurie, or make warre vpon him." The French lords nothing further saieng, much maruelled why the king of England so suerlie claue to the duke of Britains partie: but they knew not (or else at the least remembred not) that Henrie earle of Richmond was within the power and dominion of the duke of Britaine, whome king Edwards phantasie euer gaue him would make once a title to the crowne of England, as next heire to the house of Lancaster. For he knew well, that if the duke of Britaine would transport him into England (where hée had both kinsfolks and friends) with neuer so small an aid (yea, though it were but the shadow of an armie) then were he inforced newlie to begin againe a conquest, as though he had neuer woone the crowne, nor obteined the possession of the realme, which was the verie cause why he stucke so sore to the duke of Britains part.

The same night the lords returned to Amiens, and reported to their maister king Edwards answer, who therewith was not the best pleased. But pleasure or displeasure, there was no remedie but to dissemble the matter, This same night also, there came the lord Howard, and two other of the king of Englands councell, who had béene coadiutors toward the peace, to the French king to supper. The lord Howard said to the French king secretlie in his eare, that if it stood with his pleasure, he could persuade the king of England to come to Amiens, yea, peraduenture as farre as Paris, familiarlie and friendlie to solace himselfe with him, as his trustie friend and faithfull brother. The French king, to whom this motion was nothing pleasant, calling for water, washed, and rose without anie answer making: but he said to one of his councell, that he imagined in his owne conceipt, that this request would be made. The Englishmen began againe to commune of that matter, the Frenchmen politikelie brake their communication, saieng: that the king with all celeritie must march forward against the duke of Burgognie.

Although this motion séemed onelie to increase loue and continuall amitie betwéene
the

the princes; yet the Frenchmen, hauing in their perfect remembrance the innumerable damages and hurts, which they of late daies had susteined by the English nation (whereby continuall hatred increased against them in France) thought by policie and wisedome, with faire words and friendlie countenance, to put by this request, and to motion them rather to depart homeward, than to pricke them forward to Paris; where peraduenture they might be so interteined at this time, that they would at another come thither, both vndesired and vnwelcomed. This peace was said to be made onelie by the Holie-ghost, bicause that on the daie of méeting, a white dooue sat on the top of the king of Englands tent: whether she sate there to drie hir, or came thither as a token giuen by God, I referre it to your iudgment. At this treatie and méeting was not the duke of Glocester, nor other lords which were not content with this truce, but the duke came afterwards to Amiens, with diuerse other lords of England, to the French king, which both highlie feasted them, and also presented them with plate and horsses well garnished.

King Lewes, considering what gaine the Englishmen had gotten by making warre in France; and what miserie, what calamitie, and what pouertie the French nation had suffered, and manie yeares susteined, by reason of the said warres; determined clearelie rather to pacifie and interteine the English nation by faire words and great rewards (although it were to his great charge) than by too much hardinesse to put himselfe, his nobilitie & realme in hazard, by giuing them battell, as his predecessors had vnwiselie doone at Poitiers, and at Agincourt. Wherefore to buie peace, he granted king Edward for a yearelie tribute fiftie thousand crownes, to be paied at London; which, accounting a crowne at foure shillings, amounteth to ten thousand pounds. And to haue the fauour and good will of his chiefe councellors, he gaue great pensions, amounting to the summe of sixteene thousand crownes a yeere, that is to saie: to his chancellor, to the lord Hastings his chiefe chamberleine, a man of no lesse wit than vertue, and of great authoritie with his maister, and that not without cause; for he had as well in time of aduersitie, as in the faire flattering world, well and trulie serued him: and to the lord Howard, to sir Thomas Montgomerie, to sir Thomas Sentleger, to sir Iohn Cheinie maister of the kings horsses, to the marques Dorsset, sonne to the queene, and diuerse other, he gaue great and liberall rewards, to the intent to keepe himselfe in amitie with England, while he wan and obteined his purpose and desire in other places.

These persons had giuen to them great gifts, beside yearelie pensions. For Argenton his councellor affirmed of his owne knowledge, that the lord Howard had in lesse than the tearme of two yeares, for reward in monie and plate, foure and twentie thousand crownes; & at the time of this méeting, he gaue to the lord Hastings the kings chiefe chamberleine, (as the Frenchmen write) an hundred markes of siluer, made in plate, whereof euerie marke is eight ounces sterling. But the English writers affirme, that he gaue the lord Hastings foure and twentie doozen bolles, that is to saie, twelue doozen gilt, & twelue doozen vngilt, euerie cup weieng seuentéene nobles: which gift, either betokened in him a great liberall nature, or else a great and especiall confidence that he had reposed in the said lord chamberleine. Beside this, he gaue him yearelie two thousand crownes pension, the which summe he sent to him by Piers Cleret, one of the maisters of his house, giuing him in charge to receiue of him an acquittance for the receipt of the same pension, to the intent that it should appeare in time to come, that the chancelor, chamberleine, admerall, maisters of the horsses to the king of England, and manie other of his councell, had bin in fée and pensionaries of the French king, whose yearelie acquittances (the lord Hastings onelie excepted) remaine of record to be shewed in the chamber of accounts in the palace of Paris.

When Piers Cleret had paied the pension to the lord Hastings, he gentlie demanded of him an acquittance for his discharge. Which request when he denied, he then

onlie

onlie asked of him a bill of thrée lines to be directed to the king, testifieng the receipt of the pension: to the intent that the king your maister should not thinke the pension to be imbeselled.   The lord Hastings, although he knew that Piers demanded nothing but reason, answered him: "Sir this gift commeth onelie of the liberall pleasure of the king his maister, and not of my request: if it be his determinat will that I shall haue it, then put you it into my sléeue; and if not, I praie you render to him his gift againe: for neither he nor you shall haue either letter, acquittance, or scroll signed with my hand of the receipt of anie pension, to the intent to brag another daie, that the kings chamberleine of England hath béene pensionarie with the French king, & shew his acquittance in the chamber of accounts, to his dishonor."   Piers left his monie behind, and made relation of all things to his maister: which although that he had not his will, yet he much more praised the wisdome and policie of the lord Hastings, than of the other pensionaries, cōmandiug him yearlie to be paied, without anie discharge demanding.]

K. Edward
returneth into
England.
Edw. Hall
fol. Ccxxxvj.   When the king of England had receiued his monie, and his nobilitie their rewards, he trussed vp his tents, laded his baggage, and departed towards Calis.   [But yer he came there, he remembring the craftie dissimulation, and the vntrue dealing of Lewes earle of saint Paule, high constable of France, intending to declare him to the French king in his verie true likenesse and portrature, sent vnto him two letters of credence, written by the said constable, with the true report of all such words and messages as had béene to him sent, and declared by the said constable and his amdassadours. Which letters the French king gladlie receiued, and thankefullie accepted, as the cheefe instrument to bring the constable to his death; which he escaped no long season after, such is the end of dissemblers.]   When king Edward was come to Calis, and had set all things in an order, he tooke ship, and sailed with a prosperous wind into England, and was roiallie receiued vpon Blackheath by the maior of London and the magistrates, and fiue hundred commoners apparrelled in murrie, the eight and twentith daie of September, and so conueied through the citie of Westminster, where

Edw. Hall
fol. Ccxxxvj. for a while (after his long labour) he reposed himselfe [euerie daie almost talking with the queene his wife of the marriage of his daughter, whome he caused to be called Dolphinesse: thinking nothing surer than that mariage to take effect, according to the treatie.   The hope of which marriage caused him to dissemble, and doo things which afterward chanced greatlie to the French kings profit, & smallie to his.]

About the same season, the French king, to compasse his purpose for the getting of the constable into his hands, tooke truce with the duke of Burgognie for nine yeares as a contractor in the league, and not comprehended as an other princes alie. Sir Thomas
Mŏtgomerie. The king of England aduertised hereof, sent ouer sir Thomas Montgomerie to the French king, offering to passe the seas againe the next summer in his aid, to make warres on the duke Burgognie; so that the French king should paie to him fiftie thousand crownes for the losse which he should susteine in his custome, by reason that the woolles at Calis (bicause of the warres) could haue no vent, and also paie halfe the charges and halfe the wages of his souldiers and men of warre.   The French king thanked the king of England for his gentle offer, but he alledged that the truce was alreadie concluded, so that he could not then attempt anie thing against the same without reproch to his honour.

But the truth was, the French king neither loued the sight nor liked the companie of the king of England on that side the sea; but when he was here at home, he both loued him as his brother, and tooke him as his freend.   Sir Thomas Montgomerie was with plate richlie rewarded, and so dispatched.   There returned with him the lord Howard and sir Iohn Cheinie, which were hostages with the French king, till the 1475
An. Reg. 15.
Henrie earle of
Richmond. English armie were returned into England.   King Edward, hauing established all things in good order, as men might iudge, both within his realme and without, was yet troubled in his mind, for that Henrie the earle of Richmond (one of the bloud

of

of king Henrie the sixt) was aliue, and at libertie in Britaine: therefore to attempt eftsoones the mind of Francis duke of Britaine, he sent ouer vnto the said duke, one doctor Stillington, and two other his ambassadors laden with no small summe of gold.

These ambassadors, declaring their message, affirmed that the king their maister willed to haue the earle of Richmond onelie for this purpose, to ioine with him in aliance by marriage, and so to plucke vp all the leauings of discord betwéene him and the contrarie faction. The duke gentlie heard the orators. And though at the first he by excuses denied their request, yet at the length, beléeuing that king Edward would giue to the earle his eldest daughter, the ladie Elizabeth in marriage, he consented to deliuer him, and receiued of the English orators a great summe of monie. But yer they were imbarked with their preie, the duke being aduertised, that the earle of Richmond was not so earnestlie sought for, to be coupled in mariage with king Edwards daughter; but rather that his head might be chopped off with an hatchet, caused his treasuror Peter Landoise to conueie the said earle of Richmond into a sanctuarie at S. Malo, where the English ambassadors then laie, onelie staieng for a conuenient wind: who complained, that they were euill vsed, to be spoiled both of their monie and merchandize. *Ambassadors into Britaine.* *The earle of Richmond taketh sanctuarie.*

Yet bicause the matter was so handled, that it séemed the earle escaped into the sanctuarie through their owne negligence, after they had receiued him into their hands; they were soone answered: but yet promise was made, that the earle should be safelie kept, either in the sanctuarie, or else as prisoner in the dukes house, that they should not néed to feare him more than his shadow. And thus the king of England purchased for his monie the kéeping of his enimie, the space onelie of three daies and no more. King Edward was somewhat displeased with this chance, but yet trusting that the duke of Britaine would (according to promise) see the earle of Richmond safelie kept from dooing anie gréeuance to him or his subiects, put all doubts therof out of his mind, and began to studie how to kéepe a liberall princelie house, and therevpon storing his chests with monie, he imploied no small portion in good housekéeping.

¶ But hauing spoken thus much of the earle of Richmond, whome Edward Hall compareth to a shéepe betraied into the téeth and clawes of the woolfe, you shall vnderstand, that at such time as his troubles were set fresh abroach, and he knowing that he was going towards his death, for verie pensifenesse and inward thought, fell into a feruent and sore ague. In which verie season, one Iohn Cheulet, so estéemed among the princes of Britaine as few were in all the countrie, and in much credit, and well accepted with the duke, was (when these things were thus concluded) for his solace in the countrie. Who being hereof certified, was chafed with the abhomination of the fact, resorted to the court, and familiarlie came to the dukes presence, where he stood so sadlie and so palie, without anie word speaking, that the duke was much abashed, and suddenlie maruelled at his sad and frowning countenance, and demanded of him what should signifie that dumpishnesse of mind, and inward sighing, the which by his countenance manifestlie appeared and was euident? He modestlie answered; "Most noble and redoubted lord, this palenesse of visage and deadlie looke dooth prognosticate the time of my death to approach and be at hand, which if it had chanced to me before this daie, I assure you, it had much lesse hurt me. For then had I not béene reserued to féele the dolorous pangs and sorowfull sighings, which a fact by you doone (that I thought impossible to be obteined) hath printed in my stomach and in my heart deeplie grauen: so that I well perceiue, that either I shall lose my life, or else liue in perpetuall distresse and continuall miserie. *Abr. Fl. ex Edw. Hall fol.* Ccxxxvij.

"For you my singular good lord, by your vertuous acts and noble feats, haue gotten to you in manner an immortall fame, which in euerie mans mouth is extolled & aduanced aboue the high clouds. But alas me séemeth (I praie you pardon me my rudenesse) that

that now that you haue obteined so high praise and glorie, you nothing lesse regard than to kéepe and preserue the same inuiolate, considering that yon, forgetting your faith and faithfull promise made to Henrie earle of Richmond, haue deliuered the most innocent yoong gentleman to the cruell tormentors, to be afflicted, rent in péeces, and slaine. Wherefore all such as loue you, of the which number I am one, cannot choose but lament & be sorie, when they sée openlie the fame and glorie of your most re- nowmed name, by such a disloialtie and vntruth against promise, to be both blotted and stained with a perpetuall note of slander and infamie." "Peace mine owne good Iohn (quoth the duke) I praie thée, beléeue me there is no such thing like to happen to the earle of Richmond: for king Edward hath sent for him, to make of him, being his suspected enimie, his good and faire sonne in law."

"Well well (quoth Iohn) my redoubted lord, giue credence vnto me: the earle Henrie is at the verie brinke to perish, whome if you permit once to set but one foot out of your powerand dominion, there is no mortall creature able héereafter to deliuer him from death." The duke being mooued with the persuasions of Iohn Cheulet, which either little beléeued, or smallie suspected king Edward, to desire the earle for anie fraud or deceipt, or else seduced by blind auarice and loue of monie, more than honestie, fidelitie, or wisedome would require, did not consider what he vnaduisedlie did, or what he aduisedlie should haue doone, Wherefore, with all diligence he sent foorth Peter Landoise his chéefe treasuror, commanding him to intercept and slaie the earle of Richmond, in all hast possible, as before you haue heard.]

Abr. Flex. I. S. pag. 752. Sir Iohn Crosbie his gift to the citie

¶ In this yeare deceassed sir Iohn Crosbie knight, (not long before this, maior of London) and was buried in the parish church of saint Helen in Bishops gate stréet, vnto the reparing of which parish church he gaue fiue hundred marks, and thirtie pounds to be distributed to poore housholders in the ward of Bishops gate: to the reparing of the parish church at Heneworth in Middlesex fortie pounds: to the re- pairing of London wall one hundred pounds: toward the making of a new tower of stone at the southend of London bridge, if the same were begun by the maior and communaltie within ten yeares next after his deceasse, one hundred pounds: to the reparations of Rochester bridge ten pounds: to euerie the prisons in and about Lon- don liberallie. Also he gaue to the wardens and communaltie of the grocers in Lon- don two large pots of siluer chased halfe guilt, weieng thirtéene pounds and fiue ounces of Troie weight, to be occupied in their common hall, and elsewhere, at their discretions.

I. S. pag.745. Knights made by the king.

In this yeare were inhanced to the honour of knighthood, after the custome of England, in the time of peace the kings eldest son Edward prince of Wales, duke of Cornewall, and earle of Chester, his second sonne the duke of Yorke, and with them the earle of Lincolnes sonne and heire, the duke of Suffolke, the lord Thomas Greie, the quéenes sonne, and Richard his brother, the earle of Shrewesburie, the earle of Wilshire, master Edward Wooduile, the lord Neuill, the lord Barkleis sonne and heire, the lord Audelies sonne and heire, the lord saint Amand, the lord Stanleis sonne and heire, the lord Suttons sonne and heire, the lord Hastings sonne and heire, the lord Ferrers of Charleis sonne and heire, master Herbert brother to the earle of Penbroke, master Vaughan Brian chiefe iudge, Litilton one of the iudges of the common plées, master Bodringham, master Brian Stapleton, Kneuit, Pilkinton, Ludlow, Charleton &c. The same daie the king created the lord Thomas marquesse Dorset before dinner, and so in the habit of a marquesse aboue the habit of his knight- hood he began the table of knights in saint Edwards chamber. At that time he ordeined that the kings chamberleine should go with the ancient and well nurtered knight, to aduertise and teach the order of knighthood to the esquiers, being in the baine. The king himselfe came in person and did honour to all the companie with his noble councell.]

Litilton.

This

This yeare the duke of Burgognie was slaine by the Switzers, before the towne of Nancie in Lorraine, after whose death the French king wan all the townes which the said duke held in Picardie and Artois. And bicause that the towne of Bullen and countie of Bullenois apperteined by right of inheritance vnto the lord Berthram de la Toure, earle of Auuergne, the French king bought of him his right and title in the same, and recompensed him with other lands in the countie of Forests, and in other places. And bicause the forenamed towne and countie were holden of the earledome of Artois he changed the tenure, and auowed to hold the same towne & countie of our ladie of Bolongne and therof did homage to the image in the great church of Bolongne, offering there an hart of gold, weieng two thousand crownes; ordeining further, that his heires and successors at their entrie into their estates, by themselues or their deputies should offer an hart of like weight and value, as a reliefe and homage for the same towne and countie.

¶ This yeare was Robert Basset maior of London, who did sharpe correction vpon bakers, for making of light bread, he caused diuerse of them to be set on the pillorie in Cornehill. And also one Agnes Daintie a butterwife for selling of butter new and old mingled togither, being first trapped with butter dishes, was then set on the pillorie. ¶ The countesse of Oxford deceassed and was buried at Windsore. ¶ Also this yeare Richard Rawson one of the shiriffes of London, caused to be builded one house in the church yard of S. Marie hospitall without Bishops gate of London, where the maior of that citie and his brethren the aldermen vse to sit and heare the sermons in the Easter holiedaies, as in times past appeared by an inscription on the front of the same house, now by wethering defaced, which I haue read in these words: Praie for the soules of Richard Rawson late Mercer and alderman of London, and Isabell his wife, of whose goods this worke was made and founded. Anno Dom. 1488.]

By the diligence of Ralph Iosseline maior of London the wall about London was new made betwixt Algate and Creplegate: he caused the Moore field to be searched for claie, and bricke to be made and burnt there: he also caused chalke to be brought out of Kent, and in the same Moore field to be burnt into lime, for the furtherance of that worke. The maior with his companie of the drapers made all that part betwixt Bishops gate and Alhalowes church in the same wall. Bishops gate it selfe was new built by the merchants Almans of the Stilliard, and from Alhalowes church toward Moore gate a great part of the same was builded of the goods, & by the executors of sir Iohn Crosbie somtimes an alderman of London, as may appeare by his armes in two places fixed. The companie of Skinners made that part of the wall betweene Algate and Buries markes towards Bishops gate, as may appeare by their armes in thrée places fixed: the other companies of the citie made the other deale of the said wall, which was a great worke to be doone in one yeare.

Also this yeare Thomas Burdet an esquier of Arrow in Warwikeshire, sonne to sir Nicholas Burdet (who was great butler of Normandie in Henrie the sixt daies) was beheaded for a word spoken in this sort. King Edward in his progresse hunted in Thomas Burdets parke at Arrow, and slue manie of his deere, amongst the which was a white bucke, whereof Thomas Burdet made great account. And therefore when he vnderstood thereof, he wished the buckes head in his bellie that mooued the king to kill it. Which tale being told to the king, Burdet was apprehended and accused of treason, for wishing the buckes head (hornes and all) in the kings bellie: he was condemned, drawne from the Tower of London to Tiburne, and there beheaded, and then buried in the Greie friers church at London. Wherefore it is good counsell that the wiseman giueth, saieng: Kéepe thy toong & kéepe thy life, for manie times we sée, that speech offendeth & procureth mischéefe, where silence is author neither of the one nor the other, as it is trulie and in praise of silence spoken by the poet:

———nulli tacuisse nocet, nocet esse loquutum.]

Marginal notes:

1476
———
An. Reg. 16.
The death of the duke of Burgognie.

Abr. Fl. ex I. S. pag. 745.

Agnes Daintie on the pillorie.

1477
———
Part of Lōdon wall new builded.
Iohn Rouse.

Bishops gate new builded.

Burdet for a word spoken beheaded.

Enguerant.

Register of the Greie friers.

About this season, through great mishap, the sparke of priuie malice was newlie kindled betwixt the king and his brother the duke of Clarence, insomuch that where one of the dukes seruants was suddenlie accused (I can not saie whether of truth, or vntrulie suspected by the dukes enimies) of poisoning, sorcerie or inchantment, and thereof condemned, and put to execution for the same; the duke which might not suffer the wrongfull condemnation of his man (as he in his conscience iudged) nor yet forbeare but to murmur and reproue the dooing thereof, mooued the king with his dailie exclamation to take such displesure with him, that finallie the duke was cast into the Tower, and therewith adiudged for a traitor, and priuilie drowned in a butt of malmesie, the eleuenth of March, in the beginning of the seuententh yeare of the kings reigne.

Some haue reported, that the cause of this noble mans death rose of a foolish prophesie, which was, that after K. Edward one should reigne, whose first letter of his name should be a G. Wherewith the king and quéene were sore troubled and began to conceiue a greeuous grudge against this duke, and could not be in quiet till they had brought him to his end. And as the diuell is woont to incumber the minds of men which delite in such diuelish fantasies, they said afterward, that that prophesie lost not his effect, when after king Edward, Glocester vsurped his kingdome. Other alledged, that the cause of his death was for that the duke, being destitute of a wife, by the meanes of his sister the ladie Margaret, duchesse of Burgognie, procured to haue the ladie Marie, daughter and heire to hir husband duke Charles.

Which marriage king Edward (enuieng the prosperitie of his brother) both gaine said and disturbed, and thereby old malice reuiued betwixt them: which the quéene and hir bloud (euer mistrusting, and priuilie barking at the kings linage) ceassed not to increase. But sure it is, that although king Edward were consenting to his death; yet he much did both lament his infortunate chance, & repent his sudden execution: insomuch that when anie person sued to him for the pardon of malefactors condemned to death, he would accustomablie saie, & openlie speake: "Oh infortunate brother, for whose life not one would make sute." Openlie and apparantlie meaning by such words that by the meanes of some of the nobilitie he was deceiued and brought to confusion.

This duke left behind him two yoong infants begot of the bodie of his wife, the daughter of Richard late earle of Warwike: which children by destinie as it were, or by their owne merits, following the steps of their ancestors, succéeded them in like misfortune and semblable euill chance. For Edward his heire, whome king Edward had created earle of Warwike was thrée and twentie yeares after, in the time of Henrie the seauenth, atteinted of treason, and on the Tower hill lost his head. Margaret his sole daughter maried to sir Richard Pole knight, and by Henrie the eight restored to the name, title, & possessions of the earldome of Salisburie, was at length for treason committed against the said Henrie the eight atteinted in open parlement; and sixtie two yeares after hir father had suffered death in the Tower, she on the greene within the same place was beheaded. In whose person died the verie surname of Plantagenet, which from Geffrie Plantagenet so long in the bloud roiall of this realme had florished and continued.

After the death of this duke, by reason of great heat and distemperance of aire, happened so fierce & quicke a pestilence, that fiftéene yeares warre past consumed not the third part of the people, that onelie foure moneths miserablie and pitifullie dispatched & brought to their graues. So that if the number had béene kept by multiplieng of vnities, & out of them to haue raised a complet number, it would haue mooued matter of verie great admiration. But it should séeme that they were infinit, if consideration be had of the comparison, inferred for the more effectuall setting foorth of that cruell and ceaselesse contagion. And suerlie it soundeth to reason, that the pestilence should fetch awaie so manie thousands, as in iudgement by proportion of fiftéene yeares warre

one

one maie gather; and manie more too.   For euerie man knoweth that in warres, time, place, persons, and meanes are limited: time of warre begun and ended; place circumscribed; persons imbattelled, and weapons also whereby the fight is tried: so that all these haue their limitations, beyond which they haue no extent.   But the pestilence, being a generall infection of the aire, an element ordeined to mainteine life, though it haue a limitation in respect of the totall compasse of the world; yet whole climats maie be poisoned: and it were not absurd to saie, that all and euerie part of the aire maie be pestilentlie corrupted; and so consequentlie not limited: wherefore full well it maie be said of the pestilence (procuring so great a depopulation) as one saith of surfetting:

Ense cadunt multi, perimit sed crapula plures.

Auson.
1478

The councellors of the yoong duchesse of Burgognie sent to K. Edward for aid against the French king.   About the same time had the queene of England sent to the ladie Margaret duchesse of Burgognie, for the preferrement of hir brother Anthonie erle Riuers to the yoong damsell.   But the councell of Flanders, considering that he was but an earle of meane estate, and she the greatest inheritrice of all christendome at that time, gaue but deafe eare to so vnméet a request.   To which desire, if the Flemings had but giuen a liking eare by outward semblance, and with gentle words delaied the sute, she had beene both succoured and defended.   Whether king Edward was not contented with this refusall, or that he was loth to breake with the French king, he would in no wise consent to send an armie into Flanders against the French king: but yet he sent ambassadours to him with louing and gentle letters, requiring him to grow to some reasonable order & agréement with the yoong duchesse of Burgognie, or at the least to take a truce with hir at his request.

An. Reg. 18.

The ambassadours of England were highlie receiued, bountifullie feasted, and liberallie rewarded, but answer to their desire had they none; sauing that shortlie after, the French king would send ambassadours, hostages, and pledges to the king of England their maister, for the perfecting and concluding of all things depending betweene them two; so that their souereigne lord & they should haue cause to be contented and pleased.   These faire words were onelie delaies to driue time, vntill he might haue space to spoile the yoong damsell of hir townes and countries.   And beside this, to staie king Edward from taking part with hir, he wrote to him, that if he would ioine with him in aid, he should haue and inioie to him and his heires the whole countie & countrie of Flanders, discharged of homage, superioritie and resort, to be claimed by the French king, or his successors.

He also wrote that he should haue the whole duchie of Brabant, whereof the French king offered at his owne cost and charge to conquer foure of the chiefest and strongest townes within the said duchie, & them in quiet possession to deliuer to the king of England: granting further to paie him ten thousand angels toward his charges, with munitions of warre and artillerie, which he promised to lend him, with men and carriage for the conueiance of the same.   The king of England refused to make anie warres against those countries that were thus offered to him: but if the French king would make him partner of his conquest in Picardie, rendering to him part of the townes alreadie gotten, as Bologne, Monsterell, and Abuile, then he would suerlie take his part, and aid him with men at his owne costs and charges.

Large offers made to the king of England by the French king.

Thus passed faire words and golden promises betwéene these two princes: and in the meane time the yoong duchesse of Burgognie was spoiled of hir townes, castels & territories, till at length for maintenance she condescended to marrie with Maximilian sonne to the emperour Frederike, that he might kéepe the woolfe from the fold. King Edward in the nineténth yeare of his reigne began (more than he was before accustomed) to serch the forfeiture of penall lawes and statutes, as well of the chéefe of his nobilitie as of other gentlemen, being proprietaries of great possessions, or abundantlie furnished with goods; likewise of merchants, and other inferior persons.

1479
An. Reg. 19

Y y 2

By reason whereof, it was of all men iudged that he would proue hereafter a sore and a rigorous prince among his subiects.   But this his new inuented practise and couetous meaning (by reason of forreine affaires and abridgement of his daies in this transitorie life, which were within two yeares after consumed) tooke some (but not great) effect.

Abr. Fl. er I.S.
pag. 747, 748.
Pestilence.

¶ In this yeare was great mortalitie and death by the pestilence, not onelie in London, but in diuerse parts of the realme, which began in the latter end of September in the yeare last before passed, and continued all this yeare till the beginning of Nouember, which was about fourtéene moneths: in the which space died innumerable of people

Vnaduised &
vnséemelie de-
meanor punish-
ed with a fine.

in the said citie & else-where.   ¶ This yeare also the maior of London being in Paules, knéeling in his deuotions at saint Erkenwalds shrine, Robert Bifield one of the shiriffes vnaduisedlie knéeled downe nigh vnto the maior: whereof afterward the maior charged him to haue doone more than becomed him.   But the shiriffe answering rudelie and stubbornlie, would not acknowledge to haue commited anie offense: for the which he was afterward by a court of aldermen fined at fiftie pounds to be paid toward the reparations of the conduits in London, which was trulie paid.   ¶ This yeare Thomas

Conduit in
Cheape builded.

Ilam one of the shirifs of London newlie builded the great conduit in Cheape, of his owne charges.   ¶ This yeare also king Edward began his Christmasse at Waking, and at fiue daies end remooued to Greenewich, where he kept out the other part of his Christmasse with great roialtie.]

1480
An. Reg. 20.

Ambassadours were sent to and fro betwixt the king of England and France, and still the French king fed the king of England with faire words, putting him in hope to match his sonne and heire the Dolphin with the ladie Elizabeth daughter to the king of England, according to the conclusions of agréement had and made at Picquenie betwixt them, although in verie déed he meant nothing lesse.   His ambassadours euer made excuses if anie thing were amisse, and he vsed to send change of ambassadours; so that if those which had béene here before, and were returned, had said or promised anie thing (though they were authorised so to doo) which might turne to their masters hinderance, the other that came after, might excuse themselues by ignorance of that matter; affirming that they wanted commission once to talke or meddle with that matter: or if he perceiued that anie thing was like to be concluded contrarie to his mind, for a shift he would call his ambassadours home in great hast, and after send an other with new instructions nothing depending on the old.

Thus the French king vsed to dallie with king Edward in the case of this mariage, onelie to kéepe him still in amitie.   And certeinelie the king of England, being a man of no suspicious nature, thought sooner that the sunne should haue fallen from his circle, than that the French king would haue dissembled or broken promise with him.

The French
king féedeth the
king of England
with faire words
and promises.

But there is none so soone beguiled, as he that least mistrusteth; nor anie so able to deceiue, as he to whome most credence is giuen.   But as in mistrusting nothing, is great lightnesse; so in too much trusting, is to much follie: which well appeared in this matter.   For the French king, by cloking his inward determinate purpose with great dissimulation and large promises, kept him still in fréendship with the king of England, till he had wrought a great part of his will against the yoong duchesse of Burgognie.   Which king Edward would not haue suffered, if he had put anie great doubt in the French kings faire promises, considering that the crowne of France was in this meane time so much increased in dominions, to the great re-enforcement of that realme.

Abr. Fl. ex I. S.
pag. 748, 749.
Fiue théeues for
sacrilege seuere-
lie executed.

¶ On the two and twentith of Februarie were fiue notable théeues put to death, for robbing the church called saint Martins le grand in London, and other places; thrée of them were drawne to the Tower hill, hanged & burnt, the other two were pressed to death.   A sore and seuere kind of execution no doubt, but yet thought by iustice meritorious in the malefactors, for their offences of sacrelege.   Heinous enough had

it

it beene to spoile a priuat man of his goods, and by law of nations punishable with death; but much more horrible, that prophane persons with polluted hands should priuilie or openlie so touch holie & consecrated things, as to take them out of a sacred place, whereto (for holy vses) they were dedicated, & applie them to the satisfieng of the corrupt concupiscences of their owne hearts, the bottomlesse gulfe whereof bicause no booties nor spoiles could satisfie; it stood with the high praise of iustice that they and their ceaselesse desires were seuered by deserued death; wherefore it is wiselie said by the comicall poet of such gréedie guts:

Quam quis auidus poscit escam auariter,
Decipitur in transenna perítque auaritia.

Plaut. in Rud,

In this yeare king Edward required great sums of monie to be lent him. The citizens of London granted him fiue thousand marks, which were seized of the fiue and twentie wards: which fiue thousand marks was trulie repaid againe in the next yeare following. ¶ Also this yeare on Whitsundaie K. Edward the fourth created the lord Berkleie, vicount Berkeleie, at Gréenewich. ¶ In this yeare also an house on London bridge called the common siege, or priuie, fell downe into the Thames, where thorough it fiue persons were drowned. ¶ This yeare the king with his quéene kept a roiall Christmas at Windsor. *Scala temporum.*

Also this yéere was one Richard Chawrie maior of London, whome king Edward so greatlie fauoured, that he tooke him (with certeine of his brethren the aldermen, & commons of the citie of London) into the forrest of Waltham, where was ordeined for them a pleasant lodge of gréene boughs, in which lodge they dined with great chéere; & the king would not go to dinner vntill he saw them serued. Moreouer he caused the lord chamberlaine, with other lords, to cheere the said maior and his companie sundrie times whilest they were at dinner. After dinner they went a hunting with the king, and slue manie deare, as well red as fallow, whereof the king gaue vnto the maior and his companie good plentie, and sent vnto the ladie mairesse and hir sisters the aldermens wiues, two harts, six bucks, and a tun of wine to make them merrie with, which was eaten in the drapers hall. The cause of which bountie thus shewed by the king, was (as most men did take) for that the maior was a merchant of woonderous aduentures into manie and sundrie countries. By reason whereof, the king had yearelie of him notable summes of monie for his customes, beside other pleasures that he had shewed vnto the king before times. ¶ This yéere the Scots began to stir, against whom the king sent the duke of Glocester & manie others, which returned againe without any notable battell.] The king feasteth the maior and aldermen. *Fabian pag.* 512.

In this verie season Iames the third of that name king of Scots sent into England a solemne ambassage for to haue the ladie Cicilie, king Edwards second daughter, to be married to his eldest sonne Iames, prince of Scotland, duke of Rothsaie, and earle of Caricke. King Edward and his councell, perceiuing that this affinitie should be both honourable and profitable to the realme, did not onelie grant to his desire; but also before hand disbursed certeine summes of monie, to the onelie intent that the marriage hereafter should neither be hindered nor broken. With this condition, that if the said mariage by anie accidentall meane should in time to come take none effect; or that king Edward would notifie to the king of Scots, or his councell, that his pleasure was determined to haue the said marriage dissolued: then the prouost and merchants of the towne of Edenburgh, should be bound for repaiment of the said summes againe. All which things were with great deliberation concluded, passed, and sealed, in hope of continuall peace and indissoluble amitie. Ambassadors foorth of Scotland.

But king Iames was knowne to be a man so wedded to his owne opinion, that he could not abide them that would speake contrarie to his fansie: by meanes whereof, he was altogither led by the counsell and aduise of men of base linage, whome for their flatterie he had promoted vnto great dignities and honourable offices. By which

persons

persons diuerse of the nobilitie of his realme were greatlie misused and put to trouble, both with imprisonment, exactions, & death; insomuch that some of them went into voluntarie exile. Amongst whome Alexander duke of Albanie, brother to king Iames, being exiled into France, & passing through England, taried with K. Edward: and vpon occasion mooued him to make warre against his brother, the said king Iames, for that he forgetting his oth, promise, and affinitie concluded with king Edward, caused his subiects to make roads and forraies into the English borders, spoiling, burning, and killing king Edwards liege people.

King Edward, not a little displeased with this vnprincelie dooing, prouoked and set on also by the duke of Albanie, determined to inuade Scotland with an armie, as well to reuenge his owne iniuries receiued at the hands of King Iames, as to helpe to restore the duke of Albanie vnto his countrie and possessions againe. Herevpon all Preparation for the Winter season he mustered his men, prepared his ordinance, rigged his ships, and left nothing vnprouided for such a iournie: so that in the begining of the yeare, all things apperteining to the warre, and necessarie for his voiage, were in a readinesse. To be the cheefteine of his hoast, and lieutenant generall, Richard duke of Glocester was appointed by his brother king Edward; and with him were adioined as associats, Henrie the fourth earle of Northumberland, Thomas lord Stanleie lord steward of the kings house, the lord Louell, the lord Greiestocke, and diuerse other noblemen and worthie knights.

These valiant capteins came to Alnewike in Northumberland, about the beginning of Iulie, where they first incamped themselues, & marshalled their hoast. The fore-ward was led by the earle of Northumberland, vnder whose standard were the lord Scroope of Bolton, sir Iohn Middleton, sir Iohn Dichfield, and diuerse other knights, esquiers, & souldiers, to the number of six thousand and seauen hundred. In the midle-ward was the duke of Glocester, and with him the duke of Albanie, the lord Louell, the lord Greiestocke, sir Edward Wooduile, and other, to the number of fiue thousand & eight hundred men. The lord Neuill was appointed to follow, accompa-nied with thrée thousand. The lord Stanleie led the wing on the right hand of the dukes battell with foure thousand men of Lancashire & Cheshire. The lord Fitz Hugh, sir William a Parre, sir Iames Harrington, with the number of two thosand souldiers, guided the left wing. And beside all these, there were one thousand appointed to giue their attendance on the ordinance.

¶ In this yeare Edmund Shaw goldsmith and maior of London newlie builded Creplegate from the foundation, which gate in old time had bene a prison, wherevnto such citizens and other as were arrested for debt (or like trespasses) were committed, as they be now to the counters, as maie appear by a writ of king Edward the second, in these words: Rex vic' London salutem. Ex graui querela capti & detenti in prisona nostra de Creplegate, prox. li. quas coram Radulpho Sandwico, tunc custode ciuitatis nostræ London, & I. de Blackewell custode recognit. debitorum, &c. King Edward held his Christmas at Eltham, and kept his estate all the whole feast in his great chamber; and the quéene in hir chamber, where were dailie more than two thousand persons. The same yeare on Candlemas day, he with his quéene went on procession from saint Stephans chappell into Westminster hall, accompanied with the earle of Angus, the lord Greie, & sir Iames Liddall, ambassadors from Scotland. And at his procéeding out of his chamber he made sir Iohn Wood vnder-treasuror of England, & sir William Catesbie one of the iustices of the cōmon plées, knights.]

But to returne to the kings affaires concerning Scotland. The roiall armie aforesaid not intending to lose time, came suddenlie by the water side to the towne of Berwike, and there (what with force, and what with feare of so great an armie) tooke and entered the towne: but the earle of Bothwell, being capteine of the castell, would in no wise deliuer it; wherfore the capteines, vpon good and deliberate aduise, planted a strong

siege

Preparation for
warre against
Scotland.
1482
An. Reg. 22.
An armie sent
into Scotland.

Abr. Fl. ex I.S.
pag. 749.
Creplegate
builded.

Records.

An. Reg. 23.
1483
Berwike woone
by the English-
men.

siege round about it. When this siege was laid, the two dukes and all the other souldiers (except the lord Stanleie, sir Iohn Eldrington treasuror of the kings house, sir William a Parre, and foure thousand men that were left behind to keepe the siege before the castell) departed from Berwike toward Edenburgh; and in marching thitherward, they burnt and destroied manie townes and bastiles. King Iames hauing small confidence in his communaltie, and lesse trust in his nobilitie, kept himselfe within the castell of Edenburgh.

The duke of Glocester entered into the towne, and at the especiall desire of the duke of Albanie saued the towne, and the inhabitants from fire, bloud, and spoile, taking onelie of the merchants, such presents as they gentlie offered to him and his capteins, causing Gartier principall king at armes to make a publike proclamation at the high crosse in the market place of Edenburgh; by the which he warned and admonished king Iames, to kéepe, obserue, and performe, all such promises, compacts, couenants, and agreements, as he had concluded and sealed with the king of England, and also to make sufficient recompense vnto his subiects, for the tyrannie, spoile, and crueltie which he and his people had committed and doone, contrarie to the league, within the marches of his realme of England, before the first daie of August next insuing: and further without delaie to restore his brother the duke of Albanie to his estate, & all his possessions, offices, and authorities, in as large maner as he occupied & inioied the same before. Or else the duke of Glocester, lieutenant generall for the king of England, was readie at hand to destroie him, his people, and countries, with slaughter, flame, and famine.

King Iames would make no answer, neither by word nor writing, but kept himselfe close within the castell. But the lords of Scotland lieng at Hadington with a great puissance, determined first to practise with the duke of Glocester for a peace, and after by some meanes to allure the duke of Albanie from the English amitie. And vpon this motion, the second daie of August they wrote to the duke of Glocester, requiring that the mariage betwéene the prince of Scotland, and king Edwards daughter might be accomplished, according to the couenants: and further, that a peace from thencefoorth might be louinglie concluded betwéene both the realmes. The duke of Glocester answered againe vnto these demands; that for the article of the mariage, he knew not the king his brothers determinate pleasure, either for the affirmance or deniall of the same; but neuerthelesse he desired full restitution of all the sums of monie prested out in lone vpon the same mariage. And as for peace, he assured them that he wold agrée to none, except the castell of Berwike might be to him deliuered; or at the least wise, that he should vndertake that the siege lieng afore the same should not be troubled by the king of Scots, nor by anie of his subiects, nor by his or their procurement or meanes.

The Scotish lords, vpon this answer and demands of the duke of Glocester, sent to him the elect of Murreie, and the lord Dernleie, which excused the matter touching the repaiment of the monie: for that the time of the lawfull contract of the said mariage was not yet come, and no daie appointed for the monie to be paied before the contract begun. But for further assurance either for the contract to be made, or for the paiment of the monie, they promised therevnto accordinglie (as reason should require) to agrée. Secondarilie, as touching the castell of Berwike, they alledged, that it apperteined to the realme of Scotland, as the old inheritance of the same.

The duke, notwithstanding all that they could saie, would agrée to no peace, except the castell of Berwike might be deliuered to the K. of England. And so the messengers departed. The same daie the archbishop of S. Andrews, the bishop of Dunkeld, Colin earle of Argile, lord Campbell, and lord Andrew lord of Anandale chancellor of Scotland, wrote to the duke of Albanie, a solemne and an autenticall instrument, signed and sealed with their hands and seales, concerning a generall pardon to him and
his

The bishop elect of Murreie sent to the duke of Glocester.

his seruants, vpon certeine conditions to be granted; which conditions seemed to be so reasonable, that the duke of Albanie, desirous to be restored to his old estate, possessions, and natiue countrie, willinglie accepted the same.

But before he departed from the duke of Glocester, he promised both by word and writing of his owne hand, to doo and performe all such things, as he before that time had sworne and promised to king Edward : notwithstanding anie agréement now made, or after to be made with the lords of Scotland. And for performance of the effect hereof, he againe tooke a corporall oth, and sealed the writing before the duke of Glocester, in the English campe at Leuington besides Hadington, the third daie of August, in the yeare 1482. After he was restored, the lords of Scotland proclamed him great lieutenant of Scotland; and in the kings name made proclamation, that all men within eight daies should be readie at Craushaus, both to raise the siege before the castell, and for the recouering againe of the towne of Berwike.

The duke of Albanie wrote all this preparation to the duke of Glocester, requiring him to haue no mistrust in his dealings. The duke of Glocester wrote to him againe his mind verie roundlie, promising that he with his armie would defend the besiegers from all enimies that should attempt to trouble them, or else die in the quarell. To be briefe, when the lords of Scotland saw that it booted them not to assaie the raising of the siege, except they should make account to be fought withall, they determined to deliuer the castell of Berwike to the Englishmen, so that therevpon there might be an abstinence of warre taken for a season.

And herewith they sent to the duke of Glocester a charter indented, which was dated the foure and twentith daie of August, in the said yeare 1482 contracted betwéene the duke of Glocester lieutenant generall for the king of England, & Alexander duke of Albanie lieutenant for Iames king of Scots ; that an especiall abstinence of warre should be kept betwixt the realmes of England and Scotland, as well by sea as by land, to begin the eighth daie of September next comming, & to indure till the fourth daie of Nouember next following. And in the same season, the towne & castell of Berwike to be occupied and remaine in the reall possession of such, as by the king of Englands deputie should be appointed.

Herevnto the duke of Glocester agreed, and so then was the castell of Berwike deliuered to the lord Stanleie, and other thereto appointed; who therein put both Englishmen and artillerie, sufficient to defend it against all Scotland, for six months. The duke of Albanie also caused the prouost and burgesses of Edenburgh, to make a sufficient instrument obligatorie to king Edward, for the true satisfaction and contentation of the same monie, which he also sent by the said prouost to the duke of Glocester to Alnewike: the verie copie whereof hereafter followeth.

The true copie of the said instrument obligatorie.

BE it knowne to all men by these present letters, vs Walter Bertraham, prouost of the towne of Edenburgh in Scotland, and the whole fellowship, merchants, burgesses, & communaltie of the same towne, to be bound and obliged by these presents, vnto the most excellent, and most mightie prince Edward, by the grace of God king of England. That where it was communed and agreed betweene his excellencie on the oné part, and the right high & mightie prince our souereigne lord, Iames king of Scots on the other part, that mariage and matrimonie should haue beene solemnized and had betwixt a mightie and excellent prince Iames the first begotten sonne and heire apparent to our souereigne lord aforesaid, & the right noble princesse Cicilie, daughter to the said Edward k. of England; and for the said mariage to haue beene performed, certeine and diuerse great summes of monie bene paid and contented by
the

the most excellent prince, vnto our souereigne lord aforesaid, as by certeine writings betwixt the said princes therevpon made more at large plainlie appeares.

That if it be the pleasure of the said Edward king of England, to haue the said mariage to be performed and completed, according to the said communication in writing, that then it shall be well and trulie, without fraud, deceipt, or collusion observed, kept, and accomplished on the partie of our souereigne lord aforesaid, & the nobles spirituall and temporall of the realme of Scotland. And if it be not the pleasure of the said excellent prince Edward king of England, to haue the said mariage performed and completed; that then we Walter, prouost, burgesses, merchants, and commons of the aboue named towne of Edenburgh, or anie of vs, shall paie and content to the king of England aforesaid, all the summes of monie that was paied for the said mariage, at such like termes & daies immediatlie insuing after the refusall of the said mariage, and in such like maner & forme as the said summes were afore deliuered, contented and paied; that then this obligation and bond to be void, and of no strength. Prouided alwaies, that the said Edward king of England, shall giue knowledge of his pleasure and election in the premisses in taking or refusing of the said mariage, or of repaiment of the said sums of monie, to our said souereigne lord, or lords of his councell, or to vs the said prouost, merchants, or any of vs, within the realme of Scotland, being for the time, betwixt this & the feast of Alhalowes next to come.

To the which paiment well and trulie to be made, we bind and oblige vs, & euerie of vs, our heires, successors, executors, and all our goods, merchandizes, & things what soeuer they be, where soeuer, or in what place, by water or by land, on this side the sea or beyond, we shall happen to be found, anie league, anie truce or safegard made or to be made, notwithstanding. In witnesse whereof to this our present writing, and letters of bond, we, the said prouost, burgesses, merchants, and communitie, haue set our common seale of the said towne of Edenburgh, the fourth daie of August, the yeare of our Lord God, 1482. Giuen in the presence of the right mightie prince Richard duke of Glocester, Alexander duke of Albanie, the reuerend father in God Iames bishop of Dunkeld, & the right noble lord Henrie earle of Northumberland, Colin earle of Argile, Thomas lord Stanleie, maister Alexander English, and others, &c.

So that you see it was conteined in the said instrument or writing, that king Edward should intimate his pleasure vnto the said prouost and burgesses of Edenburgh, before the feast of Alsaints next following, whether he would the mariage should take place, or that he would haue the paiment of the monie. According to which article, king Edward sent Gartier his principall king of armes, and Northumberland herald, to declare his refusall of the mariage, and the election and choise of the repaiment of the monie. They came to Edenburgh eight daies before the feast of Alsaints, where (according to their commission and instructions) Gartier declared the pleasure of the king his maister vnto the prouost and burgesses of Edenburgh, to whom he openlie said as followeth.

Gartier king of armes is sent into Scotland.

The intimation of Gartier king of armes to the Edenburghers.

I Gartier king of armes, seruant, proctour and messenger vnto the most high and mightie prince, my most dread souereigne lord Edward, by the grace of God king of England and of France, and lord of Ireland, by vertue of certeine letters of procuracie here readie to be shewed to me, by my said souereigne lord made and giuen, make notice and giue knowledge vnto you prouost, burgesses, merchants and com-

Abr. Fl. ex Edw. Hall. fol. Ccxlvij.

　　　　　　　　　　　　　　　　munaltie

munaltie of the towne of Edenburgh in Scotland, that whereas it was sometime communed and agreed betweene my said souereigne lord on the one partie, and the right high & mightie prince Iames king of Scots on the other partie, that mariage and matrimonie should haue beene solemnized, and had betweene Iames the first begotten sonne of the said king of Scots, and ladie Cicilie, daughter to my said souereigne lord the king of England.

And for the said mariage to haue been performed, certeine and diuers great sums of monie beene paied and contented by my said souereigne lord, which summes of monie, in case of refusall of the said mariage, by my said souereigne lord to be made and declared, yee the said prouost, burgesses, merchants, and communaltie, and euerie one of you are bound and obliged by your letters, vnder your common seale of your towne of Edenburgh, to repaie vnto his highness vnder like forme, & at such termes as they were first paied. So that the king my souereigne lord would make notice and knowledge of his pleasure and election in taking or refusing of the said mariage, of the repaiment of the said sums of monie, before the feast of Alhalowes next to come; like as in your said letters, bearing date at Edenburgh the fourth daie of August last past, it was conteined all at large.

The pleasure and election of my said souereigne lord, for diuerse causes and considerations him moouing, is to refuse the accomplishment of the said mariage, and to haue the repaiment of all such summes of monie, as (by occasion of the said betrusted mariage) his highnesse had paied. The said repaiment to be had of you prouost, burgesses, merchants, and communaltie, and euerie of you, your heires and successours, according to your bond and obligation afore rehearsed. And therefore I giue you notice & knowledge by this writing, which I deliuer vnto you, within the terme in your said letters limited and expressed, to all intents and effects, which thereof may insue.

When Gartier had thus declared all things giuen to him in charge, the prouost and other burgesses made answer, that they now knowing the kings determinat pleasure, would (according to their bond) prepare for the repaiment of the said summes; and gentlie interteining Gartier conueied him to Berwike, from whence he departed to Newcastell, to the duke of Glocester, making relation to him of all his dooings: which duke with all speed returned to Shrithuton, and there abode. Shortlie after Gartiers departing, the duke of Albanie, thinking to obteine againe the high fauour of the king his brother, deliuered him out of captiuitie and prison, wherin he had a certeine space continued (not without the dukes assent, which besieged him in the castell of Edenburgh a little before) and set him at large, of whome outwardlie he receiued great thanks, when inwardlie nothing but reuenging & confusion was in the kings stomach fullie setled. So that shortlie after in the kings presence he was in ieopardie of his life, and all vnprouided for dread of death, constrained to take a small balinger, and to saile into France, where shortlie after riding by the men of armes, which incountered at the tilt, by Lewes then duke of Orleance, after French king, he was with mischarging of a speare by fortunes peruerse countenance pitifullie slaine and brought to death, leauing after him one onelie son named Iohn, which being banished Scotland, inhabited and maried in France, and there died.

How dolorous, how sorrowfull is it to write, and much more painefull to remember the chances and infortunities that happened within two yeares in England and Scotland, betweene naturall brethren. For king Edward, set on by such as enuied the estate of the duke of Clarence, forgetting nature and brotherlie amitie, consented to the death of his said brother. Iames king of Scots, putting in obliuion that Alexander his brother was the onelie organ and instrument, by whome he obteined

teined libertie & fréedome, seduced and led by vile and malicious persons, which maligned at the glorie and indifferent iustice of the duke of Albanie, imagined and compassed his death, and exiled him for euer. What a pernicious serpent, what a venemous toade, and what a pestiferous scorpion is that diuelish whelpe, called priuie enuie. Against it no fortresse can defend, no caue can hide, no wood can shadow, no fowle can escape, nor no beast can auoid. Hir poison is so strong, that neuer man in authoritie could escape from the biting of hir teeth, scratching of hir pawes, blasting of hir breth, & filth of hir taile. Notable therefore is the Gréeke epigram in this behalfe, touching enuie of this kind, which saith, that a worsse thing than enuie there is not in the world, and yet hath it some goodnesse in it: for it consumeth the eies and the hart of the enuious. The words in their owne toong sententiouslie sound thus:

ὁ φθόνος ἐςὶ κάκιςον, ἔχει δὲ τὶ καλὸν ἐν αὐΐῷ,
τήκα γὰρ φθονδρῶν ὄμμαΐα καὶ κραδίαν

Although king Edward reioised that his businesse came to so good a conclusion with the Scots, yet he was about the same time 'sore disquieted in his mind towards the French king, whome he now perceiued to haue dallied with him, as touching the agreement of the mariage to be had betwixt the Dolphin and his daughter the ladie Elizabeth. For the lord Howard, being as then returned out of France, certified the king (of his owne knowledge) how that he being present, saw the ladie Margaret of Austrich daughter to duke Maximilian, sonne to the emperor Frederike, receiued into France with great pompe and roialtie, and at Ambois to the Dolphin contracted and espoused. King Edward highlie displeased with such double and vniust dealing of the French king, called his nobles togither, and opened to them his gréefes; who promised him for redresse thereof, to be readie with all their powers to make warres in France at his pleasure and appointment.

But whilest he was busie in hand to make his purueiance for warres thus against France, whether it was with melancholie and anger, which he tooke with the French kings dooings and vncourteous vsage; or were it by any superfluous surfet (to the which he was verie much giuen) he suddenlie fell sicke, and was so gréeuouslie taken, that in the end he perceiued his naturall strength in such wise to decaie, that there was little hope of recouerie in the cunning of his physicians, whome he perceiued onlie to prolong his life for a small time. Wherefore he began to make readie for his passage into another world, not forgetting (as after shall appeare) to exhort the nobles of his realme (aboue all things) to an vnitie among themselues. And hauing (as he tooke it) made an attonement betwixt the parties that were knowne to be scant fréends, he commended vnto their graue wisedoms the gouernment of his sonne the prince, and of his brother the duke of Yorke, during the time of their tender yeares. But it shall not be amisse to adde in this place the words which he is said to haue spoken on his death-bed, which were in effect as followeth.

The words of king Edward vttered by him on his death-bed.

MY welbeloued and no lesse betrusted fréends, councellors, and alies, if we mortall men would dailie and hourlie with our selues reuolue, and intentiuelie in our hearts ingraue, or in our minds seriouslie ponder, the fraile and fading imbecillitie of our humane nature, and the vnstablenesse of the same: we should apparantlie perceiue, that we being called reasonable creatures, and in that predicament compared and ioined with angels, be more worthie to be named and déemed persons vnreasonable, and rather to be associate in that name with brute beasts called vnreasonable (of

Abr. Fl, ex Edw. Hall. fol. Ccxlviij. Ccxlix.

Z z 2   whose

whose life and death no creature speaketh) rather than in that point to be resembled to the angelicall societie and reasonable companie.

For while health in vs florisheth, or prosperitie aboundeth, or the glosing world laugheth, which is he, so reasonable of vs all, that can saie (if he will not er from the truth) that he once in a weeke remembreth his fatall end, or the prescribed terme of his induring; or once prouided by labour, studie, or otherwise, to set a stedfast and sure order for the securitie, profit, and continuance either of his possessions & dominions, or of his sequele and posteritie which after him shall naturallie succéed. Such is the blindnesse of our fraile and weake nature, euer giuen to carnall concupiscence and worldlie delectations, dailie darkened and seduced with that lithargious and deceiuable serpent called hope of long life, that all we put in obliuion our duetie present, and lesse remember the politike purueiance for things to come : for blindlie we walke in this fraile life, till we fall groueling, with our eies suddenlie vpon death.

The vanities of this world be to vs so agreeable, that when we begin to liue, we estéeme our life a whole world; which once ouerpassed, it sheweth no better but dust driuen awaie with a puffe of wind. I speake this to you of my selfe, and for your selues to you; sore lamenting and inwardlie bewailing, that I did not performe & finallie consummate such politike deuises, & good and godlie ordinances, in my long life and peaceable prosperitie, which then I fullie determined to haue begun, set forward, and completlie to haue finished. Which now for the extreame paines and tortures of my angrie maladie, and for the small terme of my naturall life, I can neither perform, neither yet liue to sée either to take effect, or to sort to anie good conclusion.

For God I call to record, my heart was fullie set, and my mind deliberatlie determined, so to haue adorned this realme with wholesome lawes, stacutes and ordinances; so to haue trained and brought vp mine infants and children in vertue, learning, actiuitie, and policie, that, what with their roiall puissance, & your fréendlie assistance, the proudest prince of Europe durst not once attempt to mooue anie hostilitie, against them, you, or this realme. But oh Lord, all things that I of long time haue in my mind reuolued and imagined, that stealing théefe death goeth about to subuert, and in the moment of an houre cléerelie to ouertred. Wherefore (as men saie) I now being driuen to the verie hard wall, haue perfect confidence and sure hope in the approued fidelitie, and constant integritie, which I haue euer experimented and knowne to be rooted and planted in the hearts of your louing bodies, towards me and mine.

So that I may saie and auouch, that neuer prince bearing scepter and crowne ouer realmes and regions, hath found or prooued more faithfull councellors, nor truer subiects, than I haue doone of you; nor neuer potentate nor gouernour put more affiance and trust in his vassals and seruants, than I, since the adeption of the crowne, firmelie haue fixed in your circumspect wisedoms and sober discretions. And now of very force compelled, lieng in a doutfull hope, betwéene liuing and dieng, betweene remembrance and obliuion, I doo require you, and instantlie mooue you, that as I haue found you faithfull, obedient, and to all my requests and desires (while I was here in health conuersant with you) diligent and intentiue : so after my death, my hope is with a sure anchor grounded, & mine inward conceipt vndoubtedlie resolued, that the especiall confidence and inward fidelitie, which so long hath continued betwéene vs, being together liuing, shall not wholie by my death be extinct and vanished like smoke.

For what auaileth fréendship in life, when trust deceiueth after death? What profiteth amitie in apparant presence, when confidence is fraudulentlie beguiled in absence? What loue groweth by coniunction of matrimonie, if the ofspring after doo not agree and accord? Or what profiteth princes to aduance and promote their subiects,

iects, if after their death, the bountifulnesse by them shewed, be of the receiuers of the same and their sequele neither regarded nor yet remembred? The parents make the marriage for an indissoluble amitie.   Princes promote sometime for fauour, sometime for desert, & sometime for pleasure: yet (if you will consider) the verie scope, to the which all gifts of promotions doo finallie tend, is to haue loue, fauour, faithfull counsell, and diligent seruice, of such as be by them promoted and exalted, not onelie in their owne liues, being but bréefe and transitorie: but also that they and their progenie, calling to remembrance the fauor, estimation, and aduancement, which they of so liberall and munificent a prince had receiued and obteined, should with speare and shield, toong and wit, hand and pen, continuallie studie to defend, councell and preferre, not onelie him during his life, but also to serue, assist, and mainteine his sequele and lineall succession, as the verie images and carnall portratures of his stirpe, line, and stemme, naturallie descended.

In this case am I, whome you know, not without vnspeakable trouble & most dangerous war to haue obteined the scepter and diademe of this realme and empire. During which reigne, I haue had either litle peace, or small tranquillitie: and now when I thought my selfe sure of a quiet life, and worldlie rest death hath blowne his terrible trumpet, calling and summoning me (as I trust) to perpetuall tranquillitie and eternall quietnesse. Therefore now, for the perfect and vnmoueable confidence that I haue euer had in you, and for the vnfeined loue that you haue euer shewed vnto me, I commend and deliuer into your gouernance, both this noble realme, and my naturall children, and your kinsmen. My children by your diligent ouersight and politike prouision to be taught, informed, and instructed, not onelie in the sciences liberall, vertues morall, and good literature: but also to be practised in trickes of martiall actiuitie, and diligent exercise of prudent policie. For I haue heard clarkes saie, although I am vnlettered, that fortunate is that realme where philosophers reigne, or where kings be philosophers and louers of wisedome.

In this tender age, you may writh and turne them into euerie forme and fashion. If you bring them vp in vertue, you shall haue vertuous princes. If you set them to learning, your gouernours shall be men of knowledge. If you teach them actiuitie, you shall haue valiant capteins. If they practise policie, you shall haue both politike and prudent rulers. On the other side, if by your negligence they fall to vice (as youth is to all euill prone and readie) not onelie their honor, but also your honestie shall be spotted and appalled. If they be sluggards and giuen to slouth, the publike wealth of this realme must shortlie decaie. If they be vnlearned, they may by flatterie soone be blinded, and by adulation often deceiued. If they lacke actiuitie, euerie creature (be he neuer so base of birth) shall foile and ouerthrow them like dum beasts and beastlie dastards. Therefore I desire you, and in Gods name adiure you, rather to studie to make them rich in godlie knowledge, and vertuous qualities; than to take paine to glorifie them with abundance of worldlie treasure, and mundane superfluitie.

And certeinlie, when they come to ripenesse of age, and shall peraduenture consider, that by your omission and negligent education, they haue not such graces, nor are indued with such notable qualities as they might haue béene, if you had performed the trust to you by me committed: they shall not onelie deplore and lament their vngarnished estate, and naked condition; but also it may fortune, that they shall conceiue inwardlie against you such a negligent vntruth, that the sequele thereof may rather turne to displeasure than thanks, and sooner to an ingratitude than to a reward. My kingdome also I leaue in your gouernance, during the minoritie of my children, charging you (on your honors oths and fidelitie made and sworne to me) so indifferentlie to order and gouerne the subiects of the same, both with iustice and mercie, that the wils of malefactors haue not too large a scope, nor the harts of the good people by too much extremitie be neither sorowfullie daunted, nor vnkindlie kept vnder.

Oh

Oh I am so sléepie, that I must make an end. And now before you all I commend my soule to almightie God my sauiour and redeemer, my bodie to the wormes of the earth, my kingdome to the prince my sonne: and to you my louing fréends my my heart, my trust, and my whole confidence. [And euen with that he fell on sléepe.]

Hauing thus spoken, and set things in good staie, as might be supposed, he shortlie after departed this life at Westminster the ninth of Aprill, in the yeare 1483, after he had reigned two and twentie yeares, one moneth, and eight daies. His bodie was with funerall pompe conueied to Windsore, and there buried. He left behind him issue by the quéene his wife two sonnes, Edward and Richard, with fiue daughters; Elizabeth that was after quéene married to Henrie the seauenth; Cicilie married to the vicount Welles; Briget a nunne professed in Sion or Dertford, as sir Thomas More saith; Anne married to the lord Thomas Howard, after earle of Surrie, and duke of Norffolke; Katherine wedded to the lord William Courtenie sonne to the earle of Deuonshire. Beside these he left behind him likewise a base sonne named Arthur, that was after vicount Lisle. For the description of his person & qualities I will referre you to that which sir Thomas More hath written of him in that historie, which he wrote and left vnfinished of his sonne Edward the fift and of his brother king Richard the third: which we shall (God willing) hereafter make you partaker of, as we find the same recorded among his other workes, word for word; when first we haue (according to our begun order) rehersed such writers of our nation as liued in his daies.

As first, Nicholas Kenton borne in Suffolke a Carmelit frier in Gippeswich, prouinciall of his order through England; Henrie Parker a Carmelit frier of Doncaster, preached against the pride of prelats, and for such doctrine as he set foorth, was imprisoned with his fellow Thomas Holden, and a certeine blacke frier also for the like cause; Parker was forced to recant thrée speciall articles, as Bale noteth out of Leland; Iohn Harding an esquier borne in the north parts, wrote a chronicle in English verse, and among other speciall points therein touched, he gathered all the submissions and homages had and made by the Scotish kings, euen from the daies of king Athelstan [whereby it euidentlie may appeare, how the Scotish kingdome euen in manner from the first establishing thereof here in Britaine, hath béene apperteining vnto the kings of England, and holden of them as their chéefe, & superior lords.]

William Iue a doctor of diuinitie and prebendarie of saint Paules in London; Thomas Wilton a diuine, and deane of the said church of Paules in London; Iulian Bemes, a gentlewoman indued with excellent gifts both of bodie and mind, wrote certeine treatises of hawking and hunting, delighting greatlie hir selfe in those exercises and pastimes; she wrote also a booke of the lawes of armes, and knowledge apperteining to heralds; Iohn Stamberie borne in the west parts of this realme, a Carmelit frier, and confessor to king Henrie the sixt, he was also maister of Eaton colledge, and after was made bishop of Bangor, and remooued from thence to the sée of Hereford; Iohn Slueleie an Augustine frier, prouinciall of his order; Iohn Fortescue a iudge and chancellor of England, wrote diuerse treatises concerning the law and politike gouernement.

Rochus a Chaterhouse moonke borne in London, of honest parents, and studied in the vniuersitie of Paris, he wrote diuerse epigrams; Iohn Phreas borne also in London was fellow of Balioll colledge in Oxenford, and after went into Italie, where he heard Guarinus that excellent philosopher read in Ferrara, he prooued an excellent physician and a skilfull lawier, there was not in Italie (whilest he remained there) that passed him in eloquence & knowledge of both the toongs, Gréeke and Latine; Walter Hunt a Carmelit frier, a great diuine, and for his excellencie in learning sent from the
whole

whole bodie of this realme, vnto the generall councell holden first at Ferrara, and af-ter at Florence by pope Eugenius the fourth, where he disputed among other with the Gréekes, in defense of the order and ceremonies of the Latine church; Thomas Wig-henhall a moonke of the order called Premonstratensis in the abbeie of Durham in Norffolke.

Iohn Gunthorpe went into Italie, where he heard that eloquent learned man Gua-rinus read in Ferrara, after his comming home into England he was deane of Welles, and kéeper of the priuie seale; Iohn Hambois an excellent musician, and for his notable cunning therein made doctor of musicke; William Caxton wrote a chronicle called *Fructus temporum*, and an appendix vnto Treuisa, beside diuerse other bookes and translations; Iohn Miluerton a Carmelit frier of Bristow, and prouinciall of his order through England, Ireland, aud Scotland, at length (bicause he defended such of his order as preached against endowments of the church with temporall possessions) he was brought into trouble, committed to prison in castell S. Angelo in Rome, where he continued thrée yeares, and at length was deliuered through certeine of the cardinals that were appointed his iudges; Dauid Morgan a Welsh man, treasuror of the church of Landaffe, wrote of the antiquities of Wales, & a description of the countrie.

Iohn Tiptoft, a noble man borne, a great traueller, excellentlie learned, and wrote diuerse treatises, and finallie lost his head in the yeare 1471, in time of the ciuill warre betwixt the houses of Yorke and Lancaster; Iohn Shirwood bishop of Durham; Tho-mas Kent an excellent philosopher; Robert Huggon borne in Norffolke in a towne called Hardingham, wrote certeine veine prophesies; Iohn Maxfield a learned phy-sician; William Gréene a Carmelit frier; Thomas Norton borne in Bristow an alcumist; Iohn Meare a moonke of Norwich; Richard Porland borne in Norffolke a Franciscane frier, and a doctor of diuinitie; Thomas Milling a moonke of Westminster, a doctor of diuinitie and preferred to the bishoprike of Hereford; Scogan a learned gentleman and student for a time in Oxford, of a plesant wit, and bent to merrie deuises, in res-pect whereof he was called into the court, where giuing himselfe to his naturall incli-nation of mirth & pleasant pastime, he plaied manie sporting parts, although not in such vnciuill maner as hath beene of him reported

Thus farre the prosperous reigne of Edward the fourth, sonne and
heire to Richard duke of Yorke

THE.

THE HISTORIE OF

KING EDWARD THE FIFT,

AND

KING RICHARD THE THIRD vnfinished,

Written by Maister Thomas More then one of the vnder shiriffes of London,
about the yeare of our Lord 1513, according to a copie of his owne hand,
printed among his other Works.

KING Edward the fourth of that name, after that he had liued fiftie & three yeeres,
seuen moneths, and six daies, and thereof reigned two and twentie yeares, one
moneth, & eight daies, died at Westminster the ninth daie of Aprill, the yeare of our
redemption, a thousand foure hundred fourescore and thrée; leauing much faire
issue, that is to wit, Edward the prince, a thirtéene yeares of age, Richard duke of
Yorke two yeares yoonger; Elizabeth, whose fortune and grace was after to be quéene,
wife vnto king Henrie the seuenth, and mother vnto the eight; Cicilie, not so fortunate as faire; Briget, which representing the vertue of hir, whose name she bare,
professed and obserued a religious life in Dertford, an house of close nunnes; Anne,
that was after honorablie married vnto Thomas, then lord Howard, and after earle of
Surrie; and Katharine, which long time tossed in either fortune, sometime in wealth,
oft in aduersitie, at the last, if this be the last (for * yet she liueth) is by the benignitie
of hir nephue king Henrie the eight, in verie prosperous estate, and worthie hir birth
and vertue.

This noble prince deceassed at his palace of Westminster, and with great funerall
honor and heauines of his people from thence conueied, was interred at Windsor. A
king of such gouernance & behauior, in time of peace (for in warre each part must
néeds be others enimie) that there was neuer anie prince of this land, atteining the
crowne by battell, so heartilie beloued with the substance of the people: nor hée
himselfe so speciallie in anie part of his life, as at the time of his death. Which
fauour and affection, yet after his deceasse, by the crueltie, mischiefe, and trouble of
the tempestuous world that followed, highlie toward him more increased. At such
time as he died, the displeasure of those that bare him grudge for king Henries sake
the sixt, whome he deposed, was well asswaged, & in effect quenched, in that manie
of them were dead in more than twentie yeres of his reigne, a great part of a long life:
and manie of them in the meane season growne into his fauour, of which he was
neuer strange.

He was a goodlie personage, and princelie to behold, of heart couragious, politike
in counsell, in aduersitie nothing abashed, in prosperitie rather ioifull than proud,
peace iust and mercifull, in warre sharpe and fierce, in the field bold and hardie, and
natheles no further (than wisedome would) aduenturous, whose warres who so well
considered, he shall no lesse commend his wisedome where he voided, than his manhood where he vanquished. He was of visage louelie, of bodie mightie, strong, and
cleane made: howbeit, in his latter daies with ouer liberall diet somewhat corpulent

and

and boorelie, and nathelesse not vncomelie. He was of youth greatlie giuen to fleshlie wantonnesse: from which health of bodie, in great prosperitie and fortune, without a speciall grace hardlie refraineth, the poet implieng no lesse and saieng:

Mens erit apta capi tunc cùm lætissima rerum.

Vt seges in pingui luxuriabit humo.

This fault not greatlie gréeued the people: for neither could anie one mans pleasure stretch and extend to the displeasure of verie manie, and was without violence, and ouer that in his latter daies lessed, and well left. In which time of his latter daies this realme was in quiet and prosperous estate, no feare of outward enimies, no warre in hand, nor none toward, but such as no man looked for. The people toward the prince, not in a constreined feare, but in a willing and louing obedience: among themselues the commons in good peace. The lords, whome hée knew at variance, himselfe in his death bed appeased: he had left all gathering of monie (which is the onelie thing that withdraweth the hearts of English men from the prince) nor anie thing intended he to take in hand, by which he should be driuen therto: for his tribute out of France he had before obteined; and the yeare foregoing his death, he had obteined Berwike.

And albeit that all the time of his reigne he was with his people, so benigne, courteous, and so familiar, that no part of his vertues was more estéemed: yet the condition in the end of his daies (in which manie princes by a long continued souereigntie decline into a proud port from debonair behauior of their beginning) maruellouslie in him grew and increased: so farre foorth, that in summer (the last that euer hée saw) his highnes being at Windsor in hunting, sent for the maior & aldermen of London to him for none other errand, but to haue them hunt & be merrie with him, where he made them not so statelie, but so fréendlie and familiar cheere, and sent venison from thence so freelie into the citie, that no one thing in manie daies before gat him either more hearts, or more heartie fauour amongest the common people; which oftentimes more estéeme and take for greater kindnesse a little courtesie, than a great benefit. Sée before pag. 705.

So deceassed (as I haue said) this noble king, in that time in which his life was most desired. Whose loue of his people, and their entier affection towards him, had béene to his noble children (hauing in themselues also as manie gifts of nature, as manie princelie vertues, as much goodlie towardnesse as their age could receiue) a maruellous fortresse and sure armor, if diuision and dissention of their fréends had not vnarmed them, and left them destitute, and the execrable desire of souereigntie prouoked him to their destruction: which if either kind or kindnesse had holden place, must needs haue béene their cheefe defense. For Richard the duke of Glocester, by nature their vncle, by office their protector, to their father beholden, to themselues by oth and allegiance bounden, all the bands broken that bind man and man togither, without anie respect of God or the world, vnnaturallie contriued to beréeue them, not onelie their dignitie, but also their liues.

But forsomuch as this dukes demeanor ministreth in effect all the whole matter whereof this booke shall intreat, it is therefore conuenient somewhat to shew you yer we further go, what maner of man this was, that could find in his hart such mischiefe to conceiue. Richard duke of Yorke, a noble man and a mightie, began not by warre, but by law to chalenge the crowne, putting his claime into the parlement, where his cause was either for right or fauor so farre foorth aduanced, that king Henrie his bloud (albeit he had a goodlie prince) vtterlie reiected, the crowne was by authoritie of parlement intailed vnto the duke of Yorke and his issue male in remainder, immediatlie after the death of king Henrie. But the duke not induring so long to tarrie, but intending vnder pretext of dissention and debate arising in the realme, to preuent his time, and to take vpon him the rule in king Henrie his life, Richard duke of Yorke.

was with manie nobles of the realme at Wakefield slaine, leauing thrée sonnes, Edward George, and Richard.

All thrée as they were great states of birth, so were they great and statelie of stomach, greedie and ambitious of authoritie, and impatient of partners. Edward reuenging his fathers death, depriued king Henrie, and atteined the crowne. George duke of Clarence was a goodlie noble prince, and at all times fortunate, if either his owne ambition had not set him against his brother, or the enuie of his enimies * his brother against him. For were it by the quéene and lords of hir bloud, which highlie maligned the kings kinred (as women commonlie not of malice, but of nature hate them whome their husbands loue) or were a proud appetite of the duke himselfe, intending to be king; at the least wise heinous treason was there laid to his charge: and finallie, were hée faultie, were he faultlesse, atteinted was he by parlement, and iudged to the death, and therevpon hastilie drowned in a butt of malmesie. Whose death king Edward (albeit he commanded it) when he wist it was doone, pitiouslie bewailed, and sorrowfullie repented.

Richard the third sonne, of whome we now intreat, was in wit and courage equall with either of them, in bodie and prowesse farre vnder them both, litle of stature, ill featured of limmes, crooke backed, his left shoulder much higher than his right, hard fauoured of visage, and such as is in states called warlie, in other men otherwise; he was malicious, wrathfull, enuious, and from afore his birth euer froward. It is for truth reported, that the duchesse his mother had so much adoo in hir trauell, that she could not be deliuered of him vncut; and that he came into the world with the féet forward, as men be borne outward, and (as the fame runneth also) not vntoothed, whether men of hatred report aboue the truth, or else that nature changed hir course in his beginning, which in the course of his life manie things vnnaturallie committed. So that the full confluence of these qualities, with the defects of fauour and amiable proportion, gaue proofe to this rule of physiognomie:

Distortum vultum sequitur distorsio morum.

None euill capteine was he in the warre, as to which his disposition was more méetly than for peace. Sundrie victories had he, & sometimes ouerthrowes; but neuer on default as for his owne person, either of hardinesse or politike order. Frée was he called of dispense, and somewhat aboue his power liberall: with large gifts he gat him vnstedfast fréendship, for which he was faine to pill and spoile in other places, and got him stedfast hatred. He was close and secret, a déepe dissembler, lowlie of countenance, arrogant of heart, outwardlie companiable where he inwardlie hated, not letting to kisse whome he thought to kill: despitious and cruell, not for euill will alway, but ofter for ambition, and either for the suertie or increase of his estate.

Friend and fo was much what indifferent, where his aduantage grew, he spared no mans death whose life withstoode his purpose. He slue with his owne hands king Henrie the sixt, being prisoner in the Tower, as men constantlie said, and that without commandement or knowledge of the king, which would vndoubtedlie (if he had intended that thing) haue appointed that butcherlie office to some other, than his owne borne brother. Some wise men also wéene, that his drift couertlie conueied, lacked not in helping foorth his brother of Clarence to his death: which he resisted openlie, howbeit somewhat (as men déemed) more faintlie than he that were hartilie minded to his wealth.

And they that thus deeme, thinke that he long time in king Edwards life forethought to be king; in case that the king his brother (whose life he looked that euill diet should shorten) should happen to deceasse (as in déed he did) while his children were yoong. And they déeme, that for this intent he was glad of his brothers death the duke of Clarence, whose life must néeds haue hindered him so intending, whether the same duke of Clarence had kept him true to his nephue the yoong king, or enterprised

*dward.

George duke of Clarence.

* Had not set.

The description of Richard the hird.

The death of king Henrie the sixt.

prised to be king himselfe. But of all this point is there no certeintie, and who so diuineth vpon coniectures, maie as well shoot too farre as too short.

Howbeit this haue I by credible information learned, that the selfe night, in which king Edward died, one Mistlebrooke, long yer morning, came in great hast to the house of one Pottier dwelling in Redcrosse-stréete without Creplegate : and when he was with hastie rapping quickelie letten in, he shewed vnto Pottier, that king Edward was departed. "By my truth man" quoth Pottier, "then will my maister the duke of Glocester be king." What cause he had so to thinke, hard it is to saie; whether he being toward him, anie thing knew that he such thing purposed, or otherwise had anie inckeling thereof : for he was not likelie to speake it of nought.

But now to returne to the course of this historie. Were it that the duke of Glocester had of old foreminded this conclusion, or was now at erst therevnto mooued, and put in hope by the occasion of the tender age of the yoong princes, his nephues (as opportunitie & likelihood of spéed putteth a man in courage of that he neuer intended) certeine it is that he contriued their destruction, with the vsurpation of the regall dignitie vpon himselfe. And forsomuch as he well wist and holpe to mainteine a long continued grudge and heart-burning betwéene the quéens kinred and the kings bloud, either partie enuieng others authoritie, he now thought that their diuision should be (as it was in déed) a furtherlie beginning to the pursuit of his intent.

Nay he was resolued, that the same was a sure ground for the foundation of all his building, if he might first (vnder the pretext of reuenging of old displeasure) abuse the anger and ignorance of the tone partie to the destruction of the tother; and then win to his purpose as manie as he could, and those that could not be woone, might be lost yer they looked therfore. For of one thing was he certeine, that if his intent were perceiued, he should soone haue made peace betwéene both the parties with his owne bloud. King Edward in his life, albeit that this dissention betwéene his fréends somewhat irked him : yet in his good health he somewhat the lesse regarded it : bicause he thought whatsoeuer businesse should fall betweene them, himselfe should alwaie be able to rule both the parties.

But in his last sickenesse, when he perceiued his naturall strength so sore inféebled, that he despaired all recouerie, then he, considering the youth of his children, albeit he nothing lesse mistrusted than that that hapned; yet well foreséeing that manie harmes might grow by their debate, while the youth of his children should lacke discretion of themselues, & good counsell of their freends, of which either partie should counsell for their owne commoditie, & rather by plesant aduise to win themselues fauor, than by profitable aduertisement to doo the children good, he called some of them before him that were at variance, and in especiall the lord marquesse Dorset the quéenes sonne by hir first husband.

So did he also William the lord Hastings a noble man, then lord chamberleine, against whome the quéene speciallie grudged, for the great fauour the king bare him : and also for that she thought him secretlie familiar with the king in wanton companie. Hir kinred also bare him sore, as well for that the king had made him capteine of Calis, which office the lord Riuers, brother to the quéene, clamed of the kings former promise, as for diuerse other great gifts which he receiued, that they looked for. When these lords, with diuerse other of both the parties, were come in presence, the king lifting vp himselfe, and vnderset with pillowes, as it is reported, on this wise said vnto them.

Hastings lord chamberleine maligned of the quéene & hir k.

The oration of the king on his death-bed.

My lords, my deere kinsmen and alies, in what plight I lie you see, and I feele. By which the lesse while I looke to liue with you, the more deepelie am I mooued to

care

care in what case I leaue you, for such as I leaue you, such be my children like to find you. Which if they should (as God forbid) find you at variance, might hap to fall themselues at warre, yer their discretion would serue to set you at peace. Ye see their youth, of which I reckon the onelie suertie to rest in your concord. For it sufficeth not that all you loue them, if ech of you hate other: if they were men, your faithfulnesse happilie would suffice. But childhood must be mainteined by mens authoritie, and slipper youth vnderpropped with elder counsell, which neither they can haue but ye giue it, nor ye giue it if ye gree not.

For where ech laboureth to breake that the other maketh, and for hatred of ech of others person impugneth ech others counsell, there must it needs be long yer anie good conclusion go forward. And also while either partie laboureth to be cheefe, flatterie shall haue more place than plaine and faithfull aduise: of which must needs insue the euill bringing vp of the prince, whose mind in tender youth infect, shall redilie fall to mischeefe and riot, and draw downe with his noble relme to ruine. But if grace turne him to wisedome: which if God send, then they that by euill meanes before pleased him best, shall after fall furthest out of fauour: so that euer at length euill drifts shall draw to nought, and good plaine waies prosper.

Great variance hath there long beene betweene you, not alwaie for great causes. Sometimes a thing right well intended, our misconstruction turneth vnto woorse; or a small displeasure doone vs, either our owne affection or euill toongs aggreeueth. But this wot I well, ye neuer had so great cause of hatred, as ye haue of loue. That we be all men, that we be christian men, this shall I leaue for preachers to tell you; and yet I wot neere whether anie preachers words ought more to mooue you, than his that is by & by going to the place that they all preach of.

But this shall I desire you to remember, that the one part of you is of my bloud, the other of mine alies; and ech of you with other either of kinred or affinitie; which spirituall kinred of affinitie, if the sacraments of Christs church beare that weight with vs that would God they did, should no lesse mooue vs to charitie, than the respect of fleshlie consanguinitie. Our Lord forbid, that you loue together the woorse, for the selfe cause that you ought to loue the better. And yet that happeneth, and no where find we so deadlie debate, as among them, which by nature and law most ought to agree togither. Such a pestilent serpent is ambition and desire of vaine glorie and souereigntie, which among states where she once entereth, creepeth foorth so farre, till with diuision and variance she turneth all to mischeefe: first longing to be next vnto the best, afterward equall with the best, & at last cheefe and aboue the best.

The nature of ambition.

Of which immoderat appetite of worship, and thereby of debate and dissention, what losse, what sorow, what trouble hath within these few yeares growne in this realme, I praie God as well forget, as we well remember. Which things if I could as well haue foreseene, as I haue with my more paine than pleasure prooued, by Gods blessed ladie (that was euer his oth) I would neuer haue woone the courtesie of mens knees, with the losse of so manie heads. But sithens things passed can not be gaine called, much ought we the more beware, by what occasion we haue taken so great hurt afore, that we eftsoones fall not in that occasion againe.

Now be those greefs passed, and all is (God be thanked) quiet, and likelie right well to prosper in wealthfull peace vnder your coosins my children, if God send them life and you loue. Of which two things, the lesse losse were they, by whom though God did his pleasure, yet should the realme alwaie find kings, and peraduenture as good kings.

But if you among your selues in a childs reigne fall at debate, manie a good man shall perish, and happilie he too, and ye too, yer this land find peace againe. Wherfore in these last words that euer I looke to speake with you, I exhort you and require you all, for the loue that you haue euer borne to me; for the loue that I haue euer

borne

borne vnto you; for the loue that our Lord beareth to vs all; from this time forward (all greefs forgotten) ech of you loue other. Which I verilie trust you will, if ye anie thing earthlie regard, either God or your king, affinitie or kinred, this realme, your owne countrie, or your owne suertie. And therewithall the king no longer induring to sit vp, laid him downe on his right side, his face towards them: and none was there present that could refraine from weeping.

But the lords recomforting him with as good words as they could, and answering for the time as they thought to stand with his pleasure, there in his presence, as by their words appeared, ech forgaue other, and ioined their hands togither, when (as it after appeared by their deeds) their hearts were farre asunder. As soone as the king was departed, the noble prince his sonne drew toward London, which at the time of his deceasse kept his houshold at Ludlow in Wales, which countrie being farre off from the law and recourse to iustice, was begun to be farre out of good rule, and waxen wild robbers and reauers, walking at libertie vncorrected. And for this occasion the prince was in the life of his father sent thither, to the end that the authoritie of his presence should refraine euill disposed persons from the boldnesse of their former outrages. *A counterfet and pretended reconcilement.*

To the gouernance and ordering of this yoong prince at his sending thither, was there appointed sir Anthonie Wooduile lord Riuers, and brother vnto the queene, right honourable man, as valiant of hand as politike in counsell. Adioined were there vnto him other of the same partie; and in effect euerie one as he was néerest of kin vnto the queene, so was he planted next about the prince. That drift by the queene not vnwiselie deuised, whereby hir bloud might of youth be rooted into the princes fauour, the duke of Glocester turned vnto their destruction; and vpon that ground set the foundation of all his vnhappie building. For whome soeuer he perceiued either at variance with them, or bearing himselfe their fauour, he brake vnto them some by mouth, & some by writing. *a Lord Riuers.* *The duke of Glocesters solicitations.*

Nay, he sent secret messengers saieng, that it neither was reason, nor in anie wise to be suffered, that the yoong king their maister and kinsman, should be in the hands and custodie of his moothers kinred, sequestred in maner from their companie and attendance, of which euerie one ought him as faithfull seruice as they, and manie of them farre more honourable part of kin than his moothers side. Whose bloud (quoth he) sauing the kings pleasure, was full vnméetelie to be matched with his: which now to be as who say remooued from the king, and the lesse noble to be left about him, is (quoth he) neither honourable to his maiestie nor to vs, and also to his grace no suertie, to haue the mightiest of his fréends from him; and vnto vs no little ieopardie, to suffer our well prooued euill willers to grow in ouer-great authoritie with the prince in youth; namelie, which is light of beléefe and soone persuaded.

Yée remember (I trow) king Edward himselfe, albeit he was a man of age & discretion, yet was he in manie things ruled by the bend, more than stood either with his honor, or our profit, or with the cōmoditie of any man else, except onlie the immoderate aduancement of themselues. Which, whether they sorer thirsted after their owne weale, or our wo, it were hard (I wéene) to gesse. And if some folks fréendship had not holden better place with the king, than anie respect of kinred, they might peraduenture easilie haue betrapped and brought to confusion some of vs yer this. Why not as easilie as they haue doone some other alreadie, as neere of his roiall bloud as we? But our Lord hath wrought his will, and (thanks be to his grace) that perill is past. Howbeit as great is growing, if we suffer this yoong king in our enimies hand, which without his witting might abuse the name of his commandement, to anie of our vndooing, which thing God [defend] and good prouision forbid.

Of

Of which good prouision none of vs hath anie thing the lesse néed, for the late made attonement, in which the kings pleasure had more placé than the parties willes. Nor none of vs (I beléeue) is so vnwise, ouersoone to trust a new fréend made of an old fo; or to thinke that an hourlie kindneſ, suddenlie contracted in one houre, continued yet scant a fortnight, should be déeper settled in their stomachs, than a long accustomed malice manie yeares rooted. With these words and writings, and such other, the duke of Glocester soone set on fire them that were of themselues easie to kindle, & in speciallie twaine, Edward duke of Buckingham, and William lord Hastings then chamberleine, both men of honour & of great power; the one by long succession

A consent to ∞ orke wicked-ɪesse.

from his ancestrie, the other by his office and the kings fauour. These two, not bearing ech to other so much loue, as hatred both vnto the quéenes part: in this point accorded togither with the duke of Glocester, that they would vtterlie remoue from the kings companie all his mothers fréends, vnder the name of their enimies.

Vpon this concluded the duke of Glocester, vnderstanding that the lords, which at that time were about the king, intended to bring him vp to his coronation accōpanied with such power of their fréends, that it should be hard for him to bring his purpose to passe, without the gathering and great assemblie of people and in maner of open warre, whereof the end (he wist) was doubtfull, and in which the king being on their side, his part should haue the face and name of a rebellion: he secretlie therfore by diuers means caused the queene to be persuaded and brought in the mind, that it neither were néed, and also should be ieopardous, the king to come vp strong.

For whereas now euerie lord loued other, and none other thing studied vpon, but about the coronation and honor of the king: if the lords of hir kindred should assemble in the kings name much people, they should giue the lords, betwixt whome and them had béene sometime debate, to feare and suspect, least they should gather this people, not for the kings safegard, whom no man impugned, but for their destruction, hauing more regard to their old variance, than their new attonement. For which cause they should assemble on the other partie much people againe for their defense, whose power she wist well far stretched: and thus should all the realme fall on a rore. And of all the hurt that thereof should insue, which was likelie not to be little, and the most harme there like to fall where she least would, all the world would put hir and hir kindered in the wight, and saie that they had vnwiselie and vntrulie also broken the amitie & peace that the king hir husband so prudentlie made, betwéene his kin and hirs in his death bed and which the other partie faithfullie obserued.

The queene, being in this wise persuaded, such word sent vnto hir sonne, and vnto hir brother being about the king, and ouer that the duke of Glocester himselfe and other lords the chiefe of his bend, wrote vnto the king so reuerentlie, and to the quéenes fréends there so louinglie, that they nothing earthlie mistrusting, brought the king vp in great hast, not in good spéed, with a sober companie. Now was the king in his waie to London gone from Northampton, when these dukes of Glocester and Buckingham came thither, where remained behind the lord Riuers the kings vncle, intending on the morrow to follow the king, and to be with him at Stonie Stratford [certeine] miles thence earlie yer he departed. So was there made that night much fréendlie chéere betwéene these dukes & the lord Riuers a great while, but incōtinent, after that they were openlie with great courtesie departed, and the lord Riuers lodged, the dukes secretlie with a few of their most priuie fréends set them downe in councell, wherein they spent a great part of the night.

The practices of the duke of Buckingham & Glocester.

And at their rising in the dawning of the daie, they sent about priuilie to their seruants in their Ins & lodgings about, giuing them commandement to make themselues shortlie readie, for their lords were to horsse backeward. Vpon which messages, manie of their folke were attendant, when manie of the lord Riuers seruants were vnreareadie.

readie. Now had these dukes taken also into their custodie the keies of the In, that none should passe foorth without their licence. And ouer this, in the high waie toward Stonie Stratford, where the king lay, they had bestowed certeine of their folke, that should send backe againe, and compell to returne, anie man that were gotten out of Northampton, toward Stonie Stratford, till they should giue other licence. For asmuch as the dukes themselues intended for the shew of their diligence, to be the first that should that daie attend vpon the kings highnesse out of that towne. Thus bare they folke in hand.

But when the lord Riuers vnderstood the gates closed, and the waies on euerie side beset, neither his seruants nor himselfe suffered to gone out, perceiuïng well so great a thing without his knowledge not begun for naught, comparing this manner present with this last nights chéere, in so few houres so great a change, maruellouslie misliked. Howbeit, sith he could not get awaie, and keepe himselfe close, he would not, least he should séeme to hide himselfe for some secret feare of his owne fault, whereof he saw no such cause in himselfe; he determined vpon the suertie of his owne conscience, to go boldlie to them, and inquire what this matter might meane. Whóm assoone as they saw, they began to quarrell with him and saie that he intended to set distance betweene the king and them, and to bring them to confusion, but it should not lie in his power.

And when he began (as he was a verie well spoken man) in goodlie wise to excuse himselfe, they tarried not the end of his answer, but shortlie tooke him, and put him in ward, and that doone, foorthwith went to horssebacke, and tooke the waie to Stonie Stratford, where they found the king with his companie, readie to leape on horssebacke, and depart forward to leaue that lodging for them, bicause it was too streight for both companies. And assoone as they came in his presence, they light adowne with all their companie about them. To whome the duke of Buckingham said; Go afore gentlemen, & yeomen kéepe your roomes. And thus in a goodlie araie, they came to the king, and on their knées in verie humble wise saluted his grace, which receiued them in verie ioious and amiable manner, nothing earthlie knowing nor mistrusting as yet.

The lord Riuers put in ward.

But euen by and by in his presence they piked a quarrell to the lord Richard Greie, the kings other brother by his mother, saieng, that he with the lord marquesse his brother, & the lord Riuers his vncle, had compassed to rule the king and the realme, and to set variance among the states, and to subdue and destroie the noble bloud of the Realme. Toward the accómplishing wherof they said that the lord marquesse had entered into the Tower of London, & thence taken out the kings treasure, and sent men to the sea. All which things these dukes wist well were doone for good purposes and necessarie, by the whole councell at London, sauing that somewhat they must saie.

The lord Greie is quarelled against.

Vnto which words the king answered; What my brother marquesse hath doone I cannot saie, but in good faith I dare well answer for mine vncle Riuers and my brother here, that they be innocent of anie such matter. Yea my liege (quoth the duke of Buckingham) they haue kept their dealing in these matters farre fro the knowledge of your good grace. And foorthwith they arested the lord Richard and sir Thomas Vaughan knight, in the kings presence; and brought the king and all backe vnto Northampton, where they tooke againe further councell. And there they sent awaie from the king, whom it pleased them, and set new seruants about him, such as liked better them than him. At which dealing he wept, and was nothing content; but it booted not.

And at dinner, the duke of Glocester sent a dish from his owne table vnto the lord Riuers, praieng him to be of good chéere: all should be well inough. And he thanked the duke, and praied the messenger to beare it to his nephue the lord Richard, with

the

the same message for his comfort, who he thought had more néed of comfort, as one to whome such aduersitie was strange. But himselfe had béene all his daies in vse therewith, & therefore could beare it the better. But for all this comfortable courtesie of the duke of Glocester, he sent the lord Riuers, and the lord Richard, with sir Thomas Vaughan into the north countrie, into diuerse places to prison, and afterward all to Pomfret, where they were in conclusion beheaded.

The death of the lord Riuers & other.

In this wise the duke of Glocester tooke vpon himselfe the order and gouernance of the yoong king, whome with much honor and humble reuerence he conueied vpward towards the citie. But anon, the tidings of this matter came hastilie to the queene a little before the midnight following, and that in the sorest wise; that the king hir son was taken, hir brother, hir sonne, & hir other fréends arrested, and sent no man wist whither, to be doone with God wot what. With which tidings the quéene in great flight & heauinesse, bewailing hir childes reigne, hir freends mischance, and hir owne infortune, damning the time that euer she dissuaded the gathering of power about the king, gat hir selfe in all the hast possible with hir yoonger sonne and hir daughters out of the palace of Westminster, in which she then laie, into the sanctuarie, lodging hir selfe and hir companie there in the abbats place.

The quéene taketh sanctuarie.

Now came there one in likewise not long after midnight from the lord chamberleine, to doctor Rotheram the archbishop of Yorke, then chancellor of England, to his place not farre from Westminster, and for that he shewed his seruants that he had tidings of so great importance, that his maister gaue him in charge, not to forbeare his rest, they letted not to wake him, nor he to admit this messenger in, to his bed side. Of whom he heard that these dukes were gone backe with the kings grace from Stonie Stratford vnto Northampton. Notwithstanding sir (quoth he) my lord sendeth your lordship word, that there is no feare: for he assureth you that all shall be well. I assure him (quoth the archbishop) be it as well as it will, it will neuer be so well as we haue seene it.

And therevpon, by and by after the messenger departed, he caused in all the hast all his seruants to be called vp, and so with his owne houshold about him, and euerie man weaponed, he tooke the great seale with him, and came yet before daie vnto the queene. About whom he found much heauinesse, rumble, hast and businesse, cariage and conueiance of hir stuffe into sanctuarie, chests, coffers, packs, fardels, trussed all on mens backs, no man vnoccupied, some lading, some going, some discharging, some comming for more, some breaking downe the walles to bring in the next waie, and some yet drew to them that holpe to carrie a wrong waie: such made their lucre of others losse, praising a bootie aboue beautie, to whome the poets verse may be well applied, to wit:

Tibul. lib. 2. eleg. 3.

> Ferrea non Venerem sed prædem sæcula laudant.

The desolate state of the quéene.

The quéene hir selfe sate alone alow on the rushes all desolate and dismaid, whome the archbishop comforted in best manner he could, shewing hir that he trusted the matter was nothing so sore as she tooke it for, and that he was put in good hope and out of feare by the message sent him from the lord chamberleine. Ah wo woorth him (quoth she) for he is one of them that laboreth to destroie me and my bloud. Madame (quoth he) be yée of good chéere, for I assure you, if they crowne anie other king than your sonne, whome they now haue with them, we shall on the morow crowne his brother, whome you haue here with you. And here is the great seale, which in likewise as that noble prince your husband deliuered it vnto me; so here I deliuer it vnto you, to the vse and behoofe of your sonne: and therewith he betooke hir the great seale, and departed home againe, yet in the dawning of the daie.

By which time, he might in his chamber window sée all the Thames full of boates of the duke of Glocesters seruants, watching that no man should go to sanctuarie, nor none could passe vnsearched. Then was there great commotion and murmur, as

well

well in other places about, as speciallie in the citie, the people diuerselie diuining vpon this dealing. And some lords, knights, and gentlemen, either for fauour of the quéene, or for feare of themselues, assembled in sundrie companies, and went flockmele in harnesse: and many also, for that they reckoned this demeanor attempted, not so speciallie against the other lords, as against the king himselfe in the disturbance of his coronation. But then by and by the lords assembled togither at [a certeine place.]

Toward which méeting, the archbishop of Yorke fearing that it would be ascribed (as it was indéed) to his ouermuch lightnesse, that he so suddenlie had yéelded vp the great seale to the quéene, to whome the custodie thereof nothing perteined, without especiall commandement of the king, secretlie sent for the seale againe, and brought it with him after the customable maner. And at this méeting the lord Hastings (whose truth toward the king no man doubted, nor néeded to doubt) persuaded the lords to beléeue, that the duke of Glocester was sure and fastlie faithfull to his prince, and that the lord Riuers, and lord Richard with the other knights, were for matters attempted by them against the duke of Glocester and Buckingham, put vnder arrest for their suertie, not for the kings ieopardie: and that they were also in safegard, and there no longer should remaine, than till the matter were, not by the dukes onelie, but also by all the other lords of the kings councell indifferentlie examined, & by others discretions ordered, and either iudged or appeased. Neuerthelesse he was depriued thereof shortlie after.

But one thing he aduised them beware, that they iudged not the matter too farre foorth, yer they knew the truth; nor turning their priuate grudges into the common hurt, irriting and prouoking men vnto anger, and disturbing the kings coronation, towards which the dukes were comming vp, that they might peraduenture bring the matter so farre out of ioint, that it should neuer be brought in frame againe. Which strife if it should hap (as it were likely) to come to a field, though both parties were in all other things equall; yet should the authoritie be on that side where the king is himselfe. With these persuasions of the lord Hastings, whereof part himselfe beléeued, of part he wist the contrarie, these commotions were somewhat appeased. But speciallie by that, that the dukes of Glocester and Buckingham were so néere and came so shortlie on with the king, in none other manner, with none other voice or semblance than to his coronation, causing the fame to be blowen about, that these lords and knights which were taken, had contriued the destruction of the dukes of Glocester and Buckingham, and of other noble bloud of the realme, to the end that themselues would alone demeane and gouerne the king at their pleasure.

And for the colourable proofe thereof, such of the dukes seruants as rode with the carts of their stuffe that were taken (among which stuffe, no maruell though some were harnesse, which at the breaking vp of that houshold must néeds either be brought awaie or cast awaie) they shewed vnto the people all the waies as they went; " Lo here be the barrels of harnesse that these traitors had priuilie conueied in their carriage to destroie the noble lords withall." This deuise albeit that it made the matter to wise men more vnlikelie, well perceiuing that the intendors of such a purpose would rather haue had their harnesse on their backs, than to haue bound them vp in barrels, yet much part of the common people were therewith verie well satisfied, and said it were almesse to hang them.

When the king approched néere to the citie, Edmund Shaw goldsmith, then maior, with William White, and Iohn Matthew shiriffes and all the other aldermen in scarlet, with fiue hundred horsse of the citizens, in violet, receiued him reuerentlie at Harnesie; and riding from thence accompanied him into the citie, which he entered the fourth daie of Maie, the first and last yeare of his reigne. But the duke of Glocester bare him in open sight so reuerentlie to the prince, with all semblance of lowlinesse, that from the great obloquie in which he was so late before, he was suddenlie fallen in so The kings comming to London.

great trust, that at the councell next assembled he was made the onelie man, chosen

The duke of
Glocester made
protector.
and thought most meet to be protector of the king and his realme, so that (were it
destinie or were it follie) the lambe was betaken to the woolfe to kéepe.

At which councell also, the archbishop of Yorke chancellor of England, which had
deliuered vp the great seale to the quéene, was thereof greatlie reprooued, and the seale

The bishop of
Lincolne made
lord chancellor.
taken from him, and deliuered to doctor Russell bishop of Lincolne, a wise man and a
good, and of much experience, and one of the best learned men vndoubtedlie that
England had in his time. Diuerse lords and knights were appointed vnto diuerse
roomes. The lord chamberleine and some other kept still their offices that they had
before. Now all were it so that the protector so sore thirsted for the finishing of that
he had begun, that thought euerie daie a yeare till it were atchiued; yet durst he no
further attempt, as long as he had but halfe his preie in his hand.

And why? Well did he wéet, that if he deposed the one brother, all the realme
would fall to the other, if he either remained in sanctuarie, or should happilie be shortlie

The protectors
oration.
conueied to his fathers libertie. Wherfore incontinent at the next méeting of the lords
at the councell, he proposed to them, that it was a heinous déed of the quéene, & procéeding of great malice toward the kings councellors, that she should kéepe in sanctuarie the kings brother from him, whose speciall pleasure & comfort were to haue his
brother with him. And that by hir doone to none other intent, but to bring all the
lords in obloquie and murmur of the people.

As though they were not to be trusted with the kings brother, that by the assent of
the nobles of the land, were appointed as the kings neerest fréends, to the tuition of
his owne roiall person. The prosperitie whereof standeth (quoth he) not all in kéeping from enimies, or ill viand, but partlie also in recreation, and moderate pleasure:
which he cannot (in this tender youth) take in the companie of ancient persons, but
in the familiar conuersation of those that be neither farre vnder, nor farre aboue his
age: and neuerthelesse of estate conuenient to accompanie his noble maiestie. Wherefore, with whome rather, than with his owne brother?

And if anie man thinke this consideration light (which I thinke none thinks that
loues the king) let him consider, that sometime without small things, greater cannot
stand. And verelie, it redoundeth greatlie to the dishonor both of the kings highnesse, and of all vs that béene about his grace, to haue it run in euerie mans mouth,
not in this realme onlie, but also in other lands (as euill words walke far) that the kings
brother should be faine to keepe sanctuarie. For euerie man will wéene, that no man
will so doo for naught. And such euill opinion once fastned in mens harts, hard it is to
wrest out, and may grow to more greefe than anie man can here diuine.

Wherefore me thinketh it were not worst to send vnto the quéene, for the redresse
of this matter, some honorable trustie man, such as both tendereth the kings weale

The lord
cardinall thought
the fittest man
to deale with the
quéene for the
surrendring of
hir sonne.
and the honour of his councell, and is also in fauour and credence with hir. For all
which considerations, none seemeth more méetlie, than our reuerend father here present, may lord cardinall, who may in this matter doo most good of anie man, if it
please him to take the paine; which I doubt not of his goodnesse he will not refuse
for the kings sake and ours, and welth of the yoong duke himselfe, the kings most
honorable brother, and (after my souereigne lord himselfe) my most déere nephue, considered that thereby shall be ceassed the slanderous rumor and obloquie now going, and
the hurts auoided that thereof might insue, and much rest and quiet grow to all the
realme.

And if she be percase so obstinate, and so preciselie set vpon hir owne will, that
neither his wise and faithfull aduertisement can not mooue hir, nor anie mans reason
content hir; then shall we by mine aduise, by the kings authoritie fetch him out of
that prison, and bring him to his noble presence, in whose continuall companie he shall
be so well cherished and so honorablie intreated, that all the world shall to our honour
and

and hir reproch perceiue that it was onelie malice, frowardnesse, or follie, that caused hir to kéepe him there. This is my purpose and mind in this matter for this time, except anie of your lordships anie thing perceiue to the contrarie; for neuer shall I (by Gods grace) so wed myselfe to mine owne will, but that I shall be readie to change it vpon your better aduises.

When the protector had said, all the councell affirmed, that the motion was good and reasonable; and to the king and the duke his brother, honorable; and a thing that should ceasse great murmur in the realme, if the mother might be by good means induced to deliuer him. Which thing the archbishop of Yorke, whome they all agreed also to be thereto most conuenient, tooke vpon him to mooue hir, and therein to doo his vttermost deuoir. Howbeit, if she could be in no wise intreated with hir good will to deliuer him, then thought he, and such other as were of the spiritualtie present, that it were not in anie wise to be attempted to take him out against hir will.

For it should be a thing that would turne to the great grudge of all men, and high displeasure of God, if the priuilege of that holie place should now be broken, which had so manie yeares be kept, which both kings and popes so good had granted, so manie had confirmed, and which holie ground was more than fiue hundred yeares ago (by saint Peter in his owne person in spirit accompanied with great multitudes of angels by night) so speciallie halowed, & dedicated to God (for the proofe wherof, they haue yet in the abbeie saint Peters cope to shew) that from that time hitherward, was there neuer so vndeuout a king that durst that sacred place violate, or so holie a bishop that durst it presume to consecrate. Reasons why it was not thought méet to fetch the quéens son out of sanctuarie.

And therefore (quoth the archbishop of Yorke) God forbid that anie man should for anie thing earthlie, enterprise to breake the immunitie & libertie of the sacred sanctuarie, that hath beene the safegard of so manie a good mans life. And I trust (quoth he) with God grace, we shall not need it. But for anie maner néed, I would not we should doo it. I trust that shée shall be with reason contented, and all things in good maner obteined. And if it happen that I bring it not so to passe, yet shall I toward it so farre foorth doo my best, that ye shall all well perceiue, that no lacke of my deuoire, but the mother's dread and womanish feare shall be the let.

Womanish feare, naie womanish frowardnes (quoth the duke of Buckingham.) For I dare take it vpon my soule, she well knoweth she needeth no such thing to feare, either for hir son or for hir selfe. For as for hir, here is no man that will be at war with women. Would God some of the men of hir kin were women too, & then should all be soone in rest. Howbeit there is none of hir kin the lesse loued, for that they be hir kin, but for their owne euill deseruing. And nathelesse, if we loued neither hir nor hir kin, yet were there no cause to thinke that wee should hate the kings noble brother, to whose grace we our selues be of kin. Whose honor, if she as much desired as our dishonor, and as much regard tooke to his wealth as to hir owne will, she would be as loth to suffer him to be absent from the king, as anie of vs be. For if she haue anie wit (as would God she had as good will as she hath shrewd wit) she reckoneth hir selfe no wiser than she thinketh some that be here, of whose faithfull mind she nothing doubteth, but verelie beléeueth and knoweth, that they would be as sorie of his harme as hir selfe, and yet would haue him from hir if she bide there: and we all (I thinke) contented, that both be with hir, if she come thence, and bide in such place where they may with their honors be. Now then, if she refuse in the deliuerance of him, to follow the counsell of them, whose wisdome she knoweth whose truth she well trusteth: it is easie to perceiue, that frowardnesse letteth hir and not feare. But go to, suppose that she feare (as who maie let hir to feare hir owne shadow) the more she feareth to deliuer him the more ought we feare to leaue him in hir hands. The duke of Buckinghãs words against the quéene.

For if she cast such fond doubts, that she feare his hurt: then will she feare that he shall be fet thence. For she will soone thinke, that if men were set (which God forbid) vpon so great mischiefe, the sanctuarie would little let them: which good men might (as me thinketh) without sinne somewhat lesse regard than they doo. Now then, if she doubt, least he might be fetched from hir, is it not likelie inough that she shall send him some where out of the realme? Verelie I looke for none other. And I doubt not, but shee now as sore mindeth it, as we the let thereof. And if she might happen to bring that to passe (as it were no great maistrie, we letting hir alone) all the world would saie, that we were a wise sort of councellors about a king, that let his brother be cast awaie vnder our noses.

And therefore, I insure you faithfullie for my mind, I will rather (mauger hir mind) fetch him awaie, than leaue him there, till hir frowardnesse and fond feare conueie him awaie. And yet will I breake no sanctuarie therefore. For verely, sith the priuileges of that place, and other like, haue béene of long continued, I am not he that would be about to breake them. And in good faith, if they were now to begin, **Of sanctuaries.** I would not be he that should be about to make them. Yet will I not say naie, but that it is a déed of pitie, that such men as the sea, or their euill debtors haue brought in pouertie, should haue some place of libertie, to kéepe their bodies out of danger of their cruell creditors.

And also, if the crowne happen (as it hath doone) to come in question, while either part taketh other as traitors, I will well there be some places of refuge for both. But as for théeues, of which these places be full, and which neuer fall from the craft, after they once fall thereto, it is pitie the sanctuarie should serue them. And much more, mankillers, whome God bad to take them from the altar and kill them, if their muther were wilfull. And where it is otherwise, there néed we not the sanctuaries that God appointed in the old law. For if either necessitie, his owne defense, or misfortune draweth him to that déed, a pardon serueth, which either the law granteth of course, or the king of pitie maie. Then looke me now how few sanctuarie men there be, whome anie fauourable necessitie compelled to go thither. And then sée on the other side, what a sort there be commonlie therin of them, whom wilfull vnthriftinesse hath brought to naught.

What a rabble of théeues, murtherers, and malicious heinous traitors, and that in two places speciallie; the one at the elbow of the citie, the other in the verie bowels. **Westminster and saint Martins.** I dare well auow it, weie the good that they doo, with the hurt that commeth of them, and ye shall find it much better to lacke both, than haue both. And this I saie, although they were not abused as they now be, & so long haue be, that I feare me **The abuse of sanctuaries.** euer they will be, while men be afraid to set their hands to the mendment, as though God & S. Peter were the patrones of vngratious liuing. Now vnthrifts riot & run in debt, vpon boldnesse of these places, yea, and rich men run thither with poore mens goods, there they build, there they spend, & bid there creditors go whistle them. Mens wiues run thither with their husbands plate, & saie they dare not abide with their husbands for beating. Théeues bring thither their stollen goods, and there liue thereon.

There deuise they new robberies, nightlie they steale out, they rob, and reaue, and kill, and come in againe, as though those places gaue them not onelie a safegard for the harme they haue doone, but a licence also to doo more. Howbeit, much of this mischiefe (if wise men would set their hands to it) might be amended, with great thanks to God, and no breach of the priuilege. The residue, sith so long ago, I wote néere what pope, and what prince more pitious than politike, hath granted it, & other men since, of a certeine religious feare, haue not broken it, let vs take a paine therewith, and let it a Gods name stand in force, as farre foorth as reason will, which is not fullie so farre foorth, as may serue to let vs of the fetching foorth of this noble man to his honor and wealth, out of that place, in which he neither is, nor can be a sanctuarie man.

                                                A sanctuarie

A sanctuarie serueth alwaie to defend the bodie of that man that standeth in dan- The vse of
sanctuaries.
ger abroad, not of great hurt onlie, but also of lawfull hurt: for against vnlawfull
harmes, neuer pope nor king intended to priuilege anie one place, for that priuilege
hath euerie place. Knoweth anie man, anie place wherin it is lawfull one man to
doo another wrong? That no man vnlawfullie take hurt, that libertie, the king, the
law, and verie nature forbiddeth in euerie place, and maketh (to that regard) for euerie
man euerie place a sanctuarie. But where a man is by lawfull means in perill, there néedeth he the tuition of some speciall priuilege, which is the onelie ground and cause of
all sanctuaries.

From which necessitie, this noble prince is farre, whose loue to his king, nature and
kinred prooueth; whose innocencie to all the world, his tender youth prooueth; and
so sanctuarie, as for him, neither none he néedeth, nor also none can haue. Men come
not to sanctuarie, as they come to baptisme, to require it by their godfathes, he must
aske it himselfe that must haue it, and reason; sith no man hath cause to haue it, but
whose conscience of his owne fault maketh him fane, néed to require it. What will
then hath yonder babe, which and if he had discretion to require it, if néed were, I
dare say would now be right angrie with them that kéepe him there? And I would thinke
without anie scruple of conscience, without anie breach of priuilege, to be somewhat
more homelie with them that be there sanctuarie men in déed.

For if one go to sanctuarie with another mans goods, whie should not the king,
leauing his bodie at libertie, satisfie the partie of his goods, euen within the sanctuarie? For neither king nor pope can giue anie place such a priuilege, that it shall discharge a man of his debts, being able to paie. [And with that, diuerse of the clergie
that were present (whether they said it for his pleasure, or as they thought) agréed
plainelie, that by the law of God, and of the church, the goods of a sanctuarie man
should be deliuered in paiment of his debts, and stollen goods to the owner, and onlie
libertie reserued him to get his liuing with the labor of his hands.]

Verelie (quoth the duke) I thinke you say verie truth. And what if a mans wife
will take sanctuarie, bicause she lust to run frō hir husband, I would weene if she
could alledge none other cause, he maie lawfullie without anie displeasure to saint
Peter, take hir out of saint Peters church by the arme. And if no bodie maie be
taken out of sanctuarie, that saith hée will bide there: then if a child will take sanctuarie, bicause he feareth to go to schoole, his maister must let him alone. And as
simple as that sample is, yet is there lesse reason in our case than in that; for therein,
though it be a childish feare, yet is there at the leastwise some feare, and herein is
there none at all. And verelie, I haue often heard of sanctuarie men, but I neuer
heard earst of sanctuarie children.

And therefore, as for the conclusion of my mind, who so maie haue deserued to
need it, if they thinke it for their suertie, let them kéepe it. But he can be no sanctuarie man, that neither hath wisdome to desire it, nor malice to deserue it; whose
life or libertie can by no lawfull processe stand in ieopardie. And he that taketh one
out of sanctuarie to doo him good, I saie plainlie, that he breaketh no sanctuarie.
When the duke had doone, the temporall men whole, and a good part of the spirituall
also, thinking no hurt earthlie meant toward the yoong babe, condescended in effect,
that if he were not deliuered, he should be fetched. Howbeit they thought it all best
in the auoiding of all maner of rumor, that the lord cardinall should first assaie to
get him with hir good will.

Wherevpon all the councell came vnto the Starre chamber at Westminster; and
the lord cardinall, leauing the protector with the councell in the Starchamber, departed
into the sanctuarie to the quéene, with diuers other lords with him: were it for the
respect of his honor, or that she should by presence of so manie perceiue, that this
errand was not one mans mind: or were it, for that the protector intended not in this

matter

matter to trust anie one man alone; or else, that if she finallie were determined to kéepe him, some of that companie had happilie secret instruction, incontinent (maugre hir mind) to take him, and to leaue hir no respit to conueie him, which she was likelie to mind after this matter broken to hir, if hir time would in anie wise serue hir.

When the quéene and these lords were come togither in presence, the lord cardinall shewed vnto hir, that it was thought vnto the protector, and vnto the whole councell that hir kéeping of the kings brother in that place, was the thing which highlie soun-ded, not onelie to the great rumor of the people and their obloquie; but also to the importable gréefe and displeasure of the kings roiall maiestie, to whose grace it were as singular a comfort, to haue his naturall brother in companie, as it was their both dishonour, and all theirs and hirs also, to suffer him in sanctuarie, as though the one brother stood in danger and perill of the other [and therefore more conuenient it were they should be togither, than parted asunder; that the world may well thinke and saie both of their kinred and also of them, when they shall see and heare how they kéepe continuall companie, and liue in mutuall amitie (as becometh brethren) which bringeth commodities with it, for number, infinite; and for vse, comfortable and necessarie; as it is truelie said:

Quæ ligat vnanimes fœlix concordia fratres,
O quales fructus vtilitatis habet!]

The cardinall shewed hir likewise, that the councell therefore had sent him vnto hir to require hir the deliuerie of him, that he might be brought vnto the kings presence at his libertie, out of that place, which they reckoned as a prison; and there should he be demeaned according to his estate: and she in this dooing, should both doo great good to the realme, pleasure to the councell, and profit to hir selfe, succour to hir freends that were in distresse, and ouer that (which he wist well she speciallie tendered) not onelie great comfort and honor to the king, but also to the yoong duke himselfe, whose both great wealth it were to be togither, as well for manie greater causes, as also for their both disport & recreation. Which thing the lord estéemed no slight, though it séeme light, well pondering that their youth without recreation and plaie cannot indure; nor anie stranger, for the conuenience of both their ages and estates, so méetlie in that point for anie of them, as either of them for other.

My lord (quoth the quéene) I saie not naie, but that it were verie conuenient, that this gentleman, whome yée require, were in companie of the king his brother: and in good faith, me thinketh it were as great commoditie to them both, as for yet a while to béene in the custodie of their mother, the tender age considered of the elder of them both, but speciallie the yoonger, which (besides his infancie, that also needeth good looking to) hath a while béene so sore diseased, vexed with sicknesse, and is so newlie rather a little amended, than well recouered, that I dare put no person earthlie in trust with his kéeping, but my selfe onelie, considering that there is (as physicians saie) and as we also find, double the perill in the recidiuation, than was in the first sicknesse, with which disease nature being sore laboured, forewearied and weakened waxeth the lesse able to beare out and susteine a new surfet. And albeit there might be founden other that would happilie doo their best vnto him, yet is there none that either knoweth better how to order him, than I that so long haue kept him: or is more tenderlie like to cherish him, than his owne mother that bare him.

No man denieth, good madame (quoth the cardinall) but that your grace were of all folke most necessarie about your children: and so would all the councell not onelie be content, but glad that ye were (if it might stand with your pleasure) to be in such place as might stand with their honour. But if you doo appoint your selfe to tarrie héere, then thinke they it more conuenient that the duke of Yorke were with the

king

king honourablie at his libertie, to the comfort of them both: than heere as a sanctuarie man, to their both dishonour and obloquie, sith there is not alwaie so great necessitie to haue the child to be with the mother: but that occasion may sometime be such, that it should be more expedient to keepe him elsewhere. Which in this well appeareth, that at such time as your déerest sonne then prince, and now king, should for his honor, and good order of the countrie, keepe houshold in Wales, farre out of your companie: your grace was well content therewith your selfe.

Not verie well content (quoth the queene) and yet the case is not like, for the tone was then in health, and the tother is now sicke. In which case, I maruell greatlie, The quéenes mistrust of the lord protector. that my lord protector is so desirous to haue him in his kéeping, where if the child in his sicknesse miscarried by nature, yet might he run into slander and suspicion of fraud. And where they call it a thing so sore against my childes honor, and theirs also, that he bideth in this place: it is all their honours there to suffer him bide, where no man doubteth he shall be best kept; and that is héere, while I am heere, which as yet intend not to come foorth and ieopard my selfe after other of my fréends, which would God were rather héere in suertie with me, than I were there in ieopardie with them.

Whie madame (quoth another lord) know you anie thing whie they should be in ieopardie? Naie verelie sir (quoth shee) nor whie they should be in prison neither, as The lord Howard, saith *Edw. Hall.* they now be. But it is (I trow) no great maruell though I feare, least those that haue not letted to put them in duresse without colour, will let as little to procure their destruction without cause. The cardinall made a countenance to the other lord, that he should harpe no more vpon that string; and then said he to the queene, that he nothing doubted, but that those lords of hir honorable kin, which as yet remained vnder arrest, should vpon the matter examined, doo well inough: and as toward hir noble person, neither was nor could be anie maner ieopardie.

Whereby should I trust that (quoth the quéene) in that I am giltlesse? As though they were giltie, in that I am with their enimies better loued than they? When they hate them for my sake, in that I am so néere of kin to the king? And how far they be off, if that would helpe, as God send grace it hurt not, and therefore as for me, I purpose not as yet to depart hence. And as for this gentleman my sonne, I mind that he shall be where I am, till I sée further: for I assure you, for that I see some men so greedie, without anie substantiall cause to haue him, this maketh me much the more fearder to deliuer him.

Truelie madame, quoth he, and the fearder that you be to deliuer him, the fearder bin other men to suffer you to kéepe him, least your causelesse feare might cause you further to conueie him; and manie be there that thinke he can haue no priuilege in this place, which neither can haue will to aske it, nor malice to deserue it. And therefore, they reckon no priuilege broken, though they fetch him out; which if yée finallie refuse to deliuer him, I verelie thinke they will. So much dread hath my lord his vncle, for the tender loue he beareth him, least your grace should hap to send him awaie.

A sir (quoth the quéene) hath the protector so tender zeale, that he feareth nothing The quéenes replie vpon the lord cardinall. but least he should escape him? Thinketh he that I would send him hence, which neither is in the plight to send out. And in what place could I reckon him sure, if he be not sure in this sanctuarie, whereof was there neuer tyrant yet so diuelish that durst presume to breake? And I trust God is as strong now to withstand his aduersaries as euer he was. But my sonne can deserue no sanctuarie, and therefore he can not haue it. Forsooth he hath found a goodlie glose, by which that place that may defend a théefe, may not saue an innocent. But he is in no ieopardie, nor hath no need thereof, would God he had not.

Troweth the protector (I praie God he may prooue a protector) troweth he that I

perceiue

perceiue not wherevnto his painted processe draweth? It is not honourable that the duke bide héere: it were comfortable for them both, that he were with his brother, bicause the king lacketh a plaifellow. Be you sure? I praie God send them both better plaifellowes than him, that maketh so high a matter vpon such a trifling pretext: as though there could none be founden to plaie with the king, but if his brother that hath no lust to plaie for sicknesse, come out of sanctuarie out of his safegard to plaie with him. As though princes (as yoong as they be) could not plaie but with their péeres, or children could not plaie but with their kinred, with whome for the more part they agrée much woorse than with strangers.

But the child cannot require the priuilege. Who told him so? He shall heare him aske it, and he will. Howbeit, this is a gaie matter. Suppose he could not aske it, suppose he would not aske it, suppose he would aske to go out. If I saie he shall not; if I aske the priuilege but for my selfe, I say he that against my will taketh him out, breaketh the sanctuarie. Serueth this libertie for my person onelie, or for my goods too? Yée may not hence take my horsse fro me: and may you take my child fro me? He is also my ward: for as my learned councell sheweth me, sith he hath nothing by descent holden by knights seruice, the law maketh his mother his gardian. Then may no man I suppose take my ward fro me out of sanctuarie, without the breach of the sanctuarie.

This that is héere betwéen this marke (*) & this marke (*) was not writte by him in English but is translated out of this historie which he wrote in Latine. And if my priuilege could not serue him, nor he aske it for himselfe, yet sith the law committeth to me the custodie of him, I may require it for him, except the law giue a child a gardian onelie for his goods and lands, discharging him of the cure and safe kéeping of his bodie, for which onelie both lands and goods serue. (*) And if examples be sufficient to obteine priuilege for my child, I néed not farre to séeke. For in this place in which we now be (and which is now in question whether my child may take benefit of it) mine other sonne now king was borne, and kept in his cradle and preserued to a more prosperous fortune, which I praie God long to continue. And as all you know, this is not the first time that I haue taken sanctuarie.

For when my lord my husband was banished, and thrust out of his kingdome, I fled hither, being great with child, and héere I bare the prince. And when my lord my husband returned safe againe, and had the victorie, then went I hence to welcome him home, and from hence I brought my babe the prince vnto his father, when he first tooke him in his armes. And I praie God that my sonnes palace, may be as great safegard vnto him now reigning, as this place was sometime to the kings enimie. In which place I intend to kéepe his brother, sith, &c. (*) Wherefore héere intend I to kéepe him, sith mans law serueth the gardian to kéepe the infant.

The law of nature will the moother to kéepe hir child, Gods law priuilegeth the sanctuarie, and the sanctuarie my sonne, sith I feare to put him in the protectors hands that hath his brother alreadie, and were (if both failed) inheritour to the crowne. The cause of my feare hath no man to doo to examine. And yet feare I no further than the law feareth, which (as learned men tell me) forbiddeth euerie man the custodie of them, by whose death he maie inherit lesse land than a kingdome. I can no more but whosoeuer he be that breaketh this holie sanctuarie, I praie God shortlie send him néed of sanctuarie, when he maie not come to it. For taken out of sanctuarie would I not my mortall enimie were.

The lord cardinall vseth an other waie to persuade the quéene. The lord cardinall, perceiuing that the quéene waxed euer the longer the farther off, and also that she began to kindle and chafe, and spake more biting words against the protector, and such as he neither beléeued, and was also loth to heare, he said to hir for a finall conclusion, that he would no longer dispute the matter: but if she were content to deliuer the duke to him, and to the other lords present, he durst laie his owne bodie & soule both in pledge, not onelie for his suertie, but also for his estate. And if she would giue them a resolute answer to the contrarie, he would foorthwith

depart

depart therwithall, and shift who so would with this businesse afterwards: for he neuer intended more to mooue hir in that matter, in which she thought that he & all other also (saue hir selfe) lacked either wit or truth: wit, if they were so dull that they could nothing perceiue what the protector intended: truth, if they should procure hir sonne to be deliuered into his hands, in whom they should perceiue toward the child anie euill intended.

The quéene with these words stood a good while in a great studie. And forsomuch as hir seemed the cardinall more readie to depart than some of the remnant, and the protector himselfe readie at hand; so that she verelie thought she could not kéepe him, but that he should incontinentlie be taken thense: and so conueie him else-where, neither had she time to serue hir, nor place determined, nor persons appointed, all things vnreadie, this message came on hir so suddenlie, nothing lesse looking for than to haue him fet out of sanctuarie, which she thought to be now beset in such places about, that he could not be conueied out vntaken, and partlie as she thought it might fortune hir feare to be false, so well she wist it was either néedlesse or bootlesse: wherefore if she should needs go from him, she deemed it best to deliuer him.

And ouer that, of the cardinals faith she nothing doubted, nor of some other lords neither, whome she there saw. Which as she feared least they might be deceiued: so was she well assured they would not be corrupted. Then thought she it should yet make them the more warilie to looke to him, and the more circumspectlie to sée to his suertie, if she with hir owne hands betooke him to them of trust. And at the last she tooke the yoong duke by the hand, and said vnto the lords: My lords (quoth she) and all my lords, I neither am so vnwise to mistrust your wits, nor so suspicious to mistrust your truths: of which thing I purpose to make you such a proofe, as if either of both in you, might turne both you and me to great sorow, the realme to much harme, and you to great reproch.

She falleth to a resolution touching hir sonnes deliuerie.

For lo, here is (quoth she) this gentleman, whom I doubt not but I could here kepe safe, if I would, what euer anie man say: & I doubt not also, but there be some abroad so deadlie enimies vnto my bloud, that if they wist where anie of it laie in their owne bodie, they would let it out. We haue also experience that desire of a kingdome knoweth no kinred. The brother hath beene the brothers bane: and maie the nephues be sure of their vncle? Ech of these children is the others defense while they be asunder, and ech of their liues lieth in the others bodie. Kéepe one safe and both be sure, and nothing for them both more perillous, than to be both in one place. For what wise merchant aduentureth all his goods in one ship?

All this notwithstanding, here I deliuer him and his brother in him, to keepe, into your hands, of whom I shall aske them both afore God & the world. Faithfull ye be that wot I well, & I know well you be wise. Power and strength to kéepe him (if you list) lacke ye not of your selfe, nor can lacke helpe in this cause. And if ye can not else-where, then maie you leaue him here. But onelie one thing I beséech you, for the trust which his father put in you euer, & for the trust that I put in you now, that as farre as ye thinke that I feare too much, be you well ware that you feare not as farre too little. And therewithall she said vnto the child; Fare well mine owne sweete sonne, God send you good kéeping: let me kisse you yet once yer you go, for God knoweth when we shall kisse togither againe. And therewith she kissed him and blessed him, turned hir backe and wept and went hir waie, leauing the child wéeping as fast. [Howbeit she was sorie afterwards that she had so parted from hir son (when it was past hir power to procure remedie, & no hope of helpe left against afterclaps) which is the common case of all that kind, as the prouerbe saith:

　　　　Femineus verè dolor est post facta dolere.]

When the lord cardinall, and these other lords with him, had receiued this yoong duke, they brought him into the Star chamber, where the protector tooke him in his

O dissimulation. armes and kissed him with these words: Now welcome my lord euen with all my verie heart.   And he said in that of likelihood as he thought.   Therevpon foorthwith they brought him vnto the king his brother into the bishops palace at Paules, and from thense thorough the citie honourablie into the Tower, out of the which after that daie they neuer came abroad.   (*) When the protector had both the children in his hands, he opened himselfe more boldlie, both to certeine other men, and also cheeflie to the duke of Buckingham.   Although I know that manie thought that this duke was priuie to all the protectors counsell, euen from the beginning; and some of the protectors fréends said, that the duke was the first moouer of the protector to this matter, sending a priuie messenger vnto him, streict after king Edwards death.

This that is here betwene this marke (*) & this marke (*) was not written by him in English but is translated out of his historie which he wrote in Latine.

But others againe, which knew better the subtill wit of the protector, denie that he euer opened his enterprise to the duke, vntill he had brought to passe the things before rehearsed.   But when he had imprisoned the queenes kinsfolks, & gotten both his sonnes into his owne hands, then he opened the rest of his purpose with lesse feare to them whome he thought méet for the matter, and speciallie to the duke, who being woone to his purpose, he thought his strength more than halfe increased.   The matter was broken vnto the duke by subtill folks, and such as were their craftes-masters in the handling of such wicked deuises: who declared vnto him that the yoong king was offended with him for his kinsfolks sake, and if he were euer able he would reuenge them, who would pricke him forward therevnto if they escaped (for they would remember their imprisonment) or else if they were put to death, without doubt the yoong K. would be carefull for their deaths, whose imprisonment was gréeuous vnto him.

Also that with repenting the duke should nothing auaile, for there was no waie left to redéeme his offense by benefits, but he should sooner destroie himselfe than saue the king, who with his brother and his kinsfolks he saw in such places imprisoned, as the protector might with a becke destroie them all: and that it were no doubt but he would doo it in deed, if there were anie new enterprise attempted.   And that it was likelie, that as the protector had prouided priuie gard for himselfe, so had he spials for the duke, and traines to catch him, if he should be against him; and that peraduenture from them, whome he lest suspected.   For the state of things and the dispositions of men were then such, that a man could not well tell whome he might trust, or whom he might feare.

These things and such like, being beaten into the dukes mind, brought him to that point, that where he had repented the way that he had entered; yet would he go foorth in the same; and sith he had once begun, he would stoutlie go thorough.   And therefore to this wicked enterprise, which he beléeued could not be voided, he bent himselfe, and went through; and determined, that sith the common mischéefe could not be amended, he would turne it as much as he might to his owne commoditie.   Then it was agreed, that the protector shuld haue the dukes aid to make him king, and that the protectors onelie lawfull sonne should marrie the dukes daughter, and that the protector should grant him the quiet possession of the earldome of Hereford, which he claimed as his inheritance, and could neuer obteine it in king Edwards time.

The dukes full resolution, to go thorough with his enterprise.

Besides these requests of the duke, the protector of his owne mind promised him a great quantitie of the kings treasure, and of his houshold stuffe.   And when they were thus at a point betwéene themselues, they went about to prepare for the coronation of the yoong king, as they would haue it séeme.   And that they might turne both the eies and minds of men from perceiuing of their drifts other-where, the lords being sent for from all parts of the realme, came thicke to that solemnitie.   But the protector and the duke, after that they had sent the lord cardinall, the archbishop of

Yorke

Yorke then lord chancellor, the bishop of Elie, the lord Stanleie, and the lord Hastings then lord chamberlaine, with manie other noble men (*) to common & deuise about the coronation in one place, as fast were they in an other place, contriuing the contrarie, and to make the protector king.

To which councell albeit there were adhibited verie few, and they were secret: yet began there here and there abouts, some maner of muttering among the people, as though all should not long be well, though they neither wist what they feared, nor wherefore: were it, that before such great things, mens hearts of a secret instinct of nature misgiue them; as the sea without wind swelleth of himselfe sometime before a tempest: or were it that some one man, happilie somewhat perceiuing, filled manie men with suspicion, though he shewed few men what he knew. Howbeit somewhat the dealing it selfe made men to muse on the matter, though the councell were close. For by little and little all folke withdrew from the Tower, and drew vnto Crosbies in Bishops gates stréet, where the protector kept his houshold. The protector had the resort, the king in maner desolate.

While some for their businesse made sute to them that had the dooing, some were by their fréends secretlie warned, that it might happilie turne them to no good, to be too much attendant about the king without the protectors appointment, which remooued also diuerse of the princes old seruants from him, and set new about him. Thus manie things comming togither, partlie by chance, partlie of purpose, caused at length not common people onelie, that woond with the wind, but wise men also, and some lords eke to marke the matter and muse thereon; so farre foorth that the lord Stanleie that was after earle of Derbie, wiselie mistrusted it, and said vnto the lord Hastings, that he much misliked these two seuerall councels. For while we (quoth he) talke of one matter in the tone place, little wot we wherof they talke in the tother place.

My lord (quoth the lord Hastings) on my life neuer doubt you: for while one man is there, which is neuer thense, neuer can there be thing once mooued, that should sound amisse toward me, but it should be in mine eares yer it were well out of their mouths. This ment he by Catesbie, which was of his neere secret councell, and whome he verie familiarlie vsed, and in his most weightie matters put no man in so speciall trust, reckoning himselfe to no man so liefe, sith he well wist there was no man so much to him beholden as was this Catesbie, which was a man well learned in the lawes of this land, and by the speciall fauour of the lord chamberlaine, in good authoritie, and much rule bare in all the countie of Leicester, where the lord chamberlains power cheefelie laie.

Catesbie and his conditions described.

But suerlie great pitie was it, that he had not had either more truth, or lesse wit. For his dissimulation onelie kept all that mischéefe vp. In whome if the lord Hastings had not put so speciall trust, the lord Stanleie & he had departed with diuerse other lords, and broken all the danse, for manie ill signes that he saw, which he now construes all to the best. So suerlie thought he, that there could be none harme toward him in that councell intended, where Catesbie was. And of truth the protector and the duke of Buckingham made verie good semblance vnto the lord Hastings, and kept him much in companie. And vndoubtedlie the protector loued him well, and loth was to haue lost him, sauing for feare least his life should haue quailed their purpose.

For which cause he mooued Catesbie to prooue with some words cast out a farre off, whether he could thinke it possible to win the lord Hastings vnto their part. But Catesbie, whether he assaied him, or assaied him not, reported vnto them, that he found him so fast, and heard him speake so terrible words, that he durst no further breake. And of truth, the lord chamberlaine of verie trust shewed vnto Catesbie the distrust that others began to haue in the matter. And therefore he, fearing least

3 C 2

their

their motion might with the lord Hastings minish his credence, wherevnto onelie all the matter leaned, procured the protector hastilie to rid him. And much the rather, for that he trusted by his death to obteine much of the rule that the lord Hastings bare in his countrie: the onelie desire whereof was the allectiue that induced him to be partner, and one speciall contriuer of all this horrible treason.

An assemblie of lords in the Tower.

Wherevpon soone after, that is to wit, on the fridaie [being the thirteenth of Iune] manie lords assembled in the Tower, and there sat in councell, deuising the honourable solemnitie of the kings coronation, of which the time appointed then so neere approched, that the pageants and subtilties were in making daie & night at Westminster, and much vittels killed therfore, that afterward was cast awaie. These lords so sitting togither communing of this matter, the protector came in amongst them, first about nine of the clocke, saluting them courteouslie, and excusing himselfe that he had béene from them so long, saieng merilie that he had béene a sléeper that daie.

After a little talking with them, he said vnto the bishop of Elie; My lord you haue verie good strawberies at your garden in Holborne, I require you let vs haue a messe of them. Gladlie my lord (quoth he) would God I had some better thing as readie to your pleasure as that! And therewithall in all the hast he sent his seruant for a messe of strawberies. The protector set the lords fast in communing, and therevpon praieng them to spare him for a little while, departed thense. And soone after one hoare, betwéene ten & eleuen he returned into the chamber amongst them all, changed with a woonderfull soure angrie countenance, knitting the browes, frowning and fretting, and gnawing on his lips: and so sat him downe in his place.

The Behauior of the lord protector in the assemblie of the lords.

All the lords were much dismaid and sore maruelled at this maner of sudden change, and what thing should him aile. Then, when he had sitten still a while, thus he began: What were they worthie to haue that compasse and imagine the destruction of me, being so néere of bloud vnto the king, and protector of his roiall person and his realme? At this question, all the lords sat sore astonied, musing much by whome this question should be meant, of which euerie man wist himselfe cléere. Then the lord chamberlaine (as he that for the loue betwéene them thought he might be boldest with him) answered and said, that they were worthie to be punished as heinous traitors, whatsoeuer they were. And all the other affirmed the same. That is (quoth he) yonder sorceresse my brothers wife, and other with hir (meaning the queene.)

At these words manie of the other lords were greatlie abashed, that fauoured hir. But the lord Hastings was in his mind better content, that it was mooued by hir, than by anie other whome he loued better: albeit his heart somewhat grudged, that he was not afore made of counsell in this matter, as he was of the taking of hir kinred, and of their putting to death, which were by his assent before deuised to be beheaded at Pomfret this selfe same daie, in which he was not ware that it was by other deuised, that he himselfe should be beheaded the same daie at London. Then said the protector: Ye shall all sée in what wise that sorceresse, and that other witch of hir councell Shores wife, with their affinitie, haue by their sorcerie and witchcraft wasted my bodie. And therwith he plucked vp his dublet sléeue to his elbow vpon his left arme, where he shewed a weerish withered arme, and small; as it was neuer other.

Herevpon euerie mans mind sore misgaue them, well perceiuing that this matter was but a quarell. For they well wist that the quéene was too wise to go about anie such follie. And also if she would, yet would she of all folke least, make Shores wife of hir counsell, whome of all women she most hated, as that concubine whome the king hir husband had most loued. And also, no man was there present, but well knew that his arme was euer such since his birth. Naithelesse, the lord chamberlaine (which from the death of king Edward kept Shores wife, on whome he somewhat doted in the kings life, sauing (as it is said) he that while forbare hir of reuerence toward the king,

or

else of a certeine kind of fidelitie to his fréend) answered and said: Certeinelie my lord, if they haue so heinouslie doone, they be worthie heinous punishment.

What (quoth the protector) thou seruest me I wéene with ifs and with ands, I tell thée they haue so doone, and that I will make good on thy bodie traitor: and therewith as in a great anger, he clapped his fist vpon the boord a great rap. At which token one cried, Treason, without the chamber. Therewith a doore clapped, and in come there rushing men in harnesse, as manie as the chamber might hold. And anon the protector said to the lord Hastings: I arrest thée traitor: What me my lord? (quoth he.) Yea thée traitor quoth the protector. And an other let flie at the lord Stanleie, which shrunke at the stroke, & fell vnder the table, or else his head had béene cleft to the téeth: for as shortlie as he shranke, yet ran the bloud about his eares. The lord Stanleie wounded.

Then were they all quickelie bestowed in diuerse chambers, except the lord chamberleine, whome the protector bad speed and shriue him apace, for by saint Paule (quoth he) I will not to dinner till I sée thy head off. It booted him not to aske whie, but heauilie tooke a priest at aduenture, & made a short shrift: for a longer would not be suffered, the protector made so much hast to dinner, which he might not go to, vntill this were doone, for sauing of his oth. So was he brought foorth to the gréene beside the chappell within the Tower, and his head laid downe vpon a long log of timber, and there striken off, and afterward his bodie with the head interred at Windsor beside the bodie of king Edward, both whose soules our Lord pardon. [Thus began he to establish his kingdome in bloud, growing thereby in hatred of the nobles, and also abridging both the line of his life, and the time of his regiment: for God will not haue bloudthirstie tyrants daies prolonged, but will cut them off in their ruffe; according to Dauids words: Lord Hastings lord chamberleine beheaded.

> Impio, fallaci, auidoque cædis
> Fila mors rumpet viridi in iuuenta.]

Buchan. in psal. 55.

A maruellous case is it to heare either the warnings of that he should haue voided, or the tokens of that he could not void. For the selfe night next before his death, the lord Stanleie sent a trustie messenger vnto him at midnight in all the hast, requiring him to rise and ride awaie with him, for he was disposed vtterlie no longer to bide, he had so fearfull a dreame; in which him thought that a boare with his tuskes so rased them both by the heads, that the bloud ran about both their shoulders. And forsomuch as the protector gaue the boare for his cognisance, this dreame made so fearefull an impression in his heart, that he was throughlie determined no longer to tarie, but had his horsse readie, if the lord Hastings would go with him, to ride yet so farre the same night, that they should be out of danger yer daie. The lord Stanleies dreame.

Ha good Lord (quoth the lord Hastings to this messenger) leaneth my lord thy maister so much to such trifles, and hath such faith in dreames, which either his owne feare fantasieth, or doo rise in the nights rest by reason of his daies thought? Tell him it is plaine witchcraft to beléeue in such dreames, which if they were tokens of things to come, why thinketh he not that we might be as likelie to make them true by our going, if we were caught & brought backe, as fréends faile fliers; for then had the boare a cause likelie to rase vs with his tusks, as folke that fled for some falsehood. Wherefore, either is there perill, or none there is in deed: or if anie be, it is rather in going than biding. And in case we should néeds fall in perill one waie or other, yet had I rather that men should sée that it were by other mens falsehood, than thinke it were either by our owne fault, or faint heart. And therefore go to thy maister (man) and commend me to him, & praie him be merie & haue no feare: for I insure him I am as sure of the man that he woteth of, as I am of mine owne hand. God send grace sir (quoth the messenger) and went his waie.

Certeine is it also, that in riding towards the Tower, the same morning in which he was beheded, his horsse twise or thrise stumbled with him, almost to the falling. Which Foretokens of imminent misfortune to the lord Hastings.

Which thing albeit ech man wote well dailie happeneth to them, to whom no such mischance is toward; yet hath it béene of an old rite and custome obserued, as a token oftentimes notablie foregoing some great misfortune. Now this that followeth was no warning, but an enuious scorne. The same morning yer he was vp, came a knight vnto him, as it were of courtesie, to accompanie him to the councell; but of truth sent by the protector to hast him thitherwards, with whome he was of secret confederacie in that purpose; a meane man at that time and now of great authoritie.

This knight (I say) when it happened the lord chamberleine by the waie to staie his horsse, & common a while with a priest whome he met in the Tower stréet, brake his tale, and said merilie to him; What my lord, I pray you come on, whereto talke you so long with that priest? you haue no néed of a priest yet: and therwith he laughed vpon him, as though he would say, Ye shall haue soone. But so little wist the tother what he ment, and so little mistrusted, that he was neuer merier, nor neuer so full of good hope in his life, which selfe thing is oft séene a signe of change. But I shall rather let anie thing passe me, than the vaine suertie of mans mind so neere his death [flattering himselfe with deceitfull conceipts of inward motions of life to be prolonged, euen in present cases of deadlie danger, and heauie misfortunes offering great mistrust; as he did that is noted for speaking like a foole :

Mani. lib. 4.
Astro.

Non est (crede mihi) sapientis dicere, Viuam :
Nascentes morimur, finísq; ab origine pendet.]

Vpon the verie Tower wharfe, so neare the place where his head was off soone after, there met he with one Hastings a purséuant of his owne name. And at their méeting in that place, he was put in remembrance of another time, in which it had happened them before to meet in like manner togither in the same place. At which other time the lord chamberleine had béene accused vnto king Edward by the lord Riuers the queenes brother, in such wise, as he was for the while (but it lasted not long) farre fallen into the kings indignation, & stood in great feare of himselfe. And forsomuch as he now met this purseuant in the same place, that ieopardie so well passed, it gaue him great pleasure to talke with him thereof, with whome he had before talked thereof in the same place, while he was therein.

And therefore he said : Ha Hastings, art thou remembred when I met thée here once with an heauie heart? Yea my lord (quoth he) that remember I well, and thanked be God, they gat no good, nor you no harme thereby. Thou wouldest say so (quoth he) if thou knewest as much as I know, which few know else as yet, and mo shall shortlie. That meant he by the lords of the quéenes kinred that were taken before, and should that daie be beheaded at Pomfret : which he well wist, but nothing ware that the ax hung ouer his owne head. In faith man (quoth he) I was neuer so sorie, nor neuer stood in so great dread in my life, as I did when thou and I met here. And lo how the world is turned, now stand mine enimies in the danger (as thou maiest hap to heare more hereafter) and I neuer in my life so merrie, nor neuer in so great suertie.

O good God, the blindnesse of our mortall nature, when he most feared, he was in good suertie; when he reckoned himselfe surest, he lost his life, and that within
The description
of the lord Hast-
ings.
two houres after. Thus ended this honorable man, a good knight and a gentle, of great authoritie with his prince, of liuing somewhat dissolute, plaine and open to his enimie, & secret to his friend, easie to beguile, as he that of good heart and courage forestudied no périls, a louing man, and passing well beloued : verie faithfull, and trustie inough, trusting too much. Now flew the fame of this lords death swiftlie through the citie, and so foorth further about like a wind in euerie mans eare. But the protector, immediatlie after dinner, intending to set some colour vpon the matter, sent in all the hast for manie substantiall men out of the citie into the tower.

Now at their comming, himselfe with the duke of Buckingham, stood harnessed
in

in old ill faring briganders, such as no man should wéene, that they would vouchsafe to haue put vpon their backs, except that some sudden necessitie had constreined them. And then the protector shewed them, that the lord chamberleine, and other of his conspiracie, had contriued to haue suddenlie destroied him, and the duke, there the same day in the councell. And what they intended further, was as yet not well knowne. Of which their treason he neuer had knowledge before ten of the clocke the same forenoone, which sudden feare draue them to put on for their defense such harnesse as came next to hand. And so had God holpen them, that the mischiefe turned vpon them that would haue doone it. And this he required them to report.

Euerie man answered him faire, as though no man mistrusted the matter, which of truth no man beléeued. Yet for the further appeasing of the peoples minds, he sent The protectors proclamation. immediatlie after diner in all the hast one herald of armes, with a proclamation to be made through the citie in the kings name, conteining, that the lord Hastings, with diuerse other of his traitorous purpose, had before conspired the same day to haue slaine the lord protector, and the duke of Buckingham sitting in the councell; and after to haue taken vpon them to rule the king & the realme at their pleasure, and therby to pill and spoile whome they list vncontrolled. And much matter there was in that proclamation, deuised to the slander of the lord chamberleine, as that he was an ill councellor to the kings father, intising him to manie things highlie redounding to the minishing of his honour, and to the vniuersall hurt of the realme.

The meanes whereby; namelie, his euill companie, sinister procuring, and vngra- The life and déeds of the lord chamberleine laid open. tious example, as well in manie other things, as in the vicious liuing and inordinate abusion of his bodie, with manie other, and also speciallie with Shores wife, which was one also of his most secret counsell in this most heinous treason, with whome he laie nightlie, and namelie the night last past next before his death. So that it was the lesse maruell, if vngratious liuing brought him to an vnhappie ending, which he was now put vnto by the most dred commandement of the kings highnesse, and of his honorable and faithfull councell, both for his demerits, being so openlie taken in his falslie conceiued treason, and also least the delaieng of his execution might haue incouraged other mischiefous persons, partners of his conspiracie, to gather and assemble themselues togither, in making some great commotion for his déliuerance: whose hope being now by his well deserued death politikelie repressed, all the realme should (by Gods grace) rest in good quiet and peace.

Now was this proclamation made within two houres after that he was beheaded, and it was so curiouslie indicted, & so faire written in parchment, in so well a set hand, and therewith of it selfe so long a processe, that euerie child might well perceiue that it was prepared before. For all the time, betwéene his death and the proclaming, could scant haue sufficed vnto the bare writing alone, all had it beene but in paper, and scribled foorth in hast at aduenture. So that vpon the proclaming thereof, one that was schoolemaister of Powles of chance standing by, and comparing the shortnesse of the time with the length of the matter, said vnto them that stood about him; Here is a gaie goodlie cast foule cast awaie for hast. And a merchant answered him, that it was written by prophesie.

Now then by and by, as it were for anger, not for couetise, the protector sent into Shores wife spoiled of all that she had. the house of Shores wife (for hir husband dwelled not with hir) and spoiled hir of all that euer she had, aboue the value of two or three thousand markes, and sent hir bodie to prison. And when he had a while laid vnto hir (for the maner sake) that she went about to bewitch him, and that she was of counsell with the lord chamberleine to destroie him: in conclusion, when that no colour could fasten vpon these matters, then he laid heinouslie to hir charge, that thing that hir selfe could not denie, and that all the world wist was true, and that nathelesse euerie man laughed at, to heare it then so suddenlie so highlie taken, that shee was naught of hir bodie.

And

Shores wife put to open penance. And for this cause (as a goodlie continent prince, cleane and faultlesse of himselfe, sent out of heauen into this vicious world for the amendment of mens maners) he caused the bishop of London to put hir to open penance, going before the crosse in procession vpon a sundaie with a taper in hir hand. In which she went in countenance and pase demure so womanlie; that albeit she were out of all araie, saue hir kirtle onelie, yet went she so faire and louelie, namelie while the woondering of the people cast a comelie rud in hir cheeks (of which she before had most misse) that hir great shame wan hir much praise among those that were more amorous of hir bodie, than curious of hir soule. And manie good folks also that hated hir liuing, & glad were to see sin corrected: yet pitied they more hir penance, than reioised therin, when they considered that the protector procured it, more of a corrupt intent, than anie vertuous affection.

The descriptiō of Shores wife. This woman was borne in London, worshipfullie friended, honestlie brought vp, and verie well maried, sauing somewhat too soone, hir husband an honest citizen, yoong and godlie, & of good substance. But forsomuch as they were coupled yer she were well ripe, she not verie feruentlie loued him, for whō she neuer longed, which was happilie the thing that the more easilie made hir incline vnto the kings appetite, when he required hir. Howbeit the respect of his roialtie, the hope of gaie apparell, ease, and other wanton wealth, was able soone to pearse a soft tender heart, [so that she became flexible and pliant to the kings appetite and will; being so blinded with the bright glorie of the present courtlie brauerie which shée inioied, that she vtterlie forgat how excellent a treasure good name and fame is, and of what incomparable sweetnesse, euen by the iudgement of him, whose match for wisdome the world neuer bred vp, saieng:

Eob. Hess. in Eccles. Sal.
Sunt optanda magis puræ bona nomina famæ,
Nobilis vnguenti quàm pretiosus odor.]

But when the king had abused hir, anon hir husband (as he was an honest man, and one that could his good, not presuming to touch a kings concubine) left hir vp to him altogither. When the king died, the lord chamberleine tooke hir, which in the kings daies, albeit he was sore inamoured vpon hir, yet he forbare hir; ether for reuerence, or for a certeine friendlie faithfulnesse. Proper she was and faire; nothing in hir bodie that you would haue changed, but if ye would haue wished hir somewhat higher. * Meaning when this storie was written. Thus saie they that knew hir in hir youth. Albeit some that now sée hir (for yet * she liueth) deem hir neuer to haue béene well visaged: whose iudgement seemeth me somewhat like, as though men should gesse the beautie of one long before departed by hir scalpe taken out of the charnell house.

For now is she old, leane, withered and dried vp, nothing left but riuelled skin and hard bone. And yet being euen such, who so well aduise hir visage, might gesse and deuise, which parts how filled would make it a faire face. Yet delighted not men so much in hir beautie, as in hir pleasant behauiour. For a proper wit had she, and could both read well and write, merrie in companie, readie and quicke of answer, neither mute, nor full of bable, sometime tawnting without displeasure, and not without disport. K. Edwards three concubines. The king would saie that he had thrée concubins, which in thrée diuerse properties diuerslie excelled. One the merriest, another the wiliest, the third the holiest harlot in his realme, as one whome no man could get out of the church lightlie to any place, but it were to his bed.

The other two were somewhat greater personages, and nathelesse of their humilitie content to be namelesse, and to forbeare the praise of those properties: but the meriest was this Shores wife, in whom the king therefore tooke speciall pleasure. For manie he had, but hir he loued; whose fauour to say the truth (for sin it were to beelie the diuell) she neuer abused to anie mans hurt, but to manie a mans comfort and reléefe.

reléefe.   Where the king tooke displeasure, shée would mitigate and appease his mind : where men were out of fauour, she would bring them in his grace.   For manie that had highlie offended shée obteined pardon.   Of great forfeitures she gat men remission.

Finallie, in manie weightie sutes she stood manie a man in great stead, either for none or verie small rewards, and those rather gaie than rich ; either that she was content with the déed it selfe well doone ; or for that she delighted to be sued vnto, and to shew what she was able to doo with the king ; or for that wanton women and wealthie be not alwaies couetous.   I doubt not some shall thinke this woman too slight a thing to be written of, and set among the remembrances of great matters : which they shall speciallie thinke, that happilie shall estéeme hir onelie by that they now sée hir.

But me séemeth the chance so much the more worthie to be remembred, in how much she is now in the more beggerlie condition, vnfréended and worne out of acquaintance, after good substance, after as great fauour with the prince, after as great sute and séeking to with all those, that those daies had businesse to speed, as manie other men were in their times, which be now famous onelie by the infamie of their ill déeds. Hir dooings were not much lesse, albeit they be much lesse remembred, bicause they were not so euill.   For men vse if they haue an euill turne, to write it in marble : and who so dooth vs a good turne, we write it in dust, which is not worst prooued by hir : for at this daie she beggeth of manie at this daie liuing, that at this daie had begged if she had not béene.

Now was it so deuised by the protector and his councell, that the selfe daie, in which the lord chamberleine was beheaded in the Tower of London, and about the selfe same houre, was there (not without his assent) beheaded at Pomfret, the fore-remembred lords & knights that were taken from the king at Northampton and Stonie Stratford.   Which thing was doone in the presence, and by the order of sir Richard Ratcliffe knight, whose seruice the protector speciallie vsed in that councell, and in the execution of such lawlesse enterprises, as a man that had béene long secret with him, hauing experience of the world, and a shrewd wit, short & rude in spéech, rough and boisterous of behauiour, bold in mischiefe, as far from pitie as from all feare of God. *Sir Richard Ratcliffe.*

This knight bringing them out of the prison to the scaffold, and shewing to the people about that they were traitors (not suffering them to declare & speake their innocencie, least their words might haue inclined men to pitie them, and to hate the protector and his part) caused them hastilie, without iudgement, processe, or maner of order to be beheaded, and without other earthlie gilt, but onelie that they were good men, too true to the king, and too nigh to the quéene.   Now when the lord chamberleine & these other lords and knights were thus beheaded, and rid out of the waie : then thought the protector, that when men mused what the matter meant, while the lords of the realme were about him out of their owne strengths, while no man wist what to thinke, nor whom to trust, yer euer they should haue space to dispute and digest the matter and make parties ; it were best hastilie to pursue his purpose, and put himselfe in possession of the crowne, yer men could haue time to deuise anie waie to resist. *The lord Riuers & other beheaded.*

But now was all the studie by what meanes this matter, being of it selfe so heinous, might be first broken to the people, in such wise that it might be well taken.   To this councell they tooke diuerse, such as they thought meetlie to be trusted, likelie to be induced to that part, and able to stand them in steed either by power or policie. Among whome they made of councell Edmund Shaw knight then maior of London, which vpon trust of his owne aduancement, whereof he was of a proud heart highlie desirous, should frame the citie to their appetite.   Of spirituall men they tooke such *Edmund Shaw maior of London.*

as had wit, and were in authoritie among the people for opinion of their learning, and had no scrupulous conscience. Among these had they Iohn Shaw clearke brother to the maior, and frier Penker, prouinciall of the Augustine friers both doctors of diuinitie, both great preachers, both of more learning than vertue, of more fame than learning. For they were before greatlie estéemed among the people: but after that neuer.

Of these two the one had a sermon in praise of the protector before the coronation, the other after, both so full of tedious flatterie, that no mans eares could abide them. Penker in his sermon so lost his voice, that he was faine to leaue off, and come downe in the midst. Doctor Shaw by his sermon lost his honestie, & soone after his life, for verie shame of the world, into which he durst neuer after come abroad. But the frier forced for no shame, and so it harmed him the lesse. Howbeit some doubt, and manie thinke, that Penker was not of counsell in the matter before the coronation, but after the common maner fell to flatterie after: namelie sith his sermon was not incontinentlie vpon it, but at saint Marie hospitall at the Easter after.

Doct. Shaw.
Frier Penker.

But certeine it is, that doctor Shaw was of counsell in the begining, so farre foorth that they determined that he should first breake the matter in a sermon at Paules crosse, in which he should (by the authoritie of his preaching) incline the people to the protectors ghostlie purpose. But now was all the labor and studie in the deuise of some conuenient pretext, for which the people should be content to depose the prince, and accept the protector for king. In which diuerse things they deuised. But the chéefe thing & the weightiest of all that inuention rested in this, that they should alledge bastardie, either in king Edward himselfe, or in his children, or both. So that he should séeme disabled to inherit the crowne, by the duke of Yorke, and the prince by him.

The chiefest
deuise to depose
the prince.

To laie bastardie in king Edward, sounded openlie to the rebuke of the protectors owne mother, which was mother to them both; for in that point could be no other color, but to pretend that his owne mother was an adultresse, which notwithstanding, to further this purpose he letted not. But neuerthelesse he would that point should be lesse and more fauourablie handled: not euen fullie plaine and directlie, but that the matter should be touched aslope craftilie, as though men spared in that point to speake all the truth, for feare of his displeasure. But the other point concerning the bastardie that they deuised to surmize in king Edwards children, that would he should be openlie declared and inforced to the vttermost. The colour and pretext whereof cannot be well perceiued, but if we first repeat you some things long before doone about king Edwards mariage.

After that king Edward the fourth had deposed king Henrie the sixt, and was in peaceable possession of the realme, determining himselfe to marie (as it was meet both for him selfe & the realme) he sent ouer in ambassage the erle of Warwike, with other noble men in his companie to Spaine, to treat & conclude a mariage betwéene K. Edward & the kings daughter of Spaine. In which thing the erle of Warwike found the parties so toward & willing, that he speedily (according to his instructions without any difficultie) brought the matter to very good cōclusion. Now hapned it, that in the meane season there came to make a sute by petition to the king dame Elizabeth Greie, which was after his quéene, at that time a widow, borne of noble bloud, by hir mother, duches of Bedford, yer she maried the lord Wooduile, hir father.

Sée before *pag.*
283.

Dame Elizabeth
Greie.

Howbeit, this dame Elizabeth hir selfe, being in seruice with queene Margaret, wife vnto king Henrie the sixt, was maried vnto one [Iohn] Greie an esquier, whome king Henrie made knight vpon the field that he had on [Barnet heath by saint Albons] against king Edward. But litle while inioied he that knighthood: for he was at the same field slaine. After which doone, and the earle of Warwike, being in his ambassage about the afore remembred mariage, this poore ladie made humble sute vnto the

king

king, that she might be restored vnto such small lands as hir late husband had giuen hir in iointure. Whome when the king beheld, and heard hir speake as she was both faire and of a goodlie fauor, moderate of stature, well made and verie wise: he not onelie pitied hir, but also waxed inamoured of hir. And taking hir afterward secretlie aside, began to enter in talking more familiarlie. Whose appetite when she perceiued, she vertuouslie denied him.

But that did she so wiselie, and with so good maner, and words so well set, that she rather kindled his desire than quenched it. And finallie, after manie a méeting, much wooing, and many great promises, she well espieng the kings affection toward hir so greatlie increased, that she durst somewhat the more boldlie saie hir mind, as to him whose hart she perceiued more feruentlie set, than to fall off for a word. And in con- clusion, she shewed him plaine, that as she wist hir selfe too simple to be his wife, so thought she hir selfe too good to be his concubine. The king much maruelling at hir constancie (as he that had not béen woont elsewhere to be so stiffelie said naie) so much esteemed hir continencie and chastitie, that he set hir vertue in the stéed of posses- sion and riches: and thus taking counsell of his desire, determined in all possible hast to marie hir. *A wise answer of a chast and continent ladie.*

Now after he was thus appointed, and had betwéene them twaine insured hir: then asked he counsell of his other fréends, and that in such maner, as they might then perceiue it booted not greatlie to say naie. Notwithstanding the duches of Yorke his mother was so sore mooued therewith, that she dissuaded the mariage as much as she possible might; alledging that it was his honour, profit and suertie also, to marie in a noble progenie out of his realme, wherevpon depended great strength to his estate, by the affinitie and great possibilitie of increase of his possession. And that he could not well otherwise doo, seeing that the earle of Warwike had so farre moued alreadie: which were not likelie to take it well, if all his voiage were in such wise frustrate, and his appointment deluded. And she said also, that it was not princelie to marie his owne subiect, no great occasion leading therevnto, no possessions, or other commodi- ties depending therevpon; but onlie as it were a rich man that would marie his maid, onelie for a little wanton dotage vpon hir person. *The kings mother.*

In which mariage manie mo commend the maidens fortune, than the maisters wise- dome. And yet therein (she said) was more honestie than honour in this mariage. For somuch as there is betwéene no merchant and his owne maid so great difference, as betwéene the king and this widow. In whose person, albeit there was nothing to be misliked; yet was there (she said) nothing so excellent, but that it might be found in diuerse other that were more meetlie (quoth she) for your estate, and maidens also; whereas the onelie widowhead of Elizabeth Greie, though she were in all other things conuenient for you, shuld yet suffice (as me seemeth) to refraine you from hir mariage, sith it is an vnfitting thing, and a verie blemish and high disparagement to the sacred maiestie of a prince, that ought as nigh to approch priesthood in clean- nesse as he dooth in dignitie, to be defiled with bigamie in his first mariage.

The king, when his mother had said, made hir answer, part in earnest, part in plaie merilie, as he that wist himselfe out of hir rule. And albeit he would gladlie that she should take it well, yet was at a point in his owne mind, tooke she it well or other- wise. Howbeit somewhat to satisfie hir, he said, that albeit mariage (being a spirituall thing) ought rather to be made for the respect of God, where his grace inclineth the parties to loue togither, as he trusted it was in his, than for the regard of anie tempo- rall aduantage: yet neuerthelesse, him séemed that this mariage, euen worldlie consi- dered, was not vnprofitable. For he reckoned the amitie of no earthlie nation so ne- cessarie for him, as the fréendship of his owne, which he thought likely to beare him so much the more hartie fauour, in that he disdeined not to marie with one of his owne land. *The kings answer to his mother.*

       And

And yet if outward aliance were thought so requisite, he would find the meanes to enter thereinto, much better by other of his kin, where all the parties could be contented, than to marie himselfe whome he should happilie neuer loue; and for the possibilitie of more possessions, leese the fruit and pleasure of this that he had alreadie. For small pleasure taketh a man of all that euer he hath beside, if he be wiued against his appetite. And I doubt not (quoth he) but there be (as ye say) other, that be in euerie point comparable with hir. And therefore I let not them that like them to wed them. No more is it reason, that it mislike anie man, that I marrie where it liketh me. And I am sure that my cousine of Warwike neither loueth me so little, to grudge at that I loue; nor is so vnreasonable, to looke that I should in choise of a wife, rather be ruled by his eie, than by mine owne: as though I were a ward that were bound to marie by the appointment of a gardian.

Libertie preferred before a kingdome. I would not be a king with that condition, to forbeare mine owne libertie in choise of mine owne mariage. As for possibilitie of more inheritance by new affinitie in strange lands, is oft the occasion of more trouble than profit. And we haue alreadie title by that meanes vnto so much, as sufficeth to get and kéepe well in one mans daies. That she is a widow, and hath alreadie children; by Gods blessed ladie, I am a bacheler, and haue some too, and so ech of vs hath a proofe that neither of vs is like to be barren. And therefore (madame) I praie you be content, I trust in God she shall bring foorth a yoong prince that shall please you. And as for the bigamie, let the bishop hardlie laie it in my waie when I come to take orders. For I vnderstand it is forbidden a preest, but I neuer wist it yet, that it was forbidden a prince. [This spake he as alluding to the libertie of princes, whose lust standeth oftentimes for law, and their opinion for reason, according to the saieng of the poet;

Claudi.
————tunc omnia iure tenebis
Cùm poteris rex esse.]

The duches with these words nothing appeased, and séeing the king so set thereon, that she could not pull him backe. so highlie she disdained it, that vnder pretext of hir dutie to Godward, she deuised to disturbe this mariage, and rather to helpe that he should marie one dame Elizabeth Lucie, whome the king had also not long before gotten with child. Wherefore the kings mother openlie obiected against his mariage, as it were in discharge of hir conscience, that the king was sure to dame Elizabeth Lucie and hir husband before God. By reason of which words, such obstacle Elizabeth Lucie. was made in the matter, that either the bishops durst not, or the king would not proceed to the solemnization of this wedding, till these same were clearlie purged, and the truth well and openlie testified. Wherevpon dame Elizabeth Lucie was then sent for.

And albeit that she was by the kings mother and manie other put in good comfort, to affirme that she was ensured vnto the king: yet when she was solemnlie sworne to saie the truth, she confessed that they were neuer ensured. Howbeit she said his grace spake so louing words vnto hir, that she verelie hoped he would haue married hir. And that if it had not béene for such kind words, she would neuer haue shewed such kindnesse to him, to let him so kindlie get hir with child. This examination solemnelie taken, when it was cléerelie perceiued, that there was none impe- The kings mariage. diment: the king with great feast and honourable solemnitie married dame Elizabeth Greie, and hir crowned queene that was his enimies wife, and manie times had praied full hartilie for his losse, in which God loued hir better than to grant hir hir boune.

But when the earle of Warwike vnderstood of this marriage, he tooke it so highlie that his ambassage was deluded, that for verie anger and disdaine he (at his returning) assembled a great puissance against the king, and came so fast vpon him yer he could The king fled. be able to resist, that he was faine to void the realme, and flee into Holland for succor, where he remained for the space of two yeares, leauing his new wife at Westminster The prince borne. in sanctuarie, where she was deliuered of Edward the prince, of whome we before haue spoken.

spoken. In which meane time the earle of Warwike tooke out of prison, and set vp King Henrie the sixt set vp. againe king Henrie the sixt, who was before by king Edward deposed, and that much what by the power of the erle of Warwike, which was a wise man, and a Of the earle of Warwike. couragious warriour, and of such strength, what for his lands, his aliance, and fauor with all people, that he made kings and put downe kings almost at his pleasure, and not impossible to haue atteined it himselfe, if he had not reckoned it a greater thing to make a king than to be a king.

But nothing lasteth alwaie: far in conclusion, king Edward returned, and with The earle of Warwike slaine. much lesse number than he had at Barnet on the Easter daie field, slue the earle of Warwike, with manie other great estates of that partie, & so stablie atteined the crowne againe, that he peaceablie enioied it vntill his dieng daie: and in such plight left it, that it could not be lost but by the discord of his verie friends, or falshood of his feined freends. I haue rehearsed this businesse about this marriage somewhat the more at length, bicause it might thereby the better appeare, vpon how slipperie a ground the protector builded his colour, by which he pretended king Edwards children to be bastards. But that inuention, simple as it was, it liked them to whome it sufficed to haue somewhat to saie, while they were sure to be compelled to no larger proofe than themselues list to make.

Now then (as I began to shew you) it was by the protector and his councell concluded, that this doctor Shaw should in a sermon at Pauls crosse signifie to the peo- Doc. Shaws sermon. ple, that neither king Edward himselfe, nor the duke of Clarence, were lawfullie begotten, nor were not the verie children of the duke of Yorke, but gotten vnlawfullie by other persons, in adulterie, of the duches their mother. And that also dame Elizabeth Lucie was verilie the wife of king Edward, and so the prince and all his children bastards, that were begotten vpon the quéene. According to this deuise doctor Shaw the sundaie after, at Paules crosse in a great audience (as alwaie assembled great number to his preaching) he tooke for his theame; Spuria vitilamina non agent radices altas, that is to saie; Bastard slippes shall neuer take deepe root.

Therevpon when he had shewed the great grace that God giueth, and secretlie insundeth in right generation after the lawes of matrimonie, then declared he, that commonlie those children lacked that grace, and for the punishment of their parents were (for the more part) vnhappie, which were gotten in base, and speciallie in adulterie. Of which, though some, by the ignorance of the world and the truth hid from knowledge, inherited for the season other mens lands, yet God alwaie so prouideth, that it continueth not in their bloud long: but the truth comming to light, the rightfull inheritors be restored, and the bastard slip pulled vp yer it can be rooted deepe. And so he did laie for the proofe and confirmation of this sentence certeine insamples taken out of the old testament, and other ancient histories.

Then began he to descend into the praise of the lord Richard late duke of This preacher was taught his lesson yer he came into the pulpit. Yorke, calling him father to the lord protector, and declared the title of his heires vnto the crowne, to whome it was (after the death of king Henrie the sixt) intailed by authoritie of parlement. Then shewed he that his verie right heire of his bodie lawfullie begotten was onelie the lord protector. For he declared then, that king K. Edward slandered in a sermon. Edward was neuer lawfullie married vnto the queene, but was before God husband vnto dame Elizabeth Lucie, and so his children bastards. And besides that, neither king Edward himselfe, nor the duke of Clarence, among those that were secret in the houshold, were reckoned verie suerlie for the children of the noble duke, as those that by their fauours more resembled other knowne men than him. From whose vertuous conditions he said also that the late king Edward was far off.

But the lord protector he said, the verie noble prince, the speciall paterne of knightlie prowesse, as well in all princelie behauior, as in the lineaments and fauour of his visage, represented the verie face of the noble duke his father. This is, quoth he, he, the fathers owne figure, this is his owne countenance, the verie print of his visage, the sure vndoubted image, the plaine expresse likenesse of that noble duke. Now

A maruelous de-
uise to mooue
the assemblie.

was it before deuised, that in the speaking of these words, the protector should haue comen in among the people to the sermon ward, to the end that those words méeting with his presence, might haue béen taken among the hearers, as though the Holie-ghost had put them in the preachers mouth, & should haue mooued the people euen there to crie; King Richard, king Richard: that it might haue béene after said, that he was speciallie chosen by God, and in maner by miracle. But this deuise quailed, either by the protectors negligence, or the preachers ouermuch diligence.

For while the protector found by the waie tarieng least he should preuent those words, and the doctor fearing that he should come yer his sermon could come to these words, hasted his matter thereto, he was come to them and past them, and entred into other matters yer the protector came. Whome when he beheld comming, he suddenlie left the matter with which he was in hand, and without anie deduction therevnto, out of all order, and out of all frame, began to repeat those

K. Richard
commended by
the preacher.

words againe : "This is the verie noble prince, the speciall patrone of knightlie prowesse, which as well in all princelie behauior, as in the lineaments & fauor of his visage, representeth the verie face of the noble duke of Yorke his father : this is the fathers owne figure, this is his owne countenance, the verie print of his visage, the sure vndoubted image, the plaine expresse likenesse of the noble duke, whose remembrance can neuer die while he liueth."

While these words were in speaking, the protector accompanied with the duke of Buckingham, went through the people into the place where the doctors commonlie stand in the vpper storie, where he stood to hearken the sermon. But the people were so farre frō crieng; K. Richard, that they stood as they had béene turned into

Note the course
of Gods iudge-
ment.

stones, for woonder of this shamefull sermon. After which once ended, the preacher gat him home, and neuer after durst looke out for shame, but kept him out of sight like an owle. And when he once asked one that had béene his old friend what the people talked of him, all were it that his owne conscience well shewed him that they talked no good ; yet when the tother answered him, that there was in euerie mans mouth spoken of him much shame, it so strake him to the heart, that within few daies after he withered and consumed awaie [for verie thought and inward pine, procured by irrecouerable cares, whose nature is noted by obseruation of their effects :

Ouid. lib. 3.
met.

Attenuant vigiles corpus miserabile curæ.]

Then on the tuesdaie following this sermon, there came to the Guildhall in London the duke of Buckingham, accompanied with diuerse lords and knights mo than happilie knew the message that they brought. And there in the east end of the hall, where the maior kéepeth the Hustings, the maior and all the aldermen being assembled about him, all the commons of the citie gathered before them. After silence commanded vpon great paine in the protectors name : the duke stood vp, and (as he was neither vnlearned, and of nature maruelouslie well spoken) he said vnto the people with a cleare and lowd voice in this maner of wise.

The duke of Buckinghams oration to the assemblie of the maior, aldermen, and commoners.

FRIENDS, for the zeale and heartie fauour that we beare you, we be comen to breake vnto you of a matter right great and weightie, and no lesse weightie than pleasing to God, and profitable to all the realme : nor to no part of the realme more profitable, than to you the citizens of this noble citie. For whie, that thing that we wote well ye haue long time lacked, and sore longed for, that yee would haue
                                                                                        giuen

giuen great good for, that yee would haue gone farre to fetch; that thing we be come hither to bring you without your labour, paine, cost, aduenture or ieopardie. What A notable per-thing is that? Certes the suertie of your owne bodies, the quiet of your wiues and suasion. your daughters, the safegard of your goods: of all which things in times past ye stood euermore in doubt. For who was there of you all, that would reckon himselfe lord of his own goods among so manie grens & traps as was set therefore, among so much pilling and polling, among so manie taxes and tallages, of which there was neuer end, & oftentimes no need? Or if anie were, it rather grew of riot, and vnreason-able wast, that anie necessarie or honourable charge.

So that there was dailie pilled fro good men and honest, great substance of goods, to be lashed out among vnthrifts; so far forth, that fifteenes sufficed not, nor anie vsual names of knowne taxes: but vnder an easie name of beneuolence and good will, the commissioners so much of euerie man tooke as no man could with his good will haue giuen. As though that name of beneuolence had signified, that euerie man should paie, not what himselfe of his owne good will list to grant, but what the king of his good will list to take. Which neuer asked little, but euerie thing was hawsed aboue the measure, amercements turned into fines, fines into ransoms, small trespasses into misprison, misprison into treason. Whereof (I thinke) no man looketh that we should remember you of examples by name, as though Burdet were Burdet. forgotten, that was for a word spoken in hast cruellie beheaded, by the misconstru-ing of the laws of this realme, for the princes pleasure.

With no lesse honour to Markam then cheefe iustice, that left [the benefit & Markam. dignitie] of his office, rather than he would assent to the dishonestie of those, that either for feare or flatterie gaue that iudgment. What Cooke, your owne worshipful Cooke. neighbour, alderman and maior of this noble citie, who is of you so either negli-gent that he knoweth not, or so forgetful that he remembreth not, or so hard hearted that he pittieth not that worshipful mans losse? What speake we of losse? His vtter spoile and vndeserued destruction, onelie for that it hapned those to fauour him whome the prince fauoured not. We need not (I suppose) to rehearse of these anie mo by name, sith there be (I doubt not) manie heere present, that either in themselues or in their nigh friends haue knowne, as well their goods as their persons greatlie in-dangered, either by feigned quarels, or small matters aggreeued with heinous names. And also there was no crime so great, of which there could lacke a pretext.

For sith the king, preuenting the time of this inheritance, atteined the crowne by battell: it sufficed in a rich man for a pretext of treason, to haue beene of kinred or aliance, neer familiaritie, or legier acquaintance with any of those that were at anie time the kings enimies, which was at one time and other more than halfe the relme. Thus were neither your goods in suertie, and yet they brought your bodies in ieopardie, beside the common aduenture of open warre, which albeit that it is euer the Open warre not will and occasion of much mischeefe, yet is it neuer so mischeeuous, as where any so ill as ciuill. people fall at distance among themselues; nor in none earthlie nation so deadlie and so pestilent, as when it hapneth among vs; and among vs neuer so long continued dissention, nor so manie batels in that season, nor so cruell and so deadlie fought, as was in that kings daies that dead is, God forgiue it his soule.

In whose time, and by whose occasion, what about the getting of the garland, keeping it, leesing and winning againe, it hath cost more English bloud, than hath twise the winning of France. In which inward war among our selues, hath beene so Ciuill warre the great effusion of the ancient noble bloud of this realme, that scarselie the halfe re- occasion of manie great maineth, to the great infeebling of this noble land, beside manie a good towne ransack- inconueniences, ed and spoiled by them, that haue beene going to the field or comming from thence. And peace long after not much surer than war. So that no time was therein, which rich men for their monie, and great men for their lands, or some other for some feare,

or

or some displeasure were not out of perill. For whom trusted he that mistrusted his owne brother? Whome spared he that killed his owne brother? Or who could perfectlie loue him, if his owne brother could not?

What maner of folke he most fauoured we shall for his honour spare to speake of. Howbeit this wote you well all, that who so was best, bare alwaie least rule; & more

Shores wife more sued vnto than all the ords in England

sute was in his daies to Shores wife a vile and an abhominable strumpet, than to all the lords in England: except vnto those that made hir their proctor. Which simple woman was well named & honest, till the king for his wanton lust and sinfull affection bereft hir from hir husband, a right honest substantiall yoong man among you. And in that point, which in good faith I am sorie to speake of, sauing that it is in vaine to keepe in counsell that thing that all men know, the kings greedie appetite was insatiable, and euerie where ouer all the realme intollerable.

For no woman was there anie where, yoong or old, rich or poore, whome he set his eie vpon, in whome he anie thing liked, either person or fauour, speech, pase, or countenance, but without anie feare of God, or respect of his honour, murmur or grudge of the world, he would importunelie pursue his appetite, and haue hir, to the great destruction of manie a good woman, and great dolor to their husbands, and their other freends; which being honest people of themselues, so much regard the cleannesse of their house, the chastitie of their wiues, and their children, that them were leauer to leese all that they had beside, than to haue such a villanie doone them. And all were it that with this and other importable dealing, the realme was in euerie part

He directeth his spéech to the communaltie of the citie.

annoied: yet speciallie yee heere the citizens of this noble citie, as well for that amongest you is most plentie of all such things as minister matter to such iniuries as for that you were neerest at hand, sith that neere heere abouts was commonlie his most abiding.

And yet be yee the people, whome he had as singular cause well and kindlie to

London the kings especiall chamber.

intreat, as anie part of his realme; not onelie for that the prince (by this noble citie, as his speciall chamber, & the speciall well renowmed citie of this realme) much honourable fame recciueth among all other nations: but also for that yee (not without your great cost, & sundrie perils & ieopardies in all his warres) bare euen your speciall fauor to his part. Which your kind minds borne to the house of Yorke, sith he hath nothing worthilie acquited, there is of that house that now by Gods grace better shall: which thing to shew you is the whole summe and effect of this our present errand. It shall not (I wot well) need that I rehearse you againe, that yee haue alreadie heard of him that can better tell it, and of whome I am sure yee will better beleeue it. And reason is that it so be.

I am not so proud, to looke therefore that yee should reckon my words of as great

Doct. Shaw commended by the duke of Buckinghā.

authoritie as the preachers of the word of God, namelie a man so cunning and so wise, that no man better woteth what he should saie, and thereto so good and vertuous, that he would not saie the thing which he wist he should not saie, in the pulpit namelie, into the which no honest man commeth to lie. Which honorable preacher, yee well remember, substantiallie declared vnto you at Paules crosse, on sundaie last passed, the right & title that the most excellent prince Richard duke of Glocester, now protector of this realme, hath vnto the crowne and kingdome of the same. For as the worshipfull man groundlie made open vnto you, the children of king Edward the fourth

A slanderous lie confirmed.

were neuer lawfullie begotten, forsomuch as the king (leauing his verie wife dame Elizabeth Lucie) was neuer lawfullie maried vnto the queene their mother, whose bloud, sauing that he set his voluptuous pleasure before his honor, was full vnmeetlie to be matched with his; and the mingling of whose blouds togither, hath beene the effusion of a great part of the noble bloud of this realme.

Wherby it may well seeme the mariage not well made, of which there is so much mischeefe growne. For lacke of which lawfull coupling, & also of other things which
the

the said worshipfull doctor rather signified than fullie explaned, & which things shall not be spoken for me, as the thing wherein euerie man forbereth to say that he knoweth in auoiding displeasure of my noble lord protector, bearing (as nature requireth) a filiall reuerence to the duchesse his mother. For these causes (I say) before remembred that is to wit, for lacke of other issue lawfullie of the late noble prince Richard duke of Yorke, to whose roiall bloud the crowne of England and of France is by the high authoritie of parlement intailed, the right and title of the same is by the iust course of inheritance (according to the cōmon lawes of the land) deuolued & com- men vnto the most excellent prince the lord protector, as to the verie lawfullie be- gotten sonne of the foreremembred noble duke of Yorke. The title of K. Richard to the crowne

Which thing well considered, and the great knightlie prowesse pondered, with manifold vertues, which in his noble person singularlie abound; the nobles and commons also of this realme, and speciallie in the north part, not willing anie bastard bloud to haue the rule of the land, nor the abusions before in the same vsed anie longer to continue, haue condescended and fullie determined, to make humble petition to the most puissant prince the lord protector, that it maie like his grace (at our humble request) to take vpon him the guiding and gouernance of this realme, to the wealth and increase of the same, according to his verie right and iust title. Which thing I wote it well, he will be loth to take vpon him, as he whose wisdome The dignitie and office of a king full of care & studie well perceiueth the labor and studie both of mind and bodie, that come there- with, to whomsoeuer so will occupie the roome, as I dare say hee will, if he take it. Which roome I warne you well is no childs office. And that the great wise man well perceiued, when hee said : Væ regno cuius rex puer est : Wo is that realme that hath a child to their king.

Wherefore so much the more cause haue we to thanke God, that this noble personage, which is so rightlie intituled therevnto, is of so sad age, & thereto so great wisdome ioined with so great experience, which albeit hee will bee loth (as I haue said) to take it vpon him, yet shall he to our petition in that behalfe more gratiouslie incline, if ye the worshipfull citizens of this the cheefe citie of this realme, ioine with vs the nobles in our said request. Which for your owne weale (we doubt not) but ye will : and nathelesse I heartilie pray you so to doo, whereby you shall doo great profit to all this realme beside, in choosing them so good a king, and vnto your selues speciall commoditie, to whom his maiestie shall euer after beare so much the more tender fauor, in how much he shall perceiue you the more prone and beneuolentlie minded toward his election. Wherin deere friends what mind you haue, wee require you plainlie to shew vs.

When the duke had said, and looked that the people, whome he hoped that the maior had framed before should after this proposition made, haue cried; King Richard, king Richard : all was husht and mute, and not one word answered therevnto. Wherewith the duke was maruellouslie abashed, and taking the maior neerer to him, with other that were about him priuie to that matter, said vnto them softlie, What meaneth this, that the people be so still? Sir (quoth the maior) percase they perceiue you not well. That shall we mend (quoth he) if that will helpe. And by & by somewhat lowder he rehersed to them the same matter againe in other order, and other words, so well and ornatlie, and nathelesse so euidentlie and plaine, with voice, gesture and countenance so comelie, and so conuenient, that euerie man much maruelled that heard him, and thought that they neuer had in their liues heard so euill a tale so well told [insomuch that he séemed as cunning an orator, as he, of whome the poet spake to his high praise & cōmendation, saieng:

    Quælibet eloquio causa fit apta suo.]

But were it for woonder or feare, or that each looked that other should speake first:

The election of K. Richard hardlie to be preferred.

not one word was there answered of all the people that stood before, but all was as still as the midnight, not somuch as rowning amongest them, by which they might seeme to commune what was best to do. When the maior saw this, he with other partners of that councell drew about the duke, and said that the people had not béene accustomed there to be spoken vnto, but by the recorder, which is the mouth of the citie, and happilie to him they will answer. With that the recorder, called Fitz William, a sad man, & an honest, which was so new come into that office, that he neuer had spoken to the people before, and loth was with that matter to begin, notwithstanding therevnto commanded by the maior, made rehearsall to the commons of that the duke had twise rehearsed to them himselfe.

Fitz William recorder.

But the recorder so tempered his tale, that he shewed euerie thing as the dukes words, and no part his owne. But all this noting no change made in the people, which alwaie after one stood as they had béene men amazed. Wherevpon the duke rowned vnto the maior and said; This is a maruellous obstinate silence: and therewith he turned vnto the people againe with these words; Déere friends, we come to mooue you to that thing, which peraduenture we not so greatlie néeded but that the lords of this realme, and the commons of other parties migh haue sufficed, sauing that we such loue beare you, and so much set by you, that we would not gladlie doo without you, that thing in which to be partners is your weale and honor, which (as it séemeth) either you sée not, or weie not. Wherefore we require you giue vs answer one way or other, whether you be minded, as all the nobles of the realme be, to haue this noble prince, now protector, to be your king or not.

At these words the people began to whisper among themselues secretly, that the voice was neither lowd nor distinct, but as it were the sound of a swarme of bées, till at the last in the nether end of the hall, an ambushment of the dukes seruants and Nashfields, and other belonging to the protector, with some prentisses and lads that thrust into the hall amongst the prease, began suddenlie at mens backes to crie out, as lowd as their throtes would giue; King Richard, king Richard: and threw vp their caps in token of ioy. And they that stood before, cast backe their heads maruelling therof, but nothing they said. Now when the duke and the maior saw this maner, they wiselie turned it to their purpose, and said it was a goodlie crie, & a ioifull, to heare euerie man with one voice, no man saieng naie.

K. Richard's election preferred by voices of confederacie.

Wherefore friends (quoth the duke) sith we perceiue it is all your whole mind to haue this noble man for your king (whereof we shall make his grace so effectuall report, that we doubt not but it shall redound vnto your great weale and commoditie) we require ye, that ye to morrow go with vs, and we with you vnto his noble grace, to make our humble request vnto him in maner before remembred. And therewith the lords came downe, and the companie dissolued and departed, the more part all sad: some with glad semblance that were not verie merrie, and some of those that came thither with the duke not able to dissemble their sorrow, were faine at his backe to turne their face to the wall while the dolor of their hearts burst out of their eies.

The maiors comming to Bainards castell vnto the lord protector.

Then on the morrow after, the maior with all the aldermen, and chiefe commoners of the citie, in their best maner apparelled, assembling themselues togither, resorted vnto Bainards castell, where the protector laie. To which place repaired also (according to their appointment) the duke of Buckingham, and diuerse noble men with him, beside manie knights and other gentlemen. And therevpon the duke sent word vnto the lord protector, of the being there of a great and honourable companie, to mooue a great matter vnto his grace. Wherevpon the protector made difficultie to come out vnto them, but if he first knew some part of their errand, as though he doubted and partlie mistrusted the comming of such a number vnto him so suddenlie, without anie warning or knowledge, whether they came for good or harme.

Then

Then the duke, when he had shewed this to the maior and other, that they might thereby sée how little the protector looked for this matter, they sent vnto him by the messenger such louing message againe, and therewith so humblie besought him, to vouchsafe that they might resort to his presence to propose their intent, of which they would vnto none other person anie part disclose; that at the last he came foorth of his chamber, and yet not downe vnto them, but stood aboue in a gallerie ouer them, where they might sée him, and speake to him, as though he would not yet come too néere them till he wist what they ment. And thervpon the duke of Buckingham first made humble petition vnto him on the behalfe of them all, that his grace would pardon them, and licence them to propose vnto his grace the intent of their comming, without his displeasure, without which pardon obteined, they durst not be bold to mooue him of that matter.

In which albeit they ment as much honor to his grace, as wealth to all the realme beside, yet were they not sure how his grace would take it, whome they would in no wise offend. Then the protector (as he was verie gentle of himselfe, and also longed sore to wit what they ment) gaue him leaue to propose what him liked, verelie trusting (for the good mind that he bare them all) none of them anie thing would intend vnto himward, wherewith he ought to bée gréeued. When the duke had this leaue and pardon to speake, then waxed he bold to shew him their intent and purpose, with all the causes moouing them therevnto (as ye before haue heard) and finallie to beséech his grace, that it would like him, of his accustomed goodnesse and zeale vnto the realme, now with his eie of pitie to behold the long continued distresse and decaie of the same, and to set his gratious hands to redresse and amendment thereof.

All which he might well doo, by taking vpon him the crowne and gouernance of this realme, according to his right and title lawfullie descended vnto him, and to the laud of God, profit of the land, & vnto his noble grace so much the more honour, and lesse paine, in that, that neuer prince reigned vpon anie people, that were so glad to liue vnder his obeisance, as the people of this realme vnder his. When the protector had heard the proposition, he looked verie strangelie thereat, and answered: that all were it that he partlie knew the things by them alledged to be true, yet such entire loue he bare vnto king Edward and his children, that so much more regarded his honour in other realmes about, than the crowne of anie one of which he was neuer desirous, that he could not find in his hart in this point to incline to their desire. For in all other nations, where the truth were not well knowne, it should peraduenture be thought, that it were his owne ambitious mind and deuise, to depose the prince, and take himselfe the crowne. *O singular dissimulation of king Richard.*

With which infamie he would not haue his honour stained for anie crowne, in which he had euer perceiued much more labour and paine, than pleasure to him that so would vse it, as he that would not, were not worthie to haue it. Notwithstanding, he not onlie pardoned them the motion that they made him, but also thanked them for the loue and hartie fauour they bare him, praieng them for his sake to giue and beare the same to the prince, vnder whom he was, and would be content to liue, and with his labour aud counsell (as farre as should like the king to vse him) he would doo his vttermost deuoir to set the realme in good state, which was alreadie in this little while of his protectorship (the praise giuen to God) well begun, in that the malice of such as were before occasion of the contrarie, and of new intended to be, were now partlie by good policie, & partlie more by Gods speciall prouidence, than mans prouision, repressed. *K. Richard spake otherwise than he meant.*

Vpon this answer giuen, the duke by the protectors licence, a little rowned aswell with other noble men about him, as with the maior and recorder of London. And after that (vpon like pardon desired & obteined) he shewed alowd vnto the protector,

3 E 2

that

that for a finall conclusion, that the realme was appointed K. Edwards line should not anie longer reigne vpon them, both for that they had so farre gone, that it was now no suertie to retreat, as for that they thought it for the weale vniuersall to take that waie, although they had not yet begun it.　Wherefore, if it would like his grace to take the crowne vpon him, they would humblie beseech him therevnto.　If he would giue them a resolute answer to the contrarie, which they would be loth to heare, then must they needs seeke and should not faile to find some other noble man that would.　These words much mooued the protector, which else (as euerie man may weet) would neuer of likelihood haue inclined therevnto.

But when he saw there was none other waie, but that either he must take it, or else he and his both go from it, he said vnto the lords and commons ; Sith we perceiue well that all the realme is so set, whereof we be verie sorie, that they will not suffer in any wise king Edwards line to gouerne them, whom no man earthlie can gouerne against their willes ; & we well also perceiue, that no man is there, to whome the crowne can by iust title apperteine, as to our selues, as verie right heire lawfully begotten of the bodie of our most déere father Richard late duke of Yorke, to which title is now ioined your election, the nobles and commons of this realme, which we of all titles possible take for the most effectuall : we be content and agrée fauourablie to

incline to your petition and request, and (according to the same) here we take vpon vs the roiall estate, preheminence and kingdome of the two noble realmes, England and France : the one from this daie forward by vs and our heires to rule, gouerne, and defend ; the other by Gods grace, and your good helpe, to get againe and subdue, and establish for euer in due obedience vnto this realme of England, the aduancement wherof we neuer aske of God longer to liue than we intend to procure.

With this there was a great shout, crieng ; King Richard, king Richard.　And then the lords went vp to the king (for so was he from that time called) and the people departed, talking diuerslie of the matter, euerie man as his fantasie gaue him.　But much they talked and maruelled of the maner of this dealing, that the matter was on

both parts made so strange, as though neither had euer communed with other thereof before, when that themselues wist there was no man so dull that heard them, but he perceiued well inough that all the matter was made betwéene them.　Howbeit some excused that againe, and said all must be doone in good order though : and men must sometime for the maners sake, not be aknowen what they know [though it be hard to outreach the circumspect, wise, & vigilant minded man ; as the poet saith :

————non facile est tibi

Decipere Vlyssem.]

For at the consecration of a bishop, euerie man woteth well by the paieng for his buls, that he purposeth to be one, & though he paie for nothing else.　And yet must he be twise asked whether he will be bishop or no, and he must twise saie naie, and the third time take it, as compelled therevnto by his owne will.　And in a stage plaie, all the people know right well, that one plaieng the Soldan, is percase a sowter ; yet if one should can so little good, to shew out of season what aquaintance he hath with him, and cast him by his owne name while he standeth in his maiestie, one of his tormentors might hap to breake his head (and worthie) for marring of the plaie.　And so they said, that these matters be kings games, as it were stage plaies, and for the more part plaied vpon scaffolds, in which poore men be but the lookers on.　And they that wise be will meddle no further.　For they that sometime step vp, and plaie with them, when they can not plaie their parts, they disorder the plaie, and doo themselues no good.

Thus farre Edward the fift, who was neuer king crowned, but shamefullie by his vncle slaine, as in the processe following appeereth,

RICHARD

RICHARD THE THIRD,

third sonne to Richard duke of Yorke, and vncle to Edward the fift.

(*) THE next daie the protector with a great traine went to Westminster hall, & there when he had placed himselfe in the court of the Kings bench, declared to the audience, that he would take vpon him the crowne in that place there, where the king himselfe sitteth and ministreth the law, bicause he considered that it was the chiefest dutie of a king to minister the lawes.   Then with as pleasant an oration as he could, be went about to win vnto him the nobles, the merchants, the artificers, and in conclusion all kind of men, but especiallie the lawiers of this realme.   And finallie to the intent that no man should hate him for feare, and that his deceitfull clemencie might get him the good will of the people, when he had declared the discommodities of discord, & the cōmodities of concord & vnitie, he made an open proclamation, that he did put out of his mind all enimities, and that he there did openlie pardon all offenses committed against him.

An. Reg. 1.
1483
(*) This that is here betwéene this marke & this marke (*) was not written by maister *More* in this historie written by him in English, but is translated out of this historie which he wrote in Latine.

And to the intent that he might shew a proofe therof, he commanded that one Fog, whom he had long deadlie hated, should be brought then before him, who being brought out of the sanctuarie (for thither had he fled for feare of him) in the sight of the people, he tooke him by the hand.   Which thing the common people reioised at, and praised, but wise men tooke it for a vanitie.   In his returne homeward, whome so euer he met, he saluted.   For a mind that knoweth it selfe guiltie, is in a manner deiected to a seruile flatterie [which refuseth no dutifulnesse, tend the same to neuer so hie a degrée of indignitie; which one noteth, saieng:

———————rides? maiore cachinno
Concutitur; flet, si lachrymas aspexit amici;
Frigescis? friget: si dixeris, æstuo, sudat.]

When he had begun his reigne in the moneth of Iune, after this mockish election, then was he crowned king in the verie same moneth.   And that solemnitie was furnished, for the most part, with the selfe same prouision that was appointed for the coronation of his nephue.   (*) But here to shew the manner of his coronation, as the same is inserted in this pamphlet of sir Thomas More, by maister Edward Hall and Richard Grafton (although not found in the same pamphlet) thus we find it by them reported.   (*) First, to be sure of all enimies (as he thought) he sent for fiue thousand men of the north against his coronation, which came vp euill apparelled, and worse harnessed, in rustie harnesse, neither defensible, nor scowred to the sale, which mustered in Finsburie field to the great disdaine of the lookers on.   [By which beginning it appéered to the world that he had his state in suspicion, otherwise he would not haue procured such a power to be attendant at his commandment, and that at such time as (all weapons laid aside) peacé and tranquillitie should haue béene sought after for the comforts of the peoples minds, & the safetie of his owne person; but being verie mistrustfull & fraught with carefull thoughts, he was in a maze betwéene hope and feare, according to this verie true saieng:

From this marke (*) to this (*) is not found in sir *Thomas More,* but in maister *Hall* and *Grafton.*

Sollicitæ mentes spéque metúque pauent.]

The fourth daie of Iulie he came to the Tower by water with his wife, and the fift daie he created Thomas lord Howard duke of Norfolke, and sir Thomas Howard his

sonne

sonne he created earle of Surrie, and William lord Berkeleie was then created erle of Nottingham, and Francis lord Louell was then made vicount Louell, and the king his chamberleine, and the lord Stanleie was deliuered out of ward, for feare of his sonne the lord Strange, which was then in Lancashire, gathering men (as men said) and the said lord was made steward of the king his houshold: likewise the archbishop of Yorke was deliuered, but Morton bishop of Elie was committed to the duke of Buckingham to kéepe in ward, which sent him to his manour of Brecknocke in Wales, from whence he escaped to king Richard his confusion.

Seuentéene
knights of the
Bath created by
king Richard.

The same night, the king made seuenteene knights of the Bath, whose names insue: Sir Edmund the duke of Suffolks sonne, sir George Greie, the earle of Kents sonne, sir William, the lord Zouches sonne, sir Henrie Aburgauennie, sir Christopher Willoughbie, sir William Berkeleie, sir Henrie Babington, sir Thomas Arundell, sir Thomas Bologne, sir Gerueis of Clifton, sir William Saie, sir Edmund Bedingfield, sir William Enderbie, sir Thomas Lekenor, sir Thomas of Vrmon, sir Iohn Browne, sir William Berkeleie. The next daie, being the fift daie of Iulie, the king rode through the citie of London toward Westminster with great pompe, being accompanied with these dukes, earles, lords, and knights, whose names follow. Edward

what péers &
states were at-
tendant on him
going to his co-
ronation.

prince of Wales, the kings onelie sonne. Dukes: the duke of Norffolke, the duke of Buckingham, the duke of Suffolke. Earles: the earle of Northumberland, the earle of Arundell, the earle of Kent, the earle of Surrie, the earle of Wilshire, the earle of Huntington, the earle of Nottingham, the earle of Warwike, the earle of Lincolne. Lords: the lord Lisle vicount, the lord Louell vicount, the lord Stanleie, the lord Audleie, the lord Dacres, the lord Ferrers of Chertleie, the lord Powes, the lord Scroope of Vpsall, the lord Scroope of Bolton, the lord Greie Codner, the lord Greie of Wilton, the lord Sturton, the lord Cobham, the lord Morleie, the lord Aburgauennie, the lord Zouch, the lord Ferrers of Grobie, the lord Welles, the lord Lomleie, the lord Matreuers, the lord Herbert, the lord Becham. Knights: sir Iames Tirell, sir William Kneuet, sir Thomas Aborow, sir William Stanleie, sir William Aparre, sir George Browne, sir Robert Middleton, sir Iohn Henningham, sir Nicholas Latimer, sir Thomas Montgomerie, sir Thomas Delamer, sir Gilbert Debnam, sir Terrie Robsart, sir William Brandon, sir Iohn Sauell, sir Henrie Wentford, sir Edward Stanleie, sir Henrie Sentmount, sir William Yoong, sir Thomas Bowser, sir Henrie Winkefield, sir Thomas Wortleie, sir Iohn Sentlow, sir Charles of Pilkington, sir Iames Harrington, sir Iohn Ashleie, sir Thomas Berkeleie, sir Richard Becham, sir William Hopton, sir Thomas Persie, sir Robert Dimmocke, sir Iohn Cheinie, sir Richard Ludlow, sir Iohn Eldrington, sir William Sands, sir Richard Dudleie, sir William Sentlow, sir Tho. Twaights, sir Edmund of Dudleie, sir Rafe Ashton, sir Richard Charlington, sir Thomas Greie, sir Philip Berkeleie, sir Robert Harington, sir Thomas Greffleie, sir Richard Harecourt, sir William Noris, sir Thomas Selenger, sir Richard Hodlesten, sir Iohn Conias, sir William Stoner, sir Philip Courtneie, sir William Gascoigne, sir Richard Amedilton, sir Roger Fines, sir George Véere, sir Henrie Persie, sir Iohn Wood, sir Iohn Aparre, sir Iohn Greie, sir Iohn Danbie, sir Richard Tailebush, sir Iohn Rudet, sir Iohn Herring, sir Richard Enderbie, sir Iohn Berkeleie, sir Iames Stranguish, sir Rafe Carnbrecke, sir Iohn Constable, sir Robert Eliard, sir Richard Derell, sir Iohn Gilford, sir Iohn Lekenor, sir Iohn Morleie, sir Iohn Hues, sir Iohn Bologne, sir Edmund Shaw alderman.

The solemne ce-
remonies vsed
at king Richards
coronation.

On the morow, being the sixt daie of Iulie, the king with queene Anne his wife, came downe out of the White hall into the great hall at Westminster, and went directlie into the kings Bench. And from thense, the king and the queene going vpon raie cloth barefooted, went vnto saint Edwards shrine, and all his nobilitie going with him, euerie lord in his degrée. And first went the trumpets, and then the heralds of armes in their rich coats, & next followed the crosse with a solemne procession,
                                                                                          the

the priests hauing fine surplisses and graie amisses vpon them. The abbats and bishops mitred and in rich copes, & euerie of them caried their crosiers in their hands. The bishop of Rochester bare the crosse before the cardinall. Then followed the earle of Huntington bearing a paire of gilt spurres, signifieng knighthood. Then followed the earle of Bedford bearing saint Edwards staffe for a relike.

After them came the earle of Northumberland bare-headed, with the pointlesse sword naked in his hand, which signified mercie. The lord Stanleie bare the mace of the constableship. The earle of Kent bare the second sword on the right hand of the king naked, with a point, which signified iustice vnto the temporaltie. The lord Louell bare the third sword on the left hand with a point, which signified iustice to the cleargie. The duke of Suffolke followed with the scepter in his hand, which signified peace. The earle of Lincolne bare the ball and crosse, which signified monarchie. The erle of Surrie bare the fourth sword before the king in a rich scabberd, and that is called the sword of estate. Then went thrée togither, in the middest went Garter king at armes in his rich cote : and on his left hand went the maior of London, bearing a mace : and on his right hand went the gentleman vsher of the priuie chamber. Then followed the duke of Norffolke, bearing the kings crowne betwéene his hands.

Then followed king Richard in his robes of purple veluet, and ouer his head a canopie, borne by foure barons of the cinque ports. And on euerie side of the king there went one bishop, that is to saie, the bishop of Bath, and the bishop of Durham. Then followed the duke of Buckingham bearing the kings traine, with a white staffe in his hand, signifieng the office of the high steward of England. Then there followed a great number of earles and barons before the queene. And then came the earle of Huntington, who bare the quéenes scepter, and the vicount Lisle bearing the rod with the doue. And the earle of Wilshire bare the queenes crowne. Then followed quéene Anne daughter to Richard earle of Warwike in robes like to the king, betwéene two bishops, and a canopie ouer hir head borne by the barons of the ports. On hir head a rich coronet set with stones and pearle.

Quéene Anne wife to king Richard and daughter to Richard earle of Warwike and hir traine.

After hir followed the countesse of Richmond heire to the duke of Summerset, which bare vp the quéenes traine. After followed the duchesse of Suffolke and Norffolke, with countesses, baronesses, ladies, and manie faire gentlewomen. In this order they passed through the palace, and entered the abbeie at the west end; and so came to their seats of estate. And after diuerse songs solemnelie soong, they both ascended to the high altar, and were shifted from their robes, and had diuerse places open from the middle vpward, in which places they were annointed. Then both the king and the queene changed them into cloth of gold, and ascended to their seats, where the cardinall of Canturburie, & other bishops them crowned according to the custome of the realme, giuing him the scepter in the left hand, & the ball with the crosse in the right hand; and the queene had the scepter in hir right hand, and the rod with the doue in her left hand.

The king & quéene crowned.

On euerie side of the king stood a duke, and before him stood the earle of Surrie with the sword in his hands. And on euerie side of the quéene standing a bishop, & a ladie kneeling. The cardinal soong masse, and after pax, the king and the queene descended, and before the high altar they were both houseled, with one host diuided betwéene them. After masse finished, they both offered at saint Edward his shrine, and there the king left the crowne of saint Edward, and put on his owne crowne. And so in order as they came, they departed to Westminster hall; and so to their chambers for a season : during which time the duke of Norffolke came into the hall, his horsse trapped to the ground in cloth of gold, as high marshall, and voided the hall. About foure of the clocke, the king and queene entered the hall, and the king sate in the middle, and the queene on the left hand of the table, and on euerie side of hir stood a countesse, holding a cloth of pleasance, when she list to drinke.

And

And on the right hand of the king sat the bishop of Canturburie. The ladies sat all on one side, in the middle of the hall. And at the table against them sat the chancellor and all the lords. At the table next the cupboord, sat the maior of London; and at the table behind the lords, sat the barons of the ports: and at the other tables sat noble and worshipfull personages. When all persons were set, the duke of Norffolke earle marshall, the earle of Surrie, constable for that daie, the lord Stanlie lord steward, sir William Hopton treasuror, & sir Thomas Persie controllor, came in and serued the king solemnelie, with one dish of gold, and an other of siluer, and the quéene all in gilt vessell, and the bishop all in siluer.

Sir Robert Dimmocke the kings champion his challenge in the behalfe of king Richard.

At the second course came into the hall sir Robert Dimmocke the kings champion, making proclamation, that whosoeuer would saie, that king Richard was not lawfull king, he would fight with him at the vtterance, and threw downe his gantlet, and then all the hall cried; king Richard. And so he did in thrée parts of the hall, and then one brought him a cup of wine couered, and when he had drunke, he cast out the drinke, and departed with the cup. After that, the heralds cried a largesse thrise in the hall, and so went vp to their stage. At the end of dinner, the maior of London serued the king & quéene with swéete wine, and had of each of them a cup of gold, with a couer of gold. And by that time that all was doone, it was darke night. And so the king returned to his chamber, and euerie man to his lodging.

A gaie pretense of iustice and equitie.

When this feast was thus finished, the king sent home all the lords into their countries that would depart, except the lord Stanleie, whom he reteined, till he heard what his sonne the lord Strange went about. And to such as went home, he gaue streight charge and commandement, to sée their countries well ordered, and that no wrong nor extortion should be doone to his subiects. And thus he taught other to execute iustice and equitie, the contrarie whereof he dailie exercised. He also with great rewards giuen to the Northernemen, which he sent for to his coronation, sent them home to their countrie with great thanks: whereof diuerse of them (as they be all of nature verie greedie of authoritie, & speciallie when they thinke to haue anie comfort or fauour) tooke on them so highlie, and wrought such maisteries, that the king was faine to ride thither in his first yeare, and to put some in execution, and staie the countrie, or else no small mischéefe had insued.

Sir Thomas More againe.

Now fell there mischeefs thicke. And as the thing euill gotten is neuer well kept, thorough all the time of his reigne neuer ceassed there cruell death and slaughter, till his owne destruction ended it. But as he finished his time with the best death and the most righteous, that is to wit, his owne; so began he with the most pitious and wicked, I meane the lamentable murther of his innocent nephues, the yoong king and his tender brother: whose death and finall infortune hath naitheless comen so farre in question, that some remaine yet in doubt, whether they were in his daies destroied or no. Not for that onelie that Perkin Werbecke by manie folks malice, and

Perkin Werbecke.

mo folks follie, so long space abusing the world, was as well with princes as the poorer people reputed and taken for the yoonger of these two; but for that also that all things were in late daies so couertlie demeaned, one thing pretended, and an other meant.

Close dealing is euer suspected.

Insomuch that there was nothing so plaine and openlie prooued, but that yet for the common custome of close and couert dealing, men had it euer inwardlie suspect; as manie well counterfaited iewels make the true mistrusted. Howbeit, concerning the opinion, with the occasions moouing either partie, we shall haue place more at large to intreat, if we hereafter happen to write the time of the late noble prince of famous memorie king Henrie the seauenth, or percase that historie of Perkin in anie compendious processe by it selfe. But in the meane time, for this present matter, I shall rehearse you the dolorous end of those babes, not after euerie waie that I haue heard,

but

but after that waie, that I haue so heard by such men and by such meanes, as me thinketh it were hard but it should be true.

King Richard after his coronation, taking his waie to Glocester to visit (in his new honour) the towne of which he bare the name of his old, deuised (as he rode) to fulfill the thing which he before had intended. And forsomuch as his mind gaue him, that his nephues liuing, men would not reckon that he could haue right to the realme: he thought therefore without delaie to rid them, as though the killing of his kinsmen could amend his cause, and make him a kindlie king. Whervpon he sent one Iohn Greene, (whom he speciallie trusted) vnto sir Robert Brakenberie, constable of the Tower, with a letter and credence also, that the same sir Robert should in anie wise put the two children to death. Iohn Gréene. Robert Brakenberie constable of the Tower.

This Iohn Gréene did his errand vnto Brakenberie, knéeling before our ladie in the Tower. Who plainelie answered, that he would neuer put them to death to die therefore. With which answer Iohn Gréene returning, recounted the same to king Richard at Warwike yet in his waie. Wherewith he tooke such displeasure & thought, that the same night he said vnto a secret page of his: "Ah! whom shall a man trust? Those that I haue brought vp my selfe, those that I had wéent would most suerlie serue me, euen those faile me, and at my commandement will doo nothing for me." "Sir (quoth his page) there lieth one on your pallet without, that I dare well saie, to doo your grace pleasure, the thing were right hard that he would refuse." Meaning this by sir Iames Tirrell, which was a man of right goodlie personage, and for natures gifts worthie to haue serued a much better prince, if he had well serued God, and by grace obteined as much truth and good will as he had strength and wit. The murther of the two yoong princes set abroch. Sir Iames Tirrell described.

The man had an high heart, & sore longed vpward, not rising yet so fast as he had hoped, being hindered & kept vnder by the meanes of sir Richard Ratcliffe, and sir William Catesbie, which longing for no mo parteners of the princes fauour; and namelie, not for him, whose pride they wist would beare no péere, kept him by secret drifts out of all secret trust, which thing this page well had marked and knowne. Wherefore this occasion offered, of verie speciall friendship he tooke his time to put him forward, and by such wise doo him good, that all the enimies he had (except the deuill) could neuer haue doone him so much hurt. For vpon this pages words king Richard arose (for this communication had he sitting at the draught, a conuenient carpet for such a councell) and came out into the pallet chamber, on which he found in bed sir Iames and sir Thomas Tirrels, of person like, and brethren of bloud, but nothing of kin in conditions. Authoritie loueth no partners.

Then said the king merilie to them; What sirs, be ye in bed so soone? And calling vp sir Iames, brake to him secretlie his mind in this mischéeuous matter. In which he found him nothing strange. Wherefore on the morow he sent him to Brakenberie with a letter, by which he was commanded to deliuer sir Iames all the keies of the Tower for one night, to the end he might there accomplish the kings pleasure, in such things as he had giuen him commandement. After which letter deliuered, & the keies receiued, sir Iames appointed the night next insuing to destroie them, deuising before and preparing the meanes. The prince (as soone as the protector left that name, and tooke himselfe as king) had it shewed vnto him, that he should not reigne, but his vncle shuld haue the crowne. At which word the prince sore abashed, began to sigh, and said: Alas, I would my vncle would let me haue my life yet, though I leese my kingdome. The constable of the Tower deliuereth the keies to sir Iames Tirrell vpon the kings commandement.

Then he that told him the tale, vsed him with good words, and put him in the best comfort he could. But foorthwith was the prince and his brother both shut vp, & all other remooued from them, onelie one (called Blacke Will, or William Slaughter) excepted, set to serue them and sée them sure.' After which time the The two princes shut vp in close hold.

prince neuer tied his points, nor ought rought of himselfe; but with that yoong babe his brother, lingered with thought and heauinesse, vntill this traitorous death deliuered them of that wretchednesse. For sir Iames Tirrell deuised, that they should be murthered in their beds. To the execution whereof, he appointed Miles Forrest, one of the foure that kept them, a fellow fleshed in murther before time. To him he ioined one Iohn Dighton his owne horssekéeper, a big, broad, square, and strong knaue.

The two murtherers of the two princes appointed.

Then all the other being remooued from them, this Miles Forrest, and Iohn Dighton, about midnight (the séelie children lieng in their beds) came into the chamber, & suddenlie lapping them vp among the clothes, so to bewrapped them and intangled them, keeping downe by force the fether-bed and pillowes hard vnto their mouths, that within a while, smoothered and stifled, their breath failing, they gaue vp to God their innocent soules into the ioies of heauen, leauing to the tormentors their bodies dead in the bed. Which after that the wretches perceiued, first by the strugling with the paines of death, and after long lieng still, to be thoroughlie dead, they laid their bodies naked out vpon the bed, and fetched sir Iames to sée them; which vpon the sight of them, caused those murtherers to burie them at the staire foot, meetlie déepe in the ground, vnder a great heape of stones.

The yoong K. and his brother murthered in their beds at midnight in the Tower.

Then rode sir Iames in great hast to king Richard, and shewed him all the maner of the murther; who gaue him great thanks, and (as some saie) there made him knight. But he allowed not (as I haue heard) the burieng in so vile a corner, saieng, that he would haue them buried in a better place, bicause they were a kings sonnes. Lo the honourable courage of a king. Whervpon they saie, that a priest of sir Robert Brakenberies tooke vp the bodies againe, and secretlie interred them in such place, as by the occasion of his death, which onelie knew it, could neuer since come to light. Verie truth is it, and well knowne, that at such time as sir Iames Tirrell was in the Tower, for treason committed against the most famous prince king Henrie the seauenth, both Dighton and he were examined, and confessed the murther in maner aboue written: but whither the bodies were remooued, they could nothing tell.

The murther confessed.

And thus (as I haue learned of them that much knew, and little cause had to lie) were these two noble princes, these innocent tender children, borne of most roiall bloud, brought vp in great wealth, likelie long to liue, reigne, and rule in the realme, by traitorous tyrannie taken, depriued of their estate, shortlie shut vp in prison, and priuilie slaine and murthered, their bodies cast God wot where, by the cruell ambition of their vnnaturall vncle and his despiteous tormentors. Which things on euerie part well pondered, God neuer gaue this world a more notable example, neither in what vnsuertie standeth this worldlie weale; or what mischeefe worketh the proud enterprise of an high heart; or finallie, what wretched end insueth such despiteous crueltie.

The iust iudgement of God seuerelie reuenging the murther of the innocent princes vpon the malefactors.

For first, to begin with the ministers, Miles Forrest, at S. Martins péecemeale rotted awaie. Dighton in déed yet walketh on aliue in good possibilitie to be hanged yer he die. But sir Iames Tirrell died at the Tower hill beheaded for treason. King Richard himselfe, as ye shall hereafter heare, slaine in the field, hacked and hewed of his enimies hands, haried on horsse-backe dead, his haire in despite torne and tugged like a curre dog; and the mischéefe that he tooke, within lesse than three yeares of the mischeefe that he did: and yet all (in the meane time) spent in much paine & trouble outward, much feare, anguish and sorow within. For I haue heard by credible report of such as were secret with his chamberleine, that after this abominable déed doone, he neuer had a quiet mind. [Than the which there can be no greater torment. For a giltie conscience inwardlie accusing and bearing witnesse against an offendor, is such a plague and punishment, as hell itselfe

(with

(with all the feends therein) can not affoord one of greater horror & affliction; the poet implieng no lesse in this tristichon:

> Pœna autem vehemens, ac multo sæuior illis,
> Quas & Cæditius grauis inuenit & Radamanthus,
> Nocte diéque suum gestare in pectore testem.

Pers. sat. 3.

He neuer thought himselfe sure. Where he went abroad, his eies whirled about, his bodie priuilie fensed, his hand euer vpon his dagger, his countenance and maner like one alwaies readie to strike againe, he tooke ill rest a nights, laie long waking and musing, sore wearied with care and watch, rather slumbered than slept, troubled with fearefull dreames, suddenlie sometime start vp, lept out of his bed, and ran about the chamber; so was his restlesse heart continuallie tossed and tumbled with the tedious impression and stormie remembrance of his abhominable déed. Now had he outward no long time in rest. For herevpon, soone after began the con-spiracie, or rather good confederation, betwéene the duke of Buckingham and manie other gentlemen against him. The occasion wherevpon the king and the duke fell out, is of diuerse folke in diuerse wise pretended.

The outward and inward troubles of ty-rants by meanes of a grudging conscience.

This duke (as I haue for certeine béene informed) as soone as the duke of Glocester, vpon the death of king Edward, came to Yorke, and there had solemne funerall seruice for king Edward, sent thither in the most secret wise he could, one * Persall his trustie seruant, who came to Iohn Ward a chamberer of like secret trust with the duke of Glocester, desiring that in the most close and couert maner, he might be admitted to the presence and spéech of his maister. And the duke of Glocester aduertised of his desire, caused him in the dead of the night (after all other folke auoided) to be brought vnto him in his secret chamber, where Persall (after his maisters recommendations) shewed him that he had secret sent him to shew him, that in this new world he would take such part as he would, & wait vpon him with a thousand good fellowes, if need were.

* Persiuall, saith Ed. Hall.

The messenger sent backe with thanks, & some secret instruction of the protectors mind, yet met him againe with further message from the duke his master within few daies after at Notingham: whither the protector from Yorke with manie gentlemen of the north countrie, to the number of six hundred horsses, was come on his waie to London-ward, & after secret méeting and communication had, eftsoones departed. Wherevpon at Northampton, the duke met with the protector himselfe with thrée hundred horsses, and from thence still continued with him partner of all his deuises; till that after his coronation, they departed (as it séemed) verie great fréends at Glo-cester. From whense as soone as the duke came home, he so lightlie turned from him, and so highlie conspired against him, that a man would maruell whereof the change grew. And suerlie, the occasion of their variance is of diuerse men diuerselie re-ported.

Some haue I heard say, that the duke a little before his coronation, among other things, required of the protector the duke of Herefords lands, to the which he pre-tended himselfe iust inheritor. And forsomuch as the title, which he claimed by in-heritance, was somwhat interlaced with the title to the crowne by the line of king Henrie before depriued, the protector conceiued such indignation, that he reiected the dukes request with manie spitefull and minatorie words. Which so wounded his heart with hatred and mistrust, that he neuer after could indure to looke aright on king Richard, but euer feared his owne life; so far foorth, that when the protector rode through London toward his coronation, he feined himselfe sicke, bicause he would not ride with him. And the other also taking it in euill part, sent him word to rise, and come ride, or he would make him be caried. Wherevpon he rode on with euill will, and that notwithstanding on the morow, rose from the feast, feining himselfe sicke, and king Richard said it was doone in hatred and despite of him.

Causes of the duke of Buck-ingham and K. Richards falling out.

And

The duke of
Buckingham and
king Richard
mistrust each
other.
And they said, that euer after continuallie, each of them liued in such hatred and distrust of other, that the duke verelie looked to haue beene murthered at Glocester: from which nathelesse, he in faire maner departed. But suerlie some right secret at that daie denie this: and manie right wise men thinke it vnlikelie (the déepe dissembling nature of both those men considered, and what néed in that gréene world the protector had of the duke, and in what perill the duke stood, if he fell once in suspicion of the tyrant) that either the protector would giue the duke occasion of displeasure, or the duke the protector occasion of mistrust. And verelie, men thinke, that if king Richard had anie such opinion conceiued, he would neuer haue suffered him to escape his hands. Verie truth it is, the duke was an high minded man, and euill could beare the glorie of another; so that I haue heard of some that say they saw it, that the duke, at such time as the crowne was first set vpon the protectors head, his eie could not abide the sight thereof, but wried his head another way.

But men say, that he was of truth not well at ease, and that both to king Richard well knowne, and not euill taken; nor anie demand of the dukes vncourteouslie reiected; but he both with great gifts, and high behests, in most louing and trustie maner departed at Glocester. But soone after his comming home to Brecknocke, hauing there in his custodie by the commandement of king Richard doctor Morton bishop of Elie, who (as ye before heard) was taken in the councell at the Tower, Doctor Morton
bishop of Elie,
& what pageants
he plaied. waxed with him familiar, whose wisedome abused his pride to his owne deliuerance, and the dukes destruction. The bishop was a man of great naturall wit, verie well learned, and honorable in behauior, lacking no wise waies to win fauour. He had béene fast vpon the part of king Henrie, while that part was in wealth; and nathelesse left it not, nor forsooke it in wo, but fled the realme with the queene & the prince, while king Edward had the king in prison, neuer came home, but to the field.

After which lost, and that part vtterlie subdued, the other (for his fast faith and wisedome) not onelie was content to receiue him, but also wooed him to come, and had him from thencefoorth both in secret trust, and verie speciall fauour, which he nothing deceiued. For he being (as yée haue heard) after king Edwards death, first taken by the tyrant for his truth to the king, found the meane to set this duke in his top, ioined gentlemen togither in the aid of king Henrie, deuising first the mariage betwéene him & king Edwards daughter: by which his faith he declared the good seruice to both his masters at once, with infinit benefit to the realme by the coniunction of those two blouds in one, whose seuerall titles had long disquieted the land, he fled the realme, went to Rome, neuer minding more to meddle with the world; till the noble prince king Henrie the seuenth gat him home againe, made him archbishop of The high honour
of doctor Morton. Canturburie, and chancellor of England, wherevnto the pope ioined the honour of cardinall. Thus liuing manie daies in as much honor as one man might well wish, ended them so godlie, that his death with Gods mercie well changed his life.

This man therefore (as I was about to tell you) by the long & often alternate proofe, as well of prosperitie as aduerse fortune, had gotten by great experience (the verie mother and mistresse of wisedome) a déepe insight in politike worldlie drifts. Whereby perceiuing now this duke glad to commune with him, fed him with faire words, and manie pleasant praises. And perceiuing by the processe of their communications, the dukes pride now and then belking out a little breath of enuie toward Bishop Mortons
subtill vnder-
mining of the
duke. the glorie of the king, and thereby feeling him easie to fall out if the matter were well handled: he craftilie sought the waies to pricke him forward, taking alwaies the occasion of his comming, and so kéeping himselfe so close within his bounds, that he rather séemed to follow him, than to lead him. For when the duke first began to
praise

praise and boast the king, and shew how much profit the realme should take by his reigne: my lord Morton answered thus.

Suerlie, my lord, follie were it for me to lie, for if I would sweare the contrarie, your lordship would not (I weene) beléeue; but that if the world would haue gone as I would haue wished, king Henries sonne had had the crowne, and not king Edward. But after that God had ordered him to léese it, and king Edward to reigne, I was neuer so mad that I would with a dead man striue against the quicke. So was I to king Edward a faithfull chapleine, & glad would haue béene that his child had suc-céeded him. Howbeit, if the secret iudgment of God haue otherwise prouided, I purpose not to spurne against a pricke, nor labour to set vp that God pulleth downe. And as for the late protector and now king. And euen there he left, saieng that he had alreadie medled too much with the world, and would from that daie meddle with his booke and his beads, and no further.

Then longed the duke sore to heare what he would haue said, bicause he ended with the king, and there so suddenlie stopped, and exhorted him so familiarlie betweene them twaine to be bold to saie whatsoeuer he thought; whereof he faithfullie promis-ed there should neuer come hurt, and peraduenture more good than he would weene; and that himselfe intended to vse his faithfull secret aduise & counsell, which (he said) was the onelie cause for which he procured of the king to haue him in his custodie, where he might reckon himselfe at home, and else had he béene put in the hands of them with whome he should not haue found the like fauour. The bishop right humblie thanked him, and said: In good faith my lord, I loue not to talke much of princes, as a thing not all out of perill, though the word be without fault: forsomuch as it shall not be taken as the partie ment it, but as it pleaseth the prince to con-strue it. Princes matters perillous to med-dle in.

And euer I thinke on Aesops tale, that when the lion had proclaimed that (on paine of death) there should no horned beast abide in that wood: one that had in his forehed a bunce of flesh, fled awaie a great pace. The fox that saw him run so fast, asked him whither he made all that hast? And he answered, In faith I neither wote, nor recke, so I were once hence, bicause of this proclamation made of horned beasts. What foole (quoth the fox) thou maiest abide well inough: the lion ment not by thée, for it is no horne that is in thine head. No marie (quoth he) that wote I well inough. But what and he call it an horne, where am I then? The duke laughed merilie at the tale, and said; My lord, I warrant you, neither the lion nor the bore shall pike anie matter at anie thing héere spoken: for it shall neuer come néere their eare.

In good faith sir (said the bishop) if it did, the thing that I was about to say, taken as well as (afore God) I ment it, could deserue but thanke: and yet taken as I wéene it would, might happen to turne me to little good, and you to lesser. Then longed the duke yet much more to wit what it was. Wherevpon the bishop said; In good faith (my lord) as for the late protector, sith he is now king in possession, I purpose not to dispute his title; but for the weale of this realme, whereof his grace hath now the gouernance, and whereof I am my selfe one poore member, I was about to wish, that to those good habilities whereof he hath alreadie right manie, little néeding my praise, it might yet haue pleased God, for the better store, to haue giuen him some of such other excellent vertues, meet for the rule of a realme, as our Lord hath planted in the person of your grace: and there left againe.

The duke somewhat maruelling at his sudden pauses, as though they were but parentheses, with a high countenance said: My lord, I euidentlie perceiue, and no lesse note your often breathing, and sudden stopping in your communication; so that to my intelligence, your words neither come to anie direct or perfect sentence in con-clusion, whereby either I might perceiue and haue knowledge, what your inward intent is now toward the king, or what affection you beare toward me. For the comparison Here endeth sir *Thomas Moore*, & this that fol-loweth is taken out of master *Hall.*

of

of good qualities ascribed to vs both (for the which I my selfe acknowledge and recognise to haue none, nor looke for no praise of anie creature for the same) maketh me not a little to muse, thinking that you haue some other priuie imagination, by loue or by grudge, ingrauen and imprinted in your heart, which for feare you dare not, or for childish shamefastnesse you be abashed to disclose and reueale; and speciallie to mee being your fréend, which on my honor doo assure you, to be as secret in this case, as the deafe and dumbe person is to the singer, or the tree to the hunter.

Bishop Morton buildeth vpō the dukes ambition.

The bishop being somewhat bolder, considering the dukes promise, but most of all animated and incouraged bicause he knew the duke desirous to bee exalted and magnified; and also he perceiued the inward hatred and priuie rancor which he bare toward king Richard: was now boldened to open his stomach euen to the verie bottome, intending thereby to compasse how to destroie, and vtterlie confound king Richard, and to depriue him of his dignitie roiall; else to set the duke so on fire with the desire of ambition, that he himselfe might be safe and escape out of all danger and perill. Which thing he brought shortlie to conclusion, both to the kings destruction, and the dukes confusion, and to his owne safegard, and finallie to his high promotion.

And so (as I said before) vpon trust and confidence of the dukes promise, the bishop said: My singular good lord, since the time of my captiuitie, which being in your graces custodie, I may rather call it a liberall libertie, more than a streict imprisonment, in auoiding idlenesse, mother and nourisher of all vices, in reading bookes and ancient pamphlets I haue found this sentence written, that no man is borne frée, and in libertie of himselfe onelie: for one part of dutie he oweth or should owe to his parents for his procreation, by a verie naturall instinct and filiall courtesie: another part to his fréends and kinsfolke; for proximitie of bloud and naturall amitie dooth euerie dutie chalenge and demand: but the natiue countrie, in the which he tasted first the swéet aires of this pleasant and flattering world after his natiuitie, demandeth as a debt by a naturall bond, neither to be forgotten, nor yet to be put in obliuion.

Which saieng causeth me to consider in what case this realme my natiue countrie now standeth, and in what estate and assurance (before this time) it hath continued: what gouernour we now haue, and what ruler we might haue. For I plainelie perceiue the realme being in this case, must needs decaie, and be brought to vtter confusion, and finall extermination. But one hope I haue incorporat in my brest, that is, when

The duke of Buckingham highlie commended.

I consider, and in my mind doo diligentlie remember, and dailie behold your noble personage, your iustice, and indifferencie, your feruent zeale, and ardent loue toward your naturall countrie, and in like manner, the loue of your countrie toward you, the great learning, pregnant wit, and goodlie eloquence, which so much dooth abound in the person of your grace, I must needs thinke this realme fortunate, yea twise more than fortunate, which hath such a prince in store, méet and apt to be a gouernour, in whose person (being indued with so manie princelie qualities) consisteth and resteth the verie vndoubted similitude and image of true honour.

Dispraise of the lord protector or king in esse.

But on the other side, when I call to memorie the good qualities of the late protector and now called king, so violated and subuerted by tyrannie, so changed and altered by vsurped authoritie, so clouded and shadowed by blind and insatiable ambition: yea, and so suddenlie (in manner by a metamorphosis) transformed from politike ciuilitie, to detestable tyrannie: I must needs saie, & iustlie affirme, that he is neither méet to be a king of so noble a realme, nor so famous a realme méet to be gouerned by such a tyrant [whose kingdome (if it were of more amplenesse than it is) could not long continue; neither would the Lord suffer him in his bloudthirstines to abuse the holie and diuine estate of a prince by the cruell title of tyrannie. For such he will ouerthrow, yea he will bring most horrible slaughter vpō them, as it is prophesied:

Impius ad summos quamuis ascendat honores
Aspice quas clades tempora sæua vehent.

Was

Was not his first enterprise to obteine the crowne begun and incepted by the murther of diuerse noble, valiant true, and vertuous, personages? O holie beginning to
come to a mischeeuous ending! Did he not secondarilie procéed (contrarie to all lawes
of honestie) shamefullie against his owne naturall mother, being a woman of much
honour and more vertue, declaring hir openlie to be a woman giuen to carnall affection, and dissolute liuing? Which thing if it had béene true, as it was not indéed,
euerie good & naturall child would haue rather mummed at it, than haue blasted it
abroad, and especiallie she being aliue.   Declaring furthermore his two brethren, and
his two nephues to be bastards, and to be borne in adulterie: yet was he not with all
this content.

After that he had obteined the garland, for the which he so long thirsted, he caused the
two poore innocents his nephues, committed to him for especiall trust, to be murthered
and shamefullie to be killed.   The bloud of which séelie and litle babes dailie crie to
God from the earth for vengeance.   Alas, my hart sobbeth, to remember this bloudie
butcher, and cruell monster.   What suertie shall be in this realme to anie person,
either for life or goods vnder such a cruell prince, which regardeth not the destruction
of his owne bloud, and then lesse the losse of other? And most especiallie (as often- ^{Suspicion in a}
times it chanceth) where a couetous or a cruell prince taketh suspicion, the smallest ^{prince how mis-}
swaruing that is possible (if the thing be misconstrued) may be the cause of the des- ^{chéefous it is.}
truction of manie guiltlesse persons: and in especiall of noble and wealthie personages,
hauing great possessions and riches: such a lord is Lucifer when he is entered into the
hart of a proud prince, giuen to couetousnesse and crueltie.

But now my lord to conclude what I meane toward your noble person, I saie and
affirme, if you loue God, your linage, or your natiue countrie, you must your selfe take
vpon you the crowne and imperiall diademe of this noble empire, both for the maintenance of the honour of the same (which so long hath flourished in fame and renowme)
as also for the deliuerance of your naturall countrimen, from the bondage and thraldome (woorse than the captiuitie of Aegypt) of so cruell a tyrant and arrogant op-
pressor.   For thus I dare saie, if anie forren prince or potentate, yea the Turke himselfe would take vpon him the regiment here, and the crowne, the commons would
rather admit and obeie him, than to liue vnder such a bloudsucker and child-killer.
But how much more ioifull and glad would they be to liue vnder your grace, whome
they all know to be a ruler méet and conuenient for them, and they to be louing and
obedient subiects, méet to liue vnder such a gouernour? Despise not, nor forsake not
so manifest an occasion so louinglie offered.

And if you your selfe, knowing the paine and trauell that apperteineth to the office of
a king, or for any other consideration, will refuse to take vpon you the crowne and ^{The bishop}
scepter of this realme: then I adiure you, by the faith that you owe to God, by your ^{adiureth the}
honor and by your oth made to saint George, patrone of the noble order of the garter ^{duke to release} ^{the realme by}
(whereof you be a companion) and by the loue and affection that you beare to your ^{some deuise from} ^{the present}
natiue countrie, and the people of the same; to deuise some waie, how this realme (now ^{euill state.}
being in miserie) may by your high discretion and princelie policie, be brought and
reduced to some suertie and conuenient regiment, vnder some good gouernour by you
to be appointed: for you are the verie patrone, the onelie helpe, refuge and comfort for
the poore amazed and desolate commons of this realme.

For if you could either deuise to set vp againe the linage of Lancaster, or aduance
the eldest daughter of king Edward to some high and puissant prince, not onelie the
new crowned king shall small time inioy the glorie of his dignitie; but also all ciuill
war should ceasse, all domesticall discord should sléepe, and peace, profit and quietnesse should be set foorth and imbraced.   When the bishop had thus ended his saieng,
the duke sighed, and spake not of a great while.   Which sore abashed the bishop,
and made him change colour.   Which thing when the duke perceiued, he said; Be

not

not afraid my lord, all promises shall be kept, to morrow we will common more: let vs go to supper, So that night they communed no more, not a little to the disquieting of the bishop, which now was euen as desirous to know the dukes mind and intent, as the duke longed the daie before to know his opinion and meaning.

A new conferēce betwéene the bishop and the duke.

So the next daie, the duke sent for the bishop, and rehearsed to him in maner (for he was both wittie and eloquent) all the communication had betwéene them before, and so paused a while, and after a little season, putting off his bonet, he said: O Lord God creator of all things, how much is this relme of England, and the people of the same, bounden vnto thy goodnesse! For where we now be in vexation and trouble with great stormes oppressed, sailing and tossing in a desperate ship, without good maister or gouernour: yet by thy helpe good Lord I trust yer long time passe, that we shall prouide for such a ruler, as shall be both to thy pleasure, and also to the securitie and safegard of this noble realme.

And then he put on his bonet, saieng to the bishop; My lord of Elie, whose true hart and sincere affection toward me at all times I haue euidentlie perceiued and knowen, and now most of all in our last priuie communication and secret deuising; I must néeds in hart thinke, and with mouth confesse and saie, that you be a sure fréend, a trustie councellor, a vigilant foreséer, a verie louer of your countrie, and a naturall countrieman: for which kindnes for my part, I most louinglie render to you my hartie thanks now with words, hereafter trusting to recompense and remunerate you with deeds, if life and power shall serue.

And sith, at our last communication, you haue disclosed and opened the verie secrets and priuities of your stomach, touching the duke of Glocester now vsurper of the crowne; and also haue a little touched the aduancement of the two noble families of Yorke and Lancaster: I shall likewise not onelie declare and manifest vnto you all my open acts, attempts, and doings, but also my priuie intents, and secret cogitations. To the intent that as you haue vnbuckeled the bouget of your priuie meanings, and secret purposes to me: so shall all my cloudie workings, close deuises, and secret imaginations be (as cléere as the sunne) reuealed, opened, and made lightsome to you.

The duke openeth himselfe and his secrets to the bishop.

And to begin, I declare, that when king Edward was deceassed, to whome I thought my selfe little or nothing beholden (although we two had maried two sisters) bicause he neither promoted, nor preferred me, as I thought I was worthie, and had deserued; neither fauoured nor regarded me, according to my degrée and birth (for suerlie I had by him little authoritie, and lesse rule, and in effect nothing at all: which caused me lesse to fauour his children, bicause I found small humanitie, or none in their parent) I then began to studie, and with ripe deliberation to ponder and consider, how and in wha manner this realme should be ruled and gouerned. And first I remembred an old prouerbe worthie of memorie, that often rueth the realme where children rule, and women gouerne.

The duke complaineth of want of preferment in king Edwards daies.

This old adage so sanke and settled in my head, that I thought it a great errour, and extreame mischiefe to the whole realme, either to suffer the yoong king to rule, or the quéene his mother to be a gouernesse ouer him, considering that hir brethren, and hir first children (although they were not extract of high and noble linage) tooke more vpon them, and more exalted themselues, by reason of the quéene, than did the kings brethren, or anie duke in his realme: which in conclusion turned to their confusion. Then I being persuaded with my selfe in this point, thought it necessarie both for the publike and profitable wealth of this realme, and also for mine owne commoditie and emolument, to take part with the duke of Glocester; whom (I assure you) I thought to be as cleane without dissimulation, as tractable without iniurie, as mercifull without crueltie; as now I know him perfectlie to be a dissembler without veritie, a tyrant without pitie, yea & worse than the tyrant Phalaris, destitute of all truth and clemencie.

And

And so by my meanes, at the first councell holden at London, when he was most suspected of that thing that after happened (as you my lord know well inough) he was made protector and defendor both of the king and of the realme, which authoritie once gotten, & the two children partlie by * policie brought vnder his gouernance, he being mooued with that gnawing and couetous serpent desire to reigne, neuer ceassed priuilie to exhort and require, yea and sometimes with minatorie tearmes to persuade me and other lords, as well spirituall as temporall, that he might take vpon him the crowne, till the prince came to the age of foure and twentie yeares, and were able to gouerne the realme, as a ripe and sufficient king.

* An vnhappie policie tending to slaughter & bloudshed.

Which thing when he saw me somewhat sticke at, both for the strangenesse of the example (bicause no such president had béene séene) and also bicause we remembred that men once ascended to the highest type of honour and authoritie, will not gladlie descend againe; he then brought in instruments, autentike doctors, proctors, and notaries of the law, with depositions of diuerse witnesses, testifieng king Edwards children to be bastards. Which depositions then I thought to be as true, as now I know them to be feinèd; ánd testified by persons with rewards vntrulie suborned. When the said depositions were before vs read and diligentlie heard, he stood vp bareheaded, saieng: Well my lords, euen as I and you (sage and discréet councellors) would that my nephue should haue no wrong; so I preic you doo me nothing but right. For these witnesses & saiengs of famous doctors being true, I am onelie the vndubitate heire to lord Richard Plantagenet duke of Yorke, adiudged to be the verie heire to the crowne of this relme by authoritie of parlement.

Which things so by learned men to vs for a veritie declared, caused me and other to take him for our lawfull and vndoubted prince and souereigne lord. For well we knew that the duke of Clarence sonne, by reason of the atteindor of his father, was disabled to inherit; and also the duke himselfe was named to be a bastard, as I my selfe haue heard spoken, and that vpon great presumptions more times than one: so againe, by my aid and fauour, he of a protector was made a king, and of a subiect made a gouernor. At which time he promised me on his fidelitie (laieng his hand in mine at Bainards castell) that the two yoong princes should liue, and that he would so prouide for them and so mainteine them in honorable estate, that I and all the realme ought and should be content. [But his words wanted weight, which is a foule discredit to a prince, to a péere, yea to a priuat and meane common man, as testifieth this sentence:

Dedecus est rebus cum bona verba carent.

For when he was once crowned king, and in full possession of the whole realme, he cast awaie his old conditions as the adder dooth hir skin, verifieng the old prouerbe; Honours change manners, as the parish preest remembreth that he was neuer parish clearke. For when I my selfe sued vnto him for my part of the earle of Herefords lands which his brother king Edward wrongfullie deteined and withheld from me; and also required to haue the office of the high constableship of England, as diuerse of my noble ancestors before this time haue had, and in long descent continued: in this my first sute shewing his good mind toward me; he did not onelie first delaie me, and afterward denaie me, but gaue me such vnkind words, with such tawnts & retawnts, ye in manner checke and checkemate, to the vttermost proofe of my patience: as though I had neuer furthered him, but hindered him; as though I had put him downe, and not set him vp.

The principall cause why the duke of Buckingham cōceiued such inward grudge against king Richard.

Yet all these ingratitudes and vndeserued vnkindnesses I bare closelie, & suffered patientlie, and couertlie remembred, outwardlie dissembling that I inwardlie thought: and so with a painted countenance, I passed the last summer in his last companie, not without manie faire promises, but without anie good déeds. But when I was crediblie informed of the death of the two yoong innocents, his owne naturall nephues con-

trarie

trarie to his faith and promise, to the which (God be my iudge) I neuer agréed, nor condescended; O Lord, how my veines panted, how my bodie trembled, and how my heart inwardlie grudged! insomuch that I so abhorred the sight, and much more the companie of him, that I could no longer abide in his court, except I should be openlie reuenged: the end whereof was doubtfull. And so I feined a cause to depart, and with a merrie countenance and a despitefull heart I tooke my leaue humblie of him (he thinking nothing lesse than that I was displeased) and so returned to Brecknocke to you.

The imaginations of the duke of Buckingham to depriue K. Richard.

But in that iournie (as I returned) whither it were by the inspiration of the Holie-ghost, or by melancholious disposition, I had diuerse and sundrie imaginations how to depriue this vnnaturall vncle, and bloudie butcher, from his roiall seat, and princelie dignitie. First I fantised, that if I list to take vpon me the crowne, and imperiall scepter of the realme, now was the time propice and conuenient. For now was the waie made plaine, and the gate opened, and occasion giuen: which now neglected, should peraduenture neuer take such effect and conclusion. For I saw he was disdeined of the lords temporall, abhored and accurssed of the lords spirituall, detested of all gentlemen, and despised of all the communaltie: so that I saw my chance as perfectlie as I saw mine owne image in a glasse, that there was no person (if I had béen gréedie to attempt the enterprise) could nor should haue woone the ring, or got the gole before me. And on this point I rested in imagination secretlie with my selfe two daies at Tewkesburie.

From thence so iournieng, I mused and thought that it was not best nor conuenient to take vpon me as a conqueror. For then I knew that all men, and especiallie the nobilitie, would with all their power withstand me, both for rescuing of possessions and tenures, as also for subuerting of the whole estate, laws and customes of the realme: such a power hath a conqueror, as you know well inough my lord. But at the last, in all this doubtfull case there sprang a new branch out of my head, which suerlie I thought should haue brought forth faire floures; but the sunne was so hot, that they turned to drie wéeds. For I suddenlie remembred that the lord Edmund duke of Summerset my grandfather, was with king Henrie the sixt in the two and thrée degrées, from Iohn duke of Lancaster lawfullie begotten: so that I thought sure, my mother being eldest daughter to duke Edmund, that I was next heire to king Henrie the sixt of the house of Lancaster.

Note the working of ambition in the duke.

This title pleased well such as I made priuie of my counsell, but much more it incouraged my foolish desire, and eleuated my ambitious intent; insomuch that I cléerelie iudged, and in mine owne mind was determinatlie resolued, that I was indubitate heire of the house of Lancaster, and thereupon concluded to make my first foundation, and erect my new building. But whether God so ordeined, or by fortune it so chanced, while I was in a maze either to conclude suddenlie on this title, & to set it open amongst the common people, or to keepe it secret a while, sée the chance: as I rode betweene Worcester and Bridgenorth, I incountered with the ladie Margaret countesse of Richmond, now wife vnto the lord Stanlie, which is the verie daughter and sole heire to lord Iohn duke of Summerset, my grandfathers elder brother, which was as cleane out of my mind, as though I had neuer séene hir: so that she and hir sonne the earle of Richmond be both bulworke and portcullice betwéene me and the gate, to enter into the maiestie roiall and getting of the crowne.

Now when we had communed a little concerning hir sonne, as I shall shew you after, and were departed, shée to our ladie of Worcester, and I to Shrewsburie: I then new changed, and in maner amazed, began to dispute with my selfe, little considering that thus my earnest title was turned to a tittell not so good as Est Amen. Eftsoones I imagined whether were best to take vpon me, by election of the nobilitie and communaltie, which me thought easie to be done, the vsurper king thus being in

　　　　　　　　　　　　　　　　　　　　　　　　　　　　　　hatred

hatred and abhorred of this whole realme; or to take it by power, which, standeth in fortunes chance, and difficile to be atchiued and brought to passe. Thus tumbling and tossing in the waues of ambiguitie, betwéene the stone and the sacrifice, I considered first, the office, dutie, and paine of a king, which surelie thinke I that no mortall man can iustlie and trulie obserue, except he be called, elected, and speciallie appointed by God as K. Dauid, and diuerse other haue beene.

The office of a king verie hard to discharge.

But further, I remembred that if I once tooke on me the scepter, and the gouernance of the realme; that of two extreame enimies I was dailie sure, but of one trustie friend (which now a daies be gone a pilgrimage) I was neither assured nor crediblie ascerteined; such is the worlds mutation. For I manifestlie perceiued, that the daughters of king Edward, and their alies and freends, which be no small number, being both for his sake much beloued, and also for the great iniurie & manifest tyrannie doone to them by the new vsurper, much lamented and pitied, would neuer ceasse to barke if they cannot bite at the one side of me. Semblablie, my coosine the earle of Richmond, his aids and kinsfolks, which be not of little power, will suerlie attempt like a fierce greihound, either to bite or to pearse me on the other side. So that my life and rule should euer hang by a haire, neuer in quiet, but euer in doubt of death, or deposition.

And if the said two linages of Yorke and Lancaster, which so long haue striued for the imperiall diadem, should ioine in one against me, then were I suerlie mated, and the game gotten. Wherefore I haue cléerelie determined, and with my selfe concluded, vtterlie to relinquish all such fantasticall imaginations, concerning the obteining of the crowne. But all such plagues, calamities and troubles, which I feared and suspected might haue chanced on me if I had taken the rule and regiment of this realme, I shall with a reredemaine so make them rebound to our common enimie that calleth himselfe king, that the best stopper that he hath at tenice shall not well stop without a fault.

The dukes resolution not to medle in séeking to obteine the crowne.

For (as I told you before) the countesse of Richmond in my returne from the new named king, méeting me in the high waie, praied me first for kinred sake, secondarilie for the loue that I bare to my grandfather duke Humfrie, which was sworne brother to hir father, to mooue the king to be good to hir sonne Henrie earle of Richmond, and to licence him with his fauour to returne againe into England. And if it were his pleasure so to doo, she promised that the earle hir sonne should marrie one of king Edwards daughters, at the appointment of the king, without anie thing to be taken or demanded for the said espousals, but onelie the kings fauour: which request I soone ouerpassed, and gaue hir faire words, and so departed.

But after in my lodging, when I called to memorie with a deliberate studie, and did circumspectlie ponder them, I fullie adiudged, that the Holie-ghost caused hir to mooue a thing (the end whereof she could not consider) both for the securitie of the realme, as also for the preferment of hir child, and the destruction and finall confusion of the common enimie king Richard. Which thing, she neither then thought (I am sure) as I by hir words could make coniecture, nor I my selfe cast not hir desire to be so profitable to the realme as I now doo perceiue. But such a Lord is God, that with a little sparkle he kindleth a great fire, and (to the admiration of the world) of impossibilities he maketh possibilities, of small beginnings mightie increasings, of drops great flouds.

And so finallie to declare to you the verie conclusion to the which I am both bent and set, my mind is, and my power and pursse shall helpe, that the earle of Richmond, verie heire of the house of Lancaster (in the quarrell of the which linage, both my father and grandfather lost their liues in battell) shall take to wife ladie Elizabeth eldest daughter to king Edward, by the which mariage both the houses of Yorke and Lancaster may be ioined and vnited in one, to the cleere establishment of the

The duke of Buckingham resolued to helpe to depose king Richard, and to prefer the erle of Richmond to the crowne.

title

title to the crowne of this noble relme. To which conclusion if the mothers of both parts, and especiallie the earle himselfe, and the ladie will agrée: I doubt not but the* bragging bore, which with his tuskes raseth euerie mans skin, shall not onelie be brought to confusion (as he hath deserued) but that this empire shall euer be certeine of an vndubitate heire, & then shall all ciuill and intestine warre cease, which so long hath continued to the paring of manie mens crownes, and this realme shall be reduced againe to quietnesse, renowme and glorie.

This inuention of the duke manie men thought after, that it was more imagined for the inward hatred that he bare to king Richard, than for anie fauor that he bare to the earle of Richmond. But of such doubtfull matter it is not best to iudge, for erring too farre from the mind and intent of the author. But what soeuer he intended, this deuise once opened to king Richard was the verie occasion, that he was rounded shorter by the whole head, without attaindor or iudgement. When the duke had said, the bishop which fauoured euer the house of Lancaster, was woonderous ioifull, and much reioised to heare this deuise. For now came the wind about euen as he would

haue it, sith all his imagination tended to this effect, to haue king Richard subdued, and to haue the lines of king Edward, and king Henrie the sixt againe raised and aduanced.

But lord how he reioised, to thinke how that by this marriage the linages of Yorke and Lancaster should be conioined in one, to the verie stedfastnesse of the publike wealth of this realme. And least the dukes courage should swage, or his mind should againe alter, as it did often before (as you may easilie perceiue by his owne tale) he thought to set vp all the sailes that he had, to the intent that the ship of his pretend-

The motion for
the coniunction
of the two
houses of Lan-
caster & Yorke
(deuised by the
duke) furthered.

ed purpose might come shortlie to some sure port, and said to the duke: My lord, sith by Gods prouision and your incomparable wisedome and policie, this noble coniunc-tion is first mooued, now is it conuenient, yea and necessarie, to consider what per-sonages, and what fréends we shall first make priuie of this high deuise and politike con-clusion: [which is not rashlie & without aduisement to be aduentured, for therin is danger, as the wiseman saith:

Semper habet damnum mentis temerarius ardor.]

By my truth, quoth the duke, we will begin with the ladie Richmond, the earles mother, which knoweth where he is, either in captiuitie, or at large in Bri-taine. For I heard saie, that the duke of Britaine restored him to libertie, imme-diatlie after the death of king Edward, by whose means he was restreined. Sith you will begin that waie (said the bishop) I haue an old fréend with the countesse, a man sober, secret, and well witted, called Reginald Braie: whose prudent policie I haue knowne to haue compassed things of great importance, for whome I shall secretlie send, if it be your pleasure; and I doubt not but he will gladlie come and that with a good will. So with a little diligence the bishop wrote a letter to Reginald Braie, re-quiring him to come to Brecknocke with speed, for great and vrgent causes touching his mistresse: and no other thing was declared in the letter. So the messenger rode into Lancashire where Braie was with the countesse, and lord Thomas Stanlie hir hus-band, and deliuered the letter: which when he had read, he tooke it as a signe or pre-sage of some good fortune to come.

Then he (with the messenger) came to the castell of Brecknocke, where the duke and the bishop declared what thing was deuised, both for to set the relme in a quiet stedfastnesse, as also for the high preferment of the earle of Richmond, sonne to his ladie and mistresse: willing hir first to compasse how to obteine the good will of quéene Elizabeth, and also of hir eldest daughter bearing the same name: and after secretlie to send to hir sonne into Britaine, to declare what high honor was prepared for him, if he would sweare to marrie the ladie Elizabeth assoone as he was king, and in roiall possession of the relme. Reginald Braie with a glad heart, forgetting

nothing

nothing giuen to him in charge, in great hast and with good spéed returned to the countesse his ladie and mistresse.

When Braie was departed, and this great doubtfull vessell once set abroach, the bishop thirsting for nothing more than for libertie: when he saw the duke pleasant and well minded toward him; he told the duke, that if he were in his Ile of Elie, he could make manie fréends to further their enterprise: and if he were there and had but foure daies warning, he little regarded the malice of king Richard, his countrie was so strong. The duke knew well all this to be true, but yet loth he was that the bishop should depart: for he knew well, that as long as the bishop was with him, he was sure of politike aduise, sage counsell, and circumspect procéeding. And so he gaue the bishop faire words, saieng, that he should shortlie depart, and that well accompanied for feare of enimies. Bishop Mortons deuise for to be at his owne libertie in his bishoprike of Elie.

The Bishop being as wittie as the duke was wilie, did not tarrie till the dukes companie were assembled, but secretlie disguised, in a night departed (to the dukes great displeasure) and came to his sée of Elie; where he found monie and fréends; and so sailed into Flanders, where he did the earle of Richmond good seruice, and neuer returned againe, till the erle of Richmond (after being king) sent for him, and shortlie promoted him to the see of Canturburie. Thus the bishop woond himselfe from the duke when he had most need of his aid, for if he had taried still, the duke had not made so manie blabs of his counsell, nor put so much confidence in the Welshmen, nor yet so temerariouslie set forward (without knowledge of his fréends) as he did, which things were his sudden ouerthrowe (as they that knew it did report) [and might perhaps haue béene auoided by the bishops wisdome for the dukes saftie, as his owne; sith The bishop of Elie saileth into Flanders to the earle of Richmond.

Qui sapit, ille potest alios sapuisse docere.]

When Reginald Braie had declared his message and priuie instruction to the countesse of Richmond his mistresse, no maruell though she were ioious and glad, both of the good newes, and also for the obteining of such a high fréend in hir sonnes cause as the duke was. Wherefore she willing not to sléepe this matter, but to further it to the vttermost of hir power and abilitie, deuised a means how to breake this matter to quéene Elizabeth then being in sanctuarie at Westminster. And therevpon she, hauing in hir familie at that time (for the preseruation of hir health) a certeine Welshman called Lewes, learned in physicke, which for his grauitie and experience, was well knowne, and much estéemed amongest great estates of the realme, brake hir mind to him.

For with this Lewes she vsed sometime liberallie and familiarlie to talke, and now hauing opportunitie and occasion to expresse hir hart vnto him in this weightie matter, declared that the time was come that hir sonne should be ioined in marriage with ladie Elizabeth, daughter and heire to king Edward; and that king Richard being taken and reputed of all men for the common enimie of the relme, should out of all honor and estate be deiected, and of his crowne and kingdome be cléerelie spoiled and expelled: and requiredhim to go to quéene Elizabeth (with whome in his facultie he was of counsell) not as a messenger, but as one that came fréendlie to visit and consolate hir, and (as time & place should require) to make hir priuie of this deuise; not as a thing concluded, but as a purpose by him imagined.

This physician did not linger to accomplish hir desire, but with good diligence repaired to the queene, being still in the sanctuarie at Westminster. And when he saw time propice and conuenient for his purpose, he said vnto hir: Madame, although my imagination be verie simple, and my deuise more foolish; yet for the entire affection that I beare toward you and your children, I am so bold to vtter vnto you a secret and priuie conceit that I haue cast and compassed in my fantasticall braine. When I well remembred and no lesse considered the great losse and damage that you haue Lewes the physician sheweth the quéene the whole conceipt and deuise of the matter.

sus-

susteined, by the death of your noble and louing husband; ana the great dolour and sorow that you haue suffered and tollerated, by the cruell murther of your innocent children: I can no lesse doo both of bounden duetie and christian charitie, than dailie to studie, and hourelie imagine, not onelie how to bring your hart to comfort and gladnesse, but also deuise how to reuenge the righteous quarell of you and your children on that bloudie bloudsupper, and cruell tyrant king Richard.

And first consider, what battell, what manslaughter, what mischéefe hath risen in this realme by the dissention betwéene the two noble houses of Yorke & Lancaster. Which two families (as I haue contriued) if they may be ioined in one, I thinke, yea and doubt not, but your line shall be againe restored to the pristinate estate and degrée; to your great ioie and comfort, and to the vtter confusion of your mortall enimie the vsurper king. You know verie well madame, that of the house of Lancaster, the earle of Richmond is next of bloud, who is liuing, and a lustie yoong batcheler, and to the house of Yorke your daughters now are heires. If you could agree and inuent the meane how to couple your eldest daughter with the yoong earle of Richmond in matrimonie, no doubt but the vsurper of the realme should be shortlie deposed, and your heire againe to hir right restored.

When the queene had heard this friendlie motion (which was as farre from hir thought, as the man that the rude people saie is in the moone) lord how hir spirits reuiued, and how hir heart leapt in hir bodie for ioie and gladnesse! And first giuing laud to Almightie God, as the chiefe authour of hir comfort, secondarilie to maister Lewes, as the deuiser of these good newes & tidings, she instantlie besought him, that as he had beene the first inuenter of so great an enterprise, so now he would not relinquish nor desist to follow the same: requiring him further (bicause he was apperteining to the countesse of Richmond mother to the erle Henrie) that he would with all diligent celeritie resort to hir, then lodging in hir husbands place, within the citie of London: and to declare on the quéenes behalfe to the countesse, that all the friends and fautors of king Edward hir husband, should assist and take part with the earle of Richmond hir sonne, so that he would take a corporall oth after the kingdome obteined, to espouse and take to wife the ladie Elizabeth hir daughter, or else ladie Cicilie, if the eldest daughter were not then liuing.

Maister Lewes with all dexteritie so sped his businesse, that he made and concluded a finall end and determination of this enterprise betwene the two mothers. And bicause he was a physician, and out of all suspicion and misdéeming, he was the common curror and dailie messenger betweene them, aiding and setting foorth the inuented conspiracie against king Richard. So the ladie Margaret countesse of Richmond, brought into a good hope of the preferment of hir sonne, made Reginald Braie hir most faithfull seruant, chiefe sollicitor and priuie procuror of this conspiracie; giuing him in charge secretly to inuegle and attract such persons of nobilitie to ioine with hir and take hir part, as he knew to be ingenious, faithfull, diligent, and of actiuitie. This Reginald Braie within few daies brought vnto his lure (first of all taking of euerie person a solemne oth to be true and secret) sir Giles Daubneie, sir Iohn Cheinie knight, Richard Gilford, and Thomas Rame esquiers, and diuers other. The countesse of Richmond was not so diligent for hir part, but quéene Elizabeth was as vigilant on the other side, and made friends, and appointed councellors to set forward and aduance hir businesse.

In the meane season, the countesse of Richmond tooke into hir seruice Christopher Urswike, an honest and wise priest, and (after an oth of him for to be secret taken and sworne) she vttered to him all hir mind and counsell, adhibiting to him the more confidence and truth, that he all his life had fauoured and taken part with king Henrie the sixt, and as a speciall iewell put to hir seruice by sir Lewes hir physician. So the mother, studious for the prosperitie of hir son, appointed this Christopher Urswike

wike to saile into Britaine to the earle of Richmond, and to declare and reueale to him all pacts and agréements betwene hir & the quéene agréed and concluded. But suddenlie she remembring that the duke of Buckingham was one of the first inuentors, and a secret founder of this enterprise, determined to send some personage of more estimation than hir chapleine.

Herevpon she elected for a messenger Hugh Conweie esquier, & sent him into Britaine with a great sum of monie to hir sonne, giuing him in charge, to declare to the earle the great loue and especiall fauor that the most part of the nobilitie of the realme bare toward him, the louing hearts & beneuolent minds which the whole communaltie of their owne free will frankelie offered, and liberallie exhibited to him, willing and aduising him not to neglect so good an occasion apparantlie offered; but with all speed and diligence, to addict and settle his mind & full intention how to returne home againe into England, where he was both wished and looked for: giuing him further monition and counsell, to take land and arriuall in the principalitie of Wales, where he should not doubt to find both aid, comfort and friends.

Hugh Coweie esquire sent ouer to the earle of Richmond, to informe him of his roiall preferment.

Richard Gilford, least Hugh Conweie might fortune to be taken, or stopped at Plimmouth, where he intended to take his nauigation, sent out of Kent Thomas Rame with the same instructions: and both made such diligence, and had such wind and weather, the one by land from Calis, and the other by water from Plimmouth, that within lesse than an houre both ariued in the duke of Britains court, and spake with the earle of Richmond, which (from the death of king Edward) went at pleasure and libertie, and to him counted and manifested the cause and effect of their message and ambassage. When the earle had receiued this message (which was the more pleasant, bicause it was vnlooked for) he rendered to Iesu his sauiour, his most humble & heartie thanks, being in firme credence and beléefe, that such things as hée with busie mind and laborious intent had wished & desired, could neuer haue taken anie effect, without the helpe and preferment of almightie God.

Tho. Rame sent ouer for the same purpose for feare of interception.

And now being put in comfort of his long longing, he did communicate & breake to the duke of Britaine all his secrets, and priuie messages, which were to him declared: aduertising him that he was entered into a sure and stedfast hope, to obteine and get the crowne and kingdome of the realme of England, desiring him both of his good will and friendlie helpe toward the atchiuing of his offered enterprise, promising him when he came to his intended purpose, to render to him againe equall kindnes, and condigne recompense. Although the duke of Britaine before that daie, by Thomas Hutton ambassadour from king Richard, had both by monie and praiers beene solicited and mooued to put againe into safe custodie the earle of Richmond, he neuerthelesse promised faithfullie to aid him: and his promise hée trulie performed.

The earle of Richmond maketh the duke of Britaine priuie to the matter.

Wherevpon the earle with all diligence sent into England againe Hugh Conweie, and Thomas Rame, which should declare his comming shortlie into England: to the intent that all things, which by counsell might be for his purpose prouided, should be spéedilie and diligentlie doone; and that all things doubtfull, should of his friends be prudentlie foreséene, in auoiding all engines or snares which king Richard had or might set in disturbance of his purpose: and he in the meane season would make his abode still in Britaine, till all things necessarie for his iournie were prepared, and brought in a readinesse. In the meane season, the chiefteins of the coniuration in England began togither manie enterprises: some in conuenient fortresses put strong garrisons, some kept armed men priuilie, to the intent that when they should haue knowledge of the earles landing, they would begin to stir vp the war: other did secretlie mooue and solicit the people to rise & make an insurrection: other (amongst whom Iohn Morton bishop of Elie then being in Flanders was chiefe) by priuie letters and cloked messengers did stirre and mooue to this new coniuration, all such which

Hugh Cowey and Thomas Rame returne into England and deliuer their answer.

Preparation to bring in, receiue, & erect the earle to the kingdome.

they

they certeinlie knew to haue a rooted hatred, or to beare cankered malice toward king Richard and his proceedings.

Although this great enterprise were neuer so priuilie handled, and so secretlie amongst so circumspect persons treated, compassed and conueied; yet knowledge therof came to the eares of king Richard, who with the sudden chance was not a little mooued and astonied. First bicause he had no host readie prepared; secondlie, if he should raise an armie so suddenlie, he knew not where to méet his enimies, or whither to go, or where to tarrie. Wherefore he determined to dissemble the matter as though he knew nothing, till he had assembled his host; and in the meane season either by the rumour of the common people, or by the diligence of his espials to search out all the counsels, determinations, intents, and compasses of his close aduersaries; or else by policie to intercept and take some person of the same coniuration, considering that there is no more secret nor hid espiall, than that which lurketh in dissimulation of knowledge and intelligence, or is hidden in name and shadow of counterfeit humanitie and feined kindnesse. But yet wisedome hath a deuise to auoid & shift off all such deceiuers, as the poet well saieth:

K. Richards purpose in the case of coniuration against him.

Dissimulatores vitat prudentia vafros.

The duke of Buckingham conspireth against king Richard.

And bicause he knew the duke of Buckingham to be the chiefe head and aid of the coniuration, hée thought it most necessarie to plucke him from that part, either by faire promises or open warre. Wherevpon he addressed his louing letters to the duke, full of gentle words, & most friendlie speach; giuing further in charge to the messenger that caried the letter to promise the duke (in his behalfe) golden hilles, and siluer riuers, and with all gentle and pleasant means to persuade and exhort the duke to come to the court. But the duke as wilie as the king, mistrusting the faire flattering words, and the gaie promises to him so suddenlie without any cause offered, knowing the craftie casts of king Richards bow, which in diuerse affaires before time he had séene practised, required the king to pardon him, excusing himselfe that he was so diseased in his stomach, that scant he could either take refection or rest.

The duke of Buckingham a professed enimie to king Richard.

King Richard not being content with this excuse would in no wise admit the same; but incontinent directed to the duke other letters, of a more rougher and hautier sort, not without tawnting and biting tearmes, and checking words, commanding him (all excuses set apart) to repaire without anie delaie to his roiall presence. The duke made to the messeng a determinate answer, that he would not come to his mortall enimie, whome he neither loued, nor fauoured: and immediatlie prepared open warre against him, and persuaded all his complices and partakers, that euerie man in his quarter, with all diligence should raise vp people & make a commotion. And by this means almost in one moment Thomas marques Dorset come out of sanctuarie, where since the begining of K. Richards daies he had continued, whose life by the onelie helpe of sir Thomas Louell was preserued from all danger & perill in this troublous world, gathered togither a great band of men in Yorkeshire.

Sir Edward Courtneie, and Peter his brother bishop of Excester, raised an other armie in Deuonshire and Cornewall. In Kent Richard Gilford and other gentlemen collected a great companie of souldiers, and openlie began warre. But king Richard, who in the meane time had gotten togither a great strength and puissance, thinking it not most for his part beneficiall, to disperse and diuide his great armie into small branches, and particularlie to persecute anie one of the coniuration by himselfe, determined (all other things being set aside) with his whole puissance to set on the chiefe head, which was the duke of Buckingham. And so remoouing from London, he tooke his iournie towards Salisburie, to the intent that in his iournie he might set on the dukes armie, if he might know him in anie place incamped, or in order of battell arraied.

K. Richards drift in the disposing of his armie.

The

The king was scarse two daies iournie from Salisburie, when the duke of Bucking-ham accompanied with a great power of wild Welshmen, whom he (being a man of great courage and sharpe speech) in maner against their willes had rather thereto inforced and compelled by lordlie and streict commandement, than by liberall wages and gentle demenour, which thing was the verie occasion why they left him desolate, & cowardlie forsooke him.   The duke with all his power marched through the forrest of Deane, intending to haue passed the riuer Seuerne at Glocester, & there to haue ioined his armie with the Courtneis, and other westerne men of his confederacie and affinitie. Which if he doone, no doubt but king Richard had béene in great ieopardie, either of priuation of his realme, or losse of his life, or both.

But sée the chance.   Before he could atteine to Seuerne side, by force of continuall raine and moisture, the riuer rose so high that it ouerflowed all the countrie adioining, insomuch that men were drowned in their beds, and houses with the extreame violence were ouerturned, children were caried about the fields swimming in cradels, beasts were drowned on hilles.   Which rage of water lasted continuallie ten daies, insomuch that in the countrie adioining they call it to this daie, The great water; or the duke of Buckinghams great water.   By this floud the passages were so closed, that neither the duke could come ouer Seuern to his adherents, nor they to him.   During the which time, the Welshmen lingring idelie, and without monie, vittels, or wages, suddenlie scattered and departed: and for all the dukes faire promises, threatnings, and inforcement, would in no wise either go further nor abide.

The duke (being thus left almost post alone) was of necessitie compelled to flie, and in flight was with this sudden fortune maruellouslie dismaid: and being vnpurneied what counsell he should take, and what waie he should follow, like a man in despaire, not knowing what to doo, of verie trust & confidence conueied himselfe into the house of Humfreie Banaster his seruant beside Shrewesburie, whome he had tenderlie brought vp, and whome he aboue all men loued, fauoured and trusted; now not doubting but that in his extreame necessitie he should find him faithfull, secret, and trustie, intending there couertlie to lurke, till either he might raise againe a new armie, or else shortlie to saile into Britaine to the earle of Richmond.   [But alas (good duke) the meanes (by occasion of Gods prouidence, shaking men out of their shifts of supposed safetie) failed him, and he fell infortunatlie into the hands of the foming bore, that tare him in péeces with his tuskes.]

Now when it was knowne to his adherents, which were redie to giue battell, that his host was scatred, and had left him almost alone, and was fled, & could not be found; they were suddenlie amazed & striken with sudden feare, that euery man like persons desperate shifted for himselfe & fled.   Some went to sanctuarie, and to solitarie places; some fled by sea, whereof the most part within a few daies after arriued safelie in the duchie of Britaine.   Among which number were these persons; Peter Courtneie bishop of Excester, and sir Edmund Courtneie his brother, by king Henrie the seuenth after created earle of Deuonshire; Thomas marquesse Dorset, Iohn lord Welles, sir Iohn Bourchier, sir Edward Wooduile, a valiant man in armes, brother to quéene Elizabeth, sir Robert Willoughbie, sir Giles Daubneie, sir Thomas Arundell, sir Iohn Cheinie and his two brethren, sir William Barkelie, sir William Brandon, & Thomas his brother, sir Richard Edgecombe: all these for the most part being knights, Iohn Hallowell, and Edward Poinings, a politike capteine.

At this verie season, Iohn Morton bishop of Elie, and Christopher Urswike priest, and an other companie of noble men soiourned in Flanders; and by letters and messengers procured manie enimies against king Richard, which vsing a vigilant eie, and a quicke remembrance, being newlie come to Salisburie, hauing perfect notice and knowledge how the duke was fled, and how his complices intended to passe out of the realme; first he sent men of warre to all the next ports and passages, to kéepe

streictlie

streictlie the sea coast, so that no person should passe outward, nor take land within the realme without their assent and knowledge; secondarilie he made proclamation, that what person could shew and reueale where the duke of Buckingham was, should be highlie rewarded; if he were a bondman, he should be infranchised and set at libertie; if he were of frée bloud, he should haue a generall pardon, and be rewarded with a thousand pounds.

Furthermore, bicause he vnderstood by Thomas Hutton, which (as you haue heard) was newlie returned out of Britaine, that Francis duke of Britaine not onelie refused to kéepe the earle of Richmond as a prisoner, at his contemplation, and for his sake; but also that he was readie to aid and succour the said earle, with men, monie and all things necessarie for his transporting into England; he therefore rigged and sent out ships of warre, well furnished and decked with men and artillerie, to scowre and kéepe that part of the sea that lieth ouer against Britaine, to the intent that if the earle of Richmond would aduenture to saile toward England, either he should be taken captiue, or be beaten and driuen from the coast of England. And moreouer, to the intent that euerie coast, waie, passage, and corner, should be diligentlie watched & kept, he set at euerie doubtfull and suspected place men of warre, to séeke, search, and inquire, if anie creature could tell tidings of the duke of Buckingham; or of anie of his confederation, adherents, fautors or partakers.

While this busie search was diligentlie applied and put in execution, Humfreie Banaster (were it more for feare of life and losse of goods, or allured & prouoked by the auaricious desire of the thousand pounds) he bewraied his guest and maister to Iohn Mitton then shiriffe of Shropshire; which suddenlie with a strong power of men in harnesse apprehended the duke in a little groue adioining to the mansion of Humfreie Banaster, and in great hast and euill speed conueied him apparelled in a pilled blacke cloake to the towne of Shrewesburie, where king Richard then kept his houshold. Whether this Banaster bewraried the duke more for feare than couetous, manie men doo doubt: but sure it is, that shortlie after he had betraied the duke his master; his sonne and heire waxed mad, & so died in a bores stie; his eldest daughter of excellent beautie, was suddenlie striken with a foule leprosie; his second sonne maruellouslie deformed of his lims, and made lame; his yoonger sonne in a small puddle was strangled and drowned; and he being of extreame age, arreigned, and found guiltie of a murther, and by his cleargie saued. And as for his thousand pounds, K. Richard gaue him not one farthing, saieng that he which would be vntrue to so good a maister, would be false to all other: howbeit some saie that he had a small office or a farme to stop his mouth withall. The duke being by certeine of the kings councell diligentlie vpon interrogatories examined, what things he knew preiudiciall vnto the kings person, opened and declared franklie and fréelie all the coniuration, without dissembling or glosing; trusting, bicause he had trulie and plainelie reuealed and confessed all things that were of him required, that he should haue licence to speake to the king: which (whether it were to sue for pardon and grace, or whether he being brought to his presence, would haue sticked him with a dagger as men then iudged) he sore desired and required. But when he had confessed the whole fact & conspiracie, vpon All soules daie, without arreigment or iudgement, he was at Salisburie in the open market place, on a new scaffold beheaded and put to death.

This death (as a reward) the duke of Buckingham receiued at the hands of king Richard, whome he before in his affaires, purposes and enterprises had holpen, susteined, and set forward, aboue all Gods forbode. By this all men may easilie perceiue, that he not onelie loseth both his labour, trauell, and industrie (and further staineth and spotteth his line with a perpetuall ignominie and reproch) which in euill and mischiefe assisteth and aideth an euill disposed person, considering for the most part, that he for his freendlie fauour should receiue some great displeasure or importunate chance.

Beside

Beside that, God of his iustice in conclusion appointed to him a condigne paine and affliction for his merits and deserts. [Auailable therefore, and for his best aduantage had it béene, to haue followed the wise counsell of him, that willed him, and such as he, to kéepe them from the man that hath power to slaie; so shalt thou doubt (saith he) the feare of death. And if thou come vnto him make no fault, least he take awaie thy life: remember that thou goest in the middest of snares, & that thou walkest vpon the towers of the citie. Which aduise a learned man, in good place, and necessarie seruice about the prince, neatlie comprised in these few verses:

> Vtere principibus modicè, nimis esse propinquus
> 　　Si cupis, in vitæ multa pericla rues.
> Si tua te fortuna facit seruire potenti,
> 　　Dispice ne titubes, atque repentè cadas,
> Sollicitè vigiles, laquei sunt vndíque fusi,
> 　　Turribus in summis es situs, ergo caue.]

Gu. Ha.

While these things were thus handled and ordered in England, Henrie earle of Richmond prepared an armie of fiue thousand manlie Britons, and fortie well furnished ships. When all things were prepared in a readinesse, and the daie of departing and setting forward was appointed, which was the twelfe daie of the moneth of October, the whole armie went on shipbord, and halsed vp their sailes, and with a prosperous wind tooke the sea. But toward night the wind changed, and the weather turned, and so huge and terrible a tempest so suddenlie arose, that with the verie power and strength of the storme, the ships were disparkled, seuered & separated asunder: some by force were driuen into Normandie, some were compelled to returne againe into Britaine. The ship wherein the earle of Richmond was, associat onelie with one other barke, was all night tossed and turmoiled.

The earle of Richmonds preparation of ships and souldiers to the sea.

His ships disparkled by tempest.

In the morning after, when the rage of the furious tempest was asswaged, and the ire of blustering wind was some deale appeased; about the houre of noone the same daie, the earle approched to the south part of the realme of England, euen at the mouth of the hauen of Pole, in the countie of Dorset, where he might plainelie perceiue all the sea bankes & shores garnished and furnished with men of warre and souldiers, appointed and deputed there to defend his arriuall and landing (as before is mentioned.) Wherefore he gaue streict charge, and sore commandement, that no person should once presume to take land, and go to shore, vntill such time as the whole nauie were assembled and come togither. And while he taried and lingered, he sent out a shipboate toward the land side, to know whether they, which stood there in such a number, and so well furnished in apparell defensiue were his foes and enimies, or else, his fréends and comfortors.

He séeth all the sea bankes furnished with souldiers.

He sendeth to know whether they were with him or against him.

They that were sent to inquire, were instantlie desired of the men of warre keeping the coast (which thereof were before instructed & admonished) to descend and take land, affirming that they were appointed by the duke of Buckingham there to await and tarie for the arriuall and landing of the earle of Richmond, and to conduct him safelie into the campe, where the duke not far of laie incamped with a mightie armie, and an host of great strength and power, to the intent that the duke and the earle, ioining in puissances and forces togither, might prosecute and chase king Richard being destitute of men, and in maner desperate, and so by that meanes, and their owne labours, to obteine the end of their enterprise which they had before begun.

A forged tale to intrap the earles messengers.

The earle of Richmond suspecting their flattering request to be but a fraud (as it was in déed) after he perceiued none of his ships to appeare in sight, he weied vp his anchors, halsed vp his sailes, & hauing a prosperous and streinable wind, and a fresh gale sent euen by God to deliuer him from that perill and ieopardie, arriued safe and in all securitie in the duchie of Normandie, where he (to refresh and solace his soldiers and peo-

ple)

The earle arriueth in Normandie & passeth by land into Britaine againe.

ple) tooke his recreation by the space of thrée daies, and cléerelie determined with part of his companie to passe all by land againe into Britaine. And in the meane season he sent ambassadors to the French king, called Charles the eight, which newlie succéeded his father king Lewes the eleuenth, not long before departed to God, requiring of him a safe conduct and licence to passe thorough his countrie of Normandie into Britaine.

Charles the 8. of France his beneuolence to the earle of Richmond.

This yoong king, hauing compassion of the misfortune of the earle of Richmond, not onelie gentlie granted and assigned to him a pasport; but also liberallie disbursed to him a great summe of monie for his conduct and expenses necessarie in his long iournie and passage. But the earle trusting in the French kings humanitie, aduentured to send his ships home into Britaine, and to set forward himselfe by land on his iournie, making no great hast till his messengers were returned. Which being with that benefit so comforted, and with hope of prosperous successe so incouraged, marched towards Britaine with all diligence, intending there to consult further with his louers & fréends of his affaires and enterprises. When he was returned againe into Britaine, he was certified by credible information, that the duke of Buckingham had lost his head; and that the marquesse Dorset, and a great number of noble men of England, had a little before inquired and searched for him there, and were now returned to Vannes.

The earle lamenteth and reioiseth.

When he had heard these newes thus reported, he first sorowed and lamented his first attempt and setting forward of his fréends, and in especiall of the nobilitie, not to haue more fortunatelie succéeded. Secondarilie, he reioised on the other part, that God had sent him so manie valiant and prudent capteins to be his companions in his martiall enterprises, trusting suerlie and nothing doubting in his owne opinion, but that all his businesse should be wiselie compassed, and brought to a good conclusion. Wherefore he determining with all diligence to set forward his new begun businesse, departed to Rheims, and sent certeine of his priuie seruitours to conduct and bring the marquesse and other noble men to his presence. When they knew that he was safelie returned into Britaine, Lord how they reioised! for before that time they missed him, and knew not in what part of the world to make inquirie or search for him. For they doubted and no lesse feared least he had taken land in England, & fallen into the hands of king Richard, in whose person they knew well was neither mercie nor compassion.

Wherefore in all spéedie maner they galoped toward him, and him reuerentlie saluted. Which meeting after great ioy and solace, and no small thanks giuen and rendered on both parts, they aduisedlie debated and communed of their great businesse and weightie enterprise. In the which season the feast of the Natiuitie of our sauiour Christ hap-

The English lords giue faith and promise either to other.

pened, on which daie all the English lords went with their solemnitie to the chéefe church of the citie, and there ech gaue faith and promise to other. the earle himselfe first tooke a corporall oth on his honor, promising that incontinent after he shuld be possessed of the crowne and dignitie of the realme of England, he would be conioined

The earle of Richmond sweareth to marie Elizabeth daughter to Edward the fourth, after possession of the crowne.

in matrimonie with the ladie Elizabeth daughter to king Edward the fourth. Then all the companie sware to him fealtie, and did to him homage (as though he had béene that time the crowned king, and annointed prince) promising faithfullie, and firmelie affirming, that they would not onelie loose their worldlie substance; but also be depriued of their liues and worldlie felicitie, rather than to suffer king Richard that tyrant longer to rule and reigne ouer them.

Which solemne oths made and taken, the earle of Richmond declared and communicated all these dooings to Francis duke of Britaine, desiring & most heartilie requiring him to aid him with a greater armie to conduct him into his countrie, which so sore longed and looked for his returne, and to the which he was by the more part of the nobilitie and communaltie called and desired. Which (with Gods aid, and the dukes comfort) he doubted not in short time to obteine; requiring him further to prest to him a conuenient summe of monie; affirming that all such summes of monie which he had receiued of his especiall freends, were spent and consumed iu preparation of his last iourneie made toward England; which summes of monie, after his enterprise once atchiued, he in the word of a prince faithfullie promised to repaie and restore againe. The duke promised him aid and helpe. Vpon confidence whereof he rigged his ships, and set foorth a nauie well decked with ordinance, and warlikelie furnished with all things necessarie, to the intent to saile forward shortlie, and to loose no time.

In the meane season king Richard apprehended in diuerse parts of the realme certeine gentlemen of the earle of Richmonds faction, & confederation, which either intended to saile into Britaine toward him, or else at his landing to assist and aid him. Amongst whome sir George Browne, sir Roger Clifford, and foure other were put to execution at London, and sir Thomas Sentleger which had married the duchesse of Excester the kings owne sister, and Thomas Rame, and diuerse other were executed at Excester. Beside these persons, diuerse of his houshold seruants, whome either he suspected or doubted, were by great crueltie put to shamefull death. [By the obseruation of which mens names, the place, and the action here mentioned, with the computation oftime, I find fit occasion to interlace a note (newlie receiued from the hands of one that is able to saie much by record) deliuering a summarie (in more ample sort) of their names, whome king Richard did so tyrannicallie persecute and execute: as followeth.]

King Richard (saith he) came this yeare to the citie, but in verie secret maner, whome the maior & his brethren in the best maner they could did receiue, and then presented to him in a purse two hundred nobles; which he thinkefullie accepted. And during his abode here he went about the citie, & viewed the seat of the same, & at length he came to the castell: and when he vnderstood that it was called Rugemont, suddenlie he fell into a dumpe, and (as one astonied) said; Well, I sée my daies be not long. He spake this of a prophesie told him, that when he came once to Richmond he should not long liue after: which fell out in the end to be true, not in respect of this castle, but in respect of Henrie earle of Richmond, who the next yeare following met him at Bosworth field where he was slaine. But at his being here, he did find the gentlemen of this countrie not to be best affected towards him, and after his departure, did also heare that the marquesse of Dorset, the bishop of Excester, aud sundrie other gentlemen were in a confederacie against him for the assisting of the erle of Richmond.

Wherefore he sent downe Iohn lord Scroope with a commission to keepe a session; who sat at Torington, & then & there were indicted of high treason, Thomas marquesse Dorset, Peter bishop of Excester, Thomas Sentleger, and Thomas Fulford knights as principals, and Robert Willoughbie and Thomas Arundell knights, Iohn Arundell deane of Excester, Dauid Hopton archdeacon of Excester, Oliuer abbat of Buckland, Bartholomew Sentleger, William Chilson, Thomas Gréenefield, Richard Edgecombe, Robert Burnbie, Walter Courtneie, Thomas Browne, Edward Courtneie, Hugh Lutterell, Iohn Crocker, Iohn Hallewell, and fiue hundred others were indicted as accessaries. All which fled and shifted for themselues, some into Britaine, and some else where; sauing sir Thomas Sentleger, and one sir Iohn Rame; who were brought to Excester, and there at the Carefox were beheaded.]

After this, king Richard called a parlement, in the which he atteinted the earle of Richmond and all other persons which were fled out of the realme for feare, or anie other cause, as enimies to him, and to their naturall countrie; & all their lands, goods, & possessions, were confiscate and seized to the kings vse. And yet not content with this preie, which no doubt was of no small valour and moment, he laid on the peoples necks a great tax and tallage, and suerlie necessitie to that actin maner him compelled.

For

Marginal notes:

Diuerse of the earle of Richmonds faction apprehended and executed.

Abr. Flem.

Iohn Hooker, alias Vowel.

K. Richard commeth to Excester, and is receiued with presents.

A prophesie, the memorie whereof did appall the kings spirits.

Lord Scroope by the kings commission kept a session against diuerse indicted of high treason.

More than fiue hundred indicted, whereof some escaped, and some were executed.

1484

The earle of Richmod atteinted in parlement, and all other that fled ouer sea to take his part.

For what with purging and declaring his innocencie concerning the murther of his nephues towards the world, and what with cost to obteine the loue and fauour of the communaltie (which outwardlie glosed, and openlie dissembled with him) he gaue prodigallie so manie and so great rewards, that now both he lacked, and scarse wist honestlie how to borow.

In this troublous season, nothing was more maruelled at, than that the lord Stanleie had not béene taken, and reputed as an enimie to the king; considering the working of the ladie Margaret his wife, moother to the earle of Richmond. But forsomuch as the enterprise of a woman was of him reputed of no regard or estimation; and that the lord Thomas hir husband had purged himselfe sufficientlie to be innocent of all dooings and attempts by hir perpetrated and committed; it was giuen him in charge to kéepe hir in some secret place at home, without hauing anie seruant or companie:

so that from thence foorth she should neuer send letter or messenger vnto hir sonne, nor anie of his freends or confederats, by the which the king might be molested or troubled, or anie hurt or preiudice might be attempted against his realme and communaltie. Which commandement was a while put in execution and accomplished, according to his dreadfull commandement.

Yet the wild worme of vengeance wauering in his head, could not be content with the death of diuerse gentlemen suspected of treason; but also he must extend his bloudie furie against a poore gentleman called Callingborne, for making a small rime of three of his vnfortunate councellors, which were the lord Louell, sir Richard Ratcliffe his mischeeuous minion, and sir William Catesbie his secret seducer, which méeter or rime was thus framed:

> The Cat, the Rat, and Louell our dog,
> Rule all England vnder an hog.

Meaning by the hog, the dreadfull wild boare, which was the king cognisance. But bicause the first line ended in dog, the metrician could not (obseruing the regiments of méeter) end the second verse in boare, but called the boare an hog. This poeticall schoolemaister, corrector of bréefs and longs, caused Collingborne to be abbreuiated shorter by the head, and to be diuided into foure quarters.

Here is to be noted, that beside the rime which is reported by some to be the onelie cause for which this gentleman suffered, I find in a register booke of indictments concerning fellonies and treasons by sundrie persons committed, that the said Collingborne (by the name of William Collingborne) late of Lidyard in the countie of Wilshire esquier, and other his associats were indicted in London: for that they about the tenth daie of Iulie. in this second yeare of king Richards reigne, in the parish of saint Botulphes in Portsoken ward had solicited and requested one Thomas Yate,

offering to him for his paines eight pounds, to go ouer into Britaine vnto Henrie erle of Richmond, Thomas marquesse Dorset, Iohn Cheineie esquier, and others, which in the last parlement holden at Westminster had béene atteinted of sundrie high treasons by them practised within the kings dominion.

Besides this, to declare vnto them that they should doo verie well, to returne into England with all such power as they might get before the feast of S. Luke the euangelist next insuing; for so they might receiue all the whole reuenues of the realme due at the feast of saint Michaell next before the said feast of saint Luke. And that if the said earle of Richmond and his partakers, following the counsell of the said

Collingborne, would arriue at the hauen of Pole in Dorsetshire, he the said Collingborne and other his associats would cause the people to rise in armes, and to leuie warre against king Richard, taking part with the said earle and his freends; so that all things should be at their commandements. Moreouer, to mooue the said earle to send the said Iohn Cheineie vnto the French king, to aduertise him that his ambassadors sent into England should be dallied with, onelie to driue off the time till the

winter

season were past, and that then in the beginning of summer king Richard meant to make warre into France, inuading that realme with all puissance: and so by this meanes to persuade the French king to aid the earle of Richmond and his partakers, in their quarell against king Richard.

Further, that the said William Collingborne, being confederate with the said earle and other his adherents, as well within the realme as without, the eightéenth day of Iulie, in the said second yeare, within the parish of saint Gregories in Faringdon ward within, had deuised certeine bils and writings in rime, to the end that the same being published, might stir the people to a commotion against the king. And those bils and writings in rime so deuised and written, the same Collingborne the daie and yeare last mentioned, had fastened and set vpon diuerse doores of the cathedrall church of saint Paule, for the more speedie furthering of his intended purpose. Thus farre the indictement. But whether he was giltie in part or in all, I haue not to saie. Collingborne indicted to be a libeller against king Richard.

King Richard being thus disquieted in mind, and doubtfull for the suertie of his owne estate, called to remembrance that confederations, honest bands and pacts of amitie, concluded and had betwixt princes and gouernours, are the efficient cause that realmes and common wealths are strengthened with double power, that is, with aid of fréends abroad, and their owne forces at home. Wherevpon he deuised how to conclude a league and amitie with his neighbour the king of Scots: who not long before had made diuerse incursions and roads into the realme of England. And although he had not much gotten; yet verelie he lost not much. And now euen as king Richard could haue wished, he of himselfe made sute for peace or truce to be had betwixt him and king Richard; who willinglie giuing eare to that sute, commissioners were appointed to méete about the treatie thereof, as in the historie of Scotland it maie appeare. Sée Scotland pag. 284, 285.

At length they agréed vpon a truce for thrée yeeres, and withall for a further increase of firme fréendship and sure amitie (betwixt him and the king of Scots) king Richard entered into a treatie also of aliance for the concluding of a marriage betwixt the duke of Rothsaie (eldest sonne to the king of Scots) and the ladie Anne de la Poole daughter to Iohn duke of Suffolke and the duchesse Anne, sister to king Richard: which sister he so much fauoured, that studieng by all waies and meanes possible, how to aduance hir linage, he did not onelie thus seeke to preferre hir daughter in marriage; but also after the death of his sonne, he proclaimed Iohn earle of Lincolne hir sonne and his nephue, heire apparant to the crowne of England, disheriting king Edwards daughters, whose brethren (as ye haue heard) he most wickedlie had caused to be murthered and made awaie. A truce betwixt England & Scotland with a treatie of aliance. Iohn earle of Lincolne proclaimed heire apparant to the crowne.

The king of Scots standing in néed of freends, although not so greatlie as king Richard, did willinglie consent to that motion of marriage, first broched by king Richard, insomuch that it tooke effect, and by commissioners was passed and concluded, in maner as in the historie of Scotland it likewise appeareth. But albeit that by this league and amitie thus couenanted and concluded, it might be thought, that all conspiracies, coniurations, and confederacies against king Richard had béene extinct, especiallie considering the duke of Buckingham and his alies were dispatched out of the waie, some by death, and some by flight and banishment into farre countries: yet king Richard, more doubting than trusting to his owne people and freends, was continuallie vexed and troubled in mind for feare of the earle of Richmonds returne: which dailie dread and hourelie agonie caused him to liue in dolefull miserie, euer vnquiet, and in maner in continuall calamitie. A marriage concluded betwixt the prince of Rothsaie & the duke of Suffolkes daughter.

Wherefore he intending to be reléeued, and to haue an end of all his doubtfull dangers, determined cléerelie to extirpate and plucke vp by the roots all the matter and ground of his feare and doubts. Insomuch that (after long and deliberate consultation had) nothing was for his purpose and intent thought either more necessarie or

expe-

expedient than once againe with price, praier, aad rewards, to attempt the duke of Britaine, in whose territorie the earle of Richmond then abode, to deliuer the said earle into his hands : by which onelie meanes he should be discharged of all feare and perill, and brought to rest and quietnesse both of bodie and mind. Wherefore incontinent he sent certeine ambassadors to the duke of Britaine, which tooke vpon them (beside the great and ample rewards that they brought with them into Britaine) that king Richard should yearelie paie and answer the duke of all the reuenues, rents, and profits of the seigniories, lands, and possessions, as well belonging and apperteining to the erle of Richmond, as to anie other noble or gentleman, which then were in the earles companie; if he after that time would kéepe them in continuall prison, and restraine them from libertie.

The ambassadors (furnished with these and other instructions) arriued in Britaine, and came to the dukes house; where with him they could haue no maner of communication concerning their weightie affaires : by reason that he being faint ar d weakened by a long and dailie infirmitie, began a little to wax idle and weake in his wit and remembrance. For which cause Peter Landoise his cheefe treasuror, a man both of pregnant wit and great authoritie, ruled and adiudged all things at his pleasure and commandement, for which cause (as men set in authoritie be not best beloued) he excited & prouoked against him the malice and euill will of the nobilitie of Britaine, which afterward (for diuerse great offenses by him during his authoritie perpetrate & committed) by their meanes was brought to death & confusion.

The English ambassadors mooued their message and request to Peter Landoise, and to him declared their maisters commandement, instantlie requiring and humblie desiring him (in whose power it laie to doo all things in Britaine) that he would freendlie assent to the request of king Richard : offering to him the same rewards and lands, that they should haue offered to the duke. This Peter (which was no lesse disdeined than hated almost of all the people of Britaine) thought that if he did assent & satisfie king Richards petition and desire, he should be of power and abilitie sufficient to withstand and refell the malicious attempts and disdeinfull inuentions of his enuious aduersaries. Wherefore he faithfullie promised to accomplish king Richards request & desire: so that he kept promise with him, that he might be able to withstand the cankered malice of his secret enimies.

This act that he promised to doo, was not for anie grudge or malice that he bare vnto the erle of Richmond: for (as you haue heard before) he deliuered him from the perill of death at saint Malos, when he was in great doubt of life, and ieopardie. But as cause ariseth we euer offend, and that curssed hunger of gold, and execrable thirst of lucre, and inward feare of losse of authoritie, driueth the blind minds of couetous men, & ambitious persons to euils and mischéefs innumerable, not remembring losse of good name, obloquie of the people, nor in conclusion the punishment of God for their merits and deserts. [Which vengeance of God for such falshood was more to be feared, than the gaie offers of the king to be desired; for the one was sure to fall, the other was likelie to faile. Wherefore it is wisedome to make choise of a fréend, by the rule of the wiseman to be obserued in wine, which is drunke with pleasure when it is old. Neither dooth it stand with a mans safetie to trust a fréend too farre: for occasions maie fall out wherby he shall become an enimie, as the poet saith:

Hostis erit forsan qui tuus hospes erat.]

But fortune was so fauourable to the publike wealth of the realme of England, that this deadlie and dolorous compact tooke none effect or place. For while posts ran, and letters were sent to and fro for the finishing of this great enterprise betwéene king Richard and Peter Landoise, Iohn Morton bishop of Elie (soiourning then in Flanders) was of all this craftie conueiance certified by his secret and sure fréends.

fréends. Wherefore he sent Christopher Urswike (which at that sent verie season was come out of Britaine into Flanders) to declare to the earle of Richmond how all the deceit and craftie working was conueied and compased, giuing him charge to councell and aduise the earle in all hast possible with all his companie to retire out of Britaine into France.

When these newes were brought to the earle, he then kept house in Vannes, and incontinent dispatched againe Christopher Urswike vnto Charles the French king, requiring him that he and his might safelie passe into France. Which desire being obteined, the messenger shortlie returned to his lord and prince. The earle, well perceiuing that it was expedient and necessarie, with all spéed and diligence to looke to this weightie matter, calling verie few to counsell, he made inquirie and search of all secret & by-waies, & sent before all his noble men, as though for a certeine familiaritie and kindnesse they should visit and comfort the duke, which then (for recreation and change of aire) laie on the borders and confines of France. And secretlie he gaue charge to the earle of Penbroke, which was the leader and conductor of his companie, that when they approched the marches and limits of Britaine, they should diuert and take the next waie into France.

The earle of Penbroke cŏductor of the earle of Richmonds companie.

The noble men somewhat suspicious of things newlie imagined, without any tarieng, scowring the waies as fast as their horsses could runne, came out of the duchie of Britaine into the duchie of Aniou in the dominion of France, where they taried the erles comming, which two daies after departed out of Vannes, onelie accompanied with fiue seruitors, as though he had gone secretlie to visit a familiar friend of his, in a small village adioining. No man suspected the he would depart, considering that a great multitude of Englishmen were left and continued in the citie. But after that he had passed directlie fiue miles forward, he suddenlie turned into a solitarie wood next adioining, where clothing himselfe in the simple coat of his poore seruant, made and appointed his said minister leader and maister of his small companie, & he as an humble page diligentlie followed and serued his counterfeit gouernor, neither resting nor refreshing themselues, except the baiting of their horsses, till they by waies vnknowne, now this way, now turning that way, came to their companie abiding them in Angiers.

The earles small t aine for a policie.

The earle apparelled like a page attĕdeth vpŏ one of his men as his maister.

The fourth day after the earle of Richmond was thus departed, that craftie merchant Peter Landoise, thirsting still after his preie promised by king Richard, was readie to set forward his crew of souldiers, which he priuilie had consigned, with certeine trustie capteins for that onelie purpose appointed and elected, to performe and atchiue his pretended enterprise; dissembling and feining them to be conducted and hired by him to serue the earle of Richmond, and him to conduct in his returne towards his natiue countrie: meaning no other thing but to apprehend him, and the other noble men in his retinue, which no such fraud suspected, nor yet anie treason imagined, vnware and vnprouided, and destitute of all aid, and them to cast and commit suddenlie into continuall captiuitie and bondage, to the intent that by this his wretched and naughtie act, he might satisfie the charitable request and louing desire of good king Richard, more for his owne profit than king Richards gaine.

But when this craftie dissembler Peter Landoise, which was no wilier than an old fox, perceiued that the earle was departed (thinking that to be true that he imagined) Lord how currors ran into euerie coast! how light horssemen gallopped in euerie street! to follow and deteine him, if by anie possibilitie hee could be met with and ouertaken, and him to apprehend and bring captiue into the citie of Vannes. The horssemen made such diligence, and with such celeritie set forward their iournie, that nothing was more likelie than they to haue obteined, yea and seized their preie. For the earle of Richmond was not entered into the realme of France scarse one houre, but the fol-

Peter Landoise his expectation disappointed by the priuate and vnknowne departing of the earle.

lowers

lowers came to the limits and confines of Britaine, and durst aduenture no further, but vainlie (without their desire) sorrowfullie returned.

At which season were left at Vannes about the number of three hundred English-men, which not being called to counsell, and vnware of this enterprise, but knowing of the earles sudden departure, were so incontinentlie astonied, that in maner they were all in despaire, both of him, and their owne suertie and safegard. But fortune

turned hir saile, and otherwise it happened than their feare them incumbered. For the duke of Britaine, now being somewhat recouered, was sore displeased, and nothing contented, that the earle of Richmond was in his dominion so vncourteouslie vsed and intreated, that he should be by fraud and vntruth compelled to leaue and flie out of his duchie and countrie, contrarie to his honour. Wherefore he tooke verie great dis-pleasure with Peter Landoise his treasuror, to whome (although he knew not, and was ignorant that all the drift was driuen and deuised by him) he laid the fault, and im-puted the crime.

Herevpon he sent for Edward Wooduile, and Edward Poinings, valiant esquiers of England, and deliuered vnto to them monie sufficient for their conduct, willing them to conueie the rest of the Englishmen being in Britaine, to the erle of Richmonds pre-sence. When the earle was thus furnished, and appointed with his trustie companie, and was escaped all the dangers, labirinths, and snares that were set for him : no mar-uell though he were iocund and glad of the prosperous successe that happened in his affaires. Wherefore, least he should séeme to be blotted with the note of ingratitude, he sent diuerse of his gentlemen to the duke of Britaine, the which should publish and declare to him on the behalfe of the earle, that he and his were onelie by his bene-fit and fauour conserued and deliuered from the imminent danger that they were like to be trapped in. Wherefore at that time he rendered vnto him his most hartie thanks in words, trusting and not doubting, but in time to come liberallie to recompense him with acts and déeds.

After this, the earle tooke his iournie to Charles the French king, lieng then at Langes vpon the riuer of Loire, to whome (after great thanks giuen for manifold plea-sures by him to the earle shewed) hée disclosed and manifested the cause and oc-casion of his accesse and repaire to his person. After that, hée required of him helpe and succour, to the intent that by his immortall benefit to him at that time shewed, hée might safelie returne vnto the nobilitie of his realme; of whome he was generallie called to take vpon him the crown & scepter of the realme, sith they much hated and abhorred the tyrannie of king Richard. King Charles promised him aid and comfort, and bade him be of good courage, and make good cheare; for he assured him that he would gladlie shew to him his beneuolent mind and bountifull liberalitie. Which king from thence remooued to Mountargis, leading with him the earle of Richmond, and all the noble personages of his retinue and faction.

¶ This is that Charles the French K. in whose time France was all aflant, for the state of that realme is said, that then it was verie populous in multitudes of men, for wealth and riches euerie particular region most fertile and plentifull, for glorie in armes most florishing & renowmed, a policie well directed, discipline administred, an authoritie dreadfull, and in opinion and hope most mightie; lastlie their generall con-ditions and faculties so well furnished, as perhaps it was not more happie in these mortall felicities since the daies of Charlemaine. It was newlie amplified in euerie one of the three parts wherein all Gall stood diuided by the ancients : for fortie yéers be-fore vnder Charles the seuenth (a prince for his victories obteined with great dangers called Happie) Normandie and the duchie of Guien, holden by the Englishmen, were reduced to the obedience of the French crowne. And in the last daies of Lewes the eleuenth, the earledome of Prouince, the dukedome of Burgognie, almost all
Picardie

Picardie, togither with the duchie of Britaine, were by a new mariage inuested in the power of Charles the eight.]

While the earle was thus attendant in the French court, Iohn Vere earle of Oxford, which (as you haue heard before) was by king Edward kept in prison within the castell of Hammes, so persuaded Iames Blunt capteine of the same fortresse, and sir Iohn Fortescue porter of the towne of Calis, that he himselfe was not onelie dismissed and set at libertie; but they also abandoning and leauing their fruitfull offices, did condescend to go with him into France to the earle of Richmond, and to take his part. But Iames Blunt, like a wise capteine, bicause he left his wife remaining in the castell before his departure, did fortifie the same both with new munitions, and fresh souldiers. [And here bicause the names of Vere and Fortescue are remembred, it shall not be amisse, somewhat out of due place, yet better a little out of order than altogither to omit the same, to adde a supplement for the further perfecting of a report recorded in page 329, and adding some light also to this present place touching the said persons, with others.]

¶ Know you therefore, that this sir Iohn Vere earle of Oxford (that withdrew himselfe from Barnet field, and with all spéed fled into Scotland) in the yere 1473, and the thirtéenth of Edward the fourth, did (after he had sometime soiourned there) saile into France, about the borders whereof he was continuallie houering, as hoping to win some preie (to support his estate) of such passengers as for merchandize cause or otherwise must kéepe their course a long the sea. Whose good successe therein did not deceiue his mind. For in the end (what of one and other) hée got such riches and other furniture, as he was able to support a chosen number of followers. Wherwith he (being reléeued and incouraged to aduenture to set foot in his countrie in despite of king Edward) did with his companie of 397 persons, and with his saile of ships land in the west countrie the last of September, where (partlie by force of his, and partlie through feare of the inhabitants, but mostlie by a subtill shift) he gat and entered the castell of saint Michaels mount, a place of strength, and such an harborough, as he determined to kéepe the same against all assailants. During the time of his remaine there, he would with his companie manie times descend the hill, and come abrode in the countrie, where (for his loue, for his honour, and for the hatred they bare to king Edward) he was well interteined of manie gentlemen and others of the countrie.

But this matter vnpossible long to be kept in secret, was at length brought to the knowledge of king Edward; who being somewhat mooued, thought in the beginning to withstand such mischéefe, least suffering too long, & the earle growing to strength, he might be put to as great plunge for the crowne as he had bene twise before: wherwith séeing he was possessed, he grew resolute to kéepe it both by policie and puissance, maugre the open violence and priuie practises as well of his professed as secret enimies. For he ran through the pikes yer he could obteine it, and offered his bodie to manie desperate perils in hope to get it: which if he had either feared or shunned, it is a matter of demand whether he had euer had it. For pretious things, as principalities and such like, vnlesse they be hereditarie, as they are hardlie kept, so are they not easilie gotten: for he that desireth to gather a rose, must not be tender ouer his fingers bicause of thornes; and he that would tast honie fresh out of the hiue, must not be scared with the stinging of bées, as the poet verie swéetlie noteth:

Non quisquam fruitur veris odoribus,
Hyblæos latebris nec spoliat fauos,
Si fronti caueat si timeat rubos,
Armat spina rosas, mella tegunt apes.

Wherefore king Edward gaue in charge to Bodringham, ruler or shiriffe of Cornewall to assemble such power as he could; and besieging the mount, he should either take

3 I 2

take or kill the earle of Oxford. The which the shiriffe did accordinglie, but that so feintlie and fauourablie, as he permitted the earle of Oxford (now in distresse) to re-uittell the mount, knowing that there was no waie to expell the earle from thence but by famine. These things thus doone (the king not pleased, and the earle not dis-pleased) one Fortescue (which surname is deduced from the strength of his shield, whereof that familie had first originall) was with a stronger and faithfuller companie sent by king Edward to laie siege to the castell; which he did, and long continued. For it was not easie to be had, being (of it selfe) by nature stronglie set, by policie well vittelled, and by manhood valiantlie defended: which mooued the king to assay an other means therefore, and to sée if policie might doo that which force could not.

The name of Fortescue whereupon it grew.

Deuises to withdraw the earles power from him.

For which cause, as Fortescue still continued the said siege, the K. supposed it best (if possiblie he might) to weaken the earles part, by withdrawing the strength and hearts of his people from him: which might not be doone but with rich promises and strong pardons. On which consideration he sent liberallie pardons to them, and in the end so secretlie wrought with the earles men: that if the earle (fearing the woorst, and iudging it better to trie the kings mercie, than to hazard the extreamitie of taking, in which rested nothing but assured death) had not wholie submitted himselfe to king Edward, he had beene by his owne men most dishonestlie betraied, and sud-denlie taken prisoner. Wherevpon the earle comming foorth to Fortescue, did there yeeld himselfe and the castell into the kings hands. At what time (being the fiftéenth of Februarie, which from the first entrance of the earle into that castell being the last of September, was about foure moneths and foureteené daies) the same Fortescue entred the mount, & tooke possession thereof, finding it yet sufficientlie vittelled to haue susteined an other siege more than one halfe yeare. After all things were thus quieted, the earle, the lord Beaumont, two brothers of the said earle, and Thomas Clifford, were brought vp as prisoners vnto king Edward. And now to our present historie againe.]

The earle of Oxford submit-teth himselfe & yéeldeth the castell into the kings hands.

When the earle of Richmond saw the earle of Oxenford, he was rauished with an incredible gladnesse, that he being a man of so high nobilitie, of such knowledge and practises in feates of warre, and so constant, trustie and assured (which alwaie had studied for the maintenance and preferment of the house of Lancaster) was now by Gods prouision deliuered out of captiuitie and imprisonment; and in time so neces-sarie and conuenient come to his aid, succour, and aduancement; in whome more surer than anie other he might put his trust and confidence, and take lesse paine and trauell in his owne person. For it was not hid from him, that such as euer had taken part with king Edward before this time, came to doo him seruice, either for malice they bare king Richard, or else for feare to liue vnder his cruell rule and tyrannous gouernance.

Not long after, the French king returned againe to Paris, whome the earle of Rich-mond followed, intending there to solicit his matter to the conclusion. Wherevpon he besought king Charles to take vpon him the whole tuition and defense of him and his cause, so that he and his companie being (by his means) aided and comforted, should confesse and saie, their wealth, victorie, and aduancement to haue flowed and budded foorth of his bountifulnesse and liberalitie, which they would (God willing) shortlie acquite. In the meane season, diuerse Englishmen, which either fled out of England for feare, or were at Paris to learne and studie good literature and vertuous doctrine, came voluntarilie and submitted themselues to the earle of Richmond, and vowed & sware to take his part. Amongst whom was Richard Fox a priest, a man of great wit and no lesse learning, whome the earle incontinent receiued into secret fami-liaritie, and in bréefe time erected and aduanced him to high dignities and promotions, and in conclusion made him bishop of Winchester.

Diuers English doo voluntarilie submit them-selues to the earle of Rich-mond in France.

In

In the meane season, king Richard was crediblie aduertised, what promises and oths the earle and his confederates had made and sworne togither at Reimes, and how by the earles means all the Englishmen were passed out of Britaine into France. Wherefore being sore dismaid, and in a maner desperate, bicause his craftie chieuance tooke none effect in Britaine, he imagined & deuised how to infringe and disturbe the earles purpose by an other meane; so that by the marriage of ladie Elizabeth his néece, he should pretend no claime nor title to the crowne. For he thought if that marriage failed, the earles cheefe combe had béene clearlie cut. And bicause that he being blinded with the ambitious desire of rule before this time in obteining the kingdome, had committed and doone manie curssed acts, and detestable tyranies, yet according to the old prouerbe; Let him take the bull that stale awaie the calfe: he thought all facts by him committed in times passed to be but of small moment, and not to be regarded in comparison of that mischéeuous imagination, which he now newlie began and attempted.

K. Richards deuise to infringe and defeat the earle of Richmõds purpose.

There came into his vngratious mind a thing not onelie detestable to be spoken of in the remembrance of man, but much more cruell and abhominable to be put in execution. For when he reuolued in his wauering mind, how great a founteine of mischeefe toward him should spring, if the earle of Richmond should be aduanced to the marriage of his néece: which thing he heard saie by the rumor of the people, that no small number of wise and wittie personages enterprised to compasse and bring to conclusion: he cléerelie determined to reconcile to his fauour his brothers wife quéene Elizabeth, either by faire words, or liberall promises; firmelie beléeuing hir fauour once obteined, that she would not sticke to commit (and louinglie credit) to him the rule and gouernance both of hir and hir daughters, and so by that meanes the earle of Richmond of the affinitie of his néece should be vtterlie defrauded and beguiled.

A subtill and lewd practise of king Richard to beguile the earle of Richmond.

And if no ingenious remedie could be otherwise inuented, to saue the innumerable mischeefes which were euen at hand, and like to fall if it should happen quéene Anne his wife to depart out of this present life, then he himselfe would rather take to wife his cousine and néece the ladie Elizabeth; than for lacke of that affinitie the whole realme should run to ruine, as who said, that if he once fell from his estate and dignitie, the ruine of the relme must néeds shortlie insue and follow. Wherefore he sent to the queene (being in sanctuarie) diuerse and often messengers, which first should excuse and purge him of all things before against hir attempted or procured, and after should so largelie promise promotions innumerable, and benefits, not onelie to hir, but also to hir sonne lord Thomas marquesse Dorset, that they should bring hir (if it were possible) into some wanhope, or (as men saie) into a fooles paradise.

The messengers, being men both of wit and grauitie, so persuaded the queene with great and pregnant reasons, & what with faire and large promises, that she began somewhat to relent, and to giue to them no deafe eare; insomuch that she faithfullie promised to submit and yéeld hir selfe fullie and frankelie to the kings will and pleasure. And so she putting in obliuion the murther of hir innocent children, the infamie and dishonour spoken by the king hir husband, the liuing in adulterie laid to hir charge, the bastarding of hir daughters; forgetting also the faithfull promise and open oth made to the countesse of Richmond, mother to the earle Henrie, blinded by auaricious affection, & seduced by flattering words, first deliuered into king Richards hands hir fiue daughters, as lambs once againe committed to the custodie of the rauenous woolfe.

The inconstancie of Q. Elizabeth.

After she sent letters to the marquesse hir sonne, being then at Paris with the earle of Richmond, willing him in anie wise to leaue the earle, and without delaie to repaire into England, where for him were prouided great honours, and honourable promotions; asserteining him further, that all offenses on both parts were forgotten and forgiuen

Queene Elizabeth allureth hir sonne the marquesse Dorset home out of France.

forgiuen, and both he and she highlie incorporated in the kings heart. Suerlie the inconstancie of this woman were much to be maruelled at, if all women had béene found constant; but let men speake, yet women of the verie bond of nature will follow their owne sex. [But it was no small allurement that king Richard vsed to ouercome hir (for we know by experience that women are of a proud disposition, and that the waie to win them is by promises of preferment) and therefore it is the lesse maruell that he by his wilie wit had made conquest of hir wauering will. [Besides that, it is to be presumed that she stood in feare to impugne his demands by denials, least he in his malicious mood might take occasion to deale roughlie with hir, being a weake woman, and of a timorous spirit.]

Now when king Richard had thus with glorious promises, and flattering words, pleased and appeased the mutable mind of queene Elizabeth, which knew nothing lesse than that he most intended; he caused all his brothers daughters to be conueied into his palace with solemne receiuing: as though with his new familiar and louing interteinment they should forget, and in their minds blot out the old committed iniurie, and late executed tyrannie. Now nothing was contrarie and against his diuelish purpose, but that his mansion was not void of his wife, which thing he in any wise adiudged necessarie to be doone. But there was one thing that so much feared and staied him from committing this abhominable murther, bicause (as you haue heard before) he began to counterfet the image of a good and well disposed person: and therefore he was afeard least the sudden death of his wife once openlie knowne, he should loose the good and credible opinion which the people had of him, without anie desert, conceiued and reported.

But in conclusion, euill counsell preuailed in a wit latelie minded to mischeefe, and turned from all goodnesse. So that his vngratious desire ouercame his honest feare. And first to enter into the gates of his imagined enterprise, he absteined both
A forged cõplaint of king Richard against his wife to be rid of hir.
from the bed and companie of his wife. Then he complained to diuerse noble men of the realme, of the infortunate sterilitie and barennesse of his wife, bicause she brought foorth no fruit and generation of hir bodie. And in especiall he recounted to Thomas Rotheram archbishop of Yorke (whome latelie he had deliuered out of ward and captiuitie) these impediments of his queene, and diuerse other, thinking that he would reueale to hir all these things, trusting the sequele hereof to take due effect, that she hearing this grudge of hir husband, & taking therefore an inward thought, would not long liue in this world.

Of this the bishop gathered (which well knew the complexion and vsage of the king) that the quéenes daies were short, and that he declared to certeine of his
A rumor spred abroad of the quéenes death at the procurement of king Richard.
secret freends. After this he procured a common rumor (but he would not haue the author knowne) to be published and spred abroad among the common people, that the quéene was dead; to the intent that she taking some conceit of this strange fame, should fall into some sudden sicknesse or gréeuous maladie: and to prooue if afterwards she should fortune by that or anie other waies to lease her life, whether the people would impute hir death to the thought or sicknesse, or thereof would laie the blame to him. Now when the quéene heard tell that so horrible a rumor of hir death was sprung amongst the communaltie, she sore suspected and iudged the world to be almost at an end with hir. And in that sorowfull agonie she with lamentable countenance and sorowfull cheare, repaired to the presence of the king hir husband, demanding of him what it should meane, that he had iudged hir worthie to die.

The king answered hir with faire words, and with smiling and flattering leasings comforted hir, and bid hir be of good cheere, for (to his knowledge) she should haue no other cause. But howsoeuer that it fortuned, either by inward thought and pensiuenesse of hart, or by infection of poison (which is affirmed to be most likelie)
within

within few daies after the queene departed out of this transitorie life, and was with The quéene wife to king Richard suddenlie dead.
due solemnitie buried in the church of S. Peter at Westminster. This is the same
Anne, one of the daughters of the earle of Warwike, which (as you haue heard before) at the request of Lewes the French king was maried to prince Edward, sonne
to king Henrie the sixt. The king thus (according to his long desire) losed out of
the bonds of matrimonie, began to cast a foolish fantasie to ladie Elizabeth his néece, K. Richard casteth his loue on his néece purposing to marie her.
making much sute to haue hir ioined with him in lawfull matrimonie.

But bicause all men and the maiden hirselfe most of all detested and abhorred this
vnlawfull, and in maner vnnaturall copulation; he determined to prolong and defer
the matter, till he were in a more quietnesse. For all that verie season he was
oppressed with great, weightie, and vrgent causes, and businesses on euerie side;
considering that dailie, part of the nobilitie sailed into France to the earle of Richmond: other priuilie fauoured and aided certeine of the coniuration, so that of his
short end few or none were in doubt. And the common people (for the most part)
were brought to such desperation, that manie of them had rather be reputed and
taken of him in the number of his enimies, than to abide the chance and hazard to
haue their goods taken as a spoile of victorie, by his enimies. [In such hatred they
had the wretch, wishing his hart in their hands with the hazard of their heads. For
how can people saie well or thinke well of tyrants, whose propertie it is to teare
them in peeces with their clawes, like a woolfe let loose among a fold of shéepe?
Whereto Homer had an eie when he said in pithie sense as here followeth: Hom. Odyss. lib. 19.

> Quisquis inhumanis studet intestabilis vti
> Moribus, huic omnes viuo clàm dira precantur:
> Huic omnes credunt fas insultare perempto.]

Amongst the noble men whome he most mistrusted, these were the principall. What noble men K. Richard most mistrusted.
Thomas lord Stanleie, sir William Stanleie his brother, Gilbert Talbot, and six hun-
dred other: of whose purposes although king Richard were not ignorant, yet he gaue
neither confidence nor credence to anie one of them; and least of all to the lord
Stanleie, bicause he was ioined in matrimonie with the ladie Margaret, mother to the
earle of Richmond, as afterward apparantlie yée may perceiue. For when the said
lord Stanleie would haue departed into his countrie to visit his familie, and to recreate
and refresh his spirits (as he openlie said, but the truth was, to the intent to be in a
perfect readinesse to receiue the earle of Richmond at his first arriuall in England)
the king in no wise would suffer him to depart, before he had left as an hostage in
the court George Stanleie lord Strange, his first begotten sonne and heire.

While king Richard was thus troubled and vexed with imaginations of the troublous 1485
time that was like to come: lo, euen suddenlie he heard newes, that fire was sprung out An. Reg. 3.
of the smoke, and the war freshlie begun; and that the castell of Hammes was de- The castell of Hammes de-liuered vnto the earle of Rich-mond.
liuered into the hands of the earle of Richmond, by the meanes of the earle of
Oxford; and that not onlie he, but also Iames Blunt capteine of the castell, were
fled into France to aid the earle Henrie. Wherefore he, thinking it great policie to
withstand the first brunt, sent the most part of the garrison of Calis, to recouer
againe by force the castell of Hammes. They which were in the castell, perceiuing
their aduersaries to approch, prepared munitions and engines for their defense, and
sent also to the earle of Richmond, to aduertise him of their sudden inuasion, requiring of him hastie aid and speedie succour.

The earle sleeping not this first begun assault, sent the earle of Oxford with an
elected companie of souldiers to raise the siege, and rescue the castell: which at their
first arriuing pitched their campe not far from their enimies. Now while king Thomas Bran-don entereth the castell.
Richards men gaue vigilant eie, waiting least the earle of Oxford should take anie aduantage of them that laie on that side of the castell; Thomas Brandon with thirtie
approoued men of war by a marish, which laie on the other side, entered into the castell

tell. The souldiers within greatlie incouraged, & much comforted by this new succour, and aid, grieued the enimies, by shooting from the walles more than they were accustomed to doo. Then they of the castell vexed their enimies on the fore part: and the earle of Oxford no lesse molested & vnquieted them on the other part. Which was the occasion that king Richards men offered (of their owne méere motion) licence to all being within the castell to depart in safetie, with bag and baggage, nothing excepted.

Why king Richard gaue licence to all in the castell to depart in safetie with bag and baggage.

Which condition the earle of Oxford, comming onelie for that purpose to deliuer his louing fréends out of all perill and danger, and chieflie of all, his old hostesse Iane Blunt, wife to Iames Blunt the capteine, would in no wise forsake or refuse: and so leauing the castell bare and vngarnished both of vittels and artillerie, came safelie to the earle of Richmond soiourning in Paris. During this time, king Richard was crediblie informed of his inquisitors and espials, that the earle of Richmond was with long sute in the court of France sore wearied; and desiring great aid, could obteine small reliefe: in somuch that all things went so farre backwards, that such things as were with great diligence (and no lesse deliberation) purposed and determined to be set forward, were now dashed and ouerthrowne to the ground.

King Richard either being too light of credence, or seduced and deluded by his craftie taletellers, greatlie reioised, as though he had obteined the ouer hand of his enimies with triumphant victorie, and thought himselfe neuer so suerlie deliuered of all feare and dreadfull imaginations: so that he néeded now no more once for that cause either to wake, or to breake his golden sleepe. Wherefore he called home againe his ships of warre, which he had appointed to kéepe the narrow seas, and dispatched all such souldiers as he had deputed to kéepe certeine garrisons, and to stop certeine passages (as you haue heard before.) Yet least he might for lacke of prouision be suddenlie trapped, he streightlie charged and gaue in commandement to all noblemen, and especiallie such as inhabited néere the sea coast, and on the frontiers of Wales, that (according to the vsage of the countrie) they should kéepe diligent watch and strong ward, to the intent that his aduersaries in no wise should haue anie place opportune easilie to take land, without defense or rebutting back.

K. Richard calleth home his ships of warre from the narrow seas.

For the custome of the countries adioining néere to the sea is (especiallie in the time of warre) on euerie hill or high place to erect a beacon with a great lanterne in the top, which may be séene and discerned a great space off. And when the noise is once bruted that the enimies approch neere the land, they suddenlie put fire in the lanternes, and make shouts and outcries from towne to towne, and from village to village. Some run in post from place to place, admonishing the people to be readie to resist the ieopardie, and defend the perill. And by this policie the fame is soone blowne to euerie citie and towne, in somuch that aswell the citizens as the rurall people be in short space assembled and armed to repell and put backe the new arriued enimies. [Whereas if the necessarie vse of this visible warning were neglected, the policie of the enimie might priuilie so preuaile, as that the people should sooner fall into perill irrecouerable, than they could thinke on (much lesse prouide) meanes to auoid it.]

The vse of beacons in countries néere the sea coasts.

But now to returne to our purpose. King Richard thus somewhat eased of his accustomed pensiuenesse, began to be a little more merrie, & tooke lesse thought and care for outward enimies than he was woont to doo; as who say, that he with politike prouision should withstand the destinie which hoong ouer his head, and was ordeined in briefe time suddenlie to fall. Such is the force and puissance of diuine iustice, that euerie man shall lesse regard, lesse prouide, lesse be in doubt of all things, when he is most néerest punishment, and next to his mischance for his offenses & crimes. [For though God did forbeare him a while, yet was that forbearance no acquittance, but rather a time of preparing & making vp that which wanted of the plagues that God

had

had purposed in iustice to powre vpon and ouerwhelme him for his fowle offenses, which could not scape heauie iudgment & vengeance:

Nam scelus admissum pœna seuera premit.]

About this season, while the earle of Richmond was desiring aid of the French king, certeine noble men were appointed to rule the realme of France, during the minoritie of king Charles, which amongst themselues were not of one opinion. Of which dissention, Lewes duke of Orleance was the chiefe stirrer, who bicause he had maried ladie Ioane sister to the French king, tooke vpon him aboue other the rule and administration of the whole realme. By reason of which controuersie, no one man was suffered to rule all. Wherefore the earle of Richmond was compelled to make sute to euerie one of the councell seuerallie one after another, requiring and desiring them of aid and reliefe in his weightie businesse, and so his cause was prolonged and deferred. During which time, Thomas marquesse Dorset, which was (as you haue heard) intised by his mother to returne againe into England, partlie despairing in the good successe of the earle of Richmond, and partlie ouercome and vanquished with the faire glosing promises of king Richard: secretlie in the night season stale out of Paris, and with all diligent expedition tooke his iournie toward Flanders.

Dissention among the péeres of France made the earle of Richmond renew his sute and put him to his shifts.

The marques Dorset forsaketh the earle.

When relation of his departure was made to the earle of Richmond, and the other noble men, no maruell though they were astonied and greatlie amazed. Yet that notwithstanding, they required of the French king, that it might be lawfull for them in his name, and by his commandement, to take and staie their companion, confederate, and partaker of all their counsell, in what place within his realme and territorie so euer they could find him. Which petition once obteined, they sent out currors into euerie part, amongst whom Humfreie Cheinie (plaieng the part of a good bloud hound) followed the tract of the flier so euen by the sent, that he ouertooke and apprehended him not far from Campeigne; and so what with reason, and what with faire promises, being persuaded, he returned againe to his companions.

The earle of Richmond vnburdened of this misaduenture, least by lingering of daies, and prolonging of time, he might loose the great opportunitie of things to him offered and ministred: also least he should further wound and molest the minds of his faithfull and assured fréends, which dailie did expect and tarie for his comming, determined no longer to protract and deferre the time: but with all diligence and celeritie attempted his begun enterprise. And so obteining of king Charles a small crew of men, and borrowing certeine summes of monie of him, and of diuerse other his priuate freends, for the which he left as debter (or more likelie as a pledge or hostage) lord Thomas marquesse Dorset (whome he halfe mistrusted) and sir Iohn Bourchier, he departed from the French court, and came to the citie of Rone.

The earle of Richmond hath men and monie of the French king for hostages.

While he taried there, making prouision at Harfleet in the mouth of the riuer of Sene for all things necessarie for his nauie, tidings were brought to him that king Richard (being without children, and now a widower) intended shortlie to marie the ladie Elizabeth his brothers daughter; and to prefer the ladie Cicilie hir sister to a man found in a cloud, and of an vnknowne linage and familie. He tooke theses newes as a matter of no small moment: and so (all things considered) it was of no lesse importance than he tooke it for. For this thing onelie tooke awaie from him and all his companions their hope and courage, that they had to obteine an happie enterprise. And therefore no maruell though it nipped him at the verie stomach: when he thought, that by no possibilitie he might atteine the mariage of any of K. Edwards daughters; which was the strongest foundation of his building; by reason whereof he iudged that all his fréends in England would abandon and shrinke from him.

The earle is grèeued at the newes of king Richards intended mariage with his néece.

Wherefore, making not manie of his counsell, after diuerse consultations, he determined not yet to set forward: but to tarie and attempt how to get more aid, more fréends, and more stronger succours. And amongst all other, it was thought most expedient to allure by affinitie in his aid, as a companion in armes, sir Walter Herbert, a man of an ancient stocke, & of great power among the Welsh, who had with him a faire ladie to his sister, of age ripe to be coupled with him in matrimonie. And for the atchiuing of this purpose, messengers were secretlie sent to Henrie earle of Northumberland (which had before maried another sister of sir Walter Herberts) to the intent that he should set forward all this deuise and purpose: but the waies were so narowlie watched, and so manie spies laid, that the messenger procéeded not in his iournie and businesse.

But in the meane season, there came to the earle a more ioifull message from Morgan Kidwellie, learned in the temporall law, which declared that Rice ap Thomas, a man of no lesse valiantnesse than actiuitie, and Iohn Sauage an approoued capteine, would with all their power be partaker of his quarell. And that Reginald Breie had collected and gotten togither no small summe of monie for the paiment of the wages to the souldiers and men of warre: admonishing him also to make quicke expedition, and to take his course directlie into Wales. The earle of Richmond, bicause he would no longer linger and wearie his fréends, liuing continuallie betwéene hope and feare, determined in all conuenient hast to set forward, and caried to his ships armor, weapons, vittels, aud all other ordinances expedient for warre.

After that all things were in readinesse, the earle being accompanied onelie with two thousand men, and a small number of ships, weied vp his anchors, and halsed vp his sailes in the moneth of August, and sailed from Harfléet with so prosperous a wind, that the seuenth daie after his departure, he arriued in Wales in the euening, at a place called Milford hauen, and incontinent tooke land, and came to a place called Dalle; where he heard saie that a certeine companie of his aduersaries were laid in garrison to defend his arriuall all the last winter. And the earle at the sunne rising remooued to Hereford west, being distant from Dalle not full ten miles, where he was ioifullie receiued of the people, and he arriued there so suddenlie, that he was come and entered the towne at the same time when the citizens had but knowledge of his comming.

Here he heard newes, which were as vntrue as they trulie were reported to him in Normandie; that Rice ap Thomas, and Iohn Sauage, with bodie and goods, were determined to aid king Richard. While he and his companie were some what astonied at these new tidings, there came such message from the inhabitants of the towne of Penbroke, that refreshed and reuiued their frosen hearts and daunted courages. For Arnold Butler a valiant capteine, which first asked pardon for his offenses before time committed against the earle of Richmond, and that obteined, declared to him that the Penbrochians were readie to serue and giue their attendance on their naturall and immediat lord Iasper earle of Penbroke. The earle of Richmond, hauing his armie thus increased, departed from Hereford west to the towne of Cardigan, being fiue miles distant from thence.

While the souldiers were refreshing and trimming themselues in their campe, strange tidings sproong among them without anie certeine author; that sir Walter Herbert, which laie with a great crue of men at Carmarden, was now with a great armie readie to approch and bid them battell. With which newes the armie was sore troubled, and euery man assaied his armour and prooued his weapon, and were prest to defend their enimies. And as they were in this fearfull doubt, certeine horssemen, which the earle had sent to make inquirie and search, returned and reported all the countrie to be quiet, and no let nor impediment to be laid or cast in their iournie. And euen at the same time, the whole armie was greatlie recomforted, by reason that the comming of Richard Griffith, a man of great nobilitie; the which notwithstanding that he was confederate with sir Walter Herbert, and Richard ap Thomas; yet at that verie instant
he

Sir Walter Herbert.
A mariage purposed but disappointed.
The Welshmen offer to aid the earle of Richmond.
The earle arriueth at Milford hauen.
A false rumor of ill newes.
The earle of Richmonds power made stronger by accesse of confederats.

he came to the earle of Richmond with all his companie; which were of no great number. After him the same daie came Iohn Morgan with his men.

Then the earle aduanced forward in good hast, making no repose or abode in anie one place. And to the intent to passe forward with sure and short expedition, he assaulted euerie place where his enimies had set anie men of warre; which with small force, and lesse difficultie, he brieflie did ouercome & vanquish. And suddenlie he was by his espials ascerteined, that sir Walter Herbert, and Rice ap Thomas were in harnesse before him, readie to incounter with his armie, and to stop their passage. Wherefore like a valiant capteine he first determined to set on them, and either to destroie or to take them into his fauour, and after with all his power and puissance to giue battell to his mortall enimie king Richard. But to the intent his fréends should know in what readinesse he was, and how he procéeded forward; he sent of his most secret and faithfull seruants with letters and instructions to the ladie Margaret his mother, to the lord Stanleie and his brother, to sir Gilbert Talbot, and to other his trustie fréends; declaring to them that he being succoured and holpen with the aid and reliefe of his fréends, intended to passe ouer the riuer of Seuerne at Shrewesburie, and so to passe directlie to the citie of London. *The erle sendeth secret word to his mother and other his fréends that he meant direct passage to London & their conference.*

Wherefore he required them, as his speciall trust and confidence was fixed in the hope of their fidelitie, that they would meet him by the waie with all diligent preparation; to the intent that he and they, at time and place conuenient, might communicate togither the déepenesse of all his doubtfull and weightie businesse. When the messengers wer dispatched with these commandements and admonitions, he marched forward toward Shrewesburie: and in his passing, there met and saluted him Rice ap Thomas with a goodlie band of Welshmen, which making an oth and promise to the earle, submitted himselfe wholie to his order and commandement. For the earle of Richmond two daies before made to him promise, that if he would sweare to take his part and be obedient to him, he would make him chiefe gouernour of Wales: which part as he faithfullie promised and granted, so (after that he had obteined and possessed the realme and diademe) he liberallie performed and accomplished the same. *Rice ap Thomas sweareth fealtie and seruice to the earle of Richmond.*

In the meane time the messengers, that were sent, diligentlie executed their charge, and laden with rewards of them to whom they were sent, returned to him the same day that he entered into Shrewesburie: and made relation to him that his fréends were readie in all points to doo all things for him, which either they ought or might doo. The earle Henrie brought in good hope with this pleasant message, continued foorth his intended iournie, and came to a little towne called Newport, and pitching his campe on a little hill adioining, reposed himselfe there that night. In the euening the same daie came to him sir Gilbert Talbot, with the whole power of the yoong earle of Shrewesburie then being in ward, which were accounted to the number of two thousand men. And thus his power increasing, he arriued at the towne of Stafford, and there paused

There also came sir William Stanleie accompanied with a few persons. And after that the earle and he had communed no long time togither; he reuerted to his souldiors whom he had assembled togither to serue the earle: which from thence departed to Lichfield, and lay without the walles in his campe all the night. The next morning he entered into the towne, and was with all honor like a prince receiued. A daie or two before, the lord Stanleie, hauing in his band almost fiue thousand men, lodged in the same towne. But hearing that the erle of Richmond was marching thitherward, gaue to him place, dislodging him and his, and repaired to a towne called Aderstone, there abiding the comming of the earle. And this wilie fox did this act, to auoid all suspicion on king Richards part. *The lord Stanleies deuise to auoid suspicion of K. Richard and to saue his sonnes life.*

For the lord Stanleie was afraid, least if he should séeme openlie to be a fautor or aider to the earle his sonne in law, before the day of the battell, that king Richard, which yet vtterlie did not put in him diffidence and mistrust, would put to some cruell death his sonne and heire apparant George lord Strange, whome king Richard (as you haue heard before) kept with him as a pledge or hostage, to the intent that the lord Stanleie his father should attempt nothing preiudiciall to him. King Richard at this season kéeping his house in the castle of Notingham, was informed that the earle of Richmond, with such banished men as were fled out of England to him, were now arriued in Wales, and that all things necessarie to his enterprise were vnprouided vnpurueied, and verie weake, nothing méet to withstand the power of such as the king had appointed to méet him.

K. Richard con-
temneth the earle
and his power. This rumor so inflated his mind, that in maner disdeining to heare speake of so small a companie, he determined at the first to take little or no regard to this so small a sparkle, declaring the earle to be innocent and vnwise, bicause that he rashly attempt-ed such a great enterprise with so small and thin a number of warlike persons: and therefore he gaue a definitiue sentence, that when he came to that point that he should be compelled to fight against his will, hée either should be apprehended aliue, or else by all likelihood he should of necessitie come to a shamefull confusion: and that he trusted to be shortlie doone by sir Walter Herbert, and Rice ap Thomas, which then ruled Wales with equall power and like authoritie.

But yet reuoluing and casting in his mind, that a small war begun and winked at, and not regarded, maie turne to a great broile and trouble; and that it was prudent policie not to contemne and disdeine the little power and small weakenesse of the enimie (be it neuer so small) thought it necessarie to prouide for afterclaps that might happen & chance. [For victorie dooth not alwaies follow the greatest multitude, neither is it a necessarie consequent, that the biggest bodie is indued with most force. For we see that the small viper is the huge buls deadlie bane, and a little curre dooth catch a bore boisterous and big; as the poet properlie (and to the purpose) verie well saith:

Ouid.
Parua necat morsu spatiosum vipera taurum,
A cane non magno sæpè tenetur aper.

The king sendeth
to his friends for
a chosen power
of men. Wherefore he sent to Iohn duke of Norffolke, Henrie earle of Northumberland, Thomas earle of Surrie, and to other of his especiall & trustie friends of the nobilitie, which he iudged more to preferre and estéeme his wealth and honour, than their owne riches and priuate commoditie; willing them to muster and view all their seruants and tenants, and to elect and choose the most couragious and actiue persons of the whole number, and with them to repaire to his presence with all spéed and diligence. Also hée wrote to Robert Brakenberie lieutenant of the Tower, commanding him with his power to come to his armie, and to bring with him (as fellowes in armes) sir Thomas Bourchier, & sir Walter Hungerford, and diuers other knights and esquiers, in whom he cast no small suspicion.

Now while he was thus ordering his affaires, tidings came that the earle of Rich-mond was passed Seuerne, & come to Shrewesburie without anie detriment or incum-brance. At which message he was sore mooued and broiled with melancholie and dolor, crieng out, & asking vengeance of them that (against their oth and promise) had so deceiued him. For which cause he began to haue diffidence in other, insomuch that he determined himselfe out of hand the same daie to méet with and resist his aduersaries: and in all haste sent out espials to view and espie what waie his enimies The earle is
incamped at
Litchfield. kept and passed. They diligentlie dooing their dutie, shortlie after returned, declaring to the king that the earle was incamped at the towne of Lichfield.

When he had perfect knowledge where the earle with his armie was soiourning, he hauing continuall repaire of his subiects to him, began incontinentlie without delaie to marshall and put in order his battels (like a valiant capteine and politike leder) and first he made his battels to set forward, fiue and fiue in a ranke, marching toward that
way

way where his enimies (as was to him reported) intended to passe. In the middle part The ordering of king Richards armie. of the armie, he appointed the traffike and cariage preteining to the armie. Then he (inuironed with his gard with a frowning countenance and cruell visage, mounted on a great white courser, and followed with his footmen, the wings of horssemen coasting and ranging on euerie side: and keeping this arraie, he with great pompe entered the towne of Leicester after the sunne set [full of indignation & malice, which vttered it selfe from the inward hart by the mouth, out of which flowed speaches of horrible heate, tempered with cruell threatnings, equall to his of whome it was thus said long ago:

Horrebant sæuis omnia verba minis.]

The earle of Richmond raised his campe, and departed from Lichfield to the towne The earle of Richmond re- moueth his power to Tamworth. of Tamworth thereto néere adioining, and in the mid way passing, there saluted him sir Walter Hungerford and sir Thomas Bourchier knights, and diuerse other which yeelded and submitted themselues to his pleasure. For they, being aduertised that king Richard had them in suspicion and gelousie, a llttle beyond Stonie Stratford left and forsooke priuilie their capteine Robert Brakenberie; and wandering by night, and in maner by vnknowne paths, and vncerteine waies searching, at the last came at earle Henrie. Diuerse other noble personages, which inwardlie hated king Richard woorse than a tode or a serpent, did likewise resort to him with all their power and strength, wishing and working his destruction, who otherwise would haue béene the instrument of their casting away.

There happened in this progression to the earle of Richmond a strange chance A strange chance that happened to the earle of Richmond. worthie to be noted. For albeit he was a man of valiant courage, & that his armie increased, and dailie more and more he waxed mightier and stronger; yet he was not a litle afeard, bicause he could in no wise be assured of his father in law Thomas lord Stanleie, which for feare of the destruction of the lord Strange his sonne (as you haue heard) as yet inclined to neither partie. For if he had gone to the earle, and that notified to king Richard, his sonne had béene shortlie executed. Wherefore he accompanied with twentie light horssemen lingered in his iournie, as a man musing & imagining what was best to be doone. And the more to aggrauate his pensiuenesse, it was shewed him, that king Richard was at hand with a strong power & a great armie.

While he thus heauilie dragged behind his host, the whole armie came before the towne of Tamwoorth; and when he for the deepe darknesse could not perceiue the steps of them that passed on before, and had wandered hither & thither, séeking after his companie, and yet not once hearing anie noise or whispering of them; he turned to a verie little village, being about thrée miles from his armie, taking great thought, The earle of Richmond put to a hard shift. and much fearing least he should be espied, and so trapped by king Richards scout- watch. There he taried all night, not once aduenturing to aske or demand a question of any creature, he being no more amazed with the ieopardie & perill that was passed, than with this present chance, sore feared that it shuld be a prognostication or signe of some infortunate plage afterward to succeed. As he was not merie being absent from his armie, so likewise his armie much maruelled, and no lesse mourned for his sudden absence.

The next morning earlie in the dawning of the day he returned, and by the con- duct of good fortune, espied and came to his armie, excusing himselfe not to haue gone out of the way by ignorance: but that for a policie (deuised for the nonce) he went from his campe to receiue some glad message from certeine of his priuie fréends and secret alies. This excuse made, he priuilie departed againe from his host to the The lord Stan- leie the earle of Richmond & others meet, embrace, and consult. towne of Aderston, where the lord Stanleie and sir William his brother with their bands were abiding. There the earle came first to his father in law, in a litle close, where he saluted him, and sir William his brother: and after diuerse and fréendlie imbracings, each reioised of the state of other, and suddenlie were surprised with great ioy, comfort, and

and hope of fortunate successe in all their affaires and dooings. Afterward they consulted togither how to giue battell to king Richard if he would abide, whome they knew not to be farre off with an huge host.

The principals of K. Richards power fall from him. In the euening of the same day, sir Iohn Sauage, sir Brian Sanford, sir Simon Digbie, and manie other, leauing king Richard, turned and came to the part of the earle of Richmond, with an elect companie of men. Which refusall of king Richards part, by men of such experience, did augment and increase both the good hope, and the puissance of the earle of Richmond. In the meane season, king Richard which was appointed now to finish his last labor by the very diuine iustice & prouidence of God (which called him to condigne punishment for his mischiefous deserts) marched to a place méet for two battels to incounter, by a village called Bosworth, not farre from Leicester: and there he pitched his field on a hill called Anne Beame, refreshed his souldiers, and tooke his rest.

The dreame of king Richard the third foretelling him of his end. The fame went, that he had the same night a dreadfull and terrible dreame: for it séemed to him being asleepe, that he did see diuerse images like terrible diuels, which pulled and haled him, not suffering him to take anie quiet or rest. The which strange vision not so suddenlie strake his heart with a sudden feare, but it stuffed his head and troubled his mind with manie busie and dreadfull imaginations. For incontinent after, his heart being almost damped, he prognosticated before the doubtfull chance of the battell to come; not vsing the alacritie and mirth of mind and countenance as he was accustomed to doo before he came toward the battell. And least that it might be suspected that he was abashed for feare of his enimies, and for that cause looked so pitiouslie; he recited and declared to his familiar fréends in the morning his wonderfull vision and fearefull dreame.

But I thinke this was no dreame, but a punction and pricke of his sinfull conscience: for the conscience is so much more charged and aggréeued, as the offense is greater & more heinous in degrée. [So that king Richard, by this reckoning, must needs haue a woonderfull troubled mind, because the déeds that he had doone, as they were heinous and vnnaturall, so did they excite and stirre vp extraordinarie motions of trouble and vexations in his conscience.] Which sting of conscience, although it strike not alwaie; yet at the last daie of extreame life, it is woont to shew and represent to vs our faults and offenses, and the paines and punishments which hang ouer our heads for the committing of the same, to the intent that at that instant, we for our deserts being penitent and repentant, maie be compelled (lamenting and bewailing our sinnes like forsakers of this world) iocund to depart out of this mischéefe life.

King Richard bringeth all his men into the plaine. Now to returne againe to our purpose. The next daie after, king Richard being furnished with men & all ablements of warre, bringing all his men out of their campe into the plaine, ordered his fore-ward in a maruellous length, in which he appointed both horsmen and footmen, to the intent to imprint in the hearts of them that looked a farre off, a sudden terror and deadlie feare, for the great multitude of the armed souldiers: and in the fore-front he placed the archers like a strong fortified trench or bulworke. Ouer this battell was capteine, Iohn duke of Norffolke, with whome was The duke of Norffolke and the earle of Surrie on K. Richards side. Thomas earle of Surrie his sonne. After this long vant-gard, followed king Richard himselfe with a strong companie of chosen and approoued men of warre, hauing horssemen for wings on both sides of his battell.

After that the earle of Richmond was departed from the communication of his fréends (as you haue heard before) he began to be of a better stomach, and of a more valiant courage, and with all diligence pitched his field iust by the campe of his enimies, and there he lodged that night. In the morning betimes, he caused his men to put on their armour, and apparell themselues readie to fight and giue battell; and sent vnto the lord Stanleie (which was now come with his band into a place indifferent betwéene both the armies) requiring him with his men to approch néere to his armie,

and

and to helpe to set the souldiers in arraie. But he answered that the earle should set his owne men in good order of battell, while he would arraie his companie, and come to him in time conuenient. Which answer made otherwise than the earle thought or would haue iudged, considering the oportunitie of the time & the weight of the businesse. And although he was ther withall a little vexed, & began some what to hang the head; yet he without anie time delaieng, compelled of necessitie, after this maner instructed and ordered his men. *The lord Stanleie refuseth to set the earles men in battell raie.*

He made his fore-ward somewhat single and slender, according to the small number of his people. In the front he placed the archers, of whome he made capteine Iohn earle of Oxenford. To the right wing of the battell he appointed sir Gilbert Talbot to be the leader. To the left wing, he assigned sir Iohn Sauage who had brought thither with him a crue of right able personages, clad in white coats and hoods, which mustered in the eies of their aduersaries right brimlie. The earle of Richmond himselfe, with aid of the lord Stanleie, gouerned the battell, accompanied with the earle of Penbroke, hauing a good companie of horssemen, and a small number of footmen. For all his whole number exceeded not fiue thousand men, beside the power of the Stanleies, wherof three thousand were in the field, vnder the standard of sir William Stanleie. The kings number was double so much and more. When both these armies were thus ordered, and all men readie to set forward, king Richard called his chiefteins togither, and to them said as followeth. *The earle setteth his men in order and appointeth chiefteins.*

The oration of king Richard the third to the chiefteins of his armie.

MY most faithfull and assured fellowes, most trustie & welbeloued freends, & elected capteins, by whose wisedome and policie I haue obteined the crowne, and type of this famous realme, and noble region: by whose puissance & valiantnesse I haue inioid and possessed the state roiall & dignitie of the same, maugre the ill will and seditious attempts of all my cankered enimies, and insidious aduersaries: by whose prudent & politike counsell I haue so gouerned my realme, people, subiects, that I haue omitted nothing apperteining to the office of a iust prince: nor you haue pretermitted nothing belonging to the dutie of wise and sage councellors. So that I maie saie, and trulie affirme, that your approoued fidelitie & tried constancie, maketh me to beleeue firmelie, and thinke that I am an vndoubted king, and an indubitate prince. *King Richard iustifieth himselfe and his gouernement.*

And although in the adeption and obteining of the garland, I being seduced, and prouoked by sinister councell, and diabolicall temptation, did commit a wicked and detestable act: yet I haue with streict penance and salt tears (as I trust) expiated & cleerelie purged the same offense: which abhominable crime I require you of frendship as cleerelie to forget, as I dailie remember to deplore and lament the same. If ye will euen now diligentlie call to remembrance in what case and perplexitie we doo stand; and in what doubtfull perill we be all intrapped; I doubt not but you in heart will thinke, and with mouth confesse, that if euer amitie and faith preuailed betweene prince and subiects, or betweene subiect and subiect; or if euer bond of alegiance obliged the vassall to loue and serue his naturall souereigne lord; or if anie obligation of dutie bound anie prince to aid & defend his subiects; all these loues, bonds, and duties of necessitie are now this day to be tried, shewed, and put in experience.

For if wise men saie true (as they doo not lie) there is some policie in getting, but much more in keeping; the one being but fortunes chance, & the other high wit and policie. For which cause, I with you, and you with me, must needs this day take labour and paine, to keepe and defend with force, that preheminence and possession, which by your prudent deuises I haue gotten & obteined. I doubt not but you know how the diuell (continuall enimie to humane nature, disturber of concord, & sower of sedition *He speaketh opprobrouslie of the earle of Richmond.*

sedition) hath entered into the heart of an vnknowne Welshman (whose father I neuer knew, nor him personallie saw) exciting him to aspire and couet our realme, crowne, and dignitie, and thereof cleerelie to depriue and spoile vs and our posteritie. Ye see further, how a companie of traitors, theeues, outlawes, and runnagates of our owne nation, be aiders and partakers of his feat and enterprise, readie at hand to ouercome and oppresse vs.

You see also, what a number of beggerlie Britans and faint-hearted Frenchmen be with him arriued to destroie vs, our wiues and children. Which imminent mischeefs and apparant inconueniences, if we will withstand & refell, we must liue togither as brethren, fight togither like lions, & feare not to die togither like men. And obseruing and keeping this rule and precept, beleeue me, the fearefull hare neuer fled faster before the greedie greihound, nor the sillie larke before the sparrowhawke, nor yet the simple sheepe before the rauenous woolfe; than your proud bragging aduersaries, astonied and amazed with the onelie sight of your manlie visages, will flee, run, and skir out of the field. For if you consider and wiselie ponder all things in your mind, you shall perceiue, that we haue manifest causes, and apparant tokens of triumph and victorie.

And to begin with the erle of Richmond capteine of this rebellion, he is a Welsh milkesop, a man of small courage, and of lesse experience in martiall acts and feats of warre, brought vp by my moothers meanes, and mine, like a captiue in a close cage in the court of Francis duke of Britaine; and neuer saw armie, nor was exercised in martiall affaires: by reason wherof he neither can, nor is able by his owne will or experience to guide or rule an hoast. For in the wit and policie of the capteine consisteth the cheefe adeption of the victorie, and ouerthrow of the enimies. Secondarilie feare not, but put awaie all doubts; for when the traitors and runnagates of our realme, shall see vs with banner displaied come against them, remembring their oth, promise, and fidelitie made vnto vs, as to their souereigne lord and annointed king; they shall be so pricked and stoong in the bottome of their scrupulous consciences, that they for verie remorse and dread of the diuine plague, will either shamefullie flee, or humblie submit themselues to our grace and mercie.

And as for the Frenchmen and Britans, their valiantnesse is such, that our noble progenitors, and your valiant parts haue them oftener vanquished and ouercome in one moneth, than they in the beginning imagined possiblie to compasse and finish in a whole yeare. What will you make of them? braggers without audacitie, drunckards without discretion, ribalds without reason, cowards without resisting, and in conclusion, the most effeminate and lasciuious people that euer shewed themselues in front of battell; ten times more couragious to flee & escape, than once to assault the breast of our strong & populous armie. Wherefore considering all these aduantages, expell out of your thoughts all douts, auoid out of your minds all feare; and like valiant champions aduance foorth your standards, & assaie whether your enimies can decide and trie the title of battell by dint of sword. Aduance (I say againe) forward my capteines, in whome lacketh neither policie, wisedome, nor yet puissance. Euerie one giue but one sure stripe, & suerlie the iournie is ours. What preuaileth a handfull to a whole realme?

Desiring you (for the loue that you beare to me) and the affection that you haue to your natiue and naturall countrie, and to the safegard of your prince & your selues, that you will this daie take to you your accustomed courage and couragious spirits, for the defense and safegard of vs all. And as for me, I assure you, this daie I will triumph by glorious victorie, or suffer death for immortall fame. For they be maimed and out of the palace of fame disgraded, dieng without renowme, which doo not asmuch prefer and exalt the perpetuall honour of their natiue countrie, as their owne mortall and transitorie life. Now saint George to borow, let vs set forward, and remember well, that I am he which shall with high aduancements reward and preferre the

valiant

valiant and hardie champions, and punish and torment the shamefull cowards, and dreadfull dastards.

This exhortation incouraged all such as fauoured him; but such as were present (more for dread than loue) kissed them openlie, whome they inwardlie hated. Other sware outwardlie to take part with such, whose death they secretlie compassed, and inwardlie imagined. Other promised to inuade the kings enimies, which fled and fought with fierce courage against the king. Other stood still and looked on, intending to take part with the victors and ouercommers. So was his people to him vnsure and vnfaithfull at his end, as he was to his nephues vntrue and vnnaturall in his beginning. [How then was it possible that this princes regiment could long stand, seeing the preseruation and prorogation of his reigne consisted not in the loue of his subiects? In place wherof bicause feare (yea seruile and forced feare succéeded) he was the sooner forsaken of his people, whose harts fell from him as isicles from a penthouse in a sunnie daie; and in this case the poet saith truelie, and was well worthie of credit when he craued it, saieng:

Credite quem metuit quisq; perire cupit.]

When the earle of Richmond knew by his foreriders that the king was so neere imbatelled, he rode about his armie from ranke to ranke, & from wing to wing, giuing comfortable words to all men, and that finished (being armed at all péeces, sauing his helmet) mounted on a little hill, so that all his people might sée and behold him perfectlie, to their great reioising. For he was a man of no great stature, *The person of the earle of Richmond described.* but so formed and decorated with all gifts and lineaments of nature, that he séemed more an angelicall creature, than a terrestriall personage. His countenance and aspect was chéerefull and couragious, his haire yellow like the burnished gold, his eies graie shining and quicke; prompt and readie in answering, but of such sobrietie, that it could neuer be iudged whether he were more dull than quicke in speaking (such was his temperance.) Now when he had ouerlooked his armie ouer euerie side, he paused awhile, and after with a lowd voice and bold spirit spake to his companions these, or the like words following.

The oration of King Henrie the seauenth to his armie.

If euer God gaue victorie to men fighting in a iust quarrell, or if he euer aided such as made warre for the wealth & tuition of their owne naturall and nutritiue countrie, or if he euer succoured them which aduentured their liues for the releefe of innocents, suppressing of malefactors and apparant offendors; no doubt my fellowes & freends, but he of his bountifull goodnesse will this daie send vs triumphant victorie, and a luckie iournie ouer our proud enimies, and arrogant aduersaries: for if you remember and consider the verie cause of our iust quarell, you shall apparantlie perceiue the same to be true, godlie, and vertuous. In the which I doubt not, but God will rather aid vs (yea and fight for vs) than see vs vanquished and ouerthrowne by such as neither feare him nor his laws, nor yet regard iustice or honestie.

Our cause is so iust, that no enterprise can be of more vertue, both by the lawes *The earles cause iust and right, & therefore likelie of good successe.* diuine & ciuill. For what can be a more honest, goodlie, or godlie quarrell, than to fight against a capteine, being an homicide and murtherer of his owne bloud or progenie, an extreame destroier of his nobilitie, and to his and our countrie and the poore subiects of the same a deadlie mallet, a firie brand, and a burthen intollerable? Beside him, consider who be of his band and companie: such as by murther and vntrueth committed against their owne kin and linage, yea against their prince and souereigne lord, haue disherited me and you, and wrongfullie deteine and vsurpe our

lawfull

lawfull patrimonie & lineall inheritance. For he that calleth himselfe king, keepeth from me the crowne and regiment of this noble realme and countrie, contrarie to all iustice and equitie.

Likewise, his mates and friends occupie your lands, cut downe your woods, and destroie your manors, letting your wiues and children range abroade for their liuing: which persons for their penance and punishment I doubt not, but God of his goodnes will either deliuer into our hands, as a great gaine and bootie; or cause them (being greeued and compuncted with the pricke of their corrupt consciences) cowardlie to flie, and not abide the battell. Beside this I assure you, that there be yonder in the great battell, men brought thither for feare, and not for loue; souldiers by force compelled, and not with good will assembled; persons which desire rather the destruction than saluation of their maister and capteine: and finallie, a multitude, whereof the most part will be our friends, and the least part our enimies.

For truelie I doubt which is greater, the malice of the soldiors toward their capteine; or the feare of him conceiued of his people. For suerlie this rule is infallible, that as ill men dailie couet to destroie the good; so God appointeth the good men to confound the ill. And of all worldlie goods the greatest is to suppresse tyrants, and releeue innocents; whereof the one is as much hated, as the other is beloued. If this

be true (as clearkes preach) who will spare yonder tyrant Richard duke of Glocester, vntruelie calling himselfe king, considering that he hath violated and broken both the lawes of God and man? What vertue is in him which was the confusion of his brother, and murtherer of his nephues? What mercie is in him that sleieth his trustie freends as well as his extreame enimies? Who can haue confidence in him which putteth diffidence in all men?

If you haue not read, I haue heard good clearkes saie, that Tarquine the proud for the vice of the bodie lost the kingdome of Rome; and the name of Tarquine banished the citie for euer: yet was not his fault so detestable as the fact of cruell Nero, which slue his own mother, and opened hir entrailes, to behold the place of his concep-

tion. Behold yonder Richard, which is both Tarquine and Nero: yea a tyrant more than Nero, for he hath not onlie murthered his nephue being his king and souereigne lord, bastarded his noble brethren, and defamed the wombe of his vertuous and womanlie mother; but also compassed all the meanes and waies that he could inuent, how to defile and carnallie know his owne neece, under the pretense of a cloked matrimonie, which ladie I haue sworne and promised to take to my mate and wife, as you all know and beleeue.

If this cause be not iust, and this quarell godlie; let God (the giuer of victorie) iudge and determine. We haue (thanks be giuen to Christ) escaped the secret treasons in Britaine, and auoided the subtill snares of our fraudulent enimies there, passed the troublous seas in good and quiet safegard, and without resistance haue ouergone the ample region & large countrie of Wales, and are now come to the place which we so much desired: for long we haue sought the furious bore, and now we

haue found him. Wherefore let vs not feare to enter into the toile, where we may suerlie sleie him; for God knoweth that we haue liued in the vales of miserie, tossing our ships in dangerous stormes: let vs not now dread to set vp our full sailes in faire weather, hauing with vs both God and good fortune.

If we had come to conquer Wales and had atchiued it, our praise had beene great, and our gaine more: but if we win this battell, the whole rich realme of England, with the lords and rulers of the same, shall be ours; the profit shall be ours, and the honour shall be ours. Therefore labour for your gaine, & sweat for your right. While we were in Britaine, we had small liuings and little plentie of wealth or welfare, now is the time come to get aboundance of riches, and copie of profit; which is the reward of your seruice, and merit of your paines. And this remember with your selues,

selues, that before vs be our enimies; and on either side of vs be such, as I neither suerlie trust, nor greatlie beleeue; backeward we cannot flee; so that heere we stand like sheepe in a fold, circumuented and compassed betweene our enimies and our doutfull friends.

Wherefore let all feare be set aside, and like sworne brethren let vs ioine in one; for this daie shall be the end of our trauell, and the gaine of our labour, either by honorable death or famous victorie: and as I trust, the battell shall not be so sowre, as the profit shall be sweet. Remember that victorie is not gotten with the multitudes of men, but with the courages of hearts, and valiantnesse of minds. The smaller that our number is, the more glorie is to vs if we vanquish: if we be ouercome, yet no laud is to be attributed to the victors, considering that ten men fought against one. And if we die so glorious a death in so good a quarell, neither fretting time, nor cancarding obliuion, shall be able to darken or rase out of the booke of fame either our names, or our godlie attempt. And this one thing I assure you, that in so iust and good a cause, and so notable a quarrell, you shall find me this daie rather a dead carrion vpon the cold ground, than a free prisoner on a carpet in a ladies chamber.

[margin: Victorie consisteth not in multitude but in manlinesse.]

Let vs therefore fight like inuincible giants, and set on our enimies like vntimorous tigers, & banish all feare like ramping lions. And now aduance forward true men against traitors, pitifull persons against murtherers, true inheritors against vsurpers, the scourges of God against tyrants. Displaie my banner with a good courage, march foorth like strong and robustious champions, and begin the battell like hardie conquerors. The battell is at hand, and the victorie approcheth; and if we shamefullie recule, or cowardlie flee; we and all our sequele be destroied, and dishonored for euer. This is the daie of gaine, and this is the time of losse; get this daie victorie, and be conquerors: and leese this daies battell, and be villaines. And therefore in the name of God and S. George, let euerie man couragiouslie aduance foorth his standard.

These chéerefull words he set foorth with such gesture of his bodie, & smilling countenance, as though alreadie he had vanquished his enimies, and gotten the spoile. He had scantlie finished his saieng, but the one armie spied the other. Lord how hastilie the soldiers buckled their healmes, how quicklie the archers bent their bowes and frushed their feathers, how readilie the bilmen shooke their billes, and prooued their staues, readie to approach and ioine, when the terrible trumpet should sound the bloudie blast to victorie or death! Betwéene both armies there was a great marish then (but at this present, by reason of diches cast, it is growne to be firme ground) which the earle of Richmond left on his right hand; for this intent, that it should be on that side a defense for his part, and in so dooing he had the sunne at his backe, and in the faces of his enimies. When king Richard saw the earles companie was passed the marish; he did command with all hast to set vpon them. Then the trumpets sounded, and the souldiers shouted, and the kings archers couragiouslie let flie their arrowes. The earles bowmen stood not still, but paied them home againe.

[margin: The battell betwéene king Richard, and king Henrie the seuenth, called Bosworth field.]

[margin: The policie of the earle.]

The terrible shot once passed, the armies ioined and came to hand-strokes, where neither sword nor bill was spared. At which incounter, the lord Stanleie ioined with the earle. The earle of Oxford in the meane season, fearing least while his companie was fighting, they should be compassed and circumuented with the multitude of the enimies, gaue commandement in euerie ranke, that no man should be so hardie, as to go aboue ten foot from the standard. Which commandment once knowne, they knit themselues togither, and ceassed a little from fighting. The aduersaries suddenlie abashed at the matter, and mistrusting some fraud and deceit, began also to pause and left striking; and not against the wils of manie, which had rather had the king destroied, than saued, and therefore they fought verie faintlie, or stood still.

[margin: The earle of Oxfords charge to his band of men.]

The

The earle of
Oxfords valiant-
nesse.

The earle of Oxford, bringing all his band togither on the one part, set on his enimies freshlie againe. The aduersaries perceiuing that, placed their men slender and thin before, but thicke and broad behind, beginning againe hardilie the battell. While the two fore-wards thus mortallie fought, ech intending to vanquish and conuince the other; king Richard was admonished by his explorators and espials, that the earle of Richmond (accompanied with a small number of men of armes) was not far off. And as he approched and marched toward him, he perfectlie knew his personage by certeine demonstrations and tokens, which he had learned and knowen of others that were able to giue him full information. Now being inflamed with ire, and vexed with outragious malice, he put his spurres to his horsse, and rode out of the side of the range of his battell, leauing the vant-gard fighting; and like a hungrie lion ran with speare in rest toward him. The earle of Richmond perceiued well the

The earle of
Richmond prof-
fereth to in-
counter K.
Richard bodie
to bodie.
Sir William
Brandon slaine.

king furiouslie comming toward him, and bicause the whole hope of his wealth and purpose was to be determined by battell, he gladlie proffered to incounter with him bodie to bodie, and man to man.

King Richard set on so sharplie at the first brunt, that he ouerthrew the earles standard, and slue sir William Brandon his standard-bearer (which was father to sir Charles Brandon by king Henrie the eight created duke of Suffolke) and matched hand to hand with sir Iohn Cheinie, a man of great force and strength, which would haue resisted him: but the said Iohn was by him manfullie ouerthrowen. And so he making open passage by dint of sword as he went forward, the earle of Richmond withstood his violence, and kept him at the swords point without aduantage, longer than his companions either thought or iudged: which being almost in despaire of victorie, were suddenlie recomforted by sir William Stanleie, which came to his succors

The kings armie
fleeth.

with three thousand tall men. At which verie instant, king Richards men were driuen backe and fled, & he himselfe manfullie fighting in the middle of his enimies, was slaine, and (as he worthilie had deserued) came to a bloudie death, as he had lead a bloudie life.

In the meane season, the earle of Oxford with the aid of the lord Stanleie, after no long fight, discomfited the fore-ward of king Richard, whereof a great number were slaine in the chase and fight: but the greatest number which (compelled by feare of the king, and not of their meere voluntarie motion) came to the field, gaue neuer a stroke, and hauing no harme nor damage, safelie departed, which came not thither in hope to sée the king prosper and preuaile, but to heare that he should be shamefullie confounded and brought to ruine. In this battell died few aboue the number of

Duke of Nor-
folke slaine in
the field.

a thousand persons: and of the nobilitie were slaine Iohn duke of Norffolke, which was warned by diuerse to refraine from the field, in so much that the night before he should set forward toward the king, one wrote this rime vpon his gate:

Iacke of Norffolke be not too bold,

* Richard.

For * Dikon thy maister is bought and sold.

Yet all this notwithstanding, he regarded more his oth, his honor, and promise made to king Richard, like a gentleman; and as a faithfull subiect to his prince, absented not himselfe from his maister; but as he faithfullie liued vnder him, so he manfullie died with him, to his great fame and laud. [And therfore, though his seruice was ill imploied in aid of a tyrant (whome it had béene more honorable to haue suppressed than supported) yet bicause he had vpon his fealtie vndertaken to fight in his quarell, he thought it lesse losse of life and liuing than of glorie & honour: so that he might haue said, in respect of his loialtie & promised truth testified with constancie to the death:

Ouid.

Est mihi supplicium causa fuisse pium.

There

There were slaine beside him, Walter lord Ferrers of Chartleie, sir Richard Rad- cliffe, and Robert Brakenberie lieutenant of the Tower, and not manie gentlemen more. Sir William Catesbie learned in the lawes of the realme, and one of the chéefe councellors to the late king, with diuerse other, were two daies after beheaded at Leicester. Amongst them that ran awaie, were sir Francis vicount Louell, and Humfreie Stafford, and Thomas Stafford his brother, which tooke sanctuarie in saint Iohns at Glocester. Of captiues and prisoners there were a great number. For after the death of king Richard was knowne and published, euerie man in manner vnarming himselfe, & casting awaie his abiliments of warre, meekelie submitted themselues to the obeisance and rule of the earle of Richmond: of the which the more part had gladlie so doone in the beginning, if they might haue conuenientlie escaped from king Richards espials, which hauing as cléere eies as Lynx, and open eares as Midas, ranged & searched in euerie quarter.

Amongst these was Henrie the fourth earle of Northumberland, which (whether it was by the commandement of King Richard, putting diffidence in him; or he did it for the loue and fauour that he bare vnto the earle) stood still with a great companie, and intermitted not in the battell, which was incontinentlie receiued into fauour and made of the councell. But Thomas Howard earle of Surreie, which submitted him- selfe there, was not taken to grace; bicause his father was chiefe councellor, and he greatlie familiar with king Richard, but committed to the Tower of London, where he long remained; and in conclusion deliuered, was for his truth and fidelitie after promoted to high honors, offices and dignities. On the earle of Richmonds part were slaine scarse one hundred persons, among whome the principall was sir Willam Brandon his standard-bearer. This battell was fought at Bosworth in Leicestershire, the two and twentith daie of August, in the yeare of our redemption 1485. The whole conflict indured litle aboue two houres.

King Richard (as the fame went) might haue escaped and gotten safegard by fléeing. For when they, which were next about his person, saw and perceiued at the first ioining of the battell the souldiers faintlie and nothing couragiouslie to set on their enimies; and not onlie that, but also that some withdrew themselues priuilie out of the prease and departed; they began to suspect fraud and to smell treason; and not onelie exhorted, but determinatlie aduised him to saue himselfe by flight. And when the losse of the battell was imminent and apparant, they brought to him a swift and a light horsse, to conueie him awaie. He which was not ignorant of the grudge and ill will that the common people bare toward him, casting awaie all hope of fortunate successe and happie chance to come, answered (as men saie) that on that daie he would make an end of all battels, or else there finish his life. Such a great audacitie and such a stomach reigned in his bodie.

For suerlie he knew that to be the daie, in the which it should be decided and determined whether he should peaceablie obteine and inioy his kingdome during his life, or else vtterlie forgo and be depriued of the same. With which too much hardines he being ouercome, hastilie closed his helmet, and entered fiercelie into the hard battell, to the intent to obteine that daie a quiet reigne and regiment; or else to finish there his vnquiet life, and vnfortunat gouernance. And so this miser at the same verie point had like chance and fortune, as happeneth to such which in place of right iustice and honestie, following their sensuall appetite, loue, and vse to imbrace mischiefe, tyrannie, and vnthriftinesse. Suerlie these be examples of more vehemencie, than mans toong can expresse, to feare and astonish such euill persons, as will not liue one houre vacant from dooing and exercising crueltie, mischiefe, or outragious liuing.

When the earle had thus obteined victorie, and slaine his mortall enimie, he knéeled downe and rendred to almightie God his hartie thanks, with deuout and godlie orisons; beséeching his goodnesse to send him grace to aduance and defend the catholike faith; and

and to mainteine iustice and concord amongst his subiects and people, by God now to his gouernance committed & assigned. Which praier finished, he replenished with incomparable gladnesse ascended vp to the top of a little mounteine, where he not onelie praised and lauded his valiant souldiers; but also gaue vnto them his hartie thanks, with promise of condigne recompense for their fidelitie and valiant facts, willing and commanding all the hurt and wounded persons to be cured, and the dead carcasses to be deliuered to the sepulture. Then the people reioised, and clapped their hands, crieng vp to heauen; King Henrie, king Henrie.

The lord Stanleie setteth the crowne on king Henries head.

When the lord Stanleie saw the good will and gladnesse of the people, he tooke the crowne of king Richard which was found amongst the spoile in the field, and set it on the earles head; as though he had béene elected king by the voice of the people, as in ancient times past in diuerse realmes it hath beene accustomed: and this was the first signe and token of his good lucke and felicitie, ¶ I must put you here in remembrance, how that king Richard (putting some diffidence in the lord Stanleie) had with him as an hostage the lord Strange, his eldest sonne, which lord Stanleie (as ye haue heard before) ioined not at the first with his sonne in lawes armie, for feare the king would haue slaine the lord Strange his heire.

The lord Stanlies bold answer to K. Richards purseuant.

When king Richard was come to Bosworth, he sent a purseuant to the lord Stanleie, commanding him to aduance forward with his companie, and to come to his presence; which thing if he refused to doo, he sware by Christes passion, that he would strike off his sonnes head before he dined. The lord Stanleie answered the purseuant that if the king did so, he had more sonnes aliue; and as to come to him, he was not then so determined. When king Richard heard this answer, he commanded the lord Strange incontinent to be beheaded; which was at that verie same season, when both the armies had sight ech of other. But the councellors of king Richard pondered the time and cause, knowing also the lord Strange to be innocent of his fathers offense, & persuaded the king that it was now time to fight, & no time to execute.

Proclamation made to bring in the lord Strange.

Besides that, they aduised him to kéepe the lord Strange as prisoner till the battell were ended, and then at leisure his pleasure might be accomplished. So (as God would) king Richard brake his holie oth, and the lord was deliuered to the keepers of the kings tents, to be kept as prisoner. Which, when the field was doone, and their maister slaine, and proclamation made to know where the child was, they submitted themselues as prisoners to the lord Strange, and he gentlie receiued them, and brought them to the new proclamed king; where, of him and of his father he was receiued with great ioy. After this the whole campe remooued with bag and baggage.

The shamefull cariage of K. Richards bodie to Leicester.

The same night in the euening, king Henrie with great pompe came to the towne of Leicester; where as well for the refreshing of his people & souldiers, as for preparing all things necessarie for his iournie toward London, he rested and reposed himselfe two daies. In the meane season the dead corps of king Richard was as shamefullie caried to the towne of Leicester, as he gorgeouslie (the day before) with pompe and pride departed out of the same towne. For his bodie was naked and despoiled to the skin, and nothing left about him, not so much as a clout to couer his priuie members, and was trussed behind a purseuant of arms, one Blanch Senglier, or White bore, like a hog or calfe, his head and armes hanging on the one side of the horsse, and his legs on the other side, and all besprinkled with mire and bloud he was brought to the graie friers church within the towne, and there laie like a miserable spectacle.

But suerlie considering his mischiefous acts and vngratious dooings, men maie woonder at such a caitife, who although he deserued no buriall place either in church or churchyard, chappell or chancell, but otherwise to haue bin bestowed: yet in the said church he was with no lesse funerall pompe & solemnitie interred, than he would to be doone at the buriall of his innocent nephues, whome he caused cruellie to be murthered, and vnnaturallie killed. Now when his death was knowne, few lamented

and

and manie reioiced. The proud bragging white bore (which was his badge) was K. Richards badge and cognisance euerie where defaced. violentlie rased & plucked downe from euerie signe and place where it might be espied: so ill was his life, that men wished the memorie of him to be buried with his carren corps. He reigned two yeers, two moneths, and one daie [too long by six and twentie moneths, and foure and twentie houres in most mens opinions, to whome his name and presence was as swéet and delectable, as his dooings princelie, and his person amiable.]

As he was small and little of stature, so was he of bodie greatlie deformed; the one The description of king Richard. shoulder higher than the other; his face was small, but his countenance cruell, and such, that at the first aspect a man would iudge it to sauour and smell of malice, fraud, and deceit. When he stood musing, he would bite and chaw busilie his nether lip; as who said, that his fierce nature in his cruell bodie alwaies chafed, stirred, aud was euer vnquiet: beside that, the dagger which he ware, he would (when he studied) with his hand plucke vp & downe in the sheath to the midst, neuer drawing it fullie out: he was of a readie pregnant, and quicke wit, wilie to feine, and apt to dissemble: he had a proud mind, aud an arrogant stomach, the which accompanied him euen to his death, rather choosing to suffer the same by dint of sword, than being forsaken and left helpelesse of his vnfaithfull companions, to preserue by coward-lie flight such a fraile and vncerteine life, which by malice, sicknesse, or condigne punishment was like shortlie to come to confusion.

Thus ended this prince his mortall life with infamie and dishonor, which neuer pre-ferred fame or honestie before ambition, tyrannie and mischiefe. And if he had con-tinued still protector, and suffered his nephues to haue liued and reigned, no doubt but the realme had prospered, & he as much praised & loued as he is now had in hatred: but to God, which knew his inward thoughts at the houre of his death, I remit the punish-ment of his offenses commited in his life; [which if the one be as manifold as the other, Gods iustice were not to be charged with crueltie. For by nature he is mer-cifull, slow to anger, and loth to smite: but yet euerie sinne (in respect of his righteous-nesse) being deadlie (much more heinous and horrible) how can he but by iustice (which is an essentiall vertue in him) punish it seuerelie? And if he did it with ten thousand torments, who shall be so hardie as to expostulate and reason why he so dooth?

But to leaue the tyrant as he died, you shall vnderstand that K. Henrie the seuenth caused a toome to be made and set vp ouer the place where he was buried, in the church of the graie friers at Leicester, with a picture of alabaster representing his person, dooing that honour to his enimie, vpon a princelie regard and pitifull zeale, which king Richard (mooued of an hypocriticall shew of counterfeit pitie) did to Sée pag. 324. king Henrie the sixt, whom he had first cruellie murthered, and after in the second yeare of his vsurped reigne, caused his corps to be remooued from Chertseie vnto Windsore, and there solemnlie interred. And now to conclude with this cruell tyrant king Richard, we may consider in what sort the ambitious desire to rule and gouerne in the house of Yorke, was punished by Gods iust prouidence.

For although that the right might seeme to remaine in the person of Richard duke of Yorke, slaine at Wakefield; yet maie there be a fault worthilie reputed in him, so Sée pag. 268. to séeke to preuent the time appointed him by authoritie of parlement to atteine to the crowne intailed to him and his issue; in whome also, and not onelie in himselfe, that offense (as maie bée thought) was dulie punished. For although his eldest sonne Edward the fourth, beeing a prince right prouident and circumspect for the suertie of his owne estate and his children, insomuch that not content to cut off all his armed and apparant enimies, he also of a gealous feare, made awaie his brother the duke of Clarence, and so thought to make all sure: yet Gods vengeance might not be disap- Sée pag. 346.

pointed,

pointed, for (as ye haue partlie heard) he did but further thereby the destruction of his issue, in taking awaie him that onlie might haue staied the crueltie of his brother of Glocester, who inraged for desire of the kingdome, bereft his innocent nephues of their liues & estates.

And as it thus well appeared, that the house of Yorke shewed it selfe more bloudie in séeking to obteine the kingdome, than that of Lancaster in vsurping it: so it came to passe, that the Lords vengeance appeared more heauie towards the same than toward the other, not ceassing till the whole issue male of the said Richard duke of Yorke was extinguished. For such is Gods iustice, to leaue no vnrepentant wickednesse vnpunished, as especiallie in this caitife Richard the third, not deseruing so much as the name of a man, much lesse of a king, most manifestlie appeareth. [At whom we will end, with a comparison of the like practise in Lodowike Sforce, aspiring to the dukedome of Millane, the name, armes and title wherof he tooke vpon him, hauing secretlie protested before, that he receiued them as apperteining to him by the inuestiture of the king of Romans.

Abr. Flem. ex Guic. pag. 49. Lodowike Sforce duke of Millan by vsurpation.

It was published that the death of Galeas (his late predecessor) happened by immoderate cohabitation, but the vniuersall iudgment of Italie was, that he died not of infirmities naturall, nor by incontinencie, but by poison and violent compulsion. Wherof Theodor de Pauia, one of the physicians, assisting when the king visited him, assured the king to sée most apparant and manifest signes: and if hee were dispatched by poison, there was none that doubted that his vncle was innocent, either directlie or indirectlie; as he, who not content with an absolute power to be gouernor of the state, but aspiring according to the common desires of great men, to make themselues glorious with titles and honors; and speciallie he iudged, that both for his proper suertie and the succession of his children, the death of the lawfull prince was necessarie, and therefore thought to establish in himselfe the power and name of duke. Wherin ambition and couetousnesse preuailed aboue conscience and law of nature, and the gealous desire of dominion inforced his disposition (otherwise abhorring bloud) to that vile action.

Sée page. 211.

But to end with king Richard sometimes duke of Glocester, a title of dignitie ioined with misfortune and vnluckinesse (as is noted * before.) So that for infelicitie it might well be compared vnto the name of Ione, a name vnhappie and much accursed for the kingdome of Naples. As for king Richard, better had it béene for him to haue contented his heart with the protectorship, than to haue cast vp his snout, or lifted vp his hornes of ambition so high (and that with a setled intent) as to hacke and hew downe by violent blowes all likelie impediments betwixt him and home. Better (I say) had it béene for him to haue dwelt vpon his first honor, than to haue wandered in princelinesse; and better had it béene for him neuer to haue inioied the flattering prosperitie of a king, than afterwards to fall, and neuer to recouer losse or ruine, as is noted by the poet, saieng:

Guic. pag. 12.

T. Wat. in Am. Quer. 7.

Est melius nunquam felicia tempora nosse,
Quàm post blanditias fortunæ, fata maligna
Nec reparanda pati infortunia sortis iniquæ.]

¶ In this yere 1483 died William Dudleie who (by the translation of Laurence Booth bishop of Durham and chancellor of England from the sée of Durham to the citie of Yorke) was made bishop of Durham (in place of the said Laurence) by the popes bulles. For by vertue thereof, Edward the fourth in the sixténth yeare of his reigne, and in the yeare of Christ 1476, directed his letters patents to the knights and other free men of that bishoprike, with all solemnitie to install the said William Dudleie (borne of the honorable house of the lords Dudleies) in the said bishoprike of Durham, and to deliuer him quiet possession therof, who was consecrated thereunto

Fr. Thin. The death of William Dudleie bishop of Durham, descended of the honorable house of the Dudleies.

vnto

vnto in the yeare of Christ 1477, in which he woorthilie gouerned six yeares, and died in this yeare, as before.]

Now of learned men that liued, and wrote in the daies of this vsurper and his nephue king Edward the fift, these we find recorded by Iohn Bale. First, Iohn Penketh an Augustine frier of Warington in Lancashire, a right subtill fellow in disputation, following the footsteps of his master Iohn Duns, whome he chieflie studied, he wrote diuers treatises, and made that infamous sermon at Paules crosse, in fauour of the duke of Glocester then protector, to the disheriting of Edward the fift, his lawfull king and gouernor; Iohn Kent or Caileie borne in Southwales; George Ripleie, first a chanon of Bridlington, and after a Carmelit frier in Boston, a great mathematician, rhetorician, and poet; Iohn Spine a Carmelit frier of Bristow, that procéeded doctor of diuinitie in Cambridge: and such like.

Thus farre Richard the vsurper, vnnaturall vncle to Edward the fift
and Richard duke of Yorke, brethren.

HENRIE THE SEAUENTH,

sonne to Edmund earle of Richmond, which Edmund was brother by the moothers side to Henrie the sixt.

KING Henrie hauing thus got the victorie at Bosworth, and slaine his mortall enimie there in the field, did send before his departure from Leicester, sir Robert Willoughbie knight, to the manour of Sheriffehuton in the countie of Yorke, for Edward Plantagenet earle of Warwike, sonne and heire to George duke of Clarence then being of the age of fifteene yeares; whome king Richard had kept there as prisoner during the time of his vsurped reigne. Sir Robert Willoughbie receiuing the yoong earle of the constable of that castle conueied him to London where he was shut vp in the Tower, for doubt least some vnquiet and euill disposed persons might inuent some occasion of new trouble by this yoong gentleman: and therefore king Henrie thought good to haue him sure.

An. Reg. 1.

Edward Plantagenet earle of Warewike sonne and heire to George duke of Clarence committed to the tower.

There was beside him in the castell of Sheriffehuton the ladie Elizabeth eldest daughter to king Edward the fourth, whome king Richard (as ye haue heard) meant to haue married: but God otherwise ordeined for hir, and perserued hir from that vnlawfull copulation and incestuous bed. Shortlie after, she being accompanied with a great number as well of noblemen, as honourable matrons, was with good spéed conueied to London, and brought to hir moother. Iu the meane season king Henrie remooued forward by soft iournies towards London, the people comming in from all sides to behold him, and excéedinglie reioising at his presence, as by their voices and gestures it well appeared.

King Henrie commeth to London.

At his approching néere to the citie, the maior and his brethren, with other worshipfull citizens, being clothed in violet, met him at Shordich, and reuerentlie saluted him: and so with great pompe and triumph he rode thorough the citie to the cathedrall church of S. Paule, where he offered three standards. In the one was the image of saint George, in an other was a red fierie dragon beaten vpon white and greene sarcenet,

3 M

cenet, and in the third was painted a dun cow vpon yellow tarterne. After his praiers said, and Te deum soong, he departed to the bishops palace, and there soiourned a season. Anon after, he assembled togither the sage councellors of the realme, in which councell like a prince of iust faith, and true of promise, to auoid all ciuill discord, he appointed a daie to ioine in marriage with the ladie Elizabeth, heire of the house of Yorke; with his noble personage, heire to the line of Lancaster. Which thing not onelie reioised the hearts of the nobles and gentlemen of the realme, but also gained the fauours and good wils of all the commons.

After this, with great pompe he rowed vnto Westminster, & there the thirtith daie of October he was with all ceremonies accustomed, annointed, & crowned king, by the whole assent as well of the commons as of the nobilitie, & called Henrie the seauenth of that name: which was in the yeare of the world 5452, and after the birth of our Lord 1485, in the fortie and sixt yeare of Frederike the third then emperour of Almaine, Maximillian his sonne being newlie elected king of the Romans, in the second yeare of Charles the eight then king of France, and in the fiue and twentith of king Iames then ruling the realme of Scotland. For the establishing of all things as well touching the preseruation of his owne estate, as the commendable administration of iustice and preferrement of the common wealth of his realme, he called his

high court of parlement at Westminster the seauenth daie of Nouember, wherein was atteinted Richard late duke of Glocester, calling and naming himselfe by vsurpation, king Richard the third.

Likewise there was atteinted as chéefe aiders and assistants to him in the battell at Bosworth, aduanced against the present king, Iohn late duke of Norfolke, Thomas earle of Surrie, Francis Louell knight vicount Louell, Walter Deuereux knight late lord Ferrers, Iohn lord Zouch, Robert Harrington, Richard Charleton, Richard Ratcliffe, William Berkeleie of Weleie, Robert Middleton, Iames Harrington, Robert Brakenberie, Thomas Pilkington, Walter Hopton, William Catesbie, Roger Wake, William Sapcote of the countie of Huntington, Humfrie Stafford, William Clerke of Wenlocke, Geffrie saint Germaine, Richard Watkins herald of armes, Richard Reuell of Derbishire, Thomas Pulter of the countie of Kent, Iohn Welsh otherwise called Hastings, Iohn Kendall late secretarie to the said Richard late duke of Glocester, Iohn Bucke, Andrew Rat, and William Brampton of Burford.

In which atteindor neuerthelesse there were diuerse clauses and prouisos for the benefit of their wiues and other persons, that had or might claime anie right, title, or interest lawfullie vnto anie castels, manours, lordships, townes, towneships, honours, lands, tenements, rents, seruices, fée farmes, annuities, knights fées, aduousons, reuersions, remainders, and other hereditaments; whereof the said persons atteinted were possessed or seized to the vses of such other persons: with a speciall prouiso also, that the said atteindor should not be preiudiciall to Iohn Catesbie knight, Thomas Reuell, and William Ashbie esquiers, in, of, & vpon the manour of Kirkebie vpon Wretheke in the countie of Leicester, nor in, of, and vpon anie other lands and tenements in Kirkebie aforesaid, Melton, Somerbie, Thropseghfield, and Godebie, which they had of the gift & feoffement of Thomas Dauers, & Iohn Lie. And further, notwithstanding this atteindor, diuerse of the said persons afterwards were not onelie by the king pardoned, but also restored to their lands and liuings.

Moreouer, in this present parlement, he caused proclamation to be made, that all men were pardoned and acquited of their offenses, which would submit themselues to his mercie, and receiue an oth to be true and faithfull vnto him: wherevpon manie that came out of sanctuaries and other places were receiued to grace, and admitted for his subiects. After this, he began to remember his speciall freends, of whome some he aduanced to honour and dignitie, and some he inriched with goods and possessions, euerie man according to his deserts and merits. And to begin, his vncle

Iasper

Iasper earle of Penbroke, he created duke of Bedford; Thomas lord Stanleie was created earle of Derbie; and the lord Chendew of Britaine his especiall fréend, he made earle of Bath; sir Giles Daubeneie was made lord Daubeneie; sir Robert Willoughbie was made lord Brooke. And Edward Stafford eldest sonne to Henrie late duke of Buckingham, he restored to his name, dignitie, & possessions, which by king Richard were confiscat and atteinted. Beside this, in this parlement was this notable act assented to and concluded as followeth; to the pleasure of almightie God, wealth, prosperitie, and suertie of this realme of England, and to the singular comfort of all the kings subiects of the same, in auoiding all ambiguities and questions.

An act for the establishing of the crowne in the line of Henrie the seauenth.

BE it ordeined, established, and enacted by this present parlement, that the inheritance of the crown of this realme of England, & also of France, with all the preheminence, and dignitie roiall to the same apperteining; all other seigniories to the king belonging beyond the sea, with the appurtenances thereto in anie wise due or apperteining, shall rest, remaine, and abide, in the most roiall person of our now souereigne lord king Henrie the seuenth, and in the heires of his bodie lawfullie comming, perpetuallie, with the grace of God so to indure, and in none other.

Beside this act, all atteindors of this king enacted by king Edward and king Richard were adnihilated, and the record of the same iudged to be defaced; and all persons atteinted for his cause and occasion were restored to their goods, lands, and possessions. Diuerse acts also made in the time of king Edward and king Richard were reuoked, and other adiudged more expedient for the common wealth were put in their places and concluded. After the dissolution of this parlement, the king remem- <small>The king redéemeth his hostages.</small> bring his fréends left in hostage beyond the seas, that is to wit, the marquesse Dorset, & sir Iohn Bourchier, he with all conuenient spéed redéemed them, and sent also into Flanders for Iohn Morton bishop of Elie. These acts performed, he chose to be of his councell a conuenient number of right graue and wise councellors.

¶ This did he, that he might the more roiallie gouerne his kingdome, which he ob- <small>*Abr. Flem. ex subsequentib.*</small> teined and inioied as a thing by God elected and prouided, and by his especiall fauour <small>Sée the historie</small> and gratious aspect compassed and atchiued. Insomuch that men commonlie report <small>of Englād pag. 124.</small> that seauen hundred nintie & seauen yéeres passed, it was by a heauenlie voice reuealed <small>Sée also D.</small> to Cadwalader last of king Britains, that his stocke & progenie should reigne in this <small>*Powels* historie of Wales, pag. 2.</small> land & beare dominion againe. Wherevpon most men were persuaded in their owne <small>and 376, 377, &c.</small> opinion, that by this heauenlie voice he was prouided & ordeined long before to inioy & obteine this kingdome. Which thing K. Henrie the sixt did also shew before, as it <small>Sée before in</small> were by propheticall inspiration, at such time as the earle of Penbroke presented the <small>Edward the fourth, pag. 302.</small> said Henrie (at that time a proper child) vnto Henrie the sixt, whome after he had beheld, and a good while viewed the comlinesse of his countenance, and orderlie lineaments of his bodie, he said to such peeres as stood about him: Lo, suerlie this is he, to whome both we and our aduersaries, leauing the possession of all things, shall hereafter giue roome and place: & so it came to passe by the appointment of God, to whose gouernement, gift, and disposing, all realmes and all dominions are subiect, as king Dauid confesseth, saieng:

Omnia sunt regno subdita regna Dei.]   <small>*Gu. Ha. in psal.* 103.</small>

Now although by this meanes all things séemed to be brought in good and perfect order, yet there lacked a wrest to the harpe, to set all the strings in a monocord and perfect tune, which was the matrimonie to be finished betweene the king and the ladie

Elizabeth,

Elizabeth, daughter to king Edward. Which like a good prince, according to his oth, & promise, he did both solemnize & consummate shortlie after, that is to saie, on the eightéenth daie of Ianuarie. By reason of which marriage, peace was thought to descend out of heauen into England, considering that the lines of Lancaster and Yorke were now brought into one knot, and connexed togither, of whose two bodies one heire might succeed to rule and inioie the whole monarchie and realme of England, which before was rent and diuided into factions & partakings, whereby manie a mans life was lost, great spoiles made of peoples goods, wast of wealth, worship, and honor, all which ended in this blessed and gratious connexion, authorised by God, as our Anglorum prælia saith:

Hoc Deus omnipotens pacis confecerat author,
Ciuilísque habuit tandem contentio finem.

Shortlie after, for the better preseruation of his róiall person, he constituted an ordeined a certeine number, as well of archers, as of diuerse other persons, hardie, strong, and actiue to giue dailie attendance on his person, whom he named yeomen of his gard, which president men thought that he learned of the French king when he was in France. For it is not remembered, that anie king of England before that daie vsed anie such furniture of dailie souldiers. ¶ In this same yéere a new kind of sickenes inuaded suddenlie the people of this land, passing through the same from the one end to the other. It began about the one and twentith of September, and continued vntill the latter end of October, being so sharpe and deadlie, that the like was neuer heard of to anie mans remembrance before that time.

For suddenlie a deadlie burning sweat so assailed their bodies and distempered their bloud with a most ardent heat, that scarse one amongst an hundred that sickened did escape with life: for all in maner as soone as the sweat tooke them, or within a short time after yéelded the ghost. Beside the great number which deceassed within the citie of London, two maiors successiuelie died within eight daies and six Aldermen. At length, by the diligent obseruation of those that escaped (which marking what things had doone them good, and holpen to their deliuerance, vsed the like againe.) When they fell into the same disease, the second or third time, as to diuerse it chanced, a remedie was found for that mortall maladie, which was this. If a man on the day time were taken with the sweat, then should he streight lie downe with all his clothes and garments, and continue in his sweat foure and twentie houres, after so moderate a sort as might be.

If in the night he chanced to be taken, then should he not rise out of his bed for the space of foure and twentie houres, so casting the clothes that he might in no wise prouoke the sweat, but lie so temperatlie, that the water might distill out softlie of the owne accord, and to absteine from all meat if he might so long suffer hunger, and to take no more drinke neither hot nor cold, than would moderatelie quench and asswage his thirstie appetite. Thus with lukewarme drinke, temperate heate, and measurable cloaths manie escaped: few which vsed this order (after it was found out) died of that sweat. Marie one point diligentlie aboue all other in this cure is to be obserued, that he neuer did put his hand or feet out of the bed to refresh or coole himselfe, which to doo is no lesse ieopardie than short and present death. Thus this disease comming in the first yeare of king Henries reigne, was iudged (of some) to be a token and signe of a troublous reigne of the same king, as the proofe partlie afterwards shewed it selfe.

The king standing in néed of monie to discharge such debts, and to mainteine such port as was behouefull, sent the lord treasuror with maister Reginald Braie, and others, vnto the lord maior of London, requiring of the citie a prest of six thousand marks. Wherevpon the said lord maior and his brethren, with the commons of the citie, grant-

ed

Marginalia:

King Henrie the seuenth taketh to wife Elizabeth eldest daughter of Edward the fourth. 1486

In Hen. 7.

Yeomen of the gard first brought in.

The sweating sickenesse.

A remedie for the sweating sickenesse.

The king requested a prest of six thousand markes.

ed a prest of two thousand pounds, which was leiued of the companies, and not of the wards: and in the yeare next insuing, it was well and trulie againe repaid euerie penie, to the good contentation and satisfieng of them that disbursed it. The king considering that the suertie of his roiall estate and defense of the realme consisted chéefelie in good lawes and ordinances to be had and obserued among his people sum- A parlement summoned & new lawes for the common-wealth enacted. moned eftsoones his high court of parlement, therein to deuise and establish some pro-fitable acts and statutes, for the wealth and commoditie of his people.

After this, hauing set things in quiet about London, he tooke his iournie into the North parts, there to purge all the dregs of malicious treson that might rest in the The king goeth into the North. hearts of vnquiet persons, and namelie in Yorkeshire, where the people bare more fauour vnto king Richard in his life time, than those of anie other part of the realme had commonlie doone. He kept the feast of Easter at Lincolne; where he was cer-tified that the lord Louell and Humfrie Stafford, and Thomas Stafford, his brother, were departed out of the sanctuarie at Colchester, to what place or whither, no man as yet could tell. The king little regarding the matter, kept on his iournie, and came to Yorke, where as soone as he was once setled, it was openlie shewed and declared for a truth to the king himselfe, that Frances lord Louell was at hand with a strong and A rebellion made by the lord Louell and others. mightie power of men, and would with all diligence inuade the citie.

It was also told him, that the forenamed Staffords were in Worsetershire, and had raised a great band of the countrie people and commons there, and had cast lots what Humfrie Stafford. Thomas Staf-ford. part should assault the gates, what men should scale the wals of the citie of Worces-ter, and who should let the passages for letting of rescues and aiders. The king could not beleeue this report to be true at the first, but after that, by letters of cre-dence sent from his fréends, he was fullie persuaded that it was too true, he was put in no small feare, and not without great cause. For he wiselie considered, that he neither had anie competent armie readie, nor conuenient furniture to arme them that were present: and also he was in such place, where he could not assemble anie power, but of those whome he sore mistrusted, as fréends to them that were most his eni-mies; the memorie of king Richard as yet being not amongst them forgotten nor worne out of mind.

But bicause the matter required quicke expedition, he appointed the duke of Bed- The duke of Bedford against the lord Louell in armes. ford with three thousand men not altogither the best armed (for their brest plates for the most part were of tanned leather) to march foorth against the lord Louell, and to set vpon him without anie lingering of time. The duke hasting forward, approch-ed to the campe of his enimies, & before he would assaile them, he caused the heralds to make proclamation, that all those that would depart from their armour, and sub-mit themselues as subiects vnto their naturall prince and souereigne lord, should be pardoned of all former offenses. The lord Louell vpon this proclamation, either put-ting mistrust in his souldiers, or fearing himselfe in his owne behalfe, fled priuilie in a night from his companie, and left them as a flocke of shéepe without a shéepe-heard.

Which departure of the lord when his armie vnderstood, it put the souldiers in such despaire of atchiuing anie further enterprise, that they immediatlie put off their ar-mour, and came directlie vnto the duke, euerie man humblie submitting himselfe, and desiring pardon of his offenses. So in this wise was that dangerous storme and cruell rage of those furious rebels appeased, which was doubted would haue growne to the destruction of manie a man. The lord Louell the procurer of this businesse, The lord Louell escapeth. escaping awaie got him into Lancashire, and there for a certeine space lay lurking in secret with sir Thomas Broughton knight, which in those parties was a man of no small authoritie and power.

Sir Humfreie Stafford also, hearing what had happened to the lord Louell, in great
displeasure

displeasure and sorrowe, and for feare left his enterprise, and in like manner fled, and tooke sanctuarie at Colnham, a village not past two miles from Abindon. But bicause that sanctuarie was not a sufficient defense (as was prooued before the iustices of the kings Bench) for traitours, he was taken from that place, & brought to the Tower, & after put to execution at Tiborne: but his brother Thomas that was with him, was pardoned, bicause he was thought not to haue attempted anie thing of himselfe other-

wise than by the euill counsell and persuasion of his elder brother. After that the king had quieted all these commotions and tumults, and reformed the rude and brabling people of the North parts, he returned to London.

¶ In this yeare Iohn Persiuall, one of the maior of Londons officers, and his caruer, was chosen one of the shiriffes of London. For when the maior (as the custome of London is) dooth elect one of the shiriffes of London for the yeare insuing, by taking and drinking a cup of wine to such a one as he lust to name shiriffe; the maior for the time being, whose name was sir Henrie Collet, tooke the cup of wine, and dranke vnto the aforesaid Iohn Persiuall his caruer standing barcheaded before him, and waiting vpon his boord, and called him shiriffe of London for the yeare insuing: and foorthwith the said maior caused the same Persiuall to sit downe at his owne table, and to couer his head. And the same Persiuall tooke vpon him the office of shiriualtie, and after was maior of London, and was made knight.]

In this meane time, of a small matter, and the same altogither false and fained, there was an open path made and beaten foorth, for a greater inconuenience to insue. The which matter might séeme verie strange, how such trouble and mischéefe should grow thereof, if the time were not considered, in which it happened. For in those daies manie persons, either borne in the wombe of continuall dissention, or nourished with the milke of ciuill sedition, could not forbeare their vsuall custome of moouing strife, and sowing debate, euer glad to haue anie occasion, though neuer so small, to stirre vprores of warre, and slaughter of people. Which men if they knew (a matter of weightie conceipt) the hurts thereof, they would be as earnest in seeking after peace as they are gréedie in pursuit of warre, speciallie ciuill warre: but the cause whie they are defectiue therein, is the want of méekenesse and humilitie, as the wiseman saith:

Mite cor horribili seditione vacat.

Amongst other such monsters and limmes of the diuell, there was one sir Richard Simond preest, a man of base birth, and yet well learned, but not so learned as wilie, nor so wilie as vngratious, delighting in fraud & deceit, euen from his youth. He had a scholer called Lambert Simenell, one of a gentle nature and pregnant wit, to be the organe and chéefe instrument, by the which he might conueie and bring to passe his mischéeuous attempt. The diuell chéefe master of such practises, put in the venemous braine of this disloiall and traitorous préest to deuise how he might make his scholer the foresaid Lambert to be reputed as right inheritour to the crowne of this realme: namelie, for that the fame went that king Edwards children were not dead but fled secretlie into some strange place, and there to be liuing: and that Edward earle of Warwike, sonne and heire to the duke of Clarence, either was, or shortlie should be put to death.

These rumors though they séemed not to be grounded of anie likelihood to the wiser sort of men, yet incouraged this péeuish priest to thinke the time come, that his scholer Lambert might take vpon him the person and name of one of king Edwards children. And herevpon at Oxford, where their abiding was, the said préest instructed his pupill both with princelie behauiour, ciuill maners, and good literature, declaring to him of what linage he should affirme himselfe to be descended, and omitted nothing that might serue for his purpose. Soone after, the rumor was blowne abroad, that the earle of Warwike was broken out of prison. And when the préest sir Richard
Simond

Simond heard of this, he streight intended now by that occasion to bring his inuented purpose to passe, and changing the childes name of baptisme, called him Edward, after the name of the yoong earle of Warwike, the which were both of like yeares, and of like stature.

Then he with his scholer sailed into Ireland, where he so set foorth the matter vnto the nobilitie of that countrie, that not onelie the lord Thomas Gerardine chancellor of that land deceiued though his craftie tale, receiued the counterfeit earle into his castell with all honour and reuerence; but also manie other noble men determined to aid him (with all their powers) as one descended of the bloud roiall and lineallie come of the house of Yorke, which the Irish people euermore highlie fauoured, honoured, and loued aboue all other. By this meanes euerie man through out all Ireland was willing and readie to take his part, and to submit themselues to him; alreadie reputing and calling him of all hands king. So that now they of this sect (by the aduise of the préest) sent into England certeine priuie messengers to get fréends héere. *Thomas Gerardine chancellor of Ireland interteineth the counterfeit earle verie honorabie.*

Also they sent into Flanders to the ladie Margaret, sister to king Edward, & late wife to Charles duke of Burgognie, to purchase aid and helpe at hir hands. This ladie Margaret bare no small rule in the low countries, and in verie déed sore grudged in hir heart, that king Henrie (being descended of the house of Lancaster) should reigne and gouerne the realme of England: and therefore though she well vnderstood that this was but a coloured matter; yet to worke hir malicious intention against king Henrie, she was glad to haue so fit an occasion: and therfore promised the messengers all the aid that she should be able to make in furtherance of the quarell; and also to procure all the fréends she could in other places, to bé aiders and partakers of the same conspiracie. *Margaret the duchesse of Burgognie sister to king Edward the fourth, hir malicious mind to Lancaster house.*

King Henrie aduertised of all these dooings, was greatlie vexed therewith: and therefore to haue good aduise in the matter, he called togither his councell at the Charterhouse beside his manor of Richmond, and there consulted with them, by which means best this begun conspiracie might be appeased and disappointed without more disturbance. It was therefore determined, that a generall pardon should be published to all offendors that were content to receiue the same. This pardon was so fréelie granted that no offense was excepted, no not so much as high treason committed against the kings roiall person. It was further agréed in the same councell for the time then present, that the earle of Warwike should personallie be shewed abroad in the citie, and other publike places: whereby the vntrue report falselie spred abroad, that he should be in Ireland, might be among the communaltie prooued and knowne for a vaine imagined lie. *A generall pardon excepting no offese.* *Order taken that the yoong earle of Warwike should be shewed abroad.*

In this solemne councell, diuerse & manie things for the wealth of the realme were debated and concluded. And among other it was determined, that the ladie Elizabeth wife to king Edward the fourth, should loose and forfeit all hir lands and possessions, bicause she had voluntarilie submitted hir selfe and hir daughters wholie to the hands of king Richard, contrarie to hir promise made to the lords and nobles of this realme in the beginning of the conspiracie made against king Richard, whereby she did inough to haue quailed all the purpose of them that ioined with hir in that matter. But though hir fault was greeuous, yet was it iudged by some men that she deserued not by equitie of iustice so great a losse and punishment. Howbeit, this iudgement was altogither affectionate and parciall in hir behalfe; besides that it was reasonable in great measure (all circumstances considered) for she was not lightlie induced to doo as she did, neither stood it with the frailtie of a woman to withstand the temptations of a mightie man, or rather a reaching tyrant. *Ladie Elizabeth late wife to king Edward the fourth, adiudged to forfeit all hir lands for promise-break-ing.*

But such was hir chance by hir lightnesse and inconstancie, that she wan the displeasure of manie men, and for that cause liued after in the abbeie of Bermondseie beside Southwarke a wretched and a miserable life, where not manie yeares after she deceassed and

and is buried with hir husband at Windsore. Though fortune thus ruleth manie things at hir plesure, yet one worke that this quéene accomplished cannot be forgotten: for in the life time of hir husband king Edward the fourth, she founded and erected a notable colledge in the vniuersitie of Cambridge, for the finding of scholers and students of the same vniuersitie, and endowed it with sufficient possessions for the long maintenance of the same, which at this daie is called the Quéenes colledge.

Quéenes Col-
ledge in Cam-
bridge founded
by the ladie
Elizabeth king
Edward the
fourth his wife.

When all things in this counsell were sagelie concluded and agréed to the kings mind, he returned to London; giuing in commandement, that the next sundaie insuing, Edward the yoong earle of Warwike should be brought from the Tower through the most publike streets in all London, to the cathedrall church of saint Paule, where he went openlie in procession, that euerie man might sée him, hauing communication with manie noble men, and with them especiallie that were suspected to be partakers of the late begun conspiracie; that they might perceiue how the Irishmen vpon a vaine shadowe mooued warre against the king and his realme. But this medicine little auailed euill disposed persons. For the earle of Lincolne sonne to Iohn de la Poole duke of Suffolke, and Elizabeth sister to king Edward the fourth, thought it not méet to neglect and omit so readie an occasion of new trouble.

Edward the
right earle of
Warwike shew-
ed openlie in
procession.

Wherefore they determined to vphold the enterprise of the Irishmen, and other complices of this conspiracie; so that consulting with sir Thomas Broughton, and certeine other of his most trustie freends, he purposed to saile into Flanders to his aunt the ladie Margaret duchesse of Burgognie, trusting by hir helpe to make a puissant armie, and to ioine with the companions of the new raised sedition. Therefore after the dissolution of the parlement which then was holden, he fled secretlie into Flanders vnto the said ladie Margaret; where Francis lord Louell landed certeine daies before. Héere after long consultation had how to proceed in their businesse, it was agreed, that the earle of Lincolne, and the lord Louell should go into Ireland; and there to attend vpon the duchesse hir counterfeit nephue, and to honor him as a king, and with the power of the Irishmen to bring him into England.

An ill matter
followed to the
proofe.

Now they concluded, that if their dooings had successe, then the foresaid Lambert (misnamed the earle of Warwike) should by consent of the councell be deposed, and Edward the true earle of Warwike deliuered out of prison and annointed king. King Henrie supposing that no man would haue béene so mad as to haue attempted anie further enterprise in the name of that new found & counterfeit earle, he onelie studied how to subdue the seditious conspiracie of the Irishmen. But hearing that the earle of Lincolne was fled into Flanders, he was somwhat mooued therewith, and caused soldiors to be put in a readinesse out of euerie part of his realme, and to bring them into one place assigned, that when his aduersaries should appeare, he might suddenlie set vpon them, vanquish and ouercome them.

The earle of
Lincolnes flight
into Flanders
doubted of king
Henrie.

Thus disposing things for his suertie, he went towards S. Edmunds burie, and being certified that the marquesse Dorset was comming towards his maiestie, to excuse himselfe of things that he was suspected to haue doone when he was in France, he sent the earle of Oxford to arrest the said marques by the waie, and to conueie him to the Tower of London, there to remaine till his truth might be tried. From thence the K. went foorth to Norwich, and tarrieng there Christmasse daie, he departed after to Walsingham, where he offered to the image of our ladie, and then by Cambridge he shortlie returned to London. In which meane time, the earle of Lincolne had gotten togither by the aid of the ladie Margaret about two thousand Almains, with one Martine Sward, a valiant and noble capteine to lead them.

The marques
Dorset commit-
ted to the Tower.

1487

Martin Sward a
valiant capteine
of the Almains,
assistant to the
earle of Lin-
colne.

With this power the earle of Lincolne sailed into Ireland, and at the citie of Diuelin caused yoong Lambert to be proclaimed and named king of England, after the most solemne fashion, as though he were the verie heire of the bloud roiall lineallie borne and descended. And so with a great multitude of beggerlie Irishmen, almost all naked and

and vnarmed, sauing skains and mantels, of whome the lord Thomas Gerardine was capteine and conductor, they sailed into England with this new found king, and land- The counterfeit earle of Warwike with all his abhe-reuts landeth in England. ed for a purpose at the pile of Fowdreie, within a little of Lancaster, trusting there to find aid by the meanes of sir Thomas Broughton, one of the chéefe companions of the conspiracie.

The king had knowledge of the enimies intent before their arriuall, and therefore hauing assembled a great armie (ouer the which the duke of Bedford, and the earle of Oxenford were chéefe capteins) he went to Couentrie, where he was aduertised, that the earle of Lincolne was landed at Lancaster with his new king. Héere he tooke aduise of his councellors what was best to be doone, whether to set on the enimies without further delaie, or to protract time a while. But at length it was thought best to delaie no time but to giue them battell, before they should increase their power, and therevpon he remooued to Notingham, & there by a little wood called Bowres, he pitched his field.

Shortlie after this came to him the lord George Talbot earle of Shrewesburie, the K. Henries power soone increas-ed. lord Strange, sir Iohn Cheinie, right valiant capteins, with manie other noble and expert men of warre, namelie of the countries neere adioining; so that the kings The earle of Lincolne entreth Yorkeshire. armie was woonderfullie increased. In this space the earle of Lincolne being entered into Yorkeshire, passed softlie on his iournie without spoiling or hurting of anie man, trusting thereby to haue some companie of people resort vnto him. But after he per-ceiued few or none to follow him, and that it was too late now to returne backe, he determined to trie the matter by dint of sword, and herevpon directed his waie from Yorke to Newarke vpon Trent.

But before he came there, king Henrie knowing all his enimies purposes, came the night before the daie of the battell to Newarke; and tarrieng there a little, went thrée miles further, and pitching his field, lodged there that night. The earle of Lincolne certified of his comming, was nothing abashed, but kept still on his iournie; and at a little The battell of Stoke. village called Stoke, nigh to the king and his armie, set downe his campe. The next daie the king diuided his whole power into thrée battels, and after in good arraie ap-proched nigh to the towne of Stoke. The earle likewise set foorth his armie, and incountring with the kings people in a faire plaine there, meet for the triall of such a conflict, set vpon them with a manlie courage, desiring his soldiors to remember his honour and their owne liues.

Then both the armies ioined and fought verie earnestlie, in so much that the Almains, The armies ioine. being tried and expert men of warre, were in all things, as well in strength as policie, equals and matches to the Englishmen. But as for Martine Sward their coronell, few Martine Sward a péerelesse warrior. of the Englishmen, either in valiant courage, or strength, and nimblenesse of bodie was to him comparable. On the other side, the Irishmen, although they fought manfullie, and stucke to it valiantlie; yet bicause they were (after the maner of their countrie) almost naked, without anie conuenable furniture of armour, they were striken downe and slaine like dull & brute beasts, which was a great discouragement to the residue of the companie. Thus they fought for a space so sore and so egerlie on both parts, that no man could well iudge to whome the victorie was like to incline.

But at length the kings fore-ward being full of people, and well fortified with wings, The kings power ouercommeth. which onelie both began and continued the fight, set vpon the aduersaries with such force and violence, that first they oppressed and killed such capiteins, one by one, as re-sisted their might and puissance: and after that, put all the other to flight, the which were either apprehended as prisoners in their running awaie, or else slaine and brought vnto confusion in a small moment. Now when this battell was ended, and fought out to the extremitie, then it well appeared, what high prowesse, what manfull stomachs, what hardie and couragious hearts rested in the kings aduersaries. For All the capteins of the aduerse part against the king slaine. there the cheefe capteins, the earle of Lincolne, and the lord Louell, sir Thomas Broughton,

Broughton, Martine Sward, and the lord Gerardine capteine of the Irishmen were slaine, and found dead in the verie places which they had chosen aliue to fight in, not giuing one foot of ground to their aduersaries.

Howbeit some affirme, that the lord Louell tooke his horsse, and would haue fled ouer Trent, but was not able to recouer the further side for the highnesse of the banke,

The number of
the slaine that
were against the
king.
Lambert and his
maister Simond
take.

and so was drowned in the riuer. There were killed at that battell, with their fiue capteins before rehersed, of that partie about foure thousand. Of the kings part there were not halfe of them which fought in the fore-ward, and gaue the onset slaine or hurt. Then was Lambert the yoongling, which was falslie reported to be the sonne of the duke of Clarence, and his maister sir Richard Simond priest both taken, but neither of them put to death; bicause that Lambert was but an innocent, and of yeares insufficient of himselfe to doo any such enterprise; and the other was pardoned of life, bicause he was a priest, and annointed man; but yet was committed to perpetuall prison.

Lambert was at length made one of the kings falconers, after that he had béene a turnebroch for a space in the kings kitchen. This battell was fought on a saturdaie being the sixtéenth daie of Iune, in this second yeere of his reigne. In this yéere

Morton bishop
of Elie made
archbishop of
Canturburie and
chancellor of
England.

died Thomas Bourchier archbishop of Canturburie: and Iohn Morton bishop of Elie; a man of excellent learning, vertue and policie, succeeded in his place, whom Alexander pope of Rome, the sixt of that name, created a cardinall, and the king created him also chancellor of England. Of which pope (hauing so conuenient a place to speake) it were a fault to omit the ambition, accompanied with other disorders vnbeséeming a successor of Peter (but neither personallie nor locallie) as all the brood of

*Abr. Fl. ex
Guic. pag 4, 5.*
Creation of
pope Alexander
the sixt, Otherwise called
Roderike Borgia
borne at Venice.

them brag of themselues, & will be intituled with a primasie, vsurped.

¶ This Alexander the sixt pope of that name, was sometime an ancient cardinall, and one of the greatest in all the court of Rome. One meane that raised him to the seat of the pope, was the difference betweene the cardinals Ascanius Sforce, and Iulian S. Petri ad Vincula: but the chiefest thing that accomplished his election, was, that with a new example for that time, he bought by the consent and knowledge of euerie one, partlie for monie, and partlie with promises of offices and great dignities,

Corruption of
cardinals in the
election of the
pope.

manie voices of the cardinals, who reiecting the instruction of the gospell, were not ashamed to passe to him by sale, an authoritie and power to make merchandize of the holie tresures, & that with the name of the celestiall authoritie in the most high part of the temple.

To which abhominable & too too prophane negotiation manie of them were induced by the cardinall Ascanius, but that was not more with persuasions and sutes, than with his example: for that being corrupted with the infinit desire of riches, he made the pope promise him for his hire and recompense of so great wickednesse, the office of vicechancellorship (the principallest place in the court of Rome) togither with benefices, castels, and his palace of Rome full of mooueables of great valour. But the pope for all this could not auoid; neither for the time to come, the iudgment and iustice of God; nor for the present, the infamie and iust hate of men, in whom for this election was no small impressions of astonishment and horror, not onelie for that it was intangled with meanes dishonest, but also bicause the natures and conditions of the man chosen, were (for the greatest part) knowen to manie.

Manie sentences and coniectures were made of his successe. And amongst other, Ferdinand king of Naples, dissembling openlie the griefe he had of that election, signified to the quéene his wife with teares (which he was woont to forbeare euen in the death of his children) that there was created a pope who wold be most hurtfull to Italie, and the whole common weale of Christendome. A iudgement not vnworthie of the wisedome of such a prince: for that in Alexander the sixt (for so would this new pope be called) was a subtiltie, sharpenesse, and expedition of wit most singular,

a counsell

a counsell excellent, a woonderfull efficacie in persuasion, and in all great affaires a iudgement and care incredible. But these vertues were maruellouslie defaced by his vices, for touching his maners and customes, they were verie dishonest, in his administrations he expressed little sinceritie, in his countenance no shame, in his words small truth, in his heart little faith, and in his opinion lesse religion. Of the contrarie all his actions were defiled with an insatiable couetousnesse, and immoderate ambition, a barbarous crueltie, and a burning desire to raise and make great (by what meanes soeuer) his children, who were manie in number; and amongst others, one no lesse detestable than the father, to whose cursed counsels he became a wicked instrument. Thus much (by waie of digression) of Alexander, a pope (as you heare) well qualified, and therefore forward enough to creat cardinals both in England and elsewhere of like disposition. But to returne to the storie.] *Pope Alexander the sixt corrupted with manie vices.*

After that the king had got the vpper hand of his enimies, he remooued to Lincolne, and there taried thrée dais, causing euerie of the same daies solemne processions to be made in rendering thanks to God for his fortunate victorie. Then caused he execution to be done, of such rebels & traitors as were taken in the field, either at the battell, or in the chase. And shortlie after he went into Yorkshire, & there coasted the countrie ouerthwart, searching out such as had aided his enimies and were thought to be seditious persons, whome he punished, some by imprisonment, some by fines, and some by death: according to the qualitie of their offenses, and as was thought most expedient [not by extremitie of rigor inclining to tyrannie, but by due moderation of iustice tempering execution with clemencie; according to the good rule of iustice prescribed by the wise man, saieng: *Thanks giuen to God after victorie. Execution vpon the offendors.*

   Sobria commissum plectat clementia crimen,
  Parua negat poenam culpa subire grauem.] *Gu. Ha. in eccle. cap. 10.*

About the middest of August entering into the third yere of his reigne, he came to Newcastell vpon Tine, and from thence sent in ambassage into Scotland Richard Fox, latelie before made bishop of Excester, and with him Richard Edgecombe knight, controller of his house, to conclude some peace or truce with king Iames of Scotland. The English ambassadors were honorablie receiued, and louinglie interteined of the said king, who gladlie would haue concluded a perpetuall peace with the king of England, if he might haue bene licenced so to haue doone: but his people being stedfast in their old accustomed vsage, would not agrée to anie peace, but yet were contented to gratifie their king that he should take truce with England for the tearme of seuen yeares, which was concluded. *An. Reg. 3 Fox bishop of Excester sent ambassador into Scotland. A truce with Scotland for seuen yeares.*

Then was secret promise made by king Iames, that he would not onlie obserue peace, & continue in perfect amitie with the king of England during his life, but also would renew againe this truce new taken for other seuen yeers, before the first seuen yeers were fullie expired. The king of Scots indéed was as desirous of the king of Englands friendship, as the king of England was of his: bicause that his subiects bare him much euill will, misliking with all things that either he could doo or saie. [So that his regiment was no longer liked, than they were in a good mood, which was when they were well minded; and that was neuer: for that if by gentlenesse he allured them, they esteemed him a flatterer; if by seueritie, a tyrant. And therefore it stood him vpon to strengthen himselfe against such a people, of whose pleasure & displeasure depended his estate.]

K. Henrie after the returne of his ambassadors out of Scotland, came from Newcastell to Yorke, and so toward London, and in the way being at Leicester, there came to him ambassadors from Charles the French king, which declared both the recouerie of certeine townes out of the hands of Maximilian king of Romans, which he had wrongfullie deteined from the crowne of France before that time; and also that their maister king Charles had now wars in hand against Francis duke of Britaine, *King Henrie returneth out of the north countrie.*

                 bicause

The French
kings request
for aid against
Frācis duke of
Britaine.
bicause that he succoured and mainteined diuers noble men, as the duke of Orleance and others, that were rebels and traitors, against him and the realme of France. Wherefore his request was, that for the old familiaritie that had bene betwixt them, he would either assist and helpe him, or else stand neuter betwixt them, neither helping nor yet hurting the one nor the other.

Vpon good and deliberate aduise taken in this matter, bicause it was iudged weightie, the king for answer told the French ambassadors, that he would neither spare paine nor cost, to set some reasonable staie betwixt their souereigne lord king Charles, and the duke of Britaine: so that a finall end and some perfect conclusion of friendship might be had betwixt them. And so as soone as the French ambassadors were returned home, the king sent his chapleine Christopher Urswike ouer into France to king Charles, as well to shew that he was glad of the victorie which he had against Maximilian; as to declare what a tempestuous storme of ciuill rebellion himselfe had escaped & ouercome heere in England.

King Henries
offer to make an
attonement
betwixt the
French king
and the duke

Christopher
Urswike.
But the chiefest point of Urswikes errand consisted in this, that he should intimate to the French king, how his maister king Henrie offered himselfe as a mediator betwixt him and the duke of Britaine, to make them friends: and if he perceiued that the French king gaue eare hereunto, then should he go into Britaine, to mooue the duke there to be contented, that some reasonable order might be taken for a quietnesse to be had betwixt the French king and him. Whilest Urswike was trauelling in this matter (according to his commission) the king came backe againe to London, where he was receiued of the citizens with great ioy and triumph, they being heartlie glad and greatlie reioising that he with such good successe had subdued his enimies.

The marques
Dorset deliuered
out of the Tower.

The kings loue
to his wife
quéene Eliza-
beth.
Shortlie after, he deliuered the lord Thomas marques Dorset out of the Tower, receiuing him againe to his former fauor and old familiaritie: bicause his truth and loialtie by diuerse assaies and sundrie arguments had béene throughlie tried, and sufficientlie prooued. In which meane time, the king for the great loue that he bare to his wife quéene Elizabeth, caused hir to be crowned and anointed quéene on saint Katharins day in Nouember, with all solemnitie, as in such cases apperteineth. In the meane season Christopher Urswike (according to his commission) trauelled betwéene the French king and the duke of Britaine in the king of Englands Name to make them friends. But although the French king séemed willing enough to haue peace, yet meant he nothing lesse. For he had as manie subtilties in his heart, as there be faces in the world, according to the poet.

Pectoribus fraudes tot sunt quot in orbe figuræ.

For whilest he went about with faire words, courteous letters, and swéet promises to beare the king of England in hand to labour a peace betwixt him and the Britains, he inforced his whole puissance to subdue them, and besieged the citie of Nants. And on The duke of
Orleance par-
taker with the
duke of Britaine. the other part, the duke of Orleance being withdrawne to the duke of Britaine, and one that ruled most about him, had no liking to heare of peace, but did what he could to hinder it. The English ambassador Christopher Urswike (hauing thus passed from the French king to the duke of Britaine, and backe againe to the French king) returned shortlie after into England, and shewed vnto king Henrie what he had doone betwixt them.

Immediatlie after came to the French king the lord Bernard Daubeneie a Scot borne, which on the French kings behalfe required K. Henrie to make some maner of end of those Brittish warres, whatsoeuer it were. King Henrie being desirous of the same, sent ouer againe into France, Iohn the abbat of Abingdon, sir Richard Edgecombe knight, and the forenamed Christopher Urswike, with full and perfect commission & long instructions how to procéed, in driuing of some agréement betwixt the Frenchmen and the Britons. These orators (according as they had in commandement) first went vnto the French king, and after they had communed with him, sir Richard Edgecombe,

Edgecombe, and Christopher Urswike departed streight to the duke of Britaine, in full hope to conclude a peace, vpon such offers and articles as they had to propone vnto him.

But all their hope was vaine, for the duke refused to agree vpon anie such articles and conditions as they offered; and so without concluding anie thing with the duke, they returned backe into France; and from thence signified to the king of England by letters all that they knew, or had doone. But in the meane time, Edward lord Wooduile, vncle to the quéene, sued to king Henrie that he might haue a power of men appointed to him, with the which he would steale priuilie ouer without licence or passeport, so that euerie man should thinke that he was fled the realme, without knowledge of the king, for that no warre should arise by his meanes betwixt the realmes of France and England, and yet should the duke of Britaine be aided against the power of the Frenchmen, which sought to vanquish him, that they might ioine his countrie vnto the dominion of France: which in no wise ought to be suffered, considering what annoiance & hurt the same might bring to the realme of England in time to come.

1488

Edward lord Wooduile aideth the duke of Britaine without the kings cōsent.

Although this request was vtterlie denied, and that the lord Wooduile was streightlie commanded by the king to make no such attempt; yet could not all that staie him, but that withdrawing him into the Ile of Wight, whereof he was made ruler and capteine, he there gathered togither a crue of tall & hardie personages, to the number of 400, & with prosperous wind & weather arriued in Britaine, and ioined himselfe with the Britons against the Frenchmen. The French king aduertised herof, was not well plesed in his mind towards the king of England; till K. Henrie by new messengers informed him how guiltlesse he was in the matter, and that by plaine and euident proofes. With the which excuse the French king séemed to be the better pacified, and was content to dissemble the matter.

Lord Wooduile gathereth a power in the Ile of wight.

Then the English ambassadors, renewing the league and amitie betwixt king Henrie & the French king, for the space of twelue moneths, they returned into England, and shewed the king all things that they had either heard or séene; so that he perceiued that the French king dealt craftilie in this matter of Britaine, still motioning peace when he meant nothing else but warre. He therefore called his high court of parlement, in the which it was not onelie determined that the duke of Britaine should be aided with a power of men against the wrongfull inuasions of the Frenchmen, but also there were diuerse summes of monie granted to the furnishing foorth and maintenance of the same. And immediatlie hervpon, the king sent his ambassadors into France to certifie the French king what the estates assembled in parlement here in England had decréed.

The league renewed betwéene England and France.

The king calleth a parlement.

Wherefore he required him either to surcease the warres which he had in hand against the Britons, or else not to be gréeued though he condescended to the iudgement and determination of the lords both spirituall and temporall, and commons of his realme, in taking vpon him the defense of the duke of Britaine; promising neuerthelesse that the English armie should onelie take land within the duchie of Britaine, and séeke to defend the same against all those that did inuade it, and not to make anie warre within the French dominions. This message was nothing regarded of the French king, in so much that the French armie procéeded in oppressing the Britons, destroieng the countrie, and besieging townes.

A peremptorie ambassage out of England into France.

At length on the seuen and twentith, or (as the chronicles of Aniou haue) the eight and twentith daie of Iulie, the duke of Britains armie gaue battell to the French host néere to a towne called saint Aulbin, hauing apparelled a thousand and seuen hundred of the Britons in coates with red crosses, after the English fashion, to make the Frenchmen beleeue that they had a great number of Englishmen, although they had but foure hundred onelie with the lord Wooduile. The victorie in this battell fell to the Frenchmen, so that almost all the Englishmen were slaine with the

The battell of saint Aulbin in Britaine, betwéene the duke of Britaine and the French king.

the

Lord Wooduile
staine. the lord Wooduile, beside six thousand Britons. The duke of Orleance and the prince of Orainge were taken prisoners, which were there on the Britons part. The Frenchmen lost twelue hundred men, and amongst other, that valiant Italian capteine Iames Galeot.

King Henrie
sendeth foorth
his armie against
the French. These newes being brought into England, caused king Henrie to make hast in sending foorth his armie, and therefore was the lord Brooke, with sir Iohn Cheinie, sir Iohn Middleton, sir Rafe Hilton, sir Richard Corbet, sir Thomas Leighton, sir Richard Laton, and sir Edmund Cornewall sent ouer into Britaine with all conuenient speed, hauing with them an eight thousand men, well armed and furnished in warlike wise, to aid the duke of Britaine against the Frenchmen. These lustie capteins being arriued in Britaine, after they had a little refreshed them, marched forward, and comming neere to their enimies, pitched downe their field, not farre from the Frenchmens campe.

When the
French be in-
uincible. The Frenchmen by experience knowing the Englishmen (so long as they be fresh and lustie) in maner to be inuincible, thought not good to match with them in open battell, till they were somewhat wearied lieng and lingering abroad in the field. And therefore at the first they sought to wearie them with light skirmishes, appointing their horssemen to giue them alarmes, & some skirmishes; in the which the Frenchmen, by reason of the English archers (which galled both men and horsses) were euer put to the worsse. But behold the mutabilitie of worldlie chances! Whiles this warre was thus set forward, Francis duke of Britaine departed this life, & then Francis duke of
Britaine dieth. the cheefe rulers of Britaine, falling at dissention among themselues, tendered not the defense of their countrie, but rather minded the destruction thereof.

Herevpon the Englishmen, perceiuing in what danger they were, and considering that it was in the middest of winter, a time not meet for men of warre to lie in the cold and frostie fields, they returned into England, within fiue monethes after their first setting foorth. So that finallie the French king got the vpper hand of the Britons, The duchie of
Britane incor-
porated to the
realme of
France.
Iohn Stow.
The birth of
prince Arthur. and did incorporate that duchie to his realme and crowne of France, as in the historie of France it may appeere at large· ¶ In Iuly this yeere was a prest leuied for the king in the citie of London, of foure thousand pounds, which was repaied the yeare next following. In September, the quéene was deliuered at Winchester of her first sonne, named prince Arthur; and the fiue and twentith of Nouember (next insuing) she was crowned at Westminster with all due solemnitie.

An. Reg. 4. Yée haue heard, how there was in the last parlement monie granted for the furnishing foorth of the armie into Britaine; that is to wit, it was agréed, that euerie man should be taxed after the rate of his substance, to paie the tenth penie of his goods. Which monie the most part of them that dwelled in the bishoprike of Durham, and in the parties of Yorkeshire refused vtterlie to paie: either for that they thought themselues ouercharged with the same; or were procured to shew themselues disobedient, thorough the euill counsell of some seditious persons, which conspired against The collectors
of the subsidie
complaine to
the earle of Nor-
thumberland
that they can-
not get in the
tax monie.
1489. the king, to put him to new trouble. Therefore such as were appointed collectors, after that they could not get the monie, according to their extract deliuered to them by the commissioners, they made their complaint priuilie to Henrie the fourth earle of Northumberland, chiefe ruler of the North parts.

The earle of
Northumber-
land murthered
by the northerne
rebels at the in-
stigation and
setting on of
Iohn a Chamber. The earle foorthwith signified to the king all that matter, and the king not willing to pardon them of anie one penie (least the example might doo hurt by incouraging others to shew the like stubbornes in other parts of the realme) comanded the earle either by distresse or otherwise, to leuie the monie as he should thinke most meet. The rude and beastlie people hearing of this answer from the king, by and by with great violence set vpon the earle by the exciting of a simple fellow named Iohn a Chamber, whome the erle with faire words sought to appease. But they like vnreasonable villaines, alledging all the fault to be in him, as chiefe author of the tax, furiouslie and cruellie murthered both him and diuerse of his houshold seruants. Diuerse affirme

that

that the Northerne men bare against this earle continuall grudge euer since the death of king Richard, whom they entirelie fauoured.

Although this offense was great and heinous; yet there succéeded a more mischiefe : for incontinentlie (to cloke this presumptuous murther) the Northerne men got them to armour, and assembling togither, chose them a capteine, no lesse seditious than desirous of trouble, called sir Iohn Egremond knight; and passing by the countries, they published and declared that they would bid the king battell onlie in defense of their liberties & common fréedome, of the which he went about to beereaue them. But when the matter should come to be tried with blowes, their harts so fainted that they scattered awaie, euerie man séeking to saue himselfe by flight : but that little auailed them.

: A rebellion in the north for a tax granted by parlement.

Sir Iohn Egremond capteine rebell.

For the king hearing of this businesse, sent foorth Thomas earle of Surreie (whome not long before he had deliuered out of the Tower, and receiued to his speciall fauour) with a crue of men, to chastise those rebels of the north parts, who skirmished with a certeine companie of them, and them discomfited, and took aliue Iohn a Chamber, the first beginner of this rebellion. The king himselfe road after into Yorkeshire, of whose comming the sturdie rebels were so abashed and afraid, that they fled more and lesse; which afterward were apprehended, and punished according to their demerits. Yet the king of his clemencie pardoned the innocent people, and executed the chiefe procurers. For Iohn a Chamber was hanged at Yorke on a gibbet set vpon a square paire of gallowes like an archtraitor, and his complices and lewd disciples were hanged on the lower gallowes round about their maister, to the terrible example of other.

Thomas erle of Surrie sent with a power against the north rebels.

Iohn a Chāber hanged like an archtraitor.

But sir Iohn Egremond fled into Flanders to the ladie Margaret duchesse of Burgognie, that euer enuied the prosperitie of king Henrie. After this the king returned to London, leauing the earle of Surreie to rule the north parts, and appointed sir Richard Tunstall, a man of great wit and policie, to gather the subsidie to him due of the people. This yeare the king borrowed of euerie alderman of London two hundred pounds, and of the Chamber nine thousand eightie two pounds seuenteene shillings foure pence; which he repaied againe to the vttermost, with great equitie and thankefulnes. [A vertue verie laudable in this good king, and so much the more noteworthie as it is rare; speciallie in mightie men and great estates of the world, that count what soeuer they can catch their owne, as though the pursses of their people were theirs to possesse at pleasure & vse at lust, without conscience or care of restitution. Which foule fault Ecclesiasticus noteth (affirming that all is lost that is lent them) in expresse words, saieng :

Sir Iohn Egremond flieth into Flanders.

The king boroweth a gret summe of monie of the chāber of Londō.

Reddere magnates nolunt, quæ mutua sumunt,
Mutua quæ trades interiisse scias.]

Gu. Ha. in Ecle. cap. 8.

In this season, the emperour Frederike made warre against the Flemings, namelie against Bruges and certeine townes of Flanders, which had rebelled against his sonne Maximilian king of Romans, their liege and souereigne lord; in so much that they of Bruges had not onelie slaine his officers but imprisoned him within their towne, till they had caused him to pardon all their offenses, and also to sweare neuer to remember, nor reuenge the same in time to come. But his father Frederike the emperour could not suffer such a reproch & dishonour doone to his sonne (whose fame & princelie estate as he tendered and had in gelosie; so was it his hart gréefe and immoderat vexation that he should be abused of open contemners, in such villanous sort as tended highlie to the indignitie of his person, and the aggrauating of their offense and punishment) to passe vnreuenged, & therefore scourged the countrie of Flanders with sharpe and cruell warre.

A rebellion in Flanders.

Maximilian king of Romans imprisoned at Bruges by the townesmen.

The lord of Rauenstine being driuen to take the same oth, that his master Maximilian tooke at Bruges, to shew that the warre was not begun with his assent, forsooke Maximilian his lord, and tooke the townes of Ipre and Sluis, with both the castels of the same

same hauen, and further did not onelie stir the Cantois, Brugeans, and other towns of Flanders, to rebell against their souereigne lord; but also sent to the French kings lieutenant in Picardie, the lord Cordes, to aid him to conquer such townes of Flanders, as were not of his opinion. The lord Cordes, otherwise called monsieur de Querdes, was glad to haue so good occasion to set foot in Flanders, as he that had sufficient instructions of his maister the French king, vpon anie such offred occasion so to doo, sent foorthwith to the aid of the Flemings eight thousand Frenchmen, commanding them to conquer such townes, as were in the waie betwixt France and Bruges.

The capteins, according to his deuise, besieged a little walled towne called Dixmew, to whome came foure thousand Flemings with vittels and artillerie, sent from the lord of Rauenstein. They laid siege on the north side of the towne, in a marish ground then being drie, and so déepelie ditched and rampired their campe about (on which rampire they laid their ordinance) that it was in maner impossible to enter their campe, or doo them anie displeasure or damage. The K. of England was dailie aduertised of these dooings, which nothing lesse desired than to haue the English pale inuironed with French fortresses. Wherefore to preuent that mischiefe in time, with all expedition he sent ouer to the lord Daubeneie, then his deputie of Calis, the lord Morleie, with a crue of valiant archers & souldiers, to the number of a thousand men, with priuie instructions what they should doo.

At their comming ouer it was bruted abroad, that they were sent onelie to defend the English pale, against all attempts that might vpon the sudden in anie wise be made by the Frenchmen, or Flemings: but their enterprise was all otherwise. For on a tuesday at the shutting of the gates at night, the lord Daubneie chiefeteine of the armie, the lord Morleie, sir Iames Tirrell capteine of Guisnes, sir Henrie Willoughbie, sir Gilbert Talbot, and sir Humfreie Talbot marshall of Calis, with diuerse other knights, and esquiers, and other of the garisons of Hammes, Guisnes, and Calis, to the number of two thousand men or thereabouts, issued priuilie out of Calis, & passed the water of Graueling in the morning betimes; and left there for a stale, and to kéepe the passage, sir Humfreie Talbot, with six score archers, and came to Newport, where they found the souereigne of Flanders with six hundred Almaines, and there they staied that night.

On the next daie they went toward Dixmew, and by the guiding of a prisoner, that should haue béene hanged on the next morning, they issued out of the south gate of the towne of Dixmew, and were conueied by their said guide by an high banke set with willowes; so that the Cantois could not well espie them, and so secretlie gat to the end of their enimies campe, and there paused. The lord Daubeneie commanded all men to send their horsses and wagons backe, but the lord Morleie said he would ride till he came to hand strokes. Thus they marched foorth till they came to a low banke, and no déepe ditch, where the ordinance laie; and there the archers shot altogither, euerie man an arrow, and so fell prostrate to the ground. The enimies herewith discharged their ordinance, and ouershot them.

The Almains lept ouer the ditch with their morice pikes. The Englishmen in the fore-front waded the ditch, and were holpen vp by the Almains, and set on their enimies, and tooke manie prisoners. The other Englishmen hasted by the causie to enter in at the north gate of the campe, where the lord Morleie being on horssebacke in a rich coate, was slaine with a gun. When his death was knowen, euerie man killed his prisoner, and slue all such as did withstand them, to the number of eight thousand men; in so much that of two thousand that came out of Bruges (as the Flemish chronicle reporteth) there came not home one hundred. On the English part was slaine the lord Morleie, and not an hundred more.

The Englishmen tooke their ordinance and sent it to Newport, with all the spoile and great horsses. And by the waie hearing certeine Frenchmen to be at Ostend,
they

they made thitherward: but the Frenchmen fled, and so they burned part of the towne, and came againe to Newport, where the lord Daubeneie left all the Englishmen that were hurt and returned to Calis, where he buried the bodie of the lord Morleie. The Englishmen got great riches at this field, for they that went foorth in cloth, came home in silke, and those that went out on foot, came home on great horsses. The lord Cordes being at Ipre with twentie thousand men, was sore displeased with this ouerthrow; & therefore thinking to be reuenged, besieged the towne of Newport right stronglie, and shot dailie at the wals, breaking them in manie places.

The English souldiers inriched.

Newport besieged by the Frenchmen.

But the Englishmen that were hurt at Dixmew field before, and might either stand or draw bowe, neuer came from the wals. On a daie the Frenchmen gaue a great assault to a tower, and perforce entered it, and set vp the banner of the lord Cordes. But sée the chance! During the time of the assault, there arriued a barke with foure score fresh English archers, which came streight to the tower, and did so much, that what with the helpe of such as before were wounded and hurtmen, and of the couragious harts of the new come archers incouraged greatlie by the women of the towne, crieng; Shoot Englishmen, shoot: the tower was regained out of the Frenchmens hands, and the banner of the lord Cordes rent in péeces, and in place thereof the penon of saint George set vp. Then the Frenchmen, supposing a great aid of Englishmen to haue béene come to the towne by sea, left the assault.

English archers.

And the night following, the enuious lord Cordes (which so sore longed for Calis, that he would commonlie saie that he could be content to lie seuen yeares in hell, so that Calis were in possession of the Frenchmen) brake vp his siege, and returned to Helding with shame. And the Englishmen glad of this victorie returned to Calis. This yeare Iames the third of that name king of Scots was slaine by his owne subiects, after they had vanquished him in a pight field. About the same time one Adrian an Italian was sent in ambassage from pope Innocent the eight into Scotland, to haue taken vp the variance betwixt the king there and his people. But being arriued here in England, he was informed that king Iames was slaine, and therfore taried here certeine moneths.

The malicious and foolish words of the lord Cordes.

Iames king of Scots slaine by his owne subiects.

And for that he was a man of excellent learning, vertue, and humanitie, the archbishop of Canturburie Iohn Morton so commended him to the king, that he made him first bishop of Hereford, and shortlie after, that resigned and giuen ouer, he promoted him to the bishoprike of Bath and Welles. And after that with these honors he was returned to Rome, he was aduanced by all the degrées of spirituall dignities into the college of the cardinals. And worthie sure he was of great preferment, for by his meanes, learned men were mooued to séeke out the vse of eloquent writing and speaking in the Latine toong, he being the first in the time of our fathers that taught the trade to choose and vse apt words and fit termes.

Adrian an Italian made bishop of Hereford, and after of Bath and Welles.

In the sixt yeare of king Henries reigne there came ambassadors to him from the French king the lord Francis of Lutzenburgh, Charles Marignane, and Robert Gaguine minister of the Bonnehommes of the trinitie. The effect of their comming was to haue concluded a peace with king Henrie, and that with good will the French king might dispose of the mariage of the yoong duchesse of Britaine, as he should thinke good; and to make void the contract and former mariage, which by proxie the deputie of Maximilian king of Romans had before time contracted & made with hir. But thereto would not king Henrie gaue his consent, euer harping on this string, that the maiden being once lawfullie combined in matrimonie with Maximilian, ought not to be compelled against hir will and promise (yea and contrarie to all law, right and equitie) to take anie other person than him to hir spouse and husband.

1490

An. Reg. 6.

Ambassadors from the Frèch king to the king of England.

In deed king Henrie was loth that the French king should marrie the duchesse of Britaine himselfe (as he perceiued his meaning was) and so ioine the duchie of Britaine

K. Henrie is loth that the French king should marrie the duchesse of Britaine.

taine to the crowne of France: and therefore he did what he could to hinder that bargaine. Yet at length it was agréed that a forme of a league should be drawen with conditions, clauses, and couenants. And for full concluding of the same, it was thought expedient, that the king of England should send ambassadors to the French king to finish all matters betwixt them. Wherevpon the French ambassadors being dismissed with great rewards, streightwaies Thomas erle of Ormond, and Thomas Goldenston prior of Christes church in Canturburie, were appointed by the king to follow them into France, instructed fullie in althings that he would haue on his behalfe either mooued or determined.

Lionell bishop of Concordia sent from the pope to the French king.

In this meane space, Lionell the bishop of Concordia was sent as oratour from pope Alexander the sixt to the French king for certeine matters: and amongst other things, he had in charge to conclude a peace and vnitie betwixt the French king and the king of England. He moouing this matter to the French king, found him nothing strange to incline to his motion. Wherevpon the bishop of Concordia conceiuing good hope, and therewith desirous (as became him best bearing that title) to set an attonement betwixt those two kings, tooke his iournie towards England, to the intent he might mooue king Henrie to be agréeable therevnto, and so comming to Calis, found the English ambassadors there, being so farre on their waie towards the French king; and being honorablie receiued of them into that towne, after they had communed togither, the bishop tooke the sea, and was transported ouer into England, and the ambassadors departed towards the French king.

After the bishop of Concordia had talked with king Henrie, and perceiued that (vpon reasonable conditions) he could be content to conclude a peace with all christian princes, and to liue in rest after so manie troubles afore time susteined, the said bishop returned backe into France to sollicit this purpose to some perfect conclusion. But the Frenchmen so handled the matter, that whilest they outwardlie shewed how they

The duchesse of Britaine maried to K. Charles.

desired nothing but fréendship and amitie, they allured the yoong dutchesse of Britaine to submit hirselfe wholie to their discretion, so that shortlie after she was maried to king Charles. Now the English ambassadors, after they perceiued which waie the wind would blow, returned againe to their countrie, and nothing doone or agreed vpon in their matter.

A parlement wher n king Henrie openeth the iust cause of making warres against France.

King Henrie sore troubled in his mind therwith, determining no more with peaceable messages, but with open warre to determine all controuersies betwixt him and the French king, called his high court of parlement, and there declared the cause why hée was iustlie prouoked to make warre against the Frenchmen: and therefore desired them of their beneuolent aid of men and monie toward the maintenance therof. The cause was so iust, that euerie man allowed it; and to the setting foorth of the war taken in hand for so necessarie an occasion, euerie man promised his helping hand. The king commended them for their true and faithfull hearts. And to the intent that he might spare the poorer sort of the commons (whome he euer desired to kéepe in fauor) he thought good first to exact monie of the richest sort by waie of a beneuolence.

Who first leuised the exaction of monie called a beneuolence. Sée pag. 331.

Which kind of leuieng monie was first deuised by king Edward the fourth, as it appeareth before in his historie. King Henrie following the like example, published abroad, that by their open gifts he would measure and search their beneuolent hearts and good minds toward him; so that he that gaue most, should be iudged to be his most louing fréend; and he that gaue little, to be esteemed according to his gift. By this it appeareth, that whatsoeuer is practised for the princes profit, and brought to a president by matter of record, maie be turned to the great preiudice of the people, if rulers in authoritie will so adiudge and determine it. But by this means king Henrie got innumerable great summes of monie, with some grudge of the people. for the extremitie shewed by the commissioners in diuers places.

Ye

Ye haue heard before, how the lord of Rauenstein, by the aid of Bruges & Gant, had taken the towne and two castels of Sluis, which he kept against his souereigne lord Maximilian, and getting into the hauen certeine ships and barks, robbed, spoiled, & tooke prisoners the ships and vessels of all nations that passed alongest by that coast, towards the mart at Antwerpe, or into anie part of Brabant, Zeland, or Friseland, and was euer sufficientlie vittelled out of France and Picardie. There was a little towne also two miles from Bruges towards the sea, called Dam, which was a bulworke to Bruges, and an hedspring to Sluis. The king of Romans had attempted the wining of this towne diuerse times, but missed his purpose; till at length Albert duke of Saxonie, a great fréend to the king of Romans, by policie found meanes to get it.

Albert the duke of Saxonie policie to get the towne of Dam.

This duke feining himselfe as a neuter betwixt the king of Romans, and the rebels of Flanders, required of the lords of Bruges, that he might enter peaceablie into their towne according to his estate, with a certeine number of men of armes, to communicate with them diuerse matters of great weight, and sent before his cariages and herbengers to make prouision. They of Bruges were in no doubt of him, so that his men of warre entered into the citie in good order, and he followed. They that went before, inquired for innes and lodgings, as though they would haue rested there all the night, and so went foorth still in order asking after lodgings, till they came at the gate that leadeth directlie toward Dam, distant from Bruges a Flemish mile, which is called the bulworke of Bruges.

The capteins and inhabitants of Dam suspecting no harme to come out of Bruges, thought their fréends (knowing some danger towards) had sent them aid, and so nothing mistrusting those that approched their towne, suffered them to enter, and so was the towne of Dam taken by sleight, which could not be woone by open force. This chance sore displeased them of Bruges, for now could they haue no recourse to the sea; so that they must néeds fall into ruine and decaie. The duke of Saxonie thus hauing woone the towne of Dam, sent to the king of England, that if it would please him to minister anie aid by sea, hée would besiege Sluis by land. Wherevpon the king of England, vpon due consideration of the dukes motion (as he was wise enough in all his enterprises, and no lesse fortunate in the issue of the same) would conclude nothing vpon the sudden, but (as he did alwaies) ruled his affaires by good counsell, like to the wise man commended in the holie scripture:

The duke of Saxonie sendeth for aid to king Henrie to win Sluis.

Consilio sapiens semper sua facta gubernat.

Gu. Ha. in Tob. 4.

At last he well remembring that Sluis was a rousenest, and a verie den of théeues to them that trauersed the seas towards the east parts, incontinentlie dispatched sir Edward Poinings a right valiant knight and hardie capteine, with twelue ships well furnished with bold souldiers and sufficient artillerie. Which sir Edward sailed into the hauen, and kept the lord of Rauenstein from starting by sea. The Duke of Saxonie besieged one of the castels, lieng in a church ouer against it: and the Englishmen assaulted the lesse castell, and issued out of their ships at the ebbe, neuer suffering their enimies to rest in quiet one day togither, for the space of twentie daies, and euerie day slue some of their aduersaries; and on the English part were slaine one Vere, brother to the earle of Oxford, and fiftie more.

Sir Edward Poinings a valiant capteine sent into Flanders with an armie.

One Vere brother to the earle of Oxford slaine.

The lord of Rauenstein had made a bridge of botes betwéene both the castels, to passe from the one to the other; which bridge one night the Englishmen did set on fire. Then he, perceiuing that he must lose his castels by force, and that the Flemings could not aid him, yéelded the castels to sir Edward Poinings, and the towne to the duke of Saxonie, vpon certeine conditions. Sir Edward Poinings kept the castels a while, of whom the Almains demanded their wages, bicause the duke had nothing to paie. Then these two capteins so handled them of Bruges, that they not onelie submitted themselues to their lord Maximilian; but also were contented to paie and dis-

3 O 2

patch

patch the Almains. And so sir Edward Poinings taried there a long space, aud at length returned to the king before Bullogne.

The sixt day of Aprill this present yeare, the nobles of the realme assembled in the cathedrall church of S. Paule in London, where the maior of the same citie, his brethren the aldermen, and the craftesmen in their liueries also assembled: to whome doctor Morton chancellor made an oration, declaring how the king of Spaine had woone the great and rich citie & countrie of Granado from the Turks: for ioy whereof Te Deum was soong with great solemnitie. ¶ But bicause it is requisite and necessarie in this ample volume, to set downe the report of accidents as they are to be found at large in our owne English writers: you shall heare for the furtherance of your knowledge in this matter concerning Granado, what Ed. Hall hath left noted in his chronicle. Which although it conteine diuerse actions of superstition, and popish trumperie: yet should it not offend the reader, considering that a people estranged from the true knowledge of God and sincere religion put the same in practise, as supposing principall holinesse to consist in that blind deuotion.

Abr. Fl. ex I. S. pag. 866.

Abr. Fl. ex Edw. Hall, in Hen. 7. *fo.* xxiij. &c.

Granado woone from the Turkes or Saracens.

On the sixt of Aprill (saith he) this yéere, the king commanded all the nobilitie of his realme to assemble at the cathedrall church of S. Paule in London, where (after Te Deum solemnlie soong the cardinall of Canturburie, standing on the steps before the quier doore, declared to the people, how the famous citie of Granado, which manie yeares had beene possessed of the Moores or Mauritane nation, being infidels & vnchristened people, was now of late besieged a great time by Don Ferdinando and Elizabeth his wife, king and quéene of Spaine, Arragon, and Castile. And the said infidels, by reason of siege brought to great penurie and miserie, for lacke of vittels & necessarie viands, perceiuing that all succours were clerelie stopped and excluded from them, and so brought into vtter despaire of aid, or comfort, after long consultation had amongst them, determined to render themselues and their citie to the said king vpon diuerse couenants and conditions, and therevpon sent to him diuerse senators of the citie fullie instructed of their mind and purpose.

The king of Spaine and his councell, considering and sagelie pondering that winter approched & was at hand, and that the christian host had long lied in the fieldes in sore tempests and greeuous stormes (which they gladlie suffered for Christes sake, in whose cause and quarell they made that present warre) remembring also that the citie was of such riches, fame, and estimation, that it conteined an hundred and fiftie thousand houses of name, beside other small houses and cotages; & that it was replenished with people innumerable, and furnished with three score and ten thousand good fighting men; and finallie, perceiuing that he might inioy now the possession of the same, without assault or effusion of christian bloud, by the aduice of his councell, he accepted, accorded, and agreed to their offers the twentie and fift of Nouember, in the yeare of Christs incarnation 1491, then being the daie of saint Katharine.

The citie of Granado conteined an hundred and fiftie thousand houses, besides cotages & small dwellings.

By the which composition, the roiall citie of Granado, with all the holds and fortresses of the realme, and the towers and castels of Alpussarare was rendered into the hands of the said king of Spaine; and that the king of Granado should become subiect and vassall to the king of Spaine, and to relinquish and forsake the vsurped name of a king foreuer: and that all the men of warre should frankelie depart out of the citie, and none there to remaine, but artificers and merchants: and all these things to be doone before the fiue and twentith day of Ianuarie. But the time was preuented, for the moores on the first day of Ianuarie sent six hundred notable personages out of the citie with their children for hostages into the campe of the king of Spaine, to the intent that he should put no diffidence nor mistrust in the citizens, but that he might peaceablie and quietlie with his people enter into the citie, and take possession of the same. The which hostages were distributed and lodged in the tents and pauillions of the Spanish armie.

Hostages deliuered to the K. of Spaine for his securitie.

The

The third of Ianuarie, the lord of Guitterins Cardenes, great master & gouernor of Lion, of the order of S. Iames, departed from the armie, noblie and triumphantlie accompanied with fiue hundred horsmen, and thrée thousand footmen toward the citie. And as he approched néere to the suburbs, there issued out diuers noble and valiant capteins of the Moores, making to him humble obeisance, and conducted him to a palace adioining to the citie, called the palace of Anaxaras, and from thence conueied him to the palace roiall of the same citie called Alhambra, whereof hée tooke quiet and peaceable possession, to the behoofe of the king of Spaine, whome the Moores promised and confessed to take and obeie as their king and souereigne lord. And in signe and token that they thought in their hearts, that which they promised by mouth; they prostrated and humbled themselues before the said great master, and with dolorous lamentation and salt teares deliuered tò him the keies of the said palace. _{The vanquished people humblie submit théselues to the kings vicegerent, & deliuer vp the keies of the citie.}

When he had the keies, and was also possessed of that strong and magnificent place, he first of all dispatched the house of all the Moores and pagans, and appointed a garrison of valiant and noble christians, to kéepe and defend the same: and the same day caused a masse solemnlie to be celebrate in a place of the same palace called Melchita; which done and finished, he tooke possession of all the fortresses, towers, and holds to the said citie and towne of Granado belonging or apperteining. And then he caused to be erected and set vp on the highest tower of the palace (where it might best be séene) the signe and token of the crosse, whereon Christ for vs sinners suffered his bitter passion. At the raising whereof weré present an archbishop and thrée bishops, with other prelats, which deuoutlie sang this antheme: O crux, aue spes vnica.

The said crosse was thrée times deuoutlielifted, and at euerie exaltation, the Moores being within the citie, rored, howled, & cried, prostrating themselues, groueling on the ground, & making dolorous noise and pitifull outcries. The armie incamped without the citie, séeing these things, humbled themselues méekelie before the crosse, rendering to almightie God their most humble and heartie thankes. The king of Spaine, being mounted on horssebacke, perceiuing the erection of the crosse, descended from his genet, and knéeled downe on the bare ground; and rendered to God, laud, honour, and praise; for that noble and triumphant victorie. And after that the crosse was thus set vp on the high tower, the banner of saint Iames, and the kings banners were pitched and fixed vpon the turrets and pinacles of the citie: an herald standing in the top of the high tower, proclaming and publishing these words following. _{The maner of the Spanish kings giuing of thanks for victorie.}

" Saint Iames, saint Iames, saint Iames; Castile, Castile, Castile; Granado, Granado, Granado. By high and mightie power, lord Ferdinando and Elizabeth, king and quéene of Spaine, haue woone from the infidels and Moores the citie and realme of Granado, through the helpe of our Lord God, & the most glorious virgin his mother, and the vertuous apostle S. Iames and the holie father Innocent the eight, togither with the aids and succours of the great prelats, knights, and other gentlemen borne, and commons of their realmes and countries." When the herald had finished, the artillerie sounded, the minstrels blew, the people applauded and clapped their hands, for gladnesse, that the earth séemed to tremble and quake vnderneath them. _{The Spaniards reioising & triumphing after the conquest of the Moores.}

After this ioy ended, there issued out of the citie in maner of procession, seuen hundred and mo christians, as well men, as women and children, which had bin there prisoners and liued in bonds, seruitude, and miserable captiuitie, whereof the most part were naked, wounded, and in maner famished for hunger. To whome the king (of his great liberalitie) gaue both apparell, viands and monie. These poore prisoners comming out of the citie sang this psalme; Benedictus Dominus Deus Israel, qui visitauit & fecit redemptionem pledis suæ; Blessed be the Lord God of Israel, which

hath

hath visited and redeemed his people. And so singing foorth the psalme, went to the church of saint Faith, which the king Ferdinando had caused to bée most sumptuouslie edified during the time of the siege, being distant from Granado two or thrée miles.

Now as this poore procession passed by the host, one espied his sonne, and another saw his brother; and the son perceiued the father, and the father found the daughter, which were now deliuered out of miserable seruitude and bondage. But they could not refraine nor bridle themselues from distilling of teares and sobbing, séeing their parents and kinsfolke restored to libertie & fréedome. And when these people had said their orisons in the church of saint Faith, and were come to the armie, they knéeled before the king, kissed his féet, crieng with one voice; God grant to the

The lord Euerus de Mēdoza made capteine of the house roiall. king of Spaine euerlasting life. The next daie after the lord Euerus de Mendoza, earle of Tendiglie, was by the king made capteine of the house roiall and principall tower of the citie of Granado, called Alhambra, hauing to him appointed and assigned one thousand men of armes, and two thousand footmen. Vnto the which earle, the great master deliuered the keies of the said palace and tower, and other ports and fortresses.

A great number of states with their traine enter triumphantlie into Granado to take reall possession. On saturday the eight daie of Ianuarie, in the yeare of our Lord 1492, Ferdinando, K. of Spaine & Granado, the quéene, & their eldest son Don Iohn prince of Spaine, the lord Peter of Mendoza, the archbish. of Toledo, the patriarch of Alexandria, the cardinall of Spaine, the lord Peter prince of Lion, the duke of Gaditan, the marques of Villena & Moia, the erle of Capre, the earle of Vienna of Cifnentes, and manie other earles, barons and nobles, whereof some were Englishmen (whose names I haue not) with ten thousand horssemen, and fiftie thousand footmen, with great triumph and roialtie entered into the citie of Granado, and thereof tooke reall possession & seazine, and caused masse to be soong in a great place called Melchita, where hée caused a solemne church to be builded in the honour of God and his mother. When masse was ended, the king and quéene repaired to the palace roiall of Alhambra, the which was woonderfull, both in qualitie & sumptuous building, which house was adorned with rich arras and tapestrie in euerie chamber.

The earle of Tendiglie capteine of the palace, feasted the king and queene, and all the nobilitie at his owne costes and charges. So the king of Spaine there remained till the countrie was reduced into a good conformitie and order, and diuerse fortresses and castels were made for the safegard and tuition of the realme. And bicause this victorie obteined, was to the glorie of God, and to the publike wealth of all christianitie, the

* Namelie doctor Morton, of whom mentiō is made in the beginning of this historie. * said cardinall of Canturburie declared to the people, that the king had sent him and the other nobles thither that day, not onelie to notifie and declare to them the veritie of the fact; but also to exhort them to giue lauds and praisings to almightie God, for deliuering so goodlie a citie, so plentifull a countrie, and so notable a region out of the hands of his enimies, and persecutors of his faith and religion. Which declaration ended the archbishop with the cleargie & the nobles with the communaltie, in most deuout maner went in generall procession, rendering to God for this great atchiued enterprise, glorie, honour, and most reuerent thanks.]

Abr. Fl. ex I. S. pag. 866. ¶ In the moneth of Maie next and immediatlie following this triumph, was holden a great and valiant iusting within the kings palace of Shine, now named Richmond, the which indured by the space of a moneth, sometime within the said palace and sometime without, vpon the greene before the gate of the said palace. In which

Sir Iames Parker by casualtie at iustes mortallie wounded.
Two pardoners set on the pillorie. iustes sir Iames Parker knight, running against a gentleman named Hugh Vauhan, by casualtie was so sore hurt and brused, that he died thereof. This yeare also two pardoners were set on the pillorie in Cornehill thrée market daies, for forging of false pardons, wherewith they had deceiued the people, & got much monie. And for that one of them had feined himselfe to be a priest, hee was sent to Newgate, where he died: the other was driuen out of London with shame enough. ¶ Also this yere was

Robert

Robert Fabian shiriffe of London & alderman, who made a chronicle of England & of Robert
France, beginning at the creation of the world, and ending in the third yeare of the
reigne of king Henrie the eight, which booke is now imprinted to the end of Richard
the third.]

Maximilian king of Romans, intending to be reuenged on the Frenchmen for the
manie iniuries doone to him of late (and especiallie for that king Charles had forsaken his daughter ladie Margaret, and purposed to take to wife the ladie Anne of
Britaine) bicause he was not rich enough to mainteine the warre of himselfe, he sent
his ambassadour, one Iames Contibald, a man of great wisedome, to require the king
of England to take his part against the French king, making diuers great offers on
his owne behalfe, if it should please him so to doo.

King Henrie no lesse desirous than Maximilian to put the French king to trouble,
and chieflie to aid the Britains in the extremitie of their businesse, gladlie consented
to the request of Maximilian; and promised to prepare an armie with all speed, and
in time conuenient to passe the seas with the same, and inuade the French territories.
In this verie season, Charles the French king receiued the ladie Anne of Britaine, as his
pupill into his hands, and with great solemnitie hir espoused, hauing with hir in dower,
the whole duchie of Britaine.

Now was Maximilian in great chafe toward the French king, not onelie for that he had
refused his daughter, but also had beréeued him of his assured wife the said ladie
Anne, contrarie to all right and conscience. Wherefore he sent vnto king Henrie,
desiring him with all speed to passe the seas with his armie, that they might pursue
the warre against their aduersarie, with fire, sword and bloud. King Henrie hearing
this, and hauing no mistrust in the promise of Maximilian, with all speed leuied an
armie, and rigged his nauie of ships. And when all things were readie he sent his almoner Christopher Urswike, and sir Iohn Riseleie knight vnto Maximilian, to certifie
him, that the king was in a readinesse, and would arriue at Calis, as soone as he
should be aduertised that Maximilian and his men were readie to ioine with him.

These ambassadors comming into Flanders perceiued that Maximilian was neither
purueied of men, monie, nor armor, nor of any other thing neccessarie for the setting
foorth of warre; sauing onlie that his will was good, although his power was small.
King Henrie being aduertised hereof by letters sent to him from his said ambassadors,
was sore disquieted in his mind, and was almost brought to his wits end, to consider
how his companions in arms should thus faile him at néed; but taking aduise of his
counsell, at length he determined not to stay his prepensed iournie, and therfore he so
increased his numbers before he tooke ship, that he with his owne power might be
able to match with his aduersaries. When he had thus gathered and assembled his
armie, hée sailed to Calis the sixt day of October, and there incamped himselfe for
a space, to see all his men and prouision in such readinesse, as nothing should be wanting.

In this place all the armie had knowledge by the ambassadours (which were newlie
returned out of Flanders) that Maximilian could not set foorth anie armie, for lacke
of monie: and therefore there was no succour to be looked for at his hand. But the
Englishmen were nothing dismaid therewith, as they that iudged themselues able
enough to match the Frenchmen without the helpe of anie other nation. In the meane
season, although the French king had an armie togither, both for number and furniture able to trie in battell with the Englishmen: yet he made semblance as though he
desired nothing more than peace, as the thing much more profitable to him than warre:
considering the minds of the Britains were not wholie setled.

And againe, he was called into Italie to make warre against the king of Naples,
whose kingdome he pretended to apperteine to him by lawfull succession from his father

ther king Lewes, to whome Reine duke of Aniou last king of Sicill, of the house of Aniou, had transferred his right to that kingdome (as partlie before ye haue heard) wrongfullie and without cause disinheriting his coosine, godsonne and heire, Reine

A motion on the French part for a treatie of peace with the English.

duke of Loraine and Bar. The lord Chordes hauing commission from his maister the French king to make some entrie into a treatie for peace with the king of England, wrote letters to him before he passed ouer to Calis, signifieng to him that if it might stand with his pleasure to send some of his councellors to the borders of the English pale adioining to France, there should be so reasonable conditions of peaceproffered, that he doubted not but his grace might with great honour breake vp his campe, and retire his armie home againe.

The king of England considering that Britaine was cléerelie lost, and past recouerie, and that Maximilian for lacke of monie, and mistrust which he had in his owne subiects, laie still like a dormouse dooing nothing; and herewith weieng that it should be honorable to him, and profitable to his people to determine this great warre without bloudshed, appointed the bishop of Excester, and Giles lord Daubenie to passe the

Commissioners sent ouer to Calis about the said peace.

seas to Calis, and so to commun with the lord Chordes of articles of peace, which tooke effect as after ye shall perceiue. In the meane time, whilest the commissioners were communing of peace on the marches of France, the king of England (as ye haue heard) was arriued at Calis: from whense after all things were prepared for such a

Bullogne besieged by the Englishmen the king himselfe present.

iournie, he remooued in foure battells forward, till he came néere to the towne of Bullogne, & there pitched his tents before it in a conuenient place for his purpose, meaning to assaile the towne with his whole force & puissance.

But there was such a strong garison of warlike souldiers within that fortresse, and such plentie of artillerie, and necessarie munitions of warre, that the losse of Englishmen assaulting the towne (as was doubted) should be greater damage to the realme of England, than the gaining thereof should be profit. Howbeit the dailie shot of the kings battering peeces brake the wals, and sore defaced them. But when euerie man was readie to giue the assault, a sudden rumor rose in the armie that peace was concluded: which brute as it was pleasant to the Frenchmen, so was it displesant to the Englishmen, bicause they were prest and readie at all times to set on their enimies, and brought into great hope to haue béene inriched by the spoile and gaine to haue fallen to their lots of their enimies goods, beside the glorious fame of renowmed victorie.

Why the English preferred warre before peace.

And therefore to be defrauded hereof by an vnprofitable peace, they were in great fume, and verie angrie: and namelie, for that diuerse of the capteins to set themselues and their bands the more gorgeouslie forward, had borrowed large summes of monie, and for the repaiment had morgaged their lands and possessions, and some happilie had made through sale thereof, trusting to recouer all againe by the gaines of this iournie. Wherefore offended with this sudden conclusion of peace, they spake euill, both of the king and his councell. But the king like a wise prince asswaged their displeasure in part with excusing the matter, alledging what losse and bloudshed was like to insue both of capteins and souldiers, if the assault should haue béene giuen to the vtterance, especiallie sith the towne was so well furnished with men and munitions. When he had somewhat appeased their minds with these and manie other reasons, he returned backe againe to Calis.

Polydor.
Sir Iohn Sauage slaine at this siege.

There were not manie of the English armie lost at this siege of Bullogne, & few or no men of name, sauing that valiant capteine sir Iohn Sauage knight, the which, as he and sir Iohn Riselie rode about the wals of the towne, to view in what place it might be easiliest assaulted, was compassed about by certeine Frenchmen that were issued out of the towne, and there slaine standing at defense and vtterlie refusing to yéeld himselfe as prisoner. But sir Iohn Riselie escaped by flieng awaie. When the K.

was

was thus returned to Calis, he began to smell a certeine secret smoke, which was like to turne to a great flame, without wise foresight, and good looking to. For by the craftie inuention, and diuelish imagination of the ladie Margaret duchesse of Burgognie, a new idoll was set vp in Flanders, and by a forged name called Richard Plantagenet second sonne to king Edward the fourth, as though he had béene raised from death to life.

Richard Platagenet a counterfeit of ladie Margarets imagining.

The newes hereof somewhat troubled him, so that he was with better will content to receiue the honorable conditions of peace offered of his enimie: bicause he should not be constreined at one time to make warre both at home, and also in a forren region. The conclusion of this agréement made with the Frenchmen, was this: That this peace should continue both their liues; and that the French king should pay to the king of England a certeine summe of monie in hand, according as the commissioners should appoint for his charges susteined in this iournie. Which (as the king certified the maior of London by his letters the ninth of Nouember) amounted to the summe of seuen hundred fortie and fiue thousand duckats: the which is of sterling monie, one hundred foure score and six thousand, two hundred and fiftie pounds. It was also concluded that he should yearelie (for a certeine space) paie or cause to be paid, for the monie that the K. had spent & expended in the defense of the Britans fiue & twentie thousand crowns.

The conclusion of peace betwéene the English and French.

Which yearelie tribute the French king (afterwards continuallie occupied in the wars of Italie) yearelie satisfied & paid so long as K. Henrie liued, who after he had taried a conuenient space at Calis, tooke the sea, and arriued at Douer, and so came to his manour of Gréenewich. Immediatlie after his returne thus into England, he elected into the fellowship of saint George, commonlie called the order of the garter, Alphonse duke of Calabre, sonne and heire to Ferdinando king of Naples, Christopher Urswike the kings almoner was sent to him vnto Naples with the garter, collar, mantell, and other habilments apperteining to the companions of that noble order. The which was reuerentlie receiued of the said duke, who in a solemne presence reuested himselfe with that habit, supposing by the countenance of that apparell to be able to resist his aduersarie the French king, sith he was now made a fréend and companion in order with the king of England: but that little auailed him, as after it was right apparant. [And here, bicause in sundrie actions we haue séene and obserued the French kings subtilties, his inconstancie, lacke of truth, honestie, and kinglie modestie; we maie be bold to set downe the description of his person, as we find the same readie drawne to hand; that by a view thereof we maie conclude that his properties were proportioned to his person.

Alphōse duke of Calabre made knight of the garter.

It is verie certeine (saith mine author) that king Charles from his infancie was of complexion verie delicate and of bodie vnsound and diseased, of small stature, and of face (if the aspect and dignitie of his eies had béene taken awaie) fowle and deformed, his other members bearing such equall proportion, that he séemed more a monster than a man: he was not onelie without all knowledge of good sciences, but scarselie he knew the distinct characters of letters: his mind desirous to command, but more proper to anie other thing, for that being inuironed alwaies with his familiars and fauourits, he reteined with them no maiestie or authoritie: he reiected all affaires and businesse, and yet if he did debate and consider in anie, he shewed a weake discretion and iudgement. And if he had any thing in him that caried apparance of merit or praise, yet being thoroughlie weied and sounded, it was found further off from vertue than from vice: he had an inclination to glorie, but it was tempered more with rashnesse and furie than with moderation and counsell: his liberalities were without discretion, measure or distinction: immooueable oftentimes in his purposes, but that was rather an ill grounded obstinacie than constancie. And that which manie call bountie, deserued more reasonablie in him the name of coldnesse & slackenesse of spirit.]

Abr. Fl. ex. Guic. pag. 43. The French king described.

The birth of
Henrie duke
of Yorke, after
crowned king by
the name of
Henrie the eight.

This yeare the two and twentith of Iune, was borne at Gréenewich the lord Henrie second sonne to this king Henrie the seuenth, which was created duke of Yorke, & after prince of Wales, and in conclusion succéeded his father in gouernance of this realme, by the name of Henrie the eight, father to our gratious souereigne quéene Elizabeth. But now to returne to the new found sonne of king Edward coniured by mens policies from death to life: ye shall vnderstand that the duchesse of Burgognie euer desiring to cast a scorpion in the bosome of king Henrie, not for anie displeasure by him towards hir wrought or doone; but onelie bicause he was descended of the house of Lancaster, being an enimie to hir line, began to spin a new web, like a spider that dailie weaueth when his kall is torne: for after that the earle of Lincolne, which was by hir set foorth, had missed the cushin, and lost both horsse and spurres, she could not be quiet, vntill she had practised a new deuise to put king Henrie to trouble. And as the diuell prouideth venemous sauce to corrupt stomachs, so for hir purpose she espied a certeine yoong man of visage beautifull, of countenance demure, and of wit craftie and subtill.

1492

The malice of
th' duchesse of
Burgognie to the
line of Lancaster.

Perkin War-
becke the
counterfeit duke
of Yorke.

This youths name was Peter Warbecke, one for his faintnesse of stomach of the Englishmen in derision called Perkin Warbecke, according to the dutch phrase, which change the name of Peter to Perkin, of yoonglings and little boies, which for want of age, lacke of strength, and manlike courage, are not thought worthie of the name of a man. This yoong man trauelling many countries, could speake English and diuerse other languages; & for his basenesse of birth and stocke, was almost vnknowne of all men; and driuen to séeke liuing from his childhood, was constreined to go and trauell thorough manie countries. The duchesse glad to haue got so meet an organ for the conueieng of hir inuented purpose, as one not vnlike to be taken and reputed for the duke of Yorke, sonne to hir brother king Edward, which was called Richard, kept him a certeine space with hir priuilie.

The readie wit
of Perkin to
learne all that
made for his
preferment to
honor.

Besides that, she with such diligence instructed him both in the secrets and common affaires of the realme of England, and of the linage, descent and order of the house of Yorke, that like a good scholer, not forgetting his lesson, he could tell all that was taught him promptlie without anie stackering or staie in his words. And besides that, he kept such a princelie countenance, and so counterfeit a maiestie roiall, that all men in manner did firmelie beléeue, that he was extracted of the noble house and familie of the dukes of Yorke. For suerlie, it was a gift giuen to that noble progenie, as of nature planted in the root, that all the sequels of that line and stocke did studie and deuise how to be equiualent in honour and fame with their forefathers and noble predecessors.

The emulatiō of
the dukes of
Yokre.

When the duches had framed hir cloath méet for the market, she was informed that king Henrie prepared to make warre against Charles the French king. Wherefore she, thinking that the time serued well for the setting foorth of hir malicious inuention, sent this Perkin hir new inuented mawmet, first into Portingale, and so craftilie into the countrie of Ireland; to the intent that he, being both wittie and wilie, might inuegle the rude Irishmen (being at those daies more inclined to rebellion than to reasonable order) to a new seditious commotion. Shortlie after his arriuall in Ireland, whether by his shrewd wit, or the malicious exhortation of the sauage Irish gouernours, he entred so farre in credit with the people of that Ile, that his words were taken to be as true, as he vntruelie with false demonstrations set foorth and published them.

Perkin War-
becke arriueth
in Ireland.

The French king aduertised hereof, then being in displeasure with king Henrie, sent into Ireland for Perkin, to the intent to send him against king Henrie, which was then inuading France (as yée before haue heard.) Perkin thought himselfe aloft, now that he was called to the familiaritie of kings, and therefore with all diligence sailed into France, and comming to the kings presence, was of him roiallie receiued and

after

after a princelie fashion interteined, and had a gard to him assigned, whereof was Perkin saileth into France all aflant. gouernour the lord Congreshall: and to him being at Paris, resorted sir George Neuill bastard, sir Iohn Tailor, Rowland Robinson, and an hundred English rebels. Now, after that a peace (as before is said) was concluded betwixt the French king, and the king of England, the French king dismissed Perkin, and would no longer kéepe him.

But some haue said (which were there attending on him) that Perkin, fearing least the French king should deliuer him to the king of England, beguiled the lord Congreshall, aud fled from Paris by night. But whether the French king knew of his Perkin returneth to the ladie Margaret his first founder. departure or not, the truth is, that he being in maner in despaire, returned to his first founder the ladie Margaret, of whome he was so welcomed to all outward appearance, that it séemed she could not haue reioised at anie earthlie thing more, than she did at his presence, and (as she could well dissemble) she made semblance as though she had neuer séene him before that time. Now as she had sore longed to know not once, but diuerse times in open audience, and in solemne presence, she willed him to declare and shew by what means he was preserued from death and destruction, and in what countries he had wandered and sought fréendship; and finallie, by what chance of fortune he came to hir court.

This did shée, to the intent that by the open declaration of these fained phantasies, the people might be persuaded to giue credit, and beléeue that he was the true begotten sonne of hir brother king Edward. And after this, shee assigned to him a gard of thirtie persons in murrie and blew, and highlie honoured him as a great estate, and Perkin named by the dutches of Burgognie the whtie rose of England. 1493 called him the white rose of England. The nobilitie of Flanders did to him all reuerence. [All which port and pompe exhibited in most solemne sort, he was well content to take vpon him, forgetting the basenesse of his birth, and glorieng in the counterfeit title of honour: much like the iay that would be called a swan, or like the crow that trimming hir selfe with the stolne feathers of a pecocke, would séeme Iunos bird; as the poet saith:

> ————mentito nomine cygnum
> Graculus appellat sese, cornicula plumas *M. Pal, in virg.*
> Pauonis furata cupit pauo ipsa videri.

¶ In this yeare was one Hugh Clopton maior of London, and of the staple, a *Abr. Fl. ex. I. S. paz.* 865. Stratford bridge vpon Auen builded. gentleman, borne at Clopton village, halfe a mile from Stratford vpon Auen by north, who continued (during his life) a bacheler: he builded the great and sumptuous bridge of Stratford vpon Auen, at the east end of the towne. This bridge hath fouretéene great arches, and a long cawsie with smaller arches, all made of stone, new walled on each side. At the west end of the bridge, he builded a faire large chappell. Toward the south end of that towne, & néere vnto the same a pretie house of bricke and timber, where he laie, and ended his life. He glased the chancell of the parish church in that towne, and made a waie of foure miles long, thrée miles from Alesburie towards London, and one mile beyond Alesburie.]

But to returne to Perkin: the brute of whome in England, blowne throughout the Such long and looked for alteration of states. realme, sore disquieted the people, insomuch that not onelie the meaner sort, but also manie of the nobles and worshipfull personages beléeued and published it abroad, that all was true which was reported of him. And not onelie they that were in sanctuaries but also manie other that were fallen in debt, assembled in a companie, and passed ouer the seas into Flanders, to their counterfeit duke of Yorke, otherwise rightlie named Perkin Warbecke. Truelie the realme of England was in maner diuided (with the rumor and vaine fable spred abroad of this twise borne duke) into partakings and False rumors occasions of great disquietnes. contrarie factions. And some of the noble men conspired togither, purposing to aid the foresaid Perkin, as the man whome they reputed to be the verie sonne of king

Edward;

Edward; and that the matter was not feigned, but altogither true, iust, and not imagined of any malicious pretense or euill purpose.

And bicause the thing was weightie, and required great aid and assistance, therefore they determined to send messengers vnto the ladie Margaret, to know when Richard duke of Yorke might conuenientlie come into England; to the intent that they being thereof certified, might be in a readinesse to helpe and succour him at his

An. Reg. 8. arriuall. So by the common consent of the conspirators, sir Robert Clifford knight, and William Barlcie, were sent into Flanders, which discouered to the duches all the secret intents and priuie meanings of the fréends and fautors of the new found duke. The duches gladlie receiued this message, and after shee had heard their errand, shée

Perkin counter-
feiteth the duke
of Yorke verie
cunninglie. brought the messenger to the sight of Perkin, who so well counterfeited the gesture, countenance, and maner of Richard duke of Yorke, that sir Robert Clifford beléeued verelie, that he was the second sonne of king Edward; and therefore wrote a letter of credit into England to his complices: and to put them out of doubt, he affirmed that he knew him to be king Edwards sonne by his face, and other lineaments of his bodie.

Vpon this letter, the chéefe dooers in this businesse spred the signification thereof abroad through the realme, to the intent to stirre the people to some new tumult and commotion: but it was doone by such a secret craft, that no man could tell who was the author of that rumor. The king perceiued that this vaine fable was not vanished out of the mad brains of the common people. To prouide therefore against all perils that might thereby insue, he sent certeine knights that were skilfull men of warre, with competent bands of soldiers, to kéepe the sea coasts and hauens, to vnderstand who came in and went out of the realme; doubting least some great conspiracie were in brewing against him. He also sent into the low countries certeine persons, to learne

Perkins true
linage. the truth of this forged dukes progenie, where some of them that were so sent, comming to Tournie, got knowledge that he was borne in that citie, of base linage, and named Perkin Warbecke.

The king then aduertised not onelie by his espials vpon their returne, but also from other his trustie freends, determined with all spéed to haue the fraud published, both in England and forren parts: and for the same cause sent sir Edward Poinings knight,

Ambassadors
sent to Philip
archduke of
Burgognie. & sir William Warram doctor of the laws vnto Philip archduke of Burgognie, and to his councellors (bicause he was not of age able to gouerne of himselfe) to signifie to him and them, that the yoong man, being with the ladie Margaret, had falselie and vntruelie vsurped the name of Richard duke of Yorke, which long before was murthered with his brother Edward in the Tower of London, by the commandement of their vncle king Richard, as manie men then liuing could testifie.

The ambassadors comming to the court of Philip the archduke, were honorablie interteined of him and of his councell, and willed to declare the effect of their message. William Warram made to them an eloquent oration, and in the later end somewhat inueihed against the ladie Margaret, not sparing to declare, how she now in hir later age had brought foorth (within the space of a few yeares togither) two detestable monsters, that is to saie, Lambert (of whom yée heard before) and this

The sum of
D. Warrams
spéech to the
archduke. same Perkin Warbecke, and being conceiued of these two great babes, was not deliuered of them in eight or nine moneths as nature requireth; but in one hundred and eightie moneths, for both these at the lest were fiftéene yéers of age, yer she would be brought in bed of them, and shew them openlie; and when they were newlie crept out of hir wombe, they were no infants but lustie yoonglings, and of age sufficient to bid battell to kings. Although these tawnts angred the ladie Margaret to the hart, yet Perkin was more vexed with the things declared in this oration, and especiallie bicause his cloaked iuggling was brought to light.

The duches intending to cast hot sulphur into the new kindled fire, determined with might and maine to arme and set forward prettie Perkin against the king of England.

When

When the ambassadors had doone their message, and that the archdukes councell had long debated the matter; they made answer, that to haue the king of Englands loue, the archduke and they would neither aid nor assist Perkin nor his complices in anie cause or quarrell. Yet notwithstanding if the ladie Margaret, persisting in hir rooted malice towards the king of England, would be to him aiding and helping, it was not in their power to withstand it; for bicause in the lands assigned to hir for hir dower, she might franklie and fréelie order all things at hir will and pleasure, without contradiction of anie other gouernour.

After that the ambassadors were returned with this answer, the king streight sent foorth certeine espials into Flanders, which should feigne themselues to haue fled to the duke of Yorke; and thereby search out the whole intent of the conspiracie, and after what sort they meant to proceed in the same. Others were sent also to intise sir Robert Clifford and William Barleie, to returne into England, promising to them pardon of all their offenses and high rewards for obeieng the kings request. They that were sent, did so earnestlie and prudentlie applie their businesse, that they brought all things to passe at their owne desires. For first they learned who were the chéefe conspirators, and after persuaded sir Robert Clifford to giue ouer that enterprise, which had no grounded staie to rest vpon. Albeit William Barleie at the first would not leaue off, but continued his begun attempt; till after two yeares, he repenting him of his follie, & hauing pardon granted him of the king, returned home into his natiue countrie. *An. Reg.* 9. Espials sent into Flanders from the king for a subtill policie.

When the king had knowledge of the chiefe capteins of this conspiracie (by the ouerture of his espials which were returned) he caused them to be apprehended, and brought to London before his presence. Of the which the chiefe were Iohn Ratcliffe, lord Fitz-Water, sir Simon Montford, sir Tho. Thwaits knights, William Daubenie, Robert Ratcliffe, Thomas Cressenor, and Thomas Astwood. Also certeine preests & religious men, as sir William Richford doctor of diuinitie, and sir Thomas Poines, both friers of saint Dominikes order, doctor William Sutton, sir William Worseleie deane of Paules, Robert Laiborne, and sir Richard Lesleie. Other which were guiltie, hearing that their fellowes were apprehended, fled and tooke sanctuarie. The other that were taken were condemned, of the which sir Simon Montford, Robert Ratcliffe, and William Daubenie were beheaded. The conspiring fautors of the counterfeit duke of Yorke.

Some had their pardons, and the préests also for their order sake; but yet few of them liued long after. The lord Fitz-Water pardoned of life, was conueied to Calis, and there laid in hold, & after lost his head; bicause he went about to corrupt his kéepers with rewards, that he might escape, intending (as was thought) to haue gone to Perkin. [Thus by the policie and subtile deuise of the king, practised to the point by his espials, the sinewes of this conspiracie was rent in sunder. So that the malicious ladie Margaret was not a little swolne with indignation when she saw the course of hir deuise (now that it had passed so far as that it was knowne to people on this side and beyond the seas) stopped, and the confederacie (whereto she speciallie trusted) dissolued. Yet notwithstanding, as women will not (to die for it) giue ouer an enterprise, which of an enuious purpose they attempt; so she put hir irons afresh into the fier to set hir hatred forward: whome a while we will leaue at worke, and shew some doings betwéene England and Flanders.] *Abr. Flem.*

King Henrie taking displeasure with the king of Romans, for that he kept not touch in aiding him against the French king, and partlie displeased with the Flemings, but speciallie with the ladie Margaret, for kéeping and setting forward Perkin Warbecke, not onelie banished all Flemish wares and merchandizes out of his dominions, but also restreined all English merchants from their repaire and traffike into anie of the lands and territories of the king of Romans, or of the archduke Philip, sonne to the same king of the Romans; causing the mart to be kept at Calis, of all English Flemish wares forbidden. The mart kept at Calis.

English commodities banished out of Flanders. lish merchandizes and commodities. Wherefore the said king and his sonne banished out of their lands and seigniories all English clothes, yarne, tin, lead, and other commodities of this realme. The restreint made by the king sore hindered the merchants aduenturers; for they had no occupieng to beare their charges, and to support their credit withall.

And that most greeued them, the Easterlings being at libertie, brought to the realme such wares as they were woont, & so serued their customers throughout the realme. Wherevpon there insued a riot by the seruants of the mercers, haberdashers, & cloth-workers in the citie of London, the tuesdaie before saint Edwards day. For they per-A riot made vpon the Easterlings.ceiuing what hinderance grew to their maisters, in that they were not able so well to kéepe them as before they had doone, assembled togither in purpose to reuenge their malice on the Easterlings, & so came to the Stilliard, & began to rifle & spoile such chambers & warehouses as they cold get into. So that the Easterlings had much adoo to withstand them, & kéepe them back out of their gates, which with helpe of carpenters, smiths, and other that came to them by water out of Southwarke, they shored & so fortified, that the multitude of the seruants and prentises, being assembled, could not preuaile.

At length came the maior with a number of men, defensiblie weaponed, to remooue the force; at whose approch those riotous persons fled awaie like a flocke of shéepe. But diuerse of them were apprehended, and vpon inquirie made before the kings commissioners, aboue foure score seruants & apprentises were found to be conspired togither, and sworne not to reueale it; of whome some of the chiefe beginners were committed to the Tower, and there long continued. But in conclusion, bicause none of their maisters, nor anie one housholder was found culpable, the king of his clemencie pardoned their offense, and restored them to libertie. [For he thought it no credit to his crowne to take vengeance of such sillie soules by seueritie of death, whom in clemencie pardoning he might restore to a reformed life.]

Abr. Fl. ex. I. S. pag. 867. Execution for seditious bils against the kings person. ¶ On the two & twentith of Februarie in this yeere were arreigned in the Guildhall of London foure persons, Thomas Bagnall, Iohn Scot, Iohn Heath, and Iohn Kenington, the which were sanctuarie men of saint Martins le grand in London, and latelie before were taken out of the said sanctuarie, for forging of seditious bils, to the slander of the king, & some of his councell, for the which thrée of them were iudged to die; and the fourth named Bagnall, pleaded to be restored to sanctuarie: by reason whereof he was repriued to the Tower till the next tearme: and on the six and twentith of Februarie, the other thrée with a Fleming, and a yeoman of the crowne, were all fiue executed at Tiborne. ¶ On the eight and twentith of Aprill Ione Boughton widow was burnt in Smithfield, for holding certeine opinions of Iohn Wickliffe. Vittels plentie sold good cheape. Wheat was sold at London at six pence the bushell, baie salt for thrée pence halfe penie the bushell, Nantwich salt was sold for six pence the bushell, white herings nine shillings the barrell, red herings at thrée shillings the cade, red sprots six pence the cade, & Gascoigne wine for six pound the tun.]

1494
An. Reg. 10.

Policie of K. Henrie against Robert Clifford. Shortlie after sir Robert Clifford, partlie trusting on the kings promise, and partlie mistrusting the desperat begun enterprise, returned suddenlie againe into England. The king certified before of his comming, went streight to the Tower of London the morow after the day of Epiphanie, & there taried till such time as sir Robert Clifford was there presented to his person. This was doone for a policie, that if sir Robert accused anie of the nobilitie, they might be called thither without suspicion of anie euill, and their attached and laid fast. Some thought also, that for a policie king Henrie sent sir Robert Clifford ouer as an espie, or else he would not so soone haue receiued him into fauour againe. Neuerthelesse, there were great presumptions that it was nothing so, for both was he in great danger after his begun attempt, and neuer was so much estéemed with the king afterward as he was before.

But

But this is true, vpon his comming to the kings presence, he besought him of pardon, and obteined it; and therewith opened all the maner of the conspiracie, so far as he knew, and who were aiders, fautors, and chiefe beginners of it; amongst whóme he accused sir William Stanleie, whome the king had made his chiefe chamberleine, and one of his priuie councell. The king was sorie to heare this, and could not be induced to beleeue that there was so much vntruth in him, till by euident proofes it was tried against him. Then the king caused him to be restreined from his libertie in his owne chamber within the quadrat tower, and there appointed him by his priuie councell to be examined, in which examination he nothing denied, but wiselie and sagelie agréed to all things laid to his charge if he were faultie therein. Sir William Stanleie a fauourer of Perkin.

The report is, that this was his offense. When communication was had betwixt him, and the aboue mentioned sir Robert Clifford, as concerning Perkin, which falselie vsurped the name of K. Edwards sonne; sir William Stanleie said, that if he knew certeinlie that the yoong man was the indubitate heire of king Edward the fourth, he would neuer fight or beare armour against him. This point argued, that he bare no hartie good will toward king Henrie as then. But what was the cause that he had conceiued some inward grudge towards the king; or how it chanced that the king had withdrawen his speciall fauor from him, manie haue doubted. Some indéed haue gessed, that sir William Stanlie, for the seruice which he shewed at Bosworth field thought that all the benefits which he receiued of the king to be farre vnder that which he had deserued, in preseruing not onelie the kings life; but also in obteining for him the victorie of his enimies, so that his aduersarie was slaine in the field. The offense of sir William Stanleie. Coniectures of sir William Stanleies alienated mind from king Henrie.

Wherfore desiring to be created earle of Chester, and therof denied, he began to disdeine the king. And one thing incouraged him much, which was the riches and treasure of king Richard, which he onlie possessed at the battell of Bosworth; by reason of which riches and great power of men, he set naught by the king his souereigne lord and maister. The king hauing thus an hole in his coat, doubted first what he should doo with him; for loth he was to lose the fauour of his brother the earle of Derbie: and againe to pardon him, he feared least it should be an euill example to other, that should go about to attempt the like offense. And so at length, seueritie got the vpper hand, & mercie was put backe, in so much that he was arreigned at Westminster and adiudged to die, and (according to that iudgement) was brought to the Tower hill the sixtéenth daie of Februarie, and there had his head striken off. King Henrie in a quandare.

1495
Sir William Stanleie beheaded.

[This was the end of sir William Stanleie the chiefest helper of king Henrie to the crowne at Bosworth field against king Richard the third, and who set the same crowne first vpon the kings head, when it was found in the field trampled vnder féet. He was a man (while he liued) of great power in his countrie, and also of great wealth: in somuch as the common fame ran, that there was in his castell of Holt found in readie coine, plate, and iewels, to the value of fortie thousand markes or more, and his land and fees extended to three thousand pounds by yeare. Neuerthelesse all helped not; neither his good seruice in Bosworth field, neither his forwardnesse (euen with the hazard of life) to prefer K. Henrie to the crowne, neither his faithfulnesse in cleauing to him at all brunts, neither the bond of aliance betwixt them, neither the power that he was able to make, neither the riches which he was worth, neither intercession of fréends, which he wanted not; none of these, nor all these could procure the redemption of his lost life: Abr. Flem. See pag. 446.

O fluxum decus hominum, ó variabile tempus.

¶ On the sixtéenth of Nouember was holden the sergeants feast at the bishops place of Elie in Holborne, where dined the king, queene, and all the chiefe lords of England. The new sergeants names were maister Mordant, Higham, Kingsmill, Conisbie, Butler, Yakesleie, Frowike, Oxenbridge, & Constable. In digging for to laie a new Iohn Stow. pag. 969. The king and queene dine at sergeants feast kept at Elie palace.

A wonder to be noted in a corpse that laie long in the ground.

new foundation in the church of saint Marie hill in London, the bodie of Alice Hack-neie which had béene buried in the church the space of 175 yeares, was found whole of skinne, & the ioints of hir armes pliable: which corpse was kept aboue ground foure daies without annoiance, and then buried againe. ¶ Also this yeare (as maister

Rich. Grafton.

Grafton saith) at the charges of maister Iohn Tate alderman of London was the church of saint Anthonies founded, & annexed vnto the college of Windsore, wherein was erected one notable and frée schoole to the furtherance of learning, and a number of poore people (by the name of almesmen, which were poore, aged, and decaied housholders) releeued, to the great commendation of that worthie man, who so liued in worship, that his death by his worthie dooings maketh him still aliue; for he was not forgetfull to beau-tifie the good state of this citie, in which by wealth he had tasted of Gods bles-sings.]

About this same time, diuerse men were punished that had vpon a presumptuous boldnesse spoken manie slanderous words against the kings maiestie, hoping still for

An. Reg. 11. Lord Daubenie the kings chéefe chamberleine. Sir Edward Poinings sent into Ireland with an armie.

the arriuall of the feigned Richard duke of Yorke. After the death of sir William Stanleie, Giles lord Daubenie was elected and made the kings chéefe chamberleine. Also, the K. sent into Ireland (to purge out the euill & wicked séeds of rebellion amongest the wild & sauage Irish people, sowed there by the craftie conueiance of Perkin Warbecke) sir Henrie Deane, late abbat of Langtonie (whome he made chan-cellor of that Ile) & sir Edward Poinings knight, with an armie of men. The fauou-rers of Perkin, hearing that sir Edward Poinings was come with a power to persecute them, withdrew streightwaies, and fled into the woods and marishes for the safegard of themselues.

Sir Edward Poinings according to his commission, intending to punish such as had aided and aduanced the enterprise of Perkin, with his whole armie marched forward against the wild Irishmen, bicause that all other being culpable of that offense, fled and resorted to them for succour. But when he saw that his purpose succéeded not as he would haue wished it; both bicause the Irish lords sent him no succour according to their promises; and also for that his owne number was not sufficient to furnish his enterprise, bicause his énimies were dispersed amongst woods, mounteins, and marishes; he was constreined to recule backe, sore displeased in his mind against Gerald earle of Kildare, being then the kings deputie.

Now, the cause of this his discontentment was, for that the said earle was suspected to be the meane that he had no succours sent him, and was so informed in déed by

Gerald earle of Kildare depu-tie of Ireland apprehended.

such as bare the earle no good will. And therefore suddenlie he caused the earle to be apprehended, and as a prisoner brought him in his companie into England. Which earle being examined, and sundrie points of treason laid to him, he so auoided them all, & laid the burthen in other mens necks, that he was dismissed, and sent into Ireland againe, there to be deputie and lieutenant as he was before. The king being now in

King Henries progresse into Lancashire.

some better suertie of his estate, did take his progresse into Lancashire the fiue & twentith daie of Iune, there to make merrie with his moother the countesse of Derbie, which then laie at Lathome in the countrie.

In this meane while, Perkin Warbecke, being in Flanders, sore troubled that his iuggling was discouered, yet he determined not to leaue off his enterprise, in hope at length to atteine the crowne of England: and so gathering a power of all nations, some bankrupts, some false English sanctuarie men, some théeues, robbers, and vaga-bunds, which desiring to liue by rapine, were glad to serue him. And thus furnished, he tooke such ships as his fréends had prouided for him: and departing from Flanders

Perkin attemp-teth to land in Kent in hope of victorie.

towards England, he arriued vpon the Kentish coast, & there cast anchor, purposing to prooue how the people there were affected towards him: and therefore he sent certeine of his men to land, to signifie to the countrie his arriuall with such power, that the victorie must incline to his part.

The

The Kentishmen vnderstanding that Perkin was but Perkin, and had none with him (to make account of) but strangers borne, like faithfull subiects determined to fall vpon those that were thus new come to land, and to trie if they might allure the whole number out of their ships, so to giue them battell. But Perkin wiselie considering that the maner of a multitude is not to consult, and sagelie to aduise with themselues in anie deliberate sort, but suddenlie and rashlie to run headlong into rebellion, would not set one foot out of his ship, vntill he saw all things sure. Yet he permitted some of his souldiers to go on land, which being trained foorth a pretie waie from their ships, were suddenlie compassed about and beset of the Kentishmen, and at one stroke vanquished and driuen backe to their ships. *Perkins men discomfited.*

Of these discomfited soules were taken prisoners an hundred and fortie persons, whereof fiue, Montfort, Corbet, White Belt, Quintin (or otherwise Genin) being capteins were brought to London by sir Iohn Pechie, shiriffe of Kent, railed in ropes like horsses drawing in a cart, & after vpon their arreignment confessed their offense, and were executed, some at London, and other in the townes adioining to the sea coast. And thus Perkin, missing of his purpose, fled backe into Flanders. In this verie season departed to God Cicilie duchesse of Yorke moother to king Edward the fourth, at hir castell of Berkhamstéed, a woman of small stature, but of much honour and high parentage, and was buried by hir husband in the college of Fodringeie. *Perkins capteins taken & executed. Perkin reculeth into Flanders. The death of Cicilie duchesse of Yorke moother to Edward the fourth.*

The king being aduertised that his enimies were landed, leauing off his progresse, purposed to haue returned to London; but being certified the next day of the luckie speed of his faithfull subiects, continued his progresse, & did send sir Richard Gilford both to commend the fidelitie and manhood of the Kentishmen, and also to render to them most hartie thanks for the same. He also caused order to be taken for the erecting of beacons, and watching of them. Perkin then perceiuing that he should not be receiued into England, sailed into Ireland, trusting there to augment his numbers, and then to returne towards the coast of England againe, and to take land in the West countrie, if occasion serued; but if not, then he determined to saile streight into Scotland, to séeke fréendship there. *Sir Richard Gilford.*

After he had therefore staid a while in Ireland, and perceiued that the hope of victorie consisted not in the Irish nation, being naked people, without furniture of armour or weapon, he tooke the sea againe at Corffe, and sailed into Scotland; where comming to the presence of king Iames, he forged such a painted processe to mooue him to beléeue that he was the verie sonne of king Edward: that the Scotish king, whether blinded with errour, or vsing dissimulation, that he might vnder a colourable pretext make war against England, began to haue Perkin in great honour, and caused him openlie to be called duke of Yorke. And to persuade the world that so he was indeed, he caused the ladie Catharine, daughter to Alexander earle of Huntleie, his nigh kinsman, to be espoused to him. [But yer we passe anie further, you shall sée and peruse (if you will) the said painted processe of Perkin, as it is left in record by Edward Hall for an example what working force is in words (speciallie where the hearers are easie to be seduced) and not to be ouer hastie to giue them too quicke & hastie credit. For the poet saith of gaie words void of truth: *Perkin saileth into Ireland and is in sundrie opinions. Katharine daughter to the earle of Huntleie maried to Perkin.*

    Verba nitent phaleris, at nullas verba medullis
    Intus habent.   *M. Pal. in Virg.*

The colourable oration or counterfeit tale that Perkin told the king of Scots to iustifie his false title.

I THINKE it is not vnknowne vnto you (most noble king and puissant prince) into what ruine the stocke house, and familie of Edward the fourth, of that name king of England, *Abr. Flem. ex Edw. Hall. fol. xxxviij, xxxix.*

Perkin saith that he is Edward the fourth lawfull sonne.

England, is now of late brought to and fallen in, either by Gods permission, or by diuine punishment; whose indubitate sonne (if you know not alreadie) I am, and by the power of almightie God, preserued aliue to this houre from the mightie hand of a tyrant. For my father king Edward (when he died) appointed his brother Richard duke of Glocester to be our gouernour, protector, and defendor; whome the more that he loued & studied to aduance and promote, the better he thought that he would loue, fauour, and tender his children. But alas my vnfortunate chance I may say! how hath his trust beene turned into treason, and his hope into hinderance, all men know and I feele. Our vncle was not the tutor and preseruer of our stocke and linage, but the confounder & destroier of our bloud and progenie. For that tyrant, blinded and glutted with the desire of ruling and souereigntie, commanded Edward my bro-ther & me to be slaine and dispatched out of this mortall life. Wherevpon that per-

Perkin telleth the king how he was preserued and kept aliue.

son, to whome the weightie and cruell charge was commited and giuen to oppresse and destroie vs poore innocent infants, and giltlesse babes, the more that he abhorred this heinous and butcherlie offense, the more he feared to commit it.

And so wauering in mind and doubtfull what to doo, at the length willing in part to stanch the bloudie thirst of the vnnaturall tyrant, and in part to absteine from so heinous & detestable homicide, he destroied my brother and preserued me; like the good preest Ioiada, who saued little Ioas, when all the children of the bloud roiall were command-ed by Athalia the queene to be slaine and vtterlie destroied. And further, to the intent that my life might be in suertie, he appointed one to conueie me into some strange countrie; where when I was furthest off, and had most need of comfort he forsooke me suddenlie (I thinke he was so appointed to doo) and left me desolate alone without freend or knowlege of anie releefe or refuge. And so king Richard did obteine the crowne as a preie mischeefouslie gotten by the dispatching awaie of my brother and me. So that I thus escaping, by reason of my tender infancie, forgat almost my selfe, and knew not well what I was. But after long wandering from countrie to countrie, and from citie to citie, I perceiued and learned by little and little what was my estate & de-

Perkin calleth the ladie Mar-garet duchesse of Burgognie his owne aunt.

gree; and so in conclusion came to mine owne aunt the ladie Margaret lieng in Flanders, which was sometime married to Charles duke of Burgognie, which as ioifullie receiued and welcomed me, as if I had come out of hell into heauen, as the onelie type and garland of hir noble stirpe and linage. But forsomuch as she being onelie Dowager of the duchie of Burgognie, and hauing nothing but hir dowrie proper to hir selfe, was not of power to helpe me with men and munitions of warre, as she would gladlie haue doone for the recouerie of my fathers relme & rightfull inheritance: I therefore am driuen to seeke further aid and succour.

Perkin craueth aid of the Scotish king toward the re-couerie of the crowne of Eng-land from king Henrie the seuenth.

And therefore by hir counsell and aduertisement, with this small handfull of men of warre and souldiers, I am repaired to your presence for succours; of whome (as the publike fame is spred ouer the whole world) there was neuer man by wrong or iniurie chased or driuen out of his countrie, region, or inheritance, or by extort power and tyrannie kept out of the same (as I my selfe from mine infancie haue beene) whose re-quest was frustrate and denied at your hand. Therefore, by the maiestie of your realme & countrie I desire, & heartilie with praier as I can, I beseech and exhort you to helpe and releeue me now in my extreame necessitie. And if it chance me by your aid and succour to recouer & possesse my father's realme and dignitie; not onelie I, but all the kings of our linage, which hereafter shall obteine the same, shall be so much obliged and bound vnto to you; that they must needs thinke, that dooing to you all the pleasure and benefits that they can, yet with all thanks that can be giuen your great kindnesse can neuer in full measure be recompensed.

When he had thus said, the king bad him be of good comfort, and promised him
that

that whatsoeuer he were, it should neuer repent of his comming to him.] Shortlie
after, hauing this Perkin with him in companie, he entered into England with a The Scotish king inuadeth England with a great armie in Perkin his behalfe.
puissant armie, and caused proclamation to be made, to spare all those that would
submit themselues vnto Richard duke of Yorke.   Héerewith they began the warre in
most cruell maner, with slaughter of men, burning of townes, spoiling of houses,
and committing of all other detestable enormities; so that all the countrie of
Northumberland was by them in maner wasted, and destroied.   At length, when the
souldiers were laden with spoiles, and saciate with bloud, perceiuing that no succoures
came out of England vnto the new inuented duke, contrarie to that which he had
made them to beleeue would come to passe; they determined to retire rather with
assured gaine, than to tarrie the vncertaine victorie of that counterfeit duke, and
so thereupon they withdrew backe into Scotland inriched with with preies and
booties.

It is said, that Perkin Warbecke, being returned into Scotland with the king of
Scots, vnder a cloked pretense should sore lament the great slaughter, spoile, and
damage, which had béene doone at this last roade made into England; and therefore
as one that bare a naturall loue toward his natiue countrie, besought the king of Scots, The counterfeit compassion of Perkin.
that from thensefoorth, he would no more so deface his naturall relme, and destroie
his subiects with such terrible fire, flame and hauocke; as who should saie, he being
ouercome now with compassion, did bewaile the cruell destruction of his natural
countrie of England.   But the Scotish K. told him, that he seemed to take thought
for that which appeared to be none of his, sith that not so much as one gentleman
or yeoman (for ought he could see) would once shew themselues readie to aid him
in the warre begun for his cause, and in his name, within that realme which he
pretended so cléerelie to apperteine to him.

The king of England being certified of this inuasion, prepared an armie with all
diligence to have resisted the Scots: but they were returned yer the English power
could assemble togither.   Now when the king was truelie certified that the Scotish
king was returned home, he staied all the preparations made at that time to go
against him.   But yet meaning to be reuenged of the wrongs doone to him by king
Iames and his people; he first called a parlement, and in that assemblie of three A parlement of the three estates of the realme
estates of the realme, he declared the cause of the instant warre, and how necessarie
it should be for the suertie and wealth of the realme of England to haue that warre,
pursued against those enimies that had begun it.   To this motion all the nobilitie A subsidie.
wholie agréed.   And to the maintenance of that warre, a subsidie was by whole
assent of the parlement fréelie giuen and granted.   Which paiment though it
was not great, yet manie of the common people sore grudged to pay the same,
as they that euer abhorre such taxes and exactions.   At the same parlement were
diuerse acts and statutes made, necessarie & expedient (as was thought) for the
publike weale of the realme.

In the meane season the king of Scots, perceiuing that the Englishmen would
shortlie go about to reuenge the injuries doone to them by him and his people, The king of England and Scotlād prepare for mutuall warre.
assembled eftsoones a puissant armie, that he might either defend his realme against
the English power, attempting to inuade his countrie, or else afresh to enter into the
English borders.   And thus these two mightie princes minded nothing more than the
one to indamage the other.   But the king of Englandwould not deferre one houre
by (his good will) till he were reuenged, and therefore prepared a mightie armie to
inuade Scotland, and ordeined for chéefteine thereof the lord Daubeneie.   But as this
armie was assembled, and that the lord Daubenie was forward on his iournie towards
Scotland, he was suddenlie staid and called backe againe, by reason of a new
commotion begun by the Cornishmen for the paiment of the subsidie which was
granted at the last parlement.

These

These vnrulie people the Cornishmen, inhabiting in a barren countrie and vnfruitfull, at the first sore repined that they should be so greeuouslie taxed, and burdened the kings councell as the onelie cause of such polling and pilling: and so being in their rage, menaced the chéefe authors with death and present destruction. And thus being in a rore, two persons of the affinitie, the one called Thomas Flammocke, a gentleman, learned in the lawes of the realme; and the other Michael Ioseph, a smith, men of stout stomachs and high courages, tooke vpon them to be capteins of this seditious companie. They laid the fault and cause of this exaction vnto Iohn Morton, archbishop of Canturburie, and to sir Reginald Braie; bicause they were cheefe of the kings councell. Such rewards haue they commonlie that be in great authoritie with kings and princes.

The capteins Flammocke and Ioseph exhorted the common people to put on harnesse, and not to be afeard to follow them in that quarrell, promising not to hurt anie creature, but onelie to sée them punished that procured such exactions to be laid on the people, without anie reasonable cause, as vnder the colour of a little trouble with the Scots, which (sith they were withdrawne home) they tooke to be well quieted and appeased. So these capteins bent on mischeefe, (were their outward pretense neuer so finelie coloured) yet persuaded a great number of people to assemble togither, and condescended to do as their capteins would agrée and appoint. Then these capteins praising much the hardines of the people, when all things were readie for their infortunate iournie, set forward with their armie, and came to Taunton, where they slue the prouost of Perin, which was one of the commissioners of the subsidie, and from thence came to Welles, so intending to go to London, where the king then soiourned.

When the king was aduertised of these dooings, he was somewhat astonied, and not without cause; being thus troubled with the warre against the Scots, and this ciuill commotion of his subiects at one instant. But first meaning to subdue his rebellious subiects; and after to proceed against the Scots, as occasion should serue, he reuoked the lord Daubenie which (as you haue heard) was going against the Scots, and increased his armie with manie chosen and piked warriors. Also mistrusting that the Scots might now (hauing such opportunitie) inuáde the relme againe; he appointed the lord Th. Howard erle of Surrie (which after the death of the lord Dinham was made high treasuror of England) to gather a band of men in the countie Palatine of Durham, that they with the aid of the inhabitants adioining, and the borderers, might keepe backe the Scots if they chanced to make anie inuasion. The nobles of the realme hearing of the rebellion of the Cornishmen, came to London, euerie man with as manie men of warre as they could put in a readinesse, to aid the king if need should be. In the which number were the earle of Essex, and the lord Montioy, with diuerse other.

In the meane time, Iames Twichet lord Audeleie being confederate with the rebels of Cornewall ioined with them, being come to Welles, and tooke vpon him as their chéefe capteine to lead them against their naturall lord and king. From Welles they went to Salisburie, and from thence to Winchester, and so to Kent, where they hoped to haue had great aid, but they were deceiued in that their expectation. For the erle of Kent, George lord of Aburgauenie, Iohn Brooke, lord Cobham, sir Edward Poinings, sir Richard Gilford, sir Thomas Bourchier, Iohn Peche, William Scot, and a great number of people, were not onelie prest and readie to defend the countrie, to kéepe the people in due obedience, but bent to fight with such as would lift vp sword, or other weapon against their souereigne lord: insomuch that the Kentishmen would not once come neere the Cornishmen, to aid or assist them in anie maner of wise.

Which

Which thing maruelouslie dismaid the hearts of the Cornishmen, when they saw Manie of the Cornishmen take their héels by night. themselues thus deceiued of the succours which they most trusted vpon, so that manie of them (fearing the euill chance that might happen) fled in the night from their companie, and left them, in hope so to saue themselues. The capteines of the rebels, perceiuing they could haue no helpe of the Kentishmen, putting their onelie hope in their owne puissance, brought their people to Blacke heath, a foure miles distant from London, and there in a plaine on the top of an hill, they ordered their battels, either readie to fight with the king if he would assail them, or else assault the citie of London : for they thought the king durst not haue encountered with them in battell. But they were deceiued : for the king although he had power inough about to haue fought with them before their comming so neere to the citie ; yet he thought it best to suffer them to come forward, till he had them farre off from their natiue countrie, and then to set vpon them being destitute of aid in some place of aduantage.

The citie was in a great feare at the first knowledge giuen, how the rebels were so The citie of London sore afraid of the rebels. neere incamped to the citie, euerie man getting himselfe to harnesse, and placing themselues, some at the gates, some on the walles, so that no part was vndefended. But the king deliuered the citie of that feare : for after that he perceiued how the Cornishmen were all daie readie to fight, and that on the hill ; he sent straight Iohn Earle of Oxenford, Henrie Bourchier, earle of Essex, Edmund de la Poole, earle of Suffolke, sir Rise ap Thomas, and sir Humfreie Stanleie, noble warriors, with a great companie of archers and horssemen, to enuiron the hill on the right side, and on the left, to the intent that all bywaies being stopped and foreclosed, all hope of flight should be taken from them. And incontinentlie he himselfe, being as well incouraged with manlie stomachs as furnished with a populous armie and plentie of artillerie, set forward out of the citie, and incamped himselfe in saint Georges field, where he on the fridaie at night then lodged.

On the saturdaie in the morning, he sent the lord Daubeneie with a great companie to set on them earlie in the morning, which first got the bridge at Dertford Strand, which was manfullie defended by certeine archers of the rebels, whose arrows (as is reported) were in length a full cloth yard. While the earles set on them on euerie side, the lord Blackheath field. Daubenie came into the field with his companie, and without long fighting, the Cornishmen were ouercome ; and first they tooke the lord Daubenie prisoner : but whether it were for feare, or for hope of fauour, they let him go at libertie, without hurt or detriment. There were slaine of the rebels which fought and resisted, aboue two thousand men Thrée hundred slaine, & a thousand fiue hundred taken prisoners, as Iohn Stow saith. (as Edward Hall noteth) and taken prisoners an infinite number, & amongst them the blacke smith, and other the cheefe capteins, which were shortlie after put to death. When this battel was ended, the king wanted of all his numbers but three hundred, which were slaine at that conflict.

Some affirme, that the king appointed to haue fought with them not till the mondaie, and preuenting the time set on them on the saturdaie before, taking them vnprouided, and in no arraie of battell ; and so by that policie obteined the field and victorie. The prisoners as well capteins as other, were pardoned, sauing the chéefe capteins and first beginners, to whome he shewed no mercie at all. The lord Audeleie was drawne Iames lord Audeleie ignominouslie drawne to execution and beheaded. from Newgate to the Tower-hill in a coate of his own armes, painted vpon paper reuersed and all torne, and there was beheaded the foure and twentith of Iune. Thomas Flammocke & Michael Ioseph were hanged, drawne, and quartered after the maner of traitors, & their heads and quarters were pitched vpon stakes, and set vp in London, and in other places : although at the first, the king meant to haue sent them into Cornewall, to haue béene set vp there for a terror to all others. But hearing that the Cornishmen at home were readie to begin a new conspiracie, least he should the more irritate and prouoke them by that displeasant sight, he changed his purpose, for doubt to wrap himselfe in more trouble than néeded.

While

An. Reg. 13.

The Scots in-
uade the Eng-
lish borders.

While these things were adooing in England, the king of Scots being aduertised of the
whole matter and rebellion of the Cornishmen, thought not to let passe that occasion:
and therefore he eftsoones inuaded the frontiers of England, wasting the countrie,
burning townes, and murthering the people, spareing neither place nor person: and
while his light horsmen were riding to forraie and destroie the bishoprike of Durham,
and there burned all about, he with an other part of his armie did besiege the castell

Fox bishop of
Durham owner
of Norham
castell.

of Norham. The bishop of Durham Richard Fox, being owner of that castell, had
well furnished it both with men and munitions aforehand, doubting least that would
follow which came now to passe. The bishop, after that the Scots made this inuasion,
aduertised the king (as then being at London) of all things that chanced in the
North parts; and sent in all post hast to the earle of Surrie, to come to the rescue.
The earle being then in Yorkeshire, and hauing gathered an armie, vpon knowledge
giuen to him from the bishop, with all diligence marched forward, and after him
followed other noble men out of all the quarters of the North, euerie of them bringing
as manie men as they could gather, for defense of their countrie.

What lords &
knights with
their companies
went to the
rescue of the
castell against
the Scots.

Amongst these, the chéefe leaders were, Rafe earle of Westmerland, Thomas lord
Dacres, Rafe lord Neuill, George lord Strange, Richard lord Latimer, George lord
Lumleie, Iohn lord Scroope, Henrie lord Clifford, George lord Ogle, William lord
Coniers, Thomas lord Darcie. Of knights, Thomas baron of Hilton, sir William
Persie, sir William Bulmer, sir William Gascoigne, sir Rafe Bigod, sir Rafe Bowes,
sir Thomas a Parre, sir Rafe Ellecker, sir Iohn Constable, sir Iohn Ratcliffe, sir Iohn
Sauill, sir Thomas Strangweis, and a great number of other knights and esquiers
besides. The whole armie was little lesse than twentie thousand men, beside the
nauie, whereof the lord Brooke was admerall.

When the Scots had diuerse waies assaulted and beaten the castell of Norham, but
could make no batterie to enter the same, they determined of their owne accord to
raise the siege, and returne; and that so much the sooner in verie déed, bicause they
heard that the earle of Surrie was within two daies iournie of them, with a great
puissance. Wherefore king Iames raised his siege, and returned home into his owne
realme. When the earle knew of the kings returne, he followed him with all hast
possible, trusting suerlie to ouertake him, and to giue him battell. When the earle

The earle of
Surrie entreth
Scotland de-
facing castels
and towers.

was entred Scotland, he ouerthrew and defaced the castell of Cawdestreimes, the
tower of Hetenhall, the tower of Edington, the tower of Fulden: and he sent Norreie
king at armes to the capteine of Haiton castell, which was one of the strongest places
betwixt Berwike and Edenburg, to deliuer him the castell. Which he denied to doo,
affirming that he was sure of spéedie succours.

The earle héerevpon laid his ordinance to the castell, and continuallie beat it, from
two of the clocke till fiue at night, in such wise, that they within rendered vp the
the place, their liues onelie saued. The earle caused his minors to raise & ouerthrow
the fortresse to the plaine ground. The Scotish king was within a mile of the siege,
and both knew it, and saw the smoke, but would not set one foot forward to the
rescue. While the erle laie at Haiton, the king of Scots sent to him Machemont,
and an other herald, desiring him at his election, either to fight with whole puissance
against puissance, or else they two to fight person to person; requiring that if the
victorie fell to the Scotish king, that then the earle should deliuer for his ransome, the
towne of Berwike, with the fishgarths of the same.

The valiant
hart of the erle
of Surrie re-
ioisin at his
hap likelie to
fight hand to
hand with the
K. of Scots.

The earle made answer hereto, that the towne of Berwike was the king his maisters,
and not his, the which he neither ought nor would laie to pledge, without the king of
Englands assent; but he would gage his bodie, which was more pretious to him than
all the townes of the world, promising on his honour, that if he tooke the king prisoner in that singular combat, he would release to him all his part of the fine and
ransome; and if it chanced the king to vanquish him, he would gladlie paie such ran-
                                                                                        some

some as was conuenient for the degree of an earle, and thanked him greatlie for the offer: for suerlie he thought himselfe much honored, that so noble a prince would vouchsafe to admit so poore an earle to fight with him bodie to bodie. When he had rewarded and dismissed the heralds, he set his armie in a readinesse, to abide the comming of the king of Scots, and so stood all daie.

But king Iames not regarding his offers, would neither performe the one nor the other; fearing to cope with the English nation in anie condition; and so therevpon fled in the night season with all his puissance. When the earle knew that the king was reculed, and had béene in Scotland six or seuen daies, being dailie and nightlie vexed with continuall wind and raine, vpon good and deliberate aduise returned backe to the towne of Berwike, and there dissolued his armie, tarieng there himselfe, till he might vnderstand further of the kings pleasure. In the meane time there came an ambassadour to the K. of Scots from the K. of Spaine, one Peter Hialas, a man of no lesse learning than wit & policie, to mooue and intret a peace betweene the two kings of England & Scotland [that their people might fall to their necessarie trades of aduantage with quietnesse, and friend with friend, husband with wife, father with children, and maisters with seruants dwell and accompanie: a dissolution and separation of whom one from another is procured by bloudie warre, wherein as there is no pitie, so is there is no pietie, as one saith full trulie:

An ambassadour from the K of Spaine to treat a peace betwixt England and Scotland.

Nulla fides pietásque viris qui castra sequuntur,
Nulla salus bello.]

Luc. Lib. 10.

This Spanish ambassadour so earnestlie trauelled in his message vnto the king of Scots, that at length he found him conformable to his purpose: and therefore wrote to the king of England, that it would please him to send one of his nobilitie or councell, to be associat with him in concluding of peace with the Scotish king. The king of England was neuer dangerous to agree to anie reasonable peace, so it might stand with his honour; and therefore appointed the bishop of Durham doctor Fox, to go into Scotland about that treatie which Peter Hialas had begun. The bishop (according to his commission) went honorablie into Scotland, where he and Peter Hialas at the towne of Iedworth, after long arguing and debating of matters with the Scotish commissioners, in stéed of peace concluded a truce for certeine yeares; vpon condition, that Iames king of Scots should conueie Perkin Warbecke out of his realme, seigniories, and dominions.

About the same time, king Henrie receiued the ambassadors that were sent to him from the French king, and had béene staied at Douer, till the Cornish rebels were vanquished and subdued. Also the lord of Camphire, and other oratours of Philip archduke of Austrich, and duke of Burgognie came to him for the conclusion of amitie, and to haue the English merchants to resort againe to their countrie. Which request being verie agréeable to the quietnesse and wealth of his realme, and especiallie at that time, he did fauorablie grant and agrée vnto. And so did the Englishmen resort againe into the archdukes dominions, and were receiued into Antwerpe with generall procession: so glad was that towne of their returne. Shortlie after the concluding of the truce betweene England and Scotland, Perkin Warbecke being willed of the king of Scots to depart out of the Scotish dominions, sailed with his wife and familie into Ireland, there determining with himselfe either to repaire into Flanders to his first setter vp the duches of Burgognie, or else ioine and take part with the Cornishmen.

The English merchants receiued into Antwerpe with generail procession.

Perkin is faine to packe out of Scotland.

But howsoeuer it came to passe, whilest he laie in Ireland, he had knowledge from the Cornishmen, that they were readie to renew the warre againe. Wherevpon he minding not to let passe so faire an occasion, hauing with him foure small ships, and not aboue six score men, sailed into Cornewall; and there landed in the moneth of September, and came to a towne called Bodman, and there did so prouoke the waueriing

Perkin Warbeck arriueth in Cornwall.

ing people, what with faire words and large promises, that he gathered to him aboue thrée thousand persons, which immediatlie called him their capteine, promising to

Another rebel-
lion by the Cor-
nishmen.

take his part, and follow him to the death. Then Perkin well incouraged, made pro-clamations in the name of king Richard the fourth, as sonne to king Edward the

Perkins thrée
councellors.

fourth. And by the aduise of his three councellors, Iohn Heron mercer a bankrupt, Richard Skelton a tailor, and Iohn Astelie a scriuener determined first of all to assaie the winning of Excester.

Excester as-
saulted by Per-
kin & the Cor-
nishmen.

Then hasting thither, he laid siege to it, and wanting ordinance to make batterie, studied all waies possible how to breake the gates, and what with casting of stones, heauing with iron barres, and kindling of fire vnder the gates, he omitted nothing that could be deuised for the furtherance of his purpose. The citizens, perceiuing in what danger they stood, first let certeine messengers downe by cords ouer the wall, that might certifie the king of their necessitie & trouble. And herewith taking vnto them boldnenesse of courage, determined to repell fire with fire, and caused fagots to be brought and laied to the inward parts of the gates, and set them all on fire; to the intent that the fire being inflamed on both sides the gates, might as well keepe out their enimies from entring, as shut in the citizens from fléeing out, and that they in the

The citie of Ex-
cester preserued
from fire by fire.

meane season might make trenches and rampiers to defend their enimies in stéed of gates and bulworks. Thus by fire was the citie preserued from fire.

Then Perkin of verie necessitie compelled to forsake the gates, assaulted the towne in diuerse weake and vnfortified places, and set vp ladders to take the citie. But the citizens, with helpe of such as were come foorth of the countrie adioining to their aid, so valiantlie defended the walles, that they slue aboue two hundred of Perkins soul-

The king maketh
out his power
against Perkin.

diers at that assault. The king hauing aduertisement of this siege of Excester, hasted foorth with his host, in as much speed as was possible, and sent the lord Daubeneie with certeine bands of light horssemen before, to aduertise all men of his comming at hand. But in the meane season, the lord Edward Courtneie earle of Deuonshire, and the valiant lord William his sonne, accompanied with sir Edmund Carew, sir Thomas Trenchard, sir William Courtneie, sir Thomas Fulford, sir Iohn Halewell, sir Iohn Croker, Water Courtnie, Peter Edgecombe, William saint Maure, with all spéed came into the citie of Excester, and holpe the citizens, and at the last assault was the earle hurt in the arme with an arrow, and so were manie of his companie, but verie few slaine.

When Perkin saw that he could not win the citie of Excester, sith he sawe it was so well fortified both with men and munitions, he departed from thence, and went vnto Taunton, and there the twentith day of September he mustered his men; as though he were readie to giue battell: but perceiuing his number to be minished, by the secret withdrawing of sundrie companies from him, he began to put mistrust in all the remnant. In déed when the people that followed him, in hope that no small number of the nobilitie would ioine with him, saw no such matter come to passe, they stale awaie from him by secret companies. When the king heard that he was gone to Taunton, he followed after him with all spéed. And by the way there came to him

Edward the
yoong duke of
Buckingham
and his companie
ioine with the
king.

Edward duke of Buckingham, a yoong prince of great towardnesse; and him followed a great companie of noble men, knights and esquiers, as sir Alexander Bainam, sir Maurice Barkleie, sir Robert Tame, sir Iohn Guise, sir Robert Pointz, sir Henrie Vernon, sir Iohn Mortimer, sir Thomas Tremaile, sir Edward Sutton, sir Amise Paulet, sir Iohn Birkneill, sir Iohn Sapcotes, sir Hugh Lutterell, sir Francis Cheineie, and diuerse other.

At the kings approching to the towne of Taunton, he set before him Robert lord Brooke lord steward of his house, Giles lord Daubeneie his chiefe chamberleine, and sir Rice ap Thomas. But as soone as Perkin was informed that his enimies were readie to giue him battell, he that nothing lesse minded than to fight in open field with

the

the kings puissance, dissembled all the daie time with his companie, as though no- Perkin fléeth and taketh Beaudlie sanctuarie.
thing could make him afraid: and about midnight, accompanied with thrée score horsse-
men, he departed from Taunton in post to a sanctuarie towne beside Southampton,
called Beaudlie, & there he and Iohn Heron with other registred themselues as persons
priuileged. When as king Henrie knew that Perkin was thus fled, he sent after him
the lord Daubeneie with fiue hundred horssemen toward the sea side, to apprehend
him before he should get away. Although Perkin escaped (as I haue said) vnto
sanctuarie, yet manie of his chiefe capteins were taken and presented to the king

Also the horssemen that were sent, without anie stop or staie came to saint Michaels The beautifull ladie Katharine (Perkins wife) presented to the king.
mount, and there (as chance was) found the ladie Katharine Gordon wife to Perkin,
and brought hir streight to the king. At whose beautie and amiable countenance the
king much maruelled, and thought hir a preie more méet for a prince, than for the
meane souldiers, and sent hir incontinentlie vnto London to the queene, accompanied
with a sort of sage matrones and gentlewomen, bicause she was but yoong. The
common people that had followed Perkin, after that their chéefeteine was fled, threw
awaie their armour as people amazed, and submitted themselues to the king, humblie
beséeching him of mercie, which he most gentlie granted, and receiued them to his
fauour. After this the king road to Excester, and there not onelie commended the
citizens, but also hartilie thanked them for dooing so well their duties in defending
their citie from their enimies. He also put there to execution diuerse Cornishmen,
which were the authors and principall beginners of this new conspiracie and insurrection. Neuerthelesse, he vsed maruellous clemencie also in pardoning a great number
of the rebels.

¶ For when king Henrie was come to Excester with a great armie, mooued there- *Iohn Hooker, alias Vowell.*
vnto (as you haue heard) by reason of the rebellion of Perkin Warbecke, who was
fled before the kings comming, he staied a few daies about the examination of the said
rebellion, and the executing of the chiefe and principall capteins. In the end, the
multitude of the offendors being great, and most humblie crauing for pardon, the All Perkins partakers in their shirts with halters about their necks appeare before the king.
king caused them all to be assembled in the churchyard of saint Peters, where they
all appeared bare headed, in their shirts, and with halters about their necks. His
grace was then lodged in the treasurors house, lieng fast vpon the churchyard, and
out of a faire and large window (made for the purpose) he tooke the view of them,
who shouted and cried out for pardon. At length, when the king had paused, hee
made a speach vnto them, exhorting them to obedience, and in hope he should thencefoorth find them dutifull, he pardoned them all: whereat they all made a great shout,
gaue the king thanks, and hurled awaie their halters. Yet neuerthelesse, some
returned againe, and ioined themselues with the Cornish peo le, which had not all
submitted themselues, nor sought for pardon.]

Now while he remained at Excester, he considered with himselfe, that he had
doone nothing, if he could not get into his hands the chiefe head of this trouble and
seditious businesse. Wherefore he caused the sanctuarie wherein Perkin was inclosed, Perkin in sanctuarie assaulted.
to be inuironed with two bands of light horssemen, to watch diligentlie, that Perkin should
not escape by anie meanes foorth of that place vntaken: and withall attempted by
faire promises of pardon and forgiuenes, if Perkin would submit himselfe to him and
become his man. Perkin perceiuing himselfe so shut vp, that he could no waie escape, Perkin submit- teth himselfe to the king, and is strictlie séene to.
of his owne free will came out of the sanctuarie, and committed himselfe to the kings
pleasure. When the king had thus atchiued his purpose, he returned to London, and
appointed certeine kéepers to attend on Perkin, which should not (the bredth of a
naile) go from his person; least he should conueie himselfe by anie meanes out of
the land [and set new troubles abroch by such practises as he had to fore vsed, for the
aduancement of himselfe to the estate of a king, by assuming vnto himselfe the name
of a kings sonne, when in déed hee was come of base parentage. But Iacke will bee
a gentleman,

a gentleman, the long eared asse will be taken for a leopard, & the pelting pismire for a lion, as one saith:

M. Pal. in Virg.

Nunc se asinus pardum vocat & formica leonem.]

After this, the king caused inquiries to be made, of all such as had aided with men or monie the Cornish rebels, so that diuerse persons as well in Summersetshire as Deuonshire were detected of that offense, which he minded for example sake should tast some part of due punishments for their crimes, according to the qualitie thereof.

Cŏmissioners appointed for assessing of their fines that fauoured the Cornish rebels.
1498

And therefore he appointed Thomas lord Darcie, Amise Paulet knight, and Robert Sherborne deane of Poules (that was after bishop of Chichester) to be commissioners for assessing of their fines that were found culpable. These commissioners so bestirred themselues, in tossing the coffers and substance of all the inhabitants of both those shires, that there was not one person imbrued or spotted with the filth of that abhominable crime, that escaped the paine which he had deserued: but to such yet as offended rather by constreint than of malice, they were gentle and fauourable, so that equitie therein was verie well and iustlie executed.

Abr. Fl. ex. I. S. pag. 872.
Gardens in Moore field laid wast to make archers game.
Price of haie doubled.
Sebastian Gabato his discouerie of an Iland of rich commodities.

¶ In this yeare all the gardens which had béene continued time out of mind, without Moore gate of London, were destroied, and of them was made a plaine field for archers to shoot in. Also this yéere was a great drought, by reason whereof a load of haie, which was before sold at London at fiue shillings, was this yeare sold for ten or twelue more. Also this yeare, one Sebastian Gabato, a Genoas sonne, borne in Bristow, professing himselfe to be expert in knowledge of the circuit of the world, and Ilands of the same, as by his charts and other reasonable demonstrations he shewed, caused the king to man and vittell a ship at Bristow, to search for an Iland which he knew to be replenished with rich commodites. In the ship diuerse merchants of London aduentured small stocks, and in the companie of this ship sailed also out of Bristow three or foure small ships fraight with slight and grosse wares, as course cloath, caps, lases, points, and such other.

Sir Humfrie Gilbert knight, in his booke intituled, A discouerie for a new passage to Cataia, writeth thus; " Sebastian Gabato, by his personall experience and trauell, hath described and set foorth this passage in his charts, which are yet to be séene in the quéenes maiesties priuie gallerie at White hall, who was sent to make this discouerie by king Henrie the seuenth, and entered the same fret, affirming that hee sailed verie farre westward, with a quarter of the north, on the north side of terra de Labrador, the eleuenth of Iune, vntill he came to the septentrionall latitude of $67\frac{1}{2}$ degrées, and finding the seas still open, said, that he might & would haue gon to Cataia, if the emnitie of the maister and mariners had not béene." Neuerthelesse, he went verie farre, euen to a nation inhabited with people more like beasts than men, as appeareth in the yeare 1502, and the seuentéenth of this kings reigne, when the said traueller was returned, and presented himselfe to the kings maiestie.]

An. Reg. 14.
England and Scotland liklie to go togither by the eares afresh.

In this yeare the warre had like to haue béene reuiued betwixt the realmes of England and Scotland by a small occasion, as thus. Certeine yongmen of the Scots came arriued before Norham castell, & beheld it woonderous circumspectlie, as though they would faine haue béene of counsell to know what was doone therein. The kéepers not perceiuing anie damage attempted against them for the first time, determined not to mooue anie question to them, or once to stirre out. But when they came againe the next day, and viewed it likewise, the kéepers of the castell suspecting some euill meaning, demanded of them what their intent was, and why they viewed and aduised so the castell. The Scots answered them roughlie with disdainfull words, so that the Englishmen fell to and replied with strokes; and after manie blowes giuen and receiued, diuerse Scots were wounded, and some slaine; and the residue ouermatched with multitude of the Englishmen, fled as fast as their horsses could carie them.

The

The Scotish king hereof aduertised, was highlie displeased, and in all hast signified to king Henrie by his herald Marchemont, in what sort his people (to the breach of the truce) were abused and handled. King Henrie being not in will to breake with anie of his neighbours, excused the matter, affirming that he was not of knowledge to the misdemeanor of those that had the castell in kéeping; requiring the king of Scots not to thinke the truce broken for anie thing doone without his consent; promising in the word of a king to inquire of the truth, and if the offense were found to be begun on the partie of the kéepers of the castell, he assured him that they should for no meed nor fauour escape due correction and punishment.

This answer (though it was more than reasonable) could not pacifie the king of Scots, till the bishop of Durham (that was owner of the castell of Norham) who sore lamented, that by such as he appointed kéepers there, the warre should be renewed) with sundrie letters written to the Scotish king, at length asswaged his displeasure, so that the said king wrote courteouslie to the bishop againe, signifieng that bicause he had manie secret things in his mind, which he would communicate onelie with him touching this matter now in variance; therefore he required him to take the paine to come into his countrie, trusting that he should thinke his labor well bestowed. The bishop was glad, and sent word hereof to the king his master, who willed him to accomplish the desire of the Scotish king, which he tooke to bee reasonable. *The bishop of Durham asswageth the kings displeasure by leters.*

At his comming into Scotland, he was courteouslie receiued of the king himselfe at the abbeie of Melrosse. And there, after the king had (for a countenance) complained much of the vniust slaughter of his men late committed at Norham: vpon the bishops gentle answers thervnto, he forgaue the same, and after began to talke secretlie without witnesses alone with the bishop. And first he declared what iust causes mooued him in times past to séeke amitie with the king of England: which now he desired much more to haue confirmed, for further maintenance & increase thereof. Which he doubted not but should sort to a fortunate conclusion, if the king of England would vouchsafe to giue to him in matrimonie his first begotten daughter the ladie Margaret, vpon which point he purposed latelie to haue sent his ambassadors into England, which thing he would the sooner doo if he knew the bishops mind therein to bée readie to further his sute. The bishop answered but few words sauing that when he were returned to the king his maister, he would doo the best in the matter that he could. *The bishop of Durham goeth into Scotland.*

The Scotish king desireth the ladie Margaret eldest daughter of K. Henrie the seuenth to be his wife.

When the bishop was returned into England, and come to the king, he declared to him all the communication had betwéene king Iames and him, from point to point in order. The king liked well thereof as he to whome peace was euer a souereigne solace and comfort. In this meane time Perkin Warbecke, disappointed of all hope to escape out of the Englishmens hands (which was the onelie thing that he most desired) found meanes yet at length to deceiue his kéepers, & took him to his héels. But when he came to the sea coasts, and could not passe, he was in a maruellous perplexitie: for euerie by way, lane, and corner was laid for him, and such search made, that being brought to his wits end, and cut short of his pretensed iournie, he came to the house of Bethlem, called the priorie of Shéene beside Richmond in Southerie, and betooke himselfe to the prior of that monasterie, requiring him for the honour of God, to beg his pardon of life of the kings maiestie. *1499*

Perkin Warbecke escapeth from his kéepers.

The prior, which for the opinion that men had conceiued of his vertue, was had in great estimation, pitieng the wretched state of that caitife, came to the king, and shewed him of this Perkin, whose pardon he humblie craued, and had it as fréelie granted. Incontinentlie after was Perkin brought to the court againe at Westminster, and was one day set fettered in a paire of stocks, before the doore of Westminster hall, and there stood a whole day, not without innumerable reproches, mocks and scornings. And the next daie he was caried through London, and set vpon a like

scaffold

scaffold in Cheape by the standard, with like ginnes and stocks as he occupied the daie before, and there stood all daie, and read openlie his owne confession, written with his owne hand, the verie copie whereof here insueth.

The confession of Perkin as it was written with his owne hand, which he read openlie vpon a scaffold by the standard in Cheape.

IT is first to be knowne, that I was borne in the towne of Turneie in Flanders, and my fathers name is Iohn Osbecke, which said Iohn Osbecke was controllor of the said towne of Turneie, and my moothers name is Katharine de Faro. And one of my grandsires vpon my fathers side was named Diricke Osbeck, which died. After whose death my grandmoother was married vnto Peter Flamin, that was receiuer of the forenamed towne of Turneie, & deane of the botemen that row vpon the water or riuer called le Scheld. And my grandsire vpon my moothers side was Peter de Faro, which had in his keeping the keies of the gate of S. Iohns within the same towne of Turneie. Also I had an vncle called maister Iohn Stalin, dwelling in the parish of S. Pias within the same towne, which had maried my fathers sister, whose name was Ione or Iane, with whome I dwelt a certeine season.

Perkin maketh an anatomie of his descent or linage.

And after I was led by my moother to Antwerpe for to learne Flemish, in a house of a cousine of mine, an officer of the said towne, called Iohn Stienbecke, with whome I was the space of halfe a yeare. And after that I returned againe to Turneie, by reason of warres that were in Flanders. And within a yeare following I was sent with a merchant of the said towne of Turneie, named Berlo, to the mart of Antwerpe, where I fell sicke, which sickenesse continued vpon me fiue moneths. And the said Berlo set me to boord in a skinners house, that dwelled beside the house of the English nation. And by him I was from thense caried to Barow mart; and I lodged at the signe of the old man, where I abode for the space of two moneths.

Perkins education or bringing vp.

After this, the said Berlo set me with a merchant of Middleborow to seruice for to learne the language, whose name was Iohn Strew, with whome I dwelt from Christmasse to Easter, and then I went into Portingall in companie of sir Edward Bramptons wife, in a ship which was called the queens ship. And when I was come thither, then was I put in seruice to a knight that dwelled in Lushborne, which was called Peter Vacz de Cogna, with whome I dwelled an whole yeare, which said knight had but one eie. And bicause I desired to see other countries, I tooke licence of him, and then I put my selfe in seruice with a Briton, called Pregent Meno, which brought me with him into Ireland. Now when we were there arriued in the towne of Corke, they of the towne (bicause I was arraied with some cloths of silke of my said maisters) came vnto me, & threatned vpon me that I should be the duke of Clarences sonne, that was before time at Dublin.

Perk n a notable landloper.

But forsomuch as I denied it, there was brought vnto me the holie euangelists, and the crosse, by the maior of the towne, which was called Iohn Leweline, and there in the presence of him and others, I tooke mine oth (as the truth was) that I was not the foresaid dukes sonne, nor none of his bloud. And after this came vnto me an Englishman, whose name was Stephan Poitron, and one Iohn Water, and laid to me in swearing great oths, that they knew well that I was king Richards bastard sonne: to whome I answered with like oths, that I was not. Then they aduised me not to be afeard, but that I should take it vpon me boldlie: and if I would so doo, they would aid and assist me with all their power against the king of England; & not onelie they, but they were well assured, that the earle of Desmond & Kildare should doo the same.

The Irish would haue Perkin take vpon him to be the duke of Clarences sonne.

They beare Perkin downe with oths that he is king Richards bastard.

For they forced not what part they tooke, so that they might be reuenged on the king

king of England: and so against my will made me to learne English, and taught me They call him duke of Yorke. what I should doo and saie. And after this they called me duke of Yorke, second sonne to king Edward the fourth, bicause king Richards bastard sonne was in the hands of the king of England. And vpon this the said Water, Stephan Poitron, Iohn Tiler, Hughbert Burgh, with manie others, as the foresaid earles, entered into this false quarell, and within short time others. The French K. sent an ambassador into Ireland, whose name was Loit Lucas, and maister Stephan Friham, to aduertise me to come into France. And thense I went into France, and from thense into Flanders, & from Flanders into Ireland, and from Ireland into Scotland, & so into England.

When the night of the same daie (being the fifteenth of Iune) was come, after he had stood all that daie in the face of the citie, he was committed to the Tower, there to remaine vnder safe kéeping, least happilie he might eftsoones run awaie, and escape out of the land, to put the king and realme to some new trouble. For he had a woonderfull dexteritie and readinesse to circumuent, a heart full of ouerreaching imaginations, an aspiring mind, a head more wilie (I wisse) than wittie; bold he was and presumptuous in his behauiour, as forward to be the instrument of a mischeefe, as anie deuiser of wickednesse would wish; a féend of the diuels owne forging, nursed and trained vp in the studie of commotions, making offer to reach as high as he could looke; such was his inordinate ambition, wherewith he did swell as coueting to be a princes peere: much like the tode that would match the bull in drinking, but in the end she burst in peeces and neuer dranke more; as the poet telleth the tale (by the imitation of the fabler) saieng:

————cupiens æquare bibendo *M. Pal. in Virg.*
Rana bouem, rupta nunquam bibit amplius aluo.

In this yeare was an Augustine frier called Patrike in the parties of Suffolke, the *An.* Reg. 15.
Patrike an
Augustine
Frier. which hauing a scholer named Rafe Wilford (a shoomakers sonne of London as Stow noteth) had so framed him to his purpose, that in hope to worke some great enterprise, as to disappoint the king of his crowne and seat roiall, tooke vpon him to be the earle Rafe Wilford the
counterfeit earle
of Warwike. of Warwike, insomuch that both the maister and scholer hauing counselled betwéene themselues of their enterprise, they went into Kent, & there began the yoong mawmet to tell priuilie to manie, that he was the verie earle of Warwike, and latelie gotten out of the Tower, by the helpe of this frier Patrike. To which saiengs when the frier perceiued some light credence to be giuen, he declared it openlie in the pulpit, and desired all men of helpe. But the danger of this seditious attempt was shortlie re-mooued and taken awaie, the maister and scholer being both apprehended and cast into prison and atteinted.

The scholer was hanged on Shrouetuesdaie at saint Thomas Waterings, and the frier The counterfeit
earle is execu-
ted. condemned to perpetuall prison. For at that time so much reuerence was attributed to the holie orders, that to a préest (although he had committed high treason against his souereigne lord) his life was spared, in like case as to anie other offendor in mur-ther, rape, or theft, that had receiued anie of the three higher holie orders. [The *Abr. Fl. ex*
Edw. Hall. in
Hen. 7. *fol.* lj. chéefe cause (saith Edward Hall) of this fauour was this, bicause bishops of a long The cause why
the clergie neuer
so heinouslie
offending was
so fauoured. time and season did not take knowledge, nor intermix themselues with the search & punishment of such heinous and detestable offenses: by reason whereof. they did not disgrade and depriue from the holie orders such malefactors and wicked persons, which without that ceremonie by the canon lawes could not be put to death.

Furthermore, what should a man saie, it was also vsed, that he that could but onelie read (yea although he vnderstood not what he read) how heinous or detestable a crime so euer he had committed (treason onelie excepted) should likewise as affines & alies to the holie orders be saued, and committed to the bishops prison. And to the intent that if they should escape, and be againe taken, committing like offense, that their liues

be

be no more to them pardoned: it was ordeined that murtherers should be burnt on the brawne of the left hand with an hot iron signed with this letter M. and théeues in the same place with this letter T. So that if they, which were once signed with anie of these markes or tokens did reiterate like crime & offense againe, should suffer the

Burning in the hand when enacted.
paines and punishments which they had both merited and deserued. Which decrée was enacted and established in a session of parlement kept in the time of this kings reigne, and taken (as I coniecture) of the French nation, which are woont, if they take anie such offendor, to cut off one of his eares, as a sure token and marke hereafter of his euill dooing.]

Perkin corrupted his kéepers.
Perkin Warbecke (as before ye haue heard) being now in hold, by false persuasions and great promises corrupted his kéepers, Stranguish, Blewet, Astwood, and long Roger, seruants to sir Iohn Digbie lieutenant of the Tower. Insomuch that they (as it was at their arreignment openlie prooued) intended to haue slaine their maister, and to haue set Perkin and the earle of Warwike at large. Which earle of Warwike had beene kept in prison within the Tower almost from his tender yeares, that is to saie, from the first yeare of the king, to this fiftéenth yeare, out of all companie of men &

Edward Plantagenet earle of Warwike a verie innocent.
sight of beasts, insomuch that he could not discerne a goose from a capon, and therefore by common reason and open apparance could not of himselfe séeke his owne death and destruction. But yet by the drift and offense of an other he was brought to his death and confusion.

For being made priuie of this enterprise deuised by Perkin and his complices, therevnto (as all naturall creatures loue libertie) he assented and agreed. But this craftie deuise and subtill imagination being reuealed, sorted to none effect, so that Perkin and Iohn Awater sometime maior of Corke in Ireland, one of his chéefe founders, and his sonne, were on the sixtéenth daie of Nouember arreigned and condemned at Westminster. And on the thrée and twentith daie of the same moneth, Perkin and Iohn Awater

Perkin and Iohn Awater executed at Tiburne.
were drawne to Tiburne, where Perkin standing on a little scaffold, read his confession (as before he had doone in Cheape side) taking it on his death to be true. And so he and Iohn Awater asked the king forgiuenesse, and died patientlie.

This was the reward of the feined glose and counterfeit comment of Perkin Warbecke, the which as by his false surmises in his life time had brought manie honourable personages to their deaths, and vndoone manie an honest man: so now at his death he brought other of the same sort to their not altogither vndeserued punishment. And amongest others Edward Plantagenet the forenamed erle of Warwike, which (as the fame went) consented to breake prison, and to depart out of the realme with Perkin (which in prisoners is high treason) was the one and twentith daie of the said moneth arreigned at Westminster before the earle of Oxenford then high steward of England of the said treason, which (whether it were by intisement and persuasion of other, or of his owne frée will manie doubted, bicause of his innocencie) confessed the fact,

Edward Plantagenet the yoong earle of Warwike beheaded
and submitted himselfe to the kings mercie; and vpon his confession had his iudgement, and according thervnto the eight and twentith daie of Nouember in the yeare 1499, was brought to the scaffold on the Tower hill, and there beheaded.

The fame after his death sprang abroad, that Ferdinando king of Spaine would make no full conclusion of the matrimonie to be had betweene prince Arthur and the ladie Katharine daughter to the said Ferdinando, nor send hir into England as long as this earle liued. For he imagined that so long as anie earle of Warwike liued, England should neuer be purged of ciuill warre and priuie sedition; so much was the name of Warwike in other regions had in feare and gealousie. The next yeare after there was

1500
A great plague.
a great plague, whereof men died in manie places verie sore; but speciallie and most of all in the citie of London, where died in that yeare thirtie thousand. The foure and twentith of Februarie in this fifteenth yeare of this kings reigne his third son was

Edward the kings third sonne christened.
christened and was named Edward. Also in this yeare was burned a place of the kings,

kings, called the manour of Shéene situate nigh the Thames side, which he after The manour of
builded againe sumptuouslie, and changed the name of Sheene, and called it Rich- Shéene burnt
mond; bicause his father and he were earles of Richmond: or (as some note) for that & Richmond built in place
so manie notable and rich iewels were there burnt.   He also new builded Bainards thereof.
castell in London, and repaired Greenewich.] *I. S. pag.* 874.

The king, whether to auoid the danger of so great and perilous sickenesse, then raging, or to take occasion to commen with the duke of Burgognie, did personallie take King Henr'e
his ship at Douer in the beginning of Maie, and sailed to Calis, whither the duke of the seuenth saileth to Calis.
Burgognie sent to him honourable personages in ambassage to welcome him into those
parties, and to declare that the said duke would gladlie repaire personallie to his presence with such a number as the king should appoint, so that it were within no walled
towne nor fortresse.   For hauing denied the French king to enter into anie of his fortresses to talke with him, he would be loth now to giue a president to him to desire
the like méeting.   The king interteining the ambassadours, and thanking the duke of
his courteous offer, appointed the place at saint Peters church without Calis.

Vpon tuesdaie in Whitsunweeke the archduke Philip came thither with a con- The king of
uenient companie.   The king and the queene with manie a lustie lord and ladie rode England and the duke of
thither to welcome him.   [And when the king approched, the duke at his lighting Burgognie méet
offered to hold his stirrupe, which the king in no wise would suffer to be doone. at saint Peters church without
When the king was descended from his horsse, he and the archduke imbraced each Calis.
other with most princelie familiaritie, and then the quéene and all the nobles saluted *Abr. Fl. ex*
him.]   And after most louing interteinments, bankettings, mirth, and pastime shewed *Edw. Hall, in Hen.* 7. *fol.* lij.
amongest them, there was communication of marriages, treating of further strengthen-
ing of leagues, requests of tolles in Flanders to be minished: with manie other things
touching the commoditie and traffike of both their countries.   And when all things
were set in order, the two princes tooke their leaue, and departed; the king to Calis,
and the archduke to S. Omers.   After his departing, there came as ambassadors from
the French king, the lord Gronthouse gouernour of Picardie, and the lord Meruelliers
bailiffe of Amiens, which declared to the king the getting of Millaine and taking of
the duke.   The king highlie feasted them, and rewarded them princelie at their
departing.

Soone after, when the death was slaked, the king returned againe into England *An. Reg.* 16.
about the end of Iune.   Shortlie after there came to him one Gasper Pons a Spaniard,
a man of excellent learning and most ciuill behauiour, sent from Axexander the bishop
of Rome to distribute the heauenlie grace (as he termed it) to all such as (letted by
anie forceable impediment) could not come to Rome that yeare to the Iubile, which A yeare of
was there celebrate, being the yeare after the birth of our Sauiour, 1500.   This be- Iubile.
neuolent liberalitie was not altogither fréelie giuen.   For Alexander looking to the Pope Alexander
health of mens soules, thought to doo somewhat for his owne priuat commoditie, & maketh profit of his great pardon
therefore he set a certeine price of that his grace and pardon.   And to the end that or heauenlie
the king should not hinder his purpose, he offered part of his gaines to the king. grace, as he termeth it.

And to colour the matter with some fauourable pretext, and to make men the better
willing, & more readie to giue franklie, he promised with that monie to make warre
against the Turke.   By this meanes the pope got a great masse of monie, which he
had conueied ouer vnto him by such trustie messengers (doubt you not) as he had appointed; and yet nothing doone against the Turks, which in the meane season did
much hurt to the christians. [For it was no part of his meaning (what colourable shew *Abr. Flem.*
soeuer he made of tendering the succourlesse people) to impart anie portion thereof to
so good a vse; but rather for the supportation of him and his swarme, who before
they will bate an ace of their gorgeous gallantnesse, the whole world shall be cousened.
Such is the collusion of the pope, such be the shamelesse shifts of him and his cleargie for the maintenance of their owne courtlie brauerie, which is wicked vanitie; farre
passing

passing the pompe of anie prince, were the same of neuer so rare magnificence; as he well noteth that said full trulie:

————immenso princeps non visus in orbe est,
　　Cui tanti fastus tantáue pompa fuit.
Ingreditur quando miseræ Babylonis in vrbes,
　　Cernitur hic plusquam regia pompa comes.
Huic equus est spumans ostróq; insignis & auro,
　　Altisono cuius sub pede terra fremit, &c.]

About this time died thrée bishops in England, Iohn Morton archbishop of Canturburie, Thomas Langton bishop of Winchester, and Thomas Rotheram archbishop of Yorke. After him succéeded Thomas Sauage bishop of London, a man of great honour and worthinesse: in whose place succéeded William Worham, of whome before is made mention. And Henrie Deane bishop of Salisburie, was made archbishop of Canturburie, and Richard Fox was remooued from Durham to the sée of Winchester.

Also this yeare two notable mariages were concluded, but not consummate till afterwards, as you shall heare in place conuenient. For king Henrie granted his daughter ladie Margaret to Iames the fourth king of Scots. And Ferdinando king of Spaine gaue his daughter ladie Katharine to Arthur prince of Wales, sonne and heire apparant to the king of England.

Among other articles of the mariage concluded with the Scotish king this was one, that no English men should be receiued into Scotland without letters commendatorie of their souereigne lord, or safe conduct of his warden of the marches; and the same prohibition was in like maner giuen to the Scots. This yeare the ladie Katharine of Spaine was sent by hir father king Ferdinando with a puissant nauie of ships into England, where she arriued in the hauen of Plimmouth the second daie of October then being saturdaie. Vpon the twelft of Nouember she was conueied from Lambeth through London with all triumph and honour that might be deuised to the bishops palace, the stréets being hanged, and pageants erected after the maner as is vsed at a coronation: which solemnitie Edward Hall describeth with the sumptuous shewes then glistering in the beholders eies.

¶ I passe ouer (saith he) the wise deuises, the prudent spéeches, the costlie works, the cunning portratures, practised and set foorth in seuen goodlie beautifull pageants, erected and set vp in diuerse places of the citie. I leaue also the goodlie ballades, the swéet harmonie, the musicall instruments, which sounded with heauenlie noise on euerie side of the streets. I omit further, the costlie apparell both of goldsmiths worke and imbroderie, the rich iewels, the massie chaines, the stirring horsses, the beautifull bards and the glittering trappers, both with belles and spangels of gold. I pretermit also the rich apparell of the princesse, the strange fashion of the Spanish nation, the beautie of the English ladies, the goodlie demeanure of the yoong damosels, the amorous countenance of the lustie bachelers. I passe ouer also the fine ingrained clothes, the costlie furs of the citizens, standing on scaffolds, raised from Gracechurch to Paules. What should I speake of the oderiferous scarlets, the fine veluets, the pleasant furres, the massie chaines, which the maior of London with the senat, sitting on horssebacke at the little conduit in Cheape, ware on their bodies and about their necks? I will not speake of the rich arras, the costlie tapestrie, the fine clothes both of gold and siluer, the curious veluets, the beautifull sattens, nor the pleasant silkes which did hang in euerie street where she passed, the wine that ran continuallie out of the conduits, and the graueling of the stréets néedeth not to be remembred.]

Whilest this ladie soiourned for hir recreation in the bishops palace of London, being in the meane time visited of the king, the quéene, and the kings mother, there was erected in the bodie of S. Paules church a long bridge made of timber, extending

tending from the west doore of the church to the step at the entring into the queere, which was six foot from the ground. On the said bridge or stage, euen directlie before the consistorie of the church, was a place raised like a mount for eight persons to stand vpon, compassed round about with steps to ascend and descend, which was couered with fine red worsted, and in likewise were all the railes of the said stage. On the north side of this mount was a place decked and trimmed for the king and quéene, and such other as they appointed to haue. On the south side of the same mount stood the maior and the magistrates of the citie.

When all things were prepared and set in order, vpon the fouretéenth of Nouember then being sundaie, the foresaid ladie was led to the said mount, and there prince Arthur openlie espoused hir, both being clad in white, both lustie and amorous, he of the age of fiftéene and more, and she of the age of eightéene or thereabouts, the king and queene standing priuily on their stage. After the matrimonie celebrated, the prince and his wife went vp into the queere, and there heard a solemne masse soong by the archbishop of Canturburie, associat with nineteene prelats mitred. And after the masse finished, the bride was led homewards to the bishops palace by the duke of Yorke, being then a goodlie yoong prince, and the legat of Spaine. Next after followed the ladie Cicilie sister to the quéene, supporting the traine of the spouse. The solemniza-
tion of the ma-
riage betwéene
Arthur prince of
Wales & Ka-
tharine daughter
to the king of
Spaine.

But to speake of all the solemne pompe, noble companie of lords and ladies, and what a sumptuous feast and plentifull was kept, with dansing and disguisings, words might sooner faile than matter worthie of rehearsall. Howbeit euerie daie endeth and night insueth, and so when night was come, the prince and his beautifull bride were brought and ioined togither in one bed, where they laie as man and wife all that night. ¶ Now when the morning appéered, the prince (as his familiar seruitors, which had then neither cause nor reward to lie or faine, openlie told the tale) called for drinke, which he before times was not accustomed to doo. At which thing one of his chamberleins maruelling, asked the cause of his drouth. To whome the prince answered merilie, saieng; I haue this night béene in the middest of Spaine, which is a hot region, and that iournie maketh me so drie: and if thou haddest béene vnder that hot climat, thou wouldest haue béene drier than I.] Edw. Hall,
fol. liij.

Shortlie after the king and the quéene, with the new wedded spouses went from Bainards castell by water to Westminster, on whom the maior and communaltie of London in barges gorgeouslie trimmed gaue their attendance. And there in the palace were such martiall feats, valiant iusts, vigorous turneis, and such fierce fight at the barriers, as before that time was of no man had in remembrance. Of this roiall triumph lord Edward duke of Buckingham was chiefe chalenger, and lord Thomas Greie marquesse Dorset chiefe defender, which with their aids and companions bare themselues so valiantlie, that they got great praise and honour, both of the Spaniards, and of their owne countriemen. During the time of these iusts and triumphs, were receiued into London, an earle, a bishop, and diuerse noble personages sent from the king of Scots into England, for conclusion of the mariage betwéene the ladie Margaret and him; which earle by proxie, in the name of king Iames his maister, affied and contracted the said ladie. Which affiance was published at Paules crosse, the daie of the conuersion of saint Paule: in reioising whereof Te Deum was soong, and great fiers made through the citie of London. Margaret eldest
daughter to king
Henrie affied to
Iames king of
Scots.

These things being accomplished, the ambassadors as well of Spaine as Scotland tooke their leaue of the king, & not without great rewards returned into their countries. When the ambassadors were departed, he sent his sonne prince Arthur againe into Wales, to keepe that countrie in good order; appointing to him wise and expert councellors, as sir Richard Poole his kinsman, which was his chiefe chamberleine, also sir Henrie Vernon, sir Richard Crofts, sir Dauid Philip, sir William Wall, 1502

Prince Arthur
is sent into
Wales.

sir Thomas Englefield, sir Peter Newton knights; Iohn Walleston, Henrie Marton, & doctor William Smith, president of his councell, and doctor Charles; of the which two doctors, the one was after bishop of Lincolne, and the other bishop of Hereford.

¶ This yeare Iohn Shaw (who was maior of London) caused his brethren the aldermen to ride from the Guildhall vnto the water side, when he went to Westminster to be presented in the excheker. He also caused the kitchens and other houses of *The maiors feast first kept at Guildhall.* office to be builded at the Guildhall, where since that time the maiors feasts haue béene kept, which before had béene in the grosers or tailors hall. About Easter, all the Greie friers in England changed their habit, for whereas of long time before they had vsed to weare browne russet of foure shillings, six shillings, and eight shillings *Woollen cloth of two shillings the brode yard.* the yard; now they were compelled to weare russet of two shillings the yard and not aboue, which was brought to passe by the Friers of Gréenewich. This yeare, the *Dikes of Lõdon clensed.* dike called Turnemill brooke, with all the course of Fléet dike, were so scowred downe to the Thames, that boates with fish and fewell were rowed vp to Holborne bridge, as they of old time had beene accustomed: which was a great commoditie to all the inhabitants in that part of London. Also the tower néere to the Blacke friers was taken downe by the commandement of the maior. Also this yeare were brought *Men brought from the new found islands.* vnto the king thrée men taken in the new found ilands, by Sebastian Gabato, before named in Anno 1468. These men were clothed in beasts skins, and eat raw flesh, but spake such a language as no man could vnderstand them, of the which thrée men, two of them were séene in the kings court at Westminster two yeares after, clothed like Englishmen, and could not be discerned from Englishmen.]

A few moneths before the mariage of prince Arthur, Edmund de la Poole earle of Suffolke, sonne to Iohn duke of Suffolke, and ladie Elizabeth sister to king Edward the fourth, being bold and rash withall, was indicted of murther, for sleaing of a meane person in his rage & furie. And although the king pardoned him whome he might iustlie haue put to death for that offense; yet bicause he was brought to the barre before the kings Bench, and arraigned (which fact he tooke as a great blemish to *Edmund erle of Suffolke fleeth into Flanders.* his honour) shortlie after vpon that displeasure he fled into Flanders vnto his aunt the ladie Margaret, the king not being priuie to his going ouer. Neuerthelesse, whether he was persuaded by his fréends therevnto, whom the king had willed to deale with him therein; or whether vpon trust of his innocencie: true it is that he returned againe, and excused himselfe to the king, so that he thought him to be giltlesse of anie crime that might be obiected against him.

But when the mariage betwixt the prince & the ladie Katharine of Spaine was kept at London, this erle either for that he had passed his compasse in excessiue charges and sumptuousnesse at that great triumph and solemnitie, and by reason thereof was farre run into debt; either else through the procurement of his aunt the foresaid ladie Margaret; or pricked with some priuie enuie, which could not patientlie *The discontented mind of the earle of Suffolke.* with open eies behold king Henrie (being of the aduerse faction to his linage) so long to reigne in wealth and felicitie: in conclusion with his brother Richard fled againe into Flanders. This departure of the earle sore vexed the king, doubting of some new trouble to insue thereof.

The kings woonted policie now againe practised. But yet to vnderstand the full meaning of the said earle, the king vsed his old fetch: for immediatlie after the earle was fled, he appointed sir Robert Curson, whome he had aduanced to the order of knighthood, and made capteine of Hammes castell, a valiant man and a circumspect, to dissemble himselfe one of that conspiracie; who went into Flanders, to espie what was doone there by the ladie Margaret, and hir nephue the earle of Suffolke. After that the said sir Robert Curson was thus gone into Flanders, the king, to put him out of all suspicion with the said ladie Margaret and the earle, caused the said earle, and sir Robert Curson, and fiue

persons

persons more to be accurssed at Paules crosse, the first sundaie of Nouember, as enimies to him and his realme.

To be breefe, the king by his meanes, and other such diligent inquisition as he made, tried out such as he suspected, partlie to be deuisers of mischéefe against him, and partlie to beare no sincere affection towards his person, so that he could readilie name them: whereof a great part were within few daies apprehended and taken. And amongst them William lord Courtneie, sonne to the earle of Deuonshire, which maried the ladie Katharine, daughter to king Edward the fourth; lord William de la Poole, brother to the foresaid earle of Suffolke, sir Iames Tirrell, and sir Iohn Windham. Both the Williams were rather taken of suspicion, bicause they were so neere of kin to the conspirator, than for anie prooued matter. But sir Iames Tirrell and Iohn Windam, bicause they were traitors, and so attainted, the sixt daie of Maie after their apprehension, they were on the Tower hill beheaded.

Tirrell & Windham beheaded.

When the earle of Suffolke heard what fortune thus happened to his fréends, as one in vtter despaire to haue anie good successe in his pretensed enterprise, wandred about all Germanie and France, to purchase some aid and succour, if by anie means he might. But when he perceiued no stedfast ground to catch anchor hold vpon, he submitted himselfe vnder the protection of Philip archduke of Austrich. But his brother Richard, being a politike man, so wiselie ordered himselfe in this stormie tempest, that he was not intrapped either with net or snare. The king not yet out of all doubt of ciuill sedition, bicause a great number of euill disposed persons partakers of this conspiracie, were fled into sundrie sanctuaries, deuised to haue all the gates of sanctuaries and places priuileged shut and locked vp, so that none should issue out from thence to perturbe and disquiet him.

And for that intent he wrote vnto pope Alexander, desiring him by his authoritie to adiudge all Englishmen, being fled to sanctuarie for the offense of treason as enimies to the christian faith, interdicting and prohibiting the refuge and priuilege of sanctuarie to all such, as once had enioied the libertie and protection of the same, and after that fled out, and eftsoones returned againe. Which thing after that the pope had granted, turned to the great quietnesse of the king and his realme. For manie that had offended, for feare to fall into danger, returned to the due subiection of their prince; and other that were yet frée from perill, durst not hazard themselues so boldlie as they durst haue doone before, vpon hope of such starting holes.

Sanctuaries restrained.

When the king had thus setled things to his owne contentation and pleasure, there suddenlie happened to him a lamentable chance. For that noble prince Arthur, the kings first begotten sonne, after he had béene maried to the ladie Katharine his wife, the space of fiue moneths, departed out of this transitorie life, in his castell of Ludlow and with great funerall obsequie was buried in the cathedrall church of Worcester. His brother the duke of Yorke was staied from the title of Prince by the space of a moneth, till to women it might appeare whether the ladie Katharine wife to the said prince Arthur was conceiued with child or not. [It is reported that this ladie Katharine thought and feared such dolorous chance to come: for when she had imbraced hir father, and taken hir leaue of hir noble and prudent mother, and sailed towards England, she was continuallie so tossed and tumbled hither and thither with boisterous winds, that what for the rage of the water, and contrarietie of the winds, hir ship was prohibited diuerse times to approach the shore and take land.]

The death of Arthur prince of Wales.

Edw. Hall in Hen. 7. fol. iv.

In this eightéenth yeare, the twentie fourth daie of Ianuarie, a quarter of an houre afore three of the clocke at after noone of the same daie, the first stone of our ladie chapell within the monasterie of Westminster was laid, by the hands of Iohn Islip abbat of the same monasterie, sir Reginald Braie knight of the garter, doctor Barnes maister of the rolles, doctor Wall chapleine to the kings maiestie, maister Hugh Oldham chapleine to the countesse of Darbie and Richmond the kings mother,

An. Reg. 18.

1503

King Henrie the seauenths chapell at Westminster first builded.

sir

sir Edmund Stanhope knight, and diuerse others. Vpon the same stone was this scripture ingrauen: Illustrissimus Henricus septimus rex Angliæ & Franciæ, & dominus Hiberniæ, posuit hanc petram in honore beatæ virginis Mariæ, 24 die Ianuarij; anno Domini 1502. Et anno dicti regis Henrici septimi, decimo octauo. The charges whereof amounted (as some report, vpon credible information as they saie) to foureteéne thousand pounds.

Quéene Elizabeth lieng within the Tower of London, was brought a bed of a faire daughter on Candlemasse daie, which was there christened and named Katharine; and the eleuenth of the same moneth the said queene there deceased, and was buried at Westminster, whose daughter also liued but a small season after hir mother. [King Henrie the seauenth being himselfe a brother of the tailors companie in London, as diuerse other his predecessors kings before him had béene (to wéet Richard the third, Edward the fourth, Henrie the sixt, Henrie the fift, Henrie the fourth, and Richard the second; also of dukes eleuen, earles eight and twentie, and lords eight and fortie) he now gaue to them the name and title of merchant tailors, as a name of worship to indure for euer. This yeare, about the later end of March, the prior of the Charterhouse of Shene was murthered in a cell of his owne house, by meanes of one Goodwine, a monke of the same cloister, and his adherents artificers of London. A drie summer, hauing no notable raine from Whitsuntide to the later ladie daie in haruest.

The eighteenth of Februarie, the king at his palace of Westminster created his onelie sonne Henrie prince of Wales, earle of Chester, &c: who afterward succéeded his father in possession of the regall crowne of this realme. Moreouer, this yeare also, after the deceasse of that noble queene, for hir vertue commonlie called good queene Elizabeth, departed out of this world also sir Reginald Braie knight of the garter, a verie father of his countrie, for his high wisedome and singular loue to iustice well worthie to beare that title. If anie thing had béene doone amisse contrarie to law and equitie, he would after an humble sort plainelie blame the king, and giue him good aduertisement, that he should not onelie reforme the same, but also be more circumspect in anie other the like case. Of the same vertue and faithfull plainnesse was Iohn Morton archbishop of Canturburie, which died (as is shewed aboue) two yeares before.

So these two persons were refrainers of the kings vnbrideled libertie; whereas the common people (ignorant altogither of the truth in such matters) iudged and reported, that the counsell of those two worthie personages corrupted the kings cleane and immaculate conscience, contrarie to his princelie disposition and naturall inclination; such is euer the errour of the common people. ¶ About this time died Henrie the archbishop of Canturburie, whose roome doctor William Warham bishop of London supplied. And to the sée of London William Barnes was appointed, and after his death succéeded one Richard Fitz Iames. This yeare also the lord Cassimire marquesse of Brandenburgh, accompanied with an earle, a bishop, and a great number of gentlemen well apparrelled, came in ambassage from the emperor Maximilian, and were triumphantlie receiued into London, and lodged at Crosbies place.

Their message was for thrée causes, one to comfort the king in his time of heauinesse for the losse of his wife. The second for the renewing of amitie, and the old league. The third (which was not apparant) was to mooue the king to marie the emperours daughter, the ladie Margaret, duchesse Dowager of Sauoie. The two first tooke effect: for the king vpon Passion sundaie road to Paules in great triumph, the said marquesse riding on his left hand. And there the bishop made to the king an excellent consolatorie oration concerning the death of the quéene. And there also the king openlie sware to kéepe the new reuiued league and amitie during their two liues. But the third request (whether the let was on the mans side, or on the womans) neuer sorted to anie conclusion.

The

The ladie Margaret the kings daughter, affied (as yee haue heard) to the king of Scots, was appointed to be conueied into Scotland, by the earle of Surrie: and the earle of Northumberland, as warden of the marches, was commanded to deliuer hir at the confines of both the realmes. And so héerevpon, after hir comming to Berwike, she was conueied to Lamberton kirke in Scotland, where the king of Scots, with the flower of all the nobles and gentlemen of Scotland, was readie to receiue hir: to whome the earle of Northumberland (according to his commission) deliuered hir. The said earle of Northumberland that daie, what for the riches of his coat being goldsmithes worke, garnished with pearle and stone, and what for the gallant apparell of his Henchmen, and braue trappers of his horsse, beside foure hundred tall men well horssed and apparelled in his colours, was estéemed both of the Scots and Englishmen more like a prince than a subiect. *The sumptuous araie of the earle of Northumberland.*

From Lamberton, the foresaid ladie was conueied to Edenburgh, and there the daie after, king Iames the fourth, in the presence of all his nobilitie espoused hir, and feasted the English lords, and shewed iusts and other pastimes verie honourablie, after the fashion of that countrie. And after all things were finished according to their commission, the erle of Surrie with all the English lords and ladies returned into their countrie. In this yeare the king kept his high court of parlement, in the which diuerse acts estéemed necessarie for the preseruation of the common-wealth were established: and amongst other, it was enacted, that théeues and murtherers duelie conuicted by the law to die, and yet saued by their books, should be committed to the bishops custodie. After this, a subsidie was granted, both of the temporaltie, and spiritualtie, and so that parlement ended. *The mariage betwéene the K. of Scots & ladie Margaret king Henries eldest daughter. An. Reg. 19.*

But the king now drawing into age, and willing to fill his chest with abundance of treasure, was not satisfied with this onelie subsidie, but deuised an other meane how to inrich himselfe, as thus. He considered that the Englishmen little regarded the kéeping of penall lawes, and pecuniall statutes, deuised for the good preseruation of the common-wealth. Whereof he caused inquisition to be made of those that had transgressed anie of the same lawes, so that there were but few noble men, merchants, farmers, husbandmen, grasiers, or occupiers, that could cléerlie prooue themselues faultlesse, but had offended in some one or other of the same lawes. At the first, they that were found giltie were easilie fined. But after, there were appointed two maisters and surueiors of his forfeits, the one sir Richard Empson, and the other Edmund Dudleie. *The king couetous in his old age. 1504. Richard Empson & Edmund Dudleie.*

These two were learned in the lawes of the realme, who meaning to satisfie their princes pleasure, and to sée their commission executed to the vttermost, séemed little to respect the perill that might insue. Wherevpon they being furnished with a sort of accusers, commonlie called promoters, or (as they themselues will be named) informers, troubled manie a man, whereby they wan them great hatred, and the king (by such rigorous procéedings) lost the loue and fauour which the people before time had borne towards him; so that he for setting them a worke, and they for executing of it in such extreame wise, ran into obloquie with the subiects of this realme. *Promoters.*

¶ On the thirtéenth of Nouember was holden within the palace of the archbishop of Canturburie, at Lambeth, the sergeants feast, where dined the king and all his nobles. And vpon the same day, Thomas Granger, newlie chosen shiriffe of London was presented before the barons of the kings exchequer, there to take his oth, and after went with the maior vnto the same feast, which saued him monie in his pursse; for if that day that feast had not béene kept, he must haue feasted the maior, aldermen, and others, woorshipfull of the citie. This feast was kept at the charge of ten learned men, newlie admitted to bée sergeants to the kings law, whose names were, Robert Bridnell, William Greuill, Thomas Marow, George Edgore, Iohn Moore, Iohn Cutler, Thomas Eliot, Lewes Pollard, Guie Palmis, William Fairefax. On the one *Abr. Fl. ex I. S. pag. 876. sergeants feast whereat were the king and all his nobles at dinner.*

and

Fire on London bridge. and twentith of Nouember at night, began a perillous fier at the signe of the panier vpon London bridge, néere to saint Magnus church; where six tenements were Fire. burned yer the same could be quenched. On the seuenth of Ianuarie, were certeine houses consumed with fire against saint Butolphes church in Thames street. On the Parlement. fiue and twentith of Ianuarie began a parlement at Westminster, of which was chosen speaker for the commons, maister Edmund Dudleie.]

An. Reg. 20. A new coine of siluer was ordeined of grotes and halfe grotes, which bare but halfe faces; and some péeces of the value of twelue pense were then stamped, though very Alum déere. few of that sort came abroad. In this yeare, alum, which manie yeares had bene sold for six shillings an hundred, and lower, arose to fiue nobles an hundred, and after to foure marks, &c. Sir William Capell, who for this yeare was maior, caused in Cages and stockes ordeined. Hunsditch paued. euerie ward of London a cage with a paire of stocks, therein to punish vagabunds. Also he caused all Hunsditch to be ouerpaued, which manie yeares before lay full noiouslie and perillouslie for all trauellers that way. About Christmas, the more part Prisoners of the Marshalseie brake out. of the prisoners of the Marshalseie in Southwarke brake out, and manie of them being shortlie after taken, were put to execution, speciallie those which had laine for felonie or treason. On the fiftéenth of Aprill, a monie maker, one of the coiners of the Tower, was drawne to Tiburne and there hanged.

John Hooker, aliàs Vowell. A beneuolence put into the kings head to be leuied ouer the whole land. ¶ In this twentith yeare (saith one of Excester) the king (hauing some need of monie) was by his councell aduised (by way of beneuolence) to leuie the same vpon the whole realme, as well of the cleargie as of the laitie. And for the same, commissioners were assigned accordinglie. For the cleargie, Richard Fox, sometime bishop of Excester, but now of Winchester, a verie wise, graue, and trustie councellor, was appointed chiefe commissioner, and had the chiefest dealing therein. He at daies and times appointed, assembled the cleargie before him, and (according to the trust committed vnto him) he persuaded them by all the meanes he could, to be liberall contributors to the king, considering his present néed, and who (for their causes, & the safetie of all the common-wealth) was now to vse and imploie some monie.

The cleargie of two sorts, and both desirous to spare their pursses. The cleargie was of two sorts, the one shewing themselues as they were wealthie, seemelie, & comelie; the other pretending that which was not, pouertie, barenesse, and scarsitie: but both were of one mind, and deuised all the waies they could to saue their pursses. The first being called, alledged that they were dailie at great charges and expenses in kéeping of hospitalitie, in mainteining themselues, their house and familie; besides extraordinaries which dailie did grow and increase vpon them: and by that meanes they were but bare and poore, and praied that they might be borne withall, and pardoned for that time.

The other sort alledged, that their liuings were but small and slender, and scarse able to mainteine themselues withall, which compelled them to go bare, and to liue a hard and a poore life, and therefore (they hauing nothing) praied that they might The wisdome of bishop Fox in procuring these cleargie men to be contributors to this beneuolence. be excused. The bishop when he had heard them at full, and well considered thereof, verie wittilie, and with a prettie dilemma answered them both, saieng to the first: " It is true, you are at great charges, and are well beséene in your apparell, well mounted vpon your faire palfreies, and haue your men waiting vpon you in good order; your hospitalitie is good, and your dailie expenses are large, and you are for the same well reported amongst your neighbours; all which are plaine demonstrations of your wealth and abilitie, otherwise you would not be at such voluntarie charges.

" Now hauing store to spend in such order, there is no reason, but that to your prince you should much more be well willing & readie to yéeld your selues contributorie and dutifull, and therefore you must paie." To the other sort he said: " Albeit your liuings be not of the best, yet good, sufficient, and able to mainteine you in better estate than you doo imploie it: but it appeareth that you are frugall and
thriftie

thriftie men ; and what others doo voluntarilie spend in apparell, house, and familie, you warilie doo kéepe, and haue it to lie by you; and therefore it is good reason that of your store you should spare with a good will and contribute to your prince ; They are persuaded to contribute. wherefore be contented, for you shall paie." And so by this prettie dilemma he reduced them to yeeld a good paiment to the king.]

The king after he had gotten a great masse of monie togither, hauing pitie on the people, which oppressed with the sharpe procéedings of his gréedie officers, cried 1505 daily to God for vengeance, ment to haue depriued them of their offices (as some write) & that such monie as had béene violentlie exacted, should haue béene restored and deliuered againe, if he had not bene preuented by death. And yet by his last will he commanded that it should be dulie and trulie performed, but in the meane season many mens coffers were emptied. [¶ Thomas Kneisworth maior of London *Abr. Fl. ex. I. S.*
pag 878.
Conduit at
Bishops gate
builded. for this yeare, of his owne goods, builded the conduit at Bishopsgate. He gaue to the fishmongers certeine tenements, for the which they be bound to find foure scholers that studie art; two at Oxford, and two at Cambrige, euerie of them foure pounds the yeare. They be bound also to giue to twelue aged poore people of their companie, to euerie one of them at Bartholomew tide a winter garment for euer. Also to giue to the prisoners of Ludgate and Newgate euerie yeare fortie shillings, &c. The first of Ianuarie in the night, the kings chamber was fired at Richmond, the Richmond
on fire. which might not be quenched, till manie curteins, carpets, rich beds, and much other stuffe was consumed.

In this verie season, and the yeare of our Lord 1506, Elizabeth queene of Castile *An.* Reg. 21.
1506 died without issue male, by reason whereof the inheritance of Castile (bicause that kingdome is not partible) descended to ladie Iane hir eldest daughter by king Ferdinando, the which was maried to Philip archduke of Austrich. Wherefore the yeare following, about the sixt day of Ianuarie, hauing a great nauie prepared, he intituled now king of Castile, sailed out of Flanders with his wife towards Spaine ; but by a mightie tempest of wind and foule weather, the whole nauie was dispersed and sparkled abroad in diuerse places on the coasts of England. The kings ship with two other vessels were blowne by tempest on the west part of the realme, to the port of Philip archduke
of Austrich
landeth in the
west parts of
England. Weimouth in Dorsetshire. The king being wearied with the tossing of the seas, as one not accustomed thereto, contrarie to the mind of his councellors, came on land to refresh himselfe.

When it was knowne that strange ships were arriued in that place, there came thither a great number, as well of gentlemen as commons of the countrie, to beat them backe if they prooued to be enimies. But when they perceiued that the king of Spaine was there driuen on land by force of weather, sir Thomas Trenchard knight, chéefe of that companie, went with great humblenesse vnto him, and did what he could to haue him to his house, being not farre off, and so to cause him to stay, till such time as king Henrie might be certified of his arriuall; to whome with all spéed he sent diuerse posts to aduertise him of king Philips landing. In this meane while came people in from all sides, vpon knowlege of this strange princes comming. And among other there came sir Iohn Carew, with a goodlie band of piked men. Which sir Iohn and sir Thomas Trenchard intreated the king of Castile not to depart, vntil such time as he had spoken with the king.

The king of Castile excused him by necessitie of his weightie enterprise : but when he perceiued that if he would proffer to go once aboord to his ships againe, he might be letted, and was like so to bée ; hée thought good rather to assent to their humble request and to seeme to gratifie them ; than by denieng it to procure their euil willes, and yet neuer the néer of his purpose. When king Henrie was informed of his landing, he was right glad therof, and wrote vnto sir Iohn Carew, and to sir Thomas Trenchard, that they should interteine him in the most honorable sort they could

deuise,

The king of Casti'e interteined honorablie.

deuise, till he might come himselfe in person to welcome him. Beside this, he sent the earle of Arundell with manie lords and knights to attend vpon him. Which earle (according to the kings letters) receiued him with thrée hundred horsses, all by torchlight, to the great admiration of the strangers.

King Philip séeing no remedie but that he must needs tarie, would no longer gaze after king Henries comming, but tooke his iournie toward Windsore castell, where the king laie: and fiue miles from Windsore the prince of Wales, accompanied with fiue earles, and diuerse lords and knights, and other to the number of fiue hundred persons gorgiouslie apparelled, receiued him after the most honorable fashion. And within halfe a mile of Windsore, the king, accompanied with the duke of Buckingham, and a great part of the nobilitie of this realme, welcomed him, & so conueied him to the castell of Windsore, where he was made companion of the noble order of the garter. After him came to Windsore his wife queene Iane, sister to the princesse Dowager, late wife to prince Arthur.

King Henrie desireth to haue Edmund de la Poole earle of Suffolke deliuered into his hands.

After the two kings had renewed & confirmed the league and amitie betwixt them, king Henrie desired to haue Edmund de la Poole earle of Suffolke to be deliuered into his hands. To whome the king of Castile answered that he verelie was not within his dominion: and therefore it laie not in him to deliuer him. In deed he was loth to be the author of his death that came to him for succour, and was receiued vnder his protection: yet vpon the earnest request and assured promise of king Henrie (that he would pardon him of all executions and paines of death) he granted to king Henries desire; and so incontinentlie caused the said earle secretlie to be sent for. After this, to protract time till he were possessed of his preie, king Henrie conueied the king of Castile vnto the citie of London, that he might sée the head citie of his realme.

Then he led him from Bainards castell by Cheape to Barking; and so returned by Watling street againe: during which time there was shot out of the Tower a woonderfull peale of ordinance. But he would not enter into the Tower, bicause (as ye haue heard before) he had aduowed not to enter the fortresse of anie forren prince, in the which a garrison was mainteined. From London the king brought him to Richmond, where manie notable feates of armes were prooued both of tilt, turnie, and barriers. In the meane season the erle of Suffolke, perceiuing what hope was to be had in forreine princes, and trusting that after his life to him once granted, king Henrie would bréeflie set him at his full libertie, was in maner contented to returne againe into his natiue countrie.

The king of Castiles vow inuiolablie kept.

When all pacts and couenants betwéene the kings of England aud Castile were appointed, concluded, and agréed; king Philip tooke his leaue of king Henrie, yéelding to him most heartie thanks for his high chéere and princelie interteinement. And being accompanied with diuers lords of England, he came to the citie of Excester, and so to Falmouth in Cornewall, and there taking ship sailed into Spaine, where shortlie after he died being thirtie yeares of age. He was of stature conuenient, of countenance amiable, of bodie somewhat grosse, quicke witted, bold and hardie stomached. The tempest that he suffered on the sea was huge, and woonderfull also vpon the land, insomuch that the violence of the wind blew downe an eagle of brasse, being set to shew on which part the wind blew, from a pinacle or spire of Paules church, and in the falling, the same eagle brake and battered an other eagle that was set vp for a signe at a tauerne doore in Cheapeside.

The death & de criytion of Philip king of Spaine.

Prodigious tokens or accidents haue their issue in truth.

Herevpon men that were giuen to gesse things that should happen by marking of strange tokens, déemed that the emperour Maximilian, which gaue the eagle, should suffer some great misfortune: as he did shortlie after by the losse of his sonne, the said king Philip. ¶ And suerlie these prodigious accidents are not to be omitted as matter of course; for they haue their weight, and shew their truth in the issue. Examples in this booke be diuerse, among which one is verie memorable, mentioned in the thirtie & ninth

& ninth yeare of Henrie the sixt. At what time the duke of Yorke making an oration See pag. 264. to the lords of the parlement, for the iustifieng of his title to the crowne, it chanced that a crowne which hoong in the middle of the nether house (to garnish a branch to set lights vpon) without touch of man or blast of wind suddenlie fell downe. About which season also fell downe the crowne which stood on the top of Douer castell. Which things were construed to be signes that the crowne of the realme should some waie haue a fall; and so it came to passe.

And bicause the euents of these foreshewes had their truth, as manie more of the like nature; it shall not be amisse here to ad (by waie of digression) what hath béene obserued in former ages by forren writers in and about such foretokens. *Abr. Flem. ex. Guic. pag.* 40. The consent of the heauens and of men, pronounced to Italie their calamities to come: for that such as made profession to haue iudgement either by science or diuine inspiration in the things to come, assured with one voice that there were in preparing, both more great mutations and more strange and horrible accidents, than for manie worlds before had béene discerned in anie part or circuit of the earth. There were seene in the night in Pouille thrée suns in the middest of the firmament, but manie clouds Thrée sunnes séene at once in the night. about them, with right fearefull thunders and lightnings. In the territorie of Aretze, were visiblie séene passing in the aire, infinit numbers of armed men vpon mightie horsses, with a terrible noise of drums and trumpets. The images & figures of saints did sweat in manie parts of Italie.

In euerie place of the countrie were brought foorth manie monsters of men and other creatures, with manie other things against the order of nature concurring all at one time, but in diuerse places: by means wherof the people were caried into incredible feares, being alreadie amazed with the brute of the French powers & furie of that nation, with which (according to the testimonie of histories) they had aforetime run ouer all Italie, sacked and made desolate with fire and sword the citie of Rome, and subdued in Asia manie prouinces; and generallie no part of the world which had not felt the vertue of their armes. But albeit these iudgements are oftentimes fallible, and rather coniectures vncerteine, than effects happening: yet the accidents that drew on, brought to them, in the spirits of fraile men, an absolute faith, credit, & religion. So that there is in foreshewes matter of moment worthie to be obserued, howsoeuer the world lulled asléep in the lap of securitie is touched with no feare of change. But alas the Heathen could sée the contrarie, and therefore said:

> Omnia mortali mutantur lege creata,
> Nec se cognoscunt terræ veteribus annis *Manil. lib. Astr.* 1.
> Exutas variam faciem per secula gentes.]

But to returne to our owne storie. Shortlie after the departing of king Philip, the king of England began to suspect sir George Neuill lord of Aburgauenie, and sir Thomas Greene of Gréenes Norton, as partakers in the beginning of the conspiracie with the earle of Suffolke; and so vpon that suspicion they were commanded to the Tower. But shortlie after, when they had béene tried and purged of that suspicion, he commanded them both to be set at libertie. But sir Thomas Gréene fell sicke before, and remained in the Tower, in hope to be restored to his health as well as to his libertie, but by death he was preuented. [And here bicause it is good to see the consent of histories in the report of accidents, it shall not be amisse to repeat the entier relation of a late writer stranger touching this casualtie which befell to king Philip, in such sort to be cast vpon the English coasts; as also the promise of the said king to deliuer the duke of Suffolke into the hands of king Henrie, with the cause (as it is supposed) why the king desired to haue him within his owne reach.

¶ King Philip was imbarked to saile out of Flanders into Spaine with a great armie *Abr. Fl. ex Guic. pag* 355. by sea; and to reduce his going to a more facilitie and safetie (for he feared least his King Philip saileth out of father in law by the aid of the French would hinder his passage) he practised the Flanders into

Spanish subtilties, and agréed with him to leaue vnto him the managing and policie of the most part of affaires, and that they shuld take in common the title of king of Spaine, according to the example in the queenes time: and lastlie, that the reuenues and tributes should be diuided in an order certeine & indifferent. By reason of which accord, his father in law, notwithstanding he was not assured of the obseruation, sent him into Flanders manie ships to furnish his voiage: with the which, hauing imbarked his wife, and Ferdinand his second sonne, he tooke his course into Spaine with forward winds, which, within two daies turning cleane contrarie, after his nauie had runne a

King Philip cast by casualtie of sea vpon the coasts of England.

dangerous fortune, and made a wearie resistance against the furie of the sea, his ships were cast vpon sundrie coasts of England and Britaine; his owne person with two or thrée ships being driuen with manifest perill vpon England into the hauen of Southhampton.

Whereof Henrie the seuenth then king of that nation being aduertised, sent to him with spéed manie barons to doo him honour, and desire him to come to his court, then at London: a request which Philip could not denie, the king of Englands demand beeing no lesse honourable, than his owne estate full of necessitie and nakednesse. He remained in the court of England, vntill all his nauie was reassembled, and eftsoones rigged, making in the meane while betwéene them new capitulations: wherein albeit Philip in all other things held himselfe vsed as a king, yet in this one thing

Philip promiseth to redeliuer to king Henrie the duke of Suffolke.

complained, that he was constreined as a prisoner, to consent to redeliuer to K. Henries hands the duke of Suffolke, whom he held prisoner within the castell of Namur, and whom the king of England desired much to haue in his power, for that he quarrelled the title of the crowne, pretending the right of the kingdome to apperteine to him: onelie the king of England assured Philip by the faith and word of a king, that he would not put him to death. Which he did as iustlie performe, as he had honorablie promised, keeping him in prison so long as he liued, and afterwards was beheaded vnder the reigne and commandement of his sonne.]

An. Reg. 22.

This yeare the king began to be diseased of a certeine infirmitie, which thrise euerie yeare, but specially in the springtime sore vexed him. And bicause for the

The sweting sicknesse eftsoones returneth.

most part the harme that chanceth to the prince, is parted with his subiects, the sweating sicknesse, which (as ye haue heard in the first yeare of the king first afflicted the people of this realme, now assailed them againe; howbeit by the remedie found at the beginning of it, nothing the like number died thereof now this second time, as did at the first time till the said remedie was inuented. But now the third plage equall to the pestilence insued, by the working of the maisters of the forfeitures, and such informers as were appointed thereto. By whose meanes manie a rich & wealthie person by the extremitie of the lawes of the realme were condemned and brought to great losse and hinderance.

A great part of which their vndooings procéeded by the inconuenience of such vnconscionable officers, as by the abuse of exigents outlawed those that neuer heard, nor had knowledge of the sutes commensed against them, of which hard and sharpe dealing (the harme that thereof insueth considered) if the occasion might be taken awaie by some other more reasonable forme and order of law deuised, whereby the parties might haue personall warning, it would both preserue manie an innocent man from vndeserued vexation, and danger of vnmercifull losse of goods; and also redound highlie to the commendation of the prince, and such other as chanced to be reformers of that colourable law, where they be called onelie in the counties without other knowledge giuen to them or theirs at their dwelling houses.

But now to returne. Such maner of outlawies, old recognisances of the peace, and good abearings, escapes, riots, & innumerable statutes penall, were put in execution, and called vpon by Empson and Dudleie; so that euerie man, both the spiritualtie and temporaltie, hauing either lands or substance, were inuited to that plucking
banket,

banket. For these two rauening woolues had a gard of false periured persons apperteining to them, which were impanelled in euerie quest. Learned men in the law, when they were required of their aduise, would say; To agrée is the best counsell that I can giue you. By this vndue meanes, these couetous persons filled the kings coffers, and inriched themselues. And at this vnreasonable and extort dooing, noble men grudged, meane men kicked, poore men lamented, preachers openlie at Poules crosse and other places exclamed, rebuked, and detested. Howbeit the good king in his last daies conserued and pardoned his poore subiects of such vncharitable yokes and ponderous burdens as they were laden withall.

Ed. Hall in Hen. 7 fol. 59.

Sir Gilbert Talbot knight, and Richard Bere abbat of Glastenburie, and doctor Robert Sherborne deane of Poules, were sent as ambassadors from the K. to Rome, to declare to Pius the third of that name newlie elected pope in place of Alexander the sixt deceased what ioy and gladnesse had entered the kings heart for his preferment. But he taried not the comming of those ambassadors, for within a moneth after that he was installed, he rendered his debt to nature, and so had short pleasure of his promotion [not beguiling the hopes which the cardinals conceiued of him at the time of his creation, the six & twentith day after his election, which was in short time to die. This popes name was Francis Piccolomini cardinall of Sienna, in whom was no expectation of long life, both for his extreame age, and present sickenesse: a cardinall sure of vnspotted report, and for his other conditions not vnworthie that degree; who to renew the memorie of Pius secundus his vncle, tooke vpon him the name of Pius the third.

1507

Abr. Fl. ex Guic. pag. 314.

Pag. 312.

He succéeded Alexander the sixt, who went to supper in a vineyard néere the Vatican to reioise in the delight & plesure of the fresh aire, & was suddenlie caried for dead to the bishops palace; his sonne also communicating in the same accident, but with better fortune. For the day folowing, which was the eightenth day of August, the dead corps of the pope (according to custome) was borne into the church of saint Peter, blacke, swolne, and most deformed; most manifest signes of poison. But Valentinois, what by the vigour and strength of his youth, and readie helpe of strong medicines and counterpoisons, had his life saued, remaining notwithstanding oppressed with long and greeuous sickenesse: it was assuredlie beléeued that the accident procéeded of poison, the discourse whereof (according to common report) was in this sort.

Pag. 307.

The duke Valentinois, who was to be present at that supper, had determined to poison Adrian cardinall of Cornette, reseruing that time and place to execute his bloudie resolution: for it is most certeine that in his father and him were naturall customes to vse poison, not onelie to be reuenged of their enimies, or to be assured of suspicions; but also vpon a wicked couetousnesse, to despoile rich men of their goods, whether they were cardinals or courtiers, although they had neuer doone them wrong, as hapned to the cardinall saint Ange, who was verie rich. This maner of rage they would vse also against their greatest friends & familiars, and such as had bin their most faithfull seruants, such as were the cardinals of Capua and Modeno: a recompense vnworthie the merits of good men, and not disagréeable to the disposition of such a father and sonne, whereof the one made all things lawfull by vile dispensation; and with the other nothing was dishonest wherein was opportunitie to his purposes. The duke Valentinois sent before certeine flagons with wine infected with poison, which he gaue to a seruant that knew nothing of the matter, commanding that no person should touch them.

A practise of custome by poison to an ill purpose vsed.

A commandement preiudiciall to his maister, as the ignorance of the seruant was the instrument in the euill that happened both to the father and son. Such is the sufferance of God, who in the execution of his iudgments raiseth one murtherer to kill another, & breaketh the brands of the fire vpon the head of him that first kindled

it:

The pope poi-
soned with the
wine that his
owne son had
sent to poison
the cardinall of
Cornette.

it : for the pope comming by aduenture somewhat before supper, and ouercome with the drought and immoderate heat of the time, called for drinke. And bicause his owne prouision was not yet brought from the palace, he that had the infected wine in charge, thinking it to be recommended to his keeping for a wine most excellent, gaue the pope to drinke of the same wine which Valentinois had sent; who arriuing while his father was drinking drunke also of the same wine, being but iust that they both should tast of the same cup which they had brued for the destruction of others. All the towne of Rome ran with great gladnesse to saint Peters about the dead bodie of the pope, their eies not satisfied to see ded and destroied a serpent, who with his immoderate ambition and poisoned infidelitie, togither with all the horrible examples of crueltie, luxurie, and monstruous couetousnesse, selling without distinction both holie things and prophane things, had infected the whole world.

And yet was he accompanied with a most rare, & almost perpetuall prosperitie euen from his yoong age, to the end of his life; desiring alwaies great things, and obteining most often that he desired. An example of much importance, to confound the arrogancie of those men, who presuming to know and see perfectlie with humane eies the depth of Gods iudgements, doo assure, that what happeneth either good or ill to mortall men, proceedeth either of their merits or faults: as though we saw not dailie manie good men vniustlie tormented, & wicked persons aboue their diseruings liue in ease and honour: wherein who makes an other interpretation, derogates the iustice and power of God, the greatnesse of which being not to be conteined within any scripts or tearms present, knoweth how well and largely to discerne in an other time and place the iust from the vniust, and that with rewards and eternall punish-ments. In the meane time he powreth out his vengeance vpon the imaginers of mischeefe in this life; so prouiding, as that they are caught in their owne snares, and ouertaken with such destruction as they had prepared for others, according to that saieng of the Psalmist:

Eob. Hess. & G.
Buch. in Psal. 7.

Effodit puteum, foueámque eduxit ab imo,
     Et miser in latebras incidit ipse suas.
     In verticem ipsius recurrit
     Pernicies, recidúntque fraudes.]

The lord Dau-
benie dieth.

At the same time died Giles lord Dawbenie the kings cheefe chamberleine, whose office Charles, bastard sonne, to Henrie last duke of Summerset occupied and enioied;

An. Reg. 23.
Guidebald duke
of Urbin in Italie
made knight of
the garter.

a man of good wit, and great experience. Soone after, the king caused Guidebald duke of Urbine to be elected knight of the order of the garter, in like maner as his father duke Frederike had beene before him, which was chosen and admitted into the order by king Edward the fourth. Sir Gilbert Talbot, and the other two am-bassadors being appointed to keepe on their iournie vnto pope Iulie the second, elected after the death of the said Pius the third, bare the habit and collar also vnto the said duke Guidebald; which after he had receiued the same, sent sir Balshasar Castalio, knight, a Mantuan borne, as his orator vnto king Henrie, which was for him installed, according to the ordinances of the order.

Thomas Sauage
archbishop of
Canturburie de-
ceassed.

This yeare that worthie prelate Thomas Sauage archbishop of Yorke departed this life at his castell of Cawood: a man beside the worthinesse of his birth highlie esteemed with his prince for his fast fidelitie and great wisedome. He bestowed great cost in repairing the castell of Cawood and the manor of Scrobie. His bodie was buried at Yorke, but he appointed by his testament, that his hart should be buried at Macclesfield in Cheshire, where he was borne, in a chapell there of his foundation, ioining to the south side of the church, meaning to haue founded a college there also, if his purpose had not beene preuented by death. After him succeeded doctor Ben-bridge in the archbishops see of Yorke, being the fiftie and sixt archbishop that had sat in that see.

           About

About this same time Lewes the French king, the twelfe of that name (who suc- Abr. Fl. ex Guic. pag. 184.
céeded Charles the eighth that died at Amboise the night before the eighth daie of
Aprill, of a catarrhe, which the physicians call an apoplexie, the same rising in him
with such abundance, as he beheld a match plaied at tennisse, that in a few houres
he ended at the same place his life: during the which, he had with greater importunitie than vertue troubled the whole world with great appearance of danger to
kindle eftsoones new fiers of innouation and troubles) maried his eldest daughter
named Clare, vnto Francis de Valois Dolphin of Vienne, and duke of Angolesme,
which ladie was promised vnto Charles the king of Castile: wherevpon by ambassadors sent to and fro betwixt king Henrie and the said king of Castile, a mariage
was concluded betwixt the said king of Castile, and the ladie Marie, daughter to
king Henrie, being about the age of ten yeares. For conclusion of which mariage,
the lord of Barow, & other ambassadors were sent into England from the emperor
Maximilian which with great rewards returned.

¶ William Browne mercer maior of London, this yeare deceassed, and foorthwith   1508
sir Laurence Ailmer draper was chosen and sworne, and went home in a graie cloake, Abr. Fl. ex
with the sword borne before him, on the eight and twentith daie of March. Item he I. S. pag. 879.
tooke his oth at the Tower, and kept no feast. William Capell was put in sute by the William Capell sued by the king.
king for things by him doone in his maioraltie. Also Thomas Knelsworth that had Tho. Knelsworth imprisoned.
beene maior of London, and his shiriffes, were sent to the kings Bench, till they were
put to their fines of foureteene hundred pounds. In the moneth of Iune, the citie of Norwich on fier.
Norwich was sore perished, & neere consumed with fier, that began in a Frenchmans
house named Peter Iohnson, a surgian, in the parish of saint George.

Stephan Genings merchant tailor, maior of London, founded a free grammar Fréeschoole at Wlfrunehamp-ton.
schoole at Wlfrunehampton in Staffordshire, with conuenient lodgings for the maister
and vsher, in the same place where he was borne. He gaue lands sufficient for the
maintenance, leauing the ouersight thereof to the merchant tailors in London,
who haue hitherto iustlie dealt in that matter, and also augmented the building there.
Maister Nichols, who maried the onelie daughter and heire of the aforesaid Stephan
Genings, gaue lands to mainteine the pauements of that towne. Also, Iohn Leneson
esquier, about Anno 1556, gaue lands, whereof foure pounds should be dealt euerie
yeare, on good fridaie, to the poore people of Wlfrunehampton, and six and twentie
shillings eight pence yéerelie, towards the reparation of the church there.

Moreouer, about Anno 1566, sir Iohn Ligh, a préest, which had serued in that Iohn Ligh of Wlfrunehampton, his rare example of charitie.
church there, the space of thréescore years, for fiue pounds, six shillings and eight pence
the yeare, without anie other augmentation of his liuing, who would neuer take anie
other benefice, or other preferment, gaue twentie pounds, to purchase twentie shillings the yeare lands, the same to be giuen yearelie for euer to the poore of Wlfrunehampton vpon good fridaie; & twelue pounds thirteene shillings foure pence, to purchase a marke a yeare lands, the same to be giuen to the poore of Chifnall, in the
countie of Salope, where the said Ligh was borne. This man liued nigh one hundred years. He bestowed besides his owne labour which was great (in bearing of
stones, &c.) aboue twentie pounds on the high waies about that towne of Wlfrunehampton.

This towne of Wlfrunehampton, is now corruptlie called Wolnerhampton: for in Anno Wlfrunehampton, corruptlie called Wolnerhamp-ton.
996, in king Ethelreds time (who wrote himselfe Rex Anglorum & princeps Northum-
brorum Olympiade tertia regni sûi, for so he wrote the count of his reigne then, which
was the fiftéenth yeare) it was then called Hampton, as appeareth by an old charter Ex charta regia.
written by the notary of the said king Ethelred, which charter I haue seene and
read. And for that a noble woman named Wlfrune a Widow, some time wife to
Althelme duke of Northampton, did obteine of the said king to giue lands vnto the
church

church there which she had founded, the said towne tooke the addition of the same Wlfrune, for that charter so named hir Wlfrune, and the towne Hampton.

Smart.
Hospitall of the Sauoie.

In this yeare was finished the goodlie hospitall of the Sauoie néere vnto Charing-crosse, which was a notable foundation for the poore, doone by king Henrie the seauenth, vnto the which he purchased and gaue lands for the releeuing of one hundred poore people. This was first named Sauoie place, by Peter earle of Sauoie, father to Boniface archbishop of Canturburie, about the nine and twentith yeare of king Henrie the third, who made the said Peter erle of Richmond. This house belonged since to the duke of Lancaster, and at this time was conuerted to an hospitall, still reteining the first name of Sauoie. King Henrie also builded three houses of Franciscane friers, which are called obseruants, at Richmond, Gréenewich, and Newarke; and three other of the familie of Franciscane friers which are called conuentuals, at Canturburie, Newcastell, and Southampton.]

Rec. of Canturb.
church.

Fr. Thin.
Thomas Ruthall
bishop of Dur-
ham.

¶ This yeare was Thomas Ruthall made bishop of Durham by Henrie the seauenth, touching whose place of birth (being at Cirencester now Cicester) and himselfe, I will not refuse to set downe what Leland (about the yeare 1542) hath written, not being vnfit héere to be recorded. Cirencester (saith he) in Latine called Corinium standeth on the riuer Churne. " There haue béene thrée parish churches, whereof saint Ciciles church is cleane downe, being of late but a chappell. Saint Laurence yet standeth, but it is no parish church. There be two poore almes women endued with land. There is now but one parish church in all Cirencester that is verie faire, the bodie of which church is all new worke, to the which Ruthall bishop of Durham (borne and brought vp in Cirencester) promised much, but (preuented by death) gaue nothing. One Anne Aueling aunt to doctor Ruthall by the mothers side, gaue one hundred markes to the building of that church. King Henrie the first made the hospitall of saint Iohns at Cirencester. Thus farre Leland."

The situation of
Cicester.

The bishop was
one of K. Henrie
the eights priuie
councell.

This man thus borne at Cirencester in Glocestershire, and made bishop of Durham, was after the death of king Henrie the seauenth, one of the priuie councell to king Henrie the eight; in whose court he was so continuallie attendant, that he could not steale anie time to attend the affaires of his bishoprike. But yet not altogither carelesse (though not so much as he ought to haue béene) of the place and cause from whence and for which he receiued so great reuenues, as came vnto his hands from that see. He repaired the third part of Tine bridge next vnto the south, which he might well doo; for he was accompted the richest subiect through the realme.

The king cō-
mandeth him
to write a booke
of the whole
estate of the
kingdom.

To whome (remaining then at the court) the king gaue in charge to write a booke of the whole estate of the kingdome, bicause he was knowne to the king to be a man of sufficiencie for the discharge thereof, which he did accordinglie.

Afterwards, the king commanded cardinall Woolseie to go to this bishop, and to bring the booke awaie with him to deliuer to his maiestie. But see the mishap! that a man in all other things so prouident, should now be so negligent: and at that time most forget himselfe, when (as it after fell out) he had most need to haue remembred himselfe. For this bishop hauing written two bookes (the one to answer the kings command, and the other intreating of his owne priuate affaires) did bind them both after one sort in vellame, iust of one length, bredth, and thicknesse, and in all points in such like proportion answering one another, as the one could not by anie especiall note be discerned from the other: both of which he also laid vp togither in one place of his studie.

The bishops
booke of his pri-
uat affaires vn-
aduisedlie deli-
uered in stéed of
the kings.

Now when the cardinall came to demand the booke due to the king: the bishop vnaduisedlie commanded his seruant to bring him the booke bound in white vellame lieng in his studie in such a place. The seruant dooing accordinglie, brought foorth one of those bookes so bound, being the booke intreating of the state of the bishop, and deliuered the same vnto his maister, who receiuing it (without further consi-
sideration

deration or looking on) gaue it to the cardinall to beare vnto the king. The cardinall hauing the booke, went from the bishop, and after (in his studie by himselfe) vnderstanding the contents thereof, he greatlie reioised, hauing now occasion (which he long sought for) offered vnto him to bring the bishop into the king's disgrace.

Wherefore he went foorthwith to the king, deliuered the booke into his hands, and bréefelie informed the king of the conteuts thereof; putting further into the king's head, that if at anie time he were destitute of a masse of monie, he should not need to séeke further therefore than to the cofers of the bishop, who by the tenor of his owne booke had accompted his proper riches and substance to the value of a hundred thousand pounds. Of all which when the bishop had intelligence (what he had doon, how the cardinall vsed him, what the king said, and what the world reported of him) he was striken with such gréefe of the same, that he shortlie through extreame sorrow ended his life at London, in the yeare of Christ 1523. After whose death the cardinall, which had long before gaped after the said bishoprike, in singular hope to atteine therevnto, had now his wish in effect: which he the more easilie compassed, for that he had his nets alwaies readie cast, as assuring himselfe to take a trout: following therein a prophane mans cautelous counsell, and putting the same in practise; who saith: *The bishops owne booke disaduantageable to himselfe.* *The bishop dieth of a sorowfull and pensiue conceipt.*

Casus vbiq; valet, semper tibi pendeat hamus,
　Quo minimè credis gurgite piscis erit.] *Ouid.*

The sicknesse which held the king dailie more and more increasing, he well perceiued that his end drew néere, and therefore meaning to doo some high pleasure to his people, granted of his frée motion a generall pardon to all men, for all offenses doone & committed against anie his lawes or statutes; théeues, murtherers, & certeine other were excepted. He paied also the fées of all prisoners in the gaoles in and about London, abiding there onelie for that dutie. He paied also the debts of all such persons as laie in the counters of Ludgate for fortie shillings & vnder; and some he reléeued that were condemned in ten pounds. Hervpon were processions generallie vsed euerie daie in euerie citie and parish, to praie to almightie God for his restoring to health and long continuance of the same. Neuerthelesse, he was so wasted with his long maladie, that nature could no longer susteine his life, and so he departed out of this world the two and twentith of Aprill, in his palace of Richmond, in the yéere of our Lord 1509. His corpse was conueied with all funerall pompe to Westminster, and there buried by the good queene his wife in a sumptuous chapell, which he not long before had caused to be builded. *1509 An. Reg. 24.* *The death of king Henrie the seuenth.*

He reigned thrée and twentie yeares, and more than seuen moneths, and liued two and fiftie yeares. He had by his quéene Elizabeth foure sonnes, and foure daughters, of the which thrée remained aliue behind him. Henrie his second son prince of Wales, which after him was king, Margaret quéen of Scots, and the ladie Marie promised to Charles king of Castile. He was a man of bodie but leane and spare, albeit mightie and strong therewith; of personage and stature somewhat higher than the meane sort of men, of a woonderfull beautie and faire complexion, of countenance merie and smiling, especiallie in his communication, his eies graie, his téeth single, and haire thin, of wit in all things quicke and prompt, of a princelie stomach and hautie courage. In great perils, doubtfull affaires, and matters of importance, supernaturall and in maner diuine; for he ordered all his dooings aduisedlie and with great deliberation. *What children he had.* *The description of king Henrie the seuenth.*

Besides this, he was sober, moderate, honest, courteous, bountious, and so much abhorring pride and arrogancie, that he was euer sharpe and quicke to them that were noted with that fault. He was also an indifferent and vpright iusticer, by the which one thing he allured to him the hearts of manie people, and yet to this seueritie of his he ioined a certeine mercifull pitie, which he did extend to those that had offended *Iustice mingled with mercie.*

the

the penall lawes, and were put to their fines by his iustices. He did vse his rigour onelie (as he said himselfe) to dant, bring low, and abate the high minds and stout stomachs of the wealthie and wild people, nourished vp in seditious factions and ciuill rebellions, rather than for the gréedie desire of monie; although such as were scourged with amerciaments cried out, and said it was rather for the respect of gaine, than for anie politike prouision. Indéed he left his coffers well stuffed, for he was no wastfull consumer of his riches by anie inordinat meanes.

Out of the bishop of Rochesters funerall sermon preached in Paules church at London.

To conclude, he had asmuch in him of gifts both of bodie, mind and fortune, as was possible for anie potentate or king to haue. His politike wisedome in gouernance was singular, his wit alwaie quicke and readie, his reason pithie and substantiall, his memorie fresh and holding, his experience notable, his counsels fortunate and taken by wise deliberation, his spéech gratious in diuerse languages, his person (as before ye haue heard) right comelie, his naturall complexion of the purest mixture, leagues and confederations he had with all christian princes. His mightie power was dread euerie where, not onelie within his realme but without. Also his people were to him in as humble subiection as euer they were to king; his land manie a daie in peace and tranquillitie, his prosperitie in battell against his enimies was maruellous, his dealing in time of perils and dangers was cold and sober, with great hardinesse. If anie treason were conspired against him, it came out wonderfullie. His buildings most goodlie, and after the newest cast, all of pleasure.

And so this king liuing all his time in fortunes fauour, in high honour, wealth and glorie, for his noble acts and prudent policies is woorthie to be registred in the booke of fame, least time (the consumer of all worthie things) should blot out the memorie of his name here in earth, whose soule we trust liueth in heauen, enioieng the fruition of the godhead, & those pleasures prepared for the faithfull. [In memorie of whome, his manifold vertues, with the fortunate successe of his affaires, and the gratious descent of his loines, as they procured a famous report in nations farre and néere; so haue some at the contemplation of his princelinesse, and euerie waie crowned with felicitie, made memorials of his magnificence; to the immortalitie of his high praise and vnblemishable renowme: among whome (for the truth of the report iustifiable by the contents of this historie) one commeth to mind, which may well serue for an epitaph:

Septimus Henricus factis est nomen adeptus
Præclarum claris ventura in secula famæ:
Ciuibus ille suis fuerat charissimus, hostes
Omnes iure ipsum metuebant: numinis almi
Relligiosus erat cultor, pietatis & æqui,
Versutos hominésque malos vehementiùs odit.
Viginti totos charus trésque ampliùs annos
Regibus externis in summo vixit honore:
Magnanimus, iustus rex, prudens atque modestus,
Henrico hæredi moriens sua regna reliquit,
Diuitiásque, immensum argenti pondus & auri.

Abr. Fl. ex I. S. pag. 892. Sepulture of Henrie the seuenth. Executors to Henrie the seuenth.

¶ The altar and sepulture of the same king Henrie the seuenth, wherein he now resteth, in his new chappell at Westminster, was made and finished in the yeare of our Lord 1519, by one Peter T. a painter of the citie of Florence, for the which he receiued one thousand pounds sterling for the whole stuffe and workemanship, at the hands of the king executors, Richard bishop of Winchester, Richard Fitz Iames bishop of London, Thomas bishop of Duresme, Iohn bishop of Rochester, Thomas duke of Norffolke treasuror of England, Edward earle of Worcester the kings Chamberleine, Iohn F. knight, chiefe iustice of the kings Bench, Robert R. knight chiefe iustice of the common plees, &c.]

Of

Of learned men that liued in this kings daies (as maister Bale noteth them) these are recorded. First George Rppeleie a Carmelite frier at Boston, seene in the mathematikes, he wrote diuerse treatises, and after his decease was accounted a nekromancer; Iohn Erghom borne in Yorke, a blacke frier, a doctor of diuinitie professed in Oxford, studious of prophesies, as by the title of the works which he wrote it may appeare; Iohn Persiuall a Chartreux monke; Thomas Maillorie a Welshman borne, he wrote (I wote not what) of king Arthur, and of the round table; Iohn Rousse borne in Warwikeshire, a diligent searcher of antiquities, whervpon few libraries were any where to be seene in England and Wales, where he made not search for the same, and wrote sundrie treatises of historicall arguments. He deceassed at Warwike the fourteenth of Ianuarie in the yeare 1491, and was buried in our ladie church there.

Thomas Scroope, otherwise surnamed Bradleie, descended of the noble familie of the Scroops, professed sundrie kinds of religions, as that of the order of saint Benet, and saint Dominike, and likewise he became a Carmelite, and last of all he fell to and preached the gospell in haire and sackecloth, till he vnderstood himselfe to be in the displeasure of Walden and other, that could not awaie with such singularitie in him or other, sounding (as they tooke it) to the danger of bringing the doctrine of the Romish church in misliking with the people; for then he withdrew himselfe to his house againe, and there remained twentie yeares, leading an anchors life, but yet after that time he came abroad, and was aduanced to be a bishop in Ireland, and went to *Dromorensis* the Roades in ambassage, from whence, being returned, he went barefooted vp and *episcopus.* downe in Norffolke, teaching in townes and in the countrie abroad the ten commandements, he liued till he came to be at the point of an hundred yeares old, & departed this life the fifteenth day of Ianuarie in the yeare of our Lord 1491, and was buried at Lestolfe, in Suffolke.

Iohn Tonneis, a diuine and an Augustine frier in Norwich, wrote certeine rules of grammar, and other things printed by Richard Pinson; Gefferie surnamed the Grammarian; Iohn Alcocke bishop of Elie, changed a nunrie at Cambridge into a college named Iesus college, about the yeere of Christ 1496. The chiefe cause of suppressing the nunrie is noted to be, for that the abbesse and other of the conuent liued dissolute liues; Stephan Hawes a learned gentleman, and of such reputation, as he was admitted to be one of the priuie chamber to king Henrie the seuenth; William Bintree, so called of a towne in Norffolke where he was borne, by profession a Carmelite frier in Burnham, a great diuine; William Gallion an Augustine frier in Lin, and at length became prouinciall of his order.

Robert Fabian a citizen and merchant of London, an historiographer, he was in his time in good estimation for his wisedome and wealth in the citie, so that he bare office and was shiriffe in the yeare 1493; William Celling, borne beside Feuersham in Kent, a monke of Canturburie; Thomas Bourchier descended of the noble linage of the earles of Essex, was first bishop of Elie, and after remooued from thense to Canturburie, succeeding Iohn Kemp in that archbishops see, at length created by pope Paule the second a cardinall; Philip Bromierd a Dominicke frier a diuine; Iohn Miles a doctor of both the lawes, ciuill and canon, he studied in Oxenford in the college of Brasen nose, newlie founded in the daies of this king Henrie the seuenth by William Smith bishop of Lincolne; Richard Shirborne bishop of Chichester, and imploied in ambassage to diuerse princes, as a man most méet thereto for his singular knowledge in learning and eloquence.

Robert Viduus vicar of Thakestéed in Essex, and a prebendarie canon of Welles, an excellent poet; Peter Kenighall a Carmelit frier, but borne of worshipfull linage in France, hauing an Englishman to his father, was student in Oxenford, and became a notable preacher; Iohn Morton first bishop of Elie, and after archbishop of Canturburie the sixtie and fourth in number that ruled that sée, he was aduanced to the dignitie of a cardinall, and by king Henrie the seuenth made lord chancellor, a worthie councellor and a modest, he was borne of worshipfull parents in Cheshire, & departed this life in the yeare of our Lord 1500; Henrie Medwall chapleine to the said Morton; Edmund Dudleie borne of noble parentage, studied the lawes of this land, and profited highlie in knowledge of the same, he wrote a booke intituled Arbor rei publicæ, the tree of the common wealth: of this man ye haue heard before in the life of this king, and more (God willing) shall be said in the beginning of the next king, as the occasion of the historie leadeth; Iohn Bokingham an excellent schooleman; William Blackeneie a Carmelit frier, a doctor of diuinitie, and a nekromancer.

Thus farre Henrie the seuenth, sonne to Edmund earle of Richmond.

========================

HENRIE THE EIGHT,

sonne and successor to Henrie the seuenth.

AFTER the death of the noble prince Henrie the seauenth, his sonne Henrie the eight began his reigne the two and twentith daie of Aprill in the yeare of the world 5475, after the birth of our sauiour 1509, and in the eightéenth yeare of his age, in the sixtéenth yeare of Maximilian then being emperour, in the eleuenth yeare of Lewes the twelfth that then reigned in France, and in the twentith yeare of king Iames the fourth as then ruling ouer the Scots. Whose stile was proclamed by the sound of a trumpet in the citie of London, the thrée and twentith daie of the said moneth, with much gladnesse and reioising of the people. And the same daie he departed from his manour of Richmond, to the Tower of London, where he remained closelie and secret with his councell, till the funerals of his father were finished.

Although this king now comming to the crowne, was but yoong (as before is said) yet hauing béene in his first yeares trained vp in learning, did for respect of his owne suertie and good gouernement of his people, prudentlie (by the aduise of his grandmoother the countesse of Richmond and Derbie) elect. & choose foorth of the most wise and graue personages to be of his priuie councell, namelie such as he knew to be of his fathers right déere and familiar fréends, whose names were as followeth. William Warham archbishop of Canturburie and chancellor of England, Richard Fox bishop of Winchester, Thomas Howard earle of Surrie, and treasuror of England, George Talbot earle of Shrewesburie, and lord steward of the kings houshold, Charles Summerset lord chamberleine, sir Thomas Louell, sir Henrie Wiat, doctor Thomas Ruthall, and sir Edward Poinings.

These graue and wise councellors, fearing least such abundance of riches and welth as the king was now possessed of, might mooue his yoong yeares vnto riotous forgetting of himselfe (for vnto no king at anie time before, was left greater or the like riches, as well in readie coine, as in iewels and other mooueables, as was left to him by his father) they therefore his said councellors trauelled in such prudent sort with him, that they got him to be present with them when they sat in councell; so to acquaint him with matters perteining to the politike gouernment of the realme, that by little

and

and little he might applie himselfe to take vpon him the rule and administration of publike affaires, with the which at the first he could not well indure to be much troubled, being rather inclined to follow such pleasant pastimes as his youthfull yoong yeares did more delite in, and therefore could be verie well contented, that other graue personages should take paines therein.

The same daie also that the king came to the Tower, the lord Henrie Stafford brother to the duke of Buckingham was arrested, and committed to the Tower: and the same daie also doctor Ruthall was named bishop of Durham. The fiue and twentith daie of Aprill was proclaimed, that the kings grace ratified all the pardons granted by his father, and also pardoned all such persons as were then in sute for anie offense whatsoeuer it was; treason, murther, and fellonie onelie excepted. And now, whereas the performance of the deceassed kings will was thought right expedient with all spéed to be performed, a proclamation was also set foorth and published thorough the realme, that if anie man could prooue himselfe to be hurt, and depriued of his goods wrongfullie by the commissioners of the forfeitures; he should come and present his plaint to the king, being readie to satisfie euerie one of all iniuries susteined. *A proclamation.*

After this proclamation was notified abroad, all such as had béene constreined either by right or by wrong (as Polydor saith) to paie anie thing for anie forfeitures of lawes and customes by them transgressed, came flocking to the court, & there declared their gréefs, in what sort they had wrongfullie béene compelled (as they surmised) to paie this or that summe. The councell heard euerie mans complaint, and such as were found to haue paid anie thing without plaine proofe of iust cause, they tooke such order for them, that they had their monie againe. Which being once knowne, it was a strange thing to sée how thicke other came in; yea euen those that had béene worthilie fined & punished for their disorderlie transgressions, making earnest sute for restitution, feining and forging manie things to make their cause séeme good, and to stand with equitie. *Multitudes of suters what shifts they made to be heard.*

And the better to be heard in their sute, they made friends as well with bribes and large gifts as otherwise, leauing no waies vnassaied to compasse their desires. Which gréedines in such multitude of suters, brought the commissioners, and others that had delt in the forfeitures into danger, and did themselues no good: for the councell perceiuing that it was not possible to satisfie them all, refused to heare anie further complaints or sutes for restitution: but thought it best to commit those to prison, by whom the complainants pretended themselues to haue been wronged. And herevpon was sir Richard Empson knight, and Edmund Dudleie esquier, great councellors to the late king attached, and brought to the Tower, thereby to quiet mens minds, that made such importunate sute to haue their monie againe restored, which in the late kings daies they had béene compelled to disburse, thorough the rigorous procéedings, as they alleged, of the said two councellors, and others. *Empson and Dudleie committed to the Tower.*

Trulie great exclamation was made against them, as often happeneth; that where anie thing is doone contrarie to the liking of the people, those that be dealers vnder the prince, and by his commandement procéed in the execution thereof, run in hatred of the multitude. But how so euer it was, their apprehension and committing to prison was thought by the wise to be procured by the malice of them that in the late kings daies were offended with their authoritie. Shortlie after (as Edward Hall saith) were apprehended diuerse other persons, that were called promoters, as Canbie, Page, Smith, Derbie, Wright, Simson, and Stecton; of which the more part ware papers, and stood on the pillorie. [And (as an other saith, who termeth them ringleaders of false quests in London) they rode about the citie with their faces to the horsses tailes, and papers on their heads, and after they had beene set on the pillorie in Cornehill, they were brought againe to Newgate, where they died all within seauen daies after for verie shame.] *Promoters punished.* *I. S. pag. 893.*

When

The funerall pompe and solemnitie of Henrie the seuenth.

When all things were prepared readie for the funerall of the late king, his corps with all sumptuous pompe and solemne ceremonies, was conueied from Richmond to saint Georges field, where the clergie of the citie met it: and at the bridge the maior and his brethren with manie commoners all clothed in blacke likewise met it, and gaue their attendance on the same thorough the citie, to the cathedrall church of saint Paule, where was soong a solemne dirige and masse, and a sermon made by the bishop of Rochester Iohn Fisher. The next daie the corps was had to Westminster, and there the daie following, put into the earth with all due solemnities as apperteined. [Notwithstanding this breefe remembrance of king Henries solemne funerall, might seeme sufficient in the iudgement of some, without further amplification; yet bicause it is good in others opinion (and those not of meanest wit) to set downe things of state at large, if conuenient helps thereto maie be had: therefore you shall haue the whole solemnitie of the said roiall funeral, as it is found recorded by Edward Hall.

Edw. Hall, in Hen. 8. fol. j.

After that all things (saith he) necessarie for the interrement and funerall pompe of the late king, were sumptuouslie prepared and doone: the corps of the said deceassed king was brought out of his priuie chamber into the great chamber, where he rested thrée daies, and euerie daie had there dirige and masse soong by a prelat mitred. From thense he was conueied into the hall, where he was also three daies, and had like seruice there; and so thrée daies in the chapell. And in euerie of these thrée places, was a hearse of wax garnished with baners, and nine mourners giuing their attendance all the seruice time: and euerie daie they offered, and euerie place

The corps put into a charriot sumptuouslie garnished.

hanged with blacke cloth. Vpon Wednesdaie the ninth daie of Maie, the corps was put into a charriot, couered with blacke cloth of gold, drawne with fiue great coursers all couered with blacke veluet, garnished with cushins of fine gold: and ouer the corps was an image or representation of the late king, laied on cushins of gold, and the said image was apparelled in the kings rich robes of estate, with a crowne on the head with ball and scepter in the hands: the charriot was garnished with baners and pencels of the armes of his dominions, titles and genealogies.

The order of the pompe and mourners.

When the charriot was thus ordered, the kings chappell, and a great number of prelats set forward praieng. Then followed all the kings seruants in blacke, then followed the charriot: and after the charriot nine mourners, and on euerie side were caried long torches & short, to the number of six hundred, & in this order they came to saint Georges field, from Richmond. There met with them all the préests and clerks and religious men within the citie & without, which went formost before the K. chappell. The maior and his brethren with manie commoners all clothed in blacke, met with the corps at London bridge, and so gaue their attendance on the same through the citie. And in good order the companies passed thorough the citie, whereof the stréets on euerie side were set with long torches, and on the stals stood yoong children holding tapers; & so with great reuerence the charriot was brought to the cathe-

The charriot brought into Paules church.

drall church of S. Paule, where the bodie was taken out and caried into the quire, and set vnder a goodlie hearse of wax garnished with baners, pencels, and cushins, where was soong a solemne dirige and a masse with a sermon made by the bishop of Rochester. During which time, the kings houshold and the mourners reposed them in the bishops palace.

Description of the curious hearse at Westminster.

The next daie the corps in like order was remooued towards Westminster: sir Edward Howard bearing the kings baner on a courser trapped in the armes of the deceased king. In Westminster was a curious hearse, made of nine principals, all full of lights, which were lighted at the comming of the corps, which was taken out of the charriot by six lords and set vnder the hearse; the image or the representation lieng vpon the cushin on a large pall of gold. The hearse was double railed; within the first railes sat the mourners, and within the second raile stood knights bearing baners of saints, and without the same stood officers of armes. When the mourners were

were set, Gartier king at armes, cried; For the soule of the noble prince king Henrie the seauenth late king of this realme: then the quire began Placebo, and so soong dirige: which being finished, the mourners departed into the palace, where they had a void, and so reposed for that night. The next daie were thrée masses solemnelie soong by bishops, and at the last masse was offered the kings baner and courser, his coat of armes, his sword, his target, and his helme: and at the end of masse the mourners offered vp rich palles of cloath of gold and baudekin: and when the quire sang, Libera me; the bodie was put into the earth.

The bodie of the dead king interred.

Then the lord treasuror, lord steward, lord chamberleine, the treasuror and comptrollor of the kings houshold, brake their staues and cast them into the graue. Then Gartier cried with a lowd voice; Viue le roy Henrie le huictesme, roy d'Angleterre, & de France, sire d'Irland. Then all the mourners, and all other that had giuen their attendance on this funerall obsequie, departed to the palace, where they had a great and a sumptuous feast. Woonder it were to write of the lamentation that was made for this prince amongst his seruants, and other of the wisest sort; and the ioie that was made for his death by such as were troubled by rigour of his law: yet the toward hope which in all points appeared in the yoong king did both repaire and comfort the heauie hearts of them, which had lost so wise and sage a prince: and also did put out of the minds of such as were releeued by the said kings death, all their old grudge and rancor, and confirmed their new ioie by the new grant of his pardon.

After that the funerals of the said late king were once ended, great preparation was made for the coronation of the new king, which was appointed on Midsummer daie next insuing. During the time of which preparation, the king was aduised by some of his councell to take to wife the ladie Katharine, late wife to his brother prince Arthur, least she hauing so great a dowrie as was appointed to hir, might marrie out of the realme, which should be to his hinderance. The king being hereto persuaded, espoused the said ladie Katharine the third daie of Iune, the which marriage was dispensed with by pope Iulie, at the sute of hir father king Ferdinando. On the eleuenth daie of this moneth of Iune, the king came from Gréenewich to the Tower ouer London bridge and so by Grace church, with whome came manie a gentleman richlie apparelled, but speciallie the duke of Buckingham, which had a gowne all of goldsmiths worke, verie costlie.

Ladie Katharine prince Arthur his widow married to his brother king Henrie the eight.

The duke of Buckinghams rich arraie.

On Fridaie the two and twentith day of Iune, the king with the quéene being in the Tower of London, made foure and twentie knights of the Bath. And the morow following, being saturdaie the foure and twentith of Iune, his grace with the quéene departed from the Tower through London, the streets being hanged with tapestrie and cloth of arras, very richlie; and a great part of the south side of Cheape with cloth of gold, & so was some part of Cornehill. The stréets were railed & barred on the one side, from ouer against Grace church to Bredstréet in Cheapeside, where euerie occupation stood in their liueries in order, beginning with base and meane occupations, and so ascending to the worshipfull crafts. Highest and lastlie stood the maior with the aldermen. The goldsmiths stals vnto the end of the Old change, being replenished with virgins in white, with branches of white wax: the priests and clearkes in rich copes, with crosses and censers of siluer, with censing his grace and the queene also, as they passed. The features of his bodie, his goodlie personage, his amiable visage, princelie countenance, with the noble qualities of his roiall estate, to euerie man knowen, néedeth no rehersall, considering that (for lacke of cunning) I cannot expresse the gifts of grace and of nature that God indued him with all.

Ed. Hall in Hen. 8. fol. ij.

A trim sight of virgins in white, with branches of white wax.

Yet partlie to describe his apparell, it is to be noted, his grace ware in his vppermost apparell, a robe of crimsin veluet, furred with ermins, his iacket or coat of raised gold, the placard imbrodered with diamonds, rubies, emerauds, great pearles,

K. Henries apparell at his coronatiō.

and

and other rich stones, a great bauderike about his necke of great balasses. The trapper of his horse damaske gold, with a deepe purfle of ermins. His knights and esquiers for his bodie in crimsin veluet; and all the gentlemen, with other of his chappell, and all his officers and houshold seruants were appareled in scarlet. The barons of the fiue portes bare the canopie or cloth of estate. For to recite vnto you the great estates by name, the order of their going, the number of the lords spirituall & temporall, knights, esquiers, and gentlemen, and their costlie and rich apparell of seuerall deuises and fashions, who tooke vp his horsse best, or who was richest beseene; it would aske long time, and yet I should omit manie things, and faile of the number, for they were verie manie: wherefore I passe ouer. But this I dare well saie, there was no lacke or scarsitie of cloth of tissue, cloth of gold, cloth of siluer, broderie, or of goldsmiths works: but in more plentie and aboundance than hath beene séene or read of at anie time before, and thereto manie and great numbers of chaines of gold, & bauderikes both massie and great.

The kings traine and the pompe of the same. Also before the kings highnesse rode two gentlemen richlie apparelled, and about their bodies ouerthwart, they bare two robes, the one of the duchie of Guien, and the other for the duchie of Normandie, with hats on their heads powdered with ermins, for the estate of the same. Next followed two persons of good estate, the one bearing his cloke, the other his hat, apparelled both in goldsmiths worke and broderie, their horsses trapped in burned siluer, drawen ouer with cordes of gréene silke and gold, the edges and borders of their apparell being fretted with gold of damaske. After them came sir Thomas Brandon, master of the kings horsse, clothed in tissue, brodered with roses of fine gold, and ouerthwart his bodie a great bauderike of gold, great and massie; his horsse trapped in gold, leading by a raine of silke; the kings spare horsse trapped bard wise, with harnesse brodred with bullion gold, curiouslie wrought by goldsmiths. Then next followed the nine children of honor vpon great coursers, appareled on their bodies in blue veluet, powdered with floure delices of gold, & chaines of goldsmiths worke, euerie one of their horsses trapped with a trapper of the kings title, as of England and France, Gascoigne, Guien, Normandie, Angiou, Cornewall, Wales, Ireland, &c. wrought vpon veluets, with imbroderie, and goldsmiths worke.

The quéenes traine and the sumptuousnesse of the same. Then next following in order, came the quéenes retinue, as lords, knights, esquiers, and gentlemen in their degrees, well mounted, and richlie apparelled in tissue, cloth of gold, of siluer, tinsels, and veluets imbrodered, fresh and goodlie to behold. The quéene then by name Katharine, sitting on hir litter borne by two white palfries, the litter couered and richlie appareled, and the palfries trapped in white cloth of gold; hir person apparelled in white satin imbrodered, hir haire hanging downe to hir backe of very great length, beautifull and goodlie to behold, & on hir head a coronall set with manie rich orient stones. Next after, six honorable personages on white palfries all apparelled in cloth of gold, and then a chariot couered, and the ladies therein all apparelled in cloth of gold. And another sort of ladies, and then another chariot, then the ladies next the chariot, and so in order, euerie one after their degrées in cloth of gold, cloth of siluer, tinsels, and veluet, with imbroderies. Euerie couplement of the said chariots, and the draught harnesses were powdered with ermins mixt with cloth of gold: & so with much ioy & honour they came to Westminster, where was high preparation made, aswell for the said coronation, as also for the solemne feasts and iusts therevpon to be had and doone.

The coronation of king Henrie and quéene Katharine. The morrow following being sundaie, and also Midsummer daie, this noble prince with his quéene at time conuenient, vnder their canopies borne by the barons of the fiue ports, went from the said palace to Westminster abbaie vpon cloth, called vulgarlie cloth of raie; the which cloth was cut and spoiled by the rude and common people, immediatlie after their repaire into the abbaie; where, according to the sacred

obseruance

obseruance & ancient custome, his grace with the quéene were annointed and crowned by the archbishop of Canturburie, with other prelats of the realme there present, and the nobilitie, with a great multitude of commons of the same. It was demanded of the people, whether they would receiue, obeie, and take the same most noble prince for their king? Who with great reuerence, loue, and desire, said and cried; Yea yea. After the which solemnitie and coronation finished, the lords spirituall and temporall did to him homage, and returned to Westminster hall with the quéenes grace, euerie one vnder their canopies; where, by the lord Marshall, & his tipped staues was made roome, and euerie lord, and other noble men, according to their tenures, before claimed and viewed, séene and allowed by the lords, and other of his graces councell, entred into such roome and office that daie, to execute their seruices accordinglie.

Homage doone to the king at his coronatiō both of the lords spirituall & temporall.

The kings estate on the right hand, & the queenes on the left hand, the cupboord of nine stages, their noble personages being set: first, at the bringing of the first course, the trumpets sounded. And in came the duke of Buckingham, mounted vpon a great courser, richlie trapped and imbrodered, and the lord steward in likewise on an horsse trapped in cloth of gold, riding before the seruice, which was sumptuous, with manie subtilties, strange deuises, with seuerall poses, and manie deintie dishes. At the kings feet vnder the table were certeine gentlemen; and in likewise with the queene, who there continued, during that long and roiall feast. What should I speake or write of the sumptuous, fine, and delicate meats prepared for this high and honorable coronation, prouided for aswell in the parties beyond the seas, as in manie and sundrie places within this realme, where God so aboundantlie hath sent such plentie and foison? Or of the honorable order of the seruices, the cleane handeling and breaking of meats, the ordering of the dishes, with the plentifull abundance? So that none of anie estate being there did lacke, nor no honorable or worshipfull person went vnfeasted.

The second course being serued: in at the hall doore entered a knight, armed at all points, his bases rich tissue embrodered, a great plume and a sumptuous of ostrich feathers on his helmet, sitting on a great courser, trapped in tissue, and embrodered with the armes of England, and of France, and an herald of armes before him. And passing through the hall, he presented himselfe with humble reuerence before the kings maiestie, to whome Gartier king of heralds cried and said with a lowd voice; Sir knight from whence come you, and what is your pretense? This knights name was sir Robert Dimmocke, champion to the king by tenure of his inheritance, who answered the said king of armes in effect after this maner: Sir, the place that I come from is not materiall, nor the cause of my repaire hither is not concerning anie matter of anie place or countrie, but onelie this: and therewithall commanded his herald to make an O yes. Then said the knight to the king of armes; Now shall ye heare the cause of my cōming and pretense. Then he commanded his owne herald, by proclamation to saie; If there be anie person, of what estate or degree soeuer he be, that will saie or prooue, that king Henrie the eight is not the rightfull inheritor and king of this realme, I sir Robert Dimmocke here his champion, offer my gloue, to fight in his quarell with any person to the vtterance. Which proclamation was made in sundrie places of the hall: and at euerie time his gantlet cast downe, in the maintenance thereof.

Sir Robert Dimmocke the kings champion.

The knights answer to the king of heralds.

After these seuerall proclamations doone, and offers made, the said knight or champion eftsoones repaired to the kings presence, demanding drinke; to whome the kings grace sent a cup of gold with wine, whereof after this knight had drunke, he demanded the couer of the said cup, which to him also was deliuered: that doone he departed out of the hall, with the said cup and couer as his owne. The maner of his tenure is this, that at the coronation of the king, he shall go to the armorie,

The maner of the same knights tenure.

and

and there take the kings best harnesse saue one, the best and rich bases sauing one, then of the plumes or other things for the garnishing of his creast or helme; and so to the stable, there taking the next courser or horsse to the best, with like trappers, & so furnished, to enter (as afore) and his office doone, to haue all these things with the cup of gold and couer to his owne vse. After the departure of the said champion, the king of armes with all the heralds and other officers of armes, made proclamations in seuerall places of the hall, crieng largesse. Brieflie I passe ouer this high and long solemnitie of this honorable coronation and feast, more honorable than of the great Cesar, whome manie historiographers so highlie set out and magnifie.

Sir Stephā Genings maior of London.

Now when the tables were voided, the wafers were brought. Then sir Stephan Genings that time maior of London, whome the king before he sat downe to dinner had dubbed knight, which began the earles table that daie, arose from the place where he sat, to serue the king with ipocras in a cup of gold: which cup, after his grace had dronken thereof, was with the couer giuen vnto the said sir Stephan, like as other his predecessors, maiors of the said citie, were woont to haue at the coronation of the king. Then after the surnap laied, and that the kings grace and the quéene had washed, euerie of them vnder their cloths of estate, the tables being auoided, went vnto their chambers. For the more honour and innobling of this triumphant corona-

Iusts and turnements.

tion, there were prepared both iusts and turneis to be doone in the palace of Westminster, where, for the kings grace and the quéene, was framed a faire house, couered with tapestrie, and hanged with rich clothes of arrais, and in the said palace was made a curious founteine and ouer it a castell, on the top therof a great crowne imperiall, all the imbatelling with roses and pomegranats gilded.

Vnder and about the said castell, a curious vine, the leaues and grapes thereof gilded with fine gold, the walles of the same castell coloured white & greene losengis, and in euerie losing either a rose or a pomegranat, and a sheafe of arrowes, or else H. and K. gilded with fine gold, with certeine arches and turrets gilded, to support the same castell. And the targets of the armes of the defendants, appointed for the said iusts, therevpon sumptuouslie set. And out at seuerall places of the same castell, aswell on the daie of the coronation, as on the said daies of the iusts & turneies, out of the mouthes of certeine beasts or gargels did run red, white, and claret wine.

The enterprisers of the said iusts.

The enterprisers of these iusts, was Thomas lord Howard, heire apparant to the earle of Surrie, sir Edward Howard admerall his brother, the lord Richard brother to the Marques Dorset, sir Edmund Howard, sir Thomas Kneuet, and Charles Brandon esquier. The trumpets blew to the field, the fresh yoong galants and noble men gorgeouslie apparrelled, with curious deuises of cuts and of embroderies, as well in their coates as in trappers for their horsses, some in gold, some in siluer, some in tinsels, and diuerse other in goldsmithes worke, goodlie to behold.

Goodlie shews & delightfull.

These first entred the field, in taking vp & turning their horsses netlie and freshlie. Then followed a deuise (caried by strength of men and other prouision) framed like a castell, or a turret, wrought with fine cloth of gold: the top whereof was spred with roses and pomegranats, hanging downe on euerie side of the said deuise; wherein was a ladie, bearing a shield of christall named Pallas. After whome the said lord Howard with his companions followed, armed at all points, their bases and bards, or trappers, were of gréene veluet, beaten with roses and promegranats of gold, brodred with fringes of damaske gold. The said deuise or turret, being brought before the

Pallas knights the defendants.

king, the ladie Pallas presented the said persons, whome she named hir scholers, to the kings highnes, beséeching the same to accept them as hir scholers, who were desirous to serue him, to the increase of their honours; which said scholers had about them on foot to the number of an hundred persons, freshlie apparrelled, in veluets of sundrie colours, with hose & bonets according to the same. And further, the said

ladie

ladie desired the king, that it might please his grace, that hir said scholers might be be defendants to all commers, which request was granted.

Then came in an other band of horssemen, freshlie and well apparelled in cloth of gold, in siluer, in goldsmithes worke, & broderie, to the number of three score, with trappers according to their garments, with great bauderikes, collars, and chaines of gold about their necks and trauerse their bodies, euerie man with a coife of gold on his head, and a great plume of feathers thervpon, some of one colour and some of an other, entering before into the field with drums and fifes a great number, euerie man taking vp his horsse in his best maner, as well for their ladies, as also for laud or praise to be giuen them. After whome followed a good number of footmen, in veluets and other silkes, cut and embrodered, with hose to the same accordinglie, and bonets and other furniture, after a fresh and lustie fashion. Next to them came on horssebacke eight persons, whose names were, sir Iohn Pechie, sir Edward Neuill, sir Edward Guildeford, sir Iohn Carre, sir William Parre, sir Giles Capell, sir Griffith Dun, and sir Rouland, armed also at all points, with shields of their owne armes, with rich plumes, and other deuises on their head péeces, their bases and trappers of tissue, cloth of gold, siluer and veluet; and next before them, a gentleman on horssebacke, in a coat of blue veluet, embrodered with gold, and his horsse trapped in the same sute, with a speare of gold on his thigh, and the same presented to the quéene: saieng, that it was informed those knights of his companie, how that dame Pallas had presented six of hir scholers to the king, but whether they came to learne, or to teach feats of armes they knew not.

He further declared, that his knights were come to doo feats of armes, for the loue of ladies. Wherfore he besought hir grace, to licence those knights to prooue themselues against dame Pallas scholers: and that in case hir scholers brake more speares on the said knights, by the view of the iudges, and the report of the heralds, than the same knights should doo on them; then the said scholers of Pallas knights to haue the speare of gold for their prise. And if the knights brake more speares than dame Pallas scholers, the said knights to haue the christall shield. The which request to them granted, the iusts began, where euerie man did acquite himselfe well and valiantlie: but who had the prise of other, I know not. The night cōming on, the iusts ended. The next daie approached the foresaid defenders, scholers to Pallas on horssebacke, armed *cape a pie, the one side of their bases and bards of their horsses white veluet, embrodered with roses of gold and other embroderies; the other side gréene veluet embrodered with pomegranats of gold, euerie one of them on his head péece had an heare of flat gold of damaske, and so presented themselues before the king readie to tourneie.

Then immediatlie on the other part came in the forenamed eight knights, readie armed, their bases and bards of their horsse gréene sattin, embrodered with fresh deuises of bramble branches, of fine gold curiouslie wrought, powdered all ouer. And after them a great number of hornes blowne, by men apparrelled in gréene cloth, with caps and hosen of like sute, as foresters or kéepers; & a pagent made like a parke, paled with pales of white and greene, wherein were certeine fallow deare, and in the same parke curious trees made by craft, with bushes, fernes, and other things in likewise wrought, goodlie to behold. The which parke or deuise, being brought before the quéene, had certeine gates thereof opened, the deare ran out therof into the palace, the greiehounds were let slip and killed the deare: the which deare so killed, were presented to the quéene and the ladies by the foresaid knights.

Crocheman, which the daie before brought in the speare of gold, there declared, that the same knights were seruants to Diana, and being in their pastime of hunting, newes were brought vnto them, that dame Pallas knights were come into those parts, to doo déeds of armes: wherefore they had left their hunting and chase, and repaired

Another band of horssemen richlie araied.

Eight knights armed at all points.

* From head to foot.

Dianas knights.

A conceipt or deuise of a parke with deare, &c.

also thither, to encounter with the knights of Pallas, and so to fight with them for the loue of ladies, to the vtterance: saieng, that if Pallas knights vanquished the other, or made them to leaue the field, then they to haue the deare killed, and the greiehounds that slue them.   And in case Dianas knights ouercame the other, they to haue their swords, and none other thing more.   Wherevpon the queene and ladies sent to the king to haue his aduise and pleasure in this behalfe.   His grace conceiuing that there was some grudge and displeasure betwéene them, thinking if such request were to them granted some inconuenience might insue, would not therevnto agrée: so that for the appeasing thereof it was awarded, that both parties should tourneie togither, giuing but some certeine strokes, which doone they departed: and so these iusts brake vp, and the prises giuen to euerie man after his deserts.]

The kings wisedome in preuenting an inconuenience.

Henrie the duke of Buckinghams brother created erle of Wilshire.

The king pardoned the lord Henrie brother to the duke of Buckingham, committed to the Tower (as yee haue heard) vpon suspicion of treason: but when nothing could be prooued against him, he was set at libertie, and at the parlement after created earle of Wilshire.   Also this yeare the king ordeined fiftie gentlemen to be speares, euerie of them to haue an archer, a demilance, and a custrell; and euerie speare to haue thrée great horsses to be attendant on his person, of the which band the earle of Essex was lieutenant, and sir Iohn Pechie capteine.   This ordinance continued but a while, the charges was so great; for there were none of them, but they and their horsses

A great plague in Calis.

were apparrelled and trapped in cloth of gold, siluer & goldsmithes worke.   This yeare also was a great pestilence in the towne of Calis, so that the king sent one sir Iohn Pechie with thrée hundred men to tarrie there vpon the defense of that towne

A parlement.

till the sicknesse was ceassed.   Furthermore, this yeare the king summoned his parlement in the moneth of Nouember, to begin in the moneth of Ianuarie next ensuing: whereof sir Thomas Inglefield was chosen speaker.

Empson and Dudleie atteinted of treason.

Polydor.

At this parlement sir Richard Empson knight, and Edmund Dudleie esquier late councellors vnto king Henrie the seauenth, were atteinted of high treason.   They were charged with manie offenses committed in the late kings daies, as partlie before yée haue heard; who being brought before the councell, as they were graue and wise personages, and both of them learned and skilfull in the lawes of the realme: so had they vtterance verie readie whereby to deliuer the conceipts of their minds with singular dexteritie, speciallie in a case of importance; in so much that when the said parties were conuented before the assemblie of the lords, they alleged for themselues right constantlie (in their owne defenses) much good and sufficient matter, of whome Empson (being the elder in yeares) had these words.

A speech vttered by Empson to the lords of the councell to find fauour.

I KNOW (right honorable) that it is not vnknowne to you, how profitable and necessarie lawes are for the good preseruation of mans life: without the which neither house, towne, nor citie can long continue or stand in safetie.   Which lawes heere in England, thorough negligence of magistrates, were partlie decaied, and partlie quite forgotten and worne out of vse; the mischeefe whereof dailie increasing, Henrie the seauenth a most graue and prudent prince wished to suppresse, and therefore appointed vs to see, that such lawes as were yet in vse might continue in their full force; and such as were out of vse might againe be reuiued and restored to their former state; & that also those persons which transgressed the same, might be punished according to their demerits.   Wherein we discharged our dueties in most faithfull wise, and best maner we could, to the great aduantage & commoditie (no doubt) of the whole commonwealth.   Wherfore we most humblie beseech you in respect of your honours, courtesie, goodnesse, humanitie, and iustice, not to decree any greeuous sentence
against

against vs, as though we were worthie of punishment; but rather to appoint how with thankfull recompense our paines & trauell may be be worthilie considered.

Manie of the councell thought that he had spoken well, and so as stood with great reason: but yet the greater number (supposing that the reuiuing of those lawes had procéeded rather of a couetous meaning in the king and them, than of anie zeale of of iustice, and hauing also themselues felt the smart latelie before for their owne offenses and transgressions) had conceiued such malice towards the men, that they thought it reason, that such as had béene dealers therein, were worthie to lose their heads, in like sort as they had caused others to lose their monie. Héereupon, their accusors were mainteined, and manie od matters narrowlie sought out against them, as by two seuerall indictments framed against sir Richard Empson (the copies whereof I haue séene) it may well appeare.

Most of the lords of the councell against Empson.

In the one he is charged, that to win the fauour and credit of the late king, not weieng his honor nor the prosperitie of him, or wealth of his realme, hee had (in subuersion of the lawes of the land) procured diuerse persons to be indicted of diuerse crimes and offenses surmised against them, and thereupon to be committed to prison, without due proces of law; who not suffered to come to their answers, were kept in durance, till they had compounded for their fines, to their great importable losses, and vtter impouerishment. Also diuerse vntrue offices of intrusions and alienations, made by sundrie the late kings liege people, into manors, lands, and tenements were found; it being vntrulie alleged, that they held the same of the king In capite. And when such persons as were thus vexed, offered to trauerse those offices, they could not be admitted thereto, in such due and lawfull forme as in such cases the law prouideth, till they had compounded to paie great fines and ransomes.

Matters obiected against Empson.

Wrong mainteined against the kings liege people.

Moreouer the kings wards, after they had accomplished their full age, could not be suffered to sue their liueries, till they had paied excessiue fines and ransomes, vnto their great annoiance, losse, and disquieting, and to no lesse contempt of the said king. And further, whereas diuerse persons had béene outlawed, as well at the sute of their aduersaries, as of the said late king; they could not be allowed to purchase their charters of pardon out of chancerie, according to the law of the realme, till they were driuen to answer halfe the issues and profits of all their lands and tenements by the space of two yeares, which the king receiued to his vse, by the said Richard Empsons procurement, who informed him that hée might lawfullie take the same, although he knew that it was contrarie to the lawes and customes of the realme. Wherevpon the people, vexed and molested by such hard dealings, sore grudged against the said late king, to the great perill and danger of his person and realme, and subuertion of the lawes and ancient customes thereof.

Iniurie doone to the kings wards

Also it was alleged against the said Empson, that he had sent foorth precepts directed vnto diuerse persons, commanding them, vpon great penalties, to appeare before him, and other his associats, at certeine daies and times within his house in S. Brides parish, in a ward of London, called Farringdon without: where they making their appearances, according to the same precepts, were impleaded afore him and other his said associats, of diuerse murthers, felonies, outlawries, and of the articles in the statute of prouisors conteined; also of wilfull escapes of felonies, and such like matters and articles apperteining to the plées of the crowne, and common lawes of the realme. And that doone, the said persons were committed to diuerse prisons, as the Fléet, the Tower, and other places, where they were deteined, till they had fined at his pleasure, as well for the commoditie of the said late king, as for the singular aduantage of the said sir Richard Empson.

A charge of manifest oppression and extortion.

Moreouer, whereas the said Empson, being recorder of Couentrie, and there sate with the maior and other instices of the peace, vpon a speciall gaole deliuerie within

Empson sometime recorder of Couentrie.

that citie, on the mondày before the feast of saint Thomas the apostle, in the sixtéenth yeare of the late kings reigne; a prisoner that had beene indicted of felonie, for taking out of an house in that citie, certeine goods to the value of twentie shillings, was arreigned before them. And bicause the iurie would not find the said prisoner giltie, for want of sufficient euidence (as they after alleged) the said sir Richard Empson, supposing the same euidence to be sufficient caused them to be committed to ward, wherein they remained foure daies togither, till they were contented to enter bond in fortie pounds a péece, to appeare before the king and his councell, the second returne of the tearme then next insuing, being Quindena Hilarij. Wherevpon they kéeping their daie, and appearing before the said sir Richard Empson, and other of the kings councell, according to their bonds, were adiudged to paie euerie of them eight pounds for a fine, and accordinglie made paiment thereof, as they were then thought well worthie so to doo. But now this matter so long past, was still kept in memorie, and so

Empson indicted & found guiltie.

earnest some were to inforce it to the vttermost against the said Empson, that in a sessions holden at Couentrie now in this first yeare of this kings reigne, an indictment was framed against him for this matter, and thereof he was found giltie, as if therein he had committed some great and heinous offense against the kings peace, his crowne and dignitie.

Thus haue I thought good to shew what I find hereof, to the end ye may perceiue how glad men were to find some colour of sufficient matter, to bring the said sir Richard Empson, and maister Edmund Dudleie, within danger of the lawes; whereby at length they were not onelie condemned by act of parlement, through malice of such as might séeme to seeke their destruction for priuat grudges; but in the end also they were arreigned: as first the said Edmund Dudleie in the Guildhall of London, the seuentéenth of Iulie; and sir Richard Empson, at Northampton in October next insuing: and being there condemned, was from thence brought backe againe to the Tower of London, where he remained till the time of his execution: as after yée shall heare.

The plague.
1510

This yeare the plague was great, and reigned in diuerse parts of this realme. The king kept his Christmas at Richmond. The twelfe of Ianuarie, diuerse gentlemen

The king runneth at tilt in his owne person.

prepared to iust, and the king and one of his priuie chamber called William Compton, secretlie armed themselues in the little parke of Richmond, & so came into the iustes, vnknowne to all persons. The king neuer ran openlie before, and did exceeding well. Maister Compton chanced to be sore hurt by Edward Neuill esquier, brother to the lord of Aburgauennie, so that he was like to haue died. One person there was that knew the king, and cried; God saue the king: and with that, all the people were astonied, and then the king discouered himselfe, to the great comfort of the people. The king soone after came to Westminster, and there kept his Shrouetide with great bankettings, dansings, and other iollie pastimes.

Edw. Hall in H. 8. fol. vj.
The king with other nobles disguised like Robin hoods men for disport.

And on a time the king in person, accompanied with the earles of Essex, Wilshire and other noble men, to the number of twelue, came suddenlie in a morning into the queenes chamber, all apparelled in short coates of Kentish Kendall, with hoodes on their heads & hosen of the same, euerie one of them his bow and arrowes, and a sword and a buckler, like outlawes, or Robin Hoods men. Whereat the queene, and ladies, and all other there were abashed, as well for the strange sight, as also for their sudden

A banket.

comming, and after certeine danses and pastime made, they departed. On Shrouesundaie the same yeare, the king prepared a goodlie banket in the parlement chamber at Westminster, for all the ambassadors, which then were here out of diuerse realmes and countries. The banket being readie, the king leading the queene, entered into the chamber, then the ladies, ambassadours, and other noble men followed in order.

The king caused the queene to keepe the estate, and then sate the ambassadours and ladies, as they were marshalled by the K. who would not sit, but walked from place to

place,

place, making cheare to the quéene and the strangers: suddenlie the king was gone. And shortlie after, his grace, with the earle of Essex, came in apparelled after the Turkie fashion, in long robes of baudekin, powdered with gold, hats on their heds of crimsin veluet, with great rolles of gold, girded with two swords called cimiteries, hanging by great bauderiks of gold. Then next came the lord Henrie earle of Wil- shire, and the lord Fitzwater, in two long gownes of yellow sattin, trauersed with white sattin, and in euerie band of white was a band of crimsin sattin after the fashion of Russia or Rusland, with furred hats of graie on their heads, either of them hauing an hatchet in their hands, and boots with pikes turned vp. *The king and others disguised after the Turk- ish fashion.*

And after them came sir Edward Howard then admerall, and with him sir Thomas Parre, in dublets of crimsin veluet, voided low on the backe, and before to the chanell bone, lased on the breasts with chaines of siluer, and ouer that short cloakes of crim- sin sattin, and on their heads hats after dansers fashion, with feasants feathers in them: they were apareled after the fashion of Prusia or Spruce. The torchbearers were ap- parelled in crimsin sattin and gréene, like Moreskoes, their faces blacke: and the king brought in a mummerie. After that the quéene, the lords, & ladies (such as would) had plaied, the said mummers departed, and put off the same apparell, and soone after entered into the chamber in their vsuall apparell. And so the king made great cheere to the quéene, ladies and ambassadours. The supper or banket ended, and the tables voided, the king in communication with the ambassadours, the queene with the ladies tooke their places in their degrées.

Then began the dansing, and euerie man tooke much heed to them that dansed. The king perceiuing that, withdrew himselfe suddenlie out of the place, with certeine other persons appointed for that purpose. And within a little while after there came in a drum and a fife apparelled in white damaske & gréene bonnets, and hosen of the same sute. Then certeine gentlemen followed with torches, apparelled in blue damaske, purfelled with amis greie, fashioned like an albe, and hoods on their heads, with robes and long tippets to the same of blue damaske, in visards. Then after them came a certeine number of gentlemen, whereof the king was one, apparelled all in one sute of short garments, little beneath the points, of blue veluet and crimsin, with long sléeues, all cut and lined with cloth of gold. And the vtter part of the gar- ments were powdered with castels and sheafes of arrowes of fine ducket gold; the vpper parts of their hosen of like sute and fashion, the nether parts were of skarlet, powdered with timbrels of fine gold, on their heads bonnets of damaske, with siluer flat wouen in the stole, & therevpon wrought with gold, and rich fethers in them, all with visors. *A maske where- in the king was an actor.*

After them entered six ladies, whereof two were apparelled in crimsin sattin and purple, embrodered with gold, and by viniets ran floure delices of gold, with maruellous rich & strange tiers on their heads. Then two ladies in crimsin and purple, made like long slops embrodered and fret with gold after antike fashion: and ouer that garment was a short garment of cloth of gold scant to the knee, fashioned like a tabard all ouer, with small double rolles, all of flat gold of damaske, fret with frised gold, and on their heads skarfs and wrappers of damaske gold, with flat pipes, that strange it was to behold. The other two ladies were in kirtels of crimsin & purple sattin, embroder- ed with a viniet of pomegranats of gold, all the garments cut compasse wise, hauing but demie sléeues, naked downe from the elbowes, and ouer their garments were votchets of pleasants, rolled with crimsin veluet, and set with letters of gold like characts, their heads rolled in pleasants and tipets like the Aegyptians, embrodered with gold. Their faces, necks, armes, and hands, couered in fine pleasants blacke: some call it Lumbardines, which is maruellous thin; so that the same ladies seemed to be Nigers or blacke Mores. Of these foresaid six ladies, the ladie Marie, sister vnto *Certeine ladies richlie attired and after a strange fashion.*

The ladie Marie sister to the king.

the

the king was one, the other I name not. After that the kings grace and the ladies had dansed a certeine time, they departed euerie one to his lodging.

In this yeare also came ambassadors, not onelie from the king of Arragon and Castile, but also from the kings of France, Denmarke, Scotland, and other places, which were highlie welcomed, and noblie interteined. It happened on a daie, that there were certeine noble men made a wager to run at the ring and parties were taken, and which partie atteined or tooke awaie the ring oftnest with certeine courses, should win the wager. Whereof the kings grace hearing, offered to be on the one partie with six companions. The ambassadors hearing thereof, were much desirous to see this wager tried, and speciallie the ambassadours of Spaine, who had neuer séene the king in harnesse. At the daie appointed, the king was mounted on a goodlie courser, trapped in purple veluet cut, the inner side whereof was wrought with flat gold of damaske in the stoole, and the veluet on the other side cut in letters: so that the gold appeared as though it had beene embrodered with certeine reasons or posies. And on the veluet betwéene the letters were fastened castels and sheafs of arrowes of ducket gold, with a garment, the sléeues compassed ouer his harnesse, and his bases of the same worke, with a great plume of feathers on his head péece, that came downe to the arson of his saddle, and a great companie of fresh gentlemen came in with his grace richlie armed and decked, with manie other right gorgeouslie apparelled, the trumpets before them goodlie to behold, whereof manie strangers (but speciallie the Spaniards) much reioised; for they had neuer séene the king before that time armed.

On the other side came in another band of gentlemen freshlie apparelled, and pleasant to behold, all apparelled in cloth of gold, checkered with flat gold of damaske, & poudered with roses; and so euerie man ran: but to conclude, the prise was giuen vnto the king. Euerie man did run twelue courses, the king did beare away the ring fiue times, and atteined it thrée. And these courses thus finished, the Spanish ambassadours desired to haue some of the badges or deuises, which were on the kings trapper. His grace therof knowing, commanded euerie of them to take thereof what it pleased them, who in effect tooke all or the more part; for in the beginning they thought they had beene counterfeit, and not of gold; as they were. On Maie day then next folowing in the second yeare of his reigne, his grace being yoong, and willing not to be idle, rose in the morning verie earlie to fetch maie or gréene boughs, himselfe fresh & richlie apparelled; and clothed all his knights, squiers and gentlemen in white sattin, and all his gard and yeomen of the crowne in white sarcenet; and so went euerie man with his bow and arrowes shooting to the wood, and so repaired againe to the court, euerie man with a gréene bough in his cap.

Now at his returning, manie hearing of his going on maieng, were desirous to sée him shoot, for at that time his grace shot as strong and as great a length as anie of his gard. There came to his grace a certeine man with bow and arrowes, and desired his grace to take the muster of him, and to sée him shoot; for at that time his grace was contented. The man put the one foot in his bosome, and so did shoot, and shot a verie good shoot, and well towards his marke; whereof, not onelie his grace, but all other greatlie maruelled. So the king gaue him a reward for his so dooing; which person afterwards of the people, and of them in the court, was called, Foot in bosome. The same yeare in the feast of Pentecost, holden at Gréenwich, that is to say, the thursdaie in the same wéeke, his grace with two other with him, chalenged all commers, to fight with them at the barriers with target, and casting the speare of eight foot long; and that doone, his grace with the said two aides to fight euerie of them twelue strokes with two handed swordes, with and against all commers, none excepted being a gentleman; where the K. behaued himselfe so well, and deliuered himselfe so valiantlie by his hardie prowesse and great strength, that the praise and laud was giuen to
his

Edw. Hall in Hen. 8. fol. vij. Running at the ring.

The king verie roiallie arraied runneth at the ring in the sight of the ambassadours & beareth the prise awaie.

King Henrie goeth a maieng with other of his courtiers.

The king a good archer.

The king chalengeth all commers at sundrie exercises of actiuitie.

his grace, and his aides: notwithstanding that diuerse and strong persons had assailed him and his aides.

From thense the whole court remooued to Windsor, then begining his progresse, & exercising himselfe dailie in shooting, singing, dansing, wrestling, casting of the barre, plaieng at the recorders, flute, virginals, in setting of songs, and making of ballads; he did set two full masses, euerie of them fiue parts, which were soong oftentimes in his chappell, and afterwards in diuerse other places. And when he came to Oking, there were kept both iustes and turneies: the rest of this progresse was spent in hunting, hawking, and shooting. ¶ Doctor Colet deane of Poules erected a frée schoole *Abr. Fl. ex*
I. S. pag. 894. in Poules church yard in London, and committed the ouersight thereof to the Pouls schoole. masters and wardens of the mercers, bicause himselfe was borne in London, & was sonne to Henrie Colet mercer, sometime lord maior of the citie of London. On Mid- The king apparelled like one of the gard. summer night, the king came priuilie into Cheape, in one of the cotes his gard; and on saint Peters night, the king and quéene came riding roiallie to the kings hed in Cheape, there to behold the watch of the citie.]

Now when the said progresse was finished, his grace, the quéene, with all their whole traine, in the moneth of October following, remooued to Gréenewich. The king not minded to sée yoong gentlemen vnexpert in martiall feates, caused a place to be prepared within the parke of Greenewich, for the quéene and the ladies to stand & sée the fight with battle axes that should be doone there, where the king himselfe The king fighteth with a battleaxe against an Almaine. armed, fought with one Giot a gentleman of Almaine, a tall man, and a good man of armes. And then after they had doone, they marched alwaies two and two togithers, and so did their feats and enterprises euerie man verie well. Albeit, it happened the said Giot to fight with sir Edward Howard, which Giot was by him striken to the ground. The morow after this enterprise doone, the king with the quéene came to the Tower of London. And to the intent that there should no displeasure nor malice be borne by anie of those gentlemen, which fought with the ax against other; the king gaue vnto them a certeine summe of gold, valued at two hundred markes, to make a banket among themselues withall. The which banket was made at fishmongers hall in Thames stréet, where they all met to the number of foure and twentie, all apparelled in one sute or liuerie, after Almaine fashion; that is to say, their vtter garments all of yellow sattin, yellow hosen, yellow shooes, girdels, scabberds, and bonnets with yellow feathers, their garments and hosen all cut & lined with white sattin, and their scabberds woond about with sattin. After their banket ended they went by torchlight to the Tower, & presented themselues before the king, who tooke pleasure to behold them.

From thence the eight day of Nouember, his grace remooued to Richmond, and The king (with his assistants) chalengeth all commers at tilt. willed to be declared to all noble men and gentlemen, that his grace with two aides, that is to wit, maister Charles Brandon, and maister Compton, during two daies would answer all commers; with speare at the tilt one daie, and at turneie with swords the other. And to accomplish this enterprise, on the thirtéenth day of Nouember, his grace armed at all péeces with his two aides entered the field, their bases and trappers were of cloth of gold, set with red roses, wrought with gold of broderie. The counterpart came in freshlie apparelled, euerie man after his deuise. At these iustes the king brake more staues than anie other, & therefore had the prise. At the turneie in likewise, the honour was his. The second night were diuerse strangers of Maximilian the emperours court and ambassadors of Spaine with the king at supper. When they had supped, the king willed them to go into the quéenes chamber, who so did.

In the meane season, the king with fifteene other, apparelled in Almaine iackets of A roiall mummerie. crimsin and purple sattin, with long quartered sléeues, and hosen of the same sute, their bonnets of white veluet, wrapped in flat gold of damaske, with visards and

white

white plumes, came in with a mummerie; and after a certeine time that they had plaied with the quéene and the strangers, they departed. Then suddenlie entered six minstrels richlie apparelled, plaieng on their instruments; and then followed foure-téene persons, gentlemen, all apparelled in yellow sattin, cut like Almains, bearing torches. After them came six disguised in white sattin and gréene, embrodered and set with letters and castels of fine gold in bullion, the garments were of strange fashion, with also strange cuts, euerie cut knit with points of fine gold, and tassels of the same, their hosen cut and tied in likewise, their bonnets of cloth of siluer woond with gold. The first of these six was the king, the earle of Essex, Charles Brandon, sir Edward Howard, sir Thomas Kneuet, and sir Henrie Guilford.

Then part of the gentlemen bearing torches departed, and shortlie returned, after whom came in six ladies, apparelled in garments of crimsin sattin embrodered and trauersed with cloth of gold, cut in pomegranats and yokes, stringed after the fashion of Spaine. Then the said six men dansed with these six ladies: and after that they had dansed a season, the ladies tooke off the mens visors, whereby they were knowen: whereof the quéene and the strangers much praised the king, and ended the pastime. It is to be noted, that at this time the quéene was great with child, & shortlie after this pastime, she tooke hir chamber at Richmond, for the which cause the king kept his Christmasse there. And on Newyeares daie the first daie of Ia-nuarie the quéene was deliuered of a prince to the great gladnesse of the realme, for the honour of whom fiers were made, and diuerse vessels with wine set for such as would take thereof in certeine stréets in London, and generall processions therevpon to laud God. As touching the preparation of the princes christening, I ouerpasse, which was honorablie doone, whose godfathers at the font were the archbishop of Canturburie, and the earle of Surreie, & godmother the ladie Katharine countesse of Deuonshire, daughter to king Edward the fourth: his name was Henrie.

Against the twelfe daie or the daie of the Epiphanie at night, before the banket in the hall at Richmond, was a pageant deuised like a mounteine, glistering by night as though it had béene all of gold and set with stones, on the top of which mounteine was a tree of gold, the branches and boughes frised with gold, spreading on euerie side ouer the mounteine with roses and pomegranats, the which mounteine was with vices brought vp towards the king, and out of the same came a ladie ap-parelled in cloth of gold, and the children of honour called the henchmen, which were freshlie disguised, and dansed a morice before the king; and that doone, reentred the mounteine, which then was drawen backe, and then was the wassaill or banket brought in, and so brake vp Christmasse. Shortlie after and before the quéenes churching, the K. rode to Walsingham. The quéene being churched or purified, the king and she remooued from Richmond to Westminster, where was preparation for solemne iusts in the honor of the quéene; the king being one, and with him thrée aides: his grace being called Cure loial, the lord William erle of Deuonshire called Bon voloire, sir Thomas Kneuet named Bon espoir, sir Edward Neuill called Valiant desire, whose names were set vpon a goodlie table, & the table hanged in a tree curiouslie wrought, and they were called Les quater cheualiers de la forest saluigne, these foure to run at the tilt against all commers, with other certeine articles comprised in the said table.

A place in the palace was prepared for the king and quéene, richlie hanged, the inner part with cloth of gold, & the vtter with rich cloth of arras. These iusts be-gan the thirtéenth daie of Februarie. Now after that the quéene with hir traine of ladies had taken their places, into the palace was conueied a pageant of a great quan-titie, made like a forrest with rockes, hils, and dales, with diuerse sundrie trées, floures, hathornes, ferne, and grasse, with six foresters standing within the same forrest, garnished in cotes and hoods of gréene veluet, by whome laie a great number of speares; all the trées, hearbs, and floures of the same forrest were made of gréene veluet,

veluet, gréene damaske, & silke of diuerse colours, as sattin & sarcenet. In the middest of this forrest was a castell standing made of gold, and before the castell gate sat a gentleman freshlie apparelled, making a garland of roses for the prise. This forrest was drawen as it were by strength of two great beasts, a lion and an antelop; the lion florished all ouer with damaske gold, the antelop was wrought all ouer with siluer, of damaske, his beames or hornes and tuskes of gold.

These beasts were led with certeine men apparelled like wild men, or woodhouses, their bodies, heads, faces, hands, and legs couered with gréene silke flosshed: on either of the said antelop and lion sat a ladie richlie apparelled, the beasts were tied to the pageant with great chaines of gold, as horsses be in the cart. When the pageant rested before the quéene, the forenamed foresters blew their horns, then the deuise or pageant opened on all sides, and out issued the foresaid foure knights armed at all peeces, euerie of them a speare in his hand on horssebacke with great plumes on their heads, their bases and trappers of cloth of gold, euerie of them his name embrodered on his base and trapper. On the other part with great noise aswell of trumpets as of drums entered into the field, the erle of Essex, the lord Thomas Howard with manie other cleane armed, their trappers and bases all of crimsin satin embrodered with branches of pomegranats of gold, and posies; with manie a fresh gentleman riding before them, their footmen well apparelled: and so the iusts began and endured all that daie. *The foure knights issue out of the pageant all armed.*

The morrow, being the thirtéenth of Februarie after dinner, at time conuenient, the quéene with the ladies repaired to sée the iusts, the trumpets sounded, and in came manie a noble man and gentleman richlie apparelled, taking vp their horsses; after whom followed certeine lords apparelled, they and their horsses in cloth of gold and russet tinsell: knights in cloth of gold and russet veluet; and a great number of gentlemen on foot in russet sattin and yellow, and yeomen in russet damaske and yellow, all the nether part of euerie mans hosen scarlet and yellow caps. Then came the king vnder a pauilion of cloth of gold and purple veluet embrodered, and powdered with H. and K. of fine gold, the compasse of the pauilion aboue embrodered richlie, and valansed with flat gold, beaten in wire, with an imperiall crowne in the top of fine gold, his bases and trappers of cloth of gold, fretted with damaske gold, the trapper pendant to the taile. A crane and chafron of stéele, in the front of the chafron was a goodlie plume set full of musers or trembling spangles of gold. After followed his three aids, euerie of them vnder a pauilion of crimsin damaske and purple, powdered with H. and K. of fine gold, valansed and fringed with gold of damaske: on the top of euerie pauilion a great K. of goldsmiths worke. *Gorgeous shewes in apparell.* *The king vnder a pauilion of cloth of gold and purple veluet, &c.*

The number of the gentlemen and yeomen attending on foot, apparelled in russet and yellow, was an hundred thréescore and eight. Then next these pauilions came twelue children of honour, sitting euerie of them on a great courser richlie trapped and embrodered in seuerall deuises and fashions, where lacked neither broderie nor goldsmiths worke, so that euerie child and horsse in deuise and fashion was contrarie to other, which was goodlie to behold. Then on the contrarie part entered sir Charles Brandon, first on horssebacke in a long robe of russet sattin, like a recluse or religious person, and his horsse trapped in the same sute, without drum or noise of minstrelsie, putting a bill of petition to the quéene, the effect wherof was, that if it would please hir to licence him to run in hir presence, he would doo it gladlie; and if not, then he would depart as he came. After that his request was granted, then he put off his said habit, and was armed at all péeces with rich bases and horsse also richlie trapped, and so did run his horsse to the tilt end, were diuerse men on foot apparelled in russet sattin waited on him. *Sir Charles Brandon on horssebacke in a long robe of russet sattin like a religious person.*

Next after came in alone yoong Henrie Guilford esquier, himselfe and his horsse in russet cloth of gold and cloth of siluer, closed in a deuise, or a pageant made like a castell or a turret, wrought of russet sarcenet Florence, wrought and set out in gold *Henrie Guilford esquier in russet cloth of gold, with his deuise.*

with

with his word or posie, and all his men in russet sattin & white, with hosen to the same, and their bonets of like colours, demanding also licence of the queene to run; which to him granted, he tooke place at the tilts end. Then came next the marquesse Dorset and sir Thomas Bullen like two pilgrims from saint Iames, in taberds of blacke veluet, with palmers hats on their helmets, with long Iacobs staues in their hands, their horsse trappers of blacke veluet, their taberds, hats, and trappers set with scalop shels of fine gold, and strips of blacke veluet, euerie strip set with a scalop shell, their seruants all in blacke sattin with scalop shels of gold in their breasts. Soone after came in the lord Henrie of Buckingham earle of Wilshire, himselfe and his horsse apparelled in cloth of siluer, embrodered with his posie or word, and arrowes of gold in a posie, called La maison du refuge, made of crimsin damaske brodered with roses & arrowes of gold, on the top a greihound of siluer, bearing a tree of pomegranats of gold, the branches whereof were so large that it ouerspred the pageant in all parts.

The marquesse Dorset and sir Thomas Bullen like pilgrims.

Then entered sir Giles Capell, sir Rouland with manie other knights richlie armed and apparelled. And thus began the iusts, which was valiantlie atchiued by the king and his aids, among whom his grace atteined the prise. These iusts finished, euerie man withdrew, the king was disarmed, and at time conuenient he and the queene heard euensong, and that night all the ambassadors supped with the king and had a great banket. After supper, his grace with the quéene, lords & ladies came into the White hall within the said palace, which was hanged richlie, the hall was scaffolded and railed on all parts. There was an enterlude of the gentlemen of his chapell before his grace, and diuerse fresh songs: that doone, his grace called to him a great man, or a lord of Ireland called O neall, whome in the presence of the said ambassadors he made knight: then the minstrels began to plaie, the lords & ladies began to danse. Now in the midst of this pastime, when all persons were most attentiue to behold the dansing, the king was suddenlie gone, vnknowen to the most part of the people there, vnlesse it were of the quéene and certeine other. Within a little while after his departing, the trumpets at the end of the hall began to sound.

The great O nea'l made knight.

Then was there a deuise or a pageant vpon whéels brought in, out of the which pageant issued out a gentleman richlie apparelled, that shewed how in a garden of pleasure there was an arbor of gold wherin were lords and ladies, much desirous to shew pastime to the quéene & ladies, if they might be licenced so to doo: who was answered by the quéene, how she and all other there were verie desirous to sée them and their pastime. Then a great cloth of arras that did hang before the same pageant was taken away, and the pageant brought more néere. It was curiouslie made and plesant to behold, it was solemne and rich; for euerie post or piller thereof was couered with frised gold, therein were trees of hathorne, eglantine, rosiers, vines, and other pleasant floures of diuerse colours, with gillofers, and other hearbs all made of sattin, damaske, siluer and gold, accordinglie as the naturall trees, hearbs, or floures ought to be.

A pageant deuised to run vpon whéeles.

In this arbor were six ladies, all apparelled in white satin and greene, set and embrodered full of H. and K. of Gold, knit togither with laces of gold of damaske, and all their garments were replenished with glittering spangels gilt ouer, on their heads were bonets all opened at the foure quarters, ouerfrised with flat gold of damaske, the orrellets were of rolles, wreathed on lampas doucke holow, so that the gold shewed through the lampas doucke; the fassis of their head set full of new deuised fashions.

In this garden also was the king and fiue with him apparelled in garments of purple sattin, all of cuts with H. and K. euerie edge garnished with frised gold, and euerie garment full of posies, made of letters of fine gold in bullion as thicke as they might be, and euerie person had his name in like letters of massie gold. The first Cure loial,

A goodlie shew of the king & fiue other with him.

loial, the second Bon voloire, the third Bon espoir, the fourth Valiant desire, the fift
Bon foy, the sixt Amour loial, their hosen, caps, and coats were full of posies, with
H. & K. of fine gold in bullion, so that the ground could scarse appeere, & yet was in
euerie void place spangles of gold. When time was come, the said pageant was
brought foorth into presence, and then descended a lord and a ladie by couples, and
then the minstrels which where disguised also dansed, and the lords and ladies dansed,
that it was a pleasure to behold.

In the meane season the pageant was conueied to the end of the palace, there to
tarie till the danses were finished, & so to haue receiued the lords & ladies againe; but
suddenlie the rude people ran to the pageant, and rent, tare, and spoiled the pageant
so that the lord steward nor the head officers could not cause them to absteine,
except they should haue foughten and drawen bloud, and so was this pageant broken.
Then the king with the queene and the ladies returned to his chamber, where they
had a great banket, and so this triumph ended with mirth & gladnes. At this
solemnitie a shipman of London caught certeine letters, which he sold to a goldsmith
for three pounds fourteene shillings & eight pence; by reason whereof it appéered
that the garments were of a great value. After this great ioy came a sorowfull chance,
for the yoong prince which was borne vpon Newyeares day last past, vpon the two
and twentith daie of Februarie, being then the euen of saint Matthie, departed this
world at Richmond, and from thence was caried to Westminster and buried. The
king like a wise prince tooke this dolorous chance wonderous wiselie; and the more to
comfort the quéene he dissembled the matter, and made no great mourning outwardlie:
but the queene, like a naturall woman, made much lamentation; howbeit, by the kings
good persuasion and behauiour, hir sorow was mitigated, but not shortlie.

In the moneth of Februarie this yeare came ambassadors from the king of Arragon
and Castile, to require an aid of fiftéene hundred archers to be sent to the same king,
hauing at that time war against the Moores, enimies of the christian faith. The
king hearing their message gentlie granted their request. And bicause the lord Thomas Darcie a knight of the garter, made humble sute to the king to be generall of the
crue that should be thus sent into Spaine, the king vpon trust of his approued valiancie granted his desire. There were appointed to go with him the lord Anthonie Greie
brother to the marquesse Dorset, Henrie Guilford, Weston Browne, and Willian Sidneie esquiers of the kings house, sir Robert Constable, sir Roger Hastings, and sir
Rafe Elderton, with other gentlemen to be capteins.

In this second yeare, the king being foorth on his progresse, heard euerie daie more
& more complaints of Empson and Dudleie, set foorth and aduanced no doubt by the
drift of their deadlie enimies. Wherefore, he sent writs to the shiriffes of London, to
put them to execution, and so the seuentéenth daie of August, they were both beheaded at the Tower hill, and both their bodies and heads buried, the one at the White
friers, and the other at the Blacke friers. The king about this season was much giuen
to plaie at tenisse, and at the dise, which appetite certeine craftie persons about him
perceiuing, brought in Frenchmen and Lombards to make wagers with him, & so lost
much monie; but when he perceiued their craft, he eschued their companie and let
them go.

¶ On the first daie of Maie the king accompanied with manie lustie batchelers, on
great and well dooing horsses rode to the wood to fetch Maie, where a man might
haue séene manie a horsse raised on high with carrier, gallop, turne and stop, maruellous to behold: where he & three other, as sir Edward Howard, Charles Brandon, and
Edward Neuill, which were challengers with the king, shifted themselues into coats
of gréene satin garded with crimsin veluet. On the other part the earles of Essex, of
Deuonshire, the marquesse Dorset, & the lord Howard were all in crimsin satin, garded
with a pounced gard of gréene veluet. And as they were returning on the hill, a ship

A deuise of a
ship vnder saile.
met with them vnder saile: the maister hailed the king and that noble companie, and
said that he was a mariner, and was come from many a strange port, and came thither
to sée if anie déeds of armes were to be doone in the countrie, of the which he might
make true report in other countries. An herald demanded the name of his ship; he
answered she is called Fame, & is laden with good Renowme: then said the herald, If
you will bring your ship into the baie of Hardinesse, you must double the point of
Gentlenesse, and there you shall sée a companie that will meddle with your merchandize. Then said the king, Sithens Renowme is their merchandize, let vs buie it if we
can. Then the ship shot a peale of guns, and sailed foorth before the kings companie,
full of flags and banners, till it came to the tilt yard.

At after noone, the king and his thrée fellowes entered into the field, their bards
and bases of crimsin and blue veluet, cut in quadrant cuts, embroded full of pomegranats, and all the waiters in silke of the same colour. The other partie were in
crimsin sattin and gréene veluet. Then began the trumpets to sound, and the horsses
to run, that manie a speare was burst, and manie a great stripe giuen: and for a truth

The king brake
more staues than
the rest and had
the prise giuen
him.
the king excéeded in number of staues all other euerie daie of the three daies. Wherefore on the third daie, the queene made a great banket to the king and all them that
had iusted: and after the banket doone, she gaue the chiefe prise to the king, the
second to the earle of Essex, the third to the earle of Deuonshire, and the fourth to
the lord marquesse Dorset. Then the heralds cried; My lords, for your noble feats in
armes, God send you the loue of your ladies that you most desire. The king euer
desirous to serue Mars, began another iusts the fiftéenth daie of the said moneth.
The king & his band were all in gréene silke, and the earle of Essex and his band in
blue, garded with gold, and all the speares were painted of the same colours. There
was good running and manie a speare burst: but for all the sport euerie man feared
least some ill chance might happen to the king, and faine would haue had him a looker
on rather than a dooer, and spake thereof as much as they durst: but his courage was
so noble that he would euer be at the one end.]

The lord Dar-
cie and his com-
panie readie at
Plimmouth.
In this meane time, the lord Darcie and other appointed to the viage against the
Moores, made such diligence, that they and all their people were readie at Plimmouth
by the middes of Maie, and there mustered their souldiers before the lord Brooke,
and other the kings commissioners. The lord Darcie as capteine generall, ordeined
for his prouost marshall Henrie Guilford esquier, a lustie yoong man, & welbeloued of
the king, for his manifold good seruice. On the mondaie in the Rogation wéeke,
they departed out of Plimmouth hauen with foure ships roiall, and the wind was so
fauourable to them, that the first daie of Iune, being the euen of the feast of Pentecost, he arriued at the port of Calis in south Spaine; and immediatlie by the aduise of
his councell, he dispatched messengers to the king, whom they found beside the citie
of Ciuill where he then laie, and declared to him, how the lord Darcie by the king
their maisters appointment, was come thither with sixtéene hundred archers, and laie
still at Calis to know his pleasure. The king of Castile answered them gentlie, that
the lord Darcie and all other that were come from his louing sonne were welcome, and
hartilie thanked them of their paines, requiring the messengers to returne to their
capteine, and tell him that in all hast he would send certeine of his councell to him.

*Abr. Fl. ex
Edw. Hall in
Hen. 8. fol. xij.*
¶ Herevpon they departed from the king, and made report to the lord Darcie, which
The vnrulie be-
hauiour of the
Englishmen.
kept his ship in great estate, and would not land, but onelie suffered such as were
sicke and feeble, and few other to go aland. The Englishmen which went aland, fell
to drinking of hot wines, & were scarse maisters of themselues, some ran to the
stewes, some brake hedges and spoiled orchards and vineyards, and oranges before they
were ripe, and did manie outragious déeds: wherefore the chiefe of the towne of Calis
came to complaine to the lord Darcie in his ship, which sent foorth his prouost marshall, who scarselie with paine refrained the yeoman archers, they were so hot and
　　　　　　　　　　　　　　　　　　　　　　　　　　　　　　　　　　　　　wilfull

wilfull, yet by commandement & policie they were all brought on bord to their ships.]

Then vpon saturdaie, the eight of Iune, a bishop and other of the kings councell came to Calis, and there abode till wednesdaie, being the euen of Corpus Christi; at which daie, the lord capteine tooke land, and was honorablie receiued of the king of Aragons councell, and on the morrow was highlie feasted at dinner and supper. And at after supper, the bishop declared the king his maisters pleasure, giuing to the lord capteine as heartie thankes for his pains and trauell, as if he had gone forward with his enterprise against the Moores. But whereas by the aduise of his councell, circumspectlie considering the suertie of his owne realme, vpon perfect knowledge had that the Frenchmen meant to inuade his dominions in his absence, he had altered his former determination, and taken an abstinence of war with the Moores, till an other time. *The lord Darcie honorablie receiued of the K. of Aragons councell.*

He therefore required the lord Darcie to be contented to returne home againe, promising him wages for all his soldiers; and if it should please him to come to the court, he should receiue high thanks of the king, and such chéere as there could be made him. The lord Darcie was nothing pleased with this declaration, but sith he saw there was no remedie, he said, that whatsoeuer the king had concluded, he could not be against it, considering he was sent to him: but suerlie it was against his mind to depart home, without dooing anie thing against Gods enimies, with whome he had euer a desire to fight. And as for his comming to court, he said, he could not leaue his men whome he had brought out of their countrie, without an head; and as for the kings banket, it was not the thing that he desired. *The lord Darcie discontented at the bishops declaration.*

On the next daie in the morning, monie was sent to paie the souldiers their wages for their conduction againe into England, with diuerse gifts giuen to the lord Darcie, and other gentlemen; yet notwithstanding, he was highlie displeased: howbeit, like a wiseman he dissembled the matter. The same daie, being the fourtéenth daie of Iune, and fridaie, there chanced a fraie to be begun in the towne of Calis, betwixt the Englishmen, and them of the towne; by reason than an Englishman would haue had for his monie a loafe of bread from a maid that had beene at the bakers to buie bread, not to sell, but to spend in hir mistresse house. Howbeit the Englishman followed hir, as making proffer not to be denied, in so much that the maid perceiuing what he went about, cried out; A force, a force. Then was the common bell roong, and all the towne went to harnesse, and those few Englishmen that were a land, went to their bowes. The Spaniards cast darts, and the Englishmen shot. But the capteins of England, and the lords of the councell for their part, tooke such paine, that the fraie was ceassed, and but one Englishman slaine, though diuerse were hurt: and of the Spaniards diuerse were slaine. Thus of a sparkle was kindled a flame to the spoiling of manie; which is no rare thing to see, according to the scriptum est: *A shrewd fraie begun vpon a small occasion.*
Edw. Hall.

              Concitat ingentes flammas scintilla minuta.

After this, vpon request made by the lords of Spaine, the lord Darcie and all his men the same night went aboord their ships, but Henrie Guilford, Weston Browne, and William Sidneie, yoong and lustie esquiers, desired licence to see the court of Spaine: which being granted, they went thither, where they were of the king highlie interteined. Henrie Guilford and Weston Browne were made knights by the king, who also gaue to sir Henrie Guilford à canton of Granado, and to sir Wolston Browne an egle of Sicill on a chefe, to the augmentation of their armes. William Sidneie so excused himselfe, that he was not made knight. When they had soiourned there a while, they tooke their leaue of the king and quéene and returned through France into England. *The Englishmen desire to sée the Spanish court.*

During which season, the lord Darcie made saile toward England, and arriuing at Plimmouth, came to the king at Windsore, and so this iourneie ended. During the time *The lord Darcie returneth out of Spaine.*

time that the lord Darcie was in Spaine, the ladie Margaret duches of Sauoie, and daughter vnto Maximilian the emperour, and gouernour of Flanders, Brabant, Holland, Zeland, & other the low countries apperteining to Charles the yoong prince of Castile, sent in the end of Maie to the king of England, to haue fiftéene hundred archers, to aid hir against the duke of Gelders, which sore troubled the countries aforesaid. The king tenderlie regarding the request of so noble a ladie, most gentlie granted hir request, and appointed sir Edward Poinings, knight of the garter, and comptroller of his house, a valiant capteine and a noble warriour, to be lieutenant and leader of the said fiftéene hundred archers.

The duchesse of Sauoie sēdeth to king Henrie for aid against the duke of Gelders.

This gentleman accompanied with his sonne in law the lord Clinton, sir Matthew Browne, sir Iohn Digbie, Iohn Werton, Richard Whethrill, & Shrelleie esquiers, with other gentlemen and yeomen, to the foresaid number of fiftéene hundred, tooke their ships a mile beside Sandwich, the eightéenth daie of Iulie, and landed at Armew the nineteenth daie, not without some trouble, by reason of a little storme. From thence they were conducted to Barowe, whither the ladie Regent came to welcome them. On the sundaie, being the seuen & twentith of Iulie, they departed to Rossindale, and on thursdaie the last of Iulie they came to Bulduke. And the next daie the whole armie of the Almans, Flemings, and other apperteining to the said ladie, met with the Englishmen without Bulduke, where they set foorth in order; the ladie Regent being there present, which tooke hir leaue of all the capteines, and departed to Bulduke.

The armie, to the number of ten thousand, beside the fifteene hundred English archers, passed forward; and the tenth daie of August, being saint Laurence daie, came before a little castle, standing on the higher side of the Mazé, called Brimnoist, belonging to the bastard of Gelderland. The same night, Thomas Hert, cheefe gouernour of the ordinance of the English part, made his approach; and in the morning, made batterie so, that the assault therevpon being giuen, the fortresse was woone, and the capteine with eightie and od men were slaine, and nintéene taken; of the which, eleuen were hanged. Iohn Morton, capteine of one hundred Englishmen, and one Guiot an esquier of Burgognie, crieng saint George, were the first that entered; at which assault, there was but one Englishman slaine. On thursdaie, the fourteenth of August, the armie feried ouer the riuer of Maze into Gelderland. The next daie, they came to a little towne called Aiske.

Thom. Hert gouernour of the English ordinance. The fort is woone.

The people were fled, but there was a little castell rased, and cast downe, which was newlie built vp on the side of the said riuer. Vpon the twentith daie of August, they burnt the foresaid towne of Aiske, and all the countrie about it, and came at the last to a towne called Straulle, being verie strong, double diked and walled. Within it were thrée hundred & sixtie good men of war, beside the inhabitants. At the first, they shewed good countenance of defense but when they saw their enimies approach néere vnto them with rampiers and trenches, they yeelded by composition, so that the souldiers might depart with a little sticke in their hands. But the townesmen rested prisoners, at the will of the prince of Castile. And so on S. Bartholomews day the admerall of Flanders, and sir Edward Poinings entered the towne with great triumph.

The towne of Aiske burned.

On the six and twentith daie, the armie came before Venlow, and sent an herald called Arthois, to summon the towne; but they within would not heare but shot guns at him. On the eight and twentith daie the armie remooued vnto the north side of Venlow and part went ouer the water, and made trenches to the water, & so besieged the towne as streictlie as their number would giue them leaue; but yet for all that they could doo without, they within kept one gate euer open. At length, the English capteins perceiuing that they laie there in vaine, considering the strength of the towne, and also how the armie was not of number sufficient to enuiron the same on each side, wrote to the king, who willed them with all speed to returne, and so they did. Sir

Venlow besieged by the English.

Edward

Edward Poinings went to the court of Burgognie, where he was receiued right honorablie of the yoong prince of Castile and his aunt the ladie Margaret.

Iohn Norton, Iohn Fog, Iohn Scot, and Thomas Linde, were made knights by the prince. And the ladie Margaret perceiuing the soldiers coates to be worne and foule with lieng on the ground (for euerie man laie not in a tent) gaue to euerie yeoman a coate of woollen cloth of yeallow, red, white, and greene colours, not to hir little laud & praise among the Englishmen. After that sir Edward Poinings had béene highlie feasted and more praised of all men for his valiantnesse and good order of his people, he returned with his crue into England, and had lost by war and sicknesse not fullie an hundred persons. When the Englishmen were departed, the Gelders issued out of the gates of Venlow, dailie skirmished with the Burgognians, and asked for their archers, and héerewith winter began sharplie to approach, and the riuer of Maze by aboundance of raine rose so high, that it drowned vp the trenches: so that all things considered, the capteins without determined to raise their siege, and so they did, and after they had wasted all the countrie about Venlow, they returned euerie man to his home.

The duchesse of Sauoie bestoweth new coats on the English soldiors.

In Iune the king being at Leicester, heard tidings, that one Andrew Barton a Scotishman and pirat of the sea, saieng that the king of Scots had warre with the Portingals, robbed euerie nation, and stopped the kings streames, that no merchant almost could passe. And when he tooke Englishmens goods, he bare them in hand that they were Portingals goods, and thus he hanted and robbed at euerie hauens mouth. The king displeased herewith, sent sir Edward Howard lord Admerall of England, and lord Thomas Howard, sonne and heire to the earle of Surrie in all hast to the sea, which hastilie made readie two ships, and taking sea, by chance of weather were seuered. The lord Howard lieng in the downes, perceiued where Andrew was making toward Scotland, and so fast the said lord chased him, that he ouertooke him; and there was a sore battell betwixt them. Andrew euer blew his whistle to incourage his men, but at length the lord Howard and the Englishmen did so valiantlie, that by cleane strength they entered the maine decke. The Scots fought sore on the hatches: but in conclusion Andrew was taken, and so sore wounded, that he died there. Then all the remnant of the Scots were taken with their ship called the Lion.

Andrew Barton a Scotish pirat.

A cruele fight on the sea, betwéene the said pirat and the lords Howards.

Andrew Bartõ slaine.

All this while was the lord admerall in chase of the barke of Scotland, called Iennie Pirwine, which was woont to saile with the Lion in companie, & so much did he with other, that he laid him aboord: and though the Scots manfullie defended themselues, yet the Englishmen entered the barke, slue manie, and tooke all the residue. Thus were these two ships taken, and brought to Blackewall the second of August [and all the Scots were sent vnto the bishop of Yorkes place, where they remained at the kings charge, till other direction was taken for them. After this, the king sent the bishop of Winchester, and certeine of his councell, to the archbishop of Yorkes place, where the Scots were prisoners: and there the bishop rehearsed to them, whereas peace was yet betweene England and Scotland, that they contrarie to that, as théeues & pirats, had robbed the kings subiects within his streames. Wherefore they had deserued to die by the law, and to be hanged at the low water marke. Then said the Scots; We acknowledge our offense, and aske mercie and not the law. Then a preest which was also a prisoner, said; My lords we appeale from the kings iustice to his mercie.

Abr. Fl. ex Edw. Hall in H. 8. fol. xvj. The Scots prisoners in the bishop of Yorkes place.

Then the bishop asked him if he were authorised by them to saie so, and they cried all; Yea, yea. Then (said he) you shall find the kings mercie aboue his iustice. For where you were dead by the law, yet by his mercie he will reuiue you; wherefore you shall depart out of this realme within twentie daies, vpon paine of death, if you be found after the twentith daie; and praie for the king: and so they passed into

their

their countrie.] Thus was their captiuitie conuerted into libertie, and their liues saued by the kings mercie. The king of Scots hearing of the death of Andrew Barton, and the taking of the two ships, was woonderfull wroth, and sent letters to the king requiring restitution, according to the league and amitie. The king wrote to the king of Scots againe with brotherlie salutation, of the robberies doone by the said Andrew, and that it became not a prince to laie breach of peace to his confederat, for dooing iustice vpon a pirat and theefe: and that all the Scots that were taken, had deserued to die by iustice, if he had not extended his mercie. And with this answer the Scotish herald departed.

King Henrie the eight taketh the popes part against the French king.

About this season, the French king made sharpe warre against pope Iulie: wherefore the king of England wrote to the French king, that he should leaue off to vex the pope in such wise, being his fréend and confederat. But when the French king séemed little to regard that request, the king sent him word to deliuer him his lawfull inheritance both of the duchie of Normandie and Guien, and the countries of Aniou & Maine, and also of his crowne of France; or else he would come with such a power, that by fine force he would obteine his purpose: but notwithstanding those writings, the French king still pursued his warres in Italie. Wherevpon the king of England, ioining in league with Maximilian the emperour, and Ferdinando king of Spaine, with diuerse other princes, was resolued by aduise of his councell to make warre on the French king and his countries, and made preparation both by sea and land, setting foorth ships to the sea for safegard of his merchants.

Abr. Fl. ex Guic. pag. 314. Cardinall S. Petri ad vincula made pope.

¶ The foresaid pope Iulie, the kings confederat, was (before his aduancement to the popedome) cardinall of saint Petri ad Vincula, a man mightie in freends, reputation and riches, who had drawne to him the voices of so manie cardinals, that entering the conclaue, he was with an example all new and without shutting the conclaue, elected pope the verie same night following the deceasse of his predecessor pope Pius (those that were of the contrarie opinion not daring to appose against him.) He either hauing regard to his first name Iulie, or (as coniectures were made) to signifie the greatnesse of his conceptions, or lastlie bicause he would not giue place to Alexander, no not in the excellencie of name, tooke vpon him the name of Iulie, the second of that name. Amongest all the popes that had passed, it was woondered that by so great consent, they had created for pope, a cardinall who was knowne to be of a disposition rigorous and terrible, and in whome was no expectation of rest and tranquillitie, hauing consumed his youth in continuall trauels, offended manie by necessitie, and exercised hatreds against manie great personages; a man to whose wit nothing was more familiar, than the inuention of trouble, faction, and conspiracie.

Pope Iulie a factious fellow and an enimie to peace.

But on the other side, the causes of his election to that degrée appeared cléerelie, and surmounted all other difficulties: for he had béene of long time a cardinall of great power and might, & with his magnificence, wherein he had alwaies excéeded the residue, and with the greatnesse of his spirit, by the which he did great things, he had not onelie made himselfe mightie in opinion and freends; but by times and degrées had erected high his authoritie in the court of Rome, bearing the name, title, and dignitie of the principall defendor of the ecclesiastike libertie. But that which serued most to his aduancement, was the promises immoderate and infinite which he made to the cardinals, princes, and barons, and to all others whome he might make profitable to him in that action. Besides, he had the meane to distribute monie, benefices, and spirituall dignities, as well such as were his owne, as those that were the rights of others; for such was the brute & renowme of his liberalitie, that manie made willing offers to him to dispose as he best liked of their treasures, their names, their offices, and benefices.

Indirect meanes to atteine the popedome.

They considered not that his promises were farre too great, than that being pope he
was

was either able or ought to obserue, for that he had of so long continuance inioied the name of iust and vpright, that pope Alexander himselfe (his greatest enimie) speaking ill of him in all other things, could not but confesse him to be true of his word. A praise which he made no care to defile and staine, to the end to become pope; knowing that no man more easilie beguileth an other, than he that hath the custome and name neuer to deceiue anie. Which practise of dissimulation was much frequented of those that aspired & possessed the popedom; insomuch that the same was in Alexander the sixt so notable, that it was a prouerbe ordinarilie in Rome, that the pope did neuer the thing which he said, and his sonne the duke of Valentinois seldome spake that which he ment. Which kind of people (pretend they what they will) are excluded from the rest of Sion, as the psalmist saith:

A prouerbe vpon the popes dissembling. *Guicc.* 305.

Buch in Psal. 15.

> Quem fraudis expers simplicitas iuuat,
> Vrgétque rectum propositi tenax,
>   Nec mente sæuus grata blandam
>   Edocuit simulare linguam,
>   Perpetua requie fruetur.]

In this yeare the king kept his Christmasse at Greenewich, where was such abundance of viands serued to all comers of anie honest behauiour, as hath béene few times séene. And against Newyéeres night was made in the hall a castell, gates, towers, and dungeon, garnished with artillerie and weapon after the most warlike fashion: and on the front of the castell, was written Le forteresse dangereux, and within the castell were six ladies cloathed in russet sattin, laid all ouer with leaues of gold, and euerie one knit with laces of blew silke and gold. On their heads, coifs, and caps all of gold. After this castell had béene caried about the hall, and the quéene had beheld it, in came the king with fiue other, apparelled in coats, the one halfe of russet sattin, spangled with spangles of fine gold, the other halfe of rich cloth of gold, on their heads caps of russet sattin embrodered with works of fine gold bullion.

1512 *Abr. Fl. ex Ed. Hall in Hen. 8. fol.* xv. Christmasse pastimes or delights at Gréenewich.

These six assaulted the castell. The ladies seeing them so lustie and couragious, were content so solace with them, & vpon further communication, to yéeld the castell and so they came downe & dansed a long space. And after the ladies led the knights into the castell, and then the castell suddenlie vanished out of their sights. On the daie of the Epiphanie at night, the king with eleuen other were disguised, after the maner of Italie, called a maske, a thing not seene before in England: they were apparelled in garments long and broad, wrought all with gold, with visors and caps of gold. And after the banket doone, these maskers came in, with six gentlemen disguised in silke, bearing staffe torches, and desired the ladies to danse; some were content, and some refused. And after they had dansed, and communed togither as the fashion of the maske is, they tooke their leaue and departed, and so did the quéene, and all the ladies.]

The king & fiue other assaile the castell.

Maskers disguised after the Italian fashion.

The fiue and twentith daie of Ianuarie began the parlement, where the bishop of Canturburie began his oration with this verse Iustitia & pax osculatæ sunt. Vpon which words he declared how iustice should be ministred, and peace should be nourished, and by what meanes iustice was put by, and peace turned into warre. And therevpon he shewed how the French king would doo no iustice in restoring to the king his right inheritance: wherefore for lacke of iustice peace of necessitie must be turned into warre. In this parlement was granted two fiftéens of the temporaltie, and of the clergie two tenths. After that it was concluded by the whole bodie of the realme in the high court of parlement assembled, that warre should be made on the French king and his dominions. Whervpon was woonderfull spéed made in preparing all things necessarie both for sea and land.

A parlement. The summe of the bishop of Canturburies oration in the parlement.

In this parlement was sir Robert Sheffeld knight, sometime recorder of London, speaker for the commons. During this parlement, in the moneth of March, a yeoman

Abr. Fl. ex I. S. pag. 896.

Newbolt a yeoman of the gard hanged.

of the crowne, one of the kings gard, named Newbolt, slue within the palace of Westminster a seruant of maister Willoughbies, for the which offense the king commanded to be set vp a new paire of gallowes in the same place where the said seruant lost his life; and vpon the same the said Newbolt was hanged, and there remained on the gallowes by the space of two daies. A notable example of iustice, whereby the king verefied the report that was commonlie noised abroad of him; namelie that he could not abide the shedding of mans bloud, much lesse wilfull murther. Wherein he shewed how tender he was ouer his subiects, and also how seuere against malefactors, speciallie mankillers; whome he thought vnworthie of life, that had béene the instruments of others death; according to the law:

Gu. Ha. in Mat. 5.

———— oculos oculis & dentibus esse
Pensandos dentes: sic par erit vltio culpæ.

Edw. Hall in Hen. 8. fol. xvj. Ierome Bonuise the popes collector and proctor in England a false knaue.

¶ In this season one Ierome Bonuise, which was borne in Luke, and was factor in London for merchants of that nation, and had plaied bankerupt, and was conueied out of the realme for debt, was now in such fauour with pope Iulie, that he made him his collector and proctor in England: & so he kept a great port, and resorted to the king and his councell for the popes affaires (which then was sore troubled by the French king) so that he knew both the popes councell and the kings, and falselie and vntrulie resorted by night to the French ambassadours lieng in London, and to them discouered what the king and the pope intended, which was not so closelie doone, but the king knew it: and so he was laid for, & was taken communing with one of the said ambassadours vpon London wall at midnight, and brought to the Tower, where he remained vntill by the sute of his freends he was deliuered and shortlie for shame voided the realme.]

The French king hath his hands full of troubles.

The king of Aragon also, hauing at that time warre with the French king, wrote to his sonne in law king Henrie, that if he would send ouer an armie into Biskaie, and so to inuade France on that side, for the recouerie first of his duchie of Guien; he would aid them with ordinance, horssemen, beasts, and cariages, with other necessaries apperteining to the same. The king and his councell putting their affiance in this promise of king Ferdinando, prepared a noble armie all of footmen, and small artillerie, appointing the noble lord Thomas Greie marquesse Dorset to be chéefe conductor of the same. The king dailie studieng to set foorth his warre which he had begun against the French king, caused sir Edward Howard his admerall with diligence to make readie diuerse goodlie tall ships, as the Souereigne and others, to the number of eighteene, beside other smaller vessels.

An. Reg. 4. Sir Edmund Howard lord admerall.

Noblemen appointed for the viage to Biskaie.

Therewith hauing in his companie sir Weston Browne, Griffith Downe, Edward Cobham, Thomas Windham, Thomas Lucie, William Pirton, Henrie Shirbourne, Stephan Bull, George Witwange, Iohn Hopton, William Gunston, Thomas Draper, Edmund Cooke, Iohn Burdet, and diuerse others, he tooke the sea, and scowring the same, about the middest of Maie he came before Portesmouth. About the verie selfe time the lord marquesse Dorset, and other noblemen appointed for the iournie of Biskaie, as the lord Howard sonne and heire to the earle of Surrie, the lord Brooke, the lord Willoughbie, the lord Ferrers; the lord Iohn, the lord Anthonie, and the lord Leonard Greies, all thrée brethren to the marquesse; sir Griffith ap Rice, sir Morris Berkeleie, sir William Sands, the baron of Burford, sir Richard Cornewall brother to the said baron, William Husseie Iohn Melton, William Kingston esquiers, sir Henrie Willoughbie, and diuerse others, with souldiers to the number of ten thousand.

Amongst these were fiue hundred Almans clad all in white, vnder the leading of one Guiot a gentleman of Flanders, all which (with the residue abouenamed) came to Southampton, and there mustered their bands which were appointed and trimmed in the best maner. On the sixtéenth daie of Maie they were all bestowed aboord in Spanish ships furnished with vittels, and other necessaries for that iournie. The wind
serued

serued so well for their purpose, that they came all in safetie on the coast of Biskaie The English nobles arriue on the coast of Biskaie. at the port of Passagh southwest of Fonterabie; and so the third daie of Iune they landed, and tooke the field, imbattelling themselues for their safegard right stronglie. Within thrée daies after that the armie was thus aland, there came to the marquesse an earle and an other noble man, to welcome him and his companie.

Then the lord capteine remooued his field, & tooke an other place néerer to Fontera-bie, where he laie a long time, looking euerie daie to haue aid of horssemen and artillerie of the king of Aragon, but none came. Sir Iohn Stile caused to be bought The English campe greatlie hindered for want of beasts to draw their ordinance. two hundred mulets and asses of such price as the Spaniards gained greatlie, and when they were put to carie and draw, they would not serue the turne, for they were not exercised thereto before that time; and so for want of beasts to draw such ordinance as the Englishmen had there with them, they lost the dooing of some great exploit against the Frenchmen on the frontiers of Gascoigne, for they might haue run a great waie into that countrie, being as then destitute and vnpurueied of men and munitions.

On a daie the Frenchmen made a skrie toward the English campe, but the Englishmen perceiuing them, passed the riuer that was betwixt them, and with arrowes chased the Frenchmen; so that for hast manie of their horsses foundered, and fell, yer they came to Baion: if there had béene anie horssemen amongst the Englishmen, they had sore indamaged their enimies. The king of Nauarre doubting least the English-A gentle offer by the king of Nauarre to the Englishmen. men were come into those parties for no good meaning towards him, sent to the lord marquesse a bishop, and diuerse other, offering to minister vittels vnto the English-men for their monie, if it should stand so with his pleasure. The lord marquesse thanked him for the offer, and promised that if they of Nauarre would vittell his people, they should paie them well and trulie for the same.

He said also that he would warrant their passing and repassing in safetie, and that by the Englishmen no preiudice should be doone to his realme. Herevpon were the Englishmen vittelled out of Nauarre to their great comfort. After that the armie had laine thirtie daies in the second campe, there came from the king of Aragon a bishop and other nobles of his councell. This bishop was the same that made the answer to the lord Darcie at Calis the last yeare. The effect of his message was, to The effect of the bishops message sent from the king of Aragon to the lord marquesse. desire the lord capteine and his people to take patience for a while, and they should see that such preparation should be made for the furnishing of their enterprise, as should stand with the honour of his maister and their aduancements.

The Englishmen sore discontented with their idle lieng still in the field, misliked with his excuses, supposing the same (as they prooued in déed) to be nothing but delaies. In the meane time that the Englishmen thus lingered without attempting any exploit, their vittels were much part garlike, & they eating thereof with all their meats, and drinking hot wines, & féeding also on hot fruits, procured their bloud to boile within Great death of the flix by vnwoonted diet. The lord marquesse sendeth to the K. of Spaine to performe promise. their bellies, that there fell sicke thrée thousand of the flix: & thereof died an eigh-téene hundred persons. The lord marquesse perceiuing this mischeefe, sent to the king of Spaine certeine of his capteins to know his pleasure. The king told them that shortlie the duke of Alua should ioine with them, bringing with him a mightie power; so that they might the more assuredlie procéed in their enterprise. With this answer they returned to the lord marquesse, who liked it neuer a deale; bicause he iudged that the king meant but to driue time with him, as after it prooued.

In the meane time there began a mutinie in the English campe thorough a false report, contriued by some malicious person; which was, that the capteins should be allowed eight pense for euerie common souldier; where the truth was, that they had allowed to them but onelie six pense. The lord generall aduertised that the souldiers began to gather in companies, found meanes to apprehend the cheefe beginner, and deliuered him vnto William Kingston esquier, then prouost marshall; and so was he

put

put to death to the terrour of all other. Whilest the Englishmen laie thus in campe on the borders of Biskaie towards Guien, the archers went oftentimes a forraging into the French confines almost to Baion, and burnt manie pretie villages. The king of Spaine raised an armie, and sent foorth the same vnder the leading of the duke of Alua, which came forward as though he meant to haue come to the Englishmen; who being aduertised of his approch, were maruellouslie glad thereof, in hope that then they should be imploied about the enterprise for the which they were come.

The king of Spaines armie vnder the conduct of the duke of Alua.

But the duke intending an other thing, when he was aduanced foorth within a daies iournie of them, suddenlie remooued his armie toward the realme of Nauarre, and entering the same, chased out of his realme the king of that land, and conquered the same to the king of Spains vse, as in the historie of Spaine more plainelie it dooth appeare. After that the king of Spaine was thus possessed of the kingdome of Nauarre, he sent vnto the lord marquesse, promising to ioine with him shortlie, and so to inuade the borders of France; but he came not. Wherefore the Englishmen thought themselues not well vsed: for it gréeued them much, that they should lie so long idle, sith there was so great hope conceiued at their setting foorth, that there should be some great exploit atchiued by them, thorough the aid that was promised by the king of Spaine.

The kingdom of Nauarre gotten to the K. of Spaine.

Thus whilest the armie lingered without remoouing, there chanced an affraie to rise betwixt the Englishmen and the townes-men of Sancta Maria, a village so called, wherevnto such Englishmen as fell sicke, had their resort; and therevpon the alarms brought into the campe, the Englishmen and Almans ran in great furie to the succour of their fellowes: and notwithstanding all that the capteins could doo to staie them, they slue and robbed the people without mercie. The Biskaines that could get awaie, fled ouer that water into Guien. The capteins yet so ordered the matter, that all the pillage was restored, and one and twentie souldiers were condemned, which were apprehended as they were fléeing awaie with a bootie of ten thousand duckats into Gascoigne; seauen of them were executed, and the residue pardoned of life, at the sute of certeine lords of Spaine, which were as then present.

A fraie betwéene the Englishmen & the townesmen of *Sancta Maria.*

The Frenchmen hearing of this riot came foorth of Baion to see and vnderstand the maner thereof; but perceiuing that the Englishmen had descried them, suddenlie they returned. The Englishmen followed, & comming to the towne of S. Iehan de Lucie, they burnt and robbed it, & slue the inhabitants. Diuerse other villages they spoiled on the borders of Guien; but bicause they wanted both horsses of seruice, and horsses to draw foorth their ordinance, they could not doo anie such damage as they might and would haue doone, if they had béene furnished according to their desires in that point. Thus continued the English armie in such wearisome sort till the moneth of October, and then fell the lord marquesse sicke, and the lord Howard had the chéefe gouernance of the armie.

S. Iehans burnt by the English.

Then were sent from the king of Spaine diuerse lords of his priuie councell vnto the said lord Howard, to excuse the matter for that he came not according to his promise, requiring them, that sith the time of the yeare to make warre was past, it might please them to breake vp their campe, and to diuide themselues abroad into the townes and villages of his realme till the spring time of the yeare, that they might then go forward with their first pretended enterprise. The lord Howard shewed well in words that the Englishmen could not thinke well of the king of Spaines fained excuses and vnprofitable delaies, to his small honor & their great hinderance & losse, hauing spent the king their maister so much treasure, and doone so little hurt to his aduersaries. The Spaniards gaue faire words; and so in courteous maner departed.

Then about the end of October it was agréed amongest all the lords of the English hoast that they should breake vp their campe, and so they did. The lord marquesse

The English campe in Biskaie breaketh vp.

and

and his people went to saint Sebastian, the lord Howard and his retinue to Rendre, the The armie dispersed into sundrie villages. lord Willoughbie to Garschang, and sir William Sands with manie other capteins repaired to Fonterabie, and so euerie capteine with his retinue was placed in one towne or other. The king of England aduertised of the king of Spaine his meaning, sent an herald called Windsor with letters vnto his armie, willing his men there to tarie, & promising to send ouer to them right shortlie a new supplie, vnder the guiding of the lord Herbert his chamberleine.

When this letter was read, and the contents thereof notified, the souldiers began Vnappeaceable rage amongest the English souldiers. to be so highlie displeased; and spake such outragious words, as it was maruell to heare: & not contented with words, they were bent to haue doone outragious déeds; insomuch that in their furie they had slaine the lord Howard and diuerse others, if they had not followed their intents: and herevpon they were glad to hire ships, and so imbarked themselues in the moneth of Nouember. When the lord marquesse was brought aboord, he was so weake and féeble of remembrance thorough sickenesse, that he asked where he was. In the beginning of December they landed here in England, The English armie returneth out of Biskaie. and were glad to be at home, and got out of such a countrie, where they had little health, lesse pleasure, and much losse of time. The king of Spaine séemed to be sore discontented with their departure, openlie affirming, that if they had taried vntill the next spring, he would in their companie haue inuaded France.

About the same time that the marquesse went into Spaine, that is to wit, about the The lord admerall in Britaine. middest of Maie, sir Edward Howard lord admerall of England, being on the sea afore Portesmouth, made foorth againe to the sea, and directing his course towards Britaine on Trinitie sundaie arriued at Berthram baie with twentie great ships, and suddenlie set his men on land, and there wan a bulworke, which the Britains kept and defended a while; but being ouercome, fled out of their hold, & left it to the Englishmen. Then the lord admerall passed seauen miles into the countrie, burning and wasting townes and villages, and in returning, skirmished with diuerse men of armes, and slue some of them: and notwithstanding that the Britains fought valiantlie in defense of their countrie; yet they were put to the worsse, and so the lord admerall returned to his ships.

On the thrée & twentith daie of Maie being mondaie, he landed in the morning, Conquet and diuerse other places burnt by sir Edward Howard lord admerall of England. and commanded to burne the house of the lord Piers Moguns, with the towne of Conquet, & diuerse other places, and chased the Britains into the castell of Brest: and notwithstanding all the assemblies and shewes that the Britains made, yet they suffered the English peaceablie to returne with their preies and booties. The first of Iune the Englishmen tooke land in Croiton baie, and then the lords of Britaine sent word to the lord admerall, that if he would abide, they would giue him battell. The admerall rewarded the messenger, and willed him to say to them that sent, that all that day they should find him in that place tarieng their comming.

Then to incourage diuerse gentlemen the more earnestlie to shew their valiancie, Diuers gentlemen knighted by the lord admerall. he dubbed them knights; as sir Edward Brooke, brother to the lord Cobham, sir Griffith Downe, sir Thomas Windham, sir Thomas Lucie, sir Iohn Burdet, sir William Pirton, sir Henrie Shirborne, and sir Stephan Bull. When the lord admerall saw the Frenchmen come, he comforted his men with pleasant words, therby the more to incourage them. The whole number of the Englishmen was not much aboue 25 hundred, where the Frenchmen were at the least ten thousand; and yet when they saw the order of the Englishmen, they were suddenlie astonied.

Then a gentleman of good experience and credit amongest them, aduised the other capteins not to fight; but to retire a little and take a strong ground, there to remaine till the Englishmen returned toward their ships: and then to take the aduantage. And so the capteins began to retire, which when the commons saw, they all ran awaie

as

as fast as they might, supposing that the capteins had séene or knowne some great perill at hand, bicause they were not priuie to the purpose of their capteins. The lord admerall seeing what happened, when the night came departed to his ships. After this the gentlemen of Britaine sent to the admerall for a safeconduct for diuerse persons, which they ment to send to him about a treatie. The lord admerall was of his gentlenesse content to grant their request. Then certeine lords of Britaine tooke a bote, and came to the ship of the lord admerall, where he was set with all his councell of the armie about him.

The request of the lords of Britaine to the lord admerall.

A truce required for six daies.

The request of the Britains was, that it might please him to surcease his cruell kind of warre, in burning of townes and villages: but the admerall plainlie told them, that he was sent to make warre and not peace. Then they required a truce for six daies, which would not be granted; and to their reproofe, the admerall told them, that gentlemen ought to defend their countrie by force, rather than to sue for peace. And thus (making them a banket) he sent them awaie. And after hearing that there was ships of warre on the seas, he coasted from thence alongst the countrie of Normandie, still scowring the sea, so that no enimie durst appeare. And at length he came and laie by the Ile of Wight, to see if anie enimies would appéere. During which time, diuers ships were kept in the north seas, vnder the conduct of sir Edward Ichingham, Iohn Lewes, Iohn Louedaie, and others.

Iustes at Gréenewich.

Abr. Fl. ex Edw. Hall fol. xxj.
A description of the shewes and triumphs then solemnlie held.

This yeare also in Iune, the king kept a solemne iustes at Gréenewich, the king & sir Charles Brandon taking vpon them to abide all commers. ¶ First came the ladies all in white and red silke, set vpon coursers trapped in the same sute, freated ouer with gold; after whom followed a founteine curiouslie made of russet sattin, with eight gargils spowting water: within the founteine sat a knight armed at all peeces. After this founteine followed a ladie all in blacke silke dropped with fine siluer, on a courser trapped in the same. Then followed a knight in a horsselitter, the coursers & litter apparelled in blacke with siluer drops. When the fountein came to the tilt, the ladies rode round about, and so did the founteine, and the knight within the litter. And after them were brought two goodlie coursers apparelled for the iusts: and when they came to the tilts end, the two knights mounted on the two courses abiding all commers. The king was in the founteine, and sir Charles Brandon was in the litter. Then suddenlie with great noise of trumpets entred sir Thomas Kneuet in a castell of cole blacke, and ouer the castell was written, The dolorous castell, and so he and the earle of Essex, the lord Howard, and other ran their courses with the king and sir Charles Brandon, and euer the king brake most speares, and likelie was so to doo yer he began, as in former time; the prise fell to his lot: so luckie was he and fortunat in the proofe of his prowes in martiall actiuitie, whereto from his yong yéers he was giuen, as the poet saith:

Huic erat à teneris annis ars bellica cordi.]

After this, the king hauing prepared men and ships readie to go to the sea vnder the gouernance of sir Anthonie Oughtred, sir Edward Ichingham, William Sidneie, and diuerse other gentlemen, appointed them to take the sea, and to come before the Isle of Wight, there to ioine with the lord admerall, which they did, but in their passage a gallie was lost by negligence of the maister. The king hauing a desire to see his nauie togither, rode to Portesmouth, and there appointed capteins for one of his chiefest ships called the Regent, sir Thomas Kneuet master of his horsses, & sir Iohn Carew of Deuonshire; and to the Souereigne he appointed for capteins, sir Charles Brandon, and sir Henrie Gilford; and with them in the Souereigne were put threescore of the tallest yeoman of the kings gard. Manie other gentlemen were ordeined capteins in other vessels. And the king made them a banket before their setting forward, and so commited them to God. They were in number fiue and twentie faire ships of great burden, well furnished of all things necessarie.

The king riding to Portesmouth appointeth capteins ouer his ships.

The kings nauie setteth out.

The

The French king in this meane while had prepared a nauie of thirtie nine saile in the hauen of Brest; and for chiefe he ordeined a great Carrike of Brest, apperteining to the queene his wife, called Cordelier a verie strong ship, and verie well appointed. This nauie set forward out of Brest the tenth of August, and came to Britaine baie, in the which the same day was the English fléet ariued. When the Englishmen perceiued the Frenchmen to be issued foorth of the hauen of Brest, they prepared themselues to battell, and made foorth towards their enimie, which came fiercelie forward; and comming in sight ech of other, they shot off their ordinance so terriblie togither, that all the sea coast sounded of it. The lord admerall made with the great ship of Déepe, and chased hir; sir Henrie Gilford and also sir Charles Brandon made with the great Carrike of Brest, being in the Souereigne, and laid stem to stem to the Carrike; but by negligence of the master, or else by smoke of the ordinance, or otherwise, the Souereigne was cast at the sterne of the Carrike, with which aduantage the Frenchmen shouted for ioy.

The English nauie incountereth with the French vpon the coast of Britaine.

But when sir Thomas Kneuet, who was readie to haue boorded the great ship of Déepe, saw that the Souereigne missed the Carrike, suddenlie he caused the Regent (in the which he was aboord) to make to the Carrike, and to grapple with hir a long boord. And when they of the Carrike perceiued they could not depart, they let slip an anchor, and so with the streame the ships turned, and the Carrike was on the weather side, and the Regent on the lie side. The fight was cruell betwixt these two ships, the archers on the English side, & the crossebowes on the French part dooing their vttermost to annoie each other: but finallie the Englishmen entered the Carrike, which being perceiued by a gunner, he desperatlie set fire in the gunpowder, as some say; though there were that affirmed, how sir Anthony Oughtred folowing the Regent at the sterne, bowged hir in diuerse places, and set hir powder on fire.

A cruell fight betwixt the two nauies.

The English Regent, and the French Carrik burnt togither.

But howsoeuer it chanced, the whole ship by reason of the powder was set on fire, & so both the Carrike and the Regent being grappled togither, so as they could not fall off, were both consumed by fire at that instant. The French nauie perceiuing this, fled in all hast, some to Brest, and some to the Iles adioining. The Englishmen made out boats to helpe them in the Regent: but the fire was so terrible, that in maner no man durst approch; sauing that by the Iames of Hull certeine Frenchmen that could swim were saued. Capteine of this Carrike was sir Piers Morgan, and with him he had in the same nine hundred men: and with sir Thomas Kneuet and sir Iohn Carew were seuen hundred; but all drowned and burnt. The Englishmen that night laie in Berthram baie, for the French fléet was disperst (as ye haue heard.) The lord admerall after this mischance thus happened to these two worthie ships, made againe to the sea, and scowered all alongest the coasts of Britaine, Normandie, and Picardie, taking manie French ships, and burning such as they could not well bring away with them.

The French nauie flieth.

The king of England hearing of the losse of the Regent, caused a great ship to be made, such a one as the like had neuer béene séene in England, and named it Henrie grace de Dieu. The French king about the same time sent to a knight of the Rhodes called Priour Iehan, a Frenchman borne, of the countrie of Guien, requiring him to come by the streicts of Marrocke into Britaine: the which he did, bringing with him thrée gallies of force, with diuerse foists and row-gallies, so well ordinanced and trimmed, as the like had not béene séene in these parties before his comming. He had laine on the coasts of Barbarie to defend certeine of the religion, as they came from Tripolie. This yeare in the moneth of Nouember the king called his high court of parlement, in the which it was concluded, that the king himselfe in person with an armie roiall shuld inuade France; wherevpon notice being giuen to such as shuld attend, they made their purueiance with all diligence that might be. In this parlement was granted to the king two fifteens, and foure demies; and head monie, of

The kings ship roiall called Henrie grace de Dieu.

A parlement wherein it was concluded that king Henrie in proper person should inuade France.

Abr. Fl. ex I. S. pag. 897.

Great subsidie.

of euerie duke ten markes, an earle fiue pounds, a lord foure pounds, a knight foure marks, & euerie man rated at eight hundred pounds in goods, to paie foure marks, and so after that rate, till him that was valued at fortie shillings paied twelue pence, and euerie man that tooke fortie shillings wages twelue pence, and euerie man and woman of fiftéene yeares or vpward foure pence.   The steeple and lanterne of Bow church in Cheape was this yeare finished.   By fire this yeare a great part of the kings palace of Westminster, and the chappell in the Tower of London, and manie other places in England were burned.   In Aprill, the king sent a great nauie of twelue thousand men to the sea. On Maie euen, Edmund de la Poole was beheaded on the Tower hill, his brother Richard was after slaine in France.]

Bow stéeple builded.

Kings palace at Westminster burned.

Edmund de la Poole beheaded.

1513

Edw. Hall in Hen. 8. *fol.* xxij. The description of a rich mount being a Christmasse shew.

After this parlement was ended, the king kept a solemne Christmasse at Gréenwich, with danses and mummeries in most princelie maner.   And on the Twelfe daie at night came into the hall a mount, called the rich mount.   The mount was set full of rich flowers of silke, and especiallie full of broome slips full of cods, the branches were gréene sattin, and the flowers flat gold of damaske, which signified Plantagenet. On the top stood a goodlie beacon giuing light, round about the beacon sat the king and fiue other, all in cotes and caps of right crimsin veluet, embrodered with flat gold of damaske, their cotes set full of spangles of gold.   And foure woodhouses drew the mount till it came before the quéene, and then the king and his companie descended and dansed.   Then suddenlie the mount opened, and out came six ladies all in crimsin sattin and plunket, embrodered with gold and pearle, with French hoods on their heads, and they dansed alone.   Then the lords of the mount tooke the ladies and dansed togither: and the ladies reentered, aud the mount closed, and so was conueied out of the hall.   Then the king shifted him, and came to the queene, and sat at the banket which was verie sumptuous.

Sir Charles Brandon created vicount Lisle.

After Candlemasse, the king created sìr Charles Brandon vicount Lisle.   In March following was the kings nauie of ships roiall & other set foorth to the number of fortie and two, beside other balangers vnder the conduct of the lord admerall, accompanied with sir Walter Deuereux, lord Ferrers, sir Wolstan Browne, sir Edward Ichingham, sir Anthonie Pointz, sir Iohn Wallop, sir Thomas Windham, sir Stephan Bull, William Fitz Williams, Arthur Plantagenet, William Sidneie esquiers, and diuerse other noble and valiant capteins.   They sailed to Portesmouth, and there laie abiding wind, and when the same serued their turne, they weied anchor, & making saile into Britaine, came into Berthram baie, and there laie at anchor in sight of the French nauie, which kept it selfe close within the hauen of Brest, without proffering to come abroad.

The nauie set out againe.

The English nauie purposing to set vpon the French in the hauen, are defeated by a mischãce.

The English perceiuing the maner of the French men, determined to set on them in the hauen, and making forward in good order of battell, at their first entrie one of their ships, whereof Arthur Plantagenet was capteine, fell on a blind rocke, and burst in sunder, by reason whereof, all the other staied: and so the English capteins perceiuing that the hauen was dangerous to enter without an expert lodesman, they cast about, and returned to their harborough at Berthram baie againe.   The Frenchmen perceiuing that the Englishmen meant to assaile them, moored their ships so neere to the castell of Brest as they could, and placed bulworks on the land on euerie side, to shoot at the Englishmen.   Also they trapped togither foure and twentie great hulkes that came to the baie for salt, and set them on a row, to the intent that if the Englishmen had come to assault them, they would haue set those hulks on fire, and haue let them driue with the streame amongest the English ships.

The lord admerall would haue the king present in person at the encounter, and is rebuked.

Prior Iehan also laie still in Blanke sable baie, and plucked his gallies to the shore, setting his basiliskes aud other ordinance in the mouth of the baie, which baie was bulworked on euerie side, that by water it was not possible to be woone.   The lord admerall perceiuing the French nauie thus to lie in feare, wrote to the king to come thither in person, and to haue the honour of so high an enterprise: which writing the kings

kings councell nothing allowed, for putting the king in ieopardie vpon the chance of the sea. Wherefore the king wrote to him sharplie againe, commanding him to accomplish that which apperteined to his duetie: which caused him to aduenture things further than wisedome would he should (as after yée shall heare) to his vtter vndooing and casting awaie, God hauing ordeined the means by his prouidence, which the pagans implied (though wanting the light of grace) in the name of destinie, of them counted ineuitable. [A destinie lamentable considering the qualitie of the person, with the maner of his dieng. Wherein although manie vainlie dispute, that fortune led him to so miserable an accident: yet if we will lift vp our considerations to God, we shall find that he hath reserued such a prerogatiue ouer all things which he hath created, that to him onelie belongeth the authoritie to dispose all things by the same power wherewith he hath created them of nothing.] And yet the foolish world (doting in blind ignorance, but pretending a singular insight in matters of secrecie) blusheth not to talke or rather to asseuere, casualtie, chancemedlie, misfortune, and such like foolish imaginations: whereas (indéed) the prouidence of God compasseth all things whatsoeuer, for nothing can be priuileged from the amplenesse of the same.

Guic. pag. 325.

Prior Iehan kéeping him still within his hold, as a prisoner in a dungeon, did yet sometime send out his small foists to make a shew before the English nauie, which chased them to the baie. But bicause the English ships were mightie vessels, they could not enter the baie: and therefore the lord admerall caused certeine boats to be manned foorth, which tooke one of the best foists that Prior Iehan had, and that with great danger: for the gallies and bulworks shot so freshlie all at one instant, that it was maruell how the Englishmen escaped. The lord admerall perceiuing that the Frenchmen would not come abroad, called a councell, wherein it was determined, that first they would assaile Prior Iehan and his gallies lieng in Blanke sable baie, and after to set on the residue of the French fléet in the hauen of Brest. Then first it was appointed, that the lord Ferrers, sir Stephan Bull, and other, should go aland with a conuenient number to assault the bulworkes, while the admerall entered with row barges and little gallies into the baie, and so should the Frenchmen be assailed both by water and land.

An. Reg. 5

A consultatiõ about the assault ng of Prior Iehan.

The lord admerall by the counsell of a Spanish knight called sir Alfonse Charant, affirming that he might enter the baie with little ieopardie, called to him William Fitz Williams, William Cooke, Iohn Colleie, and sir Wolstan Browne, as his chéefe and most trustie fréends, making them priuie to his intent; which was to take on him the whole enterprise, with their assistance. And so on S. Markes daie, which is the fiue and twentith of Aprill, the said admerall put himselfe in a small row barge, appointing thrée other small rowing ships, and his owne ship bote to attend him; and therewith vpon a sudden rowed into the baie, where Prior Iehan had moored vp his gallies iust to the ground: which gallies with the bulworkes on the land, shot so terriblie, that they that followed were afraid. But the admerall passed forward, & as soone as he came to the gallies, he entered & droue out the Frenchmen. William Fitz Williams within his ship was sore hurt with a quarell. The baie was shallow, and the other ships could not enter, for the tide was spent.

The admerall roweth into the baie where the Prior laie.

Which thing the Frenchmen perceiuing, they entered the gallies againe with moris pikes, and fought with the English in the gallies. The admerall perceiuing their approch, thought to haue entred againe into his row barge, which by violence of the tide was driuen downe the streame, and with a pike he was throwne ouer the boord, and so drowned, and also the forenamed Alfonse was there slaine: all the other boates and vessels escaped verie hardlie awaie: for if they had taried, the tide had failed them, and then all had béene lost. The lord Ferrers and the other capteins were right sorowfull of this chance: but when there was no remedie, they determined not to at-

Sir Edward lord Howard admerall drowned.

tempt anie further, till they might vnderstand the kings pleasure, and so they returned into England.

The Frenchmen perceiuing that the English fléet departed from the coasts of Britaine and drew towards England, did come foorth of their hauens, and Prior Iehan set foorth his gallies and foists, and drawing alongst the coasts of Normandie and Britaine coasted ouer to the borders of Sussex with all his companie, and there landed, and set fire on certeine poore cotages. The gentlemen that dwelt néere, raised the countrie, and came to the coast, and droue Prior Iehan to his gallies. The king was right sorie for the death of his admerall; but sorrow preuaileth not when the chance is past. Therefore the king hearing that the French nauie was abroad, called to him the lord Thomas Howard eldest brother to the late admerall, and sonne and heire apparant to the earle of Surrie, whome he made admerall, willing him to reuenge his brothers death. The lord Howard humblie thanked his grace of the trust that he put in him, and so immediatlie went to the sea, and scowred the same, that no Frenchman durst shew himselfe on the coast of England, for he fought with them at their owne ports.

The king hauing all his prouisions readie for the warre, and meaning to passe the sea in his owne person, for the better taming of the loftie Frenchmen, appointed that worthie councellor and right redoubted chéefteine, the noble George Talbot earle of Shrewesburie, high steward of his houshold, to be capteine generall of his fore-ward; and in his companie were appointed to go, the lord Thomas Stanleie earle of Derbie, lord Decowreie prior of saint Iohns, sir Robert Ratcliffe lord Fitzwater, the lord Hastings, the lord Cobham, sir Rice ap Thomas, sir Thomas Blunt, sir Richard Sacheuerell, sir Iohn Digbie, sir Iohn Askew, sir Lewes Bagot, sir Thomas Cornewall, and manie other knights, esquiers, and souldiers; to the number of eight thousand men. These passed the sea, and came all to Calis about the middle of Maie.

The lord Herbert called sir Charles Summerset, lord chamberleine to the king, in the end of the same moneth followed the said earle of Shrewesburie, with six thousand men: in whose companie were the erls of Northumberland Percie, of Kent Greie, of Wilshire Stafford, the lord Dudleie, the lord Delaware, and his sonne sir Thomas West, sir Edward Husseie, sir Edward Dimmocke, sir Dauid Owen, with manie other knights, esquiers, and gentlemen. After they had soiourned certeine daies in Calis, and that all their necessaries were readie, they issued foorth of the towne, so to begin their campe. And first the earle of Shrewesburie and his companie tooke the field, and after him the lord Herbert with his retinues in manner of a rere-ward. Then followed that valiant knight sir Rice ap Thomas, with fiue hundred light horssemen and archers on horssebacke, who ioined himselfe to the fore-ward, a gentleman of such spirit and hardinesse, that he is named the floure of the Welshmen, as the poet saith:

——Ricius Thomas flos Cambrobritannûm.

These two lords thus imbattelled did remooue the seuentéenth of Iune to Sandifield, & on the eightéenth they came to Marguison, on the further side of the water, as though they would haue passed streightwaies to Bullongne. But they meaning an other thing, the next daie tooke an other waie, and so coasted the countrie with such diligence, that the two and twentith of Iune they came before the strong citie of Terrouan, and pight their tents a mile from the towne. The same night (as certeine capteins were in councell within the lord Herberts tent) the baron Carew was slaine with a bullet shot out of the towne; which sudden aduenture much dismaied the assemblie, but the lord Herbert comforted them with manlie words, and so his death was passed ouer. All the countrie of Artois and Picardie fortified their holds, and made shewes as the English armie passed, but they durst not once assaile them.

The citie of Terrouan was stronglie fortified with walles, rampiers, bulworks, and large

large ditches, The lord Pontremie was gouernour within it, hauing with him six The lord Pontre-
mic capteine of
hundred horssemen, and 2500 Almans, besides the inhabitants. The walles & towers Terwine.
Terwine besieg-
were full of ordinance, which oftentimes did much displeasure to the Englishmen. ed.
The earle of Shrewesburie planted his siege on the northwest side of the towne, and
the lord Herbert on the east side, causing great trenches to be made to couer his people withall: for on that side there was no hill to succour or defend him. The Frenchmen and Almans would diuerse times issue out, but the archers were euer readie to
beat them into the citie againe. The earle of Shrewesburie got into an hollow ground
or vallie néere to the citie, and likewise the lord Herbert (by reason of his trenches)
approched likewise verie néere to the ditches.

The seuen and twentith daie of Iune being mondaie, sir Nicholas Vaux and sir
Edward Belknap hauing with them foure hundred and thrée score men set from
Guisnes to conduct foure and twentie carts laden with vittels towards the siege at
Terrouan; but the duke of Vandosme lieutenant of Picardie with eight hundred
horssemen set on them as they passed through Ard, and found them so out of order,
that notwithstanding all that the English capteins could doo to bring men into arraie,
it would not be: for the Frenchmen set on so readilie, that they kept the Englishmen
in sunder. Yet the horssemen of Guisnes, being not past foure and twentie in all,
tooke their speares and ioined with the Frenchmen right manfullie, and likewise
thrée score archers shot freshlie at their enimies; but the Frenchmen were so manie
in number, that they obteined the place, slue eight gentlemen, and diuerse archers.
Sir Nicholas Vaux and sir Edward Belknap fled toward Guisnes.

Thus were the vittels lost, and yet the Frenchmen went not awaie with cleere hands;
for those few archers that closed togither, shot so egerlie, that they slue and hurt
diuerse Frenchmen; and on the field laie foure score and seuen great horsses, which
died there in the place, and neuer went further. On the fiftéenth day of Iune the K. The king in
person passeth
departed from Gréenewich, taking his iourneie towards Douer, whither he came by ouer into France.
easie iournies, and the quéene in his companie. After he had rested a season in the
castell of Douer, and taken order for the rule of the realme in his absence, he tooke
leaue of the queene, and entring his ship the last daie of Iune, being the daie of saint
Paule: he sailed ouer to Calis, where he was receiued with great ioy by the deputie
sir Gilbert Talbot and all other there. At his entring into Calis, all the banished men
entred with him, and were restored to the libertie of the towne. The king laie in
Calis a certeine time, till all his prouisions were readie, but the armie laie in campe at
Newnham bridge.

On the one and twentith of Iulie, the kings maiestie passed foorth of Calis, and
tooke the field, diuiding the armie which he had there with him into three battels.
The lord Lisle marshall of the host was capteine of the fore-ward, and vnder him The order of
the kings armie.
thrée thousand men: sir Richard Carew with three hundred kept on the right side of
the same fore-ward as a wing thereto: and the lord Darcie with other thrée hundred
men was a wing on the left hand. The fore-riders of this battell were the Northumberland men on light geldings. The earle of Essex was lieutenant generall of the
speares, and sir Iohn Pechie was vicegouernour of all the horssemen, and sir Iohn
Burdet standard-bearer to the kings spears. An eight hundred Almans went on a
plumpe by themselues before the kings battell, and the duke of Buckingham with
six hundred men was on the kings left hand, equall with the Almans, in like maner
as sir Edward Poinings was on the right hand, with other six hundred men equall with
the Almans.

In the kings battell, where was the standard of the armes of England borne by sir
Henrie Guilford, there were thrée thousand; & the lord of Aburgauenie with eight
hundred men was wing on the right hand, and sir William Compton with the retinue
of the bishop of Winchester, and of maister * Woolseie the kings almoner, being in * This man was
afterward car-
4 A 2 number dinall.

number eight hundred was in manner of a rere-gard. Sir Anthonie Oughtred and sir Iohn Neuill with the king speares that followed were foure hundred, and so the whole armie conteined eleuen thousand and thrée hundred men. The number of the cariages were thirtéene hundred, and the number of them that attended the same were ninetéene hundred men, and all these were reckoned in the battell: but of good fighting men & souldiers appointed for the purpose, there were not full nine thousand. In this order the king with his armie marched forward through the confines of his enimies to the siege of Terrouan, entring into the French ground the fiue and twentith of Iulie being mondaie. On the morrow after as the armie marched forward, by negligence of the carters that mistooke the waie, a great curtall (called the Iohn Euangelist) was ouerthrowne in a déepe pond of water and could not quicklie be recouered.

The French armie approcheth, & their number.

The king being aduertised that the Frenchmen approched to fight with him, left the gun (bicause the maister carpenter vndertooke to weie it shortlie out of the water) & set forward, passing on by Tornohan, which he left on his right hand, and a little beyond pitched downe his field abiding for his enimies, the which (as he was informed) were not far off. On the morrow after being wednesdaie, the Reliefe of the speares, brought word that they had ascried the French armie comming forward in order of battell, to the number of eleuen thousand footmen, and foure thousand horssemen. Capteins of this armie were the lord de la Palice, the lord de Priennes, the duke of Longuile, the earle of S. Paule, the lord of Floringes, the lord of Cleremont, & Richard de la Poole a banished man, son to Iohn duke of Suffolke. They came within two miles of the kings armie, and there the footmen staied, and came no further.

The northern prickers plaie the men.

But certeine of the horssemen to the number of thrée thousand came forward, and at the end of a wood shewed themselues in open sight of the English armie. And thus they stood countenancing the Englishmen. Some of the northerne prickers made to them, and in skirmishing with them, tooke some of them prisoners. About noone the same daie, that valiant Welsh knight sir Rice ap Thomas with his retinue of horssemen being departed from the siege of Terrouan came to the king, and streightwaies was sent to the earle of Essex, which with two hundred speares was laid in a stale, if the Frenchmen had come neerer. When they were ioined togither, they drew about the hill, hauing with them sir Thomas Guilford, with two hundred archers on horssebacke, meaning to set on the Frenchmen: which perceiuing that, and doubting least more companie had followed, they suddenlie drew backe, and ioined them with their great battell.

Then the earle of Essex and the English horssemen followed them, till they came néere to the armie of France, and then scaled and sent foorth light horssemen to view the demeanor of the Frenchmen. When the Frenchmen of armes were returned to their battell, then both the horssemen and footmen withdrew in order of battell, and still the English currors followed them for the space of three leagues, and then returned to the earle, making report to him of that they had séene, who then brake vp his stale, and came to the king, declaring to him how the Frenchmen were gone backe. This was called the drie wednesdaie; for the daie was woonderfull hot, and the king with his armie stood in order of battell, from six of the clocke in the morning till three of the clocke in the after noone. And some died for lacke of moisture, and generallie euerie man was burned about the mouth with heat of the stomach; for drinke lacked, and water was not neere.

The drie wednesdaie.

After this the king remooued toward Terrouan, and as he was setting forward, the lord Walon of Flanders came to him with his horssemen, which were alreadie in the kings wages. As the armie passed, by negligence the same daie in a lane was ouerthrowne

throwne one of the kings bombards of iron, called the red gun, and there left. The king lodged that night two miles from saint Omers on the north side of the towne. On the thursdaie, being the eight and twentith of Iulie, the maister carpenter with an hundred carpenters and labourers, without knowledge of the marshall, went to weie vp the great gun that was in the pond (as ye haue heard) and by force of engins drew it vp, and carted it readie to bring awaie: but suddenlie there came an eight hundred Frenchmen with speares, crossebowes, and handguns, which set on the labourers so fiercelie, that notwithstanding their manfull defense, the most part of them were slaine and the residue taken, and both they and the péece of ordinance conueied to Bullongne.

The Frenchmen glad of this chance, assembled a great number to fetch the other gun, which laie yet in the lane. But the lord Berners being capteine of the pioners and hearing all these things, prepared to recouer that gun; and so in the morrow ment to fetch it. There were appointed to go backe to see him safe conducted, the earle of Essex with his companie of speares, sir Rice ap Thomas with his retinue, and sir Iohn Neuill with the Northumberland men. The Almans also were commanded to retire backe to the succours of them that were gone for the gun. The Almans went foorth, till they came within two miles of the place where the gun laie, and further they would not go. The Frenchmen to the number of nine or ten thousand men (as some estéemed) were abroad, and came toward the place where the Englishmen were carting the péece of ordinance.

The Northumberland horssemen hauing espied them, gaue knowledge to the residue of the Englishmen, who prepared themselues to defend their ground against the enimies: and the earle of Essex sent to the lord Walon, willing him with his companie to come to his aid: but the lord Walon sent word againe, that he was come to serue the king of England more than for one daie, and therefore he wished that all the Englishmen would returne, sith that with the great power of France they were not able to match. This answer was much displeasant to the earle of Essex and the other capteins. In this meane time the foreriders of the French part were come to the hands of the Englishmen, and so they fell in skirmish very hotlie: but at length all things considered, and speciallie the small number of the Englishmen, being not aboue seuen hundred horssemen, it was thought best that they should returne and follow the gun which they had sent forward.

Herevpon they retreited in order, and not in anie flieng manner, still following the gun. The Frenchmen perceiuing that, pricked forward to the number of two thousand horssemen, & came iust to the backs of the Englishmen, who therewith cast about, and made returne to the Frenchmen. Sir William Tiler and sir Iohn Sharpe were the first that charged, and after all the other Englishmen. The Frenchmen fled immediatlie so fast backe, that happie was he that might be formost. The whole host séeing their horssemen thus had in chase, suddenlie returned. The earle of Essex withdrew to an hill, and there caused his trumpet to blow to the standard for feare of subtile dealing; and when his men were come in, and gathered togither, he returned. On the same daie being fridaie, the nine and twentith of Iulie, the king came to Arkes, & there incamped; whither the earle of Essex came to him, and declared what had beene doone that daie, the king thanking him and other the capteins for their paines and diligence.

The king laie here at Arkes till mondaie the first of August, and then remooued to a village midwaie betwixt Terwine and saint Omers, where he lay till thursdaie the fourth of August, and came that daie in good order of battell before the citie of Terwine, & there pight vp his tents and pauillions in most roiall manner, fensing his campe right stronglie with ordinance and other warlike deuises. [The king for himselfe had a house of timber with a chimnie of iron, and for his other lodgings he had

great

great and goodlie tents of blew water worke garnished with yellow and white, diuerse roomes within the same for all offices necessarie. On the top of the pauillions stood the kings beasts holding fanes, as the lion, the dragon, the greihound, the antelope, the dun cow: all within the lodging was pointed full of the sunnes rising, the lodging was one hundred and fiue and twentie foote in length.]

The king lieng before Terwine, his great ordinance did sore beat the walles, & they within likewise shot ordinance out of the towne, and slue diuerse Englishmen in the trenches, among which shots they had one gun that euerie daie and night was ordinarilie shot at certeine houres without faile: this gun was of the Englishmen called the whistling gun, but it neuer did harme in the kings field. The siege thus lieng before the citie of Terwine, sir Alexander Bainam a capteine of the miners, caused a mine to be enterprised to enter into the towne: but the Frenchmen perceiuing that, made a countermine, and so destroied the other mine, and diuerse miners slaine within the same. The French armie houered euer a farre to take the Englishmen at aduantage, as they went a forraging; and manie a skirmish was doone, and manie good feates of armes atchiued on both sides, and diuerse prisoners taken. Among the Frenchmen were

Stradiots described and incountered of the English light horssemen.

certeine light horssemen called Stradiots with short stirrops, beuer hats, small speares, and swords like cimiteries of Turkie: diuerse times the northerne light horssmen vnder the conduct of sir Iohn Neuill skirmished with these Stradiots and tooke diuerse of them prisoners, and brought them to the king.

While the king laie thus before Terwine, the capteine of Bullongne knowing by his espials, that manie of the garrison of Calis were with the king at the siege, and also that vittels were dailie brought out of England to Calis to succour the campe, imagined a great enterprise, and sent for all the men of warre vnder his dominion and rule, and declared to them what honour they should obteine if they hurted or spoiled the out parts of Calis, the king of England on that side of the sea. The men of warre perceiuing the good courage of the capteine, assented to his purpose, and so with all diligence they, to the number of a thousand men, in the euening set forward, & came to Newnam bridge by thrée of the clocke in the morning, and found the watchmen that kept the bridge asléepe, & so entred the bulworke and slue the watchmen, and tooke the ordinance of the bridge, and then let the bridge fall, so that all entered that would.

The capteine of Bullongne kept six hundred men for a stale at the bridge, & sent the other into the marishes and medows to fetch awaie the beasts and cattell which they should find there. This was doone, and some of them came so néere the walles of Calis, that they were escried. And about a six score coupers, bakers, shipmen & other which laie without the towne, hearing the alarme, got togither, & setting on

Watchmen found sléeping serued iustlie.

those Frenchmen which were aduanced so néere the towne, slue them downe that abode, chased them that fled euen into Newnam bridge, and recouered the same, and put backe their enimies. About fiue of the clocke in the morning, the gate of Calis

Culpeper vndermar hall of Calis.

called Bullongne gate was opened, and then by permission of the deputie, one Culpeper the vnder-marshall with two hundred archers vnder a banner of saint George issued foorth.

All these in great hast came to Newnam bridge, where they found the other Englishmen that had woone the bridge of the Frenchmen, and so all togither set forward to assaile the Frenchmen that kept the stale, and tarie till the residue of their companie which were gone a forraging vnto Calis walles were come: for the other that had spoiled the marishes were returned with a great bootie. At the first, when the Frenchmen saw the Englishmen approch, they thought they had bene their owne fellowes. But when they saw the banner of saint George, they perceiued how the matter went, & so determined to defend themselues against their enimies; but the Englishmen set so fiercelie on, that

finallie

finallie the Frenchmen were discomfited, and foure and twentie of them slaine, beside twelue score that were taken prisoners, and all the ordinance and bootie againe recouered.

These prisoners were brought to Calis, & there sold in open market. [Among all *Abr. Fl. ex* other, a couper of the towne of Calis bought a prisoner of this bootie that dwelt in *Ed. Hall in.* Bullongne, and had of the prisoner an hundred crowns for his ransome. When the *H. 8. fol. xxviij.* monie was paied, the Frenchmen praied the couper to sée him safe deliuered, and to conduct him out of danger. The couper gentlie granted, and without anie knowledge *The follie of* of his friends, all alone went with the Frenchman till he came beyond the causeie, & *a couper.* there would haue departed: but the Frenchman perceiuing that the couper was aged, and that no reskue was nie, by force tooke the couper prisoner, and caried him to Bullongne, & made him paie two hundred crownes for his ransome: thus through follie was the poore couper deceiued. Wherefore it is wisedome for a man to hold fast his possession, and to supplie his want of strength by subtiltie; imitating therein the fox, which although in force he be inferior to the lion, as not able to beare the yerking of his taile, or a pelt of his paw; yet in craft he goeth beyond that boisterous beast, and so escapeth danger, which otherwise might susteine.]

On the eleuenth day of August, being thursday, the king lieng at the siege of Ter *The emperor* wine, had knowledge that Maximilian the emperour was in the towne of Aire. The *Maximilian* king prepared all things necessarie to méet with the emperour in triumph. The noble *and the king of* men of the kings campe were gorgeouslie apparelled, their coursers barded with cloth *England méet.* of gold, of damaske and broderie, their apparell all tissue, cloth of gold and siluer, and goldsmiths woorke, great chains of bauderikes of gold, and belles of bullion: but in especiall the duke of Buckingham, he was in purple sattin, his apparell and his bard full of antelops and swans of fine gold bullion, and full of spangles, & little bels of gold maruellous costlie and pleasant to behold. The K. was in a garment of great riches in iewels and stone, he was armed in a light armour. The master of his horsse followed him with a spare horsse, the henchmen followed bearing the kings péeces of harnesse, euerie one mounted on a great courser.

The one bare his helmet, the second his grangard, the third his speare, the fourth *The kings har-* his axe, and so euerie one had something belonging to a man of armes. The apparell *nesse and fur-* of the nine henchmen were white cloth of gold, and crimsin cloth of gold, richlie *niture.* embrodered with goldsmithes worke, the trappers of the coursers were mantell har- nesse coulpened, and in euerie vent a long bell of fine gold, and on euerie pendent a déepe tassell of fine gold in bullion, which trappers were verie rich. The king and the emperour met betwéene Aire and the campe, in the foulest weather that lightlie hath béene seene. The emperour gentlie interteined the king, and the king likewise him, and after a little communication had betwene them, bicause the weather was foule, they parted for that time. The emperour & all his men were at that daie all in blacke cloth, for the empresse his wife was latelie deceased.

Within a day or two after this interuiew, and that the king was returned to his *A letter of de-* campe, thither came a king at armes of Scotland called Lion, with his cote of armes *fiance sent by* on his backe, who within short time was by Gartier king of armes brought to the *the Scotish king* kings presence, where he being almost dismaid to see the king so noblie accompanied, *to king Henrie.* with few words & meetlie good countenance, deliuered a letter to the king, which his grace receiued and read it himselfe; and therewith hauing conceiued the whole con- tents thereof, made this answer immediatly to the herald.

Now we perceiue the king of Scots our brother in law, and your master to be the *The king of* same person whom we euer tooke him to be, for we neuer estéemed him to be of anie *Englands speach* truth: and so now we haue found it. For notwithstanding his oth, his promise in the *to the Scotish* word of a king, and his owne hand and seale; yet now he hath broken his faith & *kings herald* promise to his great dishonour and infamie for euer, and intendeth to inuade our realme *vttered without* in our absence, which he durst not once attempt, our owne person being present. *permeditation.*

But

But he sheweth himselfe not to be degenerat from the conditions of his forfathers, whose faiths (for the most part) haue euer béene violated, and their promises neuer obserued, further than they list. Therefore tell thy master, first, that he shall neuer be comprised in anie league wherein I am a confederat; and also that I suspecting his truth (as now the déed prooueth) haue left an earle in my realme at home, which shall be able to defend him and all his power. For we haue prouided so, that he shall not find our land destitute of people as he thinketh to doo: but this saie to thy master, that I am the very owner of Scotland, & that he holdeth it of me by homage. And insomuch as now, contrarie to his bounden dutie, he being my vassall, dooth rebell against me, with Gods helpe I shall at my returne expell him his realme, and so tell him.

Sir said the king of armes, I am his naturall subiect, and he is my naturall lord, and that he commandeth me to say, I may boldlie say with fauour, but the commandements of other I may not, nor dare say to my souereigne: but yur letters, with your honor sent, may declare your pleasure, for I may not say such words of reproch to him, to whom I owe onelie mine allegiance and faith. Then said the king, Wherfore came you hither? will you receiue no answer? Yes said Lion, but your answer requireth dooing and no writing, that is, that immediatlie you should returne home. Well said the king; I will returne to your damage and not at thy maisters summoning. Then the king commanded Gartier to take him to his tent, and to make him good cheare, which so did, and cherished him well: for he was sore abashed.

After he was departed, the king sent for all the capteins, and before them and his councell caused the letter to be read, the contents wherof were, that king Henrie had not dealt with him vprightlie in sundrie points, as in mainteining of those which had slaine his people of Scotland by sea, and also in succouring bastard Heron with his complices, which had (vnder trust of daies of méeting for iustice) slaine his warden. Also his wiues legacie was by him withholden: & moreouer, where first he had desired him in fauour of his dere cousin the duke of Gelder, not to attempt anie thing against him; yet had he sent his people to inuade the said dukes countrie, which did what in them lay to destroie and dishinherit the said duke, that had nothing offended against him.

The effect of the Scotish kings letter to K. Henrie. Sée historie of Scotland, pa. 295, and *Edw.* Hall, in *H.* 8. *fol.* xxix, xxx.

And now againe, where he had made the like request for his brother & cousine the most christian king of France: yet notwithstanding, had the king of England caused him to lose his duchie of Millaine, and at this present inuaded his realme with all his puissance, to destroie him and his subiects, whereas yet the said king of France had béene euer fréend to him, & neuer giuen him occasion thus to doo. In consideration of which iniuries receiued in his owne person, and in his friends, he must néeds séeke redresse, and take part with his brother and cousine the said king of France. Wherefore he required him to desist from further inuasion and destruction of the French dominions, which to doo if he refused, he plainlie declared by the same letters, that he would doo what he could to cause him to desist from further pursute in that his enterprise, & also giue letters of marque to his subiects for the deniall of iustice made to them by the king of England.

The letters thus sent to the king of England, were dated at Edenburgh the six and twentith daie of Iulie, and giuen vnder the signet of the said Scotish king. When the king had thus caused these letters to be read, and throughlie considered of them as apperteined, he sent them straight to the earle of Surrie, which then laie at Pomfret, and caused other letters to be deuised to the king of Scots, the effect whereof was; that although he well perceiued by the kings letters, which he had receiued from him, in what sort, vnder colour of contriued occasions and feined quarrelles, he meant to breake the peace; he did not much maruell thereat, considering the ancient accustomed manners of some his progenitors.

King Henrie his answer to the Scotish kings letters. Sée hi-torie of Scotland pag. 297 and *Edw.* Hall in *He.* 8, *fol.* 30, 31.

Howbeit

Howbeit, if loue and dread of God, nighnesse of blood, honour of the world, law *An euill deed* and reason had bound him, it might be supposed, that he would neuer so farre haue *to breake the* procéeded; wherein the pope and all princes christned might well note in him dishono- *league of peace.* rable demeanor, which had dissembled the matter, whilest he was at home in his realme: and now in his absence thus went about vpon forged causes to vtter his old rancor, which in couert manner he had long kept secret. Neuerthelesse, vpon mis- trust of such vnstedfastnesse, he had put his realme in a readinesse to resist his en- terprises, as he doubted not through Gods fauour and assistance of his confederats, he should be able to resist the malice of all schismatikes, and their adherents, being by generall councell expreslie excommunicated & interdicted, trusting in time con- uenient to remember his friends, & requite his foes.

Moreouer, he willed him to set before his eies the example of the king of Nauarre, *The king of Na-* who for assistance giuen to the French king was now a king without a realme. *uarre a king* And as touching answere to be made to the manifold griefs in the Scotish kings let- *without a realme,* ters surmised, if law or reason could haue remooued him from his sensuall opinions, *and why.* he had beene manie times alreadie answered sufficientlie to the same; vnlesse to the pretended griefs therein amongst other comprised, for denieng of a safe conduct to the Scotish ambassadour to haue beene lastly sent vnto him. Whervnto thus he answered; that the same safe conduct had béene granted, if the Scotish herald would haue taken it with him.

And finallie, as touching the Scotish kings request, to desist from further attempt *The king of* ing against the French K. he signified to him, that he knew him for no competent *Englands an-* iudge of so high authoritie, as to require him in that behalfe, and therefore God *swere to the last* willing he ment with the aid and assistance of his confederats & alies to prosecute his *clause of the* begun attempt. And as the Scotish king should doo to him, & to his realme, so it *Scotish kings* should be hereafter remembred and acquited. These letters were written in the *letter.* campe before Terwine the twelfe of August, and giuen vnder the kings signet, and therewith deliuered to Lion king of armes, who had of the king 100 angels in reward. *An hundred an-*

Then departed he with his letters into Flanders, there to take ship to saile into *gels to a Scotish* Scotland, but yer he could haue a vessell and wind for his purpose, his maister was *herald for a re-* slaine, as after ye shall heare. In this meane while the Frenchmen being assembled *ward.* and lodged in campe at Blangie on this side Amiens, the French king appointed that all the horssmen to the number of eight thousand (as Paulus Iouius recordeth) *Fourtéene hun-* should go with vittels vnto Terwine, and put the same into the towne, if by anie *dred men of* meanes they might, for that those within stood as then in great necessitie for want *armes hath Mon-* of vittels. *sieur de Langeie.*

The charge of this conueie was committed vnto Monsieur de Piennes, because he *Monsieur de Pi-* was lieutenant of those marches: notwithstanding there were amongst the number, *ennes appoin:ed* other noble men of more high degrée in honor, and also of great prowesse, fame, and *by the French* experience, furnished with sundrie bands of men at armes of long approoued vali- *king to vittell* ancie, and vsed to go awaie with victorie in manie a dangerous conflict and battell, *Terwine.* wanting at this present nothing but their old accustomed good fortune. Whilest the Frenchmen were thus prepared to come with vittels to Terwine, the emperour *The emperor* Maximilian came from Aire to the kings campe before Terwine the twelfe of August, *Maximilian* wearing a crosse of saint George as the kings souldier, & receiuing of him salarie for *weareth a crosse* seruice; which Anglorum prælia noteth as noteworthie, saieng: *of saint George* *as souldier to the* *king of England.*

Sub rege Anglorum magnus meret induperator

The emperour was honourablie receiued, and lodged in a rich tent of cloth of gold prepared for him, according as was conuenient for his estate. He taried vntill sun- daie being the foureteenth of August, and then returned to Aire: and on the morrow after came againe being mondaie the fifteenth of August, on which daie there

A fraie betwéene the Almans of the kings campe, and the Englishmen well appeased by the discret on of the capteins.

chanced a great fraie betwixt the Almans of the kings campe, and the Englishmen, insomuch that manie were slaine. The Almans ran to the kings ordinance and tooke it, and imbattelled themselues, and bent the ordinance against the king and his campe. The English prepared their bowes, and the Almans made redie their pikes: but the capteins tooke such paines in the matter, that the fraie was appeased.

Now as this trouble was in hand, the emperour came from Aire, and saw all the demeanour of both parts, and was glad to behold the discréet behauiour of the cap-

The king and the emperour consult which waies were best to besiege Terwine, to preuent the vittelling of it.

teins. After that the emperour was thus come to the kings field, the king called a councell, at the which the emperour was present, where it was debated, by what meanes they might best constreine them within to deliuer vp the towne, and especiallie how to kéepe them from vittels & other succours, which the French armie (as it was knowne) meant verie shortlie to minister vnto them. Some were of this mind, and namelie the emperour; that bridges should be made ouer the riuer, to passe ouer a part of the armie to besiege the towne on that side; where otherwise the French armie might vittell the towne at their pleasures.

Others were of a contrarie mind, doubting what might happen, if the armie should be so diuided, least the Frenchmen setting on the backe of the one part of the armie, and they within the towne to sallie out in their faces, some misfortune might happen yer the other part could passe the riuer to the succour of their fellowes. Yet at length the former purpose was allowed as most necessarie; and therefore commandement was giuen to the maister of the ordinance, that in all hast he should

Fiue bridges made in one night for the armie to passe ouer the riuer at Terwine.

cause fiue bridges to be made ouer the water for the armie to passe. The carpenters so applied their worke that night, that the bridges were made by the next morow, and all the horssemen first passed ouer, and then the king with his whole battell, and the great ordinance followed and passed ouer to the other side of the water. This was on the sixteenth daie of August being tuesdaie.

On the same morning the Frenchmen were comming with their conueie of vittels to refresh the towne, hauing appointed one part of their troops to kéepe on that side the riuer where the English armie was first incamped, and where the earle of Shrewes-burie still kept his field; that in offering the skirmish on that side, the residue of the horssemen might with more ease and safetie put the vittels and other necessarie things into the towne on the other side. Here might a man haue séene of what

Polydor. The force of sudden chance in warre.

force in wars sudden chance is oftentimes. For the king thus with his battell pass-ing the riuer, meaning to besiege the towne on euerie side, and the Frenchmen at that same instant hauing also passed the riuer with other carriages laden with vittels, purposing to reléeue the towne on that side, caused no small doubt to be conceiued of ech others meaning, on both parts, least that the one, hauing knowlege of the others purpose, had béene prepared for to hinder the same.

And yet was it nothing so, for neither the king knew of the Frenchmens approch

Edw. Hall. Polydor.

that daie, neither they of his passing ouer the water. But when the king had ad-uertisement giuen him (by the light horssemen that were sent abroad to discouer the countrie) how the Frenchmen were at hand; he prepared himselfe to the battell, and

The king with his battell of footmen.

first set foorth his horssemen, and then followed himselfe with his battell of foote-men. The French capteins being hereof aduised, determined not to fight without their footmen; and therefore with all speed sent backe their carriages, and staied with their horssemen, vntill the carriages might haue leasure to get out of danger. In the meane time the Englishmen aduanced forward, and their horssemen mounted vp the hill, where the French horssemen were in troope, with thirtie and three standards spred, & might sée the Englishmen comming, and the kings battell march-ing forward with the Almans.

There were amongest the Frenchmen certeine companies of Estradiots, which being placed before the French hoast, as they came downe the hill to skirmish with the

Englishmen

Englishmen saw where the banners of the English horssemen were comming, and The Estradiots mistaking footmen for horssemen fled first. the kings battell following vpward, weening verelie that all had béene horssemen, wherevpon they cast themselues about and fled. The Frenchmen were so fast in arraie, that the Estradiots could not enter; and so they ran still by the ends of the Frenchmens ranks. Herewith the English horssemen set on, and about an hundred archers on horsse-backe, being lighted beside their horsses, and set by an hedge all alongest a village side called Bomie, shot freshlie at their enimies; & also certeine culuerings being placed on the top of an hill were discharged amongest the thickest prease of the Frenchmen; so that finallie the French were discomfited: for those that were behind saw the fall of some of their standards, which the Englishmen ouerthrew, and their Estradiots also (in whome they had great confidence) returne.

They that were furthest off fled first, and then the Englishmen & Burgognian A great ouerthrow giuen to the French, king Henrie in person being present. horssemen, which were with them, egerlie followed the chase, in the which were taken the duke of Longuile, brother to the earle of Dunois that had married the daughter and heire to the marquesse of Rothlois, the lord of Cleremont, capteine Baiard, monsieur de Busie, and other, to the number of twelue score prisoners, and all brought to the kings presence with six standards, which were likewise taken. The Burgognians brought not their prisoners to sight. Monsieur de la Palice, and monsieur de Imbrecourt being taken of them and knowne, were put to their ransomes, and licenced maintenantlie to depart vpon their word. Thus was the power of the French horssemen by the sharpe incounter of the English horssemen, and full fight of the battels of the footmen, following in arraie at the backs of the horssemen, and the discharging of certeine culuerings amongst them, quickelie put to flight without anie great resistance.

The emperour Maximilian was present with the king, and ware saint Georges The emperor incourageth his Almans to plaie the men. crosse, greatlie incouraging the Almans to shew themselues like men, sith the place was fortunate to him and them, to trie the chance of battell in: as they might call to remembrance by the victorie there obteined against the Frenchmen a foure and twentie yeares past. This incounter chancing thus on the sixtéenth daie of August, being tuesdaie, in this fift yeare of king Henries reigne, which was the yeare after the incarnation 1513, was called the battell Des esprons, by the Frenchmen themselues, that is to saie, the battell of spurres: forsomuch as they in stéed of sword The battell of spurres. and lance vsed their spurres, with all might and maine to pricke foorth their horsses to get out of danger; so that in them was verefied the old prouerbe, One paire of heeles is worth two paire of hands.

That wing of the horssemen also, which was appointed to skirmish with the Englishmen on the other side the riuer, whilest the other might haue conueied the vittels into the towne, was fiercelie beaten backe by the martiall prowesse of the valiant erle of Shrewesburie, sir Rice ap Thomas, and other worthie capteins, which laie on that side the water. The duke of Alanson, the earle of saint Paule, and monsieur de Florenges, had the leading of those Frenchmen. They within the towne were in great hope of succour this daie, and when they saw the French power approch, they sallied foorth on that side where the lord Herbert laie, and skirmished with his people verie proudlie, but they were repelled to the gates of their towne, and manie of them slaine by the high valiancie of the said lord Herbert and his capteins.

After that the Englishmen were returned from the chase of the Frenchmen, whome Sir Iohn Pechie made baneret, and Iohn Carre knight. they had followed a thrée long miles from the field, the king made sir Iohn Pechie a baneret, and Iohn Carre knight, which was sore hurt: sir Iohn Pechie had his guidon taken, and diuerse of his men hurt, they followed so farre in the chase. After this ouerthrow of the French horssemen, the K. compassed the towne more streictlie on ech side, and the batterie was brought so nigh the wals as might be, wherwith breaches were made in sundrie places, by meanes whereof the lord Pontremie despairing any long time to kéepe the towne, fell to a composition, and yéelded it vp to the kings hands. This incounter and ouerthrow, with the giuing vp of Terwine, is extant to the knowledge of forren nations (to be read) recorded as followeth:

Francorum pugnax equitatus prælia miscet,
Succurrúntque suis, sed frustra infirmior arma,
Turba capit; palmam bellando potentior Anglus
Aufert, læthifera transfossis hostibus hasta.
Diruta turrifragis bombardis mœnia præbent
Brutigenæ ingressum facilem, Gallísque timorem
Injciunt, tandem Terrouana deditur Anglo.

Howbeit this yéelding vp of the said towne was with condition, that the souldiers might depart with horsse and armour, & that such townesmen as would there remaine, might haue their liues and goods saued. Thus (I saie) was the citie of Terwine deliuered vp to the king of England, with all the ordinance and munitions then being found within the same. This was on the eightéenth of August. The earle of Shrewesburie entered the same night, and caused the banner of saint George to be set vp in the highest place of the towne in signe of victorie. When the lord Pontremie, and all the souldiers were departed, and that the earle of Shrewesburie had searched all the towne to sée that euerie thing was sure, he called the townesmen afore him, and sware them to be true to the king of England. The foure and twen-

The citizens of
Terwine sworne
to king Henrie.
The king enter-
eth into Ter-
wine. tith of August the king himselfe entered the towne with great and roiall triumph, and dined in the bishops palace. At after noone he returned to his campe, and on the six and twentith daie of August he remooued againe to Guingate, where he first incamped after the chase of the French horssemen.

Here it was determined in councell, that the wals and fortifications of Terwine should be rased, which was doone, and the towne burned; except the cathedrall church and the palace. All the ordinance was sent to Aire to be kept there to the kings vse. After this, it was concluded that the king should laie siege to the citie

of Tornaie; wherevpon he set forward in thrée battels: the earle of Shrewesburie leading the va-ward, the king and the emperour gouerning the battell, and the lord chamberleine following with the rere-ward. The first night they incamped beside Aire Diuerse Englishmen tarieng behind at Terwine for pillage, were surprised by the Frenchmen, which slue some of them, & cast some into the fire. Those that fled escaped verie narrowlie. The king with his armie passed forward towards Tornaie,

The king goeth
to Lisle to visit
the yoong prince
of Castile. and by the waie visited the yoong prince of Castile and the ladie Margaret, gouernor of the prince, in the towne of Lislie, whilest his armie laie abroad in the fields beyond the Pont Auandien.

There was appointed to attend the king vnto Lislie the duke of Buckingham, the lord marquesse Dorset, the earle of Essex, and the lord Lisle, with diuerse other; the charge of his campe he committed for the time to his councell. Then mounted the king vpon a courser, his apparrell & bard were cloth of siluer of small quadrant cuts trauersed and edged with cut cloth of gold, and the border set full of red roses,

Sir Henrie Guil-
ford maister of
the kings horsse. his armour fresh & set full of iewels. The maister of his horsse sir Henrie Guilford, and the henchmen followed (as you haue heard before) and the coursers richlie apparelled, and so were manie capteins that waited on the king: by the waie met the king the lord Rauesten with manie noble men. And a mile without the towne there met with him the burgesses of Lisle, and presented to him the keies of the towne, saieng, that the emperor their souereigne lord had so commanded them to doo.

The king praised their obedience to their souereigne, and thanked the emperour and them for so high a present as the keies of such a towne. Neuerthelesse, he had such confidence in them, that he trusted them no lesse than his owne subiects, and so deliuered the keies to the prouost of the towne, which was well accompanied. Then met the king a great number of nobles of Flanders, Brabant, Holland, and Henaud, which noblie receiued him. After them came the countie Palatine or Palsgraue, one of the electors of the empire, with thirtie horsses, all his men gorgiouslie apparelled after the fashion of his countrie, and humblie saluted the king. At the gate of Lisle the capiteine of the towne stood with a garrison in armor well appointed, all the streets were set on both sides with burning torches and diuerse goodlie pageants pleasant to behold. Thus he passed thorough the towne with his sword and maces borne before him, and alighted at the hall doore with his sword borne, where met with him the emperour, the prince of Castile, and the ladie Margaret, and humblie saluted him. ^{The Palsgraue of Rhene & his traine come to receiue the k. of England.}

Then for reuerence of the emperour, the king caused his sword to be put vp, and his maces to be laid downe; & so was the king and all other nobles lodged and feasted according to their degrées. In the towne of Lisle was a noise that thrée gunners with handguns should haue slaine the king: for which rumor manie were attached, but nothing prooued. But when these tidings came to the campe, they were neuer merrie till they saw the king againe. Great was the cheere, with bankets, plaies, comedies, maskes, and other pastimes that were shewed to the king in the court of Burgognie, and so in solace he soiorned there sundaie and mondaie the nineteenth daie of September. On the twentith daie he sent word that his armie should remooue toward Tornaie, and so they remooued to a place conuenient betwéene Tornaie and Lisle, and certeine capiteins were appointed to kéepe the passage at the bridge of Auandien. ^{A false rumor of the kings death.}

After that the king had taried at Lisle thrée daies, and had well reposed himselfe, he tooke his leaue, and thanked the emperour and the yoong prince, the ladie Margaret & all the ladies for all his high chéere and solace; and about six of the clocke at night, he departed out of Lisle, and the noble men brought the king foorth and so returned, and then the capteine shut the gates. When the king was a mile and more out of the towne, he asked where his campe laie? And no man there could tell the waie, and guide had they none, the night was so darke & mistie. Thus the king taried a long while, and wist not whither to go; at last they met with a vitteler comming from the campe, which was their guide and brought them thither. The maister of the ordinance shot diuerse peeces of ordinance, but they were not heard; but in safetie the king with all his companie returned. ^{The king and his traine ignorant of the waie to his campe by meanes of a mist.}

On the one and twentith daie of September the king remooued his campe toward Tornaie, and lodged within thrée miles of the citie, on a corne ground by the riuer. On which night came to the king the emperour and the Palsgraue, which were lodged in rich tents, and noblie serued of all viands and things necessarie. The people about Tornaie were with their goods fled to the citie, and yet the citie had no men of warre to defend it, but with multitude of inhabitants the same was well replenished. The king commanded sir Rice and his horssemen to view one quarter, and the earle of Essex and his companie another quarter; and the lord Wallon and the lord Lignie the other quarters. Then the two and twentith daie of September, these foure capteins at one time were soone openlie with banners displaied before the towne, and there made a long stale, and returned.

Then the king sent Gartier king of armes to summon them to yeeld it ouer into his hands, to whome they made answer, that they receiued no citie of the king of England to kéepe, nor anie would they render him, with which answer he departed. Then they fortified the wals, and made prouision for vittels, corne, wine, and artillerie, and for all fortifications that might be gotten. And the citie of it selfe was strong, well walled, and turrited with good bulworks and defenses. But when they saw the king with such a puissance draw néere the citie, they were sore abashed, ^{Tornaie summoned by Gartier king of armes.}

and

The prouost of Tornaies words to the distressed townesmen. and called a generall councell. Then the prouost said; "Brethren, you know how that the king of England sent an herald to summon vs to render vp to him this citie, or else he would put it and vs to the sword, fier, and bloud. We answered we would be at defense. Now he is come in our sight to fulfill the message sent by the herald, & now is come the time of our defense.

"Howbeit in this matter standeth thrée mischéefs, one is our bounden duetie and allegiance that we owe to our souereigne lord king Lewes of France; the second the liues of vs, our wiues, children, and neighbors; the third how to defend the finall destruction of this ancient citie, now likelie to fall, which citie was neuer conquered. Now our citie is whole, your liues in safetie, your goods your owne ; determine whether you will haue war or peace." Then the common people cried all; "War, war, war." Then said the prouost, "Take compassion of wiues and children and of the old folke; consider if you haue no quicke rescue, you cannot continue against yonder puissance, although your courages were neuer so great, this the wisest of the citie and I haue considered." Then suddenlie was there in the councell a vaunt-parler, a botcher, which hearing this, called a great number of his affinitie, and went out of the councell and so out of the gates, and set fire of the suburbs on all sides. When the councell saw the minds of the commons, and that their waies might not be followed, they comforted the people, and mainteined them for their defense.

After this the king approched the citie with his whole armie, and they of the citie issued foorth to proffer the skirmish: but the archers beat them backe. Also the carriage men that came with the herbingers, saw where certeine wagons were entering the citie, vnto the which they ran, and tooke some of them. At this skirmish the horsse of the lord Iohn Graie was slaine vnder him, as he came to defend the carriage men; but he himselfe had no hurt. The king with his battell planted his *Tornaie besieged by king Henrie.* siege on the north side the citie. The earle of Shrewsburie with the foreward lodged toward the south side of the riuer, and there laie that night. The lord Herbert with the rereward incamped himselfe on the west side, and beat the wals and towers of the citie with the great ordinance. The next daie after their comming thither, being the thrée and twentith of September, the earle of Shrewesburie with the foreward passed the riuer, & planted his siege on the southside of the citie, stretching to the east end, and bent his ordinance against the walles. And thus was the citie of Tornaie besieged on all parts.

On the fiue and twentith daie of September, the king receiued letters from the earle of Surrie with the Scotish kings gantlet, whereby he was certified of the slaughter of the said king, and how all things had béene handled at the battell of *See Hall in Henrie 8. fol. 37, 38. & historie of Scotland, pag. 297, 298.* of Floddon, whereof héereafter yee shall find further mention. The king thanked God for the newes, and highlie commended the prowesse of the earle, and other the capteins: howbeit he had a secret letter, that Cheshiremen and other fled from sir Edmund Howard in the battell, which letter caused great hartburning, and manie words: but the king tooke all things in good part, and would that no man should be dispraised. On the six and twentith daie, fiers were made in the hoast, in token of that victorie against the Scots, and on the seauen and twentith daie being tuesdaie, masse was soong by them of the kings chappell, with Te Deum, and the bishop of Rochester made a sermon, declaring the death of the king of Scots, and lamenting his euill hap and periurie. But now to our purpose of the siege of Tornaie.

Abr. Fl. ex Edw. Hall in Hen. 8. fo. xliiii, xlv. The citie of Tornaie on all sides besieged. ¶ The king of England lieng afront before Tornaie, caused his great ordinance to be planted round about the citie, and diuerse trenches were cast, and rampiers made, and the lord Lisle and the lord Willoughbie were appointed to mainteine the ordinance with their bands, and the earle of Kent was lodged before the gate called port Valencien;

lencien; so that the citizens could not issue out, nor no aid could come in. The ordinance dailie beat the gates, towers, & wals, which made a great batterie: and a few Englishmen assaulted the port coquerell, but they were too few in number; and if they had béene more in number, they had taken the towne, as the Tornasins confessed after. The Citizens of Tornaie considering their estate came togither to councell, and there the prouost said in effect as followeth. "Friends and brethren of this noble citie, I cannot too much praise your truth and fidelitie to your souereigne lord the king of France; considering how manfully you haue defended this citie since the beginning of this siege. The prouosts words to the townesmen.

"But alas! although it be written on the gates grauen in stone, Iammes ton ne a perdeu ton pucellage, that is to saie; Thou hast neuer lost thy maidenhed: yet if this citie had not béene well furnished and euer at the daie appointed sure of rescue, it could not haue continued. Now you see that rescue faileth, our gates be rased, our towers beaten downe, our chiefe tower like to fall, so that if this perilous siege continue, or else if our enimies assault vs, we be not able to defend vs: wherefore now, all these things considered, I would know whether you will treat with the king of England or abide the chance." Then they which at the last councell cried War, war; now cried Peace, peace: yet all were not agréed. Then one wise man said, "Sirs if the towne be assaulted once againe with a great number, suerlie it will be taken: you saw the experience at the last assault, and then consider if it be taken by force, who is there can saie he is sure of his life: but by intreatie, the king of England is so mercifull that we may fortune to saue both life and goods." Then finallie all agréed to treat.

Then the prouost sent to the king a trumpet, desiring a safe conduct for him & certeine other to come and to speake with him: which request was to him granted. Then the prouost of the citie, accompanied with eleuen with him of the best of the citie, came to the armie, & spake with the lords of the councell, and after were led to the kings presence. The prouost knéeled downe and all his companie, and said: "Right high and mightie prince, although the citie of Tornaie is strong, well walled, well replenished with people, vittels, artillerie, yea and the people in feare and dread of nothing; yet we know that against your great puissance it can not continue long, although it were ten times as strong as it is. Wherefore we knowing by report your honor, your wisedome, your iustice, & noble hart, are content to become your subiects & vassals, so that we may haue and inioy our old lawes, customes, liberties, and franchises, vnder you; as we haue before this doone vnder other princes." The prouost with eleuen more submit themselues & yéeld vp the citie to the king.

Then said the king; We haue well heard your petition, we will common with our councell & make you answer. And when he had communed with his councell, he answered saieng: Sirs, he that asketh mercie of vs, shall not be denied; and séeing you come to treat, we remit you to our councell. Then they went into the tent of councell, & there the Tornasins fell at a point, and in conclusion they yéelded the the citie and ten thousand pounds sterling for the redemption of their liberties, and so departed to the citie, making relation of the king and his noble courage. On thursdaie the nine and twentith daie of September, the king was in his rich tent of cloth of gold vnder his cloth of estate, to whome came the citizens of the citie, and were sworne to him, and became his subiects.

Then the king appointed the lord Lisle, the lord Aburgauenie, & the lord Willoughbie to take possession, which with six thousand men entered the citie, and tooke the market place and the wals, and searched the houses for feare of treason. Then maister Thomas Woolsie the kings almoner called before him all the citizens yoong and old, and sware them to the king of England, the number whereof was foure score thousand. Thus the king of England by conquest came to the possession The possessiõ taken in the king of Englands behalfe.

of

of the citie of Tornaie. On sundaie the second daie of October, the king entered the citie of Tornaie at port founteine, and foure of the chiefe of the citie ouer him bare a canopie with all the armes of England. Euerie person was in his best apparell, the ladies & gentlewomen laie in the windowes beholding the king and his nobilitie, euerie citizen had in his hand a staffe torch. The king himselfe was richlie apparelled in rich armour on a barded courser, his henchmen bearing his péeces of war, as ax, speare, and other, their coursers were barded with the armes of England, France, Ireland, and other the kings dominions all richlie brodered. Thus the king with his nobilitie all richlie apparelled with his sword borne before him, his heralds and sergeants of armes with trumpets and minstrelsie entered the citie, and came to our ladie church, and there Te Deum was soong.

The king maketh certeine gentlemē (for their good seruice) knights.

     Then the king called to his presence Edward Guilford, William Fitz Williams, Iohn Dansie, William Tiler, Iohn Sharpe, William Husse, Iohn Sauage, Christopher Garnish, and diuerse other valiant esquiers, and gaue to them the order of knighthood, and then went to his lodging, and at after noone he came to the market place, were was prepared for him a roome. Then he caused a proclamation to be made in his name king of England & France, that no man should gréeue the citizens. During which proclamation the Tornasins scarce looked vp, nor shewed once to him any amiable countenance, which was much marked. The crie finished, the king departed to his campe, leauing the citie in safe keeping. This wéeke the king rode to sée the castell of Morton, and there his grace tooke great pleasure. The king remembring the great chéere that the prince of Castile and the ladie Margaret had made him at Lisle, which was but twelue miles English from Tornaie, desired the said prince & ladie, with diuerse other to come to him to his citie of Tornaie, and made preparation for the same, and appointed a iusts, whereof he himselfe would be one; and caused a tilt to be made in the market place.

Sir Edward Poinings made lieutenant of Tornaie.

     While thsse things were preparing, the king and his councell ordered for the sure kéeping of the citie of Tornaie, and there ordeined sir Edward Poinings knight of the order of the garter to be his lieutenant with foure hundred archers, with capteins, horssemen, and artillerie conuenient, and to haue aid of Henaud and other the kings friends adioining; and of his gard he left there foure hundred archers, and ordinance was appointed for the defense of the same. On mondaie the eleuenth daie of October the king without the towne receiued the prince of Castile, the ladie Margaret, and diuerse other nobles of their countries, and them brought into Tornaie with great triumph. The noise went that the lord Lisle made request of mariage to the ladie Margaret duches of Sauoie, and daughter to the emperour Maximilian, which before that time was departed from the king with manie rich gifts and monie borrowed: but whether he proffered mariage or not, she fauoured him highlie. There the prince and duches soiourned with great solace by the space of ten daies.

Iustes held at Tornaie for disport of the prince of Castile & the duchesse of Sauoie.

     During which time, the eightéenth daie of October began the iusts, the king and the lord Lisle answering all commers: vpon the king attended foure & twentie knights on foot in coats of purple veluet and cloth of gold. A tent of cloth of gold was set in the place for the armorie & Reliefe. The king had a base and a trapper of purple veluet both set full of S S of bullion, and the lord Lisle in the same suite, there were manie speares broken, and manie a good buffet giuen; the strangers, as the lord Walon and lord Emerie and other did right well. When the iusts were doone, the king & all the other vnhelmed them, & rode about the tilt, and did great reuerence to the ladies, and then the heralds cried to lodging. This night the K. made a sumptuous banket of an hundred dishes to the prince of Castile and the ladie Margaret, and to all other lords and ladies; and after the banket the ladies dansed, and then came in the king and eleuen in a maske, all richlie apparelled with bonets of gold, and when they had

passed

passed the time at their pleasure, the garments of the maske were cast off amongst the ladies, take who could take.

On the twentith daie of October, the prince of Castile and the ladie Margaret (with manie great gifts to them giuen) returned to Lisle and all their traine. After that the king was informed that all directions were taken, and euerie thing put in an order for the sure kéeping of the citie of Tornaie, he betooke the same to sir Edward Poinings knight, which valiantlie kept it in good order and iustice. The king & his councell before this considering, that the Frenchmen would giue them no battell, and that winter approched, which was no time to lie at siege of other townes, concluded to kéepe Tornaie safelie, and to breake vp his campe for that winter, and to begin againe warre in the spring of the yeare. This was a full conclusion taken by the king and his councell, and so the king and all his people (except such as were appointed to be with sir Edward Poinings) departed out of Tornaie the twentith daie of September: and the king and the noble men made such spéed, that shortlie they came to Calis.

Thither came the lord admerall, whome the king heartilie thanked of his paines, and there euerie man was paied his full wages and conduct monie, and ships prepared for the passage; and so the foure and twentith daie of September, the king with a priuie companie tooke ship, and the same day landed at Douer, and shortlie after all his people followed; then he with a small companie rode to Richmond in post to the queene, where was such a louing méeting, that euerie creature reioised. This season began a great mortalitie in London and other places, where much people died. All this winter the kings nauie kept the seas, and robbed and spoiled the Frenchmen on their coasts, so that they were euerie foot afflicted by the English, & wist not which way to remedie it, bearing grudge in their hearts, and wishing a generall destruction of their enimies, against whome they did swell with malignitie and indignation, both for their late ouerthrowes and losses aswell of lands as liues; the surrender of Terwin sticking in their stomachs, and the yéelding of Tornaie nipping them at the heart, which had lost the propertie, & was now forced to obeie new lords and new lawes, as our poet saith:

————dominorum serua nouorum,
* Accipit ecce nouas Henrico principe leges.

But now I must returne to speake of the dooings in the North parts, betweene the Englishmen and Scots. Whilest the king was occupied in his warres against France in the summer of this yeare (as before is mentioned) yée haue heard how the king of Scots sent his letters vnto the king, as then lieng at the siege before Terwine, and what answer was made thereto by the king. Immediatlie vpon the sending of those his letters conteining in effect a defiance, the king of Scots assembled his people to inuade the English confines: but before his whole power was come togither, the lord Humes that was lord chamberleine of Scotland, on a day in August entered England with seuen or eight thousand men, and getting togither a great bootie of cattell, thought to haue returned therewith into his countrie.

But as he came to passe through a field ouergrowne with broome, called Milfield, the English men vnder the leading of sir William Bulmer, and other valiant capteins, hauing with them not past a thousand souldiers, being laid within that field in ambushment, brake foorth vpon him: and though the Scots on foot defended themselues right manfullie, yet the English archers shot so wholie togither, that the Scots were constreined to giue place. There were of them slaine at this bickering fiue or six hundred, and foure hundred or more taken prisoners; the lord chamberleine himselfe escaped by flight, but his banner was taken. This was called by the Scots the ill rode. In the meane time was the whole power of Scotland assembled, with the which king Iames approching to the borders, and comming to Norham castell, laid siege thereto, hauing there with him an hundred thousand men.

Marginal notes:
- The prince & the duchesse returne to Lisle.
- The king returneth into England.
- A mortalitie.
- * Vrbs Tornaci.
- Lord Humes entereth the borders of England.
- Englishmen assaile the Scots.
- Scots put to flight.
- Lord chamberleine escapeth. The ill road.
- Norham castell besieged.

Norham castell
deliuered.

After he had beaten this castell with his ordinance for the space of six daies togither, the same was deliuered vp into his hands; for the capteine was so liberall of his shot and powder, spending the same so freelie before he had cause so to doo, that when it shuld haue stood him in stead, he had none left to aid him, so that in the end he yeelded himselfe without more resistance. In which meane time the earle of Surreie being

The earle of
Surrie lieute-
nant of the
north raiseth an
armie.

lieutenant of the north parts of England, in absence of king Henrie, had giuen order to assemble a power of six and twentie thousand men; and comming to Alnwike the third of September being saturdaie, taried there all the next day till the whole number of his people were come, which by reason of the foule way were staied, and could not come forward with such spéed as was appointed. This fourth daie of September then

The lord adme-
rall ioineth with
the earle of Sur-
rie his father.

being sundaie, his sonne the lord admerall, with a thousand souldiers and able men of warre, which had beene at sea, came to his father; whereof he greatlie reioised for the great wisedome, manhood, and experience, which he knew to be in him.

The lord How-
ard admerall
capteine of the
fore-ward.

Then the earle and his councell, with great deliberation appointed his battels in order, with wings, and with horsmen necessarie. First of the fore-ward was ordeined capteine the lord Howard admerall of England, as well with such as came with him from the sea, as others. First the lord Clifford, the lord Coniers, the lord Latimer, the lord Scrope of Vpsall, the lord Ogle, the lord Lomlie, sir Nicholas Appleyard maister of the ordinance, sir Stephan Bull, sir Henrie Shirburne, sir William Sidnie, sir Edward Ichingham, sir William Bulmer, with the power of the bishoprike of Durham, sir William Gascoigne, sir Christopher Ward, sir Iohn Eueringham, sir Thomas Metham, sir Walter Griffith, and manie others.

Of the wing on the right hand of the fore-ward, was capteine sir Edward Howard knight marshall of the host, & with him Brian Tunstall, Rafe Brearton, Iohn Laurence, Richard Bold, esquiers: sir Iohn Booth, sir Thomas Butler, knights: Richard Done, Iohn Bigod, Thomas Fitz Williams, Iohn Claruis, Brian Stapleton, Robert Warcop, Richard Cholmleie, with the men of Hull, and the kings tenants of Hatfield, and others. Of the wing on the left hand, was capteine sir Marmaduke Constable, with his sonnes and kinsmen, sir William Persie, and of Lancashire a thousand men. Of the rere-ward was capteine the earle of Surreie himselfe, and with him the lord Scroope of Bolton, sir Philip Tilneie, sir George Darcie, sir Thomas Berkleie, sir Iohn Rocliffe, sir Christopher Pikering, Richard Tempest, sir Iohn Stanleie, with the bishop of Elies seruants, sir Brian Stapleton, Lionell Persie, with the abbat of Whitbies tenants, Christopher Clapham, sir William Gascoigne the yoonger, sir Guie Dawneie, maister Magnus, maister Dalbies seruants, sir Iohn Normanuile, the citizens of Yorke, sir Ninian Markanuile, sir Iohn Willoughbie, with others.

Of the wing on the right hand, was capteine the lord Dacres with his power. Of the left hand wing, was capteine sir Edward Stanleie knight, with the residue of the power of the two counties palantine of Chester and Lancaster. Thus was the host appointed and diuided into wards and wings at the first, though afterward (vpon occasion) this order was somewhat altered. And now that euerie man knew what to doo, the earle of Surrie with his power comming toward the place where he thought

The strength of
the place where
king Iames laie
incamped,
called Floddon.

to find the Scotish host, was informed how king Iames being remooued six miles from Norham, laie imbattelled vpon a great mounteine called Floddon, a place of such strength, as it was not possible for the Englishmen to come néere him, but to their great disaduantage: for at the foot of the same hill on the left hand, there was a great marish ground full of réed and water.

On the right hand it was defended with a riuer called Till, the course whereof being so swift, and the chanell in some places so deepe, that it might not conuenientlie be passed. On the backe halfe there were such craggie rocks and thicke woods, that it was not possible to assaile him to anie aduantage that waie foorth. And on the forepart of the campe, where nature had left an easie entrie for men to come to the
same

come to the same, all his ordinance was planted aloft vpon the sides of such trenches, as he had caused to be cast for defense on that part.   The earle of Surrie herevpon, considering with himselfe, that vnlesse he might deuise some policie to cause the Scotish armie to descend the hill, it were not possible for him to accomplish his desire, he called about him his councell, and with them tooke aduise in this point.

At length it was concluded and determined among other things, to send Rouge Crosse, purseuant at armes, with a trumpet to the king of Scots, with a message and certeine instructions : which in substance was, to shew and declare vnto the said king of Scots, that where he (contrarie vnto his oth and league, and vnnaturallie against all reason and conscience) had entered and inuaded this his brothers realme of England, and done great hurt to the same, in casting downe castels, towers and houses, burning, spoiling, and destroieng the same, and cruellie murthering the king of England his brothers subiects; he the said earle would be readie to trie the rightfulnesse of the matter with the king in battell, by fridaie next comming at the furthest, if he of his noble courage would giue him tarieng and abode.   And the same did the said earle promise, as he was a true knight vnto God & the king of England his maister.

And before Rouge Crosse should depart with the said instructions, the lord admerall gaue him in credence to shew the said king of his comming, and part of his companie from the sea with him, and that he had sought the Scotish nauie then being on the sea, but he could not méet with them, bicause they were fled into France by the coast of Ireland.   And in as much as the said king had diuerse and manie times caused the said lord to be called at daies of truce, to make redresse for Andrew Barton a pirat of the sea, long before that vanquished by the same lord admerall, he was nowcome in his owne proper person, to be in the vant-gard of the field, to iustfie the death of the said Andrew against him and all his people, and would sée what could be laid to his charge the said daie.

Furthermore, that he nor none of his companie should take no Scotish noble man prisoner, nor anie other; but they should die if they came in his danger, vnlesse it were the kings owne person; for he said he trusted to none other courtesie at the hands of the Scots.   And in this maner he should find him in the vant-gard of the field, by the grace of God, and saint George, as he was a true knight.   Yet before the departing of Rouge Crosse, with the said instructions and credence, it was thought by the earle & his councell, that the said king would faine and imagine some other message, to send an herald of his with the same, onelie to view and ouersée the manner and order of the kings roiall armie, ordinance, and artillerie then being with the earle, whereby might haue insued great danger to the same.

And for the eschuing thereof, he had in commandement, that if anie such message were sent, not to bring anie person comming therewith within thrée or two miles of the field at the nighest, where the said earle would come, and heare what he would saie. And thus departed Rouge Crosse, with his trumpet, apparelled in his coat of armes. On mondaie the fift daie of September, the earle tooke his field at Bolton in Glendale, as he had appointed, where all the noble men and gentlemen met him with their retinues, to the number of six and twentie thousand men.   And about midnight next insuing came the trumpet which went to Rouge Crosse, and declared how the king of Scots, after the message doone to him by Rouge Crosse, according to his instructions, the said king deteined him, & sent one Ilaie an herald of his with him vnto the earle, to declare to him the kings pleasure; to whom the earle sent Yorke herald at armes, to accompanie the said Ilaie, at a village called Milo, two miles from the field, vntill the comming thither of the said earle the next morow.

On the sixt daie of September, earlie in the morning, the earle accompanied with the most part of the lords and knights, and gentlemen of the field, euerie man hauing with him but one seruant to hold his horsse, rode vnto the place: and so the

Side notes:
An herald sent from the earle of Surrie to king Iames.

The lord admerals message to the king of Scots

Andrew Barton, of whom mention before pag. 565.

A good policie.

Ilaie and Yorke heralds.

4 C 2   said

said herald met with the earle, and with blunt reuerence declared to him that he was come from his maister the king of Scots, which would know whether the earle sent anie such message by Rouge Crosse. The earle iustified the same, saieng further; that Rouge Crosse had the same message of him in writing, signed with his owne hand. Wherevpon the said Ilaie said: As to the abiding for battell betwéene that and fridaie then next following, the king his maister bade him shew to the earle, that he was as welcome as anie noble man of England vnto the said king, and that if be had béene at home in his towne of Edenburgh, there receiuing such a message from the said earle, he would gladlie haue come, and fulfilled the said earles desire.

And the herald assured the earle, on the king his masters behalfe, that the same king would abide him battel at the daie prefixed. Wherof the said earle was right ioious, and much praised the honorable agréement of the said roiall king, and esteemed the same to proceed of an high and honorable courage, promising the herald, that he and good suertie with him should be bound in ten thousand pounds sterling, to kéepe the said daie appointed; so that the king would find an earle of his, and thereto a good suertie with him to be bound in like summe, for the performance of the same. And furthermore the earle bade the herald to saie vnto his maister the king; that if he for his part kept not his appointment, then he was content that the Scots should baffull him, which is a great reproch among the Scots, and is vsed, when a man is openlie periured, and then they make of him an image painted, reuersed, with his héeles vpward, with his name, woondering, crieng, and blowing out on him with hornes, in the most despitefull manner they can, in token that he is worthie to be exiled the companie of all good creatures. Then Ilaie deliuered to the earle a little schedule written with the kings secretaries hand vnsigned, as followeth.

The tenor of the said schedule.

AS to the causes alledged of our comming into England against our band and promise (as is alledged) thereto we answere; our brother was bound as farre to vs, as we to him. And when we sware last before his ambassador, in presence of our councell; we expressed especiallie in an othe, that we would keepe to our brother, if our brother kept to vs, and not else. We sweare our brother brake first vnto vs. And since his breach we haue required diuers times him to amend; & latelie we warned our brother, as he did not vs, yet he brake. And this we take for our quarrell, and with Gods grace shall defend the same at your affixed time, which with Gods grace we shall abide.

And forsomuch as the king kept Rouge Crosse with him, who was not yet returned, the same earle caused the same Ilaie to be in the kéeping of sir Humfrie Lisle and Yorke herald in the same village, vntill the time that a seruant of the same Ilaie might ride in all hast to the king of Scots, for the deliuering of the said Rouge Crosse. Then the earle ioious of the kings answer, returned to his campe, and set forward fiue miles, to a place called Woller Haugh, in such order of battell, as euen then he should haue fought, and there lodged for that night, three little miles from the king of Scots. And betwéene the king & him was a goodlie & large corne field called Milfield, which was a conuenient & faire ground for two hosts to fight on: there either host might perceiue other. The earles desire was to procure the Scots to descend the hill into some euen ground, where he might fight with them without disaduantage of place.

But the king, though he had a great desire to fight, yet vpon diuers considerations,
by

by aduise of his councell he still kept his ground, and meant not to remooue at all out of his strength. Wherevpon the earle of Surrie not able long to continue in such grounds of disaduantage, by reason of mires, and marishes, amongst the which he lodged with his armie that was almost famished for lacke of sufficient vittels, which could not be recouered in such a barren countrie, determined to séeke all waies possible, if he might constreine the Scotish king to come downe beside the hill. He therefore The earle of Surrie remooueth his campe ouer the water of Till. raised his campe, and leauing his enimies on the left hand, and passing ouer the water of Till, he drew into a more commodious ground, at the end of Barmore wood; to the end he might refresh his souldiers somewhat hereby after they had béene toiled for the space of thrée daies togither in cloggie mires, and foule filthie waies, to their disease and wearinesse.

The earle of Surrie being thus lodged, the water of Till ran betwixt the two campes of Scots and Englishmen, diuiding them in sunder: and still by reason the one was within the shot of a culuering of the other, they ceassed not to bestow shot and pouder either at other, though without dooing anie great hurt at all. For the English campe on that part which laie toward the Scots, was couered with an hill rising from the hither banke of Till water, with an easie steepenesse to the height a miles space or thereabouts. Thomas lord Howard sonne and heire to the earle of Surrie, from the The lord Howard taketh view of the Scotish armie. top of this hill beholding all the countrie on euerie side about him, declared to his father, that if he did eftsoons remooue his campe, and passe the water of Till againe in some place a little aboue, and by fetching a small compasse come & shew himselfe on the backe halfe of his enimies, the Scotish king should either be inforced to come downe foorth of his strength and giue battell, or else be stopped from receiuing vittels or anie other thing out of Scotland.

The earle of Surrie desirous of nothing so much as to ioine with the Scots in battell, The earle of Surrie returneth againe ouer the the water of Till. after he vnderstood that his sonne had informed him nothing but truth, he raised his field; and marching a thrée miles vpward by the riuer side, passed ouer his armie in two parts at two seuerall bridges, all at one time. King Iames when he saw this manner of his enimies, and perceiuing what their meaning was, by coniecture of their dooings, thought it stood not with his honor to sit still, and suffer himselfe to be forestalled foorth of his owne realme: and againe, that it might sore diminish the opinion of his princelie power, if he seemed to remaine as it were besieged within a fortresse, hauing more confidence in strength of the place, than in the manhood of his people: wherevpon immediatlie he raised his campe, and got an hill, which he doubted least the enimie should haue taken before him.

But by such diligence as he vsed, and by reason of the great smoke which was raised and spred ouer all the countrie, by burning of the litter and cabbins wherein the Scots had lodged, purposelie set on fire to the same intent, he was got to the place whither he intended, before the Englishmen knew for anie certeintie that he was dislodged, though they were as then within a mile of him. Thus king Iames kéeping the tops of the hils, the earle of Surrie with the English armie came to the foot of the same hils, and staieng there a while for so much as he saw how the hill to the which the The valiant determination of the earle to incounter the Scots. Scots were gotten, was neither steepe nor hard to ascend, he determined to mount the same, and to fight with the Scotish hoast yer they should haue leasure to fortifie their campe.

Héerewith calling his people togither, he made vnto them a bréefe oration, declaring vnto them both what necessitie there was for them to shew their manhood, and what iust causes they had also to fight against those enimies, that against both the lawes of God and man had most cruellie inuaded the relme of England, in the quarrell of a schismatike, and one that was accurssed and excommunicated by the censures of the church. The Englishmen kindled with desire to fight, the more thorough those words of the earle, required incontinentlie to be led foorth against

the

the Scots, that they might shew what earnest wils they had to be reuenged; not onelie of new receiued wrongs, but also of ancient iniuries; for there should neither héigth of hill, nor anie other obstacle hinder them, but they would either returne with victorie, or else lose their liues in the paine.

The ordering of the English armie. The earle of Surrie conceiued no small hope of victorie in this chearefull readinesse of his souldiors, and therevpon with all spéed (as the occasion then mooued him at that instant) diuided his armie into thrée battels, or rather foure : vnto the vant-gard whereof the lord Howard was capteine, his brother sir Edmund Howard was ioined as a wing; the earle himselfe led the midle-ward, and the rere-ward was guided by sir Edward Stanleie, afterwards created lord Mounteagle. The lord Dacres with a number of horssemen was set apart by himselfe to succor where need should séeme to appeare. The ordinance was placed in the front of these battels, & in places betwéene, as was thought expedient. In this order, forward they made with manlie courages towards the Scots a good marching pase.

The Scotish kings thought at the view of the English armie. In the meane time, king Iames beholding all the demeanor of the Englishmen, from the heigth of the hill, thought with himselfe, that there was offered him that daie a goodlie occasion of victorie, if he might come to fight with the enimies at such aduantage of place and number. And therfore, being hastned forward through the strenable force of destinie, or rather Gods ordinance, he commanded his standards to be raised and spred, and euerie man to resort to his appointed place, that they might foorthwith incounter the enimies, that presumed thus to séeke battell. And héerewith turning him to the lords and capteins that stood about him, he spake vnto them manie comfortable words touching the occasion offered them at that present, to gaine both a famous victorie and to reuenge so manifold iniuries and displeasures, as they had susteined diuerse waies foorth at the Englishmens hands.

He had scarse made an end of his tale, but the soldiers with great noise and clamor cried; Forward, Vpon them; shaking their weapons in signe of an earnest desire King Iames and all the rest alight from horsse-backe. they had (as then they shewed) to buckle with the Englishmen. Wherevpon, with-out delaie, king Iames putting his horsse from him, all other as well nobles as meane men did the like, that the danger being equall, as well to the greatest as to the mean-est, and all hope of succour taken awaie, which was to be looked for by flight, they might be the more willing to shew their manhood, sith their safegard onelie rested in the The order of the Scotish hoast. edges and points of their weapons. Then was the whole armie diuided into fiue wards or regiments, to this intent that the battell wherein the king himselfe stood with his standard, might be inclosed as it were with two wings, on either side one. In the right wing, the earles of Huntleie, Crawford, and Montrosse, were placed as cheefe leaders thereof; and in the left were the earles of Lenox, and Argile, with the lord Hume, lord chamberleine of Scotland, being men of great skill in warlike affaires, as was reported.

French capiteins in the Scotish hoast. Moreouer, in euerie band (almost generallie thoroughout) there was a knight appointed for capteine and guider, and amongst them certeine French capteins, the which king Lewes had sent ouer into Scotland latelie before, to traine the Scots in the practise of warres. The ordinance was lodged in places most conuenient; though by reason they marched downe the hill, their shot did small damage to the Englishmen comming vpwards towards them, and yet they bestowed it freshlie on either side one The battell is begun, and sir Edmund Howard incoun-tred with the earles of Lenox and Argile. vpon an other. Héerwith sir Edmund Howard with his wing was got vp on the hill side, with whome the lord Hume and the two foresaid earles of Lenox and Argile incountered with such violence, that this battell of Scots with speares on foot on that part, beat downe and broke that wing of the Englishmen, in such wise that sir Edmund Howard was in maner left alone, and felled to the earth, that (had not bastard Heron come to his succours at that instant) he had béene slaine there without all remedie.

On

On the other part, the lord Dacres watching to aid where need appeered, came in on the sides of the Scots, & gaue a charge on them with his horssemen, wherby sir Edmund Howard being somewhat relieued, escaped to the English vant-gard, which was led (as before is mentioned) by his brother, lord Howard, who being now also got aloft on the hill, preassed still forward to renew the battell, & to succour those whome he saw put to the worse, so that thereby they tooke new courages, & laid about them againe. Herewith the earles of Crawford & Montrosse came with their battell of speares also on foot, and incountring with the said lord Howard, after sore fight on both sides continued, with more malicious hatred than force of the parties, both the said earles were slaine, besides a great number of other; the whole battell which they led being put to flight and chased out of the field, maimed, wounded, and slaine. And though they did what they could to the vttermost resistance, in hope to haue bathed their blades in English blood; yet the contrarie came to passe, as in stories is left recorded, to the honour of the English; namelie:

> Sustinet inflictos duris vmbonibus ictus,
> Imbuit & gladios manante cruore Britannus.

On the left hand at the same instant, sir Edward Stanleie hauing begun to incounter with the Scots on that side, forced them to come downe into a more euen ground; and brought to that point with such incessant shot of arrowes as his archers bestowed amongst them, that to auoid the danger of that sore and sharpe storme, the Scots were constreined to breake their arraie, & to fight not closed togither in order of battell, but insunder one separated from another, so that their standards began to shrinke here and there. Which thing when sir Edward Stanleie perceiued, foorthwith bringing about thrée bands, which he had kept in store for such like purpose; he inuaded the open sides of his enimies by a fresh onset, and put them in such disorder, that they were not able anie longer to abide the violence of the Englishmen mightilie preassing vpon them: so that taking themselues to flight, and running headlong downe the stiepe descent of the mounteine, they escaped to the woods and there saued themselues. But the earles of Argile and Lenox, dooing what they could to staie their people from running awaie, were slaine in the same place.

In the meane time, the king, who a little before had ioined with the earle of Surreie, perceiuing that the wings of his battell were distressed, and that his enimies began to inclose him on ech side, he bashed nothing at the matter, but with assured countenance exhorted those that were about him to sticke to him, and to remember their worthie ancestors, in committing nothing that might anie waies foorth sound to their reproch. And herewith rushing against his enimies, a new battlell more egre than the first began to arise; for that battell being well appointed and armed passed litle for the Englishmens arrowes, in so much that persing the earles battell, they entered well néere so farre within the same, that they were at point to haue ouerthrowne his standards.

There were on either part a number of tall men of bodie, chosen foorth of purpose by the capteins, for the good opinion conceiued of their hardie valiancie, & the battell betwixt them séemed long time doubtfull and variable, now one while fauourable to the one part, and an other while to the other. The king himselfe on foot euen in the foremost ranke, fought right valiantlie, incouraging his people, as well by example as exhortation, to doo their deuoirs. Neither did the earle of Surrie for his part faile in the dutie of a right worthie generall. But while the battell was thus foughten in most earnest maner about the standards with doubtfull chance of victorie, the lord Howard and sir Edward Stanleie hauing vanquished the enimies in either wing, returned to the middle-ward, and finding them there thus occupied, they set on, in two parts seuerallie, with great violence.

At the same time the lord Dacres came with his horssemen vpon the backs of the Scots;

The stout sto-mach of king Iames.

Scots; so that they being thus assailed behind and before, and on either side, were constreined (as inuironed about) to fight in a round compasse. King Iames as he beheld sir Adam Forman his standard-bearer beaten downe, thought suerlie then, there was no waie for him but death, and that euen out of hand. Wherefore to deliuer himselfe from such despitefull reproch, as was like to follow, he rushed foorth into the thickest prease of his enimies; and there fighting in most desperat wise was beaten downe and slaine. And a little beside him, there died with like obstinate wilfulnesse, or (if he list so to terme it) manhood, diuerse honorable prelats, as the archbishop of saint Andrewes, and two other bishops, besides foure abbats; also of lords and knights of honor a six and thirtie.

The lord Hume and the earle of Huntleie got horsses, and escaped awaie togither with certeine bands, placed in two the hindermost wards, which of all that daie neuer came to handstrokes, but stood still and gaue the looking on. Thus thorough the power of God, on fridaie being the ninth of September, in the yeare 1513 was Iames the fourth of that name, king of Scots, slaine at Bramxston, and his armie discomfited by the earle of Surrie, lieutenant to Henrie the eight king of England, which a little before had woone the towne of Terwine, and was then preparing to go to besiege Tornaie. There were slaine in this battell on the Scotish part, of all sorts, the number of eight thousand persons at the least: some saie twelue thousand, besides prisoners that were taken, as sir William Scot, chancellor to the said king, and sir Iohn Forman his sergeant porter, with diuerse others. Also in maner, all the Scotish ensignes were taken, and a two and twentie peeces of great ordinance, amongest the which where seauen culuerings of a large assise, and verie faire peeces. King Iames named them (for that they were in making one verie like to an other) the seauen sisters. This conflict with egernesse on both sides was continued three full houres, as Anglorum prælia saith:

Iam tres integras pugnatum est cominùs horas.

Though the victorie thus remained with the Englishmen, yet they bought it deere, loosing no small number of their people, as well of those that were slaine in the field, as of others that were taken prisoners; for the Scots fought verie stoutlie, and gaue it not ouer for a little, insomuch that there were taken and slaine about fifteene hundred men as appeared by the booke of wages, when the souldiers were paid. Manie Englishmen that followed ouer rashlie in the chase of the Scots, went so farre, that they wist not which waie to returne, and so were taken of the Scots that were in the two battels that went awaie with cleare hands, and neuer fought. Also, diuerse were taken by the lord chamberleine, which fought with the wing of sir Edmund Howard, and were caried awaie by him and his companie into Scotland, as sir Iohn Fitton esquier, and others. During the time of the fight, and the night after, manie Englishmen lost their horsses, and such stuffe as they left in their tents and pauilions, by the robbers of Tindale and Tiuidale.

When the field was doone, and that the skouts brought word that there was no more appearance of the Scots, but that they were all auoided and gone, the earle gaue thanks to God, and called to him certeine lords and gentlemen, and them made knights; as sir Edmund Howard his sonne, the lord Scroope, sir William Persie, sir Edward Gorge, and diuerse others. The earle and the lord admerall departed to Bermar wood, & there lodged that night, leauing sir Philip Tilneie knight and diuerse other worthie capteins, with a conuenient power of men, to keepe the place where the field had beene fought, for safegard of the ordinance. The bodie of the king of Scots was not found vntill the next daie, and then being found and knowne by the lord Dacres, there appeared in the same diuerse deadlie wounds, and speciallie, one with an arrow, and another with a bill. But some saie he died of two, both which
were

were inflicted vpon him to his deadlie bane (and well worthie for truce breaking) by the sword; as *Anglorum prælia* reporteth:

Vulneribus Scotus acceptis cadit ense duobus,
Perfidiæ meritas fuso dans sanguine pœnas.

Scots flie at the peale of guns.

The same daie, there appeared some Scots on a hill, but one William Blackenall that had the chéefe rule of the ordinance, caused such a peale to be shot off at them that the Scots fled; or else the lord admerall, which was come to view the field, had béene in great danger; as was supposed. But now that the Scots were fled, and withdrawne, all the ordinance was brought in safetie to Eitill, and there remained for a time. After that the earle of Surrie had taken order in all things, and set the North parts in good quiet, he returned to the quéene with the dead bodie of the Scotish king cered. When the king was returned into England from his conquest made in France of the cities of Terwine and Tornaie, he forgat not the good seruice of those that had béene with the earle of Surrie at the battell at Bramxston: wherefore he wrote to them his louing letters, with such thanks and fauourable words, that euerie man thought himselfe well rewarded.

The kings thankfulnesse signified to his good seruitors in war.

On the daie of the Purification of our ladie, at Lambeth, the king created the earle of Surrie duke of Norffolke, with an augmention of the armes of Scotland, and sir Charles Brandon vicount Lisle he created duke of Suffolke, and the lord Howard high admerall he created earle of Worcester: and after this, he also made sir Edward Stanleie (for his good seruice shewed at Bramxston field) lord Mounteagle: and in March following was maister Thomas Wolsie the kings almoner, consecrated bishop of Lincolne. This man was borne at Ipswich, and was a good philosopher, verie eloquent and full of wit: but passinglie ambitious, as by his dooings it well appeared. In the time of king Henrie the seauenth it was agréed betwixt the said king and Philip king of Castile, that Charles king Philips eldest son should marrie the ladie Marie, daughter to the said king Henrie, with a dower to hir appointed: but for want of sufficient assurance of the dower, the rest of couenants were made void, and yet had the king highlie prouided for the sending of hir ouer, now after his comming from Tornaie.

1514

Wolsie described.

This yeare the citizens of London, finding themselues gréeued with the inclosures of the common fields about Islington, Hoxton, Shorditch, and other places néere to the citie, whereby they could not be suffered to exercise their bowes, nor other pastimes in those fields, as before time they had bene accustomed, assembled themselues on a morning, and went with spades and shouels vnto the same fields, and there (like diligent workemen) so bestirred themselues, that within a short space, all the hedges about those towns were cast downe, and the ditches filled. The kings councell comming to the graie friers, to vnderstand what was meant by this dooing, were so answered by the maior and councell of the citie, that the matter was dissembled: and so when the workemen had doone their worke, they came home in quiet maner, and the fields were neuer after hedged.

Inclosures of the fields about London, cast downe & ouer throwne.

George Monox for this yeare Maior of London, of his godlie disposition reedified the decaied stéeple of the parish church of Walthamstow, in the countie of Essex, adding therevnto a side Ile, with a chappell, where he lieth buried. And on the northside of the churchyard there, he founded a faire large almeshouse for an almose priest or schoolemaister, and thirtéene poore almes folke, eight men, and fiue women, appointing to the said almes priest or schoolmaister for his yearelie wages, six pounds thirtéene shillings foure pence; and to euerie one of the said almes folke seuen pence a weeke, and fiue pounds to be bestowed yearelie amongst them in coles. And ordeined that the said almes priest should on sundaies and festiuall daies, be helping and assistant to the vicar or curat there in celebration of diuine seruice, & on the wéeke daies fréelie to applie and teach yoong children of the said parish, to the number of thirtie, in a schoolehouse by him there builded for that purpose. Moreouer, hée gaue

An. Reg. 6
Abr. Fl. ex I. S.
pag. 902.

Frée schoole at Walthamstow.

to the parish clearke there for the time being, a yearlie stipend of twentie six shillings eight pence, for euer, and a chamber by the said almes house, to the intent he should helpe the said schoolemaister to teach the said children. And hath giuen faire lands and tenements in the citie of London, for the prepetuall maintenance of the premisses to Gods glorie for euer. He also for the great commoditie of trauellers on foot, made a continuall causie of timber ouer the marshes from Walthamstow to Locke bridge towards London.

Edw. Hall in Hen. 8. fol. 46. The king and the new duke of Suffolke defenders at the tilt against all commers.

In the moneth of Maie, the king and the new duke of Suffolke were defenders at the tilt against all commers. The king was in a scopelarie mantle, an hat of cloth of siluer, and like a white hermit, and the duke apparelled like a blacke hermit, all of blacke veluet, both their berds were of damaske siluer: and when they had ridden about the tilt, & shewed themselues to the quéene, then they threw off their apparell, and sent it to the ladies for a larges. Then was the king in blacke, and the duke in white, with blacke staues, on the staues was written with white letters, Who can hold that will away: this posie was iudged to be made for the duke of Suffolke, and the duchesse of Sauoie. At these iustes were the duke of Longuile, & the lord Cleremont, and there the king & duke did so valiantlie, that they obteined the prise. At these iustes were broken an hundred and fourteene speares in a short space. The king at this season sent againe into Flanders, for the performance of the mariage of the yoong prince of Castile, and the faire ladie Marie his sister, and shewed how he had prepared all things necessarie and conuenient for such an high estate. The councell of Flanders answered, that they would not receiue hir that yeare, with manie subtill arguments; by reason wherof, the perfect loue betwene England and the low countries was much slaked.

A cap of maintenance sent to the king from the pope.

Abr. Fl. ex Guic. pag. 490. Pope Iulie compared to Anteus.

On the nineteenth daie of Maie was receiued into London a cap of maintenance & a sword, sent from pope Iulie, with a great companie of nobles and gentlemen, which was presented to the king on the sundaie then next insuing, with great solemnitie in the cathedrall church saint of Paule. Touching this pope (saith Guicciardine) disappointed of so manie hopes, we may laie him in comparison with that which is written by the poets of Anteus, that being tamed by the forces of Hercules, as often as he was throwne to the ground, so often did appeare in him a greater strength and courage; such wéening had the pope amidst his aduersities, for when he seemedmost abased and oppressed, it was then that he did most lift vp him selfe with a spirit more constant and resolute, promising better of his fortune than euer.

Guic. pag. 631.

After he had plaied all his troublesome pageants, and had got by sundrie aspiring practises I wot not what péerelesse primasie, he fell sicke. And happilie he was then more full of high conceipts and trauelling thoughts than at anie time before: for notwithstanding he had brought his fortune to be equall with his desires, & obteined the thing he aspired vnto, yet his deuises and plots did nothing diminish, but grew

The purposes of pope Iulie the second and his death.

increasing by the same meane which should haue satisfied them. He had determined in the beginning of the spring and first opening of the yeare, to send to the enterprise of Ferrara which he so much desired, and his opinion was, that that state was able to make no resistance, both for that it was naked of all succours, and bicause the Spanish armie was to ioine with his companies: he had secretlie bought of Cesar for the price of thirtie thousand duckets, the citie of Sienna for the behoofe of the duke of Urbin to whome (except Pesera) he would neuer giue anie thing of the estate ecclesiastike, to the end to reserue to himselfe the whole glorie to haue simplie and onelie studied for the exaltation of the church. He agreed to lend to Cesar fortie thousand duckats, receiuing Modona in gage. He threatned them of Lucquoie, who in the heat of the affaires of the duke of Ferrara, were become lords of Garsagnana, making instance that they would deliuer it to him.

He was out of conceit with the cardinall of Medicis, for that he thought him to
cleaue

cleaue more to the king catholike, than to him. And bicause he knew he was not _{The pope a mal} able to dispose of the citie of Florence as he thought, he studied alredie new plots, _{content.} and new practises to alter that estate. He was ill contented with the cardinall of Sion, from whome he tooke the name of legat, and inioined him to come to Rome, for that in the duchie of Millan he had appropriat to himselfe a yearelie rent of more than thirtie thousand duckats, of the estates and goods of diuerse persons. The better to assure the duke of Urbin of Sienna by intelligences of his neighbours, he had of new taken into his paie Charles Baillon, to chase out of Perousa Iohn Paule, who by affinitie was verie neere ioined to the sonnes of Pandolffe Petruccio successours to the greatnesse of their father. He would of new create duke of Genes, Octausan Fregosa, deposing Ianus from that dignitie: an action wherevnto did consent the others of the house of Fregosa, bicause for the degrée that his ancestors held in that state, it séemed best to apperteine vnto him.

He studied continuallie either how he might worke out of Italie the Spanish armie, or cut it in péeces by the aid of the Swizzers, whome aboue all others he exalted and imbraced. In this deuise hée had this intention, that the kingdome of Naples being occupied by him, Italie should remaine frée from strangers; a speach that often passed out of his mouth: and to that end hée had hindered that the Swizzers did not confederate with the king catholike. And yet, as though it had been in his power to batter all the world at one time, he continued his accustomed rigour against the French king. And notwithstanding he had hard a message from the queene, yet he stirred vp to make warre, the king of England, to whome he had _{The king of} transferred by publike decree of the councell of Lateran, the name of Christianis- _{England intituled *Christi-*} simo, whereof there was alreadie a bull written, and in it likewise was conteined the _{*anissimo* by the} priuation of the dignitie & name of the king of France, giuing his kingdome to _{pope.} who could occupie it.

In these conceptions, no lesse strange for their varietie, than great for the importance they drew, and perhaps in other thoughts more secret and singular (for in a mind so fierce and terrible, all sorts of imaginations, how great and vaine so euer they be, are not incredible) after the continuation of his sicknesse for manie daies, he declined towards death: and féeling the end of his mortalitie to hasten on, and the same to preuent the execution of his high thoughts, he caused to call togither the consistorie, which albeit he could not assist in person by reason of his disease: yet by the authoritie of it, he caused to be confirmed the bull which he had published before against such as by simonie would clime vp vnto the popedome. He _{Against climing} declared, that the election of his successor apperteined to the college of cardinals, _{to the popedome by simonie.} and not to the councell: and that the cardinals schismatikes could haue no presence or communitie there, to whom he protested there to pardon the iniuries they had doone him, and praied to God to forgiue them the wrongs they had doone to his church. After this he besought the college of cardinals, that in his fauor, and for his sake, they would grant to the duke of Urbin his nephew, the citie of Pesera in patronage or vicarage, alledging the consideration, that by meane of the duke it had béene recouered to the church after the death of Iohn Sforce. In no other matter he expressed anie priuate or particular affection.

Insomuch as Madame Felice his daughter (ioining with hir the petitions of manie _{Madame Felice} others) beseeching him with great importunitie, to create cardinal Guido de Mont- _{the popes daughter hir request.} falcon being hir brother by the mothers side, he answered roundlie, that he was not worthie of that degree. He made not his affections conformable to their desires. In that last action of life he shewed no parcialitie in worldlie causes: his present debilitie could diminish nothing of his ancient resolution, but expressed in all things the same constancie and seueritie, togither with that iudgement and force of mind which he had before his sicknesse: in which firme estate and disposition of spirit,

he

he receiued deuoutlie the offices of the church, and the one and twentith daie of Februarie he ended his course of these mortal and present paines. He was a prince of incredible constancie and courage, but so full of furie & vnrulie conceptions, that the reuerence that was borne to the church, the discord of princes, & the conditions of times, did more to staie him from his ruine, than either his moderation or his discretion; worthie no doubt of great glorie, if either he had béene a prince secular, or if that care and intention which he had to raise the church into temporall greatnesse by the meane of warre, had béene imploied to exalt it by the meane of peace in matters spirituall.

The description of pope Iulie, and his properties.

Neuerthelesse, he was lamented aboue all his predecessors, & no lesse estéemed of those, who hauing either lost the true consideration of things, or at least ignorant how to distinguish and peise them rightlie, iudged it an office more duelie apperteining to popes to increase the iurisdiction of the sée apostolike by armes and blood of christians, than by good example of holie life and due curing and correction of corrupt maners, to trauell for the sauing of those soules, for whom they glorie so much that Iesus Christ hath named them his vicars in earth: and therefore it is a good consequent that he is a branch or rather a brand of the diuell, as one concludeth against him saieng:

Antith. Christ. & Pape pag. 26, 28.

Impius est igitur natus cacodæmone papa,

Turpibus & genijs est homicida satus.]

About the same time the warres yet continuing betwéene England & France, Prior Iehan (of whom ye haue heard before in the fourth yéere of this kings reigne) great capteine of the French nauie, with his gallies and foists charged with great basilisks and other artillerie, came on the borders of Sussex in the night season, at a poore village there called Brighthelmston, & burnt it, taking such goods as he found. But when the people began to gather, by firing the becons, Prior Iehan sounded his trumpet, to call his men aboord, and by that time it was daie. Then certeine archers that kept the watch folowed Prior Iehan to the sea, and shot so fast, that they beat the gallie men from the shore; and wounded manie in the foist, to which Prior Iehan was constreined to wade and was shot in the face with an arrow, so that he lost one of his eies, and was like to haue died of the hurt: and therefore he offered his image of wax before our ladie at Bullongne, with the English arrow in the face for a miracle.

Brighthelmston in Sussex burnt.

Prior Iehan capteine of the French galies shot into the eie with an arrow.

The lord admerall offended with this proud part of the Frenchmen, in making such attempt on the English coasts, sent sir Iohn Wallop to the sea with diuers ships, which sailing to the coasts of Normandie, landed there, and burnt one and twentie villages and townes, with diuerse ships in the hauen of Treaport, Staples, and other where. Men maruelled greatlie at the manfull dooings of sir Iohn Wallop, considering he had not past an eight hundred men, and tooke land there so often. In Iune sir Thomas Louell was sent ouer to Calis with six hundred men to strengthen that towne, and other the fortesses within the English pale, for doubt of anie sudden attempt to be made by the Frenchmen; bicause monsieur de Pontremie, with a mightie armie and great ordinance was come downe néere to Ard: howbeit he taried not long, but raised his campe within a while after his comming thither, and returned without anie more dooing. The French king perceiuing what losses he had susteined by the warres against England; and doubting least one euil lucke should still follow in the necke of an other, determined to make sute for peace; and first agréeing with pope Leo, desired him to be a meane also for the procuring of some agréement betwixt him and the king of England.

Sir Iohn Wallop in Normandie.

The French king procureth the pope to be a meane for peace betweene king Henrie and him.

¶ This pope Leo, of that name the tenth, before his election, cardinall of Medicis, bare but seauen and thirtie yeeres of age, which albeit was so much the more maruellous and wonderfull, by how much the election was contrarie to custome; yet the

Abr. Fl. ex Guic. pag. 633. Creation of pope Leo the tenth.

yong

yong cardinals were the principall causers of it by their industrie, hauing long time afore secretlie agréed amongst themselues to create the first pope of their number. The most parts and nations of christendome reioised much at this election, euerie one interteining an assured expectation of his vertues, as well by the present and gréene memorie of the valor of his late father, as for an vniuersall reputation that went of his owne inclinations and liberalities. To this estimation was ioined a generall opinion of his continencie and life not atteinted, togither with a gladsome hope, that by the example of his father, he would be a furtherer of learning, and beare fauor to wits disposed to studie and knowledge. So that vnto these hopes was much helping the manner of the election, being made in his person sincerelie, and without simonie or suspicion of other corruption.

The first act of this new pope was his coronation, which was represented according to the vsage of his predecessors in the church of saint Iohn de Lateran. The pompe was so great both of his familie and his court, and also of the prelates and multitudes that were there, togither with the popular and vniuersall assemblies of people, that by the opinion and iudgement of men, the pride and maiestie of that action did farre surpasse all the celebrations doone in Rome since the tyrannies of the Goths and sauage nations. In this same solemnitie the Gonfalon of the church was caried by Alfonso de Este, who hauing obteined a suspension of his censures & paines, was come to Rome, with great hope, that by the clemencie and facilitie of the pope, he should be able to compound for his affaires. The Gonfalon of the religion of Rhodes was borne by Iulio de Medicis mounted vpon a statelie courser armed at all points: by his nature he bare an inclination to the profession of armes; but by destinie he was drawen to the life ecclesiastike, in which estate he maie serue as a wonderfull example of the variation of fortune. *[margin: Coronation of pope Leo the tenth.]*

One matter that made the memorie of that daie wonderfull, was this consideration; that the person who then in so high & rare pompe was honored with the most supreme and souereigne dignitie of the world, was the yéere before, and on the verie same daie miserablie made prisoner. The great magnificence that appéered vpon his person, and his expenses, confirmed in the generalitie and multitude of men, the expectation that was had of him; euerie one promising that Rome should be happie vnder a pope so plentifullie indued with the vertue of liberalitie, whereof that daie he had giuen an honorable experience, his expenses being aboue an hundred thousand duckats. But wise men desired in him a greater grauitie and moderation: they iudged that neither such a maiestie of pompe was conuenient for popes, neither did the condition of the present time require, that he should so vnprofitablie disperse the treasures that had beene gathered by his predecessour to other vses.] *[margin: Pope Leo a poore prisoner the verie same daie twelue moneth of his election and inthronization.]*

The vessell of amitie betwéene the king of England & the French being first broched by this popes letters, the French king by an herald at armes sent to the king of England, requiring of him a safe conduct for his ambassadors, which should come to intreat for a peace and attonement to be concluded betwixt them and their realmes. Vpon grant obteined thereof, the French king sent a commission with the president of Rone and others, to intreat of peace and aliance betwixt both the princes. And moreouer, bicause they vnderstood that the mariage was broken betwéene the prince of Castile and the ladie Marie, they desired that the said ladie might be ioined in mariage with the French king, offering a great dowrie and suerties for the same. So much was offered, that the king mooued by his councell, and namelie by Woolsie the bishop of Lincolne, consented vpon condition, that if the French king died, then she should (if it stood with hir pleasure) returne into England againe with all hir dowrie and riches. *[margin: A mariage concluded.]*

After

A peace con-
cluded betwéene
England &
Fráce.

Polydor.

After that they were accorded vpon a full peace, and that the French king should marrie this yoong ladie, the indentures were drawen, ingrossed, & sealed, and peace therevpon proclamed the seuenth daie of August; & the king in presence of the French ambassadors was sworne to kéepe the same: and likewise there was an ambassage sent out of England so see the French king sweare the same. The dowrie that was assigned vnto the bride to be receiued after hir husbands deceasse, if she suruiued him, was named to be 32000 crownes of yearlie reuenues, & to be receiued out of certeine lands assigned foorth therefore during all hir naturall life. And moreouer, it was further agreed & couenanted, that the French king should content and paie yearelie vnto king Henrie, during the space of fiue yeares, the summe of

The ladie Marie
affied to K. Lewes
of France.

one hundred thousand crownes. By conclusion of this peace was the duke of Longuile with the other prisóners deliuered, paieng their ransoms, and the said duke affied the ladie Marie in the name of his maister king Lewes.

In September following, the said ladie was conueied to Douer by the king hir brother & the queene, and on the second daie of October she was shipped, and such as were appointed to giue their attendance on hir, as the duke of Norffolke, the marquesse Dorset, the bishop of Durham, the earle of Surreie, the lord de la Ware, the lord Berners, the lord Monteagle, the foure brethren of the said marques, sir Maurice Berklie, sir Iohn Pechie, sir William Sands, sir Thomas Bulleine, sir Iohn Car, and manie other knights, esquiers, gentlemen and ladies. They had not sailed past a quarter of the sea, but that the wind arose and seuered the ships, driuing some of them to Calis, some into Flanders, and hir ship with great difficultie was brought to Bullen not without great ieopardie at the entering of the hauen, for the maister ran the ship hard on shore.

But the boats were readie, and receiued the ladie out of the ship, and sir Christopher Garnish stood in the water and tooke hir in his armes, and so caried hir to land, where the duke of Vandosme, and a cardinall, with manie other great estates receiued hir with great honor. From Bullen with easie iournies she was conueied vnto Abuile, & there entered the eighth of October [where she was receiued by the

*Edw. Hall in
He.* 8. *fol.* xlviij.

Dolphin with great honour, she was apparelled in cloth of siluer, hir horsse was trapped in goldsmiths worke verie richlie. After hir followed 36 ladies all their palfries trapped with crimsin veluet embrodered. After them followed one chariot of cloth of tissue, the second cloth of gold, & the third crimsin veluet embrodered with the kings armes & hirs, full of roses. After them followed a great number of archers, and then wagons laden with their stuffe. Great was the riches in plate, iewels, monie, apparell, and hangings that this ladie brought into France.]

The mariage so-
lemnized be-
twéene the
French king,
and the ladie
Marie sister to
K. Henrie.

On the morrow following being mondaie, and S. Denise day, the mariage was solemnized betwixt the French king and the said ladie, with all honour, ioy, & roialtie, both apparelled in goldsmiths worke. Then a great banket and sumptuous feast was made, where the English ladies were honorablie interteined, according to the dignitie of the persons, and to the contentment of them that had no dregs of malice or misliking settled in their harts. For vnpossible it is, that in a great multitude meeting togither, though all about one matter, be it of pleasure and delight, there should not be one of a repugnant disposition, and (though not apparantlie perceiued trauelling with grudge) malignant mind; as we sée some apples vnperished and othersome wormeaten, albeit one bough beare them, and one trée giue them sáp.

*Abr. Fl. ex Edw.
Hall in Hen.* 8.
fol. xlviij.
English gentle-
men discharged
of their places
and offices vnder
the quéene.

¶ On the tuesdaie being the tenth daie of October, all the Englishmen, except a few that were officers with the said quéene, were discharged; which was a great sorrow for them, for some had serued hir long in hope of preferment, & some that had honest roomes left them to serue hir, and now they were without seruice, which caused them to take thought, in so much some died by the waie returning, and some fell mad, but there was no remedie. After the English lords had doone

their

their commission, the French king willed them to take no longer paine, and so gaue to them good rewards; and they tooke their leaue of the queene and returned. Then the Dolphin of France called lord Francis duke of Valois, and by his wife duke of Britaine, for the more honour of this mariage before the Englishmen departed from Abuile, caused a solemne iusts to be proclamed, which should be kept at Paris in the moneth of Nouember next insuing.

The Dolphin causeth solemne iusts to be proclamed at Paris.

Namelie, that he with his nine aids should answer all commers, being gentlemen of name and of armes. First to run fiue courses at the tilt with peeces of aduantage, & also fiue courses at random with sharpe speares, and twelue strokes with sharpe swords; and that doone, he and his aids to fight at the barriers with all gentlemen of name and of armes. First six foines with hand speares, and after that eight strokes to the most aduantage if the speare so long held, and after that twelue strokes with the sword: and if anie man be vnhorssed or felled with fighting on foot, then his horsse and armour to be rendered to the officers of armes: and euerie man of this chalenge must set vp his armes and name vpon an arch triumphant, which shalbe made at the place where the iusts shalbe, and further shall write to what point he will answer, to one or to all.

When this proclamation was reported in England by the noble men that returned from the mariage: the duke of Suffolke, the marquesse Dorset, and his foure brethren, the lord Clinton, sir Edward Neuill, sir Giles Capell, Thomas Cheneie, and other sued to the king to be at the chalenge, which request he gratiouslie granted. Then the lords and knights prepared all things necessarie for their enterprise, and shipped there horsses and harnesse, and did so much by iournie, that they came to Paris at the end of October, which were hartilie welcomed of the king and the Dolphin: but most of all of the French queene which then laie at saint Denise, and was not yet crowned nor entered into Paris. The Dolphin desired the duke of Suffolke and the lord marquesse Dorset, to be two of his immediat aids, which thereto assented.

English nobilitie craue licence of the king to go ouer to the iusts.

Therefore was erected an arch of widnesse at the tornels beside the stréet of saint Anthonie, directlie before the bastell, on the which were set foure targets or scutchions, the one siluer, and he that set his name vnder that shield, to run at tilt according to the articles. He that put his name vnder the golden target should run with the sharpe speares and fight with sharpe swords. They that put their names to the blacke shield, should fight on foot with speares and swords for the one hand. And he that touched the tawnie shield should cast a speare on foot with a target on his arme, and after to fight with a two hand sword. On this arch aboue stood the armes of the king & the queene, and beneath them stood the armes of the Dolphin and his aids, and vnderneath stood the foure scutchions that you haue heard of, and vnder them all the armes and names of such as set their names to anie of the said foure scutchions.

Decrées for the said iusts.

While all these things were preparing, the ladie Marie of England the fift daie of Nouember, then being sundaie, was with great solemnitie crowned queene of France in the monasterie of S. Denise, and the Dolphin all the season held the crowne ouer hir head, bicause it was of great weight to hir greeuance, at which coronation were the lords of England, all according to their degrées well interteined. On mondaie the sixt daie of Nouember, the said queene was receiued into the citie of Paris after the order that followeth. First the gard of the citie met with hir without saint Denise all in coats of goldsmiths worke, with ships gilt, and after them met hir all the priests and religious, esteemed to be thrée thousand. The quéene was in a chaire couered about (but not ouer hir person) in white cloth of gold; the horsses that drew it, in cloth of gold; on hir head a coronall all of great pearles, hir necke and brest full of iewels.

The ladie Marie crowned quéene of France.

She is receiued into Paris.

Before

Before hir went a gard of Almans after their fashion, and after them all noble-men, as the Dolphin, the duke of Alanson, the duke of Bourbon, the duke of Van-dosme, the duke of Longeuile, and the duke of Suffolke, the marquesse Dorset, fiue cardinals, and a great number of estates; about hir person rode the kings gard, which were Scots. Thus was this queene receiued into Paris, and so conueied to the cathedrall church, and there offered, & from thence to the palace, where she offered at the holie chappell; and from thence she went to hir lodging for that night:

The heralds reward.

for whome was prouided a great supper, and the heralds cried a largesse, and had to them giuen a ship of siluer and gilt, and other plate, to the value of two hundred marks, and after supper began dansing and pastime. On the morow began the iusts, and the Dolphin with his aids entered the field, the apparell and bards were cloth of gold, cloth of siluer, and crimsin veluet kanteled togither all in one sute, they shewed themselues before the king and quéene, who were on a goodlie stage, and the queene stood so that all men might sée hir, and woondered at hir beautie: but the king was feeble & laie on a couch for weakenesse.

The time how lõg these iusts lasted and the maner therof.

Then entered the counter part by a raile for combring the place. These iusts con-tinued thrée daies, in the which were answered thrée hundred and fiue men of armes, and euerie man ran fiue courses, and with sharpe speares; diuerse were slaine & not spoken of. At the randon and turneie the duke of Suffolke hurt a gentleman, so that he was like to die. The Marques Dorset stroke monsieur Grue an Albanois with his speare, persed his headpéece, and put him in icopardie. The duke of Suffolke in the turneie ouerthrew a man of armes, horsse and man; and so did the lord Marquesse another, and yet the Frenchmen would in no wise praise them. At this turneie the Dol-phin was hurt in the hand, so that he could not performe his chalenge at the barriers, and put one of his aid in his roome. The next daie after began the fight at the barriers. And bicause the Dolphin was not present, the duke of Suffolke and the lord marques Dorset that daie began the field, and tooke the barriers with speares in his hand abiding all commers.

The duke of Suffolke incoun-treth a tall and strong Alman.

The Dolphin brought a man secretlie, which in all the court of France was the tallest & the strongest man, and he was an Alman, and put him in the place of an other person to haue had the duke of Suffolke rebuked. The same great Alman came to the bars fiercelie with face hid, bicause he would not be knowne, and bare his speare to the duke of Suffolke with all his strength, and the duke him receiued and for all his strength put him by strong strokes from the barriers, and with the but end of the speare strake the Alman that he staggered: but for all that the Alman strake stronglie and hardlie at the duke, and the iudges suffered manie more strokes to be foughten than were appointed; but when they saw the Alman reele and stagger, then they let fall the raile betwéene them. The lord marquesse Dorset at the same time, euen at the same barre fought with a gentleman of France that he lost his speare, and in maner withdrew. When the raile was let fall, these two noble men put vp their visers and tooke aire, and with swords, the points and edges abated, they came to the barriers.

The duke foiles the Alman.

The Alman fought sore with the duke, which imagined that he was a person set on for the nonce, but the duke by pure strength tooke him about the necke, and pomeled him so about the head that the bloud issued out of his nose, and then they were parted, and the Alman was conueied by the Dolphin least he should be knowne. These two noblemen of England that daie fought valiantlie diuerse feats, and the Frenchmen likewise noblie them defended. But it happened the lord Marquesse on a time to put for his aid his yoongest brother called the lord Edward Greie of the age of ninetéene yeare, and to him was put a gentleman of France of great stature

The yoong lord Greies prowesse.

and strength, to the intent to plucke him ouer the barres, but yet the yoong lord was of such strength, power, & policie, that he so stroke his aduersarie that he

disarmd

disarmd him, all the face bare. Thus were these enterprises finished to the laud of all parties, & the Englishmen receiued much honor and no spot of rebuke, yet they were priuilie set at & in manie ieopardies.

For the declaration of this triumph, he that saw it can tell how goodlie the coursers trotted, bounded, and quicklie turned: how valiantlie the men of armes behaued themselues, and how the duke of Bourbons band was apparrelled, and bassed in tawnie veluet, and cloth of siluer cloudie, the band of the earle of saint Paule apparrelled and barded in purple veluet all to cut on purple sattin, the infant of Arragon, sonne to Frederike last king of Naples, and his band all in cloth of gold and siluer paled. This lord was but yoong, but yet verie toward. The duke of Vandosme and his band in cloth of gold and plunket veluet. The Dolphin and his aids were euerie daie new apparrelled at his cost, one daie in siluer and gold, another in crimsin veluet and yellow veluet, and another daie in white veluet and greene, some daie mixed with sattin, some daie embrodered, some daie pounced with gold, and so euerie daie in change as the woorkers fantasie could deuise, but the Englishmen had euer on their apparrell red crosses to be knowne for loue of their countrie.

A description of the pompe and brauerie in apparell at this solemne tilt.

At this triumph the countie Galeas came into the place on a genet trapped in blew satten, and he himselfe likewise apparrelled, and ran a course with a speare, which was at the head fiue inches on euerie side square, that is twentie inches about, and at the butt nine inches square, that is six and thirtie inches, this speare was massie timber, and yet for all that he ran cleane with it a long course and slightlie auoided it to his great honour. Also there was another gentleman called Anthonie Bounarme, which came into the field all armed, and on his bodie brought in sight ten speares, that is to wit, three speares set in euerie stirrop forward, and vnder euerie thigh two speares vpward, and vnder his left arme was one speare backward, and the tenth in his hand; and when he came before the quéene, he let his horsse run, and neuer stopped till he had taken euerie speare after other and broken it on the ground, and he neuer stopped his horsse till all were broken. This gentleman was highlie praised, and so he was worthie. When all this great triumph was doone, the lords of England tooke their leaue, and were highlie thanked of the king, queene, Dolphin, and all the lords, and so departed and came into England before Christmas. ¶ In Nouember the quéene was deliuered of a prince which liued not long after.]

Anthony Bounarme with his ten speares all at once about him.

Touching the accord of peace betwéene England and France, you shall heare the report of Guicciardine, which to this place maketh passage to knowledge, as oile giueth maintenance of light to the lampe. [At the first opening of this practise for peace, there fell out manie difficulties, for that the king of England demanded Bulongne in Picardie, with a great summe of monie: but at last all the differences fell vpon the towne of Tornaie, the king of England striuing to reteine it, and the French obiecting some difficultie: in so much as the king of England dispatched in post to the French king the bishop of Tricaro, whome he charged, without imparting in what nature of particularitie consisted the difficultie, to declare to the king from him, that in regard of so great a benefit, he should not stand vpon so manie subtile difficulties, but to consider that in a prince reason shuld beare more imperie than passion.

Abr. Fl. ex Guic. pag. 675.

Difficulties about the practise of peace.

The French king, bicause he would neither doo wrong to his crowne, nor ill content his people, the towne of Tornaie being verie noble and loiall to the crowne of France, caused the matter to be debated in full councell, wherein was an assistance of the principals of his court, who aduised him with one voice to imbrace peace, yea vnder the condition offered. And yet in that time the king catholike did what he could to breake it, offering the king manie plots and deuises, but speciallie to minister to him all his means and fauours to conquer the duchie of Millan. But the

The French councell accord for peace.

answer being returned into England, that the French king stood content with the resolution of Tornaie, the peace succéeded & was concluded in the beginning of August betwéene the two kings during their liues, & a yeare after their death.

In the capitulation it was expressed, that Tornaie should remaine to the king of England, to whom the French king should paie six hundred thousand crownes, and that in such sort of distribution, that the French king should make paiment of an hundred thousand franks euerie yeare, vntill the full paiment was satisfied: that they should be bound to defend their estates mutuallie and reciprocallie with ten thousand footmen if the warre went by land, and with six thousand onelie if the warre were made by sea: that the French king should be bound to serue the king of England in all his affaires with twelue hundred lances, and the king of England likewise to minister to his seruices with ten thousand footmen: the expenses to be defraied by either of them that should haue néed of the men: both the one and the other of them named the Scotish king, the archduke, & the empire: but Cesar and the king catholike were not named: the Swizzers had a nomination, but it bare a condition, that whosoeuer would defend against the French king, the estate of Millan, Genes, or Ast, should be excluded out of the nomination.

This peace, which was made with a woonderfull readinesse, was confirmed by the marriage of the kings sister of England with the French king, vnder condition, that he should acknowledge to haue receiued foure hundred thousand crownes for hir dowrie: the contract or handfastings were made in England, where the king catholiks ambassador was not in presence, for the great hatred the king of England bare to the king his maister. And euen vpon the conclusion and resolution of this peace, came to the court of France the instrument of ratification which Cesar had made, togither with his commission, and the king catholiks, for conclusion of the marriage that was solicited betweene Ferdinando de Austrich and the second daughter of France not yet foure yeares of age: but the practise of that marriage vanished presentlie by reason of the peace that was now established: and the French king to satisfie better the king of England, gaue order that the duke of Suffolke, capteine generall of the lance-knights that were in his paie, should depart the dominions of France, in whome the honours and recompenses that the king made to him ouercame all occasions of discontentment, the bountie and liberalitie of the one being no greater than the affabilitie and disposition of the other.]

In December, one Richard Hun a merchant tailor of London, that was laid in Lollards tower by commandement of the bishop of London, called Richard Fitz Iames, and his chancellor doctor Horssie, was found dead, hanging by the necke in a girdle of silke within the said tower. That ye maie vnderstand the cause of his imprisonment, the beginning was this. The same Hun had a child that died in his house, being an infant; the curat claimed the bearing shéet for a mortuarie. Hun answered, that the infant had no propertie in the shéet. Wherevpon, the préest ascited him in the spirituall court. He taking to him counsell, sued the curat in a premunire: and when this was knowne, meanes was found, that Hun being accused of heresie, was attached, and laid in Lollards tower, where he was found dead, as ye haue heard. Much adoo was made about his death, for the bishop and the chancellor said, that he hanged himselfe.

But manie of the temporaltie affirmed, that he was murthered, greatlie lamenting the case: for he was well beloued, and namelie of the poore, which cried out against them that were suspected to haue made him awaie. He was a good almes-man, and greatly reléeued the needie. The question of his death was so farre put foorth, that vpon the suspicion he should be murthered, twelue men were charged before the coroner. After they had taken view of the bodie, the same was burned in Smithfield by the bishops appointment: notwithstanding the coroners quest indicted doctor Horssie, with one
Iohn

Iohn Spalding, otherwise called Belringer, and Charles Ioseph the summoner of the murthered; howbeit, vpon his arreignement, through great sute and corruption of monie (as manie iudged) the kings attorneie declared doctor Horssie not to be giltie.

This Christmasse on Newyeares night, the king, the duke of Suffolke, & two other were in mantels of cloath of siluer lined with blew veluet, the siluer was pounst in letters that the veluet might be séene thorough, the mantels had great capes like to the Portingall slops, and all their hosen, dublets, and coats were of the same fashion cut, and of the same stuffe. With them were foure ladies in gowns, after the fashon of Sauoie, of blew veluet, lined with cloath of gold, the veluet all cut, and mantels like tipets knit togither all of siluer, and on their heads bonets of burned gold, the foure torch-bearers were in sattin white and blew. This strange apparell pleased much euerie person, and in especiall the quéene. And thus these foure lords & foure ladies came into the quéenes chamber with great light of torches, and dansed a great season, and then put off their visors, and were all well knowne, and then the quéene hartilie thanked the kings grace for hir goodlie pastime and disport.

Ed. Hall. in H. 8. fol. lv, lvj. A gorgious & rich maske wherein the king was an actor.

Likewise on the Twelfe night, the king and the quéene came into the hall of Greene-wich, & suddenlie entered a tent of cloath of gold, and before the tent stood foure men of armes, armed at all points with swords in their hands; and suddenlie with noise of trumpets entered foure other persons all armed, and ran to the other foure, and there was a great and a fierce fight. And suddenlie came out of a place like a wood eight wildmen, all apparelled in gréene mosse, made with sleued silke, with ouglie weapons & terrible visages, and there fought with the knights eight to eight; and after long fighting, the armed knights droue the wild men out of their places, and followed the chase out of the hall: and when they were departed, the tent opened, and there came out six lords and six ladies richlie apparelled, and dansed a great time: when they had dansed their pleasure, they entered the tent againe, which was con-ueied out of the hall; then the king & the quéene were serued with a right sumptuous banket.

A tent of cloth of gold with a shew of armed men.

On the third day of Februarie, the king made a solemne iusts, and he and the mar-quesse Dorset would answer all commers, their apparell and bards were of blew veluet and cloath of siluer, all to cut in subtill knots, richlie embrodered, all the seruitours in white and blew silke. The counterpart, which were foureteen in number, richlie apparelled in veluet, cloath of gold, and embroderie, euerie man after his owne de-uise. The king was that daie highlie to be praised, for he brake thrée and twentie speares beside atteints and bare downe to ground a man of armes and his horsse: the lord marquesse and all other did valiantlie, and had much praise, for euerie man did passing well, which is seldome séene in such a case. But the king for a suertie ex-céded all other.

The king and the marquesse Dorset make a challenge at iusts.

On the fourth daie of October, the king remooued to Lambeth, and on the morow began the high court of parlement, sir Thomas Neuill was then speaker. In this par-lement were diuerse acts made, but in especiall two, which were much spoken of: the one was the act of apparell, and the other act for labourers: of these two acts was much communing, and much businesse arose. For the labourers would in no wise la-bour by the daie, but all by taske & in great, and therefore much trouble fell in the countrie, and in especiall in haruest time, for then husbandmen could skarse get workemen to helpe in their haruest. This parlement continued vntill Easter, in the which diuerse subsidies were granted to the king, toward his great costs and charges that he had béene at in his viage roiall to France.

A parlement wherein sir Thomas Neuill was proloquutor or speaker.

After Easter the nineteenth daie of the moneth of Aprill, the king deliting to set foorth yoong gentlemen, called Nicholas Carew, and Francis Brian, and caused di-uerse other yoong gentlemen to be on the counter part, and lent to them horsse and

       harnesse

harnesse to incourage all youth to séeke déeds of armes. This yeare died at Rome by poison (as was reported) the archbishop of Yorke and cardinall, called doctor Benbrike, who was the kings ambassadour there: this was a wiseman and of a iollie courage. The king then gaue the said archbishoprike to Thomas Wolsie, then bishop of Lincolne, who at that time bare all the rule about the king, and what he said was obeied in all places. Now when he was once archbishop, he studied daie and night how to be a cardinall, and caused the king, and the French king to write to Rome for him, and at their requests he obteined his purpose, as you shall heare afterward.

Doctor Benbrike archbishop of Yorke and cardinall poisoned at Rome.

At this time was much communing, and verelie (as it appeared) it was intended, that the king in person would passe the sea to Calis, and there on the marches of the same, the French king and quéene to come and sée the king their brother: and for the same iournie manie costlie works were wrought, much rich apparell prouided, and much preparation made against the next spring: but death which is the last end of all things let this iournie. For before the next spring the French king died at the citie of Paris, the first daie of Ianuarie, when had béene married to the faire ladie Marie of England foure score and two daies [whom he so feruentlie loued, that he gaue himselfe ouer to behold too much hir excellent beautie bearing then but eighteene yeares of age, nothing considering the proportion of his owne yeares, nor his decaied complexion; so that he fell into the rage of a feauer, which drawing to it a sudden flux, ouercame in one instant the life, that nature gaue ouer to preserue anie longer. He was a king iust & much beloued of his people, but touching his condition, neither before he was king, nor after he had the crowne he neuer found constancie nor stabilitie in either fortune.

The K. in person purposed to passe the seas to sée the French king his brother.

Abr. Fl. ex Guic. pag. 684.

For, rising from a small duke of Orleance with great happinesse to the crowne, and that by the death of Charles yoonger than he, and two of his sonnes, he conquered with a verie great facilitie the duchie of Millan and the kingdome of Naples, and almost all the residue of the regions of Italie, being gouerned for manie yeares by his direction: he recouered with a verie great prosperitie, the state of Genes that was in rebellion: and vanquished with no lesse glorie the armies of the Venetians, being in person at both those victories. But on the other side, euen when he was in his youth and best disposition of bodie, he was then constreined by king Lewes the eleuenth to marrie his daughter that was both barren and deformed; and yet could neuer get the good will nor countenance of his father in law.

The variablenesse of his fortune.

And after his death, such was the greatnesse of the ladie of Burbon, that he could neuer get the institution of the new king, being then in minoritie, being almost compelled to retire himselfe into Britaine: where being taken in the battell of saint Aubin, he liued two yeares in the calamitie of a prisoner. To these afflictions maie be added the siege and famine of Nauarre, the manie discomfits he had in the realme of Naples, the losse of the estate of Millan, Genes, and all the townes which he had taken from the Venetians: and lastlie the gréeuous warre he had in France against verie mightie enimies, his eies beholding into what lamentable perils his realme was brought: neuerthelesse, before he died it séemed he had conquered all his aduersities, and fortune shewed good tokens of hir reconcilement, both for that he had defended his kingdome against mightie enimies, and also established a perpetuall peace and aliance with the king of England, with whome by how much his amitie was great and assured, by so much it gaue him hope to be able to reconquer the duchie of Millan.]

The king of England being aduertised of the French kings death, caused a solemne obsequie to be kept for him in the cathedrall church of S. Paule, with a costlie hearse: at which manie nobles were present. After this he sent a letter to comfort the quéene his sister, requiring to know hir pleasure, whether she would continue

still

still in France, or returne into England. And when he was aduertised of hir mind The duke of Suffolke and others sent into France to bring the French que ne into England.
Abr. Fl. ex Guic. pag. 685. Francis the first coms to the crowne. (which was to returne into England) the duke of Suffolke, sir Richard Wingfield de- putie of Calis, and doctor West, with a goodlie band of gentlemen and yeomen, all in blacke, were sent into France, and comming to Paris, were well receiued of the new French king, Francis the first of that name [who was the next heire male of the bloud roiall and of the same line of the dukes of Orleance: he was preferred to the succession of the kingdome before the daughters of the dead king by vertue and dis- position of the law Salike, a law verie ancient in the realme of France, which exclud- eth from the roiall dignitie all women; so long as there is anie issue male of the same line.

The world had such a hope in his vertues, and such an opinion of his magnanimitie and such a conceipt of his iudgement and wit, that euerie one confessed, that of verie long time there was none raised vp to the crowne with a greater expectation. He His praisewor- thie properties. was made the more agreeable to the fansies of men, by the consideration of his age bearing then but two and twentie yeares; his excellent feiture and proportion of bodie, his great liberalitie, and generall humanitie, togither with the ripe knowledge he had in manie things. But speciallie he pleased greatlie the nobilitie, to whome he transfered manie singular and great fauours. Vnto this king Francis de Angoulesme did the foresaid English nobilitie declare the effect of their commission, which was to receiue the quéene Dowager, according to the couenants of the marriage.]

The councell of France (by the kings appointment) assigned foorth hir dowrie, and the duke of Suffolke put in officers, and then was the quéene deliuered to the duke by indenture, who behaued himselfe so towards hir, that he obteined hir good will to be The duke of Suffolke winneth the good will of the quéene Dow- ager of France. *Polydor.* *Edw. Hall.* hir husband. It was thought, that when the king created him duke of Suffolke, he perceiued his sisters good will towards the said duke; and that he meant then to haue bestowed hir vpon him; but that a better offer came in the waie. But howsoeuer it was now, he wan hir loue; so as by hir consent, he wrote to the king hir brother, méeklie beséeching him of pardon in his request, which was humblie to desire him of his good will and contentation.

The king at the first staid, but after long sute, and speciallie by meane of the French quéene hir selfe, and other the dukes fréends, it was agreed that the duke should bring hir into England vnmarried, and at his returne to marrie hir in England: but for doubt of change he married hir secretlie in Paris at the house of Clugnie, as was said. After he had receiued hir with hir dower appointed, & all hir apparell, An. Reg. 7. The French quéene married to the duke of Suffolke. iewels, and houshold stuffe deliuered, they tooke leaue of the new French king, and so passing thorough France, came to Calis; where she was honourablie interteined, and after openlie married with great honour vnto the said duke of Suffolke. Doctor West (as then nominated bishop of Elie) remained behind at Paris, to go through with the full conclusion of a new league betwixt the king of England and the new French king.

¶ The court lieng at Gréenewich, the king and the quéene, accompanied with *Edw. Hall in Hen 8. fol. lvj.* Robin hood and his two hundred men present tem-chus to the king & quéene in a ma.egame. manie lords and ladies, road to the high ground of shooters hill to take the open aire; and as they passed by the waie, they espied a companie of tall yeomen, clothed all in gréene with gréene hoods, and bowes and arrowes, to the number of two hundred. Then one of them, which called himselfe Robin hood, came to the king, desiring him to sée his men shoot; and the king was content. Then he whisteled, and all the two hundred archers shot and losed at once; and then he whisteled againe, and they like- wise shot againe; their arrowes whisteled by craft of the head, so that the noise was strange and great, and much pleased the king, the quéene, and all the companie. All these archers were of the kings gard, and had thus apparelled themselues to make so- lace to the king.

Then Robin hood desire the king and quéene to come into the greene wood, and to

sée

sée how the outlawes liued. The king demanded of the queene & hir ladies, if they durst aduenture to go into the wood with so manie outlawes. Then the queene said, that if it pleased him she was content. Then the hornes blew, till they came to the wood vnder shooters hill & there was an arbor made of boughes with a hall, and a great chamber; and an inner chamber verie well made and couered with floures & swéet hearbs, which the king much praised. Then said Robin hood; Sir, outlawes breake-fasts is venison, and therefore you must be content with such fare as we vse. Then the king and quéene sat downe, and were serued with venison and wine by Robin hood and his men, to their great contentation.

Then the king departed and his companie, and Robin hood and his men them conducted; and as they were returning, there met with them two ladies in a rich

A shew of two ladies in a rich chariot drawne with fiue horsses.

chariot drawen with fiue horsses, and euery horsse had his name on his head, and on euerie horsse sat a ladie with hir name written. On the first courser called Caude, set Humidite, or Humide. On the second courser called Memeon road ladie Ver. On the third called Pheton sat ladie Vegetiue. On the fourth called Rimphon sat ladie Pleasant. On the fift called Lampace sat sweet Odour. And in the chaire sat ladie Maie, accompanied with ladie Flora, richlie apparelled, and they saluted the king with diuerse goodlie songs, and so brought him to Gréenewich. At this maieng was a great number of people to behold it to their great solace and comfort.

The same after noone, the king, the duke of Suffolke, the marquesse Dorset, and the earle of Essex, their bardes and bases of gréene veluet and cloth of gold, came into the field on great coursers, on whome waited diuerse gentlemen in silke of the same colour. On the other side entered sixtéene lords and gentlemen, all apparelled

The king and certeine nobles ran their horsses volant.

richlie after their deuises, and so valiantlie they ran their courses appointed: & after that, they ran volant one as fast as he might ouertake another, which was a goodlie sight to sée: and when all was doone they departed, and went to a goodlie banket. This summer the king tooke his progresse westward, and visited his townes and castels there, and heard the complaints of his poore communaltie; and euer as he road he hunted and liberallie departed with venison.]

This yeare in September, the king being at his manour of Oking, after his returne

The archbishop of Yorke elected cardinall.

from his progresse which he made that yeare into the west parts, the archbishop of Yorke came thither to him. Whilest he soiourned there, a letter was brought to the said archbishop from Rome, aduertising him that he was elected cardinall, which letter incontinentlie he shewed to the king, disabling himselfe in words, though his intent was otherwise; and so the king did incourage him, and willed him to take that

A parlement at Westminster.

dignitie vpon him, and called him from thensefoorth my lord cardinall. But his hat, bull, nor other ceremonies were not yet come. In Nouember, the king assembled his high court of parlement at Westminster, wherein diuerse acts made in the sixt yeare were reformed and altered, and especiallie the act of apparell, and the act of labour-ers, as by the booke of statutes more plainelie appéereth.

At the end of this parlement, doctor Warham archbishop of Canturburie, and as then lord chancellour, perceiuing how the new lord cardinall medled further in his office of chancellorship than he could well suffer, except he should aduenture the kings displeasure; for this and for other considerations gaue vp his office of chancel-

Cardinall Wol-sie made lord chancellor.

lor into the kings hands, and deliuered to him the great seale, which incontinentlie was deliuered by the king vnto the lord cardinall, and so was he made lord chancellor. He was no sooner in that office, but he directed foorth commissions into euerie shire, for the execution of the statutes of apparell and labourers, and in all his dooings shewed himselfe more loftie and presumptuous than became him. ¶ And he himselfe on a

Edw. Hall in Hen. 8. fol. lvij.

daie called a gentleman named Simon Fitz Richard, and tooke from him an old iacket of crimsin veluet and diuerse brooches, which extreame dooing caused him greatlie to be hated: and by his example manie cruell officers for malice euill intreated diuerse

of

of the kings subiects, in so much that one Shinning, maior of Rochester, set a yoong man on the pillorie for wearing of a riuen or gathered shirt.]

In the end of Nouember, the cardinals hat was sent into England, which the gentlemen of Kent receiued, and brought to London with such triumph, as though the greatest prince in Europe had béene come to visit the king [much like that of the people at Rome in the yeare 1515, when were séene in the said citie two elephants, a nature of creatures which happilie had not béene séene in Italie since the triumphs and publike plaies of the Romans. Emanuell king of Portingall sent to pope Leo the tenth a verie honorable ambassage, and withall presented him with these huge and statelie elephants, which his ships had brought by sea from India; their entring into Rome was celebrated with a verie great concourse of people, some woondering at the strange forme and stature of the beasts, some maruelling to what vses their nature inclined them, and some coniecturing the respects and purposes of such a present, their ignorance making their woonder farre greater than their reason.]

No lesse adoo was there at the bringing of the cardinals hat, who on a sundaie (in S. Peters church at Westminster) receiued the same, with the habit, the piller, and other such tokens of a cardinall. And now that he was thus a perfect cardinall, he looked aboue all estates, which purchased him great hatred and disdaine on all sides. For his ambition was no lesse discernable to the eies of the people, than the sunne in the firmament in a cléere and cloudlesse summer daie; which procured against him the more hatred among the noble and popular sort; for that his base linage was both noted and knowne, in so much that his insatiable aspring to supereminent degrees of dignitie kindled manifest contempt and detestation among such as pretended a countenance of good will and honorable dutie vnto him, though in verie deed the same parties (if fréelie and without checke they might haue spoken their fansie) would haue intituled him a proud popeling; as led with the like spirit of swelling ambition, wherwith the rable of popes haue béene bladder like puffed and blowne vp: a diuelish and luciferian vice, in the iudgements of men abhominable, and in the sight of God most damnable; as the poet in this distichon trulie witnesseth:

Dij superi fastum, fastum mortales abhorrent,
     Hæc homini leuitas displicet atque Deo.

After the end of the parlement, sir Edward Poinings laboured to be discharged of the kéeping of Tornaie, bicause he could not haue health there: and so he was discharged, and sir William Blunt lord Mountioy was sent thither to haue that roome, and for marshall was appointed sir Sampson Norton. Immediatlie vpon their comming thither chanced a great riot, raised by the souldiers, so that to appease them, the lord Mountioy was put in ieopardie of his life. In conclusion, to quiet them sir Sampson Norton was banished the towne for euer, but what the matter was I haue not found rehearsed by anie writer. After that the citie was appeased and euerie thing thought to be forgotten diuerse of the offendors were executed, and diuerse banished the towne, some fled, and were confined both out of England and the towne.

After the parlement was ended, the king kept a solemne Christmasse at his manor of Eltham; and on the Twelfe night in the hall was made a goodlie castell, woonderouslie set out; and in it certeine ladies and knights, and when the king and queene were set, in came other knights and assailed the castell, where manie a good stripe was giuen; and at the last the assailants were beaten awaie. And then issued out knights and ladies out of the castell, which ladies were rich and strangelie disguised: for all their apparell was in braids of gold, fret with moouing spangls of siluer and gilt, set on crimsin sattin loose and not fastned: the mens apparell of the same sute made like Iulis of Hungarie; and the ladies heads and bodies were after the fashion of Amsterdam. And when the dansing was doone, the banket was serued in of two hundred dishes, with great plentie to euerie bodie.]

This

The cardinals hat receiced by the Kentish gentlemen with great solemnitie. *Guic. pag.* 682. Two elefants presented to the pope.

Gu. Ha.

The lord Mountioy made gouernour of Tornaie.

A mutinie amongst the soldiers at Tornaie.

The king kept his Christmasse at Eltham.

Courtlie pastime on the Twelf night.

The birth of Margaret daughter to the queene of Scots, and of the earle Angus afterwards maried to the earle of Lenox.

This yéere the new league accorded betwixt king Henrie & the French king was openlie proclaimed through the citie of London by a trumpet. Margaret quéene of Scots eldest sister to the K. came this yere into England, & at Harbottell castell was deliuered of a daughter, begot by hir second husband the lord Archembald Dowglasse earle of Angus. This daughter was called at the fontstone after hir mother Margaret. The said said quéene after the death of hir late husband king Iames married the said earle of Angus, without consent of hir brother king Henrie, or other of hir friends ; chéeflie (as some haue thought for hir sonnes sake, doubting if she should not haue taken hir choise at home, she should haue maried in some other place, and so haue béene sequestred from hir sonne, whose bringing vp apperteined now chéeflie vnto

Edw. Hall The queene of Scots and the earle of Angus hir husband come into England. 1518

hir. But such contention rose shortlie after in Scotland amongst the lords, that both she and hir husband were glad to séeke succor in England at hir brothers hand, who was contented to releeue them, assigning them the said castell of Harbottell to lie in with apparell and all other necessaries, till his further pleasure should be knowne. The eightéenth daie of Februarie this yeare, the ladie Marie, daughter to king Henrie the eight was borne at Gréenewich. This was she that afterwards was quéene of this realme, & married the king of Spaine. This yéere also died the king of Aragon, father to the queene; for whome was kept a solemne obsequie in the cathedrall church of Paules.

The birth of ladie Marie the kings daughter, afterwards queene.

An. Reg. 8.

As ye haue heard the last yéere how the quéene of Scots with hir husband was come for succor into England, and laie at Harbottell in Northumberland, till the kings pleasure was to send for them; so now know you that he (like a naturall brother) sent for hir and hir husband to come to his court for their solace : for the which kindnesse the earle humblie thanked the king, and promised to giue his attendance on the queene his wife to the court. Wherevpon the king sent William Blacknall esquier, clerke of his spicerie with siluer vessell, plate, and other things necessarie for the conueiance of hir, and sent to hir all manner of officers for hir estate conuenient. Now when she was readie to depart, she asked for hir husband, but he was departed into Scotland, and left hir alone; nothing remembring his promise. Which sudden departing much made hir to muse: howbeit, the lords of England greatlie incouraged hir to kéepe hir promise with the king hir brother.

The king sendeth for the queene of Scots and hir husband to his court.

The queene of Scots comming to London, and so to Greenewich.

Now when she was somewhat appeased, she set forward ; and in euerie towne she was well receiued, & so on the third day of Maie she made hir entrie into London, riding on a white palfreie (which the quéene of England had sent vnto hir) behind sir Thomas Parre richlie beséene, and with a great companie of lords and ladies she rode through the citie to Bainards castell, and from thence she was conueied to Greenewich, and there receiued ioiouslie of the king, the quéene, the French quéene hir sister, and highlie was she feasted. And when the king heard that the earle of Angus hir husband was departed, he said it was doone like a Scot. This quéene sometime was at the court, and sometime at Bainards castell, and so she continued in England all this yéere.

Three queenes in the English court at once.

The king for the honour of his sister the nineteenth and twentith daie of Maie prepared two solemne daies of iusts : and the king himselfe, and the duke of Suffolke, the earle of Essex, and Nicholas Carew esquier, tooke on them to answer all commers. The apparell of them and their horsses was blacke veluet, couered all ouer with branches of honie-suckles of fine flat gold of damaske of loose worke, euerie leafe of the branch moouing, the embroderie was verie cunning and sumptuous. On the king was attending in one sute on horssebacke, the lord marquesse Dorset, the earle of Surrie, the lord Aburgauennie, the lord Hastings, sir Iohn Pechie, the lord Ferrers, sir William Fitz Williams, and twelue other knights. All these were in frockes of blew veluet, garded with rich cloth of gold, and their horsse trappers of blew veluet fringed with gold : and on foot were fortie persons all in blew sattin garded with cloth of gold,

And

And so they entred the field with trumpets, drumslades and other minstrelsie. Then in came the counterpartie richlie apparelled, to the number of twelue· and on that daie euerie man did well, but the king did best, and so was adiudged; and so at night they ceased, and came to supper.

The king the next daie and his companie were apparelled (horsse and all) in purple The second daie of solemne iusts held by the king and others against all commers. veluet, set full of leaues of cloth of gold ingrailed with fine flat gold of dasmaske embrodered like to rose leaues, and euerie leafe fastned to other with points of damaske gold, and on all their borders were letters of gold bullion. And on the king waited fiue lords, fourtéene knights in frockes of yellow veluet, garded and bound with rich cloth of gold: and thirtie gentlemen were in like apparell on foot, and fortie officers in yellow sattin edged with cloth of gold. Thus with great triumph they entred the field. Then the counterpartie entred all clothed and barded in white sattin trauersed with cloth of gold richlie. This daie was manie a great stripe giuen. The king and sir William Kingston ranne togither; which sir William Kingstone was a strong and a tall knight, & yet the king by strength ouerthrew him to the ground. And after that the king and his aids had performed their courses, they ranne volant at all commers, which was a pleasant sight to sée. And when night approched, they all disarmed them, and went to the quéenes chamber, where was a great banket for the welcome of the quéene of Scots.

In this moneth of Maie were sent out of England twelue hundred masons and A castell builded by the king at Tornaie. carpenters, and thrée hundred laborers to the citie of Tornaie; for the king and his councell considered that the garrison that was kept there was chargeable: and therefore it was determined that there should be builded a castell to chastise the citie if they rebelled, and to minish the garrison. And therefore these workemen were sent thither, which this yéere began a strong castell, and wrought still on it. In this Iustice executed by cardinall Wolsie vpõ offendors of sundrie qualities and degrees. yéere by the cardinall were all men called to accompt that had the occupieng of the kings monie in the warres or elsewhere, not to euerie mans contentation: for some were found in arrerages, and some saued themselues by policie and briberie, and waxed rich, and some innocents were punished. And for a truth, he so punished periurie with open punishment, and open papers wearing, that in his time it was lesse vsed. He punished also lords, knights, and men of all sorts, for riots bearing and mainteining in their countries, that the poore men liued quietlie: who perceiuing that he punished the rich, complained without number, and brought manie an honest man to trouble and vexation.

Now when the cardinall at the last perceiued their vntrue surmises, and feined com- Erection of new courts by the kings commission. plaints for the most part, he then waxed wearie of hearing their causes, and ordeined by the kings commission diuerse vnder courts to heare complaints by bill of poore people. The one was kept in the White hall, the other before the kings almoner doctor Stokesleie, a man that had more learning than discretion to be a iudge, the third was kept in the lord treasurors chamber beside the starre chamber, and the fourth at the rols at the after noone. These courts were greatlie haunted for a time: but at the last the people perceiued that much delaie was vsed in these courts, and few matters ended, and when they were ended, they bound no man by the law; then euerie man was werie of them and resorted to the common law.

It was strange to sée the cardinall (a man not skilled in the laws) sit in the seat of iudgement and pronounce the law, being aided at the first by such as (according to the ancient custome) did sit as associats with him: but he would not sticke to determine sundrie causes, neither rightlie decided nor adiudged by order of law. And againe, such as were cleare cases, he would sometime prohibit the same to passe, call them into iudgement, frame an order in controuersies, and punish such as came with vntrue surmises afore the iudges, & sharpelie reprooue the negligence of the iudges them- *Edw. Hall.* selues, which had receiued such surmises, and not well considered of the controuersies of the parties. And such was the administration of the cardinall vnder a colour of *Polydor* iustice at the first: but bicause the same seemed at length to be but a verie shadow or colour in déed, it quicklie vanished awaie, he taking vpon him the whole rule himselfe, for that he saw the king made small account of anie other but onelie of him.

Grafton is contrarie to this.

Whereby it came to passe, that manie of the péeres and high estates of the realme withdrew them from the court; as first the archbishop of Canturburie, and the bishop of Winchester, which got them home into their diocesses. But yet before their departure (as good fathers of their countrie) they instantlie besought the king that he would not suffer anie seruant to exceed and passe his maister: borrowing that sentence out of the gospell of saint Iohn, where our Sauiour speaking to his disciples, saith to them; Verelie, verelie, I say vnto you, the seruant is not greater than his maister. Herevnto the king, knowing that they meant this by the cardinall, made this answer, That he would diligentlie sée, that euerie seruant should obeie, and not command. But the cardinall notwithstanding (during the time of his flattering felicitie) held out, thinking scorne to be countermanded; behauing himselfe more like a prince, than a prelat, so blinded was he with vaineglorie, and drunken with the transitorie delights of the world: obstinate impediments and most horrible hinderances to the permanent ioies of heauen, as the poet saith:

Gu. Ha. in Iac. 4.

Delicias mundi fragiles quimente sequetur,
Perdidit æterni certissima gaudia cœli.

After this, the duke of Norffolke departed home into his countrie, and last of all the duke of Suffolke also followed the other, For he hauing spent liberallie in his iournies when he went as ambassador into France, also in the solemnization of his

The duke of Suffolkes hope hindered by the cardinall.

marriage, and in housekéeping since he was maried, borrowed great summes of monie of the king, which hé hoped should haue béene forgiuen him: but the cardinall would not haue it so, to the intent that the duke being behind hand in debt, should be the more at commandement. For as wealth maketh men loftie, so dooth want make them

Edw. Hall. An ambassador from the emperour Maximilian.

lowlie. In the moneth of October, in this eight yeare of king Henrie, Matthew bishop of Sion or Sittin, a cardinall (commonlie called the cardinall of the Swizzes) came into England from the emperour Maximilian.

At the contemplation of this cardinall, the king lent to the emperour a great summe of monie. But the chiefest matter that mooued the king to be so free to Maximilian, was bicause the same monie should be imploied on men of warre against the French king, towards whome the king (or rather cardinall Woolseie) of late had conceiued a grudge, as thus. True it is, that the king bestowsd the reuenues of the see of Tornaie vpon the cardinall, at what time that sée came into the kings hands: and therefore the cardinall being desirsous to assure to himselfe the same, made sute to the French king, that he would prouide Guillard the former bishop of Tornaie of some other bishoprike in France, so that he might resigne the bishoprike of Tornaie clearelie into his hands. The French king, perceiuing how much this should make against his purpose, that vpon occasion hoped euer to recouer the possession of Tornaie, would not gratifie the cardinall herein.

The cardinall an enimine to peace.

Wherevpon the cardinall turning the kings mind at his plasure, persuaded him, that the next way to abate the French kings puissance (which in the begining of his reigne had recouered Millan, and grew euerie daie in power more than other) should bée to mainteine the emperour with monie against him, so as the Frenchmen should be chastised without the trauell of him or his people. Herevpon was Richard Pase sent first into Germanie with a great summe of monie to wage the Swizzes, which vnder the conduct of the emperor Maximilian inuaded the duchie of Millan; but without anie great gaine returned from thence, leauing Millan in the Frenchmens hands at that time. And now for a new reliefe was this cardinall of Sion sent from Millan, at whose instance monie was assigned to be deliuered, and certeine Genowaies vndertooke

tooke the exchange, which made not paiment thereof at the day, although they had receiued it of the king.

In this yeare the king kept his Christmasse at his manor of Gréenwich, & on the Twelfe night, according to the old custome, he and the queene came into the hall: and when they were set, and the quéene of Scots also, there entered into the hall a garden artificiall, called the garden of Esperance. This garden was towred at euerie corner, and railed with railes gilt, all the bankes were set with flowers artificiall of silke and gold, the leaues cut of gréene sattin, so that they séemed verie flowers. In the midst of this garden was a piller of antique worke, all gold set with pearles and stones; and on the top of the piller, which was six square, was a louer or an arch embowed, crowned with gold: within which stood a bush of roses red and white, all of silke and gold, and a bush of pomegranats of like stuffe. In this garden walked six knights, and six ladies richlie apparelled; and then they descended and dansed manie goodlie danses, and so ascended the garden againe, and were conueied out of the hall, and then the king was serued of a great banket. After this Christmasse the king exercised himselfe much in hawking.

¶ This yeare, and about this time, Richard Fox bishop of Winchester builded and founded Corpus Christi college in Oxford, and minded to haue appointed the same for a house of monks: but Hugh Oldom then bishop of Excester changed his mind from that purpose by these meanes. This Hugh Oldom albeit hée were not the best learned of himselfe, yet verie much and well affected towards learning and learned men; and was minded to haue inlarged Excester college. But being denied the preferment of a scholer, which stood then in election for a roome, his good will was withdrawne from that college, and he would haue ioined with William Smith bishop of Lincolne, who then was in building of Brasen nose college; but it tooke no effect. And then being aduertised that Richard Fox bishop of Winchester was in hand to build Corpus Christi college, hee did send his letters vnto him, and offered to ioine with him therein, who was verrie glad thereof and well contented. Now these two bishops conferring togither what maner of house they should build, and to what end and purpose.

Bishop Fox was of the mind and determination to haue made the college for religious men. But bishop Oldom (whether it was bicause he fauoured not those sects of cloistered moonks, or whether hée foresaw anie fall towards of those sects) disuaded bishop Fox what he could from that his purpose and opinion, and said vnto him; " What my lord, shall we build houses, and prouide liuelodes for a companie of bussing moonks, whose end and fall we our selues maie liue to sée? No, no it is more méet a great deale, that we should haue care to prouide for the increase of learning, and for such as who by their learning shall doo good in the church and commonwealth." To this bishop Fox at length yéelded, and so they procéeded in their buildings. Wherin Oldom reseruing to Fox the name of the founder, was contented with the name of a benefactor, and verie liberallie did contribute great masses of monie to the same: and since (according to his wish and desire) the same college hath bene and is the nursse of manie notable good scholers.]

About this season there grew a great hartburning and malicious grudge amongst the Englishmen of the citie of London against strangers; and namelie the artificers found themselues sore grieued, for that such numbers of strangers were permitted to resort hither with their wares and to exercise handie crafts to the great hinderance and impouerishing of the kings liege people. Besides that, they set nought by the rulers of the citie, & bare themselues too too bold of the kings fauor, wherof they would insolentlie boast; vpon presumption therof, & they offred manie an iniurious abuse to to his liege people, insomuch that among other accidents which were manifest, it fortuned that as a carpenter in London called Williamson had bought two stockdooues

in

Marginal notes:

Ed. Hall in Hen. 8. fol. lix. A moueable garden called the garden of Esperance, verie costlie & artificiallie wrought.

Iohn Hooker, alias Vowell. Corpus Christi college in Oxford founded by Richard Fox bishop of Winchester.

Bishop Oldom of Excester is vtterlie against Foxs mind to found a college for moonks.

Oldom giueth Fox the name of founder, & contenteth himselfe with the name of benefactor.

Hall in H. 8. fol. lix.

in Cheape, and was about to pay for them, a Frenchman tooke them out of his hand, and said they were not meate for a carpenter.

The insolent sawcinesse of the Frenchmen against the Eng- ish.

Well said the Englishman I haue bought them and now paid for them, and therefore I will haue them. Naie said the Frenchman I will haue them for my lord the am- bassadour. And so for better or woorsse, the Frenchman called the Englishman knaue, and went awaie with the stockdooues. The strangers came to the French am- bassador, and surmised a complaint against the poore carpenter. And the ambassa- dor came to the lord maior, and said so much, that the carpenter was sent to prison; and yet not contented with this, so complained to the kings councell, that the kings commandement was laid on him. And when sir Iohn Baker knight and other worship-

The diuelish malice of the Frenchmen.

full persons sued to the ambassador for him, he answered by the bodie of God that the English knaue should lose his life, for he said no Englishman should denie that the Frenchmen required, and other answer had they none.

There was also a Frenchman that had slaine a man, and should abiure the realme, and had a crosse in his hand. Then suddenlie came a great sort of Frenchmen about him, and one of them said to the constable that led him; Sir is this crosse the price to kill an Englishman. The constable was somewhat astonied & answered not. Then said another Frenchman, On that price we should be banished all by the masse. This saieng was noted to be spoken spitefullie. Howbeit, the Frenchmen were not alonelie oppressors of the Englishmen. For a Lombard called Francis de Bard, entised a mans wife in Lombard stréet to come to his chamber with hir husbands plate, which thing she did. After, when hir husband knew it, he demanded his wife, but answer

Strangers out- face Englishmē against all ho- nestie, equitie, and conscience.

was made he should not haue hir: then he demanded his plate, and in like maner answer was made that he should neither haue plate nor wife. And when he had sued an action against the stranger in the Guildhall, the stranger so faced the Englishman, that he fainted in his sute. Then the Lombard arrested the poore man for his wiues boord, while he kept hir from hir husband in his chamber.

This abuse was much noted, so that the same and manie other oppressions doone by them, increased such a malice in the Englishmens harts, that at the last it burst out. For amongst other that sore grudged at these matters, there was a broker in London called Iohn Lincolne, that busied himselfe so farre in the matter, that about

Iohn Lincolne the author of the insurrection vpō ill Maie daie.

Palme sundaie in this eight yeare of the kings reigne, he came to one doctor Henrie Standish with these words; Sir I vnderstand that you shall preach at the sanctuarie spittle on mondaie in Easter wéeke, and so it is, that Englishmen, both merchants and other are vndoone, for strangers haue more libertie in this land than Englishmen, which is against all reason, and also against the common-weale of the realme. I be- séech you therefore to declare this in your sermon, and in so dooing yée shall deserue great thanks of my lord maior, and of all his brethren: and héerewith he offered vnto the said doctor Standish a bill, conteining this matter more at large.

But doctor Standish (wiselie considering that there might more inconuenience rise thereof, than he would wish, if he should deale in such sort) both wiselie refused the bill, and told Lincolne plainlie, that he ment not to meddle with anie such matter in his sermon. Wherevpon the said Lincolne went vnto one doctor Bele a chanon of the foresaid spittle, that was appointed to preach likewise vpon the tuesdaie in Easter wéeke at the same spittle, whome he persuaded to read his said bill in the pulpit.

The gréefes particularised in Lincolns bill for the cities be- hoofe.

Which bill in effect conteined how miserablie the common artificers liued, and scarse could get anie worke to find them, their wiues & children: there were such a number of artificers strangers that tooke awaie all their liuing in manner. And also how the English merchants could haue no vtterance, for the merchant strangers bring in all silkes, cloth of gold, wine, oile, iron, and such other merchandize, that no man almost buieth of an Englishman.

Furthermore, they carie out so much English wooll, tinne, and lead, that Englishmen
who

who aduenture outward can haue no liuing: which things (said Lincolne) hath béene shewed to the councell, and cannot be heard. And further (said he) the strangers compasse the citie round about, in Southwarke, in Westminster, Temple barre, Holborne, saint Martins, saint Iohns street, Algate, Tower hill, and saint Katharins, and forestall the market, so that no good thing for them commeth to the market: which is the cause that Englishmen want and starue, & they liue aboundantlie in great pleasure. Wherfore (said Lincolne) maister doctor, sith you were borne in London, and see the oppression of the strangers, and the great miserie of your owne natiue countrie, exhort all the citizens to ioine in one against these strangers, raueners, and destroiers of your countrie. Maister doctor hearing this, said he much lamented the case, if it were as Lincolne had declared.

Yes said Lincolne, that it is, and much moore. For the Dutchmen bring ouer iron, timber, leather, and weinscot readie wrought; also nailes, locks, baskets, cupboords, stooles, tables, chests, girdles, with points, saddles & painted clothes, so that if it were wrought héere Englishmen might haue some worke and liuing by it. And besides this, they grow into such a multitude, that it is to be looked vpon: for I saw on a sundaie this Lent, six hundred strangers shooting at the popingaie with crosbowes, and they keepe such assemblies and fraternities togither, and make such a gathering to their common box, that euerie botcher will hold plée with the citie of London. Well said the doctor, I will doo for a reformation of this matter as much as a préest maie do, and so receiued Lincolns bill, and studied for his purpose. Then Lincolne verie ioious of his enterprise, went from man to man, saieng that shortlie they should heare news, and dailie excited yoong people and artificers to beare malice to the strangers. When Easter came, and doctor Bele should preach the tuesdaie in Easter wéeke, he came into the pulpit, and there declared, that to him was brought a pitifull bill, and read it in this wise.

The tenor of the bill of complaint which doctor Bele read in open audience at the Spitle.

To all you the worshipfull lords & maisters of this citie, that will take compassion ouer the poore people your neighbours, and also of the great importable hurts, losses, and hinderances, whereof proceedeth the extreame pouertie to all the kings subiects, that inhabit within this citie and suburbs of the same. For so it is, that the aliens & strangers eat the bread from the fatherlesse children, and take the liuing from all the artificers, and the intercourse from all merchants, whereby pouertie is so much increased, that euerie man bewaileth the miserie of other; for craftsmen be brought to beggerie, and merchants to needinesse. Wherefore the premisses considered, the redresse must be of the commons, knit and vnited to one part. And as the hurt and damage greeueth all men, so must all men set to their willing power for remedie, & not to suffer the said aliens so highlie in their wealth; & the naturall borne men of this region to come to confusion. ¶ Of this letter was more, but the doctor read no further.

When he had read this letter, or the chiefest part thereof, comprehending (as ye haue heard) much seditious matter, he began with this sentence, Cœlum cœli Domino, terram autem dedit filijs hominum, and vpon this text he intreated, how this land was giuen to Englishmen. And as birds defend their nests, so ought Englishmen to cherish and mainteine themselues, and to hurt and grieue aliens for respect of their common-wealth. And vpon this text Pugna pro patria, he brought in, how by Gods law it was lawfull to fight for their countrie. And thus he subtilie mooued or rather vndiscréetlie

vndiscréetlie prouoked the people to rebell against strangers. By this foolish sermon, manie a light person tooke courage, and openlie spake against strangers. And as vnhap would, there had béene diuerse euill parts plaied of late by strangers, in and about the citie of London, which kindled the peoples rancour the more furiouslie against them.

Now as the diuell would, the sundaie after at Gréenwich in the kings gallerie was Francis de Bard, who (as yée haue heard) kept an Englishmans wife and his goods, and yet he could haue no remedie; and with him were Domingo, Anthonie Caueler, and manie more strangers, and there they talking with sir Thomas Palmer knight, iested and laughed how that Francis kept the Englishmans wife, saieng that if they had the maiors wife of London they would kéepe hir. Sir Thomas said; Sirs you haue too much fauour in England. There were diuerse English merchants by, who heard them laugh, and were not content, in so much as one William Bolt a mercer said; Well you whoreson Lombards, you reioise and laugh, by the masse we will one daie haue a fling at you, come when it will. And that saieng the other merchants affirmed. This tale was reported about London, and the yoong and euill disposed people said they would be reuenged on the merchants strangers as well as on the artificers strangers. ¶ On monday the morow after, the king remooued to his manor of Richmond.]

On the eight and twentith daie of Aprill, diuerse yoong men of the citie piked quarels to certeine strangers as they passed by the streets, some they did strike, some they buffeted, and some they threw into the kennell: wherefore the maior sent some of the Englishmen to prison, as Stephan Studleie skinner, Bets, Stephanson, and diuerse other. Then suddenlie rose a secret rumour, and no man could tell how it began, that on Maie daie next the citie would rebell and slea all the aliens, insomuch that diuerse strangers fled out of the citie. This brute ran so into euerie mans eares, that it came to the knowledge of the kings councell, wherevpon the lord cardinall sent for the maior, and other of the councell of the citie, giuing them to vnderstand what he had heard.

The maior, as one ignorant of the matter, told the cardinall that he doubted not but so to gouerne the citie, as peace should be obserued. The cardinall willed him so to doo; and to take good heed, that if anie such riotous attempt was intended, he should with good policie preuent it. The maior came from the cardinals house at foure of the clocke in the after noone on Maie éeuen, and in all hast sent for his brethren to the Guildhall; yet was it almost seuen of the clocke yer the assemblie was set. Vpon conference had of the matter touching the rumour that was spred abroad of the rebellion against the strangers, some thought it necessarie that a substantiall watch should be set, of the honest citizens housholders which might withstand the euill dooers, if they went about anie misrule.

But other were of this opinion, that it was dangerous to raise men in armour, bicause it was hard to tell whome they might trust: but rather they thought it best that commandement should be giuen to euerie man through euerie ward, to shut in his doores, & to kéepe his seruants within. Before eight of the clocke the recorder was sent to the cardinall with these opinions; who hearing the same, allowed the latter for best and most surest. And then the recorder and sir Thomas More (late vndershiriffe of London, and now of the kings priuie councell) came to the Guildhall halfe an houre before nine of the clocke, and there shewed the pleasure of the kings councell; wherevpon euerie alderman sent to his ward, that no man should stirre after seauen of the clocke out of his house, but to kéepe his doores shut, and his seruants within, till nine of the clocke in the morning.

After this commandement giuen, in the euening, as sir Iohn Mundie (an alderman) came from his ward, and found two yoong men in Cheape plaieng at the bucklers and a great manie of yoong men looking on them (for the commandement was then scarse

Marginal notes:

Note the saucie, brode, shamelesse, and dishonest boasting of the strangers in their lewdnes.

An. Reg. 9.
Strangers iniurieuslie abused of diuerse yoonkers.

The cardinals aduise to the maior in this hurliburlie.

Councell taken by the maior and his brethren how to preuent the hurt at hand.

Euill Maie daie as *Edw. Hall* noteth it.

scarse knowne) he commanded them to leaue of. And for that one of them asked, why? he would haue had him to the Counter. Then all the yoong prentises stept to, and resisted the alderman, taking the yoong fellow from him, & cried; Prentises and clubs. Then out at euerie doore came clubs and weapons. The alderman fled and was in great danger. Then more people arose out of euerie quarter, and foorth came seruingmen, watermen, courtiers, and others; so that by eleuen of the clocke, there were in Cheape, six or seuen hundred; and out of Panles churchyard came thrée hundred, which knew not of the other. So out of all places they gathered, & brake vp the counters, tooke out the prisoners that the maior had thither committed for hurting the strangers, and came to Newgate, and tooke out Studleie and Petit committed thither for that cause.

The heat of the hurlieburlie.

The maior and shiriffes were present there, and made proclamation in the kings name, but nothing was obeied. Herewith being gathered in plumpes, they ran thorough saint Nicholas shambles, and at saint Martins gate there met with them sir Thomas More, and others, desiring them to go to their lodgings. And as they were thus intreating, and had almost persuaded the people to depart, they within saint Martins threw out stones, bats, and hot water; so that they hurt diuerse honest persons that were there with sir Thomas More, persuading the rebellious persons to ceasse, insomuch as at length one Nicholas Downes a sergeant of armes being there with the said sir Thomas More, & sore hurt amongst others, in a furie, cried; Downe with them. And then all the misruled persons ran to the doores and windowes of the houses with saint Martins, and spoiled all that they found.

The raging madnesse of the mutiners.

Nicholas Downes sore hurt.

After that, they ran headlong into Cornehill, & there likewise spoiled diuerse houses of the French men that dwelled within the gate of maister Mewtas house called Gréene gate. This maister Mewtas was a Picard borne, and reputed to be a great bearer of Frenchmen in their occupiengs and trades contrarie to the laws of the citie. If the people had found him, they would suerlie haue striken off his head: but when they found him not, the watermen and certeine yoong préests that were there fell to rifling, and some ran to Blanchapelton, and brake vp the strangers houses, and spoiled them. Thus from ten or eleuen of the clocke, these riotous people continued in their outragious dooings till about thrée of the clocke, at what time they began to withdraw, and went to their places of resort: and by the waie they were taken by the maior and the heads of the citie, and sent some of them to the Tower, some to Newgate, and some to the Counters, to the number of thrée hundred.

The rioters malicious purpose against one Mewtas.

Manie fled, and speciallie the watermen, preests, & seruingmen, but the prentises were caught by the backs and had to prison. In the meane time, whilest the hottest of this ruffling lasted, the cardinall was aduertised thereof by sir Thomas Parre: wherevpon the cardinall strengthened his house with men and ordinance. Sir Thomas Parre rode in all hast to Richmond, where the king laie, and informed him of the matter; who incontinentlie sent foorth hastilie to London, to vnderstand the state of the citie, and was truelie aduertised how the riot was ceassed, and manie of the misdooers apprehended. The lieutenant of the Tower sir Roger Cholmeleie (no great fréend to the citie) in a frantike furie, during the time of this vprore, shot off certeine péeces of ordinance against the citie. And though they did no great harme; yet he wan much euill will for his hastie dooing, bicause men thought he did it of malice, rather than of anie discretion.

Sir Thomas Parre informeth the king of the riot and rebellion.

About fiue of the clocke the earles of Shrewesburie and Surrie, Thomas Dokercie lord of saint Iohns, George Neuill lord of Aburgauennie, and others, which had heard of this riot, came to London with such strength as they could make vpon that sudden, and so did the Innes of court. But before they came, whether with feare of the brute of their comming, or otherwise, the riotous assemblie was broken vp, and manie of the misdooers taken (as ye haue heard.) Then were the prisoners examined and the sermon of doctor Bele called to remembrance, and he taken and sent to the

Certeine lords with their powers come to London about this riot.

Tower.

A commission of oier and determiner to inquire and punish the offendors.

Abr. Fl. ex Edw. Hall in H. 8. fol. lxij.

The cause why the citie thought the duke of Norffolke bare them an old grudge.

Tower. Herewith was a commission of oier and determiner directed to the duke of Norffolke, and to diuerse other lords, to the lord maior of London, and the aldermen, and to all the iustices of England, for punishment of this insurrection. [The citie thought the duke bare them a grudge for a lewd preest of his, which the yeare before was slaine in Cheape, insomuch that he then in his furie said; I praie God I maie once haue the citizens in my danger! And likewise the duke thought that they bare him no good will; wherefore he came into the citie with thirtéene hundred men in harnesse to keepe the oier and determiner.

Now vpon examination it could neuer be prooued of anie méeting, gathering, talking, or conuenticle, at anie daie or time before that daie; but that the chance so happened without anie matter prepensed of anie creature sauing Lincolne, and neuer an honest person in maner was taken but onelie he. Then proclamations were made, that no women should come togither to babble and talke, but all men should kéepe their wiues in their houses. All the stréets that were notable stood full of harnessed men, which spake manie opprobrious words to the citizens, which gréeued them sore: and if they would haue béene reuenged, the other had had the woorsse: for the citizens were two hundred to one, but like true subiects they suffred patientlie.] Now for the due correction (according to law) of this disorder, all the iustices with all the kings councell learned in the lawes, assembled at the house of sir Iohn Fineux lord cheefe iustice of England néere to saint Brides by Fléetestréet, to take aduise, and conclude vpon the order which they should follow in this matter, and first there was read the statute of the third yeare of Henrie the fift, the effect whereof insueth in these words following.

Sir Iohn Fineux.

The statute made in anno tertio of Henrie the fift.

BICAUSE that diuerse nations comprised within the truces concluded as well by our souereigne lord the king that now is, as by his right noble father, haue beene robbed and spoiled by the kings lieges and subiects, as well on the maine seas as within the ports and coasts of England, Ireland, & Wales, by reason whereof, the truces and safe conducts haue broken and violated, to the damage, dishonour, and slander of the king, and against his dignitie, & the manslaiers, spoilers, robbers, & violaters of the same truces and safe conducts (as before is declared) haue beene recetted, procured, counselled, vpholden, and mainteined by diuerse of the kings liege people vpon the coasts: our said souereigne lord the king by the aduise and assent abouesaid, and at the praier of the said commons, hath ordeined and established, that all such manslaiers, robbers, spoilers, breakers of truces, and safe conducts granted by the king, and the wilfull recetters, abbetters, procurers, counsellors, susteiners and mainteiners of such persons, hereafter in time to come, being anie of the lieges & subiects of this realme of England, Ireland, & Wales, are to be adiudged and determined as giltie of high treason committed against the crowne & dignitie of the king. And further, in euerie hauen and port of the sea, there shall be from hense-foorth made and assigned by the king, by his letters pattents, one lawfull officer named a conseruator of truces and safe conducts granted by the king, which officer shall dispend at the least ten pounds in land by yeare, &c: as in the statute more at large is expressed.

This statute bringeth the rioters within compasse of treason.

The which statute being read and well considered of, bicause there was diuerse leagues of truces betwixt the king and diuerse other princes, as one betwixt him and the French king, and another betwixt him and the archduke of Burgognie, and another betwixt him & and the king of Spaine (all the which truces were violated by the said insurrection) it was determined by the whole councell there assembled, that the kings sergeants and attournies should go to the lord chancellor, to haue a sight of

Diuers truces betwéne the king and sundrie forren princes.

of all the said leagues and charters of truces, to the intent they might frame their indictments according to the matter. And note that iudge Fineux said, that all such Iudge Fineux interpreteth the said statute. as were parties to the said insurrection, were guiltie of high treason, as well those that did not commit anie robberie, as those that were principall dooers therein themselues, bicause that the insurrection in it selfe was high treason, as a thing practised against the regall honour of our souereigne lord the king.

And the same law holdeth of an insurrection (said Fineux) made against the statute of laborers. For so (said he) it came to passe, that certeine persons within the countie of Kent began an insurrection, in disobedience of the statute of labourers, and were atteinted therfor of high treason, and had iudgement to be drawne, hanged, and quartered. He shewed where and when this chanced. It was further determined by the said Fineux, and all the iustices of the land, that vpon the said commission of oier and terminer in London, the iustices named in the said commis- Order for proceeding against the said offendors. sion, might not arreigne the offendors, and proceed to the triall in one selfe daie, no more than might the iustices of peace. But iustices in oier might so doo, aswell as the iustices of gaole deliuerie: and as the sufficiencie of the iurors within the citie to passe betwixt the king and the said traitors, the iustices determined, that he that had lands, and goods, to the value of an hundred marks, should be inabled to passe vpon the said indictments. And this by the equitie of the statute of Anno vndecimo Henrici septimi, the which will, that no man be admitted to passe in anie inquest in London in a plée of lands, or other action, in which the damages shall passe the value of fourtie shillings, except he be woorth in lands or goods the value of an hundred markes.

On saturdaie the second of Maie, in this ninth yeare, all the commissioners, with Manie of the offendors indicted at Guildhall. the lord maior, aldermen, and iustices, went to the Guildhall, where manie of the offendors were indicted, as well of the insurrection, as of the robberies by them committed against the truces. Herevpon they were arreigned, & pleading not guiltie, had day giuen till monday next insuing. On which daie being the fourth of Maie, the lord maior, the duke of Norfolke, the earle of Surrie and others came to sit in the Guildhall, to procéed in their oier and terminer as they were appointed. When the lords were set, the prisoners were brought through the stréets tied in ropes, some men, and some lads of thirtéene yéeres of age. Among them were diuerse not of the citie, some priests, some husbandmen, and labourers. The whole number The whole number of the rebellious rout. amounted vnto two hundred thrée score and eightéene persons.

This daie was Iohn Lincolne indicted as a principall procurer of this mischieuous insurrection, and therevpon hée was arreigned, and pleading not giltie, had daie giuen ouer till wednesdaie, or (as Hall saith) till thursday next insuing. He was What was laid to Lincolnes charge. charged with such matter (as before ye haue heard) concerning his sute vnto doctor Standish, and doctor Bele, for the reading of this bill in their sermons, and opening the matter (as before ye haue heard) all which matter with the circumstances he had confessed on sundaie the third of Maie, vnto sir Richard Cholmleie, sir Iohn Dansie, & sir Hugh Skeuington. Diuers other were indicted this mondaie, and so for that time the lords departed. The next daie the duke came againe, & the erle of Surrie with 2000 armed men, which kept the stréets. When the maior, the duke, the earles of Shrewesburie and Surrie were set, the prisoners were arreigned, and thirtéene found guiltie, and adiudged to be hanged, drawne, and quartered. For exe- Eleuen paire of gallows erected for the executing of the rebels. cution whereof were set vp eleuen paire of gallowes in diuerse places where the offenses were doone, as at Algate, at Blanchappelton, Gratious stréete, Leaden hall, and before euerie counter one, also at Newgate, at saint Martins, at Aldersgate, and at Bishopsgate.

Then were the prisoners that were iudged brought to those places of execution: and executed in most rigorous maner, in the presence of the lord Edmund Howard

Edw. Hall in Hen. 8. *fol.* lxij.

son to the duke of Norffolke, & knight marshall, who shewed no mercie, but extreme crueltie to the poore yoonglings in their execution: and likewise the dukes seruants spake manie opprobrious words, some bad hang, some bad draw, some bad set the citie on fire, but all was suffered. On thursdaie the seuenth of Maie, was Lincolne, Shirwin, and two brethren called Bets, and diuerse other adiudged to die. Then Lincolne said, My lords, I meant well: for if you knew the mischief that is insued in this realme by strangers, you would remedie it, & manie times I haue complained, and then I was called a busie fellow: now our Lord haue mercie on me. They were laid on hardles, & drawne to the standard in Cheape, and first was Iohn

Iohn Lincolne the author of ill Maie daie executed in Cheape side.

Lincolne executed. And as the other had the ropes about their neckes, there came a commandement from the king to respit the execution. Then the people cried, God saue the king, and so was the oier and terminer deferred till another daie, and the prisoners sent againe to ward: the armed men departed out of London, and all things set in quiet.

Edw. Hall in H. 8. *fol.* lxii.

On the eleuenth daie of Maie, the king came to his manor of Greenwich, where the recorder of London and diuerse aldermen came to speake with his grace, and all ware gownes of blacke colour. And when they perceiued the king comming out of his priuie chamber into his chamber of presence, they kneeled downe, and the re-

The recorder in the behalfe of the citie speaketh humblie to the K. touching the riot.

corder said: "Our most naturall, benigne, and souereigne lord, we know well that your grace is displeased with vs of your citie of London, for the great riot late doone: we ascerteine your grace, that none of vs, nor no honest person were condescending to that enormitie, and yet wee, our wiues, and children, euerie houre lament that your fauour should be taken from vs. And for so much as light and idle persons were the dooers of the same, we most humbly beseech your grace to haue mercie of vs for our negligence, and compassion of the offendors for their offence and trespasse."

The kings answer wherein their sute is denied,

"Trulie said the king, you haue highlie displeased and offended vs, and you ought to waile and be sorie for the same. And where as you saie that you the substantiall persons were not consenting to the same, it appeareth to the contrarie. For you neuer mooued to let them, nor stirred once to fight with them, which you say were so small a number of light persons. Wherefore we must thinke, and you can not denie, that you did winke at the matter, but at this time we will grant to you neither our fauour nor good will, nor to the offenders mercie, but resort to the cardinall our lord chancellour, and he shall make you an answer, and declare our pleasure." And with this answer the Londoners departed, and made relation to the maior.

The queene of Scots returneth towards Scotland,

On the eighteenth day of this moneth, the queene of Scots, which had beene at the court, and at Bainards castell, a whole yeare at the kings charge, and was richlie appointed of all things meet to hir estate, both of iewels, plate, tapistrie, arras, coine, horsses, & all other things of the kings gift & liberalitie, departed out of London toward Scotland with great riches, albeit she came into England with great pouertie, and she entered into Scotland the thirteenth daie of Iune, whome hir husband receiued at Berwike, but the Englishmen smallie regarded him. All hir charges within the realme, comming to the court and returning, were of the kings pursse.

The king cōmeth to Westminster hall, and there sitteth in iudgement himselfe.

On thursdaie the two & twentith daie of Maie, the king came into Westminster hall, for whome at the vpper end was set a cloth of estate, and the place hanged with arras. With him was the cardinall, the dukes of Norffolke and Suffolke, the earles of Shrewsburie, of Essex, of Wiltshire, & Surrie, with manie lords and other of the kings councell. The maior and aldermen, with all the chiefe of the citie were there in their best liuerie (according as the cardinall had appointed them) by nine of the clocke. Then the king commanded that all the prisoners should bee

brought

brought foorth, so that in came the poore yoonglings and old false knaues bound in ropes all along, one after another in their shirts, and euerie one a halter about his necke, to the number of foure hundred men, and eleuen women. And when all were come before the kings presence, the cardinall sore laid to the maior and communaltie their negligence, and to the prisoners he declared that they had deserued death for their offence. Then all the prisoners togither cried; Mercie gratious lord, mercie. Herewith the lords altogither besought his grace of mercie, at whose sute the king pardoned them all. Then the cardinall gaue vnto them a good exhortation, to the great gladnesse of the hearers.

The kings gratious and generall pardon.

Now, when the generall pardon was pronounced, all the prisoners showted at once, & altogither cast vp their halters into the hall roofe, so that the king might perceiue they were none of the discréetest sort. Here is to be noted, that diuerse offendors, which were not taken, hearing that the king was inclined to mercie, came well apparelled to Westminster, and suddenlie stripped them into their shirts with halters, and came in among the prisoners willinglie, to be partakers of the kings pardon. By which dooing, it was well knowne, that one Iohn Gelson yeoman of the crowne was the first that began to spoile, and exhorted other to doo the same: and bicause he fled and was not taken, he came in with a rope among the other prisoners, and so had his pardon. This companie was after called the blacke wagon. Then were all the gallowes within the citie taken downe, and manie a good praier said for the king, and the citizens tooke more héed to their seruants. But the kings mercie ministred abundant matter of communication, euerie one (speciallie the pardoned and their alies) sounding the benefit of his roial clemencie, whereby of dead men they became liuing, and had susteined the seuere sentence of law, had not mercie remitted the fault and the punishment, which breaketh the force of iudgement, as the poet trulie saith :

The blacke wagon that followed ill Maie daie.

Iudicij neruos frangit miseratio clemens.

In Iune the king had with him diuerse ambassadours, for solace of whome he prepared a costlie iustes, he himselfe & twelue more against the duke of Suffolke and other twelue. His base and bard was the one half cloth of siluer, & the other halfe blacke tinsell. On the siluer was a curious loose worke of veluet imbrodered with gold, cut on the siluer, and euerie cut ingrailed with gold, so that that side was gold, siluer, and veluet. On the blacke tinsell side was blacke veluet imbrodered with gold, and cut, and euerie cut was ingrailed with flat gold of damaske. The base and bard were brodered with great letters of massie gold bullion, full of pearles and stones, maruellous rich : all his companie were in like sute, sauing that they had no iewels. The king had on his head a ladies sleeue full of diamonds. On the king attended gentlemen, armourers, and other officers, to the number of an hundred and twentie fiue persons, all in white veluet and white sattin, horsse and harnesse for horssemen, caps and hosen for footmen, all white, at the kings cost. Thus roiallie the king and his companie with his waiters came to the tilts end.

Solemne iustes betwéene the king and others.

A gallant and glorious shew.

Then entered the duke of Suffolke, with the marques Dorset, the earls of Essex and Surrie, and eight other of his band, in bards and bases of white veluet and crimsin sattin losenged, set full of letters of C. M. of gold, for Charles and Marie, and they tooke the other end of the tilt. Then the trumpets blue, and the king and the duke ran fiercely togither, and brake manie speares, and so did all the other, that it was hard to saie who did best. But when the courses were run, they ran volant one at another, so that both by the report of sir Edward Gifford maister of the armourie, and also of the iudges and heralds, at these iustes were broken fiue hundred and six spears: and then the king the same night made the ambassadours a sumptuous banket, with manie riddels and much pastime. After this great triumph, the king appointed his ghests for his pastime this summer; but suddenlie there

The king & the duke run personallie.

came

came a plague of sickenesse, called the sweating sickenesse, that turned all his purpose.

The sweting sicknesse peremptorie and deadlie.

This maladie was so cruell, that it killed some within thrée houres, some within two houres, some merrie at dinner, and dead at supper. Manie died in the kings court, the lord Clinton, the lord Graie of Wilton, and manie knights, gentlemen, and officers. For this plague Michaelmasse tearme was adiourned. And bicause that this maladie continued from Iulie to the midst of December, the king kept himselfe euer with a small companie, and held no solemne Christmasse, willing to haue no resort for feare of infection: but much lamented the number of his people, for in some one towne halfe the people died, and in some other towne the third part, the sweat was so feruent and infectious. [By the extremitie whereof, and the multitudes with such suddennesse and present mortalitie dropping awaie: it should seeme that they little remembred, or at leastwise neglected the preseruatiue remedie vsed in the first great sweating sicknesse in *king Henrie the seuenths time, whereby as then manie a mans life was saued, so now the like benefit (by applieng of the same wholsome meanes) might haue redounded to the patients.]

Abr. Flem.

* Sée before. pag. 482.

In the beginning of this yeare, Trinitie tearme was begun at Oxenford, where it continued but one daie, and was againe adiourned to Westminster. This yeare came to Calis from pope Leo, a legat De latere, called Laurence Campeius borne in Bullogne la Grasse, commonlie called cardinall Campeius, to require the king of aid against the Turke. At the request of the king of England, and also of the French king (which sought now to be receiued into fréendship with the king of England chéeflie by cardinall Woolsies meanes) pope Leo constituted the said cardinall Woolsie his legat in England, ioining him in commission with the said Campeius, the which staid at Calis vntill the bulles were brought from Rome touching that matter. There was also another cause that staid Campeius at Calis, & that was a sute which cardinall Woolsie had mooued for the obteining of the bishoprike of Bath, which benefice cardinall Adrian Castalian inioied by the collation of king Henrie the seuenth.

1519
An. Reg. 10.
The tearme begun at Oxford and adiourned to Westminster.
Cardinall Campeius sent from the pope.
Polydor.

Edward Hall.
Causes of cardinall Campeius staieng at Calis.

This cardinall Adrian being fallen in the popes displeasure, withdrew out of the court of Rome vnto Venice: and in the meane time cardinall Campeius, at the instance of cardinall Woolsie, wrote to the pope, that cardinall Adrian might be depriued of that bishoprike, to the end that cardinall Woolsie might haue the same. Which request was accomplished, and the bulles sent vnto Calis; so that then cardinall Campeius, after he had remained at Calis thrée moneths, came ouer into England, and was receiued with all pompe & honour that might be deuised. ¶ Insomuch that cardinall Woolsie had sent to the legat (whilest he laie at Calis) red cloth to cloath his seruants, which at their comming to Calis were but meanelie apparelled. And when all things were readie, he passed the sea and landed at Douer; and so kept foorth his iournie toward London.

Abr. Fl. ex Edw. Hall in H. 8. fol. lxiiij.

At euerie towne as they passed, he was receiued with procession, and accompanied with all the lords & gentlemen of Kent. And when he came to Blackeheath, there met him the duke of Norffolke, with a great number of prelats, knights, & gentlemen, all richlie apparelled. And in the waie he was brought into a rich tent of cloath of gold, where he shifted himselfe into the robe of a cardinall, edged with ermins; and so tooke his mule riding towards London. The night before he came to London, the cardinall of Yorke, to furnish the carriages of the cardinall Campeius, sent to him twelue mulets with emptie coffers couered with red: which twelue mulets were led thorough London amongest the mulets of Campeius, which were but eight; and so these twentie mulets passed thorough the stréets, as though they had béene full of treasures, apparell, & other necessaries.

Cardinall Campeius receiued with great pompe.

Now

Now when they came into Cheape, one of the mulets brake from hir kéeper, and What trumperie was inclosed in the lord legats chests. ouerthrew the chests, and óuerturned two or thrée other mulets carriages, which fell with such a violence, that diuerse of them vnlocked; & out of some fell old hosen, broken shooes, and roasted flesh, peeces of bread, egges, and much vile baggage. At which sight the boies cried; Sée, sée my lord legats treasure: and so the muletters were ashamed, and tooke vp all their stuffe and passed foorth. About thrée of the clocke in the after noone on the twentie ninth day of Iulie the said legat entered the citie, and in Southworke met him all the clergie of London, with crosses, censors, and copes, and censed him with great reuerence. The maior and aldermen, with all the occupations of the citie in their best liueries stood in the stréets, and him highlie honoured : to whome sir Thomas More made a bréefe oration in the name of the citie.

Now when he came to Paules, there he was receiued with bishops mitred, and vnder a canopie entered the church : which canopie his seruants tooke for their fees. And when he had offered, he gaue his benediction to all the people, & tooke againe his mule, & so with all his traine aforesaid was conueied to Bath place, and there rested : where he was welcommed of cardinall of Yorke. On sundaie next insuing, these The glorious shewes or pompous port of the two cardinals going to the court. two cardinals as legats tooke their barges, & came to Gréenewich, ech of them had besides their crosses two pillers of siluer, two little axes gilt, and two cloake-bags embrodered, & the cardinals hats borne before them. And when they came to the kings hall, the cardinall of Yorke went on the right hand : and there the king roiallie apparelled and accompanied, met them euen as though both had come from Rome and so brought them both vp into his chamber of presence.

Then a solemne oration was made by an Italian, declaring the cause of the legacie to be in two articles, one for aid against Gods enimies, and the second for reformation of the clergie. And when masse was doone, they were had to a chamber, and serued of lords and knights, with much solemnitie : and after dinner they tooke their leaue of the king, and came to London, and rode through the citie togither, in great pompe and glorie to their lodgings.] This cardinall Campeius for his fréendship shewed in helping the cardinall of England to the bishoprike of Bath, was considered (besides other great rewards) with the bishoprike of Salisburie, the profits whereof he receiued, vntill the act was established, that no forrener should inioie anie spirituall benefice within this realme. But for the chéefest errand that this cardniall Campeius came, he could haue no toward answer : which was (as you haue heard) to haue leauied a summe of monie by waie of tenths in this realme, to the maintenance of the warre in defense of the christian confines against the Turke.

There were at the same time other legats sent into other parts of Christendome Sée after in the extract out of *Guicciardine.* A craftie feare of the pope. about the same matter, as into France, Spaine, and Germanie. For pope Leo calling to remembrance, that the feare conceiued of the Turkes had brought no small gaines to diuerse of his predecessors, he began to feare too. But for that such feare was now too well knowne to be vsed as an ordinarie shift of the popes, when they stood in néed of monie, this practise was at this time vsed in vaine ; so that Campeius hearing that it tooke not place in other parties, left off his earnest sute about it, and with great rewards receiued of the king and cardinall, returned to Rome, not without hope yet (by reason of promises made vnto him by his fréends) that the popes request might hereafter be granted, according to his motion. There attended him to Rome one Iohn Clearke a lawier, as ambassadour from the king.

This man obtained for the cardinall, authoritie to dispense with all men for offenses committed against the spirituall lawes, which part of his power legantine was verie profitable and gainefull. For then he set vp a court, and called it the The court of the legat erected by the cardinall. court of the legat : in the which he prooued testaments, and heard causes, to the great hinderance of all the bishops of this realme. He visited bishops, and all the
cleargie

cleargie exempt and not exempt, and vnder colour of reformation he got much treasure. For thorough bribes & rewards, notorious offendors were dispensed with, so that nothing was reformed, but came to more mischéefe. The example of his pride, caused préests and all spirituall persons to wax so proud, that they ruffled it it out in veluet and silks, which they ware both in gounes, iackets, doublets, and shooes. They vsed open lecherie, and bare themselues so stout by reason of his authorities and faculties, that no man durst reprooue any thing in them. So that we sée here verefied in proofe how forcible the examples of great men be in the inferior sort; as the wise man truelie saith:

Examples of great ones what it dooth.

Qualis erit princeps, talis præfectus habetur,
Nobilitas qualis, plebs quoque talis erit.

Gu. Ha. in Eccl. cap. 10.

[But before we inferre further processe of other accidents, it were good to heare a full discourse, for the exact vnderstanding of the popes affaires, whereabouts he addressed so manie cardinals into so manie parts of christendome, as solicitors to obteine succour against the Turke. ¶ Now followeth (saith mine author) the yeare 1518, in which the regions of Italie, contrarie to the precedent of manie yeares before, felt not the least impression or motion of war, yea there appeared the selfe same disposition in all other princes of christendome, betweene whome by the operation of the pope, though happilie more with faire reason, than with substantiall counsels, was solicited an vniuersall expedition of all christendome aginst the pride of Selim prince of the Turkes.

Abr. Fl. ex Guic. pag. 756.

The pope soliciteth all the princes of christendome against the Turke.

This man the yeare before, had so inlarged and extended his greatnesse, that comparing with his power, his ambition to be greater, pushed on with manie helpes of nature, it was worthilie to be doubted, that if he were not preuented by the inuasions of the christians, he would in his pride lift vp his victorious hands against them. For Selim discerning that Baiseth his father, reduced to extreme old age, sought to establish the succession of the empire in the person of Acomath his elder brother, drew into rebellion against him, and by force of armes, concurring the corruption of the souldiors of his gard, constreined him to resigne vp to him the authoritie of the gouernment: and not suffering his ambition to staie there, it was beleeued of all men, that for his more absolute assurance he tooke awaie his life by poison: and afterwards giuing an ouerthrow to his brother in an inconter of a battell, he confirmed fullie the seat of his empire, by depriuing him of his life in publike shew, exercising the like rage of crueltie vpon Corcu the yongest brother of all. And being not satisfied according to the tyrannie of the house of Ottomanni, with the bloud and slaughter of all his nephues, or anie others that remained of that line and stocke, he was in thought oftentimes (by the rage and furie of his disposition) to take awaie the life of Soliman his onelie sonne.

The ambition and tyrannie of Selim against his father & affines.

Of these beginnings bréeding one warre vpon another, after he had subdued the Aduliti, a people of the mountaines, he passed ouer into Persia against the Sophi, to whome he gaue battell and ouerthrew him, and in that felicitie of warre he tooke the citie of Tauris the souereigne seat of that estate, togither with the greatest part of Persia which he was constreined to abandon, not through the valour of his enimies, who for their disabilitie to support their army were retired into the mounteins and places desert, but for the vniuersall dearth and barrennesse of that yeare, he fell into an extreme want of vittels: he returned soone after this expedition to Constantinople, where after he had doone execution vpon certeine souldiers seditious, and for certeine moneths had refreshed his armie, he gaue out that he would eftsoons returne to make warre vpon Persia. But indeed he turned his forces against the Soldan king of Soria and Aegypt, a prince not onelie of most ancient reuerence and dignitie for that religion; but most mightie for the amplitude of dominion,

Selim ouerthroweth the Sophi of Persia.

most

most rich in tributes, and verie glorious by the discipline of the Mammelukes, of **The state of the Soldan king of Soria and Aegypt.** whose armes and forces that state was possessed with great reputation thrée hundred yeares.

For that empire, being ruled of the Soldans, they not by succession but by election ascended to it, and to the supreme seat of gouernement were not preferred but men of manifest vertue, and confirmed by all the degrees of warre, in the administration of prouinces and armies, and also the sinewes and strengthes of their forces stood not vpon souldiors mercenarie and forreine, but of men elected, who taken of children in the prouinces adioining, and trained vp by succession of yeares in hardnesse of fare, in suffering of labour and toile, and in the exercise of armes and all customes apperteining to the discipline and law of warre, they ascribed and inrolled them in the order of the Mammelukes. There succéeded from hand to hand in this order, not the sons of the Mammelukes that were dead, but others, who being taken of children for slaues, had their rising by the same discipline, and by the same industrie and artes, by the which their predecessours had passed from hand to hand.

These not being in number aboue seuenteene or eighteene thousand, held subiected vnder a most heauie yoke, all the people of Aegypt and Soria, whom they **By whose election the Soldans were chosen.** spoiled of the vse of all armes, and practise to manage horsses : yea such was their fiercenesse and valour, that oftentimes they made warre of themselues, for that of their numbers and by their election were chosen the Soldans, and in their power rested all authoritie to distribute the honours, offices, and profits of that most rich empire. By the oportunitie of which, hauing subdued manie nations adioining, and reduced to obedience the Arabians, and mainteined manie warres with the Turkes, they were manie times victorious, but verie seldome or neuer vanquished of others. Against these people did Selim conuert his forces, whome he ouerthrew in manie battels fought in plaine field, wherein was slaine the Soldan, and afterwards in an other **The Turke slaieth the two Soldans and subdueth all Soria and Aegypt.** battell was taken prisoner the other Soldan his successor, whome he caused to be publikelie murthered with an vnworthie kind of torment. Thus hauing satisfied his bloudie humour with such great slaughters, and also wasted the name of the Mammelukes, he procéeded to the inuasion of Cairo a most populous citie, wherein were resident the Soldans, and in short time subdued vnder his iurisdiction all Soria and Aegypt.

These drew vnto him so great an increase of impérie, such amplification of tribute and reuenue, and remoouing the impediments of so mightie enimies, and of so great reputation, that with great reason hée was to be feared of the christians. A feare which tooke his degrees of increasing by this consideration, that to so great a power and valour was ioined a settled impression of ambition to beare rule, & by manie victories, to make glorious his name to all posterities : wherein reading oftentimes the legends and actions of the great Alexander, and Iulius Cesar, he séemed to suffer **The Turks ambition hath no bounds or circumscription.** griefe and perplexitie of mind, that his actions & and exploits of warre could in no wise hold comparison with so manie great triumphs and victories. In which humour, refurnishing continuallie his armies, and building of new a great number of ships, and leuieng all prouisions necessarie for the warre, it was fered when his preparations were accomplished, that he would inuade Rhodes, the bulworke of the christians in the east parts, or else the kingdome of Hungaria, made fearefull by the valour of the inhabitants of the nation of the Turks, which at that time was in diuision amongst themselues, and made weake by the minoritie of their king, who was gouerned by the priests and barons of the realme.

Others were of opinion, that he had addressed all his thoughts to the inuasion of Italie, taking his incouragement vpon the discord of the potentates and naturall princes, whome he knew to be much shaken with the long warres of those regions.

To

To this was ioined the memorie of Mahomet his grandfather, who with a power farre lesse than his, and with a small nauie sent vpon the coasts of the realme of Naples, had woone by assault the citie of Otronto: and (sauing he was preuented by death) had both opened the way, and established the meane to persecute the regions of Italie with continuall vexations: so that the pope togither with the whole court of Rome being made astonished with so great successe, and no lesse prouident to eschew so great a danger, making their first recourse vnto the aid and succour of God, caused to be celebrated through Rome most deuout inuocations, which he did assist in presence bare-footed.

And afterwards calling vpon the helpe of men, he wrote letters to all christian princes, both admonishing them of the perill, and persuading them to lay aside all ciuill discords and contentions, and attend spéedilie to the defense of religion & their common safetie, which he affirmed would more and more take increase of most greiu-ous danger, if with the vnitie of minds, and concordances of forces, they sought not to transferre the warre into the empire of the Turks, & inuade the enimie in his owne countrie. Vpon this aduise and admonition, was taken the examination and opinion of men of warre, and persons skilfull in the discouerie of countries, the disposing of prouinces, and of the nature and vsage of the forces and weapons of that kingdome, and therevpon a resolution was set downe to make great leuies of monie by voluntarie contributions of princes, and vniuersall imposts of all people of christendome.

It was thought necessarie that Cesar accompanied with the horssemen of Hunga-ria and Polonia, nations warlike, and practised in continuall warre against the Turke, and also with the footmen of Germanie, should saile along Danubi into Bossina called ancientlie Misia, and from thence to Thracia, and so to draw neare Constantinople, the seat of the empire of Ottomanes: that the French king with all the forces of his kingdome, the Venetians, and the other potentates of Italie, accompanied with the infanterie of Swizzerland, should passe from the port of Brindisi in Albania, a passage verie easie & short, to inuade Greece, a countrie full of christian inhabitants, and for the intollerable yoke of the Turkes, most readie to rebell: that the kings of Spaine, of England, and Portugall, assembling their forces togither in Cartagenia, and the ports thereabouts, should take their course with two hundred ships full of Spanish footmen and other souldiers, to the streict of Galipoli, to make rodes vp to Constanti-nople, hauing first of all subdued the castels and forts standing vpon the mouth of the streict: and the pope to take the same course, imbarking at Ancona, with an hundred ships armed.

With these preparations, séeming sufficient to couer the land, and ouerspread the sea, it was thought that of a warre so full of deuotion and pietie, there could not be but hoped a happie end, speciallie adding the inuocation of God, and so manie seuerall inuasions made at one time against the Turkes, who make their principall foundation of defense, to fight in the plaine field. These matters were solicited with no small in-dustrie, and to stop all matter of imputation against the office of the pope, the minds of princes were throughlie sounded, and an vniuersall truce for fiue yeares betweene all the princes of christendome, published in the consistorie, vpon paine of most grieuous censure to such as should impugne it. So that the negociation continuing for all things apperteining to so great an enterprise, he assigned ambassadours to all princes: to the emperour he sent the cardinall S. Sisto, to the French king he dispatch-ed the cardinall of S. Maria in Portico, the cardinall Giles to the king of Spaine, and the cardinall Campeius to the king of England.

All cardinals of authoritie, either for their experience in affaires, or for opinion of their doctrine, or for their familiaritie with the pope. All which things albeit they were begun with great hope and expectation, and the vniuersall truce accepted of all men, and all men with no little ostentation and brauerie of words, made shew of their

readinesse

readinesse with their forces to aduance so good a cause: yet, what with the consideration of the perill estéemed vncerteine and farre off, and extending more to one prince than to another, and what by the difficulties and long tract of time that appeared, to introduce a zeale and vnion so vniuersall, priuat interests and respects particular séemed to preuaile more, than the pietie of the expedition: insomuch that the negociation stood not onelie naked of all hope and issue, but also it was followed verie lightlie, and as it were by ceremonie.

The popes negociation naked of all hope & issue.

This being one propertie in the nature of men, that those things which in their beginnings appeare fearefull, doo dailie take such degrées of diminution and vanishing, that vnles the first feares be reuiued by new accidents, they lead men in processe of time to securitie. Which propertie of negligence, both touching the affaires publike, and affection of priuate and particular men was well confirmed by the death that succéeded not long after to Selim, who, hauing by a long maladie suspended the preparations of the warre, was in the end consumed by the passions of his disease, and so passed into the other life, leauing so great an empire to Soliman his sonne, yoong in yeares and iudged to beare a wit and mind not so disposed to the warres, although afterwards the effects declared the contrarie.

The death of Selim and succession of Soliman.

At this time appeared betweene the pope and the French king a most great and streict coniunction: for the king gaue to wife to Laurence his nephue, the ladie Magdalen noblie descended of the bloud and house of Bullognie, with a yearelie reuenue of ten thousand crownes, whereof part was of the kings gift, and the residue rising of hir owne patrimonie. Besides, the king hauing borne to him a sonne, the pope required that in his baptisme, he would impose vpon him his name. By which occasion Laurence making preparations to go to marrie his new wife, for his more spéed, performed his iournie by post into France, where he was receiued with manie amities and much honour of the king, to whom he became verie gratious and of deare account, the rather for that (besides other generall respects) he made a dedication of himselfe wholie to the king, with promise to follow in all accidents, his fortune.]

Aliance betwixt the pope & the French king.

And now to returne to cardinall Woolsie, who grew so into excéeding pride, that he thought himselfe equall with the king. For when he said masse which he did oftener to shew his pompe, rather than for anie deuotion) he made dukes and earles to serue him of wine, with a say taken, and to hold to him the bason at the lauatorie. Thus was the pride of the cardinall and other priests so past the compasse of reason, that in maner all good persons abhorred and disdeined it [as altogither degenerating from the example of Christ & his poore traine, of whome in name and title they séemed to be professors, but of their maners and trade of life open defiers; yea in such manifest sort, both in apparell and diet, as also in all other respects, that few there were (if they perceiued anie thing by discretion) but saw the euident abuses of their behauiours, tending greatlie to the dishonour of the place which they possessed, as also to the no small offense of the modester sort of the cleargie, wherof some did so well like of this ruffling and masking presbyterie, that they abhorred it as strong poison in their broth.]

The excessiue pride of the cardinall.

It fortuned that the archbishop of Canturburie wrote to the cardinall, anon after that he had receiued his power legantine, the which letter after his old familiar maner he subscribed thus: Your brother William of Canturburie. With which subscription, bicause the archbishop wrote him brother, he was so much offended, as though the archbishop had doone him great iniurie, that he could not temper his mood, but in high displeasure said, that he would so worke within a while, that he should well vnderstand how he was his superiour, and not his brother. When the archbishop (being a sober wise man) heard of the messenger that bare the letter, how the cardinall tooke it not well, but so as it might seeme there was a great fault in the letter, and reported the tale as one that misliked the cardinals presumption herein: Peace (said the archbishop)

The cardinall taketh it in scorne to be called brother by the archbishop.

bishop) knowest thou not how the man is become mad with too much ioy. And thus the cardinall forgetting to hold the right path of true laud and praise, sought to be feared rather than beloued of all good men.

In this meane time the French king greatlie coueting to redeeme the citie of Tornaie out of the hands of the king of England, and knowing that he must make waie there-vnto thorough the cardinals freendship, ceassed not with high gifts to win his good will, and moreouer in often writing to him, exalted him with titles of honor, and so magnified him, that the cardinall, as one tickled with vaine-glorie more than can be imagined, thought that he could not doo pleasure enough to the French king, that did estéeme so much of him. Herevpon the French king hoping to compasse his desire, after he perceiued the cardinals good will towards him, signified his meaning vnto the said cardinall; who found meanes to breake thereof to the king, in such wise as he was contented to heare the French kings ambassadors, that should be sent hither to talke of that matter.

The French king writeth to cardinall Woolsie.

The French king then vnderstanding the king of England his pleasure, sent ouer the lord Boniuet high admerall of France, and the bishop of Paris as chéefe ambassadours, accompanied with a great sort of lustie gentlemen of the French kings court, to the number of foure score and aboue, on whome attended such a companie of other of the meaner sort, that the whole number amounted to twelue hundred one and other, which were thought to be manie for an ambassage. ¶ On mondaie the twentie seuenth daie of September, the earle of Surrie high admerall of England, in a coat of rich tissue cut on cloth of siluer, on a great courser richlie trapped, and a great whistle of gold, set with stones and pearle, hanging at a great and masse chaine baudricke wise, accompanied with an hundred and sixtie gentlemen, richlie apparelled, on goodlie horsses came to Blackeheath, and there amiablie receiued the ambassadours of France. The yoong gallants of France had coats garded with one colour, cut in ten or twelue parts verie richlie to behold: and so all the Englishmen accoupled themselues with the Frenchmen louinglie togither, and so road to London. After the two admerals followed foure and twentie of the French kings gard, accompanied with foure and twentie of the English gard. And after them a great number of archers, to the nnmber of foure hundred. And in this order they passed thorough the citie to tailors hall, and there the chéefe ambassadours were lodged, and the remnant in merchants houses about.

Ambassadors from the French king.

An vnreasonable number for an ambassage.
Abr. Fl. ex *Ed. Hall in Hen.* 8. *fol.* lxv.
The ambassadors of Frãce receiued on Blackeheath.

When these lords were in their lodgings, then the French harder men opened their wares, & made the tailors hall like the paund of a mart. At this dooing manie an Englishman grudged, but it auailed not. The last daie of September, the French ambassadours tooke their barge, and came to Gréenewich. The admerall was in a gowne of cloath of siluer raised, furred with rich sables; and all his companie almost were in a new fashioned garment, called a shemew, which was in effect a gowne cut in the middle. The gentlemen of France were brought into the kings presence, where the bishop of Paris made a solemne oration; which being ended, & answer made thereto, the king highlie interteined the admerall and his companie, and so did all the English lords and gentlemen.]

The French ambassadors come to the court.

The ambassadours after this were dailie in councell, till at length an agréement was concluded, vnder pretense of a marriage to be had betweene the Dolphin of France, and the ladie Marie, daughter to the king of England: in name of whose marriage monie, Tornaie should be deliuered vnto the French king, he paieng to the king of England for the castell which he had made in that citie, six hundred thousand crownes, to be paid in twelue yeares space, that is to saie, fiftie thousand euerie yeare during that terme. And if the marriage chanced not to take effect, then should Tornaie be againe restored to the king of England. For performance of which article, hostages should be deliuered, that is to wit, monsieur de Montmorancie, monsieur de Montpesac, monsieur

Articles of agréement for the deliuerie of Tornaie.

monsieur de Moie, monsieur de Morret.   Moreouer the French king should paie to the lord cardinall of England a thousand marks of yearelie pension, in recompense of his reuenues before time receiued of the bishoprike of Tornaie, and likewise to other of the kings councell he should also giue certeine summes of monie as yearelie pensions, in like maner as his ancestors had doone to the councellors of the kings of England before time.

The French K. agreed to call backe the duke of Albanie out of Scotland, that the suertie of K. Iames might the better be prouided for, and lesse occasion of trouble ministred to the king of England.   And further the French king was contented that the said king Iames should be receiued as a confederat in this peace.   When all things were concluded, the king and the ambassadours road to the cathedrall church of saint Paule in London from Durham place, where the cardinall of England sang the masse in most pompous maner : and after that masse was ended, doctor Pace the kings secretarie made an eloquent oration in praise of peace : and that doone, the king and his nobles with the ambassadours went to the bishops palace, and there dined, and after dinner, the king rode againe to Durham place.   That night the cardinall of Yorke made to the ambassadors a solemne banket, and them accompanied manie lords and ladies of England.   And when the banket was doone, in came six minstrels, richlie disguised, and after them followed thrée gentlemen in wide and long gownes of crimsin sattin, euerie one hauing a cup of gold in their hands. *Edw. Hall. in H. 8. fol. lxv.*

The first cup was full of angels and roials, the second had diuerse bales of dice, and the third had certeine paires of cards. These gentlemen offered to plaie at mumchance, and when they had plaied the length of the first boord, then the minstrels blew vp, and then entered into the chamber certeine ladies disguised, on whome attended twelue knights disguised bearing torches.   All these thirtie & six persons were in one sute of fine gréene sattin, all couered ouer with cloth of gold, vnder tied togither with laces of gold, and masking hoods on their heads : the ladies had tiers made of braids of damaske gold with long haire of white gold.   All these maskers dansed at one time, and after they had dansed, they put off their visors, and so were they all knowne.   The admerall and lords of France hartilie thanked the king, that it pleased him to visit them with such disport.   Then the king & his companie were banketted, and had high chéere : and so they departed euerie man to his lodging.   The eight of October at Gréenewich, was soong a solemne masse by the bishop of Durham, and after masse, doctor Tunstall, maister of the rolles, made an eloquent proposition in praise of the matrimonie to be had betwixt the Dolphin and the ladie Marie.   All that daie were the strangers feasted, and at night they were brought into the hall, where was a rocke full of all maner of stones, verie artificiallie made, and on the top stood fiue trées, the first an oliue tree, on which hanged a shield of the armes of the church of Rome; the second a pineaple trée, with the armes of the emperour; the third a rosier, with the armes of England; the fourth a branch of lillies, bearing the armes of France; and the fift a pomegranat trée, bearing the armes of Spaine : in token that all these fiue potentats were ioined togither in one league against the enimies of Christes faith. *Doctor Tunstall maister of the rolles.* *Edw. Hall in H. 8. fol. lxvj. A pageant very sumptuous and of notable deuise.*

In and vpon the middest of the rocke sate a faire ladie, richlie apparelled with a dolphin in hir lap. In this rocke were ladies and gentlemen apparelled in crimsin sattin, couered ouer with floures of purple sattin, embrodered vpon with wrethes of gold, knit togither with golden laces, and on euerie floure a hart of gold moouing. The ladies apparell was after the fashion of Inde, with kerchifes of pleasance, hatched with fine gold, and set with letters of Gréeke in gold of bullion; and the edges of their kerchifes were garnished with hanging perle. These gentlemen and ladies sat on the nether part of the rocke, and out of a caue in the said rocke came ten knights, armed at all points, and fought togither a faire tournie. And when they were

seuered

seuered and departed, the disguisors descended from the rocke, and dansed a great space: and suddenlie the rocke mooued and receiued the disguisors, and immediatlie closed againe.

Then entered a person called Report, apparelled in crimsin sattin full of toongs, sitting on a flieng horsse with wings and féet of gold called Pegasus. This person in French declared the mening of the rocke, the trées, and the tournie. After this pastime rended, the king and the ambassadours were serued at a banket with two hundred and sixtie dishes, and after that a voidee of spices with sixtie spice plates of siluer and gilt, as great as men with ease might beare. This night the cupboord in the hall was of twelue stages all of plate of gold, and no gilt plate. When that euerie man had béene plentiouslie serued, the tables were taken vp, and the king with the quéene and all the strangers departed to their lodgings.

After diuerse iusts &.feasts made for the said ambassadours by the king and lords: sir Thomas Exmew maior of London made to them a costlie dinner at Goldsmiths hall, which dinner they highlie praised, it was so well ordered. And when the time came, they tooke their leaue of the king, the quéene, and the kings councell, and deliuered into the kings possession their foure hostages (as you haue heard before.) At which departing the king gaue to the admerall of France a garnish of gilt vessell, a paire of couerd basens gilt, twelue great gilt boles, foure paire of great gilt pots, a standing cup of gold, garnished with great pearles: and to some other also, he gaue plate, to some chains of gold, to some rich apparell, and to some great horsses with rich bards, so that euerie gentleman was well rewarded; which liberalitie the strangers much praised: and after that all their trusses were readie they departed towards the sea, and tooke ship and landed at Bullogne.]

Shortlie after their departure, the earle of Worcester, lord chamberleine, the bishop of Elie, the lord of saint Iohns, sir Nicholas Vaux, sir Iohn Pechie, sir Thomas Bullen, as ambassadours from the king of England, accompanied with thrée score and ten knights, gentlemen and yeomen, to the number of foure hundred and aboue, passed the sea to Calis, and so from thense went to Paris, where they were noblie receiued, & being brought to the French kings presence, the bishop of Elie made a solemne oration touching the mariage and peace concluded. [To interteine the English ambassadours and gentlemen, the French king had made a banketting house in the bastill of Paris betwéene foure old walles. This house was couered with cords streined by craft, and éuerie cord was woond about with box, and so laid crossewise one ouer an other in fret, and at the méetings a great knop gilt with gold foile. Ouer their cords was streined woollen cloaths of light blew: this roofe was foure score foot high, and on euerie side three stages high: all the pillers of the stages were couered with antike works, & the brests of the stages curiouslie wrought with armes, viniets, and branches: the roofe was set full of starres gilt & furnished with glasses betwéene the frets. In this house was two hundred and twelue branches gilt hanged, & on euerie branch a great number of lights of white wax.

Diuerse sorts of maskes were shewed also that night: and at euerie side of the palace a great cupboord of massie plate of much greatnesse was set, the French king welcomming the lords and ambassadours with good countenance.] Here is to be remembred, that immediatlie after the conclusion of the marriage, a rumor was raised, that the Dolphin was dead before, and that this marriage was but a colourable pretext, deuised of the Frenchmen for a policie to come by their purpose: and therefore, after that the English ambassadours had beene feasted and interteined with banketting and princelie pastime, the bishop of Elie, with sir Thomas Bullen, and sir Richard Weston, were appointed to go vnto Coniacke to see the Dolphin, where they were honorablie receiued, and brought vnto the presence of the Dolphin, being a goodlie yoong child, whome they kissed and imbraced in most louing wise.

The

The earle of Worcester, and with him sir Nicholas Vaux, sir Iohn Pechie, sir Edward Belknap, and diuerse others at the same time, tooke leaue of the French king, and rode to Tornaie to sée the citie deliuered to the Frenchmen. Wherevpon, the eight of Februarie, the lord Chatillon came thither with one and twentie hundred men; and after some controuersie mooued about the deliuerie of his commission, and sealing an indenture, which the earle had there readie ingrossed, conteining the articles of agreement, in consideration whereof it was deliuered, the capteine sir Richard Ierningham was discharged, and the Frenchmen suffered to enter with drumslads and minstrelsie, but not with standards nor banners, which the Englishmen caused them to roll vp greatlie against their wils. Before they came to the gates, they sealed the indenture, confessing how they receiued the citie as a gift, and not as a right, and deliuered their commission, whereby they were authorised to receiue it, which at the first they refused to doo, affirming that it was sufficient for them to shew it.

The maner how Tornaie was deliuered to the French king.

Thus was Tornaie deliuered in this tenth yeare of the kings reigne, on the eight daie of Februarie, & the Englishmen returned into England, sore displeased in their minds. For thereby manie a tall yeoman lacked liuing, the which would not labour after their returne, but fell to robbing, pilfering, shifting, and other extraordinarie meanes of maintenance, whereas before they were staied vpon a certeintie of hope, so long as they had allowance by the king. So that this resignation of Tornaie, though it were answerable to the desire of the French king, and commodious for his people, yet that benefit of theirs bred to the English soldiors detriment and losse: who wished in their harts to haue left their liues behind them in defense of possession, rather than it should reuert into the hands of them, by whome it was surrendred & giuen vp to the English power, whom (bicause they were not able to incounter) they let in at their gates by a voluntarie motion and common consent for their better safetie, as a late writer witnesseth:

> Angligenas passis intra sua mœnia portis
> Sponte intromittens.

¶ During this time remained in the French court diuerse yoong gentlemen of England, and they with the French king rode dailie disguised through Paris, throwing egges, stones, and other foolish trifles at the people, which light demeanour of a king was much discommended and ieasted at. And when these yoong gentlemen came againe into England, they were all French, in eating drinking, and apparell, yea, and in French vices and brags, so that all the estates of England were by them laughed at: the ladies and gentlewomen were dispraised, so that nothing by them was praised, but if it were after the French turne, which after turned them to displesure, as you shall heare.

Ed. Hall in H. 8. fol. lxv i.
The light and mislikedde meanour of diuerse yoong gentlemen of England & the French king.

After the kings ambassadours were returned, and Tornaie deliuered to the Frenchmen vpon the conditions aforesaid, the hostages that were here left for the paiment of the great summes and performance of the conditions comprised in the league (of the which one was, that if the marriage tooke none effect, then the citie of Tornaie should be redeliuered vpon repaiment of the same summes) the said hostages knew not in what case they stood, but when they knew it, they were verie heauie and sorowfull: howbeit, they dissembled the matter in the best wise they could. The king vsed familiarlie these foure hostages, and on the seuenth daie of Maie prepared a disguising, and caused his great chamber at Gréenwich to be staged, and great lights to be set on pillors that were gilt, with basons gilt, and the roofe was couered with blue sattin set full of presses of fine gold and flowers: and vnder was written Iammes, the meaning whereof was, that the flower of youth could not be oppressed.

Preparation for solemne disport.

Into this chamber came the king, and the quéene, with the hostages, and there was a goodlie comedie of Plautus plaied; and that doone, there entered into the chamber

eight

A comedie of Plautus plaied before the king.

eight ladies in blacke veluet bordered about with gold, with hoopes from the wast downeward, and sléeues ruffed and plited at the elbow, and plaine in the middest, full of cuts, plucked out at euerie cut with fine camerike, & tired like the Aegyptians verie richlie. And when these ladies had passed about the place, in came eight noble personages in long gownes of taffata set with flowers of gold bullion, and vnder that apparell cotes of blacke veluet embrodered with gold all to cut, and plucked out with cuts of white sarcenet, and euerie man had buskins of blacke veluet full of agglets of gold.

A iustes.

Then the eight men dansed with the eight ladies all being visarded, and suddenlie the men cast off their large gownes, and then their vnder apparell was séene. And when all was doone, euerie lord and ladie put off their visards, and then it was knowne that the king, the duke of Suffolke, and the French quéene were there, which were present at the plaie time. On the eight daie of March was a solemne iustes, the king himselfe, and eight yoong gentlemen based and barded in blacke veluet embrodered with gold; against the duke of Suffolke, and eight of his band, all in white satten with drops of gold. And that daie they all ran excéeding well, which the strangers highlie commended.]

The soldiors of Tornaie rewarded.

Abr. Fl. ex Guic. pag. 760.

About the end of March, the king sent for all the yeomen of the gard that were come from Tornaie, and after manie good words giuen to them, he granted to euerie of them foure pence the daie without attendance, except they were speciallie commanded. ¶ And here it seemeth requisit to adde the report of a forreine chronicler touching the league of amitie and conditions of the same, knit vp in breuitie and good tearmes as followeth. Now (saith he) the differences betwéene the French and English were also reconciled. And for the more stabilitie of which agreement, it was confirmed with a contract of parentage and aliance, wherein the king of England promised to giue his onelie daughter, to whom hauing no sons, there was hope of the descending & succession of the kingdome to the Dolphin the eldest sonne of the

The portion giuē with the kings daughter of England.

crowne of France, adding for a portion foure hundred thousand duckets. Both the one and the other bore yet so tender age, that infinit accidents might happen, before perfection of yeeres would make them able to establish matrimonie. There was made betwene them a league defensiue, wherin were comprehended Cesar, and the king of Spaine, in case they would ratifie it in a certeine time.

The king of England bound himselfe to restore Tornaie, receiuing presentlie for defraiments expended vpon that towne, two hundred and three score thousand duckets, and thrée hundred thousand to bée defalked of the portion, and to paie thrée hundred thousand more in the space of twelue yeares. The French king also was bound, that if the peace and the parentage folowed not, to render vp againe into the hands of the English, the towne of Tornaie. Manie ambassadours were sent from both the realmes to negociat this league, and to receiue the ratifications and othes, by whom in the courts of both the kings the acts of the accord were dispatched with great solemnitie and ceremonie, with a resolution of an interuiew of both the kings betwéene Calis and Bullongne, immediatlie after the restitution of Tornaie.

Peace and aliance betwixt the French king and the Spanish solemnlie celebrated.

About the same time, the daughter of the French king, appointed to be married to the king of Spaine, being dead, the former peace and capitulation was eftsoones reconfirmed betwéene them, wherein was promised the marriage of the second daughter of France. Both the kings celebrated this coniunction with most great demonstrations of perfect amitie: for the king of Spaine, hauing paied in at Lions an hundred thousand duckets, ware publikelie the order of saint Michaell vpon the day of the celebration of the same, and in recompense of that honour: the French king, vpon the daie dedicated to saint Andrew, was honorablie attired in the robes and colour of the golden fléece.

About this time, Iohn Ia. Triuulce, whome neither old age reduced almost to the
last

last time, nor his vertue so oftentimes expressed in the seruice of the truce of France could anie waie aid or comfort (being both ambicious and impatient, and therefore enuied) following the French court, fell sicke at Charters, where he gaue vp to the king, his innocencie and complaints, and made to God the last reckoning of his aged daies. He was a man in the iudgement of manie, and confirmed by sundrie experiences, of singular valour in the discipline of warre, and ran a race alwaies opposed to the inconstancie of fortune, who (according to hir mutabilitie) made him feele the operation of both hir humors, sometimes reioising in hir fauour, and erst againe finding hir sowre and of a bitter tast. By his commandement were written vpon his toome these words, not disagreeable to the variable condition and course of his naturall life : *The death of Iohn Ia. Triuulce, a noble seruitour in the French affaires.*

I find the rest within my graue,
Which in my life I could not haue.]

In this yeare the twelfe of Februarie, died the emperour Maximilian, for whome the king caused a solemne obsequie to be kept in Poules church. ¶ Hée died at Luiz, a towne vpon the marches of Austrich, where he remained for his delight and pleasure in hunting the wild bore, and other chases of the field. He liued alwaies vnder one condition of fortune, who manie times fauoured him, in offering him manie faire occasions, & as often wrought against him in not suffering him to take the fruit and effect of them. He was by nature inconstant and remooueable, and had conceipts and impressions verie ill disposed and different from the iudgement of other men, ioined to an excessiue prodigalitie and dissipation of monie. *The death of the emperour Maximilian. Guic. pag. 763.*
A description of the emperors qualities.

Matters which cut off from him the effects and successe of all occasions, being otherwise a prince most perfect and instructed in the ordering of warre, secret to laie and dispose a plot, diligent to follow it, of bodie able and suffering, of mind affable and easie, and replenished with manie other excellent gifts and ornaments. Vnto some of these properties, the good seruice which he did the king of England at Terwin giueth proofe, at what time both he and his people marched vnder the English ensigne, and receiued paie as stipendarie souldiors; whose wages the king had a care to paie, as maie appeare by his coining of siluer monie, whereof was scarsitie in his campe, in respect of gold, wherewith the souldiors were well stored, as one dooth verie well make report, saieng :

Pro mercede nihil nisifuluum soluitur aurum,
Auri militibus radiantis copia totis
Tanta fuit castris, vt rex cudisse coactus
Nummum ex argento fuerit.

As soone as the emperour was dead, the French king and the king of Spaine began manifestlie to aspire to the empire, the purchase whereof albeit was a matter of right great importance, and no lesse the emulation running betwéene two so mightie princes, yet they ordered their ambition with great modestie, neither vsing words of iniurie, nor threats of armes ; but either one labouring by his authoritie, & by his meanes, to draw on his side the electors. The French king sundrie times reasoned touching the election with great comelinesse with the Spanish ambassadours, to whom he said it was a matter both agréeable and conuenient, that either of them seuerallie should séeke by honest meanes to increase the houour of his house by so great a dignitie : which for that in times before had bene transferred into the families of their predecessours, there was now the lesse occasion to bréed betwéene them two matter of iniurie, nor diminution of their amitie and good will. *The French king and the Spanish begin to aspire to the empire.*

But rather he wished, that in the action of the empire, they might follow the example and order of two yoong louers, who albeit they follow the quest of one ladie, and either one laboureth by his industrie to carie hir; yet they forbere to come to contention. The king of Spaine alluded with good right, that the empire apperteined

to

The king of Spaines claim to the empire.

to him, as hauing continued by a long succession of time in the house of Austrich, and that it had not béene the custome of the electors to depriue the issue of the emperour, without manifest cause of their disabilitie, neither was there anie in Germanie of that puissance and authoritie to make him equall to stand competitor with him in that election. And least of all did he hold it iust or likelie, that the electors would transport to a forreine or strange prince so great a dignitie continued by so manie ages in the nation of Germanie.

And albeit some particular amongst them, either through the insinuation of monie, or other propertie of corruption, might be allured to another intention, yet he hoped to stop him with force prepared in time conuenient, not doubting also but the other electors also would oppose against him, and the princes and frée townes of Germanie would not indure so vniuersall an infamie, speciallie to suffer it to be laid vpon the person of the French king, which would be no other thing than to make great the puissance of a king enimie vnto their nation, and from whome there was no suertie that the imperiall dignitie would euer returne into Germanie: he thought it would be an action easie to obteine and reduce to perfection, that which had bin solicited by his grandfather, who had alreadie compounded for recompenses and donations, and other diuidents for euerie of the electors.

The French king in hope to be emperor as well as the Spanish.

On the other side, the desire of the French king was as great, and no lesse were his hopes, which tooke their principall foundation vpon an opinion he had to corrupt the voices of the electors with his huge summes of monie: especiallie for that there were amongest them both pensionaries to him, and otherwise assured by manie good offices, who incouraging him with the facilitie of the enterprise, pushed him on to imbrace it. And for his part, as mortall men are apt to beléeue the thing they desire, so he nourished that hope with reasons rather apparant than true: he knew that commonlie it was a matter grieuous to the princes of Germanie to haue the emperors mightie; being gealous that in so great a puissance, they would not either in part or in all, quarrell the iurisdictions and authorities imperiall occupied by manie of them. In which reason he persuaded himselfe, that they would in no sort consent to the election of the Spaniard, & so of themselues to subiect themselues to an emperor more mightie than had beene since a long descent and race of emperors. A matter which in his person séemed to be qualified, for that hauing neither estates nor ancient aliances in Germanie, they had no occasion of suspicion of his greatnesse.

The same reason also made him beleeue well of the conformitie of the frée townes, in whome much lesse that the regard of the glorie of the nation would carie it from him, séeing it would helpe to peize the ballance on his side, for that with most men the motions of proper and priuate interest maie doo more, than the respect of publike and

The French king builded his hope vpon the humors of the princes of Germanie.

generall profit. He knewe it was not a little grieuous to manie noble houses of Germanie, pretending to be capable of such a dignitie, to see the empire continue so long time in one house; but much more did it discontent them to suffer that so great an estate, which of right ought sometimes to be giuen to one of them, and sometime to passe to another, should become a perpetuall descent and succession in one line: insomuch as they might call inheritance and succession that election, which durst not leaue the line of the emperors. That in that sort the empire was translated from Albert de Austrich to Frederike his brother, and from Frederike to Maximilian his sonne; and now there was deuise to passe it from Maximilian to the person of Charles his grandchild.

By these humors and indignations of the princes of Germanie, he tooke hope that the discords and gealousies amongst themselues might helpe on his cause, the rather for that it often happeneth in the contentions of men, that he that is excluded, or the partie whome he fauoureth, runneth with a naturall rashnesse rather to call in, and to aduance a third, than to giue place to him that hath opposed against his intention.

Moreouer

Moreouer, the French king was not without his hopes in the fauour of the pope, both in regard of the amitie and aliance newlie past betwixt them; and also for that he was not ignorant how inconuenient it would be to the sée apostolike to haue the imperiall crowne inuested in Charls, nor so much for his owne greatnesse, as for that by the opportunitie and neighbourhood of the realme of Naples to the estate of the church, and the adherencie of the barons of the Gebelins, he had a plaine and open passage to run vp to the gates of Rome.

But in that discourse he considered not that the same reason, which he iudged true against Charles, was also against himselfe: for that the empire being ioined to his person, he was no lesse to be feared of the pope & all others, than Charles. For that though the one of them possessed happilie more realmes and states; yet the other was not to be lesse esteemed, hauing his power not dispersed nor separate in manie places, but was prince of a realme entierlie assembled and vnited, where the obedience and fidelitie of his subiects was no lesse woonderfull, than his treasure and riches infinite. Neuerthelesse, not knowing in himselfe that which he considered in an other, he had recourse to the pope, and implored his fauor vnder the offer and protestation of his person and kingdoms, with all other deuotions of a louing son. Notwithstanding all this, the French king was abused by his vaine hope, which fed him with fansies of the empire, whereto he was not allotted nor elected.

For on the twentie eight of Iune was elected to be emperor Charles king of Castile, and nephue to the quéene, by the whole assent of the electors of the empire: namelie, the archbishop of Maience, the archbishop of Cullen, the count Palatine, and the duke of Saxon. Although the French king sent his great maister to cause him to be elected to the high maiestie of the empire; yet his ambassador and great maister of his houshold (called Gonffier lord of Boisie, and brother to William Gonffier lord Boneuet, admerall of France, which was ambassador in England the last yéere, as you haue heard) did not so his message that it tooke anie effect. The king which had sent doctor Pace his secretarie for the aduancement of his nephue the king of Castile, to the dignitie imperiall, because he had the duchie of Austrich, and manie other seigniories in Almaine, was verie ioious of this election, and caused a solemne masse to be soong at Paules the seuenth daie of Iulie: at which masse was present the cardinall Campeius, the cardinall of Yorke, the duke of Buckingham, of Norffolke, & Suffolke, with the ambassadours of Spaine, France, Venice, and Scotland.

After masse was doone, the quier sang Te Deum, and then all the lords departed to Bainards castell to dinner, and that night were solemne fires made thorough London, and great plentie of wine giuen by Italians, Dutchmen, and Spaniards for these newes. In this yeare the king with all the knights of his order being in England, rode on double horsses, with the henchmen following the king from Colbrooke to Windsore in gorgious apparell, and there he kept with great solemnitie the feast of saint George, and dined in the hall. The bishop of Winchester prelat of the order sat at the boords end alone. The king was solemnelie serued and the surnap cast like the feast of a coronation. All things were plentious to strangers that resorted thither. At the masse of Requiem were offered the banner & other habillements of honour belonging to Maximilian the emperour late deceassed.

After this feast ended, the king came to Richmond, and so to Gréenewich, and there laie all Maie. In which moneth the kings councell secretlie communed togither of the kings gentlenesse and liberalitie to all persons: by the which they perceiued that certeine yooug men in his priuie chamber, not regarding his estate or degree, were so familiar and homelie with him, that they forgat themselues. Which things although the king of his gentle nature suffered, and not rebuked nor reprooued it: yet the kings councell thought it not méet to be suffered for the kings honour, and therefore they all togither came to the king, beseeching him to haue more regard to his roialtie.

To whome the king answered, that he had chosen them of his councell, both for the maintenance of his honour, and for the defense of all things that might blemish the same: wherefore if they saw anie about him misuse themselues, he committed it vnto their reformation. Then the kings councell caused the lord chamberleine to call before them diuerse of the priuie chamber, which had béene in the French court, and banished them the court for diuerse considerations, laieng nothing particularlie to their charges, & they that had offices were commanded to go to their offices. Which discharge out of court gréeued sore the hearts of these yoong men, which were called the kings minions. Then was there foure sad & ancient knights put into the K. priuie chamber, whose names were; sir Richard Wingfield, sir Richard Ierningham, sir Richard Weston, and sir William Kingston; and diuerse officers were changed.

Certeine of the priuie chamber remooued, and others in their roome appointed.

In this summer the quéene desired the king to bring to hir manor of Hauering in the Bower in Essex the gentlemen of France being hostages, for whose welcomming she purueied all things in the most liberall manner: and especiallie she made to the king such a sumptuous banket, that the king thanked hir hartilie, & the strangers gaue hir great praise. The king lieng there did shoot, hunt, and run dailie with the hostages to their great ioy. This yéere in September the king laie at his manor of Newhall in Essex, otherwise called Beaulieu, where the king had newlie builded a costlie mansion, there to welcome the quéene, the lords, and the French gentlemen, he made to them a sumptuous banket, and all along the chamber sat a ladie & a lord, or a knight, which were plentiouslie serued.

The king and quéene at Hauering in the Bower.

Newhall in Essex called Beaulieu.

After the banket ended, with noise of minstrels entered into the chamber eight maskers with white beards, and long and large garments of blew sattin paned with sipers, poudered with spangles of bullion gold, and they dansed with ladies sadlie, and communed not with the ladies after the fashion of maskers, but behaued themselues grauelie. Wherfore the quéene plucked off their visors, and then appeared the duke of Suffolke, the earle of Essex, the marquesse Dorset, the lord Aburgauennie, sir Richard Wingfield, sir Robert Wingfield, sir Richard Weston, sir William Kingston: all these were somewhat aged, the yoongest man was fiftie at the least. The ladies had good sport to see these ancient persons maskers.

A maske of graue and ancient courtiers.

When they departed, the king and the foure hostages of France, and the earle of Deuonshire with six other yoong gentlemen entered the chamber, of the which six were all in yellow sattin, hose, shooes, and caps, and six other were in like maner in gréene: the yelow sattin was fretted with siluer of damaske, and so was the gréene verie richlie to behold: then euerie masker tooke a ladie and dansed. When they had dansed and communed a great while, their visors were taken off, and they knowne, and the king gaue manie brooches and proper gifts where he liked.] In the moneth of Nouember the king came from Lambeth to Westminster hall, and so to the Starchamber, and there were brought before him the lord Ogle, the lord Howard, sir Matthew Browne, sir William Bulmer, and Iohn Scot of Camerwell, for diuerse riots, misdemeanors, & offenses by them committed; but the king speciallie rebuked sir William Bulmer knight, bicause he being his seruant sworne, refused the kings seruice, and became seruant to the duke of Buckingham: yet at length vpon his humble crauing of mercie, still knéeling on his knées before his grace, the king pardoned him his offense: and likewise he pardoned the lord Howard, and sir Matthew Browne, their offenses: but bicause the lord Ogles matter concerned murther, he remitted him to the common law. And then he rose and went to his barge, and by the waie made Iames Yarford maior of the citie of London knight, and so returned to Lambeth.

A maske of youthfull courtiers.

The king sitteth in the Starchamber in iudgement.

The French king desirous to continue the friendship latelie begun betwixt him and the king of England, made meanes vnto the cardinall, that they might in some conuenient

nient

nient place come to an interuiew togither, that he might haue further knowlege of
of king Henrie, and likewise king Henrie of him.   But the fame went that the cardinall desired greatlie, of himselfe, that the two kings might méet, who mesuring by
his will what was conuenient, thought it should make much with his glorie, if in
France also at some high assemblie of noble men, he should be séene in his vaine Note the ambicious humor
of the cardinal
of Yorke.
pompe and shew of dignitie: hee therefore breaketh with the king of that matter, declaring how honourable, necessarie, and conuenient it should be for him to gratifie
his friend therein, and thus with his persuasions the K. began to conceiue an earnest
desire to sée the French king, and thereupon appointed to go ouer to Calis, and so in
the marches of Guisnes to meet with him.

Then were there sent vnto Guisnes, vnder the rule of sir Edward Belknap three *Edw. Hall.*
thousand artificers, which builded out of the earth on the plaine before the castell of
Guisnes, a most pleasant palace of timber, right curiouslie garnished without and
within.   Herewith were letters written to all such lords, ladies, gentlemen, and gen
tlewomen, which should giue their attendance on the king and quéene, which incontinentlie put themselues in a readinesse after the most sumptuous sort.   Also it was
appointed that the king of England, & the French king, in a campe betwéene Ard
and Guisnes, with eightéene aides, should in Iune next insuing abide all commers being gentlemen, at the tilt, at tourneie, and at barriers, whereof proclamation was
made by Orleans king of armes of France here in the court of England, and by Clarenceaux king of armes of England in the court of France, and in the court of Burgognie, and in diuerse other courts and places in Almanie and Italie.

During the time of these preparations, newes were brought to the king, that *Edw. Hall in
H. 8. fol.* lxix.
Preparation for
the interteining
of the emperour
Charles into
England.
Charles his nephue elected emperour of Almanie, would shortlie depart out of Spaine
by sea, and come by England to go to Acon or Aix (a citie of fame and renowne in
Germanie, for the ancient residence and sepulchre of Charlemaine) where he receiued
the first crowne.   Wherefore the king hearing of this determination of the emperour,
caused great prouisions to be made at euerie hauen, for the receiuing of his welbeloued
nephue and friend; & dailie prouisions were made on all sides for these noble méetings
of so high princes: and especiallie the quéene of England, and the ladie Dowager of
France, made great cost on the apparell of their ladies and gentlewomen.

On the first daie of Februarie being Candlemasse éeuen, as the king and quéene
were come from euensong at their manour of Greenwich, before the quéenes chamber A deuise of a
waggon vpon
the sudden.
there blew a trumpet suddenlie, and then entered into the quéens chamber four gentlemen apparelled in long and large garments of blew damaske bordered with gold, and
brought with them a tricke waggon, in the which sat a ladie richlie apparelled, with
a canopie ouer hir head: and on the foure corners of the waggon were foure hed
peeces called armites, euerie péece being of a sundrie deuise.   The said ladie put vp a
bill to the king, the effect whereof was, that the foure gentlemen present would (for
the loue of their ladies) answer all commers at the tilt at a daie by the king to be appointed: which daie was appointed at Shrouetide next insuing.   At which daie the
foresaid gentlemen valiantlie accomplished their enterprise, with great lauds of the
king, the quéene, and the ladies.

Moreouer, now that it was concluded, that the kings of England and France The whole
maner of the in-
teruiew comitted
to the cardinall.
should méet (as yee haue heard) then both the kings committed the order and manner
of their méeting, and how manie daies the same should continue, and what preheminence each should giue to other, vnto the cardinall of Yorke, which to set all
things in a certeintie, made an instrument, conteining an order and direction concerning the premisses by him deuised and appointed.

The

The tenour of the said instrument mad by the cardinall.

Ab. Fl. ex Fd.
Hall in H. 8.
fol. lxx.

THOMAS archbishop of Yorke and cardinall, &c.　Albeit that by the treatie and meeting of the right high, and right puissant princes, Henrie by the grace of God, king of England, and of France, lord of Ireland, my souereigne lord: and Francis by the same grace, K. of France right christened, made and concluded at London the eight daie of October, the yeare of our Lord one thousand fiue hundred and eighteene, be among other things concluded and accorded, that the same meeting shall be in place indifferent, and not subiect to any of the said princes.　Neuerthelesse we, considering the honour, profit, and vtilitie, that shall redound by the interuiew of the said two princes, and not onelie to the said two princes, their realmes and subiects, but also to all christendome, after declaration hereupon had with the said princes.

Also considering that the said illustre king of England my souereigne lord, in passing the sea with his retinue, shall susteine great costs and expenses, and dispose himselfe to great labors and dangers, leauing his realme and puissance for certeine time, we haue thought & esteemed, that he should not be wholie satisfied to the honour and dignitie of the same, right illustre king of England my souereigne lord, and should not haue in regard condigne of his labours and dangers, if the said interuiew or meeting after the first treatie shuld be in place indifferent.　Wherefore it is that we desiring to weie equallie the honor and dignitie of the said two kings, by vertue and power of the commissions to vs giuen, of whome the tenours shall bee hereafter declared: we haue made, declared, and ordeined certeine articles accepted & approoued by the same princes respectiuelie, which they will obserue, and by these presents we make, declare, and ordeine as followeth.

The first article
of the interuiew
of the two kings
& their traine.

And first we declare and ordeine, that before the end of the moneth of Maie next comming, the said illustre king of England shall come personallie to the castle of Guisnes, with his bedfellow the queene, and his sister the Dowaresse of France: & semblablie the right christened K. of France, shall come in person to his castle of Ard with the queene & his mother: and some day, houre, and time, within foure daies at the most, after the end of Maie, that shall be assigned by the commissioners of the one and the other partie, the said king of England shall issue out of his castell of Guisnes half a mile long, without that that he shall issue out of the limits of his demaine of Guisnes, and shall come towards the said castell of Ard: and there within the territorie of the said castell of Guisnes, he shall rest in some place not fortified nor walled, and neere the limits of France, that the said commissioners shall assigne (as aboue said.)

The maner of
their meeting
and mutuall
greeting.

And the said right christened king, parting from his castell of Ard, shall come toward the said king of England the same day, place, time, and houre, that shall tarie him within the demaine of Guisnes, as is said.　In the which shall not bee set or dressed anie pauilions or tents, and there the said two kings being on horssebacke, with their retinue shall see the one the other, and salute each other, and speake together familiarlie, and common in that sort and maner, and so long as shall seeme to them good.　And after the said salutation and communication finished for that time, the said illustre king of England shall returne to his castell of Guisnes, and the said right christened king to his castell of Ard.

What both the
kings were to
doo the morrow
after the first in-
teruiew.

Item, for so much that we thinke to be satisfied touching the labours, dangers, & honour of the said king of England, my souereigne lord of so much, that the said right christened king at the first speaking, he shall come forward vnto, and within his territorie of Guisnes, we will keepe the honour of the said kings: & therefore declare and ordeine, that on the morrow after the first interuiew, the same kings shall
meet

meet togither in some fit place, indifferent betweene Ard and Guisnes, that shall be assigned by the said commissioners.

And after the salutation made on the one and the other partie, the said right illustre king of England shall go to the castell of Ard, to see, salute, and visit the queene of France, and also the sister of the said christened king, with whome he shall dine priuilie. And likewise the said right christened king shall go the castell of Guisnes, to visit and salute the queene of England, and the Dowaresse of France, with whome he shall dine. In the which places the said princes shall be receiued familiarlie and amiablie, vnto mutuall loue, and also to the honour of the said princes.

Item, as the said serene princes of England & France, be like in force corporall, beautie, and gift of nature, right expert & hauing knowledge in the art militant, right cheualrous in armes, & in the flower and vigor of youth, wherby seemed to vs a right assemblie, that for to adorne and honor the same assemblie, and to shew their forces in armes, they shall take counsell & dispose themselues to doo some faire feat of armes, as well on foot as on horssebacke, against all commers: we declare and ordeine, that the place where shall be the said fight and feat of armes, shall be chosen betweene Guisnes and Ard, and assigned by the commissioners of the one and the other partie. Order for feats of cheualrie and a tiuit.e and the place thereto appointed.

And for a suertie of the persons of the said kings & their companie, the said place shall be apparelled, diched, fortified, and kept of the one and the other partie, by equall number of men of armes, respectiuely committed and deputed that to doo. And during the time of the said iusts and feats of warre, the same kings and queenes with their retinue, shall see ech other familiarlie, and conuerse and speake togither. And euerie daie towards the euening, after the iusts, triumphs, bankets, & familiar communications doone, the said kings with their retinue shall returne into their castels, that is to say, the king of England into his castell of Guisnes, & the said right christened king into his castell of Ard; and thus they shall doo dailie, during the said fight and feat of armes.

Item, we declare and ordeine, that when the same king of England and the queene his bedfellow, & the Dowaresse of France his sister, with their retinue, shall go to the territorie and entrie of the foresaid right christened king, the superioritie and preheminence shall be giuen to the said king of England, to the queene his bedfellow, and to their retinue respectiuelie, during the time that they shall tarie and be there: and semblablie when the said right christened king, and the queene his bedfellow and his right illustre ladie and moother, with their retinue shall come to the territorie and entrie of the said illustre king of England, the superioritie and preheminence shall be giuen to the said right christened king, to the queene his bedfellow, and to his moother, and to their retinue during the time that they shall continue and abide there. Order for superioritie to be giuen to the king of England and the queene within the French territorie.

Item, forsomuch as the castels and places where the said interuiew shall be, be so little and narrow, that if entrie and licence to come thither be giuen to all them that would go thither, diuers annoiances, troubles & impechments should follow: wherfore it is so, that we the cardinall aboue said, by these presents declare and ordeine, that none of the retinue of the said kings, queenes, or other lords and nobles, of what estate, qualitie, or condition that he or they be of, shall not come to the said assemblie with more great number of persons or horsse, than shall be written by letters subscribed by the said kings: the which shall conteine the estates and conditions of the persons, as well men as women, and number of seruants and horsse, except the common consent and licence of the said kings. Order for restraint of assemblies to the places appointed for the interuiew.

Item, forsomuch as peraduenture it shall come that the said princes, lords, gentlemen, and houshold seruants, shall see and conuerse togither familiarlie, to the end that it maie ingender betweene them an amitie more firme and stable, for that cause, and Order for both princes personall securitie going and comming.

and that more suerlie and agreeablie they may be togither, as well by day as by night without any danger or feare, which we desire to prouide: we declare and ordeine that two gentlemen, with sufficient companie of equall & like number, be committed and deputed, respectiuelie by the said kings for the keeping and suertie of the waies and watches, that shall be made continuallie during the assemblie of the said kings. The which gentlemen, with their companies, shall ordeine and depute explorators and spies in the vallies, forrests, woods, towns, burrowes, villages, castels, passages, and waies, and other places dangerous and suspect: from time to time, and houre to houre, as well towards Flanders, as Picardie, Artois, & England, to exploit and watch there.

And if anie be found suspect, them to repulse and take awaie, to the end that not onelie the said princes, their gentlemen, and houshold-seruants, maie suerlie and without feare visit the one the other, as said is; but also those that shall bring vittels necessarie to the said assemblie, maie without danger, trouble, impechement, or noisance go and come: the which explorators shall be bounden euerie daie in the morning and euening, to make report to the said princes or to their said councellors respectiuelie, of that which they found, and in what estate the waies be. We declare further and ordeine, that all men of armes and of warre, of the one and the other partie, shall not approch neerer than two iournies, to the place where the said interuiew shall be, except the retinue and men of war that be committed and deputed to keepe Bullongne and Calis: and that the same men of warre nor none other, during the assemblie of the said princes, shall not presume to come neerer, vnlesse by the consent, accord, and licence of the said princes.

Item, we cardinall aboue said, by expresse authoritie and power to vs giuen, by these presents, bind the said princes to doo, fulfill, and accomplish, all and euerie things aboue said herein conteined. Finallie, we declare and ordeine, that ech of the said kings on his partie, shall ratifie, confirme, and approoue all and euerie the chapters and articles aboue said, by their letters pattents sealed with their hands. And by the same letters of ratification they shall be bounden, to accomplish with good faith and word of a king, all and euerie the things aboue said: the which letters made, subscribed, and sealed, as is said, they shall giue the one the other, and shall change in the citie of London, within one moneth next after the date of these presents. Made the twelfe of March, the yeare of our Lord a thousand fiue hundred and nineteene.

The peeres of the realme receiuing letters to prepare themselues to attend the king in this iourneie, and no apparant necessarie cause expressed, why nor wherefore; séemed to grudge, that such a costilie iournie should be taken in hand to their importunate charges and expenses, without consent of the whole boord of the councell. But namelie the duke of Buckingham, being a man of a loftie courage, but not most liberall, sore repined that he should be at so great charges for his furniture foorth at this time, saieng; that he knew not for what cause so much monie should be spent about the sight of a vaine talke to be had, and communication to be ministred of things of no importance. Wherefore he sticked not to saie, that it was an intollerable matter to obeie such a vile and importunate person.

The duke indeed could not abide the cardinall, and speciallie he had of late conceiued an inward malice against him for sir Willam Bulmers cause, whose trouble was onelie procured by the cardinall; who first caused him to be cast in prison. Now such gréeuous words as the duke thus vttered against him, came to the cardinals eare; wherevpon he cast before hand all waies possible to haue him in a trip, that he might cause him to leape headlesse. But bicause he doubted his fréends, kinnesmen, and alies, and chéeflie the earle of Surrie lord admerall, which had married the dukes
daughter,

daughter, he thought good first to send him some whither out of the waie, least he might cast a trumpe in his waie. There was great enimitie bewixt the cardinall and the earle, for that on a time, when the cardinall tooke vpon him to checke the earle, he had like to haue thrust his dagger into the cardinall.

At length there was occasion offered him to compasse his purpose, by occasion of the earle of Kildare his comming out of Ireland. For the cardinall knowing he was well prouided of monie, sought occasion to fléece him of part thereof. The earle of Kildare being vnmarried, was desirous to haue an English woman to wife; and for that he was a suter to a widow contrarie to the cardinals mind, he accused him to the king, of that he had not borne himselfe vprightlie in his office in Ireland, where he was the kings lieutenant. Such accusations were framed against him when no bribes would come, that he was committed to prison, and then by the cardinals good preferment the earle of Surrie was sent into Ireland as the kings deputie, in lieu of the said earle of Kildare, there to remaine rather as an exile, than as lieutenant to the king, euen at the cardinals pleasure, as he himselfe well perceiued. *The earle of Kildare committed to ward.*

In the beginning of Aprill, the said earle passed ouer into Ireland, and had with him diuerse gentlemen that had béene in the garrison of Tornaie, and one hundred yeomen of the kings gard, and others, to the number of a thousand men, where he by his manhood and policie brought the earle of Desmond and diuerse other rebels to good conformitie and order. He continued there two yeares, in which space he had manie bickerings and skirmishes with the wild Irish. There rested yet the earle of Northumberland, whome the cardinall doubted also, least he might hinder his purpose, when he should go about to wreake his malice against the duke of Buckingham : and therefore he picked a quarell to him, for that he had seized vpon certeine wards which the cardinall said apperteined of right to the king. And bicause the earle would not giue ouer his title, he was also committed to prison, & after tooke it for a great benefit at the cardinals hands, that he might be deliuered out of his danger. *Edw. Hall.* *Good seruice doone by the earle of Surrie.* *Polydor.* *The earle of Northumberland committed to prison.*

Now in this meane while, the cardinall ceassed not to bring the duke out of the kings fauour, by such forged tales, and contriued surmises, as he dailie put into the kings head : insomuch that (through the infelicitie of his fate) diuerse accidents fell out to the aduantage of the cardinall ; which he not omitting, atchiued the thing whereat he so studiouslie (for the satisfieng of his canckered & malicious stomach) laid full aime. Now it chanced that the duke comming to London with his traine of men, to attend the king into France, went before into Kent vnto a manor place which he had there. And whilest he staid in that countrie till the king set forward, greeuous complaints were exhibited to him by his farmars and tenants against Charles Kneuet his surueiour, for such bribing as he had vsed there amongest them. Wherevpon the duke tooke such displeasure against him, that he depriued him of his office, not knowing how that in so dooing he procured his owne destruction, as after appeared.

The kings maiestie perseuering in purpose to méet with Francis the French king, remooued with the quéene, and all his court, the one & twentith day of Maie being mondaie, from his manor of Gréenwich towards the sea side : and so on the fridaie the fiue and twentith of Maie, he arriued at the citie of Canturburie, intending there to keepe his Whitsuntide. On the morrow after, the emperour being on the sea returning out of Spaine, arriued with all his nauie of ships roiall on the coast of Kent, direct to the port of Hieth the said daie by noone, where hée was saluted by the viceadmerall of England, sir William Fitz William, with six of the kings great ships well furnished, which laie for the safegard of passage betwixt Calis and Douer. Towards euening the emperour departed from his ships, and entered into his bote, and comming towards land, was met and receiued of the lord cardinall of Yorke with such reuerence as to so noble a prince apperteined. *An. Reg. 12.* *The king setteth forward towards France.*

Thus landed the emperour Charles the fift at Douer, vnder his cloth of estate of
the

The emperor
Charles the fift
landeth in
England.

the blacke eagle, all spread on rich cloth of gold. He had with him manie noble men, and manie faire ladies of his bloud. When he was come on land, the lord cardinall conducted him to the castell of Douer, which was prepared for him in most roiall maner.

The méeting of
the emperor and
K. Henrie at
Douer castell.

In the morning, the king rode with all hast to the castell of Douer to welcome the emperour, and entering into the castell, alighted. Of whose comming the emperour hauing knowledge, came out of his chamber, and met him on the staires, where either of them embraced other in most louing maner, and then the king brought the emperour to his chamber.

The emperor
and K. Henrie
kéepe Whit-
suntide at
Canturburie.

On Whitsundaie earlie in the morning, they tooke their horsses, and rode to the citie of Canturburie, the more to kéepe solemne the feast of Pentecost: but speciallie to sée the quéene of England his aunt was the emperour his intent, of whom ye may be sure he was most ioifullie receiued and welcomed.

Polydor.

Thus the emperour and his retinue, both of lords and ladies, kept their Whitsuntide with the king and quéene of England, in the citie of Canturburie with all ioy and solace. The emperour yet himselfe séemed not so much to delight in pastime and pleasure, but that in respect of his youthfull yeares, there appeared in him a great shew of grauitie: for they could by no meanes bring him to danse amongst the residue of the princes, but onelie was contented to be a looker on. Peraduenture the sight of the ladie Marie troubled him, whome he had sometime loued, and yet through fortunes euill hap might not haue hir to wife. The chiefe cause that mooued the emperour to come thus on land at this time, was to persuade that by word of mouth, which he had before done most earnestlie by letters; which was, that the king should not meet with the French king at anie interuiew: for he doubted least if the king of England & the French king should grow into some great friendship and faithfull bond of amitie, it might turne him to displeasure.

The emperor
laboureth to
hinder the
purposed inter-
ueiw.

But now that he perceiued how the king was forward on his iournie, he did what he could to procure, that no trust should be committed to the faire words of the French-men: and that if it were possible, the great friendship that was now in bréeding betwixt the two kings, might be dissolued. And forsomuch as he knew the lord cardinall to be woone with rewards, as a fish with a bait: he bestowed on him great gifts, and promised him much more, so that hée would be his friend, and helpe to bring his purpose to passe. The cardinall not able to susteine the least assault by force of such rewards as he presentlie receiued, and of such large promises as on the emperours behalfe were made to him, promised to the emperour, that he would so vse the matter, as his purpose should be sped: onelie he required him not to disalow the kings intent for interuiew to be had, which he desired in anie wise to go forward, that he might shew his high magnificence in France, according to his first intention.

Edw. Hall.

The emperour remained in Canturburie till the thursdaie, being the last of Maie, and then taking leaue of the king, and of his aunt the queene, departed to Sandwich, where he tooke his ships and sailed into Flanders.

The king land-
eth at Calis.

The same daie, the king made saile from the port of Douer and landed at Calis about eleuen of the clocke, and with him the quéene and ladies, & manie nobles of the realme. His grace was receiued into the checker, and there rested. The fourth of Iune, the king and quéene with all their traine remooued from Calis, to his princelie lodging newlie erected beside the towne of Guisnes, the most noble & roiall lodging that euer before was seene. ¶ For it was a palace, the which was quadrant, and euerie quadrant of the same palace was

Ed. Hall in H.8
fol. lxxiij.
The descriptiõ
of the new
palace before
Guisnes.

thrée hundred and twentie eight foot long of assise, which was in compasse thir-téene hundred and twelue foot about. This palace was set on stages by great cunning & sumptuous worke.

At the entering into the palace before the gate, on the plaine gréene, was builded a fountaine of imbowed worke, gilt with fine gold, and bice, ingrailed with antike works: the old god of wine called Bacchus birling the wine, which by the conduits in the earth

earth ran to all people plentiouslie with red, white, and claret wine, ouer whose head was written in letters of Romane in gold, Faicte bonne chere quiuouldra. On the other hand or side of the gate was set a piller, which was of ancient Romane worke, borne with foure lions of gold, the pillers wrapped in a wreath of gold curiouslie wrought and intrailed, and on the summit of the said piller stood an image of the blind god Cupid, with his bow and arrows of loue, readie by his séeming to strike the yoong people to loue.

The foregate of the same palace or place with great and mightie masonrie by sight was arched, with a tower on euerie side of the same port, rered by great craft, and imbattelled was the gate and tower, and in the fenesters and windowes were images resembling men of warre, readie to cast great stones. Also the same gate or tower was set with compassed images of ancient princes, as Hercules, Alexander, and other by intrailed worke, richlie limmed with gold and albine colours: and well and warilie was made ouer the gate loups, and inforced with battelments, and in the same gate a lodge for the porter, which there appeared, and other sumptuouslie apparelled like vnto kings officers. By the same gate all people passed into a large court faire and beautifull, for in this court appeared much of the outward beautie of this place, for from the first water table, to the raising or reisin péeces, were baie windowes, on euerie side mixed with cleare stories curiouslie glased, the posts or moinels of euerie window was gilt. The foregate of the said palace.The large court.

Thus the outward part of the place lumined the eies of the beholders, by reason of the sumptuous worke. Also the tower of the gate (as séemed) was builded by great masonrie, and by great engine of mans wit, for the sundrie countenances of euerie image that there appeared, some shooting, some casting, some readie to strike, and firing of gunnes, which shewed verie honorablie. Also all the said quadrants, baies, and edifices, were roiallie intrailed, as farre as vnto the same court apperteined. And direct against the gate was deuised a halpas, and at the entrie of the staire, were images of sore and terrible countenances, all armed in curious worke of argentine. The baie of the same halpas pendant by craft of timber, & vnder it antike images of gold inuironed with verdor of olifs cast in compasse, mounstring their countenances toward the entring of the palace. The staire of the said halpas was cast of passage by the wents of brode steps, so that from the first foot or lowest step, anie person might without paine go vnto the highest piace of the same halpas. The halpas.

On euerie hand was their chamber doores and enterings into the chambers of the same palace, which were long and large, and well proportioned, to receiue light and aire at pleasure: the roofes of them from place to place, and chamber to chamber were sieled, and couered with cloth of silke, of the most faire and quicke inuention that before time was séene. For the ground was white ingraild, embowed, and batoned with rich clothes of silkes, knit and fret with cuts and braids, and sundrie new casts, that the same clothes of silke shewed like bullions of fine burned gold: and the roses in losenges, that in the same roofe were in kindlie course, furnished so to mans sight, that no liuing creature might but ioy in the beholding thereof. For from the iaw péece of the said sieling (which péece was gilt with fine gold) were workes in pane paled, all the walles to the crest incountering the cleare stories, the same crest which was of large deepnesse, the worke was antike knots with bosses cast and wrought with more cunning than I can write, all which works and ouerages were gilt, and to set it the more to the glorie, the flourishing bise was comparable to the rich ammell. The chambers and lodges.

Also at the foot of the same palace was another crest all of fine set gold, whereon hanged rich & maruelous clothes of arras wrought of gold and silke, compassed of manie ancient stories, with which clothes of arras euerie wall and chamber were hanged, & all the windowes so richlie couered, that it passed all other sights before séene. In euerie chamber and euerie place conuenient were clothes of estate, great and large of cloth The hangings & other ornaments.

of gold, of tissue, and rich embroderie, with chaires couered with like cloth, with

pommels of fine gold, and great cushins of rich worke of the Turkie making, nothing lacked of honourable furnishment. Also to the same palace was reared a chappell
with two closets, the quire of the said chappell sieled with cloth of gold, and thereon
fret ingrailed bent clothes of silke, all was then silke and gold. The altars of this
chappell were hanged with rich reuesture of cloth of gold and tissue, embrodered with
perles. Ouer the hie altar was hanged a rich canopie of maruellous greatnesse, the
altar was apparelled with fiue paire of candlesticks of gold, and on the altar an
halpas, and thereon stood a crucifix all of fine gold, and on the same halpas stood
twelue images of the bignes of foure yeares of age, all gold.

All the copes and vestments were so rich as might be prepared or bought in the
citie of Florens, for they were all but of one péece, so wouen for the purpose, cloth
of tissue and powdered with red roses purpled withe fine gold. The Orfris set with

pearles and precious stones. And all the walles and deskes of this chappell were hanged with right cloth of gold, & thrée rich great crosses were there readie to be borne
at festiuall times, and basens and censers, gospellers, paxes, crewets, holie water
vessels, and other ornaments all of gold. Also in the first closet was a trauerse for

the kings person of cloth of gold, & in it his place & chaire, with cushins of cloth
of gold: before the trauerse was an altar of presence, which altar was adorned with
cloth of broderie, and rich pearles and precious stones, set in goldsmiths worke of
fine gold. On the altar was a deske or halpas, whereon stood a patible of the crucifix
of fine gold, with an image of the Trinitie, an image of the virgin Marie, and twelue
other images, all fine gold & precious stones, two paire of candlesticks of fine gold,
with the basens, crewets, paxes, and other ornaments.

The said closet was hanged with tapets embrodered with rich worke fret with
pearles and stones, the roofe of the same closet was sieled with worke of inmouled,
gilt with fine gold, and senoper, and bise. The second closet was for the queens

person, in which was a trauerse of rich cloth of gold, the altar so richlie apparelled,
that there lacked neither pearles nor stones of riches. On the altar were twelue great
images of gold, the closet hanged with cloth of gold, all other iewels missall I suppose
neuer such like were séene, and the roofe of the same closet was sieled with like worke

that the kings closet was, as is before rehearsed. And from this palace or place into
the mightie & strong fortresse & castell roiall of Guisnes, was a gallerie for the secret

passage of the kings person into a secret lodging within the same castell, the more
for the king ease. Also to this palace was all houses of offices, that to such an
honourable court should apperteine, that is to wit, the lord chamberlein, lord steward,
lord treasuror of the houshold, for the comptrollor, the office of gréene cloth,
wardrobes, iewell house, and office of houshold seruice, as ewrie, pantrie cellar,
butterie, spicerie, pitcher house, larder and poultrie, and all other offices so large and
faire, that the officers might & did maruell, as in the craft of viands, by ouens,
harthes, rered orses, chimnies, ranges, & such instruments as there were ordeined.

In this palace (as ye haue heard) was the kings grace lodged, and all the nobles after
their degrees. And for that the towne of Guisnes was little, and that all the noble
men might not there be lodged, they set vp tents in the field, to the number of twen-

tie and eight hundred sundrie lodgings, which was a goodlie sight. Thus was the
king in his palace roiall at Guisnes. Francis the French king was with all his nobles
of the realme of France come to the towne of Ard, which was prepared for his comming, manie tents, halles, and pauilions were set and pitched in the field. On the
French partie also there was at the same towne of Ard builded the French kings
lodging full well, but not finished. Much was the prouision in Picardie on euerie
part thorough all. The French king commanded his lodging to bée made a little out
of the towne of Ard, in the territorie of an old castell, which by the warre of old
time

time had béene beaten.　On the same place was edified a house of solace and sport, of

A banketting house for solace and disport.

large and mightie compasse, which was chieflie susteined by a great mightie mast, whereby the great ropes and tackle streined, the same mast was staied.　All the roofe of the same house hoong on the same mast, and with tackle was streined & borne by the supporters of the same mast or trée, the colours of the same was all blew, set with starres of gold foile, and the orbs of the heauens by the craft of colours in the roofe, were curiouslie wrought in maner like the skie or firmament, and a cressant strained somedeale towards the towne of Ard, this cressant was couered with frets and knots made of iuie bushes, and box branches, and other things that longest would be gréene for pleasure.

Now like as diuerse of the French nobilitie had visited the king of England whilest he laie in Calis, so likewise the lord cardinall, as ambassadour to the king, rode with a noble repaire of lords, gentlemen, and prelates, to the towne of Ard, where he was of the French king highlie interteined, with great thanks, for that by his meanes hée had ioined in friendship with the king of England, to his high contentation and pleasure, as hauing obteined the thing which he had long desired.　The noble port, sumptuous shew, and great traine of gentlemen, knights, lords, and number of seruants, in rich apparell & sutes of liueries attendant on the cardinall, made the French men greatlie to woonder at his triumphant dooings.

The great pompe of cardinall Woolsie.

The king of England had giuen vnto the said cardinall full authoritie, power, and libertie, to affirme and confirme, bind and vnbind, whatsoeuer should be in question betwéene him and the French king: and the like authoritie, power, and libertie, did the French king by his sufficient letters patents, grant to the same cardinall, which was accepted to be a signe of great loue, that he should commit so great a trust vnto the king of Englands subiect.　The daie of the meeting was appointed to be on the thursdaie the seauenth of Iune, vpon which daie the two kings met in the vale of Andren, accompanied with such a number of the nobilitie of both realmes, so richlie appointed in apparell, and costlie iewels, as chaines, collars of S S, & other the like ornaments to set foorth their degrees and estates, that a woonder it was to behold and view them in their order and roomes, which euerie man kept according to his appointment.

Great credit committed to the cardinall by both the kings. The interuiew of the two kings in the vale of Andren.

The two kings méeting in the field, either saluted other in most louing wise, first on horssebacke, and after alighting on foot eftsoones imbraced with courteous words, to the great reioising of the beholders: and after they had thus saluted ech other, they went both togither into a rich tent of cloath of gold, there set vp for the purpose, in the which they passed the time in pleasant talke, banketting, and louing deuises, till it drew toward the euening, and then departed for that night, the one to Guisnes, the other to Ard.　At this meeting of the two kings in open sight, I then well perceiued (saith Hall) the habillements roiall of the French king.　His garment was a chemew, of cloath of siluer, culponed with cloath of gold, of damaske, cantell wise, and garded on the borders with the Burgon bands.

Edw. Hall in H. 8. fol. lxxvij. The French kings roiall ornaments.

Ouer that he had a cloake of broched sattin, with gold of purple colour, wrapped about his bodie trauerse, beded from the shoulder to the wast, fastned in the loope of the first fould: this said cloake was richlie set with pearles and pretious stones.　This French king had on his head a coife of damaske gold set with diamonds, and his courser that he rode on was couered with a trapper of tissue, brodered with deuise, cut in fashion mantell wise, the skirts were embowed and fret with frized worke, and knit with corbelles & buttons tasseled of Turkie making, raines and headstall answering of like worke: and verelie of his person the same Francis the French king, a goodlie prince, statelie of countenance, merie of chéere, browne coloured, great eies, high nosed, big lipped, faire brested, broad shoulders, small legges, & long féet.

The description of the French kings person.

On saturdaie the ninth of Iune, in a place within the English pale were set vp in

a field

a field called the campe, two trées of much honour, the one called the Aubespine, that is to saie, the hawthorne in English, for Henrie: and the other the Framboister, which in English signifieth the raspis berie, after the signification in French. These trees were curiouslie wrought, the leaues of gréene damaske, the branches, boughs, and withered leaues of cloath of gold; and all the bodies and armes of the same cloath of gold laid on timber: they were in height from the foot to the top thirtie foure foot of assize, in compasse about an hundred twentie and nine foot, & from bough to bough fortie thrée foot: on these trées were flowers and fruits in kindlie wise, with siluer and Venice gold: their beautie shewed farre.

On the same daie the two kings came to those trées of honour, noblie accompanied in such roiall sort as was requisit. The campe was in length nine hundred foot, and in bredth thrée hundred and twentie foot ditched round about (sauing at the entries) with broad and déepe ditches. Diuerse scaffolds were reared about this campe for the ease of the nobles. On the right side of the field stood the quéene of England, and the quéene of France, with manie ladies. The campe was stronglie railed and barred on euerie end: in the entrie there were two lodgings prepared for the two kings, wherein they might arme themselues, and take their ease. Also in the same compasse there were two great cellars couched full of wine, which was liberallie bestowed on all men. The two kings, as brethren in armes, vndertooke to deliuer all persons at iusts, tournie and barriers.

With these two kings were associate by the order of armes, the duke of Vandosme, the duke of Suffolke, the countie saint Paule, the marquesse Dorset, monsieur de Roche, sir William Kingston, monsieur Brian, sir Richard Ierningham, monsieur Canaan, sir Giles Capell, monsieur Buccall, maister Nicholas Carew, monsieur Mortafilion, and maister Anthonie Kneuet. On mondaie the eleuenth of Iune, the two quéenes of England and of France came to the campe, where either saluted other right honourablie, and went into a stage for them prepared. At the houre assigned, the two kings armed at all peeces mounted on horssebacke, and with their companies entered the field; the French king on a courser barded, couered with purple sattin, broched with gold, & embrodered with corbins fethers round and buckled, the fether was blacke and hatched with gold: on his head péece he bare a sléeue. All the parteners of the French kings chalenge were in like apparell euerie thing correspondent in cloath of silke embrodered, on his person were attendant on horssebacke noble persons, and on foot foure persons all apparelled in purple sattin.

The king of England was vpon a fresh courser, the trappers of cloth of gold, of tissue, the arson mantell wise, and on the brunt of the trapper bard fashion, cut in waues of water worke, and euerie waue raw wrought and frized with damaske gold: this worke was laid loose on russet veluet, and knit togither with points of gold, which waues signified the lordship of the narrow seas. All the parteners of the kings chalenge were in the same sute, their horsses as well as their persons. Attendant on the king on horssebacke were sir Henrie Guilford maister of the kings horsse, sir Iohn Pechie deputie of Calis, sir Edward Guilford maister of the kings armie, and monsieur Moret of the French court. All these foure were apparelled in the kings liuerie, which was white on the right side, and the left side gold and russet both hose and garment: on him were attendant on foot six honourable knights, twentie esquiers, and officers to the number of an hundred and twelue persons, of the which number all the knights and gentlemen had coats, the one halfe siluer, and the other cloath of gold and russet veluet, and the other officers coats were of right sattin of the same colour, and all their hosen were of the same sute verie costlie.

Thus with honour and noble courage these two noble kings with their companies entered into the field, and them presented vnto the quéenes. After reuerence doone, they rode round about the tilt, and so tooke their places appointed, abiding the answers: which was for the first the duke of Alanson and ten men of armes on his
band,

band, on coursers barded, the bards couered with white and black veluet, fastened the one within the other, garded with Burgon bands of tinsell sattin, as well their garments as their bards. Then entered on coursers barded twelue gentlemen of the band of the lord admerall of France, their garments and bards were russet sattin, broched with gold and white and purple sattin, after the deuise of their pleasure with great plumes. When these bands were entred the field, they shewed themselues about the tilt, and did reuerence vnto the queenes. The band of the duke of Alanson tooke first place, they made them prest on both sides, the French king was the first that ran, he did valiantlie and brake speares mightilie.

Then ran the king of England to monsieur Grandeuile with great vigor; so that The king of England runneth against Grandeuile. the speares brake in the kings hand to the vantplate all to shiuers. And at the second course he gaue the said monsieur Grandeuile such a stroke, that the charnell of his headpéece, although the same was verie strong, was broken in such wise that he might run no more, wherby the king wanted three courses. Then ran the duke de Vandosme, & met his counter part right noblie, and brake speares right valiantlie. The noble duke of Suffolke charged his course, and met right valiantlie his counter part, and furnished the fiue courses right noblie togither like good men of armes. And when all parties of the chalenge had right valiantlie furnished their courses, then ran againe the two noble kings, who did so valiantlie, that the beholders had great ioy, after which courses the heralds cried Desarmee, and the trumpets sounded to lodging.

On tuesdaie the twelfe of Iune at houre conuenient the two quéenes tooke their Monsieur de Swies and his band. stages, and the band of chalenge in the field prest to answer and deliuer all commers, to whome came ten gentlemen armed on barded horsses of the band of monsieur de Swies, their bards and apparell cloath of veluet full of friers knots siluer. After they had presented them vnto the quéenes, they they tooke the end of the tilt, and so course after course they ran to the chalengers right egerlie, and the chalengers of the partie of the two kings deliuered to the end of their articles of iusts. Then entered eleuen men of armes of the band of monsieur de Tremoiell, on horsses barded with yellow veluet, losenged with friers knots of blacke veluet: and after they had saluted the quéenes, they likewise tooke the end of the tilt, and course after course ran vntill they were deliuered of their chalenges of iusts. Valiantlie this daie was finished.

On wednesdaie the thirtéenth of Iune, the two hardie kings armed at all peeces, The attire of the French king and his parteners of chalenge. entered into the field right noblie apparelled. The French king and all his parteners of chalenge were arraied in purple sattin, broched with gold and purple veluet, embrodered with little rolles of what sattin, wherein was written, Quando: their bards & garments were set full of the same, and the residue where was no rolles were poudered & set with the letter elle, as thus, L. which in French is she, which was interpreted to be, Quando elle, when she: and insuing the deuise of the first daie, it signifieth togither, Hart fastened in paine endles, when she. The king of England The king of England and the parteners of his chalenge. with all the band or parteners of his chalenge were likewise on horssebacke, apparelled in trappers of losenges russet veluet and cloath of siluer of damaske, embrodered and set in euerie losenge a branch of eglantine of gold, the apparell of the persons were of the same correspondent to the trapper. This eglantine trée is sweet, pleasant and greene, if it be kindlie and fréendlie handeled; but if it be rudelie dealt with, it will pricke and he that will pull vp the whole trée by the top, his hands will be hurt.

The two kings with their companies thus apparelled, presented themselues to the quéenes, and so tooke the end of the tilt. Then entered into the field monsieur Leskew called lord Leskin, with him came eleuen men of armes, himselfe the twelfe on horsses barded and richlie apparelled, and so rode about the tilt and saluted the

queenes.

queenes, and tooke the end of the tilt.   Monsieur de Leskew and his eleuen companions had their bases and bards all of blacke cloath of gold of damaske all cut on blacke
sattin, their garments had mantell sléeues on the left arme, to the wast behind iust to
the shoulder, which was praised for the strangenesse.   The French king ran to monsieur de Ambois, one of the band of monsieur Leskew, and the king of England
charged his course and ran to monsieur Leskew, and so furnished their courses (as
they saie) right noblie and valiantlie in breaking speares that were strong.   Thus
course after course ech with other, his counter partie did right valiantlie: but the
two kings surmounted all the rest in prowesse and valiantnesse.

This band thus furnished, entered the marquesse de Salons and his band, twelue
persons all riding on coursers barded and apparelled in white sattin and blacke, broched
with gold and siluer, with cuts and culpins much after tawnie and blacke sattin bil-
lots: & after reuerence doone to the queenes, they tooke the end of the tilt.   To the
marquesse de Salons ran the king of England, and the king of France to an other of
the same band, still course after course ran all the noble men, till the marques de
Salons and his band were deliuered, who bare them right valiantlie: then blew the
trumpets the retreit, & the two kings them vnarmed and after departed, the French
king vnto Ard, and the king of England to his castell of Guisnes.

On thursdaie the thirtéenth daie of Iune by the noonetide the two quéenes met in
the campe & tooke their places, the people were come to behold the honour, and to
sée the two kings, who all readie armed entered the field, to receiue and deliuer all
men by answer of iusts.   Then entered the earle of Deuonshire, on his band the
lord Montacute, lord Herbert, lord Leonard Greie, maister Arthur Poole, maister
Francis Brian, maister Henrie Norris, and foure other all richlie apparelled, the one
side blew veluet embrodered with a mans heart burning in a ladies hand holding a
garden pot stilling with water on the heart: the other side was white sattin embrodered with letters of gold.   This companie rode about the tilt, and did reuerence
to the queenes, and so abode at the end of the same.

The earle of Deuonshire charged his speare, and the French king likewise charged
his course to meet the same earle, and ran so hard togither, that both their speares
brake, and so mainteined their courses noblie.   Then ran the king of England to monsieur Memorancie, and him encountered, & both bare togither and gaue great strokes;
the kings most noble grace neuer disuisored nor breathed vntill he ran the fiue courses
& deliuered his counterpartie.   Dukes, marquesses, knights, esquiers, and others ran
as fast as euer they might, there was none that abode when the courses came, vntill
the earle of Deuonshire and his band were deliuered of demands.   Then entered the
lord Howard sonne to the duke of Norffolke and eleuen companions apparelled and
barded in crimsin sattin full of flames of gold, the borders ribbed with crimsin veluet,
and with much honor (after due reuerence doone to the quéenes) were brought with
heralds of armes about the tilts; and so tooke the place to them appointed: right rich
was their apparell.

Then ran the French king and incountered the same lord Edmund, they brake both
their staues valiantlie course after course, the incounter ceassed not till they had furnished their fiue courses; so was the lord Edmund deliuered by the French K.   Then
ran the king of England to a strong gentleman named Rafe Brooke and brake his
speare, and ran course after course, vntill he had finished his courses right noblie and
like a prince of most valiancie.   The residue ceassed not vntill they had ech deliuered
other of their chalenge.   On fridaie the fiftéenth daie of Iune the king of England
mounted on a courser roiall, his person armed at all peeces, his apparell and trappers
was the one side rich cloath of gold of tissue, the other side cloath of tissue of siluer,
and cloath of gold of tissue entered ound the one with the other.

                                                                              The

The ound is a worke wauing vp & downe, and all the borders as well trappers as other was garded with letters of fine gold, and all the other side that was ound was set with signes called cifers of fine gold, the which were set with great and orientall pearles. The cifers signified letters knit togither in a knot, which was to wit; God my freend, my realme and I maie. This was the deuise and reason thereof. All the kings band were apparelled in like apparell. The French K. likewise armed at all points mounted on a courser roiall, all his apparell as well bards as garments were purple veluet entered the one with the other, embrodered full of little books of white sattin, & in the bookes were written A me. About the borders of the bards and the borders of the garments a chaine of blew like iron, resembling the chaine of a well or prison chaine, which was interpreted to be Liber, a booke. Within this booke was written (as is said) A me. Put these two togither and it maketh Libera me. The chaine betokeneth prison or bonds, and so maketh togither in English, Deliuer me of bonds. Then they tooke the end of the tilt.

The French king, his furniture and deuise vpon his ornaments.

Readie was monsieur Florengis and with him twelue men of armes with coursers barded: the bards and apparell was crimsin veluet, tawnie veluet, and plunket veluet embrodered borderwise with sheepeheards hookes of cloath of siluer. When they with honour had passed about the tilt (due reuerence to the quéenes and ladies doone) the two kings had their speares readie, and then began the rushing of speares. The king of England this daie ran so freshlie and so manie courses, that one of his best coursers was dead that night, this band was deliuered man after man of their pretense of iusts. Then entered bands of monsieur de Rambeurs and monsieur de Puis, ech hauing eleuen persons in number, the one band all white sattin embrodered with blacke, and the other all blacke dropped with siluer drops; who after reuerence doone to the quéenes, at the end of the tilt tooke their places. Then began a new incounter hard and sore, manie of them bare great strokes of the kings, to their honour: and with such violence they ran, as they set their horsses in a sweating heat, and themselues meeting with full force made the fragments or broken péeces of their staues mount aloff in the air like an arow out of a bow; as the poet saith;

Monsieur Florengis and his companie.

Hastæ stridentis fractæ petit æthera cuspis.

On saturdaie the seuentéenth daie of Iune, the French king with a small number came to the castle of Guisnes about the houre of eight in the morning. The king being in his priuie chamber had thereof knowledge, who with glad hast went to receiue the same French king, and him met and welcomed in friendlie and honorable maner; and after communication betwéene them had, the king of England departed, leauing the French king there in the sumptuous place before named. Then was busie the lord chamberleine, the lord steward, and all other officers, to make readie feast and cheare. It were too long to rehearse all, for such a feast and banket was then made, that of long time before the like had not bene séene. The king of England thus departing, he tooke his horsse, and with a companie of noblemen rode to Ard, where the French quéene and other noble men receiued him with much honour.

The French king commeth to Guisnes, & the king of England goeth to Ard.

After which receiuing, he was by the said quéene and lords brought into a chamber hanged with blew veluet embrodered with flowers delice of cloth of gold, wherein was a great bed of like worke, from whence he was conueied to another chamber, in the which was a kings state. This chamber was hanged and sieled with cloth of gold, embrodered with great cordels or friers knots of cloth of siluer. In the same chamber were two cupboords, on either side one, furnished with great and goodlie plate gilt. Noble feasting and cheare was there made. After dinner the ladies dressed them to danse, and certeine yoong honourable lords of England, apparelled after the maner of Rusland or farre Eastland, whose hosen were of rich gold sattin called aureat sattin, ouerrolled to the knée with scarlet, and on their feet shooes with little pikes of white nailes after the Estland guise, their dublets of rich crimsin veluet and

The king of England interteined of the French quéene.

A maske in the French court of English lords.

cloth

cloth of gold, with wide sléeues lined with cloth of gold: ouer this they had clokes of crimsin veluet short, lined with cloth of gold, on euerie side of the clokes rings of siluer, with laces of Venice gold, and on their heads they had hats made in the towne of Danske, and purses of seales skinnes, and girdels of the same: all these yoong lords had visards on their faces, and their hats were drawne with like hatbands full of damaske gold.

Other ten lords were apparelled in long gownes of blew sattin of the ancient fashion, embrodered with reasons of gold that said Adieu iunesse, Farewell youth: they had tippets of blacke veluet, & hats hanging therby, & on their heads hie violet standing caps, and girdels of silke, and purses of cloth of gold after the ancient maner, with visards on their faces of like anciencie. After all these triumphs and braueries, great store of spices, fruits, iellies, & banketing viands were brought, which being doone and ended, the king tooke leaue of the French queene and ladies, to whome were brought thirtie horsses trapped in damaske, white and yellow, and so passed he and his traine the towne of Ard into the field and campe. Right roiailie also was the French K. interteined, and all other after their degree and state. Now when all this solemnitie was ended, the French king tooke leaue of the quéene and ladies of the court. The lord cardinall in statelie attire, accompanied with the duke of Buckingham, and other great lords, conducted forward the French king, and in their way they incountered and met the king of England and his companie right in the vallie of

Anderne, apparelled in their masking apparell, which gladded the French king. After reuerence doone, the said two kings departed for that night, the English to Guisnes, and the French to Ard.

On mondaie, the eighteenth of Iune, was such an hideous storme of wind and weather, that manie coniectured it did prognosticate trouble and hatred shortlie after to follow betwéene princes. On tuesdaie the nintéenth of Iune, the two kings came to the campe againe armed at all peeces, and there abode them that would come, so that then began the iustes afresh. On wednesdaie the twentith of Iune, the two kings began to hold tournies with all the parteners of their chalenge armed at all péeces. The quéene of France and the quéene of England were in the places for them prepared, and there was manie a goodlie battell performed: the kings dooing as well as the best, so that the beholders spake of them honor. On thursdaie the one and twentith of Iune, the two kings likewise kept the tourneies, so that all those noble men that would prooue their valiancies, were deliuered according to the articles of the tourneies, which this daie tooke end. On fridaie the 22 of Iune, the two kings with their retinue did battell on foot at the barriers, and there deliuered all such as put foorth themselues to trie their forces. On saturdaie the thrée and twentith of Iune, the lord cardinall sang an high solemne masse by note, aloft vpon a pompous stage before the two kings & quéenes, the which being finished, indulgence was giuen to all the hearers. The two kings dined in one chamber that daie, and the two quéenes in another. After dinner, the two kings with their band entered the field on foot before the barriers, & so began the fight, which continued battell after battell, till all the commers were answered. There were deliuered this day thus at the barriers by battell, an hundred and six persons: the two last battels did the kings trie. And so that saturdaie the whole chalenge was performed, and all men deliuered of the articles of iusts, tourneies, and battels on foot at the barriers, by the said two kings and their aids.

After this, there followed roiall maskes, and on the sundaie the foure and twentith of Iune, the king of England with foure companies, in euerie companie ten, trimlie appointed in masking apparell, rode to Ard: and likewise the French king accompanied with eight and thirtie persons as maskers repaired to Guisnes. They met on the waie, & each companie passed by other without any countenance making or disuisarding

Margin notes: The two kings méet. / A great and tempestuous wind prognosticating trouble. / Barriers. / The cardinall sang masse before the two kings. / Maskes.

uisarding. They were honorablie receiued, as well at the one place as the other. And when they had ended their pastime, banketting, and danses, they returned and met againe on the way homeward, and then putting off their visards, they louinglie embraced: and after amiable communication togither, they tooke leaue each of other, & for a remembrance gaue gifts either to other verie rich and princelie.

¶ During this triumph, much people of Picardie and west Flanders drew to Guisnes, to sée the king of England & his honor, to whom vittels of the court were giuen in plentie, the conduit of the gate did run wine alwaies. There were vagabonds, plowmen, labourers, and of the bragerie, wagoners and beggers, that for drunkennesse laie in routs and heapes. So great resort came thither, that knights and ladies, who were come to sée the noblenesse, were faine to lie in haie and straw, and held them thereof highlie pleased. From the court of the emperour, nor of the ladie Margarets court, nor of Flanders, Brabant, nor Burgognie came neuer a person to answer to the chalenge. By that it séemed that there was small loue betwene the emperour & the French king. Moreouer, monsieur Faiot capteine of Bullongne with monsieur Chattelon, did their deuoir to haue taken the towne of saint Omer, of which dooing was thought no goodnesse to the emperour.]

On mondaie the fiue and twentith of Iune, the king with the quéene remooued from Guisnes to Calis, where he remained till the tenth of Iulie, on which daie he rode to Graueling, and was receiued on the waie by the emperour, and so by him conueied to Graueling, where not onelie the king, but also all his traine was cheared and feasted, with so louing maner, that the Englishmen highly praised the emperours court. [When the French king and his lords had knowledge of the meeting of the emperour and the king of England in the towne of Graueling, they were therewith greatlie gréeued, as by manie things appeared. For as the Englishmen were in France disdained, and in their sutes there greatlie deferred, and had little right, and much lesse fauour: so from day to day still more and more began hartburning, and in conclusion open warre did arise betweene the two realmes.]

On wednesdaie the eleuenth of Iulie, the emperour and his aunt the ladie Margaret duchesse of Sauoy came with the king of England to the towne of Calis, and there continued in great ioy and solace, with feasting, banketting, dansing and masking vntil the fourtéenth of Iulie. ¶ For the interteining of these estates (the English lords and gentlemen displaced of their lodgings to serue the other and their traine) there was builded a banketting house eight hundred foot compasse, like a theatre, after a goodlie deuise, builded in such maner as (I thinke) was neuer séene, with sixtéene principals made of great masts, betwixt euerie mast foure and twentie foot, and all the outsides closed with boord and canuas.

Ouer it, and within round about by the sides, were made thrée scaffolds or lofts one aboue another for men and women to stand vpon. And in the midst of the same banketting house, was set vp a great piller of timber made of eight great masts, bound togither with iron bands, for to hold them togither: for it was an hundred and foure and thirtie foot of length, and cost six pounds thirteene shillings and fourepence to set it vpright. The banketing house was couered ouer with canuas, fastened with ropes and iron as fast as might be deuised. And within the said house was painted the heauens, with starres, sunne, moone, and clouds, with diuerse other things made aboue ouer mens heads: and there were great images of wickers couered, and made like great men of diuerse strange nations: and diuerse reasons were written by them of the countries that they likened to be of, with the armes of those countries hanging by them.

Also there was made as it were manie ships vnder saile, and windmils going, and about the high piller of timber that stood vpright in the middest, was made stages of timber for organs and other instruments to stand vpon, and men to plaie on them,

VOL. III.   4 L   & for

Side notes:

Ed. Hall in H.8. fol. lxxxiiij.

Knights and ladies faine to lie in haie and straw.

King Henrie departed from Guisnes to Calis, & from thence to Graueling to visit the emperour. *Ed. Hall in H. 8. fol. lxvj.*

The emperor commeth to Calis to king Henrie.

Abr. Fl. ex I. S. pag. 927. Banketting house within the towne of Calis. *Rt. Turpin.*

Goodlie workmanship within the banketting house.

& for other musicians & pageants to be plaied, when the K. of England & the emperor should be at their banket. But in the morning of the same day, the wind began
to rise, & at night blew off the canuas, and all the elements, with the starres,
sunne, moone, and clouds, and the wind blew out aboue a thousand torches, and
other lights of wax, that were prepared to giue light to the banket, & all the kings
seats that were made with great riches, besides all other things, were all dashed and
lost.]

Banketting house defaced by tempest.

The same daie at night that the states were interteined, the king and fiftéene persons were apparelled all in blacke veluet couered with cloth of gold, cut on the
veluet, fastened with knots of gold, on the which knots hoong spangles of gold like
tufts, and bonnets of the same, & clokes of crimsin sattin and cloth of gold wrapped trauerse, and their buskins of the same cloth of gold. All these lustie maskers
went to the emperours lodging, and were receiued, and in the chamber of presence
dansed and reuelled, the which at the emperours request, the king and other dis-
uisarded themselues, whereby the king was knowne: then the king tooke his leaue,
and departed for that night. On tuesdaie the twelfe of Iulie, bicause the banketting
house could not be finished, the emperour and the ladie Margaret supped with the
king & the queene at the checker, where the same night after supper reuelled ninetie
and six maskers: after the reuels was a banket, after which banket the king brought
the emperour and the ladie Margaret to the staple, and after withdrew him.

A statelie mask to solace the empe-ror & his com-panie.

This night were eight companies of maskers, and in euerie companie twelue persons all in gold, siluer and veluet, richlie apparelled, but bicause the roome was
small, the shew was the lesse. In these reuels were put in maskers apparell diuerse
gentlemen of the French court vnwéeting to the K. or anie other that bare rule. For
diuerse yoong gentlemen of the French court fauored more the French partie, than
the emperours partie; through which meanes they saw and much more heard than
they should haue doone. On fridaie the thirteenth daie of Iulie, the emperour did
intend to haue departed from Calis, but the counsell was such that he departed not
that night.

French gentle-men in maskers apparell vnwéet-ing to them that bare rule in the reuels.

On saturdaie the fouretéenth of Iulie, the emperour tooke his leaue of the queene of
England his aunt, and departed toward Graueling, being conducted on his waie by
the king of England, to a village towards Flanders called Waell, and there they
imbraced and tooke their leaue either of other in most louing maner. They did not
altogither spend the time thus while they were togither, in vaine pleasures, and sporting reuels; for the charters before time concluded were read ouer, and all the articles
of the league tripartite agréed betwixt the emperour, the king of England, and the
French king, were at full declared, to the which the French king had fullie condescended. And for the more proofe thereof, and exemplification of the same, he sent
monsieur de Roch with letters of credence to signifie to the emperour, that in the
word of a prince he would obserue, fulfill, performe and kéepe all the same articles,
for him, his realme and subiects. Shortlie after that the emperour and the king had
taken leaue each of other, and were departed, the king shipped, and with the quéene
and all other the nobilitie returned safelie into England.

The king re-turneth into England.

The king kept his Christmas at Greenwith this yeare, with much noblenesse and
open court. And the tenth daie of Februarie, in his owne person, iusted with all
commers. On Twelfe daie his grace and the earle of Deuonshire, with foure aids,
answered at the tourneie all commers, which were sixtéene persons: noble and rich
was their apparell, but in feats of armes the king excelled the rest. About this time
the king hauing regard to the common welth of his realme, considered how for the
space of fiftie yeares past and more, the nobles and gentlemen of England, being
giuen to grasing of cattell, and kéeping of shéepe, had inuented a meane how to
increase their yearlie reuenues, to the great decaie and vndooing of husbandmen of
the

1521

Polydor.

the land.   For the said nobles and gentlemen, after the maner of the Numidians, An inconueni-
more studieng how to increase their pastures, than to mainteine tillage, began to ence of turning arable ground
decaie husband tacks & tenements, and to conuert arable ground into pasture, fur- into pasture.
nishing the same with beasts and shéepe, and also deere, so inclosing the field with
hedges, ditches, and pales, which they held in their owne hands, ingrossing woolles,
and selling the same, and also shéepe and beasts at their owne prices, and as might
stand most with their owne priuate commoditie.

Hereof a thréefold euill chanced to the common wealth, as Polydor noteth.   One, The common-
for that thereby the number of husbandmen was sore diminished, the which the wealth hurt thrée waies thereby.
prince vseth chieflie in his seruice for the warres : an other, for that manie townes and
villages were left desolate, and became ruinous : the third, for that both wooll and
cloth made thereof, and the flesh of all maner beasts vsed to be eaten, was sold at far
higher prices than was accustomed.   These enormities at the first begining being not
redressed, grew in short space to such force and vigour by euill custome, that afterwards they gathered to such an vnited force, that hardly they could be remedied.
Much like a disease, which in the beginning with litle paine to the patient, and lesse
labour to the surgeon maie be cured; whereas the same by delai and negligence being
suffered to putrifie, becommeth a desperate sore, and then are medicines nothing
auailable, and not to be applied, according to his opinion that said :

> Helleborum frustra (cùm iam cutis ægra tumescit)   *Pers. sat.* 3.
> Poscentes videas : venienti occurrite morbo.

The king therefore causing such good statutes as had beene deuised and established
for reformation in this behalfe, to be reuiued and called vpon, took order by directing Commissions granted for the
foorth his commissions vnto the iustices of peace, and other such magistrats, that maintenance of
presentment should be had and made of all such inclosures, and decaie of husbandrie, tillage and laieng open of in-
as had chanced within the space of fiftie yeares before that present time.   The iustices closures.
and other magistrates, according to their commission executed the same.   And so
commandement was giuen, that the decaied houses should bée built vp againe, that
the husbandmen should be placed eftsoones in the same, and that inclosed grounds
should be laid open, and sore punishment appointed against them that disobeied.

These so good and wholesome ordinances shortlie after were defeated by meanes of Bribes.
bribes giuen vnto the cardinall : for when the nobles and gentlemen, which had for
their pleasures imparked the common fields, were loth to haue the same againe disparked, they redéemed their vexation with good summes of monie; and so had licence to keepe their parks and grounds inclosed as before.   Thus the great expectation which men had conceiued of a general redresse, prooued void : howbeit, some
profit the husbandmen in some parts of the realme got by the moouing of this
matter, where inclosures were alreadie laid open, yer mistresse monie could preuent them; and so they inioied their commons, which before had beene taken from
them.

After that this matter for inclosures was thus dispatched, the cardinall boiling in The cardinall deui-eth the de-
hatred against the duke of Buckingham, & thirsting for his bloud, deuised to make struction of the
Charles Kneuet, that had beene the dukes surueior, and put from him (as ye haue heard) duke of Buck-ingham.
an instrument to bring the duke to destruction.   This Kneuet being had in examination before the cardinall, disclosed all the dukes life.   And first he vttered, that the
duke was accustomed by waie of talke, to saie, how he meant so to vse the matter,
that he would atteine to the crowne, if king Henrie chanced to die without issue : &
that he had talke and conference of that matter on a time with George Neuill, lord
of Aburgauennie, vnto whome he had giuen his daughter in marriage; and also that
he threatened to punish the cardinall for his manifold misdooings, being without
cause his mortall enimie.

The

The cardinall imboldeneth Kneuet against the duke.

The cardinall hauing gotten that which he sought for, incouraged, comforted, and procured Kneuet, with manie comfortable words and great promises, that he should with a bold spirit and countenance obiect and laie these things to the dukes charge, with more if he knew it when time required. Then Kneuet partlie prouoked with desire to be reuenged, and partlie mooued with hope of reward, openlie confessed, that the duke had once fullie determined to deuise meanes how to make the king away, being brought into a full hope that he should be king, by a vain prophesie which one Nicholas Hopkins, a monke of an house of the Chartreux order beside Bristow, called Henton, sometime his confessor had opened vnto him.

The cardinall accuseth the duke of Buckingham to the king.

The cardinall hauing thus taken the examination of Kneuet, went vnto the king, and declared vnto him, that his person was in danger by such traitorous purpose, as the duke of Buckingham had conceiued in his heart, and shewed how that now there is manifest tokens of his wicked pretense: wherefore, he exhorted the king to prouide for his owne suertie with speed. The king hearing the accusation, inforced to the vttermost by the cardinall, made this answer; If the duke haue deserued to be punished, let him haue according to his deserts. The duke hervpon was sent for vp

Edw. Hall.

to London, & at his comming thither, was streightwaies attached, and brought to the Tower by sir Henrie Marneie, capteine of the gard, the sixteenth of Aprill. There was also attached the foresaid Chartreux monke, maister Iohn de la Car aliàs de la Court, the dukes confessor, and sir Gilbert Perke priest, the dukes chancellor.

An. Reg. 13.

After the apprehension of the duke, inquisitions were taken in diuerse shires of England of him; so that by the knights and gentlemen, he was indicted of high

The duke of Buckingham indicted of treason.

treason, for certeine words spoken (as before ye haue heard) by the same duke at Blechinglie, to the lord of Aburgauennie: and therewith was the same lord attached for concelement, and so likewise was the lord Montacute, and both led to the Tower. Sir Edward Neuill, brother to the said lord of Aburgauennie, was forbidden the kings presence. Moreouer, in the Guildhall, within the citie of London, before Iohn Brugge knight, then lord maior of the same citie, by an inquest whereof one Miles Gerrard was foreman, the said duke was indicted of diuerse points of high treason, as by the same indictment it appeareth.

The effect of the dukes indictement.

Namelie, that the said duke intending to exalt himselfe, and to vsurpe the crowne, the roiall power, and dignitie of the realme of England, and to depriue the kings maiestie thereof, that he the said duke might take vpon him the same; against his

The duke is indicted of treason in London.

allegiance, had the tenth daie of March, in the second yéere of the kings maiesties reigne, and at diuerse other times before and after, imagined and compassed the kings death and destruction at London, & at Thorneburie, in the countie of Glocester. And for the accomplishment of his wicked intent and purpose (as in the indictment is alledged) the twentie and fourth daie of Aprill, in the fourth yéere of the kings reigne he sent one of his chapleins called Iohn de la Court, to the priorie of Henton in Summersetshire, which was an house of the Chartreux monks. The effect or substance

This Hopkins had sent one of the prior of Hentons seruants to the duke the daie afore, to will him to send ouer to him his chancellor, as by an other indictment appeareth.

of whose message was, to vnderstand of one Nicholas Hopkins, a monke of the same house (who was vainelie reputed by waie of reuelation to haue foreknowledge of things to come) what should happen concerning the matters which he had imagined. Which monke, causing the said de la Court first to sweare vnto him, not to disclose his words to anie maner of person but onelie to the duke his maister: therewith declared, that his maister the said duke should haue all, willing him for the accomplishment of his purpose to séeke to win the fauour of the people. De la Court came backe with this answer, and told it to the duke at Thorneburie the morrow after, being the twentie fift of Aprill.

Also the two and twentith of Iulie in the same fourth yeare, the duke sent the same de la Court with letters vnto the said monke, to vnderstand of him further of such

such matters: and the monke told him againe for answer, that the duke should haue The monks reuelation was peremptorie to the duke. all. And being asked as well now, as before at the first time, how he knew this to be true: he said, By the grace of God. And with this answer de la Court now also returning, declared the same vnto the duke, the twentie fourth of Iulie at Thorneburie aforesaid. Moreouer, the said duke sent the same de la Court againe to the said monke with his letters, the six and twentith of Aprill, in the fift yeare of the kings reigne, when the king was to take his iournie into France; requiring to vnderstand what should become of these warres: and whether the Scotish king should in the kings absence inuade the realme or not. The monke (among other things) for answer But herein the moonke lied. of these letters, sent the duke word, that the king should haue no issue male.

Againe, the said duke the twentith daie of Februarie, in the sixt yeare of the kings reigne, being at Thorneburie, spake these words vnto Rafe earle of Westmerland; Well, there are two new dukes created here in England, but if ought but good come to the king, the duke of Buckingham should be next in bloud to sucéed to the crowne. After this, the said duke on the sixtéenth daie of Aprill, in the said sixt yeare of the kings reigne, went in person vnto the priorie of Henton, and there had conference with the foresaid monke, Nicholas Hopkins, who told him, that he should be king. Wherevnto the duke said, that if it so chanced, he would shew himselfe a The duke & the monke haue conference saith the indictment. iust and a righteous prince. The monke also told the duke, that he kew this by reuelation, and willed him in anie wise to procure the loue of the commons, the better to atteine his purposed intention.

The duke at the same time gaue, and promised to giue yearelie vnto the said priorie, six pounds, therewith to buie a tun of wine. And further he promised to giue vnto the same priorie, in readie monie twentie pounds, whereof ten pounds he gaue in hand, towards the conueieng of water vnto the house by a conduit. And to the said monke Nicholas Hopkins he gaue at that present in reward three pounds, and at an other time fortie shillings, at an other time a marke, and at an other time six shillings eight pense. After this, the twentith daie of March, in the tenth yeare of the kings reigne, he came to the same priorie, & eftsoones had conference with the said monke, to be more fullie informed by him in the matters aboue specified. At what time the monke also told him, that he should be king. The duke in talke told the monke, that he had doone verie well, to bind his chapleine Iohn de la Court, vnder the seale of confession, to kéepe secret such matter: for if the king should come to the knowledge thereof, it would be his destruction.

Likewise, the twentith daie of October, in the seuenth yeare of the kings reigne, Robert Gilbert the dukes chapleine and chancellor his errand to London. and at diuers other times, as well before as after, the said duke had sent his chancellor Robert Gilbert chapleine, vnto London, there to buie certeine cloathes of gold, siluer, and veluets, euerie time so much as amounted to the woorth of thrée hundred pounds; to the intent the said duke might bestow the same, as well vpon knights, esquiers, gentlemen of the kings house, and yeomen of his gard, as vpon other the kings subiects, to win their fauours and freendships to assist him in his euill purpose. Which cloathes the said Gilbert did buie, and brought the same vnto the said duke, who the twentith daie of Ianuarie, in the said seuenth yeare, & diuerse other daies and yeares before and after, did distribute and giue the same vnto certeine of the kings subiects for the purpose afore recited, as by the indictment it was inferred.

Furthermore, the said duke, the tenth of Iulie, in the tenth yeare of the kings Meanes that the duke vsed to make himselfe strong against the king. reigne, and diuerse other daies and times, as well before as after, did constitute more seuerall and particular officers in his castels, honours, lordships, and lands than he was accustomed to haue, to the end they might be assistant to him, vnder coulour of such offices, to bring his euill purpose to passe. Moreouer, the same duke sent vnto the king the tenth of Maie, in the ninth yeare of his reigne, for licence to reteine anie of the kings subiects, whome it should please him, dwelling within the shires of

Hereford,

Hereford, Glocester, and Summersetshire; and also, that he might at his pleasure conueie diuerse armors, and habillements for warre into Wales, to the intent to vse the same against the king as the indictment imported, for the accomplishing of his naughtie purpose, which was to destroie the king and to vsurpe the roiall gouernement and power to himselfe.

Which sute for licence to haue reteiners, and to conueie such armors and habillements of warre, the said Gilbert, the twentith daie of Maie, in the said ninth yeare, and diuerse other daies before and after, at London, and east Greéenewich did follow, labouring earnestlie, both to the king and councell, for obteining the same. On the twentith daie of Iulie in the said ninth yeare, the said duke sent the said Gilbert

A false prophesi-
eng moonke.

vnto Henton aforesaid, to vnderstand of the said moonke Nicholas Hopkins, what he heard of him: and the moonke sent him word that before Chrismas next there should be a change, & that the duke should haue the rule and gouernement of all England. And moreouer, the twentith of Februarie, in the eleuenth yeare of the kings reigne, at Blechingleie in the countie of Surrie, the said duke said vnto the said Robert Gilbert his chancellor, that he did expect and tarie for a time more conuenient to atchiue his purpose, and that it might easilie be doone, if the nobles of this realme would declare their minds togither: but some of them mistrusted, and feared to shew their minds togither: and that marred all.

He said further at the same time to the said Gilbert, that what so euer was doone by the kings father, was doone by wrong. And still he murmured against all that the

He was in a
verie ill mind if
this were true.

king then presentlie reigning did. And further he said, that he knew himselfe to be so wicked a sinner, that he wanted Gods fauour: and therefore he knew, that what so euer he tooke in hand against the king had the woorse successe. And furthermore, the said duke (to alienate the minds of the kings subiects from their dutifull obeisance towards the said king and his heires) on the twentith daie of September, in the first yeare of his reigne, being then at London, reported vnto the said Robert Gilbert, that he had a certeine writing sealed with the kings great seale, comprehending a cer-

A certeine writ-
ing legitimating
the duke of
Summerset.

teine act of parlement in the which it was enacted, that the duke of Summerset one of the kings progenitors was made legitimate: and further, that the said duke meant to haue deliuered the same writing vnto king Henrie the seuenth, but (said he) I would not that I had so doone for ten thousand pounds.

And furthermore, the same duke on the fourth of Nouember, in the eleuenth yere of the kings reigne, at east Greenwich in the countie of Kent, said vnto one Charles Kneuet esquier, after that the king had reprooued the duke for reteining William Bulmer knight into his seruice, that if he had perceiued that he should haue beene committed to the Tower (as he doubted hée should haue béene) hée would haue so wrought, that the principall dooers therein should not haue had cause of great reioising: for he would haue plaied the part which his father intended to haue put in

Sée the historie
of Richard the
third, pag. 418.

practise against king Richard the third at Salisburie, who made earnest sute to haue come vnto the presence of the same king Richard: which sute if he might haue obteined, he hauing a knife secretlie about him, would haue thrust it into the bodie of king Richard, as he had made semblance to knéele downe before him. And in speaking these words, he maliciouslie laid his hand vpon his dagger, and said, that if he were so euill vsed, he would doo his best to accomplish his pretensed purpose, swearing to confirme his word by the bloud of our Lord.

Beside all this, the same duke the tenth of Maie, in the twelfe yeare of the kings reigne, at London in a place called the Rose, within the parish of saint Laurence Poultnie in Canwike street ward, demanded of the said Charles Kneuet esquier, what was the talke amongest the Londoners concerning the kings iournie beyond the seas? And the said Charles told him, that manie stood in doubt of that iournéie, least the Frenchmen meant some deceit towards the king. Whereto the duke answered, that

it

it was to be feared, least it would come to passe, according to the words of a certeine The duke discouereth the secrecie of all the matter to his owne vndooing. holie moonke. For there is (saith he) a Chartreux moonke, that diuerse times hath sent to me, willing me to send vnto him my chancellor: and I did send vnto him Iohn de la Court my chapleine, vnto whome he would not declare anie thing, till de la Court had sworne vnto him to kéepe all things secret, and to tell no creature liuing what hée should heare of him, except it were to me.

And then the said moonke told de la Court, that neither the king nor his heires should prosper, and that I should indeuour my selfe to purchase the good wils of the communaltie of England; for I the same duke and my bloud should prosper, and haue the rule of the realme of England. Then said Charles Kneuet; The moonke maie be deceiued through the diuels illusion: and that it was euill to meddle with such matters. Well (said the duke) it cannot hurt me, and so (saith the indictment) the But the end of that ioy was heauinesse. duke séemed to reioise in the moonks woords. And further, at the same time, the duke told the said Charles, that if the king had miscaried now in his last sicknesse, he would haue chopped off the heads of the cardinall, of sir Thomas Louell knight, and of others; and also said, that he had rather die for it, than to be vsed as he had béene.

Moreouer, on the tenth daie of September, in the said eleuenth yere of this kings reigne, at Blechinglie, in the countie of Surrie, walking in the gallerie there with George Neuill knight, lord Aburgauennie, the duke murmuring against the kings councellors, and there gouernement, said vnto the said George; that if the king died, he would haue the rule of the realme in spite of who so euer said the contrarie; and withall said, that if the said lord Aburgauennie would say that the duke had spoken such words, he would fight with him, and lay his sword vpon his pate: & this he bound vp with manie great oths. These were the speciall articles & points comprised in the indictment, and laid to his charge: but how trulie, or in what sort prooued, I haue not further to say, either in accusing or excusing him, other than as I find in Hall and Polydor, whose words in effect, I haue thought to impart to the reader, and without anie parciall wresting of the same either to or fro.

Sauing that (I trust) I maie without offense saie, that (as the rumour then went) the cardinall chieflie procured the death of this noble man, no lesse fauoured and beloued of the people of this realme in that season, than the cardinall himselfe was hated and enuied. Which thing caused the dukes fall the more to be pitied and lamented, sith he was the man of all other, that chieflie went about to crosse the cardinall in his lordlie demeanor, & headie procéedings. But to the purpose. Shortlie after that the duke had béene indicted (as before ye haue heard) he was arreigned in Westminster The duke of Buckingham arreigned at Westminster. hall, before the duke of Norffolke, being made by the kings letters patents high steward of England, to accomplish the high cause of appeale of the péere or péeres of the realme, and to discerne and iudge the cause of the péeres.

There were also appointed to sit as peeres and iudges vpon the said duke of Buckingham, the duke of Suffolke, the marques Dorset, the earles of Worcester, Deuon- The names of the dukes péeres for his triall. shire, Essex, Shrewesburie, Kent, Oxford, and Derbie, the lord of saint Iohns, the lord de la Ware, the lord Fitz Warren, the lord Willoughbie, the lord Brooke, the lord Cobham, the lord Herbert, and the lord Morleie. There was made within the hall at Westminster a scaffold for these lords, and a presence for a iudge, railed and counterrailed about, and barred with degrées. When the lords had taken their place, the duke was brought to the barre, and vpon his arreignement pleaded not guiltie, and put himselfe vpon his péeres. Then was his indictment read, which the duke denied to be true, and (as he was an eloquent man) alledged reasons to falsifie the Polydor. Edw. Hall. indictment; pleading the matter for his owne iustification verie pithilie and earnestlie. The kings attourneie against the dukes reasons alledged the examinations, confessions, and proofes of witnesses.

The

The duke desired that the witnesses might bée brought foorth. And then came before him Charles Kneuet, Perke, de la Court, & Hopkins the monke of the priorie of the Charterhouse beside Bath, which like a false hypocrite had induced the duke to the treason with his false forged prophesies. Diuerse presumptions and accusations were laid vnto him by Charles Kneuet, which he would faine haue couered. The depositions were read, & the deponents deliuered as prisoners to the officers of the Tower. Then spake the duke of Norffolke, and said: My lord, the king our souereigne lord hath commanded that you shall haue his lawes ministred with fauour and right to you. Wherefore if you haue anie other thing to say for your selfe, you shall be heard. Then he was commanded to withdraw him, and so was led into Paradise, a house so named. The lords went to councell a great while, and after tooke their places.

Edw. Hall in H. 8. fol. lxxxvj.

Then said the duke of Norffolke to the duke of Suffolke; What say you of sir Edward duke of Buckingham touching the high treasons? The duke of Suffolke answered; He is giltie: & so said the marques and all the other earles and lords. Thus was this prince duke of Buckingham found giltie of high treason, by a duke, a marques, seuen earles, & twelue barons. The duke was brought to the barre sore chafing, and swet maruellouslie; & after he had made his reuerence, he paused a while. The duke of Norffolke as iudge said; Sir Edward, you haue heard how you be indicted of high treason, you pleaded thereto not giltie, putting your selfe to the péeres of the realme, which haue found you giltie. Then the duke of Norffolke wept and said; You shall be led to the kings prison, and there laid an a hardle, and so drawne to the place of execution, and there be hanged, cut downe aliue, your members cut off and cast into the fire, your bowels burnt before you, your head smitten off, and your bodie quartered and diuided at the kings will, and God haue mercie on your soule, Amen.

The duke of Buckingham conuinced of high treason.

*The duke of Buckinghams iudgement pronounced by the duke of Norffolke.
Rich. Grafton.
Iohn Stow.*

The duke of Buckingham said, My lord of Norffolke, you haue said as a traitor should be said vnto, but I was neuer anie: but my lords I nothing maligne for that you haue doone to me, but the eternall God forgiue you my death, and I doo: I shall neuer sue to the king for life, howbeit he is a gratious prince, and more grace may come from him than I desire. I desire you my lords and all my fellowes to pray for me. Then was the edge of the axe turned towards him, and he led into a barge. Sir Thomas Louell desired him to sit on the cushins and carpet ordeined for him. He said nay; for when I went to Westminster I was duke of Buckingham, now I am but Edward Bohune the most caitife of the world. Thus they landed at the Temple, where receiued him sir Nicholas Vawse & sir William Sands baronets, and led him through the citie, who desired euer the people to pray for him, of whome some wept and lamented, and said: This is the end of euill life, God forgiue him, he was a proud prince, it is pitie that hée behaued him so against his king and liege lord, whome God preserue. Thus about foure of the clocke he was brought as a cast man to the Tower.

The duke of Buckingham beheaded on a scaffold at Tower hill.

On fridaie the seuentéenth daie of Maie, about eleuen of the clocke, this duke of Buckingham, earle of Hereford, Stafford, and Northampton, with a great power was deliuered to Iohn Keime & Iohn Skeuington shiriffes, who led him to the scaffold on Tower hill, where he said he had offended the kings grace through negligence and lacke of grace, and destred all noble men to beware by him, and all men to pray for him, and that he trusted to die the kings true man. Thus méekelie with an axe he tooke his death. Then the Augustine friers tooke his bodie, and head, and buried them. Alas that euer the grace of truth was withdrawne from so noble a man, that he was not to his king in allegiance as he ought to haue béene! Such is the end of ambition, the end of false prophesies, the end of euill life, and euill counsell; but speciallie the end of malice, which grew to so huge and monstruous a fire in the hautie hart of the

proud

proud cardinall, that nothing could asswage it, but the bloud of this noble duke, against whome he had procured this processe in iudgement ended with the execution of death: the torments whereof were (as it seemeth by the sentence of the iudge) much diminished through the mercie of the king.

For though his offense was traitorous, and therfore deserued as law had prouided, and the iudge defined; yet in respect of the offendors person, the kings fauor dispensed with the rigor of iudgement, so that he was beheaded onelie, and his bodie not dismembred. ¶ This duke had begun a great and sumptuous building at his manor of Thornburie, but left the same vnfinished. He made a faire parke hard by the same building, for the which he tooke in much and fruitfull ground. Also another parke at Eastwood, one mile off, he inlarged at two times to the compasse of six miles, for the which déed, and such like, he had manie a cursse of the poore tenants.] At the time of his death (no doubt) his conscience (giuing in greater euidence than 10000 witnesses) told him whether he was iustlie condemned or no, for a mans dieng day is as a bill of information, putting him in mind of his life well or ill spent, as one saith: *Abr. Fl. ex I. S. pag. 929. Iohn Leland.*

> Pectora terribili cùm mors ferit horrida telo,
> Quomodo vita tibi sit priùs acta scies.

Gu. Ha. in eccl. cap. 11.

A conuenient collection concerning the high constables of England, which office ceassed and tooke end at the duke of Buckingham aboue mentioned.

THE death of this duke of Buckingham, being the last constable of England, dooth present apt place to me wherein to insert the names of all such honorable persons as haue béene inuested with that title of the constableship of England, an office of great account, & such as sometime was the chéefest place of a temporall subiect in the relme (the high steward excepted) whose power did extend to restreine some actions of the kings. Wherefore being now no such office (for there was neuer anie aduanced therevnto since the beheading of this duke) I thinke it not vnméet to make some memorie of those persons possessing so high a place, least both they and their office might hereafter grow in vtter obliuion: these therefore they were. *The collection of Fr. Thin in this yere 1585.*

Alfgarus Stallere, constable to Edward the Confessor, of whome thus writeth the historie of Elie in the second booke written by Richard of Elie a moonke of that house, in the time of Henrie the second, whose words although they be somewhat long, I shall not gréeue to set downe in this sort. De famosa villa Estre, alio nomine Plassie vocata, dicendum est quàm miserè ab Elie est destracta. Alfgarus quidem Stallere, quod Latinè dux dicitur, eam inuasit, & vsus est ea. Abbas verò Wolfricus & fratres, cùm sedulò frustra requirerent, Edwardum Confessorem adeunt, cui rex mandauit, vt restitueret: sed ille regijs iussis nequaquam obtemperauit. Fratres autem, cùm nec prece nec precio eius animum flectere potuissent, anathematizant eum, nec sententiam super eum vllo die prætermittebant. *Alfgarus Stallere.*

Quod ille diutiùs paruipendens, licèt magnus & potens in regno esset (vti regis constabularius) ab ecclesia eliminatus, & fidelium consortio ad correptionem (vix iam cunctis detestabilis effectus) compulsus peruenire, tandem (plurimùm obiurgatus & correptus à rege) reuersus est in se, & prece tandem nititur obtinere quod iniqua manu cunctatus non est. Illi verò hoc cognoscentes, illi annunt, demiserúntq; ei (quamuis ad suum incommodum) ita vt iureiurando postipsius vitam ab omni suorum inquietudine libera ad ecclesiam possessio rediret. Quod quidem factum est, & scripto Anglici sermonis designatum. Testes rex Edwardus & regina, &c. Which man (after the death of king Edward the Confessor and Harold the vsurper) was when the Normans entered England, as saith the said historie In ergastulo plurimis alijs ferro astrictus vsque ad mortem.

Walter of Glocester. Walter constable of England in the time of William the Conquerour, and of William Rufus succeeded Alfgarus. Here (before I saie anie more) I thinke it not amisse to set downe somewhat touchiug William Fitz Osberne, or Osbert earle of Hereford, whome manie will haue to be constable in the time of the Conquerour: which truelie I can not as yet be led to beleeue. For although that this William was the onelie man, who both persuaded, incouraged, and procured aid of others to assist William Conquerour for the obteining of England; and that this man was (as we commonlie saie) the onelie right hand, chéefe compeller, and disposer of the kingdome, after that William the Conquerour had obteined the same, being also Tribunus militum of all the armie that William Conquerour led into England, and the man that persuaded the bishop of Samborrow to compound for the title of the king of Denmarke made vnto England: yet I suppose him not to be constable, but onelie marshall of England; or at the least if he were, it could not be verie long. For that this earle was extreame old, departed the realme, and disposed all the affaires of the Norman bastard beyond the seas, and died about the yeare of our redemption 1072, being about the eight yeare of the reigne of William Conquerour.

Milo of Hereford. Milo the sonne of the said Walter, an enimie to king Stephan (who yet confirmed him in his fathers inheritance) was aduanced first to great honors by Henrie the first: who méeting Mawd the empresse at Bristow, and taking hir for lawfull quéene, did continuallie follow hir faction; for which she, in the sixt yeare of king Stephan, to honour him for his good seruice (as appeareth by the charter thereof) gaue him the earledome of Hereford, constableship of England, the castell of Bironell, & the forrest of Deane. He was lord also of Breckenocke. He translated the chanons of the monasterie of saint Iohns of Lanthonie, in the yeare of our redemption 1103, being the fourth yeare of king Henrie the first, to a place néere Glocester, then called Hide, and since Lanthonie; as Iohn Stow hath well noted out of other authors.

He married Sibilla the daughter of Bernard Newmarch, a nobleman of Normandie, who obteined by conquest the lordship of Breckenocke: by whom he had issue fiue sonnes and thrée daughters. The sonnes were Roger, Walter, Henrie, William and Mahaell. His thrée daughters were, Margaret, married to Humfreie Bohune; Bertha the second was married to Philip Bruse, created by king Stephan lord of Bruse, Gower, Bauld, & Brimble, and in his wiues right lord of Breckenocke; Lucia married to Herebert the sonne of Herebert, base sonne to Henrie the first, who was (in hir right) lord of the forrest of Deane: he died in the eight or (as others haue) the ninth yeare of king Stephan, being the yeare of our redemption 1143.

William Beauchampe. William (the sonne of Walter Beauchampe) shiriffe of Worcester, was made high constable of England by king Stephan, in the fift yeare of his reigne, being in the yeare of our redemption 1139, when the king was at Worcester: which honour he tooke from Miles of Glocester; as saith that painefull antiquarie Iohn Stow in his chronicle printed in the yeare of our Lord 1580, fol. 191.

Roger fitz Milo. Roger the sonne of Milo succéeded his father in all his inheritance, as well of the earledome, as otherwise: whereby he was in time following also constable of England, and (as it is most probable) restored to that office by Henrie the second; for that he was a great enimie to king Stephan. He went amongest others with Henrie Fitz Empresse to Dauid king of Scots, who knighted the said Henrie in the fouretéenth yeare of king Stephan: he married Cicilie the daughter of Iohn Fitz Paine, and died without issue.

Walter fitz Milo. Walter second sonne to Milo, after the death of his brother Roger was earle of Hereford, constable of England, and lord ouer Gwenthie or Wenthie: he builded in the time of Henrie the first the castels of Glocester, Bristow, and Rochester, with
the

the Tower of London: he held the land of Wenthie by long time, who hauing no heire of his bodie gaue the same land to Henrie of Hereford, and forsaking the world tooke monasticall habit on him at Lanthonie, where he was buried, dieng without issue.

Henrie of Hereford the sonne of Milo, after the enterance of Walter his brother into religion, was earle of Hereford, constable of England, and lord of Breckenocke and Deane; who was in Wenthie at a conflict slaine by his owne men, and buried at Lanthonie with Walter the constable: after whose death Henrie the second deputed Iago ap Seisell to the custodie of the land of Wenthie.

Henrie of Hereford.

William the sonne of Milo, and brother to Henrie of Hereford, was constable of England, after the death of his brother, and died without issue.

William fitz Milo.

Mahaell the yoongest sonne of Milo, after the death of William, was constable of England, who died without issue: whome I feare not to place as constable, since all histories agrée that all the sons of Milo did successiuelie inioie that office, after whome the inheritance comming to their sister, whereof the eldest called Margaret (or Margerie) was married to Humfrie Bohune, which line of the Bohunes became afterwards constables of England by inheritance.

Mahaell fitz Milo.

Humfrie de Bohune, steward to Henrie the first, (the sonne of Humfrie de Bohune, steward in house to William Rufus, sonne to Humfrie de Bohune that came in with the Conquerour) was (in the right of his wife Margerie one of the daughters and heire of the foresaid Milo) constable of England, he had issue Humfrie de Bohune.

Humfrie de Bohune.

Humfrie de Bohune, constable of England, married Margaret sister to William king of Scots and daughter to the earle of Huntington, moother to Conon earle of Britaine: he had issue Henrie. This Margaret died the third of king Iohn, being the yeare of Christ 1201. And this Humfrie also died in the time of king Iohn, as some haue: or rather (as others haue) in the time of king Richard the first.

Humfrie de Bohune.

Henrie de Bohune, the sonne of the said Humfrie and Margaret, was the first earle of Hereford of that name of the Bohunes, contrarie to that receiued error, which hitherto hath made the other Bohunes earle of Hereford: and contrarie to the printed pedegrée of the deceassed father of the earle of Essex now liuing. For this man, being the first erle of the Bohunes, was made earle of Hereford in the first yeare of king Iohn, as the charter dooth witnesse. He was also constable of England, and married Mawd, the daughter and heire of Geffrie lord Ludgarsall sometime earle of Essex, in whose right hir husband was intituled to that honor of the earledome of Essex, by whome he had issue Humfrie his heire. He died about the fourth yeare of Henrie the third, being the yeare of our redemption 1220, in his iournie as he went to Ierusalem with other noblemen.

Henrie de Bohune.

Humfrie de Bohune sonne of Henrie, being the second of that name that was erle of Hereford, was also earle of Essex and constable of England, being by all men termed La bone counte de Hereford. He married Mawd the daughter of the earle of Oxie in Normandie, he had issue Humfrie de Bohune that was taken in the yeare of Christ 1265, being the fortie & ninth of king Henrie the third at the battell of Euesham, and died in the life of his father, leauing behind him a sonne called Humfrie, heire to him and to his father, which Humfrie the father died in the yeare of our redemption 1275, being the third yeare of king Edward the first.

Humfrie de Bohune.

Humfrie de Bohune the third earle of Hereford of that name, the sonne of Humfrie Bohune slaine at the battell of Euesham, was after the death of his grandfather erle of Hereford and Essex, and constable of England, he married Mawd de Ferens, or Frenis, and had issue Humfrie, this earle died in the yeare of our redemption 1298, being the twentie sixt of Edward the first, & was buried at Walden with his wife Mawd.

Humfrie de Bohune.

Humfrie de Bohune the fourth erle of Hereford of that name, was earle of Hereford,

Humfrie de Bohune.

ford, Essex, and constable of England, he married Elizabeth the daughter to king Edward the first, and widow to Iohn earle of Holland, he had issue Iohn erle of Hereford, Humfrie earle of Hereford, and William earle of Northampton. This Humfrie taking part with Thomas earle of Lancaster was slaine at Borrobridge by a Welshman standing vnder a bridge that thrust him thorough with a speare, in the fouretéenth yeare of the reigne of king Edward the second, being the yeare of our redemption 1321.

Iohn de Bohune. Iohn de Bohune the eldest sonne of this Humfrie, being the first earle of Hereford, was after the death of his father earle of Hereford, Essex, and constable of England, he married the daughter of Edmund Fitz Alen earle of Arundell, and died without issue in the yeare of Christ 1335, being the ninth yeare of king Edward the third. He was buried in the abbeie of Stratford besides London.

Humfrie de Bohune. Humfrie de Bohune sixt earle of Hereford, being brother to Iohn de Bohune, whome he succeeded, was after the death of his brother earle of Hereford and Essex, and constable of England, he died without issue in the yeare of our Lord 1361, being the thirtie fift of king Edward the third, and was buried at the Augustine friers in London.

William de Bohune. William de Bohune seuenth erle of Hereford of that surname, being the sonne of the other Humfrie and brother to the last Humfrie, was at a parlement holden in the tenth yeare of the reigne of king Edward the third, being in the yeare of our Lord 1336, created earle of Northampton, and after the death of his brother Humfrie, he was earle of Hereford and Essex, and constable of England. He was in the eightéenth yeare of Edward the third, being the yere of Christ 1344, sent into Britaine as generall ouer the English armie, to restore Iohn de Montford to the dukedome of Britaine: which he did, putting Charles de Blois to flight. He married Elizabeth some saie Eleanor, one of the daughters and heires of Bartholomew Bladesmere baron of Bedes in Kent, by whome he had issue Humfrie.

Humfrie de Bohune. Humfrie de Bohune, the eight & last erle of Hereford of that surname of Bohune, was after the death of William his father earle of Hereford, Essex and Northampton, and constable of England. He augmented the castell of Brecnocke, first built by Bernard Newmarch. He in the eight and twentith yere of Edward the third (as Iohn Stow noteth) being the yeare of Christ 1354, reedified the frier Augustines church in London, in which he was buried. He maried Ione the daughter of Richard Fitz Alen earle of Arundell, by whome he had issue two daughters and heires, Eleanor the eldest, maried to Thomas of Woodstocke; and Marie the second, maried to Henrie of Bollingbrooke, after king of England, by the name of king Henrie the fourth.

Thomas of Woodstocke. Thomas of Woodstocke the sixt sonne to king Edward the third, was created earle of Buckingham, in the first yeare of Richard the second at his coronation, being the yeare of our Lord 1377, and after duke of Glocester, in the eight yeare of Richard the second 1385. He maried Eleanor eldest daughter of Humfreie Bohune (as before) in whose right he was earle of Essex, Northampton, and constable of England, besides which he was also lord of Brecnocke. He had issue one son & foure daughters: his sonne was Humfreie earle of Buckingham, whom K. Richard (after the murthering of his father at Calis) sent into Ireland, where he remained as prisoner vntill the time of king Henrie the fourth, which called him home: who returning into England, died of the plague without issue at Chester: after whome his moother liued not long. Of whose death thus writeth that worthie poet sir Iohn Gower knight, liuing at that time, in his booke of the historie of Richard the second, and Henrie the fourth, commonlie taken as part of his worke intituled & named, Vox clamantis:

> Interea transit moriens nec in orbe remansit,
> Humfredus dictus reddit ille Deo benedictus,
> Defuncto nato citò post de fine beato,

                                                  Mater

Mater transiuit dum nati funera sciuit,
Primo decessit * Cignus, dolor vnde repressit
Matrem cum pullo, sibi mors nec parcit in vllo.

* The duke of Glocester, bicause the swan was his cognisance.

The foure daughters, heires to Thomas of Woodstocke & their brother Humfreie, were Anne the eldest, married to Edmund Stafford erle Stafford, who had issue Humfreie erle of Stafford, Hereford, & Northampton, lord of Brecknocke, &c: which Anne after the death of erle Stafford, did the second time marie William vicont Bourchier created erle of Ewe in France: the second daughter was Philip, which died without issue: the third Ione, was maried to Gilbert lord Talbot: the fourth Isabell, was a religious person at the Minories in London. This duke of Glocester was murthered at Calis about the yeare of Christ 1398, being the 22 yeare of Richard the second, touching whose life and death, with the maner thereof, thus writeth the said sir Iohn Gower, in the same booke intituled Vox clamantis:

O quàm fortuna stabilis non permanet vna,
Exemplum cuius stat in ordine carminis huius,
Rex agit, & Cygnus patitur de corde benignus,
Ille prostratus non est de rege leuatus,
Ad Plessye captus tunc est velut hostia raptus,
Rex iubet arma geri, nec eo voluit misereri,
Cum sponsa nati lugent quasi morte grauati,
Plúsq; lupo sæuit rex dummodo fœmina fleuit,
Nil pietas munit quem tunc manus inuida punit,
Rex stetit obliquus nec erat tunc vnus amicus,
O regale genus, princeps quasi pauper egenus,
Turpiter attractus iacet & sine iure subactus,
Sunt ibi fautores regis de sorte priores,
Qui Cygnum pendent, vbi captum ducere tendent,
Sic ducendo ducem, perdit sine lumine lucem,
Anglia quæ tota tenebrescit luce remota,
Trans mare natauit, regnum qui semper amauit,
Flent centum mille, quia Cygnus præterit ille,
Calisij portus petit vnde dolus latet ortus,
Error quem regis genuit putredine legis,
Carcere conclusus subitò fuit ille reclusus,
Nescit quo fine sit vitæ siue ruinæ,
Tunc rex elatum sumpsit quasi falco volatum,
Vnde suas gentes perdit custode carentes.

A little after which followeth these verses, touching the deniall of buriall to be granted vnto him among the rest of his honourable and roiall ancestors.

Sic nece deuictum, sic corpus ab hoste relictum,
Clam de conclaui, susceperat Anglia naui,
Per mare regreditur, corpus nec adhuc sepelitur,
Námq; sepulturam, defendit rex sibi puram,
Desuper à latere, patris loca iusta tenere,
Dummodo quæsiuit, vix bassa sepulchra subiuit.

Of the maner also of whose death the said sir Iohn Gower hath set downe these three following verses:

Heu quàm tortorum quidam de sorte malorum,
Sic ducis electi plumarum pondere lecti,
Corpus quassatum iugulántq; necant iugulatum.

His wife Elenor died the third of October, in the yeare of our redemption 1399, being

being the first yeare of king Henrie the fourth, and was buried at Westminster on the south side of king Edward the third with this epitaph:

Icy gist Elenor de Bohune aysne fille & vn des heyres a honorable seigneur monseigneour Humphrey de Bohune, countie de Hereford, & de Essex, & de Northampton, & constable d'Angliterre, femme a puissant & noble prince Thomas Woodstocke, fitz a tresexcellent & trespuissant seigneiur Edwarde roy d'Angliterre pius le cõquest tierce, duc de Glocester, que morust tierce ioure de October lan du grace 1399, de que alme Dieux fait mercye.

Edward Plantagenet. Edward Plantagenet sonne to Edmund of Langleie, was by Richard the second created earle of Rutland, and duke of Albemerle, who being constable of England arriued in the thrée and twentith yeare of Richard the second, and in the yeare of our Lord 1399 in Ireland, to bring aid to the king being there in warre. Of this man is more liberall discourse in my folowing treastise of the dukes of England.

Henrie Persie. Henrie Persie lord Persie, the sixt lord, and the first earle of Northumberland of that name, was aduanced to that honourable title of earle at the coronation of king Richard the second, in the yeare of our redemption 1377. He was made high constable of England by Henrie the fourth, then elected but not crowned king of England, bicause the said earle did giue that ring to the king whereby he was wedded to the kingdome of England, to whome also the king gaue the Ile of man to beare the sword with which he entered the realme. He in the fourth yeare of king Henrie the fourth, being the yeare of Christ 1403, rebelled against the king: but after comming to the king vpon sending for, he was pardoned his life, but commited to safe custodie. After which, in the fift yeare of that king, he was at a parlement holden at London restored to his estate and dignitie, who the yeare following, being the sixt of Henrie the fourth, and the yeare of Christ 1405, againe rebelled, and after fled into Scotland, to Dauid lord Fleming who receiued him, and in the seuenth yeare of Henrie the fourth, being the yere of our redemption 1506, as saith Iohn Stow.

This Dauid persuaded the erle to flie into Wales, for which cause the Scots slue the said Dauid. After this, in the ninth yeare of Henrie the fourth, he came into England, raised the people, and was slaine at Broomeham neere to Hasewood, in a conflict had with him by Thomas Rockleie shiriffe of Yorkeshire. He married two wiues, the first was Margaret daughter to Rafe lord Neuill, by whome he had issue Henrie Persie, surnamed Hotspurre (slaine at the battell of Shrewesburie in the fourth yeare of Henrie the fourth in his fathers life) Thomas and Rafe. His second wife was Mawd, daughter to Thomas lord Lucie, and sister and heire to Anthonie lord Lucie baron of Cockermouth, being before the widow of Gilbert Humfreuill called the earle of Angus. This ladie Mawd gaue to hir husband the lordship and castell of Cockermouth, whereby the earles of Northumberland are bound still to beare the armes of Lucie.

John of Bedford. Iohn duke of Bedford the sonne and brother of kings (for so he calleth himselfe in the precept to summon Reginald lord Greie, & sir Edward Hastings knight, to determine the controuersie for bearing of the armes of Hastings earle of Penbroke in the marshals court) was earle of Richmond and Kendall, and constable of England, being aduanced to that office about the eight yeare of Henrie the fourth his father, being the yeare of our redemption 1406, of whome there is more mention in the following discourse of the protectors of England.

Humfrie Stafford. Humfrie earle of Stafford, Hereford, and Northampton, lord of Brecknocke, Holdernesse, and of Cambridge, and constable of England, and of Douer castell, in the eight yeare of Henrie the sixt, being the yeare of Christ 1430, went into France with Henrie the sixt to attend his coronation at Paris. He was created duke of Buckingham in the two and twentith yeare of Henrie the sixt, being the yeare of Christ 1444. He was slaine at the battell of Northampton in the eight and thirtith yeare of king

Henrie

Henrie the sixt, being the yeare of our Lord 1460, he maried Anne daughter to Rafe
Neuil erle of Westmerland: he had amongst manie other of his children Humfrie his
eldest sonne earle Stafford, hurt (as hath Iohn Stow) with an arrow in the right
hand at the battell of saint Albons in the three and thirtith yeare of Henrie the sixt,
being the yeare of our lord 1455, of which battell of saint Albons thus writeth Iohn
Whethamsted a learned abbat of that house:

> Dum Maius madidi flos floruit imbribus austri,
> Mollibus & Zephyrus refouerat flatibus aruos,
> Flora velut regnans herbis ditauerat hortos,
> Post glacies inopes hos fecerat & locupletes,
> Sic rapidis Stilbon prædonibus vndíq; regnum,
> Repleverat nimis, sic latè sparserat ipsos,
> Vt * villam tandem tantus peruaserat istam,
> Illorum numerus quòd vix euaderet vnus,
> Quin spolium lueret, spoliantes vel trepidaret.
> Accidit ex causa spoliatio tam grauis ista,
> Mars cœli dominus fuerat tunc, & soror eius
> In terris domina belli Bellona vocata,
> Vnde malum multis signanter partibus istis
> Contigit, & bellum fuit istic grande peractum,
> Sanguis & effusus multus, dux est iugulatus
> Illius pugnæ quæ fertur causa fuisse.
> Bello finito, strepitu quóq; pacificato,
> Indultum est prædæ, prædones quippe fuere
> Victores omnes, nulli quasi compatientes.
> Tunc rex, tunc proceres, tunc villani quòq; plures,
> Ac alij varij fuerant rebus spoliati,
> Attamen ecclesia, simul ecclesiæ bona cuncta
> Intra quæ fuerant, sub clausuráq; iacebant,
> Manserunt salua nec ei res defuit vlla.
> Laus igitur domino, laus in speciéq; patrono,
> Cuius per media stabant sua singula salua,
> Saluis & in cunctis simul abbas frater & omnis.
> Spiritus ille bonus sine fallo spiritus almus,
> Ad villam regem qui direxit venientem
> Illius ad medium, nec tunc premiserat ipsum
> Ecclesiam petere, conseruauit sua quæque.
> Sed patronus erat qui pro monachis medi arat,
> A raptore locúmq; suum seruauit, & omnem
> Ipsius ornatum fedari nec siuit ipsum.
> Si rex intrasset, secúmq; ducem sociasset,
> Valuas ecclesiæ, paruissent cuncta rapinæ,
> Nec poterat furias quisquam compescere plebis.
> Laus igitur domino, rursus rursusq; patrono,
> Stat locus iste suo saluus munimine solo,
> Saluáq; supposita, sua salua iocalia cuncta.

*Iohn Tiptoth or Tiptost knight, the son of Iohn lord Tiptost, and of Ioice his wife,
second daughter to Edmund Charleton lord Powes, was treasuror of the realme in
Michaelmasse tearme in the tenth yere of Henrie the fourth, after which he was
againe admitted to that office in the one and thirtith and two and thirtith yeare of
Henrie the sixt, from which place being once more remoqued, he was the third time
aduanced to the honor of treasuror of England in the second of Edward the fourth,

and

Marginal notes:

* S. Albons.

Edmund Beau-
ford duke of
Summerset.

Henrie the sixt.

The abbeie of
S. Albons.

O tempora,
o mores.

Rich. Plan-
tagenet duke of
Yorke.

Iohn Tiptoth or
Tiptost.

and continued the same in the third of the said king. He was created earle of Worcester in the time of king Henrie the sixt. This man in the yeare 1470, being the tenth of king Edward the fourth, tooke his part against the duke of Clarence, and Richard Neuill earle of Warwike, at what time the said duke and earle being discomfited, fled to the sea side, and thence sailed to Southhampton, where they thought to haue had the Trinitie a great ship of the earle of Warwikes, but the lord Scales the queenes brother fought with them, and inforced them to flie into France.

Wherevpon king Edward the fourth came to Southhampton and caused Tiptost earle of Worcester to sit in iudgement vpon certeine gentlemen, as Clapham and others, taken at the same skirmish of Southhampton, where the earle caused the bodies of certeine condemned men, after that they were hanged to be thrust thorough the fundament vp to the head with stakes, for the which crueltie he and others fell into indignation of the common people. Before which in the eight yeare of king Edward, he was with Iohn Dudleie made constable of the Tower, during their liues, and the longer liuer of them two.

After this in the said yeare 1470, being the tenth of Edward the fourth, in which Henrie the sixt readepted the crowne of England, which yeare of Henrie the sixt is called in the law bookes, the fourtie & ninth yere of the reigne of K. Henrie the sixt. This earle of Worcester was taken in the top of an high trée in the forest of Weibridge in Huntingtonshire, brought to London, at a parlement arrested and condemned to death, by sir Iohn Vere earle of Oxford. Whervpon he was beheaded at Tower hill, and buried in the blacke friers of London. He had three wiues, wherof the first was called Cicilie the daughter of Richard earle of Salisburie: the second Elizabeth the daughter of Robert Greindoure: the third was Elizabeth, after married to sir William Stanleie, which Iohn had by his third wife Edward lord Tiptost who died without issue, & so the inheritance went to the sisters of the said earle Iohn Tiptost.

Lord Beaumont.   And here I thinke it not amisse to say somewhat of the lord Beaumont, who being in our chronicles named constable of England (as may appeare in the fiue and twentith yeare of Henrie the sixt, in which yeare he arrested Humfrie duke of Glocester) that for any thing that I can yet sée or learne, this Beaumont was not constable by patent during his life, but for the present time to execute the princes pleasure, and therefore not méet in this discourse to haue anie speciall place amongest such as were constables of England, either by descent or patent.

Richard Wooduile.   Sir Richard Wooduile knight, earle Riuers, was high constable of England in the fourth yere of king Edward the fourth, of whom is more large mention in the following discourse of the treasurors of England in the historie of the reigne of quéene Elizabeth.

George Plantagenet.   George Plantagenet, second sonne to Richard duke of Yorke, was created amongst other estates duke of Clarence, in the yeare of our redemption 1461, being the first yeare of king Edward the fourth immediatlie vpon his coronation, and was made constable of England in the time of Edward the fourth. He in the eight of Edward the fourth, about the yeare of Christ 1468, maried Isabell the eldest daughter of Richard Neuill earle of Warwike and Salisburie, by whome he had issue Edward earle of Warwike and Salisburie, borne vpon the sea in the hauen of Calis, who was in the time of Richard the third a continuall prisoner, and so hauing béene a prisoner, and thereto borne by a certeine fatall destinie, was in the yere of our redemption 1485, being the first of king Henrie the seuenth committed to custodie in the Tower, where he continued all the rest of his life, & was beheaded at Tower hill in the fiftéenth yeare of king Henrie the seuenth, being the yeare of Christ 1499, & was buried at Birsam néere to his ancestors. Besides this Edward, this George duke of Clarence had issue a daughter called Margaret, created by king Henrie the eight

countesse

countesse of Salisburie, who maried sir Richard Poole knight of the garter, descended of the ancient familie of the Pooles in Wales.

Richard Plantagenet, the third sonne to Richard duke of Yorke, was aduanced to the title and honor of the dukedome of Glocester, in the yeare of our redemption 1461, being the first yeare of king Edward the fourth, soone after his coronation. He was high constable of England: he maried Anne second daughter to Richard Neuill earle of Warwike and Salisburie. Which Richard after the death of his brother king Edward the fourth, did by the murther of his nephues ascend to the highest gouernement of England, and was crowned king by the name of Richard the third.   *Richard Plantagenet.*

Henrie Stafford, whome our chronicles doo in manie places corruptlie terme Edward, was sonne to Humfrie earle Stafford, & was high constable of England, and duke of Buckingham. This man raising warre against Richard the third vsurping the crowne, was in the first yeare of the reigne of the said Richard, being the yeare of Christ 1483, betraied by his man Humfrie Banaster (to whome being in distresse he fled for succour) and brought to Richard the third then lieng at Salisburie, where the said duke confessing all the conspiracie, was beheaded without arreignement or iudgement, vpon the second of Nouember, in the said yere of our redemption 1483, he maried Katharine the daughter of Richard Wooduile, sister to quéene Elizabeth wife to Edward the fourth; & had issue, Edward duke of Buckingham, and Henrie earle of Wilshire, with two daughters, which were, Anne maried to George lord Hastings of whom is descended the erle of Huntington now liuing, and Elizabeth married to Richard Ratcliffe lord Fitz Waters, of whome is issued sir Henrie Ratcliffe knight, now earle of Sussex.   *Henrie Stafford.*

Edward Stafford sonne to Henrie duke of Buckingham, being also duke of Buckingham after the death of his father was constable of England, earle of Hereford, Stafford, and Northampton, being in the first yeare of Henrie the seuenth, in the yeare of our redemption 1485, restored to his fathers dignities and possessions. He is tearmed in the books of the law in the said thirtéenth yeare of Henrie the eight (where his arreignement is liberallie set downe) to be the floure & mirror of all courtesie. This man (as before is touched) was by Henrie the seuenth restored to his fathers inheritance, in recompense of the losse of his fathers life, taken awaie (as before is said) by the vsurping king Richard the third. He married Elianor the daughter of Henrie earle of Northumberland, and had issue Henrie lord Stafford (father to Henrie lord Stafford now liuing) and thrée daughters, Elizabeth married to Thomas Howard earle of Surrie, Katharine married to Rafe Neuill earle of Westmerland, and Marie married to George Neuill lord of Aburgauennie. And thus much by Francis Thin touching the succession of the constables of England.]   *Edward Stafford.*

In this meane while, were the emperour and the French king fallen at variance, so that the warre was renewed betwixt them; for the pacifieng wherof, the cardinall of Yorke was sent ouer to Calis, where the ambassadours of both those princes were appointed to come to him. He arriued there the second of August. There went ouer with him the erle of Worcester, then lord chamberleine, the lord of S. Iohns, the lord Ferrers, the lord Herbert, the bishop of Duresme, the bishop of Elie, primat of Armacane, sir Thomas Bullen, sir Iohn Pechie, sir Iohn Hussie, sir Richard Wingfield, sir Henrie Guilford, and manie other knights, esquiers, gentlemen, doctors, and learned men. Thus honourablie accompanied he rode thorough London the twentie fift daie of Iulie, and at Thomas Beckets house the maior and aldermen tooke leaue of him, praieng God to send him good spéed. Thus passed he to Canturburie, where the archbishop of Canturburie and others receiued him in his statelinesse, and brought him vnto his lodging vnder a canopie to the bishops palace. On the eight daie of   *Cardinall Woolsie sent ouer to Calis.*   *Ed. Hall in H.8. fol. lxxxvj.*

Iulie he came to Douer. On the twentith he & the other lords with their retinues tooke passage, and arriued at Calis in safetie, where the lord deputie and the councell receiued them with much honour and lodged the cardinall in the Staple hall.

Shortlie after his ariuall at Calis, thither came the chancellor of France, and the countie de Palice, with foure hundred horses as ambassadors from the French king; and likewise from the emperour came great ambassadors, either partie being furnished with sufficient commissions to treat and conclude of peace as should appeare. But yet when it came to the point, as the one partie seemed conformable to reasonable offers, so the other would not incline that waie; insomuch that they were neuer at one time agreeable to anie indifferent motion that could be made. There were also the popes ambassadors, whervpon the cardinall would haue furthered a league betwixt the emperour, the king of England, the king of France, and the pope: but the popes ambassadors wanted commission thereto, and therefore were letters sent to Rome in all hast, and the Frenchmen taried still in Calis, till answer came from thence. The cardinall rode into Flanders to speake with the emperour, which as then laie in Bruges. A mile without Bruges the emperour receiued him, and did to him as much honour as could be deuised. The chéere was great which was made to the Englishmen, and of euerie thing there was such plentie, that there was no want of things necessarie, insomuch that of the fare, both for plentifulnesse, delicatnesse, and statelinesse of seruice, a man might haue said:

Βρώμαΐα magnorum dixisses esse deorum.

The cardinall after he had soiorned in Bruges the space of thirtéene daies, and concluded diuerse matters with the emperour, and accomplished his commission, he tooke leaue of his maiestie, and by conuenient iorneis returned to Calis, where the ambassadors of France taried his comming: and immediatlie after his returne to Calis, he treated with them of peace, but not so earnestlie as he did before. In fine, nothing was concluded, but onelie that fishermen of both the princes might fréelie fish on the seas without disturbance, till the second of Februarie next. When no conclusion of agréement could be accorded, the cardinall sent to the emperour the lord of S. Iohns, and sir Thomas Bullen knight, to aduertise his maiestie what had béene doone, and likewise to the French king, as then lieng in campe with a mightie armie in the marches about Cambreie. The earle of Worcester and the bishop of Elie were sent to informe him of all things that had béene motioned, exhorting him to incline to peace, but he gaue little eare thereto: and then after they had béene a nineteene or twentie daies in his host they returned. During the continuance of the cardinall in Calis, all writs and patents were there by him sealed, and no shiriffes chosen for lacke of his presence, hauing there with him the great seale, & full power in things, as if the king had béene there in person. ¶ Ambassadors comming from the king of Hungarie towards the king of England, were receiued honourablie of the Cardinall during his abode in Calis.

After the returne of the English ambassadours, which the cardinall had sent to the emperour, and to the French king, he returned into England, hauing (as some write) concluded a new league with the emperour, and signified by waie of intendment to the French king in the treatie with his ambassadors, that the king of England meant him not so much fréendship as of late he had doone, for diuerse causes. But speciallie this was vttered, that where it was concluded that the king of Scots should be included within the league (as before yée haue heard) contrarie to that agréement, the said king refused to enter as a confederate into the same league: and this no doubt procéeded through counsell of the French king, by whom he was wholie guided. This quarrell was laid as an occasion, whie to mooue the king of England (perceiuing himselfe to be dissembled with) to withdraw his good will from the French king.

Who

Who when he vnderstood the drifts of the cardinall, and conclusion of the new league confirmed betwixt the king of England and the emperour, he condemned the cardinall of vntruth, accused him of dissimulation, abhorred his practises, as by the which he lost the fruition of the king of England his freendship, and might no longer inioy it. And herewith he determined with himselfe neuer to put confidence in anie Englishman after, nor to bestow anie gifts or pensions vpon them. For he vsed yéerelie to send to diuerse of the kings councell after the maner of his predecessors sundrie gifts and summes of monie: & bicause he had imploied more on the cardinall than on the residue, he was the more offended toward him as the head of all this iniurious dooing. Yet he found not himselfe so much gréeued, as to vtter anie bitter words towards the king: but contrarilie within a while after, directed his letters vnto him, signifieng that he meant to continue the league as his freend: but it maie be he did this after a dissembling sort, bicause he would not be at warres with two so mightie princes at one time.

In this meane while, the warre was pursued betwixt the emperour & the French king, as well on the confines towards Flanders, as beyond the mounteins in the parties of Lombardie. Tornaie was besieged by the lord Hugh de Moncada, a Spaniard, the which comming vpon the sudden, tooke manie abroad in the fields, yer they knew of his approch, and after this, comming before the citie, he inuironed it with a siege, to kéepe the citizens from stirring foorth, and sent part of his armie with the light horsemen to forlaie the stréets and passages, that no succour should come to them within. The French king assembled an armie, in hope to aid them of Tornaie with men, munitions, and vittels, the which armie assaied twise or thrise with all endeuor, to haue approched the citie: but in vaine, for with no small losse the French were repelled by the imperials, which neuerthelesse felt their part of slaughter, loosing sundrie of their capteins, as bastard Emerie, and the capteine of Gant. Finallie, the French armie brake vp, & was dispersed into fortresses. Wherevpon they of Tornaie perceiuing the succours which they hoped for, to faile them thus at néed, rendered the citie to the emperor the last of Nouember, in this 13 yeare of king Henries reigne.

¶ Pope Leo died this yeare suddenlie, on the first of December, as he laie at the village of Magliana whither he went oftentimes for his recreation. He had heard the first reapport of the taking of Millan, which stirred in him such an extreame passion of ioy, that the same night he entered into a small feauer: and for his better remedie he caused himselfe the next daie to be remooued to Rome: where he died within a verie few daies after, notwithstanding the physicians in the beginning made no great reckoning of his disease. There was great suspicion that he was poisoned by Barnabie Malespina his chamberleine, whose office was alwaies to giue him drinke. And yet though he was made prisoner through the suspicion of the fact & the vehement reasons of the same; yet the matter was dashed and the examination thereof: for that the cardinall de Medicis as soone as he came to Rome, set him at libertie, fearing to fall further in disgrace of the French king, by whose practise it was supposed that Barnabie gaue him the fatall drinke. This was but whispered secretlie, the author being no lesse doubtfull than the coniectures vncerteine.

He died (if we consider the common opinion of men) in verie great glorie and felicitie, not so much for that by the surprising of Millan he saw himselfe deliuered of dangers & expenses intollerable, which hauing drained him of all store of monie and treasure, he was constreined to aduance all meanes and maners for his supplie and reléeuing: but also that a verie few daies afore his death he receiued aduertisement of the taking of Plaisanca, and the verie daie he died, newes came to him of the winning of Parma: a matter so greatlie desired by him, that at such time as he debated to mooue warre against the Frenchmen, it is verie well remembred that he said vnto the cardinall de Medicis labouring to dissuade him, that as he was in nothing more

[margin notes:]
Hot warres betwéene the emperor and the French king.
Tornaie besieged by the emperor his men.
Edw. Hall.
Tornaie deliuered vp to the emperor.
Abr. Fl. ex Guic. pag. 813. The death of pope Leo the tenth who (as was suspected) was poisoned.
The maner and order of the popes death.

caried to the desire of that warre, than to recouer to the church those two cities; so when so euer God should blesse him with the effect of that desire, it would not gréeue him to die. He was a prince in whom were manie things worthie to be commended & blamed, and in the estate & discourse of his life he deceiued greatlie the expectation that was had of him, when he was created pope, for that in his gouernement was great discretion, but farre lesse bountie than was looked for.]

Polydor.
Cardinall Woolsie maketh meanes to be elected pope.

Guic. pag. 823.

After the death of the pope, doctor Richard Pace was sent to Rome, to make friends in the behalfe of the cardinall of Yorke, who was brought into a vaine hope thorough the kings fauour and furtherance, to be elected pope. But Adrian the sixt of that name was chosen before doctor Pace could come to Rome; and so that sute was dashed. ¶ This Adrian bishop of Derchuso (after great contention in the college of cardinals touching the election of a new pope) was preferred to the custome of lotting of voices in the conclaue, without anie affection or parcialitie of voice: he was of nation a Fleming, & in his youth hauing béene schoolemaister to Cesar, and by his meane made cardinall vnder pope Leo, did at that time gouerne Spaine in the absence of Cesar. And as there begar some voices to publish for him, so cardinall Xisto one of that election, began vnder an oration speciall, to recount and amplifie his vertues and knowledge, by whose example certeine other cardinals yeelded, and the residue from hand to hand followed, though more by constraint than councell.

The election of Adrian to the popedome woondered at, and why.

Thus was he chosen with the voices of all the cardinals, and had his creation perfected the same morning. Wherein this was to be woondered at, that euen those that had elected him could giue no reason, why amid so manie troubles & dangers in the estate ecclesiastike, they had raised to the souereigne sée a stranger, a forrener, and of long absence out of the countrie, & wherein were helping no respects of fauor, no consideration of former merits, nor anie conuersation had with anie of the other cardinals: yea they scarselie knew his name, he had neuer béene in Italie, and had no hope nor cogitation to see it: of which strauagant maner of dealing, being not able to excuse themselues, they attributed all to the working of the Holie-ghost, who is woont (for so they alleged) to inspire the hearts of the cardinals in the electing of popes: he receiued newes of his election in the towne of Victoria in Biskaie, and would not haue imposed vpon him anie other name than his owne, which he caused to be published vnder Andrian the sixt.

Pope Adrian the sixt, commeth to Rome.

Now he made his entrie into Rome the nine and twentith of August, with a great concourse of the commons and the whole court: of whome albeit his comming was desired with an vniuersall gladnesse (for that without the presence forsooth of the popes, Rome beareth more a resemblance of a sauage desart than of a citie) yet that spectacle wrought sundrie impressions and diuersities of thoughts in the minds of all men, when they considered that they had a pope for nation and languge a stranger, and for the affaires of Italie and the court altogither vnexperienced: and also for that he was not of those regions and countries, who by long conuersation were alreadie made familiar with the customes of Italie. The enuie that stirred vp in men this consideration was redoubled by the accident of the plague, which beginning in Rome at his arriuall, afflicted the citie during the whole season of Autumne, to the great calamitie and losse of the people: a matter which in the fansies of men was construed to an euill prognostication of his pontificacie.]

The description of doctor Pace.

Nowithstanding this election of Adrian (as you heare) accomplished; yet doctor Pace kept his iournie according to his commission. This Pace was a right worthie man, and one that gaue in counsell faithfull aduise. Learned he was also, and indued with many excellent good gifts of nature, courteous, pleasant, and delighting in musike, highlie in the kings fauour, and well heard in matters of weight. But the more the prince fauoured him, the more was he misliked of the cardinall, who sought onelie to beare all the rule himselfe, and to haue no partener; so that he procured that this

doctor

doctor Pace vnder color of ambassage, should be sent foorth of the realme, that his presence about the king should not win him too much authoritie and fauour at the kings hands.

This yeare was a great death in London and other places of the realme. Manie men of honour and great worship died, and amongest other, the bishop of London, doctor Fitz Iames, in whose place was doctor Tunstall elected. The earle of Surrie returned out of Ireland, and came to the court the fiue and twentith of Ianuarie. Manie complaints were made by the merchants to the king and his councell of the Frenchmen, which spoiled them by sea of their goods. For by reason that the wars were open betwixt the emperour, and the French king, manie ships of warre were abroad on both parts, and now and then the Englishmen fell into their hands, and were vsed as enimies; namelie by the Frenchmen, which naturallie hated the Englishmen. The French kings ambassadours promised restitution of euerie thing, but little was restored. In this moneth of Ianuarie therefore, the king commanded all his ships to be rigged, and made readie, which was doone with all diligence.

On the second daie of Februarie, the king as then being at Greenewich, receiued a bull from the pope, whereby he was declared Defendor of the Christian faith, & likewise his successors for euer. The cardinall of Yorke sang the high masse that daie with all the pompous solemnitie that might be, and gaue cleane remission of sinnes to all that heard it. This title was ascribed vnto the king, bicause he had written a booke against Luther in Germanie; whereunto the said Luther answered verie sharpelie, nothing sparing his authoritie nor maiestie. ¶ Of which booke published by the king, I will not (for reuerence of his roiallie) though I durst, report what I haue read: bicause we are to iudge honourablie of our rulers, and to speake nothing but good of the princes of the people. Onelie this breefe clause or fragment I will adde (least I might seeme to tell a tale of the man in the moone) that king Henrie in his said booke is reported to rage against the diuell and antichrist to cast out his fome against Luther, to raise out the name of the pope, and yet to allow his law, &c. I suppresse the rest for shame, and returne to our historie.]

In this meane time, grudges and displeasures still grew and increased betwixt the king of England and the French king, so that their greefs rankled dailie more and more, till at length the duke of Albanie returned into Scotland, contrarie to that which was couenanted by the league. The French king in deed alleaged, that he was not priuie to his going thither; and wrote to the king, that the said duke was entered Scotland without his assent: but it was otherwise iudged & knowne, that he had commission of the French king to go thither. Hereupon, the king was sore offended, and prepared for wars. Musters were made of able men, and a note taken of what substance men were. The king also sent six ships to the sea, well trimmed, manned, and vittelled. The admerall was one Christopher Coo, an expert sea man. His commission was, to safe gard the merchants, and other the kings subiects, that were greeuouslie spoiled and robbed on the sea, by Frenchmen, Scots, and other rouers.

The eight of Februarie, the lord Dacres, warden of the marches fore aneinst Scotland, entered into Scotland with fiue hundred men, by the kings commandement, & there proclamed, that the Scots should come in to the kings peace, by the first of March following, or else to stand at their perils; the duke of Albanie being then within fiue miles with a mightie power of Scots. The eleuenth of Februarie, the lord of Aburgauennie was brought from the Tower to Westminster, and there in the kings bench confessed his indictment of misprision. The lord Montacute was about the same time restored vnto the kings fauour. ¶ On the second of March, certeine noble men of the empire, arriued in England, to passe into Spaine, who were honourablie receiued; and in honour of them, great iusts and triumphs were made, which being finished and doone, they tooke their leaue and departed on their iournie.

Duncan

A Scotish rouer taken on the sea by Iohn Arundell.

Dunc̀n Campbell, a Scotish rouer, after long fight, was taken on the sea by Iohn Arundell an esquier of Cornewall, who presented him to the king. He was committed to the Tower, & there remained prisoner a long season. All the kings ships were put in a readinesse, so that by the beginning of Aprill, they were rigged and trimmed readie to make saile. ¶This yeare died the lord Brooke, sir Edward Poinings, knight of the garter, sir Iohn Pechie, and sir Edward Belknap, valiant capteins, which were suspected to be poisoned at a banket made at Ard, when the two kings met last. Wheat was sold this yeare in the citie of London, for twentie shillings a quarter, & in other places for twentie six shillings eight pence.

Great dearth of corne.

In this yeare Gawan Dowglas, bishop of Dunkell fled out of Scotland into England, bicause the duke of Albanie being come thither, had taken vpon him the whole gouernement of the king and realme there, the sequele of whose dooings the bishop sore mistrusted. The king assigned vnto this bishop an honest pension to liue on. And shortlie after, was Clarenceaux the herald sent into Scotland, vnto the duke of Albanie, to command him to auoid that realme for diuerse considerations; & if he would not, then to defie him, sith contrarie to the articles of the league concluded betwixt France & England, he was entered Scotland without his licence. The duke refused to accomplish the kings commandement, and was therefore defied by the said Clarenceaux. The sixt of March, the French king commanded all Englishmens goods being in Burdeaux, to be attached, and put vnder arrest, and reteined not onelie the monie due to be paid for the restitution of Tornaie, but also withheld the French quéenes dower.

Clarenceaux sent into Scotland.

The French K. attacheth the Englishmens goods in Burdeaux.

Polydor.

The cardinals liberalitie by vertue of his spirituall power forsooth.

The cardinall vnderstanding that he was euill spoken of, for vsing his power legantine to such aduantage as he did, in selling graces & dispensations, he thought to bestow some part therof amongst the people fréelie, without taking anie thing for the same. Wherevpon, when Lent drew neere, he appointed the preachers at Paules crosse, to declare, that it should be lawfull to all persons for that Lent, to eat milke, butter, chéese, & egs. And to the end that none should haue anie scrupulousnesse of conscience in so dooing, he by his authoritie granted remission of sins to all those that did eat white meats: knowing as it were afore hand, that the people giuen to the obseruance of their religious fast, would not easilie be brought to breake the same, contrarie to the ancient custome vsed in their countrie. Neither was he deceiued therein, for so farre were the people from receiuing or accounting this as a benefit, that they tooke it rather for a wicked & cursed déed in those that receiued it, & few or almost none could he induce to breake their old order and scrupulous trade in that behalfe.

An. Reg. 14.

The French ambassador is called before the councell.

The king, vnderstanding how his subiects were handled at Burdeaux by the French kings commandement, in breach of the league, the French ambassadour was called before the councell, and the cardinall laid sore to his charge, that contrarie to his promise at all times on the French king his maisters behalfe, affirming that he ment nothing but peace and amitie to be obserued in all points with the king of England: yet now the English merchants had not onelie their goods staied at Burdeaux, but also they and their factors were laid in prison, in full breach of all peace and amitie afore time concluded. The ambassadour in woords so well as hée could excused his maister, but in the end hée was commanded to keepe his house: and the French hostages that were appointed héere to remaine for the monie to be paid for the deliuerie of Tornaie, were committed vnto the safe kéeping of the lord of Saint Iohns, sir Thomas Louell, sir Andrew Windsor, and sir Thomas Neuill, euerie of them to haue one.

The Frenchmen in Lŏdon are all arested and put to their fines. *Polydor.*

Herewith also, all the Frenchmen in London were arrested, committed to prison, and put to their fines: but they were more courteouslie vsed than the Englishmen were in France. For after they had béene in durance ten daies, they were set at libertie, vpon finding suerties to appeare before the maior, or else before the councell at a certeine daie, and to paie the fine vpon them assessed, which fine the king pardoned to diuerse of the poorest sort. But in comparison of the Scotish nation, you

would

would haue said, the Frenchmen were in small displeasure: for not onelie those that All the Scots in England apprehended and fined. were borne in Scotland, but also diuers northernmen borne, within English ground, for enuious spite called Scots, were apprehended, imprisoned, and grieuouslie fined, although some of them by streict inquirie tried to be Englishmen, escaped without paieng the fine.

There were sent to the sea, vnder conduct of sir William Fitz Williams viceadme- The nauie setteth foorth. rall, twentie & eight goodlie ships well manned and trimmed for the warres, & seuen other ships were sent toward Scotland, which entered the Forth, and proffered to enter the Scotish ships that laie in the hauens: but the Scots ran their ships aland, and the Englishmen followed with boats, landed, and set the ships on fire, & at Leith tooke certeine prisoners, which they brought into England; and still the kings great nauie kept the narrow seas: for then was neither peace betwixt England and France, nor open warres. The king vnderstanding that the emperor would come to Calis, so to passe into England, as he went towards Spaine, appointed the lord marquesse Dorset to go to Calis, there to receiue him, and likewise the lord cardinall was appointed to receiue him at Douer.

The cardinall taking his iournie forward on the twentith of Maie, rode through Cardinall Woolsie his pompe when he receiued the emperour at Douer. London, accompanied with two earles, six and thirtie knights, and an hundred gentlemen, eight bishops, ten abbats, thirtie chapleins, all in veluet and sattin, and yeomen seuen hundred. The marquesse Dorset was gone ouer before vnto Calis: and The marques Dorset receiueth the emperour at Graueling. the fiue and twentith of Maie being sundaie, the said marquesse, with the bishop of Chichester, the lord de la Ware, and diuerse other at the water of Graueling, receiued the emperour in the name of the king of England, and with all honour brought him to Calis, where he was receiued with procession, by the lord Bernes lieutenaut of the towne, with the maior and merchants of the Staple, in the best maner that might be deuised.

On the mondaie he tooke ship at Calis, and landed at Douer, where the cardinall The emperor landeth at Douer. with thrée hundred lords, knights, and gentlemen of England was readie to receiue him, and with all honour that might be, brought him to the castell, where he was lodged. On wednesdaie, being the Ascension éeuen, the king came to Douer, and there with great ioy and gladnesse, the emperour and he met. On the fridaie in the after noone they departed from Douer, & came that night to Canturburie, so from thence by easie iournies to Gréenewich, where the quéene receiued hir nephue with all the ioy that might be. Here the emperour taried certeine daies in great solace and pleasure; and the more to honor his presence, roiall iustes and tourneies were appoint- Iustes and tourneies at Gréenwich. ed, the which were furnished in most triumphant maner: the king, and the earle of Deuonshire, and ten aids with them, kéeping the place against the duke of Suffolke, the marques Dorset, and other ten aids vpon their part.

On fridaie being the sixt of Iune, the king and the emperour with all their companies, marched toward London, where the citie was prepared for their entrie, after the maner as is vsed at a coronation, so that nothing was forgotten that might set foorth the citie. For the rich citizens well apparelled stood within railes set on the left side Edw. Hall in H. 8. fol. xcviij. of the stréetes, and the cleargie on the right side in rich copes, which censed the princes as they passed, and all the stréetes were richlie hanged with clothes of gold, siluer, veluet, and arras, and in euerie house almost minstrelsie: and in euerie stréet were these two verses written in letters of gold, both Latine and English:

Carolus, Henricus, viuant; defensor vtérq,
Henricus fidei, Carolus ecclesiæ. That is,

Long prosperitie,   ⎧ The one of the faith,
To Charles and Henrie, ⎨ The other of the church,
Princes most puissant: ⎩ Chosen defendant.

Sundrie pageants were deuised, and stages verie faire and excellent to behold, with
such

See Ed. Hall in
B. B. fol. xcvj.
& deinceps.

such melodie of instruments, and other tokens of ioy and gladnesse, that woonder it was to consider the manner thereof. The emperour was lodged at the Blacke friers, and all his nobles in the new palace of Bridewell. On Whitsundaie being the eight of Iune, the emperour and the king rode to the cathedrall church of saint Paule, and there heard masse, which was soong by the cardinall that had his trauerse, and cupboord. Before masse, two barons gaue him water, and after the gospell two earles; and at the last lauatorie, two dukes: which pride the Spaniards sore disdained. The emperour thus remained with the king certeine daies and fode to diuerse places with him, being still feasted & banketted, and had all the pleasure shewed to him that might be imagined. At Windsor they taried a whole weeke and more, where on Corpus Christi daie, the emperour ware his mantell of the garter, and sate in his owne stall. On the same daie both the princes receiued the sacrament, and after that seruice was ended, they tooke their corporall othes to kéepe and obserue the league, which was concluded betwixt them. On the morrow after, they departed from Windsor, and by soft and easie iournies they came to Winchester, on the two & twentith of Iune.

Now before the emperour was thus come to Winchester, the earle of Surrie being high admerall of England, was come to Hampton with all the kings nauie, and with him the lord Fitz Walter, the baron Curson, sir Nicholas Carew, sir Richard Wingfield, sir Richard Ierningham, Francis Brian, sir William Barentine, sir Adrian Foskew, sir Edward Donne, sir Edward Chamberleine, sir Richard Cornwall, sir Anthonie Poines, sir Henrie Shirborne, and the viceadmerall sir William Fitz Williams, sir Edmund Braie, sir Giles Capell, sir William Pirton, Iohn Cornwallis, sir Iohn Wallop, sir Edward Echingham, sir William Sidneie, Anthonie Browne, Giles Husie, Thomas Moore, Iohn Russel, Edward Bray, Henrie Owen, George Cobham, Thomas Oldhall, Thomas Louell, Robert Ierningham, Anthonie Kneuet, sir Iohn Tremaile, and sir William Skeuington the maister of the kings ordinance, & Iohn Fabian sergeant at armes, by whom this enterprice was chieflie mooued, with diuerse others, which in the end of Iune departed from Hampton, noising that they should onelie scowre the seas for safegard of the emperour and his nauie.

On the first of Iulie, the emperours nauie came before Hampton, conteining an hundred and fourescore goodlie ships. Then the emperour tooke leaue of the king, of whome he had manie great gifts, and notable summes of monie by waie of loane; & so the sixt of Iulie he tooke his ship, and made saile to Spaine, where he arriued in safetie the tenth daie after. The king borrowed of the citie of London twentie thousand pounds, and deliuered priuie seales for warrant of the repaiment. None were charged but men of good wealth. The like lone was practised through all the realme, not without grudge of manie persons that were called vpon for the same. The earle of Surrie hauing wafted the emperour ouer to the coast of Biscaie, vpon his returne finding the wind fauourable, according to his instructions, made to the coast of Britaine, and landing with his people in number seuen thousand, about fiue miles from Morleis, marched thither, and assaulting the towne, wan it.

For the maister gunner Christopher Morreis hauing there certeine falcons, with the shot of one of them, stroke the locke of the wicket in the gate, so that it flew open: and then the same Christopher and other gentlemen, with their souldiers, in the smoke of the gunnes pressed to the gates, and finding the wicket open, entered, and so finallie was the towne of Morleis woone, and put to sacke. The souldiers gained much by the pillage, for the towne was excéeding rich, and speciallie of linnen cloth. When they had rifled the towne throughlie, and taken their pleasure of all things therein, the earle caused them by sound of trumpet to resort to their standards, and after they had set fire in the towne, and burned a great part thereof, the earle retreated with his armie towards his ships, burning the villages by the waie, and all that night lay on land. On the morrow after they tooke their ships, and when they were bestowed on boord, the

earle

Note the pride
of cardinall
Woolsie.

The emperor
and the king of
England sweare
each to other to
obserue the
league made be-
twixt them.

Erle of Surrie
high admerall
of England.

The emperor
departeth out of
England to-
wards Spaine.

The king bor-
roweth 20000
pounds of the
citie.

The maner of
the winning of
Morleis in Bri-
taine by the earle
of Surrie.

earle commanded sixtéene or seuenteene ships small and great, lieng there in the hauen, to be burnt.

When the lord admerall had thus woone the towne of Morleis, he called to him certeine esquiers, and made them knights, as sir Francis Brian, sir Anthonie Browne, sir Richard Cornewall, sir Thomas Moore, sir Giles Huseie, sir Iohn Russell, sir Iohn Reinsford, sir George Cobham, sir Iohn Cornewallis, sir Edward Rigleie, and diuerse other. After this they continued a while on the coast of Britaine, and disquieted the Britains by entering their hauens, and sometimes landing and dooing diuerse displeasures to the inhabitants about the coast. After that the earle had lien a while thus on the coast of Britaine, hée was countermanded by the kings letters, who therevpon brought backe his whole fleet vnto a place called the Cow, vnder the Ile of Wight, and then went on land himselfe, discharging the more part of his people, and leauing the residue with certeine ships vnder the gouernance of the vice-admerall sir William Fitz Williams, to képe the seas against the French.

Diuerse gentlemen knighted by the erle of Surrie vp5 the winning of Morleis.

Polydor.

In this meane while, diuerse exploits were atchiued betwixt them of the garrisons in the marches of Calis, & the Frenchmen of Bullongne and Bullongnois: but still the losse ran for the most part on the French side. For the English frontiers were well and stronglie furnished with good numbers of men of warre, and gouerned by right sage and valiant capteins, which dailie made inuasions vpon the French confines, and namelie sir William Sands treasuror of the towne of Calis, and sir Edward Gilford marshall, were two that did the Frenchmen most displeasure. On the third of Iulie, three hundred French horssemen comming néere to the castell of Guisnes, kept themselues in couert, appointing eight or ten of their companie to shew themselues in sight to the Englishmen within. Wherevpon there went foorth eight archers, and fell in skirmish with those horssemen, till there came thrée other to the rescue of the Frenchmen, and skirmished with the archers on foot.

Sir William Sands and sir Edward Gilford two whips to the Frenchmen.

Herewith issued out of Guisnes twelue demilances all Welshmen, in rescue of the footmen, and then all the troope of the French horssemen brake foorth and set on the Welshmen. The footmen, so long as they had anie arrowes to bestow, shot lustilie, and in the end were driuen to defend themselues with their swords. The Welshmen keeping togither, entered into the band of the Frenchmen, brake their speares, and after fought and laid about them with their swords, so that they made a waie, and escaped from those thrée hundred French horssemen. Of the French side were slaine thrée men and fiue horsses, the English archers on foot selling their liues dearlie, were all slaine, for the Frenchmen would not take any of them prisoners, they were so angrie for losse of their fellowes.

The valiancie of the Welshmen against the French.

On the fiue and twentith of Iulie, the treasuror and marshall of Calis, with fourtéene hundred footmen, entered the French pale: and finding not monsieur de Foiat for whome they sought, they went to Whitsand baie, set the towne on fire, and assaulting the church, into the which people were withdrawne, wan it, and afterwards set fire on the steeple, bicause that diuerse, hauing shut vp themselues therein, through counsell of a priest that was with them, refused to yéeld, till the fire caused them to leape downe and so manie of them perished, and the rest were taken prisoners, and led to Calis. About two daies before this, to wit, the three and twentith daie of Iulie, one Thwaits a capteine of an English ship, with six score men, archers and others, tooke land beside Bullongne, and passing vp into the countrie thrée miles to a towne called Newcastell, forraied all the parts as he went, and in his returne set fire on that towne, and burnt a great part thereof, and came againe to his ship in safetie, notwithstanding fourscore hagbutters, and thrée hundred other men of warre of the countrie came foorth, and pursued the Englishmen verie fiercelie: but the Englishmen putting them backe, got to their ship, and lost not a man.

The lords Rosse & Dacres of the north inuade Scotland and spoile the coun-trie.

Moreouer, whilest the warres were thus followed in France, the lord Rosse, and the lord Dacres of the north, which were appointed to keepe the borders against Scotland, burnt the towne of Kelsie, and fourescore villages, & ouerthrew eighteene towers of stone, with all their barnekines. Also the king appointed the earle of Shrewesburie to be his lieutenant generall of the north parts, against the inuasion which was intended by the duke of Albanie, which earle directed his letters to all the shires lieng from Trent northward, that all men should be in a readinesse. Order was taken by the cardinall, that the true value of all mens substance might be knowne, and he

The cardinall will haue euerie man sworn to tell what he is woorth.

would haue had euerie man sworne to haue vttered the true valuation of that they were woorth, and required a tenth part thereof to bée granted towards the kings charges now in his warres, in like case as the spiritualtie had granted a fourth part, and were content to liue on the other three parts.

This demand was thought gréeuous to them of the citie of London, where the cardinall first mooued it; so that manie reasons were alleaged by them why they iudged themselues sore dealt with. In the end they brought in their billes, which

The earle of Surrie sent with an armie to inuade France.

were receiued vpon their honesties. The king in this mean time, being now entered into wars with France, thought not to suffer his enimies to rest in quiet: and therefore leauied an armie which he sent ouer to Calis, appointing the earle of Surrie to be generall of the same. When the earle was come to Calis, and had taken order in his businesse for that iournie, he set forward with his armie, being diuided into thrée battels or wards, of the which, the first was led by sir Robert Ratcliffe, lord Fitz Water, the middle ward or battell the earle himselfe guided, and with him his brother the lord Edmund Howard. The rereward was gouerned by sir William Sands, and sir Richard Wingfield, both being knights of the garter. Capteine of the horssemen was sir Edward Guilford.

The Burgog-nians ioine with the English host.

They entered into the French ground the second of September, being tuesdaie, and tooke their iournie toward Heding. By the way there came to them a great power of Burgognians from the ladie Margaret, as then regent of Flanders, according to the articles of the league. All the townes, villages, and castels in the countrie thorough the which they marched, were burned, wasted, and destroied on euerie side of their waie: as the towne and castell of Sellois, the townes of Brume bridge, Senekerke, Botingham, & Manstier, the towne and castell of Nerbins, the towne of Dauerne, the castels of Columberge, and Rew, the towne and church fortified of Boards, saint Marie de Bois, the towne of Vaus, the towne and castell of Fringes. On the sixteenth daie of September, the earle of Surrie with his armie of Englishmen and

The castell of Heding besieged by the English-men.

Burgognians, came before the castell of Heding, and planted his siege before it. The towne was entered, and part thereof burned by the Burgognians.

Within the castell was capteine monsieur de Biez, hauing prouided for defense of the place all things necessarie; so that the earle of Surrie, and other the capteins of the hoast, perceiuing they could not within anie short time win it, after they had bin before it eleuen daies, they raised their siege, chéeflie bicause they had no great battering peeces to ouerthrow the walles. For the weather was such, and the waies waxed so deepe towards the latter end of that summer, that they could not conueie with them anie great ordinance. From Heding they passed forward, and comming to Dorlens, burned the towne, and rased the castell. From thense they came vnto

The earle of Surrie returneth with his armie to Calis.

the towne of Darrier, which they burnt also and spoiled. Thus they burned and spoiled all the waie as they passed. But the weather still waxed woorse and woorse, so that manie fell sicke through intemperance thereof, and the Burgognians and Spaniards which were in the armie returned into Flanders.

Then the earle of Surrie, perceiuing that he could no longer keepe the field in that season of the yeare, turned backe towards Calis in good order of battell, and came thither the sixteenth of October. He would gladlie in déed (before the departure of

the

the Burgognians and Spaniards) haue passed the water of Somme: but other capteins considering the time of the yeare to be past, and that the whole armie conteined not aboue eightéene thousand men, iudged it more wisedome to returne, and so in the end their opinions were followed. After that the English armie was returned to Calis, the earle of Surrie sent foorth sir William Sands, sir Maurice Berkeleie, sir William Fitz Williams, and with them three thousand men, which burned Marguison, the towne of saint Iehans rode, and also Temple towne, with manie villages.

They also brought a maruellous great bootie of goods out of the countrie, which they got at this rode, as fouretéene thousand shéepe, a thousand foure hundred oxen and kine, and other great cattell, a thousand three hundred hogs, and eight hundred mares and horsses, besides prisoners. When the earle of Surrie had set things in order, and appointed foorth such as he would haue remaine in the garrisons, on that side the sea; he returned, and all the residue of the armie (sauing those that were commanded to tarie) came ouer also with the nauie, and arriued in the Thames; and so euerie man into his countrie at his pleasure. There remained also behind a companie of men of warre called aduenturers, which serued without wages, liuing onelie on that which they could catch & win of the enimies. There were foure hundred of them that went with the armie now this last time into France, and did much hurt vnto the Frenchmen: for they were by practise become expert and skilfull in the points of warre, and dailie exploited one enterprise or other, to their owne aduantage, and hinderance of the enimie.

The duke of Albanie being in this meane while established gouernour of Scotland, raised an armie of fourescore thousand men and aboue, with the which he approched to the English borders: but made no inuasion. The mistrust that he had in the Scots caused him to staie, and therefore he sent to the French king for six thousand Almans, the which he dailie looking for (& that in vaine) droue off time till the end of summer was now at hand, and then requiring a truce for certeine moneths, obteined it at the kings hand. The earle of Shrewesburie had in a readinesse eight and twentie thousand men to haue resisted him, if he had entered vpon the English confines. After that an abstinence of warre was taken betwixt England and Scotland, then in October following there came into England three personages of small behauiour (as it séemed) ambassadors out of Scotland: they were smallie regarded, and shortlie departed.

Their commission was onelie to vnderstand, whether the king had assented to the truce or not. Wherevpon it was thought that they were sent for a countenance onelie of fulfilling the promise made by the duke of Albanie at that present, when the truce was granted, than for anie true meaning to accomplish that which was promised; that is to saie, to agrée vnto some vnfeined and perfect conclusion of peace. The king héerevpon doubting their old pranks, ordeined the earle of Northumberland Henrie Persie the fift of that name, warden of the whole marches, who thankefullie receiued the honor thereof, and so he departed. But whatsoeuer matter it was that mooued him, shortlie after he began to make sute to the king, and ceassed not, till he was of that office discharged : and then the earle of Surrie lord admerall of England was made generall warden, and the lord Marquesse Dorset was made warden of the east and middle marches, and the lord Dacres of the west marches.

The earle of Northumberland was for this refusall of exercising the office of lord warden, greatlie blamed of his owne tenants, and accounted of all men to be void of the loue and desire that noblemen ought to haue to honor and chiualrie. The lord Marquesse Dorset accompanied with sir William Bulmer, and sir Arthur Darcie, with manie other of the nobilitie, the second of Aprill then being thursdaie before Easter, entered into Tiuidale, and so passing forward ten miles into Gallowaie, burnt on euerie side the townes and villages. All the night he tarried within the Scotish

ground,

Marginal notes:

A great bootie woone by the Englishmen.

The earle of Surrie returneth with his armie into England.

Aduenturers.

The duke of Albanie leuieth an armie of Scots to inuade England. *Io. ydor.*

Truce betwixt England & Scotland. *Edw. Hall.*

A meane ambassage out of Scotland.

The earle of Northumberland warden of the whole marches. 1523

The Marquesse Dorset entereth into Scotland and burneth diuerse townes there.

ground, and on the morrow being goodfridaie, he withdrew backe into England with foure thousand neat, hauing burned Grimsleie, Mowhouse, Doufford, Miles, Ackfoorth, Crowling, Nowes manour, Midder, Crowling, Marbottell, Lowbog, Seforth manor, Middell right, Primsted, Broket, Shawes, Harwell, Wide open Haugh, with others.

A parlement holden at the Blackefriers in London. *Edw. Hall in H. 8. fol. cvj.*

On the fiftéenth daie of Aprill began the parlement, which was holden as then at the Blackefriers, and that daie the masse of the Holie-ghost was soong, all the lords being present in their parlement robes. ¶ Now when masse was finished, the K. came to the parlement chamber, and there sat downe in the seat roiall or throne, and at his féet on the right side sat the cardinall of Yorke and the archbishop of Canturburie, and at the raile behind stood doctor Tunstall bishop of London, which made to the whole parlement an eloquent oration, declaring to the people the office of a king. First he must be a man of iudgement, according to the saieng of the prophet Dauid, Deus iudicium tuum regi da, &c. Also he must be a man of great learning, according

The oration of doctor Tunstall bishop of London.

to the saieng of the prophet, Erudimini qui iudicatis terram. According to which saiengs he said, that God had sent vs a prince of great iudgement, of great learning, and great experience: which according to his princelie dutie, forgat not to studie to set forward all things which might be profitable to his people and realme, least might be laid to his charge the saieng of Seneca; Es rex & non habes tempus esse rex? Art thou a king and hast no time to be a king? Which is as much to saie, as; Art thou a king, and dooest nothing profitable to thy people? Art thou a king, and séest the people haue an insufficient law? Art thou a king, and wilt not prouide remedie for the mischéefe of thy people?

These things haue mooued the kings most excellent maiestie to call this his high court of parlement, both for the remedie of mischéefs which be in the common law, as recoueries, forren vouchers & corrupt trials, and for making and ordering of new statutes, which maie be to the high aduancement of the common-wealth. Wherefore he willeth his commons to repaire to the common house, and there to elect them a speaker, or their common mouth, and to certifie the lord chancellor of the same, who should thereof make report to the kings most noble grace, and should declare his pleasure when he would haue him presented to his person. This was the cause of the parlement, as he said. But suerlie of these things no word was spoken in the whole parlement, and in effect no good act made, except the grant of a great subsidie were one. But according to this instruction the commons departed to the common house,

The oration of sir Thomas More speaker for commons.

& chose for their speaker sir Thomas More knight, & presented him on the saturday after in the parlement chamber, where he (according to the old vsage) disabled himselfe both in wit, learning, & discretion, to speake before the king, and brought in for his purpose how one Phormio desired Haniball to come to his reading, which thereto assented, and when Haniball was come he began to read De re militari, that is, of cheualrie. When Haniball perceiued him, he called him arrogant foole: bicause he would presume to teach him which was maister of cheualrie, in the feats of warre. So the speaker said, if he should speake before the king, of learning and ordering of a common-wealth and such other like, the king so well learned and of such prudence and experience might saie to him as Haniball said to Phormio. Wherefore he desired his grace that the commons might choose an other speaker.

The cardinall answered, that the king knew his wit, learning, and discretion by long experience in his seruice: wherefore he thought that the commons had chosen him as the most méetest of all; and so he did admit him. Then sir Thomas Moore gaue to the king his most humble thanks, and desired of him two petitions: the one, if he should be sent from the commons to the king on message and mistake their intent, that he might with the kings pleasure resort againe vnto the commons for the knowledge of their true meaning. The other was, if in communication and reasoning, ng, any man in the common house should speake more largelie than of dutie he ought to doo, that all such offenses should be pardoned, and that to be entered of record. Which two petitions were granted; and so thus began the parlement and continued as you shall heare.]

This yeare was the citie and the whole Ile of the Rhodes conquered by the Turke, and all the christians displaced: whereof Guicciardin hath discoursed as followeth. ¶ The end of this yeare (saith he) was made no lesse wretched and vnhappie, than *Abr. Fl. ex Guic. pag.* 840. Rhodes taken by Soliman Ottoman. slanderous to all christian princes for the losse of the Ile of Rhodes: which Soliman Ottoman tooke by violence, notwithstanding it was defended by the knights of Rhodes, called in other times more ancient the knights of saint Iohn of Ierusalem. And abiding in that place since they were chased out of Ierusalem, notwithstanding they laie betweene two so mightie princes as the Turke & the Soldan; yet their valour had preserued it of long time, and to the right woorthie glorie of their order, they had remained as an assured rampier of christian religion in those seas: & yet they were not without their imputations & notes of infamie, for that hauing a continuall custome for the better defending of those shoares, to spoile the vessels of the infidels, they were thought sometimes to make pillage of christian ships.

The Turke sent into the Iland a woonderfull great armie, which remaining there manie moneths with no lesse horrour to good men for their cruelties, than terrour to all men for their huge numbers, at last he came thither in person. And drawing to his desire of conquest and glorie, the respect of profit and riches which the victorie would yéeld, he lost not one minute of time to vex them. Wherein his industrie was The Turkes great industrie equiualent to his valour. nothing inferiour to his valour, for sometimes he cast monstrous mines and trenches, sometimes he raised platformes of earth and wood, whose height ouertopped the wals of the towne, and sometimes he afflicted them with most furious and bloudie assaults: insomuch that as these works and engines were not performed without a woonderfull butcherie & slaughter of his souldiors; so also the defense of them was so dangerous to the liues of them within, that manie numbers were diminished, manie bodies maimed and made vnseruiceable, & the residue sore terrified by the calamitie of their companions and fréends, to whom they could giue no other propertie of compassion, than to mourne with them in their common miserie.

Their aduersitie was so much the more intollerable, by how much their trauels were without fruit, their words without comfort, and their valour disfauoured of fortune, & lastlie their store of gunpowder was consumed, which is not the least necessitie for the defense of a place. They saw before their eies huge breaches made into their The manifold calamities & mines inforced by this warre. walles with the artilleries of their enimies, they discerned seuerall mines wrought into manie parts of the towne, and they found by lamentable experience, that the lesse good they did, the more painfullie they laboured, for that their fortune had reduced them to these termes of extremitie, that in abandoning one place to relieue another, they put both in danger, not hauing numbers sufficient to furnish the seruice, and lesse expectation of rescue amid perils so raging and desperate: so that, what for that their necessities were greater than their hopes, & their defense lesse able by the continuall diminution of their numbers, & lastlie holding it no breach of honour to preserue by wisdome and composition, that they could no longer defend by their valour and prowes, they gaue place to their destinie, and capitulated with the Turke as followeth. That the great maister of their order should leaue the towne to him : that as well he as all his knights should depart in safetie, with libertie to carie with them as much of their goods as they could. And for assurance of this capitulation, the Turke should withdraw out of those seas, his fléet or nauie, and retire his armie by land fiue miles from Rhodes. By vertue of which capitulation Rhodes remained to the Turkes, and the christians passed into Sicilie, and so into Italie, kéeping their Rhodes renderd vp to the Turkes faith and profession vnuiolated. They found in Sicilie an armie by sea compounded of a cera certeine number of vessels, with great releefe of vittels and munitions, and readie to hoise saile at the next wind to reuittle Rhodes. The slownesse of this rescue was laid to the popes fault.

Solimans contempt of christian religion.

After they were departed, Soliman for a more contempt of christian religion, made his entrie into the citie vpon the daie of the birth of the sonne of God : which daie being celebrated in the churches of christians with noise of musike & holie inuocations, he conuerted all the churches of Rhodes dedicated to the seruice of Iesus Christ, into Mosqueis (so they call their temples) which after all the christian rites and ceremonies were abolished, they made dedicatorie to Mahomet. Good cause had the christians herevpon with heauie hearts to make their complaint to God by the president of the psalmist, lamenting the libertie of the enimies exercising the vehemencie of his rage against Gods people ; & full well with swolne eies testifieng the sorrow of their soules might (sadlie sounding the dumps of their threnomina) saie :

Buc. in psal. 74.

        ———perde funditùs:
    Hostes proteruos, qui tuum sacrarium
    Manu nefanda polluunt,
    Clangunt sonora buccina, non quæ tuas
    Laudes canat, ludibrio
    Sed festa acerbo quæ profanet ; in tuis
    Vexilla figunt turribus, &c.

To vnderstand more of this historie touching the taking of Rhodes, what mooued the Turke to couet the same, his letter comminatorie to Philip de Villiers who tooke part against him, with other accidents and circumstances belonging to this martiall

Ed. Hall in H. 8. fol. cvij, cviij, & deinceps.

action ; read the report of Edward Hall, which is verie copious and plentifull in this behalfe. And now will we returne to our owne affaires here in England.] About this time the bishop of Durham departed this life, & the king gaue that bishoprike to the

Cardinall Woolsie made bishop of Durham.

cardinall, who resigned the bishoprike of Bath to doctor Iohn Clerke maister of the rolles, and sir Henrie Marneie that was vicechamberleine, was made lord priuie seale, and shortlie after was created lord Marneie. In the end of this yeare, doctor Blith bishop of Chester was attached for treason, but he acquited himselfe. About this time the cardinall exercised his authoritie (which he pretended by his power legantine, verie largelie, not onelie in proouing of testaments in his court, calling the executors and administrators before him, of what diocesse soeuer they were, but also by prouisions he gaue all benifices belonging to spirituall persons, and ran thereby within danger of the premunire, as afterward was laid to his charge.

The cardinall exerciseth his authoritie verie largelie. Polydor.

But after that he perceiued his owne follie and rash dooing herein, contrarie to the lawes, which would not permit that anie such things as were mooued within the prouince of Canturburie, might be concluded without the authoritie of the archbishop, he sent them againe to Poules, and sate himselfe at Westminster with his cleargie of the prouince of Yorke. And euen as there was much adoo amongst them of the common house about their agréement to the subsidie, so was there as hard hold for a while amongst them of the clergie in the conuocation house. Namelie Richard bishop of Winchester, & Iohn bishop of Rochester held sore against it, but most of all sir Rowland Philips vicar of Croidon, and one of the canons of Poules, béeing reputed a notable preacher in those daies, spake most against that paiment.

The cleargie grant halfe of all their spirituall reuenues for one yeare.

But the cardinall taking him aside, so handled the matter with him, that he came no more into the house, willinglie absenting himselfe to his great infamie, and losse of that estimation which men had of his innocencie. Thus the belwedder giuing ouer his hold, the other yéelded, and so was granted the halfe of all their spirituall reuenues for one yeare, to bée paid in fiue yeres following, that the burthen might the more easilie be borne. The parlement being begun (as ye haue heard) the cardi-

An. Reg. 15.

nall on the nine and twentith day of Aprill came into the common house, and there
                                        shewing

shewing the great charges that the king necessarilie was at, and dailie must be at in maintenance of his warres against the French and Scots, demanded the summes of eight hundred thousand pounds to bée raised of the fift part of euerie mans goods and lands, that is to wit, foure shillings of euerie pound.

A great subsidie demanded by the cardinall in the cõmon house.

This demand was inforced on the morrow after, by sir Thomas Moore then speaker of the parlement: but he spake not so much in persuading the house to grant it, but other spake as earnestlie against it, so that the matter was argued to and fro, and handled to the vttermost. There were that proued how it was not possible to haue it leuied in monie, for men of lands and great substance had not the fift part of the same in coine. And sith the king by the loane had receiued two shillings of the pound, which by this rate amounted to 400000 pounds: and now to haue foure shillings of the pound, it would amount in the whole vnto twelue hundred thousand pounds, which is first and last six shillings of the pound, being almost a third part of euerie mans goods, which in coine might not be had within this realme.

Hard hold about grant of the great subsidie.

For the proofe whereof was alleaged, that if there were in England but twentie thousand parishes, and euerie parish should giue an hundred markes, that were but fiftéene hundred thousand markes, which is but an hundred thousand pounds; and there be not verie manie parishes in England one with another, able to spare an hundred markes, out of cities and townes. And where it is written, that in England there be fortie thousand parish churches, it was prooued that there were not thirtéene thousand at this daie. Hard hold there was about this demand, and certeine wise and discréet persons were sent to the cardinall, to mooue him to be a meane to the king, that a lesse summe might be accepted: but he answered that he would rather haue his toong plucked out of his head with a paire of pinsers, than to mooue the king to take anie lesse summe: and so with that answer they departed, reporting to the house the cardinals words. Then euerie daie was reasoning, but nothing concluded.

There are not 10000 parishes in England as *Stow* hath trulie noted. The obstinate answer of the cardinall to the motion of the common house in the parlement.

Wherevpon the cardinall came againe into the lower house, and desired that he might reason with them that were against the demand: but he was answered that the order of that house was to heare, and not to reason, except amongst themselues. There he began to shew arguments of the great wealth of the realme, so that it might be thought, that he repined and disdained that anie man should be wealthie but himselfe. After he was gone, the commons debated the matter according to their former maner, and so in the end concluded of two shillings in the pound, from twentie pounds vpwards, and from fortie shillings to twentie pounds, of euerie twentie shillings twelue pence, and vnder fortie shillings of euerie head of sixtéene yeeres and vpward foure pence to be paid in two yeares. When this was notified to the cardinall, he was much therwith offended, so that to please him, at length, the gentlemen of fiftie pounds land and vpward, by the liberall motion of sir Iohn Huseie, a knight of Lincolnshire, were burdened with twelue pence more of the pound of the same lands, to be paid in thrée yeares.

Sir Iohn Huseie.

The cardinall to mooue them thereto, bare them in hand that the lords had agreed to foure shillings of the pound, which was vntrue: for they had granted nothing, but staid till they might vnderstand what the commons would doo. The king therefore hauing knowledge of this, and such other notable lies vttered by the cardinall, reprooued him therefore verie sharpelie, and said that yer it were long he would looke to things himselfe without anie substitute. A maruellous matter to consider how much the cardinall was cooled herewith, and how lowlie for a while he bare himselfe, so that thereby it well appeared how the maisters sharpenesse now and then, dooth much to refraine the euill nature of the seruant. But the cardinall within a few daies after, pacifieng the kings displeasure toward him, became nothing the better.

Polydor. Cardinall Woolsie reprooued by the king.

After that the foresaid grant was passed and accorded, the parlement was proroged

till

Edw. Hall in H. 8. fol. cx.

The cardinall dissolueth the archbishop of Canturburies conuocation.

till the tenth of Iune. During which prorogation, the common people said to the burgesses; Sirs, we heare say you will grant foure shillings of the pound, we aduise you to doo so that you may go home: with manie euill words and threatnings. In this season the cardinall by his power legantine dissolued the cōuocation at Pouls called by the archbishop of Canturburie, calling him and all the cleargie to his con-uocation at Westminster, which was neuer séene before in England (saith Hall) whereof maister Skelton a merrie poet wrote:

> Gentle Paule lay downe thy sweard,
> For Peter of Westminster hath shauen thy beard.

When the parlement was begun againe, the gentlemen that saw themselues charged with twelue pence more of the pound for their lands, did so much, that it was granted, that men of fiftie pounds and vpward in goods, should also pay twelue pence of euerie pound in the fourth yeare: which could not bee brought about but with great adoo, and much grudging of the burgesses and commons. The one and thirtith of Iulie, the parlement was adiourned to Westminster, & there continuing till the thirtéenth of August, was that day at nine of the clock at night dissolued. During

Arthur Plantagenet created vicount Lisle.

the time of this parlement, the seuen and twentith of Aprill, was sir Arthur Plan-tagenet, bastard sonne to king Edward the fourth, at Bridewell created vicount Lisle, in right of his wife, which was wife to Edmund Dudleie beheaded.

The king of Denmarke ar-riueth in England.

In this yeare the fiftéenth of Iune, Christerne king of Denmarke, with his wife, and a small traine with them, landed at Douer, where he was noblie receiued by the earle of Deuonshire, the bishops of Excester and Rochester, and diuerse knights and esquiers which brought them to Gréenwich, where the king and quéene receiued them

Sée Edw. Hall in H. 8. fol. cxj.

with all honor. Now after he had remained at the court certeine daies, he was brought to London, & lodged at Bath place. He saw the watch on saint Peters eeuen, being brought vnto the kings head in Cheape, accompanied with the duke of Suffolke, the earles of Oxford, Essex, and Kent, and diuerse other lords and ladies. The citie

The citie of London banketteth the K. of Denmarke.

made to him and to his wife a costlie banket that night, and after he had passed the time a while in London, he resorted againe to the king, and had of him great gifts, and so likewise had his wife of the quéene hir aunt, & then taking their leaue they de-

The king of Denmarke de-parteth out of England into Flanders. *Polydor.*

parted, and were conueied to Douer. And thus after this king had béene in England two and twentie daies, he tooke shipping, and sailed againe into Flanders, where he remained as a banished man out of his owne countrie.

The earle of Kildare restored to his office of deputiship in Ireland.

About the same time, the earle of Kildare being restored to the cardinals fauour, and taking to wife the ladie Elizabeth Graie, was sent ouer againe into Ireland to occupie his former office, where by the assistance of his faithfull friend Hugh Hinke archbishop of Dublin, and chancellour of that land, hée brought the countrie into

Edw. Hall.

reasonable good order, so far as the rebellious dooings of the wild Irish would permit. In this meane while, the warre was earnestlie pursued betweene England & France, & England and Scotland, insomuch that each part did what in them lay to hurt other. On the borders toward Scotland lay the earle of Surrie high admerall of England, and the marques Dorset, with his brethren, sir William Compton, & sir William Kingston, with diuerse other knights and esquiers sent to them by the king, which dailie

Scotland sore spoiled.

inuaded the realme of Scotland and threw downe the castell of Wederborne, the castell of west Nesgate, the castell of Blackater, the tower of Mackwalles, the the tower of east Nesgate, & manie other, and burnt to the number of thirtie and seuen villages, and haried the countrie from the east marches to the west, and neuer had skirmish.

For the Scots, albeit they shewed themselues in plumps, waiting some aduantage, they durst not yet approch to the maine battell of the Englishmen, so that in all this iournie there were but few Englishmen lost. When the lords perceiued that the Scots ment not to make anie inuasion into England this yeare, they tooke order for the fortifieng

tifieng of the frontiers, and so returned.　It was thought that the cardinall perceiuing *Polydor.*
in what fauour sir William Compton was with the king, and doubting least the same
might diminish his authoritie, deuised to send him thus into the warres against the
Scots.　For the said sir William could not well brooke the cardinals presumption, in
taking vpon him so highlie, to the derogation of the kings supreme gouernement, and
therfore the cardinall in his absence thought to woorke him out of fauour: but it
would not be.　For shortlie after was sir William Compton called home to the court
againe.

　The Frenchmen burned a ship fraught with stone in the hauen of Calis, vpon hope The Frenchmen meaning to destroy Calis
to haue destroied the hauen; but they missed the chanell in bringing in the ship, hauen, are disappointed by missing the chanell.
and so after that the ship was consumed with fire, the stones were recouered out of the
water, and brought into Calis, which serued the Englishmen to good vse.　Diuerse
enterprises were atchiued betwixt them of the garrisons French and English in those
marches.　In Iulie the lord Sands treasuror of Calis, with other capteins & souldiors,
to the number of twelue hundred, entered into the confines of their enimies, and
came before Bullongne, where they had a great skirmish, & put their enimies to the A rode made into the Frēch ground.
woorse: and after marching into the countrie, tooke diuerse churches and other places
which the Frenchmen had fortified, as the church of Odersall, the steeple of Odingham,
and the castell of Hardingham, and so after they had beene within the enimies countrie
almost two nights and two daies, they came backe to Calis, hauing not lost past a
dozen of their men.

　The king of England being aduertised that the duke of Albanie would returne
shortlie into Scotland by sea, and bring with him a power of Frenchmen, prepared a
fléet of tall and strong ships méet to encounter with the same duke and his power, and
appointed for admerall, sir William Fitz Williams, & with him sir Francis Brian, sir
Anthonie Poines, sargeant Rot, Iohn Hopton, William Ganston, Anthonie Kneuet,
Thomas West, and other, which vsed great diligence to haue met with the said duke
of Albanie.　And as they laie on the French coast, the foure and twentith of August
being sundaie, at seauen of the clocke in the morning, they landed in the hauen of The English fléet landeth in Treiport hauen.
Treiport, and assaulted the Frenchmen that were in certeine bulworks on the shore,
and did what they could to impeach the Englishmens landing.

　But the Englishmen incouraged by their capteins, did so valiantlie (although they
were but an handfull of men in comparison of their enimies, as seuen hundred to
six thousand) that in the end they repelled the Frenchmen, and wan their bulworks
of them, and in the same found diuerse peeces of ordinance, which they seized.　And
perceiuing that the Frenchmen fled to the towne of Treiport, they followed, and
shot at them right egerlie, so that manie of the Frenchmen were slaine and wounded,
yer they could get to the towne.　The Englishmen assaulted the gates but could not The English set fire on the suburbes of Treiport.
breake them open: yet they set fire on the suburbes, & also burnt seuen ships which
laie in the hauen.　The English capteins perceiuing how the people of the countrie
came downe in great numbers to the rescue of the towne, caused their men to get
togither such spoiles as they might bring awaie in that sudden: and then after they had
béene on land fiue houres, with like spéed as they came, they retired backe againe *Polydor.*
to their ships, not without some losse and damage of men both hurt & slaine; as it
often hapneth, when those be not found vnprouided which a man vnaduisedlie
assaileth.

　In this season the king hauing put an armie of men in a readinesse, caused the same
to be transported ouer to Calis, & appointed the duke of Suffolke to haue the leading
thereof, and to make a iourneie into France.　The duke (according to his commission) *Polydor.* *Edw. Hall*
came to Calis the foure and twentith of August, and there abiding the armie, caused
all things to be prepared necessarie for the same, as vittels, munition, and such like.
There were appointed to attend him in this iourneie, the lord Montacute, and his

brother sir Arthur Pole, the lord Herbert sonne to the earle of Worcester, the lord Ferrers, the lord Marneie, the lord Sandes, the lord Barkleie, the lord Powes, and the baron Curson: of knights sir Richard Wingfield chancellour of the duchie of Lancaster, sir Iohn Véer, sir Edward Neuill, sir William Kingston, sir Richard Weston, sir Andrew Winsor, sir Robert Wingfield, sir Anthonie Wingfield, sir Edward Guilford, sir Edward Greuile, sir Edward Chamberleine, sir Thomas Lucie, sir Euerard Digbie, sir Adrian Foscew, sir Richard Cornewall, sir William Courtneie, sir William Sidneie, sir Henrie Owen, and manie others.

The whole armie (as appéered by the musters taken thereof) consisted in six hundred demilances, two hundred archers on horssebacke, three thousand archers on foot, and fiue thousand bill men. To these also were adioined seuentéene hundred, which were taken out of the garisons and crewes of Hammes, Guisnes, & Calis, so that in all they were ten thousand and fiue hundred, well armed and appointed for the warre. Beside them, there were also two thousand six hundred labourers and pioners. When this armie was come ouer to Calis, and all things readie for the iournie, they issued out of Calis and tooke the fields. The vant-gard was led by the lord Sandes. Capteine of the right wing was sir William Kingston, & on the left sir Euerard Digbie. The marshall of Calis sir Edward Guilford was capteine of all the horssemen. The duke himselfe gouerned the battell, and sir Richard Wingfield was capteine of the rere-ward.

While the armie laie without Calis, they dailie came into the towne. And so it happened that a simple felow cut a pursse, as he made to buie apples, which incontinent was taken, and brought to the maiors house to ward. Which thing diuerse Welshmen perceiuing, and not knowing what apperteined to iustice, ran in great companies to the maiors house, & would haue broken the house. The officers of the towne intreated, but the Welshmen more & more approched. The number of the Welshmen was so great, that the watch of Calis strake alarum. Then the lord deputie and the lord Sands did all that in them laie, to bring them to conformitie. But they were so rude, that they nothing them regarded: the priests brought foorth the sacrament, which also was not regarded. Wherefore the lord Ferrers was straightlie commanded to appease their rage, for with him they came thither, which with great paine and intreatie them appeased. And then all the Welshmen were commanded to the field, and to depart the towne, and so were all other capteins: and afterwards diuerse of the head rioters were apprehended and sore punished for example.

The first enterprise that the duke attempted, was the winning of a castell called Bell castell, to which the lord Sands, and the lord Ferrers being sent, did so much by the power of battrie, that after the wals were beaten, those that were appointed to giue the assalt, prepared them therto. Which when the French men within perceiued, they yéelded the place into the Englishmens hands, and themselues to the mercie of the duke, which receiued them as prisoners, and deliuered the castell to Sir William Skeuington, the which he caused to be rased downe to the ground the seauen and twentith of September. In this season was the duke of Burbon high constable of France reuolted from seruice of the French king to the seruice of the emperour and the king of England. For after it was knowne that this duke had his mind alienated from the French king, sir Iohn Russell (that was afterward created erle of Bedford) was sent into France vnto the said duke.

This gentleman being verie faire spoken, & well languaged, in disguised apparell, ordered himselfe so wiselie and fortunatlie in his iornie, that in couert manner he came to the duke, and so persuaded him, that he continued in his former determina-tion, and auoided the realme of France, as in the French historie ye maie more at large perceiue. The more to incourage the English souldiers, there was a proclamation made in the host the eight and twentith of September, how the said duke of Burbon

was

was become enemie to the French king, and friend to the king of England; so that hauing in his wages ten thousand Almans, he was readie to inuade France in another part, the more to let & disturb the French kings purposes. For the accomplishing wherof there was sent to him monie in no small summes. After this proclamation the nine and twentith of September, the duke of Suffolke remooued to Ard, and so forward into Picardie. At Cordes betwéene Terwine and saint Omers, there came to him the lord of Isilstein, and with him of Spaniards, Almans, Cleueners, and others, thrée thousand footmen, and fiue hundred horssemen. ^{The Spaniards}

The Spaniards ioine with the English armie.

The duke being thus furnished with new aid, marched forward in wet weather, and made bridges, and mended the waies where he passed as well as he might, sending out diuerse companies of his men of warre, to take townes, and fetch in booties on euerie side. The Frenchmen were so afraid of the Englishmen, that they fled out of their houses, and left the townes and villages void, conueieng such goods as they could awaie with them, but oftentimes they left good store behind them, so that the Englishmen gained greatlie, and namely at Anchor, which was a rich towne, and vpon the Englishmens approch the inhabitants fled out of it, and then the Englishmen entred. They tooke also the castell of Bounegard, and put therein a garison, whereof was capteine the lord Leonard Greie, brother to the marquesse Dorset, to conduct vittellers to the armie, which now was farre from anie succours of the English part.

The castell of Bounegard manned by the Englishmen.

The duke passed forward till he came to the towne of Braie, in the which were sixtéene hundred men of warre, vnder the gouernance of capteine Adrian, and beside his retinue, there came to the succours of the towne, monsieur Pontdormie, the vicount Lauerdam, the vicount Tourraine, monsieur Applingcourt, and monsieur Dampneie, with fiue hundred horssemen, so that in the towne beside the inhabitants were two thousand good men of warre. This towne standeth on the riuer of Some foure and twentie English miles from Arras, and foureteene of the same miles aboue Amiens. On the twentith of October, the duke caused his ordinance to be brought afore it by foure of the clocke in the morning, the which was so well applied in making batterie to the walles of the towne, that by nine of the clocke the towne was made assaultable; and then the Englishmen, Flemings & Burgognians made forward, and by the good comfort of the lord Sandes and other capteins, they got the diches, and after entred vpon the walles. The Frenchmen stood at defense with pikes, crossebowes, handguns, and halbards, but they were too weake, for on all parts entred the Englishmen, and suddenlie the Frenchmen fled, and the Englishmen followed.

The towne of Braie besieged.

On the further side of the towne there was a bulworke fortified with ordinance verie stronglie to defend the passage ouer the water of Some, which is there diuided into diuerse branches. The French horssemen being withdrawne to the passage, defended it till the footmen were got ouer the bridge, and then they plucked awaie the plankes of the bridge, so that no man should follow: but the Englishmen cast plankes on the bridge and got ouer, in which passing diuerse were drowned: but such diligence and inforcement was vsed, that they all passed both horsmen and footmen. Then was the bulworke fiercelie assaulted, and finallie taken by the Englishmen, with all the ordinance. There was also taken capteine Adrian and capteine Utterlieu. The English horssemen followed the Frenchmen, and slue & tooke manie of them. Sir Robert Ierningham brake a speare on the lord Pontdormie. The lord Leonard Greie did valiantlie that day, which was come from the castell of Bounegard, and was here at the winning of Braie, which was taken in maner aboue rehearsed the twentith of October.

Braie won by assault.

The Frenchmen when they perceiued that they should not be able to defend, had laid a traine of gunpowder to set it on fire, in hope to haue destroied manie of the Englishmen as they should be occupied in gathering the spoile; but by reason that they

A traine of gunpowder laid.

4 P 2

they

they followed their enimies, and got ouer the passage, the fire tooke and set the towne on fire yer the Englishmen returned. Yet much wine was saued which laie in cellars, and stood the Englishmen in good steed. The one and twentith day of October the armie and all the ordinance passed ouer the riuer, and came to a towne called Kappe.

Kappe taken.

All the inhabitants were fled, but they had left good plentie of wine & other riches behind them. The garison that laie at anchor knowing that the duke was passed the water of Some, rased the towne and castell there called Bounegard, and came to the armie now being lodged at Kappe.

Roie yéelded to the duke of Suffolke.

The duke sent to them of Roie, requiring to haue the towne deliuered to him, which they granted to doo, bicause they had no garison of souldiers within to defend the towne. Thither was sent sir Richard Cornewall, with foure hundred men, which receiued the towne and kept it in good quiet, till the duke came thither with his whole armie. On the fiue and twentith daie of October, the duke remooued to a village

Lihome taken.

called Lihome where the souldiers had great pillage. The next daie they went to

Montdedier besieged.

Dauenker, and the seuen and twentith daie they came before the towne of Montdedier, in the which were a thousand footmen, and fiue hundred horssemen vnder the gouernance of monsieur de Roch baron, purposing to defend the towne to the vttermost. But after that sir William Skeuington had made batterie from foure of the clocke in the next morning till eight in the same forenoon, with such force that the wals were

Montdedier yéelded.

ouerthrowne and made assaultable, they within yeelded the towne into the dukes hands, with condition they might go with bag and baggage.

The Frenchmen made such hast, and were so glad to be gone, that they left much houshold stuffe behind them, and great plentie of wine. The Englishmen also would not suffer them to beare their standards vnspred, but rent the same in péeces: wherewith the lord Roch baron was highlie displeased, but he could not amend it. The duke remained in Montdedier till the last of October, and then remooued to Roie,

Knights made by the duke of Suffolke in France.

where he rested a while with all his armie. On Alhallowes daie, the duke of Suffolke in the chiefe church of Roie made knights, the lord Herbert, the lord Powes, Oliuer Manners, Arthur Poole, Richard Sandes, Robert Ierningham, Robert Salisburie, Edmund Beningfield, Richard Corbet, Thomas Wentworth, William Storton, Walter Mantell, George Warram, Edward Seimor, that was after duke of Summerset. The morow after the armie remooued to a place called Néele.

The souldiers being thus led from place to place, began to murmur among themselues & to grudge, bicause of the winter season, being nothing meet for their pur-

Mutinie amongst the English souldiers.

pose to kéepe the fields: it grieued them that the Burgognians being prouided of wagons, made shift to send the spoile and pillage home into their countrie being at hand, & they to want such meanes to make the best of those things which they got, so that (as they tooke it) they beat the bush & others had the birds. This grudge was yet by gentle words ceassed for a time. On the sixt daie of Nouember the whole armie came to a village called Veane, and there rested for that night, and on the morow after

Iohn Dudlie and Robert Utreight knighted.

they returned againe ouer the water of Some, and came to a place called Beaufford. At this passage the duke made Iohn Dudleie and Robert Utreight knights.

On the eight of Nouember the duke remooued to a place called Mont saint Martine, and from thence was sent the lord Sands to the king in post, to aduertise him in what case the armie stood, and the armie remooued to Permont, and there rested for a time. The Welshmen still murmured that they might not returne home now that the winter was thus farre entered. But there were a sort of men of warre, to

Sir Iohn Wallop.

the number of a thousand persons vnder the leading of sir Iohn Wallop, which had little wages or none, liuing only on their aduentures, & were therefore called aduen-

Aduenturers or Kréekers.

turers, and of some they were called Kréekers, which had as good will to be still abroad, as the Welshmen had desire to returne home. For these Kréekers by spoiling of townes, taking of prisoners, & other such practisés of warlike exploits, made their

haunts

haunts, and dailie brought to the campe, horsses, mares, vittels, cloth, corne, and other necessaries, which might not haue béene missed.

After great raines and winds which had chanced in that season, there followed a sore frost, which was so extreame, that manie died for cold, and some lost fingers, some lost toes, and manie lost nailes beside their fingers, so extreame was the rigour of that frost. ¶ The thirteenth daie of Nouember the duke remooued to a place within two miles of Boghan castell, and still it froze. The Welshmen in the morning set out a shout, and cried; Home, home. The Kréekers hearing that, cried; Hang, hang. Hereof businesse was like to haue insued, but by policie it was ceassed. Sir Edward Guilford capteine of the horssemen viewing the castell of Boghan, perceiued that the marishes (wherewith it was inuironed) were so hard frozen, that great ordinance might passe ouer the same. Which he signified to the duke, & therewith the duke was contented that he should trie what successe would come of giuing the attempt to win it. So was the ordinance brought ouer the marish ground, wherof they within being aduertised, immediatlie after thrée shots of canon discharged against them, they yéelded the castell, and all the artillerie within it, of the which there was good store, as thrée score & sixtéene péeces great and small. The kéeping of this castell was deliuered to the senescall of Henegow.

In this meane while the lord Sands was come to the court, and informed the king of the state of the armie. The king had before his comming heard that his people in the said armie were in great miserie, both by reason of the intemperat weather, & vnseasonable time of the yeare, the lacke of vittels, & such other discommodities: wherefore he caused a new power of six thousand men to be prepared and sent vnto the duke of Suffolke for a reléefe, vnder the leading of the lord Montioie. But yer this power could be put in order to passe the sea, and before the duke could haue knowledge againe from the king of his further pleasure, he was constreined to breake vp his armie, and returned by Valencennes, and so through Flanders vnto Calis. He left at Valencennes all the great artillerie. The king was somewhat displeased with the breaking vp of the armie thus contrarie to his mind, but hearing the resonable excuses which the duke & the capteins had to alleage, he was shortlie after pacified. And so after they had remained in Calis a certeine time, vntill their fréends had asswaged the kings displeasure, they returned, and all things were well taken, and they receiued into as much fauour as before.

But now to returne to the dooings in other parts, as betwixt the Englishmen and Scots, which chanced in this meane while that the duke of Suffolke was thus in France. Ye shall vnderstand, that the Scots hearing that the warre was thus turned into France, thought that nothing should be attempted against them, and therefore waxed more bold, and began to rob and spoile on the marches of England. Wherefore the king sent againe thither the earle of Surrie treasuror and high admerall of England, the which with all speed comming to the west borders, sent for an armie of six thousand men, with the which entering Scotland by the drie marishes, he ouerthrew certeine castels, piles, and small holds, till he came through the dales to Iedworth, wherein laie a great garrison of Scots, which skirmished with the Englishmen right sharpelie at their first comming, but yet at length the towne, abbeie, and castell were woone, spoiled, and burned.

After this the earle incamped within the Scotish ground from the two and twentith of September till the fiue and twentith of the same moneth, & then returned backe againe into England. During which time the lord Dacres wan the castell of Ferniherst. The French king perceiuing that the Scots did not worke anie notable trouble to the Englishmen to staie them from the inuading of France (& the cause was (as he tooke it) for that they lacked the duke of Albanie, whome they named their gouernour) he therefore prouided a nauie of ships to haue transported him ouer into

Scotland;

[marginal notes]
A bitter and nipping frost.

Boghan castell assaulted and yéelded.

The duke of Suffolke breaketh vp his armie and commeth to Calis.

The Scots spoile the English marches.

The earle of Surrie inuadeth Scotland.

Iedworth burnt.

The castell of Ferniherst woon by the lord Dacres.

Scotland; so that all things were redie for his iournie. But the Englishmen were redie on the sea vnder the conduct of sir William Fitz Williams to stop his passage if he had set forward, wherefore he caused his ships to be brought into Brest hauen, and bruted it abroad, that he would not go into Scotland that yeare.

The king of England being certified that the duke meant not to depart out of France of all that yeare, about the middest of September, commanded that his ships *See the historie of Scoland, pag. 309. &* sic *deinceps.* should be laid vp in hauens till the next spring. The duke of Albanie being thereof aduertised, boldie then tooke his ships, and sailed into Scotland with all conuenient spéed, as in the Scotish historie ye maie read more at large. Shortlie after his arriuall there, he wrought so with the Scots, that an armie was leauied, with the which he approched to the borders of England, & lodged at Cawdestreame, readie to enter into England. The king of England hauing aduertisement giuen to him from time to time of the proceedings of his aduersaries, with all diligence caused to be assembled the people of the North parts beyond Trent, in such numbers that there were three thousand gentlemen bearing coats of armes with their powers and strength, which were all commanded to repaire to the earle of Surrie with spéed. The noble marquesse Berwike cheeflie Dorset was appointed with six thousand men to kéepe Berwike, least the Scots should laie siege thereto.

Berwike cheeflie regarded.

The duke of Albanie hearing of the preparation which the earle of Surrie made against him, sent to him an herald, promising him of his honour to giue him battell; and if he tooke him prisoner, he would put him to courteous ransome, & his bodie to be safe. To whome the earle answered, that much he thanked the duke of his offer, promising him to abide battell if he durst giue it; & that if the said duke chanced to be taken by him or his, he would strike off his head, and send it for a present to his maister the king of England, and bade him that he should trust to none other. At this answer the duke and the Scots tooke great despite. The earle of Surrie being at Alnewicke, there came to him the earles of Northumberland and Westmerland, the lords Clifford, Dacres, Lumleie, Ogle, & Darcie, with manie knights, esquiers, gentlemen, and other souldiers and men of warre, to the number of fortie thousand. And from the court there came the maister of the horsse, sir Nicholas Carew, sir Francis Brian, sir Edward Bainton, and others.

The castell of Warke assaulted by the Scots.

The last of October being saturdaie, in the night before the same daie, the duke of Albanie sent two or thrée thousand men ouer the water to besiege the castell of Warke, which comming thither with their great ordinance, beat the castell verie sore, and wan the vttermost ward called the Barnekins. On sundaie and mondaie being the first and second of Nouember, they continued their batterie, and then thinking that the place was assaultable, couragiouslie set on the castell, and by strength entered the second ward. Sir William Lisle that was capteine of this castell, perceiuing the enimies to haue woone the false braies, and that nothing remained but onelie the inner ward or dungeon, incouraged his men to the best of his power, with words of great comfort and manhood, and therewith issued foorth with those few that he had left about him (for he had lost manie at other assaults) and what with couragious shooting, and manfull fighting, the enimies were driuen out of the place, and of **The Scots & French driuen backe from Warke castell.** them were slaine, and namelie of those Frenchmen which the duke had brought foorth of France, to the number of thrée hundred, which laie there dead in fight when the earle of Surrie came thither, besides such as died of wounds, and were drowned.

Then the Scots and Frenchmen remooued their ordinance ouer the water in all hast, and by that time that they were got ouer, the earle of Surrie was come with fiue thousand horssemen, and all his great armie followed. He was sorie that his enimies were gone, and much praised sir William Lisle for his valiancie. The earle would gladlie haue followed his enimies into their owne borders, but his commission was onelie to defend the realme, and not to inuade Scotland; and therefore he staid, not

onelie

onelie vnto the great displeasure of himselfe, but also of manie a lustie gentleman, that would gladlie haue séene further proofe of the Scotish mens manhood. Shortlie after, the quéene of Scots, moother to the king, sent to hir brother the king of England, for an abstinence of warre, vntill further communication might be had about the conclusion of some good agréement betwixt the two realmes of England and Scotland, which request to hir was granted; and so the English armie brake vp, and the earle of Surrie returned to the court.

¶ In this season the emperour Charles sent to the king of England two mules *Edw. Hall. in* trapped in crimsin veluet curiouslie embrodered, all the buckles, stirrops and all such *H. 8. fol. Cxvj.* other garnishings were siluer and gilt of maruellous cunning worke. He sent also by the emperour eleuen genets full goodlie to behold trapped with russet veluet richlie wrought, and *to the king.* foure speares, and two iauelins of strange timber & worke richlie garnished, and fiue brace of greihounds : and to the queene he sent two mules with rich trappers, and high chaires after the Spanish fashion. All these presents were thankefullie receiued both of the king and quéene.]

Whilest the earle of Surrie was in the marches of Scotland, and the duke of Suffolke in France (as before ye haue heard) the cardinall sent out commissions in the moneth of October, that euerie man being worth fortie pounds, should paie the whole subsidie before granted, out of hand, not tarrieng till the daies of paiment limited. This An anticipation. was called an anticipation, that is to meane, a thing taken before the time appointed, and was a new tearme not knowne before those daies : but they paied swéetelie for their learning. ¶ In December were taken certeine traitors in Couentrie, one called Francis Philip, schoolemaister to the kings henchmen, and one Christopher Pickering clearke of the larder, and one Anthonie Mainuile gentleman, which by the persuasion of the said Francis Philip, intended to haue taken the kings treasure of his subsidie, as the collectors of the same came towards London, and then to haue raised men and taken the castell of Kilingworth, and to haue arreared warre against the king. The said Francis, Christopher, and Anthonie, were hanged, drawne, and quartered at Tiborne the eleuenth of Februarie, and the other were sent to Couentrie, and there executed.

In this yeare the king sent the lord Morleie, sir William Huseie knight, & doctor Lée The archduke his almoner to don Ferdinando the archduke of Austrich, with the order of the gar- of Austrich ter, which in the towne of Nuremberge receiued the same, where all the princes of the garter. Germanie were then assembled at a diet or councell. In this meane while, diuerse enterprises and feats of warre were practised and atchiued by them of the garrisons in the marches of Calis, and the Frenchmen of Bullogne, and the borders thereabouts : but the Frenchmen commonlie were put to the worse. Amongest other exploits, it Brereton capchanced that one Brereton a gentleman, and capteine of a number of the aduenturers, teine of the as he went about to spoile the towne of Wast, was taken by the French horssemen, and taken & slaine. sold vnto the pezants of the countrie, the which vnmercifullie slue him and sixtéene more that were taken with him, after that the men of warre had deliuered them, and were departed. But this murther was reuenged shortlie by other of the aduenturers, which comming vnto the same towne of Wast, tooke thirtie eight prisoners of the inhabitants, & slue of them thirtie and six, & burned the towne.

In this yeare thorough books of ephemerides, and prognostications, foreshewing 1524 much hurt to come by waters & flouds, many persons vittelled themselues and went to Bolton prior of high grounds for feare of drowning : speciallie one Bolton prior of saint Bartholomewes mewes buildeth in Smithfield, builded him an house vpon Harow on the hill, onelie for feare of this a house at Harow floud, and thither he went and made prouision of all things necessarie for the space of auoid flouds two moneths. This great raine and waters should haue fallen in Februarie, but no such prognosticated thing happened, whereby the follie of men was shewed. The astronomers for their that yeare. excuse did saie, that in their computation they had miscounted in their number an

hundred

A legat from
Rome to treat
a peace be-
twéene king
Henrie and the
French king.
hundred yeares. A legat was sent from the pope to the king to mooue him to peace: but the king declared to him the whole circumstance of his title, for the which he made wars against the Frenchmen, and thereof deliuered notes to the said legat, the which departed with the same backe to Rome in post. He had béene first with the French king, and with the emperour, but could not bring them to anie good conformitie, as his desire was to haue doone; so that his trauell was without frute in maner, as it appeared.

Manie enterprises, skirmishes, forreis, and other feats of warre were attempted and put in vse betwixt the Englishmen of Calis, Guisnes, and other fortresses there in those marches, and the Frenchmen of Bullogne, and other of the garrisons in the frontiers of Picardie, and still sir William Fitz Williams as then capteine of Guisnes, sir Robert Ierningham capteine of Newnam bridge, sir Iohn Wallop, and sir Iohn Gage were those that did to the Frenchmen most damage. Also monsieur de Bees being capteine of Bullogne, did for his part what he could to defend the frontiers there, and to annoie his enimies. Yet one daie in Maie, sir William Fitz Williams, and sir Robert Ierningham, with seuen hundred men (accounting in that number the Kreekers) went to Bullogne, and there skirmished with the Frenchmen, whilest
Christopher Coo a capteine of foure English ships tooke land, and fought with them of base Bullogne on the one side, as the Kréekers assailed them on an other.

There was a sharpe bickering, and in the end the Frenchmen were driuen backe, and diuerse of them slaine & taken, speciallie by the Kréekers, that wan the barriers of them, & so when the tide was turned, Christopher Coo with his men withdrew to his ships, & the Kréekers returned to sir William Fitz Williams, who staid for them, and then gathering his men togither by sound of a trumpet, sent foorth such as might fetch the drifts of beasts and cattell in the countrie néere adioning, & with the same returned backe in safetie. On the eight of August monsieur de Bées accompanied with diuerse French lords and men of war, to the number of eight hundred footmen, and as manie horssemen, came verie earlie in a morning to a village called Bonnings, within the English pale, and leauing there thrée hundred horssemen in ambush, road to Kalkewell, and there appointed to tarrie with other thrée hundred men, and the residue of the horssemen and footmen with banner displaied went foorth and forraied all the countrie.

Sir Robert Ierningham also with foure score horssemen issued foorth of Calis, to vnderstand the demeanor of the Frenchmen: but being not able to resist the great number of the Frenchmen, he was chased, and saued himselfe by flight. But this displeasure was shortlie after reuenged by the said Robert, the which comming to Marguison the twelfe of August with three hundred footmen, and thrée score horssemen, he skirmished with the Frenchmen that stood at defense, chased them into the church, and fired them out of the same, so that the Frenchmen leapt out of the church to their destruction, for of thrée hundred there were saued but thrée score
The Scots enter
England and rob
the market folks
going to Ber-
wike faire.
aliue. On the one and twentith of Maie being Trinitie sundaie, fiue hundred Scotishmen in the morning verie earlie, entred by seuerall foords into England, and laie couertlie by the high waies, in purpose to haue surprised such market men as came to the faire that day kept at Berwike. They tooke diuerse, but finallie being espied, the alarme rose, and they were fought with right sharplie, who defended themselues with such manhood in drawing backe to their aduantage, that if the yoong lord of Fulberie had not come to the succours of the Englishmen, the Scots had gone awaie with their bootie. Notwithstanding in the end they were glad to séeke refuge by flight, loosing 200 of their number, which were taken in the chase.

On the fift of Iulie next insuing, sir Iohn a Fenwike, Leonard Musgraue, and bastard Heron, with diuerse other English capteins, hauing with them nine hundred men of war, entred the Mers, minding to fetch out of the same some bootie, and
                                                                                                    encountring

encountring with the Scots being in number two thousand, after sore and long fight, caused them to leaue their ground and to flie, so that in the chase were taken two hundred Scots, and manie slaine, & amongst them were diuerse gentlemen. But sir Rafe a Fenwike, Leonard Musgraue, and the bastard Heron, with thirtie other Englishmen well horssed, followed so farre in the chase, that they were past rescues of their companie, whereof the Scots being aduised, suddenlie returned, and set on the Englishmen, which oppressed with the multitude of their enimies, were soone ouercome, and there was taken sir Rafe a Fenwike, Leonard Musgraue, and six other: and bastard Heron, with seauen other were slaine. The residue by chance escaped. The other Englishmen with their 200 prisoners returned safelie into England.

The Scots put to flight and slaine.

On the seuenth of Iulie, the Englishmen fought with like fortune against the Scots that were entered England at the west marches. For in the beginning they put the Scots to the worse, and tooke thrée hundred of them prisoners: but afterwards, bicause the Englishmen that had taken those prisoners, withdrew out of the field with the same prisoners, the Scots perceiuing the number of the Englishmen to be diminished, gaue a new onset on the Englishmen, and them distressed. After this, the Scots sued for a truce, and had it granted to indure till the feast of saint Andrew. This yeare the first of September was doctor Thomas Haniball maister of the rolles receiued into London with earles, and bishops, and diuerse other nobles and gentlemen, as ambassadors from pope Clement, which brought with him a rose of gold for a token to the king. And on the daie of the natiuitie of our ladie, after a solemne masse song by the cardinall of Yorke, the said present was deliuered to the king: which was a trée forged of fine gold, & wrought with branches, leaues, and floures resembling roses. This trée was set in a pot of gold which had three feet of antike fashion. The pot was of measure halfe a pint, in the vppermost rose was a faire saphire loupe persed, the bignesse of an acorne, the trée was of heigth halfe an English yard, and a foot in bredth.

The popes ambassadour presenteth the king with a golden rose.

This yeare in Iulie the lord Archembald Douglas earle of Angus, which had maried the quéene of Scots sister to the king of England, escaped out of France (where he had remained for a season, in maner as a banished man) and came into England to the king, as then being at Gréenewich, and was of him courteouslie receiued. Sir Anthonie Fitz Herbert one of the Iustices of the common plées, sir Rafe Egerton knight, and doctor Denton deane of Lichfield, being sent in the begining of this yeare into Ireland as commissioners, behaued themselues so sagelie, that they reformed diuers wrongs, brought sundrie of the wild Irish by faire means vnto obedience, and made (by the kings authoritie) the earle of Kildare deputie of the land; before whome the great Onele bare the sword. And the lord Piers Butler earle of Ormond, which before was deputie, was now made high treasurer of Ireland. In September the said commissioners returned.

Commissioners sent into Ireland to reforme the countrie.

The earle of Kildare made deputie of Ireland.

During all this season, there were dailie attempts made and practised by the Englishmen in the lowe countries, namelie the English horssemen; & the aduenturers rested not, but dailie made inuasions vpon the French confines. But the aduenturers about the beginning of winter made an enterprise to fetch some bootie from a village lieng towards Mutrell. They were not fullie two hundred men, and of those there were fiue and twentie horssemen. The Frenchmen by chance the same time were abroad vnder the conduct of the earle of Dammartine, which was going to S. Omers with fiftéene hundred horssemen, and eight hundred footmen, and perceiuing where the aduenturers were comming, made towards them, and after long & cruell fight ouercame them, and slue most part of them, for that in defending themselues most stoutlie, they had slaine and wounded a great number of the Frenchmen yer they could be ouercome, keeping themselues close togither, and might not be

The end of the Kréekers.
broken so long as they had anie arrowes to shoot. This was the end of the aduenturers otherwise called Kréekers, being as hardie men as euer serued prince.

In December there came to London diuerse ambassadors out of Scotland, about a
peace to be had, and a marriage concluded betwéene the king of Scots, and the ladie
Marie daughter to the king of England, as in the Scotish historie yee shall find more
Sée the historie of Scotland, pag. 312.
at large expressed. Before the feast of Christmasse, the lord Leonard Graie, and the
lord Iohn Graie, brethren to the marquesse Dorset, sir George Cobham, sonne to
the lord Cobham, William Carie, sir Iohn Dudleie, Thomas Wiat, Francis Pointz,
Francis Sidneie, sir Anthonie Browne, sir Edward Seimor, Oliuer Manners, Perciuall
Hart, Sebastian Nudigate, and Thomas Caien, esquiers of the kings household, enterprised a chalenge of feats of armes against the feast of Christmas, which was
proclaimed by Winsore the herald, and performed at the time appointed after the best
Sée these tri- umphs in *Edw. Hall, pag.* Cxxxiij.
maner, both at tilt, tourneie, barriers, and assault of a castell erected for that purpose
in the tiltyard at Gréenewich, where the king held a roiall Christmasse that yeare,
with great mirth and princelie pastime.

1525

The friers ob- seruants im- pugne the cardi- nals authoritie.
In the moneth of Ianuarie, the cardinall by his power legantine, would haue
visited the friers obseruants, but they in no wise would thereto condescend, wherefore nineteene of the same religion were accurssed at Paules crosse, by one of their
owne religion, called frier Forrest. Iohn Iokin steward of houshold to the French
kings mother, this yéere whilest the French king was in Italie, came into England,
& was receiued in secret maner into the house of one doctor Larke, a prebendarie of
S. Stephans, and oftentimes talked with the cardinall about the affaires betwixt the
kings of England and France, motioning waies for a peace to be concluded. When
this was knowne abroad, as at the length it was, monsieur de Prate the emperours
ambassador misliked such couert dooings, and sore grudged thereat. The foure
and twentith of Ianuarie, the president of Rone called monsieur Brinion, came to
London as ambassador from the French king, and was lodged with the said Iohn
Iokin.

Ambassadors from the empe- rour and their requests.
On sundaie the fift of March were receiued into London monsieur de Beuer lord of
Campher, admerall of Flanders, and maister Iohn de la Coose, president of Malins,
& maister Iohn de la Gache, as ambassadours from the ladie Margaret in the name of
the emperour. These ambassadors required thrée things in their suit. First they
demanded the ladie Marie the kings onelie daughter to be deliuered out of hand, and
she to be named empresse, and to take possession of all the lowe countries, and to be
gouernour of the same. Also that all such sums of monie as the king should giue
with hir in mariage for a dower to be made to hir, should be paid incontinentlie.
Thirdlie, that the king of England himselfe should passe the sea, and make warre in
France the next summer. The two first demands were not agréed to for certeine
causes, and as to this last, the king said he would take aduisement.

Newes of the siege of Pauia & the taking of the French king prisoner.
On Thursdaie the ninth of March, at seauen of the clocke in the morning, there
came a gentleman in post from the ladie Margaret gouernesse of Flanders, which
brought letters conteining how that the foure and twentith of Februarie, the siege of
Pauia (where the French king had lien long) was raised by force of battell, and the
French king himselfe taken prisoner. The same day the president of Rone, & Iohn
Iokin were going to the court (for they had not yet spoken with the king) and in
Holburne in their waie heard these tidings, whervpon they returned to their lodging right sorowfull, and within short space after returned to the regent of France.
It was thought the king would haue agréed with the French king, if this chance had
not hapned, for all the people of England grudged against Flanders, for the euill
demeanour of the Flemings in time of the warre. Also the king was displeased with
them for inhancing his coine there, which caused much monie to be conueied out of
this realme dailie ouer into that countrie. Bounfires and great triumph was made in
London

London for the taking of the French king, on saturdaie the eleuenth of March; and on the morow after being sundaie the twelfe of March, the king came to Paules, and there heard a solemne masse, and after the same was ended, the quéere sang Te Deum, and the minstrels plaid on euerie side.

¶ Here it is conuenient to adde the battell of Pauia, wherein the French king was taken prisoner, most notablie discoursed by Guicciardine, in the fiftéenth booke of his historie: the principall matter wherof, to make the report of Pauia and the French king more perspicuous, it were good to inferre. On the night (saith mine author) before the fiue and twentith of Februarie, a daie dedicated by the christians to the apostle saint Matthew, and also the daie of the natiuitie of the emperour, the imperialles determined to march to Mirabell, where laie incamped certeine companies of horssemen and footmen. In this march they stood vpon this intention, that if the French men mooued, then they had set at libertie the siege of Pauia: and if they mooued not, then to aduenture the fortune of the battell. Therefore the better to aduance this determination, all the beginning of the night they gaue manie alarmes, the more to kéepe trauelled and wearie the French men, making semblance as though they would charge them on that side towards Paw, Thesin, and saint Lazarus. *Abr. Fl. ex Guic. pag. 902, & sic deinceps. The battell of Pauia, wherein the French king is taken prisoner.*

About midnight euerie souldior, by the commandement of the capteins, put on a white cassakin ouer his armor, to be knowne from the Frenchmen. They were cast into two squadrons of horssemen, & foure of footmen. In the first were six thousand footmen equallie compounded of lanceknights, Spaniards, and Italians: this squadron was led by the marquesse of Guast: the second stood onelie vpon certeine bands of Spanish footmen vnder the charge of the marquesse of Pisquairo: the third and fourth squadron were of lanceknights, commanded by the viceroy and the duke of Burbon. They arriued at the parke walles certeine houres before daie, and by the working of their masons, and readie willes of their souldiers, they cast downe to the earth thrée score fadome of wall: by which breach, being entred within the parke, the first squadron drew towards Mirabell, and the residue of the armie tooke the waie to the campe.

As soon as the king vnderstood that they were entred into the parke, thinking they would draw to Mirabell, he issued out of his lodging to fight in plaine and open field, desiring to draw the battell rather to that place than to anie other, for the aduantages which it gaue to the horssemen: he commanded to turne the artilleries toward the enimies, which beating them in flanke, brought great damage to the reregard. But in the meane while, the battell of the imperialles gaue a furious charge vpon the kings squadron, which ordinarilie was the battell: but as the Spaniards went, it was the reregard. The king fought valiantlie, & abode with great courage the violence of his enimies, who with the furie of their harquebuziers forced his men to giue ground, till the rescue of the Switzers came, when the Spaniards were repelled, as well by them as by the horssemen that charged them in flanke. But the viceroy being called in by the marquesse of Pisquairo, who broght to the fight his lanceknights, they were easilie broken, not without great slaughter of the Switzers, who that daie did nothing answer the opinion of valor which aforetimes they had woont so honorablie to expresse in battelles. *Whie the French king desired to fight in plaine and open field.*

The king kept alwaies the middle of the battell, being inuironed with a great gard of men at armes. And albeit he did what he could to conteine and confirme his people: yet after he had fought long with his owne hands, his horsse being slaine vnder him, himselfe lightlie hurt in the face and in the hand, he was stricken downe to the earth, and taken prisoner by fiue souldiers that knew not what he was. In which misfortune the viceroy pressing into the throng his maiestie disclosed him selfe to him, who with great reuerence kissed his hand, and receiued him prisoner in the emperours name. At the same time the marquesse of Guast with the first squadron *The maner how the French king was vanquished and taken prisoner.*

4 Q 2　　　　　　　　　　　　　　　　　　　　had

had defeated the horssemen that were at Mirabell. And Anthonie de Leua, who (as was said) had to that end cast downe to the earth so great a quantitie and space of wall, as an hundred and fiftie horssemen might sallie foorth in front, issued out of Pauia; & so charged the French behind, that he put them wholie to flight. And in that feare they were almost all stripped and trussed, except the reregard of the horssemen, which being led by monsieur de Alanson from the beginning of the battell, retired almost whole.

The number of the French that were slaine in this battell. It is holden for certeine, that in this battell were slaine more than eight thousand men of the French campe, part by sword, and part of bodies drowned in the riuer of Thesin, séeking their safetie by swimming. Of this generall number were about twentie of the most noble and apparant lords of France, as the admerall, the lord Iames Chebanes, the lord Palissa, and Trimouille, the master of the horsse, monsieur de Aubignie, monsieur de Boissie, and monsieur de la Escud, who being taken gréeuouslie wounded by his enimies, gaue to them his life in stéed of a ransome. The prisoners that were taken were the king of Nauarre, the bastard of Sauoie, the lord Montmerancie, Saint Paule, Brion, Auall, monsieur de Chandion, monsieur de Imbercourt, Galeas Visconte, Frederike Bossolo, Barnabie Visconte, Guidanes, with manie gentlemen, and almost all the capteins that escaped the slaughter of the sword. There was also taken prisoner Ierome Leandro bishop of Brunduso the popes nuntio; but by commandement of the viceroy, he was eftsoones set at libertie: as also monsieur Saint Paule and Frederike Bossolo committed to the castell of Pauia, brake prison a little after, by the corruption of the Spaniards that The number of the slaine on the imperialles side. had them in charge. Of the imperialles side the vniuersall slaughter excéeded not seauen hundred bodies; and not one capteine of name except Ferrand Castriot marquesse of Angeo, the marquesse of Pisquairo was wounded in two places, & Anthonie de Leua lightlie hurt in the leg. The preie and spoile of this battell was so great, as there had not beene séene in Italie more rich souldiors.

Of so great an armie there was preserued but the reregard of foure hundred lances, commanded by monsieur de Alanson, they neuer came to the fight, neuer suffered charge, nor neuer were followed, but leauing behind them their baggage, they retired whole to Piemont, their feare making them more hastie to flie, than carefull of their honor. And as one calamitie followeth another, so the losse of the battell was no sooner reapposted at Millaine, than Theodor Triuulce, who laie there in garrison with foure hundred lances, departed and tooke his waie to Musocquo, all the souldiors folowing him by troops: insomuch as the same daie that the king lost the battell, all The French king led prisoner to the rocke of Pisqueton. the dutchie of Millaine was made frée from the iurisdiction of the French. The daie after the victorie, the king was led prisoner to the rocke of Pisqueton, for that the duke of Millaine, in regard of his proper suretie, consented hardlie that the person of the king should be kept within the castell of Millaine: he was garded with great gelousie and watch; but in all other things (except his libertie) he was vsed and honored as apperteined to the state and maiestie of a king.

Guic. pag. 904. Now (saith mine author, speaking to the readers of his historie) you haue séene set downe the ouerthrow of the French armie in the battell of Pauia: a wretched successe where was so great expectation of victorie. You haue séene a mightie king deliuered vp prisoner into the hands of him, with whom he contended for glorie and emperie: a spectacle most tragicall amongst all the calamities that fortune bringeth vpon mans mortalitie. You haue séene the most part of the nobilitie, and honorable capteins of France, slaine in the seruice and presence of their king: a matter that made more lamentable his owne condition and aduersitie. You haue séene the residue of that armie, so vniuersallie perplexed with feare and confusion, that the same thing that should haue reteined them in so great afflietion, made them the lesse assured, and further off from confidence.

When word came to the emperour of all the former accidents, the eies of euerie man
were

were set to behold with what propertie of affection he would receiue his gladsome Guic. pag. 915.
news, and to what ends his thoughts were disposed: who so farre as exterior demon- *The moderation and temperance*
strations made shew, expressed great tokens of a mind much moderated, and verie *of the emperour*
apt to resist easilie the prosperitie of fortune: yea the signes and inclinations appeer- *vpon the newes of the victorie.*
ing so much the more incredible, by how much he was a prince mightie & yong, and
as yet had neuer tasted but of felicitie.　For after he was informed truelie of so great
a victorie, whereof he had the reapport the tenth of March, togither with letters of
the French kings owne hand, written rather in the spirit and condition of a prisoner,
than with the courage of a king, he went foorthwith to the church to make his holie
oblations to God with manie solemnities.　And the morning folowing he receiued with
signes of right great deuotion the sacrament of the eucharist, and so went in procession to our ladies church out of Madrill, where was his court at that time.

His temperance and moderation was aboue the expectation of his estate, and farre
contrarie to the course of the time in matters of that nature: for he would not suffer
anie bels to be roong, nor bounfires to be made, nor anie other manner of publike demonstrations, such as are vsed for glorie or gladnesse, alledging with a mind more
vertuous than insolent, that such propertie of feasting and reioising was due to victories *A most excellent*
obteined against infidels, but ought to haue no shew where one christian ouercame *conceipt and saieng of the*
another.　Neither were the actions and gestures of his person and speaches differing *emperour.*
from so great a temperance and continencie of mind, which he well expressed in the
answers he made to the congratulations of the ambassadours and great men that were
about him: to whome he said he was not glad of the accident according to the glorious operation of flesh and bloud, but his reioising was in that God had so manifestlie
aided him: which he interpreted to be an assured signe that he stood in his grace and
fauour, though not through his owne merit, yet by his celestiall election.　The
French king being in the custodie of the viceroy of Naples (who much comforted him *Ed. Hall in H.8.*
and praised his valiantnesse, and praied him to be content, for he should haue a gen- *fol. Cxxxvj.*
tle end) desired to write to his mother, which was to him granted.　His verie words
were these.

The French kings letter to his mother the regent of France.

TO aduertise you of my infortunat chance: nothing is left but the honour and the *This he wrote*
life that is saued.　And seeing some other news shall recomfort you, I haue desired *being the emper-*
to write to you this letter, the which liberallie hath beene granted to me: beseeching *ors prisoner.*
you to regard the extremitie of your selfe, in insuing your accustomed wisedome.
For I hope that at length God will not forget me, to you recommending your little
infants and mine, supplieng you to giue safe conduct, to passe and returne from
Spaine, to this bearer that goeth toward the emperor, to know in what wise I shall
be intreated.　And thus right humbly to your good grace I haue me recommended.
This subscribed by your humble and obedient sonne Francis.

In this estate of aduersitie the people set before their eies all that feare and despaire *Guic. pag.* 625.
could imagine: they doubted least so great a calamitie were not the beginning of a *The manifold*
further ruine & subuersion: they saw their king prisoner, and with him either taken *passions or per-*
or slaine in the battell the chiefteins of the kingdome, which in the imagination of *plexities of the people in ge-*
their sorrowes they held a losse irreparable: they beheld their capteins discomfited, *nerall.*
and their souldiers discouraged: a calamitie which stopped in them all hope to be
readdressed or reassured: they saw the realme made naked of monie and treasure, and
inuironed with most mightie enimies: an affliction which most of all caried their
thoughts into the last cogitation of desperat ruine: for the king of England, notwithstanding that he had holden manie parlées and treaties, and shewed in manie things a
variation of mind, yet not manie daies before the battell, he had cut off all the
negociations

negociations which he had interteined with the king, and had published that he would descend into France, if the things of Italie tooke anie good successe.

So that the Frenchmen feared least in so great an oportunitie, the emperour and he would not leuie warre against France, either for that there was no other head or gouernour than a woman, and the little children of the king, of whom the eldest had not yet run eight yeares accomplished: or else bicause the enimies had with them the duke of Burbon, for his owne particular a puissant prince, and for his authoritie in the realme of France verie popular and strong in opinion, a mightie instrument to stirre up most dangerous emotions. Besides, the ladie regent, as well for the loue she bare to the king, as for the dangers of the realme was not without hir passions both proper and particular: for being full of ambition, and most gréedie of the gouernment, shée feared that if the kings deliuerie drew any long tract of time, or if anie new difficultie hapned in France, she should be constreined to yéeld vp the administration of the crowne to such as should be delegate and assigned by the voices of the kingdome. Neuerthelesse amid so manie astonishments and confusions, she drew hir spirits to hir, and by hir example were recomforted the nobles that were of counsell with hir, who tooke spéedie order to man the frontiers of the realme, and with diligence to leuie a good prouision of monie.

The ladie regent, in whose name all expeditions and dispatches went out, wrote to the emperour letters full of humilitie and compassion, wherin she forgat not by degrées vehement and inducing to solicit a negociation of accord: by vertue whereof, hauing a little after deliuered don Hugo de Moncado, shée sent him to the emperour, to offer him that hir sonne should renounce and disclaime from all rights of the kingdome of Naples, and the estate of Millan, with contentment to refer to the censure and arbitration of the law, the titles and rights of Burgundie, which if it apperteined to the emperour, he should acknowledge it for the dowrie of his sister: that he should render to monsieur Burbon his estate togither with his moouables and goods which were of great valour, and also the fruits and reuenues which had beene leuied by the commissioners deputed out of the regall chamber: that he should giue to him his sister in mariage, and deliuer vp to him Prouence, if iudgement of the interest and right were made of his side.

And for the more facilitie and spéedie passage of this negociation, rather than for anie desire she had to nourish hir inclination to the warre, she dispatched immediatlie ambassadours into Italie, to recommend to the pope and the Venetians the safetie of hir sonne. To whome she offered, that if for their proper securitie they would contract with hir, and raise armes against the emperour, she would for hir particular aduance fiue hundred lances, togither with a great contribution of monie. But amid these trauels and astonishments, the principall desire as well of hir, as of the whole realme of France, was, to appease and assure the mind of the king of England, iudging trulie that if they could reduce him to amitie and reconcilement, the crowne of France should remaine without quarrell or molestation. Where, if he on the one side, and the emperour on the other, should rise in one ioint force, hauing concurrent with them the person of the duke of Burbon, and manie other opportunities and occasions, it could not be but all things would be full of difficulties and dangers.

Of this the ladie regent began to discerne manie tokens and apparances of good hope: for notwithstanding the king of England immediatlie after the first reapports of the victorie, had not onelie expressed great tokens of gladnesse and reioising, but also published that he would in person passe into France: and withall had sent ambassadours to the emperour to solicit and treat of the moouing of warre iointlie togither: yet procéeding in deed with more mildnesse than was expected of so furious shewes and tokens, he dispatched a messenger to the ladie regent, to send to him an expresse ambassadour: which accordinglie was accomplished, and that with fulnesse of authoritie and commission, such as brought with it also all sorts of submissions & implorations

tions which she thought apt to reduce to appeasement the mind of that king so highlie displeased.　He reposed himselfe altogither vpon the will and counsell of the cardinall of Yorke, who séemed to restreine the king and his thoughts to this principall end, that bearing such a hand vpon the controuersies and quarrels that ran betwéene other princes, all the world might acknowledge to depend vpon him and his authoritie the resolution and expectation of all affaires.

And for this cause he offered to the emperour at the same time to descend into France, with a puissant armie, both to giue perfection vnto the aliance concluded betwéene them before; and also to remooue all scruple and gelousie, he offered present-lie to consigne vnto him his daughter, who was not as yet in an age and disposition able for mariage.　But in these matters were very great difficulties, partlie depending vpon himselfe, and partlie deriuing from the emperour, who now shewed nothing of that readinesse to contract with him which he had vsed before: for the king of England demanded almost all the rewards of the victorie, as Normandie, Guien, and Gascoigne, with the title of king of France.　And that the emperour, notwithstanding the inequalitie of the conditions should passe likewise into France, and communicate equallie in the expenses and dangers.　The inequalitie of these demands troubled not a little the emperour, to whome they were by so much the more grieuous, by how much he remembred that in the yeares next before, he had alwaies deferred to make warre euen in the greatest dangers of the French king.　So that he persuaded him-selfe that he should not be able to make anie foundation vpon that confederation.

And standing in a state no lesse impouerished for monie and treasure, than made wearie with labours and perils, he hoped to draw more commodities from the French king by the meane of peace, than by the violence of armes and warres, speciallie ioining with the king of England.　Besides, he made not that accompt which he was woont to doo of the mariage of his daughter, both for hir minoritie in age, and also for the dowrie for the which he should stand acceptable for so much as the emperour had receiued by waie of loane of the king of England: he séemed by manie tokens in nature to nourish a woonderfull desire to haue children, and by the necessitie of his condition he was caried with great couetousnesse of monie: vpon which two reasons he tooke a great desire to marie the sister of the house of Portugall, which was both in an age able for mariage, and with whome he hoped to receiue a plentifull portion in gold and treasure, besides the liberalities of his owne people offered by waie of beneuolence in case the mariage went forward: such was their desire to haue a quéene of the same nation and language, and of hope to procreat children.

For these causes the negociation became euerie daie more hard and desperat betwéene both those princes, wherein was also concurrent the ordinarie inclination of the cardinall of Yorke towards the French king, togither with the open complaints he made of the emperour, as well for the interests and respects of his king, as for the small reputation the emperour began to hold of him.　He considered that afore the battell of Pauia; the emperour neuer sent letters vnto him which were not written with his owne hand, and subscribed, your sonne and coosine Charles: but after the battell, he vsed the seruice of secretaries in all the letters he wrote to him, infixing nothing of his owne hand but the subscription, not with titles of so great reuerence and submission, but onelie with this bare word Charles.　In this alteration of affection in the emperour, the king of England tooke occasion to receiue with gratious words and demonstrations, the ambassadour sent by the ladie regent, to whome he gaue comfort to hope well in things to come.　And a little afterward, estranging his mind wholie from the affaires which were in negociation betwéene him and the emperour, he made a confederation with the ladie regent, contracting in the name of hir sonne, wherein he would haue inserted this expresse condition, that for the kings ransome and deliuerie, should not be deliuered to the emperour anie thing that at that time should be vnder the power or possession of the crowne of France.

Shortlie

Guic. pag. 930.
The person of the French king led prisoner into Spaine.

Shortlie after, the viceroy & the other capteins imperiall were induced vpon vrgent reasons to transport the person of the French king into a surer hold, than where presentlie he was kept, iudging that for the ill disposition of others, they could not without perill kéepe him garded in the duchie of Millan: in which feare ioined to their continuall desire so to doo, they resolued to conueie him to Genes, and from thense by sea to Naples, where his lodging was prepared within the new castell. This determination brought no little gréefe to the king, who from the beginning of his captiuitie, had vehementlie desired to be carried into Spaine: perhaps he had opinion (measuring happilie an other man by his owne nature, or else running with the common errour of mortall men being easilie beguiled in things they desire) that if once he were brought to the presence of the emperour, he doubted not of some easie passage for his libertie, either through the emperours benignitie, or by the conditions he meant to offer. The viceroy was of the same desire for the augmentation of his owne glorie.

Monsieur Montmerancie sent to the ladie regent.

But being reteined for feare of the French armie by sea, they dispatched by common consent monsieur Montmerancie to the ladie regent: who granted to him six light gallies of those that laie in the port of Marseilles vpon promise to haue them restored as soone as the king was arriued in Spaine. With these gallies he returned to Portofino, where the kings person was alredie arriued, and ioining them to sixtéene gallies of the emperour, which was the nauie appointed at first to conduct him to Naples, he reduced them all into one fléet, and armed them all with footmen of the Spanish. The capteins imperials and the duke of Burbon were persuaded, that the kings person should be led to Naples: but of the contrarie, setting vp saile the seuenth of Iune, they tooke such course that the eight daie they arriued with a happie voiage at Rosa a hauen of Catalognia: their comming brought no small ioy to the emperour, who vntill that daie had vnderstood nothing at all of that resolution.

The emperor commandeth that the French king should be receiued with honour in all places where he should passe.

Now as soone as he was made assured of the kings being there, he dispatched commandements vnto all places where he should passe, to receiue him with great honours: onelie till it should be otherwise determined, he gaue order to kéepe him in the castell of Sciatiua néere to Valence, a castell ancientlie vsed by the kings of Aragon for the garding of great personages, and wherein had béene kept prisoner for manie yeares the duke of Calabria. But the deliberation to kéepe him in that place, séeming farre too rigorous to the viceroy, and nothing agréeable to the promises he had made to the king in Italie, he woone so much of the emperour, that till he had taken an other counsell, the kings person might remaine néere Valence in a place apt for hunting and other delights of the field. There he left him lodged with sufficient gard vnder the charge of capteine Alarcon, in whose custodie he had alwaies remained since his vnfortunate daie.

From thence the viceroy, togither with Montmerancie, went to the emperour to make reapport of the state of Italie, and the discourse of things which till that daie had béene debated with the king, with whome he persuaded the emperour with manie reasons to draw to accord, for that he could not haue a faithfull amitie and coniunction with the Italians. The emperour after he had heard the viceroy and Montmerancie, determined to conueie the king into Castillo to the castell of Madrill, a place farre remooued from the sea and the confines of France, where being honored with ceremonies & reuerences agréeable to so great a prince, he should neuerthelesse be kept vnder carefull and strait gard, with libertie to take the aire abroad certeine times of the daie, mounted onelie vpon a mule. The emperour could neuer be brought to admit the king to his presence, if first the accord were not either established, or at least in an assured hope of resolution.

And to the end there might be interposed in the negociation a personage honorable, & almost equall with the king, Montmerancie was sent in great diligence into France, to bring the duchesse of Alanson the kings sister and a widow, with fulnesse of authoritie

authoritie to debate and contract. And to the end this negociation of accord were not hindered by new difficulties, there was made a little afterwards a truce vntill the end of December, betweene the emperour and such as administred the gouernment of France. Moreouer the emperour gaue order that one part of those gallies which were come with the viceroy, should returne into Italie to bring the duke of Burbon into Spaine, without whose presence and priuitie he gaue out that he would make no conuention: and yet the gallies what for want of monie, and other impediments, were prepared but with slow diligence.

Whiles the case of the French king was in demand, but not yet determined, by means of sundrie ouerthwarts that ouerthrew the foundation of euerie purpose tending to his deliuerance; it fortuned that the French king falling sicke in the castell of Madrill, and hauing in vaine desired the presence of the emperour, was caried by his discontentment and melancholie into such extremitie and danger of his life, that the physicians appointed for his cure, told the emperour that they stood desperate of his recouerie, if himselfe in person came not to comfort him with some hope of his deliuerie. The emperour obeieng more compassion than the reason of things, was not curious to condescend to performe so good an office, and as he prepared to visit him accordinglie, his high chancellor seeking to turne him from the iorneie, told him with manie strong reasons, that he could not go to him in honour, but with intention to deliuer him presentlie and without anie couenant: otherwise as it would be a humanitie not roiall but mercenarie, so it would disclose a desire to recouer him, not mooued of charitie, but pushed on by his proper interest, as not to loose by his death the occasion of the profit hoped for by the victorie.

This counsell assuredlie was graue and honourable touching the man that gaue it, and no lesse worthie to be followed by so great a prince as the emperour: and yet being more caried by the reasons of others, he tooke post to go to him. But for the danger of the king being almost at the extremitie, the visitation was short, and yet for the time accompanied with gratious words ful of hope that he would deliuer him immediatlie vpon his returning to health: in so much that whether it was by the comfort that he breathed into him (in the sicknesse of captiuitie the promise of libertie excéedeth all medicines) or by the benefit of his youth, which with the fauour of nature was stronger than the maladie, he began after this visitation to resume so good disposition, that within few daies he was out of danger, notwithstanding he could not recouer his former health but with verie slowe time.

And now neither the difficulties that were shewed on the emperours side, nor the hopes which were giuen by the Italians, nor anie other nature of impediments whatsoeuer, could staie the voiage of the ladie Alanson into Spaine. For that as nothing was more hard or heauie to the Frenchmen than to leaue off the practises and negociations of accord begun with those that had power to restore their king: so nothing was more easie to the emperour, than féeding the French with hopes, to draw their minds from taking armes; and by that meane so to kéepe the Italians in suspense, as not to dare to enter into new deliberations. And in that cunning maner, sometimes vsing delaies, and sometimes pressing forward the affaires, he thought to keepe the minds of all men confused and intangled. The ladie Alanson was receiued by the emperour with verie gratious demonstrations and hopes: but the effects fell out both hard and heauie. For when she ministred speech to him for the mariage of his sister the widowe with the king: he made answer; that it was a matter which could not be doone without the consent of the duke of Burbon.

The other particularities were debated by deputies of both parts, wherein, as the emperour insisted obstinatlie to haue the dutchie of Burgognie restored as apperteining to him: so the French refused to consent, vnlesse he would accept it for dowrie; or else to referre it to the sentence of the law and iustice to decide the true title. And

Side notes:
A truce for a time betwéene the emperour and the gouernors of Fráce.

The French king extremelie sicke in the castell of Madr.ll. *Guic. pag.* 837.

The emperor visiteth the French king in durance.

The ladie Alanson treateth with the emperour for the kings deliuerie.

albeit they could easilie haue condescended to the residue, yet for that they were so
farre off for the demand of Burgognie, the ladie Alanson returned at last into France,
without winning anie other grace, than a fauour to sée the king hir brother; who
growing more and more into distrust of his deliuerie, desired hir at hir departing to admonish his mother, and all the councell from him, to looke carefullie to the profit of the
crowne of France, without hauing anie consideration of him, as if he liued not. But
notwithstanding the departure of the ladie Alanson, the sollicitations for the kings
deliuerie did not ceasse, for that there remained behind the president of Paris, and
the bishops of Ambrum and Tarbe, who had till then followed the negociation but with
verie little hope, sith the emperour would not harken to anie condition, if first Burgognie
were not rendred, which the king would not be brought to restore, but in a last
necessitie.

The French
king is carefull
ouer the crowne
of France.

Guic. 961, &
deinceps.
The treatie of
Madrill touch-
ing the deliuerie
of the French
king.

After this infortunate accident of the French king insued manie troublesome and
intricate matters, among which the case of the French king was descanted vpon, and
a sollicitation of peace resolued, which conteined these couenants following. That
betwéene the emperour and the French king should be a peace perpetuall, in which
should be comprehended all such as should be named by their common consent. That
the French king by the sixt daie of the next moneth of March, should be set at
libertie vpon the marches in the coast of Fontarabie. That within six weeks after he
should consigne to the emperour the dutchie of Burgognie, the countie of Charrolois,
the iurisdiction of Noiers, the castell Chainro, dependancies of the said dutchie, the
vicountie of Flussona, the resort of S. Laurence de la Roche, a dependant of Franch
countie, togither with all the appurtenances as well of the said dutchie as vicountie, all
which for hereafter should be separate and exempted from the souereigntie of the
realme of France. That at the same and verie instant that the king should be
deliuered, there should be put into the emperours hands the Dolphin of France, and
with him either the duke of Orleance the kings second sonne, or else twelue principall
lords of France, whom the emperour did name.

What was left
to the ladie
regents election
in this capitula-
tion.

It was left to the election of the ladie regent, either to deliuer the kings second
sonne, or the twelue barons, and they to remaine as hostages vntill restitution were
made of the lands and places aforesaid, and the peace sworne and ratified, togither
with all the articles by the estates generall of France, and inregistred in all the courts
of parlement of the kingdome with forme and solemnities necessarie. For the
accomplishing wherof, there was set downe a terme of foure moneths: at which time
returning the hostages, there should be put into the emperors hands the duke de
Angolesme the kings third son, to the end to traine him vp with the emperour, the
better to interteine and assure the peace. That the French king should renounce and
giue vp to the emperour all his rights to the realme of Naples, togither with all such
titles and preeminences as were to come to him by the inuestiture of the church. That
he should doo the like touching his interest in the state of Millaine, of Genes, of Ast,
and likewise of Arras, Tourneie, of the Ile, and of Dowaie. That he should render
vp the towne and castell of Hedin as a member of the countie of Artois, with all
the munitions, artilleries, and mooueables that were in it when it was last taken. That
he should disclaime and yeeld vp all souereigntie in Flanders and Artois, and all other
places or péeces which the emperour possessed.

Couenants con-
cerning the
emperour, and
of him to be
kept and per-
formed.

That on the other side, the emperour should resigne and giue vp to him all the right,
title, and quarrell which he pretended to anie place possessed by the Frenchmen, and
especiallie the townes and castelldomes of Perone, Montdidier, Roie, the counties of
Bullongne, Guines, & Ponthiew, with other towns standing vpon the one and other
shore of the riuer of Some. That there should be betwéene them a league and
confederation perpetuall for the defense of their estates, with oblation to aid one another
when néed required, with 500 men at armes, and ten thousand footmen: that the
emperour

emperour should promise to giue in marriage to the king the ladie Elianor his sister, whome, as soone as the dispensation should be obteined from the pope, he should contract or handfast with words obligatorie for the present, and afterwards she should be led into France, to consummate the marriage at the same time that according to the capitulations the hostages were to be deliuered: that she should haue for hir portion two hundred thousand crowns, with iewels according to hir estate, the one moitie of the monie to be paid within sixtéene moneths, and the other halfe in one yeare after.

Furthermore, that a mariage should be made betwéene the Dolphin & the daughter of the K. of Portugall, daughter to the ladie Elianor, at such time as their age will suffer: that the French king should doo all that he could to induce the ancient K. of Nauarre to giue vp to the emperour the rights of that kingdome, which in case he would not performe, then the king not to aid him with anie succours. That the duke of Guelders, and the countie of Zulffe, and the principall townes of those estates, should promise with sufficient securitie, to giue themselues to the emperour, after his death. That the king should giue no succour to the duke of Wittenberge, nor like-wise to Robert de la March. That he should furnish and rigge for the emperour, both when he should passe into Italie, and two moneths after being so required, twelue gallies, foure ships, & foure gallions, all well munitioned and appointed, ex-cept men of war, & the said vesselles to be rendred thrée moneths after accompting from the daie of his imbarking: that in place of the armie by land which the king offered for Italie, he should paie him two hundred thousand crownes in monie, the one halfe within sixtéene moneths, and the other halfe within a yéere after.

These couenãts restraine a great part of the French kings roiaitie.

Againe, that at the time when the hostages should be deliuered, he should be bound to giue bils of exchange for the paie of six thousand footmen for six moneths imme-diatlie after the emperous arriuall in Italie: that he should also furnish for his seruice fiue hundred lances paied, with a band of artillerie. That he should saue harmelesse the emperour of his promise made to the king of England by pensions, which the French king should paie to him, the arerages whereof amounted to fiue hundred thou-sand crownes, or else to deliuer so much in readie monie to the emperour. That they should both ioine to beséech the pope to call a generall councell with all spéed, to the end to consult vpon an vniuersall peace amongst christians, to aduance an enterprise against the infidels and heretikes, and to grant to all the croisade for thrée yeares. That within six weeks the king should restore the duke of Burbon in most ample forme, into all his estates, goods moouable and vnmoouable, and fruits and reuenues receiued: nor to molest him for anie thing past, nor constraine him to dwell or go to the realme of France. That it should be lawfull to the said duke of Burbon, to de-mand by the waie of law and iustice, the earledome of Prouence. That in like sort all those that had followed him should reenter in safetie into their goods and states, and namelie the bishop of Autun, and monsieur de saint Valier.

The king of England includ-ed in this peace.

Moreouer, that the prisoners taken in the warre should be deliuered on both parts within fiftéene daies. That there should be restitution made to the ladie Margaret of Austrich of all that she possessed afore the warre. That the prince of Orange should be set at libertie with restauration to the principalitie of Orange, and all that he pos-sessed by the death of his father, which had béene taken from him for following the faction of the emperour. That the like should be doone to other barons. That there should be made restitution to the marquesse of Salusse of his estate. That the king as soone as he arriued in the first towne of his realme, should ratifie this capitulation, and be bound to procure the Dolphin to ratifie it when he should come to the age of fouretéene yeares. Manie were named by common consent, and cheeflie the Switzers. Onelie there was not one of the potentates of Italie, except the pope, whom they named as conseruator of the accord, and that more for maner sake and ceremonie,

The prince of Orange included also in this peace.

　　　　　　　　　　　　　　　　　　than

than in effect and true meaning. Lastlie, it was expressed in the said capitulation, that in case the king for anie occasion, would not accomplish these matters promised; he should returne true prisoner.

This accord for the parts it conteined, brought no small astonishment to all Christendome. For when it was vnderstood, that the first execution thereof consisted in the deliuerie of the king, all mens opinions were, that being in his libertie, he would not deliuer vp Burgongnie, as being a member of too great importance for the realme of France. And except a few, who had counselled the emperour to it, all his court had the same iudgement, and namelie the Chancellor, who reprehended and detested the matter with so great vehemencie, that notwithstanding he was commanded to signe the capitulation (according to the office of chéefe chancellors) yet he refused to doo it, alledging; that in such matters, dangerous and hurtfull as that was, he ought not to vse the authoritie that was giuen him : neither could he be altered from this opinion, notwithstanding the emperour was angrie with him: who séeing him so resolute in his opinion, signed it himselfe, and within few daies after went to Madrill, to confirme the aliance, and make a foundation of amitie and good will with the king, whome he interteined in familiar and priuat sort.

Great were the ceremonies and demonstrations of amitie betwéene them: oftentimes they shewed themselues togither in places publike : and as often did they passe in secret familiar discourses. They went togither in one coch vnto a castell not halfe a daiés iournie from thence, where was quéene Eleanor, whom the king married. And yet in all these great signes of peace and amitie, he was obserued with as carefull and streict gard as before, without anie aduantage of libertie. So that he was embraced as a brother, and garded as a prisoner. A matter which made manifest to the world, that it was an accord full of discord, an aliance without amitie, and that vpon euerie occasion their ancient gelousies and passions would be stronger in them, than the regard of that aliance, made more by force than freendship. Manie daies were spent in these offices and ceremonies of amitie, when was brought from the ladie regent the ratification, togither with the declaration, that with the Dolphin of France they would rather giue in hostage the kings second son, than the twelue barons.

Then the king departed from Madrill, taking his waie to the frontier of his realme, where was to be exchanged his person for his sonnes, who bare verie small age. There was sent to accompanie him the viceroy the worker and author of his deliuerie, to whome the emperour had giuen the citie of Ast, with other estates in Flanders and in the kingdome of Naples. The king of England hearing that the French king should now be deliuered, sent to him a knight of his chamber, called sir Thomas Chenie, to signifie to him the great ioy and gladnesse, which he conceiued for his restitution to libertie, and the conclusion of the generall peace. For which kindnesse & courteous remembrance, the French king thought himselfe much bound (as he confesseth himselfe here after) to the king of England, & thanked him greatlie hereafter.

After much a doo and manie remoouings, the French king was come on the confines of Fontarabie, a towne apperteining to the emperour, standing vpon the Ocean sea, and is a frontier betwéene Biskaie and the duchie of Guien. And on the othe side, the ladie regent was ariued with the children of France, at Baion, not manie leagues from Fontarabie. The torments of the gowt tooke hir by the waie, which was the cause that she had lingred some time longer than the daie appointed of permutation. But at last, the eighteenth daie of March, the French king accompanied with the viceroy and capteine Alarcon with fiftie horsse, was presented vpon the shore of the riuer that diuideth the realme of France from the kingdome of Spaine. And on the other side, vpon the shore opposite appéered monsieur Lawtrech with the kings children and like number of horsse. There was in the middest of the riuer a great barke made fast with anchors, in which was no person. The king was rowed néere

to

Whie this accord set all Christendome in a woondering.

The French king marrieth the emperors sister according to a clause in the capitulation.

The king of England glad o. the French kings deliuerance.

Guic. pag. 966. The maner of the deliuerie of the French king.

to this barke in a little boat, wherein he was accompained with the viceroy, capteine Alarcon, and eight others, all armed with short weapons: and on the other side of the barke were likewise brought in a little boat, monsieur Lawtrech with the ostages & eight others, weaponed according to the others,

After this the viceroy went into the barke with the king, and all his companie: and also monsieur Lawtrech with his eight that accompanied him, so that they were within the barke a like number of both parts, Alarcon and his eight being with the viceroy, and Lawtrech and the others with the person of the king. And when they were all thus within the barke, Lawtrech fetched out of the boat into the barke, the Dolphin, who being giuen to the viceroy and by him committed to capteine Alarcon, was foorthwith bestowed in their boate, and after him followed the little duke of Orleance, who was no sooner entred the barke, than the French king leaped out of the barke into his boat, which he did with such quicknesse and celeritie, that the exchange or permutation was thought to be doone at one selfe instant; so welcome to him was libertie, without the which nothing is swéet, nothing is comfortable, as the poet saith:

> Libertas perdulce bonum, bona cætera reddit.

Assoone as the king was on the other side of the shore, his new libertie making him fearefull of ambush, he mounted vpon a Turkish horsse of a woonderfull swiftnesse, which was perpared for the purpose: and running betweene feare and gladnesse vpon the spurre, he neuer staied till he came to S. Iohn de Lus, a towne of his obedience, foure leagues from the place. And being there readilie relieued with a fresh horsse, he ran with the same swiftnesse to Baion, where, after he had passed ouer the offices of court doone to him by his people, he dispatched with great diligence a gentleman to the king of England, to whom he wrote with his owne hand letters of his deliuerie, charging the messenger vnder verie louing commission, to tell the king of England, that as he acknowledged the effect of his libertie to be wrought wholie by him and his operations, so in recompense, he offered to remaine to him a perpetuall and assured friend, and to be guided in all his affaires by his counsell. And afterwards he sent an óther solemne ambassage into England, to ratifie the peace which his mother had made with him, as one that reapposed a verie great foundation in the amitie of that king.

When the French king was gotten into Baion, being required by a gentleman of the viceroys, to ratifie the accord according to the obligation of his word, being come into a place frée and assured, he deferred it from one daie to another, interposing reasons and excuses generall: wherin, to the end to hold still the emperour in hope, he sent to aduertise him by a man especiall, that he forbare for the present to accomplish the ratification, not by omission or willing negligence, but vpon this necessitie, that before he procéeded reallie to such an act, he was to labour to reappease and reduce the minds of his subiects ill contented with the obligations he had made, tending to the diminution of the crowne of France. Neuerthelesse, he would in his time resolue all difficulties, and obserue with fidelitie all that he had promised to him, both in substance and circumstance. By this dealing, no lesse doubtfull for the manner, than dangerous in meaning, might easilie be comprehended what were his intentions, the same being more manifestlie detected at the arriuall of the messengers sent to him not manie daies after, by the pope and Venetians, in whome was no great need of industrie or labour, to sound out the plaine course of his inclination.

For, after he had receiued them with manie demonstrations and offices of court, he interteined them seuerallie and apart with sundrie spéeches of compassion, such as tended to manifest complaints against the inhumanitie of the emperour: who he said did neuer administer to him during his captiuitie, anie one office apperteining to the ranke

The French king with the viceroy are imbarked.

The French K. is not a litle glad of his libertie.

The king of England the procurer of the French kings libertie.

Guic. pag. 968. The French king is not verie hastie to ratifie the accord.

The French king complaineth vpon the emperour to the messengers sent from the pope and the Venetians.

ranke of a prince, nor at anie time shewed himselfe touched with that affection and commiseration which one prince ought to expresse in the calamities of another: and much lesse would vse anie course of common comfort, either to relieue the heauinesse of his condition with anie propertie of apt consolation, or once to enter into consideration, that the same accident that had fallen vpon him, might also be as heauilie heaped vpon his owne head. In this complaint, he alleaged the example of Edward king of England called of some Edward Long-shanke. To whome when was presented as prisoner Iohn king of the Frenchmen, taken by the prince of Wales his son in the battell of Poitiers, he did not onelie receiue him with great comfort and compassion of his afflicted case, but also, all the time of his imprisonment within the realme of England, he let him go at libertie vnder a frée gard.

Furthermore he had dailie familiar conuersation with him, he would oftentimes haue him to accompanie him on hunting, to communicate in the open aire and solace of the field, and was not curious to call him to eat with him at his table. And by these humanities much lesse that he lost his prisoner, or ranged him to an accord lesse fauourable; but of the contrarie, by the operation of those graces and good offices, there grew betwéene them such a familiaritie and confidence, that the French king, after he had continued manie yeares in France, made a voluntarie voiage into England, to honour and gratifie vnder that propertie of office, the liberalitie and frankenesse of the king. He alleged that as there was onelie remembrance of two kings of France that had beene taken prisoners in battell, king Iohn and himselfe, so the diuersitie of the examples was also worthie of singular memorie, séeing vpon the one was exercised all facilitie and mildnesse of the victor, and to the other were ministred all those rigours and seuerities, which tyrants in the height and pride of their fortune are woont to vse. Herevnto he added manie circumstances discouering the discontentment of his mind, wherevpon insued practises wherewith the emperour was not well pleased. To be short, after that this peace was accorded, and the French king deliuered, the emperour maried the ladie Isabell daughter to Emanuell king of Portugall, and had with hir eleuen hundred thousand ducats. Thus farre the French affaires intermixed (as you heare) with our owne, and verie needfull to be added, which here we will end, and returne to England.]

Cardinall Woolsie being still most highlie in the kings fauour, obteined licence to erect a college at Oxford, and another at Ipswich, the towne where he was borne, the which foundations he began rather of a vaine desire of glorie and worldlie praise, than vpon the instinction of true religion and aduancement of doctrine, and therfore sith he was not mooued therto in respect of true godlinesse and bountifull liberalitie, he went about to cloth Peter and rob Paule: for he first got licence of the king to suppresse certeine small monasteries, and after got a confirmation of the pope, that he might imploie the goods, lands, and reuenues belonging to those houses, to the maintenance of those his two colleges, whereby not onelie he, but also the pope were euill spoken of through the whole realme. In March the king sent Cuthbert Tunstall bishop of London, and sir Richard Wingfield chancellour of the duchie of Lancaster, & knight of the garter, into Spaine, to common with the emperour for great causes, concerning the taking of the French king, and for warres to be made into France on euerie side.

The king being determined thus to make wars in France, & to passe the sea himselfe in person, his councell considered that aboue all things great treasure and plentie of monie must néedes be prouided. Wherfore, by the cardinall there was deuised strange commissions, and sent in the end of March into euerie shire, and commissioners appointed, and priuie instructions sent to them how they should proceed in their sittings, and order the people to bring them to their purpose: which was, that the

sixt

sixt part of euerie mans substance should be paid in monie or plate to the king with- The sixt part of euerie mans substance demanded. out delaie, for the furniture of his war. Hereof followed such cursing, weeping, and exclamation against both king & cardinall, that pitie it was to heare. And to be bréefe, notwithstanding all that could be said or doone, forged or deuised by the commissioners to persuade the people to this contribution, the same would not be granted. And in excuse of their deniall it was alledged, that wrong was offered, and the ancient customes & lawes of the realme broken, which would not anie man to be charged with such paiment, except it were granted by the estates of the realme in parlement assembled. The like answer was made by them of the spiritualtie, of whome was demanded the fourth part of their goods.

Monsieur de Prate the emperours ambassador, whether offended for admitting of The emperors ambassador departeth out of England without leaue taking of the king. Iohn Iokin into the realme (as before ye haue heard) or for some other cause, the ninth of Aprill departed out of England, not taking leaue of the king, nor of the cardinall, and so much did by safe conduct, that he passed through France in post, and came to the emperour before the ambassadors of England came thither. And whether it was by his report, or otherwise, the accustomed fauour that the emperour shewed to the Englishmen, began then to decaie, as was well perceiued, whatsoeuer the matter was. This yeare at Whitsuntide died Thomas duke of Norffolke, and Death of the duke of Norffolke: was honourablie buried at Thetford. The cardinall trauelled earnestlie with the *An. Reg.* 17. maior and aldermen of London, about the aid of monie to be granted, and likewise the commissioners appointed in the shires of the realme, sat vpon the same: but the burthen was so gréeuous, that it was generallie denied, and the commons in euerie place so mooued, that it was like to grow to rebellion.

In Essex the people would not assemble before the commissioners in no houses, but The commissioners for the tax resisted. in open places, and in Huntingtonshire diuerse resisted the commissioners, and would not suffer them to sit, which were apprehended and sent to the Fléet. The duke of Suffolke sitting in commission about this subsidie in Suffolke, persuaded by courteous meanes the rich clothiers to assent therto: but when they came home, and went about to discharge and put from them their spinners, carders, fullers, weauers, and other arti- A rebellion in Suffolke by the grieuousnesse of the subsidie. ficers, which they kept in worke afore time, the people began to assemble in companies. Whereof when the duke was aduertised, he commanded the constables that euerie mans harnes should be taken from him. But when that was knowne, then the rage of the people increased, railing openlie on the duke, and sir Robert Drurie, and threatned them with death, and the cardinall also. And herewith there assembled togither after the maner of rebels foure thousand men of Lanam, Sudberie, Hadleie, and other townes thereabouts, which put themselues in harnesse, and rang the bels alarme, and began still to assemble in great number.

The duke of Suffolke perceiuing this, began to gather such power as he could, but that was verie slender. Yet the gentlemen that were with the duke, did so much that all the bridges were broken, so that the assemblie of those rebels was somewhat letted. The duke of Norffolke being thereof aduertised, gathered a great power in Norffolke, The duke of Norffolke cōmeth with a power against the rebels in Suffolke. and came towards the commons, & sending to them to know their intent, receiued answer, that they would liue and die in the kings causes, and be to him obedient. Hereupon he came himselfe to talke with them, and willing to know who was their capteine, that he might answer for them all: it was told him by one Iohn Gréene a man of fiftie yeares of age, that Pouertie was their capteine, the which with his cou- Pouertie and Necessitie capteins of the rebellion. sine Necessitie, had brought them to that dooing. For whereas they and a great number of other in that countrie, liued not vpon themselues, but vpon the substantiall occupiers, now that they through such paiments as were demanded of them, were not able to mainteine them in worke, they must of necessitie perish for want of sustenance.

The duke hearing this matter, was sorie for their case, and promised them, that if they would depart home to their dwellings, he would be a meane for their pardon to the

king.

king. Wherevpon they were contented to depart. After this, the duke of Norffolke, and the duke of Suffolke came to Burie, and thither resorted much people of the countrie in their shirts, with halters about their neckes, meekelie desiring pardon for their offenses. The dukes so wiselie demeaned themselues, that the commons were appeased, and the demaund of monie ceased in all the realme, for well it was perceiued

that the commons would pay none. Then went the two dukes to London, and brought with them the chiefe capteins of the rebellion, which were put in the Fléet. The king then came to Westminster to the cardinals palace, and assembled there a great councell, in the which he openlie protested, that his mind was neuer to aske anie thing of his commons which might sound to the breach of his lawes, wherefore he willed to know by whose meanes the commissions were so streictlie giuen foorth, to demand the sixt part of euerie mans goods.

The cardinall excused himselfe, and said, that when it was mooued in councell how to leuie monie to the king vse; the kings councell, and namelie the iudges, said, that he might lawfullie demand anie summe by commission, and that by the consent of the whole councell it was doone, and tooke God to witnes that he neuer desired the hinderance of the commons, but like a true councellor deuised how to inrich the king. The king indéed was much offended that his commons were thus intreated, & thought it touched his honor, that his councell should attempt such a doubtfull matter in his name, and to be denied both of the spiritualtie and temporaltie. Therefore he would no more of that trouble, but caused letters to be sent into all shires, that the matter should no further be talked of: & he pardoned all them that had denied the demand openlie or secretlie. The cardinall, to deliuer himselfe of the euill will of the commons, purchased by procuring & aduancing of this demand, affirmed, and caused it to be bruted abrode, that through his intercession the king had pardoned and released all things.

Those that were in the Tower and Fléet for the rebellion in Suffolke, and resisting the commissioners aswell there as in Huntington shire and Kent, were brought before the lords in the Star chamber, and there had their offenses opened and shewed to them : and finallie the kings pardon declared, and thereon they were deliuered. ¶ In this season a great number of men of warre laie at Bullongne, and in other places thereabout, which diuerse times attempted to indamage the Englishmen, and to spoile the English pale : but they could neuer spoile the marishes where the greatest part of the cattell belonging to the inhabitants was kept.

Tindale men with aid of the Scots, did much hurt in England by robberies, which they exercised : and therefore were sent thither, sir Richard Bulmere, and sir Christopher Dacres, to restreine their dooings. Diuerse came to them, and submitted themselues : but the greatest théeues kept them in the mounteins of Cheuiot, and did much hurt, yet at length they seuered, and manie of them were taken.

The cardinall by his power legantine sent one of his chapleins called doctor Iohn Allen, to visit the religious houses of this realme about this season, which doctor practised amongst them greatlie to his profit, but more to the slander both of himselfe and of his maister.

On the eightéenth daie of Iune, at the manor place of Bridewell, the kings sonne (which he had begot of Elizabeth Blunt, daughter to sir Iohn Blunt knight) called Henrie Fitzroie, was created first earle of Notingham, and after on the selfe same daie he was created duke of Richmond and Summerset. Also the same daie the lord Henrie Courtneie earle of Deuonshire, and coosine germane to the king, was created marquesse of Excester : and the lord Henrie Brandon sonne to the duke of Suffolke and the French queene, a child of two yeares old, was created earle of Lincolne : and sir Thomas Manners lord Roos was created earle of Rutland, and sir Henrie Clifford earle of Cumberland, and the lord Fitzwater sir Robert Ratcliffe was
created

created vicount Fitzwater, and sir Thomas Bullen treasuror of the kings houshould was created vicount Rochefort.

The French kings mother as then regent of France, procured a safe conduct for an ambassador to be sent into England to treat of peace, and therewith sent Iohn Iokin called monsieur de Vaux, which (as yée haue heard) in the last yeare was kept secret in maister Larks house. By his procurement a truce was granted to indure from the thirtéenth of Iulie for fortie daies betwéene England and France both by sea and land. In the later end of Iulie came into England the chéefe president of Rone with sufficient authoritie to conclude anie agréement that should be granted. At his sute the king was contented that a truce should be taken, to endure from the foureteenth of August, till the first of December. This yeare the king sent doctor Henrie Standish bishop of saint Asse, and sir Iohn Baker knight into Denmarke, to intreat with the nobles of that countrie for the reduction of their king Christierne to his realme and former dignitie: but the Danes hated him so much for his crueltie, that they could not abide to heare of anie such matter, and so these ambassadors returned without speeding of their purpose for the which they were sent.

A truce betwéene England & France for fortie daies.

Ambassadors sent into Denmarke.

But the French ambassadors did so much both by offers and intreaties, that the king condescended to a peace, which being concluded, was proclamed in London with a trumpet the eight of September. By the couenants of this peace the king of England should receiue at certeine daies twentie hundred thousand crownes, which then amounted in sterling monie to the summe of foure hundred thousand pounds sterling, of which one paiment of fiftie thousand pounds was paid in hand. In October were sent into France, sir William Fitzwilliam treasuror of the kings house, and doctor Tailor, as ambassadors from the king of England to the ladie regent, whome they found at the citie of Lion, where, of hir they were honorablie receiued: and in their presence the said ladie regent tooke a corporall oth in solemne wise, and according to the custome in such cases vsed, to performe all the articles and couenants passed and concluded in the league and treatie of peace by hir commissioners.

A peace proclamed betwéene England & Fráce.

The ladie regent sworne to performe the articles of the league.

The emperour was nothing pleased, in that the king of England had thus concluded peace with the Frenchmen, and therefore the English merchants were not so courteouslie dealt with, as they had béene afore time. In this winter was great death in London, so that the terme was adiourned: and the king kept his Christmasse at Eltham, with a small number, and therefore it was called the still Christmasse. ¶ In Ianuarie was a peace concluded betwixt the realmes of England and Scotland for thrée yeares and six moneths. The cardinall about this time comming to the court, which then laie (as before yée haue heard) at Eltham, tooke order for altering the state of the kings house. Manie officers and other seruants were discharged, and put to their pensions and annuities. In which number were fourescore and foure yeomen of the gard, which before hauing twelue pence the daie with checke, were now allowed six pence the daie without checke, and commanded to go home into their countries. Diuers ordinances were made at that season by the cardinall, touching the gouernance of the kings house, more profitable than honorable, as some said, and were called long after, The statues of Eltham.

A winters death.

Th: still Christmasse.

1526

The cardinall altereth the state of the kings houshold.

The statutes of Eltham.

On Shrouetuesdaie there was a solemne iusts held at the manor of Gréenewich, the king & eleuen other on the one part, and the marquesse of Excester with eleauen other on the contrarie part. ¶ At those iusts by chance of shiuering of a speare sir Francis Brian lost one of his eies. The eleuenth of Februarie being sundaie, the cardinall with great pompe came to the cathedrall church of Paules, where he sat in pontificalibus vnder his cloth of estate of rich cloth of gold, and there doctor Barnes an Augustine frier bare a fagot for certeine points of heresie alleaged against him; and two merchants of the Stiliard bare fagots for eating of flesh on a fridaie: and there the bishop of Rochester doctor Fisher made a sermon against Martine Luther, which

Doct. Barnes and two merchants of the Stiliard beare fagots.

certeine yeares before, that is to wit, about the yeare a thousand fiue hundred and eightéene, had begun to preach and write against the authoritie of the pope.

Ye must here note, that the emperour being at Windsor in the fourtéenth yeere of the kings reigne couenanted, amongst other things, to take to wife the ladie Marie daughter to the king of England: but now vpon considerations his mind changed, for the which the Englishmen sore murmured against him. On the nine and twentith of Aprill being sundaie, the cardinall soong a solemne masse in the kings chappell at Gréenewich, and after the same was ended, the king sware in presence of the ambassadors of France, and of the ambassadors of Rome, of the emperour of Venice, and of Florence, to obserue and kéepe the peace and league concluded betwixt and his louing brother, and perpetuall alie the French king, during his life and one yeare after.

An. Reg. 18.

King Henrie sworne to performe the league concluded.

A secret league betwixt the pope and certeine states of Italie.

In this meane while, there was a secret league concluded betwixt the pope, the Venecians, the Florentins, and Francis Sforza duke of Millan: into the which league the French king also entered, after he was returned into France. There was also place left to the king of England to enter into the same league, and likewise to all other kings and princes: and if the king of England would, he should be admitted as protector of the same. But the emperour might not be admitted, till he had deliuered the French kings children (hauing a reasonable summe of monie for the same) and had restored the duke of Millan to his whole duchie. It was thought indéed, that the emperour being wrongfullie informed against this duke, rather through enuie of some of the emperours capteins, than for anie cause ministred by the duke, dealt verie streightlie with him, and meant to defeat him of his duchie. For redresse wherof, and also to prouide that the emperor should not grow too strong in Italie to the danger of other estates, this league was deuised: by force whereof he might be brought to reason, if he would refuse conuenient offers and indifferent waies of agréement.

Read *Guic. lib.* 18.

This league was concluded the two and twentith of Maie in this yeare. What followed thereof, ye may read more at large in the histories of Italie and France, where the warres are more at large touched, which chanced in that season betwixt the emperour, and the confederats, and how the imperiall armie tooke the citie of Rome, and besieging the pope in castell saint Angelo, constreined him to yéeld, and agree to certeine propositions put vnto him. ¶ Who being by his aduersitie made naked of all helpe present, and lesse expectation to be rescued where was so great want of valour and order, was driuen to run the race of his fortune, compounding the sixt daie of Iune with the imperials almost vnder the same conditions with the which he might haue accorded before. That the pope should paie to the armie foure hundred thousand duckets in this order: one hundred thousand presentlie to be defraied of the gold, monie, and treasure reserued in the castell: fiftie thousand within twentie daies, and two hundred and fiftie thousand within two moneths: assigning to him for these defraiments, an impost of monie to be charged vpon the whole church state. That he should deliuer into the power of the emperour, to reteine them so long as he thought good, the castell S. Angelo, the rockes of Ostia, of Ciuita Vecchia, of Ciuita Castelano, togither with the cities of Parma, Plaisanca, and Modena.

Abr. Fl. ex *Guic. pag.* 1067.

The pope being abandoned of all hopes, compoundeth with the imperials.

Furthermore, that the pope togither with all those cardinals that were with him, which were thirtéene in number, should remaine prisoners within the castell, vntill the first paiment of an hundred and fiftie thousand duckets were satisfied. That afterwards they should go to Naples or to Caietta, to expect what the emperour would determine of them. That for assurance of the paiments, whereof the third part apperteined to the Spaniards, he should deliuer in for ostages, the archbishops of Siponto and Pisa, the bishops of Pistoia & Verona, togither with Iames Saluiatio, Simon de Ricasola, and Laurence brother to cardinall Rodolffo. That Ranso de Cero, Albert Pio,

A hard article and to be maruelled how the pope and his cardinals might brooke it.

Pio, Oratio Baillon, the knight Casalo, the ambassadour of England, with all others that were saued within the castell, except the pope and the cardinals, should depart in suertie. That the pope should giue absolution to the Colonnois of the censures they had incurred. And that when he should be led out of Rome, a legat should remaine there for him with authoritie to dispose and administer iustice.

During the popes captiuitie, Rome was sore afflicted with the plague, in so much *Guic. pag.* 1072. that the rage thereof so greatlie increased, that the castell of saint Angelo was visited, The castell to the great danger of the life of the pope; about whom died certeine speciall men where the pope that did seruice to his person: who amid so manie afflictions and aduersities, and no was prisoner in- other hope remaining to him than in the clemencie of the emperour, appointed for fected with the legat with the consent of the capteins, cardinall Alexander of Farneso, who notwith- plague. standing being issued out of the castell, and Rome, refused vnder that occasion to go in the said legation. The capteins desired to carie the person of the pope with the thirtéene cardinals that were with him, to Caietto: but he laboured against that resolution with great diligence, petitions, and art.]

¶ In the month of Maie was a proclamation made against all vnlawfull games, ac- *Ed. Hall in H.8.* cording to the statutes made in this behalfe, and commissions awarded into euerie *fol.* Cxlix. shire for the execution of the same; so that in all places, tables, dice, cards, and bouls were taken and burnt. Wherfore the people murmured against the cardinall, saieng: that he grudged at euerie mans plesure, sauing his owne. But this proclamation small time indured. For when yoong men were forbidden boules and such other games: some fell to drinking, some to feretting of other mens conies, some to stealing of deere in parks, and other vnthriftinesse.]

This yeare in the citie of London a great grudge was conceiued against merchants Great grudge strangers, for that they by vertue of licences, which they had purchased to bring against strangers woad into the realme, contrarie to a statute thereof prouided, brought ouer such for procuring li- plentie thereof, and vttered it aswell in the citie, as abroad in the countrie, so franklie, woad. that Englishmens woad laie vnbought. At length the maior called a common coun- *Edw. Hall. H.8.* cell in the moneth of August, and there were manie billes laied against the strangers, *fol.* Cliiij. and at last it was enacted, that no citizen nor freeman shuld buy nor sell in no place, nor exchange nor meddle with certeine strangers, called Anthonie Bonuice, Laurence Bonuice, Anthonie Viuald, Anthonie Caueler, Francis de Bard, Thomas Calnecant, and a great sort more, whose names I let passe. And if anie person did meddle or occupie with them contrarie to this act, he should loose his fréedome and libertie in the citie of London. By which act the strangers were so brideled, that they came to a reasonable point and conclusion.

In this season the angell noble was iust the sixt part of an ounce Troie, so that six Valuation of angels were iust an ounce, which was fourtie shillings sterling; & the angell was certeine coins worth two ounces of siluer: so that six angels were worth twelue ounces, which was as angels, rials, but fourtie shillings in siluer. By reason of the good weight and low valuation of the crowns, &c. English coine, merchants dailie carried ouer great store, bicause the same was much inhanced there. So that, to méet with this inconuenience, in September proclamation was made through all England, that the angell should go for seuen shillings foure pence, the roiall for eleuen shillings, & the crowne for foure shillings foure pence. On the fift of Nouember following, by proclamation againe, the angell was inhanced to seuen shillings six pence, and so euerie ounce of gold should be fiue and fourtie shillings, and an ounce of siluer at thrée shillings and nine pence in value.

The king kept a solemne Christmasse at Gréenewich with reuellers, maskes, dis- *Edw. Hall in* guisings, & bankets: and the thirtith daie of December, was an enterprise of iusts *H. 8. fol.* Cliiij. made at the tilt by six gentlemen, against all commers, which valiantlie furnished the same, both with speare and sword: and like iusts were kept the third daie of Ianuarie, where were thrée hundred speares broken. That same night, the king and manie

　　　　　　　　　　　　　　　　　　　　　　　　　yoong

yoong gentlemen with him, came to Bridewell, and there put him and fiftéene other, all in masking apparell, and then tooke his barge, and rowed to the cardinals place, where were at supper a great companie of lords and ladies, and then the maskers dansed, and made goodlie pastime: and when they had well dansed, the ladies plucked awaie their visors, and so they were all knowen, and to the king was made a great banket.

1527
An ambassadour from the emperour.

Abr. Fl. ex Edw. Hall in H. 8. fol. Cliiij.
A plaie at Graies In.

The argument of the plaie.

On the fourtéenth of Ianuarie came to the court don Hugo de Mendoza, a man of a noble familie in Spaine: he came as ambassadour from the emperour to the king, with large commission, for the emperour put it to the kings determination, whether his demands which he required of the French king were reasonable or not. This noble man tarried here two yéeres. ¶ This Christmasse was a goodlie disguising plaied at Graies In, which was compiled for the most part by maister Iohn Roo, sergeant at the law manie yeares past, and long before the cardinall had any authoritie. The effect of the play was, that lord gouernance was ruled by dissipation and negligence, by whose misgouernance and euill order ladie publike weale was put from gouernance: which caused rumor populi, inward grudge and disdaine of wanton souereignetie, to rise with a great multitude, to expell negligence and dissipation, and to restore publike welth againe to hir estate, which was so doone.

The cardinall is offended at it and punisheth the author and actors of the same.

This plaie was so set foorth with rich and costlie apparell, with strange deuises of maskes & morrishes, that it was highlie praised of all men, sauing of the cardinall, which imagined that the play had beene deuised of him, and in a great furie sent for the said maister Roo, and tooke from him his coife, and sent him to the Fléet; and after he sent for the yoong gentlemen, that plaied in the plaie, and them highlie rebuked and threatned, and sent one of them called Thomas Moile of Kent to the Fléet, but by means of friends maister Roo and he were deliuered at last. This plaie sore displeased the cardinall, and yet it was neuer meant to him, as you haue heard. Wherfore manie wisemen grudged to sée him take it so hartilie, and euer the cardinall said that the king was highlie displeased with it, and spake nothing of himselfe. But what will you haue of a guiltie conscience but to suspect all things to be said of him (as if all the world knew his wickednesse) according to the old verse:

Conscius ipse sibi de se putat omnia dici.]

Ambassadors frō the Frēch king.

Edw. Hall pag. Clv.
A iustes.

The second of March were receiued into London the bishop of Tarbe, Francis vicount of Thurane, and master Anthonie Vescie second president of Paris, as ambassadours from the French king. They were lodged in Tailors hall. On Shrouetuesdaie the king himselfe in a new harnesse all gilt, of a strange fashion that had not béene seene, and with him eight gentlemen all in cloth of gold of one sute, embrodered with knots of siluer, and the marques of Excester, and eight with him in blew veluet and white sattin, like the waues of the sea, these men of armes came to the tilt, and there ran manie fresh courses, till two hundred fourescore and six speares were broken, and then they disarmed and went to the queenes chamber, where for them was prouided a costlie banket.

Sute by the French ambassadors for the ladie Marie to be married to the duke of Orleance.

Edw. Hall in H. 8. fol. Clv.
The dogged nature of the French for a matter of nothing.

The French ambassadours sued (as was said) to haue the ladie Marie daughter to the K. of England, giuen in mariage to the duke of Orleance, second sonne to their master the French king: but that matter was put in suspense for diuerse considerations. And one was, for that the president of Paris doubted whether the mariage betweene the king and hir mother (she being his brothers wife) was lawfull or not. ¶ While the French ambassadors laie thus in London, it happened one euening as they were comming from the Blacke friers, from supper to the Tailors hall, two boies were in a gutter casting downe rubbish, which the raine had driuen there, and vnwares hit a lackeie belonging to the vicount of Thurane, and hurt him nothing, for scantlie touched it his cote. But the French lords tooke the matter highlie, as a thing doone in despite, & sent word to the cardinall. Who being too hastie of credence, sent for

sir

sir Thomas Seimor knight, lord maior of the citie, and in all hast commanded him vpon his allegiance, to take the husband, wife, children, and seruants of the house, and them to imprison, till he knew further of the kings pleasure, and that the two boies apprentises should be sent to the Tower: which commandement was accomplished without anie fauor. For the man, and his wife, and seruants, were kept in the counter till the sixt daie of Maie, which was six wéekes full, and their neighbours of gentlenesse kept their house in the meane time, and one of the apprentises died in the Tower, and the other was almost lame. Of the crueltie of the cardinall, and of the pride of the Frenchmen, much people spake, & would haue béene reuenged on the Frenchmen, if wise men in the citie had not appeased it with faire words.] *The cardinal crueltie.*

On the foureteenth daie of March were conueied from London to Gréenwich by the earle of Rutland and others, the lord Gabliel de Salamanca earle of Ottonburgh, Iohn Burgraue of Siluerberge, and Iohn Faber a famous clearke, after bishop of Vien, as ambassadors from don Ferdinando, brother to the emperour, newlie elect king of Hungarie and Beame, after the death of his brother in law king Lewes, which was slaine by the Turke the last summer, as you haue heard before. This companie was welcomed of the high officers, and after brought into the kings presence, all the nobilitie being present, and there after great reuerence made, master Faber made a notable oration, taking his ground of the gospell, Exijt seminator seminare semen suum, and of that he declared how Christ and his disciples went foorth to sow, and how their seed was good that fell into the good ground, and brought foorth good fruit, which was the christian faith : and then he declared how contrarie to that sowing, Mahomet had sowne séed, which brought foorth euill fruit. He also shewed from the beginning, how the Turkes haue increased in power, what realmes they had conquered, what people they had subdued euen to that daie. *Ambassadors from the king of Hungarie.* *An oration made by maister Faber.*

He declared further what acts the great Turke then liuing had doone, and in especiall he noted the getting of Belgrad, and of the Rhodes, and the slaieng of the king of Hungarie, to the great rebuke (as he said) of all the kings christened. He set foorth also what power the Turke had, what diuersities of companies, what armor, what capteins he had, so that he thought, that without a maruellous great number of people he could not be ouerthrowne. Wherefore he most humblie besought the king, as S. Georges knight, and defendor of the faith, to assist the king his master in that godlie warre and vertuous purpose. To this oration the K. by the mouth of sir Thomas Moore answered, that much he lamented the losse that happened in Hungarie, and if it were not for the wars which were betweene the two great princes, he thought that the Turke would not haue enterprised that act. Wherefore he with all his studie would take paine, first, to set an vnitie and peace throughout all christendome; and after that, both with monie and men, he would be redie to helpe toward that glorious warre, as much as any other prince in christendome. After this doone, the ambassadours were well cherished, and diuerse times resorted to the court, and had great cheare and good rewards, and so the third daie of Maie next insuing, they tooke their leaue and departed homeward. *The kings answer by the mouth of sir Thomas Moore.*

In the winter season of this yeare fell great abundance of raine, and namelie in September, Nouember, and December. And on the sixtéenth of Ianuarie it rained so abundantlie, that great flouds thereby insuing, destroied corne fields, pastures, and drowned manie sheepe and beasts. Then was it drie till the twelfe of Aprill, and from thence it rained euerie day or night till the third of Iune, & in Maie it rained thirtie hours continuallie without ceasing, which caused great flouds, & did much harme, namelie in corne, so that the next yeare it failed within this realme, and great dearth insued. *A verie wet season for a long time by continuall raine.*

¶ This

An. Reg. 19.
*Edw. Hall
in H. 8. fo. Clvj.*
A caueat to the
cardinall by a
libell set vp in
London.

¶ This time a bill was set vp in London, much contrarie to the honour of the cardi-nall, in the which the cardinall was warned that he should not counsell the king to marrie his daughter into France: for if hée did, he should shew himselfe enimie to the king and the realme, with manie threatning words. This bill was deliuered to the cardinall by sir Thomas Seimor maior of the citie, which thanked him for the same, & made much search for the author of that bill, but he could not be found, which sore displeased the cardinall. And vpon this occasion the last daie of Aprill at night he caused a great watch to be kept at Westminster, and had there cart guns readie charged, & caused diuerse watches to be kept about London, in Newington, S. Iohns stréet, Westminster, saint Giles, Islington, and other places néere London:

The citizens of
London are
hated of the
cardinall and he
also of them.

which watches were kept by gentlemen & their seruants, with housholders, and all for feare of the Londoners bicause of this bill. When the citizens knew of this, they said that they maruelled why the cardinall hated them so, for they said that if he mistrusted them, he loued them not: and where loue is not, there is hatred: and they affirmed that they neuer intended anie harme toward him, and mused of this chance. For if fiue or six persons had made alarm in the citie, then had entred all these watchmen with their traine, which might haue spoiled the citie without cause. Wherefore they much murmured against the cardinall and his vndiscréet dooings.]

The French
ambassadors in
the name of their
maister sweare
to obserue the
league.
*See Edw. Hall
in H. 8. fol. Clv.
& deinceps.*

The French ambassadors at Greenwich on sunday the fift of Maie, sware in the name of their maister the French king to obserue the peace and league concluded betwéene them, for tearme of two princes liues. These ambassadours had great cheare, and iustes were enterprised for the honour and pleasure of them a the kings commandement by sir Nicholas Carew, sir Robert Ierningham, sir Anthonite Browne, and Nicholas Haruie esquier chalengers. Against whom ran the marques of Excester, and thirtéen with him as defendants. When these ambassadours should returne, they had great rewards giuen them of the king, and so tooke their leaue and departed.

Ambassadors
into France.

Shortlie after the king sent sir Thomas Bullen vicount Rochford, and sir Anthonie Browne knight, as ambassadours from him into France, which came to Paris to the bishop of Bath that laie there for the king as legier.

Then these thrée went to the court, and saw the French king in person sweare to kéepe the league & amitie concluded betwéene him & the king of England. Also the

An ambassage
to the emperor.

king sent sir Francis Poins knight ambassadour from him to Charles the emperour, and with him went Clarenceaux king of armes, to demand the one halfe of the treasure and ordinance which was taken at Pauia, forsomuch as that warre was made as well at the kings charge as at the emperours. Also they were commanded to demand one of the French kings sonnes, which lay in hostage with the emperour, that is to wit, the duke of Orleance to be deliuered to the king of England; and further that he shuld call backe his armie out of Italie. And if it were so that he refused these reasonable requests, then should they in the kings name denounc,

English mer-
chants.

open warre against him. The English merchants liked the matter nothing at all that there should bée anie warres betwixt the emperour and the king of England. And where they were desired by the cardinall to kéepe their marts at Calis, they would not

*Abr. Fl. ex
Guic. pag.* 1060.
The duke of
Burbon incamp-
eth neere
Rome.

assent thereto.

¶ In this meane time great warres were managed betweene the pope and other princes, amongest whom the duke of Burbon (of whom you haue heard often mention before in sundrie actions) leuieng a great power, led the same towards Rome, and incamped within the medow néere to the citie, from whence with the insolencie of a souldier hee sent a trumpet to demand passage of the pope through the citie of Rome, to go with his armie to the realme of Naples. The morning following vpon the point of the daie, by the consideration of his case and the aduersities thereof, he found there remained no other hope for his affaires, than to be resolute to reléeue the afflictions of his armie, and according to the opportunitie that was offered by the citie of Rome, either to die or to vanquish. In which resolution pushed on more and more

by

by the murmurs and exclamations of his souldiers, in whom he could not discerne which was greater, either their insolencies or their necessities, he drew néere the suburbs by the waie of the mounteine and Santo Spirito, where he began to giue a furious assault. Wherein he séemed to haue the fauour of fortune, who made him present his armie in more suertie by the benefit of a thicke mist, which being risen before daie, and increased with degrees of fog and thicknesse, became such a couer to his whole campe, that his souldiers were not discerned till they were néere the place where they began to giue the assault.

The duke of Burbon through a last despaire of his estate aduanced before all his companies, either for that he had no other expectation of refuge, in case he returned not victorious, or else by his owne example he thought to call on with a greater courage the lanceknights, who it séemed went not resolutelie to the seruice. But such was his destinie to determine his life & his glorie togither, or rather such the reward of his wilfull forwardnes, which for the most part heapeth wretched effects The duke of
Burbon slain at vpon such as seeke not to accompanie their valour with counsell and discretion. In the assault of
Rome. the beginning of the assault he was striken with a bullet of an harquebuze, of which wound he fell downe dead to the earth, receiuing iustlie vpon his bodie and life the price of the action, which contrarie to all iustice and pietie he went about to execute. But much lesse that his death did abate or diminish, séeing it did inflame and redouble the courage of his souldiers, who fighting with a woonderfull constancie the space of two houres, made waie at last by their hands and weapons to enter the suburbs, wherin they were not onelie holpen by the weaknesse of the rampires which were great and generall, but also they found helpe in the slender resistance which the defendants made.

An experience of right good doctrine to such as haue not as yet gotten by the The morall of benefit of examples past, the knowledge of things present, " who in that action maie the foresaid ac-
tion woorth the discerne what propertie of difference is betwéene the vertue of souldiours exercised noting. and trained in war, and armies newlie and hastilie leuied, and compounded of the multitude of a people more wilfull than skilfull; and by so much lesse apt to be drawen vnder discipline, by how much more by their nature and custome they are seldome conformable to anie good order." For there was at the defense of the suburbs one part of the youth of Rome, vnder the ensignes of the people; notwithstanding that manie of the Gebelins & faction of Colonno desired, or at least did not feare the victorie of the imperials. They hoped in regard of their faction, to receiue no harme or offense by the victors : the same being the cause whie they procéeded so coldlie in the defense. Neuerthelesse, for that according to the rules of warre, it is a hard matter to take townes without artilleries, there died of the assailants, partlie by that want, and partlie through their wilfull forwardnesse, about a thousand footmen; who hauing once by their valor made the waie open to enter in, all the defendants fled before them as men whose feare was far aboue anie other sense or passion in them.

In which disorder, some tooke the waie which his fortune and not his wit laid out Rome taken for him : some in the astonishment séeking to flie, who durst no more fight, were and sacked. slaine by the enimie afore he could resolue vpon the waie of his safetie; some either better prepared, or more happilie preserued, found that safetie in running away, which they could not but doubt if they had longer endured the fight : and some with that resolution which their present calamitie would suffer, ran by heapes towards the castell, where in place of rescue they found a feare conformable to their owne : insomuch as all things being reduced to confusion and manifest flight, the suburbs were entierlie aban- doned & left a preie to the victors. And the person of the pope, who expecte with great The pope with deuotion in the palace of Vatican what would be the issue of the assault, hearing that certeine cardi-
nals flie to the the enimies were entred, had also (with the others) his passions of feare & frailtie, and castell of saint
Angelo. in in that timorous contemplation of his owne perill, he fled with certeine cardinalles to the castell.

His feare kept him from being resolute in a perill that was so desperate, neither did he thinke, that with the presence and maiestie of his person, though it was couered with the vaile of the highest dignitie on earth, he was able to put by the danger, which the valor and fidelitie of his souldiers could not defend with their weapons. There he consulted with the cardinalles, whether it were more for his safetie to remaine there, or during the furie of the astonishment, to retire with the light horssemen of his gard into some place of more suertie by the waie of Rome. But he, who was appointed by destinie, to be an example of the calamities that maie thunder vpon popes, and how fraile is the authoritie and maiestie of that sée, being certified by the relation of Berard de Padoa, who was fled from the armie imperiall, that the duke of Burbon was dead, and that the whole armie standing abated in courage for the death of their capteine, desired to come to accord with him. In which matter they sent out men to parlee with the principalles there, he wretchedlie left there all his councelles to go awaie, both he and his capteins remaining no lesse irresolute in the prouisions for defense, than they had beene slow in the expeditions.

So that the daie following, the Spaniards neither séeing order nor councell to defend the quarter beyond Tiber, entred the place without anie resistance. And from thence, not finding anie impediments to stop their victorie, the same euening they entred the citie of Rome by the bridge Xisto; where, except such as reapposed in the confidence of their faction, and certeine cardinalles, who for that they bare a name to embrace the emperours quarrell, beléeued to find more suertie than the others, all the residue of the court and citie (as happeneth in accidents so furious) was conuerted into fléeing and confusion. But the souldiours being within the citie, which they knew wanted nothing to make them right glorious, and well satisfied of all things apperteining to their desires, they began to omit no time to execute the thing they had so dearlie bought. Euerie one ran to pillage with the same vnbridled libertie, which in such cases maketh souldiors both insolent and impious.

There was small care or regard borne either to the name of fréends, factions or fauourers; and much lesse was respected the authoritie of cardinalles and prelats, or dignitie of temples and monasteries; and lastlie, not reserued from violation, the holie reliks brought thither from all parts of the world; yea euen things sacred, and speciallie dedicated, were profaned from their shrines and holie places, and made subiect to the furious wils and discretion of the souldiours. It is not onelie impossible to reaccount, but also to imagine the calamities of that citie raised to a woonderfull greatnesse, and appointed by Gods ordinance to suffer manie fortunes and directions, hauing beene sacked by the Goths within ix. C. and lxxx yeares. It is hard to particulate the greatnesse of the preie, both for the generall wealth and riches which the gréedie hands of the souldiours had made vp in heaps, and for other things more rare and pretious drawne out of the store-houses of merchants and courtiers. But the matter which made the spoile infinit in value, was the qualitie and great number of prisoners redéemed with most rich and huge ransomes.

And to make vp a full tragedie of miserie and infamie, the lanceknights being so much the more insolent and cruell, by how much they bare hatred to the name of the church of Rome, tooke prisoners certeine prelats, whom with great contempt and indignitie they set vpon asses and leane mules, and with their faces reuersed to the crowp of the beasts, they led them thorough the citie of Rome, apparelled with the habits and markes of their dignitie: yea they passed manie of them to cruell torments, who either died in the furie of the action, or at least with the painefulnesse thereof they liued not long after, first yéelding a ransome, and afterwards rendering their liues. The generall slaughter as well at the assault as in the rage of sacking, was

about

about foure thousand bodies. All the palaces of the cardinalles were sacked, except some particulars, who to saue the merchants that were retired thither with their goods, togither with the persons and goods of manie others reserued of the generall calamitie, made promise of great summes of monie. To whom notwithstanding was vsed this iniquitie, that some of them that had compounded with the Spaniards, were afterwards sacked by the lanckeuights, or at least constreined to a second ransome.

The ladie marquesse of Mantua compounded for hir palace for the summe of fiftie thousand duckats, which were paied by the merchants and others retired thither: of which summe the rumor ran, that Ferrand hir sonne had ten thousand for his share. The cardinall of Sienna dedicated in a perpetuall deuotion to the name of the emperor, after he had agreed with the Spaniards, as well for him selfe as for his palace, was afterwards made prisoner by the lanceknights, who made bootie and preie of his palace; and afterwards leading him all naked with buffets and bastanadoes into the borough, he was driuen to redéeme his life out of their hands, with a promise of fiue thousand duckats. The cardinalles Minerua and Ponsero passed vnder almost the like calamitie, who being prisoners to the lanceknights, were rated at a ransome which they paied, after they had béene in a vile spectacle caried in procession thorough the towne of Rome. Compositions with the souldiours to saue certeine places vnsacked.

This furie of souldiours executed in a place of so great riches and profit, could endure no dispensation of anie sort or qualitie of men, seeing the prelats and cardinalles, Spanish and Germans, who made themselues assured that the souldiours of their nation would spare them from oppression and taxation, were taken and passed by the same measure of miserie and calamitie as others did. Right pitifull were the criengs and lamentations of the women of Rome: and no lesse woorthie of compassion, the calamitie of nunnes and virgins professed, whom the souldiours rauished by troopes out of their houses to satisfie their lust, no age, no sex, no dignitie or calling was frée from the violation of souldiours, in whom it was doubtfull whether bare more rule, the humor of crueltie to kill, or the appetite of lust to defloure, or lastlie, the rage of couetousnesse to rob and spoile: yea in the violation of these women might be discerned a confirmation of the iudgements of God hidden from mortall men, for that he suffered to be deliuered vp to the vilenesse of men, barbarous and bloodie, the renowmed chastitie of women professed and virgins. The shamefull and lamentable abuse which the souldiors offered to the female sex.

To this compassion was ioined the infinite clamors of men forced against all law of humanitie, partlie to wrest from them vnreasonable ransomes, and partlie to disclose their goods which they had hidden from the rauine of the souldiors. All holie things, sacraments and reliks of saints, whereof the churches were full, being despoiled of their ornaments, were pulled downe, and laid vpon the earth, suffring no small prophanations, by the vile hands of the lanceknights. And whatsoeuer remained vpon the preies and spoilings of the imperialles, which were things but base and vile, were raked and caried awaie by the pezants and tenants of the lands of the Colonnois, whose insolencie caried them into Rome during the generall furie. Onelie the cardinall of Colonno arriuing the daie after, preserued in his compassion the honor of manie women that happilie were fled for rescue into his house. The rumor went that the valuation and price of this sacke in gold, siluer, and iewels, amounted to more than a millian of duckats, but the matter of ransomes conteined a greater quantitie.] The value of this sacke in gold, siluer, and iewels.

When Rome was thus taken by the imperials, and the pope brought into captiuitie, therewith the king was so incensed against the emperour by the instigation of the cardinall, that he had determined not to spare anie treasure for the popes deliuerance. There rose a secret brute in London that the kings confessor doctor Longland, and diuerse other great clerks had told the king that the marriage betweene him and the ladie Katharine, late wife to his brother prince Arthur was not lawfull: wherevpon the king should sue a diuorse, and marrie the duchesse of Alanson sister to the French The kings marriage brought in question.

king at the towne of Calis this summer: and that the vicount Rochford had brought with him the picture of the said ladie. The king was offended with those tales, and sent for sir Thomas Seimor maior of the citie of London, secretlie charging him to sée that the people ceassed from such talke.

But what so euer the commons talked, it was determined that the cardinall should go ouer into France as high ambassadour for the king, and to take with him twelue score thousand pounds, to be emploied on the warres to be made by the confederats against the emperour, if he would not condescend to such demands as the English ambassadours on the kings behalfe should exhibit vnto him. The third of Iulie this triumphant cardinall passed thorough London with twelue hundred horsse towards the sea side, and comming vnto Canturburie rested there, and there declared to the people what had chanced vnto the pope, and caused the moonks of Christes church to sing their Letanie after this maner: Sancta Maria ora pro Clemente papa, &c. Then he exhorted the people to fast and praie for the popes deliuerance, accordinglie as he had alreadie sent commissions vnto all the bishops within the realme to follow that order, which was to fast three daies in the weeke, and to vse in euerie parish solemne processions. The eleuenth of Iulie the cardinall tooke shipping at Douer, and landed the same daie at Calis, from whense he departed the two and twentith of Iulie, and with him was the bishop of London Cutbert Tunstall, the lord Sands chamberleine to the king, the earle of Derbie, sir Henrie Guilford, sir Thomas Moore, with manie other knights and esquiers, in all to the number of twelue hundred horsse, and of carriages there were foure score wagons, and three score mules and sumpter horsses.

He that is desirous to vnderstand with what honour this triumphant cardinall was receiued in all places as he passed thorough Picardie by order giuen by the French king, maie read thereof at large in the chronicles of maister Edward Hall. At Amiens he was receiued by the French king himselfe, and by his moother with all other chéefe péeres of France. There was nothing forgot that might doo him honour or pleasure. But to the effect of his businesse. After he had shewed his commission, they fell in councell, and in the end grew to a full conclusion of a league to be accorded and established betwixt the kings of England and France: the couenants and articles whereof were drawne and written vp in a faire charter, which was sealed in solemne wise, and deliuered vnto the cardinals by the kings owne hand.

After this, it was agréed, that Odet de Fois, commonlie called monsieur de Lawtrech, should go into Italie with a puissant armie to procure the popes deliuerance, & expell the emperours power out of all the partie of Italie, if he refused such reasonable offers & articles of agréement as were drawen, & should be exhibited to him. In this armie went sir Robert Ierningham, Iohn Carew of Hakam, & 80 other English gentlemen, which were sent by the cardinall from Amiens. When the armie was assembled, the cardinall deliuered the monie which he had brought out of England with him in barrels, with the which the armie was paid two moneths before hand, & the surplusage was deliuered to sir Robert Ierningham, which was called treasuror of the wars. This armie was called in Latine, Exercitus Angliæ & Gallorum regum pro pontifice Romano liberando congregatus, that is to saie, The armie of the kings of England and France, gathered for the deliuerance of the bishop of Rome: and so was it reputed.

In this meane time the English ambassadors, sir Francis Poins and Clarenceaux the herald, were come into Spaine, and there to the emperour in the towne of Vale Doliffe the sixt of Iulie deliuered the kings letters, and further declared their message as they had in commandement. The emperor made to them a courteous answer for that time, and said he would take counsell in the matter, and then shuld they receiue further answer, and in the meane time they might repose them. Within a daie or two after he called to him doctor Lée that was the kings ambassadour legier there with him,

him, & the said sir Francis Poins, and said to them; My lords we haue perceiued the king your maisters demands, which are weightie and of great importance. Wherefore we intend with all spéed to write to the king our vncle, and when we haue receiued answer from him, we shall deliuer you of such things as you require, praieng you in the meane time to take patience.

The emperour protracted time of purpose, bicause he was loth to answer directlie to such grieuous and most irkesome complaints, bicause he gessed by the course of things that the French king would shortlie be constrained to agrée to those conditions of peace, which he at the first had offered. But the French king & the cardinall being togither at Amiens, amongst other things determined there betwixt them in counsell, deuised further what articles of offer should be sent to the emperour, which if he refused, then open defiance to be made vnto him in name of both the kings. The articles were these in effect.

1 First that the French king should paie for his ransome 25000 crownes: one writer calleth it two millians. 2 Also that he should release all the pension that he had in Naples, with all the right of the same. 3 Also that he should neuer claime title to the dutchie of Millane. 4 Also he should release the superioritie of Flanders for euer, and the right which he had to the citie of Torneie. 5 Also he should release all the homages of all persons within those countries. 6 Also to withdraw his armie out of Italie. 7 Also to forsake the aid of the Switzers against the emperour. 8 Also to take no more part with Robert de la March against the emperor. 9 Also neuer to aid the king of Nauarre against him, although he had maried the kings sister. 10 Also neuer to aid the duke of Gelderland, nor to chalenge the same dutchie. 11 Also to aid the emperor with ships and men to his coronation. 12 Also to marie the ladie Elenor quéene of Portugall sister to the emperor. 13 Also that the Dolphine should marie the said quéenes daughter. 14 Also that if the French king had anie children male by the said quéene, then the dutchie of Burgognie to remaine to the said child being male. 15 Also that the French king should be fréend to the emperour & his fréends, and enimie to his enimies. Articles proponed to the emperor being in number fiftéene.

These with manie other articles, which were not openlie knowne, were sent to the bishop of Tarbe, and to the vicount of Thuraine ambassadours with the emperour from the French king. Other articles were also sent to the English ambassadours being in Spaine, as to to mooue the emperour to some reasonable end with the French king: and that the king of England would release vnto him all the summes of monie due to him, as well by the emperour Maximilian his grandfather as himselfe, and take the French king as debtor for the same. If he would not agrée to these offers, then was it accorded, that the French king should marrie the ladie Marie daughter to the king of England, and they both to be enimies to the emperour. When all these things were concluded, the cardinall tooke his leaue of the French king & his moother, and with great rewards returned, comming to Richmond, where the king then laie, the last of September. Articles sent to the English ambassadors in Spaine. The cardinall returneth out of France.

In October, there came ambassadours from the French king into England, the lord Annas de Montmerancie, great maister of the said French kings house, the bishop of Baion chéefe president of Rone, and Monsieur de Humiers accompanied with sixtie gentlemen well appointed. These ambassadours were receiued with all honour that might be deuised. On Alhallowes daie the king comming to the cathedrall church of saint Paule, where the cardinall sang masse, sware before the high altar in the presence of the French ambassadours to kéepe and performe the league. On sundaie the tenth of Nouember, the king being elected knight of the order of S. Michaell, receiued at Gréenewich the said order by the hands of the great maister of France, and monsieur Humiers that were companions of the same order: in like case as the French king the same daie at Paris receiued the order of the garter by the hands of the lord Lisle, Ambassadors from the French king. The king of England receiueth the order of saint Michaell.

　　　　　　　　　　　　　　doctor

doctor Tailor, maister of the rolles, sir Nicholas Carew knight maister of the kings horsses, sir Anthonie Browne knight, and sir Thomas Wriothesleie knight, otherwise called Gartier king of armes, the which were sent thither with the whole habit, collar, and other habillements of the order as apperteined.

After that the French ambassadors had béene highlie feasted, banketed, and interteined, with all honor and pastime conuenient, the great maister and all his companie tooke leaue of the king, and with great rewards returned into France, leauing the bishop of Baion behind them, who abode ambassador legier in England. In this moneth of Nouember, Arthur Bilneie, Geffrei Lome, and one Garret that spake against the popes authoritie, were abiured by the cardinall. ¶ By reason of the great wet that fell in the sowing time of the corne, and in the beginning of the last yeare, now in the beginning of this, corne so failed, that in the citie of London for a while bread was scant, by reason that commissioners appointed to sée order taken in shires about, ordeined that none should be conueied out of one shire into an other.

Which order had like to haue bred disorder, for that euerie countrie and place was not prouided alike, and namelie London, that maketh hir prouision out of other places, felt great inconuenience hereby, till the merchants of the Stiliard, and others out of the Dutch countries, brought such plentie, that it was better cheape in London than in anie other part of England, for the king also reléeued the citizens in time of their néed with a thousand quarters by waie of lone of his own prouision. The scarsitie at the first was more than the dearth. For in the beginning of their want, wheat was onelie at fifteene shillings a quarter, & from thence it rose to twentie shillings, and after to six and twentie shillings eight pence the quarter, till remedie by outward prouision was procured and had. In this meane while the lord Lautrech with his armie was entred into Italie, where how he sped, and what came of that expedition, yée shall find in the histories of France and Italie, and therefore in this place I passe it ouer. Sir Francis Poins knight, in the end of December, returned out of Spaine into England, leauing Clarenceaux behind him to bring further answer.

The emperour at the request of this sir Francis Poins, who made the same in name of his maister the king of England, was contented to release twelue articles, which were reputed most preiudiciall to the French king, onelie to gratifie the king of England: but the cardinall kept the king still in displeasure toward the emperor, for the fauour which he bare to the French king, whose onelie purposes he sought to aduance. The articles which were drawne at Amiens when the cardinall was there, were exhibited to the emperor by the French ambassadors, and bicause he refused the same, word was sent to Clarenceaux king of armes, to make defiance to the emperor. Wherevpon on the wednesdaie the two and twentith of Ianuarie, Guien king of armes to the French king, and Clarenceaux king of armes to the king of England, being in the citie of Burges in Spaine, came to the court of Charles the elect emperour, about nine of the clocke in the morning, and there did request of his maiestie, that it would please him to appoint them an houre of audience.

The lord de Chaoux by ordinance from his maiestie gaue them answer, that it should be about ten of the clocke before noone the same daie. And at the same houre his maiestie came into the great hall of his court accompanied with diuerse prelats, dukes, marquesses, earles, barons, and other great lords and good personages, of diuerse nations of his kingdome and seigniories in great number. The emperour sitting in a chaire prepared according to his dignitie, the two kings of armes of France & England being in the nether end of the hall, holding vpon their left arms each one his coat of armes, did make thrée solemne reuerences accustomed, with knée to the ground. And when they were at the lowest staire before his imperiall maiestie, Clarenceaux king of armes of England, hauing the words in both their names, speake as followeth.

                                                                    " Sir

" Sir, following the three edicts inuiolablie kept and obserued by your predecessors emperours of Rome, kings, princes, and capteins, Guien king of armes of the most christened king; and also Clarenceaux king of armes to the king of England our so
souereigne & naturall lords : we presenting our selues before your sacred maiestie, for to declare certeine things from the said kings our maisters : beseech your maiestie, that hauing regard to the said lawes according to your benignitie and mercie, that it would please you to giue vs sure accesse and good intreating in your countries, lands, and seigniories, attending your answer, with sure conduct to returne vnto the countries, lands, and seigniories of our said souereigne lords." The emperour then bad them saie on whatsoeuer the kings your maisters haue giuen you in charge : your priuileges shall be kept, none shall doo you anie displeasure within my kingdomes or territories. After this, Guien read a writing signed with the hand of the said Guien king of armes.

A copie of the said writing read as followeth.

SIR, the most christened king my souereigne and naturall lord hath commanded me to saie to you, that he hath conceiued a maruellous greefe and displeasure of that, that in place of amitie, which he so much desired to haue with you, the former enmitie in full force still remaineth. By the which he séeth and perceiueth, that the euils and inconueniences long since begun, shall continue and augment, not onelie vnto you, and vnto him, with your vassals and subiects, but also vnto all christendome : and that the forces and youths which the one and the other ought to imploie against the enimies of the faith, shall be spent to the effusion of christian bloud, and in offense vnto God : and that you and he endowed with so manie gratious gifts, shall not inioy the benefits, which it pleased the son of God to leaue to vs, by his testament, which is peace, whereof all goodnesse procéedeth; and in place of the same shall haue war, wherof foloweth all calamities, dangers, inconueniences, pouerties, and miseries.

Héerewith you shall submit your selfe vnto them whome yée may command, and shall hazard the bloud and substance of your subiects in the pursses of strangers. Euerie one as for himselfe ought to haue regard thereto, and for the short time that we haue here to liue, not to go about to depriue himselfe of that tranquillitie, ioy, good regard and pastime, that the princes may haue by peace : and by following the warre, to be in pouertie, heauinesse, and hazard of losse of goods, honours, and liues : and that worst is, after they haue had euill daies in this world, to be in danger of eternall paine in the world to come, thorough them that haue béene the cause thereof, and that would not yéeld vnto reason.

The king my souereigne lord is readie to put himselfe for his part in all deuoir, and more than so, to haue peace and amitie with you : and by this means peace shall be procured throughout all christendome, whereby men might doo God good seruice, in making warre on the Infidels, which will be so thankfull to him, that it will put off the punishment of faults, which haue béene committed héeretofore by reason of the warres, which haue too long indured betwéene you two, and not yet like to ceasse, considering the termes which you hold and séeke to mainteine ; sith on the one part, certeine aduowing themselues on you, haue assailed and taken by force the citie of Rome, which is the place of the holie and apostolike sée, where they haue committed and done all the mischéefe that might be deuised.

The churches and relikes were prophaned, the pope holding saint Peters seat, as vicar of God on earth, taken and put out of his libertie. By means whereof, they that haue committed and executed the said execrable deeds and wickednesse, with their

their authors and fautors, be fallen and run in paines of right; and they that hold them captiues, beare themselues on you; and he that dooth keepe them, hath béene and is of the principall capteins, of whome you haue béene serued in your warres in Italie and other parts. And on the other side, the difference which at this time resteth betweene you and the king my souereigne and naturall lord, is principallie vpon the ransome and recouerie of the princes his sonnes, which you hold for hostages of the same. He hath oftentimes offered, and yet dooth offer to paie to you, and giue to you, not onelie that which may be said to be reasonable, and in such cases accustomed, but also more largelie.

You ought not to stand vpon things which by force and constraint he hath promised, the which iustlie and honesthe he maie not performe nor accomplish: you had a great deale more gained, to haue taken the said ransome which was offered vnto you, than to continue the warre, and to giue occasion of all the euils and inconueniences that dailie happen thereby thorough christendome. You sée the king of England, with whome he hath brotherlie amitie for euer, and also the Venetians, Florentines, and duke of Bar, and other princes and potentats, following and holding the partie of the said christian king, for that they sée he yéeldeth to reason, and by reason you will not thereto incline, the vniuersall peace can not be concluded in christendome. The enimies of the faith gaine countries: all Italie is in armes, bloud and rapine, and the apostolicall sée in trouble: so that if on your part you séeke not remedie, and that things doo thus continue as they haue begun, it is to be feared that God will be angrie.

The herald mooueth the emperor with the king of Englands example, &c.

And for as much (sir) as to the declarations which the aboue said princes haue offered vnto you, and the presentations which the said christian king hath made vnto you, you haue refused to giue eare, thereby to come to some accord with him, and to content your selfe with a ransome more than reasonable: also for that you will not render vnto his good brother, perpetuall alie and confederat, the king of England, that which is his, set the pope at libertie, and leaue Italie in peace and tranquillitie, he hath commanded me to declare, signifie, and notifie vnto you, his great gréefe and displeasure, with his said good brother the king of England, that they will hold and take you for their enimie, declaring all maner of treaties and couenants heretofore passed betweene them and you, in all that concerneth your profit & vtilitie to be nothing; and that for his part he will not obsèrue nor kéepe the same.

The herald commeth to the verie drift of his message.

Naie he hath resolued by all meanes that he may imagine with his good fréends, alies, & confederats, & with all his forces to indamage you, your countries, lands, and vassals by warre, or otherwise, in such sort as he maie deuise vntill the time that you haue restored vnto him his children, with honest meanes and couenants touching his ransome, deliuered the pope, rendered vnto the king of England that you hold of him, and acquited the summe which you owe him, and suffer his alies and confederats to liue in peace, rest, and tranquillitie, and protesteth before God and all the world, that he dooth not wish nor desire the warre, but that it wholie displeaseth him, and is not therefore the cause of the euill that is or maie come thereof, considering that he hath put, and will put himselfe vnto all reason, as he hath offered and signified vnto you and to all other christian princes, and yet dooth.

What the king of Englãd desireth of the emperour in the French kings behalfe.

And of all this he calleth God (who knoweth all things) to witnesse: And for that vnder colour of the publication of the pretended tretie of Madrill made, he being yet prisoner in Spaine, diuerse of your subiects, and of them of the king of Englands, and of his haue carried their merchandizes and other goods into the kingdomes, streicts, and seignories the one of the other, whereby maie insue great damages, if of them no mention should be made in this present declaration and signification: my souereigne lord and the said king of England be contented that libertie be giuen vnto all subiects being in the said kingdomes, countries, streicts, and seigniories, to retire

The king of Englands meaning and the French kings for the returne of the emperours subiects out of their countries, and contrariwise.

and

and depart from thence with all their goods and merchandizes within fortie daies after this intimation made. Prouided that you shall doo the like vnto their subiects in all & euerie their merchandizes. Giuen the eleuenth daie of Nouember 1527, & signed Guien king of armes.

The emperour after the defiance giuen by Guien, spake in this sort : I doo vnderstand that which you haue read from the king your maister, & I doo much maruell why he dooth defie me, for he being my prisoner by right warre, and I hauing his faith by reason he can not doo it. It is vnto me a noueltie to be defied of him, séeing it is six or seuen yeares that he hath warred against me, and yet giuen me no defiance. And sith that by the grace of God I haue defended my selfe from him (as he hath seene, and euerie one else) without that he hath giuen me anie warning, or considering the reason and iustification whereon I doo rest my selfe, for the which I thinke I haue not otherwise deserued towards God : I hope that at this time now you aduertise me of it, being aduertised I shall defend my selfe the better, in such sort that the king your maister shall doo me no hurt : for sith he dooth defie me, I am halfe assured.

The emperors words to Guien the French kings herald.

And touching that which you spake of the pope, none hath béene more sorrowfull than I of that which was doone, and it was without my knowledge or commandement : and that which hath béene doone, was doone by vnrulie people, without obedience to anie of my capteins. And yet I aduertise you, that the pope long since is set at libertie, and yesterdaie I had certeine newes of it. And touching the sonnes of your maister, he knoweth that I haue them for pledges ; and also my lords his ambassadors know well, that the fault hath not lien in me that they haue not béene deliuered. And as for that of the king of England my good brother and vncle, I beléeue if it be so as you doo say, that he is not well informed of things passed : and if he were, yet could I not saie as your writing conteineth, I desire to send him my reasons for to aduertise him of all the truth. And I beleeue when he shall know it, that he will be vnto me as he hath béene.

How the emperor was affectioned for the pope in his captiuitie.

The emperor seemeth loth to incur the K. of Englands displeasure.

I neuer denied the monie which I borowed of him, and I am readie to paie it as by reason & right I am bound : and thanked be God I haue enough to doo it. Neuerthelesse, if he will make warre against me, it will be to my great displeasure, & I can not but defend my selfe. I praie to God that he giue me no more occasion than I thinke I haue giuen vnto him. And to the rest, for that your writing is great, and the paper sheweth it selfe to be gentle ; séeing that they haue written what they would, you shall giue me the writing, whereby more particularlie I maie answer in another paper, wherein shall be nothing but truth. This answer being made by his maiestie with his owne mouth vnto Guien king of armes, the said Guien tooke his cote of armes that he had on his left arme (as before is said) and put it on, and then Clarenceaux king of armes of England said vnto his maiestie, not by writing, but by mouth, as followeth.

The English heralds message deliuered by word of mouth.

SIR, the king my souereigne lord hath commanded me to say vnto you, that séeing the necessitie of peace in the christian religion, as well by reason of the inforcements manie yéers past, begun by the great Turke enimie vnto our faith, which by force of armes hath taken awaie from the christians the citie and Ile of Rhodes, one of the principall bulworks of christendome and in Hungarie the fortresse of Belgrad, and part of the countrie there, as also by heresies and new sects, of late risen in

diuerse

The report of the herald falleth out iustifiable by *Guicciardines* discourse, *lib.* 18.
diuerse places of christendome; and likewise knowing the great warres being kindled in all parts, by meanes of which all christendome is in trouble, confusion, and maruellous diuision, and not long since by your people and ministers and souldiers in your armie, and vnder your capteins the holie citie of Rome hath béene sacked and robbed, the person of our holie father the pope taken prisoner, and kept by your people, the cardinals likewise taken and put to ransome, the churches robbed, bishops, priests, and people of religion put to the sword, and so manie other euils, cruelties, and inhumane facts committed by your people, that the aire and the land are infected therewith.

The king of England fauoured the French king.
And it is verie like, that God is verrie greatlie stirred and prouoked vnto ire. And to speake after the maner of men, if by amendment it be not pacified, innumerable euils and inconueniences shall happen vnto all christendome. And for that the root and increasement of the said warre, proceedeth of the contentions and debates betwéene you, and the most christened king his good brother and perpetuall alie: to make an end of which debates, the king my souereigne lord hath sent his ambassadors and others, vnto the most christened king his good brother, with whome he hath doone so much, that for the loue that he hath borne him, he hath made vnto you so great offers, and so reasonable, that you cannot, nor ought reasonablie to refuse them, as conditions and offers for his ransome excéeding the ransome accustomed of all kings. And if in this, the consideration of peace had not béene, an euill example might thereof grow for other kings and christened princes subiect vnto the like fortune.

The herald vseth an argument drawne from benefits receiued to mooue the emperour.
Of which offers and conditions he hath likewise aduertised you by his ambassadours, praied and besought you for the honour of God, and the wealth of all christendome, for the benefits and pleasures that he hath doone vnto you diuerse waies, and that in time of your great néed, that it would please you to accept the said offers, and make an end of the said warres, that haue too long endured. Likewise as a christened prince bound to the protection of the pope, and sée apostolike, and consequentlie to the deliuerance of his holinesse (whom you cannot, nor ought to kéepe prisoner without great offense) that you would restore his holinesse vnto a full and entier libertie. Also he hath oftentimes shewed by diuerse obligations, and other meanes, how you are indebted vnto him in diuerse great summes of monie, that he hath giuen and lent you in your necessitie, requiring you to make paiment.

Of all which things you haue made no account from time to time, but deferred it, and held in suspense the ambassadours of the king my souereigne, without hauing regard to Gods honour, and the necessitie of all christendome, and the reuerence that ye ought to haue vnto the holie seate and person of our holie father the pope, the vicar of God on earth, or vnto the pleasures that you haue receiued of him, or vnto your The herald of England sheweth the emperour what is the king of Englands present determination if his offers be refused. faith and promise that you so oftentimes haue made. And for this cause the king my said souereigne, by honest reason and iustice constreined, by great and ripe deliberation of his councell, hoping for a finall conclusion, hath caused againe to be presented offers more large and to greater aduantage than the others before, to put you in deuoir, and to auoid and take awaie all occasion to deferre and dissemble to come to reason.

Which offers, and the augmenting of the same haue béene made and made againe, with all demonstrations and honest resons that haue beene possible. And in the end there hath béene made vnto you instance for the deliuerie of our holie father, whom you haue restreined or caused to be restreined, in place of deliuerie, which is very strange, & against the true estate & dutie of a christian prince. So that the king my souereigne, & the most christian king his brother and perpetuall alie, can no longer indure it with their honours and dutie towards God and the church. And séeing you will not condescend to reason, nor accept the said offers being more than reasonable, nor satisfie the king my said souereigne of the debts by you due, as you are bound, he hath concluded with the said most christened king his good brother & perpetuall alie, & other of his confederats,

derats, to doo his endeuour to constreine you by force & might of armes to deliuer our holie father, & likewise the children of France, whom you hold, in paieng you a reasonable ransome, and to satisfie him of that you owe him.

Therefore the king my souereigne lord, as a true and constant prince, willing to kéepe inuiolablie his faith, which he hath promised vnto the said christian prince, and other his alies, and not willing to leaue the person of our said holie father the pope in captiuitie, as also will not the said christian king : they two doo summon you at this time for all, to accept these last offers, for the deliuerance of the said children of France, and for the wealth of an vniuersall peace, & to deliuer the person of our said holie father, & also to paie spéedilie and without anie more delaie, the debts by you due vnto the king my souereigne. And if you refuse these finall offers, and also to de-liuer the person of our said holie father, and paie the said debtes, as a good christian prince and louer of peace is bound to doo; the king my souereigne, and the said chris-tian king his good brother, not without great sorrow and displeasure, doo declare to be your enimies, and so hereafter doo hold and repute you for such one, denouncing vnto you warre by sea and land, and defieng you with all their forces. *[The disposition of the king of England to the pope and the French king.]*

Neuerthelesse, considering that there be diuerse of your subiects, and great quan-titie of their goods in the realmes of England and France, and other lands & lordships of the said princes : likewise there be diuerse of the subiects of the kings of England and France, and of their goods in your kingdomes, countries, lands, and lordships, the which may receiue aswell of the one part as of the other, great and vnrecouerable hurts and damages, if without aduertisements and monition they should be taken and deteined, the kings maiestie my souereigne, and the most christian king of France his good brother be willing that libertie be giuen vnto your subiects being in their king-domes, countries, and lordships, for to retire and depart with all their goods and merchandize, within fourtie daies after this intimation, so that the like libertie and permission be in like sort granted to their subiects. ¶ To this defiance of the king at armes of England the emperours maiestie did answer in these words. *[The defiance in-timated to the emperor by the herald of Eng-land.]* *[Libertie granted to the emperors subiects in Eng-land and France to returne to their owne countries, and the like de-manded on the contrarie parts]*

The emperours answer to the English heralds oration.

I DOO vnderstand that which you haue declared, and I cannot thinke that if the king of England were throughlie aduertised of things as they haue passed, and of the reason to which I haue yéelded, he would not saie that which you haue said, and there-fore mine intention is to aduertise him. As to that which you spake of the pope, I was neuer consenting to his destruction, which was neuer doone by my commande-ment : & I giue you to vnderstand, that he is deliuered, and I am sorie for the harmes that were doone at the time when he was taken, of the which I take my selfe not to be in fault, as I haue told the king at armes of France. And as to the deliuerance of the French kings sons, where means haue béene made for their deliuerance, I haue béene readie to giue eare thereto, and the fault resteth not in me, for that the peace hath not beene concluded.

But now that you tell me that the king your maister will force me to deliuer them, I will answer thereto in other sort than hitherto I haue doone, and I trust to kéepe them in such wise, that by force I shall not néed to deliuer them : for I am not accus-tomed to be forced in things which I doo. As to the debt which the king of England hath lent me, I haue neuer denied it, neither doo I denie it, but am readie to paie it as right requireth, as I haue caused it to be declared vnto him, and I my selfe haue shewed no lesse to his ambassadors, and deliuered my saieng by writing, and I cannot beleeue that for such things (which I refuse not to accomplish) he will make war against me, and if he will so doo it will grieue me, but yet I must defend my selfe : and I *[The emperors modestie in this point notable.]*

praie God that the king your maister giue me not greater occassion to make him war than I haue giuen him. You shall deliuer me in writing, that which you haue said, to the which I will answer by writing particularlie.

This answer made by the emperour to the king of armes Clarenceaux, the said Clarenceaux tooke his coat of armes, which he had lieng on his left arme, (as before is said) and put it vpon him. The emperour herewith commanded him to deliuer by writing into the hands of the lord of Buclans all that he had vttered by word of mouth, as is aboue expressed. Which Clarenceaux promised to doo, & so he did afterwards, signed with his owne hand, word for word. Clarenceaux hauing thus doone his dutie, incontinentlie withdrew: but before his departure, the lord of Buclans said to him, and also to Guien, these words insuing. Behold here this writing in my hand, conteining the articles of the composition betwéene the emperour and the pope.

¶ That the pope should be no partie against the emperour, neither in the affaires of Millane, nor in the kingdome of Naples. That he should accord vnto the emperour the croisade in Spaine, and a tenth of the reuenues ecclesiastike through all his dominions. That to assure the obseruation of these things, Ostia should remaine in the hands of the emperour, and Ciuita Vecchia which Andrea Dore had left to him before. That he should assigne ouer to him Ciuita Castellana, a towne which had refused to receiue the imperials, Mario Perusquo procuror of the fiske being entred within the rocke by secret commission from the pope, notwithstanding he made semblance of the contrarie. That he should also deliuer ouer to him the rocke of Furlie, and to put into his hands for ostages Hyppolito and Alexander his nephues, and till they were come from Parma the emperour to be possessed of the cardinals Pisani, Triuulco, and Gaddi, whome they led to the realme of Naples.

Furthermore, that he should make present paiment to the lanceknights of three score thousand ducates, and to the Spaniards thirtie & fiue thousand. That in so dooing they should let him come out at libertie with all the cardinals, and they to go out of Rome and out of the castell, alwaies interpreting to libertie when soeuer they should be conueied in safetie to Orbietto, Spoletto, or Perousa. That within fiftéene daies after his going out of Rome he should paie the like quantitie of monie to the lanceknights, and afterwards the residue within thrée moneths to the Spaniards & lanceknights iointlie, according to their shares and portions. Which residue togither with the summes paid amounted to more than thrée hundred and fiftie thousand ducats.]

This is the true copie (said the lord of Buclans) of the capitulation, made touching the deliuerance of the pope, and how he is deliuered, and departed from castell saint Angelo, the tenth of December last past: put it in your relation. The said king of armes answered; We will so doo: and so for that time they parted. ¶ Here, bicause mention is made of the popes deliuerance out of prison, it shall not be amisse to set downe the maner thereof as it is reported by Guicciardine. All things hauing their orderlie expedition, & the resolution set downe, that the tenth of December the Spaniards should accompanie him into a place of suertie, he fearing some variation either for the ill mind which he knew don Hugo bare to him, or for anie other accident that might happen, the night before he stale secretlie out of the castell in the closing of the euening, disguised in the attire of a merchant. Lewis de Gonsaguo who was in the paie of the emperour, taried for him in the meadowes with a strong companie of harquebuziers, and with that gard did accompanie him to Montfalcon, where dismissing almost all his bands of footmen, he was led by the same Lewis euen to Orbietto, into which citie he entred by night without the companie of anie one cardinall. An example worthie of consideration, and perhaps neuer happened since the church was great, that a pope should in that sort fall from so great a puissance and reuerence,

reuerence, his eies to behold the losse and sacke of Rome, his person to be turned ouer into captiuitie, and his whole estate reduced to the disposing of an other, and within few moneths after, to be restored & established in his former greatnesse. So great towards princes christian is the authoritie of the pope, and the respect which mortall men doo beare to him.

At the same instant that the heralds were at the emperors court, the emperour called before him the said Guien king at armes of France, and said to him as followeth. Sith it is reason that you enioy your priuileges, you ought also to doo your dutie; and therefore I praie you declare to your maister, yea euen to his owne person that which I shall tell you, which is this: that since the treatie of Madrill, contrarie to the same, diuerse of my subiects haue béene taken going about their businesses, and other also going to serue me in Italie, which haue béene deteined prisoners, euill intreated, and by force thrust into the gallies: and bicause I haue of his subiects the which I might likewise take, yée shall aduertise him, that if he deliuer vnto me mine, I will deliuer his; if not, as he shall intreat mine, I will intreat his; and that he send me answer hereof within fortie daies: if not, I will take the refusall for an answer. *(margin: The emperors words to the French herald.)*

The king of armes Guien asked if his maiestie ment this concerning the merchants? Wherevnto the emperor answered: This is beside that which is conteined in your writing, touching the merchants, to which point (said he) I will answer by writing. And herewith Guien making thrée obeisances, said; Sir I will gladlie doo it. Then said the emperor, Tell the king your maister further, that I beléeue that he hath not béene aduertised of that which I told to his ambassador in Granado, which toucheth him néere. For I told him in such a case so noble a prince, that if he had vnderstood the same, he would haue made me an answer. He shall do well to know it of his ambassador. For by that he shall vnderstand, that I haue kept better faith to him in that I haue promised at Madrill than he to me, and I praie you so tell him, and faile not hereof. Guien answered, Without doubt sir I will doo it: and so making his obeisance he departed. *(margin: This the emperor inferreth to iustifie his owne dealings by waie of comparison.)*

The emperor appointed Iohn le Alemant the baron of Buclans to see that no displeasure nor euill speach were vsed to the said kings of armes, but that they should be well vsed: which was doone to their good contentation. After this, the seauen and twentith of Ianuarie, the said kings of armes came to the said lord of Buclans, who by the emperours appointment deliuered an answer vnto either of them in writing, accordinglie as the emperor had promised, the copies whereof are set foorth at large in the annales of Aquitaine, and for bréefenesse here omitted. To conclude, the French king tooke such displeasure with the emperours answers made vnto his king of armes Guien, whereby he was charged to doo otherwise than by his faith giuen he ought to haue doone, that the eight and twentith daie of March being in the citie of Paris, accompanied with a great number of the princes of his bloud, cardinals and other prelats and nobles of his realme, and also the ambassadors of diuerse princes and potentates, he called before him Nicholas Perenot lord of Granuelle, vnto whom he said in effect as followeth. *(margin: The heralds receiue the emperors answer in writing.)* *(margin: The seauen & twentith saith* Guic. pag. *1091.)*

The French kings oration before an honourable assemblie at Paris.

MY lord ambassadors, it hath gréeued me, and dooth gréeue me, that I haue béene constreined to handle you not so courteouslie and gratiouslie as for the good and honourable behauiour, which you haue shewed in dooing your dutie being here with me, you haue deserued at my hands, sith I must néeds saie, yée haue acquit your selfe in euerie behalfe, as well to the honor of your maister, as good contentation of each man else, so that I am assured the fault resteth not in you, whie things haue nōt come *(margin: This speach of the kings dooth wholie concerne the emperor and sauoureth of displeasure.)*

to

to better end and purpose than they haue doone, for the good zeale and affection, which I haue euer prooued in you to the aduancement of peace and quieting of things, wherein I doubt not but you haue doone your duetie to the full.

But being informed what your maister the elect emperor, against all right and law, as well diuine as humane, had commanded to be doone vnto my ambassadors, and likewise to the other of the league remaining with him, for the furtherance of things toward a peace, and contrarie to all good customs, which hither to haue béene obserued betwixt princes, not onelie christians, but also infidels, me thought I could not otherwise doo, for the behoofe of mine owne ambassadours, arrested and against reason kept in ward, but to doo the same to you, although I had no mind to vse you euill, for the reasons aboue said, for the which, and for the dutie you haue shewed in dooing that apperteined, I assure you my lord ambassador, that beside that I doubt not but your maister will recompense you for the same, yée may be assured that where particularlie in anie thing I may pleasure you, I will doo it with as good a will as you can require me.

What induced the French king to vse some discourtesie against the emperors ambassadors.

And to make answer to that which your maister by word of mouth hath said vnto Guien and Clarenceaux kings of armes of the king my good brother and perpetuall and best alie, and of me vpon the intimation of the warre which hath béene made by vs, consisting in eight points, I will that each one vnderstand it. First, as to the which he saith he maruelleth that he hauing me a prisoner by iust warre, and hauing also my faith, I should defie him, and that in reason I neither may nor ought to doo it; I answer thereto, that if I were his prisoner here, and that he had my faith, he had spoken true : but I know not that the emperor hath euer at anie time had my faith, that may in anie wise auaile him. For first in what warre so euer I haue béene, I know not that I haue either séene him or encountred with him.

The king answereth the emperours words vttered to Guien his herald.

When I was prisoner, garded with foure or fiue hundred harquebuzers, sicke in my bed, and in danger of death, it was an easie matter to constreine me, but not verie honorable to him that should doo it : and after that I returned into France, I know not anie that hath had power to compell me to it : and to doo it willinglie without constraint, it is a thing which I waie more, than so lightlie to bind my selfe thereto. And bicause I will not that my honor come in disputation, although I know well that euerie man of warre knoweth sufficientlie, that a prisoner garded is not bound to anie faith, nor can bind himselfe thereto in anie thing : I doo neuerthelesse send to your master this writing signed with mine owne hand, the which my lord ambassadour I praie you read, and afterwards promise me to deliuer it vnto your master, and not to anie other. And herewith the king caused it to be deliuered to the said ambassador by master Iohn Robertet, one of the secretaries of the estate, and of his chamber.

The French K. saith that constraint and necessitie made him tractable to the emperor.

The ambassador tooke the writing in his hand, and after excused himselfe to the king, saieng : That as to him, by the letter which his master & souereigne lord had written vnto him now lastlie, his commission was alreadie expired, and that he had no further commandement nor instructions from his maiestie, but to take leaue of the king with as much spéed as he might, and to returne home. Which he most humblie besought him to permit him to doo, without further charge or commission, although he knew that he was at his commandement, and that he might at his pleasure constreine him, as seemed to him good. Herevnto the king answered ; My lord ambassador, sith you will not take vpon you to read this writing, I will cause it to be read in this companie, to the end that euerie one may vnderstand and know that I am cleered in that, whereof against trueth he goeth about to accuse me.

The emperors ambassador refuseth to read the French kings letters sent to his souereigne.

Beside that, if you afterwards will not beare it, & deliuer it to him, I will send one of my heralds here present to go in companie with you : for whom you shall procure a good & auailable safe conduct, that he maie passe vnto your master, protesting & demanding,

The French king deliuereth his mind with a corage, as vtter enimie to the emperour.

demanding, that an act maie be registred before this companie, that if he will not it should come to his knowledge, that I am discharged, in that I doo my best to cause him to vnderstand it accordinglie as I ought to doo, and in such sort as he can not pretend cause of ignorance. ¶ After the king had ended these words, he called to him the said Robertet, and commanded him to reade the said writing with a lowd voice, which was doone word for word.

The copie of the said writing directed to the emperour.

WE Francis, by the grace of God, king of France, lord of Genes, &c. To you Charles, by the same grace, chosen emperour of Rome, and king of Spaine. We doo you to wit, that being aduertised, that in all the answers that you haue made to our ambassadors and heraulds, sent to you for the establishing of peace, in excusing your selfe, without all reason you haue accused vs, saieng, that we haue plight you our faith, and that thereupon (besides our promise) we departed out of your hands and power. In defense of our honour, which hereby might be burthened too much against all truth, we thought good to send you this writing; by which we giue you to vnderstand, that notwithstanding that no man being in ward is bound to keepe faith, and that the same might be a sufficient excuse for vs: yet for the satisfieng of all men, and our said honor (which we mind to keepe, and will keepe, if it please God, vnto the death) that if ye haue charged, or will charge vs, not onelie with our said faith, and deliuerance, but that euer we did anie thing that became not a gentleman that had respect to his honor; that ye lie falslie in your throat: and as oft as ye saie it, ye lie: and we determine to defend our honor to the vttermost drop of our bloud. Wherefore, seeing ye haue charged vs against all truth, write no more to vs hereafter: but appoint vs the field, and we will bring you the weapons. Protesting, that if after this declaration ye write into anie place, or vse anie words against our honor, that the shame of the delaie of the combat shall light on you, seeing that the offering of combat is the end of all writing. Made at our good towne and citie of Paris, the eight and twentith daie of March. In the yere of our Lord, one thousand fiue hundred twentie and eight, before Easter. Thus signed. Francis.

The French kings allegations in defense of his honor charged with vntruth.

The French king giueth the emperor the lie: see Guic. pag. 1091.

After that Robertet had read this writing there in presence of the emperours ambassadors, the king made futher replie vnto the points conteined in the emperours answers to the defiance: and withall to conclude, told the said ambassador, that his master the emperor had constreined him by such message as he had sent to him, to make the answer in truth, which he had made: and further willed him to deliuer vnto the emperour the writing which he had signed with his hand, and to saie to him, that he tooke him for so honorable a prince, that considering the matter wherewith he charged him, and the answer that he made, he would not faile but to answer him like a gentleman, and not by writing like an aduocate. For if he otherwise doo (said the king) I will answer his chancellor by an aduocate, and a man of his estate, and a more honest man than he.

This Robertet was one of the secretaries to the estate.

Shortlie after, the emperors ambassadors returned home into Spaine in safetie, and well intreted. And vpō their returne, the ambassadors of France were set at libertie, and deliuered beyond Fonterabie, & so came safelie home into France. Then a French herald, appointed to accompanie the ambassadour Grandeuill, brought the writing of the combat vnto the emperor, bicause Grandeuill refused to medle with it. To the which the emperor fiue moneths after, or thereabouts, sent an answer by one of his heralds; who being arriued at Paris, meant vpon the sudden to present his letters vnto the French king. But the king getting intelligence thereof, the tenth of September, sitting

The emperor answereth the French kings letters.

sitting within his great hall of his palace at Paris aforesaid, before the table of marble in a roiall seat, addressed and set vp for him sixtéene steps in height, appointed to giue audience to the said herald.

On his right hand sate in chaires the king of Nauarre, the duke of Alanson and Berrie, the earle of Foix and Arminacke. And on the same side sate also vpon a bench, the duke of Vandosme a peere of France, lieutenant generall, and gouernor of Picardie, don Hercules de Est, eldest sonne to the duke of Ferrar, duke of Chartres and Montarges, who latelie before had maried the ladie Rener, a daughter of France, the duke of Albanie regent and gouernor of Scotland, the duke of Longueille, great chamberleine of France. And néere to them vpon another bench sate the presidents and councellors of the court of parlement; and behind them manie gentlemen, doctors, and learned men. On the left hand were set in chaires prepared for them, the cardinall Saluarie the popes legat, the cardinall of Burbon, and duke of Laon, a peere of France, the cardinall of Sens chancellor of France, the cardinall of Lorrain, the archbishop of Narbon, the ambassadors of the kings of England and Scotland, of the segniorie of Venice, of Millan, of the Cantons, of the Suisses, and of Florence.

On an other bench sate the bishop of Transiluania, ambassador for the king of Hungarie, the bishop and duke of Langres, one of the peeres of France, the bishop & earle of Noion, an other of the peeres of France, th'archbishop of Lion, primat of all France, the archbishop of Burges primate of Aquitaine, the archbishops of Aux and Rouen, the bishops of Paris, Meaux, Lizeux, Mascon, Limoges, Vabres,

Conserans and Terbe. And behind them sate the masters of the requests, and the councellors of the great councell. On either side the kings seate stood the earle of Beaumout great master and marshall of France, the lord de Brion admerall of France lieutenant generall, and gouernor of Burgognie. And behind the same seat were manie knights of the order, that is to wit, the earle of Lauall, lieutenant generall and gouernor of Britaine, the lord of Montmerancie, the lord Daubignie capteine of an hundred lances, and of the Scotish gard, the earle of Brienne, Lignie, and Roussie, the lord of Fleuranges marshall of France, the lord of Ruffoie, the lord of Genoilliac great esquier and master of the artillerie of France, Lois monsieur de Elenes, the lord of Humiers, and the earle of Carpie.

Behind them was the earle of Estamps prouost of Paris, and with him manie gentlemen of the kings chamber: among the which was the earle of Tancaruill, the lord of Guien, the son of the earle of Roussie, the son of the lord of Fleuranges, the lord de la Rochpot, the lord Donartie great master of the waters and forrests, the lord of Lude, the lord of Ianlie, the lord de Villebon, bailie of Rouen, the baron of Chasteau Morant, the lord de la Loue, the vicount de la Motheaugroing, and the lord of Vertes. And beside these, the masters and officers of the houshold & gentlemen waiters, with the more part of the two hundred gentlemen or pensioners, as we terme them. At the entrie into the said throne or tribunall seat, were the capteins of the gards, and the prouost of the houshold. And before the king knéeled the vshers of the chamber vpon the one knée: and at the foot of the step that went vp to the kings seate were the prouosts of the merchants and escheuins of the towne of Paris. Beneath in the hall (the gates whereof were still open) there was an infinite number of people of all nations: and in presence of them all the king made this declaration.

The cause wherefore I haue made this assemblie, is, for that the emperour elect hath sent to me an herald of armes, who (as I coniecture, and as the same herald hath said, and as his safe conduct importeth) hath brought me letters patents and autentike, concerning the suertie of the field for the combat that should be betwixt the said elected emperour and me. And forasmuch as the said herald, vnder colour to bring the

the suertie of the field, may vse certeine fictions, dissimulations, or hypocrisies, to shift off the matter, whereas I desire expedition, and to haue it dispatched out of hand; so that by the same an end of the warres, which haue so long continued, may be had, to the ease and comfort of all christendome, to auoid the effusion of bloud, and other mischéefes which come thereof: I haue wished it knowne to all christendome, to the end that euerie one may vnderstand the truth, from whence procéedeth the mischéefe and the long continuance thereof.

I haue also caused this assemblie to be made, to shew that I haue not without great cause enterprised such an act; for the right is on my side: and if I should otherwise haue doone, mine honor had béene greatlie blemished. A thing which my lords that are of my bloud, and other my subiects would haue taken in euill part. And knowing the cause of the combat, and my right, they will beare with it, as good and loiall subiects ought to doo, trusting by Gods helpe to procéed in such sort therein, that it shall plainelie appéere if the right be on my side or not: and how, against truth, I haue béene accused for a breaker of my faith, which I would be loth to doo, nor at anie time haue meant so to doo. The kings my predecessors and ancestors, whose pictures are ingrauen and set héere in order within this hall, which in their daies haue successiuelie atchiued glorious acts, and greatlie augmented the realme of France, would thinke me vnworthie, and not capable to be their successor, if against mine honor I should suffer my selfe to be charged with such a note by the emperour, and should not defend my person and honor in the manner and forme accustomed.

Further cause whie the said assemblie was procured.

And herewith he declared the whole case as it stood. First, how being taken at Pauia by fortune of war, he neuer gaue his faith to anie of his enimies, & consenting to be led into Spaine, caused his owne gallies to be made readie to conueie him thither, where at his arriuall, he was committed to ward within the castell of Madrill, garded with a great number of harqubeuziers & others. Which vncourteous dealing found in the emperor, so much gréeued him, that he fell sicke, and laie in danger of death. Wherevpon the emperour comming to visit him after his recourie of health, an accord was made betwixt the deputies of the emperour and the ambassadours of the ladie his moother then regent of France: which accord was so vnreasonable, that no prince being in libertie would haue consented thereto, nor for his deliuerance haue promised so great a ransome. Which tretie yet they constrained him (as he said) to sweare to performe, being prisoner, against the protestation which he diuerse times had made, yea as yet being sicke, and in danger of recidiuation; and so consequentlie of death.

The French king in presence of all his estates auereth that he neuer gaue his faith to anie of his enimies, ergo not to the emperour.

After this, he was conueied foorth on his iournie homewards, still garded & not set at libertie. And it was told him, that after he came into France, it was conuenient that he should giue his faith, for that it was knowne well enough, that what he did or promised in Spaine, it nothing auailed. And further he remembred not that the emperour had told him at anie time, that if he performed not the contents of the treatie, he would hold him for a breaker of his faith, & though he had, he was not in his libertie to make anie answer. Two things therefore said he, in this case are to be considered. One, that the tretie was violentlie wroong out from them that could not bind his person, and the which (as to the residue) had béene accomplished by his moother, deliuering his sonnes in hostage. The other thing was his pretended faith, on which they can make no ground, sith he was not set at libertie. And herevnto he shewed manie reasons, to prooue that his enimies could not pretend in right that they had his faith.

The king proseccuteth the discourtesie of the emperour in his declaration.

Further he said, that in matter of combat there was the assailant, which ought to giue suertie of the field, and the defendant the weapons. Herewith also he caused a letter to be read, which the emperour had written to maister Iohn de Caluimont president of Burdeaux, the said kings ambassadour in the court of the said emperour: the tenor of which letter imported, that the emperour put the said ambassadour in remembrance

The field, that is, a place where they may safelie come to fight in listes before indifferent iudges.

Guic. pag. 1091. membrance of spéech which he had vttered to the said ambassadour in Granado, repeating the same in substance as followeth. That the king his maister had doone naughtilie in not keeping his faith which he had of him, acording to the treatie of Madrill: and if the king would saie the contrarie, I will (said the emperour) mainteine the quarrell with my bodie against his. And these be the same words that I spake to the king your maister in Madrill, that I would hold him for a lewd and naughtie man, if he brake the faith which I had of him, &c.

Then after the said letter had béene read, he caused also his answer made by way of a cartell to be read, the tenor whereof ye haue heard before. That doone, he continued his tale, in declaring what order he had obserued to procure the emperour to the combat, without all shifting delaies: so as if the herald now come from the emperour would vse anie talke, other than to deliuer him an authentike writing for suertie of the field, and not obserue the contents of his safe conduct, he meant not to giue him audience. And herevpon was the herald called to come in, and declare his message. Who apparelled in his cote of armes, made his appéerance before the king there sitting, accompanied (as ye haue heard.) Vnto whome the king said.

The French kings talke and communication to the emperors ambassador vttered with indignation. Herald, dooest thou bring the suertie of the field, such one as thy maister, being the assailant, ought to deliuer vnto the defendant, being such a personage as I am? The herald herevnto said: Sir, maie it please you to giue me licence to doo mine office? Then said the king; Giue me the pattent of the field, and saie what thou wilt. The herald beginning his tale, The sacred. Tush (said the king) shew me the pattent of the field, for I hold thy master for so noble a prince, that he hath not sent thée without the suertie of the field, sith I haue demanded it; and thou knowest that thy safe conduct conteineth no lesse but that thou shouldest bring it. The herald answered, that he trusted he had brought that which might content his maiestie.

The king replied & said: Herald, giue me the pattent of the field, giue it me: and if it be sufficient, I will receiue it, and after saie what thou wilt. The herald said he had in commandement not to deliuer it, except he might declare that which he had first to saie. The king said: Thy maister can not giue lawes to vs in France. To conclude he told the herald, that he peraduenture might speake things that his maister would not auouch, and that he had not to deale with him, but with his maister. The The herald requireth libertie to depart. herald then required that he might haue licence to depart: which the king granted. And withall the king commanded that it might be registred what had passed in this behalfe, for a testimonie that the fault rested not in him in that he receiued not the pattent. The herald likewise for his discharge, required a copie in writing of that which had passed, and the same was granted.

Thus far haue I ouerpassed the common bounds of my purpose, in speaking so largelie of this matter of combat, bicause of the rarenesse thereof, chancing betwixt two so mightie princes, although it came not to the effect of triall. And now to re- 1528 turne to that which followed further vpon the defiance, denounced to the emperor by The emperor defied by the kings of England and France. the two kings of armes, Guien and Clarenceaux. Ye shall vnderstand, that the lords and nobilitie, to the number of seuen hundred in whose presence it was giuen, tooke it so offensiuelie, that drawing foorth their swords, they sware that the same should be reuenged: for otherwise they protested, that the infamie would redound to them and their heires for euer. Herewith the warre was proclaimed through all Spaine with baners displaied, in which were painted a red sword, with a burning cresset against the French king and his partakers, but not mentioning the king of England by expresse name. But it was recited in the proclamation, that the king of England had menaced and defied the emperour in the French kings quarell.

English merchants staied in Spaine. Then were the English merchants in Spaine attached, and their goods put in safetie, till it might be knowne how the emperours subiects were ordered in England. Then likewise were all the ships of the emperours subiects here arrested: and in semblable

maner

maner all the Englishmen and their goods and ships were arrested by the ladie regent in the low countries. The common people in England much lamented, that warre should arise betwéene the emperour and the king of England, speciallie bicause the emperours dominions had holpen and reléeued them with graine in time of their necessitie & want. But cheefelie this matter touched merchants which hanted the emperors dominions. Yet at length were those of the low countries set at libertie, and their goods to them deliuered, in fauour of intercourse of merchandize. But forsomuch as the Spaniards were still deteined, the ladie regent also deteined the ships and goods of the English merchants though she set their persons at libertie.

By this meanes the trade of merchandize was in maner fore-let here in England, and namelie the clothes laie on their hands, whereby the commonwealth suffered great decaie, and great numbers of spinners, carders, tuckers, and such other that liued by clothworking, remained idle, to their great impouerishment. And as this warre was displeasant to the Englishmen, so was it as much or more displeasant to the townes and people of the low countries, & in especiall to the townes of Antuerpe & Barrow, where the marts are kept. So that at length there came ambassadours from the ladie regent, the which associating themselues with don Hugo de Mendoza ambassadour for the emperour, came to the king at Richmond the twentie and ninth of March, and there mooued their sute so effectuallie, that an abstinence of warre was granted, till time that a further communication might be had: and vpon this point letters were sent into Spaine, France, and Flanders, and so this matter continued vntill answers were brought from thense againe. *[margin: An abstinence of war granted vpon sute made to the king of England.]*

[margin: The incōmoditie rising of lacke of intercourse for traficke.]

The emperours ambassadours intreated not so earnestlie to mooue the king to haue peace with their maister, but the French ambassadours sollicited the king as earnestlie to enter into the warre against him, and suerlie they had the cardinall on their side. But yet the king wiselie considering with other of his councell, what damage should insue therby vnto his subiects, and speciallie to the merchants and clothiers, would not consent so easilie to the purpose of the Frenchmen, though he had twentie thousand pounds sterling out of France, of yearelie pension, to continue fréend & alie to the French king. But he protested euer that he would sée the relme of France defended to his power, and studie no lesse to haue a peace concluded, which might be as honourable to the French king as to himselfe, and beneficiall vnto their people, of whome by warres, might be made both slaughter and bloudshed, which are companions vnseparable of battell; as the poet well saith:

Hinc breuiter diræ mortis aperta via est.

On the two and twentith of Februarie the king created at Windsor sir Piers Butler of Ireland, erle of Osserie. ¶ Also a Dutch craire of Armew chased a French craire vp the Thames from Margate to the Tower wharfe, and there as they fought sir Edmund Walsingham lieutenant of the Tower perceiuing them, called his men togither, and entering the ships tooke both the capteins. The kings councell tooke vp the matter betwixt them, for the Fleming chalenged the Frenchman as a lawfull prise. An abstinence of the warre was taken in the beginning of this yeare betwixt Flanders, and the countries of Picardie on this side the riuer of Some to begin the first of Maie & indure till the last of Februarie. By means of this truce all the Englishmen might lawfullie passe into the low countries, but not into Spaine: which sore gréeued the merchants that haunted those parties. It was further agréed, that if no generall peace could be had, during the time of this truce: then all the merchants should haue respit two moneths after to passe into their owne countries with their wares and merchandizes in safetie. *[margin: Creation of the earle of Osserie. Sir Edmund Walsingham. A truce and the benefit insuing from the same.]*

In the end of Maie began in the citie of London the disease called the sweating sickenesse, which afterwards infected all places of the realme, and slue manie within fiue or six houres after they sickened. This sickenesse, for the maner of the taking *[margin: The sweating sickenesse, whereof died both courtiers and others,]* of the patients, was an occasion of remembring that great sweat which raged in the reigne of this kings grandfather; and happilie men caused the same remedie then vsed to be reuiued. By reason of this sickenesse, the tearme was adiourned, and the circuit of the assises also. There died diuerse in the court of this sicknesse, as sir Francis Poins, which had béene ambassadour in Spaine, and diuerse others. The king for a space remooued almost euerie daie till he came to Tintinghangar, a place of the abbat of saint Albons, and there he with the quéene, and a small companie about them, remained till the sickenesse was past. In this great mortalitie died sir William Compton knight, and William Carew esquier; which were of the kings priuié chamber.

Sir William Compton.

Abr. Fl. ex I.S. pag. 959. A prisoner brake fro̅ the sessions house. *Register of Greie friers.*

¶ A prisoner brake from the sessions hall at Newgate when the sessions was doone, which prisoner was brought downe out of Newgate in a basket, he séemed so weake: but now in the end of the sessions he brake thorough the people vnto the Greie friers church, and there was kept six or seauen daies yer the shiriffes could speake with him, and then bicause he would not abiure and aske a crowner, with violence they tooke him thense, and cast him againe in prison, but the law serued not to hang him.]

Doctor Longland bishop of Lincolne.

Ye heaue heard how the people talked a little before the cardinals going ouer into France the last yeare, that the king was told by doctor Longland bishop of Lincolne and others, that his mariage with queene Katharine could not be good nor lawfull. The truth is, that whether this doubt was first mooued by the cardinall, or by the said Longland, being the kings confessor, the king was not onelie brought in doubt, whether it was a lawfull marriage or no; but also determined to haue the case examined, cléered, and adiudged by learning, law, and sufficient authoritie. The

Why the cardinall was suspected to be against the marriage.

cardinall verelie was put in most blame for this scruple now cast into the kings conscience, for the hate he bare to the emperor, bicause he would not grant to him the archbishoprike of Toledo, for the which he was a suter. And therefore he did not onlie procure the king of England to ioine in fréendship with the French king, but also sought a diuorse betwixt the king and the quéene, that the king might haue had in marriage the duchesse of Alanson, sister vnto the French king: and (as some haue

Polydor.

thought) he trauelled in that matter with the French king at Amiens, but the duchesse would not giue eare therevnto.

Edw. Hall.

But howsoeuer it came about, that the king was thus troubled in conscience concerning his mariage, this followed, that like a wise & sage prince, to haue the doubt

The king is desirous to be resolued by the opinions of the learned touching his marriage.

cléerelie remooued, he called togither the best learned of the realme, which were of seuerall opinions. Wherfore he thought to know the truth by indifferent iudges, least peraduenture the Spaniards, and other also in fauour of the quéene would saie, that his owne subiects were not indifferent iudges in this behalfe. And therefore he wrote his cause to Rome, and also sent to all the vniuersities in Italie and France, and to the great clearkes of all christendome, to know their opinions, and desired the court of Rome to send into his realme a legat, which should be indifferent, and of a great and profound iudgement, to heare the cause debated. At whose request the whole

Cardinall Campeius sent into England.

consistorie of the college of Rome sent thither Laurence Campeius, a préest cardinall, a man of great wit and experience, which was sent hither before in the tenth yeare of this king, as yée haue heard, and with him was ioined in commission the cardinall of Yorke and legat of England.

The matter touching the kings marriage debated.

This cardinall came to London in October, and did intimate both to the king & queene the cause of his comming: which being knowne, great talke was had thereof. The archbishop of Canturburie sent for the famous doctors of both the vniuersities to Lambeth, and there were euerie daie disputations and communings of this matter. And bicause the king meant nothing but vprightlie therein, and knew well that the quéene was somewhat wedded to hir owne opinion, and wished that she should do nothing without counsell, he bad hir choose the best clearks of his realme to be of hir counsell, and licenced them to doo the best on hir part that they could, according to

the

the truth. Then she elected William Warham archbishop of Canturburie, and Ni- The quéene chooseth law-yers for hir part. cholas Weast bishop of Elie, doctors of the laws; and Iohn Fisher bishop of Ro-chester, and Henrie Standish bishop of saint Assaph, doctors of diuinitie, and manie other doctors and well learned men, which for suertie like men of great learning de-fended hir cause, as farre as learning might mainteine and hold it vp.

This yeare was sir Iames Spenser maior of London, in whose time the watch in *Polydor.* London on Midsummer night was laid downe. About this time the king receiued into Doctor Stephā Gardner. 1529 Doctor Pace falleth out of his wits. fauour doctor Stephan Gardiner, whose seruice he vsed in matters of great secrecie and weight, admitting him in the roome of doctor Pace, the which being continuallie abroad in ambassages, and the same oftentimes not much necessarie, by the cardinals appointment, at length he tooke such gréefe therewith, that he fell out of his right wits. The place where the cardinals should sit to heare the cause of matrimonie An. Reg. 21. *Edw. Hall.* betwixt the king and the quéene, was ordeined to be at the Blacke friers in London, where in the great hall was preparation made of seats, tables, and other furniture, according to such a solemne session and roiall apparance. The court was platted in *Abr. Fl. ex I. S. pag.* 959. The maner of the session, euerie per-onage of acount in his place. tables and benches in manner of a consistorie, one seat raised higher for the iudges to sit in. Then as it were in the midst of the said iudges aloft aboue them three degrées high, was a cloth of estate hanged, with a chaire roiall vnder the same, wherein sat the king; and besides him, some distance from him sat the quéene, and vnder the iudges feet sat the scribes and other officers: the chéefe scribe was doctor Stéeuens, and the caller of the court was one Cooke of Winchester.

Then before the king and the iudges within the court sat the archbishop of Cantur-burie Warham, and all the other bishops. Then stood at both ends within, the counsellors learned in the spirituall laws, as well the kings as the quéenes. The doctors of law for the king (whose names yée haue heard before) had their conuenient roomes. Thus was the court furnished. The iudges commanded silence whilest their commission was read, both to the court and to the people assembled. That doone the The king and quéene called into the court. scribes commanded the crier to call the king by the name of king Henrie of England, come into the court, &c. With that the king answered and said, Héere. Then called he the queene by the name of Katharine quéene of England come into the court, &c. Who made no answer, but rose out of hir chaire.

And bicause shée could not come the king directlie, for the distance seuered betweene them, shée went about by the court, and came to the king, kneeling downe at his féet, to whome she said in effect as followeth: Sir (quoth she) I desire you to doo me Queene Katha-rines lamentable and pi hie speech in pre-sence of the court. iustice and right, and take some pitie vpon me, for I am a poore woman, and a stranger, borne out of your dominion, hauing héere no indifferent counsell, & lesse assurance of fréendship. Alas sir, what haue I offended you, or what occasion of displeasure haue I shewed you, intending thus to put me from you after this sort? I take God to my iudge, I haue beene to you a true & humble wife, euer conformable to your will and pleasure, that neuer contraried or gainesaid any thing thereof, and being alwaies contented with all things wherein you had any delight, whether little or much, without grudge or displeasure, I loued for your sake all them whome you loued, whether they were my fréends or enimies.

I haue béene your wife these twentie yeares and more, & you haue had by me diuerse children. If there be anie iust cause that you can alleage against me, either of dishonestie, or matter lawfull to put me from you; I am content to depart to my shame and rebuke: and if there be none, then I praie you to let me haue iustice at your hand. The king your father was in his time of excellent wit, and the king of The quéene iustifieth the mariage. Spaine my father Ferdinando was reckoned one of the wisest princes that reigned in Spaine manie yeares before. It is not to be doubted, but that they had gathered as wise counsellors vnto them of euerie realme, as to their wisedoms they thought méet, who déemed the marriage betwéene you and me good and lawfull, &c. Wherefore, I

4 X 2   humblie

humblie desire you to spare me, vntill I may know what counsell my freends in Spaine will aduertise me to take, and if you will not, then your pleasure be fulfilled. ¶ With that she arose vp, making a lowe curtesie to the king, and departed from thence.

The king being aduertised that shée was readie to go out of the house, commanded the crier to call hir againe, who called hir by these words; Katharine quéene of England, come into the court. With that (quoth maister Griffith) madame, you be called againe. On on (quosh she) it maketh no matter, I will not tarrie, go on your waies. And thus she departed, without anie further answer at that time, or anie other, and neuer would appeare after in anie court. The king perceiuing she was departed, said these words in effect: For as much (quoth he) as the quéene is gone, I will in hir absence declare to you all, that shée hath béene to me as true, as obedient, and as conformable a wife, as I would wish or desire. She hath all the vertuous qualities that ought to be in a woman of hir dignitie, or in anie other of a baser estate, she is also surelie a noble woman borne, hir conditions will well declare the same.

With that quoth Wolseie the cardinall: Sir, I most humblie require your highnesse, to declare before all this audience, whether I haue béene the chéefe and first moouer of this matter vnto your maiestie or no, for I am greatlie suspected heerein. My lord cardinall (quoth the king) I can well excuse you in this matter, marrie (quoth he) you haue béene rather against me in the tempting héereof, than a setter forward or moouer of the same. The speciall cause that mooued me vnto this matter, was a certeine scrupulositie that pricked my conscience, vpon certeine words spoken at a time when it was, by the bishop of Baion the French ambassador, who had béene hither sent, vpon the debating of a marriage to be concluded betweene our daughter the ladie Marie, and the duke of Orleance, second son to the king of France.

Vpon the resolution and determination whereof, he desired respit to aduertise the king his maister thereof, whether our daughter Marie should be legitimate in respect of this my marriage with this woman, being sometimes my brothers wife. Which words once conceiued within the secret bottome of my conscience, ingéndered such a scrupulous doubt, that my conscience was incontinentlie accombred, vexed, and disquieted; whereby I thought my selfe to be greatlie in danger of Gods indignation. Which appeared to be (as me seemed) the rather, for that he sent vs no issue male: and all such issues male as my said wife had by me, died incontinent after they came into the world, so that I doubted the great displeasure of God in that behalfe.

Thus my conscience being tossed in the waues of a scrupulous mind, and partlie in despaire to haue anie other issue than I had alredie by this ladie now my wife, it behooued me further to consider the state of this realme, and the danger it stood in for lacke of a prince to succéed me, I thought it good in release of the weightie burthen of my weake conscience, & also the quiet estate of this worthie relme, to attempt the law therin, whether I may lawfullie take another wife more lawfullie, by whom God may send me more issue, in case this my first copulation was not good, without anie carnall concupiscence, and not for anie displeasure or misliking of the queenes person and age, with whome I would be as well contented to continue, if our mariage may stand with the laws of God, as with anie woman aliue.

In this point consisteth all this doubt that we go about now to trie, by the learning wisedome, and iudgement of you our prelats and pastors of all this our realme and dominions now héere assembled for that purpose; to whose conscience & learning I haue committed the charge and iudgement: according to the which I will (God willing) be right well content to submit my selfe, and for my part obeie the same. Wherein, after that I perceiued my conscience so doubtfull, I mooued it in confession to you my lord of Lincolne then ghostlie father. And for so much as then you your selfe were in

some

some doubt, you mooued me to aske the counsell of all these my lords : wherevpon I mooued you my lord of Canturburie, first to haue your licence, in as much as you were metropolitane, to put this matter in question, and so I did of all you my lords : to which you granted vnder your seales, héere to be shewed. That is truth, quoth the archbishop of Canturburie. After that the king rose vp, and the court was adiorned vntill another daie.

Héere is to be noted, that the quéene in presence of the whole court most gréeuouslie *The quéene* accused the cardinall of vntruth, deceit, wickednesse, & malice, which had sowne *accuseth cardi-* *nall Wolsie.* dissention betwixt hir and the king hir husband; and therefore openlie protested, that she did vtterlie abhorre, refuse, and forsake such a iudge, as was not onelie a most malicious enimie to hir, but also a manifest aduersarie to all right and iustice, and therewith did *She appeleth to* she appeale vnto the pope, committing hir whole cause to be iudged of him. But *the pope.* notwithstanding this appeale, the legats sat weekelie, and euerie daie were arguments brought in on both parts, and proofes alleaged for the vnderstanding of the case, and still they assaied if they could by anie meanes procure the quéene to call backe hir appeale, which she vtterlie refused to doo. The king would gladlie haue had an end *The king mis-* in the matter, but when the legats draue time, and determined vpon no certeine point, *of seeking de-* he conceiued a suspicion, that this was doone of purpose, that their dooings might *laies.* draw to none effect or conclusion.

The next court daie, the cardinals set againe, at which time the councell on both sides were there readie to answer. The kings councell alleaged the matrimonie not to *The present* be lawfull at the beginning, bicause of the carnall copulation had betwéene prince *mariage whie* Arthur and the quéene. This matter was verie vehementlie touched on that side, and *full.* to prooue it, they alleaged manie reasons and similitudes of truth : and being answered negatiuelie againe on the other side, it séemed that all their former allegations were doubtfull to be tried, and that no man knew the truth. And thus this court passed from sessions to sessions, and daie to daie, till at certeine of their sessions the king sent the two cardinals to the queene (who was then in Bridewell) to persuade with hir by their wisdoms, and to aduise hir to surrender the whole matter into the kings hands by hir owne consent & will, which should be much better to hir honour, than to stand to the triall of law, and thereby to be condemned, which should séeme much to hir dishonour.

The cardinals being in the queenes chamber of presence, the gentleman vsher *Quéene Katha-* aduertised the quéene that the cardinals were come to speake with hir. With that she *rine and the car-* *dinals haue com-* rose vp, & with a skeine of white thred about hir necke, came into hir chamber of *munication in hir* presence, where the cardinals were attending. At whose comming, quoth she, What *priuie chamber.* is your plesure with me ? If it please your grace (quoth cardinall Wolseie) to go into your priuie chamber, we will shew you the cause of our comming. My lord (quoth she) if yée haue anie thing to saie, speake it openlie before all these folke, for I feare nothing that yee can saie against me, but that I would all the world should heare and sée it, and therefore speake your mind. Then began the cardinall to speake to hir in Latine. Naie good my lord (quoth she) speake to me in English.

Forsooth (quoth the cardinall) good madame, if it please you, we come both to know *The quéene* your mind how you are disposed to doo in this matter betwéene the king and you, and *refuseth to make* *sudden answer* also to declare secretlie our opinions and counsell vnto you : which we doo onelie for *to so weightie a* verie zeale and obedience we beare vnto your grace. My lord (quoth she) I thanke *matter as the* *diuorse.* you for your good will, but to make you answer in your request I cannot so suddenlie, for I was set among my maids at worke, thinking full little of anie such matter, wherein there néedeth a longer deliberation, and a better head than mine to make answer, for I néed counsell in this case which toucheth me so nécre, & for anie counsell or fréendship that I can find in England, they are not for my profit. What thinke you my lords, will anie Englishman counsell me, or be fréend to me against the K.

pleasure

pleasure that is his subiect? Naie forsooth. And as for my counsell in whom I will put my trust, they be not here, they be in Spaine in my owne countrie.

And my lords, I am a poore woman, lacking wit, to answer to anie such noble persons of wisedome as you be, in so weightie a matter, therefore I praie you be good to me poore woman, destitute of freends here in a forren region, and your counsell also I will be glad to heare. And therewith she tooke the cardinall by the hand, and led him into hir priuie chamber with the other cardinall, where they tarried a season talking with the quéene. Which communication ended, they departed to the king, making to him relation of hir talke. Thus this case went forward from court to court, till it came to iudgement, so that euerie man expected that iudgment would be giuen the next day. At which daie the king came thither, and set him downe in a chaire within a doore, in the end of the gallerie (which opened directlie against the iudgement seat) to heare the iudgement giuen, at which time all their proceedings were red in Latine.

The king & quéenes matter commeth to iudgement.

That doone, the kings councell at the barre called for iudgement. With that (quoth cardinall Campeius) I will not giue iudgement till I haue made relation to the pope of all our procéedings, whose counsell and commandement in this case I will obserue: the case is verie doubtfull, and also the partie defendant will make no answer here, but dooth rather appeale from vs, supposing that we be not indifferent. Wherfore I will adiourne this court for this time, according to the order of the court of Rome. And with that the court was dissolued, and no more doone. This protracting of the conclusion of the matter, king Henrie tooke verie displeasantlie. Then cardinall Campeius tooke his leaue of the king and nobilitie, and returned towards Rome.]

Cardinall Campeius refuseth to giue iudgement.

Whilest these things were thus in hand, the cardinall of Yorke was aduised that the king had set his affection vpon a yoong gentlewoman named Anne, the daughter of sir Thomas Bullen vicount Rochford, which did wait vpon the quéene. This was a great griefe vnto the cardinall, as he that perceiued aforehand, that the king would marie the said gentlewoman, if the diuorse tooke place. Wherfore he began with all diligence to disappoint that match, which by reason of the misliking that he had to the woman, he iudged ought to be auoided more than present death. While the matter stood in this state, and that the cause of the queene was to be heard and iudged at Rome, by reason of the appeale which by hir was put in: the cardinall required the pope by letters and secret messengers, that in anie wise he should defer the iudgement of the diuorse, till he might frame the kings mind to his purpose.

The kings affection and good will to the ladie Anne Bullen.

The secret working and dissimulation of cardinall Woolseie.

Howbeit he went about nothing so secretlie, but that the same came to the kings knowledge, who tooke so high displeasure with such his cloked dissimulation, that he determined to abase his degrée, sith as an vnthankefull person he forgot himselfe and his dutie towards him that had so highlie aduanced him to all honor and dignitie. When the nobles of the realme perceiued the cardinall to be in displeasure, they began to accuse him of such offenses as they knew might be proued against him, and thereof they made a booke conteining certeine articles, to which diuerse of the kings councell set their hands. The king vnderstanding more plainlie by those articles, the great pride, presumption, and couetousnesse of the cardinall, was sore mooued against him; but yet kept his purpose secret for a while. Shortlie after, a parlement was called to begin at Westminster the third of Nouember next insuing.

The king cōceiueth displeasure against the cardinall.

Edw. Hall.

Articles exhibited against the cardinall.

In the meane time the king, being informed that all those things that the cardinall had doone by his power legantine within this realme, were in the case of the premunire and prouision, caused his atturneie Christopher Hales to sue out a writ of premunire against him, in the which he licenced him to make his atturneie. ¶ And further the seuentéenth of Nouember the king sent the two dukes of Norffolke and Suffolke to the cardinals place at Westminster, who (went as they were commanded) and finding

The cardinall sued in a premunire.

Abr. Fl. ex I. S. pag. 966, 967.

finding the cardinall there, they declared that the kings pleasure was that he should surrender vp the great seale into their hands, and to depart simplie vnto Asher, which was an house situat nigh vnto Hampton court, belonging to the bishoprike of Winchester. The cardinall demanded of them their commission that gaue them such authoritie, who answered againe, that they were sufficient commissioners, and had authoritie to doo no lesse by the kings mouth. Notwithstanding, he would in no wise agrée in that behalfe, without further knowledge of their authoritie, saieng; that the great seale was deliuered him by the kings person, to inioy the ministration thereof, with the roome of the chancellor for the terme of his life, whereof for his suertie he had the kings letters patents. The cardinall is loth to part from the great seale.

This matter was greatlie debated betwéene them with manie great words, in so much that the dukes were faine to depart againe without their purpose, and rode to Windsore to the king, and made report accordinglie; but the next daie they returned againe, bringing with them the kings letters. Then the cardinall deliuered vnto them the great seale, and was content to depart simplie, taking with him nothing but onelie certeine prouision for his house: and after long talke betwéene him and the dukes, they departed with the great seale of England, and brought the same to the king. Then the cardinall called all his officers before him, and tooke accompt of them for all such stuffe, whereof they had charge. And in his gallerie were set diuerse tables, wherevpon laie a great number of goodlie rich stuffe, as whole pééces of silke of all colours, veluet, sattin, damaske, taffata, grograine, and other things. Also, there laie a thousand peeces of fine Holland cloth. The cardinall discharged of the great seale.
The cardinall calleth all his officers to accounts.

There was laid on euerie table, bookes reporting the contents of the same, and so was there inuentaries of all things in order against the kings comming. He caused to be hanged the walles of the gallerie on the one side with cloth of gold, cloth of tissue, cloth of siluer, and rich cloth of bodken of diuerse colours. On the other side were hanged the richest sute of coapes of his owne prouision made for his colleges of of Oxford and Ipswich, that euer were séene in England. Then had he two chambers adioining to the gallerie, the one most commonlie called the gilt chamber, and the other the councell chamber, wherein were set vp two broad and long tables vpon trestles, whervpon was set such a number of plate of all sorts, as was almost incredible.

In the gilt chamber were set out vpon the table nothing but gilt plate, and vpon a cupbord and in a window was set no plate but gold, verie rich: and in the councell chamber was all white and parcell gilt plate, and vnder the table in baskets was all old broken siluer plate, and bookes set by them purporting euerie kind of plate, and euerie parcell, with the contents of the ounces thereof. Thus were all things prepared, giuing charge of all the said stuffe, with all other remaining in euerie office, to be deliuered to the king, to make answer to their charge: for the order was such, that euerie officer was charged with the receipt of the stuffe belonging to his office by indenture. To sir William Gascoigne, being his treasuror, he gaue the charge of the deliuerie of the said goods, and therwithall, with his traine of gentlemen and yeomen, he tooke his barge at the priuie staires, and so went by water vnto Putneie, where when he was arriued, he tooke his mule, & euerie man tooke their horsses, and rode streight to Asher, where he and his familie continued the space of three or foure weekes, without either beds, shéets, table cloths, or dishes to eat their meat in, or wherwith to buie anie: the cardinall was forced to borow of the bishop of Carleill, plate and dishes, &c. The cardinall of Yorke goeth to Asher, and hath his plentie turned into penurie.

After this, in the kings bench his matter for the premunire, being called vpon, two atturneis, which he had authorised by his warrant signed with his owne hand, confessed the action, and so had iudgement to forfeit all his lands, tenements, goods, and cattels, and to be out of the kings protection: but the king of his clemencie sent Iohn Scute, and Edmund Iennie.
The cardinall condemned in a premunire.

to

to him a sufficient protection, and left to him the bishoprikes of Yorke and Winches-

ter, with plate and stuffe conuenient for his degrée. The bishoprike of Duresme was giuen to doctor Tunstall bishop of London, and the abbeie of saint Albons to the prior of Norwich. Also the bishoprike of London being now void, was bestowed on doctor Stokesleie, then ambassadour to the vniuersities beyond the sea for the kings mariage.

The ladie Margaret duches of Sauoy aunt to the emperour, and the ladie Lois duchesse of Angolesme mother to the French king, met at Cambreie in the beginning of the moneth of Iune, to treat of a peace, where were present doctor Tunstall bishop of London, and sir Thomas Moore then chancellor of the duchie of Lancaster, commissioners for the king of England. At length through diligence of the said ladies a peace was concluded betwixt the emperour, the pope, and the kings of England and France. All these met there in the beginning of Iulie, accompanied with diuerse great princes and councellors, on euerie part. And after long debating on both sides, there was a good conclusion taken the fift daie of August. In the which

was concluded, that the treatie of Madrill should stand in his full strength and vertue, sauing the third and fourth, and the eleuenth and fourtéenth articles, which touch the duchie of Burgognie and other lordships.

1 Item, it was agréed, that the French king should haue his children againe, paieng to the emperour two millians of crownes of gold, whereof hée should paie at the deliuering of the children, twelue hundred thousand crownes.

2 Item, that the French king should acquit the emperour against the king of England, of fourescore and ten thousand crowns, which the emperour owght to the king of England, and the king of England to deliuer all such bonds and gages as he had of the emperours.

3 Item, as touching the remnant, which was fiue hundred and ten thousand crownes, the emperour should haue fiue and twentie thousand crownes rent yearelie, for which he should haue the lands of the duchesse of Vandosme, lieng in Flanders and Brabant bound.

4 Item, that Flanders and diuerse other countries, should not be hold in chiefe, nor haue resort to the crowne of France.

5 Item, that the realme of Naples, the duchie of Millan, and the countie of Ast, should for euer remaine to the emperour.

6 Item, that the French king should withdraw all such souldiors as he had, out of Italie.

7 Item, that the ladie Eleanor should be brought into France, with the French kings children, and in time conuenient should be maried to the French king.

8 Item, that the French king should aid the emperour with twelue gallies to go into Italie.

9 Item, that all prisoners on both parties should be acquited.

10 Item, that the French king should not aid Robert de la March, against the bishop of Luke.

11 Item, that all the goods mooueable and vnmoouable, of Charles duke of Burbon, should be restored to his heires, they paieng to lord Henrie, marquesse of Dapenete, and earle of Nassaw, lord chamberleine to the emperour, ten thousand ducats, which he lent to the said duke of Burbon.

12 Item, that Iohn earle of Panthieure, should be remitted to all such goods, as were earle Rene his fathers.

13 Item, the lord Laurence de Gorowood, great master to the emperour, should be restored to the lordships of Chalmont, & Monteualle, which he bought of the duke of Burbon, or to haue his monie againe.

14 Item

14 Item, Philip de Chalon prince of Orenge and viceroy of Naples, to be restored to all his lands in Burgognie.

15 Item, that the duches of Vandosme, and Lois earle of Nauers, should haue all such right and actions, as they should haue had before the warre began.

In the emperours countries, when all things were written, sealed, and finished, there was a solemne masse soong in the cathedrall church of Cambreie, the two ladies ambassadors of the king of England, sitting in great estate: and after masse the peace was proclamed betwéene the thrée princes, and Te Deum soong, and monie cast to the people, and great fires made through the citie. The same night the French king came into Cambreie, well and noblie accompanied, and saluted the ladies, and to them made diuerse bankets: and then all persons departed into their countrie, glad of this concord. This peace was called the womens peace, for bicause that notwith- The womens peace. standing this conclusion, yet neither the emperour trusted the French king, nor he neither trusted nor loued him, and their subiects were in the same case. This procla- mation was proclamed solemnelie by heralds with trumpets in the citie of London, which proclamation much reioised the English merchants, repairing into Flanders, Brabant, Zealand, and other the emperors dominions. For during the wars, mer- chants were euill handled on both parties, which caused them to be desirous of peace.] On the foure & twentith of Nouember, was sir Thomas Moore made lord chancellor, Sir Thomas & the next day led to the chancerie by the dukes of Norffolke and Suffolke, and there Moore lord sworne. chancellor.

At the daie appointed the parlement began, on which daie the king came by water *Edw. Hall. in H.* to his place of Bridewell, and there he and his nobles put on their robes of parlement, *8. fol.* clxxxvij. and so came to the Blacke friers church, where a masse of the Holie-ghost was so- An oration made lemnelie soong by the kings chappell: and after the masse, the king with all the lords in the audience of the parlement of parlement and commons, which were summoned to appeare at that daie, came into by sir Thomas the parlement chamber, where the king sate in his throne or seat roiall: and sir Tho- Moore. mas Moore his chancellor, standing on the right hand of the king behind the barre, made an eloquent oration.

In this oration he declared, that like as a good shéepheard, which not alonelie keep- eth and attendeth well his shéepe, but also foreseeth and prouideth for all things which either may be hurtfull or noisome to his flocke, or maie preserue and defend the same against all perils that may chance to come: so the king which was the shéep- heard, ruler and gouernour of his realme, vigilantlie foreséeing things to come, consi- dered how diuers laws before this time were made, now by long continuance of time and mutation of things, verie insufficient and vnperfect: and also by the fraile con- dition of man, diuerse new enormities were sproong amongest the people, for the which no law was yet made to reforme the same. Which was the verie cause whie at that time the king had summoned his high court of parlement. And hée resembled the king to a shéepheard or heardman for this cause: for if a prince be compared to his riches, he his but a rich man; if a prince be compared to his honour, he is but an ho- nourable man: but compare him to the multitude of his people, and the number of his Wherein the flocke ,then he is a ruler, a gouernor of might & puissance, so that his people maketh person of the him a prince, as of the multitude of shéepe commeth the name of a shéepheard. reputed a ruler. And as you sée that amongst a great sort of shepe some be rotten & faultie, which the good shéepheard sendeth from the good sheepe: so the great wedder which is of late fallen (as you all know) so craftilie, so scabbedlie, yea and so vntrulie iugled with the king, that all men must néedes ghesse and thinke, that he thought in himselfe that he had no wit to perceiue his craftie dooing; or else that he presumed that the king would not sée nor know his fraudulent iugling and attempts. But he was deceiued: for his graces sight was so quicke and penetrable, that hée saw him, yea and saw through him, both within and without, so that all things to him was open, and according to his desert he hath had a gentle correction.

Which small punishment the king will not to be an example to other offendors, but clearelie declareth, that whosoeuer hereafter shall make like attempt, or commit like offense, shall not escape with like punishment. And bicause you of the common house be a grosse multitude, and can not speake all at one time : therefore the kings pleasure is, that you shall resort to the nether house, & there amongst your selues, according to the old and ancient custome, to choose an able person to be your common mouth and speaker : and after your election so made, to aduertise his grace thereof, which will declare to you his pleasure, what day he will haue him present in this place. After this

doone, the commons resorted to the nether house, and they chose for their speaker Thomas Audleie esquier, and attournie of the duchie of Lancaster : and the same daie was the parlement adiorned to Westminster.

On the sixt daie of the same moneth, the king came to the parlement chamber, and all the lords in their robes. And there the commons of the nether house pre-

sented their speaker, which there made an eloquent oration, which consisted in two points. The first point was, that he much praised the king for his equitie and iustice, mixed with mercie and pitie, so that none offense was forgotten and left vnpunished, nor in the punishment the extremitie nor the rigor of the law cruellie extended : which should be a cause to bridle all men from doing like offenses, & also a comfort to offendors to confesse their crime and offense, and an occasion of amendment and reconciliation. The second point was, that he disabled himselfe, both for lacke of wit, learning, and discretion to so high an office, beseeching the king to cause his commons to resort eftsoones to their common house, and there to choose an other speaker for that parlement.

To this the king (by the mouth of the lord chancellor) answered ; that where he disabled himselfe in wit and learning, his owne ornate oration there made testified the contrarie. And as touching his discretion and other qualities, the king himselfe had well knowne him and his doings since he was in his seruice, to be both wise and discreet : and so for an able man he accepted him, and for the speaker he him ad-

mitted. When the commons were assembled in the nether house, they began to commune of their griefes, wherewith the spiritualtie had before time greeuouslie oppressed them, both contrarie to the law of the realme, and contrarie to all right : and in speciallie they were sore mooued with six great causes.

1 The first for the excessiue fines, which the ordinaries tooke for probats of testaments, insomuch that sir Henrie Guilford knight of the garter, and controllor of the kings house, declared in the open parlement on his fidelitie, that he and others being executors to sir William Compton knight, paied for the probat of his will to the cardinall and the archbishop of Canturburie a thousand markes sterling. After this declaration were shewed so manie extortions doone by ordinaries for probats of willes, that it were too much to rehearse.

2 The second was the great polling and extreame exaction, which the spirituall men vsed in taking of corps, presents, or mortuaries. For the children of the defunct should all die for hunger, and go a begging, rather than they would of charitie giue to them the seelie cow which the dead man owght, if he had but onelie one ; such was the charitie then.

3 The third cause was, that priests being surueiors, stewards and officers to bishops, abbats, and other spirituall heads, had and occupied farmes, granges, and grasing in euerie countrie, so that the poore husbandmen could haue nothing but of them ; and yet for that they should paie deerlie.

4 The fourth cause was, that abbats, priors, and spirituall men kept tan-houses,
and

and bought and sold wooll, cloth, and all maner of merchandize, as other temporall merchants did.

5 The fift cause was, bicause that spirituall persons promoted to great benefices, and hauing their liuings of their flocke, were lieng in the court in lords houses, and tooke all of the parishioners, and nothing spent on them at all: so that for lacke of residence both the poore of the parish lacked refreshing, and vniuersallie all the parishioners lacked preaching and true instruction of Gods word, to the great perill of their soules.

6 The sixt cause was, to sée one priest little learned, to haue ten or twelue benefices, & to be resident vpon none; and to know manie well learned scholars in the vniuersities which were able to preach & teach to haue neither benefice nor exhibition.

These things before this time might in no wise be touched, nor yet talked of by anie man, except he would be made an heretike, or lése all that he had. For the bishops were chancellors, and had all the rule about the king, so that no man durst once presume to attempt anie thing contrarie to their profit or commoditie. But now, when God had illuminated the eies of the king, and that their subtile dooings were once espied; then men began charitablie to desire a reformation: and so at this parlement men began to shew their grudges. Wherevpon the burgesses of the parlement appointed such as were learned in the law, being of the common house, to draw one bill of the probats of testaments, another for mortuaries, and the third for non residence, pluralities, and taking of farmes by spirituall men. The learned men tooke much paines, and first set foorth the bill of mortuaries, which passed the common house, and was sent vp to the lords. To this bill the spirituall lords made a faire face; saieng; that suerlie priests and curats tooke more than they should, and therefore it were well done to take some reasonable order: thus they spake, bicause it touched them little. *The bishops sticke hard against these billes.*

But within two daies after was sent sent vp the bill concerning probats of testaments; at the which the archbishop of Canturburie in especiall, and all other bishops in generall both frowned and grunted, for that touched their profit. Insomuch as doctor Iohn Fisher bishop of Rochester said openlie in the parlement chamber these words: My lords, you sée dailie what billes come hither from the common house, and all is to the destruction of the church. For Gods sake sée what a realme the kingdome of Boheme was; and when the church went downe, then fell the glorie of the kingdome: now with the commons is nothing but Downe with the church; and all this me séemeth is for lacke of faith onlie. When these words were reported to the commons of the nether house, that the bishop should saie, that all their dooings were for lacke of faith, they tooke the matter gréeuouslie, for they imagined that the bishop estéemed them as heretikes, and so by his slanderous words would haue persuaded the temporall lords, to haue restrained their consent from the said two billes, which they before had passed, as you haue heard before. *The saieng of Iohn Fisher bishop of Rochester.*

Wherefore the commons, after long debate, determined to send the speaker of the parlement to the kings highnesse, with a gréeuous complaint against the bishop of Rochester. And so on a daie, when the king was at leasure, Thomas Audleie speaker for the commons, and thirtie of the cheefe of the common house, came to the kings presence in his palace at Westminster, which before was called Yorke place; and there verie eloquentlie declared what a dishonor to the king and the realme it was, to saie, that they which were elected for the wisest men of all the shires, cities, and boroughs, within the realme of England, should be declared, in so noble and open presence, to lacke faith: which was equiualent to saie, that they were infidels, and no christians, as ill as Turkes, or Saracens, so that what paine or studie soeuer they tooke for the common wealth, or what acts or lawes soeuer they made or stablished, should be taken as lawes made by Painims and heathen people, and not woorthie to be kept by *A complaint made to the king against the bishop of Rochester.*

christian

christian men. Wherefore he most humbly besought the kings highnesse to call the said bishop before him, and to cause him to speake more discréetlie of such a number as was in the common house.

The king was not well contented with the saieng of the bishop, yet he gentlie answered the speaker, that he would send for the bishop, and send them word what answer he made, and so they departed againe. After this the king sent for the arch-bishop of Canturburie and six other bishops, and for the bishop of Rochester also, and there declared to him the grudge of the commons; to the which the bishop answered, that he meant the dooings of the Bohemians was for lacke of faith, and not the dooings of them that were in the common house. Which saieng was con-

The bishops excuse to the kings maiestie.

firmed by the bishops being present, who had him in great reputation: and so by that onelie saieng the king accepted his excuse, and thereof sent word to the commons by sir William Fitz Williams knight, treasuror of his houshold; which blind

Hard hold be-twéene the lords spirituall and temporall about the probats of willes and mor-tuaries.

excuse pleased the commons nothing at all. After diuerse assemblies were kept be-twéene certeine of the lords, and certeine of the commons, for the billes of probats of testaments, and the mortuaries; the temporaltie laid to the spiritualtie their owne lawes and constitutions; and the spiritualtie sore defended them by prescription & vsage, to whom this answer was made by a gentleman of Greies inne : The vsage hath euer béene of théeues to rob on Shooters hill, ergo is it lawfull?

With this answer the spirituall men were sore offended, because their dooings were called robberies. But the temporall men stood still by their saiengs, insomuch that the said gentleman said to the archbishop of Canturburie, that both the exaction of probats of testaments, and the taking of mortuaries, as they were vsed, were open robberie and theft. After long disputation, the temporall lords began to leane to the

The loane of monie released to the king, which he borow-ed in anno reg. 15.

commons : but for all that the billes remained vnconcluded for a while. In the meane season, there was a bill assented to by the lords, and sent downe to the commons : the effect whereof was, that the whole realme by the said act did release to the king, all such summes of monie as he had borrowed of them at the loane, in the fiftéenth yeare of his reigne (as you haue heard before.) This bill was sore argued in the com-mon house, but the most part of the commons were the kings seruants, and the other were so laboured to by other, that the bill was assented vnto.

When this release of the loane was knowen to the commons of the realme, Lord so they grudged & spake ill of the whole parlement. For almost euerie man counted it his debt, and reckoned suerlie of the paiment of the same. And therefore some made their willes of the same, and some other did set it ouer to other for debt, and so manie men had losse by it, which caused them sore to murmur, but there was no remedie. The king like a good and discréet prince, séeing that his commons in the parlement house had released the loane, intending somewhat to requite the same, grant-ed to them a generall pardon of all offenses; certeine great offenses and debts onelie excepted : also he aided them for the redresse of their griefes against the spiritualtie, and caused two new billes to be made indifferentlie, both for the probats of testaments

The matter of testaments and mortuaries mo-derated by the king.

and mortuaries; which billes were so reasonable, that the spirituall lords assented to them all, though they were sore against there mindes, & in especiall the probats of testaments sore displeased the bishops, and the mortuaries sore displeased the parsons and vicars.

After these acts thus agréed, the commons made another act for pluralities of bene-fices, non residence, bieng selling and taking of farmes by spirituall persons. Which act so displeased the spiritualtie, that the priests railed on the commons of the com-mon house, and called them heretikes and schismatikes, for the which diuerse priests were punished. This act was sore debated aboue in the parlement chamber, and the

All against the cleargie both head and taile.

lords spirituall would in no wise consent. Wherefore the king perceiuing the grudge of his commons, caused eight lords and eight of his commons to méet in the Star

chamber

chamber at an after noone, and there was sore debating of the cause, in so much that the temporall lords of the vpper house, which were there, tooke part with the commons, against the spirituall lords; and by force of reason caused them to assent to the bill with a little qualifieng. Which bill the next daie was wholie agreed to in the lords house, to the great reioising of the laie people, and to the great displeasure of the spirituall persons. During this parlement was brought downe to the commons the booke of articles, which the lords had put to the king against the cardinall, the chiefe wherof where these.

1 First, that he without the kings assent had procured to be a legat, by reason where- of he tooke awaie the right of all bishops and spirituall persons. Articles exhibited against the cardinall of Yorke.

2 Item, in all writings which he wrote to Rome, or anie other forren prince, he wrote Ego & rex meus, I and my king: as who would saie, that the king were his seruant.

3 Item, that he hath slandered the church of England in the court of Rome. For his suggestion to be legat was to reforme the church of England, which (as he wrote) was Facta in reprobum sensum.

4 Item, he without the kings assent carried the kings great seale with him into Flanders, when he was sent ambassador to the emperour.

5 Item, he without the kings assent, sent a commission to sir Gregorie de Cassado, knight, to conclude a league betwéene the king & the duke of Ferrar, without the kings knowledge.

6 Item, that he hauing the French pockes presumed to come and breath on the king.

7 Item, that he caused the cardinals hat to be put on the kings coine.

8 Item, that he would not suffer the kings clerke of the market to sit at saint Albons.

9 Item, that he had sent innumerable substance to Rome, for the obteining of his dignities, to the great impouerishment of the realme.

These articles, with manie more, read in the common house, and signed with the cardinals hand, was confessed by him. And also there was shewed a writing sealed with his seale, by the which he gaue to the king all his mooueables and vnmooueables. On the daie of the Conception of our ladie, the king at Yorke place at West- Creation of earles at Yorke place. minster, in the parlement time, created the vicount Rochford erle of Wilshire, and the vicount Fitz Water was created earle of Sussex, and the lord Hastings was created earle of Huntington. When all things were concluded in the parlement house, the king came to the parlement chamber the 17 daie of December, and there put his roiall assent to all things doone by the lords and commons, and so proroged his court of parlement till the next yeare. After the parlement was thus ended, the king remooued to Gréenewich, and there kept his Christmasse with the queene in great triumph: with great plentie of viands, and diuerse disguisings and enterludes, to the great reioising of his people.

The king, which all this while, since the doubt was mooued touching his marriage, absteined from the quéenes bed, was now aduertised by his ambassadors, whom he had sent to diuerse vniuersities for the absoluing of his doubt, that the said vniuersities were agreed, and cléerelie concluded, that the one brother might not by Gods law marrie the other brothers wife, carnallie knowen by the first marriage, & that neither the pope nor the court of Rome could in anie wise dispense with the same. For ye must vnderstand, that amongst other things alleged for disproofe of the mariage to A speciall argument in disproofe of the marriage. be lawfull, euidence was giuen of certeine words, which prince Arthur spake the morrow after he was first married to the quéene, whereby it was gathered, that he knew hir carnallie the night then passed. The words were these, as we find them in the chronicle of master Edward Hall.

In

In the morning after he was risen from the bed, in which he had laine with hir all night, he called for drinke, which he before time was not accustomed to doo. At which thing, one of his chamberleines maruelling, required the cause of his drought. To whome he answered merilie, saieng; I haue this night béene in the middest of Spaine, which is a hot region, and that iournie maketh me so drie. and if thou haddest beene vnder that hot climat, thou wouldest haue béene drier than I. Againe, it was alleged, that after the death of prince Arthur, the king was deferred from the title and creation of prince of Wales almost halfe a yeare, which thing could not haue béene doubted, if she had not béene carnallie knowen. Also she hir selfe caused a bull to be purchased, in the which were these words Velforsan cognitam, that is, and peraduenture carnallie knowen: which words were not in the first bull granted by pope Iulie at hir second mariage to the king, which second bull with that clause was onelie purchased to dispense with the second matrimonie, although there were carnall copulation before, which bull néeded not to haue béene purchased, if there had béene no carnall copulation, for then the first bull had béene sufficient. To conclude, when these & other matters were laid foorth to prooue that which she denied, the carnall copulation betwixt hir and prince Arthur, hir counsellors left that matter, and fell to persuasions of naturall reason. And lastlie, when nothing else would serue, they stood stiffe in the appeale to the pope, and in the dispensation purchased from the court of Rome, so that the matter was thus shifted off, and no end likelie to be had therein.

The king therefore vnderstanding now that the emperour and the pope were appointed to méet at the citie of Bononie aliàs Bologna, where the emperour should be crowned, sent thither in ambassage from him the earle of Wilshire, doctor Stokesleie, elected bishop of London, and his almoner doctor Edward Lée, to declare both vnto the pope and emperour, the law of God, the determinations of vniuersities in the case of his mariage, and to require the pope to doo iustice according to truth, and also to shew to the emperour, that the king did mooue this matter onelie for discharge of his conscience, and not for anie other respect of pleasure or displeasure earthlie. These ambassadours comming to Bononie were honorablie receiued, and first dooing their message to the pope, had answer of him, that he would heare the matter disputed when he came to Rome, and according to right he would doo iustice.

(margin: Ambassadors sent to Italie out of England about this intricate matter of the marriage.)

The emperour answered, that he in no wise would be against the lawes of God, & if the court of Rome would iudge that the matrimonie was not good, he could be content: but he solicited both the pope and cardinals, to stand by the dispensation, which he thought to be of force inough to prooue the mariage lawfull. With these answers the ambassadors departed and returned homewards, till they came on this side the mounteins, and then receiued letters from the king, which appointed the earle of Wilshire to go in ambassage to the French king which then laie at Burdeaux, making shift for monie for redéeming of his children: and the bishop of London, was appointed to go to Padoa, and other vniuersities in Italie, to know their full resolutions and determinate opinions in the kings case of matrimonie: and the kings almoner was commanded to returne home into England, and so he did.

(margin: The emperours answer to the ambassadors.)

(margin: The earle of Wilshire ambassador to the French king, & others sent to other places.)

¶ You haue heard before how the cardinall was attainted in the premunire, and how he was put out of the office of the chancellor, & laie at Asher. In this Lent season the king by the aduise of his councell licenced him to go into his diocesse of Yorke, & gaue him commandement to kéepe him in his diocesse, and not to returne southward without the kings speciall licence in writing. So he made great prouision to go northward, and apparelled his seruants newlie, and bought manie costlie things for his houshold: and so he might well inough, for he had of the kings gentlenesse the bishoprikes of Yorke and Winchester, which were no small things. But at this time diuerse of his seruants departed from him to the kings seruice, and in especiall Thomas Crumwell

(margin: Abr. Flem. ix Edw. Hall in H. 8. fol. cxcj. cxcij.)

(margin: 1530)

(margin: The cardinall licenced to repaire into Yorkeshire.)

one

one of his chiefe counsell, and chiefe dooer for him in the suppression of abbeies. Thomas Crumwell aduanced to the kings seruice.
After that all things necessarie for his iournie were prepared, he tooke his waie northward till he came to Southwell, which is in his diocesse, and there he continued this yeare, euer grudging at his fall, as you shall heare hereafter. But the lands which he had giuen to his colleges in Oxford and Ipswich, were now come to the kings hands, by his atteindor in the premunire : and yet the king of his gentlenesse and for fauour that he bare to good learning, erected againe the college in Oxford, and where it was The kings college in Oxford otherwise called Christs church. named the cardinals college, he called it the kings college, & indowed it with faire possessions, and put in new statutes and ordinances. And for bicause the college of Ipswich was thought to be nothing profitable, therefore he left that dissolued.

In this yeare the emperour gaue to the lord master of saint Iohnes of Ierusalem, and his brethren the Iland of Malta lieng betwéene Sicill and Barbarie, there to imploie themselues vpon Christs enimies, which lord master had no place sure to inhabit there, since he was put frō the Rhodes by the Turke that besieged Vienna, but missed of his expectation. For the christians defended the same so valiantlie against the said Turke and his power, that he lost manie of his men by slaughter; The number of the Turks that died at the siege of Vienna. manie also miscarried by sicknesse and cold : so that there perished in all to the number of fourescore thousand men, as one of his bassats did afterward confesse, which was to him a great displeasure; and in especiallie bicause he neuer besieged citie before, but either it was yéelded or taken. In the time of this siege a metrician did make these two verses in memorie of the same :

Cæsar in Italiam quo venit Carolus anno,
Cincta est ripheis nostra Vienna Getis.]

In the beginning of this yeare was the hauing and reading of the new testament An. Reg. 22. in English translated by Tindall, Ioie, and others, forbidden by the king with the aduise of his councell, and namelie the bishops, which affirmed that the same was not The new testament translated into English. trulie translated, and that therein were prologs and prefaces sounding to heresie, with vncharitable railing against bishops and the cleargie. The king therefore commanded the bishops, that they calling to them the best learned men of the vniuersities, should cause a new translation to be made, that the people without danger might read the same for their better instruction in the lawes of God, and his holie word. Diuerse persons that were detected to vse reading of the new testament, and other bookes in English set foorth by Tindall, and such other as were fled the realme, were punished by order taken against them by sir Thomas Moore then lord chancellor, who held greatlie against such bookes, but still the number dailie increased.

¶ In this yeare in Maie, the bishop of London caused all his new testaments which *Ed. Hall in H.8. fol.* Cxcij. he had bought with manie other bookes, to be brought into Paules churchyard in London, and there were openlie burned. In the end of this yeare, the wild Irish- Tindals testaments burned. men, knowing the earle of Kildare to be in England, entered his land, and spoiled and burnt his countrie, with diuerse other countries. And the erle of Osserie being The wild Irish spoile the earle of Kildares countrie, &c. the kings deputie made little resistance, for lacke of power. Wherfore the king sent the earle of Kildare into Ireland, & with him sir William Skeuington knight, master of the kings ordinance, and diuerse gunners with him, which so politikelie ordered themselues, that their enimies were glad to offer amends, and to treat for truce : & so sir William Skeuington the next yeere returned into England, leauing there the earle of Kildare for the kings deputie.

Now I will returne to the execution of the treatie of Cambreie, in the which it The execution of the treatie accorded vpon at Cambreie. was agréed, that the ladie Eleanor and the French kings children should be deliuered when the ransome appointed was paied as you haue heard in the last yeare. Wherefore the French king gathered monie of his subiects with all speed, and when the monie was readie, he sent the great master of France called Annas de Memorancie and diuerse other nobles to Baion with the monie, and to receiue the ladie and the

children

children. And thither came to them the great constable of Castile and monsieur Prat for the emperour, & there the crowns were weied and touched: and what fault soeuer the Spaniards found in them they would not receiue a great number of them, and so they carried the children backe from Fontarbie into Spaine. Thus the great master of France and his companie laie still at Baion, without hauing his purpose performed, from March till the end of Iune, and longer had lien if the king of England had not sent sir Francis Brian to Baion to warrant the paiement: wherevpon the daie of deliuerance was appointed to be on saint Peters daie in Iune.

At which daie the great master, with one and thirtie mulets laden with the crownes came to the one side of the riuer of Audaie, which riuer departeth Spaine and France, and there taried till the first daie of Iulie: on which daie the ladie Eleanor and the children were put in two great boates, hauing onelie twelue gentlemen of Spaine with them: and in like maner the great master with two great boats, in the which the mony was, and twelue gentlemen with him. All these boats met at a bridge made in the middest of the riuer. The constable of Spaine and his twelue gentlemen with the great master of France and his twelue gentlemen on the bridge: and after a little salutation, the Frenchmen entered into the two boats where the ladie and the two children were; and the Spaniards into the two boats where the monie was, and then ech part hasted to land. Thus were the French kings wife and children deliuered into his hands, for which deliuerance was great ioy and triumph made in France: and also in Iulie were fiers made in London and diuerse other places for the same consideration and cause.]

¶ Now will we leaue France, and returne to England, renewing the remembrance of cardinall Wolseie, who after great sute made to the king, was licenced to remooue from Asher to Richmond, which place he had a little before repared with great costs, for the king made an exchange thereof with him for Hampton court. The cardinall hauing licence of the king to repaire to Richmond, made hast thither, and lodged there in the lodge of the great parke, which was a verie pretie house, there he laie vntill the beginning of Lent. Then he remooued into the charter-house of Richmond, where he laie in a lodging which doctor Collet made for himselfe, vntill he remooued northward, which was in the Passion weeke after, and euerie daie he resorted to the charterhouse there, and would sit with one of the most ancient fathers, who persuaded him to despise the vaine glorie of the world.

Then prepared the cardinall for his iournie into the north, and sent to London for liuerie clothes for his seruants, and so rode from Richmond to Hendon, from thence to a place called the Rie, the next daie to Raistone, where he lodged in the priorie; the next daie to Huntingdon, and there lodged in the abbeie; the next daie to Peterborow, and there lodged in the abbeie, where he abode all the next wéeke, & there he kept his Easter, his traine was in number an hundred and thréescore persons. Vpon Maundie thursdaie he made his maundie, there hauing nine and fiftie poore men, whose féet he washed, and gaue euerie one twelue pence in monie, three els of good canuas, a paire of shoes, a cast of red herrings, and three white herrings, and one of them had two shillings.

On thursdaie next after Easter, he remooued to master Fitz Williams, sometime a merchant-tailor of London, and then of the kings councell; the next wéeke he remooued to Stamford, the next daie to Grantham, the next daie to Newarke, and lodged in the castell that night and the next daie also: from thence he rode to Southwell, where he continued most part of all that summer, vntill the latter end of grasse time, and then he rode to Scrobie, where he continued vntill Michaelmasse, and then to Cawood castell within seuen miles of Yorke, whereof we will speake more hereafter. On the sixtéenth of Maie, a man was hanged in chaines in Finsburie

field, for murthering doctor Miles vicar of saint Brides. The fourth and fift of Nouember

uember was a great wind, that blew downe manie houses and trées, after which wind A great wind. followed so high a tide, that it drowned the marshes on Essex side and Kent, with the Ile of Thanet, and other places, destroieng much cattell. The nineteenth of September, in the citie of London, a proclamation was made for the restreining of the popes authoritie in England, as followeth.

A proclamation published in England in the behalfe of the kings prerogatiue roiall against the pope.

THE kings highnes streictlie chargeth and commandeth, that no maner of person, of what estate, degree, or condition soeuer he or they be of, doo purchase or attempt to purchase from the court of Rome or elswhere, nor vse & put in execution, diulge, or publish anie thing hertofore within this yeare passed purchased, or to be purchased hereafter, conteining mater preiudiciall to the high authoritie, iurisdiction, and prerogatiue roiall of this his said realme, or to the let, hinderance, or impechment of his graces noble & vertuous intended purposes in the premisses, vpon paine of incurring his highnesse indignation, and imprisonment, and further punishment of their bodies for their so dooing at his graces pleasure, to the dreadfull example of all other.

Some iudged, that this proclamation was made, bicause the queene (as was said) What was surmised to be the cause of this proclamation. had purchased a new bull for ratification of hir marriage. Others thought that it was made, bicause the cardinall had purchased a bull to cursse the king, if he would not restore him to his old dignities, and suffer him to correct the spiritualtie, the king not to meddle with the same. In déed manie coniectured, that the cardinall grudging at his fall from so high dignities, sticked not to write things sounding to the kings reproch, both to the pope, and other princes; for that manie opprobrious words were spoken to doctor Edward Kéerne the kings orator at Rome, and that it was said to him, that for the cardinals sake the king should haue the worse spéed in the sute of his matrimonie.

¶ Cardinall Wolseie lieng at Cawood, held there an honourable and plentifull house *Abr. Fl. ex I. S. pag.* 970. The cardinall at his maner of Cawood kéepeth a bountifull house. for all commers, and also built & repared the castell, which was greatlie in decaie, hauing artificers and labourers aboue thrée hundred persons dailie in wages. At length being therevnto persuaded by the doctors of the church of Yorke, he determined to be installed there at Yorke minster, the next mondaie after Alhallowes daie, against which time due preparation was made for the same, but not in such sumptuous wise, as his predecessors before him had vsed. For wheras the cardinall was not abashed to send to the king, requiring him to lend him the mitre and pall which he was woont to weare when he soong masse in anie solemne assemblie: the king vpon sight of his letters, could not but maruell at the proud presumptuousnes of the man, saieng: What a thing is this, that pride shuld thus reigne in a person that is quite vnder foot.

The daie being once knowne vnto the worshipfull gentlemen of the countrie, and The cardinall knoweth not that he was to be arrested of treason. other, as abbats, and priors, and notice of his installation, they sent in such prouision of vittels, that it is almost incredible, all which was vnknowne to the cardinall, for as much as he was preuented and disappointed of his purpose, by the reason that he was arrested of high treason, as yée shall héereafter heare. So that most part of this former prouision that I speake of, was sent vnto Yorke the same daie of his arrest, and the next daie following: for his arrest was kept as close as could be. The order of his arrest was thus. It was appointed by the king & councell, that sir Walter Walsh knight, one of the kings priuie chamber, should be sent downe with a commission into the north vnto the earle of Northumberland (who was sometime brought vp in house with the cardinall) and they twaine being iointlie in commission to arrest the cardinall of high treason, maister Walsh tooke his horsse at the court gate, about ncone, vpon Alhallowes daie, toward the earle of Northumberland.

And now haue I occasion to declare what happened about the same time, which peraduenture signified the troubles following to the cardinall. The cardinall sitting at dir ner vpon Alhallowes daie, hauing at his boords end diuerse chapleins sitting at dinner, yée shall vnderstand that the cardinals great crosse stood in a corner at the tables end, leaning against the hanging, and when the boords end was taken vp, and a conuenient time for the chapleins to arise, one doctor Augustine a Venecian, and physician to the cardinall, rising from the table with the other, hauing vpon him a great gowne of boisterous veluet, ouerthrew the crosse, which trailing downe along the

tappet, with the point of one of the crosses, brake doctor Bonars head that the bloud ran downe, the companie there standing greatlie astonied with the chance.

The cardinall perceiuing the same, demanded what the matter meant of their sudden amaze? and they shewed him of the fall of his crosse vpon doctor Bonars head. Hath it (quoth he) drawne anie bloud? Yea forsooth my lord (quoth they.) With that he cast his eies aside, & shaking his head, said Malum omen, & therewith saieng grace, rose from the table, & went to his chamber. Now marke the signification how

the cardinall expounded this matter at Pomfret after his fall. First, yée shall vnderstand, that the crosse which he bare as archbishop of Yorke, signified himselfe; and Augustine the physician who ouerthrew the crosse, was onelie he that accused the cardinall, whereby his enimies caught an occasion to ouerthrow him: it fell vpon doctor Bonars head, who was maister of the cardinals faculties and spirituall iurisdictions, and was then damnified by the ouerthrow of the crosse: yea, and more ouer, drawing bloud of him, betokened death, which shortlie after did insue.

About the time of this mischance, the same verie daie and season, maister Walsh tooke his horsse at the court as nigh as could be iudged. Now the appointed time drew neere of his installation, and sitting at dinner vpon the fridaie next before the mondaie on the which daie he intended to be installed at Yorke, the earle of North-

umberland and maister Walsh, with a great companie of gentlemen of the earles house, & of the countrie, whome he had gathered togither in the kings name, came to the hall at Cawood, the officers being at dinner, and the cardinall not fullie dined, being then in his fruits. The first thing that the earle did after he had set order in the hall, he commanded the porter at the gates to deliuer him the keies thereof. Who would in no wise obeie his commandement, though he were roughlie threatened, and streictlie commanded in the kings name to make deliuerie of them to one of the earles seruants.

Sir (quoth he) seeing that yee doo but intend to set one of your seruants in my place to kéepe the gates, I know no seruant that yée haue but I am as able as he to doo it, and kéepe the gates to your purpose (whatsoeuer it be) also the keies were deliuered me by my lord and maister, wherefore I praie you to pardon me, for whatsoeuer yée shall command me to doo in the ministration of mine office, I shall doo it with a good will. With that (quoth the earle) hold him a booke (& commanding him to laie his hand thereon:) Thou shalt sweare (quoth he) that thou shalt well and trulie kéepe the gates to the kings vse, and to doo all such things as we shall command: and that yée shall let passe neither in nor out at these gates, but such as yée be commanded by vs. And with this oth he receiued the keies at the earles hands.

Of all these doings knew the cardinall nothing, for they stopped the staires, so that none went vp to the cardinals chamber, and they that came downe could no more go vp againe. At last one escaped, who shewed the cardinall that the earle was in the hall. Whereat the cardinall maruelled, and would not beléeue him, but commanded a gentleman to bring him the truth, who going downe the staires, saw the earle of Northumberland, and returned, and said it was verie he. Then (quoth the cardinall)

                                                   I am

I am sorie that we haue dined, for I feare our officers be not prouided of anie store of good fish to make him some honorable chéere, let the table stand (quoth he.) With that he rose vp, and going downe the staires, he encountered the earle comming vp with all his taile. And as soone as the cardinall espied the earle, he put off his cap, and said, My lord ye be most hartilie welcome, and so imbraced each other.

Then the cardinall tooke the earle by the hand, and had him vp into the chamber, whome followed all the number of the earles seruants. From thence he led him into his bed-chamber, and they being there all alone, the earle said vnto the cardinall with a soft voice, laieng his hand vpon his arme: My lord I arrest you of high treason. With which words the cardinall being maruellouslie astonied, standing both still a good space. At last (quoth the cardinall) What authoritie haue you to arrest me? Forsooth my lord (quoth the erle) I haue a commission so to doo. Where is your commission (quoth he) that I may sée it? Naie sir that you may not (said the erle.) Well then (quoth the cardinall) I will not obeie your rest. But as they were debating this matter betwéene them in the chamber, as busie was maister Walsh in arresting doctor Augustine at the doore of the palace, saieng vnto him, Go in traitor or I shall make thée. *The action of arrest which the cardinall taketh in ill part.*

At the last maister Walsh being entred the cardinals chamber, began to plucke off his hood, and after knéeled downe to the cardinall. Vnto whom the cardinall said, Come hither gentlemen, & let me speake with you: Sir, héere my lord of Northumberland hath arrested me, but by whose authoritie he sheweth not, if yée be ioined with him I praie you shew me. Indéed my lord (quoth maister Walsh) he sheweth you the truth. Well then (quoth the cardinall) I praie you let me see it. Sir I beséech you (quoth maister Walsh) hold vs excused: there is annexed to our commission certeine instructions, which you may not see. Well (quoth the cardinall) I trow yée are one of the kings priuie chamber, your name is Walsh, I am content to yéeld to you, but not to my lord of Northumberland without I see his commission: the worst in the kings priuie chamber is sufficient to arrest the greatest péere of the realme by the kings commandement, without anie commission, therefore put your commission and authoritie in execution, spare not, I will obeie the kings will; I take God to iudge, I neuer offended the king in word nor deed. *The cardinall desireth to see the commission of the arest.*

Then the earle called into the chamber diuerse gentlemen of his owne seruants, and after they had taken the cardinals keies from him, they put him in custodie of the earles gentlemen, and then they went about the house to set all things in an order. Then sent they doctor Augustine awaie to London with as much spéed as they could, who was bound vnto the horsse like a traitor, But it was sundaie toward night yer the cardinall was conueied from Cawood, who lodged that night in the abbeie of Pomfret. The next daie he remooued toward Doncaster, and was there lodged at the Blacke friers. The next daie he was remooued to Shefield parke, where the earle of Shrewsburie with his ladie, and a traine of gentlemen and gentlewomen receiued him with much honour. Then departed all the great number of gentlemen that conducted him thither. *The cardinall committed to the custodie of the earls gentlemen.*

The cardinall being thus with the earle of Shrewsburie, continued there eightéene daies after, vpon whome the earle appointed diuerse gentlemen to attend continuallie, to sée that he should lacke nothing, being serued in his owne chamber as honorablie as he had béene in his owne house, and once euerie daie the earle would repaire to him and commune with him. After the cardinall had thus remained with the earle of Shrewsburie about a fortnight, it came to passe at a certeine time as he sat at dinner in his owne chamber, hauing at his boords end a messe of gentlemen and chapleins to kéepe him companie, toward the end of his dinner, when he was come to eating his fruits, his colour was perceiued often to change, whereby he was iudged not to be in good health. *The cardinall honourablie receiued and serued at the earle of Shrewsburies house.*

Wherevpon

The cardinall
sickneth sitting
at the table.

Wherevpon one of his gentlemen said, Sir, me séemes you are not well at ease. To whom he answered with lowd voice, Forsooth no more I am, for I am (quoth he) taken suddenlie with a thing about my stomach, that lieth there along as cold as a whetstone, which is no more but wind, I praie you go to the apothecarie, & inquire of him if he haue anie thing that will breake wind vpward. Then went he to the earle and shewed him what estate the cardinall was in, and what he desired. With that, the earle caused the apothecarie to be called before him, & demanded of him if he had anie thing that would breake wind vpward in a mans bodie. And he answered he had such géere. Then (quoth the earle) fetch me some. Then the apothecarie fetched a white confection in a faire paper, & shewed it to the earle, who commanded one to giue the assaie thereof before him, and then the same to be brought to the cardinall, who receiued it vp all at once into his mouth.

The cardinall
falleth into a
flux that cost
him his life.

But immediatlie after suerlie, he auoided much wind vpward: Lo (quoth he) ye may see that it was but wind, and now I am well eased, I thanke God, and so rose from the table, and went to his praiers. And that doone, there came on him such a loosenesse that it caused him to go to the stoole. And not long after the earle of Shrewesburie came into the gallerie to him, with whome the cardinall met: and then sitting downe vpon a bench, the earle asked him how he did, and he most lamentablie answered him, and thanked him for his good interteinment. Sir (quoth the earle) if ye remember, ye haue often wished to come before the king, to make your answer; and I haue written to the king in that behalfe, making him priuie of your lamentation that yée inwardlie haue receiued for his displeasure, who accepteth all your dooings therein as friends be accustomed to doo in such cases: wherefore I would aduise you to plucke vp your hart, and be not agast of your enimies, I doubt not but this your iournie to his highnesse shall be much to your aduancement.

Sir William
Kingston is sent
to fetch vp the
cardinall before
the king.

The king hath sent for you that worshipfull knight master Kingston, and with him foure and twentie of your old seruants, now of the gard, to the intent yée may safelie come to his maiestie. Sir (quoth the cardinall) I trow master Kingston is constable of the Tower. Yea, what of that (quoth the erle) I assure you he is elected by the king for one of your friends. Well quoth the cardinall, as God will, so be it, I am subiect to fortune, being a true man, readie to accept such chances as shall follow, and there an end; I praie you where is master Kingston. Quoth the earle, I will send for him. I praie you so doo (quoth the cardinall) at whose message he came. And as soone as the cardinall espied him, he made hast to encounter him, and at his comming he knéeled to him, and saluted him in the kings behalfe, whome the cardinall bareheaded offered to take vp, and said: I praie you stand vp, knéele not me, I am but a wretch replet with miserie, not esteeming my selfe but as a vile abiect, vtterlie cast awaie, without desert, as God knoweth.

Talke betwixt the
said sir William
& the cardinall.

Then said master Kingston with humble reuerence: Sir, the king hath him commended vnto you. I thanke his highnesse quoth the cardinall, I trust he be in health. Yea (quoth master Kingston) and he commanded me to saie to you, that you should assure your selfe that he beareth you as much good will as euer he did, and willeth you to be of good chéere. And where report hath béene made, that ye should commit against him certeine heinous crimes, which he thinks to be vntrue, yet he can doo no lesse than send for you to your triall, & to take your iournie to him at your owne pleasure, commanding me to be attendant vpon you. Therefore sir I praie you, when it shall be your owne pleasure to take your iournie, I shall be readie to giue attendance. Master Kingston (quoth he) I thanke you for your newes, and sir, if I were as lustie as I haue béene but of late, I would ride with you in post, but I am diseased with a flux that maketh me verie weake, but I shall with all spéed make me readie to ride with you to morrow.

When

When night came, the cardinall waxed verie sicke with the laske, the which caused The cardinall extremelie ill. him continuallie to go to the stoole all that night, in so much that he had that night fiftie stooles: therefore in consideration of his infirmities, they caused him to tarrie all that day: and the next daie he tooke his iournie with master Kingston, and them of the gard, till he came to an house of the earle of Shrewesburies called Hardwike hall, where he laie all night verie euill at ease. The next daie he rode to Notingham, and there lodged that night more sicke: and the next daie he rode to Leicester abbeie, and by the waie waxed so sicke that he was almost fallen from his mule; so that it was night before he came to the abbeie of Leicester, where at his comming in at the gates, the abbat with all his conuent met him with diuerse torches light, whom they honorablie receiued and welcomed.

To whome the cardinall said: father abbat, I am come hither to lay my bones among you, riding so still vntill he came to the staires of the chamber, where he allighted from his mule, and master Kingston led him vp the staires, and as soone as he was in his chamber he went to bed. This was on the saturday at night, and then increased he sicker and sicker, vntill mondaie, that all men thought he would haue died: so on tuesdaie saint Andrewes euen, master Kingston came to him and bad him good morrow, for it was about six of the clocke, and asked him how he did? Sir (quoth he) I tarrie but the pleasure of God, to render vp my poore soule into his hands. Not so sir (quoth master Kingston) with the grace of God, yée shall liue and doo verie well, if yee will be of good cheere. Nay in good sooth master Kingston, my disease is such, that I can not liue: for I haue had some experience in physicke.

Thus it is, I haue a flux with a continuall feuer, the nature whereof is, that if there The cardinall affirmeth by his owne experience in physicke that he can not liue. be no alteration of the same within eight daies, either must insue excoriation of the intrailes, or fransie, or else present death, and the best of them is death, and (as I suppose) this is the eight daie, & if yée sée no alteration in me, there is no remedie, saue (though I may liue a daie or twaine after) but death must insue. Sir (quoth maister Kingston) you be in much pensiuenes, doubting that thing, that in good faith yée néed not. Well, well, master Kingston (quoth the cardinall) I sée the matter how The cardinall ascribeth his fall to the iust iudgement of God. it is framed: but if I had serued God as diligentlie as I haue doone the king, he would not haue giuen me ouer in my greie haires: but it is the iust reward that I must receiue for the diligent paines and studie that I haue had to doo him seruice, not regarding my seruice to God, but onelie to satisfie his pleasure.

I praie you haue me most humblie commended vnto his roiall maiestie, & beseech him in my behalfe to call to his princelie remembrance all matters procéeding betwéene him & me from the beginning of the world, and the progresse of the same, &c. Master Kingston farewell, I can no more saie, but I wish all things to haue good success, my time draweth on fast. And euen with that he began to draw his spéech at Manifest indication of death in the cardinall. length, & his toong to faile, his eies being set, whose sight failed him. Then they did put him in remembrance of Christ his passion, & caused the yeomen of the gard to stand by to sée him die, and to witnesse of his words at his departure: & incontinent the clocke stroke eight, and then he gaue vp the ghost, and departed this present life: which caused some to call to remembrance how he said the daie before, that at eight of the clocke they should loose their master.

Here is the end and fall of pride and arrogancie of men exalted by fortune to digni- Example of pride and arrogancie. tie: for in his time he was the hautiest man in all his procéedings aliue, hauing more respect to the honor of his person, than he had to his spirituall profession, wherin should be shewed all meekenes, humilitie, and charitie. [An example (saith Guic- *Guic. pag.* 1139. ciardin, who handleth this storie effectuallie, and sheweth the cause of this cardinals ruine) in our daies woorthie of memorie, touching the power which fortune and enuie hath in the courts of princes.] He died in Leicester abbeie, & in the church of the same abbeie was buried. Such is the suertie of mans brittle state, doubtfull in

birth

birth, & no lesse féeble in life, which is as vncerteine, as death most certeine, and the meanes thereof manifold, which as in number they excéed; so in strangenesse they passe: all degrees of ages & diuersities of sexes being subiect to the same. In consideration whereof, it was notablie said by one that wrote a whole volume of infirmities, diseases, and passions incident to children:

> A primo vitæ diuersos stamine morbos
> Perpetimur, diris afficimúrque malis:
> Donec in occasum redeat qui vixit ab ortu,
> Antea quàm discat viuere, vita cadit.

Sebast. Austa-rius.

The description of cardinall Wolseie, set downe by *Edmund Campian.*

This cardinall (as Edmund Campian in his historie of Ireland describeth him) was a man vndoubtedly borne to honor: I thinke (saith he) some princes bastard, no butchers sonne, excéeding wise, faire spoken, high minded, full of reuenge, vitious of his bodie, loftie to his enimies, were they neuer so big, to those that accepted and sought his fréendship woonderfull courteous, a ripe schooleman, thrall to affections, brought a bed with flatterie, insatiable to get, and more princelie in bestowing, as appeareth by his two colleges at Ipswich and Oxenford, the one ouerthrowne with his fall, the other vnfinished, and yet as it lieth for an house of students, considering all the appurtenances incomparable thorough Christendome, whereof Henrie the eight is now called founder, bicause he let it stand. He held and inioied at once the bishopriks of Yorke, Duresme, & Winchester, the dignities of lord cardinall, legat, & chancellor, the abbeie of saint Albons, diuerse priories, sundrie fat benefices In commendam, a great preferrer of his seruants, an aduancer of learning, stout in euerie quarell, neuer happie till this his ouerthrow. Wherein he shewed such moderation, and ended so perfectlie, that the houre of his death did him more honor, than all the pompe of his life passed. Thus far Campian. Here it is necessarie to adde that notable discourse, which I find in Iohn Stow, concerning the state of the cardinall, both in the yeares of his youth, and in his settled age: with his sudden comming vp from preferment to preferment; till he was aduanced to that step of honor, which making him insolent, brought him to confusion.

Abr. Fl. ex I. S. pag. 904, 905. &c.
The ascending of Thomas Wolseie, Bachellor of art at fiftéene yeares old.

¶ This Thomas Wolseie was a poore mans sonne of Ipswich, in the countie of Suffolke, & there borne, and being but a child, verie apt to be learned, by the meanes of his parents he was conueied to the vniuersitie of Oxenford, where he shortlie prospered so in learning, as he was made bachellor of art, when he passed not fiftéene yeares of age, and was called most commonlie thorough the vniuersitie the boie bachellor. Thus prospering in learning, he was made fellow of Mawdeline college, and afterward appointed to be schoolemaster of Mawdelin schoole, at which time the

Schoolemaster to the marquesse Dorsets children.

lord marquesse Dorset had thrée of his sonnes there at schoole, committing vnto him as well their education as their instruction. It pleased the said lord marquesse against a Christmas season to send as well for the schoolemaster, as for his children home to his house for their recreation, in that pleasant and honorable feast.

Then being there, the lord their father, perceiuing them tō be right well imploied in learning for their time, he hauing a benefice in his gift, being at that time void, gaue

Thomas Wolseie gat a benefice.

the same to the schoolemaster in reward of his diligence at his departure after Christmas to the vniuersitie, and hauing the presentation thereof, repaired to the ordinarie for his induction, and being furnished of his instruments, made spéed to the benefice

Thomas Wolseie set in the stocks by Sir Iames Paulet.

to take possession, and being there for that intent, one sir Iames Paulet knight dwelling thereabouts, tooke occasion against him, and set the schoolemaster by the héeles during his pleasure, which after was neither forgotten nor forgiuen.

Wolseies imprisonment reuenged.

For when the schoolemaster mounted to the dignitie to be chancellor of England, he sent for master Paulet, & after manie sharpe words, inioined him to attend vntill he were dismissed, and not to depart out of London without licence obteined; so that he continued there within the middle Temple the space of fiue or six yeares, and laie

then

then in the Gate house next the stréet, which he reedified verie sumptuouslie, garnish- Gatehouse of the middle Temple new builded.
ing the same all ouer the outside with the cardinals armes, with his hat, cognisances, and other deuises in so glorious a sort, that he thought thereby to haue appeased his old displeasure.

Now after the deceasse of the lord marquesse, this same schoolemaster considering himselfe to be but as imple beneficed man, and to haue lost his fellowship in the college, which was much to his reléefe, thought not long to be vnprouided of some other helpe, and in his trauell thereabouts, he fell in acquaintance with one sir Iohn Sir Iohn Naphant treasuror of Calis, Thomas Wolsie his chapleine.
Naphant, a verie graue & ancient knight, who had a great roome in Calis vnder king Henrie the seuenth: this knight he serued, and behaued himselfe so discreetlie, that he obtained the especiall fauor of his master, insomuch that he committed all the charge of his office vnto his chapleine, and (as I vnderstand) the office was the treasurorship of Calis, who was in consideration of his great age discharged of his roome, and returned againe into England, and thorough his instant labor, his chapleine was Thomas Wolsie was chapleine to Henrie the seuenth.
promoted to be the kings chapleine, and when he had once cast anchor in the port of promotion, how he wrought, I shall somewhat declare.

He hauing there a iust occasion to be in the sight of the king dailie, by reason he said masse before him in his closet, and that being doone, he spent not the daie in idlenesse, but would attend vpon those whom he thought to beare most rule in the coun- cell, the which at that time was doctor Fox, bishop of Winchester, secretarie, and lord of the priuie seale: and also sir Thomas Louell knight a sage councellor, master of the wards, and constable of the Tower: these graue councellors in processe of time perceiued this chapleine to haue a verie fine wit, and thought him a méet person to be preferred to wittie affaires. It chanced at a certeine season that the king had an vrgent occasion to send an ambassador vnto the emperor Maximilian, who laie at that present in the low countrie of Flanders, not farre from Calis.

The bishop of Winchester, and sir Thomas Louell, whome the king counselled and debated with vpon this ambassage, saw they had a conuenient occasion to prefer the kings chapleine, whose wit, eloquence, and learning, they highly commended to the king. The king commanded them to bring his chapleine before his presence, with whome he fell in communication of great matters, and perceiuing his wit to be verie fine, thought him sufficient, commanding him therevpon to prepare himselfe to his iournie; and hauing his depeach, he tooke his leaue of the king at Richmond about noone; & so comming to London about foure of the clocke, where the barge of Graues Thomas Wolsie ambassador to the emperor.
end was readie to lanch foorth, both with a prosperous tide and wind, without anie abode he entered the barge.

Hauing so doone, he passed foorth with such spéed, that he arriued at Graues end within little more than thrée houres, where he tarried no longer than his post horsses were a prouiding, and then trauelled so spéedily that he came to Douer the next morning, whereas the passengers were readie vnder saile to Calis, into the which passenger, without tarrieng, he entered, and sailed foorth with them, that long before noone he arriued at Calis, and hauing post horsses, departed from thense with The cardinall verie expedite and readie in his ambassage.
such speed, that he was that night with the emperor, and disclosed the whole summe of his ambassage to the emperor, of whome he required speedie expedition, the which was granted him by the emperor; so that the next daie he was cléerlie dispatched with all the kings requests fullie accomplished.

At which time he made no longer delaie, but tooke post horsses that night, and rode toward Calis, conducted thither with such persons as the emperor had appointed; and at the opening of the gates of Calis, he came thither, where the passengers were as readie to returne into England, as they were before at his iournie forward, insomuch that he arriued at Douer by ten of the clocke before noone, and hauing His returne into England after his ambassage discharged.
post horsses, came to the court at Richmond the same night, where he taking some rest

rest vntill the morning, repaired to the king at his first comming from his bedchamber to his closet, whom when the king saw, he checked him, for that he was not on his iournie: Sir (quoth he) if it may please your highnesse, I haue alreadie béene with the emperor, and dispatched your affaires (I trust to your graces contentation) and with that presented vnto the king his letters of credence from the emperor.

The king mar-
uelleth at the
cardinals spéedie
returne.

The king being in a great maze and woonder of his speedie returne and procéedings, dissembled all his woonder, and demanded of him whether he incountered not his pursiuant the which he sent vnto him, supposing him not to be out of London, with letters concerning a verie necessarie matter, neglected in their consultation: Yea forsooth (quoth the chapleine) I met with him yesterdaie by the waie, and hauing no vnderstanding by your graces letters of your pleasure, haue notwithstanding béene so bold vpon mine owne discretion (perceiuing that matter to be verie necessarie in that behalfe) to dispatch the same. And forsomuch as I haue excéeded your graces commission, I most humblie require your graces pardon. The king reioising not a little, said; We doo not onelie pardon you thereof, but also giue you our princelie thanks, both for the procéeding therein, and also for your good and speedie exploit, commanding him for that time to take his rest, and repaire againe after dinner for the further relation of his ambassage.

Thomas Wolseie
deane of Lin-
colne. Thomas
Wolseie the
kings almoner.

The ambassador, when he saw time, repaired before the king and councell, where he declared the effect of all his affaires so exactlie, with such grauitie and eloquence, that all the councell that heard him, commended him, estéeming his expedition to be almost beyond the capacitie of man. The king gaue him at that time the deanrie of Lincolne. From thense forward he grew more and more into estimation and authoritie, and after was promoted by the king to be his almoner. After the death of king Henrie the seuenth, and in the florishing youth of king Henrie the eight, this almoner handled himselfe so politiklie, that he soone found the meanes to be made one of the

Thomas Wolseie
of the priuie
councell vnto
Henrie the eight.

kings councell, and to grow in fauor with the king, to whome the king gaue an house at Bridewell in Fleetstréet, sometime sir Richard Empsons, where he kept house for his familie; and so dailie attended vpon the king, and in his especiall fauor, who had great sute made vnto him.

His sentences & wittie persuasions in the councell chamber were alwaies so pithie, that the councell (as occasion mooued them) continuallie assigned him to be the expositor to the king in all their procéedings, in whome the king receiued such a leaning fantasie, for that he was most earnest and readiest of all the councell to aduance the kings will and pleasure: the king therefore estéemed him so highlie, that all the other councellors were put from the great fauor that they before were in, insomuch that the king committed all his will vnto his disposition, which the almoner perceiuing,

The cardinall
presumeth too
farre vpon a
conceit and
flattering opinion
of his owne qua-
lities and the
kings fauor.

tooke vpon him therefore to discharge the king of the weightie and troublesome businesse, persuading the king that he should not néed to spare anie time of his pleasure for anie businesse that should happen in the councell.

And whereas the other councellors would diuerse times persuade the king to haue sometime recourse into the councell chamber, there to heare what was doone; the almoner would persuade him to the contrarie, which delited him much: and thus the almoner ruled all them that were before him, such did his policie and wit bring to passe. Who was now in high fauor but master almoner? And who ruled all vnder the king, but master almoner? Thus he perseuered in fauor, vntill at last in came presents, gifts, and rewards so plentifullie, that he lacked noting that might either please his fantasie, or inrich his coffers.

And thus proceeding in fortunes blisfulnesse, it chanced the warres betwéene the realmes of England and France to be open, insomuch as the king was fullie persuaded in his most roiall person to inuade his forren enimies with a puissant armie; wherefore it was necessarie that this roiall enterprise should be speedilie prouided and furnished,

nished, in euerie degree of things apt & conuenient for the same, for the expedition wherof the king thought no mans wit so méet for policie and painefull trauell, as was his almoner, to whome therefore he committed his whole trust therein, and he tooke vpon him the whole charge of all the businesse, and brought all things to good passe in a decent order, as all maner of vittels, prouisions, and other necessaries conuenient for so noble a voiage and armie. *The cardinall taketh vpon him the managing of all the kings affaires.*

All things being by him perfected, the king aduanced to his roiall enterprise, passed the seas, and marched forward in good order of battell, vntill he came to the strong towne of Terwine, to the which he laid his siege, and assailed it verie stronglie continuallie with such vehement assaults, that within short space it was yéelded vnto his maiestie, vnto the which place the emperor Maximilian repaired vnto the king with a great armie like a mightie prince, taking of the king his graces wages: which is a rare thing, and but seldome seene, an emperor to fight vnder a kings banner. *Sée before pag. 586.*

Thus after the king had obteined this puissant fort and taken the possession thereof, and set all things there in due order, for the defense and preseruation thereof to his vse, he departed thense, and marched toward the citie of Torneie, and there laid his siege in like maner, to the which he gaue so fierce & sharpe assault, that they were constreined of fine force to render the towne vnto his victorious maiestie : at which time the king gaue the almoner the bishoprike of the same see, towards his paines and diligence susteined in that iournie. Now when the king had established all things ageéeable to his will and pleasure, and furnished the same with noble capteines & men of warre for the safegard to the towne, he returned againe into England, taking with him diuerse noble personages of France being prisoners, as the duke of Longuile, and vicount Clarimont, with other which were taken there in a skirmish. *Thomas Wolseie bishop of Torneie in Fráce.*

After whose returne, immediatlie the sée of Lincolne fell void, by the death of doctor Smith late bishop there, the which benefice his grace gaue to his almoner, late bishop of Torneie elect, who was not negligent to take possession therof, and made all the spéed he could for his consecration ; the solemnization whereof ended, he found meanes that he gat the possession of all his predecessors goods into his hands. It was not long after that doctor Benbrike archbishop of Yorke died at Rome, being there the kings ambassador, vnto the which sée the king immediatlie presented his late and new bishop of Lincolne; so that he had thrée bishopriks in his hands in one yeere giuen him. *Thomas Wolseie bishop of Lincolne.* *Sée pag. 610.*

Then prepared he for his translation from the see of Lincolne, vnto the sée of Yorke, after which solemnization doone, he being then an archbishop Primas Angliæ, thought himselfe sufficient to compare with Canturburie, and therevpon erected his crosse in the court, and euerie other place, as well within the precinct and iurisdiction of Canturburie, as in anie other place. And forsomuch as Canturburie claimeth a superoritie ouer Yorke, as ouer all other bishopriks within England, and for that cause claimeth as a knowledge of an ancient obedience of Yorke, to abate the aduancing of his crosse, in presence of the crosse of Canturburie : notwithstanding, the archbishop of Yorke nothing minding to desist from bearing thereof, in maner as I said before, caused his crosse to be aduanced, as well in the presence of Canturburie as elsewhere. Wherefore Canturburie being mooued therewith, gaue vnto Yorke a certeine checke for his presumption, by reason whereof, there ingendered some grudge betwéene Yorke and Canturburie; Yorke intending to prouide some such meanes, that he would be rather superior in dignitie to Canturburie, than to be either obedient or equall to him. Wherefore he obteined to be made priest cardinall, and Legatus de latere : vnto whome the pope sent a cardinals hat with certeine buls for his authoritie in that behalfe. Yet you shall vnderstand, that the pope sent him this woorthie hat of dignitie, as a iewell of his honor and authoritie, the which was conueied in a varlets budget, who seemed to all men to be but a person of small estimation. *Thomas Wolseie archbishop of Yorke.* *Note the pride of Wolseie and his ambition.* *The two archbishops at strife for the prerogatiue.* *Thomas Wolseie cardinall, sée pag. 612*

Wherefore Yorke being aduertised of the basenes of this messenger, & of the peoples opinion, thought it meete for his honor, that this iewell should not be conueied by so simple a person, and therefore caused him to be stopped by the waie immediatlie after his arriuall in England, where he was newlie furnished in all maner of apparell, with all kind of costlie silks, which séemed decent for such an high ambassador, and that doone, he was incountered vpon Blackeheath, and there receiued with a great assemblie of prelats, and lustie gallant gentlemen, and from thense conducted thorough London with great triumph. Then was great and spéedie preparation made in Westminster abbeie, for the confirmation and acceptance of this high order and dignitie, the which was executed by all the bishops and abbats about or nigh London, with their rich miters and copes, and other ornaments, which was doone in so solemne wise, as had not béene seene the like, vnlesse it had béene at the coronation of a mightie prince or king. Obteining this dignitie, he thought himselfe méet to beare rule among the temporall power, & among the spirituall iurisdiction : wherfore, remembring as well the taunts susteined of Canturburie, as hauing respect to the aduancement of worldlie honor & promotion, he found the meanes with the king, that he was made lord chancellor of England, and Canturburie which was chancellor dismissed, who had continued in that roome long since before the deceasse of Henrie the seuenth. Now being in possession of the chancellorship, and indued with the promotions of the archbishop, & cardinall De Latere, hauing power to correct Canturburie, and all other bishops and spirituall persons, to assemble his conuocation when he would assigne, he tooke vpon him the correction of matters in all their iurisdictions, and visited all the spirituall houses, hauing in euerie diocesse all maner of spirituall ministers, as commissaries, scribes, apparators, and all other officers to furnish his courts, and presented by preuention whome he pleased vnto all benefices thoroughout all this realme.

And to the aduancing further of his legantine iurisdiction and honor, he had masters of his faculties, masters Ceremoniarum, and such other, to the glorifieng of his dignitie. Then had he his two great crosses of siluer, the one of his archbishoprike, the other of his legacie, borne before him whither soeuer he went or rode, by two of the tallest priests that he could get within the realme. And to increase his gaines, he had also the bishoprike of Durham, and the abbeie of saint Albons in commendation. And after, when doctor Fox bishop of Winchester died, he surrendred Durham into the kings hands, and tooke to him Winchester. Then had he in his hand (as it were in farme) the bishopriks of Bath, Worcester, & Hereford, for so much as the incumbents of them were strangers, and made their abode continuallie beyond the seas in their owne countries, or else at Rome, from whence they were sent in legation to this realme vnto the king, and for their reward at their departure, king Henrie the seuenth gaue them those bishopriks.

But they being strangers, thought it more méet for the assurance to suffer the cardinall to haue their benefices for a conuenient sum of monie paid them yearelie, where they remained, than either to be troubled with the charges of the same, or to be yearelie burthened with the conueiance of their reuenues vnto them: so that all the spirituall liuings and presentations of these bishopriks were fullie in his disposition, to prefer whom he listed. He had also a great number dailie attending vpon him, both of noblemen & woorthie gentlemen, with no small number of the tallest yeomen that he could get in all the realme, insomuch that well was that nobleman and gentleman, that could preferre a tall yeoman to his seruice.

Ye shall vnderstand, that he had in his hall continuallie three boords, kept with three seuerall principall officers, that is to saie a steward which was alwaies a priest; a treasuror a knight; and a comptrollor an esquier; also a cofferer being a doctor; three marshals; three yeomen vshers in the hall, besides two groomes, and almoners.

Then

The cardinall in allh i actions stande.h vpon his reputation.

Thomas Wolseie lord chancellor arrogateth all that he may to himselfe by vertue of his promotions.

Thomas Wolseie biohop of Winchester, he had also thrée other bishopriks in his hand as it were in farme.

What kind of persons he reteined in his seruice.

The order of the cardinals house, and first of his hall.

Then in the hall kitchin, two clearks of the kitchin; a clearke comptrollor; a surueior The hall kitchin. of the dressor; a clearke of the spicerie, the which togither kept also a continuall messe in the hall. Also in his hall kitchin he had of master cooks two, and of other cooks, laborers and children of the kitchin, twelue persons; foure yeomen of the scul-lerie, and foure yeomen of the siluer scullerie; two yeomen of the pastrie, with two other pastelers vnder the yeomen.

Then in his priuie kitchin a master cooke, who went dailie in veluet or in sattin, with The priuie kichin. a chaine of gold, with two other yeomen and a groome: in the scalding house, a kichin. yeoman and two groomes: in the pantrie two persons: in the butterie two yeomen, The scalding house. two groomes, and two pages: and in the yewrie likewise: in the cellar thrée yeomen, The pantrie. and thrée pages: in his chandrie two: in the wafarie two: in the wardrobe of beds, The butterie. the maister of the wardrobe, and ten other persons: in the landrie, a yeoman, a The cellar. groome, thirtie pages, two yeomen purueiors, & one groome: in the bake-house, a The chandrie yeoman and two groomes: in the wood-yard a yeoman, and a groome: in the barne wafarie, &c. one: in the garden a yeoman and two groomes: porters at the gate, two yeomen, and two groomes: a yeoman of his barge: and a maister of his horsse: a clearke of the stable, a yeoman of the same: the sadler: the ferrier: a yeoman of his chariot: a sumpter man: a yeoman of his stirrop: a muleter: sixtéene groomes of his stable, euerie of them kept foure geldings.

In the almorie a yeoman and a groome: in his chappell he had a deane, a great Thomas Wol-diuine, and a man of excellent learning: a subdeane: a repeater of the quire: a gos- seies chappell peller: a pistler: of singing priests ten: a maister of the children: seculars of the office there. chappell, singing men twelue: singing children ten, with one seruant to await vpon the children: in the reuestrie a yeoman, and two groomes, ouer and besides diuerse reteiners that came thither at principall feasts. For the furniture of his chappell, it The furniture of passeth my capacitie to declare the number of costlie ornaments and rich iewels that his chappell. were to be occupied in the same continuallie: there hath béene séene in procession, about the hall, foure and fortie verie rich coapes of one sute worne, besides the rich crosses and candlestickes, and other ornaments to the furniture of the same.

He had two crossebearers, and two pillerbearers in his great chamber; and in his Officers of cre-priuie chamber these persons: first the chiefe chamberleine, and vicechamberleine: dit about Thomas of gentlemen vshers, besides one in his priuie chamber, he had twelue dailie waiters; priuie chamber. and of gentemen waiters in his priuie chamber he had six, and of lords nine or ten, who had each of them two men allowed them to attend vpon them, except the earle of Darbie, who had allowed fiue men: then had he of gentlemen, of cupbearers, caruers, and sewers, both of the priuie chamber, and of the great chamber, with gen-tlemen dailie waiters there, fortie persons: of yeomen vshers six: of groomes in his chamber eight: of yeomen in his chamber fiue and fortie dailie: he had also almes men sometime more in number than other sometime.

There was attending on his boord of doctors and chapleins, besides them of his Attendants on chappell, sixtéene dailie: a clearke of his closet: secretaries two: and two clearks his boord. of his signet: and foure counsellers learned in the law. And forsomuch as it was necessarie to haue diuerse officers of the Chancerie to attend vpon him, that is to saie, Officers of the the clerke of the crowne: a riding clearke: a clearke of the hamper: and a chafer of Chancerie. the wax: then a clearke of the checke, aswell vpon the chapleins, as of the yeoman of his chamber: he had also foure footmen which were garnished in rich running coats, His footmen. whensoeuer he rode in anie iourneie: then had he an herald of armes: and a sargeant His herald at of armes: a physician: an apothecarie: foure minstrels: a kéeper of his tents: an armes & other armorer: an instructor of his wards: two yeomen of the wardrobe of his robes: officers. and a keeper of his chamber continuallie in the court: he had also in his house the surueior of Yorke, and a clearke of the gréene cloth.

5 A 2

All

All these were dailie attending, downe lieng and vprising, and at meales: he kept in his great chamber a continuall boord for the chamberers and gentlemen officers, hauing with them a messe of the yoong lords, and another of gentlemen. Besides all these, there was neuer an officer, gentleman, or worthie person, but he was allowed in the house, some thrée, some two, and all other one at the least, which grew to a great number of persons. Thus farre out of the checker roll, besides other officers,

Thomas Wolseie twise ambassador to the emperour Charles. seruauts, reteiners, and suters, that most commonlie dined in the hall. After that he was thus furnished, he was sent twise in ambassage to the emperour Charles the fift, for diuerse vrgent causes touching the kings maiestie, it was thought, that so noble a prince (the cardinall) was most méet to be sent: wherfore being readie to take vpon him the charge thereof, hée was furnished in all degrées and purposes, most like a great prince.

For first he procéeded foorth furnished like a cardinall: his gentlemen being verie manie in number, were clothed in liuerie coats of crimsin veluet of the best, with chaines of gold about their necks, and his yeomen and meane officers in coats of fine scarlet, garded with blacke veluet an hand broad. Thus furnished, he was twise sent into Flanders to the emperour then lieng in Bruges, whome he did most highlie interteine, discharging all his charges and his mens. There was no house within the towne of Bruges, wherein anie gentleman of the cardinals was lodged, or had recourse,

The emperors munificence notable and worthie his imperiall person. but that the owners were commanded by the emperours officers, that they, vpon paine of their liues, should take no monie for any thing that the cardinals seruants did take of anie kind of vittels, no although they were disposed to make anie costlie bankets.

Commanding furthermore their said hostes, to sée that they lacked no such things as they honestlie required for their honestie and pleasure. Also the emperours officers euerie night went through the towne from house to house, whereas anie English gentlemen did repast or lodge, and serued their liueries for all night, which was doone in this maner. First, the officers brought into the house a cast of fine manchet, and of siluer two great pots with white wine, and sugar to the weight of a pound: white lights and yellow lights of wax: a boll of siluer with a goblet to drinke in, and euerie night a staffetorch: this was the order of the liueries euerie night. And in the morning, when the same officers came to fetch awaie their stuffe, then would they account with the hostes for the gentlemens costs spent in the daie before. Thus the emperour interteined the cardinall and all his traine for the time of his ambassage there. And that doone, he returned into England with great triumph.

The maner of his going to Westminster hall dailie in the terme time. Now of his order in going to Westminster hall dailie in the tearme. First yer he came out of his priuie chamber, he heard seruice in his closet, and there said his seruice with his chapleine; then going againe to his priuie chamber, he would demand if his seruants were in a readinesse, and furnished his chamber of presence, and waiting chamber. Being thereof then aduertised, he came out of his priuie chamber about eight of

His owne apparell of crimsin and other sumptuous stuffe. the clocke, apparelled all in red, that is to say, his vpper garment either of fine scarlet, or else fine crimsin taffata, but most comonlie of fine crimsin sattin ingrained, his pillion of fine scarlet, with a necke set in the inner side with blacke veluet, and a tippet of sables about his necke, holding in his hand an orenge, whereof the substance within was taken out, and filled vp againe with the part of a sponge, wherein was vinegar and other confections against the pestilent aires, the which he most commonlie held to his nose when he came among anie prease, or else that he was pestered with manie suters.

The tokens and marks of his dignities borne before him. Before him was borne first the broad seale of England, and his cardinals hat, by a lord, or some gentleman of worship, right solemnlie: & as soone as he was once entered into his chamber of presence, his two great crosses were there attending to be borne before him: then cried the gentlemen vshers, going before him bare headed, and
said

said: On before my lords and maisters, on before, make waie for my lords grace. Thus went he downe through the hall with a sergeant of armes before him, bearing a great mace of siluer, and two gentlemen carieng two great pillers of siluer. And when he came at the hall doore, there was his mule, being trapped all in crimsin veluet, with a saddle of the same stuffe, & gilt stirrups. Then was there attending vpon him when he was mounted, his two crosse-bearers: & his piller-bearers in like case vpon great horsses, trapped all in fine scarlet. Then marched he forward with a traine of noble men and gentlemen, hauing his footmen foure in number about him, bearing ech of them a gilt pollax in their hands.

Thus passed he foorth vntill he came to Westminster hall doore, and there lighted, His behauior in the court of Chancerie & Starchamber. and went vp after this maner into the Chancerie, or into the Starre-chamber: howbeit, most commonlie he would go into the Chancerie, and staie a while at a barre made for him beneath the Chancerie on the right hand, and there commune sometime with the iudges, and some time with other persons: and that doone, he would repaire into the Chancerie, and sitting there vntill eleuen of the clocke, hearing of sutes, and determining of other matters, from thence he would diuers times go into the Starre-chamber, as occasion serued. There he neither spared high nor low, but iudged euerie state according to his merits and deserts.

He vsed also euerie sundaie to resort to the court, then being for the most part of His order of going to and coming from the court. all the yeare at Gréenewich, with his former triumphs, taking his barge at his owne staires, furnished with yeomen standing upon the bails, and his gentlemen being within about him, and landed againe at the thrée cranes in the Vintrie: and from thense he rode vpon his mule with his crosse, his pillers, his hat and broad seale carried afore him on horssebacke through Thames street, vntill he came to Billingsgate, and there tooke his barge againe, and so was rowed to Gréenewich, where he was receiued of the lords and chiefe officers of the kings house, as the treasuror, comptrollor and others, and so conueied vnto the kings chamber. Then the court was woonderfullie furnished with noblemen and gentlemen: and after dinner among the lords, hauing some consultation with the king or with the councell, he would depart homeward with the like triumph.

Thus in great honour, triumph, and glorie, he reigned a long season, ruling all things within the realme apperteining vnto the king. His house was resorted to with noblemen and gentlemen, feasting and banketting ambassadors diuerse times, and all The cardinals house like a princes court for all kind of brauerie & sumptuousnesse. other right noblie. And when it pleased the king for his recreation to repaire to the cardinals house (as he did diuerse times in the yeare) there wanted no preparations or furniture: bankets were set foorth with maskes and mummeries, in so gorgeous a sort and costlie maner, that it was an heauen to behold. There wanted no dames or damosels meet or apt to danse with the maskers, or to garnish the place for the time: then was there all kind of musike and harmonie, with fine voices both of men and children.

On a time the king came suddenlie thither in a maske with a dozen maskers all in A maske and banket, the king in person present at the cardinals house. garments like shéepheards, made of fine cloth of gold, and crimosin sattin paned, & caps of the same, with visards of good physnomie, their haires & beards either of fine gold-wire silke, or blacke silke, hauing sixtéene torch-bearers, besides their drums and other persons with visards, all clothed in sattin of the same color. And before his entring into the hall, he came by water to the water gate without anie noise, where were laid diuerse chambers and guns charged with shot, and at his landing they were shot off, which made such a rumble in the aire, that it was like thunder: it made all the noblemen, gentlemen, ladies, and gentlewomen, to muse what it should meane, comming so suddenlie, they sitting quiet at a solemne banket, after this sort.

First yée shall vnderstand, that the tables were set in the chamber of presence iust The cardinals statelie sitting at table like a prince. couered, & the lord cardinall sitting vnder the cloth of estate, there hauing all his seruice.

seruice alone: and then was there set a ladie with a noble man, or a gentleman and a gentlewoman throughout all the tables in the chamber on the one side, which were made and ioined as it were but one table, all which order and deuise was doone by the lord Sandes then lord chamberleine to the king, and by sir Henrie Gilford comptroller of the kings maiesties house. Then immediatlie after the great chamberleine, and the said comptrollor, sent to looke what it should meane (as though they knew nothing of the matter) who looking out of the windowes into the Thames, returned againe and shewed him, that it séemed they were noblemen and strangers that arriued at his bridge, comming as ambassadours from some forren prince.

With that (quoth the cardinall) I desire you, bicause you can speake French, to take the paines to go into the hall, there to receiue them according to their estates, and to conduct them into this chamber, where they shall sée vs, and all these noble personages being merie at our banket, desiring them to sit downe with vs, and to take part of our fare. Then went he incontinent downe into the hall, whereas they receiued them with twentie new torches, and conueied them vp into the chamber, with such a noise of drums and flutes, as seldome had béene heard the like. At their entring into the chamber two and two togither, they went directlie before the cardinall, where he sate and saluted him reuerentlie.

To whom the lord chamberleine for them said: Sir, for as much as they be strangers, and can not speake English, they haue desired me to declare vnto you, that they hauing vnderstanding of this your triumphant banket, where was assembled such a number of excellent dames, they could doo no lesse vnder support of your grace, but to repaire hither, to view as well their incomparable beautie, as for to accompanie them at mum-chance, and then to danse with them: and sir, they require of your grace licence to accomplish the said cause of their cōming. To whom the cardinall said he was verie well content they should so doo. Then went the maskers, and first saluted all the dames, and returned to the most worthie, and there opened their great cup of gold filled with crownes and other péeces of gold, to whom they set certeine péeces of gold to cast at.

Thus perusing all the ladies and gentlewomen, to some they lost, and of some they woone: and marking after this maner all the ladies, they returned to the cardinall with great reuerence, powring downe all their gold so left in their cup, which was aboue two hundred crownes: At all (quoth the cardinall) and so cast the dice and wan them, whereat was made a great noise and ioy. Then quoth the cardinall to the lord chamberleine, I praie you (quoth he) that you would shew them, that me séemeth there should be a nobleman amongst them, who is more meet to occupie this seat and place than I am, to whome I would most gladlie surrender the same according to my dutie, if I knew him.

Then spake the lord chamberleine to them in French, and they rounding him in the eare, the lord chamberlein said to my lord cardinall: Sir (quoth he) they confesse, that among them there is such a noble personage, whom, if your grace can appoint him out from the rest, he is content to disclose himselfe, and to accept your place. With that the cardinall taking good aduisement among them, at the last (quoth he) me séemeth the gentleman with the blacke beard, should be euen he: and with that he arose out of his chaire, and offered the same to the gentleman in the blacke beard with his cap in his hand. The person to whom he offered the chaire was sir Edward Neuill, a comelie knight, that much more resembled the kings person in that maske than anie other.

The king perceiuing the cardinall so deceiued, could not forbeare laughing, but pulled downe his visar and master Neuils also, and dashed out such a pleasant countenance and chéere, that all the noble estates there assembled, perceiuing the king to be

there

there among them, reioised verie much.   The cardinall eftsoons desired his highnesse to take the place of estate.   To whom the king answered, that he would go first and shift his apparell, and so departed into my lord cardinals chamber, and there new apparelled him : in which time the dishes of the banket were cleane taken vp, and the tables spred againe with new cleane perfumed cloths, euerie man and woman sitting still, vntill the king with all his maskers came among them againe all new apparelled.

Then the king tooke his seat vnder the cloth of estate, commanding euerie person to sit still as they did before : in came a new banket before the king, and to all the rest throughout all the tables, wherein were serued two hundred diuerse dishes, of costlie deuises and subtilties.   Thus passed they foorth the night with banketting, dansing, and other triumphs, to the great comfort of the king, and pleasant regard of the nobilitie there assembled.   And thus spent this cardinall his time from daie to daie, and yeare to yeare, in such wealth, ioie, triumph, and glorie, hauing alwaies on his side the kings especiall fauour, vntill fortune enuied his prosperitie, and ouerthrew all the foundations of his glorie; which as they were laid vpon sand, so they shroonke and slipt awaie, whereby insued the ruine of his estate, euen to the verie losse of his life, which (as a man of a guiltie conscience, and fearing capitall punishment due by law for his vndutifull demeanour against his souereigne) Edward Hall saith (vpon report) he partlie procured, willinglie taking so great a quantitie of a strong purgation, as nature was therewith oppressed, and vnable to digest the same ; so that in fine he gaue vp the ghost, and was buried in Leicester abbeie : of whome to saie more I will surceasse, concluding onelie with a description which I find of him not impertinent for this place, sith wholelie concerning his person.

¶ This cardinall (as you may perceiue in this storie) was of a great stomach, for he compted himselfe equall with princes, & by craftie suggestion gat into his hands innumerable treasure : he forced little on simonie, and was not pittifull, and stood affectionate in his owne opinion : in open presence he would lie and saie vntruth, and was double both in speech and meaning : he would promise much & performe little : he was vicious of his bodie, and gaue the clergie euill example : he hated sore the citie of London & feared it : it was told him that he should die in the waie toward London, wherefore he feared least the commons of the citie would arise in riotous maner and so slaie him, yet for all that he died in the waie toward London, carrieng more with him out of the world than he brought into it; namellie a winding shéete, besides other necessaries thought méet for a dead man, as christian comelinesse required.   This ruine of the cardinall was not so much as once dreampt vpon, when I. Leland the famous antiquarie wrote this welwishing octastichon vnto the said Wolseie (being then in the flowre of his glorie, and the pearle of his pride) as hereafter followeth.

A new banket
vpon the sudden
of 200 dishes.

*Ab. Fl. ex
Edw. Hall
Clxxxxiiij.*
The description
of the cardinall.

*Ad. Tho. Wol-
uesegū archie-
piscopum Isuro-
canum.*

Sic tuus Henricus, regum qui gloria, florens,
  Perpetuo studio te colat, ornet, amet :
Sic pia coniungat proceres concordia magnos,
  Vt iusto belli fulmine Turca ruat :
Sic vastas operum tantorum deniq; moles
  Absoluas, summo templa dicata Deo.
Sis bonus (ô fœlix) mihi ! tutela Camænæ
  Dicéris meritò præsidiúmq; meæ.

After the cardinall was dead, the king remooued from Hampton court Gréenwich, where he with quéene Katharine kept a solemne Christmasse, and on the Twelfe night he set in the hall in his estate, whereas were diuerse enterludes, rich maskes and disports, and after that a great banket.   Now after Christmas he came to his manour of Westminster, which before was called Yorke place : for after that the cardinall was attainted in the premunire, & was gone northward, he made a feoffement of the same

The king and
quéene kept a
solemne Christ-
masse at Gréen-
wich.

place

place to the king, and the chapiter of the cathedrall church of Yorke by their writing confirmed the same feoffement, & then the king changed the name and called it the kings manor of Westminster, and no more Yorke place.

The whole cleargie of England euer supported and mainteined the power legantine of the cardinall, wherefore the kings learned councell said plainlie that they were all in the premunire: the spirituall lords were called by processe into the kings Bench to answer, but before their daie of appearance they in their conuocation concluded an humble submission in writing, and offered the king a hundred thousand pounds to be their good lord, & also to giue them a pardon of all offenses touching the premunire by act of parlement, the which offer with much labour was accepted, and their pardon promised. In this submission the cleargie called the king supreame head of the church of England, which thing they neuer confessed before, wherevpon manie things followed after, as you shall heare.

When the parlement was begun the sixt daie of Ianuarie, the pardon of the spirituall persons was signed with the kings hand, and sent to the lords, which in time conuenient assented to the bill, and sent it to the commons in the lower house. Now when it was read, diuerse froward persons would in no wise assent to it except all men were pardoned, saieng that all men which had anie thing to doo with the cardinall were in the same case. The wiser sort answered, that they would not compell the king to giue them his pardon, & beside that it was vncharitablie doone of them to hurt the cleargie, and doo themselues no good: wherefore they aduised them to consent to the bill, and after to sue to the king for their pardon, which counsell was not followed, but they determined first to send the speaker to the king yer they would assent to the bill.

Wherevpon Thomas Audleie speaker for the commons, with a conuenient number of the common house, came to the kings presence, and there eloquentlie declared to the king, how the commons sore lamented and bewailed their chance, to thinke or imagine themselues to be out of his gratious fauor, bicause that he had gratiouslie giuen his pardon of the premunire to his spirituall subiects and not to them: wherefore they most humblie besought his grace of his accustomed goodnesse and clemencie to include them in the same pardon. The king wiselie answered that he was their prince and souereigne lord, and that they ought not to restraine him of his libertie, nor to compell him to shew his mercie; for it was at his pleasure to vse the extremitie of his laws or mitigate and pardon the same: wherefore sith they denied to assent to the pardon of the spirituall persons, which pardon (he said) he might giue without their assent by his great seale, he would be well aduised yer he pardoned them, bicause he would not be noted to be compelled to it.

With this answer the speaker and the commons departed verie sorowfull and pensiue, and some light persons said that Thomas Crumwell, which was newlie come to the fauour of the king, had disclosed the secrets of the commons, which thing caused the king to be so extreame. The king like a good prince considered how sorowfull his commons were of the answer that he made them, and thought that they were not quiet: wherefore of his owne motion he caused a pardon of the premunire to be drawne, and signed it with his hand, and sent it to the common house by Christopher Hales his atturneie, which bill was soone assented to. Then the commons louinglie thanked the king, and much praised his wit, that he had denied it to them when they vnworthilie demanded it, and had bountifullie granted it when he preceiued that they sorrowed and lamented.

While the parlement sat, on the thirtith daie of March at afternoone, there came into the common house the lord chancellor and diuerse lords of the spiritualtie and temporaltie, to the number of twelue, and there the lord chancellor said: You of this worshipfull house (I am sure) be not so ignorant, but you know well, that the king

our

our souereigne lord hath married his brothers wife, for she was both wedded and bedded with his brother prince Arthur, and therefore you may suerlie saie that he hath married his brothers wife. If this marriage be good or no manie clerkes doo doubt. Wherefore the king like a vertuous prince willing to be satisfied in his conscience, & also for the suertie of his realme, hath with great deliberation consulted with profound clerkes, & hath sent my lord of London here present, to the chiefe vniuersities of all christen- _{Namelie Ed-} dome, to know their opinion and iudgement in that behalfe. And although that the _{mund Bonner.} vniuersities of Cambridge and Oxford had béene sufficient to discusse the cause, yet bicause they be in his realme, and to auoid all suspicion of parcialitie he hath sent into the realme of France, Italie, the popes dominions and Venecians, to know their iudgement in that behalfe, which haue concluded, written, and sealed their determinations according as you shall heare read. Then sir Brian Tuke tooke out of a box certeine writings sealed, and read them word by word as after insueth, translated out of Latine into the English toong.

Determinations of diuerse vniuersities touching the vnlawfulnesse of the king marriage, and first the determination of the vniuersitie of Orleance.

NOT long since there were put foorth to vs the college of doctors, regents of the vniuersitie of Orleance, these two questions that follow. The first, whether it be lawfull by the law of God for the brother to take to wife that woman whom his brother hath left? The second, if this be forbidden by the law of God, whether this prohibition of the law of God may be remitted by the pope his dispensation? We the foresaid college of doctors regents, according to our custome and vsage came manie times togither, and did sit diuerse times vpon the discussing of these foresaid doubts and questions, and did examine and weigh as much as we might diuerse and manie places, both of the old testament and the new, and also the interpretors and declarers both of the law of God and the canon law.

After we had weighed & considered all things exactlie, with good leisure and deliberation we haue all determined and concluded, that these foresaid mariages cannot be attempted, nor enterprised, except a man doo wroong, and plaine contrarie to the law of God : yea and that although it be doone by pardon and sufferance of the pope. And in witnesse of this conclusion and determination, we haue caused this present publike writing to be signed by the scribe of our said vniuersitie, and to be strengthened & fortified with the seale of the same. Enacted in the chapell of our ladie, the annuntiation, or the good tidings that she had of Christes comming in Orleance, the yeare of our Lord 1529, the 5. daie of Aprill.

The determination of the facultie of decrees of the vniuersitie of Paris.

IN the name of the Lord so be it. There was put foorth before vs the deane _{Lawiers of} and college of the right councelfull facultie of decrées of the vniuersitie of Paris, _{Paris.} this question? Whether that the pope might dispense, that the brother might marrie the wife that his brother hath left, if mariage betweene his brother now dead and his wife were once consummate? We the deane and college of the said facultie after manie disputations and reasons made of both sides vpon this matter, and after great and long turning and searching of bookes, both of the law of God, and the popes law, and of the law ciuill, we counsell and saie that the pope hath no power to dispense in this foresaid case. In witnesse whereof we haue caused this present writing to be strengthened with the seale of our facultie and with the signe of our

scribe

scribe or chiefe bedle. Yeuen in the congregation or assemble at saint Iohn Late-renense in Paris the second daie of Maie 1530.

The determination of ciuilians and canonists of the vniuersitie of Aniou.

Aniou.

NOT long time since there were proposed vnto vs the rector and doctors regents in law canon and ciuill of the vniuersitie of Aniou, these two questions here following, that is to wit; Whether it is vnlawfull by the law of God & the law of nature for a man to marrie the wife of his brother, that is departed without children, so that the marriage was consummate? And againe, whether it is lawfull for the pope to dispense with such marriage? We the aforesaid rector and doctors haue according to our custome and vsage manie times communed togither, and sitten to dispute these questions, and to find out the certeintie of them. And after that we had discussed and examined manie and diuerse places, aswell of the law of God as of the law of man, which séemed to perteine to the same purpose, and after we had brought reasons for both parties, and examinedt hem: all things faithfullie and after good conscience considered, and vpon sufficient deliberation and aduisement taken, we define and determine that neither by the law of God nor of nature, it is permitted for any christian man, no not euen with the authoritie of the sée apostolike, or with anie dispensation granted by the pope, to marrie the wife that his brother hath left, although his brother be departed without children, after that the marriage is once finished and consummate. And for witnes of the aforesaid things, we haue commanded the scribe of our said vniuersi-tie to signe this present publike instrument, and it to be fortified with the great seale of our vniuersitie. Enacted in the church of saint Peter in Aniou, the yeare of our Lord 1530, the 7 daie of Maie.

The determination of the facultie of diuinitie in the vniuersitie of Paris.

Paris.

THE deane and the facultie of the holie diuinitie of the vniuersitie of Paris, to all them to whom this present writing shall come, wisheth safetie in our sauiour Iesu Christ, which is the verie true safetie. Where of late there is risen a great con-trouersie of great difficultie, vpon the marriage betweene the most noble Henrie the eight king of England defendor of the faith, and lord of Ireland, &c: and the no-ble ladie Katharine quéene of England, daughter to the catholike king Ferdinand, which marriage was not onelie contract betwéene hir and hir former husband, but also con-summate and finished by carnall intermedling.

This question also was proposed to vs to discusse and examine according to iustice and truth, that is to saie; Whether to marie hir that one brother dead without children hath left, being so prohibited by the law of God and nature, that it can not be law-full by the popes dispensation, that any christian man shuld marrie the wife that his brother hath left? We the foresaid deane and facultie calling to our remembrance, how vertuous and how holie a thing, and how agréeable to our profession, vnto our dutie of loue and charitie it is for vs to shew the waie of iustice and right, of vertue and honestie, to them which desire to lead and passe ouer their life in the law of our Lord with sure and quiet conscience; could not but be readie to satisfie so honest and iust requests: wherevpon after our old woont, we came togither vpon our oth in the church of S. Maturine, and there for the same cause had a solemne masse with deuout praier to the Holie-ghost.

And also we tooke an oth, euerie man to deliuer and to studie vpon the foresaid
                question

question, as should be to the pleasure of God & according to conscience. And after diuerse & manie sessions or sittings, which were had and continued in the church of saint Maturine, and also in the college called Sorbon, from the eight daie of Iune to the second daie of Iulie ; when we had searched and examined through and through, with as much diligence as we could, and with such reuerence and religion or conscience as becommeth in such a matter, both the bookes of holie scripture, and also the most approoued interpretors of the same : finallie the generall and synodall councels, decrées and constitutions of the sacre and holie church, which by long custome hath béene receiued and approbate.

We the foresaid deane and facultie, disputing vpon the foresaid question, and making answer to the same, and that after the iudgement and full consent of the most part of the said facultie, haue concluded and determined, that the foresaid marriage with the brothers wife, departing without children, be so forbidden both by the law of God & of nature, that the pope hath no power to dispense with such mariages, whether they be contract or to be contract. And for credence, beléefe, and witnesse of this our assertion and determination, we haue caused the seale of our facultie, with our notaries signe, to be put vnto this present writing. Dated in our generall congregation that we kéepe by an oth at saint Maturines, the yeare of our Lord 1530, the second daie of Iulie.

The determination of the vniuersitie of Burges in Berrie or Biturs.

WE the deane and facultie of diuinitie in the vniuersitie of Burges (bicause we will *Burges.* doo according to the example of S. Paule doctor of the gentiles, which dooth likewise) will begin our writing with praier for all the belooued of God, among whome you most deare readers, vnto whome we write, be called: grace, peace, and quietnesse of conscience come to you from God the father, and from our Lord Iesu Christ. While we were gathered together all into one place (in the octaues of Whitsuntide) both in bodie and mind, and were sitting in the house of the said deane, there was a question put to vs againe, which had béene proposed to vs oftentimes before, being no small question, which was this: Whether the brother taking the wife of his brother now dead, and the marriage once consummate and perfect, dooth a thing vnlawfull or no?

At the last when we had sought for the truth of the thing, and had perceiued and found it out by much labour and studie of euerie one of vs by himselfe, and by much and often turning of holie bookes, euerie one of vs not corrupt, whereby we might the lesse obeie the truth, began as the holie ghost did put in his mind, to giue euerie man one arbitrement and sentence, which was this. I haue well perceiued in verie truth, without regard or respect of anie person, that those persons which be rehearsed in the 18 chapter of the Leuiticall law, be forbidden by the verie law of nature to contract matrimonie togither, and that this law can in no wise be released by anie authoritie of anie man, by the which there is made an abhominable discouering of his brothers foulenesse. And this is the signe of our common bedell or notarie, and the seale of our foresaid facultie put vnto this present writing the 10 daie of Iune, in the yeare of our Lord 1530. And bicause the foot of our writing shall be of one forme and fashion with the head, as we began with praier, so let vs end after the example of S. Paule that we spake of before, and saie, the grace and fauour of our Lord Iesu Christ, the charitie and loue of God and the communication of the holie ghost be with you all, Amen.

The determination of the diuines in the popes vniuersitie of Bononie.

Bononie.   GOD best and mightiest taught first the old law and testament with his owne mouth, to forme and fashion according to loue and charitie the maners and life of men. And secondarilie the same God did take afterwards manhood vpon him for to be the redéemer of man, and so made the new law or new testament, not onlie to forme and fashion according to loue and charitie the life and maners of men, but also to take awaie and to declare doubts, the which did arise in manie cases, which when they be once cléerelie determined, shall helpe greatlie to perfect vertue and goodnesse, that is to saie, to perfect loue aud charitie.

Wherefore we thought it euermore, that it should be our part to follow these most holie doctrines and lawes of our father of heauen, and that we lightned by the light of God aboue & of the holie ghost, should giue our sentence and iudgement in high and doubtfull matters, after that we haue once leisurelie and sufficientlie taken aduisement vpon the cause, and haue cléerelie searched out and opened the thing by many reasons and writings of holie fathers, as well for the one part as for the other, dooing nothing (as néere as we can) rashlie or without deliberation. Therefore where certeine great and noble men did instantlie desire vs, that we would with all diligence possible looke for this case that after insueth, & afterwards to giue our iudgement vpon the same, according to most equitie, right, and conscience, sticking onelie to the truth.

All the doctors of diuinitie of this vniuersitie, when we had euerie one by himselfe examined the matter at home in our houses, came all togither into one place, and there treated vpon it manie daies with as much cunning and learning as we could, we anon looked on the case togither, we examined it togither, we compared all things togither, we handling euerie thing by it selfe, did trie them euen as you would saie by line and rule, we brought foorth all maner of reasons which we thought could be brought for the contrarie part, and afterward solued them, yea euen the reasons of the most reuerend father cardinall Caietane, yea and moreouer the Deuteronomie dispensation of stirring vp the brothers séed, and shortlie all other maner of reasons and opinions of the contrarie part, as manie as séemed to belong to this purpose.

And this question that was asked of vs, was this: Whether it was forbidden onelie by the ordinance of the church, or else by the law of God, that a man might not marrie the wife left of his brother departed without children? And if it were commanded by both the lawes not to be doone, whether the pope may dispense with anie man to make such mariage? The which question now that we haue examined both by our selfe secretlie, and also openlie as diligentlie and exactlie as we could pcssiblie, and discussed it after the best manner that our wits would serue: we determine, giue iudgement, and saie, and as stiflie as we can we witnesse, and without anie doubt doo stedfastlie hold, that this marriage should be horrible, accurssed, and to be cried out vpon, and vtterlie abhominable not onelie for a christian man, but for an infidell, vnfaithfull or heathen.

And that it is prohibited vnder gréeuous paines and punishments by the law of God, of nature, and of man, and that the pope, though that he almost may doo all things, vnto whome Christ did giue the keies of the kingdome of heauen, hath no power to giue a dispensation to anie man for to contract such mariage for anie maner of cause, consideration or suggestion: and all we be readie at all times & in all places to defend & mainteine the truth of this our conclusion. In witnesse whereof we haue made this present writing, and haue fortified the same both with the seale of our vniuersitie, and also with the seale of our college of doctors of diuinitie, and haue subscribed & signed it with our generall and accustomed subscription in the cathedrall church of Bononie, the tenth daie of Iune, the yeare of our Lord 1530.

The

The determination of the facultie of diuinitie in the vniuersitie of Padua in Italie.

THEY that haue written for the maintenance of the catholike faith, affirme that *Padua.* God (best and mightiest) did giue the precepts & commandements of the old law with his owne mouth, to be an example for vs, wherein we might sée how we should order our life and maners, and this God had doone before he became man : and after that he had put vpon him our manhood, & was become redéemer or buier of mankind, he made the new law or testament, and of his méere liberalitie did giue it vs, not onelie for the cause aforsaid; but also to take awaie and declare all maner of doubts and questions that might arise, the which once opened and declared, what their verie true meaning is, to the intent that thereby we might be made perfectlie good, which be greatile fruitfull vnto vs and wholesome.

And séeing that this was the mind of God in making these lawes, it hath béene our intent, and euermore shall be, as it becommeth christian men, to follow these most solemne ordinances of the most high woorkemaister God, & the helpe of his light, that is aboue the capacitie of nature, to vtter our iudgment in all maner of doubts and hard questions. After we had once considered the thing after the best maner, and had by sufficient leisure made it cleere by manie euident reasons of both parties, and by manie authorities of the fathers of the church, determining nothing (as neere as we can) rashlie or without conuenient deliberation. Séeing therefore that certeine great orators or ambassadors did humblie require and praie vs, that we would vouchsafe to search out with all the diligence we could this case following, and afterwards to giue our sentence vpon the same, plainelie and simplie looking onelie on the truth.

After the doctors of diuinitie of this vniuersitie came togither, and after that we had euerie man examined the thing particularlie in our owne houses, and had beaten it with all learning and cunning that we were able : anon when we were togither, we considered, examined, and weied all things by themselues, and brought in all maner of reasons, which we thought might by anie meanes be made to the contrarie, and without all colour or cloke did wholie and cléerlie dissolue them and take them awaie. And amongst all, the dispensation by the law of Deuteronomie, of stirring vp the brothers seed, and all maner other reasons and determinations to the contrarie, that séemed to vs to perteine anie thing to that purpose, we vtterlie confuted and dispatched them.

The question that is put vnto vs is this; Whether to marrie the wife of our brother departed without children, is forbidden onelie by the law of the church, or by the law of God also ? And if it be forbidden by both these laws, whether the pope maie dispense with anie man for such matrimonie or no ? Which question now that we haue discussed it, and as farre as we could, haue made it cléere, both priuatlie euerie man by himselfe, and after all togither openlie, we saie, iudge, decrée, witnesse, and for a truth affirme, that such marriage is no marriage; yea and that it is abhorred and curssed of euerie christian man, and to be abhominate as a grieuous sinne; and that it is as cleere as can be forbidden vnder most cruell penalties by the lawes of nature, of God, and of man; and that the pope, vnto whome the keies of the kingdome of heauen be committed by Christ the sonne of God, hath no power to dispense by the right of law for anie cause, suggestion, or excuse, that anie such matrimonie should be contracted.

For those things which be forbidden by the law of God, be not vnderneath his power, but aboue it; nor he is not the vicar of God as concerning those things, but onelie in such things as God hath not determined himselfe in his law; but hath left them to the determination and ordinance of man. And to mainteine the truth of this our sentence and conclusion, and for the most certeine and vndoubted defense of the same, we all of one mind and accord shall at all times and in euerie place be readie.

In

In witnesse whereof we haue made this writing, and haue authorised it with the accustomed seale of our vniuersitie and also of our college of diuines. Dated at Padua in the church of the heremites of saint Augustine the first daie of Iulie, in the yeare of our Lord 1530.

The determination of the vniuersitie of Tholose.

THERE was treated in our vniuersitie of Tholose a verie hard question; Whether it be lawfull for the brother to marrie hir which had béene wife to his brother now departed, & that without children? There was besides this an other thing that troubled vs verie sore; Whether, if the pope which hath the cure of Christs flocke, would by his dispensation (as men call it) suffer this, that then at the least wise it might be lawfull? The rector of the vniuersitie called to counsell all the doctors regents, that were at that time at Tholose for to shew their minds on this question, and that not once, but twise: for he iudged that counsell giuing ought not to be hasted nor doone vpon head, and that we had need of time and space to doo anie thing conuenientlie and as it ought to be.

At the last there came togither into one place all the best learned and cunningest doctors, both of holie diuinitie, and also doctors that were best learned in both lawes; yea, and finallie, as manie as had anie experience in anie matter, and were able to doo anie thing either by iudgement and discretion, or by eloquence or their excellent wits; and there did sweare that they would obeie the sacred and holie councels, and would follow the decrees of the fathers, which no man that hath anie good conscience will violat or breake. And so euerie man said his mind, & the matter was debated and reasoned diffuselie and at large for both parts.

In conclusion, we fell so fast to this point, that this was the sentence and determination that our vniuersitie, with one voice of all, did determine and conclude with most pure and cléere conscience, and defiled with no maner of leuen of corruption: That it is lawfull for no man, neither by the law of God, nor by the law of nature, to take hir to wife that his brother hath left: and séeing that it maie not be doone by the law of God nor of nature, we answered all, that the pope can loose no man from that law, nor dispense with him. And as for that thing can not be contrarie to our sentence and verdict, that the brother in old time was compelled by the law of Deuteronomie to marrie the brothers wife departed without issue. For this law was but a shadow and a figure of things to come, which vanished awaie as soone as euer the light and truth of the gospell appeared. And bicause these things be thus, we haue giuen our sentence after this forme aboue, and haue commanded the same to be signed by our notarie which is our secretarie, and to be fortified and authorised by the putting to of our authenticall seale of our vniuersitie aforesaid, at Tholose the calends or first daie of October, the yeare of our Lord 1530.

After these determinations were read, there were shewed aboue an hundred books drawn by doctors of strange regions, which all agreed the kings marriage to be vnlawfull, which were not read, for the daie was spent. Then the chancellor said: " Now you of this common house maie report in your countries what you haue séene and heard, & then all men shall openlie perceiue, that the king hath not attempted this matter of will and pleasure, as some strangers report, but onlie for the discharge of his conscience and suertie of the succession of his realme: this is the cause of our repaire hither to you, and now will we depart.

When these determinations were published, all wise men in the realme much abhorred that marriage: but women, and such as were more wilfull than wise or learned, spake
against

against the determination, and said that the vniuersities were corrupt and intised so to doo, which is not to be thought. The king himselfe sore lamented his chance, and made no maner of mirth nor pastime as he was woont to doo. He dined and resorted to the quéene as he was accustomed, and diminished nothing of hir estate, and much loued and cherished their daughter the ladie Marie: but in no wise he would not come to hir bed. When Easter began to draw neere, the parlement for that time ended, and was proroged till the last daie of March, in the next yéere. In the parlement aforesaid An act of poisoning. was an act made, that whosoeuer did poison any person, should be boiled in hot water to the death: which act was made, bicause one Richard Roose, in the parlement time had poisoned diuerse persons at the bishop of Rochesters place, which Richard, according to the same act, was boiled in Smithfield the teneber wednesdaie following, to the terrible example of all other.

When the vniuersitie aforesaid, and a great number of clearks and well learned men An. Reg. 23. had determined the kings marriage to be vnlawfull, detestable, and against Gods law (as you haue heard) the king willing the quéene to haue knowledge of the same, sent to hir diuerse lords of the councell, the last daie of Maie, being the wednesdaie in Whitsun wéeke: the which lords, in hir chamber at Gréenewich, declared to hir Message sent to the quéene from the king. all the determinations (as you haue heard) and asked hir whether she would (for the quietnesse of the kings conscience) put the matter to foure prelats, and foure temporall lords of this realme, or abide by hir appeale? The quéene answered: "The king my father which concluded my marriage, I am sure, was not so ignorant but he asked councell of clearks and well learned men before he married me the second time: for if he had had anie doubt in my marriage, he would not haue disbursed so great a tresure as he did, & then all the doctors in a maner agréed my mariage to be good, insomuch that the pope himselfe, which knew best what was to be doone, did both dispense and ratifie the second marriage, against whose dooings I maruell that any person will speake or write.

"And as to the determination of the vniuersitie, I am a woman, and lacke wit and learning to answer to them, but to God I commit the iudgement of that, whether they haue doone iustlie or parciallie: for this I am sure, that neither the kings father, nor my father would haue condescended to our marriage, if it had beene declared to be vnlawfull. And where you saie that I should put the cause to eight persons of this realme for quietnesse of the kings conscience, I pray God send his grace a quiet conscience. And this shall be your answer: that I saie I am his lawfull wife, and to him lawfullie married, and by the order of holie church I was to him espoused as his true wife (although I was not so woorthie) and in that point I will abide till the court of Rome, which was priuie to the beginning, haue made thereof a determination and finall ending." With this answer the lords departed to the king, which was sorie to heare of hir wilfull opinion, and in especiall that she more trusted in the popes law, than in kéeping the precepts of God.]

Forsomuch as merchant strangers, bringing their wares into the realme, did receiue readie monie for them, and euer deliuered the same monie to other merchants by exchange, not emploieng it vpon the commodities of the realme, a proclamation was set A proclamation for merchant strangers. foorth and made, that no person should make anie exchange, contrarie to the meaning of a statute ordeined in the time of king Richard the second: by reason whereof, clothes and other commodities of this realme shortlie after were well sold, till they fell to exchange againe, and that this proclamation was forgotten. After Whitsuntide, the king & the queene remooued to Windsor, and there continued till the fourtéenth of Iulie, on the which daie the king remooued to Woodstocke, and left the quéene at Windsor, where she remained a while, & after remooued to the More, and from thence to Estamstéed, whither the king sent to hir diuerse lords, to aduise hir to be conformable to the law of God, shewing sundrie reasons to persuade hir to their purpose,

purpose, and one among the rest vsed for that present this communication, as I find it left in writing, in the behoofe of the king.

¶ " Madam, the kings highnesse hath commanded vs repairing vnto you, on his highnesse behalfe to shew vnto you thus much, that his maiestie hauing heretofore sent vnto you a great number of his councellors and learned men, to declare what great iniuries and wrongs by your procurement and solicitation were and yet be doone vnto his maiestie and this his realme, in citing his highnesse in his owne person, or by his proctor to appeare at Rome, to make answer to your sute, contrarie to the determination of all lawes, as not onelie the famous vniuersities of christendome, as Paris and Orleance; but also as the most part of the learned men here or else where in that facultie affirme, and as maister deane learned in that facultie can and will testifie vnto you, on his conscience, if it shall please you to heare him, and contrarie also to his estate roiall, and to the priuileges and prerogatiues of this his graces realme.

" His highnesse perceiuing your grace not to regard their aduertisements in right and iustice, but still to preseuere and continue, and rather increase your iniurious procurements and solicitations in that behalfe, is not a little gréeued & displeased with your continuance and prosecution of this iniurie and manifest wrong towards his maiestie, and this his graces realme. The continuance of which your vnkind dealing hath compelled his highnesse not onelie to absteine from the sight of you, but also to forebeare to receiue anie of your tokens, which doo nothing else but renew and refresh his displeasure, inforcing him also to an indignation, to see tokens offered and sent by hir, who continueth in prosecuting of so notable an iniurie and manifest wrong towards his maiestie, & this his realme, perceiuing also what boldnesse other outward princes might take to misintreat his highnesse, when they should vnderstand how his maiestie suffreth himselfe to be wronged by his pretended subiect, and so notable wrong to be doone to this his realme.

" And vpon this cause and ground, like as the kings highnesse these certeine moneths past, hath disseuered your grace from his presence, so he intendeth yet to continue, and hath commanded vs to shew you, that his pleasure is ye shalbe at your libertie, & (as ye shall thinke most commodious) repaire to either of these thrée places, his manour of Oking, his manour of Estamsteed, or the monasterie of Bisham, and there to continue without further molesting of his highnesse with your sutes or requests to the contrarie, as wherewith ye shall not preuaile; but more and more molesting and troubling his highnesse, procure his further displeasure towards you.

" And though percase the pope shall desist, as perceiuing now the matter of right he will, yet the kings highnesse cannot digest in his stomach this iniurie doone, not to be amended or reformed at your graces procurement, but your grace rather suing and instanting the contrarie. And this is the charge, madam, which the kings highnesse hath committed vnto vs, to be spoken vnto you on his highnesse behalfe. And to saie to you as of my selfe, concerning the iustnesse of the kings cause, as I haue heretofore said, I shall now repeat and rehearse againe vnto your grace ; which is, that your grace being knowne by prince Arthur, ye be not lawfull wife to the kings highnesse our souereigne lord in my conscience." This speach ended, others of the companie vsed their persuasorie talke to the quéene: whose words notwithstanding did so little mooue hir, that she stood stiffelie in hir first opinion, that she was his true and lawfull wife, and from the same would not by anie meanes be remooued.]

The priests of London being called afore the bishop that would haue had them contributaries to the paiment of the hundred thousand pounds, granted to the king for his pardon of the premunire, kept such a stir in breaking into the chapiter house (where the bishop sat) all at once and striking and buffeting the bishops seruants which gaue them euill language, that the bishop was faine to giue them his blessing, and suffer them to depart in quiet for that time. But after, vpon complaint made to the lord
chancellor,

chancellor, diuerse of them and of their partakers were arrested, and committed to prison, to the number of fiftéene priests, and fiue laie men, some to the Tower, and some to the Fleet, and to other places, where they remained long after. ¶ Thomas *Iohn Stow.* Bilneie, bachellor of law, was burnt at Norwich the nineteenth of August, and the fourth of December sir Rées Griffin was beheaded at the Tower hill, and his man named Iohn Hewes was drawne to Tiburne, and there hanged and quartered.

The fiue and twentith of Maie, betwéene London and Grauesend, were taken two great fishes called whorlepooles, male and female. ¶ In this season, there was in the realme much preaching, one learned man holding against an other, namelie in the matter of the kings mariage. After Christmas, the parlement began to sit againe, in the which the commons found themselues sore gréeued with the crueltie of ordinaries, that called men before them Ex officio. At length a booke was drawne of all the griefes of the commons, for the cruell demeanor of the cleargie, and the same deliuered to the K. by the speaker, humblie beséeching him in the name of all the commons, to take such direction therein, as to his high wisedome might séeme most expedient. The king answered, that he would take aduise, and heare the partie accused speake. He was not so readie to gratifie the commons in their requests, as some thought that he would haue béene, if they had not sticked and refused to passe a statute, which he had sent to them touching wards and primer seasons.

1532
Crueltie of ordinaries.

After this, was the parlement proroged till the tenth of Aprill. In this parlement was an act made, that bishops should paie no more annates or monie for their bulles to the pope : for it was prooued that there had béene paid for bulles of bishops, since the fourth yeare of Henrie the seuenth an hunderd thréescore thousand pounds sterling, beside other dispensations & pardons. When the parlement was begun againe after Easter, there was a motion made to helpe the king with monie toward his charges about the edifieng of houses, piles, and other fortifications, vpon the borders fore against Scotland, both for better habitation to be had there, & also for the restraint of the Scots that vsed to make inuasions. There was therefore a fiftéenth granted, but not enacted at this session, bicause that suddenlie began a pestilence in Westminster, wherfore the parlement was proroged, as ye shall heare in the next yeare.

The parlemēt proroged.
Annates forbidden to be paid.
A fiftéenth granted.

In this yeare was an old toll demanded in Flanders of Englishmen called the toll of the hound, which is a riuer and a passage. The toll is twelue pence of a fardell. It had béene often demanded, but neuer paied, insomuch that king Henrie the seuenth for the demand of that toll, prohibited all his subiects to kéepe anie mart at Antwerpe or Barrow, till it was promised that vpon their returne the said toll should neuer be demanded. The king sent doctor Knight, and others to Calis, whither came the emperours commissioners, and there (vpon talke) the matter was put in suspension for a time. The king hauing purchased of the cardinall after his attendure in the premunire his house at Westminster, called Yorke place, and got a confirmation of the cardinals feoffement thereof made of the chapter of the cathedrall church of Yorke, purchased this yeare also all the medows about saint Iames, and there made a faire mansion and a parke for his greater commoditie & pleasure. And bicause he had a great affection to the said house at Westminster, he bestowed great cost in going forward with the building thereof, and changed the name, so that it was after called the kings palace of Westminster.

A toll demanded in the low countries.
Yorke place or white Hall now the palace of Westminster.
S. Iames.

The fourtéenth daie of Maie, the parlement was proroged till the fourth of Februarie next comming. After which prorogation, sir Thomas Moore chancellor of England, after long sutes made to the king to be discharged of his office, the sixtéenth of Maie he deliuered to the king at Westminster the great seale of England, and was with the kings fauour discharged, which seale the king kept till mondaie in Whitsunwéeke, on which daie he dubbed Thomas Audleie speaker of the parlement, knight,

An. Reg. 24.
The parlemēt proroged.
Sir Thomas Moore deliuereth vp the great seale.

and

Sir Thomas Audleie lord kéeper of the great seale.

and made him lord kéeper of the great seale, and so he was called. ¶ The king being informed, that the pope and the French king should meet in the beginning of the next spring at Marseiles, he thought good for diuerse considerations, to speake with the French king in his owne person, before the pope and he should come togither: wherevpon it was concluded, that in October following, both the princes should méet betwéene Calis and Bullongne. Wherefore the king of England sent out his letters to his nobles, prelats, and seruants, commanding them to be readie at Canturburie the six and twentith of September, to passe the seas with him, for the accomplishment of the interuiew betwixt him and the French king.

The ladie Anne Bullongne created marchiones of Penbroke.

On the first of September being sundaie, the K. being come to Windsor, created the ladie Anne Bullongne marchionesse of Penbroke, and gaue to hir one thousand pounds land by the yeare; and that solemnitie finished, he rode to the college, where after that seruice was ended, a new league was concluded and sworne betwene the the king, and the French king, Messire Pomoraie the French ambassador being pre-sent.

The king passeth ouer to Calis.

On the tenth of October, the king came to Douer, and on the eleuenth daie in the morning at thrée of the clocke hée tooke shipping at Douer rode, and before ten of the same daie, he with the ladie marchionesse of Penbroke landed at Calis, where he was receiued with all honour, and lodged at the Eschecker. There came to him whilest he laie in Calis, diuerse lords from the French court, and amongst other the lord great maister of France, and the archbishop of Roane, which were honorablie of him receiued, and with them he tooke a daie and place of méeting with the king their maister.

Wherevpon the one and twentith of October, he marched out of Calis, accompa-nied with the dukes of Norffolke and Suffolke, the marquesses of Dorset and Excester, the erles of Arundell, Oxford, Surreie, Essex, Darbie, Rutland, Huntington, and Sussex, with diuerse vicounts, barons, knights of the garter, and other of the nobi-litie and gentlemen freshlie apparelled, and richlie trimmed; and comming to the

The interuiew betwixt the kings of England and France.

place appointed, he there met with the French king, who was come to receiue him with all honor that might be: and after salutations and embracings vsed in most louing maner, the king of England went with the French K. to Bullongne; and by the waie was incountered by the French kings thrée sons, and other great lords that attended them, with welcomming the king of England; he them gentlie receiued, and so all this noble companie came to Bullongne, where the king of England and his nobles were so noblie interteined, feasted, banketed, and cheared, that woonder it was to consider the great plentie of viands, spices, wines, and all other prouision necessarie for man and horsse, so that there was no more but aske and haue; and no man durst take anie monie, for the French king paid for all.

The fiue and twentith of October, whilest the king laie thus in Bullongne, the French king called a chapiter of the companions of his order named S. Michaell, of whome the king of England was one, and so there elected the dukes of Norffolke and

The dukes of Norffolke and Suffolke elected into the order of S. Michaell.

Suffolke to be companions of the same order: and being brought to the chapiter, they had their collars deliuered to them, and were sworne to the statutes of the order, their obeisance to their souereigne lord alwaie reserued. Thus the two kings laie in Bul-longne, mondaie, tuesdaie, wednesdaie, and thursdaie: and on fridaie the fiue and twentith of October, they departed out of Bullongne to Calis. Without the towne of Calis about the distance of two miles, the duke of Richmond the kings base son,

The duke of Richmond.

with a great companie of noble men, which had not béene at Bullongne, met them, and saluting the French king, embraced him in most honorable and courteous maner.

Thus they passed forward, and came to Newnham bridge, and so to Calis, where was such prouision made for the receiuing of them, as well for lodgings, plate, and all such other furniture of houshold, as also of all sorts of viands, wines, and other neces-saries, that it séemed woonderfull: in so much as the proportion assigned to the French

lords

lords oftentimes was so abundant, that they refused a great part thereof. The French kings traine was twelue hundred horsses, or rather aboue. But there was lodging inough in Calis, not onlie for them, but also for manie other, so that there were aboue eight thousand persons lodged within the towne in that season. The French king comming thither on the fridaie, tarried there till tuesdaie the thirtith of October, and then departed; the king of England accompanieng him out of the towne, till he came to enter into the French ground, and there either tooke leaue of other with right princelie countenance, louing behauiour, and so hartie words, that all men reioised that saw them.

Whilest the two kings laie in Calis, the lord Annas de Montmorancie earle of Beaumont, great master of the French kings house, & Philip de Chabot erle of Newblanke, great admerall of France, were admitted into the order of the garter, the king calling a chapiter for that purpose, of the knights of that order, at the which the French king was present, and ware a blew mantell, because he was one of the same order. Whilest the king was in the French kings dominion, he had the vpper hand, and likewise had the French king in his dominion. And as the French king paid all the Englishmens charges at Bullongne: so did the king of England at Calis. There rose about the same season such sore weather, storms and rigorous winds, continuing for the more part at north and northwest, that the king staied at Calis for a conuenient wind till tuesdaie the thirténth of Nouember at midnight, and then taking his ship, landed at Douer the next daie about fiue of the clocke in the morning. And herewith vpon his returne, he married priuilie the ladie Anne Bullongne the same daie, being the fourteenth daie of Nouember, and the feast daie of saint Erkenwald; which marriage was kept so secret, that verie few knew it till Easter next insuing, when it was perceiued that she was with child.

When the king should passe ouer the sea, he considered that the Scots would happilie attempt somewhat to the preiudice of his subiects in his absence, which sticked not (he being within the realme) to rob both by sea and land. Wherefore to resist their malice, he appointed sir Arthur Darcie with thrée hundred men to go vnto Berwike, to defend the borders from inuasions of the Scots, who shortlie after by the middle marches entred the realme, and came to a place called Fowberie, and fiering certeine villages in their waie, returned. The erle of Angus as then was at Berwike as a banished man; and the said sir Arthur determined to reuenge this displeasure: and thereupon with foure hundred men made a rode into Scotland, and set a village on fire. Then immediatlie assembled togither eight hundred Scots, and began to approch néere to the English men, who perceiuing them, caused their trumpet to blow the retreit, and the erle and twentie with him shewed himself on an hill, euen in the face of the Scots, and the trumpet blew at their backs, so that the Scots thought that there had been two companies, which caused the Scots to flie, and the Englishmen followed and slew a great number of them, and tooke manie of them prisoners.

After Christmasse sir Thomas Audleie lord kéeper of the great seale was made high chancellor of England. And when the parlement began, because the office of the speaker was void, Humfreie Wingfield of Greis inne was chosen speaker. In this parlement was an act made, that no person should appeale for anie cause out of this realme to the court of Rome, but from the commissarie to the bishop, and from the bishop to the archbishop, and from the archbishop to the king; and all causes of the king to be tried in the vpper house of the conuocation. It was also enacted the same time, that quéene Katharine should no more be called queene, but princesse Dowager, as the widow of prince Arthur. ¶ In the season of the last summer died William Warham archbishop of Canturburie, and then was named to that sea Thomas Cranmer the kings chapleine, a man of good learning, and of a vertuous life, which latelie before had béene ambassador from the king to the pope.

5 C 2

After

Quéene Anne.

After that the king perceiued his new wife to be with child, he caused all officers necessarie to be appointed to hir, and so on Easter euen she went to hir closet openlie as quéene; and then the king appointed the daie of hir coronation to be kept on Whitsundaie next following: and writings were sent to all shiriffs, to certifie the names of men of fortie pounds to receiue the order of knighthood, or else to make fine. The assesment of the fine was appointed to Thomas Cromwell, maister of the kings iewell house, & councellor to the king, a man newlie receiued into high fauour. He so vsed the matter, that a great summe of monie was raised to the kings vse by those fines. The matter of the quéenes appeale wherevnto she still sticked, and by no means could be remooued from it, was communed of, both in the parlement house, and also in the conuocation house, where it was so handled, that manie were of opinion, that not onelie hir appeale, but also all other appeales made to Rome were void and of none effect: for that in ancient councels it had béene determined, that a cause rising in one prouince should be determined in the same.

An. Reg. 25.

This matter was opened with all the circumstances to the ladie Katharine Dowager (for so was she then called) the which persisted still in hir former opinion, and would reuoke by no means hir appeale to the court of Rome. Wherevpon the archbishop of Canturburie accompanied with the bishops of London, Winchester, Bath, Lincolne, and diuers other learned men in great number, rode to Dunstable, which is six miles from Ampthill, where the princesse Dowager laie, and there by one doctor Lée, she was cited to appeare before the said archbishop in cause of matrimonie in the said towne of Dunstable, and at the daie of appearance she appeared not, but made de-

The ladie Katharine Dowager called peremptorilie.

fault, and so she was called peremptorie euerie daie fiftéene daies togither, and at the last, for lacke of appearance, by the assent of all the learned men there present, she was diuorsed from the king, and the mariage declared to be void and of none effect. Of this diuorse and of the kings mariage with the ladie Anne Bullongne men spake diuerselie; some said the king had doone wiselie, and so as became him to doo in discharge of his conscience. Other otherwise iudged, and spake their fansies as they thought good: but when euerie man had talked inough, then were they quiet, and all rested in good peace.

In Maie pope Clement sent an orator to the king, requiring him to appeare personallie at the generall councell which he had appointed to be kept the yeere following. But when his commission was shewed, at the earnest request of the king, there was neither place nor time specified for the keeping of that councell; and so with an vncerteine answer to an vncerteine demand he departed, but not vnrewarded. The

Ambassadors to the French king.

king vnderstanding that the pope, the emperor, & the French king shuld méet at Nice in Iulie folowing, appointed the duke of Norffolke, the lord Rochford brother to quéene Anne, sir William Pawlet controllor of his house, sir Anthonie Browne, and sir Francis Brian knights, to go in ambassage to the French king, and both to accompanie him to Nice, and also to commune with the pope there concerning his staie in the kings diuorse. These worthie personages made their prouision readie; and so with the number of eight score horsses they went to Douer, and passing ouer to Calis, tooke their waie through France, to accomplish their ambassage as they had in commandement.

Proclamation for the coronation of quéene Anne.

In the beginning of Maie, the king caused open proclamations to be made, that all men that claimed to doo anie seruice, or execute anie office at the solemne feast of the coronation by the waie of tenure, grant, or prescription, should put their grant thrée wéekes after Easter in the Starrechamber before Charles duke of Suffolke, for that time high steward of England, and the lord chancellor and other commissioners.

The seuerall claimes of diuerse honorable and worshipfull persons.

The duke of Norffolke claimed to be erle marshall, and to exercise his office at that feast; the erle of Arundell claimed to be high butler, and to exercise the same; the erle of Oxford claimed to be chamberleine; the vicount Lisle claimed to be pantler;

the

the lord Aburgauennie to be chiefe larderer; and the lord Braie claimed to be almoner, and sir Henrie Wiat knight claimed to be ewrer. All these noble personages desired their offices with their fées.

Beside these, the maior of London claimed to serue the quéene with a cup of gold, and a cup of assaie of the same, and that twelue citizens should attend on the cupboord, and the maior to haue the cup and cup of assaie for his labor: which petition was allowed. The fiue ports claimed to beare a canopie ouer the quéens head the daie of the coronation with foure guilt belles, and to haue the same for a reward, which to them was allowed. Diuerse other put in petie claimes which were not allowed, bicause they séemed onlie to be doone at the kings coronation. All this season great purueiance was made of all maner of vittels: & lords, knights & esquiers were sent for out of all countries, which came to London at their daie with a great number of people.

The receiuing, conueieng, and coronation of quéene Anne, wife to the high & mighty prince king Henrie the eight. *Edw. Hall.* CCxij.

¶ After that the kings highnesse had addressed his gratious letters to the maior and communaltie of the citie, signifieng to them, that his pleasure was to solemnize and celebrate the coronation of his most deare and welbeloued wife quéene Anne, at Westminster the Witsundaie next insuing, willed them to make preparation, as well to fetch hir grace from Greenwich to the Tower by water, as to sée the citie ordered and garnished with pageants in places accustomed, for the honor of hir grace. When she shuld be conueied from the Tower to Westminster, there was a common councell called, and commandement was giuen to the haberdashers (of which craft the maior sir Stephan Pecocke then was) that they should prepare a barge for the bachelors, with a wafter and a foist, garnished with banners and streamers likewise, as they vse to doo when the maior is presented at Westminster on the morrow after Simon and Iude. Also all other crafts were commanded to prepare barges, and to garnish them, not alonelie with their banners accustomed, but also to decke them with targets by the sides of the barges, and to set vp all such séemelie banners and bannerets as they had in their halles, or could get meet to furnish their said barges, and euerie barge to haue minstrelsie: according to which commandements great preparation was made for all things necessarie for such a noble triumph.

The kings letters to the maior of London, touching the coronation.

The cities preparation.

The nineteenth daie of Maie, the maior and his brethren all in scarlet, and such as were knights had collars of S S, and the remnant hauing good chains, and the counsell of the citie with them, assembled at saint Marie hill, and at one of the clocke descended to the new staire to their barge, which was garnished with manie goodlie banners and streamers, and richlie couered. In which barge were shalmes, shagbushes, and diuerse other instruments, which continuallie made goodlie harmonie. After that the maior and his brethren were in their barge, séeing that all the companies to the number of fiftie barges were readie to wait vpon them, they gaue commandement to the companies, that no barge should rowe néerer to another than twise the length of the barge vpon a great paine. And to sée the order kept, there were thrée light wheries prepared, and in euerie one of them two officers to call on them to kéepe their order, after which commandement giuen, they set foorth in order as hereafter is described.

Hir comming by water from Gréenewich on thursdaie.

First before the maiors barge was a foist or wafter full of ordinance, in which foist was a great dragon continuallie moouing and casting wild fire: and round about the said foist stood terrible monsters and wild men casting fire, and making hideous noises. Next after the foist a good distance came the maiors barge: on whose right hand was the bachelors barge, in the which were trumpets and diuerse other melodious instruments; the deckes of the said barge and the sailyards, with the top castels were hanged with rich cloth of gold and silke: at the foreship and the sterne were two great banners rich, beaten with the armes of the king and the quéene, and on the top

The maiors barge with the conceits and deuises thereof.

castell

castell also was a long streamer newlie beaten with the said armes. The sides of the barge was set full of flags and banners of the deuises of the companie of the haberdashers, and merchants aduenturers, and the cords were hanged with innumerable penselles, hauing little belles at the ends, which made a goodlie noise and a goodlie sight, wauering in the wind. On the outside of the barge were thrée dozen scutchions in mettall of arms of the king and the queene, which were beaten vpon square bucram diuided, so that the right side had the kings colours, and the left side the queenes, which scutchions were fastened on the clothes of gold and siluer, hanging on the decks on the left hand.

On the left hand of the maior was another foist, in the which was a mount, and on the same stood a white falcon crowned, vpon a roote of gold inuironed with white roses and red, which was the quéens deuise; about which mount sat virgins singing and plaieng sweetlie. Next after the maior followed his fellowship the haberdashers; next after them the mercers, then the grocers, and so euerie companie in his order, and last of all the maior and shiriffes officers, euerie companie hauing melodie in his barge by himselfe, and goodlie garnished with banners, and some garnished with silke, and some with arras and rich carpets, which was a goodlie sight to behold: and in this order they rowed to Gréenwich, to the point next beyond Gréenwich, and there they turned backeward in another order, that is to wit, the maior and shiriffs officers first, and the meanest craft next, and so ascending to the vttermost crafts in order, and the maior last, as they go to Paules at Christmas, and in that order they rowed downeward to Gréenwich towne, and there cast anchor, making great melodie.

At thrée of the clocke the queene appéered in rich cloth of gold, entring into hir barge accompanied with diuerse ladies and gentlewomen: and incontinent the citizens set forwards in their order, their minstrelles continuallie plaieng, and the bachelors barge going on the quéens right hand, which she tooke great pleasure to behold. About the quéenes barge were manie noble men, as the duke of Suffolke, the marques Dorset, the erle of Wilshire hir father, the erles of Arundell, Darbie, Rutland, Worcester, Huntington, Sussex, Oxford, and manie bishops and noble men, euerie one in his barge, which was a goodlie sight to behold. She thus being accompanied rowed toward the tower: and in the meane waie the ships which were commanded to lie on the shore for letting of the barges, shot diuerse peales of guns, and yer she was landed, there was a maruellous shot out of the tower as euer was heard there. And at hir landing there met with hir the lord chamberlaine with the officers of armes, and brought hir to the king, which receiued hir with louing countenance at the posterne by the water side, and then she turned backe againe, and thanked the maior and the citizens with manie goodlie words, and so entred into the tower. After which entrie the citizens all this while houered before the tower, making great melodie, and went not on land, for none were assigned to land but the maior, the recorder, and two aldermen. But for to speake of the people that stood on either shore to behold the sight, he that saw it not would scarse beleeue it.

On fridaie at dinner serued the king all such as were appointed by his highnesse to be knights of the bath, which after dinner were brought to their chambers, and that night were bathed and shriuen, according to the old vsage of England, and the next daie in the morning the king dubbed them according to the ceremonies thereto belonging, whose names insue; the marques Dorset, the erle of Darbie, the lord Clifford, the lord Fitzwater, the lord Hastings, the lord Mounteagle, sir Iohn Mordant, the lord Vaux, sir Henrie Parker, sir William Winsore, sir Francis Weston, sir Thomas Arundell, sir Iohn Hulston, sir Thomas Poinings, sir Henrie Sauell, sir George Fitzwilliam, sir Iohn Tindall, sir Thomas Iermeie.

To

To the intent that the horsses should not slide on the pauement, nor that the people should not be hurt by horsses, the high stréets where the queene should passe were all grauelled from the tower to temple barre, and railed on the one side, within which railes stood the crafts along in their order from Grace church, where the merchants of the stilliard stood till the little conduit in Cheape, where the aldermen stood: and on the other side of the stréet stood the constables of the citie, apparelled in veluet and silke, with great staues in their hands, to cause the people to kéepe roome and good order. And when the stréets were somwhat ordered, the maior clothed in a gowne of crimsin veluet, and a rich collar of SSS, with two footmen clad in white and red damaske, rode to the tower to giue his attendance on the quéene, on whome the shiriffs with their officers did wait till they came to tower hill, where they taking their leaue, rode downe the high stréets, commanding the constables to sée roome and good order kept, and so went and stood by the aldermen in Cheape. The receiuing and conueieng of the quéen through London.

The maior in a gowne of crimsin veluet.

Now before the quéen and hir traine should come, Cornehill and Gratious stréet were hanged with fine scarlet, crimsin, and other grained cloths, and in some place with rich arras, tapistrie, and carpets; and the most part of the Cheape was hanged with cloth of tissue, gold, veluet, and manie rich hangings, which made a goodlie shew, and all the windowes were replenished with ladies and gentlewomen, to behold the quéene and hir traine as they should passe by. The first of the queenes companie that set forward were twelue Frenchmen, which were belonging to the French ambassador clothed in coates of blew veluet, with sléeues of yellow and blew veluet, and their horsses trapped with close trappers of blew sarsenet powdered with white crosses: after them marched gentlemen, esquires and knights two and two: after them the iudges, and after them the knights of the bath in violet gownes, with hoods purfled with miniuer like doctors; after them abbats, then barons; after them bishops, then earls and marquesses; then the lord chancellor of England; after him the archbishop of Yorke, and the ambassador of Venice, after him the archbishop of Canturburie and the ambassador of France, after rode two esquiers of honor with robes of estat rolled and worne bauldrike-wise about their necks, with caps of estate, representing the dukes of Normandie & Aquitaine: after them rode the maior of London with his mace and garter in his cote of armes, which maior bare his mace to Westminster hall. The attire of certeine Frenchmen belonging to the French ambassador.

After all these rode the lord William Howard with the marshalles rod, deputie to his brother the duke of Norffolke marshall of England, which was ambassador then in France: and on his right hand rode Charles duke of Suffolke, for that daie high constable of England, bearing the verder of siluer apperteining to the office of con-stableship, and all the lords for the most part were clothed in crimsin veluet, and all the queenes seruants or officers of armes in scarlet. Next before the queene rode hir chancellor bareheaded, the sargeants and officers of armes rode on both the sides of the lords. Then came the quéene in a litter of white cloth of gold, not couered, nor bailed, which was lead by two palfries clad in white damaske downe to the ground, head and all, led by hir footmen. She had on a circot of white cloth of tissue, and a mantell of the same furred with ermine, hir haire hanged downe, but on hir head shee had a coife with a circlet about it full of rich stones. Ouer hir was borne a canopie of cloth of gold, with foure guilt staues and foure siluer belles. For the bearing of which canopie were appointed sixtéene knights, foure to beare it one space on foot, and other foure another space, according to their owne appointment. The two dukes of Norffolke and Suffolke in their offices.

Quéene Annes attire verie sumptuous and roiall.

Next after the quéene rode the lord Borough hir chamberleine, next after him William Coffin maister of the horsses, leading a spare horsse with a side saddle trapped downe with cloth of tissue. After him rode seauen ladies in crimsin veluet turned vp with cloth of gold and of tissue, and their horsses trapped with cloth of gold, after them two chariots couered with red cloth of gold. In the first chariot were two ladies,

Thrée chariots with goodlie ladie and gentlewomen.

ladies, which were the old dutchesse of Norffolke, and the old marchionesse Dorset. In the second chariot were foure ladies all in crimsin veluet. Then rode seauen ladies in the same sute, their horsses trappers and all. Then came the third chariot all white, with six ladies in crimsin veluet; next after them came the fourth chariot all red with eight ladies also in crimsin veluet: after whom followed thirtie gentlewomen all in veluet and silke in the liuerie of their ladies, on whom they gaue their attendance. After them followed the gard in cotes of goldsmiths worke.

Sundrie pageants with the descriptions of their deuises.

Thus they rode foorth till the came to Fanchurch, where was made a pageant all with children, apparelled like merchants, which welcommed hir to the citie, with two proper propositions both in French and English. And from thence she rode to Gratious church corner, where was a costlie and a maruelous cunning pageant made by the merchants of the Stilliard, for there was the mount Parnassus with the founteine of Helicon, which was of white marble, and foure streames without pipe did rise an ell high, and met togither in a little cup aboue the founteine, which founteine ran abundantlie racked Rhenish wine till night. On the mounteine sat Apollo, and at his feet sat Calliope, and on euerie side of the mounteine sat foure muses plaieng on seuerall sweet instruments, and at their féet epigrams and poeses were written in golden letters, in the which euerie muse according to hir propertie praised the quéene.

The quéene from thence passed to Leaden hall, where was a goodlie pageant with a type and a heauenlie roofe, and vnder the type was a roote of gold set on a little mounteine inuironed with red roses and white: out of the type came downe a falcon all white & sat vpon the roote, and incontinent came downe an angell with great melodie, and set a close crowne of gold on the falcons head. And in the same pageant sat saint Anne with all hir issue beneath hir, and vnder Marie Cleoph sat hir foure children,

An oration made to the quéene by one of the children in the pageant.

of the which children one made a goodlie oration to the queene of the fruitfulnes of saint Anne and of hir generation, trusting that like fruit should come of hir. Then she passed to the conduit in Cornehill, where were thrée graces set in a throne, afore whom was the spring of grace continuallie running wine. Afore the founteine sat a poet declaring the properties of euerie grace: and that doone euerie ladie by hir selfe, according to hir propertie, gaue to the quéene a seuerall gift of grace.

The conduit in Cheape runneth wine white and claret.

That doone, she passed by the great conduit in Chéepe, which was newlie painted with armes of deuises: out of the which conduit by a goodlie founteine set at the one end ran continuallie wine both white and claret all that afternoone, and so she rode to the Standard which was richlie painted with images of kings and quéenes, and hanged with banners of armes, and in the top was maruellous sweet harmonie both of song and instrument. Then she went forward to the crosse, which was newlie guilt, till she came where the aldermen stood, and then master Baker the recorder came to hir with low reuerence, making a proper and briefe proposition, and gaue to hir in the

The recorder presenteth a 1000 marks in gold to the quéene for a gratuitie in the cities behalfe.

name of the citie a thousand marks in a purse of gold, which she thankefullie accepted with manie goodlie words, and so rode to the little conduit, where was a rich pageant full of melodie and song.

In this pageant was Pallas, Iuno and Venus, and before them stood Mercurie, which in the name of the thrée goddesses gaue to hir a ball of gold diuided in thrée, signifieng thrée gifts which the thrée goddesses gaue to hir, that is to saie, wisedome, riches, and felicitie. As she entered into Paules gate there was a pretie pageant, in which sat thrée ladies richlie clothed, and in a circle on their head was written Regina Anna prosperè procede & regna. The ladie in the middes had a tablet, in the which was written Veni amica coronaberis, and vnder the tablet sat an angell with a close crowne, and the ladie sitting on the right hand had a tablet of siluer in which was written, Domine dirige gressus meos, & the third ladie had a tablet of gold with letters azure written, Confido in Domino, & vnder their féet was written in legible letters:

Regina Anna nouum regis de sanguine natum
Cùm paries, populis aurea secla tuis.

And

And these ladies cast downe wafers, on the which the two verses were written. From thence she passed to the east end of Paules churchyard against the schoole, where stood on a scaffold two hundred children well apparelled, which said to hir diuerse goodlie verses of poets translated into English, to the honour of the king and hir, which she highlie commended. And when she came to Ludgate, the gate was newlie garnished with gold & bise. And on the leads of saint Martins church stood a goodlie queere of singing men and children, which soong new balads made in praise of hir. After that she was passed Ludgate, she procéeded toward Fléetstréet, where the conduit was newlie painted, and all the armes and angels refreshed, & the chime melodiouslie sounding. Vpon the conduit was made a towre with foure turrets, and in euerie turret stood one of the cardinall vertues with their tokens and properties, which had seuerall spéeches, promising the queene neuer to leaue hir, but to be aiding and comforting hir: and in the middest of the towre closelie was such seuerall solemne instruments, that it séemed to be an heauenlie noise, and was much regarded and praised: and beside this the said conduit ran wine claret and red all the after-noone.

So she with all hir companie and the maior rode foorth to Temple barre, which was newlie painted and repared, where stood also diuerse singing men and children, till she came to Westminster hall, which was richlie hanged with cloth of arras, and new glased. And in the middest of the hall she was taken out of hir litter, & so led vp to the higher deske vnder the cloth of estate, on whose left hand was a cupbord of ten stages maruellous rich and beautifull to behold: and within a little season was brought to the quéene with a solemne seruice in great standing spice plates, a void of spice and subtilties with ipocras and other wines, which she sent downe to hir ladies, and when the ladies had dranke, she gaue hartie thanks to the lords and ladies, with the maior and other that had giuen their attendance on hir, and so withdrew hir selfe with a few ladies to the Whitehall and so to hir chamber, and there shifted hir, and after went into hir barge secretlie to the king to his manour of Westminster, where she rested that night.

On sundaie the maior clad in crimsin veluet and with his collar, and all the aldermen and shiriffes in scarlet, and the counsell of the citie tooke their barge at the crane by seauen of the clocke and came to Westminster, where they were welcomed & brought into the hall by master treasuror and others of the kings house, and so gaue their attendance till the quéene should come foorth. Betwéene eight and nine she same into the hall, and stood vnder the cloth of estate, and then came in the kings chappell, and the moonks of Westminster all in rich copes, and manie bishops and abbats in copes and miters which went into the middest of the hall, and there stood a season. Then was there a raie cloth spred from the quéenes standing in the hall through the palace and sanctuarie, which was railed on both sides to the high altar of Westminster. After that the raie cloth was cast, the officers of armes appointed the order accustomed..

First went gentlemen, then esquiers, then knights, then the aldermen of the citie in their cloks of scarlet, after them the iudges in their mantels of scarlet and coiffes. Then followed the knights of the bath being no lords, euerie man hauing a white lace on his left sléeue, then followed barons and vicounts in their parlement robes of scarlet. After them came earls, marquesses and dukes in their robes of estate of crimsin veluet furred with ermine poudered according to their degrées. After them came the lord chancellor in a robe of scarlet open before, bordered with lettise: after him came the kings chapell and the moonks solemnelie singing with procession, then came abbats and bishops mitered, then sargeants and officers of armes, then after them went the maior of London with his mace and garter in his cote of armes, then went the marquesse Dorset in a robe of estate which bare the scepter of gold, and the earle of Arundell which bare the rod of iuorie with the doue both togither

Then went alone the earle of Oxford high chamberleine of England which bare the crowne, after him went the duke of Suffolke in his robe of estate also for that daie being high steward of England, hauing a long white rod in his hand, and the lord William Howard with the rod of the marshalship, and euerie knight of the garter had on his collar of the order. Then proceeded foorth the quéene in a circot and robe of purple veluet furred with ermine in hir here coiffe and circlet as she had the saturdaie, and ouer hir was borne the canopie by foure of the fiue ports, all crimsin with points of blue and red hanging on their sléeues, and the bishops of London and Winchester bare vp the laps of the queenes robe. The queenes traine which was verie long was borne by the old duches of Norffolke: after hir folowed ladies being lords wiues, which had circots of scarlet with narow sléeues, the brest all lettise with bars of borders according to their degrées, and ouer that they had mantels of scarlet furred, and euerie mantell had lettise about the necke like a neckercher likewise poudered, so that by the pouderings their degree was knowen. Then followed ladies being knights wiues in gownes of scarlet, with narow sléeues without traines, onlie edged with lettise, and likewise had all the queenes gentlewomen.

When she was thus brought to the high place made in the middest of the church, betwéene the quéere and the high altar, she was set in a rich chaire. And after that she had rested a while, she descended downe to the high altar and there prostrate hir selfe while the archbishop of Canturburie said certeine collects: then she rose, and the bishop annointed hir on the head and on the brest, and then she was led vp againe, where after diuerse orisons said, the archbishop set the crowne of saint Edward on hir head, and then deliuered hir the scepter of gold in hir right hand, and the rod of iuorie with the doue in the left hand, and then all the quéere soong Te Deum, &c. Which doone, the bishop tooke off the crowne of saint Edward being heauie and set on the crowne made for hir. Then went she to saint Edwards shrine and there offered, after which offering doone she withdrew hir into a little place made for the nones on the one side of the quéere.

Now in the meane season euerie duches had put on their bonets a coronall of gold wrought with flowers, and euerie marquesse put on a demie coronall of gold, euerie countesse a plaine circlet of gold without flowers, and euerie king of armes put on a crowne of coper and guilt, all which were worne till night. When the quéene had a little reposed hir, the companie returned in the same order that they set foorth, and the quéene went crowned and so did the ladies aforesaid. Hir right hand was susteined by the earle of Wilshire hir father, and hir left hand by the lord Talbot deputie for the earle of Shrewesburie and lord Forinfall his father. Now when she was out of the sanctuarie and appéered within the palace, the trumpets plaied maruellous freshlie, then she was brought to Westminster hall, & so to hir withdrawing chamber: during which time the lords, iudges, maior and aldermen put off their robes, mantels and clokes, and tooke their hoods from their necks and cast them about their shoulders, and the lords sat onlie in their circots, and the iudges and aldermen in their gownes. And all the lords that serued that daie serued in their circots and their hoods about their shoulders: also diuerse officers of the kings house being no lords had circots and hoods of scarlet edged with mineuer, as the treasuror, controllor, & master of the iewell house, but their circots were not guilt.

While the queene was in hir chamber, euerie lord and other, that ought to doo seruice at coronations, did prepare them acording to their dutie, as the duke of Suffolke high steward of England which was richlie apparelled, his doublet and iacket set with orient pearle, his gowne of crimsin veluet imbrodered, his courser trapped with a cloth trapper head and all to the ground of crimsin veluet, set full of letters of gold

gold of goldsmiths worke, hauing a long white rod in his hand; on his left hand rode the lord William, deputie for his brother as earle marshall with the marshals rod, whose gowne was crimsin veluet, and his horsse trapper purple veluet cut on white sattin imbrodered with white lions. The earle of Oxenford was high chamberleine, the earle of Essex caruer, the earle of Sussex sewer, the earle of Arundell cheefe butler, on whom twelue citizens of London did giue their attendance at the cupbord. Twelue citizens of London attendant at the cupboord. The earle of Darbie cupbearer, the vicount Lisle pantler, the lord of Aburgaine chéefe larder, the lord Braie almoner for him and his coparteners, and the maior of Oxford kept the buttrie bar, and Thomas Wiat was chéefe eurer for sir Henrie Wiat his father.

When all things were redie, the quéene vnder hir canopie came to the hall, and washed and sat downe in the middest of the table vnder the cloth of estate. On the The maner of sitting at the table. right side of the chaire stood the countesse of Oxford widow, and on the left side stood the countessse of Worcester all the dinner season, which diuerse times in the dinner time did hold a fine cloth before the quéenes face when she list to spet or doo otherwise at hir pleasure. At the tables end sat the archbishop of Canturburie on the right hand of the quéene, and in the middest betwéene the archbishop and the countesse of Oxford stood the earle of Oxford with a white staffe all dinner time, and at the quéenes féet vnder the table sat two gentlewomen all dinner time. When all these things were thus ordered, in came the duke of Suffolke and the lord William Howard The bringing in of the first course. on horssebacke, and the sergeants of armes before them, and after them the sewer, and then the knights of the bath bringing in the first course which was eightéene dishes, besides subtilties and ships made of wax maruellous gorgious to behold, all which time of seruice the trumpets standing in the window at the nether end of the hall plaied melodiouslie.

When hir grace was serued of two dishes, then the archbishops seruice was set downe, whose sewer came equall with the third dish of the quéenes seruice on his left hand. After that the quéene and the archbishop was serued, the barons of the ports began the table on the right hand next the wall, next them at the table sat the masters How the seuera tables were furnished. and clearks of the Chancerie, and beneath them at the table other doctors and gentlemen. The table next the wall on the left hand by the cupbord, was begun by the maior and aldermen, the chamberleine and the councell of the citie of London, and beneath them sat substantiall merchants, and so downeward other worshipfull persons. At the table on the right hand in the middest of the hall sat the lord chancellor, and other temporall lords on the right side of the table in their circots : and on the left side of the same table sat bishops and abbats in their parlement robes : beneath them sat the iudges, sargeants, & the kings councell, beneath them the knights of the bath. At the table on the left hand, in the middle part, sat dutchesses, marquesses, countesses, baronesses, in their robes, and other ladies in circots, and gentlewomen in gownes. All which ladies and gentlewomen sat on the left side of the table along, and none on the right side.

When all were thus set, they were incontinent serued, and so quicklie that it was maruell : for the seruitors gaue such good attendance, that meat or drinke nor any thing else néeded not to be called for, which in so great a multitude was maruell. As touching the fare, there could be deuised no more costlier dishes nor subtilties. The The maior o Londons seruice. maior of London was serued with thrée and thirtie dishes at two courses, and so were all his brethren, and such as sat at his table. The quéene had at hir second course foure and twentie dishes, and thirtie at the third course : & betwéene the two last courses, the kings of armes cried larges, in thrée parts of the hall : and after stood in their place, which was in the bekins at the kings bench. And on the right hand out of the cloister of S. Stephans, was made a little closet, in which the king with diuerse ambassadors stood to behold the seruice. The duke of Suffolke and the lord

William

William rode often times about the hall, chering the lords, ladies, and the maior and his brethren. After they all had dined, they had wafers and ipocras, and then they washed, and were commanded to rise, and to stand still in their places, before the table or on the formes till the queene had washed.

When she had taken wafers and ipocras, the table was taken vp, and the earle of Rutland brought vp the surnap, and laid it at the boords end, which immediatlie was drawne, and cast by master Rode, marshall of the hall: and the quéene washed, and after the archbishop, and when the surnap was drawne off, she arose and stood in the middest of the palace hall: to whome the earle of Sussex in a goodlie spice plate brought a void of spice and comfets. After him the maior of London brought a standing cup of gold, set in a cup of assaie of gold, and after that she had droonke, she gaue the maior the cup, with the cup of assaie, bicause there was no leiar, accord-

ing to the claime of the citie, thanking him and all his brethren, for their paine. Then she vnder hir canopie departed to hir chamber, and at the entrie of hir chamber, she gaue the canopie with bels and all, to the barons of the ports, according to their claime, with great thanks. Then the maior of London bearing his cup in his hand, with his brethren, went through the hall to their barge, and so did all other noble men and

gentlemen, for it was six of the clocke. On mondaie were the iusts at the tilt, before the kings gate, where the maior and his brethren had a goodlie standing: but there were verie few speares broken, by reason the horsses would not cope. On wednesdaie, the king sent for the maior and his brethren to Westminster, and there he himselfe gaue to them hartie thanks, with manie goodlie words. On Midsummer daie after, the ladie Marie the French quéene died in Suffolke, who was the late wife to Lewes the twelfe, & after married to Charles duke of Suffolke, & was buried at S. Edmundsburie. The K. kept his progresse about London, bicause of the quéene.] The seuenth of September being sundaie, betwéene thrée & foure of the clocke in the afternoone, the queene was deliuered of a faire yoong ladie, on which daie the duke of Norffolke came home to the christening, which was appointed on the wednesdaie next following, and was accordinglie accomplished on the same daie, with all such solemne ceremonies as were thought conuenient. The godfather at the font, was the lord archbishop of Cantar-burie, the godmothers, the old dutches of Norffolke, & the old marchionesse Dorset widow; and at the confirmation the ladie marchionesse of Excester was godmother: the child was named Elizabeth.

Vpon the daie of the christening, the maior sir Stephan Peacocke, in a gowne of crimsin veluet, with his collar of SS, and all the aldermen in scarlet, with collars and chaines, and all the councell of the citie with them, tooke their barge after dinner, at one of the clocke, and the citizens had another barge, and so rowed to Gréenwich, where were manie lords, knights, and gentlemen assembled. All the walles betweene the kings palace & the friers were hanged with arras, and all the waie strawed with gréene rushes: the friers church was also hanged with arras.

The font was of siluer, and stood in the middest of the church, thrée steps high, which was couered with a fine cloth, and diuerse gentlemen with aperns and towels about their necks gaue attendance about it, that no filth should come in the font, ouer it hoong a square canopie of crimsin sattin, fringed with gold, about it was a raile couered with red saie: betweene the quier and the bodie of the church was a close place with a pan of fire, to make the child readie in. When all these things were ordered, the child was brought to the hall, and then euerie man set forward; first the

citizens two and two, then gentlemen, esquiers and chapleins, next after them the aldermen and the maior alone: next the maior the kings councell, the kings chappell in copes: then barons, bishops, earles, then came the earle of Essex, bearing the couered basins gilt, after him the marquesse of Excester with the taper of virgin wax, next him the marquesse Dorset bearing the salt.

                                                   Behind

Behind him the ladie Marie of Norffolke, bearing the créesome which was verie rich of pearle and stone, the old dutches of Norffolke bare the child in a mantell of purple veluét, with a long traine furred with ermine. The duke of Norffolke with his marshall rod went on the right hand of the said dutches, and the duke of Suffolke on the left hand, and before them went the officers of armes. The countesse of Kent bare the long traine of the childs mantell, and betwéene the countesse of Kent and the child went the earle of Wilshire on the right hand, and the earle of Darbie on the left hand, supporting the said traine: in the middest ouer the said child was borne a canopie, by the lord Rochford, the lord Husée, the lord William Howard, and by the lord Thomas Howard the elder, after the child followed manie ladies and gentlewomen. When the child was come to the church doore, the bishop of London met it with diuerse bishops and abbats mitred.

A canopie borne ouer the yoong princesse.

When the ceremonies and christening were ended, Garter chéefe king of armes cried alowd, God of his infinite goodnesse send prosperous life & long to the high and mightie princesse of England Elizabeth: & then the trumpets blew. Then the archbishop of Canturburie gaue to the princesse a standing cup of gold: the dutches of Norffolke gaue to hir a standing cup of gold, fretted with pearle: the marchionesse of Dorset gaue thrée gilt bolles, pounced with a couer: and the marchionesse of Excester gaue thrée standing bolles grauen, all gilt with a couer. Then was brought in wafers, comfets, & ipocrasse in such plentie, that euerie man had as much as he would desire. Then they set forwards, the trumpets going before in the same order towards the kings palace, as they did when they came thitherwards, sauing that the gifts that the godfather and the godmothers gaue, were borne before the child by foure persons, that is to saie. First sir Iohn Dudleie bare the gift of the ladie of Excester, the lord Thomas Howard the yoonger bare the gift of the ladie of Dorset, the lord Fitzwater bare the gift of the ladie of Norffolke, and the earle of Worcester bare the gift of the archbishop of Canturburie, & all the one side as they went was full of staffe torches to the number of fiue hundred, borne by the gard and other of the kings seruants, and about the child were borne manie other proper torches by gentlemen.

Rich gifts giuen to the princesse.

Who bare the gifts presented to the princesse.

In this order they brought the princesse to the Q. chamber, & tarried there a while with the maior & his brethren the aldermen, and at the last the dukes of Norffolke & Suffolke came out frō the K. thanking them hartilie, who commanded them to giue thanks in his name: which being doone with other courtesies they departed, & so went to their barges. From that time forward (God himselfe vndertaking the tuition of this yoong princesse, hauing predestinated hir to the accomplishment of his diuine purpose) she prospered vnder the Lords hand, as a chosen plant of his watering, & after the reuolution of certeine yeares with great felicitie and ioy of all English hearts atteined to the crowne of this realme, and now reigneth ouer the same: whose heart the Lord direct in his waies, and long preserue hir in life, to his godlie will and pleasure, and the comfort of all true and faithfull subiects. Of the blessed natiuitie of this most gratious virgine quéene, as also of hir baptisme and confirmation in the christian faith, with all the solemnities and ceremonies recorded in our English annales, hir education, hir knowledge in diuerse languages, hir peaceable gouernement, and manie other trim discourses C. O. in his Eirenarchia, or Elisabetha, hath made honorable mention, saieng:

Angl. præt.

Septembris (Deus hoc voluit) quæ septima lux est
Consecrata venit Domino voluentibus annis,
Parturijt coniux Henrici principis Anna,
Vi dolor increuit, præscripto sedula nutrix
Perstat in officio, matronáque nobilis instat
Auxilium latura suum, cùm pondus in auras
Maturum genetrix enixa puerpera languet,
Certa tamen veræq; salutis signa debantur.

Septimo Septembris, videlicet die Dominico nascitur Elisabetha.

Postquam

Postquam pulchellæ faciei prodijt infans
Compositis membris, speciosam vt cæra liquescens
Fingitur in formam, populo mirante, periti
Artificis manibus: tensis adsidera palmis
Fœmina conclamat senior, Benedicite Christo
Præsentes Domino, ô vos benedicite Christo,
Virgo beat matrem, virgo modò nata patrémque,
Britannos omnes posthâc hæc virgo beabit,
Hæc sola est nostræ spes & solatia gentis.
Rex pater inuisit celeri sua gaudia passu
Matrem & filiolam, verbis solatus amicis
Languidam adhuc illā, partúsq; doloribus ægram, &c.]

Edw. Hall.
Ccxviij.
Pauier a contem-
ner of the gos-
pel, & his
shamefull end.

¶ This yéere also, one Pauier the towne clerke of the citie of London hanged him-selfe, which suerly was a man that in no wise could abide to heare the gospell should be in English. And I my selfe heard him once saie to me and other that were by, swearing a great oth, that if he thought the kings highnesse would set foorth the scrip-ture in English, and let it be read of the people by his authoritie, rather than he would so long liue, he would cut his owne throat, but he brake promise, for (as you haue heard) he hanged himselfe: but of what mind and intent he so did, maie be soone gathered. For God had (no doubt) appointed him to that iudgement, no lesse heauie than his offense was heinous; namelie the contempt of Gods word, the know-ledge whereof Dauid desired, preferring it before gold and siluer, yea before pearles & pretious stones in richnesse; and before honie and the honiecombe in swéetnes, as the paraphrase noteth, saieng:

Eob. Hess. in
psal. 119.

Quàm tua verba meo sapiunt iucunda palato!
Nulla màgis fingi dulcia mella queant.
Iustitia dòctrinæ tuæ mihi charior auro est,
Hac etiam argentum vilius instar habet.]

Guic. pag. 1182.
&c.

¶ About this time the pope, by lingering sickenes, (whose gréefe in the first appre-hension was the pains of the stomach, which drawing with them to passions of a feuer and other accidents, kept him long time vexed and tormented) sometimes séeming to be reduced to the point of death, and sometimes so eased and reléeued, that he gaue

Death of pope
Clement the se-
uenth.

to others but not to himselfe a kind of hope of recouering, being no longer able to make resistance against his maladie, exchanged his life the fiue and twentith of Sep-tember, leauing behind him in the castell of saint Angeo manie rich stones and iewels, more than was expected of him, and in the chamber of the sée apostolike infinit offices, contrarie to custome and good order, but in the treasurie a verie small store of monie, wherin he beguiled the opinion of all men. He was raised from base degrée to the place of the popedome with woonderfull felicitie, but in managing the place he prooued a verie great variation of fortune, wherein if both the properties of fortune be euenlie balanced the one with the other, the woorser fortune without all comparison was farre more familiar with him than the better.

Pope Clement
more infortunate
than fortunate.

For as there could háppen to him no greater infelicitie than the aduersitie of his imprisonment (for that with his owne eies he beheld with so great a ruine and destruc-tion the sacke of Rome; a desolation which his fortune suffered him to bewaile with pitie and compassion, but not to turne awaie or remedie the harme) so also by him mooued the generall desolation of his naturall countrie, to the which by how much more he was bound by perpetuall obligations, by so much greater was his aduersitie to be a chiefe instrument in the ruine of the place where he had taken his first being.

He died hated of all the court, suspected to most princes, and for the discourse of his life, he left behind him a renowme rather hatefull than acceptable: for he was ac-

counted

counted couetous, of little fidelitie, and naturallie farre off from dooing pleasures to
men. And in that humor albeit during his time of pope he created one and thirtie How manie cardinals he created during his popedome.
cardinals; yet vpon none of them did he impose that dignitie to content himselfe but
was drawne as it were by the violent law of necessitie and to please others: yea he
called to that dignitie the cardinall of Medicis, not of his proper and frée election,
but at the contemplation and persuasion of others, and at that time when being oppressed with a dangerous maladie, if he had died, he had left his friends and kindred
in the state of beggers and depriued of all aid. Neuerthelesse he was in counsell verie
graue, and in his actions much foreséeing; touching passions and affections a conqueror of himselfe, and for the facultie of his mind & spirit of great capacitie and
power, if timorousnesse had not oftentimes corrupted his iudgement.

Immediatlie after his death the cardinals going the same night into the conclaue, Creation of pope Paule the third a Roman borne.
elected in his place with full voice, Alexander of the familie of Farnesa, a Roman by
nation, and for his time the most ancient cardinall of the court: in which election
their voices seemed conformable to the iudgement and instance that Clement had
made, the person elected being most woorthie to be preferred before all the other to
so souereigne a degrée: for that he was both furnished with doctrine and good
learning, and fullie replenished with good apparances and customes. And for the
cardinals, they were so much the more forward to passe the election in his person, by
how much for the greatnesse of his age, being alreadie vpon the thréescore and seuenth
yeare, and supposed to beare a weake and vnsound complexion (which opinion he
nourished with art) they hoped he would not sit long in the seat; whereby the dignitie
of the place and primasie might fall to one of them, whose eies looked for the glorie
which their hearts lusted, being vtterlie estranged from God and godlinesse, as altogither addicted to the wanton desires of temporall delites, that they might passe
their daies in delicasie; as one noteth trulie of all that viperous generation, saieng: *Antith. Christi & papæ, pag.* 16.

> Omnibus idem animus celsas mirarier arces,
> Idem animus fluxis est inhiare bonis,
> De grege quid fiat nihili gens impia curans,
> Spectat magnificas ambitiosa domos:
> Elysios horum nullus contendit ad agros,
> Nil cœleste iuuat, terrea sola placent.]

About this season, the craftie practises of one Elizabeth Barton, named the holie Elizabeth Barton.
maid of Kent, came to light and were discouered: so that she and hir adherents in
Nouember folowing were brought to the Starchamber, & there before the kings councell confessed their feined hyprocrisie and dissembled holinesse, traitorous purposes
and intents. The names of those hir adherents, which were presented with hir before
the lords in the Starchamber were as followeth: Richard Master priest, parson of Aldington in Kent: Edward Bocking doctor in diuinitie, a moonke of Canturburie:
Richard Dering, moonke also of Canturburie: Edward Twaites gentleman: Thomas
Laurence register to the archdeacon of Canturburie: Henrie Gold parson of Alder-
marie, bachellor of diuinitie: Hugh Rich frier obseruant: Richard Risbie: and Thomas Gold gentleman. They were adiudged vpon their confession aforesaid, to stand Penance at Pauls crosse.
at Pauls crosse in the sermon time, where they with their owne hands should seuceral-
lie deliuer ech of them to the preacher that should be appointed, a bill, declaring their
subtill, craftie, and superstitious dooings. Which thing they did the sundaie next following, standing vpon a stage at the crosse erected for that purpose. But for their
treasons commited, the order was respited till the parlement next following, in the
which they were attainted, and suffered (as after ye shall heare.)

In this meane time, the Scots were not quiet, but stil robbed the kings subiects The Scots meoue warre.
both by sea and land: wherevpon the king caused them to be requited, not onelie
by the borderers and other to them associate, which entring by the marches, burnt

manie

manie of their strong piles, but also he set foorth certeine ships which entered into their streames, and fetched out manie of those prises, which they had taken out of their hauens and créekes, mawger all their heads. Yet was there no warre proclaimed, but still commissioners sat and communed of agréement, and amends to be made on either part. Now in the end when the Scots had much demanded, and little or nothing granted, they for that time being wearie of warre, desired peace, which was concluded to indure both the kings liues. And so the twentith daie of Maie in the yeare following, it was openlie proclamed, to the comfort of all them that delited in peace and godlie quietnesse.

At the suit of the ladie Katharine Dowager, a cursse was sent from the pope, which curssed both the king and the realme. This cursse was set vp in the towne of Dunkirke in Flanders (for the bringer thereof durst no nearer approch) where it was taken downe by one William Locke a mercer of London. Bicause it was knowne that the ladie Katharine Dowager had procured this cursse of the pope, all the order of the court was broken: for the duke of Suffolke being sent to hir as then lieng at Bugden beside Huntingdon, according to that he had in commandement, discharged a great sort of hir houshold seruants, and yet left a conuenient number to serue hir like a princesse, which were sworne to serue hir not as quéene but as princesse Dowager. Such as tooke that oth she vtterlie refused, and would none of their seruice, so that she remained with the lesse number of seruants about hir.

After Christmas the parlement began, wherein the forenamed Elizabeth Barton and other hir complices were attainted of treason, for sundrie practised deuises and tales by them aduanced, put in vse, and told, sounding to the vtter reproch, perill, and destruction of the kings person, his honour, fame and dignitie: for they had of a diuelish intent put in the heads of manie of the kings subiects, that to the said Elizabeth Barton was giuen knowledge by reuelation from God and his saints, that if the king procéeded to the diuorse, and maried another, he should not be king of this realme one moneth after, and in the reputation of God not one daie nor houre.

This Elizabeth first through sickenesse, being oftentimes brought as it were into a transe, whereby hir visage and countenance became maruellouslie altered at those times when shee was so vexed, at length, by the incouraging, procurement, and information of the forenamed Richard Master parson of Aldington, she learned to counterfeit such maner of transes (after she came to perfect health) as in hir sickenes by force of the disease she had bene acquainted with: so that she practised, vsed, and shewed vnto the people diuerse maruellous and sundrie alterations of the sensible parts of hir bodie, craftilie vttering in hir said feigned and false transes, diuerse and manie counterfeit, vertuous, and holie words, tending to the rebuke of sin, and reproouing of such new opinions as then began to rise.

And to bring the people the more in beliefe with hir hypocriticall dooings, she was counselled to saie in those hir trances, that she should neuer be perfectlie whole till she had visited an image of our ladie, at a place called Court at Stréet, within the parish of Aldington aforesaid. Thither was she brought, and by the meanes of the said Richard Master, and Edward Bocking, that was now made of counsell in the matter, there assembled about two thousand persons at the daie appointed of hir thither com-

ming, to sée the miracle. At which daie, being brought before all that assemblie and multitude of people, shee falselie feigned and shewed vnto the people in the chappell of our ladie there in Court at Street, manie alterations of hir face, and other outward sensible parts of hir bodie, and in those transes she vttered woonderous words, as she was before subtilie and craftilie induced, and taught by the said Edward Bocking and Richard Master.

And amongst other things she vttered, that it was the pleasure of God, that the said Bocking should be hir ghostlie father, and that she should be a religious woman.

And

And within a while, after such feigned and counterfeit transes, she appeared to the people to be suddenlie relieued from hir sicknesse and afflictions, by the intercession and meane of the image of our ladie, being in the same chappell. By reason of which hyprocritcall dissimulation, the said Elizabeth was brought into a maruellous fame, credit, and good opinion of a great multitude of the people of this realme. And to increase the same, by counsell of the said Edward Bocking, she became a nun in the priorie of saint Sepulchres at Canturburie, to whome the said Edward Bocking had commonlie his resort, not without suspicion of incontinencie, pretending to be hir ghostlie father by Gods appointment. And by conspiracie betwene hir & him, she still continued in practising hir dissembled transes, alledging that in the same she had reuelations from almightie God and his saints, and amongst other, that which (as before we haue mentioned) touched the kings mariage, as ye haue heard.

Elizabeth Barton becommeth a nun.

This matter proceeded so farre, that there was a booke written by hir complices, and namelie by Thomas Laurence, register to the archbishop of Canturburie, of hir feigned and counterfeit miracles, reuelations, and hypocriticall holinesse. All things were handled so craftilie, that not onelie the simple, but also the wise and learned sort were deceiued by the same, insomuch that William Warham the late archbishop of Canturburie, and Iohn Fisher bishop of Rochester, and diuerse others, being informed thereof, gaue credit thereto. All which matters and manie other had bene traitorouslie practised and imagined amongst the parties manie yeres, chieflie to interrupt the diuorse and to destroie the king, and to depriue him from the crowne and dignitie roiall of this realme, as in the act of their attaindor made more at large it maie appeare, and likewise in the chronicles of maister Edward Hall. Therefore to conclude with hir and hir adherents, on the one and twentith of Aprill next following, she with diuerse of them before condemned, was drawen to Tiburne, and there executed, as iustlie they had deserued; where and when she made this confession following, euen at the present time that she suffered, in the hearing of the people.

The archbishop of Canturburie and the bishop of Rochester giue credit to hir hypocritical practises. Elizabeth Barton executed.

The words of Elizabeth Barton, otherwise called the holie maid of Kent at the houre of hir death in maner of a confession.

HITHER am I come to die, and I haue not beene the onelie cause of mine owne death, which most iustlie I haue deserued, but also I am the cause of the death of all these persons which at this time here suffer: and yet to say the truth, I am not so much to be blamed, considering that it was wel knowen vnto these learned men, that I was a poore wench, without learning, and therefore they might haue easilie perceiued, that the things that were doone by me, could not proceed in any such sort, but their capacities and learning could right well iudge from whence they proceeded, and that they were altogither feined: but bicause the things which I feined were profitable vnto them, therefore they much praised mee, and bare me in hand that it was the holie ghost, and not I that did them, and then I being puft vp with their praises, fell into a certeine pride and foolish fantasie with my selfe, and thought I might feine what I would, which thing hath brought me to this case, and for the which now I crie God and the kings highnes most hartilie mercie, and desire all you good people to praie to God to haue mercie on me, and on all them that suffer here with me.

In this parlement also was made the act of succession, for the establishing of the crowne, to the which euerie person being of lawfull age should bée sworne. On mondaie the thrée & twentith of March in the parlement time, were solemnlie receiued into London ambassadours from Iames the fift king of Scots, the bishop of Aberdine, the abbat of Kinlos, and Adam Otterborne the kings attourneie, with di-

The act of establishing the crowne Ambassadors foorth of Scotland.

uerse gentlemen on them attendant, which were brought to the tailors hall, and there lodged. And on the daie of the Annunciation, they were brought to the kings palace at Westminster, where they shewed their commission and message, for the which the king appointed them daies to counsell. During the parlement time, euerie sundaie at Paules crosse preached a bishop, declaring the pope not to be supreme head of the church.

The popes supremacie de-nied in sermons.

The thirtith of March was the parlement proroged, and there euerie lord, knight, and burges, and all other were sworne to the act of succession, and subscribed their hands to a parchment fixed to the same. The parlement was proroged till the third of Nouember next. After this were commissioners sent into all parts of the realme, to take the oth of all men and women to the act of succession. Doctor Iohn Fisher, and sir Thomas More knight, and doctor Nicholas Wilson parson of saint Thomas apostles in London, expreslie denied at Lambeth before the archbishop of Canturburie, to receiue that oth. The two first stood in their opinion to the verie death (as after ye shall heare) but doctor Wilson was better aduised at length, and so dissembling the matter escaped out of further danger.

The lords sworne to the succession.

¶ In this yéere it chanced that two merchant strangers fell in loue with a harlot, which was called Woolfes wife, and this harlot had often hanted the strangers cham-bers. And so on a time the said harlot appointed these strangers to come to West-minster, and she had prepared for them a bote, in the which bote was but one man to row which was a strong theefe, and in the end of the bote laie Woolfe hir husband, couered with a leather that botemen vse to couer their cushins with, and so these strangers sat them downe mistrusting nothing. Now when this boteman had brought them as farre as a place called the turning tree, suddenlie stepped vp the said Woolfe, and with his dagger thrust the one of them through: the other cried out to safe his life, and offred great sums of monie to the boteman and him to saue his life. But no proffers would be heard, nor mercie would they extend, but as cruell murtherers without pitie slue the other also, and bound them face to face, and so threw them into the Thames in the foresaid place, where they were long after before they were found. But immediatlie the harlot Woolfes wife went to the strangers chambers, & tooke from thence so much as she could come by. And at the last she and hir husband (as they deserued) were apprehended, arreigned, and hanged at the aforesaid turning trée.]

Ab. Fl. ex Edw. Hall. 224. Woolfes wife a notable harlot.

The end of vn-lawful loue and lust.

The reward of murther committed through co-uetousnesse.

An. Reg. 26. The lord Dacres of the north arreigned.

On the ninth of Iulie was the lord Dacres of the north arreigned at Westminster of high treason, where the duke of Norffolke sate as iudge, and high steward of Eng-land. The said lord Dacres being brought to the barre, with the axe of the Tower before him, after his indictment read, so improoued the same, answering euerie part and matter therein conteined, and so plainlie and directlie confuted his accusers, which were there readie to auouch their accusations, that to their great shames, and his high honor, he was found that day by his péeres not guiltie, whereof the commons not a little reioised, as by their shout and crie made at those words, not guiltie, they fréelie testified.

The two and twentith of Iulie was Iohn Frith burned in Smithfield, for the opinion of the sacrament: and with him the same time, and at the same stake, suffered also one Andrew Hewet, a yoong man, by his occupation a tailor. The eleuenth of Au-gust were all the places of the obseruant friers suppressed, as Gréenwich, Canturburie, Richmont, Newarke, and Newcastell, and in their places were set Augustine friers, and the obseruant friers were placed in the roomes of the graie friers. ¶ The one and twentith of September, doctor Tailor master of the rolles, was discharged of that of-fice, and Thomas Cromwell sworne in his place the nineteenth of October. Moreouer the third of Nouember, the parlement began againe, in the which was concluded the act of supremacie, which authorised the kings highnes, to be supreme head of the church of England, and the authoritie of the pope abolished out of the realme. ¶ In

Iohn Frith burned.

John Stow. Frieries sup-pressed.

The parlement againe begin-neth.

the

the same parlement also was giuen to the king, the first fruits and tenths of all spi- The admerall of France cō- meth in ambass- age into Eng- land.
rituall dignities and promotions. This yeare came the great admerall of France into
England, ambassadour from the French king, and was honorablie receiued.

In this time died the earle of Kildare, prisoner in the Tower, and his sonne Thomas 1535
Fitzgaret began to rebell, and tooke all the kings ordinance, and sent to the emperour, requiring him to take his part: also he slue the bishop of Dublin, and robbed
all such as would not obeie him. In the beginning of this yeare, the duke of Norf- An. Reg. 27.
folke and the bishop of Elie went to Calis, and thither came the admerall of France.
On the two & twentith of Aprill the prior of the Charterhouse at London, the prior *Iohn Stow.* Certeine priors
of Beuall, the prior of Exham, Reinalds a brother of Sion, & Iohn vicar of Thistle- arreigned and
worth, were arreigned and condemned of treason: and therevpon drawne, hanged and executed for treason.
quartered at Tiburne the fourth of Maie: their heads and quarters were set ouer the
bridge & gates of the citie, one quarter excepted, which was set vp at the Charterhouse at London. ¶ On the eight of Maie, the king commanded that all belonging
to the court should poll their heads, & to giue example, caused his owne head to be
polled, and his beard from thenceforth was cut round, but not shauen, which fashion
the courtiers imbraced, and would (no doubt) haue put in practise, though they had
not beene therevnto bound by precept: for the people imitate the prince, as the poet
long ago well noted, saieng:

Regis ad exemplum totus componitur orbis.

¶ The fiue and twentith daie of Maie, was in saint Paules church at London ex- *Iohn Stow. pag.* 1004.
amined nineteene men and six women borne in Holland, whose opinions were, first, Hollanders con-
that in Christ is not two natures, God and man: secondlie, that Christ tooke neither demned for heretikes.
flesh nor bloud of the virgin Marie: thirdlie, that children borne of infidels shall be
saued: fourthlie, that baptisme of children is to none effect: fiftlie, that the
sacrament of Christs bodie is but bread onelie: sixtlie, that he, who after his baptisme sinneth wittinglie, sinneth deadlie, and cannot be saued. Fourteene of them
were condemned, a man & a woman of them were burned in Smithfield, the other
twelue were sent to other townes there to be burnt.]

On the nineteenth of Iune were three moonkes of the Charterhouse hanged, drawne, Moonks of the Charterhouse
and quartered at Tiburne, and their heads and quarters set vp about London, for de- executed.
nieng the king to be supreme head of the church: their names were, Exmew, Mid-
dlemoore, and Nudigate. Also the one and twentith of the same moneth, and for The bishop of Rochester be-
the same cause, doctor Iohn Fisher bishop of Rochester was beheaded for denieng of headed.
the supremacie, and his head set vpon London bridge, but his bodie buried within
Barking churchyard. This bishop was of manie sore lamented, for he was reported
to be a man of great learning, and of a verie good life. The pope had elected him a
cardinall, and sent his hat as far as Calis, but his head was off before his hat was on:
so that they met not. On the sixt of Iulie was sir Thomas Moore beheaded for the Sir Thomas Moore behead-
like crime, that is to wit, for denieng the king to be supreme head. And then the ed.
bodie of doctor Fisher was taken vp, and buried with sir Thomas Moores in the
Tower. This man was both learned and wise, and giuen much to a certeine pleasure
in merie taunts and ieasting in most of his communication, which maner he forgat
not at the verie houre of his death.

¶ I cannot tell (saith master Hall) whether I should call him a foolish wise man, *Abr. Fl. ex Edw. Hall.*
or a wise foolish man, for vndoutedlie he beside his learning, had a great wit, but it *fol.* CCxxvj.
was so mingled with taunting and mocking, that it seemed to them that best knew
him, that hee thought nothing to be well spoken except he had ministred some mocke
in the communication. Insomuch as at his comming to the Tower, one of the officers
demanded his vpper garment for his fee, meaning his gowne: and he answered, he
should haue it, and tooke him his cap, saieng it was the vppermost garment that he
had. Likewise euen going to his death at the Tower gate, a poore woman called vnto

5 E 2
him,

Sir Thomas
Moore a scoffer
& mocker at
the verie houre
of his death.

him, and besought him to declare what he had doone with euidenses of hirs in the time that he was in office (which after he was apprehended shée could not come by) and that he would intreat shée might haue them againe, or else she was vndoone. He answered, good woman, haue patience a little while, for the king is so good vnto me that euen within this halfe houre he will discharge me of all businesse, and helpe thée himselfe.

Also when he went vp the staiers on the scaffold, he desired one of the shirifes officers to giue him his hand to helpe him vp, and said; When I come downe againe, let me shift for my selfe as well as I can. Also the hangman knéeled downe to him, asking him forgiuenesse of his death (as the maner is) to whome he said, I for-giue thée, but I promise thee thou shalt neuer haue honestie by striking off my head, my necke is so short. Also euen when he should laie downe his head on the blocke, he hauing a great graie beard, stroked out his beard, and said to the hangman, I praie you let me laie my beard ouer the blocke, least you should cut it. Thus with a mocke he ended his life.

God had in most bountifull sort powred his blessings vpon this man, induing him with eloquence, wisedome and knowledge: but the grace of God withdrawne from him, he had the right vse of none, no not of reason as it should be rightlie vsed. God had extraordinarilie blessed his children, and namelie his thrée daughters, to whome he had giuen an admirable dexteritie in the science of toongs and arts, as Iohn Leland our reuerend antiquarie noteth in a proper and learned epigramme, saieng :

*I. Lelandi
Moriades, siue
Charitæa corona.*

Desine facundas nimiùm laudare diserti
  Natas Hortensi maxima Roma tui :
Candida tres Charites nam Mori cura politi
  Obscurant multis nomina vestra modis.
Non illis studium Milesia vellera dextra
  Carpere, non facili ducere fila manu :
Sed iuuat eloquij crebro monumenta Latini
  Versare, & doctis pingere verba notis,
Nec minùs authores Græcos euoluere, Homerum
  Et quem dicendi gloria prima manet.
Vt nec Aristotelis dicam quo pectore libros
  Scrutentur, sophiæ mystica dona deæ.
Turpe viris posthàc erit ignorare Mineruæ
  Artes, grex adeò quas muliebris amet.

Spirituall graces
doo not neces-
sarilie concurre
or depend vpon
temporall.

And yet was not the will of God for the infusing of spirituall graces, so linked to that of temporall, as because the one was granted, therefore the other must not be de-nied. For the blessings of God which be outward, are common to the wicked with the good: the sun shineth vpon all, the raine is kept from none: naie, God with a sparing hand reacheth out those things to the faithfull, which with full gripes he filleth out and powreth into the laps and bosoms of infidels and epicures: insomuch that the prophet Dauid noting no lesse, with a kind of indignation opened his mouth saieng ; I was grieued at the wicked, I doo also see the vngodlie in such prosperitie, these florish in the world, these haue riches in possessions, and I said; Then haue I cleansed my heart in vaine, and washed my hands in innocencie : yea, and I had almost said euen as they ; but lo, then should I haue condemned the generation of Gods children. But the end of these men, being set in slipperie places, are cast downe and destroied, yea suddenlie doo they consume and come to a fearfull end : euen like as a dreame when one awaketh, so dooth God make their image to vanish out of the citie.

Sir Thomas
More in some
cases com-
mended.

And albeit the fall of this sir Thomas More was reprochfull, issuing from a trea-sonable offense: yet as in pagans manie times there is somwhat which may teach
                                                                                                                  christians

christians lessons for their lerning to their shame: so in this papist was one praise-worthie propertie among the rest most eminent, which I will note to the rebuke of protestants. ¶ The reuerend father doctor Elmer bishop of London, in a sermon at Paules crosse by him made in a solemne audience assembled at the parlement time 1584, teaching diuerse points of doctrine, and the duties of sundrie degrées, said, that it was commendable for noble men and gentlemen, and a great furtherance to the loue of religion, to be deuout: he brought an example of sir Thomas More, a man for his zeale (saith the bishop) to be honored, but for his religion to be abhorred.

Abr. Flem. out of a sermon made at Paules crosse by doctor Elmer bishop of London on the eighteenth of October 1584.

This knight would diuerse times put on a surplesse, and helpe the préest in pro-per person to saie seruice: insomuch that vpon a time being at Chelsie, and busie about that exercise, the duke of Norffolke then liuing, came to the said sir Thomas, then lord chancellor of England, about speciall affaires: and being informed that sir Thomas was at the church; thither went the duke, expecting the end of seruice. In the end, the duke and the lord chancellor met, and after mutuall gréeting the duke said thus: "What! is my lord chancellor become a parish clarke? What will the kings maiestie saie to this geere, when he shall vnderstand that the lord chancellor of Eng-land, a speciall péere of the realme, and in highest roome of honor in the land next the prince is become a parish clarke?" Now trulie (saith sir Thomas) I thinke, and verelie beléeue, that his highnesse will be so farre to misdéeme or mislike me herein, that when he shall heare of the care which I haue to serue both his maister and mine, he will accept and take me for a faithful seruant. And thus much of him.]

Whether it were mattins or euen-song it makes no matter.

Sir Thomas More deuoutle giuen in his kind.

This yéere in the time that the king went his progresse to Glocester, and to other places westward, the king of Scots was installed knight of the garter at Winsore by his procurator the lord Erskin: and in October following, Stephen Gardner (which after the cardinals death was made bishop of Winchester) was sent ambassador into France, where he remained thrée yeeres after. ¶ In August the lord Thomas Fitz-gerard, sonne to the earle of Kildare, was taken in Ireland, and sent to the tower of London.

The king of Scots knight of the garter.

The bishop of Winchester am-bassador into France. *1. Stow.*

In the moneth of October, doctor Lée and other were sent to visit the abbeies, priories, and nunries in England, who set all those religious persons at libertie that would forsake their habit, and all that were vnder the age of foure and twentie yéeres, and the residue were closed vp that would remaine. Further, they tooke order that no men should haue accesse to the houses of women, nor women to the houses of men, except it should be to heare their seruice. The abbat or prior of the house, where anie of the brethren was willing to depart, was appointed to giue to euerie of them a priests gowne for his habit, and fortie shillings in monie, the nunnes to haue such apparell as secular women ware, and to go whither them liked best. ¶ The eleuenth of Nouember was a great procession at London for ioie of the French kings recouerie of health from a dangerous sicknesse. ¶ In December a surueie was taken of all chanteries, and the names of them that had the gift of them.

Visitation of re-ligious houses.

The princesse Dowager lieng at Kimbalton, fell into hir last sicknesse, whereof the king being aduertised, appointed the emperors ambassador that was legier here with him named Eustachius Caputius, to go to visit hir, and to doo his commenda-tions to hir, and will hir to be of good comfort. The ambassador with all diligence did his dutie therein, comforting hir the best he might: but she within six daies after, perceiuing hir selfe to wax verie weake and féeble, and to féele death approching at hand, caused one of hir gentlewomen to write a letter to the king, commending to him hir daughter and his, beseeching him to stand good father vnto hir: and further desired him to haue some consideration for hir gentlewomen that had serued hir, and to sée them bestowed in marriage. Further, that it would please him to appoint that hir seruants might haue their due wages, and a yéeres wages beside. This in effect

1536

The ladie Ka-tharine Dowager deceaseth.

effect was all that she requested, and so immediatly herevpon she departed this life the eight of Ianuarie at Kimbalton aforesaid, and was buried at Peterborow. ¶ The nine and twentith of Ianuarie quéene Anne was deliuered of a child before hir time, which was borne dead.

Religious houses giuen to the king.
I. Stow. On the fourth of Februarie the parlement began, in the which (amongst other things) enacted, all religious houses of the value of three hundred marks and vnder, were giuen to the king, with all the lands and goods to them belonging. The number of these houses were thrée hundred seauentie and six; the value of their lands yearlie aboue two and thirtie thousand pounds; their moouable goods one hundred thousand; the religious persons put out of the same houses, amounted to the number William Tindall burnt. of aboue 10000. This yéere was William Tindall burnt at a towne betwixt Bruxels and Maclin called Villefort. This Tindall, otherwise called Hichins, was borne in the marches of Wales, and hauing a desire to translate and publish to his countrie diuerse books of the bible in English, and doubting to come in trouble for the same, if he should remaine here in England, got him ouer into the parties of beyond the sea, where he translated not onelie the new testament into the English toong, but also the fiue bookes of Moses, Iosua, Iudicum, Ruth, the books of the kings, and Paralipomenon, Nehemias, or the first of Esdras, and the prophet Ionas.

Beside these translations, he made certeine tretises, and published the same, which were brought ouer into England, and read with great desire of diuerse, and of many sore despised and abhorred, so that proclamations were procured foorth for the condemnation and prohibiting his books (as before you haue heard.) Finallie, he was apprehended at Antwerpe by meanes of one Philips an Englishman, and then scholer at Louaine. After he had remained in prison a long time, and was almost forgotten, the lord Cromwell wrote for his deliuerance; but then in all hast, because he would not recant anie part of his doctrine, he was burned (as before you haue heard.) Of whose conuersation and doctrine, innocent in the world, and sincere for truth, as also of his death and martyrdome, read the martyrologie of Iohn Fox our ecclesiasticall chronographer Anno 1536. sub Hen. 8.

An. Reg. 28. On Maie daie were solemne iusts kept at Gréenwich, and suddenlie from the iusts the king departed, not hauing aboue six persons with him, and in the euening came to Westminster. Of this sudden departing manie mused, but most chéeflie the Abr. Fl. ex I. Stow. 1006. Quéene Anne committed to the tower. quéene. ¶ On the next morrow, the lord Rochford brother to the quéene, and Henrie Norris were brought to the tower of London prisoners. Also the same daie about fiue of the clocke in the after noone, queene Anne of Bullongne was brought to the tower of London, by sir Thomas Audleie lord chancellor, the duke of Norffolke, Thomas Cromwell secretarie, and sir William Kingston constable of the tower; and Hir imprecation at the tower gate on hir knees. when she came to the tower gate, entring in she fell on hir knées before the said lords, beseeching God to helpe hir, as she was not guiltie of that whereof she was accused, and then desired the said lords to beséech the kings grace to be good vnto hir, and so they left hir there prisoner. On the fiftéenth of Maie quéene She is arreigned in the tower. Anne was arreigned in the tower of London on a scaffold for that purpose, made in the kings hall, before the duke of Norffolke, who sate vnder the cloth of estate as high steward of England, with the lord chancellor on his right hand, the duke of Suffolke on his left hand, with marquesses and lords, &c: and the earle of Surrie sat before the duke of Norffolke his father, as earle marshall of England. The kings commission being read, the constable of the tower, and the lieutenant brought the queene to the barre, where was made a chaire for hir to sit downe in, and there hir indictement was read, wherevnto she made so wise and discréet answers, that she seemed fullie to cleere hir selfe of all matters laid to hir charge: but being tried by hir péeres, whereof the duke of Suffolke was chiefe, she was by them found guiltie, and had iudgement pronounced by the duke of Norffolke.

Immediatlie

Immediatlie the lord Rochford the queenes brother was likewise arreigned and condemned: the lord maior of London, his brethren the aldermen, the wardens and foure persons mo of euerie the twelue principall companies being present. The seauenteenth of Maie, the lord Rochford brother to the quéene, Henrie Norris, Marke Smeton, William Brierton, and Francis Weston, all of the kings priuie chamber, about matters touching the quéene were beheaded on the tower hill: the lord Rochfords bodie with the head was buried in the chappell of the tower, the other foure in the churchyard there. On the ninetéenth of Maie quéene Anne was on a scaffold (made for that purpose) vpon the gréene within the tower of London, beheaded with the sword of Calis, by the hands of the hangman of that towne: hir bodie with the head was buried in the quéere of the chappell in the tower.]

The lord Rochford condemned.

Quéene Anne and diuerse others beheaded.

The words of queene Anne at hir death.

GOOD christian people, I am come hither to die, for according to the law, and by the law I am iudged to die, and therfore I will speake nothing against it. I am come hither to accuse no man, nor to speake anie thing of that whereof I am accused & condemned to die, but I praie God saue the king and send him long to reigne ouer you, for a gentler, nor a more mercifull prince was there neuer, and to me he was euer a good, a gentle, and a souereigne lord. And if anie person will meddle of my cause, I require them to iudge the best. And thus I take my leaue of the world, and of you all, and I hartilie desire you all to praie for me, Oh Lord haue mercie on, to God I commend my soule, Iesu receiue my soule: diuerse times repeting those words, till that hir head was striken off with the sword.

Now bicause I might rather saie much than sufficientlie inough in praise of this noble quéene, as well for hir singular wit and other excellent qualities of mind, as also for hir fauouring of learned men, zeale of religion, and liberalitie in distributing almes in reliefe of the poore, I will refer the reader vnto master Fox his volume of Acts and Monuments, where he commendeth hir mild nature in taking admonition, prooueth hir marriage lawfull, defendeth hir succession, ouerthroweth the sinister iudgements, opinions and obiections of backebiters against that vertuous quéene, sheweth hir faith and trust in Christ at hir death, and finallie how the protestants of Germanie forsooke king Henrie for the death of so good a princesse. ¶ Anglorum prælia saith, that this good quéene was forwarned of hir death in a dreame, wherein Morpheus the god of sléepe (in the likenesse of hir grandfather) appéered vnto hir, and after a long narration of the vanities of this world (how enuie reigneth in the courts of princes, maligning the fortunate estate of the vertuous, how king Henrie the eight and his issue should be the vtter ouerthrow and expulsion of poperie out of England, and that the gouernment of quéene Elizabeth should be established in tranquillitie & peace) he saith vnto hir in conclusion by waie of prophesie, as our poet hath recorded:

I. Fox in martyrologio.

Ang. prælia.

Forti sis animo, tristis si nuncius adsum,
Insperata tuæ velox necis aduenit hora,
Intra triginta spacium moriere dierum:
Hoc magnum mortis solamen habeto futuræ,
Elizabetha suis præclarè filia gestis
Nomen ad astra feret patris, matrísque, suúmque.]

Anne mors prædicitur. Pla. in Phe. Socratis tale quiddam somniauit.

Immediatlie after hir death, in the weeke before Whitsuntide, the king married the ladie Iane Seimer, daughter to sir Iohn Seimer knight, which at Whitsuntide was openlie shewed as quéene. And on the tuesdaie in Whitsunweeke, hir brother

The king marieth ladie Iane Seimer.

sir

A parlement.

sir Edw. Seimer was created vicount Beauchampe, and sir Water Hungerford, lord Hungerford. The eight of Iune began the parlement, during the which the lord

The lord Th. Howard atteinted of treason.

Thomas Howard, without the kings assent, affied the ladie Margaret Duglas, daughter to the quéene of Scots, and neece to the king, for which act he was atteinted of treason, and an act made for like offendors, and so he died in the tower, and she remained long there as prisoner. In the time of this parlement the bishops and all the cleargie of the realme held a solemne conuocation at Paules church in London, where after much disputation and debating of matters, they published a

A booke published concerning religion by the king.

booke of religion, intituled Articles deuised by the kings highnesse, &c. In this booke is speciallie mentioned but thrée sacraments. Also beside this booke certeine iniunctions were giuen foorth, wherby a number of their holie daies were abrogated,

I. Stow. Triumph at Westminster.

& speciallie those that fell in haruest time. ¶The nine & twentith of Iune, the king held a great iusting and triumph at Westminster, where were ordeined two lighters made like ships to fight vpon the water, one of the which brake in the midst, wherby one Gates a gentleman, & seruant to M. Kneuet was drowned in his harnesse. In the other a gun brake hir chamber, & maimed two of the mariners.] Thomas Cromwell secretarie vnto the king, and maister of the rols, was made lord

Aduancement of the lord Cromwell.

kéeper of the priuie seale, and the ninth of Iulie the lord Fitzwaren was created erle of Bath, and the morrow after the said lord Cromwell was created lord Cromwell. The eightéenth of Iulie he was made knight, and vicar general vnder the king ouer the spiritualtie, and sat diuerse times in the conuocation amongst the

The death of the kings base sonne.

bishops as head ouer them. The two and twentith of Iulie, Henrie duke of Richmont and Summerset, earle of Northampton, base sonne to the king, begot of the ladie Tailebois then called Elizabeth Blunt, departed this life at saint Iames, and was buried at Thetford in Norffolke, of whome you shall find more in the treatise of the dukes of this land.

In September, Thomas Cromwell lord priuie seale and vicegerent, sent abroad vnder the kings spirituall priuie seale certeine iniunctions, commanding that the persons and curats should teach their parishioners the Pater noster, the Aue & Creed,

The people grudged at the iniunctions established by act of parlement.

with the ten commandements, and articles of the faith in English. These articles and iniunctions being established by authoritie of parlement, and now to the people deliuered, bred a great misliking in the harts of the common people, which had béene euer brought vp and trained in contrarie doctrine. And herewith diuerse of the cleargie as moonks, priests, and others, tooke occasion herby to speake euill of the late procéedings of the king, touching matters of religion, affirming that if spéedie remedie were not in time prouided, the faith would shortlie be vtterlie destroied, and all praier and diuine seruice quite abolished and taken awaie.

Manie sinister reports, slanderous tales, and feigned fables were blowne abroad, and put into the peoples eares, and diuerse of the nobilitie did also what they could to stir the commons to rebellion, faithfullie promising both aid and succour against the king. The people thus prouoked to mischiefe, and deceiued through ouer light cre-

A traitorous conspiracie.

dence, incontinentlie as it were to mainteine that religion, which had so manie yeares continued, and béene estéemed, they stiffelie and stoutlie conspired togither, and in a part of Lincolneshire they first assembled, and shortlie after ioined into an armie, being (as it was supposed) of men apt for the warres, in number about twentie thousand. Against these rebels with all the hast that might be, the king in his proper person vpon intelligence therof had marched towards them, being furnished with a

The Lincolnshire men in armes against the king.

warlike armie, perfectlie appointed of all things that to such a companie should apperteine.

The rebels hearing that his person was present with his power to come thus against them, began to feare what would follow of their dooings: and such nobles and gentlemen as at the first fauoured their cause, fell from them and withdrew, so that
they

they being destitute of capteines, at length put certeine petitions in writing, which they exhibited to the king, professing that they neuer intended hurt towards his roiall person. The king receiued their petitions, which consisted in choise of coun- The petitions of cellors, suppression of religious houses, maintenance of the seruice of almightie God, the rebels re- the statute of vses, the release of the fifteenth, and receiuing of the first fruits, king and of with such other matters as nothing apperteined to them: wherevpon he made them consisted. answer in pithie sentence, reprouing them of their presumptuous follie and rebellious attempt, to meddle in anie such matters and weightie affaires, the direction whereof onelie belonged to him, and to such noble men and councellors as his pleasure should be to elect and choose to haue the ordering of the same.

Wherfore he aduised them to remember their rash and inconsiderate dooings, and that now in anie wise they should resort home to their houses, and no more to as- semble contrarie to his lawes and their owne allegiance; and also to cause the pro- uokers of this mischiefe to be deliuered to the hands of his lieutenant, and further to submit themselues wholie to such punishment as he and his nobles should thinke them worthie to receiue: for otherwise he would not suffer that iniurie at their hands to go vnreuenged. After the Lincolneshire men had receiued the kings answer thus The Lincoln- made to their petitions, each mistrusting other, who should be noted the greatest shiremen giue meddler, suddenlie they began to shrinke, and got them home to their houses with- ouer their re- out longer abode. bellious enterprise.

Herewith the duke of Suffolke the kings lieutenant was appointed to go with the armie, to see the countrie set in quiet, accompanied with the lord admerall, sir Francis Brian, and sir Iohn Russell that were ioined with him also in commission for the ordering of things there within the countie of Lincolne. The duke entered the citie of Lincolne the seuentéenth of October. On the ninetéenth all the inhabitants The rebels sub- of Louth (according to order giuen by the duke) came to Lincolne, and there in the mit themselues castell made their submission, holding vp their hands, and crieng for the kings mercie. and receiue a And herwith were chosen foorth Nicholas Melton, capteine Cobler, & thirteene more, fealtie to the which were commanded to ward, and all the residue were new sworne to the king, re- king. nouncing their former oth receiued in time of their rebellion, and then departed home to their houses in the kings peace. After this were proclamations made abrode in the countrie in euerie market towne by the heralds of armes, Summerset and Winsore, that the capteins and souldiers of the dukes armie should not take anie mans goods, cattels, or vittels, except they paied or agréed with the owners of the same.

And further commandement was giuen, that all inhabitants and dwellers within the townes and villages about, should repaire to the citie of Lincolne, with all maner of vittels as well for men as horsses, where they should receiue paiment at reasonable prices for the same. After this, there was likewise proclamation made for the appre- hending of all such lewd persons, as had sowne anie false rumours abrode in the coun- False rumors trie (the cheefe occasion of this rebellion) bruting that the king pretended to haue the occasion of the gold in the hands of his subiects brought into the tower to be touched, and all rebellions. their cattell vnmarked, the chalices, goods, and ornaments of parish churches, fines for christenings, weddings, and burierrgs, licences to eat white meat, bread, pig, goose or capon, with manie other slanderous, false, and detestable tales and lies, forged of diuelish purpose to incourage the people to rebellion. If therefore anie man could apprehend such as had béene the setters foorth and sowers of such se- ditious reports, they that brought them in, should be so rewarded, as they should thinke their labour well bestowed.

Moreouer, if there were anie assemblies made in anie part of the realme without the kings licence, by any vnrulie persons, and would not depart to their houses vpon warning by his graces proclamations, they should not looke for further mercie at the kings hand, but to be prosecuted with fire and sword to the vttermost. To conclude, by the wise and sage direction taken in appeasing the countrie by that noble duke, all things were quieted in those parties. Diuerse of the principall offendors were sent vnto London. He that tooke vpon him as cheefe capteine of the rout, was the same that called himselfe capteine Cobler: but he was indeed a moonke named doctor Makarell, which afterwards with diuerse others was executed.

But now in the meane time, whilest the duke was sent forwards into Lincolneshire within six daies after the king was trulie informed, that there was a new stir begun in the north parts by the people there, which had assembled themselues into an huge armie of warlike men & well appointed, both with capteins, horsses, armor, and artillerie, to the number of fortie thousand men, which had incamped themselues in Yorkeshire. These men declared by their proclamations solemnlie made, that this their rising and commotion should extend no further, but onelie to the maintenance and defense of the faith of Christ, and deliuerance of holie church, sore decaied and oppressed, and also for the furtherance as well of priuate as publike matters in the realme, touching the wealth of all the kings poore subiects.

They named this their seditious voiage, an holie and blessed pilgrimage: they had also certeine banners in the field, in which was painted Christ hanging on the crosse on the one side, and a chalice with a painted cake in it on the other side, with diuers other banners of like hypocrisie and feigned holinesse. The souldiers had also imbrodered on the sléeues of their cotes in stéed of a badge, the similitude of the fiue wounds of our sauiour, and in the middest thereof was written the name of our Lord. Thus had the rebels host of sathan with false and counterfeit signes of holinesse set out themselues, onelie to deceiue the simple people in that their wicked and rebellious enterprise against their liege lord and naturall prince, whome by the law of nations and by Gods commandements they were bound in conscience to obeie, and so farre to be from lifting vp the least finger of their hand, as rather to put life and goods in hazard for his sake, to testifie their allegiance.

The spéedie diligence and loiall dutie which was found at that present in the worthie councellour George earle of Shrewesburie, is not to be forgotten, who immediatlie after he vnderstood how the northerne men were thus vp in armes, considering how much it imported to stop them of their passage before they should aduance too far forwards, whereby they might both increase in power, and put all other parts of the realme in hazard, through feare or hope to incline to their wicked purposes, he sent abroad with all spéed possible to raise such power of his seruants, tenants, and fréends, as by anie means he might make, and withall dispatched one of his seruants to the king, both to aduertise him what he had doone, and also to purchase his pardon, for making such leuie of power, before he had receiued his maiesties commision so to doo.

I haue heard by relation of men of good credit that were there present: that when such knights and gentlemen as were of his councell, and other of his especiall fréends were come vnto him, he put foorth this question to them; Whether his fact in raising a power of armed men without the kings commission (although he had doone it to resist the rebels) were treason or not? Wherevnto when answer was made by some that were knowne to haue skill in the laws of the realme, how that by no means it could be intended treason, sith his intent was good, and no euill thereby meant, but contrarilie the aduancement of the kings seruice dutifullie sought: Yée are fooles (quoth the earle) I know it in substance to be treason, and I would thinke my selfe in an hard case, if I thought I had not my pardon comming.

Such a reuerend regard had this noble earle vnto his bounden allegiance towards his prince, that whatsoeuer seemed but as it were to sound in anie behalfe to the breach thereof, it so troubled his loial mind, that he could not be satisfied, till as it were in confessing his fault: where according to the truth there was none at all. He had signi-

signified his assured fidelitie in crauing pardon, where otherwise he might haue looked for thanks, which indéed he receiued with his pardon, according to his petition, and a commission to procéed as he had begun. Moreouer, whereas there were diuerse speaches amongst the soldiors in the armie, vttered by some not altogither happilie well disposed, that the said earle had so good liking of the northerne mens cause, that when it came to the point of triall, he would surelie ioine with them against that part, which he yet pretended to mainteine.

To put that matter out of doubt, he caused the multitude of his soldiours to come before him, and there declared to them, that he vnderstood what lewd talke had béene raised of his meaning among them in the campe, as if he had fauoured the part of the rebels: " But (saith he) whatsoeuer their colourable pretense may be, true it is, that traitors they are in this their wicked attempt. And whereas my ancestors haue béene euer true to the crowne, I meane not to staine my bloud now in ioining with such a sort of traitors, but to liue and die in defense of the crowne, if it stood but vpon a stake: and therefore those that will take my part in this quarrel, I haue to thanke them, and if there be anie that be otherwise minded, I would wish them hence." And herewith he caused his chapleine to minister an oth to him, which he receiued to the effect aforesaid, in the presence of them all.

What the earle said to them that talked lewdlie of him in the campe.

And verelie this was thought to be doone not without great cause that mooued him thereto: for whereas the more part of his souldiours consisted of the countrie people, who with forged tales and wicked surmises were easilie led to beléeue whatsoeuer was reported in fauor of the rebels, and disfauor of such as were then chiefe councellors to the king, against whome they pretended to rise (although there was no reasonable occasion leading them therevnto) it was greatlie to be suspected, least they might thorough some traitorous practise haue béene induced to forget their dutifull allegiance to their souereigne, and souldiorlike obedience to their leaders, insomuch that the capteins of the rebels were persuaded (and some of them reported no lesse) that they might haue fought with the duke of Norffolke, and the earle of Shrewesburie, on this hither side of the riuer of Dun, euen with their owne men, not néeding to haue brought a man of their armie with them.

He was prouided of ill souldiors that so vndutifullie to deale with him would be induced.

Therefore it was thought, that the oth which the earle of Shrewesburie in that sort receiued before all his people there openlie in field, serued to great purpose; to put out of his soldiours wauering heads all such lewd expectation that he would turne to the enimies, staieng thereby their fickle minds; sith they were now assured, that he being their chiefteine meant no dissimulation. A matter trulie of no small importance, considering the fauor which the commons bare towards him, and the opinion they had conceiued of his high prowesse; so that which waie he inclined, it was thought verelie the game were likelie to go. But now after the king was aduertised of that perilous commotion of the northerne men, he appointed not onlie the said earle of Shrewesburie to raise a power to resist them: but also ordeined the duke of Norffolke his lieutenant generall, with the marquesse of Excester, and the said earle of Shrewesburie, the earles of Huntington and Rutland, accompanied with a mightie power to go against them.

The oth of the earle of Shrewesburie in presence of the people necessarie.

The duke of Norffolke the kings lieutenant.

These lords raising such retinues of souldiers and men of warre as were to them assigned, made forward to the place where the armie of the rebels was then incamped, which was beyond the towne of Doncaster, in the high waie towards Yorke. But first the said earle of Shrewesburie, with the earles of Huntington, and Rutland, and such other that were next adioining to those parties, with their powers assembled out of the shires of Salop, Stafford, Leicester, Rutland, Notingham, and Derbie, came to a place in Notingham shire called Blithlow, and there taking the musters of their people, streightwaies passed foorth to Doncaster, and appointed certeine bands of their men, to lie in places where anie foords or passages laie ouer the riuer of Dun,

that

that runneth by the northside of Doncaster, to staie the enimies if they should attempt to come ouer. Shortlie after came the duke of Norffolke, and finallie the marquesse of Excester with a iollie companie of westerne men, well and perfectly appointed.

When these capteins and sage councellors being here assembled, vnderstood the manner of the northerne men, their number, and readinesse to battell, they first practised with great policie, to haue pacified the matter without bloudshedding: but the northerne men were so bent to mainteine their wilfull enterprise, that there was no hope to take vp the matter without battell: therefore a daie was set, on the which they should trie the quarrell betwixt them with dint of sword. But sée the chance. The night before the daie assigned for this bloudie and vnnaturall battell, t haue béene fought betwixt men of one nation, and subiects to one king; there fell a raine not great to speake of, but yet as it were by miracle, the riuer of Dun rose suddenlie on such a height, that seldome had béene séene there the like hugenesse of water: so that the daie when the houre of battell should come, it was not possible for the one armie to come at the other, and so the appointment made betwéene both the armies for triall of the matter by force of armes, was by Gods good prouidence disappointed, and manie an innocent mans life perserued, that should haue died, if their purposes had taken place.

After this by the great wisedome and policie of the nobles and capteins, a comunication was had, and an agréement made vpon the kings pardon, obteined for all the capteins and chiefe dooers in this insurrection, and promise made that they should be gentlie heard, to declare such things as they found themselues gréeued with: and that vpon their articles presented to the king, their reasonable petitions should be granted, as by him & his councell it should be thought expedient, whereby all troubles might be quieted, and ech thing brought to a good conclusion. Herewith euerie man departed, and those which before came as hot as fire to fight, letted of their desperat purpose, by Gods mercifull prouidence, returned now peaceablie to their houses without anie more businesse.

At the selfe same time that these northerne men were lodged néere to Doncaster, and the kings power readie to stop them of their passage (as before ye haue heard) there was an other armie readie to haue marched southwards thorough Lancashire: but by the faithfull diligence of the earle of Derbie, who with the forces of Lancashire and Cheshire was appointed to resist them, they were likewise kept backe and brought to quiet; notwithstanding they were a verie great number assembled togither of the commons out of Cumberland, Westmerland, and of the north parts of Lancashire. The earle of Sussex was sent downe by the king, to ioine in assistance with the earle of Derbie; who causing diuerse of the chiefe procurers of that rebellion in those parties to be apprehended and arreigned, they being found giltie had iudgement, and were executed, as the abbats of Walleie, Sauleie, and others.

In time of this rebellion, a priest that by a butcher dwelling within fiue miles of Windsor had been procured to preach in fauor of the rebels, and the butcher (as well for procuring the priest thereto, as for words spoken as he sold his meat in Windsor) were hanged: the priest on a tree at the foot of Windsor bridge, and the butcher on a paire of new gallowes set vp before the castell gate, at the end of the same bridge. The words which the butcher spake were these. When one bad him lesse for the carcase of a sheepe than he thought he could make of it: Naie by Gods soule (said he) I had rather the good fellowes of the north had it, and a score more of the best I haue, than I would so sell it. This priest and butcher being accused on a mondaie in the morning whilest the kings armie was in the field, and the king himselfe lieng at Windsor, they confessed their faults vpon their examinations, and by the law martiall they were adiudged to death, and suffered as before is mentioned. This yeare in December, the

Thames

Thames was frosen ouer: insomuch that the king and quéene rode thorough London to Gréenewich. A great frost.

In Christmas the king by his messengers and heralds sent downe into the north his generall pardons to all the offendors; and shortlie after Aske that had béene the principall procurer, & as it were chiefe capteine of the northerne rebels, came to London, and now was both pardoned and receiued into fauor, receiuing of the kings bounteous liberalitie, apparell, and diuerse other rewards, whereof he was most vnworthie: for there liued not (as Hall saith) a verier wretch, as well in person as conditions and déeds, speciallie towards the kings maiestie, as after appeared. ¶ Sir Rafe Euers kept Scarbrow castell in the north, being six wéeks besieged by the rebels, twentie daies whereof he and all his companie (which were his onelie friends, seruants, and tenants, and serued for good will to him) were forced to susteine themselues with bread and water, and yet he kept the same to the end of that rebellion; and so deliuered it to king Henrie, who sent him soone after to serue in the borders against Scotland, where in great credit he continued his seruice, kéeping the Scots without dooing hurt to England, and with such obedience of them, as within twentie miles of the borders of Scotland fore against him, there was not a Scot but at his commandement: and so continued, till he was killed in the yeare 1545.]

Generall pardons.
1537
Aske rewarded.

Abr. Fl. ex I. S.
pag. 1610
Sir Rafe Euers
his good seruice
in the north.

The twelfe of Nouember, sir Thomas Newman priest bare a faggot at Paules crosse, for singing masse with good ale. On the third of Februarie, Thomas Fitzgaret sonne and heire to the earle of Kildare was beheaded, and fiue of his vncles were drawne, hanged, and quartered at Tiborne for treason. In the same moneth Nicholas Musgraue, Thomas Tilbie, with others, began a new rebellion at Kirkbie Stephan in Westmerland, who hauing got togither eight thousand men, besieged the citie of Carleill, from whence they were beaten with the onlie power of the citie: and in returning from thense, the duke of Norffolke, who then was lieutenant of the north, incountered with them, tooke the capteins, and according to the law martiall areigned seuentie and foure of them, whome he hanged on Carleill wals: but Musgraue escaped. Penance at
Paules crosse.
The earle of
Kildare ex-
ecuted.
Tibie.
A new rebellion.

In the same moneth of Februarie began a new commotion, by the procurement of sir Francis Bigod, who being intised to that mischieuous enterprise by certeine wicked persons, forgat his dutie to his prince, although he had béene a man (as Hall saith) that vndoubtedlie loued God, and reuerenced his prince with a right obedient and louing feare: but such are men when God leaueth them, and that they will take in hand things which Gods most holie word vtterlie forbiddeth. This last rebellion began in Setrington, Pikering, Leigh, and Scarbrow; but it was quickelie suppressed, and the said sir Francis Bigod apprehended, and brought to the Tower. The said sir Francis & one Halam, hauing raised a great companie of rebels, meant to haue taken the towne of Hull, there to haue fortified themselues, and to haue assembled more power; but by the wisedome of sir Rafe Ellerkar, & the maior of the towne of Hull, the said Halam, & thréescore other of the rebels without anie slaughter were taken, which Halam was afterwards hanged in chaines, and two other with him, at the said towne of Hull. Sir Francis Bigod fled, & could not be heard of for a time, but at length he was also apprehended. Sir Francis
Bigod procureth
a new commo-
tion.

The purpose
of the rebels.

Moreouer, about the latter end of this twentith and eight yeare, the lord Darcie, Aske, sir Robert Constable, sir Iohn Bulmer and his wife, sir Thomas Persie brother to the erle of Northumberland, sir Stephan Hamilton, Nicholas Tempest esquier, William Lomleie, began eftsoones to conspire, although euerie of them before had receiued their pardons: and now were they all taken and brought to the Tower of London as prisoners. This yeare Robert Packington a mercer of London, a man both rich, wise, and of good credit, dwelling at the signe of the leg in Cheapside, on a morning going (as his custome was) about foure of the clocke to heare masse, in the church then called S. Thomas of Acres, & now the Mercers chappell, as he crossed Aske & others
practise to raise
a new rebellion.

Robert Pack-
ington mur-
thered.

ouer

ouer the stréet from his house to thé church, was suddenlie murthered with a gun, the cracke whereof was heard of the neighbors, and of a great number of laborers that stood at Soper lane end, and saw the said Packington go foorth of his house: but there was such a thicke mist that morning, as the like had not béene séene, by couert whereof the murtherer found shift the more easilie to escape.

Manie were suspected, but none found in fault, albeit forsomuch as he was one that would speake his mind freelie, and was at the same time one of the burgesses of the parlement for the citie of London, and had talked somewhat against the couetousnesse and crueltie practised by the cleargie, it was mistrusted least by some of them he came thus to his end. At length the murtherer in déed was condemned at Banburie in Oxfordshire, to die for a fellonie which he afterwards committed: and when he came to the gallowes on which he suffered, he confessed that he did this murther, and till that time he was neuer had in anie suspicion thereof. ¶ The nine and twentith of March, were twelue of the Lincolneshire rebels drawne to Tiburne, and there hanged and quartered, fiue of them were priests, the residue laie men. One of the priests was doctor Makarell, and an other was the vicar of Louth.

Rich. Grafton.
The inuention
of casting pipes.

About this season the maner of casting pipes of lead for the conueiance of water vnder the ground, without occupieng of soulder to the same, was inuented by Robert Brocke clearke, then one of the kings chapleins, an inuention right necessarie for the sauing of expenses: for two men and a boie will doo that in one daie, which before could not be doone by manie men in manie daies. Robert Cooper goldsmith was the first that made the instruments, and put this inuention in practise. ¶ In the verie beginning of this yeare, certeine commissioners being sent into Summersetshire to take vp corne, the people began to make an insurrection: but by the wisedome and diligence of yoong master Paulet & others the same was suppressed, and the beginners thereof, to the number of thréescore, were apprehended & condemned, and fourtéene of them were hanged and quartered, one of the number being a woman, the residue were saued by the kings mercifull pardon.

An. Reg. 29.

Execution.

In Iune the lord Darcie & the lord Huseie were arreigned at Westminster before the marquesse of Excester then high steward, where they were found guiltie, and had iudgement, as in cases of high treason. Shortlie after also were arreigned sir Robert Constable, sir Thomas Persie, sir Francis Bigod, sir Stephan Hamilton, sir Iohn Bulmer, and his wife, or rather (as some report) his paramour: also William Lomleie, Nicholas Tempest, William Thurst abbat of Founteins, Adam Sudburie abbat of Ierueux, William Wold prior of Birlington, also the abbat of Riuers, and Robert Aske. They were all found guiltie of high treason, and all put to death. Sir Robert Constable was hanged in chains ouer Beuerleie gate at Hull, and Robert Aske was also hanged in chains on a tower at Yorke, and Margaret Cheineie sir Iohn Bulmers paramour burnt in Smithfield in London. The other suffered at Tiburne.

Arcignment.

Execution.

In the latter end of Iune, was the lord Darcie beheaded at the Tower hill, and shortlie after the lord Huseie was likewise beheaded at Lincolne. This yeare at saint Georges feast, was the lord Cromwell made knight of the garter. In October on saint Edwards euen, which falleth on the twelft of that moneth, at Hampton court the quéene was deliuered of hir sonne named Edward, for whose birth great ioie was made thorough the realme, with thanksgiuing to almightie God, who had sent such a yoong prince to succéed his father in the crowne of this realme (as afterwards he did) by the name of king Edward the sixt. His godfathers at the fontstone were the archbishop of Canturburie & the duke of Norffolke, the ladie Marie was his godmoother, and at the bishopping, the duke of Suffolke was his godfather. On the eightéenth of October he was made prince of Wales, duke of Cornewall, and erle of Chester.

The birth of
king Edward
the sixt.

But as ioie is often mixed with sorrow, so at that time it came to passe by the death of his moother, that noble and vertuous ladie queene Iane, which departed out of this life

The death of
quéene Iane.

life the fourteenth daie of this moneth of October, to the great griefe of the whole realme: but namelie the king hir husband tooke it most grieuouslie of all other, who remoouing to Westminster, there kept himselfe close a great while after. The eight of Nouember, the corps of the quéene was caried to Windsor, with great solemnitie, and there buried in the midst of the quire in the castell church. There was also a solemne hearse made for hir in Paules church, and funerall exequies celebrated, as well as in all other churches within the citie of London. Thus was the king left againe a widower, and so continued the space of two yeares togither. Vpon the death of which quéene Iane, and the birth of prince Edward hir son this distichon following was made: *Iohn Fox in Acts & Monuments.*

Phœnix Iana iacet nato Phœnice, dolendum
Sæcula Phœnices nulla tulisse duas.

These verses were thought to be made by master Armigill Wade.

The king held his Christmas at Gréenewich, and as well he as all the court ware mourning apparell, till the morrow after Candlemas daie, & then he and all other changed. This yeare Edward Seimer vicount Beauchampe the quéenes brother was created earle of Hertford, & sir William Fitzwilliams lord high admerall was created earle of Southampton, ¶ and master Paulet was made vicetreasuror, sir Iohn Russell comptrollor of the king house, master Henedge, master Long, master Kneuet of the kings priuie chamber, knights: master Coffin, master Listar, & master Seimer the quéenes brother, knights. On Allhallowes euen, the lord Thomas Howard, brother to the duke of Norffolke, died prisoner in the Tower of London, and was buried at Thetford, and then the ladie Margaret Dowglas was pardoned, and released out of the Tower. The foure and twentith of Februarie, being sundaie, the rood of Boxleie in Kent, called the rood of grace, made with diuerse vices, to mooue the eies and lips, was shewed at Paules crosse by the preacher, which was the bishop of Rochester, and there it was broken and plucked in peeces.

1538

Creation of officers. Abr. Fl. ex I. S. pag. 1011, 1012.

Lord Thomas Howard deceassed.

Rood of grace shewed at Paules.

The fiue and twentith of Februarie, sir Iohn Allen priest, and also an Irish gentleman of the Garets were hanged & quartered at Tiburne. The second of March, the image of the rood, called saint Sauior at Bermonseie abbeie in Southworke, was taken downe by the kings commandement. The one and twentith of March, Henrie Harfam customer of Plimmouth, and Thomas Ewell, were hanged and quartered at Tiburne.] In Maie a frier obseruant called frier Forrest was apprehended, for that he was knowne in secret confessions to haue declared to manie of the kings liege people, that the king was not supreame head of the church, where he had by his oth neuerthelesse affirmed him so to be. Wheruppon in his examination, that point being laid to his charge, he answered that he tooke his oth with his outward man, but his inward man neuer consented thereuuto. But being further accused of diuerse hereticall and damnable opinions that he held & mainteined contrarie to the scripture, at length being not able to defend the same, he submitted himselfe to the punishment of the church.

Saint Sauior in Southworke.

An. Reg. 30. Frier Forrest.

Now when vpon this his submission, hauing more libertie than before he had to talke with whome he would, and other hauing libertie to talke with him, he was incensed by some such as had conference with him, that when his formall abiuration was sent him to read and peruse, he vtterlie refused it, and obstinatelie stood in all his heresies and treasons. Wherevpon he was condemned, & afterwards on a paire of new gallowes prepared for him in Smithfield, he was hanged by the middle and armeholes all quicke, and vnder the gallowes was made a fire wherewith he was consumed and burnt to death. There were diuerse of the councell present at his death readie to haue granted him pardon, if anie sparke of repentance would haue appeared in him. There was also a pulpit prepared, in which that renowmed preacher Hugh Latimer, then bishop of Worcester, by manifest scriptures

Frier Forrest burnt.

tures

tures confuted the friers errors, and with manie godlie exhortations mooued him to repentance, but he would neither heare nor speake.

A little before the execution, an huge and great image was brought to the gallowes.
This image was fetched out of Wales, which the Welshmen had in great reuerence :
A prophesie. and it was named Daruell Gatheren.   They had a prophesie in Wales, that this image
should set a whole forest on fire, which prophesie was now thought to take effect, for
he set this frier Forrest on fire, and consumed him to nothing.   The frier when he saw
the fire come, caught hold on the ladder, which he would not let go, but in that sort
vnpatientlie tooke his death, so as if one might iudge him by his outward man, he appeared (saith Hall) to haue small knowledge of God, and lesse trust in him at his
Ric. Graf. in ending : otherwise he would haue béene persuaded to patience, and a christian fare-
fol. pag. 1237. well to the world. ¶ Vpon the gallows that he died on, was set vp in great letters
these verses here following :

> Dauid Daruell Gatheren,
> As saith the Welshmen,
> Fetched outlawes out of hell :
> Now is he come with speare and shield,
> In harnesse to burne in Smithfield,
> For in Wales he maie not dwell.
> And Forrest the frier,
> That obstinate lier,
> That wilfullie shall be dead :
> In his contumacie,
> The gospell dooth denie,
> The king to be supreme head.]

In Iulie was Edmund Cuningsbie atteinted of treason, for counterfeiting the kings
signe manuell, and in August was Edward Clifford for the same cause atteinted, and
Execution. both put to execution as traitors at Tiburne.   In September by the speciall motion of
Certeine images the Lord Cromwell, all the notable images, vnto the which were made anie especiall
take away and pilgrimages and offerings, were vtterlie taken awaie, as the images of Walsingham,
remooued from Ipswich, Worcester, the ladie of Wilsdon, with manie other, and likewise the shrines
their places. of counterfeit saints, as that of Thomas Becket, and others.   And euen foorthwith,
by meanes of the said Cromwell, all the orders of friers and nuns, with their cloisters
Ab. Fl. ex I. S. and houses, were suppressed and put downe. ¶ As for the images of our ladie of
pag. 1013. Walsingham, and Ipswich, were brought vp to London, with all the iewels that hoong
about them, and diuerse other images both in England & Wales, wherevnto anie common pilgrimage was vsed, for auoiding of idolatrie, all which were burnt at Chelsie
by the lord priuie seale.

Hangman On the first of September being sundaie, one Gratnell hangman of London and two
hanged. other were hanged at the wrestling place by Clearken well, for robbing a booth in
Bartholomew faire, at which execution were aboue twentie thousand people, as Edward
Hall himselfe (then a present beholder) iudged.   This moneth of September, Thomas
Cromwell lord priuie seale, vicegerent to the kings highnesse, sent foorth iniunctions
The bible in to all bishops & curats through the realme, charging them to see that in euerie parish
euerie church to church, the bible of the largest volume, printed in English, were placed for all men
be read. to read on : and that a booke of register were also prouided and kept in euerie parish
Register booke church, wherein shall be written euerie wedding, christening, and burieng, within
in euerie church the same parish for euer.
to be kept.

Saint Augustines abbeie at Canturburie was suppressed, and the shrine & goods
taken to the kings treasurie, as also the shrine of Thomas Becket in the priorie of
Christs church was likewise taken to the kings vse, and his bones, scull and all, which
                                                                                     was

was there found, with a peece broken out by the wound of his death, were all burnt Thomas Becket in the same church by the lord Cromwell. The moonks there were commanded to burnt. change their habits, &c. The one and twentith of October, the church of Thomas Becket in London called the hospitall of saint Thomas of Acres was suppressed. Nicholas Gibson groser, for this yeare shiriffe of London, builded a free schoole at Ratcliffe, néere vnto London, appointing to the same, for the instruction of thréescore Frée schoole poore mens children, a schoolemaster and vsher, with a stipend of ten pounds by the at Ratcliffe. yere to the master, and six pounds thirteene shillings foure pence to the vsher. He also builded there certeine almes houses for fouretéene poor and aged persons who quarterlie receiue six shillings eight pence a peece for euer.]

In this season sute was made to the king by the emperour, to take to wife the duchesse of Millan: but shortlie after that sute brake off, bicause (as was thought) the emperours councell ment by a cautell to haue brought the king in mind to sue for a licence of the pope. Then the duke of Cleue began to sue to the king, that it would please him to match with his sister the ladie Anne, which after tooke effect. In Nouember, one Iohn Nicholson, otherwise called Lambert, a priest, was accused of he- Iohn Nicholson resie, for holding opinion against the bodilie presence in the sacrament of the altar. aliàs Lambert. He appealed to the kings maiestie, who fauourablie consented to heare him at a daie appointed, against which daie, in the kings palace at Westminster, within the kings hall, there was set vp a throne or seat roiall for the king, with scaffolds for all the lords, and a stage for Nicholson to stand vpon.

This Nicholson was esteemed to be a man well learned, but that daie he vttered no such knowledge (saith Hall) as was thought to be in a man of that estimation. Diuerse arguments were ministred to him by the bishops, but namelie the king pressed him sore, and in the end offered him pardon if he would renounce his opinion: but he would not consent thereto, and therefore he was there condemned, and had iudgement, and so shortlie after he was drawne into Smithfield, and there burnt to ashes. The third of Nouember, Henrie Courtneie marques of Excester and earle of Deuon- The marques shire, Henrie Poole lord Montacute, and sir Edward Neuill brother to the lord of Excester condemned. Aburgauennie, were sent to the tower, being accused by sir Geffrie Poole, brother to the lord Montacute, of high treason. They were indicted for deuising to mainteine, promote, & aduance one Reginald Poole, late deane of Excester, enimie to the king beyond the sea, & to depriue the king. The marques, and the lord Montacute were arreigned the last of December at Westminster before the lord Audleie that was chancellor, and for that present time high steward of England, and there they found him giltie.

The third daie after were arreigned sir Edward Neuill, sir Geffreie Poole, two *I. Stow.* priests called Crofts and Collins, & one Holland a mariner, & all atteinted. ¶ The *pag. 1019.* sixteenth of Nouember, was the blacke friers in London suppressed, the next daie the Frierie suppressed. white friers, the graie friers, and the moonks of the Charterhouse, and so all the other immediatlie, the foure and twentith of Nouember, the bishop of Rochester preached at Paules crosse, & there shewed the bloud of Hales, and affirmed the same to be no Bloud of Hales bloud, but honie clarified, and coloured with saffron, as it had béene euidentlie shewed at Pauls prooued before the king and his councell. Also foure anabaptists, thrée men, and one Anabaptists. woman, all Dutch, bare fagots at Paules crosse the same daie. The nintéenth of Nouember, a man and a woman Dutch anabaptists, were burnt in Smithfield.]

The ninth of Ianuarie, the lord marques, and the lord Montacute, with sir Ed- 1539 ward Neuill lost their heads on the Tower hill. The two priests and Holland were The lord marques executed. drawne to Tiburne, and there hanged and quartered. Sir Geffreie Poole had his pardon. ¶ On Ashwednesdaie, Iohn Ihons, Iohn Potter, & William Manering, were hanged in the princes liueries (bicause they were the princes seruants) on the southside of Paules churchyard, for killing Roger Cholmeleie esquier in that place, of malice

Sir Nicholas Carew executed.

prepensed. The third of March, sir Nicholas Carew of Bedington in the countie of Surrie knight of the garter, and maister of the kings horsse, condemned before of treason, was beheaded on the Tower hill, where he made a godlie confession, both of his fault, and superstitious faith, giuing God thanks, for that his hap was to be prisoner in the Tower, where he first sauored the pleasant tast of Gods holie word, meaning the bible in English, which there he read by the exhortation of one Thomas Philips then kéeper of that prison, and sometime a citizen and point-maker of London, who had béene in some trouble for religion, and examined before doctor Stokeslie bishop of London, and sir Thomas More, but through his wise demeanor and mild answers, he escaped their hands.

Creation of new officers.

The ninth of March, the king created sir William Paulet knight treasuror of his house, lord saint Iohn, and sir Iohn Russell comptroller of his household, lord Russell. Also either then or shortlie after, was sir William Par created lord Par. The new abbeie of white moonks at the Tower hill, and the Minories, nuns without Algate, were suppressed on the last of March. The same time the king caused all the

Bulworks & blockhouses builded.

hauens to be fensed with bulworks, and blockehouses, and riding to Douer, he tooke order to haue bulworks made alongst the sea coasts, and sent commission to haue generall musters made through the realme. Moreouer on Easter daie there were thréescore saile discouered that laie in the Downes, and for that it was neither knowne what they were, nor what they intended to doo, all the able men in Kent rose and mustered in armour the same daie. The eight and twentith of Aprill began a parlement

An. Reg. 31.
A parlement.
Attaindors.

at Westminster, in the which Margaret countesse of Salisburie, Gertrude wife to the marques of Excester, Reginald Poole cardinall, brother vnto the lord Montacute, sir

Execution.

Adrian Foskew, & Thomas Dingleie knight of saint Iohns, and diuerse other were atteinted of high treason, which Foskew and Dingleie the tenth of Iulie were beheaded.

The statute of the six articles.
An inquest of inquirie.

In this parlement the act of the six articles was established. Of some it was named the bloodie statute, as it prooued indéed to manie. And euen shortlie after the making thereof, when the first inquest for inquirie of the offendors of the same statute sat in London at the mercers chappell, those that were of that inquest were so chosen foorth for the purpose, as there was not one amongst them that wished not to haue the said statute put in execution to the vttermost, insomuch that they were not contented onelie to inquire of those that offended in the six articles conteined in that statute, but also they deuised to inquire of certeine branches (as they tooke the matter) belonging to the same, as of those that came seldome to heare masse, that held not vp their hands at the sacring time, who tooke no holie bread nor holie water, who vsed to read the bible in churches, or in communication séemed to despise preests, or images in the churches, &c. To conclude, they inquired so diligentlie of them that had so offended in anie of those articles or the branches, that they indicted & presented to the number of fiue hundred persons and aboue, so that if the king had not granted his pardon, for that he was informed by the lord Audleie then lord chancellor that they were indicted of malice, a great manie of them which alreadie were in prison, had died for it in Smithfield, in friena a faggot. But although the king at that present granted his gratious

The extreme procéeding in execution of the six articles.

pardon, and forgaue all those offenses : yet afterwards, during the time that this statute stood in force, which was for the space of eight years insuing, they brought manie an honest and simple person to death. For such was the rigor of that law, that if two witnesses, true or false, had accused anie, and aduouched that they had spoken against the sacrament, there was no waie but death ; for it booted him not to confesse that his faith was contrarie, or that he said not as the accusers reported, for the witnesses (for the most part) were beléeued.

Prouision for defense of the realme.

The king being informed that the pope by instigation of cardinall Poole, had mooued and stirred diuers great princes and potentats of christendome to inuade the

realme

realme of England; without all delaie rode himselfe toward the sea coasts, and sent diuerse of his nobles and councellors to surueie all the ports and places of danger on the coast, where anie meet and conuenient landing place might be doubted, as well in the borders of England, as also of Wales: in which dangerous places he caused bulworks and forts to be erected. And further, he caused the lord admerall earle of Southampton to prepare in a readinesse his nauie of ships for defense of the coasts. Beside this, he sent forth commissions to haue generall musters taken through the realme, to vnderstand what number of able men he might make account of: and further to haue the armor and weapons séene and viewed. Nothing left he vndoone that tended to the foreséeing and preuenting of a mischiefe to insue, which in a prince is counted a virtue, because such prouidence and circumspection is reputed no lesse in a priuat & ordinarie man, as the poet Plautus saith;

Virtus est, vbi occasio admonet, dispicere.

Sir William Forman knight, at that present maior of London, was commanded to certifie the names of all the able men within the citie and liberties thereof, betwéene the ages of thrée score and of sixtéene, with the number of armors and weapons of all kinds of sorts. Wherevpon the said maior and his brethren ech one in his ward, by the oth of the common councell and constable, tooke the number of men, armor, and weapons. And after well considering of the matter, by view of their bookes, they thought it not expedient to admit the whole number certified for apt and able men: and therefore assembling themselues againe, they chose forth the most able persons, and put by the residue, speciallie such as had no armor, nor for whom anie could be prouided. But when they were crediblie aduertised by Thomas Cromwell lord priuie seale (to whome the citie was greatlie beholden) that the king himselfe would see the people of the citie muster in a conuenient number, and not to set forth all their power, but to leaue some at home to kéepe the citie; then eftsoons euerie alderman repaired to his ward, and there put aside all such as had iacks, cotes of plate of maile, and *Preparation in* brigandines, and appointed none but such as had white armor, except such as should *London for a* beare morish pikes, which ware no armor but sculles, and there was no stranger *muster to be* (although he were a denisine) permitted to be in this muster. *ed before the* *king.*

Euerie man being of anie abilitie, prouided him selfe a cote of white silke, and garnished their basenets with turues like caps of silke, set with owches, furnished with chaines of gold and feathers, or caused their armor to be guilt, and likewise their halberds and pollaxes. Some, and especiallie certeine goldsmiths, had their whole armor of siluer bullion. The lord maior, the recorder, the aldermen, and euerie other officer beside were gorgeouslie trimmed as for their degrees was thought séemelie. The maior had sixteene tall fellowes on foot attending on him with guilt halberds, apparelled in white silke doublets, and their hose and shooes were likewise white, cut after the Almaine guise, pounsed and pulled out with red sarsenet: their ierkins were of white leather cut, and chains about their necks, with feathers and brooches in their caps. The recorder and euerie alderman had about him foure halberders trimmed also in warlike sort. The chamberleine of the citie, the councellors & aldermens deputies were appointed to be wiflers on horssebacke, which aloft on their armor ware white damaske cotes, mounted on good horsses well trapped, with great chaines about their necks, and proper iauelins or battell axes in their hands, and caps of veluet richlie trimmed.

The wiflers on foot, being in number foure hundred proper light persons, were clad *The wiflers.* in white ierkins of leather cut, with white hose and shooes, euerie man with a iauelin or slaughsword in his hand, to kéepe the people in arraie. They had chaines about their necks, and fethers in their caps. The minstrels were in white, with the armes of *The minstrels.* the citie, and so was euerie other person at this muster without anie diuersitie; the lord maior, recorder, and aldermen, onélie excepted, who had crosses of veluet or satin

     pirled

pirled with gold. The standard bearers were the tallest men of euerie ward, for whome were made thirtie new standards of the deuise of the citie, beside baners. Euerie alderman mustred his own ward in the fields, to sée that euerie man were in furniture prouided as was requisite.

Euerie alderman with his ward in order of battell.

The eight of Maie being the daie appointed for to shew themselues before the king, euerie alderman in order of battell with those of his ward came into the fields at Mile end, and then all the gunners seuered themselues into one place, the pikes into another, and the archers into an other, and likewise the bilmen, and there cast themselues in rings, and other formes of battell, which was a beautifull sight to behold: for all the fields from white Chapell to Mile end, and from Bednall greene to Ratcliffe & Stepnie, were all couered with armour, men, and weapons, and especiallie the battell of pikes séemed to be as it had béene a great forrest. Then was euerie part diuided into thrée battels, a for-ward, a midle-ward, and a rere-ward.

The order of the Londoners in their musters.

About seauen of the clocke marched forward the light péeces of ordinance, with stone and powder. After them followed the drums and fifes, and immediatlie after them a guidon of the armes of the citie. Then followed master Sadler capteine of the gunners on horssebacke armed, and in a cote of veluet, with a chaine of gold, and foure halberders about him apparelled as before is recited. Then followed the gunners foure in a ranke, euerie one going fiue foot in sunder, which shot altogither in diuerse places verie liuelie, and in speciallie before the kings maiestie, which at that time sat in his new gatehouse at his palace of Westminster, where he viewed all the whole companie. In like maner passed the other companies of all the thrée battels in good and séemelie order. The foremost capteine at nine of the clocke in the morning, by the little conduit came and entered into Paules churchyard, and from thense directlie to Westminster, and so through the sanctuarie, and round about the parke of S. Iames, and vp into the field, comming home through Holborne, and as the first capteine entered againe to the little conduit, the last of the muster entered Paules churchyard, which was then about foure of the clocke in the afternoone. The number, beside the wiflers, and of other waiters was fiftéene thousand.

The king taketh view of the Londoners in their musters.

The number of Londoners in this muster.

¶ The eight of Iulie, Griffith Clearke, vicar of Wandsworth, with his chapleine and his seruant, & frier Waire, were all foure hanged and quartered at S. Thomas Waterings. The tenth of Iulie sir Adrian Fortescue, and Thomas Dingleie were beheaded. The ninth of September, the nunnerie of Clerkenwell and diuerse others were suppressed.] This yeare the sixtéenth of September came to London duke Frederike of Bauiere, the Palsgraue of the Rhine, and the eightéenth of the same moneth came to London the marshall of Hans Frederike prince elector of Saxonie, and the chancellor of William duke of Cleue, Gulicke, Gelderland, and Berghen. The Palsgraue was receiued and conducted to Windsore by the duke of Suffolke, and the other were accompanied with other noble men, and the thrée and twentith of the same moneth they all came to Windsore, where eight daies togither they were continuallie feasted, and had pastime shewed them, in hunting and other pleasures, so much as might be. The Palsegraue shortlie after departed homewards and was princelie rewarded, & at that present was the marriage concluded betwixt the king and the ladie Anne, sister vnto duke William of Cleue, and great preparation was made for the receiuing of hir. ¶ The twelfe of October the nunnerie of Haliwell, & foorthwith the priorie of S. Marie oueries in Southworke, and S. Bartholmews in Smithfield, were suppressed, & all their lands & goods taken to the kings vse. Thomas Huntlow of London for this yeare shiriffe, gaue the habardashers certeine tenements, for the which they be bound to giue to ten poore almes people of the same companie, euerie one of them eight pence euerie fridaie for euer: and also at euerie quarter dinner kept by the masters, to be giuen to euerie one of those ten poore people a penie loafe, a pottell

Iohn Stow. Vicar of Wandsworth and other executed.

Clerkenwell and other suppressed. The Palsgraue & other strangers come ouer into England.

The mariage concluded betwixt king Henrie & the ladie Anne Cleue. I. Stow. pag. 1016. Thom. Huntlow his charitie.

of

of ale, a péece of beefe worth foure pence in a platter, with porage, and foure pence in monie.]

The fouretéenth of Nouember, Hugh Feringdon abbat of Reding, and two priests, the one called Rug, and the other Onion, attainted of high treason for denieng the supremacie of the king ouer the church of England, were drawne, hanged, and quartered at Reding. The same daie was Richard Whiting abbat of Glastenburie likewise hanged and quartered on Towre hill beside his monasterie, for the same matter and other treasons whereof he had beene conuicted. The first of December was Iohn Bech abbat of Colchester put to death for the like offense. In December were appointed to wait on the kings person fiftie gentlemen called pensioners, or speares, vnto whome was assigned the sum of fiftie pounds yeerelie a péece, for the maintenance of them-selues and two horsses, or one horsse and a gelding of seruice. *Pensioners in-stituted.*

The eleuenth daie of December at the turne pike on this side Graueling, was the ladie Anne of Cleue receiued by the lord deputie of the towne of Calis, and with the speares and horssemen belonging to the retinue there. When she came within little more than a mile of the towne of Calis, she was met by the erle of Southampton high admerall of England, who had in his companie thirtie gentlemen of the kings hous-hold, as sir Francis Brian, sir Thomas Seimer, and others, beside a great number of gentlemen of his owne retinue clad in blue veluet, and crimsin satin, and his yeomen in damaske of the same colours. The mariners of his ship were apparelled in satin of Bridges, cotes & slops of the same colour. The lord admerall brought hir into Calis by Lanterne gate. There was such a peale of ordinance shot off at hir entrie, as was maruellous to the hearers. The maior presented hir with an hundred markes in gold, the merchants of the staple with an hundred souereignes of gold in a rich purse. She was lodged in the kings place called the Checker, and there she laie fiftéene daies for want of prosperous wind. *Ladie Anne of Cleue is receiu-ed into Calis.*

During which time, goodlie iusts and costlie bankets were made to hir, for hir solace and recreation. And on S. Iohns daie in Christmasse, she with fiftie saile tooke passage about noone, and landed at Dele in the Downes about fiue of the clocke, where sir Thomas Chenie lord Warden of the ports receiued hir. She taried there a certeine space in a castell newlie built, and thither came the duke of Suffolke, and the dutches of Suffolke, and the bishop of Chichester with a great number of knights and esquiers, and ladies of Kent and other, which welcomed hir grace, and brought hir that night vnto Douer castell, where she rested till mondaie, on which daie (notwithstanding it was verie foule and stormie weather) she passed towards Canturburie, and on Baram downe met hir the archbishop of Canturburie, with the bishops of Elie, S. Asse, S. Dauies, and Douer, and so brought hir to S. Augustins without Canturburie, where she laie that night. The next daie she came to Sittingburne, and laie there that night. As she passed towards Rochester on Newyeares euen, on Reinam downe met hir the duke of Norffolke, and the lord Dacres of the south, and the lord Montioie, with a great companie of knights and esquiers of Norffolke and Suffolke, with the barons of the escheker which brought hir to Rochester, where she laie in the palace all Newyeares daie. On which daie, the king (longing to sée hir) accompanied with no more but eight persons of his priuie chamber, both he and they all apparelled in marble cotes, priuilie comming to Rochester, suddenlie came to hir presence, wherof at the first she was somewhat astonied, but after he had spoken to hir and welcomed hir, she with louing countenance and gratious behauiour him receiued, and welcomed him on hir knées, whom he gentlie tooke vp and kissed, and all that after noone communed and deuised with hir, supped that night with hir, and the next daie he departed to Gréene-wich, and she came forward to Dartford. *She landeth in Kent.* *1540* *The king com-meth to sée hir at Rochester.*

On the morrow the third daie of Ianuarie being saturdaie, in a faire plaine of Blacke-heath, more neere to the foot of Shooters hill, than the ascendent of the same, called

Blackheath

Blackheath hill, was pitched a pauilion of rich cloth of gold, and diuerse other tents and pauilions, in which were made fiers and perfumes for hir and such ladies as were

appointed to receiue hir: and from the tents to the parke gate of Greenewich, all the bushes and firs were cut downe, and a large open waie made for the shew of all persons. And first next to the parke pale on the east side stood the merchants of the stilliard, and on the west side stood the merchants of Genoa, Florence and Venice, and the Spaniards in cotes of veluet. Then on both sides the waie stood the merchants of the citie of London, and the aldermen, with the councellors of the said citie, to the number of a hundred and threescore which were mingled with the esquiers; then the fiftie gentlemen pensioners: and all these were apparelled in veluet and chaines of gold, trulie accounted to the number of twelue hundred & aboue, beside them that came with the king and hir, which were six hundred in veluet cotes and chaines of gold. Behind the gentlemen stood the seruingmen in good order well horssed and apparelled, that who so euer had well viewed them, might haue said, that they for tall and comelie personages, and cleane of lim and bodie, were able to giue the greatest prince in christendome a mortall breakefast, if he had béene the kings enimie.

About twelue of the clocke, hir grace with all the companie which were of hir owne nation, to the number of an hundred horsse, accompanied with the dukes of Norffolke and Suffolke, the archbishop of Canturburie and other bishops, lords, and knights, which had receiued and conueied hir, came downe Shooters hill towards the tents, and a good space from the tents met hir the earle of Rutland appointed lord chamberlaine to hir grace, sir Thomas Denise hir chancellor, and all hir councellors and officers, amongst whome doctor Daie (appointed to be hir almoner) made to hir an eloquent oration in Latine, presenting to hir on the kings behalfe all the officers and seruants: which oration was answered vnto by the duke hir brothers secretarie, there being present:

which doone the ladie Margaret Dowglas, daughter to the quéene of Scots, the ladie marquesse Dorsset, daughter to the French quéene, being néeces to the king, and the dutches of Ritchmond the countesses of Rutland and Hereford, with diuers other ladies and gentlewomen, to the number of threescore and fiue, saluted and welcomed hir grace, who alighted out of hir chariot in the which she had rid all hir long iourneie, and with courteous demeanor and louing countenance, gaue to them hartie thanks, and kissed them all, and after all hir councellors and officers kissed hir hand: which doone, she with all the ladies entered the tents, and there warmed them a space.

When the king knew that she was arriued in hir tent, he with all diligence set out through the parke. And first issued the kings trumpets, then the kings officers sworne of his councell, next after came the gentlemen of his priuie chamber, after them followed barons, the yoongest first, and sir William Hollis lord maior of London rode with the lord Par that was the yoongest baron. Then followed the bishops, and immediatlie after them the earles, and then the duke of Bauiere, and countie Palatine of the Rhine, with the liuerie of the Toison or golden fléece about his necke.

Then came the ambassadours of the French king and emperour, next to whome followed the lord priuie seale lord Cromwell, and the lord chancellour, then Gârter king at armes, and the other officers and sargeants of armes gaue their attendance on each side the lord. The lord marquesse Dorset bare the sword of estate, and after him a good distance followed the kings highnesse, mounted on a goodlie courser. To

speake of the rich and gorgeous apparell that was there to be séene that daie, I haue thought it not greatlie necessarie, sith each man may well thinke it was right sumptuous, and as the time then serued, verie faire and costlie, as they that are desirous to vnderstand the same may read in maister Halles chronicle more at large, which in this part I haue thought good to abridge.

After the king followed the lord chamberleine, then came sir Anthonie Browne maister of his horsses, a goodlie gentleman, and of personage verie séemelie, richlie

mounted

mounted, leading the kings horsse of estate by a long reine of gold. Then followed his pages of honour riding on great coursers, and lastlie followed sir Anthonie Wingfield capteine of the gard, and then the gard well horssed, and in their rich cotes. In this order rode the king till he came to the last end of the ranke of the pensioners, & there euerie person that came with him placed himselfe on the one side or the other, the king standing in the middest.

When hir grace vnderstood that the king was come, she came foorth of hir tent, and at the doore therof, being set on a faire and beutifull horsse richlie trapped, she rode foorth towards the king, who perceiuing hir to approch, came forward somewhat beyond the crosse on Blackheath, and there staied till she came néerer, & then putting off his cap, he made forward to hir, and with most louing countenance and princelie behauiour saluted, welcomed, and imbraced hir, to the great reioising of the beholders: and she likewise not forgetting hir dutie, with most amiable aspect and womanlie behauiour receiued him with manie apt words and thanks, as was most to purpose. Whilest they were thus talking togither, the fiftie pensioners with the gard departed to furnish the hall at Gréenewich. After the king had talked with hir a small while, he put hir on his right hand, and so with their footmen they rode togither, and with their companies being thus met, returned in this manner through the rankes of the knights and esquiers (which stood still all this while and remooued not.) *The méeting of the king & the ladie Anne of Cleue on Blackeheath.*

First hir trumpets set forward being twelue in number, beside two ketle drums on horssebacke; then followed the kings trumpeters, then the kings councellors, then the gentlemen of the priuie chamber, after them the gentlemen of hir graces countrie in cotes of veluet, and all on great horsses. Then the maior of London with the yoongest baron, then all the barons: next them the bishops, then the earles, with whom rode the earles of Ouerstein and Waldec hir countrimen, then the dukes of Norffolke and Suffolke, and the archbishop of Canturburie, and duke Philip of Bauier: next followed the ambassadors, then the lord priuie seale, and the lord chancellor, then the lord marquesse Dorset that bare the sword: next followed the king himselfe equallie riding with the ladie Anne, and behind him rode sir Anthonie Browne with the kings horsse of estate, as yée haue heard, and behind him rode sir Iohn Dudleie maister of hir horsses, leading hir spare horsse trapped in rich tissue downe to the ground; after them followed henxmen and pages of honor. *The kings trumpets and the ladie Anne of Cléeues.* *The king and the ladie Anne ride togither.*

Then followed the ladie Margaret Dowglas, the ladie marquesse Dorset, the dutches of Richmond and Suffolke, the countesses of Rutland and Hertford, and other countesses. Then came hir chariot in which she had rid all hir iournie, well carued and gilt with the armes of hir countrie curiouslie wrought & couered with cloth of gold, all the horsses were trapped with blacke veluet, and on them rode pages of honor, in which chariot rode two ancient ladies of hir countrie: next after the chariot, followed six ladies and gentlewomen of hir countrie verie beautifull and richlie apparelled, and with them rode six ladies of England. Then followed an other chariot, gilt and furnished, then ten English ladies, and next them an other chariot couered with blacke cloth and therein rode foure gentlewomen that were hir chamberers. Then followed all the remnant of the ladies, gentlewomen and damosels in great number: and last of all came an other chariot all blacke, with thrée launders apperteining to hir grace; next after followed an horslitter of cloth of gold and crimsin veluet vpon veluet paled, with horsses trapt accordinglie, which the king had sent to hir. Then followed the seruingmen of hir traine, all clothed in blacke, mounted on great horsses, euerie one in due place and decent order, so that it was verie magnificall and more than princelie brauerie that then was exhibited to the beholders eies, as the poet saith: *Hir chariot wherein she rode all hir iourneie.*

Cernitur hîc plusquam regia pompa comes.

In this order they rode through the rankes and through the parke, till they came at the

the late friers wall, where all men alighted except the king, the two maisters of the horsse, and the henxmen, which rode to the hall doore, & the ladies rode to the court gate, & as they passed they might behold on the wharfe, how the citizens of London were rowing vp and downe on the Thames right before them, euerie craft with his barge garnished with banners, flags, streamers, pencels, and targets, painted and beaten with the kings armes, some with hir armes, and some with the armes of their craft and mysterie.

There was also a barge called the bachellors barke, richlie decked, on the which waited a foist that shot great peeces of artillerie, and in euerie barge was great store of instruments of diuerse sorts, and men and children singing and plaieng altogither, as the king and the ladie Anne passed by on the wharfe. When the king and she were

The king wel-
commeth hir to
Greenwich.

within the vtter court, they alighted from their horsses, and the king louinglie imbraced hir, kissed hir, & bad hir welcome to hir owne, leading hir by the left arme through the hall, which was furnished beneath the harth with the gard and aboue the harth with the fiftie pensioners, with their battell axes ; and so the king brought hir vp to hir priuie chamber, where he left hir for that time. Assoone as the king and she were entered the court, a great peale of artillerie was shot off from the tower of Gréenwich, and there about.

When the kings companie and hirs were once come within the parke (as before yée haue heard) then all the horssemen on Blackeheath brake their araie, and had licence to depart to London or otherwhere to their lodgings.

The mariage is
solemnized be-
twixt king Hen-
rie & the ladie
Anne of Cleue.

On the tuesdaie following, being the daie of the Epiphanie the mariage was solemnized betwixt the king and the said ladie. She was fetched from hir chamber by the lords, so that she going betweene the earle of Ouersteine, and the grand master Hosconder, which had the conduct and order to sée the mariage performed, she passed through the kings chamber & all the lords before hir, till shée came into the gallerie, where the king was readie, staieng for hir, to whome she made thrée low obeisances and courtesies. Then the archbishop of Canturburie receiued them, and married them togither, and the earle of Ouersteine did giue hir. When the mariage was celebrate they went hand in hand into the kings closet, and there hearing masse, offered their tapers, and after Masse was ended, they had wine and spices. And that doone, the king departed to his chamber, and all the ladies waited on hir to hir chamber, the duke of Norffolke going on hir right hand, and the duke of Suffolke on hir left.

After nine of the clocke, the king hauing shifted his apparell, came to his closet, & she likewise in hir haire, & in the same apparell she was married in she came to hir closet with hir sargeant at armes, & all hir officers before hir like a quéene, & so the king and she went openlie in procession, and offered and dined togither. After they had supped togither, there were bankets and maskes, and diuerse disports shewed, till time came, that it pleased the king and hir to take rest. On the sundaie after were

Iusts and tor-
nements.

kept solemne iusts, which greatlie contented the strangers. This daie she was apparelled after the English manner, with a French hood, which became hir excéeding well. When the earle of Ouersteine and the other lords and ladies which had giuen their attendance on hir grace all that iourneie, had béene highlie feasted and interteined of the king and other of the nobles, they tooke leaue, and had great gifts giuen to them, both in monie and plate, and so returned toward their countrie, leauing behind them the erle of Waldecke, and diuerse gentlemen and damosels to remaine with hir, till she were better acquainted in the realme.

The king and
the ladie Anne
remooue to
Westminster.

The fourth of Februarie, the king and she remooued to Westminster by water, on whome the lord maior & his brethren, with twelue of the chéefe companies of the citie, all in barges gorgeouslie garnished with baners, penons, and targets, richlie couered, and furnished with instruments, sweetlie sounding, gaue their attendance : and by the waie, all the ships shot off, and likewise from the tower, a great peale of ordinance
went

went off lustilie. The twelfe of Februarie, the duke of Norffolke was sent in ambassage to the French king, of whome he was well interteined, and in the end of the same moneth he returned againe into England. The duke of Norffolke ambassador into France.

After Christmas, the priorie church of S. Marie Oueris in Southworke was purchased of the king by the inhabitants of the Borow, D. Gardener bishop of Winchester putting to his helping hand: they made thereof a parish church, and the little church of Marie Magdalen ioining to the same priorie, was made all one church, and saint Margarets in Southworke a parish, was admitted to the same parish. ¶ The twelfe of March, Henrie Bourcher erle of Essex riding a yoong horsse, was cast, & brake his necke, at his manour in Essex: he was the eldest earle in England. The nintéenth of March, Iohn Vere erle of Oxford, high chamberleine of England, deceassed at his manour in Essex. The tenth of Aprill, sir William Peterson priest, late commissarie of Calis, and sir William Richardson priest of S. Maries in Calis, were both there drawne, hanged, and quartered in the market place for denieng obstinatelie the kings supremacie.] S. Marie Oueries made a parish church. Iohn Stow. Erle of Essex deceassed. Earle of Oxford deceassed. Priests at Calis executed.

The third sundaie in Lent one doctor Barnes preached at Paules crosse, and in his sermon inueighed against the bishop of Winchester, for doctrine by him preached in the same place, the first sundaie of that Lent, intreating of iustification. Among other taunts that Barnes vttered against the bishop, this was one, that if he & the bishop were both at Rome, he knew that great sums of monie would not saue his life, where but for the bishop, there was no great feare, but small intreatance would serue. The bishop offended herewith, complained of Barnes to the K. and had him examined, & at length by the kings commandement he came to the bishops house, where the matter was so handled at this time, that Barnes with two other preachers, the one named Hierome, and the other Garret (of whom hereafter more shall be said) were appointed to preach at S. Marie spittle by London in the Ester wéeke. In that sermon which Barnes made before all the people, he asked the bishop forgiuenesse for speaking so vnreuerentlie of him in his former sermon, and required the bishop (if he did forgiue him) in token thereof to hold vp his hand, which like as it was long before he did, so (as manie thought afterward) it was but a feigned forgiuenesse. D. Barnes.

The twelfe of Aprill began a parlement, and sir Nicholas Hare was restored to the office of speaker, who togither with sir Humfreie Browne knight, and William Connesbie esquier, the thrée and twentith of Februarie last past, had bin called before the lords into the Starchamber, for being of counsell with sir Iohn Shelton knight, in making a fraudulent will of his lands, to the hinderance of the kings prerogatiue, and contrarie to the statute of Anno 27, for the which offense they were all at that time dismissed of their offices and seruices to the king, and the two knights were immediatlie sent to the tower, and thrée daies after Connesbie was committed thither also. They remained there in ward about ten daies. and were then deliuered. Sir Humfreie Browne was the kings sargeant at law, sir Nicholas Hare was one of the kings councellors, and speaker of the parlement, who being then depriued, was now againe thereto restored. William Connesbie was attorneie of the dutchie of Lancaster. In this parlement, were fréelie granted without contradictions, foure fiftéenes and a subsidie of two shillings of lands, and twelue pence of goods, toward the kings great charges of making Bulworkes. Sir Iohn Shelton, sir Nicholas Hare, sir Humfreie Browne fraudulent lawiers punished.

The eighteenth of Aprill at Westminster was Thomas lord Cromwell created earle of Essex, and ordeined great chamberleine of England, which office the earles of Oxford were woont euer to inioie; also Gregorie his sonne was made lord Cromwell. The foure and twentith of Aprill, Thomas lord Audleie, & chancellor of England, with sir Anthonie Browne, maister of the kings horsses, were made knights of the right honourable order of the garter. On Maie daie, was a great triumph of iusting at Westminster, which iusts had beene proclaimed in France, Flanders, Scotland, and Spaine, for all commers that would, against the challengers of England; which were, Aduancement of Thomas Cromwell.

sir Iohn Dudleie, sir Thomas Seimer, sir Thomas Poinings, sir George Carew knights, Anthonie Kingston, and Richard Cromwell esquiers, which said challengers came into the lists that daie richlie apparelled, and their horsses trapped all in white veluet, with certeine knights and gentlemen riding afore them, apparelled all in white veluet, and white sarsenet, and all their seruants in white dublets, and hozen cut after the Burgonion fashion : and there came to iust against them the said daie, of defendants fortie six, the earle of Surrie being the formost, lord William Howard, lord Clinton, and lord Cromwell, sonne and heire to Thomas Cromwell earle of Essex, and chamberleine of England, with other, which were richlie apparelled.

And that day, sir Iohn Dudleie was ouerthrowne in the field, by mischance of his horsse, by one master Breme defendant, neuerthelesse he brake diuerse speares valiantlie after that. And after the said iusts were doone, the said challengers rode to Durham place, where they kept open houshold, and feasted the king and quéene, with hir ladies, and all the court. The second of Maie, Anthonie Kingston & Richard Cromwell were made knights at the said place. The third of Maie, the said challengers did tournie on horssebacke with swords, & against them came nine and twentie defendants ; sir Iohn Dudleie, and the earle of Surrie running first, who in the first course lost both their gantlets : and that daie, sir Richard Cromwell ouerthrew master Palmer in the field off his horsse, to the great honor of the challengers. On the fift of Maie, the said challengers fought on foot at the barriers, and against them came thirtie defendants, which fought valiantlie : but sir Richard Cromwell ouerthrew that daie at the barriers master Culpeper in the field.

The said challengers brake vp their houshold, after they had kept open hospitalitie, and feasted the king, quéene, and all the lords, beside all the knights and burgesses of the common house in time of the parlement, and the maior, aldermen, and all their wiues to their no small honor, though great expense. In the parlement which began the eighteenth of Aprill last past, the religion of saint Iohns in England, commonlie called the order of knights of the Rhodes, was dissolued ; & on the ascension day, being the fift of Maie, sir William Weston knight, prior of saint Iohns departed this life for thought (as was reported) which he tooke to the heart, after he heard of that dissolution of his order. ¶ For the king tooke all the lands that belonged to that order into his hands, to the augmentation of his crowne, and gaue vnto euerie of the challengers aboue written for a reward of their valiantnesse, a hundred marks, and a house to dwell in of yearelie reuenues out of the said lands for euer.]

The same moneth were sent to the Tower doctor Samson, bishop of Chichester, and doctor Wilson, for reléeuing certeine traitorous persons : and for the same offense was one Richard Farmer, a grocer of London, a rich and welthie man, and of good estimation in the citie, committed to the Marshalseie, & after at Westminster hall arreigned, and atteinted in the premunire ; so that he lost all his goods. ¶ The ninth daie of Iulie, Thomas lord Cromwell, late made earle of Essex (as before you haue heard) being in the councell chamber, was suddenlie apprehended & committed to the Tower of London : the which manie lamented, but more reioised, and speciallie such as either had béene religious men, or fauoured religious persons, for they banketed & triumphed togither that night, manie wishing that that daie had béene seuen yeares before ; and some fearing that he should escape, although he were imprisoned, could not be merie.

Other who knew nothing but truth by him, both lamented him, and heartilie praied for him. But this is true, that of certeine of the cleargie he was detestablie hated, and speciallie such as had borne swinge and by his meanes were put from it : for in déed he was a man that in all his dooings seemed not to fauor anie kind of poperie, nor could not abide the snuffing pride of some prelats, which vndoubtedlie (whatsoeuer else was the cause of his death) did shorten his life, and procured the
end

end that he was brought vnto: which was, that the ninteenth daie of the said moneth he was atteinted by parlement, and neuer came to his answer: which law manie reported that he caused first to be made, howbeit the plaine truth thereof I know not. The articles for which he died appeare in the records, where his attaindor is written, which are too long here to be rehearsed; but to conclude he was there atteinted of heresie and high treason, and the eight & twentith of Iulie was brought to the scaffold on the Tower hill, where he said these words following.

The words of the lord Cromwell spoken at his death.

I AM come hither to die, and not to purge my selfe, as may happen some thinke that I will, for if I should so doo, I were a verie wretch and a miser. I am by the law condemned to die, and thanke my Lord God, that hath appointed me this death for mine offense. For since the time that I came to yeares of discretion I haue liued a sinner, and offended my Lord God, for the which I aske him hartilie forgiuenesse. And it is not vnknowne to manie of you, that I haue beene a great traueller in the world, and being but of a base degree, was called to high estate. And since the time I came therevnto, I haue offended my prince, for the which I aske him hartilie forgiuenesse, and beseech you all to praie to God with me, that he will forgiue me. O Father forgiue me, O Sonne forgiue me, O Holie ghost forgiue me, O three persons and one God forgiue me. And now I praie you that be here, to beare me record, I die in the catholike faith, not doubting in anie article of my faith, no nor doubting in anie sacrament of the church. Manie haue slandered me, and reported that I haue beene a bearer of such as haue mainteined euill opinions, which is vntrue: but I confesse, that like as God by his holie spirit dooth instruct vs in the truth, so the diuell is readie to seduce us, and I haue beene seduced: but beare me witnesse, that I die in the catholike faith of the holie church, and I hartilie desire you to praie for the kings grace, that he may long liue with you in health and prosperitie, & after him that his sonne prince Edward, that goodlie impe may long reigne ouer you. And once againe I desire you to praie for me, that so long as life remaineth in this flesh, I wauer nothing in my faith.

Then made he his praier, which was long, but not so long as godlie and learned, and after committed his soule to the hands of God, and so patiently suffered the stroke of the ax, by a ragged and butcherlie miser, which ill fauouredlie performed the office. This man being borne in Putneie, a village in Surreie by the Thames side, foure miles distant from London, was sonne to a Smith, after whose deceasse, his mother was married to a Shereman. But notwithstanding the basenesse of his birth and lacke of maintenance was at the beginning (as it happeneth to manie others) a great let and hinderance for vertue to shew hir selfe: yet through a singular excellencie of wit, ioined with an industrious diligence of mind, and helpe of knowledge, gathered by painefull trauell, and marking the courses of states and gouernements as well of his natiue countrie at home, as in forren parties abrode, he grew to such a sufficient ripenesse of vnderstanding and skill, in ordering of weightie affaires, that he was thought apt and fit for anie roome or office wherto he should be admitted.

Which being perceiued of cardinall Wolseie, then archbishop of Yorke, he tooke him into his seruice, and making him his solicitor, imploied him about businesse oftentimes of most importance, wherein he acquited himselfe with such dexteritie, as answered alwaies the credit committed to him. After the cardinals fall, he was aduanced to the kings seruice, behauing himselfe so aduisedlie in matters which he tooke in hand, that within a small time he rose to high authoritie, and was admitted to be

See Iohn Fox in the Acts & Monuments.

A description of the birth of Thomas Cromwell and other circumstances.

Thomas Cromwell in most authoritie vnder of the king.

of the priuie councell, bearing most rule of all other vnder the king, as partlie ye haue heard: so that by him it well appeared, that the excellencie of heroicall vertues, which aduance men to fame and honor, resteth not onelie in birth and bloud, as a priuilege appropriate and alonelie annexed vnto noble houses, but remaineth at the disposition of almightie God the giuer & disposer of all gifts, who raiseth the poore manie times from the basest degrée, and setteth him vp with princes, according to the saieng of Ecclesiastes:

Qui iacuit tetro quandóque in carcere vinctus,
Parta suis meritis regia sceptra tulit.

Neuerthelesse, concerning the lord Cromwell earle of Essex, if we shall consider his comming vp to such high degree of honor as he atteined vnto, we maie doubt whether there be cause more to maruell at his good fortune, or at his woorthie and industrious demeanor. But sith in the booke of Acts and Monuments ye maie find a

sufficient discourse hereof, we néed not to spend more time about it, saue onelie as master Fox hath trulie noted, such was his actiuitie and forward ripenesse of nature, so readie and pregnant of wit, so discreet and well aduised in iudgement, so eloquent of toong, so faithfull and diligent in seruice, of such an incomparable memorie, so bold of stomach and hardie, and could doo so well with his pen, that being conuersant in the sight of men, he could not long continue vnespied, nor yet vnprouided of fauor and helpe of friends, to set him forward in place and office.

Thankefull he was and liberall, not forgetting benefits receiued, as by his great

courtesie shewed to Friscobald the Italian it well appeared: a fauourer of the poore in their sutes, and readie to reléeue them that were in danger to be oppressed by their mightie aduersaries: a fauorer of the gospell, and an enimie to the pride of prelates, verie stout, and not able well to put vp iniuries, which wan him shrewd enimies that ceassed not (as was thought) to séeke his ouerthrow, till at length they had bróught to passe that they wished. Carefull he was for his seruants, and readie to doo them good, so that fearing the thing which came to passe, he prouided well for the more part of them, notwithstanding nis fall. And thus much for the lord Cromwell. The morrow after Midsummer daie, the king caused the queene to remooue to Richmont, supposing it to be more for hir health, and more for hir pleasure.

The sixt of Iulie, certeine lords came downe into the nether house, & expresselie declared causes, for the which the kings marriage was not to be taken lawfull: & in conclusion, the matter was by the conuocation cléerelie determined, that the king might lawfullie marrie where he would, and so might she. And thus were they cléerelie diuorsed, and by the parlement it was enacted, that she should be taken no more for queene, but called the ladie Anne of Cleue. In this yeare, the lord Leonard Greie,

brother vnto Thomas marquesse Dorset, being the kings lieutenant in Ireland, was reuoked home, and vpon his comming to London was sent to the Tower. In Iulie the prince of Salerne, and the lord Lois Dauola came into England to sée the king, & after they were departed, don Frederike, marquesse of Padula, brother to the duke of Ferrara, the prince of Macedonie, the marquesse of Terra Noua, & monsieur de Flagie, with other, came from the emperors court into England to sée the king, the which on Marie Magdalens daie came to the court at Westminster, and after they had béene highlie feasted, and noblie interteined, they were richlie rewarded as the other, and so departed.

The eight and twentith of Iulie (as you haue heard before) the lord Cromwell

was beheaded, and likewise with him the lord Hungerford of Heitesburie, who at the houre of his death séemed vnquiet, as manie iudged him rather in a frensie than otherwise: he suffered for buggerie. The thirteenth of Iulie were drawne on hurdels from the Tower to Smithfield, Robert Barns doctor of diuinitie, Thomas Garard, and William Ierom bachellors in diuinitie; Ierom was vicar of Stepnie, and Garard was

person

person of Honie lane: also Powell Fetherston, and Abell priests. The first thrée were drawne to a stake, there before set vp, and then burned. The other three were drawne to the gallowes, and hanged, beheaded and quartered. The thrée first (as is found in their atteindor) were executed for diuerse heresies, but none alledged, whereat (saith Hall) I haue much maruelled, that their heresies were so manie, and not one alledged as a speciall cause of their death. And verelie at their deaths they asked the shiriffs what was their offense for which they were condemned? Who answered, they could not tell: but most men said it was for preaching against the doctrine of Stephan Gardiner bishop of Winchester, who chieflie (as the same Hall saith) procured their deaths. The last thrée, to wit, Powell, Fetherston, and Abell, suffered for treason, as in their atteindor was speciall mention made, to wit, for denieng the kings supremacie, and affirming his mariage with the ladie Katharin Dowager to be good.

The fourth of August, Thomas Empson sometime a moonke of Westminster, which had béene in prison for treason in Newgate now for the space of thrée yeares and more, came before the iustices of gaole deliuerie at Newgate, and for that he would not aske the kings pardon, nor be sworne to be true to him, his moonks garment was plucked from his backe, and he repriued, till the king were informed of his malicious obstinacie: and this was the last moonke that was séene in his clothing in England till queene Maries daies. The fourth of August were drawne from the Tower of London to Tiburne, Giles Heron gentleman, Clement Philpot gentleman, late of Calis, and seruant to the lord Lisle, Darbie Genning, Edmund Brindholme priest, chapleine to the said lord Lisle, William Horne late a laie brother of the Charterhouse of London, and another offendor: which six persons were there hanged and quartered, and had béene atteinted of treason by parlement. The same daie also was one Charles Carew gentleman hanged for robbing of the ladie Carew.

The eight of August was the ladie Katharine Howard néece to the duke of Norffolke, and daughter to the lord Edmund Howard shewed openlie as quéene at Hampton court. The eleuenth of September a stranger was hanged in Moore field, named Iames Rination, who had slaine his maister, one Capon a Florentine in a garden, for his harlot. In the latter end of this summer, was vnuiersallie through the most parts of this realme great death by a strange kind of hot agues and fluxes, and some pestilence, in which season was such a drought, that wels and small riuers were cleane dried vp, so that much cattell died for lacke of water, and the Thames was so shalow, & the fresh water of so small strength that the salt water flowed aboue London bridge, till the raine had increased the fresh waters.

On the two and twentith of September, Rafe Egerton, seruant to the lord Audleie, lord chancellor, and one Thomas Harman seruant to one master Flightwood, were drawne, hanged, and quartered, the one for counterfeiting and antidating of the kings seale in a signet, wherewith he sealed licences for denizens, vnder the name of the clearkes of the chancerie: and the other, that is to saie Harman, for writing them. One Tuckefield, being of their faction, robbed the lord Audleies chappell and fled, who being afterward apprehended at Calis, which towne he would haue betraied, he slue himselfe with a dagger. In the end of this yeare, the French king made a strong castell at Ard, and also a bridge ouer into the English pale, which bridge the crew of Calis did beat downe, and the Frenchmen built it vp againe, but the Englishmen beat it downe againe. After this, the K. sent about fiftéene hundred workemen to fortifie the towne of Guisnes, and sent with them fiue hundred men of warre to gard them.

It was reported in France, that a mightie armie was come ouer foorth of England with great ordinance: which brute caused the French king to send to the frontiers of Picardie the duke of Vandosme, and other capteins with all spéed to defend the same.

Thomas Empson an obstinate moonke.

Execution for treason.

Harlots cause manie murthers.

A death and a drought.
I. S tow.

A castell built at Ard.

Guisnes fortified.

The earles of Surrie and Southampton sent to Calis.

same. The king of England hearing thereof, sent the earles of Surrie, and Southampton, and the lord Russell, high admerall into the marches of Calis, to set order there, and after them he likewise sent two hundred light horssemen of the borders of Scotland, whom the Frenchmen called Stradiots. The lords hauing set order in

Richard Mekins burnt. See Iohn Fox in the Acts & Monuments.

things, shortlie returned. A boie, one Richard Mekins, not past fiftéene years of age, was burnt in Smithfield, for speaking against the sacrament, and contrarie to the statute of the six articles. The bishop of London was thought in great fault, for procuring that terrible execution, seeing the yoong fellow was but an ignorant foole without learning, and gladlie recanted that wherewith he was charged.

1541

An. Reg. 33.

A new rebellion practised in Yorkshire.

About the latter end of this yeare, doctor Samson bishop of Chichester, and doctor Wilson, which had béene committed to the tower (as before ye haue heard) were now pardoned of the king, and set againe at libertie. In the beginning of this yeare, fiue priests in Yorkeshire began a new rebellion, with the assent of one Leigh, a gentleman, and nine temporall men, all which persons were apprehended, and in diuers places put to execution. The said Leigh and two other, the one named Tatersall a clothier, & the other Thornton a yeoman, on the seuentéenth of Maie,

Sir Iohn Neuill executed.

The countesse of Salisburie beheaded.

Execution of two of the gard.

were drawne through London to Tiburne, and there executed. And sir Iohn Neuill knight, and ten other persons, died for the same cause at Yorke. The same daie, Margaret countesse of Salisburie, that had remained a long time prisoner in the tower, was beheaded there within the tower. She was the last of the right line and name of Plantagenet.. The ninth of Iune for example sake, two of the kings gard, the one named Damport, and the other Chapman, were. hanged at Greenwich by the friers wall, for robberies which they had committed.

Abr. Fl. ex I. S. pag. 1020.

Sir Edmund Kneuet arreigned for striking in the court.

¶On the tenth of Iune, sir Edmund Kneuet knight, of Norffolke, was arreigned before the kings iustices (sitting in the great hall at Gréenewich) maister Gage, comptroller of the kings household, maister Southwell, sir Anthonie Browne, sir Anthonie Winkefield, maister Wrisleie, and Emund Peckham, cofferer of the kings houshold, for striking of one maister Clere of Norffolke, seruant with the earle of Surrie,

The order of euerie officer about that execution.

within the kings house in the tenis court. There was first chosen to go vpon the said Edmund, a quest of gentlemen, and a quest of yeomen, to inquire of the said stripe, by the which inquests he was found giltie, and had iudgement to lose his right hand. Wherevpon was called to doo the execution, first the sergeant surgion with his instruments apperteining to his office: the sergeant of the woodyard with the mallet, and a blocke wherevpon the hand should lie: the maister cooke for the king, with the knife: the sergeant of the larder, to set the knife right on the ioint: the sergeant ferrer, with the searing irons to seare the veines: the sergeant of the poultrie, with a cocke, which cocke should haue his head smitten off vpon the same blocke, and with the same knife: the yeoman of the chandrie, with seare cloths: the yeoman of the skullerie, with a pan of fire to heate the irons, a chafer of water to coole the ends of the irons, and two formes for all officers to set their stuffe on: the sergeant of the cellar, with wine, ale, and béere: the yeoman of the yewrie in the sergeants stead, who was absent, with bason, ewre, and towels.

Iudgement vpon Kneuet to lose his hand.

Thus euerie man in his office readie to doo the execution, there was called foorth sir William Pickering knight marshall, to bring in the said Edmund Kneuet; and when he was brought to the bar, the chiefe iustice declared to him his tresspasse, and the said Kneuet confessing himselfe to be giltie, humblie submitted him to the kings mercie: for this offense he was not onelie iudged to lose his hand, but also his

He is pardoned.

bodie to remaine in prison, and his lands and goods at the kings pleasure. Then the said sir Edward Kneuet desired that the king of his benigne grace would pardon him of his right hand, and take the left, for (quoth he) if my right hand be spared, I maie hereafter doo such good seruice to his grace, as shall please him to appoint. Of this submission and request the iustices foorthwith informed the king, who of his goodnesse,

considering

considering the gentle heart of the said Edmund, and the good report of the lords, granted him his pardon, that he should lose neither hand, lands, nor goods, but should go frée at libertie.

The lord Leonard Greie being inditced of certeine points of treason by him committed, as was alledged against him, during the season that he was the kings lieutenant in Ireland, to wit, for deliuering his nephew Girald Fitzgerard brother vnto Thomas Fitzgerard before executed, and also for that he caused certeine Irishmen to inuade the lands of the kings friends, whome he fauoured not: on the fiue and twentith of Iune he was arreigned at Westminster in the kings bench, and appointed to be tried by knights, because he was a lord by name, and no lord of the parlement; but he discharged the iurie, and confessed the indictement, wherevpon he had iudgement, and on the eight and twentith of Iune being saint Peters euen, he was beheaded at tower hill, where he ended his life verie quietlie and godlie. The lord Leonard Greie beheaded.

This noble man as he was come of high linage, so was he a right valiant and hardie personage, hauing in his time doone his prince and countrie good seruice, both in Ireland, France, and other places, greatlie to his commendation, although now his hap was thus to loose his head, as conuicted by law, and his renowme (ouercast with a cloud of disgrace) vanished, as future chances befell, to the abolishing of the present honor which sometime he inioied. Howbeit, his estimation he might haue preserued vnblemished, had prouident circumspection vndertaken the direction of his dooings, and that he had borne his eies in his forehead, to foresee all afterclaps, which a wise man will in no case neglect:

Nam sapiens in fronte oculos habet, omnia spectans,
    Omnia prudenti cum ratione videns.

The same daie that he suffered, there was executed at saint Thomas Waterings thrée gentlemen, Iohn Mantell, Iohn Frowds, and George Roidon: they died for a murther committed in Sussex (as their indictement imported) in companie of Thomas Fines lord Dacres of the south. The truth whereof was thus. The said lord Dacres, through the lewd persuasion of some of them, as hath béene reported, meaning to hunt in the parke of Nicholas Pelham esquire at Laughton, in the same countie of Sussex, being accompanied with the said Mantell, Frowds, and Roidon, Iohn Cheinie and Thomas Isleie gentlemen, Richard Middleton and Iohn Goldwell yeomen, passed from his house of Hurstmonseux, the last of Aprill in the night season, toward the same parke, where they intended so to hunt; and comming vnto a place called Pikehaie in the parish of Hillingleie, they found one Iohn Busbrig, Iames Busbrig, and Richard Summer standing togither; and as it fell out through quarelling, there insued a fraie betwixt the said lord Dacres and his companie on the one partie, and the said Iohn and Iames Busbrig and Richard Summer on the other: insomuch that the said Iohn Busbrig receiued such hurt, that he died thereof the second of Maie next insuing. The true report of the cause wherevpon the murther of Iohn Busbrig insued.

Wherevpon, as well the said lord Dacres as those that were there with him, and diuerse other likewise that were appointed to go an other waie to méet them at the said parke, were indicted of murther: and the seauen and twentith of Iune the lord Dacres himselfe was arreigned before the lord Audleie of Walden then lord chancellor, sitting that daie as high steward of England, with other péeres of the realme about him, who then and there condemned the said lord Dacres to die for that transgression. And afterward the nine and twentith of Iune being saint Peters daie, at eleuen of the clocke in the forenoone, the shiriffs of London, accordinglie as they were appointed, were readie at the tower to haue receiued the said prisoner, and him to haue lead to execution on the Tower hill. But as the prisoner should come forth of the tower, one Heire a gentleman of the lord chancellors house came, and in the kings name commanded to staie the execution till two of the clocke in the afternoone, which caused manie to The lord Dacres arreigned before the lord Audleie.
thinke

thinke that the king would haue granted his pardon. But neuerthelesse, at three of the clocke in the same afternoone, he was brought forth of the tower, and deliuered to the shiriffs, who lead him on foot betwixt them vnto Tiburne, where he died. His

Lord Dacres executed at Tiburne.

bodie was buried in the church of saint Sepulchers. He was not past foure and twentie yéeres of age, when he came through this great mishap to his end, for whome manie sore lamented, and likewise for the other thrée gentlemen, Mantell, Frowds, and Roidon. But for the said yoong lord, being a right towardlie gentleman, and such a one, as manie had conceiued great hope of better proofe, no small mone and lamentation was made; the more indéed, for that it was thought he was induced to attempt such follie, which occasioned his death, by some light heads that were then about him.

The first of Iulie a Welshman a minstrell was hanged and quartered for singing of

The king goeth in progresse into Yorkeshire.

songs, which were interpreted to be prophesies against the king. This summer the king tooke his progresse to Yorke, and passed through Lincolneshire, where was made to him an humble submission by the temporaltie, and confessing their faults, they

Gifts giuen to him by them of Lincolneshire.

humblie thanked him for his pardon, which he had granted them. The towne of Stanford gaue to him twentie pounds, the citie of Lincoln fortie pounds, Boston fiftie pounds, that part of the shire which is called Linseie gaue thrée hundred pounds, and Kesterne and the church of Lincolne presented him with fiftie pounds. At his entring into Yorkeshire, he was met with two hundred gentlemen of the same shire, in cotes of veluet, and foure thousand tall yeomen and seruing men well horssed, which on their knees made their submission, by the mouth of sir Robert Bowes, and gaue to

Gifts giuen him by them of Yorkeshire.

the king nine hundred pounds. On Barnesdale the archbishop of Yorke, with thrée hundred priests and more met the king, and making a like submission, gaue to him six hundred pounds. The like submission was made by the maiors of Yorke, Newcastell, and Hull, and ech of them gaue to the king an hundred pounds.

After he had béene at Yorke twelue daies, he came to Hull, where he deuised cer-

Hull fortified.

teine fortifications. This doone, he passed ouer the water of Humber, and so through Lincolneshire, returned toward the south parts, and at Alhallowen tide came to Hampton court. About the same time, the king had knowledge that the quéene liued dissolutelie, in vsing the vnlawfull companie of one Francis Diram, with whome

Diram and Culpeper quéene Katharins paramours.

she had béene too familiar before hir mariage with the king; & not meaning to forgo his companie now in time of hir marriage, without regard had either to the feare of God, or the king hir husband, the last summer being in progresse with the king at Pomfret, the seuen and twentith of August, she reteined the said Francis Diram in hir seruice, to the intent she might vse his companie in such vnlawfull sort the more fréelie: and not satisfied with him, she also vsed the vnlawfull companie of Thomas Culpeper esquire, one of the gentlemen of the kings priuie chamber, as well at Pomfret afore-

At Lincolne (saith *Hall*) in August, wher she gaue to him a rich cap and a chaine.

said on the nine and twentith and last of August aforesaid, and on the first of September, as at diuerse other times and places before and after. Wherevpon, the thirtéenth of Nouember, sir Thomas Wriothesleie knight the kings secretarie, came to Hampton court vnto the said quéene, and called all hir ladies, gentlewomen, and seruants into hir great chamber, & there openlie in presence of them all, declared hir offenses committed in abusing of hir bodie before hir mariage, & therwith he discharged

Quéene Katharine detected of incontinent liuing.

hir houshold. The morrow after she was conueied to Sion, the ladie Bainton and certeine gentlewomen and some of hir seruants being appointed to wait vpon hir there, till the kings pleasure might be further knowen. Culpeper, Diram, and others were had to the tower. Diram in his examination being charged with the familiaritie which had béene betwixt them, before she was married to the king, confessed that he and the said quéene had made a precontract togither, and that he concealed it for hir preferment in marriage to the king, after he vnderstood the king began to cast a liking towards hir.

The first of December, Culpeper and Diram were arreigned at the Guildhall in London,

don, before the lord maior sitting there in iudgement as chéefe iudge, hauing the lord chancellor vpon his right hand, and the duke of Norffolke vpon his left hand, the duke of Suffolke the lord priuie seale, the earles of Sussex and Hereford, with diuerse other of the councell sitting there as iudges in commission that daie: the prisoners in the end confessed the indictement, and had iudgement to die, as in cases of treason.

The tenth of December, the said Culpeper and Diram were drawen from the tower vnto Tiburne and there Culpeper had his head striken off, and Diram was hanged, dismembred and headed. Culpepers bodie was buried in S. Sepulchers church, but both their heads were set on London bridge. The two and twentith of December were arreigned in the Kings bench at Westminster, the ladie Margaret Howard, wife to the lord William Howard, Katherine Tilneie, & Alice Restwold gentlewomen, Ioane Bulmer, wife to Anthonie Bulmer gentleman, Anne Howard, wife to Henrie Howard esquier, and brother to the late queene, Malein Tilneie widow, Margaret Benet, wife to Iohn Benet gentleman, Edward Walgraue gentleman, William Ashbie gentleman; all these were condemned of misprision of treason, for concealing the queenes misdemeanour. And the same daie in the afternoone, the lord William Howard, and Damport a gentleman were likewise arreigned, and condemned of the same offense, and as well these as the other were adiudged to lose their goods, & the profits of their lands during life, and to remaine in perpetuall prison.

Culpeper and Diram executed.

Attaindors.

The sixtéenth of Ianuarie the parlement began at Westminster, in the which the lords and commons exhibited certeine petitions to the king. First, that he would not vex himselfe with the quéenes offense, and that she and the ladie Rochford might be attainted by parlement: and to auoid protracting of time, they besought him to giue his roiall assent thereto, vnder his great seale, without staieng for the end of the parlement. Also, that Diram and Culpeper before attainted by the common law, might also be attainted by parlement, & that Agnes duches of Norffolke, and Katharine countesse of Bridgewater hir daughter, which for concealing the said offense, were committed to the towre, and indicted of misprision, & the lord William Howard arreigned of the same, might likewise be attainted. Also, that who soeuer had spoken or doone anie thing in detestation of hir naughtie life, should be pardoned.

A parlement.
1542

The petitiõs of the lords & commons of the parlement to the king.

To these petitions the king granted, thanking the commons, for that it appéered they tooke his griefe to be theirs: wherevpon the quéene and the ladie Rochford were attainted by both the houses. On the tenth of Februarie, the quéene was conueied from Sion to the towre, by water, the duke of Suffolke, the lord priuie seale, and the lord great chamberleine, hauing the conduction of hir. The next daie after being saturdaie, and the eleuenth of Februarie, the king did send his roiall assent by his great seale, and then all the lords were in their robes, and the common house called vp, & there the act was read, and his assent declared. And so on the thirtéenth daie, those two ladies were beheaded on the greene within the towre with an ax, where they confessed their offenses, and died repentant.

The quéene and other attainted by parlemen.
The quéene sent to the towre.

She is beheaded.

Before this, on the thrée and twentith daie of Ianuarie was the king proclamed king of Ireland, as it was enacted both by authoritie of the parlement here, and also of an other parlement holden at Dublin in Ireland, there begun the thirteenth of Iune last past, before sir Anthonie Saintleger knight, and the kings deputie there, where as till that time the kings of England were onlie intituled lords of Ireland. In the beginning of March died sir Arthur Plantagenet vicount Lisle, bastard sonne to Edward the fourth, in the towre of London vnattainted, when he should haue béene deliuered and set at libertie.

The king proclamed king of Ireland.

The occasion of his trouble for the which he was committed to the towre, rose vpon suspicion that he should be priuie to a practise, which some of his men (as Philpot and Brindholme executed the last yeare as before ye haue heard) had consented vnto, for the betraieng of Calis to the French, whilest he was the kings lieutenant there. But

The occasion of sir Arthur Plantagenets trouble.

after that by due triall it was knowne that he was nothing guiltie to the matter, the king appointed sir Thomas Wriotheslie his maiesties secretarie, to go vnto him, and to deliuer to him a ring, with a rich diamond for a token from him, & to will him to be of good chéere. For although in that so weightie a matter, he would not haue doone lesse to him if he had béene his owne son; yet now vpon through triall had, sith it was manifestlie proued that he was void of all offense, he was sorie that he had béene occasioned so farre to trie his truth: and therefore willed him to be of good chéere and comfort, for he should find that he would make accompt of him as of his most true and faithfull kinsman, and not onelie restore him to his former libertie, but otherwise forth be readie to pleasure him in what he could. Master secretarie set foorth this

The lord Lisle
dieth thorough
immoderate ioy. message with such effectuall words, as he was an eloquent and well spoken man, that the lord Lisle tooke such immoderate ioy thereof, that his hart being oppressed therwith, he died the night following through too much reioising. After his deceasse, the twelfe of the same moneth of March, sir Iohn Audeleie sonne and heire to the said lord Lisles wife, was at Westminster created vicount Lisle. ¶ The seuentéenth of March one Margeret Dauie a yoong woman, being a seruant, was boiled in Smithfield for poisoning of hir mistres with whome she dwelt, and diuerse other persons.

George Ferrers
a burges of the
parlement ar-
rested, and what ?
mischiefe in-
sued. In the Lent season, whilest the parlement yet continued, one George Ferrers gentleman, seruant to the king, being elected a burgesse for the towne of Plimmouth in the countie of Deuonshire, in going to the parlement house, was arrested in London by a processe out of the Kings bench, at the sute of one White, for the sum of two hundred markes or thereabouts, wherein he was late afore condemned, as a suertie for the debt of one Weldon of Salisburie: which arrest being signified to sir Thomas Moile knight, then speaker of the parlement, and to the knights and burgesses there, order was taken, that the sargeant of the parlement, called S. Iohn, should foorthwith repaire to the counter in Bredstréet (whither the said Ferrers was caried) and there demand deliuerie of the prisoner.

The sargeant (as he had in charge) went to the counter, and declared to the clearks there what he had in commandement. But they and other officers of the citie were so farre from obeieng the said commandement, as after manie stout words they forciblie resisted the said sargeant, whereof insued a fraie within the counter gates, betwéene the said Ferrers and the said officers, not without hurt of either part: so that the said sargeant was driuen to defend himselfe with his mace of armes, & had the crowne there-of broken by bearing off a stroke, and his man striken downe. During this brall, the

The shiriffes
and officers
denie the deli-
uerie of the
burgesse. shiriffes of London, called Rowland Hill, and Henrie Suckliffe came thither, to whome the sargeant complained of this iniurie, and required of them the deliuerie of the said burgesse, as afore. But they bearing with their officers, made little accompt either of his complaint or of his message, reiecting the same contemptuouslie, with much proud language, so as the sargeant was forced to returne without the prisoner, wheras if they had obeied authoritie, and shewed the seruice necessarilie required in their office and person, they might by their discretion haue appeased all the broile, for wisedome assuageth the outrage & vnrestreinable furiousnes of war, as the poet saith:

Instrumenta feri vincit sapientia belli.

The sargeant thus hardlie intreated, made returne to the parlement house, and find-ing the speaker, and all the burgesses set in their places, declared vnto them the whole case as it fell, who tooke the same in so ill part, that they altogither (of whome there were not a few, as well of the kings priuie councell, as also of his priuie chamber) would sit no longer without their burges, but rose vp wholie, and repaired to the vpper house,

The speaker of
the parlement
declareth all
the matter to
the lords. where the whole case was declared by the mouth of the speaker, before sir Thomas Audleie knight then lord chancellor of England, and all the lords and iudges there assembled, who iudging the contempt to be verie great, referred the punishment thereof to the order of the common house. They returning to their places againe, vpon new

debate

debate of the case, tooke order, that their sargeant should eftsoones repaire to the shiriffe of London, and require deliuerie of the said burgesse, without anie writ or warrant had for the same, but onelie as afore.

And yet the lord chancellor offered there to grant a writ, which they of the common house refused, being in a cléere opinion, that all commandements and other acts of procéeding from the nether house, were to be doone and executed by their sargeant without writ, onelie by shew of his mace, which was his warrant. But before the sargeants returne into London, the shiriffes hauing intelligence how heinouslie the matter was taken, became somwhat more mild, so as vpon the said second demand, they deliuered the prisoner without anie deniall. But the sargeant hauing then further in commandement from those of the nether house, charged the said shiriffes to appeere personallie on the morrow, by eight of the clocke before the speaker in the nether house, and to bring thither the clearks of the counter, and such officers as were parties to the said affraie, and in like manner to take into his custodie the said White, which wittinglie procured the said arest, in contempt of the priuilege of the parlement. *The shiriffes deliuer the burgesse and are charged to apéere before the speaker.*

Which commandement being doone by the said sargeant accordinglie, on the morrow the two shiriffes, with one of the clearks of the counter (which was the chiefe occasion of the said affraie) togither with the said White, appeered in the common house, where the speaker charging them with their contempt and misdemeanor aforesaid, they were compelled to make immediat answer, without being admitted to anie counsell. Albeit, sir Roger Cholmeleie, then recorder of London, and other of the councell of the citie there present, offered to speake in the cause, which were all put to silence, and none suffered to speake, but the parties themselues: wherevpon in conclusion, the said shiriffes and the same White, were committed to the Tower of London, and the said clearke (which was the occasion of the affraie) to a place there called litle ease, and the officer of London which did the arrest called Tailor, with foure other officers to Newgate, where they remained from the eight & twentith vntill the thirtith of March, and then they were deliuered, not without humble sute made by the maior of London & other their fréends. *The shiriffes committed to the Tower.*

And for somuch as the said Ferrers being in execution vpon a condemnation of debt, and set at large by priuilege of parlement, was not by law to be brought againe into execution, and so the partie without remedie for his debt, as well against him as his principall debter; after long debate of the same by the space of nine or ten daies togither, at last they resolued vpon an act of parlement to be made, and to reuiue the execution of the said debt against the said Welden which was principall debter, and to discharge the said Ferrers. But before this came to passe, the common house was diuided vpon the question: howbeit in conclusion, the act passed for the said Ferrers, woone by fourtéene voices. *An act passeth for George Ferrers.*

The king then being aduertised of all this procéeding, called immediatlie before him the lord chancellor of England and his iudges, with the speaker of the parlement, and other of the grauest persons of the nether house, to whome he declared his opinion to this effect. First commending their wisedomes in mainteining the priuileges of their house (which he would not haue to be infringed in anie point) he alleged that he being head of the parlement, and attending in his owne person vpon the businesse thereof, ought in reason to haue priuilege for him and all his seruants attending there vpon him. So that if the said Ferrers had béene no burgesse, but onlie his seruant, yet in respect thereof he was to haue the priuilege as well as anie other. *Priuilege of a burgesse of the parlement or of anie seruant to such like officers belonging.*

For I vnderstand (quoth he) that you not onelie for your owne persons, but also for your necessarie seruants, euen to your cookes and horssekéepers, inioie the said priuilege; in somuch as my lord chancellor here present hath informed vs, that he being speaker of the parlement, the cooke of the Temple was arrested in London, and in execution

vpon

vpon a statute of the staple. And for somuch as the said cooke, during all the parlement, serued the speaker in that office, he was taken out of execution, by the priuilege of the parlement. And further we be informed by our iudges, that we at no time stand so highlie in our estate roiall, as in the time of parlement, wherein we as head, and you as members, are conioined and knit togither into one bodie politike, so as whatsoeuer offense or iniurie (during that time) is offered to the meanest member of the house, is to be iudged as doone against our person, and the whole court of parlement. Which prerogatiue of the court is so great (as our learned councell informeth vs) as all acts and processes comming out of anie other inferiour courts must for the time cease and giue place to the highest.

The king counted it presumption to arrest the burgesse.

And touching the parties, it was a great presumption in him, knowing our seruant to be one of this house, and being warned thereof before, would neuerthelesse prosecute this matter out of time, and therevpon was well worthie to haue lost his debt (which I would not wish) and therefore doo commend your equitie, that hauing lost the same by law, haue restored him to the same against him who was his debter. And if it be well considered, what a charge hath it béene to vs and you all, not onelie in expense of our substance, but also in losse of time, which should haue béene imploied about the affaires of our realme, to sit here welnigh one whole fortnight about this one priuat case, he may thinke himselfe better vsed than his desert. And this may be a good example to other to learne good maners, & not to attempt anie thing against the priuilege of this court, but to take their time better. This is mine opinion, and if I erre, I must referre my selfe to the iudgement of our iustices here present, and other learned in our lawes.

Sir Edward Montacute lord chiefe iustice.

Whervpon sir Edw. Montacute lord chiefe iustice, verie grauelie told his opinion, cōfirming by diuers reasons all that the king had said, which was assented vnto by all the residue, none speaking to the contrarie. The act in déed passed not the higher house, for the lords had not time to consider of it, by reason of the dissolution of the parlement, the feast of Easter then approching. Bicause this case hath béene diuerslie reported, and is commonlie alleged as a president for the priuilege of the parlement; I haue endeuored my selfe to learne the truth thereof, and so set it forth with the whole circumstance at large according to their instructions, who ought best both to know and remember it.

An. Reg. 34.
A lone.

This yeare in Maie the king tooke a lone of monie of all such as were valued at fiftie pounds and vpward in the subsidie bookes. The lord priuie seale, the bishop of Winchester, sir Iohn Baker, and sir Thomas Wriothesleie were commissioners about this lone in London, where they so handled the matter, that of some head citizens they obteined a thousand markes in prest to the kings vse. They that laid forth anie summe in this wise, had priuie seales for the repaiment thereof within two yeares next insuing.

Submission of the Irish nobilitie.

Diuerse of the Irish nobilitie came this yeare into England, and made their submission to the king as in the Irish chronicle it is more particularlie touched. Also wars fell out betwixt England and Scotland, the causes whereof (as appeereth by a declaration set forth by the king of England at this present) in effect were these.

The causes of the wars betwixt England & Scotland.

First there were diuerse of the English rebels, such as had moued the commotion in the north and Lincolneshire, that fled into Scotland, and were there mainteined: and although request had béene made that they might be deliuered, yet it would not be granted.

Moreouer, where the king of Scots had promised to repaire vnto Yorke the last yeare, and there to méet his vncle the king of England, wherevpon the king of England to his great charges had made preparation for their méeting there; the same was not onelie disappointed, but also at the kings being at Yorke, in lieu thereof an inuasion was made by the Scots, as it were in contempt and despite of the king of England, who notwithstanding imputing the default of méeting to the aduise of his nephues councell,

councell, and the inuasion to the lewdnesse of his subiects, was contented to giue courteous audience vnto such ambassadors as the same king of Scots sent into England, which came to the king at Christmas last, and with manie swéet and pleasant words excused that which was doone amisse, & sought to persuade kindnesse and perfect amitie in time to come. And for the better accomplishment thereof, they offered to send commissioners to the borders, there to determine the debate betwixt them of the confines, if it would please the king likewise to send commissioners for his part, which to doo he gratiouslie condescended, desirous to make triall of his nephue in some correspondence of deeds, to the faire and pleasant messages in words which he had receiued from him.

Herevpon commissioners were sent from either king, the which met and talked. But where the Englishmen chalenged a peece of ground, vndoubtedlie vsurped by the Scots, being for the same shewed such euidence as more substantiall, or more autentike can not be brought forth for anie ground within the realme; the same was neuerthelesse by the Scots denied and reiected, onelie for that it was made (as they alleged) by Englishmen, and yet was it so ancient, as it could not be counterfeited now, and the value of the ground so little, and of so small weight, as no man would attempt to falsifie a writing for such a matter. But yet this deniall notwithstanding, the English commissioners departed from the Scotish commissioners as fréends, taking order, as hath béene accustomed, for good rule vpon the borders in the meane time to be obserued.

After their departure, the lord Maxwell warden of the west marches in Scotland, made proclamation in deed for good rule to be kept: but neuerthelesse added therwith, that the borderers of Scotland shuld withdraw their goods from the borders of England, and incontinentlie after the Scotish borderers, on the fourth of Iulie entered into England suddenlie, & spoiled the kings subiects, contrarie to the league, and euen after the plaine maner of warre. Wherevpon the king of England greatlie maruelling, was driuen to furnish his borders with a garrison for defense of the same, as mistrusting a further mischiefe intended by the enimie, whose treacherie & loose dealing became a whetstone to the kings wrath, and set him in a heat of indignation, as the poet saith:

> Iam Scotus Henrici iustam irritauerat iram
> Fœdifragus.

Then was Iames Leirmouch master of the Scotish kings houshold sent into England with letters deuised in the best maner, offering a good redresse of all attempts: and yet neuerthelesse at the entrie of the said Leirmouth into England, a great number of Scots then not looked for, made a rode into England, to the great annoiance of the English borders, which dealing, though it much mooued the king of England to take displeasure against the Scots, yet he gaue gentle audience to Leirmouth at his comming vnto him, and by his faire words and promises was partlie pacified. But in the meane time, the déeds of the Scotish borderers were as extreame as might be. And in a rode made by sir Robert Bowes for reuenge thereof, the same sir Robert, and manie other with him, were taken prisoners, and could not be deliuered, nor admitted to paie their fine and ransome, as hath beene euer accustomed betwixt them on the borders.

And where at the same time, an assurance was made on both sides for a season, at the sute of the said Leirmouth, the Scots ceased not to make sundrie inuasions into England, in such wise, as the king no longer trusting to their faire words, but weieng their déeds, put an armie in a readinesse for defense of his subiects, as the due meane to atteine such a peace, as for the safetie of his people and dominions, he thought it stood with his honour to procure. After which preparation made, and knowledge thereof had, the king of Scots made new sute to haue the matter taken vp by treatie. Wherevpon the king caused the armie to staie about Yorke, and appointed the duke of Norffolke his lieutenant generall, the lord priuie seale, the bishop of Durham, & sir

Anthonie

[marginal notes]
The wilfull obstinatnesse of the Scotish comissioners.

Iames Leirmouth.

King Henrie forced to take armes against the Scots.

Anthonie Browne master of his horsses, to treat & conclude with the ambassadors of Scotland some friendlie peace, vpon reasonable and indifferent conditions, as should be thought requisit, for the auoiding of warres, then by sundrie inuasions of the Scots made open and manifest. But after they had viewed ech others commissions, and began to propone articles, the Scotish commissioners to protract time, at the first seemed to like such articles as the English commissioners had proponed, and made semblance as if there were no doubt, but that in case their king & ours might méet, all matters shuld be quietlie compounded and ended: and so taking it as for a thing sure and certeine, they onlie desired six daies to obteine answer from their master, and our armie for that time to staie: wherevnto the English commissioners accorded.

The double dealing of the Scots in the negotiation about an agrée-ment.

After those six daies was sent a commission out of Scotland, to conclude a méeting preciselie, at such a place as they knew well could not in the winter season be obserued nor kept. Wherewith when the English commissioners séemed nothing content, the Scotish commissioners shewed forth instructions, wherein libertie was giuen to them to excéed their commission in the appointing of a place, & to consent to anie other by the English commissioners thought méet and conuenient. But when the English commissioners refused to deale with men wanting sufficient commission to warrant their dooings, the Scotish commissioners required other six daies respit, to send for a larger commission, which being granted, at the end of those six daies, they brought forth a commission made in good forme, and without exception or restraint of place: but therewith they shewed instructions conteining a like restraint, as in the former commission was expressed. And thus driuing forth the matter by trifling, vpon purpose onelie to win time, they hoped thereby through the winter comming on, that the English armie should not be able much to annoie their countrie for that yeare. And so their talke brake vp without any conclusion of agréement at all; and forthwith was the armie set forward, a good part whereof had lien all this time of the treatie in Yorke, and in the countries thereabouts.

The English armie entreth into Scotland.

When the whole power was assembled, the duke of Norffolke then lieutenant generall, accompanied with the earles of Shrewsburie, Derbie, Cumberland, Surreie, Hertford, Angus, Rutland, and the lords of the north parts, and sir Anthonie Browne master of the horsses, sir Iohn Gage controllor of the kings house, and others, hauing with them twentie thousand men well and warlike appointed, entred Scotland the one and twentith of October, and tarried there eight daies, without hauing anie battell offered vnto them, in which space they burnt these townes and villages, Paxton, Ramrige, Stine, Gradin, Shilles, lang Ednem, Newton, Skitshell, Newthorne, Smellem spittle, the two Merdens, Siedericke, and the two Broxlawes, Floris, and the Faire croft, Ednem spittle, Roxborough, Kelseie and the abbeie, long Spronstow, Riden, and Hadenston. For they had determined with fire and sword to take vtter reuenge, crieng out, as the poet saith;

Vindice ferro opus esse, opus esse & vindice flamma,
Acclamant omnes.

Now while the duke was at Farnton, the fourth daie after his comming into Scotland, there came to speake with him halfe a mile from the campe, the bishop of Orkeneie, and Iames Leirmouth sent from the king of Scots to intreat of peace, but they agréed not. Finallie, after the Englishmen had lien so long within Scotland as they might recouer vittels, at length for necessitie they returned to Berwike. In all which iourneie the standard of the earle of Southampton, late lord priuie seale (which died at Newcastell before their entring into Scotland) was borne in the fore-ward, because he was appointed capteine of the same.

The earle of Southamptons standard.

The king of Scots, hearing that the English armie was returned, raised a power of fiftéene thousand men forth of all parts of his realme, vnder the guiding of the

lord

lord Maxwell (or rather of Oliuer Sincler, as the Scots affirme) boasting to tarrie as long in England, as the duke of Norffolke had tarried in Scotland. And so on fridaie being saint Katharins euen, they passed ouer the water of Eske, and burnt certeine houses of the Greues on the verie border. Thomas bastard Dacres, with Iacke of Musgraue sent word to sir Thomas Wharton lord Warden for the king vpon the west marches, to come forward to succour them. But in the meane while the Scots entring verie fierclie, the aforesaid two valiant capteins, bastard Dacres and Musgraue, manfullie set vpon the Scots with one hundred light horsses, and left a stale on the side of a hill, wherewith the Scots were woonderfullie dismaied, thinking that either the duke of Norffolke with his whole armie had béene come to those west marches, or that some other great power had beene comming against them, when they saw onelie sir Thomas Wharton with three hundred men marching forward toward them. But so it fortuned at that time vndoubtedlie as God would haue it, that the Scots fled at the first brunt, whome the Englishmen followed, and tooke prisoners at their pleasure; for there was small resistance, or none at all shewed by the Scots.

Aongst others that were taken, we find these men of name, the earle of Cassill and Glencarne, the lord Maxwell admerall of Scotland, and warden of the west marches, the lord Fleming, the lord Sumerwell, the lord Oliphant, the lord Greie, sir Oliuer Sincler the kings minion, Iohn Rosse lord of Gragie, Robert Erskin, son to the lord Erskin, Carre lard of Gredon, the lord Maxwelles two brethren, Iohn Lesleie bastard son to the earle of Rothus, George Hume lard of Hemitton, Iohn Mateland lard of Wike castell, Iames Pringell, Iames Sincler brother to Oliuer Sincler, Iohn Carmell capteine of Craiforth, Patrike Hebborne esquire, Iohn Seton esquire son in law to the lord Erskin, William Seton esquire, Iohn Steward cousin to the king, Iohn Morrowe esquire, Henrie Droumont esquire, Iames Mitton esquire, Iohn Cormurth esquire capteine of Gainsforth, Iames Mitton esquire, and other esquiers and gentlemen (beside the earles and lords before mentioned) to the number of two hundred and aboue, and more than eight hundred other persons of meaner calling; so that some one Englishman, yea some women had thrée or foure prisoners. They tooke also foure and twentie peeces of ordinance, foure carts laden with speares, and ten pauilions, with other things of price; so that this might well be said to be the handie worke of God, and the verse of the psalme verified:

Contemplans dixi, Hæc est mutatio dextræ
Numinis excelsi mortalia cuncta gubernans.

The king of Scots tooke such griefe and inward thought for his ouerthrow, and also for the murther of an English herald that was slaine at Dunbar, by one Léech an Englishman (the which for the rebellion in Lincolnshire was fled into Scotland) that he fell into a hot ague, and thereof died, although manie reported that he was at the bickering, and receiued there his deaths wound, and fled therewith into Scotland. But of his death, and of the birth of his daughter ye may see more in the historie of Scotland.

Of these prisoners before named, one and twentie of them were brought to London, and on the nineteenth of December entred into the citie by Bishops gate, and so were conueied to the tower, where they remained for the space of two daies: and vpon saint Thomas daie the apostle, being the one and twentith of December, they were conueied to Westminster, sir Iohn Gage constable of the tower riding before them, and the lieutenant of the same tower riding behind them. They rode two and two togither, and eight of them being earls and lords, had new gowns of blacke damaske furred with blacke conie, cotes of blacke veluet, and doublets of sattin, with shirts and other apparell bought new for them at the kings charges.

Thus

Marginal notes:

An armie of Scots inuade England.

The error of the Scots

The Scots flie:

Scotish lords taken at Solem Mosse.

The number of prisoners and artillerie taken.

The death of the king of Scotland.

Foure and twentie hath *Hall.*

Scots prisoners brought to London.

The Scots prisoners before the councel in the Star chamber.

Thus being solemnelie conueied through the stréets of London vnto Westminster, they came before the councell sitting in the Starchamber, and there the lord chancellor declared to them their vntruth, vnkindnesse, and false dissimulation, declaring further how the king had cause of war against them, both for denieng of their homages, and also for their traitorous inuasions made into his realme without defiance, and for keeping his subiects prisoners without redemption, contrarie to the ancient laws of the marches; for which dooings, God (as they might perceiue) had scourged them. Howbeit the K. more regarding his honor than his princelie power, was content to shew them kindnesse for vnkindnesse, and right for wrong. And although he might kéepe them in streict prison by iust law of armes, yet he was content that they should haue libertie to be with the nobles of his realme in their houses, and so according to their estates, they were appointed to dukes, earles, bishops, knights, and gentlemen, whichso interteined them, that they confessed themselues neuer to be better vsed, nor to haue had greater cheere in all their life times.

The earle of Cassils was appointed to be with the archbishop of Canturburie, the earle of Glencarne with the duke of Norffolke, the lord Fleming with the lord priuie seale, the lord Maxwell with sir Anthonie Browne, the lord Sumerwell with the lord chancellor, the lord Oliphant with sir Thomas Lée, Oliuer Sincler with the duke of Suffolke, Robert Erskin with the bishop of Westminster, the lord Monteth with sir Antonie Wingfield, the lord Monketh with sir Rafe Sadler, George Hume with the earle of Hertford, the lord of Gragie with sir Thomas Cheineie, the lard of Gredon with maister Gostwike, Henrie Maxwell with sir Richard Long, Thomas Craiford with sir Arthur Darcie, Patrike Hebborne with sir Thomas Wriotheslie, Iames Pringell with sir Richard Rich, Iohn Matland with sir Edward North, the lord Greie, Iames Sincler, and Iohn Lislie, were appointed to men of such credit, as were thought méet to answer for their safe kéeping.

The two and twentith of December, tidings came of the king of Scots death, and vpon S. Iohns daie in Christmas weeke the foresaid lords of Scotland were brought to the court, which was then at Greenwich, where they had great cheare, and went before the king to the chappell, and were lodged within the court. Herevpon ye must consider, that whereas the king of Scots had left no issue behind him in life but onelie one daughter, the king and his councell perceiuing a meane now offered, whereby without warre the two realmes might be vnited, these Scotish lords hauing first made the motion themselues, for a mariage to be had betwixt prince Edward and their

A motion of a mariage betwéene prince Edward and the yong Scotish quéene.

yoong queene, the king required their helpe vnto the furtherance of that matter, which might be a great benefit to themselues & their countrie. This they promised faithfullie to doo, and aswell by themselues as by their friends, to bring the same to effect, so much as the king could require. Wherevpon the king was not onelie contented to release them home, but also highlie rewarded them with rich and costlie gifts of sundrie sorts, in most bountifull wise, as *Anglorum prælia* noteth verie well, saieng:

Præterea ex auro captiuos torquibus ornat,
Et sumptum, vestes, argentum donat & aurum.

The thirtith of December they departed from the court, and the morrow after, eight of them dined with sir Iohn Cotes then lord maior of London, and the rest with the shiriffes, and had verie great cheare. On Newyeares daie they departed from London homewards towards Scotland, and rode to Enfield to sée the prince, and there dined that day, greatlie reioising, as by their words and countenance it seemed, to behold so proper and towardlie an impe. From thence they kept on their iournie till they came to the north parts, where they found the duke of Suffolke the kings lieutenant there, and with him remained till such pledges were come forth of Scotland, as it was couenanted they should leaue behind them.

The Scots depart into their owne countrie.

1543

The

The duke then after he had receiued the hostages, permitted them to depart, and so they returned into Scotland, where they were gladlie welcomed by their kinsmen and friends. With them went also the earle of Angus, who had béene banished The munificence of king Henrie to the earle of Angus. Scotland, and hauing remained here in England a long time, receiued of the kings fée, a thousand marks by yeare; and likewise his brother sir George Dowglas, who had fiue hundred markes yearelie likewise of the kings gift. They were now both restored home into their countrie, and that (as was said) by the kings last will. The said earle of Angus, and diuerse of the lords that had béene prisoners here in England, were made of the priuie councell of the realme by the earle of Arraine, that was chosen gouernour to the yoong quéene, and of the realme, as next heire apparent: notwithstanding that the archbishop of saint Andrews, and cardinall of the sée of Rome, enimie mortall vnto the king of England for the popes cause (and partlie set Archbishop of S. Andrew deadlie enimie to K. Henrie. on by the French king) had forged a will, expressing how the king had made him go-uernour (associat with two earles of his affinitie) as well of the queene as realme, con-trarie to the lawes of Scotland. Wherevpon the said earle of Arraine, according to his right (as he pretended) with the helpe of his friends, tooke vpon him the autho- The earle of Arraine. sir Robert Bowes deliuered. ritie of gouernor, and put the said cardinall in prison, and deliuered sir Robert Bowes, and the other English prisoners, by their bonds, according to the custome of the marches.

All this yeare was neither perfect peace nor open warre betwixt England and France, but the merchants ships were taken and robbed on both parts, and at length mer-chants goods were seized, and the ambassadors of both realms staied. Howbeit, shortlie after the ambassadors were deliuered: but the merchants still were robbed, and no warre proclaimed. In the end of this yeare came from the gouernor of Scot- Ambassadors from Scotland. land as ambassadors, sir William Hamilton, and Iames Leirmouth the secretarie of Scotland, whose message was so meanlie liked, that they were faine to send an herald into Scotland for other ambassadors, and so came hither the earle of Glencarne, and sir George Dowglas: but whatsoeuer their answer was, sir George returned in post, and within twentie daies came backe againe with an answer that was well liked of. But shortlie after they brake promise, and went from that which they had couenanted, greatlie to their reproch.

Wood was sold verie deare in the winter season of this yeere, and likewise vittels A dearth. both flesh and fish grew to an high price towards the spring, by reason (as was thought) of the vntemperate wet summer last past, causing great death among cattell. A quar-ter of mutton was sold for two shillings, or seuen grotes, a lambe at thrée shillings, or thrée and foure pence, which afore that time was esteemed scarse woorth sixteene pence. Against Easter at a court of aldermen kept in the Guildhall the twentith of A necessarie & wholsome ord-nance for mode-ration in diet. March 1542, it was enacted by the lord maior and his brethren, that the maior and shiriffs should be serued at their tables but with one course at dinner and supper in their houses; the maior to haue but seuen dishes at the most at one messe for his owne table, and the sheriffs and euerie other alderman but six dishes, vpon paine to forfeit for euerie dish fortie shillings at euerie time when they offended in this ordi-nance. Also that the sargeants and yeomen of their houses should haue but thrée dishes at dinner or supper, the sword bearers messe onlie excepted, which should be allowed to haue one dish more. It was also enacted, that from the feast of Easter then next insuing, neither the maior nor his brethren should buie anie crane, swan, or bustard, vpon paine to forfeit for euerie foule by them so bought, twentie shillings, the offense to be tried by oth, if it should be presented.

In the beginning of this yeare, on Trinitie sundaie, was a new league sworne be- *An. Reg. 35.* twéene the king and the emperour at Hampton court, either of them to be friends to A league be-twixt the king of England and the emper-our. the others friends, and enimies to the others enimies. ¶ In this yeare also a procla-mation was made, whereby the people were licenced to eate whit meats in Lent, but

streictlie *Abr. Fl. ex I. S. pag.* 1026.

Whit meats li-
cenced to be
eaten in Lent,
and noble men
punished for
breaking the
law.
Summerset an
herald killed, &
the offender
dieth as a traitor.

First iron péeces
cast.

Creations of
earles and ba-
rons.

The king ma-
rieth the ladie
Katharine Par.

Corporations,
fraternities, &
comunalties paid
more as well of
their lands as
goods as ap-
peareth by the
statute.

Articles de-
manded of the
French king.

streictlie forbidden the eating of flesh. Wherevpon shortlie after the earle of Surrie, with diuerse lords, knights, and gentlemen, were imprisoned for eating of flesh in the same Lent, contrarie to the said proclamation. The eight of Maie, one Léech, some-times bailie of Louth, who had killed Summerset one of our heralds of armes at Dun-bar in Scotland, was drawne to Tiburne, and there hanged and quartered. And the twelfe of Iune, Edward Leech his brother, and with him a priest, for the same fact were likewise executed at Tiburne.

This yeare the first cast péeces of iron that euer were made in England, were made at Buckesteed in Sussex, by Rafe Hoge, and Peter Bawd.] The third of Iune came to the court from the realme of Ireland, thrée Irish lords, Obrin, Macke William a Burgh, and Macke Gilpatrike. In Iulie the said Obrin was created earle of Townon, Macke William a Burgh, earle of Claurickford, and sir Dunon Obrin was made baron of Ebrankie, and so with rewards they tooke leaue and returned. The same moneth also, the Scotish ambassadors returned with great rewards. The twelfe of Iulie, at Hampton court, the king maried the ladie Katharine Par, widow, late wife vnto the lord Latimer deceased, and then she was nominated quéene, and so proclamed.

In the parlement holden this yeare at Westminster, a subsidie was granted to the king, to be paied in thrée yeares. Euerie Englishman being woorth in goods twentie shillings & vpward to fiue pounds, paied foure pence of euerie pound. From fiue pounds to ten pounds, eight pence. From ten pounds to twentie pounds, sixtéene pence. From twentie pounds and vpward, of euerie pound two shillings. Strangers as well denizens as other, being inhabitants, doubled this summe: and euerie stranger not being an inhabitant, that was sixteene yéeres of age and vpwards, paid foure pence for euerie poll. And for lands, fées, and annuities, euerie one borne within the kings dominions, paid eight pence of the pound, from twentie shillings to fiue pounds. And from fiue pounds to ten pounds, sixtéene pence. From ten pounds to twentie pounds, two shillings. And from twentie pounds and vpwards, thrée shil-lings; strangers still doubling this summe. The cleargie granted a subsidie of six shillings the pound, to be paied of their benefices in perpetuities in three yeares in-suing: and euerie priest hauing no perpetuitie, but an annuall stipend, paid yearelie (during the said thrée yeares) six shillings and eight pence.

About the same time, the king and the emperour sent Garter and Toison Dor, kings at armes, to demand the performance of certeine articles of the French king, which if he denied, they were commanded then to defie him, but he would not suffer them to come within his land, & so they returned. Whervpon the king caused the said demands to be declared to the French ambassador at Westminster. And in Iulie the king sent ouer six thousand men, vnder the leading of sir Iohn Wallop, appointed to haue the generall conduction of them, accompanied with diuerse other knights, esquiers and gentlemen right hardie and valiant. Sir Thomas Seimer was marshall of that armie, sir Robert Bowes treasuror, sir Richard Cromwell capteine of the horssemen, and sir George Carew his lieutenant. There were likewise sir Thomas Palmer, sir Iohn Reinsforth, sir Iohn saint Iohn, and sir Iohn Gascoigne, knights, that were capteines of the footmen. They were appointed to ioine with the em-perours power, and so to make warre into France. They departed from Calis the two and twentith of Iulie. The third of August open warre was proclamed in London betwixt the emperour and the king of England on the one part, and the French king on the other, as enimie mortall to them both, and to all other christian princes beside, as he that had confederated himselfe with the Turke.

The armie that was sent ouer vnder the leading of sir Iohn Wallop, passed foorth from the marches of Calis, and keeping alongst betwixt the borders of the French and Burgonion pales and confines, and ioining with the emperors forces, Spaniards, Wallons, and Dutch, came at length before Landerseie, a towne latelie fortified by the French,

French, within the borders of the emperors dominions, to the which they laid a strong _{Landerseie be-sieged.} siege. At length the emperour hauing dispatched his wars against the duke of Cleue, who had submitted himselfe vnto him, came now to the siege of Landerseie, with a mightie power of sundrie nations, so that the towne was sore constreined and in danger to have béene lost, if at that present the French king had not likewise with an huge armie of Frenchmen, Switzers, Lantsquenets, Italians, and others, come to _{The French king commeth to the rescue of Landerseie.} the rescue, pitching downe his campe, making countenance as if he ment presentlie to giue battell: and verelie it was thought that two such powers as were there at that time so néere togither, should neuer haue departed without battell. The emperor thinking suerlie to fight, raised his siege, and drew his people into the field. The Frenchmen thereby espieng their aduantage, put as well fresh men as vittels, and all kind of munition necessarie into the towne, and in the meane while kept the emperours people occupied with hot skirmishes.

But now after the towne was thus reléeued, which thing the French king onelie wished to accomplish, the next daie when the emperor was readie with his armie ranged in battell to haue fought with his aduersaries, the French king put his armie also in order; but hauing no mind to come forward, he trifled foorth that daie, and in the night following, secretlie departed with as much haste as was possible. When the next morning had discouered the Frenchmens flight (for manie so termed this their sudden retire) it was no néed to bid diuerse troops of the emperours armie to hie after them: but some made too much haste. For the French king suspecting _{The French king retireth backe with his armie.} what would insue, appointed his eldest sonne Henrie the Dolphin to remaine behind with the rereward, accompanied with diuerse noble capteins, which ordered their people in their retire with such warinesse and héedful skill, as the reason of warre required, that such of the emperours campe as aduentured ouer rashlie, and shewed themselues more forward than wise, fell within danger of such ambushments as were by the waie couertlie laid in places of aduantage: and so diuerse were taken, as sir George Carew, sir Thomas Palmer knight porter of Calis, Edward Bellingham, and others. But neuerthelesse a great number of such Frenchmen as could not make waie, and kéepe pase with their maine troops, were snapped vp, slaine, and taken in no small numbers by their enimies, who followed them as egre as tigers, and as the describer of that pursute saith:

Imbuit & gladios menante cruore Britannus.

This was after Alhalowentide, so that now by reason the winter was farre entred, and the weather waxing extreame foule, and contrarie to an armie that should lie in the fields, the emperour brake vp his campe and licenced the most part of his people _{The emperor breaketh vp his campe.} to depart home into their countries, for all hope to win Landerseie at that time was cleane cut off, sith it was vittelled and newlie furnished with fresh men and munition. After that the warres were once open betwixt England and France, sundrie enterprises were attempted by the parties on either side in the marches of Calis and Bullognois, in which, for the most part, the Englishmen got the vpper hand of their enimies.

At one time the Frenchmen, to the number of eight hundred, comming in the night season to enter into the English pale by the turne pike at Hammes, in purpose to make some spoile in the countrie there, were assailed vpon the sudden by sir George Summerset, and sir William Walgraue, latelie before come ouer with two hundred men out of Suffolke, to strengthen the English pale against the enimies, and at this time did behaue themselues so valiantlie, that they disappointed the enimies of their purpose. For whereas they were entered into a lane inclosed with hedges on either side, sixtéene archers getting into the grounds on the backe side of the hedges lieng alongst the lane, through which the Frenchmen were marching, placed themselues as they saw their aduantage, and so bestowed their shot, that they galled the Frenchmen in such wise, that they were forced to recule in so great disorder, that other of the Englishmen comming vpon them, easilie slue and tooke of them no small number.

Beside this, at sundrie times the Englishmen inuading the countrie of Bullognois, wasted the townes and villages, brought awaie great booties of goods and cattell, to the great impouerishing of the countrie. They burnt at one time the towne of Audinghen, and tooke the stéeple of the church there, into the which were fled six score pezzants with their wiues and children, whome the Englishmen threw downe headlong out of the steeple, bicause they had most stubbornelie refused to yéeld.

In this yeare a great death of the pestilence reigned in London, and therefore Michaelmasse terme was adiourned to S. Albons, and there kept till the end thereof. The

eightéenth of December the archbishop of Canturburies palace at Canturburie was burnt, and therein was burnt his brother in law, and other men.

In Christmasse weeke came to the king lieng at Hampton court, Ferdinando Gonzaga viceroie of Sicilie, prince of Malfeta, duke of Iuano, the emperours capteine generall. The chiefest cause of his comming was, to appoint what time the emperours armie should be readie to inuade France. He had great chéere, and at his departure was rewarded with a hundred and fiftie thrée ounces of gold in plate, and foure thousand and thrée ounces in guilt plate, all verie curiouslie wrought, and all the time of his being here, his charges were borne by the king. The sundaie before Christmas, the lord William Par brother to the quéene, who had married the daughter & heire of Henrie Bourchier erle of Essex, at Hampton court was created earle of

Essex, & sir Will. Par knight vncle to them both, was made lord Par of Horton, & chamberleine to the quéene.

On New yeares daie, was sir Thomas Wriothesleie the kings secretarie made lord Wriothesleie of Tichfield. ¶This yeare chanced foure eclipses, one of the sunne the fourtéenth of Ianuarie, and three of the moone. On the seuenth of March, Germaine Gardner, and Larke person of Chelseie were executed at Tiburne, for denieng the kings supremacie, & with whome was executed for other offenses one Singleton. And shortlie after Ashbeie was likewise executed for the supremacie. In this yeare sir Iohn Allen (who had bin twise maior of London, & of councell to the king) departing out of this life, did giue to the citie of London a rich collar of gold, to be worne by the maior: which collar was first worne by sir William Laxton on S. Edwards daie, to the election of the new maior, who gaue to euerie ward in London twentie pounds to be distributed to the poore housholders, besides to one hundred and twentie persons, thrée score men euerie of them a gowne of brode cloth, and a blacke cap, and thréescore women, to euerie of them a gowne of the like cloth, and a white kerchiefe. Humfreie Monmouth, and Iohn Cotes which were shiriffes in his maioraltie,

in the beginning of their yeare put awaie twelue sargeants and twelue yeomen, till they were forced by a court of common councell to take them againe.]

In this meane while was the cardinall of Scotland deliuered forth of prison, and shortlie after got into his hands againe all such conclusions as were made touching the marriage betwixt the quéene of Scots and prince Edward, procuring in maner all the lords and nobles of the realme to renounce that which they had promised to the king of England, as well diuerse of those whome the said king had released home out of captiuitie, as others. Wherwith the king tooke such sore displeasure, that he prepared an armie to passe into Scotland by sea, and ordeined the lord Edward

Seimer, earle of Hertford to be lieutenant of the north parts, and to haue the leading of the same armie: who went thither in March, as well for defense of the borders, as to foresee all things in order for the armie that should thus go into Scotland, whereof he was appointed generall.

When all things were in a readinesse for the nauie which was rigged to set forward towards Scotland, and that the soldiers were come which were appointed to go

with

with sir Iohn Dudleie lord Lisle, and high admerall of England in that voiage, they The lord admerall Dudleie setteth foorth from London towards Scotland. were imbarked, and so the two and twentith of March the said lord admerall, with sir Nicholas Pointz, and diuerse other knights and capteins departed from the port of London towards the north parts; and comming to Newcastell, found the erle of Hertford readie with such power as was appointed to be there at a daie assigned, forth of those countries that lie from Trent northwards. And now wanted nothing to further their iournie, but a conuenient wind; which caused them to staie certeine daies at the said towne of Newcastell, and in the villages thereabouts.

After that the earle of Hertford, and the lord admerall, accompanied with the earle An. Reg. 36. of Shrewesburie, the lords Cobham, Clinton, Coniers, Stinton, the lord William Howard, and manie other right valiant knights, gentlemen, and capteines, had lien with the armie and nauie readie at Newcastell a certeine time, looking for a prosper-The armie setteth forward by sea towards Scotland.ous wind to set forward on their purposed iournie, at length the same came about verie fit to serue their turne, and then with all spéed the soldiers were bestowed aboord, euerie companie in their appointed vessels: and herewith vp went the sailes, and forth they got into the maine seas, making their course directlie towards the Forth, a gulfe or riuer in Scotland, able to beare vessels fiftie miles vp within the countrie. There were at the least two hundred saile which the lord admerall had caused to come together, according to his commission, rigged, trimmed, and furnished with all things necessarie for the conduction of such an armie, estéemed to be about ten thousand The number of the English armie. men.

The third of Maie they arriued in the Forth, entring betwéene two Ilands, the The English armie landeth in Scotland. Bas and the Maie. The next daie being the fourth of Maie, the whole armie was landed two miles by west the towne of Lith, at a place called Grantham crag. And forthwith the lord lieutenant putting his people in good order of warre, marched on towards the said towne of Lith. The lord admerall led the fore-ward, the lord lieutenant the battell, and the earle of Shrewesburie gouerned the rere-ward. Before they came to the towne of Lith, they found in their waie readie to impeach their passage six thousand horssemen beside footmen. At first the Scots made towards The Scots offer to impeach the Englishmens passage. the Englishmen, as if they had ment to set vpon the voward: but being manfullie assailed by the harquebutters, fiue hundred in number, and shrewdlie by them curried and galled, they had no mind to come forward, but perceiuing how willing the Englishmen were to incounter with them, after certeine shot on both sides, they made a sudden retreat, and leauing their artillerie behind them, they fled to Eden-The Scots flie to Edenburgh.burgh.

The first man that fled (as the talke went) was the cardinall, who perceiuing the deuotion which the Englishmen had to sée his holinesse, had no mind to tarie. With him also fled the gouernour, the earles of Huntleie, Murreie, and Bothwell: as for their soldiers, they were disparkled, and feared the English forces as the lambe dooth the wolfe, the doe the dog, or the hart the lion: to vse the words of Anglorum prælia verie fitlie describing this battell, and saieng:

Exhorrent, vt dama canes, vt cerua leones.

The Englishmen thus hauing put their enimies to flight, & seized vpon their artil-The English armie entreth into Lith.lerie, made streight to the towne of Lith, and entered it without anie great resistance, wherein they incamped themselues the same night to their most ease and aduantage, and afterwards landed their vittels and great artillerie. They found also in this towne such plentie of riches as they looked not to haue found in anie one towne of Scotland.

The sixt of Maie they went towards Edenburgh, and as they approched néere The prouost of Edenburghs request. the towne, the prouost of the same towne accompanied with one or two burgesses, and two or three officers at armes, desired to speake with the kings lieutenant, and in the name of all the towne, said that the keies of the towne should be deli-

uered

The earle of Hertfords answer.

uered vnto his lordship, conditionallie that they might go with bag & baggage, and the towne to be saued from fire. Wherevnto answer was made by the said lord lieutenant, that where the Scots had so manifestlie broken their promises confirmed by oths and seales, and certified by the whole parlement, as was euidentlie knowne to the world, he was sent thither by the kings highnesse to take vengeance of their detestable falsehood, to declare and shew the force of his highnesse sword to all such as should make anie resistance vnto his graces power sent thither for that purpose. And therefore he told them resolutelie, that vnlesse they would yéeld vp their towne franklie without condition, and cause man, woman, and child, to issue foorth into the fields, submitting them to his will and pleasure, he would put them to the sword, and their towne to the fire. The prouost answered it were better to stand to their defense.

Sir Christopher Morice.

Wherevpon charge was giuen to the said prouost and officer at armes, vpon their perill to depart. And foorthwith the lord lieutenant sent to the voward, commanding that they should march toward the towne, which right hardilie they did, and the English gunners manfullie assailed the gates; namelie sir Christopher Morice master of the ordinance, insomuch that the Scots were beaten from their ordinance, and the gate called Canogate beaten open with shot of the great artillerie, and therewith the English entering the same gate by fine force, beat downe & slue a great number of

Edenburgh entered by force.

Scots, and continuallie without staieng was the great ordinance drawne vp the stréet to the castell gates: but those that were within the castlell shot so freelie at the Englishmen thus approching with their great artillerie, that diuerse were slaine, the artillerie of the castell beat so directlie alongest the high stréet, as the Englishmen came vp the same. At length also one of the Englishmens culuerings was striken, and dismounted, and therevpon they were forced to retire backe and giue ouer their enterprise of making batterie to the castell, wanting pioners, baskets, and other things necessarie for such a purpose.

This daie the Englishmen set fire in diuerse parts of the towne, but they had not leasure to mainteine it, by reason of the smoke rising and troubling them so extremelie, that no great hurt could be doone that daie, for that the night also came on, and so they departed backe againe to their campe at Lith. But the next daie, a certeine number of Englishmen vnder the leading of doctor Leigh, went againe to Edenburgh, and did what they could, vtterlie to destroie the whole towne with fire, and so continued all that daie & the two daies next following. During all this violence offered by the English to the enimie, & nothing left but despaire of life, the women and children beholding this desolation, made such outragious exclamations and wofull lamentations, that heauen it selfe rang with their noise, as verie pithilie is described by Chr. O. in his report, saieng:

Fœminei sexus gemitus ad sydera grandi

Tolluntur strepitu, puerorum clamor in auras,

Nil nisi triste fuit, faciésque miserrima rerum.

The lord Euers brought a power of horssemen from the borders.

In the meane time, foure thousand light horssemen, vnder the leading of the lord Euers, came from our borders, as order was taken afore, and ioined themselues with the armie thus lieng in Lith, where after their comming, they did such exploits, in riding and wasting the countrie, that within seuen miles euerie waie of Edenburgh, they left few places, either pile, village, or house vnburnt. And beside this, they brought great numbers of cattell dailie into the armie, and met with much good stuffe, which the inhabitants of Edenburgh had for the safetie of the same conueied out of the towne.

Knights created at Lith by the earle of Hertford.

The names of the knights made at Lith after the burning of Edenburgh by the earle of Hertford, generall of the kings armie there, on sundaie the eleuenth of Maie, in the six & thirtith yeare of the reigne of king Henrie the eight, in the

yeare

yeare 1544, as they were deliuered to me by sir Gilbert Dethike knight, aliàs Garter, king of armes, are as followeth: The lord Clinton, the lord Coniers, sir William Wroughton, sir Thomas Holcroft, sir Edward Dorrell, sir Iohn Luttrell, sir Iohn Ienins, sir Thomas Waterton, sir Charles Howard, sir George Blunt, sir Peter Mewtas, sir Edward Warner, sir Rafe Bulmer, sir Hugh Cholmeleie, sir Thomas Leigh, aliàs doctor Leigh, sir Richard Leigh, sir Peter Leigh, sir Iohn Leigh of Booth, sir Laurence Smith, sir William Vauasour, sir Richard Shirburne, sir Robert Stapleton, sir Thomas Holt, sir William Dauenport, sir Rafe Leicester, sir Humfrie Bradborne, sir Thomas Maliuereie, sir Francis Hothome, sir Iohn Massie, sir Leonard Beckwith, sir Thomas Cokaine, sir Peter Freshwell, sir Richard Egerton, sir Anthonie Neuill, sir Iohn Neuill, sir William Ratcliffe, sir George Bowes, sir Brian Brereton, sir William Brereton, sir Roger Brereton, sir Edward Waren, sir Brian Leiton, sir Robert Wurseleie, sir Thomas Talbot, sir Hugh Caluerleie, sir Iohn Clere, sir Richard Holland, sir Thomas Venables, sir Iohn Constable, sir Edmund Trafford, sir Iohn Atherton, sir Richard Cholmeleie, sir Philip Egerton, sir Hugh Willoughbie, sir Thomas Constable, sir William Woodhouse, sir Edmund Sauage, and sir Thomas Gerard.

On the fourtéenth daie the Englishmen brake downe the pire of the hauen of Lith, and burnt euerie sticke of it. This doone, and hauing shipped their great artillerie, and taken foorth all such Scotish ships as were méet to serue, appointing them to attend on their ships, they tooke vpon them to returne home by land. Amongst other ships which the Englishmen had in Lith hauen, there were two of notable fairenesse, the one called the Salamander, giuen by the French king at the marriage of his daughter into Scotland, the other called the Vnicorne, made by the late Scotish king. The balast of these two ships was cannon shot, which they found in the towne, to the number of fourescore thousand. The rest of the Scotish ships being taken awaie togither with their owne ships, which they brought with them, were for the more part pestered with the spoile and booties of the souldiors & mariners. On the fiftéenth of Maie, their armie and their fleet departed from Lith both in one houre, the towne being set on fire and burned to the ground.   *Lith burnt.*

The English armie incamped that night at a place called Seaton, seuen miles from Lith, where they burnt the castell, and destroied the orchards and gardens with the more despite, for that the lord Seaton owner of the place, was the chiefe laborer to *The lord Seaton.* helpe the lord cardinall out of prison. The same daie was Haddington burnt, with a *Haddington burnt.* great nunrie and house of friers there. The next night they incamped beside Dunbar, where they had an alarum giuen them, but in the morning they burnt the towne of Dunbar, and marched foorth, though somewhat staid by the waie, by reason of the *Dunbar burnt.* mist and fog, which was verie thicke, continuing all the forenoone, and bicause also they vnderstood how the lords of Seton & Hume with the lard of Bouclough, and others, had assembled a power of men of warre, and were minded to impeach their passage at a streict named the Pease.

But after that the mist brake vp, which was about two of the clocke in the afternoone, the Englishmen came forward, and passed the same streict without anie resistance. For the Scotish lords perceiuing that they were not of power sufficient to incounter with the Englishmen, minded not to put their people in their danger, but wiselie retired, suffering the Englishmen to passe at their pleasure, who that night lodged at Ranton, eight miles distant from our borders, where hauing ouerthrowne a pile which stood there, they dislodged the next morrow, and the same daie being the eightéenth of Maie, they entred into Berwicke: so ending their voiage with great ioie *The end of the voiage.* and gladnesse, not hauing lost past fortie persons in all this iournie.

The names of the chiefe townes, castels, and places burnt in this voiage, were *Townes burnt in the same voiage.* these: the burow and towne of Edenburgh, with the abbeie called holie Rood house, and the kings palace adioining to the same. The towne of Lith burnt, and the hauen

and

and pire destroied, the castle and village of Cragmiller, the abbeie of Newbottle, part of Muskelburow towne, with the chappell of our ladie of Lauret, Preston towne and the castell, Seton castell, Hadington towne, with the friers and nunrie, a castell of Oliuer Sinclers, the towne of Dunbar, Lanreston with the grange, Drilaw, Wester crag, Enderligh, the pile, and the towne, Broughton, Thester fields, Crawnend, Dudiston, Stan house, the Ficket, Beuerton, Tranent, Shenston, Markle, Trapren, Kirkland hill, Hatherwike, Belton, east Barnes, Bowland, Butterden, Quickewood, Blackeburne, Ranton, Bildie and the Tower, Kinkorne, saint Minees, the quéenes ferrie, part of Petin Waines, and the burnt Iland, were burned by the fleet on the sea.

Sée more heereof in Scotland.

For during the continuance of the armie at Lith, the ships laie not idle, but scowring the riuer, burnt diuerse places, and left neither ship, craier, nor bote belonging to anie village, towne, créeke, or hauen, vpon either side of the foord, betwéene Sterling and the mouth of the riuer, vnburned, or brought awaie, which space conteineth fiftie miles in length. About the same time the earle of Lenox fled out of Scotland into the relme of England, where he was right gladlie receiued by king Henrie, and shortlie he obteined in marriage the ladie Marie Dowglas, néece to the king of England, and returned soone after into Scotland by sea, accompanied with a good competent crue of English. But finding no such friendship among his countrie men as he looked to haue doone, he was constreined to returne, without atchiuing the enterprise which he had taken in hand, in hope of such assistance by his friends, as now failed him at néed.

Abr. Fl. ex I. Stow. 1029.

Base monie coined.
Irish in warlike manner passe through the citie.

Procession in English.

¶ In the moneth of Maie proclamation was made for the inhancing of gold to eight & fortie shillings, & siluer foure shillings the ounce. Also the K. caused to be coined base monie, which was since that time called downe, the fift yeare of Edward the sixt, and called in the second of quéene Elizabeth. In the same moneth also passed through the citie of London in warlike maner, to the number of seauen hundred Irishmen, hauing for their weapons, darts, and handguns, with bagpipes before them : and in saint Iames parke besides Westminster they mustered before the king. In Iune the letanie or procession was set foorth in English, with commandement by the king to be generallie vsed in parish churches.] About the same time that the armie before remembred, was set forward into Scotland vnder the guiding of the earle of Hertford, as before yée haue heard, the king by aduise of his councell tooke order for the leuieng of a mightie armie, to passe ouer into France, according to the appointment taken with his confederate, fréend and colleague, the emperour, against the French king, at that present common aduersarie to them both, and not long before had entered in league with the Turks, as Ch. Oc. noteth :

An armie leuied to inuade France.

————cum dira fœdera Turcis
Iunxerat, heu nimiùm res est indigna relatu,
Christicolam facere hoc, qui relligionis amantem
Se profitens, titulum pietatis venditat orbi.

Thrée battels apointed with their seuerall lieutenants.

There were appointed thrée battels the voward vnder the leading of the duke of Norffolke, the battell vnder the guiding of the duke of Suffolke, which also was reckoned to be the kings battell, bicause his maiestie ment to be present with the same in person, and the rere-ward was led by the lord Russell lord priuie seale. Those of the fore-ward were appareled in blew cotes garded with red, and had caps and hosen after the same sute, partie blue and partie red, their caps made fit for their sculs, which were put into the same. The battell in cotes, caps, and hosen, after the like fashion, but their colours were red and yellow.

The duke of Norffolke & the lord priuie seale.

The duke of Norffolke and the lord priuie seale, accompanied with diuerse other noble men, as the earle of Surreie sonne to the said duke of Norffolke marshall of the field, the earle of Oxford, the lord Greie of Wilton lieutenant of Hammes, whose name euen then began to grow famous, the lord Ferres of Charteleie, and sir Richard

Deuereux

Deuereux his sonne and heire, that brought with them a great number of Welshmen, sir Thomas Cheineie lord warden of the cinque ports, the lord Mountioie a towardlie yoong gentleman, well learned, and for his time perfect in all points and qualities fit for a noble man, sir Francis Brian knight, one of the kings priuie chamber, and no lesse affectioned to his seruice, than of him fauoured and well estéemed, sir Thomas Poinings capteine of Guisnes, and diuerse others beside, no lesse worthie to be re-membred for their valure and merits, if time would permit to rehearse them, passed ouer to Calis about Whitsuntide, and from thence marching forward to France, left Bullongne on their right hand, & kéeping foorth towards Muttrell, ioined with an armie which the emperour had raised for that purpose, vnder the leading of the countie de Buren, admerall of the low countries, and so these armies being vnited in one, ‹The countie de Buren.› came before Muttrell, and there laid siege to that towne, being well manned and fur-nished with all things necessarie for defense, as well in vittels as munition. The chéefe capteine of which towne was monsieur de Biez one of the marshals of France, ‹Monsieur de Biez.› and gouernour also in the absence of monsieur de Vandosme of Picardie, who being within Bullongne & hearing how the English armie was passed by, and drew towards Muttrell, he left Bullongne, and with all speed got him into Muttrell, not mistrusting anie thing of that policie which the king of England went about, which was, to send this armie to besiege Muttrell, to the end the Frenchmen might be kept occupied further off, while he with the residue of his power should come and besiege Bullongne, which towne standing most commodious for his purpose, he ment by force to bring vnder his subiection.

Herevpon was the duke of Suffolke appointed with the kings armie to passe ouer, ‹The duke of Suffolke.› accompanied with the earle of Arundell marshall of the field, the lord saint Iohn, and the bishop of Winchester, sir Iohn Gage comptroller of the kings house, sir Anthonie Browne maister of the kings horsse, with diuerse other worthie capteins, all which the ninteenth of Iulie came before Bullongne, incamped on the eastside of the said towne aloft vpon the hill, and after for his more safetie remooued into a vallie, where ‹Bullongne besieged.› after manie sharpe skirmishes they first entered the base towne, being left and forsaken by the inhabitants, which hauing set fire on their fishing nets, and other such bag-gage, vnder couert of the smoke, got them vp into the high towne, before the Eng-lishmen could espie them. After this, the Old man, otherwise called Le toure dordre, standing without the towne for a direction to them that were to enter the hauen, and now being kept by sixtéene souldiers, was yéelded vp by them, vpon presenting the canon before it.

The Frenchmen within the towne, being despoiled of those two places, yet spared not to shoot off from their walles and bulworkes, dooing what damage they might deuise, and namelie from the castell and gréene bulworke they did much hurt to the English-men with their shot, whereof they made no spare, till at length they were forced to be quiet: for the Englishmen so applied them with such plentie of their shot, that the Frenchmen had no oportunitie to doo them anie great hurt with their artillerie. The ‹The king pass-eth the seas to Bullongne.› fourtéenth of Iulie, the king in person, accompanied with diuers of the nobilitie, passed the seas from Douer to Calis; and the six and twentith of the same moneth incamped himselfe before Bullongne on the north side, within lesse than three quarters of a mile of the towne, where he remained, till the towne was surrendered into his hands. The king being then in campe, it was a matter of ease to discerne which was he, for none of the rest came néere him in talnesse by the head: as for his proportion of lims, it was answerable to his goodlie stature and making: a memorable de-scription whereof, as also of his artificall armour, I find reported as followeth:

Rex capite Henricus reliquos supereminet omnes,
Heros præualidus seu fortia brachia spectes,
Seu suras quas fuluo opifex incluserat auro,

Siue virile ducis præstanti pectore corpus,
Nulla vi domitum, nullo penetrabile ferro, &c.

Beside the trenches which were cast, and brought in maner round about the town, there was a mount raised vpon the east side, and diuerse péeces of artillerie planted aloft on the same, the which togither with the morter péeces, sore annoied them within, & battered downe the steeple of our ladies church. To conclude, the batterie was made in most forcible wise in thrée seuerall places, and the walles, towers, and castell were were vndermined, and the towne within so beaten with shot out of the campe, and from the mount and trench by the morter péeces, that there were verie few houses left whole therein. The towne thus standing in great distresse, there were two hundred Frenchmen and Italians, which interprised vnder the conduct of Ioncurtio to enter the town in couert of the night, which exploit they so warilie atchiued, that by meanes of a priest that could speake the English toong, they passed by the scouts, & through the watch, so as the most part of them were got ouer the trenches yer it was knowne what they were: to the number of six score of them got into the towne, but the residue after they were once descried, being intercepted, were taken or slaine. Although this small succour somewhat relieued them within, and put them in some hope to defend the towne somewhat longer against the kings power: yet at length when a péece of the castell was blowne vp, and the breaches made, as was thought reasonable, the assault was giuen by the lord admerall Dudleie, that was come thither from the sea, which he had scowred after his returne foorth of Scotland.

Bullongne assaulted.

This assault was couragiouslie giuen, and to speake a truth, no lesse manfullie defended: so that when the assailants had perceiued in what state the breaches stood, and what prouision they within had made for defense of their towne, which vndoubtlie was great (for nothing was by them omitted, that might either aduantage the defendants, or annoie their assailants) those that were appointed in this sort to giue the assault, were called backe, and so they retired, but not without losse on both sides, and namelie of them within. For during the time of the assault, the great artillerie did beat still vpon them that presented themselues at the breaches to repell the assailants, and so diuerse of their valiant capteins and braue souldiers were slaine at this assault, & among other, capteine Philip Corse. Shortlie after, the capteins within the towne, doubting to be eftsoones assaulted, and perceiuing themselues in extreame danger to lose the towne by force, if they prouided not the sooner, by rendering it to saue themselues: they sent foorth two of their chiefe capteins, monsieur Semblemont, and monsieur de Haies, which declared vnto the king, that monsieur de Veruine gouernour of the towne, with his retinue, was contented to deliuer the towne vnto his grace, with condition that they might passe with bag and baggage. Which request the king, like a noble and mercifull prince, fréelie granted: and so the next daie, the duke of Suffolke rode into Bullongne, vnto whome in the kings name the keies of the towne were deliuered, & in the afternoone departed out of Bullongne all the French-

Bullongne deliuered.

men with heauie hearts, to the number of six thousand, as C. O. witnesseth, saieng:

Sex hinc exierant Gallorum millia gentis.

The number of them that went forth of Bullonge.

The number of the men of warre that were strong and able to serue, were of horssemen sixtie seuen, of footmen fiftéene hundred, thréescore and three, of the which number eight hundred were harquebutters, of hurt men foure score and seuen, of women and children nintéene hundred and twentie seuen, beside a great number of aged & sicke persons, not able to depart with the others. The last person that came foorth was monsieur de Veruine himselfe, who vpon his approch to the place where the king stood, alighted from his horsse, and came to the king, and after hée had talked with him a space, the king tooke him by the hand, and he reuerentlie kneeling vpon his knées, kissed his hand, and afterward mounted vpon his horsse, and so departed, following his companie.

The

The eight of September, the king hauing the sword borne before him by the lord The king en-
tereth into Bul-
longne. marques Dorset, like a puissant conqueror rode into Bullongne, and the trumpetters standing on the walles, sounded their trumpets at the time of his entering, to the great comfort of the beholders. In the entering, there met him the duke of Suffolke, and deli-uered to him the keies of the towne, and so he rode foorth to his lodging that was pre-pared for him on the south side of the towne. Within two daies after, the king rode about the towne within the walles, and appointed that our ladie church of Bullongne should bée taken downe, and in the place thereof a mount to bée made, for the more strengthen-ing of the towne. Finallie after he had set things in order for the safe kéeping of this his towne of Bullongne, by his princely force thus woone out of the possession of his aduersaries hands, he appointed the lord Lisle high admerall of the seas, to be his deputie of the same towne, and then determining not to staie there any longer, he The king re-
turneth into
England. tooke the seas, & returned into England, landing at Douer the first of October.

In this meane time, whilest the king of England laie (as ye haue heard) with his siege about Bullongne, and the duke of Norffolke, and lord priuie seale about Mutterell, the emperour inuaded France by Champeigne, winning diuerse castels and townes, as Comersis, Lignie, saint Desir, Chausteau, Thierie, and others. But at the length, meanes were made by treatie to haue the matter taken vp, as in the end it was, and a peace concluded without consent of the king of England, although there was place The emperor
concludeth a
peace with the
French king. left for him and other princes to enter into this agréement of peace. But the king of England hauing now defraied no small quantitie of treasure in these warres, beside the trauell of his owne person and his people, and hauing the thing now in a maner sure in his possession, which he chieflie went abont to obteine, that is to wit, the strong towne of Bullongne, he would not agrée vnto anie peace, except he might inioy that towne, at that instant readie to be deliuered into his hands. And euen now after it was to him deliuered, hearing that for certeine, the peace was concluded betwixt the emperour and the French king, he determined to breake vp his camps : but neuerthe-lesse to kéepe Bullongne in his possession, in despite of all his aduersaries. But here, before we procéed anie further, we haue thought good somewhat to speake touching the siege which all this while continued afore Mutterell, where the Englishmen and Burgonians inforced themselues by all waies and meanes they could deuise, how to constreine their enimies within the towne. On the other part, monsieur de Biez, and those that were with him in gard of the same towne, left nothing vndoone that might serue for their defense, and make to the annoiance of their enimies.

There were with monsieur de Biez within the towne, an hundred men at armes of The number of
the men of war
in Muttrell. the retinue of the constable of France, vnder the leading of the lord de la Guich an expert man of war. There were also with the lord of Genlie, foure ensignes of French footmen. Count Berenger a Neapolitane with a thousand footmen Italians. Capteine Francisco de Chiaramont, a Neapolitane also, with the like number of Italian footmen. So that the towne might séeme sufficientlie furnished with men, and they wanted neither shot nor powder requisit, so that there was no spare thereof when occasion serued on either part.

The duke of Norffolke and the lord priuie seale caused a mount to be raised, and aloft A mount raised. thereon were certeine péeces of artillerie planted to shoot into the towne. Moreouer they compassed the walles so on ech hand with their seuerall camps and trenches, that hardlie might anie escape either in or out vnespied. Sir Francis Brian was appointed Sir Francis
Brian. with certeine bands, conteining about the number of a thousand men, to lodge in a campe fortified by himselfe, ouer against one part of the towne, to stop certeine passages on that side, that no succours should enter by the same to reléefe of them within. There were skirmishes dailie betwixt them that sallied forth of the gates, and the Englishmen that watched and warded in the trenches, and other places, insomuch

5 L2

that

that diuerse lost their liues, and some were irrecouerablie wounded, as Anglorum prælia witnesseth, saieng :

Confossi sæuo moriuntur vulnere multi
Disperso cerebro, faciei nulla figura.

On a daie as sir Thomas Poinings soldiours were warding in one of the trenches, an Italian secretlie comming forth of the towne, fetched awaie the said sir Thomas Poinings his ensigne ; and notwithstanding the pursute that was made after him, he escaped and got into the towne with it, to the great displeasure of the whole campe. But as the enimies sometimes went awaie with the aduantage of their attempted enterprises, so ofttimes againe they paid for their aduenturing ouer rashlie aboue the common price of the market.

But here I cannot but lament the negligence vsed in that season : for there is not one English writer to be found extant, that hath written anie thing effectuallie of the exploits atchiued in that iornie ; so as we are driuen to borrow of the aduersaries that haue written thereof, wanting other helps of our owne nation to furnish our booke héerin according to our wished purpose. But neuerthelesse, to giue occasion to those that yet liue, and can best doo it, to set forth hereafter a more perfect discourse therof, I haue thought it not amisse to recite in part what I haue read and learned of such things as then were accounted worthie of relation, and now like to be buried in the dimme booke of obliuion, vnlesse some fauourer of notable euents chancing in the assiegement of those two townes, Bullongne and Muttrell, will put to his helping hand to report the same to posteritie.

Among other stratagems, one I remember, deuised and put in practise by the lord Mountioie, as thus. The enimies had espied a place of aduantage without the towne, where vnder fauour of the shot of certeine peeces of great artillerie lodged vpon some platforms or bulworks within the towne, they might lie without the walles betwixt the Englishmens trenches and the towne ditches, and there couer themselues within a litle trench or counterscarpe made for the purpose, and out of the same be readie with their harquebusses to shoot at the Englishmen, so soone as anie of them should once shew his head out of the trenches, to the great danger of them that warded in the same.

The lord Mountioie perceiuing this, deuised with himselfe how to rouse the enimies out of that lurking place, and withall came to the duke of Norfolke, and desired licence to put the deuise (which he had alreadie forecast in his mind) in practise. But the duke being not willing that he should put himselfe in such danger, was loth to grant thereto, but rather persuaded with him not to attempt it : for (said he) my lord, yée may doo the king better seruice than so to hazard your life, and cast your selfe awaie, as it is verie like you should, in aduenturing vpon such a desperat peece of seruice, and therfore I would not wish you to meddle therewith, for we shall otherwise prouide for the matter well inough. But the lord Mountioie still persisted in his sute verie earnestlie, declaring that he doubted not (by Gods helpe) but to atchiue his purpose to his good contentation without anie great danger, if that were executed which he tooke to be necessarie for the accomplishment of his deuise : and that was to haue certeine peeces

of the great ordinance shot off that waie forth, at what time the wind stood méet to carrie the smoke full vpon the place where the Frenchmen laie. At length vpon his earnest sute, the duke gaue him licence to trie what he could doo, commanding the great ordinance to be laid and charged readie to shoot off as he should appoint it. Herewith the lord Mountioie taking with him fouretéene of his owne soldiers (of the which number one of them forsooke to go through with him when it came to the point) immediatlie vpon the shooting off of the artillerie, & that all the ground about was couered ouer with smoke, he came to the place where those Frenchmen laie vnder co-

uert

uert of their trench, and so displaced them, that they had no liking eftsoones to lodge so neere vnto such vnfriendlie neighbors.

Manie other valiant and politike feats (no doubt) were atchiued during this siege, & happilie as worthie the rehearsall as this. But sith it was the inuention of so noble a yoong gentleman, I haue estéemed it not impertinent to speake thereof, and withall to lament the losse of the inuentor, who being taken awaie shortlie after in his returne homewards, by vntimelie death, was like (if he had liued to greater yéers of experience) to haue prooued comparable in valor to anie of his noble progenitors. But now to speake of other incidents that chanced whilest this siege remained before Muttrell, you must vnderstand that the most part of the vittels that was spent in the campe was brought to them either from the kings campe at Bullongne, or else from S. Omers, to conueie the same so far off, it was néedfull to haue the carriage garded with good troops and bands both of horssemen and footmen: for the French fortresses were stronglie furnished with great numbers of men of war, which vpon occasions were readie to take aduantages offered.

And as it fortuned at one time among other, there was a conuoie of certeine wagons loden with vitels appointed to come from saint Omers, the same being garded with diuerse bands of Englishmen and Burgonions, sent thither for that purpose, the which marching forward from saint Omers, kept not so good order as had béene requisit: whereof certeine companies of French horssemen that were abroad being aware, set vpon the Burgonions that were attendant vpon the foremost carriages, and finding them in some disorder, easilie discomfited them, followed, and slue them in the chase, till they came to the hindermost carriages, where six hundred Englishmen that attended on the same, impaled themselues with their wagons, so as the Frenchmen could take no aduantage: but with shot of the English archers were so curried and galled that they were driuen to retire and that in such hast, as they left diuerse of their companie captiues in the Englishmens hands beside those that were faire laid to take their last sléepe there on the ground. Neuerthelesse, of the Burgonions there were slaine foure hundred, and much good vittels lost, the bottoms of the hogsheads and other vessels being beaten out, and manie a good Flemish mare killed or taken. For the Frenchmen found small resistance (as before ye haue heard) till they approched to the Englishmen, by whose accustomed manhood, some part of the vittels of that conuoie was saued, to the reléefe of the campe, which notwithstanding by losse of the ersidue suffered great want for the time.

Moreouer, somewhat towards the latter end of this siege, the earle of Surreie son vnto the duke of Norffolke and marshall of his field, accompanied with the lord warden of the cinque ports, and diuerse other valiant capteins English & Burgonions marched forth into the countrie towards Abuile, where they tooke and burnt a proper towne called saint Requiers: and after comming to another towne called Rieu, they found no bodie at home but women and children, for the men were departed out of it before their comming thither. When they had taken their pleasure in sacking all such goods as they found there fit to be carried awaie, they spared the towne from fire, and so departed. And thus after they had béene two daies and two nights abroad in the countrie, they returned home to the campe with a great bootie of beasts, sheepe, and other things which they had got in that voiage.

But now to conclude with this siege of Muttrell, after the king had woone Bullongne, and vnderstood how the emperor had agréed with his aduersarie the French king, he resolued to haue his armie to raise that siege which thus had lien before Muttrell, and with all couenient spéed to draw toward Calis. And because it was signified that the Dolphin of France Henrie was comming forward with a great power, which had béene raised by his father the French king to resist the emperor, and now was sent vnder the conduct of the said Dolphin to the succours of them that were besieged in

Muttrell,

The lord Mountioie a noble yoong gentleman.

The English archers gall the French horssemen.

Saint Requiers burnt by the Englishmen. Rieu sacked.

The siege at Muttrell broken vp.

Muttrell, the king sent the earle of Arundell, sir Iohn Gage, George Carew, sir Iohn Reinsford, and others, with a chosen number of lustie soldiors vnto Muttrell, to reinforce his armie there, that in leuieng the campe, and withdrawing backe, they might be the better able to withstand anie attempt which the enimies might put in execution to their annoiance. And verelie this was doone with good aduise and necessarie consideration, for the Englishmen that had lien so long time at the siege before Muttrell, wanting such behoouefull refreshment as those were stored with that laie before Bullongne, hauing the seas open, and all things at pleasure brought vnto them forth of England, were sore weakened and decaied by death and sicknesse, and now in raising their campe had manie things to looke vnto, as well for the conueieng of their ordinance, trusse, and baggage, as their feeble and diseased persons: so that if the Dolphin with his armie might haue made such spéed forward as to haue ouertaken them with his maine power before they had come to Bullongne, it was to be feared least he might haue put them in danger of a plaine distresse. But with such timelie foresight as was vsed the siege was raised, and the armie retired first to Bullongne, and after to Calis without losse, although the French horssemen in great number followed, and sundrie times made proud proffers to giue the charge vpon the hindermost companies; but nothing was doone to make great account of, except certeine skirmishes that were procured, and alarums giuen, as in such cases it fortuneth.

The Dolphin notwithstanding that the siege was thus raised from Muttrell, yer he could come thither, yet he kept forward his iourneie, to prooue what he might doo to recouer Bullongne, which towne the king of England (as ye haue heard) had left in the keeping of the lord Lisle high admerall. The same towne being then weake, God knoweth, on all sides through batterie and minings, which by the kings power had béen made, to bring it into his subiection, and the trenches not cast downe, nor the ordinance mounted.

The Dolphin being come before the towne, sent certeine bands of his best soldiors by night to giue a camisado to the base towne. They that thus were sent, entred the same the ninth of October, about two of the clocke in the morning, where they tooke the stand watches, and slue (beside a great number of sicke and weake persons) as well soldiors as other, before they could araie themselues, or well get out of their beds. But after, the Frenchmen and Italians fell to rifling and breaking vp of coffers, scattering here and there abrode, and began fall to their vittels, which they found there in good plentie. The Englishmen that were driuen vp to the gates of the high towne, got weapons that were throwne downe vnto them foorth of the same, & assembling togither, fiercelie entred in amongst the prease of their enimies. And herewith there sallied foorth of the high towne sir Thomas Poinings with a band of two hundred soldiors, the which togither with the other so bestirred themselues, that they manfullie beat backe the enimies, slue to the number of eight hundred of them, and chased the residue out of the towne, which fled ouer the sands vp to the hill, where the Dolphin himselfe stood with a great troope of horssemen about him, and durst not once come downe to the rescue of his people, for feare of the great artillerie that with plentie of bullets saluted the enimies, after that the breake of the daie had once discouered them in sight. Amongst other that were slaine in this repulse of the Frenchmen, le segneur de Foquessolles, another of the marshall de Biez his sons in law, and seneschall of Bullongne was one.

Thus the Dolphin, perceiuing that it would nothing auaile him to make anie further attempt against Bullongne, passed foorth toward Guisnes, & shortlie after through want of vittels, and sicknesse which sore infested his campe, breake vp his armie, and returned into France: so that the proud enterprises of the vainglorious and most insolent French turned to their owne great shame, as C. O. trulie saith:

Sic Galli in magnum cesserunt dedecus ausa.

But shortlie after Christmas came downe an armie of fourtéene thousand, vnder the conduction

conduction of monsieur de Biez, the which the six and twentith of Ianuarie incamped Monsieur de Biez cōmeth before Bullongne with an armie. on the west side of Bullongne beyond the hauen, where they laie ten daies: but on the sixt of Februarie, the earle of Hertford, the lord admerall, as then lord lieutenant of the towne of Bullongne, the lord Greie of Wilton, sir Thomas Poinings & others, hauing assembled out of the garisons on that side the seas, to the number of foure thousand footmen, & seuen hundred horsmen, whereof an hundred or foure score were Albanoises, issued foorth of Bullongne about foure of the clocke in the morning, and comming to the place where the king had incamped during the time of the siege, they staid there, and put themselues in order of battell: and about six of the clocke, it being then a low water, capteine Edward Breie, with three hundred shot, was appointed to passe ouer, and to giue the enimies an alarum in their campe.

At which instant the trumpets sounded, and the drums stroke vp in the English armie, and herewith they being diuided into three battels, and to ech one his gard of two hundred horssemen, beside the od hundred that attended as a defense to the residue, they shewed themselues to their enimies. The Frenchmen perceiuing this, packed The Frenchmen dislodge out of their campe. awaie with all haste possible, marching toward Hardilo in two battels. Wherevpon the English capteins leauing their footmen behind them, and taking onelie with them the horssemen, followed with all spéed after their enimies, and comming to the bridge commonlie called pont de Bricque, which certeine English carpenters garded with a number of harquebutters, and foure small field peeces, had forced and repared the same that night: and so the horssemen finding it sufficientlie repared, passed ouer, and comming to S. Estienne, they found there fiue hundred Dutch horsmen, commonlie called Swart rutters, that were lodged there to kéepe that passage: but being surprised on the sudden by the English horssemen, and sharpelie assailed, they were wholie distressed, and the most part of them taken prisoners, and therewith left with the followers of the armie, were after slaine, bicause they knew not where to bestow them.

But now the hill of saint Estienne being thus gained by the English horsmen, they put themselues in order of battell againe, appointing an hundred of their men at armes to follow and kéepe aloofe as a stale to relieue their fellowes in time of need, when they saw them in anie danger. The lords, to incourage euerie one to doo his dutie, rode vp and downe about the troops, & vsing manie comfortable words, desired them, The comfortable words of the English capteins. that although they were but an handfull in comparison to the number of their enimies, they would yet in regard of the honour of the realme of England, make a proffer of an onset to the enimies, that they might perceiue that there they were to giue them battell, and to follow, as they should sée them their capteins and gouernors to lead them the waie. Herewith forward they make towards the enimie, and ouertaking The English horssemen charge the French battels. them three miles on the hitherside of Hardilo sands, they valiantlie gaue the charge, and thrusting in betwixt the two French battels, ouerthrew their cariages, tooke their ordinance and munitions, slue and bare downe manie of them that preased foorth to defend the same.

Monsieur de Biez being in the fore ward, brought backe the strongest and best The valiant order of monsieur de Biez. armed men he had to resist his enimies, ranging them in order so, as he ment to haue inclosed the English horssemen betwixt his battels and the sea, and so to haue distressed them. But this purpose being espied first of all by the lord admerall, the Englishmen by his valiant incouragement gaue a new charge, and breaking through The lord admerall his redie cōceiuing the meaning of the enimies. their ranks by force, came backe againe vnto their hundred men of armes that kept aloofe, and there staied till their footmen might come to them, who by this time were aduanced within sight of them, but distant yet by the space of two English miles, or little lesse.

Monsieur de Biez, perceiuing that the English footmen began thus to approch, made forward againe with his armie, so fast as was possible for his people to march, drawing

drawing still his armed men and best souldiors to the hindermost ranks, there to be readie to withstand the Englishmen, as they should offer to assaile them: and in this order the Frenchmen made away, and rested not till they came to Hardilo sands, being a place of such strength and aduantage, by reason of the streict, that after they were once got thither, they might account themselues out of all danger, and therefore there they staid, and dispatched an herald vnto the chiefteins of the English armie, to signifie vnto them, that there they ment to abide and to giue them battell, if they would aduance forward to fight with them: but yet they would not in anie wise come foorth of their strength vnto some euen ground, although they were earnestlie required therevnto. Wherevpon the Englishmen, to light them a candle that they might sée where they were, set all the villages & houses about on a light fire, continuing the same all that afternoone, and most part of the night following, and the next morning betwixt foure and fiue of the clocke, they came backe againe vnto Bullongne with all their spoiles and prisoners.

Artillerie gained. They tooke in this incounter seuen peeces of artillerie, two of brasse and fiue of iron; also the peeces of aduantage of the armour of monsieur de Biez, beside apparell, plate, and furniture in great plentie, as well taken in the field, as also in their campe, where they left their tents standing, & all their prouision of vittels wholie vnremoued. The same péeces of armour were sent ouer into England to the king for a witnesse of the good successe that had thus happened to his people in this famous enterprise, in the atchiuing whereof there were not past halfe a dozen Englishmen slaine, besides those that were hurt, which neither were manie, as vnder halfe a score at the most.

1545
Iohn Stow.
Whilest such things were in dooing about Bullongne, and other places (as before ye haue heard in this twentie and sixt yeare) the ships of the west countrie and other coasts of this realme wafted abroad on the seas, and tooke to the number of thrée *Great prises of French goods taken by the westerne ships.* hundred & od French ships, so that the Graie friers church in London was laid full of wine, the Austine friers and Blacke friers full of herring, and other fish that was taken, as the same should haue béene conueied into France. About the same season the king demanded a beneuolence of his subiects spirituall and temporall, towards *Abr. Fl. ex I.S. pag. 1000.* the maintenance of the warres against the Frenchmen and Scots. ¶ On the twelfe of Ianuarie, the lord chancellour, the duke of Suffolke, and other of the kings councell, began to sit at Bainards castell, where they first called before them the maior and aldermen, &c. And bicause Richard Read alderman would not agree to paie as they set him; he was commanded vpon paine to serue the king in his warres of Scotland, who departed from London the thrée and twentith of Ianuarie.

Sir William Roch sent to the Fléet. Also sir William Roch alderman, for words of displeasure taken by the kings councell, was by them sent to the fléet, where he remained till passion sundaie. On the six and twentith of Ianuarie, there camped on the west side of Bullongne beyond the hauen, an armie of French, to the number of eightéene thousand, where they laie ten daies, and the sixt of Februarie were put to flight by the earle of Hertford, and sir Iohn Dudleie lord admerall, then deputie of Bullongne. On the thirteenth of *Execution for false accusation.* Februarie, a priest was set on the pillorie in Cheape, and burnt in both chéekes with the letters F. and A. and a paper on his head, wherein was written, For false accusing: which iudgement was giuen by the lord chancellor in the Starre chamber, a notable example of iustice. Great cause haue I to wish the like to the like accuser, who neuer yet repented, but contrariwise sweareth and forsweareth that he neuer did anie such act against his brother.]

The discomfiture gotten by the Scots at Halidon rig. In the beginning of March sir Rafe Euers lord warden of the marches after manie fortunate rodes and forraies made into Scotland, assembled now about foure thousand men, & entering with the same into Scotland, was incountered at Halidon rig by the earle of Arraine and other Scotishmen, which so beset the Englishmen with thrée

battels

battels on ech side, that in the end they slue the said lord warden, with the lord Ogle, and The valiant sir Rafe Euers slaine. a great number of other gentlemen and commons, beside prisoners, which they tooke, so that few escaped the Scotishmens hands. Among other prisoners taken, Richard Read, alderman of London prisoner. Read an alderman of London aforesaid was one. The death of sir Rafe Euers was greatlie bemoned: for he had shewed great proofe of his valiant prowesse at sundrie times before: namelie in this yeare past, as at the taking and burning of the towne of Iedworth, which enterprise was atchiued the tenth of Iune, beside diuerse other exploits fortunatelie brought to passe by his high valiancie and manhood, till his hap was at this present to finish his daies: whose life though then it tooke end, yet shall not his fame & good report (purchased by martiall courage, policie, and dangerous aduentures) perish or decaie; as the poet trulie saith:

Parta labore volat vastum bona fama per orbem,
Hæc veluti Phœbus non moritura manet.

This yeare on saint Georges daie sir Thomas Wriothesleie lord chancellor of Eng- *An.* Reg. 37. *Rich. Grafton.* land was made knight of the garter. Also Trinitie terme was adiourned by reason of the warres, but the escheker and the court of the tenths were open, for those that were accomptable in either of the said courts. The thirteenth of Iune Robert Luken ser- Anne Askew and others are reigned and acquited. uant to sir Humfrie Browne one of the iustices of the kings Bench, Anne Askew gentlewoman, otherwise called Anne Kime, wife to one Kime, a gentleman of Lin- colneshire, and Ione Sautereie, wife to Iohn Sautereie of London, were arreigned in the Guildhall of London, for speaking against the sacrament of the altar (as they tearmed it) contrarie to the statute of the six articles: but because no witnesse ap- peared against the women, nor against Luken, one onelie excepted, who was thought to accuse him rather of malice, than otherwise, they were by twelue honest substan- tiall men of the citie (sworne to passe vpon their indictments) cléerelie acquited and discharged.

The same daie also was a pewterer named Thomas Daie discharged, by the pardon Thomas Daie pewterer. granted in the last parlement, after he had remained in prison in Newgate the space of thrée yeares now past, condemned long before the date of the same pardon, for the article of auricular confession comprised within the same statute. About the same time, to wit the seuenth of Iune a great armie of Frenchmen came downe to Bullongne and néere to the hauen incamped themselues. In this armie were reckoned to be Martin de Bellaie. twelue thousand lanceknights, twelue thousand French footmen, six thousand Italians, foure thousand of legionarie soldiours of France, & a thousand or twelue hundred men of armes, beside seuen or eight hundred light horsmen. After some skirmishes not greatlie to their aduantage, they began yet to build a fort, which at length they ac- The new fort before Bullogne. *I. S. pag.* 1031. complished, as after shall appeare. ¶ About the fiue & twentith of Iune, was a great tempest in Derbishire, where thorough trées were ouerturned, & diuerse churches, chappels, and houses were vncouered. Also in Lancashire, there fell halestones as big Hailestones figured like mens heads. as mens fists, which had diuerse prints in them, some like mens faces, some like gun holes, &c.]

The same moneth also the lord Lisle admerall of England with the English fléet The English fléet commeth before New- hauen. entered the mouth of Saine, and came before Newhauen, where a great nauie of the Frenchmen laie, to the number of a two hundred ships, and six and twentie gallies, wherof the pope (as was reported) had sent twentie well furnished with men and monie, to the aid of the French king. The Englishmen being not past an hundred and thréescore saile, and all great ships, determined not to set vpon the Frenchmen where they laie: but yet approching néere vnto them, shot off certeine péeces of or- dinance at them, and thereby caused the gallies to come abroad, which changed shot againe with the Englishmen. The gallies at the first had great aduantage, by reason of the great calme. Twise either part assaulted other with shot of their great ar- tillerie, but suddenlie the wind rose so high, that the gallies could not indure the rage of the seas, and so the Englishmen for feare of flats were compelled to enter the maine seas, and so sailed vnto Portsmouth where the king laie, for he had knowledge by his espials that the Frenchmen intended to land in the Ile of Wight, wherefore he repaired to that coast, to sée his realme defended.

After this, the eighteenth of Iulie the admerall of France monsieur Danebalte hoised vp sailes, and with his whole nauie came foorth into the seas, and arriued on the coast of Sussex before bright Hamstéed, and set certeine of his soldiors on land, to burne and spoile the countrie: but the beacons were fired, & the inhabitants thereabouts came down so thicke, that the Frenchmen were driuen to flie with losse of diuerse of their numbers: so that they did little hurt there. Immediatlie herevpon they made to the point of the Ile of Wight, called saint Helens point, and there in good order vpon their arriuall they cast anchors, and sent dailie sixtéene of their gallies to the verie hauen of Portesmouth. The English nauie lieng there in the same hauen, made them readie, and set out toward the enimies, and still the one shot hotlie at the other: but the wind was so calme, that the kings ships could beare no saile, which greatlie grieued the minds of the Englishmen, and made the enimies more bold to approch with their gallies, and to assaile the ships with their shot euen within the hauen.

The twentith of Iulie, the whole nauie of the Englishmen made out, & purposed to set on the Frenchmen, but in setting forward, thorough too much follie, one of the kings ships called the Marie Rose was drowned in the middest of the hauen, by reason that she was ouerladen with ordinance, and had the ports left open, which were verie low, and the great artillerie vnbreeched; so that when the ship should turne, the water entered, and suddenlie she suncke. In hir was sir George Carew knight and foure hundred soldiours vnder his guiding. There escaped not past fortie persons of all the whole number. On the morrow after about two thousand of the Frenchmen landed in the Ile of Wight, where one of their chiefe capteins named le cheualier Daux, a Prouencois was slaine with manie other, and the residue with losse and shame driuen backe againe to their gallies.

The king perceiuing the great Armada of the Frenchmen to approch, caused the beacons to be fired, and by letters sent into Hamptonshire, Summersetshire, Wiltshire, and into diuerse other countries adioining, gaue knowledge to such as were appointed to be readie for that purpose, to come with all spéed to incounter the enimies. Wherevpon they repaired to his presence in great numbers well furnished with armor, weapon, vittels, and all other things necessarie, so that the Ile was garnished, and all the frontiers alongest the coasts fortified with excéeding great multitudes of men. The French capteins hauing knowledge by certeine fishermen, whom they tooke, that the king was present, & so huge a power readie to resist them, they disanchored and drew along the coast of Sussex, and a small number of them landed againe in Sussex, of whome few returned to their ships: for diuerse gentlemen of the countrie, as sir Nicholas Pelham, and others, with such power as was raised, vpon the sudden, tooke them vp by the waie and quickelie distressed them.

When they had searched euerie where by the coast, and saw men still readie to receiue them with battell, they turned sterne, and so got them home againe without anie act atchiued woorthie to be mentioned. The number of the Frenchmen was great, so that diuerse of them that were taken prisoners in the Ile of Wight, and in Sussex, did report that they were thréescore thousand. The French king aduertised the emperor most vntrulie by letters, that his armie had gotten the Ile of Wight with the ports of Hamton, and Portesmouth, and diuerse other places. In August following, the earle of Hertford entered againe into Scotland with twelue thousand men, and destroied all the townes in the middle marches, burned Coldingham abbeie, and passed to the west marches, sore annoieng and indamaging the Scots, and yet neither

they

The French fléet landeth in the Ile of Wight.
The Frenchmn land in Sussex.

The Marie Rose drowned by negligence.

Frenchmen distressed in the Ile of Wight.

The number in the French nauie.

The earle of Hertford forraieth the middle marches of Scotland.

they, nor the Frenchmen that were sent into Scotland this yeare to the aid of the Scots, vnder the leading of monsieur de Lorges, Montgomerie his father, durst once come foorth into the field to incounter with him.

Also in the beginning of this moneth the citie of London set foorth a thousand sol- The Londoners diors of archers, harquebutters, pikes, and bils, which went to Douer, and so passed set foorth a ouer vnto Calis, to serue the king in his wars on that side the seas. In the same power into moneth that valiant capteine sir Thomas Poinings knight, lord Poinings, and the kings The death of lieutenant of his towne and marches of Bullogne departed this life, after he had to the valiant lord his great honor atchiued manie woorthie enterprises in seruice of his prince against the Poinings. enimies, so that his death was much lamented. A gentleman vndoubtedlie deseruing to be had in perpetuall memorie: and pitie it is, that diuerse such valiant feats as he in his life time atchiued, were not committed to writing, to remaine for examples sake to posteritie:

Also in the same moneth at Guilford died the noble and valiant duke of Suffolke The death of Charles Brandon lord great maister of the kings houshold, a right hardie gentleman, the duke of and yet not so hardie, as almost of all estats and degrees of men, high & low, rich and Suffolke. poore, hartilie beloued, & his death of them greatlie lamented: his bodie was ho- norablie buried at Windsore, at the kings costs. This man in his daies had doone to His just com- the king and realme right agreeable seruices, as well in peace, as in wars, both in mendation. England, France, Scotland, and Ireland, he died the kings generall lieutenant of his armie then appointed to resist the Frenchmen, if they durst haue landed.

But now, whereas in this meane time we haue spoken nothing of the dooings in Scotland, where the warre was still continued, the king of France sent thither cer- teine bands of Frenchmen, vnder the gouernement of monsieur de Lorges, to aid the Monsieur de Scots against the Englishmen; and the king of England waged manie strangers, and Lorges sent into sent them with certeine Englishmen to the borders, for defense of the same against certeine French the inuasions of the enimies: for after the arriuall of the Frenchmen, a great armie of bands. Scots was raised, and approched néere to the borders, where for a certeine time they incamped, so that manie thought some notable enterprise would haue béene attempted. But after they had laine in campe a certeine time, they brake vp, and departed with- out attempting anie further exploit.

Shortlie after the earle of Hertford lieng on the borders, as lieutenant of the north The earle of parts of England, calling to him an armie of twelue thousand men, or thereabouts, Hertford in- what of Englishmen and strangers, entred Scotland with the same, and burnt a great uadeth Scotland. part of the Mers, and Teuidale, as Kelsaie abbeie and the towne; Melrosse abbeie & Driborne abbeie, also Iedworth abbeie, and diuerse other places, townes, and villages, to the number of fiue score. Kelsaie abbeie was defended a while by thrée hundred Scots, but in the end the most part of them were slaine, & taken by the strangers and others that gaue the assault. Thus the earle of Hertford sore indamaged the Scots by this inuasion, and yet neither they, nor the Frenchmen their assistants, durst come foorth into the field once to incounter with him.

On the sixtéenth of September a number of Scots and Frenchmen attempted to enter into England on the east borders. But the Englishmen perceiuing them about to passe by a certeine streict, set vpon them, and slue and tooke of them to the num- ber of seuen score. Among the prisoners that were taken, the lord of Humes sonne, and a French capteine were accompted chiefest. Also in another rode made into the west borders, the lord Maxwels sonne, and diuerse others were taken. But at an Ouerthrowes on- other time about the same season also, certeine Englishmen to the number of fiue hun- both sides, be- dred, making their entrie by the west borders into Scotland, were discomfited by the twixt the Eng- Scots, and the more part of them either taken or slaine. Thus were they occupied as lish and Scots. well on the borders betwixt England and Scotland, in this season, as also in the marches of Calis, Guisnes, and Bullognois, where the garrisons lieng in those places,

made

made continuall rodes & forraies into the marches of the enimies countrie, and oftentimes chanced to incounter with some of their troops.

The capteine of Ard, monsieur de Dampiere, hauing got for a supplie from the French campe at Bullogne, the companie of the men of armes that belonged to the duke of Orleance, led by his lieutenant monsieur de Tauannes, chanced on a daie to incounter with the Englishmen guided by that valiant baron the lord Greie of Wilton, capteine of the towne of Guisnes, who being accompanied with a number of valiant gentlemen & soldiers, distressed their enimies, & slue the capteine of Ard the foresaid lord de Dampiere there in field. Diuerse other skirmishes and incounters chanced in that summer, on the further side the seas. And moreouer, now after that the French nauie was withdrawen (as ye haue heard) from the coasts about Portesmouth, that martiall chiefteine, sir Iohn Dudleie, lord Lisle, & high admerall of England, hauing all his ships, men, munition, & furniture readie, set forward from Portesmouth hauen, to haue fought with the Frenchmen, if they had still kept the seas, but they were withdrawne home into Harborough.

Wherevpon the lord admerall meaning to reuenge their brauados, and presumptuous attempts made at Portesmouth, and in the Ile of Wight, approched to the coasts of Normandie, and landed with six thousand men at Treport, burnt the suburbes of that towne, with the abbeie, and certeine villages and houses thereabouts. Also they destroied thirtie ships, and a barke there found in the hauen: and after they had wrought their pleasures, they returned to the sea, and so home, not hauing lost past fourtéene persons in the execution of this whole enterprise. Of this great spoile & ouerthrow giuen at Treport, by the kings admerall, I find these verses remembred:

Treporte oppidum Galliæ maritimum à Iohanne Dudleio prefecto regiæ classis d ripitur & flammis absumitur.

　　　　　　　　———Treportem passibus æquis
Ordine seruato (qui mos est militis) intrant:
Obuius vt quisque est, is stricto sternitur ense,
Ast alius volucri traiectus membra sagitta,
Occidit exanguis, fœdátque cruore plateas.
Dum reclusa alius vult prospectare fenestra,
Nec conferre pedem, nec aperto prælia Marte
Commiscère audet, glandis transfigitur ictu.
Omne genus telorum ad cædem immittitur atram.

In this meane while monsieur de Biez, being incamped néere to Bullogne with such a puissant armie (as before you haue heard) busied about the building of a fort, there was not such diligence vsed therin, as was promised on his part in accomplishing the same, to the French kings great displeasure (as some write) who had meant with that armie (if this fort had béene finished at the appointed time) to haue gone to besiege the towne and castell of Guisnes: but now the time being prolonged, and not without some suspicion least monsieur de Biez cared not how long the warres indured in that sort, so as he might command ouer so manie princes and great lords as were there vnder his gouernance, at length before the fort were fullie finished, he remooued to mount Lambert with the more part of the armie, pretending as though he meant to fight with the Englishmen, the which (as he said) he vnderstood were purposed to come with a conuoie of vittels from Calis to Bullogne.

Whilest he there remained, manie princes and great lords came from the court, that laie at an abbeie called forrest Montier, eleuen leagues from Bullogne beyond Muttrell, on the waie towards Abuille, in hope that battell should haue followed betwixt the English and French armies. Among other that came thither are these remembred as principall, monsieur Danguien, monsieur Daumalle, monsieur le duc de Neuers, monsieur le conte de Lauall, and monsieur de la Trimouille. Monsieur Daumalle eldest sonne to the duke of Guise, being lodged in the vantgard that was gouerned by monsieur de Brissac, chanced on a daie to be present at a skirmish, where
　　　　　　　　　　　　　　　　　　　　　　　　　　　　　　shewing

shewing himselfe verie forward, he was striken through the sight of his helmet, with a light horssemans staffe, that pearsing in betwixt his nose and his eie, entred halfe a foot into his head, as monsieur de Langeie writeth, and breaking off a two fingers beneath the iron, the same iron remained still within his head: but yet escaping out of the Englishmens hands, he came backe to the campe, had the truncheon and iron pulled out of his head, and being dressed was conueied in a litter to Piquignie, where he laie for two or three daies in such danger, that no man looked that he should haue escaped with life.

Martin de Bel-laie, seigneur Langeie in his memoires.

There were manie of these skirmishes, wherin the Englishmen bare themselues so valiantlie, that the Frenchmen went awaie oftentimes with losse of manie of their noble men and best souldiers. At one time they lost the lord Menaintuille brother to the lord de Tillebonne, being slaine with stroke of lance and pike. At another time they lost likewise a yoong lord of Picardie called le seigneur de Fretoie. At length, after their new fort or bastillion was brought in some strength, they furnished it in most defensible wise with men, munition and vittels, naming it Monpleastre. Here-with monsieur de Biez departing from mount Lambert with part of the armie, came downe towards Calis, and entring into the English pale beside Grauelin, wan certeine bulworks, and incountring diuerse new bands of Leicestershiremen and others, latelie before sent ouer, distressed them, and after burnt certeine villages, forraied the countrie almost to Marke, and afterwards in great hast with their bootie and pillage they turned. This enterprise was exploited by the French men about S. Matthews daie in September.

Monsieur de Biez forraieth the English pale about Calis.

There were with monsieur de Biez at this enterprise the lord of Brissac, who go-uerned the vauntgard, and had with him his owne companie of men of armes, and the light horssemen of whome he had the generall conduct. There was also the com-panie of men at armes that belonged to the constable of France, led by the lord Guich, & fiftie men of armes vnder the gouernance of the lord of Hellcie, the com-panie also of the lord of Boisie, the companie of the lord Escars, and that of the lord de la Roch du Maine, & others. There was also monsieur de Taies generall of the French footmen, and manie yoong princes and lords of high estate, as monsieur Francis de Bourbon, duc Danglien, Francis de Lorraine, duke Daumalle latelie re-couered of his hurt, the duke of Neuers, and the earle de Lauall that in this voiage was hurt with an harquebush shot in the arme.

Martin de Bel-laie.

The three and twentith of Nouember, a parlement began at Westminster, in the which was granted to the king a subsidie of the spiritualtie of six shillings the pound, to be paid in two yeares next insuing: and of the temporaltie two shillings and eight pence of the pound in goods, and foure shillings of the pound in lands, to be paid likewise within two yeares. Also in this parlement all colleges, chanteries, and hospitals were committed to the king, to order, by altering or transposing the same as to him should seeme expedient, which at the prorogation of the same parlement he promised should be doone to the glorie of God, and the common profit of the realme. The foure and twentith of December, the said parlement was proroged, on which daie the king comming into the house, to giue his roiall assent vnto such acts as were passed, the speaker made vnto him an eloquent oration, to the which although the custome hath euer béene that the lord chancellor should make answer, it pleased the king at that present to make the answer himselfe, which he vttered as here ensueth.

A parlement. A subsidie grant-ed.

The kings oration in the parlement house.

ALTHOUGH my chancellor, for the time being, hath before this time vsed verie eloquentlie and substantiallie, to make answer to such orations as hath béene set foorth

in

in this high court of parlement; yet is he not so able to open and set foorth my mind and meaning, and the secrets of my heart, in so plaine and ample manner, as I my selfe am and can doo. Wherefore I taking vpon me to answer your eloquent oration maister speaker, saie, that where you in the name of our welbeloued commons, haue both praised and extolled me, for the notable qualities that you haue conceiued to be in me: I most hartilie thanke you all, that you haue put me in remembrance of my dutie, which is to indeuour my selfe to obteine and get such excellent qualities, and necessarie vertues, as a prince or gouernour should or ought to haue, of which gifts I recognise my selfe both bare and barren, but of such small qualities as God hath indued me withall, I render to his goodnesse my most humble thanks, intending with all my wit and diligence to get and acquire to me such notable vertues and princelie qualities, as you haue alledged to be incorporated in my person. These thanks for your louing admonition and good counsell first remembred, I eftsoones thanke you. Againe, bicause that you considering our great charge, not for our pleasure, but for your defense, not for our gaine, but to our great cost, which we haue latelie susteined, aswell in defense of our and your enimies, as for the conquest of that fortresse, which was to this realme most displesant and noisome, and shalbe (by Gods grace) hereafter to our nation most profitable and pleasant, haue fréelie of your owne minds granted to vs a certeine subsidie, here in an act specified, which verelie we take in good part, regarding more your kindnesse, than the profit thereof, as he that setteth more by your louing harts than by your substance. Beside this hartie kindnesse, I cannot a little reioise, when I consider the perfect trust and confidence, which you haue put in me, as men hauing vndoubted hope and vnfeined beléefe in my good dooings and iust proceedings for you, without my desire or request, haue committed to mine order and disposition all chanteries, colleges, hospitals, and other places specified in a certeine act, firmlie trusting that I will order them to the glorie of God, and the profit of the common-wealth. Surelie if I (contrarie to your expectation) should suffer the ministers of the church to decaie, or learning (which is so great a iewell) to be minished, or poore and miserable to be vnreléeued, you might saie that I being put in so speciall a trust, as I am in this case, were no trustie fréend to you, nor charitable to mine euen christian, neither a louer to the publike wealth, nor yet one that feared God, to whome accompt must be rendered of all our dooings. Doubt not I praie you, but your expectation shall be serued, more godlie and goodlie than you will wish or desire, as hereafter you shall plainlie perceiue.

Now sith I find such kindnesse on your part towards me, I cannot choose but loue and fauour you, affirming that no prince in the world more fauoureth his subiects than I doo you; nor no subiects or commons more loued and obeied their souereigne lord, than I perceiue you doo me, for whose defense my treasure shall not be hidden, nor if necessitie require, my person shall not be vnaduentured. Yet although I wish you, and you with me, to be in this perfect loue and concord, this fréendlie amitie cannot continue, except both you my lords' temporall, and my lords spirituall, and you my louing subiects, studie and take paine to amend one thing, which surelie is amisse, and farre out of order, to the which I most hartilie require you: which is, that charitie and concord is not among you, but discord and dissention beareth rule in euerie place. Saint Paule saith to the Corinthians, and the thirtéenth chapter: Charitie is gentle, charitie is not enuious, charitie is not proud, and so foorth in the said chapter. Behold then what loue and charitie is among you, when the one calleth an other heretike and anabaptist, and he calleth him againe papist, hypocrite, and pharisie? Be these tokens of charitie amongst you? Are these signes of fraternall loue betweene you? No, no, I assure you that this lacke of charitie amongst your selues will be the hinderance and asswaging of the feruent loue betwéene vs, as I said before, except this wound be salued, and cleerelie made whole. I must néeds iudge the fault and occasion of this
discord

The kings thanks to his commons.

The kings promises for the well disposing of chantries and colleges.

Charitie and concord in commonwealths be things most necessarie: but in matters of religion, charitie and concord is not enough, without veritie and true worship of God.

discord to be partlie by negligence of you the fathers and preachers of the spiritualtie: for if I know a man which liueth in adulterie, I must iudge him a lecherous and a carnall person: if I sée a man boast and brag himselfe, I cannot but déeme him a proud man. I sée here dailie that you of the cleargie preach one against another, teach one contrarie to another, inueigh one against an other without charitie or discretion: some be too stiffe in their old Mumpsimus, other be too busie and curious in their new Sumpsimus: thus all men almost be in varietie and discord, and few or none preacheth trulie and sincerelie the word of God, according as they ought to doo. Shall I iudge you charitable persons dooing this? No, no, I cannot so doo. Alas, how can the poore soules liue in concord, when you preachers sow amongst them in your sermons debate and discord? Of you they looke for light, and you bring them to darkenesse. Amend these crimes I exhort you, and set foorth Gods word, both by true preaching and good example giuing: or else I, whome God hath appointed his vicar and high minister here, will sée these diuisions extinct, and these enormities corrected according to my verie dutie, or else I am an vnprofitable seruant, and an vntrue officer. Although I saie the spirituall men be in some fault, that charitie is not kept amongst you; yet you of the temporaltie be not cleare and vnspotted of malice and enuie: for you raile on bishops, speake slanderouslie of preests, and rebuke and taunt preachers, both contraie to good order and christian fraternitie. If you know suerlie that a bishop or preacher erreth, or teacheth peruerse doctrine, come and declare it to some of our councell, or to vs, to whome is committed by God the high authoritie to reforme and order such causes and behauiors, and be not iudges your selues, of your owne fantasticall opinions and vaine expositions, for in such high causes you may lightlie erre. And although you be permitted to read holie scriptures, and to haue the word of God in your mother toong, you must vnderstand, that it is licenced you so to doo, onelie to informe your owne consciences, and to instruct your children and familie, and not to dispute, and make scripture a railing and a taunting stocke against priests and preachers, as manie light persons doo. I am verie sorie to know and heare, how vnreuerentlie that most pretious iewell the word of God is disputed, rimed, soong, and iangled in euerie alehouse and tauerne, contrarie to the true meaning and doctrine of the same: and yet I am euen as much sorie, that the readers of the same follow it in dooing so faintlie and coldlie. For of this I am sure, that charitie was neuer so faint amongst you, and vertuous and godlie liuing was neuer lesse vsed, nor God himselfe amongst christians was neuer lesse reuerenced, honored, or serued. Therfore (as I said before) be in charitie one with an other, like brother and brother: loue, dread, and serue God, to the which I as your supreame head and souereigne lord exhort and require you, and then I doubt not, but that loue and league that I spake of in the beginning, shall neuer be dissolued or broken betwéene vs. And to the making of laws which we haue now made and concluded, I exhort you the makers to be as diligent in putting them in execution, as you were in making & furthering of the same: or else your labour shall be in vaine, & your common-wealth nothing reléeued. Now to your petition, concerning our roiall assent to be giuen to such acts as haue passed both houses, they shall be read openlie that ye may heare them.

Then were they openlie read, and to manie his grace assented, and diuerse he assented not vnto. Thus the kings oration was to his subiects there present such comfort, that the like ioie could not be vnto them in this world. And thus the acts read (as the manner is) and his assent giuen, his grace rose and departed. Manie proper feats of armes were exploited and doone in this meane while, betwixt the parties English and French about Bullongne. On the morrow after the feast of the Epiphanie, there came a con- ——— **1546** uoie of vittels towards the French fort, garded with thrée or foure thousand lancequenetz vnder their coronell the Reingraue and certeine French horssemen. The earle of Surreie *The Reingraue.* then

then lieutenant of Bullongne aduertised thereof, made out with such power as he might conuenientlie spare of them within Bullongne and the Old man, to cut off those vittels: but comming to encounter with the enimies at saint Estiens, he was put to flight: sir Edward Poinings capteine of a band called the kings gard of Bullongne was slaine in that conflict with fifteene or sixteene other capteins, beside officers and common soldiors. About the same time the Frenchmen made a voiage vnto the Isle of Brasill with a ship called the barke Ager, which they had taken from the Englishmen before: and in their waie they met with a little craior of the which one Golding was master, a proper man and an hardie. The barke perceiuing the craier to be an Englishman, shot at hir and bowged hir. Wherevpon straitwaies the craier drew to the great barke, and six or seauan of the Englishmen leapt into hir. In the meane time while the Frenchmen, without regard of perill towards themselues, looked ouer hatches to behold how the craier sunke there at hand before them, not mistrusting anie thing, that the Englishmen might doo against them, it fortuned that those Englishmen which got vp into the barke, found in the end thereof a great number of lime pots, which they with water quenched, or rather (as the nature thereof is) set them on fire, and threw them so thicke at the Frenchmen which were there aboord, that they blinded them, in such wise as those few Englishmen that entered the ship vanquished the Frenchmen, and driuing them vnder hatches, shut the same, and brought the barke awaie with them home into England. In the latter end of March the brothell houses called the Stues on the banke side in Southworke were conuerted from such filthie vses by the kings commandement, the bawds and ruffians being put out, and other persons of honest behauior placed in their rooms to inhabit in the same houses. This was doone by proclamation and sound of trumpet by an herald of armes.

¶ On the seuen and twentith of Aprill being tuesdaie in Easter weeke William Foxleie pot-maker for the mint of the Tower of London fell asleepe, and so continued sleeping, and could not be wakened with pricking, cramping, or otherwise burning whatsoeuer, till the first daie of the next terme, which was full foureteene daies, and as manie nights or more, for that Easter terme beginneth not before seauenteene daies after Easter. The cause of his thus sleeping could not be knowen, though it were diligentlie searched for by the kings physicians and other learned men, yea the king himselfe examining the said William Foxleie, who was in all points found at his waking to be but as if he had slept but one night: he was liuing in the Tower of London in the yeere of our Lord God 1579.

This yeere by meanes made by the emperor, commissioners were appointed to meet & treat of some accord betweene the realmes of England & France, so that the king of England sent ouer to Guisnes, Cutbert Tunstall bishop of Duresme, sir William Paget his secretarie, and doctor Tregonell: and the French king sent to Ard a bishop, the chiefe president of Rouen, and a notarie, but no conclusion followed of their trauell. Wherevpon the king of England hauing perfect knowledge how the Frenchmen intended to build a fortresse at saint Iohns rode betweene Bullongne and Calis, to the great annoiance of both those places, if they might haue compassed their purpose; he meant to preuent that deuise of his aduersaries, sending ouer the earle of Hertford and the lord Lisle high admerall of England, with manie valiant capteins, which got the rode but two daies before the Frenchmen had appointed to be there. But when they vnderstood that the Englishmen had so preuented them, they staied about Hardilow where monsieur de Biez their generall gaue order to incampe, and durst not once come forward to assaie the English forces: so that without anie impeachment by land, the Englishmen built certeine fortresses, to wit, two at the same place of saint Iohns rode, otherwise called Hamble Thew, and an other about a two miles from thence at a place called Blacke Nesse. There was in the earle of Hertfords campe beside Englishmen diuerse strangers, Almains, Spaniards and Italians. And because it is not much
impertinent

impertinent to the matter, we haue thought good here to set downe the whole number of all the kings forces at that present in his paie that were there vnder the said earle of Hertford the kings generall lieutenant. First the earle had two hundred, the lord William Sturton thrée hundred, the lord Iohn Greie brother to the marques Dorset two hundred, the lord Braie one hundred sir, Thomas Seimer knight marshall of the host one hundred, sir Henrie Kneuet capteine of the horssemen one hundred, sir Iohn Harrington treasuror of the armie one hundred, sir Thomas Wiat master of the ordinance one hundred, sir Mauris Barkleie thrée hundred, sir Thomas Holcoft two hundred, sir Walter Dennis two hundred, sir George Blewet two hundred, sir Richard Greenefield two hundred, sir George Cornewall two hundred, sir Iohn Lutterell one hundred, sir Edmund Hussie one hundred, Gorge Throkmorton two hundred, capteine Broughton two hundred, capteine Palmer two hundred, capteine Chancie two hundred, capteine Windam two hundred, capteine Stukeleie one hundred, capteine Blewet one hundred, capteine Sidnam one hundred, capteine Bret one hundred, capteine Dier one hundred, capteine Euans one hundred, Spaniards fiftéene hundred, Italians two hundred, Cleueners thrée hundred; lancequenets vnder the gouernment of their coronell Conrade Phenning, commonlie called Courtpennie, thrée thousand. The summe of all the soldiors in Bullongne & Bullongnois were 93000. Here you must note, that whilest the English armie laie thus in the field till the forts of Hamble Thew and Blacke Nesse were in building, the French gallies were on the seas, and now and then came and approched néere to the shore, where the English armie laie in campe, at the which they shot off their ordinance: and the Englishmen answered them againe with the like. They came also before Calis and shot off at the towne. But the lord admerall being there, made out to encounter them, notwithstanding they did first much hurt, and tooke awaie diuerse of the English vessels laden with vittels.

The eighteenth daie of Maie there were foure of the kings ships, and foure pinases abroad on the seas afore the hauen of Hamble Thew, and there came eightéene of the French gallies to set vpon them, and so there was great shooting betweene them: and at length one of their gallies was taken, in the which were aboord fourtéene score soldiors and seauen score rowers: the rest of their gallies packed awaie. Moreouer, whilest the campe laie thus at Hamble Thew, it chanced that on a daie a mutinie rose among the lancequenets against their capteine, so that they got themselues into order of battell, seized vpon the great artillerie, and shewed countenance as if they would haue set vpon the residue of the whole campe. Herevpon euerie soldior was commanded to repaire to his ensigne, and the Spaniards came and ioined with the Englishmen, readie to take such part as they did. At length by the diligence of the chiefteines, and good countenance of the English soldiors and Spaniards the tumult was staied, and six of the principall beginners were hanged.

The one and twentith of Maie the French armie came and incamped beyond Bullonge at the church on the hill: and the morrow after the earle of Hertford marched with his power to a place within two miles of them, and certeine footmen and horssemen went foorth and skirmished with them; and in the meane time the artillerie ceassed not to shoot off, as well from the French campe and fortresse as from Bullongne and the Old man. This daie were slaine fourtéene Frenchmen and two taken prisoners; and thrée of the English part were likewise taken, and so the earle of Hertford returned to his campe, and left the lancequenets vpon the hill, incamped before the enimies faces, not two miles distant from them, in which place a fort was begun to be raised, which was after called the fort of Bullongne Berg. The next daie, to wit, the thrée and twentith of Maie the soldiors of Bullongne and the lancequenets skirmished with the Frenchmen, slue and tooke of them seuen score and aboue, of the which there were fortie that were in cotes of veluet, and diuerse also with chaines.

A French gallie taken.

A mutinie in the English campe.

A great skirmish.

Here you must vnderstand, that now in this meane while by the motion of diuerse princes, a méeting was had of sundrie commissioners, appointed to treat of some peace, to be concluded betwixt the two kings of England and France. Herevpon there came to Guisnes for the king of England the earle of Hertford, the bishop of Winchester, sir Iohn Dudleie vicount Lisle baron of Maupas, and high admerall of England, sir William Paget the kings secretarie, and doctor Nicholas Wootton deane of Canturburie. For the French king there came to Ard monsieur Claude Danebault admerall of France, being also one of the foure marshals of that realme, the bishop of Eureux, monsieur Reimund chiefe president of Rone, the secretarie Bouchetell. Diuerse times they met betwixt Ard and Guisnes, and after long debating of matters,

*A peace con-
cluded and pro-
clamed.*

and diuerse breakings off: yet at length the seauenth of Iune a peace was concluded, and proclamed as well in the court as in the citie of London on Whitsundaie the thirtéenth of Iune, with sound of trumpet, according to the manner: and in like sort the same daie it was proclamed at Paris and at Rone. The chiefest article of which peace was this, that the French king paieng to the king of England 800000 crownes within the terme of eight yeares, should haue Bullongne againe to him restored, which in the meane time should remaine in the hands and possession of the king of England, as a pledge and gage for assurance of the said moneie.

*I. Stow, pag.
1033.
Iohn Fox in Acts
& Monuments.*

*D. Crome re-
canteth at Paules
crosse.*

On the seuen & twentith of Iune doctor Crome recanted at Paules crosse: which recantation was vrged vpon this occasion. When the chanteries & colleges were giuen by act of parlement into the kings hands (as is aboue remembred) which was about the moneth of December 1545, the next lent following doctor Crome preaching in the mercers chappell, among other reasons and persuasions, to rouse the people from the vaine opinion of purgatorie, inferred this, grounding vpon the said act of parlement: that if trentals and chanterie masses could auaile the soules in purgatorie, then did the parlement not well in giuing awaie monasteries, colleges, & chante-ries, which serued principallie to that purpose. But if the parlement did well (as no man could denie) in dissoluing them & bestowing the same vpon the king, then is it a plaine case, that such chanteries and priuat masses doo nothing conferre to re-léeue them in purgatorie. This Dilemma of doctor Crome, no doubt, was insoluble: but notwithstanding the charitable prelats (for all the kings late exhortation vnto charitie) were so charitable to him that they brought him Coram nobis, and so handled

*Abr. Fle. ex
manuscripto ab
Henr. Tenant
tradito.*

him that they made him recant his words. ¶On the sixtéenth of Iune were letters patents deliuered to sir Thomas Cheinie treasuror of the kings houshold, and lord warden of the cinque ports, wherby he was authorised to be the kings agent in chris-tening the Dolphins daughter of France named Elizabeth. A true copie of which letters patents is here recorded, bicause the said action hath beene ignorantlie trans-ferred from the said sir Thomas Cheinie to sir Henrie Kneuet: as appeareth in Ho-linsheds chronicle published 1577, pag. 1608.

A true copie of the kings letters patents to sir Thomas Cheinie.

HENRICUS octauus Dei gratia Angliæ, Franciæ, & Hiberniæ rex, fidei defensor, & in terra ecclesiæ Anglicanæ & Hibernicæ supremum caput. Prædilecto & fideli con-siliario nostro Thomæ Cheinie sacri ordinis nostri garterij militi, domino gardiano quinque portuum, & hospitij nostri the saurario salutem. Cúm illustrissima princeps ac consanguinea nostra charissima domina Katharina illustrissimi principis consangui-nei & filij nostri charissimi Henrici Franciæ Delphini christianissimi principis Francisci Francorum regis fratris, amici & confœderati nostri perpetui, filij primogeniti coniunx præclarissima, nuper (diuina cooperante clementia) prolem fœminam enixa sit: nos summoperè cupientes pacis, amicitiæ, & vnionis vinculum inter præfatum christianis-
simum

simum Francorum regem & nos iam nuper redintegratum, firmioribus quibus possu-
mus nexibus astringi, admaiorem ipsius corroborationem & firmitatem, ac vt dicto
illustrissimo filio nostro in hac parte gratificemur, etiam compaternitatis fœdus duxi-
mus adijciendum.   Quocirca ad leuandum de sacro fonte vice & nomine nostro dictam
prolem ex præfata illustrissima domina Katharina dicti illustrissimi principis coniuge,
& consanguinea nostra charissima natam, illique nomen Elisabethæ imponendum, & ipsam nomine Elisabethæ in illius baptismo nominandā, cæteráq; omnia & singula in
præmissis, & circa ea necessaria seu quouismodo oportuna nomine nostro faciendum &
exercendum, etiamsi maiora existant superiùs expressis, & mandatum de se exigant
magis speciale quàm superiùs est insertum : te commissarium ac ambassiatorem & pro-
curatorem nostrum specialem ordinamus, facimus, & constituimus per præsentes : pro-
mittentes nos ratum, gratum, firmum habituros quicquid per te gestum & procuratum
siue actum fuerit in præmissis.   In cuius rei testimonium has literas nostras fieri feci-
mus patentes.   Teste me ipso apud Greenewich sextodecimo die Iunij anno regni nostri
tricesimo octauo.   Henrie Rex.

    The king hauing passed ouer the aforesaid letters patents to sir Thomas, and he in
forwardnesse to execute his charge, to the intent that his retinue and attendants
should no waies offensiuelie behaue themselues against the French, with whom the
king was verie carefull to continue and mainteine the peace interchangeablie agreed
vpon and concluded, his maiestie to preuent and cut off all occasions that might anie
waie impeach, interrupt, or violate this peace, commanded the lords of his councell
to direct letters with all expedition to the said sir Thomas, then vpon his voiage into
France, conteining a prescript forme of demeanor, which the gentlemen & yeomen attendant vpon him in France should vse, during the time of their abode in those forren
parts : a copie of which letter, being a testimoniall of the king of Englands inclinable
mind to peace hereafter followeth out of the verie originall, as the same was subscribed
by the lords.

*A copie of the said letters sent in post to sir Thomas Cheinie being vpon his voiage
into France.*

    AFTER our right hartie commendations to your good lordship.   The kings maiestie
hath willed vs to signifie vnto you, that his highnesse expresse pleasure and commandement is, ye should in his maiesties name declare to such gentlemen as accompanie you
into France, that they haue in remembrance so to vse & behaue themselues among
the Frenchmen as well on the waie as at the court, in such sort as they by communication vpon feats of the warre passed giue no occasion of priuat displeasure.   Wherein
therefore it shall be expedient, that either they saie nothing, vnlesse they be prouoked ;
or in that case call the things happened fortune de la guerre, without comparison of
things chanced on our part or on theirs, but turne the communication to reioise in
peace.   In the conditions whereof they shall pretend ignorance, without speaking of
the keeping still of Bullogne, or deliuerance of it againe, but as shall please the
princes for the continuance of peace, wherein by Gods grace the crueltie of warre
shall be conuerted into extreamitie of friendship, to the weale and commoditie of both
realmes.
    And forsomuch as there want not in the world naughtie men of the state of moonks
and friers, who for malice of the alteration of their estate here, would gladlie defame
our religion towards God, as though we had with them cast out all ; his highnesse expresse pleasure and commandement is, that considering at this first entrie of you,
the behauiour of your companie shall be much marked and noted in matters of reli-

        gion

gion and circumstances: of the same they should therfore haue so much the more regard both to their communications and also behauiors, and not onelie in speech to forbeare to dispute or intermedle with the state of their policy there, but also in their diet on the fish daie and deuout hearing of masse, follow the order of the kings maiesties relme, so as their conuersation & behauior maie be cōfusion to such as would defame this realme in the contrarie. Thus fare your good lordship right hartilie well. From Greenewich the ninteenth of Iune 1546. Your lordships assured louing friends, Thomas Wriothesleie, canc. W: Saint-Iohn. I: Russell. Cutb: Duresme. Steph: Winton. Anthonie Brenne. William Petres. This letter was thus indorsed. ¶ To our assured louing friend sir Thomas Cheinie knight of the order, treasuror of the kings maiesties houshold, and lord warden of the cinque ports, presentlie in speciall commission from the kings maiestie into France. Hast, post hast for thy life, to Douer, Calis, or where he shall chance to be: hast, hast.

Henrie Tenant.

Thus farre of sir Thomas Cheinie, imploied about the kings affaires in France; namelie the christening of the Dolphins daughter: wherein we haue béene the more copious in words, bicause it hath béen published, that sir Henrie Kneuet was thereunto personallie deputed: which to be vntrue, both the letters patents and the letter missiue doo sufficientlie prooue: both which we receiued at the hands of an * ancient seruitor attendant vpon the same sir Thomas at his béeing in France to execute his charge in the kings behalfe. Of which woorthie knight when we come to the yeare and daie of his death, we will deliuer further report to his high commendation, but yet none otherwise than as by warranted intelligence we shall be directed.]

A combat be-tweene Iulian Romerou, and Morow.

The same time was a combat fought before the French king betwixt two Spaniards, Iulian Romerou, and one Morow. They both serued the king of England in the last wars against France: but Morow had reuolted from his seruice to the French kings, and for certeine spéeches which he had vttered, was chalenged to fight the said combat by the said Iulian, for whome sir Henrie Kneuet vndertooke that he should stand to his chalenge, and trie it with his aduersarie, which he now did, and vanquished him in lists, the fight being appointed on horssebacke. Incontinentlie after, sir Henrie

The death of sir Henrie Kne-uet.

Kneuet sickned and died at Corbell, and was buried in Paris within the church of S. Paule. Moreouer, for the full establishment of the peace, and to receiue the French kings oth, the vicount Lisle lord admerall, with the bishop of Duresme, and diuerse other lords, and gentlemen, to the number of one hundred and aboue, all in veluet cotes and chaines of gold, with fiue and fortie yeomen right séemelie appointed, went

The lord ad-merall Dudleie went into France to receiue the Frēch kings oth

into France, departing from Bullogne the tenth of Iulie, and came to Mellune a towne beyond Paris, where the French king then laie, by whome and the Dolphin his sonne they were roiallie receiued, feasted, and banketted: and hauing doone that for the which he was sent, the said lord admerall Dudleie the first of August tooke his leaue of the French king, who rewarded him with a cupboord of plate all gold, valued at 1500 pounds. The lords also and gentlemen had chaines of gold giuen to them, and the yeomen had two hundred crownes bestowed amongst them, and so the lord admerall returned into England. This lord admerall, during the time that he had to deale with the French, so valiantlie demeaned himselfe, and was such a terror and astonishment to the enimie, as it is left written of him, that they durst not quéech in his presence, but were like a sort of timorous cattell, giuing roome to the raging lion ranging ouer the pastures with hir yoonglings, and making the verie heauens to ring with hir roring, after she hath filled hir selfe with bulles flesh, and laid hir selfe downe to rest being wearie with eating; the comparison verie aptlie followeth.

Vtque iracundo cedunt armenta leoni,
Pascua cum plenus bacchante furore peragrat
Solus cum catulis, cœlum, & rugitibus implens

Conspicitur,

Conspicitur, postquam taurorum carnibus atra
Sit saturata fames, lassúsque recumbit edendo :
Tantus terror erat Gallis Dudleius Heros.

In the same moneth of August monsieur Danebalt high admerall of France, ac-companied with the bishop of Eureux, the earle of Nauteuill knight of the order, the earle of Villiers, the chiefe president of Roan, secretarie Bouchetell, monsieur de Canaples knight of the order, monsieur de Taies knight of the order, monsieur de Maillerie viceadmerall of France, monsieur de Desse, the baron de la Gard, with di-uerse other lords and capteines of honor, beside two hundred gentlemen well appoint-ed, leused from Déepe with twelue gallies and a right faire ship called the Sacre of Déepe and so making saile he staied not anie where to take land, till he came into the Thames, where at Blackewall he was receiued into the kings barge by the earles of Darbie and Essex, who brought him to Gréenewich, where he landed, and lodged there that night. An ambassage forth of France.

The next daie he came vp with all his gallies, and landed at the Tower wharfe. Vpon all the banks by the water side were laid péeces of artillerie, which shot off freelie, and so likewise did all the artillerie in the ships, but speciallie from the Tower was shot a maruellous great peale of ordinance. From whence being landed, they rode thorough London in great triumph (the maior and the crafts standing in the streets in verie good order) vnto the bishops palace by Paules, where the French ad-merall lodged till Bartholomew euen, on which daie he was conueied toward Hampton court, where in the waie the prince hauing with him the archbishop of Yorke, the earles of Hertford and Huntington, and aboue two thousand horsse, met him and imbrased him in such courteous and honorable wise, that all the beholders greatlie reioised, and much maruelled at the said princes high wit and great audacitie, and so the French admerall came to the court, giuing the prince the vpper hand as they rode. And at the vtter gate of the court, the lord chancellor, and all the kings councell re-ceiued him, and brought him to his lodging. The kings ships that laie in the riuer betwixt Grauesend & Detford, shot off lustilie, & like-wise the French galleis halsed them againe. The french ad-merall receiued by prince Ed-ward.

On Bartholomew daie the king admitting him to his presence, welcomed him, and in great triumph went to the chappell, where the king receiued his oth to performe the articles of the league, as it was couenanted. To speake of the bankettings, hunt-ings, and such like honorable sorts of interteinements, it were much to vtter, and hard to beléeue. But on fridaie following, being the seuen and twentith of August, he being rewarded with a cupboord of plate, to the value of twelue hundred pounds, returned to London, and on the sundaie next insuing tooke his gallies and departed. Beside the kings gifts he had giuen to him by the citie of London two flaggons guilt, and two other that were parcell guilt, valued at one hundred thirtie six pounds, beside wine, wax, and torches. There were diuerse of his companie also that went not awaie vnrewarded, hauing both plate, and also manie horsses, and greihounds giuen them. The admerall of France re-ceiueth an oth. His gifts that he had of the king & others.

Although this peace pleased both the English and French nations, yet suerlie both mistrusted the continuance therof. And verelie the old prouerbe séemed to be throughlie verefied, which saith, that what the eie séeth, the hart rueth : for the Frenchmen still longed for Bullogne, and the Englishmen meant not willinglie to giue it ouer. For during the French admerals being in England, monsieur de Chatillon cap-teine of Montplaisier began to make a new bastilion euen at the verie mouth of the hauen, naming it Chatillons garden. Wherevpon that noble gentleman the lord Greie of Wilton, shortlie after appointed to be deputie of the towne and countie of Bullogne, perceiuing the great inconuenience that this new building would bring to the towne if it went forwards, did aduertise the king thereof, earnestlie beséeching his grace, that the matter might be throughlie considered of. Sir Thomas Palmer was the messenger. The lord Greie of Wilton. Sir Thomas Palmer.

The

The king vpon the intelligence, asked his councels aduise, which onelie went wholie, that the conditions of the peace were not in anie wise to be infringed. This resolued, secretarie Paget then knight, and afterwards lord, was commanded accordinglie to draw a letter to the lord Greie, the which the king himseife did signe, willing that the messenger should further know of his pleasure before he departed. Wherevpon sir Thomas Palmer, hauing his dispatch at the secretaries hands, did get word to be giuen to the king, who presentlie sent for him into his priuie chamber, and betwixt them two, vsed these words : Palmer, you haue there a letter from vs to the lord Greie, that he doo in no wise deale in the matter that he hath by you aduertised vs of. Notwithstanding, I will that you deliuer him this message from vs.

King Henries message to the lord Greie by sir Thomas Palmer.

" Bid him call to mind how that his brethren and himselfe not a short time, but euen from tender yeares, nor farre off, but still neere to our person, we haue brought him vp, which (tell him) not vniustlie, if that be in him that we conceiue dooth bréed in vs an od trust of feruencie to serue vs of him, more than a common seruant or subiect. By that token will him whatsoeuer I haue written to the contrarie, that he presentlie impeach the fortification of Chatillons garden, and raise it if it be possible : and this my message shall be his cléering therein, & the seruice gratefullie accepted." Sir Thomas Palmer somewhat astonied hereat, considering the weightinesse of the cause, and the contrarietie of the letter and message, began to put the king in mind of the small credit that his bare errand of right was like to haue, so flat against that which his maiesties letters imported. But the king cutting off his tale ; " Deliuer thou the message (quoth he) at his choise then be the executing thereof."

Sir Thomas thus dispatched, with great spéed arriued at Bullogne immediatlie vpon the opening of the gates at after noone. His letters and message deliuered, the lord Greie streight assembled the councell, shewed them the kings letters, which read, he caused sir Thomas to pronounce before them the message also. Euerie man was to saie his aduise : it went roundlie through the boord without anie question, that the letter was to be followed, the message not to be staied on. The lord Greie hauing heard, and not replieng anie thing, willed sir Thomas to be called in againe, bad him repeat his message, and therwhilest made a clearke of the councell to write the same Verbatim. This doone, he praied the whole table to set their hands vnto it, which they did, and the lord Greie taking the same into his hands, without further opening, declaring his resolution, brake vp councell, commanded streight the gates to be shut, gaue priuie warning, that certeine bands with armour and weapon, and likewise pioners should that night by an houre be in a readiness.

Chatillons garden ouerthrowne and rased downe.

The houre came, himselfe with the warned companie issued out, passed ouer the water, and without anie alarum of the enimie, did ouerthrow in thrée or foure houres, what in two or three moneths had bin raised, and so in great quietnesse returned into the towne. Presentlie he dispatched sir Thomas Palmer backe againe to the king with the newes, whose returne was so sudden, as the king himselfe being in the chamber of presence, & séeing him, said alowd : What? Will he doo it or no? Sir Thomas giuing no other answer, but presenting his letters, and saieng, that thereby his maiestie should know, The king againe in earnest mood, Naie tell vs I saie, whether he will doo it or not? Then sir Thomas told him that it was doone, and the whole fortification cleane rased. Whereat the king taking great ioy, presentlie called to certeine of the lords of the councell that were by, and said : How saie you my lords, Chatillons garden the new fort is laid as flat as this floore. One streight amongst

The lord Greies seruice verie honorablie accepted of the king.

them gaue iudgement, that he that had doone it, was worthie to lose his head. The king streight replied, he had rather lose a dozen such heads as his was so that iudged, than one such seruants as he had doone it : and herewith he commanded, that the lord Greies pardon should presentlie be made, the which with a letter of great thanks, and promise of reward, was returned by the said sir Thomas Palmer to the said lord Greie ;
                                                             but

but the reward failed, the king not continuing long after in life: the like hap whereof had oftentimes happened vnto diuerse of his worthie ancestors vpon their due deserts to haue béene considered of, and therefore the case the lesse strange.

This haue I set downe the more willinglie, for that I haue receiued it from them, which haue heard it reported, not onlie by the lord Greis owne mouth, but also by the relation of sir Thomas Palmer, and others that were present: the same not tending so much to the lord Greies owne praise, as to the betokening of the kings noble courage, and the great secret trust which he worthilie reposed in the said lord Greie. Here is to be noted also, lest any man should mistake the matter, as if the king dealt indirectlie herein, that his maiestie knowing how the Frenchmen in going about to build this fort, did more than they might by the couenants of the peace; and therefore was resolued at the first aduertisement thereof, to haue it rased. But yet for that it might happilie haue béene signified ouer vnto the Frenchmen, before my lord Greie could haue accomplished the feat, he therefore wiselie wrote one thing in his letters, wherevnto manie might be priuie, and sent secret knowledge by words contrarie to the contents of the same letters, so as if the messenger were trustie, his pleasure might not be discouered to the hinderance or disappointing of the same. But now to our purpose.

The French king after this, bicause as yet hée would not séeme to breake the peace, commanded the trenches and new fortifications made about this fortresse, called Chatillons garden thus cast downe, to be filled by his owne people, and so it rested during the life king Henrie: but afterwards it was begun againe, and finished, as after ye shall heare. About Michaelmas in this present yeare, Thomas duke of Norffolke, ^{The duke of} and Henrie earle of Surrie that was his sonne and heire, vpon certeine surmises of ^{Norffolke cō-} treason, were committed to the tower of London, and immediatlie after Christmas, ^{mitted to the} the thirtéenth of Ianuarie, the king then lieng in the extremities of death, the said ^{tower.} earle was arreigned in the Guildhall of London, before the lord maior, the lord chancellor, and diuerse other lords and iudges being there in commission. Where if he had tempered his answers with such modestie as he shewed token of a right perfect and readie wit, his praise had béene the greater. Some things he flatlie denied, seeking to weaken the credit of his accusers by certeine circumstances: other he excused with interpretations of his meaning, to proue the same to be far otherwise than was alleged against him.

And one speciall matter amongest other wherewith he was charged, was, for bearing certeine arms that were said to belong to the king, and to the prince. The bearing whereof he iustified and maintened, that (as he tooke it) he might beare them as belonging to diuerse of his ancestors, and withall affirmed, that he had the opinion of heralds therein. But yet to his indictment he pleaded not giltie: and for that he was no lord of the parlement, he was inforced to stand to the triall of a common inquest of his countrie, which found him giltie, and therevpon he had iudgement of death: and shortlie after, to wit, the 19 of Ianuarie, he was beheaded on the tower hill. ¶ In ^{The earle of} this moneth of Ianuarie, the church of the late graie friers in London was opened, ^{Surrie behead-} and masse soong there: and that daie preached at Paules crosse the bishop of Roches- ^{ed.} ter, who declared the kings gift to the citie of London, for the relieuing of the poore ^{I. S. pag. 1034.} people, which was by patent vnder his great seale. Saint Bartholomews spittle, the ^{King Henrie} church of the graie friers, and two parish churches, the one of saint Nicholas in the ^{his gift to the citie of London:} shambles, the other saint Ewine in Newgate market, all to be made one parish church of the graie friers church; and in lands he gaue for the maintenance of the same 500 markes by yeare for euer, & this church to be named Christs church, founded by king Henrie the eight.]

The duke was atteinted by parlement, and the atteindor after reuersed in the first ^{The duke at-} yeare of quéene Marie. The euill hap as well of the father, as of the sonne, was ^{teinted.}

greatlie

^{1547.}

greatlie lamented of manie, not onelie for the good seruice which the duke had doone in his daies in defense of this realme, but also for that the earle was a gentleman well learned, and knowne to haue an excellent wit, if he had béene thankefull to God for the same, and other such good gifts as he had indued him withall. The king now

The king maketh his testament.

lieng at the point of death, made his last will and testament, wherein he not onelie yéelded himselfe to almightie God; but also tooke order, that during the minoritie of his sonne prince Edward, his executors should be councellors and aiders to him in all things, as well concerning priuat as publike affaires. They were sixtéene in number, whose names were as hereafter followeth.

His executors.

Thomas Cranmer archbishop of Canturburie, Thomas Wriothesleie lord chancellor, sir William Paulet knight of the order, lord Saint-Iohn, & great master of the houshold: sir Edward Seimer knight of the order, earle of Hertford, and high chamberleine of England: sir Iohn Russell knight of the order, lord priuie seale: sir Iohn Dudleie knight of the order, vicount Lisle, & baron of Maupas, high admerall of England: Cutbert Tunstall bishop of Durham: sir Anthonie Browne knight of the order, and master of the horsse: sir Edmund Montacute knight chiefe iustice of the cōmon plees: sir Thomas Bromleie knight, one of the iustices of the kings bench: sir Edward North knight, chancellor of the augmentation: sir William Paget knight of the order: sir Anthonie Dennie knight: sir William Herbert knight: sir Edward Wotton knight, treasuror of Calis: Nicholas Wotton deane of Canturburie and Yorke.

The decease of king Henrie the eight.

So soone as the noble king had finished his last will and testament, as afore is said, he shortlie therevpon yeelded vp his spirit to almightie God, departing this world the eight and twentith daie of Ianuarie, in the eight and thirtith yeare of his reigne, and in the yeare of our Lord 1546, after the accompt of the church of England; but after the accompt which we follow in this booke 1547, beginning our yeare the first of Ianuarie. He reigned thirtie and seuen yeares, nine moneths and od daies. His bodie (according to his will in that behalfe) was conueied to Windsor with all funerall pompe, and in the college there interred. Of this tresnoble and trespuissant monarch, I find these few verses, which maie serue in good stead of an epitaph or funerall inscription:

Henricus octauus post 38. annos moritur.

Henricus princeps propè lustra peregerat octo,
Et populum magna prudens cum laude regebat,
Ex quo magna soli tractauit sceptra Britanni:
Cùm Deus omnipotens, morbo obrepente, moneret
Hinc emigrandum de vita. Proh dolor ingens!
Quot pia plebs lachrymis quàm tristibus ora rigauit?
Quàm grauiter regni proceres planxere cubantem?
Anglia tota iacet mœrens, lugubris & amens,
Nil opis apportant medici, nil profuit herba,
Quœ solet humanis membris adferre salutem,
Pharmaca nil prosunt, præbetur potio frustra:
Heu nulla tristis mors est medicabilis arte.

The description of king Henrie the eight.

This noble prince was right fortunate in all his dooings, so that commonlie whatsoeuer he attemted, had good successe, as well in matters of peace as of wars. Of personage he was tall and mightie, in his latter daies somwhat grosse, or as we tearme it, bourlie: in wit and memorie verie perfect: of such maiestie tempered with humanitie, as best became so noble and high an estate: a great fauorer of learning, as he that was not ignorant of good letters himselfe: he was of great magnificence and liberalitie, insomuch that Iohn Leland that woorthie antiquarie, hauing tasted of his roiall bountifulnesse, hath left no lesse testified to the world in a proper epigram, which I will not omit, least I should wilfullie conceale a manifest protestation of his thankfulnesse left witnessed vnto the world in writing:

Antè

Antè suos Phœbus radios ostendere mundo
     Desinet, & claras Cynthia pulchra faces :
Antè fluet rapidum tacitis sine piscibus æquor,
     Spinifer & nullam sentis habebit auem :
Antè sacræ quercus cessabunt spargere ramos,
     Floráq; sollicita pingere prata manu :
Quàm rex diue tuum labatur pectore nostro
     Nomen, quod studijs portus & aura meis.

Ad Henricum octauum, regem Angliæ, maximum studiosorum amatorem.

And the same Iohn Leland, who deseruedlie had tasted the fruits of the kings largesse, was not vnacquainted with the fame of his renowme, which had made it selfe knowne by restles flight to nations far and neare, some to their smart hauing felt the valor of his forces, and others submitting themselues for feare of vtter desolation. Wherevpon he became a terror to his enimies, and yet none more desirous of peace than he, if by anie other meanes (besides violence) the same might haue béene obteined. Sufficient cannot be said in his high & merited commendation, considering that as his victories were singular, so were they also manifold; and hard it is for the pen of a cunning rhetorician to paint him out according to his dignitie: howbeit the said Iohn Leland hath left in writing a proper epigram, deuised in praise of this most excellent king, by way of comparison, to his immortall commendation, as here followeth :

Comparatio in gloriam Henrici octaui regis potentissimi.

Quantum puniceis nouo rosetis
Cedunt vere suis rubeta spinis :
Quantum lilio amœnioris horti
Gemmæ omnes aliæ nitore cedunt :
Quantum cætera punicis decoro
Malis poma quidem rubore cedunt :
Quantum coniferis breues myricæ
Concedunt quoq; gloria cupressis :
Quantum stelligero repressa tellus
Cælo mole sua & nigrore cedit :
Tantum omnes alij, celebritate,
Fama, nomine, gloriáq; vera
(Vt mittam ingenij valentioris
Lumen, flumina, fulmen atq; vires
Rari iudicij tui perennes)
Concedunt tibi principes sereni,
Henrice, ô patriæ tuæ columna
Talis, qualis erat celebris illa
Olim quam extulit Henricus triumphans.

Of lerned men that liued in the daies of this most famous prince, we find manie, as first Iohn Colet deane of Paules, and founder of the schoole there, he was borne in London of honest parents; William Lillie borne in the town of Odiham in Hampshire, and was the first schoolemaster of Paules schoole after it was erected; Thomas Linacer, or rather Linaker, borne in Darbie, a learned physician, and well séene in the toongs; Iohn Skelton a pleasant poet, Richard Pace that succeeded Iohn Colet in the roome of deane of Paules, Iohn Fisher bishop of Rochester of whome ye haue heard before, Thomas More borne in London of whome mention likewise is made in the life of this famous king; William Horman borne in Salisburie viceprouost of Eaton college, a learned man, as by his works it appeareth; Iohn Frith borne in London, William Tindall, of which two persons ye haue heard likewise in the historie of this king; Robert Wakefield excellentlie seene in toongs, Iohn Rastall a citizen and stationer of London, Christopher Saint German an excelleut lawier, Robert Barnes of whom also we haue made mention before.

Sir Thomas Eliot knight, Edward Lée archbishop of Yorke, Iohn Leland a diligent searcher of antiquities, Anne Askew wrote certeine treatises concerning hir examinations, sir Iohn Bourchier knight lord Berners translated the chronicles of sir Iohn Froissard out of French into English, William Chubs, Henrie Standish a frier minor and bishop of saint Assaph wrote against Erasmus for his translation of the new testament, to his small praise as he handled the matter; Thomas surnamed Philomelus a Londoner an excellent poet, William Grocine verie expert in both toongs Gréeke and Latine, Thomas Spenser a Carmelitie frier borne in Norwich, Henrie Bullocke, William Latimer, Yoong a moonke of Ramseie, Arnold of London wrote certeine collections touching historicall matters, Thomas Lupset a Londoner a learned yoong man departed this life in the six and thirtith yeare of his age about the yeare of our Lord 1532, he wrote sundrie vertuous treatises; William Melton chancellor of Yorke, Iohn Sowle a Carmelite frier of London and a doctor of diuinitie, Iohn Batemanson a Charterhouse moonke & prior of his house at London, Richard Whitford.

Thomas Attour borne in Norffolke and fellow with Bilneie in suffering persecution vnder cardinall Wolseie, Henrie Bradshaw borne in Chester where he was professed a blacke moonke wrote the life of saint Werbourgh and a certeine chronicle, Iohn Palsgraue a citizen of London wrote instructions for the perfect vnderstanding of the French toong, Iohn Skuish a Cornishman wrote certeine abbreuiations of chronicles with a treatise of the warres of Troie, Anthonie Fitzherbert a iudge wrote an abridgement of the lawe, Iohn Littleton wrote also of the principles of the law but he liued before this season, Wilfride Holme wrote a treatise of the rebellion in Lincolneshire and in the North after the maner of a dialog, Iohn Constable an excellent poet and rhetorician, Iohn Hilier, Edward Fox student in the kings college in Cambridge was aduanced to the bishops sée of Hereford and was imploied in diuerse ambassages from king Henrie the seuenth both into Germanie and Italie.

Iohn Lambert aliàs Nichols borne in Norffolke, of whome yee haue heard in the historie of this king, how he suffered for the controuersie of the sacrament; George Fulberie, Iohn Hooker, Thomas Lanquet wrote an epitome of chronicles and also of the winning of Bullongne, Iohn Shepre, Leonard Cox wrote diuerse treatises, one in English rhetorike whereof Bale maketh no mention; Thomas Soulmon borne in the Ile of Gernseie verie studious in histories as by his writings and notes it appeareth, Iohn Longland bishop of Lincolne, Maurice Chancie a Charterhouse moonke, Cutbert Tunstall bishop of Duresme, Richard Samson, Alban Hill a Welshman an excellent physician, Richard Croke verie expert in the Gréeke toong, Robert Whittington borne in Staffordshire néere to Lichfield wrote diuerse treatises for the instruction of Grammarians, Iohn Aldrige bishop of Carleill, Iohn Russell gathered a treatise intituled Super iure Cæsaris & Papæ, he wrote also commentaries in Cantica; William Roie, Simon Fish a Kentishman borne wrote a booke called the supplication of beggers.

Iohn Powell and Edward Powell Welshmen wrote against Luther, Edward died in Smithfield for treason in denieng the kings supremacie in the yeare 1540; Iohn Houghton gouernour of the Charterhouse moonks in London died likewise for treason in the yeare a thousand fiue hundred thirtie and fiue; Iohn Rickes being an aged man, forsaking the order of a frier Minor, which he had first professed, imbraced the gospell; George Bullen lord Rochford, brother to quéene Anne, wrote diuerse songs and sonets; Francis Bigod knight borne in Yorkeshire wrote a booke against the cleargie intituled De impropriationibus, and translated certeine bookes from Latine into English, he died for rebellion in the yeare a thousand fiue hundred thirtie and seauen; Richard Wise, Henrie Morleie lord Morleie, wrote diuerse treatises, as comedies and tragedies, the life of sectaries, and certeine rithmes; William Boteuille aliàs Thin restored Chaucers workes by his learned and painfull corrections.

Iohn Smith sometime schoolemaister of Heiton, Richard Turpine borne of a worshipfull familie

familie in England & seruing in the garrison of Calis wrote a chronicle of his time, he died in the yéere a thousand fiue hundred fortie and one, and was buried in saint Nicholas church in Calis; Sir Thomas Wiat knight, in whose praise much might be said, as well for his learning as other excellent qualities meet for a man of his calling, he greattlie furthered to inrich the English toong, he wrote diuerse matters in English méeter, and translated the seauen penitentiall psalmes, and (as some write) the whole psalter, he died of the pestilence in the west countrie, being on his iourneie into Spaine, whither he was sent ambassadour from the king vnto the emperour, in the yeare a thousand fiue hundred fortie and one; Henrie Howard earle of Surrie, sonne to the duke of Norffolke, delighted in the like studies with sir Thomas Wiat wrote diuerse treatises also in English méeter, he suffered at Tower hill, as in the historie of this king before yée haue heard.

Iohn Field a citizen and lawyer of London wrote sundrie treatises, as his owne answers vnto certeine articles ministred to him by sir Thomas More, the bishop of Rochester, Rastall, and others; when he was in prison for religion, he wrote also a treatise of mans fréewill, De seruo hominis arbitrio, and collections of the common lawes of the land, &c: Tristram Reuell, Henrie Brinklow a merchant of London wrote a a little booke, which he published vnder the name of Roderike Mors, and also a complaint vpon London, &c: Robert Shingleton borne of a good familie in Lancashire wrote a treatise of the seauen churches, and other things, as of certeine prophesies, for the which (as some write) he suffered at London, being conuict of treason in the yeare 1544: William Parreie a Welshman wrote a booke intituled Speculum iuuenum.

Of strangers that liued here in this kings daies and for their works which they wrote were had in estimation, these we find recorded by maister Bale: Barnard Andreas a Frenchman, borne in Tolouse an Augustin Frier, and an excellent poet; Adrian de Castello, an Italian of Corneto a towne in Thuscaine, he was commended vnto king Henrie the seuenth by the archbishop Morton, and therevpon was first made bishop of Hereford, and after resigning that sée, was aduanced to Bath and Welles; Andreas Ammonius an Italian of the citie of Luca, secretarie to the king, wrote diuerse treatises; Iames Calco an Italian also of Pauia in Lumbardie, by profession a Carmelite frier, an earnest defender of the diuorse betwixt the king and the ladie Katharine Dowager, disproouing the marriage betwixt them to be in anie wise lawfull.

Thus farre the right high and renowmed Henrie the eight, sonne and successor to Henrie the seuenth.

EDWARD THE SIXT,

sonne and successor to Henrie the eight.

AFTER it had pleased almightie God to call to his mercie that famous prince king An. Reg. 1. Henrie the eight, the parlement as yet continuing, and now by his death dissolued, the executours of the said king, and other of the nobilitie, assembling themselues togither, did first by sound of trumpet in the palace of Westminster, and so through

London, cause his sonne and heire prince Edward to be proclamed king of this realme by the name of Edward the sixt, king of England, France, and Ireland, defender of the faith, and of the churches of England and Ireland the supreame head, he being yet but nine yeares and od moneths of age: he was thus proclamed the eight and twentith of Ianuarie, in the yeare of the world 5513, and after the birth of our Lord 1547, according to the accompt of them that begin the yeare at Christmasse: but after the accompt of the church of England, in the yeare 1546, about the nine and twentith yeare of the emperor Charles the fift, the three and thirtith of Francis the first of that name king of France, and in the fift yeare of the reigne of Marie quéene of Scotland.

1547

Shortlie herevpon the earle of Hertford with other of the lords resorted to Hatfield, where the yoong king then laie, from whence they conducted him with a great and right honorable companie to the Tower of London. During the time of his abode there, for the good gouernement of the realme, the honour and suertie of his maiesties person, his vncle Edward earle of Hertford, was by order of the councell, and the assent of his maiestie (as one most meetest to occupie that roome) appointed gouernour of his roiall person, and protector of his realmes, dominions and subiects, and so proclamed the first of Februarie by an herald at armes, and sound of trumpet through the citie of London in the vsuall places thereof, as it was thought expedient.

The sixt daie of Februarie the earle of Hertford lord protector adorned king Edward with the order of knighthood, remaining then in the Tower, and therewith the king standing vp, called for Henrie Hubblethorne lord maior of the citie of London, who comming before his presence, the king tooke the sword of the lord protector, and dubbed the said Hubblethorne knight, he being the first that euer he made. The seauenteenth of Februarie the lord protector was created duke of Summerset, the earle of Essex was created marquesse of Northampton, the lord Lisle high admerall of England was created earle of Warwike and high chamberlaine of England, sir Thomas Wriothesleie lord chancellour was created earle of Southampton, sir Thomas Seimer was aduanced to the honour of lord of Sudleie and high admerall of England, which office the earle of Warwike then resigned, sir Richard Rich was made lord Rich, and sir William Willoughbie was created lord Willoughbie of Parrham, sir Edmund Sheffield was made lord Sheffield of Butterwike; and as saith a late writer of this action:

Vt quisque est ditione potentior, auctus honore,
Et noua virtutis sumens insignia fulget.

At the same time great preparation was made for the kings coronation, so that the foure and twentith of Februarie next insuing, his maiestie came from the Tower, and so rode through London vnto Westminster, with as great roialtie as might be, the stréets being hoong, and pageants in diuerse places erected, to testifie the good willes of the citizens, reioising that it had pleased God to deale so fauourablie with the English nation to grant them such a towardlie yoong prince to their king and souereigne thus to succéed in place of his noble father. ¶ Now as he rode through London toward Westminster, and passed on the south part of Pauls churchyard, an Argosine came from the battlements of the stéeple of Paules church vpon a cable, being made fast to an anchor by the deanes gate, lieng on his breast, aiding himselfe neither with hand nor foot, and after ascended to the middest of the cable where he tumbled and plaied manie pretie toies, whereat the king and the nobles had good pastime.

The morrow after being Shrouesundaie and the fiue and twentith of Februarie, his coronation was solemnized in due forme and order, with all the roialtie and honour which therevnto apperteined. Shortlie after the coronation, to wit, the sixt of March, the erle of Southampton, lord chancellour of England, for his too much repugnancie (as was reported) in matters of councell to the residue of the councellors about the
king,

king, was not onelie depriued of his office of chancellor, but also remooued from his The lord chancellor discharged of his roome. place and authoritie in councell, and the custodie of the great scale was taken from him, and deliuered vnto sir William Paulet lord Saint-Iohn, that was lord great maister of the kings housbold.

Also shortlie after his coronation, the kings maiestie by the aduise of his vncle the lord protector and other of his priuie councell, minding first of all to séeke Gods honor and glorie, and therevpon intending a reformation, did not onelie set foorth by certeine commissioners, sundrie iniunctions for the remoouing of images out of all churches, to the suppressing and auoiding of idolatrie and superstition within his realmes and dominions, but also caused certeine homilies or sermons to be drawne by Homilies. sundrie godlie & learned men, that the same might be read in churches to the people, which were afterward by certeine of these commissioners sent foorth as visitors, accompanied with certeine preachers, thoroughout the realme, for the better instruction of the people, published and put in vse. At Easter next following, he set out also an The communion in both kinds. order thorough all the realme, that the supper of the Lord should be ministred to the laie people in both kinds. ¶ On the fiftéenth of Maie doctor Smith recanted at Paules *I. S. pag.* 1036. D. Smith recanted. crosse.]

All these things doone concerning religion (as before is said) the lord protector and the rest of the councell, calling to mind the euill dealing and craftie dissimulation of the Scots, concerning the matter of marriage betwixt the kings maiestie, and the quéene of Scotland (which marriage as ye haue heard, in the fiue and thirtith yeare of king Henrie the eight, was by authoritie of parlement in Scotland fullie concluded) thought it not to stand with the kings honor to be in such maner by them deluded, and withall considering how greatlie it shuld turne to the quietnesse and safetie of both realmes to haue these two princes conioined in matrimonie, they did deuise sundrie waies and meanes how the same might be brought to passe, and the rather (as some doo write) for that king Henrie (before his death) had *Rich. Grafton.* giuen them in speciall charge by all indeuours to procure that the said marriage might take place, as wholie wishing by the coniunction of those two yoong princes, the vniting of the two kingdoms in perpetuall amitie and faithfull league of loue; as our poet saith:

Optat coniugio duo regna coire fideli,
Aeternam pacem hinc æternàque fœdera iungi.

But the lords of Scotland were so inueigled and corrupted by the French king, and abused by cardinall Beton, archbishop of saint Andrewes, and other of their clergie, that they not onelie shranke from that which they had promised, but also sought to destroie those that fauored the king of Englands part: wherevpon a great and puissant armie was now prepared to passe by land into Scotland, and likewise a nauie to passe by sea to attend vpon the same: whereof the great gallie and foure and twentie tall ships were thoroughlie furnished with men and munition for the warres, besides manie merchants ships and other small vessels, which serued for carriage of vittels, and other necessaries.

But now to shew what noble men and other were ordeined officers, and assigned to haue the conduction as well of the armie by land, as of the fleete by sea; ye shall Chiefteines in the armie. vnderstand, that first the duke of Summerset, lord protector, tooke vpon him to go himselfe in person, as generall of the whole armie, and capteine also of the battell or middle-ward, wherin were foure thousand footmen. The marshall erle of Warwike appointed lord lieutenant of the same armie, led the foreward conteining thrée thousand footmen. The lord Dacres gouerned in the rere-ward, wherein were other thrée thousand footmen. The lord Greie of Wilton was ordeined high marshall of the said armie & capteine generall of all the horssemen, being in number

number six thousand. Sir Rafe Sadler knight treasuror of the armie. Sir Francis Brian knight, capteine of the light horssemen, in number two thousand.

Sir Rafe Vane knight lieutenant of all the men of armes and demilances. Sir Thomas Darcie knight capteine of all the kings maiesties pensioners, and men at armes. Sir Richard Leigh knight deuiser of the fortifications. Sir Peter Mewtas knight capteine of the harquebutters, which were in number six hundred. Sir Peter Gamboa knight, capteine of two hundred harquebutters on horssebacke. Sir Francis Fleming knight was master of the ordinance. Sir George Blaag & sir Thomas Holcroft commissioners of the musters. Edward Shelleie, the lord Greies lieuteuant of the men of armes of Bullongne, who was the first that gaue the onset in the daie of battell, and died most honorablie in the same. Iohn Brenne capteine of the pioners being in number a thousand foure hundred. Thomas Audeleie and Edward Chamberleine harbengers of the field.

The lord Edward Clinton admerall of the fléet: sir William Woodhouse knight his viceadmerall. There were in the armie of great ordinance fiftéene peeces, and of carriages nine hundred carts, beside manie wagons, whereof the commissarie generall was George Ferrers. As soone as the armie by land was in a readinesse, and set forward to come to Berwike at a daie appointed, the nauie likewise tooke the sea, and by the helpe of Gods good guiding had so prosperous speed in their passage, that they arriued at Berwicke in time conuenient, whither vpon the thirtith of August being tuesdaie, the lord protector came, and laie in the castell with sir Nicholas Strelleie knight, capteine there. The next daie commandement was giuen that euerie man should prouide himselfe for foure daies vittels to be caried foorth with them in carts.

On thursdaie the first of September the lord protector, not with manie more than with his owne band of horssemen, rode to a towne standing on the sea coast, a six miles from Berwike within Scotland called Aimouth, whereat there runneth a riuer into the sea, which he caused to be sounded, and finding the same well able to serue for an hauen, caused afterwards a fortresse to be raised there, appointing Thomas Gower, that was marshall of Berwike, to be capteine thereof. On fridaie, all sauing the councell departed the towne of Berwike, and incamped a two flight shoots off, by the sea side, toward Scotland. And the same daie the lord Clinton with his fléet tooke the seas from Berwike, to the end that in case the wind should not serue them to keepe course with the armie by land; yet were it but with the driuing of tides, they might vpon anie néed of munition or vittels be still at hand, or not long from them.

The same daie the earle of Warwike, and sir Rafe Sadler treasuror of the armie, came to Berwike from Newcastell, where they had staid till then, for the full dispatch of the rest of the armie, and the next daie the earle of Warwike incamped in field with the armie.

On which daie a proclamation with sound of trumpet was made by an herald in thrée seuerall places of the campe, signifieng the cause of the comming of the kings armie at that present into Scotland, which in effect was, to aduertise all the Scotish nation, that their comming was not to depriue them of their liberties, but to aduance the marriage alreadie concluded and agréed vpon betwixt the kings maiestie of England and their quéene, and no hostilitie ment to such as should shew themselues furtherers thereof. On the fourth of September being sundaie, the lord protector came from out of the towne, and the armie raised, and marched that daie a six miles, and camped by a village called Rostan in the baronrie of Boukendall.

The order of their march was this. Sir Francis Brian capteine of the light horssemen, with foure hundred of his band, tended to the skout a mile or two before. The carriages kept along the sea coast, and the men at armes and demilances diuided into thrée troops, answering the thrée wards, rid in arraie directlie against the cariages a

two

two flight shoots asunder from them. The thrée foot battels kept order in place betwixt them both. The fore-ward foremost, the battell in the middest, the rere-ward
hindermost, ech ward hauing his troope of horssemen and gard of ordinance, his aid
of pioners for amendment of waies, where néed should be. The fift of September The Peaths.
they marched an eight miles, vntill they came to the Peaths, a clough or vallie, running for a six miles west streight eastward, and toward the sea a twentie score brode
from banke to banke aboue, and a fiue score in the bottome, wherein runnes a little
riuer. Stéepe is this vallie on either side, and déepe in the bottome.

The Scots had cast trenches ouerthwart the side waies on either side, in manie places,
to make the passage more cumbersome: but by the pioners the same were soone filled,
and the waie made plaine, that the armie, carriage, & ordinance were quite set ouer
soone after sun set, & there they pitched downe their campe. Whilest the armie was
thus passing ouer this cumbersome passage, an herald was sent from the lord protector, An English
herald sent from
to summon a castell, that stood at the end of the same vallie, a mile from the place the lord pro-
where they passed downe towards the sea. Matthew Hume capteine thereof, a bro- tector to sum-
thers sonne of the lord Humes, vpon his summons required to speake with the lord mon a castell.
protector. It was granted, and he came, whome the lord protector handled in such
sort with effectuall words, putting him in choise whether he would yeeld, or stand to
the aduenture, to haue the place woone of him by force, that he was contented to
render all at his graces pleasure.

And so being commanded to go fetch his companie out of the house, he went and
brought them, being in all one and twentie persons. The capteine and six other
were staied and commanded to the kéeping of the marshall, the residue were suffered to depart whither they thought good. After this surrender, the lord Iohn
Greie brother to the marques Dorset, was appointed to seize & take possession of the
house, being capteine of a great number of demilances, as for his approoued worthinesse and valiancie right well he might, agréeable to the deserued report remaining of
him in print in forren spéech as followeth:

――――Graius heros
Ob summam belli cataphractis præfuit artem.

The spoile was not rich sure, but of white bread, oten cakes, and Scotish ale indifferent good store, and soone bestowed among my lords soldiors; for swords, bucklers, pikes, pots, pans, yarne, linnen, hempe, and heaps of such baggage, which the
countrie people there about had brought into that pile, to haue it in more suretie, the
soldiors would scarse vouchsafe to stoope and take the same vp.

In the meane time the lord protector appointed the house to be ouerthrowne, which The castell of
by the capteine of the pioners was doone, though with some trauell, by reason the Dunglas ouer-
walles were so thicke, and the foundation so déepe, and thereto set vpon so craggie a throwne,
a plot. Tuesdaie the sixt of September, the armie dislodged and marched forward.
In the waie as they should go, a mile and an halfe from Dunglas northward were two Thornton.
piles or holds, Thornton & Anderwike, set both on craggie foundations, & diuided a Anderwike.
stones cast a sunder by a déepe gut, wherein ran a little riuer. Thornton belonged to
the lord Hume, and was kept by one Thom Trotter, who vpon summons giuen him Thom Trotter.
to render the house, lockt vp a sixteene poore soules like the soldiors of Dunglas fast
within the house, tooke the keies with him, commanding them to defend the place
till his returne, which should be on the morrow, with munition and reléefe: and
this doone, he and his prickers prickt (as saith master Patten) quite their waies.

Anderwike perteined to the lord of Hambleton, and was kept by his son and heire, The lord of
whome of customs they call the master of Hambleton, & eight more gentlemen for the Hambleton.
most part, as was reported. The lord protector at his comming nigh, sent vnto both
these places, which vpon summons refusing to render, were streight assailed;
Thornton by batterie of foure great péeces of ordinance, and certeine of sir Peter
Mewtas

Mewtas hackbutters, and Anderwike by a sort of the same hackbutters, who so well bestirred them, that where these keepers had rammed vp their outer doores, cloied and stopt their staires within, and kept themselues for defense of their house about the battlements, the hackbutters got in, and fired them vnderneath, whereby being greatlie troubled with smoke, they cried for mercie, which the lord protector meant to grant them; but yer the messenger came, the hackbutters were got vp to them, & killed eight of them aloft: one leapt ouer the walles, and running more than a furlong, was after slaine without in a water.

The pile of Anderwike woone.

All this while at Thornton was the assault on the English part, and the defense by them within stoutlie continued: but at length when they perceiued in what danger they stood, and how little able they were to helpe themselues, or to annoie the assailants, they pluckt in a banner which they had hoong forth, in token of defiance, and put foorth a white linnen clout tied to a stickes end, crieng all with one tune for mercie: but hauing answer by the whole voices of the assailers that they were traitors, and that it was too late, they pluckt in their sticke, and set vp againe their banner of defiance, and shot off, hurled stones, & did what else they could with great courage of their side, & small hurt of the assailants. Wherefore perceiuing that they could not long kéepe out, being on the one side battered, and mined on the other, kept in with hackbutters on ech side, and some of the Englishmen being got into the house below, for they hauing shopt vp themselues also in the highest of their house, pluckt in againe their banner, and cried eftsoones for mercie, but being answered generallie by the assailants, that they should neuer looke for it, they fell to make this petition, that if they should needs die, they might rather suffer by hanging, and so reconcile themselues to God, than to die in malice with so great danger of their soules.

Sir Miles Partrige.

Thornton yéelded.

The piles of Thornton and others defaced.

This sute was so furthered to the dukes grace by sir Miles Partrige that was néere at hand when they made this sute, that it was granted; and they comming foorth, humbled themselues, and without more hurt they were but commanded to the prouost marshall, who kept them for a time, and were after released. The house was shortlie after so blowen with pouder, that more than the one halfe of it fell streight downe to dust and rubbish, the rest stood all to shaken with rifts and chinks. Anderwike also was burned, and all the houses of office, and stacks of corne about them both. While this was in dooing the dukes grace, in turning but about, saw the fall of Dunglas, which likewise was vndermined and blowen vp with pouder.

This doone, about noone the armie marched, and passing by Dunbar, the castell sent them diuerse shots of artillerie, but all in vaine. The Scotish prickers shewed themselues in the field with proffer of skirmish, but to no great purpose, one of them being killed with a shot of one of Barteuils men an hackbutter on horssebacke. The armie hauing marched that daie a ten miles, lodged at night néere vnto Tantallon, and had a blind alarum. Marching the next morning a two miles, they came to a riuer called Lin, where there is a stone bridge, named Linton bridge of a towne thereby on the right hand as the armie marched, and standing eastward vpon the same riuer: the horssemen and carriages passed thorough the water, for it was not verie deepe, and the footmen ouer the bridge. The passage was streict for an armie, and therfore the longer in setting ouer.

Cantallon.

Linton bridge.

Beyond this bridge about a mile westward vpon the same riuer, on the south side standeth a proper castell called Hailes, perteining to the earle of Bothwell, but kept as then by the gouernors appointment, who held the earle in prison. Out of this castell as the lord protector passed forward in following the fore-ward, there were roundlie shot off (but without hurt) six or seuen péeces, the which before that (though some of the armie had beene verie nigh) yet kept they all couert. In the meane time rose a thicke mist, which caused a great disorder in the rere-ward, by reason they could not

Hailes castell.

sée

sée about them.　The earle of Warwike therefore doubting least the enimies, who had béen pricking vp and downe néere to the armie, and offered skirmish the same morning, should now by occasion of the mist attempt some feat to the annoiance of the Englishmen in their passage, his lordship himselfe scant with sixtéene horsses (whereof Barteuill, and Iohn de Ribaud Frenchmen were two, seuen or eight light horssemen more, and the rest being his owne seruants) returned toward the passage to sée the arraie againe.

The Scotish horssemen perceiuing our horssemen to haue passed on before, and thinking (as the truth was) that some capteine of honor did staie for the looking to the order of this rere-ward, they kéeping the south side of the riuer, did call ouer to some of the armie, to know whether there were anie noble man nigh there? They were asked whie they asked? One of them answered, that he was such a one whose name the Englishmen knew to be honorable among the Scots, and would come in to the dukes grace, so that he might be sure to come in safetie.　Some yoong soldiers nothing suspecting the craftie falshood of the Scots, told him that the earle of Warwike was nigh there, by whose tuition he should be safelie brought to my lord protectors presence.　They had cand their lesson & fell to their practise, which was this. Hauing come ouer the water, in the waie as the earle should passe, they had cowched about two hundred of their prickers, and had sent fortie beside to search where my lord was, whome when they had found, part of them prickt verie nigh, whome ten or twelue of the earles small companie did boldlie incounter, and droue them well-nigh home to their ambush, fléeing perchance not so much for feare as for falshood, to bring them within their danger.　But hereby informed that the earle was so nigh, they sent out a bigger number, and kept the rest more secret vpon this purpose, that they might either by a plaine onset distresse him, or else by fainting of flight to have trained him within danger of their ambush.　And thus instructed, they came pricking toward his lordship apase.　Whie (quoth he) & will not these knaues be ruled? Giue me my staffe.　The which then with so valiant a courage he charged at one (as it was thought) Dandie Car, a capteine among them, that he did not onelie compell Car to turne, and himselfe chased him aboue twelue score togither, all the waie at the speares point, so that if Cars horsse had not beene excéeding good and wight, his lordship had surelie run him through in this race, but also with his little band caused all the rest to flee amaine. After whome as Henrie Wane, a gentleman of the said earles, and one of his companie did fiercelie pursue foure or fiue Scots, suddenlie turned, and set vpon him, and though they did not altogither escape his hands free, yet by hewing and mangling his head, bodie, and manie places else, they did so cruellie intreat him, as if rescue had not come the sooner, they had slaine him outright.　Here was Barteuill run at sideling, and hurt in the buttocke, and one of the Englishmen slaine : of Scots againe none slaine, but thrée taken prisoners, wherof one was Richard Maxwell, and hurt in the thigh; who had béene long in England not long before, and had receiued right manie benefits, both of the late kings liberalitie, and of the earle of Warwike, and of manie other nobles and gentlemen in the court beside.

But to conclude, if the earle of Warwike had not thus valiantlie incountred them, yer they could haue warned their ambush how weaklie he was garded, he had béene beset round about by them yer he could haue bin aware of them, or rescued of other. Whereas hereby his lordship vndoubtedlie shewed his woonted valor, saued his companie, and discomfited the enimie.　As Barteuill the Frenchman that daie had right honestlie serued, so did the lords right honorablie acquite it: for the earle of Warwike did get him a surgion, and dressed he was, streight after laid and conueied in the lord protectors owne chariot.　The rest that were hurt were here also drest, Scots and others.

Sidenotes:

A subtile practise of the Scots.

The manlie courage of the earle of Warwike.

Dandie Car.

Henrie Wane.

Barteuill hurt.

Richard Maxwell taken.

The armie hauing marched that same daie nine miles, incamped at night by a towne
standing on the Frith called Lang Nuddreie. The next morning being thursdaie the
eight of September, in time of the dislodging of the English campe, signe was made
to some of the ships (whereof the most part and chiefest laie a ten or twelue miles in
the Forth, beyond vs, ouer against Lieth & Edenborough) that the lord admerall
should come a shore, to speake with the lord protector. In the meane time, somewhat
earlie as our gallie was comming toward vs, about a mile and more beyond our campe,
the Scots were verie busie, wafting here on shore toward them with a banner of saint
George that they had, so to traine them to come on land there: but the earle of Warwike soone disappointed the policie, for making toward that place where the lord admerall should come on shore, the Englishmen on the water by the sight of his presence, did soone discerne their friends from their foes.

The lord admerall herevpon came to land, and riding backe with the earle vnto the
Order taken
for the placing
of the ships.   lord protector, order was taken, that the great ships should remoue from before
Lieth, and come to lie before Muskelborough; and the Scotish campe which laie
there in field alreadie assembled, to resist the English power that marched thus towards them. The smaller vessels that were vittelers were appointed to lie néerer to
the armie. The lord admerall herevpon, being returned to the water, & the armie
marching onward a mile or two, there appéered aloft on a hill, that laie longwise east
and west, and on the south side of them, vpon a six hundred of their horssemen
The Scotish
prickers shew
themselues.   prickers, wherof some within a flight shoot, directlie against the Englishmen, shewed
themselues vpon the same hill, & more further off.

Toward these, ouer a small bridge that laie ouer a little riuer there, verie hardlie
did ride about a dozen harquebutters on horssebacke, and held them at baie so nie to
their noses, that whether it were by the goodnesse of the same harquebutters, or the
badnesse of them, the Scots did not onelie not come downe to them, but also verie
courteouslie gaue place, and fled to their fellowes. The armie went on, but so much
the slowlier, bicause the waie was somewhat narrow, by meanes of the Forth on the
one side, and certeine marishes on the other. The Scots kept alwaies pase with them,
till there were shot off two field peeces twise, wherewith there was a man killed, and
the leg of one of their horsses striken off, which caused them to withdraw, so that
the Englishmen saw no more of them, till they came to the place where they meant to
incampe, for there they shewed themselues againe aloft on the fore remembred hill,
standing as it were to view and take muster of the armie: but when the lord Greie
made towards them, minding to know their commission, they wiselie went their waie,
and would not once abide the reasoning.

Little else was doone that daie, but that George Ferrers, one of the duke of Summersets gentlemen, and one of the commissioners of the cariages in the armie,
perceiuing where certeine Scots were got into a caue vnder the earth, stopping some
Scots smothered
in a caue.   of the vents, and setting fire on the other, smothered them to death, as was thought
it could be none other, by coniecture of the smoke breaking forth at some of the
other vents. The English ships also taking their leaue from before Lieth, with a score
of shot or more, and as they came by saluting the Scots in their campe also, with as
manie, came and laie according to appointment. The armie hauing marched this daie
Salt Preston.   about a fiue miles, incamped at Salt Preston by the Forth. On fridaie the ninth of
September, the English armie lieng in sight & view of the Scotish campe, that laie
two miles or therabouts from them, had the Forth on the north, and the hill last re-
Fauxside Braie.   membered on the south, the west end whereof is called Fauxside Braie, on the which
standeth a sorie castell, and halfe a score houses of like worthinesse by it, and had
westward before the Englishmen, the Scots lieng in campe. About a mile from the
English campe were the Scots horsemen verie busie, pranking vp and downe, & faine
would haue béene a counsell with the Englishmens doings; who againe, bicause the
                                                                                            Scots

Scots seemed to sit to receiue them, did diligentlie prepare that they might soone go to them, and therefore kept within their campe all that daie.

　The lord protector and the councell sitting in consultation, the capteines and officers prouiding their bands, store of vittels, and furniture of weapons, for furtherance whereof our vessels of munition and vittels were here alreadie come to the shore. The Scots continued their brauerie on the hill, the which the Englishmen not being so well able to beare, made out a band of light horssemen, and a troope of demilances to backe them: the Englishmen and strangers that serued among them, got vp aloft on the hill, and thereby of euen ground with the enimie rode streight toward them with good spéed and order, whom at the first the Scots did boldlie countenance and abide: but after, when they perceiued that our men would néeds come forward, they began to pricke, and would faine haue béene gone, yer they had told their errand. But the Englishmen hasted so spéedilie after, that euen streight they were at their elbowes, and did so stoutlie then bestirre them, that what in the onset at the first, The Scots horssemen discomfited and put to flight. and after in the chase, which lasted a thrée miles welnie to as far as the furthest of their campe on the south side, they had killed of the Scots within a thrée houres, Scots slaine. aboue the number of thirtéene hundred, and taken the maister of Hume, the lords Prisoners taken. Humes sonne and heire, two priests and six gentlemen, whereof one by sir Iaques Granado, and all vpon the highest and welnéere nighest of the hill toward the Scots, within the full sight of their whole campe.

　On the English part one Spanish haquebutter hurt, and taken sir Rafe Bulmer Englishmen taken. knight, Thomas Gower marshall of Berwike, and Robert Crouch, all capteins of seuerall bands of the English light horssemen, and men of right good courage and approued seruice, & at this time distressed by their owne too much forwardnesse, and not by the enimies force. To conclude, of fiftéene hundred horssemen for skirmish, and fiue hundred footmen to lie close in ambush, and to be readie at néed, which came that morning out of their campe, there returned not home aboue seuen hundred, and diuerse of those sore hurt, and among other, the lord Hume himselfe, for hast The lord Hume hurt with a fall in the chase. in the flight, had a fall from his horsse, and burst the canell bone of his necke, that he was faine to be caried streight to Edenborough, and finallie there departed this life of that hurt. So that it is true which C. O. saith, that in this skirmish manie a good rider was dismounted, their horsses with emptie saddles and loose bridles running vp hill and downe dale, as if they had beene starke mad, and to conclude (saith he)

　　　——— equi lapsurus inhæsit
　　　Tergo alius summo tellurem vertice pulsans.
　Then after this, the lord protector, and the earle of Warwike, and other of the councell, with a small gard, mounting vp the hill where the slaughter had béene made, about halfe a mile southeast from the Scotish campe, tooke full view thereof, the plot where they laie, so chosen for strength, as in all their countrie (some thought) not a better, saue on the south by a great marish, & on the north by the Forth, which side they fenced with two field péeces, and certeine haquebutters a crooke, lieng vnder a turffe wall, Edenborough on the west at their backes, and eastward betwéene the Englishmen and them stronglie defended by the course of a riuer called Eske, running north into the Forth, which as it was not verie déepe of water, so were the bankes of it so high and stéepe, as a small sort of resistants might haue béene able to kéepe downe a great number of commers vp. About a twelue score from the Forth, ouer the same riuer, is there a stone bridge, which they did kéepe also well garded with ordinance.

　When the lord protector, and the earle of Warwike had viewed euerie thing, as they thought expedient, they returned home towards their campe, alongst before the campe of the enimies, within lesse than two flight shoots, entring into a lane of

　　　　　　　　　　　　　　　　　　　thirtie

thirtie foot broad, fensed on either side with a wall of turffe, an ell of height. The Scots did often shoot at them in the waie as they passed thus homewards, without hurt, sauing the killing of an horsse among thrée hundred, the rider escaping else

A Scotish herald deliuereth a message to the duke of Summerset.

harmelesse. And as the dukes grace was passed welnie halfe the waie homewards, a Scotish herald with a cote of his princes armes vpon him (as the maner is) and with him a trumpetter, ouertooke them.

The herald declaring this message to the lord protector, pretended to come from the gouernour, to inquire of prisoners taken, and therewith to proffer honest conditions of peace. And after he had told his tale, then began the trumpetter, and said, how he was sent from the earle of Huntleie: " My lord my maister (saith he) hath willed me to shew your grace, that bicause this matter maie be the sooner ended, and with lesse hurt, he will fight with your grace for the whole quarell, twentie to twentie, ten to ten, or else himselfe alone with your grace man to man." The lord protector hauing kept with him the lord lieutenant, had heard them both throughlie, and then in answering, spake somewhat with lowder voice, than they had doone their messages. Wherevpon they that were the riders by, thinking that his grace would haue it no secret, were somewhat the bolder to come néerer, the words whereof

The lord protectors answer.

were vttered so expeditelie with honour, and so honourablie with expedition, that the standers by were mooued to doubt whether they might rather note in them the promptnesse of a singular prudence, or the boldnesse of a noble courage: and they were thus.

" Your gouernour maie know, that the speciall cause of our comming hither was not to fight, but for the thing that should be the weale, both of vs and you. For God we take to record, we mind no more hurt to the realme of Scotland, than we doo to the realme of England, and therefore our quarell being so good, we trust God will prosper vs the better. But as for peace, he hath refused such conditions at our hands, as we will neuer proffer againe: and therefore let him looke for none, till this waie we make it: and thou trumpetter, saie to thy maister, he seemeth to lacke wit so to make this chalenge to me, being of such estate, by the sufferance of God, as to haue so weightie a charge of so pretious a iewell, the gouernance of a kings person, & then the protection of all his realmes, whereby in this case I haue no power of my selfe, which if I had, as I am true gentleman, it should be the first bargaine I would make: but there be a great sort amongst vs his equals, to whome hee might haue made this chalenge without refusall."

The earle of Warwikes request and message to the earle of Huntleie.

Then quoth the lord lieutenant to them both, " He sheweth his small wit to make this chalenge to my lords grace, and he so meane, but if his grace will giue me leaue, I shall receiue it: and trumpetter bring me word thy maister will so doo, and thou shalt haue of me an hundred crownes." " Naie (quoth my lords grace) the earle of Huntleie is not meet in estate with you, my lord: but herald saie to the gouernor, and him also, that we haue béene a good season in this countrie, and are here now but with a sober companie, and they a great number, and if they will méet vs in field, they shall be satisfied with fighting inough: and herald bring me word if they will so doo, and by my honour I will giue the a thousand crownes. Ye haue a proud sort among you, but I trust to sée your pride abated shortlie, and of the erle Huntleies too: I wis he is a glorious yoong gentleman."

This said, the earle of Warwike continued his request, that he might receiue this chalenge: but the lord protector would in no wise grant it. These messengers had

The order of war touching heralds violated.

their answers, and therewith leaue to depart. The Scots in midst of this message, dooing contrarie to the order of warre, which as it granteth safetie to heralds and trumpetters, to passe betwixt armie and armie: so during the time of anie such message, as this was, hostilitie on both parts ought to ceasse, but it skilled not. On the morow after, they had their guns taken from them (as saith maister Patten) and put into their hands that could vse them with more good maner. But now concerning

ing

ing the message of the herald, it was thought that he was sent therewith, not for that it was beléeued of them, that it would be accepted; but rather that whilest he was dooing his errand, he might surueie the English power: or else for that vpon refusall of the offer, they might vse the victorie (whereof they accounted themselues assured) with more crueltie.

Of nothing they doubted more, than least the Englishmen would haue béene gone The vaine doubt of the Scots. backe, and gotten to the water, before they should haue incountered them, and therefore they had appointed to haue giuen the English armie a camisado in the night before the daie of the battell: but peraduenture, vnderstanding that the Englishmen had warning of their intention, and were prouided for them if they had come, they staied and came not at all. But in the morning, they were vp verie timelie, and being put in order of battell, they marched streight towards the English campe, against whome then, though they saw the English horssemen readilie to make: yet could not be persuaded, but that it was for a policie to staie them, till the English footmen and cariages might fullie be bestowed a shipboord, and that for the same purpose the English ships were come backe from before Lieth.

In the night of this daie, the dukes grace appointed, that earlie in the next morning Ordinance pláted against the enimie. part of the ordinance should be planted in the lane (wherof mention before is made) vnder the turfe of the wall, next to their campe, and some also to be set vpon the hill nie to Vndreske church afore-remembered: and this to the intent we should with our shot cause them either whollie to remooue their campe, or else much to annoie them in that place where they laie. It was not the least of the Englishmens meaning also to win from them certeine of their ordinance, that laie néerest vnto this church. And herewith the same morning, being the tenth of September, and Saturday, some-Saturday, the tenth of September, the daie of the battell. what before eight of the clocke, the English armie dislodged, & marched streight toward the church of Vndreske, as well for intent to haue incamped neere the same, as for placing their ordinance, and other considerations afore remembred.

The Scots either for feare of the Englishmens departing, or hope of their spoiling, were out of their campe comming toward them, passed the riuer, gathered in araie, and well néere at this church, yer the Englishmen were halfe waie to it, so quite disappointing the Englishmens purpose. Which at the first séemed verie strange in their eies, as altogither beside their expectation, as they that thought they would neuer haue forsaken their strength, to méet them in the field. But after it was knowne that they did not onelie thus purpose to doo, but also to haue assailed them in their campe, as they laie if they had not béene stirring the timelier, and hauing caused all their tents to be let flat downe to the ground, yer they came out, bicause none should lie lurking behind them in their campe, and as well the nobles as other, leauing their horsses behind them (except such as were appointed to serue on horsse-backe) marched on with their souldiors on foot.

They came spéedilie forwards on both sides, the one till then no whit aware of the The Englishmen & Scots march the one armie toward the other. The gallie. The Irish archers. others intent: but the Scots indeed with a rounder pase betweene two hillocks, betwixt the Englishmen and the church, mustred somewhat brim, at whome as they staied, the English gallie shot off, & slue the maister of Greime, with fiue and twentie others néere by him, and therewith so skard foure thousand Irish archers, brought by the earle of Argile, that where (as it was said) they should haue béene a a wing to the fore-ward, they could neuer after be made to come forward. Hervpon did their armie hastilie remooue, and from thence declining southward, tooke their direct waie toward Fauxside braie. Of this, sir Rafe Vane, lieutenant of all the English horssemen, first of all, or with the first, noting it, quicklie aduertised the lord protector, who thereby did readilie conceiue their meaning, which was to win the hill, and thereby the wind and sunne, the gaine of which thrée things (as is thought) whether partie in fight of battell can hap to obteine, hath his force doubled against his enimie.

In

In all this enterprise, they vsed for haste so little the helpe of horsse, that they plucked foorth their ordinance by draught of men, which at that present began freelie to shoot off towards the English armie, whereby it was perceiued they ment

more than a skirmish. Herewith euerie man began to applie himselfe in his charge and dutie which he had to doo. And herewith the lord protector, and other of the councell on horssebacke as they were, fell streight in consultation. The sharpenesse of whose ciscumspect wisedoms, as it quicklie espied out the enimies intents, so did it among other things promptlie prouide therin remedie, to preuent them (as néedfull it was) for the time asked no leisure.

Their deuise was, that the lord Greie of Wilton, marshall of the armie, with his band of Bulleners, and with the lord protectors band, and the earle of Warwikes, all to the number of eightéene hundred horssemen, on the left hand on the east halfe, and sir Rafe Vane, with sir Thomas Darcie capteine of the pensioners, and men of armes, and the lord Fitzwaters, with his band of demilances, all to the number of sixtéene hundred, to be readie and euen with the lord marshall, on the west halfe. And thus all these togither afore to incounter the enimies afront, whereby either to breake their araie, and that waie to weaken their power by disorder, or at the least to stop them of their gate, and force them to staie, while the fore-ward might wholie haue the hilles side, and the battell and rere-ward be placed in grounds next that in order, and best for aduantage. And after this, that the same horssemen should retire vp to the hilles side to come downe in order afresh, and infest them on both sides, whilest the foot battels should occupie them in fight afront.

Which enterprise, though it séemed right dangerous to the assailers, yet was it not more wiselie deuised by the councell, than valiantlie and willinglie executed of the lord marshall, & the others. For euen there taking their leaues of the councell, the said lord marshall requiring onelie, that if it went not well with him, the dukes grace would be good to his wife & children, he said he would méet those Scots, and so with their bands the foresaid capteins tooke their waie, and made towards the enimie. By this time were the fore-wards on either part aduanced within two flight shoots in sunder. The Scots came on so fast, that it was thought of the most part of the English-men, they were rather horssemen than footmen. The Englishmen againe were led the more with speed, to shew that they were as willing as the Scots to trie the battell. The master of the ordinance to their great aduantage pluckt vp the hill at that instant certeine péeces, and soone after planted two or thre canons of them welnigh vpon the top there, wherby hauing so much the helpe of the hill, he might ouer the Eng-lishmens heads shoot niest at the enimie. As the lord protector had so circumspectlie taken order for the araie and station of the armie, and for the execution of euerie mans office beside, he being perfectlie appointed in faire armour, accompanied onelie with sir Thomas Chaloner knight, one of the clearkes of the kings priuie councell, got him to the hight of the hill, to tarrie by the ordinance, where hée might best surueie the whole field, and succour with aid where most he saw néed, and also by his presence to be a defense to the thing that stood weakest in place, and also most in daunger, the which how much it stood in stead, anon ye shall heare further.

As he was halfe vp the hill, the erle of Warwike was ware the enimies were all at a sudden staie, and stood still a good while, so that it séemed to him that they per-ceiuing now their owne follie in leauing their ground of aduantage, had no will to come anie further forward, but gladlie would haue bin whence they came. The rea-sons were these. First bicause at that time, beside the full muster of the English foot-men, of whome they thought there had béene none there in field, but all to haue béene either shipt, or a shipping; then they saw plaine that the Englishmen were sure to haue the gaine of the hill, and they the ground of disaduantage out of their hold, and put from their hope: and hereto, for that their herald gaue the lord protector

no

no warning, the which by him (if they had ment to fight it out) who would not haue presumed that for the estimation of their honor, they would little haue stucke to haue sent; and he againe, and it had beene but for his thousand crowns, would right gladlie haue brought? Well yet how so euer their meaning changed, finallie considering belike the state they stood in, that as they had left their strength too soone, so now to be too late to repent, vpon a change of countenance, they made hastilie forward againe, and (as it séemed) with no lesse stoutnesse of courage, than stronglie in order, whose maner, armour, weapon, and order in fight in those daies and also before (though now somewhat changed as well as amongest other nations) was as insueth.

Harquebutters had they few, and appointed their fight most commonlie alwaies on foot. They vsed to come to the field well furnished, with iacke and skull, dagger, buckler, and swords, all notablie brode and thin, of excéeding good temper, and vniuersallie so made to slice, as hard it is to deuise the better: hereto euerie man his pike, and a great kercher wrapped twise or thrise about his necke, not for cold but for cutting. In their araie toward the ioining with the enimie, they thrust so nie in the fore-ranke, shoulder to shoulder, togither with their pikes in both hands, streight afore them, and their followers in that order so hard at their backes, laieng their pikes ouer their foregoerrs shoulders, that if they doo assaile vndisseuered, no force can well withstand them. The order of the Scots in warres both touching their furniture and diposition.

Standing at defense, they thrust shoulders likewise so nie togither, the fore-ranks well nie to knéeling stoope low before, for their fellowes behind, holding their pikes in both hands, and therwith in their left their bucklers, the one end of their pike against their right foot, the other against the enimie breast high, their followers crossing their pike points with them before, and thus each with other, so nie as place and space will suffer, through the whole rankes so thicke, that as easilie shall a bare finger pearse through the skin of an angrie hedgehog, as anie incounter the front of their pikes. Thus prouided, they (I meane the Scots) addressed themselues to incounter inflamed with a heat of furious hatred, but not aduised whether the cause were iust or vniust, for the which they were vp in armes: which foolish madnesse the poet pointeth at, and painteth out, saieng:

Arma Scotus poscit, valida contendere vi vult,
Is nec habet pensi sit id æquum an prorsus iniquum.

The lord marshall notwithstanding, whome no danger detracted from dooing his enterprise, with the companie and order afore appointed, came full in their faces from the hill side towards them. Herewith waxed it verie hot on both sides, with pitifull cries, horrible rore, and terrible thundering of guns, beside the daie darkened aboue head with smoke of the artillerie, the sight and appeerance of the enimie euen at hand before, the danger of death on euerie side else, the bullets, pellets and arrowes flieng each where so thicke, and so vncerteinelie lighting, that no where was there anie suretie of safetie, euerie man striken with a dreadfull feare, not so much perchance of death, as of hurt, which things though they were but certeine to some, yet doubted of all, assured crueltie at the enimies hands, without hope of mercie, death to flie, and danger to fight. The incounter is verie hot betwéene both sides.

The whole face of the field on both sides vpon this point of ioining, both to the eie and to the eare so heauie, so deadlie, lamentable, furious, outragious, terrible, confuse, and so quite against the quiet nature of man, as if to the nobilitie the regard of their honor and fame, to the knights and capteines the estimation of their worship and honestie, and generallie to them all the naturall motion of bounden dutie, their owne safetie, hope of victorie, and the fauour of God, that they trusted vpon for the equitie of their quarrell, had not béene a more vehement cause of courage, than the danger of death was cause of feare, the verie horrour of the thing had béene able to haue made anie man to forget both prowesse and policie. But the lord marshall and the The face of the field at the point of ioining.

the others, with present mind and courage warilie and quicklie continued their course towards them. The enimies were in a fallow field, whereof the furrowes laie sidelong toward the Englishmen, next to whome by the side of the same furrowes, & a stones cast from the Scots, was there a crosse ditch or slough, which the Englishmen must needs passe to come to them, wherein manie that could not leape ouer stucke fast, to no small danger of themselues, and some disorder of their fellowes.

The enimie perceiuing the Englishmen fast to approch, disposed themselues to abide the brunt, and in this order stood still to receiue them. The earle of Angus next to the Englishmen in the Scotish foreward as capteine of the same, with an eight thousand men, and fore or fiue péeces of ordinance on his right hand, and a foure hundred horssemen on his left. Behind him westward, the gouernour with ten thousand Inland men (as they call them) the choisest soldiers counted of their countrie. And the earle of Huntleie in the rere-ward, welnie euen with the battell on the left side with eight thousand. The foure thousand Irish archers as a wing to them both,

last indéed in order, & first (as they said) that ran awaie. The battell and also the rare-ward were garded likewise with their ordinance according.

Edward Shelleie lieutenant vnder the lord Greie of his band of Bulleners, was the first that passed ouer the slough. The lord Greie himselfe next, with the lord Iohn Greie and others in the foremost ranke, and so then after two or thrée rankes of their former bands. But badlie yet could they make their rase, by reason the furrowes laie trauerse to their course. That notwithstanding, and though also they were nothing likelie well to be able thus afront to come within them to doo them hurt, as well bicause the Scotishmens pikes were as long or longer than their staues, as also for that their horsses were all naked without bards, whereof though there were right manie among them, yet not one put on, for as much as at their comming forth in the morning, they looked for nothing lesse than for battell that daie : yet did those worthie gentlemen, the lord Greie of Wilton, the lord Iohn Greie and maister Shelleie with the residue, so valiantlie & stronglie giue the charge vpon them, that whether it were by their prowesse or power, the left side of the enimies that his lordship did set vpon (though their order remained vnbroken) was yet compelled to swaie a good waie backe, and giue ground largelie, and all the residue of them beside to stand much amazed.

Beside this, as the Englishmen were welnie at their enimies, they stood verie braue and bragging, shaking their pike points, & crieng ; Come lounds, come héeretikes, come heretikes ; and such like rhetorike they vsed. But though (saith master Patten) they meant but small humanitie, yet shewed they thereby much ciuilitie both of faire plaie, to warne yer they stroke, and of formall order, to chide yer they fought. The English capteines that were behind, perceiuing at eie, that both by the vnéeuennesse of the ground, by the sturdie order of the enimie, and for that their fellowes were so nie and streight before them, they were not able to anie aduantage to mainteine this

onset, did therefore according to the deuise in that point appointed, turned themselues, and made a soft retire vp toward the hill againe. Howbeit, to confesse the truth, some of the number that knew not the prepensed policie of the counsell in this case, made of a sober aduised retire, an hastie, rash, and vnaduised flight : howbeit, without capteine or standard, & vpon no cause of néed, but of a méere vndiscretion and madnesse. A madnesse indéed, for first the Scots were not able to pursue, bicause they were footmen ; and then if they could, what hope by flight so farre from home in their enimies land, where was no place of refuge?

The valiant lord Greie, Edward Shelleie, little Preston, Brampton, and Ierningham, Bulleners, Ratcliffe, the lord Fitzwaters brother, sir Iohn Cleres sonne and heire, Rawleie a gentleman of right commendable prowesse, Digs of Kent, Ellerker a pensioner,

Segraue : of the duke of Summersets band, Standleie, Woodhouse, Conisbie, Horgill, Norris, Denis, Arthur, and Atkinson, with other in the fore-ranke, not being able in

this

this earnest assault, both to tend to their fight afore, and to the retire behind : the Scots againe well considering herby how weake they remained, caught courage afresh, ran sharplie forward vpon them, and without anie mercie, slue the most part of them that abode furthest in prease a six more of Bulleners, and other than before are named, in all to the number of twentie six, and most part gentlemen. My lord Greie yet and my lord Iohn Greie, and likewise my lord Edward Seimer (as some grace was) returned againe ; but neither all in safetie, nor without euident markes they had bin there : for the lord Greie with a pike through the mouth was rased a long from the tip of the toong, and thrust that waie verie dangerouslie more than two inches in the necke ; and the other two had their horsses vnder them with swords sore wounded. Like as also a little before this onset, sir Thomas Darcie vpon his approch to the enimies, was striken glansing wise on the right side, with a bullet of one of their field péeces, and thereby his bodie brused with the bowing in of his armour, his sword hilts broken, and the forefinger of his right hand beaten flat. Euen so vpon the parting of this fraie, was sir Arthur Darcie slasht at with swords, and so hurt vpon the wedding finger of his right hand also, as it was counted for the first part of curing to haue it quite cut awaie. *The lord Greie hurt.*

About the same time, certeine of the Scots ran on hastilie to the kings standard of the horssemen (the which sir Andrew Flammocke bare) and laieng fast hold vpon the staffe therof, cried, A king, a king, that if both his strength, his hart, and his horsse had not beene good, and herewith somewhat aided at this pinch by sir Rafe Coppinger a pensioner, both he had béene slaine, and the standard lost, which the Scots neuerthelesse held so fast, that they brake and bare awaie the nether end of the staffe to the burrell, and intended so much to the gaine of the standard, that sir Andrew (as hap was) scaped home all safe, and else without hurt. At this businesse also the lord Fitzwaters, both earle of Sussex and lord chamberleine to the * quéenes maiestie, capteine there of a number of demilances was vnhorst, but soone mounted againe, scaped yet in great danger, and his horsse all hewen. Hereat further were Caluerleie the standard-bearer of the men at armes, and Clement Paston a pensioner, thrust each of them into the leg with pikes, and Don Philip a Spaniard into the knée, diuerse others maimed and hurt, and manie horsses sore wounded beside. *Sir Andrew Flammocke.* *The lord Fitz-waters.* ** Quéene Elizabeth.* *Caluerleie & . Clement Paston.* *Don Philip a Spaniard.*

By this time had the English fore-ward accordinglie gotten the full vantage of the hilles side, and in respect of their march stood sideling toward the enimie : who neuerthelesse were not able in all parts to stand full square in arraie : by reason that at the west end of them vpon their right hand, and toward the enimie, there was a square plot inclosed with turffe (as their maner of fensing in those parts, as well as in diuerse other is) one corner whereof did let the square of the same arraie. The battell in good order next them, but so as in continuance of arraie, the former part thereof stood vpon the hils side, the taile vpon the plaine, and the rere-ward wholie vpon the plaine. So that the placing and countenance of the English armie in this wise, they shewed themselues in maner to compasse in the Scots battels, that they should no waie escape them : but how little able they were to doo it with power and number, you may easilie coniecture. *The placing of the Englih vant-gard.* *The battell.* *The rere-ward.*

Those horssemen that were so repelled, and in their comming backe vnorderlie brake their arraie from the residue, ran so hastilie through the ranks of the English fore-ward as it stood, that it did both disorder manie, feared manie, and was a great incouragement to the enimie. The worthie earle of Warwike, who had the guiding of this fore-ward, right valiantlie had conducted the same to their standing, and there did verie noblie incourage and comfort them with such chéerefull words, offering to liue and die among them, that doubtlesse his presence, demening himselfe in such manlike sort, stood the whole companie in great sted. Neither wanted there the chearefull diligence of those capteines, with whome his honor was furnished in that fore-ward *The presence of the earle of War-wike greatlie in-couraged the souldiers.*

likewise to incourage their bands, nor the worthie behauiour of other in the battell and rere-ward, euerie one according to his calling, shewing such proofe of his dutie, as the most part certeinlie deserued to haue their names registred in the kalendar of fame, where no rust of cankered obliuion might fret out the remembrance of their commendable demeanours: and therefore if anie among them should haue shewed anie lacke of courage, their dispraise had béene the more, sith by others they saw such worthie example giuen, and were to stand vpon this resolution, to haue harts hardened against all hazzards in a iust cause, whereof they hoped almightie God had vndertaken the managing and direction, vnto whome they had committed the same; as the poet truelie saith:

Iusta Deo commissa Anglorum causa tonanti,
Audaces animos fecit impauidósque pericli.

But sith there were so manie that did well, & therfore deseruing a longer processe to be made of their high valiancies shewed in that dangerous seruice, than this volume may permit, I will procéed to the battell. The Scots were somewhat disordred with their comming out about the slaughter of the Englishmen, the which they did so earnestlie follow, that they tooke not one to mercie. The dukes grace placing himselfe (as yée haue heard) on the hill of Fauxside braie, and therewith perceiuing the great disorder of the stragling horssemen, that had in the retire broken arraie, hemmed them in from further straieng, whome sir Rafe Vane, and others of the capteins soone after with great dexteritie brought into good order and arraie againe, and with all the rest of the strengths of the whole armie, by the policie of the lords, and diligence of euerie capteine and officer beside, were so fitlie and aptlie applied in their feat, that where this repulse giuen by the enimie to the horssemen was doubted of manie, to turne to the whole losse of the field, the same was wrought and aduanced according as it was deuised, to the great certeintie of gaine and victorie. For first at this slough, where most of the horssemen had stood, sir Peter Mewtas capteine of all the harquebutters a foot did verie valiantlie conduct & place a good number of his men, in maner hard at the faces of the enimes, wherevnto sir Peter Gamboa a Spaniard, capteine of two hundred harquebutters, Spaniards, and Italians on horssebacke did readilie bring his men also, who with the hot continuance of their shot in both parts, did so stoutlie staie the enimies, that they could not well come further forward: then the archers that marched in arraie on the right hand of the footmen, and next to the enimies, pricked them sharpelie with arrowes as they stood. Therewith the master of the ordinance, to their great annoiance, did gall them with haile shot and other out of the great ordinance, directlie from the hill top, and certeine other gunners with their peeces a flanke from the rere-ward, most of the artillerie and missiue engines then wholie thus at once, with great puissance and vehemencie occupied about them, herewith the full sight of the Englishmen, all shadowed from them before by the horssemen, and dust raised, whome then they were ware in such order to be so néere vpon them, and to this the perfect arraie of the horssemen againe comming couragiouslie to set on them afresh, miserable men, perceiuing themselues then all too late, how much too much they had ouershot themselues, began suddenlie to shrinke.

Their gouernour and other the principall capteins that had brought them to the bargaine, tooke their horsses and fled amaine, which other perceiuing did quicklie follow, and with the formost of that crue their Irishmen, and therewith turned all the whole rout, cast downe their weapons, ran out of their wards, off with their iackes, and with all that euer they might, betooke them to the race that their gouernour began. The Englishmen at the first had found them (as what could scape so manie eies) and sharpelie and quicklie with an vniuersall outcrie, They flie, they flie, pursued after in chase so egerlie, and with such fiercenesse, that they ouertooke manie, and spared indéed but few, that when they were once turned, it was a woonder to see how soone, and

Sir Rafe Vane.

Sir Peter Mewtas.

Sir Peter Gamboa.

The archers.

The maister of the ordinance.

The Scots flie and are sharplie pursued.

and in how sundrie sorts they were scattered. The place they stood on like a wood of staues strewed on the ground, as rushes in a chamber, vnpassable (they laie so thicke) for either horsse or man. Here at the first had they let fall all their pikes, and after that, euerie where scattered swords, bucklers, daggers, iackes, and all things else that was of anie weight, or might be any let to their course; which course among them, thrée waies speciallie they made, some along the sands by the Frith towards Lith, some streight towards Edenburgh, whereof part through the parke there (in the walles whereof, though they be round about of flint stone, yet were there manie holes alreadie made) and part of them by the high waie that leadeth along by the abbaie of Holie-rood house; and the residue and most part of them towards Daketh, which waie by means of the marish our horssemen were worst able to follow. *The enimies cast awaie their munition and furniture the lightlier to flie and be gone.*

Sundrie shifts, some shrewd, some sorie, made they in their running : diuerse of them in their courses, as they were ware they were pursued but of one, would suddenlie start backe, and lash at the legs of the horsse, or foine him in the bellie, and sometime did they reach at the rider also, whereby Clement Paston in the arme, and diuerse in other parts of their bodies otherwise in this chase were hurt. Some other laie flat in a furrow as they were dead, thereby past by of the Englishmen vntouched, and (as was reported) the earle of Angus confessed he couched in that sort till his horsse hapt to be brought him. Other some were found to staie in the riuer, couring downe his bodie vnder the root of some willow tree, with scant his nose aboue water for breath. Some for lightnesse cast awaie shoos and doublets, and ran in their shirts, and some were séene in this race all breathlesse to fall flat downe, and haue run themselues to death. *The earle of Angus.*

Before this, at the time of the onset, which the English horssemen gaue, there came eastward fiue hundred of the Scotish horsmen vp along this Fauxside braie, streight vpon the English ordinance and cariage. The lord protector (as yée haue heard) most speciallie for doubt hereof, placing himselfe by the same, caused a péece or two to be turned toward them, with a few shots whereof they were soone turned also and fled to Daketh. But had they kept on their purpose, they were prouided for accordinglie. For one parson Keble a chapleine of his graces, and two or thrée other, by and by discharged foure or fiue of the carts of munition, and therewith bestowed pikes, billes, bowes and arrowes, to as manie as came; so that of carters and other, there were soone weaponed about a thousand, whome parson Keble and the other did verie handsomlie dispose in arraie, and made a pretie muster. *Parson Keble one of the lord protectors chapleins.*

To returne now after this notable strewing of their footmens weapons, began a pitifull sight of the dead corpses, lieng dispersed abrode, some their legs off, some but hought, and left lieng halfe dead, some thrust quite through the bodie, others their necks halfe a sunder, manie their heads clouen, with other thousand kinds of killing After that, and further in chase all for the most part killed, either in the head, or in the necke, for the horssemen could not well reach them lower with their swords. And thus with bloud and slaughter of the enimie, this chase was continued fiue miles in length, westward from the place of their satnding, which was in the fallow fields of Vndreske, vntill Edenburgh parke, and well nigh to the gates of the towne it selfe, and vnto Lith, and in breadth nie foure miles, from the Forth sands vp toward Daketh southwards: in all which space, the dead bodies laie as thicke as a man may note cattell grasing in a full replenished pasture. The riuer ran all red with bloud (a signe of great slaughter) so that in the same chase were slaine to the number of ten thousand men, some saie aboue fouretéene thousand, as I doo find by this report concerning the battell: *The maner of the slaughter.* *The number of Scots slaine.*

Millia bis septem sunt morte absumpta Scotorum,
Cætera pars certam quærit fugiendo salutem.

5 Q 2

To

To conclude, considering the smalnesse of the Englishmens number, and shortnesse of the time (which was scant fiue houres, from one till well nigh six) the mortalitie was so great (as it was thought) the like afore time had not béene séene. One great cause whie the Englishmen spared so few of them, was thought to be their tyrannous vow by them made (which the Englishmen certeinly heard of) that whensoeuer they fought and ouercame, they would kill so manie, and spare so few: a sure proofe whereof they plainelie had shewed at the first onset giuen, where they killed all, and saued not a man that came within their danger. An other respect was, to reuenge their great and cruell tyrannie shewed at Paniar hough, where they slue the lord Euers, whome otherwise they might haue taken prisoner and saued, and cruellie killed as manie else of our men as came into their hands. An other occasion also was their armor among them so little differing, all clad alike in iacks couered with white leather, doublets of the same, or of fustian, and most commonlie all white hosen, not one with either chaine, brooch, ring, or garment of silke, vnlesse chains of latten drawne foure of fiue times along the vpper stocks, or to vse master Pattens words, the thighs of their hosen and doublet sleeues for cutting.

(margin: The causes why so few Scots were taken. The Scotishmens vow. Paniar hough. The apparell of the Scots.)

This lacke for difference in apparell was the chiefest cause that so manie of their great men and gentlemen were killed, and so few saued. The outward shew, the resemblance or signe, whereby a stranger might discerne a poore man from a gentleman, was not among them to be séene: as for words and goodlie profers of great ransoms, were as rife in the mouths of the one as the other. And it came here to passe, that after at the examination and counting of the prisoners, there were found taken aboue twentie of their common countrie people, to one of their gentlemen, whome no man need to doubt the Englishmen had rather haue spared than the other, if they could haue séene anie difference betweene them in taking. And yet verelie considering the case as it stood, the Englishmen shewed more grace, and tooke more to mercie, than the respects before mentioned might séeme to haue required. For beside the earle of Huntleie, who in good armor appointed likest a gentleman of anie among them, but could not then escape bicause he lacked his horsse, and hapned to be taken by sir Rafe Vane, and beside the lord of Yester, Hobbie Hambleton capteine of Dunbar, the master of Sanpoole, the lard of Wimmes taken by Iohn Bren, a brother of the earle of Cassils, and besides one Montrell, taken by Cornelius comptrollor of the ordinance in the armie, and one Camals an Irish gentleman, and beside manie other Scotish gentlemen more, taken by diuerse others.

(margin: The earle of Huntleie taken. Other prisoners taken.)

The prisoners reckoned in the marshals booke were numbred to aboue fiftéene hundred. Touching the slaughter, sure they killed not so manie, as for the time & oportunitie they might, if they had minded crueltie. For the lord protector mooued with pitie at the sight of the dead bodies, and rather glad of victorie than desirous of slaughter, soone after (by gesse) fiue of the clocke, staid the standard of his horssemen at the furthest part of their campe westward, & caused the trumpets to sound a retreat. Whereat also sir Rafe Sadler treasuror (whose great diligence at that time, and readie forwardnesse in the chiefest of the fraie before, did woorthilie merit no small commendation) caused all the footmen to staie; and then with much trauell & great paine made them to be brought in some order againe: which was a thing not easilie doone, by reason they all as then were somewhat busie in applieng their market, the spoile of the Scotish campe, where was found good prouision of white bread, ale, otencaks, otemeale, mutton, butter in pots, chéese, and in diuerse tents good wine also, and in some tents among them was found some siluer plate and chalices, which with good deuotion ye maie be sure were plucked out of their cold clowts, and thrust into their warme bosoms.

(margin: The number of the prisoners. The lord protector not desirous of slaughter. Sir Rafe Sadler. The spoile of the Scotish campe.)

The plot of their campe called Edmonston edge, nigh Gilberton a place of the lord of Brimstons, halfe a mile beyond Muskelburgh, and foure miles on this side Edenburgh, occupied

occupied in largenesse with diuerse tents and tenticles, that stood in sundrie places out of square, about a miles compasse, wherein as the Englishmen vpon the sound of the retreat somewhat assembled, they all with a lowd and entire outcrie and hallowing, in signe of gladnesse and victorie, made an vniuersall noise aad showt, the shrilnesse A showt in signe of victorie. whereof (as after was reported) was heard vnto Edenburgh.   It was a woonder to sée, but (as they saie) manie hands make light woorke, how soone the dead bodies were stripped out of their garments starke naked, euen from as farre as the chase went, vnto the place of the onset, whereby the personages of the enimies might by the waie easilie be viewed and considered, the which for the talnesse of their stature, cleannesse of The feature of the Scotishmens personages. skin, bignesse of bone, with due proportion in all parts was such, as the beholders, if they had not séene it, would not haue beleeued that there had béene so many of that sort in all their countrie.   Among them laie manie priests, and kirkmen, as they call Priests or kirk-men. them, of whome it was bruted that there was a whole band of thrée or foure thousand, but it was found afterwards not to be altogither so.

Among other banners, standards, and pennons, a banner of white sarsenet was found, vnder which it was said these kirkmen came, wherevpon was painted a woman A baner of a papists deuise. with hir haire about hir shoulders, knéeling before a crucifix, & on hir right hand a church, after that written in great Romane letters, Afflictæ sponsæ ne obliuiscaris.   It was said that this was the abbat of Dunfirmlings banner, but whether it was his or the bishop of Dunkels, the gouernours brother, who (as was said) were both in the field, his meaning was, to signifie that the church made intercession to Christ hir husband, What was the signification and meaning of the baner so in-scribed. not now to forget hir his spouse, being at that time afflicted and persecuted by the Englishmen. But whose deuise soeuer it was, it maie séeme, that this church comming thus to battell, full appointed with weapon, and garded with such a sort of deacons to fight, howsoeuer in painting he had set hir out, a man might well thinke, that in condition, he had rather framed hir like a curst queane, that would plucke hir husband by the pate, except she had hir will; than like a meeke spouse, that went about humblie by submission and praier to desire hir husbands helpe, for redresse of things amisse.

But now to leaue this prelat with his Afflicta sponsa, and to make an end with this battell.   There was vpon Fauxside braie, a little castell or pile, which was verie busie A little castle or pile verie busie with the Eng-lish. all the time of the battell, as anie of the Englishmen came nigh it, to shoot at them, with such artillerie as they had; which was none other than of handguns and har-quebuts, & of them not a dozen neither.   Little hurt they did, but as they saw their fellowes in the field thus driuen and beaten awaie before their faces, they plucked in their péeces, and couched themselues within all mute: but by and by the house was set on fire, and they for their good wils burned and smoothered within.   Thus (saith master Patten) through the fauour of Gods bountie, by the valiancie and policie of the lord protector, by the forward indeuour of all the nobles and councell there beside, and by the willing diligence of euerie capteine officer, and true subiect else, they most valiantlie wan the victorie ouer their enimies, of whom such slaughter was made in the field, as ye haue heard, amongest whome (as the prisoners reported) beside the lord Fleming, the lard of Loghenware, the master of Greim, the master of Arskin, What men of name and ac-count were slaine in the battell and taken prisoners. the master of Oglebie, the master of Auendale, the master of Rouen, and manie other of noble birth amongest them, there were of lards, lards sons, and other gentle-men slaine aboue twentie six hundred, & among the prisoners also there were manie gentlemen, speciallie of name these; the earle of Huntleie lord chancellor of the realme, the lord of Yester, Hobbie Hamilton capteine of Dunbar, the master of San-poole, the lord of Wimmes, and a brother of the earle of Cassils.   Two thousand by lurking and lieng (as they had béene dead) scaped awaie in the night all maimed and hurt.   Herewith of weapons and armor more was found than the Englishmen did

vouch-

Armor and
weapons caried
into England. vouchsafe to giue carriage for: & yet were there conueied thense by ship into Eng-land, of iacks speciallie and swords, aboue thirtie thousand.

This night the Englishmen with great gladnesse and thanksgiuing to God (as good cause they had) about seauen of the clocke pitched their campe at Edgebuckling braie, beside Pinkerslough, and a mile beyond the place they camped at before. Now after the battell, among other questions, one was mooued who killed the first man that Ieronimo an
Italian. daie in the field, the glorie whereof one Ieronimo an Italian would gladlie haue had, a gentleman sure that had serued that daie right valiantlie: howbeit it was after well Cutbert Mus-
graue. tried, that Cutbert Musgraue, a gentleman of the earle of Warwiks, deserued the praise of killing the first enimie that died that daie, who right hardilie slue a guner at his péece in the Scots fore-ward, yer euer they began anie whit to turne. As for the ordinarie soldiors, it was a pleasure vnto them to make rehearsall of their aduentures past, and to record what dangers (in maner ineuitable) they had escaped, according to the poets report in that case, saieng:

———res est meminisse laboris
Præteriti iucunda: graue effugisse periclum
Summa recordari secuta mente voluptas.

The next daie being sundaie the eleuenth of September, somewhat before noone, the armie remooued, & marching along the Forth side toward Lieth, about three of the clocke in the after noone pitched their field, a pricke shot on this side that towne on the southeast halfe, somewhat shadowed from Edenburgh by a hill, but yet the The English
armie incampeth
by Lieth. most part of it laie within the full sight and shot of the castell there, and in distance somewhat aboue a quarter of a mile. The lord marshall, and the most part of the horssemen were bestowed and lodged in the towne of Lieth. The dukes grace, the lord lieutenant, and the rest of the armie in the campe. On tuesdaie the thirteenth of September, the smaller vessels of the English fléet burned Kinkorne, and a towne or two standing on the north shore of the Forth against Lieth.

In the after noone the dukes grace rowed vp the Forth a six or seuen miles west-ward, as it runneth into the land, and tooke in his waie an Iland there called saint S. Cooms ins. Cooms ins, which lieth foure miles beyond Lieth, and a good waie neerer the north shore than the south, yet not within a mile of the néerest. It is but halfe a mile about, and had in it an abbeie, but the moonks were gone: fresh water inough, and store of conies, and is so naturallie strong, that but by one waie it can be entred; the plot whereof the lord protector considering, did quicklie cast to haue it kept, whereby all traffike of merchandize, all commodities else comming by the Forth into their land, and vtterlie the whole vse of the Forth it selfe, with all the hauens vpon it, should quite be taken from them.

The castell of
Daketh. The next daie the lord protector riding backe againe eastward, to view diuerse things and places, tooke Daketh in his waie, where a house of George Dowglas did stand, and comming somewhat néere it, he sent Summerset his herald with a trumpet to know who kept it, and whether the keepers would hold or yéeld it to his grace? Answer was made, that there were three score persons within, whome their maister lieng there saturdaie at night after the battell, did will that they, the house, and all that was in it, should be at his graces commandement. Wherevpon the chiefest came, and in name of all the rest humbled himselfe to the dukes will. From thense his grace passed to the place where the battell had béene stricken, and so by Muskle-burgh returned backe to the campe.

Blacke Nesse
an hauen towne
on the south
shore of Scot-
land. On thursdaie being the fiftéenth of this moneth, the lord Clinton high admerall, taking with him the gallie whereof Richard Brooke was capteine, and foure or fiue other smaller vessels besides, as well appointed with munition and men, rowed vp the Forth a ten miles westward, to an hauen towne standing on the south shore called
Blacke

Blacke Nesse, whereat toward the water side is a castell of a pretie strength; as nigh wherevnto as the depth of the water would suffer, the Scots for safegard had laid the Marie Willoughbie, and the Anthonie of Newcastell, two tall ships, which with extreme iniurie they had stollen from the Englishmen before time, when no war was betwixt vs: with these laie there also an other large vessell called the Bosse, and seauen more, wherof part laden with merchandize. The lord Clinton and his com- Thrée ships of panie with right hardie approch, after a great conflict betwixt the castell and his name woone from the Scots. vessels, by fine force wan from them those thrée ships of name, and burnt all the residue before their faces.

The sixtéenth of September the lard of Brimston a Scotish gentleman came to the dukes grace from their counsell for cause of communication, and returned againe to them, hauing with him Norreie an herald and king at armes of ours, who found them with the old quéene at Sterling. On saturdaie the seauentéenth of September, Sir Iohn Lut- sir Iohn Luttrell in the afternoone departed toward saint Cooms ins, hauing with trell. S. Cooms ins him an hundred harquebutters, fiftie pioners, & two row barks well furnished with kept with a gar- munition, and thrée score and-ten mariners to remaine there, & kéepe that from in- rison of Eng- lishmen. uasion of the enimies, against whom the English were so sharplie whetted, that when they came to incounter, they gaue proofe of their manhood by wounds and bloudshed, according to the report of C. O. in these verses following:

————Anglorum pectora Mauors
Belliger exacuit, crescunt ad vulnera vires.

In the time whilest the armie laie thus in the campe betwéene Lieth and Eden- burgh, manie lards and gentlemen came in to the lord protector to require his pro- tection, the which his grace to whome he thought good did grant. This daie came The earle of Bothwell. the earle of Bothwell to his grace, who hauing beene kept in prison by the gouernour, the night after the battell was set at libertie, and comming thus to the lord protector, was friendlie welcomed and interteined; and hauing this night supped with his grace, he departed.

Lieth was set on fire this saturdaie, whereas it was meant, that there should haue Lieth burned. beene but one house onelie burnt, belonging to one Barton that had plaied a slipperie part with the lord protector. But the soldiors being set a worke to fire that house, fired all the rest. Six great ships also that laie in the hauen, which for their age and decaie were not so apt for vse, were likewise set on fire and burnt. On sundaie the eightéenth of September, the lord protector (for considerations moouing him to pitie) hauing all this while spared Edenburgh from hurt, did so leaue it, but Lieth and the ships burning, soone after seauen of the clocke in the morning, caused the The armie dis- campe to dislodge, and as they were raised and on foot, the castell shot off a peale, lodged. with chambers hardlie and all, of foure and twentie péeces. Passing that daie seauen miles, they camped earlie for that night at Crainston by a place of the lard of Crainston. Brimstons.

The same morning the lord protector made maister Andrew Dudleie knight, brother to the earle of Warwike, dispatched my lord admerall and him by ships full fraught with men and munition toward the winning of an hold in the east side of Scotland called Broughticrag, which stood in such sort in the mouth of the riuer of Taie, as that be- Broughticrag. ing gotten, both Dundée, saint Iohns towne, and diuerse other townes standing vpon the same riuer the best of the countrie in those parts, set vpon the Taie, should either become subiect vnto this hold, or else be compelled to forgo the whole vse of the riuer, for hauing anie thing comming in or outward. The lord admerall, and the said sir Andrew sped themselues with such good successe and diligence in that enter- prise, that on the wednesdaie following, being the one and twentith of September, after certeine of their shot discharged against that castell, the same was yeelded vnto them,

Broughticrag
yéelded to the
Englishmen.

them, the which sir Andrew did then enter, and after kept, as capteine to his high praise and commendation.

Lawder.

But now to the armie. On mondaie the nineteenth of September, they marched ten miles, and incamped a little on this side a market towne called Lawder. Here as they were setled in their lodging, the herald Norrie returned from the Scotish councell, with the lard of Brimston, and Rose their herald, who vpon their sute to the lord protector, obteined that fiue of their councell should haue his graces safe conduct, that at anie time and place within fiftéene daies, during his abode in their countrie, or at Berwike, the same fiue might come and commune with fiue of the English councell, touching matters in controuersie betwéene them. Rose the herald departed earlie with his safe conduct, the campe raised, and that daie they went seauen miles till as far as Hume

Hume castell.

castell, where they camped on the west side of a rockie hill that they call Hare crag, standing about a mile westward from the castell.

Here they did so much by shewing that they ment indeed to win the castell by force, if otherwise they might not haue it, causing a certeine number of harque-butters vpon appointment before to beset the castell, and to watch that none should

Hume castell be-
sieged and
and yéelded vp
to the lord pro-
tector.

passe in or out, that in the end, the ladie of the house, and other that were within in charge with it, yéelded it vp to the lord protectors hands: for the ladie doubting the losse of hir son that was prisoner with the Englishmen, hauing the first daie béene with the lord protector, and got respit till the next daie at noone, in the meane time consulted with hir sonne, and other hir friends the kéepers of the castell, returned at the time appointed the next daie, being the one and twentith of that moneth, and made sute for a longer respit till eight of the clocke at night, and therewith safe conduct for Andrew Hume hir second son, and Iohn Hume lard of Coldan Knows, a kinsman of hir husbands, capteins of this castell, to come and speake with his grace in the meane while. It was granted hir. Wherevpon these capteins about thrée of the clocke came to the lord protector, and after other couenants (with long debating on both parts) agréed vpon, she and these capteins concluded to giue their assent to render the castell, so far foorth as the rest of the keepers would therewith be contented, for two or thrée within (said they) were also in charge with kéeping it as well as they,

Summerset the
dukes herald.

for knowledge of whose minds the duke sent Summerset his herald with this ladie to the castell vnto them; who as the herald had made them priuie to the articles, would faine haue had leisure for foure and twentie hours longer, to send to their lord to Edenburgh, where he laie hurt (as before you haue heard) and in danger of death, which followed of the fall that he caught at the fridaies skirmish before the battell, to know his will and plesure in this point of rendering vp the castell: but being wiselie and sharplie called vpon by the herald, they agréed to the couenants afore by

The conditions
of the sur-
rendring of
Hume castell.

their ladie and capteins concluded on: whereof part (as the sequele shewed) were these. That they should depart thense the next daie in the morning by ten of the clocke with bag and baggage, as much as they could carie, leauing all munition and vittels behind them in the castell. Howbeit, to be assured of them, the lord protector prouiding ech waie to be readie for them, caused eight péeces of ordinance fensed with baskets of earth to be planted on the southside toward the castell within power of batterie, and the harquebutters to continue their watch and ward.

On thursdaie morning being the two and twentith of September, the lord Greie was appointed to receiue the rendring of the castell into his hands, and sir Edward

The lord Greie
receiueth the
possession of
Hume castell.

Dudleie now lord Dudleie after to be capteine there. They both departed to it, and at the time set Andrew Hume, and foure other of the chiefest there with him came out, and yéelding the castell, deliuered the keies to the said lord Greie: his lordship causing the residue to come out then, sauing six or seuen to keepe their baggage within, who all were in number seuentie and eight, entred the same with maister

Dudleie,

Dudleie, and diuerse other gentlemen with him. He found there indifferent good store of vittels and wine, & of ordinance two bastard culuerings, one sacre, also thrée falconets of brasse, and of iron eight péeces beside. The keeping of this castell the lord Greie betaking vnto sir Edward Dudleie, accordinglie returned to the campe. This doone, the next daie being fridaie, and the thrée and twentith of September, they dislodged, and went that morning to Rockesburgh, incamping in a great fallow field, betwixt Rockesburgh and Kelseie, standing eastward a quarter of a mile off. Here at Rockesburgh they began to build a fort within the compasse of an old ruinous castell, the plot and site whereof standeth naturallie verie strong, vpon a hill east and west of an eight score in length, and thrée score in breadth, drawing to a narrownesse at the east end, the whole ground whereof the old walles did yet inuiron. Beside the heigth and hardnesse to come to, it is stronglie fensed on either side with the course of two great riuers, Tiuet on the north, and Twéed on the south, both which ioining somwhat nigh togither at the west end of it. Tiuet by a large compasse about the fields (in which the campe laie) at Kelseie, dooth fall into this Twéed, which with great depth and swiftnesse runneth from thense eastward into the sea at Berwike. Ouer this betwixt Kelsei and Rockesburgh there hath béene a great stone bridge with arches, the which the Scots in times past haue all to broken, because the Englishmen should not that waie come to them. *The situation of Rockesburgh.*

Soone after the lord protector surueie of the plot, and determination to doo as much in déed for making it defensible, as shortnesse of the time & season of the yéere could suffer (which was) that one great trench of twentie foot broad with depth according, and a wall of like depth, bredth, and heigth, should be made crosse within the castell from the one side wall to the other, and fortie foot from the west end: and that a like trench and wall should likewise be cast a trauerse within, about a coits cast from the east end, and hereto that the castell walles on either side where néed was, should be mended with turffe, and made with lowps, as well for shooting directlie forward as for flanking at hand: the worke of which deuise did make that (beside the safegard of these trenches and walles) the keepers should also be much defended from the enimies force by both the end walles of the castell: the pioners were set a worke, and diligentlie applied in the same. *The determinatiõ in what sort Rockesburgh should be fortified.*

The lard of Sesseforth, and manie other lards and gentlemen of Tiuidall and the Mers, hauing come and communed with the lord protector and the councell, made an assurance, or as it were a truce for that daie, till the next daie at night; and on the next daie, while assurance lasted, these lards and gentlemen being the chiefest in the whole Mers and Tiuidale, came in againe, whome the dukes grace with wisedome and policie without bloudshed did win then vnto the kings obedience, for the which they did willinglie then receiue an oth: whose names in part insue. The lard of Sesseforth, the lard of Fernihurst, the lard of Grænehead, the lard of Hunthill, the lard of Huntleie, the lard of Markeston by Merside, the lard of Boniedworth, the lard of Ormeston, the lard of Mailestaine, the lard of Warmeseie, the lard of Linton, the lard of Egerston, the lard of Marton, the lard of Mow, the lard of Reddell, the lard of Reamerside. George Trombull, Iohn Holliburton, Robert Car of Greiden, Adam Kirton, Andrew Kirton, Andrew Meither, Sander Spur of Erleston, Marke Car of Littleden, George Car of Faldenside, Alexander Makdowell, Charles Rotherford, Thomas Car of the Yere, Iohn Car of Meinthorne, Walter Holiburton, Richard Hanganside, Andrew Car, Iames Dowglas of Cauers, Iames Car of Mersington, George Hoppringle, William Ormeston of Enmerden, Iohn Grimslow. Manie more there were beside, but ouerpassed by maister Patten, for that they remained in the register with these, as he saith. The duke of Summerset tendred the furtherance of the worke so much, that he forbare not to laie his owne hand to the spade and shouell, thereby to incourage others: *Scots that came to the kings obeisance.* *Lards.* *Gentlemen.* *The diligence of the duke of Summerset to further the fortification to Rockesburgh* so asthere were but few lords, knight, and gentlemen in the field, but with spade, shouell, ormattocke did therein their parts.

The fiue and twentith of September being sundaie, the Scots began to bring vittels to the campe, & were so well intreated and paied for the same, that during the time of the Englishmens sbode there, they wanted not of the commodities which their countrie could minister. The eight and twentith of September a Scotish herald accompanied with certeine Frenchmen, that were perchance more desirous to marke the armie than to wit of their welfare, came and declared that within a seauen-night after, their commissioners, to whome safe conduct had béene granted, should come and commune with our councell at Berwike; whose comming the earle of Warwike, and sir Rafe Sadler with other the commissioners appointed, did so long while there abide. But what the Scots ment by breaking promise I cannot saie, howbeit come they did not, & therfore escaped not the iust note of dissimulation, howsoeuer else they could colour the matter in their owne excuse.

Creation of banerets, knights, &c.
Banerets.

Knights.
Edward Seimer the duke of Summersets son.

Sir Francis Fleming.

The same daie after noone, the duke of Summerset adorned with titles of dignitie diuerse lords, knights, and gentlemen, the names and promotions of whom master Patten hath set downe out of the heralds booke, as followeth: Sir Rafe Sadler treasuror, sir Francis Brian capteine of the light horssemen, sir Rafe Vane lieutenant of all the horssemen: these knights were made banerets, a dignitie aboue a knight, and next to a baron. The lord Greie of Wilton high marshall, the lord Edward Seimer the duke of Summersets son, the lord Thomas Howard, the lord Waldike a Cleuelander, sir Thomas Dacres, sir Edward Hastings, sir Edmund Bridges, sir Iohn Thin, sir Miles Patridge, sir Iohn Conweie, sir Giles Poole, sir Rafe Bagnoll, sir Oliuer Laurence, sir Henrie Gates, sir Thomas Chaloner, sir Francis Fleming master of the ordinance, sir Iohn Gresham, sir William Skipwith, sir Iohn Buts, sir George Blaag, sir William Francis, sir Francis Knolles, sir William Thornburrow, sir George Howard sir Iames Wilford, sir Rafe Coppinger, sir Thomas Wentworth, sir Iohn Meruen, sir Nicholas Strange, sir Charles Sturton, sir Hugh Askue, sir Francis Salmin, sir Richard Tounleie, sir Marmaduke Conestable, sir George Audleie, sir Iohn Holcroft, sir Iohn Southworth, sir Thomas Danbie, sir Iohn Talbot, sir Rowland Clarke, sir Iohn Horsleie, sir Iohn Forster, sir Christopher Dies, sir Peter Negro, sir Alanzo de Vile, sir Henrie Husseie, sir Iames Granado Brabander, sir Walter Bonham, sir Robert Brandling maior of Newcastell, and made knight there at the duke of Summersets returne.

Order taken for defense of the fort gained and built in this voiage.

But now that Rockesburgh was sufficientlie made defensible (the which to sée it séemed the duke of Summerset had vowed before he would thence depart) his grace and the councell did first determine that my lord Greie should remaine vpon the borders there as the kings lieutenant, and then tooke order for the forts: that sir Andrew Dudleie capteine of Broughticrag had left with two hundred soldiers of harquebutters & others, and a sufficient number of pioners for his works: sir Edward Dudleie capteine of Hume castell thréescore harquebutters, fortie horssemen and a hundred pioners: sir Rafe Bulmer capteine of Rockesburgh thrée hundred soldiers of harquebutters and others, and two hundred pioners. As things were thus concluded, and warning giuen

The armie returneth homewards.
The danger of the soldiers in passing the riuer of Twéed.

ouer night on this wednesdaie being Michaelmasse euen, on the next morrow being Michaelmasse daie euerie man fell to packing apase and got them homewards, passing ouer the Twéed there with some trouble and danger also, by reason of raine that latelie fell before, & had raised the streame, which being swift of it selfe, and the chanell vneuen in the bottome with great stones made the passage cumbersome, so that manie as well horssemen as footmen were in no small perill as they passed thorough, and one or two drowned, and manie cariages ouerthrowne, and in great hazzard of losing.

The duke of Summerset rode streight to Newcastell, and thence homewards. The earle

earle of Warwike, my lord Greie, and sir Rafe Sadler, with diuerse other rode to Berwike to abide the comming of the Scotish commissioners. In the meane time of their tarieng there, the earle of Warwike made six knights; sir Thomas Neuill the lord Neuils brother, sir Andrew Corbet, sir Anthonie Strelleie, sir Arthur Manering, sir Richard Verneie, sir Iohn Berteruille. After that the earle of Warwike had taried for the comming of the Scots the full terme of the appointment, which was vntill the fourth of October, and perceiued they came not, the next daie he departed homewards.

Here ye haue to vnderstand also, that in part of the meane time whilest the duke of Summerset was in dooing of these exploits in Scotland (as ye haue heard rehearsed) the earle of Lenox, and the lord Wharton warden of the west marches, with an armie of fiue thousand men, entred Scotland on that side, and first passing two miles after a daie and a nights defense, they wan the church of Annan, tooke seuentie & two prisoners keepers of the same, burnt the spoile for cumber of cariage, and caused the church to be blowen vp with powder, passing thence a sixteene miles within the land, they wan the castell of Milke, the which they left furnished with munition and men, and so returned. But of this ye shall find more in the historie of Scotland, by the sufferance of God, where we intreat of the dooings there in this yeare. *An inuasion made into Scotland. Annan church woone.*
The castell of Milke weone.

Thus much haue I collected out of master Pattens booke. or rather exemplified the same, not much digressing from his owne words, except where I haue bin forced to abridge his worke in some places, wishing to haue inserted the whole, if the purpose of this volume would haue so permitted, as well for the full vnderstanding of euerie particular point, by him remembred, as also for his pleasant and apt maner of penning the same. Whilest the lord protector was abrode thus in wars against the Scots, the lords of the councell that remained at home, chiefelie by the good and diligent calling on and furtherance of the archbishop of Canturburie, and others of the cleargie, tooke order for the aduancement of religion, causing the bookes of homilies and the paraphrase of Erasmus to be set foorth and had in churches. *The homilies & paraphrase of Erasmus.*

At the comming backe of the lord protector from his iournie into Scotland, the citizens of London determined to haue receiued him with great triumph: but he hearing thereof, forbad them in anie wise so to doo: for (said he) "if anie thing hath beene doone to the honour of the realme, it was Gods dooing," and therefore willed them to giue him the praise. Neuerthelesse the maior and aldermen, with certeine of the commoners in their liueries and their hoods, hearing of his approch to the citie, the eight daie of October met him in Finnesburie field, where he tooke each of them by the hand, and thanked them for their good wils. The lord maior did ride with him till they came to the pound in Smithfield, where his grace left them, and rode to his house of Shene that night, and the next daie to the king to Hampton court. The fourth daie of Nouember began a parlement, called and holden at Westminster, which continued till the foure and twentith of December next following, & was then proroged. In this parlement, all colleges, chanteries, and free chappels were giuen to the king, and the statute of the six articles was repealed, with diuerse others tending to the like end. Moreouer, during this parlement visiters being appointed to visit in London, the sixteenth of Nouember began to take downe the images in Paules church; and shortlie after all the images in euerie church, not onelie through London, but also throughout the whole realme, were pulled downe and defaced. *The lord protectors returne.*

A parlement.

The lord protector and others of the councell, considering now in what sort they had got foothold in Scotland, by reason of such peeces as they had taken and fortified within the realme, did deuise for the more suertie of those places, which they had alreadie got, and the better to bring the rest of the countrie vnto reason, to haue some holds also more within the land, and therefore first they caused a fort to be builded at 1548
An. Reg. 2.

                                                     Lowder,

Lowder, where sir Hugh Willoughbie was appointed capteine with a conuenient garrison of soldiers to kéepe it. Beside this, it was thought expedient to fortifie the towne of Hadington, wherevpon the lord Greie lieutenant of the north parts, with sir Thomas Palmer, and sir Thomas Holcroft, were appointed to go thither with a conuenient number of men of warre & pioners to sée that towne fensed with trenches, rampiers, and bulworks, as should séeme to his lordship necessarie and behoouefull;

who therefore entring into Scotland the eightéenth of Aprill, passed forth to Hadington, where he began to fortifie, and there remained to sée the worke brought to some perfection. During his abode there, diuerse exploits were both valiantlie attempted and luckilie atchiued by his martiall conduct and politike direction, as occasions offred might moue him, which I would gladlie haue set downe at large, if I could haue come to the true vnderstanding thereof; but sith I cannot get the same, in such full manner as I haue wished, that yet which I haue learned by true report (as I take it) I haue thought good to impart to the reader.

The eight and twentith of Maie, his lordship wan the castell of Yester, after he had beaten it right sore with terrible batterie of canon shot for the time it lasted, and therewith hauing made a reasonable breach for the soldiers to enter, they within yéelded with condition to haue their liues saued: which the lord Greie was contented

to grant to them all, one onelie excepted, who during the siege vttered vnséemelie words of the king, abusing his maiesties name with vile and most opprobrious termes. They all comming foorth of the castell in their shirts, humbled themselues to my lord Greie (as became them) and vpon strait examination who should be the railer that was

excepted out of the pardon, it was knowne to be one Newton a Scot: but he to saue himselfe, put it to one Hamilton, and so these two gentlemen accusing one an other, the truth could not be decided otherwise than by a combat, which they required, and my lord Greie therevnto assented, and pronounced iudgement so to haue it tried: which he did the rather, bicause all men doo séeme resolute in the triall of truth (as in a verie good cause) by losse of life to gaine an endlesse name; as one saith:

Mors spernenda viris vt fama perennis alatur.

At the appointed time they entered the lists, set vp for that purpose in the market place of Hadington, without other apparell sauing their doublets and hosen, weaponed

with sword, buckler and dagger. At the first entrie into the lists, Hamilton kneeling downe, made his heartie praier to God, that it might please him to giue victorie vnto the truth, with solemne protestation that he neuer vttered anie such words of king Edward of England, as his aduersarie charged him with. On the other side Newton being troubled (as it séemed) with his false accusation, argued vnto the beholders his guiltie conscience. Now were the sticklers in a readinesse, and the combattors with their weapons drawne fell to it, so that betwixt them were striken six or seuen blowes right lustilie. But Hamilton being verie fierce and egre, vpon trust of his innocencie, constreined Newton to giue ground almost to the end of the lists; and if he had driuen him to the end indéed, then by the law of armes he had woone the victorie. Newton perceiuing himselfe to be almost at point to be thus ouercome,

stept forwards againe, and gaue Hamilton such a gash on the leg, that he was not able longer to stand, but fell therewith downe to the ground, and then Newton falling on him, incontinentlie slue him with a dagger.

There were gentlemen present that knowing as they tooke it for certeine, how Newton was the offendor (although fortune had fauoured him in the combat) would gladlie haue ventured their liues against him man for man, if it might haue béene granted:

but he chalenging the law of armes, had it granted by my lord Greie, who gaue him also his owne gowne beside his own backe, and a chaine of gold which he then ware. Thus was he well rewarded how so euer he deserued: but he escaped not so,

for afterwards as he was riding betwixt the borders of both the realms, he was slaine
and

and cut in péeces. On the fourth of Iune, the towne of Dawketh was burnt, and the castell woone by force, where fourteene Scots were slaine, and thrée hundred taken prisoners, amongst whome were these men of name; the maister of Morton, son in law to sir George Dowglasse, the lard of Blengaruie, the lard of Wedderburne, and one Alexander Hume, a man of good reputation among them. The same daie the English horssemen burnt all the mils round about Edenburgh, within the compasse of six miles on each side the towne. The seuenth of Iune they burnt Muskelburgh. Now after that my lord Greie had fortified Hadington, and furnished it with vittels, and munition sufficient, the twelfe of Iune he departed from thence homewards, leauing there in garrison about two thousand footmen, and fiue hundred horssemen.

Muskelburgh burnt

In this meane time, Henrie the French king succeeding his father Francis the first (who departed this life the last of March in the yere last past, to wit, 1547) made prouision of an armie, with a nauie of ships and gallies, to passe into Scotland to the aid of the quéene and other of his faction. And first he had sent thither monsieur de la Chapelle de Biron, a gentleman of good account, to assist the gouernour with his aduise and counsell, which gouernour desirous to recouer the castell of Broughticrag, and loth to sée it possessed by the Englishmen, raised a power of eight thousand men, and with eight péeces of artillerie came before that fortresse, meaning to win it by siege; but by the valiant prowes of sir Andrew Dudleie, and the hardie manhood of such English souldiors as serued there vnder him, the Scots were repelled, and driuen to leuie their siege with dishonor.

The French king prepareth an armie in aid of the Scots.

Broughticrag besieged.

Yet not thus contented, the earle of Argile with an armie of his Irish Scots, or Heiland men (if I maie so call them) after this likewise came and besieged the place, but glad to take truce for a time with sir Andrew. Before the tearme of the same truce was expired, there came new succours to him, and thereupon the earle in the end was constrained to leuie his siege, and suffer the Englishmen to become maisters of a little hill not farre off from the castell, where afterwards they builded a fortresse. But to returne to the French armie which was prepared to passe into Scotland, ye shall vnderstand that when their ships and prouisions were once readie, and the capteins with their bands come downe to Brest in Britaine, where the nauie was rigged to receiue them, monsieur de Desse generall of all the armie, reckoned to conteine seuen or eight thousand men, imbarked himselfe with all his people, and sailed foorth on his iournie, till they arriued in the Forth, and there tooke land at Lieth the sixteenth of Iune.

Monsieur de Desse general of the French armie. He landeth at Lieth.

Shortlie after, hauing got their great artillerie on land, and taken aduise with the lord gouernour & other of the Scotish nobilitie, whome they found at Edenburgh, how to proceed in prosecuting the war against the Englishmen, it was resolued that without delaie they shuld trie their forces about the recouerie of Hadington, and go to besiege that towne, before they attempted anie further exploit. The gouernour and other of the Scotish lords, hauing with them seuen or eight hundred light horssemen, offred to go with them, to the better aduancing forward of that enterprise. Herevpon setting forward, and comming to Muskelburgh, the capteins with a certeine number of horssemen and footmen, as well of Scots as Frenchmen, were appointed to go before to view the said towne of Hadington. Vpon their approch neere to the towne, there issued foorth certeine Englishmen and Italians, that were of Tiberios band, which skirmished with them right stoutlie, till at length the Frenchmen and Scots retired backe to Lauret a little from Muskelburgh (where their armie incamped for that night) and the Englishmen and Italians returned backe to the fortresse.

The Frenchmen resolue to besiege Hadington.

The next daie the Frenchmen and Scots with their whole power came before Hadington, where they were welcomed with a right sharpe and hot skirmish, in which was slaine with an harquebuse shot, one of the French capteins called Villeneufue.

The French armie commeth before Hadington.

I i

The Reinsgraue. In the meane time whilest this skirmish continued, the Reinsgraue with his Almans incamped himselfe on the one side of the towne, where the maister of the ordinance in the French armie, named monsieur Duno, caused trenches to be cast for the safe placing of the artillerie: the Englishmen still kept them occupied on each side the towne with shirmishing, to the annoiance of the aduersaries. To conclude, they incamped before the towne, cast trenches, lodged their ordinance, & laid their siege to the most aduantage, so far as they might be suffered. Shortlie after that this siege was planted, there came to the aid of the French, the earle of Argile, with a great number of Irish Scots, and monsieur de la Chapelle brought an eight or nine hundred Scotish pioners, which began a trench on the left hand of the abbeie gate, and likewise a trauerse to couer their souldiors that should watch and ward, from danger of the shot ont of the towne on that side.

The valiancie
of the Englishmen.

The Reinsgraue.

They plant
their artillerie.

The earle of
Argile.
Monsieur de la
Chapelle.

Piero Strozzi
hurt.

Hadington
battered.

The Englishmen with often issues gaue their aduersaries small rest, procuring manie hot skirmishes, as occasion serued. At one of the which skirmishes Piero Strozzi, coronell of three ensigns of Italians, was striken with a musket shot. Yet monsieur de Desse inforcing the siege to the vttermost of his power, caused one night with helpe of baskets filled with earth, six peeces of artillerie to be planted in batterie fast at the towne side, which at the breake of daie began to shoot off, and discharged that present daie thrée hundred and fortie shots. But after they perceiued that they did litle hurt to the fortifications of the towne in that place where this batterie was laid: the next night, the baskets & péeces of artillerie were remooued lower, and not past three score pases from the ditches of the towne, where the next daie two hundred shots were discharged against the rampire. To conclude, they made such breaches in sundrie places for easie entrie into the towne, that it was greatlie maruelled whie they durst not assaie to giue a general assault.

They lodged so neare within the verie ditches, that there were deuised certeine plummets of lead, tied with cords to a truncheon of a staffe, like to an handstaffe of a flaile, wherewith the souldiors that watched and warded within the towne on the rampire, slue diuerse of the Frenchmen being their lodged within their ditches. Thus notwithstanding that the Frenchmen with their artillerie had broken downe the fortifications, so as the breaches were made verie reasonable and easie for them to enter; yet durst they not presume once to giue the assault: for the Englishmen although their powder was sore spent, and that for want of matches they were constreined to teare their shirts, and vse the same in sted of matches; yet they shewed themselues so valiant in defending the towne thus beaten & made weake on each hand, that there was no hope left to their aduersaries to win it of them by force. Although the French power on the one side, and eight thousand Scots on an other had so inuironed it, that the Englishmen within were driuen to the most hard shifts, for want of things necessarie & requisite or their maintenance and defense of that towne.

Succours entring the towne.

But yet whilest they remained thus in such distresse and necessitie of things, two hundred Englishmen vnder the conduct of capteine Windham, Warham Seintleger, and Iohn Car of Warke, found meanes one night to passe through all the watches on that side where the Scots laie, and entering the towne, and bringing with them great plentie of powder, and other necessaries, greatlie relieued them within, & so incouraged them, that they séemed to make small account of their enimies forces. Herevpon within few daies after, the Scots (fiue or six hundred light horssemen onelie excepted) brake vp their campe and returned home. After this, my lord Greie remaining at Berwike, ment to make a voiage himselfe in person for the reliefe of them that were thus besieged in Hadington. Now when all things were so farre in a readinesse as the next daie he ment to haue set forward, letters were brought that night from the court, willing him to performe that seruice by a deputie, and to staie himselfe till the comming

ming of the earle of Shrewesburie, who was appointed with an armie to come verie shortlie as generall into those parties.

My lord Greie herevpon appointed in his stead sir Robert Bowes, and sir Thomas Sir Robert Bowes sent to succour Hadington Palmer, to go thither, who comming to Dunglas, left there certeine bands of footmen, and with the horssemen being in number thirtéene hundred (whereof seuen hundred lances were appointed vnder the charge of sir Thomas Palmer) they rode forward to accomplish their enterprise: but the French capteins hauing knowledge of their comming, they prouided the best they could to repell them, appointing foure venlins or ensignes of lanceknights to kéepe a standing watch that night in the trenches, and the like number of French ensignes to watch about their campe. All the other of their bands were commanded to take rest, but yet with their armour on their backs.

Their generall monsieur de Desse himselfe, monsieur de Mailleraie admerall of their fléet, monsieur Dandelot coronell of the French footmen, Piero Strozzi coronell of the Italians, the Reinsgraue coronell of the lanceknights, and all other the noble men and capteins of honour among them were all night long in armour, trauelling vp and downe, some on horssebacke, and some on foot, to visit the watches and skouts, set in places and waies by the which they suspected that the Englishmen ment to come. The lord Hume. The lord Hume riding abrode to learne what he might of the Englishmens demeanour earlie in the morning returned to the campe, and certified monsieur de Desse, that they were at hand. Herewith were the Scotish and French horssemen that kept the scout called in, and monsieur Dandelot with great expedition ranged his battell of Dandelot. footmen in order, and so likewise did the Reinsgraue his Almans.

The Englishmen diuided into two bands came and shewed themselues in the sight of the towne, and charging such Scots and Frenchmen as came foorth to incounter them, gaue them the ouerthrow at two seuerall charges: but finallie presuming too farre vpon their good lucke thus chancing to them in the beginning, followed in chase those that fled before them, vntill at length they were inclosed and shut vp betwixt the French footmen on the one side, and the Almans on the other. And herewith the Scotish horsmen vnder the conduct of the lords, Humes & Dune, & the French horssemen led by monsieur de Étauges their generall, being assembled togither eftsoones, Monsieur Étauges. after they had beene so repelled, were now readie to come forward againe: and perceiuing their footmen so to haue inuironed the Englishmen, that they were not able to recouer themselues, nor to get out of danger, but by disordring their ranks to take The English horssemen discomfited. them to flight, followed amaine, so that those which escaped the Frenchmens hands were taken by the Scots that pursued them in chase, so that few were saued that were not either slaine or taken. My lord Greie lost thréescore and twelue great horsses, and an hundred geldings, with all the men vpon them, armed with his lordships owne furniture, onelie foure or fiue of his men came home, of the which Thomas Cornwallis now groome porter to the *quéenes maiestie was one, Robert Car esquier an other then * Quéene Elizabeth. page to my said lord Greie.

The vnaduised rashnesse of sir Thomas Palmer was thought to be the chiefe occasion of this distresse of those horssemen, who after they had doone sufficientlie for that time, would needs haue them to giue a new charge, and so were discomfited. After this ouerthrow and chase of our horssemen, the armie that was leuied to passe into Scotland was hasted forward with all spéed possible: for although before the comming of the English horssemen, the French, vpon aduertisement giuen that they meant to come, The Frenchmen remooue their campe. had plucked backe their great artillerie, and sent the same vnto Edenburgh, kéeping onelie with them six field-péeces, and herewith remooued their campe further off from the towne: yet by forestalling vitels and all other necessarie things from them within, they were driuen to such distresse, that they must of force haue left the towne to the enimies, if some power had not come within a while to remooue the siege that laie thus to annoie them.

When

When therefore the armie was come to Newcastell, & the earle of Shrewesburie generall lieutenant of the same was there arriued, they passed forward to Berwike, and from thense marched streight towards Hadington. The number of the Englishmen and strangers was reported at the point of fifteene thousand, whereof thrée thousand were Almans vnder the conduct of a right worthie and expert chiefteine, named Conrad Phenning, commonlie called Cortpenie. Beside this armie by land, there was also furnished foorth a fléet by sea, vnder the conduct of the lord Clinton high admerall of England, and other capteins of great experience in affaires and seruice by sea. This fléet was appointed so to kéepe course with the armie by land, that the one might be euer in sight of the other. Monsieur de Desse aduertised of the comming forward of this armie, durst not abide their comming, but raised his field, and retired with his armie toward Edenburgh: howbeit they were no sooner dislodged, but that a great troope of the English horssemen were got within sight of them, and coasted them all the waie as they marched for the space of seuen or eight miles, in maner to as farre as Muskelburgh, where the Frenchmen staied, and incamped in a place chosen foorth to their most aduantage.

The earle of Shrewesburie, and the lord Greie with the armie comming vnto Hadington, were ioifullie receiued of the capteins and soldiours within: where it might appeare how valiantlie they had defended that tòwne during the siege, being so destitute of all things necessarie for their reléefe; and the fortifications so weake, that if the noble prowesse of their woorthie generall sir Iames Wilford, and the incomparable manhood of the rest of the capteins and soldiours had not supplied all other wants, it was thought impossible that they should haue defended the place so long a time against such forces as had beene there imploied against them. But such was the vndanted valiancie of that noble crue and garrison, that euen the verie enimies themselues could not but yéeld high commendations to the capteins and soldiours for the hardie forwardnesse and manhood, which at all times they had found and tried in them at all points of seruice, when they came to deale with them. And verelie their fame deserueth to be had in memorie for euer, not onelie for their woorthie atchiued exploits, doone by force of hand, to the beating backe and repelling of the enimies, but also for their patient susteining of hunger, thirst, continuall watching, nakednesse, sicke-

nesse, and all other such calamities and miseries, as want of things necessarie for the reléefe and maintenance of mans life is woont to bring, to those that are inclosed in such wise by the enimie. All which extremities they were well content to susteine, so that it might turne to the benefit and renowme of their countrie, in comparison whereof they esteemed all things else verie vile and contemptible, were the same neuer so good, as the poet saith:

Tantus amor patriæ mortalia pectora tangit,
Natalisque soli, præ quo bona cætera sordent.

The noble earle of Shrewesburie could not forbeare to shed teares, to vnderstand and perceiue that such woorthie soldiours should suffer such great distresse, whose valiant hearts could not be quailed with anie afflictions. Thus with mournefull imbracings intermixed with pitifull regards they met. The earle entering the towne, furnished it with new bands of men, good store of vittels, munition, and all other things conuenient, and as then thought requisit. Thus hauing refreshed the towne,

within two daies after he passed foorth towards the enimies, appointing by the aduise of that noble chiefteine the lord Greie, certeine bands of horssemen to kéepe themselues close togither in ambush, and to send a few to the French campe, to trie if they might traine the Frenchmen out of their strength. And as they wished, it partlie came to passe: for diuerse of their horssemen issued foorth of their campe, and proffered the skirmish. The Englishmen suffered themselues to be chased, vntill they had got their enimies within danger of their ambush, and then whirling about, gaue

them the charge, inforcing them to make their careir backe, with more than an easie
                                                                gallop;

gallop; so that hauing the Frenchmen thus in chase, they slue and tooke diuerse, and among the prisoners were two capteins, Pierre Longue, and one Lucinet. The others that escaped, returned with this losse to their campe.

In the meane time, whilest these things were thus in dooing, there came to the aid of the Frenchmen fouretéene or fiftéene thousand Scots, accounting herewith the Irish Scots which came with the earle of Argile. These Scots were scarse lodged, when suddenlie the earle of Shrewesburie & the lord Greie came with their armie diuided into three battels of footmen, garded with two troops of horssemen, presenting themselues before the faces of their enimies in the same place, where their auant currors the daie before had shewed themselues to draw foorth the Frenchmen. Here the armie thus ranged in arraie of battell, staied aboue the space of an houre, looking if the enimies durst haue come foorth to haue giuen battell: but when they perceiued that by no meanes the Frenchmen meant to forsake their strength, they returned backe to their campe. The English nauie being entered now into the Forth, was not idle: for comming to Brent Iland they set fire on foure ships, which they found there, and after passing by Lieth saluted them within the towne with cannon shot, and after intending to burne saint Minets, were repelled from thense by the lord of Dune, and after returned to attend on the armie. The earle of Shrewesburie, and my lord Greie hauing executed so much as their commission would beare, and refreshed Hadington with all things néedfull, departed homewards; and comming to Dunglas, began there to build a fortresse. The English Almans as the armie passed by Dunbar, burned the towne. These Almans also, and certeine bands of Englishmen, as well horssemen as footmen, were left at Dunglas, vntill the fort there begun was in some strength. The earle of Shrewesburie with the rest of the armie came backe into England. My lord Greie remaining on the borders lieutenant of the north parts, after the earle of Shrewesburie was returned home, assembled all the horssemen then lieng on the borders, and being backed with the Almane footmen, entered againe with the same horssemen into Scotland, burning and wasting in the countries of Tiuidall, and Liddesdall, for the space of twentie miles, both house, corne, haie, and all other things that came within their reach, and after returned without incounter.

The ninth of October being tuesdaie, monsieur de Desse, with his Frenchmen and Almans, came in the morning long before daie to Hadington, meaning to haue woone the towne by stealth. And verelie the enterprise was gouerned in such secret maner, that the Frenchmen had killed the English scouts, and were entered the base court, yer anie alarum was raised: and hauing slaine the watch, some of them ran to a place behind a church, where the Englishmen had their vittels and munitions, and some thrust vp to the towne gate, inforsing with great violence to breake it open, crieng with noise and shouts, Victorie, victorie, whereof in déed they accounted themselues then assured. And questionles the Englishmen being thus wakened out of their sléeps on the sudden, were in some great disorder; so that manie of them came running foorth without either armour or apparell, their shirts excepted; & others ran they wist not well whither, nor where to take héed. But yet as the Frenchmen were thronged togither at the gate to breake it open, a Frenchman (as their writers doo report) that serued within the towne, but as other saie Tiberio capteine of the Italians, with his match light gaue fier to a double canon, that laie readie bent against the gate, so that the same shooting off, made such a lane among the Frenchmen, that they were glad to giue place, and with such a fearefull crie, that those which were behind, not vnderstanding what losse their fellowes before had susteined, brake their arraie and fled amaine.

The Englishmen herewith passed through a priuie posterne into the base court, and comming vpon them with their halberds, and blacke bils, slue of them great plentie, and droue the rest that escaped ouer the wall in such hast, that happie was he that could tumble ouer first. Monsieur de Desse yet gathering them togither againe, gaue

that

Side notes:

The armie of the Scots come to ioine with the Frenchmen.

The earle of Shrewesburie preferrth the enimies battell.

The Frenchmen durst not come foorth of their campe.

Ships burned.

A fortresse built at Dunglas.

The lord Greie entereth againe into Scotland.

A camisado giuen to Hadington.

The Frenchmen repelled.

that morning thrée sharpe assaults to the towne, but was repelled with great losse, for they caried awaie with them sixtéene carts and wagons laden with hurt persons and dead carcasses, besides thrée hundred that were found in the base court, which they could not come to, after they were beaten out, to take awaie with them. And thus was monsieur de Desse constreined to returne, repenting himselfe of that his bold attempted enterprise, hauing lost no small number of his Frenchmen and Almans, being slaine in the place. In this meane time, the kings maiestie summoned his high court of parlement, to be holden vpon prorogation at Westminster the fourth of Nouember, where it continued till the fourtéenth of March next insuing.

A parlement.

In the meane time, the proceedings for the Scotish wars was not forgotten, wherevpon in the deepe of the winter, there were conueied certeine bands of the English lancequenets, and some number of Englishmen, both horssemen and footmen by sea vnto Broughticrag; and passing from thence vnto Dundée, a two miles from thence, entred the towne, and began to fortifie it: but shortlie after by the comming of the French armie with monsieur de Desse, they left it, first spoiling the houses, and after set them on fire at their departure. The Reinsgraue coronell of the Almans, and monsieur de Etauges, being sent by monsieur de Desse before, entered Dundee, and lodged within it. Within two daies after their comming thither, they tooke certeine of their bands, and goingf oorth did view and surueie the new fort, which the Englishmen had begun to make on the hill, a small distance from the castell. But the Englishmen and their Almans issuing foorth against them, were at their elbowes yer they were halfe well aduised that they were got so neare them, whereby being driuen hastilie to retire, they hardlie escaped out of danger, being so hotlie pursued, that if the Reinsgraue had not shewed his approoued valiancie, guided with no lesse policie than manhood, the whole troope had béene (as was thought) vtterlie distressed.

Dundée spoiled.

The Reinsgraue constreined to retire.

In Christmasse this yéere the castell of Hume was recouered out of the Englishmens hands, through treson of certeine assured Scots, that vsing to bring vittels to the Englishmen that kept it, had marked all the manner of the scouts and watches, with the places of the wall where the clime was most easie. Wherevpon in the night season, certeine of the Scots secretlie comming into the ditches, got vp to the height of the walls, and entring the place, slue and tooke vpon the sudden all that were within it. The sixtéenth of Ianuarie, sir Thomas Seimer baron of Sudleie, lord admerall, and brother to the duke of Summerset lord protector, was arrested and sent to the tower, and after by authoritie of parlement he was attainted, and the twentith of March next insuing, in the third yeare of this kings reigne beheaded at tower hill. Moreouer in this parlement, the vse of the masse was clearlie prohibited, and a booke for the vniformitie of diuine seruice, and right administration of the sacraments, was set foorth and established.

1549

Sir Thomas Seimer sent to the tower.

An. Reg. 3.

The masse abolished.

Yée haue heard how the Frenchmen fortified the towne of Dundee, where monsieur de Etauges, with his companie of horssemen lieng in garrison chanced in a skirmish to be taken by the Englishmen that laie in Broughticrag, to the great reioising of them that tooke him, and no lesse gréefe of the French and Scots, for the tried valiancie that was throughlie knowne to rest in him. Moreouer, the Englishmen that kept the towne of Hadington all this while against the enimies, could not come by anie vittels, but onelie by a conuoie of some conuenient power to gard the cariages that brought the same from the borders. And as it fortuned at one time when the conuoie came and passed by Dunbar, a skirmish was proffered by the French which laie within that castell in garrison. And as sir Iames Wilford that was there amongst other vpon this occasion (according to his woonted valiancie) shewed himselfe verie forward and egre against the enimie, he was inclosed by an ambush, which the Frenchmen had laid on ech side the stréet within the towne, that he could by no means escape out of their hands, but hauing his horsse there slaine vnder him, was taken prisoner euen by a

Monsieur de Etauges taken prisoner.

Gascoigne

Gascoigne of the countrie of Basque named Pellicque, that woone no small commend- Sir Iames Wilford taken prisoner. ation for that his good hap, in taking such a prisoner, whose name for his often approoued prowesse was verie famous euen among the enimies, who saw well inough a resolutenesse in the man rather by perillous aduentures to purchase the perpetuitie of renowme, than by defect of courage or negligent seruice to loose both life and fame. Which persuasion should enter into the hart of euerie seruitor in the field, if they will be counted right valiant indeed, considering that he which in his life time dooth performe nothing worthie memorie, is like a plaier entering vpon the stage, but shewing nothing either in spéech or in action, as the poet verie fitlie saith:

> Qui nullum facinus tota memorabile vita
> Ediderint, obscuri homines migrare videntur
> Hinc, vt qui structa nil dixerit histrio scena.

Some haue written that he was taken through default of those that were appointed to follow him, sith he vndertooke to charge the enimie, in hope that by them he should haue béene assisted. But suerlie those that had the charge of this conuoie, doubting by aduenturing too far, to put all in hazard, thought it wisedome rather to suffer the losse of one than to ieopard the whole; not perceiuing which waie to remedie the matter at that prsent. Now after that the generall of Hadington was thus taken prisoner, to the great griefe vndoubtedlie, not onelie of all the garrison there, but also of all such as tendered the aduancement of the kings maiesties seruice, sir Iames Crofts was Sir Iames Crofts generall of Hadington. thought a man most méet to supplie the place, and therefore by the lord protector and others of the councell was ordeined generall of that towne of Hadington, and the garrison there, in which roome he bare himselfe so worthilie, as if I should not be suspected of flatterie, for that he liueth yet, and in such credit (as the world knoweth) I might mooue my selfe matter to saie rather much than sufficientlie inough in his due and right deserued commendation.

The king by the aduise of his councell meaning to prosecute the wars in Scotland with great forces, reteined a new power of lancequenets, and other strangers, vnder the conduct of diuers & sundrie capteines: but in the meane time the French king meaning to breake with the king of England, thought to haue stolen the fortresse of Bullognberg, so that a chosen power of men of warre, to the number of seuen thousand, vnder the conduct of monsieur de Chatillon, being sent downe about that exploit on Maie daie at night, came forward with their ladders, and all other furniture méet for the purpose, approching about the houre of midnight néere to the fort, within the which were not at that time manie aboue thrée hundred and fiftie soldiers, vnder the gouernement of sir Nicholas Arnalt knight generall of that péece, a cap- Sir Nicholas Arnalt capteine of Bullognberg. teine of great courage, and no lesse diligence in his charge.

And as it chanced, there were among the Frenchmen thrée or foure Englishmen, which hauing matched themselues in marriage with women of that countrie, after the peace was concluded betwixt France and England, were discharged out of the king of Englands wages; and remaining with their wiues, got interteinement among the Frenchmen, and were with monsieur de Chatillon, now comming towards this enterprise. Wherevpon one of the same Englishmen named Carter, that had aforetime Carter an Englishman seruing amõg the Frenchmen, but to their disaduantage. giuen intelligence to the said sir Nicholas of the Frenchmens dooings so farre as he might learne and vnderstand the same, would gladlie haue aduertised sir Nicholas Arnalt of the Frenchmens purpose at this time: but monsieur de Chatillon kept the matter so secret, that Carter nor any of the other Englishmen had knowledge thereof, till they were now marching forward, so that Carter could not get awaie from them, till they were approched within lesse than a quarter of a mile of Bullognberg, and then slipping aside from among them, came running so fast as he might towards the fort, crieng; Bowes, bowes, as lowd as his voice would serue, & so gaue the alarum to them within the fort.

One.

One of the soldiers called Morgaine Deaton, that chanced to be there at hand in scout with three or foure other, streight knew him, and brought him to the draw-bridge, where sir Nicholas Arnalt caused him to be drawen vp betwixt two pikes, vnto whome he declared how the Frenchmen were at hand, meaning to assaile his fort now vpon the sudden, in hope so to surprise it. Herewith it néeded not to will sir Nicholas to bestirre him, to cause euerie man to make readie, and place themselues as was thought most expedient. And vndoubtedlie the noble courage of that worthie gentleman, furthered much, to cause euerie capteine and soldier vnder him, to put awaie all feare, and to haue a regard to doo his dutie, for the receiuing of the enimies; so as they séemed glad of the occasion, whereby they might shew proofe of their accustomed manhood against the enimie, that thus came to steale on them without warning, in purpose to kill euerie man that fell into their hands, if their intention had taken place, making now such hast forward, that before the Englishmen could be well readie with their armour and weapons in their appointed places, the Frenchmen were got to the ditches, and appointing thrée thousand of their numbers, the most part gentlemen and double paies, with targets, battell axes, and pistols, to haue the first scale, saluted them within vpon their verie approch, with seuen hundred harquebuts shot at the first volée.

Sir Nicholas Arnalts valiantnesse.

The Frenchmen assaile Bullognberg.

The Englishmen by order giuen by sir Nicholas, kept themselues close, till the Frenchmen by their scaling ladders, which they brought with them, and had quickelie raised against the walles, began to mount vp, and enter vpon them; at which instant, off went the flankers. Those of sir Nicholas Arnalts monts discharged verie well at the first, but at the second volee the morters burst. Albeit there were two brasse peeces that were planted aloft on the same mont, of the which the one discharged fiue & twentie shot by the maister, and the other seuen and twentie by his maiestie. Sir Nicholas Arnalt here being accompanied with his capteins and soldiers about him, stood at defense so stoutlie as was possible, dooing so valiantlie, that their fame deserueth to liue for euer. There were burst vpon the faces of the enimies (ouer and beside the shot that was bestowed among them) to the number of fiftéene hundred pikes and blacke bils. The Frenchmen verelie stucke to it to the vttermost, and did what laie in the verie last point of their powers to enter vpon the Englishmen, supplieng still the places of their dead and wearie men with fresh succors.

The number of pikes and bils broken vpon the Frenchmen.

Carter that came to bring word of their comming, with a pike in his hand, stood at the place of the bulworke where they thus gaue the assault, & fought right valiantlie, giuing manie wounds, and receiuing some againe: for he was hurt both in the thigh and arme, who suerlie of a priuat soldier (if he were priuat and ordinarie) séemed verie seruiceable at all assaies, considering into what desperat aduentures and hazzards he did as it were cast himselfe, estéeming lesse the losse of life and lim, than the reproch and dishonor of his countrie, the glorie & renowme wherof (aboue all worldlie things which are but temporall) all men are naturallie bound with might & maine both to séeke and saue; as one verie well saith:

Carter an hardie soldier and a good seruitor.

Nascimur vt patriam vitáque operáque iuuemus.

Sir Nicholas Arnalt himselfe was hurt with a pike in the nose. Capteine Warren standing on the same bulworke with sir Nicholas, receiued two shots in his corselet, and one of them droue two or three links of his chaine into his necke. Capteine Broughton had there sixtéene of his armed men, euerie of them hauing their corselets persed through. The number of the Englishmen that were slaine, was reckoned to be fiue and twentie, and hurt eight and fiftie. Of Frenchmen there were slaine a great number, beside those that were hurt, and at length through shot, casting downe of stones and timber vpon their heads, scalding water and handblowes they were repelled, retiring out of the trenches shortlie after the breake of the daie, hauing continued the assault from midnight till that time, still renewing their forces, in hope to atchiue
their

The Frenchmen repelled.

their wished preie : but being thus beaten off, they gathered togither their dead men, and lading fiftéene waggons with their carcasses, they returned backe, without making anie further attempt at that time. Fiftéene wagons laden with French carcasses.

And so by the high valiancie of sir Nicholas Arnalt, and the other capteins that serued in that fort vnder him, and chieflie by the assistance of almightie God, the giuer of all victories, the enimies were repelled, to their great dishonor, and the péece reserued to the immortall renowme of the defendants. Within a daie or two after, the generall of the Frenchmen sent to know of prisoners taken ; but sir Nicholas Arnalt answered the messenger, "that he knew of no warre : and therefore if anie had attempted to make a surprise of his péece by stealth, they were serued accordinglie to their malicious meanings. Indéed (said he) we haue taken none of your men, but we haue got some of your braue guilt armour & weapons. Well (said the messenger) it is not the cowle that maketh the moonke, and no more is it the braue armour or weapon that maketh the man of warre : but the fortune of warre is such, sometime to gaine, and sometime to lose." Sir Nicholas receiuing him into the fort, made him good chéere, a n dgaue him fiftie crownes in reward, and so he departed.

But concerning the liberalitie of sir Nicholas, I might here speake further thereof, how bountifullie he rewarded the souldiers for their great manhood shewed at that time, in defending so sharpe an assault, to their great honour, and no lesse confusion of the aduersaries. The daie after the said assault, there came to Bullognberg from Guisnes, a supplie of thrée or foure hundred men, vnder the leading of sir William Cobham, now lord Cobham and others. Within a while after, sir Nicholas Arnalt sent forth thrée hundred footmen, and fiue and twentie horssemen, conducted by the said sir William Cobham, capteine Mutton of the Old man, & capteine More of Bulognberg, with certeine cariages, to go vnto a wood not farre off, called the north wood, to fetch fagots and brush, to repare and mainteine the rampires. The lord Cobham with a new supplie of souldiers.

These capteins with their bands being passed forward, about two miles in distance from the fort, met with certeine of their scouts that were sent forth that morning, who told them that they had discouered the tract of a great number of horssemen. Whervpon the Englishmen now being almost come to the wood side, retired with all spéed : and herewith the French horssemen brake out of the wood, and following them, fell in skirmish with them. The Englishmen casting themselues in a ring, kept them off with their pikes, wherewith they impailed themselues, and hauing their small troope lined with shot, they also galled the Frenchmen right sore therewith, as they still approched them. Neuerthelesse, those horssemen gaue three manie onsets vpon the Englishmen, with the number of a thousand horsse at two of the first onsets, and the third they gaue with all their whole power, being estéemed a fiftéene hundred horssemen in all.

But such was the valiant prowesse of the English souldiers, incouraged with the comfortable presence of sir William Cobham, and other their capteins, that conducted them in such order as stood most for their safegard, exhorting them with such effectuall words as serued best to purpose, that the enimie to conclude was repelled with losse of seuentie of their great horsses that laie dead there in the field, within the space of halfe a mile. There were also foure thousand French footmen that came forward, but could not reach, and so marching about the fort, returned in vaine, after they once perceiued that the Englishmen were safelie retired within their fort. The councell thus perceiuing the French kings purpose, which he had conceiued to worke some notable damage to this realme, as well in support of his friends in Scotland, as in hope to recouer those peeces which the English held at Bullongne, and in those marches, doubted also of some inuasion meant by him to be attempted into this realme, bicause of such great preparation as he had made, for leuieng of his forces both by sea and land. The great valiacie of the Englishmen vnder the conduct of their noble capteins.

                                         The

*The preparation
for warre as
well in England
as France.*

The councell therefore made likewise prouision to be readie to resist all such attempts, as anie waie foorth might be made, to the annoiance of the realme. But as things fell out, the same stood in good stead, not against the forren enimie, but against a number of rebellious subiects at home, the which forgetting their dutie and allegiance, did as much as in them laie (what soeuer their pretense was) to bring this noble realme and their naturall countrie vnto destruction. But first, for that it maie appeare, that the duke of Summerset then protector, and other of the councell, did not without good ground and cause mainteine the warres against the Scots, I haue thought good to set downe an epistle exhortatorie, as we find the same in the great chronicle of Richard Grafton, sent from the said protector and councell vnto the Scots, to mooue them to haue consideration of themselues, and of the estate of their countrie, by ioining in that friendlie bond and vnitie with England, as had beene of the kings part and his fathers continuallie sought, for the benefit of both realmes, the copie of which exhortation here insueth.

*Rich. Grafton
in fol. 1294.*

*The lord pro-
tectors right
honorable stile.*

Edward by the grace of God, duke of Summerset, earle of Hertford, vicount Beauchampe, lord Seimer, vncle to the kings highnesse of England, gouernor of his most roiall person, and protector of all his realmes, dominions, & subiects, lieutenant generall of all his maiesties armies, both by land and sea, treasuror and earle marshall of England, gouernor of the Iles of Gerneseie and Ierseie, and knight of the most noble order of the garter, with others of the councell of the said most high and noble prince Edward, by the grace of God of England, France, and Ireland king, defender of the faith, and in earth vnder Christ the supreame head of the churches of England and Ireland. To the nobilitie and councellors, gentlemen and commons, and all other the inhabitants of the realme of Scotland, greeting and peace.

*The epistle ex-
hortatorie sent
to the Scots.*

CONSIDERING with our selues the present state of things, and weieng more déepelie the maner and tearmes wherein you and we doo stand, it maketh vs to maruell what euill & fatall chance dooth so disseuer your hearts, and maketh them so blind and vnmindfull of your profit, and so still conciliate and heape to your selues most extreame mischiefs, the which we whome ye will néeds haue your enimies, go about to take awaie from you, and perpetuallie to ease you therof. And also by all reason & order of necessitie, it should be rather more conuenient for you to séeke and require moderate agréements of vs, whome God hath hitherto according to our most iust, true, and godlie meanings and intents, prospered and set forward, with your affliction and miserie, than that we being superiours in the field, maisters of a great part of your realme, should seeke vpon you. Yet to the intent that our charitable minds and brotherlie loue should not cease, by all meanes possible to prouoke and call you to your owne commoditie and profit, euen as the father to the son, or the elder brother to the yoonger; and as the louing physician would doo to the mistrustfull and ignorant patient : we are content to call and crie vpon you to looke on your estate, to auoid the great calamitie that your countrie is in, to haue vs rather brothers than enimies, and rather countrimen than conquerors. And if your gouernor or capteins shall reteine and kéepe from you this our exhortation, as heretofore they haue doone our proclamation, tending to the like effect, for their owne priuat wealth & commoditie, not regarding though you be still in miserie, so they haue profit and gouernance ouer you, and shall still abuse you with feined and forged tales : yet this shall be a witnesse before God and all christian people betweene you and vs, that we professing the gospell of Iesus Christ, according to the doctrine thereof, doo not cease to call and prouoke you from the effusion of your owne bloud, from the destruction of the realme of Scotland, from perpetuall

*Herein appear-
eth the lord
protectors care
for their good
estate.*

petuall enimitie and hatred, from the finall destruction of your nation, and from seruitude to forren nations, to libertie, to amitie, to equalitie with vs, to that which your writers haue alwaies wished might once come to passe.

Who that hath read the stories in times past, and dooth marke & note the great battels past fought betwixt England & Scotland, the incursions, rodes, & spoiles, which haue béene doone on both parties: the realme of Scotland fiue times woone by one king of England, the Scotish kings some taken prisoners, some slaine in battell, some for verie sorrow and discomfort vpon losse, dieng and departing the world: and shall perceiue againe, that all nations in the world, that nation onelie beside England, speaketh the same language: and as you and we be annexed and ioined in one Iland, so no people are so like in maners, forme, language, and all conditions as we are: shall not he thinke it a thing verie vnméet, vnnaturall, and vnchristian, that there should be betwixt vs so mortall war, who in respect of all other nations, be and should be like as two brethren of one Iland of Great Britaine? And though he were a stranger to both, what should he thinke more meet, than if it were possible one kingdome to be made in rule, which is one in language, and to be diuided in rulers, which is all one in countrie? Scotland woone fiue times by one king of England.

And for so much as two successors cannot concurre and fall into one, by no other maner of meanes than by marriage, whereby one bloud, one linage, one parentage is made of two, and an indefensible right giuen of both to one, without the destruction and abolishing of either. If God should grant that whatsoeuer you would wish, other than that which now not by fortune hath chanced, but by his infinit mercie and most inscrutable prouidence, as carefull for you he hath giuen vnto you. The which thing that you should also thinke to come of his disposition, and not by blind fortune, how vnlike hath it beene, and how suddenlie hath it turned, that the power of God might be shewed: your last king being a prince of much excellencie and yoong, whom you know after a promise broken contrarie to his honor, & misfortune by Gods iust iudgement following vpon it, God either by sorrow or by some meanes otherwise at his inscrutable pleasure, did take awaie from you, had thrée children, did not almightie God (as it were) to shew his will and pleasure to be, that the long continued warre and enimitie of both the nations should be taken awaie, and knit in perpetuall loue and amitie, take the two men-children of those babes being distant the one from the other, and in diuerse places, both as it were at one time, and within the space of foure and twentie houres, leauing but one maiden-child and princesse? The case of the coniunctiõ in mariage of the two yoong princes touched.
The course of Gods iust iudgement in this example notable.

When the most wise and victorious prince late our king and maister, king Henrie the eight, in other of his mariages not most fortunate, had by his most lawfull and most vertuous wife, quéene Iane, his other two wiues before that mariage departed this world, and neuer surmise nor question made of that mariage, since that time to this daie, nor so much as all hir life time, name or motion to or of anie other wife, one prince of so high expectation, of so great gifts of God, the right and vndoubted heire of the realme of England and his maiestie onelie of male issue left behind him to succéed the imperiall crowne. If nothing else had béene doone, what can anie wise or anie christian man that thinketh the world to be gouerned by Gods prouidence and not by fortune, thinke otherwise, but that it was Gods pleasure it should be so, that these two realmes should ioine in mariage, and by a godlie sacrament, make a godlie, perpetuall and most friendlie vnitie & concord, whereby such benefits as of vnitie and concord commeth, may through his infinit grace come vnto these realmes. Or if anie man of you or of anie nation doubteth hereof, except you looked for miracles to be doone herein, and yet if ye marke all the possibilities of the natures of the two princes, the children alreadie had, the doubtfull chance, least each of them should haue a sonne, or both daughters, or not of méet ages, with other circumstances both of the partie of this realme of England, and that of Scotland, which hath not The lord protector inforceth by pithie persuasions a perpetuall vnitie betwéene the two realms by the foresaid mariage.

chanced

chanced in eight hundred yeares, it must néeds be reckoned a great maruell and a miracle.

But let it be no miracle, séeing that God dooth not now speake in oracles, as amongest the Iewes he did: and present prophesies now adaies be but either not certeine, or else not plaine: what more certeine can be had of Gods will in this case, than the before rehearsed dooth bring? But if God himselfe should speake, what could he speake more, than he speaketh in these? Call you them prouidences or chances, if The lord protector still vrgeth peace and amitie. you be still afflicted and punished? Maie he not saie: I of mine infinite mercie and loue to your nation, had prouided a right heire and a prince to the one, and a right heire and princesse to the other, to be ioined in my holie lawes, and by the lawe of nature and the world to haue made an vnitie, concord and peace, in the which Isle of both the realmes you refused it; you loued better dissention than vntitie, discord than agréement, warre than peace, hatred than loue and charitie. If you doo' then therefore smart for it, whome can you blame but your owne election?

But because some of those, who make therevnto impediments, cannot but confesse, that there appeareth Gods prouidence herein, and oportunitie and occasion giuen to vnitie of both the realmes, yet may hereafter say, and heretofore haue said, that the fault herein is, that we séeke not equalitie, nor the mariage, but a conquest: we would not be friends but the lords. Although our proclamation at the last warres dooth inough declare the contrarie, yet here we protest and declare vnto you and all christian people, to be the kings maiesties mind our maisters, by our aduise and counsell not to conquer, but to haue in amitie; not to win by force, but to conciliate by loue; not to spoile and kill, but to saue and kéepe; not to disseuer and diuorse, but to ioine in mariage, from high to low both the realms, to make of one Isle one realme, in loue, amitie, concord, peace and charitie, which if you refuse, and driue vs to conquer, who is guiltie of the bloudshed? Who is the occasion of the warre? Who maketh the battels, the burning of houses, and the deuastation which shall follow?

The Scots by the consent of a parlement granted their great seale for the confirmation of a mariage to be had betwéen Marie the heire of Scotland, & prince Edward heire of England. Can it be denied but that we haue the great seale of Scotland granted by the parlement of Scotland, for the mariage which should be made, with assurances and pledges, vntill the performance? And thus in the time that the late king of most famous memorie our souereigne lord king Henrie the eight did reigne, and in the time of the same your gouernour, who now is the earle of Arrane, who then being a chiefe dooer and laborer therin, for the high and inestimable benefit of that realme, so soone as he was by the late cardinall of saint Andrews and others, with certeine vaine feares and hopes & gréedinesse of dignitie peruerted, reuolted from his first agréement, and put all the realme to the losse of such holds and fortresses as are now taken from you, and to the losse of a foughten field, for the which we are sorie, if otherwise peace might haue bin concluded, for his owne priuat lucre and retchlesnesse of that noble realme. And what end can you looke for of these manner of proceedings, but such successe as heretofore hath béene experimented & assaied? We offer loue, we offer What offers are made to the Scots. equalitie and amitie, we ouercome in warre, and offer peace: we win holds, and offer no conquest: we get in your land, and offer England.

What can be more offered and more proffered, than intercourse of merchandizes, and interchange of mariages, the abolishing of all such our lawes, as prohibiteth the same, or might be impediment to the mutuall amitie. We haue offered not onelie to leaue the authoritie, name, title, right or chalenge of conquerour, but to receiue that which is the shame of men ouercommed, to leaue the name of the nation, and the glorie of anie victorie (if anie we haue had, or should haue of you) and to take the indifferent Britaine was the first name of England and Scotland. old name of Britains againe, because nothing should be left on our part to be offered, nothing on your part vnrefused, whereby ye might be inexcusable. And all the world might testifie all other meanes, not being able to doo anie thing, after manie other waies and remedies attempted, battell of vs to be taken as an extreame refuge, to atteine

teine right and reason among christian men: if anie man may rightfullie make battell for his espouse and wife. The daughter of Scotland was by the great seale of Scotland promised to the sonne & heire of England.

If it be lawfull by Gods lawe to fight in a good quarrell, and for to make peace, this is to make an end of all warres, and to conclude an eternall and perpetuall peace; which to confirme, we shall fight, and you to breake, is it not easie to discerne who hath the better part? God and the sword hath alreadie, and shall hereafter (if there be no remedie) trie it. Who so willeth the mariage to go forward; who so mindeth the peace and tranquillitie of both the realmes; who willeth no conquest to be had, but amitie and loue to go forward, we refuse no man: let him bring his name and his pledge of good seruice in this quarrell, he shall not onelie be receiued to the amitie; but shall haue sufficient defense against the aduersaries, and recompense of his liuing, if he susteine anie losse. We neither doo nor intend to put anie man from his lands, taxes, or offices, vnlesse he will néeds resist, and so compell vs therevnto. *A verie good, lawfull, and bountifull offer.*

What face hath this of conquest? We intend not to disherit your queene, but to make hir heires inheritors also to England. What greater honour can ye séeke vnto your quéene, than the mariage offered? What more méeter mariage than this with the kings highnes of England? What more sure defense in the nonage of your quéene for the realme of Scotland, than to haue England your patrone and garrison? We séeke not to take from you your lawes nor customes; but we seeke to redresse your oppressions, which of diuerse ye doo susteine. In the realme of England, diuerse lawes and customes be according to the ancient vsage thereof. And likewise, France, Normandie, and Gascoigne haue sundrie kind of orders. Haue all the realmes and dominions that the emperour now hath, one custome and one sort of lawes? These vaine feares and fantasies of expulsion of your nation, of changing the lawes, of making a conquest, be driuen into your heads, of those, who in deed had rather you were all conquered, spoiled, and slaine, than they would lose anie point of their will, of their desire of rule, of their estimation, which they know in quietnesse would be be séene what it were, as it were in a calme water. *The case of the foresaid mariage still vrged.* *The lord protector telleth the Scots who they be that put doubts into their heads, &c.*

Now in this tumult of disorder, when the realme is tossed vp and downe with waues and surges of battell, famine, and other mischiefes which the warre bringeth, they thinke they cannot be espied; but looke on them you that haue wit and prudence, and consider the state of your quéene and realme, you will not kéepe hir sole and vnmaried, the which were to you great dishonor. If you maried hir within the relme, that cannot extinguish the title which we haue to the crowne of Scotland. And what dissention, enuie, grudge, and malice that shall bréed among you, is easie to perceiue. You will marrie hir out of the realme, our title remaineth, you be subiects to a forren prince of another countrie, and of another language, and vs ye haue your enimies, euen at your elbow, your succours farre off from you: and be we not in the bowels now of the realme? Haue we not a great part thereof, either in subiection or in amitie and loue? Who shall come into your realme, but he shall be met with, and fought with, if néede be, euen of your owne nation, who be faithfull and true to the realme of England in the waie of this most godlie vnion by mariage.

And if anie forren power, prince, or potentate, or whosoeuer be your aider to nourish still discord, send you an armie also, how shall they oppresse you, fill your houses, waste your grounds, spend and consume your vittels, hold you in subiection, & regard you as slaues, which without them could not liue, & will take your quéene to bestow as they lust, & speciallie if their ruler or king (as perchance he may be) in other warres be otherwise occupied, to be a preie to vs, & a true conquest, then it should be too late to saie; We will haue a mariage and no conquest, We wish peace & *Further inducements to make the Scots forward in this mariage.*

amitie, We are wearie of battell and miserie. The stubborne ouercommed must suffer the victors pleasure, and pertinacitie will make the victorie more insolent, whereof you your selfe haue giuen the cause, if they send monie and capteines, but no souldiers. First if they be capteins, who ruleth and who dooth obeie? Who shall haue the honor of the enterprise, and if it be well atchiued? But whether it be well atchiued or no, which number is that which shall be slaine? Whose bloud shall be shed? Their monie peraduenture shalbe consumed, & their commandements obeied. But whose bodies

shall smart for it? Whose lands shall be wasted? Whose houses burned? What realme made desolate? Remember what it is to haue a forren power within you, a strong power of your enimies vpon you, you (as it were) the campe & plaine betwixt them to fight on, and to be troden vpon, both of the victor, and of the ouercommed. And imagine you sée before your eies your wiues & daughters in danger of wantonnesse & insolencie of the soldiors, the proud looks of the capteins & soldiors, whom you call to helpe you, the contempt you shall bring your nation in, then take heed least indeed that follow which you feare, that is, that you shall be by them conquered, that ye shall be by them put from your holds, lands, taxes & offices, that your laws by them

shall be altered, that your nation shall be by them destroied. Consider in this realme, did not the Britons call in the Saxons for helpe, & by them were put out? Where be the Picts, once a gret nation betwixt you and vs? How did the nation of France put out the Galles out of all France? How got the Turk first all Grecia, & now of late all Hungarie, but being called in for to aid & helpe? And did not the Goths by like meanes get all Italie, and the Lombards one part therof now called Lombardie? What looke you for more? Néedie soldiors, & hauing their weapons in their hands, and knowing that you cannot liue without them, what will not they command you

to doo? What will they not incroch vpon you? What will they not thinke they may doo? And what will they thinke that you dare doo? This forren helpe is your confusion, that succour is your detriment, the victorie so had is your seruitude: what is then to be thought of losse taken with them? The strangers and forren soldiors shall oppresse you within, our power and strength without; and of your owne nation, so manie as loue quietnesse, godlines, and wealth of your realme, shall helpe also to

scourge and afflict you. Is it not better to compose and acquite all this calamitie and trouble by marriage, to end all sorrows and battels by such and so honorable a peace? Hath not the emperor Spaine & Burgundie by title of marriage? How holdeth the French king Britaine now latelie annexed to that crowne, but by title of marriage? How haue all the great princes of the world happilie and with quiet made of two kingdoms one, of diuerse lordships one, of nations alwaies at warre with themselues, or else in doubtfull peace, one well gouerned kingdome, rule, and dominion, but by that godlie, most quiet, and most amiable composition of marriage? Two

meanes there be of making one rule, wherto title is pretended, and perfect agréement betwixt two nations, either by force or superioritie, which is conquest; or by equalitie and loue, which is by parentage & mariage; you hate the one, that is conquest; and by refusing the other, you inforce vpon you hatred & malice.

You will not haue peace, you will not haue aliance, you will not haue concord; and conquest commeth vpon you whether you will or no. And yet if all things were considered, we feare it will appeere that it were better for you to be conquered of vs, than succoured of strangers, lesse losse to your goods, lesse hurt to your lands, lesse dishonor to your realme; this nation which is one in toong, one in countrie and birth, hauing so little diuersitie to occupie the whole, than other powers come in to you, neither like in language, nor yet like in behauior, who should rule ouer you,

and take you to be but their slaues. But we eftsoons and finallie declare and protest vnto you, that although for the better furtherance of this godlie purpose of vniting the realmes, and for the sure defense of them which fauour the marriage, we are compelled

pelled for the time to keepe holds, and to make fortifications in your realme : yet the kings maiesties mind and determinat pleasure is, with our aduise and counsell to be as before is declared, that where fauour may be shewed, not to vse rigor, if by conditions you will recciue this amitie offered, not to follow conquest : for we desire loue, vnitie, concord, peace and equalitie. Let neither your gouernor nor your kirkemen, nor those, who so often haue falsified their faith and promise, and by treacherie and falshood be accustomed to proroge the time, féed you foorth with faire words, and bring you into the snare from whence they cannot deliuer you. They will peraduenture prouide for themselues with pensions in some other realme, and set soldiors strangers in your holds to kéepe you in subiection, vnder the pretense to defend them against vs. But who prouideth pensions for you? How are you defended when they are fled away? Who conquereth you when the strange capteins haue your holds, when your land is wasted, and the realme destroied, and the more part kept from you? Who will set by the mariage of the quéene to buie a title with the war of England; to marrie the name, an other mightie king holding the land? If we two being made one by amitie, be most able to defend vs against all nations, and hauing the sea for wall, the mutuall loue for garrison, & God for defense, should make so noble and well agréeing monarchie, that neither in peace we may be ashamed, nor in war afraid of anie worldlie or forren power : whie should not you be as desirous of the same, and haue as much cause to reioise at it as we? If this honor of so noble a monarchie doo not moue you to take and accept amitie, let the griefe and the danger of the aforenamed losses feare you to attempt that thing which shall displease God, increase warre, danger your realme, destroie your land, vndoo your children, wast your grounds, desolate your countries, and bring all Scotland either to famine & miserie, or to subiection and seruitude of an other nation. We require but your promised quéene, your offered agréement of vnitie, the ioining of both the nations, which God of his infinite clemencie and tender loue that he hath declared to beare to both the nations, has offered vnto us both, and in manner called vs both vnto it, whose calling and prouocation we haue, and will folow to the best of our powers, and in his name, and with his aid, admonition, exhortation, requests, and ambassages, not being able to doo it, and to find stablenesse in promises, we shall not willing, but constreined pursue the battell, chastise the wicked & malicious by the angrie angels of God, fire and sword.

An item to the Scotish gouernor and kirkemen, &c.

What England & Scotland might do being made one by amitie.

Nothing required of the Scots that was not promised by them.

Fire & sword Gods angrie angels.

Wherefore we require and exhort you all, who haue loue to the countrie, pitie of that realme, a true hart to your quéene and mistresse, regard of your honors and promises made by the great seale of Scotland, and who fauoureth the peace, loue, vnitie, and concord, and that most profitable marriage to ent.. and come to vs; and declaring your true and godlie harts thervnto, to aid vs in this most godlie purpose and enterprise. To be witnesse of our dooings we refuse no man, temporall nor spirituall, lord ne lard, gentleman nor other, who will aid this our purpose, and minish the occasion of slaughter and destruction, to whom we shall kéepe the promises heretofore declared, and further sée reward and recompense made according to the desert.

An argument of vpright mening that refuseth no witnesse.

And for a more sure proofe and plainer token of the good mind and will which we beare vnto you, that which neuer yet was granted to Scotland in anie league, truce, or peace betwixt England and Scotland, because yée shall haue proofe of the beginning of loue and amitie of both the realmes : the kings highnes considering the multitude of them which are come to his maiesties deuotion, and of them that be well-willers and aiders of this godlie enterprise, hath by our aduise and counsell granted, and by these presents doth grant, that from henceforth all maner of merchants and other Scotishmen, who will enter their names with one of the wardens of the marches, & there professe to take part with vs in this before named godly purpose,

The kings grant as a proofe of the beginning of loue betwéene England and Scotland.

to

to his owne commoditie, & to serue all such as be of the same agréement, may law-fullie and without anie trouble and vexation enter into anie port, créeke, or hauen of England, and there vse their traffike of merchandize, buie and sell, bring in the com-modities of Scotland, and take and carrie foorth the commodities of England, as li-berallie and as fréelie, and with the same and none other custome or paiments therefore, than Englishmen and the kings subiects do at this present : minding further vpon the successe hereof to gratifie so the furtherers of this most godlie enterprise and vnion, than all the world may be witnesse of the great zeale and loue which his highnesse dooth beare toward you and your nation. And all this the kings highnesse, by our aduise and counsell, hath willed to be declared vnto you ; and giuen in commande-ment vnto vs, and all his lieutenants, wardens, rulers, and other head officers, minis-ters, and subiects, to sée executed and doone, according to the true purport, effect, and meaning thereof. Fare you well.

The Scots reiect the benefit of this exhortation. Although this admonition and wholsome exhortation might haue mooued the Scots to haue regarded their owne state, yet it little auailed, as by the sequele it ap-peared. For hauing both great promises made by the French, and now considering there-with the hurlie burlies and tumults that sproong vp in England, they continued in their obstinat purposes, not to yéeld vnto such reasonable motions as had béene offered, if they would haue shewed themselues conformable thereto, and not haue so stubbornlie denied to submit themselues to that which of right they were bound vnto. So that herein they shewed themselues verie peruerse and wilfull, reiecting not onelie the good aduise that the duke gaue them, but also not so much as once thinking what might insue to their great mischéefe vpon their refusall, and what benefit re-dound to them by admitting the offer : naie, they were of opinion and beléefe, that if so braue a bootie might befall England, it would be an occasion of great ruth and wretchednesse to Scotland : as one of late hath affirmed in his poeticall supposall :

——— si hæc præda Britannis
Cederet, ô miseræ Scotiæ miserabile regnum,
Genti infelici nihil est nisi flere relictum.

But now to let the Scots alone for a time, we will returne to the rebellion which followed in this yéere, to the whole diappointing of the plot laid by the councell, for the present subduing of the Scots, as it was verie like that it should haue so come to passe, if none other let had come. So it was, that the kings ma-A proclamation for the laieng open of inclo-sures. iestie, by the aduise of his vncle the lord protector, and other of the councell, thought good to set foorth a proclamation against inclosures, and taking in of fields and commons that were accustomed to lie open, for the behoofe of the inhabitants dwelling neere to the same, who had greeuouslie complained of gentle-men and others for taking from them the vse of those fields and commons, and had inclosed them into parks and seuerall pasture for their priuat commodities and pleasures, to the great hinderance and vndooing manie a poore man.

The meaning of the foresaid pro-clamation. This proclamation tending to the benefit and reléefe of the poore, appointed that such as had inclosed those commons, should vpon a paine by a daie assigned laie them open againe. But how well soeuer the setters foorth of this proclamation meant, thinking thereby peraduenture to appease the grudge of the people that found themselues grieued with such inclosures ; yet verelie it turned not to the wished effect, but rather ministered occasion of a foule and dangerous disorder. For whereas there were few that obeied the commandement, the vnaduised people pre-suming vpon their proclamation, thinking they should be borne out by them that had set it foorth rashlie without order, tooke vpon them to redresse the matter : and assembling themselues in vnlawfull wise, chose to them capteins and leaders, brake
open

open the inclosures, cast downe ditches, killed vp the deare which they found in parkes, spoiled and made hauocke, after the maner of an open rebellion. First they began to plaie these parts in Summersetshire, Buckinghamshire, Northamptonshire, Kent, Essex, and Lincolneshire. Commotions in Summersetshire and other places.

　　In Summersetshire they brake vp certeine parks of sir William Herbert, and the lord Sturton: but sir William Herbert assembling a power togither by the kings commission, slue and executed manie of those rebellious people. In other places also, by the good diligence and policie vsed by the councell, the rebels were appeased and quieted. But shortlie after, the commons of Deuonshire and Cornewall rose by waie of rebellion, demanding not onelie to haue inclosures laied open, and parkes disparked: but also thorough the instigation and pricking forward of certeine popish priests, ceased not by all sinister and subtill meanes, first vnder Gods name & the kings, and vnder the colour of religion, to persuade the people to assemble in routs, to choose capteins to guide them, and finallie to burst out into open rebellion. Their chiefe capteins were these, Humfrie Arundell esquier, gouernour of the Mount, Iames Rosogan, Iohn Rosogan, Iohn Paine, Thomas Vnderhill, Iohn Soleman, and William Segar. Moreouer, of priests which were principall stirrers, and some of them chiefe gouernors of the camps, and after executed, there were to the number of eight, whose names we find to be as follow: Robert Bocham, Iohn Thompson, Roger Barret, Iohn Wolcocke, William Alsa, Iames Mourton, Iohn Barrow, Richard Benet, besides a multitude of other priests which ioined with them. Rebellion in Deuonshire. *Iohn Fox* in Acts & Monuments.

The names of the capteins of the rebels.

　　The whole companies of these rebels amounted little lesse than to the number of ten thousand stout and valiant personages, able indéed (if their cause had béene good and fauoured of the Lord and giuer of victories) to haue wrought great feats. But being (as they were) ranke and malicious traitors, the almightie God confounded their deuises, and brought them to their deserued confusion. A strange case, that those mischéefous and wicked traitors could not be warned by the euill successe of their diuellish attempted outrage, in the yeare last past: at what time certeine seditious persons in Cornewall fell vpon one of the kings commissioners named master Bodie, sent thither with others for the reformation of matters in religion, in like manner as other were sent at the same time into other shires of the realme, for the which murther a priest being apprehended, arreigned, and condemned, was drawne into Smithfield, and there hanged and quartered the seauenth daie of Iulie, in the said last yeare before mentioned, to wit, 1548. Other of his complices and associats were executed and put to death in diuerse other parts of the realme. The number of the rebels in Deuonshire.

　　But now touching these other that rose in this present summer. At the first they were in great hope that the other disordered persons, which stirred in other parts of the realme, would haue ioined with them, by force to haue disappointed and vndoone that which the prince by law and act of parlement, in reformation of religion, had ordeined and established. But afterwards perceiuing how in most places such mischéefous mutinies and diuelish attempts, as the commons had begun, partlie by force and partlie by policie were appeased, or that their cause being but onelie about plucking downe of inclosures, and inlarging of commons, was diuided from theirs; so that either they would not, or could not ioine with them in aid of their religious quarrell: they began somewhat to doubt of their wicked begun enterprise. Notwithstanding now, sith they had gone so farre in the matter, they thought there was no shrinking backe: and therefore determining to proceed, they fell to new deuises, as first before all things to bring into their hands all such places of force, wealth, and defense, as might in anie respect serue for their aid and furtherance. Herevpon the second of Iulie, they came before the citie of Excester, incamping about the same in great numbers, and vsed all waies and meanes they could deuise how to win it by force, sometimes assaulting it right sharplie, sometimes firing the gates, other- Their hope in others failed them.

Excester besieged.

whiles

whiles vndermining the wals, and at other times (as occasions serued) procuring skirmishes.

Finallie, nothing was left vndoone which the enimie could imagine to serue his purpose for the winning of that citie. And albeit there wanted not lustie stomachs among the citizens to withstand this outward force of the enimie: yet in processe of time, such scarsitie of bread and vittels increased, that the people waxed wearie & loth to abide such extremitie of famine. Howbeit the magistrats (though it grieued them to sée the multitude of the citizens in such distresse) yet hauing a speciall regard of their dutie toward the prince, and loue to the common-wealth, left no waies vnsought to quiet the people, & staie them in their dutifull obedience to resist the enimies: so that comforting the people with faire promises, and reléeuing their necessities verie liberallie, so farre as their power might extend, did in such sort vse the matter, that euerie of them within resolued with one generall consent to abide the end, in hope of some spéedie reléefe. And in the meane while, when their corne and meale was consumed, the gouernors of the citie caused bran aud meale to be moulded vp in cloth, for otherwise it would not sticke togither.

Also they caused some excursions to be made out of the citie, to take and fetch into the citie such cattell as were found pasturing abroad néere to the wals, which being brought in, were distributed among the poore. To conclude, into such extremitie were the miserable citizens brought, that albeit mans nature can scarselie abide to féed vpon anie vnaccustomed food; yet these sillie men were glad to eat horsse flesh, and to hold themselues well content therewith. Whilest the siege thus remained before Excester, the rebels spoiled and robbed the countrie abroad, and laieng their traitorous heads togither, they consulted vpon certeine articles to be sent vp to the king. But herein such diuersitie of heads and wits was among them, that for euerie kind of braine there was one maner of article: so that neither appeared anie consent in their diuersitie, nor yet anie constancie in their agréement. Some séemed more tollerable, others altogither vnreasonable, some would haue no iustices, some no state of gentlemen. The priests euer harped vpon one string, to ring the bishop of Rome into England againe, and to hallow home cardinall Poole their countriman. After much a doo, at length a few articles were agréed vpon, to be directed vnto the king, with the names of certeine of their heads set therevnto, the copie whereof here insueth.

The great loialtie of the citizens of Excester.

Sée Iohn Fox in the Acts & Monuments.

The articles of the commons of Deuonshire and Cornewall, sent to the king, with answers afterward following vnto the same.

Sacrament of baptisme.

FIRST, forsomuch as man, except he be borne of water, and the Holie-ghost, can not enter into the kingdome of God, and forsomuch as the gates of heauen be not open without this blessed sacrament of baptisme; therefore we will that our curats shall minister this sacrament at all times of need, as well on the wéeke daies, as on the holie daies.

Confirmation

2 Item, we will haue our children confirmed of the bishop, whensoeuer we shall within the diocesse resort vnto him.

Consecrating of the Lords bodie.

3 Item, forsomuch as we constantlie beléeue, that after the priest hath spoken the words of consecration being at masse, there celebrating and consecrating the same, there is verie reallie the bodie and bloud of our Sauiour Iesus Christ God and man, and that no substance of bread and wine remaineth after, but the verie selfe same bodie that was borne of the virgin Marie, and was giuen vpon the crosse for our redemption: therefore we will haue masse celebrated as it hath béene in times past, without anie man communicating with the priests, forsomuch as manie rudelie presuming vnworthilie to

receiue

receiue the same, put no difference betweene the Lords bodie & other kind of meat; some saieng that it is bread before and after, some saieng that it is profitable to no man except he receiue it: with manie other abused termes.

4 Item, we will haue in our churches reseruation.

5 Item, we will haue holie bread and holie water in the remembrance of Christs pretious bodie and bloud. Reseruation of the lords bodie consecrated. Holie bread and holie water.

6 Item, we will that our priests shall sing or saie with an audible voice, Gods seruice in the quier of the parish churches, and not Gods seruice to be set foorth like a Christmasse plaie.

7 Item, forsomuch as priests be men dedicated to God for ministring and cele- The single life of priests. brating the blessed sacraments, and preaching of Gods word, we will that they shall liue chast without marriage, as saint Paule did, being the elect and chosen vessell of God, saieng vnto all honest priests; Be you followers of me.

8 Item, we will that the six articles, which our souereigne lord king Henrie the The six articles to be renewed. eight set forth in his latter daies, shall be vsed and so taken as they were at that time.

9 Item, we praie God saue king Edward, for we be his both bodie and goods.

For the pacifieng of these rebels, were appointed by the king and his councell, sir The capteins appointed to go against the Deuonshire rebels. Iohn Russell knight lord priuie seale, the lord Greie of Wilton, sir William Herbert after earle of Penbroke, sir Iohn Paulet, sir Hugh Panlet, sir Thomas Speake, and others, with a conuenient power of men of warre both on horssebacke and foot. Amongst others, there were certeine strangers that came with my lord Greie, as cap- Strangers. teine Germane an Hennower, with a band of horssemen, most part Albanoises and Italians. Also capteine Paule Baptist Spinola an Italian borne of a noble house in Genoa, with a band of Italian footmen. But now the lord priuie seale that was or- deined by the king and his councell, generall of that armie, vpon his first approching *Ric. Grafton.*
A proclamation. towards them, sent vnto them the kings maiesties proclamation: the effect whereof was, that all such persons as were vnlawfullie assembled, and did not within thrée daies next after the proclaming thereof, yéeld and submit themselues to the lord priuie seale (the kings lieutenant) they should from thenceforth be déemed, accepted, and taken for rebels against his roiall person, and his imperiall crowne and dignitie.

And further, the kings maiestie, for a more terrour to the rebels, and the incourage- ment of such other his louing subiects, as should helpe and aid to apprehend anie of the said rebels, he by his said proclamation granted and gaue all the offices, fées, goods and possessions, which the said rebels had at and before their apprehension. This pro- clamation notwithstanding, the rebels continued in their wicked deuises & traitorous purposes, hastening to the hazzards of their owne deaths & vndooings, as the poet saith of the foolish fish swiming to the hidden hooke:

Occultum visus decurrere piscis ad hamum. *Hor. Epist.*
lib. 1.

Wherevpon yet once againe the kings maiestie, for the auoiding of the shedding of christian bloud, sent vnto them a most gentle and louing message in writing, thereby to reduce them againe to their dutifull obedience: but all would not serue nor auaile to mooue their obstinate minds to leaue off their desperate and diuelish enterprise. The message was as followeth.

The kings message to the rebels of Cornewall and Deuonshire.

ALTHOUGH knowledge hath beene giuen to vs, and our deerest vncle the duke of Summerset gouernor of our person, and protector of all our realms, dominions, and subiects,

subiects, and to the rest of our priuie councell, of diuerse assemblies made by you, which ought of dutie to be our louing subiects, against all order of law, and otherwise than euer anie louing or kind subiects haue attempted against their naturall and liege souereigne lord: yet we haue thought it méet, at this verie first time, not to condemne and reiect you, as we might iustlie doo; but to vse you as our subiects, thinking that the diuell hath not that power in you, to make you of naturall borne Englishmen, so suddenlie to become enimies to your owne natiue countrie, of our subiects to make you traitors, or vnder pretense to relieue your selues, to destroie your selues, your wiues, children, lands, possessions, and all other commodities of this your life. This we saie, that we trust, that although ye be ignorantlie seduced, ye will not be vpon knowledge, obstinate.

And though some amongst you (as euer there is some cockle amongst good corne) forget God, neglect their prince, estéeme not the state of the realme, but as carelesse & desperat men delite in sedition, tumults & wars: yet neuerthelesse the greater part of you will heare the voice of vs your naturall prince, and will by wisedom and counsell be warned, and cease your euils in the beginning, whose ends will be euen by God almighties order your owne destruction. Wherfore as to you our subiects by ignorance seduced, we speake and be content to vse our princelie authoritie like a father to his children, to admonish you of your faults, not to punish them; to put you in remembrance of your duties, not to auenge your forgetfulnesse. First, your disorder to

rise in multitudes, to assemble your selues against our other louing subiects, to arraie yourselues to the war, who amongst you all can answer for the same to almightie God, charging you to obeie vs in all things? Or how can anie English good hart answer vs, our lawes, and the rest of our verie louing and faithfull subiects, who in déed by their obedience make our honour, estate, and degrée?

Ye vse our name in your writings, and abuse the same against our selfe. What iniurie herein doo you vs, to call those which loue vs, to your euill purposes, by the authoritie of our name? God hath made vs your king by his ordinance and prouidence, by our bloud and inheritance, by lawfull succession, and our coronation: but not to this end, as you vse our name. We are your most naturall souereigne lord & king Edward the sixt, to rule you, to preserue you, to saue you from all your outward enimies, to sée our lawes well ministred, euerie man to haue his owne, to suppresse disordered people, to correct traitors, théeues, pirats, robbers, & such like, yea to keepe our realms from other princes, from the malice of the Scots, of Frenchmen, of the bishop of Rome. Thus good subiects, our name is written, thus it is honored and obeied, this maiestie it hath by Gods ordinance, not by mans. So that of this your offense we cannot write too much. And yet doubt not but this is inough from a prince to all reasonable people, from a roiall king to all kindharted & louing subiects, frō the puissant K. of England, to euerie naturall Englishman.

Your pretense, which you saie, moueth you to doo thus, and wherewith you séeke to excuse this disorder, we assure you is either false, or so vaine, that we doubt not, that after that ye shall hereby vnderstand the truth thereof, ye will all with one voice acknowlege your selues ignorantlie led, and by errour seduced. And if there be anie one that will not, then assure you the same be ranke traitors, enimies of our crowne, seditious people, heretikes, papists, or such as care not what cause they haue to prouoke an insurrection, so they may doo it, nor in deed can wax so rich with their owne labors & with peace, as they can doo with spoiles, with wars, with robberies and such like, yea with the spoile of your owne goods, with the liuing of your labors, the sweat of your bodies, the food of your owne households, wiues and children: such they be, as for a time vse pleasant persuasions to you, and in the end will cut your throtes for your owne goods.

You

You be borne in hand, that your children, though necessitie chance, shall not be Baptisme. christened but vpon the holie daies: how false this is, learne you of vs. Our booke which we haue set foorth by free consent of our whole parlement in the English toong teacheth you the contrarie, euen in the first leafe, yea the first side of the first leafe of that part which intreateth of baptisme. Good subiects (for to other we speake not) looke and be not deceiued. They which haue put this false opinion into your eares, they meane not the christening of children, but the destruction of you our christened subiects. Be this knowne vnto you, that our honor is so much, that we may not be found faultie of one iote or word: proue it, if by our laws you may not christen your children when ye be disposed vpon necessitie, euerie daie or houre in the wéeke, then might you be offended: but seeing you may doo it, how can you beléeue them that teach you the contrarie? What thinke you they meane in the rest, which moue you to breake your obedience against vs, your king & souereigne, vpon these so false tales & persuasions in so euident a matter? Therfore all you which will acknowledge vs your souereigne lord, and which will heare the voice of vs your king, may easilie perceiue how you be deceiued, and how subtillie traitors and papists, with their falsehood séeke to atchiue and bring their purpose to passe with your helpe. Euerie traitor will be glad to dissemble his treason, and féed it secretlie; euerie papist his poperie, and nourish it inwardlie; and in the end make you our subiects partakers of treason and poperie, which in the beginning was pretended to be a commonweale and holinesse.

And how are you seduced by them, which put in your heads the blessed sacrament Sacrament of of Christes bodie, should not differ from other common bread? If our lawes, procla- the bodie, &c. mations, and statutes be all to the contrarie, whie shall anie priuat man persuade you against them? We doo our selfe in our owne hart, our councell in all their profession, our lawes and statutes in all purposes, our good subiects in all our dooings most highlie estéeme that sacrament, and vse the communion thereof to our most comfort. We make so much difference thereof from other common bread, that we thinke no profit of other bread, but to mainteine our bodies: but this blessed bread we take to be the verie food of our soules to euerlasting life. How thinke you, good subiects, shall not we being your prince, your lord, your king by Gods appointment, with truth more preuaile, than certeine euill persons with open falsehood? Shall anie seditious person persuade you that the sacrament is despised, which is by our lawes, by our selfe, by our councell, and by all our good subiects estéemed, vsed, participated, and dailie receiued? If euer ye were seduced, if euer deceiued, if euer traitors were beléeued, if euer papists poisoned good subiects, it is now. It is not the christening of children, nor the reuerence of the sacrament, nor the health of your soules that they shoot at, good subiects: it is sedition, it is high treason, it is your destruction they séeke. How craftilie, how pitiouslie, how cunninglie so euer they doo it, with one rule iudge yée the end, which of force must come of your purposes.

Almightie God forbiddeth vpon paine of euerlasting damnation, disobedience to Disobedience vs your king, and in his place we rule in earth. If we should be slow, would God to a king is diserre? If your offense be towards God, thinke you it is pardoned without repentance? obedience to Is Gods iudgement mutable? Your paine is damnation, your iudge is incorruptible, almightie God. your fault is most euident. Likewise are ye euill informed in diuerse other articles, as for confirmation of your children, for the masse, for the maner of your seruice of mattins and euensong. Whatsoeuer is therein ordered, hath beene long debated, and consulted by manie learned bishops, doctors, and other men of great learning in this realme concluded, in nothing so much labour and time spent of late time, nothing so fullie ended. As for seruice in the English toong hath manifest reasons for it, and yet perchance séemeth to you a new seruice, and yet in déed is none other but Seruice in the the old. The selfe same words in English which were in Latin, sauing a few things English toong.

taken out, so fond that it had béene a shame to haue heard them in English, as all they can iudge which list to report the truth.

The difference is, that we ment godlie, that you our subiects should vnderstand in English, being our naturall countrie toong, that which was heretofore spoken in Latine, then seruing onelie them which vnderstand Latine, & now for all you that be borne English. How can this with reason offend anie reasonable man, that he should vnderstand what anie other saith, and so to consent with the speaker? If the seruice in the church were good in Latine, it remaineth good in English: for **Knowledge is better than ignorance.** nothing is altered, but to speake with knowledge, that before was spoken with ignorance: and to let you vnderstand what is said for you, to the intent you maie further it with your owne deuotion, an alteration to the better, except knowledge be woorse than ignorance. So that whosoeuer hath mooued you to mislike this order, can giue you no reason, nor answer yours, if ye vnderstand it.

Wherefore you our subiects, remember we speake to you, being ordeined your prince and king by almightie God, if anie wise we could aduance Gods honour more than we doo, we would doo it, and sée that ye become subiects to Gods ordinance. Obeie vs your prince, and learne of them which haue authoritie to teach you, which haue power to rule you, and will execute our iustice, if we be prouoked. Learne not of them whose fruits be nothing but wilfulnesse, disobedience, obstinacie, & de**The masse.** struction of the realme. For the masse, we assure you, no small studie & trauell hath béene spent by all the learned clergie therin, and to auoid all contention thereof, it is brought euen to the verie vse as Christ left it, as the apostles vsed it, as holie fathers deliuered it: indeed somwhat altered from that which the popes of Rome for their lucre brought to it. And although you maie heare the contrarie of some popish and euill men, yet our maiestie, which for our honour maie not be blemished nor stained, assureth you, that they deceiue you, abuse you, and blow these opinions into your heads for to furnish their owne purposes.

Confirmation of Children. And so likewise iudge you of confirmation of children, and let them answer you this one question. Thinke they that a child, christened is damned, bicause he dieth before bishoping? Marke good subiects, what inconuenience hereof commeth. Our doctrine therefore is founded vpon true learning, and theirs vpon shamelesse errors. To conclude, beside our gentle maner of information to you, whatsoeuer is conteined in our booke, either for baptisme, sacrament, masse, confirmation and seruice in the church, is by parlement established, by the whole cleargie agréed, yea by the bishops of the realme deuised, & further by Gods word confirmed. And how dare you trust, yea how dare you giue eare without trembling, to anie singular person to disalow a parlement; a subiect to persuade against our maiestie, or anie man of his single arrogancie against the determination of the bishops and all the cleargie, anie inuented argument against the word of God?

But now you our subiects, we resort to a greater matter of your vnkindnesse, a great vnnaturalnes, and such an euill, that if we thought it had not béene begun of ignorance, and continued by persuasion of certeine traitors amongst you, which we thinke few in number, but in their dooings busie, we could not be persuaded but to vse our sword and doo iustice: and as we be ordeined of God for to redresse your errors by auengement. But loue and zeale yet ouercommeth our iust anger, but how long that will be, God knoweth, in whose hand our heart is; and rather for your owne causes, being our christened subiects, we would ye were persuaded than vanquished, taught than ouerthrowne, quietlie pacified than rigorouslie persecuted. Ye require to haue **Six articles.** the statute of six articles reuiued. And know you what ye require? Or know ye what ease ye haue with the losse of them? They were lawes made, but quicklie repented; too bloudie they were to be borne of our people, yet at the first in deed made of some necessitie. Oh subiects how are ye trapped by euil persons? We of pitie,

bicause

bicause they were bloudie, tooke them awaie, and you now of ignorance will aske them againe. You know full well that they helped vs to extend rigour, and gaue vs cause to draw our sword verie often.

And since our mercie mooued vs to write our lawes with milke and equitie, how are ye blinded to aske them in bloud? But leauing this maner of reasoning, and re-sorting to the truth of our authoritie, we let you wit, the same hath béene adnulled by parlement with great reioice of our subiects, and not now to be called in question. And dareth anie of you with the name of a subiect, stand against an act of parlement, a law of the realme? What is our power if lawes should be thus neglected? Or what is your suertie if lawes be not kept? Assure you most suerlie, that we of no earthlie thing vnder the heauen make such reputation as we doo of this one, to haue our lawes obeied, & this cause of God to be throughlie mainteined, from the which we will neuer remoue a heares bredth, nor giue place to anie creature liuing: but therein will spend our whole roiall person, our crowne, treasure, realme, and all our state, whereof we assure you of our high honor. For herein resteth our honor, herein doo all kings knowledge vs a king. And shall anie one of you dare breath or thinke against our kingdome and crowne? The authoritie of a parlement.

In the end of this your request (as we be giuen to vnderstand) ye would haue them stand in force till our full age. To this we thinke, that if ye knew what ye spake, ye would not haue vttred the motion, nor neuer giuen breath to such a thought. For what thinke you of our kingdome? Be we of lesse authoritie for our age? Be we not your king now as we shall be? Shall ye be subiects hereafter, and now are ye not? Haue we not the right we shall haue? If ye would suspend and hang our dooings in doubt vntill our full age, ye must first know, as a king we haue no difference of yeares, but as a naturall man and creature of God we haue youth, and by his sufferance shall haue age. We are your rightfull king, your liege lord, the souereigne prince of England, not by our age, but by Gods ordinance; not onelie when we shall be one and twentie yeares of age, but when we were of ten yéers. We possesse our crowne not by yeares, but by the bloud and descent from our father king Henrie the eight. If it be considered, they which mooue this matter, if they durst vtter themselues, would denie our kingdome.

But our good subiects know their prince, and will increase, not diminish his honor, inlarge his power not abate it, knowledge his kingdome, not deferre it to certeine yeares. All is one, to speake against our crowne, and to denie our kingdome, as to require that our lawes maie be broken vnto one and twentie yeares. Be we not your crowned, annointed, and established king? Wherein be we of lesse maiestie, of lesse authoritie, or lesse state, than our progenitors kings of this realme, except your vn-kindnes, your vnnaturalnesse will diminish our estimation? We haue hitherto since the death of our father, by the good aduise and counsell of our deare and intirelie be-loued vncle the duke of Summerset, and gouernor and protector, kept our estate, mainteined our realme, preserued our honour, defended our people from all enimies. We haue hitherto béene feared and dread of our enimies, yea of princes, kings, and nations. Yea herein we be nothing inferiour to anie our progenitors, which grace we acknowledge to be giuen vs from God, and how else, but by good obedience, good counsell of our magistrates, and by the authoritie of our kingdome?

England hitherto hath gained honour during our reigne: it hath woone of the enimie, and not lost. It hath béene maruelled that wée of so yoong yeares haue reigned so noblie, so roiallie, so quietlie. And how chanceth that you our louing subiects of that our countrie of Cornewall and Deuonshire, will giue occasion to slander this our realme of England, to giue courage to the enimie, to note our realme of the euill of rebellion, to make it a preie to our old enimies, to diminish our honour which God hath giuen, our father left, our good vncle and councell preserued vnto vs? What greater euill could ye commit, than euen now when our forren enimie in

Scotland

Scotland, and vpon the sea séeketh to inuade vs, to doo our realme dishonour, than to arise in this maner against our law, to prouoke our wrath, to aske our vengeance, and to giue vs an occasion to spend that force vpon you, which we meant to bestow vpon our enimies, to begin to slaie you with that sword that we drew forth against Scots, and other enimies, to make a conquest of our owne people, which otherwise should haue beene of the whole realme of Scotland?

Thus farre we haue descended from our high maiestie, for loue to consider you in your simple ignorance, and haue béene content to send you an instruction like a father, who of iustice might haue sent you your destructions like a king to rebels. And now we let you know, that as you sée our mercie abundantlie, so if ye prouoke vs further, we sweare to you by the liuing God, ye shall féele the power of the same God in our sword, which how mightie it is, no subiect knoweth; how puissant it is, no priuat man can iudge; how mortall, no Englishman dare thinke. But suerlie, suerlie, as your lord and prince, your onlie king and maister, we saie to you, repent your selues, and take our mercie without delaie: or else we will foorthwith extend our princelie power, and execute our sharpe sword against you, as against infidels and Turks, and rather aduenture our owne roiall person, state, and power, than the same should not be executed.

And if you will proue the example of our mercie, learne of certeine which latlie did arise, as they perceiuing pretended some griefes, and yet acknowledging their offenses, haue not onelie most humblie their pardon: but féele also by our order, to whome onelie all publike order apperteineth, present redresse of their griefes. In the end, we admonish you of your duties to God, whome ye shall answere in the daie of the Lord, & of your duties towards vs, whom ye shall answere by our order, and take our mercie whilest God so inclineth vs, least when ye shall be constrained to aske, we shall be too much hardened in heart to grant it you. And where ye shall heare now of mercie, mercie, and life; ye shall then heare of iustice, iustice, and death. Written the eight of Iulie, in the third yeare of our reigne.

A godlie and princelie admonition.

Although the rebels receiued this princelie message, & wholesome admonition from the kings maiestie, yet would they not reforme themselues, as dutiful subiects ought to haue doone, but stood still in their wicked begun rebellion, offering to trie it at the weapons point. There wanted not priestes and other busie bodies among them, such as by all waies and meanes possible sought to kindle the coles of malice and hatred betwixt the king and his subiects; which as the maner is among all the like wicked disposed people, contriued to raise and strew abroad false forged tales, and feined rumors, giuing it out, that the people should be constreined to paie a ratable taske for their sheepe and cattell, and an excise for euerie thing that they should eate or drinke. These and such other slanderous brutes were spred abroad by those children of Beliall, whereby the cankered minds of the rebels might the more be hardened and made stiffe from plieng vnto anie reasonable persuasion, that might be made to moue them to returne vnto their dutifull obedience, as by the lawes both of God and man they were bounden: and so it came to passe. For the rebellious rout were growne to an obstinacie, séeming so far from admitting persuasions to submission, that they became resolute in their pestilent actions; wilfullie following the woorst, which they knew full well would redound to their detriment; and auoiding the best, which they doubted not might turne to their aduantage, agreable in sense and meaning vnto that of the poet:

False rumors.

Hor. in Epist. lib. 1.

Quæ nocüere sequar, fugiam quæ profore credam.

Herevpon when no hope was left to procure them by anie quiet meanes to laie downe armes, the lord priuie seale, and the lord Greie, with their forces, although not comparable with the rebels in number, about the latter end of Iulie set vpon them, and by great manhood put them from their ground, notwithstanding they

fought

fought verie stoutlie, & gaue it not ouer for a little: and although they were thus driuen to giue place at this first onset, yet they got togither againe, and aboad a new charge, defending their ground, & dooing what they could to beat backe and repell those that came to assaile them. But neuerthelesse through the power of the almightie God fauouring the rightfull cause, the rebels were distressed, and followed in chase with great slaughter for the space of two miles. This was about the beginning of August. The rebels put from their ground.

Their chiefe capteines, to wit, Humfreie Arundell, Whinsland, Holms, and Burie, were taken and brought vp to London. There were taken also others of their capteins, as Thomas Vnderhill, Iohn Soleman, William Segar, Tempson, and Barret, which two last were priests; also Boier and Henrie Lée, two maiors, all the which were executed in one place or other, as they had well deserued. The said Boier being maior of Bodmin in Cornewall, (as Grafton reporteth) had béene a busie fellow among the rebels, to set them forward in mischiefe: howbeit some that loued him sought to excuse him, as if he had béene forced hereto against his will by the rebels, who would haue killed him, and burnt his house, if he had not consented to them. But howsoeuer it was, sir Anthonie Kingston that was prouost marshall in the kings armie vnder the lord priuie seale, wrote his letter vnto the said maior, signifieng to him, that he and other with him would come and dine with him such a daie. The maior séeming to be glad thereof, made the best purueiance he could to receiue them, and at the time appointed, sir Anthonie Kingston came with his companie, and were right hartilie welcomed of the maior. But before they sat downe to dinner, calling the maior aside, he told him that there must be execution doone in that towne, and therefore willed him that a paire of gallowes might be framed and set vp with spéed, so that they might be readie by that time that they should make an end of dinner. *Iohn Fox.*
The capteins of the rebels taken. Sir Anthonie Kingston prouost marshall.

The maior with all diligence caused the same to be doone: so that when dinner was ended, sir Anthonie calling the maior to him, and asking whether the gallowes were set vp accordinglie as he had willed, the maior answered that they were readie. Wherewith sir Anthonie taking the maior by the hand, desired him to bring him to the place where they stood, and comming thither and beholding them, he said to the maior; Thinke you maister maior that they be strong inough? Yea sir, quoth he, that they are. Well then said sir Anthonie, get you euen vp vnto them, for they are prouided for you. The maior greatlie abashed herewith, said; I trust you meane no such thing to me. Sir said he, there is no remedie, ye haue béene a busie rebell, and therefore this is appointed for your reward: and so without respit or staie, there was the maior hanged. The maior of Bodmin hanged.

At the same time, & neere the same place dwelled a miller that had beene a great dooer in that rebellion, for whom also sir Anthonie Kingston sought: but the miller being thereof warned, called a good tall fellow that he had to his seruant, and said vnto him: I haue businesse to go from home, if anie therefore come to aske for me, saie thou art the owner of the mill and the man for whome they shall so aske, and that thou hast kept this mill for the space of thrée yeares, but in no wise name me. The seruant promised his maister so to doo. And shortlie after came sir Anthonie Kingston to the millers house, and calling for the miller, the seruant came forth, and answered that he was the miller. "How long, quoth sir Anthonie, hast thou kept this mill? he answered thrée yeares. Well then said he, come on, thou must go with me, and caused his men to laie hands on him, and to bring him to the next trée, saieng to him; Thou hast béene a busie knaue, and therefore here shalt thou hang. Then cried the fellow out, and said that he was not the miller, but the millers man. Well then, said sir Anthonie, thou art a false knaue to be in two tales, therefore said he, hang him vp: and so incontinentlie hanged he was in déed." After he was dead, one that was present, told sir Anthonie; Suerlie sir this was but the millers man. What A millers man hanged for his maister.

then

This was a hard proceeding, though the partie had béene nocent.

then said he, could he euer haue doone his maister better seruice than to hang for him.

Manie other were executed by order of the marshall law, & a great part of the countrie abandoned to the spoile of the souldiers, who were not slouthfull to gleane what they could find for the time their libertie lasted. ¶ Thus far the report of this rebellious broile, wherevpon it first kindled, by what meanes the same sparkled and became a flame, and what deuises were vsed to extinguish & quench it. Wherein we sée how prone the people are to rise by routs vpon occasions of discontentments; how hastie and headie to vndertake dangerous enterprises, how wilfull and obstinate to persist in their pernicious proceedings, how cold-harted and hopelesse when they see the course of their plots of perilous policie either interrupted, vndermined, or ouerthrowne; and finallie, what a reprochfull reward redoundeth both to the ringleaders in rebellions, as also what falleth to the shares of all such as shake hands and become confederats to the furthering and strengthening of riots, mutinies, insurrections, commotions, and hurlieburlies. Wherby the state is disquieted, & (that more is) the prince drawne into a conceipt of suspecting his subiects loialties; besides a wicked president to posterities, without feare of shame, remorse of concience, regard to allegiance, or foresight of afterclaps, to attempt the like. Now it resteth, that for the further truth and knowledge hereof, we adde a new report (new I meane, in respect of the publication, hauing not heretofore béene printed) though old enough, and sufficientlie warranted by the reporter, who vpon his owne notice hath deliuered no lesse in writing, than himselfe vpon verie good and infallible grounds obserued, and hath left testified in the discourse following; wherein there is not one word either added, or inuerted: but all things (from point to point) agreeable to the written copie.

Abr. Fl. introduction into the next narration being a new addition, touching this rebellion.

The addition following being a large discourse, was neuer heretofore published.

The description of the citie of Excester, and of the sundrie assaults giuen to the same: collected and gathered by Iohn Vowell (alias Hooker) gentleman and chamberleine of the same.

Dumnonia, the countrie of vallies.

Deuonia, Deuonshire.

EXCESTER or Exeter is a famous and an ancient citie, being the metropole and Emporium of the west parts of England, situated and lieng in the prouince sometime called Dumnonia, that is to saie, the countrie of vallies: for whereas are manie hilles (as that countrie is full of hilles and mounteins) there are manie vallies. But now corruptlie it is named Deuonia, or Deuonshire, and not Daneshire of the Danes, as some would haue it. Of the first foundation thereof, by reason of the sundrie inuasions of forren nations, who with their hostilities and cruell warres did burne and destroie the same, there remaineth no certeine memoriall, neither among the records of the said citie, ne yet in anie one other writer.

But most certeine it is, that it was first builded and founded by the Britons or Brutes. For the names which they gaue and vsed, are yet at this present had in remembrance, as well among the chronographers of this land, as also among the Cornish people, who were sometimes one with this prouince; but now in a countie of themselues, and next bordering to this, and in the same diocesse. And they are the remanent of the bloud of Brutus. For when Cadwallader king of this land, by reason of a great famine and pestilence was driuen to forsake the same, & to flie into little Britaine named Armorica, which is now vnder the dition of the French king: diuers & the most part of his people fled, some into Wales, and some into Cornwall, where euer since they and after them their posteritie haue remained and continued.

Corinia. Baleus lib. 1. Centuriarum. Lelandus in Genethliaco.

The old chronographers, searchers, and writers of antiquities doo find, that this citie was called Corinia, and thereof the cathedrall church of the same was (as Bale saith) named Ecclesia Coriniensis: which name, if it were first giuen by Corinus (as Leland writeth) who after the arriuall of Brutus into this land, was made the first

duke

duke of this whole west countrie of Deuon and Cornewall, which were both comprised vnder the name of Corinia, and wherof this citie euer hath beene and is the metropole, and alwaies parcell sometime of the kingdome, then of the duchie, and after of the earledome, and now againe of the duchie of Cornwall : then out of doubt this citie is of no lesse antiquitie than the said names doo import. It was also called Augusta. Of this name there were diuerse cities so named by the Romans ; but this onelie was named Augusta Britannorum, and so called (as some thinke) by the Romans at the conclusion of the peace made at the siege of this citie betwéene king Aruiragus and Vespasian coronell of the Romane armie vnder Claudius Augustus. The Britons in their toong or language doo call this citie by sundrie names ; the first and eldest in remembrance is cair Penhulgoile, that is to saie, the prosperous chiefe ^{Penhulgoile.} towne in the wood, as dooth appeere by Geffreie of Monmouth, and Ponticus Virunnius. It was also called Pennehaltecaire, that is, the chiefe citie or towne vpon the hill ; as ^{Pennehaltecaire.} dooth appéere in a trauerse betweene the bishop, deane, and chapiter of this citie of the one partie ; and the maior, bailiffe, and communaltie of the other partie, concerning their liberties. But the names which the Cornish people doo at these presents remember & reteine, are speciallie thrée, Pennecaire, Caireruth, Caireiske. Pennecaire ^{Pennecaire the} signifieth, and is to saie, the chéefe citie. Caireruth signifieth the red or reddish citie, ^{cheefe citie, Caireruth the} so called and taking the name of the ground and soile wherevpon it is situated, which ^{red citie, Caire-} is a red earth. Caireiske is the citie of Iske, being so called of the riuer, which the ^{iske the citie of Exe.} Britons name Iske, and floteth fast by the same. And of this name Houeden in his ^{Houeden.} chronicle maketh mention, saieng thus : Anno Domini 877 exercitus Danorum ab Wareham nocte quadam, fœdere dirupto, ad Exeancestre diuerterunt, quod Britanicè dicitur Caireiske.

Ptolomeus the famous astronomer, who was about the yéere of our Lord 162, Coell ^{Ptolomeus inta-} being king of this land, nameth this citie Isca ; and the riuer Isaca. And Bale the ^{butis. Baleus centur.} searcher of antiquities following the same opinion, dooth also name the citie Isca, ^{l b.} and the inhabitants therein Iscans. But vnder correction be it spoken, a man maie well thinke that Ptolomeus being in Alexandria, and so farre distant from this land, was misinformed, or the print mistaken. For it was most likelie that the riuer should be named Isca according to the British spéech wherein it was called Isca ; and which name by transposing of the two middle letters, dooth at this present remaine being now named Icsa or Exa. But whatsoeuer the censures and opinions of Ptolomeus and of Bale, who wrote onelie vpon report, be herein, it is certeine, that the names which the Brutes or Britons gaue, were of longest continuance. And this citie was called by their denominations, by the space of fiftéene hundred yéeres, vntill the comming of the Saxons, the Picts, and the Scots into this realme, which was about the yéere of our Lord foure hundred and fiftie. For they, where, and whensoeuer they ^{New lords new} preuailed in anie place, did for the most part alter and change the names of all places ^{names.} & townes, accounting it a great renowme, as also a perpetuall memoriall of their chiualrie, to giue new names, either of their owne deuises, or of their owne natiue countries ; for so is it writen of them : Picti, Scoti, Angli, Daci, & Normanni in hac insula rerum potiti, cuncta immutârunt, pro tropheis habentes, locis à se deuictis noua imponere nomina. The Saxons therfore of all other cities & townes (few excepted) so of this also they changed and altered the old names aud called it Monketon ; and ^{Monketon.} by which name it was so called by the space of three hundred and od yéeres, and vntill the time of king Athelstane, for he about the yéere of our Lord nine hundred thirtie and two, being much gréeued and vnquieted with the rebellion of the Cornish people because they refused and denied to acknowledge him for their lawfull king, did bend his force, & conduct his armie against them. And hauing subdued and preuailed ouer them, he returned to this citie : and while he rested here, he repared the same ; and ^{Ex veteri libro.} the walles which before were but mightie ditches of earth, and the banks set with

great

great poles of timber now destroied, he builded all of square stone, as it is recorded :
Hanc vrbem primus Athelstanus in potestatem Anglorum fugatis Britonibus reductam,
turribus muniuit, & muro ex quadratis lapidibus tandem cinxit. And then he altered
and changed the former names, and called it after the name of the riuer Esseterra,
or Exeterra, that is to saie, Exeter. For so is it written, Est Exonia vrbs Deuoniæ
comitatus, loco præcelso ad occidentem versus posita : abluitúrq; flumine Exi, à quo
nomen habet. Others name it of the riuer floting by it, which they saie is named
Excestrum, & thus they write : Clarissima vrbium est Excestria, quæ ab amni Excestro
qui eandem præterfluit est sic nuncupata. I find it also written in an old chronicle,
that it is named Exancestria or Exancestre : which shuld seeme to be so called by the
Saxons. For the most part of the cities, townes, & forts, which they builded or reedified, did end in cestre :as Glocestre, Lecestre, Manchestre, Winchestre, Oscestre,
Worcestre, Colchestre, Cicestre, Ilcestre, Bicestre, & this citie of Excestre, with
others. For Caire in British & Cestre in Saxonish are one thing, & doo signifie in
English a fort, towre, or castell. This citie (as is before said) being walled about
with stone by king Athelstane is not altogither foure square, but declineth somewhat
toward a roundnesse, and conteineth in circuit or compasse sixtéene hundred whole
pases, after fiue foot to a pase; which accounting after the Italian maner one thousand
pases to a mile, it is a mile and halfe about, & somewhat more. The situation of this
citie is verie pleasant and delicate, being set vpon a little hill among manie hilles. For
the whole countrie round about is mounteinous and full of hilles. It is pendant towards the south and west parts, after and in such sort, that be the streets neuer so
foule or filthie, yet with a shoure of raine they are clensed and made sweet. And
albeit hilles are commonlie drie, yet nature is so beneficiall to this litle hill, that it is
in euerie quarter full of water springs : & by that meanes the whole citie is throughlie
furnished with wels and tirpits ; the great good benefit and commoditie whereof hath
well appéered in sundrie times of necessitie, and especiallie in the time of the late
commotion, which was in the yeere of our Lord 1549. For albeit the enimie, by
breking and spoiling of the pipes or canales, whereby water was conueied to the
founteins of the citie, from certeine springs distant not a mile from the same, did
abridge them of that water : yet most comfortablie they did inioy without impeachment the wels and tirpits within the walles, which abundantlie floted with waters to
the satisfieng of all people therein.

 There are also within this citie certeine founteins or conduits, wherevnto, through
certeine canales or pipes of lead, the waters from certeine springs, rising in the fields
not far from the citie, are brought and conueied. And these waters are of most price
because by the carriage thereof they are purified, and made lighter than are the other
waters springing within the citie : and by that means more meet for dressing of meats.
Of these conduits two are speciall, the one of them standeth and is within the cemeterie or churchyard of the cathedrall church of the said citie, and is called saint Peters
conduit: the other being of great antiquitie standeth in the middle of the citie, at the
méeting of foure principall streets of the same, and whereof sometimes it tooke
his name, being called the conduit at Quatrefois or Carfox; but now the great
conduit.

 At the higher end of the citie is a verie old and ancient castell, named Rugemont,
that is to saie the red hill, taking that name of the red soile or earth wherevpon it is
situated. The site or situation of it is eminent and aboue both the citie and countrie adioining : for they doo all lie as it were vnder the lée thereof. It hath a goodlie and pleasant prospect towards the seas : for betweene that and it is no hill at all. It is stronglie
ditched round about, and was first builded (as some thinke) by Iulius Cesar : but rather and in truth by the Romans after him when they had their recourse to it for their
defense, refuge, and abode, manie yeares. The same was sometimes the palace of
                                                                        such

*Polydorus hist.
lib. 5. Exeter.*

*Baleus centur.
lib. in Britannie
descriptione.*
Excester.
Exeancester.

Caire, } a fort.
Cestre }

The site of Ex-
cester and cir-
cuit.

The citie is full
of water springs.

The rebels
breake and
spoile the pipes
of lead for wa-
ters.

The conduits for
water.

Saint Peters
conduit.

The great con-
duit.

Castell Ruge-
mont.

The site of the
castell.

The castell
builded by the
Romans.

such kings, as vnto whome the kingdome of Westsex or Westsaxons was alotted vnto : and after them, it was the habitation of the earles of Cornewall, and last of all of the dukes of Excester. It was alwaies parcell, and of the inheritance of the earle-dome, but now of the duchie of Cornewall : it is in great ruine and decaie, and not easilie to be gotten with force, if it were reedified and inuironed.

At the lower end and part of this citie, without the wals, floteth a goodlie and a pleasant riuer, which the Britons called Isk; Ptolomeus by misinformation nameth it Isaca : but the other old writers named it Esse, Exe, Exa, or Excestrum : and these names be reteined at these presents. It hath his head or spring in a certeine moore or desert distant from the citie néere about foure and twentie miles, called Exmoore. It floweth into the maine seas about eight miles from the citie, at a place named Ex-mouth, and by the waie it is increased with sundrie riuers, brooks & lakes, the chiefe of which are Créedie and Collome. It is well stored and is plentifull of samon, trout, peale, dace, pike, and other like freshwater fishes : which albeit they be verie good and delicate, and especiallie the samon and pike : yet they are the lesse estéemed, bicause the seas being so néere doo furnish the citie & countrie verie abundantlie with sundrie kinds of sea fishes most delicate. *The riuer of Exe.* *Exe riseth in Exmoore.*

The maine seas are not distant from the citie aboue eight miles, out of which com-meth an arme seruing for the port of the same : which (as dooth appeare by certeine old and ancient records) did sometimes flow vp to the verie wals of the citie, where boats and vessels were woont to be laden and vnladen of all kind of wares and mer-chandizes, at a proper place appointed for the same : which at these presents kéepeth his old and ancient name, and is called the watergate. The decaie thereof hapned about the yeare of our Lord 1312, by one Hugh Courtneie the third of that name, and earle of Deuon : who being offended and incensed against this citie, his wrathfull humor could not be satisfied, vntill by some meanes he did impaire and annoie the state of the commonwealth of the same. And séeing that among other commodities, the vse of the hauen and watercourse to the citie to be one of the chiefest, he was neuer quiet vntill he had destroied the same : wherefore minding to performe what he had conceiued, he did in the yeare of our Lord 1313, the fift yeare of king Edward the second, enterprise & begin his pretended deuise and mischéefe. *The hauen of Excester.* *The decaie of the hauen of Excester. Hugh Court-neie the first destroier of the hauen.*

And first whereas the ladie Isabella de Fortibus, countesse of Aumerle and of Deuon, his ancestrix had builded certeine wéers vpon the riuer of Exe (the propertie and seig-norie whereof did apperteine to the citie) the one of the west side of the riuer of Exe in Exminster parish, and the other of the east side of the same riuer in the parish of Topesham ; leauing betwéene the said two wéers a certeine aperture or open space of thirtie foot, thorough which all boats and vessels without let or hinderance might haue and had their vsuall passage and repassage, to and from the citie vnto the seas : the said earle to abridge and destroie this great benefit and commoditie, did leuie and build a new wéere in the said aperture or open roome, stopping, filling, and quirting the same, with great trees, timber, and stones, in such sort, that no vessell nor vessels could passe or repasse.

After him Edward Courtneie earle of Deuon, and nephue to the said Hugh, did not onelie mainteine and continue the dooings of his ancestor, by his dailie reparing and defending the same : but also to worke an vtter destruction for euer of anie passage or repassage to be had thensefoorth to and from the said citie ; vnder pretense to build and make certeine mils, did erect two other weeres, the one at saint Iames ouerthwart the whole riuer, and the other at Lampreford : by meanes whereof not onelie the citie did susteine the whole losse of the hauen, but the whole countrie also was surrounded about it, and in processe of time altogither, and as it is at these presents couered with salt waters. For which gréefs and iniuries vpon complaints made thereof, diuerse & sundrie writs and commissions of inquirie were awarded and granted by the king; *Edward Court-neie.*

and the said earles by sundrie inquisitions and verdicts found giltie. And yet notwithstanding, such was their power and authoritie, and such was the iniquitie of those daies, as no iustice could take place, nor law haue his due course against them.

Furthermore also the foresaid Hugh, to incroch the gaine and commoditie of the lading & vnlading of merchandizes within the port & riuer to himselfe, did build a keie and a crane in the riuer at his towne of Topesham, distant from the citie about thrée miles: and by power did inforce and compell all maner of merchants arriuing within that port to vnlade & lade all their wares and merchandizes brought within that port (to be laden and vnladen) there onelie. And from thense, euer since, all wares and merchandizes haue béene caried and recaried to and from the citie by horsse, cart, and waine, though to the gaine of the earle and his tenants, yet to the great trouble and hinderance of the citie and merchants of the same. Neuerthelesse, the port hath euermore and yet dooth kéepe his old and ancient name, being called the port of the citie of Excester: and alwaies hath béene and presentlie is paied a tribute vnto the citie, by the name of the towne custome, for all kind of wares and merchandizes, discharged within that port or riuer, or the members thereof.

And although the watercourse thus being destroied can hardlie be restored to his old pristinate and naturall estate; for that thorough long continuance the old course can not be discerned: yet now at length after manie attempts and with great expenses, a watercourse and passage begun in the yeare 1564, is recouered, and by certeine sluces, boats, and vessels of fifteene or sixtéene tuns are conueied and brought vp to the citie, and there discharged at the old and ancient place, called the watergate: & where is builded a verie faire large keie or wharfe, as also an engine called a crane fit for the purpose.

Within the citie were somtimes but few parish churches, vntill the time of Innocentius the third: who when in the yeare 1198 he had established the doctrine of transubstantiation, and had made it an article of the symbole, as appeareth in the decretals, Titulo de summa trinitate, canone Firmiter: then his next successor Honorius the third, in the yeare 1218 did not onelie confirme the same, but also by decree did establish reseruation, candlelight, and praieng for the dead, as dooth appeare, Decret. tit. de celebratione missarum, canone Sane cum, & Sane cum creatura: by which meanes the number of sacrificing & massing priests did not onelie increase, but churches also and chapels began in all places and euerie where to be builded and erected.

And among others in this citie in the yeare 1222 and the sixt yeare of king Henrie the third, the parish churches were limited, and increased to the number of nintéene churches within the citie and suburbs, and were called by the name of the christianitie euen to this daie. Euerie of which in times past was a sufficient and competent liuing to mainteine a massing sacrificer; for such and so great was the blind deuotion of the people then in that Romish religion: but the same now being abolished, and the gospell preached, the liuelihoods are so small, as not sufficient for the most part to mainteine a poore clerke or scholar, & by reason thereof, the most part of them doo lie void and vacant, without incumbent.

Besides these parish churches, there was also a monasterie, sometimes of moonks of saint Benets order, but since a cathedrall church, being of a verie faire and sumptuous building of fréestone and with beautifull pillers of graie marble. It standeth and is situated in the east part of the citie; and (as some report) was first founded and built by king Etheldred, the third sonne to king Ethelwolphus. Some thinke that king Edgar did it. True it is that euerie of them builded a house for religious persons within this citie, of which the one was spoiled and burned by the Danes, and the other in processe of time was vnited to the monasterie, which is now the cathedrall church. But the cathedrall church it selfe was founded & builded by king Athelstane, the sonne to king Edward the elder; for so is it recorded in the historie of the same
                                                                                        church,

church, the words whereof are these : Atthelstanus subiugatis Cornugualensibus, re- The cathedrall church was first
uersus est ad ciuitatem, quæ antiquitùs Monketon vocabatur, nunc autem Exeter : a monasterie
ac ibi sedens, anno Dom. 932, non tam lacerata eiusdem ciuitatis mœnia reparabat, and founded by king Athelstane.
quin & mansum quoddam dedit ad fundandum monasterium pro monachis, Deo & *Chronica ecclesic.*
sancto Petro famulantibus.

    This king besides his great charges and expenses in building of this church, which
at the first was but small, and that part which is now called the Ladie chapell, he placed
therein moonkes of S. Benets order, prouided liuelihoods for them, and appointed a
ruler or gouernour ouer them, and who was called by the name of an abbat, towards
whose diet and liuelihood he gaue Morkeshull and Tresurors béere : and whichat
these presents doo remaine to the said church and are annexed to the dignitie of the
treasurorship of the same. The church being thus begun, kings, princes, & noble
men were from time to time gladlie and willinglie verie liberall contributors to the absoluing and finishing of the same. For about foure score years after king Athelstane, King Canutus
king Knoght who was also named Cahutus or Canutus, at the earnest sute of one of confirmeth the
his dukes named Atheldred, did confirme and grant to Athelwood then abbat of the priuileges of the
said church, and to his successors manie and sundrie priuileges and liberties, vnder his monasteries.
letters patents, dated the second yeare of his reigne, Anno Domini, 1019.

    After him about thirtie yeares, king Edward the confessor remooued the moonkes K. Edward the
vnto Westminster, and made this church a cathedrall church, and remooued the bishops confessor re-
sée which was then at Crediton vnto this citie, making Leofricus bishop therof, and mooued the moonks vnto
whom he and his wife quéene Edith did put in possession of the same, as appeareth by his Westminster,
letters patents dated the eight yeare of his reigne, Anno Dom. 1050. Howbeit the and made this a cathedrall
moonke of Burie, Polydorus, and others doo affirme and write, that this should be doone church.
about the twelfe yeare of William the conqueror, for thus they doo write : Habitum Leofricus the first bishop of
est Londini, sub Lanfranco, antistitum & sacerdotum comitium, in quo decretum Excester.
est, quòd aliquot sedes episcopales, quæ in oppidulis & pagis anteà fuerant, in *Polyd. hist. li.* 19
vrbibus & locis celeberrimis collocarentur, vnde factum est vt Bathonia, Lincolnia, *Chronica chroni-*
Sarisburia, Exonia, Cestria, & Cicestria vrbes, huiusmodi nouis episcoporum domicilijs *corum. lib.* 7.
sunt nobilitatæ.

    But the reuerence of these writers reserued, this cannot be true concerning this The charter of
church, bicause the words of the charter thereof doo witnesse the contrarie, and de- the church.
clare expresselie, how that king Edward and queene Edith his wife did put Leofricus
the first bishop in possession, the one by the one hand and the other by the other hand,
leading him betweene them vp to the high altar, and there put his hands vpon the same.
And yet it may be true, that at the foresaid councell, this remoouing and placing
of this bishop might be ratified and confirmed. Likewise William the conqueror, The conqueror
in the third yeare of his reigne 1069, did not onelie confirme the former charter, but confirmeth the charters of the
also at the instance and request of William Warewest, then his chapleine, but after- church, and
wards bishop of the same sée, did giue vnto it the seigniories of Plimpton, Brampton, inlargeth the possessions of
and S. Stephans in Excester, which the said William Warewest being afterwards bishop it.
did distribute, giuing Plimpton to the religious canons, whome he placed there :
Brampton was annexed to the deanerie, but S. Stephans was reserued alwaies to the
bishop, and to his successors, whereby they are barons, and so lords in the parlement
house.

    It was also inlarged from time to time with great possessions, reuenues, buildings,
riches, priuileges, and sundrie other commodities, by kings, princes, prelats, bishops,
and sundrie others. And this one thing is to be noted, that albeit there were about The cathedrall
foure hundred yeares distant from the first foundation and building thereof, vnto the church was foure hundred yeres
ending and finishing of the same; yet it is so vniformelie and decentlie compact and in building.
builded in one mould, as though it had beene doone at one instant. The bishop is
distinct from the chanons both in house and reuenue: his liuelihoods being no part

5 X 2

nor

nor parcell of that which apperteineth to the deane and chapter. It was sometimes of great reuenues and large possessions, but the more part thereof hath béene consumed and exhausted by a wastfull bishop. The bishop and chanons haue verie faire houses, which are situated about the church & cemiterie, and are inclosed euerie night by shutting fast of certeine gates, by which occasion it is called a close, A claudendo: and which gates are to be shut euerie night (except at certeine times) and to be opened euerie morning at certeine hours appointed, as it appeareth by a composition made for the same betwéene the communaltie of Excester, and the bishop and deane of the same. In the middle of the cemiterie or churchyard is a verie faire founteine or conduit of water conueied by certeine pipes of lead from out of the same féelds, as is the cities conduit. And albeit the springs of both waters are in the same field, and not farre distant: yet this dooth excell the other. Out of this well or founteine waters are conueied to sundrie of the chanons houses, as also of late vnto the bishops house, and yet it serueth besides the whole close and citie. The citie it selfe is verie populous, and was sometimes chéefelie inhabited with clothiers & clothworkers of broad clothes, seruing much for the Spanish and south countries; and which in those daies were of such goodnesse & substance, that the names of them doo remaine in those countries: but now it is chéeflie inhabited with merchants kersie-clothiers, and all sorts of artificers, among whome the merchants are the chéefe & welthiest.

S. Peters conduit.

The inhabitants of this citie.

The gouernement of this citie was sometimes by foure bailiffes, which before the conquest were called portgreues, that is, the chéefest lords or rulers of the towne: for porta is taken for a towne, and greue in Saxonie is Dominus or maior: but after the conquest they were after the French toong named Prouostres, that is to saie Præfecti or rulers, and now stewards. Not long after the conquest there was ordered and constituted a senate of six and thirtie persons, but of later yeares by king Henrie the seauenth of foure & twentie persons, out of which number yearelie there was and is chosen one to be the chéefest gouernour for the yeare following; and is called by the name of a maior, whome the Saxons called Meregreue, that is, Maior dominus, or the chéefe ruler. This maior associated with the foure prouosts or bailiffes, hath the hearing, decerning, and determining in all ciuill causes betwéene partie and partie, and for which they kéepe wéekelie vpon euerie mondaie a court in the Guildhall of the said citie: but the bailiffes reteining their old and ancient custome, doo kéepe the like courts, and in the like causes distinctlie from the maior by themselues, at all time and times (the mondaies and festiuall daies excepted) as it shall please them to assigne, and with their court is called by the name of the prouost court.

The gouernment of this citie.

Portegreue.

Prouostres.

Maier or Meregreue.

The maiors court.

The prouost court.

Thus the maior and bailiffes both iointlie and seuerallie haue iurisdiction to decerne and determine in ciuill matters. But if the matters doo touch and concerne the prince, the crowne, the common peace, anie criminall matter, or the publike state of the citie and common-wealth of the same, then the same are decided by the maior and iustices, or by the maior and common councell, or by the maior himselfe, or by some other officer or officers, according to the nature and qualitie of the cause and offense. But bicause it requireth a large and speciall course, to describe the gouernement of this citie and common-wealth of the same, the charge of euerie officer, the diuersitie of officers, their seuerall iurisdictions, and a number of other things incident vnto their charges: there is a particular booke imprinted, and at large the same is set out, in such order as is requisite, and apperteining to the gouernement: whereby euerie man may know his office and charge, and what to him dooth apperteine. And let it suffice, that partlie through good gouernement, and partlie of a good inclination, the people of this citie haue béene alwaies dutifull and obedient to the king and the lawes: and haue in great awe and reuerence their gouernours and magistrats for the time being. And this one thing is not so strange as worthie to be noted, that euen from the beginning, from time to time they haue béene carefull for their common-wealth, and vigilant

The good inclination and dutifulnesse of the citizens.

gilant

gilant for the preseruation of the same.   And as in times of peace and quietnesse the same hath béene well gouerned: so in times troublesome and vnquiet, it hath béene most valiantlie defended against the inuasions and assaults of the enimies, as by sundrie histories it may appeare: whereof for example these few may serue.

1 First Aruiragus king of this land, then named Britaine, minding to staie the land in his ancient estate, fréedome and libertie, did withdraw and denie to paie vnto the Romans the tribute which they did require and demand: wherefore Claudius the emperor sent Vespasian then duke of the Romane armie, into this realme with a great hoast, either to recouer the tribute, or to subdue the land.   This Vespasian is he, who in the foure and twentith yeare after this his iourneie, did destroie Ierusalem.   Wherfore this duke landing in Torrebaie, then named Totonesium littus, came to this citie, laid siege vnto it, and gaue continuall assaults therevnto, for eight daies continuallie togither.   Aruiragus the king, being then in the east parts of the land, and hearing of this, with a great armie and power marcheth towards this citie to remooue the siege, and incountereth with the enimie.   The Romane after long fight, and not able to preuaile, is contented to come to parlée, and in the end a composition was concluded, as it dooth appeare, and is set downe and written by sundrie historiographers.   The chronicle of the cathedrall church of the said citie hath these words: Anno Domini 49, Vespasianus cum Romano exercitu ciuitatem nunc vocatam Exeter, octo diebus obsedit, sed minimè præualuit, Aruirago rege ciuibus auxilium præstante.

Claudius Nero the emperor sendeth Vespasian into Britaine.

Vespasian landeth in Torrebaie, and laieth siege to this citie.

King Aruiragus rescueth this citie and incountereth the enimie.

Annales ecclesiæ cathed.

Geffreie of Monmouth hath these words: Vespasianus à Claudio missus est, vt Aruiragum vel pacificaret, vel Romanæ subiectioni restitueret.   Cùm igitur in portu in Rutupi applicare voluisset Vespasianus, obuiauit ei Aruiragus, atque prohibuit ne portum ingrederetur.   Retraxit itaque se Vespasianus à portu illo, retortisque velis in littore Totonesio applicuit.   Nactus deinde tellurem Caier Penhulgoite, quæ nunc Exonia vocatur obsessurus; eandem adiuit, cúmque octo diebus eandem obsedisset, superuenit Aruiragus cum exercitu suo, præliúmque commisit: die illa, valde laceratus fuit vtrorúmque exercitus, sed neuter est victoria potitus, mane autem facto, mediante Genwissa regina, concordes effecti sunt.   Matthew of Westminster writeth: Aruiragus Britannorum rex, in tantam prolapsus est superbiã, quòd Romanæ potestatis noluit diutiùs subiectioni parere.   Vespasianus igitur à Claudio missus cùm in Rutupi portu applicare incepisset, Aruiragus illi obuius prohibuit ne ingrederetur.   At Vespasianus retortis velis in Totonesio littore applicuit, & ciuitatem quæ Britannicè Caier Penhulgoite, nunc autem Exonia appellatur, obsedit: elapsis inde septem diebus Aruiragus superuenit, præliúmque commisit, & vtrorúmq; exercitu valde lacerato, mediante Genwissa Claudij filia, duces amici facti sunt.

Galfridus Monumetensis.

Flores historiarum.

In the historie intituled, Noua historia de gestis Anglorum à Britonibus vsque ad Henricum sextum, is written the like in effect: Vespasianus à Claudio missus est vt Aruiragum pacificaret, vel Romanæ ditioni restitueret, cui obuians Aruiragus, prohibuit ne terram suam ingrederetur, timens Vespasianus armatorum cohortem, retraxit sese, retortísq; velis in Totonesio littore est appulsus, atque vrbem Exoniæ obsedit, post septem dies superuenit Aruiragus, prælium committitur, laceratúrque vtrorúmque exercitus, sed neuter potitur victoria, demum mediante Genewissa regina, reconciliati sunt.   It was also in manie troubles and great perplexities, in the vncerteine and troublesome states of this realme, when sometimes the Romans, sometimes the Picts, sometimes the Scots, sometimes the Saxons, and sometimes the Danes made their incursions and warres within this land, by reason whereof the records and memorials in those daies for the most part were lost and consumed.

Noua historia.

2 And yet Matthew of Westminster writeth that it was besieged by Penda king of Mertia, in the yeare of our Lord 632, in the time of Cadwallin one of the last kings of the Britons.   The historie is this, Edwin the Saxon king of the Northumbers, hauing wars against Cadwillin or Cadwallo, did so preuaile and had such conquests ouer

Flores historiarum.

Penda king of Mertia.

Edwin king of Northumberland.

King Cadwallo is driuen to flée into Ireland.

ouer him, that Cadwallo was driuen to forsake his realme of Wales, and to flie into Ireland, where he being, was verie carefull and pensifull how to recouer his countrie againe. Wherefore he repareth his armie and gathereth a new force, and gaue sundrie attempts to atchiue to his purpose: but all was in vaine, for he could neuer set foot on land in his countrie. But Edwin was alwaies at hand and in a readinesse to stop and

Pellitus a witch dooth foretell to king Edwin of things to come.

resist the same, for this Edwin had about him in his seruice a man named Pellitus, who was a magician and verie skilfull in necromancie, and who by his art and science did foreshew and declare vnto Edwin what things were a dooing and attempted against him.

Cadwallo hauing continuallie euill successe, was in vtter despaire and distrust to preuaile against Edwin, and therefore as one giuing ouer all, saileth ouer the seas into

King Cadwallo saileth into Armorica.

Armorica now called little Britaine, vnto Salomon the king thereof, and vnto him dooth disclose his miserable estate and fortune, as also greatlie complaineth of Pellitus and of his sorceries. When these two kings had throughlie consulted and debated the matter, it was at length concluded and thought best, that some one man being bold and wittie should be sent ouer to the court of king Edwin, & to giue the aduenture to kill Pellitus. Wherevpon the matter being discouered to Brienus nephue to king Cad-

Brienus the kings nephue is sent to kill Pellitus.

wallo, he taketh vpon him to enterprise the matter, and to couer himselfe from all suspicion, apparelleth himselfe in a poore beggers wéed, and so saileth ouer into England, and trauelleth foorthwith towards king Edwins court, who then laie at Yorke, and there ioineth and accompanieth himselfe among the poore people, whose custome and maner was, to lie about the kings gates at dinner and supper times, waiting for the almesse vsuallie giuen and woont to be distributed amongst the poore.

Pellitus being the kings almoner, and hauing the charge to distribute the said almesse, commeth foorth and setteth the poore folke in order. Brienus being there and

Brienus killeth Pellitus.

amongst them, watcheth his time to worke his purpose, and thrusting himselfe in the middle of the presse of the people, suddenlie with his poinado or weapon which for the purpose he had prepared, thrusteth Pellitus into the bodie, & gaue him a deadlie wound whereof he died, and forthwith (the thing in such a thrust not perceiued) shifteth himselfe awaie priuilie, and through woods, hils, thickets, and dales out of the common waie, commeth to this citie of Excester, & declareth vnto the citizens (who were then Britons) what he had doone: whereof they were verie glad and ioifull, and in good hope that their king Cadwallo should yet againe returne; and therefore vpon good aduise doo prepare and make readie both themselues and the citie, aswell for the resisting of the enimie, as for the receiuing, succouring and aiding of their king.

King Penda aduertised of this murther, and vnderstanding the whole course of the matter and practise, taketh in griefe the iniurie thus doone to his neighbor and coun-

King Penda besiegeth Excester.

triman king Edwin. And therefore to reuenge the same mustereth his subiects and gathereth a great armie; and vnderstanding that Brienus was come to this citie marcheth towards the same, and in the end laieth his siege round about it, minding the vtter subuersion thereof. But the citizens manfullie withstanding his force, did defend and kéepe both themselues and their citie, vntill that king Cadwallo, who before was aduertised both of the fact of Brienus and of this preparation of Penda, did with his force and armie come to the citie, who did not onelie rescue the same; but also ioining the battell with his enimie gaue him the ouerthrow, and so deliuered his countrie, and recouered himselfe and his kingdome.

3 It was also in greater troubles in the time of king Alured or Alfred the fourth sonne to king Ethelwolphus. For Polydorus and others doo write, that in the fift

Polyd. lib 5.

yeare of the said kings reigne, the Danes concluded a peace with the said king, and gaue hostages for the true kéeping thereof. And yet notwithstanding most perfidiouslie and falselie contrarie to the same, they assembled themselues, and vpon a sudden marched to this citie, and perforce entered and tooke the same: Daci etenim qui religionem

gionem & fidem pro suo commodo postponendam ducebant, Londino se mouent, & maximis itineribus Exoniam proficiscuntur, vrbémq; per vim capiunt. But long they inioied not the same, for after that winter passed, the king to be reuenged marcheth with a great power to this citie, which the Danes vnderstanding and thinking themselues too weake to withstand the K. as also vtterlie distrusting the citizens, shifted themselues awaie, of which some fled vnto Dartmouth and there tooke shipping, and who for the most part were drowned in a tempest at the seas. Some fled to Chipen- *The Danes are ouerthrowne and their capteins are slaine.* ham or (as some saie) to Bristow, but the King followed and pursued these so sharplie, that he neuer left nor gaue ouer, vntill he had ouercome and slaine the capteins Hubbert and Hungar.

Likewise in the nineteenth yeare of the reigne of the said king, the Danes contrarie to their faith, pledges, and promises, did againe come to this citie, and laid siege to the same: Danorum exercitus anno 877, ab Wareham nocte quadam, fœdere dirupto, *Noua chronica.* ad Exeancestre, quod Britannicè dicitur Caieriske diuerterunt, at audito regis aduentu, ad puppes fugerunt, & in mari prædantes manebant.

5 It was also besieged by the said Danes in the nineteénth yeere of king Egelred, in the yéere of our Lord 1001. For the Danes, which were in Normandie, being aduertised of the good lucke, successe, and great spoiles which their companions and countriemen in England had, and their téeth set on edge therewith, suddenlie prepared shipping, and came ouer the coasts and landed in Deuon, and forthwith marched and tooke their course towards the citie of Excester; thinking to haue found the citizens napping & to haue taken them suddenlie and vnawares; sed ciuibus viriliter resistenti- *Flores histo-* bus recesserunt. The people & cōmons of Deuon, Cornewall, Summerset & Dorset, *riarum.* aduertised hereof, assembled themselues, & minding to rescue the citie, as also to incounter & aduenture the field with the Danes, met with them at a place néere the citie called Pinneho, and ioined battell with them, betwéene whome the fight was cruell and the slaughter great. And thus dooth Houeden testifie, whose words be these: *Houeden:* Memoratus paganorum exercitus de Normannia in Angliam reuectus, ostium fluuij *The battell at* Exe ingreditur, & mox ad extinguendam vrbem Exeancestre egreditur, sed dum murum *Pinneho.* illius destruere moliretur, ac ciuibus vrbem viriliter defendentibus repellitur, vnde nimis exasperatus more solito villas succendendo, agros depopulando, hominésque cædendo per Domnoniam vagatur, quare Domnonenses in vnum congregati, in loco qui dicitur Pinho certamen cum eis ineunt.

King Sweno being in Denmarke, and aduertised hereof, as also giuen to vnderstand how king Elfred aliàs Etheldred or Egelred had caused all the Danes in the realme to be suddenlie slaine in one night, being much gréeued therewith, did prepare and prouide a great armie for the reuenge thereof. And in the yeare of our Lord 1002, he *King Sweno* landed in sundrie and diuerse parts of this realme, vsing great hostilitie, and making *inuadeth and spoileth the* great spoiles, and brought the whole land to an vnspeakeable miserie and distresse: *land.* but at length, receiuing a tribute for a peace, he returned home into his owne countrie. Howbeit the citizens of Excester hearing of this crueltie vsed in the east parts, made themselues strong: and doubting of so mightie an enimie, did make themselues readie, and prepared the citie to withstand him, if he should haue attempted anie force or hostilitie against them.

But the Dane being gone and returned home, and knowing nothing of this prepa- *Hugh earle of* ration, one Hugh then earle of Deuon (as princes lacke no fawners) sent his letters *Deuon as a false mā to his* into Denmarke to king Sweno, certifieng him both of the state and wealth of this *countrie, dooth* citie, as also of the great preparation which had bene made to withstand him, per- *betraie the citie.* suading him not to susteine such an iniurie. And as coles will be soone kindled: euen so the Dane vpon this aduertisement was in a great heat, and foorthwith arreareth his armie, and repareth all **things** in readinesse to crosse the seas anew to worke his will against this citie. 6 **And** accordinglie when time serued, in the yeare following, being

ing

ing the yeare of our Lord 1003, he tooke the seas and landed vpon the coasts of Deuon

King Sweno by the treclærie of the earle of Deuon besiegeth the citie.
and Cornewall, and marched foorthwith to this citie, and laid his siege against the same in the beginning of the moneth of August, and continued the same vntill the kalends of September: during which time were sundrie sharpe, fierce, and cruell assaults giuen by the Dane, and as valiantlie resisted by the citizens.

But in continuance of time, when they saw themselues dailie more and more to be weakened, vittels to faile, the fire round about them, their walles beaten downe, themselues slaughtered and murthered, and the enimie to increase and be strong, and in all

King Eldred as one forlorne forsaketh his countrie.
these distresses, their king Eldred being fled into Normandie, to haue no care of them, nor to prepare anie rescue, aid, or helpe for them: it was not to be maruelled, if in so heauie a distresse they were amazed and astonished. And yet considering with themselues that Sweno was a Dane, a cruell enimie, a bloudie murtherer, an usurping ty-rant, hauing no other title to the crowne of England, but the sword, did with one con-

The stoutnes and courage of the citizens.
sent agrée and conclude, neuer to yéeld nor giue ouer whilest anie were left liuing able to withstand the same, wishing rather to die manfullie for their common wealth, than to liue in reproch and infamie; and by death to reape an immortall fame, than by life to become ignominious & infamous, and in the end also to be the miserable slaues of a cruell and vsurping tyrant.

When therefore after manie assaults, all or the most part of the ablest men were

King Sweno en-tereth and taketh the citie, & vt-terlie destroieth it.
Wil. Malm.
spent and consumed, and none or few left aliue to withstand so mightie and so manie enimies: the Dane on the seuen and twentith daie of August, with force entered the citie, and after that he had serued and satisfied his bloudie appetits, in deflowring the women, murthering the children, and making hauocke of all the people, hée spoiled the citie, burned the houses, rased the walles, bet downe the temples, and left no-thing to be doone which might by fire, sword, and spoiles be consumed: and this is so witnessed by sundrie writers. Reinulph of Chester writeth thus: Daci cum suo

Rein. Cest.
rege Sweno Excestriam venerunt, & vrbem funditùs destruxerunt, nulla re incolumi relicta, quæ aut ferro aut igni vastari poterat: & omnia spolia cineribus tantùm relictis secum deportauerunt. Huntington hath these words: Daci irâ exarserunt sicut

Hen. Hunt.
ignis quem velit aliquis sanguine extinguere: aduolantes igitur quasi multitudo locus-tarum, quidam Excestriam venerunt, & vrbem funditùs destruxerunt: & omnia spoliæ cineribus tantum relictis secum deportauerunt.

Houeden.
Houeden thus saith: Rex Danorum Sweni periurium & proditionem Normannici comitis, quem Emma Domnaniæ præfecerat, ciuitatem Exon infregit, spoliauit, & murum ab orientali vsq; ad occidentalem portam destruxit, & cum ingenti præda naues

William the Conquerour be-siegeth the citie. A league be-twéene the gen-tlemen & the citizens to resist the Conquerour.
repitijt. 7 It was also besieged by William the Conquerour in the first yeare of his reigne Anno 1068. For when he first entred this land, and by dint of sword sought the conquest thereof; the citizens of this citie, and the noble and gentlemen of all the countrie about, entered into one common league, conclusion and promise, to ioine togither and to withstand the enimie to the vttermost. And this confederacie being confirmed by a publike oth, preparation on all parts was made accordinglie, for the accomplishing of the same. But the conquerour hauing preuailed, and subdued in a maner the whole land, was aduertised that this citie stood vpon their gard, and would not yéeld nor submit themselues vnto him. Wherevpon he sent his armie from Lon-don and besieged the same, and perceiuing the siege to continue, marched and came

The records of the citie.
himselfe vnto the same, but rather came no further than Salisburie. In the meane time the citizens were aduertised how the whole realme had yeelded, and seeing also how their confederats did dailie shrinke awaie from them, and by that meanes they to grow weaker & weaker, and therefore the lesse able to withstand so great a force, and to keepe out so puissant an armie as was round about them; and considering also, that small mercie or fauor should they find if the citie by force were taken; did by way of intreatie offer submission, and desire peace, which in the end they obteined: and so

                                             paieng

paieng a grieuous fine, they and the citie were restored. But yet in token of his conquest, the king altered and changed the gates of the castell, and tooke an oth of all the citizens to be his liege and true subiects.

Houeden in his historie maketh mention, that Githa king Harolds mother should be within this citie, during the time that this siege and assault lasted : and perceiuing the bent of the people to submit and yeeld themselues, secretlie conueied hirselfe awaie. For these be his words : Hyeme minuente, rex Wilhelmus de Normannia in Angliam redijt, & Anglis importabile tributum imposuit : deinde in Dunmoniam hostiliter profectus est ad ciuitatem Excestriam, quam ciues & nonnulli Anglici ministri contra illum retinebant : & obsedit, & infregit. Githa verò comitissa, mater scilicet Haroldi regis Anglorum, & soror Swani regis Danorum, cum multu de ciuitate fugiens, euasit & Flandriam petijt, ciues autem dextris acceptis regi se dederunt.   8 Also in the second yeare of king Stephan Anno 1137, the lords and péeres of the realme, remembring the oth which they had before made to king Henrie the first, to whom they sware to be true to Mawd the kings onelie daughter and heire, and to hir heires, and yet contrarie to the same had sworne themselues to king Stephan, began to repent themselues, & consulted how to restore Mawd the empresse, and to expell Stephan. Wherefore they assembled themselues in armor, & diuided themselues into sundrie cities, townes and castels.

Houeden.
Polychron. li. 7.

Githa king Harolds mother laie in the citie during the siege and secretlie fleeth awaie into Flanders.

Among whom one Baldwin Rideuers then erle of Deuon, with force entered and tooke this citie. But the king so sharpelie followed and pursued him, that he draue him from hence into the Ile of Wight, which was then his lordship. But the king when he had receiued the citie into his faith, marched with his armie to the said Ile, & tooke the same, as also the earle himselfe, whome he foorthwith banished. But Mawd the empresse afterwards remembring this citie for such their seruice as she well liked, did inlarge the liberties of this citie, for whome yearelie euer after was an anniuersarie kept at the charges of the citie.

Baldwin Rideuers earle of Deuon entred into this citie, and resisteth against king Stephan. Baldwin the earle is taken and banished. Q. Mawd is friendlie to the citie.

It was also in great troubles in the eleuenth yere of king Richard the second, Anno 1387. For a controuersie being fallen betwéene the king & his two vncles, the dukes of Yorke & Glocester, none were then so highlie in the kings fauour, as were Robert Vere marques of Dublin, and Michaell de la Poole earle of Suffolke, & others of their faction. To these the king gaue in commandement, to collect and muster an armie, as it were for his defense, against his said vncles : which when they had partlie doone, whether it were bicause they mistrusted their owne parts, or whether they doubted of the sequele of their dooings, they left their iourneie towards London, as it was first appointed and came towards this citie. The two dukes who stood vpon their owne gard and defense, hauing aduertisement hereof followed and persuaded them with all haste and spéed : and hauing ouertaken them at this citie, they ioined the fight with the marques and the earle. But they trusting more to their feet than to their hands, secretlie gaue the slip and fled awaie, making no staie before they came to Scotland ; and from thence into Flanders, where they died.

Polydor. li. 20.

The marques of Dublin and the earle of Suffolke come to Exon and are pursued by the dukes of York and Glocester.

10 It was moreouer in troubles in the tenth yere of king Edward the fourth Anno 1469, when the states of this king, and of king Henrie the sixt were doubtfull, and the whole realme diuided : some following king Henrie, and some king Edward. In time of which troubles the duches of Clarence, the lord Dineham, the lord Fitzwaren, and the baron of Carew, who followed and tooke part with king Henrie, came to this citie, being accompanied and stipated with a thousand fighting men. The duches was great with child, and lodged in the bishops palace, but the lords were in other houses within the close among the chanons, and here staied themselues. But sir Hugh Courtneie knight, who then fauoured and was on the part of king Edward, hearing of this assemblie, raiseth an armie of his friends and alies, approcheth therewith vnto this citie, besiegeth it, breaketh the bridges and stoppeth all the

The duches of Clarēce with others commeth to Exon being great with child & lieth in the bishops palace.

Sir Hugh Courtneie laieth siege to the ci.ie.

The maior is
required to deli-
uer the keies of
the citie, and
refuseth so to
doo.
waies leading to the same, and by which means no vittels could bée brought to the markets : and being thus incamped about this citie, sendeth to the maior, requiring him either to open the gates and to giue him entrie, or to deliuer vnto him the gentlemen that were therein. On the other side, the gentlemen which were within, they either mistrusting the maior and citizens, or not willing to stand to his courtesie, and be vnder his gouernment, required the keies of the citie gates to be deliuered vnto their custodie, and that all things to be doone by their order and appointment.

In these doubts and perplexities consulting what were best to be doone, they did at length resolue & conclude neither to yeeld to the requests of them who were without, nor yet to satisfie the demands of them which were within the citie : but pacifieng both parties with such good words, and in such good order as they might, did reserue to themselues the kéeping and safe custodie of the citie, being the chamber of the king, and parcell of the reuenues of the crowne, to the onlie vse of the king and

The maior and
citizens doo for-
tifie the citie.
crowne, as to them in dutie and allegiance did apperteine. And therefore forthwith they rampired vp the citie gates, fortified the walles, appointed souldiers, and did set all things in such good order as in that case was requisit ; leauing nothing vndoone which might be for the preseruation of the state & commonwealth of the citie.

But yet for want of forecasting, in processe of time the prouision within the citie waxed short, and vittels to be scant ; whereof it was doubted there would insue some famine, which the common people neither could nor would indure, if some remedie were not in due time had and prouided. The magistrats did their best indeuor euerie waie, aswell by diligence in following, as by counselling, in persuading euerie man to continue firme and true to the publike state, and their owne priuate common-weale. And albeit the common people were vnpatient to abide troubles, and loth to indure the present state of want and famine ; yet they had that respect to their owne truth, faith, and safetie, as euerie man yeelded himselfe contented to abide and indure the time of their deliuerance : and by the good will of God it followed, and the same tooke good effect.

The siege raised,
and the citie de-
liuered.
For about twelue daies after this sturre begun, by waie of intreatie and mediation of certeine chanons of the cathedrall church of this citie, the siege was remoued and raised ; wherevpon verie shortlie after did insue the field of Edgecourt, where the

The duke of Cla-
rence and the
Earle of War-
wike came from
Edgecourt field
to this citie, and
from hence to
Dartmouth.
duke of Clarence and the earle of Warwike being put to the worst, did flée vnto this citie, and made their entrie into the same the third daie of April, 1470, and laie in the bishops palace for a few daies, vntill they had caused to be prouided ships at Dartmouth for their passage ouer into Calis.

The king being aduertised which waie his enimies were gone, followed and pursued them with an armie of fortie thousand men, and came to this citie the fourtéenth of Aprill 1470. hauing with him in his companie sundrie & diuerse great lords and estates, as namelie the bishop of Elie lord treasuror of England, the duke of Norffolke earle marshall of England, the duke of Suffolke, the earle of Arundell, the earle of Wiltshire son to the duke of Buckingham, the earle of Shrewesburie, the earle Riuers, the lord Hastings, the lord Greie of Codner, the lord Audleigh, the lord Saie, the lord Sturton, the lord Dacres, the lord Mountioie, the lord Stanleie, the lord Ferris, & the baron of Dudleigh, with a number of knights and gentlemen. But they all came too late : for the duke and the earle were both departed and gon to the seas before their comming.

Perkin War-
becke commeth
to Excester and
besiegeth it.
Wherefore the king, after that he had rested and reposed himselfe here thrée daies, he departed and returned to London. 11 It was also in great troubles, being besieged in the twelfe yeare of king Henrie the seuenth : by one Perkin Warbecke, 1470, who in the beginning of the moneth of September came to this citie, and incamped about it with his whole armie with ordinance battered the walls, fired the gates, vndermined

it,

it, and with mightie ladders scaled them, and left nothing vndoone which might be to compasse their attempt : thinking and supposing that small would be the resistance against them. But such was the noble courage and valiant stomach of the citizens, that they manfullie resisted and defended those forces, and indured the same to the vttermost, vntill that the king being aduertised thereof, did send the lord Edward Courtneie, earle of Deuon and the lord William his sonne, with sundrie others well appointed, who came and rescued the citie, but in certeine conflicts the said earle and others were hurt ; notwithstanding the enimie had the repulse, and was driuen to raise his campe and to depart.

12 Finallie & last of all, it was besieged in the third yeare of king Edward the sixt; 1549, by the commons of Deuon and Cornewall : the historie whereof, for so much as hitherto it hath not béene fullie and at large set forth by anie man, & whereat I Iohn Hooker the writer herof was present, and Testis oculatus of things then doone, I will somewhat at large discourse & set downe the whole course & maner of the same. It is apparant and most certeine, that this rebellion first was raised at a place in Deuon named Sampford Courtneie, which lieth westwards from the citie about sixtéene miles; vpon mondaie in the Whitsunwéeke being the tenth daie of Iune 1549. The cause thereof (as by the sequele it did appeare) was onelie concerning religion ; which then by act of parlement was reformed, and to be put in execution on Whitsundaie the ninth of Iune. The which daie being now come, and the statute made for the same to be put in execution throughout the whole realme : it was accordinglie with all obedience receiued in euerie place, and the common people well inough contented therewith euerie where ; sauing in this west countrie, and especiallie at the said Sampford Courtneie.

For albeit, the daie appointed by statute, they had heard and were present at the diuine seruice said, and had according to the new reformed order, and could not in anie respect, find fault, or iustlie reprehend the same : yet (as old bottels which would not receiue new wine) would rather wallow in the old dreggs and puddels of old superstition, than to be fed and refreshed with the wholsome and heauenlie manna. Wherefore they confederated themselues, vtterlie to renounce, reiect and cast off the same, not onelie to the great offense of God, whome they ought in all truth and veritie to reuerence and honor ; and to the great displeasure of the king, whome in all dutifulnesse they ought to haue obeied : but also to the raising of open rebellion, the cause of the spoile of the whole countrie, and the vndooing of themselues, their wiues, and children ; as in sequele and in the end it fell out and came to passe.

And here dooth appeare what great detriments doo come and insue to the church of God, and what great trouble to the publike and commonweale : when as learned preachers doo want to teach and instruct the people ; and well persuaded magistrats to gouerne the common state. For these people lacking the one, & not stored with the other, were left to themselues, and to their owne dispositions : and thereby partlie of ignorance, but more of a froward and rebellious disposition, they doo now vtterlie condemne to accept, and doo openlie resist to receiue the reformed religion, now put and to be put in vse and execution. For vpon the said mondaie, the priest being come to the parish church of Sampford, & preparing himselfe to saie the seruice according to the booke & reformed order set foorth, & as he had doone the daie before : some of the parishioners, namelie one William Vnderhill a tailor, and one Segar a laborer, and others who had consulted and determined before of the matter, went to the priest, and demanded what he ment to doo, and what seruice he would saie? Who answered that according to the lawes set forth, he would saie the same seruice as he had doone the daie before. Then they said, that he should not so doo, saieng further, that they would kéepe the old and ancient religion, as their forefathers before them had doone ; and as king Henrie the eight by his last will and testament had taken

5 Y 2   order,

order, that no alteration of religion should be made, vntill king Edward his sonne were come vnto his full age. And therefore, for somuch as he was now but a child, and could doo nothing, they also would not haue anie change.

The priest was compelled, because he would be compelled to saie masse.

In the end, all the parishoners ioining and taking parts togither, were all of the same mind, willing and charging the priest that he should vse and saie the like seruice as in times past he was woont to doo: who in the end, whether it were with his will, or against his will, he relied to their minds, and yéelded to their wills: and forthwith rauisheth himselfe in his old popish attire, and saith masse, and all such seruices as in times past accustomed. These newes, as a cloud caried with a violent wind, and as a thunder clap sounding at one instant through the whole countrie, are caried and noised euen in a moment throughout the whole countrie: and the common people so well allowed and liked thereof, that they clapped their hands for ioie, and agréed in one mind, to haue the same in euerie of their seuerall parishes.

The iustices resort to Sampford and doo no good.

The iustices of peace dwelling not far from Sampford, being aduertised how disorderlie, & contrarie to the lawes, things had béene doone in the church of Sampford; and how that the common people were clustered and assembled togither, to continue and to mainteine their lewd & disordered behauiour: such of them, namelie, sir Hugh Pollard knight, Anthonie Haruie, Alexander Wood, and Marke Slader esquiers came & met at Sampford, minding to haue had conference with the chiefe plaiers in this enterlude, aswell for the redresse of the disorder alreadie committed, as also to persuade and pacifie the rest of the people. But they partlie vnderstanding before hand of the iustices comming, were so addicted and wholie bent to their follies, that they fullie resolued themselues, wilfullie to mainteine what naughtilie they had begun. And therfore, when the iustices were come to the place, and requested to talke with them, they refused it; vnlesse the said gentlemen would leaue all their men behind, and go with them into a certeine seuerallclose not far off; and so they would be contented to conferre with them.

These gentlemen were afraid of their owne shadowes.

The gentlemen, albeit they and their men were the greater number, and sufficient to haue repressed the small companie of the commoners then & there assembled: yet whether it were because they thought in such a case to vse all the best & quietest waie for the pacifieng of them; or whether some of them being like affected as they were, did not like the alteration, as it was greatlie suspected: they yéelded, and according to the motion made, they left their men in the towne, & went into the foresaid close & there hauing had conference a pretie while togither, did in the end depart without anie thing doone at all. Whereof as there appéered some weakenesse in the said iustices which were so white liuered, and they would not, nor durst not to represse the rages of the people (which they might haue done) so therof also insued such a scab as passed their cure, and such a fire as they were not able to quench. For the commons hauing now their willes, were set vpon a pin, that the game was theirs, and that they had woone the garland before they had runne the race; nothing forecasting what might insue, nor yet accounting what follie it is to triumph before the victorie. Wherfore they assemble & confederat themselues throughout the whole shire in great troops and companies, and doo associat and flocke vnto them the Cornish people, minding to ioine togither, and foolishlie to mainteine what rashlie they had begun.

Sir Peter Carew and sir Gawen Carew sent into Deuon.

The king and councell then occupied in the weightie causes concerning the state of Scotland, being aduertised of this towards rebellion, & respecting the speedie redresse thereof, sent foorthwith for sir Peter Carew knight, who then was in Lincolneshire, and for sir Gawen Carew, who was then attendant at the court: and to them commandement was giuen, that foorthwith, and with all spéed they should hasten and depart into Deuon, and there to vse, by the aduise of the iustices, all the best meanes and waies that they might for the appeasing of this rebellion, quieting of the people, and pacifieng of the countrie; and to cause euerie man quietlie to returne to his home,

and

and to refer the causes of their griefs and complaints (if they had anie) vnto the king and councell: and if they then refused so to doo, they to vse such other good means and waies as might be for the suppressing of them. And the councell being dailie more and more aduertised, that these begun rebellions did more and more increase; and doubting of the sequele thereof, by reason that in other places of the realme the like tumults were begun, though not for the like causes; doo direct and giue an order to the lord Russell, then lord priuie seale, and after earle of Bedford, that he also should follow and dispatch himselfe into Deuon; and he had a commission to deale in such order as he might best doo for the pacifieng of the said tumults and vprores.

The foresaid two knights, hauing receiued their commission vnder the kings hand, came in post into the countrie, and making their repaire to this citie, doo foorthwith send for sir Péers Courtneie then shiriffe and the iustices of the peace of the countrie; and vnderstanding, that a great companie of the commons were assembled at Crediton, which is a towne distant about seauen miles from Excester, and that among them were the Sampford men: & who were the chiefe of them tooke councell & aduise what was best to be doone, and what waie méetest to be taken. In the end it was concluded, that the said sir Peter and sir Gawen with others should ride to Crediton, & there to haue conference and spéeches with the said commons, and to vse all the good waies and meanes they might to pacifie & appease them, they then supposing, and being persuaded, that by good spéeches and gentle conferences they should haue béene able to haue compassed and persuaded the said commons. But the people being by some secret intelligence aduertised of the comming of the gentlemen towards them, and they fullie resolued not to yéeld one iote from their determinations, but to mainteine their cause taken in hand, doo arme and make themselues strong, with such armors and furnitures as they had; they intrench the high waies and make a mightie rampire at the townes end, and fortifie the same, as also the barns next adioining to the said rampires with men and munition, hauing persed the walles of the barns with loopes and holes for their shot.

The foresaid gentlemen knowing nothing hereof, rode on their iourneie, and being come almost to the towne, they were aduertised how the waies were stopped and rampired, and that they could not ride into the towne Whervpon they alighted from their horsses, and after a little conference had, they agréed to go into the towne on foot, nothing thinking lesse that they should be stopped or denied to go in on foot. But when they came to the rampires they found the contrarie: for they not onelie were denied to come néere the rampire, but vtterlie were refused to be talked withall: no offers of persuasiòns nor motions of conference at all could be allowed. For the sun being in cancer, & the midsummer moone at full, their minds were imbrued in such follies, and their heads caried with such vanities, that as the man of Athens they would heare no man speake but themselues, and thought nothing well said but what came out of their owne mouths.

The gentlemen vpon such checks, taking the matter in euill part, to be so vnreuerentlie and discourteouslie intreated, with one consent doo agree to make waie ouer the rampire. But in the aduenture thereof they were so galled both by them which kept the rampires, and speciallie by such as were within the barnes, that they were faine to retire and giue place, with the losse of some, and the hurt of manie. In which distresse, a certeine seruingman named Fox, and reteining to sir Hugh Pollard, suddenlie set one of the barnes on fire: whervpon not onelie such as were therein, but all they also which were in the rampires fled and ran awaie. And then the gentlemen hauing recoured the rampire went into the towne; but there they found none except a few poore and old people, the residue trusting better to their héeles than to their armes were fled to a further place: and then they returned againe to Excester without anie thing doone.

The

The iusticiaries doo assemble all at Excester.

Sir Peter Carew by the aduise of the iustices rideth to Kitton.

The people at Kirton doo arme themselues & rampire vp the waies.

The barnes at the townes end at Kirton are set on fire.

The noise of this fire and burning was in post hast, and as it were in a moment carried and blazed abroad throughout the whole countrie; and the common people vpon false reports, and of a gnat making an elephant, noised and spread it abroad, that the gentlemen were altogither bent to ouer-run, spoile, and destroie them. And in this rage, as it were a swarme of wasps they cluster themselues in great troops and multitudes, some in one place, and some in an other, fortifieng and intrenching themselues as though the enimie were readie to inuade and assaile them. And among other places one was at a village belonging to the lord Russell named S. Marie Clift distant from Excester about two miles, where the commons of the countrie thereabout had begun to fortifie the towne for their defense & safetie.

An assemblie of the people at Clift Marie or bishops Clift.

The cause and pretense of their dooings herein, was not onelie the burning of the barnes at Crediton aforesaid, which all the commons generallie did vse for a cloke of this their rising and rebellion: but this one thing also increased their disposition. It happened that a certeine gentleman named Walter Raleigh dwelling not far from thense, as he was vpon a side holie daie riding from his house to Excester, ouertooke an old woman going to the parish church of saint Marie Clift, who had a paire of beads in hir hands, and asked hir what she did with those beads? And entring into further spéeches with hir concerning religion, which was reformed & as then by order of law to be put in execution, he did persuade with hir that she should as a good christian woman and an obedient subiect yéeld therevnto; saieng further, that there was a punishment by law appointed against hir, and all such as would not obeie and follow the same, and which would be put in execution vpon them.

A cause whie they rose at bishops Clift.

This woman nothing liking, nor well digesting this matter, went foorth to the parish church, where all the parishioners were then at the seruice: and being vnpatient, and in an agonie with the spéeches before passed betwéene hir and the gentleman, beginneth to vpbraid in the open church verie hard and vnséemelie spéeches concerning religion, saieng that she was threatned by the gentleman, that except she would leaue hir beads, and giue ouer holie bread and holie water, the gentlemen would burne them out of their houses and spoile them, with manie other spéeches verie false and vntrue, and whereof no talke at all had passed betwéene the gentleman and hir. Notwithstanding she had not so soon spoken, but that she was beléeued: and in all hast like a sort of wasps they fling out of the church, and get them to the towne which is not far from thense, and there began to intrench and fortifie the towne, sending abroad into the countrie round about, the news aforesaid, and of their dooings in hand, flocking, and procuring as manie as they could to come and to ioine with them.

And they fearing or mistrusting, least the gentlemen which were then at Excester, would come vpon them, they first fortified the bridge, which lieth at the end of the towne towards the citie, and laid great trées ouerthwart the same, as also planted certeine peeces of ordinance vpon the same, which they had procured and fetched from Topsham a towne not far from thense. But before they came into the towne, they ouertooke the gentleman maister Raleigh aforesaid, and were in such a choler, and so fell in rages with him, that if he had not shifted himselfe into the chappell there, and had béene rescued by certeine mariners of Exmouth which came with him, he had béene in great danger of his life, and like to haue béene murdered. And albeit he escaped for this time, yet it was not long before he fell into their hands, and by them imprisoned and kept in prison in the towre and church of saint Sidwelles, without the east gate of the citie of Excester, during the whole time of the commotion, being manie times threatned to be executed to death. But to the matter.

The towne a Clift is fortified, and the bridge rampired.

Walter Raleigh esquier in danger of the rebelles.

These the dooings of the commons being aduertised to sir Peter Carew, who then was in Excester, assembleth all the iustices & the gentlemen, & conferreth with them what were best to be doone; and in the end, concluded & agréed that he, sir Gawen Carew, sir Thomas Denis, sir Hugh Pollard, and sundrie others should ride to Clift,

and

and there to vse all the best meanes they might, for the pacifieng and quieting of Sir Peter Carew and others ride to Clift. them. And accordinglie in the next morning being sundaie they all rode thither: and being come almost to the bridge, they perceiued the same to be rampired, & no waie to be open for them to passe into the towne. Wherevpon sir Peter Carew alighted from his horsse, and mistrusting nothing, was going on foot toward the bridge. But such was the rancor and malice conceiued against him, partlie for religion, and Sir Peter Carew like to be slaine. partlie for the burning of the barns at Crediton, which was laid altogither to his fault, that the gunner whose name was Iohn Hamon an alien and a smith, and dwelling then at Woodburie, not far from Clift, by the procurement and abetting of some there, hauing charged his peece of ordinance there lieng, leuelled the same, to haue shot and discharged it at him: which he had doone, if one Hugh Osborne seruant then to sergeant Prideox had not let him and staied his hand.

The gentlemen perceiuing they could not passe into the towne, doo send in a messenger vnto the towne, aduertising them that they were come to talke friendlie with them, as also to satisfie them if they had anie cause of griefe, or were by anie bodie misused. They at this message and motion staggered a while and cast manie doubts: but in the end they sent word that they were contented, that if sir Thomas Denis, sir Hugh Pollard, and Thomas Yard esquier, would come into the towne to them and leaue their men behind them, as also would take order, and giue their faith and promise that no hurt should be doone or offered to be doone vnto them, whiles they were thus in conference togither: that then vpon these conditions they would be contented The conference of the gentlemen with the commoners at Clift. to talke with them. Vpon which promise made and assured vnto them, the foresaid thrée gentlemen went into the towne about ten of the clocke in the forenoone, and there taried and spent the most part of the daie in much talke and to no purpose: as in the end it fell out.

The other knights and gentlemen, which in the meane while taried without, and waited a long time euen vntill the daie did draw toward night, began to mislike of the matter, some speaking one thing and some an other; yea and some of them in plaine spéeches said they would ride ouer the water and issue into the towne. But the friends and seruingmen of the two knights, respecting the promise made before their entrie into the towne, but especiallie their masters safetie, which by breach of promise might be put in perill, did vtterlie mislike and were grieued with those spéeches, and whereof A mutinie towards among the seruing-men. This man was named Richard Carwithian seruant to sir Peter Carew. began a little quarrelling among themselues, but foorthwith pacified and quieted. And yet some one or two of the companie rode to the waters side, and with their staues searched the depth thereof: for at that bridge the water at euerie tide (by reason that the seas are so néere) swelleth vp and reboundeth. Which thing when they in the towne did sée, foorthwith cried out alarum, and made much adoo; and some of them began and grew into such rages, that the gentlemen within the towne began to distrust their safetie.

Neuerthelesse the conference and talke herewith ended, and they came awaie; who as soone as they were come to Sir Peter Carew, they were demanded what they had doone, and how they had sped: who answered; Well inough: & giuing no other answer they rode all togither to Excester, deferring the discouerie of their dooings vntill their comming thither. The same night they supped all togither, & after supper ended, and all the seruingmen auoided out of that roome, sir Peter Carew demanded The agréement offered by the commoners. of them what they had doone, and what agréement they had made: who answered that the commons had promised, and were contented to kéepe themselues in good & quiet order, and to procéed no further in their attempts: so that the king and the councell would not alter the religion, but suffer it to remaine and tarie in the same state as king Henrie the eight left it, & vntill the king himselfe came to his full age. Sir Peter Carew and all the residue nothing liking this answer, being farre from their expectation, were for the time in a great dumpe or studie; but in the end misliked

and

and discommended both the matter and the maner of their dealings : insomuch that sir Peter Carew, and sir Péerce Courtneie, then shiriffe of Deuon, openlie, sharpelie, and in plaine termes inueied against them for their slender, or rather sinister dealings in so weightie a cause : wherein they all ought rather to haue vsed all meanes to haue suppressed their outrages, than to haue mainteined their follies : and therefore as there was a blame in them, so was there a plaine rebellion in the other.

But though the two knights would haue excused the matter, and haue purged their sinceritie herein ; yet on ech side words were so multiplied, that they brake asunder without anie further dealings, and euerie man shifted for himselfe, some one waie some an other waie. The commons vnderstanding hereof stop all the high waies, casting great trenches, and laieng great trées ouerthwart the same, and doo watch & ward the same : and by that meanes sundrie gentlemen suspecting no such matter, and making waie to their appointed places, were intrapped, taken, and put in prison ; and manie of them kept in durance, during the whole time of the commotion, & abode great hardnesse, and were in perill of life and limme : manie were taken bicause they would be taken, & found fauour ; & manie forsaking their houses and home, were driuen to sequester and hide themselues in woods & secret places. In the citie none or verie few remained or taried, sauing six or seuen persons then knowne of : for by conference had before with the maior, it was knowne that the citie was vnprouided of sufficient vittels, méet for such a companie as the foresaid gentlemen were.

The gentlemeu which taried and remained in the citie ; namelie, sir Roger Blewet knight, Iohn Beauchampe, Bartholomew Fortescute, Iohn Courtneie, & Iohn Peter customer, esquiers, and others, did verie good seruice as well in their persons, as in their good aduises and counsels, sauing such as secretlie kept themselues close in certeine houses then vnknowne. Sir Peter Carew verie earlie in the next morning tooke his horsse, and the high waies being then not stopped he escaped and rode vnto George Henton, a place of sir Hugh Paulets in Summersetshire : where was the lord Russell, being then newlie come from London, and vnto him he gaue to vnderstand, how all things had passed : who foorthwith dispatched and sent him awaie to the king and councell to aduertise them of the same. The king at the first hearing of the matter, was verie much grieued, & in great perplexitie in two respects ; the one bicause at this instant the like tumults and rebellions (though for an other cause) were now raised and begun in other places ; the other was bicause he was inforced to leaue and giue ouer the appointed attempt for the conquest of Scotland, and to imploie now those soldiors and strangers, whome he had reteined for that seruice, for the quenching of this fire kindled at home.

Neuerthelesse minding to follow the first, and to appease the last, he sent verie courteous letters, gratious proclamations, and manie mercifull offers vnto all the commons of these parties, to haue pacified and satisfied them, if they had had so much grace so to haue accepted it. The commons being now entered in their follies, and hauing driuen the gentlemen to the flight, doo openlie shew themselues traitors & rebels : and therefore assembling themselues doo appoint out capteins to direct & order both themselues, and all their procéedings, and as the common prouerbe is, Like lips like lettice, as is their cause, so are the rulers, the one being not so bold and euill, as they wicked or woorse. The capteins then are these : Vnderhill a tailor, Maunder a shoomaker, Seager a labourer, and Aisheredge a fishdriuer, with sundrie other such like, the woorst men and the reffuse of all others, thought most méet in this seruice. Howbeit it was not long before, that certeine gentlemen and yeomen of good countenance and credit both in Deuon and Cornewall were contented, not onelie to be associats of this rebellion : but also to carrie the crosse before this procession, and to be capteins and guiders of this wicked enterprise, as namelie in Deuon sir Thomas Pomeroie knight, Iohn Burie and one Coffin gentlemen : & in Cornewall Humfrie Arundell

Arundell and Winneslade esquiers, & Holmes a yeoman, with sundrie others, who for the most part were in the end executed and put to death: and their facts to the memoriall of their perpetuall infamie recorded in chronicles.

The principall & chiefe capteins in Deuon being fullie resolued by their owne power and authoritie to mainteine & continue the religion, according to the Romish church, & vtterlie to impugne the reformation therof, established by act of parlement; & to support the authoritie of the idoll of Rome (whome they neuer saw) in contempt of their true and lawfull king, whome they knew and ought to obeie: these I saie sent their messengers vnto the maior of this citie, whose name was Iohn Blackaller, to mooue and praie him to ioine with them, they thinking that they hauing by these meanes the libertie to haue frée accesse to and from the citie, and the helpe of the citizens, should not want monie or armor, or anie thing else to serue their turne: the maior foorthwith aduertised vnto his brethren this motion. And albeit some and the chiefest of them did like & were well affected to the Romish religion: yet respecting their dutie to God, their obedience to the king, their fidelitie to their countrie, and safetie of themselues, gaue their full resolute and direct answer, that they would not ioine nor deale with them at all.

The rebels send to the maior of the citie to ioine with them.

The maior & citizens refuse to ioine or to deale with the rebels.

This answer was nothing liked, and therefore sent they their second messenger, requiring and commanding them to mainteine the old catholike religion with them, and to doo as they did; or else they would besiege them, and perforce compell them thervnto. The maior and his brethren returned their former answer, adding moreouer that they in their dooings were wicked & bad men; & they did & would repute them for enimies and rebels against God, their king, and countrie: and so renounced them. The one side therefore as they prepare to besiege the citie, and to worke all the extremities they can, by force to take that which by words they can not obteine: so on the other side the maior and his brethren vpon good aduise, garded and watched the citie with sufficient men, armed both by daie and by night. The rebels (according to their determination) relieng themselues vpon a vaine hope, thinking that notwithstanding the answer before made; yet because the most part of the citizens were of their opinions, and of the like affections in religion, would not resist them: as also that they had manie friends within the citie, more readie to ioine with them, than to follow the maior, if they might haue the choise what to doo: they came being in number about two thousand persons, to the citie, vpon the second of Iulie 1549, first making proclamation that if the citie would not yeeld, and ioine with them, they would enter with force and take the spoile of it, & so then they vpon the deniall compassed the same round about, and gained vnto them at the first all the suburbs.

Preparation is made on both sides to withstand the one the other.

The citie of Exon besieged.

And hereof they conceiued such a vaine hope to haue their full desire vpon the citie, that not onelie the number in hope did dailie more & more increase, but also manie of them brought their wiues, horsses, and paniers; persuading themselues, and promising them, by such a daie and vpon such a daie to enter into the citie, and then to measure veluets and silks by the bow, and to lade their horsses home with plate, monie, and other great riches. The maior and his brethren forecasting the perils which might in such a case insue, doo prouide all things necessarie and méet wherewith to defend themselues, and to annoie the enimie. The citie therefore is viewed for armor, men are mustered, soldiers are reteined, capteins in euerie ward appointed, warders for the daie and watchmen for the night assigned, great péeces of ordinance laid in euerie gate, and placed in all conuenient places of the wals; mounts in sundrie places erected, as well for laieng of ordinance, as for sauing of the soldiers & watchmen from the enimies shot: and nothing was left vndoone, which in anie respect that present state and necessitie required.

The vaine persuasions of the rebels to haue the spoile of the citie.

The citie is viewed for armor and all things are prepared for defense of the citie.

The rebels likewise intrench the high waies, plash downe trées, breake downe bridges, kéepe watches and wards in euerie place; so that no man could passe to or from the citie.

The rebels stop vp all the waies comming to the citie.

from the citie without their sufferance. The markets are stopped, vittels are kept from it, and all dealings and intercourses shut and cut off: and hauing (as they bragged) penned and shut vp the townesmen in a coope or mew, they plant their ordinance against euerie gate, and in all other such places as best to serue their turne, and to hurt them within: they burnt the gates, they brake vp the pipes and conduits, aswell for the taking awaie of the water comming to the citie, as also to haue the led to serue for their shot and pellets. But for the burning of the gates, there followed rather a benefit than a hurt thereof: for foorthwith there were made certeine rampiers within the gate, which were farre stronger and of more defense than the gates, as also there were fiers continuallie kept euerie night betwéene the rampiers and the gates: and as for water, the citie so standeth vpon a little hill, that it is full of springs in euerie quarter within the same, and by that means full and plentifull of euerie good and swéet waters. Also they in sundrie places did vndermine the wals, minding thereby with gunpowder and with other matters fit for fier to haue blowne vp the wals, and so to haue entered in that waie: but herein they were also preuented by this means and in this maner.

The citie it selfe (as is before said) is set vpon a little hill, and lieth verie stéeping towards two of the gates. And at one of these named the west gate, the said rebels had vndermined on the one side, and filled the place with certeine barels of powder, pitch, and other stuffe, méet and apt to receiue fier, and had appointed the night when the same should be set on fier, and so to haue blowne the wals vp. At the same time there was a certeine tinner in the citie, whose dwelling was at Teingemouth, named Iohn Newcombe, who depended much vpon the goodwill and fréendship of maister William Hurst one of the aldermen of the citie; and he vnderstanding of such an vndermining to be in working, aduertised the same to maister Hurst, and maketh him priuie how he would preuent the same, which was doone in this maner.

For whereas he by a noise vnder the ground did suspect the vndermining to be in working, he tooke a pan of water, and did put the same on the ground, & by shaking of the water in the pan, he by remoouing the pan from place to place, came at length to the verie place, whereat the miners were working, and foorthwith he countermined against the same, and wrought so néere vnto it, vntill that he might and did sée & looke into it. That doone, he caused all the wals and tirpits in the citie towards euerie stréet, hauing a fall that waie to be drawne at one time, and euerie man to fill therewith a great tub of water at his foredoore; which being doone, he caused them all at one instant to be cast out and emptied, which water running in great abundance towards the said west gate, was conueied into the place countermined, & so entered and drowned the place, which before was mined: at which time also by the goodnesse of God, there fell a great showre, as the like for the time had not béene séene manie years before, and which at that instant greatlie serued this turne.

The rebels perceiuing themselues disappointed of their purpose, gaue ouer to deale anie further in those attempts. howbeit otherwise they left nothing vndoone which might be to annoie the citizens. For sometimes they made alarums, as though they with all might and maine would haue giuen the scale: and indeed they had prouided ladders for the same purpose. Sometimes they by policies would séeke to come to the gates to burne them, and herein they vsed this stratagem. They prouided carts laden with old haie, & driuing the whéeles before them would come to the gate without danger, and so set fier in the gate. But notwithstanding they escaped not scot-frée, for both at the west gate and at the south gate, their commings being perceiued, the great port péeces were charged with great bags of flintstones and haileshot: and as they were approching vnto the gates, the gates were secretlie opened, and the said port péeces discharged, and so they were spoiled diuerse of them, & by that means they had small pleasure to follow those deuises; as also the citizens to preuent the

same,

The rebels plant their ordinance against the citie & breake vp the conduit pipes, and burne one of the gates.

The gates of the citie were kept open continuallie and rampired within side, as also fiers kept burning all night in the same.

The citie being full of water springs they want no water.

The citie wals at the west gate were vndermined, but by countermining the same was preuented.

The vndermininings of the wals how it was found and destroied.

A prettie stratagem of the rebels.

same, did from thencefoorth kéepe the gates open. Likewise they would kéepe themselues close in sundrie houses, in the suburbs neere the wals, and would so watch the garrets, that if anie within the citie would looke out at the garrets, was in the danger of their shot, and some thereby were killed, and manie hurt. Vpon which occasion the citizens set some part of the suburbs on fier, and some part which was next to the wals they beat and brake down, and so draue the rebels out of those holes. Besides this, they had in sundrie places their great ordinance, so set and placed, that in certeine stréets and places none could go but in perill and danger of their shot, which their deuises were choked, by making of certeine mounts to shadowe the streets from the same. Diuerse other deuises they practised to the continuall annoiance of the citie, which though they were greeuous and dangerous, yet not to be compared vnto the perils which were within the walles among themselues, and whereof had insued the confusion of the whole citie, had not the Lord God of his goodnesse kept and preserued the same. For the serpent of diuision, and the fier of malice, was entered into the citie, manie being inuenomed with the one, but more scaulded with the other. The citie gates kept alwaies open.
The suburbs burned and the houses beaten downe.
The citie diuided within it selfe into two factions of religion.

In the citie there were two sorts of people, the one and the greater number were of the old stampe, and of the Romish religion. The other being of the lesser number were of a contrarie mind and disposition, for they wholie relied themselues to the reformed religion, and to the kings procéedings, and indeuoured themselues to obeie and follow the same. The first were so addicted to their owne fantasies, and their bottels were so farre seasoned with the old wines, that they cannot abide to heare of anie other religion, than as they were first nuzled in. Wherefore to kéepe and obserue that, was their onelie endeuor, and in respect whereof they regarded not king nor Keisar, passed not for kin nor fréendship, regarded not countrie nor commonwealth, but were wholie of the opinion of the rebels, and would haue no reformation in religion; and how so euer all other things fared, that must néeds remaine as in times past had beene vsed. The affection and disposition of the Romish faction.

The magistrates and chéefeteins of the citie, albeit they were not as yet fullie resolued and satisfied in religion, yet they not respecting that, but chéefelie their dutifulnesse to the king and commonwealth, nothing like the rebellion, nor beare with the same, but they doo all things to defend the citie and themselues against their rebellious attempts, and likewise doo their best indeuour to keepe their owne citizens in peace and quietnesse. Wherevpon the fauourers of the old Romish religion, being inwardlie gréeued, that they could not haue their will, nor obteine to haue the gates to be opened, that those good and religious men (as they termed them) might come in, they vsed priuat conferences with them, sometimes by secret conferences ouer the wals, somtimes by priuat letters priuilie conueied too and fro, by messengers lurking and attending for the same, sometimes by open spéeches in times of truce, and manie times by bils and letters bound fast about arrowes, and so shot to and fro: and by these and other such like means they discouered ech one to the other their purposes and wicked deuises and practises: all which tended to this effect, to betraie the citie, and to set vp the religion. The discretion and great circumspection of the magistrates.
The secret conferences of the papists.

Howbeit, these things were not so secretlie doone, but the same were knowne, & manifest arguments and proofes thereof did appeare. And among sundrie some one of them being one of good credit and countenance, and of the number of the common councell, whose name was Iohn Wolcot a merchant, was so farre inchanted herein, that vpon a certeine daie he being (as his course came about) a capteine for the daie, and to ward one of the gates that daie, presuming that partlie by reason of his charge that daie, and partlie for that he was one of the common councell, he might doo more than in déed did apperteine to him, he vpon his first comming to the west gate in the morning met with certeine of his confederats, and after conference had with them, A fond enterprise of an expert citizen.

them, went suddenlie out at the wicket of the gate (which gate as then was not rampired) and carrieng the keies with him, went vnto the rebels, and had a long coference with them. But it tooke small effect, for he promised (as it after appeared) more than he could performe, which turned to his great discredit: both for that he himselfe verie hardlie escaped their hands who were bent to haue kept and reteined him, as they did the two others, who went out with him: as also when he came in, was both checked and blamed for his dooings.

At an other time the maior vpon an occasion assembled all the commoners vnto the Guildhall, euerie man being in his armor, and the papists being then the greater number, some one of them named Richard Tailor a clothier, thinking by making of a tumult or an vprore they should be too hard for the others, and so atteine to their purposes, hauing his bowe bent, did nocke his arrow, minding to haue striken the man to whome he leuelled the shot: but gaging his hand, and missing his marke, he stroke his owne and best fréend Iohn Peter the kings customer, a gentleman of good countenance and credit, who had died thereof, had not the arrow lighted vpon one of his rib bones: a great muttering was like to haue bred a tumult, but the matter knowne it was appeased. Also at an other time there was a practise made with the souldiers, who had the charge and custodie of the castell, that they should receiue in at the posterne of the said castell, a certeine number of the rebels; wherevnto the said souldiers through corruption had giuen their consent. The daie and time were appointed for the same: but whether the same by secret aduertisement were discouered, or whether the matter were mistrusted, or whether it pleased God to mooue the harts of certeine men to take the view of the castell, & of the maner of the souldiers vsages there: it is most certeine that by the repaire & resort of certeine men, vnder the colour to walke and sée the trecherie, it was espied, and the practises discouered, and their whole deuises preuented. Likewise manie times and often there were truces made, and sundrie parlees and conferences had with the rebels, which were procured to the onlie end that they might compasse their deuises. And this was a common practise with them, that when soeuer the parlée was appointed, there should be hostages or pledges put in on both parties: and they as men vpon whom the greatest weight of the matter did depend, would require to haue the best and most chosen citizens, to be hostages with them, in stéed and for the safetie of those which they would send to the parlée for them, who for the most part were the reffuse, the scumme, and the rascals of the whole countrie, and yet such they were in this case, as who ruled the rost and bore the whole or chiefest swaie; and the worsse the man, the greater his authoritie among them, which was good inough for so wicked a matter taken in hand, according as the common adage is: Dignum patella operculum, Like lips like lettice.

But during the time of these truces and parlées, there being then a time and scope of libertie to talke and conferre with them euerie man at his pleasure, there wanted no deuises vnder colour of freendlie conferences, to deuise how to compasse their intents: howbeit it pleased the eternall God, so to carrie and rule the hearts of the magistrats, that albeit being nuzled in the Romish religion they were affected therevnto, yet they so much respected their dutie to their prince, and the safetie to their commonwealth, that they openlie professed they would neuer yéeld the citie so long as they liued, and were able to kéepe and defend the same.

For the maior himselfe maister William Hurst, maister Iohn Buller, maister Iohn Britnall, maister William Periam, & others of the ancientest of the citie, were by sundrie means, waies, deuises, and reasons, persuaded to conioine themselues in this rebellion with commoners. They all with one mind and one voice gaue a flat answer that in the citie they had been brought vp, there they had gotten their liuings, there they had sworne their fidelitie and allegiance to their king and prince, there they
had

This Tailor died after in prison for debt.

What man purposeth God disposeth.

A wicked practise to receiue the rebels into the castell.

The chiefest rulers & capteins among the commons were the worst men.

Great practise vsed to procure the citizens to ioine with the rebels.

The faithfull and flat determination of the citizens to refuse the conioining with the rebels.

had faithfullie hitherto serued him, and there would so continue so long as they could to the vttermost of their powers, all which their promises & auowries (the Lord be praised) they performed.

But to the matter. Sundrie other trecheries & deuises were practised, which particularlie to recite were verie tedious & to no purpose. The last but the most perillous practise was this. When these malecontents saw themselues to be preuented in all their deuises, which before they had but secretlie and priuatlie practised, now they conioining themselues togither doo openlie shew and declare themselues, being persuaded that bicause they were the greater number, and that also the most part of the poore people were wearie, and for want of vittels would not indure to be pinned in anie longer, that therefore manie would ioine against a few, and that the game would go on their side. _{The last and perilous practise of the rebels.}

And so on a sundaie, being but two daies before the deliuerie of the citie, about eight of the clocke in the forenoone, a companie of them in euerie quarter of the citie, hauing their consorts in a readines to ioine & serue with them (if need so required) get into the streets, walking with their weapons and in their armour, as to fight with their enimies, and crie out; "Come out these heretikes and twopenie bookemen; Where be they? By Gods wounds & bloud we will not be pinned in to serue their turne; We will go out and haue in our neighbors, they be honest, good, and godlie men." Their pretense and meaning being then, that if anie of the contrarie side had come out, they would haue quarelled with them, and haue taken occasion to set vpon him and raise a new tumult. _{A pestilent practise.}

But by the prouidence and goodnesse of God it so fell out, that some being in their houses, and some at their parish churches, the maior and magistrates were first aduertised herof, before the others heard anie thing of the matter: and they according to their wisedoms pacified the matter, and sent Iohn Vincent, Iohn Sharke, and others the belwedders of this flocke vnto their houses. Howbeit in the south gate stréet and at the south gate, there was a little stur, which being soone stopped there insued no hurt therof, other than a broken pate or two: for as it fell out, the warders of that gate at that time were against them and of the greater companie. These and manie other like practises were dailie and continuallie vsed on the one side, which in the end came to no effect, bicause the Lord kept the citie. _{The papists were disappointed of their purposes.}

The others on the other side being altogither bent to honor God, obeie the king, and to serue in their commonwealth, were fullie resolued to kéepe and defend the citie, whose cause being iust and good, was sufficient of it selfe to kéepe them in that mind: and yet their courage was the more, for that they saw the good bent of the maior and magistrates; who, howsoeuer they were affected otherwise in religion, yet they were wholie bent and determined to kéepe and defend the citie: and therefore they seeing the industrie, carefulnesse, seruice, and painefulnesse, of these men, doo fauour, incourage, and countenance them, and (to saie the truth) by the industrie and good seruice of them, the citie was cheeflie kept and preserued. _{The determination of the honest & good citizens.}

For there was no seruice to be doone within, nor exploit to be aduentured without vpon the enimie (as manie times there were sallies giuen) but these were the chiefest and commonlie the onelie dooers: for which cause the contrarie side maruelouslie maligned at them, and sought by all means how to impeach and indanger them. Which thing being dailie perceiued more and more by sundrie argument, and as wise men séeking how to preuent the same, did manie and sundrie times confer among themselues herein, and in the end made a couenant and a faithfull promise among themselues (being then about the number of one hundred persons) that they would stand firmelie and faithfullie to the defense and kéeping of the citie to their vttermost powers. _{The best citizens confederated.}

And if it so fell out, that the rebell and enimie should haue accesse and entrie into the citie, that then they should all meet at the lord Russels (now the earle of Bedfords) house

house, and there to issue out at the posterne of the garden, and to giue the aduenture to passe and to escape awaie, as also if they were resisted that then they to stand togither to their defense. And for this purpose they had then named some one man to be their capteine for this enterprise. And in the meane time, to doo all things circumspectlie for the preseruation of the citie, & by a particular couenant among themselues, did take order, that during the whole beseeging of the citie and their aboad therein, a certeine number by course and besides the ordinarie set watch, should watch, ward, and walke about continuallie both by daie and night, by which means no sleight nor treacherie could be practised, but that they should haue an inkeling and vnderstanding thereof, and which in déed stood and came to such effect that it was the chiefest (if not the onelie) cause of the preseruation of the citie for that time. For there was no seruice, no diligence, no care, nor anie thing wanting or left vndoone, which by these men was not doone.

The carefulnesse of the good citizens.

Howbeit the diuell, the author of all diuision and strife, who cannot abide anie vnitie, concord and agréement in good causes, did here also hurle in a bone among these men, whereof had insued a great detriment to the common state, and an ouerthrow to themselues, had it not in due time béene preuented. There were two gentlemen within this citie, and both of this companie, the one was borne of a honorable house and parentage, named Iohn Courtneie a yoonger sonne to sir William Courtneie of Porederham knight, and a man of verie good knowledge and experience in seruice. The other also was a man of verie good seruice, practise, and experience, his name was Barnard Duffeld, & seruant to the lord Russell, and kéeper of his house in Excester. Both of these were verie forward and carefull in this present seruice against the rebels. But there fell an emulation betwéene them, which albeit it be verie commendable in good things, & he praisewoorthie who can best excell therein : yet when the same shall tend to a diuision of a publike state, the dissolution of a commonwealth, the breach of common societie, or the maintenance of anie euill, it is vtterlie to be shunned and lamented.

A variance betwéene Iohn Courtneie & Barnard Duffeld.

It happened vpon an occasion offered, that certeine of this companie vpon a time issued out at the forsaid posterne and made a sallie vpon the enimies, and had such good successe, that some of them they slue, some they tooke prisoners, as also spoiled them of their goods, and brought awaie with them some of their ordinance, namelie basses and slings : howbeit they all scaped not scotfrée, for some of them were taken, some also were hurt, as namelie Iohn Drake, who the yeare before was the receiuer of the citie was shot through the chéekes with an arrow, which he brought into the citie with him, and one Iohn Simons a cooke was so hurt that he died thereof.

A sallie made vpon the rebels.

But among them all one Iohn Goldsmith being of that companie and seruant to Richard Heliard of the same goldsmith, and a Fleming borne, had the best successe : for in the same skirmish he was taken prisoner by one of the rebels, who offered in taking of him with his bill to haue slaine him. With that this Iohn Goldsmith fell downe & yeelded himselfe, hauing then in his hand his péece or handgun charged, & suddenlie the other not mistrusting nor marking the same, he discharged into his verie bellie and so slue him, tooke the spoile of him, and brought the same into the citie with him.

This skirmish though it were not cléere gaines to this companie, yet it so incouraged them, that from time to time they consulted, and in the end determined to make a fresh sallie and to giue a new aduenture : wherevpon there fell and grew a disagréement betwéene the two foresaid Iohn Courtneie & Barnard Duffeld, the one affirming that the same was not to be permitted in anie fort or citie, which stood vpon defense or gard, without a verie speciall order of the generall or chéefe capteine, or some vrgent necessitie, especiallie in that present distresse and extremitie, wherein the citie as then did stand. But Barnard Duffeld being verie loth to loose anie part of his credit, or to

desist

desist from that he with others had determined, could by no meanes be persuaded to to the contrarie, but plainelie affirmeth that what he had determined should be performed.

Wherevpon the foresaid Iohn Courtneie resorted to the maior, aduertiseth vnto him the matter, & dealeth so fullie and with such persuasions with him, that the maior assembleth his brethren, and sendeth for the foresaid Duffeld : who being come, the matter was at full debated and discoursed, and in the end concluded that it was verie hurtfull and dangerous to that present state, that anie such issuing out should be granted or permitted : and therefore praied the said Duffeld to staie his determination, and to be contented. But he being vnpatient, & thinking his credit to be stained, if he should be debarred or denied to doo that which he had faithfullie promised, did vtterlie refuse to yéeld to this the maiors request, as also by continuing of talkes, fell out in foule and disordered speaches. Wherevpon to auoid a further inconuenience, he was commanded to ward. The daughter of this Duffeld, whose name was Francis, hearing that hir father was in ward, and taking in greefe that so great an iniurie (as she tearmed it) should be doone to hir father, came more hastilie than aduisedlie vnto the maior, somewhat late in the euening, & required to haue hir father out of the ward. Which thing being denied vnto hir, shée waxed so warme that not onelie she vsed verie vnseemelie tearmes and speaches vnto the maior, but also contrarie to the modestie and shamefastnes required in a woman, speciallie yoong and vnmarried, ran most violentlie vpon him, and strake him in the face. This was taken in so euill a part, and fearing that it had béene a set match of some further inconueniences, the common bell was foorthwith roong out : and also a rumour spread that the maior was beaten, or killed.

A broile towards.

Francis the daughter of Barnard Duffeld strake the maior in the face.

The whole commons immediatlie in great troops, & the most part in armor, ran to the Guildhall, where the maior was, who though he was safe, yet were they so gréeued with this iniurie, that they would in all hast haue run to the lord Russels house, where she was then gone, and haue fetched hir out : but the maior forecasting what inconueniences might insue, and respecting the necessitie of the present state, was not onlie contented patientlie to wrap vp these iniuries, but also earnestlie requested the commoners to doo the like : who being so pacified, he went home, and they conducted him into his owne doores. The chanons of the cathedrall church which at that time were resident in their houses within the close there, namelie archdeacon Pollard, treasuror Southron, chancellor Luson, and master Holwell, with others of the said church, who ioined with the maior and citizens in this seruice for the safegard of the citie, and did keepe both watches and wards, and their men readie at all times to serue in euerie alarum and skirmish : they at the hearing of this disordered part were verie much gréeued therewith, and they likewise forthwith assembled all their men, and being well armed and appointed, they went to the maior, who was then gone home to his house, and then and there verie friendlie did comfort him, and offred to stand by him and to assist him in all the best seruice they were able to doo for his defense and safetie of the citie.

The said archdeacon offred, that in proper person he would herein stand in his behalfe against all persons whatsoeuer, that would attempt or offer to doo him anie wrong. And in the end after sundrie friendlie and good speaches, they departed to their homes. And the said archdeacon, euerie daie after, would either come or send to the maior. This maior being a merchant, and onelie exercised in that trade, had small reach in matters of policie or martiall affaires : he was maior of the citie thrée times, and in euerie yeare there grew some troubles in the citie, but he had such a speciall care & regard to his charge and gouernment, that he would neuer attempt nor doo anie thing therein, but by the aduise and counsell of wise, graue and expert

men :

men : and God so blessed him that he prospered and had good successe in all his dooings.

Besides these and sundrie other former perils, the which the citie manie and oftentimes stood in, and by the goodnes and prouidence of God still ouercomed, there befell and happened a third one, which excéeded all the rest, and whereof the greatest danger and perill was feared : and this was famine, or penurie, which of all other turmoils and perils is most dangerous, & no other plague to be compared to it. For no force is feared, no lawes obserued, no magistrate obeied, nor common societie estéemed, where famine ruleth. For as the poet saith : Nescit plebs ieiuna timere. The store

Vittels wax scant within the citie. of vittels within the citie, for want of prouision in due time, and, by reason of the restreint of the markets, vpon a sudden was verie slender and small, and the same in verie short time spent and consumed. And albeit there were good store of drie fish, rise, prunes, raisins, and wine, at verie reasonable prices, yet bread which as the prophet saith, Confirmat cor hominis, Strengtheneth mans hart, that wanted : neither was anie to be had. And in this extremitie the bakers and housholders were driuen

Bread made of bran and of puffins. to séeke vp their old store of puffins and bran, wherewith they in times past were woont to make horssebread, and to feed their swine and poultrie, and this they moulded vp in clothes, for otherwise it would not hold togither, and so did bake it vp and the people well contented therewith. For (as Plutarch writeth) Fames reddit omnia dulcia, nihílq; contemnit esuriens : Hunger maketh all things swéet, and the hungrie bellie shunneth nothing.

But when this also was spent, and nothing now left, and the common people being not acquainted with so hard a diet as famine prescribeth, were verie vnpatient to indure the continuall barking of their hungrie bellies, and therefore they were verie soone & easie to be persuaded, or rather of themselues contented to yéeld vnto the enimie, to be fed for a time with the stollen fat of his flesh pot, than to abide for a short time a little penurie in hope of a deliuerie, and then to be filled with saturitie and plentie. But the magistrats and graue senators, who in all other causes had shewed themselues wise, carefull and discreet ; and who hauing receiued sundrie iniuries, did yet without rigour, reuenge or malice, wrap the same vp, respecting rather the com-

The godlie and politike dealings of the magistrates with the poore. mon state than their owne priuat cause ; so in this matter also being of a great importance doo verie wiselie & politikelie deale with the said people : who the poorer they were, the better they were considered, and the more carefullie prouided for. First,

The poore are wéekelie liberallie relieued. there was a generall collection set and rated throughout the whole citie for their reliefe and therby they were liberallie euerie weeke considered : which thing being some increase to their stocke and store, was the better to their content. Then all such vit-

All vittels fetched into the citie were distributed amõg the poore. tels as were to be had within the citie, they either had it freelie, or for a verie small price.

Besides this, manie times when anie cattell came néere vnto the walles of the citie, some shift was made to haue them, or by skirmishing & issuing out for them, or by some other means. And this also what so euer it was, was altogither diuided among them. And as for the prisoners fast fettered in the goals, they had also their portions, as

The prisoners in the goale did and were driuen to eate horsses. farre as it would stretch : notwithstanding in the end, for want they were fed with horsseflesh, which they liked and were well contented withall. For as the prouerbe is,

The gentle intreating of the poorer sort. Hunger findeth no faults but all things are swéet. Besides, if anie wrong were offered or iniurie doone to anie of them, it was foorthwith vpon complaint redressed : but if anie of them did disorder themselues, it was borne withall, and they in all gentle and courteous meanes intreated : as also from time to time persuaded with good words patientlie to abide and be contented : not mistrusting but that God shortlie would send a deliuerance.

And thus, and by these means, in hope almost against hope, they continued dutifull and obedient, from the second daie of Iulie 1549, vntill the sixt daie of August then

folowing,

folowing, the same being fiue whole wéekes, vpon which daie they were deliuered by the comming and entrie into the citie of the lord Russell : and which daie in memoriall for euer to endure is kept for a high and holie feast amongst the citizens yearelie vpon the sixt daie of August. Immediatlie vpon which deliuerance of the citie, the first care that euerie man had, was to shift and to make prouision for vittels, wherof some hungrie bellies were so gréedie, that ouercharging their emptie stomachs too hastilie, they died therewith.

The lord Russell after that the citie had béene besieged fiue wéekes turneth to this citie vpon the sixt of August, and deliuereth the same.

Thus hauing declared something of the state of the citie, and of the dooings therein during the time of this rebellion, though much more might be therein said, let vs now returne to the lord priuie seale, who after the departure of sir Peter Carew to the court, remooued from George Henneton, and came to Honiton, minding from thence to haue passed vnto Excester, if waie had béene open. But being aduertised that the citie was besieged, and that all the waies leading thitherwards were stopped, he remained still in Honiton. Sir Peter Carew in the meane time, according to the former order betwéene them taken, was ridden to London, and being before the king, declareth the whole matter at large. Which the king, not liking the disloialtie of his people, promised to séeke a spéedie remedie : and so commanded him to the councell for the same : and being before them, and hauing at full discoursed the state of the matter, the duke of Summerset being much greeued with the matter, would haue reiected the whole on sir Peter, charging him that by reason he had caused the houses to be burnt at Crediton, it was the onelie cause of the commotion. But therevnto he answered the necessitie of that seruice, as also declared that he had doone nothing but by a good warrant, and therewith shewed foorth the kings letters vnder his hand and priuie signet.

Sir Peter Carew aduertiseth the king & councel of the rebellió.

The duke of Summerset charged Sir Peter Carew of the rebellió.

The lord Rich then lord chancellor replied and said, that the kings letters were no sufficient warrant vnlesse he had his commission vnder the brode seale : and therefore if he had right, he should by the lawes be hanged for his dooings. But to this sir Peter answered so stoutlie, and charged the duke so déepelie, that in the end he was willed to returne into the countrie, being promised that sufficient helpe both of men & monie should be with spéed sent downe into the countrie. And to this effect he had both the kings and the councels letters vnto the lord priuie seale, and so tooke his iournie backe againe into the countrie, and deliuered his letters to the said lord Russell, who in hope of the supplie promised, staied and remained somtimes at Mohonesotre, but most commonlie at Honiton, still looking for that supplie and furniture that was promised. But hauing long looked for the same in vaine, he was dailie more and more forsaken of such of the common people, as who at the first serued and offered their seruice vnto him. And hauing but a verie small gard about him, he liued in more feare than he was feared : for the rebels dailie increased, and his companie decreased and shrunke awaie, and he not altogither assured of them which remained.

The king his letters vnder his priuie signet counted to be no sufficiét warrant. The stout answer of sir Peter Carew. Sir Peter Carew being promised of helpe returneth home.

The lord Russell is almost left forsaken.

Wherefore distrusting himselfe, & by a false rumor being aduertised that the citie was taken, & in the possession of the rebels ; as also how that there was a new sturre or rebellion begun about Sarisburie ; he tooke aduise and counsell of the gentlemen and such as were with him what were best to be doone. The gentlemen of Dorsetshire were of the mind, and gaue him aduise, that it were best for him to returne into Dorsetshire, and there to remaine for a time ; because it was a place of a more safetie, vntill such time as he were better prouided. And accordinglie the next daie following he tooke his iournie, & rode backe againe with the said Dorsetshire gentlemen. Sir Peter Carew then being at Mohorosoton, and aduertised hereof, tooke his horsse and came against the said lord Russell, & met him vpon Blacke downe, where was a long conference betweene them both : and in the end he so persuaded the lord, and with such pithie reasons he caried him, that leauing his former determination, he dooth returne againe into Honiton ; & where he continued thenceforth, sauing one night spent at Oterie saint Marie, where as it fell out he was

The lord Russell distrusting himselfe, is vpon his departure from out of Deuon ; but by sir Peter Carew is recouered backe againe.

in more feare than perill. At his being in Honiton, and dailie waiting and looking for the promised helpe and supplie which came not; he was in an agonie, & of a heauie chéere: not onelie for the want of the men & monie which he had long in vaine looked for, but also because he had spent all that he had brought with him, and could not tell how otherwise to helpe and prouide to supplie his present need: but as it fell out all happened for the best.

The merchants of Exon procure and borow monie to helpe the lord Russell. For it chanced that there were then three merchants of the citie, following and attending vpon him; Thomas Prestwood not long before maior of the citie, Iohn Bodlie, and Iohn Periam, men of great wealth. These men vnderstanding of the heauinesse and griefe of his lordship, make their resort vnto him, and promise to helpe and relieue his agonie and want: and forthwith did procure vpon their credit from the merchants of Bristow, Linne, Tawnton, and elsewhere, such a masse of monie, as which when he had receiued, his griefe was eased. For forthwith he so prouided and furnished himselfe with such necessaries, and with a greater number of men; that he was now in the better safetie, as also the better able to incounter with the enimie: and it was not long after, but that he had a further supplie from the king, euen to his content. And being now somewhat reuiued, newes was brought vnto him, that the rebels vnderstanding of his distressed state, were comming, and marching toward Honiton to assaile him; and were come as far as Fenington bridge, which is about thrée milés. Wherevpon, he tooke aduise with sir Peter Carew, sir Gawen Carew & others what were best to be doone. And in the end, after manie spéeches, it was con- The lord Russell marcheth towards Fenington bridge. cluded that they should march towards them, and giue the onset vpon them, & ac- cordinglie, without further delaies or much talke, it was doone out of hand. For vpon the next morning being a holie daie, they set forth, and came to the bridge aforesaid, where the rebels were indéed: some at the bridge, but the greatest companie in a me- dow beneath the bridge: who, as soone as they perceiued the lord Russell and the gen- tlemen with all their troope to be come, they make themselues readie to the fight. But the riuer & the bridge being betwéene them, the lord Russell vseth all the policies that he can, how to recouer the bridge; which by bold aduenturing he did in the end: but Sir Gawen Carew is hurt at Fenington bridge. with the hurt of sundrie of his companie, amongst whome sir Gawen Carew was one, being hurt with an arrow in the arme.

And hauing recouered the bridge, and the riuer, all the rebels (such as were escaped) were gathered togither in a medow néere adioining in the lower side of the bridge, vpon whome they so fiercelie followed, and gaue the onset; that though not without good store of blowes and bloudshed, they in the end gaue the enimie the ouerthrow, The rebels are ouerthrowne at Fenington. and had the vpper hand. And thinking that the victorie was cleere with them, and that the enimie was cleane gone, the souldiers and seruingmen gaue themselues all to the spoile; and being in the middle of their game, and they nothing thinking lesse than of anie more enimies to be comming towards, euen suddenly march towards a new crue of Cornishmen, to the number of two hundred, or two hundred and fortie persons, vnder the conduct of one Robert Smith of saint Germans in Cornewall The Cornish rebels gaue an onset, and are ouerthrowne at Fenington; their capteine flieth awaie. gentleman; and who taking these spoilers napping, manie of them paied deerelie for their wares. The lord Russell forthwith setteth all his companie in good araie, as the others did the like, and gaue the onset vpon them: betwéene whome the fight for the time was verie sharpe and cruell. For the Cornishmen were verie lustie and fresh and fullie bent to fight out the matter: neuerthelesse in the end they were ouer- throwne, and their capteine, whose combe was cut, sheweth a faire paire of héeles and fled awaie. In these two fights, there were reported to be slaine about thrée hundred re- bels, which were verie tall men, lustie, and of great courage; and who in a good cause might haue doone better seruice.

The lord Russels companie followed the chase néere thrée miles, & he himselfe then throughlie minded and bent to haue passed through to the citie. But one Ioll his
foole

foole, who was then in hast come from Honiton, and where he had heard, as also by the waie as he came did heare bels ringing in sundrie parish churches, and supposing the same to be alarum, came with a foule mouth to my lord, and cried that all the countrie behind him were vp, and comming vpon him. Which his report (considering the cruell fights past) was credited, and thought that a new companie was in preparing to follow the former quarels. Wherevpon they all retired and returned againe to Honiton; and from thense his lordship sent his comfortable letters secretlie by a boy apointed and accustomed for the same, vnto the maior of his successe, as also aduertising him of his determination that he would be shortlie with him for the deliuerance of the citie. Which letters (the citie being then but in a doubtfull and dismaied estate) came in verie good season; and yet in the end scarselie credited by some men, because his comming was not so spéedie as was looked for.

Within verie short time after this ouerthrowe was giuen, the lord Greie of Wilton with a crue of horssemen, and one Spinola an Italian with three hundred shot, came to my lord; who being aduertised of the ouerthrow of the enimie, and that there were slaine about three hundred persons of them, they were in a great chafe, and much bewailed their euill lucke, that they had not come sooner to haue béene partakers of that seruice. My lord being now of a verie good comfort & courage, aswell for the good successe which he had ouer the enimie, & that his long looked supplie was come, sendeth his other letters to the maior, comforting him, as also as before promising him to be with him verie shortlie; willing him that he should now take but a little patience for a little time. And accordinglie about six daies after, on saturdaie the third of August, in good order he set foorth out of Honiton, and marched towards Excester, his companie being aboue a thousand of good fightingmen; and leauing the direct high waie, draweth ouer the downs towards Woodburie, and there lodged and pitched his campe that night, at a windmill apperteining to one Gregorie Carie gentleman. Which when the rebels of saint Marie Clift heard of, forthwith, with all their force and power came forth, and marched onwards vntill they came to the foresaid mill where they offer the fight: and notwithstanding they were of verie stout stomachs, & also verie valiantlie did stand to their tackels, yet in the end they were ouerthrowne and the most part of them slaine.

Side note: The lord Greie and Spinola come with a supplie to the lord Russell.

Side note: The lord Russell marcheth towards Excester for their deliuerance.

Side note: The rebels are ouerthrowne at the windmill.

Where after the victorie thus gotten, one Miles Couerdale then the preacher, and attending vpon my lord in this iournie made a sermon, and caused a generall thanksgiuing to be made vnto God: but before all was ended, there began a new alarum; and forthwith euerie man to horsse & to harnesse againe. The rebels which remained in the towne of saint Marie Clift, hearing of the euill successe befallen to their neighbours, and they doubting that their turne would be next to receiue the like; doo spread abroad the newes, and request to be aided and assisted. Wherevpon, forthwith in great troopes resorted vnto them a number of their companions out of euerie quarter, to the number (as it was said) of six thousand men: and in all hast, they make themselues and all things in a readinesse to abide the brunt. Vpon the next morning being sundaie, my lord minding to follow on his course, commandeth the trumpet to sound, & euerie man to make readie to march forwards. And about nine of the clocke in the same morning, they come to Clift; where the armie is diuided into three parts, and in thrée seuerall places doo appoint to make entrie into the towne. For in so manie places they had fortified the towne, and made great rampires for their defense.

Side note: Miles Couerdale preacher.

Side note: The kings armie marcheth towards bishops Clift.

These rampires were after some bickering recouered, and sir William Francis of Summersetshire was named to be the first that gaue the aduenture, & made the entrie. The commons being driuen from the said rampires, ran all into the towne; and there ioine themselues togither to abide the pulse. And as the kings armie was in good order marching into the towne, one of the chiefe capteins of these rebels, named sir Thomas Pomeroie knight, kept himselfe in a furze close, and perceiuing the armie to

Side note: Sir William Francis first entreth the rampire.

be past him, and hauing then with him a trumpeter, and a drumslade, commanded the trumpet to be sounded, and the drumme to be striken vp. At which sound, the lord priuie seale, and his companie were amazed, supposing verelie that there had beene an ambush behind them to haue intrapped and inclosed them. Wherevpon, they forthwith retire backe in all the hast they may: which when they in the towne perceiued, they follow after, and neuer staied vntill they came to the wagons then being in the high waie; & which now by flieng and retiring of the armie, are the formost and next to the towne. And these being laden with munition, armour, and treasure, they take and bring into the towne, where they rifle as much as they could, sauing the péeces of the ordinance, which with the shot and pouder they bestowed in places conuenient, and emploied the same against my lord and his companie.

The armie hauing recouered the hill, did there pause a while, and finding themselues to be deceiued, march backe againe towards the towne: but before they came thither, it was aduertised vnto my lord, that the towne and euerie house therein was fortified and full of men, and that it was not possible for anie to passe that waie without great perill and danger, except the towne were set on fire. Wherevpon order was giuen, that as they passed and entered into the towne, notwithstanding it was my lords owne, they should set the houses on fire. Sir William Francis being in the fore-ward was formost, and leauing the waie which he tooke before, tooke now an other waie, the which waie was both deepe and narrow. The enimies being vpon the banks vpon euerie side of the waie, with their stones so beat him, that they stroke his headpéece fast to his head and whereof he died. The armie being come into the towne, they set fire on euerie house as they passed by. But the rebelles conioining themselues in the middle of the towne, doo stand at their defense, where the fight was very fierce and cruell; and bloudie was that daie: for some were slaine with the sword, some burned in the houses, some shifting for themselues were taken prisoners, and manie thinking to escape ouer the water were drowned: so that there were dead that daie one with an other about a thousand men.

The towne thus being recouered, and the ouerthrow giuen, the lord Greie desireth to passe ouer the riuer, and to be in the open field, which is a great heath named Clift heath: & this he could not doo, but he must passe ouer either the water or the bridge, both which were somewhat dangerous, for the water was somewhat mirie and muddie, as also at that time verie deepe, by reason of the flowing of the seas, which causeth the same at euerie tide to swell. Howbeit one Iohn Yard a gentleman, and who had dwelled thereabouts, knowing the said water, gaue the first aduenture ouer, and found waie neere vnto a mill aboue the bridge; and after him others doo followe. But this was not for all the rest of the armie, who must needs passe ouer the bridge, which as then they could not doo, by reason that the same was so ouerlaid with great trées and timber, as also there stood the gunner with his péece readie charged. Wherevpon proclamation was made, that whosoeuer would aduenture and make waie ouer the bridge, should haue foure hundred crownes for his labor. Then one foorthwith more respecting the gaine, than forecasting the perill, gaue the aduenture: but the gunner rewarded him, for he discharged his péece vpon him, and slue him. And then before he could againe charge his péece, one of the companie, who before was passed ouer the water, came and entred the bridge at the further end, and comming behind him slue him; who foorthwith calleth companie vnto him, and casteth aside all the trees and timber, and maketh the bridge cléere, and so the whole armie passeth ouer the bridge into the heath.

The lord Greie as soone as he was passed ouer the water, he rode foorthwith to the top of the hill, which is in the middle of the heath: and from thense did make a view of all the countrie about him: and looking backe towards Woodburie, he saw and espied vpon Woodburie hill a great companie assembled; & marching forward, &

                                                              suspecting

suspecting that they were a new supplie appointed to follow and come vpon them, and aduertised the lord Russell therof.   Whervpon it was concluded, that the prisoners whom they had before taken at the windmill and in the towne, who were a great number, and which if they were newlie set vpon, might be a detriment and a perill vnto them, should be all killed : which foorthwith was doone, euerie man making a dispatch of his prisoners ; and then the night approching, there they incamped themselues for that night. *All the prisoners before taken are committed to the sword.*

The rebelles, which were and laie about Excester, were aduertised out of hand of this the euill successe of their neighbors, wherefore they with as manie as they could get, in all hast came to Clift heath : and in the lower side thereof next to the high waie, doo intrench and fortifie a place fast by a hedge, and secretlie there, in the night, doo place their ordinance, & make themselues in readinesse to abide the brunt : and as soone as the daie light serued, discharge and shoot off their péeces vnto the armie incamped about the top of the hill.   The lords and capteins to end the quarrell, doo determine to giue the onset vpon them ; and according to the nature of warres, doo politikelie diuide themselues into thrée parts, and euerie one hath his place assigned and order appointed vnto him.

The lord Russell, hauing no waie open before him, causeth his pioners to make waie ouer the hedges & inclosed grounds, and by that meanes dooth at legnth recouer vpon the verie backe of the enimies : and they were so intrapped on euerie side, that they could not by anie meanes escape, but must yeeld or fight.   The one they would not, and in the other they preuailed not.   For notwithstanding valiantlie and stoutlie they stood to their tackle, and would not giue ouer as long as life and lim lasted : yet in the end they were all ouerthrowen, and few or none left aliue.   Great was the slaughter, and cruell was the fight ; and such was the valor and stoutnesse of these men, that the lord Greie reported himselfe, that he neuer in all the wars that he had béen in did know the like. *The rebelles are ouerthrown vpon Clift heath.*

This fight being doone, and all things set in good order, the whole armie marched vnto Topsham, which was about a mile off, and laie in that towne all that night, and carried with them in a horslitter the bodie or corps of sir William Francis, and from thense carried it to Excester, where it was buried in martiall manner verie honorablie in the bodie of the cathedrall church of saint Peters. When the rebels who laie about the citie heard how their neighbors had sped, and from time to time had the worse side, and were still ouerthrowen : then as men despairing to preuaile, secretlie gaue ouer the siege and ran apase euerie man his waie.   The gentlemen, which were kept prisoners in the churches and in other places about the citie, being now at libertie, came straight to the walles about midnight, & gaue knowledge thereof to the watch ; and they foorthwith did the like vnto the maior.   The ioie and comfort wherof was so great, and the desire of fresh vittels so much persed, that manie not abiding till the daielight, gat and shifted themselues out of the gates, but more for vittels than for spoile, and yet they were glad of both : howbeit some did not long enioie the same, for manie being more gréedie of meat than measurable in féeding, did so ouercharge themselues in surffetting, that they died thereof. *Sir William Francis buried at Excester.* *The rebels forsake the citie.*

The next morrow being tuesdaie and the sixt of August, the lord priuie seale thinking it long before he came to the citie, commanded the trumpets verie earlie to sound, and euerie man to make readie and to prepare awaie.   And accordinglie all things being doone, he marcheth towards Excester, and about eight of the clocke being tuesdaie the sixt of August 1549 he came to the same, to the great ioy & comfort of the long captiuated citizens, who were no more glad of their deliuerie, than was his lordship and all good subiects ioyfull of his victorie.   But at his comming he entred not into the citie : for being aduertised from the maior that the citie was altogither vnfurnished of vittels, order was taken that no stranger, nor one nor other should *The lord Russell commeth to Excester.*

should enter into the citie, but lie in the campe for a time. Then his lordship pitched
his tents without the wals in S. Iohns fields, next to Southing haie, & vpon the cities
wals next to the posterne of his house was the kings standard of the red dragon set vp.

As soone as he was entred into his tent, the maior & all his brethren in most séemelie
& decent order went vnto him, who most louinglie embrased them, most thankefullie
accepted them, and most highlie commended them for their truth, dutie, and seruice,
which vpon his fidelitie and honor he did promise should be well considered by the

kings maiestie, and which in the end was performed. For the king being aduertised
thereof, he did not onelie thankefullie accept and highlie commend their seruices, but
also rewarded and considered the same, both by confirmation of their charters, inlarging of their liberties, and augmenting of their reuenues, in giuing vnto them the
manor of Exilond, which as was said was sometimes their ancient inheritance, but by
power of the earles of Deuon by force taken, and by wrong and iniurie kept from
them.

Immediatlie after his comming, sir William Herbert then master of the kings
horsses, and after earle of Penbroke, came with a thousand Welshmen: who though
they came too late to the fraie; yet soone inough to the plaie. For the whole countrie
was then put to the spoile, and euerie soldier sought for his best profit: a iust plague
of the Lord vpon rebels and disloiall persons. But the citie being as yet altogither
destitute of vittels, and the Welshmen at their first comming séeing the same, they
did by their speciall industries & trauels fraught & furnish the same within two daies
with corne, cattels, and vittels, verie plentifullie, to the great reléefe and comfort of

the people therin, & to the benefit of themselues. The lord priuie seale remained and
continued in this citie aboue twelue daies before he remooued: setting all things in
good order, rewarding the good & punishing the euill. To sir Peter Carew he gaue
all Wineslades land, to sir Gawen Carew Humfrie Arundels lands, to William Gibbes
esquier Beries lands, and to manie others which had doone good seruices he gaue prisoners, both bodies, goods, and lands.

On the other side he commanded forches and gallowes to be set vp in sundrie
places, as well within the citie as also in the countrie; and did command and cause
manie to be executed and put to death, especiallie such as were noted to be chiefe and
busie dooers & ringleaders in this rebellion. Among them all there was no one so exalted as was Welsh the vicar of saint Thomas neere the Exbridge at Excester, who
was preferred and presented to that benefice by the lord Russell patrone thereof. This
man had manie good things in him, he was of no great stature, but well set and
mightilie compact: he was a verie good wrestler, shot well both in the long bow as
also in the crossebow, he handled his handgun and péece verie well, he was a verie
good woodman and a hardie, and such a one as would not giue his head for the polling
nor his beard for the washing, he was a companion in anie exercises of actiuitie, & of a
courteous and gentle behauiour, he descended of a good honest parentage, being borne
at Penuerin in Cornewall; and yet in this rebellion an archcapteine and a principall

dooer. He was charged with thrée principall crimes. The first was, that he did not
onelie persuade the people to the contemning of the reformed religion, according to
the kings procéedings, and to keepe and obserue the Romish and popish religion: but
also did erect, kéepe, and vse the same in his parish church. Secondarilie, he was a
capteine and a principall dealer in the cause of the rebellion, which was chieflie di-

rected by him, his order, & aduise. Thirdlie, he caused one Kingwell a tinner of Chag-
ford, and seruant to master Iohn Charels of Tauestoke to be hanged, bicause secretlie
he had conueied letters betwéene my lord and his master, and was earnest in the reformed religion, which was then termed the kings procéedings, & an enimie to the
popish state. And being a sharpe inueier against the one, and an earnest mainteiner
of the other, it procured vnto him great hatred and malice: when the rebellion was
                                                                                          begun

begun he sought by all the meanes he could how to escape awaie: but he was so narrowlie watched, that he could neuer haue anie oportunitie so to doo.

They used all the deuises they could to recouer him to their opinions, sometimes with faire words, sometimes with threatenings, and sometimes with imprisonments: but still he inueied against them, calling them rebels and traitors both against God and the king, and foreprophesied vnto them that destruction and confusion would be the end & reward of their dooings. Thus when they could not reclame him to their disposition, then by the order and iudgement of this vicar Welsh, he was fetched out of the prison, and foorthwith brought foorth before Caiphas and Pilat, and condemned to be hanged: which was executed vpon him foorthwith, and he brought to an elme tree in Exilond, without the west gate of the citie, before the house of one Nicholas Caue, and there hanged. The like crueltie or rather tyrannie was doone at Sampford Courteneie, where when a certeine Frankelin a gentleman, named William Hellions, who comming to Sampford to haue some communication with them for the staie of their rebellion, and for the pacifieng of them in their due obedience, was at the townes end taken prisoner, & caried to the churchhouse, where he so earnestlie reprooued them for their rebellion, & so sharplie threatened them an euill successe; that they all fell in a rage with him, and not onlie with euill words reuiled him: but also as he was going out of the churchhouse & going downe the staires, one of them named Githbridge with a bill strake him in the necke, and immediatlie notwithstanding his pitifull requests and lamentations, a number of the rest fell vpon him, slue him, and cut him into small peeces: and though they counted him for an heretike, yet they buried him in the church-yard there, but contrarie to the common maner, laieng his bodie north and south.

These things being called to remembrance and obiected against this vicar, although some men in respect of his vertues and good gifts did pitie and lament his case, and would haue gladlie beene sutors for his pardon: yet the greatnesse of his lewdnesse and follies considered, they left him vnto his deserts: & so was by order of the marshall law condemned to death. And yet this one thing by the waie I must speake in his commendation. There was among the rebels a stranger and an alien, who was a verie skilfull gunner, & could handle his peece verie well, and did much harme vnto the citie, & among others slue one Smith standing at a doore in northgate street with a great shot from saint Dauids hill. This fellow tooke vpon him, that he would set the whole citie on fire, and it should be cleane burned within foure houres, doo they what they could. This his offer was so well liked, that the daie and time was appointed when this should be doone.

The rebels appoint to set fire on the citie and to burne it.

The vicar hearing thereof, assembleth vnto him as manie men as he could make and haue, & came to this companie when this fire should be kindled, and was so hot and earnest against their attempts, that he would in no wise suffer so lewd an act and wicked a thing to be doone. For (saith he) doo you what you can by policie, force, or dint of sword to take the citie, I will ioine with you, and doo my best: but to burne a citie which shall be hurtfull to all men and good to no man, I will neuer consent therevnto, but will here stand with all my power against you. And so stout he was in this matter, that he stopped them from their further enterprising of so wicked a fact. But to the matter. The execution of this man was committed to Barnard Duffeld, who being nothing slacke to follow his commission, caused a paire of gallowes to be made, and to be set vp vpon the top of the said vicars parish church of S. Thomas: and all things being readie and the stage perfected for this tragedie, the vicar was brought to the place, and by a rope about his middle drawne vp to the top of the tower: and there in chains hanged in his popish apparell, and had a holie water bucket and sprinkle, a sacring bell, a paire of beads, & such other like popish trash hanged about him, and there he with the same about him remained a long time. He made a verie

The vicar of saint Thomas letteth and will not consent to the burning of the citie.

The vicar is hanged in chaines vpon the top of the tower with his popish trash and ornaments about him.

verie small or no confession, but verie patientlie tooke his death, he had béene a good member in his common-wealth, had not the weeds ouergrowne the good corne, and his foule vices ouercommed his vertues.

The lord priuie seale remaining still in Excester was continuallie occupied in setting things in order, he was verie seuere and sharpe against such offendors as were chiefe and principall ringleders of this rebellion: but to the common sort who were led and carried, and who did humble themselues, he was pitifull and mercifull, and did dailie pardon infinite numbers. And his lordship thinking verelie that all things were now quieted, & the rebels pacified, suddenlie newes were brought vnto him that there assembled at Sampford Courtneie, both Deuonshiremen and Cornishmen, and who were fullie bent to mainteine their quarrell and abide the battell. These newes so troubled and tickled my lord, that all businesse set apart, he commandeth foorthwith the trumpet to be sounded, and the drumme to be striken vp, and all his armie to be foorthwith mustered: which was then the greater, by reason of the Welshmen and gentlemen of the countrie and of the commoners, who vpon submission had obteined pardon, and increased to the number of eight or ten thousand men, and foorthwith he marcheth towards Sampford Courtneie, where sir William Herbert requested to haue the fore-ward for that daie, which was granted him.

And being come thither, albeit the great companie of so manie good souldiers and well appointed might haue dismaied them, being nothing nor in order, nor in companie, nor in experience, to be compared vnto the others: yet they were at a point they would not yéeld to no persuasions, nor did, but most manfullie did abide the fight: and neuer gaue ouer, vntill that both in the towne and in the field they were all for the most taken or slaine. At which time one ap Owen a Welsh gentleman, more boldlie than aduisedlie giuing the aduenture to enter the rampier at the townes end, was there slaine by the rebels, and after carried backe to Exon, where after the maner of wars he was honorablie buried in the bodie of saint Peters church, few of the kings side besides him then slaine: and so of a traitorous beginning they made a shamefull ending. Neuerthelesse manie escaped and they fled towards Summersetshire: after whom was sent sir Peter Carew, and sir Hugh Paulet then knight marshall: with a great companie attending vpon them, and followed them as far as to king Weston in the countie of Summerset: where they ouertooke them and ouerthrew them, and also tooke one Coffin a gentleman their capteine prisoner and brought him vnto Excester.

The lord Russell himselfe minding to make all things sure, taketh his iorneie, and marcheth into Cornewall; and following his former course, causeth execution to be doone vpon a great manie, and especiallie vpon the chéefe belwedders and ringleaders: but the chéefe and principall capteins he kept as prisoners, and brought them with him to Excester. And when this lord had set all things in good order, he returned to Excester, & remained there for a time; but after departed towards London, where he was receiued with great ioy and thanks: and being come before the king, he forgat not to commend vnto his maiestie the good seruice of this citie in this rebellion, which (as is before said) was liberallie rewarded and considered. After his departure, and according to his order and appointment, the chéefe capteins and principall heads of this rebellion, whome he left in prison in the kings goale at Excester, were caried to London and commanded to the tower, and in their due time were afterwards executed to death, namelie Humfreie Arundell esquier, Wineslade esquier, Iohn Berrie and Coffin gentlemen, and Holmes yeoman; which Coffin and Holmes were seruants to sir Iohn Arundell knight. Of the number of them who were slaine, there is no certeintie knowne, but manie more be found lacke then numbred: howbeit it was accounted by such as continued in the whole seruice of this commotion to be about foure thousand men. But what number was of the contrarie side dispatched, nothing is reported,

albeit

The rebels assembled at Sampford Courtneie.

The rebels ouerthrowne at Sampford Courtneie.

Sir Peter Carew pursueth the rebels which fled to king Weston.

The lord priuie seale taketh his iorneie into Cornewall.

The lord priuie seale taketh his iorneie towards London and is honourablie receiued.

The chéefe capteins of the rebels are caried to London and there put to death.

albeit it be well knowne that they escaped not scotfrée, and especiallie the Burgonians, who were abhorred of the one partie, and nothing fauoured of the other. Thus much concerning the description of the citie, and of the sundrie inuasions and assaults against the same, and especiallie of the last rebellion or commotion in the yeare of our Lord 1549, wherein much more might be spoken, but this may suffice for this matter. And for as much as the cathedrall church of this citie, called by the name of S. Peters, is a parcell of the citie, and compassed within the wals of the same, though in respect of certeine priuileges distinct from the iurisdiction thereof; I thought it good to subnect herevnto the description of the said church, and of the antiquitie of the same.

The antiquitie, foundation, and building of the cathedrall church of saint Peters in Excester.

AFTER that corrupt religion and superstition was crept and receiued into the church, and the people become deuout therein, then began the erecting of religious houses and monasteries in euerie countrie. And as this was vniuerall throughout all christendome vnder the gouernement of the Romane bishop: so also was it generallie doone throughout all England, in which generalitie this citie was of a particularitie; for in this citie from time to time as opportunitie serued sundrie religious houses and monasteries were erected and builded, of which there were thrée within the site, circuit, and place now called the close of S. Peters, and which in time accrued and were vnited in one. The first was a house for women called moniales or nuns, which is now the deanes house or Kalendar haie. The other was a house of moonks, supposed to be builded by king Ethelred, the third sonne to king Ethelwolph, and these two were vnited by bishop Leofricus vnto the cathedrall church. The third was a house for moonks of the order of S. Benet, which was builded and founded by king Athelstane, about the yeare of our Lord 932: and this is that part of the cathedrall church now called the ladie chappell. For the said king, hauing driuen out of this citie the Britons then dwelling therein, and minding to make a full conquest both of them and of this their countrie which they then inhabited, did so fiercelie follow and pursue them euen into Cornewall, that in the end he conquered them, and had the victorie. After which he returned to this citie, and here staieng and soiourning for a time, did reedifie the citie, incompassed it with a stone wall, and founded the cathedrall church, which he then appointed for a monasterie for moonks of S. Benets order. For so is it written: Hanc vrbem rex Adelstanus primus in potestatem Anglorum, effugatis Britonibus redactam turribus muniuit, & muro ex quadratis lapidibus cinxit, ac antiquitùs vocatam Munketon nunc Exester vocari voluit: ac ibi sedens mansum quoddam dedit ad fundandum monasterium pro monachis Deo & sancto Petro famulantibus. Besides the charges which he was at the building of the said church, he gaue also lands and reuenues vnto them sufficient for maintenance and liuelihoods, whereof Morkeshull and Treasurors béere are parcell, and which now are appendant and apperteining to the treasuror of the cathedrall church.

After the time of king Athelstane, the Danes with great hostilitie and crueltie hauing ouerrun this whole land, they also came to this citie, and in spoiling the same, did also ransacke and spoile the said church, whose continuall inuasions the moonks being not able to indure, fled and forsooke their house and home, and sought places of better safetie. By which means this monasterie for sundrie yeares was left destituted, vntill the time of king Edgar; who on a time made a progresse into these west parts, to visit his father in law Odogarus then earle of Deuon, and founder of the abbeie of Tauistoke, whose daughter he had married. And being come to this

The religious houses within the precinct of the cemeterie of S. Peters.

King Athelstan builded the wals of the citie of stone.

Ex pamphleto monasterij S. Iohannis Baptistæ Exon.

Ex chronica ecclesiæ cathred. Exon.

The Danes spoile the church of S. Peters.

The moonks forsake their monasterie. Flores historiarum.

King Edgar restoreth the abbat and moonks to their house.

citie, did here rest and staie himselfe, where when he saw the distressed state of the said church, & pitieng the same, caused search and inquirie to be made of the moonks which were scattered and yet left: and when he had gotten them togither, he restored them vnto their house and liuelihoods, and appointed Sidemannus who was afterwards

Sidemannus abbat of this church, and after bishop of this diocesse.

bishop of this diocesse to be abbat of the same. And from thensfoorth they continued togither (though sometimes in troubles) vntill that king Swanus or Sweno the Dane, with a mightie and a huge armie came to this citie, besieged, tooke, spoiled, and destroied it with sword and fier. Howbeit not long after it was restored againe

K. Canutus restoreth both lands & priuileges to the church.

by king Cahutus or Canutus, who being aduertised of the great cruelties which his father Sweno had doone to the said monasterie, did at the request of Atheldredus one of his dukes, make restitution vnto Athelwoldus then abbat of all their lands, liuings aud priuileges: as dooth appeare by his charter dated in the yeare of our Lord 1019.

After this, about thirtie yeares, king Edward the Confessor came to this citie, and he by the aduise and at the motion of Leofricus bishop of Crediton, and who sometimes was lord chancellor of England vnder the said king, and one of his priuie councell, partlie for the better safetie of the bishop and his successors, who lieng and hauing their houses in the countrie, were subiect to manie and sundrie perils, and partlie to prouide a more conuenient place for the moonks, did remooue the bishops

The bishops sée remooued from Crediton to Exon. Leofricus the first bishop of Excester.

sée from Crediton, and remooued the moonks vnto Westminster: and he the king in his owne person, togither with quéene Edith his wife, did install the said Leofricus in possession of this his new church and sée. The bishop thus remooued from the old, and placed in the new sée and church, dooth endow the same with all those lands and liuelihoods which he had of the gift of the said king, and which before did apperteine to his former church, and to reduce and make his sanctuarie to his mind, pulleth downe the two monasteries néere adioining, the one being of moonks and the other of nuns, and addeth and vniteth them vnto his owne church, and hauing brought all things to effect according to his mind, deuiseth and maketh lawes, orders, and ordinances for the good gouernment of his church and cleargie.

After the death of Leofricus, all his successors for the most part procure the augmentation and increase of this their new erected see and church, some in liuelihoods, some in liberties and priuileges, some in buildings, and some in one thing, and some in another. William Warewest the third bishop of this church, who had sometimes

The king at the request of William Warewest bishop, giueth Plimpton, Brampton, & S. Stephans to the church of Excester.

béene chapleine to the Conqueror, and to his two sonnes William and Henrie, was in such fauor and good liking with the Conqueror, that at his request he gaue vnto him and to this his church, Plimpton, Brampton, and S. Stephans, in Excester, which gift his said sonnes being kings of England did ratifie and confirme. And then the said bishop, hauing the ordering and distributing thereof, giueth Plimpton to the regular moonkes there, for whom he had founded and builded a monasterie, and wherein he himselfe shortlie after leauing and yéelding vp his bishoprike, became and was a moonke. Brampton was reserued to the church, and which afterwards was annexed to the deanerie. And S. Stephans with the fee to the same apperteining, he reserued to himselfe and to his successors, & whereby they are barons and lords of the parlement. This bishop in the yeare of our Lord 1112, first began to inlarge his

The foundation of the quier of S. Peters church.

cathedrall, and laid the foundation of that part, which is now the chore or quier: for before that time it was no bigger than that, which since and now is called the ladie chapell. After him William Brewer the bishop made and established in the yeare of

Bishop William Brewer instituteth the deane & foure and twentie prebendaries.

our Lord 1235, a deane and a chapter of foure and twentie prebendaries: and for the deane (whome he appointed, and whose name was Serlo) and for his successors, he gaue and impropriated Brampton and Coliton Rawleigh, and for the prebendaries he purchased lands, alloting and assigning to euerie of them Pro pane & sale the like portion of foure pounds.

                     Peter

Peter Quiuell the bishop finding the chancell of his church to be fullie builded and ended, beginneth to found and build the lower part or the bodie of his church, in the yeare of our Lord 1284, from the chancell of his church vnto the west end of the said church. This man first appointed a chanter and a subdeane to be in his church. To the one of them he impropriated Paineton and Chudleie, and to the other the personage of Egloschaile in Cornewall. After him Iohn Grandisson, in the yeare of our Lord 1340, did increase the length of the bodie of the church from the funt westwards, as also vaulted the roofe of the whole church, and did fullie end and finish the same. And albeit from the time of king Athelstane the first founder in the yeare of our Lord 932, vntill the daie of the death of this bishop Grandisson, which was in the yeare 1369, there were about 437 yeares distant, and in the meane time this church was continued in building by sundrie persons: yet it is so decentlie and vniformelie compacted, as though it had béene builded at one verie time and instant.

The bodie of saint Peters church first founded.
The chanter and subdeane first constituted in this church.
Bishop Grandisson a great benefactor to the church.
The church of S. Peters was in building 437 yeares.

The successour of this Grandisson, who was named Thomas Brentingham, finished and ended the north tower of the church. After this, about the yeare of our Lord 1400, and in the time of bishop Stofford, the cloister was added to the church, and builded at the most part of the charges of the deane and chapter. And not long after Edmund Lacie bishop began to build the chapter house, which being not ended in his time, his next successor George Neuill, in the yeare of our Lord 1456, did fullie end and absolue the same: and which is a verie farie, beautifull, and a sumptuous worke. And thus much concerning the antiquitie, foundation, and building of this cathedrall church. Thus far Iohn Hooker.

The cloister builded.
The building of the chapter house.

About the same time that this rebellion (whereto all the foresaid discourse tendeth) began in the west, the like disordered hurles were attempted in Oxfordshire, and Buckinghamshire: but they were spéedilie appeased by the lord Greie of Wilton, who comming downe that waie to ioine with the lord priuie seale, chased the rebels to their houses, of whome two hundred were taken, and a dozzen of the ringleaders to him deliuered, wherof certeine afterwards were executed. Moreouer, in diuerse other parts of the realme, namelie in the south and east parts, did the people (as before ye haue heard (assemble themselues in rebellious maner, committing manie foule disorders: but yet by good policie and holesome persuasions they were appeased, except in Norffolke, where after there was a rumour spred, that the commons in Kent had throwne downe the diches and hedges, wherewith certeine pasture grounds were inclosed, and had laid the same open. Diuerse seditious persons and busie fellowes began to complaine that the like had not béene doone in Norffolke, and ceased not to practise how to raise the people to an open rebellion; meaning not onelie to laie open parkes and inclosures, but to attempt other reformations, as they termed them, to the great danger of ouerthrowing the whole state of the common-wealth.

Iohn Fox.
Common rebellion.
Norffolke.

They chieflie declared a spitefull rancor and hatered conceiued against gentlemen, whome they maliciouslie accused of inordinat couetousnesse, pride, rapine, extortion, and oppression, practised against their tenants and others, for the which they accounted them worthie of all punishment. Herevpon diuerse of them, namelie the inhabitants of Atilborough, and other of their neighbors, conceiuing no small displeasure, for that one Gréene of Wilbie had taken in a parcell of the common pasture, as was supposed, belonging to the towne of Atilborough, and adioining to the common pasture of Harsham riotouslie assembled togither, and threw downe certeine new diches made by the said Gréene, to inclose in the said parcell of commons.

Beginning of the rebellion in Norffolke.

This was doone before Midsummer, and so it rested till the sixt of Iulie, at which time there should be a publike plaie kept at Wimondham, a towne distant from Norwich six miles, which plaie had béene accustomed yearelie to be kept in that towne,

A conference to further this rebellion in a meeting at a publike plaie.

        continuing

continuing for the space of one night and one daie at the least. Wherevpon the wicked contriuers of this vnhappie rebellion, tooke occasion by the assembling of such numbers of people as resorted thither to sée that plaie, to enter further into their wicked enterprise: and vpon conference had, they immediatlie assembled at Morleie a mile from Wimondham, & there they cast downe certeine diches of maister Hubbords on the tuesdaie, and that night they repaired to Wimondham againe, where they practised the like feats. But as yet they tooke no mans goods by violence.

Iohn Flower-
dew.

Robert Ket.

Herevpon one Iohn Flowerdew of Hetherset gentleman, finding himselfe grieued with the casting downe of some diches, came vnto some of the rebels, and gaue to them fortie pence to cast downe the fenses of an inclosure belonging to Robert Ket, aliàs Knight, a tanner of Wimondham (which pasture lieth néere to the faire Wounge at Wimondham aforsaid) which they did. And that night consulting togither, the next morning they tooke their iourneie to Hetherset, by the procurement of the said Robert Ket, in reuenge of the displeasure which he had conceiued against the said Flowerdew, and set them in hand to plucke vp and cast downe hedges and diches, wherewith certeine pasture grounds belonging to the said Flowerdew were inclosed.

Ket chosen to
be capteine of
the rebels.

Here was somwhat adoo. For maister Flowerdew did what he could to haue caused them to desist from that attempt, in somuch that manie sharpe words passed betwixt Ket and the said maister Flowerdew. But Ket being a man hardie and forward to anie desperat attempt that should be taken in hand, was streight entered into such estimation with the commons thus assembled togither in rebellious wise, that his will was accomplished: and so those hedges and diches belonging to the pasture grounds of maister Flowerdew were throwne downe and made plaine. Herevpon was Ket chosen to be their capteine and ringleader, who being resolued to set all on six and seuen, willed them to be of good comfort, and to follow him in defense of their common libertie, being readie in the common-welths cause to hazard both life and goods.

Herewith they passed the water betwixt Cringelford and Eiton, and comming to Bowthorpe, cast downe certeine hedges and diches in that place, and their number being now greatlie increased, they incamped there that night. Here sir Edmund Windam knight, being high shiriffe of Norffolke and Suffolke, came and proclamed them rebels, commanding them to depart in the kings maiesties name. With which proclamation they were greatlie offended, and attempted to haue got him into their hands: but he being well horssed, valiantlie brake through them that had compassed him in: howbeit he escaped from them and got into Norwich, being not past a mile off. The same night there came a great number of lewd people vnto them, as well out of the citie of Norwich as out of the countrie, with weapon, armour, and artillerie.

The citizens of
Norwich.

The daie before that Ket came to this place, a great number of the meaner sort of the citizens of Norwich had throwne downe a quickset hedge, and filled vp the diches, wherewith the foresaid commons were on the one side inclosed, to kéepe in the cattell of the citizens that had the same going before their common neatherd: and so that fense which by good and prouident aduise of their forefathers, had béene raised and madè for the common profit of the whole citie, was thus by a sort of lewd persons defaced and cast downe at that present. And scarse had they throwne downe the dich in the vpper end of this pasture, but that a companie of euill disposed persons stale out of the citie, and got them to Kets campe. The maior of the citie named Thomas Cod aduertised hereof, doubting what might follow of this mischiefous begun rebellion, thought good to trie if he might persuade the rebels to giue ouer their traitorous enterprises: and therfore taking certeine of the aldermen with him, he went to Kets campe, vsing what persuasions he could to reduce them vnto their dutifull obedience, & to depart home to their houses. But his trauell was in vaine, and therefore et urned backe to the cite wthout hope to doo anie good with that vnrulie rout.

Thomas Cod.

After

After whose departure, they considering in what danger they stood to be surprised, if they should scatter abroad in such sort as till then they had doone, séeking to wast and spoile the countrie about them, without kéeping togither in anie warlike order, thought it stood most with their suertie to draw into one place, and to fortifie the same for their further strength. Vpon this resolution they determined to go with all spéed vnto Mousehold, a place as they tooke it meet for their purpose, and therefore sent to the maior of Norwich, requesting him of licence to passe through the citie, bicause it was their néerest waie, promising not to offer anie iniurie or violence to anie person, but quietlie to march through the citie vnto their place appointed. But the maior did not onlie denie them passage, but also with sharpe and bitter speach reprouing their rebellious dooings, told them what would follow thereof, if they gaue not ouer in time from further proceeding in such wicked attempts.

The rebels request licence to passe thorough Norwich.

The next daie being thursdaie, sir Roger Woodhouse with seuen or eight of his houshold seruants, came to them, bringing with him two carts laden with beere, and one cart laden with other vittels: for a recompense whereof he was stripped out of his apparell, had his horsses taken from him, and whatsoeuer else he had, the rebels accounting the same a good preie, he himselfe was cruellie tugged and cast into a dich of one Mores of nether Arleham by Heilesdonbridge: where the same daie the rebels, being disappointed of their purpose to passe through Norwich, found meanes to passe, and comming to maister Corbets house of Sprowston, intended to haue burnt the same house. But yet being persuaded to spare it from fire, they spoiled his goods, defaced a douehouse of his, which had beene a chappell, and afterwards got them to Mousehold, and comming to S. Leonards hill, on which the erle of Surrie had built a statelie house called mount Surrie, they inkennelled themselues there on the same hill; and in the woods adioining that lie on the west and the south side of the same hill, as the commons or pasture called Mousehold heath lieth on the east side, which conteineth foure or fiue miles in length, & thrée or foure in bredth.

Sir Roger Woodhouse.

Mount Surrie.

Mousehold.

They put sir Roger Woodhouse, and other prisoners whom they had caught in streict ward within the foresaid house of mount Surrie, on the which they seized, and spoiled whatsoeuer they found within it. In the meane time, the maior of Norwich taking aduise with his brethren the aldermen, what was best to doo in this case, whether presentlie to issue foorth, and distresse the rebels now in the beginning, least time might giue them meane to increase their power: or rather to staie till they had aduertised the councell of the whole matter. In the end they agréed that this last aduise was most surest, and so they dispatched a post with all spéed to the court. Beside this great campe (as they termed it) at Mousehold, there was a lesser at Rising chase neare to Lin: but the rebels there, by the good diligence and circumspect policie of the iustices and gentlemen of those parts, were spéedilie repressed, and driuen from thence. Notwithstanding afterwards they assembled togither at Watton, & there ramained about a fortnight, stopping also the passage at Thetford and Brandon ferrie, within nine miles of the said Watton: and at length came and ioined themselues with these other at Mousehold, by appointment of their generall capteine (as they tooke him) the foresaid Robert Ket.

Rising chase.

Watton.

Moreouer, there came flocking from Suffolke and other parts, a great multitude of lewd disposed persons, raised by firing of beacons, and ringing of bels. Also a number of rascals & naughtie lewd persons stale out of the citie of Norwich, and went to campe. And thus being got togither in great multitudes, they added one wickednesse to another, as hauing no staie of themselues after their downefall nor holding them content with the committing of one villanous trespasse and horrible transgression, according vnto the poets words to the like purpose:

Quisnam hominum est, quem tu contentum videris vno
Flagitio?———

Now

Now to cloke their malicious purpose with a counterfeit shew of holinesse, they caused one Coniers vicar of saint Martins in Norwich to saie seruice morning and euening, to praie to God for prosperous spéed in that their vngodlie enterprise. Moreouer they went about to ioine to their cause diuerse honest men, and right commendable for religion, doctrine, vertue, and innocencie of life; amongst whome were Robert Watson a preacher, Thomas Cod maiŏr of Norwich, and Thomas Alderich of Mangréene hall. These thrée, although sore against their willes, were constreined to be present with them in all matters of counsell, and to take vpon them (as associats with capteine Ket) the administration and order of euerie thing: which happened well for manie. For when either Ket himselfe, or anie other of the capteins, through setting on of the outragious multitude, purposed anie mischéefe (as often it came to passe) in one place or other, through their graue aduise, and approoued industrie, their furie was sundrie times staied and calmed. Although Ket bent to all vngratiousnes, would diuerse times grant foorth commissions, abusing now and then the names of honest men thereby, appointing his vnthriftie mates to fetch in vittels to furnish their campe withall. The tenor of one of the which commissions here insueth.

The forme of a warrant granted out by the rebels to take vp vittels.

WE the kings friends & deputies, doo grant licence to all men, to prouide and bring into the campe at Mousehold, all maner of cattell, and prouision of vittels, in what place soeuer they may find the same: so that no violence or iniurie bee doone to any honest or poore man. Commanding all persons as they tender the kings honor and roiall maiestie, and the releefe of the common welth, to be obedient to vs the gouernors, and to those whose names insue.

Signed   Robert Ket

Then followed in order a long list of names, for the number of the gouernors was great, as they that beside the chéefe capteins had chosen out of euerie hundred two, and there were six and twentie hundreds. By vertue of such commissions, manie that were of good worship and credit in the countrie, whom the rebels in their rage had condemned, were fetched from their houses, and other places where they might be found, and being brought to the campe, were committed to prison. Also the ditches and hedges, wherewith the commons abrode in the countrie were inclosed, were throwne downe, & manie were warned and called foorth from sundrie parts, to come and take part with them in these tumultuous vprores. And all these things were doone, the maior, maister Watson, and maister Aldrich not onlie holding their peace and winking thereat, but also sometime after a maner giuing their consent to the same. For to haue resisted them had béene but follie, and the waie to haue put themselues in danger of destruction, and their countrie too.

The honest citizens of Norwich in this meane while remained in great perplexitie, hearing nothing from the king nor his councell. They therefore being vncerteine what to doo, abode in the citie, till they might vnderstand what order it should please the king to take for the quieting of these troubles. The cause why the councell was thus slacke in prouiding remedie against the Norffolke rebels, was: for that they were busie in quieting the troubles in the inner part of the realme about London, and other places (as before ye haue heard) by meanes whereof the power of these Norffolke rebels still increased, so that there were assembled togither into Kets campe, to the number of sixtéene thousand vngratious vnthrifts, who by the aduise of their capteins fortified themselues, and made prouision of artillerie, powder and other abiliments, which they fetched out of ships, gentlemens houses, and other places where any was to be found, and

withall

Counterfeit religion.

Gentlemen imprisoned.

The number of the rebels.

withall spoiled the countrie of all the cattell, riches and coine, on which they might laie hands.

But bicause manie (as in such case is euer seene) did prouide for themselues, and hid that which they got, laieng it vp for their owne store, and brought it not foorth to further the common cause, Ket and the other gouernors (for so would they be called) thought to prouide a remedie, and by common consent it was decréed, that a place should be appointed, where iudgements might bée exercised, as in a iudiciall hall. Wherevpon they found out a great old oke, where the said Ket, and the other gouernors or deputies might sit and place themselues, to heare and determine such quareling matters as came in question. Afore whom sometime would assemble a great number of the rebels, and exhibit complaints of such disorders, as now and then were practised among them ; and there they would take order for the redressing of such wrongs and iniuries as were appointed, so that such gréedie vagabounds as were readie to spoile more than séemed to stand with the pleasure of the said gouernors, and further than there commissions would beare, were committed to prison. This oke they named the trée of reformation.

Rebels and theeues cannot kéepe togither without ministration of iustice.

The tree of reformation.

The maior, maister Aldrich and others, whome they had receiued into the number of their gouernours, would oftentimes go vp into this tree, and make diuerse pithie orations to persuade the outragious multitude to giue ouer their riotous rapines and spoilings. There were also certeine diuines which did vse all waies possible to withdraw them from their wicked attempts, and to reduce them to peace and quietnesse, although this was not doone without danger of their liues. Neuerthelesse, these in the daie time vsed to preach in the churches, and in the night to watch with armour vpon their backes leauing nothing vndoone that might séeme to apperteine vnto the dutie of godlie and vertuous diuines, or faithfull and obedient subiects. Among these was doctor Matthew Parker, afterward archbishop of Canturburie, whose wisedome, faithfulnesse, and integritie was most apparant.

Doctor Parker.

He comming on a daie into the campe with his brother Thomas Parker, that was after maior of Norwich, found them before the tree at common praier, the foreremembred Coniers vicar of saint Martins in Norwich saieng the Letanie. Wherevpon doctor Parker thinking the time to serue for his purpose, went vp into the tree, where he made a sermon, diuiding it into thrée seuerall parts. In the first he exhorted them to vse with moderation those vittels which they had prouided & brought into their campe, and not riotouslie nor lauishlie to wast and consume them. In the second he aduised them in no wise to séeke reuenge of priuat displeasures, and not to chaine or kéepe in irons those persons whom they held in ward, nor to take anie mans life from him. Lastlie, he wished that they should haue regard to themselues, & leaue off their rash begun enterprise, giuing eare to such heralds or other messengers as came from the king, and to shew such honour vnto his maiestie now in his yoong and tender yeares, as they might inioy him hereafter being growne vp in vertue, to their great ioy, comfort, and gladnesse. As he was handling this matter, with manie good and effectuall reasons, hauing the auditorie attentiue to his words, one lewd fellow among the rest cried out and said ; "How long shall we suffer this hireling doctor, who being waged by gentlemen, is come hither with his toong, which is sold and tied to serue their appetite? But for all his prating words, let vs bridle them, and bring them vnder the orders of our law."

He preacheth to the rebels.

The rebels threaten doctor Parker.

Then began the multitude to stur and make a noise, threatening the preacher, some of them saieng; It were well, that for his faire told tale we should bring him downe with a mischiefe, with arrowes and iauelings. This spéech brought doctor Parker in no small feare, and the more, for that he heard a noise and clattering of weapons vnder him, so that he looked for present death among them. But herein he was deceiued; for there was not a man that stood next him within the compasse of the trée, would

would him anie harme. And immediatlie the foresaid vicar of S. Martins that executed the office of the minister, began with helpe of some singingmen that were present, the canticle Te Deum, wherewith the vnrulie multitude seemed partlie to quiet
themselues. Which occasion doctor Parker perceiuing to serue his turne, thought
not longer to tarie amongst them, but quietlie got him downe from the trée, and with
his brother made hast towards the citie. But before he came to Pockthorp gate, there
were of the rebels that came to him, and began to question with him about his
licence, whereby he was authorised to preach : but he perceiuing that there was no
reason to be conceiued of them, slipt his waies and left his brother to argue the matter
with them.

Yet the next daie he entring into saint Clements church, tooke occasion to expound
somewhat out of one of the lessons that was read that daie, concerning these wicked
hurliburlies ; manie of the rebels comming about him, but not interrupting him a
whit, hearing the end of his exhortation, although they séemed greatlie therewith offended. But as he came out of the church, they followed him, and told him that (as
they vnderstood) he had three or foure able geldings to serue the king : and therefore
charged him that after dinner they might be readie for them to occupie. But doctor
Parker made them no great answer, but calling to him his horssekéeper, commanded
him to plucke off the shooes from some of his geldings, and to pare their hooues vnto
the quicke ; and that he should annoint the other with neruall as if they had béene
lamed with trauell. The rebels perceiuing this, when they saw the same geldings had
forth as it had béene to pasture, made no further businesse. Wherevpon doctor Parker shortlie after, feining as if he went abroad to walke two miles off from the citie,
at Crinkleford bridge found his horses readie as he had appointed, with his seruants,
and mounting vp, tooke his iourneie towards Cambridge, with as much spéed as was
possible, escaping thither out of all danger, although by the waie they met with
and saw diuerse of the rebels plaieng their parts in their woonted outragious maner.
Thus did doctor Parker escape the hands of the wicked rebels, who despising his
wholesome admonitions, did afterwards by Gods iust iudgement proue his words to be
most true.

But in the meane time proceeding from one mischiefe to another, after they had practised to spoile the gentlemen of the countrie of their goods, they began to attach their
bodies, and by force to bring them into their campe, so that such as escaped their
hands, were glad to flée, and hide themselues in woods and caues, where they might
best kéepe themselues out of their aduersaries reach and intended dangers. But to
speake of all the horrible practises by these vngratious people exercised, it would be
too long a processe. What shifts they found to cloake their dooings, and that euen
vnder the kings authoritie, it is woonderfull. For whereas there were certeine commissions directed vnto diuerse gentlemen in the countrie, to take order for the appeasing of these tumults ; they getting the same into their hands, tooke vpon them
the authoritie committed to the gentlemen vnto whome the same commissions were
sent ; and taking off the seales from the other, fastened the same vnto their counterfeit writings. To conclude, they grew to such vnmeasurable disorder, that they
would not in manie things obeie neither their generall capteine, nor anie of their gouernors, but ran headlong into all kind of mischiefe, & made such spoile of vittels
which they brought out of the countrie adioining vnto their campe, that within few
daies they consumed (beside a great number of béefes) twentie thousand muttons,
also swans, géese, hens, capons, ducks, & other foules so manie as they might laie
hands vpon. And furthermore, they spared not to breake into parks, and kill what
déere they could. Such hauocke they made of all that came in their waie, and such
number of shéepe speciallie they brought into their campe, that a good fat weather
was sold for a groat. The woods, groues, and trées that were destroied I passe ouer
and

and make no mention thereof.   Herewith, what crueltie was shewed by them in fet- tering and menacing such gentlemen as they caught, and committed to prison for some misliking they had conceiued of them, it was a miserable case to behold.   Some there were whom they brought foorth, as it had béene to iudgement before the tree of refor- mation, there to be tried afore the gouernors, as if they had béene guiltie of some heinous and gréeuous crime.   And when it was asked of the commons, what should be doone with those prisoners, they would crie with one voice; Hang them, hang them.   And when they were asked why they gaue so sharpe iudgement of those whome they neuer knew, they would roundlie answer, that other cried the same crie; and therefore they ment to giue their assent with other, although they could yéeld no reason, but that they were gentlemen, & therefore not woorthie to liue.

Whilest the rebels thus raged abroad in the countrie at Hengham eleuen miles from Norwich, sir Edmund Kenuet knight, with a small companie of his owne meniall ser- uants, set vpon the nightwatch of the rebels that were placed there, & brake through, ouerthrowing diuerse of them: and hauing some of his owne men also vnhorssed by the rebels, and in danger to be hewen in peeces among them, yet he recouered them, & escaped their hands through great manhood.   After which good nights seruice, as they would haue it esteemed, they repaired to their great capteine Ket, to shew their hurts receiued, & to complaine of their griefes.   It was talked among them, that they would go to sir Edmund Kneuets house called Buckenham castell, to assault it, and to fetch him out of it by force.   But it was doubted of some, least it were too strong for them; and other feared sharpe stripes, if they should attempt that exploit, being at the least twelue miles from their maine campe: and so that enterprise went not forward, the most part thinking it best to sléepe in whole skins.

There was at London the same time a citizen of Norwich, one Leonard Southerton fled from thence for feare of his life, whome the councell sent for, to come to speake with them : and being asked what he knew touching the state of the rebels, he de- clared to them from point to point the maner of all their outragious procéedings: but yet that as he vnderstood, there were manie among them that would laie aside their armour, if they might be assured of the kings pardon: and therefore if it would please the king to set foorth a proclamation, that all such as would depart from the campe and be quiet, should haue their pardon for all that was past, he doubted not but that those routs should be dispersed.   His aduise was allowed, and therevpon was an herald sent with all speed in companie with the said Southerton vnto Norwich; & comming into the campe the last of Iulie, and standing before the trée of reformation, apparelled in his cote of armes, pronounced there before all the multitude, with lowd voice, a frée pardon to all that would depart to their homes, and laieng aside their armour, giue ouer their traitorous begun enterprise.

After he had made an end of his proclamation, in maner all the multitude cried, God saue the king.   And manie of them falling downe vpon their knées, could not forbeare with teares gushing from their eies, but commend the kings great and vn- speakable mercie thus freelie offered vnto them, which vndoubtedlie they had at that time all of them receiued, if the wicked speech of some of the rascall sort, and namelie the traitorous persuasions of that wicked caitife Ket himselfe, had not staied them from their dutifull inclinations.   But after that Ket had with lowd voice before declared, that kings & princes were accustomed to grant pardons to such as are offendors, and not to others; he trusted that he néeded not anie pardon, sith he had doone nothing but that belonged to the dutie of a true subiect: and herewith he besought them not to forsake him, but to remember his promise, sith he was readie to spend his life in the quarell.   The herald herevpon called him traitor, and commanded Iohn Petibone the swordbearer of Norwich to attach him for treason.   Then began a great hurlie burlie among the multitude, so that the herald, perceiuing they began to shrinke from their former purpose of receiuing the kings pardon, departed from them with these words; All ye that be the kings friends, come awaie with me. The maior & maister Alderich, with a great number of other gentlemen & honest yeomen that were readie to obeie the kings commandement, followed him.

The maior being thus returned to the citie, caused the gates to be shut, and such gentlemen as had béen committed to prison within the castell, or other places in the citie, he caused to be set at libertie, & with their aduise tooke order how the rebelles might be kept out. But as he was busie about such matters, certeine of the citizens that fauored the rebelles had receiued a great multitude of them into the citie, which did put the citizens in such feare, that it was thought the most suretie for the gentlemen that had béene now released out of prison, to be shut vp againe, least the rebelles finding them abroad, should haue murthered them. Yet after this, when the rebels were departed out of the citie againe, the maior & aldermen fell in hand to rampire vp the gates, to plant ordinance, and to make all necessarie prouision that for them was possible.

At length they fell to shooting off their artillerie as well from the citie as from the campe, dooing their best to annoie ech other. But when the rebelles saw that they did little hurt to the citie with their great ordinance lieng vpon the hill, they remoued the same downe to the foot of the same hill, and from thense began to beat the walles. Notwithstanding, shortlie after they made sute for a truce to indure for a time, that they might passe to and fro through the citie, to fetch in vittels, whereof some want began to pinch them in the campe. The maior and aldermen flatlie denied their request, protesting that they would not permit anie traitors to haue passage through their citie.

The rebels sore kindled in wrath with this answer, and deniall of their sute, came running downe from the hill, and assaulting the gates, were beaten off with shot of arrowes and other weapons. And yet such rage appéered among the rebels, that the boies and yoong lads shewed themselues so desperat in gathering vp the arrowes, that when they saw and felt the same sticking in some part of their bodies, they would plucke them foorth, and deliuered them to their bow-men, that they might bestow the same again at the citizens. In all this broile (a thing note worthie) the seditious sort minding nothing more than the compassing of their purpose, had as little staie of themselues in this their outrage, as a bull at the sight of a cow, or a stoned horsse at the view of a mare; according vnto the old saieng of the poet:

Non facile est taurum visa retinere iuuenca,

Fortis equus visæ semper adhinnit equæ.

In the meane time, whilest they were thus busie vpon one side of the citie, an alarum rose at the defendants backes, crieng that the rebels were entred the citie on the contrarie side: and so euerie man shrinking awaie, and running thither to repell the enemie there, that part was left void of defendants where the first assault began. Whereof the rebels being aduised rushed into the riuer that runneth before bishops gate, got to the gates, and breaking them open, entred without anie great resistance For all the citizens were withdrawne to their houses and other places, where they hoped best to hide themselues from the furie of their enimies.

The rebels hauing thus entred the citie by force, conueied all the guns and artillerie, with other furniture of warre out of the citie into their campe. The herald that was yet abiding in the citie, to see if the rebels would before the daie prefixed for their pardons, being not yet expired, giue ouer their enterprise, came with the maior into the market place, and in the hearing of a great multitude of people that were come

foorth and stood about him, he eftsoons gaue commandement in the kings name, that they should laie armes aside, and get them home to their houses: which to so

manie

manie as did, he pronounced a generall pardon, and to the rest extreme punishment by death.

The rebels that stood by and heard him, when he had once made an end of his proclamation, bade him get him thense with a mischiefe: for it was not his faire offers, nor his swéet flattering words that should beguile them, sith they made no account of such manner of mercie, that vnder a colour of pardon, should cut off all their safetie and hope of preseruation. The herald perceiuing how obstinatelie they were bent, and set on all mischiefe, and that it was vnpossible to bring them from their outragious treason, either through feare of punishment or hope of pardon, departed; without hauing brought that to passe for which he was sent. Immediatlie after his departure, the rebels sought for Leonard Southerton, purposing to haue apprehended him, and committed him to prison, for accompanieng the herald thitherwards. But he hauing knowledge of their meaning, hid himselfe from them. *The traitorous refusall of the rebels to accept the kings pardon.*

After this, there were by Kets commandement apprehended diuerse persons, as the maior, Robert Watson, William Rogers, Iohn Homerston, William Brampton, and manie others, which were brought out of the citie, and committed to prison in mount Surrie. Ket perceiuing well that he must either now obteine a bloodie victorie by force against his countrie, or else to tast such an end as his vngratious attempts did well deserue, got togither so manie wicked persons as he might procure to come vnto him from ech side, with great rewards and faire promises: so that it was a strange matter to consider what a multitude of vnthrifts and rascalles came to him vpon the sudden. *Prisoners committed to ward in mout Surrie.* *Kets power increaseth.*

The citizens of Norwich were sore displeased, that their maior (being an honest man, and one greatlie beloued among them) should be imprisoned, and so remaine in danger of life among the rebels: for they threatned him sore, & iesting at his name, would saie one to another; Let vs all come togither to morrow, for we shall sée a * cods hed sold in the campe for a penie. Wherevpon the citizens fearing least through the malice and rage of the rebels, their maior might chance to be made awaie among them, procured maister Thomas Alderich (whose authoritie was great among them) to be a meane for his deliuerance: who comming to Ket with sharpe and bitter words reproued him for his cruell dealing; by imprisoning so honest a man as the maior was, and withall commanded him to release him: which either for shame, or rather through feare of a guiltie conscience that pricked him, he caused incontinentlie to be doone: who therevpon might now and then go and come at his pleasure to and fro the citie. But bicause he could not still remaine in the citie, but was constreined to continue for the most part in the campe, he appointed Augustine Steward to be his deputie, who with the assistance of Henrie Bacon, and Iohn Atkinson, shiriffes, gouerned the citie right orderlie, and kept the most part of the citizens in due obeisance. * *Alluding to the maior whose name was Cod.* *The maior of Norwich set at libertie.* *Augustine Steward.*

The councell aduertised now vpon the heralds returne, that there was no waie to reduce these Norffolke rebels vnto quiet otherwise than by force, appointed the marquesse of Northampton with fiftéene hundred horssemen to go downe vnto Norwich to subdue those stubborne traitors that so vndutifullie refused the kings mercifull pardon, fréelie offered by his officer at armes, and others. There went with the lord marquesse diuerse honorable and worshipfull personages, as the lord Sheffeld, the lord Wentworth, sir Anthonie Dennie, sir Henrie Parker, sir Richard Southwell, sir Rafe Sadler, sir Iohn Clere, sir Rafe Rowlet, sir Richard Lée, sir Iohn Gates, sir Thomas Paston, sir Henrie Bedingfield, sir Iohn Suliard, sir William Walgraue, sir Iohn Cuts, sir Thomas Cornewallis knights, togither with a great manie of other knights, esquiers and gentlemen, and a small band of Italians, vnder the leading of a capteine named Malatesta. *The lord marquesse of Northampton sent into Norffolke to represse the rebels.*

The lord marquesse being approched within a mile of Norwich, sent sir Gilbert Dethicke knight, now Garter, then Norrie, king at armes, vnto the citie, to summon *Norwich summoned.*

6 C 2

them

them within to yéeld it into his hands, or vpon refusall to proclame warre against them. Herevpon Augustine Steward the maiors deputie sent to the maior that was in the campe with Ket, aduertising him what message he had receiued from the marquesse. The maior sent word againe, that nothing was more greeuous vnto him, than to sée into what miserie the citie and countrie about were brought by the rage of these commotions; and declaring in what case he stood, being kept by force among the rebels, wheras otherwise he would (according to his dutie) haue come to his honor. But as for the citie, he had committed the gouernance vnto Augustine Steward, who should be readie to surrender it into his lordships hands : and that if Ket would giue him leaue, he would come himselfe to his honor, submitting all things wholie to this lordships order and disposition.

This message being brought backe by the said Norrie, Augustine Steward the maiors deputie with the shiriffs, and a great number of the citizens, came to the lord marquesses campe, and deliuered vp the sword to his lordship, declaring how the maior himselfe would gladlie haue come, if he could haue got from the rebels : and that although a great rowt of the lewd citizens were partakers with the rebelles, yet a number of the substantiall & honest citizens would neuer consent to their wicked doings, but were readie to receiue his lordship into their citie. The lord marquesse

Sir Richard Southwell.

giuing good woords to the citizens, and willing them to be of good comfort, sith he trusted to appease these troubles verie shortlie, deliuered the sword vnto sir Richard Southwell, who bare it before the lord marquesse as he passed foorth towards the citie, entring the same by saint Stephans gate. And incontinentlie was proclamation made that they should all resort into the market place, where they consulted togither how they might best defend the citie against the enimies, and to represse their furie. Herevpon was order giuen for the placing of watch and ward about the gates and the wals, as might séeme expedient. The lord marquesse supped that night and lodged in the maiors deputies house; but his lordship as well as other kept their armour on their backs all that night, for doubt of some sudden assault to be made against the citie by the rebels. Here it chanced that the strangers either by appointment or

The strāgers offer skirmish to the rebels.

otherwise, went foorth, and offered skirmish to the rebels vpon Magdalen hill.

The rebels came foorth with their horssemen : but it séemed that they were better practised to fetch in booties, than to make their manage or careire, and therefore not able to match the strangers, which being perceiued of their fellowes that were footmen, they put foorth their archers before their horssemen, and such numbers herewith came swarming foorth of their campe, meaning to compasse in those strangers, that they perceiuing the maner and purpose of the enimies, cast themselues in a ring, and retired backe into the citie againe. But they left one of their companie behind them, a gentleman that was an Italian, who more valiantlie than warilie ventured too farre among the enimies, and through euill hap being ouerthrowne beside his horsse, he was inuironed about with a great multitude of those rebels, that tooke him prisoner, and

An Italian hanged by the rebels.

like vile wretches spoiling him of his armor and apparell, hanged him ouer the wals of mount Surrie. Which act well shewed what courtesie might be looked for at such cruell traitors hands, that would thus vnmercifullie put such a gentleman and worthie souldior to death : for whose ransome, if they would haue demanded it, they might haue had no small portion of monie to haue satisfied their gréedie minds. But it séemed that their beastlie crueltie had bereft them the remembrance of all honest consideration and dutifull humanitie.

The marquesse of Northampton causing (as before ye haue heard) diligent watch to be kept vpon the walles, and at the gates, appointed the same to be visited right often, that through negligence no mishap should follow. Moreouer, besides the watch at the gates and walles, the residue of the soldiors making a mightie huge fire in the market place, so as all the stréets were full of light, they remained there all

that

that night in their armour, readie vpon anie occasion to resist the enimies if they should make anie attempt. Sir Edward Warner marshall of the field gaue the watch-word, sir Thomas Paston, sir Iohn Clere, sir William Walgraue, sir Thomas Cornwallis, and sir Henrie Bedingfield were appointed to the defense of other parts of the citie. And now when euerie thing was thought to be safelie prouided for, and that the lord marquesse and other were laid to take their rest, the rebels about the middest of the night began to shoot off their great artillerie towards the citie, so thicke as was possible: but the bullets passed ouer their heads that were lodged in the citie, without dooing anie great hurt at all. Sir Edward Warner.

The lord marquesse, by reason of the often alarums that were giuen, whilest the enimies thus ceased not to rage with continuall shot of ordinance, was called vp by the marshall sir Edward Warner; and comming into the market place, accompanied with the nobles and gentlemen of the armie, fell in councell with them, how to foreseé that the citie in such danger might be safelie defended against the enimies with such small power as he had there with him. It was therefore determined, that all the gates which were on the contrarie part of the towne from the rebels campe, and likewise the ruinous places of the walles should be rampired vp, that if the enimies should chance to giue an assault to the citie, they might more easilie be repelled.

But as these things were in dooing, and almost brought to end, in a manner all the whole multitude of the rebelles came out of their cabins, running downe in most furious maner to the citie, and with great shouts and yelling cries went about to set fire on the gates, to clime ouer the walles, to passe the riuer, and to enter the citie at such places where the walles were through age decaied and ruinous. The soldiors that were there with the lord marquesse, did shew their vttermost indeuor to beat backe the enimies. This fight in most cruell wise continued for the space of thrée houres without ceasing, the rebels forcing themselues to the vttermost of their powers to enter perforce vpon them, and they within the citie shewed no lesse courage to repell them backe. The hardie manhood of diuerse knights, and other men of worship was here right apparent. It was strange to seé the desperat boldnesse of the rebelles, that when they were thrust through the bodies or thighs, and some of them houghsinewed, would yet seeke reuenge in striking at their aduersaries, when their hands were scarse able to hold vp their weapon: thinking themselues somewhat satisfied if the humor of their enuie and deadlie spite might be fed but with a drop of their aduersaries bloud; with such a malignant spirit (tending wholie to vengeance) these desperat rebels were possessed, according to the poets spéech in the like sense and meaning: The desperatnesse of rebelles.

Inuidiosa dabit minimus solatia sanguis.

But such was the valiancie of the gentlemen and soldiers, which were there with the lord marquesse, that in the end the enimies which were alreadie entered the citie, were beaten out againe, and driuen backe to their accustomed kennell holes with losse of three hundred of their numbers. They within the towne hauing thus repelled the enimies, & accounting themselues in more safetie than before, for the rest of the night that yet remained, which was not much, they gaue themselues to refresh their wearied bodies with some sléepe. The next daie, the lord marquesse was informed by some of the citizens, that there were no small number in Kets campe that would gladlie come from him, if they might be sure of their pardon; and that at Pockethorpe gate there were foure or fiue thousand, that wished for nothing more than for pardon: and that if the same were offered them, there were no doubt (as they beléeued) but that they would submit themselues to the kings mercie. Iuuenal. sat.13. The rebels beaten backe.

The marquesse was glad to vnderstand so much, & incontinentlie dispatched Norreie king at armes with a trumpetter, to assure them on the kings behalfe, that they should be pardoned for all offenses past, and that had béene committed in time of this re-

bellion,

bellion, if they would laie armes aside. Norreie and the trumpet comming to the gate, found not a man there: but the trumpetter sounding his trumpet, there came running downe from the hill a great multitude of their people, & amongst other as chiefe, one Flotman, whome Norreie commanded to staie. Wherevpon the said Flotman asked him what was the matter, and wherefore he had called them togither by sound of trumpet? Go thy waies (said he) & tell thy companie from my lord marquesse of Northampton, the kings maiesties lieutenant, " that he commandeth them to ceasse from committing anie further outrage: and if they will (saith he) obeie his commandement, all that is past, shall be forgiuen and pardoned."

Flotman:

Pardon offered to the rebels.

Flotman hauing heard Norreies declaration, as he was an outragious and busie fellow, presumptuouslie made answer, that he cared not a pins point for my lord marquesse, and withall, like a rebellious traitor, railed vpon his lordship, and mainteined, that he and the rest of the rebels were earnest defendors of the kings roiall maiestie, and that they had taken weapon in hand not against the king, but in his defense, as in time it should appeare, as they that sought nothing but to mainteine his maiesties roiall estate, the libertie of their countrie, and the safetie of their commonwealth, &c. To conclude, he vtterlie refused the kings pardon, and told Norreie certeinelie, that they would either restore the common-wealth from decaie, into the which it was fallen, being oppressed thorough the couetousnesse and tyrannie of the gentlemen; either else would they like men die in the quarrell.

Flotmans presumptuous and traitorous allegations.

Scarselie had he made an end of his tale, when suddenlie a fearefull alarum was raised thoroughout the citie: for whilest Flotman was thus in talke with the king of armes at Pockethorpe gate, the rebels in great rage entring the citie by the hospitall, went about to bring all things to destruction: but being incountered néere to the bishops palace, by the lord marquesse his men, there insued a bloudie conflict betwixt them, which continued long with great fiercenesse and eger reuenge on both parts. There died about seuen score of the rebels, and of the soldiers that serued against them some number, beside a great multitude that were hurt and wounded on both parts. But the pitifull slaughter of the lord Sheffeld, who hauing more regard to his honor than safetie of life, desirous to shew some proofe of his noble valiancie, entering amongst the enimies, as he fought right hardilie, though not so warilie as had béene expedient, fell into a dich as he was about to turne his horsse: & herewith being compassed about with a number of those horrible traitors, was slaine amongest them: although he both declared what he was, and offered largelie to the vilans, if they would haue saued his life. But the more noble he shewed himselfe to be, the more were they kindled in outragious furie against him. And as he pulled off his head péece, that it might appeare what he was, a butcherlie knaue named Fulks, who by occupation was both a carpenter & a butcher, slat him in the head with a club, and so most wretchedlie killed him. A lamentable case, that so noble a yoong gentleman, indued with so manie commendable qualities, as were to be wished in a man of his calling, should thus miserablie end his daies by the hands of so vile a vilan.

The rebels enter the citie.

The lord Sheffeld wofullie slaine.

Diuerse other gentlemen and woorthie soldiers came to the like end among those outragious rebels, and amongst other, Robert Woluaston, that was appointed to kéepe the doore of Christs church, was killed by the same Fulks, who tooke him for sir Edmund Kneuet, against whome the rebels bare great malice, for that he sought to annoie them so farre as by anie meanes he might, as partlie ye haue heard. But the slaughter of that noble man the lord Sheffeld, sore discouraged the residue of the soldiers that were come with the lord marquesse. And on the other part, the rebels were aduanced thereby, in greater hope to preuaile against them, and thereupon preassed forward with such hardinesse, that they caused the lord marquesse and his people to giue place, and to forsake the citie, euerie man making the best shift he could to saue himselfe. But yet diuerse gentlemen of good account and worship

Alexander Newel.

remaining

remaining behind, and abiding the brunt, were taken prisoners, as sir Thomas Cornewallis, and others, whome the rebels afterwards kept in streict durance, vntill the daie came of their ouerthrow by the kings power, vnder the conduction of the earle of Warwike.

The lord marquesse and the residue that escaped, made the best shift they could *The marquesse maketh shift to escape danger.* to get out of danger; and at length, he and the most part of them that went foorth with him, came to London. The rebels hauing thus repelled the lord marquesse & his power, set fire on the citie, whereby manie faire buildings were consumed and burnt. It happened yet well the same time, that there fell great abundance of raine, the which holpe in part to quench the rage of the fire. Neuertheles, all the houses on either side of Holmes stréet, and the hospitall of the poore; also Bishops gate, Pockthorpe gate, Magdalene gate, and Bearestréet gate, with manie other houses in other parts of the citie, were burned, and fowlie defaced with fire. The citizens were brought into such extreame miserie, that they knew not which waie to turne them. Some there were that fled out of the citie, taking with them their gold and siluer, and such short ware as they might conueie awaie with them, abandoning wife and children, to rest at the mercie of the rebels. Other hid their goods in wels, priuies, and other such secret places out of the waie.

The rebels entering into the houses of such as were knowne to be wealthie men, spoiled and bare awaie all that might be found of anie value. But to speake of all the cruell parts which they plaied, it would be tedious to expresse the same, their dooings were so wicked and outragious. There was shooting, howling, and wringing among *The miserable estate of Norwich.* them, wéeping, and crieng out of women and children. To be short, the state of the citie at that present was most miserable. The maiors deputie kept himselfe close in his house, and might behold all this mischiefe and destruction of the citie, but durst not come abroad, nor go about to staie them: at length, a great multitude of the rebels that were come downe frō their campe, entering by saint Augustines gate, came straight to his house, and stroue to breake open the doores: but when they could not easilie bring their purpose to passe that waie foorth, they began to fire the house. Whereupon for feare to be burned within his owne lodging, he set open the doores, *The aldermans deputie roughlie handled to tell where the lord marquesse had hidden himselfe.* and in came those vnmannerlie ghests, tooke him, plucked his gowne beside his backe, called him traitor, and threatened to kill him, if he would not tell them where the lord marquesse of Northampton had hidden himselfe.

And when he had told them that vndoubtedlie he and all his companie were gone, they were in a great rage, and with terrible noise and rumbling they sought euerie corner of the house for him, and taking what they found, they departed. But yet manie of them afterwards partlie pacified for a péece of monie, and other things which they receiued of the maior, and partlie reprooued for the wrongfull robberies by some that were in credit among them, they brought againe such packs and fardels as they had trussed vp togither, and threw them into the shops of those houses, out of the which they had taken the same before: but yet there were diuers of the citizens that were spoiled of all that they had by those rebels, that entered their houses vnder a colour to séeke for the marquesse of Northamptons men. Namelie, the houses of those citizens that were fled, were spoiled and ransacked most miserablie, for they reputed and called them traitors and enimies to their king and countrie, that thus had forsaken their houses and dwellings in time of such necessitie: yet manie of the citizens bring- *Reléefe ministred to the rebels for feare of force.* ing foorth bread, beere, and other vittels vnto the rebels to refresh them with, somewhat calmed their furious rage, and so escaped their violent hands, although no small number were so fléesed (as before yee haue heard) that they haue liued the woorse for it all the daies of their life since that time.

But now the rebels hauing thus got possession of the citie, & chased awaie the kings people, they tooke order to haue the gates kept hourelie with watch and ward of the
citizens

citizens themselues, thretning them with most shamefull death, if they omitted the same. These vnrulie persons were so farre stept into all kind of beastlie outrage, that when it rained, they would kenell vp themselues in the churches, abusing the place appointed for the seruice and worshipping of the almightie God, in most prophane and wicked manner, and neither praier nor yet threats of men or women that aduised them to modestie could take place. The kings maiestie aduertised therefore, that there was no waie to tame their diuelish and traitorous outrage, but by force: with the aduise of his councell caused a power to be put in a readinesse, as well of his owne subiects as of strangers, namelie lancequenets, which were come to serue his maiestie against the Scots.

But now it was thought expedient to vse their seruice against these rebels, whose power and desperate boldnesse was so farre increased, that without a maine armie, guided by some generall of great experience, and noble conduct, it would be hard and right dangerous to subdue them: wherein violence and force was to be vsed, sith they had shewed themselues in an extremitie of stubbornesse, like buls that by baiting are to be tamed, or like stifnecked stalions which with bit & bridle must be managed; as one saith:

Asper equus duris contunditur ora lupatis.

Heerevpon that noble chéefteine and valiant erle of Warwike, latelie before appointed to haue gone against the Scots and Frenchmen into Scotland, was called backe, and commanded to take vpon him the conduction of this armie against the Norffolke rebels: for such was the opinion then conceiued of that honorable earle, for the high manhood, valiant prowesse, and great experience in all warlike enterprises, sufficientlie tried, and knowne to rest in him, that either they might be vanquished and ouercome by him, or by none other.

Capteine Ket and his rebellious armie, hauing some aduertisement by rumors spred, of this preparation and comming of an armie against them; they were not slacke to make themselues strong and readie to abide all the hazard that fortune of warre might bring. The earle of Warwike then, after that his men and prouisions were readie, did

set forward, and came vnto Cambridge, where the lord marquesse of Northampton and other met his lordship. Héere also diuerse citizens of Norwich came to him, and falling downe vpon their knees before him, besought him to be good lord vnto them; and withall declared their miserable state, great gréefe and sorrow, which they had conceiued for the wretched destruction of their countrie: beséeching him to haue pitie vpon them. And if in such extremitie of things as had happened vnto their citie, they had through feare or ignorance committed anie thing contrarie to their dutifull allegiance, that it might please his honor to pardon them their offenses in such behalfe, sith if anie thing were amisse on their parts, the same came to passe sore against their wils, and to their extreame greefe and sorrow.

The earle of Warwike told them, that he knew indéed in what danger they had béene among those vnrulie ribalds; and as for anie offense which they had committed, he knew not: for in leauing their citie sith matters were growne to such extremitie, they were to be borne with, but in one thing they had ouershot themselues: for that in the beginning they had not sought to represse those tumults, sith if they had put themselues in defense of their countrie, to resist the rebels at the first, such mischiefs as were now growne, might easilie haue béene auoided. But neuerthelesse, vpon this

their humble submission, he granted them all the kings mercifull pardon, and commanding them to prouide themselues of armour and weapon, appointed them to march foorth with the armie, wearing certeine laces or ribons about their necks for a difference, that they might be knowne from others. There were in this armie vnder the

earle of Warwike diuerse men of honor and great worship, as lords, knights, esquiers, and gentlemen in great numbers. First the lord marquesse of Northampton, and
sundrie

sundrie of them that had béene with him before, desirous to be reuenged of his late repulse, the lords Willoughbie, Powes and Braie, Ambrose Dudleie, sonne to the said earle, and at this present worthilie adorned with the title (which his father then bare) of earle of Warwike, and his brother lord Robert Dudleie now erle of Leicester; also Henrie Willoughbie esquier, sir Thomas Tresham, sir Marmaduke Constable, William Deuereux sonne to the lord Ferrers of Chartleie, sir Edmund Kneuet, sir Thomas Palmer, sir Andrew Flammocke, and diuerse other knights, esquiers, and gentlemen: all which plaid their parts as time and occasion was ministred vnto them to giue triall of their manhood.

The earle of Warwike, and such as were come with him to Cambridge, marched directlie from thence towards Norwich, and came vnto Wimondham the two and twentith of August, where and by the waie the most part of all the gentlemen of Norffolke that were at libertie, came vnto him. The next daie betimes he shewed himselfe vpon the plaine, betwixt the citie of Norwich and Eiton wood, and lodged that night at Intwood, an house belonging to sir Thomas Tresham knight, a two miles distant from Norwich. Héere they rested that daie and night following, not once putting off their armour, but remaining still in a readinesse, if the enimies should haue made anie sudden inuasion against them. The earle of Warwike in the meane time sent the afore remembred king of armes Norreie, to summon the citie, either to open the gates that he might quietlie enter; or else to looke for warre at his hands that would then assaie to win it by force, and such reward as rebels (that wilfullie withstand their so uereigne) ought to receiue.

Norwich summoned.

When Ket vnderstood that the herald was come to the gates, he appointed the maiors deputie Augustine Steward, and Robert Rug, two of the chéefest citizens, to go to him and to know his errand. They passing foorth at a posterne, and hearing his message, made answer, that they were the miserablest men that were then liuing, as they themselues beleeued, sith that hauing suffered such calamities as they could not but tremble at in calling to remembrance, they could not now haue libertie to declare the loiall dutie which they bare & ought to beare to the kings highnesse: so that they accompted themselues most vnfortunate, sith their hap was to liue in that season, in which they must either ieopard losse of life, or the estimation of their good name, although they trusted the kings maiestie would be gratious lord vnto them, sith they had giuen no consent vnto such wicked rebellion as was thus raised against his highnesse, but with losse of goods and perill of life so farre as in them laie, had doone what they could to kéepe the citizens in good order and dutifull obedience.

What answer was made to the herald by the citizens of Norwich, whom Ket assigned thervnto.

One thing more they would humblie desire of my lord of Warwike, that whereas there was no small number of Kets armie in the citie without armour or weapon, and as it should seeme irkesome and wearie of that which had béene alreadie doone, it might please him once againe to vouchsafe to offer them the kings pardon, and if he should thus doo, they had great hope that the rebels would gladlie accept it, and so the matter might be pacified without more bloudshed. Norreie returned to the earle of Warwike, and declared what answer he had receiued. The earle desirous of nothing more than to haue the matter thus taken vp, as well for other considerations, as for feare least the gentlemen remaining prisoners with the rebels, should be vnmercifullie murthered by their kéepers, if they came to the vttermost triall of battell, he resolued to prooue if it would thus come to passe. And héerevpon was Norreie with a trumpet sent to offer them a generall pardon, who being entered the citie, met about fortie of the rebels on horssebacke, riding two and two togither verie pleasant and merrie, and so passing from S. Stephans gate vnto Bishops gate, the trumpetter sounded his trumpet, and with that, a great multitude of the rebels came thronging downe togither from the hill: to whome the horsmen spéedilie riding, commanded that they should diuide themselues, and stand in order vpon either side the waie. And as Norreie and the

Norreie the herald deliuereth his answer to the earle of Warwike.

Norreie king of armes sent to offer the rebels their pardon.

trum-

trumpetter, with two of the chéefe citizens entred betwixt them, they were receiued with great noise and clamour, for euerie of them putting off their hats or caps, cried; God saue king Edward, God saue king Edward.

Norreie and the two citizens, highlie commending them herein, requested them to kéepe their place and order wherein they stood for a while: and then Norreie passing foorth about two hundred and fiftie pases, came to the top of the hill, and putting on his coate armour, staied awhile (for Ket was not yet come) and at length began to declare vnto them in what maner diuers times since first they had taken armes in hand, the kings maiestie by sundrie persons, as well heralds, as other, had sought to reduce them from their vnlawfull and rebellious tumults, vnto their former dutie and obedience; and yet neuerthelesse, they had shewed themselues wilfull and stubborne, in refusing his mercifull pardon freelie offered vnto them, and despised the messengers which his grace had sent vnto them to pronounce the same. He willed them therefore to call themselues now at length to remembrance, and to behold the state of the common-wealth, which they so often to no purpose had still in their mouths, and neuerthelesse by them miserablie defaced, & brought in danger of vtter ruine and decaie.

Norreie the herald maketh a long discourse to the rebels, for the reducing of them to good order.

And herewith discoursing at large of the horrible, wicked, and heinous murthers, riots, burnings, and other crimes by them committed, he willed them to consider into what sea of mischeefes they had throwne themselues, and what punishment they ought to looke for as due to them for the same; sith as well the wrath of God as the kings armie was hanging ouer their heads, and readie at hand, which they were not able to resist. For his grace had resolued no longer to suffer so great and presumptuous a mischéefe as this, to be suffered in the middle of his realme: and therefore had appointed the right honourable earle of Warwike, a man of noble fame and approoued valiancie, to be his generall lieutenant of that his roiall armie, to persecute them with fire and sword; and not to leaue off, till he had vtterlie dispersed and scattered that wicked and abhominable assemblie. And yet such was the excéeding greatnesse of the kings bountifull mercie and clemencie, that he that was by him appointed to be a reuenger of their heinous treasons committed against his maiestie, if they continued in their obstinate wilfulnesse, should be also the interpretor and minister of his gratious and free pardon, to so manie as would accept it. Which vnlesse they now imbrased, the said earle had made a solemne vow, that they should neuer haue it offered to them againe; but that he would persecute them till he had punished the whole multitude according vnto their iust deserts.

Tke kings purpose in sending the earle of Warwike against them.

Manie that heard him, hauing due consideration of their miserable estate, were touched with some remorse of conscience, fearing at length to tast the reuenge of such horrible crimes as they had been partakers of with others in committing the same. But the more part finding themselues highlie offended with his words, began to iangle (as they had doone before vnto other that had béene sent to offer them pardon) that he was not the kings herald, but some one made out by the gentlemen in such a gaie coate, patched togither of vestments and church-stuffe, being sent onelie to deceiue them, in offering them pardon, which would prooue nought else but halters; and therefore it were well doone, to thrust an arrow into him, or to hang him vp. Although other séemed dutifullie to reuerence him, and diuerse that had served in Scotland and at Bullongne, remembring that they had séene him there and knew him, told and persuaded their fellowes, that he was the kings herald indeed. Wherevpon they became more mild, and offered him no further iniurie: but yet they could not be persuaded that this pardon tended to anie other end, but to bring them to destruction; and that in stéed of pardon, there was prepared for them nought else but a barrell full of halters.

How the rebels were affected after the heralds discourse was ended.

The herald is grudged at & mistrusted of some, &c.

Such lewd speech was amongst them, sauouring altogither of malicious mistrust, and most wilfull treason. Norreie neuerthelesse departing from thense, accompanied

with

with Ket, eame to another place, where he made the like proclamation : for the multitude was such that he could not be heard of them all in one place. Héere, before he had made an end of his tale, there was a vile boie (as some write) that turned vp his bare taile to him, with words as vnseemelie as his gesture was filthie : with which spitefull reproch thus shewed towards the kings maiesties officer at armes, one (which in companie of some other that were come ouer the water to view things) being greatlie offended, with an harquebuse shot stroke that vngratious lad through the bodie a little aboue the reins. *Alexander Neuill.*

The iust reward ward of a rake-hell boie.

Which when some of the rebels had séene, a dozen of their horssemen came gallopping out of the wood, crieng ; " We are betraied fréends, we are betraied, if you looke not about you : do you not see how our fellowes are slaine with guns before our faces ? What may we hope if we disarme our selues, that are thus vsed being armed ? This herald goeth about nothing else, but to bring vs within danger of some ambush, that the gentlemen may kill and beate vs all downe at their pleasure." Héerevpon they all shranke awaie, and fled, as they had béene out of their wits : yet did their great capteine Robert Ket accompanie Norreie, meaning (as hath béene said) to haue gone to the earle of Warwike himselfe, to haue talked with him : but as he was almost at the foot of the hill, there came running after him a great multitude of the rebels, crieng to him, and asking him whither he went ; We are readie (said they) to take such part as you doo, be it neuer so bad : and if he would go anie further, they would (as they said) suerlie follow him.

Ket meant to haue talked with the earle of Warwike.

Norreie then perceiuing such numbers of people following them, desired Ket to staie them : who returning backe to them, they were incontinentlie appeased, and so they all returned with him backe to their campe. When the earle of Warwike vnderstood that they were thus altogither set on mischéefe, and neither with praier, proffer of pardon, threatening of punishment, nor other meanes they could be reduced to quietnesse, he determined to procéed against them by force. And héerevpon bringing his armie vnto saint Stephans gate, which the rebels stopped vp, with the letting downe of the portculice, he commanded those that had charge of the artillerie, to plant the same against the gate, and with batterie to breake it open.

S. Stephans gate.

As these things were in hand, he vnderstood by Augustine Steward the maiors deputie, that there was an other gate on the contrarie side of the citie, called the Brasen gate, which the rebels had rammed vp, but yet not so, but that it might be easilie broken open. Herewith were the pioners called, and commanded to breake open that gate also : which being doone, the soldiers entered by the same into the citie, and slue diuerse of those rebels that stood readie to defend and resist their entrie. In the meane time had the gunners also broken in sunder with their shot the portculice, and néere hand the one halfe of the other gate, by the which the marques of Northampton, and capteine Drurie, aliàs Poignard (that being sent from London met my lord of Warwike by the waie) entered with their bands, and droue backe the rebels with slaughter, that were readie there to resist them.

The Brasen gate.

Moreouer, the maiors deputie caused Westwike gate to be set open : at the which the earle of Warwike himselfe entring with all his armie, and finding in manner no resistance, came to the market place. Here were taken a thréescore of the rebels, the which according to the order of martiall law were incontinentlie executed, according to the qualitie of their offense, confessing (no doubt) in conscience, that their punishment was proportioned to their trespasse, and that in dieng the death (were the same neuer so extreame & dredfull) they had but their desert ; and therefore might well saie with the poet :

Supplicia & scelerum pœnas expendimus omnes.

Virgil.

Shortlie after, the carriages belonging to the armie were brought into the citie by the same gate, and passing through the citie, by negligence & want of order giuen to

6 D 2

them.

them that attended on the same cariage, they kept on forward till they were got out at Bishops gate towards Mousehold. Whereof the rebels being aduised, they came downe, & setting vpon the carters, and other that attended on the cariages, put them to flight, and droue awaie the carts laden with artillerie, powder, and other munition, bringing the same into their campe, and greatlie reioising thereof, bicause they had no great store of such things among them: but yet capteine Drurie with his band comming in good time to the rescue, recouered some of the carts from the enimies, not without some slaughter on either side. Moreouer, the enimies as yet being not fullie driuen out of the citie, placed themselues in crosse stréets, & were readie to assaile the soldiers as they saw their aduantage, part of them standing at S. Michaels, part at S. Stephans, and part at S. Peters, and some of them also stood in Wimers stréet.

Here they assailing such as vnaduisedlie were entered within their danger, they slue diuerse, and among other three or foure gentlemen, before they could be succoured from anie part. The erle of Warwike aduertised hereof, passed foorth with all his forces to remoue the enimie, and comming to S. Andrew in Iohns stréet, was receiued with a sharpe storme of arrowes: but capteine Drurie his harquebusiers galled them so with their shot, that they were glad to giue place, and so fled amaine. There were slaine a hundred and thirtie, and diuerse of them shrinking aside into churchyards and other places vnder the walles, were taken and executed. All the rest got them vp to their campe at Mousehold, and so the citie was rid of them for that time. Then did the erle of Warwike take order for the safe keeping of the citie, appointing watch and ward to be kept on the walles, and in euerie street. Also that all the gates should be rammed vp, except one or two that stood towards the enimies, at the which were planted certeine péeces of the great artillerie.

But the rebels vnderstanding that the earle of Warwike wanted powder and other things apperteining to the vse of the great ordinance, and withall perceiuing that the Welshmen which were appointed to the gard of the said great péeces of artillerie were no great number, and therefore not able to resist anie great force that should come against them, they came down the hill vpon the sudden as it were wholie togither in most outragious maner. And withall one Miles that was a verie perfect gunner, and maruellous skilfull in the feat of shooting of great artillerie, and at that time remaining among the rebels, shot off a péece; and slue one of the kings principall gunners, that was attending vpon those péeces of artillerie, which stood thus before the gate. Whom when the rebels perceiued thus to be slaine, they made forward with more courage, and gaue such a desperate onset vpon them that garded the said artillerie, that their small number, being not able to withstand their aduersaries great and huge multitude pressing in such furious rage vpon them, that they were constreined to flée backe, and to leaue the artillerie for a preie vnto the enimies, who seizing vpon the same, conueied them awaie with certeine carts laden with all manner of munition for wars vp to their campe: a matter (as was thought) of no small importance, sith the enimies thereby were furnished now with such things, whereof before they stood most in néed, and now hauing store thereof, they spared not liberallie to bestow it against the citie, beating downe not onlie the highest top of Bishops gate, but also a great part of the wals on that side.

And here trulie the good seruice of capteine Drurie is not to be forgotten, who now as earst being readie to reuenge this iniurie, following vpon the enimies, put them to flight, and recouered much of that which they had taken from the earls souldiers. The earle of Warwike after this cut off the entries at the gates, and rampired them vp, placed at the bridges and turnings of the waies and streets diuers bands of soldiers to kéepe the passages, brake downe the White friers bridge, and at Bishops gate he appointed the lord Willoughbie with a great number of soldiers to defend that part, &

in

in this sort he made prouision to defend the citie from the rebels, if they should attempt to make anie surprise vpon the sudden.

The next daie yet they passing ouer the riuer, set fire on certeine houses at Connesfoorth, burning the more part of all the houses of two parishes: and so great was the rage of the fire, that catching hold vpon an house wherein the merchants of Norwich vse to laie vp such wares and merchandize as they conueie to their citie from Yermouth, the same house with great store of wheat and other riches was miserablie consumed and defaced. Thus whilest euerie thing séemed to chance and fall out in fauour of the rebels, there were some in the earle of Warwiks armie, that despairing of the whole successe of their iourneie, came to the earle of Warwike, and began to persuade with him, that sith the citie was large, and their companies small (for in déed the whole appointed numbers as yet were not come, neither of strangers nor Englishmen) it was vnpossible to defend it against such an huge multitude as were assembled togither in Kets campe, and therefore besought him to regard his owne safetie, to leaue the citie, and not to hazard all vpon such an vncerteine maine chance. Councell giuen to the erle of Warwike to abandon the citie.

The earle of Warwike as he was of a noble and inuincible courage, valiant, hardie, and not able to abide anie spot of reproch, whereby to lose the least péece of honour that might be, made this answer: " Whie (saith he) and doo your harts faile you so soone? Or are you so mad withall, to thinke that so long as anie life resteth in me, that I will consent to such dishonour? Should I leaue the citie, heaping vp to my selfe and likewise to you such shame and reproofe as worthilie might be reputed an infamie to vs for euer? I will rather suffer whatsoeuer either fire or sword can worke against me." These words being vttered with such a courage as was maruellous to consider, he drew out his sword. Which other of the honorable and worshipfull that were then present likewise did, whome he commanded that each one should kisse others sword, according to an ancient custome vsed amongst men of war in time of great danger: and herewith they made a solemne vow, binding it with a solemne oth, that they should not depart from thence, till they had either vanquished the enimies, or lost their liues in manfull fight for defense of the kings honour. The earles answere.

Whilest these things were in dooing, the rebels brake into the citie on that side, where was no suspicion of their entring at all; but being come almost to the bridges, they were incountered by the soldiers, beaten backe, and chased out by the same waie they came. The next daie being the six and twentith of August, there came to the earle 1400 lancequenets. The rebels notwithstanding that such reinforcement of the earles power might haue somewhat discouraged them, yet trusting altogither to certeine vaine prophesies, which they had among them, and set out in verses by such wisards as were there with them in the campe, they had conceiued such a vaine hope of prosperous successe in their businesse, that they little esteemed anie power that might come against them. Among other of those same verses, were these two: Lancequenets come to the earle of Warwike.
The rebels trust in vaine prophesies.

The countrie gnuffes, Hob, Dick, and Hick,
   with clubs and clowted shoone,
Shall fill vp Dussin dale with bloud
   of slaughtered bodies soone.

Upon hope therefore of this and other vaine prophesies, the rebels through the diuels procurement, that had nourished and pricked them forward all this while in their wicked procéedings, determined to remoue thither, to the end that they might with more spéed make an end of the matter, before they should be driuen to disperse themselues by famine. For the earle of Warwike had taken order to haue the passages stopped, in such wise as no vittels could easilie be conueied to their campe, the want whereof began alreadie to pinch them. Herevpon setting fire on their cabins, which they had raised and built here and there of timber and bushes (the smoke whereof couered all the grounds about them) they came downe with their ensignes into the The rebels remoue.

vallie

vallie called Dussin dale, where with all spéed that might be they intrenched themselues about, and raising a rampire of a good height, set stakes also round about them,
to kéepe off the horssemen.

The earle of Warwike perceiuing their dooings, the next daie being the seuen and
twentith of August with all his horssemen, and the Almans with capteine Druries
band, issued foorth of the citie, marching streight towards the enimies. Yet before
he approched in sight of them, he sent sir Edmund Kneuet & sir Thomas Palmer
knights, with others, to vnderstand of them, whether now at length they would submit themselues, & receiue the kings pardon; which if they would doo, he offered to
grant it freelie to all the whole multitude, one or two of them onelie excepted: but
they with generall voices refusing it, the earle fell in hand to incourage his people
vnto the battell, and hauing appointed as well the horssemen as footmen in what order
they should giue the charge, they passed forward in approching the enimies. The rebels beholding them thus to come forward, put themselues in order of battell, in such
manner, that all the gentlemen which had béene taken prisoners, and were kept in
irons for starting awaie, were placed in the fore ranke of their battell, coupled two and
two togither, to the end they might be killed by their owne friends that came to seeke
their deliuerance: but yet as God would haue it, the most part of them were saued.
Miles the maister gunner among the rebels, leuieng a péece of ordinance, shot it off,
and stroke him that caried the kings standard in the thigh, and the horsse through the
shoulder.

The earle of Warwike and others sore grieued therewith, caused a whole volie of
artillerie to be shot off at the rebels: and herewith capteine Drurie with his owne
band, & the Almans or lanceknights, whether ye list to call them, on foot, getting
néere to the enimies, hailsed them with their harquebut shot so sharplie, and thrust
forward vpon them with their pikes so stronglie, that they brake them in sunder.
The gentlemen, who (as we haue said) were placed in the fore ranke, found meanes
(as good hap was) to shrinke aside, and escaped the danger for the more part, although
some indeed were slaine by the Almans, and other that knew not what they were.
The light horssemen of the kings part herewith gaue in amongst them so roundlie,
that the rebels not able to abide their valiant charge, were easilie put to flight, and
with the foremost their grand capteine Robert Ket gallopped awaie so fast as his
horsse would beare him. The horssemen following in chase, slue them downe on
heapes, euer still as they ouertooke them; so that the chase continuing for the space
of thrée or foure miles, there were slaine to the number of thrée thousand fiue hundred
at the least: beside a great multitude that were wounded as they fled here and there
ech waie foorth, as séemed best to serue their turne for their most spéedie escape out of
danger. Yet one part of them that had not beene assailed at the first onset, séeing
such slaughter made of their fellowes, kept their ground by their ordinance, and
shranke not: determining as men desperatlie bent, not to die vnreuenged, but to fight
it out to the last man.

They were so inclosed with their carts, carriages, trenches (which they had cast)
and stakes pitched in the ground to kéepe off the force of horssemen, that it would
haue béene somewhat dangerous to haue assailed them within their strength. But
sure they were that now they could not escape, séeing no small part of their whole
numbers were cut off and distressed, and they inuironed on ech side, without hope of
succour or reléefe of vittels, which in the end must néeds haue forçed them to come
foorth of their inclosure to their vndoubted ouerthrow and destruction. The earle of
Warwike yet pitieng their case, and loth that the king should loose so manie stout
mens bodies as were there amongst them, which might doo his maiestie and their
countrie good seruice, if they could be reclamed from this their desperat follie vnto
due obedience, sent Norreie vnto them, offering them pardon of life if they would
throw

The earle of
Warwike goeth
foorth to giue
the enimies bat-
tell.

Pardon offered.

The number of
the rebels slaine.

throw downe their weapons and yéeld: if not, he threatned that there should not a Pardon eftsoones offered. man of them escape the deserued punishment. Their answer was, that if they might be assured to haue their liues saued, they could be contented to yeeld : but they could haue no trust that promise should be kept with them. For notwithstanding all such faire offers of pardon, they tooke it that there was nothing meant but a subtill practise, to bring them into the hands of their aduersaries the gentlemen, that had prepared a barrell of ropes and halters, with which they purposed to trusse them vp : and there-fore they would rather die like men than to be strangled at the wils and pleasures of their mortall enimies.

The earle of Warwike right sorie to sée such desperat minds among them, sent to the citie, and caued the most part of the footmen which he had left there to defend the same, to come foorth now in battell arraie, that they might helpe to distresse those wilfull rebels that thus obstinatelie refused the kings pardon. And hauing brought as well them as the Almans and the horssemen in order of battell againe, and readie now to set vpon the rebels, he eftsoones sent vnto them to know that if he should come himselfe and giue his word, that they should haue their pardon, whether they Pardon once againe offered. would receiue it or not. Herevnto they answered, that they had such confidence in his honor, that if he would so doo, they would giue credit thereto, and submit them-selues to the kings mercie. Incontinentlie herevpon he went vnto them, and com-manded Norreie to read the kings pardon fréelie granted to all that would yéeld. They yéeld to the earle of Warwike. Which being read, euerie man threw downe his weapon, and with one whole and entier voice cried ; God saue king Edward, God saue king Edward. And thus thorough the prudent policie, and fauourable mercie of the erle of Warwike, a great number of those offendors were preserued from the gates of death, into the which they were readie to enter.

Thus were the Norffolke rebels subdued by the high prowesse, wisedome, and poli-cie of the valiant earle of Warwike, and other the nobles, gentlemen, & faithfull sub- Gentlemen slaine in this rebellion. iects there in the kings armie: but not without losse of diuers personages of great worship, beside other of the meaner sort, namelie master Henrie Willoughbie esquier, a man so well beloued in his countrie for his liberalitie in housekéeping, great courtesie, vpright dealing, assured stedfastnes in friendship, & modest staiednes in behauiour, that the countries where his liuings laie lament the losse of so woorthie a gentleman euen to this daie. There died also master Lucie esquier, master Forster esquier, and master Throckmorton of Northamptonshire, gentlemen of no small credit and worship in their countries. The battell being thus ended, all the spoile gotten in the field was giuen to the soldiers, who sold the most part thereof openlie in the market place of Norwich. The next daie the earle of Warwike was aduertised that Ket, being crept Ket taken. into a barne, was taken by two seruants of one master Riches of Swanington, and brought to the house of the same Riches. Herevpon were twentie horssemen sent thither to fetch him, who brought him to Norwich. The same daie examinations were taken of them that were the principall beginners and setters foorth of this vn-happie rebellion, and diuerse being found giltie were hanged, and nine of the chiefest Execution. procurers of all the mischiefe (Robert Ket and his brother William onelie excepted) were hanged vpon the oke of reformation, Miles the gunner & two of their prophets being three of that number.

Some others of them were drawne, hanged, and quartered, & their heads and quar-ters set vp in publike places for a terror to others. But yet the earle of Warwike The earle of Warwike shew-eth mercie. spared manie, where some would gladlie haue persuaded him, that there might haue béene a great number more executed. But his lordship perceiuing them importunate in that vncharitable sute, told them (as it were in fauour of life of those sillie wretches, whose miserable case he séemed to pitie) that measure must be vsed in all things, & in
punishing

punishing of men by death (saith he) " we ought alwaies to beware that we passe not the same.   I know well that such wicked dooings deserue no small reuenge, and that the offendors are woorthie to be most sharplie chastised.   But how farre yet shall we go? Shall we not at length shew some mercie? Is there no place for pardon? What shall we then doo? Shall we hold the plough our selues; plaie the carters and labour the ground with our owne hands." These and such like words tasting altogither of mercie and compassion in that noble earle, did quench the cruell desire of reuenge in them that were altogither kindled in wrath and wished nothing more than to see the whole multitude executed: but now moued with the earles wise and mercifull answer to their rigorous sute, they became more mild and mercifull towards the miserable creatures.

This also is not to be forgotten, that when information was giuen against some of the rebels, for that they had beene busie fellowes, & great dooers in time of those vprores, so as it was thought of some, that it stood with good reason to haue them punished by death, when the earle of Warwike vnderstood by credible report of Norreie king at armes, that vpon the offer of the kings pardon, they were the first that threw downe their weapons, and submitted themselues to the kings mercie, the earle would not in anie wise consent that they should die, but protested frankelie that he would kéepe promise with them, and that he would be as good to them as his word : and so

The slaine carcases buried. they had their liues saued.   The same daie was order giuen by the earle that the bodies of them that were slaine in the field should be buried.   On the morrow being the nine and twentith of August, the earle of Warwike, with the nobles and gentlemen of the armie, and others in great numbers, both men and women, went to saint Peters church, and there gaue praises and thanks to God for the victorie obteined.   And this doone he with all the armie departed out of the citie, and returned homewards with high commendation of citizens & others, that acknowledged the said earle to be the defendor of their liues, and recouerer of their wiues, children, houses and liuings.

It was afterwards ordeined, that vpon the same daie in the which the rebles were thus subdued, the citizens yearelie should repaire to their churches, and there to heare seruice, and to haue a sermon abrode, to the which they should come togither, to giue thanks to God for their deliuerance as that daie, and this is obserued till these our times.

The two Kets executed. Robert Ket and his brother William Ket were brought vp to London, where they were committed to the tower, and shortlie after arreigned of their treason and found guiltie, were brought to the tower againe, where they continued till the nine and twentith of Nouember, on which daie they were deliuered to sir Edmund Windham high shiriffe of Norffolke and Suffolke, to be conueied downe into Norffolke, where Robert Ket was hanged in chains vpon the top of Norwich castell : and William Ket his brother on the top of Windmondham stéeple, in which towne they had both dwelled, and conspired with others to go forward with their wicked rebellion.

William Ket a dissembling traitor. This William Ket (as was thought) had beene sure of his pardon, if he had not plaied the traitorous hypocrite : for vpon his submission at the first to my lord marquesse of Northampton, at his comming downe to suppresse this rebellion, he was sent to his brother to persuade him and the rest to yéeld, and receiue the kings pardon : but he (like a dissembling wretch, although he promised to my lord to doo what he could in that behalfe) vpon his comming to his brother into the rebels campe, & beholding the great multitude that were there about him, he did not onelie not dissuade him and them from their traitorous rebellion, but incouraged them to persist and continue in their dooings, declaring what a small number of souldiers the marquesse brought with him, nothing able to resist such a puissance as was there assembled.   So that if it had not beene thorough the wicked persuasion of him, and some others at that time, not onelie Robert Ket himselfe, but also all the multitude beside, would

haue

haue submitted themselues, and receiued the kings pardon, to the preseruation of manie a good mans life that after died in the quarrell.

But now to returne somewhat backe to the dooings in Scotland. In the meane while that such hurls were in hand here in England, ye shall vnderstand that in the beginning of this summer, the king by aduise of his councell sent foorth a nauie by sea towards Scotland, the which arriuing in the Forth, and comming before Lieth, saluted the towne with cannon shot, & remaining there ten or twelue daies, tooke in the meane time the Ile of Insketh, leauing therein foure ensignes of Englishmen, and Insketh taken. one of Italians, with certeine pioners to fortifie the place. But the Frenchmen (as in the Scotish historie yée shall find more at large) after the departure of the English nauie, recouered that Ile againe out of the Englishmens possession (after they had kept it sixtéene daies) with the slaughter of capteine Cotton their generall, capteine Ap- plebie, & one Iasper that was capteine of the Italians, beside others. After the re- Monsieur de Desse returneth into France. couering of this Ile, monsieur de Desse returned into France, leauing his charge to monsieur de Thermes latelie before there arriued: who after the departure of the said Desse, with a campe volant did what he could to stop the Englishmen within Hading- ton from vittels. But notwithstanding the earle of Rutland being lieutenant of the The earle of Rutland. north, did not onlie vittell it, but put the French armie in danger of an ouerthrow, as it was thought must néeds haue folowed, if they had not with more spéed than is vsed in a common march slipt awaie after they perceiued the English armie so neare at their elbowes.

Moreouer, beside these inordinate vprores and insurrections aboue mentioned, about M. Fox. the latter end of the said moneth of Iulie, in the same yeare, which was 1549, an An other re- bellion or tumult other like sturre or commotion began at Semer in the northriding of Yorkeshire, and begun in Yorke- shire. continued in the eastriding of the same, and there ended. The principall dooers and raisers vp whereof, was one William Ombler of Easthesserton yeoman, and Thomas The chiefe Dale parish clearke of Semer, with one Stéeuenson of Semer, neighbour to Dale and stirrers of this nephue to Ombler, which Stéeuenson was a meane or messenger betwéene the said rebellion. Ombler and Dale, being before not acquainted togither, and dwelling seuen miles one from the other: who at last by the trauell of the said Stéeuenson, and their owne euill dispositions, inclined to vngratiousnesse and mischiefe, knowing before one the others mind by secret conference, were brought to talke togither on saint Iames daie, Anno 1549.

The causes moouing them to raise this rebellion, were these. First & principally The causes their traitorous harts grudging at the kings most godlie procéeding, in aduancing moouing the Yorkshiremen and reforming the true honour of God and his religion. An other cause also was, to rebellion. for trusting to a blind and a fantasticall prophesie, wherwith they were seduced, thinking the same prophesie shuld shortlie come to passe, by hearing the rebellions of Norffolke, of Deuonshire, and other places. The tenour of which prophesie and purpose togither of the traitors was, that there should no king reigne in England, the A blind prophe- noblemen and gentlemen to be destroied, and the realme to be ruled by foure gouer- sie among the nours, to be elécted and appointed by the commons, holding a parlement in commo- northerne men. tion, to begin at the south and north seas of England, supposing that this rebellion in the north, and the other of the Deuonshire men in the west, méeting (as they in- The deuise of tended) at one place, to be the meane how to compasse this their traitorous diuelish the rebels how deuise. And therfore laieng their studies togither, how to find out more companie to to compasse ioine with them in that detestable purpose, and to set forward the sturre, this deuise their purpose. they framed: to sturre in two places, the one distant seuen miles from the other, and at the first rush to kill and destroie such gentlemen and men of substance about them as were fauourers of the kings proceedings, or which would resist them.

But first of all for the more spéedie raising of men, they deuised to burne beacons, & thereby to bring the people togither, as though it were to defend the sea coasts: and hauing the ignorant people assembled, then to powre out their poison, first beginning with the rudest and poorest sort, such as they thought were pricked with pouertie, and were vnwilling to labor, and therefore the more readie to follow the spoile of rich mens goods, blowing into their heads that Gods seruice was laid aside, and new inuentions neither good nor godlie put in place, and so feeding them with faire promises, to reduce into the church againe their old ignorance and idolatrie, thought by that means soonest to allure them to rage and run with them in this commotion. And furthermore, to the

The deuise of the rebels that they might be feared.

intent they would giue the more terror to the gentlemen at the first rising, least they should be resisted, they deuised that some should be murthered in churches, some in their houses, some in seruing the king in commission, and other as they might be caught, and to picke quarels at them by alteration of seruice on the holie daies: and thus was the platforme cast of their deuise, according as afterward by their confession at their examinations was testified, and remaineth in true record.

Thus they being togither agréed, Ombler and Dale, with others, by their secret appointment, so laboured the matter in the parish of Semer, Wintringham, and the townes about, that they were infected with the poison of this confederacie, in such sort that it was easie to vnderstand wheruͣto they would incline, if a commotion were begun, the accomplishment whereof did shortlie follow. For although by the words of one drunken fellow of that conspiracie named Caluerd, at the alehouse in Wintringham, some suspicion of that rebellion began to be smelled before by the lord president and gentlemen of those parties, and so preuented in that place where the rebels thought to begin: yet they gaue not ouer so, but drew to another place at Semer by the seacoast, and there by night rode to the beacon at Straxton, and set it on fire, and so gathering togither a rude rout of rascals out of the townes neare about, being on a sturre, Ombler, Thomas Dale, Barton, and Robert Dale, hasted foorthwith with the rebels to maister Whites house to take him: who notwithstanding being on horssebacke, minding, to haue escaped their hands, Dale, Ombler, and the rest of the rebels tooke him, and Clopton his wiues brother, one Sauage a merchant of Yorke, and one Berrie seruant to sir Walter Mildmaie. Which foure without cause or quarell, sauing to fulfill their seditious prophesie in some part, and to giue a terror to other gentlemen, they cruellie murthered, after they had caried them one mile from Semer towards the Wold, and there after they had stripped them of their clothes & purses, left them naked behind them in the plaine fields for crowes to feed on: vntill Whites wife and Sauages wife, then at Semer, caused them to bée buried.

The rebels increase their number & rebellious band.

Long it were and tedious to recite what reuell these rebels kept in their raging madnesse, who ranging about the countrie from towne to towne, to inlarge their vngratious and rebellious band, taking those with force which were not willing to go, & leauing in no towne where they came anie man aboue the age of sixtéene yeares, so increased this number, that in short time they had gathered three thousand to fauour their wicked attempts, and had like to haue gathered more, had not the Lords goodnesse through prudent circumspection of some interrupted the course of their furious

The kings pardon offered, receiued, refused.

beginning. For first came the kings gratious and frée pardon, discharging & pardoning all them and the rest of the rebels, of all treasons, murthers, felonies, & other offenses doone to his maiestie before the one & twentith of August, 1549. Which pardon although Ombler contemptuouslie reading, persisted still in his wilfull obstinacie, dissuaded also the rest from the humble accepting of the kings so louing & liberall pardon: yet notwithstanding with some it did good, who of likelihood submitted themselues, assuredlie belieuing if they perseuered in their enterprise, there was no way with them but one, namelie deserued death, wherewith there was no dispensing after the contempt of the princes pardon and refusall of his mercie; so that in this heauie case they might verie well complaine and saie:

Funditùs occidimus, nec habet fortuna regressum.

Virgil.

To

To make short, it was not long after this, but Ombler as he was riding from towne to towne, twelue miles from Hummanbie, to charge all the conestables and inhabitants where he came, in the kings name to resort to Hummanbie : by the waie he was espied, and by the circumspect diligence of Iohn Word the yoonger, Iames Aslabeie, Rafe Twinge, and Thomas Conestable gentlemen, hée was had in chase, and at last by them apprehended, and brought in the night in sure custodie vnto the citie of Yorke, to answer vnto his demerits.   After whome within short time, Thomas Dale, Henrie Barton, the first chiefteins and ringleaders of the former commotion, with Iohn Dale, Robert Wright, William Pecocke, Weatherell, and Edmund Buttrie, busie stirrers in this sedition, as they trauelled from place to place, to draw people to their faction, were likewise apprehended, committed to ward, lawfullie conuicted, and lastlie executed at Yorke the one and twentith of September, in the yere of our Lord 1549.   Ex actis iudicij publici a registro exceptis & notatis.

Ombler capteine of the rebels taken.

The names of the rebels taken and executed at Yorke.

Whilest these wicked commotions and tumults through the rage of the vndiscréet commons were thus raised in sundrie parts of the realme, to the great hinderance of the common-wealth, losse and danger of euerie good and true subiect, sundrie wholsome and godlie exhortations were published, to aduertise them of their dutie, and to laie before them their heinous offenses ; with the sequele of the mischiefs that necessarilie followed thereof, the which if they should consider togither, with the punishment that hanged ouer their heads, they might easilie be brought to repent their lewd begun enterprises, and submit themselues to the kings mercie.   Among other of those admonitions, one was penned and set forth by sir Iohn Chéeke which I haue thought good here to insert, as a necessarie discourse for euerie good English subiect.   Wherein to a reader of iudgement and capacitie, such learning and wisedome, with a true loiall subiects heart bewraieth it selfe to haue béene setled in that gentleman; as the verie reading of this treatise is able to turne a rebellious mind to méekenesse: if reason be not altogither led awaie captiue by lust.

¶ The hurt of sedition how greeuous it is to a common-wealth, set out by sir Iohn Cheeke knight, in the yeare 1549.

The true subiect to the rebell.

Among so manie and notable benefits, wherewith God hath alreadie and plentifullie indued vs, there is nothing more beneficiall, than that we haue by his grace kept vs quiet from rebellion at this time.   For we see such miseries hang ouer the whole state of the common-wealth, through the great misorder of your sedition, that it maketh vs much to reioise, that we haue béene neither partners of your doings, not conspirers of your counsels.   For euen as the Lacedemonians for the auoiding of drunkennesse did cause their sons to behold their seruants when they were drunke, that by beholding their beastlinesse, they might auoid the like vice: euen so hath God like a mercifull father staied vs from your wickednesse, that by beholding the filth of your fault, we might iustlie for offense abhorre you like rébels, whome else by nature we loue like Englishmen.   And so for our selues, we haue great cause to thanke God, by whose religion and holie word dailie taught vs, we learne not onelie to feare him trulie, but also to obeie our king faithfullie, and to serue in our owne vocation like subiects honestlie. And as for you, we haue suerlie iust cause to lament you as brethren, and yet iuster cause to rise against you as enimies, and most iust cause to ouerthrow you as rebels. For what hurt could be doone either to vs priuatlie, or to the whole common-wealth generallie, that is now with mischiefe so brought in by you, that euen as we sée now

What the Lacedemonians did to make their sons detest drunkennesse.

the flame of your rage, so shall we necessarilie be consumed hereafter with the miserie of the same. Wherefore consider your selues with some light of vnderstanding, and marke this gréeuous and horrible fault, which ye haue thus vilelie committed, how heinous it must néeds appeare to you, if ye will reasonablie consider that which for my duties sake, and my whole countries cause, I will at this present declare vnto you. Ye which be bound by Gods word not to obeie for feare like men-pleasers, but for conscience sake like christians, haue contrarie to Gods holie will, whose offense is euerlasting death, and contrarie to the godlie order of quietnesse, set out to vs in the kings maiesties lawes, the breach whereof is not vnknowne to you, taken in hand vncalled of God, vnsent by men, vnfit by reason, to cast awaie your bounden duties of obedience, and to put on you against the magistrats, Gods office committed to the magistrats, for the reformation of your pretensed iniuries. In the which dooing ye haue first faulted grieuouslie against God, next offended vnnaturallie our soueraigne lord, thirdlie troubled miserablie the whole common-wealth, vndoone cruellie manie an honest man, and brought in an vtter miserie both to vs the kings subiects, and to your selues being false rebels. And yet ye pretend that partlie for Gods cause, and partlie for the common-wealths sake, ye doo arise, when as your selues cannot denie; but ye that seeke in word Gods cause, doo breake in déed Gods commandements; and ye that séeke the common-wealth, haue destroied the common-wealth: and so ye marre that ye would make, and brake that ye would amend, because ye neither seeke anie thing rightlie, nor would amend anie thing orderlie.

Rebellion a verie gréeuous and horrible offense against God, the prince, and the state.

He that faulteth, faulteth against Gods ordinance, who hath forbidden all faults, and therefore ought againe to be punished by Gods ordinance, who is the reformer of faults. For he saith, Leaue the punishment to me, and I will reuenge them. But the magistrate is the ordinance of God, appointed by him with the sword of punishment to looke streightlie to all euill dooers. And therefore that that is doone by the magistrate is doone by the ordinance of God, whome the scripture oftentimes dooth call God, because he has the execution of Gods office. How then doo you take in hand to reforme? Be ye kings? By what authoritie? Or by what occasion? Be ye the kings officers? By what commission? Be ye called of God? By what tokens declare ye that? Gods word teacheth vs, that no man should take in hand anie office, but he that is called of God like Aaron. What Moses I praie you called you? What Gods minister bad you rise?

The authoritie of the magistrats great and peremptorie.

Ye rise for religion. What religion taught you that? If ye were offered persecution for religion, ye ought to flie: so Christ teacheth you, and yet you intend to fight. If ye would stand in the truth, ye ought to suffer like martyrs, and you would sleie like tyrants. Thus for religion you kéepe no religion, and neither will follow the counsell of Christ, nor the constancie of martyrs. Why rise ye for religion? Haue ye anie thing contrarie to Gods booke? Yea, haue ye not all things agréeable to Gods word? But the new is different from the old, and therefore ye will haue the old. If ye measure the old by truth, ye haue the oldest; if ye measure the old by fansie, then it is hard: because mens fansies change, to giue that is old. Ye will haue the old still. Will ye haue anie older than that as Christ left, & his apostles taught, & the first church after Christ did vse? Ye will haue that the chanons doo establish. Why that is a great deale yoonger than that ye haue, of later time, and newlier inuented. Yet that is it that ye desire. Why then ye desire not the oldest. And doo you preferre the bishops of Rome afore Christ, mens inuentions afore Gods law, the newer sort of worship before the older? Ye séeke no religion, ye be deceiued, ye séeke traditions. They that teach you, blind you, that so instruct you, deceiue you. If ye séeke what the old doctors saie, yet looke what Christ the oldest of all saith. For he saith; Before Abraham was made I am. If ye seeke the truest way, he is the verie truth; if ye

Rebellion vnlawfull in defense of true religion, *Ergo* much more vnlawfull in maintenance of false religion, &c.

ye séeke the readiest waie, he is the verie waie; if ye séeke euerlasting life, he is the verie life. What religion would ye haue other now, than his religion?

You would haue the bibles in againe. It is no maruell, your blind guides would lead you blinde still. Why, be ye howlets and backs, that ye cannot looke on the light? Christ saith to euerie one, Search ye the scriptures, for they beare witnesse of Christ. You saie, Pull in the scriptures, for we will haue no knowledge of Christ. The apostles of Christ will vs to be so readie, that we maie be able to giue euerie man an account of our faith. Ye will vs not once to read the scriptures, for feare of knowing of our faith. Saint Paul praieth that euerie man may increase in knowledge: ye desire that our knowledge might decaie againe. A true religion ye séeke belike, and worthie to be fought for. For without the sword indéed nothing can helpe it, neither Christ, nor truth, nor age can mainteine it. But why should ye not like that which Gods word establisheth, the primitiue church hath authorised, the greatest learned men of this realme haue drawen, the whole consent of the parlement hath confirmed, the kings maiestie hath set foorth? Is it not trulie set out? Can ye deuise anie truer than Christes apostles vsed? Ye thinke it is not learnedlie doone. Dare ye commons take vpon you more learning, than the chosen bishops and clearks of this realme haue? Thinke ye follie in it? Ye were woont to iudge your parlement wisest, & now will ye suddenlie excell them in wisdome? Or can ye thinke it lacketh authoritie, which the king, the parlement, the learned, the wise haue iustlie approoued? Learne, learne, to know this one point of religion, that God will be worshipped as he hath prescribed, and not as we haue deuised; and that his will is wholie in his scriptures, which be full of Gods spirit, and profitable to teach the truth, to reprooue lies, to amend faults, to bring one vp in righteousnesse, that he that is a Gods man may be perfect & readie to all good works. What can be more required to serue God withall? And thus much for religion, rebels.

The necessarie benefit and vse of the bible, and contrariwise.

A principall point of religion for rebels speciallie to learne.

The other rable of Norffolke rebelles, ye pretend a common-wealth. How amend ye it? By killing of gentlemen, by spoiling of gentlemen, by imprisoning of gentlemen? A maruellous tanned common-wealth. Whie should ye thus hate them? For their riches or for their rule? Rule they neuer tooke so much in hand as ye doo now. They neuer resisted the king, neuer withstood his councell, be faithfull at this daie when ye be faithlesse, not onelie, to the king, whose subiects ye be, but also to your lords whose tenants ye be. Is this your true duetie, in some of homage, in most of fealtie, in all of allegiance; to leaue your duties, go backe from your promises, fall from your faith, and contrarie to law and truth to make vnlawfull assemblies, vngodlie companies, wicked and detestable campes, to disobeie your betters, and to obeie your tanners, to change your obedience from a king to a Ket, to submit your selues to traitors, and breake your faith to your true king and lords? They rule but by law, if otherwise, the law, the councell, the king taketh awaie their rule. Ye haue orderlie sought no redresse, but ye haue in time found it. In countries some must rule, some must obeie, euerie man maie not beare like stroke: for euerie man is not like wise. And they that haue séene most, and be best able to beare it, and of iust dealing beside, be most fit to rule. It is an other matter to vnderstand a mans owne gréefe, and to know the common-wealths sore; and therfore not they that know their owne case, as euerie man doth, but they that vnderstand the common-welths state, ought to haue in countries the preferment of ruling. If ye felt the paine that is ioined with gouernance, as ye see and like the honor, ye would not hurt others to rule them, but rather take great paine to be ruled of them. If ye had rule of the kings maiestie committed vnto you, it were well doone ye had ruled the gentlemen: but now ye haue it not, and cannot beare their rule, it is to thinke the kings maiestie foolish and vniust, that hath giuen certeine rule to them. And séeing by the scripture, ye ought not to speake

The rebelles of Norffolke pretended the common-wealth the cause of their rising.

Whie all must not looke to beare like rule.

euill

Magistrates are to be honored both in speech and maners.

euill of anie magistrate of the people, why doo ye not onelie speake euill of them whome the kings maiestie hath put in office, but also iudge euill of the king himselfe, and thus seditiouslie in field stand with your swords drawen against him?

If riches offend you, because yee wish the like, then thinke that to be no common-wealth, but enuie to the common-wealth. Enuie it is to appaire an other mans estate, without the amendment of your owne. And to haue no gentlemen, bicause ye be none your selues, is to bring downe an estate, and to mend none. Would ye haue all alike rich? That is the ouerthrow of labour, and vtter decay of worke in this realme.

To haue all de-grees alike, & no inequalitie how inconue-nient.

For who will labour more, if when he hath gotten more, the idle shall by lust with-out right take what him lust from him, vnder pretense of equalitie with him. This is the bringing in of idlenesse, which destroieth the common-wealth; and not the amendment of labour, that mainteineth the common-wealth. If there should be such equalitie, then ye take awaie all hope from yours to come to anie better estate than you now leaue them. And as manie meane mens children doo come honestlie vp, and are great succour to all their stocke: so should none be hereafter holpen by you, but bicause ye seeke equalitie, whereby all can not be rich. Ye would that (belike) whereby euerie man should be poore; and thinke beside that riches and inheritance be Gods

Riches and in-heritance from whom, to whom, and to what end giuen.

prouidence, and giuen to whome of his wisdome he thinketh good: to the honest for the increase of their godlinesse, to the wicked for the heaping vp of their damnation, to the simple for a recompense of other lackes, to the wise for the greater setting out of Gods goodnesse. Whie will your wisdome now stop Gods wisdome, and prouide by your lawes, that God shall not inrich them, whome he hath by prouidence appointed as him liketh? God hath made the poore, & hath made them to be poore that he might shew his might, and set them aloft when he listeth for such cause as to him seemeth, & plucke downe the rich to this state of pouertie by his power, as he disposeth to order them. Whie doo not we then being poore beare it wiselie, rather than by lust seeke riches vniustlie, and shew our selues content with Gods ordinance, which we must either willinglie obeie, and then we be wise, or else we must vnprofitablie striue with-all, and then we be mad?

The vncon-scionable wish-ing of equalitie how hurtfull.

But what meane yee by this equalitie in the common-wealth? If one be wiser than an other, will ye banish him, because yee intend an equalitie of all things? If one be stronger than an other, will yee slaie him, bicause ye seeke an equalitie of all things? If one be well fauourder than an other, will yee punish him, because yee looke for an equalitie of all things? If one haue better vtterance than an other, will ye pull out his toong to saue your equalitie? And if one be richer than an other, will ye spoile him to mainteine an equalitie? If one be elder than an other, will ye kill him for this equalities sake? How iniurious are ye to God himselfe, who intendeth to bestow his gifts as he himselfe listeth: and ye seeke by wicked insurrections to make him giue them commonlie alike to all men as your vaine fansie liketh? Whie would ye haue an equalitie in riches & in other gifts of God? There is no meane sought. Either by ambition ye seeke lordlinesse much vnfit for you; or by couetousnesse ye be vnsatiable, a thing likelie inough in ye; or else by follie ye be not content with your estate, a fansie to be plucked out of you.

The precept of S. Peter teach-ing the right waie to riches and honor.

But if we being wearie of pouertie would seeke to inrich our selues, we should go a farre other waie to worke than this, and so should we rightlie come to our desire. Dooth not S. Peter teach vs afore God a right waie to honour, to riches, to all neces-sarie and profitable things for vs? He saith, Humble your selues that God might exalt you, and cast all your care on him, for he careth for you. He teacheth the waie to all good things at Gods hand, is to be humble, and you exalt your selues. Ye seeke things after such a sort, as if the seruant should anger his master, when he seeketh to haue a good turne of him. Ye would haue riches (I thinke) at Gods hand who giueth all riches, and yet ye take the waie cleane contrarie to riches. Know ye not that he that

exalteth

exalteth himselfe, God will throw him downe? How can ye get it then by thus setting out your selues? Ye shuld submit ye by humilitie one to another, and ye set vp your selues by arrogancie aboue the magistrates. See herein how much ye offend God. Remember ye not that if ye come nigh to God, he will come nigh vnto you? If then ye go from God, he will go from you. Dooth not the psalme saie, He is holie with the holie, and with the wicked man he is froward? Euen as he is ordered of men, he will order them againe. If ye would follow his will, and obeie his commandements, ye should eat the fruits of the earth, saith the prophet; if not, the sword shall deuour you. Ye might haue eaten the fruits of this seasonable yéere, if ye had not by disobedience rebelled against God. Now not onelie ye can not eat that which your selues did first sowe by labour, and now destroie by sedition; but also if the kings maiesties sword came not against you, as iust policie requireth, yet the iust vengeance of God would light among you, as his word promiseth, and your cruell wickednesse deserueth.

For whatsoeuer the causes be that haue mooued your wild affections herin, as they be vniust causes, & increase your faults much, the thing it selfe, the rising I meane, must néeds be wicked and horrible before God, and the vsurping of authoritie, and taking in hand of rule, which is the sitting in Gods seat of iustice, and a proud climbing vp into Gods high throne, must néeds be not onelie cursed newlie by him, but also hath béene often punished afore of him. And that which is doone to Gods officer, God accounteth it doone to him. For they despise not the minister, as he saith himselfe, but they despise him: and that presumption of chalenging Gods seat, dooth shew you to haue bin Lucifers, and sheweth vs that God will punish you like Lucifers. Wherefore rightlie looke, as ye dulie haue deserued, either for great vengeance for your abhominable transgression, or else earnestlie repent, with vnfeined minds, your wicked dooings; and either with example of death be content to dehort other, or else by faithfulnesse of obedience declare how great a seruice it is to God, to obeie your magistrats faithfullie, and to serue in subiection trulie.

The act of rebellion aggrauated, & prooued most wicked and horrible.

An exhortation to rebels.

Well, if ye had not thus grieuouslie offended God, whome ye ought to worship, what can ye reasonablie thinke it, to be no fault against the king, whom ye ought to reuerence? Ye be bound by Gods word to obeie your king, and is it no breach of dutie to withstand your king? If the seruant be bound to obeie his maister in the familie, is not the subiect bound to serue the king in his realme? The child is bound to the priuat father, and be we not all bound to the common-wealths father? If we ought to be subiect to the king for Gods cause, ought we not then I praie you to be faithfullie subiect to the king? If we ought dutifullie to shew all obedience to heathen kings, shall we not willinglie and trulie be subiect to christian kings? If one ought to submit himselfe by humilitie to another, ought we not all by dutie to be subiect to our king? If the members of our naturall bodie all follow the head, shall not the members of the politicall bodie all obeie the king? If good maners be content to giue place the lower to the higher, shall not religion teach vs alwaie to giue place to the highest? If true subiects will die gladlie in the kings seruice, should not all subiects thinke it dutie to obeie the king with iust seruice. But you haue not onelie disobeied like ill subiects, but also taken stoutlie rule vpon you like wicked magistrates.

Disobedience to the prince is a most abhominable sinne, and that we are bound by dutie to obeie.

Ye haue béene called to obedience by counsell of priuat men, by the aduise of the kings maiesties councell, by the kings maiesties frée pardon. But what counsell taketh place, where sturdinesse is law and churlish answers be counted wisdome? Who can persuade where treason is aboue reason, and might ruleth right, and it is had for lawfull whatsoeuer is lustfull, and commotioners are better than commissioners, and common wo is named common-wealth? Haue ye not broken his lawes, disobeied his councell, rebelled against him? And what is the common-wealth worth, when the law which is indifferent for all men, shall be wilfullie and spitefullie broken of headstrong men, that séeke against laws to order lawes; that those may take place not what

A notable and rhetoricall clause, and to the purpose.

what consent of wise men hath appointed, but what the lust of rebels hath deter-

mined? What vnthriftinesse is in ill seruants, wickednes in vnnaturall children, sturdinesse in vnrulie subiects, crueltie in fierce enimies, wildnes in beastlie minds, pride in disdainfull harts; that floweth now in you, which haue fled from housed conspiracies, to incamped robberies, and are better contented to suffer famine, cold, trauell, to glut your lusts than to liue in quietnesse to saue the common-wealth, and thinke more libertie in wilfullnesse, than wisedome in dutifulnesse, and so run headlong not to the mischiefe of other, but to the destruction of your selues, and vndoo by follie that ye intend by mischiefe, neither séeing how to remedie that ye iudge faultie, nor willing to saue your selues from miserie: which stifneckednesse cannot doo, but honestie of obedience must frame.

If authoritie would serue vnder a king, the councell haue greatest authoritie; if wisedome and grauitie might take place, they be of most experience; if knowledge of the common-wealth could helpe, they must by dailie conference of matters vnder-stand it best: yet neither the authoritie that the kings maiestie hath giuen them, nor the grauitie which you know to be in them, nor the knowledge which with great trauell they haue gotten, can mooue you either to kéepe you in the dutie ye ought to doo, or to auoid the great disorder wherin ye be. For where disobedience is thought stoutnesse, and sullennes is counted manhood, and stomaching is courage, and prating is iudged wisedome, and the eluishest is most méet to rule; how can other iust authoritie be obeied, or sad counsell be followed, or good knowledge of matters be heard, or commandements of counsellors be considered? And how is the king obeied, whose wisest be withstanded, the disobedientest obeied, the high in authoritie not weied, the vnskilfullest made chiefe capteins, to the noblest most hurt intended, the braggingest braller to be most safe? And euen as the viler parts of the bodie would contend in knowledge & gouernement with the fiue wits: so doo the lower parts of the common-wealth enterprise as high a matter, to striue against their dutie of obedience to the councell.

But what talke I of disobedience so quietlie? Haue not such mad rages run in your heads, that forsaking and bursting the quietnesse of the common peace, ye haue heinouslie and traitorouslie incamped your selues in field, and there like a bile in a bodie, naie like a sinke in a towne, haue gathered togither all the nastie vagabonds and idle loiterers to beare armour against him, whome all godlie and good subiects will liue and die withall. If it be a fault when two fight togither, and the kings peace broken, and punishment to be sought therefore; can it be but an outragious and a detestable mischiefe, when so manie rebels in number, malicious in mind, mischiefous in enterprise, fight not among themselues, but against all the kings true and obedient subiects; and séeke to proue whether rebellion may beat downe honestie, and wick-ednesse may ouercome truth or no? If it be treason to speake heinouslie of the kings maiestie, who is not hurt thereby, and the infamie returneth to the speaker againe; what kind of outragious & horrible treason is it, to assemble in campe an armie against him, and so not onelie intend an ouerthrow to him, and also to his common-wealth; but also to cast him into an infamie, through all outward and strange nations, and per-suade them that he is hated of his people, whome he can not rule; and that they be no better than vilans, which will not with good orders be ruled?

What death can be deuised cruell enough for those rebels, who with trouble séeke death, and can not quench the thirst of their rebellion, but with the bloud of true subiects; and hate the kings mercifull pardon, when they miserablie haue transgressed, and in such an outrage of mischiefe will not by stubbornesse acknowledge themselues to haue faulted, but intend to broile the common-wealth with the flame of their treason, and as much as lieth in them not onelie to annoie themselues, but to destroie all others? He that is miscontented with things that happen, and bicause he cannot beare the

miserie

miserie of them, renteth his heare, and teareth his skin, & mangleth his face, which A desperat malecontents behauiour. easeth not his sorrow, but increaseth his miserie; maie he not be iustlie called mad and fantasticall, and woorthie whose wisedome should be suspected? And what shall we saie of them, who being in the common-wealth, feeling a sore greeuous vnto them, and easie to haue béene amended, sought not the remedie, but haue increased the gréefe, and like frantike beasts raging against their head, doo teare and deface as much as lieth in them his whole authoritie in gouernement, and violentlie take to themselues that rule vpon them, which he by policie hath granted vnto other?

And who weieng well the heauinesse of the fault, maie not iustlie saie and hold Rebels and traitors worse than brute beasts. them to be worse herein than any kind of brute beasts? For we sée that the sheepe will obeie the shepheard, and the neat be ruled by the neatherd, and the horsse will know his keeper, and the dog will be in aw of his maister, and euerie one of them féed there, and of that, as his kéeper and ruler dooth appoint him, & goeth from thence, and that, as he is forbidden by his ruler. And yet we haue not heard of, that anie heard or companie of these haue risen against their heardman or gouernour, but be alwaies contented not onelie to obeie them, but also to suffer them to take profit of them. And we sée furthermore, that all heards, & all sorts, be more egre in fiercenesse against all kind of strangers, than they be against their owne rulers, & will easilier offend him who hath not hurt them, than touch their ruler who séeketh profit on them.

But ye that ought to be gouerned by your magistrates, as the heards by the heard- The application of the former comparisons impliyeng obedience. man, and ought to be like shéepe to your king, who ought to be like a shéepeheard vnto you, euen in the time when your profit was sought, and better redresse was intended, that your vpstirs and vnquietnesse could obteine, haue beyond the crueltie of all beasts fowlie risen against your ruler, and shewed your selues worthie to be ordered like beasts, who in kind of obedience will fall from the state of men. A dog stoopeth when he is beaten of his maister, not for lacke of stomach, but for naturall obedience: you being not striken of your head but fauoured, not kept downe but succoured and remedied by law, haue violentlie against law not onelie barked like beasts, but also bitten like helhounds. What? Is the mischiefe of sedition either not knowne vnto you, or not feared? Haue not examples aforetimes both told the end of rebels, and the wickednesse of rebellion it selfe? But as for old examples, let them passe for a while, as things well to be considered. But at this present one thing more to be weied.

Looke vpon your selues, after ye haue wickedlie stept into this horrible kind of The presumptuous & arrogant vsurped rule of the rebels noted to the impeachment of princelie prerogatiue. treason, doo ye not sée how manie bottomlesse whirlepooles of mischiefe yee be gulft withall, and what lothsome kinds of rebellion ye be faine to wade through? Ye haue sent out in the kings name, against the kings will, precepts of all kinds, & without commandement commanded his subiects, and vnrulilie haue ruled where yée listed to command, thinking your owne fansies the kings commandements, and rebels lusts in things to be right gouernement of things, not looking what should follow by reason, but what your selues follow by affection. And is it not a dangerous and a cruell kind of treason, to giue out precepts to the kings people? There can be no iust execution of lawes, reformation of faults, giuing out of commandements, but from the king. For in the king onelie is the right herof, & the authoritie of him deriued by his appointment to his ministers. Ye hauing no authoritie of the king, but taking it of your selues, what thinke ye your selues to be? Ministers ye be none, except ye be the diuels ministers, for he is the author of sedition.

The kings maiestie intendeth to mainteine peace, and to oppresse warre; ye stirre vp The rebels outragious and intollerable demeanor descried. vprores of people, hurliburlies of vagabonds, routs of robbers. Is this anie part of the kings ministerie? If a vagabond would doo what he lust, and call himselfe your seruant, and execute such offices of trust, whether yée would or no, as ye haue com-

mitted

mitted vnto another mans credit, what would euerie one of you saie or doo herein? Would ye suffer it? Ye wander out of houses, ye make euerie daie new matters as it pleaseth you, ye take in hand the execution of those things, God by his word forbidding the same, which God hath put the magistrates in trust withall. What can ye saie to this? Is it sufferable thinke ye? If ye told a priuat message in another mans name, can it be but a false lie I praie you? And to tell a feined message to the common-wealth, and that from the king, can it be honest thinke ye? To command is more than to speake: what is it then to command so traitorous a lie? This then which is in word a deceitfull lie, and in déed a traitorous fact, noisome to the common-wealth, vnhonourable to the king, mischiefous in you, how can ye otherwise iudge of it, but to be an vnheard of and notable disobedience to the king: and therefore by notable example to be punished, and not with gentlenesse of pardon to be forgiuen? Ye haue robbed euerie honest house, and spoiled them vniustlie, and pitiouslie wronged poore men being no offendors, to their vtter vndooing, and yet ye thinke ye haue not broken the kings lawes. The kings maiesties law and his commandement is, that euerie man should safelie keepe his owne, and vse it reasonablie to an honest gaine of his liuing: ye violentlie take and carie awaie from men without cause, all things whereby they should mainteine, not onelie themselues, but also their familie, & leaue them so naked, that they shall féele the smart of your curssed enterprise, longer than your owne vnnaturall & vngodlie stomachs would well vouchsafe. By iustice ye should neither hurt nor wrong man, and your pretensed cause of this monstruous sturre is to increase mens wealth. And yet how manie, and saie truth, haue ye decaied and vndoone, by spoiling and taking awaie their goods? How should honest men liue quietlie in the common-wealth at anie time, if their goods, either gotten by their owne labor, or left to them by their friends, shall vnlawfullie and vnorderlie, to the féeding of a sort of rebels, be spoiled and wasted, and vtterlie scattered abrode? The thing that ye take is not your right, it is an other mans owne. The maner of taking against his will is vnlawfull, & against the order of euerie good common-wealth. The cause why ye take it is mischiefous and horrible, to fat your sedition. Ye that take it be wicked traitors, and common enimies of all good order.

Their disobedience notorious.

The rebels offend against the law of iustice & equitie.

The former matter vehementlie vrged.

If he that desireth an other mans goods or cattell, doo fault: what dooth he (thinke you) whose desire taking followeth, and is led to and fro by lust, as his wicked fansie void of reason dooth guide him? Hée that vseth not his owne well and charitablie, hath much to answer for: and shall they be thought not vniust, who not onelie take awaie other mens, but also misuse and wast the same vngodlie? They that take things priuilie awaie, and steale secretlie and couertlie other mens goods, be by law iudged worthie death: and shall they that without shame spoile things openlie, and be not affeard by impudencie to professe their spoile, be thought either honest creaturs to God, or faithfull subiects to their king, or naturall men to their countrie? If nothing had mooued you but the example of mischeefe, and the foule practise of other mooued by the same, ye should yet haue absteined from so licentious and vilanous a shew of robberie, considering how manie honester there be, that being loth their wickednesse should be blazed abrode, yet be found out by prouidence, and hanged for desert. What shall we then thinke or saie of you? Shall we call you pickers, or hid theeues; naie more than théeues, daie théeues, heard stealers, shire spoilers, and vtter destroiers of all kinds of families, both among the poore and also among the rich. Let vs yet further see. Be there no mo things wherein ye haue broken the kings laws, and so vilelie disobeie him, flat contrarie to your bounden dutie and allegiance?

The rebels are still charged with their rapines, and violentlie inferred wrongs.

Ye haue not onelie spoiled the kings true subiects of their goods, but also ye haue imprisoned their bodies, which should be at libertie vnder the king, and restreined them of their seruice, which by dutie they owe the king, and appaired both strength and health, wherewith they liue and serue the king. Is there anie honest thing more desired

Libertie desired aboue all things.

desired than libertie? Ye haue shamefullie spoiled them thereof. Is there anie thing more dutifull than to serue their lord and maister? But as that was desired of the one part, so was it hindered and stopped on your part. For neither can the king be serued, nor families kept, nor the common-wealth looked vnto, where fréedome of libertie is stopped, and diligence of seruice is hindered; and the helpe of strength and health abated. Mens bodies ought to be frée from all mens bondage and crueltie, and onelie in this realme be subiect in publike punishment to our publike gouernour, and neither be touched of * headlesse capteins, nor holden of brainlesse rebels. For the gouerne- ment of so pretious a thing ought to belong vnto the most noble ruler, and not iustlie to be in euerie mans power, which is iustlie euerie liuing mans treasure. For what goods be so deare to euerie man, as his owne bodie is, which is the true vessell of the mind, to be measurablie kept of euerie man for all exercises & seruices of the mind? If ye may not of your owne authoritie meddle with mens goods, much lesse you may of your owne authoritie take order with mens bodies.

* Fit epithets and terms for head and taile of this rebellion.

For what be goods in comparison of health, libertie, and strength, which be all setled and fastened in the bodie? They that strike other, doo greatlie offend, and be iustlie punishable: and shall they that cruellie and wrongfullie torment mens bodies with irons and imprisonments, be thought not of others but of themselues honest, and plaine, and truedealing men? What shall we say by them, who in a priuat businesse will let a man to go his iourneie in the kings high waie? Doo they not (thinke ye) plaine wrong? Then in a common cause not onelie to hinder them, but also to deale cruellie with them, and shut them from dooing their seruice to the king, and their dutie to the common-wealth, is it not both disobedience, crueltie, and mischiefe thinke ye? What an hinderance is it, to haue a good garment hurt, anie iewell appaired, or anie estéemed thing to be decaied? And séeing no earthlie thing a man hath is more pretious than his body, to cause it to be cruellie tormented with irons, feebled with cold, weakened with ordering: can it be thought anie other thing but wrong to the sufferer, crueltie in the dooer, & great disobedience and transgression to the king? How then be ye able to defend it? But séeing ye so vnpitifullie vexe men, cast them in prison, lade them with irons, pine them with famine, contrarie to the rule of nature, contrarie to the kings maiesties lawes, contrarie to Gods holie ordinances, hauing no matter but pretensed and fained gloses, ye be not onelie disobedient to the king like rebels, but withstanding the law of nature like beasts, and so worthie to die like dogs, except the kings maiestie, without respect of your deseruing, doo mercifullie grant you of his goodnesse that which you cannot escape by iustice.

The offense of excluding the kings subiects from the benefit of libertie aggra- uated.

A pithie con- clusion inferred vpon the pre- misses, in forme of sentence de- finitiue.

Yet ye being not content with this, as small things enterprise great matters, and as though ye could not satisfie your selues, if ye should leaue anie mischiefe vndoone, haue sought bloud with crueltie, and haue slaine of the kings true subiects manie, thinking their murder to be your defense, when as ye haue increased the fault of your vile rebellion, with the horror of bloudshed, and so haue burdened mischiefe with mischiefe, whilest it come to an importable weight of mischiefe. What could we doo more, in the horriblest kind of faults, vnto the greatest transgressours and offendors of God and men, than to looke strictlie on them by death, and so to rid them out of the common-wealth by seuere punishment, whome ye thought vnworthie to liue among men for their dooings? And those who haue not offended the king, but defended his realme, and by obedience of seruice sought to punish the disobedient, and for safegard of euerie man put themselues vnder dutie of law, those haue ye miserablie and cruellie slaine, and bathed you in their bloud, whose dooings ye should haue followed, & not to haue appaired the common-wealth, both by destruction of good men, and also by increase of rebels. And how can that common-wealth by anie meanes indure, wherin euerie man without authoritie, may vnpunished slea whome he list, and that in such case as those who be slaine shew themselues most noble of courage, and most readie to

The rebels charged with the murder and bloudshed of the kings liege people.

A licentious common-wealth cannot indure.

6 F

serue

serue the king and the common-wealth, and those as doo slea be most vilanous and traitorous rebels that anie common-wealth did euer susteine?

For a citie and a prouince be not the faire houses and the strong walles, nor the defense of anie engine, but the liuing bodies of men, being able in number and strength to mainteine themselues by good order of iustice, & to serue for all necessarie & behouable vses in the common-wealth. And when as mans bodie being a part of the whole common-wealth, is wrongfullie touched anie way, and speciallie by death, then suffereth the common-wealth great iniurie, and that alwaies so much the more, how honester and nobler he is, who is iniuriouslie murdered. How was the lord Sheffeld handled among you, a noble gentleman, and of good seruice, both fit for counsell in peace, and for conduct in war, considering either the grauitie of his wisedome, or the authoritie of his person, or his seruice to the common-wealth, or the hope that all men had in him, or the néed that England had of such, or among manie notablie good, his singular excellencie, or the fauor that all men bare toward him, being loued of euerie man, and hated of no man?

Considered ye who should by dutie be the kings subiects, either how ye should not haue offended the K. or after offense haue required the kings pardon, or not to haue refused his goodnesse offered, or at length, to haue yéelded to his mercie, or not to haue slaine those who came for his seruice, or to haue spared those who in danger offered ransome. But all these things forgotten by rage of rebellion, because one madnesse cannot be without infinit vices, ye slew him cruellie, who offered himselfe manfullie, nor would not so much as spare him for ransome, who was worthie for noblenesse to haue had honour, & hewed him bare whome ye could not hurt armed, and by slauerie slue nobilitie, in deed miserablie, in fashion cruellie, in cause diuelishlie. Oh with what cruell spite was violentlie sundred so noble a body from so godlie a mind? Whose death must rather be reuenged than lamented, whose death was no lacke to himselfe, but to his countrie, whose death might euerie way béene better borne, than at a rebels hand. Violence is in all things hurtfull, but in life horrible. What should I speake of others in the same case, d'uerse and notable, whose death for manhood and seruice can want no woorthie praise, so long as these vglie sturrers of rebellion can be had in mind. God hath himselfe ioined mans bodie and his soule togither, not to be departed asunder, afore he euer disseuer them himselfe, or cause them to be disseuered by his minister.

And shall rebels and heedlesse camps, being armed against God, and in field against their king, thinke it no fault to shed bloud of true subiects, hauing neither office of God, nor appointment of ministers, nor cause of rebellion? He that stealeth anie part of a mans substance, is woorthie to lose his life. What shall we thinke then of them, who spoile men of their liues, for the maintenance whereof not onelie substance & riches be sought for, but also all common-welths be deuised? Now then, your owne consciences should be made your iudges, & none other set to giue sentence against ye. Séeing ye haue beene such bloudshedders, so heinous manquellers, so horrible murderers, could ye doo anie other than plainlie confesse your foule and wicked rebellion to be gréeuous against God, and traitorous to the king, and hurtfull to the common-wealth? So manie gréeuous faults meeting togither in one sinke, might not onelie haue discouraged, but also driuen to desperation, anie other honest or indifferent mind.

But what féele they, whose hearts so déepe mischéefe had hardened, and by vehemencie of affection be made vnshamefast, and stop all discourse of reason, to let at large the full scope of their vnmeasurable madnesse? Priuat mens goods séeme little to your vnsatiable desires, yée haue waxed gréedie now vpon cities, and haue attempted mightie spoiles, to glut vp (and yée could) your wasting hunger. Oh how much haue they néed of, that will neuer be contented, and what riches can suffice anie that

will

will attempt high enterprises aboue their estate? Ye could not mainteine your camps with your priuat goods, with your neighbours portion, but yée must also attempt cities, bicause ye sought great spoiles with other mens losses, and had forgotten how yee liued at home honestlie with your owne, and thought them worthie death that would disquiet yée in your house, and plucke awaie that which yée by right of law thought to be your owne. Héerein sée what yée would haue doone, spoiled the kings maiesties subiects, weakened the kings strength, ouerthrowne his townes, taken awaie his munition, drawne his subiects to like rebellion, yea and as it is among forren enimies in sacking of cities, no doubt thereof, yee would haue fallen to slaughter of men, rauishing of wiues, deflouring of maidens, chopping of children, fiering of houses, beating downe of stréets, ouerthrowing of altogither.

For what measure haue men in the increase of madnesse, when they can not at the beginning staie themselues from falling into it. And if the besetting but of one house to rob it, be iustlie deemed worthie death: what shall we thinke of them that besiege whole cities for desire of spoile? We liue vnder a king to serue him at all times when he shall néed our strength: and shall ye then not onlie withdraw your selues, which ought as much to be obedient as we be, but also violentlie plucke other awaie too, fro the dutie vnto the which by Gods commandement all subiects be strictlie bound, and by all lawes euerie nation is naturallie led? The townes be not onlie the ornament of the realme, but also the seat of merchants, the place of handicrafts, that men scattered in villages, and néeding diuerse things, maie in little roome know where to find the lacke. To ouerthrow them then, is nothing else but to wast your owne commodities, so that when ye would buie a necessarie thing for monie, ye could not tell where to find the same.

Munition serueth the king not onelie for the defense of his owne, but also for the inuasion of his enimie. And if ye will then so strictlie deale with him, that ye will not let him so much as defend his owne, ye offer him double iniurie; both that ye let him from dooing anie notable fact abrode, and also that ye suffer not him quietlie to inioie his owne at home. But herein hath notablie appéered what cities haue faithfully serued and suffred extreme danger, not onelie of goods, but also of famine & death, rather than to suffer the kings enimies to enter: and what white liuered cities haue not onlie not withstood them, but also with shame fauored them, and with mischiefe aided them. And I would I might praise herein all cities alike! which I would doo, if all were like worthie. For then I might shew more faith in subiects than strength in rebelles; and testifie to men to come, what a generall faith euerie citie bare to the kings maiestie, whose age although it were not fit to rule, yet his subiects hearts were willing to obeie, thinking not onelie of the hope, which all men conceiue hereafter to be in him, but also of the iust kind of gouernment, which in his minoritie his councell dooth vse among them. And here, how much and how worthilie maie Excester be commended, which being in the middest of rebels, vnuittelled, vnfurnished, vnprepared for so long a siege, did noblie hold out the continuall and dangerous assault of the rebell? For they sustained the violence of the rebell, not onlie they had plentie enough of vittels, but also eleuen or twelue daies after the extreme famine came on them, and liuing without bread, were in courage so manfull, & in dutie so constant, that they thought it yet much better to die the extreme death of hunger, shewing truth to their king, and loue to their countrie, than to giue anie place to the rebell, and fauor him with aid, although they might haue doone it with their lesse danger. Whose example if Norwich had followed, & had not rather giuen place to traitor Ket, than to kéepe their dutie; and had not sought more safegard than honestie, and priuat hope more than common quietnesse: they had ended their rebellion sooner, and escaped themselues better, and saued the losse of the worthie lord Shefféeld, in whome was more true seruice for his life, than in them for their

goods

goods. And although this can not be spoken against a certeine honest sort that were amongst them, whose praise was the greater, bicause they were so few: yet the greater number was such, that they not onelie obeied the rebell for feare, but also folowed him for loue, and did so traitorouslie order the kings band vnder my lord marquesse, that they suffered more damage out of their houses by the towns men, than they did abrode by the rebelles. Whose fault as the kings maiestie maie pardon, so I would either the example might be forgotten, that no citie might hereafter follow the like, or the déed be so abhorred, that others hereafter would auoid the like shame, & learne to be

noble by Excester, whose truth dooth not onelie deserue great praises, but also great reward.

Who then that would willinglie defend ye, can say anie thing for ye, which haue so diuerslie faulted, so traitorouslie offended, not onlie against priuat men seuerallie, but

also generallie against whole townes, and that after such a sort, as outward enimies full of deadlie feud could not more cruellie inuade them? And thus the kings maiestie dishonored, his councell disobeied, the goods of the poore spoiled, the houses of the wealthie sacked, honest mens bodies imprisoned, worthie mens personages slaine, cities besieged and threatned, and all kind of things disordered, can ye without teares and repentance heare spoken of, which without honestie and godlinesse ye practised, and not find in your hearts now to returne to dutie, which by witchcraft of sedition were drowned in disorder? Haue ye not in disorder first gréeuouslie offended God, next traitorouslie risen against your king, and so neither worthie euerlasting life, as long

as ye so remaine, nor yet ciuill life being in such a breach of common quietnesse? If euerie one of these cannot by themselues plucke you backe from this your lewd and outragious enterprises, yet let them altogither stir ye; or at least be a fearfull example to others, to beware by your vnmeasurable follie, how they doo so far prouoke God, or offend man: and find by your mistemper to be themselues better ordered, and learne still to obeie, bicause they would not repent, and so to liue with honestie, that they would neither willinglie offend Gods law, nor disobeie mans.

But and ye were so much bleared, that you did thinke impossible things, and your reason gaue ye against all reason, that ye neither displeased God herein, nor offended the king, yet be ye so blind, that ye vnderstand not your owne case, nor your neighbors miserie, nor the ruine of the whole common-wealth, which dooth euidentlie follow

your so foule and detestable sedition? Doo ye not sée how for the maintenance of these vngodlie rablements, not onlie cities and villages, but also shires and countries be vtterlie destroied? Is not their corne wasted, their cattell fetcht awaie, their houses rifled, their goods spoiled, and all to féed your vprising without reason and to mainteine this tumult of rebellion inuented of the diuell, continued by you, and to be

ouerthrowen by the power of Gods mightie hand? And whie should not so hurtfull wasting and harrieng of countries be iustlie punished with great seueritie, séeing robbing of houses, and taking of purses, doo by law deserue the extremitie of death? How manie suffer iniurie when one hundred of a shire is spoiled? And what iniurie thinke ye is doone, when not onelie whole shires be destroied, but also euerie quarter of the realme touched? Haue ye not brought vpon vs all pouertie, weaknesse, and hatred within the realme, & discourage, shame, and damage without the realme? If ye misera-

blie intended not onelie to vndoo other, but also to destroie your selues, and to ouerthrow the whole realme, could ye haue taken a readier waie to your owne ruine than this is?

And first if ye be anie thing reasonable, lift vp your reason, and weigh by wisdome, if not all things, yet your owne cases, and learne in the beginning of matters to foresee the end, and iudge aduisedlie yer ye enter into anie thing hastilie. See ye not this

yeare the losse of haruest? And thinke ye can grow to wealth that yéere when ye lose your thrift and profit? Barns be poore mens storehouses, wherein lieth a great

part

part of euerie mans owne liuing, his wiues and childrens liuing, wherwith men main-teine their families, paie their rents: and therefore be alwaies thought most rich when they haue best crops. And now when there is neither plentie of haie, nor sufficient of straw, nor corne inough, and that through the great disorder of your lewd rebellion, can ye thinke ye doo well, when ye vndoo your selues, and iudge it a common-welth when the commons is destroied, and séeke your hap by vnhappinesse, and esteeme your owne losse to be your owne forwardnes, and by this iudgement shew your selues, how little ye vnderstand other mens matters, when ye can scarselie consider the weightiest of your owne? Hath not the haie this yeare, as it rose from the ground, so rotted to the ground againe: and where it was woont by mens seasonable labor to be taken in due time, and then serue for the maintenance of horsse and cattell wherwith we liue, now by your disordered mischéefe hath béene by mens idlenesse and vndutifulnesse let alone vntouched, and so neither serueth the poore to make monie of, nor anie cattell to liue with. The corne was sowne with labour, and the ground tilled for it with labour, and looked to be brought home againe with labour: and for lacke of honest laborers it is lost on the ground; the owners being loiterers, and séeking other mens, haue lost their owne, and hoping for mounteins, lacked their present thrift, neither obteining that they sought, nor séeking that they ought. Haie rotting on the ground. Losse of corne for lacke of reap-ing.

And how shall men liue when the maintenance of their prouision is lacking? For labouring and their old store is wasted by wildnesse of sedition, and so neither spare the old nor saue the new. How can men be fed then or beasts liue, when as such wastfull negligence is miserablie vsed? And mispending the time of their profit, in shamefull disorder of inobedience, they care not greatlie what becommeth of their owne, bicause they intend to liue by other mens? Haie is gone, corne is wasted, straw is spoiled; what reckoning of haruest can ye make, either for the aid of others, or for the reléefe of your selues? And thus haue ye brought in one kind of miserie, which if yée saw before, as ye be like to féele after, although ye had hated the common-welth, yet for loue of your selues ye would haue auoided the great enormitie thereof, into the which ye wilfullie now haue cast your selues. The losse of one yeares haruest verie hurtfull.

An other no lesse is, that such plentie of vittels as was abundantlie in euerie quarter for the reléefe of vs all, is now wastfullie and vnthriftfullie spent, in mainteining you vnlawfull rebels, and so with disorder all is consumed, which with good husbandrie might long haue indured. For, so much as would haue serued a whole yeare at home with diligence and skilfull héed of husbandrie, that is wilfullie wasted in a moneth in the campe, through the rauening spoile of vilanie. For what is vnordered plentie, but a wastfull spoile, whereof the inconuenience is so great, as ye be worthie to féele, and bringeth in more hardnes of liuing, greater dearth of all things, & occasioneth manie causes of diseases? The price of things must needs increase much, when the number of things waxeth lesse, and by scarsitie be inhansed, & compelleth men to abate their liberalitie in house, both to their owne, and also to strangers. And where the rich wanteth, what can the poore find, who in a common scarsitie liueth most scarselie, and féeleth quickliest the sharpnesse of staruing, when euerie man for lacke is hunger-bitten. Which if ye had well remembred before, as ye now maie after perceiue, ye would not I thinke so stiffe-neckedlie haue resisted and indangered your selues in the storme of famine, whereof ye most likelie must haue the greatest part, which most stubbornlie resisted, to your owne shame and confusion. Wastfull spend-ing of vittels by the rebels incon-uenient to the whole state. A necessitie of inhansing the price of things.

Experience teacheth vs, that after a great dearth commeth a great death; for that when men in great want of meat eat much ill meat, they fill their bodies wiht ill humors, and cast them from their state of health, into a subiection of sickenesse: bicause the good bloud in the bodie is not able to kéepe his temper, for the multitude of the ill humors that corrupteth the same. And so grow great & deadlie plagues, and destroie great numbers of all sorts, sparing no kind that they light on, neither respecting the After great dearth commeth a great death, a reason why.

poore

A briefe rehearsall or summarie of mischiefes issuing from rebellion.

poore with mercie, nor the rich with fauour. Can ye therefore thinke herein, when ye see decaie of vittels, the rich pinch, the poore famish, the following of diseases, the greatnesse of death, the mourning of widowes, the pitifulnesse of the fatherlesse, and all this miserie to come thorough your vnnaturall misbehauiour, that ye haue not dangerouslie hurt the commons of your countrie with a dolefull and vncurable wound? These things being once felt in the common-wealth, as they must néeds be, euerie man séeth by and by what followeth: euen a great diminishment of the strength of the realme, when the due number that the realme dooth mainteine is made lesse, and thereby we be made rather a preie for our enimies, than a safétie for our selues.

A great decaie of people.

And how can there be but a great decaie of people at the length, when some be ouerthrowne in warre, some suffer for punishment, some pine for famine, some die with the campes diet, some be consumed with sickenesse? For although ye thinke your selues able to match with a few vnprepared gentlemen, and put them from their houses, that ye might gaine the spoile: doo ye iudge therefore your selues strong inough, not onelie to withstand a kings power, but also to ouerthrow it? Is it possible that ye should haue so mad a frensie in your head, that ye should thinke the number ye sée so strong, that all ye sée not should not be able to preualie to the contrarie? With what reason could ye thinke, that if ye bode the hot brunt of battell, but ye must néeds feele the smart, speciallie the kings power comming against you: which if ye feare not, belike ye know not the force thereof? And so much the greater number is lost in the realme, that both the ouercommer and the ouercommed be parties, although vnlike, of one realme: and what losse is not onelie of either side, but but of both, that dooth plainlie redound to the whole.

Rebels can not preuaile against the princes power.

A necessarie consequent that rebels are seuerelie to be punished, and that such punishment is good and necessarie.

Then where so great and so horrible a fault is committed, as woorse can not be mentioned of from the beginning, and bringeth in withall such penurie, such weakenes, such disorder in the common-wealth, as no mischiefe besides could doo the like: can anie man thinke with iust reason, that all shall escape vnpunished that shall escape the sword, and not manie for terrour and examples sake should be looked vnto, who haue béene either great dooers in such a disordered vilanie, or great counsellors to such an outgrowne mischiefe; séeing the onelie remedie of redressing wilfull faults is a iust and seuere punishment of such, whose naughtie déeds good men ought to abhorre for duties sake, and ill men maie dread for like punishments sake, and a frée licence to doo mischiefe vnpunished is so dangerous, that the sufferance of one is the occasion of the fall of a great number, and womanish pitie to one is a deceitfull crueltie to the whole, intising them to their owne destruction by sufferance, which would haue auoided the danger by sore punishment.

Against foolish pitie forbearing and forgiuing a wilfull offendor.

And in such a barrennesse of vittels, as must néeds come after so rauening a spoile, it must néeds be, that some (though few) shall be so nipt with egernesse of famine, that they shall not recouer againe themselues out of so fretting a danger. So in a generall weakenesse, where all shall be féebled, some must needs die, and so diminish the number, and abate such strength as the realme defended it selfe withall before. Which occasion of neuer so few, comming of so great a cause, if ye should make iust amends for, not of recompense which ye could not, but of punishment which ye ought; how manie, how diuerse and how cruell deaths ought euerie one of ye often suffer? How manie came to the camps from long labour to sudden ease, and from meane fare to stroieng of vittels: and so fell in a maner vnwares to such a contrarie change, that nature hir selfe abiding neuer great and sudden changes, can not beare it without some grounds entered of diseases to come, which vncircumspect men shall sooner féele than thinke of, and then will scarselie iudge the cause, when they shall be vexed with the effect?

Rebels punishable with manie deaths.

Idlenesse and meat of other mens charge.

It is little maruell that idlenesse and meat of an other mans charge will soone feed vp & fat like men: but it is great maruell if idlenesse and other mens meat doo not abate

abate the same by sickenesse againe, and speciallie comming from the one, and going to the other: contrarie in those who violentlie séeke to turne in a moment the whole realme to the contrarie. For while their mind changeth from obedience to vnrulinesse, and turneth it selfe from honestie to wildnesse, and their bodies go from labour to idlenesse, from small fare to spoile of vittels, and from beds in the night to cabins, and from swéet houses to stinking camps, it must néeds be by changing of affections which alter the bodie, and by vsing of rest that filleth the bodie, and by glutting of meats which weakeneth the bodie, & with cold in the nights which accraseth the bodie, and with corrupt aire which infecteth the bodie, that there follow some grieuous tempest not onelie of contagious sickenesse, but also of present death to the bodie.

The greatest plucke of all is, that vehemencie of plague, which naturallie followeth the dint of hunger, which when it entereth once among men, what darts of pangs, what throwes of paines, what showts of death dooth it cast out? How manie fall, not astoined with the sickenesse, but fretted with the paine? How beateth it downe not onelie small townes, but also great countries? This when ye sée light first on your beasts which lacke fodder, and after fall on men whose bodies gape for it, and sée the scarsenesse of men to be by this your foule enterprise, and not onelie other men touched with plagues, but also your owne house stoong with death, and the plague also raised of your rising, to fire your selues: can ye thinke you to be anie other but mankillers of other, and murtherers of your selues, and the principals of the ouer-throw of so great a number, as shall either by sword or punishment, famine, or some plague or pestilence be consumed and wasted out of the common-wealth?

And séeing he that decaieth the number of cottages or plowes in a towne, seemeth to be an enimie to the common-wealth: shall we not count him, not onelie an enimie, but also a murtherer of his countrie, who by harebrained vnrulinesse causeth vtter ruine and pestilent destruction of so manie thousand men? Grant this follie then and ouersight to be such as woorthilie ye maie count it, and I shall go further in declaring of other great inconueniences, which your dangerous and furious misbehauiour hath hurtfullie brought in; séeing diuerse honest and true dealing men, whose liuing is by their owne prouision, hath come so before hand by time, that they haue béene able well to liue honestlie in their houses, & paie beside the rents of their farmes trulie, and now haue by your crueltie and abhorred insurrections lost their goods, their cattell, their haruest, which they had gotten before, and wherwith they intended to liue here-after, & now be brought to this extremitie that they be neither able to liue, as they were woont at home before; nor to paie their accustomeable rent at their due time. Whereby they be brought into trouble and vnquietnesse, not onlie musing what they haue lost by you, but also cursing you by whome they haue lost it, and also in danger of loosing their holds at their lords hands, except by pitie they shew more mercie, than the right of the law will grant by iustice.

And what a griefe is it to an honest man, to labor trulie in youth, and to gaine paine-fullie by labour, wherewith to liue honestlie in age, and to haue this, gotten in long time, to be suddenlie caught awaie by the violence of sedition, which name he ought to abhorre by it selfe, although no miserie of losse followed to him thereby. But what greater griefe ought seditious rebels to haue themselues, who if they be not striken with punishment, yet ought to pine in conscience, and melt awaie with the griefe of their owne faults, when they sée innocents and men of true seruice hindered and bur-dened with the hurt of their rebellion, & who in a good common-wealth should for honesties sake prosper, they by these rebels onlie meanes be cast so behind the hand, as they can not recouer easilie againe by their owne truth, that which they haue lost by those traitors mischiefe? And if vniust men ought not so to be handled at anie mans hands, but onelie stand to the order of a law: how much more should true and faith-full subiects, who deserue praise, féele no vnquietnesse, nor be vexed with sedition,

The force of pestilence follow-ing famine.

The plague & pestilence oc-casioned by re-bellion.

Rebels enimies & murtherers of their countrie.

Further mis-cheifes of vn-charitablenes issuing from rebellion.

The fruits of honest mens trauels long in gathering, quickelie spoiled by rebellion.

An argument from equitie & vpright dealing euen with the vniust.

who be obedientlie in subiection, but rather séeke iust amends at false rebels hands, and by law obteine that they lost by disorder, and so constreine you to the vttermost to paie the recompense of wrongfull losses, bicause ye were the authors of these wrongfull spoiles.

Then would ye soone perceiue the common-wealths hurt, not when other felt it who deserued it not, but when you smarted who caused it, and stood not & looked vpon other mens losses which ye might pitie, but tormented with your owne which ye would lament. Now I am past this mischiefe, which ye will not hereafter denie, when ye shall praise other mens foresight rather than your wicked dooings, in bewailing the end of your furie, in whose beginning ye now reioise. What saie ye to the number of vagabonds and loitering beggers, which after the ouerthrow of your campe, and scattering of this seditious number, will swarme in euerie corner of the realme and not onelie lie loitering vnder hedges, but also stand sturdilie in cities, and beg boldlie at euerie doore, leauing labour which they like not, and following idlenesse which they should not? For euerie man is easilie and naturallie brought from labour to ease, from the better to the woorse, from diligence to slothfulnesse: and after warres it is commonlie séene, that a great number of those which went out honest, returne home againe like roisters, and as though they were burnt to the wars bottome, they haue all their life after an vnsauorie smacke thereof, & smell still toward daiesleepers, pursepickers, highwaierobbers, quarrelmakers, yea and bloudsheders too.

Multitudes of vagabonds and roges procured by rebellions.

To what shifts soldiers fall after discamping and ceassing from warres.

Doo we not sée commonlie in the end of warres more robbing, more begging, more murdering than before, and those to stand in the high waie to aske their almes, whome ye be affraid to saie naie vnto honestlie, least they take it awaie from you violentlie, and haue more cause to suspect their strength, than pitie their need? Is it not then dailie heard, how men be not onelie pursued, but vtterlie spoiled, & few maie ride safe by the kings highwaie, except they ride strong, not so much for feare of their goods, which men estéeme lesse, but also for danger of their life, which euerie man loueth.

Against loitering lubbers that can not awaie with labour.

Worke is vndoone at home and loiterers linger in stréets, lurke in alehouses, range in highwaies, valiant beggers plaie in towns and yet complaine of néed, whose staffe if it be once hot in their hand, or sluggishnesse bred in their bosome, they will neuer be allured to labour againe, contenting themselues better with idle beggerie, than with honest and profitable labour. And what more noisome beasts be there in a commonwealth? Drones in hiues sucke out the honie, a small matter, but yet to be looked on by good husbands. Caterpillers destroie the fruit, an hurtfull thing, and well shifted for by a diligent ouerséer. Diuerse vermine destroie corne, kill pulleine, engines and snares be made for them.

A loiterer described.

But what is a loiterer? A sucker of honie, a spoiler of corne, a stroier of fruit, a waster of monie, a spoiler of vittels, a sucker of bloud, a breaker of orders, a seeker of breakes, a queller of life, a basiliske of the commonwealth, which by companie and sight dooth poison the whole countrie, and staineth honest minds with the infection of his veneme, and so draweth the commonwealth to death and destruction. Such is the fruits of your labour and trauell for your pretensed commonwealth, which iustice would no man should taste of but your selues, that yée might trulie iudge of your owne mischiefe, and fraie other by example from presuming the like. When we

The sight of manie flies in a yeare a naturall prognostication of a plague like to follow.

sée a great number of flies in a yeare, we naturallie iudge it like to be a great plague, and hauing so great a swarming of loitering vagabonds, readie to beg and brall at euerie mans doore, which declare a greater infection, can we not looke for a greeuouser and perillouser danger than the plague is? Who can therefore otherwise déeme, but this one deadlie hurt, wherewith the commonwelth of our nation is wounded, beside all other is so pestilent, that there can be no more hurtfull thing in a well gouerned estate, nor more throwne into all kind of vice and vnrulinesse: and therefore this your sedition

is

is not onelie most odious, but also most horrible, that hath spotted the whole countrie with such a staine of idlenesse.

There can be none end of faults, if a man rehearse all faults that doo necessarilie follow this vnrulie sturdinesse. For not onelie vagabonds wandering and scattering themselues for mischeefe, shall run in a mans eies, but also disorder of euerie degrée *Disorder in euerie degrée caused by rebellion.* shall enter into a mans mind, and shall behold hereby the commonwealth miserablie defaced by you, who should as much as other haue kept your selues in order in it. Neither be the magistrats dulie obeied, nor the lawes iustlie feared, nor degrées of men considered, nor maisters well serued, nor parents truelie reuerenced, nor lords remembred *Magistrats disobeied, and neglect of dutie in generall by rebellion.* of their tenants, nor yet either naturall or ciuill law much regarded. And it is plainlie vnpossible that that countrie shall well stand in gouernement, and the people growe to *Obseruing of order in euerie estate supporteth a commonwealth, & contrariwise the hurt of disorder.* wealth, where order in euerie state is not fitlie obserued : and that bodie cannot be without much gréefe of inflammation, where anie lest part is out of ioint, or not duelie set in his owne naturall place.

Wherefore order must be kept in the common-wealth like health in the bodie, and all the drift of policie looketh to this end, how this temper may be safelie mainteined, without anie excesse of vnmeasurablenesse, either of the one side, or of the other. And easie inough it is to keepe the same, when it is once brought into the meane, and to hold it in the staie it is found in : but when it bursteth out once with a vehemencie, and hath gotten into an vnrulie disorder, it spreadeth so fast, and ouerfloweth all honest mens resisting so violentlie, that it will be hard to recouer the breach of long time againe, except with great and wise counsell, which no doubt shall be in season vsed, there be woonderfull remedies sought therefore. And euen as a man falling, is *An argument drawne from comparison.* easier holden vp by staie, than when he is fallen downe he is able to rise againe : so is the commonwealth slipping, by the foresight of wisedome better kept from ruine ; than when it is once fallen into anie kind of miserie, the same may be called againe to the old and former state. Doo we not euidentlie know, that a man may better kéepe his arme or his leg from breaking or falling out of ioint, afore hurt come to it ; than after the hurt it may safelie and quietlie be healed, and restored to the former strength and health againe ? And now through your seditious means, things that *A topsie turuie of all things by rebellion.* were afore quiet and in good order, laws feared and obeied, subiects ruled and kept in dutie, be all now in a great disorder, and like (if it be not holpen) to grow to wildnesse, and a beastlinesse ; séeing that neither common dutie can be kept, which nature prescribeth, nor common law can be regarded, which policie requireth. How *The necessitie of order, and therefore S. Paule said well ; Let all things be doone in order.* can yée kéepe your owne if yée kéepe no order ? Your wiues and children, how can they be defended from other mens violence, if yee will in other things breake all order ? By what reason would yée be obeied of yours as seruants, if yée will not obeie the king as subiects ? How would yee haue others deale orderlie with you, if yée will vse disorder against all others ? Seeing then there is such a confusion now of things, such a turmoile of men, such a disorder of fashions ; who can looke to liue quietlie a great while, who can thinke but that yée haue miserablie tossed the commonwealth, and so vexed all men with disorder, that the inconuenience hereof cannot onelie nip others, but also touch you ?

But now sée how that not onelie these vnlooked for mischeefes haue heauilie growne *Rebels are against their owne profit.* on yée, but also those commodities, which yée thought to haue holpen your selues and others by, be not onelie hindered, but also hurt thereby. The kings maiestie by the aduise, &c : intended a iust reformation of all such things as poore men could trulie shew themselues oppressed with, thinking equalitie of iustice to be the diademe of his *Equalitie of iustice.* kingdome, and the safegard of his commons. Which was not onelie intended by wisedome, but also set on with speed, and so entered into a due considering of all states, that none should haue iust cause to grudge against the other, when as euerie thing rightfullie had, nothing could be but vnrightfullie grudged at. And this would

haue

haue béene doone, not onelie with your glad and willing assent: but also béene doone by this daie almost throughout the whole realme: so that quietlie it had béene obteined without inconuenience, and spéedilie without delaie. And whatsoeuer had béene doone by the kings maiesties authoritie, that would by right haue remained for euer, and so taken in law, that the contrarie partie neither could by iustice, neither would by boldnesse haue enterprised the breach thereof.

Rebels hurt themselues.

But least wicked men should be wealthie, and they whose hearts be not truelie bent to obedience, should obteine at the kings hands that they deserued not in a common-wealth, yée haue maruellouslie and worthilie hurt your selues, and gréeuouslie pro-uided (except the kings goodnesse be more vnto you than your owne deserts can claime) that yée be not so much worthie as to be benefited in anie kind, as yée be worthie to lose that yée haue on euerie side. Ye haue thought good to be your owne reformers

Priuat men are not to inforce a reformation.
Rebellion hurt-eth the whole realme.

belike, not onelie vnnaturallie mistrusting the kings iustice, but also cruellie and vnciuillie dealing with your owne neighbours. Wherein I would as yée haue hurt the whole realme, so yée had not enterprised a thing most dangerous to your selues, & most contrarie to the thing yée intended. If yée had let things alone, thought good by your selues to be redressed, and dutifullie looked for the performance of that, the kings maiestie promising reformation, they should not haue béene vndoone at this time, as in a great sort of honest places they be; nor whole countries, who for their quiet-nesse be most worthie to be looked on, should haue béene vnprouided for at this daie.

The benefit of rebellion in one respect.

But this commoditie hath happened by the waie, that it is euidentlie knowne by your mischeefe, and others dutie, who be most true to the king, and most worthie to be doone for, and who be most pernicious and traitorous rebels. And it is not to be doubted, but they shall be considered with thanks, and find iust redresse without deserued miserie, & you punished like rebels, who might haue had both praise & profit like subiects.

For that as yée haue valiantlie doone of your selues, thinke yée it will stand anie longer, than men feare your rage, which cannot indure long; and that yée shall not then bide the rigor of the law for your priuat iniuries, as yée vsed the furie of your braines in other mens oppressions? Will men suffer wrong at your hands, when law can redresse it, & the right of the commonwealth will mainteine it, and good order in countries will beare it? Yée amend faults as ill surgions heale sores, which when they

Reformation intended by re-bels, like sores cured by ill sur-gions.

seeme to be whole aboue, they rankle at the bottome, and so be faine continuallie to be sore, or else be mended by new breaking of the skin. Your redresse séemeth to you perfect and good, yee haue pulled downe such things as yee would, yee thinke now all is well: yée consider no further, yee seeke not the bottome, yée see not the sore, that yée haue doone it by no law, yee haue redressed it by no order, what then? If it be no otherwise searched than by you, it will not tarie long so: either it will be after continuallie as it was afore your comming, or else it must be (when all is doone) amended by the king.

Thus haue yée both lacked in the time, and mist in the dooing, and yet besides that ye haue done, which is by your dooing to no purpose. Yée haue doone the things with such inconueniences, as hath béene both before rehearsed, and shall be after declared; that better it had béene for you, neuer to haue enioied the commoditie, if

Gréefes insuing to the rebels vpon this rebel-lion.

there be anie; than to suffer the greefs that will insue, which be verie manie. In euerie quarter some men (whom yee set by) will be lost, which euerie one of you (if ye haue loue in ye) would rather haue lacked the profit of your inclosures, than cause such destruction of them, as is like by reason & iudgement necessarilie to follow. What commonwealth is it then, to doo such abhominable enterprises after so vile a sort, that yée hinder that good yée would doo, and bring in that hurt yée would not, and so find that yée séeke not, and follow that yée lose, and destroie your selues by follie; rather than yée would be ordered by reason, and so haue not so much amended your

old

old sores, as brought in new plagues, which yée your selues that deserue them will lament, and we which haue not deserued them may cursse you for? For although the kings maiestie, &c: intended for your profits a reformation in his commonwealth: yet his pleasure was not, nor no reason gaue it, that euerie subiect should busilie inter-meddle with it of their owne head, but onelie those whome his councell thought most méet men for such an honest purpose.

Reformation ought to be no priuat mans but the princes action.

The kings maiestie, &c: hath godlie reformed an vncleane part of religion, and hath brought it to the true forme of the first church that followed Christ, thinking that to be truest, not what later mens fansies haue of themselues deuised, but what the apostles and their felowes had at Christes hand receiued, and willeth the same to be knowne and set abroad to all his people. Shall euerie man now that listeth and fansieth the same, take in hand vncalled, to be a minister, and to set foorth the same, hauing no authoritie? Naie, though the thing were verie godlie that were doone, yet the person must néeds doo ill that enterpriseth it, bicause he dooth a good thing after an ill sort, and looketh but on a little part of dutie, considering the thing, and leaueth a great part vnaduised, not considering the person: when as in a well and iustlie doone matter, not onelie these two things ought well to be weighed, but also good occasion of time, and reasonable cause of the dooing, ought also much to be set before euerie dooers eies. Now in this your déed, the manner is vngodlie, the thing vnsufferable, the cause wicked, the person seditious, the time traitorous: and can ye possiblie by anie honest defense of reason, or anie good conscience religiouslie grounded, denie that this mali-cious and horrible fault, so wickedlie set on, is not onelie sinfull afore God, and traitor-ous to the king, but also deadlie and pestilent to the whole common-wealth of our countrie, and so not onelie ouerfloweth vs with the miserie, but also ouerwhelmeth you with the rage thereof?

What things in a well and iustlie doone matter ought well to be weighed.

Yet further see and ye be not wearie with the multitude of miseries, which ye haue maruellouslie mooued, what a yoke ye wilfullie doo bring on your selues, in stirring vp this detestable sedition, and so bring your selues into a further slauerie, if ye vse your selues into a further slauerie, if ye vse your selues often thus inobedientlie. When common order of the law can take no place in vnrulie and disobedient subiects, and all men will of wilfulnesse resist with rage, and thinke their owne violence to be the best iustice; then be wise magistrats compelled by necessitie to séeke an extreame remedie, where meane waies helpe not, and bring in the martiall law where none other law serueth. Then must ye be contented to bide punishment without processe, con-demnation without witnesse, suspicion is then taken for iudgement, and displeasure may be isut cause of your execution, and so without fauor ye find strictnesse, which without rule seeke violence. Ye thinke it a hard law and vnsufferable. It is so indéed, but yet good for a medicine.

The yoke that rebels wilfullie bring vpon themselues.

Desperate sicknesse in physicke must haue desperate remedies, for meane medicines will neuer helpe great griefes. So if ye cast your selues into such sharpe diseases, ye must néeds looke for sharpe medicines againe at your physicians hands. And worthie ye be to suffer the extremitie in a commonwealth, which seeke to doo the extremitie, and by reason must receiue the like ye offer, and so be contented to bide the end wil-linglie which set on the beginning willfullie. For no greater shame can come to a com-mon-welth, than that those subiects which should be obedient euen without a law, can not be contented to be ordered by the law, and by no means kept within their dutie, which should euerie waie offend rather than in their dutie. It is a token that the subiects lacke reason, when they forsake law, and thinke either by their multitude to find pardon, which cannot iustlie stretch to all, or else by strength to beare the stroke, which cannot prosper against a king.

Desperat remedies for desperat diseases.

Rebels worthie to suffer extremitie of punishment.

The greatest shame that can come to a common-wealth.

They must néeds little consider themselues, who bring in this necessitie, rather to stand to the pleasure of a mans will, than to abide the reason of the law; and to be

indangered

indangered more when an other man listeth, than when himselfe offendeth. And this must necessarilie folow if your rebellion thus continue: and while ye séeke to throw downe the yoke, which ye fansie your selues burdened withall, ye bring your selues in a greater bondage, leauing safetie and folowing danger, and putting your selues vnder the iustice of them whose fauour ye might easilie haue kept, if ye would willinglie and dutifullie haue serued. Now the gentlemen be more in trust, bicause the commons be vntrustie, and they get by seruice, which ye loose by stubbornesse, and therefore must needs, if ye thus continue, haue more authoritie from the king: bicause ye would be in lesse subiecticn to the king, and that as ye will not doo of your selues, ye must be compelled to doo by others, and that ye refuse tō doo willinglie, thinke ye must be drawne to doo the same constreinedlie. Which when it commeth to passe, as wisedome séeth in your faults that it must néeds, what gaine ye then, or what profit can arise to you by rising, which might haue found ease in sitting still? And what shall ye be at length the better for this turmoile, which beside diuerse other incommodities rehearsed, shall be thus clogged with the vnsufferable burden of the martiall law.

Yet there is one thing behind, which me thinketh your selues should not forget, séeing that ye haue giuen the cause, ye should dulie looke for the effect. Ye haue spoiled, imprisoned, and threatened gentlemen to death, and that with such hatred of mind, as may not well be borne. The cause therof I speake not on, which tried, will happilie be not so great: but sée the thing, set murther aside, it is the heinousest fault to a priuat man. What could more spitefullie haue béene doone against them, than ye haue vsed with crueltie? Can this doo anie other but breed in their stomachs great grudge of displeasure toward you, and ingender such an hatred as the weaker and the sufferer must néeds beare the smart thereof.

The kings best kind of gouernment is so to rule his subiects, as a father ordereth his children, and best life of obedient subiects is one to behaue himselfe to an other, as though they were brethren vnder the king their father. For loue is not the knot onelie of the common-wealth, whereby diuerse parts be perfectlie ioined togither in one politike bodie, but also the strength and might of the same, gathering togither into a small roome with order, which scattered would else bréed confusion and debate. Dissention we sée in small houses, and thereby may take example to great common- wealths, how it not onelie decaieth them from wealth, but also abateth them from strength. Thinke small examples to take place in great matters, and the like though not so great to follow in them both, and thereby learne to iudge of great things vnknowne, by small things perceiued. When brethren agrée not in a house, goeth not the weakest to the walles; and with whome the father taketh part withall, is not he likest to preuaile? Is it not wisedome for the yoonger brother, after the good will of the parents, to seeke his eldest brothers fauour, who vnder them is most able to doo for him? To séeke them both with honestie is wisedome, to loose them both by sullen- nesse is madnesse.

Haue there not béene dailie benefits from the gentlemen to you, in some more, and in some lesse, but in none considered, which they haue more friendlie offered, than you haue gentlie requited? This must ye lose, when ye will not be thankefull, and learne to gaine new good will by desert, when ye forsake the old friendship vnprouoked. And ye must thinke that liuing in a common-wealth togither, one kind hath néed of an other: and yet a great sort of you more néed of one gentleman, than one gentleman of a great sort of you. And though all be parts of one common-wealth, yet all be not like worthie parts, but all being vnder obedience, some kind in more subiection one one waie, and some kind in more seruice an other waie. And séeing ye be lesse able by monie and liberalitie to deserue good will than others be, and your onelie kind of desert is to shew good will, which honest men doo well accept as much worth as

monie,

monie, haue ye not much hindered & hurt your selues herein, losing that one kind of humanitie which ye haue onelie left, and turning it into crueltie, which ye ought most to abhor, not onelie bicause it is wicked of it selfe, but also most noisome to you.

I can therefore for my part thinke no lesse herein, if ye follow your stiffenesse still, & must néeds iudge that ye haue wilfullie brought on your selues such plagues, as the like could not haue fallen on you, but by your selues. Seeing then thus manie waies ye haue hurt the common-welth of this whole countrie within, by destruction of shires, losing of haruest, wasting of vittels, decaieng of manhood, vndooing of farmers, increasing of vagabonds, mainteining of disorders, hindring of redresses, bringing in of martiall law, and bréeding continuall hatred among diuerse states : what thinke ye, I praie you? Iudge ye not that ye haue committed an odious and detestable crime against the whole common-wealth, whose furtherance ye ought to haue tendered by dutie, and not to haue sought the hurt thereof with your owne damage ? *A bréefe enumeration of the inconueniences flowing from this rebellion.*

Besides all these inward griefes, which euerie one seuerallie must néeds féele with miserie, there happeneth so manie outward mischances among strangers to vs with disdaine ; that if there were nothing ill within the realme which we should féele, yet the shame which dooth touch vs from other countries, should not onelie mooue, but also compell you hartilie to forethinke this your rebellious sedition. For what shall strangers thinke, when they shall heare of the great misorder which is in this realme with such confusion, that no order of law can kéepe you vnder, but must be faine to be beaten downe with a kings power? Shall they not first thinke the kings maiestie, in whose mind God hath powred so much hope for a child, as we may looke for gifts in a man ; either for his age to be little set by, or for lacke of qualities not to be regarded, or for default of loue to be resisted, and no notable grace of God in him considered, nor the worthinesse of his office looked vpon, nor naturall obedience due to him remembred ? *Outward mischances insuing vpon rebellions to the shame of the land and estate wherin they be raised.* *King contemned.*

Shall they not next suppose, small estimation to be giuen to the rulers, to whom vnder the king we owe due obedience, that can not in iust and lawfull matters be heard, nor men to haue that right iudgement of their wisedome, as their iustice in rule, and foresight in counsell requireth : but rather prefer their owne fansies before others experience, and déeme their owne reason to be common-wealth, and other mens wisedome to be but dreaming ? Shall they not trulie saie the subiects to be more vnfaithfull in disobedience, than other subiects worse ordered be ; and licence of libertie to make wild heads without order, and that they neither haue reason that vnderstand not the mischiefe of sedition, nor dutie which follow their beastlinesse, nor loue in them which so little remember the common-wealth, nor naturall affection which will dailie séeke their owne destruction ? *Rulers little estéemed.* *Subiects disordered.*

Thus the whole countrie lacking the good opinion of other nations, is cast into great shame by your vnrulinesse, and the proceedings of the countrie, be they neuer so godlie, shall be ill spoken of, as vnfit to be brought into vse ; and good things hereby that deserue praise, shall bide the rebuke of them that list to speake ill, and ill things vntouched shall be boldlier mainteined. Nothing may with praise be redressed, where things be measured by changeable disorder, rather than by necessarie vse ; and that is thought most politike, that men will be best contented to doo, and not that which men should be brought vnto by dutie. And with what dutie or vertue in ye, can ye quench out of memorie this foule enterprise, or gather a good report againe to this realme, who haue so vilelie with reproch slandered the same, and diuerslie discredited it among others, and abated the good opinion which was had of the iust gouernement and ruled order vsed heretofore in this noble realme, which is now most grieuous, bicause it is now most without cause. *The whole countrie ill spoken of.* *Nothing redresseable by disorder chanceable.*

If

If this outward opinion (without further inconuenience) were all, yet it might well be borne, and would with ease decaie as it grew: but it hath not onlie hurt vs with voice, but indangered vs in déed, and cast vs a great deale behind the hand, where else we might haue had a iollie foredeale. For that oportunitie of time which seldome chanceth, and is alwaies to bée taken, hath béene by your froward meanes lost this yeare, and so vainlie spent at home for bringing downe of you, which should else profitablie haue béene otherwise bestowed, that it hath béene almost as great a losse to vs abrode, to lacke that we might haue obteined, as it was combrance at home, to go

about the ouerthrow of you, whose sedition is to be abhorred. And we might both conuenientlie haue inuaded some, if they would not reasonablie haue growne to some kind of friendship, and also defended others which would beside promise for times sake vniustlie set vpon vs, and easilie haue made this stormie time a faire yeare vnto vs, if our men had beene so happie at home, as our likelihood abrode was fortunat.

But what is it (I praie) either to let slip such an occasion by negligence, or to stop it by stubbornnesse, which once past awaie, can be by no means recouered; no not though with diligence ye go about to reinforce the same againe? If ye would with

wickednes haue forsaken your faith to your naturall countrie, and haue sought craftie means to haue vtterlie betraied it to our common enimies: could ye haue had anie other spéedier waie than this is, both to make our strength weake, and their weakenesse strong? If ye would haue sought to haue spited your countrie, and to haue pleased your enimie, and follow their counsell for our hinderance: could he haue had deuised of them anie thing more shamefull for vs, and ioifull to them? If they which

lie like spials, and hearken after likelihoods of things to come, bicause they declare oportunitie of times to the enimie, are to be iudged common enimies of the countrie; what shall we reasonablie thinke of you, who doo not secretlie bewraie the counsels of other, but openlie betraie the common-wealth with your owne déeds, and haue as much as lieth in you, sought the ouerthrow of it at home: which if ye had obteined at Gods hand, as he neuer alloweth so horrible an enterprise, how could yée haue defended it from the ouerthrow of others abrode?

For is your vnderstanding of things so small, that although ye sée your selues not vnfit to get the vpper hand of a few gentlemen, that ye be able to beat downe afore the kings power: ye and by chance ye were able to doo that, would ye iudge your

selues by strength mightie enough, to resist the power of outward nations, that for praise sake would inuade ye? Naie, thinke trulie with your selues, that if yée doo ouercome, ye be vnsure both by strength abrode, and displeasure of honest men at home, and by the punishment of God aboue. And now ye haue not yet gotten in déed, that your vaine hope looketh for by fansie: thinke how certeinlie ye haue wounded the common-wealth with a sore stroke, in procuring our enimies by our weakenesse to séeke victorie, and by our outward miserie to séeke outward glorie with inward dishonor. Which howsoeuer they get, thinke it to belong of you, who haue offered them victorie before they began warre: bicause ye would declare to men hereafter (belike) how dangerous it is to make sturres at home, when they doo not onelie make our selues weake, but also our enimies strong.

Beside these, there is another sort of men desirous of aduantage, and disdainefull of our wealth, whose gréefe is most our greatest hap, and be offended with religion, bicause they be drowned in superstition, men zealed toward God, but not fit to iudge, meaning better without knowledge, than they iudge by their meaning, woorthier whose ignorance should be taken awaie, than their will should be followed; whome we should more rebuke for their stubbornesse, than despise for their ignorance. These seeing superstition beaten downe, and religion set vp, Gods word taking place, traditions kept in their kind, difference made betwéene Gods commandements and mans learning,

ing, the truth of things sought out according to Christes institution, examples taken of the primitiue churches vse, not at the bishop of Romes ordinance, and true worship taught, and wil-worship refused, doo by blindnesse rebuke that as by truth they should follow, and by affection follow that as by knowledge they should abhorre, thinking vsage to be truth, and scripture to be error, not weieng by the word, but misconstruing by custome.

And now things be changed to the better, and religion trulier appointed, they sée matters go awrie, which hurteth the whole realme, and they reioise in this mischéefe as a thing worthilie happened, mistaking the cause, and slandering religion, as though there were no cause whie God might haue punished, if their vsed profession might still haue taken place. They sée not that where Gods glorie is truliest set foorth, there the diuell is most busie for his part, and laboureth to corrupt by lewdnesse, that as is gotten out by the truth, thinking that if it were not blemished at the first, the residue of his falsehood should after lesse preuaile. So he troubleth by biwaies, that he cannot plainlie withstand and vseth subtiltie of sophistrie, where plaine reason faileth, and persuadeth simple men that to be a cause, which in déed can not be tried and taken for a cause. So he causeth religion which teacheth obedience, to be iudged the cause of sedition; & the doctrine of loue, the séed of dissention; mistaking the thing, but persuading mens minds, and abusing the plaine meaning of the honest to a wicked end of religious ouerthrow.

Religion beareth the blame and is counted the cause of rebellion, but amisse.

The diuels sophistrie.

The husbandman had not so soone throwne séed in his ground, but steppeth vp the enimie, and hee soweth cockle too, and maketh men doubt whether the good husband had doone well or no, and whether he had sowne there good séed or bad. The fansifull Iewes in Egypt would not beléeue Ieremie, but thought their plague and their miserie to come by his means; and leauing of idolatrie to be the cause of penurie, wherfore by wilfull aduise they intended to forsake the prophets councell, and thought to serue God most trulie by their rooted & accustomed idolatrie. When the christian men were persecuted in the primitiue church, & dailie suffered martyrdome for Christs profession, such faire season of weather was for thrée or foure yeares togither, that the heathen iudged thereupon God to be delighted with their crueltie, and so were persuaded that with the bloud of the martyrs they pleased God highlie. Such fansies light now in papists, and irreligious mens heads, and ioine things by chance happening togither, and conclude the one to be the cause of the other, and then delight in true worshippers hurt, bicause they iudge cursedlie the good to be bad, and therefore reioise in the punishment of the godlie, For they being fleshlie, iudge by outward things, and perceiue not the inward, for that they lacke the spirit and so iudge amis, not vnderstanding God, what diuersitie he suffereth to blind still the wilfull, and how through all dangers he saueth his forechosen.

Examples.

The Iewes ascribe their miserie to a false cause.

The heathens fond opinion of gods fauouring their crueltie against christians.

And thus ye haue giuen a large occasion to stubborne papists, both to iudge amisse, and also to reioise in this wicked chance, contented with our mischéefe, not liking our religion, and thinking God dooth punish for this better change, and haue thereby an euill opinion of Gods holie truth, confirmed in them by no sure scripture, but by following of mischance, which they ought to thinke to come for the pride and stubbornnesse of the people, who dooth not accept Gods glorie in good part, nor giue no due praise to their Lord and maker. What should I saie more? Ye hurt euerie waie, the dangers be so great, and the perils so manie, which doo dailie follow your diuelish enterprise, that the more I seeke in the matter, the more I continuallie see to saie. And what words can worthilie declare this miserable beastlines of yours, which haue intended to diuide the realme, and arme the one part for the killing of the other? For euen as concord is not onelie the health, but also the strength of the realme: so is sedition not onelie the weaknesse but also the apostume of the realme, which when it breaketh inwardlie, putteth the state in great danger of recouerie, and corrupteth the whole commonwealth with the rotten furie that it hath béene long putrified withall. For it

The papists by rebellion haue an euill opinion of Gods holie truth.

The hurts issuing from rebellion out of count.

Concord and discord with their differing effects.

is not in sedition as in other faults, which being mischéefous of themselues, haue some notable hurt alwaies fast adioined to them: but in this one is there a whole hell of faults, not seuerallie scattered, but clustered on a lumpe togither, and comming on so thicke, t hat it is vnpossible for a region armed with all kinds of wisedome, and strength thereto, to auoid the dangers that issue out thereof.

The mischiefs springing frō sedition.

When sedition once breaketh out, sée ye not the lawes ouerthrowne, the magistrates despised, spoiling of houses, murthering of men, wasting of countries, increase of disorder, diminishing of the realms strength, swarming of vagabonds, scarsitie of laborers, and all those mischiefes plentiouslie brought in, which God is woont to scourge seuerelie withall, warre, dearth, and pestilence? And séeing ye haue theft & murther, plague & famine, confusion and idlenesse linked togither, can ye looke for anie more mischéefe in one shamefull enterprise, than ye euidentlie sée to grow herein?

Forren war farre better than sedition at home.

As for warre, although it be miserable, yet the one part getteth somewhat, and reioiseth in the spoile, snd so goeth lustier awaie: and either increaseth his countrie with riches, or inhanseth himselfe with glorie: but in sedition both parts loose, the ouercommer cannot flie, the ouercommed cannot spoile; the more the winner winneth, the more he looseth; the more that escape, the more infamous men liue; all that is gained is scarcelie saued; the winning is losse, the losse is destruction, both wast themselues, and the whole most wasted; the strengthening of themselues, the decaie of the countrie; the striuing for the victorie, is a preie to the enimie: and shortlie to saie, the hellish turmoile of sedition so farre passeth the common miserie of warre, as to slaie himselfe is more heinous, than to be slaine of another.

The praise and benefits of peace.

O noble peace, what wealth bringest thou in, how doo all things flourish in field and in towne, what forwardnesse of religion, what increase of learning, what grauitie in counsell, what deuise of wit, what order of maners, what obedience of laws, what reuerence of states, what safegard of houses, what quietnesse of life, what honor of countries, what friendship of minds, what honestie of pleasure hast thou alwaies mainteined, whose happinesse we knew not, while now we féele thy lacke, and shall learne by miserie to vnderstand plentie, and so to auoid mischiefe by the hurt that it bringeth, and learne to serue better, where rebellion is once knowen; and so to liue trulie, and kéepe the kings peace.

The rebels neglect the right meanes of redressing things amisse, and follow their owne fansies.

What good state were ye in afore ye began, not pricked with pouertie, but sturred with mischiefe, to séeke your destruction, hauing waies to redresse all that was amisse? Magistrats most readie to tender all iustice, and pitifull in hearing the poore mens causes, which sought to amend matters more than you can deuise, and were readie to redresse them better than ye could imagine: and yet for a headinesse ye could not be contented; but in despite of God, who commandeth obedience, and in contempt of the king, whose lawes doo seeke your wealth, and to ouerthrow the countrie, which naturallie we should loue, ye would proudlie rise, and

The state of a countrie or land in time of sedition and tumult.

doo ye wot not what, and amend things by rebellion to your vtter vndooing. What state leaue ye vs in now, besieged with enimies, diuided at home, made poore with spoile and losse of our haruest, vnordered and cast downe with slaughter and hatred, hindered from amendments by our owne diuelish hast, indangered with sickenesse by reason of misorder, laid open to mens pleasures for breaking of the lawes, and féebled to such faintnesse that scarselie it will be couered.

Reasons to withdraw the rebels from their enterprises of rebellion, and to allure them to loialtie.

Wherefore for Gods sake haue pittie on your selues, consider how miserablie ye haue spoiled, destroied, and wasted vs all: and if for desperatnesse ye care not for your selues, yet remember your wiues, your children, your countrie, and forsake this rebellion. With humble submission acknowledge your faults, and tarie not the extremitie of the kings sword, leaue off with repentance, and turne to your duties, aske God forgiuenesse, submit ye to your king, be contented for a common-wealth one or two to die. And ye capteins for the residue sacrifice your selues, ye shall so best atteine the kings gratious pardon, saue the assemblie, and helpe the common-wealth, & to declare

your

your dooings to procéed of no stubbornesse; but all this mischiefe to grow out of ignorance, which séeing the miserie, would redresse the fault, & to recouer best the blot of your disorder, and staie the great miseries which be like to follow. Thus if ye doo not, thinke trulie with your selues, that God is angrie with you for your rebellion, the kings sword drawne to defend his countrie, the crie of the poore to God against ye, the readinesse of the honest in armor to vanquish ye, your death to be at hand, which ye cannot escape, hauing God against ye, as he promiseth in his word, the kings power to ouerthrow ye, gathered in the field, the commonwelth to beate ye downe with stripes and with cursses, the shame of your mischiefe to blemish ye for euer.

¶ Thus far this necessarie treatise touching rebellion, penned by sir Iohn Chéeke, a gentleman euerie waie in complet sort satisfieng the report blazed abroad of him. For if there were no more testimonies extant in the world, but this onelie treatise discours- ing Kets rebellion; it were enough to warrant no lesse true, than in common spéech and writing is left witnessed of him. And suerlie it appeareth, that as in this gentle- man there was an extraordinarie heape of laudable gifts; so was there also in him the right vse of them all. Wherby he grew in such fauor with king Henrie the eight, that partlie for his absolute knowledge in toongs, speciallie the Gréeke and Latineand also for his integritie of life and religion; he was chosen schoolemaister to yoong prince Edward, to traine him vp in the right vnderstanding, both of forren languages, & the purenes of Gods seruice. Insomuch that by his industrie such effects followed (God aboue prospering his actions) that the yoong prince, when he came to the king- dome was mindfull of him, and among other I will not saie gratuities, where cause of desert maketh challenge of some recompense) tokens of beneuolence, aduanced him to the dignitie of knighthood; as hereafter in due place maie appeare. Of this woor- thie man, whose praise though neuer so excessiue (if meet for a man) is equiualent vnto his merits, Iohn Leland, vpon presenting vnto him a booke, taketh occasion to write this epigram, comprising in summe no lesse than is here vnder in English re- membred:

Si vis Thespiadum choro probari,
Fac vt consilio libelle nostro
Facundo studeas placere Checo,
Quem Pandioniæ colunt Athenæ,
Et quem Roma colit diserta multùm,
Quem rex maximus omnium supremúsque
Henricus reputans virum probatum,
Spectatúmque satis, reconditæque
Censorem solidum eruditionis,
Eduardum bene filium suúmque
Hæredem puerum, illi ad alta natum,
Sic concredidit, vtriusque linguæ
Flores vt legeret venustiores,
Exercens facili manum labore,
Et Christi imbiberet suaue nectar.
Fœlicem arbitror hunc diem fuisse,
Tanto discipulo dedit magistrum.
Qui talem, &c.]

During the time of these commotions and sturs here within the realme, to the great danger of the state; the French king hauing knowledge thereof, ment not to omit the oportunitie offered, to recouer out of the Englishmens hands those fortresses which they held

held at Bullongne and in Bullongnois. Wherevpon he gaue summons to the gentlemen and men of armes, and others of his realme, to put themselues in order with all
their furniture, that they might be readie to attend him in his armie in Bullongnois by
a daie appointed. And about the same time, that is to saie, in the beginning of August;
the French king purposing to surprise the Iles of Gerneseie, and Ierseie, appointed
certeine gallies and ships of warre to passe thither; but being receiued by the king of
Englands nauie that laie there, and other of the Iland, they were 'beaten backe and
repelled, with the losse of a thousand men (as some write) and so were constreined to
retire without atchiuing their enterprise.

Iohn Fox.

The French
king is ashamed
that anie report
should passe of
his euill successe.
Credible word was brought out of France to the lord protector, that into one towne
in one vessell were brought at the least thrée score gentlemen to be buried, & also an
inhibition giuen out by the French king, not to speake of the euill successe of that
iournie. In the meane time, the French king being come downe vnto Abuile, departed
from thence the sixtéenth of August, and comming vnto Rue, lodged there that night,
and the next daie came to Monstreull, where he found the conestable and monsieur
Daumalle. The next daie being the eightéenth of August, he came to his armie
lodged foure leagues on this side Monstreull at a village called Neufcaste'l, neere to the
The French
king perseuereth
in his former
purpose, and
martiall action.
forrest of Ardelo, vpon the waie that leadeth to Bullongne. The same daie were certeine pioners sent to Pont de Bricque to repare the bridge there, and to make the waies
easie for the artillerie to passe. The next daie the said king with his armie passed by
Bullongne berg, and camped that night on a little hill betwixt that forrest and the forrest of Suren.

In this place he caused trenches to be cast about a plot of ground, after the maner of
a fortresse, within the which he left certeine bands of men of warre to be a safegard
vnto such as should passe to and fro with vittels to furnish his campe. He staied not
there past a daie & a halfe, but remoued to Ardenton, a mile or little more beyond
Marguisen; from thence he came with his armie, and lodged on a hill, somewhat more
than a mile & a halfe from Hambleteuue. The French king hauing viewed the forts,
caused fiue and twentie péeces of artillerie to be planted against that fort, which was
built in a place called the Almaine campe, but the Frenchmen named it Le fort de Selaque,
Charles Sturton,
and George
Willoughbie.
*Les chroniques
de Aquitaine.*
The fort called
Almaine campe
woone.
distant from Hambleteuue about a quarter of a mile. The artillerie had not gone off
little more than the space of two houres, but that Charls Sturton capteine of that péeec,
and George Willougbie a gentleman associat with him, came foorth to parlée with the
Conestable, offering to yéeld the fort into his hand, vpon condition they might depart
with bag and baggage. But as they were thus in hand to make their composition, the
Frenchmen thrust forward to the rampiers, and entered in plumps into the fortresse,
slue fourescore persons, & tooke the rest prisoners. There might be in all within that
péece two hundred and thirtie persons, men and women. This happened the foure
and twentith of August, being Bartholomew daie.

This doone, the king caused part of the artillerie to be planted against the castell
of Hambleteuue, situated at the one end of the towne néere to the sea side. Towards
night monsieur de Vandosme gaue an approch to the said castell, and they within by
The lord Greie.
The castell of
Hambleteuue
lost.
commandement of the lord Greie retired to the maine fort to helpe to furnish the same,
wanting numbers sufficient to defend it. The next daie being the fiue and twentith
of August, the king caused approches to be made vnto the great fort, and the morrow
after the batterie began most furiouslie. The same daie after dinner, the king sum-
momoned them within to yéeld; but the lord Iohn Greie being generall (although he
saw how weake the péece was of it selfe, & the lacke of sufficient numbers of men to
resist such a puissant force, as the French king had there with him) would not yet
hearken vnto anie talke, nor suffer the herald to come néere; for that he should not
perceiue the weakenesse of the péece: and so he was commanded to get him thence with
Hambleteuue
summoned.
spéed, or else they would cause him to be packing smallie to his ease. The French
king

king sore offended herewith, that his herald was so vncourteouslie vsed, caused the batterie to be reinforced with great diligence, which dismounting their ordinance within, and beating downe their rampiers, made such breaches, that my lord Iohn and the capteins within perceiued they were not able by anie meanes to defend the place anie longer. Herevpon they offered to render the fort to the king vpon composi-tion: which in the end fell out to be thus, that the souldiers should depart with their liues saued, and that their generall (for honor sake) should haue one horsse to ride on in his corslet, without sword or dagger, and likewise two other capteins with him: but as for the other souldiers, with the women and children, should depart on foot in their shirts, leauing all their goods and substance behind them. After it was agreed that the fort should be thus surrendered, there entered monsieur de Chatillon that was after admerall of France, and monsieur de Desse, latelie returned out of Scotland. The French souldiers entring by stealth into the fort by the breaches, committed foule disorders, not onelie in ransacking the houses, but also in spoiling the souldiers by force, intreating them in most rigorous maner.

Hambleteuue rendered to the French king.

The French writers confesse, that it was pitie to sée the poore men and women so miserablie handled and abused as they were by the outragious soldiors that thus entred the fort, and sacked all that they could laie hands vpon. Monsieur de Desse saued a great number of women and yoong maidens from the cruell hands of their aduer-saries, causing them to passe foorth by the breach, and presented them to the king, who appointed that they should be conueied in safetie, with all that they had about them, till they had gotten out of danger. Monsieur de Chatillon, by the kings com-mandement, caused all the rest within the fort to come forth, who passing thrée and thrée in a range came before the king, who stood there to behold them, with the whole armie placed so in order on either side the waie as they should come, that they might passe betwixt their ranks, as it were through a lane. They that came foorth in this sort might be (as the French writers record) about seuen or eight hundred in all of men and women, wherof there were manie hurt and maimed; some with halfe a shirt on to couer them, and diuerse starke naked. The lord Iohn Greie being mounted on a curtaile, passing by the French king, and saluting him, was courteouslie of him embraced.

The French writers report of their owne coun-triemens crueltie and sauagenesse.

The number that came foorth of Hambleteuue.

The morrow after was the fort of Blacknesse or Blaconnesse rendered to the French king, with like conditions as they of Hambleteuue had rendered theirs. This was on the tuesdaie the seuen and twentith of August. The nine and twentith of August sir Nicholas Arnault conueieng all the artillerie, munition, vittels, and goods out of Bullongne berg, caused fire to be set on that fort, and retired with all his soldiors and other people vnto Bullongne. Whervpon shortlie after the Frenchmen seized vpon the said place of Bullongne berg, & kept it. The French king leauing monsieur de Chatillon within Hambleteuue with the old bands of the French footmen, returned towards Bullongne, & approching within a mile and a halfe of the Old man, meant to build there a fort on the sea side: but what through such sharpe skirmishes as the Englishmen continuallie were redie to make with his men, and what through the abundance of raine which fell in that season, he was constreined to breake vp his campe, and leauing strong garrisons both of horssemen and footmen in all those places, which he had in that season woone out of the Englishmens hands, he returned himselfe with the princes of his bloud into France.

Causes that com-pelled the French king to breake vp his campe.

In this meane time whilest the French king was thus occupied, to vse the oportuni-tie of time in recouering of those fortresses in Bullongnois out of the Englishmens hands, the kings maiestie and his councell were busie still in quieting his rebellious subiects here in England: and finallie for meane of a full pacification, and to set all things in good frame and quiet rest, the king published his graces most generall and frée pardon to all rebelles, so that they would foorthwith (vpon publication of the

The kings gene-rall pardon.

same

same pardon) returne euerie man to his house and countrie; which they gladlie did: and so these seditious and most dangerous troubles were brought to end and pacified.

¶ Also in this busie time Marie Steward queene of Scots was conueied by sea out of Scotland into France, and there on the ninetéenth daie of Aprill 1549, was married in our ladie church in Paris (with great triumph and solemnitie) to Francis the Dolphin, eldest sonne vnto king Henrie the second of that name French king. This conueieng of the yoong quéene is reported by one to haue béene priuilie wrought, at such time as the councell of England were in some expectation and hope to obteine hir. Neuer-thelesse the subtill aduise of the French, and the trecherous forwardnesse of the Scots, vtterlie disappointed the honest and honorable purpose of the English. Now when the yoong quéene and hir traine, with the gard of hir person (be they whome you will) were vnder saile, the English nauie was abroad, and lieng in wait to haue intercepted hir course, meant not onlie to skirmish, but also to recouer the yong quéene from the French in spite of their hearts, had not the king of England and the most of his councell flatlie forbidden them to attempt anie warlike incounter, for certeine iust and weightie causes to them knowne. But the Scots smarted for this their vaine lightnesse, as in former times for like practises of their vile lewdnesse, as C. O. saith:

> Sic leuiora leui pluma promissa Scotorum
> Infamem reddunt gentem, dant sanguine pœnas
> perfidiæ quandóq; suæ velut antè dederunt.

In this troublesome yéere also Edmund Bonner bishop of London preached a sermon at Paules crosse, for the which he was accused vnto the councell by William Latimer parson of saint Laurence Pountneie, and Iohn Hooper sometime a white moonke, and so conuented before the archbishop of Canturburie, and other commissioners at Lam-beth, on the twentith daie of that same moneth, and sent to the Marshalsea. On the first of October he was depriued of his bishoprike, for disobeieng the kings order in religion.]

Now after that these hurlie burlies were throughlie quieted, manie of the lords of the realme, as well councellors as other, misliking the gouernment of the protector, began to withdraw themselues from the court. and resorting to London, fell to secret con-sultation for redresse of things, but namelie for the displacing of the lord protector. And suddenlie vpon what occasion manie maruelled, but few knew. Euerie lord and councellor went through the citie weaponed, and had their seruants likewise weaponed, attending vpon them in new liueries, to the great woondering of manie. And at the last a great assemblie of the said councellors was made at the earle of Warwiks lodg-ing, which was then at Elie place in Holborne, whither all the confederats in this matter came priuilie armed; and finallie concluded to possesse the towre of London, which by the policie of sir William Paulet lord treasuror of England was peaceablie obteined, & who by order of the said confederats immediatlie remooued sir Iohn Markam then lieutenant of the towre, and placed in that roome sir Leonard Chamberleine. And after that the said councell was broken vp at Elie place, the earle of Warwike remooued foorthwith into the citie of London, and laie in the house of one Iohn Yorke a citizen of London, who was then chiefe maister of the mint, kept at Suffolke place in Southworke. The lord protector hearing of the maner of the assemblie of this councell, and of the taking of the towre, which séemed to him verie strange and

doubtfull, did presentlie the said night remooue frō Hampton court, taking the king with him, vnto the castell of Windsore, and there began to fortifie the same, and withall wrote a letter to that noble gentleman the lord Russell lord priuie seale re-maining as yet in the west countrie, aduertising him of these troubles as followeth.

A letter

A letter of the lord protectors to the lord Russell lord priuie seale, concerning troubles working against him.

AFTER our right hartie commendations to your good lordship. Here hath of late Iohn Fox in the Acts and Monuments.
risen such a conspiracie against the kings maiestie & vs, as neuer hath béene séene, the which they can not mainteine, with such vaine letters and false tales surmised, as was neuer ment nor intended on vs. They pretend and saie, that we haue sold Bullongne to the French, and that we doo withhold wages from the soldiers, & other such tales and letters they doo spread abroad (of the which if anie one thing were true, we would not wish to liue) the matter now being brought to a maruellous extremitie, such as we would neuer haue thought it could haue come vnto, especiallie of those men towards the kings maiestie and vs, of whome we haue deserued no such thing, but rather much fauour and loue. But the case being as it is, this is to require & praie you, to hasten you hither to the defense of the kings maiestie, in such force and power as you maie, to shew the part of a true gentleman, and of a verie friend: the which thing we trust God shall reward, and the kings maiestie in time to come, and we shall neuer be vnmindfull of it too. We are sure you shall haue other letters from them, but as ye tender your dutie to the kings maiestie, we require you to make no staie, but immediatlie repaire with such force as ye haue to his highnesse in his castell of Windsor, and cause the rest of such force as ye maie make to follow you. And so we bid you right hartilie farewell. From Hampton court the sixt of October.

A letter of the lord protectors to the lord priuie seale.

Your lordships assured louing friend
Edward Summerset.

An answer to the lord protctors letter.

TO this letter of the lord protectors sent the sixt of October, the lord Russell returning answer againe vpon the eight of the said moneth, first lamented the heauie dissention fallen betwéene the nobilitie and him, which he tooke for such a plague, as a greater could not be sent of almightie God vpon this realme being the next waie (said he) to make vs of conquerors, slaues; and like to induce vpon the whole realme an vniuersall thraldome and calamitie, vnlesse the mercifull goodnesse of the lord doo helpe, and some wise order be taken in staieng these great extremities. And as touching the dukes request in his letters, forsomuch as he had heard before of the broile of the lords, and feared least some conspiracie had beene meant against the kings person, he hasted forward with such companie as he could make, for the suertie of the king as to him apperteined. Now perceiuing by the lords letters sent vnto him the same sixt daie of October, these tumults to rise vpon priuat causes betwéene him and them, he therefore thought it expedient, that a conuenient power should be leuied, to be in a readinesse to withstand the woorst (what perils soeuer might insue) for the perseruation both of the king and state of the realme from inuasion of forren enimies, and also for the staieng of bloudshed, if anie such thing should be intended betwixt the parties in the heat of this faction. And this he thinking best for the discharge of his allegiance, humblie besought his grace to haue the same also in speciall regard and consideration; first, that the kings maiestie be put in no feare; and that if there be anie such thing, wherein he hath giuen iust cause to them thus to procéed, he would so conforme himselfe, as no such priuat quarrels doo redound to the publike disturbance of the realme: certifieng moreouer the duke, that if it were true which he vnderstood by the letters of the lords, that he should send about proclamations and letters for raising vp of the commons, he liked not the same. Notwithstanding he trusted well that his wisedome would take such a waie, as no effusion of bloud should follow.

The effect of the lord Russels letter answering the lord protector.

And

The contents of the second answer of the lord Russell to the lord protector.

And thus much being conteined in his former letters the eight of October, in his next letters againe written the eleuenth of October, the said lord Russell reioising to heare of the most reasonable offers of the lord protector made to the lords, wrote vnto him and promised to doo, what in the vttermost power of him (and likewise of sir William Herbert ioined togither with him) did lie, to worke some honorable reconciliation betwéene him & them : so as his said offers being accepted and satisfied, some good

The good lord Russell a solicitor for peace betwéene the lord protector and the lords.

conclusion might insue, according to their good hope and expectation : signifieng moreouer, that as touching the leuieng of men, they had resolued to haue the same in readinesse for the benefit of the realme, to occurre all inconueniences whatsoeuer, that either by forren inuasion or otherwise might happen : & so hauing their power at hand to draw néere, wherby they might haue the better oportunitie to be solicitors and meanes for this reformation on both parts, &c. And thus much for the answer of the lord Russell to the lord protectors letters.

The lords of the councell assembled against the lord protector.

But now to procéed and go forward with the matter of the lords, who togither with the earle of Warwike (vpon what occasion God knoweth) were assembled at London (as ye haue heard) against the lord protector. When the king with his councell at Hampton court heard therof, first secretarie Peter with the kings message was sent vnto them, whome the lords notwithstanding deteined still with them, making as yet no answer to the message. Wherevpon the lord protector wrote as followeth.

A letter of the lord protectors to the councell at London.

The protectors letter to the lords.

MY lords we commend vs heartilie vnto you. And wheras the kings maiestie was informed that you were assembled in such sort as you doo, and now remaine, and was aduised by vs and such other of his councell as were then here about his person, to send master secretarie Peter vnto you with such a message, as whereby might haue insued the suertie of his maiesties person, with the preseruation of his realme and subiects, and the quiet both of vs and your selues, as master secretarie can well declare to you : his maiestie and we of his councell here doo not a little maruell, that you staie still with you the said master secretarie, & haue not as it were vouchsafed to send answer to his maiestie, neither by him nor yet by anie other. And for our selues we doo much more maruell and are sorie, as both we and you haue good cause to be, to see the maner of your dooings bent with force of violence, to bring the kings maiestie & vs to these extremities.

No word hitherto sent from the lords to the lord protector what they required of him to doo.

Which as we intend, if you will take no other waie but violence, to defend (as nature and allegiance dooth bind vs) to extremitie of death, and to put all to Gods hand, who giueth victorie as it pleaseth him : so if that anie reasonable conditions & offers would take place (as hitherto none hath béene signified vnto vs from you, nor we doo not vnderstand, what you doo require or séeke, or what you doo meane) and that you doo séeke no hurt to the kings maiesties person, as touching all other priuat matters, to auoid the effusion of christian bloud, and to perserue the kings maiesties person, his realme and subiects, you shall find vs agréeable vnto anie reasonable conditions that you will require. For we doo estéeme the kings wealth and tranquillitie of the realme more than all other worldlie things, yea than our owne life. Thus praieng you to send vs your determinate answer herein by master secretarie Peter, or if you will not let him go, by this bearer, we beséech God to giue both you and vs grace to determinate this matter, as maie be to Gods honor, the preseruation of the king, and the quiet of vs all : which maie be, if the fault be not in you. And so we bid you most hartilie farewell. From the kings maiesties castell of Windsor the seuenth of October, 1549.

Your lordships louing friend
Edward Summerset.

After

After the receipt of these letters, the lords séeming not greatlie to regard the offers The lords continue in their intended purpose against the lord protector. conteined therein, persisted in their intended purpose; and continuing still in London conferred with the maior of London and his brethren, first willing them to cause a good and substantiall watch by night, and a good ward by daie to be kept for the safegard of the citie, and the ports and gates thereof: which was consented vnto, and the companies of London in their turnes warned to watch and ward accordinglie. Then the said lords and councellors demanded of the lord maior and his brethren fiue hundred men to aid them, to fetch the lord protector out of Windsor from the king. But therevnto the maior answered, that he could grant no aid without the assent of the common councell of the citie: whervpon the next daie a common councell was summoned to the Guildhall in London. But in this meane time the said lords of the councell assembled themselues at the lord maiors house in London, who was then sir Henrie Amcotes fishmonger, and Iohn Yorke and Richard Turke shiriffes of the said A proclamation published against the lord protector. citie. And there the said councell agréed and published foorthwith a proclamation against the lord protector, the effect of which proclamation was as followeth.

1 That the lord protector, by his malicious and euill gouernement, was the occasion of all the sedition that of late hath happened within the realme.

2 The losse of the kings peeces in France.

3 That he was ambitious and sought his owne glorie, as appeared by his building of most sumptuous and costlie buildings, and speciallie in the time of the kings warres, and the kings soldiers vnpaied.

4 That he estéemed nothing the graue councell of the councellors.

5 That he sowed sedition betweene the nobles, the gentlemen, and commons.

6 That the nobles assembled themselues togither at London, for none other purpose, but to haue caused the protector to haue liued within his limits, and to haue put such order for the kings maiestie as apperteined, whatsoeuer the protectors dooings were, which (as they said) were vnnaturall, ingrate, and traitorous.

7 That the protector slandered the councell to the king, and did what in him laie to cause variance betwéene the king and his nobles.

8 That he was a great traitor, and therefore the lords desired the citie and commons to aid them to take him from the king. And in witnesse and testimonie of the Witnesses to the contents of the said proclamation. contents of the said proclamation the lords subscribed their names and titles as followeth.

The lord Rich lord chancellor, the lord S. Iohn lord great maister and president of the councell, the lord marquesse of Northampton, the earle of Warwike lord great chamberleine, the earle of Arundell lord chamberleine, the earle of Shrewesburie, the earle of Southampton Wriothesleie, sir Thomas Cheinie knight treasuror of the kings house and lord warden of the cinque ports, sir Iohn Gage knight conestable of the tower, sir William Peter knight secretarie, sir Edward North knight, sir Edward Montague chéefe iustice of the common plees, sir Rafe Sadler, sir Iohn Baker, sir Edward Wootton, doctor Wootton deane of Canturburie, sir Richard Southwell.

After the foresaid proclamation was proclamed, the lords or the most of them continuing and lieng in London, came the next daie to the Guildhall, during the time that the lord maior and his brethren sat in their court or inner chamber, and entered and communed a long while with them, and at the last the maior and his brethren The kings letter read to the citizens. came foorth vnto the common councell, where was read the kings letter sent vnto the maior and citizens, commanding them to aid him with a thousand men, as hath maister Fox, and to send the same to his castell at Windsore: and to the same letter was adioined the kings hand, and the lord protectors. On the other side, by the mouth The recorder an enimie to the lord protector. of the recorder it was requested, that the citizens would grant their aid rather vnto the lords: for that the protector had abused both the kings maiestie, and the whole realme, and without that he were taken from the king, & made to vnderstand his follie, this realme was in a great hazard: and therefore required that the citizens would willinglie assent to aid the lords with fiue hundred men: herevnto was none other answer made but silence. But the recorder (who at that time was a worthie gentleman called maister Brooke) still cried vpon them for answer.

At the last stepped vp a wise and good citizen, named (as maister Fox saith(George Stadlow, and said thus. In this case it is good for vs to thinke of things past to auoid the danger of things to come. I remember (saith he) in a storie written in Fabians chronicle, of the warre betwéene the king and his barons, which was in the time of king Henrie the third, and the same time the barons as (our lords doo now) commanded aid of the maior and citie of London, and that in a rightfull cause for the commonweale, which was for the execution of diuerse good lawes, wherevnto the king before had giuen his consent, and after would not suffer them to take place, and the citie did aid the lords. Now it came to an open battell, wherein the lords preuailed, and tooke the king and his sonne prisoners, and vpon certeine conditions the lords restored againe the king and his sonne to their liberties. And among all other conditions, this was one, that the king should not onelie grant his pardon to the lords, but also to the citizens of London, which was granted, yea and the same ratified by act of parlement. But what followed?

Was it forgotten? No suerlie, nor yet forgiuen during the kings life. The liberties of the citie were taken awaie, strangers appointed to be our heads and gouernours, the citizens giuen awaie bodie and goods, and from one persecution to another were most miserablie afflicted: such it is to enter into the wrath of a prince, as Salomon saith; The wrath and indignation of a prince is death. Wherefore forsomuch as this aid is required of the kings maiestie, whose voice we ought to hearken vnto (for he is our

high shepheard) rather than vnto the lords: and yet I would not wish the lords to be clearlie shaken off, but that they with vs, and we with them may ioine in sute, and make our most humble petition to the kings maiestie, that it would please his highnesse, to heare such complaint against the gouernement of the lord protector as may be iustlie alledged and prooued. And I doubt not but this matter will be so pacified that neither shall the king nor yet the lords haue cause to séeke for further aid, neither we to offend anie of them both. After this tale the commons staied, and the lord maior & his brethren for that time brake vp, and afterward communed with the lords.

The lords sat the next daie in councell in the Star chamber, and from thence they sent sir Philip Hobbie with their letters of credence to the kings maiestie, beséeching his highnesse to giue credit to that which the said Philip should declare vnto his maiestie in their names: & the king gaue him libertie to speake, and most gentlie heard all that he had to saie. And trulie he did so wiselie declare his message, and so grauelie told his tale in the name of the lords, yea therewithall so vehementlie and gréeuouslie against the protector, who was also there present by the king, that in the end, the lord protector was commanded from the kings presence, and shortlie was committed to ward in a tower within the castell of Windsore called Beauchamps tower.

And soone after were staied sir Thomas Smith, sir Michaell Stanhope, and sir Iohn Thin knights, master Whalleie, master Fisher, Woolfe of the priuie chamber, Graie of Reading, and diuerse other gentlemen that attended vpon the lord protector. And the same daie the lords of the councell came to Windsore to the king, and the next daie they brought from thence the lord protector, and the other that there were staied, and conueied them through the citie of London, with as much woonderment as might be, vnto the tower, where they remained prisoners.

¶ Touching the manner of the dukes comming to the tower from Windsore, I find that it was on the fouretéenth of October in the after noone, at which time he was brought on horssebacke through Holburne, in at Newgate, and so to the tower of London, accompanied with diuerse lords and gentlemen with thrée hundred horsse: the

lord

lord maior, sir Rafe Warren, sir Iohn Gresham, maister recorder, sir William Locke, The lord protec-
and both the shiriffes, and other kinghts, sitting on their horsses against Soper lane, tonr committed
with all the officers with halberds, and from Holburne bridge to the tower, certeine to the tower.
aldermen or their deputies on horssebacke in euerie street, with a number of housholders standing with billes as he passed.] Shortlie after the lords resorted to the tower,
and there charged the protector with sundrie articles, as followeth.

Articles obiected against the lord protector.

IN primis, you tooke vpon you the office of a protector and gouernour, vpon
condition expresselie and speciallie, that you would doo nothing in the kings affaires
publikelie or priuatlie, but by the assent of the late kings executors.

2 Also you, contrarie to the said condition, of your owne authoritie, did saie and
let iustice, and subuerted the lawes, as well by your letters as by your commandements.

3 Also you caused diuerse persons, being arested and imprisoned for treason, murther, manslaughter and felonie to be discharged and set at large, against the kings
lawes and statutes of this realme.

4 Also you haue made and ordeined lieutenants for the kings armies, and other
weightie affaires vnder your owne writing and seale.

5 Also you haue communed with the ambassadors of other realmes, discoursing
alone with them in the weightie causes of this realme.

6 Also you haue sometime rebuked, checked and tawnted, as well priuatlie as
openlie, diuerse of the kings most honorable councellors, for shewing and declaring
their aduises and opinions against your purposes in the kings weightie affaires, saieng
somtimes to them, that you need not to open matters vnto them, and would therefore
be otherwise aduised: and that you would, if they were not agréeable to your opinion,
put them out, and take other at your pleasure.

7 Also you had and held against the law in your owne house, a court of requests,
and thereby did inforce diuerse the kings subiects to answer for their free holds and
goods, and determined the same to the subuersion of the same lawes.

8 Also you being no officer, without the aduise of the councell, or the more part of
them, did dispose of the offices of the kings gift for monie, and granted leases
and wards of the kings, and gaue presentations to the kings benefices and bishopriks,
hauing no authoritie so to doo. And further, you did meddle with the selling of the
kings lands.

9 Also you commanded multiplication and alcumistrie to be practised to abuse the
kings coine.

10 Also you caused a proclamation to be made concerning inclosures, whereby the
common people haue made diuerse insurrections, and leuied open war, and distreined
and spoiled diuerse of the kings subiects, which proclamation went foorth against the
will of the whole councell.

11 Also you haue caused a commission with certeine articles therevnto annexed, to
be made out concerning inclosures of commons, high waies, decaieng of cottages,
and diuerse other things, giuing the commissioners authoritie to heare and determine
the same causes, to the subuersion of the laws and statutes of this realme: whereby
much sedition, insurrection, and rebellion haue risen and growne among the kings
subiects.

12 Also you haue suffered the rebels and traitors to assemble and to lie in campe and
armor against the king, his nobles, and gentlemen, without anie spéedie subduing or
repressing of them.

6 I 2

13 Also.

13 Also you did comfort and incourage diuerse of the said rebels, by giuing of them diuerse sums of your owne monie, and by promising to diuerse of them, fées, rewards, and seruices.

14 Also you in fauor of the said rebels did against the lawes cause a proclamation to be made, that none of the said rebels and traitors should be sued or vexed by anie person, for anie their offenses in the said rebellion, to the cleare subuersion of the same lawes.

15 Also you haue said in time of the rebellion, that you liked well the dooings and proceedings of the said rebels and traitors, and said that the couetousnesse of the gentlemen gaue occasion to the common people to rise: saieng also, that better it is for the commons to die, than perish for lacke of liuing.

16 Also you said that the lords of the parlement were loth to incline themselues to reformation of inclosures and other things; therefore the people had good cause to reforme the things themselues.

17 Also you after the report and declaration of the defaults and lacks reported to you by such as did surueie Bullongne and the péeces there, would neuer amend the same defaults.

18 Also you would not suffer the péeces beyond the seas, called Newhauen and Blacknesse, to be furnished with men and vittels; although you were aduertised of the defaults therein by the capteins of the same péeces and others, and were thereto aduertised by the kings councell: wherby the French king being the kings open enimie, was incouraged and comforted to win the said péeces, to the kings great losse, and dishonour of his realme.

19 Also you declared and published vntrulie, as well to the kings maiestie, as other the yoong lords attendant vpon his graces person, that the lords of the councell at London minded to destroie the king, and you required the king neuer to forget it, but to reuenge it: and likewise you required the yoong lords to put the king in remembrance thereof, to the intent to make sedition & discord betwéene the king and his lords.

20 Also where the kings maiesties priuie councell, of their loue and zeale that they did beare vnto the king and his realme, did consult at London to haue communed with you, to the intent to moue you charitablie to amend your dooings and misgouernement: you hearing of the said assemblie, did cause to be declared by letters in diuerse places the said lords to be high traitors to the king, to the great disturbance of the realme.

And thus much for these troubles of the lord protector, and articles against him obiected; to the end (as was doubted) that the same should haue cost him his life. But such was the pleasure of almightie God, disposing mens hearts as séemeth to him best; that at length, to wit, the sixt of Februarie next, he was deliuered; and that night he supped at sir Iohn Yorks one of the shiriffes of London, also the proclamation before set foorth against him was reuoked & called in. And thus being againe restored, though not to his former office, yet vnto libertie, he continued therein for the space of two yeares and two daies, till new troubles (as after shall appeare) chanced to him, which as they were to heauie for him either to cast off, or carrie awaie; so were his loders more readie to aggrauate his burthen, than willing to ease him anie waie of the weight. So that this his exaltation & raising to dignitie, in respect of the short continuance thereof as also for the enuie wherewith it was assailed, had béene better not to haue happened, than with such infelicitie in so short a time to haue ended. But this fall from honor & aduancement with losse of life (than the which nothing more pretious, nothing more delicious) gréeued him the lesse: bicause he might perceiue (as some suspected) that rather of enuie than otherwise (reseruing the

course

course of Gods iudgement and vengeance to the secrecie of his owne counsels) the same was deuised, prosecuted, & finallie practised:

> Nam quo quisque magis pius est, studiosior æqui,
> Charior & regi, & quo quisque potentior extat,
> Sentiet à prauis se tanto odiosius iri
> Deute Theonino rosum, quod fortè latenter
> Fiet & occultè, linguæ ne sentiat ictum
> Læthalem, donec stamen trux Atropos occet,
> Et vi Parcarum cœnum voluatur in imum.]

¶ The seuentéenth of October, king Edward came from Hampton court to his place in Southworke, and there dined, and after dinner he made maister Yorke one of the shiriffes knight, and then rode thorough the citie to Westminster. The lord maior of London for this yeare named sir Rowland Hill, was a man of great charitie and compassion, euident and effectuall testimonies whereof he hath left in the world; some of whose good deeds partlie in his remembrance & partlie for others example are descruedlie recorded. This man caused to be made a causeie, commonlie called Ouerlane pauement in the high waie from Stone to Nantwich, in length foure miles, for horsse and man, with diuerse lanes on both sides the same causeie. He caused likewise a causeie to be made from Dunchurch to Bransen in Warwikeshire, more than two miles of length, and gaue twentie pounds in monie towards the making of Roitton bridge, thrée miles from Couentrie. He made the high waie to Kilborne néere to London. He made foure bridges, two of them of stone, conteining eighteene arches in them both, the one ouer the riuer of Seuerne, called Achambridge; the other Ternebridge, for that the water of Terne runneth vnder it; the other two of timber at Stoke, and built a good part of Stoke church. He builded one notable frée schoole at Draiton in Shropshire, with maister and vsher, and sufficient stipends for them both, besides conuenient lodgings for the same. He also purchased a frée faire to the said towne, with a frée market wéekelie, & also a frée market for cattell euerie fouretéene daies. He gaue to the hospitall of Christs church in London in his life time fiue hundred pounds in readie monie, and a hundred pounds at his deccasse.]

But now to returne to other dooings. Whilest these hurls and tumults were in hand, to the danger of the whole state, the wars against the Scots were nothing followed, according to the former purposed meaning of the councell: so that it seemed necessarie to giue ouer the kéeping of Hadington, the same being in deed more chargeable (as was thought) than profitable, sith the garrison there could not be vitteled but with a great power to conduct the cariages in safetie, the enimies being still readie to take their aduantage to distresse them vpon anie opportunitie offered. It was therefore resolued, that the earle of Rutland should go thither to sée the fortifications raised, and to conduct from thence the men & ordinance in safetie home into England. Héerevpon the said earle with the Almans, and other souldiours then remaining on the borders, marched thither, and caused the bulworks, rampiers, and trenches to be rased and filled flat with the ground, and bringing from thence all the men, artillerie and munition, bag and baggage, returned vnto Barwike without incounter, in peaceable and quiet maner.

Shortlie after this, the kings maiestie called his high court of parlement, which began at Westminster, the foure and twentith daie of Nouember in this third yeare of his reigne, and there continued the same vntill the first daie of Februarie next following, which was in the beginning of the fourth yeare of his reigne. Among other things there enacted and concluded, one statute was made for the punishment of rebels, and vnlawfull assemblies: the which law was made by occasion of the late rebellion that happened in manner through the realme the yeare passed, & was not thought nor meant to haue touched anie noble man, speciallie such as the duke of Summerset

was

Abr. Fl. er I. S. 1044, 1045.

K. Edward rode through London.

Charitable déeds of sir Rowland Hill.

Frée schoole at Draiton in Shropshire.

His gift to Christs hospitall.

Hadington rased.

A parlement.

An act for vnlawfull assemblies.

was, which after (as it shall appeare) it did, and by that statute he was condemned within two yeares next after.

Abr. Fl. ex I. Stow. 1045. States created. Peter Gambo and another capteine murthered.

Gauaro and other hanged.

¶ The nineteenth of Ianuarie, sir Iohn Russell lord priuie seale, was created earle of Bedford : and lord saint Iohn Lord great maister, was created earle of Wilshire : and sir William Paget, comptroller of the kings house, was made lord Paget. On the same daie at night, were murthered by saint Pulchres church against the kings head without Newgate of London two capteins, that had serued the king at Bullongne and else-where, the one was sir Peter Gambo, the other Filicirga. Which murther was committed by Charles Gauaro a Flemming who came post from Barwike to doo that act. On the morrow, he with thrée of his companie was taken in Smithfield by the lord Paget, and sent to Newgate, and the foure and twentith of Ianuarie they were all foure, Charles Gauaro, Balthasar Gauaro, Nicholas Disalueron, and Francis Deualasco, had in a cart to Smithfield. And by the waie at the place where the murther was doone, Charles Gauaro had his right hand striken off on the cart wheele, and then all hanged in Smithfield; who being exhorted to reconcile himselfe to God and the world by confessing his fault, by repenting himselfe of the offense, and asking forgiuenesse, that he might with a disburthened conscience resigne his soule into the hands of God, obstinatlie and desperatlie answered, that he would neuer repent him of the déed.]

1550
———
An. Reg. 4.

About the same time, monsieur de Thermes that succeeded monsieur de Desse in gouernement as generall of the French forces in Scotland, came before Broughticrag, where he did so much by batterie & other kinds of inforcement, that giuing an assault both with his Frenchmen and certeine Scots ioined with him, the twentith of Februarie, the fort was entered by fine force, and all within it either taken or slaine. Sir Iohn Lutterell gouernour of that peece remained prisoner amongst the Frenchmen. More-

Sir Iohn Lut-terell prisoner. Erle of Warwike in highest authoritie.

ouer, now after the end of the parlement, the earle of Warwike, hauing then highest authoritie, and the rest of the lords of the councell, calling to remembrance how the last yeare in the time of rebellion, the French king had entered Bullongnois, and woone diuerse of the English forts there, being of great importance for defense of the towne and countrie, the default whereof was imputed to the negligent gouernment of the lord protector: and for so much as they well vnderstood that the French king vpon further practise had placed a capteine called the Reingraue, with diuerse regiments of Almaine lancequenets, and certeine ensignes also of Frenchmen, to the num-

Morguison the midwaie be-tweene Bullen and Calis.

ber of foure or fiue thousand at the towne of Morguison, being the midwaie betwéene Bullongne and Calis, to the great perill and danger as well of the countie of Bullongnois, as also of Calis, Guisnes, and all the low countrie.

The king therefore for the defense of the said Frontiers, caused all the strangers which had serued that yeare against the rebels, being to the number of two thousand, to be transported ouer the sea to the marches of Calis. And now at Christmas last

It is agréed among the lords to infest and annoie the French.

past, by order of the said earle, and of the councellors aforesaid, Francis earle of Huntington, and sir Edward Hastings his brother, sir Iames Croft, sir Leonard Chamberleine and diuerse other capteins and souldiers, to the number of thrée thousand, were sent ouer to the marches of Calis, to ioine with the said strangers, minding with as conuenient speed as they might to remooue the campe, and otherwise to annoie the French. But in the meane time through the diligent trauell of certeine persons, speciallie of one Guidoti an Italian, and a Florentine borne, there was a motion made for a treatie to be had by certeine commissioners, appointed betwixt the kings of England and France, for the conclusion of some peace, vpon such reasonable conditions and articles as might be thought expedient for the present time; and to stand with the honor and commmoditie of both the princes.

Commissioners sent to treat of peace.

This motion tooke such effect, that about the seuenth daie of Februarie, certeine commissioners, appointed for this treatie, that is to wit, Iohn the earle of Bedford, the

the lord Paget, sir William Peter the kings chéefe secretarie, and sir Iohn Mason, arriued at Calis: by reason of whose comming, the earle of Huntington, and the armie sent ouer before for the defense of the frontiers were countermanded from anie attempt, so that little or nothing was doone in that voiage, sauing certeine skirmishes at diuerse times, not much materiall to be written of. These commissioners being thus arriued, passed from Calis to Bullongne, there to méet with the commissioners appointed for the French king, where as a certeine house was newlie erected for the said treatie to be had, which was vpon the side of Bullongne hauen next to France, where after diuerse méetings & conferences of the commissioners of either partie, a finall peace was at last concluded betwixt both the realmes. But chéeflie among other things, for the restitution of Bullongne and Bullongnois to the Frenchmen, which were vpon certeine conditions following.

First, that the French should yeeld and paie to the king of England a certeine summe of monie, and the same to be paid at two paiments, as it was then agréed: and for the same summe the king of England should render the towne of Bullongne, and all the forts thereto adioining, which he then inioied, with all such artillerie and munition as was there found at the taking of the same to the French king. And for the sure paiment of the said sums, the French king sent into England for hostages and pledges, the counte de Anguien, Lewes the duke of Vandosme his brother, the Vidame of Chartres, and the duke de Aumale and others. And on S. Markes daie next following, being the fiue and twentith daie of Aprill, about eight of the clocke in the morning, the Englishmen did deliuer to the Frenchmen the possession of Bullongne, and the castels and forts in the countie of Bullognois, according to the agréements and articles of peace afore mentioned. And the fifteenth daie next following the French king entered into the said Towne of Bullongne with trumpets blowne, & with all the roiall triumph that might be, where he offered one great image of siluer of our ladie in the church there, which was called our ladie church: the which image he had caused speciallie to be made in the honor of the said ladie, and caused the same to be set vp in the place where the like image before did stand, the which before was taken awaie by the Englishmen at the winning of the towne.

¶ On Candlemasse daie, William lord S. Iohn earle of Wilshire, lord great maister, and president of the councell, was made lord treasuror. Iohn Dudleie earle of Warwike, lord great chamberleine, was made lord great maister. William Parre marquesse of Northampton, was made lord great chamberleine. Lord Wentworth was made lord chamberleine of the household. Sir Anthonie Wingfield capteine of the gard was made comptrollor of the kings house. And sir Thomas Darcie knight, was made vicechamberleine & capteine of the gard. And the earle of Arundell late lord chamberleine, with the earle of Southampton were put off the councell, and commanded to kéepe their houses in London. ¶ On the 10 of Februarie, one Bell a Suffolke man was hanged and quartered at Tiburne, for moouing a new rebellion in Suffolke and Essex. This time, the lord maior of London and the aldermen purchased all the liberties of Southworke, which were in the kings hands.

Soone after the aforesaid agréement betwéene England and France was concluded, vpon the fore remembred capitulations, bicause of suspicion of displeasure and hatred that was thought to remaine betwéene the earle of Warwike and the duke of Summerset, latelie before deliuered out of the tower, a meane was found that their friendship should be renewed through aliance, and a mariage was concluded betweene the earle of Warwikes eldest sonne, and the duke of Summersets eldest daughter: the which marriage was solemnized at Shene, the king being then present. After the solemnitie of this marriage, there appeared outwardlie to the world great loue and fréendship betwéene the duke and the earle, but by reason of carietales and flatterers the loue continued not long, howbeit manie did verie earnestlie wish loue and amitie

to

A peace concluded with France vpon certeine conditions.

Bullongne giuen vp to the French.

He entereth.

Abr. Fl. ex I. S. pag. 1046.
New officers created of the nobilitie.

The liberties of Southworke purchased.

The duke of Summerset deliuered out of the tower.

A marriage to compose strife and establish amitie.

Rich. Grafton.
Rebellion in Kent executed.
Priests children legitimate.
Usurie forbidden.
Abr. Fl. ex I. S. pag. 1047, 1048.
Alderman of Southworke.

to continue betwéene them. ¶ About this time was a new rebellion in Kent, but it was soone suppressed, and certeine of the chiefe were apprehended and put to death, namelie Richard Lion, Goddard Goram, and Richard Ireland. This yeare was a parlement holden at Westminster, where among other things by the authoritie of the said parlement, priests children were made legitimate, and vsurie for the loane of monie forbidden.]

¶ On wednesdaie in Whitsunweeke, at a court of aldermen kept at the Guildhall, sir Iohn Aliffe knight, and maister of Blackwell hall, was sworne alderman of the Bridge ward without, to haue iurisdiction of the borough of Southworke, and thus was he the first alderman that euer was there, who made vp the number of six and twentie aldermen of London, whereas before that time had beene but fiue and twentie.

Terme adiourned.
S. Barnabie kept holie.
High altar in Paules pulled downe.
No watch at Midsummer.

Trinitie tearme was adiourned till Michaelmasse, for that the gentlemen should kéepe the commons from commotion. The eleuenth of Iune being S. Barnabies daie, was kept holiedaie all London ouer: and the same daie at night, the high altar in Paules church was pulled downe, and a table set where the altar stood, with a veile drawne beneath the steps; and on the sundaie next a communion was soong at the same table, and shortlie after all the altars in London were taken downe, and tables placed in their roomes. This yeare was no such watch at Midsummer as had béene accustomed.

Earle of Southampton deceassed.
Charitable déeds of Andrew Iude.
Fréeschoole at Tunbridge.
Almes houses.

The thirtith of Iulie Thomas lord Wriothesleie erle of Southampton, knight of the garter, and one of the executors to king Henrie the eight, deceassed at Lincolne place in Holborne, and was buried in S. Andrewes church there. Sir Andrew Iude for this yeare maior of London, and skinner, erected one notable fréeshoole at Tunbridge in Kent, wherein he brought vp and nourished in learning great store of youth, as well bred in that shire, as brought from other countries adioining. A noble act and correspondent to those that haue beene doone by like worshipfull men, and other in old time within the same citie of London. He also builed almesse houses for six poore almesse people, nigh to the parish church of saint Helens within Bishopsgate of London, & gaue land to the companie of the skinners in the same citie, amounting to the value of thréescore pounds thrée shillings eight pence the yeare: for the which they be bound to paie twentie pounds to the schoolemaister, and eight pounds to the vsher of his free schoole at Tunbridge yearelie for euer, and foure shillings the wéeke to the six poore almesse people at S. Helens aforesaid, eight pence the péece wéekelie, and fiue and twentie shillings foure pence the yeare in coles amongst them for euer.

1551
An Reg. 5.
Arden murthered.
Arden described.
Loue and lust.
A paire of siluer dice worke much mischiefe.

About this time there was at Feuersham in Kent a gentleman named Arden, most cruellie murthered and slaine by the procurement of his owne wife. The which murther, for the horriblenesse thereof, although otherwise it may séeme to be but a priuate matter, and therefore as it were impertinent to this historie, I haue thought good to set it foorth somewhat at large, hauing the instructions deliuered to me by them, that haue vsed some diligence to gather the true vnderstanding of the circumstances. This Arden was a man of a tall and comelie personage, and matched in marriage with a gentlewoman, yoong, tall, and well fauoured of shape and countenance, who chancing to fall in a familiaritie with one Mosbie a tailor by occupation, a blacke swart man, seruant to the lord North, it happened this Mosbie vpon some misliking to fall out with hir: but she being desirous to be in fauour with him againe, sent him a paire of siluer dice by one Adam Foule dwelling at the Floure de lice in Feuersham.

After which he resorted to hir againe, and oftentimes laie in Ardens house: in somuch that within two yeares after, he obteined such fauour at hir hands, that he laie with hir, or (as they terme it) kept hir, in abusing hir bodie. And although (as it was said) Arden perceiued right well their mutuall familiaritie to be much greater than their honestie, yet bicause he would not offend hir, and so loose the benefit which he hoped to gaine at some of hir fréends hands in bearing with hir lewdnesse, which he might haue lost if he should haue fallen out with hir: he was contented to winke at hir

hir filthie disorder, and both permitted, and also inuited Mosbie verie often to lodge in Arden winkeu at his wiues lewdnesse, & why! his house. And thus it continued a good space, before anie practise was begun by them against maister Arden. She at length inflamed in loue with Mosbie, and loathing hir husband, wished and after practised the meanes how to hasten his end.

There was a painter dwelling in Feuersham, who had skill of poisons, as was reported. She therefore demanded of him, whether it were true that he had such skill in that feat or not? And he denied not but that he had indéed. Yea (said she) but I would haue such a one made, as should haue most vehement and speedie operation to dispatch the eater thereof. That can I doo (quoth he) and forthwith made hir such a one, and willed hir to put it into the bottome of a porrenger, & then after to powre milke on it. Which circumstance she forgetting, did cleane contrarie, putting in the milke first, and afterward the poison. Now maister Arden purposing that daie to ride to Canturburie, his wife brought him his breakefast, which was woont to be milke and butter. He hauing receiued a spoonefull or two of the milke, misliked the tast and colour thereof, and said to his wife; Mistresse Ales what milke haue you giuen me here? Wherewithall she tilted it ouer with hir hand, saieng, I wéene nothing can please you. Then he tooke horsse and road towards Canturburie, and by the waie fell into extreme purging vpwards and downewards, and so escaped for that time. Ardens wife attempteth means to make awaie hir husband. Arden is poisoned by his wife but recouereth.

After this, his wife fell in acquaintance with one Gréene of Feuersham, seruant to sir Anthonie Ager, from which Gréene maister Arden had wrested a péece of ground on the backeside of the abbeie of Feuersham, and there had blowes and great threats passed betwixt them about that matter. Therefore she knowing that Gréene hated hir husband, began to practise with him how to make him awaie; and concluded, that if he could get anie that would kill him, he should haue ten pounds for a reward. This Gréene hauing dooings for his master sir Anthonie Ager, had occasion to go vp to London, where his maister than laie, and hauing some charge vp with him, desired one Bradshaw a goldsmith of Feuersham that was his neighbor, to accompanie him to Grauesend, and he would content him for his pains. This Bradshaw, being a verie honest man, was content, and road with him. And when they came to Rainham downe, they chanced to sée three or foure seruingmen that were comming from Léeds: and therewith Bradshaw espied comming vp the hill from Rochester, one blacke Will, a terrible cruell ruffian with a sword and a buckler, and an other with a great staffe on his necke. She deuiseth another waie to dispatch hir husband Arden. A notorious murthering ruffian.

Then said Bradshaw to Gréene; We are happie that here commeth some companie from Léeds, for here commeth vp against vs as murthering a knaue as anie is in England: if it were not for them we might chance hardlie to escape without losse of our monie and liues. Yea thought Gréene (as he after confessed) such a one is for my purpose, and therefore asked; Which is he? Yonder is he quoth Bradshaw, the same that hath the sword and buckler: his name is blacke Will. How know you that, said Gréene? Bradshaw answered, I knew him at Bullongne, where we both serued, he was a soldier, and I was sir Richard Cauendishes man, and there he committed manie robberies and heinous murthers on such as trauelled betwixt Bullongne and France. Marke how the diuell will not let his organs or instruments let slip either occasió or opportunitie to commit most heinous wickednesse.

By this time the other companie of seruingmen came to them, and they going all togither, met with blacke Will and his fellow. The seruingmen knew blacke Will, & saluting him, demanded of him whither he went? He answered; By his bloud (for his vse was to sweare almost at euerie word) I know not, nor care not, but set vp my staffe, and euen as it falleth I go. If thou (quoth they) wilt go backe againe to Grauesend, we will giue thée thy supper. By his bloud (said he) I care not, I am content, haue with you: and so he returned againe with them. Then blacke Will tooke acquaintance of Bradshaw, saieng; Fellow Bradshaw how doost thou? Bradshaw vnwilling to renew acquaintance, or to haue ought to doo with so shameles a ruffian, said; A desperat villaine. An honest man is ashamed to renew old acquaintance with a knaue.

said; Why doo ye know me? Yea that I doo (quoth he) did not we serue in Bullongne togither? But ye must pardon me (quoth Bradshaw) for I haue forgotten you.

Then Greene talked with blacke Will, and said; When ye haue supped, come to mine hosts house at such a signe and I will giue you the sacke and sugar. By his bloud (said he) I thanke you, I will come and take it I warrant you. According to his promise he came, and there they made good cheare. Then blacke Will & Greene went and talked apart from Bradshaw, and there concluded togither, that if he would kill

master Arden, he should haue ten pounds for his labor. Then he answered, By his wounds that I will if I maie know him. Marie to morrow in Poules I will shew him thee, said Gréene. Then they left their talke, & Gréene bad him go home to his hosts house. Then Greene wrote a letter to mistresse Arden, & among other things put in these words: We haue got a man for our purpose, we maie thanke my brother Bradshaw. Now Bradshaw not knowing anie thing of this, tooke the letter of him, and

in the morning departed home againe, and deliuered the letter to mistresse Arden, and Greene & blacke Will went vp to London at the tide.

At the time appointed, Gréene shewed blacke Will maister Arden walking in Poules. Then said blacke Will, What is he that goeth after him? Marie said Gréen, one of his

men. By his bloud (said blacke Will) I will kill them both. Naie (said Gréene) doo not so, for he is of counsell with vs in this matter. By his bloud (said he) I care not for that, I will kill them both. Naie said Gréene in anie wise doo not so. Then blacke Will thought to haue killed maister Arden in Poules churchyard, but there were so manie gentlemen that accompanied him to dinner, that he missed of his purpose. Gréene shewed all this talke to maister Ardens man, whose name was Michaell, which

euer after stood in doubt of blacke Will, lest he should kill him. The cause that this Michaell conspired with the rest against his maister, was: for that it was determined, that he should marrie a kinswoman of Mosbies.

After this, maister Arden laie at a certeine parsonage which he held in London, and therefore his man Michaell and Gréene agréed, that blacke Will should come in the night to the parsonage, where he should find the doores left open, that he might come in and murther maister Arden. This Michaell hauing his maister to bed, left open the doores according to the appointment. His maister than being in bed, asked him if he had shut fast the doores, and hée said yea: but yet afterwards, fearing least blacke

Will would kill him as well as his maister, after he was in bed himselfe, he rose againe and shut the doores, bolting them fast. So that blacke Will comming thither, and finding the doores shut, departed, being disappointed at that time. The next daie blacke Will came to Gréene in a great chafe, swearing and staring bicause he was so deceiued, and with manie terrible oths threatened to kill maister Ardens man first, wheresoeuer he met him. No (said Gréene) doo not so, I will first know the cause of shutting the doores.

Then Greene met and talked with Ardens man, and asked of him, why he did not leaue open the doors, according to his promise? Marie (said Michaell) I will shew you the cause. My maister yesternight did that he neuer did before: for after I was in bed, hée rose vp and shut the doores, and in the morning rated me for leauing them vnshut. And herewith Gréene & blacke Will were pacified. Arden being redie to go homewards,

his maid came to Gréene & said; This night will my maister go downe. Wherevpon it was agréed that blacke Will should kill him on Reinam downe. When maister Arden came to Rochester, his man still fearing that blacke Will would kill him with his maister, pricked his horsse of purpose, and made him to halt, to the end he might protract the time, and tarie behind. His maister asked him whie his horsse halted, he said, I know not. Well (quoth his maister) when ye come at the smith here before (betwéene Rochester and the hill foot ouer against Cheetam) remooue his shoo, and search him, and then come after me. So maister Arden rode on: and yer he came at

the

the place where blacke Will laie in wait for him, there ouertooke him diuers gentle- Blacke Will misseth his pur-pose.
men of his acquaintance, who kept him companie : so that blacke Will mist here also
of his purpose.

After that maister Arden was come home, hee sent (as he vsuallie did) his man to
Shepeie to sir Thomas Cheinie, then lord warden of the cinque ports, about certeine
businesse, and at his comming awaie, he had a letter deliuered sent by sir Thomas
Cheinie to his maister. When he came home, his mistresse tooke the letter and kept
it, willing hir man to tell his maister, that he had a letter deliuered him by sir Thomas
Cheinie, and that he had lost it; adding that he thought it best that his maister
should go the next morning to sir Thomas, bicause he knew not the matter: he said
he would, and therefore he willed his man to be stirring betimes. In this meane while, Ardens wife visiteth, suc-coureth, em-boldneth, and direc'eth Black Will &c : how to accomplish his bloudie pur-pose.
blacke Will, and one George Shakebag his companion, were kept in a storehouse of
sir Anthonie Agers at Preston, by Greenes appointment: and thither came mistresse
Arden to sée him, bringing and sending him meat and drinke manie times. He therfore lurking there, and watching some opportunitie for his purpose, was willed in anie
wise to be vp earlie in the morning, to lie in wait for maister Arden in a certeine
broome close, betwixt Feuersham & the ferrie (which close he must néeds passe) there
to doo his feat. Now blacke Will stirred in the morning betimes, but mist the waie,
& taried in a wrong place.

Maister Arden & his man comming on their waie earlie in the morning towards
Shornelan, where sir Thomas Cheinie laie: as they were almost come to the broome Note here the force of feare and a troubled conscience.
close, his man alwaies fearing that blacke Will would kill him with his maister, feined
that he had lost his pursse; Why said his maister, thou foolish knaue, couldst thou
not looke to thy pursse but loose it ? What was in it ? Thrée pounds said he. Why
then go thy waies backe againe like a knaue (said his maister) and séeke it, for being
so earlie as it is, there is no man stirring, and therefore thou maist be sure to find it,
and then come and ouertake me at the ferrie. But neuerthelesse, by reason that blacke
Will lost his way, maister Arden escaped yet once againe. At that time, blacke Will
yet thought hée should haue béene sure to haue met him homewards: but whether
that some of the lord wardens men accompanied him backe to Feuersham, or that Blacke Will yet againe disap-pointed.
being in doubt, for that it was late to go through the broome close, and therfore tooke
another waie, blacke Will was disappointed then also.

But now saint Valentines faire being at hand, the conspirators thought to dispatch
their diuelish intention at that time. Mosbie minded to picke some quarrell to maister A prepensed quarel against Arden by the conspirators.
Arden at the faire to fight with him: for he said he could not find in his heart to mur-
ther a gentleman in that sort as his wife wished: although she had made a solemne
promise to him, and he againe to hir, to be in all points as man and wife togither, and
therevpon they both receiued the sacrament on a sundaie at London, openlie in a church
there. But this deuise to fight with him would not serue, for maister Arden both
then and at other times had béene greatlie prouoked by Mosbie to fight with him, but
he would not. Now Mosbie had a sister that dwelt in a tenement of maister Ardens Ardens wife, blacke Will, & the knot of vilans méet and conclude vpon their former prepensed mis-chiefe.
néere to his house in Feuersham: and on the faire éeuen, blacke Will was sent for to
come thither, and Gréene bringing him thither, met there with mistresse Arden;
accompanied with Michaell hir man, and one of hir maids. There were also Mosbie
and George Shakebag, and there they deuised to haue killed him in maner as afterwards
he was. But yet Mosbie at the first would nor agree to that cowardlie murthering of
him, but in a furie floong awaie, and went vp the abbeie stréet toward the flower de
lice, the house of the aforenamed Adam Foule, where he did often host. But before
he came thither now at this time, a messenger ouertooke him, that was sent from
mistres Arden, desiring him of all loues to come backe againe to helpe to accomplish
the mater he knew of. Herevpon he returned to hir againe, and at his comming backe,
she fell downe vpon hir knées to him, and besought him to go through with the matter;

as

O importunate & bloudie minded strumpet !

as if he loued hir he would be content to doo, sith as shee had diuerse times told him, he néeded not to doubt, for there was not anie that would care for his death, nor make anie great inquirie for them that should dispatch him.

Thus she being earnest with him, at length hee was contented to agrée vnto that horrible deuise, and therevpon they conueied blacke Will into maister Ardens house, putting him into a closet at the end of his parlour. Before this, they had sent out of the house all the seruants, those excepted which were priuie to the deuised murther.

The practise to kill Arden is now set abroch.

Then went Mosbie to the doore, and there stood in a night gowne of silke girded about him, and this was betwixt six and seuen of the clocke at night. Master Arden hauing béene at a neighbors house of his, named Dumpkin, & hauing cleared certeine reckonings betwixt them, came home: and finding Mosbie standing at the doore, asked him if it were supper time ? I thinke not (quoth Mosbie) it is not yet readie. Then let vs go and plaie a game at the tables in the meane season, said maister Arden. And so they went streight into the parlor: and as they came by through the hall, his wife was walking there, and maister Arden said; How now mistresse Ales ? But she made

Here the confederats ioine their practises.

small answer to him. In the meane time on cheined the wicket doore of the entrie. When they came into the parlor, Mosbie sat downe on the bench, hauing his face toward the place where blacke Will stood. Then Michaell maister Ardens man stood at his masters backe, holding a candle in his hand, to shadow blacke Will, that Arden might by no meanes perceiue him comming foorth. In their plaie Mosbie said thus (which séemed to be the watchword for blacke Wils comming foorth) Now maie I take

The watch-word to the principall murtherer.

you sir if I will. Take me (quoth maister Arden) which waie ? With that blacke Will stept foorth, and cast a towell about his necke, so to stop his breath and strangle him. Then Mosbie hauing at his girdle a pressing iron of fourtéene pounds weight, stroke him on the hed with the same, so that he fell downe, and gaue a great grone, insomuch that they thought he had béene killed.

Arden slaine outright.

Then they bare him awaie, to laie him in the counting house, & as they were about to laie him downe, the pangs of death comming on him, he gaue a great grone, and stretched himselfe, and then blacke Will gaue him a great gash in the face, and so killed him out of hand, laid him along, tooke the monie out of his pursse, and the rings from his fingers, and then comming out of the counting house, said; Now the feat is doone, giue me my monie. So mistres Arden gaue him ten pounds: and he comming

Blacke Will receiueth ten pounds for his reward of Ardens wife, for murdering hir husband.

to Gréene, had a horsse of him, and so rode his waies. After that blacke Will was gone, mistresse Arden came into the counting house, and with a knife gaue him seuen or eight picks into the brest. Then they made cleene the parlor, tooke a clout, and wiped where it was bloudie, and strewed againe the rushes that were shuffled with strugling, and cast the clout with which they wiped the bloud, and the knife that was bloudie, wherewith she had wounded hir husband, into a tub by the wels side; where afterwards both the same clout and knife were found. Thus this wicked woman, with hir complices, most shamefullie murdered hir owne husband, who most entirelie loued hir all his life time. Then she sent for two Londoners to supper, the one named Prune, and the other Cole, that were grosers, which before the murder was committed, were bidden to supper. When they came, she said: I maruell where maister Arden is; we will not tarie for him, come ye and sit downe, for he will not be long. Then Mosbies sister was sent for, she came and sat downe, and so they were merie.

Marke what a countenance of innocencie and ignorance she bore after the murdering of hir husband.

After supper, mistres Arden caused hir daughter to plaie on the virginals, and they dansed, and she with them, and so séemed to protract time as it were, till maister Arden should come, and she said, I maruell where he is so long; well, he will come anon I am sure. I praie you in the meane while let vs plaie a game at the tables. But the Londoners said, they must go to their hosts house, or else they should be shut out at doores, and so taking their leaue, departed. When they were gone, the seruants that were not priuie to the murder, were sent abroad into the towne; some to
séeke

séeke their maister, and some of other errands, all sauing Michaell and a maid, Mosbies sister, and one of mistres Ardens owne daughters. Then they tooke the dead bodie, and caried it out, to laie it in a field next to the church-yard, and ioining to his garden wall, through the which he went to the church. In the meane time it began to snow, and when they came to the garden gate, they remembred that they had forgotten the kaie, and one went in for it, and finding it, at length brought it, opened the gate, and caried the corps into the same field, as it were ten pases from the garden gate, and laid him downe on his backe streight in his night gowne, with his slippers on: and betwéene one of his slippers and his foot, a long rush or two remained. When they had thus laid him downe, they returned the same way they came through the garden into the house.

The workers of this mischiefe carie out Arden slaine into the field.

They being returned thus backe againe into the house, the doores were opened, and the seruants returned home that had béene sent abroad: and being now verie late, she sent foorth hir folks againe to make inquirie for him in diuerse places; namelie, among the best in the towne where he was woont to be, who made answer, that they could tell nothing of him. Then she began to make an outcrie, and said; Neuer woman had such neighbors as I haue, and herewith wept: in somuch that hir neighbors came in, and found hir making great lamentation, pretending to maruell what was become of hir husband. Wherevpon, the maior and others came to make search for him. The faire was woont to be kept partlie in the towne, and partlie in the abbeie; but Arden for his owne priuat lucre & couetous gaine had this present yeare procured it to be wholie kept within the abbeie ground which he had purchased; & so reaping all the gaines to himselfe, and bareauing the towne of that portion which was woont to come to the inhabitants, got manie a bitter cursse. The maior going about the faire in this search, at length came to the ground where Arden laie: and as it happened, Prune the groser getting sight of him, first said; Staie, for me thinke I sée one lie here. And so they looking and beholding the bodie, found that it was maister Arden, lieng there throughlie dead, and viewing diligentlie the maner of his bodie & hurts, found the rushes sticking in his slippers, and marking further, espied certeine footsteps, by reason of the snow, betwixt the place where he laie, and the garden doore.

This she did to colour hir wickednesse which by no meanes was excuseable.

Arden a couetous man and a preferrer of his priuat profit before common gaine.

Ardens dead bodie is descried by one of his acquaintance.

Then the maior commanded euerie man to staie, and herewith appointed some to go about, & to come in at the inner side of the house through the garden as the waie laie, to the place where maister Ardens dead bodie did lie; who all the waie as they came, perceiued footings still before them in the snow: and so it appeared plainlie that he was brought along that waie from the house through the garden, and so into the field where he laie. Then the maior and his companie that were with him went into the house, and knowing hir euill demeanor in times past, examined hir of the matter: but she defied them and said, I would you should know I am no such woman. Then they examined hir seruants, and in the examination, by reason of a péece of his heare and bloud found néere to the house in the waie, by the which they caried him foorth and likewise by the knife with which she had thrust him into the brest, and the clout wherewith they wiped the bloud awaie which they found in the tub, into the which the same were throwen; they all confessed the matter, and hir selfe beholding hir husbands bloud, said; Oh the bloud of God helpe, for this bloud haue I shed.

Footsteps all alongst from the dead bodie of Arden to his dwelling house.

A péece of Ardens heare and his bloud spilt in the house espied, as also a bloudie knife and a clout found.

Then were they all attached, and committed to prison, and the maior with others went presentlie to the flower de lice, where they found Mosbie in bed: and as they came towards him, they espied his hose and pursse stained with some of maister Ardens bloud. And when he asked what they meant by their comming in such sort, they said; Sée, here ye may vnderstand wherefore, by these tokens, shewing him the bloud on his hose and pursse. Then he confessed the déed, and so he and all the other that had conspired the murder, were apprehended and laid in prison, except Gréene, blacke Will, and the painter, which painter and George Shakebag, that was
also

Some of Ardens bloud vpon Mosbies pursse.

also fled before, were neuer heard of. Shortlie were the sessions kept at Feuersham, where all the prisoners were arreigned and condemned, And therevpon being examined wither they had anie other complices, mistres Arden accused Bradshaw vpon occasion of the letter sent by Gréene from Graues end, (as before ye haue heard)

which words had none other meaning, but onelie by Bradshaws describing of blacke Wils qualities; Gréene iudged him a méete instrument for the execution of their pretended murder. Whereto notwithstanding (as Gréene confessed at his death certeine yeares after) this Bradshaw was neuer made priuie; howbeit, he was vpon this accusation of mistres Arden, immediatlie sent for to the sessions, and indicted, and declaration made against him, as a procuror of blacke Will to kill maister Arden, which procéeded wholie by misvnderstanding of the words conteined in the letter which he brought from Greene.

Then he desired to talke with the persons condemned, and his request was granted. He therefore demanded of them if they knew him, or euer had anie conuersation

with him, & they all said no. Then the letter being shewed and read, he declared the verie truth of the matter, and vpon what occasion he told Gréene of blacke Will: neuerthelesse, he was condemned, and suffered. These condemned persons were diuerslie executed in sundrie places, for Michaell maister Ardens man was hanged in

chaines at Feuersham, and one of the maids was burnt there, pitifullie bewailing hir case, and cried out on hir mistres that had brought hir to this end, for the which she would neuer forgiue hir. Mosbie & his sister were hanged in Smithfield at London; mistres Arden was burned at Canturburie the foure and twentith of March. Gréene came againe certeine yeares after, was apprehended, condemned, & hanged in chaines in the high waie betwixt Ospring & Boughton against Feuersham; blacke Will was

burnt on a scaffold at Flishing in Zeland. Adam Foule that dwelt at the floure de lice in Feuersham was brought into trouble about this matter, and caried vp to London, with his legs bound vnder the horsse bellie, and committed to prison in the Marshalseie: for that Mosbie was heard to saie; Had it not béene for Adam Foule, I had not come to this trouble: meaning that the bringing of the siluer dice for a token to him from mistresse Arden, as ye haue heard, occasioned him to renew familiaritie with hir againe. But when the matter was throughlie ripped vp, & that Mosbie had cléered him, protesting that he was neuer of knowledge in anie behalfe to the murder, the mans innocencie preserued him.

This one thing séemeth verie strange and notable, touching maister Arden, that in the place where he was laid, being dead, all the proportion of his bodie might be séene two yeares after and more, so plaine as could be, for the grasse did not grow where his bodie had touched: but betwéene his legs, betweene his armes, and about the hollownesse of his necke, and round about his bodie, and where his legs, armes, head, or anie other part of his bodie had touched, no grasse growed at all of all that time. So that manie strangers came in that meane time, beside the townesmen, to see the print of his bodie there on the ground in that field. Which field he had (as some haue reported) most cruellie taken from a woman, that had béene a widow to one Cooke, and after maried to one Richard Read a mariner, to the great hinderance of hir and hir husband the said Read: for they had long inioied it by a lease, which they had of

it for manie yeares, not then expired: neuerthelesse, he got it from them. For the which, the said Reads wife not onelie exclaimed against him, in sheading manie a salt téere, but also curssed him most bitterlie euen to his face, wishing manie a vengeance to light vpon him, and that all the world might woonder on him. Which was thought then to come to passe, when he was thus murthered, and laie in that field from midnight till the morning: and so all that daie, being the faire daie till night, all the which daie there were manie hundreds of people came woondering about him. And

thus

thus far touching this horrible and heinous murder of maister Arden.　To returne then where we left.

About this time the kings maiestie calling his high court of parlement, held the same at Westminster the three and twentith daie of Ianuarie, in this fift yéere of his reigne, and there continued it, vntill the fiftéenth daie of Aprill in the sixt yeare of his said reigne.　In this parlement the booke of common praier, which in some part had béene corrected and amended, was newlie confirmed & established.　¶ In the end of this parlement, namelie the fifteenth of Aprill the infectious sweating sicknesse began at Shrewesburie, which ended not in the north part of England vntill the end of September.　In this space what number died, it cannot be well accounted: but certeine it is, that in London in few daies nine hundred and sixtie gaue vp the ghost. It began in London the ninth of Iulie, and the twelfth of Iulie it was most vehement: which was so terrible, that people being in best helth, were suddenlie taken, and dead in foure and twentie houres, and twelue, or lesse, for lacke of skill in guiding them in their sweat.　And it is to be noted, that this mortalitie fell chéeflie or rather vpon men, and those also of the best age, as betwéen thirtie & fortie yeers.　The spéedie riddance of life procured by this sicknes, did so terrifie people of all sorts, that such as could make shift, either with monie or freendship, changed their soile, and leauing places of concourse, betooke them (for the time) to abodes, though not altogither so-litarie, yet lesse frequented: to conclude, manifold meanes were made for safetie of life.　The first wéeke died in London eight hundred persons.

The manner of this sweat was such, that if men did take anie cold outwardlie, it stroke the sweat in, and immediatlie killed them.　If they were suffered to sléepe, commonlie they swooned in their sleepe and departed, or else died immidiatlie vpon their waking.　But the waie to escape danger was close keeping moderatlie with some aire and a little drinke, and the same to be posset-ale, and so to kéepe them thirtie houres, & then was the danger past; but beware of sudden cold.　Before men had learned the manner of keeping, an infinit number perished.　This disease at that time followed Englishmen & none other nation; for in Antwerpe and other countries, our Englishmen being there amongst diuerse other nations, onelie our Englishmen were sicke thereof, and none other persons.　The consideration of which thing made this nation much afraid thereof, who for the time began to repent and giue almes, and to remember God from whom that plague might well séeme to be sent among vs.　But as the disease in time ceased, so our deuotion in short time decaied.]　At this time also the king with the aduise of his priuie councell, and hauing also great conference with merchants and others, perceiuing that by such coins and copper monies, as had beene coined in the time of the king his father, and now were commonlie currant in the realme; and indéed a great number of them not worth halfe the value that they were currant at, to the great dishonor of the kings maiestie & the realme, and to the de-ceit & no little hinderance of all the kings maiesties good subiects, did now purpose not onelie the abasing of the said copper monies, but also meant wholie to reduce them into bullion, to the intent to deliuer fine and good monies for them.　And therefore in the moneth of Iulie by his graces proclamation, he abased the péece of twelue pence, commonlie called a teston vnto nine pence, and the péece of foure pence vnto three pence.　And in August next following, the peece of nine pence was abased to six pence, and the peece of thrée pence vnto two pence, and the pennie to an halfe-pennie.

On the eleuenth daie of October, there was a great creation of dukes and earles, as the lord marquesse Dorset was created duke of Suffolke, the earle of Warwike made duke of Northumberland, and the earle of Wilshire made marquesse of Win-chester, & sir William Herbert maister of the horsse; he also made William Cicill his secretarie knight, maister Iohn Chéeke one of his schoolemaisters knight, maister

Henrie

A parlement.

Booke of com-
mon praier con-
firmed.
*Abr. Fl. ex I.S.
pag. 1049.*
Sweating sicke-
nesse.

Iohn Caius.

Of this sweat
died Henrie &
Charles sons of
Charles Bran-
don, the elder
first, and the
yoonger after:
so that they
both died dukes
of Suffolke.

Rich. Grafton.

Remedie against
the danger of the
sweating sick-
nesse.

The imbasing of
the coine.

Two falles of
monie.

Creation of ho-
norable estates.

I. S. pag. 1050.

Henrie Dudlie knight, & maister Henrie Neuill knight. The sixtéenth daie of the said moneth being fridaie, the duke of Summerset was againe apprehended, & his wife also, and committed to the tower; with him also were cōmitted sir Michaell Stanhope, sir Thomas Arundell, sir Rafe Vane, sir Miles Partrige & other for suspicion of treason and felonie, whereof they were all shortlie after indicted. And so standing indicted, the second daie of December next following, the said duke was brought out of the tower of London with the ax of the tower borne before him, with a great number of billes, gleaues, halberds & pollaxes attending vpon him, & so came into Westminster hall, where was made in the middle of the hall a new scaffold,

where all the lords of the kings councell sate as his iudges: and there was arreigned and charged with manie articles both of felonie and treason. And when after much mild speech he had answered not guiltie, he in all humble manner put himselfe to be tried by his péeres: who after long consultation among themselues, gaue their verdict that he was not guiltie of the treason, but of the felonie. The people there present (which was a great number) hearing the lords saie not guiltie, which was to the treason. thinking most certeinlie that he was cléerelie acquited; and

chieflie for that immediatlie vpon the pronouncing of those words, he that caried the ax of the tower departed with the ax, they made such an outcrie and ioie, as the like hath not beene heard. Which was an euident declaration of their good willes and hartie fauors vnto him, whose life they greatlie desired to haue saued, for that he had deserued right well of most (though the good gentleman had some priuat enimies) and had béene as a man maie iustlie saie:

Solamen magnum patriæ, solamen amicis.

But neuerthelesse, he was condemned to the death, whereof shortlie after he tasted. The felonie that he was condemned of, was vpon the statute made the last yeare against rebelles, and vnlawfull assemblies, wherein amongst other things is one branch, that whosoeuer shall procure the death of anie councellor, that euerie such attempt or procurement shall be felonie. And by force of that statute, the duke of Summerset, being accompanied with certeine others, was charged that he purposed and attempted the death of the duke of Northumberland, the lord marquesse, the lord of Penbroke, and others of the priuie councell, which by statute was felonie.

After the duke was thus condemned, he was againe returned to the tower, and landed at the crane of the vinetree, and so passed through London, where were both exclamations: the oné cried for ioie that he was acquitted, the other cried out that he was condemned. But howsoeuer they cried, he was conueied to the

tower of London, where he remained vntill the two and twentith daie of Ianuarie next folowing. The duke being condemned (as is aforesaid) the people spake diuerslie, and murmured against the duke of Northumberland, and against some other of the lords, for the condemnation of the said duke: and also (as the common fame went) the kings maiestie tooke it not in good part. Wherefore as well to remooue fond talke out of mens mouths, as also to recreat and refresh the troubled spirits of the yoong king; who (as saith Grafton) séemed to take the

trouble of his vncle somewhat heauilie: it was deuised, that the feast of Christs natiuitie, commonly called Christmasse then at hand, should be solemnlie kept at Gréenwich with open houshold, and franke resort to court (which is called kéeping of the hall) what time of old ordinarie course there is alwaies one appointed to make sport in the court, called commonlie lord of misrule: whose office is not vnknowne to such as haue beene brought vp in noble mens houses, and among great house-keepers, which

vse liberall feasting in that season. There was therfore by order of the councell, a wise gentleman & learned named George Ferrers, appointed to that office for this yeare; who being of better credit & estimation than cōmonlie his predecessors had beene before, receiued all his commissions and warrants by the name of the maister of the kings pastimes. Which gentleman so well supplied his office, both in shew of

sundrie

sundrie sights and deuises of rare inuentions, and in act of diuerse interludes, and matters of pastime plaied by persons, as not onelie satisfied the common sort, but also were verie well liked and allowed by the councell, and other of skill in the like pastimes: but best of all by the yoong king himselfe, as appéered by his princelie liberalitie in rewarding that seruice.

¶ On mondaie the fourth of Ianuarie, the said lord of merie disports came by water to London, and landed at the tower wharffe, entred the tower, and then rode through tower street, where he was receiued by Vause lord of misrule to Iohn Mainard one of the shiriffes of London, and so conducted through the citie with a great companie of yoong lords & gentlemen to the house of sir George Barne lord maior, where he with the chéefe of his companie dined, and after had a great banket: and at his departure, the lord maior gaue him a standing cup with a couer of siluer and guilt of the value of ten pounds for a reward, and also set a hogshed of wine, and a barrell of beere at his gate, for his traine that followed him. The residue of his gentlemen & seruants dined at other aldermens houses, and with the shiriffes, and then departed to the tower wharffe againe, & so to the court by water, to the great commendation of the maior and aldermen, and highlie accepted of the king and councell.]

Abr. Fl. ex I. Stow 1055.

The shiriffes lord of misrule.

This Christmas being thus passed and spent with much mirth and pastime, wherewith the minds and eares of murmurers were méetlie well appeased, according to a former determination as the sequele shewed: it was thought now good to procéed to the execution of the iudgement giuen against the duke of Summerset, touching his conuiction & atteindor of the fellonie before mentioned. Wherevpon, the two and twentith daie of Ianuarie, then next following being fridaie, he was brought out of the tower, and according to the manner, deliuered to the shiriffes of London; and so with a great companie of the gard & others with weapons, was brought to the scaffold where he should suffer, without changing either voice or countenance, other than he was accustomed to vse at other times.

1552

The executiõ of the duke of Summerset.

The same morning earelie, the conestables of euerie ward in London (according to a precept directed from the councell to the maior) strictlie charged euerie houshold of the same citie, not to depart anie of them out of their houses, before ten of the clocke of that daie: meaning thereby to restreine the great number of people that otherwise were like to haue béen at the said execution. Notwithstanding, by seauen of the clocke, the tower hill was couered with a great multitude, repairing from all parts of the citie, as well as out of the suburbs. And before eight of the clocke, the duke was brought to the scaffold, inclosed with the kings gard, the shiriffes officers, the warders of the tower, & other with halberds: where as he nothing changing neither voice or countenance, but in a maner with the same gesture which he commonlie vsed at home, knéeling downe vpon both his knees, and lifting vp his hands, commended himselfe vnto God. After he had ended a few short praiers, standing vp againe, and turning himselfe toward the east side of the scaffold, nothing at all abashed (as it séemed vnto those that stood by) neither with the sight of the ax, neither yet of the hangman, nor of present death, but with the like alacritie and chéerefulnesse of mind and countenance as before times he was accustomed to heare the causes & supplications of other, & speciallie of the poore (towards whome as it were with a certeine fatherlie loue to his children he alwaies shewed himselfe most attentiue) he vttered these words to the people.

Meanes to restraine the multitude from the dukes execution.

Iohn Fox. The dukes behauiour at his death.

The words of the duke of Summerset at his death.

DEERELIE beloued friends, I am brought hither to suffer death, albeit I neuer offended against the king, neither by word nor deed, and haue beene alwaies as faithfull and true vnto this realme, as anie man hath beene. But forsomuch as I am by law condemned to die, I doo acknowledge my selfe as well as others, to be subiect there-vnto. Wherefore to testifie mine obedience which I owe vnto the lawes, I am come hither to suffer death, wherevnto I willinglie offer my selfe with most hartie thanks vnto God, that hath giuen me this time of repentance, who might thorough sudden death haue taken awaie my life, that I neither should haue acknowledged him nor my selfe.

Moreouer (deerelie beloued friends) there is yet somewhat that I must put you in mind of, as touching christian religion, which so long as I was in authoritie, I alwaies diligentlie set foorth, and furthered to my power. Neither doo I repent me of my dooings, but reioise therein, sith now the state of christian religion commeth most neere vnto the forme and order of the primitiue church. Which thing I esteeme as a great benefit giuen of God, both to you and me, most hartilie exhorting you all, that this which is most purelie set foorth vnto you, you will with like thankefulnesse accept and embrace, and set out the same in your liuing: which thing if you doo not, without doubt, greater mischiefe and calamitie will follow

Great feare among the peo-ple assembled on the tower hill. *Rich. Grafton. Iohn Stow.* When he had spoken these words, suddenlie there was a great noise heard, where-vpon the people were streight driuen into a great feare, few or none knowing the cause. Wherefore I thinke it good to write what I saw (saith Iohn Stow) concerning that matter. The people of a certeine hamlet which were warned to be there by seauen of the clocke to giue their attendance on the lieutenant, now came thorough the posterne, and perceiuing the duke to be alreadie on the Scaffold, the foremost began to run, crieng to their fellowes to follow fast after. Which suddennes of these men, being weaponed with bils and halberds, & this running caused the people which first saw them, to thinke some power had come to haue rescued the duke from execu-tion, and therefore cried Awaie awaie. Wherevpon the people ran, some one waie some an other, manie fell into the tower ditch, and they which tarried, thought some pardon had beene brought: some said it thundered, some that the ground mooued, but there was no such matter.

Abr. Fl. ex Io. Foxi mar-tyrologio. ¶ This amazement of the people is in other words recorded by Iohn Fox in the storie of this dukes troubles & death: which bicause they be effectuall I thinke good to interlace. When the duke had ended his speech (saith he) suddenlie there was a ter-A sudden noise & feare of the people at the death of the duke of Sum-merset. rible noise heard: wherevpon there came a great feare on all men. This noise was as it had beene the noise of a great storme or tempest, which to some seemed to be heard from aboue: like as if a great deale of gunpowder being inclosed in an armorie, and hauing caught fire, had violentlie broken out. But to some againe it seemed as though it had beene a great multitude of horssemen running togither, or comming vpon them; such a noise was then in the eares of all men, albeit they saw nothing. Whereby it happened, that all the people being amazed without any euident cause, and without anie violence or stroke striken, they ran awaie, some into the ditches and puddles, and some into the houses thereabout. Other some being affraid with the horrour and noise, fell downe groueling vnto the ground with their pollaxes & halberds, and most part of them cried out: Iesus saue vs, Iesus saue vs. Those which tarried still in their places, * Namelie *Iohn Fox* the writer of this report. for feare knew not where they were. And * I my selfe which was there present among the rest, being also affraid in this hurlie burlie, stood still altogither amazed, looking when anie man would knocke me on the head. It happened here, as the euangelists write, it did to Christ, when the officers of the high priests & Phariseis comming with wepons to take him, being astonied ran backe, & fell to the ground.

The like storie you shall read of Caius Marius in *Valerius Maxi-mus* the second booke and fift chapter. In the meane time, whilest these things were thus in dooing, the people by chance spied one sir anthonie Browne riding vnto the scaffold: which was the occasion of a new noise. For when they saw him comming, they coniectured that which was not true,

but

but notwithstanding which they all wished for, that the king by that messenger had sent his vncle pardon: and therfore with great reioising and casting vp their caps, they cried out; Pardon, Pardon is come: God saue the king. Thus this good duke, although he was destitute of all mans helpe, yet he saw before his departure, in how great loue and fauour he was with all men. And trulie I doo not thinke, that in so great slaugh-ter of dukes as hath béene in England within this few yeares, there was so manie weeping eies at one time: and not without cause. For all men did sée in the decaie of this duke, the publike ruine of all England, except such as indeed perceiued nothing.] The duke in the meane time standing still, both in the same place and mind wherin he was before, shaking his cap which he held in his hand, made a signe vnto the people that they should kéepe themselues quiet: which thing being doone, & silence obteined, he spake to them the second time in this maner. The great fa-uour of the peo-ple to the duke of Summerset.

The second speech of the duke of Summerset to the people.

DEERELIE beloued friends, there is no such matter in hand, as you vainlie hope or beleeue. It seemeth thus good to almightie God, whose ordinance it is meet & necessarie that we be all obedient vnto. Wherfore I praie you all to be quiet, and without tumult: for I am euen now quiet, and let vs ioine in praier vnto the Lord, for the perseruation of our noble king, vnto whose maiestie I wish continuall health, with all felicitie and abundance & all maner of prosperous successe: wherevnto the people cried out, Amen. Moreouer, I wish vnto all his councellors the grace and fauour of God, whereby they may rule althings vprightlie with iustice, vnto whome I exhort you all in the Lord to shew your selues obedient, the which is also verie necessarie for you, vnder the paine of condemnation, and also most profitable for the preseruation and safegard of the kings maiestie. And forsomuch as heretofore I haue had oftentimes affaires with diuerse men, & that it is hard to please euerie man that hath beene offended or iniuried by me, I most humblie require and aske them forgiuenesse: but especiallie almightie God, whome thoroughout all my life I haue most greeuouslie offended. And vnto all other, whatsoeuer they be that haue offended me, I doo with my whole heart forgiue them.

And once againe (dearelie beloued in the Lord) I require that you will keepe your selues quiet and still, least thorough your tumult you might cause me to haue some trouble, which in this case would nothing at all profit me, neither be anie pleasure vnto you. For Albeit the spirit be willing and readie, the flesh is fraile and wauer-ing, and thorough your quietnesse I shall be much more the quieter: but if that you fall vnto tumult, it will be great trouble & no gaine at all vnto you. Moreouer, I desire you to beare me witnesse, that I die heere in the faith of Iesus Christ, desir-ing you to helpe me with your praiers, that I maie perseuere constant in the same vnto my liues end.

Then he turning himselfe about knéeled downe vpon his knées, vnto whome doctor Cox, which was there present, to counsell and aduertise him, deliuered a certeine scroll into his hand, wherein was conteined a briefe confession to God. Which being read, he stood vp againe on his féet, without anie trouble of mind as it appeared, and first bad the shiriffes farewell, then the lieutenant of the tower, & certeine other that were on the scaffold, taking them all by the hands. Then he gaue the executioner monie, which doone, he put off his gowne, and knéeling downe againe in the straw, vntied his shirt strings: and then the executioner comming to him, turned downe his collar round about his necke, and all other things which did let and hinder him. Then he couering his face with his owne handkerchiefe, lifting vp his eies vnto Doctor Cox the dukes ghostlie father.

heauen, where his onelie hope remained, laid himselfe downe along, shewing no maner of trouble or feare; neither did his countenance change, but that before his eies were couered there began to appéere a red colour in the middest of his cheeks.

Abr. F. out of Iohn Fox in the Acts and Monuments.

The godlie end of the duke of Summerset.

¶ Thus this most méeke and gentle duke lieng along and looking for the stroke, bicause his doublet couered his necke he was commanded to rise vp and put it off: & then laieng himselfe downe againe vpon the blocke, and calling thrise vpon the name of Iesus, saieng: Lord Iesu saue me, as he was the third time repeating the same, euen as the name of Iesu was in vttering, in a moment he was bereft both of head and life; and slept in the Lord Iesus, being taken awaie from all the dangers and euils of this life, and resting now in the peace of God: in the preferment of whose truth and gospell he alwaies shewed himselfe an excellent instrument and member, and therefore hath receiued the reward of his labours. Thus gentle reader thou hast the true historie of this worthie and noble duke, and if anie man report it otherwise, let it be counted as a lie.]

This duke was in high fauour and estimation with king Henrie the eight, of whome he receiued sundrie high & great preferments, by reason that the said king had married ladie Iane his sister, by whome he had issue king Edward the sixt. He was not onelie courteous, wise and gentle, being dailie attendant at the court; but forward and fortunate in seruise abroad, as may well appeare in his sundrie voiages, both into France and Scotland. He was of nature verie gentle and pitifull, not blemished by any thing so much, as by the death of the admerall his naturall brother, which could not haue beene brought to passe in that sort, without his consent. But of this good duke (to let passe multitude of words) maister Fox hath written no lesse trulie than commendablie, & no lesse commendablie than deseruedlie, and no lesse deseruedlie than profitablie in his historie, whereto I refer the reader for further knowledge. Neuerthelesse of this vertuous duke by waie of application I saie as somtime one said (verie aptlie as some thinke) of the gratious ladie * An Bullen.

The duke of Summerset described.

* Who as it is supposed and proued since (saith Sleidan) was vniustlie condemned.

Discite vos viui, quid dira calumnia possit,
Inuidia alterius vitæ comes arcta beatæ,
Et falsis linguæ commista venena susurris.

The protectors of England collected out of the ancient and moderne chronicles, wherin is set downe the yeare of Christ, and of the king in which they executed that function.

The collectiō of Francis Thin in the yeare 1585.

VPON the death of this duke of Summerset protector of England, it shall not be vnfitting in this place to set downe all the protectors (whereof I can as yet haue intelligence) who haue béene gouernors, regents, gardians, or deputies of the realme, and of the kings person during his minoritie and time of his insufficiencie of gouernement; or else of his absence being out of the realme: whereof I haue made an especiall title in my Pantographie of England, in which this my collection of the protectors, although perhaps I shall not set downe all (for Barnardus non videt omnia) yet it is better to haue halfe a loafe than no bread, knowledge of some than of none at all. Thus therefore I begin.

Euendoline.

Euendoline the daughter of Corineus duke of Cornewall (after the procurement of warre against hir husband wherein he was slaine) was by common consent (for that hir sonne Madrane which she had by Locrine was insufficient by reason of his minoritie to gouerne the kingdome) made by the Britons ruler of the Ile, in the yeare of the world 2894, and so continued the same by the space of fiftéene yéeres, vntill hir sonne came to lawfull age.

Martia.

Martia (the widow of Guenteline the king) by reason that Sicilius hir sonne was

not

not of age conuenient to weld the scepter (as one being but seuen yeares old) obteined the gouernement both of the realme and of hir sonnes person, which she most worthilie deserued, being a woman of rare vertue and iudgement.

Eldred, Ethelred, or Edred (for all these diuersities are found in authors) brother _{Eldred.} to Edmund king of England, while the sonnes of Edmund (Edwine and Edgar) were for their minorities insufficient to dispose the kingdome, was appointed protector to his nephues, in the yeare of Christ 940, who about six or seuen yeares after his protectorship tooke on him the kingdome at Kingstone on Easter daie, in the yeare of Christ, as hath Iohn Stow 946, as others haue nine hundred fortie seuen.

Emma the quéene of England, the widow of king Etheldred, and of Canutus, _{Emma.} both kings of England iointlie, with Goodwine earle of Kent had the gouernement of the realme vnder Hardiknute king of England, who began his reigne in the yeare of Christ 1041.

Harold the sonne of Goodwine at the death of king Edward the Confessor (which _{Harold.} fell in the yeare of Christ 1066, and the three and twentith yeare of the same king) was by the testament of the said king Edward appointed regent of the yong Edgar Atheling (named heire in the life of the said Edward) and of the kingdome, after the death of king Edward, during the minoritie of the said Edgar. Beside which the like commending of the kingdome to this harold, in respect of the quéenes honour, as that before of the successours right, is set downe by one that liued at that time, and wrote the life of king Edward, of erle of Goodwine, and of his children, in these words. Porrectâq; manu (meaning king Edward lieng on his death bed, and speaking in the behalfe of Editha the quéene, sister to this Harold) ad prædictum nutricium suum fratrem Haroldum; Hanc inquit cum omni regno tutandam tibi commendo, vt pro domina & sorore vt est fideli serues & honores obsequio, vt quoad vixerit á me adepto non priuetur honore debito. Commendo pariter etiam eos, qui natiuam terram suam reliquerunt causa amoris meie, mihíque hæctenus fideliter sunt obsequuti: vt suscepta ab eis si ita volunt fidelitate eos tuearis & retineas, aut tua defensione conductos cum omnibus quæ sub me acquisiuerunt cum salute ad propria transfretari facias, &c. But he, when king Edward was dead, vsurped the crowne to himselfe, and shortlie after lost both his life and his kingdome.

Odo bishop of Baieux, and William Fitzosborne the first, being earle of Kent, and _{Odo bishop of Baieux, and William Fitzosborne earle of Hereford.} chiefe iustice of England, and the second being earle of Hereford, were gouernours of the realme, in the yeare of our Lord 1067, and the first yeare of William the Conquerour, when he went into Normandie after the conquest and indifferent quieting of the realme.

Lanfranke archbishop of Canturburie, as appeareth by Matthew Parker, writing in _{Lanfranke archbishop of Canturburie.} this sort in the life of the said Lanfranke: Absente Gulielmo omnia Lanfranco mandabantur, qui summa prudentia cuncta moderatus, proceres & plebem in officio tranquillè sine vlla motu atque tumultu continebat, adeò vt si quæ defectionis suspicio nascebatur, ad eam illicò compescendam maximus & potentissimus quisque opem & adiumentum illi imperanti præstitit.

Sir Richard Lucie knight, chiefe iustice of England was protector of the realme in _{Sir Richard Lucie chéefe iustice of England.} the twelfe yeare of the reigne of king Henrie the second, being the yeare of our Lord 1166, in the absence of the king when he was in Normandie, and in the parts beyond the seas. Which Lucie in the thirtéenth yeare of the same king, being the yeare of our redemption 1167, did valiantlie resist, and politikelie driue backe the carle of Bullongne inuading the realme. Hée built the abbeie of Leosnes or Westwood in the parish of Erith in Kent (and not in Southfléet as some haue written) in the yeare of Christ 1178, being about the foure and twentith yeare of king Henrie the second, and further built the castell of Angier in Essex, in the diocesse of the bishop of London. He had issue Godfreie bishop of Winchester, and thrée

daughters,

daughters, who after the death of Godfreie their brother were his heires: the eldest daughter of which sir Richard Lucie, was maried to Robert the first called Fitz-water: the second daughter Auelina, was maried to Riuers, of whome issued Iohn de Riuers: the third daughter Rose, was maried to Richard Warraine, son to king Iohn, as appeareth by a déed (belonging to my selfe, who had the rectorie of Leosnes) beginning thus: Rosa de Douer quondam vxor venerabilis viri Richardi filij regis de Chilham.

Hugh Pudsie bishop of Durham.

Hugh Pusaz de Puteaco or Pudsie, nephue to king Stephan, being bishop of Durham, and erle of Northumberland, and William Longcampe bishop of Elie, had the gouernement of the realme for Richard the first, vpon his departure foorth of the realme to take his iournie into the holie land. For in his absence he appointed this Hugh to haue the rule of the north parts, as chiefe iustice & warden of the realme from Humber to Scotland, deliuering to him also the keeping of the castell of Winchester, the other parts of the realme, with the custodie of the tower, he assigned to the gouernement of William Longchampe bishop of Elie, whome he made chiefe iustice and warden of those east, south and west parts, making him also his chancellour: who being a man of great diligence and knowledge in the administration of things, was yet verie factious and desirous of rule, honour and riches, farre aboue all measure. And with these two bishops hée linked in authoritie by commission Hugh lord Bardolph, William Marshall the great, earle of Chepstow Strigull or Penbroke, Geffreie Fitzpeter, and William Brewer, barons, men of great honor, wisedome & discretion. This the king did in the yeare of Christ 1190, and the first yeare of his reigne.

Walter de Constantijs archbishop of Roane.

Walter de Constantijs sometime chancellor of England, bishop of Lincolne, and now archbishop of Roane, vpon the misdemeanor of the proud bishop of Elie William Longchampe, about the yeare 1192, had the custodie and gouernement of the realme committed vnto him, whilest king Richard the first remained still in the holie warres: who being called from that place in the yeare of Christ 1193 (with Eleanor mother to the king) to come to king Richard then imprisoned in Austria, the archbishop of Canturburie Hubert succeeded him in the yeare 1194, whome the said archbishop of Roane procured to be installed in the see of Canturburie, which Walter de Constantijs (as hath Eueresden) was made bishop of Lincolne in the yeare 1183, and the next yeare after bishop of Roane.

Hubert archbishop of Canturburie.

Hubert Walter, or Walter Hubert (for such a transmutation of the name is vsed amongst historiographers) was made (vpon the discharge and going of Walter archbishop of Roane beyond the seas to king Richard) gouernor and protector of the realme, before the returne of Richard the first into England after the said kings imprisonment (by the duke of Austria and the emperour) procured by Sauaricus bishop of Glastenburie and Welles, & kinsman to the emperour, wherof our moderne printed chronicles nor our ancient writers, except one, make any mention. This Hubert died at his manor of Tenham, and was buried at Canturburie in the south wall, in the yeare of our redemption 1205, the third idés of Iulie, being the seuenth yeare of king Iohn.

Eleanor the widow of Henrie the second.

Eleanor widow to Henrie the second, and mother to Richard the first, was made protectresse of England, after the departure of hir son into France, when he had beene deliuered out of prison: in which office she continued during the life of hir sonne, which he ended in Poitiers in those French warres, by a hurt receiued from one that discharged a crossebow against him, on a fridaie as he besieged Chalons. Touching whose death (sith I am now in hand with the same) it shall not be amisse to set downe such seuerall verses composed by seuerall men in seuerall sorts, as I haue read, and are not yet made common to the world, which verses be these, concerning his death and place of buriall, as hereafter followeth:

Pictauus

> Pictauus exta ducis sepelit, tellúsque Chalucis
> Corpus dat claudi sub marmore fontis Ebraudi,
> Neustria túq; tegis cor inexpugnabile regis,
> Sic loca per trina se sparsit tanta ruina,
> Nec fuit hoc funus cui sufficeret locus vnus.

Whereof also another composed these following verses somewhat eloquentlie, as saith Matthew Paris (and so in truth they were, considering that age which mostlie vsed a riming kind of Latine verses, induced into the west part of the world by the barbarous Gothes) in his greater historie of the life of king Richard in manner and forme following:

> Ad Chalùs cecidit rex regni cardo Richardus,
> His ferus, his humilis, his agnus, his leopardus,
> Casus erat lucis, Chalus per secula nomen
> Non intellectum fuerat, sed nominis omen
> Non patuit, res clausa fuit, sed duce cadente
> Prodijt in lucem, pro casu lucis adeptæ.

Chalus quasi casus lucis.

Besides which verses of two seuerall men, it pleaseth my pen to ad also the third mans dooing, aswell for that the number of thrée is the holie number, as for that there is nothing so sweet, but that varietie dooth refresh it: yet especiallie sith it is delightfull to sée the seuerall inuentions of manie wits, this third poet therefore, exclaming against the daie in which the said king Richard the first receiued his deaths wound (being on a fridaie) dooth thus write:

> O veneris damnosa dies! ô sydus amarum!
> Ille dies tua nox fuit & Venus illa venenum,
> Illa dedit læthum, sed pessimus ille dierum,
> Primus ab yndecimo, quo yitæ victricus ipsum
> Clausit vtraq; dies: homicida tyrannide mira
> Transigitur, clausus exclusum, tectus opertum,
> Prouidus incautum, miles inimicus inermem.

This quéene Eleanor the protectresse died in the yere of Christ 1205, being the seuenth of king Iohn.

Gefferie Fitzpeter lord Ludgersall, who was by Richard the first made chiefe iustice of England, after the remouing of Hubert the archbishop of Canturburie, and was in the first yeare of king Iohn girded by him with the sword of the earldome of Essex, was also protector of the realme. Who being a man of great power and authoritie, was by nature gentle, by birth noble, in the lawes cunning, in reuenues great, and to all a good iusticer. This man was a bridle to king Iohn, to restreine his insolencie; since he was confedarat and alied in friendship & bloud with all the nobilitie of England: & for that cause was greatlie feared of the K. who said of him, as he did before of the archbishop Hubert, that he then did fullie reigne, when they two were dead. For turning to those which stood by him, when news was brought vnto him of the death of Fitz Geffreie, he sware by Gods feet, that he was then king & lord of England, and not before. Which words he would not vse, when the archbishop Hubert died; because this man was yet liuing, whome the king (as is alreadie said) greatlie feared. And therefore vpon the death of the archbishop, he did onelie saie that he began to reigne; but now vpon this mans departure out of the world, he said he was become a full Lord & absolute king of England. This Geffreie Fitzpeter died in the yeare of our redemption 1212, being about the fourtéenth yeare of the reigne of the said miserablie afflicted king Iohn, who died in the yeare of Christ 1216: whose death I haue beene the willinger here to mention; because I would set downe his epitaph (not else before set downe in our English chronicles) as I find the same of ancient report:

Geffreie Fitzpeter earle of Essex.

Hoc

Hoc in sarcophago sepelitur regis imago,
Qui moriens multum sedauit in orbe tumultum,
Et cui connexa dum vixit probra manebant,
Hunc mala post mortem timor est nefata sequantur.
Qui legis hæc metuens dum cernis te moriturum,
Discito quid rerum pariat tibi meta dierum.

This Geffreie Fitzpeter maried Beatrice, daughter and heire of William lord Saie, by whome he had issue, Geffreie Mandeuile earle of Essex, & Mawd maried to Humfreie de Bohune, by whome the Bohunes became earles of Essex.

William Mar-
shall earle of
Penbroke. William Marshall surnamed the great, being erle of Penbroke, was made protector of the realme, & person of the king, after that the king (being nine yeares of age) was crowned in the yeare of our Lord 1216. Which office this William (being also marshall of England) vsed so honorablie, that he recouered a great part of the nobilitie (which tooke part with Lewes son of the French king against king Iohn father to this Henrie) to assist the yoong king Henrie against the said Lewes: who in the time of the said Iohn had obteined a great part of the kingdome of England. By which meanes the said Lewes was expelled, and the kingdome wholie recouered to the vse of the said yoong king Henrie the third.

This William Marshall maried Isabell daughter and heire to Richard Strangbow earle of Penbroke, who made him a happie father in the multitude of his children. For by hir he had fiue sonnes, all which were in succession marshalls of England, and earles of Penbroke; and fiue daughters. The sonnes were William, Richard, Gilbert, Walter, and Anselme; who all dieng without issue, the inheritance was deuolued to the fiue sisters; which were, Mawd the eldest, maried to Hugh Bigod, in hir right earle marshall; Ione the second, maried to Waraine Monthensie, in hir right also earle of Penbroke, as hath Nicholas Triuet; Isabell the third, maried to Gilbert de Clare earle of Glocester; Sibill the fourth, maried to William Ferrers erle of Darbie; & Eue the fift daughter, maried to William de Berehuse, or de Brause. This William the great died in the yeare of our redemption 1219, being the third (as hath Nicholas Triuet) or the fourth (as hath Matthew Westminster) yeare of the reigne of the said king Henrie the third, and was buried at the new temple, on Ascension daie, being the seuenteenth calends of Aprill: of whome was made this epitaph by Geruasius Melcke-leie, taking vpon him the person of the earle marshall.

Sum quem Saturnum sibi sentit Hibernia, Solem
Anglia, Mercurium Normannia, Gallia Martem.

Which signifieth that he was a sharpe corrector and ruler of the Irish, an honor & glorie to the English, a councellor and dispatcher of the affaires of Normandie, a warlike knight and inuincible capteine against the Frenchmen.

Peter de la
Roches. Petrus de rupibus, or Peter of the Roch, being bishop of Winchester, was after the death of William Marshall earle of Penbroke aduanced to the protectorship of the king; because that the yoong king was almost destitute of anie of his owne kindred that might woorthilie haue the rule of his person. For his mother quéene Isabell was newlie maried to Hugh Brune earle of March in France. This bishop of Winchester (who was both a wise and a stout prelat) being now in possession of the king, and mistrusting that he had entred into a more weightie office than he might well discharge, if all things were not doone according to the fansie of the nobilitie, procured diuerse graue and honorable men to be preferred to the kings councell, and to be associats to him in the administration of the weale publike; and so entred into the administration of his new atchiued honor. Which yet he did not long inioie.

But as the bishop was at the first carefull to plant such of the nobilitie about the king, for the support of the realme; so yet himselfe being a Gascoine, did after in the riper yeares of the king prefer to offices about the king such Gascoins as both were
of

of his owne bloud and kindred; and by their extraordinarie dealing procured the nobilitie with an hard and vndutifull course to appose themselues against the king. This Peter was aduanced to the seat of Winchester, in the yeare of our redemption 1204, being about the sixt yeare of king Iohn. After which he went to Rome, and being a prelat more fit to fight than to preach, for Mars than for the muses; did returne from Rome in the yeare of Christ 1205, being about the seuenth yeare of king Iohn. He remained bishop about two and thirtie yeares, and died at his manour house of Fernham, on the fift ides of Iune, in the yeare of our Lord (as haue Matthew Paris and Matthew Westminster) 1238, being the two & twentith yeare of Henrie the third. Who somewhat before his death, about the one and thirtith yeare of his bishoprike, went into the holie land with the bishop of Excester. He builded, and indued with possessions manie religious houses: amongst which he founded Tich-field in Hampshire; of which Peter de la Roches, or of the rocks, Matthew Paris maketh a more large discourse.

Hubert de Burow, conestable of Douer castle, earle of Kent, and chiefe iustice of England, being of great account in the realme for his probitie and goodnesse, was made protector of the king and kingdome, in the yeare of our redemption 1221, being the fift yeare of king Henrie the third. This man in the yeare of Christ 1221 (being the same yeare in the which he was made protector) maried at Yorke, Margaret, sister to Alexander king of Scots. And here I thinke it not amisse to saie somewhat touching the issue of this Hubert of Burow, who in a certeine namelesse booke (caried about in the hands of all men) treating of the nobilitie (created since the inuasion of William Conqueror) is said to die without issue: which cannot possiblie be so, if that be true which I haue séene: which I am led by manie reasons to beléeue to be most true.

For I haue read of two children which this Hubert had, whereof the one being a sonne, was called Richard de Burow, who was knighted by Henrie the third (as it séemeth to me) after the death of his father: if this Richard be not the same Iohn, of whome Matthew Paris writeth, that in the yeare of Christ 1229, Rex Anglorum Henricus, in die Pentecostes Iohannem filium Huberti Angliæ iusticiary cingulo militari donauit tertio nonas Iunij. The other child was a daughter called Margaret, maried to Richard heire to the earldome of Glocester, as noteth Iohn Beuer in these words: Richardus hæres comitis Glouerniæ Margaretam filiam Hoberti de Burgo comitis Cantiæ in vxorem accepit. This Hubert of Burow was a verie old man, who after manie persecutions by the king, and after so manie chances of both fortunes, departed this world on the fourth ides of Maie in the yeare of our redemption 1243, being the seuen and twentith yeare of the reigne of king Henrie the third at his manour of Banstud, or Bansted. Whose bodie was honorablie caried to London, and there buried in the church of the frier preachers, to whom in his life he had giuen great gifts; and amongst other things, his goodlie place which stood not far from the palace of earle Richard of Cornewall (as I with some probable reasons coniecture) néere vnto Westminster, which afterward the archbishop of Yorke did procure. His wife the countesse of Kent, being likewise verie old, a woman that kept verie great hospitalitie, and that was well beloued, died in the yeare of Christ 1259, being the three and fortith yeare of Henrie the third, about sixteene years after the death of the earle hir husband.

Walter Greie archbishop of Yorke was made protector of the realme in this sort. The French king hauing vniustlie giuen the earldome of Poitiers to his brother Adulphus; Hugh Brune earle of March (the greatest of the nobilitie in that prouince) would not doo homage vnto Adulphus, but wrote his letters to his son in law king Henrie the third (whose mother Eleanor he had married) that if he would come into those parts, he should haue both aid of men, and furniture of war for the perfect restoring of those dominions to the crowne of England. For which cause Henrie the third assembling

[margin: Hubert de Barow earle of Kent.]

[margin: Walter Greie archbishop of Yorke.]

bling his power, did with his brother Richard (then latelie returned frō Ierusalem) depart the realme in the yéere of our redemption 1242, being the six & twentith yeare of his gouernment into Poitiers, & left the administration of the kingdome to Walter Greie archbishop of Yorke, whilest he should remaine in those parts. Which office the said archbishop held also in the yéere of Christ 1243, being the seuen and twentith yéere of king Henrie the third. Of this man is more mention made in my collection of the chancellors of England; in this place onelie further setting downe, that this Walter died in the yeere of Christ 1255, being about the nine and thirtith yeare of this Henrie the third, as hath Anonymus M. S.

Eleanor wife to king Henrie.
Eleanor daughter to Reimond earle of Prouince, wife to king Henrie the third and quéene of England, with Richard earle of Cornewall the kings brother (to whose custodie was committed Edward Longshanks, being after king of England by the name of Edward the first, son to the said king Henrie) were (in the yéere of our redemption 1253, being the seuen and thirtith yeere of the reigne of king Henrie the third) appointed gouernors and protectors of the realme in the kings absence, whilest he went into Gascoine, whither he went to pacifie the nobilitie and to kéepe the same in safetie from the French. And because my pen hath here fallen vpon Richard earle of Cornwall, I determine to say somewhat of him in this place, not hauing other occasion offered to me therefore. This Richard the son of king Iohn was borne in the yeare of Christ 1208, being the tenth yeare of the reigne of king Iohn. He was made (and so called) earle of Poitiers by Henrie the third, about the ninth yéere of his reigne, in the yéere of Christ 1225, who also that yéere with his vncle William earle of Sarisburie went into Poitiers, where he was ioifullie receiued: he putteth the earle of March to flight, he recouereth that which was lost to Gascoine, he went into the holie land, refuseth the kingdome of Apulia offered vnto him, he is chosen emperor, and receiueth that honor at Colen, being there crowned king of the Romans: he subdued Alfonsus competitor with him for the empire, he after returneth into England: he is an enimie to Simon Montfort and the barons rebelling against his brother king Henrie the third; he is taken prisoner by the barons, and is afterward deliuered: he was created knight and earle of Cornwall in the yeare of our redemption 1225, as hath Matthew Westminster, but as saith William Packington, he was created earle of Cornwall in the yeare of Christ 1227. He married foure wiues, if that Elisabeth his first wife and Isabell the widow of Gilbert de Clare were not all one woman. But leauing that to further knowledge, I doo for this time make them but one person; for so in truth it must be, whatsoeuer otherwise shall be shewed in mistaking their names. Elizabeth that was his first wife, as noteth Leland, was buried in the quéere of Belland, being that woman which is called Isabell, and was the daughter of William Marshall earle of Penbroke surnamed the great: and the widow of Gilbert de Clare earle of Glocester was maried to this erle of Cornwall, in the yeare of our Lord 1231 being the fiftéenth yeare of king Henrie the third.

This Isabell died in the yeare of our redemption 1240, being the foure and twentith yeare of the reigne of king Henrie the third, after this manner. For she being great with child, and néere to the time of hir deliuerance, fell into Morbum ictericum, or the hicket, and deliuering a child into the world, which had life, and was baptised by the name of Nicholas, they both presentlie died therevpon. Which thing when the earle vnderstood being then on his iourneie into Cornwall, he burst out in teares, and greatlie lamented that losse. Wherefore hastilie returning, and leauing his former iourneie, he honorablie, buried his wife at * Belland of Beauleu, an house of religion builded by king Iohn from the foundation, and replenished with Charterhouse moonks.

* Bellum locum a religious house in Hampshire, as is by some supposed.

His second wife was Sinthia or Sanclia, daughter to Reimond earle of Prouince, and sister to the queene of England, wife to king Henrie the third, brother to the said Richard earle of Cornwall, who maried the said Sinthia in the yeare of our redemption

tion 1243, being the seuen and twentith yéere of the reigne of king Henrie the third. Leland also appointeth to him the third wife, which was Beatrix de Famastais, whom he calleth quéene of Almaine, & wife to king Richard, brother to Henrie the third. Which ladie died in the yere of our redemption 1277, being the sixt yéere of Edward the first, and was buried at the friers minors in Oxford.   This noble Richard erle of Cornwall died in Februarie at Berkhamsted, in the yeare of Christ 1271, in the fiue and fiftith yeare of king Henrie the third, as saie Matthew Paris and Matthew West-minster : but Nicholas Triuet referreth his death to the yeare 1270, being the foure and fiftith yéere of Henrie the third : and the chronicle belonging to Guesham to the yeare 1272, being the six and fiftith yeare of Henrie the third.   After whose death his hart was buried in the friers minors of Oxford, and his bodie committed to the earth in the monasterie of Hales (being Charterhouse moonks) which he had builded at his charge of 10000 marks, which at this daie at fiue shillings the ounce of siluer amounteth to the summe of twentie thousand pounds.   He had two sonnes, the one called Henrie by his first wife Isabell; the other called Edmund de Almania by his second wife Sinthia.   Henrie was slaine by Simon and Guie of Montfort sonnes of the last Simon Montfort earle of Leicester, in the life of his father Richard in Italie at Viterbo, in the yere of our redemption 1270.   Which fact being doone in saint Syluesters church as he was at masse, occasioned the townesmen to paint the maner of his death on the wall of the church : and that picture being beheld by a certeine versifier, he was vrged therevpon to compose these following verses :

Regis Theutonici Richardi clara propago,
Sternitur Henricus, velut hæc designat imago,
Dum redit à Tropoli, regum fultus comitiua,
In crucis obsequio patitur sub gente nociua,
Irruit in templum, post missam, stirps Guenelonis
Perfodit gladius hunc Simonis atque Guidonis,
Disposuit Deus vt per eos vir tantus obiret,
Ne reuocatis his, gens Anglica tota periret,
Anno milleno Domini cum septuageno,
Atque duceno, Carolo sub rege sereno,
Vrbe Viterbina fit in eius carne ruina,
Cœli regina precor vt sit ei medicina.

His bones were brought into England, and buried in the monasterie of Hales, where his father was after also buried : but his hart was bestowed in a guilt cup, and placed beside the chaine of saint Edward the Confessor in Westminster abbeie.   The other sonne to this Richard earle of Cornwall was Edmund of Almaine, who after the death of his father was inuested with the honor of the earledome of Cornwall, being borne at Berkhamsted in the yéere of our redemption 1250, being the foure and thirtith yeare of the reigne of king Henrie the third, to whome his vncle Bonifacius bishop of Canturburie was godfather, and called him Edmund in the honor of saint Edmund archbishop of Canturburie and Confessor.   This Edmund earle of Cornwall married the daughter of Richard earle of Clare, of whom shall be more spoken when we come to treat of him as protector of England.

Boniface the archbishop of Canturburie, with others which follow, were protec-tors of the realme after this maner, as I haue gathered.   It was ordeined in the parle-ment of Oxford called Parlementum insanum, that the king should choose foorth twelue persons of the realme, and the communaltie of the land other twelue, the which hauing regall authoritie in their hands, might as gardians of the kingdome take in charge vpon them the gouernment of the realme, & should from yeare to yeare prouide for the due election of iustices, chancellors, treasurors, and other officers, and further prouide to sée the safe kéeping of the castels belonging to the crowne.

Boniface arch-bishop of Can-turburie.

These

These foure and twentie persons appointed to that function, began to order all things at their owne plesure : in the meane time not forgetting to vse things chieflie to their owne aduantage, as well in prouiding excheats and wards for their children and kinsfolks, as also in bestowing of patronages of churches belonging to the kings gift, vnto their owne liking So that these prouiders which shuld haue made carefull and beneficiall prouisions for the realme, made spéedie and plentifull prouision for them and theirs, insomuch that neither king nor Christ could get anie thing from these protectors. There be that write, how that there were but twelue or thirtéene chosen to be gouernors at this time (which for this present I déeme to be the truer opinion) whose names are as follow : Boniface archbishop of Canturburie, the bishop of Worcester, Roger Bigod earle of Norffolke and marshall of England, Simon de Montfort earle of Leicester, Richard de Clare earle of Glocester, Humfreie Bohune earle of Hereford, Richard Fitzalane earle of Arundell, sir Iohn Mansell chiefe iustice of England, sir Roger lord Mortimer, sir Hugh Bigod, sir Peter de Sauoie, sir Iames Audleie, and sir Peter de Montfort. To these (as some saie) was authoritie onlie giuen to punish all such as trespassed in the breach of anie of the constitutions of the parlement of Oxford. Others say that they were made rulers & protectors of the realme, and to dispose thereof, because the king was much misseled in the gouernment of the kingdome by the peruerse councell of his flatterers. Which twelue gouernors I suppose did not long continue: for being euerie one priuatlie for himselfe, and so not iointlie for the common-wealth, they grew diuided, and what the one labored to set vp, the other sought to pull downe.

Boniface arch-
bishop of Can-
turburie.   Boniface archbishop of Canturburie the second time, & the bishop of Worcester, with sir Philip Basset, or rather sir Hugh Bigod made chiefe iustice of England by the barons, were appointed in the yéere of our redemption 1260, being the fortie and fourth of king Henrie the third, to haue the gouernment of the realme in the absence of the king, whilest he remained in France at Paris about the affaires of Normandie : at what time a peace was made betwéene the kings of England and France.

Gilbert de Clare.   Gilbert de Clare the second of that name that was earle of Glocester and Hertford, was the sonne of Richard de Clare erle of Glocester and Hertford, which died in the yeere of our redemption 1262, being the fortie & sixt yeare of the reigne of king Henrie the third, and was buried at Tewkesburie, with a great image of siluer and gilt vpon his toome, and the same sword and spurres which he did weare in his life time. Of which Richard these verses were composed for his probitie and rarenesse of vertuous maners and conditions, and set vpon his toome :

Hic pudor Hyppoliti, Paridis gena, sensus Vlyssis,
Æneæ pietas, Hectoris ira iacet.

This Gilbert (I saie) the sonne of the said Richard was after the death of Henrie the third (which happened in the yeare of our Lord 1277, & in the seuen & fiftith yeare of the reigne of the said king Henrie) in the absence of king Edward the first in the holie warres made gouernour of the realme, vntill the returne of the said king Edward into England, to which function he was appointed by king Henrie the third, lieng on his death-bed: who caused the said Gilbert to sweare to kéepe the peace of the land to the behoofe of Edward his sonne. Which he did most faithfullie, vntill the second daie of August, in the second yeare of the said king, in which the said king Edward landed in England, being in the yeare of our redemption 1274, at what time the king was honorablie interteined of the said Gilbert, and Iohn earle of Warraine (a supporter to him in the charge of the kingdome) at the castell of Tunbridge in Kent, and Rigate in Surrie, which Gilbert with the other péers of the land, immediatlie after the death of king Henrie the third, assembling at the new temple brake the old seale of king Henrie, made a new seale in the name of king Edward, and
appointed

appointed faithfull officers for the sure kéeping and obseruing of the treasure, the riches, the peace, and the lawes of the kingdoms.

This Gilbert had two wiues, his first wife was Alice the daughter of Hugh le Brune erle of March, by whom he had issue a daughter, that was countesse of Fife in Scotland: his second wife was Ione the daughter of king Edward the first, called Ione of Acres, by whome he had one sonne, called Gilbert the third, earle of Glocester and Hertford, who married Mawd the daughter of Richard earle of Vlster in the yeare of Christ 1308 at Waltham, by whome he had issue a sonne, Iohn borne in the yeare of Christ 1312, being in the sixt yeare of Edward the second, that died without issue; after the death of which Gilbert the third, his lands and earldomes of Glocester and Hertford came to the sister of the said Gilbert the third, who was slaine in the battell of Striueling against the Scots in the seuenth (or as others haue the eight) yeare of king Edward the second, whome the Scots would gladlie haue kept for ransome if they had knowne him: but he had forgotten to put on his cote of armes to shew what he was, after which he was brought into England and was buried at Tewkesburie, vpon whose death the two earledomes of Glocester and Hertford were so dispersed, that there was neuer anie to this daie, that iointlie succéeded or possessed them both. Thus hauing digressed from Gilbert the second, in treating of his sonne Gilbert the third, let vs againe returne to him. He besides his sonne Gilbert the third, had by his wife Ione thrée daughters; Elenor, first married to Hugh Spenser, second sonne to Hugh Spenser earle of Glocester, and after his death to William Zouch; Margaret married to Piers de Gaueston earle of Cornewall and after to Hugh Audeleie; and Elizabeth or Isabell married in the yeare of our Lord 1308, being the first yeare of Edward the second, to Iohn the sonne of Richard earle of Vlster. This Gilbert the second, before the marriage of his second wife, was on the fiftéenth kalends of August diuorsed from Alice his first wife, in the yeare of our redemption 1271, being the six and fiftith yeare of the reigne of king Henrie the third; and after in Westminster church the last of Aprill married his second wife, about the eightéenth yeare of Edward the first being the yeare of Christ 1290, which Gilbert the second, being taken awaie by vntimelie death, departed this world in the yeare of our redemption 1195 (being the thrée and twentith of the reigne of the said Edward the first) who was in word & déed, in commandement and authoritie the greatest person of the kingdome, next to king Edward the first: for which cause he well deserued to haue his sepulture among his worthie ancestors.

Edmund earle of Cornewall, of whome there is somewhat spoken before, being the sonne of Richard king of Almaine, and earle of Cornewall brother to Henrie the third, married Margaret the daughter of Richard de Clare erle of Glocester, he was made protector of the Realme by Edward the first in the fouretéenth yeare (as some saie) or in the fiftéenth, as others saie (for there is so much disagréement amongst authors for the accounts of yeares, as it passeth anie one man to reconcile them in all points) when the said king went into Aragon to reconcile the two kings of Arragon & Naples. He continued in this office in the yeare of Christ 1287, or 1288, as hath Treuet, being the sixteenth yeare of Edward the first, in which he subdued Rise ap Merdach the Welsh prince, rebelling against Edward the first, and ouerthrew the castell of Druffillane (as hath the said Nicholas Treuet) he was lord of Wallingford, did much cost thereupon, and died without issue, as hath Matthew Westminster, in the yeare of Christ 1300: but as hath Thomas Walsingham 1301, leauing the king of England his heire. Yet are there some pedegrées and other authors, and those not the meanest, which saie that he had a daughter, Isabell married to Morice Fitz Harding lord Barkleie: so that these authors, which saie that he died without issue, are to be vnderstood of the issue male, & not of the heire generall: for they account him to die without issue, which leaueth no posteritie to continue his title of honor. The which their meaning they make more piaine, in that they saie that after his issulesse death, the

Edmund erle of Cornewall.

earledome

earledome came to the crowne. And here bicause there is mention made of Walling-ford, I will set downe what Leland hath written touching the same, bicause I desire to make common, and to preserue all whatsoeuer monuments of Leland that come vnto my hands: thus therefore he writeth of Wallingford in his commentaries of England, written in the yeare of our redemption 1542, being the foure and thirtith yeare of king Henrie the eight in these words.

The towne of Wallingford hath béene a verie notable thing and well walled. The dich of the towne, and the crest wherevpon the wals stand, be yet manifestlie perceiued, and begin from the castell, going in compasse a good mile and more, and so continueth to Wallingford bridge, a large thing of stone ouer the Thames. There remaine yet the names of these stréets amongst others. Thamesstreet, Fishstréet, Woodstréet, Goldsmiths row. And by the patents and donation of Edmund earle of Cornewall and lord of the honour of Wallingford, it appeereth that there were fourtéene parish churches in Wallingford: and there be men yet aliue that can shew the places and churchyards where they stood, at this time there are but thrée parish churches. The towne and the castell was sore defaced by the Danes warres, yet they méetlie florished in the time of Richard king of the Romans earle of Cornewall, and brother to Henrie the third, he did much cost vpon the castell which ioineth to the north gate of the towne, and hath thrée diches (as vpon the crests of the same may appéere) large and déepe, about each of the two first diches (on the crests of the ground cast out) runneth an embattelled wall now sore in ruine, and for the most part defaced. All the goodlie buildings, with the tower and dungeon, be within the third dich. There is also a collegiat chapell amongest the buildings within the third dich. Edmund earle of Cornewall son to Richard king of Romans was the first founder and indower of this college. Prince Edward the blacke (as one told me) augmented this college. There is a deane, foure priests, six clerkes, and foure choristers. The late deane be-fore doctor London that now is, builded a faire stéeple of stone at the west end of the collegiat chapell, to the making whereof he defaced (as it is said without licence) a peece of the kings lodging on the east end of the chapell. The deane hath a faire lodging of timber within the castell, and to it is ioined a place for the ministers of the chapell. Thus much Leland for Wallingford, & thus much I for Edmund earle of Cornewall and lord of Wallingford.

Edward of Carnaruan prince of Wales, sonne to Edward the first, was in the yeare of our redemption 1295 being the fiue and twentith yeare of Edward the first, pro-tector of England, in the absence of his father in Flanders, who because he was of tender yeares, had as tutors and gouernours appointed vnto him Richard bishop of Durham (Eulogium hath the bishop of London) William Montacute, with diuerse other knights, as Reignold Greie, Iohn Giffard, & Alane Plunket, being wise, discreet and expert soldiers.

Piers or Peter de Gauestone a Gascoine borne, whome king Edward the second so tenderlie loued as that he preferred him before all men, was appointed gardian of the realme in the first yeare of the said king Edward the second, being the yeare of our redemption 1308, when the king went into France and there aboad to marrie Isabell daughter to Philip king of France, before that the said Edward was crowned king of England, as hath Radulphus Higden. Of this Piers I will here saie litle, bicause I haue spoken more largelie of him in my pantographie of England.

Iohn de Drokensford bishop of Bath and Wels, was in the yeare of our redemption 1313, being the sixt yeare of king Edward the second, made protector of the realme in the absence of the said king Edward the second, and his wife quéene Isabell, who went into France to solemnize the coronation of Philip (sonne to Philip king of France) who was at that instant created king of Nauarre. This Drokensford was the four-téenth bishop of Bath & Wels. Great contention was there betwéene him and the

deane

deane and priests of that church. He succéeded in the bishoprike Walter Houelshaw. This Drokensford held the bishoprike about ninetéene yeares, he beautified the same with manie goodlie buildings, procured manie priuileges vnto it, and greatlie exalted his kindred. He was buried at Welles before the high altar of saint Iohn Baptist.

Henrie Lascie or Lacie earle of Lincolne, and of Salisburie, baron of Halton and of Pontfrait, corruptlie called Pomefret, and constable of Chester, was made protector of the realme in the fift yeare of Edward the second, being the yeare of our redemption 1310, whilest the king remained in the warres of Scotland. Which Henrie died shortlie after in the same yeare, and was buried in the new worke of Paules, who carried for his armes the purple lion cōtrarie to the cote his ancestors had borne before. This man had doone great seruice in the warres in the time of Edward the first, he married Margaret the daughter and heire of William Longespée earle of Salisburie, and had by hir a daughter named Alice, married to Thomas Plantagenet earle of Lancaster, Leicester, and Darbie. This Henrie (as I haue learned of other and read in Leland) had issue a bastard sonne, and hauing amongst manie other lordships the manour of Grantcester besides Camebridge, he gaue the same with other lands vnto that bastard, and commanded that the same Lacie so set vp iu Grantcester, should for himselfe and his successors euer name their sonnes and heires by the names of Henrie, which hitherto hath béene religiouslie obserued amongst them. And this was the originall of the houses of the Lacies in Grantcester, as Leland learned of him which was then heire of those lands. *(margin: Henrie Lacie earle of Lincolne.)*

Gilbert de Clare the third earle of Glocester of that name, after the death of Henrie Lacie, was chosen gouernour of the realme (the king being still in Scotland) during the time that the king shuld make his abode in that countrie. Of this man see before in the discourse of his father Gilbert the second earle of Glocester and Hertford, and protector of the realme. *(margin: Gilbert de Clare earle of Glocester.)*

Edward prince of Wales and duke of Aquitane, comming out of France with Isabell in the second yeare of Edward the second, his father was after his landing in England and the taking of his father made gardian of England vnder his father, which office he did not long continue: for deposing his father from the kingdome in the yeare of Christ 1326 he assumed the crowne himselfe in his fathers life. *(margin: Edwrd prince of Wales.)*

Walter Reinolds archbishop of Canturburie was with others appointed gardian of England on this sort. Edward the third as before atteining to the crowne in the yeare of our redemption 1327, or as some others more trulie saie 1326, being fourteene years of age did then begin his reigne. But bicause he was so yoong (not being of power or policie to weld so great a charge) it was decréed in this first yeare of his reigne, that twelue gouernors of the greatest lords within the realme should possesse the gouernement, vntill he came to riper yeares, whose names were as insueth: Walter archbishop of Canturburie, the archbishop of Yorke, the bishop of Winchester, the bishop of Hereford, Henrie earle of Lancaster, Thomas Brotherton earle marshall, Edmund of Woodstocke earle of Kent, Iohn earle of Warren, the lord Thomas Wake, the lord Henrie Persie, the lord Oliuer de Ingham, and the lord Iohn Rosse, who were sworne of the kings councell and charged with the gouernement of the kingdome as they would answere for the same. But this ordinance continued not long, for in the second yeare of this king, Isabell the kings mother and the lord Roger Mortimer tooke the whole rule into their hands, in such sort that the king and his councellors were in all affaires of state, and otherwise, onelie gouerned by their direction. Of this Walter Reinolds the archbishop, bicause he was sometime chancellor, and sometime treasuror, is more mention made in the large volume of the liues of the chancellours. *(margin: Walter Reinolds archbishop of Canturburie.)*

Iohn of Eltham earle of Cornewall sonne to Edward the second, had (in the fourth yeare of king Edward the third being the yeare of our redemption 1330) the gouernement of the realme committed vnto him, whilest king Edward the third had passed *(margin: Iohn of Eltham earle of Cornewall.)*

the

the seas onelie fifteene horsses in his companie, apparelled in clokes like vnto merchants, which office the said Iohn of Eltham executed vntill the returne of the said king, and before that also when the said Edward the third, in the second yeare of his reigne, did before this time go into France to doo his homage. He was made earle of Cornewall in the second yeare of king Edward the third, being the yeare of Christ 1328, and died at Barwike, others saie at S. Iohns towne in Scotland, in the moneth of October 1336, being the tenth yeare of Edward the third, and was honorablie buried at Westminster; for the solemnization of whose buriall the king came out of Scotland about the feast of the Epiphanie.

Edward the Blacke prince.

Edward the Blacke prince, eldest sonne to Edward the third, being about the age of nine yeares, was in the twelfe yéere of his father, being the yeare of our redemption 1338, or as saith Matthew Parker 1337, made gardian of England in the absence of his father, being as then sailed into Flanders to procure the Flemmings to aid him against the French king. Vnder which prince as some write (or rather as I for the time take it) equall in commission to him it séemeth that Iohn archbishop of Canturburie had the cheefest rule of the land, bicause that king Edward after his returne into England, which was about the fouretéenth or the fiftéenth of his reigne, charged the said bishop with certeine of the negligences which he vsed in collections of monie, whilest he had the chiefe rule of the land, when he was in the wars of France. Wherefore the words of Matthew Parker in the life of the said Iohn Stratford (saieng that the king held a parlement in which Omnem regni curam & gubernationem archiepiscopo cōmisit) must néeds be intended that he had that charge vnder or equallie with the said Blacke prince, as chéefest councellor to support the tender yeares of his sonne.

Iohn Stratford.

After which also in the yeare of our redemption, as hath the same Matthew Parker 1342, being about the sixteenth of the said Edward the third, the king committed the care & gouernement of the kingdome to the said archbishop, whilest the king was beyond the seas in the warres: for thus writeth the said Parker, fol. 257. Ac paulò post nulla purgatione indicta (speaking of the said bishop vniustlie accused to the king) aut recepta, omnibus penè parlamenti ordinibus pro archiepiscopo deprecantibus, rex eum sua sponte legitimè purgatum & excusatum pronuntiauit, eúmque multo magis charum quàm antè habuit, omnibúsque gerendis in Anglia rebus se in militia absente præfecit. Of which archbishop, being sometime chancellor and treasuror of England, shall be set downe a more large discourse in my large booke of the liues of the chancellors.

Lionell duke of Clarence.

Lionell third sonne to Edward the third, was in the ninth yere of the riegne of the said king Edward the third, being the yeare in which the word became flesh 1345, made gardian of England, in the absence of his father, who as then was sailed into the parts (beyond the seas) of Flanders. Of this man there is more spoken in my following treatise of the dukes of England.

Henrie lord Persie.

Henrie lord Persie, & Rafe lord Neuill, when Edward the third was sailed into Normandie, were in the twentith yere of the reigne of the said Edward the third, being the yeare of our redemption 1346, appointed to be gardians of the realme in his absence with the archbishop of Yorke, the bishop of Lincolne, and Thomas Hatfield bishop of Durham.

Thomas of Woodstocke.

Thomas of Woodstocke being verie yoong was made custos or gardian of England, in the yere that God tooke on him the forme of a seruant 1359, being the three and thirtith of the reigne of the said king Edward the third, when he sailed into France with 1100 ships. Of this man is more spoken in my discourse of the dukes of England, set downe in the time of quéene Elizabeth: and in my treatise of the conestables of England, set downe in the time of Henrie the eight pag. 867.

Iohn

Iohn of Gant duke of Lancaster, fourth sonne of Edward the third, bicause the king his father was féeble and sicklie (being now about thrée score & fiue yeares of age, though Bodinus in his Methodo historiæ saie that he died in his climactericall yeare of thrée score and thrée: for the truth is, that the said Edward the third was fourtéene yeares old when he began to reigne, and he reigned about one and fiftie yeares, which make of his age thrée score and fiue yeares) but especiallie for the sorrow which the king inwardlie conceiued for the death of that worthie prince his son, commonlie surnamed the Blacke prince. This Iohn of Gaunt (after the death of the said Blacke prince, which died in the yeare of Christ 1376, being the fiftith yeare of the reigne of Edward the third, whose death was déemed to be hastned by the said Iohn of Gaunt aspiring to the crowne, the plot whereof though it tooke not effect in the life of the said Iohn, yet it was performed in his sonne Henrie of Bullingbrooke, who deposed Richard the second) was appointed by his father Edward the third to haue the rule of the realme vnder him, the which he continued during his fathers life, which was not a full yeare after that he had made the said Iohn of Gaunt gouernour of England. After which death of king Edward the third, when Richard the second, a child of eleuen yeares of age began his reigne, in the yeare of our redemption 1377, in the first yeare of the said Richard the second, after his coronation, the said Iohn of Gaunt duke of Lancaster, & Edmund of Langleie earle of Cambridge brother to the said Iohn of Gaunt, were appointed to haue the gouernement of the kings person, and the administration of the common-wealth. But shortlie after, in the same yere of the king, in the yeare of our redemption 1378, the said Iohn of Gaunt gaue vp the same office. Of this man is more said in my treatise of the dukes of England.

Iohn of Gant duke of Lancaster.

William Courtneie bishop of London (but shortlie after his protectorship aduanced vnto the sée of Canturburie, in the yeare of Christ 1381, about the ninth of Ianuarie, being about the fourth of Richard the second, was made gouernor of the realme in this maner. After (as is before said) that the duke of Lancaster had wiselie weied the fickle estate of the realme, and considered that by the euill gouernment of the nobilitie, and inconstant mind of the yoong king, there must néeds fall a change of the estate, & doubting that if any thing succéeded otherwise than the nobles liked, the cause and negligence might be imputed to him, as one who cheeflie had the gouernment in his hands (and thanks howsoeuer the state was ruled he looked for none) did in the end after a few months authoritie (wholie misliking the maners of the court, which commonlie are not of the best in the minoritie of princes) surrender his protectorship, and obteined licence of the king to depart, and so got him quietlie to his castell of Kenelworth, permitting others to haue the whole swaie of the kingdome.

William Courtneie bishop of London.

Notwithstanding all which, in the second yeare of Richard the second, about the yeare of Christ 1379 being not altogither carelesse of the kings well dooing; this duke before his departing to Kenelwoorth, caused certeine graue persons with his full consent, to be ordeined, which should haue the gouernement of the kings person, and administration of the common-wealth. The names of whome were, William Courtneie before mentioned, Edmund Mortimer earle of March, Rafe Ergume bishop of Salisburie, and William lord Latimer, with others, of whome for the most part the people had conceiued a good opinion: yet bicause the said bishop of Salisburie, and the lord Latimer were associat to the rest, and of equall authoritie with them, the commons murmured greatlie against them. The cause for which they so misliked the lord Latimer, was for that he had sometimes bin too much fauouring to dame Alice Piers, concubine to king Edward the third, to whome the said lord Latimer was chiefe chamberleine, & therefore was of him best beloued, which two persons, the lord Latimer, and dame Alice, were by parlement in the fiftith yeare of Edward the third remooued from the king, for that they miscounselled him, but especiallie sith much mischiefe grew in the realme by the same Alice Piers. For she being now exalted in pride by ouermuch loue of K. Edward the third, would beyond the modestie and maner of women, sit in iudgement with the kings iustices, be with the doctors in the consistorie, turne sentences to what side she would, and require manie things dishonest in themselues, and dishonourable to the king, Of which woman, an old written chronicle belonging to the house of Euesham, hath deliuered to me these words: Alicia Piers regis concubina supra modum mulierum nimis & supergressa, sui etiam sexus & fragilitatis fœmineæ immemor, nunc iuxta iusticiarios regios nunc in foro ecclesiastico iuxta doctores sedendo, & pro defensione causarum suadere, & etiam contra iura postulare minimè verebatur, vnde propter scandalum petierunt ab illo (which was the king) penitùs amoueri in parlemento tento anno Domini 1376 & 50 Ed. 3. Thus that author.

And here before I go anie further with my protectors, bicause some curious heads that find not all these matters in the records of the tower, which they dailie turne with a churlish hand, or else thinke that nothing maie be knowne out of the walles of their office, will séeme to séeke a knot in a rush, and saie that I in compasse of some few lines haue written a contrarietie, in saieng that Iohn of Gaunt thirsted after the kingdome, and for that cause hastened the death of his elder brother prince Edward the blacke as Richard the third did the death of his brother George duke of Clarence, which intent could not possiblie be in Iohn of Gaunt, as appeareth by my owne following words: where I saie that he gaue ouer the protectorship of his nephue, bicause he would auoid all suspicion of euill gouernement: which hée would neuer haue doone if he had so ment, that place being so apt for the execution of his purpose, and might giue occasion to him that neuer ment anie such matter before, to attempt it being in that place, as Richard duke of Yorke did attempt, but not performe it, in the time of Henrie the sixt; and as Richard duke of Glocester, being in the same office of protectorship, did not onelie attempt it, but brought to perfection. Wherevnto I answer that all this is no contrarietie, but onelie a manifest shew and confirmation, the one part of my words to the other. For sith he could not in the life of his father Edward the third before the crowning of king Richard the second (as Richard the third did) atteine the crowne, he would not now attempt it (the king being once crowned, and in full possession of the kingdome) so rashlie and vnaduisedlie (as did Richard duke of Yorke against Henrie, for which he was in the end slaine) least that thereby his part might séeme to carie the face of a rebellion, as in truth it should haue doone. For whosoeuer either for colour of God, benefit to their countrie, or for whatsoeuer cause, lift vp the sword against a crowned king, sitting at the sterne of gouernement, being one of the gods of the earth, the same must needs tend vnto a rebellion, which Iohn of Gaunt would not seeme to execute, & for that cause leauing off his purpose at that time, he did in the end also leaue the whole matter to his son to performe, especiallie sith he afterward perceiued Richard the second so much to fauor and further him with monie, munition, and men, to recouer the kingdome of Castile & Arragon in Spaine, in the right of the wife of the said Iohn of Gaunt. To whom and to his wife (as hath Henrie Knighton) king Richard the second gaue a seuerall crowne of gold to honour them withall, & to shew how intierlie he loued them when they both went into Spaine. And for these causes the said Iohn of Gaunt refused the oportunitie of time & place in the king his nephues minoritie to execute it. But did he cease it so? No. For that sparke although it were a litle cooled, was not vtterlie quenched, bicause he hastened the same in his son, whom he not onelie persuaded, but furthered (after the banishment of his said sonne Henrie of Bullingbrooke by Richard the second in the life of the said Iohn of Gaunt) to returne into England, and after his death to chalenge by sword the earldome of Lancaster his right inheritance, and vnder the same to reuenge the death of the duke of Glocester and others: and by that means, when Richard

the

the second was out of the realme of England in Ireland, the said Henrie Bullingbrooke sonne of Iohn of Gaunt entered the realme, put downe the king, and got the crowne which his father sought. Thus this much digressing from the protectors, and to returne to that course which I haue in hand, I will leaue the discourse of policies to obteine kingdoms, bicause they be no balles for me to bandie, and follow on my former intent as meeter for my simplicitie.

Thomas Beauchampe earle of Warwike was in the third yeare of Richard the second, being the yeare of our redemption 1380, made protector in this sort. In the parlement holden the same yeare, at the speciall sute of the lords, and of the commons, the bishops and barons chosen (as you haue heard) before by Iohn of Gaunt to be protectors of the realme, were remoued, and the earle of Warwike especiallie elected to that function, to remaine continuallie with the king as chéefe gouernor of his roiall person; & one that should giue answer to all forreners repairing thither, vpon what cause soeuer their comming were; hauing further as ample gouernment of the kingdome giuen vnto him, as the other remoued gouernors had. Being placed in that office by the duke of Lancaster, he died the sixt ides of Aprill, in the yeare of Christ 1401, being the third yeare of Henrie the fourth. He maried Margaret, the daughter of William lord Ferrers of Grobie; by whome he had issue, Richard earle of Warwike. Thomas Beauchampe earle of Warwike.

Thomas Fitzalane otherwise called Arundell bishop of Elie, the two and twentith that inioied that seat, being two and twentie yeares of age, and the son of Richard Fitzalane earle of Arundell & Warren, was with others made protector of England in this sort. At a parlement holden at London in the tenth yeare of Richard the second, being the yeare of Christ 1386, were certeine gouernors of the kingdome elected, because the treasure of the realme had beene imbesiled & lewdlie wasted, nothing to the profit of the king and kingdome, by the couetous and euill gouernment of the deposed officers, which were Michaell de la Poole earle of Suffolke lord chancellor, Iohn Fortham bishop of Durham lord treasuror, & diuerse other persons that ruled about the king. Thomas Arundell bishop of Elie.

Now the gouernors elected by this parlement were in number thirtéene; and by name Thomas Arundell bishop of Elie, then made lord chancellor; Iohn Gilbert bishop of Hereford made lord treasuror; and Nicholas abbat of Waltham at that time made kéeper of the priuie seale; William Courtneie archbishop of Canturburie, Alexander Neuill archbishop of Yorke, Edmund Langleie duke of Yorke, Thomas of Woodstocke duke of Glocester, William bishop of Winchester, Thomas bishop of Excester, Richard Fitzalane erle of Arundell, Iohn lord Deuereux, and Reinold lord Cobham of Starborow. These were thus by parlement chosen to haue vnder the king the whole ouersight and gouernment of the realme, as by their commission in the statutes of the tenth yeare of the said Richard the second it dooth in the printed booke appeare.

Edmund Langleie duke of Yorke, vncle vnto Richard the second, was in the eighteenth yeare of the said Richard, being about the yeare of our redemption 1395, ordeined lord gardian of England, in the kings absence in the realme of Ireland. This protector caused a parlement to be assembled at Westminster: where he dealt so effectuallie, notwithstanding the vntowardnesse of the burgesses, that a tenth was granted by the cleargie, and a fifteenth by the temporaltie; but not without protestation, that those paiments were granted of a méere fréewill, for the loue they bare to the king, and to haue the affaires in Ireland to succéed the better. After this, about foure yeares; king Richard the second in the two and twentith yeare of his reigne, in the yeare of Christ 1399, making another voiage into Ireland (being the last and most vnhappie that euer was to him, for before his returne he had in effect lost his realme, which after his comming he lost in deed) did againe in his absence substitute this Edmund of Langleie duke of Yorke.

                                   Edmund

Edmund duke of Yorke as cheefe gouernor of England. Who in the absence of the king, assembled a power of men against Henrie of Bullingbrooke, now entered into the land to challenge the dukedome of Lancaster after the death of his father Iohn of Gaunt, and vnder that colour to vsurpe the crowne. Which Edmund passing into Wales in the thrée and twentith yeare of Richard the second, was receiued into the castell of Barkleie, & there remained yntill the comming of Henrie of Bullingbrooke. Whom when he perceiued (for the power which the said duke of Lancaster had assembled from all parts of the realme) that he was not of sufficiencie to resist; he came foorth into the church that stood without the castell, and there fell to parlée with the duke of Lancaster; after which he did neuer forsake the duke of Lancaster, vntill he came to the crowne. Who, if he had faithfullie stood vnto his nephue, might perhaps haue saued vnto him both his crowne and life. Of this man is more said in my treatise of the dukes of England.

Ione de Na-
mures widow to
Henrie the
fourth.

Ione de Namures sometime dutches of Britaine, (widow to Philip Montfort, as saith Hypodigma; but Walsingham in his historie calleth him Iohn duke of Britaine; being also the widow of king Henrie the fourth) was substitute gouernor of the realme by hir son in law king Henrie the fift, king of England, in the third yeare of his reigne, being the yeare from the birth of the Messias 1415, when the said Henrie the fift tooke his iournie into France to conquer the same. This woman in the seuenth yeare of Henrie the fift, which was in the yeare of Christ 1419, being suspected (as saith Iohn Stow) to practise witchcraft against the king, was committed to the custodie of Iohn Wellam, or rather Iohn Pelham, who appointed nine seruants to attend vpon hir, and brought hir to Peuenseie castell to be gouerned vnder his prouidence. But shortlie after cléering hir selfe, she was deliuered. This ladie died at Hauering at the bowre in Essex the ninth of Iulie in the seuentéenth yeare of the reigne of king Henrie the sixt, being the yeare of Christ one thousand foure hundred thirtie and seuen, and was buried at Canturburie with hir husband king Henrie the fourth.

Iohn de Plan-
tagenet duke of
Bedford.

Iohn duke of Bedford son to Henrie the fourth, & brother to K. Henrie the fift, was in the fourth yeare of the reigne of the said Henrie, being the yeare of our redemption 1416, by parlement appointed regent of the realme, to inioie the same office so long as the king was imploied in the French wars. Which place he possessed accordinglie; and in the ninth yeare of the victorious prince, king Henrie the fift, being gardian of England, he with Henrie Beauford bishop of Winchester vncle to Henrie the fift, and Iaqueline duches of Holland remaining then in England, were godfathers, and god-mother to Henrie, after king by the name of Henrie the sixt, the son of Henrie the fift; Henrie Chichleie archbishop of Canturburie baptising the child. In the tenth and last yeare of Henrie the fift, this Iohn with a strong power conueied quéene Katharine wife to Henrie the fift, from Southampton into France. This man being duke of Bedford, earle of Richmond and of Kendall, conestable of England, and warden of the marches of Scotland, died the fourtéenth daie of September at Rone in Normandie, who (hauing also béene regent of France, a most valiant gentleman, and one that kept the parts beyond the seas in great obedience to the crowne of Eng-land) had for his yearelie pension 20000 crownes at the least. After whose death all things went backeward, and the English lost all that they had beyond the seas, Calis, & those dominions onlie excepted.

This man (I saie) died in the yeare of our redemption 1435, being the thirtéenth yeare of the vnfortunat gouernment of the deposed king Henrie the sixt, and was honorablie buried at Rone in our ladie church there. Touching whome it shall not gréeue me to set downe the answer of a French king latelie in our age made to one of his nobilitie; saieng vnto the king (then being in the said ladie church of Rone, and beholding the toome of this Iohn of Bedford) that it were conuenient that the same toome were defaced and pulled downe; since he was the onelie man that wrought the
greatest

greatest damage that euer happened vnto France. To whom the king said; Hold thy peace foole, God forbid that euer we should doo such reproch to him being dead; whome the proudest of our nation durst not looke in the face when he was liuing. This duke Iohn maried the second yeare of Henrie the sixt, in the yeare of Christ 1423, Anne the daughter of Iohn duke of Burgognie, who died in the tenth yeare of Henrie the sixt, in the yeare of Christ 1433, after which he maried Iaques daughter to Peter earle of S. Paule in the same yeare, and yet died without issue. Of this man is mention made in my former discourse of the conestables of England, pag. 668.

Humfreie duke of Glocester brother to Henrie the fift, and vncle to Henrie the sixt was in the tenth and last yeare of Henrie the fift, being the yeare of our Lord 1422, made regent of England, vpon the remouing and departure of Iohn duke of Bedford with quéene Katharine, wife to Henrie the fift into France. In which yeare (happening the lamentable death of that woorthie prince king Henrie the fift) the said Henrie vpon his death-bed appointed this Humfreie to be protector of the realme; which he did exercise in the time of the minoritie of Henrie the sixt, from the time of his first enterance into the kingdome. Who at that time taking vpon him that function, called vnto him graue and wise councellors; with whose support he might with better honor to the realme, and benefit to the subiects, rule the ship of this kingdome, sailing in the dangerous waues of the kings infancie. By which meanes holding the sterne thereof, directed by the course of iustice, he did most honorablie during his life discharge the dutie of so weightie an office. Who in the fourteenth yeare of Henrie the sixt, being the yeare of our Lord 1439, did with fiue hundred saile land at Calis, and for eleuen daies spoiled the low countries and so by Calis returned againe into England. This man in the fiue & twentith yeare of king Henrie sixt, being the yeare of Christ 1447, was in his castell of Vies in Wilshire, & comming from thence to the parlement was lodged in the hospitall, and arrested by Iohn lord Beaumont high conestable of England. But on the foure and twentith daie of Februarie he died for sorrow as some said, and as Iohn Stow hath noted, bicause he might not come to his answer. Other write that he was murdered in the night by the quéens procurement, to the great griefe of the commons, and in time following to the vtter destruction of the king and the quéene. He was duke of Glocester, and also in the right of his wife duke of Holland and Zeland, earle of Penbroke, lord chamberleine of England, and protector of the realme, being highlie estéemed of learned men, himselfe also not meanlie furnished with knowledge, hauing rare skill in astrologie, wherof beside manie other things he compiled a singular treatise, obteining the name of Tabula directionum, touching whose death I haue read these verses following in Iohn Whethamsted:

Aemula sors varijs signanter honoribus altis
Causauit miserè mala multos flere ruinæ,
Læsus erat Iulius, vndis mersus Ptolomeus,
Pulsus Tarquinius, exul factúsque Tydeus,
Dux nimis properè iam dictus tempora vitæ
Compleuit tristis, heu indignatio regis
Causa fuit magna, maior detractio falsa,
Plebis & iunctæ fallacis & insidiosæ,
Nam regis patrius, quamuis & proximus hæres,
Tunc fueratque suus consultor in ordine primus,
Vir prudensque pius, vir doctus & ingeniosus,
Non tamen erubuit, nec pertimuit, ve pepercit
Hunc accusare falsè de proditione,
Discere quódque suam clàm vellet tollere vitam

Et

Et sibi surripere violenter iura coronæ.
Diuitis argentum, proprium qui captat in vsum,
Desiderat medium quo vindicet aptiùs ipsum,
Sic regem plures comitantes collaterales
Sectantur prædam, mediat fraus, dat dolus ipsam,
Fidior in regno regi duce non fuit isto,
Plúsque fide stabilis aut maior amator honoris,
Et tamen vt prædo voto potiretur iniquo,
Fraudem consuluit, cum fraude dolum sociauit,
Sícque ducem falsi maculans cum proditione
Obtinuit votum, prædator erátque bonorum
Illius, & tristis obijt dux criminis expers.

Which duke Humfrie was buried at saint Albons, dieng without issue, after he had married two wiues; whereof the first wife was Iacoba or Iaqueline (daughter and sole heire of William of Bauier) being then the lawfull wife to Iohn duke of Brabant then liuing, which wife this Humfrie married in England in the yéere of our redemption 1424 being the third yéere of king Henrie the sixt, vpon which grew great warres, and Humfrie duke of Glocester challenged the combat of the duke of Burgognie, taking part with his cousine Iohn duke of Brabant. But in the end the duke of Glocester left his wife at Mons & returned into England, and shée vnto Gaunt, and so into Holland, & the combat staid by means of the duke of Bedford brother to the duke of Glocester. But after (as it séemeth) the duke of Glocester was diuorsed from this dutchesse, and then married Eleanor Cobham (whome he had tenderlie loued as his paramour before that) in the yeere of our redemption 1428, being the sixt yéere of the reigne of king Henrie the sixt. This woman in the nineteenth yeere of the said Henrie the sixt (vpon the taking of Henrie Bullingbrook for practising necromancie, thereby to consume the king) fled in the night to Westminster for sanctuarie, which caused hir to be suspected of treason. Wherevpon Bullingbrook confessing that he wrought the same at the procurement of the said Eleanor, desirous to know to what estate she would come vnto, the same dame Eleanor did oftentimes for the same fact appéere before the bishop, and in the end was conuicted. After which in the twentith of Henrie the sixt she did gréeuous penance therefore, and so escaped with hir life. And here bicause I haue said somewhat of Iaqueline dutchesse of Holland, I thinke it not amisse to adde a little more of hir, being a woman of great beautie, and desire of change in performing the pleasures of the flesh: wherefore I will set downe what I haue séene written vnder the pictures of hir and hir husband Francis in this sort.

The subscription vnder the pictures of the ladie Iaqueline, and of Francis
hir husband.

IACOBA Dei gratia comitissa Hannoniæ, Hollandiæ, & Zelandiæ, domina Frisiæ, Zutbeuerlandiæ, terræ Brilensis, Vorensis, &c: Gulielmi Bauariensis ducis filia & hæres vnica, quæ primò desponsata fuit Philippo Burgundiorum duci: postea Delphino Francorum regis filio: tertiò Iohanni duci Brabantiæ Antonij filio: deinde Humfrido Glocestriæ duci Henrici quarti Angliæ regis filio: & postremò Franconi Bursaliensi comiti Osteruandiæ matrimonio copulatur. Quæ obijt absque liberis 8 Idus Octobris, anno Domini 1463 sepulta apud Hagam comitis in Hollandia.
Beside which was this written in Dutch:
Vrowen Iacoba van Byeren Grauenne van Hollant starfe Anno Domini 1463.

The

The subscription vnder the picture of hir husband Francone or Francis
was in this sort.

FRANCISCUS Dei gratia comes de Osteruant (erfginodht) in comitatibus Hollandiæ, Hannoniæ, Zelandiæ, & Friselandiæ, dominus de Boursalia de Viorne, Zuylen,
Hochstraten, Kortkene, de la Veer, Flishing, Zandenburge, terræ Brilensis, Sent-
martinsdike, quo loco fundauit cœnobium canonicorum, &c : & regi Edwardo quarto
fideliter assistebat, necnon equestris ordinis diui Antonij.

Beside which also was this written in the Dutch toong. Here vranck van Boselen
graue van Osteruant starfe Anno Domini 1470.

Thomas Beaufort duke of Excester (appointed to that office by Henrie the fift on his Thomas Beau-
fort duke of
Excester.
death-bed) was with Henrie Beaufort bishop of Winchester great vncle to king Henrie
the sixt in the yéere of our redemption 1422, being the first yeere of the reigne of king
Henrie the sixt (then but nine months old) made protector and gardian of the person
of the yoong king, to see him tenderlie and carefullie brought vp and instructed in
all such parts as were to be required in the person of a monarch. Which office he
left about the fourth yeere of king Henrie the sixt, and died on Newyéeres daie at his
manor of Gréenwich in the said fift yéere of Henrie the sixt, being the yeere of
our redemption 1446: he married Margaret the daughter of Thomas Neuill of
Hornesbie.

Richard Beauchampe earle of Warwike son of the former Thomas Beauchampe, Richard Beau-
champe earle of
Warwike.
being beyond the seas, and there deputie for Iohn duke of Bedford (being regent of
France) did (whilest the said regent was come ouer into England) obteine manie castels
in his deputieship; who being thus imploied in the forren warres, was in his absence
out of his countrie (for his singular wisdome and valor) ordeined by the thrée
estates of the realme of England in open parlement, to be gouernor of the person of
the yoong king Henrie the sixt, in the place of Thomas Beaufort duke of Excester
latelie deceased: which Richard did not yet foorthwith hasten his returne into England,
but remained in France for a season, inlarging the fame of his martiall exploits. This his
election to the protectorship of the kings person, was in the fift yéere of Henrie the
sixt, being the yéere of our redemption 1426. He died in the yeere of our Lord
1439, being the seuentéenth yéere of the deposed king Henrie the sixt, at Rone in
Normandie the last daie of Maie, as hath Iohn Stow; and the fourth of October next
following his corps was honorablie conueied, as well by land as by water from Rone to
Warwike, and there honorablie buried in the college of our ladie church founded by
his noble ancestors. He maried two wiues, the first Elisabeth daughter and heire of
Thomas lord Barkleie, by whome he had thrée daughters, Margaret maried to Iohn
lord Talbot earle of Shrewesburie, Eleanor maried to Thomas lord Rosse, and Elizabeth
married to George Neuill lord Latimer. His second wife was Isabell the daughter and
heire of Richard lord Spenser, by whome he had issue Henrie duke of Warwike, and
Anne married to Richard Neuill earle of Salisburie.

Richard Plantagenet duke of Yorke, sonne to Richard earle of Cambrige, and Richard Plan-
tagenet duke of
Yorke.
father to Edward the fourth king of England, notwithstanding that he made
challenge to the crowne against Henrie the sixt, then in possession thereof, as
heire to the house of Yorke, & was to be preferred before the house of Lancaster;
and notwithstanding that he was by parlement appointed to weare the crowne
after the death of Henrie the sixt: yet after all this, in the thrée and thirtith yeere
of the same king, being the yéere of our redemption 1455 (such was the imperfection
of the king to gouerne) he was appointed protector of the realme, ruling the
same at his owne disposition. Which office he did not long inioie, and that most worthilie: for the next yéere after being the foure and thirtith of king Henrie the sixt,
and the yeere of our redemption 1456, he was depriued from the same, and queene
Margaret

Margaret wife to Henrie the sixt tooke againe the absolute regiment into hir hands: which duke after in the nine and thirtith of king Henrie the sixt, being the yéere of our redemption 1460, the thirtith daie of December, being lord of Wakefield, was there with his sonne the earle of Rutland slaine at the battell commonlie called the battell of Wakefield; of which I haue read these verses in Whethamsted once abbat of saint Albons:

This was doone 1561, counting the yeare to be-gin at Christmas as some doo, or at Ianuarie as others doo.

> Anno milleno centum quater quoque seno,
> Terdenóque die, duodeno mense Decembre,
> Infra Eboracensem iuxta Wakefield comitatum
> Dux dominus villæ fertur pugnans habuisse
> Conflictum grandem contra gentem borealem,
> Ac proceres plures præerant quæ gentibus ipsis.
> Quod docuit, quia sors quod res fortuna secundas,
> Vitat habere moras, cecidit dux natus & eius,
> Ac comes insignis sors belli, sors fuit ipsis
> Obuia, sícque fatis regni fuerat breuis hæres
> Omen & id lætum tulerat mutamine mœstum
> Deflendum multis, ius regni, ius fuit eius.

He maried Cicilie daughter to Rafe Neuill first earle of Westmerland, by whome he had issue Edward duke of Yorke, earle of March, and after king of England by the name of Edward the fourth: George Plantagenet duke of Clarence, Richard Planta-genet duke of Glocester, after king of England by the name of Richard the third: thrée daughters, Anne maried to Henrie Holland duke of Excester, Elisabeth married to Iohn de la Poole duke of Suffolke, and Margaret maried to Charles duke of Bur-gognie.

George Plan-tagenet duke of Clarence.

George Plantagenet duke of Clarence, and conestable of England, sonne of the foresaid duke of Yorke and brother to king Edward the fourth, with Richard Neuill earle of Warwike (who set vp and pulled downe kings at his pleasure) were after the flight of Edward the fourth out of England into Burgognie to his brother in law (in the tenth yeare of the reigne of the said king Edward, being the yeare of our re-demption 1470, when Henrie the sixt had by their means readepted the kingdome) made gouernors of the land, which office they inioied not long.   For the said Edward the fourth returning into England, in the eleuenth yeare of his reigne, being the yeare of our redemption 1471, reconciled to him the duke of Clarence, did againe put downe king Henrie the sixt, and slue the said earle of Warwike (flieng awaie) at Barnet field (on Easter day) by one of the men of his campe.   After this, on the fif-téenth daie of Ianuarie began a parlement, in the eightéenth yere of the reigne of king Edward the fourth, being the yeare of our redemption 1478, where this duke of Clarence was atteinted of treason, and the eleuenth of March following he ended his life in a but of malmeseie, and was buried at Teukesburie beside his wife, who being with child died by poison a little before him.   Of this man sée more in my discourse of the conestables of England pag. 670.

Richard Plan-tagenet duke of Glocester.

A digression concerning the conestables of England not men*t*ioned be-fore in pag. 663.

Richard Plantagenet third sonne to Richard duke of Yorke, was conestable of England and gouernour of the person of the king, of whome is more spoken in my discourse of the conestables of England pag. 671.   But here mentioning the conestables of England, I thinke it better now than not at all, to mention also some imperfection and default in my former discourse of the said conestables, set downe by me before in pag. 663.   Which default of mine in that place grew by reason of ouermuch hast, which I vsed in sudden seeking for the same, whereby (according to the old prouerbe) I brought foorth a blind whelpe.   For in the former description I haue omitted diuerse the which were conestables of England, the names of which were Henrie the first in the life of his father, Nigellus, and Robert de Oilie, with others of that line in descent, which

Nigellus

Nigellus I can not as yet learne to be anie other but Nigellus de Oilie, brother to Robert de Oilie that came in with the Conqueror, who gaue Oxfordshire vnto the said Robert. Nigellus de Oilie constable of England.

Besides which, if it shall séeme to anie that I haue in my former treatise rashlie written I know not what, & that here I make Henrie the first conestable in his father the Conquerors time, & by contrarietie therevnto did before make Walter conestable also in the Conquerors and William Rufus his time: let them know that there is no contrarietie herein. For Walter might first be conestable, & then Henrie the first, and both they in the Conquerors time, this office being taken from the first, and giuen to the latter by the Conqueror. After whose death William Rufus might take it from his brother Henrie, bicause he would not make him too great in England, for doubt least he might hereby put the crowne in hazard, being fauoured of the people as one borne in England, and for that cause might restore that office to Walter. Againe it maie be, that some men reading that I haue before set downe, that Mawd the empresse gaue the conestableship to Milo the son of Walter in the sixt of king Stephan, and that king Stephan tooke that office from Milo in the first yere of his reigne, aud gaue it to Walter Beauchampe, will condemne me therefore of like vnaduised writing: bicause it seemeth thereby that Stephan tooke it from Milo before that Milo had it. Which is not so, for I can proue with some reason and authoritie, that Milo had it a little before the death of king Henrie the first, and also after his death in part of the first yeare of king Stephan, being witnesse to a deed by king Stephan, made and dated the first of his reigne, to which he subscribed his name Milo Constabularius, After which, king Stephan might in that yeare take that office from him, and so he did. Which Mawd the empresse vnderstanding, and finding Milo (now fallen from king Stephan) one which assisted hir, she the better to confront Stephan, gaue the conestableship to Milo (accounting hir selfe as quéene) in the sixt of Stephan.

This being thus spoken in defense of that which before I haue written pag. 664, let vs go to our other matter concerning the conestables not mentioned before in the said discourse, wherein I find my selfe in a maruellous laberinth (out of which I doubt that the best antiquaries cannot loose themselues, no not he which thinketh and saith that he can controll all men, for I suppose he will be lame in this matter) how all these could be conestables, vnlesse that in the time of Henrie the first, and of king Stephan, as it is most likelie, there was chopping & changing, putting in and taking out, setting vp and pulling downe one man in diuerse yeares of one and the selfe same king: for king Stephan was sometime a king, and sometime as no king, and then againe a king. And so likewise was it with Mawd the empresse at the same time, bearing hir selfe sometime as queene, and then deiected as no quéene. But be it as it will be, I will here set downe what I find in ancient charters and pedegrées touching the conestables of England not before mentioned, leauing the same to others (either to order for succession of time, or to amend for truth of matter) who peraduenture reading these things, which I haue seene and will here set downe, can bestow them in better order than I can, which I earnestlie praie them to doo, whereby truth maie be brought to light and perfection; which as yet touching these conestables set downe in this place, séemeth to be obscured and confused vntill the time that Roger Fitz Miles had that office: for from his time the same is without all controuersie sufficientlie knowne. Wherefore, here before I enter into the descent of the de Oilies, who were conestables of England, I will set downe a strange note of thrée persons witnesses to a déed, dated Primo Stephani, anno Dom. 1136, who doo all subscribe their names as conestables. Which charter being the same wherein king Stephan gaue the manor of Sudton or Sutton to the house of Winchester, the same was amongst other witnesses thus signed, Robertus de Veer constabularius, Milo constabularius, Brientius filius comitis constabularius: all who could not be conestables of England at one time. Wherfore sauing correction

correction I suppose that it is out of all controuersie, that neither the first nor the last of these three were conestables of England, but of some other places, as of Douer or other castels. And so to that which I haue further to saie of the kings conestables in one descent and succession of the de Oilies, being tearmed the kings conestables, both in ancient charters and pedegrées, whereof Nigellus before mentioned séemeth to be one.

This Nigellus was conestable of England in the yeare of our redemption one thousand one hundred and one, being the first yeere of king Henrie the first, as may appeare by a déed of confirmation made by Henrie the first touching the cathedrall church of Norwich, whereof I thinke good to saie somewhat to bring in the proofe

The foundation of the cathedral church of Norwich.

that this Nigellus was constable. This church was built for the most part in the time of William Rufus, by Herebert de Losinga the first Bishop of Norwich, who translated the sée from Tetford vnto Norwich, in the yeare of Christ 1094, which church being finished and consecrated to the holie trinitie, was afterward confirmed by Henrie the first, and Mawd his wife, in the first yeare of the said Henrie, being the yeare of our redemption 1101, to the charter whereof signed by king Henrie & Mawd his wife, were manie bishops, noblemen and abbats witnesses, amongst whome are these two set downe; Nigellus Constabularius, and Rogerus Cancellarius, of which Nigellus thus writeth Leland in his commentaries on the song of the swan in the word Isidis insulæ: Erat Roberto frater Nigellus nomine, de quo fama non admodum multa refert, which I suppose is this Nigellus de Oilie the conestable, as I before said.

Robert de Oilie constable of England.

Robert de Oilie, sonne of the said Nigellus, did succéed his father, and was as may appeare by some authors (who tearme him accordinglie) great constable of England. This man together with his wife Edith were the founders of the religious house of Osneie, touching whome I shall not greeue to set downe what I haue gathered out of Leland and others. This Edith obteined of hir husband to build a church in the Ile of Osneie in Oxfordshire, to our sauiour Christ, about the yeare of our redemption

The foundation of the abbeie of Osneie or Owsneie in the yeare of Christ 1129, being about the thirtith yeare of Henrie the first, as some write.

1129, being about the nine and twentith yeare of king Henrie the first, which church did after grow to be of great renowme and building, the occasion of building whereof is set downe by others in this sort. Edith being in great estimation with Henrie, first married the said Robert de Oilie by the kings procurement, which Robert began the priorie of the blacke chanons of Osneie by Oxford, amongst the Iles made by the riuer of Isis or Owse. This Edith vsed oftentimes to walke out of Oxford castell with hir gentlewomen for to solace and recreate hir selfe. At what time at a certeine place, as often as she came by the same, certeine pies assembled themselues in a tree, where they chattered and as it were spake vnto hir. This ladie much maruelling at the matter, happening so continuallie at one time in one place after one order, and with one maner of foules, was manie times astonished and feared therewith, esteeming it a verie strange woonder. Whervpon she sent for one Radulph or Rafe a chanon of saint Frediswide in Oxford, a man of vertuous life & hir confessor, asking his counsell vpon the same. To whom he answered (after that he had séene the order of those pies onelie chattering at hir comming thither) that she should build some church or monasterie in that place. Wherevpon she intreated hir husband to build a priorie, and so he did, making that Radulph the first prior of that house. All which matter, that is the comming of Edith to Osneie, Radulph wating on hir, and the trée with the pies were all extant (at the generall dissolution of the abbeies in the time of Henrie the eight) to be séene painted on the north side of the high altar, in the arch of the wall ouer Ediths toome in Osneie priorie, vpon which toome there laie a stone image of Edith in the habit of a vowesse holding a hart in hir right hand. This Robert de Oilie was buried in Osneie in the verie middle of the presbiterie, vnder a flat marble stone; wherevpon was a flowred crosse portraid, which Robert had issue Henrie de Oilie, baron of Hochnorton, & the kings conestable, which maried Margerie the daughter

of

of Humfreie de Bohune, by whome that Henrie had issue Henrie de Oilie baron of Hochnorton, and the kings conestable which died without issue. Thus this much by waie of digression, touching the conestables of England, left out in my former discourse of those officers. And so againe to the protectors.

Katharine the daughter of Ferdinando king of Spaine, and wife to king Henrie the eight, was (in the absence of the said king beyond the seas in the warres of Turwine and Turneie) made regent of the realme, in the yeare of Christ 1513, and the fift yeare of king Henrie the eight, she had béene the widow of Arthur prince of Wales eldest sonne vnto king Henrie the seauenth, and eldest brother to king Henrie the Eight, who after the death of that Arthur was by dispensation of the pope married to Henrie after king, by the name of Henrie the eight, being yoonger brother of the said Arthur, from which king Henrie she was afterward not onelie diuorsed, in the one and twentith of his reigne, being the yeare of Christ 1529, but after by parlement also in the foure and twentith of the kings reigne, in the yeare of Christ 1532, disgraced from the name of quéene, and from thencefoorth appointed onlie to be called the princesse dowager of prince Arthur, about fiue yeeres after which she died on the eight of Ianuarie, being the yeare of our redemption 1535, which was the seauen and twentith yeare of king Henrie the eight, and was honourablie buried in the abbeie of Peterborow, for which cause afterward in the generall dissolution of the abbeies, when all those houses were spoiled, this abbeie was not onelie for hir buriall there spared and not defaced, but also further honored with a greater title, and turned into a bishoprike, by the said king Henrie the eight.

Katharine quéene of England.

Katharine Par, the daughter of sir Thomas Par, lord of Kirkbie Kendall, and wife to king Henrie the eight, was by patent made protectresse of the realme of England, when king Henrie the eight went in person to the wars of Bullongne, on the thirtéenth of Iulie in the yeare of our redemption 1544, being the six & thirtith yeare of the triumphant reigne of the said king. This ladie Katharine being the lord Latimers widow, was maried to the king at Hampton court, on the twelfe of Iulie being the fiue aud thirtith yeare of his reigne, and the yeare of Christ 1543, who hauing no issue by the king, was after the kings death married to Thomas Seimer knight, lord Seimer of Sudleie and high admerall of England.

Edward Seimer knight, vicount Beauchampe earle of Hertford, & after duke of Summerset, was protector of the kings person, and of the kingdome, in the first yeare of king Edward the sixt, his nephue, which was in the yeare of our redemption 1546, the king being then but nine yeares old. Of this man is more spoken in my following discourse of all the dukes of England by creation or descent since the conquest, with which duke of Summerset, the last in office of protectorship, Francis Thin knitteth vp this simple discourse of the protectors of England of the kings person.

¶ On the 17 of Februarie, on which daie were receiued the bookes of the reliefe of all the wards of London, towards the new hospitals, by the kings commissioners, the councell dined at maister Coopers the shiriffe, and after dinner maister Thomas Curteis alderman came thither to speake with the lord chancellor for a matter he had depending afore him in the chancerie, but for his misdemeanour in words and signes to the lord chancellor at that time, the said maister Curteis was committed to ward in the Fléet.]
The six and twentith of Februarie, sir Rafe Vane and sir Miles Patridge were hanged on the Tower hill; & sir Michaell Stanhope with sir Thomas Arundell were beheaded there. The last of April, through negligence of the gunpowder makers, a certeine house néere the tower of London, with thrée last of powder was blowne vp and burnt, the gunpowder makers being fiftéene in number, were all slaine.
The sixtéenth of Maie was a goodlie muster of horssemen made before the king, in the parke at Gréenwich, vnder the kings banner his band of pensioners, in number

Abr. Fl. ex I. S. 1051.
Curteis, alderman of London committed to ward for vnreuerend words and signes to the lord chancellor.
An. Reg. 6
Sir Rafe Vane & other executed.
House blowne vp with gunpowder.
Muster of horssemen before the king in Gréenwich parke.

Dukes.

ber a hundred and fiftie, euerie pensioner two great horsses and a gelding, the lord Braie their lieutenant. The duke of Northumberland, great maister of the kings houshold vnder the white lion & the ragged staffe fiftie. The duke of Suffolke vnder the vnicorne in the starre a hundred and ten. The lord marquesse of Winchester, high

Marquesses.

treasuror, vnder his banner the falcon, one hundred men. The marquesse of North-ampton high chamberleine vnder the maidenhead a hundred. The earle of Bedford

Earles.

lord priuie seale vnder the gote a hundred. The erle of Warwike maister of the kings horsses vnder the white lion fiftie. The erle of Huntington vnder his banner fiftie. The earle of Rutland vnder the peacocke fiftie. The earle of Penbroke vnder the

Lords.

greene dragon fiftie. The lord Darcie vnder the maidens bodie fiftie. The lord Cob-ham vnder the Saracens head, fiftie. The lord Clinton lord admerall vnder the anchor, fiftie. Tke lord warden of the fiue ports, vnder the rose in the sunne beames, one hundred.

Rich. Grafton.
Doctor Ridleie preached before the king, mercie and charitie.

Not long after the death of the said duke of Summerset and his complices, it chanced the reuerend father in God maister doctor Ridleie then bishop of London, to preach before the kings maiestie at Westminster. In the which sermon he made a fruitfull and godlie exhortation to the rich, to be mercifull vnto the poore and also to mooue such as were in authoritie, to trauell by some charitable waie & meane, to comfort and reléeue them. Wherevpon the kings maiestie being a prince of such towardnesse and vertue for his yeares, as England before neuer brought forth, and the same also being so well reteined and brought vp in all godlie knowledge, as well by his déere vncle the late protector, as also by his vertuous and learned scholemaisters, was so carefull of the good gouernement of the realme, and chieflie to doo and prefer such things as most speciallie touched the honor of almightie God. And vnderstanding that a great number of poore people did swarme in this realme, and chieflie in the citie of London, and that no good order was taken for them, did suddenlie and of himselfe send to the said bishop as soone as his sermon was ended, willing him not to depart,

The verie re-port of bishop Ridleie, wherin we may sée what fruits followed vpon his ser-mon: *Ergo* the hearing of the word preached is profitable.

vntill that he had spoken with him (and this that I now write was the verie report of the said bishop Ridleie) who according to the kings commandement gaue his attend-ance. And so soone as the kings maiestie was at leasure, he called for him, and made him to come vnto him in a great gallerie at Westminster, where (to his knowledge) and the king also told him so, there was present no more persons than they two, and therefore made him sit downe in one chaire, and he himselfe in another, (as it seemed) were before the comming of the bishop there purposelie set, & caused the bishop (maugre his teeth) to be couered, and then entered communication with him in this sort.

First giuing him most hartie thanks for his sermon and good exhortation, he therein rehearsed such speciall things as he had noted, and that so manie, that the bishop said; "Trulie, trulie (for that was commonlie his oth) I could neuer haue thought that excellencie to haue béene in his grace, that I beheld and saw in him." At the last, the

A most noble and vertuous saieng of king Edward to bi-shop Ridleie.

kings maiestie much commended him for his exhortation for the reliefe of the poore. "But my lord (saith he) ye willed such as are in authoritie to be carefull therof, and to deuise some good order for their reliefe, wherein I thinke you meane me, for I am in highest place, and therefore am the first that must make answere vnto God for my negligence, if I should not be carefull therein, knowing it to be the expresse com-mandement of almightie God, to haue compassion of his poore and néedie members, for whome we must make an accompt vnto him. And trulie my lord, I am before all things most willing to trauell that waie, and I doubt nothing of your long and approued wisedome and learning, who hauing such good zeale as wisheth helpe vnto them, but that also you haue had some conference with others, what waies are best to be taken therein, the which I am desirous to vnderstand, and therefore I praie you saie your mind."

                                                       The

The bishop thinking least of that matter, and being amazed to heare the wisdome and earnest zeale of the king, was (as he said himselfe) so astonied, that he could not well tell what to saie: but after some pause, said that as he thought at this present for some entrance to be had, it were good to practise with the citie of London, bicause the number of the poore there are verie great, & the citizens are manie & also wise; and he doubted not but they were also both pitifull & mercifull, as the maior & his brethren, & other the worshipfull of the said citie. And that if it would please the kings maiestie to direct his gratious letter vnto the maior of London, willing him to call vnto him such assistants as he should thinke méet, to consult of this matter, for some order to be taken therein, he doubted not but good should follow thereof. And he himselfe promised the king to be one himselfe that shouid earnestlie trauell therein.

The king forthwith not onelie granted his letter, but made the bishop tarie vntill the same was written, and his hand and signet set therevnto, and commanded the bishop not onelie to deliuer the said letter himselfe, but also to signifie vnto the maior, that it was the kings speciall request and expresse commandement, that the maior should therein trauell, and as soone as he might conuenientlie giue him knowledge how farre he had proceeded therein. The bishop was so ioious of the hauing of this letter, and that he had now an occasion to trauell in that good matter, wherein he was maruellous zealous, that nothing could more haue pleased and delighted him: wherefore the same night he came to the maior of London, who then was sir Richard Dobs knight, and deliuered the kings letter, and shewed his message with effect.

The maior not onelie ioiouslie receiued this letter, but with all spéed agreed to set forward this matter, for he also fauoured it verie much. And the next daie being mondaie, he desired the bishop of London to dine with him: and against that time, the maior promised that he would send for such men, as he thought méetest to talke of this matter, and so he did. And sent first for two aldermen and six commoners, and afterward were appointed more, to the number of foure and twentie. And in the end after sundrie méetings (for by meane of the good diligence of the bishop it was well followed) they agréed vpon a booke that they had deuised, wherein first they considered of nine special kinds and sorts of poore people, and those same they brought in these thrée degrees:

Thrée degrées of poore.
{ The poore by impotencie.
　Poore by casualtie.
　Thriftlesse poore.

1 The poore by impotencie are also diuided into three kinds, that is to saie:
{ 1 The fatherlesse poore mans child.
　2 The aged, blind, and lame.
　3 The diseased person, by leprosie, dropsie, &c.

2 The poore by casualtie are of thrée kinds, that is to saie:
{ 4 The wounded souldier.
　5 The decaied housholder.
　6 The visited with gréeuous disease.

3 The thriftles poore are three kinds in like wise, that is to saie:
{ 7 The riotor that consumeth all.
　8 The vagabond that will abide in no place.
　9 The idle person, as the strumpet and others.

For these sorts of poore were prouided thrée seuerall houses. First for the innocent and fatherlesse, which is the beggers child, and is in déed the séed and breeder of beggerie, they prouided the house that was late Graie friers in London, and now is called Christes hospitall, where the poore children are trained in the knowledge of God, and some vertuous exercise to the ouerthrowe of beggerie. For the second degrée is prouided the hospitall of saint Thomas in Southworke, & saint Bartholomew in west Smithfield, where are continuallie at least two hundred diseased persons, which are not onelie there lodged and cured, but also fed and nourished. For the third degrée they

pro-

[margin notes:] The citizens of London mooued to be assistants in this charitable action.

The readines of the lord maior to prefer this good déed.

Degrées of poore.

Christes hospitall.

S. Thomas hospitall.

Bridewell.

Reliefe for the decaied housholder and lazer.

prouided Bridewell, where the vagabond and idle strumpet is chastised and compelled to labour, to the ouerthrow of the vicious life of idlenes. They prouided also for the honest decaied housholder, that he should be relieued at home at his house, and in the parish where he dwelled by a weekelie reliefe and pension. And in like manner they prouided for the lazer to keepe him out of the citie from clapping of dishes, and ringing of bels, to the great trouble of the citizens, and also to the dangerous infection of manie, that they should be relieued at home at their houses with seuerall pensions.

Now after this good order taken, and the citizens by such meanes as were deuised, willing to further the same, the report therof was made vnto the kings maiestie: and his grace for the aduancement hereof, was not onelie willing to grant such as should be the ouerseers and gouernors of the said houses a corporation and authoritie for the gouernement thereof: but also required that he might be accounted as the chiefe founder and patrone thereof. And for the furtherance of the said worke, and continuall maintenance of the same, he of his meere mercie and goodnesse granted, that where before certeine lands were giuen to the maintenance of the house of the Sauoie, founded by king Henrie the seuenth, for the lodging of pilgrims and strangers, and that the same was now made but a lodging of loiterers, vagabonds, and strumpets that laie all daie in the fields, and at night were harboured there, the which was rather the maintenance of beggerie, than the reliefe of the poore, gaue the same lands, being first surrendred into his hands by the maister and fellowes there (which lands were of the yearelie value of six hundred pounds) vnto the citie of London, for the maintenance of the foundation aforesaid.

K. Edward the sixt founder of the hospitals in Lōdon.

And for a further reliefe, a petition being made to the kings maiestie for a licence to take in mortmaine, or otherwise without licence, lands to a certeine yearelie value, and a space left in the patent for his grace to put in what summe it would please him; he looking on the void place, called for pen and inke, and with his owne hand wrote this summe, in these words (foure thousand marks by yeare) and then said in the hearing of his councell: "Lord God I yeeld thee most hartie thanks, that thou hast giuen mee life thus long, to finish this worke to the glorie of thy name." After which foundation established, he liued not aboue two daies, whose life would haue beene wished equall to the patriarchs, if it might haue pleased God so to haue protracted the same. But he was too good a prince for so bad a people, and therefore God remooued him, and translated him to his owne kingdome, foreseeing the euent of something which in his secret counsell he had purposed, against a nation that knew not the benefit of the acceptable time of grace: wherein God by this peerelesse princes means ment all good to this land, as might be gathered by the reformation of religion, wherin the kings care was exceeding great, as his desire to establish Gods glorie was zealous: according to that notable allusion of Iohn Leland recorded in praise of this most excellent prince, as followeth in this epigram:

A blessed king.

Allusio ad etymon nominis Eaduerdi.

Quisquis Eaduerdum Romano expresserat ore,
     Custodem fidei dixerit esse sacræ.
Hoc ego crediderim puero feliciter orto
     A superis nomen cœlitus esse datum.
Est pater antiquæ fidei defensor amicus,
     Degener & nullo tempore natus erit.

Sir William Chester. Iohn Calthrop draper.

But to returne where we left. By example of the charitable act of this vertuous yoong king, sir William Chester knight and alderman of London, and Iohn Calthrop citizen and draper of the said citie, at their owne proper costs and charges made the bricke walles and way on the backeside that leadeth from the said new hospitall, vnto the hospitall of saint Bartholomewes, and also couered and vauted the towne dich from Aldersgate to Newgate, which before was verie noisome and contagious to the said hospitall.

                                                          This

This hospitall being thus erected and put in good order, there was one Richard *Richard Castel* Castell aliàs Casteller, shoomaker, dwelling in Westminster, a man of great trauell *shoomaker.* and labor in his facultie with his owne hands, and such a one as was named the cocke of Westminster, for that both winter and summer he was at his worke before foure of the clocke in the morning. This man thus trulie and painfullie labouring for his liuing, God blessed and increased his labours so abundantlie, that he purchased lands and tenements in Westminster, to the yearelie value of fortie and foure pounds. And hauing no child, with the consent of his wife (who suruiued him, & was a vertuous & good woman) gaue the same lands wholie to Christs hospitall aforesaid, to the reliefe of the innocent and fatherlesse children, and for the succor of the miserable, sore and sicke, harbored in the other hospitals about London, whose example God grant manie to follow.

¶ The third of August, at Midlenton eleuen miles from Oxford, a woman brought *I. Stow, 1053.* foorth a child which had two perfect bodies from the nauill vpward, and were so *A monster.* ioined togither at the nauill, that when they were laid in length, the one head & bodie was eastward, and the other west: the legs for both the bodies grew out at the midst where the bodies ioined, and had but one issue for the excrements of both bodies: they liued eighteene daies, and were women children. The eight of August were taken at *Great fishes.* Quinborow thrée great fishes called dolphins: & the weeke following at Blackewall were six more taken, and brought to London, the least of them was more than anie horsse.]

Much about this season there were thrée notable ships set foorth and furnished for the great aduenture of the vnknowne voiage into the east by the north seas. The *Sebastian* great dooer and incourager of which voiage was Sebastian Gabato an Englishman, *Gabato.* borne at Bristow, but was the sonne of a Genowaie. These ships at the last arriued in the countrie of Moscouia, not without great losse and danger, and namelie of their capteine, who was a woorthie and aduenturous gentleman, called sir Hugh Willoughbie knight, who being tossed and driuen by tempest, was at the last found in his ship frozen to death and all his people. But now the said voiage and trade is greatlie aduanced, and the merchants aduenturing that waie, are newlie by act of parlement incorporated and indued with sundrie priuileges and liberties.

About the beginning of the moneth of Maie next following, there were thrée not- *Thrée mariages* able mariages concluded, & shortlie after solemnized at Durham place. The first was *betwéene great* betwéene the lord Gilford Dudleie, the fourth sonne of the duke of Northumberland, *estates.* and the ladie Iane, eldest daughter to Henric duke of Suffolke, & the ladie Francis his wife, was the daughter of Marie second sister to king Henrie the eight, first maried to Lewes the French king, and after to Charles Brandon duke of Suffolke. The second mariage was betwéene the lord Herbert, son and heire to William earle of Penbroke, and the ladie Katharine, second daughter of the said ladie Francis, by the said Henrie duke of Suffolke. And the third was betwéene Henrie lord Hastings, sonne and heire to Francis earle of Huntington, and ladie Katharine yoongest daughter to the forenamed duke of Northumberland.

These mariages were compassed & concluded chieflie vpon purpose to change & alter *The euill end* the order of succession to the crowne, made in the time of king Henrie the eight, *whereto the* from the said kings daughters, Marie and Elizabeth, and to conueie the same imme- *knitting of these* diatlie after the death of king Edward to the house of Suffolke, in the right of the *couples in ma-* said ladie Francis: wherein the said yoong king was an earnest traueller in the time *riage tended.* of his sickenesse, & all for feare that if his sister Marie, being next heire to the *The kings feare* crowne, should succéed, that she would subuert all his lawes and statutes made con- *fell out to be* cerning religion, whereof he was most carefull: for the continuance whereof he sought *true.* to establish a meet order of succession, by the aliance of great houses by waie of marriage, which neuerthelesse were of no force to serue his purpose. For tending to
the

the disheriting of the rightfull heirs, they proued nothing prosperous to the parties: for two of them were soone after made frustrate, the one by death, the other by diuorse.

The kings sickenesse increaseth.

In the meane while, the king became euerie daie more sicke than other of a consumption in his lungs, so as there was no hope of his recouerie. Wherevpon those that then bare chiefe authoritie in councell, with other prelats and nobles of the realme, called to them diuerse notable persons, learned as well in diuinitie as in the lawes of the land, namelie bishops, iudges, & other, who fell to consultation vpon this so weightie cause, and lastly concluded vpon the deuise of king Edwards will, to declare the said ladie Iane, eldest néece to king Henrie the eight, and wife to the said lord Gilford, to be rightfull heire in succession to the crowne of England, without re-

The euill minded consultation of councellors.

spect had to the statute made in the fiue and thirtith yeare of king Henrie the eight: the true meaning of which statute they did impugne and ouerthrow by diuerse subtill sinister constructions of the same, to disherit the said kings daughters, to whome the succession of the crowne of England of right apperteined, as well by the common lawes of this realme, as also by the said statute made in the said fiue and thirtith yeare of king Henrie, as aforesaid. To which new order of succession, all the said kings councell, with manie bishops, lords, doctors and iudges of the realme subscribed

Sir Iames Hales the od man.

their names, without refusall of anie, except sir Iames Hales knight, one of the iustices of the common plées, who being called to this councell, would in no wise giue his assent, either by word or writing, as ye shall heare more in the historie of quéene Marie.

The death of king Edward the sixt.

Now when these matters were thus concluded, and after confirmed by a number of hands, as aforesaid, then the noble prince king Edward the sixt, by long lingering sickenesse and consumption of his lungs aforesaid, approched to his death, and departed out of this life the sixt daie of Iulie, in the seuenth yeare of his reigne, and seuentéenth of his age, after he had reigned and noblie gouerned this realme six yeares, fiue moneths, and eight daies. And a little before his departing, lifting vp his eies to God, he praied as followeth.

The praier of king Edward the sixt at his death.

LORD God, deliuer me out of this miserable and wretched life, take me among thy chosen: howbeit not my will, but thy will be doone. Lord I commit my spirit to thee, oh Lord thou knoweth how happie it were for mee to be with thee: yet for thy chosens sake if it be thy will, send me life and helth, that I maie trulie serue thee. Oh my Lord blesse thy people, and saue thine inheritance. Oh Lord God, saue thy chosen people of England. Oh my Lord God defend this realme from papistrie, and mainteine thy true religion, that I and my people maie praise thy holie name. And therewithall he said, I am faint, Lord haue mercie vpon me, and take my spirit.

The commendation of king Edward.

Thus did this good yoong king yéeld vp to God his ghost the sixt daie of Iulie (as before is mentioned) whome if it had pleased God to haue spared with longer life, not vnlike it was, but he should haue so gouerned this English common-wealth, that he might haue béene comparable with any of his noble progenitors: so that the losse of so towardlie a yoong king, greatlie discomforted the whole English nation, that looked for such a reformation in the state of the common-wealth at his hands, as was to be wished for of all good subiects: which bred such a liking in them toward him, that euen among verie traitorous rebels his name yet was had in reuerence, although otherwise they neuer so much forgat their dutie both towards him and other, appointed to gouerne vnder him, through a malicious and most wilfull error; as if his tender yeares

had

had not sufficientlie warranted his roiall authoritie, but that the same had béene vsurped by others against his will and pleasure.

And as he was intirelie beloued of his subiects, so with the like affection of kindnes he loued them againe; of nature and disposition méeke, much inclined to clemencie, euer hauing a regard to the sparing of life. There wanted in him no promptnes of wit, grauitie of sentence, ripenesse of iudgement, as his age might beare, fauour and loue of religion was in him from his childhood, his skill and knowledge in sciences, besides his other excellent vertues, were such, that to them he séemed rather borne than brought vp. It maie séeme verie strange, that in his yoong years (as maister Fox reporteth of him) he could tell and recite all the ports, hauens, and créekes, not within his owne realme onelie, but also in Scotland, and likewise in France, what comming in there was, how the tide serued in euerie of them; moreouer, what burthen, and what wind serued for the comming into each hauen: also of all his iustices, magistrates, & gentlemen that bare any authoritie within his realme, he knew their names, their houskeeping, their religion and conuersation what it was. He had a singular respect to iustice, a vertue most commendable in a prince, and chieflie to the dispatch of poore mens sutes. Hée perfectlie vnderstood the Latine toong, the French the Gréeke, Italian, and Spanish, neither was he ignorant (saith Cardanus) in Logike, in the principles of naturall philosophie, or in musicke.

Sée *Iohn Fox* in the Acts & Monuments vnder the title of Edward the sixt.

The noble memorie of king Edward and his rare wit.

To conclude, his towardlinesse was such in all heroicall vertues, noble gifts, and markable qualities conuenient for his princelie estate, that so much was hoped for in his roiall person (if he had liued till triall might haue béene had of the proofe) as was to be looked for in anie one prince that euer had rule ouer this noble realme. ¶ The eight of Iulie, the lord maior of London was sent for to the court, then at Gréenwich, and to bring with him six aldermen, as manie merchants of the Staple, and as manie merchant aduenturers, vnto whom by the councell was secretlie declared the death of king Edward, & also whom he had ordeined to the succession of the crowne by his leters patents, to the which they were sworne, and charged to kéepe it secret.] But now to procéed with the dooings that followed. Immediatlie after the death of this so worthie a prince king Edward, the aforesaid ladie Iane was proclamed queene of this realme by the sound of trumpet, that is to saie, the ninth daie of Iulie, at which proclamation were present the lords of the councell, the maior of London, with others.

I. Stow. 1058. K. Edwards death opened.

Ladie Iane proclamed quéene.

¶ The eleauenth of Iulie. Gilbert Pot, drawer to Ninion Sanders Vintener, dwelling at S. Iohns head within Ludgate, who was accused by the said Sanders his maister was set vpon the pillorie in Cheape, with both his eares nailed, and cleane cut off, for words speaking at time of the proclamation of ladie Iane. At the which execution was a trumpet blowne, and a herald read his offense, in presence of one of the shiriffes, &c. About fiue of the clocke the same daie in the afternoone, Ninion Sanders, master to the said Gilbert Pot, and Iohn Owen a gunner, comming from the tower of London, by water in a wherrie, and shooting London bridge, towards the blacke friers, were drowned at saint Marie Locke, and the whirriemen saued by their ores.]

I. Stow. 1059. Gilbert Pot punished in Cheape.

Men drowned at London bridge.

The ladie Marie, a little before lieng at Honesdon in Hartfordshire, hauing intelligence of the state of the king hir brother, and of the secret practise against hir: by the aduise of hir fréends, with all spéed tooke hir iorneie toward hir house of Keningall in Norffolke, intending there to remaine, vntill she could make hir selfe more strong of hir freends and alies, and withall wrote vnto the lords of the councell in forme as followeth.

A letter of the ladie Marie sent to the lords of the councell, wherein she claimeth the crowne now after the decease of hir brother king Edward.

MY lords we gréet you well, and haue receiued sure aduertisement, that our dearest brother the king our late souereigne lord is departed to Gods mercie: which newes, how they be wofull to our heart, he onelie knoweth, to whose will and pleasure we must and doo humblie submit vs, and all our wils. But in this so lamentable a case, that is to wit, now after his maiesties departure and death, concerning the crowne & gouernance of this realme of England, with the title of France, and all things thereto belonging: that hath béene prouided by act of parlement, and the testament and last will of our dearest father, besides other circumstances aduancing our right; you know, the realme, and the whole world knoweth, the rolles and records appeare by the authoritie of the king our said father, and the king our said brother, and the subiects of this relme, so that we verelie trust that there is no true subiect that is, can, or would pretend to be ignorant thereof: and of our part we haue our selues caused, and as God shall aid and strength vs, shall cause our right and title in this behalfe to be published and proclamed accordinglie. And albeit this so weightie a matter séemeth strange, that the dieng of our said brother vpon thursdaie at night last past, we hitherto had no knowledge from you thereof: yet we consider your wisedomes and prudence to be such, that hauing eftsoones amongst you debated, pondered, and well weighed this present case with our estate, with your owne estate, the commonwealth, and all our honors, we shall and may conceiue great hope and trust, with much assurance in your loialtie and seruice, and therefore for the time interpret and take things not to the worst, and that ye yet will like noblemen worke the best. Neuerthelesse, we are not ignorant of your consultations to vndoo the prouisions made for our preferment, nor of the great bands and prouisions forcible, wherevnto ye be assembled and prepared, by whome, and to what end, God and you know, and nature can feare some euill. But be it that some consideration politike, or whatsoeuer thing else hath mooued you thereto, yet doubt you not my lords, but we can take all these your dooings in gratious part, being also right readie to remit and fullie pardon the same, with that fréelie to eschew bloudshed & vengeance against all those that can or will intend the same, trusting also assuredlie you will take and accept this grace and vertue in good part, as apperteineth, and that we shall not be inforced to vse this seruice of other our true subiects and freends, which in this our iust and rightfull case God (in whome our whole affiance is) shall send vs. Wherefore my lords, we require you, and charge you, and euerie of you of your allegiance which you owe to God and vs, and to none other, for our honor, and the suertie of our realme, onelie imploie your selues and foorthwith vpon receipt hereof cause our right and title to the crowne and gouernment of this realme, to be proclamed in our citie of London, and such other places as to your wisedoms shall séeme good, and as to this case apperteineth, not failing hereof, as our verie trust is in you: and this our letter signed with our owne hand shall be your sufficient warrant in this behalfe. Yeuen vnder our signet at our manor of Keningall the ninth of Iulie 1553.

The ladie Maries challenge to the crowne by right of succession.

She certifieth the lords that she knoweth what is intended against hir.

She chargeth the lords vpon their loialties to cause hir right to the regiment to be proclamed.

To this letter of the ladie Marie, the lords of the councell answered againe as followeth.

MADAM, we haue receiued your letters the ninth of this instant, declaring your supposed title, which you iudge your selfe to haue to the imperiall crowne of this realme, and all the dominions thereto belonging. For answer wherof, this is to aduertise

tise you, that forsomuch as our souereigne ladie quéene Iane is, after the death of our The lords ad-uertise the ladie Marie that the ladie Iane is queene. souereigne lord Edward the sixt, a prince of most noble memorie, inuested and pos-sessed with the iust and right title of the imperiall crowne of this realme, not onelie by good order of old ancient good lawes of this realme; but also by our late soue-reigne lords letters patent, signed with his owne hand, and sealed with the great seale of England, in presence of the most part of the nobles, councellors, iudges, with diuers others graue and sage personages, assenting and subscribing to the same: we must therefore, as of most bound dutie and allegiance, assent vnto hir said grace and to none other, except we should (which faithfull subiects cannot) fall into grée-uous and vnspeakable enormities. Wherefore we can no lesse doo, but for the quiet both of the realme and you also, to aduertise you, that forsomuch as the diuorse made betwéene the king of famous memorie king Henrie the eight, and the ladie Katharine your mother, was necessarie to be had, both by the euerlasting lawes of God, and also by the ecclesiasticall lawes, and by the most part of the noble and learned A subtill shift to prooue the ladie Marie illegiti-mate. vniuersities of christendome, and confirmed also by the sundrie acts of parlements, remaining yet in their force, and thereby you iustlie made illegitimate, and vnherita-able to the crowne imperiall of this realme; and the rules, dominions, and possessions of the same: you will vpon iust consideration hereof, and of diuers other causes law-full to be alledged for the same, and for the iust inheritance of the right line, and godlie orders taken by the late king Edward the sixt, and greatest personages afore-said, surcease, by anie pretense to vex and molest anie of our souereigne ladie quéene Iane hir subiects, from the true faith and allegiance due vnto hir grace; assuring you, that if you will for respect shew your selfe quiet and obedient (as you ought) you shall find vs all, and seuerall, readie to doo you anie seruice that we with dutie may, and to be glad of your quietnesse, to preserue the common state of this realme, where-in you may be otherwise gréeuous vnto vs, to your selfe, and to them. And thus we bid you most hartilie well to fare. From the tower of London this ninth of Iulie.

Your ladiships freends shewing
your selfe an obedient subiect,

Thomas Canturburie, the marquesse of Winchester, Iohn Bedford, William North-ampton, Thomas Elie chancellor, Iohn Northumberland, Henrie Suffolke, Henrie Arundell, Francis Shrewesburie, William Penbroke, Cobham, R. Rich, Huntington, Darcie, Cheineie, R. Cotton, Iohn Gates, William Peter, William Cecill, Iohn Chéeke, Iohn Mason, Edward North, Robert Bowes.

ALL these aforesaid, except onelie the duke of Northumberland, and sir Iohn Gates were either by speciall fauour, or speciall or generall pardon, discharged for this offense against hir committed, after hir comming to be quéene. But now vpon Ladie Marie remooueth frō Keningall to Fremingham, castell. the receipt of this answer, vnderstanding by hir fréends that she could not lie in suer-tie at Keningall, being a place open & easie to be approched, she remooued from thence vnto hir castell of Fremingham, standing in a wood countrie, & not so easie to be in-uaded by hir enimies. So soone as the councell heard of hir sudden departure, and considering that all came not to passe as they supposed; they caused spéedilie a power of men to be gathered togither. And first they agréed that the duke of Suffolke father to the new made quéene, should haue the conduct and leading of the armie.

¶ But afterward it was deuised and decréed vpon further considerations, and by Abr. Fl. ex I. S. 1059. the speciall means of the ladie Iane his daughter, who taking the matter heauilie, with wéeping teares, made request to the whole councell, that hir father might tarrie at home in hir companie. Whervpon the councell persuaded with the duke of Northum- The councell persuade the duke to vnder-take this enter-prise. berland, to take that voiage vpon him, saieng, that no man was so fit therefore: bi-cause that he had atchiued the victorie in Norffolke once alreadie, and was therefore so feared, that none durst once lift vp their weapon against him: besides that, he was the best man of warre in the realme, as well for the ordering of his campes and souldiers, both in battell and in their tents, as also by experience, knowlege and wisdome he could both animate his armie with wittie persuasions, and also pacifie and allaie his enimies pride with his stout courage, or else to dissuade them (if néed were) from their enterprise. Finallie said they, this is the short and the long, the quéene will in no wise grant, that hir father shall take it vpon him: wherefore (quoth they) we thinke it good, if it may please your grace, it lieth in you to remedie the matter. With these & the like persuasions the duke was allured to put himselfe desperatlie vpon hazzard:

Non morte horrenda non vllis territus armis.

Insomuch that he reioined vpon their talke, and said: Well then, sith yee thinke it good, I and mine will go, not doubting of your fidelitie to the queenes maiestie, which now I leaue in your custodie. So that night he sent for both lords, knights, and other that should go with him, and caused all things to be prepared accordinglie. Then went the councell in to the ladie Iane, and told hir of their conclusion, who humblie thanked the duke for reseruing hir father at home, and beséeched him to vse his diligence: whereto he answered, that he would doo what in him laie. The morrow following, great preparation was made, the duke earlie in the morning called for his owne harnesse, and saw it made readie at Durham place, where he appointed all his

Carts laden with munitiō.

retinue to méet. The same daie carts were laden with munition and artillerie, and field péeces were set forward.

The same forenoone the duke mooued eftsoones the councell to send their powers after him, as it was before determined, the same to méet with him at Newmarket, and

The dukes words to the lords of the councell.

they promised they would. He said further to some of them; My lords, I and these other noble personages, with the whole armie that now go foorth, as well for the behalfe of you & yours, as for the establishing of the quéenes highnesse, shall not onelie aduenture our bodies and liues amongst the bloudie strokes and cruell assaults of our aduersaries in the open fields: but also we doo leaue the conseruation of our selues, children, and families at home here with you, as altogither committed to your truth and fidelities: whome, if we thought ye would through malice, conspiracie, or dissention leaue vs your fréends in the briers, and betraie vs; we could as well sundrie waies foresee and prouide for our owne safegard, as anie of you by betraieng vs can doo for yours. But now vpon the onelie trust and faithfulnesse of your honors, whereof we thinke our selues most assured, we doo hazzard our liues. Which trust and promise if yée shall violate, hoping thereby of life and promotion: yet shall not God

He meaneth the the new quéen after depriued and executed.

count you innocent of our blouds, neither acquite you of the sacred and holie oth of allegiance, made fréelie by you to this vertuous ladie the queenes highnesse, who by your and our intisement is rather of force placed therein, than by hir owne séeking and request. Consider also, that Gods cause, which is the preferment of his word, & feare of papists entrance, hath beene (as ye haue here before alwaies laid) the originall ground wherevpon ye euen at the first motion granted your goodwils and consents therevnto, as by your hand writings appeareth; and thinke not the contrarie, but if ye meane deceit, though not foorthwith, yet hereafter God will reuenge the same.

I can saie no more, but in this troublesome time wish you to vse constant hearts, abandoning all malice, enuie, and priuat affections. And therewithall the first course

The conclusion of the dukes talke to the lords.

for the lords came vp, wherefore the duke shut vp his talke with these words, I haue not spoken to you in this sort vpon anie mistrust I haue of your truths, of which alwaies I haue euer hitherto conceiued a trustie confidence, but I haue put you in remembrance thereof, what chance of variance so euer might grow amongst you in mine absence: and this I praie you, wish me not worsse good spéed in this iorneie,

than

than yée would haue to your selues. My lord, saith one of them, if yée mistrust anie of vs in this matter, your grace is farre deceiued, for which of vs can wash his hands cleane thereof? And if we should shrinke from you as from one that were culpable, which of vs can excuse himselfe to be giltlesse? Therefore herein your doubt is too farre cast. I praie God it be (quoth the duke) let vs go to dinner: and so they sat downe. After dinner the duke went in to the quéene, where his commission was by that time sealed, for his lieutenantship of the armie, and then tooke his leaue of hir and so did certeine other lords also.

Then as the duke came through the councell chamber, he tooke his leaue of the earle of Arundell, who praied God be with his grace, saieng he was sorie it was not his chance to go with him and beare him companie, in whose presence he could find in his heart to spend his bloud euen at his féet. Then the earle of Arundell tooke Thomas Louell the dukes boie by the hand, and said; Farewell gentle Thomas with all my heart. Then the duke, with the lord marquesse of Northampton, the lord Greie, and diuerse other tooke their barge, and went to Durham place, and to White hall where that night they mustered their men: and the next daie in the morning the duke departed with the number of six hundred men, or thereabouts. And as they rode through Shordich, said the duke to the lord Greie; The people prease to see vs, but not one saith God spéed vs. The same daie sir Iohn Gates and other went out after the duke.] ·

[margin: The earle of Arundell professeth himselfe sorie that he goeth not with the duke of Northumberland.]

Now as the duke went forward on his waie (with his commission from the whole councell, and his warrant vnder the broad seale of England, without mistrust of that which after fortuned to his owne destruction, as in the historie of quéene Marie shall appeare, accompanied with no small number of lords and gentlemen, hauing notwithstanding his times prescribed, and his iourneies appointed by the councell, to the intent he would not seeme to doo any thing but vpon warrant) what a doo there was, what stirring on euerie side, what sending, what riding and posting, what letters, messages, & instructions went to and fro, what talking among the souldiers, what hartburning among the people, what faire pretenses outwardlie, inwardlie what priuie practises there were, what speeding and sending foorth ordinance out of the tower, yea euen the same daie that quéene Marie at euen was proclaimed quéene, what rumors, and comming downe of souldiers as there was from all quarters, a world it was to see, and a processe to declare, enough to make (as saith master Fox) a whole volume, euen as big as an Ilias.

[margin: Much a do on all sides during this stir broched betwéene the duke and the ladie Marie.]

The greatest helpe that made for the ladie Marie, was the short iourneies of the duke, which by commission were assigned vnto him before, as aboue is mentioned: and happilie not without the politike forecast of some in fauour of the ladie Marie: for the longer the duke lingered in his voiage, the ladie Marie the more increased in puissance, the hearts of the people being mightilie bent vnto hir. Whervpon she in the meane time remaining at Fremingham, and hearing of this preparation against hir, gathered togither such power of the noblemen & other hir fréends in that countrie, as she could get. And first of all, the noblemen that came vnto hir aid, were the earles of Sussex, Bath, and Oxford, the lord Wentworth, sir Thomas Cornewallis, sir Henrie Ierningham, sir William Walgraue, with diuerse other gentlemen and commons of the counties of Norffolke and Suffolke. Here (as master Fox noteth) the Suffolke men being the first that resorted to hir promised hir their aid and helpe to the vttermost of their powers, so that she would not go about to alter the religion which hir brother had established, and was now vsed and exercised through the realme. To this condition she agréed, with such promise, as no man would haue doubted that anie innouation of matters in religion should haue followed, by hir sufferance or procurement during hir reigne: but how soone shée forgat that promise, it shall shortlie after plainelie appeare.

[margin: The old prouerbe verefied Delaie bréedeth danger.]

[margin: Suffolke men the the first that resorted to the ladie Marie.]

In

Assistants to the ladie Marie. In this meane season, the lord Windsor, sir Edmund Peckham, sir Robert Drurie, and sir Edward Hastings, raised the commoners of the shire of Buckingham; vnto whóme sir Iohn Williams, which afterward was lord Williams of Thame, and sir Leonard Chamberleine, with the cheefe power of Oxfordshire. And out of Northamptonshire came sir Thomas Tresham, and a great number of gentlemen out of diuerse parts, whose names were too long to rehearse. These capteins with their companies being thus assembled in warlike manner, marched forward towards Norffolke to the aid of the ladie Marie, and the further they went, the more their power increased.

Abr. Fl. ex I. S. pag. 1062. ¶ About this time six ships well manned, that were appointed to lie before Yarmouth, and to haue taken the ladie Marie if she had fled that waie, were by force of weather driuen into the hauen, where one maister Ierningham was raising power on the ladie Maries behalfe, who hearing therof, came thither. Wherupon the capteins tooke a bote *Aid by wind and* and went to the ships, but the sailers and souldiers asked master Ierningham what he *wether for queene Marie that was bent against hir.* would haue, and whether he would haue their capteins or no, and he said yea. Marrie said they, ye shall haue them or we will throw them into the bottome of the sea. But the capteins said foorthwith, that they would serue quéene Marie willinglie, and so brought foorth their men, and conueied with them their great ordinance. Of the comming of these ships the ladie Marie was woonderfull ioious, & afterward doubted little the dukes puissance: but when newes thereof was brought to the tower, each man there began to draw backward: and ouer that, word of a greater mischeefe was brought to the tower: that is to saie, that the noblemens tenants refused to serue their lords against quéene Marie.

The duke of Northumberland writeth for more succours. The duke thought long for his succors, and wrote somewhat sharpelie to the councell at the tower in that behalfe, as well for lacke of men as munition, but a slender answer had he againe. And from that time forward, certeine of the councell, to wit, the erle of Penbroke, and sir Thomas Cheineie lord warden, and other, sought to get out *Doctor Ridleie persuadeth the people in the title of queene Iane, &c* of the tower to consult in London, but could not. On the sixteenth of Iulie, being sundaie, doctor Ridleie bishop of London, by commandement of the councell, preached at Paules crosse, where he vehementlie persuaded the people in the title of the ladie Iane, late proclamed quéene, and inueied earnestlie against the title of ladie Marie, &c. The same sixteenth of Iulie, the lord treasuror was gone out of the tower to his house in London at night, and foorthwith aboue seauen of the clocke the gates of the tower vpon a sudden were shut vp, and the keies borne vp to the ladie Iane, which was for feare of some packing in the lord treasuror: but he was fetched againe to the tower about twelue of the clocke in the night.]

The lords of the councell suspecting that all would go against them, proclamed the ladie Marie queen. The lords of the councell, being in this meane while at London, after they vnderstood how the better part of the realme were inclined, and hearing euerie daie newes of great assemblies, began to suspect the sequell of this enterprise. So that prouiding for their owne suertie, without respect of the duke (who now was at Burie) they fell to a new councell, and lastlie by assent made proclamation at London in the name of the ladie Marie, by the name of Marie quéene of England, France & Ireland, defender of the faith, & of the churches of England & Ireland supreme head. Of which proclamation, after the duke of Northumberland, being then at Burie, was aduertised by letters of discomfort from the councell, he incontinentlie, according to the new order receiued from them, returned with his power againe to Cambridge. Now so sudden change of minds foorthwith appeared in his armie, that they which before séemed most forward in that quarrell, began first to flie from him, & so euerie man shifting for himselfe, he that late before was furnished of such multitude of souldiers, was suddenlie forsaken of all sauing a few, whose perils were ioined with his.

Learned men that wrote in the reigne of king Edward. But now before I proceed anie further in the historie of quéene Marie, who was now receiued and proclamed quéene, as then to succeed hir brother, I will speake somewhat of the learned men that wrote & published anie pamphlets or treatises in his daies, as

in

in deed there were manie: but for that the more part of them died in quéene Maries time, or in the quéenes maiesties time that now is, or else are yet liuing, I doo omit those here, meaning to speake of them hereafter, if God shall permit, as occasion maie serue. For the residue that ended their liues in this kings daies, these I find: Dauid Clapham a lawyer and well séene in the Latine toong, wrote sundrie treatises; Robert Talbot a prebendarie of Norwich, verie skilfull in antiquities; Edward Hall a counsellor in the common law, but excellentlie séene in histories, wrote a notable chronicle of the vnion of the two houses of Yorke & Lancaster.

Furthermore Richard Tracie of Todington in Glocestershire, an esquier, and verie well learned, sonne to William Tracie; doctor Ioseph an excellent preacher: George Ioie a Bedfordshire man, that wrote diuerse treatises concerning diuinitie, and died either in the last yeare of king Edward, or in the beginning of quéene Maries reigne, as appéareth by master Bale; Alexander Barkleie a Scot, a notable poet, and a good rhetorician, departed this life in the yeare one thousand fiue hundred fiftie and two: William Hugh a Yorkeshireman, wrote, besides other things, a notable treatise called the troubled mans medicine, he deceassed by the bursting of a veine, in the yeare one thousand fiue hundred fortie and nine; Thomas Sternehold borne in Southhampton, turned into English méeter seuen & thirtie psalmes chosen foorth of Dauids psalter, Of strangers that liued and died here in this kings daies, excellentlie learned, and renowmed for such treatises as they published to the world, Marteine Bucer and Paulus Fagius are most famous. To end now with this part of the booke concerning king Edward, I haue thought good to set downe Ierom Cardans verses, written as an epitaph of him (and recorded by master Fox in his historie) as here followeth:

Flete nefas magnum, sed toto flebilis orbe
     Mortales, vester corruit omnis honor.
Nam regum decus, & iuuenum flos, spésque bonorum,
     Deliciæ secli, & gloria gentis erat,
Dignus Apollineis lachrymis, doctæque Mineruæ:
     Flosculus heu miserè concidit ante diem.
Te cumulo dabimus musæ, supremáque flentes
     Munera, Melpomene tristia fata canet.

Carmen epitaphicum Cardani in obitum regis Edouardi.

Thus farre the good and vertuous yoong prince Edward the sixt, successor to Henrie the eight of most famous memorie.

END OF VOL. III.

BROOKE, PRINTER PATER-NOSTER ROW.